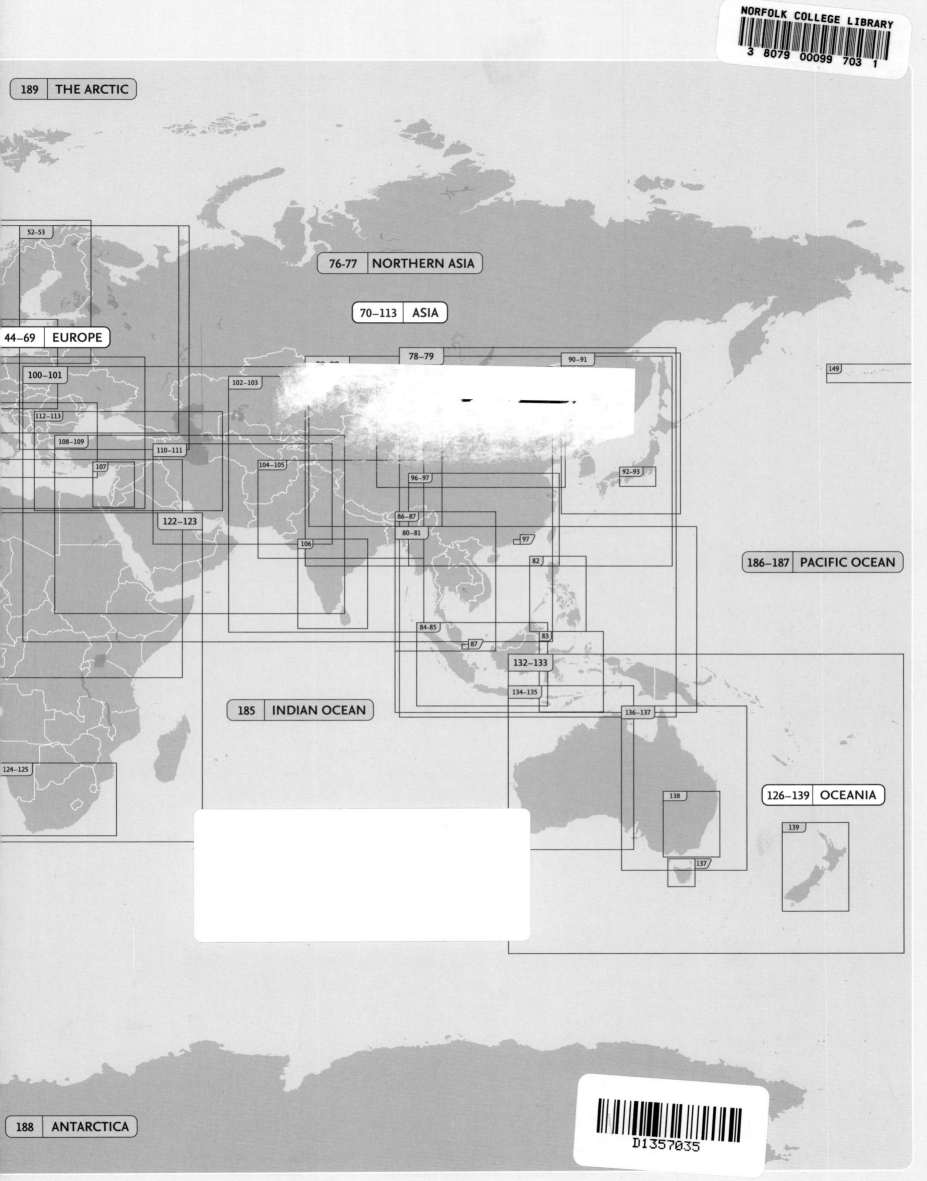

189 | THE ARCTIC

52–53

76-77 | NORTHERN ASIA

70–113 | ASIA

44–69 | EUROPE

78–79

90–91

149

100–101

102–103

112–113

108–109

110–111

104–105

92–93

107

96–97

122–123

86–87

80–81

106

97

82

186–187 | PACIFIC OCEAN

84–85

83

87

132–133

134–135

185 | INDIAN OCEAN

136–137

124–125

138

126–139 | OCEANIA

139

137

188 | ANTARCTICA

Find your map

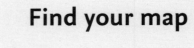

D1357035

Collins World Atlas – Complete Edition

Collins
An imprint of HarperCollins Publishers
Westerhill Road,
Bishopbriggs, Glasgow G64 2QT

First published 2008
Reprinted with changes 2009, 2011

Printed in Thailand.

ISBN 978-0-00-726965-5

All mapping in this title is generated
from Collins Bartholomew™ digital databases.
Collins Bartholomew™, the UK's leading independent geographical
information supplier, can provide a digital, custom, and premium
mapping service to a variety of markets.
For further information:
Tel: +44 (0) 141 306 3752
e-mail: collinsbartholomew@harpercollins.co.uk

or visit our website: www.collinsbartholomew.com

www.CollinsMaps.com
Discover the world through maps

Collins World Atlas

COMPLETE EDITION

Collins

Contents

Title	Scale	Page
Map Symbols		4

World		**5–43**
Time Zones and International Organizations		5
Landscapes		6–7
Countries		8–9
Earthquakes and Volcanoes		10–11
Climate and Weather		12–13
Land Cover		14–15
Population		16–17
Urbanization and Cities		18–19
Communications		20–21
Social Indicators		22–23
Economy and Wealth		24–25
Conflict		26–27
Global Issues		28–29
Environmental Threats		30–31
Change		32–33
Satellite images		34-41
Venice		34–35
Namib Desert		36
Kamchatka Peninsula		37
Kuala Lumpur		38
Cape Canaveral		39
Songhua River		40
Spider Crater		41
Useful Facts and Web Links		42–43

Europe		**44–69**
Landscapes		46–47
Countries		48–49
Northern Europe	1:8 750 000	50–51
Western Russian Federation	1:6 500 000	52–53
Scandinavia and the Baltic States	1:4 300 000	54–55
Inset: Iceland	1:6 000 000	
Inset: Faroe Islands	1:4 300 000	
Northwest Europe	1:4 300 000	56–57
England and Wales	1:1 730 000	58–59
Scotland	1:1 730 000	60
Inset: Shetland Islands	1:1 730 000	
Ireland	1:1 730 000	61
Belgium, Netherlands, Luxembourg and Northwest Germany	1:1 730 000	62–63
Southern Europe and the Mediterranean	1:8 750 000	64–65
France	1:4 300 000	66
Spain and Portugal	1:4 300 000	67
Italy and the Balkans	1:4 300 000	68–69

Asia		**70–113**
Landscapes		72–73
Countries		74–75
Northern Asia	1:17 300 000	76–77
Eastern and Southeast Asia	1:17 300 000	78–79
Southeast Asia	1:13 000 000	80–81
Philippines	1:5 500 000	82
Inset: Palau	1:1 000 000	
Central Indonesia	1:5 500 000	83
West Indonesia and Malaysia	1:5 500 000	84–85
Myanmar, Thailand, Peninsular Malaysia and Indo-China	1:6 000 000	86–87
Inset: Singapore	1:550 000	
Eastern Asia	1:13 000 000	88–89
Japan, North Korea and South Korea	1:6 000 000	90–91
Japan – Central Honshū	1:1 100 000	92–93
Northern China and Mongolia	1:6 000 000	94–95
Southeast China	1:6 000 000	96–97
Inset: Hong Kong	1:700 000	
West China	1:6 000 000	98–99
Central and Southern Asia	1:17 300 000	100–101
Southern Asia	1:11 000 000	102–103
Northern India, Nepal, Bhutan and Bangladesh	1:6 000 000	104–105
Southern India and Sri Lanka	1:6 000 000	106
Middle East	1:2 600 000	107
Southwest Asia	1:11 000 000	108–109
The Gulf, Iran, Afghanistan and Pakistan	1:6 000 000	110–111
Eastern Mediterranean, the Caucasus and Iraq	1:6 000 000	112–113

Contents

Title	Scale	Page
Africa		**114–125**
Landscapes		116–117
Countries		118–119
Northern Africa	1:14 000 000	120–121
Inset: Cape Verde	1:14 000 000	
Central and Southern Africa	1:14 000 000	122–123
Republic of South Africa	1:4 300 000	124–125
Oceania		**126–139**
Landscapes		128–129
Countries		130–131
Australia, New Zealand and Southwest Pacific	1:17 300 000	132–133
Western Australia	1:7 000 000	134–135
Eastern Australia	1:7 000 000	136–137
Inset: Tasmania	1:7 000 000	
Southeast Australia	1:4 300 000	138
New Zealand	1:4 500 000	139
North America		**140–169**
Landscapes		142–143
Countries		144–145
Canada	1:14 000 000	146–147
Alaska	1:6 000 000	148–149
Western Canada	1:6 000 000	150–151
Eastern Canada	1:6 000 000	152–153
United States of America	1:10 000 000	154–155
Western United States	1:6 000 000	156–157
Inset: Hawaiian Islands	1:6 000 000	
Southwest United States	1:3 000 000	158–159
Central United States	1:6 000 000	160–161
Eastern United States	1:6 000 000	162–163
Northeast United States	1:3 000 000	164–165
Mexico and Central America	1:6 300 000	166–167
Central America and the Caribbean	1:12 000 000	168–169
South America		**170–179**
Landscapes		172–173
Countries		174–175
Northern South America	1:12 000 000	176–177
Inset: Galapagos Islands	1:12 000 000	
Southern South America	1:12 000 000	178
Southeast Brazil	1:6 000 000	179
Oceans and Poles		**180–189**
Features		182–183
Atlantic Ocean and Indian Ocean	1:43 000 000	184–185
Pacific Ocean	1:43 000 000	186–187
Antarctica	1:22 500 000	188
The Arctic	1:22 500 000	189
Geographical Information Section		**190–336**
World Statistics		190–196
World States and Territories		197–217
Geographical Dictionary		218–248
Index		249–335
Acknowledgements		336

Map Symbols

Southern Europe

Japan

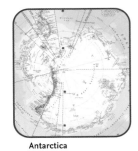

Antarctica

Settlements

Population	National capital	Administrative capital	Other city or town
over 10 million	BEIJING ✶	Karachi ◉	New York ◉
5 million to 10 million	JAKARTA ✶	Tianjin ◉	Nova Iguaçu ◉
1 million to 5 million	KĀBUL ✶	Sydney ◉	Kaohsiung ◉
500 000 to 1 million	BANGUI ✶	Trujillo ◉	Jeddah ◉
100 000 to 500 000	WELLINGTON ✶	Mansa ◉	Apucarana ◉
50 000 to 100 000	PORT OF SPAIN ✶	Potenza ◉	Arecibo ◉
10 000 to 50 000	MALABO ✶	Chinhoyi ◦	Ceres ◦
under 10 000	VALLETTA ✶	Ati ◦	Venta ◦

⬤ Built-up area

Boundaries

—————— International boundary

▬·▬·▬·▬ Disputed international boundary or alignment unconfirmed

—————— Administrative boundary

·········· Ceasefire line

Miscellaneous

----------- National park

············· Reserve or Regional park

✿ Site of specific interest

〰〰〰〰 Wall

Land and sea features

⋮⋮⋮ Desert

▾ Oasis

⦂⦂⦂ Lava field

1234 △ Volcano
height in metres

◯ Ice cap or Glacier

⌐⌐⌐ Escarpment

≈≈≈≈ Coral reef

⌇*1234* Pass
height in metres

Lakes and rivers

◯ Lake

◌ Impermanent lake

◌ Salt lake or lagoon

◌ Impermanent salt lake

◌ Dry salt lake or salt pan

123 Lake height
surface height above
sea level, in metres

—————— River

—————— Impermanent river or watercourse

‖ Waterfall

| Dam

∣ Barrage

Relief

Contour intervals and layer colours

Height metres		feet
5000		16404
3000		9843
2000		6562
1000		3281
500		1640
200		656
0		0
below sea level		
0		0
200		656
2000		6562
4000		13124
6000		19686

Depth

1234 ▲ Summit
height in metres

-123 Spot height
height in metres

123 Ocean deep
depth in metres

Transport

——➤----	Motorway (tunnel; under construction)
——➤----	Main road (tunnel; under construction)
——➤----	Secondary road (tunnel; under construction)
-----------	Track
━━➤----	Main railway (tunnel; under construction)
——➤----	Secondary railway (tunnel; under construction)
——➤----	Other railway (tunnel; under construction)
——————	Canal
✈	Main airport
✈	Regional airport

Satellite imagery - The thematic pages in the atlas contain a wide variety of photographs and images. These are a mixture of terrestrial and aerial photographs and satellite imagery. All are used to illustrate specific themes and to give an indication of the variety of imagery available today. The main types of imagery used in the atlas are described in the table below. The sensor for each satellite image is detailed on the acknowledgements page.

Main satellites/sensors

Satellite/sensor name	Launch dates	Owner	Aims and applications	Internet links	Additional internet links
Landsat 1, 2, 3, 4, 5, 7	July 1972–April 1999	National Aeronautics and Space Administration (NASA), USA	The first satellite to be designed specifically for observing the Earth's surface. Originally set up to produce images of use for agriculture and geology. Today is of use for numerous environmental and scientific applications.	landsat.gsfc.nasa.gov	asterweb.jpl.nasa.gov
					earth.jsc.nasa.gov
					earthnet.esrin.esa.it
SPOT 1, 2, 3, 4, 5 (Satellite Pour l'Observation de la Terre)	February 1986–March 1998	Centre National d'Etudes Spatiales (CNES) and Spot Image, France	Particularly useful for monitoring land use, water resources research, coastal studies and cartography.	www.spotimage.fr	earthobservatory.nasa.gov
					eol.jsc.nasa.gov
					gs.mdacorporation.com
Space Shuttle	Regular launches from 1981	NASA, USA	Each shuttle mission has separate aims. Astronauts take photographs with high specification hand held cameras. The Shuttle Radar Topography Mission (SRTM) in 2000 obtained the most complete near-global high-resolution database of the earth's topography.	science.ksc.nasa.gov/shuttle/countdown www.jpl.nasa.gov/srtm	modis.gsfc.nasa.gov
					seawifs.gsfc.nasa.gov
					topex-www.jpl.nasa.gov
IKONOS	September 1999	GeoEye	First commercial high-resolution satellite. Useful for a variety of applications mainly Cartography, Defence, Urban Planning, Agriculture, Forestry and Insurance.	www.geoeye.com	visibleearth.nasa.gov
					www.usgs.gov

Time Zones

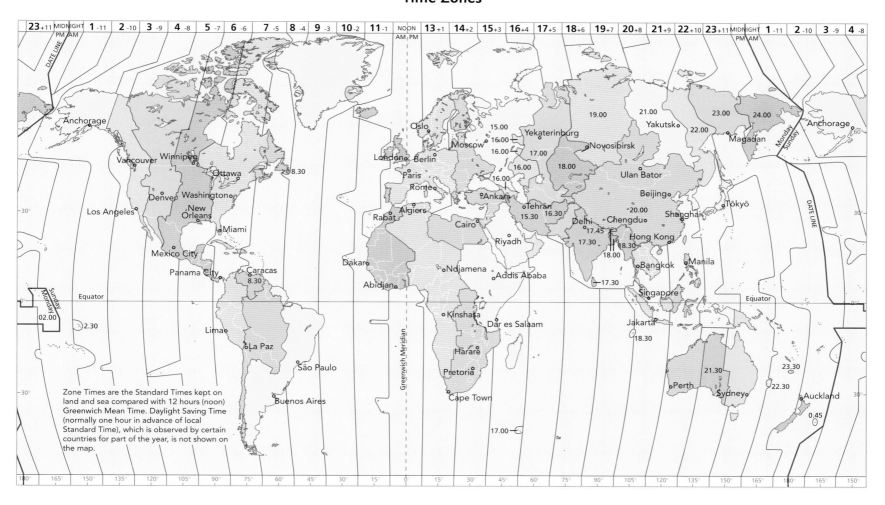

| 23 +11 MIDNIGHT PM AM | 1 -11 | 2 -10 | 3 -9 | 4 -8 | 5 -7 | 6 -6 | 7 -5 | 8 -4 | 9 -3 | 10 -2 | 11 -1 | NOON AM PM | 13 +1 | 14 +2 | 15 +3 | 16 +4 | 17 +5 | 18 +6 | 19 +7 | 20 +8 | 21 +9 | 22 +10 | 23 +11 MIDNIGHT PM AM | 1 -11 | 2 -10 | 3 -9 | 4 -8 |

DATE LINE

Anchorage

Vancouver Winnipeg
Ottawa
8.30
Denver Washington
New Orleans
Los Angeles
Miami
Mexico City
Panama City
Caracas 8.30
Sunday Monday 02.00
2.30
Lima
La Paz
São Paulo
Buenos Aires

Oslo
London Berlin
Paris
Rome
Rabat Algiers
Dakar
Abidjan
Cairo
Riyadh
Ndjamena
Addis Ababa
Kinshasa
Dar es Salaam
Harare
Pretoria
Cape Town

15.00
16.00
Moscow 16.00
16.00
16.00
Ankara
Tehrān 15.30 16.30
Delhi 17.45
17.30
18.00
17.30

Yekaterinburg
Novosibirsk
17.00
18.00
Ulan Bator
Beijing
-20.00
Chengdu
Shanghai
Hong Kong
Bangkok Manila
Singapore
Jakarta 18.30
Perth 21.30
Sydney 22.30

19.00
21.00
Yakutsk 22.00
23.00 24.00
Magadan

Monday Sunday Anchorage

DATE LINE

Tōkyō

23.30
Auckland
0.45

Greenwich Meridian

Equator   Equator

Zone Times are the Standard Times kept on land and sea compared with 12 hours (noon) Greenwich Mean Time. Daylight Saving Time (normally one hour in advance of local Standard Time), which is observed by certain countries for part of the year, is not shown on the map.

17.00

| 180° | 165° | 150° | 135° | 120° | 105° | 90° | 75° | 60° | 45° | 30° | 15° | 0 | 15° | 30° | 45° | 60° | 75° | 90° | 105° | 120° | 135° | 150° | 165° | 180° | 165° | 150° |

International Organizations

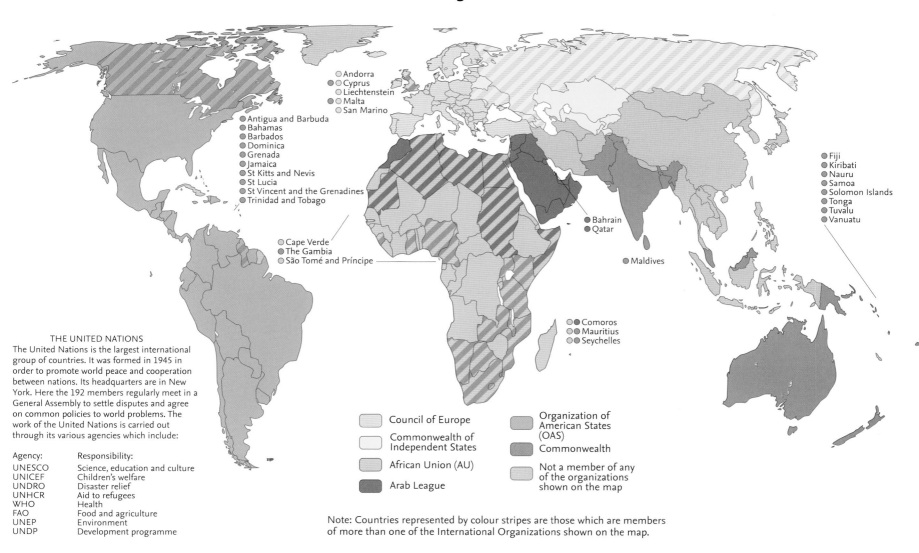

Andorra
Cyprus
Liechtenstein
Malta
San Marino

Antigua and Barbuda
Bahamas
Barbados
Dominica
Grenada
Jamaica
St Kitts and Nevis
St Lucia
St Vincent and the Grenadines
Trinidad and Tobago

Cape Verde
The Gambia
São Tomé and Príncipe

Bahrain
Qatar

Maldives

Comoros
Mauritius
Seychelles

Fiji
Kiribati
Nauru
Samoa
Solomon Islands
Tonga
Tuvalu
Vanuatu

THE UNITED NATIONS
The United Nations is the largest international group of countries. It was formed in 1945 in order to promote world peace and cooperation between nations. Its headquarters are in New York. Here the 192 members regularly meet in a General Assembly to settle disputes and agree on common policies to world problems. The work of the United Nations is carried out through its various agencies which include:

Agency:	Responsibility:
UNESCO	Science, education and culture
UNICEF	Children's welfare
UNDRO	Disaster relief
UNHCR	Aid to refugees
WHO	Health
FAO	Food and agriculture
UNEP	Environment
UNDP	Development programme

Council of Europe

Commonwealth of Independent States

African Union (AU)

Arab League

Organization of American States (OAS)

Commonwealth

Not a member of any of the organizations shown on the map

Note: Countries represented by colour stripes are those which are members of more than one of the International Organizations shown on the map.

World
Landscapes

The Earth's physical features, both on land and on the sea bed, closely reflect its geological structure. The current shapes of the continents and oceans have evolved over millions of years. Movements of the tectonic plates which make up the Earth's crust have created some of the best-known and most spectacular features. The processes which have shaped the Earth continue today with earthquakes, volcanoes, erosion, climatic variations and man's activities all affecting the Earth's landscapes.

The total topographic range of the Earth's surface is nearly 20 000 metres, from the highest point Mount Everest, to the lowest point in the Mariana Trench. Major mountain ranges include the Himalaya, the Andes and the Rocky Mountains, each of which gives rise to some of the world's greatest rivers. In contrast, the deserts of the Sahara, Australia, the Arabian Peninsula and the Gobi cover vast areas and each provides unique landscapes.

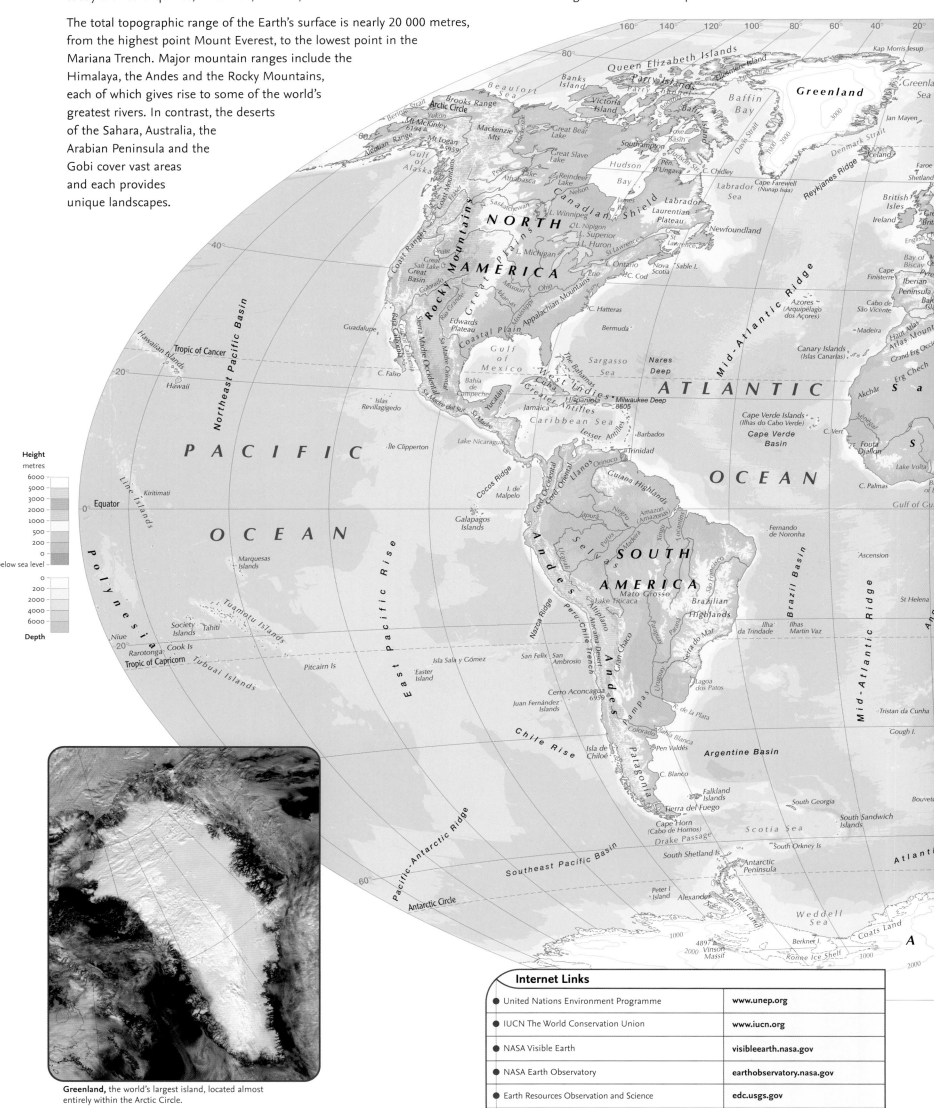

Height
metres
6000
5000
3000
2000
1000
500
200
0
below sea level

Depth
0
200
2000
4000
6000

Greenland, the world's largest island, located almost entirely within the Arctic Circle.

Internet Links

● United Nations Environment Programme	**www.unep.org**
● IUCN The World Conservation Union	**www.iucn.org**
● NASA Visible Earth	**visibleearth.nasa.gov**
● NASA Earth Observatory	**earthobservatory.nasa.gov**
● Earth Resources Observation and Science	**edc.usgs.gov**

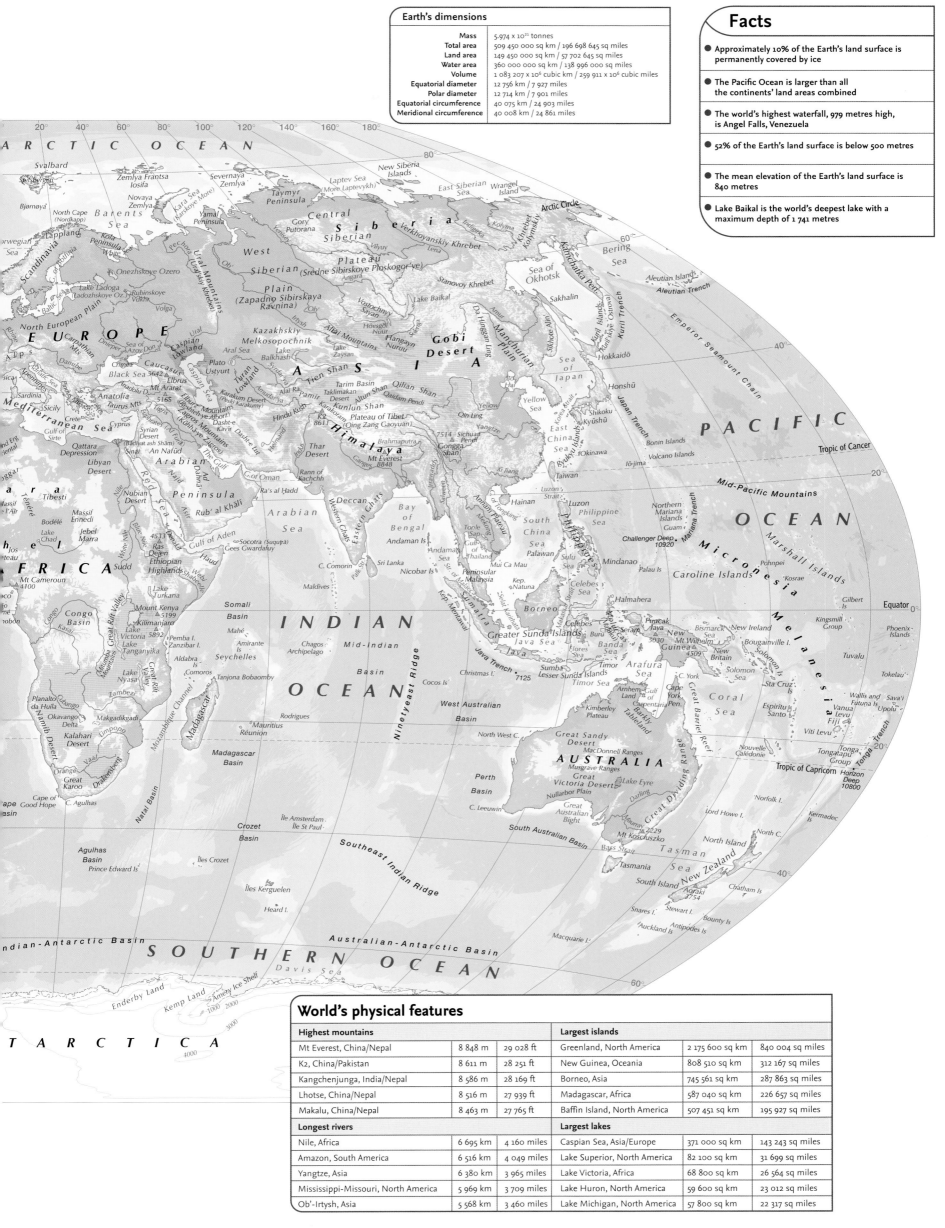

Earth's dimensions

Mass	5.974 x 10²¹ tonnes
Total area	509 450 000 sq km / 196 698 645 sq miles
Land area	149 450 000 sq km / 57 702 645 sq miles
Water area	360 000 000 sq km / 138 996 000 sq miles
Volume	1 083 207 x 10⁶ cubic km / 259 911 x 10⁶ cubic miles
Equatorial diameter	12 756 km / 7 927 miles
Polar diameter	12 714 km / 7 901 miles
Equatorial circumference	40 075 km / 24 903 miles
Meridional circumference	40 008 km / 24 861 miles

Facts

- Approximately 10% of the Earth's land surface is permanently covered by ice

- The Pacific Ocean is larger than all the continents' land areas combined

- The world's highest waterfall, 979 metres high, is Angel Falls, Venezuela

- 52% of the Earth's land surface is below 500 metres

- The mean elevation of the Earth's land surface is 840 metres

- Lake Baikal is the world's deepest lake with a maximum depth of 1 741 metres

World's physical features

Highest mountains			Largest islands		
Mt Everest, China/Nepal	8 848 m	29 028 ft	Greenland, North America	2 175 600 sq km	840 004 sq miles
K2, China/Pakistan	8 611 m	28 251 ft	New Guinea, Oceania	808 510 sq km	312 167 sq miles
Kangchenjunga, India/Nepal	8 586 m	28 169 ft	Borneo, Asia	745 561 sq km	287 863 sq miles
Lhotse, China/Nepal	8 516 m	27 939 ft	Madagascar, Africa	587 040 sq km	226 657 sq miles
Makalu, China/Nepal	8 463 m	27 765 ft	Baffin Island, North America	507 451 sq km	195 927 sq miles
Longest rivers			**Largest lakes**		
Nile, Africa	6 695 km	4 160 miles	Caspian Sea, Asia/Europe	371 000 sq km	143 243 sq miles
Amazon, South America	6 516 km	4 049 miles	Lake Superior, North America	82 100 sq km	31 699 sq miles
Yangtze, Asia	6 380 km	3 965 miles	Lake Victoria, Africa	68 800 sq km	26 564 sq miles
Mississippi-Missouri, North America	5 969 km	3 709 miles	Lake Huron, North America	59 600 sq km	23 012 sq miles
Ob'-Irtysh, Asia	5 568 km	3 460 miles	Lake Michigan, North America	57 800 sq km	22 317 sq miles

The current pattern of the world's countries and territories is a result of a long history of exploration, colonialism, conflict and politics. The fact that there are currently 195 independent countries in the world – the most recent, Kosovo, only being created in February 2008 – illustrates the significant political changes which have occurred since 1950 when there were only eighty-two. There has been a steady progression away from colonial influences over the last fifty years, although many dependent overseas territories remain.

The shapes of countries and the pattern of international boundaries reflect both physical and political processes. Some borders follow natural features – rivers, mountain ranges, etc – others are defined according to political agreement or as a result of war. Some are still subject to dispute between two or more countries, and many remain undefined on the ground.

Facts

- The longest single continuous land border stretches for 6 416 kilometres between Canada and the USA

- Both China and the Russian Federation have land borders with 14 different countries

- Vatican City, the smallest independent country, was created in 1929 as an enclave within Rome, the capital of Italy

- All countries of the world are members of the United Nations except Kosovo, Taiwan and Vatican City

Internet Links

United Nations	www.un.org
Foreign and Commonwealth Office	www.fco.gov.uk
International Boundaries Research Unit	www.dur.ac.uk/ibru
Permanent Committee on Geographical Names	www.pcgn.org.uk
U.S. Board on Geographic Names	geonames.usgs.gov

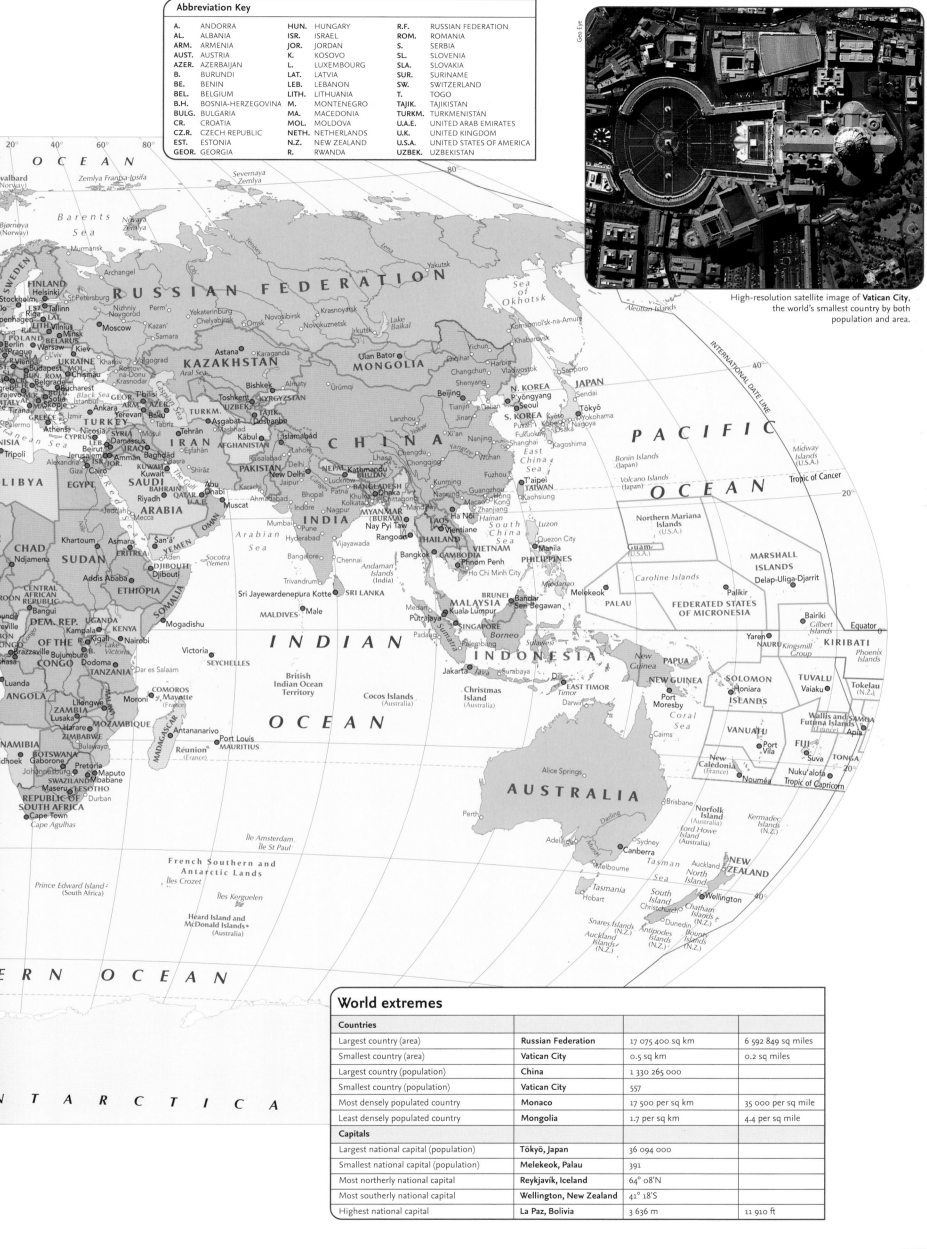

Abbreviation Key

A.	ANDORRA	HUN.	HUNGARY	R.F.	RUSSIAN FEDERATION
AL.	ALBANIA	ISR.	ISRAEL	ROM.	ROMANIA
ARM.	ARMENIA	JOR.	JORDAN	S.	SERBIA
AUST.	AUSTRIA	K.	KOSOVO	SL.	SLOVENIA
AZER.	AZERBAIJAN	L.	LUXEMBOURG	SLA.	SLOVAKIA
B.	BURUNDI	LAT.	LATVIA	SUR.	SURINAME
BE.	BENIN	LEB.	LEBANON	SW.	SWITZERLAND
BEL.	BELGIUM	LITH.	LITHUANIA	T.	TOGO
B.H.	BOSNIA-HERZEGOVINA	M.	MONTENEGRO	TAJIK.	TAJIKISTAN
BULG.	BULGARIA	MA.	MACEDONIA	TURKM.	TURKMENISTAN
CR.	CROATIA	MOL.	MOLDOVA	U.A.E.	UNITED ARAB EMIRATES
CZ.R.	CZECH REPUBLIC	NETH.	NETHERLANDS	U.K.	UNITED KINGDOM
EST.	ESTONIA	N.Z.	NEW ZEALAND	U.S.A.	UNITED STATES OF AMERICA
GEOR.	GEORGIA	R.	RWANDA	UZBEK.	UZBEKISTAN

High-resolution satellite image of **Vatican City**, the world's smallest country by both population and area.

World extremes

Countries			
Largest country (area)	**Russian Federation**	17 075 400 sq km	6 592 849 sq miles
Smallest country (area)	**Vatican City**	0.5 sq km	0.2 sq miles
Largest country (population)	**China**	1 330 265 000	
Smallest country (population)	**Vatican City**	557	
Most densely populated country	**Monaco**	17 500 per sq km	35 000 per sq mile
Least densely populated country	**Mongolia**	1.7 per sq km	4.4 per sq mile
Capitals			
Largest national capital (population)	**Tōkyō, Japan**	36 094 000	
Smallest national capital (population)	**Melekeok, Palau**	391	
Most northerly national capital	**Reykjavík, Iceland**	64° 08'N	
Most southerly national capital	**Wellington, New Zealand**	41° 18'S	
Highest national capital	**La Paz, Bolivia**	3 636 m	11 910 ft

Earthquakes and volcanoes hold a constant fascination because of their power, their beauty, and the fact that they cannot be controlled or accurately predicted. Our understanding of these phenomena relies mainly on the theory of plate tectonics. This defines the Earth's surface as a series of 'plates' which are constantly moving relative to each other, at rates of a few centimetres per year. As plates move against each other enormous pressure builds up and when the rocks can no longer bear this pressure they fracture, and energy is released as an earthquake. The pressures involved can also melt the rock to form magma which then rises to the Earth's surface to form a volcano. The distribution of earthquakes and volcanoes therefore relates closely to plate boundaries. In particular, most active volcanoes and much of the Earth's seismic activity are centred on the 'Ring of Fire' around the Pacific Ocean.

Facts

● Over 900 earthquakes of magnitude 5.0 or greater occur every year

● An earthquake of magnitude 8.0 releases energy equivalent to 1 billion tons of TNT explosive

● Ground shaking during an earthquake in Alaska in 1964 lasted for 3 minutes

● Indonesia has more than 120 volcanoes and over 30% of the world's active volcanoes

● Volcanoes can produce very fertile soil and important industrial materials and chemicals

Earthquakes

Earthquakes are caused by movement along fractures or 'faults' in the Earth's crust, particularly along plate boundaries. There are three types of plate boundary: constructive boundaries where plates are moving apart; destructive boundaries where two or more plates collide; conservative boundaries where plates slide past each other. Destructive and conservative boundaries are the main sources of earthquake activity.

The epicentre of an earthquake is the point on the Earth's surface directly above its source. If this is near to large centres of population, and the earthquake is powerful, major devastation can result. The size, or magnitude, of an earthquake is generally measured on the Richter Scale.

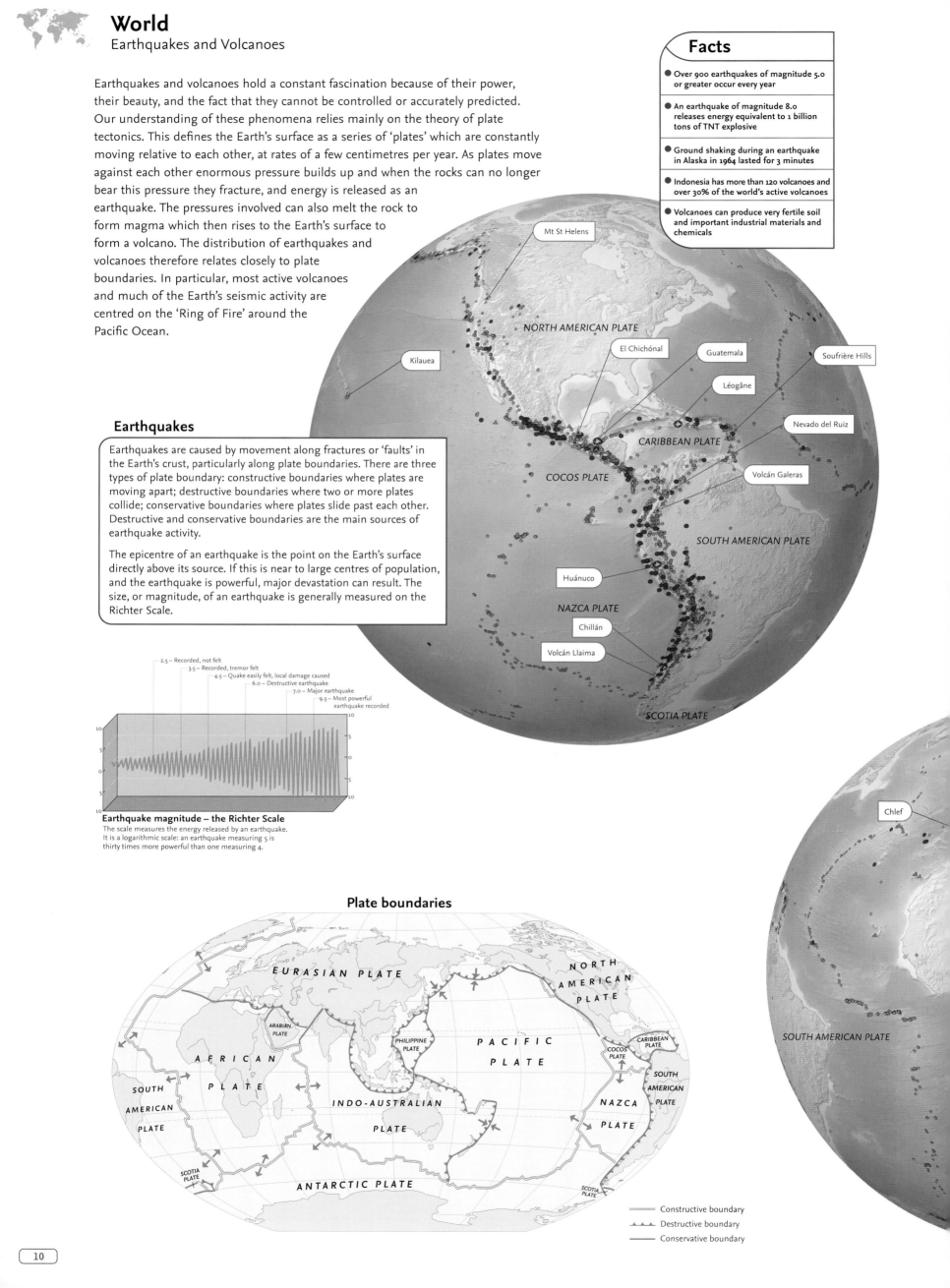

2.5 – Recorded, not felt
3.5 – Recorded, tremor felt
4.5 – Quake easily felt, local damage caused
6.0 – Destructive earthquake
7.0 – Major earthquake
9.5 – Most powerful earthquake recorded

Earthquake magnitude – the Richter Scale
The scale measures the energy released by an earthquake. It is a logarithmic scale: an earthquake measuring 5 is thirty times more powerful than one measuring 4.

Plate boundaries

Constructive boundary
Destructive boundary
Conservative boundary

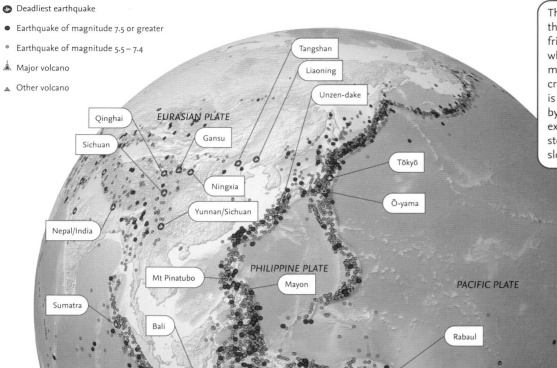

Legend

- Deadliest earthquake
- Earthquake of magnitude 7.5 or greater
- Earthquake of magnitude 5.5 – 7.4
- Major volcano
- Other volcano

Map labels (top globe)

Tangshan
Liaoning
Unzen-dake
Qinghai
EURASIAN PLATE
Gansu
Sichuan
Tōkyō
Ningxia
Ō-yama
Yunnan/Sichuan
Nepal/India
PHILIPPINE PLATE
PACIFIC PLATE
Mt Pinatubo
Mayon
Sumatra
Bali
Rabaul
Gunung Galunggung
INDO-AUSTRALIAN PLATE
ANTARCTIC PLATE

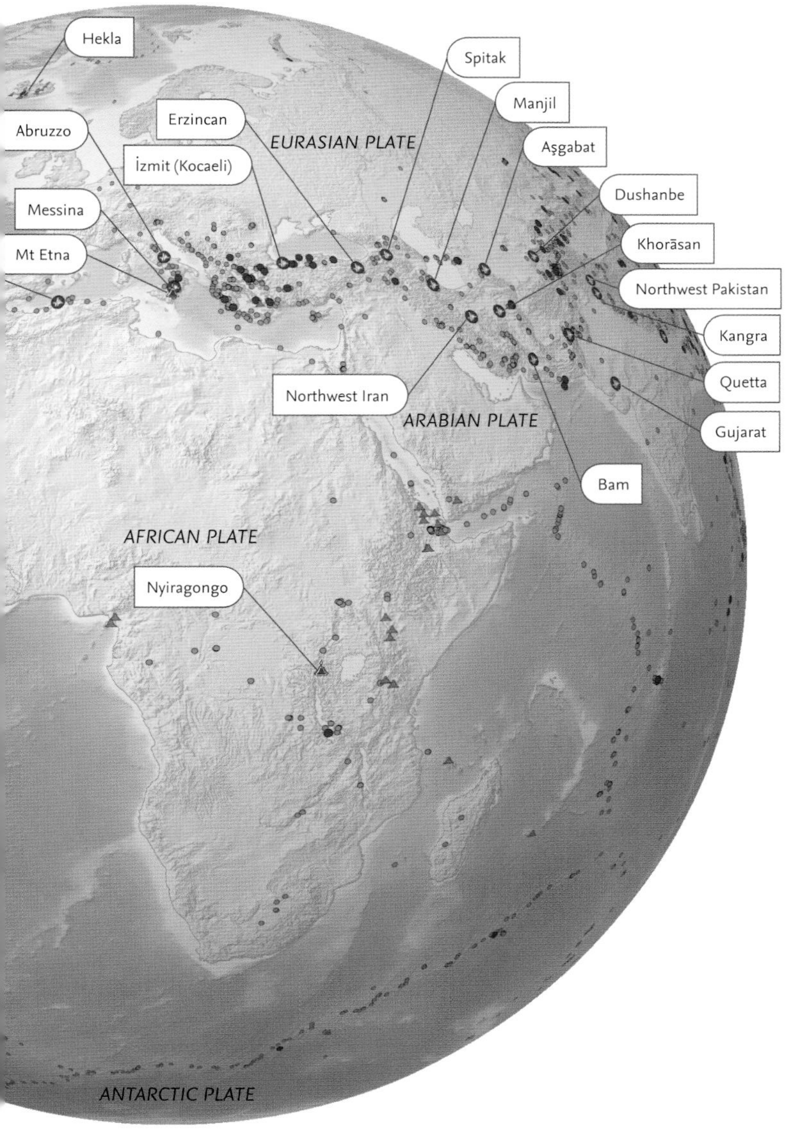

Map labels (bottom globe)

Hekla
Spitak
Abruzzo
Erzincan
Manjil
İzmit (Kocaeli)
EURASIAN PLATE
Aşgabat
Messina
Dushanbe
Mt Etna
Khorāsan
Northwest Pakistan
Kangra
ARABIAN PLATE
Northwest Iran
Quetta
Gujarat
Bam
AFRICAN PLATE
Nyiragongo
ANTARCTIC PLATE

Volcanoes

The majority of volcanoes occur along destructive plate boundaries in the 'subduction zone' where one plate passes under another. The friction and pressure causes the rock to melt and to form magma which is forced upwards to the Earth's surface where it erupts as molten rock (lava) or as particles of ash or cinder. This process created the numerous volcanoes in the Andes, where the Nazca Plate is passing under the South American Plate. Volcanoes can be defined by the nature of the material they emit. 'Shield' volcanoes have extensive, gentle slopes formed from free-flowing lava, while steep-sided 'continental' volcanoes are created from thicker, slow-flowing lava and ash.

Major volcanic eruptions since 1980

Volcano	Country	Date
Mt St Helens	USA	1980
El Chichónal	Mexico	1982
Gunung Galunggung	Indonesia	1982
Kilauea	Hawaii, USA	1983
Ō-yama	Japan	1983
Nevado del Ruiz	Colombia	1985
Mt Pinatubo	Philippines	1991
Unzen-dake	Japan	1991
Mayon	Philippines	1993
Volcán Galeras	Colombia	1993
Volcán Llaima	Chile	1994
Rabaul	Papua New Guinea	1994
Soufrière Hills	Montserrat	1997
Hekla	Iceland	2000
Mt Etna	Italy	2001
Nyiragongo	Democratic Republic of the Congo	2002

Deadliest earthquakes since 1900

Year	Location	Deaths
1905	Kangra, India	19 000
1907	west of Dushanbe, Tajikistan	12 000
1908	Messina, Italy	110 000
1915	Abruzzo, Italy	35 000
1917	Bali, Indonesia	15 000
1920	Ningxia Province, China	200 000
1923	Tōkyō, Japan	142 807
1927	Qinghai Province, China	200 000
1932	Gansu Province, China	70 000
1933	Sichuan Province, China	10 000
1934	Nepal/India	10 700
1935	Quetta, Pakistan	30 000
1939	Chillán, Chile	28 000
1939	Erzincan, Turkey	32 700
1948	Aşgabat, Turkmenistan	19 800
1962	northwest Iran	12 225
1970	Huánuco Province, Peru	66 794
1974	Yunnan and Sichuan Provinces, China	20 000
1975	Liaoning Province, China	10 000
1976	central Guatemala	22 778
1976	Tangshan, Hebei Province, China	255 000
1978	Khorāsan Province, Iran	20 000
1980	Chlef, Algeria	11 000
1988	Spitak, Armenia	25 000
1990	Manjil, Iran	50 000
1999	İzmit (Kocaeli), Turkey	17 000
2001	Gujarat, India	20 000
2003	Bam, Iran	26 271
2004	off Sumatra, Indian Ocean	225 000
2005	northwest Pakistan	74 648
2008	Sichuan Province, China	> 60 000
2009	Abruzzo region, Italy	308
2009	Sumatra, Indonesia	> 1 100
2010	Léogâne, Haiti	222 570

Internet Links

USGS National Earthquake Hazards Program	earthquake.usgs.gov/regional/neic
USGS Volcano Hazards Program	volcanoes.usgs.gov
British Geological Survey	www.bgs.ac.uk
NASA Natural Hazards	earthobservatory.nasa.gov/NaturalHazards
Volcano World	volcano.oregonstate.edu

World
Climate and Weather

The climate of a region is defined by its long-term prevailing weather conditions. Classification of Climate Types is based on the relationship between temperature and humidity and how these factors are affected by latitude, altitude, ocean currents and winds. Weather is the specific short term condition which occurs locally and consists of events such as thunderstorms, hurricanes, blizzards and heat waves. Temperature and rainfall data recorded at weather stations can be plotted graphically and the graphs shown here, typical of each climate region, illustrate the various combinations of temperature and rainfall which exist worldwide for each month of the year. Data used for climate graphs are based on average monthly figures recorded over a minimum period of thirty years.

World Statistics: see pages 190–196

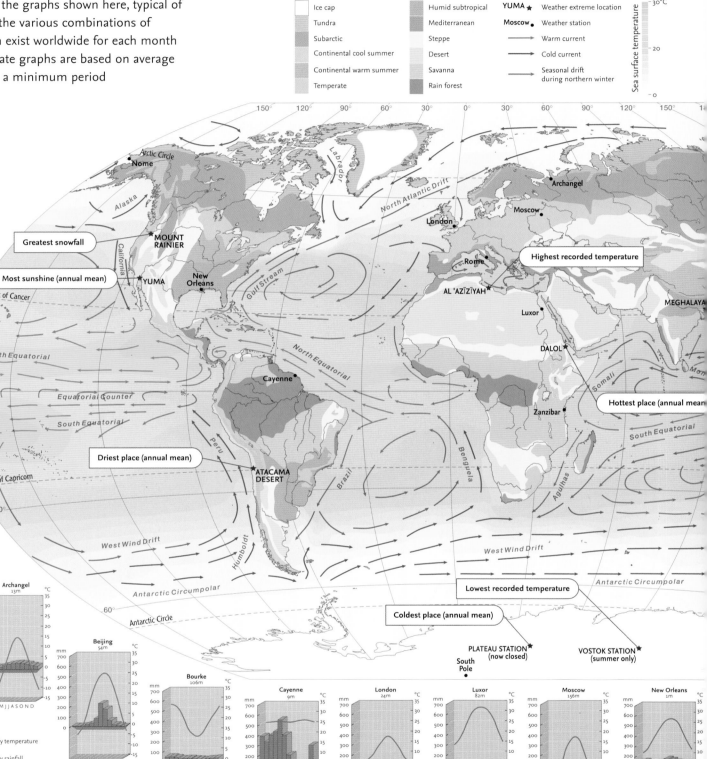

Major climate regions, ocean currents and sea surface temperatures

Ice cap
Tundra
Subarctic
Continental cool summer
Continental warm summer
Temperate
Humid subtropical
Mediterranean
Steppe
Desert
Savanna
Rain forest

YUMA ★ Weather extreme location
Moscow ● Weather station
→ Warm current
→ Cold current
→ Seasonal drift during northern winter

Sea surface temperature
30°C
20
0

Average monthly temperature
Average monthly rainfall
13m Height above sea level

Climate change

In 2004 the global mean temperature was over 0.6°C higher than that at the end of the nineteenth century. Most of this warming is caused by human activities which result in a build-up of greenhouse gases, mainly carbon dioxide, allowing heat to be trapped within the atmosphere. Carbon dioxide emissions have increased since the beginning of the industrial revolution due to burning of fossil fuels, increased urbanization, population growth, deforestation and industrial pollution.

Annual climate indicators such as number of frost-free days, length of growing season, heat wave frequency, number of wet days, length of dry spells and frequency of weather extremes are used to monitor climate change. The map opposite shows how future changes in temperature will not be spread evenly around the world. Some regions will warm faster than the global average, while others will warm more slowly.

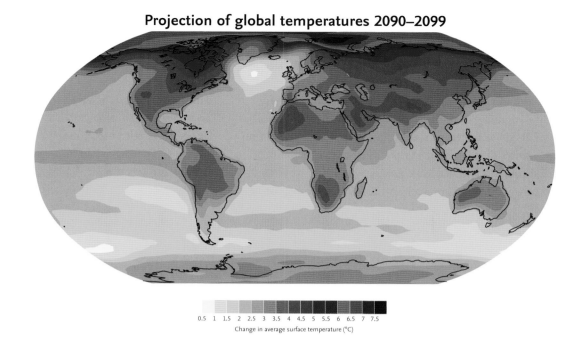

Projection of global temperatures 2090–2099

0.5 1 1.5 2 2.5 3 3.5 4 4.5 5 5.5 6 6.5 7 7.5

Change in average surface temperature (°C)

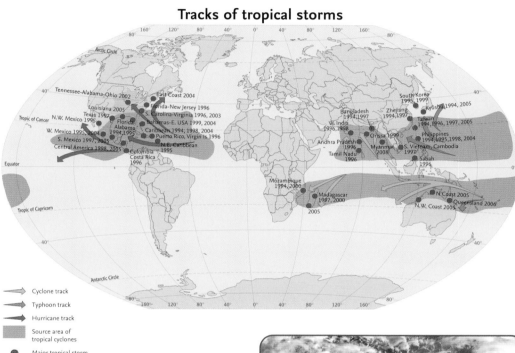

Facts

- Arctic Sea ice thickness has declined 40% in the last 40 years
- El Niño and La Niña episodes occur at irregular intervals of 2–7 years
- Sea levels are rising by one centimetre per decade
- Precipitation in the northern hemisphere is increasing
- Droughts have increased in frequency and intensity in parts of Asia and Africa

Tracks of tropical storms

Tennessee-Alabama-Ohio 2002
East Coast 2004
Louisiana 2005
Texas 1997
S. Carolina-Virginia 1996, 2003
Florida-New Jersey 1996
N.W. Mexico 1995
Florida 1996
Bahamas-E. USA 1999, 2004
Alabama 1994, 1995
Caribbean 1994, 1998, 2004
W. Mexico 1995, 2004
S. Mexico 1997, 2005
Puerto Rico, Virgin Is 1996
Central America 1998, 2005
N.E. Caribbean 1995
Colombia 1996
Costa Rica 1996
South Korea 1996, 1999
Kyushu 1994, 2005
Bangladesh 1994, 1997
Zhejiang 1994, 1997
Taiwan 1994, 1996, 1997, 2005
W. India 1996, 1998
Orissa 1999
Philippines 1994, 1995, 1998, 2004
Andhra Pradesh 1996
Myanmar 2008
S. Vietnam, Cambodia 1997
Tamil Nadu 1996
Sabah 1996
Mozambique 1994, 2000
Madagascar 1997, 2000
2005
N. Coast 2005
N.W. Coast 2006
Queensland 2006

→ Cyclone track
→ Typhoon track
→ Hurricane track
▨ Source area of tropical cyclones
● Major tropical storm (1994–2008)
▨ Tornado high risk areas

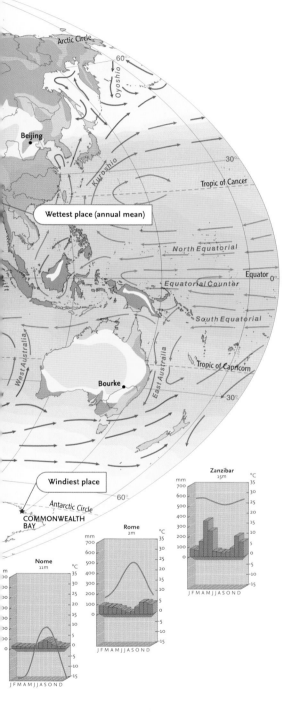

Wettest place (annual mean)

Beijing

Oyoshio
Kuroshio

Tropic of Cancer
North Equatorial
Equator
Equatorial Counter
South Equatorial
Tropic of Capricorn

West Australia
East Australia

Bourke

Windiest place

Antarctic Circle
COMMONWEALTH BAY

Nome
11m

Rome
2m

Zanzibar
15m

Tropical storms

Tropical storms are among the most powerful and destructive weather systems on Earth. Of the eighty to one hundred which develop annually over the tropical oceans, many make landfall and cause considerable damage to property and loss of life as a result of high winds and heavy rain. Although the number of tropical storms is projected to decrease, their intensity, and therefore their destructive power, is likely to increase.

Tropical storm Dina, January 2002.

Weather extremes

Highest recorded temperature	**57.8°C/136°F** Al'Azīzīyah, Libya (September 1922)
Hottest place - annual mean	**34.4°C/93.9°F** Dalol, Ethiopia
Driest place - annual mean	**0.1mm/0.004 inches** Atacama Desert, Chile
Most sunshine - annual mean	**90%** Yuma, Arizona, USA (over 4000 hours)
Lowest recorded temperature	**-89.2°C/-128.6°F** Vostok Station, Antarctica (July 1983)
Coldest place - annual mean	**-56.6°C/-69.9°F** Plateau Station, Antarctica
Wettest place - annual mean	**11 873 mm/467.4 inches** Meghalaya, India
Greatest snowfall	**31 102 mm/1 224.5 inches** Mount Rainier, Washington, USA (February 1971 – February 1972)
Windiest place	**322 km per hour/200 miles per hour** (in gales) Commonwealth Bay, Antarctica

Internet Links

● Met Office	www.metoffice.gov.uk
● BBC Weather Centre	www.bbc.co.uk/weather
● National Oceanic and Atmospheric Administration	www.noaa.gov
● National Climatic Data Center	www.ncdc.noaa.gov
● United Nations World Meteorological Organization	www.wmo.ch

The oxygen- and water-rich environment of the Earth has helped create a wide range of habitats. Forest and woodland ecosystems form the predominant natural land cover over most of the Earth's surface. Tropical rainforests are part of an intricate land-atmosphere relationship that is disturbed by land cover changes. Forests in the tropics are believed to hold most of the world's bird, animal, and plant species. Grassland, shrubland and deserts collectively cover most of the unwooded land surface, with tundra on frozen subsoil at high northern latitudes. These areas tend to have lower species diversity than most forests, with the notable exception of Mediterranean shrublands, which support some of the most diverse floras on the earth. Humans have extensively altered most grassland and shrubland areas, usually through conversion to agriculture, burning and introduction of domestic livestock. They have had less immediate impact on tundra and true desert regions, although these remain vulnerable to global climate change.

World land cover

Evergreen needleleaf forest	Grasslands
Evergreen broadleaf forest	Permanent wetlands
Deciduous needleleaf forest	Croplands
Deciduous broadleaf forest	Urban and built-up
Mixed forest	Cropland/Natural vegetation mosaic
Closed shrublands	Snow and Ice
Open shrublands	Barren or sparsely vegetated
Woody savannas	Water bodies
Savannas	

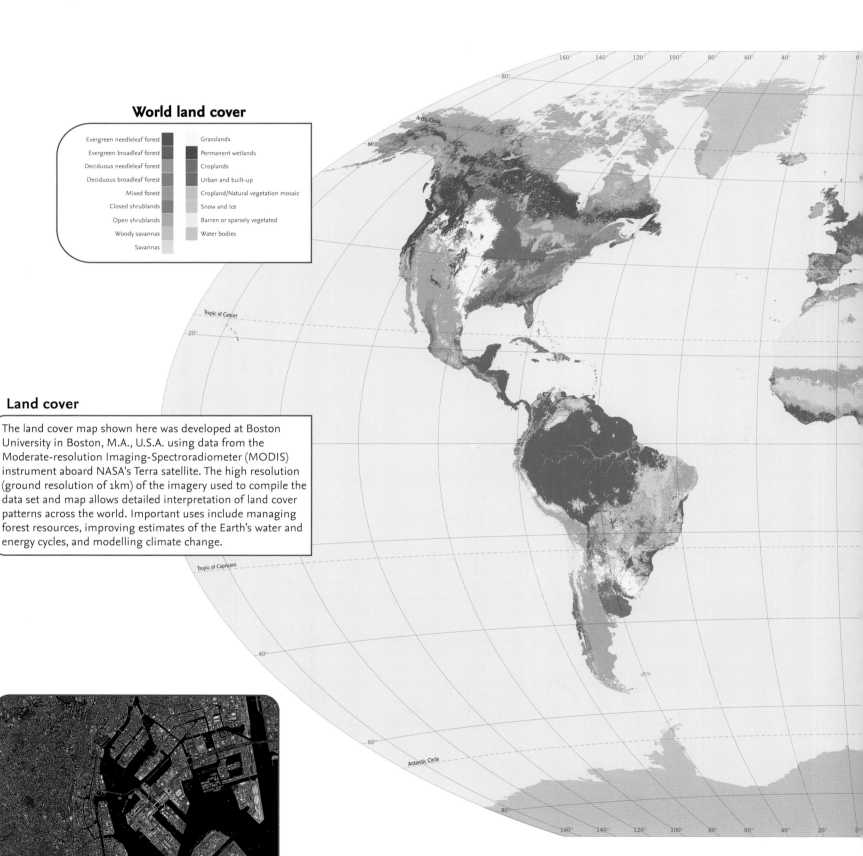

Land cover

The land cover map shown here was developed at Boston University in Boston, M.A., U.S.A. using data from the Moderate-resolution Imaging-Spectroradiometer (MODIS) instrument aboard NASA's Terra satellite. The high resolution (ground resolution of 1km) of the imagery used to compile the data set and map allows detailed interpretation of land cover patterns across the world. Important uses include managing forest resources, improving estimates of the Earth's water and energy cycles, and modelling climate change.

Urban, Tōkyō, capital of Japan and the largest city in the world.

Land cover composition and change

The continents all have different characteristics. There are extensive croplands in North America and eastern Europe, while south of the Sahara are belts of grass/shrubland which are at risk from desertification. Tropical forests are not pristine areas either as they show signs of human activity in deforestation of land for crops or grazing.

Cropland, near Consuegra, Spain.

Barren/Shrubland, Mojave Desert, California, United States of America.

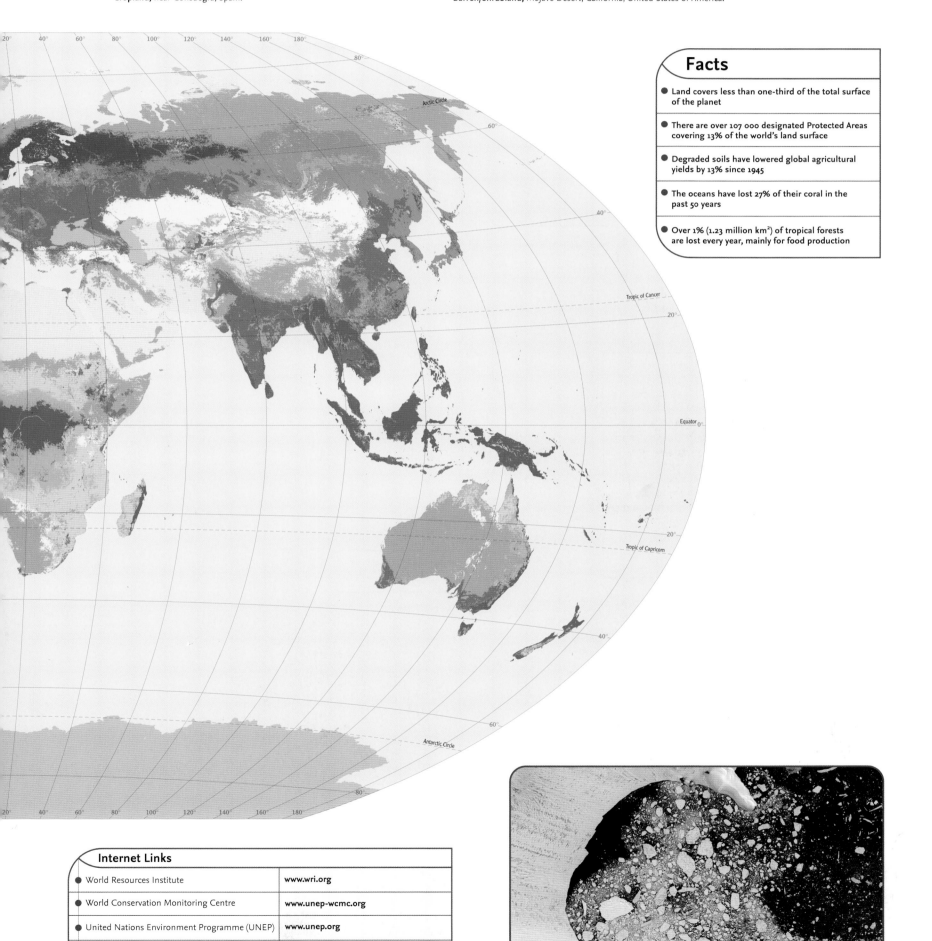

Facts

- Land covers less than one-third of the total surface of the planet

- There are over 107 000 designated Protected Areas covering 13% of the world's land surface

- Degraded soils have lowered global agricultural yields by 13% since 1945

- The oceans have lost 27% of their coral in the past 50 years

- Over 1% (1.23 million km²) of tropical forests are lost every year, mainly for food production

Internet Links

● World Resources Institute	**www.wri.org**
● World Conservation Monitoring Centre	**www.unep-wcmc.org**
● United Nations Environment Programme (UNEP)	**www.unep.org**
● IUCN The World Conservation Union	**www.iucn.org**
● Land Cover at Boston University	**www-modis.bu.edu/landcover/index.html**

Snow and ice, Larsen Ice Shelf, Antarctica.

World
Population

After increasing very slowly for most of human history, world population more than doubled in the last half century. Whereas world population did not pass the one billion mark until 1804 and took another 123 years to reach two billion in 1927, it then added the third billion in 33 years, the fourth in 14 years and the fifth in 13 years. Just twelve years later on October 12, 1999 the United Nations announced that the global population had reached the six billion mark. It is expected that another 2.5 billion people will have been added to the world's population by 2050.

World Statistics: see pages **190–196**

World population distribution
Population density, continental populations (2005)
and continental population change (2000–2005)

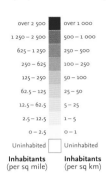

Inhabitants (per sq mile)	Inhabitants (per sq km)
over 2 500	over 1 000
1 250 – 2 500	500 – 1 000
625 – 1 250	250 – 500
250 – 625	100 – 250
125 – 250	50 – 100
62.5 – 125	25 – 50
12.5 – 62.5	5 – 25
2.5 – 12.5	1 – 5
0 – 2.5	0 – 1
Uninhabited	Uninhabited

World population change

Population growth since 1950 has been spread very unevenly between the continents. While overall numbers have been growing rapidly since 1950, a massive 89 per cent increase has taken place in the less developed regions, especially southern and eastern Asia. In contrast, Europe's population level has been almost stationary and is expected to decrease in the future. India and China alone are responsible for over one-third of current growth. Most of the highest rates of growth are to be found in Sub-Saharan Africa and, until population growth is brought under tighter control, the developing world in particular will continue to face enormous problems of supporting a rising population.

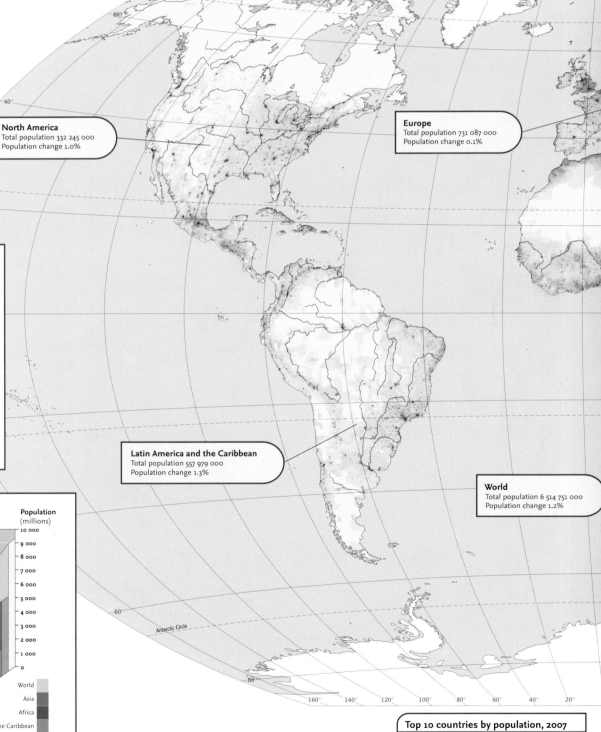

North America
Total population 332 245 000
Population change 1.0%

Europe
Total population 731 087 000
Population change 0.1%

Latin America and the Caribbean
Total population 557 979 000
Population change 1.3%

World
Total population 6 514 751 000
Population change 1.2%

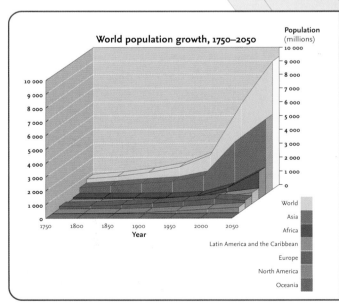

World population growth, 1750–2050

Population (millions)

World
Asia
Africa
Latin America and the Caribbean
Europe
North America
Oceania

Top 10 countries by population, 2007		
Rank	Country	Population
1	China	1 313 437 000
2	India	1 169 016 000
3	United States of America	305 826 000
4	Indonesia	231 627 000
5	Brazil	191 791 000
6	Pakistan	163 902 000
7	Bangladesh	158 669 000
8	Nigeria	148 093 000
9	Russian Federation	142 499 000
10	Japan	127 967 000

The island nation of **Singapore,** the world's second most densely populated country.

Facts

● The world's population is growing at an annual rate of 77 million people per year

● Today's population is only 5.7% of the total number of people who ever lived on the Earth

● It is expected that in 2050 there will be more people aged over 60 than children aged less than 14

● More than 90% of the 70 million inhabitants of Egypt are located around the River Nile

● India's population reached 1 billion in August 1999

Asia
Total population 3 938 020 000
Population change 1.3%

Africa
Total population 922 011 000
Population change 2.3%

Oceania
Total population 33 410 000
Population change 1.4%

Top 10 countries by population density, 2007
(persons per square kilometre)

Rank	Country	Population density
1	**Bangladesh**	1 102
2	Taiwan	632
3	**South Korea**	486
4	Netherlands	395
5	**India**	381
6	Belgium	343
7	**Japan**	339
8	Sri Lanka	294
9	**Philippines**	293
10	Vietnam	265

*Only countries with a population of over 10 million are considered

Kuna Indians inhabit this congested island off the north coast of Panama.

World
Urbanization and Cities

The world is becoming increasingly urban but the level of urbanization varies greatly between and within continents. At the beginning of the twentieth century only fourteen per cent of the world's population was urban and by 1950 this had increased to thirty per cent. In the more developed regions and in Latin America and the Caribbean over seventy per cent of the population is urban while in Africa and Asia the figure is forty per cent. In recent decades urban growth has increased rapidly to fifty per cent and there are now nearly 400 cities with over 1 000 000 inhabitants. It is in the developing regions that the most rapid increases are taking place and it is expected that by 2030 over half of urban dwellers worldwide will live in Asia. Migration from the countryside to the city in the search for better job opportunities is the main factor in urban growth.

World Statistics: see pages **190–196**

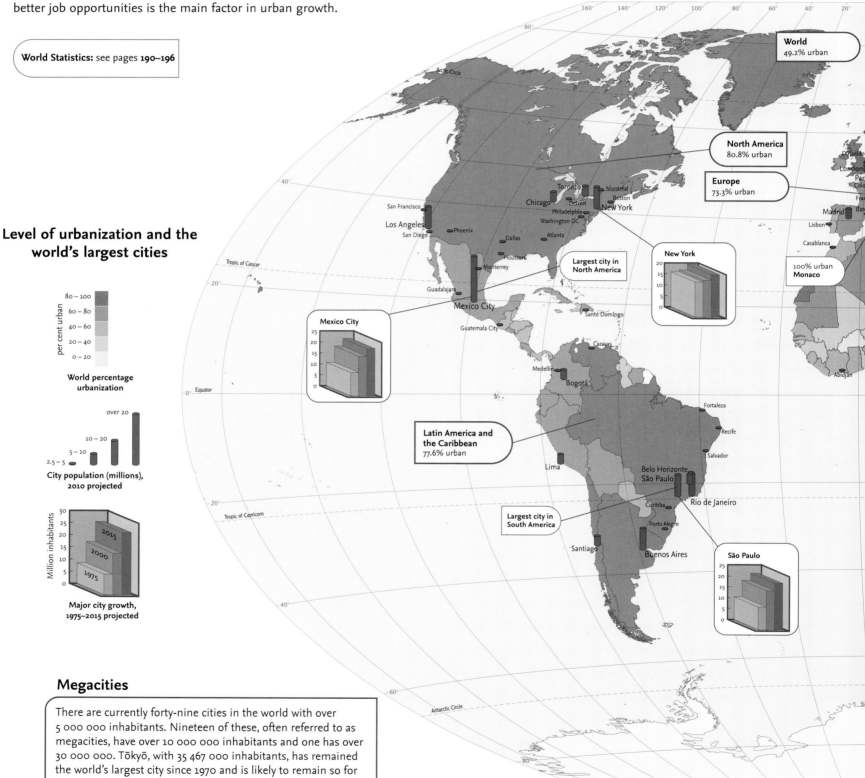

Level of urbanization and the world's largest cities

per cent urban

- 80 – 100
- 60 – 80
- 40 – 60
- 20 – 40
- 0 – 20

World percentage urbanization

over 20
10 – 20
5 – 10
2.5 – 5

City population (millions), 2010 projected

Million inhabitants

30
25
20
15
10
5
0

2015
2000
1975

Major city growth, 1975–2015 projected

Megacities

There are currently forty-nine cities in the world with over 5 000 000 inhabitants. Nineteen of these, often referred to as megacities, have over 10 000 000 inhabitants and one has over 30 000 000. Tōkyō, with 35 467 000 inhabitants, has remained the world's largest city since 1970 and is likely to remain so for the next decade. Other cities expected to grow to over 20 000 000 by 2015 are Mumbai, São Paulo, Delhi and Mexico City. Eleven of the world's megacities are in Asia, all of them having over 10 000 000 inhabitants.

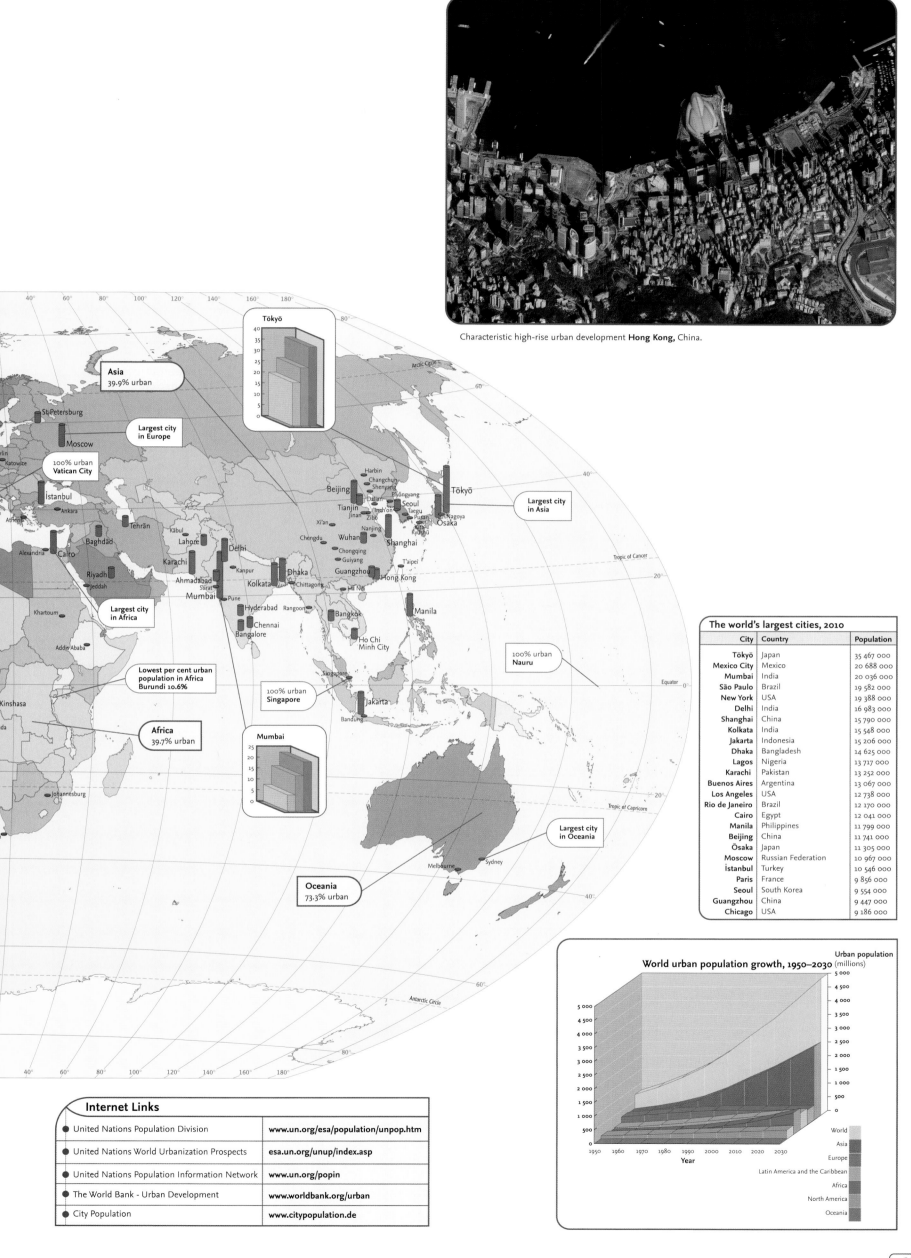

Characteristic high-rise urban development **Hong Kong,** China.

Asia
39.9% urban

Largest city in Europe

100% urban Vatican City

Largest city in Asia

Largest city in Africa

Lowest per cent urban population in Africa Burundi 10.6%

100% urban Nauru

100% urban Singapore

Africa
39.7% urban

Oceania
73.3% urban

Largest city in Oceania

Tōkyō

Mumbai

The world's largest cities, 2010

City	Country	Population
Tōkyō	Japan	35 467 000
Mexico City	Mexico	20 688 000
Mumbai	India	20 036 000
São Paulo	Brazil	19 582 000
New York	USA	19 388 000
Delhi	India	16 983 000
Shanghai	China	15 790 000
Kolkata	India	15 548 000
Jakarta	Indonesia	15 206 000
Dhaka	Bangladesh	14 625 000
Lagos	Nigeria	13 717 000
Karachi	Pakistan	13 252 000
Buenos Aires	Argentina	13 067 000
Los Angeles	USA	12 738 000
Rio de Janeiro	Brazil	12 170 000
Cairo	Egypt	12 041 000
Manila	Philippines	11 799 000
Beijing	China	11 741 000
Ōsaka	Japan	11 305 000
Moscow	Russian Federation	10 967 000
İstanbul	Turkey	10 546 000
Paris	France	9 856 000
Seoul	South Korea	9 554 000
Guangzhou	China	9 447 000
Chicago	USA	9 186 000

World urban population growth, 1950–2030

Urban population (millions)

World
Asia
Europe
Latin America and the Caribbean
Africa
North America
Oceania

Internet Links

United Nations Population Division	www.un.org/esa/population/unpop.htm
United Nations World Urbanization Prospects	esa.un.org/unup/index.asp
United Nations Population Information Network	www.un.org/popin
The World Bank - Urban Development	www.worldbank.org/urban
City Population	www.citypopulation.de

Increased availability and ownership of telecommunications equipment since the beginning of the 1970s has aided the globalization of the world economy. Over half of the world's fixed telephone lines have been installed since the mid-1980s and the majority of the world's internet hosts have come on line since 1997. There are now over one billion fixed telephone lines in the world. The number of mobile cellular subscribers has grown dramatically from sixteen million in 1991 to well over one billion today.

The internet is the fastest growing communications network of all time. It is relatively cheap and now links over 140 million host computers globally. Its growth has resulted in the emergence of hundreds of Internet Service Providers (ISPs) and internet traffic is now doubling every six months. In 1993 the number of internet users was estimated to be just under ten million, there are now over half a billion.

Facts

- The first transatlantic telegraph cable came into operation in 1858

- Fibre-optic cables can now carry approximately 20 million simultaneous telephone calls

- The internet is the fastest growing communications network of all time and now has over 267 million host computers

- Bermuda has the world's highest density of internet and broadband subscribers

- Sputnik, the world's first artificial satellite, was launched in 1957

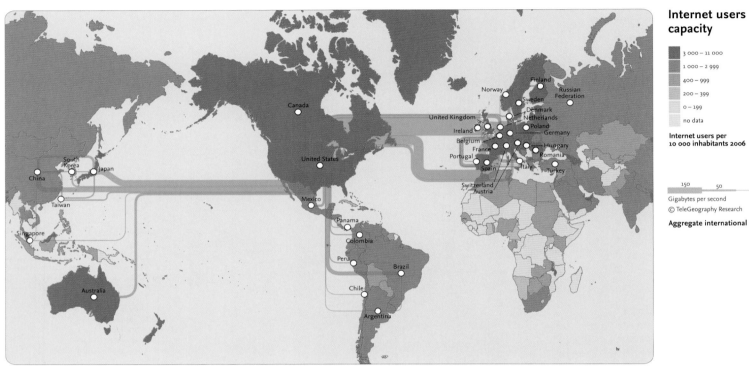

Internet users and capacity

Internet users per 10 000 inhabitants 2006

- 3 000 – 11 000
- 1 000 – 2 999
- 400 – 999
- 200 – 399
- 0 – 199
- no data

150   50   15

Gigabytes per second

© TeleGeography Research   www.telegeography.com

Aggregate international internet capacity 2007

The Internet

The Internet is a global network of millions of computers around the world, all capable of being connected to each other. Internet Service Providers (ISPs) provide access via 'host' computers, of which there are now over 267 million. It has become a vital means of communication and data transfer for businesses, governments and financial and academic institutions, with a steadily increasing proportion of business transactions being carried out on-line. Personal use of the Internet – particularly for access to the World Wide Web information network, and for e-mail communication – has increased enormously and there are now estimated to be over half a billion users worldwide.

Top Broadband Economies 2006
Countries with the highest broadband penetration rate – subscribers per 100 inhabitants

	Top Economies	Rate
1	Denmark	29.3
2	Netherlands	28.8
3	Iceland	27.3
4	South Korea	26.4
5	Switzerland	26.2
6	Finland	25.0
7	Norway	24.6
8	Sweden	22.7
9	Canada	22.4
10	United Kingdom	19.4
11	Belgium	19.3
12	USA	19.2
13	Japan	19.0
14	Luxembourg	17.9
15	France	17.7
16	Austria	17.7
17	Australia	17.4
18	Germany	15.1
19	Spain	13.6
20	Italy	13.2

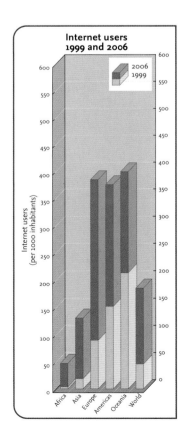

Internet users 1999 and 2006

2006
1999

Internet users (per 1000 inhabitants)

Africa Asia Europe Americas Oceania World

Internet Links

Internet Links	
OECD Information and Communication Technologies	www.oecd.org
TeleGeography Research	www.telegeography.com
International Telecommunication Union	www.itu.int

Satellite communications

International telecommunications use either fibre-optic cables or satellites as transmission media. Although cables carry the vast majority of traffic around the world, communications satellites are important for person-to-person communication, including cellular telephones, and for broadcasting. The positions of communications satellites are critical to their use, and reflect the demand for such communications in each part of the world. Such satellites are placed in 'geostationary' orbit 36 000 km above the equator. This means that they move at the same speed as the earth and remain fixed above a single point on the earth's surface.

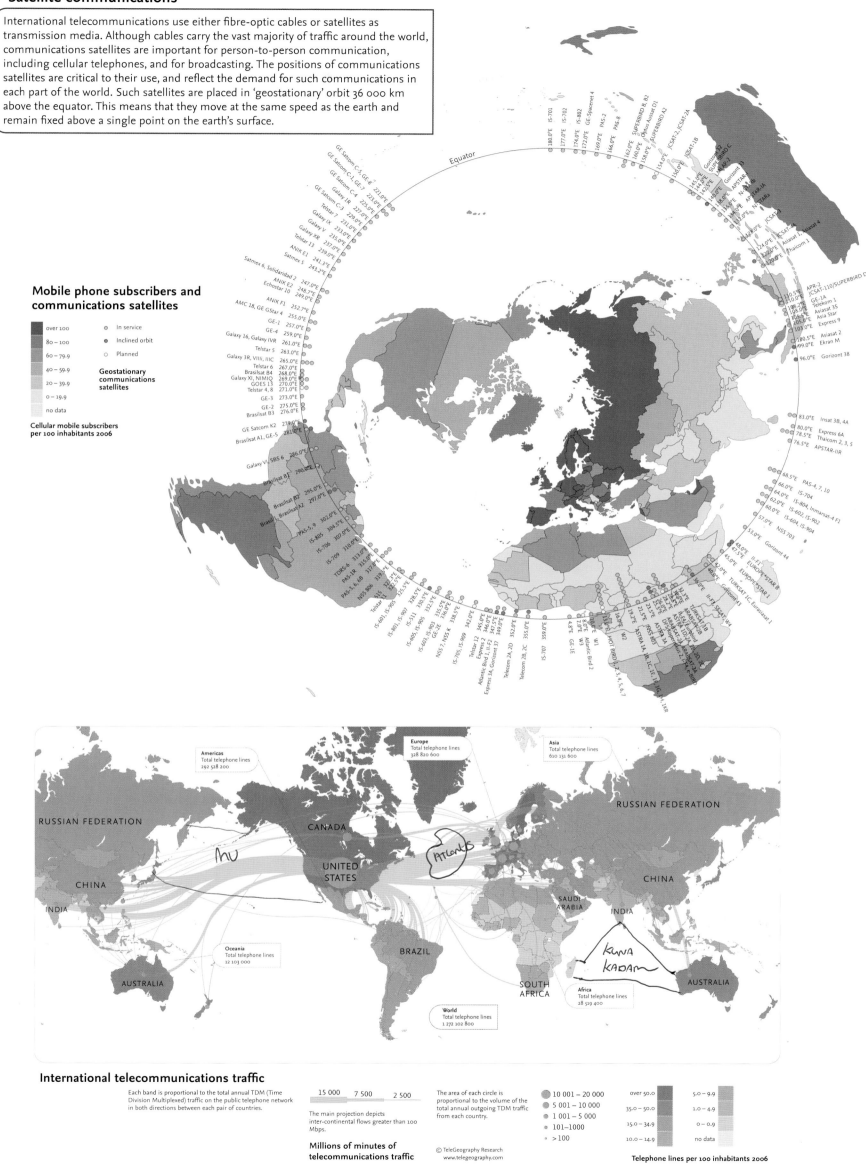

Mobile phone subscribers and communications satellites

- over 100
- 80 – 100
- 60 – 79.9
- 40 – 59.9
- 20 – 39.9
- 0 – 19.9
- no data

- ◉ In service
- ● Inclined orbit
- ○ Planned

Geostationary communications satellites

Cellular mobile subscribers per 100 inhabitants 2006

International telecommunications traffic

Each band is proportional to the total annual TDM (Time Division Multiplexed) traffic on the public telephone network in both directions between each pair of countries.

15 000 7 500 2 500

The main projection depicts inter-continental flows greater than 100 Mbps.

Millions of minutes of telecommunications traffic

The area of each circle is proportional to the volume of the total annual outgoing TDM traffic from each country.

- 10 001 – 20 000
- 5 001 – 10 000
- 1 001 – 5 000
- 101–1000
- >100

- over 50.0
- 35.0 – 50.0
- 15.0 – 34.9
- 10.0–14.9
- 5.0 – 9.9
- 1.0 – 4.9
- 0 – 0.9
- no data

© TeleGeography Research
www.telegeography.com

Telephone lines per 100 inhabitants 2006

Americas
Total telephone lines
292 528 200

Europe
Total telephone lines
328 820 600

Asia
Total telephone lines
610 131 600

Oceania
Total telephone lines
12 103 000

Africa
Total telephone lines
28 519 400

World
Total telephone lines
1 272 102 800

RUSSIAN FEDERATION

CANADA

UNITED STATES

CHINA

INDIA

BRAZIL

SOUTH AFRICA

SAUDI ARABIA

AUSTRALIA

Countries are often judged on their level of economic development, but national and personal wealth are not the only measures of a country's status. Numerous other indicators can give a better picture of the overall level of development and standard of living achieved by a country. The availability and standard of health services, levels of educational provision and attainment, levels of nutrition, water supply, life expectancy and mortality rates are just some of the factors which can be measured to assess and compare countries.

While nations strive to improve their economies, and hopefully also to improve the standard of living of their citizens, the measurement of such indicators often exposes great discrepancies between the countries of the 'developed' world and those of the 'less developed' world. They also show great variations within continents and regions and at the same time can hide great inequalities within countries.

World Statistics: see pages 190–196

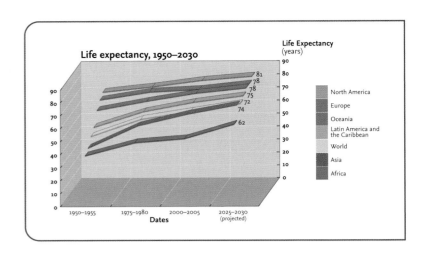

Life expectancy, 1950–2030

Life Expectancy (years)

North America
Europe
Oceania
Latin America and the Caribbean
World
Asia
Africa

Under-five mortality rate, 2006 and life expectancy by continent, 2005–2010

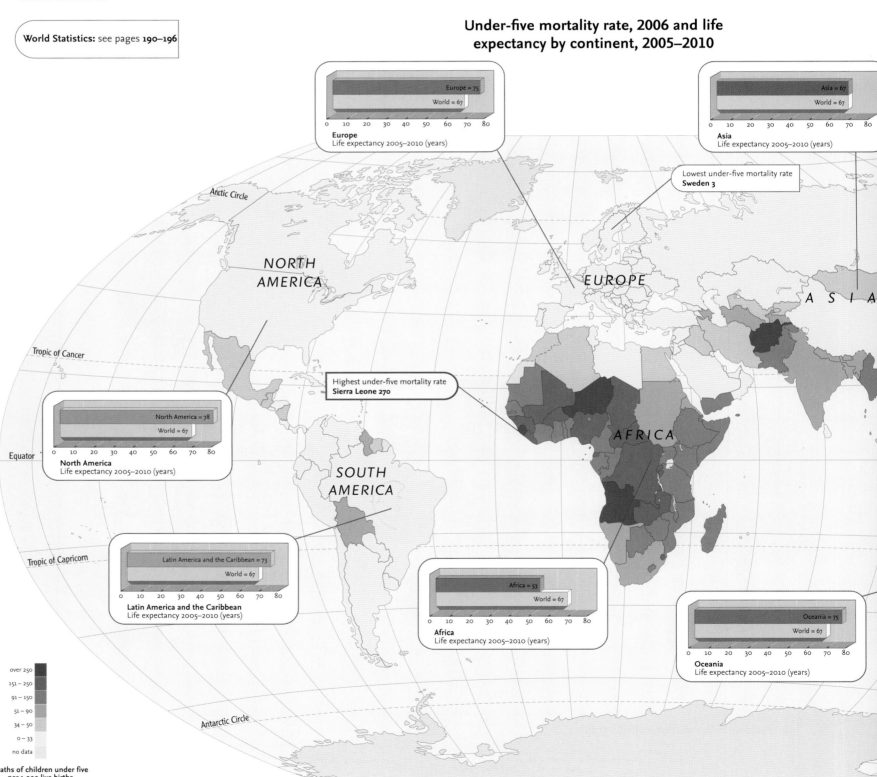

Europe = 75
World = 67
Europe
Life expectancy 2005–2010 (years)

Asia = 67
World = 67
Asia
Life expectancy 2005–2010 (years)

Lowest under-five mortality rate
Sweden 3

North America = 78
World = 67
North America
Life expectancy 2005–2010 (years)

Highest under-five mortality rate
Sierra Leone 270

Latin America and the Caribbean = 73
World = 67
Latin America and the Caribbean
Life expectancy 2005–2010 (years)

Africa = 53
World = 67
Africa
Life expectancy 2005–2010 (years)

Oceania = 75
World = 67
Oceania
Life expectancy 2005–2010 (years)

NORTH AMERICA
EUROPE
ASIA
SOUTH AMERICA
AFRICA

Arctic Circle
Tropic of Cancer
Equator
Tropic of Capricorn
Antarctic Circle

over 250
151 – 250
91 – 150
51 – 90
34 – 50
0 – 33
no data

Deaths of children under five per 1 000 live births

Facts

- Of the 11 countries with under-5 mortality rates of more than 200 per 1000 live births, 10 are in Africa

- Many western countries believe they have achieved satisfactory levels of education and no longer closely monitor levels of literacy

- Children born in Nepal have only a 12% chance of their birth being attended by trained health personnel; for most European countries the figure is 100%

- The illiteracy rate among young women in the Middle East and north Africa is almost twice the rate for young men

Health and education

Perhaps the most important indicators used for measuring the level of national development are those relating to health and education. Both of these key areas are vital to the future development of a country, and if there are concerns in standards attained in either (or worse, in both) of these, then they may indicate fundamental problems within the country concerned. The ability to read and write (literacy) is seen as vital in educating people and encouraging development, while easy access to appropriate health services and specialists is an important requirement in maintaining satisfactory levels of basic health.

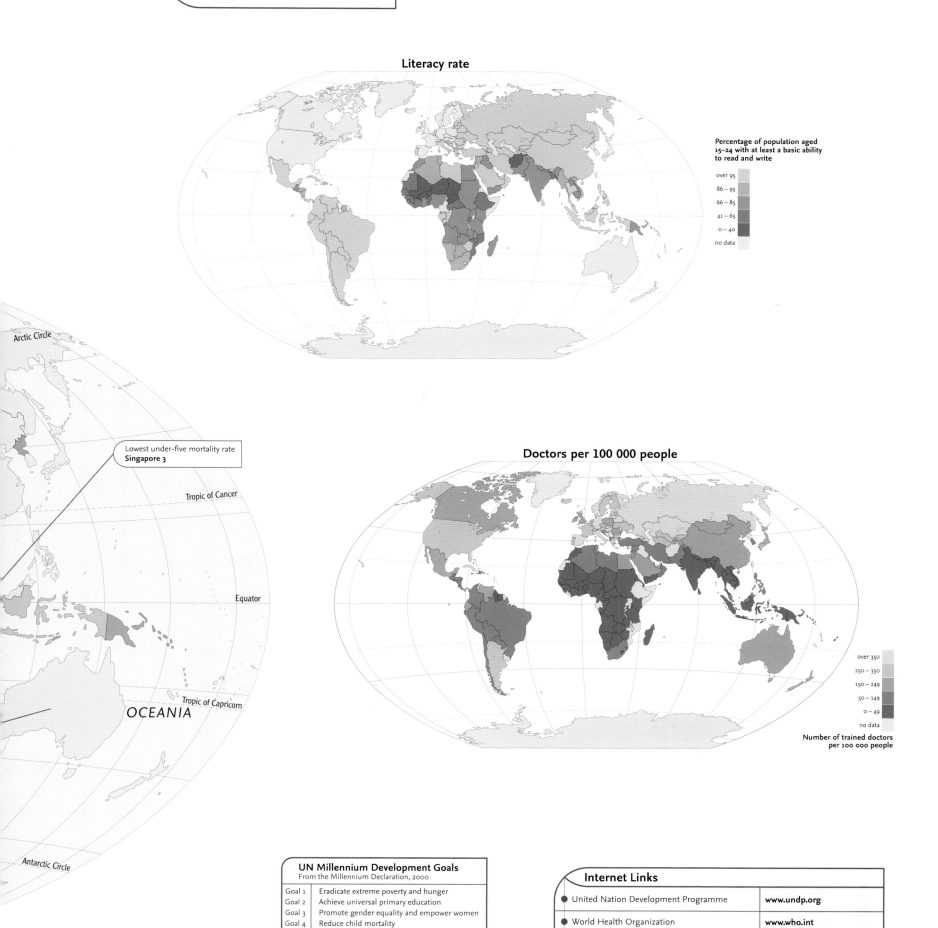

Literacy rate

Percentage of population aged 15–24 with at least a basic ability to read and write

- over 95
- 86 – 95
- 66 – 85
- 41 – 65
- 0 – 40
- no data

Lowest under-five mortality rate
Singapore 3

Arctic Circle
Tropic of Cancer
Equator
Tropic of Capricorn
OCEANIA
Antarctic Circle

Doctors per 100 000 people

- over 350
- 250 – 350
- 150 – 249
- 50 – 149
- 0 – 49
- no data

Number of trained doctors per 100 000 people

UN Millennium Development Goals
From the Millennium Declaration, 2000

Goal 1	Eradicate extreme poverty and hunger
Goal 2	Achieve universal primary education
Goal 3	Promote gender equality and empower women
Goal 4	Reduce child mortality
Goal 5	Improve maternal health
Goal 6	Combat HIV/AIDS, malaria and other diseases
Goal 7	Ensure environmental sustainability
Goal 8	Develop a global partnership for development

Internet Links

United Nation Development Programme	**www.undp.org**
World Health Organization	**www.who.int**
United Nations Statistics Division	**unstats.un.org**
United Nations Millennium Development Goals	**www.un.org/millenniumgoals**

The globalization of the economy is making the world appear a smaller place. However, this shrinkage is an uneven process. Countries are being included in and excluded from the global economy to differing degrees. The wealthy countries of the developed world, with their market-led economies, access to productive new technologies and international markets, dominate the world economic system. Great inequalities exist between and within countries. There may also be discrepancies between social groups within countries due to gender and ethnic divisions. Differences between countries are evident by looking at overall wealth on a national and individual level.

World Statistics: see pages 190–196

Facts

- The City, one of 33 London boroughs, is the world's largest financial centre and contains Europe's biggest stock market

- Half the world's population earns only 5% of the world's wealth

- During the second half of the 20th century rich countries gave over US$1 trillion in aid

- For every £1 in grant aid to developing countries, more than £13 comes back in debt repayments

- On average, The World Bank distributes US$30 billion each year between 100 countries

Personal wealth

A poverty line set at $1 a day has been accepted as the working definition of extreme poverty in low-income countries. It is estimated that a total of 1.2 billion people live below that poverty line. This indicator has also been adopted by the United Nations in relation to their Millennium Development Goals. The United Nations goal is to halve the proportion of people living on less than $1 a day in 1990 to 14.5 per cent by 2015. Today, over 80 per cent of the total population of Ethiopia, Uganda and Nicaragua live on less than this amount.

28 001 – 72 000
16 001 – 28 000
9 001 – 16 000
1 751 – 9 000
751 – 1 750
0 – 750
no data

US$

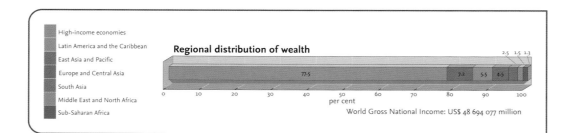

High-income economies
Latin America and the Caribbean
East Asia and Pacific
Europe and Central Asia
South Asia
Middle East and North Africa
Sub-Saharan Africa

Regional distribution of wealth

77.5   7.2   5.5   4.5   2.5 1.5 1.3

0   10   20   30   40   50   60   70   80   90   100
per cent

World Gross National Income: US$ 48 694 077 million

Percentage of population living on less than $1 a day

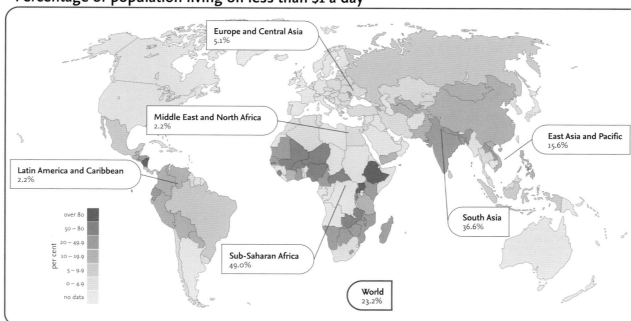

Europe and Central Asia
5.1%

Middle East and North Africa
2.2%

East Asia and Pacific
15.6%

Latin America and Caribbean
2.2%

South Asia
36.6%

Sub-Saharan Africa
49.0%

over 80
50 – 80
20 – 49.9
10 – 19.9
5 – 9.9
0 – 4.9
no data

per cent

World
23.2%

The world's biggest companies		
Rank	Name	Sales (US$ millions)
1	Wal-Mart Stores	351 139
2	ExxonMobil	347 254
3	Royal Dutch/Shell Group	318 845
4	BP	274 316
5	General Motors	207 349
6	Toyota Motor	204 746
7	Chevron	200 567
8	DaimlerChrysler	190 191
9	ConocoPhillips	172 451
10	Total	168 357

Rural homesteads, **Sudan** – most of the world's poorest countries are in Africa.

Gross National Income per capita

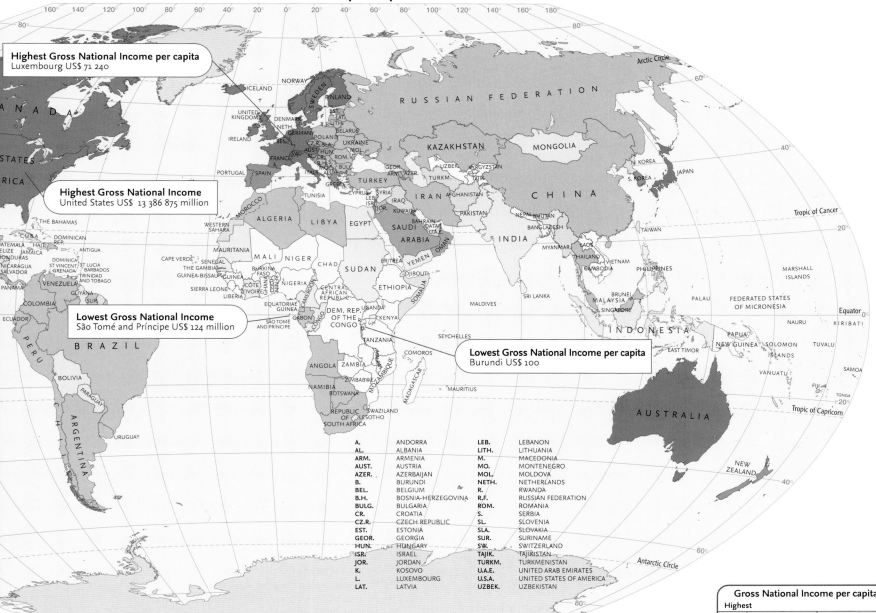

Highest Gross National Income per capita
Luxembourg US$ 71 240

Highest Gross National Income
United States US$ 13 386 875 million

Lowest Gross National Income
São Tomé and Príncipe US$ 124 million

Lowest Gross National Income per capita
Burundi US$ 100

A.	ANDORRA	LEB.	LEBANON
AL.	ALBANIA	LITH.	LITHUANIA
ARM.	ARMENIA	M.	MACEDONIA
AUST.	AUSTRIA	MO.	MONTENEGRO
AZER.	AZERBAIJAN	MOL.	MOLDOVA
B.	BURUNDI	NETH.	NETHERLANDS
BEL.	BELGIUM	R.	RWANDA
B.H.	BOSNIA-HERZEGOVINA	R.F.	RUSSIAN FEDERATION
BULG.	BULGARIA	ROM.	ROMANIA
CR.	CROATIA	S.	SERBIA
CZ.R.	CZECH REPUBLIC	SL.	SLOVENIA
EST.	ESTONIA	SLA.	SLOVAKIA
GEOR.	GEORGIA	SUR.	SURINAME
HUN.	HUNGARY	SW.	SWITZERLAND
ISR.	ISRAEL	TAJIK.	TAJIKISTAN
JOR.	JORDAN	TURKM.	TURKMENISTAN
K.	KOSOVO	U.A.E.	UNITED ARAB EMIRATES
L.	LUXEMBOURG	U.S.A.	UNITED STATES OF AMERICA
LAT.	LATVIA	UZBEK.	UZBEKISTAN

Measuring wealth

One of the indicators used to determine a country's wealth is its Gross National Income (GNI). This gives a broad measure of an economy's performance. This is the value of the final output of goods and services produced by a country plus net income from non-resident sources. The total GNI is divided by the country's population to give an average figure of the GNI per capita. From this it is evident that the developed countries dominate the world economy with the United States having the highest GNI. China is a growing world economic player with the fourth highest GNI figure and a relatively high GNI per capita (US$2 000) in proportion to its huge population.

Internet Links	
● United Nations Statistics Division	**unstats.un.org**
● The World Bank	**www.worldbank.org**
● International Monetary Fund	**www.imf.org**
● Organisation for Economic Co-operation and Development	**www.oecd.org**

Gross National Income per capita		
Highest		
Rank	Country	US$
1	Luxembourg	71 240
2	Norway	68 440
3	Switzerland	58 050
4	Denmark	52 110
5	Iceland	49 960
6	San Marino	45 130
7	Ireland	44 830
8	United States	44 710
9	Sweden	43 530
10	Netherlands	43 050
Lowest		
Rank	Country	US$
156	Niger	270
157	Rwanda	250
158	Sierra Leone	240
159	Malawi	230
160=	Eritrea	190
160=	Guinea-Bissau	190
161	Ethiopia	170
162=	Dem. Rep. Congo	130
162=	Liberia	130
163	Burundi	100

Geo-political issues shape the countries of the world and the current political situation in many parts of the world reflects a long history of armed conflict. Since the Second World War conflicts have been fairly localized, but there are numerous 'flash points' where factors such as territorial claims, ideology, religion, ethnicity and access to resources can cause friction between two or more countries. Such factors also lie behind the recent growth in global terrorism.

Military expenditure can take up a disproportionate amount of a country's wealth – Eritrea, with a Gross National Income (GNI) per capita of only US$190 spends twenty-four per cent of its total GDP on military activity. There is an encouraging trend towards wider international cooperation, mainly through the United Nations (UN) and the North Atlantic Treaty Organization (NATO), to prevent escalation of conflicts and on peacekeeping missions.

Military spending, 2006 and conflicts, 1946–2003

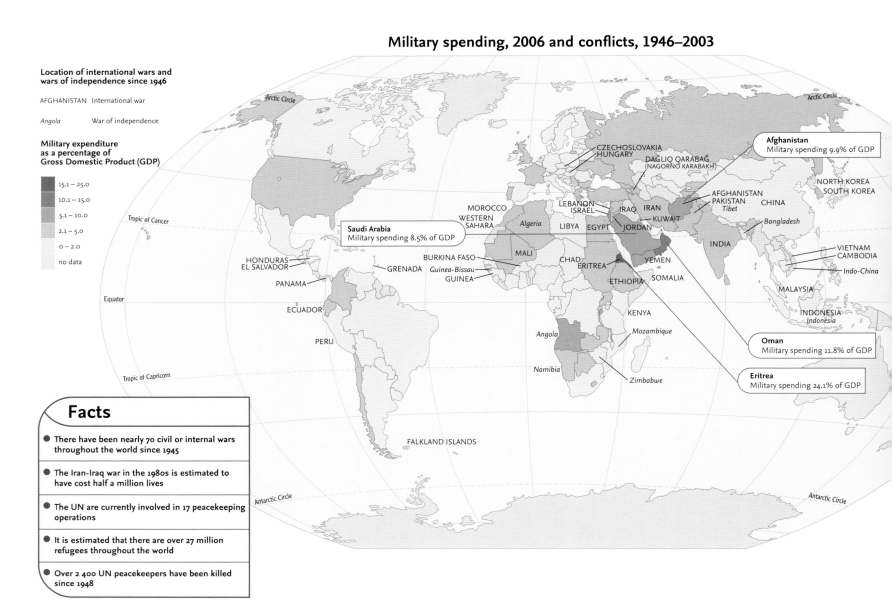

Location of international wars and wars of independence since 1946

AFGHANISTAN   International war

Angola   War of independence

Military expenditure as a percentage of Gross Domestic Product (GDP)

- 15.1 – 25.0
- 10.1 – 15.0
- 5.1 – 10.0
- 2.1 – 5.0
- 0 – 2.0
- no data

Saudi Arabia
Military spending 8.5% of GDP

Afghanistan
Military spending 9.9% of GDP

Oman
Military spending 11.8% of GDP

Eritrea
Military spending 24.1% of GDP

Facts

- There have been nearly 70 civil or internal wars throughout the world since 1945

- The Iran-Iraq war in the 1980s is estimated to have cost half a million lives

- The UN are currently involved in 17 peacekeeping operations

- It is estimated that there are over 27 million refugees throughout the world

- Over 2 400 UN peacekeepers have been killed since 1948

Spratly Islands

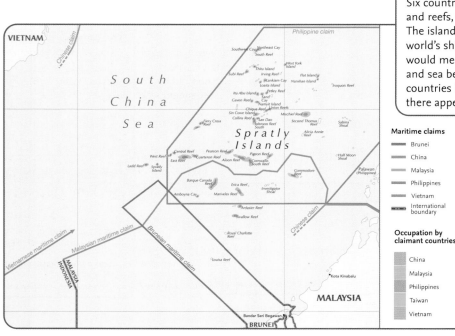

The Spratly Islands in the South China Sea are an excellent example of how apparently insignificant pieces of land can become the source of conflict. Six countries claim ownership of some or all of these remote, tiny islands and reefs, the largest of which covers less than half a square kilometre. The islands are strategically important – approximately a quarter of all the world's shipping trade passes through the area – and ownership of the group would mean access to 250 000 square kilometres of valuable fishing grounds and sea bed believed to be rich in oil and gas reserves. Five of the claimant countries have occupied individual islands to endorse their claims, although there appears little prospect of international agreement on ownership.

Maritime claims
- Brunei
- China
- Malaysia
- Philippines
- Vietnam
- International boundary

Occupation by claimant countries
- China
- Malaysia
- Philippines
- Taiwan
- Vietnam

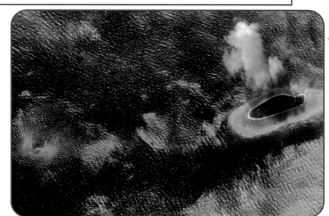

A small island and reef in the disputed **Spratly Islands** in the South China Sea.

United Nations peacekeeping

United Nations peacekeeping was developed by the Organization as a way to help countries torn by conflict create the conditions for lasting peace. The first UN peacekeeping mission was established in 1948, when the Security Council authorized the deployment of UN military observers to the Middle East to monitor the Armistice Agreement between Israel and its Arab neighbours. Since then, there have been a total of 63 UN peacekeeping operations around the world.

UN peacekeeping goals were primarily limited to maintaining ceasefires and stabilizing situations on the ground, so that efforts could be made at the political level to resolve the conflict by peaceful means. Today's peacekeepers undertake a wide variety of complex tasks, from helping to build sustainable institutions of governance, to human rights monitoring, to security sector reform, to the disarmament, demobilization and reintegration of former combatants.

United Nations peacekeeping operations 1948–2008
Current peacekeeping operations are named on the map

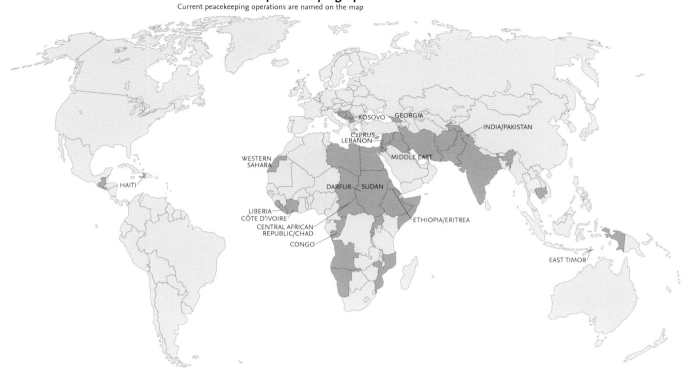

Middle East politics
Changing boundaries in Israel/Palestine since 1922

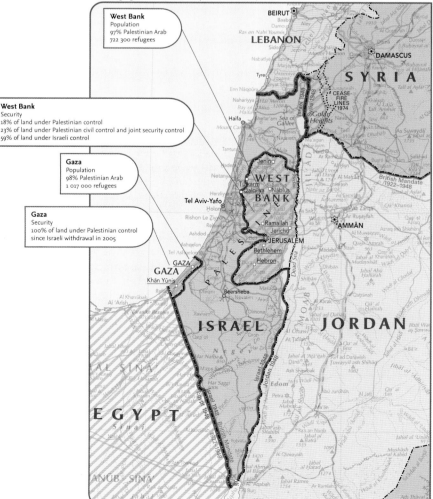

West Bank
Population
97% Palestinian Arab
722 300 refugees

West Bank
Security
18% of land under Palestinian control
23% of land under Palestinian civil control and joint security control
59% of land under Israeli control

Gaza
Population
98% Palestinian Arab
1 017 000 refugees

Gaza
Security
100% of land under Palestinian control
since Israeli withdrawal in 2005

The Middle East

The on-going Israeli/Palestinian conflict reflects decades of unrest in the region of Palestine which, after the First World War, was placed under British control. In 1947 the United Nations (UN) proposed a partitioning into separate Jewish and Arab states – a plan which was rejected by the Palestinians and by the Arab states in the region. When Britain withdrew in 1948, Israel declared its independence. This led to an Arab-Israeli war which left Israel with more land than originally proposed under the UN plan. Hundreds of thousands of Palestinians were forced out of their homeland and became refugees, mainly in Jordan and Lebanon. The 6-Day War in 1967 resulted in Israel taking possession of Sinai and Gaza from Egypt, West Bank from Jordan, and the Golan Heights from Syria. Sinai was subsequently returned to Egypt and Gaza has been under Palestinian control since Israel withdrew in 2005. The West Bank remains occupied by Israel. The situation is complex with poor prospects for peace and for mutually acceptable independent states being established.

Internet Links	
● United Nations Peace and Security	**www.un.org/peace**
● United Nations Refugee Agency	**www.unhcr.org**
● NATO	**www.nato.int**
● BBC News	**news.bbc.co.uk**
● International Boundaries Research Unit	**www.dur.ac.uk/ibru**
● International Peace Research Institute	**www.prio.no**

With the process of globalization has come an increased awareness of, and direct interest in, issues which have global implications. Social issues can now affect large parts of the world and can impact on large sections of society. Perhaps the current issues of greatest concern are those of national security, including the problem of international terrorism, health, crime and natural resources. The three issues highlighted here reflect this and are of immediate concern.

The international drugs trade, and the crimes commonly associated with it, can impact on society and individuals in devastating ways; scarcity of water resources and lack of access to safe drinking water can have major economic implications and cause severe health problems; and the AIDS epidemic is having disastrous consequences in large parts of the world, particularly in sub-Saharan Africa.

Soldiers in **Colombia**, a major producer of cocaine, destroy an illegal drug processing laboratory.

The drugs trade

The international trade in illegal drugs is estimated to be worth over US$400 billion. While it may be a lucrative business for the criminals involved, the effects of the drugs on individual users and on society in general can be devastating. Patterns of drug production and abuse vary, but there are clear centres for the production of the most harmful drugs – the opiates (opium, morphine and heroin) and cocaine. The 'Golden Triangle' of Laos, Myanmar and Thailand, and western South America respectively are the main producing areas for these drugs. Significant efforts are expended to counter the drugs trade, and there have been signs recently of downward trends in the production of heroin and cocaine.

The international drugs trade

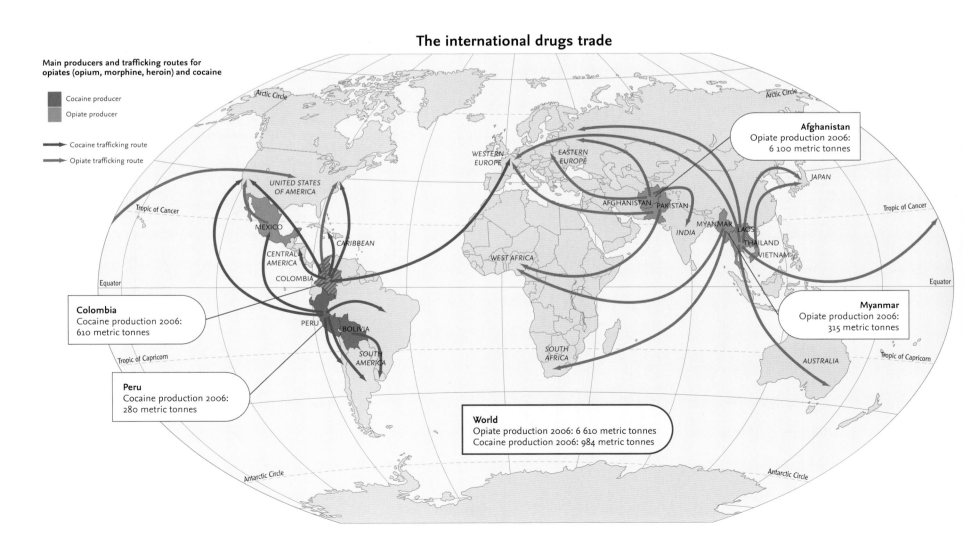

Main producers and trafficking routes for opiates (opium, morphine, heroin) and cocaine

- Cocaine producer
- Opiate producer

→ Cocaine trafficking route
→ Opiate trafficking route

Afghanistan
Opiate production 2006: 6 100 metric tonnes

Colombia
Cocaine production 2006: 610 metric tonnes

Peru
Cocaine production 2006: 280 metric tonnes

World
Opiate production 2006: 6 610 metric tonnes
Cocaine production 2006: 984 metric tonnes

Myanmar
Opiate production 2006: 315 metric tonnes

AIDS epidemic

With over 30 million people living with HIV/AIDS (Human Immunodeficiency Virus/Acquired Immune Deficiency Syndrome) and more than 20 million deaths from the disease, the AIDS epidemic poses one of the biggest threats to public health. The UNAIDS project estimated that 2.5 million people were newly infected in 2007 and that 2.1 million AIDS sufferers died. Estimates into the future look bleak, especially for poorer developing countries where an additional 45 million people are likely to become infected by 2010. The human cost is huge. As well as the death count itself, more than 11 million African children, half of whom are between the ages of 10 and 14, have been orphaned as a result of the disease.

Population living with HIV/AIDS, 2005

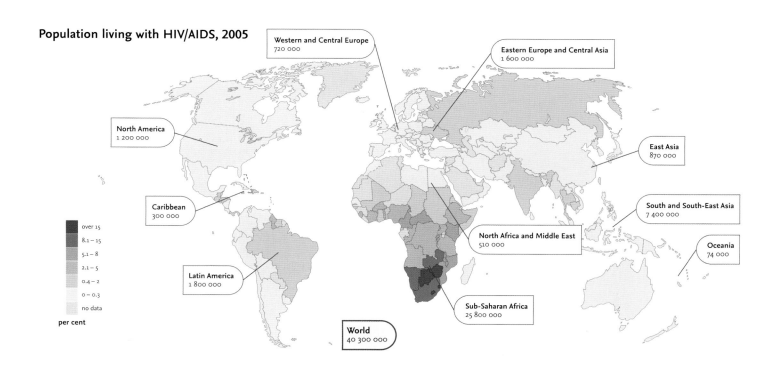

Western and Central Europe
720 000

Eastern Europe and Central Asia
1 600 000

North America
1 200 000

East Asia
870 000

Caribbean
300 000

South and South-East Asia
7 400 000

North Africa and Middle East
510 000

Oceania
74 000

Latin America
1 800 000

Sub-Saharan Africa
25 800 000

World
40 300 000

over 15
8.1 – 15
5.1 – 8
2.1 – 5
0.4 – 2
0 – 0.3
no data

per cent

Water resources

Water is one of the fundamental requirements of life, and yet in some countries it is becoming more scarce due to increasing population and climate change. Safe drinking water, basic hygiene, health education and sanitation facilities are often virtually nonexistent for impoverished people in developing countries throughout the world. WHO/UNICEF estimate that the combination of these conditions results in 6 000 deaths every day, most of these being children. Currently over 1.2 billion people drink untreated water and expose themselves to serious health risks, while political struggles over diminishing water resources are increasingly likely to be the cause of international conflict.

Domestic use of **untreated water** in Kathmandu, Nepal

Access to safe water, 2004
Percentage of population using improved drinking water

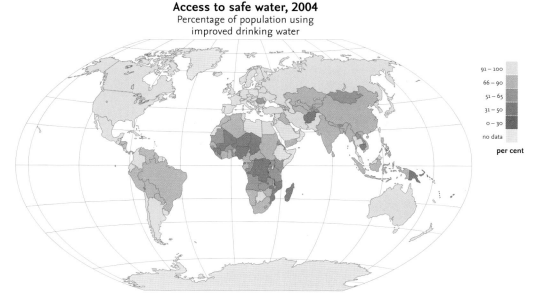

91 – 100
66 – 90
51 – 65
31 – 50
0 – 30
no data

per cent

The Earth has a rich and diverse environment which is under threat
from both natural and man-induced forces. Forests and woodland
form the predominant natural land cover with tropical rain forests –
currently disappearing at alarming rates – believed to be home
to the majority of animal and plant species. Grassland and scrub
tend to have a lower natural species diversity but have suffered
the most impact from man's intervention through conversion
to agriculture, burning and the introduction of livestock.
Wherever man interferes with existing biological and environmental
processes degradation of that environment occurs to varying degrees.
This interference also affects inland water and oceans where pollution,
over-exploitation of marine resources and the need for fresh water
has had major consequences on land and sea environments.

Facts

- The Sundarbans stretching across the Ganges delta is the largest area of mangrove forest in the world, covering 10 000 square kilometres (3 861 square miles) and forming an important ecological area, home to 260 species of birds, the Bengal tiger and other threatened species

- Over 90 000 square kilometres of precious tropical forest and wetland habitats are lost each year

- The surface level of the Dead Sea has fallen by more than 25 metres over the last 50 years

- Climate change and mismanagement of land areas can lead to soils becoming degraded and semi-arid grasslands becoming deserts – a process known as desertification

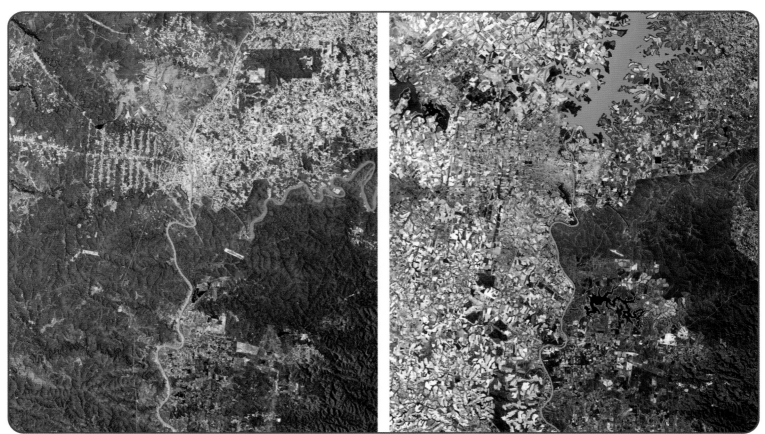

Deforestation and the creation of the **Itaipu Dam** on the Paraná river in Brazil have had a dramatic effect on the landscape and ecosystems of this part of South America. Some forest on the right of the images lies within Iguaçu National Park and has been protected from destruction.

Environmental change

Whenever natural resources are exploited by man, the
environment is changed. Approximately half the area of
post-glacial forest has been cleared or degraded, and the
amount of old-growth forest continues to decline.
Desertification caused by climate change and the impact of
man can turn semi-arid grasslands into arid desert. Regions
bordering tropical deserts, such as the Sahel region south of
the Sahara and regions around the Thar Desert in India, are
most vulnerable to this process. Coral reefs are equally
fragile environments, and many are under threat from
coastal development, pollution and over-exploitation of
marine resources.

Water resources in certain parts of the world are becoming
increasingly scarce and competition for water is likely to
become a common cause of conflict. The Aral Sea in central
Asia was once the world's fourth largest lake but it now ranks
only sixteenth after shrinking by almost 40 000 square
kilometres. This shrinkage has been due to climatic change
and to the diversion, for farming purposes, of the major rivers
which feed the lake. The change has had a devastating effect
on the local fishing industry and the exposure of chemicals
on the lake bed has caused health problems for the local
population.

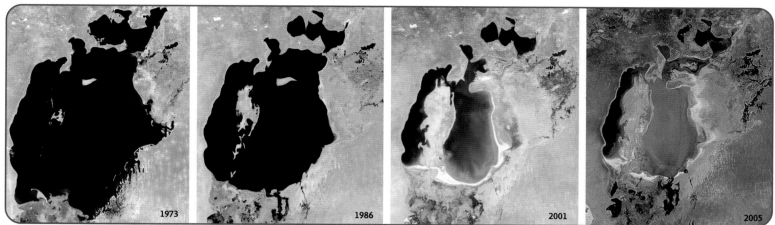

Aral Sea, Kazakhstan/ Uzbekistan 1973–2005 Climate change and the diversion of rivers have caused its dramatic shrinkage.

Environmental Impacts

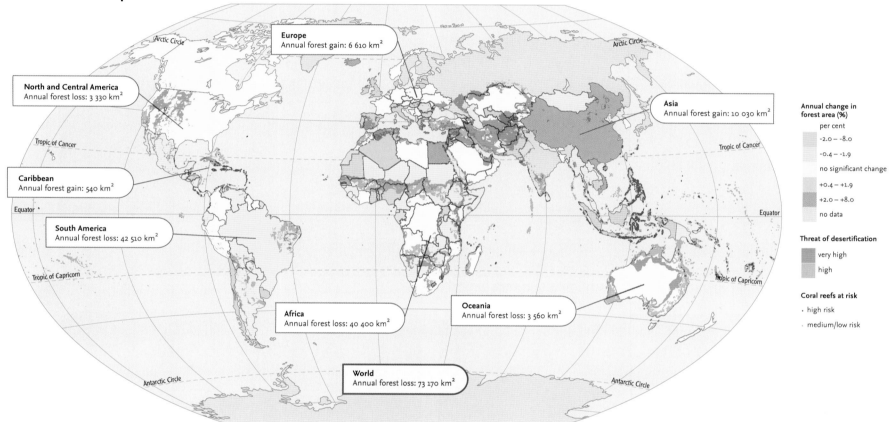

Europe
Annual forest gain: 6 610 km²

North and Central America
Annual forest loss: 3 330 km²

Asia
Annual forest gain: 10 030 km²

Caribbean
Annual forest gain: 540 km²

South America
Annual forest loss: 42 510 km²

Africa
Annual forest loss: 40 400 km²

Oceania
Annual forest loss: 3 560 km²

World
Annual forest loss: 73 170 km²

Annual change in forest area (%)
per cent

- -2.0 − -8.0
- -0.4 − -1.9
- no significant change
- +0.4 − +1.9
- +2.0 − +8.0
- no data

Threat of desertification
- very high
- high

Coral reefs at risk
- high risk
- medium/low risk

Internet links	
● UN Environment Programme	**www.unep.org**
● IUCN World Conservation Union	**www.iucn.org**
● UNESCO World Heritage Sites	**whc.unesco.org**

Environmental protection

Top 10 protected areas by size

Rank	Protected area	Country	Size (sq km)	Designation
1	Northeast Greenland	Greenland	972 000	National Park
2	Rub' al-Khālī	Saudi Arabia	640 000	Wildlife Management Area
3	Phoenix Islands	Kiribati	410 500	Protected Area
4	Great Barrier Reef	Australia	344 400	Marine Park
5	Papahānaumokuākea Marine National Monument	United States	341 362	Coral Reef Ecosystem Reserve
6	Qiangtang	China	298 000	Nature Reserve
7	Macquarie Island	Australia	162 060	Marine Park
8	Sanjiangyuan	China	152 300	Nature Reserve
9	Galápagos	Ecuador	133 000	Marine Reserve
10	Northern Wildlife Management Zone	Saudi Arabia	100 875	Wildlife Management Area

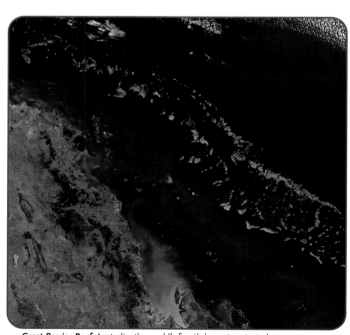

Great Barrier Reef, Australia, the world's fourth largest protected area.

Many parts of the world are undergoing significant changes which can have widespread and long-lasting effects. The principal causes of change are environmental factors – particularly climatic – and the influence of man. However, it is often difficult to separate these causes because man's activities can influence and exaggerate environmental change. Changes, whatever their cause, can have significant effects on the local population, on the wider region and even on a global scale. Major social, economic and environmental impacts can result from often irreversible changes – deforestation can affect a region's biodiversity, land reclamation can destroy fragile marine ecosystems, major dams and drainage schemes can affect whole drainage basins, and local communities can be changed beyond recognition through such projects.

Facts

- Earth-observing satellites can now detect land detail, and therefore changes in land use, of less than 1 metre extent

- Hong Kong International Airport, opened in 1998 and covering an area of over 12 square kilometres, was built almost entirely on reclaimed land

- The UN have estimated that 7 billion people could be short of water by the year 2050

- Approximately 35% of cropland in Asia is irrigated

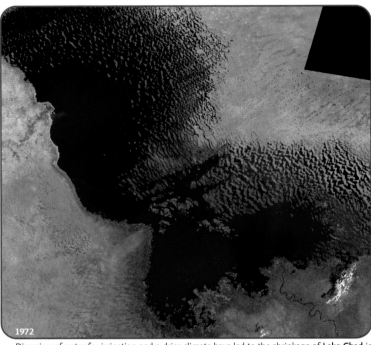
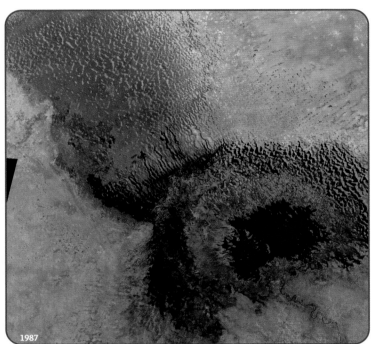

Diversion of water for irrigation and a drier climate have led to the shrinkage of **Lake Chad** in Africa.

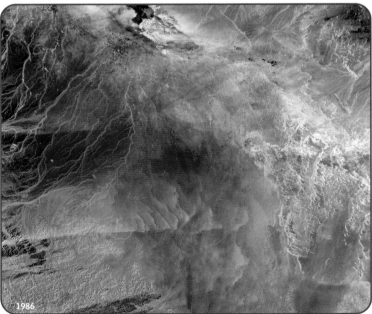
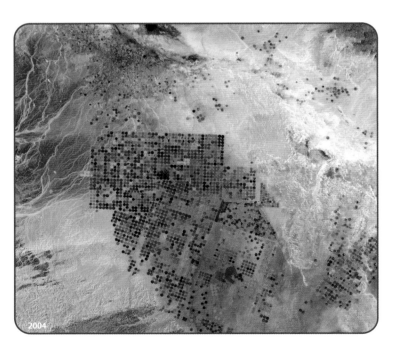

'Centre-pivot' irrigation has transformed the **Arabian Desert** near Tubarjal.

Effects of change

Both natural forces and human activity have irreversibly changed the environment in many parts of the world. Satellite images of the same area taken at different times are a powerful tool for identifying and monitoring such change. Climate change and an increasing demand for water can combine to bring about dramatic changes to lakes and rivers, while major engineering projects, reclamation of land from the sea and the expansion of towns and cities, create completely new environments. Use of water for the generation of hydro-electric power or for irrigation of otherwise infertile land leads to dramatic changes in the landscape and can also be a cause of conflict between countries. All such changes can have major social and economic impacts on the local population.

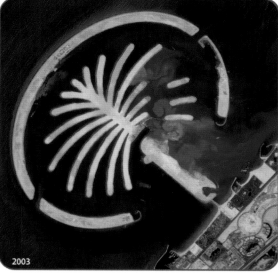

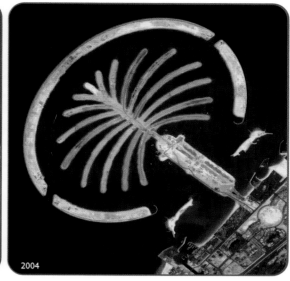

The first of three 'Palm Islands' being reclaimed from the sea off **Dubai.**

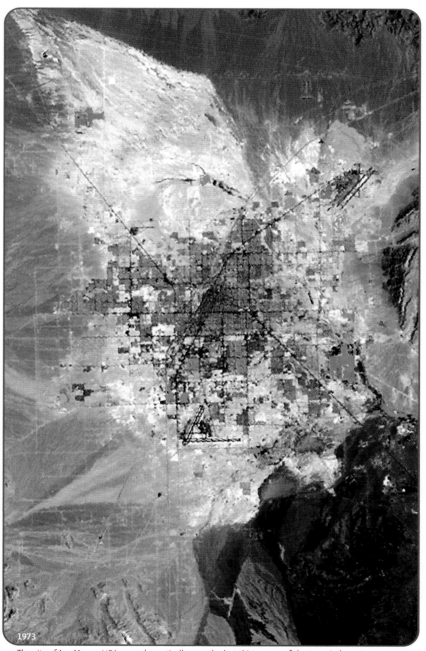

The city of **Las Vegas,** USA grew dramatically over the last thirty years of the twentieth century.

Internet Links	
● NASA Visible Earth	**visibleearth.nasa.gov**
● NASA Earth Observatory	**earthobservatory.nasa.gov**
● USGS Earthshots	**earthshots.usgs.gov**

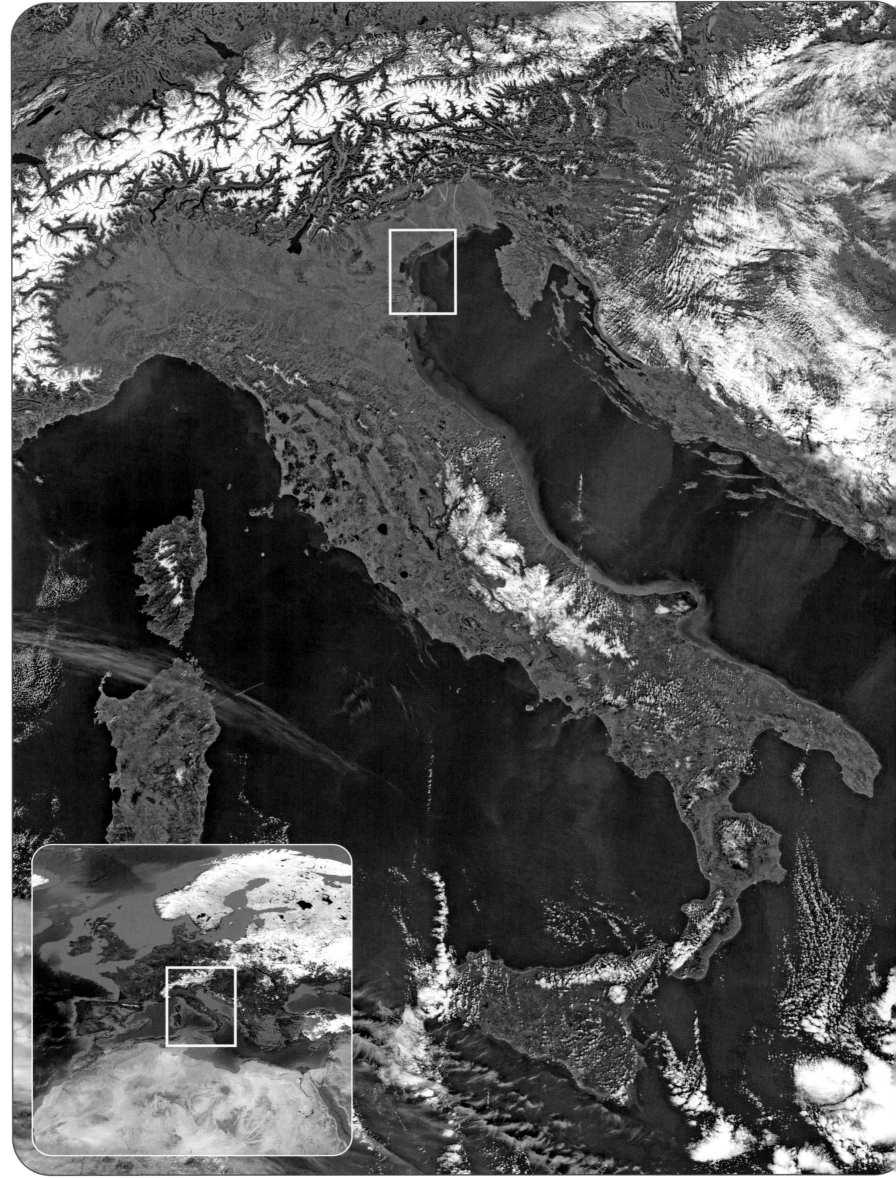

This sequence of satellite images at progressively higher resolutions illustrates the value of such imagery in observing and monitoring features on the Earth. From world, continental and regional views to detailed images picking out individual features on the ground less than 1 m (3.3 feet) in size, images like this can be used for many scientific, environmental and planning purposes.

Satellite sensors commonly collect many types of data which allow very detailed analysis of vegetation and climatic conditions. The fact that Earth-observing satellites regularly revisit the same location adds to this the valuable ability to monitor change over time.

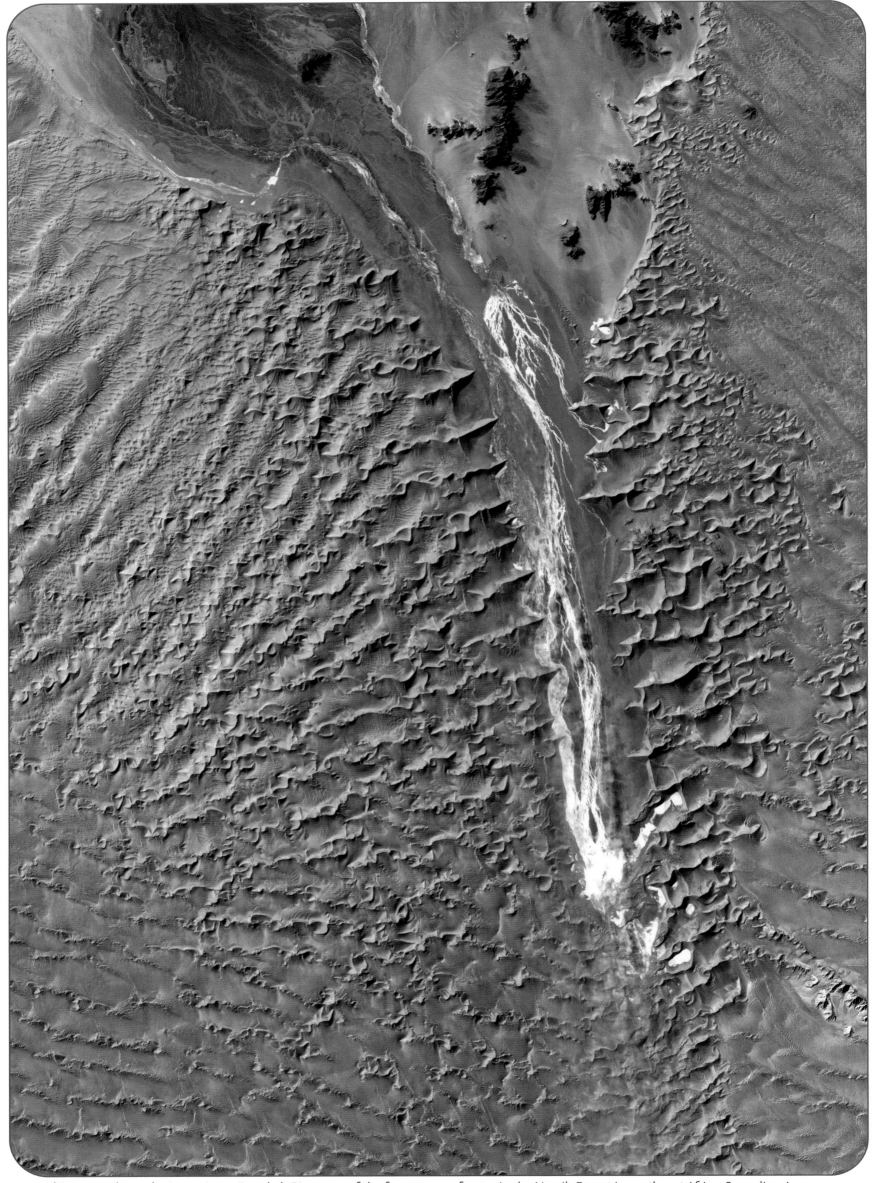

This image shows the intermittent Tsauchab River, one of the few sources of water in the Namib Desert in southwest Africa. Sporadic rains can turn the river into a raging torrent within twenty-four hours. Like other ephemeral rivers flowing into the desert it ends in a vlei, or mud flat – the clearing in the sand dunes at the top of this image.

This early springtime image of the Kamchatka Peninsula shows the distinctive feature still largely snow covered. The snow allows this complex mountainous landscape to be clearly seen. The eastern edge of the peninsula is marked by numerous active volcanoes – this region forms part of the Pacific 'Ring of Fire', a zone of volcanic and seismic activity circling the Pacific Ocean.

In the centre of this high resolution satellite image are the Petronas Twin Towers in Kuala Lumpur, Malaysia. Reaching a height of 452 metres (1483 feet) it is one of the tallest structures in the world.

The numerous space-rocket launch pads and the Space Shuttle landing strip, 4.8 km (3 miles) in length, can be easily identified in this ASTER satellite image of the John F. Kennedy Space Center located on Cape Canaveral on the east coast of Florida, USA.

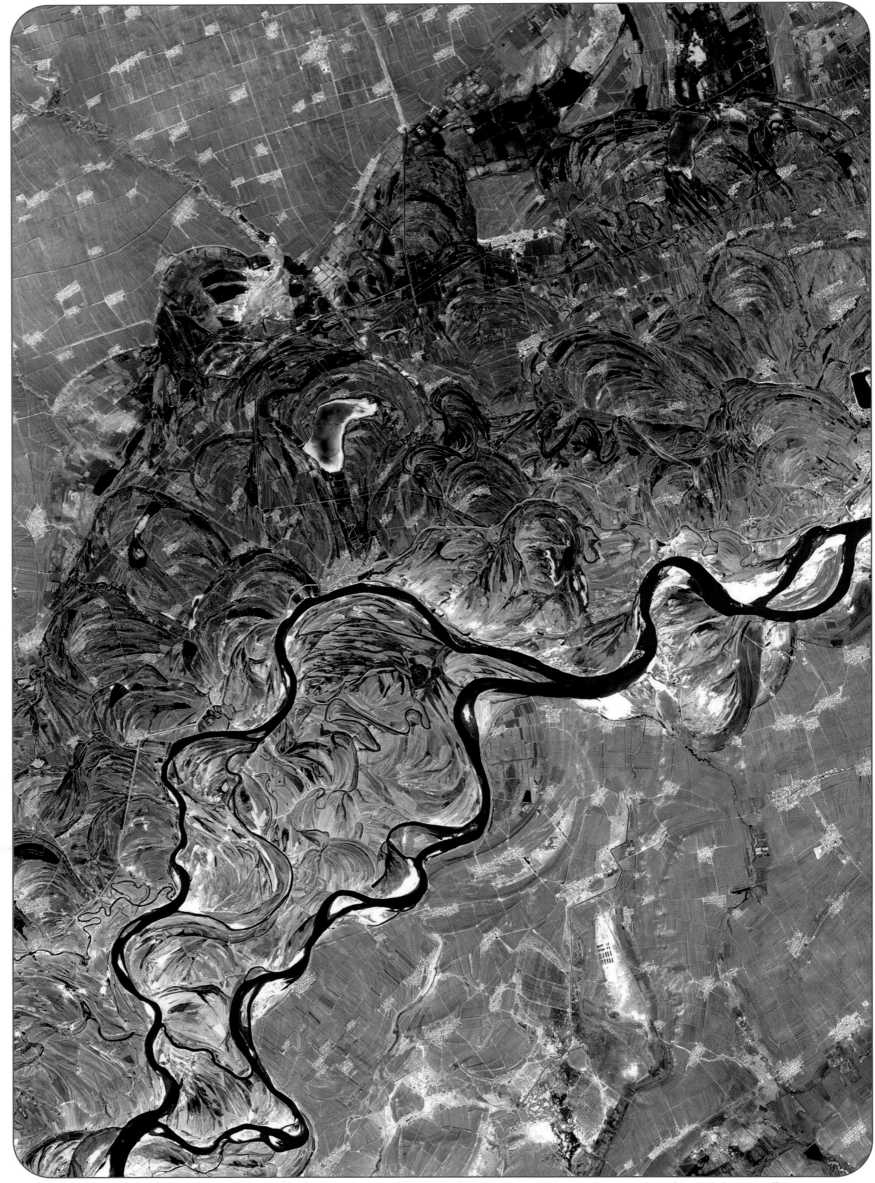

The Songhua river flows eastwards across the flat Manchurian Plain in northeastern China. The river's course has changed dramatically over time and changes are evident through the pattern of old meanders and oxbow lakes (formed when meanders are cut off by the deposition of material). This is a good example of how environmental change can sometimes be detected in a single image.

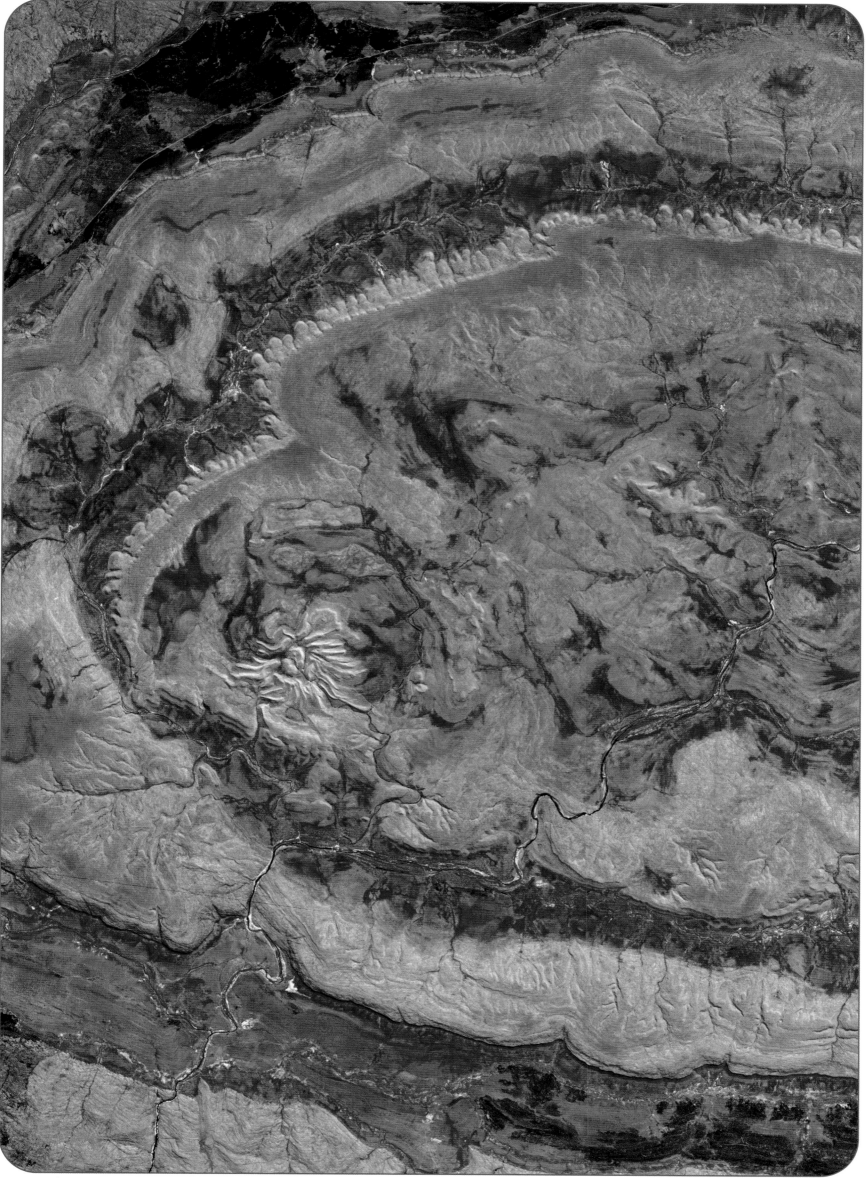

In the Kimberly region of northern Western Australia a strange rock formation known as the Spider long puzzled geologists until they found shatter cones — cone shaped, grooved rocks known only to appear in craters left by meteor or asteroid impacts. Spider Crater rests in a depression 13 by 11 km (8 by 7 miles) across, the spider's "legs" formed from tough sandstone that has resisted weathering.

ENVIRONMENT

The Earth has a rich environment with a wide range of habitats. Forest and woodland form the predominant natural land cover and tropical rain forests are believed to be home to the majority of the world's bird, animal and plant species. These forests are part of a delicate land-atmosphere relationship disturbed by changes in land use. Grassland, shrubland and deserts cover most of the unwooded areas of the earth with low-growing tundra in the far northern latitudes. Grassland and shrubland regions in particular have been altered greatly by man through agriculture, livestock grazing and settlements.

ORGANIZATION	WEB ADDRESS	THEME
NASA Earth Observatory	earthobservatory.nasa.gov	Observing the earth
USGS Earthquakes Hazards Center	earthquake.usgs.gov	Monitoring earthquakes
Scripps Institution of Oceanography	sio.ucsd.edu	Exploration of the oceans
Visible Earth	visibleearth.nasa.gov	Satellite images of the earth
USGS Volcanoes Hazard Program	volcanoes.usgs.gov	Volcanic activity
UNESCO World Heritage Centre	whc.unesco.org	World Heritage Sites
British Geological Survey	www.bgs.ac.uk	Geology
The World Conservation Union	www.iucn.org	World and ocean conservation
World Rainforest Information Portal	www.rainforestweb.org	Rainforest information and resources
United Nations Environment Programme	www.unep.org	Environmental protection by the UN
World Conservation Monitoring Centre	www.unep-wcmc.org	Conservation and the environment
World Resources Institute	www.wri.org	Monitoring the environment and resources
IUCN Red List	www.iucn.redlist.org	Threatened species

OCEANS

Between them, the world's oceans cover approximately 70 per cent of the earth's surface. They contain 96 per cent of the earth's water and a vast range of flora and fauna. They are a major influence on the world's climate, particularly through ocean currents – the circulation of water within and between the oceans. Our understanding of the oceans has increased enormously over the last twenty years through the development of new technologies, including that of satellite images, which can generate vast amounts of data relating to the sea floor, ocean currents and sea surface temperatures.

ORGANIZATION	WEB ADDRESS	THEME
International Maritime Organisation	www.imo.org	Shipping and the environment
General Bathymetric Chart of the Oceans	www.ngdc.noaa.gov/mgg/gebco	Mapping the oceans
National Oceanography Centre, Southampton	www.soc.soton.ac.uk	Researching the oceans
Scott Polar Research Institute	www.spri.cam.ac.uk	Polar research

CLIMATE

The Earth's climate system is highly complex. It is recognized and accepted that man's activities are affecting this system, and monitoring climate change, including human influences upon it, is now a major issue. Future climate change depends critically on how quickly and to what extent the concentration of greenhouse gases in the atmosphere increase. Change will not be uniform across the globe and the information from sophisticated mathematical climate models is invaluable in helping governments and industry to assess the impacts climate change will have.

ORGANIZATION	WEB ADDRESS	THEME
BBC Weather Centre	www.bbc.co.uk/weather	Worldwide weather forecasts
University of East Anglia Climatic Research Unit	www.cru.uea.ac.uk	Climatic research in the UK
Met Office	www.met-office.gov.uk	Weather information and climatic research
National Climatic Data Center	www.ncdc.noaa.gov	Global climate data
NOAA/National Weather Service National Hurricane Center	www.nhc.noaa.gov	Tracking hurricanes
National Oceanic and Atmospheric Administration	www.noaa.gov	Monitoring climate and the oceans
United Nations World Meteorological Organization	www.wmo.ch	The world's climate
El Niño	www.elnino.noaa.gov	El Niño research and observations

POPULATION

The world's population reached six billion in 1999. Rates of population growth vary between continents, but overall, the rate of growth has been increasing and it is predicted that by 2050 another three billion people will inhabit the planet. The process of urbanization, in particular migration from countryside to city, has led to the rapid growth of many cities. It is estimated that by 2008, for the first time in history, more people will be living in urban areas than in rural areas. There are now almost 400 cities with over one million inhabitants and nineteen with over ten million.

ORGANIZATION	WEB ADDRESS	THEME
UK National Statistics	www.statistics.gov.uk/census2001	The UK 2001 census
City Populations	www.citypopulation.de	Statistics and maps about population
US Census Bureau	www.census.gov	US and world population
United Nations World Urbanization Prospects	esa.un.org/unpp/index.asp	Population estimates and projections
United Nations Population Information Network	www.un.org/popin	World population statistics
UN Population Division	www.un.org/esa/population/unpop.htm	Monitoring world population

COUNTRIES

The present picture of the political world is the result of a long history of exploration, colonialism, conflict and negotiation. In 1950 there were eighty-two independent countries. Since then there has been a significant trend away from colonial influences and although many dependent territories still exist, there are now 195 independent countries. The newest country is Kosovo which gained independence from Serbia in February 2008. The shapes of countries reflect a combination of natural features, such as mountain ranges, and political agreements. There are still areas of the world where boundaries are disputed or only temporarily settled as ceasefire lines.

ORGANIZATION	WEB ADDRESS	THEME
European Union	europa.eu	Gateway to the European Union
Permament Committee on Geographical Names	www.pcgn.org.uk	Place names research in the UK
The World Factbook	www.cia.gov/library/publications/the-world-factbook/index.html	Country profiles
US Board on Geographic Names	geonames.usgs.gov	Place names research in the USA
United Nations	www.un.org	The United Nations
International Boundaries Research Unit	www.dur.ac.uk/ibru	International boundaries resources and research
Organisation for Economic Co-operation and Development	www.oecd.org	Economic statistics
World Bank	www.worldbank.org/data	World development indicators

TRAVEL

Travelling as a tourist or on business to some countries, or travelling within certain areas can be dangerous because of wars and political unrest. The UK Foreign Office provides the latest travel advice and security warnings. Some areas of the world, particularly tropical regions in the developing world, also carry many risks of disease. Advice should be sought on precautions to take and medications required.

ORGANIZATION	WEB ADDRESS	THEME
UK Foreign Office	www.fco.gov.uk	Travel, trade and country information
US Department of State	www.state.gov	Travel advice
World Health Organization	www.who.int	Health advice and world health issues
Centers for Disease Control and Prevention	www.cdc.gov/travel	Advice for travellers
Airports Council International	www.airports.org	The voice of the world's airports
Travel Daily News	www.traveldailynews.com	Travel and tourism newsletter

ORGANIZATIONS

Throughout the world there are many international, national and local organizations representing the interests of individual countries, groups of countries, regions and specialist groups. These can provide enormous amounts of information on economic, social, cultural, environmental and general geographical issues facing the world. The following is a selection of such sites.

ORGANIZATION	WEB ADDRESS	THEME
United Nations	www.un.org	The United Nations
United Nations Educational, Scientific and Cultural Organization	www.unesco.org	International collaboration
United Nations Children's Fund	www.unicef.org	Health, education, equality and protection for children
United Nations High Commissioner for Refugees	www.unhcr.org	The UN refugee agency
Food and Agriculture Organization	www.fao.org	Agriculture and defeating hunger
United Nations Development Programme	www.undp.org	The UN global development network
North Atlantic Treaty Organization	www.nato.int	North Atlantic freedom and security
European Environment Agency	www.eea.europa.eu	Europe's environment
European Centre for Nature Conservation	www.ecnc.nl/	Nature conservation in Europe
Europa - The European Union On-line	europa.eu	European Union facts and statistics
World Health Organisation	www.who.int	Health issues and advice
Association of Southeast Asian Nations	www.aseansec.org	Economic, social and cultural development
International Water Management Institute	www.iwmi.cgiar.org	Water and land resources management
The Joint United Nations Convention on AIDS	www.unaids.org	The AIDS crisis
African Union	www.africa-union.org	African international relations
LakeNet	www.worldlakes.org/searchlakes.asp	Lakes around the world
The Secretariat of the Pacific Commmunity	www.spc.int	The Pacific community
The Maori world	www.maori.org.nz	Maori culture
US National Park Service	www.nps.gov	National Parks of the USA
Parks Canada	www.pc.gc.ca	Natural heritage of Canada
The Panama Canal	www.pancanal.com	Explore the Panama Canal
The Caribbean Community Secretariat	www.caricom.org	Caribbean Community
Organization of American States	www.oas.org	Inter-American cooperation
The Latin American Network Information Center	lanic.utexas.edu	Latin America
World Wildlife Fund	www.worldwildlife.org	Global environmental conservation
Amazon Conservation Team	www.amazonteam.org	Conservation in tropical America

Europe

The generally densely vegetated continent of Europe contains some dramatic geographical features. Its northern and western limits are marked by the complex coastlines of Iceland, Scandinavia and northwestern Russian Federation, while the British Isles sit on the flat, wide continental shelf. Europe's mountain ranges divide the continent – in the southwest, the Pyrenees separate France from the drier Iberian Peninsula, the wide arc of the Alps separates Italy from the rest of western Europe, the Carpathian Mountains, appearing as a dark curve between the Alps and the Black Sea, mark the edge of the vast European plains, and the Caucasus, stretching between the Black Sea and the Caspian Sea, create a prominent barrier between Europe and Asia. Two of Europe's greatest rivers are also clearly visible on this image – the Volga, Europe's longest river, flowing south from the Ural Mountains into the Caspian Sea and the Dnieper flowing across the plains into the northern Black Sea.

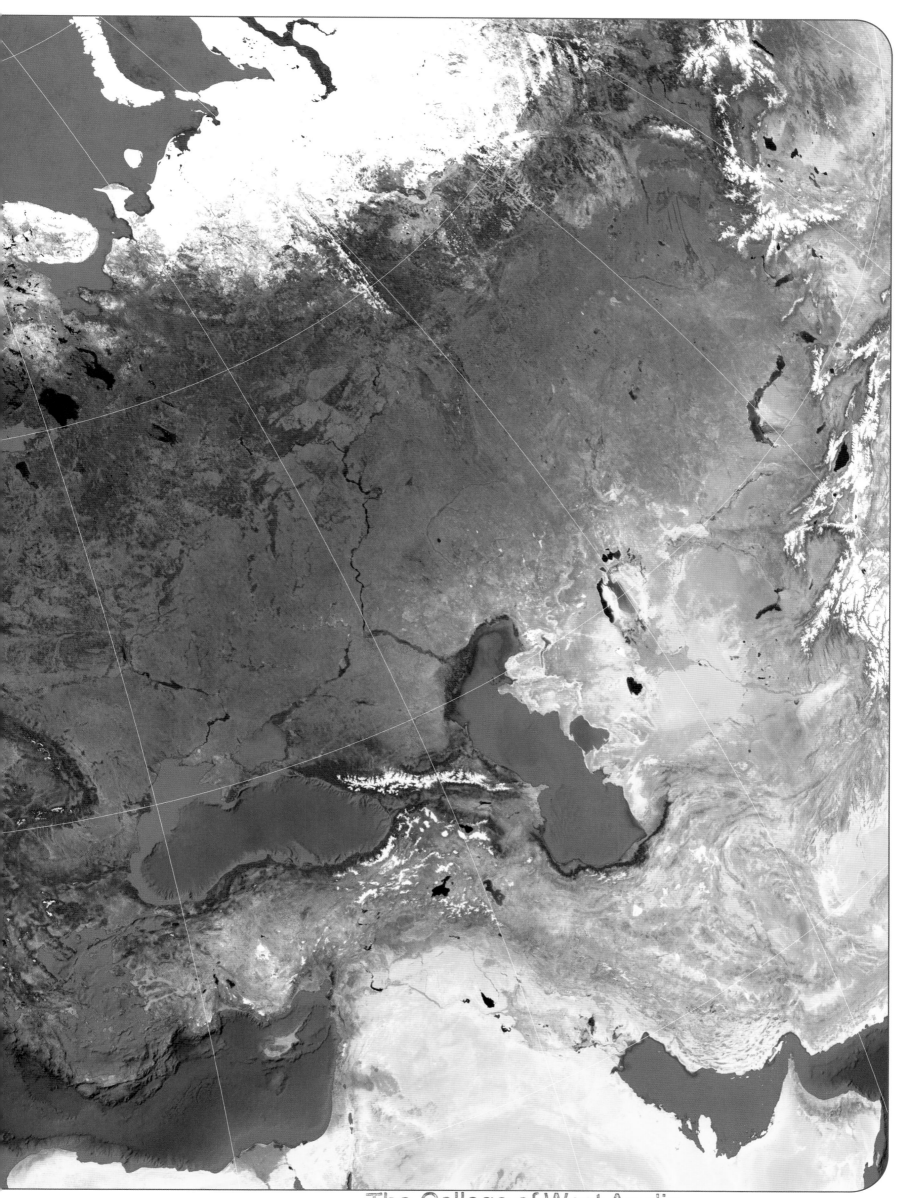

45

Europe
Landscapes

Europe, the westward extension of the Asian continent and the second smallest of the world's continents, has a remarkable variety of physical features and landscapes. The continent is bounded by mountain ranges of varying character – the highlands of Scandinavia and northwest Britain, the Pyrenees, the Alps, the Carpathian Mountains, the Caucasus and the Ural Mountains. Two of these, the Caucasus and Ural Mountains, define the eastern limits of Europe, with the Black Sea and the Bosporus defining its southeastern boundary with Asia.

Across the centre of the continent stretches the North European Plain, broken by some of Europe's greatest rivers, including the Volga and the Dnieper and containing some of its largest lakes. To the south, the Mediterranean Sea divides Europe from Africa. The Mediterranean region itself has a very distinct climate and landscape.

Facts

- The Danube flows through 7 countries and has 7 different name forms

- Lakes cover almost 10% of the total land area of Finland

- The Strait of Gibraltar, separating the Atlantic Ocean from the Mediterranean Sea and Europe from Africa, is only 13 kilometres wide at its narrowest point

- The highest mountain in the Alps is Mont Blanc, 4 808 metres, on the France/Italy border

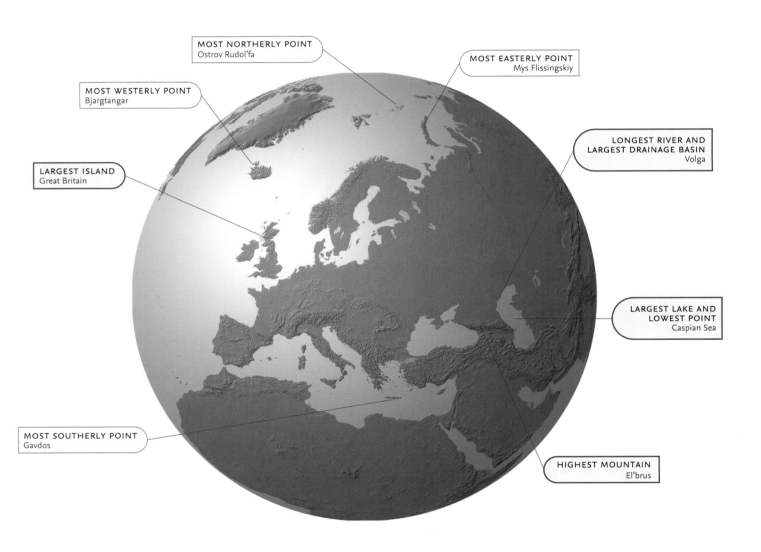

MOST NORTHERLY POINT
Ostrov Rudol'fa

MOST EASTERLY POINT
Mys Flissingskiy

MOST WESTERLY POINT
Bjargtangar

LONGEST RIVER AND
LARGEST DRAINAGE BASIN
Volga

LARGEST ISLAND
Great Britain

LARGEST LAKE AND
LOWEST POINT
Caspian Sea

MOST SOUTHERLY POINT
Gavdos

HIGHEST MOUNTAIN
El'brus

ATLANTIC

OCEAN

Europe's greatest physical features

Highest mountain	El'brus, Russian Federation	5 642 metres	18 510 feet
Longest river	Volga, Russian Federation	3 688 km	2 292 miles
Largest lake	Caspian Sea	371 000 sq km	143 243 sq miles
Largest island	Great Britain, United Kingdom	218 476 sq km	84 354 sq miles
Largest drainage basin	Volga, Russian Federation	1 380 000 sq km	532 818 sq miles

Europe's extent

Total Land Area	9 908 599 sq km / 3 825 710 sq miles
Most northerly point	Ostrov Rudol'fa, Russian Federation
Most southerly point	Gavdos, Crete, Greece
Most westerly point	Bjargtangar, Iceland
Most easterly point	Mys Flissingskiy, Russian Federation

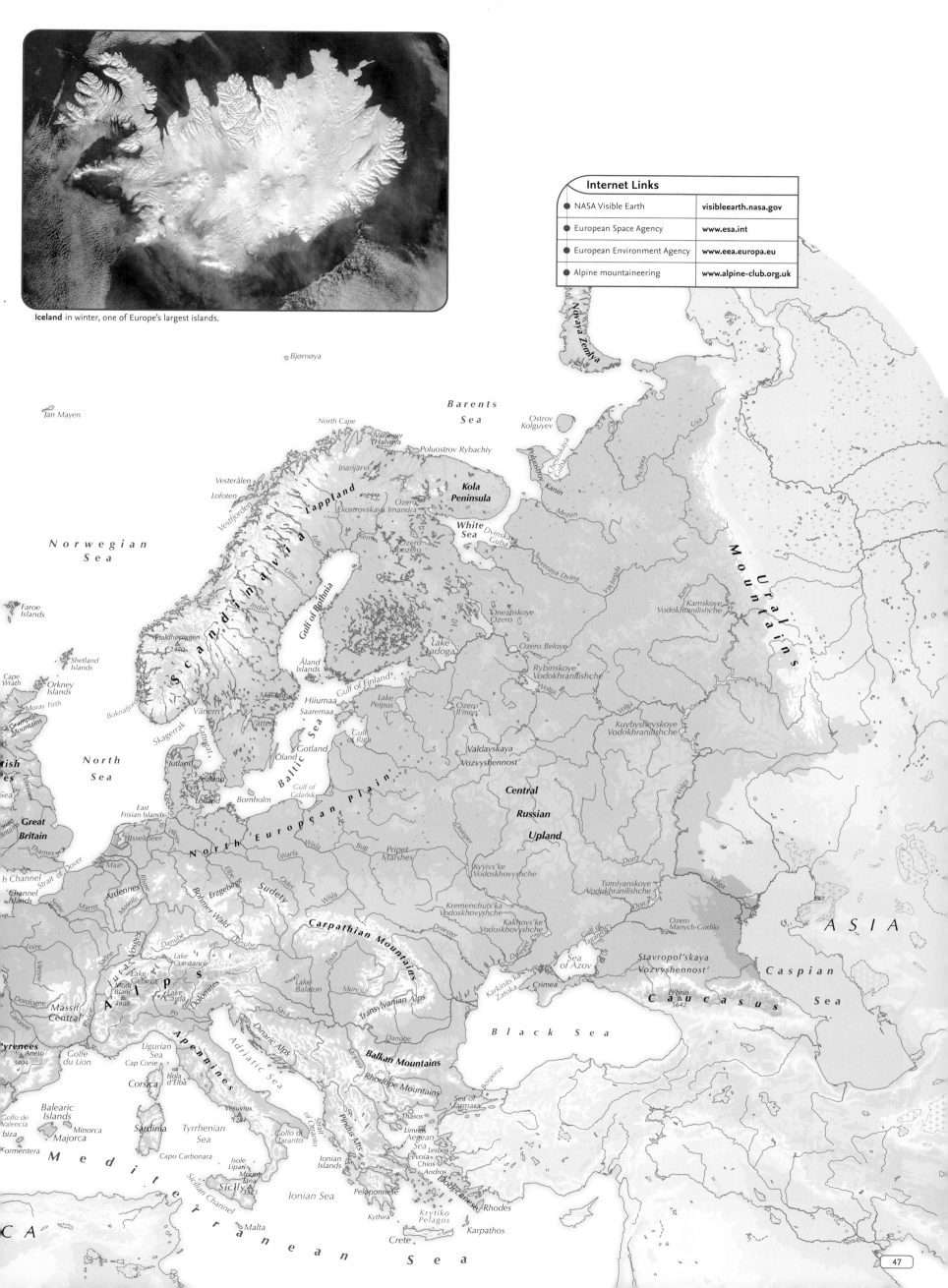

Iceland in winter, one of Europe's largest islands.

Novaya Zemlya

Bjørnøya

Jan Mayen

Barents Sea

North Cape

Varanger Halvøya

Poluostrov Rybachiy

Ostrov Kolguyev

Poluostrov Kanin

Cheshskaya Guba

Inarijärvi

Vesterålen

Lofoten

Lappland

Ozero Ekostrovskaya Imandra

Kola Peninsula

Usa

White Sea

Dvinskaya Guba

Mezen

Pechora

Norwegian Sea

Vestfjorden

Tulo

Kem'

Ozero Topozero

Severnaya Dvina

Vychegda

Kama

U r a l M o u n t a i n s

Galdhøpiggen 2470

Ume

Indals

S c a n d i n a v i a

Gulf of Bothnia

Onezhskoye Ozero

Kamskoye Vodokhranilishche

Faroe Islands

Boknafjord

Vänern

Ångerman

Lake Ladoga

Ozero Beloye

Rybinskoye Vodokhranilishche

Volga

Shetland Islands

Cape Wrath

Orkney Islands

Moray Firth

Grampian Mountains

Skagerrak

Vättern

Malaren

Åland Islands

Gulf of Finland

Lake Peipus

Ozero Il'men

Kuybyshevskoye Vodokhranilishche

North Sea

Kattegat

Hiiumaa Saaremaa

B a l t i c S e a

Gulf of Riga

Valdayskaya Vozvyshennost'

Jutland

Öland Gotland

Central

ish es

Zealand

Fyn

Lolland

Bornholm

Gulf of Gdańsk

Russian

Great Britain

Thames

East Frisian Islands

N o r t h E u r o p e a n P l a i n

Warta

Wisła

Bug

Pripet Marshes

Dnieper

Upland

Weser

IJsselmeer

h Channel

Strait of Dover

Channel Islands

Maas

Elbe

Erzgebirge

Sudety

Oder

Wisła

Tsimlyanskoye Vodokhranilishche

Marne

Ardennes

Rhine

Moselle

Böhmer Wald

Carpathian Mountains

Dniester

Kyyivs'ke Vodoskhovyshche

Don

Loire

Vienne

Saône

Danube

Inn

Lake Constance

Jura

Vosges

Danube

Tisza

Kremenchuts'ka Vodoskhovyshche

Kakhovs'ke Vodoskhovyshche

Don

Volga

Dordogne

Lake Geneva

Mont Blanc 4808

A l p s

Dolomites

Lake Garda

Lake Balaton

Sava

Mureşul

Transylvanian Alps

Dniester

Gulf of Taganrog

Ozero Manych-Gudilo

A S I A

Garonne

Massif Central

Rhône

Po

Dinaric Alps

Danube

Sea of Azov

Stavropol'skaya Vozvyshennost'

C a s p i a n

renees

Aneto 3404

Golfe du Lion

Ligurian Sea

Cap Corse

A p e n n i n e s

A d r i a t i c   S e a

Morava

Balkan Mountains

Karkinits'ka Zatoka

Crimea

C a u c a s u s

Elbrus 5642

S e a

Golfe du Lion

Isola d'Elba

Rhodope Mountains

B l a c k   S e a

Bosporus

Corsica

Balearic Islands

Golfo de Valencia

iza

Minorca

Majorca

Sardinia

Tyrrhenian Sea

Vesuvius 1281

Golfo di Taranto

Pindus Mts

Sea of Marmara

Thasos

Limnos

Aegean Sea

Lesbos

Chios

Evvoia

Formentera

Capo Carbonara

Isole Lipari

Mount Etna 3323

Strait of Otranto

Ionian Islands

Andros

Dodecanese

Rhodes

M e d i t e r

Sicilian Channel

Sicily

Ionian Sea

Peloponnese

Kythira

Krytiko Pelagos

Karpathos

CA

Malta

Crete

r a n e a n   S e a

Europe
Countries

The predominantly temperate climate of Europe has led to it becoming the most densely populated of the continents. It is highly industrialized, and has exploited its great wealth of natural resources and agricultural land to become one of the most powerful economic regions in the world.

The current pattern of countries within Europe is a result of numerous and complicated changes throughout its history. Ethnic, religious and linguistic differences have often been the cause of conflict, particularly in the Balkan region which has a very complex ethnic pattern. Current boundaries reflect, to some extent, these divisions which continue to be a source of tension. The historic distinction between 'Eastern' and 'Western' Europe is no longer made, following the collapse of Communism and the break up of the Soviet Union in 1991.

Facts

- The European Union was founded by six countries: Belgium, France, Germany, Italy, Luxembourg, and the Netherlands. It now has 27 members

- The newest members of the European Union, Bulgaria and Romania joined in 2007

- Europe has the 2 smallest independent countries in the world – Vatican City and Monaco

- Vatican City is an independent country entirely within the city of Rome, and is the centre of the Roman Catholic Church

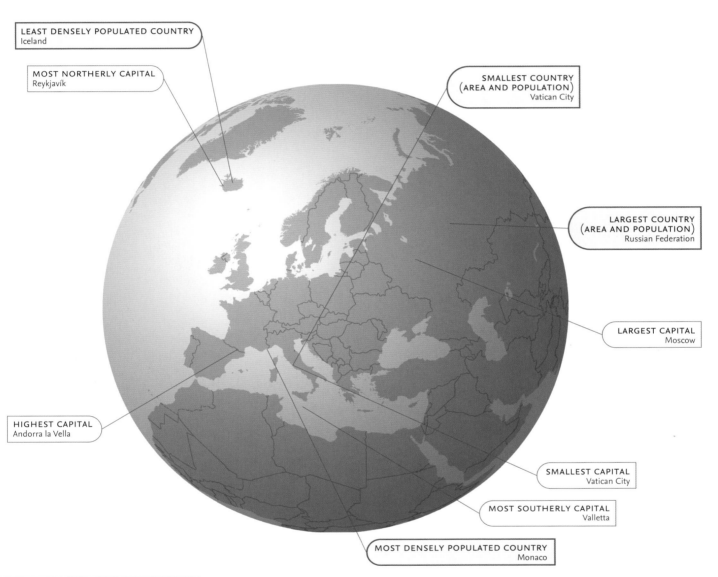

LEAST DENSELY POPULATED COUNTRY
Iceland

MOST NORTHERLY CAPITAL
Reykjavík

SMALLEST COUNTRY
(AREA AND POPULATION)
Vatican City

LARGEST COUNTRY
(AREA AND POPULATION)
Russian Federation

LARGEST CAPITAL
Moscow

HIGHEST CAPITAL
Andorra la Vella

SMALLEST CAPITAL
Vatican City

MOST SOUTHERLY CAPITAL
Valletta

MOST DENSELY POPULATED COUNTRY
Monaco

Bosporus, Turkey, a narrow strait of water which separates Europe from Asia.

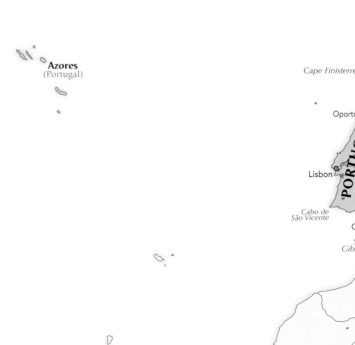

Reykjavík **ICELAND**

ATLANTIC

'Rockall'
(U.K.)

OCEAN

IRELA
D

Bay
Bis

Azores
(Portugal)

Cape Finisterre   A Coruña
Bi

Oporto   Douro   Salamanca

PORTUGAL   Madri

SPAI

Tagus

Lisbon

Cabo de
São Vicente   Seville   Córdoba

Cádiz   Cár   Málaga

Str. of
Gibraltar   Gibraltar

A

Europe's capitals

Largest capital (population)	Moscow, Russian Federaton	10 452 000
Smallest capital (population)	Vatican City	557
Most northerly capital	Reykjavík, Iceland	64° 39'N
Most southerly capital	Valletta, Malta	35° 54'N
Highest capital	Andorra la Vella, Andorra	1 029 metres 3 376 feet

Europe's countries

Largest country (area)	Russian Federation	17 075 400 sq km	6 592 849 sq miles
Smallest country (area)	Vatican City	0.5 sq km	0.2 sq miles
Largest country (population)	Russian Federation	143 202 000	
Smallest country (population)	Vatican City	557	
Most densely populated country	Monaco	17 000 per sq km	34 000 per sq mile
Least densely populated country	Iceland	3 per sq km	7 per sq mile

Internet Links	
● European Union	europa.eu
● UK Foreign and Commonwealth Office	www.fco.gov.uk
● CIA World Factbook	www.cia.gov/library/publications/the-world-factbook/index.html

Europe

Northern Europe

Conic Equidistant Projection

1:6 500 000

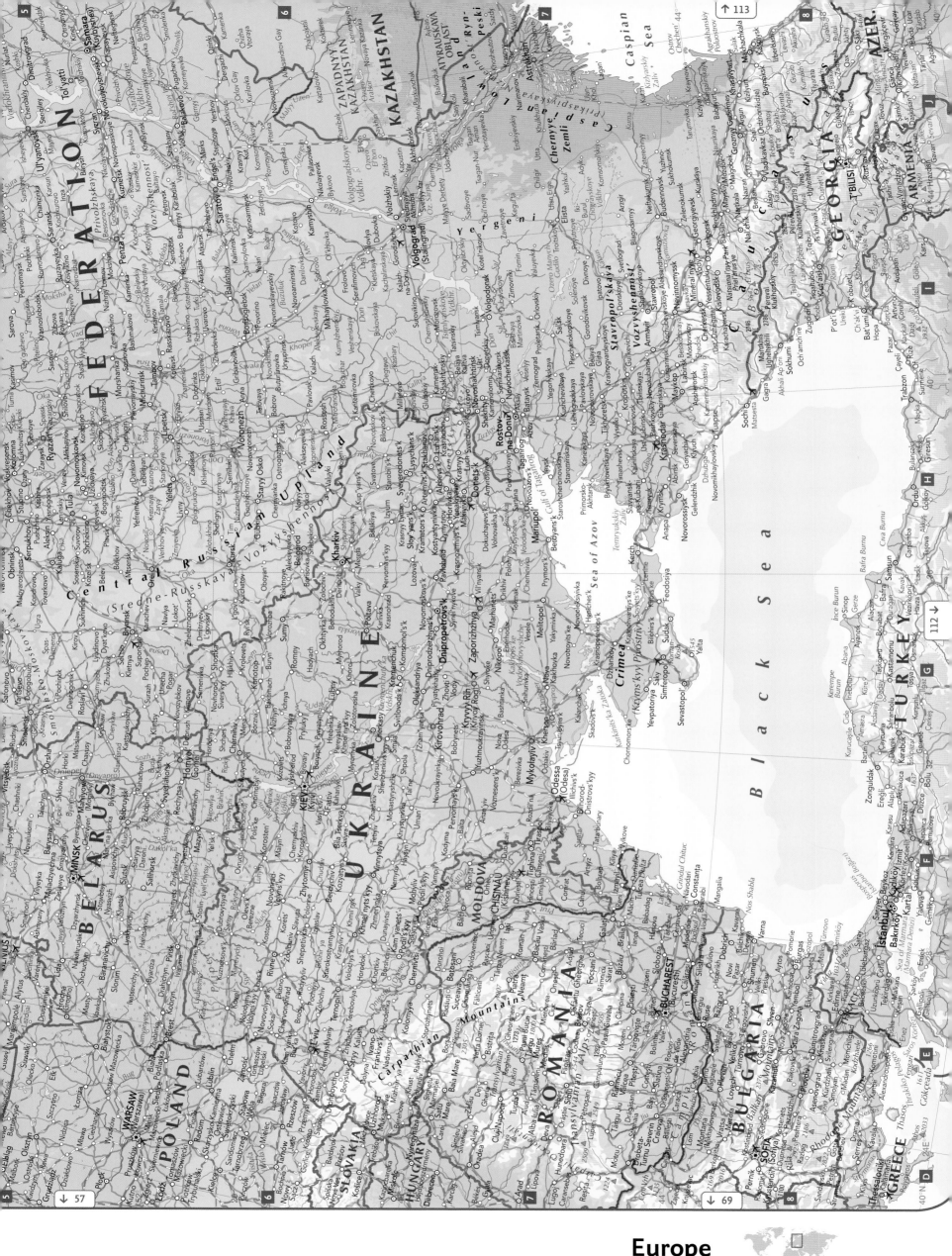

112 →

Europe
Western Russian Federation

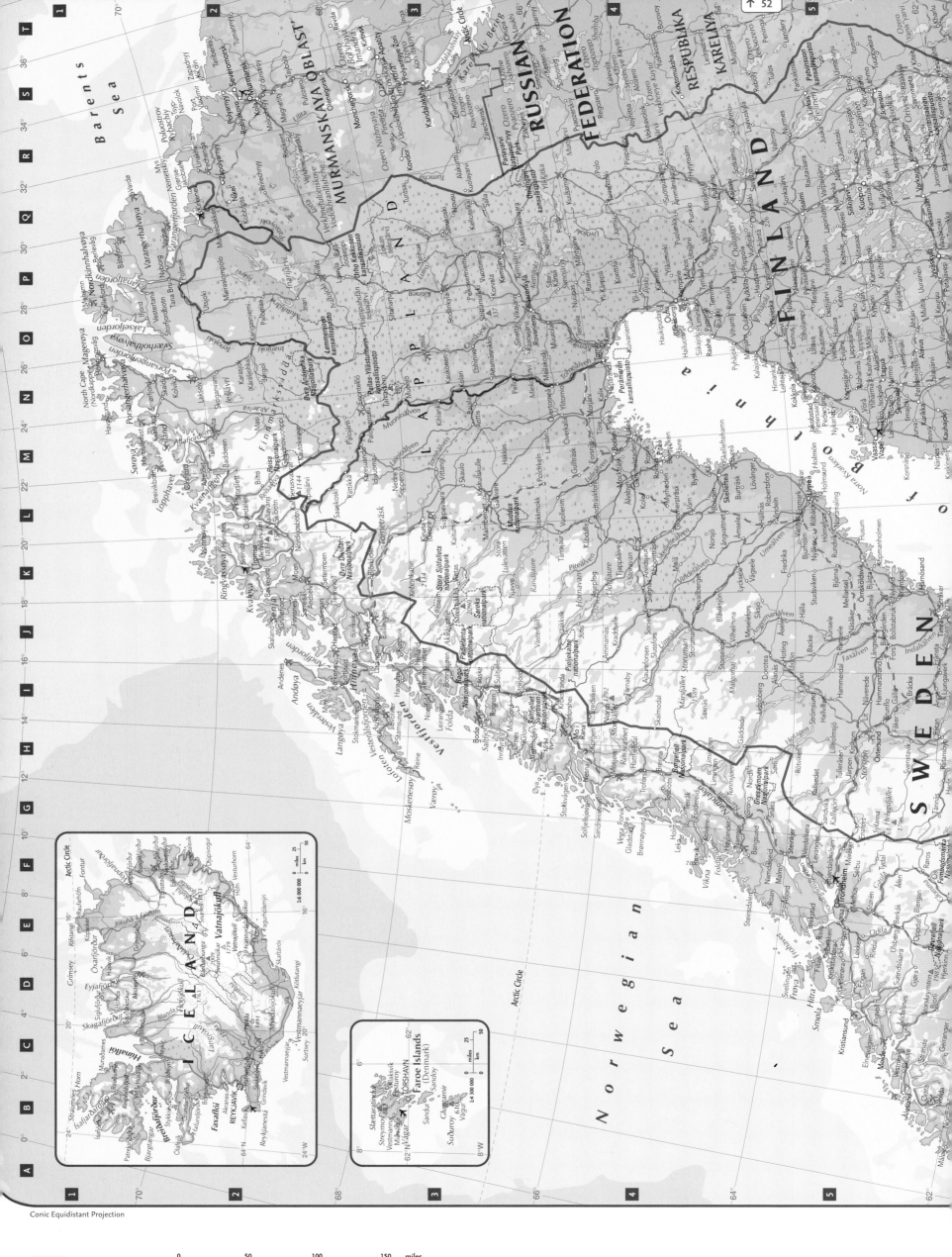

Conic Equidistant Projection

1:4 300 000

Europe
Scandinavia and the Baltic States

ATLANTIC

OCEAN

British

Isles

North Sea

Sea

UNITED

KINGDOM

Outer Hebrides

Orkney
Islands

ULSTER

CONNAUGHT

IRELAND

LEINSTER

MUNSTER

*Irish
Sea*

*Celtic
Sea*

Cardigan Bay

St George's Channel

Great

Britain

DUBLIN
(Baile Átha Cliath)

Isle of
Man
(U.K.)

Snowdonia
National Park

Peak District
National Park

Manchester

Leeds

BIRMINGHAM

LONDON

Bristol Channel

Exmoor
National Park

Dartmoor
National Park

Isle of
Wight

English Channel
(La Manche)

NETH

AMSTERDAM

THE HAGUE
('s-Gravenhage)
(Den Haag)

Rotterdam

Antwerp

BRUSSELS
(Bruxelles)

BELGIUM

ARTOIS

PICARDY

Baie de Seine

Guernsey
(U.K.)
ST PETER
PORT

Channel Islands
(Îles Normandes)

Jersey
(U.K.)
ST HELIER

*Golfe
de
St-Malo*

NORMANDY

Collines de Normandie

PARIS

BRITTANY

BRIE

ANJOU

FRANCE

POITOU

Conic Equidistant Projection

1:4 300 000

0   50   100   150   miles

0   50   100   150   200   250 km

↓ 66

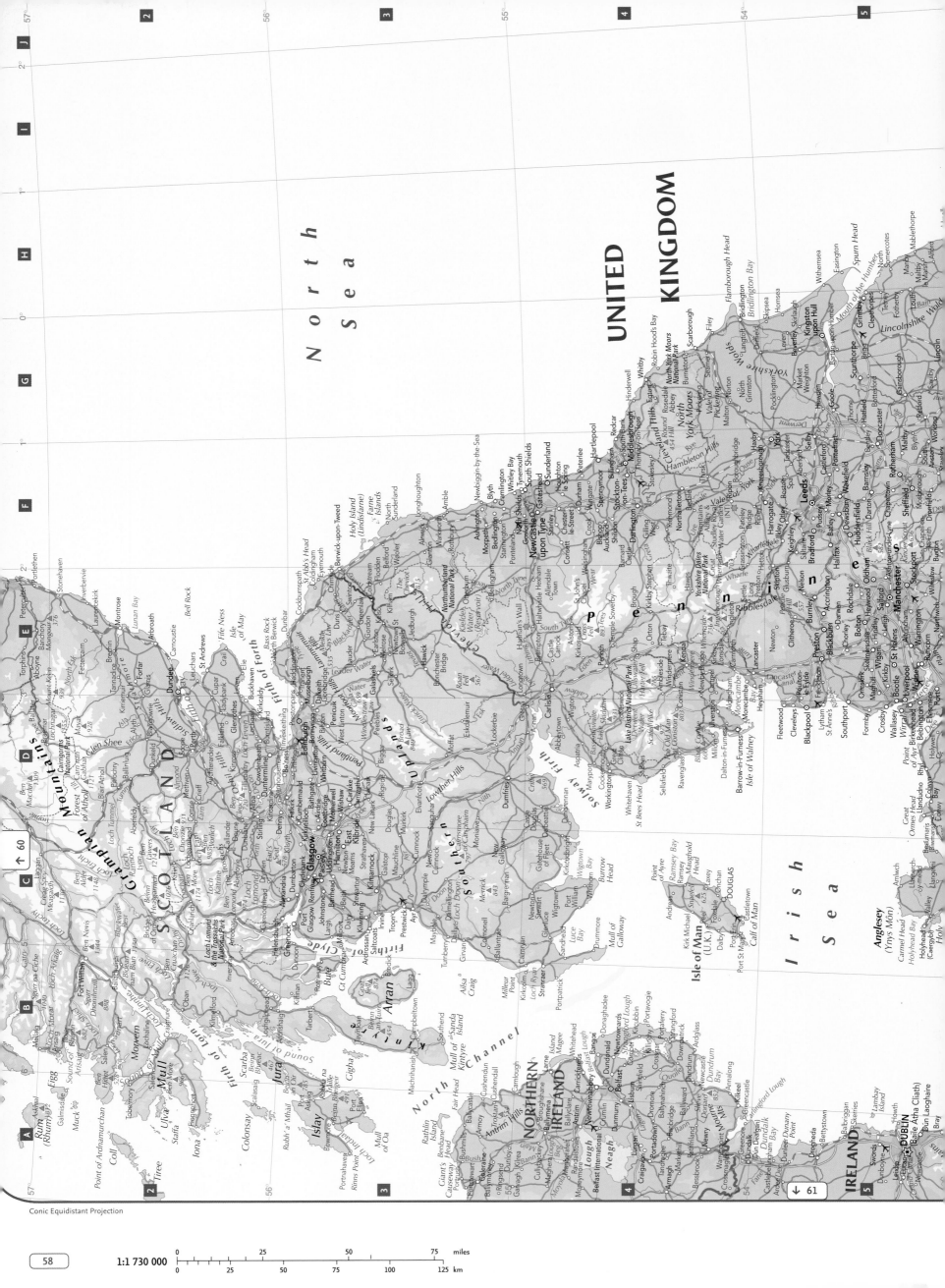

Europe
England and Wales

Europe
Scotland

Conic Equidistant Projection

1:1 730 000

Conic Equidistant Projection

1:1 730 000

Conic Equidistant Projection

1:8 750 000

← 56

Conic Equidistant Projection

Europe
France

1:4 300 000

Europe
Spain and Portugal

Conic Equidistant Projection

1:4 300 000

miles
0   50   100   150
0   50   100   150   200   250 km

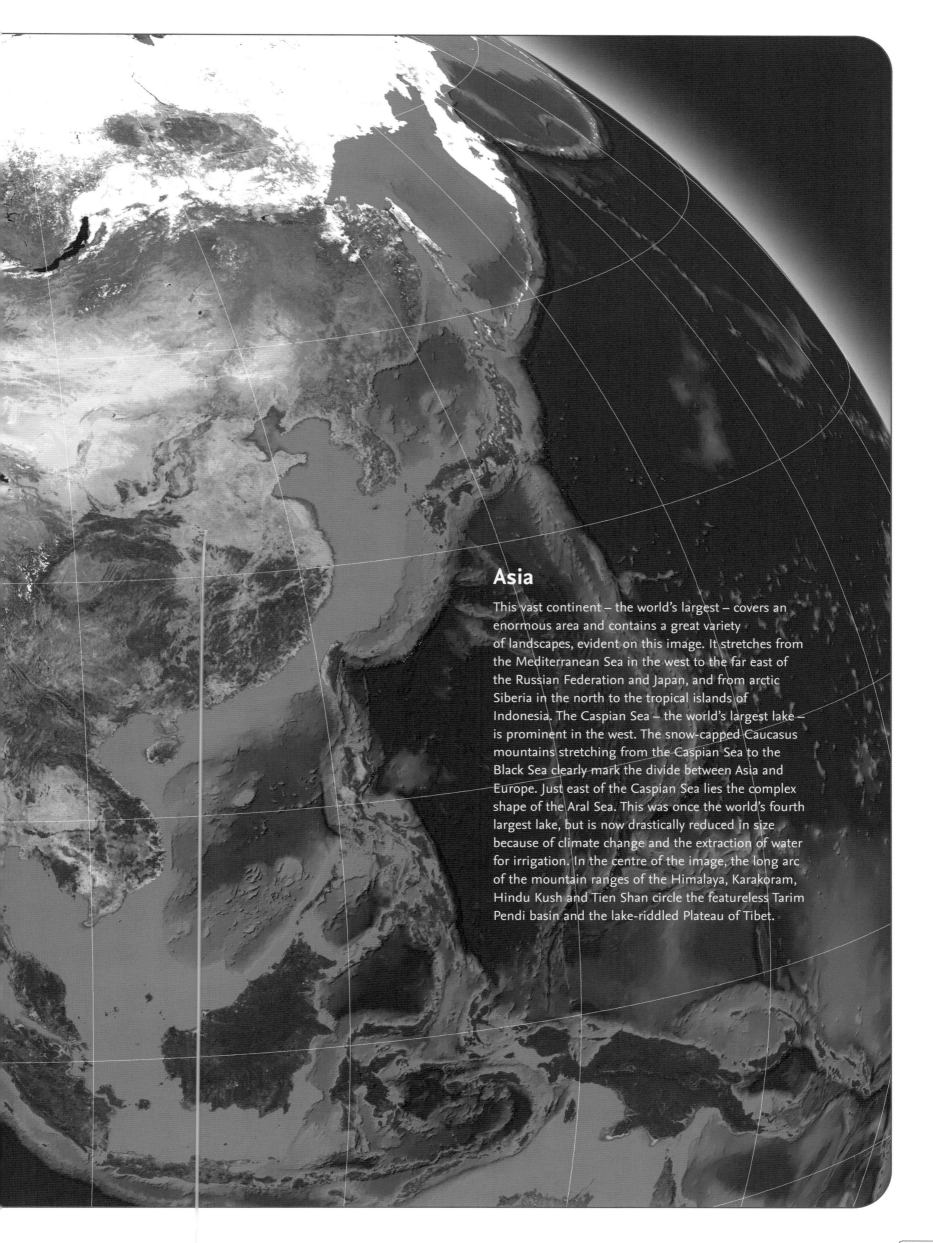

Asia

This vast continent – the world's largest – covers an
enormous area and contains a great variety
of landscapes, evident on this image. It stretches from
the Mediterranean Sea in the west to the far east of
the Russian Federation and Japan, and from arctic
Siberia in the north to the tropical islands of
Indonesia. The Caspian Sea – the world's largest lake –
is prominent in the west. The snow-capped Caucasus
mountains stretching from the Caspian Sea to the
Black Sea clearly mark the divide between Asia and
Europe. Just east of the Caspian Sea lies the complex
shape of the Aral Sea. This was once the world's fourth
largest lake, but is now drastically reduced in size
because of climate change and the extraction of water
for irrigation. In the centre of the image, the long arc
of the mountain ranges of the Himalaya, Karakoram,
Hindu Kush and Tien Shan circle the featureless Tarim
Pendi basin and the lake-riddled Plateau of Tibet.

Asia
Landscapes

Asia is the world's largest continent and occupies almost one-third of the world's total land area. Stretching across approximately 165° of longitude from the Mediterranean Sea to the easternmost point of the Russian Federation on the Bering Strait, it contains the world's highest and lowest points and some of the world's greatest physical features. Its mountain ranges include the Himalaya, Hindu Kush, Karakoram and the Ural Mountains and its major rivers – including the Yangtze, Tigris-Euphrates, Indus, Ganges and Mekong – are equally well-known and evocative.

Asia's deserts include the Gobi, the Taklimakan, and those on the Arabian Peninsula, and significant areas of volcanic and tectonic activity are present on the Kamchatka Peninsula, in Japan, and on Indonesia's numerous islands. The continent's landscapes are greatly influenced by climatic variations, with great contrasts between the islands of the Arctic Ocean and the vast Siberian plains in the north, and the tropical islands of Indonesia.

The **Yangtze**, China, Asia's longest river, flowing into the East China Sea near Shanghai.

Internet Links

● NASA Visible Earth	visibleearth.nasa.gov
● NASA Earth Observatory	earthobservatory.nasa.gov
● Peakware World Mountain Encyclopedia	www.peakware.com
● The Himalaya	www.alpine-club.org.uk

Asia's physical features

Highest mountain	Mt Everest, China/Nepal	8 848 metres	29 028 feet
Longest river	Yangtze, China	6 380 km	3 965 miles
Largest lake	Caspian Sea	371 000 sq km	143 243 sq miles
Largest island	Borneo	745 561 sq km	287 861 sq miles
Largest drainage basin	Ob'-Irtysh, Kazakhstan/Russian Federation	2 990 000 sq km	1 154 439 sq miles
Lowest point	Dead Sea	-421 metres	-1 381 feet

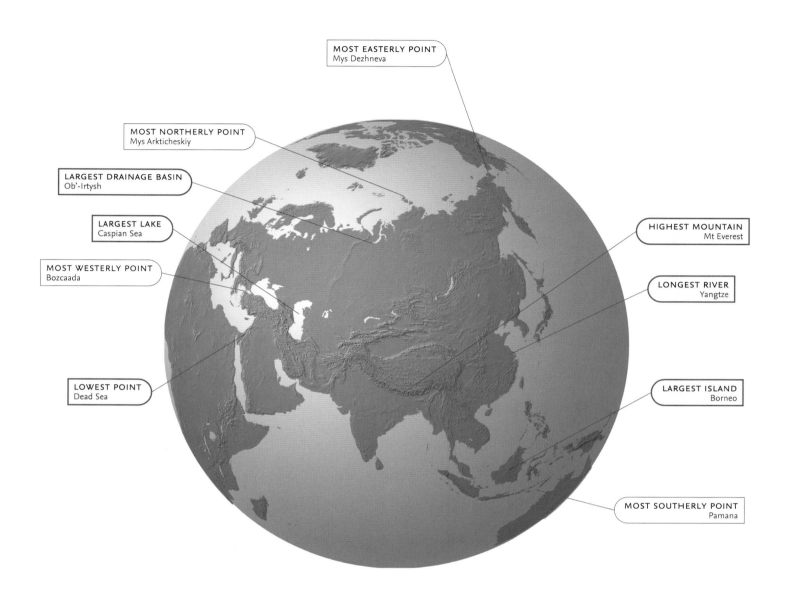

MOST EASTERLY POINT
Mys Dezhneva

MOST NORTHERLY POINT
Mys Arkticheskiy

LARGEST DRAINAGE BASIN
Ob'-Irtysh

LARGEST LAKE
Caspian Sea

MOST WESTERLY POINT
Bozcaada

LOWEST POINT
Dead Sea

HIGHEST MOUNTAIN
Mt Everest

LONGEST RIVER
Yangtze

LARGEST ISLAND
Borneo

MOST SOUTHERLY POINT
Pamana

Asia's extent

TOTAL LAND AREA	45 036 492 sq km / 17 388 686 sq miles
Most northerly point	Mys Arkticheskiy, Russian Federation
Most southerly point	Pamana, Indonesia
Most westerly point	Bozcaada, Turkey
Most easterly point	Mys Dezhneva, Russian Federation

Facts

- 90 of the world's 100 highest mountains are in Asia

- The Indonesian archipelago is made up of over 13 500 islands

- The height of the land in Nepal ranges from 60 metres to 8 848 metres

- The deepest lake in the world is Lake Baikal, Russian Federation, with a maximum depth of 1 741 metres

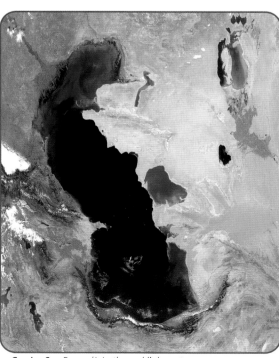

Caspian Sea, Europe/Asia, the world's largest expanse of inland water.

Asia
Countries

With approximately sixty per cent of the world's population, Asia is home to numerous cultures, people groups and lifestyles. Several of the world's earliest civilizations were established in Asia, including those of Sumeria, Babylonia and Assyria. Cultural and historical differences have led to a complex political pattern, and the continent has been, and continues to be, subject to numerous territorial and political conflicts – including the current disputes in the Middle East and in Jammu and Kashmir.

Separate regions within Asia can be defined by the cultural, economic and political systems they support. The major regions are: the arid, oil-rich, mainly Islamic southwest; southern Asia with its distinct cultures, isolated from the rest of Asia by major mountain ranges; the Indian- and Chinese-influenced monsoon region of southeast Asia; the mainly Chinese-influenced industrialized areas of eastern Asia; and Soviet Asia, made up of most of the former Soviet Union.

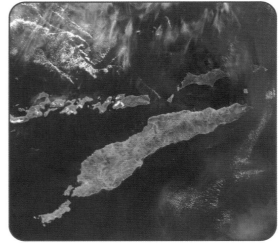

Timor island in southeast Asia, on which East Timor, Asia's newest independent state, is located.

Internet Links

UK Foreign and Commonwealth Office	www.fco.gov.uk
CIA World Factbook	www.cia.gov/library/publications/the-world-factbook/index.html
Asian Development Bank	www.adb.org
Association of Southeast Asian Nations (ASEAN)	www.aseansec.org
Asia-Pacific Economic Cooperation	www.apec.org

Asia's countries

Largest country (area)	Russian Federation	17 075 400 sq km	6 592 849 sq miles
Smallest country (area)	Maldives	298 sq km	115 sq miles
Largest country (population)	China	1 313 437 000	
Smallest country (population)	Palau	20 000	
Most densely populated country	Singapore	6 770 per sq km	17 534 per sq mile
Least densely populated country	Mongolia	2 per sq km	5 per sq mile

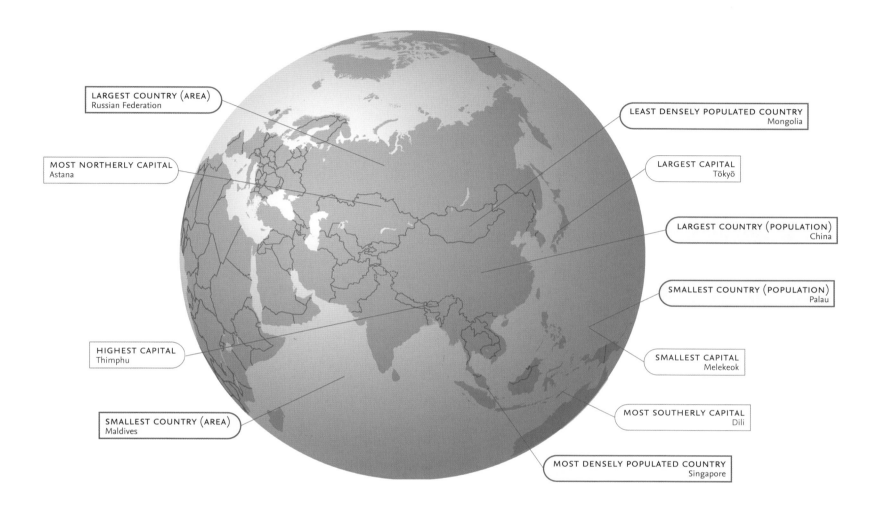

LARGEST COUNTRY (AREA)
Russian Federation

MOST NORTHERLY CAPITAL
Astana

HIGHEST CAPITAL
Thimphu

SMALLEST COUNTRY (AREA)
Maldives

LEAST DENSELY POPULATED COUNTRY
Mongolia

LARGEST CAPITAL
Tōkyō

LARGEST COUNTRY (POPULATION)
China

SMALLEST COUNTRY (POPULATION)
Palau

SMALLEST CAPITAL
Melekeok

MOST SOUTHERLY CAPITAL
Dili

MOST DENSELY POPULATED COUNTRY
Singapore

Melekeok
PALAU

Jayapura

New Guinea

Asia's capitals

Largest capital (population)	Tōkyō, Japan	35 676 000
Smallest capital (population)	Melekeok, Palau	391
Most northerly capital	Astana, Kazakhstan	51° 10'N
Most southerly capital	Dili, East Timor	8° 35'S
Highest capital	Thimphu, Bhutan	2 423 metres 7 949 feet

Facts

- Over 60% of the world's population live in Asia
- Asia has 11 of the world's 20 largest cities
- The Korean peninsula was divided into North Korea and South Korea in 1948 approximately along the 38th parallel

Beijing, capital of China, the most populous country in the world.

Conic Equidistant Projection

1:17 300 000

| 0 | | 200 | | 400 | | 600 | miles |
| 0 | 200 | 400 | 600 | 800 | 1000 km |

OCEAN

Severnaya
Zemlya
Ostrov
Oktyabr'skoy
Revolyutsii

Ostrov
Bol'shevik

New Siberia Islands
(Novosibirskiye Ostrova)

East Siberian Sea
(Vostochno-Sibirskoye More)

Wrangel Island
(Ostrov
Vrangelya)

Chukchi
Sea

Point
Hope

Arctic Circle

Seward Peninsula

U.S.A.

Nome

Aleutian Islands

Bering
Sea

Laptev
Sea
(More Laptevykh)

Ostrov
Bennetta

Ostrov
De-Longa

Khrebet Kolymskiy

Koryakskoye Nagor'ye

Kamchatka Peninsula
(Poluostrov Kamchatka)

Petropavlovsk-
Kamchatskiy

Khrebet Cherskogo

Yakutsk

S   I   B   I   R   I   A

Verkhoyanskiy Khrebet

Central Siberian
Plateau

(Sredne-Sibirskoye
Ploskogor'ye)

R U S S I A N   F E D E R A T I O N

Sea
of
Okhotsk
(Okhotskoye More)

Sakhalin

Kuril Islands
(Kuril'skiye Ostrova)

ADMINISTERED BY
RUSSIAN FEDERATION,
CLAIMED BY JAPAN

Stanovoy Khrebet

Stanovoye
Nagor'ye

Khabarovsk

Sikhote-Alin'

Komsomol'sk

Lake Baikal
(Ozero Baykal)

Irkutsk

Chita

Bratskoye
Vodokhranilishche

MANCHURIA

Harbin

Daqing

Qiqihar

Vladivostok

Hokkaido

Sapporo

PACIFIC
OCEAN

Sea
of
Japan
(East Sea)

JAPAN

Changchun

Shenyang

PYONGYANG

NORTH
KOREA

SEOUL

SOUTH
KOREA

Sendai

TOKYO
Yokohama

Nagoya

Kyōto
Ōsaka
Kōbe

Hiroshima

Kyūshū

Fukuoka

ULAN BATOR
(Ulaanbaatar)

M O N G O L I A

Gobi   Desert

INNER MONGOLIA

C H I N A

BEIJING
(Peking)

Tianjin

Baotou

Datong

Hohhot

Bo Hai

Yellow
Sea
(Huang Hai)

Dalian
(Lüda)

Great Wall

RUSSIAN FEDERATION

MONGOLIA

ULAN BATOR (Ulaanbaatar)

Gobi Desert

INNER MONGOLIA

CHINA

KAZAKHSTAN

XINJIANG

BEIJING (Peking)

NORTH KOREA

PYONGYANG

SOUTH KOREA

SEOUL (Sŏul)

J A P A N

TŌKYŌ

Hokkaidō

Sapporo

Sea of Okhotsk (Okhotskoye More)

Kamchatka Peninsula (Poluostrov Kamchatka)

Kuril'skiye Ostrova (Kuril Islands)

Sakhalin

Sea of Japan (East Sea)

Yellow Sea (Huang Hai)

East China Sea (Dong Hai)

Bo Hai

TAIWAN

T'AIPEI

Hong Kong

Shanghai

Guangzhou

Wuhan

Chongqing

MYANMAR (BURMA)

Mandalay

INDIA

DHAKA (Dacca)

BHUTAN

Taiwan Strait

ADMINISTERED BY RUSSIAN FEDERATION, CLAIMED BY JAPAN

Tropic of Cancer

TAIWAN: The People's Republic of China claims Taiwan as its province.

200   400   600 miles

200   400   600   800   1000 km

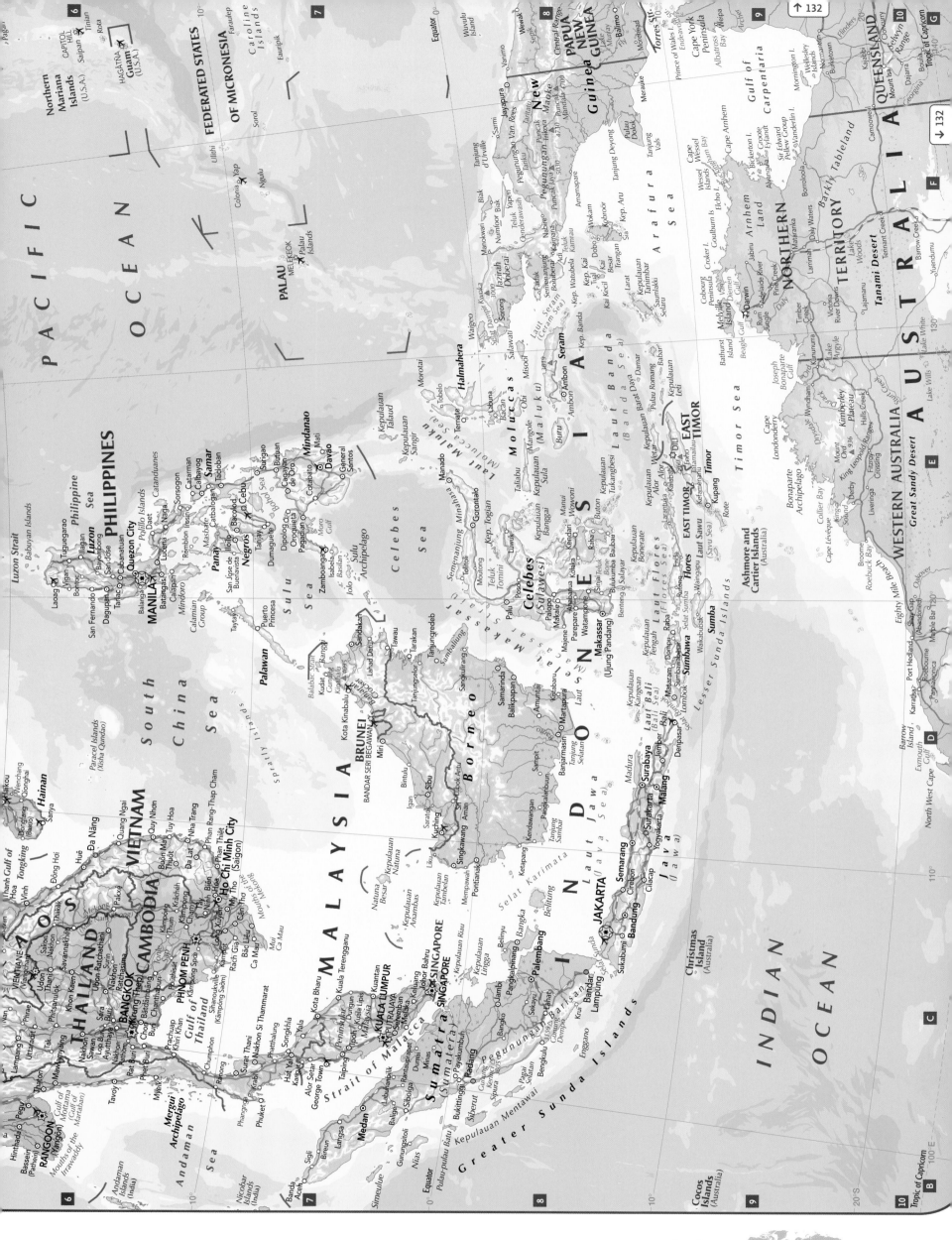

Asia

Eastern and Southeast Asia

A 116° **B** 120° **C** North Island 124° **D** 128°

1

Dongsha Qundao (China)   Pratas Reef

Luzon

North Island Mabudis
Itbayat
Batan Islands
Basco
Ibuhos   Batan
Sabtang

2

20°

South

Strait

Balintang Channel

Babuyan
Babuyan Islands

Calayan

Dalupiri
Fuga   Camiguin
Didicas

Mayraira Point
Cape Bojeador
Bangui
Pasuquin
Laoag
Batac   Dingras
Paoay   Vintar
Espiritu   Sicapoo
Cabugao   2234
Vigan   Bangued
Santa Maria   Mount Chico
Candon   Sapocoy 687
Candon Point   Bontoc   Roxas
Santa Cruz   Tagudin   Callang
Bangar   Luna   Mount
Lingayen   Tabayoc

Claveria
San Vicente   Escarpada Point
Aparri   Buguey
Lal-Lo   Iligan Point
Cabutunan Point
Valley Head

Mount Cagua
Baguio Point

Cabagan
Tuguegarao
Enrile
Cresta 1653
Lubuagan

Divilacan Bay
Estagno Point
Aubarede Point
Palanan Point
Palanan

PALAU

134° 30'

1:1 000 000
0   10 miles
0   10 km

Ngajangel
Ngariungs
Kayangel Atoll
Kayangel Passage
8°   8°
Kossol
Reef
Kossol Passage

Ngaregur
Konrei
Ngemegei Passage
Arekalong
Peninsula

Aiwokako Passage   Ngardmau
Bay   Ulimang
Pkulagalid Point   Ngardmau   200
Toagel Mlungui   Gulitel   Keklau
(West Passage)   Makelulu
Pkurengel   218
Komebail   Mukeru   Namai Bay
Lagoon   7° 30'   7° 30'
Arakabesan   MELEKEOK
Malakal   Koror
Koror   Auluptagel

PHILIPPINES

A
B
C
D

1

2

Celebes

Sea

Sulu Archipelago

MALAYSIA

Tabin
Wildlife
Reserve

Semporna

Maratua

Kakaban

Muaras Reef

Sepinang

KALIMANTAN
TIMUR

Borneo

Teluk Suleman

Tanjung
Mangkalihat

Balabac

Semenanjung Minahasa

GORONTALO

Manado

Bitung

Tanjung Kandi

SULAWESI UTARA

Gorontalo

Tomini
Teluk

Taman Nasional
Bogani Nani Wartabone

Kepulauan
Togian

SULAWESI TENGAH

Palu

Celebes
(Sulawesi)

SULAWESI
BARAT

Makassar
(Ujung Pandang)

SULAWESI
SELATAN

SULAWESI
TENGGARA

Kendari

Buton

Muna

Kabaena

Tanjung Koku

Kepulauan
Salabangka

Kepulauan
Langkesi

Kepulauan
Tukangbesi

Taman Nasional
Wakatobi

Laut Flores
(Flores Sea)

Kepulauan
Sabalana
Banawaya

Kepulauan
Taka'Bonerate

Kakabia

Tanahjampea

Pulau-pulau
Pasitelu

Kepulauan
Bonerate

Batuata

Moromaho

Kepulauan
Sula

Kepulauan
Banggai

Peleng

Banggai

Taliabu

Mangole

Kepulauan
Obi

Obi

Moluccas
(Maluku)

Selat Obi

Bacan

MALUKU
UTARA

Ternate

Tidore

Halmahera

Morotai

Kepulauan
Nanusa

Kepulauan
Talaud

Kepulauan
Karkaralong

Sangir

Kepulauan Sangir

Kepulauan
Asia

Kepulauan
Ayu

Waigeo

PAPUA
(IRIAN JAYA)

Raja Ampat
Marine
Reserve

Misool

Kepulauan
Rajaampat

Salawati

Batanta

MALUKU

Buru

Ambon

Seram

Taman Nasional
Manusela

Laut Seram
(Ceram Sea)

Kepulauan
Gorong

Kepulauan Banda

Bandaneira

Laut Banda

Laut Banda

Kepulauan
Penyu

Kepulauan
Lucipara

(Banda Sea)

Manuk

Serua

Nila

Gunungapi

Kepulauan Barat Daya

Damar

Pulau
Romang

Terbang Utara
Terbang Selatan

Wetar

Kisar

Kepulauan
Leti

Kepulauan
Sermata

Kepulauan
Babar

Yamdena

Kepulauan
Alor

Alor

East Timor

EAST TIMOR

DILI

Flores

Kepulauan Solor

Lomblen

Sumba

NUSA TENGGARA TIMUR

Kupang

Laut Sawu
(Savu Sea)

Rote

Savu

INDONESIA

3

4

5

Timor

Sea

AUSTRALIA

Cape
Van Diemen

120°E
124°
128°

Mercator Projection

→ 81

Asia
Central Indonesia

1:5 500 000

0   50   100   150   200 miles

0 50 100 150 200 250 300 km

83

China Sea

Laut

PHILIPPINES

Sulu Sea

*Celebes
Sea*

BRUNEI

SABAH

MALAYSIA

SARAWAK

KALIMANTAN
TIMUR

KALIMANTAN BARAT

B o r n e o

KALIMANTAN
TENGAH

KALIMANTAN SELATAN

SULAWESI
TENGAH

SULAWESI
BARAT

Celebes
(Sulawesi)

Equator

INESIA

Laut   Jawa

(J a v a   S e a)

Laut Bali
(Bali Sea)

*Laut
Flores*
(Flores Sea)

JAWA TENGAH

Semarang

Surabaya

JAWA TIMUR

Surakarta

YOGYAKARTA

Malang

BALI

Bali

Denpasar

Lombok

Sumbawa

NUSA TENGGARA BARAT

Asia
West Indonesia and Malaysia

Asia

Myanmar, Thailand, Peninsular Malaysia and Indo-China

Albers Conic Equal Area Projection

1:13 000 000

| 0 | 200 | 400 | | miles |
| 0 | 200 | 400 | 600 | 800 km |

Asia
Eastern Asia

Conic Equidistant Projection

1:6 000 000

| 0 | 100 | 200 | miles |

| 0 | 100 | 200 | 300 | 400 | km |

Asia

Japan, North Korea and South Korea

Sea

of

Japan

(East Sea)

2

ISHIKAWA

TOYAMA

Noto-hantō
Kokutei-kōen

Toyama-wan

Ikuji-hana

Chūbu-Sangaku
Kokuritsu-kōen

3

FUKUI

GIFU

O

Wakasa-wan

Wakasa-wan Kokutei-kōen

KYŌTO

SHIGA

Biwa-ko
Kokutei-kōen

Biwa-ko

Kyōto

AICHI

Nagoya

75

HYŌGO

ŌSAKA

Ōsaka

Kōbe

NARA

MIE

Ise-wan

Enshū-nada

4

Harima-nada

Ōsaka-wan

Awaji-shima

HYŌGO

Wakayama

Yoshino-Kumano
Kokuritsu-kōen

P A C

WAKAYAMA

34°N

O C

5
A   135°E   B   136°   C   137°   D

Conic Equidistant Projection

0   10   20   30   40   50   60 miles

0   10 20 30 40 50 60 70 80 90 100 km

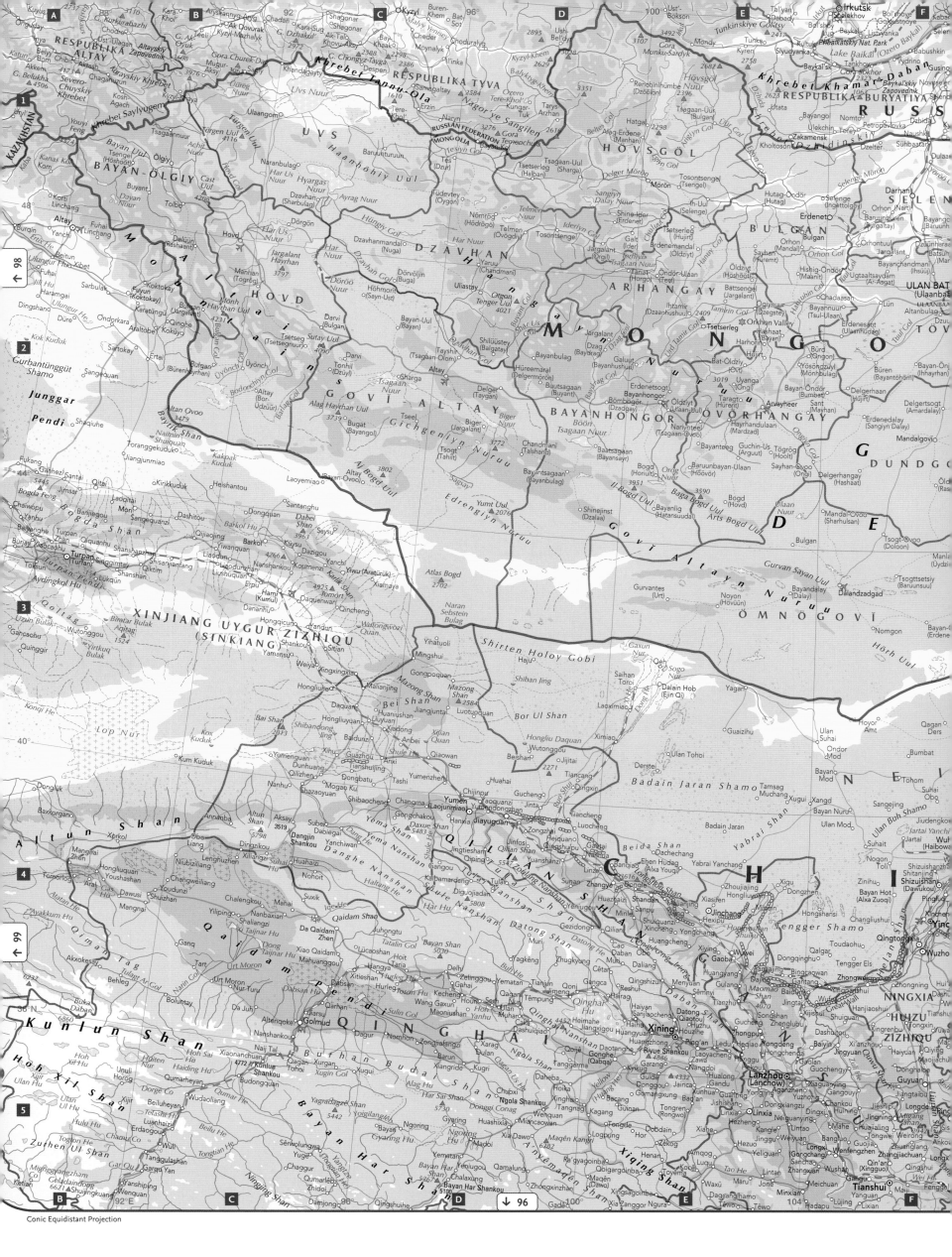

Conic Equidistant Projection

1:6 000 000

→ 90

→ 91

Asia
Northern China and Mongolia

Conic Equidistant Projection

1:6 000 000

Asia
Southeast China

Conic Equidistant Projection

1:6 000 000

| 0 | | 100 | | 200 | miles |
| 0 | 100 | 200 | 300 | 400 | km |

1:17 300 000

Albers Conic Equal Area Projection

| 0 | 200 | 400 | 600 | miles |

| 0 | 200 | 400 | 600 | 800 | 1000 km |

Asia
Central and Southern Asia

↑ 76

↓ 109

Albers Equal Area Conic Projection

1:11 000 000

| 0 | 100 | 200 | 300 | 400 | 500 miles |

| 0 | 100 | 200 | 300 | 400 | 500 | 600 | 700 | 800 km |

AFGHANISTAN

XINJIANG

KHYBER
PAKHTUNKHWA

GILGIT-BALTISTAN

BALTISTAN

AKSAI CHIN

CLAIMED BY INDIA
UNDER CHINESE
ADMINISTRATION

KABUL

ISLAMABAD
Rawalpindi

Peshawar

JAMMU
AND KASHMIR
ZANSKAR

LADAKH

HAZARAJAT

HARAZAT

Kandahar

KHAROTI

Lahore

PUNJAB

PUNJAB

HIMACHAL
PRADESH

Amritsar

Ludhiana

Chandigarh

Dehra
Dun

UTTARAKHAND

PAKISTAN

BALOCHISTAN

Multan

Faisalabad

HARYANA

Meerut

Delhi
NEW
DELHI

Ghaziabad

Faridabad

Moradabad

Bareilly

UTTAR PRA

Bikaner

Jaipur

Agra

Kanpur

RAJASTHAN

Jodhpur

Ajmer

Gwalior

SINDH

Hyderabad

Jhansi

Karachi

Kota

Udaipur

I N D I A

Tropic of Cancer

Bhopal

Ahmadabad
Gandhinagar

MADHYA PRADESH

GUJARAT

Rajkot

Indore

Jabalpur

Vadodara
(Baroda)

Bhavnagar

Arabian Sea

Surat

Nagpur

Administrative divisions in India
numbered on the map:

1. DADRA AND NAGAR HAVELI (C5)
2. DAMAN AND DIU (B5, C5)

Nashik

Amravati

MAHARASHTRA

Aurangabad

Conic Equidistant Projection

1:6 000 000

0   100   200   miles

0   100   200   300   400 km

↓ 106

Asia
Northern India, Nepal, Bhutan and Bangladesh

Asia
Southern India and Sri Lanka

↓ 103

Conic Equidistant Projection

1:6 000 000

Administrative divisions in India
numbered on the map:

1. DADRA AND NAGAR HAVELI (B1)
2. DAMAN AND DIU (A1, B1)
3. PUDUCHERRY (C4)

Albers Conic Equal Area Projection

1:11 000 000

| 0 | 100 | 200 | 300 | 400 | 500 miles |

| 0 | 100 | 200 | 300 | 400 | 500 | 600 | 700 | 800 km |

Asia
Southwest Asia

109

Asia
The Gulf, Iran, Afghanistan and Pakistan

Black Sea

Administrative divisions in Russian Federation
numbered on the map:

1. RESPUBLIKA KALMYKIYA - KHALM'G-TANGCH (G1)
2. RESPUBLIKA DAGESTAN (G2)
3. CHECHENSKAYA RESPUBLIKA (G2)
4. RESPUBLIKA INGUSHETIYA (G2)
5. RESPUBLIKA SEVERNAYA OSETIYA - ALANIYA (G2)
6. KABARDINO-BALKARSKAYA RESPUBLIKA (F2)
7. KARACHAYEVO-CHERKESSKAYA RESPUBLIKA (F2)
8. RESPUBLIKA ADYGEYA (F1)

SERBIA
KOSOVO
MACEDONIA
(F.Y.R.O.M.)
ROMANIA
BUCHAREST
(Bucureşti)
BULGARIA
SOFIA
(Sofiya)
UKRAINE
Crimea

GREECE
ATHENS
(Athína)
Thessaloniki

Istanbul
ANKARA
TURKEY
ANADOLU (ANATOLIA)

Aegean
Sea

Izmir
(Smyrna)

Taurus Mountains

Crete
(Kriti)

Mediterranean Sea

Rhodes
(Rodos)

CYPRUS
NICOSIA
(Lefkosía)

Aleppo
(Halab)

SYRIA

LEBANON
BEIRUT
(Beyrouth)

DAMASCUS
(Dimashq)

Homs

ISRAEL
JERUSALEM
Tel Aviv-Yafo
WEST BANK
GAZA

JORDAN
AMMAN

LIBYA

Alexandria
(Al Iskandarīyah)

CAIRO
(Al Qāhirah)
Gīza
(Al Jīzah)

EGYPT

Western Desert
(Aş Şaḥrā' al Gharbīyah)

Great Sand Sea

Eastern Desert
(Aş Şaḥrā' ash Sharqīyah)

Red Sea

Gulf of Suez

Gulf of Aqaba

Sinai

SA

Conic Equidistant Projection

112

1:6 000 000

0 100 200 miles
0 100 200 300 400 km

Asia

Eastern Mediterranean, the Caucasus and Iraq

Africa

This image of Africa clearly shows the change in vegetation through the equatorial regions from the vast, dry Sahara desert covering much of the north of the continent, through the rich forests of the Congo basin – the second largest drainage basin in the world – to the high plateau of southern Africa. Lake Victoria dominates central east Africa and the Nile and its delta create a distinctive feature in the desert in the northeast. The path of the Great Rift Valley can be traced by the pattern of linear lakes in east Africa, to Ethiopia, and along the Red Sea. The dark fan-shaped feature in central southern Africa is the Okavango Delta in Botswana – one of the world's most ecologically sensitive areas. To the east of the continent lies Madagascar, and in the Indian Ocean northeast of this is the Mascarene Ridge sea feature stretching from the Seychelles in the north to Mauritius and Réunion in the south.

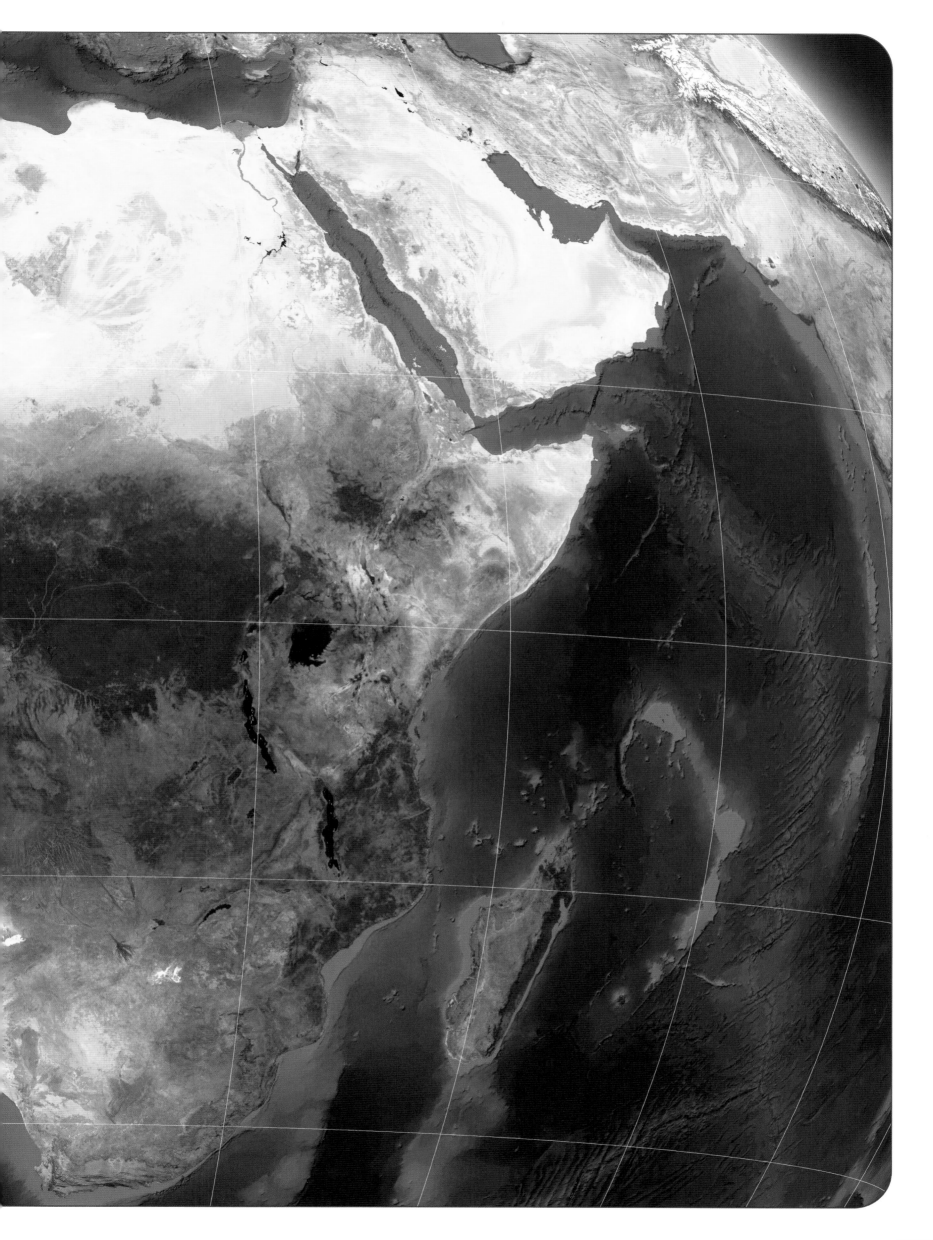

Africa
Landscapes

Some of the world's greatest physical features are in Africa, the world's second largest continent. Variations in climate and elevation give rise to the continent's great variety of landscapes. The Sahara, the world's largest desert, extends across the whole continent from west to east, and covers an area of over nine million square kilometres. Other significant African deserts are the Kalahari and the Namib. In contrast, some of the world's greatest rivers flow in Africa, including the Nile, the world's longest, and the Congo.

The Great Rift Valley is perhaps Africa's most notable geological feature. It stretches for nearly 3 000 kilometres from Jordan, through the Red Sea and south to Mozambique, and contains many of Africa's largest lakes. Significant mountain ranges on the continent are the Atlas Mountains and the Ethiopian Highlands in the north, the Ruwenzori in east central Africa, and the Drakensberg in the far southeast.

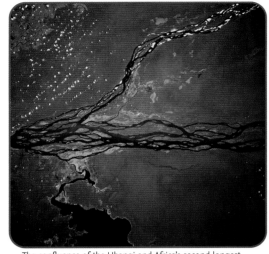

The confluence of the Ubangi and Africa's second longest river, the **Congo**.

Africa's extent

TOTAL LAND AREA	30 343 578 sq km / 11 715 655 sq miles
Most northerly point	La Galite, Tunisia
Most southerly point	Cape Agulhas, South Africa
Most westerly point	Santo Antão, Cape Verde
Most easterly point	Raas Xaafuun, Somalia

Internet Links

● NASA Visible Earth	**visibleearth.nasa.gov**
● NASA Astronaut Photography	**eol.jsc.nasa.gov**
● Peace Parks Foundation	**www.peaceparks.org**

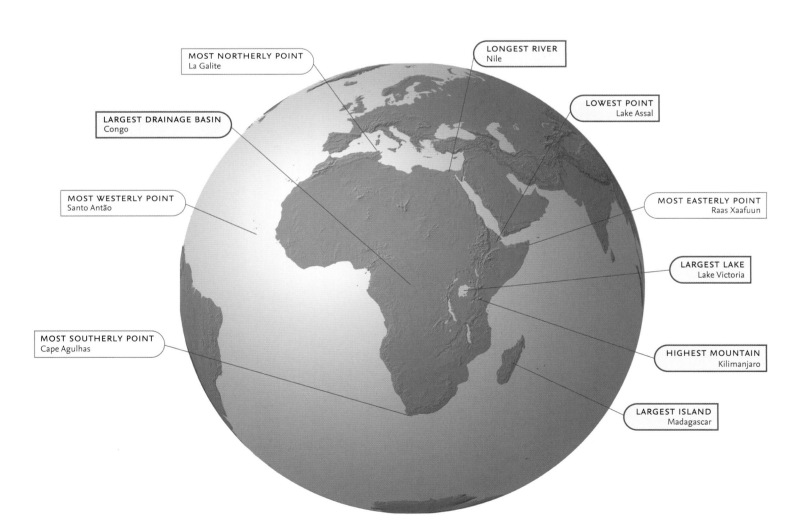

MOST NORTHERLY POINT
La Galite

LONGEST RIVER
Nile

LOWEST POINT
Lake Assal

LARGEST DRAINAGE BASIN
Congo

MOST WESTERLY POINT
Santo Antão

MOST EASTERLY POINT
Raas Xaafuun

LARGEST LAKE
Lake Victoria

MOST SOUTHERLY POINT
Cape Agulhas

HIGHEST MOUNTAIN
Kilimanjaro

LARGEST ISLAND
Madagascar

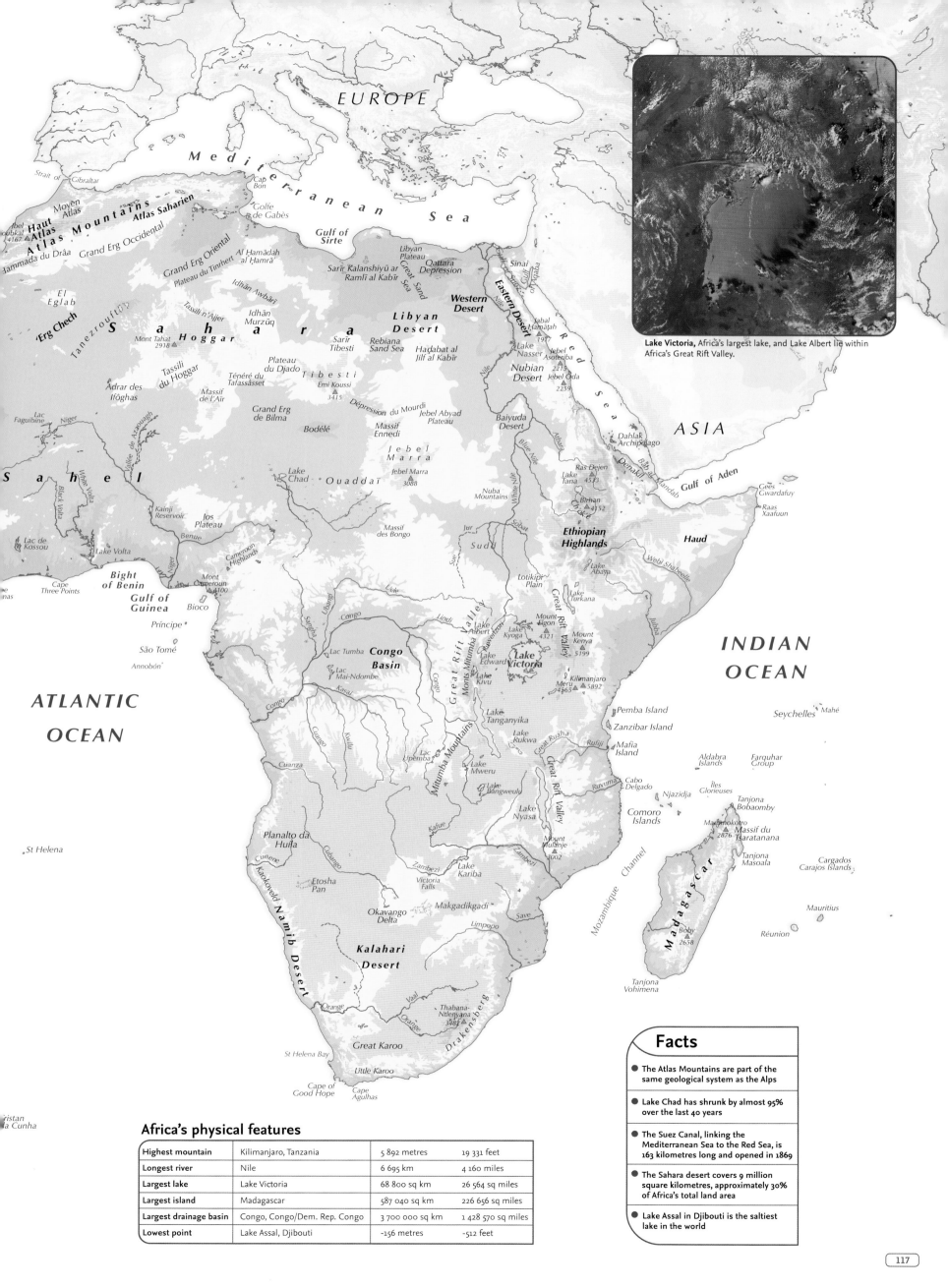

Lake Victoria, Africa's largest lake, and Lake Albert lie within Africa's Great Rift Valley.

Africa's physical features

Highest mountain	Kilimanjaro, Tanzania	5 892 metres	19 331 feet
Longest river	Nile	6 695 km	4 160 miles
Largest lake	Lake Victoria	68 800 sq km	26 564 sq miles
Largest island	Madagascar	587 040 sq km	226 656 sq miles
Largest drainage basin	Congo, Congo/Dem. Rep. Congo	3 700 000 sq km	1 428 570 sq miles
Lowest point	Lake Assal, Djibouti	-156 metres	-512 feet

Facts

- The Atlas Mountains are part of the same geological system as the Alps

- Lake Chad has shrunk by almost 95% over the last 40 years

- The Suez Canal, linking the Mediterranean Sea to the Red Sea, is 163 kilometres long and opened in 1869

- The Sahara desert covers 9 million square kilometres, approximately 30% of Africa's total land area

- Lake Assal in Djibouti is the saltiest lake in the world

Africa
Countries

Africa is a complex continent, with over fifty independent countries and a long history of political change. It supports a great variety of ethnic groups, with the Sahara creating the major divide between Arab and Berber groups in the north and a diverse range of groups, including the Yoruba and Masai, in the south.

The current pattern of countries in Africa is a product of a long and complex history, including the colonial period, which saw European control of the vast majority of the continent from the fifteenth century until widespread moves to independence began in the 1950s. Despite its great wealth of natural resources, Africa is by far the world's poorest continent. Many of its countries are heavily dependent upon foreign aid and many are also subject to serious political instability.

Facts

- Africa has over 1 000 linguistic and cultural groups

- Only Liberia and Ethiopia have remained free from colonial rule throughout their history

- Over 30% of the world's minerals, and over 50% of the world's diamonds, come from Africa

- 9 of the 10 poorest countries in the world are in Africa

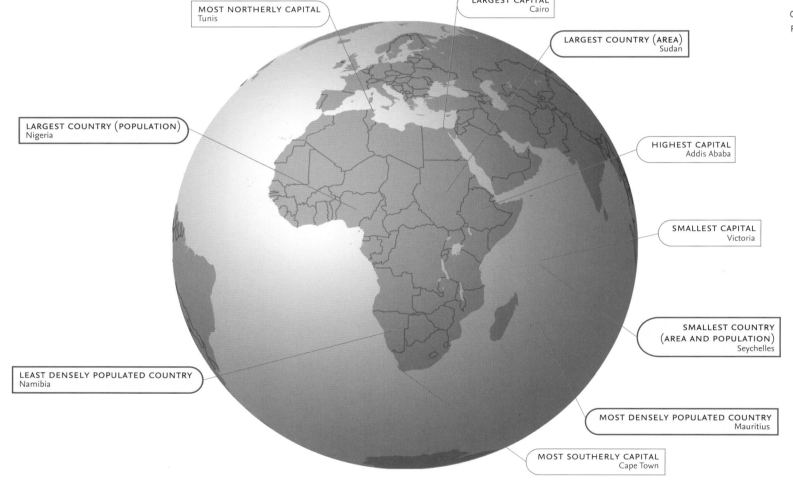

MOST NORTHERLY CAPITAL
Tunis

LARGEST CAPITAL
Cairo

LARGEST COUNTRY (AREA)
Sudan

LARGEST COUNTRY (POPULATION)
Nigeria

HIGHEST CAPITAL
Addis Ababa

SMALLEST CAPITAL
Victoria

SMALLEST COUNTRY
(AREA AND POPULATION)
Seychelles

LEAST DENSELY POPULATED COUNTRY
Namibia

MOST DENSELY POPULATED COUNTRY
Mauritius

MOST SOUTHERLY CAPITAL
Cape Town

Madeira
(Portugal)

Canary Islan
(Spain)

Laâyoune

WESTERN
SAHARA

Nouâdhibou

MAURITAN

Nouakchott

St-Louis

CAPE
VERDE

Dakar
Praia

SENEGAL

Kaolack

Banjul

THE GAMBIA

Bissau

GUINEA-
BISSAU

GUINE

Conakry

Freetown

SIERRA
LEONE

Monrovia

LIBE

Ascension
(U.K.)

Internet Links	
UK Foreign and Commonwealth Office	www.fco.gov.uk
CIA World Factbook	www.cia.gov/library/publications/the-world-factbook/index.html
Southern African Development Community	www.sadc.int
GeoEye	www.GeoEye.com

EUROPE

Strait of Gibraltar

Mediterranean Sea

Tangier
Rabat
Casablanca
Beni Mellal
arrakech
Béchar

Oran
Sidi Bel Abbès
Fès

Algiers
Ech Chélif
Bejaïa
Annaba
Constantine
Tunis
Skikda

Sfax
Gabès
Laghouat

MOROCCO

TUNISIA
Tripoli
Mişrātah

Gulf of Sirte
Benghazi

Al Baydā'

Alexandria
Port Said
Tanţa
Cairo
Giza
Suez

ALGERIA

Atlas Mountains

LIBYA

S a h a r a

Libyan Desert

EGYPT

Al Minyā
Asyūţ
Qina
Luxor
Aswān
Lake Nasser

Nile

Red Sea

ASIA

Cape Town, legislative capital of the Republic of South Africa and the most southerly African capital city.

MALI

NIGER

Gao
Mopti
gou
amako
-Dioulasso

BURKINA FASO
Ouagadougou
Tamale

Niamey

Agadez

Zinder

CHAD

Lake Chad

Sokoto
Kano
Zaria

Maiduguri

Ndjamena
Maroua

Abéché

Port Sudan

Omdurman
Khartoum
Wad Medani
El Obeid

SUDAN

Gedaref

Blue Nile

White Nile

ERITREA
Asmara

Mek'elē

DJIBOUTI
Bahir Dar
Djibouti
Dirē Dawa
Berbera
Hargeysa

Gulf of Aden

CÔTE D'IVOIRE
Bouaké
amoussoukro
Kumasi
Abidjan

GHANA
TOGO
BENIN
Parakou
NIGERIA
Ibadan
Abuja
Ogbomosho
Lagos
Porto-Novo
Accra
Cape Coast
Lomé

Kumo
Ngaoundéré

Moundou

Sarh

CENTRAL AFRICAN REPUBLIC

Bossángoa
Bouar

Wau

Juba

Addis Ababa

ETHIOPIA

Dire

SOMALIA

Mogadishu

Kismaayo

EQUATORIAL GUINEA
Malabo
SÃO TOMÉ AND PRÍNCIPE
São Tomé

Gulf of Guinea

Onitsha
Warri
Uyo
Port Harcourt
CAMEROON
Douala
Yaoundé
Nkongsamba

Bangui

DEMOCRATIC REPUBLIC OF THE CONGO

UGANDA
Kisangani
Kampala

KENYA

Mount Kenya 5199

Kisumu
Nakuru
Nairobi

Port-Gentil
Libreville
GABON
Franceville

CONGO

Mbandaka

Congo

Kasai

RWANDA
Bukavu
Kigali
BURUNDI
Bujumbura

Lake Victoria

Mwanza

Arusha
Kilimanjaro 5892

Mombasa

INDIAN OCEAN

Victoria

SEYCHELLES

ATLANTIC OCEAN

Pointe-Noire
Brazzaville
Kinshasa
CABINDA (Angola)
Matadi
Bandundu
Kikwit

Kananga
Mbuji-Mayi

Kamina

Kigoma
Kalemie

Tabora
Dodoma

TANZANIA

Iringa

Lake Tanganyika

Zanzibar Island
Zanzibar
Dar es Salaam

Aldabra Islands

Luanda

Cuanza

Mbeya

Kasama
Mansa

ANGOLA

Lobito
Benguela
Huambo

Lubango

Namibe

Likasi
Lubumbashi
Solwezi
Ndola
Chingola
Kabwe

MALAWI
Lake Nyasa
Chipata

Pemba

Moroni
COMOROS

Antsiranana

MAYOTTE (France)

St Helena (U.K.)

St Helena, Ascension and Tristan da Cunha (U.K.)

ZAMBIA
Mongu
Lusaka

Livingstone

Lilongwe
Blantyre

Tete
Nampula

Nacala

Mahajanga

NAMIBIA
Windhoek

Etosha Pan

BOTSWANA
Gaborone

Okavango Delta
Francistown

Cubango

Chitungwiza
Harare

ZIMBABWE
Gweru
Bulawayo

Mutare

MOZAMBIQUE

Beira

Quelimane

Mozambique Channel

MADAGASCAR

Toamasina

Antananarivo

Namib Desert
Zambezi

Inhambane

Xai-Xai

Toliara

Fianarantsoa

Port Louis
MAURITIUS

Réunion (France)

Johannesburg
Carletonville
Soweto
Pretoria (Tshwane)
Maputo
Mbabane
SWAZILAND

Kimberley
Bloemfontein
LESOTHO
Maseru
Durban

Orange

REPUBLIC OF SOUTH AFRICA

Cape Town
Khayelitsha
Cape of Good Hope
Cape Agulhas

East London
Port Elizabeth

Tristan da Cunha (U.K.)

Africa's capitals

Largest capital (population)	Cairo, Egypt	11 893 000
Smallest capital (population)	Victoria, Seychelles	25 500
Most northerly capital	Tunis, Tunisia	36° 46'N
Most southerly capital	Cape Town, Republic of South Africa	33° 57'S
Highest capital	Addis Ababa, Ethiopia	2 408 metres 7 900 feet

Africa's countries

Largest country (area)	Sudan	2 505 813 sq km	967 500 sq miles
Smallest country (area)	Seychelles	455 sq km	176 sq miles
Largest country (population)	Nigeria	131 530 000	
Smallest country (population)	Seychelles	81 000	
Most densely populated country	Mauritius	599 per sq km	1 549 per sq mile
Least densely populated country	Namibia	2 per sq km	6 per sq mile

1:14 000 000

Africa
Central and Southern Africa

Lambert Azimuthal Equal Area Projection

1:4 300 000

miles
km

Africa
Republic of South Africa

125

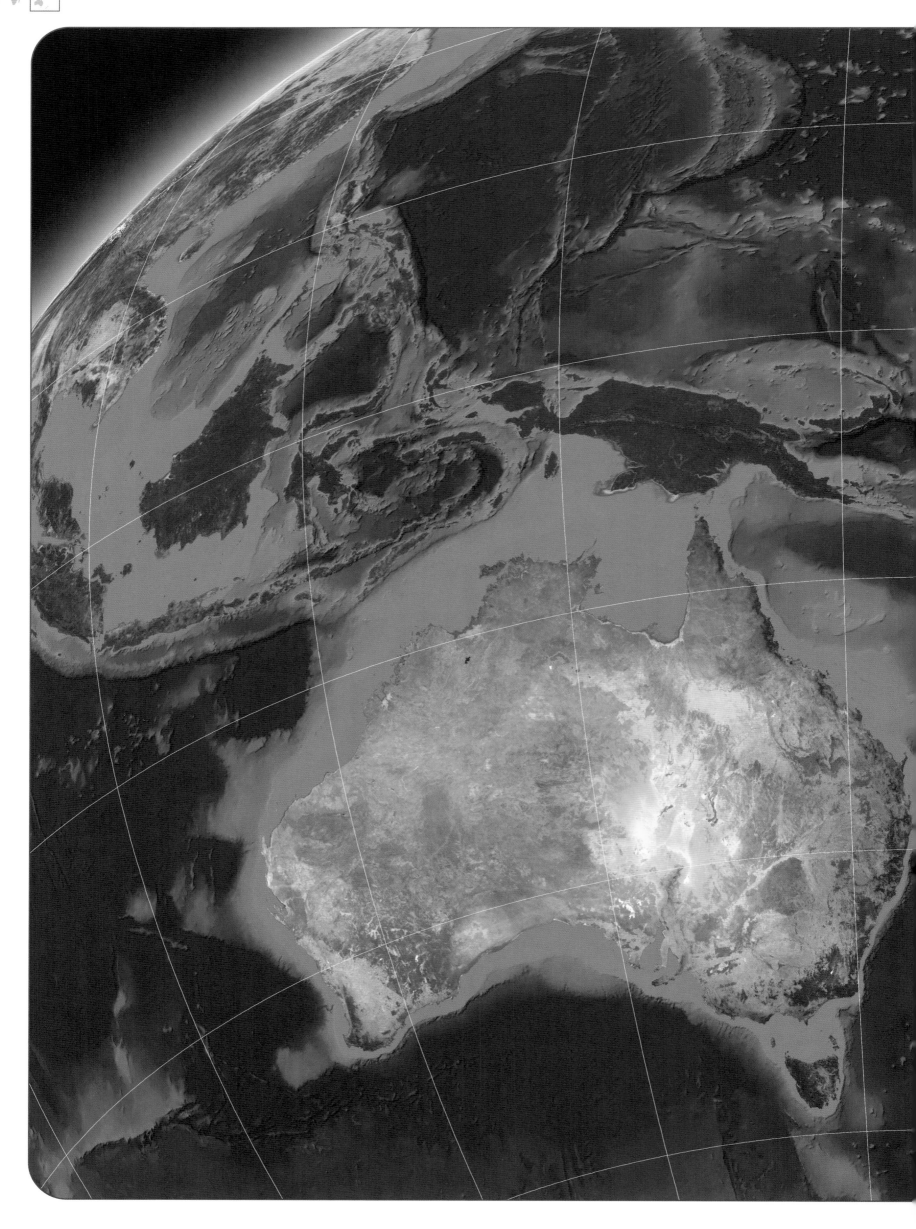

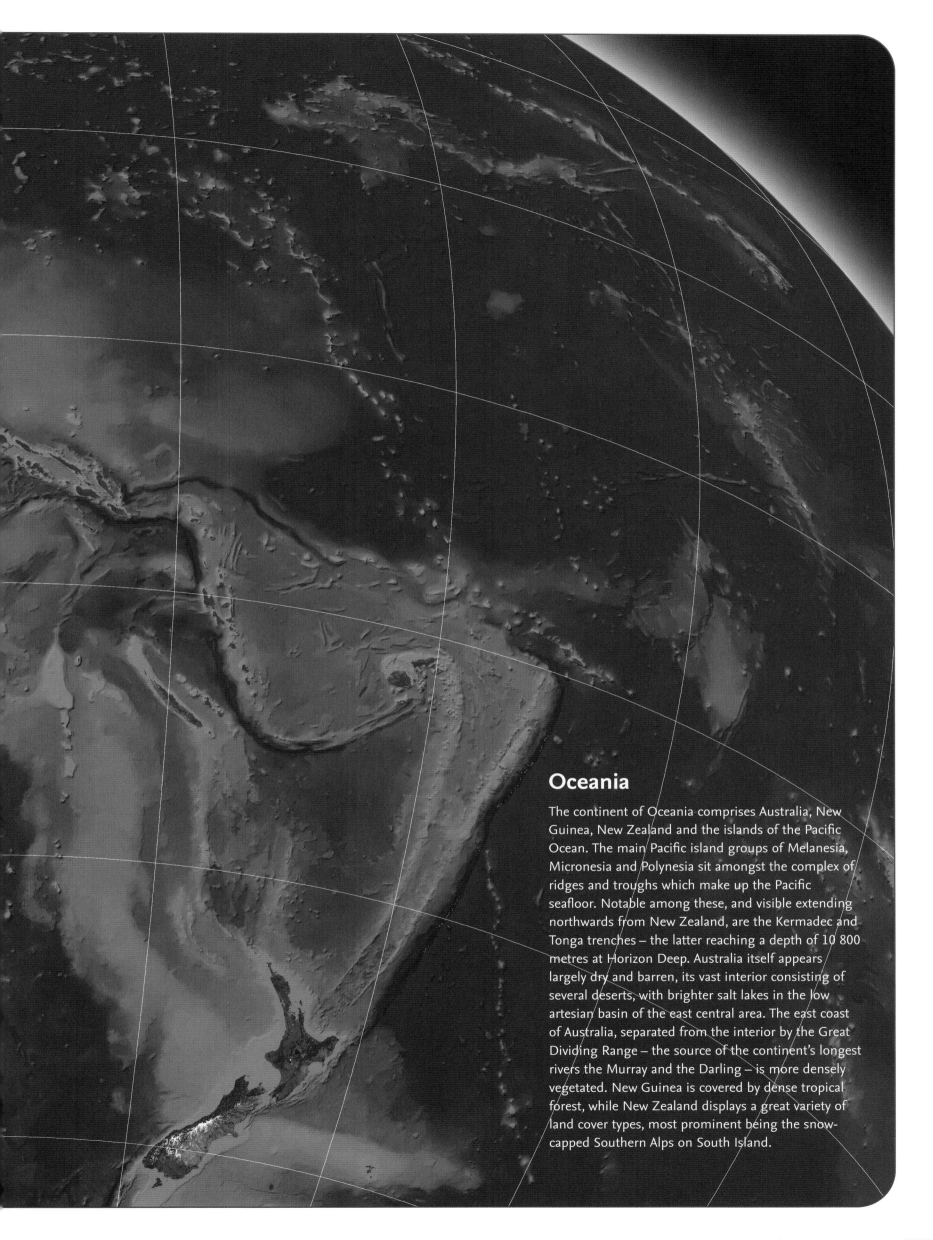

Oceania

The continent of Oceania comprises Australia, New Guinea, New Zealand and the islands of the Pacific Ocean. The main Pacific island groups of Melanesia, Micronesia and Polynesia sit amongst the complex of ridges and troughs which make up the Pacific seafloor. Notable among these, and visible extending northwards from New Zealand, are the Kermadec and Tonga trenches – the latter reaching a depth of 10 800 metres at Horizon Deep. Australia itself appears largely dry and barren, its vast interior consisting of several deserts, with brighter salt lakes in the low artesian basin of the east central area. The east coast of Australia, separated from the interior by the Great Dividing Range – the source of the continent's longest rivers the Murray and the Darling – is more densely vegetated. New Guinea is covered by dense tropical forest, while New Zealand displays a great variety of land cover types, most prominent being the snow-capped Southern Alps on South Island.

Oceania
Landscapes

Oceania comprises Australia, New Zealand, New Guinea and the islands of the Pacific Ocean. It is the smallest of the world's continents by land area. Its dominating feature is Australia, which is mainly flat and very dry. Australia's western half consists of a low plateau, broken in places by higher mountain ranges, which has very few permanent rivers or lakes. The narrow, fertile coastal plain of the east coast is separated from the interior by the Great Dividing Range, which includes the highest mountain in Australia.

The numerous Pacific islands of Oceania are generally either volcanic in origin or consist of coral. They can be divided into three main regions - Micronesia, north of the equator between Palau and the Gilbert islands; Melanesia, stretching from mountainous New Guinea to Fiji; and Polynesia, covering a vast area of the eastern and central Pacific Ocean.

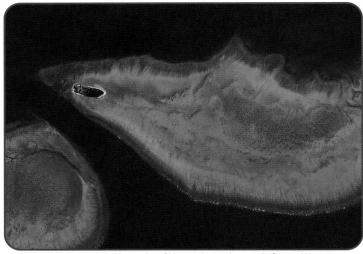

Heron Island, surrounded by coral reefs, lies at the southern end of Australia's Great Barrier Reef.

Facts

- Australia's Great Barrier Reef is the world's largest coral reef and stretches for over 2 000 kilometres

- The highest point of Tuvalu is only 5 metres above sea level

- New Zealand lies directly on the boundary between the Pacific and Indo-Australian tectonic plates

- The Mariana Trench in the Pacific Ocean contains the earth's deepest point – Challenger Deep, 10 920 metres below sea level

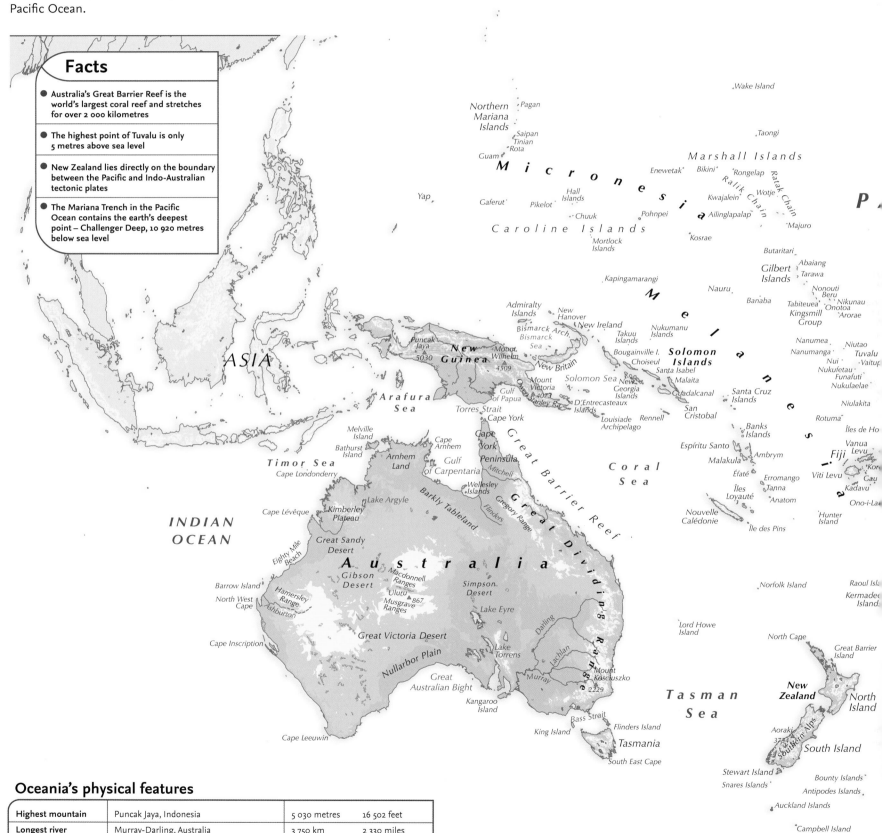

Oceania's physical features

Highest mountain	Puncak Jaya, Indonesia	5 030 metres	16 502 feet
Longest river	Murray-Darling, Australia	3 750 km	2 330 miles
Largest lake	Lake Eyre, Australia	0–8 900 sq km	0–3 436 sq miles
Largest island	New Guinea, Indonesia/Papua New Guinea	808 510 sq km	312 166 sq miles
Largest drainage basin	Murray-Darling, Australia	1 058 000 sq km	408 494 sq miles
Lowest point	Lake Eyre, Australia	-16 metres	-53 feet

Internet Links	
● NASA Visible Earth	visibleearth.nasa.gov
● NASA Astronaut Photography	eol.jsc.nasa.gov
● Great Barrier Reef Marine Park Authority	www.gbrmpa.gov.au

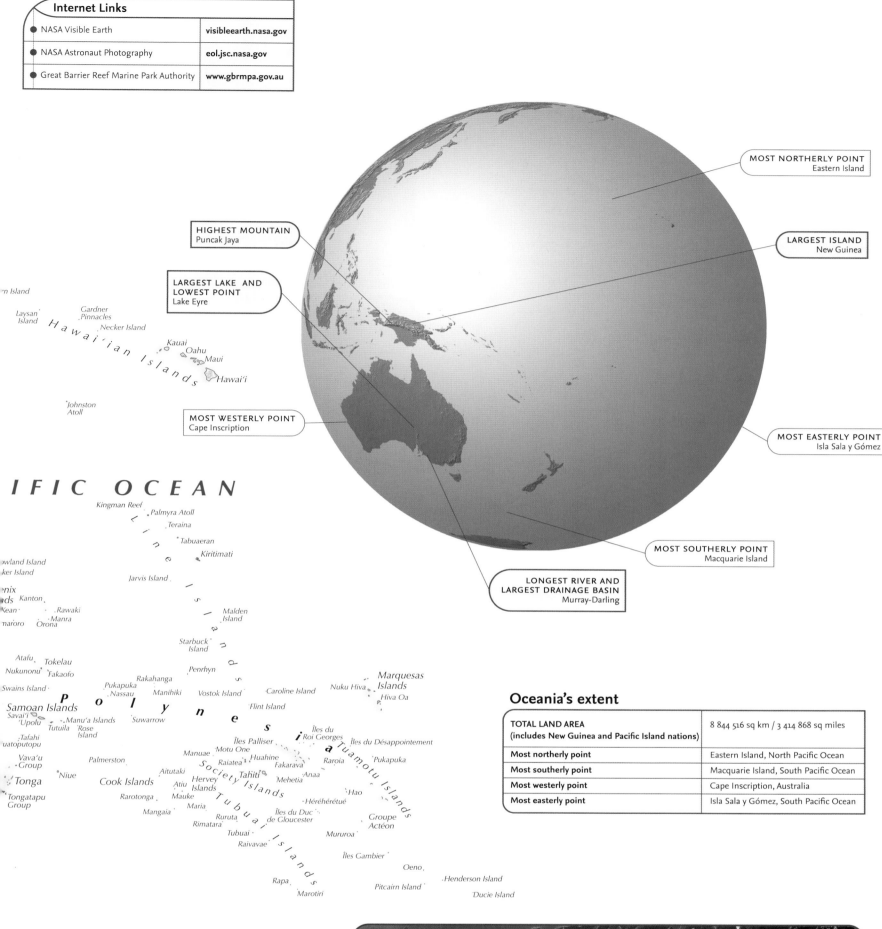

MOST NORTHERLY POINT
Eastern Island

HIGHEST MOUNTAIN
Puncak Jaya

LARGEST ISLAND
New Guinea

LARGEST LAKE AND LOWEST POINT
Lake Eyre

MOST WESTERLY POINT
Cape Inscription

MOST EASTERLY POINT
Isla Sala y Gómez

MOST SOUTHERLY POINT
Macquarie Island

LONGEST RIVER AND LARGEST DRAINAGE BASIN
Murray-Darling

rn Island

Laysan Island

Gardner Pinnacles

Necker Island

H a w a i ' i a n   I s l a n d s

Kauai
Oahu
Maui
Hawai'i

'Johnston Atoll

IFIC OCEAN

Kingman Reef
Palmyra Atoll
Teraina
Tabuaeran
Kiritimati

L i n e   I s l a n d s

owland Island
ker Island

Jarvis Island

enix
ds *Kanton*
Kean *Rawaki*
Manra
naroro *Orona*

Malden Island

Starbuck Island

Atafu *Tokelau*
Nukunonu *Fakaofo*
Swains Island

Penrhyn

Pukapuka *Rakahanga*
Nassau *Manihiki*

Vostok Island

Caroline Island

Flint Island

Marquesas Islands
Nuku Hiva
Hiva Oa

P o l y n e s i a

Samoan Islands
Savai'i
'Upolu *Manu'a Islands*
Tutuila *Rose Island*

Suwarrow

Îles du Roi Georges
Îles du Désappointement

'Tafahi
uatoputopu

Vava'u
·Group
'Niue

Manuae *'Motu One*
*Raiatea' *Huahine*
Aitutaki *Fakarava*

Raroia
Pukapuka

T u a m o t u   I s l a n d s

Palmerston

Cook Islands
Atiu
Rarotonga *Mauke*
Mangaia

Society Islands
Tahiti
Mehetia
Anaa
'Hao

Hervey Islands

Tonga
Tongatapu Group

Maria
Rimatara
Tubuai
Raivavae

Ruruta'
Îles du Duc de Gloucester

Mururoa

'Héréhérétué

Groupe Actéon

T u b u a i   I s l a n d s

Rapa
Marotiri

Îles Gambier

Oeno
Henderson Island
Pitcairn Island
'Ducie Island

Oceania's extent

TOTAL LAND AREA (includes New Guinea and Pacific Island nations)	8 844 516 sq km / 3 414 868 sq miles
Most northerly point	Eastern Island, North Pacific Ocean
Most southerly point	Macquarie Island, South Pacific Ocean
Most westerly point	Cape Inscription, Australia
Most easterly point	Isla Sala y Gómez, South Pacific Ocean

nam Islands
land

ERN OCEAN

Banks Peninsula, Canterbury Plains and the **Southern Alps**, South Island, New Zealand.

Oceania
Countries

Stretching across almost the whole width of the Pacific Ocean, Oceania has a great variety of cultures and an enormously diverse range of countries and territories. Australia, by far the largest and most industrialized country in the continent, contrasts with the numerous tiny Pacific island nations which have smaller, and more fragile economies based largely on agriculture, fishing and the exploitation of natural resources.

The division of the Pacific island groups into the main regions of Micronesia, Melanesia and Polynesia – often referred to as the South Sea islands – broadly reflects the ethnological differences across the continent. There is a long history of colonial influence in the region, which still contains dependent territories belonging to Australia, France, New Zealand, the UK and the USA.

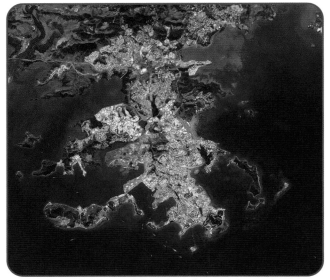

Nouméa, capital of the French dependency of New Caledonia in the southern Pacific Ocean.

Facts

- Over 91% of Australia's population live in urban areas

- The Maori name for New Zealand is Aotearoa, meaning 'land of the long white cloud'

- Auckland, New Zealand, has the largest Polynesian population of any city in Oceania

- Over 800 different languages are spoken in Papua New Guinea

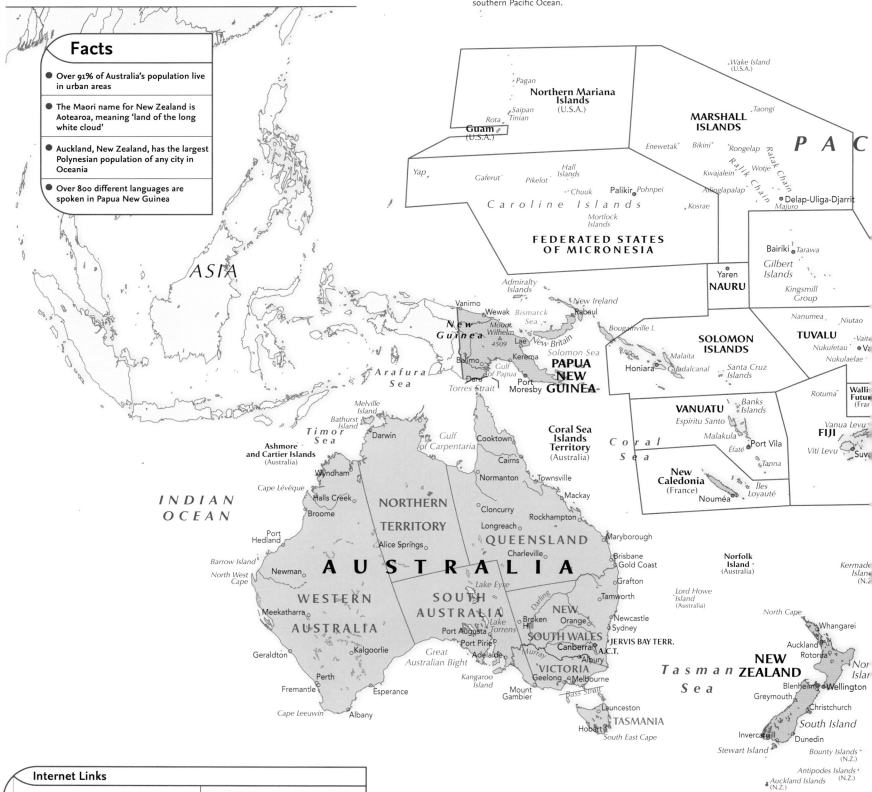

Internet Links

UK Foreign and Commonwealth Office	www.fco.gov.uk
CIA World Factbook	www.cia.gov/library/publications/the-world-factbook/index.html
Geoscience Australia	www.ga.gov.au

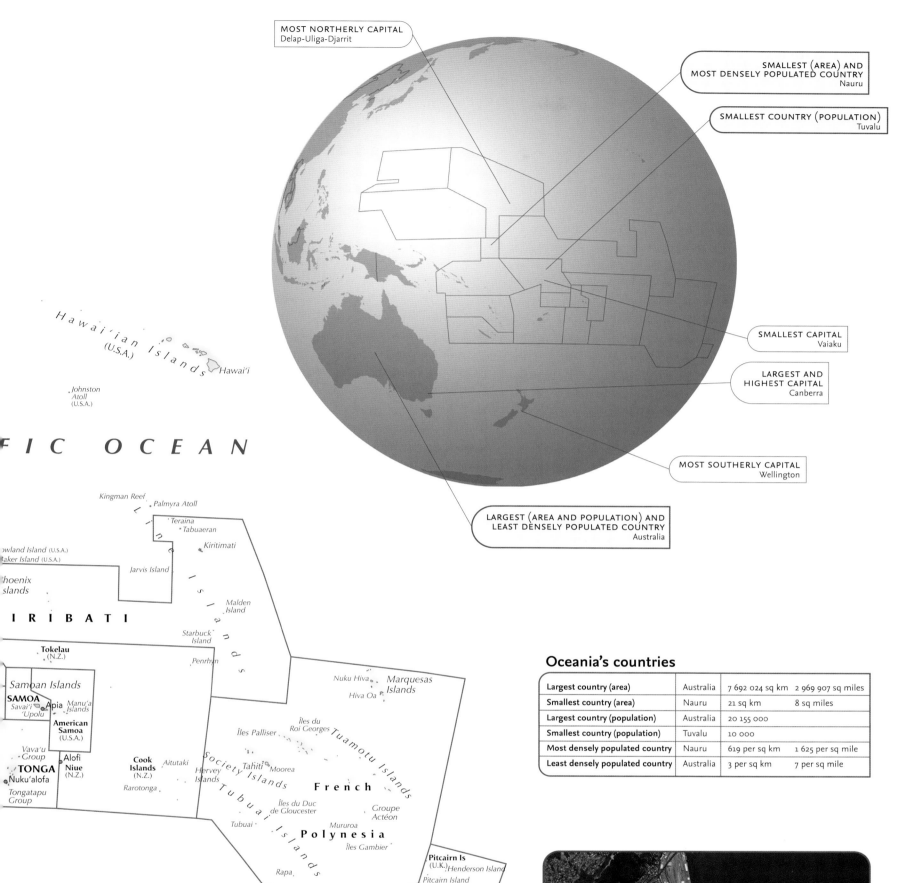

MOST NORTHERLY CAPITAL
Delap-Uliga-Djarrit

SMALLEST (AREA) AND
MOST DENSELY POPULATED COUNTRY
Nauru

SMALLEST COUNTRY (POPULATION)
Tuvalu

SMALLEST CAPITAL
Vaiaku

LARGEST AND
HIGHEST CAPITAL
Canberra

MOST SOUTHERLY CAPITAL
Wellington

LARGEST (AREA AND POPULATION) AND
LEAST DENSELY POPULATED COUNTRY
Australia

Hawai'ian Islands
(U.S.A.)
Hawai'i

Johnston
Atoll
(U.S.A.)

F I C   O C E A N

Kingman Reef
Palmyra Atoll
Teraina
Tabuaeran
Kiritimati

owland Island (U.S.A.)
aker Island (U.S.A.)

hoenix
slands

Jarvis Island

Malden
Island

I R I B A T I

Starbuck
Island

Tokelau
(N.Z.)

Penrhyn

Nuku Hiva   *Marquesas*
            Islands
Hiva Oa

Samoan Islands
SAMOA   Manu'a
Savai'i Apia Islands
'Upolu

Îles du
Roi Georges

Îles Palliser

American
Samoa
(U.S.A.)

Vava'u
Group
Alofi
TONGA   Niue
Nuku'alofa (N.Z.)
Tongatapu
Group

Cook
Islands
(N.Z.)
Aitutaki

Rarotonga

Tahiti Moorea
Hervey
Islands

Society Islands

Tuamotu Islands

F r e n c h

Îles du Duc
de Gloucester

Groupe
Actéon

Tubuai Islands

Tubuai

Mururoa

P o l y n e s i a

Îles Gambier

Rapa

Pitcairn Is
(U.K.) Henderson Island
Pitcairn Island

tham Islands

O C E A N

Oceania's countries

Largest country (area)	Australia	7 692 024 sq km	2 969 907 sq miles
Smallest country (area)	Nauru	21 sq km	8 sq miles
Largest country (population)	Australia	20 155 000	
Smallest country (population)	Tuvalu	10 000	
Most densely populated country	Nauru	619 per sq km	1 625 per sq mile
Least densely populated country	Australia	3 per sq km	7 per sq mile

Oceania's capitals

Largest capital (population)	Canberra, Australia	381 000	
Smallest capital (population)	Vaiaku, Tuvalu	516	
Most northerly capital	Delap-Uliga-Djarrit, Marshall Islands	7° 7'N	
Most southerly capital	Wellington, New Zealand	41° 18'S	
Highest capital	Canberra, Australia	581 metres	1 906 feet

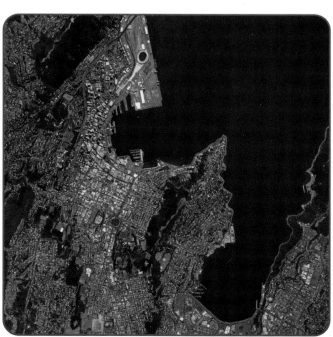

Wellington, capital of New Zealand.

INDONESIA

Borneo

Celebes Sea

Celebes (Sulawesi)

PAPUA

NEW GUINEA

New Guinea

EAST TIMOR

Timor Sea

INDIAN OCEAN

Arafura Sea

Torres Strait

Gulf of Carpentaria

Cape York Peninsula

Coral Sea Islands Territory (Australia)

Ashmore and Cartier Islands (Australia)

Arnhem Land

NORTHERN TERRITORY

Kimberley Plateau

Great Sandy Desert

Tanami Desert

Barkly Tableland

Great Barrier Reef

WESTERN AUSTRALIA

Gibson Desert

Simpson Desert

QUEENSLAND

Great Dividing Range

Tropic of Capricorn

Great Victoria Desert

SOUTH AUSTRALIA

NEW SOUTH WALES

Nullarbor Plain

Great Australian Bight

A.C.T.

VICTORIA

Bass Strait

TASMANIA

Lambert Azimuthal Equal Area Projection

1:17 300 000

	miles
0 200 400 600	
0 200 400 600 800 1000 km	

160°　　　　　　　G　170°　　　　　　H　180°　　　　　I　170°　　　　J

1

Howland Island (U.S.A.)
Baker Island (U.S.A.)

YAREN
Nauru
Banaba
(Ocean Island)
Aranuka
Nonouti

NAURU

Takuu
Islands
Nukumanu
Islands

Ontong
Java Atoll
Choiseul

Roncador Reef

**SOLOMON
ISLANDS**

w Georgia
Sound
Santa
Isabel
Buala
Malu'u
Stewart
Islands
HONIARA
Florida
Islands
Malaita
Maramasike
Ulawa Island
w Georgia
Islands
Kirakira
Auavu
Santa
Ana
San Cristobal
(Makira)
Guadalcanal
Rennell

Banaba
(Ocean Island)

Beru
Nikunau
Tabiteuea
Onotoa
Arorae
Tamana
Kingsmill Group

K I R I B A T I

Phoenix
Islands
Kanton
McKean
Rawaki
Phoenix Islands Protected Area
Nikumaroro
Orona
Manra

Nanumea
Nanumanga
Niutao
Nui
Vaitupu
Nukufetau
Funafuti　VAIAKU
Nukulaelae

TUVALU

Niulakita

Swains Island

Tokelau
(New Zealand)
Atafu
Nukunonu
Fakaofo

Pukapuka
(Danger Islands)
Nassau

2

Duff
Islands
Nupani
Swallow Islands
Ndeni
Santa Cruz Islands
(Solomon Islands)
Utupua
Vanikoro
Islands
Cherry
Island
Tikopia
Mitre
Island

Indispensable
Reefs

al Sea

Rotuma
(Fiji)

Wallis and
Futuna Islands
(France)
Îles
Wallis
MATĀ'UTU

SAMOA

Savai'i
'Upolu
APIA
Manu'a
Islands

**American
Samoa**
(U.S.A.)
Tutuila　FAGATOGO
Rose
Island

Suwarrow

10°

Torres Islands
Banks
Islands
Uréparapara
Vanua Lava
Santa María Island

Îles de Hoorn

Cook Islands
(New Zealand)

Niuafo'ou
210
Tafahi
Niuatoputapu

Espíritu Santo
Mount
Tabwémasana
1879
Aoba
Maéwo

VANUATU

Pentecost Island
Norsup
Ambrym
Malakula
Epi
1270

Îles Chesterfield
(France)

Récifs
d'Entrecasteaux
Émaé
Shepherd
Islands
PORT VILA
Éfaté

Great Sea Reef
Yasawa
Group
Labasa
(Lagilasa)
Bligh
Water
Vanua Levu
Tomanivi
Mt Victoria
Taveuni
Lautoka
Koro
Northern
Lau Group

Vava'u
Group

3

Grand Passage
Grand Récif
de Cook
Îles Belep

Nouvelle Calédonie
Ouvéa
Récif des
Français
Koumac
Lifou
Îles Loyauté
(France)
New Caledonia
(France)
Bourail
Tadin
Maré
Yaté
NOUMÉA
Île des Pins

Grand Récif
du Sud

Erromango

Tanna
361
Futuna

Anatom
(Aneityum)

Hunter
Island
100

FIJI
Viti Levu
SUVA
Kadavu Passage
Kadavu

Koro
Sea
Gau
Moala
Kabara
Matuku
Southern
Lau Group

Vatoa
Tofua
500
Ceva-i-Ra
(Conway Reef)

Doi
Ono-i-Lau
Ata

Ha'apai
Group

TONGA
NUKU'ALOFA
Tongatapu
Group

ALOFI
Niue
(New Zealand)

Palmerston

P A C I F I C

Minerva Reefs

O C E A N

Tropic of Capricorn

4

20°

Norfolk Island
(Australia)
KINGSTON

Raoul Island
Kermadec Islands
(New Zealand)
Macauley Island
Curtis Island
Havre Rock
L'Espérance Rock

160°

Lord Howe Island
(Australia)

Three Kings
Islands
Maria van Diemen
North
Cape
Cape
Awanui

Whangarei
Takapuna
North Island
Great Barrier Island

**NEW
ZEALAND**

Auckland
Manukau
Hamilton
Tokoroa
Te Kuiti
Tauranga
East Cape
Whakatane
New
Plymouth
Mount Taranaki
(Mount Egmont)
Taupo
Mount
Ruapehu
Gisborne
Wairoa
Mahia Peninsula
Hawera
Wanganui
Napier
Hastings
Palmerston North
Levin
Masterton
Cape Farewell
Tasman
Bay
Picton
Lower Hutt
Nelson
WELLINGTON
Blenheim
**South
Island**
Westport
Hokitika
Greymouth
Aoraki
(Mount Cook)
3724
Southern Alps
Mount Aspiring
3030
Mount
Christina
2502
Queenstown
Ashburton
Christchurch
Banks Peninsula
Timaru
Gore
Oamaru
Cape Providence
Foveaux
Strait
Dunedin
Invercargill
Stewart Island
South West Cape
Snares
Islands

an Sea

Chatham Islands
(New Zealand)
Chatham Island
Waitangi
Pitt Island

30°

5

6

Bounty Islands
(New Zealand)

Antipodes Islands
(New Zealand)

Auckland Islands
(New Zealand)

40°

160°　　　　G　170°　　　　H　180°　　　I　170°　　　J　160°　　　K　150° W　L

↑ 81

Lambert Azimuthal Equal Area Projection

1:7 000 000

| 0 | | 100 | | 200 | | 300 | miles |

| 0 | 100 | 200 | 300 | 400 | 500 km |

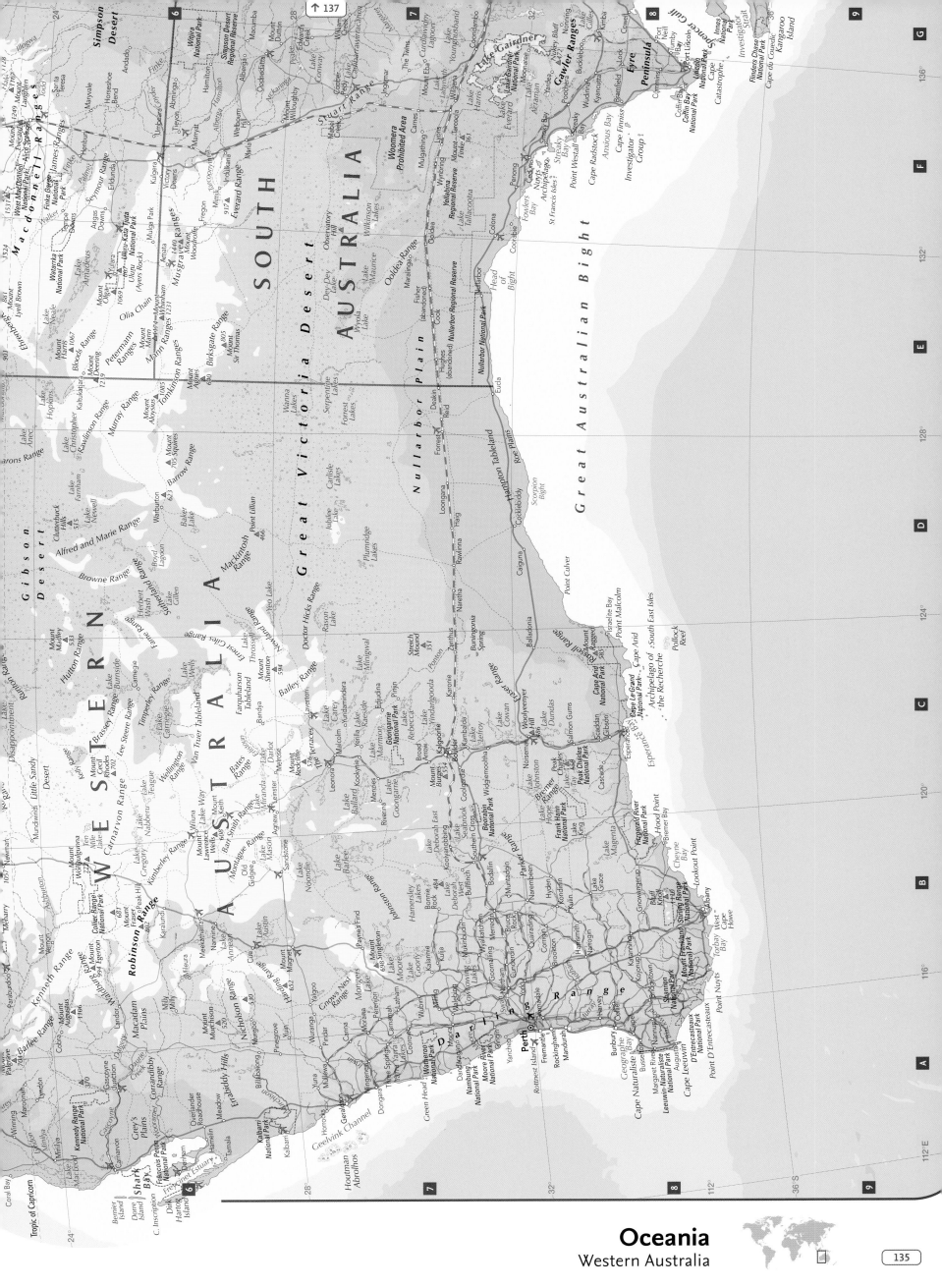

Oceania
Western Australia

Lambert Azimuthal Equal Area Projection

1:7 000 000

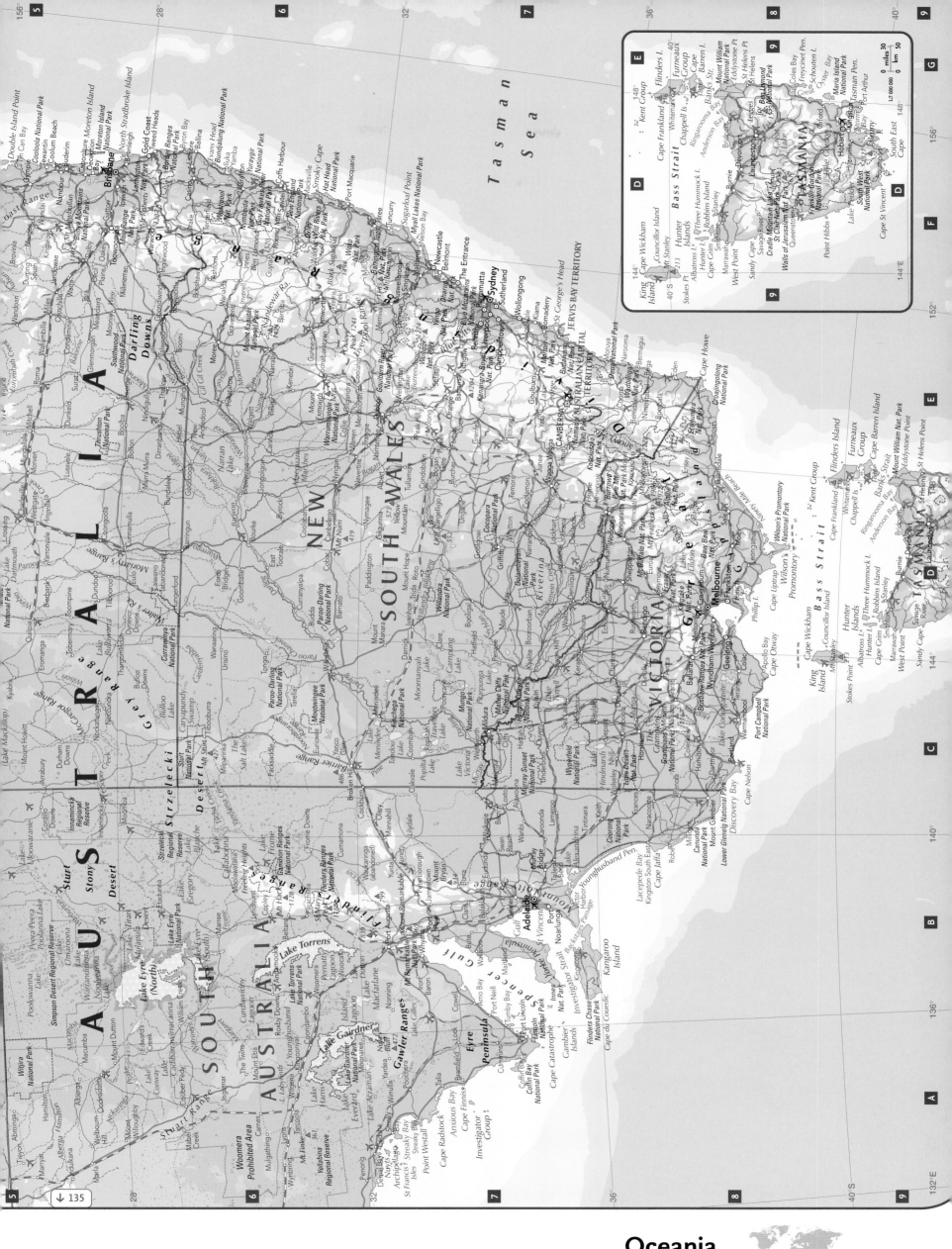

Oceania
Eastern Australia

QUEENSLAND

Darling Downs

AUSTRALIA

NEW SOUTH WALES

VICTORIA

Tasman Sea

Bass Strait

JERVIS BAY TERRITORY

AUSTRALIAN CAPITAL TERRITORY

Oceania
Southeast Australia

1:4 300 000

Lambert Azimuthal Equal Area Projection

miles
0   50   100   150
0   50   100   150   200   km

NEW

ZEALAND

Tasman

Sea

North

Island

South

Island

PACIFIC

OCEAN

Conic Equidistant Projection

1:4 500 000

| 0 | 50 | 100 | 150 | miles |

| 0 | 50 | 100 | 150 | 200 | 250 km |

Oceania

New Zealand

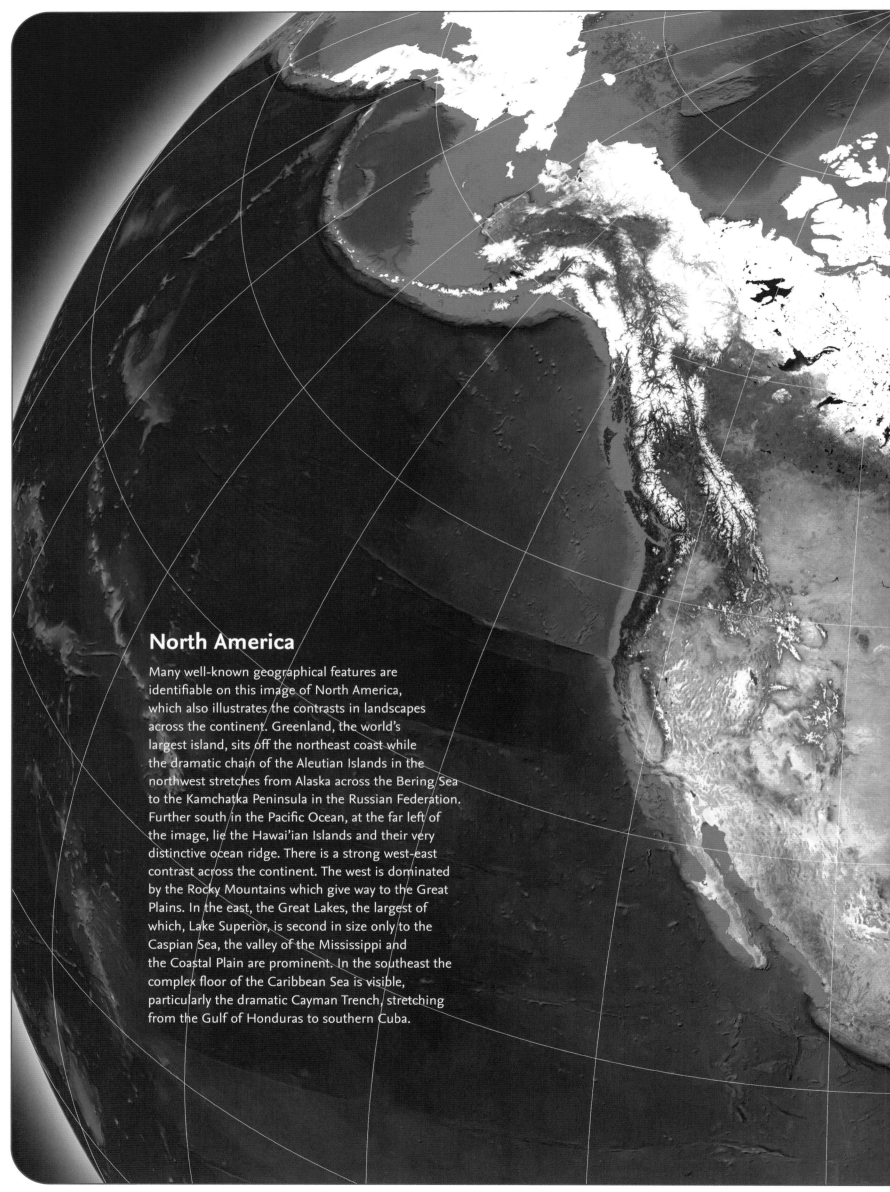

North America

Many well-known geographical features are identifiable on this image of North America, which also illustrates the contrasts in landscapes across the continent. Greenland, the world's largest island, sits off the northeast coast while the dramatic chain of the Aleutian Islands in the northwest stretches from Alaska across the Bering Sea to the Kamchatka Peninsula in the Russian Federation. Further south in the Pacific Ocean, at the far left of the image, lie the Hawai'ian Islands and their very distinctive ocean ridge. There is a strong west-east contrast across the continent. The west is dominated by the Rocky Mountains which give way to the Great Plains. In the east, the Great Lakes, the largest of which, Lake Superior, is second in size only to the Caspian Sea, the valley of the Mississippi and the Coastal Plain are prominent. In the southeast the complex floor of the Caribbean Sea is visible, particularly the dramatic Cayman Trench, stretching from the Gulf of Honduras to southern Cuba.

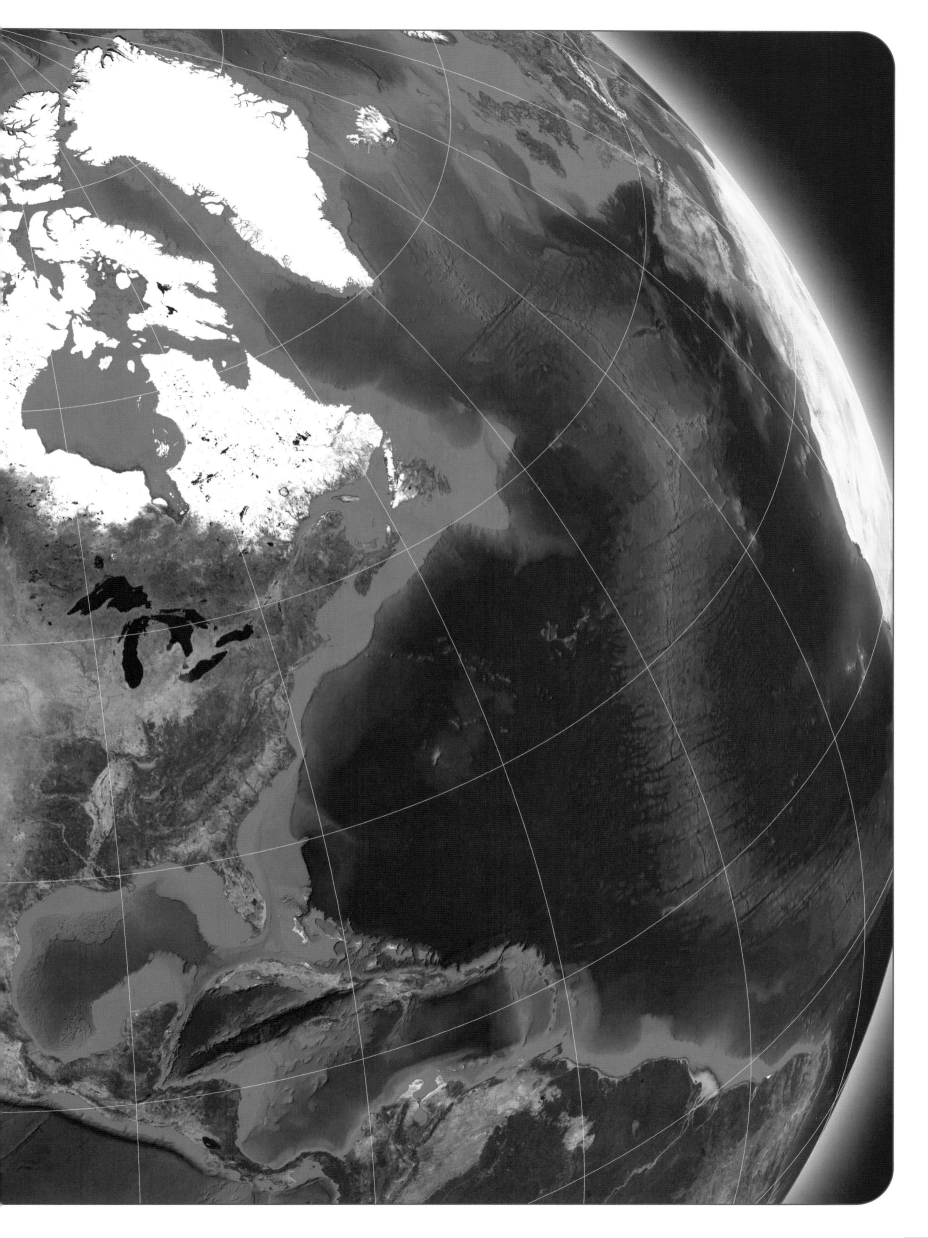

North America, the world's third largest continent, supports a wide range of landscapes from the Arctic north to sub-tropical Central America. The main physiographic regions of the continent are the mountains of the west coast, stretching from Alaska in the north to Mexico and Central America in the south; the vast, relatively flat Canadian Shield; the Great Plains which make up the majority of the interior; the Appalachian Mountains in the east; and the Atlantic coastal plain.

These regions contain some significant physical features, including the Rocky Mountains, the Great Lakes – three of which are amongst the five largest lakes in the world – and the Mississippi-Missouri river system which is the world's fourth longest river. The Caribbean Sea contains a complex pattern of islands, many volcanic in origin, and the continent is joined to South America by the narrow Isthmus of Panama.

Internet Links	
● NASA Visible Earth	**visibleearth.nasa.gov**
● U.S. Geological Survey	**www.usgs.gov**
● Natural Resources Canada	**www.nrcan-rncan.gc.ca**
● SPOT Image satellite imagery	**www.spotimage.fr**

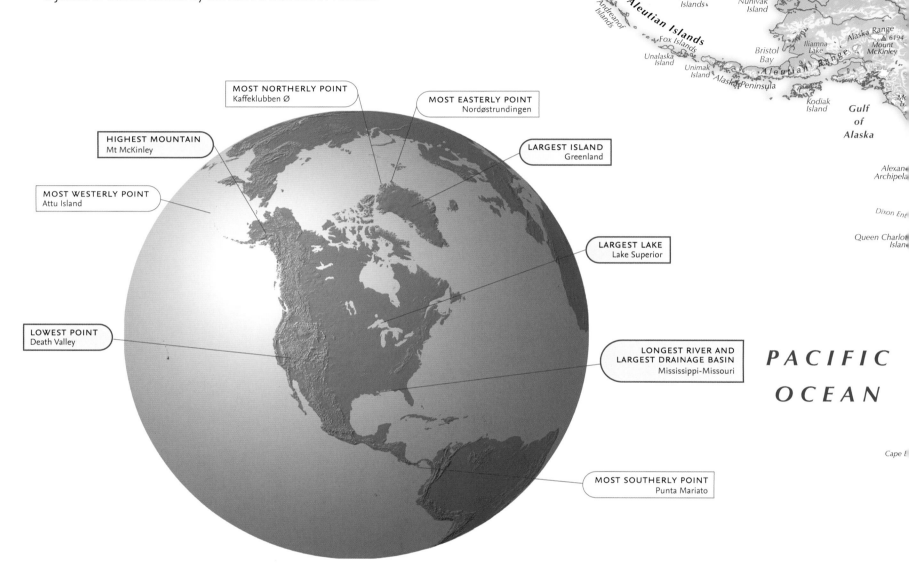

MOST NORTHERLY POINT
Kaffeklubben Ø

MOST EASTERLY POINT
Nordøstrundingen

HIGHEST MOUNTAIN
Mt McKinley

LARGEST ISLAND
Greenland

MOST WESTERLY POINT
Attu Island

LARGEST LAKE
Lake Superior

LOWEST POINT
Death Valley

LONGEST RIVER AND
LARGEST DRAINAGE BASIN
Mississippi-Missouri

MOST SOUTHERLY POINT
Punta Mariato

PACIFIC

OCEAN

Chukchi Sea

Bering Strait

Seward Peninsula

Norton Sound

Pribilof Islands

Nunivak Island

Yukon

Andreanof Islands

Aleutian Islands

Fox Islands

Iliamna Lake

Alaska Range

△ 6194
Mount McKinley

Unalaska Island

Bristol Bay

Aleutian Range

Unimak Island

Alaska Peninsula

Kodiak Island

Gulf of Alaska

Alexander Archipelago

Dixon Entrance

Queen Charlotte Islands

Cape

North America's physical features

Highest mountain	Mt McKinley, USA	6 194 metres	20 321 feet
Longest river	Mississippi-Missouri, USA	5 969 km	3 709 miles
Largest lake	Lake Superior, Canada/USA	82 100 sq km	31 699 sq miles
Largest island	Greenland	2 175 600 sq km	839 999 sq miles
Largest drainage basin	Mississippi-Missouri, USA	3 250 000 sq km	1 254 825 sq miles
Lowest point	Death Valley, USA	-86 metres	-282 feet

North America's longest river system, the **Mississippi-Missouri,** flows into the Gulf of Mexico through the Mississippi Delta.

North America's extent

TOTAL LAND AREA (including Hawai'ian Islands)	24 680 331 sq km / 9 529 076 sq miles
Most northerly point	Kaffeklubben Ø, Greenland
Most southerly point	Punta Mariato, Panama
Most westerly point	Attu Island, USA
Most easterly point	Nordøstrundingen, Greenland

The **Panama Canal**, Panama, linking the Pacific Ocean to the Atlantic Ocean.

Facts

- Devon Island, Canada, is the world's largest uninhabited island
- Canada has the longest coastline of any country in the world
- Lake Superior is the world's largest freshwater lake
- Over 320 000 square kilometres of the USA is protected for conservation purposes

North America
Countries

North America has been dominated economically and politically by the USA since the nineteenth century. Before that, the continent was subject to colonial influences, particularly of Spain in the south and of Britain and France in the east. The nineteenth century saw the steady development of the western half of the continent. The wealth of natural resources and the generally temperate climate were an excellent basis for settlement, agriculture and industrial development which has led to the USA being the richest nation in the world today.

Although there are twenty-three independent countries and fourteen dependent territories in North America, Canada, Mexico and the USA have approximately eighty-five per cent of the continent's population and eighty-eight per cent of its land area. Large parts of the north remain sparsely populated, while the most densely populated areas are in the northeast USA, and the Caribbean.

Internet Links

● UK Foreign and Commonwealth Office	www.fco.gov.uk
● CIA World Factbook	www.cia.gov/library/publications/the-world-factbook/index.html
● U.S. Board on Geographic Names	geonames.usgs.gov
● NASA Astronaut Photography	eol.jsc.nasa.gov

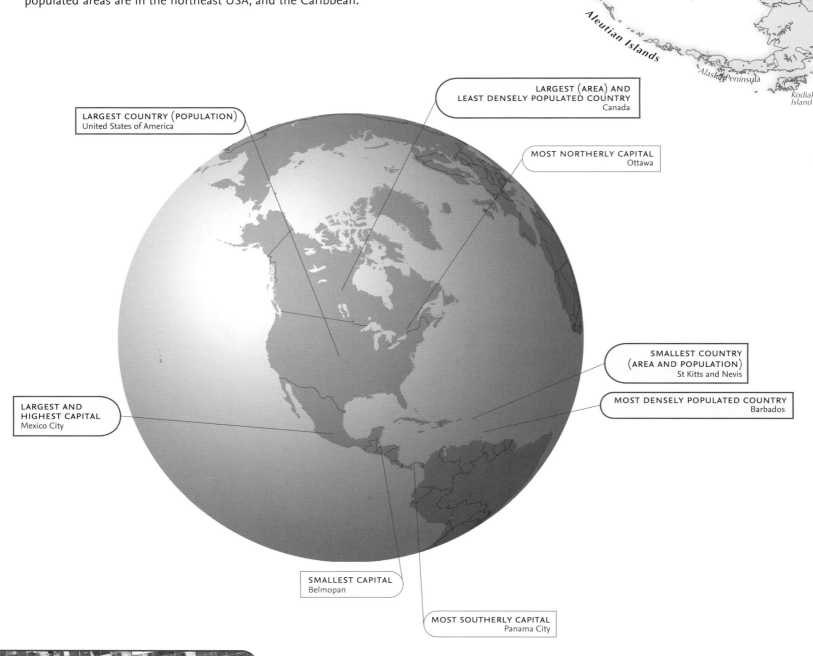

LARGEST COUNTRY (POPULATION)
United States of America

LARGEST (AREA) AND
LEAST DENSELY POPULATED COUNTRY
Canada

MOST NORTHERLY CAPITAL
Ottawa

SMALLEST COUNTRY
(AREA AND POPULATION)
St Kitts and Nevis

MOST DENSELY POPULATED COUNTRY
Barbados

LARGEST AND
HIGHEST CAPITAL
Mexico City

SMALLEST CAPITAL
Belmopan

MOST SOUTHERLY CAPITAL
Panama City

Point Hope
Bering Strait
St Lawrence Island
Nome
U.
Yukon
ALASKA
Mount McKinley 6194
Fair
Anchorage
Alaska Peninsula
Valdez
Kodiak Island
Gulf of Alaska
Alexand
Archipelag
Queen Charlott
Island

False-colour satellite image of the **Mexico-USA** boundary at Mexicali.

North America's countries

Largest country (area)	Canada	9 984 670 sq km	3 855 103 sq miles
Smallest country (area)	St Kitts and Nevis	261 sq km	101 sq miles
Largest country (population)	United States of America	298 213 000	
Smallest country (population)	St Kitts and Nevis	43 000	
Most densely populated country	Barbados	628 per sq km	1 627 per sq mile
Least densely populated country	Canada	3 per sq km	8 per sq mile

North America's capitals

Largest capital (population)	Mexico City, Mexico	19 028 000	
Smallest capital (population)	Belmopan, Belize	13 500	
Most northerly capital	Ottawa, Canada	45° 25'N	
Most southerly capital	Panama City, Panama	8° 56'N	
Highest capital	Mexico City, Mexico	2 300 metres	7 546 feet

The Bahamas, a chain of islands in the North Atlantic Ocean, lying southeast of Florida, USA.

Facts

- The Panama Canal, opened in 1914, cut the journey between the Atlantic and the Pacific by over 14 000 km

- Mexico City is the highest city in North America and houses approximately 18% of Mexico's population

- The state of Alaska was bought by the USA from Russia in 1867

- The territory of Nunavut is Canada's newest administrative division, created in 1999 from the eastern part of Northwest Territories

Lambert Conformal Conic Projection

1:14 000 000

0   200   400   miles

0   200   400   600   800 km

North America
Canada

States in the U.S.A.
numbered on the map:

1. CONNECTICUT (K5)
2. MASSACHUSETTS (K5)
3. NEW HAMPSHIRE (K5)
4. RHODE ISLAND (K5)
5. VERMONT (K5)

Lambert Conformal Conic Projection

1:6 000 000

Conic Equidistant Projection

1:6 000 000

Lambert Conformal Conic Projection

1:10 000 000

| 0 | 100 | 200 | 300 | 400 | miles |
| 0 100 | 200 | 300 | 400 | 500 | 600 | 700 | km |

Lambert Conformal Conic Projection

1:6 000 000

| 0 | 100 | 200 | miles |

| 0 | 100 | 200 | 300 | 400 | km |

North America
Western United States

Lambert Conformal Conic Projection

1:3 000 000

↑ 156

↑ 151
↓ 156

Lambert Conformal Conic Projection

1:6 000 000

miles
km

North America
Central United States

States in the U.S.A.
numbered on the map:

1. CONNECTICUT (F3)
2. DELAWARE (F4)
3. MASSACHUSETTS (F3)
4. RHODE ISLAND (G3)

↓ 160

Lambert Conformal Conic Projection

1:6 000 000

| 0 | 100 | 200 | miles |

| 0 | 100 | 200 | 300 | 400 km |

↓ 161

→ 169

North America
Eastern United States

Lambert Conformal Conic Projection

1:3 000 000

0   50   100   miles

0   50   100   150   200   km

North America
Northeast United States

North America
Mexico and Central America

Lambert Conformal Conic Projection

1:6 300 000

Lambert Conformal Conic Projection

1:12 000 000

| 0 | 200 | 400 | miles |

| 0 | 200 | 400 | 600 | 800 km |

North America
Central America and the Caribbean

↓ 176

South America

The Andes mountains stretch along the whole length of the west coast of South America, widening into the high plains of the Altiplano in Bolivia and Peru in the centre of the continent. Lake Titicaca, the world's highest large navigable lake, lies on the Altiplano, straddling the Bolivia-Peru border. Running parallel to the Andes, just off the west coast, is the Peru-Chile Trench which marks the active boundary between the Nazca and South American tectonic plates. Movement between these plates gives rise to numerous volcanoes in the Andes. The Amazon river runs across almost the whole width of the continent in the north, meeting the Atlantic Ocean in its wide delta on the northeast coast. The vast Amazon basin is one of the most ecologically diverse areas of the Earth. In the south, the wide continental shelf stretches eastward from the tip of the continent to the Falkland Islands and South Georgia on the bottom edge of the image.

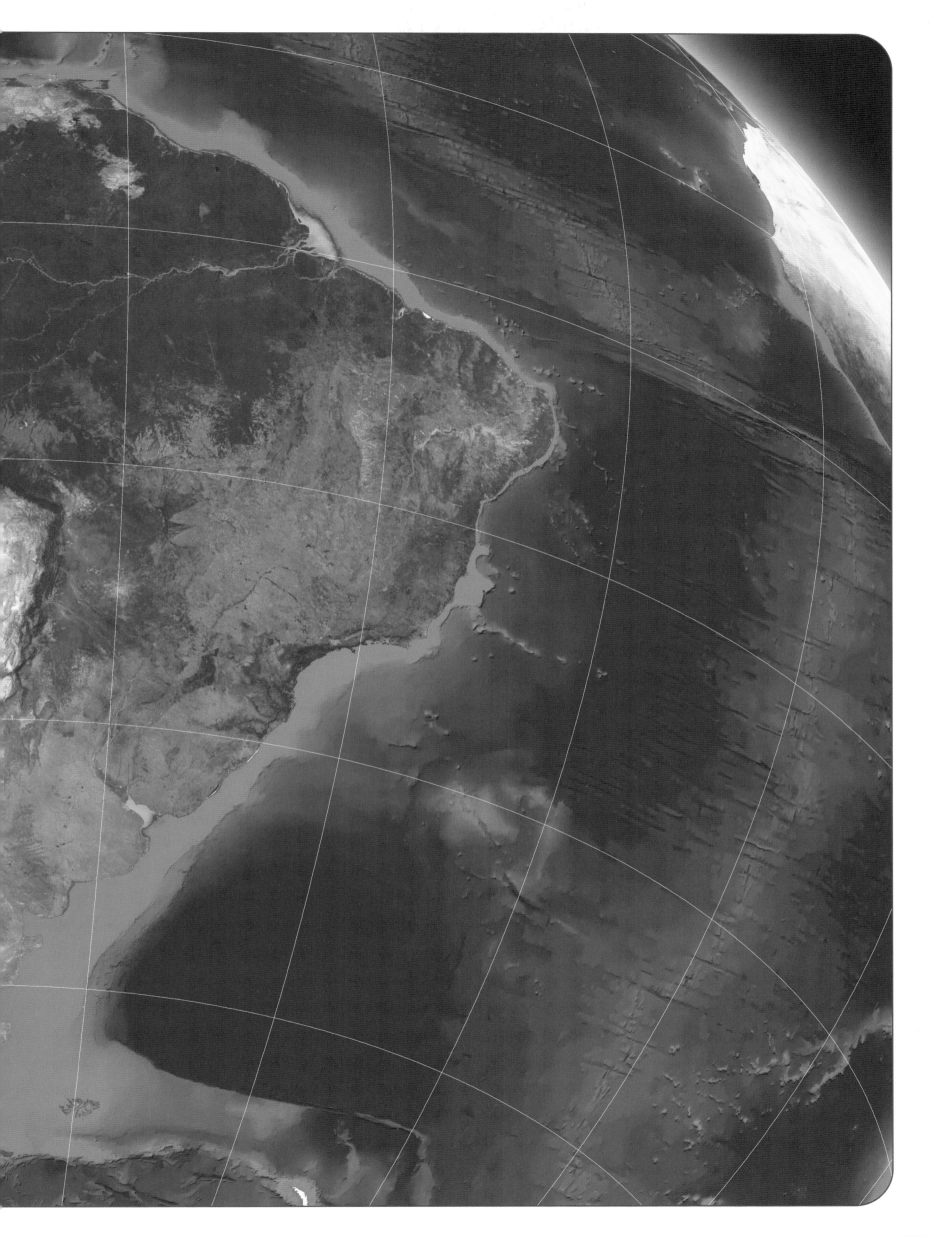

South America is a continent of great contrasts, with landscapes varying from the tropical rainforests of the Amazon Basin, to the Atacama Desert, the driest place on earth, and the sub-Antarctic regions of southern Chile and Argentina. The dominant physical features are the Andes, stretching along the entire west coast of the continent and containing numerous mountains over 6 000 metres high, and the Amazon, which is the second longest river in the world and has the world's largest drainage basin.

The Altiplano is a high plateau lying between two of the Andes ranges. It contains Lake Titicaca, the world's highest navigable lake. By contrast, large lowland areas dominate the centre of the continent, lying between the Andes and the Guiana and Brazilian Highlands. These vast grasslands stretch from the Llanos of the north through the Selvas and the Gran Chaco to the Pampas of Argentina.

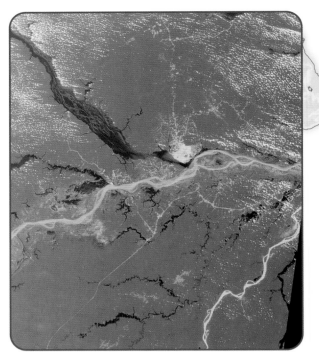

Confluence of the **Amazon** and **Negro** rivers at Manaus, northern Brazil.

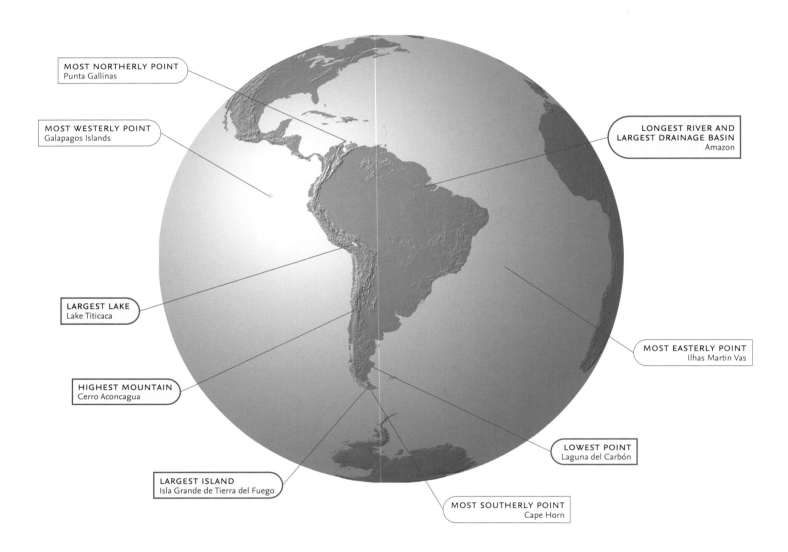

MOST NORTHERLY POINT
Punta Gallinas

MOST WESTERLY POINT
Galapagos Islands

LONGEST RIVER AND
LARGEST DRAINAGE BASIN
Amazon

LARGEST LAKE
Lake Titicaca

MOST EASTERLY POINT
Ilhas Martin Vas

HIGHEST MOUNTAIN
Cerro Aconcagua

LOWEST POINT
Laguna del Carbón

LARGEST ISLAND
Isla Grande de Tierra del Fuego

MOST SOUTHERLY POINT
Cape Horn

South America's physical features

Highest mountain	Cerro Aconcagua, Argentina	6 959 metres	22 831 feet
Longest river	Amazon	6 516 km	4 049 miles
Largest lake	Lake Titicaca, Bolivia/Peru	8 340 sq km	3 220 sq miles
Largest island	Isla Grande de Tierra del Fuego, Argentina/Chile	47 000 sq km	18 147 sq miles
Largest drainage basin	Amazon	7 050 000 sq km	2 722 005 sq miles
Lowest point	Laguna del Carbón, Argentina	-105 metres	-345 feet

NORTH AMERICA

Caribbean Sea

Facts

- Water flow along the Amazon is over 1 500 times that of the River Thames
- Cerro Aconcagua, 6 959 metres, is the highest point in the western hemisphere
- The Amazon rainforest supports approximately half of all the world's living species
- The Pantanal in Brazil is the largest area of wetland in the world
- The world's driest desert is the Atacama, where only 1mm of rain may fall as infrequently as once every 5–20 years

Punta Gallinas
Golfo de Venezuela
Isla de Margarita
Orinoco Delta
Waini Point
Gulf of Panama
Golfo del Darién
Lake Maracaibo
Orinoco
Point Isère
Cabo Corrientes
Cordillera Occidental
Cordillera Central
Cordillera Oriental
Llanos
Meta
Cerro Yavi 2285
Guiana Highlands
La Gran Sabana
Cabo Orange
Isla de Malpelo
Guaviare
Pakaraima Mountains
Ilha de Maracá
Maroni
Mouths of the Amazon
Volcán Cotopaxi 5896
Caquetá
Japurá
Putumayo
Orinoco
Branco
Negro
Amazon Basin
Represa de Balbina
Ilha de Marajó
Baía de São Marcos
alapagos Islands
Punta Santa Elena
6310
Chimborazo
Amazon
Yavari
Marañón
Iça
Japurá
Purus
Selvas
Madeira
Tapajós
Amazon
Tocantins
Represa Tucuruí
Cabo de São Roque
Golfo de Guayaquil
Punta Negra
Ucayali
Juruá
Purus
Madeira
Juruena
Teles Pires
Xingu
Araguaia
Tocantins
Parnaíba
São Francisco
Nevado de Huascarán 6768
Iparaná
Guaporé
Mamoré
Iriri
Barragem de Sobradinho
Chapada Diamantina
Cabo Santo Antonio
Lago de San Luis
San Miguel
Paraguai
Pantanal
Represa Serra da Mesa
São Francisco
Velhas
Lake Titicaca
Yungas
Bañados del Izozog
Brazilian Highlands
Ponta da Baleia
Altiplano
Lago de Poopó
Gran Chaco
Paraguai
Grande
Paranaíba
Salar de Uyuni
Pileomayo
Teuco
Paraná
Paranapanema
Cabo de São Tomé
Atacama Desert
Nevado Ojos del Salado 6908
Cerro Bonete 6872
Salado
Iguaça Falls
Iguaçu
Ilha de São Sebastião
Salinas Grandes
Cerro Aconcagua 6959
Uruguay
Negro
Lagoa dos Patos
Sierras de Córdoba
Salado
Paraná
Lagoa Mirim
Desaguadero
Serrado Mar
Punta Lavapié
Colorado
Río de la Plata
Punta Norte
Punta Sur
Negro
Bahía Blanca
Golfo San Matías
Península Valdés
Isla de Chiloé
Chubut
Golfo de San Jorge
Archipiélago de los Chonos
Golfo de Penas
Lago San Martín
Lago Argentino
Bahía Grande
West Falkland
East Falkland
Falkland Islands
Strait of Magellan
Isla Grande de Tierra del Fuego
Isla de los Estados
Cape Horn
Drake Passage
Scotia Sea
South Georgia

PACIFIC OCEAN

ATLANTIC OCEAN

A n d e s
Cordillera Occidental
Cordillera Oriental
Altiplano
Pampas
Patagonia

Punta de Coles
Punta Tetas
Punta Ballena
Islas Desventuradas
Archipiélago Juan Fernández
Punta Galera

Isla Grande de Tierra del Fuego,
South America's largest island, situated at the southernmost tip of the continent.

South America's extent

TOTAL LAND AREA	17 815 420 sq km / 6 878 534 sq miles
Most northerly point	Punta Gallinas, Colombia
Most southerly point	Cape Horn, Chile
Most westerly point	Galapagos Islands, Ecuador
Most easterly point	Ilhas Martin Vas, Atlantic Ocean

South America
Countries

French Guiana, a French Department, is the only remaining territory under overseas control on a continent which has seen a long colonial history. Much of South America was colonized by Spain in the sixteenth century, with Britain, Portugal and the Netherlands each claiming territory in the northeast of the continent. This colonization led to the conquering of ancient civilizations, including the Incas in Peru. Most countries became independent from Spain and Portugal in the early nineteenth century.

The population of the continent reflects its history, being composed primarily of indigenous Indian peoples and mestizos – reflecting the long Hispanic influence. There has been a steady process of urbanization within the continent, with major movements of the population from rural to urban areas. The majority of the population now lives in the major cities and within 300 kilometres of the coast.

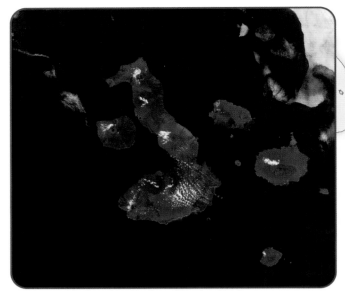

Galapagos Islands, an island territory of Ecuador which lies on the equator in the eastern Pacific Ocean over 900 kilometres west of the coast of Ecuador.

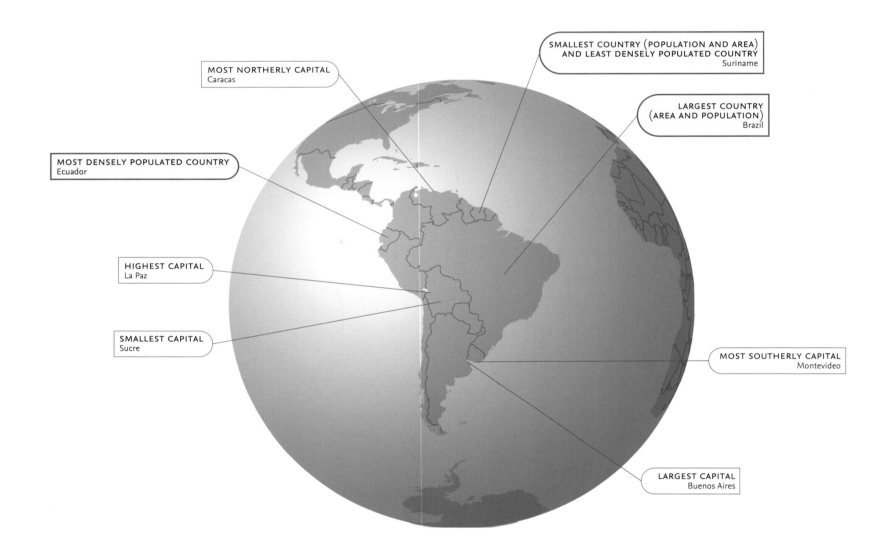

MOST NORTHERLY CAPITAL
Caracas

SMALLEST COUNTRY (POPULATION AND AREA) AND LEAST DENSELY POPULATED COUNTRY
Suriname

LARGEST COUNTRY (AREA AND POPULATION)
Brazil

MOST DENSELY POPULATED COUNTRY
Ecuador

HIGHEST CAPITAL
La Paz

SMALLEST CAPITAL
Sucre

MOST SOUTHERLY CAPITAL
Montevideo

LARGEST CAPITAL
Buenos Aires

South America's countries

Largest country (area)	Brazil	8 514 879 sq km	3 287 613 sq miles
Smallest country (area)	Suriname	163 820 sq km	63 251 sq miles
Largest country (population)	Brazil	186 405 000	
Smallest country (population)	Suriname	449 000	
Most densely populated country	Ecuador	48 per sq km	124 per sq mile
Least densely populated country	Suriname	3 per sq km	7 per sq mile

Internet Links

● UK Foreign and Commonwealth Office	www.fco.gov.uk
● CIA World Factbook	www.cia.gov/library/publications/the-world-factbook/index.html
● Caribbean Community (Caricom)	www.caricom.org
● Latin American Network Information Center	lanic.utexas.edu

NORTH AMERICA

Caribbean Sea

Punta Gallinas

Barranquilla
Cartagena
Maracaibo Cabimas Maracay Caracas
Monteria   Barquisimeto Valencia Cumaná
San Cristóbal   Ciudad
VENEZUELA   Bolívar
Medellin   Tunja   Puerto   Georgetown
Ibagué   Bogotá   Ayacucho   Paramaribo
Cali   **COLOMBIA**   **GUYANA**   Cayenne
Neiva   Guaviare   Boa Vista   **SURINAME** **French
Pasto   Guiana**
Esmeraldas   Caquetá   *Mouths of
                                          the Amazon*
Quito   Putumayo   Orinoco   *Represa
ECUADOR   Japurá   de Balbina*   Belém
Manta   Manaus   Santarém   Parnaíba
Galápagos Islands Guayaquil Iquitos Amazon   São   Fortaleza
(Ecuador)   Cuenca   Marañón   Tonantins   Luís
        Sullana   Carauari   Teresina
        Tarapoto   Natal
Chiclayo   João Pessoa
        Cruzeiro do Sul   **B   R   A   Z   I   L**   Floresta
Trujillo   Pucallpa   Porto   Recife
        Rio Branco   Velho   Juàzeiro
PERU   Maceió
    Huancayo Puerto   Aracaju
Callao Lima   Maldonado   *Lago
        Cusco   de San Luis*   Salvador
        Ica   Trinidad   Ilhéus
        Juliaca   *Lake   Brasília
        Arequipa   Titicaca* **BOLIVIA** Goiânia   Teófilo
            La Paz   Otôni
        Arica Cochabamba   Campo   Patos de Minas
            Sucre Santa Cruz   Grande   Uberaba   Belo
        Iquique   Potosí   Ribeirão Horizonte Vitória
                Tarija   *Pantanal*   Preto
                    PARAGUAY Pedro Juan Araçatuba   Campinas
                        Caballero   São   Nova Iguaçu
            Antofagasta   San Salvador   Maringá Paulo Rio de Janeiro
                    de Jujuy   Asunción Foz do Iguaçu Curitiba
            Copiapó   San Miguel   Formosa   Joinville
                    de Tucumán   Resistencia Encarnación Florianópolis
                Catamarca   Corrientes Posadas
                    La Rioja   Santa   Porto Alegre
            *Islas   Maria
            Desventuradas* San   Córdoba Santa Fé   *Lagoa   Rio Grande
            (Chile)   Juan   Paraná   dos Patos*
                Valparaíso Mendoza San Luis Rosario Concordia
        Archipiélago Santiago   Paysandú
        Juan Fernández   San Rafael   Buenos Aires **URUGUAY**
        (Chile)   Talca   La Plata Montevideo
                    ARGENTINA   *Río de la Plata*
            Concepción Chillán Santa
                    Rosa
                Valdivia   Bahía
                        Blanca Mar del Plata
                Neuquén

**PACIFIC
OCEAN**

**ATLANTIC
OCEAN**

*Islas
Desventuradas
(Chile)*

Puerto Montt
Isla de Chiloé
                Trelew
Archipiélago
de los Chonos   Comodoro
                Rivadavia *Golfo de
                    San Jorge*

                    Punta Medanosa
                **Falkland
                Islands**
                (U.K.)

Bahía Grande
            Río Gallegos
Puerto Natales   Stanley

Punta Arenas   *Isla Grande
            de Tierra del Fuego*
                Ushuaia
        Cape Horn

Cerro
Aconcagua
6959
Desaguadero
Patagonia
Negro
Viedma
Colorado

South America's capitals

Largest capital (population)	Buenos Aires, Argentina	13 349 000
Smallest capital (population)	Sucre, Bolivia	231 000
Most northerly capital	Caracas, Venezuela	10° 28'N
Most southerly capital	Montevideo, Uruguay	34° 52'S
Highest capital	La Paz, Bolivia	3 630 metres 11 909 feet

Falkland Islands, an overseas UK territory
in the South Atlantic Ocean.

South Georgia
(U.K.)

Facts

● South America is often referred to as
'Latin America', reflecting the historic
influences of Spain and Portugal

● The largest city in each South American
country is the capital, except in Brazil
and Ecuador

● South America has only two landlocked
countries – Bolivia and Paraguay

● Chile is over 4 000 kilometres long
but has an average width of only
177 kilometres

A **B** **C** **D** **E** **F**

PACIFIC

OCEAN

NICARAGUA

MANAGUA

COSTA RICA

SAN JOSÉ

PANAMA

PANAMA CITY

Gulf of Panama

COLOMBIA

BOGOTÁ

Medellín

Cali

QUITO

ECUADOR

Guayaquil

PERU

LIMA

Callao

BOLIVIA

LA PAZ

SUCRE

CHILE

ARGENTINA

VENEZUELA

CARACAS

Maracaibo

GRENADA

TRINIDAD AND TOBAGO

Guiana Highlands

Equator

Tropic of Capricorn

Galapagos Islands

(Islas Galápagos)

(Ecuador)

Isla Fernandina

Isla Isabela

Isla San Salvador

Isla Santa Cruz

Isla Santa María

Isla San Cristóbal

Baquerizo Moreno

1:12 000 000

0 miles 100

0 km 150

Equator

90°W 90°

0 miles 200 400

0 km 200 400 600 800

A T L A N T I C

O C E A N

GEORGETOWN
New Amsterdam
PARAMARIBO
Nieuw
Nickerie Onverwacht
Apoera
Brokopondo
St-Laurent-
du-Maroni
Albina
Organabo
Sinnamary
Kourou
CAYENNE
SURINAME
Wilhelmina
Gebergte
Juliana Top
Cottica
French
Guiana

Pointe Isère
Pointe Béhague
Regina
Cabo Orange
Parque Nacional
de Cabo Orange

Serra
Tumucumaque
Parque Nacional
Montanhas do
Tumucumaque
Ferreira-
Gomes
Terezinha
Araguari

Calçoene
Ilha de Maracá
Amapá

Mouths of the
Amazon

Macapá
Ilha Caviana
Ilha Mexiana

Equator 0°

B R A Z I L

Belém
São Luís
Fortaleza
(Ceará)

Fernando de Noronha
(Brazil)

Teresina
Natal

João Pessoa
Recife
(Pernambuco)
Olinda
Maceió

BRASÍLIA
Goiânia

Brazilian Highland

Salvador
(Bahia)

Belo
Horizonte
Vitória
Vila Velha

Campinas
São
Paulo
Nova
Iguaçu
Rio de
Janeiro

Ilha da Trindade
(Brazil)

South America
Northern South America

South America
Southern South America

1:12 000 000

Lambert Azimuthal Equal Area Projection

ATLANTIC

OCEAN

South America
Southeast Brazil

Lambert Azimuthal Equal Area Projection

1:6 000 000

0   100   200   miles
0   100   200   300   400   km

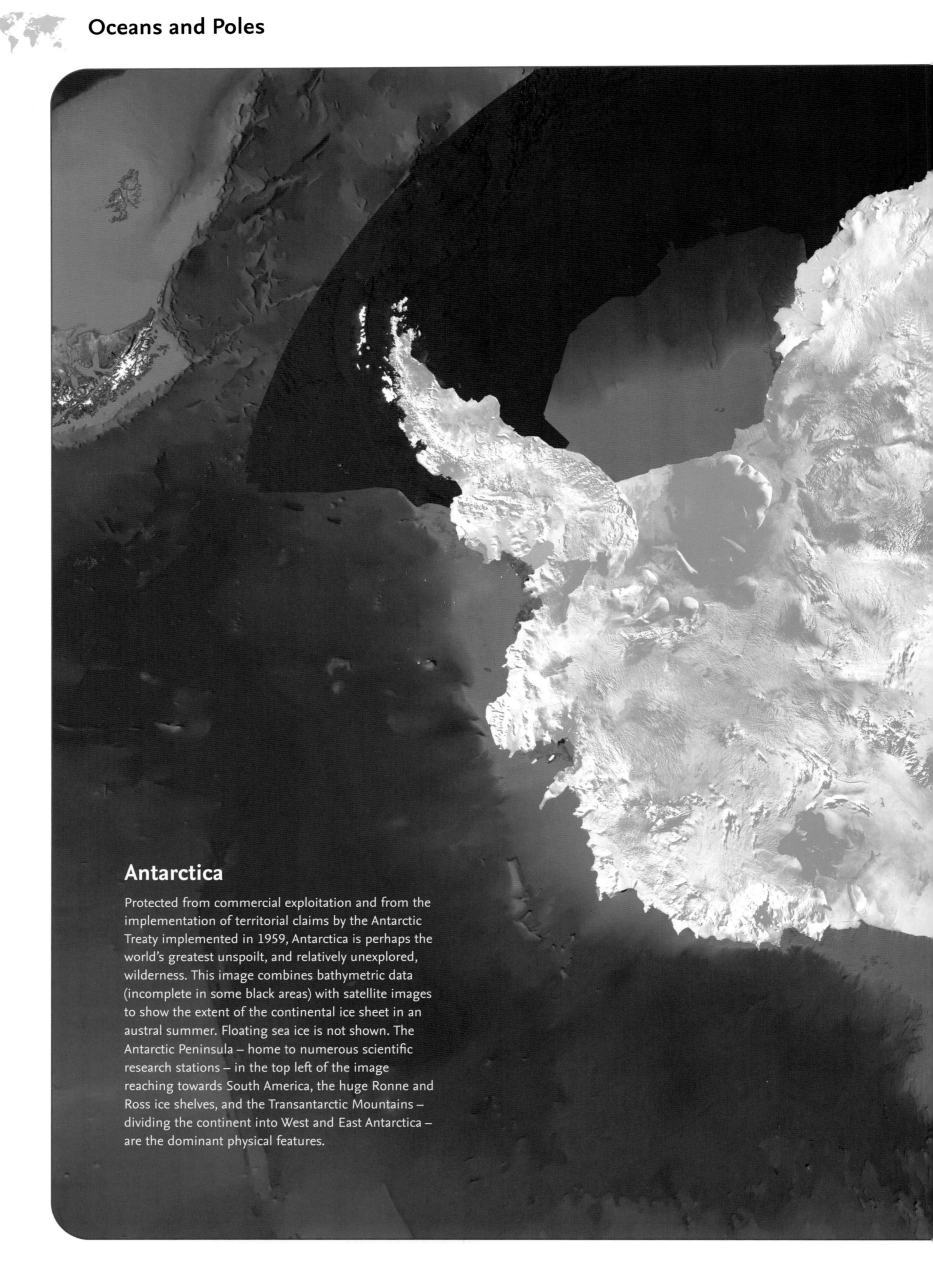

Antarctica

Protected from commercial exploitation and from the
implementation of territorial claims by the Antarctic
Treaty implemented in 1959, Antarctica is perhaps the
world's greatest unspoilt, and relatively unexplored,
wilderness. This image combines bathymetric data
(incomplete in some black areas) with satellite images
to show the extent of the continental ice sheet in an
austral summer. Floating sea ice is not shown. The
Antarctic Peninsula – home to numerous scientific
research stations – in the top left of the image
reaching towards South America, the huge Ronne and
Ross ice shelves, and the Transantarctic Mountains –
dividing the continent into West and East Antarctica –
are the dominant physical features.

Oceans and Poles
Features

Between them, the world's oceans and polar regions cover approximately seventy per cent of the earth's surface. The oceans contain ninety-six per cent of the Earth's water and a vast range of flora and fauna. They are a major influence on the world's climate, particularly through ocean currents. The Arctic and Antarctica are the coldest and most inhospitable places on the Earth. They both have vast amounts of ice which, if global warming continues, could have a major influence on sea level across the globe.

Our understanding of the oceans and polar regions has increased enormously over the last twenty years through the development of new technologies, particularly that of satellite remote sensing, which can generate vast amounts of data relating to, for example, topography (both on land and the seafloor), land cover and sea surface temperature.

The oceans

The world's major oceans are the Pacific, the Atlantic and the Indian Oceans. The Arctic Ocean is generally considered as part of the Atlantic, and the Southern Ocean, which stretches around the whole of Antarctica is usually treated as an extension of each of the three major oceans.

One of the most important factors affecting the earth's climate is the circulation of water within and between the oceans. Differences in temperature and surface winds create ocean currents which move enormous quantities of water around the globe. These currents re-distribute heat which the oceans have absorbed from the sun, and so have a major effect on the world's climate system. El Niño is one climatic phenomenon directly influenced by these ocean processes.

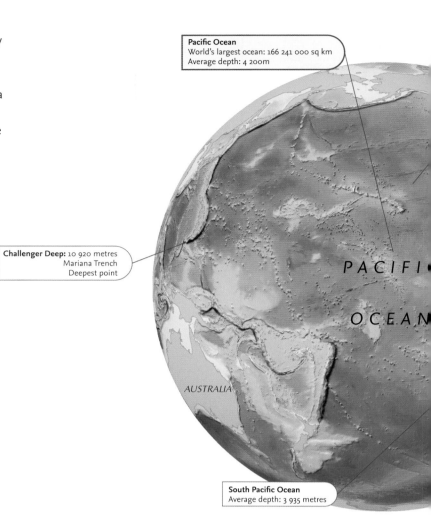

Pacific Ocean
World's largest ocean: 166 241 000 sq km
Average depth: 4 200m

Challenger Deep: 10 920 metres
Mariana Trench
Deepest point

PACIFIC

OCEAN

AUSTRALIA

South Pacific Ocean
Average depth: 3 935 metres

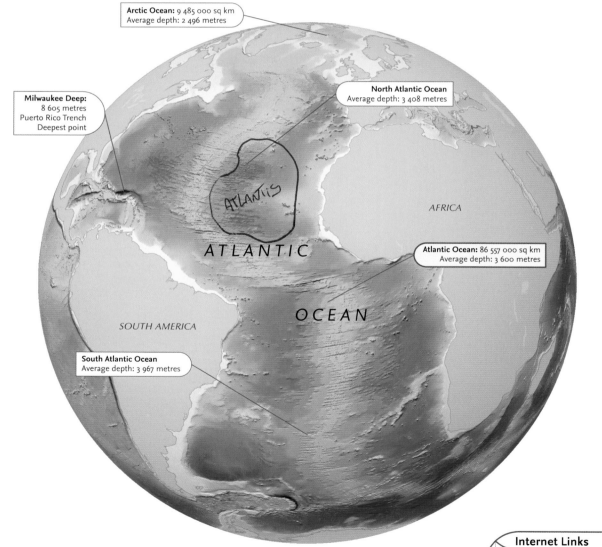

Arctic Ocean: 9 485 000 sq km
Average depth: 2 496 metres

Milwaukee Deep:
8 605 metres
Puerto Rico Trench
Deepest point

North Atlantic Ocean
Average depth: 3 408 metres

ATLANTIS

AFRICA

ATLANTIC

Atlantic Ocean: 86 557 000 sq km
Average depth: 3 600 metres

OCEAN

SOUTH AMERICA

South Atlantic Ocean
Average depth: 3 967 metres

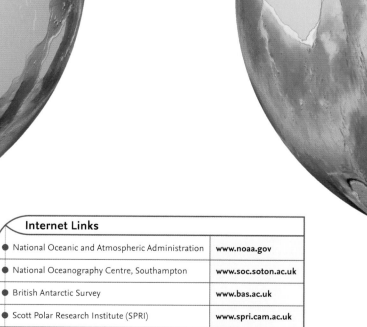

Indian Ocean: 73 427 000 sq km
Average depth: 4 000 metres

AFRICA

Internet Links

National Oceanic and Atmospheric Administration	www.noaa.gov
National Oceanography Centre, Southampton	www.soc.soton.ac.uk
British Antarctic Survey	www.bas.ac.uk
Scott Polar Research Institute (SPRI)	www.spri.cam.ac.uk
The National Snow and Ice Data Center (NSIDC)	nsidc.org

North Pacific Ocean
Average depth: 4 573 metres

NORTH
AMERICA

Polar regions

Although a harsh climate is common to the two polar regions, there are major differences between the Arctic and Antarctica. The North Pole is surrounded by the Arctic Ocean, much of which is permanently covered by sea ice, while the South Pole lies on the huge land mass of Antarctica. This is covered by a permanent ice cap which reaches a maximum thickness of over four kilometres. Antarctica has no permanent population, but Europe, Asia and North America all stretch into the Arctic region which is populated by numerous ethnic groups. Antarctica is subject to the Antarctic Treaty of 1959 which does not recognize individual land claims and protects the continent in the interests of international scientific cooperation.

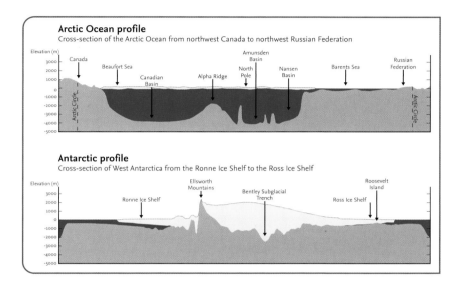

Arctic Ocean profile
Cross-section of the Arctic Ocean from northwest Canada to northwest Russian Federation

Antarctic profile
Cross-section of West Antarctica from the Ronne Ice Shelf to the Ross Ice Shelf

Facts

- If all of Antarctica's ice melted, world sea level would rise by more than 60 metres

- The Arctic Ocean produces up to 50 000 icebergs per year

- The Mid-Atlantic Ridge in the Atlantic Ocean is the earth's longest mountain range

- The world's greatest tidal range – 21 metres – is in the Bay of Fundy, Nova Scotia, Canada

- The Circumpolar current in the Southern Ocean carries 125 million cubic metres of water per second

Antarctica's physical features

Highest mountain: Vinson Massif	4 897 m	16 066 ft
Total land area (excluding ice shelves)	12 093 000 sq km	4 669 107 sq miles
Ice shelves	1 559 000 sq km	601 930 sq miles
Exposed rock	49 000 sq km	18 919 sq miles
Lowest bedrock elevation (Bentley Subglacial Trench)	2 496 m below sea level	8 189 ft below sea level
Maximum ice thickness (Astrolabe Subglacial Basin)	4 776 m	15 669 ft
Mean ice thickness (including ice shelves)	1 859 m	6 099 ft
Volume of ice sheet (including ice shelves)	25 400 000 cubic km	6 094 628 cubic miles

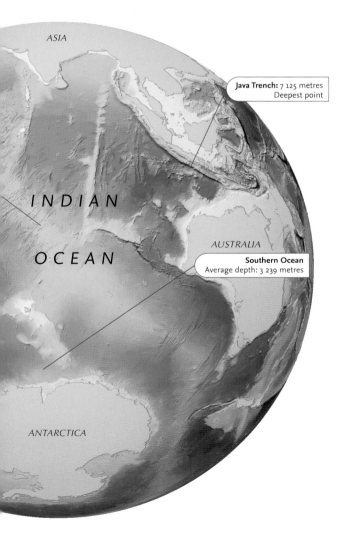

ASIA

Java Trench: 7 125 metres
Deepest point

INDIAN

OCEAN

AUSTRALIA

Southern Ocean
Average depth: 3 239 metres

ANTARCTICA

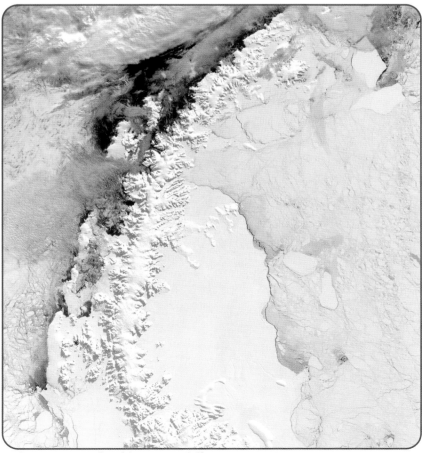

The **Antarctic Peninsula** and the **Larsen Ice Shelf** in western Antarctica.

Pacific Ocean

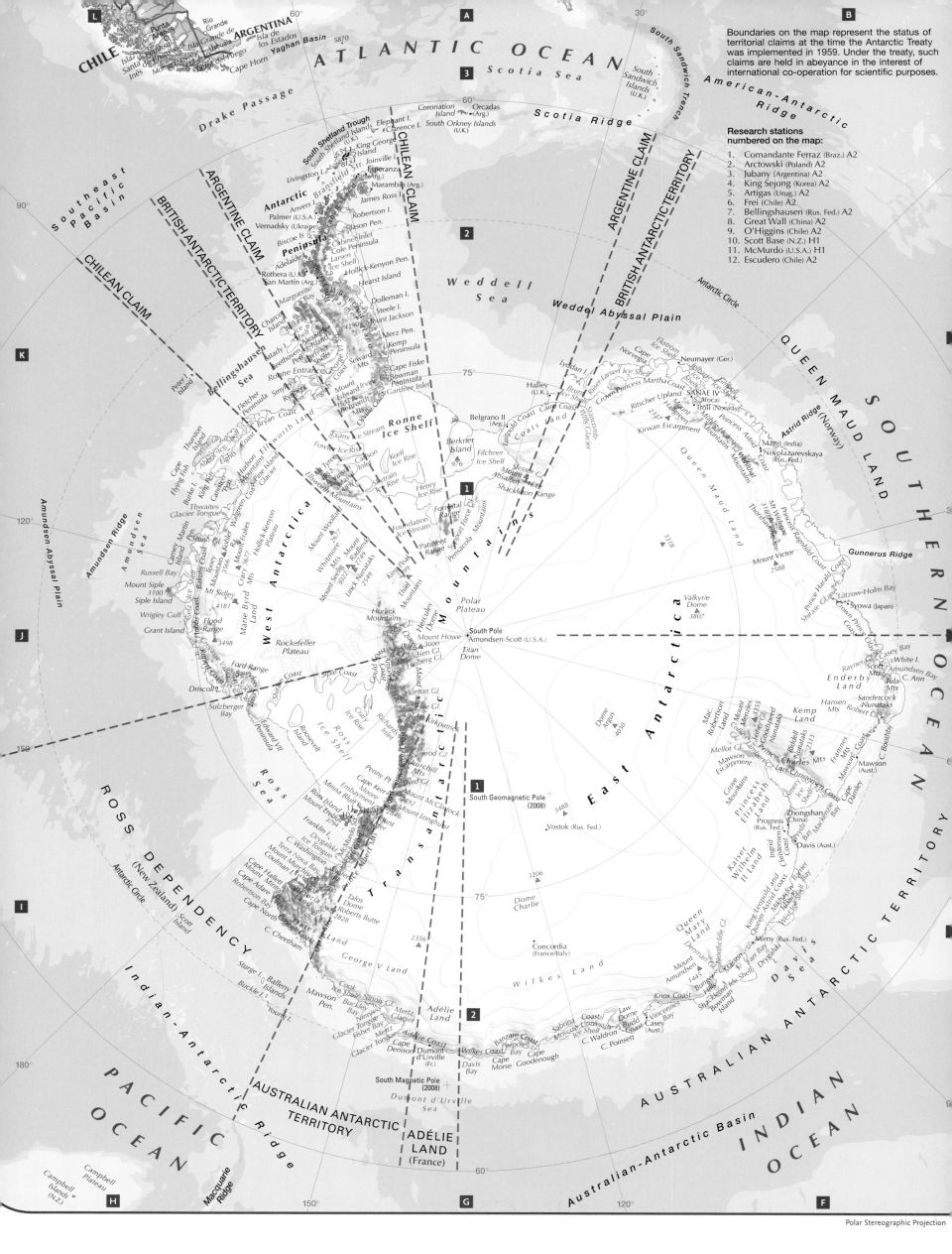

Boundaries on the map represent the status of territorial claims at the time the Antarctic Treaty was implemented in 1959. Under the treaty, such claims are held in abeyance in the interest of international co-operation for scientific purposes.

Research stations numbered on the map:

1. Comandante Ferraz (Braz.) A2
2. Arctowski (Poland) A2
3. Jubany (Argentina) A2
4. King Sejong (Korea) A2
5. Artigas (Urug.) A2
6. Frei (Chile) A2
7. Bellingshausen (Rus. Fed.) A2
8. Great Wall (China) A2
9. O'Higgins (Chile) A2
10. Scott Base (N.Z.) H1
11. McMurdo (U.S.A.) H1
12. Escudero (Chile) A2

1:22 500 000

0   200   400   600   800   1000 miles
0   200   400   600   800   1000   1200   1400   1600 km

Polar Stereographic Projection

The Arctic

1:22 500 000

Polar Stereographic Projection

189

See page 196 for explanatory table and sources

	Population						Economy					
	Total population	Population change (%)	% urban	Total fertility	Population by age (%) 0–14	Population by age (%) 60 or over	2050 projected population	Total Gross National Income (GNI) (US$M)	GNI per capita (US$)	Debt service ratio (% GNI)	Total debt service (US$)	Aid receipts (% GNI)	Military spending (% GDP)
WORLD	6 671 226 000	1.2	49.2	2.6	28.2	10.4	9 075 903 000	48 694 077	7 448	...	...	...	2.5
AFGHANISTAN	27 145 000	3.9	24.3	7.1	46.5	4.4	97 324 000	8 092	...	0.1	9 260 000	35.7	9.9
ALBANIA	3 190 000	0.6	45.0	2.1	27.0	12.0	3 458 000	9 295	2 930	1.4	132 034 000	3.5	1.6
ALGERIA	33 858 000	1.5	60.0	2.4	29.6	6.5	49 500 000	101 206	3 030	12.4	13 351 425 000	0.2	2.7
ANDORRA	75 000	0.4	91.1	...	...	...	58 000	...	...	...	...	...	...
ANGOLA	17 024 000	2.8	37.2	6.4	46.5	3.9	43 501 000	32 646	1 970	10.8	4 296 094 000	0.4	5.4
ANTIGUA AND BARBUDA	85 000	1.2	38.4	...	...	...	112 000	929	11 050	...	...	0.4	...
ARGENTINA	39 531 000	1.0	90.6	2.3	26.4	13.9	51 382 000	201 347	5 150	9.1	18 993 819 000	0.1	0.9
ARMENIA	3 002 000	-0.2	64.1	1.4	20.8	14.5	2 506 000	5 788	1 920	2.6	167 008 000	3.3	2.8
AUSTRALIA	20 743 000	1.0	92.7	1.8	19.6	17.3	27 940 000	742 254	35 860	...	...	...	1.8
AUSTRIA	8 361 000	0.4	65.8	1.4	15.5	22.7	8 073 000	329 183	39 750	...	...	...	0.8
AZERBAIJAN	8 467 000	0.8	49.9	1.8	25.8	9.2	9 631 000	15 639	1 840	1.4	241 872 000	1.2	3.3
THE BAHAMAS	331 000	1.2	90.0	2.0	28.3	9.3	466 000	...	...	...	...	...	0.7
BAHRAIN	753 000	1.8	90.2	2.3	27.1	4.5	1 155 000	14 022	19 350	...	...	...	3.0
BANGLADESH	158 665 000	1.7	25.0	2.8	35.5	5.7	242 937 000	70 475	450	1.0	684 513 000	1.9	1.1
BARBADOS	294 000	0.3	52.9	1.5	18.9	13.2	255 000	...	...	...	...	...	...
BELARUS	9 689 000	-0.6	71.6	1.2	15.2	18.6	7 017 000	33 760	3 470	2.0	733 327 000	0.2	1.7
BELGIUM	10 457 000	0.2	97.3	1.7	16.8	22.4	10 302 000	405 419	38 460	...	...	...	1.1
BELIZE	288 000	2.1	48.6	2.9	36.8	5.9	442 000	1 114	3 740	12.3	134 775 000	0.7	...
BENIN	9 033 000	3.0	46.1	5.4	44.2	4.3	22 123 000	4 665	530	1.8	82 763 000	8.0	...
BHUTAN	658 000	1.4	9.1	2.2	38.4	7.0	4 393 000	928	1 430	1.1	10 105 000	10.2	...
BOLIVIA	9 525 000	1.8	64.4	3.5	38.1	6.7	14 908 000	10 293	1 100	4.0	430 341 000	5.4	1.5
BOSNIA-HERZEGOVINA	3 935 000	0.1	45.3	1.2	16.5	19.2	3 170 000	12 689	3 230	4.6	589 095 000	4.2	1.6
BOTSWANA	1 882 000	1.2	52.5	2.9	37.6	5.1	1 658 000	10 358	5 570	0.6	54 861 000	0.7	3.0
BRAZIL	191 791 000	1.3	84.2	2.3	27.9	8.8	253 105 000	892 639	4 710	6.0	62 144 534 000	0.0	1.5
BRUNEI	390 000	2.1	77.6	2.3	29.6	4.7	681 000	10 287	26 930	...	...	...	2.4
BULGARIA	7 639 000	-0.7	70.5	1.3	13.8	22.4	5 065 000	30 669	3 990	8.7	2 743 215 000	...	2.3
BURKINA FASO	14 784 000	2.9	18.6	6.0	47.2	4.2	39 093 000	6 249	440	0.8	51 765 000	14.0	1.4
BURUNDI	8 508 000	3.9	10.6	6.8	45.0	4.2	25 812 000	815	100	4.5	39 523 000	52.8	5.5
CAMBODIA	14 444 000	1.7	19.7	3.2	37.1	5.6	25 972 000	6 990	490	0.4	30 584 000	7.7	1.7
CAMEROON	18 549 000	2.0	52.9	4.3	41.2	5.6	26 891 000	18 060	990	2.9	518 897 000	9.3	1.4
CANADA	32 876 000	0.9	81.1	1.5	17.6	17.9	42 844 000	1 196 626	36 650	...	...	...	1.2
CAPE VERDE	530 000	2.2	57.6	3.4	39.5	5.5	1 002 000	1 105	2 130	2.9	31 361 000	12.6	0.7
CENTRAL AFRICAN REPUBLIC	4 343 000	1.8	43.8	4.6	43.0	6.1	6 747 000	1 499	350	4.7	70 406 000	9.0	1.1
CHAD	10 781 000	2.9	25.8	6.2	47.3	4.7	31 497 000	4 708	450	1.3	67 834 000	5.5	0.9
CHILE	16 635 000	1.0	87.7	1.9	24.9	11.6	20 657 000	111 869	6 810	10.9	13 792 891 000	0.1	3.6
CHINA	1 313 437 000	0.6	40.5	1.7	21.4	10.9	1 402 062 000	2 620 951	2 000	1.0	27 876 906 000	0.1	1.9
COLOMBIA	46 156 000	1.3	77.4	2.2	31.0	7.5	65 679 000	141 982	3 120	7.2	10 639 506 000	0.8	3.5
COMOROS	839 000	2.5	36.3	4.3	42.0	4.3	1 781 000	406	660	0.9	3 616 000	7.6	...
CONGO	3 768 000	2.1	54.4	4.5	47.1	4.5	13 721 000	3 806	1 050	2.7	101 220 000	...	1.1
CONGO, DEM. REPUBLIC OF THE	62 636 000	3.2	32.7	6.7	47.3	4.3	177 271 000	7 742	130	3.9	319 345 000	25.2	0.0
COSTA RICA	4 468 000	1.5	61.7	2.1	28.4	8.3	6 426 000	21 894	4 980	2.8	597 316 000	0.1	...
CÔTE D'IVOIRE	19 262 000	1.8	45.8	4.5	41.9	5.3	33 959 000	16 578	880	0.8	126 329 000	1.6	1.6
CROATIA	4 555 000	-0.1	59.9	1.4	15.5	22.1	3 686 000	41 348	9 310	18.5	7 680 306 000	0.5	1.6
CUBA	11 268 000	0.0	76.0	1.5	19.1	15.3	9 749 000	...	...	...	...	...	...
CYPRUS	855 000	1.1	69.5	1.6	19.9	16.8	1 174 000	17 948	23 270	...	...	...	1.4
CZECH REPUBLIC	10 186 000	0.0	74.5	1.2	14.6	20.0	8 452 000	131 404	12 790	...	...	...	1.7
DENMARK	5 442 000	0.2	85.5	1.8	18.8	21.1	5 851 000	283 316	52 110	...	...	...	1.4
DJIBOUTI	833 000	1.7	84.6	4.0	41.5	4.7	1 547 000	864	1 060	2.6	22 564 000	14.0	...
DOMINICA	67 000	-0.3	72.7	...	...	...	98 000	300	4 160	6.9	21 255 000	7.0	...
DOMINICAN REPUBLIC	9 760 000	1.5	60.1	2.8	32.7	6.2	12 668 000	27 954	2 910	4.5	1 345 913 000	0.2	0.5
EAST TIMOR	1 155 000	3.5	7.8	6.5	41.1	5.0	3 265 000	865	840	...	...	24.7	...
ECUADOR	13 341 000	1.1	62.8	2.6	32.4	8.3	19 214 000	38 481	2 910	10.5	4 157 073 000	0.5	2.3
EGYPT	75 498 000	1.8	42.3	2.9	33.6	7.1	125 916 000	100 912	1 360	2.1	2 201 406 000	0.8	2.7
EL SALVADOR	6 857 000	1.4	60.1	2.7	34.0	7.6	10 823 000	18 096	2 680	6.2	1 133 017 000	0.9	0.6
EQUATORIAL GUINEA	507 000	2.4	50.0	5.4	44.4	6.0	1 146 000	4 216	8 510	0.1	4 307 000	0.5	...
ERITREA	4 851 000	3.2	20.8	5.1	44.8	4.0	11 229 000	888	190	1.2	12 682 000	12.0	24.1
ESTONIA	1 335 000	-0.4	69.6	1.5	15.2	21.6	1 119 000	15 302	11 400	...	...	...	1.4
ETHIOPIA	83 099 000	2.5	16.2	5.3	44.5	4.7	170 190 000	12 874	170	1.2	163 799 000	14.7	2.6
FIJI	839 000	0.6	53.2	2.8	31.7	6.4	934 000	3 098	3 720	0.5	16 360 000	2.0	1.2
FINLAND	5 277 000	0.3	60.9	1.8	17.3	21.3	5 329 000	217 803	41 360	...	...	...	1.4
FRANCE	61 647 000	0.5	76.7	1.9	18.2	21.1	63 116 000	2 306 714	36 560	...	...	...	2.4
GABON	1 331 000	1.5	85.2	3.1	40.0	6.2	2 279 000	7 032	5 360	1.1	84 901 000	0.4	1.2
THE GAMBIA	1 709 000	2.6	26.1	4.7	40.1	6.0	3 106 000	488	290	6.6	33 137 000	14.8	0.5
GEORGIA	4 395 000	-0.8	51.5	1.4	18.9	17.9	2 985 000	7 008	1 580	3.6	268 375 000	4.9	3.1

	Social Indicators					Environment				Communications			
Child mortality rate	Life expectancy	Literacy rate (%)	Access to safe water (%)	Doctors per 100 000 people	Forest area (%)	Annual change in forest area (%)	Protected land area (%)	CO₂ emissions (metric tonnes per capita)	Main telephone lines per 100 people	Cellular phone subscribers per 100 people	Internet users per 10 000 people	International dialling code	Time zone
72	**67.2**	**87.6**	**83**	**152**	**30.3**	**0.2**	**10.8**	**4.3**	**19.7**	**42.0**	**1 853**	**...**	**...**
257	43.8	34.3	39	19	1.3	-3.1	0.3	...	0.3	8.1	172	93	+4.5
17	76.4	99.4	96	139	29.0	0.6	0.7	1.2	11.3	60.4	1 498	355	+1
38	72.3	90.1	85	85	1.0	1.2	5.1	6.0	8.5	63.0	738	213	+1
3	...	...	100	259	35.6	0.0	9.7	...	51.3	96.9	3 257	376	+1
260	42.7	72.2	53	8	47.4	-0.2	10.0	0.5	0.6	14.3	60	244	+1
11	...	...	91	17	21.4	0.0	0.0	5.1	45.5	133.6	6 424	1 268	-4
16	75.3	98.9	96	301	12.1	-0.4	6.3	3.7	24.2	80.5	2 091	54	-3
24	72.0	99.8	92	353	10.0	-1.5	8.1	1.2	19.7	10.5	575	374	+4
6	81.2	...	100	249	21.3	-0.1	9.5	16.2	48.8	97.0	4 713	61	+8 to +10.5
5	79.8	...	100	324	46.7	0.1	28.3	8.5	43.4	112.8	5 131	43	+1
88	67.5	99.9	77	354	11.3	0.0	2.4	3.8	14.0	39.2	979	994	+4
14	73.5	...	97	106	51.5	0.0	0.1	6.3	40.2	77.3	3 188	1 242	-5
10	75.6	97.0	...	160	0.6	3.8	3.4	23.8	26.3	122.9	2 844	973	+3
69	64.1	63.6	74	23	6.7	-0.3	0.7	0.2	0.8	13.3	31	880	+6
12	77.3	...	100	121	4.0	0.0	0.1	4.4	50.1	87.8	5 948	1 246	-4
13	69.0	99.8	100	450	38.0	0.1	5.2	6.6	34.7	61.4	5 647	375	+2
4	79.4	...	...	418	22.0	0.0	3.2	9.7	45.2	92.6	5 260	32	+1
16	76.1	...	91	105	72.5	0.0	36.0	2.8	12.3	44.1	1 236	501	-6
148	56.7	45.3	67	6	21.3	-2.5	22.0	0.3	0.9	12.1	144	229	+1
70	65.6	...	62	5	68.0	0.3	31.5	0.7	3.8	9.8	357	975	+6
61	65.6	97.3	85	73	54.2	-0.5	20.0	0.8	7.1	30.8	620	591	-4
15	74.9	99.8	97	134	43.1	0.0	0.5	4.0	25.3	48.3	2 428	387	+1
124	50.7	94.0	95	29	21.1	-1.0	30.1	2.4	7.8	46.8	455	267	+2
20	72.4	96.8	90	206	57.2	-0.6	17.8	1.8	20.5	52.9	2 255	55	-2 to -5
9	77.1	98.9	...	101	52.8	-0.7	53.3	24.1	21.0	78.9	4 169	673	+8
14	73.0	98.2	99	338	32.8	1.4	10.0	5.5	31.3	107.6	2 166	359	+2
204	52.3	33.0	61	4	29.0	-0.3	14.0	0.1	0.7	7.5	59	226	GMT
181	49.6	73.3	79	5	5.9	-5.2	5.7	0.0	0.4	2.0	77	257	+2
82	59.7	83.4	41	16	59.2	-2.0	22.8	0.0	0.2	7.9	31	855	+7
149	50.4	...	66	7	45.6	-1.0	8.6	0.2	0.8	18.9	223	237	+1
6	80.7	...	100	209	33.6	0.0	4.8	20.0	64.5	57.6	6 789	1	-3.5 to -8
34	71.7	96.3	80	17	20.7	0.4	...	0.6	13.8	21.0	636	238	-1
175	44.7	58.5	75	4	36.5	-0.1	15.3	0.1	0.3	2.5	32	236	+1
209	50.7	37.6	42	3	9.5	-0.7	9.0	0.0	0.1	4.7	60	235	+1
9	78.6	99.0	95	109	21.5	0.4	3.9	3.9	20.2	75.6	2 524	56	-4
24	73.0	98.9	77	164	21.2	2.2	15.3	3.9	27.8	34.8	1 035	86	+8
21	72.9	98.0	93	135	58.5	-0.1	24.7	1.2	17.0	64.3	1 449	57	-5
68	65.2	...	86	7	2.9	-7.4	...	0.1	2.3	4.5	256	269	+3
126	55.3	97.4	58	25	65.8	-0.1	14.1	1.0	0.4	12.3	170	242	+1
205	46.5	70.4	46	7	58.9	-0.2	8.4	0.0	0.0	7.4	30	243	+1 to +2
12	78.8	97.6	97	172	46.8	0.1	21.1	1.5	30.7	32.8	2 761	506	-6
127	48.3	60.7	84	9	32.7	0.1	12.1	0.3	1.4	22.0	163	225	GMT
6	75.7	99.6	100	237	38.2	0.1	5.9	5.3	40.1	96.5	3 698	385	+1
7	78.3	100.0	91	591	24.7	2.2	1.4	2.3	8.6	1.4	213	53	-5
4	79.0	99.8	100	298	18.9	0.2	9.0	9.1	48.3	102.8	4 222	357	+2
4	76.5	...	100	343	34.3	0.1	15.9	11.5	28.3	116.4	3 469	420	+1
5	78.3	...	100	366	11.8	0.6	6.0	9.8	56.9	107.0	5 823	45	+1
130	54.8	...	73	13	0.2	0.0	...	0.5	1.6	6.4	136	253	+3
15	...	...	97	49	61.3	-0.6	46.8	1.5	29.4	58.7	3 722	1 767	-4
29	72.2	94.2	95	188	28.4	0.0	25.0	2.1	9.9	51.1	2 217	1 809	-4
55	60.8	...	58	...	53.7	-1.3	6.1	0.2	0.2	4.9	12	670	+9
24	75.0	96.4	94	148	39.2	-1.7	24.6	2.3	13.1	63.2	1 154	593	-5
35	71.3	84.9	98	212	0.1	2.6	5.3	2.2	14.3	23.9	795	20	+2
25	71.9	88.5	84	127	14.4	-1.7	1.0	0.9	14.8	55.0	1 000	503	-6
206	51.6	94.9	43	25	58.2	-0.9	17.1	11.5	2.0	19.3	155	240	+1
74	58.0	...	60	3	15.4	-0.3	4.2	0.2	0.8	1.4	219	291	+3
7	71.4	99.8	100	316	53.9	0.4	43.9	14.0	34.1	125.2	5 736	372	+2
123	52.9	49.9	22	3	11.9	-1.1	16.4	0.1	0.9	1.1	21	251	+3
18	68.8	...	47	34	54.7	0.0	0.9	1.3	13.3	15.9	936	679	+12
4	79.3	...	100	311	73.9	...	8.9	12.6	36.3	107.8	5 560	358	+2
4	80.7	...	100	329	28.3	0.3	10.2	6.2	55.8	85.1	4 957	33	+1
91	56.7	96.0	88	29	84.5	...	13.3	1.1	2.6	54.4	576	241	+1
113	59.4	...	82	4	41.7	0.4	...	0.2	3.0	26.0	529	220	GMT
32	71.0	...	82	391	39.7	...	3.9	0.9	12.5	38.4	749	995	+4

See page 196 for explanatory table and sources

	Population						Economy					
	Total population	Population change (%)	% urban	Total fertility	Population by age (%) 0 – 14	60 or over	2050 projected population	Total Gross National Income (GNI) (US$M)	GNI per capita (US$)	Debt service ratio (% GNI)	Total debt service (US$)	Aid receipts (% GNI)	Military spending (% GDP)
GERMANY	82 599 000	-0.1	88.5	1.4	14.3	25.1	78 765 000	3 032 617	36 810	...	...	...	1.3
GHANA	23 478 000	2.0	46.3	3.8	39.0	5.7	40 573 000	11 778	510	2.0	261 043 000	9.2	0.7
GREECE	11 147 000	0.2	61.4	1.3	14.3	23.0	10 742 000	305 308	27 390	...	...	...	3.2
GRENADA	106 000	0.0	42.2	2.3	...	...	157 000	495	4 650	2.2	15 321 000	5.6	...
GUATEMALA	13 354 000	2.5	47.2	4.2	43.2	6.1	25 612 000	33 725	2 590	1.6	550 958 000	1.4	0.4
GUINEA	9 370 000	2.2	36.5	5.4	43.7	5.6	22 987 000	3 713	400	5.0	164 764 000	5.0	2.0
GUINEA-BISSAU	1 695 000	3.0	35.6	7.1	47.5	4.7	5 312 000	307	190	11.5	33 831 000	27.9	4.0
GUYANA	738 000	-0.2	38.5	2.3	29.3	7.4	488 000	849	1 150	3.8	32 940 000	20.1	...
HAITI	9 598 000	1.6	38.8	3.5	37.5	6.0	12 996 000	4 044	430	1.3	56 732 000	13.4	...
HONDURAS	7 106 000	2.0	46.4	3.3	39.2	5.6	12 776 000	8 844	1 270	3.6	325 235 000	6.6	0.6
HUNGARY	10 030 000	-0.3	65.9	1.3	15.7	20.8	8 262 000	109 461	10 870	29.4	30 827 896 000	...	1.2
ICELAND	301 000	0.8	93.0	2.1	22.0	15.8	370 000	15 078	49 960	...	...	...	0.0
INDIA	1 169 016 000	1.5	28.7	2.8	32.1	7.9	1 592 704 000	909 138	820	2.0	17 878 568 000	0.2	2.7
INDONESIA	231 627 000	1.2	47.9	2.2	28.3	8.4	284 640 000	315 845	1 420	5.9	20 434 246 000	0.4	1.2
IRAN	71 208 000	1.4	68.1	2.0	28.7	6.4	101 944 000	205 040	2 930	1.2	2 555 530 000	0.1	4.8
IRAQ	28 993 000	1.8	66.8	4.3	41.0	4.5	63 693 000	...	...	...	...	...	...
IRELAND	4 301 000	1.8	60.4	2.0	20.2	15.1	5 762 000	191 315	44 830	...	...	...	0.5
ISRAEL	6 928 000	1.7	91.7	2.8	27.8	13.3	10 403 000	142 199	20 170	...	...	...	8.4
ITALY	58 877 000	0.1	67.5	1.4	14.0	25.6	50 912 000	1 882 544	31 990	...	...	...	1.7
JAMAICA	2 714 000	0.5	52.2	2.4	31.2	10.2	2 586 000	9 504	3 560	8.8	824 547 000	0.4	0.6
JAPAN	127 967 000	0.0	65.7	1.3	14.0	26.3	112 198 000	4 934 676	38 630	...	...	...	0.9
JORDAN	5 924 000	3.0	79.3	3.1	37.2	5.1	10 225 000	14 653	2 650	4.7	688 206 000	3.9	4.9
KAZAKHSTAN	15 422 000	0.7	55.9	2.3	23.1	11.3	13 086 000	59 175	3 870	20.3	14 531 967 000	0.3	0.9
KENYA	37 538 000	2.7	41.6	5.0	42.8	4.1	83 073 000	21 335	580	1.9	432 974 000	4.5	1.6
KIRIBATI	95 000	1.6	50.2	...	...	...	177 000	124	1 240	...	...	-37.6	...
KOSOVO*	2 069 989	...	...	...	...	...	...	...	...	...	...	...	...
KUWAIT	2 851 000	2.4	96.4	2.2	24.3	3.1	5 279 000	77 660	30 630	...	...	...	4.8
KYRGYZSTAN	5 317 000	1.1	33.7	2.5	31.5	7.6	6 664 000	2 609	500	3.5	96 608 000	11.8	3.1
LAOS	5 859 000	1.7	21.6	3.2	40.9	5.3	11 586 000	2 890	500	5.6	169 326 000	12.1	...
LATVIA	2 277 000	-0.5	65.9	1.3	14.7	22.5	1 678 000	18 525	8 100	16.9	3 279 260 000	...	1.6
LEBANON	4 099 000	1.1	88.0	2.2	28.6	10.3	4 702 000	22 640	5 580	19.8	4 433 178 000	3.2	4.1
LESOTHO	2 008 000	0.6	18.2	3.4	38.6	7.5	1 601 000	1 957	980	2.5	47 040 000	4.0	2.4
LIBERIA	3 750 000	4.5	47.9	6.8	47.1	3.6	10 653 000	469	130	0.2	809 000	54.4	...
LIBYA	6 160 000	2.0	86.9	2.7	30.1	6.5	9 553 000	44 011	7 290	...	...	0.1	1.5
LIECHTENSTEIN	35 000	0.9	21.8	...	...	...	44 000	...	...	...	...	...	...
LITHUANIA	3 390 000	-0.5	66.6	1.3	16.7	20.7	2 565 000	26 917	7 930	15.3	4 215 870 000	...	1.2
LUXEMBOURG	467 000	1.1	92.4	1.7	18.9	18.3	721 000	32 904	71 240	...	...	...	0.8
MACEDONIA (F.Y.R.O.M.)	2 038 000	0.1	59.7	1.4	19.6	15.5	1 884 000	6 260	3 070	8.4	522 292 000	3.2	2.0
MADAGASCAR	19 683 000	2.7	27.0	4.8	44.0	4.8	43 508 000	5 343	280	1.2	67 571 000	13.9	1.0
MALAWI	13 925 000	2.6	17.2	5.6	47.3	4.7	29 452 000	3 143	230	2.9	90 044 000	30.5	0.5
MALAYSIA	26 572 000	1.7	65.1	2.6	32.4	7.0	38 924 000	146 754	5 620	5.2	7 630 086 000	0.2	2.0
MALDIVES	306 000	1.8	29.7	2.6	40.7	5.1	682 000	903	3 010	3.9	34 588 000	4.4	...
MALI	12 337 000	3.0	33.7	6.5	48.2	4.2	41 976 000	5 546	460	1.5	80 175 000	13.4	2.2
MALTA	407 000	0.4	92.1	1.4	17.6	18.8	428 000	6 216	15 310	...	...	...	0.6
MARSHALL ISLANDS	59 000	2.2	66.7	...	...	...	150 000	195	2 980	...	...	28.5	...
MAURITANIA	3 124 000	2.5	64.3	4.4	43.0	5.3	7 497 000	2 325	760	3.5	97 426 000	6.8	2.5
MAURITIUS	1 262 000	0.8	43.8	1.9	24.6	9.6	1 465 000	6 812	5 430	4.8	308 955 000	0.3	0.2
MEXICO	106 535 000	1.1	76.0	2.2	31.0	7.8	139 015 000	815 741	7 830	6.8	56 068 050 000	0.0	0.4
MICRONESIA, FED. STATES OF	111 000	0.5	30.0	3.7	39.0	4.9	99 000	264	2 390	...	...	41.4	...
MOLDOVA	3 794 000	-0.9	46.3	1.4	18.3	13.7	3 312 000	3 650	1 080	8.9	334 842 000	6.0	0.3
MONACO	33 000	0.3	100.0	...	...	...	55 000	...	...	...	...	...	...
MONGOLIA	2 629 000	1.0	57.0	1.9	30.5	5.7	3 625 000	2 576	1 000	1.6	48 462 000	7.8	1.3
MONTENEGRO*	598 000	-0.3	...	1.8	...	...	...	2 481	4 130	0.5	13 260 000	4.2	...
MOROCCO	31 224 000	1.2	58.8	2.4	31.1	6.8	46 397 000	65 793	2 160	5.3	3 404 801 000	1.8	3.7
MOZAMBIQUE	21 397 000	2.0	38.0	5.1	44.0	5.2	37 604 000	6 453	310	0.9	55 018 000	23.3	0.0
MYANMAR	48 798 000	0.9	30.6	2.1	29.5	7.5	63 657 000	...	...	...	86 428 000	...	...
NAMIBIA	2 074 000	1.3	33.5	3.2	41.5	5.3	3 060 000	6 573	3 210	...	...	2.3	2.9
NAURU	10 000	0.3	100.0	...	...	...	18 000	...	...	...	...	...	...
NEPAL	28 196 000	2.0	15.8	3.3	39.0	5.8	51 172 000	8 790	320	1.6	139 842 000	6.3	1.9
NETHERLANDS	16 419 000	0.2	66.8	1.7	18.2	19.2	17 139 000	703 484	43 050	...	...	...	1.5
NEW ZEALAND	4 179 000	0.9	86.0	2.0	21.3	16.7	4 790 000	111 958	26 750	...	...	...	1.0
NICARAGUA	5 603 000	1.3	58.1	2.8	38.9	4.9	9 371 000	5 163	930	2.4	122 997 000	13.9	0.7
NIGER	14 226 000	3.5	23.3	7.2	49.0	3.3	50 156 000	3 665	270	5.0	181 178 000	11.0	1.1
NIGERIA	148 093 000	2.3	48.3	5.3	44.3	4.8	258 108 000	90 025	620	6.8	6 805 053 000	11.1	0.7
NORTH KOREA	23 790 000	0.3	61.7	1.9	25.0	11.2	24 192 000	...	...	...	...	...	...

* See Serbia for figures prior to formation of independent states

Social Indicators					Environment				Communications				
Child mortality rate	Life expectancy	Literacy rate (%)	Access to safe water (%)	Doctors per 100 000 people	Forest area (%)	Annual change in forest area (%)	Protected land area (%)	CO_2 emissions (metric tonnes per capita)	Main telephone lines per 100 people	Cellular phone subscribers per 100 people	Internet users per 10 000 people	International dialling code	Time zone
4	79.4	...	100	362	31.7	0.0	21.3	9.8	65.9	103.6	4 667	49	+1
120	60.0	70.7	75	9	24.2	-2.0	15.1	0.3	1.6	23.1	270	233	GMT
4	79.5	98.9	...	440	29.1	0.8	3.2	8.7	55.4	98.6	1 838	30	+2
20	68.7	...	95	50	12.2	0.0	3.5	2.0	26.7	44.6	1 864	1 473	-4
41	70.3	82.2	95	90	36.3	-1.3	32.2	1.0	10.5	55.6	1 022	502	-6
161	56.0	46.6	50	9	27.4	-0.5	6.1	0.2	0.3	2.4	52	224	GMT
200	46.4	...	59	17	73.7	-0.5	9.1	0.2	0.4	9.2	226	245	GMT
62	66.8	...	83	48	76.7	0.0	2.3	2.0	14.7	37.5	2 130	592	-4
80	60.9	...	54	25	3.8	-0.7	0.3	0.2	1.7	13.9	751	509	-5
27	70.2	88.9	87	83	41.5	-3.1	19.4	1.1	9.7	30.4	467	504	-6
7	73.3	...	99	316	21.5	0.7	5.7	5.7	33.4	99.0	3 475	36	+1
3	81.8	...	100	347	0.5	3.9	3.9	7.6	63.5	108.7	6 530	354	GMT
76	64.7	76.4	86	51	22.8	...	4.8	1.2	3.6	14.8	1 072	91	+5.5
34	70.7	98.7	77	16	48.8	-2.0	11.0	1.7	6.6	28.3	469	62	+7 to +9
34	71.0	97.4	94	105	6.8	0.0	6.2	6.4	31.2	21.8	2 554	98	+3.5
46	59.5	84.8	81	54	1.9	0.1	...	...	4.0	15.5	16	964	+3
5	78.9	...	...	237	9.7	1.9	1.2	10.4	49.9	112.6	3 423	353	GMT
5	80.7	99.8	100	391	8.3	0.8	14.9	10.5	43.9	122.7	2 774	972	+2
4	80.5	99.8	...	606	33.9	1.1	6.4	7.7	46.3	135.1	5 291	39	+1
31	72.6	...	93	85	31.3	-0.1	14.8	4.0	12.9	93.7	2 942	1 876	-5
4	82.6	...	100	201	68.2	...	9.3	9.8	43.0	79.3	6 827	81	+9
25	72.5	99.0	97	205	0.9	0.0	10.7	3.1	10.5	74.4	1 365	962	+2
29	67.0	99.8	86	330	1.2	-0.2	2.7	13.3	19.8	52.9	842	7	+5 to +6
121	54.1	80.3	61	13	6.2	-0.3	11.8	0.3	0.8	20.9	789	254	+3
64	...	...	65	30	3.0	0.0	...	0.3	5.1	0.7	215	686	+12 to +14
...	...	...	...	...	...	...	...	...	...	...	...	381	+1
11	77.6	99.7	...	153	0.3	2.7	0.0	40.4	18.7	91.5	2 953	965	+3
41	65.9	99.7	77	268	4.5	0.3	3.1	1.1	8.6	23.7	560	996	+6
75	64.4	78.5	51	59	69.9	-0.5	16.3	0.2	1.5	16.7	116	856	+7
9	72.7	99.8	99	291	47.4	0.4	16.1	3.1	28.6	95.1	4 665	371	+2
30	72.0	...	100	325	13.3	0.8	0.4	4.1	18.9	30.6	2 628	961	+2
132	42.6	...	79	5	0.3	2.7	0.2	...	3.0	20.0	287	266	+2
235	45.7	67.4	61	2	32.7	-1.8	15.9	0.1	0.2	4.9	...	231	GMT
18	74.0	98.0	...	129	0.1	0.0	0.1	10.3	8.1	65.8	436	218	+2
3	...	...	...	...	43.1	0.0	57.4	...	57.2	81.8	6 398	423	+1
8	73.0	99.7	...	403	33.5	0.8	5.5	3.9	23.2	138.1	3 169	370	+2
4	78.7	...	100	255	33.5	0.0	16.7	24.9	52.4	116.8	7 201	352	+1
17	74.2	98.7	...	219	35.8	0.0	7.2	5.1	24.1	69.6	1 315	389	+1
115	59.4	70.2	50	9	22.1	-0.3	2.6	0.2	0.7	5.5	58	261	+3
120	48.3	76.0	73	1	36.2	-0.9	15.7	0.1	0.8	3.3	45	265	+2
12	74.2	97.2	99	70	63.6	-0.7	18.2	7.0	16.8	75.5	5 423	60	+8
30	68.5	98.2	83	78	3.0	0.0	...	2.5	10.9	87.9	664	960	+5
217	54.5	24.2	50	4	10.3	-0.8	2.1	0.1	0.6	10.9	64	223	GMT
6	79.4	96.0	100	293	1.1	0.0	21.4	6.1	50.1	86.0	3 173	356	+1
56	...	...	87	47	...	0.0	...	...	8.3	1.1	...	692	+12
125	64.2	61.3	53	14	0.3	-3.4	...	0.9	1.1	33.6	95	222	GMT
14	72.8	94.5	100	85	18.2	-0.5	4.8	2.6	28.5	61.5	2 548	230	+4
35	76.2	97.6	97	171	33.7	-0.4	5.2	4.3	18.3	52.6	1 898	52	-6 to -8
41	68.5	...	94	60	90.6	0.0	32.7	...	11.2	12.7	1 439	691	+10 to +11
19	68.9	99.7	92	269	10.0	0.2	1.4	2.0	24.3	32.4	1 735	373	+2
4	...	...	100	586	0.0	0.0	...	...	96.8	51.6	5 634	377	+1
43	66.8	97.7	62	267	6.5	-0.8	14.0	3.4	5.9	28.9	1 157	976	+8
10	74.5	...	...	...	...	...	...	...	58.9	107.3	4 434	382	+1
37	71.2	70.5	81	48	9.8	0.2	1.2	1.4	4.1	52.1	1 985	212	GMT
138	42.1	47.0	43	2	24.6	-0.3	5.7	0.1	0.3	11.6	90	258	+2
104	62.1	94.5	78	30	49.0	-1.4	5.4	0.2	0.9	0.4	18	95	+6.5
61	52.9	92.3	87	30	9.3	-0.9	5.2	1.2	6.8	24.4	397	264	+1
30	...	...	...	...	0.0	0.0	...	...	...	...	...	674	+12
59	63.8	70.1	90	5	25.4	-1.4	15.4	0.1	2.2	4.2	114	977	+5.75
5	79.8	...	100	329	10.8	0.3	12.4	8.7	46.6	106.9	10 998	31	+1
6	80.2	...	...	223	31.0	0.2	24.2	7.7	44.1	94.0	7 877	64	+12
36	72.9	86.2	79	164	42.7	-1.3	16.4	0.7	4.4	32.7	277	505	-6
253	56.9	36.5	46	3	1.0	-1.0	7.1	0.1	0.2	3.4	28	227	+1
191	46.9	84.2	48	27	12.2	-3.3	6.2	0.8	1.3	24.1	595	234	+1
55	67.3	...	100	297	51.4	-1.9	2.6	3.4	4.4	...	...	850	+9

See page 196 for explanatory table and sources

	Population						Economy					
	Total population	Population change (%)	% urban	Total fertility	Population by age (%) 0 – 14	Population by age (%) 60 or over	2050 projected population	Total Gross National Income (GNI) (US$M)	GNI per capita (US$)	Debt service ratio (% GNI)	Total debt service (US$)	Aid receipts (% GNI)	Military spending (% GDP)
NORWAY	4 698 000	0.6	80.5	1.9	19.6	20.0	5 435 000	318 919	68 440	...	...	...	1.5
OMAN	2 595 000	2.0	78.6	3.0	34.5	4.2	4 958 000	27 887	11 120	5.1	310 065 000	...	11.8
PAKISTAN	163 902 000	1.8	34.8	3.5	38.3	5.8	304 700 000	126 711	800	1.8	2 282 421 000	1.7	3.8
PALAU	20 000	0.4	68.2	...	...	...	21 000	161	7 990	...	...	23.5	...
PANAMA	3 343 000	1.7	57.8	2.6	30.4	8.8	5 093 000	16 442	5 000	21.5	3 458 784 000	0.2	...
PAPUA NEW GUINEA	6 331 000	2.0	13.2	3.8	40.3	3.9	10 619 000	4 603	740	5.8	293 913 000	5.5	0.5
PARAGUAY	6 127 000	1.8	58.5	3.1	37.6	5.6	12 095 000	8 461	1 410	4.5	420 751 000	0.6	0.8
PERU	27 903 000	1.2	74.6	2.5	32.2	7.8	42 552 000	82 201	2 980	4.4	3 745 566 000	0.4	1.2
PHILIPPINES	87 960 000	1.9	62.6	3.2	35.1	6.1	127 068 000	120 190	1 390	10.7	13 680 640 000	0.4	0.9
POLAND	38 082 000	-0.2	62.0	1.2	16.3	16.8	31 916 000	312 994	8 210	11.1	36 044 403 000	...	2.0
PORTUGAL	10 623 000	0.4	55.6	1.5	15.9	22.3	10 723 000	189 017	17 850	...	...	...	2.1
QATAR	841 000	2.1	92.3	2.7	21.7	2.6	1 330 000	...	...	...	...	...	...
ROMANIA	21 438 000	-0.5	54.7	1.3	15.4	19.3	16 757 000	104 382	4 830	7.3	8 678 183 000	...	1.9
RUSSIAN FEDERATION	142 499 000	-0.5	73.3	1.3	15.3	17.1	111 752 000	822 328	5 770	5.2	50 222 974 000	...	4.0
RWANDA	9 725 000	2.8	21.8	5.9	43.5	3.9	18 153 000	2 341	250	1.2	30 612 000	23.6	2.7
SAMOA	187 000	0.9	22.5	3.9	40.7	6.5	157 000	421	2 270	7.0	29 506 000	11.3	...
SAN MARINO	31 000	0.8	88.7	...	...	...	30 000	1 291	45 130	...	...	...	...
SÃO TOMÉ AND PRÍNCIPE	158 000	1.6	37.9	3.9	39.5	5.7	295 000	124	800	7.8	9 337 000	18.0	...
SAUDI ARABIA	24 735 000	2.2	88.5	3.4	37.3	4.6	49 464 000	331 041	13 980	...	...	...	8.5
SENEGAL	12 379 000	2.5	51.0	4.7	42.6	4.9	23 108 000	9 117	760	2.2	202 197 000	9.3	1.6
SERBIA	7 788 448	0.1	52.3*	1.8	18.3*	18.5*	9 426 000*	29 961	4 030	8.5	2 679 730 000	5.1	2.1
SEYCHELLES	87 000	0.5	50.2	...	...	...	99 000	751	8 870	24.8	181 083 000	2.0	1.8
SIERRA LEONE	5 866 000	2.0	40.2	6.5	42.8	5.5	13 786 000	1 353	240	2.4	33 899 000	25.7	1.0
SINGAPORE	4 436 000	1.2	100.0	1.3	19.5	12.2	5 213 000	128 816	28 730	...	...	...	4.7
SLOVAKIA	5 390 000	0.0	58.0	1.3	16.7	16.2	4 612 000	51 807	9 610	7.8	4 125 305 000	...	1.7
SLOVENIA	2 002 000	0.0	50.8	1.3	13.9	20.5	1 630 000	37 445	18 660	...	...	...	1.7
SOLOMON ISLANDS	496 000	2.3	17.1	3.9	40.6	4.2	921 000	333	690	1.3	4 276 000	60.6	...
SOMALIA	8 699 000	2.9	35.9	6.0	44.1	4.2	21 329 000	...	...	...	19 000	...	...
SOUTH AFRICA, REPUBLIC OF	48 577 000	0.6	57.9	2.6	32.6	6.8	48 660 000	255 389	5 390	2.2	5 472 200 000	0.3	1.4
SOUTH KOREA	48 224 000	0.3	80.8	1.2	18.6	13.7	44 629 000	856 565	17 690	...	...	...	2.7
SPAIN	44 279 000	0.8	76.7	1.4	14.3	21.4	42 541 000	1 206 169	27 340	...	...	...	1.0
SRI LANKA	19 299 000	0.5	21.0	1.9	24.1	10.7	23 554 000	26 001	1 310	3.6	957 927 000	3.0	2.4
ST KITTS AND NEVIS	50 000	1.3	31.9	...	...	...	59 000	406	8 460	12.3	46 585 000	1.2	...
ST LUCIA	165 000	1.1	31.3	2.2	28.8	9.7	188 000	833	5 060	4.1	34 456 000	2.2	...
ST VINCENT AND THE GRENADINES	120 000	0.5	60.5	2.2	29.2	8.9	105 000	395	3 320	7.0	35 627 000	1.0	...
SUDAN	38 560 000	2.2	40.8	4.2	39.2	5.6	66 705 000	30 086	800	0.8	292 431 000	6.0	2.2
SURINAME	458 000	0.6	77.2	2.4	30.1	9.0	429 000	1 918	4 210	...	...	4.1	...
SWAZILAND	1 141 000	0.6	23.9	3.5	41.0	5.4	1 026 000	2 737	2 400	1.7	44 704 000	1.3	1.9
SWEDEN	9 119 000	0.5	83.4	1.8	17.5	23.4	10 054 000	395 411	43 530	...	...	...	1.4
SWITZERLAND	7 484 000	0.4	67.5	1.4	16.5	21.8	7 252 000	434 844	58 050	...	...	...	0.9
SYRIA	19 929 000	2.5	50.3	3.1	36.9	4.7	35 935 000	30 333	1 560	0.6	186 679 000	0.1	3.8
TAIWAN	22 880 000	...	...	...	19.8	9.2*	...	...	...	...	...	...	...
TAJIKISTAN	6 736 000	1.5	24.2	3.4	39.0	5.1	10 423 000	2 572	390	5.0	136 859 000	8.8	2.2
TANZANIA	40 454 000	2.5	37.5	5.2	42.6	5.1	66 845 000	13 404	350	0.9	113 148 000	14.5	1.1
THAILAND	63 884 000	0.7	32.5	1.9	23.8	10.5	74 594 000	193 734	3 050	7.3	14 685 762 000	-0.1	1.1
TOGO	6 585 000	2.7	36.3	4.8	43.5	4.9	13 544 000	2 265	350	0.7	15 432 000	3.6	1.6
TONGA	100 000	0.5	34.0	3.8	35.9	8.8	75 000	225	2 250	1.4	3 203 000	9.6	1.1
TRINIDAD AND TOBAGO	1 333 000	0.4	76.2	1.6	21.5	10.7	1 230 000	16 612	12 500	...	...	0.1	...
TUNISIA	10 327 000	1.1	64.4	1.9	25.9	8.6	12 927 000	30 091	2 970	8.8	2 520 202 000	1.5	1.4
TURKEY	74 877 000	1.3	67.3	2.1	29.2	8.0	101 208 000	393 903	5 400	10.1	40 511 288 000	0.1	2.9
TURKMENISTAN	4 965 000	1.3	45.8	2.5	31.8	6.2	6 780 000	...	...	2.6	254 770 000	0.3	...
TUVALU	11 000	0.4	57.0	...	...	...	12 000	...	...	...	...	...	...
UGANDA	30 884 000	3.2	12.4	6.5	50.5	3.8	126 950 000	8 996	300	1.2	114 694 000	16.9	2.1
UKRAINE	46 205 000	-0.8	67.3	1.2	14.9	20.9	26 393 000	90 740	1 940	9.0	9 388 953 000	0.5	2.1
UNITED ARAB EMIRATES	4 380 000	2.9	85.5	2.3	22.0	1.6	9 056 000	...	...	...	...	...	2.0
UNITED KINGDOM	60 769 000	0.4	89.2	1.8	17.9	21.2	67 143 000	2 455 691	40 560	...	...	...	2.6
UNITED STATES OF AMERICA	305 826 000	1.0	80.8	2.1	20.8	16.7	394 976 000	13 386 875	44 710	...	...	...	4.1
URUGUAY	3 340 000	0.3	93.0	2.1	24.3	17.4	4 043 000	17 591	5 310	30.3	5 689 614 000	0.1	1.2
UZBEKISTAN	27 372 000	1.4	36.4	2.5	33.2	6.2	38 665 000	16 179	610	5.4	923 830 000	0.9	0.5
VANUATU	226 000	2.4	23.7	3.7	39.9	5.1	375 000	373	1 690	1.0	3 725 000	13.6	...
VATICAN CITY	557	0.1	100.0	...	...	...	1 000	...	...	...	...	...	...
VENEZUELA	27 657 000	1.7	88.1	2.6	31.2	7.6	41 991 000	163 959	6 070	5.5	9 964 936 000	0.0	1.1
VIETNAM	87 375 000	1.3	26.7	2.1	29.5	7.5	116 654 000	58 506	700	1.5	918 307 000	3.1	...
YEMEN	22 389 000	3.0	26.3	5.5	46.4	3.6	59 454 000	16 444	760	1.3	225 869 000	1.6	6.0
ZAMBIA	11 922 000	1.9	36.5	5.2	45.8	4.6	22 781 000	7 413	630	1.6	153 699 000	14.3	2.3
ZIMBABWE	13 349 000	1.0	35.9	3.2	40.0	5.4	15 805 000	4 466	340	7.0	83 389 000	...	0.0

* Figures are for Serbia and Montenegro (including Kosovo) prior to formation of independent states

Social Indicators					Environment				Communications				
Child mortality rate	Life expectancy	Literacy rate (%)	Access to safe water (%)	Doctors per 100 000 people	Forest area (%)	Annual change in forest area (%)	Protected land area (%)	CO₂ emissions (metric tonnes per capita)	Main telephone lines per 100 people	Cellular phone subscribers per 100 people	Internet users per 10 000 people	International dialling code	Time zone
4	80.2	...	100	356	30.7	0.2	5.1	19.1	44.3	108.6	8 168	47	+1
12	75.6	97.3	...	126	0.0	0.0	0.1	12.5	10.3	69.6	1 222	968	+4
97	65.5	65.1	91	66	2.5	-2.1	7.4	0.8	3.3	22.0	764	92	+5
11	...	...	85	109	87.6	0.4	0.0	11.9	...	...	...	680	+9
23	75.5	96.1	90	168	57.7	-0.1	10.3	1.8	14.9	66.1	669	507	-5
73	57.2	66.7	39	5	65.0	-0.5	7.9	0.4	1.1	1.3	183	675	+10
22	71.8	95.9	86	117	46.5	-0.9	5.8	0.7	5.3	51.3	413	595	-4
25	71.4	97.1	83	117	53.7	-0.1	13.6	1.2	8.5	30.9	2 581	51	-5
32	71.7	95.1	85	116	24.0	-2.1	10.7	1.0	4.3	50.8	548	63	+8
7	75.6	...	...	220	30.0	0.3	24.2	8.0	29.8	95.5	3 658	48	+1
5	78.1	99.6	...	324	41.3	1.1	5.1	5.6	40.2	116.0	3 025	351	GMT
21	75.6	95.9	100	221	0.0	0.0	0.0	69.2	27.2	109.6	3 455	974	+3
18	72.5	97.8	57	189	27.7	...	2.2	4.2	19.4	80.5	5 224	40	+2
16	65.5	99.7	97	417	47.9	...	6.6	10.6	30.8	105.7	1 802	7	+2 to +12
160	46.2	77.6	74	2	19.5	6.9	8.0	0.1	0.2	3.4	55	250	+2
28	71.5	99.3	88	70	60.4	0.0	2.8	0.8	10.9	25.4	446	685	-11
3	...	...	...	251	1.6	0.0	...	...	77.8	64.4	5 704	378	+1
96	65.5	95.4	79	47	28.4	0.0	...	0.6	4.7	11.5	1 811	239	GMT
25	72.8	95.8	...	140	1.3	0.0	42.3	13.7	15.7	78.1	1 866	966	+3
116	63.1	49.1	76	8	45.0	-0.5	10.9	0.4	2.4	25.0	545	221	GMT
8	74.0	99.4*	...	...	26.4*	...	3.2*	...	25.9	63.3	1 334	381	+1
13	...	99.1	88	132	88.9	0.0	17.2	6.6	25.4	86.5	3 567	248	+4
270	42.6	47.9	57	7	38.5	-0.7	4.0	0.2	0.5	2.2	19	232	GMT
3	80.0	99.5	100	140	3.4	0.0	7.3	12.3	42.3	109.3	4 362	65	+8
8	74.7	...	100	325	40.1	0.1	19.8	6.7	21.6	90.6	4 176	421	+1
4	77.9	99.8	...	219	62.8	0.4	6.5	8.1	42.6	92.6	6 362	386	+1
73	63.6	...	70	13	77.6	-1.7	1.0	0.4	1.6	1.3	163	677	+11
145	48.2	...	29	4	11.4	-1.0	0.3	...	1.2	6.1	111	252	+3
69	49.3	93.9	88	69	7.6	0.0	6.0	9.4	10.0	83.3	1 075	27	+2
5	78.6	...	92	181	63.5	-0.1	3.7	9.7	49.8	83.8	7 275	82	+9
4	80.9	...	100	320	35.9	1.7	8.2	7.7	42.4	106.4	4 283	34	+1
13	72.4	95.6	79	43	29.9	-1.5	17.5	0.6	9.0	25.9	169	94	+5.5
19	...	...	100	118	14.7	0.0	0.1	2.7	59.3	23.7	2 428	1 869	-4
14	73.7	...	98	518	27.9	0.0	29.3	2.3	32.6	65.7	6 169	1 758	-4
20	71.6	...	...	88	27.4	0.8	18.6	1.7	19.0	73.6	840	1 784	-4
89	58.6	77.2	70	16	28.4	-0.8	4.6	0.3	1.7	12.7	946	249	+3
39	70.2	94.9	92	45	94.7	0.0	12.9	5.1	18.0	70.8	712	597	-3
164	39.6	88.4	62	18	31.5	0.9	3.2	0.9	4.3	24.3	408	268	+2
3	80.9	...	100	305	66.9	...	9.6	5.9	59.5	105.9	7 697	46	+1
5	81.7	...	100	352	30.9	0.4	28.2	5.5	66.9	99.0	5 807	41	+1
14	74.1	92.5	93	140	2.5	1.3	0.7	3.7	16.6	24.0	794	963	+2
...	...	...	...	...	...	...	...	...	63.6	102.0	6 368	886	+8
68	66.7	99.8	59	218	2.9	0.0	13.6	0.8	4.3	4.1	30	992	+5
118	52.5	78.4	62	2	39.9	-1.1	36.4	0.1	0.4	14.8	100	255	+3
8	70.6	98.0	99	30	28.4	-0.4	19.7	4.3	10.9	62.9	1 307	66	+7
108	58.4	74.4	52	6	7.1	-4.5	10.7	0.4	1.3	11.2	507	228	GMT
24	73.3	99.3	100	34	5.0	0.0	24.4	1.2	13.7	29.8	302	676	+13
38	69.8	99.5	91	79	44.1	-0.2	5.5	24.7	24.9	126.4	1 248	1 868	-4
23	73.9	94.3	93	70	6.8	1.9	1.5	2.3	12.4	71.9	1 268	216	+1
26	71.8	95.6	96	124	13.2	0.2	1.6	3.2	25.4	71.0	1 773	90	+2
51	63.2	99.8	72	317	8.8	0.0	2.3	8.7	8.2	4.4	132	993	+5
38	...	...	100	...	33.3	0.0	...	...	10.3	15	4 673	688	+12
134	51.5	76.6	60	5	18.4	-2.2	25.6	0.1	0.4	6.7	251	256	+3
24	67.9	99.8	96	297	16.5	0.1	3.3	6.9	26.8	106.7	1 206	380	+2
8	78.7	97.0	100	202	3.7	0.1	0.3	37.8	28.1	118.5	3 669	971	+4
6	79.4	...	100	166	11.8	0.4	20.0	9.8	56.2	116.6	6 316	44	GMT
8	78.2	...	100	549	33.1	0.1	14.6	20.6	57.2	77.4	6 983	1	-5 to -10
12	76.4	98.6	100	365	8.6	1.3	0.3	1.7	28.3	66.8	2 055	598	-3
43	67.2	...	82	289	8.0	0.5	2.0	5.3	6.7	9.3	630	998	+5
36	70.0	...	60	11	36.1	0.0	1.0	0.4	3.2	5.9	346	678	+11
...	...	...	...	...	0.0	0.0	...	...	...	...	...	39	+1
21	73.7	97.2	83	194	54.1	-0.6	69.9	6.6	15.8	69.0	1 521	58	-4.5
17	74.2	93.9	85	53	39.7	2.0	5.0	1.2	18.8	18.2	1 721	84	+7
100	62.7	75.2	67	22	1.0	0.0	0.0	1.0	4.5	13.8	125	967	+3
182	42.4	69.5	58	7	57.1	-1.0	39.9	0.2	0.8	14.0	422	260	+2
105	43.5	97.7	81	6	45.3	-1.7	14.6	0.8	2.6	6.5	932	263	+2

Definitions

Indicator	Definition
Population	
Total population	Interpolated mid-year population, 2005.
Population change	Percentage average annual rate of change, 2005–2010.
% urban	Urban population as a percentage of the total population, 2005.
Total fertility	Average number of children a woman will have during her child-bearing years, 2005–2010.
Population by age	Percentage of population in age groups 0–14 and 60 or over, 2005.
2050 projected population	Projected total population for the year 2050.
Economy	
Total Gross National Income (GNI)	The sum of value added to the economy by all resident producers plus taxes, less subsidies, plus net receipts of primary income from abroad. Data are in U.S. dollars (millions), 2006. Formerly known as Gross National Product (GNP).
GNI per capita	Gross National Income per person in U.S. dollars using the World Bank Atlas method, 2006.
Debt service ratio	Debt service as a percentage of GNI, 2006.
Total debt service	Sum of principal repayments and interest paid on long-term debt, interest paid on short-term debt and repayments to the International Monetary Fund (IMF), 2006.
Aid receipts	Aid received as a percentage of GNI from the Development Assistance Committee (DAC) countries of the Organization for Economic Co-operation and Development (OECD), 2006.
Military spending	Military-related spending, including recruiting, training, construction and the purchase of military supplies and equipment, as a percentage of Gross National Income, 2006.
Social Indicators	
Child mortality rate	Number of deaths of children aged under 5 per 1 000 live births, 2006.
Life expectancy	Average life expectancy, at birth in years, male and female, 2005–2010.
Literacy rate	Percentage of population aged 15–24 with at least a basic ability to read and write, 2005.
Access to safe water	Percentage of population using improved drinking water, 2004.
Doctors	Number of trained doctors per 100 000 people, 2004.
Environment	
Forest area	Percentage of total land area covered by forest, 2005.
Change in forest area	Average annual percentage change in forest area, 2000-2005.
Protected land area	Percentage of total land area designated as protected land, 2006.
CO_2 emissions	Emissions of carbon dioxide from the burning of fossil fuels and the manufacture of cement, divided by the population, expressed in metric tons per capita, 2004.
Communications	
Telephone lines	Main (fixed) telephone lines per 100 inhabitants, 2006.
Cellular phone subscribers	Cellular mobile subscribers per 100 inhabitants, 2006.
Internet users	Internet users per 10 000 inhabitants, 2006.
International dialling code	The country code prefix to be used when dialling from another country.
Time zone	Time difference in hours between local standard time and Greenwich Mean Time.

Main Statistical Sources	Internet Links
● United Nations Department of Economic and Social Affairs (UDESA) World Population Prospects: The 2006 Revision. World Urbanization Prospects: The 2005 Revision.	www.un.org/esa/population/unpop
● UNESCO Education Data Centre	stats.uis.unesco.org
● UN Human Development Report 2004	hdr.undp.org
● World Bank World Development Indicators online	www.worldbank.org/data
● OECD: Development Co-operation Report 2007	www.oecd.org
● UNICEF: The State of the World's Children 2008	www.unicef.org
● Food and Agriculture Organization (FAO) of the UN: Global Forest Resources Assessment 2005	www.fao.org
● World Resources Institute Biodiversity and Protected Areas Database	www.wri.org
● International Telecommunications Union (ITU)	www.itu.int

World States and Territories

All 195 independent countries and all populated dependent and disputed territories are included in this list of the states and territories of the world; the list is arranged in alphabetical order by the conventional name form. For independent states, the full name is given below the conventional name, if this is different; for territories, the status is given. The capital city name is given in conventional English form with selected alternative, usually local, form in brackets.

Area and population statistics are the latest available and include estimates. The information on languages and religions is based on the latest information on 'de facto' speakers of the language or 'de facto' adherents of the religion. This varies greatly from country to country because some countries include questions in censuses while others do not, in which case best estimates are used. The order of the languages and religions reflects their relative importance within the country; generally, languages or religions are included when more than one per cent of the population are estimated to be speakers or adherents.

ABBREVIATIONS

CURRENCIES

CFA	Communauté Financière Africaine
CFP	Comptoirs Français du Pacifique

Membership of selected international organizations is shown by the abbreviations below; dependent territories do not normally have separate memberships of these organizations.

ORGANIZATIONS

APEC	Asia-Pacific Economic Cooperation
ASEAN	Association of Southeast Asian Nations
CARICOM	Caribbean Community
CIS	Commonwealth of Independent States
Comm.	The Commonwealth
EU	European Union
NATO	North Atlantic Treaty Organization
OECD	Organisation for Economic Co-operation and Development
OPEC	Organization of the Petroleum Exporting Countries
SADC	Southern African Development Community
UN	United Nations

AFGHANISTAN

Islamic Republic of Afghanistan

Area Sq Km	652 225	Languages	Dari, Pushtu, Uzbek, Turkmen
Area Sq Miles	251 825	Religions	Sunni Muslim, Shi'a Muslim
Population	27 145 000	Currency	Afghani
Capital	Kābul	Organizations	UN

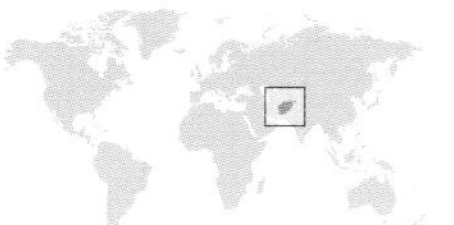

A landlocked country in central Asia with central highlands bordered by plains in the north and southwest, and by the Hindu Kush mountains in the northeast. The climate is dry continental. Over the last twenty-five years war has disrupted the economy, which is highly dependent on farming and livestock rearing. Most trade is with the former USSR, Pakistan and Iran.

ALBANIA

Republic of Albania

Area Sq Km	28 748	Languages	Albanian, Greek
Area Sq Miles	11 100	Religions	Sunni Muslim, Albanian Orthodox, Roman Catholic
Population	3 190 000	Currency	Lek
Capital	Tirana (Tiranë)	Organizations	UN

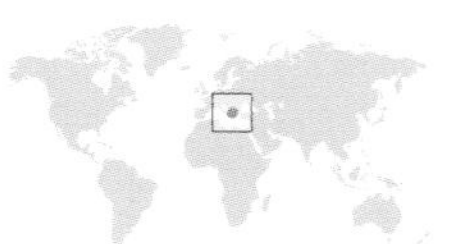

Albania lies in the western Balkan Mountains in southeastern Europe, bordering the Adriatic Sea. It is mountainous, with coastal plains where half the population lives. The economy is based on agriculture and mining. Albania is one of the poorest countries in Europe and relies heavily on foreign aid.

ALGERIA

People's Democratic Republic of Algeria

Area Sq Km	2 381 741	Languages	Arabic, French, Berber
Area Sq Miles	919 595	Religions	Sunni Muslim
Population	33 858 000	Currency	Algerian dinar
Capital	Algiers (Alger)	Organizations	OPEC, UN

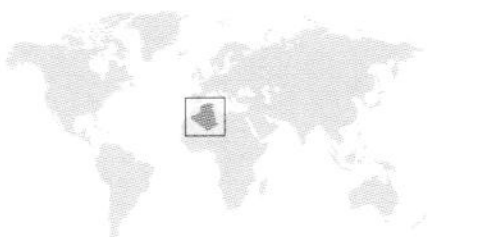

Algeria, the second largest country in Africa, lies on the Mediterranean coast of northwest Africa and extends southwards to the Atlas Mountains and the dry sandstone plateau and desert of the Sahara. The climate ranges from Mediterranean on the coast to semi-arid and arid inland. The most populated areas are the coastal plains and the fertile northern slopes of the Atlas Mountains. Oil, natural gas and related products account for over ninety-five per cent of export earnings. Agriculture employs about a quarter of the workforce, producing mainly food crops. Algeria's main trading partners are Italy, France and the USA.

American Samoa

United States Unincorporated Territory

Area Sq Km	197	Languages	Samoan, English
Area Sq Miles	76	Religions	Protestant, Roman Catholic
Population	67 000	Currency	United States dollar
Capital	Fagatogo		

Lying in the south Pacific Ocean, American Samoa consists of five main islands and two coral atolls. The largest island is Tutuila. Tuna and tuna products are the main exports, and the main trading partner is the USA.

ANDORRA

Principality of Andorra

Area Sq Km	465	Languages	Spanish, Catalan, French
Area Sq Miles	180	Religions	Roman Catholic
Population	75 000	Currency	Euro
Capital	Andorra la Vella	Organizations	UN

A landlocked state in southwest Europe, Andorra lies in the Pyrenees mountain range between France and Spain. It consists of deep valleys and gorges, surrounded by mountains. Tourism, encouraged by the development of ski resorts, is the mainstay of the economy. Banking is also an important economic activity.

ANGOLA

Republic of Angola

Area Sq Km	1 246 700	Languages	Portuguese, Bantu, local languages
Area Sq Miles	481 354	Religions	Roman Catholic, Protestant, traditional beliefs
Population	17 024 000	Currency	Kwanza
Capital	Luanda	Organizations	OPEC, SADC, UN

Angola lies on the Atlantic coast of south central Africa. Its small northern province, Cabinda, is separated from the rest of the country by part of the Democratic Republic of the Congo. Much of Angola is high plateau. In the west is a narrow coastal plain and in the southwest is desert. The climate is equatorial in the north but desert in the south. Over eighty per cent of the population relies on subsistence agriculture. Angola is rich in minerals (particularly diamonds), and oil accounts for approximately ninety per cent of export earnings. The USA, South Korea and Portugal are its main trading partners.

Anguilla

United Kingdom Overseas Territory

Area Sq Km	155	Languages	English
Area Sq Miles	60	Religions	Protestant, Roman Catholic
Population	13 000	Currency	East Caribbean dollar
Capital	The Valley		

Anguilla lies at the northern end of the Leeward Islands in the eastern Caribbean. Tourism and fishing form the basis of the economy.

ANTIGUA AND BARBUDA

Area Sq Km	442	Languages	English, Creole
Area Sq Miles	171	Religions	Protestant, Roman Catholic
Population	85 000	Currency	East Caribbean dollar
Capital	St John's	Organizations	CARICOM, Comm., UN

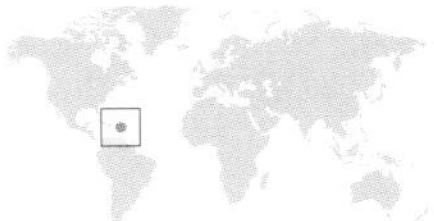

The state comprises the islands of Antigua, Barbuda and the tiny rocky outcrop of Redonda, in the Leeward Islands in the eastern Caribbean. Antigua, the largest and most populous island, is mainly hilly scrubland, with many beaches. The climate is tropical, and the economy relies heavily on tourism. Most trade is with other eastern Caribbean states and the USA.

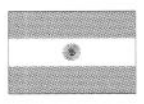

ARGENTINA

Argentine Republic

Area Sq Km	2 766 889	Languages	Spanish, Italian, Amerindian languages
Area Sq Miles	1 068 302	Religions	Roman Catholic, Protestant
Population	39 531 000	Currency	Argentinian peso
Capital	Buenos Aires	Organizations	UN

Argentina, the second largest state in South America, extends from Bolivia to Cape Horn and from the Andes mountains to the Atlantic Ocean. It has four geographical regions: subtropical forests and swampland in the northeast; temperate fertile plains or Pampas in the centre; the wooded foothills and valleys of the Andes in the west; and the cold, semi-arid plateaus of Patagonia in the south. The highest mountain in South America, Cerro Aconcagua, is in Argentina. Nearly ninety per cent of the population lives in towns and cities. The country is rich in natural resources including petroleum, natural gas, ores and precious metals. Agricultural products dominate exports, which also include motor vehicles and crude oil. Most trade is with Brazil and the USA.

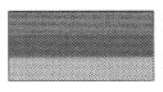

ARMENIA

Republic of Armenia

Area Sq Km	29 800	Languages	Armenian, Azeri
Area Sq Miles	11 506	Religions	Armenian Orthodox
Population	3 002 000	Currency	Dram
Capital	Yerevan (Erevan)	Organizations	CIS, UN

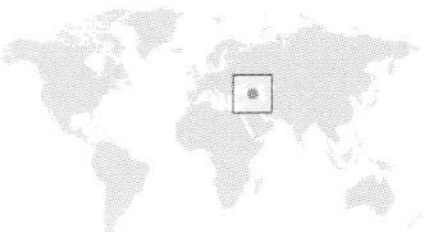

A landlocked state in southwest Asia, Armenia lies in the south of the Lesser Caucasus mountains. It is a mountainous country with a continental climate. One-third of the population lives in the capital, Yerevan. Exports include diamonds, scrap metal and machinery. Many Armenians depend on remittances from abroad.

Aruba

Self-governing Netherlands Territory

Area Sq Km	193	Languages	Papiamento, Dutch, English
Area Sq Miles	75	Religions	Roman Catholic, Protestant
Population	104 000	Currency	Aruban florin
Capital	Oranjestad		

The most southwesterly of the islands in the Lesser Antilles in the Caribbean, Aruba lies just off the coast of Venezuela. Tourism, offshore finance and oil refining are the most important sectors of the economy. The USA is the main trading partner.

AUSTRALIA

Commonwealth of Australia

Area Sq Km	7 692 024	Languages	English, Italian, Greek
Area Sq Miles	2 969 907	Religions	Protestant, Roman Catholic, Orthodox
Population	20 743 000	Currency	Australian dollar
Capital	Canberra	Organizations	APEC, Comm., OECD, UN

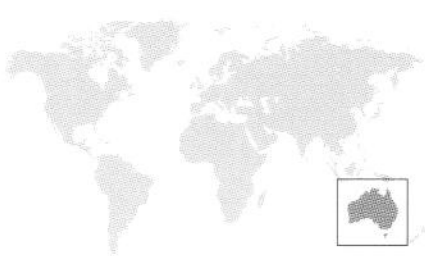

Australia, the world's sixth largest country, occupies the smallest, flattest and driest continent. The western half of the continent is mostly arid plateaus, ridges and vast deserts. The central eastern area comprises the lowlands of river systems draining into Lake Eyre, while to the east is the Great Dividing Range, a belt of ridges and plateaus running from Queensland to Tasmania. Climatically, more than two-thirds of the country is arid or semi-arid. The north is tropical monsoon, the east subtropical, and the southwest and southeast temperate. The majority of Australia's highly

urbanized population lives along the east, southeast and southwest coasts. Australia has vast mineral deposits and various sources of energy. It is among the world's leading producers of iron ore, bauxite, nickel, copper and uranium. It is a major producer of coal, and oil and natural gas are also being exploited. Although accounting for only five per cent of the workforce, agriculture continues to be an important sector of the economy, with food and agricultural raw materials making up most of Australia's export earnings. Fuel, ores and metals, and manufactured goods, account for the remainder of exports. Japan and the USA are Australia's main trading partners.

Australian Capital Territory (Federal Territory)
Area Sq Km (Sq Miles) 2 358 (910) Population 329 500 Capital Canberra

Jervis Bay Territory (Territory)
Area Sq Km (Sq Miles) 73 (28) Population 611

New South Wales (State)
Area Sq Km (Sq Miles) 800 642 (309 130) Population 6 844 200 Capital Sydney

Northern Territory (Territory)
Area Sq Km (Sq Miles) 1 349 129 (520 902) Population 207 700 Capital Darwin

Queensland (State)
Area Sq Km (Sq Miles) 1 730 648 (668 207) Population 4 070 400 Capital Brisbane

South Australia (State)
Area Sq Km (Sq Miles) 983 482 (379 725) Population 1 558 200 Capital Adelaide

Tasmania (State)
Area Sq Km (Sq Miles) 68 401 (26 410) Population 489 600 Capital Hobart

Victoria (State)
Area Sq Km (Sq Miles) 227 416 (87 806) Population 5 110 500 Capital Melbourne

Western Australia (State)
Area Sq Km (Sq Miles) 2 529 875 (976 790) Population 2 061 500 Capital Perth

AUSTRIA
Republic of Austria

Area Sq Km	83 855	Languages	German, Croatian, Turkish
Area Sq Miles	32 377	Religions	Roman Catholic, Protestant
Population	8 361 000	Currency	Euro
Capital	Vienna (Wien)	Organizations	EU, OECD, UN

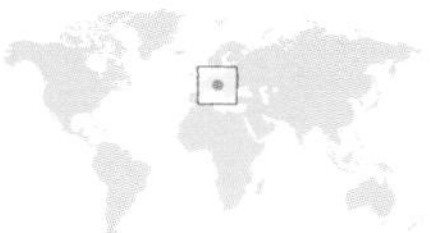

Two-thirds of Austria, a landlocked state in central Europe, lies within the Alps, with lower mountains to the north. The only lowlands are in the east. The Danube river valley in the northeast contains almost all the agricultural land and most of the population. Although the climate varies with altitude, in general summers are warm and winters cold with heavy snowfalls. Manufacturing industry and tourism are the most important sectors of the economy. Exports are dominated by manufactured goods. Germany is Austria's main trading partner.

AZERBAIJAN
Republic of Azerbaijan

Area Sq Km	86 600	Languages	Azeri, Armenian, Russian, Lezgian
Area Sq Miles	33 436	Religions	Shi'a Muslim, Sunni Muslim, Russian and Armenian Orthodox
Population	8 467 000	Currency	Azerbaijani manat
Capital	Baku	Organizations	CIS, UN

Azerbaijan lies to the southeast of the Caucasus mountains, on the Caspian Sea. Its region of Naxçıvan is separated from the rest of the country by part of Armenia. It has mountains in the northeast and west, valleys in the centre, and a low coastal plain. The climate is continental. It is rich in energy and mineral resources. Oil production, onshore and offshore, is the main industry and the basis of heavy industries. Agriculture is important, with cotton and tobacco the main cash crops.

THE BAHAMAS
Commonwealth of the Bahamas

Area Sq Km	13 939	Languages	English, Creole
Area Sq Miles	5 382	Religions	Protestant, Roman Catholic
Population	331 000	Currency	Bahamian dollar
Capital	Nassau	Organizations	CARICOM, Comm., UN

The Bahamas, an archipelago made up of approximately seven hundred islands and over two thousand cays, lies to the northeast of Cuba and east of the Florida coast of the USA. Twenty-two islands are inhabited, and two-thirds of the population lives on the main island of New Providence. The climate is warm for much of the year, with heavy rainfall in the summer. Tourism is the islands' main industry. Offshore banking, insurance and ship registration are also major foreign exchange earners.

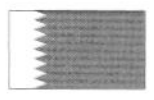

BAHRAIN
Kingdom of Bahrain

Area Sq Km	691	Languages	Arabic, English
Area Sq Miles	267	Religions	Shi'a Muslim, Sunni Muslim, Christian
Population	753 000	Currency	Bahraini dinar
Capital	Manama (Al Manāmah)	Organizations	UN

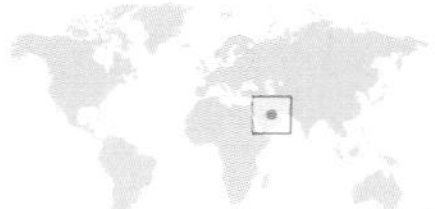

Bahrain consists of more than thirty islands lying in a bay in The Gulf, off the coasts of Saudi Arabia and Qatar. Bahrain Island, the largest island, is connected to other islands and to the mainland of Arabia by causeways. Oil production and processing are the main sectors of the economy.

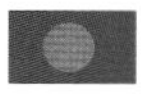

BANGLADESH
People's Republic of Bangladesh

Area Sq Km	143 998	Languages	Bengali, English
Area Sq Miles	55 598	Religions	Sunni Muslim, Hindu
Population	158 665 000	Currency	Taka
Capital	Dhaka (Dacca)	Organizations	Comm., UN

The south Asian state of Bangladesh is in the northeast of the Indian subcontinent, on the Bay of Bengal. It consists almost entirely of the low-lying alluvial plains and deltas of the Ganges and Brahmaputra rivers. The southwest is swampy, with mangrove forests in the delta area. The north, northeast and southeast have low forested hills. Bangladesh is one of the world's most densely populated and least developed countries. The economy is based on agriculture, though the garment industry is the main export sector. Storms during the summer monsoon season often cause devastating flooding and crop destruction. The country relies on large-scale foreign aid and remittances from workers abroad.

BARBADOS

Area Sq Km	430	Languages	English, Creole
Area Sq Miles	166	Religions	Protestant, Roman Catholic
Population	294 000	Currency	Barbados dollar
Capital	Bridgetown	Organizations	CARICOM, Comm., UN

The most easterly of the Caribbean islands, Barbados is small and densely populated. It has a tropical climate and is subject to hurricanes. The economy is based on tourism, financial services, light industries and sugar production.

BELARUS
Republic of Belarus

Area Sq Km	207 600	Languages	Belorussian, Russian
Area Sq Miles	80 155	Religions	Belorussian Orthodox, Roman Catholic
Population	9 689 000	Currency	Belarus rouble
Capital	Minsk	Organizations	CIS, UN

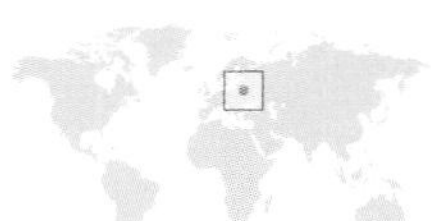

Belarus, a landlocked state in eastern Europe, consists of low hills and plains, with many lakes, rivers and, in the south, extensive marshes. Forests cover approximately one-third of the country. It has a continental climate. Agriculture contributes one-third of national income, with beef cattle and grains as the major products. Manufacturing industries produce a range of items, from construction equipment to textiles. The Russian Federation and Ukraine are the main trading partners.

BELGIUM
Kingdom of Belgium

Area Sq Km	30 520	Languages	Dutch (Flemish), French (Walloon), German
Area Sq Miles	11 784	Religions	Roman Catholic, Protestant
Population	10 457 000	Currency	Euro
Capital	Brussels (Bruxelles)	Organizations	EU, NATO, OECD, UN

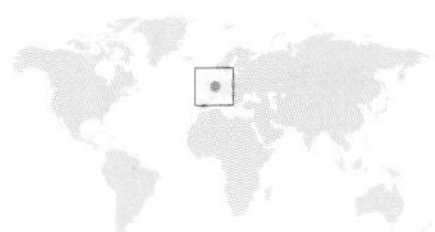

Belgium lies on the North Sea coast of western Europe. Beyond low sand dunes and a narrow belt of reclaimed land, fertile plains extend to the Sambre-Meuse river valley. The land rises to the forested Ardennes plateau in the southeast. Belgium has mild winters and cool summers. It is densely populated and has a highly urbanized population. With few mineral resources, Belgium imports raw materials for processing and manufacture. The agricultural sector is small, but provides for most food needs. A large services sector reflects Belgium's position as the home base for over eight hundred international institutions. The headquarters of the European Union are in the capital, Brussels.

BELIZE

Area Sq Km	22 965	Languages	English, Spanish, Mayan, Creole
Area Sq Miles	8 867	Religions	Roman Catholic, Protestant
Population	288 000	Currency	Belize dollar
Capital	Belmopan	Organizations	CARICOM, Comm., UN

Belize lies on the Caribbean coast of central America and includes numerous cays and a large barrier reef offshore. The coastal areas are flat and swampy. To the southwest are the Maya Mountains. Tropical jungle covers much of the country and the climate is humid tropical, but tempered by sea breezes. A third of the population lives in the capital. The economy is based primarily on agriculture, forestry and fishing, and exports include raw sugar, orange concentrate and bananas.

BENIN
Republic of Benin

Area Sq Km	112 620	Languages	French, Fon, Yoruba, Adja, local languages
Area Sq Miles	43 483	Religions	Traditional beliefs, Roman Catholic, Sunni Muslim
Population	9 033 000	Currency	CFA franc
Capital	Porto-Novo	Organizations	UN

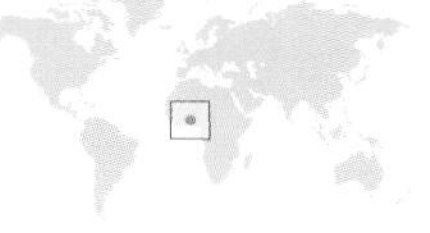

Benin is in west Africa, on the Gulf of Guinea. The climate is tropical in the north, equatorial in the south. The economy is based mainly on agriculture and transit trade. Agricultural products account for two-thirds of export earnings. Oil, produced offshore, is also a major export.

Bermuda
United Kingdom Overseas Territory

Area Sq Km	54	Languages	English
Area Sq Miles	21	Religions	Protestant, Roman Catholic
Population	65 000	Currency	Bermuda dollar
Capital	Hamilton		

In the Atlantic Ocean to the east of the USA, Bermuda comprises a group of small islands with a warm and humid climate. The economy is based on international business and tourism.

BHUTAN
Kingdom of Bhutan

Area Sq Km	46 620	Languages	Dzongkha, Nepali, Assamese
Area Sq Miles	18 000	Religions	Buddhist, Hindu
Population	658 000	Currency	Ngultrum, Indian rupee
Capital	Thimphu	Organizations	UN

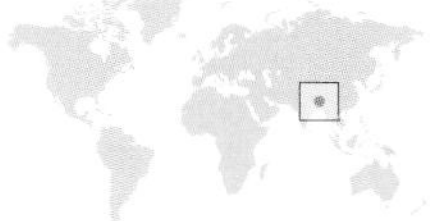

Bhutan lies in the eastern Himalaya mountains, between China and India. It is mountainous in the north, with fertile valleys. The climate ranges between permanently cold in the far north and subtropical in the south. Most of the population is involved in livestock rearing and subsistence farming. Bhutan is the world's largest producer of cardamom. Tourism is an increasingly important foreign currency earner.

BOLIVIA
Republic of Bolivia

Area Sq Km	1 098 581	Languages	Spanish, Quechua, Aymara
Area Sq Miles	424 164	Religions	Roman Catholic, Protestant, Baha'i
Population	9 525 000	Currency	Boliviano
Capital	La Paz/Sucre	Organizations	UN

Bolivia is a landlocked state in central South America. Most Bolivians live on the high plateau within the Andes mountains. The lowlands range between dense rainforest in the northeast and semi-arid grasslands in the southeast. Bolivia is rich in minerals (zinc, tin and gold), and sales generate approximately half of export income. Natural gas, timber and soya beans are also exported. The USA is the main trading partner.

BOSNIA-HERZEGOVINA
Republic of Bosnia and Herzegovina

Area Sq Km	51 130	Languages	Bosnian, Serbian, Croatian
Area Sq Miles	19 741	Religions	Sunni Muslim, Serbian Orthodox, Roman Catholic, Protestant
Population	3 935 000	Currency	Marka
Capital	Sarajevo	Organizations	UN

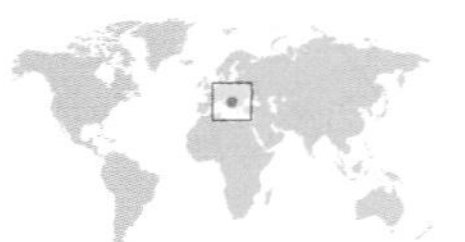

Bosnia-Herzegovina lies in the western Balkan Mountains of southern Europe, on the Adriatic Sea. It is mountainous, with ridges running northwest-southeast. The main lowlands are around the Sava valley in the north. Summers are warm, but winters can be very cold. The economy relies heavily on overseas aid.

BOTSWANA
Republic of Botswana

Area Sq Km	581 370	Languages	English, Setswana, Shona, local languages
Area Sq Miles	224 468	Religions	Traditional beliefs, Protestant, Roman Catholic
Population	1 882 000	Currency	Pula
Capital	Gaborone	Organizations	Comm., SADC, UN

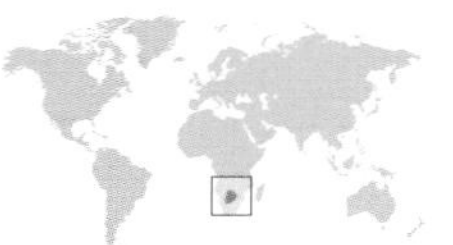

Botswana is a landlocked state in southern Africa. Over half of the country lies within the Kalahari Desert, with swamps to the north and salt-pans to the northeast. Most of the population lives near the eastern border. The climate is subtropical, but drought-prone. The economy was founded on cattle rearing, and although beef remains an important export, the economy is now based on mining. Diamonds account for seventy per cent of export earnings. Copper-nickel matte is also exported. Most trade is with other members of the Southern African Customs Union.

BRAZIL
Federative Republic of Brazil

Area Sq Km	8 514 879	Languages	Portuguese
Area Sq Miles	3 287 613	Religions	Roman Catholic, Protestant
Population	191 791 000	Currency	Real
Capital	Brasília	Organizations	UN

Brazil, in eastern South America, covers almost half of the continent, and is the world's fifth largest country. The northwest contains the vast basin of the Amazon, while the centre-west is largely a vast plateau of savanna and rock escarpments. The northeast is mostly semi-arid plateaus, while to the east and south are rugged mountains, fertile valleys and narrow, fertile coastal plains. The Amazon basin is hot, humid and wet; the rest of the country is cooler and drier, with seasonal variations. The northeast is drought-prone. Most Brazilians live in urban areas along the coast and on the central plateau. Brazil has well-developed agricultural, mining and service sectors, and the economy is larger than that of all other South American countries combined. Brazil is the world's biggest producer of coffee, and other agricultural crops include grains and sugar cane. Mineral production includes iron, aluminium and gold. Manufactured goods include food products, transport equipment, machinery and industrial chemicals. The main trading partners are the USA and Argentina. Despite its natural wealth, Brazil has a large external debt and a growing poverty gap.

BRUNEI
Brunei Darussalam

Area Sq Km	5 765	Languages	Malay, English, Chinese
Area Sq Miles	2 226	Religions	Sunni Muslim, Buddhist, Christian
Population	390 000	Currency	Brunei dollar
Capital	Bandar Seri Begawan	Organizations	APEC, ASEAN, Comm., UN

The southeast Asian oil-rich state of Brunei lies on the northwest coast of the island of Borneo, on the South China Sea. Its two enclaves are surrounded by the Malaysian state of Sarawak. Tropical rainforest covers over two-thirds of the country. The economy is dominated by the oil and gas industries.

BULGARIA
Republic of Bulgaria

Area Sq Km	110 994	Languages	Bulgarian, Turkish, Romany, Macedonian
Area Sq Miles	42 855	Religions	Bulgarian Orthodox, Sunni Muslim
Population	7 639 000	Currency	Lev
Capital	Sofia (Sofiya)	Organizations	EU, NATO, UN

Map page 185

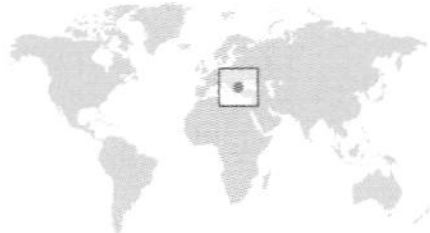

Bulgaria, in southern Europe, borders the western shore of the Black Sea. The Balkan Mountains separate the Danube plains in the north from the Rhodope Mountains and the lowlands in the south. The economy has a strong agricultural base. Manufacturing industries include machinery, consumer goods, chemicals and metals. Most trade is with the Russian Federation, Italy and Germany.

BURKINA FASO
Democratic Republic of Burkina Faso

Area Sq Km	274 200	Languages	French, Moore (Mossi), Fulani, local languages
Area Sq Miles	105 869	Religions	Sunni Muslim, traditional beliefs, Roman Catholic
Population	14 784 000	Currency	CFA franc
Capital	Ouagadougou	Organizations	UN

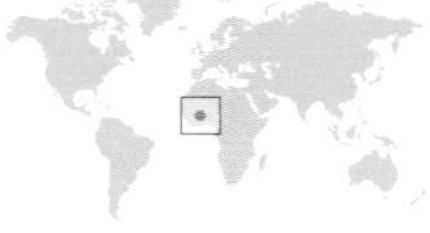

Burkina Faso, a landlocked country in west Africa, lies within the Sahara desert to the north and semi-arid savanna to the south. Rainfall is erratic, and droughts are common. Livestock rearing and farming are the main activities, and cotton, livestock, groundnuts and some minerals are exported. Burkina Faso relies heavily on foreign aid, and is one of the poorest and least developed countries in the world.

BURUNDI
Republic of Burundi

Area Sq Km	27 835	Languages	Kirundi (Hutu, Tutsi), French
Area Sq Miles	10 747	Religions	Roman Catholic, traditional beliefs, Protestant
Population	8 508 000	Currency	Burundian franc
Capital	Bujumbura	Organizations	UN

The densely populated east African state of Burundi consists of high plateaus rising from the shores of Lake Tanganyika in the southwest. It has a tropical climate and depends on subsistence farming. Coffee is its main export, and its main trading partners are Germany and Belgium. The country has been badly affected by internal conflict since the early 1990s.

CAMBODIA
Kingdom of Cambodia

Area Sq Km	181 000	Languages	Khmer, Vietnamese
Area Sq Miles	69 884	Religions	Buddhist, Roman Catholic, Sunni Muslim
Population	14 444 000	Currency	Riel
Capital	Phnom Penh	Organizations	ASEAN, UN

Cambodia lies in southeast Asia on the Gulf of Thailand, and occupies the Mekong river basin, with the Tônlé Sap (Great Lake) at its centre. The climate is tropical monsoon. Forests cover half the country. Most of the population lives on the plains and is engaged in farming (chiefly rice growing), fishing and forestry. The economy is recovering slowly following the devastation of civil war in the 1970s.

CAMEROON
Republic of Cameroon

Area Sq Km	475 442	Languages	French, English, Fang, Bamileke, local languages
Area Sq Miles	183 569	Religions	Roman Catholic, traditional beliefs, Sunni Muslim, Protestant
Population	18 549 000	Currency	CFA franc
Capital	Yaoundé	Organizations	Comm., UN

Cameroon is in west Africa, on the Gulf of Guinea. The coastal plains and southern and central plateaus are covered with tropical forest. Despite oil resources and favourable agricultural conditions Cameroon still faces problems of underdevelopment. Oil, timber and cocoa are the main exports. France is the main trading partner.

CANADA

Area Sq Km	9 984 670	Languages	English, French
Area Sq Miles	3 855 103	Religions	Roman Catholic, Protestant, Eastern Orthodox, Jewish
Population	32 876 000	Currency	Canadian dollar
Capital	Ottawa	Organizations	APEC, Comm., NATO, OECD, UN

The world's second largest country, Canada covers the northern two-fifths of North America and has coastlines on the Atlantic, Arctic and Pacific Oceans. In the west are the Coast Mountains, the Rocky Mountains and interior plateaus. In the centre lie the fertile Prairies. Further east, covering about half the total land area, is the Canadian Shield, a relatively flat area of infertile lowlands around Hudson Bay, extending to Labrador on the east coast. The Shield is bordered to the south by the fertile Great Lakes-St Lawrence lowlands. In the far north climatic conditions are polar, while the rest has a continental climate. Most Canadians live in the urban areas of the Great Lakes-St Lawrence basin. Canada is rich in mineral and energy resources. Only five per cent of land is arable. Canada is among the world's leading producers of wheat, of wood from its vast coniferous forests, and of fish and seafood from its Atlantic and Pacific fishing grounds. It is a major producer of nickel, uranium, copper, iron ore, zinc and other minerals, as well as oil and natural gas. Its abundant raw materials are the basis for many manufacturing industries. Main exports are machinery, motor vehicles, oil, timber, newsprint and paper, wood pulp and wheat. Since the 1989 free trade agreement with the USA and the 1994 North America Free Trade Agreement, trade with the USA has grown and now accounts for around seventy-five per cent of imports and around eighty-five per cent of exports.

Alberta (Province)
Area Sq Km (Sq Miles) 661 848 (255 541) Population 3 435 511 Capital Edmonton

British Columbia (Province)
Area Sq Km (Sq Miles) 944 735 (364 764) Population 4 338 106 Capital Victoria

Manitoba (Province)
Area Sq Km (Sq Miles) 647 797 (250 116) Population 1 180 004 Capital Winnipeg

New Brunswick (Province)
Area Sq Km (Sq Miles) 72 908 (28 150) Population 748 582 Capital Fredericton

Newfoundland and Labrador (Province)
Area Sq Km (Sq Miles) 405 212 (156 453) Population 508 548 Capital St John's

Northwest Territories (Territory)
Area Sq Km (Sq Miles) 1 346 106 (519 734) Population 41 777 Capital Yellowknife

Nova Scotia (Province)
Area Sq Km (Sq Miles) 55 284 (21 345) Population 933 793 Capital Halifax

Nunavut (Territory)
Area Sq Km (Sq Miles) 2 093 190 (808 185) Population 30 947 Capital Iqaluit

Ontario (Province)
Area Sq Km (Sq Miles) 1 076 395 (415 598) Population 12 726 336 Capital Toronto

Prince Edward Island (Province)
Area Sq Km (Sq Miles) 5 660 (2 185) Population 138 632 Capital Charlottetown

Québec (Province)
Area Sq Km (Sq Miles) 1 542 056 (595 391) Population 7 676 097 Capital Québec

Saskatchewan (Province)
Area Sq Km (Sq Miles) 651 036 (251 366) Population 987 939 Capital Regina

Yukon (Territory)
Area Sq Km (Sq Miles) 482 443 (186 272) Population 31 032 Capital Whitehorse

CAPE VERDE
Republic of Cape Verde

Area Sq Km	4 033	Languages	Portuguese, Creole
Area Sq Miles	1 557	Religions	Roman Catholic, Protestant
Population	530 000	Currency	Cape Verde escudo
Capital	Praia	Organizations	UN

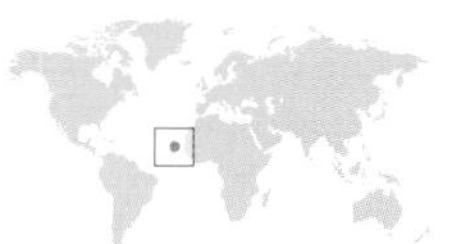

Cape Verde is a group of semi-arid volcanic islands lying off the coast of west Africa. The economy is based on fishing and subsistence farming but relies on emigrant workers' remittances and foreign aid.

Cayman Islands
United Kingdom Overseas Territory

Area Sq Km	259	Languages	English
Area Sq Miles	100	Religions	Protestant, Roman Catholic
Population	47 000	Currency	Cayman Islands dollar
Capital	George Town		

A group of islands in the Caribbean, northwest of Jamaica. There are three main islands: Grand Cayman, Little Cayman and Cayman Brac. The Cayman Islands are one of the world's major offshore financial centres. Tourism is also important to the economy.

CENTRAL AFRICAN REPUBLIC

Area Sq Km	622 436	Languages	French, Sango, Banda, Baya, local languages
Area Sq Miles	240 324	Religions	Protestant, Roman Catholic, traditional beliefs, Sunni Muslim
Population	4 343 000	Currency	CFA franc
Capital	Bangui	Organizations	UN

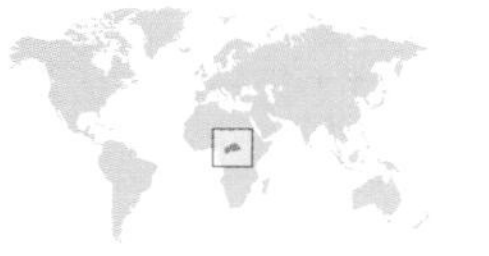

A landlocked country in central Africa, the Central African Republic is mainly savanna plateau, drained by the Ubangi and Chari river systems, with mountains to the east and west. The climate is tropical, with high rainfall. Most of the population lives in the south and west, and a majority of the workforce is involved in subsistence farming. Some cotton, coffee, tobacco and timber are exported, but diamonds account for around half of export earnings.

CHAD
Republic of Chad

Area Sq Km	1 284 000	Languages	Arabic, French, Sara, local languages
Area Sq Miles	495 755	Religions	Sunni Muslim, Roman Catholic, Protestant, traditional beliefs
Population	10 781 000	Currency	CFA franc
Capital	Ndjamena	Organizations	UN

Chad is a landlocked state of north-central Africa. It consists of plateaus, the Tibesti mountains in the north and the Lake Chad basin in the west. Climatic conditions range between desert in the north and tropical forest in the southwest. With few natural resources, Chad relies on subsistence farming, exports of raw cotton, and foreign aid. The main trading partners are France, Portugal and Cameroon.

CHILE
Republic of Chile

Area Sq Km	756 945	Languages	Spanish, Amerindian languages
Area Sq Miles	292 258	Religions	Roman Catholic, Protestant
Population	16 635 000	Currency	Chilean peso
Capital	Santiago	Organizations	APEC, UN

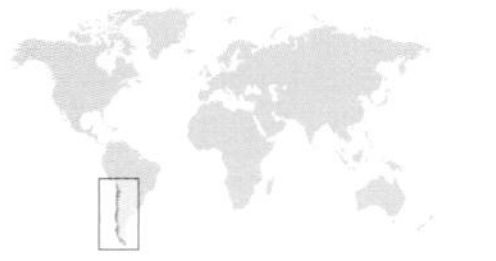

Chile lies along the Pacific coast of the southern half of South America. Between the Andes in the east and the lower coastal ranges is a central valley, with a mild climate, where most Chileans live. To the north is the arid Atacama Desert and to the south is cold, wet forested grassland. Chile has considerable mineral resources and is the world's leading exporter of copper. Nitrates, molybdenum, gold and iron ore are also mined. Agriculture (particularly viticulture), forestry and fishing are also important to the economy.

CHINA
People's Republic of China

Area Sq Km	9 584 492	Languages	Mandarin, Wu, Cantonese, Hsiang, regional languages
Area Sq Miles	3 700 593	Religions	Confucian, Taoist, Buddhist, Christian, Sunni Muslim
Population	1 313 437 000	Currency	Yuan, Hong Kong dollar, Macao pataca
Capital	Beijing (Peking)	Organizations	APEC, UN

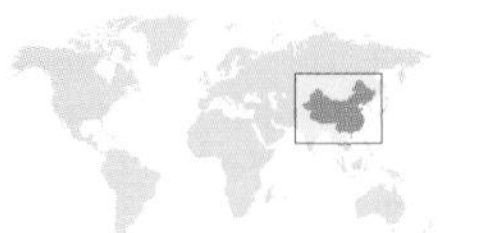

China, the world's most populous and fourth largest country, occupies a large part of east Asia, borders fourteen states and has coastlines on the Yellow, East China and South China Seas. It has a huge variety of landscapes. The southwest contains the high Plateau of Tibet, flanked by the Himalaya and Kunlun Shan mountains. The north is mountainous with arid basins and extends from the Tien Shan and Altai Mountains and the vast Taklimakan Desert in the west to the plateau and Gobi Desert in the centre-east. Eastern China is predominantly lowland and is divided broadly into the basins of the Yellow River (Huang He) in the north, the Yangtze (Chang Jiang) in the centre and the Pearl River (Xi Jiang) in the southeast. Climatic conditions and vegetation are as diverse as the topography: much of the country experiences temperate conditions, while the southwest has an extreme mountain climate and the southeast enjoys a moist, warm subtropical climate. Nearly seventy per cent of China's huge population lives in rural areas, and agriculture employs around half of the working population. The main crops are rice, wheat, soya beans, peanuts, cotton, tobacco and hemp. China is rich in coal, oil and natural gas and has the world's largest potential in hydroelectric power. It is a major world producer of iron ore, molybdenum, copper, asbestos and gold. Economic reforms from the early 1980's led to an explosion in manufacturing development concentrated on the 'coastal economic open region'. The main exports are machinery, textiles, footwear, toys and sports goods. Japan and the USA are China's main trading partners.

Anhui (Province)
Area Sq Km (Sq Miles) 139 000 (53 668) Population 61 140 000 Capital Hefei

Beijing (Municipality)
Area Sq Km (Sq Miles) 16 800 (6 487) Population 15 360 000 Capital Beijing (Peking)

Chongqing (Municipality)
Area Sq Km (Sq Miles) 23 000 (8 880) Population 27 970 000 Capital Chongqing

Fujian (Province)
Area Sq Km (Sq Miles) 121 400 (46 873) Population 35 320 000 Capital Fuzhou

Gansu (Province)
Area Sq Km (Sq Miles) 453 700 (175 175) Population 25 920 000 Capital Lanzhou

Guangdong (Province)
Area Sq Km (Sq Miles) 178 000 (68 726) Population 91 850 000 Capital Guangzhou (Canton)

Guangxi Zhuangzu Zizhiqu (Autonomous Region)
Area Sq Km (Sq Miles) 236 000 (91 120) Population 46 550 000 Capital Nanning

Guizhou (Province)
Area Sq Km (Sq Miles) 176 000 (67 954) Population 37 250 000 Capital Guiyang

Hainan (Province)
Area Sq Km (Sq Miles) 34 000 (13 127) Population 8 260 000 Capital Haikou

Hebei (Province)
Area Sq Km (Sq Miles) 187 700 (72 471) Population 68 440 000 Capital Shijiazhuang

Heilongjiang (Province)
Area Sq Km (Sq Miles) 454 600 (175 522) Population 38 180 000 Capital Harbin

Henan (Province)
Area Sq Km (Sq Miles) 167 000 (64 479) Population 93 710 000 Capital Zhengzhou

Hong Kong (Special Administrative Region)
Area Sq Km (Sq Miles) 1 075 (415) Population 6 936 000 Capital Hong Kong

Hubei (Province)
Area Sq Km (Sq Miles) 185 900 (71 776) Population 57 070 000 Capital Wuhan

Hunan (Province)
Area Sq Km (Sq Miles) 210 000 (81 081) Population 63 200 000 Capital Changsha

Jiangsu (Province)
Area Sq Km (Sq Miles) 102 600 (39 614) Population 74 680 000 Capital Nanjing

Jiangxi (Province)
Area Sq Km (Sq Miles) 166 900 (64 440) Population 43 070 000 Capital Nanchang

Jilin (Province)
Area Sq Km (Sq Miles) 187 000 (72 201) Population 27 150 000 Capital Changchun

Liaoning (Province)
Area Sq Km (Sq Miles) 147 400 (56 911) Population 42 200 000 Capital Shenyang

Macao (Special Administrative Region)
Area Sq Km (Sq Miles) 17 (7) Population 477 000 Capital Macao

Nei Mongol Zizhiqu Inner Mongolia (Autonomous Region)
Area Sq Km (Sq Miles) 1 183 000 (456 759) Population 23 860 000 Capital Hohhot

Ningxia Huizu Zizhiqu (Autonomous Region)
Area Sq Km (Sq Miles) 66 400 (25 637) Population 5 950 000 Capital Yinchuan

Qinghai (Province)
Area Sq Km (Sq Miles) 721 000 (278 380) Population 5 430 000 Capital Xining

Shaanxi (Province)
Area Sq Km (Sq Miles) 205 600 (79 383) Population 37 180 000 Capital Xi'an

Shandong (Province)
Area Sq Km (Sq Miles) 153 300 (59 189) Population 92 390 000 Capital Jinan

Shanghai (Municipality)
Area Sq Km (Sq Miles) 6 300 (2 432) Population 17 780 000 Capital Shanghai

Shanxi (Province)
Area Sq Km (Sq Miles) 156 300 (60 348) Population 33 520 000 Capital Taiyuan

Sichuan (Province)
Area Sq Km (Sq Miles) 569 000 (219 692) Population 82 080 000 Capital Chengdu

Tianjin (Municipality)
Area Sq Km (Sq Miles) 11 300 (4 363) Population 10 430 000 Capital Tianjin

Xinjiang Uygur Zizhiqu Sinkiang (Autonomous Region)
Area Sq Km (Sq Miles) 1 600 000 (617 763) Population 20 080 000 Capital Ürümqi

Xizang Zizhiqu Tibet (Autonomous Region)
Area Sq Km (Sq Miles) 1 228 400 (474 288) Population 2 760 000 Capital Lhasa

Yunnan (Province)
Area Sq Km (Sq Miles) 394 000 (152 124) Population 44 420 000 Capital Kunming

Zhejiang (Province)
Area Sq Km (Sq Miles) 101 800 (39 305) Population 48 940 000 Capital Hangzhou

Taiwan: The People's Republic of China claims Taiwan as its 23rd Province

Christmas Island
Australian External Territory

Area Sq Km	135	Languages	English
Area Sq Miles	52	Religions	Buddhist, Sunni Muslim, Protestant, Roman Catholic
Population	1 508	Currency	Australian dollar
Capital	The Settlement		

The island is situated in the east of the Indian Ocean, to the south of Indonesia. The economy was formerly based on phosphate extraction, although reserves are now nearly depleted. Tourism is developing and is a major employer.

Cocos Islands (Keeling Islands)
Australian External Territory

Area Sq Km	14	Languages	English
Area Sq Miles	5	Religions	Sunni Muslim, Christian
Population	621	Currency	Australian dollar
Capital	West Island		

The Cocos Islands consist of numerous islands on two coral atolls in the eastern Indian Ocean between Sri Lanka and Australia. Most of the population lives on West Island or Home Island. Coconuts are the only cash crop, and the main export.

COLOMBIA
Republic of Colombia

Area Sq Km	1 141 748	Languages	Spanish, Amerindian languages
Area Sq Miles	440 831	Religions	Roman Catholic, Protestant
Population	46 156 000	Currency	Colombian peso
Capital	Bogotá	Organizations	UN

A state in northwest South America, Colombia has coastlines on the Pacific Ocean and the Caribbean Sea. Behind coastal plains lie three ranges of the Andes mountains, separated by high valleys and plateaus where most Colombians live. To the southeast are grasslands and the forests of the Amazon. The climate is tropical, although temperatures vary with altitude. Only five per cent of land is cultivable. Coffee (Colombia is the world's second largest producer), sugar, bananas, cotton and flowers are exported. Coal, nickel, gold, silver, platinum and emeralds (Colombia is the world's largest producer) are mined. Oil and its products are the main export. Industries include the processing of minerals and crops. The main trade partner is the USA. Internal violence – both politically motivated and relating to Colombia's leading role in the international trade in illegal drugs – continues to hinder development.

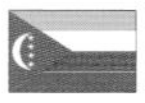

COMOROS
Union of the Comoros

Area Sq Km	1 862	Languages	Comorian, French, Arabic
Area Sq Miles	719	Religions	Sunni Muslim, Roman Catholic
Population	839 000	Currency	Comoros franc
Capital	Moroni	Organizations	UN

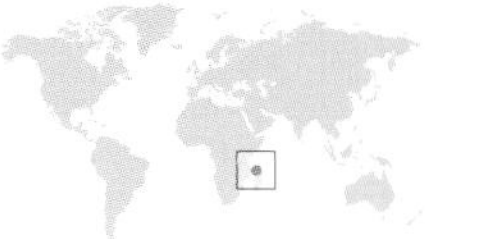

This state, in the Indian Ocean off the east African coast, comprises three volcanic islands of Njazidja (Grande Comore), Nzwani (Anjouan) and Mwali (Mohéli), and some coral atolls. These tropical islands are mountainous, with poor soil and few natural resources. Subsistence farming predominates. Vanilla, cloves and ylang-ylang (an essential oil) are exported, and the economy relies heavily on workers' remittances from abroad.

States and Territories

CONGO

Republic of the Congo

Area Sq Km	342 000	Languages	French, Kongo, Monokutuba, local languages
Area Sq Miles	132 047	Religions	Roman Catholic, Protestant, traditional beliefs, Sunni Muslim
Population	3 768 000	Currency	CFA franc
Capital	Brazzaville	Organizations	UN

Congo, in central Africa, is mostly a forest or savanna-covered plateau drained by the Ubangi-Congo river systems. Sand dunes and lagoons line the short Atlantic coast. The climate is hot and tropical. Most Congolese live in the southern third of the country. Half of the workforce are farmers, growing food and cash crops including sugar, coffee, cocoa and oil palms. Oil and timber are the mainstays of the economy, and oil generates over fifty per cent of the country's export revenues.

CONGO, DEMOCRATIC REPUBLIC OF THE

Area Sq Km	2 345 410	Languages	French, Lingala, Swahili, Kongo, local languages
Area Sq Miles	905 568	Religions	Christian, Sunni Muslim
Population	62 636 000	Currency	Congolese franc
Capital	Kinshasa	Organizations	SADC, UN

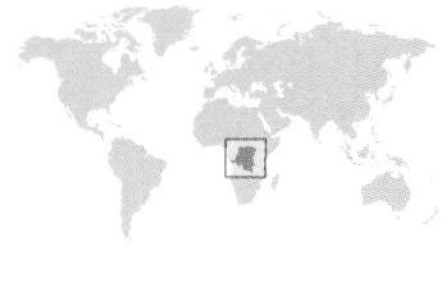

This central African state, formerly Zaire, consists of the basin of the Congo river flanked by plateaus, with high mountain ranges to the east and a short Atlantic coastline to the west. The climate is tropical, with rainforest close to the Equator and savanna to the north and south. Fertile land allows a range of food and cash crops to be grown, chiefly coffee. The country has vast mineral resources, with copper, cobalt and diamonds being the most important.

Cook Islands

New Zealand Overseas Territory

Area Sq Km	293	Languages	English, Maori
Area Sq Miles	113	Religions	Protestant, Roman Catholic
Population	13 000	Currency	New Zealand dollar
Capital	Avarua		

These consist of groups of coral atolls and volcanic islands in the southwest Pacific Ocean. The main island is Rarotonga. Distance from foreign markets and restricted natural resources hinder development.

COSTA RICA

Republic of Costa Rica

Area Sq Km	51 100	Languages	Spanish
Area Sq Miles	19 730	Religions	Roman Catholic, Protestant
Population	4 468 000	Currency	Costa Rican colón
Capital	San José	Organizations	UN

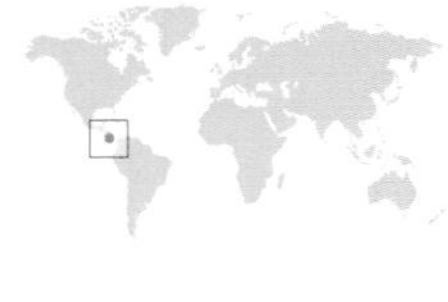

Costa Rica, in central America, has coastlines on the Caribbean Sea and Pacific Ocean. From tropical coastal plains, the land rises to mountains and a temperate central plateau, where most of the population lives. The economy depends on agriculture and tourism, with ecotourism becoming increasingly important. Main exports are textiles, coffee and bananas, and almost half of all trade is with the USA.

CÔTE D'IVOIRE (Ivory Coast)

Republic of Côte d'Ivoire

Area Sq Km	322 463	Languages	French, Creole, Akan, local languages
Area Sq Miles	124 504	Religions	Sunni Muslim, Roman Catholic, traditional beliefs, Protestant
Population	19 262 000	Currency	CFA franc
Capital	Yamoussoukro	Organizations	UN

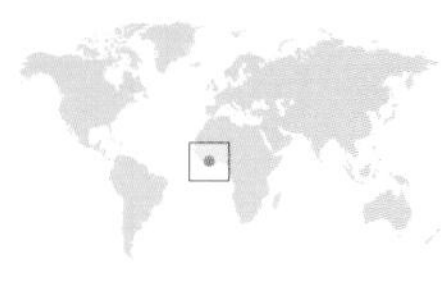

Côte d'Ivoire (Ivory Coast) is in west Africa, on the Gulf of Guinea. In the north are plateaus and savanna; in the south are low undulating plains and rainforest, with sand-bars and lagoons on the coast. Temperatures are warm, and rainfall is heavier in the south. Most of the workforce is engaged in farming. Côte d'Ivoire is a major producer of cocoa and coffee, and agricultural products (also including cotton and timber) are the main exports. Oil and gas have begun to be exploited.

CROATIA

Republic of Croatia

Area Sq Km	56 538	Languages	Croatian, Serbian
Area Sq Miles	21 829	Religions	Roman Catholic, Serbian Orthodox, Sunni Muslim
Population	4 555 000	Currency	Kuna
Capital	Zagreb	Organizations	NATO, UN

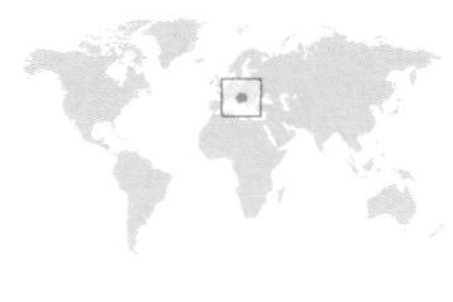

The southern European state of Croatia has a long coastline on the Adriatic Sea, with many offshore islands. Coastal areas have a Mediterranean climate; inland is cooler and wetter. Croatia was once strong agriculturally and industrially, but conflict in the early 1990s, and associated loss of markets and a fall in tourist revenue, caused economic difficulties from which recovery has been slow.

CUBA

Republic of Cuba

Area Sq Km	110 860	Languages	Spanish
Area Sq Miles	42 803	Religions	Roman Catholic, Protestant
Population	11 268 000	Currency	Cuban peso
Capital	Havana (La Habana)	Organizations	UN

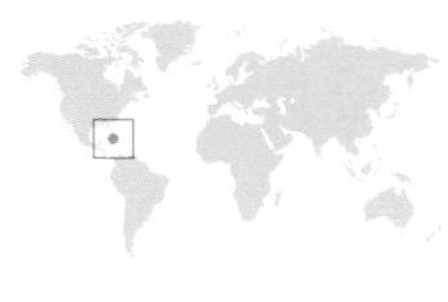

The country comprises the island of Cuba (the largest island in the Caribbean), and many islets and cays. A fifth of Cubans live in and around Havana. Cuba is slowly recovering from the withdrawal of aid and subsidies from the former USSR. Sugar remains the basis of the economy, although tourism is developing and is, together with remittances from workers abroad, an important source of revenue.

CYPRUS

Republic of Cyprus

Area Sq Km	9 251	Languages	Greek, Turkish, English
Area Sq Miles	3 572	Religions	Greek Orthodox, Sunni Muslim
Population	855 000	Currency	Euro
Capital	Nicosia (Lefkosia)	Organizations	Comm., EU, UN

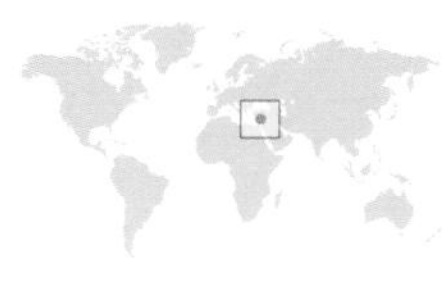

The eastern Mediterranean island of Cyprus has effectively been divided into two since 1974. The economy of the Greek-speaking south is based mainly on specialist agriculture and tourism, with shipping and offshore banking. The ethnically Turkish north depends on agriculture, tourism and aid from Turkey. The island has hot dry summers and mild winters. Cyprus joined the European Union in May 2004.

CZECH REPUBLIC

Area Sq Km	78 864	Languages	Czech, Moravian, Slovakian
Area Sq Miles	30 450	Religions	Roman Catholic, Protestant
Population	10 186 000	Currency	Czech koruna
Capital	Prague (Praha)	Organizations	EU, NATO, OECD, UN

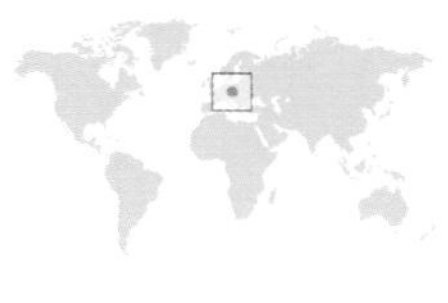

The landlocked Czech Republic in central Europe consists of rolling countryside, wooded hills and fertile valleys. The climate is continental. The country has substantial reserves of coal and lignite, timber and some minerals, chiefly iron ore. It is highly industrialized, and major manufactured goods include industrial machinery, consumer goods, cars, iron and steel, chemicals and glass. Germany is the main trading partner. The Czech Republic joined the European Union in May 2004.

DENMARK

Kingdom of Denmark

Area Sq Km	43 075	Languages	Danish
Area Sq Miles	16 631	Religions	Protestant
Population	5 442 000	Currency	Danish krone
Capital	Copenhagen (København)	Organizations	EU, NATO, OECD, UN

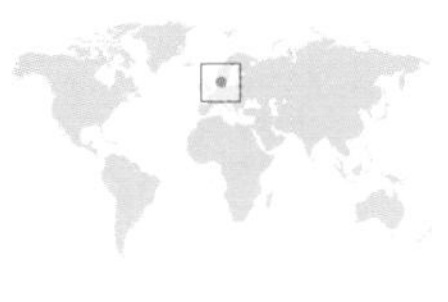

In northern Europe, Denmark occupies the Jutland (Jylland) peninsula and nearly five hundred islands in and between the North and Baltic Seas. The country is low-lying, with long, indented coastlines. The climate is cool and temperate, with rainfall throughout the year. A fifth of the population lives in and around the capital, Copenhagen (København), on the largest of the islands, Zealand (Sjælland). The country's main natural resource is its agricultural potential: two-thirds of the total area is fertile farmland or pasture. Agriculture is high-tech, and with forestry and fishing employs only around six per cent of the workforce. Denmark is self-sufficient in oil and natural gas, produced from fields in the North Sea. Manufacturing, largely based on imported raw materials, accounts for over half of all exports, which include machinery, food, furniture and pharmaceuticals. The main trading partners are Germany and Sweden.

DJIBOUTI

Republic of Djibouti

Area Sq Km	23 200	Languages	Somali, Afar, French, Arabic
Area Sq Miles	8 958	Religions	Sunni Muslim, Christian
Population	833 000	Currency	Djibouti franc
Capital	Djibouti	Organizations	UN

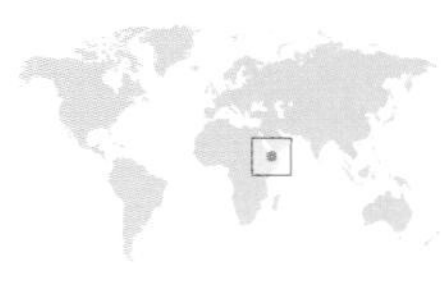

Djibouti lies in northeast Africa, on the Gulf of Aden at the entrance to the Red Sea. Most of the country is semi-arid desert with high temperatures and low rainfall. More than two-thirds of the population live in the capital. There is some camel, sheep and goat herding, but with few natural resources the economy is based on services and trade. Djibouti serves as a free trade zone for northern Africa, and the capital's port is a major transhipment and refuelling destination. It is linked by rail to Addis Ababa in Ethiopia.

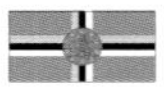

DOMINICA

Commonwealth of Dominica

Area Sq Km	750	Languages	English, Creole
Area Sq Miles	290	Religions	Roman Catholic, Protestant
Population	67 000	Currency	East Caribbean dollar
Capital	Roseau	Organizations	CARICOM, Comm., UN

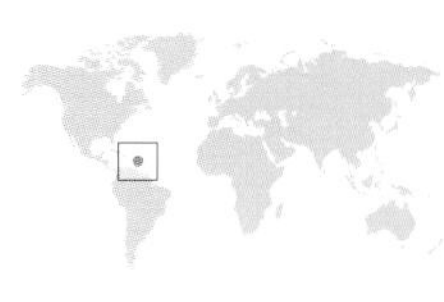

Dominica is the most northerly of the Windward Islands, in the eastern Caribbean. It is very mountainous and forested, with a coastline of steep cliffs. The climate is tropical and rainfall is abundant. Approximately a quarter of Dominicans live in the capital. The economy is based on agriculture, with bananas (the major export), coconuts and citrus fruits the most important crops. Tourism is a developing industry.

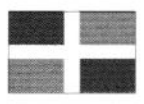

DOMINICAN REPUBLIC

Area Sq Km	48 442	Languages	Spanish, Creole
Area Sq Miles	18 704	Religions	Roman Catholic, Protestant
Population	9 760 000	Currency	Dominican peso
Capital	Santo Domingo	Organizations	UN

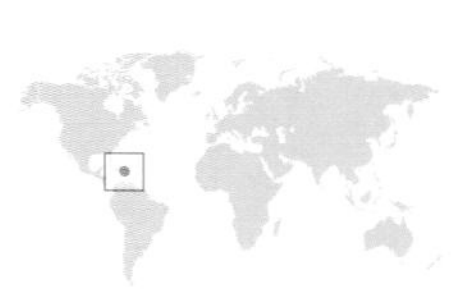

The state occupies the eastern two-thirds of the Caribbean island of Hispaniola (the western third is Haiti). It has a series of mountain ranges, fertile valleys and a large coastal plain in the east. The climate is hot tropical, with heavy rainfall. Sugar, coffee and cocoa are the main cash crops. Nickel (the main export), and gold are mined, and there is some light industry. The USA is the main trading partner. Tourism is the main foreign exchange earner.

EAST TIMOR

Democratic Republic of Timor-Leste

Area Sq Km	14 874	Languages	Portuguese, Tetun, English
Area Sq Miles	5 743	Religions	Roman Catholic
Population	1 155 000	Currency	United States dollar
Capital	Dili	Organizations	UN

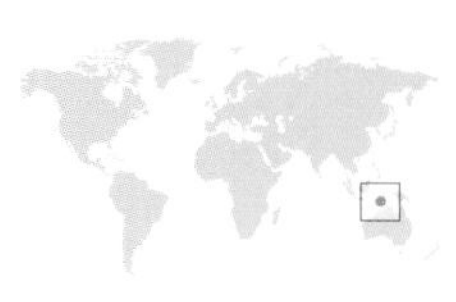

The island of Timor is part of the Indonesian archipelago, to the north of western Australia. East Timor occupies the eastern section of the island, and a small coastal enclave (Ocussi) to the west. A referendum in 1999 ended Indonesia's occupation, after which the country was under UN transitional administration until full independence was achieved in 2002. The economy is in a poor state and East Timor is heavily dependent on foreign aid.

ECUADOR

Republic of Ecuador

Area Sq Km	272 045	Languages	Spanish, Quechua, and other Amerindian languages
Area Sq Miles	105 037	Religions	Roman Catholic
Population	13 341 000	Currency	United States dollar
Capital	Quito	Organizations	OPEC, UN

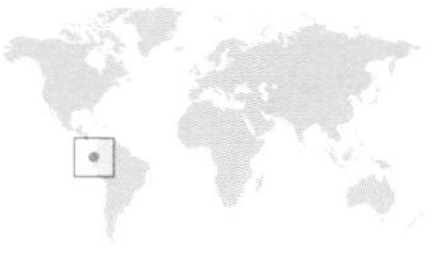

Ecuador is in northwest South America, on the Pacific coast. It consists of a broad coastal plain, high mountain ranges in the Andes, and part of the forested upper Amazon basin to the east. The climate is tropical, moderated by altitude. Most people live on the coast or in the mountain valleys. Ecuador is one of South America's main oil producers, and mineral reserves include gold. Most of the workforce depends on agriculture. Petroleum, bananas, shrimps, coffee and cocoa are exported. The USA is the main trading partner.

EGYPT

Arab Republic of Egypt

Area Sq Km	1 000 250	Languages	Arabic
Area Sq Miles	386 199	Religions	Sunni Muslim, Coptic Christian
Population	75 498 000	Currency	Egyptian pound
Capital	Cairo (Al Qāhirah)	Organizations	UN

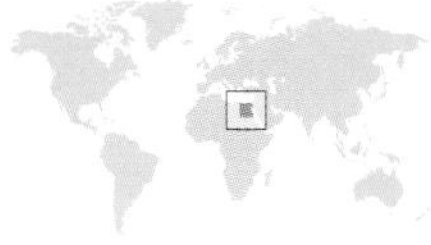

Egypt, on the eastern Mediterranean coast of north Africa, is low-lying, with areas below sea level in the Qattara depression. It is a land of desert and semi-desert, except for the Nile valley, where ninety-nine per cent of Egyptians live. The Sinai peninsula in the northeast of the country forms the only land bridge between Africa and Asia. The summers are hot, the winters mild and rainfall is negligible. Less than four per cent of land (chiefly around the Nile floodplain and delta) is cultivated. Farming employs about one-third of the workforce; cotton is the main cash crop. Egypt imports over half its food needs. There are oil and natural gas reserves, although nearly a quarter of electricity comes from hydroelectric power. Main exports are oil and oil products, cotton, textiles and clothing.

EL SALVADOR

Republic of El Salvador

Area Sq Km	21 041	Languages	Spanish
Area Sq Miles	8 124	Religions	Roman Catholic, Protestant
Population	6 857 000	Currency	El Salvador colón, United States dollar
Capital	San Salvador	Organizations	UN

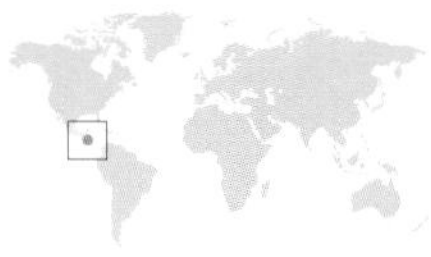

Located on the Pacific coast of central America, El Salvador consists of a coastal plain and volcanic mountain ranges which enclose a densely populated plateau area. The coast is hot, with heavy summer rainfall; the highlands are cooler. Coffee (the chief export), sugar and cotton are the main cash crops. The main trading partners are the USA and Guatemala.

EQUATORIAL GUINEA

Republic of Equatorial Guinea

Area Sq Km	28 051	Languages	Spanish, French, Fang
Area Sq Miles	10 831	Religions	Roman Catholic, traditional beliefs
Population	507 000	Currency	CFA franc
Capital	Malabo	Organizations	UN

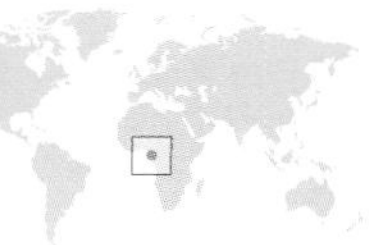

The state consists of Rio Muni, an enclave on the Atlantic coast of central Africa, and the islands of Bioco, Annobón and the Corisco group. Most of the population lives on the coastal plain and upland plateau of Rio Muni. The capital city, Malabo, is on the fertile volcanic island of Bioco. The climate is hot, humid and wet. Oil production started in 1992, and oil is now the main export, along with timber. The economy depends heavily on foreign aid.

ERITREA

State of Eritrea

Area Sq Km	117 400	Languages	Tigrinya, Tigre
Area Sq Miles	45 328	Religions	Sunni Muslim, Coptic Christian
Population	4 851 000	Currency	Nakfa
Capital	Asmara	Organizations	UN

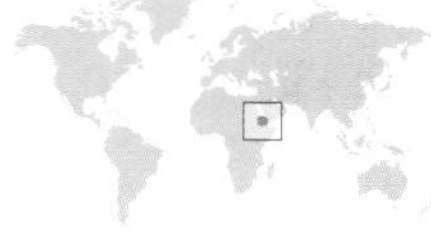

Eritrea, on the Red Sea coast of northeast Africa, consists of a high plateau in the north with a coastal plain which widens to the south. The coast is hot; inland is cooler. Rainfall is unreliable. The agriculture-based economy has suffered from over thirty years of war and occasional poor rains. Eritrea is one of the least developed countries in the world.

ESTONIA

Republic of Estonia

Area Sq Km	45 200	Languages	Estonian, Russian
Area Sq Miles	17 452	Religions	Protestant, Estonian and Russian Orthodox
Population	1 335 000	Currency	Euro
Capital	Tallinn	Organizations	EU, NATO, UN

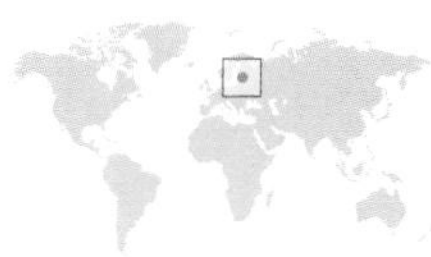

Estonia is in northern Europe, on the Gulf of Finland and the Baltic Sea. The land, over one-third of which is forested, is generally low-lying with many lakes. Approximately one-third of Estonians live in the capital, Tallinn. Exported goods include machinery, wood products, textiles and food products. The main trading partners are the Russian Federation, Finland and Sweden. Estonia joined the European Union in May 2004.

ETHIOPIA

Federal Democratic Republic of Ethiopia

Area Sq Km	1 133 880	Languages	Oromo, Amharic, Tigrinya, local languages
Area Sq Miles	437 794	Religions	Ethiopian Orthodox, Sunni Muslim, traditional beliefs
Population	83 099 000	Currency	Birr
Capital	Addis Ababa (Ādīs Ābeba)	Organizations	UN

A landlocked country in northeast Africa, Ethiopia comprises a mountainous region in the west which is traversed by the Great Rift Valley. The east is mostly arid plateau land. The highlands are warm with summer rainfall. Most people live in the central–northern area. In recent years civil war, conflict with Eritrea and poor infrastructure have hampered economic development. Subsistence farming is the main activity, although droughts have led to frequent famines. Coffee is the main export and there is some light industry. Ethiopia is one of the least developed countries in the world.

Falkland Islands

United Kingdom Overseas Territory

Area Sq Km	12 170	Languages	English
Area Sq Miles	4 699	Religions	Protestant, Roman Catholic
Population	3 000	Currency	Falkland Islands pound
Capital	Stanley		

Lying in the southwest Atlantic Ocean, northeast of Cape Horn, two main islands, West Falkland and East Falkland and many smaller islands, form the territory of the Falkland Islands. The economy is based on sheep farming and the sale of fishing licences.

Faroe Islands

Self-governing Danish Territory

Area Sq Km	1 399	Languages	Faroese, Danish
Area Sq Miles	540	Religions	Protestant
Population	49 000	Currency	Danish krone
Capital	Thorshavn (Tórshavn)		

A self-governing territory, the Faroe Islands lie in the north Atlantic Ocean between the UK and Iceland. The islands benefit from the North Atlantic Drift ocean current, which has a moderating effect on the climate. The economy is based on deep-sea fishing.

FIJI

Sovereign Democratic Republic of Fiji

Area Sq Km	18 330	Languages	English, Fijian, Hindi
Area Sq Miles	7 077	Religions	Christian, Hindu, Sunni Muslim
Population	839 000	Currency	Fiji dollar
Capital	Suva	Organizations	Comm., UN

The southwest Pacific republic of Fiji comprises two mountainous and volcanic islands, Vanua Levu and Viti Levu, and over three hundred smaller islands. The climate is tropical and the economy is based on agriculture (chiefly sugar, the main export), fishing, forestry, gold mining and tourism.

FINLAND

Republic of Finland

Area Sq Km	338 145	Languages	Finnish, Swedish
Area Sq Miles	130 559	Religions	Protestant, Greek Orthodox
Population	5 277 000	Currency	Euro
Capital	Helsinki (Helsingfors)	Organizations	EU, OECD, UN

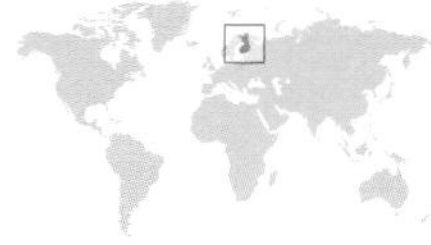

Finland is in northern Europe, and nearly one-third of the country lies north of the Arctic Circle. Forests cover over seventy per cent of the land area, and ten per cent is covered by lakes. Summers are short and warm, and winters are long and severe, particularly in the north. Most of the population lives in the southern third of the country, along the coast or near the lakes. Timber is a major resource and there are important minerals, chiefly chromium. Main industries include metal working, electronics, paper and paper products, and chemicals. The main trading partners are Germany, Sweden and the UK.

FRANCE

French Republic

Area Sq Km	543 965	Languages	French, Arabic
Area Sq Miles	210 026	Religions	Roman Catholic, Protestant, Sunni Muslim
Population	61 647 000	Currency	Euro
Capital	Paris	Organizations	EU, NATO, OECD, UN

France lies in western Europe and has coastlines on the Atlantic Ocean and the Mediterranean Sea. It includes the Mediterranean island of Corsica. Northern and western regions consist mostly of flat or rolling countryside, and include the major lowlands of the Paris basin, the Loire valley and the Aquitaine basin, drained by the Seine, Loire and Garonne river systems respectively. The centre-south is dominated by the hill region of the Massif Central. To the east are the Vosges and Jura mountains and the Alps. In the southwest, the Pyrenees form a natural border with Spain. The climate is temperate with warm summers and cool winters, although the Mediterranean coast has hot, dry summers and mild winters. Over seventy per cent of the population lives in towns, with almost a sixth of the population living in the Paris area. The French economy has a substantial and varied agricultural base. It is a major producer of both fresh and processed food. There are relatively few mineral resources; it has coal reserves, and some oil and natural gas, but it relies heavily on nuclear and hydroelectric power and imported fuels. France is one of the world's major industrial countries. Main industries include food processing, iron, steel and aluminium production, chemicals, cars, electronics and oil refining. The main exports are transport equipment, plastics and chemicals. Tourism is a major source of revenue and employment. Trade is predominantly with other European Union countries.

French Guiana

French Overseas Department

Area Sq Km	90 000	Languages	French, Creole
Area Sq Miles	34 749	Religions	Roman Catholic
Population	202 000	Currency	Euro
Capital	Cayenne		

French Guiana, on the north coast of South America, is densely forested. The climate is tropical, with high rainfall. Most people live in the coastal strip, and agriculture is mostly subsistence farming. Forestry and fishing are important, but mineral resources are largely unexploited and industry is limited. French Guiana depends on French aid. The main trading partners are France and the USA.

French Polynesia

French Overseas Country

Area Sq Km	3 265	Languages	French, Tahitian, Polynesian languages
Area Sq Miles	1 261	Religions	Protestant, Roman Catholic
Population	263 000	Currency	CFP franc
Capital	Papeete		

Extending over a vast area of the southeast Pacific Ocean, French Polynesia comprises more than one hundred and thirty islands and coral atolls. The main island groups are the Marquesas Islands, the Tuamotu Archipelago and the Society Islands. The capital, Papeete, is on Tahiti in the Society Islands. The climate is subtropical, and the economy is based on tourism. The main export is cultured pearls.

GABON
Gabonese Republic

Area Sq Km	267 667	Languages	French, Fang, local languages
Area Sq Miles	103 347	Religions	Roman Catholic, Protestant, traditional beliefs
Population	1 331 000	Currency	CFA franc
Capital	Libreville	Organizations	UN

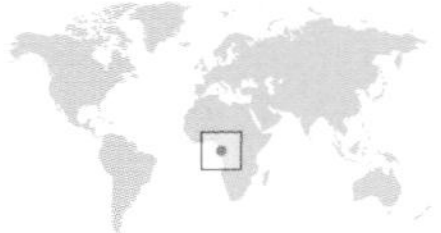

Gabon, on the Atlantic coast of central Africa, consists of low plateaus and a coastal plain lined by lagoons and mangrove swamps. The climate is tropical and rainforests cover over three-quarters of the land area. Over seventy per cent of the population lives in towns. The economy is heavily dependent on oil, which accounts for around seventy-five per cent of exports; manganese, uranium and timber are the other main exports. Agriculture is mainly at subsistence level.

THE GAMBIA
Republic of the Gambia

Area Sq Km	11 295	Languages	English, Malinke, Fulani, Wolof
Area Sq Miles	4 361	Religions	Sunni Muslim, Protestant
Population	1 709 000	Currency	Dalasi
Capital	Banjul	Organizations	Comm., UN

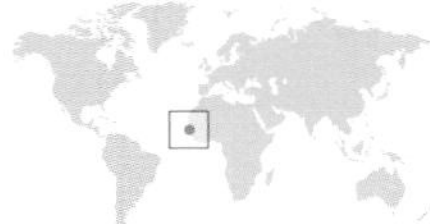

The Gambia, on the coast of west Africa, occupies a strip of land along the lower Gambia river. Sandy beaches are backed by mangrove swamps, beyond which is savanna. The climate is tropical, with most rainfall in the summer. Over seventy per cent of Gambians are farmers, growing chiefly groundnuts (the main export), cotton, oil palms and food crops. Livestock rearing and fishing are important, while manufacturing is limited. Re-exports, mainly from Senegal, and tourism are major sources of income.

Gaza
Semi-autonomous region

Area Sq Km	363	Languages	Arabic
Area Sq Miles	140	Religions	Sunni Muslim, Shi'a Muslim
Population	1 586 008	Currency	Israeli shekel
Capital	Gaza		

Gaza is a narrow strip of land on the southeast corner of the Mediterranean Sea, between Egypt and Israel. This Palestinian territory has limited autonomy from Israel, but hostilities between Israel and the indigenous Arab population continue to restrict its economic development.

GEORGIA
Republic of Georgia

Area Sq Km	69 700	Languages	Georgian, Russian, Armenian, Azeri, Ossetian, Abkhaz
Area Sq Miles	26 911	Religions	Georgian Orthodox, Russian Orthodox, Sunni Muslim
Population	4 395 000	Currency	Lari
Capital	T'bilisi	Organizations	CIS, UN

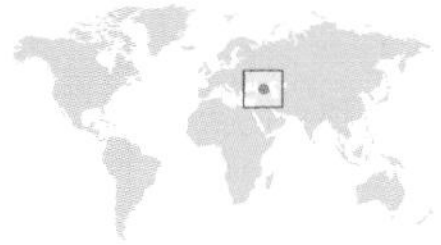

Georgia is in the northwest Caucasus area of southwest Asia, on the eastern coast of the Black Sea. Mountain ranges in the north and south flank the Kura and Rioni valleys. The climate is generally mild, and along the coast it is subtropical. Agriculture is important, with tea, grapes, and citrus fruits the main crops. Mineral resources include manganese ore and oil, and the main industries are steel, oil refining and machine building. The main trading partners are the Russian Federation and Turkey.

GERMANY
Federal Republic of Germany

Area Sq Km	357 022	Languages	German, Turkish
Area Sq Miles	137 847	Religions	Protestant, Roman Catholic
Population	82 599 000	Currency	Euro
Capital	Berlin	Organizations	EU, NATO, OECD, UN

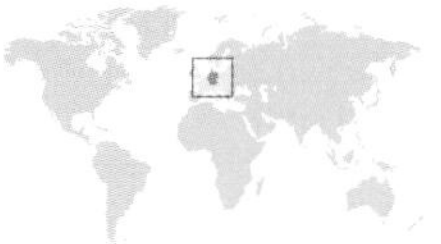

The central European state of Germany borders nine countries and has coastlines on the North and Baltic Seas. Behind the indented coastline, and covering about one-third of the country, is the north German plain, a region of fertile farmland and sandy heaths drained by the country's major rivers. The central highlands are a belt of forested hills and plateaus which stretch from the Eifel region in the west to the Erzgebirge mountains along the border with the Czech Republic. Farther south the land rises to the Swabian Alps (Schwäbische Alb), with the high rugged and forested Black Forest (Schwarzwald) in the southwest. In the far south the Bavarian Alps form the border with Austria. The climate is temperate, with continental conditions in eastern areas. The population is highly urbanized, with over eighty-five per cent living in cities and towns. With the exception of coal, lignite, potash and baryte, Germany lacks minerals and other industrial raw materials. It has a small agricultural base, although a few products (chiefly wines and beers) enjoy an international reputation. Germany is the world's third ranking economy after the USA and Japan. Its industries are amongst the world's most technologically advanced. Exports include machinery, vehicles and chemicals. The majority of trade is with other countries in the European Union, the USA and Japan.

	Area Sq Km (Sq Miles)	Population	Capital
Baden-Württemberg (State)	35 752 (13 804)	10 736 000	Stuttgart
Bayern (State)	70 550 (27 240)	12 469 000	Munich (München)
Berlin (State)	892 (344)	3 395 000	Berlin
Brandenburg (State)	29 476 (11 381)	2 559 000	Potsdan
Bremen	404 (156)	663 000	Bremen
Hamburg (State)	755 (292)	1 744 000	Hamburg
Hessen (State)	21 114 (8 152)	6 092 000	Wiesbaden
Mecklenburg-Vorpommern (State)	23 173 (8 947)	1 707 000	Schwerin
Niedersachsen (State)	47 616 (18 385)	7 994 000	Hannover
Nordrhein-Westfalen (State)	34 082 (13 159)	18 058 000	Düsseldorf
Rheinland-Pfalz (State)	19 847 (7 663)	4 059 000	Mainz
Saarland (State)	2 568 (992)	1 050 000	Saarbrücken
Sachsen (State)	18 413 (7 109)	4 274 000	Dresden
Sachsen-Anhalt (State)	20 447 (7 895)	2 470 000	Magdeburg
Schleswig-Holstein (State)	15 761 (6 085)	2 833 000	Kiel
Thüringen (State)	16 172 (6 244)	2 335 000	Erfurt

GHANA
Republic of Ghana

Area Sq Km	238 537	Languages	English, Hausa, Akan, local languages
Area Sq Miles	92 100	Religions	Christian, Sunni Muslim, traditional beliefs
Population	23 478 000	Currency	Cedi
Capital	Accra	Organizations	Comm., UN

A west African state on the Gulf of Guinea, Ghana is a land of plains and low plateaus covered with savanna and rainforest. In the east is the Volta basin and Lake Volta. The climate is tropical, with the highest rainfall in the south, where most of the population lives. Agriculture employs around sixty per cent of the workforce. Main exports are gold, timber, cocoa, bauxite and manganese ore.

Gibraltar
United Kingdom Overseas Territory

Area Sq Km	7	Languages	English, Spanish
Area Sq Miles	3	Religions	Roman Catholic, Protestant, Sunni Muslim
Population	29 000	Currency	Gibraltar pound
Capital	Gibraltar		

Gibraltar lies on the south coast of Spain at the western entrance to the Mediterranean Sea. The economy depends on tourism, offshore banking and shipping services.

GREECE
Hellenic Republic

Area Sq Km	131 957	Languages	Greek
Area Sq Miles	50 949	Religions	Greek Orthodox, Sunni Muslim
Population	11 147 000	Currency	Euro
Capital	Athens (Athina)	Organizations	EU, NATO, OECD, UN

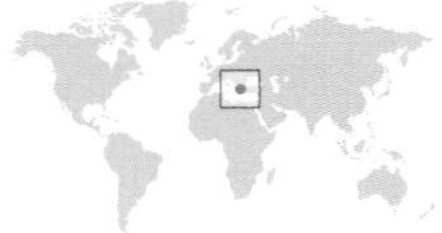

Greece comprises a mountainous peninsula in the Balkan region of southeastern Europe and many islands in the Ionian, Aegean and Mediterranean Seas. The islands make up over one-fifth of its area. Mountains and hills cover much of the country. The main lowland areas are the plains of Thessaly in the centre and around Thessaloniki in the northeast. Summers are hot and dry while winters are mild and wet, but colder in the north with heavy snowfalls in the mountains. One-third of Greeks live in the Athens area. Employment in agriculture accounts for approximately twenty per cent of the workforce, and exports include citrus fruits, raisins, wine, olives and olive oil. Aluminium and nickel are mined and a wide range of manufactures are produced, including food products and tobacco, textiles, clothing, and chemicals. Tourism is an important industry and there is a large services sector. Most trade is with other European Union countries.

Greenland
Self-governing Danish Territory

Area Sq Km	2 175 600	Languages	Greenlandic, Danish
Area Sq Miles	840 004	Religions	Protestant
Population	58 000	Currency	Danish krone
Capital	Nuuk (Godthåb)		

Situated to the northeast of North America between the Atlantic and Arctic Oceans, Greenland is the largest island in the world. It has a polar climate and over eighty per cent of the land area is covered by permanent ice cap. The economy is based on fishing and fish processing.

GRENADA

Area Sq Km	378	Languages	English, Creole
Area Sq Miles	146	Religions	Roman Catholic, Protestant
Population	106 000	Currency	East Caribbean dollar
Capital	St George's	Organizations	CARICOM, Comm., UN

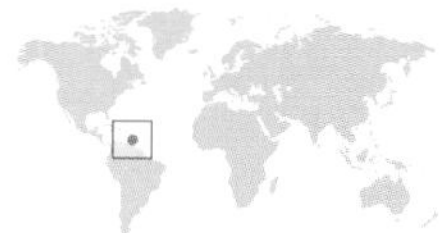

The Caribbean state comprises Grenada, the most southerly of the Windward Islands, and the southern islands of the Grenadines. Grenada has wooded hills, with beaches in the southwest. The climate is warm and wet. Agriculture is the main activity, with bananas, nutmeg and cocoa the main exports. Tourism is the main foreign exchange earner.

Guadeloupe
French Overseas Department

Area Sq Km	1 780	Languages	French, Creole
Area Sq Miles	687	Religions	Roman Catholic
Population	445 000	Currency	Euro
Capital	Basse-Terre		

Guadeloupe, in the Leeward Islands in the Caribbean, consists of two main islands (Basse-Terre and Grande-Terre, connected by a bridge), Marie-Galante, and a few outer islands. The climate is tropical, but moderated by trade winds. Bananas, sugar and rum are the main exports and tourism is a major source of income.

Guam
United States Unincorporated Territory

Area Sq Km	541	Languages	Chamorro, English, Tagalog
Area Sq Miles	209	Religions	Roman Catholic
Population	173 000	Currency	United States dollar
Capital	Hagåtña		

Lying at the south end of the Northern Mariana Islands in the western Pacific Ocean, Guam has a humid tropical climate. The island has a large US military base and the economy relies on that and on tourism.

GUATEMALA
Republic of Guatemala

Area Sq Km	108 890	Languages	Spanish, Mayan languages
Area Sq Miles	42 043	Religions	Roman Catholic, Protestant
Population	13 354 000	Currency	Quetzal, United States dollar
Capital	Guatemala City	Organizations	UN

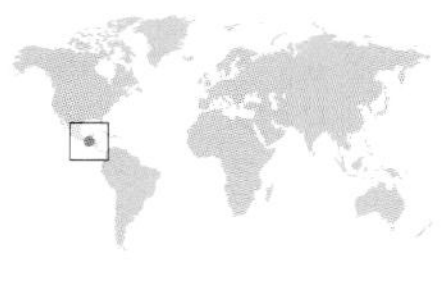

The most populous country in Central America after Mexico, Guatemala has long Pacific and short Caribbean coasts separated by a mountain chain which includes several active volcanoes. The climate is hot tropical in the lowlands and cooler in the highlands, where most of the population lives. Farming is the main activity and coffee, sugar and bananas are the main exports. There is some manufacturing of clothing and textiles. The main trading partner is the USA.

Guernsey
United Kingdom Crown Dependency

Area Sq Km	78	Languages	English, French
Area Sq Miles	30	Religions	Protestant, Roman Catholic
Population	63 923	Currency	Pound sterling
Capital	St Peter Port		

Guernsey is one of the Channel Islands, lying off northern France. The dependency also includes the nearby islands of Alderney, Sark and Herm. Financial services are an important part of the island's economy.

GUINEA
Republic of Guinea

Area Sq Km	245 857	Languages	French, Fulani, Malinke, local languages
Area Sq Miles	94 926	Religions	Sunni Muslim, traditional beliefs, Christian
Population	9 370 000	Currency	Guinea franc
Capital	Conakry	Organizations	UN

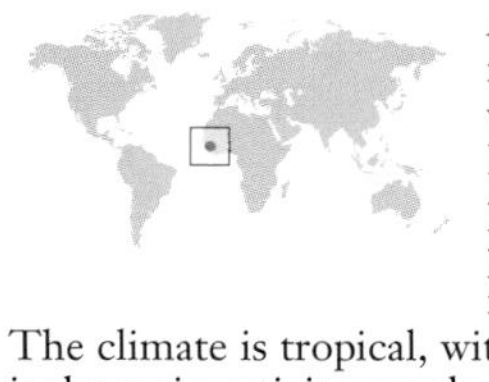

Guinea is in west Africa, on the Atlantic Ocean. There are mangrove swamps along the coast, while inland are lowlands and the Fouta Djallon mountains and plateaus. To the east are savanna plains drained by the upper Niger river system. The southeast is hilly. The climate is tropical, with high coastal rainfall. Agriculture is the main activity, employing nearly eighty per cent of the workforce, with coffee, bananas and pineapples the chief cash crops. There are huge reserves of bauxite, which accounts for more than seventy per cent of exports. Other exports include aluminium oxide, gold, coffee and diamonds.

GUINEA-BISSAU
Republic of Guinea-Bissau

Area Sq Km	36 125	Languages	Portuguese, Crioulo, local languages
Area Sq Miles	13 948	Religions	Traditional beliefs, Sunni Muslim, Christian
Population	1 695 000	Currency	CFA franc
Capital	Bissau	Organizations	UN

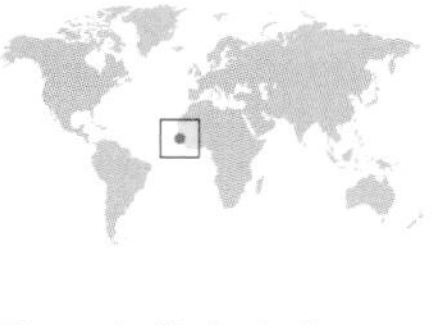

Guinea-Bissau is on the Atlantic coast of west Africa. The mainland coast is swampy and contains many estuaries. Inland are forested plains, and to the east are savanna plateaus. The climate is tropical. The economy is based mainly on subsistence farming. There is little industry, and timber and mineral resources are largely unexploited. Cashews account for seventy per cent of exports. Guinea-Bissau is one of the least developed countries in the world.

GUYANA
Co-operative Republic of Guyana

Area Sq Km	214 969	Languages	English, Creole, Amerindian languages
Area Sq Miles	83 000	Religions	Protestant, Hindu, Roman Catholic, Sunni Muslim
Population	738 000	Currency	Guyana dollar
Capital	Georgetown	Organizations	CARICOM, Comm., UN

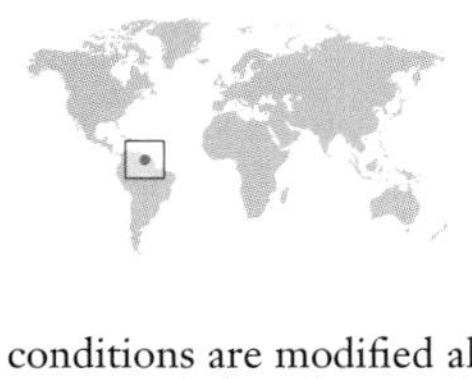

Guyana, on the northeast coast of South America, consists of highlands in the west and savanna uplands in the southwest. Most of the country is densely forested. A lowland coastal belt supports crops and most of the population. The generally hot, humid and wet conditions are modified along the coast by sea breezes. The economy is based on agriculture, bauxite, and forestry. Sugar, bauxite, gold, rice and timber are the main exports.

HAITI
Republic of Haiti

Area Sq Km	27 750	Languages	French, Creole
Area Sq Miles	10 714	Religions	Roman Catholic, Protestant, Voodoo
Population	9 598 000	Currency	Gourde
Capital	Port-au-Prince	Organizations	CARICOM, UN

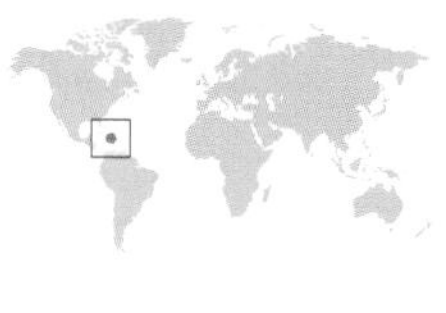

Haiti, occupying the western third of the Caribbean island of Hispaniola, is a mountainous state with small coastal plains and a central valley. The Dominican Republic occupies the rest of the island. The climate is tropical, and is hottest in coastal areas. Haiti has few natural resources, is densely populated and relies on exports of local crafts and coffee, and remittances from workers abroad.

HONDURAS
Republic of Honduras

Area Sq Km	112 088	Languages	Spanish, Amerindian languages
Area Sq Miles	43 277	Religions	Roman Catholic, Protestant
Population	7 106 000	Currency	Lempira
Capital	Tegucigalpa	Organizations	UN

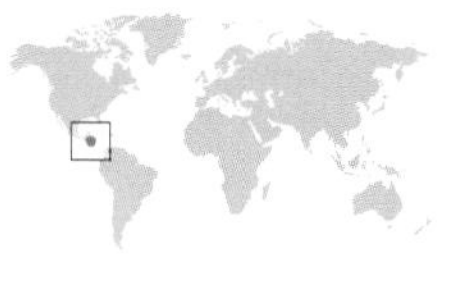

Honduras, in central America, is a mountainous and forested country with lowland areas along its long Caribbean and short Pacific coasts. Coastal areas are hot and humid with heavy summer rainfall; inland is cooler and drier. Most of the population lives in the central valleys. Coffee and bananas are the main exports, along with shellfish and zinc. Industry involves mainly agricultural processing.

HUNGARY
Republic of Hungary

Area Sq Km	93 030	Languages	Hungarian
Area Sq Miles	35 919	Religions	Roman Catholic, Protestant
Population	10 030 000	Currency	Forint
Capital	Budapest	Organizations	EU, NATO, OECD, UN

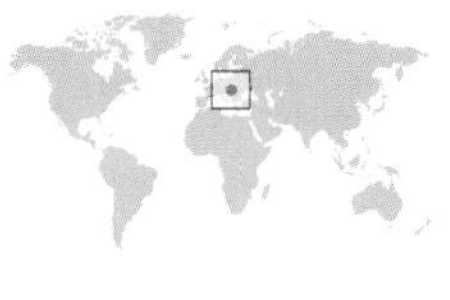

The Danube river flows north-south through central Hungary, a landlocked country in eastern Europe. In the east lies a great plain, flanked by highlands in the north. In the west low mountains and Lake Balaton separate a smaller plain and southern uplands. The climate is continental. Sixty per cent of the population lives in urban areas, and one-fifth lives in the capital, Budapest. Some minerals and energy resources are exploited, chiefly bauxite, coal and natural gas. Hungary has an industrial economy based on metals, machinery, transport equipment, chemicals and food products. The main trading partners are Germany and Austria. Hungary joined the European Union in May 2004.

ICELAND
Republic of Iceland

Area Sq Km	102 820	Languages	Icelandic
Area Sq Miles	39 699	Religions	Protestant
Population	301 000	Currency	Icelandic króna
Capital	Reykjavík	Organizations	NATO, OECD, UN

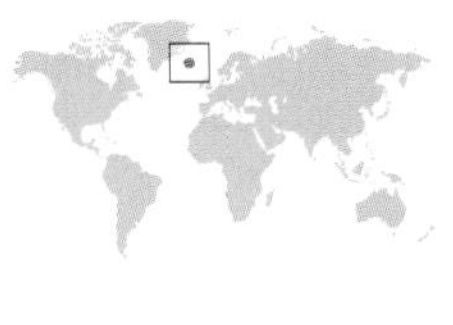

Iceland lies in the north Atlantic Ocean near the Arctic Circle, to the northwest of Scandinavia. The landscape is volcanic, with numerous hot springs, geysers, and approximately two hundred volcanoes. One-tenth of the country is covered by ice caps. Only coastal lowlands are cultivated and settled, and over half the population lives in the Reykjavik area. The climate is mild, moderated by the North Atlantic Drift ocean current and by southwesterly winds. The mainstays of the economy are fishing and fish processing, which account for seventy per cent of exports. Agriculture involves mainly sheep and dairy farming. Hydroelectric and geothermal energy resources are considerable. The main industries produce aluminium, ferro-silicon and fertilizers. Tourism, including ecotourism, is growing in importance.

INDIA
Republic of India

Area Sq Km	3 064 898	Languages	Hindi, English, many regional languages
Area Sq Miles	1 183 364	Religions	Hindu, Sunni Muslim, Shi'a Muslim, Sikh, Christian
Population	1 169 016 000	Currency	Indian rupee
Capital	New Delhi	Organizations	Comm., UN

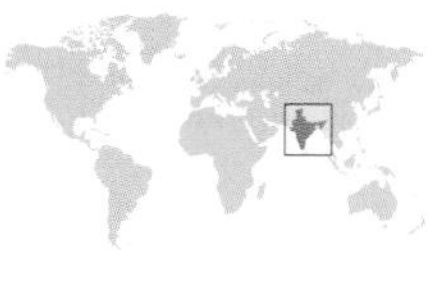

The south Asian country of India occupies a peninsula that juts out into the Indian Ocean between the Arabian Sea and Bay of Bengal. The heart of the peninsula is the Deccan plateau, bordered on either side by ranges of hills, the western Ghats and the lower eastern Ghats, which fall away to narrow coastal plains. To the north is a broad plain, drained by the Indus, Ganges and Brahmaputra rivers and their tributaries. The plain is intensively farmed and is the most populous region. In the west is the Thar Desert. The mountains of the Himalaya form India's northern border, together with parts of the Karakoram and Hindu Kush ranges in the northwest. The climate shows marked seasonal variation: a hot season from March to June; a monsoon season from June to October; and a cold season from November to February. Rainfall ranges between very high in the northeast Assam region to negligible in the Thar Desert. Temperatures range from very cold in the Himalaya to tropical heat over much of the south. Over seventy per cent of the huge population – the second largest in the world – is rural, although Delhi, Mumbai (Bombay) and Kolkata (Calcutta) all rank among the ten largest cities in the world. Agriculture, forestry and fishing account for a quarter of national output and two-thirds of employment. Much of the farming is on a subsistence basis and involves mainly rice and wheat. India is a major world producer of tea, sugar, jute, cotton and tobacco. Livestock is reared mainly for dairy products and hides. There are major reserves of coal, reserves of oil and natural gas, and many minerals, including iron, manganese, bauxite, diamonds and gold. The manufacturing sector is large and diverse – mainly chemicals and chemical products, textiles, iron and steel, food products, electrical goods and transport equipment; software and pharmaceuticals are also important. All the main manufactured products are exported, together with diamonds and jewellery. The USA, Germany, Japan and the UK are the main trading partners.

INDONESIA
Republic of Indonesia

Area Sq Km	1 919 445	Languages	Indonesian, local languages
Area Sq Miles	741 102	Religions	Sunni Muslim, Protestant, Roman Catholic, Hindu, Buddhist
Population	231 627 000	Currency	Rupiah
Capital	Jakarta	Organizations	APEC, ASEAN, OPEC, UN

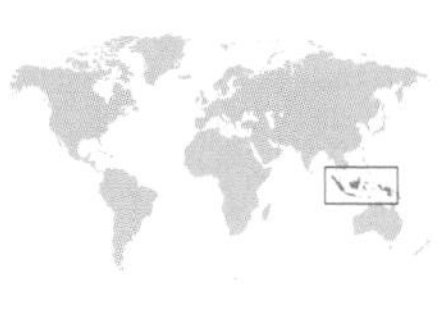

Indonesia, the largest and most populous country in southeast Asia, consists of over thirteen thousand islands extending between the Pacific and Indian Oceans. Sumatra, Java, Sulawesi (Celebes), Kalimantan (two-thirds of Borneo) and Papua (formerly Irian Jaya, western New Guinea) make up ninety per cent of the land area. Most of Indonesia is mountainous and covered with rainforest or mangrove swamps, and there are over three hundred volcanoes, many active. Two-thirds of the population lives in the lowland areas of the islands of Java and Madura. The climate is tropical monsoon. Agriculture is the largest sector of the economy and Indonesia is among the world's top producers of rice, palm oil, tea, coffee, rubber and tobacco. Many goods are produced, including textiles, clothing, cement, tin, fertilizers and vehicles. Main exports are oil, natural gas, timber products and clothing. Main trading partners are Japan, the USA and Singapore. Indonesia is a relatively poor country, and ethnic tensions and civil unrest often hinder economic development.

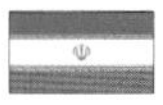

IRAN
Islamic Republic of Iran

Area Sq Km	1 648 000	Languages	Farsi, Azeri, Kurdish, regional languages
Area Sq Miles	636 296	Religions	Shi'a Muslim, Sunni Muslim
Population	71 208 000	Currency	Iranian rial
Capital	Tehrān	Organizations	OPEC, UN

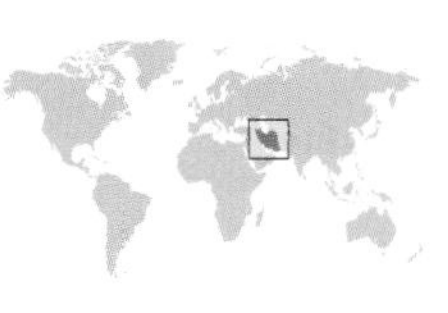

Iran is in southwest Asia, and has coasts on The Gulf, the Caspian Sea and the Gulf of Oman. In the east is a high plateau, with large salt pans and a vast sand desert. In the west the Zagros Mountains form a series of ridges, and to the north lie the Elburz Mountains. Most farming and settlement is on the narrow plain along the Caspian Sea and in the foothills of the north and west. The climate is one of extremes, with hot summers and very cold winters. Most of the light rainfall is in the winter months. Agriculture involves approximately one-third of the workforce. Wheat is the main crop, but fruit (especially dates) and pistachio nuts are grown for export. Petroleum (the main export) and natural gas are Iran's leading natural resources. Manufactured goods include carpets, clothing, food products and construction materials.

IRAQ

Republic of Iraq

Area Sq Km	438 317	Languages	Arabic, Kurdish, Turkmen
Area Sq Miles	169 235	Religions	Shi'a Muslim, Sunni Muslim, Christian
Population	28 993 000	Currency	Iraqi dinar
Capital	Baghdād	Organizations	OPEC, UN

Iraq, in southwest Asia, has at its heart the lowland valley of the Tigris and Euphrates rivers. In the southeast, where the two rivers join, are the Mesopotamian marshes and the Shaṭṭ al 'Arab waterway leading to The Gulf. The north is hilly, while the west is mostly desert. Summers are hot and dry, and winters are mild with light, unreliable rainfall. The Tigris-Euphrates valley contains most of the country's arable land. One in five of the population lives in the capital, Baghdad. The economy has suffered following the 1991 Gulf War and the invasion of US-led coalition forces in 2005. The latter resulted in the overthrow of the dictator Saddam Hussein, but there is continuing internal instability. Oil is normally the main export.

IRELAND

Republic of Ireland

Area Sq Km	70 282	Languages	English, Irish
Area Sq Miles	27 136	Religions	Roman Catholic, Protestant
Population	4 301 000	Currency	Euro
Capital	Dublin (Baile Átha Cliath)	Organizations	EU, OECD, UN

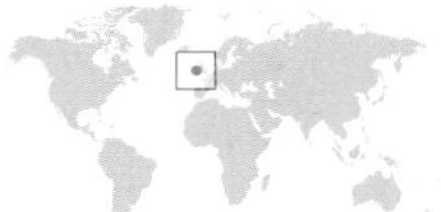

The Irish Republic occupies some eighty per cent of the island of Ireland, in northwest Europe. It is a lowland country of wide valleys, lakes and peat bogs, with isolated mountain ranges around the coast. The west coast is rugged and indented with many bays. The climate is mild due to the modifying effect of the North Atlantic Drift ocean current and rainfall is plentiful, although highest in the west. Nearly sixty per cent of the population lives in urban areas, Dublin and Cork being the main cities. Resources include natural gas, peat, lead and zinc. Agriculture, the traditional mainstay, now employs less than ten per cent of the workforce, while industry employs nearly thirty per cent. The main industries are electronics, pharmaceuticals and engineering as well as food processing, brewing and textiles. Service industries are expanding, with tourism a major earner. The UK is the main trading partner.

Isle of Man

United Kingdom Crown Dependency

Area Sq Km	572	Languages	English
Area Sq Miles	221	Religions	Protestant, Roman Catholic
Population	79 000	Currency	Pound sterling
Capital	Douglas		

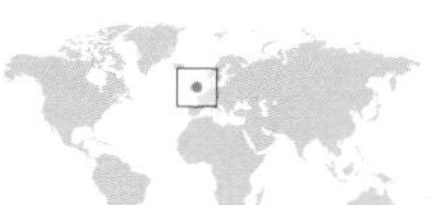

The Isle of Man lies in the Irish Sea between England and Northern Ireland. The island is self-governing, although the UK is responsible for its defence and foreign affairs. It is not part of the European Union, but has a special relationship with the EU which allows for free trade. Eighty per cent of the economy is based on the service sector, particularly financial services.

ISRAEL

State of Israel

Area Sq Km	20 770	Languages	Hebrew, Arabic
Area Sq Miles	8 019	Religions	Jewish, Sunni Muslim, Christian, Druze
Population	6 928 000	Currency	Shekel
Capital	Jerusalem (Yerushalayim) (El Quds) De facto capital. Disputed.	Organizations	UN

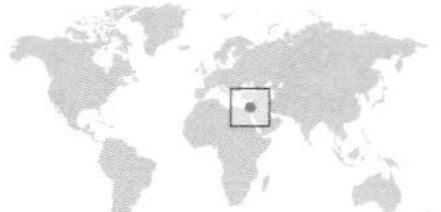

Israel lies on the Mediterranean coast of southwest Asia. Beyond the coastal Plain of Sharon are the hills and valleys of Samaria, with the Galilee highlands to the north. In the east is a rift valley, which extends from Lake Tiberias (Sea of Galilee) to the Gulf of Aqaba and contains the Jordan river and the Dead Sea. In the south is the Negev, a triangular semi-desert plateau. Most of the population lives on the coastal plain or in northern and central areas. Much of Israel has warm summers and mild, wet winters. The south is hot and dry. Agricultural production was boosted by the occupation of the West Bank in 1967. Manufacturing makes the largest contribution to the economy, and tourism is also important. Israel's main exports are machinery and transport equipment, software, diamonds, clothing, fruit and vegetables. The country relies heavily on foreign aid. Security issues relating to territorial disputes over the West Bank and Gaza have still to be resolved.

ITALY

Italian Republic

Area Sq Km	301 245	Languages	Italian
Area Sq Miles	116 311	Religions	Roman Catholic
Population	58 877 000	Currency	Euro
Capital	Rome (Roma)	Organizations	EU, NATO, OECD, UN

Most of the southern European state of Italy occupies a peninsula that juts out into the Mediterranean Sea. It includes the islands of Sicily and Sardinia and approximately seventy much smaller islands in the surrounding seas. Italy is mountainous, dominated by the Alps, which form its northern border, and the various ranges of the Apennines, which run almost the full length of the peninsula. Many of Italy's mountains are of volcanic origin, and its active volcanoes are Vesuvius, near Naples, Etna and Stromboli. The main lowland area, the Po river valley in the northeast, is the main agricultural and industrial area and is the most populous region. Italy has a Mediterranean climate, although the north experiences colder, wetter winters, with heavy snow in the Alps. Natural resources are limited, and only about twenty per cent of the land is suitable for cultivation. The economy is fairly diversified. Some oil, natural gas and coal are produced, but most fuels and minerals used by industry are imported. Agriculture is important, with cereals, vines, fruit and vegetables the main crops. Italy is the world's largest wine producer. The north is the centre of Italian industry, especially around Turin, Milan and Genoa. Leading manufactures include industrial and office equipment, domestic appliances, cars, textiles, clothing, leather goods, chemicals and metal products. There is a strong service sector, and with over twenty-five million visitors a year, tourism is a major employer and accounts for five per cent of the national income. Finance and banking are also important. Most trade is with other European Union countries.

JAMAICA

Area Sq Km	10 991	Languages	English, Creole
Area Sq Miles	4 244	Religions	Protestant, Roman Catholic
Population	2 714 000	Currency	Jamaican dollar
Capital	Kingston	Organizations	CARICOM, Comm., UN

Jamaica, the third largest Caribbean island, has beaches and densely populated coastal plains traversed by hills and plateaus rising to the forested Blue Mountains in the east. The climate is tropical, but cooler and wetter on high ground. The economy is based on tourism, agriculture, mining and light manufacturing. Bauxite, aluminium oxide, sugar and bananas are the main exports. The USA is the main trading partner. Foreign aid is also significant.

Jammu and Kashmir

Disputed territory (India/Pakistan/China)

Area Sq Km	222 236	Population	13 000 000
Area Sq Miles	85 806	Capital	Srinagar

A disputed region in the north of the Indian subcontinent, to the west of the Karakoram and Himalaya mountains. The 'Line of Control' separates the northwestern, Pakistani-controlled area and the southeastern, Indian-controlled area. China occupies the Himalayan section known as the Aksai Chin, which is also claimed by India.

JAPAN

Area Sq Km	377 727	Languages	Japanese
Area Sq Miles	145 841	Religions	Shintoist, Buddhist, Christian
Population	127 967 000	Currency	Yen
Capital	Tōkyō	Organizations	APEC, OECD, UN

Japan lies in the Pacific Ocean off the coast of eastern Asia and consists of four main islands – Hokkaidō, Honshū, Shikoku and Kyūshū – and more than three thousand smaller islands in the surrounding Sea of Japan, East China Sea and Pacific Ocean. The central island of Honshū accounts for sixty per cent of the total land area and contains eighty per cent of the population. Behind the long and deeply indented coastline, nearly three-quarters of the country is mountainous and heavily forested. Japan has over sixty active volcanoes, and is subject to frequent earthquakes and typhoons. The climate is generally temperate maritime, with warm summers and mild winters, except in western Hokkaidō and northwest Honshū, where the winters are very cold with heavy snow. Only fourteen per cent of the land area is suitable for cultivation, and its few raw materials (coal, oil, natural gas, lead, zinc and copper) are insufficient for its industry. Most materials must be imported, including about ninety per cent of energy requirements. Yet Japan has the world's second largest industrial economy, with a range of modern heavy and light industries centred mainly around the major ports of Yokohama, Ōsaka and Tōkyō. It is the world's largest manufacturer of cars, motorcycles and merchant ships, and a major producer of steel, textiles, chemicals and cement. It is also a leading producer of many consumer durables, such as washing machines, and electronic equipment, chiefly office equipment and computers. Japan has a strong service sector, banking and finance being particularly important, and Tōkyō has one of the world's major stock exchanges. Owing to intensive agricultural production, Japan is seventy per cent self-sufficient in food. The main food crops are rice, barley, fruit, wheat and soya beans. Livestock rearing (chiefly cattle, pigs and chickens) and fishing are also important, and Japan has one of the largest fishing fleets in the world. A major trading nation, Japan has trade links with many countries in southeast Asia and in Europe, although its main trading partner is the USA.

Jersey

United Kingdom Crown Dependency

Area Sq Km	116	Languages	English, French
Area Sq Miles	45	Religions	Protestant, Roman Catholic
Population	88 200	Currency	Pound sterling
Capital	St Helier		

One of the Channel Islands lying off the west coast of the Cherbourg peninsula in northern France. Financial services are the most important part of the economy.

JORDAN

Hashemite Kingdom of Jordan

Area Sq Km	89 206	Languages	Arabic
Area Sq Miles	34 443	Religions	Sunni Muslim, Christian
Population	5 924 000	Currency	Jordanian dinar
Capital	'Ammān	Organizations	UN

Jordan, in southwest Asia, is landlocked apart from a short coastline on the Gulf of Aqaba. Much of the country is rocky desert plateau. To the west of the mountains, the land falls below sea level to the Dead Sea and the Jordan river. The climate is hot and dry. Most people live in the northwest. Phosphates, potash, pharmaceuticals, fruit and vegetables are the main exports. The tourist industry is important, and the economy relies on workers' remittances from abroad and foreign aid.

KAZAKHSTAN

Republic of Kazakhstan

Area Sq Km	2 717 300	Languages	Kazakh, Russian, Ukrainian, German, Uzbek, Tatar
Area Sq Miles	1 049 155	Religions	Sunni Muslim, Russian Orthodox, Protestant
Population	15 422 000	Currency	Tenge
Capital	Astana (Akmola)	Organizations	CIS, UN

Stretching across central Asia, Kazakhstan covers a vast area of steppe land and semi-desert. The land is flat in the west, with large lowlands around the Caspian Sea, rising to mountains in the southeast. The climate is continental. Agriculture and livestock rearing are important, and cotton and tobacco are the main cash crops. Kazakhstan is very rich in minerals, including coal, chromium, gold, molybdenum, lead and zinc, and has substantial reserves of oil and gas. Mining, metallurgy, machine building and food processing are major industries. Oil, gas and minerals are the main exports, and the Russian Federation is the dominant trading partner.

KENYA
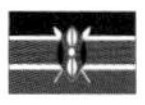

Republic of Kenya

Area Sq Km	582 646	Languages	Swahili, English, local languages
Area Sq Miles	224 961	Religions	Christian, traditional beliefs
Population	37 538 000	Currency	Kenyan shilling
Capital	Nairobi	Organizations	Comm., UN

Kenya is in east Africa, on the Indian Ocean. Inland beyond the coastal plains the land rises to plateaus interrupted by volcanic mountains. The Great Rift Valley runs north-south to the west of the capital, Nairobi. Most of the population lives in the central area. Conditions are tropical on the coast, semi-desert in the north and savanna in the south. Hydroelectric power from the Upper Tana river provides most of the country's electricity. Agricultural products, mainly tea, coffee, fruit and vegetables, are the main exports. Light industry is important, and tourism, oil refining and re-exports for landlocked neighbours are major foreign exchange earners.

KIRIBATI

Republic of Kiribati

Area Sq Km	717	Languages	Gilbertese, English
Area Sq Miles	277	Religions	Roman Catholic, Protestant
Population	95 000	Currency	Australian dollar
Capital	Bairiki	Organizations	Comm., UN

Kiribati, in the Pacific Ocean, straddles the Equator and comprises coral islands in the Gilbert, Phoenix and Line Island groups and the volcanic island of Banaba. Most people live on the Gilbert Islands, and the capital, Bairiki, is on Tarawa island in this group. The climate is hot, and wetter in the north. Copra and fish are exported. Kiribati relies on remittances from workers abroad and foreign aid.

KOSOVO

Republic of Kosovo

Area Sq Km	10 908	Languages	Albanian, Serbian
Area Sq Miles	4 212	Religions	Sunni Muslim, Serbian Orthodox
Population	2 069 989	Currency	Euro
Capital	Prishtinë (Priština)		

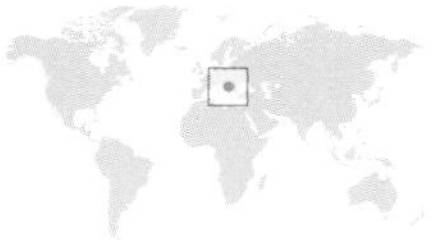

Kosovo, traditionally an autonomous southern province of Serbia, was the focus of ethnic conflict between Serbs and the majority ethnic Albanians in the 1990s until international intervention in 1999, after which it was administered by the UN. Kosovo declared its independence from Serbia in February 2008. The landscape is largely hilly or mountainous, especially along the southern and western borders.

KUWAIT

State of Kuwait

Area Sq Km	17 818	Languages	Arabic
Area Sq Miles	6 880	Religions	Sunni Muslim, Shi'a Muslim, Christian, Hindu
Population	2 851 000	Currency	Kuwaiti dinar
Capital	Kuwait (Al Kuwayt)	Organizations	OPEC, UN

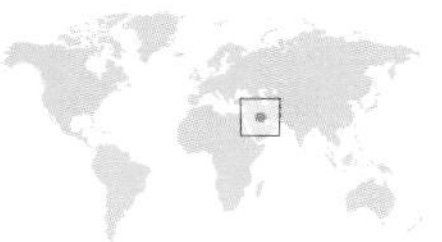

Kuwait lies on the northwest shores of The Gulf in southwest Asia. It is mainly low-lying desert, with irrigated areas along the bay, Kuwait Jun, where most people live. Summers are hot and dry, and winters are cool with some rainfall. The oil industry, which accounts for eighty per cent of exports, has largely recovered from the damage caused by the Gulf War in 1991. Income is also derived from extensive overseas investments. Japan and the USA are the main trading partners.

KYRGYZSTAN

Kyrgyz Republic

Area Sq Km	198 500	Languages	Kyrgyz, Russian, Uzbek
Area Sq Miles	76 641	Religions	Sunni Muslim, Russian Orthodox
Population	5 317 000	Currency	Kyrgyz som
Capital	Bishkek (Frunze)	Organizations	CIS, UN

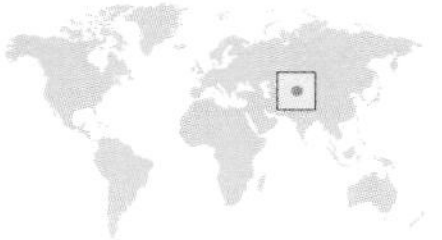

A landlocked central Asian state, Kyrgyzstan is rugged and mountainous, lying to the west of the Tien Shan mountain range. Most of the population lives in the valleys of the north and west. Summers are hot and winters cold. Agriculture (chiefly livestock farming) is the main activity. Some oil and gas, coal, gold, antimony and mercury are produced. Manufactured goods include machinery, metals and metal products, which are the main exports. Most trade is with Germany, the Russian Federation, Kazakhstan and Uzbekistan.

LAOS

Lao People's Democratic Republic

Area Sq Km	236 800	Languages	Lao, local languages
Area Sq Miles	91 429	Religions	Buddhist, traditional beliefs
Population	5 859 000	Currency	Kip
Capital	Vientiane (Viangchan)	Organizations	ASEAN, UN

A landlocked country in southeast Asia, Laos is a land of mostly forested mountains and plateaus. The climate is tropical monsoon. Most of the population lives in the Mekong valley and the low plateau in the south, where food crops, chiefly rice, are grown. Hydroelectricity from a plant on the Mekong river, timber, coffee and tin are exported. Laos relies heavily on foreign aid.

LATVIA

Republic of Latvia

Area Sq Km	63 700	Languages	Latvian, Russian
Area Sq Miles	24 595	Religions	Protestant, Roman Catholic, Russian Orthodox
Population	2 277 000	Currency	Lats
Capital	Rīga	Organizations	EU, NATO, UN

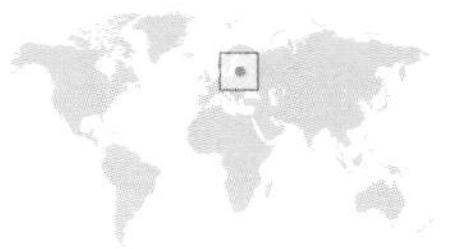

Latvia is in northern Europe, on the Baltic Sea and the Gulf of Riga. The land is flat near the coast but hilly with woods and lakes inland. The country has a modified continental climate. One-third of the people live in the capital, Rīga. Crop and livestock farming are important. There are few natural resources. Industries and main exports include food products, transport equipment, wood and wood products and textiles. The main trading partners are the Russian Federation and Germany. Latvia joined the European Union in May 2004.

LEBANON

Republic of Lebanon

Area Sq Km	10 452	Languages	Arabic, Armenian, French
Area Sq Miles	4 036	Religions	Shi'a Muslim, Sunni Muslim, Christian
Population	4 099 000	Currency	Lebanese pound
Capital	Beirut (Beyrouth)	Organizations	UN

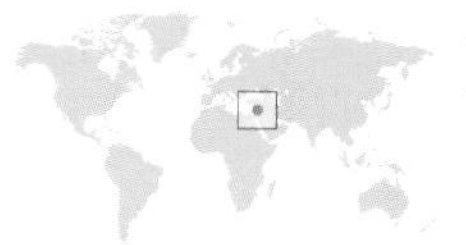

Lebanon lies on the Mediterranean coast of southwest Asia. Beyond the coastal strip, where most of the population lives, are two parallel mountain ranges, separated by the Bekaa Valley (El Beq'a). The economy and infrastructure have been recovering since the 1975–1991 civil war crippled the traditional sectors of financial services and tourism. Italy, France and the UAE are the main trading partners.

LESOTHO

Kingdom of Lesotho

Area Sq Km	30 355	Languages	Sesotho, English, Zulu
Area Sq Miles	11 720	Religions	Christian, traditional beliefs
Population	2 008 000	Currency	Loti, South African rand
Capital	Maseru	Organizations	Comm., SADC, UN

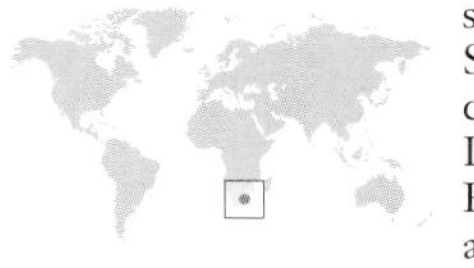

Lesotho is a landlocked state surrounded by the Republic of South Africa. It is a mountainous country lying within the Drakensberg mountain range. Farming and herding are the main activities. The economy depends heavily on South Africa for transport links and employment. A major hydroelectric plant completed in 1998 allows the sale of water to South Africa. Exports include manufactured goods (mainly clothing and road vehicles), food, live animals, wool and mohair.

LIBERIA

Republic of Liberia

Area Sq Km	111 369	Languages	English, Creole, local languages
Area Sq Miles	43 000	Religions	Traditional beliefs, Christian, Sunni Muslim
Population	3 750 000	Currency	Liberian dollar
Capital	Monrovia	Organizations	UN

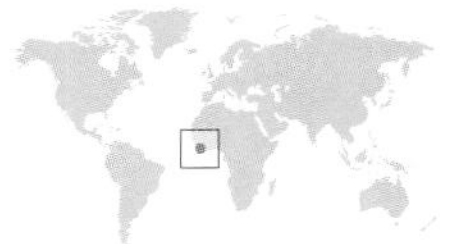

Liberia is on the Atlantic coast of west Africa. Beyond the coastal belt of sandy beaches and mangrove swamps the land rises to a forested plateau and highlands along the Guinea border. A quarter of the population lives along the coast. The climate is hot with heavy rainfall. Liberia is rich in mineral resources and forests. The economy is based on the production and export of basic products. Exports include diamonds, iron ore, rubber and timber. Liberia has a huge international debt and relies heavily on foreign aid.

LIBYA

Great Socialist People's Libyan Arab Jamahiriya

Area Sq Km	1 759 540	Languages	Arabic, Berber
Area Sq Miles	679 362	Religions	Sunni Muslim
Population	6 160 000	Currency	Libyan dinar
Capital	Tripoli (Ṭarābulus)	Organizations	OPEC, UN

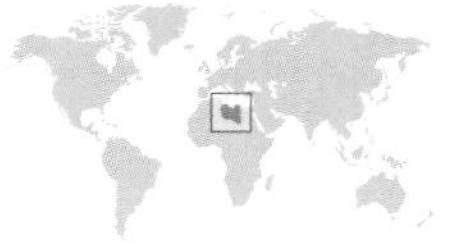

Libya lies on the Mediterranean coast of north Africa. The desert plains and hills of the Sahara dominate the landscape and the climate is hot and dry. Most of the population lives in cities near the coast, where the climate is cooler with moderate rainfall. Farming and herding, chiefly in the northwest, are important but the main industry is oil. Libya is a major producer, and oil accounts for virtually all of its export earnings. Italy and Germany are the main trading partners.

LIECHTENSTEIN

Principality of Liechtenstein

Area Sq Km	160	Languages	German
Area Sq Miles	62	Religions	Roman Catholic, Protestant
Population	35 000	Currency	Swiss franc
Capital	Vaduz	Organizations	UN

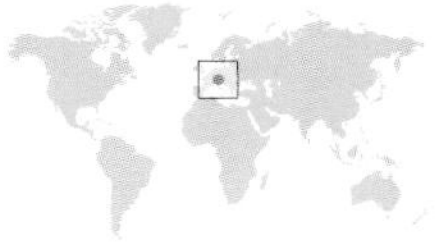

A landlocked state between Switzerland and Austria, Liechtenstein has an industrialized, free-enterprise economy. Low business taxes have attracted companies to establish offices which provide approximately one-third of state revenues. Banking is also important. Major products include precision instruments, ceramics and textiles.

LITHUANIA

Republic of Lithuania

Area Sq Km	65 200	Languages	Lithuanian, Russian, Polish
Area Sq Miles	25 174	Religions	Roman Catholic, Protestant, Russian Orthodox
Population	3 390 000	Currency	Litas
Capital	Vilnius	Organizations	EU, NATO, UN

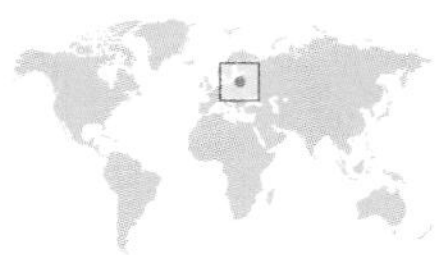

Lithuania is in northern Europe on the eastern shores of the Baltic Sea. It is mainly lowland with many lakes, rivers and marshes. Agriculture, fishing and forestry are important, but manufacturing dominates the economy. The main exports are machinery, mineral products and chemicals. The Russian Federation and Germany are the main trading partners. Lithuania joined the European Union in May 2004.

LUXEMBOURG

Grand Duchy of Luxembourg

Area Sq Km	2 586	Languages	Letzeburgish, German, French
Area Sq Miles	998	Religions	Roman Catholic
Population	467 000	Currency	Euro
Capital	Luxembourg	Organizations	EU, NATO, OECD, UN

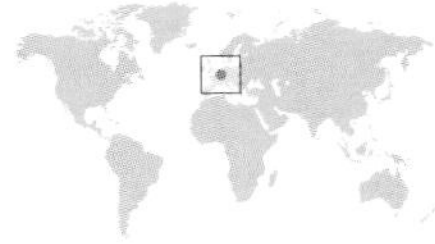

Luxembourg, a small landlocked country in western Europe, borders Belgium, France and Germany. The hills and forests of the Ardennes dominate the north, with rolling pasture to the south, where the main towns, farms and industries are found. The iron and steel industry is still important, but light industries (including textiles, chemicals and food products) are growing. Luxembourg is a major banking centre. Main trading partners are Belgium, Germany and France.

MACEDONIA (F.Y.R.O.M.)

Republic of Macedonia

Area Sq Km	25 713	Languages	Macedonian, Albanian, Turkish
Area Sq Miles	9 928	Religions	Macedonian Orthodox, Sunni Muslim
Population	2 038 000	Currency	Macedonian denar
Capital	Skopje	Organizations	NATO, UN

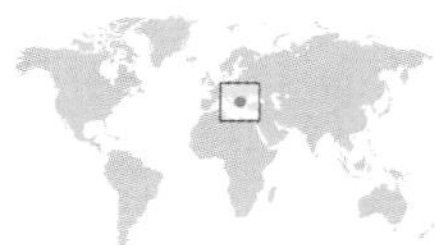

The Former Yugoslav Republic of Macedonia is a landlocked state in southern Europe. Lying within the southern Balkan Mountains, it is traversed northwest-southeast by the Vardar valley. The climate is continental. The economy is based on industry, mining and agriculture, but conflicts in the region have reduced trade and caused economic difficulties. Foreign aid and loans are now assisting in modernization and development of the country.

States and Territories

MADAGASCAR
Republic of Madagascar

Area Sq Km	587 041	Languages	Malagasy, French
Area Sq Miles	226 658	Religions	Traditional beliefs, Christian, Sunni Muslim
Population	19 683 000		
Capital	Antananarivo	Currency	Malagasy franc
		Organizations	SADC, UN

Madagascar lies off the east coast of southern Africa. The world's fourth largest island, it is mainly a high plateau, with a coastal strip to the east and scrubby plain to the west. The climate is tropical, with heavy rainfall in the north and east. Most of the population lives on the plateau. Although the amount of arable land is limited, the economy is based on agriculture. The main industries are agricultural processing, textile manufacturing and oil refining. Foreign aid is important. Exports include coffee, vanilla, cotton cloth, sugar and shrimps. France is the main trading partner.

MALAWI
Republic of Malawi

Area Sq Km	118 484	Languages	Chichewa, English, local languages
Area Sq Miles	45 747	Religions	Christian, traditional beliefs, Sunni Muslim
Population	13 925 000		
Capital	Lilongwe	Currency	Malawian kwacha
		Organizations	Comm., SADC, UN

Landlocked Malawi in central Africa is a narrow hilly country at the southern end of the Great Rift Valley. One-fifth is covered by Lake Nyasa. Most of the population lives in rural areas in the southern regions. The climate is mainly subtropical, with varying rainfall. The economy is predominantly agricultural, with tobacco, tea and sugar the main exports. Malawi is one of the world's least developed countries and relies heavily on foreign aid. South Africa is the main trading partner.

MALAYSIA
Federation of Malaysia

Area Sq Km	332 965	Languages	Malay, English, Chinese, Tamil, local languages
Area Sq Miles	128 559	Religions	Sunni Muslim, Buddhist, Hindu, Christian, traditional beliefs
Population	26 572 000		
Capital	Kuala Lumpur/ Putrajaya	Currency	Ringgit
		Organizations	APEC, ASEAN, Comm., UN

Malaysia, in southeast Asia, comprises two regions, separated by the South China Sea. The western region occupies the southern Malay Peninsula, which has a chain of mountains dividing the eastern coastal strip from wider plains to the west. East Malaysia, consisting of the states of Sabah and Sarawak in the north of the island of Borneo, is mainly rainforest-covered hills and mountains with mangrove swamps along the coast. Both regions have a tropical climate with heavy rainfall. About eighty per cent of the population lives in Peninsular Malaysia. The country is rich in natural resources and has reserves of minerals and fuels. It is an important producer of tin, oil, natural gas and tropical hardwoods. Agriculture remains a substantial part of the economy, but industry is the most important sector. The main exports are transport and electronic equipment, oil, chemicals, palm oil, wood and rubber. The main trading partners are Japan, the USA and Singapore.

MALDIVES
Republic of the Maldives

Area Sq Km	298	Languages	Divehi (Maldivian)
Area Sq Miles	115	Religions	Sunni Muslim
Population	306 000	Currency	Rufiyaa
Capital	Male	Organizations	Comm., UN

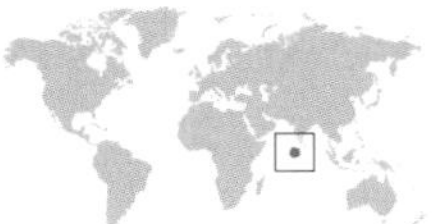

The Maldive archipelago comprises over a thousand coral atolls (around two hundred of which are inhabited), in the Indian Ocean, southwest of India. Over eighty per cent of the land area is less than one metre above sea level. The main atolls are North and South Male and Addu. The climate is hot, humid and monsoonal. There is little cultivation and almost all food is imported. Tourism has expanded rapidly and is the most important sector of the economy.

MALI
Republic of Mali

Area Sq Km	1 240 140	Languages	French, Bambara, local languages
Area Sq Miles	478 821	Religions	Sunni Muslim, traditional beliefs, Christian
Population	12 337 000		
Capital	Bamako	Currency	CFA franc
		Organizations	UN

A landlocked state in west Africa, Mali is low-lying, with a few rugged hills in the northeast. Northern regions lie within the Sahara desert. To the south, around the Niger river, are marshes and savanna grassland. Rainfall is unreliable. Most of the population lives along the Niger and Falémé rivers. Exports include cotton, livestock and gold. Mali is one of the least developed countries in the world and relies heavily on foreign aid.

MALTA
Republic of Malta

Area Sq Km	316	Languages	Maltese, English
Area Sq Miles	122	Religions	Roman Catholic
Population	407 000	Currency	Euro
Capital	Valletta	Organizations	Comm., EU, UN

The islands of Malta and Gozo lie in the Mediterranean Sea, off the coast of southern Italy. The islands have hot, dry summers and mild winters. The economy depends on foreign trade, tourism and the manufacture of electronics and textiles. Main trading partners are the USA, France and Italy. Malta joined the European Union in May 2004.

MARSHALL ISLANDS
Republic of the Marshall Islands

Area Sq Km	181	Languages	English, Marshallese
Area Sq Miles	70	Religions	Protestant, Roman Catholic
Population	59 000	Currency	United States dollar
Capital	Delap-Uliga-Djarrit	Organizations	UN

The Marshall Islands consist of over a thousand atolls, islands and islets, within two chains in the north Pacific Ocean. The main atolls are Majuro (home to half the population), Kwajalein, Jaluit, Enewetak and Bikini. The climate is tropical, with heavy autumn rainfall. About half the workforce is employed in farming or fishing. Tourism is a small source of foreign exchange and the islands depend heavily on aid from the USA.

Martinique
French Overseas Department

Area Sq Km	1 079	Languages	French, Creole
Area Sq Miles	417	Religions	Roman Catholic, traditional beliefs
Population	399 000	Currency	Euro
Capital	Fort-de-France		

Martinique, one of the Caribbean Windward Islands, has volcanic peaks in the north, a populous central plain, and hills and beaches in the south. Tourism is a major source of foreign exchange, and substantial aid is received from France. The main trading partners are France and Guadeloupe.

MAURITANIA
Islamic Arab and African Republic of Mauritania

Area Sq Km	1 030 700	Languages	Arabic, French, local languages
Area Sq Miles	397 955	Religions	Sunni Muslim
Population	3 124 000	Currency	Ouguiya
Capital	Nouakchott	Organizations	UN

Mauritania is on the Atlantic coast of northwest Africa and lies almost entirely within the Sahara desert. Oases and a fertile strip along the Senegal river to the south are the only areas suitable for cultivation. The climate is generally hot and dry. About a quarter of Mauritanians live in the capital, Nouakchott. Most of the workforce depends on livestock rearing and subsistence farming. There are large deposits of iron ore which account for more than half of total exports. Mauritania's coastal waters are among the richest fishing grounds in the world. The main trading partners are France, Japan and Italy.

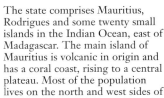

MAURITIUS
Republic of Mauritius

Area Sq Km	2 040	Languages	English, Creole, Hindi, Bhojpurī, French
Area Sq Miles	788	Religions	Hindu, Roman Catholic, Sunni Muslim
Population	1 262 000		
Capital	Port Louis	Currency	Mauritius rupee
		Organizations	Comm., SADC, UN

The state comprises Mauritius, Rodrigues and some twenty small islands in the Indian Ocean, east of Madagascar. The main island of Mauritius is volcanic in origin and has a coral coast, rising to a central plateau. Most of the population lives on the north and west sides of the island. The climate is warm and humid. The economy is based on sugar production, light manufacturing (chiefly clothing) and tourism.

Mayotte
French Departmental Collectivity

Area Sq Km	373	Languages	French, Mahorian
Area Sq Miles	144	Religions	Sunni Muslim, Christian
Population	186 026	Currency	Euro
Capital	Dzaoudzi		

Lying in the Indian Ocean off the east coast of central Africa, Mayotte is geographically part of the Comoro archipelago. The economy is based on agriculture, but Mayotte depends heavily on aid from France.

MEXICO
United Mexican States

Area Sq Km	1 972 545	Languages	Spanish, Amerindian languages
Area Sq Miles	761 604	Religions	Roman Catholic, Protestant
Population	106 535 000	Currency	Mexican peso
Capital	Mexico City	Organizations	APEC, OECD, UN

The largest country in Central America, Mexico extends south from the USA to Guatemala and Belize, and from the Pacific Ocean to the Gulf of Mexico. The greater part of the country is high plateau flanked by the western and eastern ranges of the Sierra Madre mountains. The principal lowland is the Yucatán peninsula in the southeast. The climate varies with latitude and altitude: hot and humid in the lowlands, warm on the plateau and cool with cold winters in the mountains. The north is arid, while the far south has heavy rainfall. Mexico City is the second largest conurbation in the world and the country's centre of trade and industry. Agriculture involves a fifth of the workforce; crops include grains, coffee, cotton and vegetables. Mexico is rich in minerals, including copper, zinc, lead, tin, sulphur, and silver. It is one of the world's largest producers of oil, from vast reserves in the Gulf of Mexico. The oil and petrochemical industries still dominate the economy, but a variety of manufactured goods are produced, including iron and steel, motor vehicles, textiles, chemicals and food and tobacco products. Tourism is growing in importance. Over three-quarters of all trade is with the USA.

MICRONESIA,
Federated States of

Area Sq Km	701	Languages	English, Chuukese, Pohnpeian, local languages
Area Sq Miles	271		
Population	111 000	Religions	Roman Catholic, Protestant
Capital	Palikir	Currency	United States dollar
		Organizations	UN

Micronesia comprises over six hundred atolls and islands of the Caroline Islands in the north Pacific Ocean. A third of the population lives on Pohnpei. The climate is tropical, with heavy rainfall. Fishing and subsistence farming are the main activities. Fish, garments and bananas are the main exports. Income is also derived from tourism and the licensing of foreign fishing fleets. The islands depend heavily on aid from the USA.

MOLDOVA
Republic of Moldova

Area Sq Km	33 700	Languages	Romanian, Ukrainian, Gagauz, Russian
Area Sq Miles	13 012	Religions	Romanian Orthodox, Russian Orthodox
Population	3 794 000	Currency	Moldovan leu
Capital	Chişinău (Kishinev)	Organizations	CIS, UN

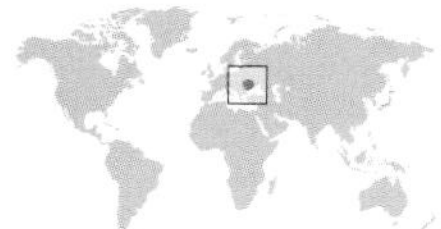

Moldova lies between Romania and Ukraine in eastern Europe. It consists of hilly steppe land, drained by the Prut and Dniester rivers. Moldova has no mineral resources, and the economy is mainly agricultural, with sugar beet, tobacco, wine and fruit the chief products. Food processing, machinery and textiles are the main industries. The Russian Federation is the main trading partner.

MONACO
Principality of Monaco

Area Sq Km	2	Languages	French, Monégasque, Italian
Area Sq Miles	1	Religions	Roman Catholic
Population	33 000	Currency	Euro
Capital	Monaco-Ville	Organizations	UN

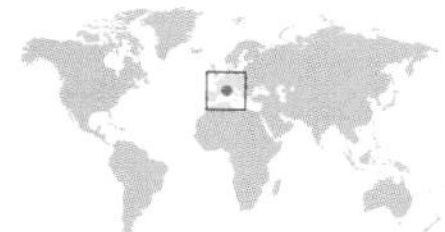

The principality occupies a rocky peninsula and a strip of land on France's Mediterranean coast. Monaco's economy depends on service industries (chiefly tourism, banking and finance) and light industry.

MONGOLIA

Area Sq Km	1 565 000	Languages	Khalka (Mongolian), Kazakh, local languages
Area Sq Miles	604 250	Religions	Buddhist, Sunni Muslim
Population	2 629 000	Currency	Tugrik (tögrög)
Capital	Ulan Bator (Ulaanbaatar)	Organizations	UN

Mongolia is a landlocked country in eastern Asia between the Russian Federation and China. Much of it is high steppe land, with mountains and lakes in the west and north. In the south is the Gobi desert. Mongolia has long, cold winters and short, mild summers. A quarter of the population lives in the capital, Ulaanbaatar. Livestock breeding and agricultural processing are important. There are substantial mineral resources. Copper and textiles are the main exports. China and the Russian Federation are the main trading partners.

MONTENEGRO

Area Sq Km	13 812	Languages	Serbian (Montenegrin), Albanian
Area Sq Miles	5 333	Religions	Montenegrin Orthodox, Sunni Muslim
Population	598 000	Currency	Euro
Capital	Podgorica	Organizations	UN

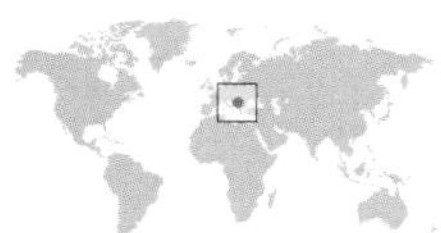

Montenegro, previously a constituent republic of the former Yugoslavia, became an independent nation in June 2006 when it opted to split from the state union of Serbia and Montenegro. Montenegro separates the much larger Serbia from the Adriatic coast. The landscape is rugged and mountainous, and the climate Mediterranean.

Montserrat
United Kingdom Overseas Territory

Area Sq Km	100	Languages	English
Area Sq Miles	39	Religions	Protestant, Roman Catholic
Population	6 000	Currency	East Caribbean dollar
Capital	Brades	Organizations	CARICOM

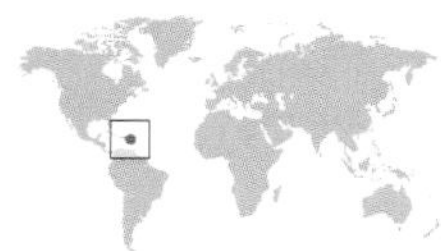

An island in the Leeward Islands group in the Lesser Antilles, in the Caribbean. From 1995 to 1997 the volcanoes in the Soufrière Hills erupted for the first time since 1630. Over sixty per cent of the island was covered in volcanic ash and Plymouth, the capital was, virtually destroyed. Many people emigrated, and the remaining population moved to the north of the island. Brades has replaced Plymouth as the temporary capital. Reconstruction is being funded by aid from the UK.

MOROCCO
Kingdom of Morocco

Area Sq Km	446 550	Languages	Arabic, Berber, French
Area Sq Miles	172 414	Religions	Sunni Muslim
Population	31 224 000	Currency	Moroccan dirham
Capital	Rabat	Organizations	UN

Lying in the northwest of Africa, Morocco has both Atlantic and Mediterranean coasts. The Atlas Mountains separate the arid south and disputed region of western Sahara from the fertile west and north, which have a milder climate. Most Moroccans live on the Atlantic coastal plain. The economy is based on agriculture, phosphate mining and tourism; the most important industries are food processing, textiles and chemicals.

MOZAMBIQUE
Republic of Mozambique

Area Sq Km	799 380	Languages	Portuguese, Makua, Tsonga, local languages
Area Sq Miles	308 642	Religions	Traditional beliefs, Roman Catholic, Sunni Muslim
Population	21 397 000	Currency	Metical
Capital	Maputo	Organizations	Comm., SADC, UN

Mozambique lies on the east coast of southern Africa. The land is mainly a savanna plateau drained by the Zambezi and Limpopo rivers, with highlands to the north. Most of the population lives on the coast or in the river valleys. In general the climate is tropical with winter rainfall, but droughts occur. The economy is based on subsistence agriculture. Exports include shrimps, cashews, cotton and sugar, but Mozambique relies heavily on aid, and remains one of the least developed countries in the world.

MYANMAR (Burma)
Union of Myanmar

Area Sq Km	676 577	Languages	Burmese, Shan, Karen, local languages
Area Sq Miles	261 228	Religions	Buddhist, Christian, Sunni Muslim
Population	48 798 000	Currency	Kyat
Capital	Rangoon (Yangôn)/ Nay Pyi Taw	Organizations	ASEAN, UN

Myanmar (Burma) is in southeast Asia, bordering the Bay of Bengal and the Andaman Sea. Most of the population lives in the valley and delta of the Irrawaddy river, which is flanked by mountains and high plateaus. The climate is hot and monsoonal, and rainforest covers much of the land. Most of the workforce is employed in agriculture. Myanmar is rich in minerals, including zinc, lead, copper and silver. Political and social unrest and lack of foreign investment have affected economic development.

NAMIBIA
Republic of Namibia

Area Sq Km	824 292	Languages	English, Afrikaans, German, Ovambo, local languages
Area Sq Miles	318 261	Religions	Protestant, Roman Catholic
Population	2 074 000	Currency	Namibian dollar
Capital	Windhoek	Organizations	Comm., SADC, UN

Namibia lies on the southern Atlantic coast of Africa. Mountain ranges separate the coastal Namib Desert from the interior plateau, bordered to the south and east by the Kalahari Desert. The country is hot and dry, but some summer rain in the north supports crops and livestock. Employment is in agriculture and fishing, although the economy is based on mineral extraction – diamonds, uranium, lead, zinc and silver. The economy is closely linked to the Republic of South Africa.

NAURU
Republic of Nauru

Area Sq Km	21	Languages	Nauruan, English
Area Sq Miles	8	Religions	Protestant, Roman Catholic
Population	10 000	Currency	Australian dollar
Capital	Yaren	Organizations	Comm., UN

Nauru is a coral island near the Equator in the Pacific Ocean. It has a fertile coastal strip and a barren central plateau. The climate is tropical. The economy is based on phosphate mining, but reserves are near exhaustion and replacement of this income is a serious long-term problem.

NEPAL
Republic of Nepal

Area Sq Km	147 181	Languages	Nepali, Maithili, Bhojpuri, English, local languages
Area Sq Miles	56 827	Religions	Hindu, Buddhist, Sunni Muslim
Population	28 196 000	Currency	Nepalese rupee
Capital	Kathmandu	Organizations	UN

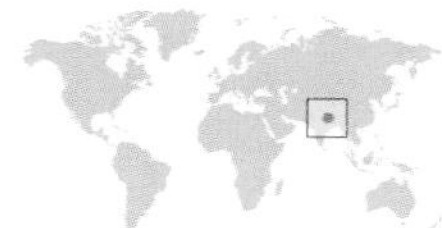

Nepal lies in the eastern Himalaya mountains between India and China. High mountains (including Everest) dominate the north. Most people live in the temperate central valleys and subtropical southern plains. The economy is based largely on agriculture and forestry. There is some manufacturing, chiefly of textiles and carpets, and tourism is important. Nepal relies heavily on foreign aid.

NETHERLANDS
Kingdom of the Netherlands

Area Sq Km	41 526	Languages	Dutch, Frisian
Area Sq Miles	16 033	Religions	Roman Catholic, Protestant, Sunni Muslim
Population	16 419 000	Currency	Euro
Capital	Amsterdam/ The Hague	Organizations	EU, NATO, OECD, UN

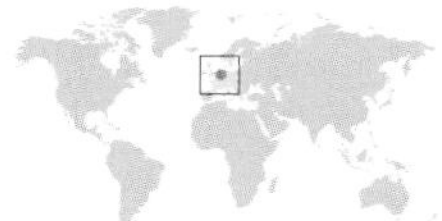

The Netherlands lies on the North Sea coast of western Europe. Apart from low hills in the far southeast, the land is flat and low-lying, much of it below sea level. The coastal region includes the delta of five rivers and polders (reclaimed land), protected by sand dunes, dykes and canals. The climate is temperate, with cool summers and mild winters. Rainfall is spread evenly throughout the year. The Netherlands is a densely populated and highly urbanized country, with the majority of the population living in the cities of Amsterdam, Rotterdam and The Hague. Horticulture and dairy farming are important activities, although they employ less than four per cent of the workforce. The Netherlands ranks as the world's third agricultural exporter, and is a leading producer and exporter of natural gas from reserves in the North Sea. The economy is based mainly on international trade and manufacturing industry. The main industries produce food products, chemicals, machinery, electrical and electronic goods and transport equipment. Germany is the main trading partner, followed by other European Union countries.

Netherlands Antilles
Self-governing Netherlands Territory - dissolved October 2010

Area Sq Km	800	Languages	Dutch, Papiamento, English
Area Sq Miles	309	Religions	Roman Catholic, Protestant
Population	192 000	Currency	Netherlands Antilles guilder
Capital	Willemstad		

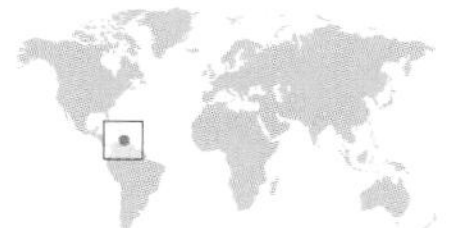

The territory comprises two island groups: Curaçao and Bonaire off the coast of Venezuela, and Saba, Sint Eustatius and Sint Maarten in the Lesser Antilles. Tourism, oil refining and offshore finance are the mainstays of the economy. The main trading partners are the USA, Venezuela and Mexico. The territory was dissolved in October 2010, being broken up into five separate direct dependencies of the Netherlands (though not fully independent). Curaçao and Sint Maarten are now self-governing Netherlands territories (the same as Aruba); Bonaire, Saba and Sint Eustatius have become special municipalities of the Netherlands, with a similar status to Dutch cities.

New Caledonia
French Overseas Collectivity

Area Sq Km	19 058	Languages	French, local languages
Area Sq Miles	7 358	Religions	Roman Catholic, Protestant, Sunni Muslim
Population	242 000	Currency	CFP franc
Capital	Nouméa		

An island group lying in the southwest Pacific, with a sub-tropical climate. New Caledonia has over one-fifth of the world's nickel reserves, and the main economic activity is metal mining. Tourism is also important. New Caledonia relies on aid from France.

NEW ZEALAND

Area Sq Km	270 534	Languages	English, Maori
Area Sq Miles	104 454	Religions	Protestant, Roman Catholic
Population	4 179 000	Currency	New Zealand dollar
Capital	Wellington	Organizations	APEC, Comm., OECD, UN

New Zealand comprises two main islands separated by the narrow Cook Strait, and a number of smaller islands. North Island, where three-quarters of the population lives, has mountain ranges, broad fertile valleys and a central plateau with hot springs and active volcanoes. South Island is also mountainous, with the Southern Alps running its entire length. The only major lowland area is the Canterbury Plains in the centre-east. The climate is generally temperate, although South Island has colder winters. Farming is the mainstay of the economy. New Zealand is one of the world's leading producers of meat (beef, lamb and mutton), wool and dairy products; fruit and fish are also important. Hydroelectric and geothermal power provide much of the country's energy needs. Other industries produce timber, wood pulp, iron, aluminium, machinery and chemicals. Tourism is the fastest growing sector of the economy. The main trading partners are Australia, the USA and Japan.

NICARAGUA

Republic of Nicaragua

Area Sq Km	130 000	Languages	Spanish, Amerindian languages
Area Sq Miles	50 193	Religions	Roman Catholic, Protestant
Population	5 603 000	Currency	Córdoba
Capital	Managua	Organizations	UN

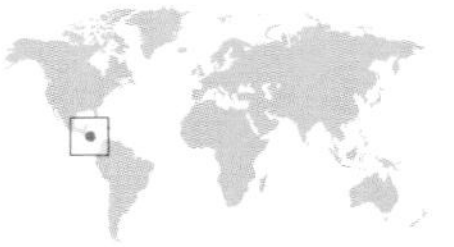

Nicaragua lies at the heart of Central America, with both Pacific and Caribbean coasts. Mountain ranges separate the east, which is largely rainforest, from the more developed western regions, which include Lake Nicaragua and some active volcanoes. The highest land is in the north. The climate is tropical. Nicaragua is one of the western hemisphere's poorest countries, and the economy is largely agricultural. Exports include coffee, seafood, cotton and bananas. The USA is the main trading partner. Nicaragua has a huge national debt, and relies heavily on foreign aid.

NIGER

Republic of Niger

Area Sq Km	1 267 000	Languages	French, Hausa, Fulani, local languages
Area Sq Miles	489 191	Religions	Sunni Muslim, traditional beliefs
Population	14 226 000	Currency	CFA franc
Capital	Niamey	Organizations	UN

A landlocked state of west Africa, Niger lies mostly within the Sahara desert, but with savanna in the south and in the Niger valley area. The mountains of the Massif de l'Aïr dominate central regions. Much of the country is hot and dry. The south has some summer rainfall, although droughts occur. The economy depends on subsistence farming and herding, and uranium exports, but Niger is one of the world's least developed countries and relies heavily on foreign aid. France is the main trading partner.

NIGERIA

Federal Republic of Nigeria

Area Sq Km	923 768	Languages	English, Hausa, Yoruba, Ibo, Fulani, local languages
Area Sq Miles	356 669	Religions	Sunni Muslim, Christian, traditional beliefs
Population	148 093 000	Currency	Naira
Capital	Abuja	Organizations	Comm., OPEC, UN

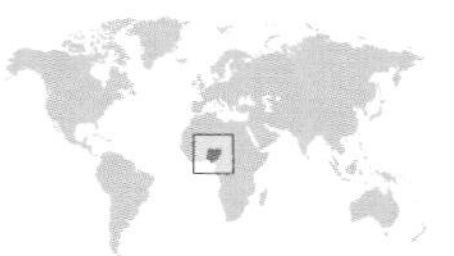

Nigeria is in west Africa, on the Gulf of Guinea, and is the most populous country in Africa. The Niger delta dominates coastal areas, fringed with sandy beaches, mangrove swamps and lagoons. Inland is a belt of rainforest which gives way to woodland or savanna on high plateaus. The far north is the semi-desert edge of the Sahara. The climate is tropical, with heavy summer rainfall in the south but low rainfall in the north. Most of the population lives in the coastal lowlands or in the west. About half the workforce is involved in agriculture, mainly growing subsistence crops. Agricultural production, however, has failed to keep up with demand, and Nigeria is now a net importer of food. Cocoa and rubber are the only significant export crops. The economy is heavily dependent on vast oil resources in the Niger delta and in shallow offshore waters, and oil accounts for over ninety per cent of export earnings. Nigeria also has natural gas reserves and some mineral deposits, but these are largely undeveloped. Industry involves mainly oil refining, chemicals (chiefly fertilizers), agricultural processing, textiles, steel manufacture and vehicle assembly. Political instability in the past has left Nigeria with heavy debts, poverty and unemployment.

Niue

Self-governing New Zealand Territory

Area Sq Km	258	Languages	English, Nivean
Area Sq Miles	100	Religions	Christian
Population	2 000	Currency	New Zealand dollar
Capital	Alofi		

Niue, one of the largest coral islands in the world, lies in the south Pacific Ocean about 500 kilometres (300 miles) east of Tonga. The economy depends on aid and remittances from New Zealand. The population is declining because of migration to New Zealand.

Norfolk Island

Australian External Territory

Area Sq Km	35	Languages	English
Area Sq Miles	14	Religions	Protestant, Roman Catholic
Population	2 523	Currency	Australian dollar
Capital	Kingston		

In the south Pacific Ocean, Norfolk Island lies between Vanuatu and New Zealand. Tourism has increased steadily and is the mainstay of the economy and provides revenues for agricultural development.

Northern Mariana Islands

United States Commonwealth

Area Sq Km	477	Languages	English, Chamorro, local languages
Area Sq Miles	184	Religions	Roman Catholic
Population	84 000	Currency	United States dollar
Capital	Capitol Hill		

A chain of islands in the northwest Pacific Ocean, extending over 550 kilometres (350 miles) north to south. The main island is Saipan. Tourism is a major industry, employing approximately half the workforce.

NORTH KOREA

Democratic People's Republic of Korea

Area Sq Km	120 538	Languages	Korean
Area Sq Miles	46 540	Religions	Traditional beliefs, Chondoist, Buddhist
Population	23 790 000	Currency	North Korean won
Capital	P'yŏngyang	Organizations	UN

Occupying the northern half of the Korean peninsula in eastern Asia, North Korea is a rugged and mountainous country. The principal lowlands and the main agricultural areas are the plains in the southwest. More than half the population lives in urban areas, mainly on the coastal plains. North Korea has a continental climate, with cold, dry winters and hot, wet summers. Approximately one-third of the workforce is involved in agriculture, mainly growing food crops on cooperative farms. Various minerals, notably iron ore, are mined and are the basis of the country's heavy industries. Exports include minerals (lead, magnesite and zinc) and metal products (chiefly iron and steel). The economy declined after 1991, when ties to the former USSR and eastern bloc collapsed, and there have been serious food shortages.

NORWAY

Kingdom of Norway

Area Sq Km	323 878	Languages	Norwegian
Area Sq Miles	125 050	Religions	Protestant, Roman Catholic
Population	4 698 000	Currency	Norwegian krone
Capital	Oslo	Organizations	NATO, OECD, UN

Norway stretches along the north and west coasts of Scandinavia, from the Arctic Ocean to the North Sea. Its extensive coastline is indented with fjords and fringed with many islands. Inland, the terrain is mountainous, with coniferous forests and lakes in the south. The only major lowland areas are along the southern North Sea and Skagerrak coasts, where most of the population lives. The climate is modified by the effect of the North Atlantic Drift ocean current. Norway has vast petroleum and natural gas resources in the North Sea. It is one of western Europe's leading producers of oil and gas, and exports of oil account for approximately half of total export earnings. Related industries include engineering (oil and gas platforms) and petrochemicals. More traditional industries process local raw materials, particularly fish, timber and minerals. Agriculture is limited, but fishing and fish farming are important. Norway is the world's leading exporter of farmed salmon. Merchant shipping and tourism are major sources of foreign exchange.

OMAN

Sultanate of Oman

Area Sq Km	309 500	Languages	Arabic, Baluchi, Indian languages
Area Sq Miles	119 499	Religions	Ibadhi Muslim, Sunni Muslim
Population	2 595 000	Currency	Omani riyal
Capital	Muscat (Masqat)	Organizations	UN

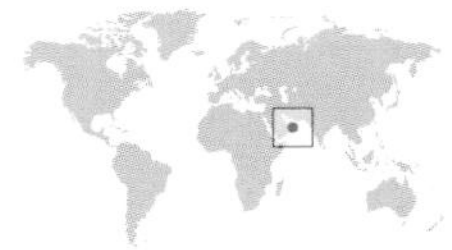

In southwest Asia, Oman occupies the east and southeast coasts of the Arabian Peninsula and an enclave north of the United Arab Emirates. Most of the land is desert, with mountains in the north and south. The climate is hot and mainly dry. Most of the population lives on the coastal strip on the Gulf of Oman. The majority depend on farming and fishing, but the oil and gas industries dominate the economy with around eighty per cent of export revenues coming from oil.

PAKISTAN

Islamic Republic of Pakistan

Area Sq Km	803 940	Languages	Urdu, Punjabi, Sindhi, Pushtu, English
Area Sq Miles	310 403	Religions	Sunni Muslim, Shi'a Muslim, Christian, Hindu
Population	163 902 000	Currency	Pakistani rupee
Capital	Islamabad	Organizations	Comm., UN

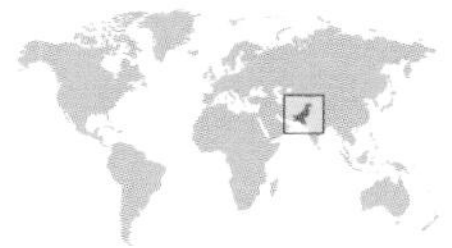

Pakistan is in the northwest part of the Indian subcontinent in south Asia, on the Arabian Sea. The east and south are dominated by the great basin of the Indus river system. This is the main agricultural area and contains most of the predominantly rural population. To the north the land rises to the mountains of the Karakoram, Hindu Kush and Himalaya mountains. The west is semi-desert plateaus and mountain ranges. The climate ranges between dry desert, and arctic tundra on the mountain tops. Temperatures are generally warm and rainfall is monsoonal. Agriculture is the main sector of the economy, employing approximately half of the workforce, and is based on extensive irrigation schemes. Pakistan is one of the world's leading producers of cotton and a major exporter of rice. Pakistan produces natural gas and has a variety of mineral deposits including coal and gold, but they are little developed. The main industries are textiles and clothing manufacture and food processing, with fabrics and ready-made clothing the leading exports. Pakistan also produces leather goods, fertilizers, chemicals, paper and precision instruments. The country depends heavily on foreign aid and remittances from workers abroad.

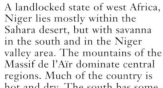

PALAU

Republic of Palau

Area Sq Km	497	Languages	Palauan, English
Area Sq Miles	192	Religions	Roman Catholic, Protestant, traditional beliefs
Population	20 000	Currency	United States dollar
Capital	Melekeok	Organizations	UN

Palau comprises over three hundred islands in the western Caroline Islands, in the west Pacific Ocean. The climate is tropical. The economy is based on farming, fishing and tourism, but Palau is heavily dependent on aid from the USA.

PANAMA

Republic of Panama

Area Sq Km	77 082	Languages	Spanish, English, Amerindian languages
Area Sq Miles	29 762	Religions	Roman Catholic, Protestant, Sunni Muslim
Population	3 343 000	Currency	Balboa
Capital	Panama City	Organizations	UN

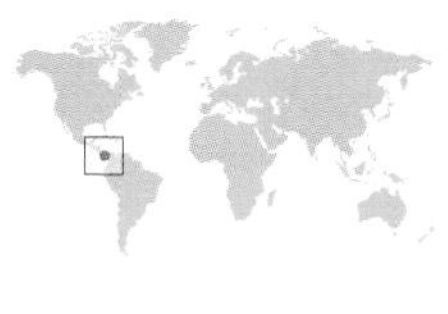

Panama is the most southerly state in central America and has Pacific and Caribbean coasts. It is hilly, with mountains in the west and jungle near the Colombian border. The climate is tropical. Most of the population lives on the drier Pacific side. The economy is based mainly on services related to the Panama Canal: shipping, banking and tourism. Exports include bananas, shrimps, coffee, clothing and fish products. The USA is the main trading partner.

PAPUA NEW GUINEA

Independent State of Papua New Guinea

Area Sq Km	462 840	Languages	English, Tok Pisin (Creole), local languages
Area Sq Miles	178 704	Religions	Protestant, Roman Catholic, traditional beliefs
Population	6 331 000	Currency	Kina
Capital	Port Moresby	Organizations	APEC, Comm., UN

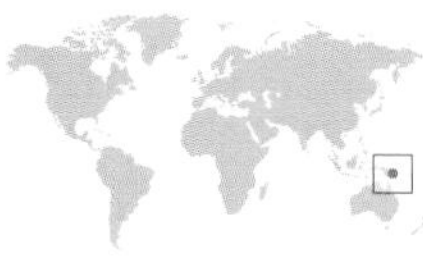

Papua New Guinea occupies the eastern half of the island of New Guinea and includes many island groups. It has a forested and mountainous interior, bordered by swampy plains, and a tropical monsoon climate. Most of the workforce are farmers. Timber, copra, coffee and cocoa are important, but exports are dominated by minerals, chiefly gold and copper. The country depends on foreign aid. Australia, Japan and Singapore are the main trading partners.

PARAGUAY

Republic of Paraguay

Area Sq Km	406 752	Languages	Spanish, Guaraní
Area Sq Miles	157 048	Religions	Roman Catholic, Protestant
Population	6 127 000	Currency	Guaraní
Capital	Asunción	Organizations	UN

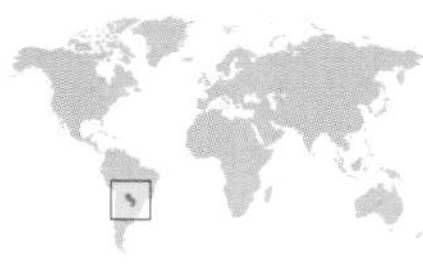

Paraguay is a landlocked country in central South America, bordering Bolivia, Brazil and Argentina. The Paraguay river separates a sparsely populated western zone of marsh and flat alluvial plains from a more developed, hilly and forested region to the east and south. The climate is subtropical. Virtually all electricity is produced by hydroelectric plants, and surplus power is exported to Brazil and Argentina. The hydroelectric dam at Itaipú is one of the largest in the world. The mainstay of the economy is agriculture and related industries. Exports include cotton, soya bean and edible oil products, timber and meat. Brazil and Argentina are the main trading partners.

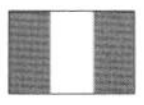

PERU

Republic of Peru

Area Sq Km	1 285 216	Languages	Spanish, Quechua, Aymara
Area Sq Miles	496 225	Religions	Roman Catholic, Protestant
Population	27 903 000	Currency	Nuevo sol
Capital	Lima	Organizations	APEC, UN

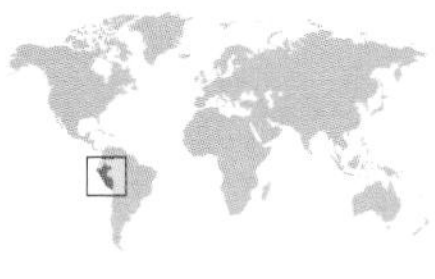

Peru lies on the Pacific coast of South America. Most Peruvians live on the coastal strip and on the plateaus of the high Andes mountains. East of the Andes is the Amazon rainforest. The coast is temperate with low rainfall while the east is hot, humid and wet. Agriculture involves one-third of the workforce and fishing is also important. Agriculture and fishing have both been disrupted by the El Niño climatic effect in recent years. Sugar, cotton, coffee and, illegally, coca are the main cash crops. Copper and copper products, fishmeal, zinc products, coffee, petroleum and its products, and textiles are the main exports. The USA and the European Union are the main trading partners.

PHILIPPINES

Republic of the Philippines

Area Sq Km	300 000	Languages	English, Filipino, Tagalog, Cebuano, local languages
Area Sq Miles	115 831	Religions	Roman Catholic, Protestant, Sunni Muslim, Aglipayan
Population	87 960 000	Currency	Philippine peso
Capital	Manila	Organizations	APEC, ASEAN, UN

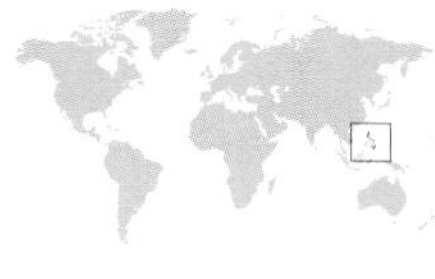

The Philippines, in southeast Asia, consists of over seven thousand islands and atolls lying between the South China Sea and the Pacific Ocean. The islands of Luzon and Mindanao account for two-thirds of the land area. They and nine other fairly large islands are mountainous and forested. There are active volcanoes, and earthquakes and tropical storms are common. Most of the population lives in the plains on the larger islands or on the coastal strips. The climate is hot and humid with heavy monsoonal rainfall. Rice, coconuts, sugar cane, pineapples and bananas are the main agricultural crops, and fishing is also important. Main exports are electronic equipment, machinery and transport equipment, garments and coconut products. Foreign aid and remittances from workers abroad are important to the economy, which faces problems of high population growth rate and high unemployment. The USA and Japan are the main trading partners.

Pitcairn Islands

United Kingdom Overseas Territory

Area Sq Km	45	Languages	English
Area Sq Miles	17	Religions	Protestant
Population	48	Currency	New Zealand dollar
Capital	Adamstown		

An island group in the southeast Pacific Ocean consisting of Pitcairn Island and three uninhabited islands. It was originally settled by mutineers from HMS *Bounty* in 1790.

POLAND

Polish Republic

Area Sq Km	312 683	Languages	Polish, German
Area Sq Miles	120 728	Religions	Roman Catholic, Polish Orthodox
Population	38 082 000	Currency	Złoty
Capital	Warsaw (Warszawa)	Organizations	EU, NATO, OECD, UN

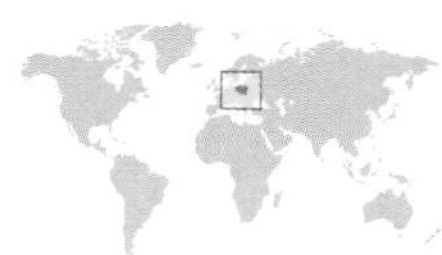

Poland lies on the Baltic coast of eastern Europe. The Oder (Odra) and Vistula (Wisła) river deltas dominate the coast. Inland, much of the country is low-lying, with woods and lakes. In the south the land rises to the Sudeten Mountains and the western part of the Carpathian Mountains, which form the borders with the Czech Republic and Slovakia respectively. The climate is continental. Around a quarter of the workforce is involved in agriculture, and exports include livestock products and sugar. The economy is heavily industrialized, with mining and manufacturing accounting for forty per cent of national income. Poland is one of the world's major producers of coal, and also produces copper, zinc, lead, sulphur and natural gas. The main industries are machinery and transport equipment, shipbuilding, and metal and chemical production. Exports include machinery and transport equipment, manufactured goods, food and live animals. Germany is the main trading partner. Poland joined the European Union in May 2004.

PORTUGAL

Portuguese Republic

Area Sq Km	88 940	Languages	Portuguese
Area Sq Miles	34 340	Religions	Roman Catholic, Protestant
Population	10 623 000	Currency	Euro
Capital	Lisbon (Lisboa)	Organizations	EU, NATO, OECD, UN

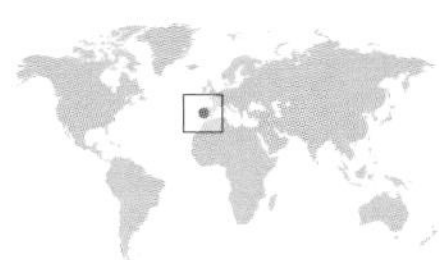

Portugal lies in the western part of the Iberian peninsula in southwest Europe, has an Atlantic coastline and is bordered by Spain to the north and east. The island groups of the Azores and Madeira are parts of Portugal. On the mainland, the land north of the river Tagus (Tejo) is mostly highland, with extensive forests of pine and cork. South of the river is undulating lowland. The climate in the north is cool and moist; the south is warmer, with dry, mild winters. Most Portuguese live near the coast, and more than one-third of the total population lives around the capital, Lisbon (Lisboa). Agriculture, fishing and forestry involve approximately ten per cent of the workforce. Mining and manufacturing are the main sectors of the economy. Portugal produces kaolin, copper, tin, zinc, tungsten and salt. Exports include textiles, clothing and footwear, electrical machinery and transport equipment, cork and wood products, and chemicals. Service industries, chiefly tourism and banking, are important to the economy, as are remittances from workers abroad. Most trade is with other European Union countries.

Puerto Rico

United States Commonwealth

Area Sq Km	9 104	Languages	Spanish, English
Area Sq Miles	3 515	Religions	Roman Catholic, Protestant
Population	3 991 000	Currency	United States dollar
Capital	San Juan		

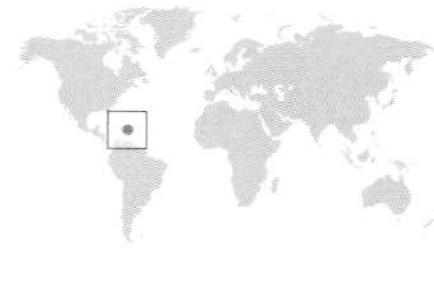

The Caribbean island of Puerto Rico has a forested, hilly interior, coastal plains and a tropical climate. Half of the population lives in the San Juan area. The economy is based on manufacturing (chiefly chemicals, electronics and food), tourism and agriculture. The USA is the main trading partner.

QATAR

State of Qatar

Area Sq Km	11 437	Languages	Arabic
Area Sq Miles	4 416	Religions	Sunni Muslim
Population	841 000	Currency	Qatari riyal
Capital	Doha (Ad Dawḩah)	Organizations	OPEC, UN

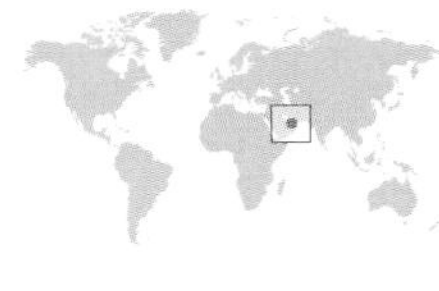

Qatar occupies a peninsula in southwest Asia that extends northwards from east-central Saudi Arabia into The Gulf. The land is flat and barren with sand dunes and salt pans. The climate is hot and mainly dry. Most people live in the area of the capital, Doha. The economy is heavily dependent on oil and natural gas production and the oil-refining industry. Income also comes from overseas investment. Japan is the largest trading partner.

Réunion

French Overseas Department

Area Sq Km	2 551	Languages	French, Creole
Area Sq Miles	985	Religions	Roman Catholic
Population	807 000	Currency	Euro
Capital	St-Denis		

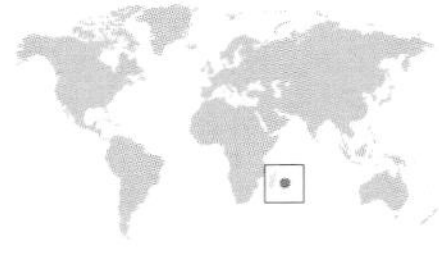

The Indian Ocean island of Réunion is mountainous, with coastal lowlands and a warm climate. The economy depends on tourism, French aid, and exports of sugar. In 2005 France transferred the administration of various small uninhabited islands in the seas around Madagascar from Réunion to the French Southern and Antarctic Lands.

ROMANIA

Area Sq Km	237 500	Languages	Romanian, Hungarian
Area Sq Miles	91 699	Religions	Romanian Orthodox, Protestant, Roman Catholic
Population	21 438 000	Currency	Romanian leu
Capital	Bucharest (București)	Organizations	EU, NATO, UN

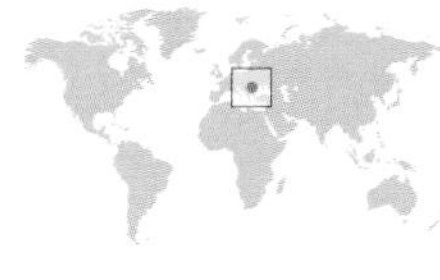

Romania lies in eastern Europe, on the northwest coast of the Black Sea. Mountains separate the Transylvanian Basin in the centre of the country from the populous plains of the east and south and from the Danube delta. The climate is continental. Romania has mineral resources (zinc, lead, silver and gold) and oil and natural gas reserves. Economic development has been slow and sporadic, but measures to accelerate change were introduced in 1999. Agriculture employs over one-third of the workforce. The main exports are textiles, mineral products, chemicals, machinery and footwear. The main trading partners are Germany and Italy.

RUSSIAN FEDERATION

Area Sq Km	17 075 400	Languages	Russian, Tatar, Ukrainian, local languages
Area Sq Miles	6 592 849	Religions	Russian Orthodox, Sunni Muslim, Protestant
Population	142 499 000	Currency	Russian rouble
Capital	Moscow (Moskva)	Organizations	APEC, CIS, UN

The Russian Federation occupies much of eastern Europe and all of northern Asia, and is the world's largest country. It borders fourteen countries to the west and south and has long coastlines on the Arctic and Pacific Oceans to the north and east. European Russia lies west of the Ural Mountains. To the south the land rises to uplands and the Caucasus mountains on the border with Georgia and Azerbaijan. East of the Urals lies the flat West Siberian Plain and the Central Siberian Plateau. In the south-east is Lake Baikal, the world's deepest lake, and the Sayan ranges on the border with Kazakhstan and Mongolia. Eastern Siberia is rugged and mountainous, with many active volcanoes in the Kamchatka Peninsula. The country's major rivers are the Volga in the west and the Ob', Irtysh, Yenisey, Lena and Amur in Siberia. The climate and vegetation range between arctic tundra in the north and semi-arid steppe towards the Black and Caspian Sea coasts in the south. In general, the climate is continental with extreme temperatures. The majority of the population (the eighth largest in the world), and industry and agriculture are concentrated in European Russia. The economy is dependent on exploitation of raw materials and on heavy industry. Russia has a wealth of mineral resources, although they are often difficult to exploit because of climate and remote locations. It is one of the world's leading producers of petroleum, natural gas and coal as well as iron ore, nickel, copper, bauxite, and many precious and rare metals. Forests cover over forty per cent of the land area and supply an important timber, paper and pulp industry. Approximately eight per cent of the land is suitable for cultivation, but farming is generally inefficient and food, especially grains, must be imported. Fishing is important and Russia has a large fleet operating around the world. The transition to a market economy has been slow and difficult, with considerable underemployment. As well as mining and extractive industries there is a wide range of manufacturing industry, from steel mills to aircraft and space vehicles, shipbuilding, synthetic fabrics, plastics, cotton fabrics, consumer durables, chemicals and fertilizers. Exports include fuels, metals, machinery, chemicals and forest products. The most important trading partners include Germany, the USA and Belarus.

RWANDA

Republic of Rwanda

Area Sq Km	26 338	Languages	Kinyarwanda, French, English
Area Sq Miles	10 169	Religions	Roman Catholic, traditional beliefs, Protestant
Population	9 725 000	Currency	Rwandan franc
Capital	Kigali	Organizations	Comm., UN

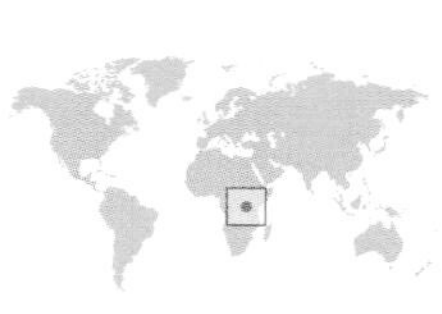

Rwanda, the most densely populated country in Africa, is situated in the mountains and plateaus to the east of the western branch of the Great Rift Valley in east Africa. The climate is warm with a summer dry season. Rwanda depends on subsistence farming, coffee and tea exports, light industry and foreign aid. The country is slowly recovering from serious internal conflict which caused devastation in the early 1990s.

St-Barthélemy

Area Sq Km	21	Languages	French
Area Sq Miles	8	Religions	Roman Catholic
Population	6 852	Currency	Euro
Capital	Gustavia		

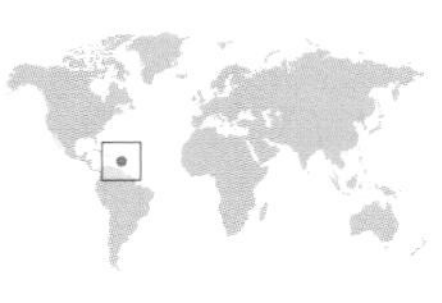

An island in the Leeward Islands in the Lesser Antilles, in the Caribbean south of St-Martin. It was separated from Guadeloupe politically in 2007. Tourism is the main economic activity.

St Helena, Ascension and Tristan da Cunha

United Kingdom Overseas Territory

Area Sq Km	307	Languages	English
Area Sq Miles	119	Religions	Protestant, Roman Catholic
Population	7 000	Currency	St Helena pound, Pound sterling
Capital	Jamestown		

St Helena along with Ascension and Tristan da Cunha are isolated island groups lying in the south Atlantic Ocean. St Helena is a rugged island of volcanic origin. The main activity is fishing, but the economy relies on financial aid from the UK. Main trading partners are the UK and South Africa.

ST KITTS AND NEVIS

Federation of St Kitts and Nevis

Area Sq Km	261	Languages	English, Creole
Area Sq Miles	101	Religions	Protestant, Roman Catholic
Population	50 000	Currency	East Caribbean dollar
Capital	Basseterre	Organizations	CARICOM, Comm., UN

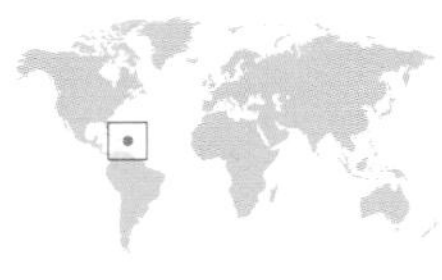

St Kitts and Nevis are in the Leeward Islands, in the Caribbean. Both volcanic islands are mountainous and forested, with sandy beaches and a warm, wet climate. About three-quarters of the population lives on St Kitts. Agriculture is the main activity, with sugar the main product. Tourism and manufacturing (chiefly garments and electronic components) and offshore banking are important activities.

ST LUCIA

Area Sq Km	616	Languages	English, Creole
Area Sq Miles	238	Religions	Roman Catholic, Protestant
Population	165 000	Currency	East Caribbean dollar
Capital	Castries	Organizations	CARICOM, Comm., UN

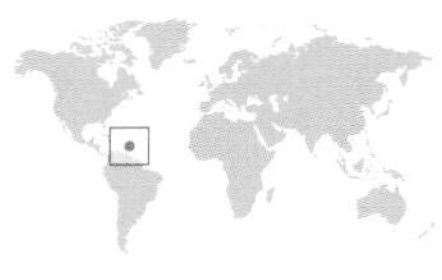

St Lucia, one of the Windward Islands in the Caribbean Sea, is a volcanic island with forested mountains, hot springs, sandy beaches and a wet tropical climate. Agriculture is the main activity, with bananas accounting for approximately forty per cent of export earnings. Tourism, agricultural processing and light manufacturing are increasingly important.

St-Martin

Area Sq Km	54	Languages	French
Area Sq Miles	21	Religions	Roman Catholic
Population	33 102	Currency	Euro
Capital	Marigot		

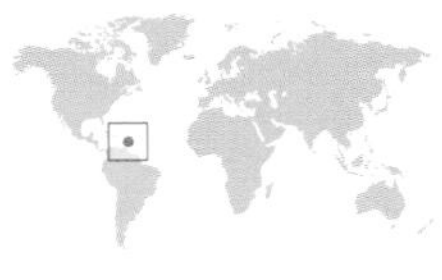

The northern part of St-Martin, one of the Leeward Islands, in the Caribbean. The other part of the island is part of the Netherlands Antilles (Sint Maarten). It was separated from Guadeloupe politically in 2007. Tourism is the main source of income.

St Pierre and Miquelon

French Territorial Collectivity

Area Sq Km	242	Languages	French
Area Sq Miles	93	Religions	Roman Catholic
Population	6 000	Currency	Euro
Capital	St-Pierre		

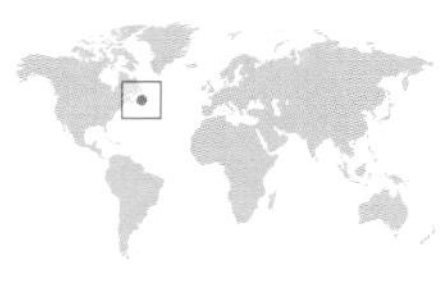

A group of islands off the south coast of Newfoundland in eastern Canada. The islands are largely unsuitable for agriculture, and fishing and fish processing are the most important activities. The islands rely heavily on financial assistance from France.

ST VINCENT AND THE GRENADINES

Area Sq Km	389	Languages	English, Creole
Area Sq Miles	150	Religions	Protestant, Roman Catholic
Population	120 000	Currency	East Caribbean dollar
Capital	Kingstown	Organizations	CARICOM, Comm., UN

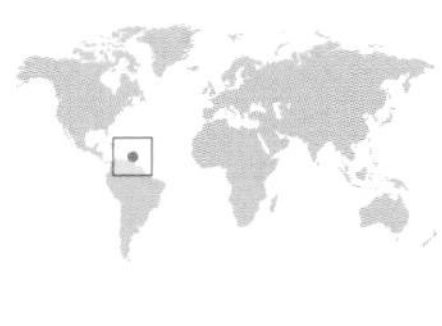

St Vincent, whose territory includes islets and cays in the Grenadines, is in the Windward Islands, in the Caribbean. St Vincent itself is forested and mountainous, with an active volcano, Soufrière. The climate is tropical and wet. The economy is based mainly on agriculture and tourism. Bananas account for approximately one-third of export earnings and arrowroot is also important. Most trade is with the USA and other CARICOM countries.

SAMOA

Independent State of Samoa

Area Sq Km	2 831	Languages	Samoan, English
Area Sq Miles	1 093	Religions	Protestant, Roman Catholic
Population	187 000	Currency	Tala
Capital	Apia	Organizations	Comm., UN

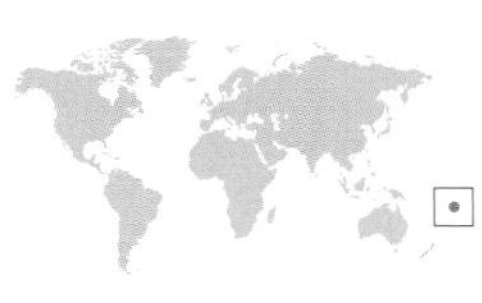

Samoa consists of two larger mountainous and forested islands, Savai'i and Upolu, and seven smaller islands, in the south Pacific Ocean. Over half the population lives on Upolu. The climate is tropical. The economy is based on agriculture, with some fishing and light manufacturing. Traditional exports are coconut products, fish and beer. Tourism is increasing, but the islands depend on workers' remittances and foreign aid.

SAN MARINO

Republic of San Marino

Area Sq Km	61	Languages	Italian
Area Sq Miles	24	Religions	Roman Catholic
Population	31 000	Currency	Euro
Capital	San Marino	Organizations	UN

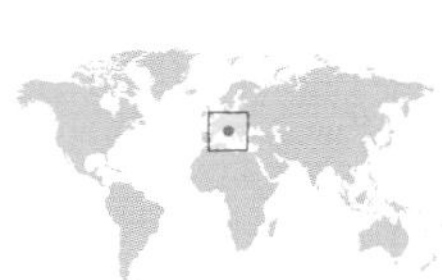

Landlocked San Marino lies in northeast Italy. A third of the people live in the capital. There is some agriculture and light industry, but most income comes from tourism. Italy is the main trading partner.

SÃO TOMÉ AND PRÍNCIPE

Democratic Republic of São Tomé and Príncipe

Area Sq Km	964	Languages	Portuguese, Creole
Area Sq Miles	372	Religions	Roman Catholic, Protestant
Population	158 000	Currency	Dobra
Capital	São Tomé	Organizations	UN

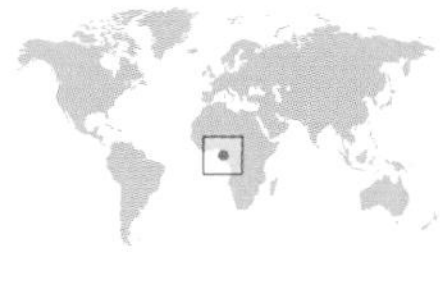

The two main islands and adjacent islets lie off the coast of west Africa in the Gulf of Guinea. São Tomé is the larger island, with over ninety per cent of the population. Both São Tomé and Príncipe are mountainous and tree-covered, and have a hot and humid climate. The economy is heavily dependent on cocoa, which accounts for around ninety per cent of export earnings.

SAUDI ARABIA

Kingdom of Saudi Arabia

Area Sq Km	2 200 000	Languages	Arabic
Area Sq Miles	849 425	Religions	Sunni Muslim, Shi'a Muslim
Population	24 735 000	Currency	Saudi Arabian riyal
Capital	Riyadh (Ar Riyāḍ)	Organizations	OPEC, UN

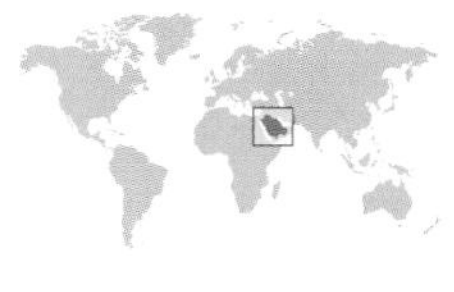

Saudi Arabia occupies most of the Arabian Peninsula in southwest Asia. The terrain is desert or semi-desert plateaus, which rise to mountains running parallel to the Red Sea in the west and slope down to plains in the southeast and along The Gulf in the east. Over eighty per cent of the population lives in urban areas. There are around four million foreign workers in Saudi Arabia, employed mainly in the oil and service industries. Summers are hot, winters are warm and rainfall is low. Saudi Arabia has the world's largest reserves of oil and significant natural gas reserves, both onshore and in The Gulf. Crude oil and refined products account for over ninety per cent of export earnings. Other industries and irrigated agriculture are being encouraged, but most food and raw materials are imported. Saudi Arabia has important banking and commercial interests. Japan and the USA are the main trading partners.

SENEGAL

Republic of Senegal

Area Sq Km	196 720	Languages	French, Wolof, Fulani, local languages
Area Sq Miles	75 954	Religions	Sunni Muslim, Roman Catholic, traditional beliefs
Population	12 379 000	Currency	CFA franc
Capital	Dakar	Organizations	UN

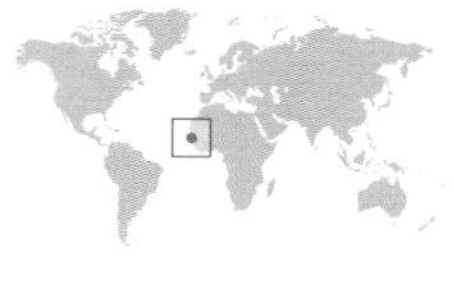

Senegal lies on the Atlantic coast of west Africa. The north is arid semi-desert, while the south is mainly fertile savanna bushland. The climate is tropical with summer rains, although droughts occur. One-fifth of the population lives in and around Dakar, the capital and main port. Fish, groundnuts and phosphates are the main exports. France is the main trading partner.

SERBIA
Republic of Serbia

Area Sq Km	77 453	Languages	Serbian, Hungarian
Area Sq Miles	29 904	Religions	Serbian Orthodox, Roman Catholic, Sunni Muslim
Population	7 788 448	Currency	Serbian dinar
Capital	Beograd (Belgrade)	Organizations	UN

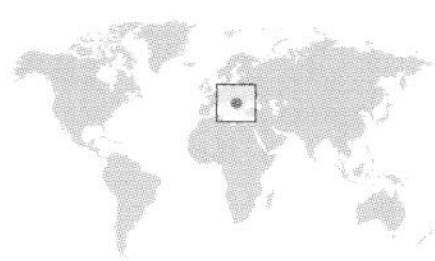

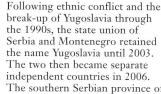

Following ethnic conflict and the break-up of Yugoslavia through the 1990s, the state union of Serbia and Montenegro retained the name Yugoslavia until 2003. The two then became separate independent countries in 2006. The southern Serbian province of Kosovo declared its independence from Serbia in February 2008. The landscape is rugged, mountainous and forested in the south, while the north is low-lying and drained by the Danube river system.

SEYCHELLES
Republic of Seychelles

Area Sq Km	455	Languages	English, French, Creole
Area Sq Miles	176	Religions	Roman Catholic, Protestant
Population	87 000	Currency	Seychelles rupee
Capital	Victoria	Organizations	Comm., SADC, UN

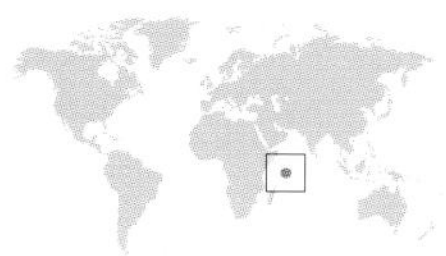

The Seychelles comprises an archipelago of over one hundred granitic and coral islands in the western Indian Ocean. Over ninety per cent of the population lives on the main island, Mahé. The climate is hot and humid with heavy rainfall. The economy is based mainly on tourism, fishing and light manufacturing.

SIERRA LEONE
Republic of Sierra Leone

Area Sq Km	71 740	Languages	English, Creole, Mende, Temne, local languages
Area Sq Miles	27 699	Religions	Sunni Muslim, traditional beliefs
Population	5 866 000	Currency	Leone
Capital	Freetown	Organizations	Comm., UN

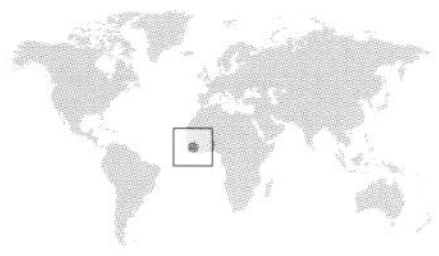

Sierra Leone lies on the Atlantic coast of west Africa. Its coastline is heavily indented and is lined with mangrove swamps. Inland is a forested area rising to savanna plateaus, with mountains to the northeast. The climate is tropical and rainfall is heavy. Most of the workforce is involved in subsistence farming. Cocoa and coffee are the main cash crops. Diamonds and rutile (titanium ore) are the main exports. Sierra Leone is one of the world's poorest countries, and the economy relies on substantial foreign aid.

SINGAPORE
Republic of Singapore

Area Sq Km	639	Languages	Chinese, English, Malay, Tamil
Area Sq Miles	247	Religions	Buddhist, Taoist, Sunni Muslim, Christian, Hindu
Population	4 436 000	Currency	Singapore dollar
Capital	Singapore	Organizations	APEC, ASEAN, Comm., UN

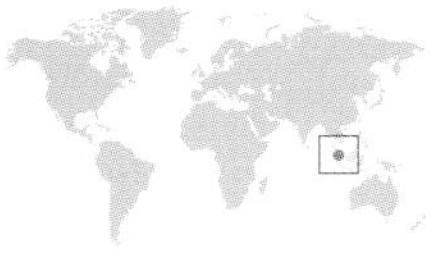

The state comprises the main island of Singapore and over fifty other islands, lying off the southern tip of the Malay Peninsula in southeast Asia. Singapore is generally low-lying and includes land reclaimed from swamps and the sea. It is hot and humid, with heavy rainfall throughout the year. There are fish farms and vegetable gardens in the north and east of the island, but most food is imported. Singapore also lacks mineral and energy resources. Manufacturing industries and services are the main sectors of the economy. Their rapid development has fuelled the nation's impressive economic growth during recent decades. Main industries include electronics, oil refining, chemicals, pharmaceuticals, ship repair, food processing and textiles. Singapore is also a major financial centre. Its port is one of the world's largest and busiest and acts as an entrepôt for neighbouring states. Tourism is also important. Japan, the USA and Malaysia are the main trading partners.

SLOVAKIA
Slovak Republic

Area Sq Km	49 035	Languages	Slovakian, Hungarian, Czech
Area Sq Miles	18 933	Religions	Roman Catholic, Protestant, Orthodox
Population	5 390 000	Currency	Slovakian koruna
Capital	Bratislava	Organizations	EU, NATO, OECD, UN

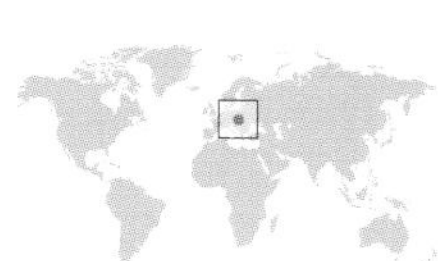

A landlocked country in central Europe, Slovakia is mountainous in the north, but low-lying in the southwest. The climate is continental. There is a range of manufacturing industries, and the main exports are machinery and transport equipment, but in recent years there have been economic difficulties and growth has been slow. Slovakia joined the European Union in May 2004. Most trade is with other EU countries, especially the Czech Republic.

SLOVENIA
Republic of Slovenia

Area Sq Km	20 251	Languages	Slovenian, Croatian, Serbian
Area Sq Miles	7 819	Religions	Roman Catholic, Protestant
Population	2 002 000	Currency	Euro
Capital	Ljubljana	Organizations	EU, NATO, UN

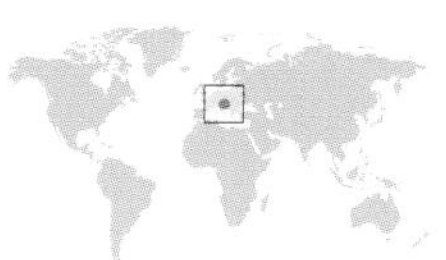

Slovenia lies in the northwest Balkan Mountains of southern Europe and has a short coastline on the Adriatic Sea. It is mountainous and hilly, with lowlands on the coast and in the Sava and Drava river valleys. The climate is generally continental inland and Mediterranean nearer the coast. The main agricultural products are potatoes, grain and sugar beet; the main industries include metal processing, electronics and consumer goods. Trade has been re-orientated towards western markets and the main trading partners are Germany and Italy. Slovenia joined the European Union in May 2004.

SOLOMON ISLANDS

Area Sq Km	28 370	Languages	English, Creole, local languages
Area Sq Miles	10 954	Religions	Protestant, Roman Catholic
Population	496 000	Currency	Solomon Islands dollar
Capital	Honiara	Organizations	Comm., UN

The state consists of the Solomon, Santa Cruz and Shortland Islands in the southwest Pacific Ocean. The six main islands are volcanic, mountainous and forested, although Guadalcanal, the most populous, has a large lowland area. The climate is generally hot and humid. Subsistence farming, forestry and fishing predominate. Exports include timber products, fish, copra and palm oil. The islands depend on foreign aid.

SOMALIA
Somali Republic

Area Sq Km	637 657	Languages	Somali, Arabic
Area Sq Miles	246 201	Religions	Sunni Muslim
Population	8 699 000	Currency	Somali shilling
Capital	Mogadishu (Muqdisho)	Organizations	UN

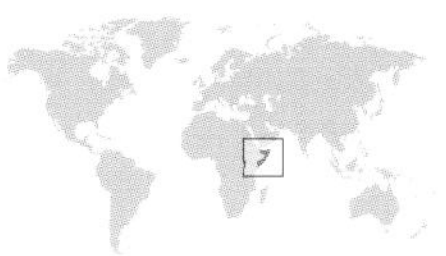

Somalia is in northeast Africa, on the Gulf of Aden and Indian Ocean. It consists of a dry scrubby plateau, rising to highlands in the north. The climate is hot and dry, but coastal areas and the Jubba and Webi Shabeelle river valleys support crops and most of the population. Subsistence farming and livestock rearing are the main activities. Exports include livestock and bananas. Frequent drought and civil war have prevented economic development. Somalia is one of the poorest, most unstable and least developed countries in the world.

SOUTH AFRICA, REPUBLIC OF

Area Sq Km	1 219 090	Languages	Afrikaans, English, nine other official languages
Area Sq Miles	470 693	Religions	Protestant, Roman Catholic, Sunni Muslim, Hindu
Population	48 577 000	Currency	Rand
Capital	Pretoria (Tshwane)/ Cape Town	Organizations	Comm., SADC, UN

The Republic of South Africa occupies most of the southern part of Africa. It surrounds Lesotho and has a long coastline on the Atlantic and Indian Oceans. Much of the land is a vast plateau, covered with grassland or bush and drained by the Orange and Limpopo river systems. A fertile coastal plain rises to mountain ridges in the south and east, including Table Mountain near Cape Town and the Drakensberg range in the east. Gauteng is the most populous province, with Johannesburg and Pretoria its main cities. South Africa has warm summers and mild winters. Most of the country has the majority of its rainfall in summer, but the coast around Cape Town has winter rains. South Africa has the largest economy in Africa, although wealth is unevenly distributed and unemployment is very high. Agriculture employs approximately one-third of the workforce, and produce includes fruit, wine, wool and maize. The country is the world's leading producer of gold and chromium and an important producer of diamonds. Many other minerals are also mined. The main industries are mineral and food processing, chemicals, electrical equipment, textiles and motor vehicles. Financial services are also important.

SOUTH KOREA
Republic of Korea

Area Sq Km	99 274	Languages	Korean
Area Sq Miles	38 330	Religions	Buddhist, Protestant, Roman Catholic
Population	48 224 000	Currency	South Korean won
Capital	Seoul (Sŏul)	Organizations	APEC, OECD, UN

The state consists of the southern half of the Korean Peninsula in eastern Asia and many islands lying off the western and southern coasts in the Yellow Sea. The terrain is mountainous, although less rugged than that of North Korea. Population density is high and the country is highly urbanized; most of the population lives on the western coastal plains and in the river basins of the Han-gang in the northwest and the Naktong-gang in the southeast. The climate is continental, with hot, wet summers and dry, cold winters. Arable land is limited by the mountainous terrain, but because of intensive farming South Korea is nearly self-sufficient in food. Sericulture (silk) is important, as is fishing, which contributes to exports. South Korea has few mineral resources, except for coal and tungsten. It has achieved high economic growth based mainly on export manufacturing. The main manufactured goods are cars, electronic and electrical goods, ships, steel, chemicals and toys, as well as textiles, clothing, footwear and food products. The USA and Japan are the main trading partners.

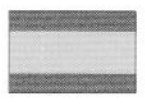

SPAIN
Kingdom of Spain

Area Sq Km	504 782	Languages	Spanish, Castilian, Catalan, Galician, Basque
Area Sq Miles	194 897	Religions	Roman Catholic
Population	44 279 000	Currency	Euro
Capital	Madrid	Organizations	EU, NATO, OECD, UN

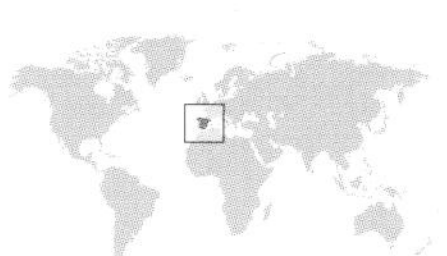

Spain occupies the greater part of the Iberian peninsula in southwest Europe, with coastlines on the Atlantic Ocean and Mediterranean Sea. It includes the Balearic Islands in the Mediterranean, the Canary Islands in the Atlantic, and two enclaves in north Africa (Ceuta and Melilla). Much of the mainland is a high plateau drained by the Douro (Duero), Tagus (Tajo) and Guadiana rivers. The plateau is interrupted by a low mountain range and bounded to the east and north also by mountains, including the Pyrenees, which form the border with France and Andorra. The main lowland areas are the Ebro basin in the northeast, the eastern coastal plains and the Guadalquivir basin in the southwest. Over three-quarters of the population lives in urban areas. The plateau experiences hot summers and cold winters. Conditions are cooler and wetter to the north, and warmer and drier to the south. Agriculture involves about ten per cent of the workforce, and fruit, vegetables and wine are exported. Fishing is an important industry, and Spain has a large fishing fleet. Mineral resources include lead, copper, mercury and fluorspar. Some oil is produced, but Spain has to import most energy needs. The economy is based mainly on manufacturing and services. The principal products are machinery, transport equipment, motor vehicles and food products, with a wide variety of other manufactured goods. With approximately fifty million visitors a year, tourism is a major industry. Banking and commerce are also important. Approximately seventy per cent of trade is with other European Union countries.

SRI LANKA
Democratic Socialist Republic of Sri Lanka

Area Sq Km	65 610	Languages	Sinhalese, Tamil, English
Area Sq Miles	25 332	Religions	Buddhist, Hindu, Sunni Muslim, Roman Catholic
Population	19 299 000	Currency	Sri Lankan rupee
Capital	Sri Jayewardenepura Kotte	Organizations	Comm., UN

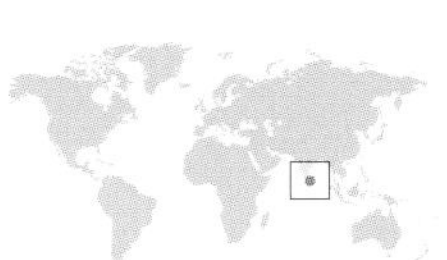

Sri Lanka lies in the Indian Ocean off the southeast coast of India in south Asia. It has rolling coastal plains, with mountains in the centre-south. The climate is hot and monsoonal. Most people live on the west coast. Manufactures (chiefly textiles and clothing), tea, rubber, copra and gems are exported. The economy relies on foreign aid and workers' remittances. The USA and the UK are the main trading partners.

SUDAN
Republic of the Sudan

Area Sq Km	2 505 813	Languages	Arabic, Dinka, Nubian, Beja, Nuer, local languages
Area Sq Miles	967 500	Religions	Sunni Muslim, traditional beliefs, Christian
Population	38 560 000	Currency	Sudanese pound (Sudani)
Capital	Khartoum	Organizations	UN

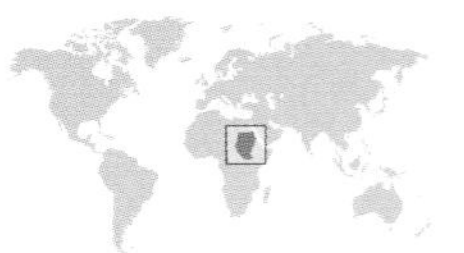

Africa's largest country, the Sudan is in the northeast of the continent, on the Red Sea. It lies within the upper Nile basin, much of which is arid plain but with swamps to the south. Mountains lie to the northeast, west and south. The climate is hot and arid with light summer rainfall, and droughts occur. Most people live along the Nile and are farmers and herders. Cotton, gum arabic, livestock and other agricultural products are exported. The government is working with foreign investors to develop oil resources, but civil war in the south and ethnic cleansing in Darfur continue to restrict the growth of the economy. Main trading partners are Saudi Arabia, China and Libya.

SURINAME
Republic of Suriname

Area Sq Km	163 820	Languages	Dutch, Surinamese, English, Hindi
Area Sq Miles	63 251	Religions	Hindu, Roman Catholic, Protestant, Sunni Muslim
Population	458 000	Currency	Suriname guilder
Capital	Paramaribo	Organizations	CARICOM, UN

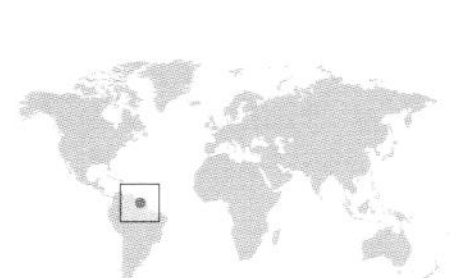

Suriname, on the Atlantic coast of northern South America, consists of a swampy coastal plain (where most of the population lives), central plateaus, and highlands in the south. The climate is tropical, and rainforest covers much of the land. Bauxite mining is the main industry, and alumina and aluminium are the chief exports, with shrimps, rice, bananas and timber also exported. The main trading partners are the Netherlands, Norway and the USA.

SWAZILAND
Kingdom of Swaziland

Area Sq Km	17 364	Languages	Swazi, English
Area Sq Miles	6 704	Religions	Christian, traditional beliefs
Population	1 141 000	Currency	Emalangeni, South African rand
Capital	Mbabane	Organizations	Comm., SADC, UN

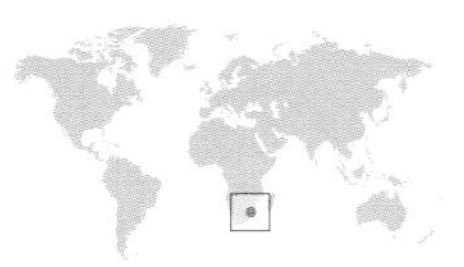

Landlocked Swaziland in southern Africa lies between Mozambique and the Republic of South Africa. Savanna plateaus descend from mountains in the west towards hill country in the east. The climate is subtropical, but temperate in the mountains. Subsistence farming predominates. Asbestos and diamonds are mined. Exports include sugar, fruit and wood pulp. Tourism and workers' remittances are important to the economy. Most trade is with South Africa.

SWEDEN
Kingdom of Sweden

Area Sq Km	449 964	Languages	Swedish
Area Sq Miles	173 732	Religions	Protestant, Roman Catholic
Population	9 119 000	Currency	Swedish krona
Capital	Stockholm	Organizations	EU, OECD, UN

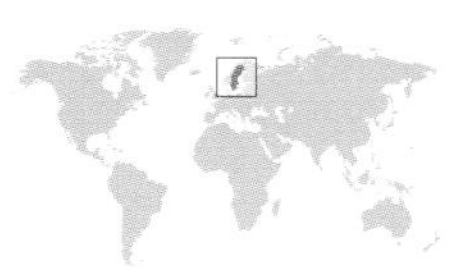

Sweden occupies the eastern part of the Scandinavian peninsula in northern Europe and borders the Baltic Sea, the Gulf of Bothnia, and the Kattegat and Skagerrak, connecting with the North Sea. Forested mountains cover the northern half, part of which lies within the Arctic Circle. The southern part of the country is a lowland lake region where most of the population lives. Sweden has warm summers and cold winters, which are more severe in the north. Natural resources include coniferous forests, mineral deposits and water resources. Some dairy products, meat, cereals and vegetables are produced in the south. The forests supply timber for export and for the important pulp, paper and furniture industries. Sweden is an important producer of iron ore and copper. Zinc, lead, silver and gold are also mined. Machinery and transport equipment, chemicals, pulp and wood, and telecommunications equipment are the main exports. The majority of trade is with other European Union countries.

SWITZERLAND
Swiss Confederation

Area Sq Km	41 293	Languages	German, French, Italian, Romansch
Area Sq Miles	15 943	Religions	Roman Catholic, Protestant
Population	7 484 000	Currency	Swiss franc
Capital	Bern	Organizations	OECD, UN

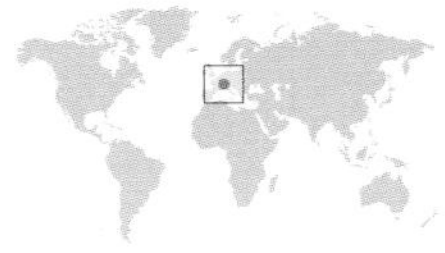

Switzerland is a mountainous landlocked country in west central Europe. The southern regions lie within the Alps, while the northwest is dominated by the Jura mountains. The rest of the land is a high plateau, where most of the population lives. The climate varies greatly, depending on altitude and relief, but in general summers are mild and winters are cold with heavy snowfalls. Switzerland has one of the highest standards of living in the world, yet it has few mineral resources, and most food and industrial raw materials are imported. Manufacturing makes the largest contribution to the economy. Engineering is the most important industry, producing precision instruments and heavy machinery. Other important industries are chemicals and pharmaceuticals. Banking and financial services are very important, and Zürich is one of the world's leading banking cities. Tourism, and international organizations based in Switzerland, are also major foreign currency earners. Germany is the main trading partner.

SYRIA
Syrian Arab Republic

Area Sq Km	185 180	Languages	Arabic, Kurdish, Armenian
Area Sq Miles	71 498	Religions	Sunni Muslim, Shi'a Muslim, Christian
Population	19 929 000	Currency	Syrian pound
Capital	Damascus (Dimashq)	Organizations	UN

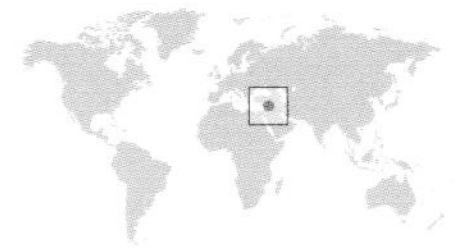

Syria is in southwest Asia, has a short coastline on the Mediterranean Sea, and stretches inland to a plateau traversed northwest-southeast by the Euphrates river. Mountains flank the southwest borders with Lebanon and Israel. The climate is Mediterranean in coastal regions, hotter and drier inland. Most Syrians live on the coast or in the river valleys. Cotton, cereals and fruit are important products, but the main exports are petroleum and related products, and textiles.

TAIWAN
Republic of China

Area Sq Km	36 179	Languages	Mandarin, Min, Hakka, local languages
Area Sq Miles	13 969	Religions	Buddhist, Taoist, Confucian, Christian
Population	22 880 009	Currency	Taiwan dollar
Capital	T'aipei	Organizations	APEC

The east Asian state consists of the island of Taiwan, separated from mainland China by the Taiwan Strait, and several much smaller islands. Much of Taiwan is mountainous and forested. Densely populated coastal plains in the west contain the bulk of the population and most economic activity. Taiwan has a tropical monsoon climate, with warm, wet summers and mild winters. Agriculture is highly productive. The country is virtually self-sufficient in food and exports some products. Coal, oil and natural gas are produced and a few minerals are mined, but none of them are of great significance to the economy. Taiwan depends heavily on imports of raw materials and exports of manufactured goods. The main manufactures are electrical and electronic goods, including television sets, personal computers and calculators, textiles, fertilizers, clothing, footwear and toys. The main trading partners are the USA, Japan and Germany. The People's Republic of China claims Taiwan as its 23rd Province.

TAJIKISTAN
Republic of Tajikistan

Area Sq Km	143 100	Languages	Tajik, Uzbek, Russian
Area Sq Miles	55 251	Religions	Sunni Muslim
Population	6 736 000	Currency	Somoni
Capital	Dushanbe	Organizations	CIS, UN

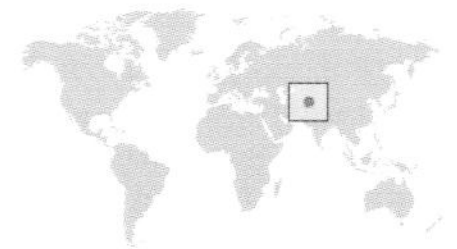

Landlocked Tajikistan in central Asia is a mountainous country, dominated by the mountains of the Alai Range and the Pamir. In the less mountainous western areas summers are warm, although winters are cold. Agriculture is the main sector of the economy, chiefly cotton growing and cattle breeding. Mineral deposits include lead, zinc, and uranium. Processed metals, textiles and clothing are the main manufactured goods; the main exports are aluminium and cotton. Uzbekistan, Kazakhstan and the Russian Federation are the main trading partners.

TANZANIA
United Republic of Tanzania

Area Sq Km	945 087	Languages	Swahili, English, Nyamwezi, local languages
Area Sq Miles	364 900	Religions	Shi'a Muslim, Sunni Muslim, traditional beliefs, Christian
Population	40 454 000	Currency	Tanzanian shilling
Capital	Dodoma	Organizations	Comm., SADC, UN

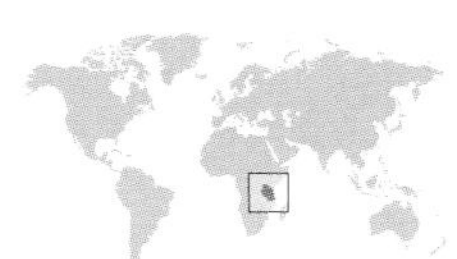

Tanzania lies on the coast of east Africa and includes the island of Zanzibar in the Indian Ocean. Most of the mainland is a savanna plateau lying east of the Great Rift Valley. In the north, near the border with Kenya, is Kilimanjaro, the highest mountain in Africa. The climate is tropical. The economy is predominantly based on agriculture, which employs an estimated ninety per cent of the workforce. Agricultural processing and gold and diamond mining are the main industries, although tourism is growing. Coffee, cotton, cashew nuts and tobacco are the main exports, with cloves from Zanzibar. Most export trade is with India and the UK. Tanzania depends heavily on foreign aid.

THAILAND
Kingdom of Thailand

Area Sq Km	513 115	Languages	Thai, Lao, Chinese, Malay, Mon-Khmer languages
Area Sq Miles	198 115	Religions	Buddhist, Sunni Muslim
Population	63 884 000	Currency	Baht
Capital	Bangkok (Krung Thep)	Organizations	APEC, ASEAN, UN

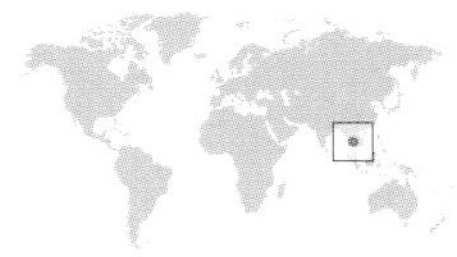

The largest country in the Indo-China peninsula, Thailand has coastlines on the Gulf of Thailand and Andaman Sea. Central Thailand is dominated by the Chao Phraya river basin, which contains Bangkok, the capital city and centre of most economic activity. To the east is a dry plateau drained by tributaries of the Mekong river, while to the north, west and south, extending down most of the Malay peninsula, are forested hills and mountains. Many small islands line the coast. The climate is hot, humid and monsoonal. About half the workforce is involved in agriculture. Fishing and fish processing are important. Thailand produces natural gas, some oil and lignite, minerals (chiefly tin, tungsten and baryte) and gemstones. Manufacturing is the largest contributor to national income, with electronics, textiles, clothing and footwear, and food processing the main industries. With around seven million visitors a year, tourism is the major source of foreign exchange. Thailand is one of the world's leading exporters of rice and rubber, and a major exporter of maize and tapioca. Japan and the USA are the main trading partners.

TOGO
Republic of Togo

Area Sq Km	56 785	Languages	French, Ewe, Kabre, local languages
Area Sq Miles	21 925	Religions	Traditional beliefs, Christian, Sunni Muslim
Population	6 585 000	Currency	CFA franc
Capital	Lomé	Organizations	UN

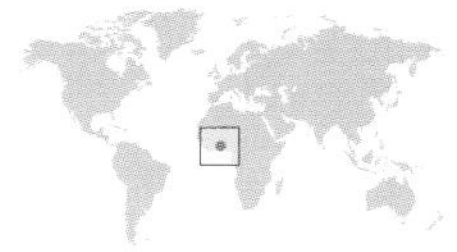

Togo is a long narrow country in west Africa with a short coastline on the Gulf of Guinea. The interior consists of plateaus rising to mountainous areas. The climate is tropical, and is drier inland. Agriculture is the mainstay of the economy. Phosphate mining and food processing are the main industries. Cotton, phosphates, coffee and cocoa are the main exports. Lomé, the capital, is an entrepôt trade centre.

Tokelau
New Zealand Overseas Territory

Area Sq Km	10	Languages	English, Tokelauan
Area Sq Miles	4	Religions	Christian
Population	1 000	Currency	New Zealand dollar

Tokelau consists of three atolls, Atafu, Nukunonu and Fakaofa, lying in the Pacific Ocean north of Samoa. Subsistence agriculture is the main activity, and the islands rely on aid from New Zealand and remittances from workers overseas.

TONGA
Kingdom of Tonga

Area Sq Km	748	Languages	Tongan, English
Area Sq Miles	289	Religions	Protestant, Roman Catholic
Population	100 000	Currency	Pa'anga
Capital	Nuku'alofa	Organizations	Comm., UN

Tonga comprises some one hundred and seventy islands in the south Pacific Ocean, northeast of New Zealand. The three main groups are Tongatapu (where sixty per cent of Tongans live), Ha'apai and Vava'u. The climate is warm and wet, and the economy relies heavily on agriculture. Tourism and light industry are also important to the economy. Exports include squash, fish, vanilla beans and root crops. Most trade is with New Zealand, Japan and Australia.

TRINIDAD AND TOBAGO
Republic of Trinidad and Tobago

Area Sq Km	5 130	Languages	English, Creole, Hindi
Area Sq Miles	1 981	Religions	Roman Catholic, Hindu, Protestant, Sunni Muslim
Population	1 333 000		
Capital	Port of Spain	Currency	Trinidad and Tobago dollar
		Organizations	CARICOM, Comm., UN

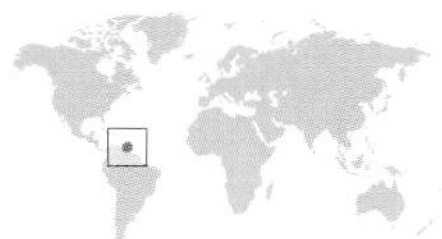

Trinidad, the most southerly Caribbean island, lies off the Venezuelan coast. It is hilly in the north, with a central plain. Tobago, to the northeast, is smaller, more mountainous and less developed. The climate is tropical. The main crops are cocoa, sugar cane, coffee, fruit and vegetables. Oil and petrochemical industries dominate the economy. Tourism is also important. The USA is the main trading partner.

TUNISIA
Tunisian Republic

Area Sq Km	164 150	Languages	Arabic, French
Area Sq Miles	63 379	Religions	Sunni Muslim
Population	10 327 000	Currency	Tunisian dinar
Capital	Tunis	Organizations	UN

Tunisia is on the Mediterranean coast of north Africa. The north is mountainous with valleys and coastal plains, has a Mediterranean climate and is the most populous area. The south is hot and arid. Oil and phosphates are the main resources, and the main crops are olives and citrus fruit. Tourism is an important industry. Exports include petroleum products, textiles, fruit and phosphorus. Most trade is with European Union countries.

TURKEY
Republic of Turkey

Area Sq Km	779 452	Languages	Turkish, Kurdish
Area Sq Miles	300 948	Religions	Sunni Muslim, Shi'a Muslim
Population	74 877 000	Currency	Lira
Capital	Ankara	Organizations	NATO, OECD, UN

Turkey occupies a large peninsula of southwest Asia and has coastlines on the Black, Mediterranean and Aegean Seas. It includes eastern Thrace, which is in southeastern Europe and is separated from the rest of the country by the Bosporus, the Sea of Marmara and the Dardanelles. The Asian mainland consists of the semi-arid Anatolian plateau, flanked to the north, south and east by mountains. Over forty per cent of Turks live in central Anatolia and on the Marmara and Aegean coastal plains. The coast has a Mediterranean climate, but inland conditions are more extreme with hot, dry summers and cold, snowy winters. Agriculture involves about forty per cent of the workforce, and products include cotton, grain, tobacco, fruit, nuts and livestock. Turkey is a leading producer of chromium, iron ore, lead, tin, borate, and baryte while coal is also mined. The main manufactured goods are clothing, textiles, food products, steel and vehicles. Tourism is a major industry, with nine million visitors a year. Germany and the USA are the main trading partners. Remittances from workers abroad are important to the economy.

TURKMENISTAN
Republic of Turkmenistan

Area Sq Km	488 100	Languages	Turkmen, Uzbek, Russian
Area Sq Miles	188 456	Religions	Sunni Muslim, Russian Orthodox
Population	4 965 000	Currency	Turkmen manat
Capital	Aşgabat (Ashkhabad)	Organizations	UN

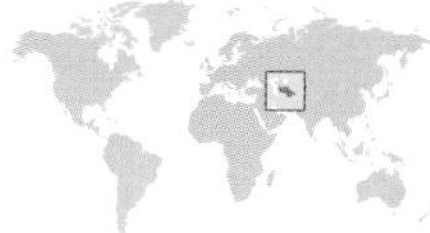

Turkmenistan, in central Asia, comprises the plains of the Karakum Desert, the foothills of the Kopet Dag mountains in the south, the Amudar'ya valley in the north and the Caspian Sea plains in the west. The climate is dry, with extreme temperatures. The economy is based mainly on irrigated agriculture (chiefly cotton growing), and natural gas and oil. Main exports are natural gas, oil and cotton fibre. Ukraine, Iran, Turkey and the Russian Federation are the main trading partners.

Turks and Caicos Islands
United Kingdom Overseas Territory

Area Sq Km	430	Languages	English
Area Sq Miles	166	Religions	Protestant
Population	26 000	Currency	United States dollar
Capital	Grand Turk (Cockburn Town)		

The state consists of over forty low-lying islands and cays in the northern Caribbean. Only eight islands are inhabited, and two-fifths of the people live on Grand Turk and Salt Cay. The climate is tropical, and the economy is based on tourism, fishing and offshore banking.

TUVALU

Area Sq Km	25	Languages	Tuvaluan, English
Area Sq Miles	10	Religions	Protestant
Population	11 000	Currency	Australian dollar
Capital	Vaiaku	Organizations	Comm., UN

Tuvalu comprises nine low-lying coral atolls in the south Pacific Ocean. One-third of the population lives on Funafuti, and most people depend on subsistence farming and fishing. The islands export copra, stamps and clothing, but rely heavily on foreign aid. Most trade is with Fiji, Australia and New Zealand.

UGANDA
Republic of Uganda

Area Sq Km	241 038	Languages	English, Swahili, Luganda, local languages
Area Sq Miles	93 065		
Population	30 884 000	Religions	Roman Catholic, Protestant, Sunni Muslim, traditional beliefs
Capital	Kampala		
		Currency	Ugandan shilling
		Organizations	Comm., UN

A landlocked country in east Africa, Uganda consists of a savanna plateau with mountains and lakes. The climate is warm and wet. Most people live in the southern half of the country. Agriculture employs around eighty per cent of the workforce and dominates the economy. Coffee, tea, fish and fish products are the main exports. Uganda relies heavily on aid.

UKRAINE

Area Sq Km	603 700	Languages	Ukrainian, Russian
Area Sq Miles	233 090	Religions	Ukrainian Orthodox, Ukrainian Catholic, Roman Catholic
Population	46 205 000		
Capital	Kiev (Kyiv)	Currency	Hryvnia
		Organizations	CIS, UN

The country lies on the Black Sea coast of eastern Europe. Much of the land is steppe, generally flat and treeless, but with rich black soil, and it is drained by the river Dnieper. Along the border with Belarus are forested, marshy plains. The only uplands are the Carpathian Mountains in the west and smaller ranges on the Crimean peninsula. Summers are warm and winters are cold, with milder conditions in the Crimea. About a quarter of the population lives in the mainly industrial areas around Donets'k, Kiev and Dnipropetrovs'k. The Ukraine is rich in natural resources: fertile soil, substantial mineral and natural gas deposits, and forests. Agriculture and livestock rearing are important, but mining and manufacturing are the dominant sectors of the economy. Coal, iron and manganese mining, steel and metal production, machinery, chemicals and food processing are the main industries. The Russian Federation is the main trading partner.

UNITED ARAB EMIRATES
Federation of Emirates

Area Sq Km	77 700	Languages	Arabic, English
Area Sq Miles	30 000	Religions	Sunni Muslim, Shi'a Muslim
Population	4 380 000	Currency	United Arab Emirates dirham
Capital	Abu Dhabi (Abū Ẓabī)	Organizations	OPEC, UN

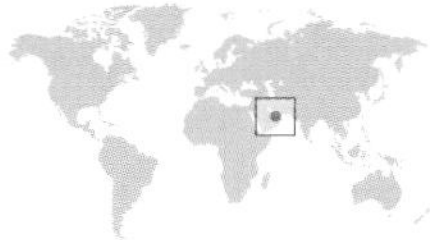

The UAE lies on the Gulf coast of the Arabian Peninsula. Six emirates are on The Gulf, while the seventh, Fujairah, is on the Gulf of Oman. Most of the land is flat desert with sand dunes and salt pans. The only hilly area is in the northeast. Over eighty per cent of the population lives in three of the emirates - Abu Dhabi, Dubai and Sharjah. Summers are hot and winters are mild, with occasional rainfall in coastal areas. Fruit and vegetables are grown in oases and irrigated areas, but the Emirates' wealth is based on hydrocarbons found in Abu Dhabi, Dubai, Sharjah and Ras al Khaimah. The UAE is one of the major oil producers in the Middle East. Dubai is an important entrepôt trade centre The main trading partner is Japan.

Abu Dhabi (Emirate)
Area Sq Km (Sq Miles) 67 340 (26 000) | Population 1 292 119 | Capital Abu Dhabi (Abū Ẓabī)

Ajman (Emirate)
Area Sq Km (Sq Miles) 259 (100) | Population 189 849 | Capital Ajman

Dubai (Emirate)
Area Sq Km (Sq Miles) 3 885 (1 500) | Population 1 200 309 | Capital Dubai

Fujairah (Emirate)
Area Sq Km (Sq Miles) 1 165 (450) | Population 118 617 | Capital Fujairah

Ra's al Khaymah (Emirate)
Area Sq Km (Sq Miles) 1 684 (650) | Population 197 571 | Capital Ra's al Khaymah

Sharjah (Emirate)
Area Sq Km (Sq Miles) 2 590 (1 000) | Population 724 859 | Capital Sharjah

Umm al Qaywayn (Emirate)
Area Sq Km (Sq Miles) 777 (300) | Population 45 756 | Capital Umm al Qaywayn

UNITED KINGDOM
United Kingdom of Great Britain and Northern Ireland

Area Sq Km	243 609	Languages	English, Welsh, Gaelic
Area Sq Miles	94 058	Religions	Protestant, Roman Catholic, Muslim
Population	60 769 000	Currency	Pound sterling
Capital	London	Organizations	Comm., EU, NATO, OECD, UN

The United Kingdom, in northwest Europe, occupies the island of Great Britain, part of Ireland, and many small adjacent islands. Great Britain comprises England, Scotland and Wales. England covers over half the land area and supports over four-fifths of the population, at its densest in the southeast. The English landscape is flat or rolling with some uplands, notably the Cheviot Hills on the Scottish border, the Pennines in the centre-north, and the hills of the Lake District in the northwest. Scotland consists of southern uplands, central lowlands, the Highlands (which include the UK's highest peak) and many islands. Wales is a land of hills, mountains and river valleys. Northern Ireland contains uplands, plains and the UK's largest lake, Lough Neagh. The climate of the UK is mild, wet and variable. There are few mineral deposits, but important energy resources. Agricultural activities involve sheep and cattle rearing, dairy farming, and crop and fruit growing in the east and southeast. Productivity is high, but approximately one-third of food is imported. The UK produces petroleum and natural gas from reserves in the North Sea and is self-sufficient in energy in net terms. Major manufactures are food and drinks, motor vehicles and parts, aerospace equipment, machinery, electronic and electrical equipment, and chemicals and chemical products. However, the economy is dominated by service industries, including banking, insurance, finance and business services. London, the capital, is one of the world's major financial centres. Tourism is also a major industry, with approximately twenty-five million visitors a year. International trade is also important, equivalent to one-third of national income. Over half of the UK's trade is with other European Union countries.

England (Constituent country)
Area Sq Km (Sq Miles) 130 433 (50 360)   Population 50 431 700   Capital London

Northern Ireland (Province)
Area Sq Km (Sq Miles) 13 576 (5 242)   Population 1 724 400   Capital Belfast

Scotland (Constituent country)
Area Sq Km (Sq Miles) 78 822 (30 433)   Population 5 094 800   Capital Edinburgh

Wales (Principality)
Area Sq Km (Sq Miles) 20 778 (8 022)   Population 2 958 600   Capital Cardiff

UNITED STATES OF AMERICA
Federal Republic

Area Sq Km	9 826 635	Languages	English, Spanish
Area Sq Miles	3 794 085	Religions	Protestant, Roman Catholic, Sunni Muslim, Jewish
Population	305 826 000	Currency	United States dollar
Capital	Washington D.C.	Organizations	APEC, NATO, OECD, UN

The USA comprises forty-eight contiguous states in North America, bounded by Canada and Mexico, plus the states of Alaska, to the northwest of Canada, and Hawaii, in the north Pacific Ocean. The populous eastern states cover the Atlantic coastal plain (which includes the Florida peninsula and the Gulf of Mexico coast) and the Appalachian Mountains. The central states occupy a vast interior plain drained by the Mississippi-Missouri river system. To the west lie the Rocky Mountains, separated from the Pacific coastal ranges by intermontane plateaus. The Pacific coastal zone is also mountainous, and prone to earthquakes. Hawaii is a group of some twenty volcanic islands. Climatic conditions range between arctic in Alaska to desert in the intermontane plateaus. Most of the USA has a temperate climate, although the interior has continental conditions. There are abundant natural resources, including major reserves of minerals and energy resources. The USA has the largest and most technologically advanced economy in the world, based on manufacturing and services. Although agriculture accounts for approximately two per cent of national income, productivity is high and the USA is a net exporter of food, chiefly grains and fruit. Cotton is the major industrial crop. The USA produces iron ore, copper, lead, zinc, and many other minerals. It is a major producer of coal, petroleum and natural gas, although being the world's biggest energy user it imports significant quantities of petroleum and its products. Manufacturing is diverse. The main industries are petroleum, steel, motor vehicles, aerospace, telecommunications, electronics, food processing, chemicals and consumer goods. Tourism is a major foreign currency earner, with approximately forty-five million visitors a year. Other important service industries are banking and finance, Wall Street in New York being one of the world's major stock exchanges. Canada and Mexico are the main trading partners.

Alabama (State)
Area Sq Km (Sq Miles) 135 765 (52 419)   Population 4 599 030   Capital Montgomery

Alaska (State)
Area Sq Km (Sq Miles) 1 717 854 (663 267)   Population 670 053   Capital Juneau

Arizona (State)
Area Sq Km (Sq Miles) 295 253 (113 998)   Population 6 166 318   Capital Phoenix

Arkansas (State)
Area Sq Km (Sq Miles) 137 733 (53 179)   Population 2 810 872   Capital Little Rock

California (State)
Area Sq Km (Sq Miles) 423 971 (163 696)   Population 36 457 549   Capital Sacramento

Colorado (State)
Area Sq Km (Sq Miles) 269 602 (104 094)   Population 4 753 377   Capital Denver

Connecticut (State)
Area Sq Km (Sq Miles) 14 356 (5 543)   Population 3 504 809   Capital Hartford

Delaware (State)
Area Sq Km (Sq Miles) 6 446 (2 489)   Population 853 476   Capital Dover

District of Columbia (District)
Area Sq Km (Sq Miles) 176 (68)   Population 581 530   Capital Washington

Florida (State)
Area Sq Km (Sq Miles) 170 305 (65 755)   Population 18 089 888   Capital Tallahassee

Georgia (State)
Area Sq Km (Sq Miles) 153 910 (59 425)   Population 9 363 941   Capital Atlanta

Hawaii (State)
Area Sq Km (Sq Miles) 28 311 (10 931)   Population 1 285 498   Capital Honolulu

Idaho (State)
Area Sq Km (Sq Miles) 216 445 (83 570)   Population 1 466 465   Capital Boise

Illinois (State)
Area Sq Km (Sq Miles) 149 997 (57 914)   Population 12 831 970   Capital Springfield

Indiana (State)
Area Sq Km (Sq Miles) 94 322 (36 418)   Population 6 313 520   Capital Indianapolis

Iowa (State)
Area Sq Km (Sq Miles) 145 744 (56 272)   Population 2 982 085   Capital Des Moines

Kansas (State)
Area Sq Km (Sq Miles) 213 096 (82 277)   Population 2 764 075   Capital Topeka

Kentucky (State)
Area Sq Km (Sq Miles) 104 659 (40 409)   Population 4 206 074   Capital Frankfort

Louisiana (State)
Area Sq Km (Sq Miles) 134 265 (51 840)   Population 4 287 768   Capital Baton Rouge

Maine (State)
Area Sq Km (Sq Miles) 91 647 (35 385)   Population 1 321 574   Capital Augusta

Maryland (State)
Area Sq Km (Sq Miles) 32 134 (12 407)   Population 5 615 727   Capital Annapolis

Massachusetts (State)
Area Sq Km (Sq Miles) 27 337 (10 555)   Population 6 437 193   Capital Boston

Michigan (State)
Area Sq Km (Sq Miles) 250 493 (96 716)   Population 10 095 643   Capital Lansing

Minnesota (State)
Area Sq Km (Sq Miles) 225 171 (86 939)   Population 5 167 101   Capital St Paul

Mississippi (State)
Area Sq Km (Sq Miles) 125 433 (48 430)   Population 2 910 540   Capital Jackson

Missouri (State)
Area Sq Km (Sq Miles) 180 533 (69 704)   Population 5 842 713   Capital Jefferson City

Montana (State)
Area Sq Km (Sq Miles) 380 837 (147 042)   Population 944 632   Capital Helena

Nebraska (State)
Area Sq Km (Sq Miles) 200 346 (77 354)   Population 1 768 331   Capital Lincoln

Nevada (State)
Area Sq Km (Sq Miles) 286 352 (110 561)   Population 2 495 529   Capital Carson City

New Hampshire (State)
Area Sq Km (Sq Miles) 24 216 (9 350)   Population 1 314 895   Capital Concord

New Jersey (State)
Area Sq Km (Sq Miles) 22 587 (8 721)   Population 8 724 560   Capital Trenton

New Mexico (State)
Area Sq Km (Sq Miles) 314 914 (121 589)   Population 1 954 599   Capital Santa Fe

New York (State)
Area Sq Km (Sq Miles) 141 299 (54 556)   Population 19 306 183   Capital Albany

North Carolina (State)
Area Sq Km (Sq Miles) 139 391 (53 819)   Population 8 856 505   Capital Raleigh

North Dakota (State)
Area Sq Km (Sq Miles) 183 112 (70 700)   Population 635 867   Capital Bismarck

Ohio (State)
Area Sq Km (Sq Miles) 116 096 (44 825)   Population 11 478 006   Capital Columbus

Oklahoma (State)
Area Sq Km (Sq Miles) 181 035 (69 898)   Population 3 579 212   Capital Oklahoma City

Oregon (State)
Area Sq Km (Sq Miles) 254 806 (98 381)   Population 3 700 758   Capital Salem

Pennsylvania (State)
Area Sq Km (Sq Miles) 119 282 (46 055)   Population 12 440 621   Capital Harrisburg

Rhode Island (State)
Area Sq Km (Sq Miles) 4 002 (1 545)   Population 1 067 610   Capital Providence

South Carolina (State)
Area Sq Km (Sq Miles) 82 931 (32 020)   Population 4 321 249   Capital Columbia

South Dakota (State)
Area Sq Km (Sq Miles) 199 730 (77 116)   Population 781 919   Capital Pierre

Tennessee (State)
Area Sq Km (Sq Miles) 109 150 (42 143)   Population 6 038 803   Capital Nashville

Texas (State)
Area Sq Km (Sq Miles) 695 622 (268 581)   Population 23 507 783   Capital Austin

Utah (State)
Area Sq Km (Sq Miles) 219 887 (84 899)   Population 2 550 063   Capital Salt Lake City

Vermont (State)
Area Sq Km (Sq Miles) 24 900 (9 614)   Population 623 908   Capital Montpelier

Virginia (State)
Area Sq Km (Sq Miles) 110 784 (42 774)   Population 7 642 884   Capital Richmond

Washington (State)
Area Sq Km (Sq Miles) 184 666 (71 300)   Population 6 395 798   Capital Olympia

West Virginia (State)
Area Sq Km (Sq Miles) 62 755 (24 230)   Population 1 818 470   Capital Charleston

Wisconsin (State)
Area Sq Km (Sq Miles) 169 639 (65 498)   Population 5 556 506   Capital Madison

Wyoming (State)
Area Sq Km (Sq Miles) 253 337 (97 814)   Population 515 004   Capital Cheyenne

URUGUAY
Oriental Republic of Uruguay

Area Sq Km	176 215	Languages	Spanish
Area Sq Miles	68 037	Religions	Roman Catholic, Protestant, Jewish
Population	3 340 000	Currency	Uruguayan peso
Capital	Montevideo	Organizations	UN

Uruguay, on the Atlantic coast of central South America, is a low-lying land of prairies. The coast and the River Plate estuary in the south are fringed with lagoons and sand dunes. Almost half the population lives in the capital, Montevideo. Uruguay has warm summers and mild winters. The economy is based on cattle and sheep ranching, and the main industries produce food products, textiles, and petroleum products. Meat, wool, hides, textiles and agricultural products are the main exports. Brazil and Argentina are the main trading partners.

UZBEKISTAN
Republic of Uzbekistan

Area Sq Km	447 400	Languages	Uzbek, Russian, Tajik, Kazakh
Area Sq Miles	172 742	Religions	Sunni Muslim, Russian Orthodox
Population	27 372 000	Currency	Uzbek som
Capital	Tashkent	Organizations	CIS, UN

A landlocked country of central Asia, Uzbekistan consists mainly of the flat Kyzylkum Desert. High mountains and valleys are found towards the southeast borders with Kyrgyzstan and Tajikistan. Most settlement is in the Fergana basin. The climate is hot and dry. The economy is based mainly on irrigated agriculture, chiefly cotton production. Uzbekistan is rich in minerals, including gold, copper, lead, zinc and uranium, and it has one of the largest gold mines in the world. Industry specializes in fertilizers and machinery for cotton harvesting and textile manufacture. The Russian Federation is the main trading partner.

VANUATU
Republic of Vanuatu

Area Sq Km	12 190	Languages	English, Bislama (Creole), French
Area Sq Miles	4 707	Religions	Protestant, Roman Catholic, traditional beliefs
Population	226 000		
Capital	Port Vila	Currency	Vatu
		Organizations	Comm., UN

Vanuatu occupies an archipelago of approximately eighty islands in the southwest Pacific. Many of the islands are mountainous, of volcanic origin and densely forested. The climate is tropical, with heavy rainfall. Half of the population lives on the main islands of Éfaté and Espíritu Santo, and the majority of people are employed in agriculture. Copra, beef, timber, vegetables, and cocoa are the main exports. Tourism is becoming important to the economy. Australia, Japan and Germany are the main trading partners.

VATICAN CITY
Vatican City State or Holy See

Area Sq Km	0.5	Languages	Italian
Area Sq Miles	0.2	Religions	Roman Catholic
Population	557	Currency	Euro
Capital	Vatican City		

The world's smallest sovereign state, the Vatican City occupies a hill to the west of the river Tiber within the Italian capital, Rome. It is the headquarters of the Roman Catholic church, and income comes from investments, voluntary contributions and tourism.

VENEZUELA
Republic of Venezuela

Area Sq Km	912 050	Languages	Spanish, Amerindian languages
Area Sq Miles	352 144	Religions	Roman Catholic, Protestant
Population	27 657 000	Currency	Bolívar fuerte
Capital	Caracas	Organizations	OPEC, UN

Venezuela is in northern South America, on the Caribbean. Its coast is much indented, with the oil-rich area of Lake Maracaibo at the western end, and the swampy Orinoco Delta to the east. Mountain ranges run parallel to the coast, and turn southwestwards to form a northern extension of the Andes. Central Venezuela is an area of lowland grasslands drained by the Orinoco river system. To the south are the Guiana Highlands, which contain the Angel Falls, the world's highest waterfall. Almost ninety per cent of the population lives in towns, mostly in the coastal mountain areas. The climate is tropical, with most rainfall in summer. Farming is important, particularly cattle ranching and dairy farming; coffee, maize, rice and sugar cane are the main crops. Venezuela is a major oil producer, and oil accounts for about seventy-five per cent of export earnings. Aluminium, iron ore, copper and gold are also mined, and manufactures include petrochemicals, aluminium, steel, textiles and food products. The USA and Puerto Rico are the main trading partners.

VIETNAM
Socialist Republic of Vietnam

Area Sq Km	329 565	Languages	Vietnamese, Thai, Khmer, Chinese, local languages
Area Sq Miles	127 246		
Population	87 375 000	Religions	Buddhist, Taoist, Roman Catholic, Cao Dai, Hoa Hao
Capital	Ha Nôi		
		Currency	Dong
		Organizations	APEC, ASEAN, UN

Vietnam lies in southeast Asia on the west coast of the South China Sea. The Red River delta lowlands in the north are separated from the huge Mekong delta in the south by long, narrow coastal plains backed by the mountainous and forested terrain of the Annam Highlands. Most of the population lives in the river deltas. The climate is tropical, with summer monsoon rains. Over three-quarters of the workforce is involved in agriculture, forestry and fishing. Coffee, tea and rubber are important cash crops, but Vietnam is the world's second largest rice exporter. Oil, coal and copper are produced, and other main industries are food processing, clothing and footwear, cement and fertilizers. Exports include oil, coffee, rice, clothing, fish and fish products. Japan and Singapore are the main trading partners.

Virgin Islands (U.K.)
United Kingdom Overseas Territory

Area Sq Km	153	Languages	English
Area Sq Miles	59	Religions	Protestant, Roman Catholic
Population	23 000	Currency	United States dollar
Capital	Road Town		

The Caribbean territory comprises four main islands and over thirty islets at the eastern end of the Virgin Islands group. Apart from the flat coral atoll of Anegada, the islands are volcanic in origin and hilly. The climate is subtropical, and tourism is the main industry.

Virgin Islands (U.S.A.)
United States Unincorporated Territory

Area Sq Km	352	Languages	English, Spanish
Area Sq Miles	136	Religions	Protestant, Roman Catholic
Population	111 000	Currency	United States dollar
Capital	Charlotte Amalie		

The territory consists of three main islands and over fifty islets in the Caribbean's western Virgin Islands. The islands are hilly, of volcanic origin, and the climate is subtropical. The economy is based on tourism, with some manufacturing, including a major oil refinery on St Croix.

Wallis and Futuna Islands
French Overseas Collectivity

Area Sq Km	274	Languages	French, Wallisian, Futunian
Area Sq Miles	106	Religions	Roman Catholic
Population	15 000	Currency	CFP franc
Capital	Matâ'utu		

The south Pacific territory comprises the volcanic islands of the Wallis archipelago and the Hoorn Islands. The climate is tropical. The islands depend on subsistence farming, the sale of licences to foreign fishing fleets, workers' remittances from abroad and French aid.

West Bank
Disputed territory

Area Sq Km	5 860	Languages	Arabic, Hebrew
Area Sq Miles	2 263	Religions	Sunni Muslim, Jewish, Shi'a Muslim, Christian
Population	2 676 284		
		Currency	Jordanian dinar, Isreali shekel

The territory consists of the west bank of the river Jordan and parts of Judea and Samaria. The land was annexed by Israel in 1967, but some areas have been granted autonomy under agreements between Israel and the Palestinian Authority. Conflict between the Israelis and the Palestinians continues to restrict economic development.

Western Sahara
Disputed territory

Area Sq Km	266 000	Languages	Arabic
Area Sq Miles	102 703	Religions	Sunni Muslim
Population	480 000	Currency	Moroccan dirham
Capital	Laâyoune		

Situated on the northwest coast of Africa, the territory of the Western Sahara is now effectively controlled by Morocco. The land is low, flat desert with higher land in the northeast. There is little cultivation and only about twenty per cent of the land is pasture. Livestock herding, fishing and phosphate mining are the main activities. All trade is controlled by Morocco.

YEMEN
Republic of Yemen

Area Sq Km	527 968	Languages	Arabic
Area Sq Miles	203 850	Religions	Sunni Muslim, Shi'a Muslim
Population	22 389 000	Currency	Yemeni riyal
Capital	Şan'ā'	Organizations	UN

Yemen occupies the southwestern part of the Arabian Peninsula, on the Red Sea and the Gulf of Aden. Beyond the Red Sea coastal plain the land rises to a mountain range and then descends to desert plateaus. Much of the country is hot and arid, but there is more rainfall in the west, where most of the population lives. Farming and fishing are the main activities, with cotton the main cash crop. The main exports are crude oil, fish, coffee and dried fruit. Despite some oil resources Yemen is one of the poorest countries in the Arab world. Main trading partners are Thailand, China, South Korea and Saudi Arabia.

ZAMBIA
Republic of Zambia

Area Sq Km	752 614	Languages	English, Bemba, Nyanja, Tonga, local languages
Area Sq Miles	290 586		
Population	11 922 000	Religions	Christian, traditional beliefs
Capital	Lusaka	Currency	Zambian kwacha
		Organizations	Comm., SADC, UN

A landlocked state in south central Africa, Zambia consists principally of high savanna plateaus and is bordered by the Zambezi river in the south. Most people live in the Copperbelt area in the centre-north. The climate is tropical, with a rainy season from November to May. Agriculture employs approximately eighty per cent of the workforce, but is mainly at subsistence level. Copper mining is the mainstay of the economy, although reserves are declining. Copper and cobalt are the main exports. Most trade is with South Africa.

ZIMBABWE
Republic of Zimbabwe

Area Sq Km	390 759	Languages	English, Shona, Ndebele
Area Sq Miles	150 873	Religions	Christian, traditional beliefs
Population	13 349 000	Currency	Zimbabwean dollar
Capital	Harare	Organizations	SADC, UN

Zimbabwe, a landlocked state in south-central Africa, consists of high plateaus flanked by the Zambezi river valley and Lake Kariba in the north and the Limpopo river in the south. Most of the population lives in the centre of the country. There are significant mineral resources, including gold, nickel, copper, asbestos, platinum and chromium. Agriculture is a major sector of the economy, with crops including tobacco, maize, sugar cane and cotton. Beef cattle are also important. Exports include tobacco, gold, ferroalloys, nickel and cotton. South Africa is the main trading partner. The economy has suffered recently through significant political unrest and instability.

abrasion

A

abrasion The wearing away of the landscape by rivers, **glaciers**, the sea or wind, caused by the load of debris that they carry. *See also* **corrasion**.

abrasion platform *See* **wave-cut platform**.

acid rain Rain that contains a high concentration of pollutants, notably sulphur and nitrogen oxides. These pollutants are produced from factories, power stations burning **fossil fuels,** and car exhausts. Once in the **atmosphere**, the sulphur and nitrogen oxides combine with moisture to give sulphuric and nitric acids which fall as corrosive rain.

administrative region An area in which organizations carry out administrative functions; for example, the regions of local health authorities and water companies, and commercial sales regions.

adult literacy rate A percentage measure which shows the proportion of an adult population able to read. It is one of the measures used to assess the level of development of a country.

aerial photograph A photograph taken from above the ground. There are two types of aerial photograph – a vertical photograph (or 'bird's-eye view') and an oblique photograph where the camera is held at an angle. Aerial photographs are often taken from aircraft and provide useful information for map-making and surveys. *Compare* **satellite image**.

afforestation The conversion of open land to forest; especially, in Britain, the planting of coniferous trees in upland areas for commercial gain. *Compare* **deforestation**.

agglomerate A mass of coarse rock fragments or blocks of lava produced during a volcanic eruption.

agribusiness Modern **intensive farming** which uses machinery and artificial fertilizers to increase **yield** and output. Thus agriculture resembles an industrial process in which the general running and managing of the farm could parallel that of large-scale industry.

agriculture Human management of the **environment** to produce food. The numerous forms of agriculture fall into three groups: **commercial agriculture, subsistence agriculture** and **peasant agriculture**. *See also* **agribusiness**.

aid The provision of finance, personnel and equipment for furthering economic development and improving standards of living in the **Third World**. Most aid is organized by international institutions (e.g. the United Nations), by charities (e.g. Oxfam) (*see* **non-governmental organizations** (NGOs); or by national governments. Aid to a country from the international institutions is called *multilateral aid*. Aid from one country to another is called *bilateral aid*.

air mass A large body of air with generally the same temperature and moisture conditions throughout.

Warm or cold and moist air masses usually develop over large bodies of water (**oceans**). Hot or cold and dry air masses develop over large land areas (**continents**).

alluvial fan A cone of **sediment** deposited at an abrupt change of slope; for example, where a post-glacial stream meets the flat floor of a **U-shaped valley**. Alluvial fans are also common in arid regions where streams flowing off **escarpments** may periodically carry large loads of sediment during **flash floods**.

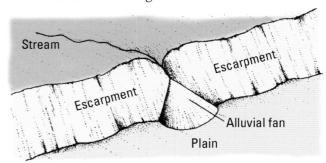

alluvial fan

alluvium Material deposited by a river in its middle and lower course. Alluvium comprises **silt**, sand and coarser debris eroded from the river's upper course and transported downstream. Alluvium is deposited in a graded sequence: coarsest first (heaviest) and finest last (lightest). Regular floods in the lower course create extensive layers of alluvium which can build up to a considerable depth on the **flood plain**.

alp A gentle slope above the steep sides of a glaciated valley, often used for summer grazing. *See also* **transhumance**.

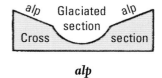

alp

anemometer An instrument for measuring the velocity of the wind. An anemometer should be fixed on a post at least 5 m above ground level. The wind blows the cups around and the speed is read off the dial in km/hr (or knots).

anemometer

antarctic circle Imaginary line that encircles the South Pole at **latitude** 66° 32'S

anthracite A hard form of **coal** with a high carbon content and few impurities.

anticline An arch in folded **strata**; the opposite of **syncline**. *See* **fold**.

anticyclone An area of high atmospheric pressure with light winds, clear skies and settled **weather**. In summer, anticyclones are associated with warm and sunny conditions; in winter, they bring frost and fog as well as sunshine.

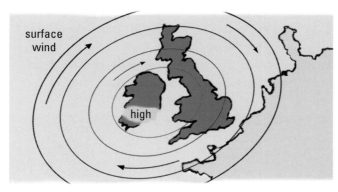

anticyclone

aquifer *See* **artesian basin**.
arable farming The production of cereal and root crops – as opposed to the keeping of livestock.
archipelago A group or chain of islands.
arctic circle Imaginary line that encircles the North Pole at **latitude** 66° 32'N
arête A knife-edged ridge separating two **corries** in a glaciated upland. The arête is formed by the progressive enlargement of corries by **weathering** and **erosion**. *See also* **pyramidal peak**.

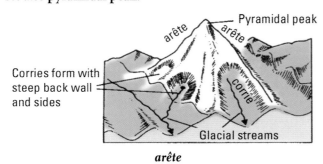

arête

artesian basin This consists of a shallow **syncline** with a layer of **permeable rock**, e.g. chalk, sandwiched between two impermeable layers, e.g. clay. Where the permeable rock is exposed at the surface, rainwater will enter the rock and the rock will become saturated. This is known as an *aquifer*. Boreholes can be sunk into the structure to tap the water in the aquifer.
asymmetrical fold Folded **strata** where the two limbs are at different angles to the horizontal.

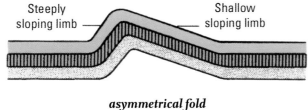

asymmetrical fold

atmosphere The air which surrounds the Earth, and consists of three layers: the *troposphere* (6 to 10 km from the Earth's surface), the *stratosphere* (50km from the Earth's surface), and the *mesosphere* and *ionosphere*, an ionised region of rarefied gases (1000km from the Earth's surface). The atmosphere comprises oxygen (21%), nitrogen (78%), carbon dioxide, argon, helium and other gases in minute quantities.
attrition The process by which a river's load is eroded through particles, such as pebbles and boulders, striking each other.

B

backwash The return movement of seawater off the beach after a wave has broken. *See also* **longshore drift** and **swash**.
bar graph A graph on which the values of a certain variable are shown by the length of shaded columns, which are numbered in sequence. *Compare* **histogram**.

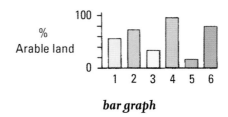

bar graph

barchan A type of crescent-shaped sand dune formed in desert regions where the wind direction is very constant. Wind blowing round the edges of the dune causes the crescent shape, while the dune may advance in a downwind direction as particles are blown over the crest.

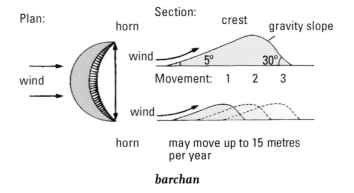

barchan

barograph An aneroid **barometer** connected to an arm and inked pen which records pressure changes continuously on a rotating drum. The drum usually takes a week to make one rotation.

barometer

barometer An instrument for measuring atmospheric pressure. There are two types, the *mercury barometer* and the *aneroid barometer*. The mercury barometer consists of a glass tube containing mercury which fluctuates in height as pressure varies. The aneroid barometer is a small metal box from which some of the air has been removed. The box expands and contracts as the air pressure changes. A series of levers joined to a pointer shows pressure on a dial.

barrage A type of dam built across a wide stretch of water, e.g. an estuary, for the purposes of water management. Such a dam may be intended to provide water supply, to harness wave energy or to control flooding, etc. There is a large barrage across Cardiff Bay in South Wales.

basalt A dark, fine-grained extrusive **igneous rock** formed when **magma** emerges onto the Earth's surface and cools rapidly. A succession of basalt **lava flows** may lead to the formation of a **lava plateau.**

base flow The water flowing in a stream which is fed only by **groundwater**. During dry periods it is only the base flow which passes through the stream channel.

batholith A large body of igneous material intruded into the Earth's **crust**. As the batholith slowly cools, large-grained **rocks** such as **granite** are formed. Batholiths may eventually be exposed at the Earth's surface by the removal of overlying rocks through **weathering** and **erosion.**

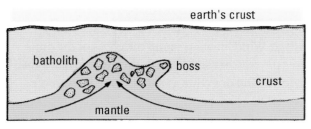

batholith

bay An indentation in the coastline with a **headland** on either side. Its formation is due to the more rapid **erosion** of softer rocks.

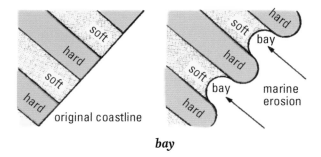

bay

beach A strip of land sloping gently towards the sea, usually recognized as the area lying between high and low tide marks.

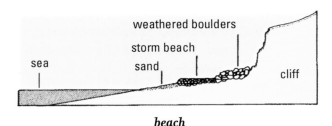

beach

bearing A compass reading between 0 and 360 degrees, indicating direction of one location from another.

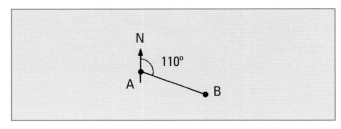

bearing *The bearing from A to B is 110°.*

Beaufort wind scale An international scale of wind velocities, ranging from 0 (calm) to 12 (hurricane).

bedrock The solid rock which usually lies beneath the soil.

bergschrund A large **crevasse** located at the rear of a **corrie** icefield in a glaciated region, formed by the weight of the ice in the corrie dragging away from the rear wall as the **glacier** moves downslope.

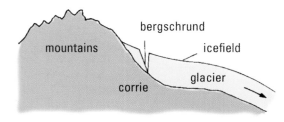

bergschrund

biodiversity The existence of a wide variety of plant and animal species in their natural environment.

biogas The production of methane and carbon dioxide, which can be obtained from plant or crop waste. Biogas is an example of a renewable source of energy (*see* **renewable resources, nonrenewable resources**).

biomass The total number of living organisms, both plant and animal, in a given area.

biome A complex community of plants and animals in a specific physical and climatic region. *See* **climate.**

biosphere The part of the Earth which contains living organisms. The biosphere contains a variety of **habitats,** from the highest mountains to the deepest oceans.

birth rate The number of live births per 1000 people in a population per year.

canyon

bituminous coal Sometimes called house coal – a medium-quality **coal** with some impurities; the typical domestic coal. It is also the major fuel source for **thermal power stations**.

block mountain *or* **horst** A section of the Earth's **crust** uplifted by faulting. Mt Ruwenzori in the East African Rift System is an example of a block mountain.

blowhole A crevice, **joint** or **fault** in coastal rocks, enlarged by marine **erosion**. A blowhole often leads from the rear of a cave (formed by wave action at the foot of a **cliff**) up to the cliff top. As waves break in the cave they erode the roof at the point of weakness and eventually a hole is formed. Air and sometimes spray are forced up the blowhole to erupt at the surface.

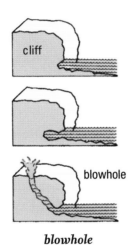

blowhole

bluff *See* **river cliff**.

boreal forest *See* **taiga**.

boulder clay *or* **till** The unsorted mass of debris dragged along by a **glacier** as *ground moraine* and dumped as the glacier melts. Boulder clay may be several metres thick and may comprise any combination of finely ground 'rock flour', sand, pebbles or boulders.

breakwater *or* **groyne** A wall built at right angles to a beach in order to prevent sand loss due to **longshore drift**.

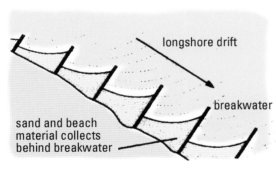

breakwater or groyne

breccia Rock fragments cemented together by a matrix of finer material; the fragments are angular and unsorted. An example of this is volcanic breccia, which

is made up of coarse angular fragments of **lava** and **crust** rocks welded by finer material such as ash and **tuff**.

bush fallowing *or* **shifting cultivation** A system of **agriculture** in which there are no permanent fields. For example in the **tropical rainforest**, remote societies cultivate forest clearings for one year and then move on. The system functions successfully when forest **regeneration** occurs over a sufficiently long period to allow the soil to regain its fertility.

bushfire An uncontrolled fire in forests and grasslands.

business park An out-of-town site accommodating offices, high-technology companies and light industry. *Compare* **science park**.

butte An outlier of a **mesa** in arid regions.

C

caldera A large crater formed by the collapse of the summit cone of a **volcano** during an eruption. The caldera may contain subsidiary cones built up by subsequent eruptions, or a crater lake if the volcano is extinct or dormant.

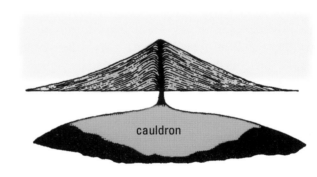

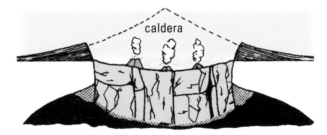

caldera

canal An artificial waterway, usually connecting existing **rivers**, **lakes** or **oceans**, constructed for navigation and transportation.

canyon A deep and steep-sided river valley occurring where rapid vertical **corrasion** takes place in arid regions. In such an **environment** the rate of **weathering** of the valley sides is slow. If the **rocks** of the region are relatively soft then the canyon profile becomes even more pronounced. The Grand Canyon of the Colorado River in the USA is the classic example. See diagram overleaf.

capital city

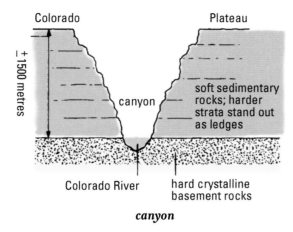

canyon

capital city Seat of government of a country or political unit.

catchment **1.** In **physical geography**, an alternative term to **river basin**.
2. In **human geography**, an area around a town or city – hence 'labour catchment' means the area from which an urban workforce is drawn.

cavern In **limestone** country, a large underground cave formed by the dissolving of limestone by subterranean streams. *See also* **stalactite, stalagmite**.

cay A small low **island** or bank composed of sand and coral fragments. Commonly found in the Caribbean Sea.

CBD (Central Business District) This is the central zone of a town or city, and is characterized by high accessibility, high land values and limited space. The visible result of these factors is a concentration of high-rise buildings at the city centre. The CBD is dominated by retail and business functions, both of which require maximum accessibility.

CFCs (Chlorofluorocarbons) Chemicals used in the manufacture of some aerosols, the cooling systems of refrigerators and fast-food cartons. These chemicals are harmful to the **ozone** layer.

chalk A soft, whitish **sedimentary rock** formed by the accumulation of small fragments of skeletal matter from marine organisms; the rock may be almost pure calcium carbonate. Due to the **permeable** and soluble nature of the rock, there is little surface **drainage** in chalk landscapes.

channel *See* **strait**.

chernozem A deep, rich soil of the plains of southern Russia. The upper **horizons** are rich in lime and other plant nutrients; in the dry **climate** the predominant movement of **soil** moisture is upwards (*contrast* with **leaching**), and lime and other chemical nutrients therefore accumulate in the upper part of the **soil profile**.

chloropleth map *See* **shading map**.

cirrus High, wispy or strand-like, thin **cloud** associated with the advance of a **depression**.

clay A soil composed of very small particles of

sediment, less than 0.002 mm in diameter. Due to the dense packing of these minute particles, clay is almost totally impermeable, i.e. it does not allow water to drain through. Clay soils very rapidly waterlog in wet weather.

cliff A steep rockface between land and sea, the profile of which is determined largely by the nature of the coastal rocks. For example, resistant rocks such as **granite** (e.g. at Land's End, England) will produce steep and rugged cliffs.

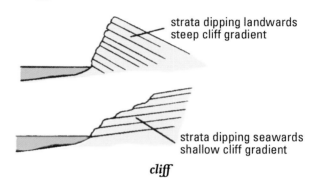

cliff

climate The average atmospheric conditions prevailing in a region, as distinct from its **weather**. A statement of climate is concerned with long-term trends. Thus the climate of, for example, the Amazon Basin is described as hot and wet all the year round; that of the Mediterranean Region as having hot dry summers and mild wet winters. *See* **extreme climate, maritime climate**.

clint A block of **limestone**, especially when part of a **limestone pavement**, where the surface is composed of clints and **grykes**.

cloud A mass of small water drops or ice crystals formed by the **condensation** of water vapour in the

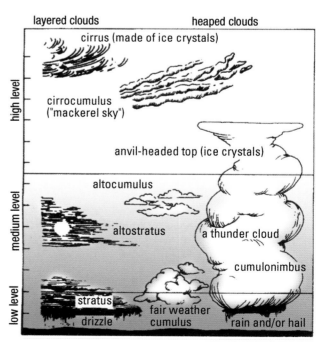

cloud

atmosphere, usually at a considerable height above the Earth's surface. There are three main types of cloud: **cumulus, stratus** and **cirrus**, each of which has many variations.

coal A **sedimentary rock** composed of decayed and compressed vegetative matter. Coal is usually classified according to a scale of hardness and purity ranging from **anthracite** (the hardest), through **bituminous coal** and **lignite** to **peat**.

cold front *See* **depression.**

commercial agriculture A system of **agriculture** in which food and materials are produced specifically for sale in the market, in contrast to **subsistence agriculture.** Commercial agriculture tends to be capital intensive. *See also* **agribusiness.**

Common Agricultural Policy (CAP) The policy of the European Union to support and subsidize certain crops and methods of animal husbandry.

common land Land which is not in the ownership of an individual or institution, but which is historically available to any member of the local community.

communications The contacts and linkages in an **environment**. For example, roads and railways are communications, as are telephone systems, newspapers, and radio and television.

commuter zone An area on or near to the outskirts of an urban area. Commuters are among the most affluent and mobile members of the urban community and can afford the greatest physical separation of home and work.

concordant coastline A coastline that is parallel to mountain ranges immediately inland. A rise in sea level or a sinking of the land cause the valleys to be flooded by the sea and the mountains to become a line of islands. *Compare* **discordant coastline.**

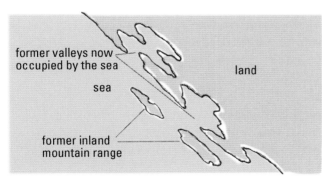

concordant coastline

condensation The process by which cooling vapour turns into a liquid. **Clouds**, for example, are formed by the condensation of water vapour in the **atmosphere**.

coniferous forest A forest of **evergreen** trees such as pine, spruce and fir. Natural coniferous forests occur considerably further north than forests of broad-leaved **deciduous** species, as coniferous trees are able to withstand harsher climatic conditions. The **taiga** areas of the northern hemisphere consist of coniferous forests.

conservation The preservation and management of the natural **environment**. In its strictest form, conservation may mean total protection of endangered species and habitats, as in nature reserves. In some cases, conservation of the man-made environment, e.g. ancient buildings, is undertaken.

continent One of the earth's large land masses. The world's continents are generally defined as Asia, Africa, North America, South America, Europe, Oceania and Antarctica.

continental climate The climate at the centre of large landmasses, typified by a large annual range in temperature, with precipitation most likely in the summer.

continental drift The theory that the Earth's continents move gradually over a layer of semi-molten rock underneath the Earth's **crust**. It is thought that the present-day continents once formed the supercontinent, **Pangaea,** which existed approximately 200 million years ago. *See also* **Gondwanaland, Laurasia** *and* **plate tectonics.**

continental shelf The seabed bordering the continents, which is covered by shallow water – usually of less than 200 metres. Along some coastlines the continental shelf is so narrow it is almost absent.

contour A line drawn on a map to join all places at the same height above sea level.

conurbation A continuous built-up urban area formed by the merging of several formerly separate towns or cities. Twentieth-century **urban sprawl** has led to the merging of towns.

coombe *See* **dry valley.**

cooperative A system whereby individuals pool their **resources** in order to optimize individual gains.

core **1.** In **physical geography**, the core is the innermost zone of the Earth. It is probably solid at the centre, and composed of iron and nickel.
2. In **human geography**, a central place or central region, usually the centre of economic and political activity in a region or nation.

corrasion The abrasive action of an agent of **erosion** (rivers, ice, the sea) caused by its load. For example the pebbles and boulders carried along by a river wear away the channel bed and the river bank. *Compare* with **hydraulic action**.

corrie, cirque *or* **cwm** A bowl-shaped hollow on a mountainside in a glaciated region; the area where a valley **glacier** originates. In glacial times the corrie contained an icefield, which in cross section appears as in diagram *a* overleaf. The shape of the corrie is determined by the rotational erosive force of ice as the glacier moves downslope (diagram *b*).

corrosion

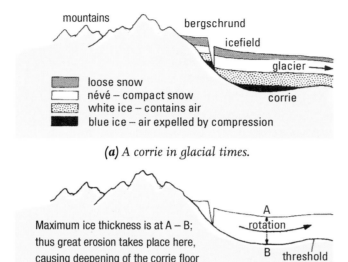

(a) A corrie in glacial times.

Maximum ice thickness is at A – B;
thus great erosion takes place here,
causing deepening of the corrie floor
below the level of the threshold

(b) Erosion of a corrie.

corrosion **Erosion** by solution action, such as the dissolving of **limestone** by running water.

crag Rocky outcrop on a valley side formed, for example, when a **truncated spur** exists in a glaciated valley.

crag and tail A feature of lowland **glaciation**, where a resistant rock outcrop withstands **erosion** by a **glacier** and remains as a feature after the **Ice Age**. Rocks of volcanic or metamorphic origin are likely to produce such a feature. As the ice advances over the crag, material will be eroded from the face and sides and will be deposited as a mass of boulder clay and debris on the leeward side, thus producing a 'tail'.

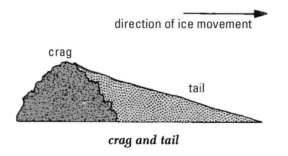

crag and tail

crevasse A crack or fissure in a **glacier** resulting from the stressing and fracturing of ice at a change in **gradient** or valley shape.

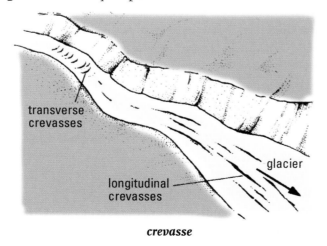

crevasse

cross section A drawing of a vertical section of a line of ground, deduced from a map. It depicts the **topography** of a system of **contours**.

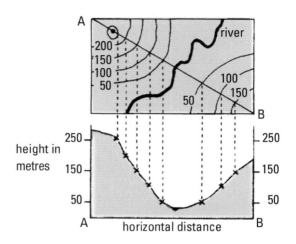

cross section Map and corresponding cross section.

crust The outermost layer of the Earth, representing only 0.1% of the Earth's total volume. It comprises continental crust and oceanic crust, which differ from each other in age as well as in physical and chemical characteristics. The crust, together with the uppermost layer of the **mantle**, is also known as the *lithosphere*.

culvert An artificial drainage channel for transporting water quickly from place to place.

cumulonimbus A heavy, dark **cloud** of great vertical height. It is the typical thunderstorm cloud, producing heavy showers of rain, snow or hail. Such clouds form where intense solar radiation causes vigorous convection.

cumulus A large **cloud** (smaller than a **cumulonimbus**) with a 'cauliflower' head and almost horizontal base. It is indicative of fair or, at worst, showery **weather** in generally sunny conditions.

cut-off *See* **oxbow lake**.

cyclone *See* **hurricane**.

D

dairying A **pastoral farming** system in which dairy cows produce milk that is used by itself or used to produce dairy products such as cheese, butter, cream and yoghurt.

dam A barrier built across a stream, river or **estuary** to create a body of water.

death rate The number of deaths per 1000 people in a population per year.

deciduous woodland Trees which are generally of broad-leaved rather than **coniferous** habit, and which shed their leaves during the cold season.

deflation The removal of loose sand by wind **erosion** in desert regions. It often exposes a bare rock surface beneath.

developing countries

deforestation The practice of clearing trees. Much deforestation is a result of development pressures, e.g. trees are cut down to provide land for agriculture and industry. *Compare* **afforestation**.

delta A fan-shaped mass consisting of the deposited load of a river where it enters the sea. A delta only forms where the river deposits material at a faster rate than can be removed by coastal currents. While deltas may take almost any shape and size, three types are generally recognized, as shown in the following diagrams.

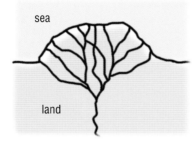

Arcuate delta, e.g. Nile. Note bifurcation of river into distributaries in delta

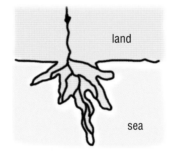

Bird's foot delta, e.g. Mississippi

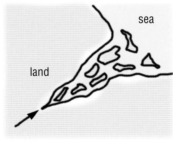

Estuarine delta, e.g. Amazon

delta

denudation The wearing away of the Earth's surface by the processes of **weathering** and **erosion**.

depopulation A long-term decrease in the population of any given area, frequently caused by economic migration to other areas.

deposition The laying down of **sediments** resulting from **denudation**.

depression An area of low atmospheric pressure occurring where warm and cold air masses come into contact. The passage of a depression is marked by thickening cloud, rain, a period of dull and drizzly weather and then clearing skies with showers. A depression develops as in the diagrams on the right.

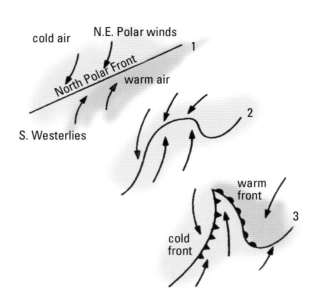

depression *The development of a depression.*

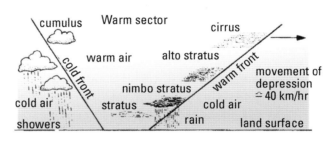

depression *Characteristics.*

desert An area where all forms of **precipitation** are so low that very little, if anything, can grow.

Deserts can be broadly divided into three types, depending upon average temperatures:

(a) *hot deserts:* occur in tropical latitudes in regions of high pressure where air is sinking and therefore making rainfall unlikely. *See* **cloud**.

(b) *temperate deserts:* occur in mid-latitudes in areas of high pressure. They are far inland, so moisture-bearing winds rarely deposit rainfall in these areas.

(c) *cold deserts:* occur in the northern latitudes, again in areas of high pressure. Very low temperatures throughout the year mean the air is unable to hold much moisture.

desertification The encroachment of **desert** conditions into areas which were once productive. Desertification can be due partly to climatic change, i.e. a move towards a drier climate in some parts of the world (possibly due to **global warming**), though human activity has also played a part through bad farming practices. The problem is particularly acute along the southern margins of the Sahara desert in the Sahel region between Mali and Mauritania in the west, and Ethiopia and Somalia in the east.

developing countries A collective term for those nations in Africa, Asia and Latin America which are

dew point

undergoing the complex processes of modernization, **industrialization** and **urbanization**. *See also* **Third World**.

dew point The temperature at which the **atmosphere**, being cooled, becomes saturated with water vapour. This vapour is then deposited as drops of dew.

dip slope The gentler of the two slopes on either side of an escarpment crest; the dip slope inclines in the direction of the dipping **strata**; the steep slope in front of the crest is the **scarp slope**.

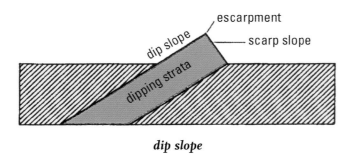

dip slope

discharge The volume of run-off in the channels of a **river basin**.

discordant coastline A coastline that is at right angles to the mountains and valleys immediately inland. A rise in sea level or a sinking of the land will cause the valleys to be flooded. A flooded river valley is known as a **ria**, whilst a flooded glaciated valley is known as a **fjord**. *Compare* **concordant coastline**.

discordant coastline

distributary An outlet stream which drains from a larger river or stream. Often found in a **delta** area. *Compare* **tributary**.

doldrums An equatorial belt of low atmospheric pressure where the **trade winds** converge. Winds are light and variable but the strong upward movement of air caused by this convergence produces frequent thunderstorms and heavy rains.

dormitory settlement A village located beyond the edge of a city but inhabited by residents who work in that city (*see* **commuter zone**).

drainage The removal of water from the land surface by processes such as streamflow and infiltration.

drainage basin *See* **river basin**.

drift Material transported and deposited by glacial action on the Earth's surface. *See also* **boulder clay**.

drought A prolonged period where rainfall falls below the requirement for a region.

dry valley *or* **coombe** A feature of **limestone** and **chalk** country, where valleys have been eroded in dry landscapes.

dune A mound or ridge of drifted sand, occurring on the sea coast and in deserts.

dyke **1.** An artificial **drainage** channel.
2. An artificial bank built to protect low-lying land from flooding.
3. A vertical or semi-vertical igneous intrusion occurring where a stream of **magma** has extended through a line of weakness in the surrounding **rock**. *See* **igneous rock**.

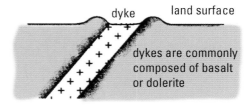

dyke Cross section of eroded dyke, showing how metamorphic margins, harder than dyke or surrounding rocks, resist erosion.

E

earthquake A movement or tremor of the Earth's crust. Earthquakes are associated with plate boundaries (*see* **plate tectonics**) and especially with subduction zones, where one plate plunges beneath another. Here the crust is subjected to tremendous stress. The rocks are forced to bend, and eventually the stress is so great that the rocks 'snap' along a **fault** line.

eastings The first element of a **grid reference**. *See* **northing**.

ecology The study of living things, their interrelationships and their relationships with the **environment**.

ecosystem A natural system comprising living organisms and their **environment**. The concept can be applied at the global scale or in the context of a smaller defined environment. The principle of the ecosystem is constant: all elements are intricately linked by flows of energy and nutrients.

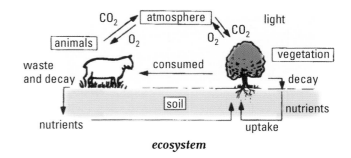

ecosystem

El Niño The occasional development of warm ocean surface waters along the coast of Ecuador and Peru. Where this warming occurs the tropical Pacific trade winds weaken and the usual up-welling of cold, deep ocean water is reduced. El Niño normally occurs late in the calendar year and lasts for a few weeks to a few months and can have a dramatic impact on weather patterns throughout the world.

emigration The movement of population out of a given area or country.

employment structure The distribution of the workforce between the **primary, secondary, tertiary** and **quaternary sectors** of the economy. Primary employment is in **agriculture**, mining, forestry and fishing; secondary in manufacturing; tertiary in the retail, service and administration category; quaternary in information and expertise.

environment Physical surroundings: **soil**, vegetation, wildlife and the **atmosphere**.

equator The great circle of the Earth with a **latitude** of 0°, lying equidistant from the poles.

erosion The wearing away of the Earth's surface by running water (rivers and streams), moving ice (**glaciers**), the sea and the wind. These are called the *agents* of erosion.

erratic A boulder of a certain rock type resting on a surface of different geology. For example, blocks of **granite** resting on a surface of carboniferous **limestone**.

escarpment A ridge of high ground as, for example, the **chalk** escarpments of southern England (the Downs and the Chilterns).

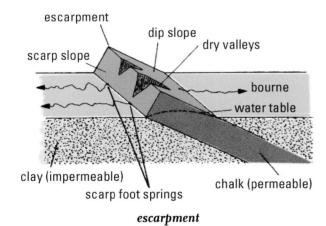

escarpment

esker A low, winding ridge of pebbles and finer **sediment** on a glaciated lowland.

estuary The broad mouth of a river where it enters the sea. An estuary forms where opposite conditions to those favourable for **delta** formation exist: deep water offshore, strong marine currents and a smaller **sediment** load.

ethnic group A group of people with a common identity such as culture, religion or skin colour.

evaporation The process whereby a substance changes from a liquid to a vapour. Heat from the sun evaporates water from seas, lakes, rivers, etc., and this process produces water vapour in the **atmosphere**.

evergreen A vegetation type in which leaves are continuously present. *Compare* **deciduous woodland**.

exfoliation A form of **weathering** whereby the outer layers of a **rock** or boulder shear off due to the alternate expansion and contraction produced by diurnal heating and cooling. Such a process is especially active in **desert** regions.

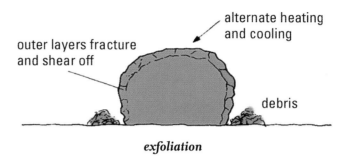

exfoliation

exports Goods and services sold to a foreign country (*compare* **imports**).

extensive farming A system of **agriculture** in which relatively small amounts of capital or labour investment are applied to relatively large areas of land. For example, sheep ranching is an extensive form of farming, and yields per unit area are low.

external processes Landscape-forming processes such as **weather** and **erosion**, in contrast to internal processes.

extreme climate A climate that is characterized by large ranges of temperature and sometimes of rainfall. *Compare* **temperate climate, maritime climate**.

F

fault A fracture in the Earth's crust on either side of which the **rocks** have been relatively displaced. Faulting occurs in response to stress in the Earth's crust; the release of this stress in fault movement is experienced as an **earthquake**. *See also* **rift valley**.

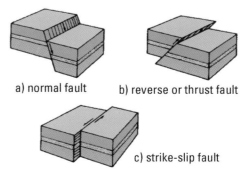

fault The main types.

fell

fell Upland rough grazing in a **hill farming** system, for example in the English Lake District.

fjord A deep, generally straight inlet of the sea along a glaciated coast. A fjord is a glaciated valley which has been submerged either by a post-glacial rise in sea level or a subsidence of the land.

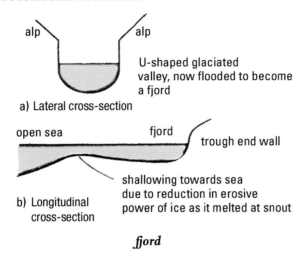

a) Lateral cross-section

alp alp

U-shaped glaciated valley, now flooded to become a fjord

open sea   fjord

trough end wall

shallowing towards sea due to reduction in erosive power of ice as it melted at snout

b) Longitudinal cross-section

fjord

flash flood A sudden increase in river **discharge** and overland flow due to a violent rainstorm in the upper **river basin**.

flood plain The broad, flat valley floor of the lower course of a river, levelled by annual flooding and by the lateral and downstream movement of **meanders**.

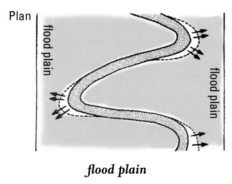

Plan

flood plain

flood plain

flood plain

flow line A diagram showing volumes of movement, e.g. of people, goods or information between places. The width of the flow line is proportional to the amount of movement, for example in portraying commuter flows into an urban centre from surrounding towns and villages.

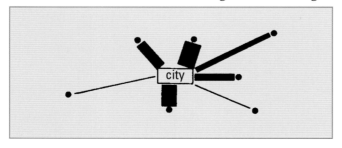

city

***Flow line** Commuter flows into a city.*

fodder crop A crop grown for animal feed.

fold A bending or buckling of once horizontal rock **strata**. Many folds are the result of rocks being crumpled at plate boundaries (*see* **plate tectonics**), though **earthquakes** can also cause rocks to fold, as can igneous **intrusions**.

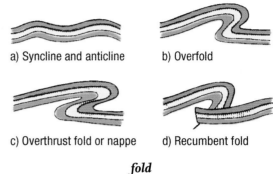

a) Syncline and anticline   b) Overfold

c) Overthrust fold or nappe   d) Recumbent fold

fold

fold mountains Mountains which have been formed by large-scale and complex folding. Studies of typical fold mountains (the Himalayas, Andes, Alps and Rockies) indicate that folding has taken place deep inside the Earth's **crust** and upper **mantle** as well as in the upper layers of the crust.

fossil fuel Any naturally occurring carbon or hydrocarbon fuel, notably coal, oil, peat and natural gas. These fuels have been formed by decomposed prehistoric organisms.

free trade The movement of goods and services between countries without any restrictions (such as quotas, tariffs or taxation) being imposed.

freeze-thaw A type of physical **weathering** whereby **rocks** are denuded by the freezing of water in cracks and crevices on the rock face. Water expands on freezing, and this process causes stress and fracture along any line of weakness in the rock. **Nivation** debris accumulates at the bottom of a rock face as **scree**.

front A boundary between two air masses. *See also* **depression**.

G

GDP *See* **Gross Domestic Product**.

geosyncline A basin (a large **syncline**) in which thick marine sediments have accumulated.

geothermal energy A method of producing power from heat contained in the lower layers of the Earth's **crust**. New Zealand and Iceland both use superheated water or steam from geysers and volcanic **springs** to heat buildings and for hothouse cultivation and also to drive steam turbines to generate electricity. Geothermal energy is an example of a renewable resource of energy (*see* **renewable resources, nonrenewable resources**).

glaciation A period of cold **climate** during which time **ice sheets** and **glaciers** are the dominant forces of **denudation**.

HDI (human development index)

glacier A body of ice occupying a valley and originating in a **corrie** or icefield. A glacier moves at a rate of several metres per day, the precise speed depending upon climatic and **topographic** conditions in the area in question.

global warming *or* **greenhouse effect** The warming of the Earth's atmosphere caused by an excess of carbon dioxide, which acts like a blanket, preventing the natural escape of heat. This situation has been developing over the last 150 years because of (a) the burning of **fossil fuels**, which releases vast amounts of carbon dioxide into the **atmosphere**, and (b) **deforestation**, which results in fewer trees being available to take up carbon dioxide (*see* **photosynthesis**).

globalization The process that enables financial markets and companies to operate internationally (as a result of deregulation and improved communications). **Transnational corporations** now locate their manufacturing in places that best serve their global market at the lowest cost.

GNI (gross national income) *formerly* **GNP (gross national product)** The total value of the goods and services produced annually by a nation, plus net property income from abroad.

Gondwanaland The southern-hemisphere super-continent, consisting of the present South America, Africa, India, Australasia and Antarctica, which split from **Pangaea** *c.*200 million years ago. Gondwanaland is part of the theory of **continental drift**. *See also* **plate tectonics**.

GPS (global positioning system) A system of earth-orbiting satellites, transmitting signals continuously towards earth, which enable the position of a receiving device on the earth's surface to be accurately estimated from the difference in arrival of the signals.

gradient **1.** The measure of steepness of a line or slope. In mapwork, the average gradient between two points can be calculated as:

$$\frac{\text{difference in altitude}}{\text{distance apart}}$$

2. The measure of change in a property such as density. In **human geography** gradients are found in, for example, **population density**, land values and **settlement** ranking.

granite An **igneous rock** having large crystals due to slow cooling at depth in the Earth's **crust**.

green belt An area of land, usually around the outskirts of a town or city on which building and other developments are restricted by legislation.

greenfield site A development site for industry, retailing or housing that has previously been used only for agriculture or recreation. Such sites are frequently in the **green belt**.

greenhouse effect *See* **global warming**.

Greenwich Meridian *See* **prime meridian**.

grid reference A method for specifying position on a map. *See* **eastings** and **northings**.

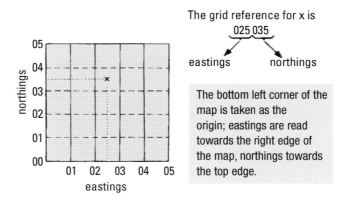

The grid reference for x is
025 035
eastings   northings

The bottom left corner of the map is taken as the origin; eastings are read towards the right edge of the map, northings towards the top edge.

Gross Domestic Product (GDP) The total value of all goods and services produced domestically by a nation during a year. It is equivalent to **Gross National Income (GNI)** minus investment incomes from foreign nations.

groundwater Water held in the bedrock of a region, having percolated through the **soil** from the surface. Such water is an important **resource** in areas where **surface run-off** is limited or absent.

groyne *See* **breakwater**.

gryke An enlarged joint between blocks of **limestone** (**clints**), especially in a **limestone pavement**.

gulf A large coastal indentation, similar to a **bay** but larger in extent. Commonly formed as a result of rising sea levels.

H

habitat A preferred location for particular species of plants and animals to live and reproduce.

hanging valley A tributary valley entering a main valley at a much higher level because of deepening of the main valley, especially by glacial erosion.

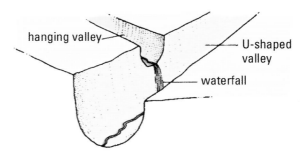

hanging valley

HDI (human development index) A measurement of a country's achievements in three areas: longevity, knowledge and standard of living. Longevity is measured by life expectancy at birth; knowledge is measured by a combination of the adult literacy rate and the combined gross primary, secondary and tertiary school enrolment ratio; standard of living is measured by **GDP** per capita.

headland

headland A promontory of resistant **rock** along the coastline. *See* **bay**.

hemisphere Any half of a globe or sphere. The earth has traditionally been divided into hemispheres by the **equator** (northern and southern hemispheres) and by the **prime meridian** and **International Date Line** (eastern and western hemispheres).

hill farming A system of **agriculture** where sheep (and to a lesser extent cattle) are grazed on upland rough pasture.

histogram A graph for showing values of classed data as the areas of bars.

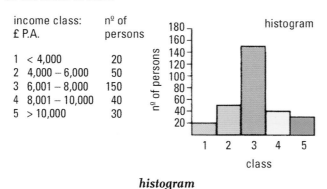

income class: £ P.A.	nº of persons
1 < 4,000	20
2 4,000 – 6,000	50
3 6,001 – 8,000	150
4 8,001 – 10,000	40
5 > 10,000	30

histogram

horizon The distinct layers found in the **soil profile**. Usually three horizons are identified – A, B and C, as in the diagram below.

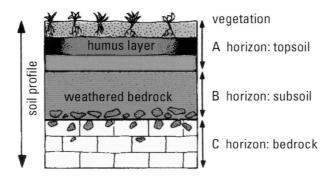

horizon A typical soil profile.

horst *See* **block mountain**.

horticulture The growing of plants and flowers for commercial sale. It is now an international trade, for example, orchids are grown in Southeast Asia for sale in Europe.

human geography The study of people and their activities in terms of patterns and processes of population, **settlement**, economic activity and **communications**. *Compare* **physical geography**.

hunter/gatherer economy A pre-agricultural phase of development in which people survive by hunting and gathering the animal and plant **resources** of the natural **environment**. No cultivation or herding is involved.

hurricane, cyclone *or* **typhoon** A wind of force 12 on the **Beaufort wind scale**, i.e. one having a velocity of more than 118 km per hour. Hurricanes can cause great damage by wind as well as from the storm waves and floods that accompany them.

hydraulic action The erosive force of water alone, as distinct from **corrasion**. A river or the sea will erode partially by the sheer force of moving water and this is termed 'hydraulic action'.

hydroelectric power The generation of electricity by turbines driven by flowing water. Hydroelectricity is most efficiently generated in rugged **topography** where a head of water can most easily be created, or on a large river where a dam can create similar conditions. Whatever the location, the principle remains the same – that water descending via conduits from an upper storage area passes through turbines and thus creates electricity.

hydrological cycle The cycling of water through sea, land and **atmosphere**.

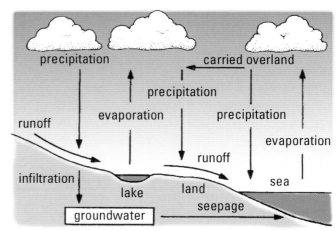

hydrological cycle

hydrosphere All the water on Earth, including that present in the **atmosphere** as well as in oceans, seas, **ice sheets**, etc.

hygrometer An instrument for measuring the relative humidity of the **atmosphere**. It comprises two thermometers, one of which is kept moist by a wick inserted in a water reservoir. Evaporation from the wick reduces the temperature of the 'wet bulb' thermometer, and the difference between the dry and the wet bulb temperatures is used to calculate relative humidity from standard tables.

I

Ice Age A period of **glaciation** in which a cooling of **climate** leads to the development of **ice sheets, ice caps** and valley **glaciers**.

ice cap A covering of permanent ice over a relatively small land mass, e.g. Iceland.

joint

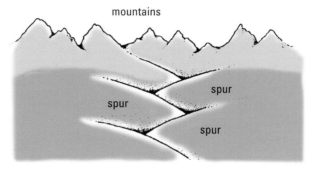

interlocking spurs A V-shaped valley with interlocking spurs.

ice sheet A covering of permanent ice over a substantial continental area such as Antarctica.
iceberg A large mass of ice which has broken off an **ice sheet** or **glacier** and left floating in the sea.
igneous rock A **rock** which originated as **magma** (molten rock) at depth in or below the Earth's **crust**. Igneous rocks are generally classified according to crystal size, colour and mineral composition. *See also* **plutonic rock**.

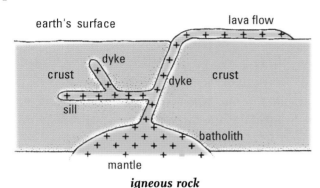

igneous rock

immigration The movement of people into a country or region from other countries or regions.
impermeable rock A rock that is non-porous and therefore incapable of taking in water or of allowing it to pass through between the grains. *Compare* **impervious rock**. *See also* **permeable rock**.
impervious rock A non-porous rock with no cracks or fissures through which water might pass.
imports Goods or services bought into one country from another (*compare* **exports**).
industrialization The development of industry on an extensive scale.
infiltration The gradual movement of water into the ground.
infrastructure The basic structure of an organization or system. The infrastructure of a city includes, for example, its roads and railways, schools, factories, power and water supplies and drainage systems.
inner city The ring of buildings around the **Central Business District (CBD)** of a town or city.
intensive farming A system of **agriculture** where relatively large amounts of capital and/or labour are invested on relatively small areas of land.
interglacial A warm period between two periods of **glaciation** and cold **climate**. The present interglacial began about 10,000 years ago.
interlocking spurs Obstacles of hard **rock** round which a river twists and turns in a V-shaped valley. **Erosion** is pronounced on the concave banks, and this ultimately causes the development of spurs which alternate on either side of the river and interlock as shown in the diagram top right.

International Date Line An imaginary line which approximately follows 180° **longitude**. The area of the world just east of the line is one day ahead of the area just west of the line.
international trade The exchange of goods and services between countries.
intrusion A body of **igneous rock** injected into the Earth's **crust** from the **mantle** below. *See* **dyke, sill, batholith**.
ionosphere *See* **atmosphere**.
irrigation A system of artificial watering of the land in order to grow crops. Irrigation is particularly important in areas of low or unreliable rainfall.
island A mass of land, smaller than a continent, which is completely surrounded by water.
isobar A line joining points of equal atmospheric pressure, as on the meteorological map below.

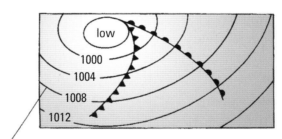

isobar, indicating atmospheric pressure in millibars

isobar

isohyet A line on a meteorological map joining places of equal rainfall.
isotherm A line on a meteorological map joining places of equal temperature.

J

joint A vertical or semi-vertical fissure in a **sedimentary rock**, contrasted with roughly horizontal bedding planes. In **igneous rocks** jointing may occur as a result of contraction on cooling from the molten state. Joints should be distinguished from **faults** in that they are on a much smaller scale and there is no relative displacement of the rocks on either side of the joint.

kame

Joints, being lines of weakness are exploited by **weathering**.

K

kame A short ridge of sand and gravel deposited from the water of a melted glacier.

karst topography An area of **limestone** scenery where **drainage** is predominantly subterranean.

kettle hole A small depression or hollow in a glacial outwash plain, formed when a block of ice embedded in the outwash deposits eventually melts, causing the **sediment** above to subside.

L

laccolith An igneous **intrusion**, domed and often of considerable dimensions, caused where a body of viscous **magma** has been intruded into the **strata** of the Earth's **crust**. These strata are buckled upwards over the laccolith.

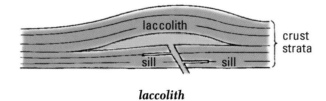

laccolith

lagoon **1.** An area of sheltered coastal water behind a bay bar or **tombolo**.
2. The calm water behind a coral reef.

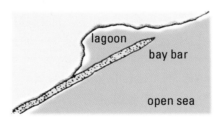

lagoon

lahar A landslide of volcanic debris mixed with water down the sides of a volcano, caused either by heavy rain or the heat of the volcano melting snow and ice.

lake A body of water completely surrounded by land.

land tenure A system of land ownership or allocation.

land use The function of an area of land. For example, the land use in rural areas could be farming or forestry, whereas urban land use could be housing or industry.

landform Any natural feature of the Earth's surface, such as mountains or valleys.

laterite A hard (literally 'brick-like') soil in tropical regions caused by the baking of the upper **horizons** by exposure to the sun.

latitude Distance north or south of the equator, as measured by degrees of the angle at the Earth's centre:

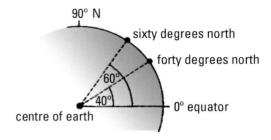

latitude

Laurasia The northern hemisphere supercontinent, consisting of the present North America, Europe and Asia (excluding India), which split from **Pangaea** *c.* 200 million years ago. Laurasia is part of the theory of **continental drift**. *See also* **plate tectonics**.

lava **Magma** extruded onto the Earth's surface via some form of volcanic eruption. Lava varies in viscosity (*see* **viscous lava**), colour and chemical composition. Acidic lavas tend to be viscous and flow slowly; basic lavas tend to be nonviscous and flow quickly. Commonly, **lava flows** comprise basaltic material, as for example in the process of sea-floor spreading (*see* **plate tectonics**).

lava flow A stream of **lava** issuing from some form of volcanic eruption. *See also* **viscous lava**.

lava plateau A relatively flat upland composed of layer upon layer of approximately horizontally bedded lavas. An example of this is the Deccan Plateau of India.

leaching The process by which soluble substances such as mineral salts are washed out of the upper soil layer into the lower layer by rain water.

levée The bank of a river, raised above the general level of the **flood plain** by **sediment** deposition during flooding. When the river bursts its banks, relatively coarse sediment is deposited first, and recurrent flooding builds up the river's banks accordingly.

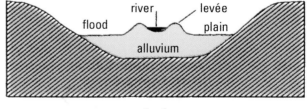

levée

lignite A soft form of **coal**, harder than **peat** but softer than **bituminous coal**.

limestone Calcium-rich **sedimentary rock** formed by the accumulation of the skeletal matter of marine organisms.

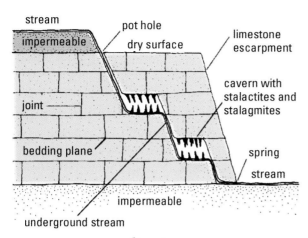

limestone

limestone pavement An exposed **limestone** surface on which the joints have been enlarged by the action of rainwater dissolving the limestone to form weak carbonic acid. These enlarged joints, or **grykes**, separate roughly rectangular blocks of limestone called **clints**.

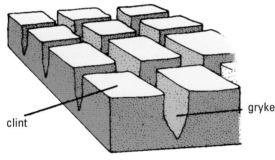

limestone pavement

location The position of population, settlement and economic activity in an area or areas. Location is a basic theme in **human geography**.

loess A very fine **silt** deposit, often of considerable thickness, transported by the wind prior to **deposition**. When irrigated, loess can be very fertile and, consequently, high **yields** can be obtained from crops grown on loess deposits.

longitude A measure of distance on the Earth's surface east or west of the Greenwich Meridian, an imaginary line running from pole to pole through Greenwich in London. Longitude, like **latitude**, is measured in degrees of an angle taken from the centre of the Earth.

The precise location of a place can be given by a **grid**

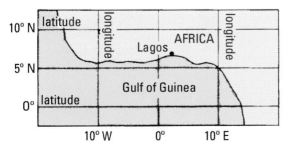

longitude A grid showing the location of Lagos, Nigeria.

reference comprising longitude and latitude. *See also* **map projection, prime meridian**.

longshore drift The net movement of material along a beach due to the oblique approach of waves to the shore. Beach deposits move in a zig-zag fashion, as shown in the diagram. Longshore drift is especially active on long, straight coastlines.

As waves approach, sand is carried up the beach by the **swash**, and retreats back down the beach with the **backwash**. Thus a single representative grain of sand will migrate in the pattern A, B, C, D, E, F in the diagram.

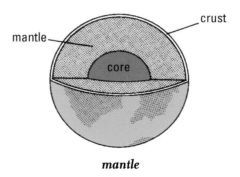

longshore drift

M

magma Molten rock originating in the Earth's **mantle**; it is the source of all **igneous rocks**.

malnutrition The condition of being poorly nourished, as contrasted with **undernutrition**, which is lack of a sufficient quantity of food. The diet of a malnourished person may be high in starchy foods but is invariably low in protein and essential minerals and vitamins.

mantle The largest of the concentric zones of the Earth's structure, overlying the **core** and surrounded in turn by the **crust**.

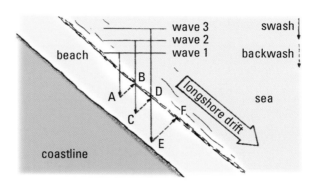

mantle

manufacturing industry The making of articles using physical labour or machinery, especially on a large scale. *See* **secondary sector**.

map Diagrammatic representation of an area – for example part of the earth's surface.

map projection

map projection A method by which the curved surface of the Earth is shown on a flat surface map. As it is not possible to show all the Earth's features accurately on a flat surface, some projections aim to show direction accurately at the expense of area, some the shape of the land and oceans, while others show correct area at the expense of accurate shape.

One of the projections most commonly used is the *Mercator projection*, devised in 1569, in which all lines of **latitude** are the same length as the equator. This results in increased distortion of area, moving from the equator towards the poles. This projection is suitable for navigation charts.

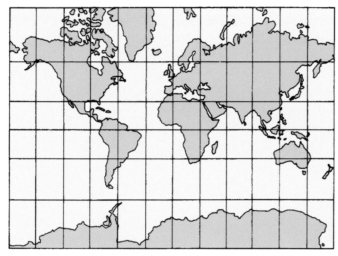

***map projection** Mercator projection.*

The *Mollweide projection* shows the land masses the correct size in relation to each other but there is distortion of shape. As the Mollweide projection has no area distortion it is useful for showing distributions such as population distribution.

The only true representation of the Earth's surface is a globe.

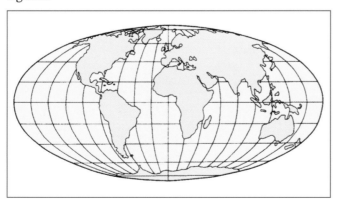

***map projection** Mollweide projection.*

marble A whitish, crystalline **metamorphic rock** produced when **limestone** is subjected to great heat or pressure (or both) during Earth movements.

maritime climate A **temperate climate** that is affected by the closeness of the sea, giving a small annual range of temperatures – a coolish summer and a mild winter – and rainfall throughout the year. Britain has a maritime climate. *Compare* **extreme climate**.

market gardening An intensive type of **agriculture** traditionally located on the margins of urban areas to supply fresh produce on a daily basis to the city population. Typical market-garden produce includes salad crops, such as tomatoes, lettuce, cucumber, etc., cut flowers, fruit and some green vegetables.

maximum and minimum thermometer An instrument for recording the highest and lowest temperatures over a 24-hour period.

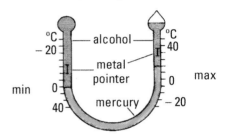

maximum and minimum thermometer

meander A large bend, especially in the middle or lower stages of a river's course. *See* **flood plain**. A meander is the result of lateral **corrasion**, which becomes dominant over vertical corrasion as the **gradient** of the river's course decreases. The characteristic features of a meander are summarized in the diagrams below. *See also* **oxbow lake**.

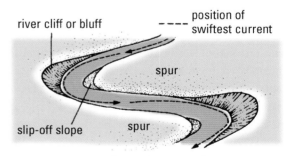

***meander** A river meander.*

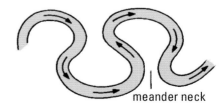

***meander** Fully formed meanders.*

mesa A flat-topped, isolated hill in arid regions. A mesa has a protective cap of hard **rock** underlain by softer, more readily eroded **sedimentary rock**. A **butte** is a relatively small outlier of a mesa.

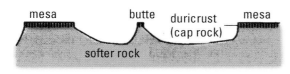

mesa

mesosphere *See* **atmosphere**.

metamorphic rock A **rock** which has been changed by intensive heat or pressure. Metamorphism implies an increase in hardness and resistance to **erosion**. Shale, for example, may be metamorphosed by pressure into **slate**; **sandstone** by heat into **quartzite**, **limestone** into **marble**. Metamorphism of pre-existing rocks is associated with the processes of **folding, faulting** and **vulcanicity**.

migration A permanent or semipermanent change of residence.

monoculture The growing of a single crop.

monsoon The term strictly means 'seasonal wind' and is used generally to describe a situation where there is a reversal of wind direction from one season to another. This is especially the case in South and Southeast Asia, where two monsoon winds occur, both related to the extreme pressure gradients created by the large land mass of the Asian continent.

moraine A collective term for debris deposited on or by **glaciers** and ice bodies in general. Several types of moraine are recognized: *lateral* moraine forms along the edges of a valley glacier where debris eroded from the valley sides, or weathered from the slopes above the glacier, collects; *medial* moraine forms where two lateral moraines meet at a glacier junction; *englacial* moraine is material which is trapped within the body of the glacier; and *ground* moraine is material eroded from the floor of the valley and used by the glacier as an abrasive tool. A *terminal* moraine is material bulldozed by the glacier during its advance and deposited at its maximum down-valley extent. *Recessional* moraines may be deposited at standstills during a period of general glacial retreat.

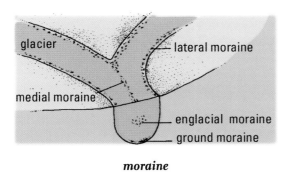

moraine

mortlake *See* **oxbow lake**.

mountain A natural upward projection of the Earth's surface, higher and steeper than a hill, and often having a rocky summit.

northings

N

national park An area of scenic countryside protected by law from uncontrolled development. A national park has two main functions:
    (a) to conserve the natural beauty of the landscape;
    (b) to enable the public to visit and enjoy the
    countryside for leisure and recreation.

natural hazard A natural event which, in extreme cases, can lead to loss of life and destruction of property. Some natural hazards result from geological events, such as **earthquakes** and the eruption of **volcanoes**, whilst others are due to weather events such as **hurricanes**, floods and droughts.

natural increase The increase in population due to the difference between **birth rate** and **death rate**.

neap tides *See* **tides**.

névé Compact snow. In a **corrie** icefield, for example, four layers are recognized: blue and white ice at the bottom of the ice mass; névé overlying the ice and powder snow on the surface.

new town A new urban location created (a) to provide overspill accommodation for a large city or **conurbation**; (b) to provide a new focus for industrial development.

newly industrialized country (NIC) A **developing country** which is becoming industrialized, for example Malaysia and Thailand. Some NICs have successfully used large-scale development to move into the industrialized world. Usually the capital for such developments comes from outside the country.

nivation The process of **weathering** by snow and ice, particularly through **freeze-thaw** action. Particularly active in cold **climates** and high altitudes – for example on exposed slopes above a **glacier**.

nomadic pastoralism A system of **agriculture** in dry grassland regions. People and stock (cattle, sheep, goats) are continually moving in search of pasture and water. The pastoralists subsist on meat, milk and other animal products.

non-governmental organizations (NGOs) Independent organizations, such as charities (Oxfam, Water Aid) which provide aid and expertise to economically developing countries.

nonrenewable resources Resources of which there is a fixed supply, which will eventually be exhausted. Examples of these are metal ores and **fossil fuels**. *Compare* **renewable resources**.

North and South A way of dividing the industrialized nations, found predominantly in the North from those less developed nations in the South. The gap which exists between the rich 'North' and the poor 'South' is called the *development gap*.

northings The second element of a **grid reference**. *See* **eastings**.

nuclear power station

nuclear power station An electricity-generating plant using nuclear fuel as an alternative to the conventional **fossil fuels** of **coal**, oil and gas.

nuée ardente A very hot and fast-moving cloud of gas, ash and rock that flows close to the ground after a violent ejection from a volcano. It is very destructive.

nunatak A mountain peak projecting above the general level of the ice near the edge of an **ice sheet**.

nutrient cycle The cycling of nutrients through the **environment**.

O

ocean A large area of sea. The world's oceans are the Pacific, Atlantic, Indian and Arctic. The Southern Ocean is made up of the areas of the Pacific, Atlantic and Indian Oceans south of latitude 60°S.

ocean current A movement of the surface water of an ocean.

opencast mining A type of mining where the mineral is extracted by direct excavation rather than by shaft or drift methods.

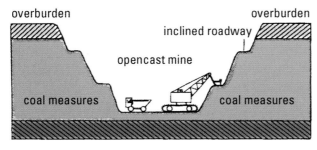

opencast mining

organic farming A system of farming that avoids the use of any artificial fertilizers or chemical pesticides, using only organic fertilizers and pesticides derived directly from animal or vegetable matter. Yields from organic farming are lower, but the products are sold at a premium price.

overfold *See* **fold**.

oxbow lake, mortlake *or* **cut-off** A crescent-shaped lake originating in a **meander** that was abandoned when erosion breached the neck between bends, allowing the stream to flow straight on, bypassing the meander. The ends of the meander rapidly silt up and it becomes separated from the river.

ozone A form of oxygen found in a layer in the **stratosphere**, where it protects the Earth's surface from ultraviolet rays.

P

Pangaea The supercontinent or universal land mass in which all continents were joined together approximately 200 million years ago. *See* **continental drift**.

passage *See* **strait**.

pastoral farming A system of farming in which the raising of livestock is the dominant element. *See also* **nomadic pastoralism**.

peasant agriculture The growing of crops or raising of animals, partly for subsistence needs and partly for market sale. Peasant agriculture is thus an intermediate stage between subsistence and commercial farming.

peat Partially decayed and compressed vegetative matter accumulating in areas of high rainfall and/or poor **drainage**.

peneplain A region that has been eroded until it is almost level. The more resistant rocks will stand above the general level of the land.

per capita income The **GNI** (gross national income) of a country divided by the size of its population. It gives the average income per head of the population if the national income were shared out equally. Per capita income comparisons are used as one indicator of levels of economic development.

periglacial features A periglacial landscape is one which has not been glaciated *per se*, but which has been affected by the severe **climate** prevailing around the ice margin.

permafrost The permanently frozen subsoil that is a feature of areas of **tundra**.

permeable rock Rock through which water can pass via a network of pores between the grains. *Compare* **pervious rock**. *See also* **impermeable rock**.

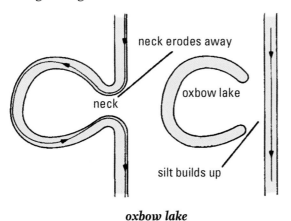

oxbow lake

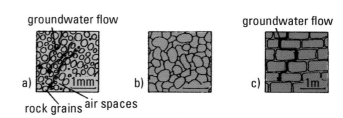

permeable rock (a) *Permeable rock,* (b) *impermeable rock,* (c) *pervious rock.*

population change

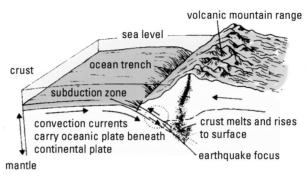

b) Destructive plate boundary
plate tectonics

pervious rock Rock which, even if non-porous, can allow water to pass through via interconnected joints, bedding planes and fissures. An example is **limestone**. *Compare* **permeable rock**. *See also* **impervious rock**.

photosynthesis The process by which green plants make carbohydrates from carbon dioxide and water, and give off oxygen. Photosynthesis balances **respiration**.

physical feature *See* **topography**.

physical geography The study of our **environment**, comprising such elements as geomorphology, hydrology, pedology, meteorology, climatology and biogeography.

pie chart A circular graph for displaying values as proportions:

The journey to work: mode of transport.
(Sample of urban population)

Mode	No.	%	Sector° (% x 3.6)
Foot	25	3.2	11.5
Cycle	10	1.3	4.7
Bus	86	11.1	40.0
Train	123	15.9	57.2
Car	530	68.5	246.6
Total	774	100	360
		per cent	degrees

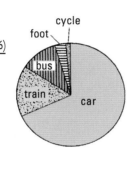

pie chart

plain A level or almost level area of land.

plantation agriculture A system of **agriculture** located in a tropical or semi-tropical **environment**, producing commodities for export to Europe, North America and other industrialized regions. Coffee, tea, bananas, rubber and sisal are examples of plantation crops.

plateau An upland area with a fairly flat surface and steep slopes. Rivers often dissect plateau surfaces.

plate tectonics The theory that the Earth's **crust** is divided into seven large, rigid plates, and several smaller ones, which are moving relative to each other over the upper layers of the Earth's **mantle**. *See* **continental drift**. **Earthquakes** and volcanic activity occur at the boundaries between the plates.

plucking A process of glacial **erosion** whereby, during the passage of a valley **glacier** or other ice body, ice forming in cracks and fissures drags out material from a **rock** face. This is particularly the case with the backwall of a **corrie**.

plug The solidified material which seals the vent of a **volcano** after an eruption.

plutonic rock **Igneous rock** formed at depth in the Earth's **crust**; its crystals are large due to the slow rate of cooling. **Granite**, such as is found in **batholiths** and other deep-seated intrusions, is a common example.

podzol The characteristic **soil** of the **taiga** coniferous forests of Canada and northern Russia. Podzols are leached, greyish soils: iron and lime especially are leached out of the upper horizons, to be deposited as *hardpan* in the B **horizon**.

pollution Environmental damage caused by improper management of **resources**, or by careless human activity.

population change The increase of a population, the components of which are summarized in the following diagram.

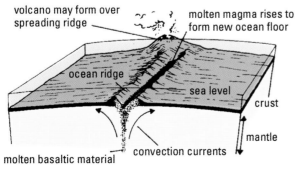

a) Constructive plate boundary
plate tectonics

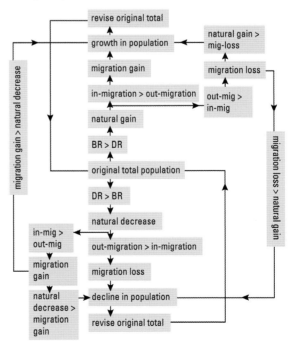

BR= birth rate   DR= death rate
population change

population density

population density The number of people per unit area. Population densities are usually expressed per square kilometre.

population distribution The pattern of population location at a given **scale**.

population explosion On a global **scale**, the dramatic increase in population during the 20th century. The graph below shows world **population growth**.

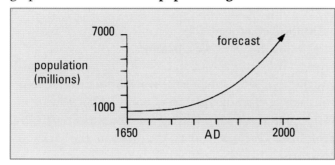

population explosion

population growth An increase in the population of a given region. This may be the result of natural increase (more births than deaths) or of in-migration, or both.

population pyramid A type of **bar graph** used to show population structure, i.e. the age and sex composition of the population for a given region or nation.

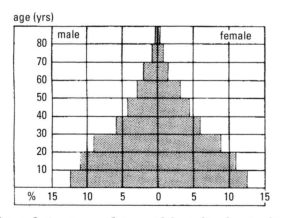

a) **population pyramid** *Pyramid for India, showing high birth rates and death rates.*

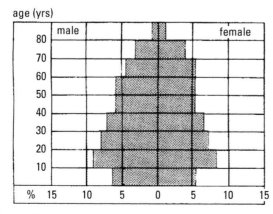

b) **population pyramid** *Pyramid for England and Wales, showing low birth and death rates.*

pothole **1.** A deep hole in limestone, caused by the enlargement of a **joint** through the dissolving effect of rainwater.

2. A hollow scoured in a river bed by the swirling of pebbles and small boulders in eddies.

precipitation Water deposited on the Earth's surface in the form of e.g. rain, snow, sleet, hail and dew.

prevailing wind The dominant wind direction of a region. Prevailing winds are named by the direction from which they blow.

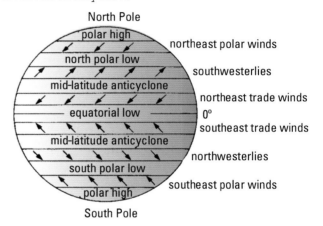

primary sector That sector of the national economy which deals with the production of primary materials: **agriculture**, mining, forestry and fishing. Primary products such as these have had no processing or manufacturing involvement. The total economy comprises the primary sector, the **secondary sector**, the **tertiary sector** and the **quaternary sector**.

primary source *See* **secondary source**.

prime meridian *or* **Greenwich Meridian** The line of 0° longitude passing through Greenwich in London.

pumped storage Water pumped back up to the storage lake of a **hydroelectric power** station, using surplus 'off-peak' electricity.

pyramidal peak A pointed mountain summit resulting from the headward extension of **corries** and **arêtes.** Under glacial conditions a given summit may develop corries on all sides, especially those facing north and east. As these erode into the summit, a formerly rounded profile may be changed into a pointed, steep-sided peak.

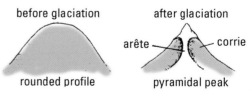

pyramidal peak

pyroclasts Rocky debris emitted during a volcanic eruption, usually following a previous emission of gases and prior to the outpouring of **lava** – although many eruptions do not reach the final lava stage.

ribbon lake

Q

quality of life The level of wellbeing of a community and of the area in which the community lives.

quartz One of the commonest minerals found in the Earth's **crust**, and a form of silica (silicon+oxide). Most **sandstones** are composed predominantly of quartz.

quartzite A very hard and resistant **rock** formed by the metamorphism of **sandstone**.

quaternary sector That sector of the economy providing information and expertise. This includes the microchip and microelectronics industries. Highly developed economies are seeing an increasing number of their workforce employed in this sector. *Compare* **primary sector, secondary sector, tertiary sector**.

R

rain gauge An instrument used to measure rainfall. Rain passes through a funnel into the jar below and is then transferred to a measuring cylinder. The reading is in millimetres and indicates the depth of rain which has fallen over an area.

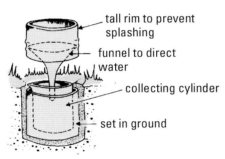

- tall rim to prevent splashing
- funnel to direct water
- collecting cylinder
- set in ground

rain gauge

raised beach *See* **wave-cut platform**.

range A long series or chain of mountains.

rapids An area of broken, turbulent water in a river channel, caused by a stratum of resistant **rock** that dips downstream. The softer rock immediately upstream and downstream erodes more quickly, leaving the resistant rock sticking up, obstructing the flow of the water. *Compare* **waterfall**.

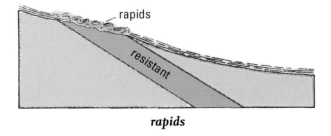

rapids

resistant

rapids

raw materials The **resources** supplied to industries for subsequent manufacturing processes.

reef A ridge of rock, sand or coral whose top lies close to the sea's surface.

regeneration Renewed growth of, for example, forest after felling. Forest regeneration is crucial to the long-term stability of many **resource** systems, from **bush fallowing** to commercial forestry.

region An area of land which has marked boundaries or unifying internal characteristics. Geographers may identify regions according to physical, climatic, political, economic or other factors.

rejuvenation Renewed vertical **corrasion** by rivers in their middle and lower courses, caused by a fall in sea level, or a rise in the level of land relative to the sea.

relative humidity The relationship between the actual amount of water vapour in the air and the amount of vapour the air could hold at a particular temperature. This is usually expressed as a percentage. Relative humidity gives a measure of dampness in the **atmosphere**, and this can be determined by a **hygrometer**.

relief The differences in height between any parts of the Earth's surface. Hence a relief map will aim to show differences in the height of land by, for example, **contour** lines or by a colour key.

remote sensing The gathering of information by the use of electronic or other sensing devices in satellites.

renewable resources Resources that can be used repeatedly, given appropriate management and conservation. *Compare* **non-renewable resources**.

representative fraction The fraction of real size to which objects are reduced on a map; for example, on a 1:50 000 map, any object is shown at 1/50 000 of its real size.

reserves Resources which are available for future use.

reservoir A natural or artificial lake used for collecting or storing water, especially for water supply or **irrigation**.

resource Any aspect of the human and physical **environments** which people find useful in satisfying their needs.

respiration The release of energy from food in the cells of all living organisms (plants as well as animals). The process normally requires oxygen and releases carbon dioxide. It is balanced by **photosynthesis.**

revolution The passage of the Earth around the sun; one revolution is completed in 365.25 days. Due to the tilt of the Earth's axis ($23\frac{1}{2}°$ from the vertical), revolution results in the sequence of seasons experienced on the Earth's surface. *See* diagram overleaf.

ria A submerged river valley, caused by a rise in sea level or a subsidence of the land relative to the sea. *See* diagram overleaf.

ribbon lake A long, relatively narrow lake, usually occupying the floor of a U-shaped glaciated valley. A ribbon lake may be caused by the *overdeepening* of a section of the valley floor by glacial **abrasion**.

Richter scale

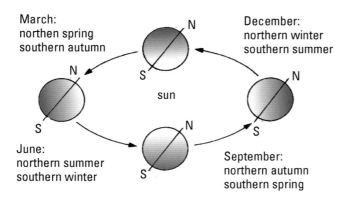

revolution *The seasons of the year.*

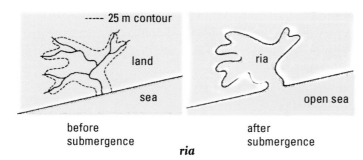

ria

Richter scale A scale of **earthquake** measurement that describes the magnitude of an earthquake according to the amount of energy released, as recorded by **seismographs**.

rift valley A section of the Earth's **crust** which has been downfaulted. The **faults** bordering the rift valley are approximately parallel. There are two main theories related to the origin of rift valleys. The first states that tensional forces within the Earth's crust have caused a block of land to sink between parallel faults. The second theory states that compression within the Earth's crust has caused faulting in which two side blocks have risen up towards each other over a central block.

The most complex rift valley system in the world is that ranging from Syria in the Middle East to the river Zambezi in East Africa.

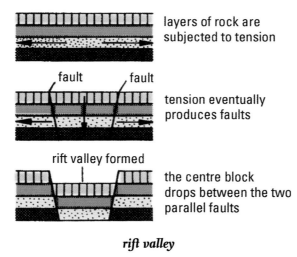

rift valley

river A large natural stream of fresh water flowing along a definite course, usually into the sea.

river basin The area drained by a river and its tributaries, sometimes referred to as a **catchment** area.

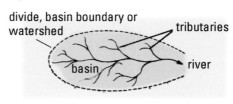

river basin

river cliff *or* **bluff** The outer bank of a **meander**. The cliff is kept steep by undercutting since river **erosion** is concentrated on the outer bank. *See* **meander** and **river's course**.

river's course The route taken by a river from its source to the sea. There are three major sections: the upper course, the middle course and the lower course.

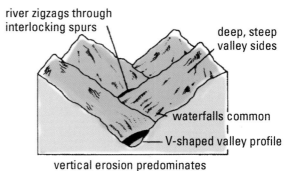

river's course *Upper course.*

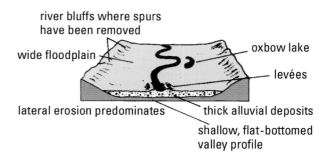

river's course *Lower course.*

river terrace A platform of land beside a river. This is produced when a river is **rejuvenated** in its middle or lower courses. The river cuts down into its **flood plain**, which then stands above the new general level of the river as paired terraces.

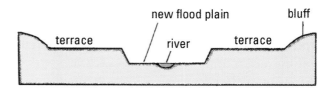

river terrace *Paired river terraces above a flood plain.*

roche moutonnée An outcrop of resistant **rock** sculpted by the passage of a **glacier**.

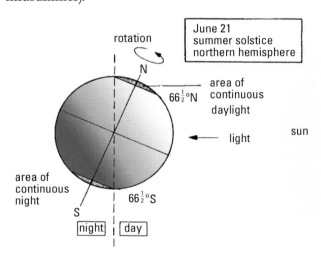

upstream side smoothed and striated by abrasion

passage of ice

downstream side jagged due to plucking

chattermarks – hollows chiselled out by rocks embedded in ice

roche moutonnée

rock The solid material of the Earth's **crust**. *See* **igneous rock, sedimentary rock, metamorphic rock**.

rotation The movement of the Earth about its own axis. One rotation is completed in 24 hours. Due to the tilt of the Earth's axis, the length of day and night varies at different points on the Earth's surface. Days become longer with increasing latitude north; shorter with increasing latitude south. The situation is reversed during the northern midwinter (= the southern midsummer).

June 21 summer solstice northern hemisphere

rotation

N

area of continuous daylight

$66\frac{1}{2}°$N

light

sun

area of continuous night

$66\frac{1}{2}°$S

S

night | day

rotation The tilt of the Earth at the northern summer and southern winter solstice.

rural depopulation The loss of population from the countryside as people move away from rural areas towards cities and **conurbations**.

rural–urban migration The movement of people from rural to urban areas. *See* **migration** and **rural depopulation**.

S

saltpan A shallow basin, usually in a desert region, containing salt which has been deposited from an evaporated salt lake.

sandstone A common **sedimentary rock** deposited by either wind or water.

Sandstones vary in texture from fine- to coarse-grained, but are invariably composed of grains of **quartz**, cemented by such substances as calcium carbonate or silica.

satellite image An image giving information about an area of the Earth or another planet, obtained from a satellite. Instruments on an Earth-orbiting satellite, such as Landsat, continually scan the Earth and sense the brightness of reflected light. When the information is sent back to Earth, computers turn it into *false colour images* in which built-up areas appear in one colour (perhaps blue), vegetation in another (often red), bare ground in a third, and water in a fourth colour, making it easy to see their distribution and to monitor any changes. *Compare* **aerial photograph**.

savanna The grassland regions of Africa which lie between the **tropical rainforest** and the hot **deserts**. In South America, the *Llanos* and *Campos* regions are representative of the savanna type.

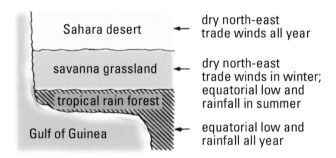

Sahara desert

dry north-east trade winds all year

savanna grassland

dry north-east trade winds in winter; equatorial low and rainfall in summer

tropical rain forest

equatorial low and rainfall in summer

Gulf of Guinea

equatorial low and rainfall all year

savanna The position of the savanna in West Africa.

scale The size ratio represented by a map; for example, on a map of scale 1:25 000, the real landscape is portrayed at 1/25 000 of its actual size.

scarp slope The steeper of the two slopes which comprise an **escarpment** of inclined **strata**. *Compare* **dip slope**.

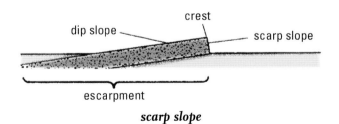

crest

dip slope

scarp slope

escarpment

scarp slope

science park A site accommodating several companies involved in scientific work or research. Science parks are linked to universities and tend to be located on **greenfield** and/or landscaped sites. *Compare* **business park**.

scree *or* **talus** The accumulated **weathering** debris below a **crag** or other exposed rock face. Larger boulders will accumulate at the base of the scree, carried there by greater momentum. *See* diagram overleaf.

sea level

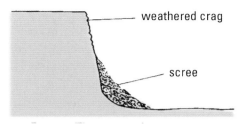

scree or talus

sea level The average height of the surface of the oceans and seas.

secondary sector The sector of the economy which comprises manufacturing and processing industries, in contrast with the **primary sector** which produces **raw materials**, the **tertiary sector** which provides **services**, and the **quaternary sector** which provides information.

secondary source A supply of information or data that has been researched or collected by an individual or group of people and made available for others to use; census data is an example of this. A *primary source* of data or information is one collected at first hand by the researcher who needs it; for example, a traffic count in an area, undertaken by a student for his or her own project.

sediment The material resulting from the **weathering** and **erosion** of the landscape, which has been deposited by water, ice or wind. It may be reconsolidated to form **sedimentary rock**.

sedimentary rock A rock which has been formed by the consolidation of **sediment** derived from pre-existing rocks. **Sandstone** is a common example of a rock formed in this way. **Chalk** and **limestone** are other types of sedimentary rock, derived from organic and chemical precipitations.

seif dune A linear sand dune, the ridge of sand lying parallel to the prevailing wind direction. The eddying movement of the wind keeps the sides of the dune steep.

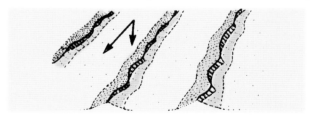

seif dunes

seismograph An instrument which measures and records the seismic waves which travel through the Earth during an **earthquake**.

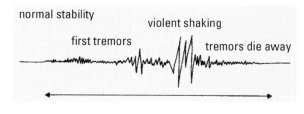

seismograph A typical seismograph trace.

seismology The study of **earthquakes**.

serac A pinnacle of ice formed by the tumbling and shearing of a **glacier** at an ice fall, i.e. the broken ice associated with a change in **gradient** of the valley floor.

service industry The people and organizations that provide a service to the public.

settlement Any location chosen by people as a permanent or semi-permanent dwelling place.

shading map *or* **choropleth map** A map in which shading of varying intensity is used. For example, the pattern of **population densities** in a region.

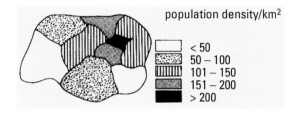

shading map

shanty town An area of unplanned, random, urban development often around the edge of a city. The shanty town is a major element of the structure of many **Third World** cities such as São Paulo, Mexico City, Nairobi, Kolkata and Lagos. The shanty town is characterized by high-density/low-quality dwellings, often constructed from the simplest materials such as scrap wood, corrugated iron and plastic sheeting – and by the lack of standard services such as sewerage and water supply, power supplies and refuse collection.

shifting cultivation *See* **bush fallowing**.

shoreface terrace A bank of **sediment** accumulating at the change of slope which marks the limit of a marine **wave-cut platform**.

 Material removed from the retreating cliff base is transported by the undertow off the wave-cut platform to be deposited in deeper water offshore.

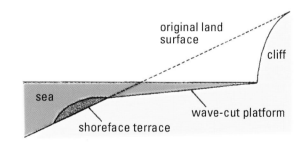

shoreface terrace

silage Any **fodder crop** harvested whilst still green. The crop is kept succulent by partial fermentation in a *silo*. It is used as animal feed during the winter.

sill 1. An igneous intrusion of roughly horizontal disposition. *See* **igneous rock**.
2. (Also called **threshold**) the lip of a **corrie**.

stack

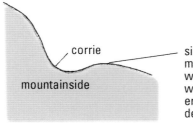

sill

silt Fine **sediment**, the component particles of which have a mean diameter of between 0.002 mm and 0.02 mm.

sinkhole *See* **pothole**.

slash and burn *See* **tropical rainforest**.

slate Metamorphosed shale or **clay**. Slate is a dense, fine-grained **rock** distinguished by the characteristic of *perfect cleavage*, i.e. it can be split along a perfectly smooth plane.

slip The amount of vertical displacement of **strata** at a **fault**.

smog A mixture of smoke and fog associated with urban and industrial areas, that creates an unhealthy **atmosphere**.

snow line The altitude above which permanent snow exists, and below which any snow that falls will not persist during the summer months.

socioeconomic group A group defined by particular social and economic characteristics, such as educational qualifications, type of job, and earnings.

soil The loose material which forms the uppermost layer of the Earth's surface, composed of the *inorganic fraction*, i.e. material derived from the **weathering** of bedrock, and the *organic fraction* – that is material derived from the decay of vegetable matter.

soil erosion The accelerated breakdown and removal of soil due to poor management. Soil erosion is particularly a problem in harsh **environments**.

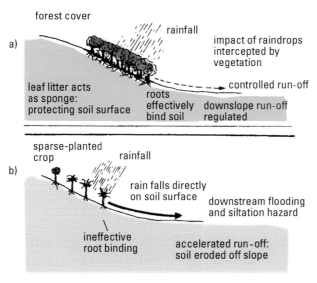

soil erosion a) *Stable environment, b) unstable environment.*

soil profile The sequence of layers or **horizons** usually seen in an exposed soil section.

solar power Heat radiation from the sun converted into electricity or used directly to provide heating. Solar power is an example of a renewable source of energy (*see* **renewable resources**).

solifluction A process whereby thawed surface soil creeps downslope over a permanently frozen **subsoil** (**permafrost**).

spatial distribution The pattern of locations of, for example, population or **settlement** in a region.

spit A low, narrow bank of sand and shingle built out into an **estuary** by the process of **longshore drift**.

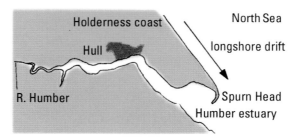

spit *Spurn Head, a coastal spit.*

spring The emergence of an underground stream at the surface, often occurring where **impermeable rock** underlies **permeable rock** or **pervious rock** or **strata**.

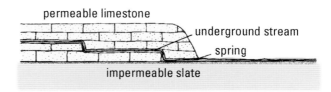

spring *Rainwater enters through the fissures of the limestone and the stream springs out where the limestone meets slate.*

spring tides *See* **tides**.

squatter settlement An area of peripheral urban settlement in which the residents occupy land to which they have no legal title. *See* **shanty town**.

stack A coastal feature resulting from the collapse of a natural arch. The stack remains after less resistant **strata** have been worn away by **weathering** and marine **erosion**.

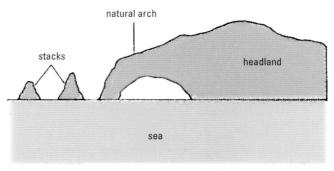

stack

stalactite

stalactite A column of calcium carbonate hanging from the roof of a **limestone** cavern. As water passes through the limestone it dissolves a certain proportion, which is then precipitated by **evaporation** of water droplets dripping from the cavern roof. The drops splashing on the floor of a cavern further evaporate to precipitate more calcium carbonate as a **stalagmite.**

stalagmite A column of calcium carbonate growing upwards from a cavern floor. *Compare* **stalactite.** Stalactites and stalagmites may meet, forming a column or pillar.

staple diet The basic foodstuff which comprises the daily meals of a given people.

Stevenson's screen A shelter used in weather stations, in which thermometers and other instruments may be hung.

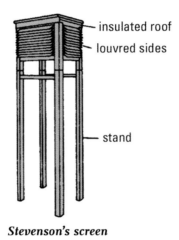

Stevenson's screen

strait, channel *or* **passage** A narrow body of water, between two land masses, which links two larger bodies of water.

strata Layers of **rock** superimposed one upon the other.

stratosphere The layer of the **atmosphere** which lies immediately above the troposphere and below the mesosphere and ionosphere. Within the stratosphere, temperature increases with altitutude.

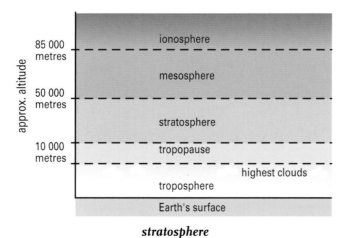

stratosphere

stratus Layer-cloud of uniform grey appearance, often associated with the warm sector of a **depression**. Stratus is a type of low **cloud** which may hang as mist over mountain tops.

striations The grooves and scratches left on bare **rock** surfaces by the passage of a **glacier.**

strip cropping A method of **soil** conservation whereby different crops are planted in a series of strips, often following **contours** around a hillside. The purpose of such a sequence of cultivation is to arrest the downslope movement of soil. *See* **soil erosion.**

subduction zone *See* **plate tectonics.**

subsistence agriculture A system of **agriculture** in which farmers produce exclusively for their own consumption, in contrast to **commercial agriculture** where farmers produce purely for sale at the market.

subsoil *See* **soil profile.**

suburbs The outer, and largest, parts of a town or city.

surface run-off That proportion of rainfall received at the Earth's surface which runs off either as channel flow or overland flow. It is distinguished from the rest of the rainfall, which either percolates into the soil or evaporates back into the **atmosphere.**

sustainable development The ability of a country to maintain a level of economic development, thus enabling the majority of the population to have a reasonable standard of living.

swallow hole *See* **pothole.**

swash The rush of water up the beach as a wave breaks. *See also* **backwash** and **longshore drift.**

syncline A trough in folded **strata**; the opposite of **anticline**. *See* **fold.**

T

taiga The extensive **coniferous forests** of Siberia and Canada, lying immediately south of the arctic **tundra.**

talus *See* **scree.**

tarn The postglacial lake which often occupies a **corrie.**

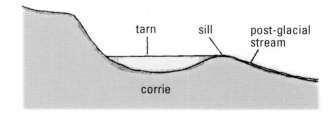

temperate climate A climate typical of mid-latitudes. Such a climate is intermediate between the extremes of hot (tropical) and cold (polar) climates. Compare **extreme climate**. *See also* **maritime climate.**

terminal moraine *See* **moraine.**

terracing A means of **soil** conservation and land utilization whereby steep hillsides are engineered into a

tropical rainforest

series of flat ledges which can be used for **agriculture**, held in places by stone banks to prevent **soil erosion**.

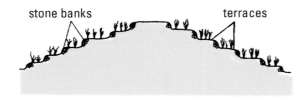

terracing

tertiary sector That sector of the economy which provides **services** such as transport, finance and retailing, as opposed to the **primary sector** which provides **raw materials**, the **secondary sector** which processes and manufactures products, and the **quaternary sector** which provides information and expertise.

thermal power station An electricity-generating plant which burns **coal**, oil or natural gas to produce steam to drive turbines.

Third World A collective term for the poor nations of Africa, Asia and Latin America, as opposed to the 'first world' of capitalist, developed nations and the 'second world' of formerly communist, developed nations. The terminology is far from satisfactory as there are great social and political variations within the 'Third World'. Indeed, there are some countries where such extreme poverty prevails that these could be regarded as a fourth group. Alternative terminology includes '**developing countries**', 'economically developing countries' and 'less economically developed countries' (LEDC). **Newly industrialized countries** are those showing greatest economic development.

threshold *See* **sill** (sense 2).

tidal range The mean difference in water level between high and low tides at a given location. *See* **tides**.

tides The alternate rise and fall of the surface of the sea, approximately twice a day, caused by the gravitational

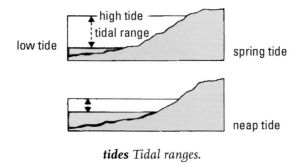

tides Tidal ranges.

pull of the moon and, to a lesser extent, of the sun.

till *See* **boulder clay**.

tombolo A **spit** which extends to join an island to the mainland.

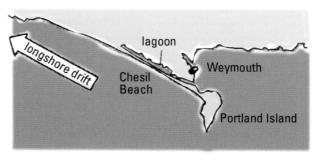

tombolo Chesil Beach, England.

topography The composition of the visible landscape, comprising both physical features and those made by people.

topsoil The uppermost layer of **soil**, more rich in organic matter than the underlying **subsoil**. *See* **horizon**, **soil profile**.

tornado A violent storm with winds circling around a small area of extremely low pressure. Characterized by a dark funnel-shaped cloud. Winds associated with tornadoes can reach speeds of over 300 mph (480 km/h).

trade winds Winds which blow from the subtropical belts of high pressure towards the equatorial belt of low pressure. In the northern hemisphere, the winds blow from the northeast and in the southern hemisphere from the southeast.

transhumance The practice whereby herds of farm animals are moved between regions of different climates. Pastoral farmers (*see* **pastoral farming**) take their herds from valley pastures in the winter to mountain pastures in the summer. *See also* **alp**.

transnational corporation (TNC) A company that has branches in many countries of the world, and often controls the production of the primary product and the sale of the finished article.

tributary A stream or river which feeds into a larger one. *Compare* **distributary**.

tropical rainforest The dense forest cover of the equatorial regions, reaching its greatest extent in the Amazon Basin of South America, the Congo Basin of

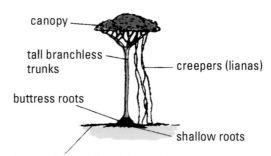

Intense bacterial activity breaks down fallen leaves, etc., to return nutrients to soil surface for immediate uptake by roots. Soils themselves are infertile: the nutrient cycle is concentrated in the vegetation and top few inches of soil.

a forest giant in the tropical rainforest

troposphere

Africa, and in parts of South East Asia and Indonesia. There has been much concern in recent years about the rate at which the world's rainforests are being cut down and burnt. The burning of large tracts of rainforest is thought to be contributing to **global warming**. Many governments and **conservation** bodies are now examining ways of protecting the remaining rainforests, which are unique **ecosystems** containing millions of plant and animal species.

tropics The region of the Earth lying between the *tropics of Cancer* ($23\frac{1}{2}°$N) and *Capricorn* ($23\frac{1}{2}°$S). *See* **latitude**.

troposphere *See* **atmosphere**.

trough An area of low pressure, not sufficiently well-defined to be regarded as a **depression**.

truncated spur A spur of land that previously projected into a valley and has been completely or partially cut off by a moving **glacier**.

tsunami A very large, and often destructive, sea wave produced by a submarine **earthquake**. Tsunamis tend to occur along the coasts of Japan and parts of the Pacific Ocean, and can be the cause of large numbers of deaths.

tuff Volcanic ash or dust which has been consolidated into **rock**.

tundra The barren, often bare-rock plains of the far north of North America and Eurasia where subarctic conditions prevail and where, as a result, vegetation is restricted to low-growing, hardy shrubs and mosses and lichens.

typhoon *See* **hurricane**.

U

undernutrition A lack of a sufficient quantity of food, as distinct from **malnutrition** which is a consequence of an unbalanced diet.

urban decay The process of deterioration in the **infrastructure** of parts of the city. It is the result of long-term shifts in patterns of economic activity, residential **location** and **infrastructure**.

urban sprawl The growth in extent of an urban area in response to improvements in transport and rising incomes, both of which allow a greater physical separation of home and work.

urbanization The process by which a national population becomes predominantly urban through a **migration** of people from the countryside to cities, and a shift from agricultural to industrial employment.

U-shaped valley A glaciated valley, characteristically straight in plan and U-shaped in **cross section**. *See* diagram. *Compare* **V-shaped valley**.

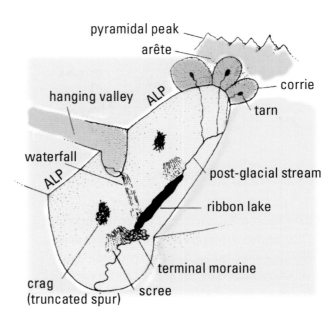

U-shaped valley

V

valley A long depression in the Earth's surface, usually containing a river, formed by **erosion** or by movements in the Earth's **crust**.

vegetation The plant life of a particular region.

viscous lava **Lava** that resists the tendency to flow. It is sticky, flows slowly and congeals rapidly. *Non-viscous* lava is very fluid, flows quickly and congeals slowly.

volcanic rock A category of **igneous rock** which comprises those rocks formed from **magma** which has reached the Earth's surface. **Basalt** is an example of a volcanic rock.

volcano A fissure in the Earth's **crust** through which **magma** reaches the Earth's surface. There are four main types of volcano:

  (a) *Acid lava cone* – a very steep-sided cone composed entirely of acidic, **viscous lava** which flows slowly and congeals very quickly.

  (b) *Composite volcano* – a single cone comprising alternate layers of ash (or other **pyroclasts**) and lava.

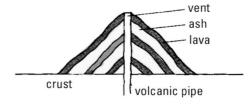

volcano *Composite volcano.*

  (c) *Fissure volcano* – a volcano that erupts along a linear fracture in the crust, rather than from a single cone.

  (d) *Shield volcano* – a volcano composed of very basic, non-viscous lava which flows quickly and congeals slowly, producing a very gently sloping cone.

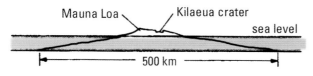

volcano Shield volcano.

V-shaped valley A narrow, steep-sided valley made by the rapid erosion of rock by streams and rivers. It is V-shaped in cross-section. *Compare* **U-shaped valley**.

vulcanicity A collective term for those processes which involve the intrusion of **magma** into the **crust**, or the extrusion of such molten material onto the Earth's surface.

W

wadi A dry watercourse in an arid region; occasional rainstorms in the desert may cause a temporary stream to appear in a wadi.

warm front *See* **depression**.

waterfall An irregularity in the long profile of a **river's course**, usually located in the upper course. *Compare* **rapids**.

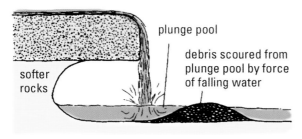

waterfall

watershed The boundary, often a ridge of high ground, between two **river basins**.

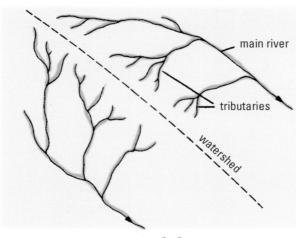

watershed

water table The level below which the ground is permanently saturated. The water table is thus the upper level of the **groundwater**. In areas where **permeable rock** predominates, the water table may be at some considerable depth.

wind vane

wave-cut platform *or* **abrasion platform** A gently sloping surface eroded by the sea along a coastline.

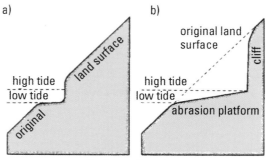

wave-cut platform a) Early in formation,
b) later in formation.

weather The day-to-day conditions of e.g. rainfall, temperature and pressure, as experienced at a particular location.

weather chart A map or chart of an area giving details of **weather** experienced at a particular time of day. Weather charts are sometimes called *synoptic charts*, as they give a synopsis of the weather at a particular time.

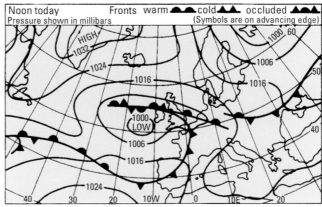

weather chart

weather station A place where all elements of the weather are measured and recorded. Each station will have a **Stevenson's screen** and a variety of instruments such as a **maximum and minimum thermometer**, a **hygrometer**, a **rain gauge**, a **wind vane** and an **anemometer**.

weathering The breakdown of rocks *in situ*; contrasted with **erosion** in that no large-scale transport of the denuded material is involved.

wet and dry bulb thermometer *See* **hygrometer**.

wind vane An instrument used to indicate wind direction. It consists of a rotating arm which always points in the direction from which the wind blows.

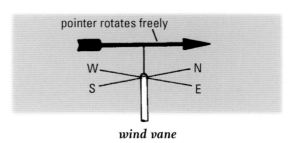

wind vane

yardang

Y

yardang Long, roughly parallel ridges of **rock** in arid and semi-arid regions. The ridges are undercut by wind **erosion** and the corridors between them are swept clear of sand by the wind. The ridges are oriented in the direction of the prevailing wind.

yield The productivity of land as measured by the weight or volume of produce per unit area.

Z

Zeugen *Pedestal rocks* in arid regions; wind **erosion** is concentrated near the ground, where **corrasion** by wind-borne sand is most active. This leads to undercutting and the pedestal profile emerges.

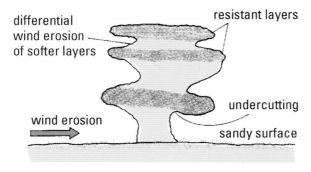

Zeugen

Introduction to the index

The index includes all names shown on the reference maps in the atlas. Each entry includes the country or geographical area in which the feature is located, a page number and an alphanumeric reference. Additional entry details and aspects of the index are explained below.

Name forms

The names policy in this atlas is generally to use local name forms which are officially recognized by the governments of the countries concerned. Rules established by the Permanent Committee on Geographical Names for British Official Use (PCGN) are applied to the conversion of non-roman alphabet names, for example in the Russian Federation, into the roman alphabet used in English.

However, English conventional name forms are used for the most well-known places for which such a form is in common use. In these cases, the local form is included in brackets on the map and appears as a cross-reference in the index. Other alternative names, such as well-known historical names or those in other languages, may also be included in brackets on the map and as cross-references in the index. All country names and those for international physical features appear in their English forms. Names appear in full in the index, although they may appear in abbreviated form on the maps.

Referencing

Names are referenced by page number and by grid reference. The grid reference relates to the alphanumeric values which appear on the edges of each map. These reflect the graticule on the map – the letter relates to longitude divisions, the number to latitude divisions. Names are generally referenced to the largest scale map page on which they appear. For large geographical features, including countries, the reference is to the largest scale map on which the feature appears in its entirety, or on which the majority of it appears.

Rivers are referenced to their lowest downstream point – either their mouth or their confluence with another river. The river name will generally be positioned as close to this point as possible.

Alternative names

Alternative names appear as cross-references and refer the user to the index entry for the form of the name used on the map.

For rivers with multiple names – for example those which flow through several countries – all alternative name forms are included within the main index entries, with details of the countries in which each form applies.

Administrative qualifiers

Administrative divisions are included in entries to differentiate duplicate names – entries of exactly the same name and feature type within the one country – where these division names are shown on the maps. In such cases, duplicate names are alphabetized in the order of the administrative division names.

Additional qualifiers are included for names within selected geographical areas, to indicate more clearly their location.

Descriptors

Entries, other than those for towns and cities, include a descriptor indicating the type of geographical feature. Descriptors are not included where the type of feature is implicit in the name itself, unless there is a town or city of exactly the same name.

Insets

Where relevant, the index clearly indicates [inset] if a feature appears on an inset map.

Alphabetical order

The Icelandic characters Þ and þ are transliterated and alphabetized as 'Th' and 'th'. The German character ß is alphabetized as 'ss'. Names beginning with Mac or Mc are alphabetized exactly as they appear. The terms Saint, Sainte, etc, are abbreviated to St, Ste, etc, but alphabetized as if in the full form.

Numerical entries

Entries beginning with numerals appear at the beginning of the index, in numerical order. Elsewhere, numerals are alphabetized before 'a'.

Permuted terms

Names beginning with generic geographical terms are permuted - the descriptive term is placed after, and the index alphabetized by, the main part of the name. For example, Mount Everest is indexed as Everest, Mount; Lake Superior as Superior, Lake. This policy is applied to all languages. Permuting has not been applied to names of towns, cities or administrative divisions beginning with such geographical terms. These remain in their full form, for example, Lake Isabella, USA.

Gazetteer entries

Selected entries have been extended to include gazetteer-style information. Important geographical facts which relate specifically to the entry are included within the entry.

Abbreviations

admin. dist.	administrative district	IL	Illinois	Phil.	Philippines
admin. div.	administrative division	imp. l.	impermanent lake	plat.	plateau
admin. reg.	administrative region	IN	Indiana	P.N.G.	Papua New Guinea
Afgh.	Afghanistan	Indon.	Indonesia	Port.	Portugal
AK	Alaska	Kazakh.	Kazakhstan	pref.	prefecture
AL	Alabama	KS	Kansas	prov.	province
Alg.	Algeria	KY	Kentucky	pt	point
AR	Arkansas	Kyrg.	Kyrgyzstan	Qld	Queensland
Arg.	Argentina	l.	lake	Que.	Québec
aut. comm.	autonomous community	LA	Louisiana	r.	river
aut. reg.	autonomous region	lag.	lagoon	reg.	region
aut. rep.	autonomous republic	Lith.	Lithuania	res.	reserve
AZ	Arizona	Lux.	Luxembourg	resr	reservoir
Azer.	Azerbaijan	MA	Massachusetts	RI	Rhode Island
b.	bay	Madag.	Madagascar	Rus. Fed.	Russian Federation
Bangl.	Bangladesh	Man.	Manitoba	S.	South, Southern
B.C.	British Columbia	MD	Maryland	S.A.	South Australia
Bol.	Bolivia	ME	Maine	salt l.	salt lake
Bos.-Herz.	Bosnia-Herzegovina	Mex.	Mexico	Sask.	Saskatchewan
Bulg.	Bulgaria	MI	Michigan	SC	South Carolina
c.	cape	MN	Minnesota	SD	South Dakota
CA	California	MO	Missouri	sea chan.	sea channel
Cent. Afr. Rep.	Central African Republic	MS	Mississippi	Sing.	Singapore
CO	Colorado	MT	Montana	Switz.	Switzerland
Col.	Colombia	Mont.	Montenegro	Tajik.	Tajikistan
CT	Connecticut	mt.	mountain	Tanz.	Tanzania
Czech Rep.	Czech Republic	mts	mountains	Tas.	Tasmania
DC	District of Columbia	N.	North, Northern	terr.	territory
DE	Delaware	nat. park	national park	Thai.	Thailand
Dem. Rep. Congo	Democratic Republic of the Congo	N.B.	New Brunswick	TN	Tennessee
depr.	depression	NC	North Carolina	Trin. and Tob.	Trinidad and Tobago
des.	desert	ND	North Dakota	Turkm.	Turkmenistan
Dom. Rep.	Dominican Republic	NE	Nebraska	TX	Texas
E.	East, Eastern	Neth.	Netherlands	U.A.E.	United Arab Emirates
Equat. Guinea	Equatorial Guinea	NH	New Hampshire	U.K.	United Kingdom
esc.	escarpment	NJ	New Jersey	Ukr.	Ukraine
est.	estuary	NM	New Mexico	U.S.A.	United States of America
Eth.	Ethiopia	N.S.	Nova Scotia	UT	Utah
Fin.	Finland	N.S.W.	New South Wales	Uzbek.	Uzbekistan
FL	Florida	N.T.	Northern Territory	VA	Virginia
for.	forest	NV	Nevada	Venez.	Venezuela
Fr. Guiana	French Guiana	N.W.T.	Northwest Territories	Vic.	Victoria
F.Y.R.O.M.	Former Yugoslav Republic of Macedonia	NY	New York	vol.	volcano
g.	gulf	N.Z.	New Zealand	vol. crater	volcanic crater
GA	Georgia	OH	Ohio	VT	Vermont
Guat.	Guatemala	OK	Oklahoma	W.	West, Western
HI	Hawaii	OR	Oregon	WA	Washington
H.K.	Hong Kong	PA	Pennsylvania	W.A.	Western Australia
Hond.	Honduras	Para.	Paraguay	WI	Wisconsin
i.	island	P.E.I.	Prince Edward Island	WV	West Virginia
IA	Iowa	pen.	peninsula	WY	Wyoming
ID	Idaho			Y.T.	Yukon

1

1st Three Mile Opening *sea chan.* Australia **136** D2
2nd Three Mile Opening *sea chan.* Australia **136** C2
3-y Severnyy Rus. Fed. **51** S3
5 de Outubro Angola *see* **Xá-Muteba**
9 de Julio Arg. **178** D5
25 de Mayo *Buenos Aires* Arg. **178** D5
25 de Mayo *La Pampa* Arg. **178** C5
70 Mile House Canada **150** F5
100 Mile House Canada **150** F5
150 Mile House Canada **150** F4

A

Aabenraa Denmark **55** F9
Aachen Germany **62** G4
Aalborg Denmark **55** F8
Aalborg Bugt *b.* Denmark **55** G8
Aalen Germany **63** K6
Aalesund Norway *see* **Ålesund**
Aaley Lebanon *see* **Aley**
Aalst Belgium **62** E4
Aanaar Fin. *see* **Inari**
Aarhus Denmark *see* **Århus**
Aarlen Belgium *see* **Arlon**
Aars Denmark **55** F8
Aarschot Belgium **62** E4
Aasiaat Greenland **147** M3
Aath Belgium *see* **Ath**
Aba China **96** D1
Aba Dem. Rep. Congo **122** D3
Aba Nigeria **120** D4
Abacaxis *r.* Brazil **177** G4
Ābādān Iran **110** C4
Abadan Turkm. **110** E2
Ābādeh Iran **110** D4
Ābādeh Ţashk Iran **110** D4
Abadla Alg. **64** D5
Abaeté Brazil **179** B2
Abaetetuba Brazil **177** I4
Abagaytuy Rus. Fed. **95** I1
Abagnar Qi *Nei Mongol* China *see* **Xilinhot**
Abag Qi *Nei Mongol* China *see* **Xin Hot**
Abaiang *atoll* Kiribati **186** H5
Abajo Peak U.S.A. **159** I3
Abakaliki Nigeria **120** D4
Abakan Rus. Fed. **88** G2
Abakanskiy Khrebet *mts* Rus. Fed. **88** F2
Abalak Niger **120** D3
Abana Turkey **112** D2
Abancay Peru **176** D6
Abariringa *atoll* Kiribati *see* **Kanton**
Abarkūh, Kavīr-e *des.* Iran **110** D4
Abarqū Iran **110** D4
Abarshahr Iran *see* **Neyshābūr**
Abashiri Japan **90** G3
Abashiri-wan *b.* Japan **90** G3
Abasolo Mex. **161** D7
Abau P.N.G. **136** E1
Abaya, Lake Eth. **122** D3
Ābaya Hāyk' *l.* Eth. *see* **Abaya, Lake**
Ābay Wenz *r.* Eth. **122** D2 *see* **Blue Nile**
Abaza Rus. Fed. **88** G2
Abba Cent. Afr. Rep. **122** B3
'Abbāsābād Iran **110** D3
'Abbāsābād Iran **110** E2
Abbasanta *Sardinia* Italy **68** C4
Abbatis Villa France *see* **Abbeville**
Abbe, Lake Djibouti/Eth. **108** F7
Abbeville France **62** B4
Abbeville *AL* U.S.A. **163** C6
Abbeville *GA* U.S.A. **163** D6
Abbeville *LA* U.S.A. **161** E6
Abbeville *SC* U.S.A. **163** D5
Abbey Canada **151** I5
Abbeyfeale Ireland **61** C5
Abbeytown U.K. **58** D4
Abborrträsk Sweden **54** K4
Abbot, Mount Australia **136** D4
Abbot Ice Shelf Antarctica **188** K2
Abbotsford Canada **150** F5
Abbott *NM* U.S.A. **157** G5
Abbott *VA* U.S.A. **164** E5
Abbottabad Pak. **111** I3
'Abd al 'Azīz, Jabal *hill* Syria **113** F3
'Abd al Kūrī *i.* Yemen **108** H7
'Abd Allah, Khawr *sea chan.* Iraq/Kuwait **110** C4
Abd al Ma'asīr *well* Saudi Arabia **107** D4
Ābdānān Iran **110** B3
'Abdollāhābād Iran **110** D3
Abdulino Rus. Fed. **51** Q5
Abéché Chad **121** F3
Abe-gawa *r.* Japan **93** E4
Abellinum Italy *see* **Avellino**
Abel Tasman National Park N.Z. **139** D5
Abengourou Côte d'Ivoire **120** C4
Åbenrå Denmark *see* **Aabenraa**
Abensberg Germany **63** L6
Abeokuta Nigeria **120** D4
Aberaeron U.K. **59** C6
Aberchirder U.K. **60** G3
Abercorn Zambia *see* **Mbala**
Abercrombie *r.* Australia **138** D4
Aberdare U.K. **59** D7
Aberdaron U.K. **59** C6
Aberdaugleddau U.K. *see* **Milford Haven**
Aberdeen Australia **138** E4
Aberdeen *H.K.* China **97** [inset]
Aberdeen S. Africa **124** G7
Aberdeen U.K. **60** G3
Aberdeen U.S.A. **160** D2
Aberdeen Lake Canada **151** L1
Aberdovey U.K. **59** C6
Aberdyfi *Wales* U.K. *see* **Aberdovey**
Aberfeldy U.K. **60** F4
Aberford U.K. **58** F5
Aberfoyle U.K. **60** E4
Abergavenny U.K. **59** D7
Abergwaun U.K. *see* **Fishguard**
Aberhonddu U.K. *see* **Brecon**
Abermaw U.K. *see* **Barmouth**
Abernathy U.S.A. **161** C5
Aberporth U.K. **59** C6
Abersoch U.K. **59** C6
Abertawe U.K. *see* **Swansea**
Aberteifi U.K. *see* **Cardigan**
Aberystwyth U.K. **59** C6
Abeshr Chad *see* **Abéché**
Abez' Rus. Fed. **51** S2
Āb Gāh Iran **111** E5
Abhā Saudi Arabia **108** F6
Abhar Iran **110** C2
Abiad, Bahr el *r.* Sudan/Uganda **108** D6 *see* **White Nile**

▶**Abidjan** Côte d'Ivoire **120** C4
Former capital of Côte d'Ivoire.

Abijatta-Shalla National Park Eth. **122** D3
Ab-i-Kavīr *salt flat* Iran **110** E3
Abiko Japan **93** G3
Abilene *KS* U.S.A. **160** D4
Abilene *TX* U.S.A. **161** D5
Abingdon U.K. **59** F7
Abingdon U.S.A. **164** D5
Abington Reef Australia **136** E3
Abinsk Rus. Fed. **112** E1
Abitau Lake Canada **151** J2
Abitibi, Lake Canada **152** E4
Ab Khūr Iran **110** E3
Abminga Australia **135** F6
Abnūb Egypt **112** C6
Åbo Fin. *see* **Turku**
Abohar India **104** C3
Aboisso Côte d'Ivoire **120** C4
Aboite U.S.A. **164** C3
Abomey Benin **120** D4
Abongabong, Gunung *mt.* Indon. **84** B1
Abong Mbang Cameroon **120** E4
Aborlan *Palawan* Phil. **82** B4
Abō-tōge *pass* Japan **92** D2
Abou Déia Chad **121** E3
Abovyan Armenia **113** G2
Aboyne U.K. **60** G3
Abqaiq Saudi Arabia **110** C5
Abraham's Bay Bahamas **163** F8
Abramov, Mys *pt* Rus. Fed. **52** I2
Abrantes Port. **67** B4
Abra Pampa Arg. **178** C2
Abreojos, Punta *pt* Mex. **166** B3
'Abri Sudan **108** D5
Abrolhos Bank *sea feature* S. Atlantic Ocean **184** F7
Abruzzo, Parco Nazionale d' *nat. park* Italy **68** E4
Absalom, Mount Antarctica **188** B1
Absaroka Range *mts* U.S.A. **156** F3
Abtar, Jabal al *hills* Syria **107** C2
Abtsgmünd Germany **63** J6
Abū ad Ḑuhūr Syria **107** C2
Abū al Abyaḑ *i.* U.A.E. **110** D5
Abū al Ḩusayn, Qā' *imp. l.* Jordan **107** D3
Abū 'Alī *i.* Saudi Arabia **110** C5
Abū 'Āmūd, Wādī *watercourse* Jordan **107** C4
Abū 'Arīsh Saudi Arabia **108** F6
Abu 'Aweigīla *well* Egypt *see* **Abū 'Uwayqilah**
Abu Deleiq Sudan **108** D6

▶**Abu Dhabi** U.A.E. **110** D5
Capital of the United Arab Emirates.

Abū Du'ān Syria **107** D1
Abu Gubeiha Sudan **108** D7
Abū Ḩafnah, Wādī *watercourse* Jordan **107** D3
Abu Haggag Egypt *see* **Ra's al Ḩikmah**
Abū Ḩallūfah, Jabal *hill* Jordan **107** C4
Abu Hamed Sudan **108** D6

▶**Abuja** Nigeria **120** D4
Capital of Nigeria.

Abū Jifān *well* Saudi Arabia **110** B5
Abū Jurdhān Jordan **107** B4
Abū Kamāl Syria **113** F4
Abukuma-gawa *r.* Japan **93** G1
Abukuma-kōchi *plat.* Japan **93** G2
Abu Matariq Sudan **121** F3
Abū Mīnā *tourist site* Egypt **112** C5
Abumombazi Dem. Rep. Congo **122** C3
Abu Musa *i.* The Gulf **110** D5
Abū Mūsá, Jazīreh-ye *i.* The Gulf *see* **Abu Musa**
Abunã *r.* Bol. **176** E5
Abunã Brazil **176** E5
Ābune Yosēf *mt.* Eth. **108** E7
Abū Nujaym Libya **121** E1
Abū Qa'ṭūr Syria **107** C2
Abū Rawthah, Jabal *mt.* Egypt **107** B5
Aburazaka-tōge *pass* Japan **92** C3
Aburo *mt.* Dem. Rep. Congo **122** D3
Abu Road India **104** C4
Abū Rujmayn, Jabal *mts* Syria **107** D2
Abu Rûtha, Gebel *mt.* Egypt *see* **Abū Rawthah, Jabal**
Abū Sawādah *well* Saudi Arabia **110** C5
Abu Simbil Egypt *see* **Abū Sunbul**
Abū Sunbul Egypt **108** D5
Abū Ṭarfā', Wādī *watercourse* Egypt **107** A5
Abut Head *hd* N.Z. **139** C6
Abū 'Uwayqilah *well* Egypt **107** B4
Abuyog *Leyte* Phil. **82** D4
Abu Zabad Sudan **108** C7
Abū Ẓabī U.A.E. *see* **Abu Dhabi**
Abūzam Iran **110** C4
Abū Zanīmah Egypt **112** D5
Abu Zenîma Egypt *see* **Abū Zanīmah**
Abyad Sudan **108** C7
Abyaḑ, Jabal al *mts* Syria **107** C2
Abyār al Hakīm *well* Libya **112** A5
Abydos Australia **134** B5
Abyei Sudan **108** C8
Abyssinia *country* Africa *see* **Ethiopia**
Academician Vernadskiy *research station* Antarctica *see* **Vernadsky**
Academy Bay Rus. Fed. *see* **Akademii, Zaliv**
Acadia *prov.* Canada *see* **Nova Scotia**
Acadia National Park U.S.A. **162** G2
Açailândia Brazil **177** I5
Acajutla El Salvador **167** H6
Acamarachi *mt.* Chile *see* **Pili, Cerro**
Acambaro Mex. **167** E4
Acampamento de Caça do Mucusso Angola **123** C5
Acancéh Mex. **167** H4
Acandí Col. **176** C2
A Cañiza Spain **67** B2
Acaponeta Mex. **168** C4
Acapulco Mex. **168** E5
Acapulco de Juárez Mex. *see* **Acapulco**
Acará Brazil **177** I4
Acarai Mountains *hills* Brazil/Guyana **177** G3
Acaraú Brazil **177** J4
Acaray, Represa de *resr* Para. **178** E3
Acarigua Venez. **176** E2
Acatlán Mex. **168** E5
Acatzingo Mex. **167** F5
Acayucán Mex. **167** G5
Accho Israel *see* **'Akko**
Accomac U.S.A. **165** H5
Accomack U.S.A. *see* **Accomac**

▶**Accra** Ghana **120** C4
Capital of Ghana.

Accrington U.K. **58** E5
Aceh *admin. dist.* Indon. **84** B1
Ach *r.* Germany **63** L6
Achacachi Bol. **176** E7
Achaguas Venez. **176** E2
Achalpur India **104** D5
Achampet India **106** C2
Achan Rus. Fed. **90** E2
Achayvayam Rus. Fed. **77** S3
Achchen Rus. Fed. **148** D2
Acheh *admin. dist.* Indon. *see* **Aceh**
Acheng China **90** B3
Achhota India **106** D1
Achi Japan **92** D3
Achicourt France **62** C4
Achill Ireland **61** C4
Achillbeg Island Ireland **61** C4
Achill Island Ireland **61** B4
Achiltibuie U.K. **60** D2
Achim Germany **63** J1
Achin *admin. dist.* Indon. *see* **Aceh**
Achinsk Rus. Fed. **76** K4
Achit Rus. Fed. **51** R4
Achit Nuur *l.* Mongolia **94** B1
Achkhoy-Martan Rus. Fed. **113** G2
Achna Cyprus **107** A2
Achnasheen U.K. **60** D3
Acıgöl *l.* Turkey **69** M6
Acıpayam Turkey **69** M6
Acireale *Sicily* Italy **68** F6
Ackerman U.S.A. **161** F5
Ackley U.S.A. **160** E3
Acklins Island Bahamas **163** F8
Acle U.K. **59** I6

▶**Aconcagua, Cerro** *mt.* Arg. **178** B4
Highest mountain in South America.

Acopiara Brazil **177** K5
A Coruña Spain **67** B2
Acoyapa Nicaragua **166** [inset] I7
Acqui Terme Italy **68** C2
Acra U.S.A. **165** H2
Acragas *Sicily* Italy *see* **Agrigento**
Acraman, Lake *salt flat* Australia **137** A7
Acre *r.* Brazil **176** E6
Acre Israel *see* **'Akko**
Acre, Bay of Israel *see* **Haifa, Bay of**
Acri Italy **68** G5
Ács Hungary **57** Q7
Actaeon Group *is* Fr. Polynesia *see* **Actéon, Groupe**
Actéon, Groupe *is* Fr. Polynesia **187** K7
Acton Canada **164** E2
Acton U.S.A. **158** D4
Actopán Mex. **167** F4
Acungui Brazil **179** A4
Acunum Acusio France *see* **Montélimar**
Ada *MN* U.S.A. **160** D2
Ada *OH* U.S.A. **164** D3
Ada *OK* U.S.A. **161** D5
Ada *WI* U.S.A. **164** B2
Adabazar *Sakarya* Turkey *see* **Adapazarı**
Adaja *r.* Spain **67** D3
Adak *AK* U.S.A. **149** [inset]
Adak Island *AK* U.S.A. **149** [inset]
Adalia Turkey *see* **Antalya**
Adam Oman **109** I5
Adam, Mount *hill* Falkland Is **178** E8
Adamantina Brazil **179** A3
Adams *IN* U.S.A. **164** C4
Adams *KY* U.S.A. **164** D4
Adams *MA* U.S.A. **165** I2
Adams *NY* U.S.A. **165** G2
Adams, Mount U.S.A. **156** C3
Adams Center U.S.A. **165** G2
Adams Lake Canada **150** G5
Adams Mountain *AK* U.S.A. **149** O5
Adam's Peak Sri Lanka **106** D5
Adams Peak U.S.A. **158** C2
Adamstown Pitcairn Is **187** L7
'Adan Yemen *see* **Aden**
Adana Turkey **107** B1
Adana *prov.* Turkey **107** B1
Adana Yemen *see* **Aden**
Adang, Teluk *b.* Indon. **85** G3
Adapazarı Turkey **69** N4
Adare Ireland **61** D5
Adare, Cape Antarctica **188** H2
Adavale Australia **137** D5
Adban Afgh. **111** H2
Ad Dabbah Sudan *see* **Ed Debba**
Ad Ḑabbīyah *well* Saudi Arabia **110** C5
Ad Dafinah Saudi Arabia **108** F5
Ad Dahnā' *des.* Saudi Arabia **108** G5
Ad Dakhla W. Sahara **120** B2
Ad Damir Sudan *see* **Ed Damer**
Ad Dammām Saudi Arabia *see* **Dammam**
Addanki India **106** C3
Ad Dār al Ḩamrā' Saudi Arabia **108** E4
Ad Darb Saudi Arabia **108** F6
Ad Dawādimī Saudi Arabia **108** F5
Ad Dawḩah Qatar *see* **Doha**
Ad Dawr Iraq **113** F4
Ad Daww *plain* Syria **107** C2
Ad Dayr Iraq **113** G5
Ad Dibdibah *plain* Saudi Arabia **110** B5
Ad Ḑiffah *plat.* Egypt *see* **Libyan Plateau**

▶**Addis Ababa** Eth. **122** D3
Capital of Ethiopia.

Addison U.S.A. **165** G2
Ad Dīwānīyah Iraq **113** G5
Addlestone U.K. **59** G7
Addo Elephant National Park S. Africa **125** G7
Addoo Atoll Maldives *see* **Addu Atoll**
Addu Atoll Maldives **103** D12
Ad Duwayd *well* Saudi Arabia **113** F5
Ad Duwaym Sudan *see* **Ed Dueim**
Ad Duwayris *well* Saudi Arabia **110** C6
Adegaon India **104** D5
Adel *GA* U.S.A. **163** D6
Adel *IA* U.S.A. **160** E3

▶**Adelaide** Australia **137** B7
Capital of South Australia.

Adelaide *r.* Australia **134** E3
Adelaide Bahamas **163** E7
Adelaide Island Antarctica **188** L2
Adelaide River Australia **134** E3
Adele Island Australia **134** C3
Adélie Coast Antarctica **188** G2
Adélie Coast *reg.* Antarctica *see* **Adélie Land**
Adélie Land *reg.* Antarctica **188** G2
Adelong Australia **138** D5
Aden Yemen **108** F7
Aden, Gulf of Somalia/Yemen **108** G7
Adena U.S.A. **164** E3
Adenau Germany **62** G4
Adendorf Germany **63** K1
Aderbissinat Niger **120** D3
Aderno *Sicily* Italy *see* **Adrano**
Adesar India **104** B5
Adhan, Jabal *mt.* U.A.E. **110** E5
Adh Dhāyūf *well* Saudi Arabia **113** G6
'Adhfā' *well* Saudi Arabia **113** F5
'Ādhirīyāt, Jibāl al *mts* Jordan **107** C4
Adi *i.* Indon. **81** I7
Ādī Ārk'ay Eth. **108** E7
Adige *r.* Italy **68** E2
Ādīgrat Eth. **122** D2
Adilabad India **106** C2
Adilcevaz Turkey **113** F3
Adin U.S.A. **156** C4
Adīrī Libya **121** E2
Adirondack Mountains U.S.A. **165** H1
Ādīs Ābeba Eth. *see* **Addis Ababa**
Adi Ugri Eritrea *see* **Mendefera**
Adıyaman Turkey **112** E3
Adjud Romania **69** L1
Adlavik Islands Canada **153** K3
Admiralty Inlet Canada **147** H3
Admiralty Island *AK* U.S.A. **149** N4
Admiralty Island National Monument-Kootznoowoo Wilderness *nat. park* U.S.A. **146** E4
Admiralty Islands P.N.G. **81** L7
Ado-Ekiti Nigeria **120** D4
Adogawa Japan **92** C3
Ado-gawa *r.* Japan **92** C3
Adok Sudan **108** D8
Adolfo L. Mateos Mex. **157** E8
Adolphus U.S.A. **164** B5
Adonara *i.* Indon. **83** B5
Adoni India **106** C3
Adorf Germany **63** M4
Adorf (Diemelsee) Germany **63** I3
Ado-Tymovo Rus. Fed. **90** F2
Adour *r.* France **66** D5
Adra Spain **67** E5
Adramyttium Turkey *see* **Edremit**
Adramyttium, Gulf of Turkey *see* **Edremit Körfezi**
Adrano *Sicily* Italy **68** F6
Adrar Alg. **120** C2
Adrar *hills* Mali *see* **Ifôghas, Adrar des**
Adraskand *r.* Afgh. **111** F3
Adré Chad **121** F3
Adrian *MI* U.S.A. **164** C3
Adrian *TX* U.S.A. **161** C5
Adrianople Turkey *see* **Edirne**
Adrianopolis Turkey *see* **Edirne**
Adriatic Sea Europe **68** E2
Adua Eth. *see* **Ādwa**
Adunara *i.* Indon. *see* **Adonara**
Adusa Dem. Rep. Congo **122** C3
Aduwa Eth. *see* **Ādwa**
Adverse Well Australia **134** C5
Ādwa Eth. **122** D2
Adycha *r.* Rus. Fed. **77** O3
Adyk Rus. Fed. **53** J7
Adzopé Côte d'Ivoire **120** C4
Aegean Sea Greece/Turkey **69** K5
Aegina *i.* Greece *see* **Aigina**
Aegyptus *country* Africa *see* **Egypt**
Aela Jordan *see* **Al 'Aqabah**
Aelana Jordan *see* **Al 'Aqabah**
Aelia Capitolina Israel/West Bank *see* **Jerusalem**
Aelōnlaplap *atoll* Marshall Is *see* **Ailinglaplap**
Aenus Turkey *see* **Enez**
Aerzen Germany **63** J2
Aesernia Italy *see* **Isernia**
A Estrada Spain **67** B2
Afabet Eritrea **108** E6
Afanas'yevo Rus. Fed. **52** L4
Affreville Alg. *see* **Khemis Miliana**
Afghānestān *country* Asia *see* **Afghanistan**
Afghanistan *country* Asia **111** G3
Afgooye Somalia **122** E3
'Afīf Saudi Arabia **108** F5
Afiun Karahissar Turkey *see* **Afyon**
Åfjord Norway **54** G5
Aflou Alg. **64** E5
Afmadow Somalia **122** E3
Afogados da Ingazeira Brazil **177** K5
Afognak *AK* U.S.A. **148** I4
Afognak Island *AK* U.S.A. **148** I4
A Fonsagrada Spain **67** C2
Afonso Cláudio Brazil **179** C3
Āfrēra Terara *vol.* Eth. **108** F7
Africa Nova *country* Africa *see* **Tunisia**
'Afrīn Syria **107** C1
'Afrīn, Nahr *r.* Syria/Turkey **107** C1
Afşin Turkey **112** E3
Afsluitdijk *barrage* Neth. **62** F2
Afton U.S.A. **156** F4
Afuá Brazil **177** H4
'Afula Israel **107** B3
Afyon Turkey **69** N5
Afyonkarahisar Turkey *see* **Afyon**
Aga Germany **63** M4
Aga Rus. Fed. **95** H1
Aga *r.* Rus. Fed. **95** H1
Aga-Buryat Autonomous Okrug *admin. div.* Rus. Fed. *see* **Aginskiy Buryatskiy Avtonomnyy Okrug**
Agadès Niger *see* **Agadez**
Agadez Niger **120** D3
Agadir Morocco **120** C1
Agadyr' Kazakh. **102** D2
Agalega Islands Mauritius **185** L6
Agalta *nat. park* Hond. **166** [inset] I6
Agalta, Sierra de *mts* Hond. **166** [inset] I6
Agana Guam *see* **Hagåtña**
Aganzhen *Gansu* China **94** E5
Agara Georgia **113** F2
Agartala India **105** G5
Agashi India **106** B2
Agate Canada **152** E4
Agathe France *see* **Agde**
Agathonisi *i.* Greece **69** L6
Agats Indon. **81** J8
Agatsuma Japan **93** E2
Agatsuma-gawa *r.* Japan **93** F2
Agatti *i.* India **106** B4
Agattu Island *AK* U.S.A. **148** [inset]
Agattu Strait *AK* U.S.A. **148** [inset]
Agboville Côte d'Ivoire **120** C4
Ağcabädi Azer. **113** G2
Ağdam (abandoned) Azer. **113** G3
Ağdaş Azer. **113** G2
Agdash Azer. *see* **Ağdaş**
Agde France **66** F5
Agdzhabedi Azer. *see* **Ağcabädi**
Agedabia Libya *see* **Ajdābiyā**
Agematsu Japan **92** D3
Agen France **66** E4
Ageo Japan **93** F3
Ageneys S. Africa **124** D5
Aggteleki *nat. park* Hungary **57** R6
Aghil Pass China **104** D1
Agiabampo Mex. **166** C3
Agiguan *i.* N. Mariana Is *see* **Aguijan**
Ağın Turkey **112** E3
Aginskiy Buryatskiy Avtonomnyy Okrug *admin. div.* Rus. Fed. **95** H1
Aginskoye Rus. Fed. **95** H1
Aginskoye Rus. Fed. **88** G1
Aginum France *see* **Agen**
Agios Dimitrios Greece **69** J6
Agios Efstratios *i.* Greece **69** K5
Agios Georgios *i.* Greece **69** J6
Agios Nikolaos Greece **69** K7
Agios Theodoros Cyprus **107** B2
Agiou Orous, Kolpos *b.* Greece **69** J4
Agirwat Hills Sudan **108** E6
Agisanang S. Africa **125** G4
Agnes, Mount *hill* Australia **135** E6
Agnew Australia **135** C6
Agnibilékrou Côte d'Ivoire **120** C4
Agnita Romania **69** K2
Agniye-Afanas'yevsk Rus. Fed. **90** E2
Ago Japan **92** C4
Agose Japan **93** F3
Ago-wan *b.* Japan **92** C4
Agra India **104** D4
Agrakhanskiy Poluostrov *pen.* Rus. Fed. **113** G2
Agram Croatia *see* **Zagreb**
Ağrı Turkey **113** F3
Agria Gramvousa *i.* Greece **69** J7
Agrigan *i.* N. Mariana Is *see* **Agrihan**
Agrigento *Sicily* Italy **68** E6
Agrigentum *Sicily* Italy *see* **Agrigento**
Agrihan *i.* N. Mariana Is **81** L3
Agrinio Greece **69** I5
Agropoli Italy **68** F4
Agryz Rus. Fed. **51** Q4
Ağsu Azer. **113** H2
Agta Point Phil. **82** C3
Agua, Volcán de *vol.* Guat. **168** F6
Agua Brava, Laguna *lag.* Mex. **166** D4
Água Clara Brazil **178** F2
Aguada Mex. **167** H5
Agua de Correra Mex. **167** E5
Aguadilla Puerto Rico **169** K5
Aguadulce Panama **166** [inset] J7
Agua Escondida Arg. **178** C5
Agua Fria *r.* U.S.A. **159** G5
Agua Fria National Monument *nat. park* U.S.A. **159** G4
Aguamilpa, Presa *l.* Mex. **166** D4
Aguanaval *r.* Mex. **161** C7
Aguanga U.S.A. **158** E5
Aguanish *r.* Canada **153** J4
Aguanqueterique Hond. **166** [inset] I6
Agua Nueva Mex. **166** D3
Aguapeí *r.* Brazil **179** A3
Agua Prieta Mex. **166** C2
Aguaro-Guariquito, Parque Nacional *nat. park* Venez. **176** E2
Aguaruto Mex. **166** D3
Aguascalientes Mex. **168** D4
Aguascalientes *state* Mex. **166** E4
Agudos Brazil **179** A3
Águeda Port. **67** B3
Aguemour *reg.* Alg. **120** D2
Agui Japan **92** C4
Aguié Niger **120** D3
Aguijan *i.* N. Mariana Is **81** L4
Aguilar U.S.A. **157** G5
Aguilar de Campóo Spain **67** D2
Águilas Spain **67** F5
Aguililla Mex. **166** E5

▶**Agulhas, Cape** S. Africa **124** E8
Most southerly point of Africa.

Agulhas Basin *sea feature* Southern Ocean **185** J9
Agulhas Negras *mt.* Brazil **179** B3
Agulhas Plateau *sea feature* Southern Ocean **185** J8
Agulhas Ridge *sea feature* S. Atlantic Ocean **184** I8
Agusan *r. Mindanao* Phil. **82** D4
Agutaya Phil. **82** C4
Agutaya *i.* Phil. **82** C4
Ağva Turkey **69** M4
Agvali Rus. Fed. **113** G2
Ahaggar *plat.* Alg. *see* **Hoggar**
Āhangarān Iran **111** F3
Ahar Iran **110** B2
Ahaura N.Z. **139** C6
Ahaus Germany **62** H2
Ahipara Bay N.Z. **139** D2
Ahiri India **106** D2
Ahklun Mountains *AK* U.S.A. **148** G4
Ahlen Germany **63** H3
Ahmadabad India **104** C5
Aḩmadābād Iran **111** E3
Aḩmad al Bāqir, Jabal *mt.* Jordan **107** B5
Aḩmadī Iran **110** E5
Ahmadnagar India **106** B2
Ahmadpur East Pak. **111** H4
Ahmar *mts* Eth. **122** E3
Ahmar Mountains Eth. *see* **Ahmar**
Ahmedabad India *see* **Ahmadabad**
Ahmednagar India *see* **Ahmadnagar**
Ahome Mex. **166** C3
Ahorn Germany **63** K4
Ahr *r.* Germany **62** H4
Ahram Iran **110** C4
Ahrensburg Germany **63** K1
Āhtāri Fin. **54** N5
Ahtme Estonia **55** O7
Ahu China **97** H1
Āhū Iran **110** C4
Ahuacatlán Mex. **166** D4
Ahuachapán El Salvador **167** H6
Ahualulco *Jalisco* Mex. **166** E4
Ahualulco *San Luis Potosí* Mex. **167** E4
Ahun France **66** F3
Ahuzhen China *see* **Ahu**
Ahvāz Iran **110** C4
Ahwa India **106** B1
Ahwāz Iran *see* **Ahvāz**
Ai *i. Maluku* Indon. **83** D4
Ai-Ais Namibia **124** C4
Ai-Ais Hot Springs and Fish River Canyon Park *nature res.* Namibia *see* **Ai-Ais Hot Springs Game Park**
Ai-Ais Hot Springs Game Park *nature res.* Namibia **124** C4
Ai-Ais/Richtersveld Transfrontier Park Namibia/S. Africa **124** C5
Aibag Gol *r.* China **95** G3
Aichi *pref.* Japan **92** D4
Aichi-kōgen Kokutei-kōen *park* Japan **92** D3
Aichilik *r. AK* U.S.A. **149** L1
Aichwara India **104** D4
Aid U.S.A. **164** D4
Aigialousa Cyprus **107** B2
Aigina *i.* Greece **69** J6
Aigio Greece **69** J5
Aigle de Chambeyron *mt.* France **66** H4
Aigües Tortes i Estany de Sant Maurici, Parc Nacional d' *nat. park* Spain **67** G2
Ai He *r.* China **90** B4
Aihua China *see* **Yunxian**
Aihui China *see* **Heihe**
Aijal India *see* **Aizawl**
Aikawa *Kanagawa* Japan **93** F3
Aikawa Japan **91** E5
Aiken U.S.A. **163** D5
Ailao Shan *mts* China **96** D3
Aileron Australia **134** F5
Aileu East Timor **83** C5
Ailigandi Panama **166** [inset] K7
Ailinglabelab *atoll* Marshall Is *see* **Ailinglaplap**
Ailinglaplap *atoll* Marshall Is **186** H5
Ailly-sur-Noye France **62** C5
Ailsa Craig Canada **164** E2
Ailsa Craig *i.* U.K. **60** D5
Ailt an Chorráin Ireland **61** D3
Aimangala India **106** C3
Aimere *Flores* Indon. **83** B5
Aimorés, Serra dos *hills* Brazil **179** C2
Aïn Beïda Alg. **68** B7
'Aîn Ben Tili Mauritania **120** C2
'Ain Dâlla *spring* Egypt *see* **'Ayn Dāllah**
Aïn Defla Alg. **67** H5
Aïn Deheb Alg. **67** G6
Aïn el Hadjel Alg. **67** H6
'Ain el Maqfī *spring* Egypt *see* **'Ayn al Maqfī**
Aïn el Melh Alg. **67** I6
Aïn Mdila *well* Alg. **68** B7
Aïn-M'Lila Alg. **64** F4
Aïn Oussera Alg. **67** H6
Aïn Salah Alg. *see* **In Salah**
Aïn Sefra Alg. **64** D5
Ainsworth U.S.A. **160** D3
Aintab Turkey *see* **Gaziantep**
Aïn Taya Alg. **67** H5
Aïn Tédélès Alg. **67** G6
Aïn Temouchent Alg. **67** F6
'Ain Tibaghbagh *spring* Egypt *see* **'Ayn Tabaghbugh**
'Ain Timeira *spring* Egypt *see* **'Ayn Tumayrah**
'Ain Zeitûn Egypt *see* **'Ayn Zaytūn**
Aiquile Bol. **176** E7
Air *i.* Indon. **84** D2
Airai Palau **82** [inset]
Airaines France **62** B5
Airbangis *Sumatera* Indon. **84** B2
Airdrie Canada **150** H5
Airdrie U.K. **60** F5
Aire *r.* France **62** E5
Aire, Canal d' France **62** C4
Aire-sur-l'Adour France **66** D5
Aïr et du Ténéré, Réserve Naturelle Nationale de l' Niger **122** A2
Air Force Island Canada **147** K3
Airgin Sum *Nei Mongol* China **95** G3
Airhitam *r.* Indon. **85** E3
Airhitam, Teluk *b.* Indon. **85** E3
Air Muda, Tasik *l.* Malaysia **84** C1
Airpanas *Maluku* Indon. **83** C4
Air Pedu, Tasik *l.* Malaysia **84** C1
Aisatung Mountain Myanmar **86** A2
Aisch *r.* Germany **63** L5
Ai Shan *hill Shandong* China **95** J4
Aishihik Y.T. Canada **149** M3
Aishihik Lake Y.T. Canada **149** M3
Aisne *r.* France **62** C5
Aïssa, Djebel *mt.* Alg. **64** D5
Aitamännikkö Fin. **54** N3
Aitana *mt.* Spain **67** F4
Aït Benhaddou *tourist site* Morocco **64** C5
Aiterach *r.* Germany **63** M6
Aitkin U.S.A. **160** E2
Aitō Japan **92** C3
Aiud Romania **69** J1
Aiwokako Passage Palau **82** [inset]
Aix France *see* **Aix-en-Provence**
Aix-en-Provence France **66** G5
Aix-la-Chapelle Germany *see* **Aachen**
Aix-les-Bains France **66** G4
Aiyina *i.* Greece *see* **Aigina**
Aiyion Greece *see* **Aigio**
Aizawl India **105** H5
Aizkraukle Latvia **55** N8
Aizpute Latvia **55** L8
Aizu-Wakamatsu Japan **91** E5
Ajaccio *Corsica* France **66** I6
Ajalpán Mex. **167** F5
Ajanta India **106** B1
Ajanta Range *hills* India *see* **Sahyadriparvat Range**
Ajaureforsen Sweden **54** I4
Ajax Canada **164** F2
Ajayameru India *see* **Ajmer**
Ajban U.A.E. **110** D5
Aj Bogd Uul *mt.* Mongolia **102** I3
Aj Bogd Uul *mts* Mongolia **94** C2
Ajdābiyā Libya **121** F1

a-Jiddét des. Oman see Ḩarāsīs, Jiddat al
Ajiro Japan 93 F3
'Ajlūn Jordan 107 B3
'Ajman U.A.E. 110 D5
Ajmer India 104 C4
Ajmer-Merwara India see Ajmer
Ajnala India 104 C3
Ajo U.S.A. 159 G5
Ajo, Mount U.S.A. 159 G5
Ajrestan Afgh. 111 G3
Ajuchitlán Mex. 167 E5
Ajuy Panay Phil. 82 C4
Ajyyap Turkm. 110 D2
Akabane Japan 92 D4
Akabori Japan 93 F2
Akademii, Zaliv b. Rus. Fed. 90 E1
Akademii Nauk, Khrebet mt. Tajik. see Akademiyai Fanho, Qatorkŭhi
Akademiyai Fanho, Qatorkŭhi mt. Tajik. 111 H2
Akagera National Park Rwanda 122 D4
Akagi Gunma Japan 93 F2
Akagi-yama vol. Japan 93 F2
Akaishi-dake mt. Japan 93 E3
Akaishi-sanmyaku mts Japan 93 D4
Akalkot India 106 C2
Akama, Akra c. Cyprus see Arnauti, Cape
Akamagaseki Japan see Shimonoseki
Akan Kokuritsu-kōen Japan 90 G4
Akaroa N.Z. 139 D6
Akas reg. India 96 B3
Akāshat Iraq 113 E4
Akashi Japan 92 A4
Akashi-kaikyō str. Japan 92 A4
Akashina Japan 93 D2
Akbalyk Kazakh. 98 B3
Akbarābād Iran 113 I5
Akbarpur Uttar Prad. India 104 E4
Akbarpur Uttar Prad. India 105 E4
Akbaur Kazakh. 98 A2
Akbaytal, Pereval pass Tajik. 111 I2
Akbaytal Pass Tajik. see Akbaytal, Pereval
Akbez Turkey 107 C1
Akbulak Kazakh. 98 B2
Akbulak Kazakh. 98 D2
Akçadağ Turkey 112 E3
Akçakale Turkey 107 D1
Akçakoca Turkey 69 N4
Akçakoca Dağları mts Turkey 69 N4
Akçakoyunlu Turkey 107 C1
Akçalı Dağları mts Turkey 107 A1
Akchâr reg. Mauritania 120 B3
Akchatau Kazakh. 98 A3
Akchi Kazakh. see Akshiy
Akdağlar mts Turkey 69 M6
Akdağmadeni Turkey 112 D3
Akdere Turkey 107 A1
Akechi Japan 92 D3
Akelamo Halmahera Indon. 83 C3
Akelamo Halmahera Indon. 83 D2
Akeno Ibaraki Japan 93 G2
Akeno Yamanashi Japan 93 E3
Åkersberga Sweden 55 K7
Akersloot Neth. 62 E2
Aketi Dem. Rep. Congo 122 C3
Akgyr Erezi hills Turkm. 110 D1
Akhali-Afoni Georgia see Akhali Ap'oni
Akhali Ap'oni Georgia 113 F2
Akhḑar, Al Jabal al mts Libya 121 F1
Akhḑar, Jabal mts Oman 110 E6
Akhiok AK U.S.A. 148 I4
Akhisar Turkey 69 L5
Akhnoor India 104 C2
Akhsu Azer. see Ağsu
Akhta Armenia see Hrazdan
Akhtarīn Syria 107 C1
Akhtubinsk Rus. Fed. 53 J6
Akhty Rus. Fed. 113 G2
Akhtyrka Ukr. see Okhtyrka
Aki Japan 91 D6
Akiachak AK U.S.A. 148 G3
Akiéni Gabon 122 B4
Akimiski Island Canada 152 E3
Akiruno Japan 93 F3
Akishma r. Rus. Fed. 90 D1
Akita Japan 91 F5
Akiyama-gawa r. Japan 93 F2
Akjoujt Mauritania 120 B3
Akkajaure l. Sweden 54 J3
Akkani Rus. Fed. 148 E2
Akkem Rus. Fed. 98 D2
Akkerman Ukr. see Bilhorod-Dnistrovs'kyy
Akkeshi Japan 90 G4
'Akko Israel 107 B3
Akkol' Akmolinskaya Oblast' Kazakh. 102 D1
Akkol' Almatinskaya Oblast' Kazakh. 98 A3
Akkol' Atyrauskaya Oblast' Kazakh. 53 K7
Akku Kazakh. 102 E1
Akkul' Kazakh. see Akkol'
Akkuş Turkey 112 E2
Akkyr, Gory hills Turkm. see Akgyr Erezi
Aklavik N.W.T. Canada 149 N1
Aklera India 104 D4
Ak-Mechet Kazakh. see Kyzylorda
Akmeņrags pt Latvia 55 L8
Akmeqit Xinjiang China 99 B5
Akmola Kazakh. see Astana
Akmolinsk Kazakh. see Astana
Ak-Moyun Kyrg. 98 B4
Akobo Sudan 121 G4
Akobo Wenz r. Eth./Sudan 122 D3
Akokan Niger 120 D3
Akola India 106 C1
Akom II Cameroon 120 E4
Akongkür Xinjiang China 98 B4
Akonolinga Cameroon 120 E4
Akordat Eritrea 108 E6
Akören Turkey 112 D3
Akot India 104 D5
Akpatok Island Canada 153 I1
Akqi Xinjiang China 98 B4
Akra, Jabal mt. Syria/Turkey see Aqra', Jabal al
Akranes Iceland 54 [inset]
Åkrehamn Norway 55 D7
Akrérèb Niger 120 D3
Akron CO U.S.A. 160 C3
Akron IN U.S.A. 164 B3
Akron OH U.S.A. 164 E3
Akrotiri Bay Cyprus 107 A2
Akrotirion Bay Cyprus see Akrotiri Bay
Akrotiriou, Kolpos b. Cyprus see Akrotiri Bay
Akrotiri Sovereign Base Area military base Cyprus 107 A2

▶Aksai Chin terr. Asia 104 D2
Disputed territory (China/India).

Aksaray Turkey 112 D3
Aksay Gansu China 98 F5
Aksay Kazakh. 51 Q5
Ak-Say r. Kyrg. 109 M1
Aksay Rus. Fed. 53 H7
Aksayqin Hu l. Aksai Chin 99 B6
Akşehir Turkey 69 N5
Akşehir Gölü l. Turkey 69 N5
Akseki Turkey 112 C3
Aksha Rus. Fed. 95 H1
Akshiganak Kazakh. 102 B2
Akshiy Kazakh. 102 E3
Akshukur Kazakh. 113 H2
Aksu Xinjiang China 98 C4
Aksu Xinjiang China 98 C4
Aksu Almatinskaya Oblast' Kazakh. 98 B3
Aksu Kazakh. 102 E1
Aksu r. Kazakh. 98 B3
Aksu r. Tajik. see Oqsu
Aksu r. Turkey 69 N6
Aksuat Kazakh. 102 F2
Aksu-Ayuly Kazakh. 102 D2
Aksubayevo Rus. Fed. 53 K5
Aksu He r. China 98 C4
Āksum Eth. 108 E7
Aksüme Xinjiang China 98 C3
Aksuyek Kazakh. 98 A3
Aktag mt. Xinjiang China 99 D5
Aktam Xinjiang China 98 B5
Aktas Dağı mt. Turkey 113 G3
Aktash Rus. Fed. 98 D2
Aktau Karagandinskaya Oblast' Kazakh. 98 A2
Aktau Kazakh. 100 E2
Akto Xinjiang China 98 B5
Aktobe Kazakh. 100 E1
Aktogay Karagandinskaya Oblast' Kazakh. 102 E2
Aktogay Vostochnyy Kazakhstan Kazakh. 102 E2
Aktsyabrski Belarus 53 F5
Ak-Tüz Kyrg. 98 A4
Aktyubinsk Kazakh. see Aktobe
Akulivik Canada 147 K3
Akune Japan 91 C6
Akun Island AK U.S.A. 148 F5
Akure Nigeria 120 D4
Akuressa Sri Lanka 106 D5
Akureyri Iceland 54 [inset]
Akusha Rus. Fed. 53 J8
Akutan AK U.S.A. 148 F5
Akutan Island AK U.S.A. 148 F5
Akutan Pass sea channel AK U.S.A. 148 F5
Akwanga Nigeria 120 D4
Akxokesay Qinghai China 99 E5
Akyab Myanmar see Sittwe
Akyatan Gölü salt l. Turkey 107 B1
Akyazı Turkey 69 N4
Akzhal Karagandinskaya Oblast' Kazakh. 98 A3
Akzhal Vostochnyy Kazakhstan Kazakh. 98 C2
Akzhar Vostochnyy Kazakhstan Kazakh. 98 C3
Akzhartas Kazakh. 98 A3
Akzhaykyn, Ozero salt l. Kazakh. 102 C3
Ål Norway 55 F6
'Alā, Jabal al hills Syria 107 C2
Alabama r. U.S.A. 163 C6
Alabama state U.S.A. 163 C5
Alabaster AL U.S.A. 163 C5
Alabaster MI U.S.A. 164 D1
Al 'Abţīyah well Iraq 113 G5
Al Abyār Libya 120 F1
Alaca Turkey 112 D2
Alacahan Turkey 112 E3
Alaçam Turkey 112 D2
Alaçam Dağları mts Turkey 69 M5
Alacant Valencia Spain see Alicante
Alaçatı Turkey 69 L5
Alacrán, Arrecife rf Mex. 167 H4
Aladağ Turkey 112 D3
Ala Dağlar mts Turkey 113 F3
Ala Dağları mts Turkey 112 D3
Al 'Adam Libya 112 A5
Ala'er Xinjiang China 98 C4
Al Aflāj reg. Saudi Arabia 110 B6
Alaganik AK U.S.A. 149 K3
Alag-Erdene Hövsgöl Mongolia 94 D1
Alag Hayrhan Uul mt. Mongolia 94 C2
Alag Hu l. Qinghai China 94 D5
Alagir Rus. Fed. 113 G2
Alagnak r. AK U.S.A. 148 H4
Alagoinhas Brazil 179 D1
Ala Gou r. China 98 E4
Alah r. Mindanao Phil. 82 D5
Alahanpanjang Sumatera Indon. 84 C3
Alahärmä Fin. 54 M5
Al Aḩmadī Kuwait 110 C4
Alai Range mts Asia 111 H2
Ālaivān Iran 110 D3
Ālājah Syria 107 B2
Alajärvi Fin. 54 M5
Al 'Ajrūd well Egypt 107 B4
Alajuela Costa Rica 166 [inset] I7
Alakanuk AK U.S.A. 148 F3
Al Akhḑar Saudi Arabia 112 E5
Alakol', Ozero salt l. Kazakh. 102 F2
Alaktak AK U.S.A. 148 I1
Ala Kul salt l. Kazakh. see Alakol', Ozero
Alakurtti Rus. Fed. 54 Q3
Al 'Alamayn Egypt 112 C5
Al 'Alayyah Saudi Arabia 108 F6
Alama Somalia 122 E3
Al 'Amādīyah Iraq 113 F3
Alamagan i. N. Mariana Is 81 L3
Alamaguan i. N. Mariana Is see Alamagan
Al 'Amārah Iraq 113 G5
'Alam ar Rūm, Ra's pt Egypt 112 B5
'Alāmarvdasht watercourse Iran 110 D4
Alameda U.S.A. 158 B3
'Alam el Rûm, Râs pt Egypt see 'Alam ar Rūm, Ra's
Al Amghar waterhole Iraq 113 G5
Alamicamba Nicaragua 166 [inset] I6
Alaminos Luzon Phil. 82 B2
Al 'Āmirīyah Egypt 112 C5
Alamítos, Sierra de los mt. Mex. 166 E3
Alamo GA U.S.A. 163 D5
Alamo NV U.S.A. 159 F3
Alamo Dam U.S.A. 159 G4
Alamogordo U.S.A. 157 G6
Alamo Heights U.S.A. 161 D6
Alamos Sonora Mex. 166 C2
Alamos Sonora Mex. 166 C3
Alamos r. Mex. 167 E3
Alamos, Sierra mts Mex. 166 C3
Alamosa U.S.A. 157 G5
Alamos de Peña Mex. 166 D2
Alampur India 106 C3
Alan Myanmar see Aunglan
Alanäs Sweden 54 I4
Åland is Fin. see Åland Islands
Aland r. Germany 63 L1
Aland India 106 C2
Al Andarīn Syria 107 C2
Åland Islands Fin. 55 K6
Alando Xizang China 99 F7
Alandur India 106 D3
Alang Kalimantan Indon. 85 G1
Alangalang, Tanjung pt Indon. 85 G3
Alang Besar i. Indon. 84 C2
Alanggantang i. Indon. 84 D3
Alanson U.S.A. 164 C1
Alanya Turkey 112 D3
Alaplı Turkey 69 N4
Alappuzha India see Alleppey
Alapuzha India see Alleppey
Al 'Aqabah Jordan 107 B5
Al 'Aqīq Saudi Arabia 108 F5
Al 'Arabīyah as Sa'ūdīyah country Asia see Saudi Arabia
Alarcón, Embalse de resr Spain 67 E4
Al 'Arīsh Egypt 107 A4
Al Arţāwīyah Saudi Arabia 108 G4
Alas Sumbawa Indon. 85 G5
Alas, Selat sea chan. Indon. 85 G5
Alaşehir Turkey 69 M5
Alashiya country Asia see Cyprus
Al Ashmūnayn Egypt 112 C6
Alaska state U.S.A. 149 L3
Alaska, Gulf of AK U.S.A. 149 K4
Alaska Highway Canada/U.S.A. 149 L3
Alaska Maritime National Wildlife Refuge nature res. AK U.S.A. 149 [inset]
Alaska Peninsula AK U.S.A. 148 G5
Alaska Peninsula National Wildlife Refuge nature res. AK U.S.A. 148 H4
Alaska Range mts AK U.S.A. 149 J3
Alas Purwo, Taman Nasional nat. park Indon. 85 F5
Älät Azer. 113 H3
Alat Uzbek. see Olot
Alataw Shankou pass China/Kazakh. see Dzungarian Gate
Alatna AK U.S.A. 148 I2
Alatna r. AK U.S.A. 148 I2
Al Atwā' well Saudi Arabia 113 F5
Alatyr' Rus. Fed. 53 J5
Alatyr' r. Rus. Fed. 53 J5
Alausí Ecuador 176 C4
Alaverdi Armenia 113 G2
'Alavī Iran 110 C3
Alavieska Fin. 54 N4
Alavus Fin. 54 M5
Alawbum Myanmar 86 B1
Alawoona Australia 137 C7
Alay Kyrka Toosu mts Asia see Alai Range
Al 'Ayn Oman 110 E6
Al 'Ayn U.A.E. 110 D5
Alayskiy Khrebet mts Asia see Alai Range
Al 'Azīzīyah Iraq 113 G4

▶Al 'Azīzīyah Libya 120 E1
Highest recorded shade temperature in the world.

Al Azraq al Janūbī Jordan 107 C4
Alba Italy 68 C2
Alba U.S.A. 164 C1
Al Bāb Syria 107 C1
Albacete Spain 67 F4
Al Badī' Saudi Arabia 110 B6
Al Bādiyah al Janūbīyah hill Iraq 113 G5
Al Bahrayn country Asia see Bahrain
Alba Iulia Romania 69 J1
Al Bajā' well U.A.E. 110 C5
Albājī Iran 110 C4
Al Bakhrā well Saudi Arabia 110 B5
Albanel, Lac l. Canada 153 G4
Albania country Europe 69 H4
Albany Australia 135 B8
Albany r. Canada 152 E3
Albany GA U.S.A. 163 C6
Albany IN U.S.A. 164 C3
Albany KY U.S.A. 164 C5
Albany MO U.S.A. 160 E3

▶Albany NY U.S.A. 165 I2
Capital of New York state.

Albany OH U.S.A. 164 D4
Albany OR U.S.A. 156 C3
Albany TX U.S.A. 161 D5
Albany Downs Australia 138 D1
Albardão do João Maria coastal area Brazil 178 F4
Al Bardī Libya 112 B5
Al Bāridah hills Saudi Arabia 107 D5
Al Başrah Iraq see Basra
Al Baţḩa' marsh Iraq 113 G5
Al Bāţinah reg. Oman 110 E5
Albatross Bay Australia 136 C2
Albatross Island Australia 137 [inset]
Al Bawītī Egypt 112 C5
Al Bayḑā' Libya 108 B3
Al Bayḑā' Yemen 108 G7
Albay Gulf Luzon Phil. 82 C3
Albemarle U.S.A. 163 D5
Albemarle Island Galápagos Ecuador see Isabela, Isla
Albemarle Sound sea chan. U.S.A. 162 E5
Albenga Italy 68 C2
Alberche r. Spain 67 D4
Alberga Australia 137 A5
Alberga watercourse Australia 137 A5
Albergaria-a-Velha Port. 67 B3
Albert Australia 138 C4
Albert France 62 C5
Albert, Lake Dem. Rep. Congo/Uganda 122 D3
Albert, Parc National nat. park Dem. Rep. Congo see Virunga, Parc National des
Alberta prov. Canada 150 H4
Alberta U.S.A. 165 G5
Albert Kanaal canal Belgium 62 F4
Albert Lea U.S.A. 160 E3
Albert Nile r. Sudan/Uganda 121 G4
Alberto de Agostini, Parque Nacional nat. park Chile 178 B8
Alberton S. Africa 125 I4
Alberton U.S.A. 156 E3
Albert Town Bahamas 163 F8
Albertville Dem. Rep. Congo see Kalemie
Albertville France 66 H4
Albertville U.S.A. 163 C5
Albestroff France 62 G6
Albi France 66 F5
Albia U.S.A. 160 E3
Al Bīḑah des. Saudi Arabia 110 C5
Albina Suriname 177 H2
Albino Italy 68 C2
Albion CA U.S.A. 158 B2
Albion IL U.S.A. 160 F4
Albion IN U.S.A. 164 C3
Albion MI U.S.A. 164 C2
Albion NE U.S.A. 160 D3
Albion NY U.S.A. 165 F2
Albion PA U.S.A. 164 E3
Al Biqā' valley Lebanon see El Béqaa
Al Bi'r Saudi Arabia 112 E5
Al Birk Saudi Arabia 108 F6
Al Biyāḑh reg. Saudi Arabia 108 G5
Alborán, Isla de i. Spain 67 E6
Ålborg Denmark see Aalborg
Ålborg Bugt b. Denmark see Aalborg Bugt
Albro Australia 136 D4
Al Budayyi' Bahrain 110 C5
Albufeira Port. 67 B5
Al Buḩayrāt al Murrah lakes Egypt see Bitter Lakes
Albuquerque U.S.A. 157 G6
Albuquerque, Cayos de is Caribbean Sea 166 [inset] J6
Al Burayj Syria 107 C2
Al Buraymī Oman 110 D5
Al Burj Jordan 107 B5
Alburquerque Spain 67 C4
Albury Australia 138 C6
Al Buşayrah Syria 113 F4
Al Busayţā' plain Saudi Arabia 107 D4
Al Bushūk well Saudi Arabia 110 B4
Alcácer do Sal Port. 67 B4
Alcalá de Henares Spain 67 E3
Alcalá la Real Spain 67 E5
Alcamo Sicily Italy 68 E6
Alcañiz Spain 67 F3
Alcántara Spain 67 C4
Alcantara Lake Canada 151 I2
Alcaraz Spain 67 E4
Alcázar de San Juan Spain 67 E4
Alcazarquivir Morocco see Ksar el Kebir
Alchevs'k Ukr. 53 H6
Alcobaça Brazil 179 D2
Alcoi Spain see Alcoy-Alcoi
Alcoota Australia 134 F5
Alcova U.S.A. 156 G4
Alcoy Spain see Alcoy-Alcoi
Alcoy-Alcoi Spain 67 F4
Alcúdia Spain 67 H4
Aldabra Islands Seychelles 123 E4
Aldama Chihuahua Mex. 166 D2
Aldama Tamaulipas Mex. 167 F4
Aldan Rus. Fed. 77 N4
Aldan r. Rus. Fed. 77 N3
Alde r. U.K. 59 I6
Aldeboarn Neth. 62 F1
Aldeburgh U.K. 59 I6
Alder Creek U.S.A. 165 H2
Alderney i. Channel Is 59 E9
Alder Peak U.S.A. 158 C4
Aldershot U.K. 59 G7
Al Dhafrah reg. U.A.E. 110 D6
Aldingham U.K. 58 D4
Aldridge U.K. 59 F6
Aleg Mauritania 120 B3
Alegre Espírito Santo Brazil 179 C3
Alegre Minas Gerais Brazil 179 B2
Alegrete Brazil 178 E3
Alegros Mountain U.S.A. 159 I4
Aleknagik AK U.S.A. 148 H4
Aleknagik, Lake AK U.S.A. 148 H4
Aleksandra, Mys hd Rus. Fed. 90 E1
Aleksandriya Ukr. see Oleksandriya
Aleksandro-Nevskiy Rus. Fed. 53 I5
Aleksandropol Armenia see Gyumri
Aleksandrov Rus. Fed. 52 H4
Aleksandrov Gay Rus. Fed. 53 K6
Aleksandrovsk Rus. Fed. 51 R4
Aleksandrovsk Ukr. see Zaporizhzhya
Aleksandrovskiy Rus. Fed. see Aleksandrovsk
Aleksandrovskoye Rus. Fed. 113 F1
Aleksandrovsk-Sakhalinskiy Rus. Fed. 90 F2
Aleksandry, Zemlya i. Rus. Fed. 76 F1
Alekseyevka Akmolinskaya Oblast' Kazakh. see Akkol'
Alekseyevka Pavlodarskaya Oblast' Kazakh. 98 A2
Alekseyevka Vostochnyy Kazakhstan Kazakh. see Terekty
Alekseyevka Amurskaya Oblast' Rus. Fed. 90 B1
Alekseyevka Belgorodskaya Oblast' Rus. Fed. 53 H6
Alekseyevka Belgorodskaya Oblast' Rus. Fed. 53 H6
Alekseyevskaya Rus. Fed. 53 I6
Alekseyevskoye Rus. Fed. 52 K5
Aleksin Rus. Fed. 53 H5
Aleksinac Serbia 69 I3
Alèmbé Gabon 122 B4
Ålen Norway 54 G5
Alençon France 66 E2
Alenquer Brazil 177 H4
'Alenuihāhā Channel U.S.A. 157 [inset]
Alep Syria see Aleppo
Aleppo Syria 107 C1
Alert Canada 147 L1
Alerta Peru 176 D6
Alès France 66 G4
Aleşd Romania 69 J1
Aleshki Ukr. see Tsyurupyns'k
Aleşkirt Turkey see Eleşkirt
Alessandria Italy 68 C2
Alessio Albania see Lezhë
Ålesund Norway 54 E5
Aleutian Basin sea feature Bering Sea 186 H2
Aleutian Islands U.S.A. 146 A4
Aleutian Range mts AK U.S.A. 148 H4
Aleutian Trench sea feature N. Pacific Ocean 186 I2
Alevina, Mys c. Rus. Fed. 77 Q4
Alevişik Turkey see Samandağı
Alexander U.S.A. 160 C2
Alexander, Kap c. Greenland see Ullersuaq
Alexander, Mount hill Australia 136 B2
Alexander Archipelago is AK U.S.A. 149 M4
Alexander Bay b. Namibia/S. Africa 124 C5
Alexander Bay S. Africa 124 C5
Alexander City U.S.A. 163 C5
Alexander Island Antarctica 188 L2
Alexandra Australia 138 B6
Alexandra N.Z. 139 B7
Alexandra, Cape S. Georgia 178 I8
Alexandra Channel India 87 A4
Alexandra Land i. Rus. Fed. see Aleksandry, Zemlya
Alexandreia Greece 69 J4
Alexandretta Turkey see İskenderun
Alexandria Afgh. see Ghaznī
Alexandria Canada 165 H1

▶Alexandria Egypt 112 C5
5th most populous city in Africa.

Alexandria Romania 69 K3
Alexandria S. Africa 125 H7
Alexandria Turkm. see Mary
Alexandria U.K. 60 E5
Alexandria IN U.S.A. 164 C3
Alexandria KY U.S.A. 164 C4
Alexandria LA U.S.A. 161 E6
Alexandria VA U.S.A. 165 G4
Alexandria Arachoton Afgh. see Kandahār
Alexandria Areion Afgh. see Herāt
Alexandria Bay U.S.A. 165 H1
Alexandria Prophthasia Afgh. see Farāh
Alexandrina, Lake Australia 137 B7
Alexandroupoli Greece 69 K4
Alexis r. Canada 153 K3
Alexis Creek Canada 150 F4
Aley Lebanon 107 B3
Aleyak Iran 110 E2
Aleysk Rus. Fed. 88 E2
Alf Germany 62 H4
Al Farwānīyah Kuwait 110 B4
Al Fas Morocco see Fès
Al Fatḩah Iraq 113 F4
Al Fāw Iraq 113 H5
Al Fayyūm Egypt 112 C5
Alfeld (Leine) Germany 63 J3
Alfenas Brazil 179 B3
Alford U.K. 58 H5
Alfred ME U.S.A. 165 J2
Alfred NY U.S.A. 165 G2
Alfred and Marie Range hills Australia 135 D6
Alfred M. Terrazas Mex. 167 F4
Al Fujayrah U.A.E. see Fujairah
Al Fuqahā' Libya 121 E2
Al Furāt r. Iraq/Syria 107 D2 see Euphrates
Alga Kazakh. 102 A2
Ålgård Norway 55 D7
Algarrobo del Aguilla Arg. 178 C5
Algarve reg. Port. 67 B5
Algeciras Spain 67 D5
Algemesí Spain 67 F4
Algena Eritrea 108 E6
Alger Alg. see Algiers
Alger U.S.A. 164 C1

▶Algeria country Africa 120 C2
2nd largest country in Africa.

Algérie country Africa see Algeria
Algermissen Germany 63 J2
Algha Kazakh. see Alga
Al Ghāfāt Oman 110 E6
Al Ghammās Iraq 113 G5
Al Ghardaqah Egypt see Al Ghurdaqah
Al Ghawr plain Jordan/West Bank 107 B4
Al Ghayḑah Yemen 108 H6
Alghero Sardinia Italy 68 C4
Al Ghurdaqah Egypt 108 D4
Al Ghuwayr well Qatar 110 C5

▶Algiers Alg. 67 H5
Capital of Algeria.

Algoa Bay S. Africa 125 G7
Algoma U.S.A. 164 B1
Algona U.S.A. 160 E3
Algonac U.S.A. 164 D2
Algonquin Park Canada 165 F1
Algonquin Provincial Park Canada 165 F1
Algorta Spain 67 E2
Algueirao Moz. see Hacufera
Al Habakah well Saudi Arabia 113 F5
Al Ḩabbānīyah Iraq 113 F4
Al Ḩadaqah well Saudi Arabia 110 B4
Al Ḩadd Bahrain 110 C5
Al Hadhālīl plat. Saudi Arabia 113 F5
Al Ḩadīdīyah Syria 107 C2
Al Ḩadīthah Iraq 113 F4
Al Hadīthah Saudi Arabia 107 C4
Al Ḩaḑr Iraq see Hatra
Al Ḩafár well Saudi Arabia 113 F5
Al Ḩaffah Syria 107 C2
Al Haggounia W. Sahara 120 B2
Al Ḩajar al Gharbī mts Oman 110 E5
Al Ḩajar ash Sharqī mts Oman 110 E6
Al Ḩamād plain Asia 112 E5
Al Ḩamādah al Ḩamrā' plat. Libya 120 E2
Alhama de Murcia Spain 67 F5
Al Ḩamar Saudi Arabia 110 B6
Al Ḩamīdīyah Syria 107 B2
Al Ḩammām Egypt 112 C5
Al Ḩanākīyah Saudi Arabia 108 F5
Al Haniyah esc. Iraq 113 G5
Al Hariq Saudi Arabia 110 B6
Al Ḩarrah Egypt 112 C5
Al Harūj al Aswad hills Libya 121 E2
Al Hasa reg. Saudi Arabia 110 C5
Al Ḩasakah Syria 113 F3
Al Hawi salt pan Saudi Arabia 107 D5
Al Hawjā' Saudi Arabia 112 E5
Al Ḩawţah reg. Saudi Arabia 110 B6
Al Ḩayy Iraq 113 G4
Al Ḩayz Egypt 112 C5
Al Hazīm Jordan 107 C4
Al Ḩazm Saudi Arabia 112 E5
Al Ḩazm al Jawf Yemen 108 F6
Al Ḩibāk des. Saudi Arabia 109 H6
Al Hījānah Syria 107 C3
Al Ḩillah Iraq see Hillah
Al Ḩillah Saudi Arabia 108 G5
Al Ḩinnāh Saudi Arabia 122 E1
Al Ḩinw mt. Saudi Arabia 107 D4
Al Hirrah well Saudi Arabia 110 C6
Al Hīshah Syria 107 D1
Al Ḩismā plain Saudi Arabia 112 D5
Al Ḩişn Jordan 107 B3
Al Hoceima Morocco 67 E6
Al Ḩudaydah Yemen see Hodeidah
Al Ḩufrah reg. Saudi Arabia 112 E5
Al Hufūf Saudi Arabia see Hofūf
Al Hūj hills Saudi Arabia 112 E5
Al Husayfīn Oman 110 E5
Al Huwwah Saudi Arabia 110 B6
Ali Xizang China 99 B6
'Alīābād Afgh. 111 H2
'Alīābād Golestān Iran 110 D2
'Alīābād Hormozgan Iran 110 D4
'Alīābād Khorāsān Iran 111 F4
'Alīābād Kordestān Iran 110 B2
'Alīābād, Kūh-e mt. Iran 110 C3
Aliağa Turkey 69 L5
Aliakmonas r. Greece 69 J4
Aliambata East Timor 83 C5
Alibag India 106 B2
Äli Bayramlı Azer. 113 H3
Alicante Spain 67 F4
Alice r. Australia 136 C2
Alice watercourse Australia 136 D5
Alice U.S.A. 161 D7
Alice, Punta pt Italy 68 G5
Alice Arm B.C. Canada 149 O5
Alice Springs Australia 135 F5
Alice Town Bahamas 163 E7
Aliceville U.S.A. 161 F5
Alichur Tajik. 111 I2
Alichur r. Tajik. 111 I2
Alicia Mindanao Phil. 82 C5
Alick Creek r. Australia 136 C4
Alifu Atoll Maldives see Ari Atoll
Al Ifzi'iyyah i. U.A.E. 110 C5
Aliganj India 104 D4
Aligarh Rajasthan India 104 D4
Aligarh Uttar Prad. India 104 D4
Alīgūdarz Iran 110 C3
Alihe Nei Mongol China 95 J1
Alījūq, Kūh-e mt. Iran 110 C4
'Alī Kheyl Afgh. 111 H3
Al Imārāt al 'Arabīyah at Muttaḩidah country Asia see United Arab Emirates
Alimia i. Greece 69 L6
Alimpaya Point Mindanao Phil. 82 C5
Alindao Cent. Afr. Rep. 122 C3
Alindau Sulawesi Indon. 83 A3
Alingsås Sweden 55 H8
Aliova r. Turkey 69 M5
Alipura India 104 D4
Alipur Duar India 105 G4
Alirajpur India 104 C5
Al 'Irāq country Asia see Iraq
Al 'Īsāwīyah Saudi Arabia 107 C4
Al Iskandarīyah Egypt see Alexandria
Al Iskandarīyah Iraq 113 G4
Al Ismā'īlīyah Egypt 112 D5
Al Ismā'īlīyah governorate Egypt 107 A4
Alitak Bay AK U.S.A. 148 I4
Aliveri Greece 69 K5
Aliwal North S. Africa 125 H6
Alix Canada 150 H4
Al Jafr Jordan 107 C4
Al Jāfūrah des. Saudi Arabia 110 C5
Al Jaghbūb Libya 112 B5
Al Jahrah Kuwait 110 B4
Al Jamalīyah Qatar 110 C5
Al Jarāwī well Saudi Arabia 107 D4
Al Jauf Saudi Arabia see Dumat al Jandal
Al Jawb reg. Saudi Arabia 110 C6
Al Jawf Libya 121 F2
Al Jawsh Libya 120 E1
Al Jaza'ir country Africa see Algeria
Al Jaza'ir Alg. see Algiers
Aljezur Port. 67 B5
Al Jībān reg. Saudi Arabia 110 C5
Al Jil well Iraq 113 F5
Al Jilh esc. Saudi Arabia 110 B5
Al Jithāmīyah Saudi Arabia 113 F6
Al Jīzah Egypt see Giza
Al Jīzah Jordan 107 B4
Al Jubayl hills Saudi Arabia 110 B5
Al Jubaylah Saudi Arabia 110 B5
Al Jufrah Libya 121 E2
Al Julayqah well Saudi Arabia 110 C5
Aljustrel Port. 67 B5
Al Juwayf depr. Syria 107 C3
Al Kahfah Al Qaşīm Saudi Arabia 108 F4
Al Kahfah Ash Sharqīyah Saudi Arabia 110 C5
Alkali Lake Canada 150 F5
Al Karak Jordan 107 B4
Al'katvaam Rus. Fed. 148 B3
Al Kāẓimīyah Iraq see Kādhimain
Al Khābūrah Oman 110 E6
Al Khalīl West Bank see Hebron
Al Khāliş Iraq 113 G4
Al Khārijah Egypt 108 D4
Al Kharj reg. Saudi Arabia 110 B6
Al Kharrārah Qatar 110 C5
Al Kharrūbah Egypt 107 A4
Al Khaşab Oman 110 E5
Al Khatam reg. U.A.E. 110 D5
Al Khawkhah Yemen 108 F7
Al Khawr Qatar 110 C5
Al Khizāmī well Saudi Arabia 110 C5
Al Khums Libya 121 E1
Al Khunfah sand area Saudi Arabia 112 E5
Al Khunn Saudi Arabia 122 E1
Al Kifl Iraq 113 G4
Al Kir'ānah Qatar 110 C5
Al Kiswah Syria 107 C3
Alkmaar Neth. 62 E2
Al Kūbrī Egypt 107 A4
Al Kūfah Iraq see Kūfah
Al Kumayt Iraq 113 G4
Al Kuntillah Egypt 107 B5
Al Kusūr hills Saudi Arabia 107 D4
Al Kūt Iraq 113 G4
Al Kuwayt country Asia see Kuwait
Al Kuwayt Kuwait see Kuwait
Al Labbah plain Saudi Arabia 113 F5
Al Lādhiqīyah Syria see Latakia
Allagadda India 106 C3
Allahabad India 105 E4
Al Lajā lava field Syria 107 C3
Allakaket AK U.S.A. 148 I2
Allakh-Yun' Rus. Fed. 77 O3
Allanmyo Myanmar see Aunglan
Allanridge S. Africa 125 H4
Allapalli India 106 D2
'Allāqī, Wādī al watercourse Egypt 108 D5
'Allâqi, Wâdi el watercourse Egypt see 'Allāqī, Wādī al

Allardville Canada 153 I5
Alldays S. Africa 125 I2
Allegan U.S.A. 164 C2
Allegheny r. U.S.A. 164 F3
Allegheny Mountains U.S.A. 164 D5
Allegheny Reservoir U.S.A. 165 F3
Allen, Lough l. Ireland 61 D3
Allen, Mount AK U.S.A. 149 L3
Allendale U.S.A. 163 D5
Allendale Town U.K. 58 E4
Allende Coahuila Mex. 167 E2
Allende Nuevo León Mex. 167 E3
Allendorf (Lumda) Germany 63 I4
Allenford Canada 164 E1
Allenstein Poland see Olsztyn
Allensville U.S.A. 164 B5
Allentown U.S.A. 165 H3
Alleppey India 106 C4
Aller r. Germany 63 J2
Alliance NE U.S.A. 160 C3
Alliance OH U.S.A. 164 E3
Al Lībīyah country Africa see Libya
Allier r. France 66 F3
Al Lihābah well Saudi Arabia 110 B5
Allinge-Sandvig Denmark 55 I9
Al Lişāfah well Saudi Arabia 110 B5
Al Lisān pen. Jordan 107 B4
Alliston Canada 164 F1
Al Līth Saudi Arabia 108 F5
Al Liwā' oasis U.A.E. 110 D6
Alloa U.K. 60 F4
Allons U.S.A. 164 C5
Allora Australia 138 F2
Allu Sulawesi Indon. 83 A4
Allur India 106 D3
Alluru Kottapatnam India 106 D3
Al Lussuf well Iraq 113 F5
Alma Canada 153 H4
Alma MI U.S.A. 164 C2
Alma NE U.S.A. 160 D3
Alma WI U.S.A. 160 F2
Al Ma'ānīyah Iraq 113 F5
Alma-Ata Kazakh. see Almaty
Almada Port. 67 B4
Al Madāfi' plat. Saudi Arabia 112 E5
Al Ma'danīyāt well Iraq 113 G5
Almaden Australia 136 D3
Almadén Spain 67 D4
Al Madīnah Saudi Arabia see Medina
Al Mafraq Jordan 107 C3
Al Maghrib country Africa see Morocco
Al Maghrib reg. U.A.E. 110 D6
Al Mahākik reg. Saudi Arabia 110 C6
Al Mahdum Syria 107 C1
Al Maḩiā depr. Saudi Arabia 112 E6
Al Maḩwīt Yemen 108 F6
Al Malsūnīyah reg. Saudi Arabia 110 C5
Almalyk Uzbek. see Olmaliq
Al Manadir reg. Oman 110 D6
Al Manāmah Bahrain see Manama
Al Manjūr well Saudi Arabia 110 B6
Almanor, Lake U.S.A. 158 C1
Almansa Spain 67 F4
Al Manşūrah Egypt 112 C5
Almanzor mt. Spain 67 D3
Al Mariyyah U.A.E. 110 D6
Al Marj Libya 121 F1
Almas, Rio das r. Brazil 179 A1
Al Maţarīyah Egypt 112 D5
Almatinskaya Oblast' admin. div. Kazakh. 98 B3

▶Almaty Kazakh. 102 E3
Former capital of Kazakhstan.

Al Mawşil Iraq see Mosul
Al Mayādīn Syria 113 F4
Al Mazār Egypt 107 A4
Almaznyy Rus. Fed. 77 M3
Almeirim Brazil 177 H4
Almeirim Port. 67 B4
Almelo Neth. 62 G2
Almenara Brazil 179 C2
Almendra, Embalse de resr Spain 67 C3
Almendralejo Spain 67 C4
Almere Neth. 62 F2
Almería Spain 67 E5
Almería, Golfo de b. Spain 67 E5
Al'metievsk Rus. Fed. see Al'met'yevsk
Al'met'yevsk Rus. Fed. 51 Q5
Älmhult Sweden 55 I8
Almina, Punta pt Spain 67 D6
Al Mindak Saudi Arabia 108 F5
Al Minyā Egypt 112 C5
Almirós Greece see Almyros
Al Mish'āb Saudi Arabia 110 C4
Almodôvar Port. 67 B5
Almoloya Mex. 167 E5
Almond r. U.K. 60 F4
Almont U.S.A. 164 D2
Almonte Spain 67 C5
Almora India 104 D3
Al Mu'ayzīlah hill Saudi Arabia 107 D5
Al Mubarrez Saudi Arabia 108 G4
Al Muḑaibī Oman 109 I5
Al Muḑairib Oman 110 E6
Al Muḩarraq Bahrain 110 C5
Al Mukallā Yemen see Mukalla
Al Mukhā Yemen see Mocha
Al Mukhaylī Libya 108 B3
Al Munbaţiḩ des. Saudi Arabia 110 C6
Almuñécar Spain 67 E5
Al Muqdādīyah Iraq 113 G4
Al Mūrītānīyah country Africa see Mauritania
Al Murūt well Saudi Arabia 113 E5
Almus Turkey 112 E2
Al Musannāh ridge Saudi Arabia 110 B4
Al Musayyib Iraq 110 B3
Al Muwaqqar Jordan 107 C4
Almyros Greece 69 J5
Almyrou, Ormos b. Greece 69 K7
Alnwick U.K. 58 F3

▶Alofi Niue 133 J3
Capital of Niue.

Aloja Latvia 55 N8
Alon Myanmar 86 A2
Along India 105 H3
Alongshan China 90 A2
Alonnisos i. Greece 69 J5
Alor i. Indon. 83 C5
Alor, Kepulauan is Indon. 83 C5
Alor, Selat sea chan. Indon. 83 B5
Alor Setar Malaysia 84 C1
Alor Star Malaysia see Alor Setar
Alost Belgium see Aalst
Aloysius, Mount Australia 135 E6
Alozero Rus. Fed. 54 Q4
Alpen Germany 62 G3
Alpena U.S.A. 164 D1
Alpercatas, Serra das hills Brazil 177 J5
Alpha Australia 136 D4
Alpha Ridge sea feature Arctic Ocean 189 A1
Alpine AZ U.S.A. 159 I5
Alpine NY U.S.A. 165 G2
Alpine TX U.S.A. 161 C6
Alpine WY U.S.A. 156 F4
Alpine National Park Australia 138 C6
Alps mts Europe 66 H4
Al Qa'āmīyāt reg. Saudi Arabia 108 G6
Al Qaddāḩīyah Libya 121 E1
Al Qadmūs Syria 107 C2
Al Qaffāy i. U.A.E. 110 D5
Al Qāhirah Egypt see Cairo
Al Qā'īyah Saudi Arabia 108 F5
Al Qā'īyah well Saudi Arabia 110 B5
Al Qal'a Beni Hammad tourist site Alg. 67 I6
Al Qalībah Saudi Arabia 112 E5
Al Qāmishlī Syria 113 F3
Al Qar'ah Libya 112 B5
Al Qar'ah well Saudi Arabia 110 B5
Al Qar'ah lava field Syria 107 C3
Al Qardāḩah Syria 107 C2
Al Qarqar Saudi Arabia 107 C4
Al Qaryatayn Syria 107 C2
Al Qaşab Ar Riyāḑ Saudi Arabia 110 B5
Al Qaşab Ash Sharqīyah Saudi Arabia 110 C6
Al Qaţīf Saudi Arabia 110 C5
Al Qaţn Yemen 108 G6
Al Qaţrānah Jordan 107 C4
Al Qaţrūn Libya 121 E2
Al Qāyşūmah well Saudi Arabia 113 F5
Al Qubbah Libya 121 F1
Alqueva, Barragem de 67 C4
Al Qumur country Africa see Comoros
Al Qunayţirah (abandoned) Syria 107 B3
Al Qunfidhah Saudi Arabia 108 F6
Al Qurayyāt Saudi Arabia 107 C4
Al Qurnah Iraq 113 G5
Al Quşaymah Egypt 107 B4
Al Quşayr Egypt 108 D4
Al Quşayr Syria 107 C2
Al Qūşīyah Egypt 112 C6
Al Qūşūrīyah Saudi Arabia 110 B6
Al Quţayfah Syria 107 C3
Al Quwayʿ Saudi Arabia 110 B6
Al Quwayīyah Saudi Arabia 108 G5
Al Quwayrah Jordan 107 B5
Al Rabbād reg. U.A.E. 110 D6
Alroy Downs Australia 136 B2
Alsace admin. reg. France 63 H6
Alsace reg. France 66 H2
Alsager U.K. 59 E5
Al Samīt well Iraq 113 F5
Alsask Canada 151 I5
Alsatia reg. France see Alsace
Alsek r. AK U.S.A. 149 M4
Alsfeld Germany 63 J4
Alsleben (Saale) Germany 63 L3
Alston U.K. 58 E4
Alstonville Australia 138 F2
Alsunga Latvia 55 L8
Alta Norway 54 M2
Alta, Mount N.Z. 139 B7
Altaelva r. Norway 54 M2
Altafjorden sea chan. Norway 54 M1
Alta Floresta Brazil 177 G5
Alta Gracia Nicaragua 166 [inset] I7
Altai Mountains Asia 88 F3
Altamaha r. U.S.A. 163 D6
Altamira Brazil 177 H4
Altamira Costa Rica 166 [inset] I7
Altamira Mex. 167 F4
Altamirano Chiapas Mex. 167 G5
Altamura Italy 68 G4
Altan Chitinskaya Oblast' Rus. Fed. 95 G1
Altan Chitinskaya Oblast' Rus. Fed. 95 G1
Altanbulag Mongolia 94 F2
Altan Emel Nei Mongol China 95 I1
Altan Ovoo mt. China/Mongolia 94 B2
Altan Shiret Nei Mongol China 95 G4
Altan Xiret Nei Mongol China see Altan Shiret
Alta Paraiso de Goiás Brazil 179 B1
Altar Mex. 166 C2
Altar r. Mex. 157 F7
Altar, Desierto de des. Mex. 166 B1
Altata Mex. 166 D3
Altavista U.S.A. 164 F5
Altay Xinjiang China 98 E3
Altay Govĭ-Altay Mongolia 94 C2
Altay Mongolia 94 D2
Altay Mongolia 94 C2
Altay, Respublika aut. rep. Rus. Fed. 94 A1
Altayskiy Rus. Fed. 102 G1
Altayskiy Khrebet mts Asia see Altai Mountains
Altayskiy Zapovednik nature res. Rus. Fed. 94 B1
Altdorf Switz. 66 I3
Altea Spain 67 F4
Alteidet Norway 54 M1
Altenahr Germany 62 G4
Altenberge Germany 63 H2
Altenburg Germany 63 M4
Altenkirchen (Westerwald) Germany 63 H4
Altenqoke Qinghai China 94 C4
Altın Köprü Iraq 113 G4
Altınoluk Turkey 69 L5
Altınözü Turkey 107 C1
Altıntaş Turkey 69 N5
Altiplano plain Bol. 176 E7
Altmark reg. Germany 63 L2
Altmühl r. Germany 63 L6
Alto, Monte hill Italy 68 D2
Alto Chicapa Angola 123 B5
Alto Cuchumatanes mts Guat. 167 H6
Alto del Moncayo mt. Spain 67 F3
Alto de Pencoso hills Arg. 178 C4
Alto Garças Brazil 177 H7
Alto Madidi, Parque Nacional nat. park Bol. 176 E6
Alton CA U.S.A. 158 A1
Alton IL U.S.A. 160 F4
Alton MO U.S.A. 161 F4
Alton NH U.S.A. 165 J2
Altona Canada 150 F3
Altoona U.S.A. 165 F3
Alto Parnaíba Brazil 177 I5
Alto Taquarí Mato Grosso Brazil 177 H7
Altotonga Mex. 167 F5
Altötting Germany 57 N6
Altrincham U.K. 58 E5
Alt Schwerin Germany 63 M1
Altūn Kūbrī Iraq see Altin Köprü
Altun Shan mt. Qinghai China 98 F5
Altun Shan mts China 99 D5
Alturas U.S.A. 156 C4
Altus U.S.A. 161 D5
Al 'Ubaylah Saudi Arabia 122 F1
Alucra Turkey 112 E2
Alūksne Latvia 55 O8
Alūm Iran 110 C3
Alum Bridge U.S.A. 164 E4
Al 'Uqaylah Libya 121 E1
Al 'Uqaylah Saudi Arabia see An Nabk
Al Uqşur Egypt see Luxor
Alur India 106 C3
Al 'Urayq des. Saudi Arabia 112 E5
Al 'Urdun country Asia see Jordan
Alur Setar Malaysia see Alor Setar
'Ālūt Iran 110 B3
Aluva India see Alwaye
Al 'Uwayjā' well Saudi Arabia 110 C6
Al 'Uwaynāt Libya 108 B5
Al 'Uwayqīlah Saudi Arabia 113 F5
Al 'Uzayr Iraq 113 G5
Alva U.S.A. 161 D4
Alvand, Kūh-e mt. Iran 110 C3
Alvarado Mex. 167 G5
Alvarado TX U.S.A. 167 F1
Alvarães Brazil 176 F4
Alvaton U.S.A. 164 B5
Alvdal Norway 54 G5
Älvdalen Sweden 55 I6
Alvesta Sweden 55 I8
Ålvik Norway 55 E6
Alvik Sweden 54 J5
Alvin U.S.A. 161 E6
Alvorada do Norte Brazil 179 B1
Älvsbyn Sweden 54 L4
Al Wafrah Kuwait 110 B4
Al Wajh Saudi Arabia 108 E4
Al Wakrah Qatar 110 C5
Al Waqbā well Saudi Arabia 110 B4
Alwar India 104 D4
Al Wari'ah Saudi Arabia 108 G4
Al Wāţiyah well Egypt 112 B5
Alwaye India 106 C4
Al Widyān plat. Iraq/Saudi Arabia 113 F4
Al Wusayţ well Saudi Arabia 110 B4
Alxa Youqi Nei Mongol China see Ehen Hudag
Alxa Zuoqi Nei Mongol China see Bayan Hot
Al Yamāmah Saudi Arabia 110 B5
Al Yaman country Asia see Yemen
Alyangula Australia 136 B2
Al Yāsāt i. U.A.E. 110 C5
Alyth U.K. 60 F4
Alytus Lith. 55 N9
Alzette r. Lux. 62 G5
Alzey Germany 63 I5
Amacayacu, Parque Nacional nat. park Col. 176 D4
Amadeus, Lake salt flat Australia 135 E6
Amadjuak Lake Canada 147 K3
Amadora Port. 67 B4
Amaga-dake mt. Japan 93 E3
Amagasaki Japan 92 B4
Amagi-san vol. Japan 93 E4
Amagi-tōge pass Japan 93 E4
Amagiyugashima Japan 93 E4
Amagoi-dake mt. Japan 92 C3
Amahai Seram Indon. 83 D3
Amakazari-yama mt. Japan 93 D2
Amakusa-nada b. Japan 91 C6
Åmål Sweden 55 H7
Amalia S. Africa 125 G4
Amaliada Greece 69 I6
Amalner India 104 C5
Amamapare Indon. 81 J7
Amambaí Brazil 178 E2
Amambaí, Serra de hills Brazil/Para. 178 E2
Amami-Ō-shima i. Japan 91 C7
Amami-shotō is Japan 91 C8
Amamula Dem. Rep. Congo 122 C4
Amanab P.N.G. 81 K7
Amangel'dy Kazakh. 102 C1
Amankeldi Kazakh. see Amangel'dy
Amantea Italy 68 G5
Amanzimtoti S. Africa 125 J6
Amapá Brazil 177 H3
Amapala Hond. 166 [inset] I6
Amara Iraq see Al 'Amārah
Amarante Brazil 177 J5
Amarapura Myanmar 86 B2
Amardalay Mongolia see Delgertsogt
Amareleja Port. 67 C4
Amargosa Brazil 179 D1
Amargosa watercourse U.S.A. 158 E3
Amargosa Desert U.S.A. 158 E3
Amargosa Range mts U.S.A. 158 E3
Amargosa Valley U.S.A. 158 E3
Amarillo U.S.A. 161 C5
Amarillo, Cerro mt. Arg. 178 C4
Amarkantak India 105 E5
Amarpur Madh. Prad. India 104 E5
Amasia Turkey see Amasya
Amasine W. Sahara 120 B2
Amasra Turkey 112 D2
Amasya Turkey 112 D2
Amata Australia 135 E6
Amatenango Mex. 167 G5
Amatique, Bahía de b. Guat. 166 [inset] H6
Amatitán Mex. 166 E4
Amatlán de Cañas Mex. 166 D4
Amatsu-Kominato Japan 93 G3
Amatulla India 105 H4
Amau P.N.G. 136 E1
Amay Belgium 62 F4
Amazar Rus. Fed. 90 A1
Amazar r. Rus. Fed. 90 A1

▶Amazon r. S. America 176 F4
Longest river and largest drainage basin in South America and 2nd longest river in the world.
Also known as Amazonas or Solimões

Amazon, Mouths of the Brazil 177 I3
Amazonas r. S. America 176 F4 see Amazon
Amazon Cone sea feature S. Atlantic Ocean 184 E5
Amazônia, Parque Nacional nat. park Brazil 177 G4
Ambajogai India 106 C2
Ambala India 104 D3
Ambalangoda Sri Lanka 106 D5
Ambalavao Madag. 123 E6
Ambam Cameroon 122 B3
Ambar Iran 110 E4
Ambarnyy Rus. Fed. 54 R4
Ambasa India see Ambassa
Ambasamudram India 106 C4
Ambassa India 105 G5
Ambathala Australia 137 D5
Ambato Ecuador 176 C4
Ambato Boeny Madag. 123 E5
Ambato Finandrahana Madag. 123 E6
Ambatolampy Madag. 123 E5
Ambatomainty Madag. 123 E5
Ambatondrazaka Madag. 123 E5
Ambejogai India see Ambajogai
Ambelau i. Maluku Indon. 83 C3
Amberg Germany 63 L5
Ambergris Cay i. Belize 167 I5
Ambérieu-en-Bugey France 66 G4
Amberley Canada 164 E1
Ambgaon India 106 D1
Ambianum France see Amiens
Ambikapur India 105 E5
Ambil i. Phil. 82 C3
Ambilobe Madag. 123 E5
Ambition, Mount B.C. Canada 149 O4
Amble U.K. 58 F3
Ambler AK U.S.A. 148 H2
Ambler r. AK U.S.A. 148 H2
Ambleside U.K. 58 E4
Amblève r. Belgium 62 F4
Ambo India 105 F5
Amboasary Madag. 123 E6
Ambodifotatra Madag. 123 E5
Ambohimahasoa Madag. 123 E6
Ambohitra mt. Madag. 123 E5
Amboina Maluku Indon. see Ambon
Ambon Maluku Indon. 83 D3
Ambon i. Maluku Indon. 83 C3
Amboró, Parque Nacional nat. park Bol. 176 F7
Ambositra Madag. 123 E6
Ambovombe Madag. 123 E6
Amboy U.S.A. 159 F4
Ambre, Cap d' c. Madag. see Bobaomby, Tanjona
Ambrim i. Vanuatu see Ambrym
Ambriz Angola 123 B4
Ambrizete Angola see N'zeto
Ambrosia Lake U.S.A. 159 J4
Ambrym i. Vanuatu 133 G3
Ambunten Jawa Indon. 85 F4
Ambunti P.N.G. 81 K7
Ambur India 106 C3
Amchitka Island AK U.S.A. 149 [inset]
Amchitka Pass sea channel AK U.S.A. 149 [inset]
Am-Dam Chad 121 F3
Amded, Oued watercourse Alg. 120 D2
Amdo Xizang China 99 E6
Ameca Jalisco Mex. 166 D4
Amecameca Mex. 167 F5
Ameland i. Neth. 62 F1
Amelia Court House U.S.A. 165 G5
Amellu Uttar Prad. India 99 C8
Amenia U.S.A. 165 I3
Amer, Erg d' des. Alg. 122 A1
Amereli India see Amreli
American, North Fork r. U.S.A. 158 C2
Americana Brazil 179 B3
American-Antarctic Ridge sea feature S. Atlantic Ocean 184 G9
American Falls U.S.A. 156 E4
American Falls Reservoir U.S.A. 156 E4
American Fork U.S.A. 159 H1

▶American Samoa terr. S. Pacific Ocean 133 J3
United States Unincorporated Territory.

Americus U.S.A. 163 C5
Amersfoort Neth. 62 F2
Amersfoort S. Africa 125 I4
Amersham U.K. 59 G7
Amery Canada 151 M3
Amery Ice Shelf Antarctica 188 E2
Ames U.S.A. 160 E3
Amesbury U.K. 59 F7
Amesbury U.S.A. 165 J2
Amet India 104 C4
Amethi India 105 E4
Amfissa Greece 69 J5
Amga Rus. Fed. 77 O3
Amgalang Nei Mongol China 95 I1
Amgu Rus. Fed. 90 E3
Amguema Rus. Fed. 148 C2
Amguema r. Rus. Fed. 148 C1
Amguid Alg. 120 D2
Amgun' r. Rus. Fed. 90 E1
Amherst Canada 153 I5
Amherst Myanmar see Kyaikkami
Amherst MA U.S.A. 165 I2
Amherst OH U.S.A. 164 D3
Amherst VA U.S.A. 164 F5
Amherstburg Canada 164 D2
Amherst Island Canada 165 G1
Ami Japan 93 G2
Amiata, Monte mt. Italy 68 D3
Amida Turkey see Diyarbakır
Amidon U.S.A. 160 C2
Amiens France 62 C5
'Amīj, Wādī watercourse Iraq 113 F4
Amik Ovası marsh Turkey 107 C1
'Amīnābād Iran 110 D4
Amindivi atoll India see Amini
Amindivi Islands India 106 B4
Amini atoll India 106 B4
Amino Eth. 122 E3
Amino Japan 92 B3
Aminuis Namibia 124 D2
Amīrābād Iran 110 B3
Amirante Islands Seychelles 185 L6
Amirante Trench sea feature Indian Ocean 185 L6
Amisk Lake Canada 151 K4
Amistad, Represa de resr Mex./U.S.A. see Amistad Reservoir
Amistad Reservoir Mex./U.S.A. 167 E2
Amisus Turkey see Samsun
Amite U.S.A. 161 F6
Amity Point Australia 138 F1
Amla India 104 D5
Amlash Iran 110 C2
Amlekhganj Nepal 105 F4
Åmli Norway 55 F7
Amlia Island AK U.S.A. 149 [inset]
Amlwch U.K. 58 C5

▶'Ammān Jordan 107 B4
Capital of Jordan.

Ammanazar Turkm. 110 D2
Ammanford U.K. 59 D7
Ämmänsaari Fin. 54 P4
'Ammār, Tall hill Syria 107 C3
Ammarnäs Sweden 54 J4
Ammaroo Australia 136 A4
Ammassalik Greenland 189 J2
Ammerland reg. Germany 63 H1
Ammern Germany 63 K3
Ammochostos Cyprus see Famagusta
Ammochostos Bay Cyprus 107 B2
Am Nābiyah Yemen 108 F7
Amne Machin Range mts China see A'nyêmaqên Shan
Amnok-kang r. China/N. Korea see Yalu Jiang
Amo Jiang r. China 96 D4
Amol Iran 110 D2
Amorbach Germany 63 J5
Amorgos i. Greece 69 K6
Amory U.S.A. 161 F5
Amos Canada 152 F4
Amourj Mauritania 120 C3
Amoy China see Xiamen
Ampah Kalimantan Indon. 85 F3
Ampana Sulawesi Indon. 83 B3
Ampani India 106 D2
Ampanihy Madag. 123 E6
Amparai Sri Lanka 106 D5
Amparo Brazil 179 B3
Ampasimanolotra Madag. 123 E5
Ampenan Lombok Indon. 85 G5
Amphitheatre Australia 138 A6
Amphitrite Group is Paracel Is 80 E3
Ampibaku Sulawesi Indon. 83 B3
Ampoa Sulawesi Indon. 83 B3
Amqog Gansu China 94 E5
Amraoti India see Amravati
Amravati India 106 C1
Amrawad India 104 D5
Amreli India 104 B5
Amri Pak. 111 H5
Amring India 105 H4
'Amrīt Syria 107 B2
Amritsar India 104 C3
Amroha India 104 D3
Amsden U.S.A. 164 D3
Åmsele Sweden 54 K4
Amstelveen Neth. 62 E2

▶Amsterdam Neth. 62 E2
Official capital of the Netherlands.

Amsterdam S. Africa 125 J4
Amsterdam U.S.A. 165 H2
Amsterdam, Île i. Indian Ocean 185 N8
Amstetten Austria 57 O6
Am Timan Chad 121 F3
Amu Co l. Xizang China 99 E6
Amudar'ya r. Asia 111 F2
Amudaryo r. Asia see Amudar'ya
Amukta Island AK U.S.A. 148 E5
Amukta Pass sea channel AK U.S.A. 148 D5
Amund Ringnes Island Canada 147 I2
Amundsen, Mount Antarctica 188 F2
Amundsen Abyssal Plain sea feature Southern Ocean 188 J2
Amundsen Basin sea feature Arctic Ocean 189 H1
Amundsen Bay Antarctica 188 D2
Amundsen Coast Antarctica 188 J1
Amundsen Glacier Antarctica 188 I1
Amundsen Gulf Canada 146 F2
Amundsen Ridges sea feature Southern Ocean 188 J2
Amundsen-Scott research station Antarctica 188 C1
Amundsen Sea Antarctica 188 K2
Amuntai Kalimantan Indon. 85 F3
Amur r. China/Rus Fed 90 D2
also known as Heilong Jiang (China)
Amur r. Rus. Fed. 90 F1
'Amur, Wadi watercourse Sudan 108 D6
Amurang Sulawesi Indon. 83 C2
Amur Oblast admin. div. Rus. Fed. see Amurskaya Oblast'
Amursk Rus. Fed. 90 E2
Amurskaya Oblast' admin. div. Rus. Fed. 90 C1
Amurskiy Liman strait Rus. Fed. 90 F1
Amurzet Rus. Fed. 90 C3
Amvrosiyivka Ukr. 53 H7
Amyderya r. Asia see Amudar'ya
Am-Zoer Chad 121 F3
An Myanmar 86 A3
Anaa atoll Fr. Polynesia 187 K7
Anabanua Sulawesi Indon. 83 B3
Anabar r. Rus. Fed. 77 M2
Anacapa Islands U.S.A. 158 D4
Anaconda U.S.A. 156 E3
Anacortes U.S.A. 156 C2
Anacuao, Mount Phil. 82 C2
Anadarko U.S.A. 161 D5
Anadolu reg. Turkey 112 D3
Anadolu Dağları mts Turkey 112 E2
Anadyr' Rus. Fed. 148 B2
Anadyrskaya Nizmennost' lowland Rus. Fed. 148 B2
Anadyrskiy Liman b. Rus. Fed. 148 B2
Anadyrskiy Zaliv b. Rus. Fed. 148 C3
Anafi i. Greece 69 K6
Anagé Brazil 179 C1
'Ānah Iraq 113 F4
Anaheim U.S.A. 158 E5
Anahim Lake Canada 150 E4
Anáhuac Nuevo León Mex. 167 E3
Anahuac U.S.A. 161 E6
Anaimalai Hills India 106 C4
Anaiteum i. Vanuatu see Anatom
Anajás Brazil 177 I4
Anakapalle India 106 D2
Anakie Australia 136 D4
Anaktuvuk r. AK U.S.A. 149 J1
Anaktuvuk Pass AK U.S.A. 149 J1
Analalava Madag. 123 E5
Anamã Brazil 176 F4
Anambas, Kepulauan is Indon. 84 D2
Anamosa U.S.A. 160 F3
Anamur Turkey 107 A1
Anan Nagano Japan 93 D3
Anan Japan 91 D6
Anand India 104 C5
Anandapur India 105 F5
Anan'ev Kyrg. 98 B4
Anano i. Indon. 83 C4
Anantapur India 106 C3
Ananthapur India see Anantapur
Anantnag India 104 C2
Anant Peth India 104 D4
Anantpur India see Anantapur
Ananyev Ukr. see Anan'yiv
Anan'yiv Ukr. 53 F7
Anapa Rus. Fed. 112 E1
Anápolis Brazil 179 A2
Anār Fin. see Inari
Anār Iran 110 D4
Anardara Afgh. 111 F3
Anatahan i. N. Mariana Is 81 L3
Anatajan i. N. Mariana Is see Anatahan
Anatolia reg. Turkey see Anadolu
Anatom i. Vanuatu 133 G4
Añatuya Arg. 178 D3
Anayapazari Turkey see Gülnar
An Baile Breac Ireland 61 B6
Anbei Gansu China 94 D3
An Blascaod Mór Ireland see Great Blasket Island
An Bun Beag Ireland 61 D2
Anbūr-e Kālārī Iran 110 D5
Anbyon N. Korea 91 B5
Ancenis France 66 D3
Anchorage AK U.S.A. 149 J3
Anchorage Island atoll Cook Is see Suwarrow
Anchor Bay U.S.A. 164 D2
Anchor Point AK U.S.A. 149 J4
Anchuthengu India see Anjengo
Anci Hebei China see Langfang
An Clochán Liath Ireland 61 D3
An Cóbh Ireland see Cobh
Ancona Italy 68 E3
Ancud, Golfo de g. Chile 178 B6
Ancyra Turkey see Ankara
Anda Heilong. China see Daqing
Anda Heilong. China 90 B3
Anda i. Indon. 83 C1
Andacollo Chile 178 B4
Andado Australia 136 A5
Andahuaylas Peru 176 D6
An Daingean Ireland 61 B5
Andal India 105 F5
Åndalsnes Norway 54 E5
Andalucía aut. comm. Spain 67 D5
Andalusia aut. comm. Spain see Andalucía
Andalusia U.S.A. 163 C6
Andaman Basin sea feature Indian Ocean 185 O5
Andaman Islands India 87 A4
Andaman Sea Indian Ocean 87 A5
Andaman Strait India 87 A4
Andamooka Australia 137 B6
Andapa Madag. 123 E5
Andarāb reg. Afgh. 111 H3
Ande China 96 E4
Andegavum France see Angers
Andelle r. France 62 B5
Andenes Norway 54 J2
Andenne Belgium 62 F4
Andéramboukane Mali 120 D3
Anderlecht Belgium 62 E4
Andermatt Switz. 66 I3
Andernos-les-Bains France 66 D4
Anderson r. N.W.T. Canada 149 O1
Anderson AK U.S.A. 149 J2
Anderson IN U.S.A. 164 C3
Anderson SC U.S.A. 163 D5
Anderson TX U.S.A. 161 E6
Anderson Bay Australia 137 [inset]
Anderson Lake Canada 150 F5
Andes mts S. America 178 C4
Andfjorden sea chan. Norway 54 J2
Andhíparos i. Greece see Antiparos
Andhra Lake India 106 B2
Andhra Pradesh state India 106 C2
Andijon Uzbek. 102 D3
Andikíthira i. Greece see Antikythira
Andilamena Madag. 123 E5
Andilanatoby Madag. 123 E5
Andimeshk Iran 110 C3
Andímilos i. Greece see Antimilos
Andípsara i. Greece see Antipsara
Andir He r. China 99 C5
Andırın Turkey 112 E3
Andirlangar Xinjiang China 99 C5
Andizhan Uzbek. see Andijon
Andkhvoy Afgh. 111 G2
Andoany Madag. 123 E5
Andoas Peru 176 C4
Andogskaya Gryada hills Rus. Fed. 52 H4
Andol India 106 C2
Andong China see Dandong
Andong S. Korea 91 C5
Andongwei Shandong China 95 I5
Andoom Australia 136 C2
Andorra country Europe 67 G2

▶Andorra la Vella Andorra 67 G2
Capital of Andorra.

Andorra la Vieja Andorra see Andorra la Vella
Andover U.K. 59 F7
Andover NY U.S.A. 165 G2
Andover OH U.S.A. 164 E3
Andøya i. Norway 54 I2
Andrade U.S.A. 159 F5
Andradina Brazil 179 A3
Andranomavo Madag. 123 E5
Andranopasy Madag. 123 E6
Andreafsky r. AK U.S.A. 148 G3
Andreafsky, East Fork r. AK U.S.A. 148 G3
Andreanof Islands U.S.A. 186 I2
Andreapol' Rus. Fed. 52 G4
Andreas Isle of Man 58 C4
André Félix, Parc National d' nat. park Cent. Afr. Rep. 122 C3
Andrelândia Brazil 179 B3
Andrew Canada 151 H4
Andrew Bay Myanmar 86 A3
Andrews SC U.S.A. 163 E5
Andrews TX U.S.A. 161 C5
Andria Italy 68 G4
Androka Madag. 123 E6
Andropov Rus. Fed. see Rybinsk
Andros i. Bahamas 163 E7

Andros i. Greece **69** K6
Androscoggin r. U.S.A. **165** K2
Andros Town Bahamas **163** E7
Andrott i. India **106** B4
Andselv Norway **54** K2
Andújar Spain **67** D4
Andulo Angola **123** B5
Anec, Lake salt flat Australia **135** E5
Āneen-Kio terr. N. Pacific Ocean see **Wake Island**
Anéfis Mali **120** D3
Anegada, Bahía b. Arg. **178** D6
Anegada Passage Virgin Is (U.K.) **169** L5
Aného Togo **120** D4
Aneityum i. Vanuatu see **Anatom**
'Aneiza, Jabal hill Iraq see **'Unayzah, Jabal**
Anemourion tourist site Turkey **107** A1
Anepmete P.N.G. **81** L8
Anet France **62** B6
Anetchom, Île i. Vanuatu see **Anatom**
Aneto mt. Spain **67** G2
Ānewetak atoll Marshall Is see **Enewetak**
Aney Niger **120** E3
Aneytioum, Île i. Vanuatu see **Anatom**
Anfu China **97** G3
Angalarri r. Australia **134** E3
Angamos, Punta pt Chile **178** B2
Ang'angxi Heilong. China **95** J2

▶**Angara** r. Rus. Fed. **88** G1
Part of the Yenisey-Angara-Selenga, 3rd longest river in Asia.

Angarsk Rus. Fed. **88** I2
Angas Downs Australia **135** F6
Angat Luzon Phil. **82** C3
Angatuba Brazil **179** A3
Angaur i. Palau **82** [inset]
Ånge Sweden **54** I5
Angel, Salto waterfall Venez. see **Angel Falls**
Ángel de la Guarda, Isla i. Mex. **166** B2
Angeles Luzon Phil. **82** C3

▶**Angel Falls** waterfall Venez. **176** F2
Highest waterfall in the world.

Ängelholm Sweden **55** H8
Angellala Creek r. Australia **138** C1
Angels Camp U.S.A. **158** C2
Ångermanälven r. Sweden **54** J5
Angers France **66** D3
Anggana Kalimantan Indon. **85** G3
Angikuni Lake Canada **151** L2
Angiola U.S.A. **158** D4
Angkor tourist site Cambodia **87** C4
Anglesea Australia **138** B7
Anglesey i. U.K. **58** C5
Angleton U.S.A. **161** E6
Anglo-Egyptian Sudan country Africa see **Sudan**
Angmagssalik Greenland see **Ammassalik**
Ang Mo Kio Sing. **87** [inset]
Ango Dem. Rep. Congo **122** C3
Angoche Moz. **123** D5
Angohrān Iran **110** E5
Angol Chile **178** B5
Angola country Africa **123** B5
Angola IN U.S.A. **164** C3
Angola NY U.S.A. **164** F2
Angola Basin sea feature S. Atlantic Ocean **184** H7
Angora Turkey see **Ankara**
Angostura Mex. **157** F8
Angoulême France **66** E4
Angra dos Reis Brazil **179** B3
Angren Uzbek. **102** D3
Ang Thong Thai. **87** C4
Anguang Jilin China **95** J2

▶**Anguilla** terr. West Indies **169** L5
United Kingdom Overseas Territory.

Anguilla Cays is Bahamas **163** E8
Anguille, Cape Canada **153** K5
Angul India **106** E1
Anguli Nur l. China **95** H3
Anguo Hebei China **95** H4
Angus Canada **164** F1
Angutia Char i. Bangl. **105** G5
Angutikada Peak AK U.S.A. **148** H2
Anholt i. Denmark **55** G8
Anhua China **97** F2
Anhui prov. China **97** H1
Anhumas Brazil **177** H7
Anhwei prov. China see **Anhui**
Aniak AK U.S.A. **148** H3
Aniak r. AK U.S.A. **148** H3
Aniakchak National Monument and Preserve nat. park U.S.A. **146** C4
Animaki-san hill Japan **93** G2
Anin Myanmar **86** B4
Anini Arun. Prad. India **99** F7
Anitaguipan Point Samar Phil. **82** D4
Anitápolis Brazil **179** A4
Anıtlı Turkey **107** A1
Aniva Rus. Fed. **90** F3
Aniva, Mys c. Rus. Fed. **90** F3
Aniva, Zaliv b. Rus. Fed. **90** F3
Anizy-le-Château France **62** D5
Anjadip i. India **106** B3
Anjalankoski Fin. **55** O6
Anjengo India **106** C4
Anji China **97** H2
Anjihai Xinjiang China **98** D3
Anjir Avand Iran **110** D3
Anjō Japan **92** D4
Anjoman Iran **110** E3
Anjou reg. France **66** D3
Anjouan i. Comoros see **Nzwani**
Anjozorobe Madag. **123** E5
Anjuman reg. Afgh. **111** H3
Anjuthengu India see **Anjengo**
Ankang China **97** F1

▶**Ankara** Turkey **112** D3
Capital of Turkey.

Ankaratra mt. Madag. **123** E5
Ankazoabo Madag. **123** E6
Ankeny U.S.A. **160** E3
An Khê Vietnam **87** E4
Ankleshwar India **104** C5
Anklesvar India see **Ankleshwar**
Ankola India **106** B3
Ankouzhen Gansu China **94** F5
Anling Henan China see **Yanling**
An Lôc Vietnam **87** D5
Anlong China **96** E3
Anlu China **97** G2
Anmoore U.S.A. **164** E4
An Muileann gCearr Ireland see **Mullingar**
Anmyŏn-do i. S. Korea **91** B5
Ann, Cape Antarctica **188** D2
Ann, Cape U.S.A. **165** J2
Anna Rus. Fed. **53** I6
Anna, Lake U.S.A. **165** G4
Annaba Alg. **68** B6
Annaberg-Buchholtz Germany **63** N4
An Nabk Saudi Arabia **107** C4
An Nabk Syria **107** C2
An Nafūd des. Saudi Arabia **113** F5
An Najaf Iraq see **Najaf**
Annaka Japan **93** E2
Annalee r. Ireland **61** E3
Annalong U.K. **61** G3
Annam reg. Vietnam **80** D3
Annam Highlands mts Laos/Vietnam **86** D3
Annan U.K. **60** F6
Annan r. U.K. **60** F6
'Annān, Wādī al watercourse Syria **107** D2
Annanba Gansu China **94** C4
Annandale U.S.A. **165** G4
Anna Plains Australia **134** C4

▶**Annapolis** U.S.A. **165** G4
Capital of Maryland.

Annapurna Conservation Area nature res. Nepal **105** F3

▶**Annapurna I** mt. Nepal **105** E3
10th highest mountain in the world and in Asia.

Ann Arbor U.S.A. **164** D2
Anna Regina Guyana **177** G2
An Nás Ireland see **Naas**
An Nāşirīyah Iraq see **Nāşirīyah**
An Naşrānī, Jabal mts Syria **107** C3
Annean, Lake salt flat Australia **135** B6
Anne Arundel Town U.S.A. see **Annapolis**
Annecy France **66** H4
Anne Marie Lake Canada **153** J3
Annen Neth. **62** G1
Annette Island AK U.S.A. **149** O5
An Nimārah Syria **107** C3
An Nimāş Saudi Arabia **108** F6
Anning China **96** D3
Anniston U.S.A. **163** C5
Annobón i. Equat. Guinea **120** D5
Annonay France **66** G4
An Nu'mānīyah Iraq **113** G4
An Nuşayrīyah, Jabal mts Syria **107** C2
Anō Japan **92** C4
Anonima atoll Micronesia see **Namonuito**
Anoón de Sardinas, Bahía de b. Col. **176** C3
Anorontany, Tanjona hd Madag. **123** E5
Ano Viannos Kriti Greece see **Viannos**
Anpu Gang b. China **97** F4
Anqing China **97** H2
Anqiu Shandong China **95** I4
An Ráth Ireland see **Charleville**
Anren China **97** G3
Ans Belgium **62** F4
Ansai Shaanxi China **95** G4
Ansbach Germany **63** K5
Anser Group is Australia **138** C7
Anshan Liaoning China **95** J3
Anshun China **96** E3
Anshunchang China **96** D2
An Sirhān, Wādī watercourse Saudi Arabia **112** E5
Ansley U.S.A. **160** D3
Anson U.S.A. **161** D5
Anson Bay Australia **134** E3
Ansongo Mali **120** D3
Ansonville Canada **152** E4
Ansted U.S.A. **164** E4
Ansu Hebei China see **Xushui**
Ansudu Indon. **81** J7
Antabamba Peru **176** D6
Antakya Turkey **107** C1
Antalaha Madag. **123** F5
Antalya Turkey **69** N6
Antalya prov. Turkey **107** A1
Antalya Körfezi g. Turkey **69** N6

▶**Antananarivo** Madag. **123** E5
Capital of Madagascar.

An tAonach Ireland see **Nenagh**

▶**Antarctica** **188**
Most southerly and coldest continent, and the continent with the highest average elevation.

Antarctic Peninsula Antarctica **188** L2
Antas r. Brazil **179** A5
An Teallach mt. U.K. **60** D3
Antelope Island U.S.A. **159** G1
Antelope Range mts U.S.A. **158** E2
Antequera Spain **67** D5
Anthony NM U.S.A. **166** D1
Anthony Lagoon Australia **136** A3
Anti Atlas mts Morocco **64** C6
Antibes France **66** H5
Anticosti, Île d' i. Canada **153** J4
Anticosti Island Canada see **Anticosti, Île d'**
Antifer, Cap d' c. France **59** H9
Antigo U.S.A. **160** F2
Antigonish Canada **153** J5
Antigua i. Antigua and Barbuda **169** L5
Antigua Guat. see **Antigua Guatemala**
Antigua country West Indies see **Antigua and Barbuda**
Antigua and Barbuda country West Indies **169** L5
Antigua Guatemala Guat. **167** H6
Antiguo-Morelos Mex. **167** F4
Antikythira i. Greece **69** J7
Antikythiro, Steno sea chan. Greece **69** J7
Anti Lebanon mts Lebanon/Syria see **Sharqī, Jabal ash**
Antimilos i. Greece **69** K6
Antimony U.S.A. **159** H2
An tInbhear Mór Ireland see **Arklow**
Antioch Turkey see **Antakya**
Antioch U.S.A. **158** C2
Antiocheia ad Cragum tourist site Turkey **107** A1
Antiochia Turkey see **Antakya**
Antiparos i. Greece **69** K6
Antipodes Islands N.Z. **133** H6
Antipsara i. Greece **69** K5
Antium Italy see **Anzio**
Antlers U.S.A. **161** E5
Antofagasta Chile **178** B2
Antofagasta de la Sierra Arg. **178** C3
Antofalla, Volcán vol. Arg. **178** C3
Antoing Belgium **62** D4
António Enes Moz. see **Angoche**
Antri India **104** D4
Antrim U.K. **61** F3
Antrim Hills U.K. **61** F2
Antrim Plateau Australia **134** E4
Antropovo Rus. Fed. **52** I4
Antsalova Madag. **123** E5
Antseranana Madag. see **Antsirañana**
Antsirabe Madag. **123** E5
Antsirañana Madag. **123** E5
Antsla Estonia **55** O8
Antsohihy Madag. **123** E5
Anttis Sweden **54** M3
Anttola Fin. **55** O6
An Tuc Vietnam see **An Khê**
Antwerp Belgium **62** E3
Antwerp U.S.A. **165** H1
Antwerpen Belgium see **Antwerp**
An Uaimh Ireland see **Navan**
Anuc, Lac l. Canada **152** G2
Anuchino Rus. Fed. **90** D4
Anugul India see **Angul**
Anupgarh India **104** C3
Anuradhapura Sri Lanka **106** D4
Anveh Iran **110** D5
Anvers Island Antarctica **188** L2
Anvik AK U.S.A. **148** G3
Anvik r. AK U.S.A. **148** G3
Anvil Range mts Y.T. Canada **149** N3
Anxi Fujian China **97** H3
Anxi Gansu China **94** C3
Anxiang China **97** G2
Anxin Hebei China **95** H4
Anxious Bay Australia **135** F8
Anyang Guangxi China see **Du'an**
Anyang Henan China **95** H4
Anyang S. Korea **91** B5
Anyar Jawa Indon. **84** D4
A'nyêmaqên Shan mts China **94** D5
Anyuan Jiangxi China **97** G3
Anyuan Jiangxi China **97** G3
Anyue China **96** E2
Anyuy r. Rus. Fed. **90** E2
Anyuysk Rus. Fed. **77** R3
Anzac Alta Canada **151** I3
Anzac B.C. Canada **150** F4
Anze Shanxi China **95** H4
Anzhero-Sudzhensk Rus. Fed. **76** J4
Anzi Dem. Rep. Congo **122** C4
Anzio Italy **68** E4
Aoba Japan **93** F3
Aoba i. Vanuatu **133** G3
Aoba-yama hill Japan **92** B3
Aogaki Japan **92** B3
Aoga-shima i. Japan **91** E6
Aohan Qi Nei Mongol China see **Xinhui**
Ao Kham, Laem pt Thai. **87** B5
Aoki Japan **93** E2
Aomen China see **Macao**
Aomen Tebie Xingzhengqu aut. reg. China see **Macao**
Aomori Japan **90** F4
A'ong Co l. Xizang China **99** C6
Ao Phang Nga National Park Thai. **87** B5

▶**Aoraki** mt. N.Z. **139** C6
Highest mountain in New Zealand.

Aoraki/Mount Cook National Park N.Z. **139** C6
Aôral, Phnum mt. Cambodia **87** D4
Aorangi mt. N.Z. see **Aoraki**
Aorangi mt. N.Z. see **Aoraki**
Aosta Italy **68** B2
Aotearoa country Oceania see **New Zealand**
Aouk, Bahr r. Cent. Afr. Rep./Chad **121** E4
Aoukâr reg. Mali/Mauritania **120** C2
Aoulef Alg. **120** D2
Aoyama Japan **92** C4
Aozou Chad **121** E2
Apa r. Brazil **178** E2
Apache Creek U.S.A. **159** I5
Apache Junction U.S.A. **159** H5
Apaiang atoll Kiribati see **Abaiang**
Apalachee Bay U.S.A. **163** C6
Apalachicola U.S.A. **163** C6
Apalachicola r. U.S.A. **163** C6
Apalachin U.S.A. **165** G2
Apamea Turkey see **Dinar**
Apan Mex. **167** F5
Apaporis r. Col. **176** E4
Apar, Teluk b. Indon. **85** G3
Aparecida do Tabuado Brazil **179** A3
Aparima N.Z. see **Riverton**
Aparri Luzon Phil. **82** C2
Apatity Rus. Fed. **54** R3
Apatzingán Mex. **168** D5
Apavawook Cape AK U.S.A. **148** E3
Ape Latvia **55** O8
Apeldoorn Neth. **62** F2
Apelern Germany **63** J2
Apennines mts Italy **68** C2
Apensen Germany **63** J1
Apex Mountain Y.T. Canada **149** M3
Aphrewn r. AK U.S.A. **148** F3
Api mt. Nepal **104** E3
Api i. Vanuatu see **Epi**
Api, Tanjung pt Indon. **83** B3
Apia atoll Kiribati see **Abaiang**

▶**Apia** Samoa **133** I3
Capital of Samoa.

Apiacas, Serra dos hills Brazil **177** G6
Apiaí Brazil **179** A4
Apipilulco Mex. **167** F5
Apishapa r. U.S.A. **160** C4
Apiti N.Z. **139** E4
Apizaco Mex. **167** F5
Apizolaya Mex. **166** E3
Aplao Peru **176** D7
Apo, Mount vol. Mindanao Phil. **82** D5
Apo East Passage Phil. **82** C3
Apoera Suriname **177** G2
Apolda Germany **63** L3
Apollo Bay Australia **138** A7
Apollonia Bulg. see **Sozopol**
Apolo Bol. **176** E6
Aporé Brazil **179** A2
Aporé r. Brazil **179** A2
Apostle Islands U.S.A. **160** F2
Apostolens Tommelfinger mt. Greenland **147** N3
Apostolos Andreas, Cape Cyprus **107** B2
Apoteri Guyana **177** G3
Apo West Passage Phil. **82** C3
Apozai Pak. **111** H4
Appalachian Mountains U.S.A. **164** D5
Appalla i. Fiji see **Kabara**
Appennines mts Italy **68** D2
Appennino mts Italy see **Apennines**
Appennino Abruzzese mts Italy **68** E3
Appennino Tosco-Emiliano mts Italy **68** D3
Appennino Umbro-Marchigiano mts Italy **68** E3
Appingedam Neth. **62** G1
Applecross U.K. **60** D3
Appleton MN U.S.A. **160** D2
Appleton WI U.S.A. **164** A1
Apple Valley U.S.A. **158** E4
Appomattox U.S.A. **165** F5
Aprilia Italy **68** E4
Aprunyi India **96** B2
Apsheronsk Rus. Fed. **113** E1
Apsheronskaya Rus. Fed. see **Apsheronsk**
Apsley Canada **165** F1
Apt France **66** G5
Apucarana Brazil **179** A3
Apucarana, Serra da hills Brazil **179** A3
Apulum Romania see **Alba Iulia**
Apurahuan Palawan Phil. **82** B4
Apurashokoru i. Palau **82** [inset]
Aq''a Georgia see **Sokhumi**
'Aqaba Jordan see **Al 'Aqabah**
Aqaba, Gulf of Asia **112** D5
'Aqaba, Wâdi el watercourse Egypt see **'Aqabah, Wādī al**
'Aqabah, Birkat al well Iraq **110** A4
'Aqabah, Wādī al watercourse Egypt **107** A4
Aqadyr Kazakh. see **Agadyr'**
Aqal Xinjiang China **98** B4
Aqdoghmish r. Iran **110** B2
Aqitag mt. Xinjiang China **94** B3
Aqköl Akmolinskaya Oblast' Kazakh. see **Akkol'**
Aqköl Atyrauskaya Oblast' Kazakh. see **Akkol'**
Aqmola Kazakh. see **Astana**
Aqqan Xinjiang China **99** C5
Aqqan Xinjiang China **99** D5
Aqqikkol Hu salt l. China **99** E5
Aqra', Jabal al mt. Syria/Turkey **107** B2
'Aqran hill Saudi Arabia **107** D4
Aqsay Kazakh. see **Aksay**
Aqsayqin Hit terr. Asia see **Aksai Chin**
Aqshī Kazakh. see **Akshiy**
Aqshuqyr Kazakh. see **Akshukur**
Aqsū Kazakh. see **Aksu**
Aqsūat Kazakh. see **Aksuat**
Aqsū-Ayuly Kazakh. see **Aksu-Ayuly**
Aqtaū Kazakh. see **Aktau**
Aqtöbe Kazakh. see **Aktobe**
Aqtoghay Kazakh. see **Aktogay**
Aquae Grani Germany see **Aachen**
Aquae Gratianae France see **Aix-les-Bains**
Aquae Sextiae France see **Aix-en-Provence**
Aquae Statiellae Italy see **Acqui Terme**
Aquarius Mountains U.S.A. **159** G4
Aquarius Plateau U.S.A. **159** H3
Aquaviva delle Fonti Italy **68** G4
Aquidauana Brazil **178** E2
Aquila Mex. **166** E5
Aquiles Mex. **166** D2
Aquincum Hungary see **Budapest**
Aquiry r. Brazil see **Acre**
Aquisgranum Germany see **Aachen**
Aquitaine reg. France **66** D5
Aquitania reg. France see **Aquitaine**
Aqzhayqyn Köli salt l. Kazakh. see **Akzhaykyn, Ozero**
Ara India **105** F4
Āra Ārba Eth. **122** E3
Arab Afgh. **111** G4
Arab, Bahr el watercourse Sudan **121** F4
'Arab, Khalîg el b. Egypt see **'Arab, Khalīj al**
'Arab, Khalīj al b. Egypt **112** C5
'Arabah, Wādī al watercourse Israel/Jordan **107** B5
Arabian Basin sea feature Indian Ocean **185** M5
Arabian Gulf Asia see **The Gulf**
Arabian Peninsula Asia **108** G5
Arabian Sea Indian Ocean **109** K6
Araç Turkey **112** D2
Araça r. Brazil **176** F4
Aracaju Brazil **177** K6
Aracati Brazil **177** K4
Aracatu Brazil **179** C1
Araçatuba Brazil **179** A3
Aracena Spain **67** C5
Aracruz Brazil **179** C2
Araçuaí Brazil **179** C2
Araçuaí r. Brazil **179** C2
'Arad Israel **107** B4
Arad Romania **69** I1
'Arādah U.A.E. **110** D6
Arafune-yama mt. Japan **93** E2
Arafura Sea Australia/Indon. **132** D2
Arafura Shelf sea feature Australia/Indon. **186** E6
Aragarças Brazil **177** H7
Ara-gawa r. Japan **93** E1
Ara-gawa r. Japan **93** F3
Aragón r. Spain **67** F2
Araguaçu Brazil **179** A1
Araguaia r. Brazil **179** A1
Araguaia, Parque Indígena res. Brazil **177** H6
Araguaia, Parque Nacional do nat. park Brazil **177** H6
Araguaiana Brazil **179** A1
Araguaína Brazil **177** I5
Araguari Brazil **179** A2
Araguari r. Brazil **177** H3
Araguatins Brazil **177** I5
Arai Brazil **179** B1
Arai Niigata Japan **93** E2
Arai Shizuoka Japan **92** D4
'Arâif el Naga, Gebel hill Egypt see **'Urayf an Nāqah, Jabal**
Árainn Mhór i. Ireland see **Arranmore Island**
Araiosos Brazil **177** J4
Arak Alg. **120** D2
Arāk Iran **110** C3
Arak Syria **107** D2
Arakai-yama mt. Japan **93** F1
Arakamchechen, Ostrov i. Rus. Fed. **148** D2
Arakan reg. Myanmar **86** A2
Arakan Yoma mts Myanmar **86** A2
Araki-gawa r. Japan **92** D2
Arakkonam India **106** C3
Araks r. Armenia see **Araz**
Araku India **106** D2
Aral Qinghai China **99** E5
Aral Kazakh. see **Aral'sk**
Aral Tajik. see **Vose**

▶**Aral Sea** salt l. Kazakh./Uzbek. **102** B2
4th largest lake in Asia.

Aral'sk Kazakh. **102** B2
Aral'skoye More salt l. Kazakh./Uzbek. see **Aral Sea**
Aralsor, Ozero l. Kazakh. **53** K6
Aral Tengizi salt l. Kazakh./Uzbek. see **Aral Sea**
Araltobe Xinjiang China **94** B2
Aramac Australia **136** D4
Aramac Creek watercourse Australia **136** D4
Aramah plat. Saudi Arabia **110** B5
Aramberri Mex. **161** D7
Aramia r. P.N.G. **81** K8
Aran r. India **106** C2
Aranda de Duero Spain **67** E3
Arandai Indon. **81** I7
Aranđelovac Serbia **69** I2
Arandis Namibia **124** B2
Arang India **105** E5
Arani India **106** C3
Aran Islands Ireland **61** C4
Aranjuez Spain **67** E3
Aranos Namibia **124** D3
Aransas Pass U.S.A. **161** D7
Arantangi India **106** C4
Aranuka atoll Kiribati **133** H1
Aranyaprathet Thai. **87** C4
Arao Japan **91** C6
Araouane Mali **120** C3
Arapaho U.S.A. **161** D5
Arapgir Turkey **112** E3
Arapiraca Brazil **177** K5
Arapis, Akra pt Greece see **Arapis, Akrotirio**
Arapis, Akrotirio pt Greece **69** K4
Arapkir Turkey see **Arapgir**
Arapongas Brazil **179** A3
Araquari Brazil **179** A4
'Ar'ar Saudi Arabia **113** F5
Araracuara Col. **176** D4
Araraj Bihar India **99** D8
Araranguá Brazil **179** A5
Araraquara Brazil **179** A3
Araras Brazil **177** H5
Ararat Armenia **113** G3
Ararat Australia **138** A6
Ararat, Mount Turkey **113** G3
Araria India **105** F4
Araripina Brazil **177** J5
Aras Turkey **113** F3
Aras r. Turkey see **Araz**
Ar-Asgat Mongolia see **Ugtaaltsaydam**
Arashima-dake mt. Japan **92** C3
Arataca Brazil **179** D1
Aratürük Xinjiang China see **Yiwu**
Arauca Col. **176** D2
Arauca r. Venez. **176** E2
Aravalli Range mts India **104** C4
Aravete Estonia **55** N7
Arawa P.N.G. **132** F2
Araxá Brazil **179** B2
Araxes r. Asia see **Araz**
Arayıt Dağı mt. Turkey **69** N5
Araz r. Azer. **113** H2
also spelt Araks (Armenia), Aras (Turkey), formerly known as Araxes
Arbailu Iraq see **Arbīl**
Arbat Iraq **113** G4
Arbela Iraq see **Arbīl**
Arberth U.K. see **Narberth**
Arbīl Iraq **113** G3
Arboga Sweden **55** I7
Arborfield Canada **151** K4
Arborg Canada **151** L5
Arbroath U.K. **60** G4
Arbuckle U.S.A. **158** B2
Arbu Lut, Dasht-e des. Afgh. **111** F4
Arcachon France **66** D4
Arcade U.S.A. **165** F2
Arcadia FL U.S.A. **163** D7
Arcadia LA U.S.A. **161** E5
Arcadia MI U.S.A. **164** B1
Arcanum U.S.A. **164** C4
Arcas, Cayos is Mex. **167** H4
Arcata U.S.A. **156** B4
Arc Dome mt. U.S.A. **158** E2
Arcelia Mex. **168** D5
Archangel Rus. Fed. **52** I2
Archer r. Australia **79** G9
Archer Bend National Park Australia **136** C2
Archer City U.S.A. **161** D5
Arches National Park U.S.A. **159** I2
Archipiélago Los Roques nat. park Venez. **176** E1
Ärçivan Azer. **113** H3
Arckaringa watercourse Australia **137** A6
Arco U.S.A. **156** E4
Arcos Brazil **179** B3
Arcos de la Frontera Spain **67** D5
Arctic Bay Canada **147** J2
Arctic Institute Islands Rus. Fed. see **Arkticheskogo Instituta, Ostrova**
Arctic Lagoon AK U.S.A. **148** F2
Arctic Mid-Ocean Ridge sea feature Arctic Ocean **189** H1
Arctic National Wildlife Refuge nature res. AK U.S.A. **149** K1
Arctic Ocean **189** B1
Arctic Red r. N.W.T. Canada **149** N2
Arctic Red River N.W.T. Canada see **Tsiigehtchic**
Arctic Village AK U.S.A. **149** K1
Arctowski research station Antarctica **188** A2
Arda r. Bulg. **69** L4
also known as Ardas (Greece)
Ardabīl Iran **110** C2
Ardahan Turkey **113** F2
Ardakān Iran **110** D3
Årdalstangen Norway **55** E6
Ardara Ireland **61** D3
Ardas r. Bulg. see **Arda**
Arḑ aş Şawwān plain Jordan **107** C4
Ardatov Nizhegorodskaya Oblast' Rus. Fed. **53** I5
Ardatov Respublika Mordoviya Rus. Fed. **53** J5
Ardee Ireland **61** F4
Ardennes plat. Belgium **62** E5
Ardennes, Canal des France **62** E5
Arden Town U.S.A. **158** C2
Arderin hill Ireland **61** E4
Ardestān Iran **110** D3
Ardglass U.K. **61** G3
Ardila r. Port. **67** C4
Ardlethan Australia **138** C5
Ardmore U.S.A. **161** D5
Ardnamurchan, Point of U.K. **60** C4
Ardon Rus. Fed. **113** G2
Ardrishaig U.K. **60** D4
Ardrossan U.K. **60** E5
Ardvasar U.K. **60** D3
Areia Branca Brazil **177** K4
Arekalong Peninsula Palau **82** [inset]
Arel Belgium see **Arlon**
Arelas France see **Arles**
Arelate France see **Arles**
Aremberg hill Germany **62** G4
Arena rf Phil. **82** C4
Arena, Point U.S.A. **158** B2
Arena, Punta pt Mex. **166** C4
Arena de la Ventana, Punta pt Mex. **166** C3
Arenal, Volcán vol. Costa Rica **166** [inset] I7
Arena Point Luzon Phil. **82** C3
Arenas de San Pedro Spain **67** D3
Arendal Norway **55** F7
Arendsee (Altmark) Germany **63** L2
Areopoli Greece **69** J6
Areponapuchi Mex. **166** D3
Arequipa Peru **176** D7
Arere Brazil **177** H4
Arévalo Spain **67** D3
Arezzo Italy **68** D3
'Arfajah well Saudi Arabia **107** D4
Argadargada Australia **136** B4
Argalant Mongolia **95** G2
Argan Xinjiang China **98** E4
Arganda del Rey Spain **67** E3
Argao Cebu Phil. **82** C4
Argatay Mongolia see **Bayanjargalan**
Argel Alg. see **Algiers**
Argentan France **66** D2
Argentario, Monte hill Italy **68** D3
Argentera, Cima dell' mt. Italy **68** B2
Argenthal Germany **63** H5

▶**Argentina** country S. America **178** C5
2nd largest and 3rd most populous country in South America, and 8th largest in the world.

Argentine Abyssal Plain sea feature S. Atlantic Ocean **184** E9
Argentine Basin sea feature S. Atlantic Ocean **184** F8
Argentine Republic country S. America see **Argentina**
Argentine Rise sea feature S. Atlantic Ocean **184** E8
Argentino, Lago l. Arg. **178** B8
Argenton-sur-Creuse France **66** E3
Argentoratum France see **Strasbourg**
Argeș r. Romania **69** L2
Arghandab r. Afgh. **111** G4
Argi r. Rus. Fed. **90** C1
Argolikos Kolpos b. Greece **69** J6
Argos Greece **69** J6
Argos U.S.A. **164** B3
Argostoli Greece **69** I5
Arguís Spain **67** F2
Argun' r. China/Rus. Fed. **89** M2
Argun Rus. Fed. **113** G2
Argungu Nigeria **120** D3
Argunskiy Khrebet mts Rus. Fed. **95** I1
Argus Range mts U.S.A. **158** E4
Arguut Mongolia see **Guchin-Us**
Argyle Canada **153** I6
Argyle, Lake Australia **134** E4
Argyrokastron Albania see **Gjirokastër**
Arhangay prov. Mongolia **94** E2
Ar Horqin Qi Nei Mongol China see **Tianshan**
Århus Denmark **55** G8
Arhymot Lake AK U.S.A. **148** G3
Ariaga i. Indon. **83** C1
Ariah Park Australia **138** C5
Ariamsvlei Namibia **124** D5
Ariana Tunisia see **L'Ariana**
Ariano Irpino Italy **68** F4
Ari Atoll Maldives **103** D11
Aribinda Burkina Faso **120** C3
Arica Chile **176** D7
Arid, Cape Australia **135** C8
Arida Japan **92** B4
Arida-gawa r. Japan **92** B4
Arigiyn Gol r. Mongolia **94** E1
Arigza China **96** C1
Arīḩā Syria **107** C2
Arīḩā West Bank see **Jericho**
Arikaree r. U.S.A. **160** C3
Arima Trin. and Tob. **169** L6
Arimine-ko resr Japan **92** D2
Ariminum Italy see **Rimini**
Arinos Brazil **179** B1
Ario de Rosáles Mex. **167** E5
Aripuanã Brazil **177** G6
Aripuanã r. Brazil **176** F5
Aripuanã, Parque Indígena res. Brazil **176** F6
Ariquemes Brazil **176** F5
Aris Namibia **124** C2
Arisaig U.K. **60** D4
Arisaig, Sound of sea chan. U.K. **60** D4
'Arīsh, Wādī al watercourse Egypt **107** A4
Aristazabal Island Canada **150** D4
Arixang Xinjiang China see **Wenquan**
Ariyalur India **106** C4
Arizaro, Salar de salt flat Arg. **178** C2
Arizona Arg. **178** C5
Arizona state U.S.A. **157** F6
Arizpe Mex. **166** C2
'Arjah Saudi Arabia **108** F5
Arjasa Jawa Indon. **85** F4
Arjeplog Sweden **54** J3
Arjuni Chhattisgarh India **106** D1
Arjuni India **104** E5
Arkadak Rus. Fed. **53** I6
Arkadelphia U.S.A. **161** E5
Arkaig, Loch l. U.K. **60** D4
Arkalyk Kazakh. **102** C1

Arkansas r. U.S.A. 161 F5
Arkansas state U.S.A. 161 E5
Arkansas City AR U.S.A. 161 F5
Arkansas City KS U.S.A. 161 D4
Arkatag Shan mts China 99 E5
Arkell, Mount Y.T. Canada 149 N3
Arkenu, Jabal mt. Libya 108 B5
Arkhangel'sk Rus. Fed. see Archangel
Arkhara Rus. Fed. 90 C2
Arkhipovka Rus. Fed. 90 D4
Árki i. Greece see Arkoi
Arklow Ireland 61 F5
Arkoi i. Greece 69 L6
Arkona Canada 164 E2
Arkona, Kap c. Germany 57 N3
Arkonam India see Arakkonam
Arkport U.S.A. 165 G2

▶Arkticheskiy, Mys c. Rus. Fed. 189 E1
Most northerly point of Asia.

Arkticheskogo Instituta, Ostrova is Rus. Fed. 76 J2
Arkul' Rus. Fed. 52 K4
Arlandag mt. Turkm. 110 D2
Arles France 66 G5
Arlington S. Africa 125 H5
Arlington NY U.S.A. 165 I3
Arlington OH U.S.A. 164 D3
Arlington SD U.S.A. 160 D2
Arlington VA U.S.A. 165 G4
Arlington Heights U.S.A. 164 A2
Arlit Niger 120 D3
Arlon Belgium 62 F5
Arm r. Canada 151 J5
Armadale Australia 135 A8
Armadores i. Indon. 83 C1
Armagh U.K. 61 F3
Armant Egypt 108 D4
Armavir Armenia 113 G2
Armavir Rus. Fed. 113 F1
Armenia country Asia 113 G2
Armenia Col. 176 C3
Armenopolis Romania see Gherla
Armeria Mex. 168 D5
Armidale Australia 138 E3
Armington U.S.A. 156 F3
Armit Lake Canada 151 N1
Armori India 106 D1
Armour U.S.A. 160 D3
Armoy U.K. 61 F2
Armstrong r. Australia 134 E4
Armstrong Canada 152 C4
Armstrong, Mount Y.T. Canada 149 N3
Armstrong Island Cook Is see Rarotonga
Armu r. Rus. Fed. 90 E3
Armur India 106 C2
Armutçuk Dağı mts Turkey 69 L5
Armyanskaya S.S.R. country Asia see Armenia
Arnaoutis, Cape Cyprus see Arnauti, Cape
Arnaud r. Canada 153 H2
Arnauti, Cape Cyprus 107 A2
Årnes Norway 55 G6
Arnett U.S.A. 161 D4
Arnhem Neth. 62 F3
Arnhem, Cape Australia 136 B2
Arnhem Land reg. Australia 134 F3
Arno r. Italy 68 D3
Arno Bay Australia 137 B7
Arnold U.K. 59 F5
Arnold's Cove Canada 153 L5
Arnon r. Jordan see Mawjib, Wādī al
Arnprior Canada 165 G1
Arnsberg Germany 63 I3
Arnstadt Germany 63 K4
Arnstein Germany 63 J5
Arnstorf Germany 63 M6
Aroab Namibia 124 D4
Aroland Canada 152 D4
Arolsen Germany 63 J3
Aroma Sudan 108 E6
Arona Italy 68 C2
Aropuk Lake AK U.S.A. 148 G3
Arorae i. Kiribati 133 H2
Arore i. Kiribati see Arorae
Aroroy Masbate Phil. 82 C3
Aros r. Mex. 166 C2
Arossi i. Solomon Is see San Cristobal
Arpa Kyrg. 98 A4
Arqalyq Kazakh. see Arkalyk
Arquipélago da Madeira aut. reg. Port. 120 B1
Arrabury Australia 137 C5
Arrah India see Ara
Arraias Brazil 179 B1
Arraias, Serra de hills Brazil 179 B1
Ar Ramādī Iraq see Ramādī
Ar Ramlah Jordan 107 B5
Ar Ramthā Jordan 107 C3
Arran i. U.K. 60 D5
Arranmore Island Ireland 61 D3
Ar Raqqah Syria 107 D2
Arras France 62 C4
Ar Rass Saudi Arabia 108 F4
Ar Rastān Syria 107 C2
Ar Rayyān Qatar 110 C5
Arrecife Canary Is 120 B2
Arretium Italy see Arezzo
Arriagá Mex. 168 F5
Arriaga Mex. 167 E4
Ar Rifā'ī Iraq 113 G5
Ar Rihāb salt flat Iraq 113 G5
Ar Rimāl reg. Saudi Arabia 122 F1
Arrington U.S.A. 165 F5
Ar Riyāḍ Saudi Arabia see Riyadh
Arrochar U.K. 60 E4
Arrojado r. Brazil 179 B1
Arrow, Lough l. Ireland 61 D3
Arrowsmith, Mount N.Z. 139 C6
Arroyo Grande U.S.A. 158 C4
Arroyo Seco Querétaro Mex. 167 F4
Ar Rubay'iyah Saudi Arabia 110 B5
Ar Rummān Jordan 107 B3
Ar Ruq'ī well Saudi Arabia 110 B4
Ar Ruṣāfah Syria 107 D2
Ar Ruṣayfah Jordan 107 C3
Ar Rustāq Oman 110 E6
Ar Ruṭbah Iraq 113 F4
Ar Ruwaydah Saudi Arabia 110 B5
Ar Ruwayḍah Saudi Arabia 110 B6
Ar Ruwayḍah Syria 107 C2
Års Denmark see Aars
Ars Iran 110 B2
Arseno Lake Canada 150 H1
Arsen'yev Rus. Fed. 90 D3
Arshaly Kazakh. 98 C2
Arsk Rus. Fed. 52 K4
Arta Djibouti 122 E2
Arta Greece 69 I5
Arteaga Coahuila Mex. 167 E3
Arteaga Michoacán Mex. 166 E5
Artem Rus. Fed. 90 D4
Artemisa Cuba 163 D8
Artemivs'k Ukr. 53 H6
Artemovsk Ukr. see Artemivs'k
Artenay France 66 E2
Artesia AZ U.S.A. 159 I5
Artesia NM U.S.A. 157 G6
Arthur Canada 164 E2
Arthur NE U.S.A. 160 C3
Arthur TN U.S.A. 164 D5
Arthur, Lake U.S.A. 164 E3
Arthur's Pass National Park N.Z. 139 C6
Arthur's Town Bahamas 163 F7
Arti Rus. Fed. 51 R4
Artigas research station Antarctica 188 A2
Artigas Uruguay 178 E4
Art'ik Armenia 113 F2
Artillery Lake Canada 151 I2
Artisia Botswana 125 H3
Artois reg. France 62 B4
Artois, Collines d' hills France 62 B4
Artos Dağı mt. Turkey 113 F3
Artova Turkey 112 E2
Artsakh aut. reg. Azer. see Dağlıq Qarabağ
Arts Bogd Uul mts Mongolia 94 E2
Artsiz Ukr. see Artsyz
Artsyz Ukr. 69 M2
Artur de Paiva Angola see Kuvango
Artux Xinjiang China 98 B5
Artvin Turkey 113 F2
Artyk Turkm. 110 E2
Aru, Kepulauan is Indon. 134 F1
Arua Uganda 122 D3
Aruanã Brazil 179 A1

▶Aruba terr. Caribbean Sea 169 K6
Self-governing Netherlands territory.

Arumã Brazil 176 F4
Arunachal Pradesh state India 105 H4
Arundel U.K. 59 G8
Arun Gol r. China 95 K2
Arun Qi Nei Mongol China see Naji
Aruppukkottai India 106 C4
Arus, Tanjung pt Indon. 83 B2
Arusha Tanz. 122 D4
Arut r. Indon. 85 E3
Aruwimi r. Dem. Rep. Congo 122 C3
Arvada U.S.A. 156 G5
Arvagh Ireland 61 E4
Arvayheer Mongolia 94 E2
Arviat Canada 151 M2
Arvidsjaur Sweden 54 K4
Arvika Sweden 55 H7
Arvonia U.S.A. 165 F5
Arwā' Saudi Arabia 110 B6
Arwād i. Syria 107 B2
Arwala Maluku Indon. 83 C4
Arxan Nei Mongol China 95 I2
Arxan Xinjiang China 98 D4
Aryanah Tunisia see L'Ariana
Arys' Kazakh. 102 C3
Arzamas Rus. Fed. 53 I5
Arzanah i. U.A.E. 110 D5
Arzberg Germany 63 M4
Arzew Alg. 67 F6
Arzgir Rus. Fed. 113 G1
Arzila Morocco see Asilah
Aš Czech Rep. 63 M4
Asaba Japan 93 D4
Asaba Nigeria 120 D4
Asad, Buḥayrat al resr Syria 107 D1
Asadābād Afgh. 111 H3
Asadābād Iran 110 C3
Asagi Japan 92 A3
Asahan r. Indon. 84 B2
Asahi Aichi Japan 92 D3
Asahi Chiba Japan 93 G3
Asahi Fukui Japan 92 C3
Asahi Gifu Japan 92 D2
Asahi Ibaraki Japan 93 G2
Asahi Kanagawa Japan 93 F3
Asahi Mie Japan 92 C3
Asahi Nagano Japan 93 D2
Asahi Toyama Japan 92 D2
Asahi-dake vol. Japan 90 F4
Asahikawa Japan 90 F4
Asaka Japan 93 F3
Asakawa Japan 93 G1
Asake-gawa r. Japan 92 C3
'Asal Egypt 107 A5
Āsalē l. Eth. 122 E2
Asālem Iran 110 C2
'Asalūyeh Iran 110 D5
Asamaga-take hill Japan 92 C4
Asama-yama vol. Japan 93 E2
Asan-man b. S. Korea 91 B5
Asansol India 105 F5
Asao Japan 93 F3
Asar Nei Mongol China 95 I2
Asashina Japan 93 E2
Āsayita Eth. 122 E2
Asbach Germany 63 H4
Asbestos Mountains S. Africa 124 F5
Asbury Park U.S.A. 165 H3
Ascalon Israel see Ashqelon
Ascea Italy 68 F4
Ascensión Bol. 176 F7
Ascensión Chihuahua Mex. 166 D2
Ascensión Nuevo León Mex. 167 F3
Ascension atoll Micronesia see Pohnpei
Ascension i. S. Atlantic Ocean 184 H6
Aschaffenburg Germany 63 J5
Ascheberg Germany 63 H3
Aschersleben Germany 63 L3
Ascoli Piceno Italy 68 E3
Asculum Italy see Ascoli Piceno
Asculum Picenum Italy see Ascoli Piceno
Ascutney U.S.A. 165 I2
Āseb Eritrea see Assab
Åseda Sweden 55 I8
Åsele Sweden 54 J4
Asenovgrad Bulg. 69 K3
Aşfar, Jabal al mt. Jordan 107 C3
Aşfar, Tall al hill Syria 107 C3

▶Aşgabat Turkm. 110 E2
Capital of Turkmenistan.

Asha Rus. Fed. 51 R5
Ashahi-dake mt. Japan 92 D2
Ashburn U.S.A. 163 D6
Ashburton watercourse Australia 134 A5
Ashburton N.Z. 139 C6
Ashburton Range hills Australia 134 F4
Ashdod Israel 107 B4
Ashdown U.S.A. 161 E5
Asheboro U.S.A. 162 E5
Asher U.S.A. 161 D5
Ashern Canada 151 L5
Asheville U.S.A. 162 D5
Asheweig r. Canada 152 D3
Ashford Australia 138 E2
Ashford U.K. 59 H7
Ash Fork U.S.A. 159 G4
Ashgabat Turkm. see Aşgabat
Ashibetsu Japan 90 F4
Ashigawa Japan 93 E3
Ashikaga Japan 93 F2
Ashington U.K. 58 F3
Ashino-ko l. Japan 93 F3
Ashio Japan 93 F2
Ashio-sanchi mts Japan 93 F2
Ashiwada Japan 93 E3
Ashiya Japan 92 B4
Ashizuri-misaki pt Japan 91 D6
Ashkelon Israel see Ashqelon
Ashkhabad Turkm. see Aşgabat
Ashkum U.S.A. 164 B3
Ashkun reg. Afgh. 111 H3
Ashland AL U.S.A. 163 C5
Ashland ME U.S.A. 162 G2
Ashland NH U.S.A. 165 J2
Ashland OH U.S.A. 164 D3
Ashland OR U.S.A. 156 C4
Ashland VA U.S.A. 165 G5
Ashland WI U.S.A. 160 F2
Ashland City U.S.A. 164 B5
Ashley Australia 138 D2
Ashley MI U.S.A. 164 C2
Ashley ND U.S.A. 160 D2

▶Ashmore and Cartier Islands terr. Australia 134 C3
Australian External Territory.

Ashmore Reef Australia 134 C3
Ashmore Reefs Australia 136 D1
Ashmyany Belarus 55 N9
Ashqelon Israel 107 B4
Ash Shabakah Iraq 113 F5
Ash Shaddādah Syria 113 F3
Ash Shallūfah Egypt 107 A4
Ash Sham Syria see Damascus
Ash Shanāfiyah Iraq 113 G5
Ash Shaqīq well Saudi Arabia 113 F5
Ash Sharāh mts Jordan 107 B4
Ash Sharawrah Saudi Arabia 108 G6
Ash Shāriqah U.A.E. see Sharjah
Ash Sharqāṭ Iraq 113 F4
Ash Shaṭrah Iraq 113 G5
Ash Shaṭṭ Egypt 107 A5
Ash Shawbak Jordan 107 B4
Ash Shaybānī well Saudi Arabia 113 F5
Ash Shaykh Ibrāhīm Syria 107 D2
Ash Shiblīyāt hill Saudi Arabia 107 C5
Ash Shiḥr Yemen 108 G7
Ash Shu'āybah Saudi Arabia 113 F6
Ash Shu'bah Saudi Arabia 108 F4
Ash Shurayf Saudi Arabia see Khaybar
Ashta India 104 D5
Ashtabula U.S.A. 164 E3
Ashtarak Armenia 113 G2
Ashti Mahar. India 104 D5
Ashti Mahar. India 106 B2
Ashti Mahar. India 106 C2
Ashtiān Iran 110 C3
Ashton S. Africa 124 E7
Ashton U.S.A. 156 F3
Ashton-under-Lyne U.K. 58 E5
Ashuanipi r. Canada 153 I3
Ashuanipi Lake Canada 153 I3
Ashur Iraq see Ash Sharqāṭ
Ashville U.S.A. 163 C5
Ashwaubenon U.S.A. 164 A1
Asi r. Asia 112 E3 see 'Āṣī, Nahr al
'Āṣī r. Lebanon/Syria see Orontes
'Āṣī, Nahr al r. Asia 112 E3
also known as Asi or Orontes
Āsīā Bak Iran 110 C3
Asid Gulf Masbate Phil. 82 C3
Asientos Mex. 166 E4
Asifabad India 106 C2
Asika India 106 E2
Asilah Morocco 67 C6
Asinara, Golfo dell' b. Sardinia Italy 68 C4
Asino Rus. Fed. 76 J4
Asipovichy Belarus 53 F5
Asīr Iran 110 D5
'Asīr reg. Saudi Arabia 108 F5
Asisium Italy see Assisi
Askale Pak. 104 C2
Aşkale Turkey 113 F3
Asker Norway 55 G7
Askersund Sweden 55 I7
Askim Norway 55 G7
Askī Mawşil Iraq 113 F3
Askino Rus. Fed. 51 R4
Askival hill U.K. 60 C4
Asl Egypt see 'Asal
Aslanköy r. Turkey 107 B1
Asmar reg. Afgh. 111 H3

▶Asmara Eritrea 108 E6
Capital of Eritrea.

Āsmera Eritrea see Asmara
Åsnen l. Sweden 55 I8
Asō Japan 93 G3
Aso-Kuju Kokuritsu-kōen Japan 91 C6
Asom state India see Assam
Asonli India 96 B2
Asop India 104 C4
Asori Indon. 81 J7
Āsosa Eth. 122 D2
Asotin U.S.A. 156 D3
Aspang-Markt Austria 57 P7
Aspara Kazakh. 98 A4
Aspatria U.K. 58 D4
Aspen U.S.A. 156 G5
Asperg Germany 63 J6
Aspermont U.S.A. 161 C5
Aspiring, Mount N.Z. 139 B7
Aspro, Cape Cyprus 107 A2
Aspromonte, Parco Nazionale dell' nat. park Italy 68 F5
Aspron, Cape Cyprus see Aspro, Cape
Aspur India 111 I6
Asquith Canada 151 J4
As Sa'an Syria 107 C2
Assab Eritrea 108 F7
As Sabsab well Saudi Arabia 110 C5
Assad, Lake resr Syria see Asad, Buḥayrat al
Aş Şadr U.A.E. 110 D5
Aş Şafā lava field Syria 107 C3
Aş Şafāqis Tunisia see Sfax
Aş Şaff Egypt 112 C5
As Safīrah Syria 107 C1
Aş Şaḥrā' al Gharbīyah des. Egypt see Western Desert
Aş Şaḥrā' ash Sharqīyah des. Egypt see Eastern Desert
Assake-Audan, Vpadina depr. Kazakh./Uzbek. 113 J2
'Assal, Lac l. Djibouti see Assal, Lake
Assal, Lake Djibouti 108 F7
Aş Şāliḥīyah Syria 113 F4
As Sallūm Egypt 112 B5
As Salmān Iraq 113 G5
As Salṭ Jordan 107 B3
Assam state India 105 G4
Assamakka Niger 120 D3
As Samāwah Iraq 113 G5
As Samrā' Jordan 107 C3
Aş Şanām reg. Saudi Arabia 108 H5
As Sarīr reg. Libya 121 F2
Assateague Island U.S.A. 165 H4
As Sawādah reg. Saudi Arabia 110 B6
Assayeta Eth. see Āsayita
As Sayḥ Saudi Arabia 110 B6
Assen Neth. 62 G1
Assenede Belgium 62 D3
Assesse Belgium 62 F4
As Sidrah Libya 121 E1
As Sīfah Oman 110 E6
Assigny, Lac l. Canada 153 I3
As Sikak Saudi Arabia 110 C5
Assiniboia Canada 151 J5
Assiniboine r. Canada 151 L5
Assiniboine, Mount Canada 150 H5
Assis Brazil 179 A3
Assisi Italy 68 E3
Aßlar Germany 63 I4
Aş Şubayḥīyah Kuwait 110 B4
Aş Şufayrī well Saudi Arabia 110 B4
As Sukhnah Syria 107 D2
As Sulaymānīyah Iraq see Sulaymānīyah
As Sulaymī Saudi Arabia 108 F4
Aş Şulb reg. Saudi Arabia 110 C5
Aş Şummān plat. Saudi Arabia 110 B5
Aş Şummān plat. Saudi Arabia 110 C6
As Sūq Saudi Arabia 108 F5
As Sūrīyah country Asia see Syria
Aş Şuwar Syria 113 F4
As Suwaydā' Syria 107 C3
As Suways Egypt see Suez
As Suways governorate Egypt 107 A4
Assynt, Loch l. U.K. 60 D2
Astacus Kocaeli Turkey see İzmit
Astakida i. Greece 69 L7
Astakos Greece 69 I5
Astalu Island Pak. see Astola Island

▶Astana Kazakh. 102 D1
Capital of Kazakhstan.

Astaneh Iran 110 C2
Astara Azer. 113 H3
Āstārā Iran 108 G2
Asterabad Iran see Gorgān
Asti Italy 68 C2
Astillero Peru 176 E6
Astin Tag mts China see Altun Shan
Astipálaia i. Greece see Astypalaia
Astola Island Pak. 111 F5
Astor Pak. 99 A6
Astor r. Pak. 111 I3
Astorga Spain 67 C2
Astoria U.S.A. 156 C3
Åstorp Sweden 55 H8
Astrabad Iran see Gorgān
Astrakhan' Rus. Fed. 53 K7
Astrakhan' Bazar Azer. see Cälilabad
Astravyets Belarus 55 N9
Astrida Rwanda see Butare
Astrid Ridge sea feature Antarctica 188 C2
Asturias aut. comm. Spain 67 C2
Asturias, Principado de aut. comm. Spain see Asturias
Asturica Augusta Spain see Astorga
Astypalaia i. Greece 69 L6
Asubulak Kazakh. 98 C2
Asuka Japan 92 B4
Asuke Japan 92 D3
Asuncion i. N. Mariana Is 81 L3

▶Asunción Para. 178 E3
Capital of Paraguay.

Asuwa-gawa r. Japan 92 C2
Aswad Oman 110 E5
Aswān Egypt 108 D5
Aswān Egypt see Aswān
Asyūṭ Egypt 112 C6
Asyūṭ Egypt see Asyūṭ
Ata i. Tonga 133 I4
Atacama, Desierto de des. Chile see Atacama Desert
Atacama, Salar de salt flat Chile 178 C2

▶Atacama Desert Chile 178 C3
Driest place in the world.

Atafu atoll Tokelau 133 I2
Atafu i. Tokelau 186 I6
Atago-san hill Japan 92 B3
Atago-yama hill Japan 93 F3
'Aṭā'iṭah, Jabal al mt. Jordan 107 B4
Atakent Turkey 107 B1
Atakpamé Togo 120 D4
Atalándi Greece see Atalanti
Atalanti Greece 69 J5
Atalaya Panama 166 [inset] J7
Atalaya Peru 176 D6
Ataléia Brazil 179 C2
Atambua Indon. 134 D2
Atami Japan 93 F3
Atamyrat Turkm. 111 G2
Ataniya Turkey see Adana
Atapupu Timor Indon. 83 C5
'Ataq Yemen 108 G7
Atâr Mauritania 120 B2
Atari Pak. 111 I4
Atascadero U.S.A. 158 C4
Atasu Kazakh. 102 D2
Atatan He r. China 99 E5
Ataúro, Ilha de i. East Timor 83 C5
Atáviros mt. Greece see Attavyros
Atayurt Turkey 107 A1
Atbara Sudan 108 D6
Atbara r. Sudan 108 D6
Atbasar Kazakh. 102 C1
At-Bashy Kyrg. 98 A4
Atchafalaya Bay LA U.S.A. 167 H2
Atchison U.S.A. 160 E4
Atchueelinguk r. AK U.S.A. 148 G3
Atebubu Ghana 120 C4
Atema-yama mt. Japan 93 E1
Ateransk Kazakh. see Atyrau
Āteshān Iran 110 D3
Āteshkhāneh, Kūh-e hill Afgh. 111 F3
Atessa Italy 68 F3
Ath Belgium 62 D4
Athabasca r. Canada 151 I3
Athabasca, Lake Canada 151 I3
Athalia U.S.A. 164 D4
'Athāmīn, Birkat al well Iraq 110 A4
Atharan Hazari Pak. 111 I4
Athboy Ireland 61 F4
Athenae Greece see Athens
Athenry Ireland 61 D4
Athens Canada 165 H1

▶Athens Greece 69 J6
Capital of Greece.

Athens AL U.S.A. 163 C5
Athens GA U.S.A. 163 D5
Athens MI U.S.A. 164 C2
Athens OH U.S.A. 164 D4
Athens PA U.S.A. 165 G3
Athens TN U.S.A. 162 C5
Athens TX U.S.A. 161 E5
Atherstone U.K. 59 F6
Atherton Australia 136 D3
Athies France 62 C5
Athina Greece see Athens
Athínai Greece see Athens
Athleague Ireland 61 D4
Athlone Ireland 61 E4
Athnā', Wādī al watercourse Jordan 107 D3
Athni India 106 B2
Athol N.Z. 139 B7
Athol U.S.A. 165 I2
Atholl, Forest of reg. U.K. 60 E4
Athos mt. Greece 69 K4
Ath Thamad Egypt 107 B5
Ath Thāyat mt. Saudi Arabia 107 C5
Ath Thumāmī well Saudi Arabia 110 B5
Athy Ireland 61 F5
Ati Chad 121 E3
Aṭīābād Iran 110 E3
Atico Peru 176 D7
Atigun Pass AK U.S.A. 149 J1
Atikameg Canada 150 H4
Atikameg r. Canada 152 E3
Atik Lake Canada 151 M4
Atikokan Canada 147 I5
Atikonak Lake Canada 153 I3
Atimonan Luzon Phil. 82 C3
Atiquizaya El Salvador 167 H6
Atitlán Guat. 167 H6
Atitlán, Parque Nacional nat. park Guat. 167 H6
Atjeh admin. dist. Indon. see Aceh
Atka Rus. Fed. 77 Q3
Atka AK U.S.A. 149 [inset]
Atka Island AK U.S.A. 149 [inset]
Atkarsk Rus. Fed. 53 J6
Atkinson Point pt N.W.T. Canada 149 O1
Atkri Papua Indon. 83 D3

▶Atlanta GA U.S.A. 163 C5
Capital of Georgia.

Atlanta IN U.S.A. 164 B3
Atlanta MI U.S.A. 164 C1
Atlantic IA U.S.A. 160 E3
Atlantic NC U.S.A. 163 E5
Atlantic City U.S.A. 165 H4
Atlantic-Indian-Antarctic Basin sea feature S. Atlantic Ocean 184 H10
Atlantic-Indian Ridge sea feature Southern Ocean 184 H9

▶Atlantic Ocean 184
2nd largest ocean in the world.

Atlantic Peak U.S.A. 156 F4
Atlantis S. Africa 124 D7
Atlas Bogd mt. Mongolia 94 D3
Atlas Méditerranéen mts Alg. see Atlas Tellien
Atlas Mountains Africa 64 C5
Atlas Saharien mts Alg. 64 E5
Atlas Tellien mts Alg. 67 H6
Atlin Lake B.C./Y.T. Canada 149 N4
Atlixco Mex. 167 F5
Atmakur India 106 C3
Atmautluak AK U.S.A. 148 G3
Atmore U.S.A. 163 C6
Atnur India 106 C2
Atocha Bol. 176 E8
Atoka U.S.A. 161 D5
Atotonilco el Alto Mex. 166 E4
Atouat mt. Laos 86 D3
Atouila, Erg des. Mali 120 C2
Atoyac de Álvarez Mex. 167 E5
Atqan Xinjiang China see Aqqan
Atqasuk AK U.S.A. 148 H1
Atrato r. Col. 176 C2
Atrek r. Iran/Turkm. 110 D2
also known as Etrek
Atropatene country Asia see Azerbaijan
Atsonupuri vol. Rus. Fed. 90 G3
Atsugi Japan 93 F3
Atsumi Aichi Japan 92 D4
Atsumi-hantō pen. Japan 92 D4
Aṭ Ṭafīlah Jordan 107 B4
Aṭ Ṭā'if Saudi Arabia 108 F5
Attalea Turkey see Antalya
Attalia Turkey see Antalya
At Tamīmī Libya 112 A4
Attapu Laos 86 D4
Attavyros mt. Greece 69 L6
Attawapiskat Canada 152 E3
Attawapiskat r. Canada 152 E3
Attawapiskat Lake Canada 152 D3
Aṭ Ṭawīl mts Saudi Arabia 113 E5
At Taysīyah plat. Saudi Arabia 113 F5
Attendorn Germany 63 H3
Attersee l. Austria 57 N7
Attica IN U.S.A. 164 B3
Attica NY U.S.A. 165 F2
Attica OH U.S.A. 164 D3
Attigny France 62 E5
Attikamagen Lake Canada 153 I3
Attleborough U.K. 59 I6
Attopeu Laos see Attapu
Attu Greenland 147 M3
Attu AK U.S.A. 148 [inset]
Aṭ Ṭubayq reg. Saudi Arabia 107 C5

▶Attu Island AK U.S.A. 148 [inset]
Most westerly point of North America.

At Tūnisīyah country Africa see Tunisia
Aṭ Ṭūr Egypt 112 D5
Attur India 106 C4
Aṭ Ṭuwayyah well Saudi Arabia 113 F6
Atuk Mountain hill AK U.S.A. 148 E3
Åtvidaberg Sweden 55 I7
Atwari Bangl. 99 E8
Atwater U.S.A. 158 C3
Atwood U.S.A. 160 C4
Atwood Lake U.S.A. 164 E3
Atyashevo Rus. Fed. 53 J5
Atyrau Kazakh. 100 E2
Atyraū admin. div. Kazakh. see Atyrauskaya Oblast'
Atyrau Oblast admin. div. Kazakh. see Atyrauskaya Oblast'
Atyrauskaya Oblast' admin. div. Kazakh. 51 Q6
Aua Island P.N.G. 81 K7
Aub Germany 63 K5
Aubagne France 66 G5
Aubange Belgium 62 F5
Aubarede Point Luzon Phil. 82 C2
Aubenas France 66 G4
Aubergenville France 62 B6
Auboué France 62 F5
Aubrey Cliffs mts U.S.A. 159 G4
Aubry Lake N.W.T. Canada 149 P2
Auburn r. Australia 137 E5
Auburn Canada 164 E2
Auburn AL U.S.A. 163 C5
Auburn CA U.S.A. 158 C2
Auburn IN U.S.A. 164 C3
Auburn KY U.S.A. 164 B5
Auburn ME U.S.A. 165 J1
Auburn NE U.S.A. 160 E3
Auburn NY U.S.A. 165 G2
Auburn Range hills Australia 136 E5
Aubusson France 66 F4
Auch France 66 E5
Auche Myanmar 86 B1
Auchterarder U.K. 60 F4

▶Auckland N.Z. 139 E3
5th most populous city in Oceania.

Auckland Islands N.Z. 133 G7
Auden Canada 152 D4
Audenarde Belgium see Oudenaarde
Audo mts Eth. 122 E3
Audo Range mts Eth. see Audo
Audruicq France 62 C4
Audubon U.S.A. 160 E3
Aue Germany 63 M4
Auerbach Germany 63 M4
Auerbach in der Oberpfalz Germany 63 L5
Auersberg mt. Germany 63 M4
Auezov Kazakh. 98 C2
Augathella Australia 137 D5
Augher U.K. 61 E3
Aughnacloy U.K. 61 F3
Aughrim Ireland 61 F5
Augrabies S. Africa 124 E5
Augrabies Falls S. Africa 124 E5
Augrabies Falls National Park S. Africa 124 E5
Au Gres U.S.A. 164 D1
Augsburg Germany 57 M6
Augusta Australia 135 A8
Augusta Sicily Italy 68 F6
Augusta AR U.S.A. 161 F5
Augusta GA U.S.A. 163 D5
Augusta KY U.S.A. 164 C4

▶Augusta ME U.S.A. 165 K1
Capital of Maine.

Augusta MT U.S.A. 156 E3
Augusta Auscorum France see Auch
Augusta Taurinorum Italy see Turin
Augusta Treverorum Germany see Trier
Augusta Vindelicorum Germany see Augsburg
Augustine Island AK U.S.A. 148 I4
Augusto de Lima Brazil 179 B2
Augustus, Mount Australia 135 B6
Auke Bay AK U.S.A. 149 N4
Aukštaitijos nacionalinis parkas nat. park Lith. 55 O9
Aulavik National Park Canada 146 G2
Auld, Lake salt flat Australia 134 C5
Auliye Ata Kazakh. see Taraz
Aulnoye-Aymeries France 62 D4
Aulon Albania see Vlorë
Aulong i. Palau 82 [inset]
Ault France 62 B4
Auluptagel i. Palau 82 [inset]
Aumale Alg. see Sour el Ghozlane
Aumale France 62 B5
Aundh India 106 B2
Aundhi India 106 D1
Aunglan Myanmar 86 A3
Auob watercourse Namibia/S. Africa 124 E4
Aupaluk Canada 153 H2
Auponhia Maluku Indon. 83 C3
Aur i. Malaysia 84 D2
Aura Fin. 55 M6
Auraiya India 104 D4
Aurangabad Bihar India 105 F4
Aurangabad Mahar. India 106 B2
Aure r. France 59 F9
Aurich Germany 63 H1
Aurigny i. Channel Is see Alderney

Aurilândia Brazil **179** A2
Aurillac France **66** F4
Aurkuning *Kalimantan* Indon. **85** E3
Aurora *Mindanao* Phil. **82** C5
Aurora *CO* U.S.A. **156** G5
Aurora *IL* U.S.A. **164** A3
Aurora *MO* U.S.A. **161** E4
Aurora *NE* U.S.A. **160** D3
Aurora *UT* U.S.A. **159** H2
Aurora Island Vanuatu *see* **Maéwo**
Aurukun Australia **136** C2
Aus Namibia **124** C4
Au Sable U.S.A. **164** D1
Au Sable Point U.S.A. **164** D1
Auskerry *i.* U.K. **60** G1
Austin *IN* U.S.A. **164** C4
Austin *MN* U.S.A. **160** E3
Austin *NV* U.S.A. **158** E2

▶**Austin** *TX* U.S.A. **161** D6
Capital of Texas.

Austin, Lake *salt flat* Australia **135** B6
Austintown U.S.A. **164** E3
Austral Downs Australia **136** B4
Australes, Îles *is* Fr. Polynesia *see* **Tubuai Islands**

▶**Australia** *country* Oceania **132** C4
Largest and most populous country in Oceania, and 6th largest in the world.

Australian-Antarctic Basin *sea feature* S. Atlantic Ocean **186** C9
Australian Antarctic Territory *reg.* Antarctica **188** G2
Australian Capital Territory *admin. div.* Australia **138** D5
Austria *country* Europe **57** N7
Austvågøy *i.* Norway **54** I2
Autazes Brazil **177** G4
Autesiodorum France *see* **Auxerre**
Authie *r.* France **62** B4
Autlán Mex. **166** D5
Autti Fin. **54** O3
Auvergne *reg.* France **66** F4
Auvergne, Monts d' *mts* France **66** F4
Auxerre France **66** F3
Auxi-le-Château France **62** C4
Auxonne France **66** G3
Auyuittuq National Park Canada **147** L3
Auzangate, Nevado *mt.* Peru **176** D6
Ava *MO* U.S.A. **161** E4
Ava *NY* U.S.A. **165** H2
Avalik *r. AK* U.S.A. **148** H1
Avallon France **66** F3
Avalon U.S.A. **158** D5
Avalon Peninsula Canada **153** L5
Ávalos Mex. **167** E3
Avān Iran **113** G3
Avarau *atoll* Cook Is *see* **Palmerston**
Avaré Brazil **179** A3
Avaricum France *see* **Bourges**

▶**Avarua** Cook Is **187** J7
Capital of the Cook Islands, on Rarotonga.

Avawam U.S.A. **164** D5
Avaz Iran **111** F3
Aveiro Port. **67** B3
Aveiro, Ria de *est.* Port. **67** B3
Āvej Iran **110** C3
Avellino Italy **68** F4
Avenal U.S.A. **158** C3
Avenhorn Neth. **62** E2
Avenio France *see* **Avignon**
Aversa Italy **68** F4
Avesnes-sur-Helpe France **62** D4
Avesta Sweden **55** J6
Aveyron *r.* France **66** E4
Avezzano Italy **68** E3
Aviemore U.K. **60** F3
Avignon France **66** G5
Ávila Spain **67** D3
Avilés Spain **67** D2
Avion France **62** C4
Avis U.S.A. **165** G3
Avlama Dağı *mt.* Turkey **107** A1
Avlama Dağı *mts* Turkey **107** A1
Avlona Albania *see* **Vlorë**
Avnyugskiy Rus. Fed. **52** J3
Avoca Australia **138** A6
Avoca *r.* Australia **138** A5
Avoca Ireland **61** F5
Avoca *IA* U.S.A. **160** E3
Avoca *NY* U.S.A. **165** G2
Avola *Sicily* Italy **68** F6
Avon *r. England* U.K. **59** E6
Avon *r. England* U.K. **59** E7
Avon *r. England* U.K. **59** F8
Avon *r. Scotland* U.K. **60** F3
Avon U.S.A. **165** G2
Avondale U.S.A. **159** G5
Avonmore *r.* Ireland **61** F5
Avonmore U.S.A. **164** F3
Avonmouth U.K. **59** E7
Avranches France **66** D2
Avre *r.* France **62** C5
Avsuyu Turkey **107** C1
Avuavu Solomon Is **133** G2
Avveel Fin. *see* **Ivalo**
Avvil Fin. *see* **Ivalo**
A'waj *r.* Syria **107** B3
Awaji Japan **92** B4
Awaji-shima *i.* Japan **92** A4
Awakino N.Z. **139** E4
'Awālī Bahrain **110** C5
Awang *Lombok* Indon. **85** G5
Awano Japan **93** F2
Awanui N.Z. **139** D2
Awara Japan **92** C2
Awarawar, Tanjung *pt* Indon. **85** F4
Āwarē Eth. **122** E3
'Awāriḍ, Wādī al *watercourse* Syria **107** D2
Awarua Point N.Z. **139** B7
Āwash Eth. **122** E3
Āwash *r.* Eth. **122** E2
Awa-shima *i.* Japan **91** E5
Āwash National Park Eth. **122** D3
Awasib Mountains Namibia **124** B3
Awat *Xinjiang* China **98** C4
Awatere *r.* N.Z. **139** E5
Awbārī Libya **120** E2
Awbeg *r.* Ireland **61** D5
'Awdah *well* Saudi Arabia **110** C6
'Awdah, Hawr al *imp. l.* Iraq **113** G5
Aw Dheegle Somalia **121** H4
Awe, Loch *l.* U.K. **60** D4
Aweil Sudan **121** F4
Awka Nigeria **120** D4
Awo *r.* Indon. **83** B3
Awserd W. Sahara **120** B2
Awu *vol.* Indon. **83** C2
Awuna *r. AK* U.S.A. **148** I1
Axe *r. England* U.K. **59** D8
Axe *r. England* U.K. **59** E7
Axedale Australia **138** B6
Axel Heiberg Glacier Antarctica **188** I1
Axel Heiberg Island Canada **147** I2
Axim Ghana **120** C4
Axminster U.K. **59** E8
Axum Eth. *see* **Āksum**
Ay France **62** E5
Ay Kazakh. **98** C3
Ayabe Japan **92** B3
Ayachi, Jbel *mt.* Morocco **64** D5
Ayacucho Arg. **178** E5
Ayacucho Peru **176** D6
Ayadaw Myanmar **86** A2
Ayagoz Kazakh. **102** F2
Ayagoz *watercourse* Kazakh. **98** B3
Ayaguz Kazakh. *see* **Ayagoz**
Ayakkum Hu *salt l.* China **99** E5
Ayaköz Kazakh. *see* **Ayagoz**
Ayakulik *AK* U.S.A. **148** I4
Ayama Japan **92** C4
Ayan Rus. Fed. **77** O4
Ayancık Turkey **112** D2
Ayang N. Korea **91** B5
Ayaş Turkey **112** D2
Ayase Japan **93** F3
Āybak Afgh. **111** H2
Aybas Kazakh. **53** K7
Aydar *r.* Ukr. **53** H6
Aydarko'l ko'li *l.* Uzbek. **102** C3
Aydere Turkm. **110** E2
Aydın Turkey **69** L6
Aydıncık Turkey **107** A1
Aydın Dağları *mts* Turkey **69** L5
Aydingkol Hu *marsh* China **98** E4
Āydyň Turkm. **110** D2
Āyelu Terara *vol.* Eth. **108** F7
Ayer U.S.A. **165** J2
Ayers Rock *hill* Australia *see* **Uluṟu**
Ayeyarwady *r.* Myanmar *see* **Irrawaddy**
Aygulakskiy Khrebet *mts* Rus. Fed. **98** D2
Aygyrzhal Kazakh. **98** C2
Ayila Ri'gyü *mts Xizang* China **99** B6
Áyios Dhimítrios Greece *see* **Agios Dimitrios**
Áyios Evstrátios *i.* Greece *see* **Agios Efstratios**
Áyios Nikólaos Greece *see* **Agios Nikolaos**
Áyios Yeóryios *i.* Greece *see* **Agios Georgios**
Aykol *Xinjiang* China **98** C4
Aylesbury N.Z. **139** D6
Aylesbury U.K. **59** G7
Aylett U.S.A. **165** G5
Ayllón Spain **67** E3
Aylmer *Ont.* Canada **164** E2
Aylmer *Que.* Canada **165** H1
Aylmer Lake Canada **151** I1
Aynabulak Kazakh. **98** B3
'Ayn al 'Abd *well* Saudi Arabia **110** C4
'Ayn al Baidā' Saudi Arabia **107** C4
'Ayn al Bayḍā' *well* Syria **107** C2
'Ayn al Ghazalah *well* Libya **112** A4
'Ayn al Maqfī *spring* Egypt **112** C6
'Ayn Dāllah *spring* Egypt **112** B6
Aynī Tajik. **111** H2
'Ayn 'Īsá Syria **107** D1
'Ayn Tabaghbugh *spring* Egypt **112** B5
'Ayn Tumayrah *spring* Egypt **112** B5
'Ayn Zaytūn Egypt **112** B5
Ayod Sudan **108** D8
Ayon, Ostrov *i.* Rus. Fed. **77** R3
'Ayoûn el 'Atroûs Mauritania **120** C3
Ayr Australia **136** D3
Ayr Canada **164** E2
Ayr U.K. **60** E5
Ayr *r.* U.K. **60** E5
Ayr, Point of U.K. **58** D5
Ayrag Nuur *salt l.* Mongolia **94** C1
Ayrancı Turkey **112** D3
Ayre, Point of Isle of Man **58** C4
Aytos Bulg. **69** L3
Ayu *i. Papua* Indon. **83** D2
Ayu, Kepulauan *atoll Papua* Indon. **83** D2
A Yun Pa Vietnam **87** E4
Ayutthia Thai. *see* **Ayutthaya**
Ayutla *Guerrero* Mex. **167** F5
Ayutla *Jalisco* Mex. **166** D4
Ayutthaya Thai. **87** C4
Ayvacık Turkey **69** L5
Ayvalı Turkey **112** E3
Ayvalık Turkey **69** L5
Azai Japan **92** C3
Azak Rus. Fed. *see* **Azov**
Azalia U.S.A. **164** C4
Azamgarh India **105** E4
Azaouâd *reg.* Mali **120** C3
Azaouagh, Vallée de *watercourse* Mali/Niger **120** D3
Azaran Iran *see* **Hashtrud**
Azärbaycan *country* Asia *see* **Azerbaijan**
Azärbayjan *country* Asia *see* **Azerbaijan**
Azare Nigeria **120** E3
A'zāz Syria **107** C1
Azbine *mts* Niger *see* **L'Aïr, Massif de**
Azdavay Turkey **112** D2
Azerbaijan *country* Asia **113** G2
Azerbaydzhanskaya S.S.R. *country* Asia *see* **Azerbaijan**
Azhikal India **106** B4
Aziscohos Lake U.S.A. **165** J1
'Azīzābād Iran **110** E4
Aziziye Turkey *see* **Pınarbaşı**
Azogues Ecuador **176** C4
Azores *terr.* N. Atlantic Ocean **184** G3
Azores-Biscay Rise *sea feature* N. Atlantic Ocean **184** G3
Azotus Israel *see* **Ashdod**
Azov Rus. Fed. **53** H7
Azov, Sea of Rus. Fed./Ukr. **53** H7
Azovs'ke More *sea* Rus. Fed./Ukr. *see* **Azov, Sea of**
Azovskoye More *sea* Rus. Fed./Ukr. *see* **Azov, Sea of**
Azraq, Bahr el *r.* Sudan **108** D6 *see* **Blue Nile**
Azraq ash Shīshān Jordan **107** C4
Azrou Morocco **64** C5
Aztec U.S.A. **159** I3
Azuaga Spain **67** D4
Azuchi Japan **92** C3
Azuero, Península de *pen.* Panama **166** [inset] J8
Azul *r.* Mex. **167** H5
Azul, Cordillera *mts* Peru **176** C5
Azul Meridional, Parque Nacional *nat. park* Hond. **166** [inset] I6
Azuma *Gunma* Japan **93** F2
Azuma *Gunma* Japan **93** F2
Azuma *Ibaraki* Japan **93** G3
Azuma-san *vol.* Japan **91** F5
Azumaya-san *mt.* Japan **93** E2
Azumi Japan **93** D2
Azusa-ko *resr* Japan **92** D2
'Azza Gaza *see* **Gaza**
Azzaba Alg. **68** B6
Az Ẓahrān Saudi Arabia *see* **Dhahran**
Az Zaqāzīq Egypt **112** C5
Az Zarbah Syria **107** C1
Az Zarqā' Jordan **107** C3
Az Zāwiyah Libya **121** E1
Az Zawr, Ra's *pt* Saudi Arabia **113** H6
Azzeffāl *hills* Mauritania/W. Sahara **120** B2
Az Zubayr Iraq **113** G5
Az Zuqur *i.* Yemen **108** F7

B

Ba, Sông *r.* Vietnam **87** E4
Baa Indon. **83** B5
Baabda Lebanon **107** B3
Baai *r.* Indon. **85** G2
Ba'albek Lebanon **107** C2
Ba'al Ḥazor *mt.* West Bank **107** B4
Baan Baa Australia **138** D3
Baardheere Somalia **122** E3
Baatsagaan Mongolia **94** D2
Bab India **104** D4
Bābā, Kūh-e *mts* Afgh. **111** H3
Baba Burnu *pt* Turkey **69** L5
Babadağ *mt.* Azer. **113** H2
Babadag Romania **69** M2
Babadurmaz Turkm. **110** E2
Babaeski Turkey **69** L4
Babahoyo Ecuador **176** C4
Babai India **104** D5
Babai *r.* Nepal **105** E3
Babak Phil. **82** D5
Bābā Kalān Iran **110** C4
Bāb al Mandab *strait* Africa/Asia **108** F7
Babana *Sulawesi Barat* Indon. **83** A3
Babanusa Sudan **108** C7
Babao *Qinghai* China *see* **Qilian**
Babao *Yunnan* China **96** E4
Babar *i. Maluku* Indon. **83** D4
Babar, Kepulauan *is Maluku* Indon. **83** D4
Babati Tanz. **123** D4
Babau *Timor* Indon. **83** B5
Babayevo Rus. Fed. **52** G4
Babayurt Rus. Fed. **113** G2
Babbage *r. Y.T.* Canada **149** M1
B'abdā Lebanon *see* **Baabda**
Babeldaob *i.* Palau **82** [inset]
Bab el Mandeb, Straits of Africa/Asia *see* **Bāb al Mandab**
Babelthuap *i.* Palau *see* **Babeldaob**
Babi, Pulau *i.* Indon. **84** B2
Babian Jiang *r.* China **96** D4
Babine *r.* Canada **150** E4
Babine Lake Canada **150** E4
Babine Range *mts* Canada **150** E4
Bābol Iran **110** D2
Bābol Sar Iran **110** D2
Babongo Cameroon **121** E4
Baboon Point S. Africa **124** D7
Baboua Cent. Afr. Rep. **122** B3
Babruysk Belarus **53** F5
Babstovo Rus. Fed. **90** D2
Babu China *see* **Hezhou**
Babuhri India **104** B4
Babusar Pass Pak. **111** I3
Babuyan *Palawan* Phil. **82** B4
Babuyan *i.* Phil. **82** C2
Babuyan Channel Phil. **82** C2
Babuyan Islands Phil. **82** C2
Bacaadweyn Somalia **122** E3
Bacabáchi Mex. **166** C3
Bacabal Brazil **177** J4
Bacalar Mex. **167** H5
Bacalar Chico, Boca *sea chan.* Mex. **167** I5
Bacan *i. Maluku* Indon. **83** C3
Bacang *Qinghai* China **94** E5
Bacanora Mex. **166** C2
Bacarra *Luzon* Phil. **82** C2
Bacău Romania **69** L1
Baccaro Point Canada **153** I6
Băc Giang Vietnam **86** D2
Bacha China **90** D2
Bach Ice Shelf Antarctica **188** L2
Bach Long Vi, Đao *i.* Vietnam **86** D2
Bachu *Xinjiang* China **98** B5
Bachuan China *see* **Tongliang**
Back *r.* Australia **136** C3
Back *r.* Canada **151** M1
Bačka Palanka Serbia **69** H2
Backbone Mountain U.S.A. **164** F4
Backbone Ranges *mts N.W.T.* Canada **149** O3
Backe Sweden **54** J5
Backstairs Passage Australia **137** B7
Bắc Liêu Vietnam **87** D5
Bắc Ninh Vietnam **86** D2
Bacnotan *Luzon* Phil. **82** C2
Baco, Mount *Mindoro* Phil. **82** C3
Bacoachi Mex. **166** C2
Bacoachi *watercourse* Mex. **157** F7
Bacobampo Mex. **166** C3
Bacolod *Negros* Phil. **82** C4
Bacqueville, Lac *l.* Canada **152** G2
Bacqueville-en-Caux France **59** H9
Bacubirito Mex. **166** D3
Baculin Bay *Mindanao* Phil. **82** D5
Baculin Point *Mindanao* Phil. **82** D4
Bād Iran **110** D3
Bada China *see* **Xilin**
Bada *mt.* Eth. **122** D3
Bada *i.* Myanmar **87** B5
Badabayhan Turkm. **111** F2
Bad Abbach Germany **63** M6
Badagara India **106** B4
Badain Jaran *Nei Mongol* China **94** E4
Badain Jaran Shamo *des. Nei Mongol* China **94** E3
Badajoz Spain **67** C4
Badami India **106** B3
Badampaharh India **105** F5
Badanah Saudi Arabia **113** F5
Badaojiang China *see* **Baishan**
Badarpur India **105** H4
Badas Brunei **85** F1
Badas, Kepulauan *is* Indon. **84** D2
Badaun India *see* **Budaun**
Bad Axe U.S.A. **164** D2
Bad Bederkesa Germany **63** I1
Bad Bergzabern Germany **63** H5
Bad Berleburg Germany **63** I3
Bad Bevensen Germany **63** K1
Bad Blankenburg Germany **63** L4
Bad Camberg Germany **63** I4
Badderen Norway **54** M2
Bad Driburg Germany **63** J3
Bad Düben Germany **63** M3
Bad Dürkheim Germany **63** I5
Bad Dürrenberg Germany **63** M3
Bademli Turkey *see* **Aladağ**
Bademli Geçidi *pass* Turkey **112** C3
Bad Ems Germany **63** H4
Baden Austria **57** P6
Baden Switz. **66** I3
Baden-Baden Germany **63** I6
Baden-Württemberg *land* Germany **63** I6
Bad Essen Germany **63** I2
Bad Grund (Harz) Germany **63** K3
Bad Harzburg Germany **63** K3
Bad Hersfeld Germany **63** J4
Bad Hofgastein Austria **57** N7
Bad Homburg vor der Höhe Germany **63** I4
Badia Polesine Italy **68** D2
Badin Pak. **111** H5
Bad Ischl Austria **57** N7
Bādiyat ash Shām *des.* Asia *see* **Syrian Desert**
Bad Kissingen Germany **63** K4
Bad Königsdorff Poland *see* **Jastrzębie-Zdrój**
Bad Kösen Germany **63** L3
Bad Kreuznach Germany **63** H5
Bad Laasphe Germany **63** I4
Badlands *reg. ND* U.S.A. **160** C2
Badlands *reg. SD* U.S.A. **160** C3
Badlands National Park U.S.A. **160** C3
Bad Langensalza Germany **63** K3
Bad Lauterberg im Harz Germany **63** K3
Bad Liebenwerda Germany **63** N3
Bad Lippspringe Germany **63** I3
Bad Marienberg (Westerwald) Germany **63** H4
Bad Mergentheim Germany **63** J5
Bad Nauheim Germany **63** I4
Badnawar India **104** C5
Badnera India **106** C1
Bad Neuenahr-Ahrweiler Germany **62** H4
Bad Neustadt an der Saale Germany **63** K4
Badnor India **104** C4
Badong China **97** F2
Ba Đông Vietnam **87** D5
Badou *Shandong* China **95** I4
Badou Togo **120** D4
Bad Pyrmont Germany **63** J3
Badrah Iraq **113** G4
Bad Reichenhall Germany **57** N7
Badr Ḥunayn Saudi Arabia **108** E5
Bad Sachsa Germany **63** K3
Bad Salzdetfurth Germany **63** K2
Bad Salzuflen Germany **63** I2
Bad Salzungen Germany **63** K4
Bad Schwalbach Germany **63** I4
Bad Schwartau Germany **57** M4
Bad Segeberg Germany **57** M4
Bad Sobernheim Germany **63** H5
Badu Island Australia **136** C1
Badulla Sri Lanka **106** D5
Bad Vilbel Germany **63** I4
Bad Wilsnack Germany **63** L2
Bad Windsheim Germany **63** K5
Badzhal Rus. Fed. **90** D2
Badzhal'skiy Khrebet *mts* Rus. Fed. **90** D2
Bad Zwischenahn Germany **63** I1
Bae Colwyn U.K. *see* **Colwyn Bay**
Baesweiler Germany **62** G4
Baeza Spain **67** E5
Bafatá Guinea-Bissau **120** B3
Baffa Pak. **111** I3
Baffin Basin *sea feature* Arctic Ocean **189** K2
Baffin Bay *sea* Canada/Greenland **147** L2

▶**Baffin Island** Canada **147** L3
2nd largest island in North America, and 5th in the world.

Bafia Cameroon **120** E4
Bafilo Togo **120** D4
Bafing *r.* Africa **120** B3
Bafoulabé Mali **120** B3
Bafoussam Cameroon **120** E4
Bāfq Iran **110** D4
Bafra Turkey **112** D2
Bafra Burnu *pt* Turkey **112** D2
Bāft Iran **110** E4
Bafwaboli Dem. Rep. Congo **122** C3
Bafwasende Dem. Rep. Congo **122** C3
Baga Bogd Uul *mts* Mongolia **94** E2
Bagac Bay *Luzon* Phil. **82** C3
Bagaha India **105** F4
Bagahak, Gunung *hill* Malaysia **85** G1
Bagalkot India **106** B2
Bagalkote India *see* **Bagalkot**
Bagamoyo Tanz. **123** D4
Bagan China **96** C1
Bagan Datoh Malaysia *see* **Bagan Datuk**
Bagan Datuk Malaysia **84** C2
Baganga *Mindanao* Phil. **82** D5
Baganian Peninsula *Mindanao* Phil. **82** C5
Bagan Serai Malaysia **84** C1
Bagansiapiapi *Sumatera* Indon. **84** C2
Baganuur Mongolia **95** G2
Bagar *Xizang* China **99** F7
Bagata Dem. Rep. Congo **122** B4
Bagdad U.S.A. **159** G4
Bagdarin Rus. Fed. **89** K2
Bagé Brazil **178** F4
Bagenalstown Ireland **61** F5
Bagerhat Bangl. **105** G5
Bageshwar India **104** D3
Baggs U.S.A. **156** G4
Baggy Point U.K. **59** C7
Bagh India **104** C5
Bàgh a' Chaisteil U.K. *see* **Castlebay**
Baghak Pak. **111** G4
Baghbaghū Iran **111** F2

▶**Baghdād** Iraq **113** G4
Capital of Iraq.

Bāgh-e Malek Iran **110** C4
Bagherhat Bangl. *see* **Bagerhat**
Bāghīn Iran **110** E4
Baghlān Afgh. **111** H2
Baghrān Afgh. **111** G3
Baginda, Tanjung *pt* Indon. **84** D3
Bağırsak *r.* Turkey **107** C1
Bağırsak Deresi *r.* Syria/Turkey *see* **Sājūr, Nahr**
Bagley U.S.A. **160** E2
Bagley Icefield *AK* U.S.A. **149** J4
Baglung Nepal **105** E3
Bagnères-de-Luchon France **66** E5
Bagnuiti *r.* Nepal **99** D8
Bago Myanmar *see* **Pegu**
Bago *Negros* Phil. **82** C4
Bagong China *see* **Sansui**
Bagor India **111** I5
Bagrationovsk Rus. Fed. **55** L9
Bagrax *Xinjiang* China *see* **Bohu**
Bagrax Hu *l.* China *see* **Bosten Hu**
Baguio *Luzon* Phil. **82** C2
Baguio *Mindanao* Phil. **82** D5
Baguio Point *Luzon* Phil. **82** C2
Bagur, Cabo *c.* Spain *see* **Begur, Cap de**
Bagzane, Monts *mts* Niger **120** D3
Bahādorābād-e Bālā Iran **110** E4
Bahadurganj Nepal **99** C8
Bahalda India **105** F5
Bahāmabād Iran *see* **Rafsanjān**
Bahamas, The *country* West Indies **163** E7
Bahara Pak. **111** G5
Baharampur India **105** G4
Bahardipur Pak. **111** H5
Bahariya Oasis *oasis* Egypt *see* **Baḥrīyah, Wāḥāt al**
Bahau *r.* Indon. **85** G2
Bahau Malaysia **84** C2
Bahaur *Kalimantan* Indon. **85** F3
Bahawalnagar Pak. **111** I4
Bahawalpur Pak. **111** H4
Bahçe *Adana* Turkey **107** B1
Bahçe *Osmaniye* Turkey **112** E3
Baher Dar Eth. *see* **Bahir Dar**
Baheri India **104** D3
Bahia Brazil *see* **Salvador**
Bahia *state* Brazil **179** C1
Bahía, Islas de la *is* Hond. **166** [inset] I5
Bahía Asunción Mex. **157** E8
Bahía Blanca Arg. **178** D5
Bahia Honda Point *Palawan* Phil. **82** B4
Bahía Kino Mex. **166** C2
Bahía Laura Arg. **178** C7
Bahía Negra Para. **178** E2
Bahía Tortugas Mex. **166** B3
Bahir Dar Eth. **122** D2
Bahl India **104** C3
Bahlā Oman **110** E6
Bahomonte *Sulawesi* Indon. **83** B3
Bahraich India **105** E4
Bahrain *country* Asia **110** C5
Bahrain, Gulf of Asia **110** C5
Bahrām Beyg Iran **110** C2
Bahrāmjerd Iran **110** E4
Baḥrīyah, Wāḥāt al *oasis* Egypt **112** C6
Bahuaja-Sonene, Parque Nacional *nat. park* Peru **176** E6
Bahubulu *i.* Indon. **83** B3
Baia Mare Romania **69** J1
Baiazeh Iran **110** D3
Baicang China **105** G3
Baicheng *Henan* China *see* **Xiping**
Baicheng *Jilin* China **95** J2
Baicheng *Xinjiang* China **98** C4
Baidoa Somalia *see* **Baydhabo**
Baidoi Co *l. Xizang* China **99** D6
Baidu China **97** H3
Baidunzi *Gansu* China **94** F4
Baidunzi *Gansu* China **98** F4
Baie-aux-Feuilles Canada *see* **Tasiujaq**
Baie-Comeau Canada **153** H4
Baie-du-Poste Canada *see* **Mistissini**
Baie-St-Paul Canada **153** H5
Baie-Trinité Canada **153** I4
Baie Verte Canada **153** K4
Baigou He *r.* China **95** I4
Baiguan China *see* **Shangyu**
Baiguo *Hubei* China **97** G2
Baiguo *Hunan* China **97** G3
Baihanchang China **96** C3
Baihar India **104** E5
Baihe *Jilin* China **90** C4
Baihe *Shaanxi* China **97** F1
Bai He *r.* China **95** I3
Baiji Iraq *see* **Bayjī**
Baijiantan *Xinjiang* China **98** D3

▶**Baikal, Lake** *l.* Rus. Fed. **94** F1
Deepest and 2nd largest lake in Asia, and 8th largest in the world.

Baikouquan *Xinjiang* China **98** D3
Baikunthpur India **105** E5
Bailang *Nei Mongol* China **95** J2
Baile an Bhuinneánaigh Ireland *see* **Ballybunion**
Baile an Chinnéidigh Ireland *see* **Newtown Mount Kennedy**
Baile Átha Cliath Ireland *see* **Dublin**
Baile Átha Luain Ireland *see* **Athlone**
Baile Mhartainn U.K. **60** B3
Baile na Finne Ireland **61** D3
Băileşti Romania **69** J2
Bailey Range *hills* Australia **135** C7
Bailianhe Shuiku *resr* China **97** G2
Bailieborough Ireland **61** F4
Bailingmiao *Nei Mongol* China **95** G3
Bailleul France **62** C4
Baillie *r.* Canada **151** J1
Baillie Islands *N.W.T.* Canada **149** O1
Bailong *Gansu* China *see* **Hadapu**
Bailong Jiang *r.* China **96** E1
Baima *Qinghai* China **96** D1
Baima *Xizang* China *see* **Baxoi**
Baima Jian *mt.* China **97** H2
Baimuru P.N.G. **81** K8
Bain *r.* U.K. **58** G5
Bainang *Xizang* China *see* **Norkyung**
Bainbridge *GA* U.S.A. **163** C6
Bainbridge *IN* U.S.A. **164** B4
Bainbridge *NY* U.S.A. **165** H2
Bainduru India **106** B3
Baingoin *Xizang* China **99** E7
Baini China *see* **Yuqing**
Baiona Spain **67** B2
Baiqên China **96** D1
Baiquan China **90** B3
Bā'ir Jordan **107** C4
Bā'ir, Wādī *watercourse* Jordan/Saudi Arabia **107** C4
Bairab Co *l.* China **99** C6
Bairat India **104** D4
Baird U.S.A. **161** D5
Baird, Mount *Y.T.* Canada **149** N2
Baird Inlet *AK* U.S.A. **148** F3
Baird Mountains *AK* U.S.A. **148** H2

▶**Bairiki** Kiribati **186** H5
Capital of Kiribati, on Tarawa atoll.

Bairin Qiao *Nei Mongol* China **95** I3
Bairin Youqi *Nei Mongol* China *see* **Daban**
Bairin Zuoqi *Nei Mongol* China *see* **Lindong**
Bairnsdale Australia **138** C6
Bais *Negros* Phil. **82** C4
Baisha *Chongqing* China **96** E2
Baisha *Hainan* China **97** F5
Baisha *Sichuan* China **97** F2
Baishan *Guangxi* China *see* **Mashan**
Baishan *Jilin* China **90** B4
Baishan *Jilin* China *see* **Baishanzhen**
Bai Shan *mt. Gansu* China **98** F4
Baishanzhen China **90** B4
Baishi Shuiku *resr Liaoning* China **95** J3
Baishui *Shaanxi* China **95** G5
Baishui *Sichuan* China **96** E1
Baishui Jiang *r.* China **96** E1
Baisogala Lith. **55** M9
Baitadi Nepal **104** E3
Baitang China **96** C1
Bai Thương Vietnam **86** D3
Baixi China *see* **Yibin**
Baixiang *Hebei* China **95** H4
Baixingt *Nei Mongol* China **95** J3
Baiyanghe *Xinjiang* China **98** E4
Baiyashi China *see* **Dong'an**
Baiyin *Gansu* China **94** F4
Baiyü China **96** C2
Baiyuda Desert Sudan **108** D6
Baiyu Shan *mts* China **95** F4
Baja Hungary **68** H1
Baja, Punta *pt* Mex. **166** B2
Baja California *pen.* Mex. **166** B2
Baja California *state* Mex. **166** B2
Baja California Sur *state* Mex. **166** B3
Bajan Mex. **167** E3
Bajau *i.* Indon. **84** D2
Bajaur *reg.* Pak. **111** H3
Bajawa *Flores* Indon. **83** B5
Baj Baj India **105** G5
Bājgīrān Iran **110** E2
Bājil Yemen **108** F7
Bajo Boquete Panama **166** [inset] J7
Bajo Caracoles Arg. **178** B7
Bajoga Nigeria **120** E3
Bajoi China **96** D2
Bajrakot India **105** F5
Baka, Bukit *mt.* Indon. **85** F3
Bakala Cent. Afr. Rep. **121** F4
Bakanas Kazakh. **102** E3
Bakanas *watercourse* Kazakh. **98** B3
Bakar Pak. **111** H5
Bakaucengal *Kalimantan* Indon. **85** G3
Bakayan, Gunung *mt.* Indon. **85** G2
Bakel Senegal **120** B3
Baker *CA* U.S.A. **158** E4
Baker *ID* U.S.A. **156** E3
Baker *LA* U.S.A. **161** F6
Baker *MT* U.S.A. **156** G3
Baker *NV* U.S.A. **159** F2
Baker *OR* U.S.A. **156** D3
Baker *WV* U.S.A. **165** F4
Baker, Mount *vol.* U.S.A. **156** C2
Baker Butte *mt.* U.S.A. **159** H4

▶**Baker Island** *terr.* N. Pacific Ocean **133** I1
United States Unincorporated Territory.

Baker Island *AK* U.S.A. **149** N5
Baker Lake *salt flat* Australia **135** D6
Baker Lake Canada **151** M1
Baker Lake *l.* Canada **151** M1
Baker's Dozen Islands Canada **152** F2
Bakersfield U.S.A. **158** D4
Bakersville U.S.A. **162** D4
Bâ Kêv Cambodia **87** D4
Bakhardok Turkm. *see* **Bokurdak**
Bākharz *mts* Iran **111** F3
Bakhasar India **104** B4
Bakhirevo Rus. Fed. **90** C2
Bakhmach Ukr. **53** G6
Bakhma Dam Iraq *see* **Békma, Sadd**
Bakhmut Ukr. *see* **Artemivs'k**
Bākhtarān Iran *see* **Kermānshāh**
Bakhtegan, Daryācheh-ye *l.* Iran **110** D4
Bakhtiari Country *reg.* Iran **110** C3
Bakhty Kazakh. **98** C3
Bakı Azer. *see* **Baku**
Baki **122** E2
Bakırköy Turkey **69** M4
Bakkejord Norway **54** K2
Bakloh India **104** C2
Bako Eth. **122** D3
Bako National Park Malaysia **85** E2
Bakongan *Sumatera* Indon. **84** B2
Bakouma Cent. Afr. Rep. **122** C3
Baksan Rus. Fed. **113** F2

▶**Baku** Azer. **113** H2
Capital of Azerbaijan.

Baku Dem. Rep. Congo **122** D3
Bakung *i.* Indon. **84** D2
Bakutis Coast Antarctica **188** J2
Baky Azer. *see* **Baku**
Balâ Turkey **112** D3
Bala U.K. **59** D6
Bala, Cerros de *mts* Bol. **176** E6
Balabac Phil. **82** B4
Balabac *i.* Phil. **82** B5
Balabac Strait Malaysia/Phil. **85** G1
Balabalangan, Kepulauan *atolls* Indon. **85** G3
Baladeh *Māzandarān* Iran **110** C2
Baladeh *Māzandarān* Iran **110** C2
Baladek Rus. Fed. **90** D1
Balaghat India **104** E5

Balaghat Range *hills* India 106 B2
Bālā Ḩowz Iran 110 E4
Balaiberkuak *Kalimantan* Indon. 85 E3
Balaikarangan *Kalimantan* Indon. 85 E2
Balaipungut *Sumatera* Indon. 84 C2
Balairiam *Kalimantan* Indon. 85 E3
Balaka Malawi 123 D5
Balakän Azer. 113 G2
Balakhna Rus. Fed. 52 I4
Balakhta Rus. Fed. 88 G1
Balaklava Australia 137 B7
Balaklava Ukr. 112 D1
Balakleya Ukr. *see* **Balakliya**
Balakliya Ukr. 53 H6
Balakovo Rus. Fed. 53 J5
Bala Lake *l.* U.K. 59 D6
Balaman India 104 E4
Balan India 104 B4
Balancán Mex. 167 H5
Balanda Rus. Fed. *see* **Kalininsk**
Balanda *r.* Rus. Fed. 53 J6
Balan Dağı *hill* Turkey 69 M6
Balanga *Luzon* Phil. 82 C3
Balangir India *see* **Bolangir**
Balantak *Sulawesi* Indon. 83 B3
Balaözen *r.* Kazakh./Rus. Fed. *see* **Malyy Uzen'**
Balarampur India *see* **Balrampur**
Balase *r.* Indon. 83 B3
Balashov Rus. Fed. 53 I6
Balasore India *see* **Baleshwar**
Balaton, Lake Hungary 68 G1
Balatonboglár Hungary 68 G1
Balatonfüred Hungary 68 G1
Balauring Indon. 83 B5
Balbina Brazil 177 G4
Balbina, Represa de *resr* Brazil 177 G4
Balbriggan Ireland 61 F4
Balchik Bulg. 69 M3
Balclutha N.Z. 139 B8
Balcones Escarpment U.S.A. 161 C6
Bald Knob U.S.A. 164 E5
Bald Mountain U.S.A. 159 F3
Baldock Lake Canada 151 L3
Baldwin Canada 164 F1
Baldwin *FL* U.S.A. 163 D6
Baldwin *MI* U.S.A. 164 C2
Baldwin *PA* U.S.A. 164 F3
Baldwin Peninsula *AK* U.S.A. 148 G2
Baldy Mount Canada 156 D2
Baldy Mountain *hill* Canada 151 K5
Baldy Peak U.S.A. 159 I5
Bal'dzhikan Rus. Fed. 95 G1
Bale Indon. 84 C3
Bâle Switz. *see* **Basel**
Baléa Mali 120 B3
Baleares *is* Spain *see* **Balearic Islands**
Baleares, Islas *is* Spain *see* **Balearic Islands**
Baleares Insulae *is* Spain *see* **Balearic Islands**
Balearic Islands *is* Spain 67 G4
Balears *is* Spain *see* **Balearic Islands**
Balears, Illes *is* Spain *see* **Balearic Islands**
Baleh *r.* Malaysia 85 F2
Baleia, Ponta da *pt* Brazil 179 D2
Bale Mountains National Park Eth. 122 D3
Baleno *Masbate* Phil. 82 C3
Baler *Luzon* Phil. 82 C3
Baler Bay *Luzon* Phil. 82 C3
Baleshwar India 105 F5
Balestrand Norway 55 E6
Baléyara Niger 120 D3
Balezino Rus. Fed. 51 Q4
Balfate Hond. 166 [inset] I6
Balfe's Creek Australia 136 D4
Balfour Downs Australia 134 C5
Balgatay Mongolia *see* **Shilüüstey**
Balgo Australia 134 D5
Balguntay *Xinjiang* China 98 D4
Bali India 104 C4
Bali *i.* Indon. 85 F5
Bali *prov.* Indon. 85 F5
Bali, Laut *sea* Indon. 85 F4
Bali, Selat *sea chan.* Indon. 85 F5
Balia India *see* **Ballia**
Baliangao *Mindanao* Phil. 82 C4
Baliapal India 105 F5
Bali Barat, Taman Nasional *nat. park Bali* Indon. 85 F5
Balige *Sumatera* Indon. 84 B2
Baliguda India 106 D1
Balihan *Nei Mongol* China 95 I3
Balıkesir Turkey 69 L5
Balīkh *r.* Syria/Turkey 107 D2
Balikpapan *Kalimantan* Indon. 85 G3
Balikpapan, Teluk *b.* Indon. 85 G3
Balimbing Phil. 82 B5
Balimila Reservoir India 106 D2
Balimo P.N.G. 81 K8
Balin *Nei Mongol* China 95 J1
Baling Malaysia 84 C1
Balingen Germany 57 L6
Balingian *Sarawak* Malaysia 85 F2
Balingian *r.* Malaysia 85 F2
Balinqiao *Nei Mongol* China *see* **Bairin Qiao**
Balintang Channel Phil. 82 C2
Balintore U.K. 60 F3
Bali Sea Indon. *see* **Bali, Laut**
Baliungan *i.* Phil. 82 C5
Balk Neth. 62 F2
Balkanabat Turkm. 110 D2
Balkan Mountains Bulg./Serbia 69 J3
Balkassar Pak. 111 I3
Balkhash Kazakh. 102 D2

▶**Balkhash, Lake** Kazakh. 102 D2
3rd largest lake in Asia.

Balkhash, Ozero *l.* Kazakh. *see* **Balkhash, Lake**
Balkuduk Kazakh. 53 J7
Ballachulish U.K. 60 D4
Balladonia Australia 135 C8
Balladoran Australia 138 D3
Ballaghaderreen Ireland 61 D4
Ballan Australia 138 B6
Ballangen Norway 54 J2
Ballantine U.S.A. 156 F3
Ballantrae U.K. 60 E5
Ballarat Australia 138 A6
Ballard, Lake *salt flat* Australia 135 C7
Ballarpur India 106 C2
Ballater U.K. 60 F3
Ballé Mali 120 C3
Ballena, Punta *pt* Chile 178 B3
Balleny Islands Antarctica 188 H2
Ballia India 105 F4
Ballina Australia 138 F2
Ballina Ireland 61 C3
Ballinafad Ireland 61 D3
Ballinalack Ireland 61 E4
Ballinamore Ireland 61 E3
Ballinasloe Ireland 61 D4
Ballindine Ireland 61 D4
Ballinger U.S.A. 161 D6
Ballinluig U.K. 60 F4
Ballinrobe Ireland 61 C4
Ballston Spa U.S.A. 165 I2
Ballybay Ireland 61 F3
Ballybrack Ireland *see* **An Baile Breac**
Ballybunion Ireland 61 C5
Ballycanew Ireland 61 F5
Ballycastle Ireland 61 C3
Ballycastle U.K. 61 F2
Ballyclare U.K. 61 G3
Ballyconnell Ireland 61 E3
Ballygar Ireland 61 D4
Ballygawley U.K. 61 E3
Ballygorman Ireland 61 E2
Ballyhaunis Ireland 61 D4
Ballyheigue Ireland 61 C5
Ballykelly U.K. 61 E2
Ballylynan Ireland 61 E5
Ballymacmague Ireland 61 E5
Ballymahon Ireland 61 E4
Ballymena U.K. 61 F3
Ballymoney U.K. 61 F2
Ballymote Ireland 61 D3
Ballynahinch U.K. 61 G3
Ballyshannon Ireland 61 D3
Ballyteige Bay Ireland 61 F5
Ballyvaughan Ireland 61 C4
Ballyward U.K. 61 F3
Balmartin U.K. *see* **Baile Mhartainn**
Balmer India *see* **Barmer**
Balmertown Canada 151 M5
Balmorhea U.S.A. 161 C6
Baloa *Sulawesi* Indon. 83 B3
Balochistan *prov.* Pak. 111 G4
Balok, Teluk *b.* Indon. 85 D3
Balombo Angola 123 B5
Balonne *r.* Australia 138 D2
Balontohe *i.* Indon. 83 C2
Balotra India 104 C4
Balpyk Bi Kazakh. 98 B3
Balqash Kazakh. *see* **Balkhash**
Balqash Köli *l.* Kazakh. *see* **Balkhash, Lake**
Balrampur India 105 E4
Balranald Australia 138 A5
Balş Romania 69 K2
Balsam Lake Canada 165 F1
Balsas Brazil 177 I5
Balsas Mex. 167 F5
Balsas *r.* Mex. 166 E5
Balta Ukr. 53 F7
Baltasound U.K. 60 [inset]
Baltay Rus. Fed. 53 J5
Bălţi Moldova 53 E7
Baltic U.S.A. 164 E3
Baltic Sea *g.* Europe 55 J9
Balţîm Egypt 112 C5
Baltim Egypt *see* **Balţîm**
Baltimore S. Africa 125 I2
Baltimore *MD* U.S.A. 165 G4
Baltimore *OH* U.S.A. 164 D4
Baltinglass Ireland 61 F5
Baltistan *reg.* Pak. 104 C2
Baltiysk Rus. Fed. 55 K9
Balu India 96 B3
Baluarte, Arroyo *watercourse* U.S.A. 161 D7
Baluch Ab *well* Iran 110 E4
Balui *r.* Malaysia 85 F2
Balumundam *Sumatera* Indon. 84 B2
Baluran, Gunung *mt.* Indon. 85 F3
Baluran, Taman Nasional *nat. park* Indon. 85 F4
Balurghat India 105 G4
Balut *i.* Phil. 82 D5
Balve Germany 63 H3
Balvi Latvia 55 O8
Balya Turkey 69 L5
Balyaga Rus. Fed. 95 G1
Balykchy Kyrg. 102 E3
Balykshi Kazakh. 100 E2
Balyktyg-Khem *r.* Rus. Fed. 94 D1
Balyqshy Kazakh. *see* **Balykshi**
Bam Iran 110 E4
Bām Iran 110 E2
Bama China 96 E3

▶**Bamako** Mali 120 C3
Capital of Mali.

Bamba Mali 120 C3
Bambang *Luzon* Phil. 82 C2
Bambannan *i.* Phil. 82 C5
Bambari Cent. Afr. Rep. 122 C3
Bambel *Sumatera* Indon. 84 B2
Bamberg Germany 63 K5
Bamberg U.S.A. 163 D5
Bambili Dem. Rep. Congo 122 C3
Bambio Cent. Afr. Rep. 122 B3
Bamboesberg *mts* S. Africa 125 H6
Bamboo Creek Australia 134 C5
Bambouti Cent. Afr. Rep. 122 C3
Bambuí Brazil 179 B3
Bambulung *Kalimantan* Indon. 85 F3
Bamda China 96 C2
Bamenda Cameroon 120 E4
Bāmīān Afgh. 111 G3
Bamiancheng *Liaoning* China 95 K3
Bamiantong China *see* **Muling**
Bamingui Cent. Afr. Rep. 122 C3
Bamingui-Bangoran, Parc National du *nat. park* Cent. Afr. Rep. 122 B3
Bāmkeri *Papua* Indon. 83 D3
Bâmnak Cambodia 87 D4
Bamnet Narong Thai. 86 C4
Bamoa Mex. 166 C3
Bamor India 104 D4
Bamori India 106 C1
Bam Posht *reg.* Iran 111 F5
Bam Posht, Kūh-e *mts* Iran 111 F5
Bampton U.K. 59 D8
Bampūr Iran 111 F5
Bampūr *watercourse* Iran 111 E5
Bamrūd Iran 111 F3
Bam Tso *l.* China 105 G3
Bamyili Australia 134 F3
Banaba *i.* Kiribati 133 G2
Banabuiu, Açude *resr* Brazil 177 K5
Bañados del Izozog *swamp* Bol. 176 F7
Banagher Ireland 61 E4
Banahao, Mount *vol. Luzon* Phil. 82 C3
Banalia Dem. Rep. Congo 122 C3
Banamana, Lagoa *l.* Moz. 125 K2
Banamba Mali 120 C3
Banámichi Mex. 166 C2
Banana Australia 136 E5
Bananal, Ilha do *i.* Brazil 177 H6
Bananga India 87 A6
Banapur India 106 E2
Banas *r.* India 104 D4
Banawaya *i.* Indon. 83 A4
Banaz Turkey 69 M5
Ban Ban Laos 86 C3
Banbar *Xizang* China 99 F7
Ban Bo Laos 86 C3
Banbridge U.K. 61 F3
Ban Bua Chum Thai. 86 C4
Ban Bua Yai Thai. 86 C4
Ban Bungxai Laos 86 D4
Banbury U.K. 59 F6
Ban Cang Vietnam 86 C2
Banc d'Arguin, Parc National du *nat. park* Mauritania 120 B2
Ban Channabot Thai. 86 C3
Banchory U.K. 60 G3
Bancoran *i.* Phil. 82 B5
Bancroft Canada 165 G1
Bancroft Zambia *see* **Chililabombwe**
Banda Dem. Rep. Congo 122 C3
Banda India 104 E4
Banda, Kepulauan *is Maluku* Indon. 83 D4
Banda, Laut *sea* Indon. 83 D4
Banda Aceh *Sumatera* Indon. 84 A1
Banda Banda, Mount Australia 138 F3
Banda Daud Shah Pak. 111 H3
Bandahara, Gunung *mt.* Indon. 84 B2
Bandama *r.* Côte d'Ivoire 120 C4
Bandaneira *Maluku* Indon. 83 D4
Bandān Kūh *mts* Iran 111 F4
Bandar India *see* **Machilipatnam**
Bandar Moz. 123 D5
Bandar Abbas Iran *see* **Bandar-e 'Abbās**
Bandaragung *Sumatera* Indon. 84 D4
Bandarban Bangl. 105 H5
Bandar-e 'Abbās Iran 110 E5
Bandar-e Anzalī Iran 110 C2
Bandar-e Deylam Iran 110 C4
Bandar-e Emām Khomeynī Iran 110 C4
Bandar-e Lengeh Iran 110 D5
Bandar-e Ma'shur Iran 110 C4
Bandar-e Nakhīlū Iran 110 D5
Bandar-e Pahlavī Iran *see* **Bandar-e Anzalī**
Bandar-e Shāh Iran *see* **Bandar-e Torkeman**
Bandar-e Shāhpūr Iran *see* **Bandar-e Emām Khomeynī**
Bandar-e Shīū' Iran 110 D5
Bandar-e Torkeman Iran 110 D2
Bandar Lampung *Sumatera* Indon. 84 D4
Bandarpunch *mt.* India 104 D3

▶**Bandar Seri Begawan** Brunei 85 F1
Capital of Brunei.

Banda Sea Indon. *see* **Banda, Laut**
Band-e Amīr *l.* Afgh. 111 G3
Band-e Amīr, Daryā-ye *r.* Afgh. 111 G2
Band-e Bābā *mts* Afgh. 111 F3
Bandeira Brazil 179 C1
Bandeirante Brazil 179 A1
Bandeiras, Pico de *mt.* Brazil 179 C3
Bandelierkop S. Africa 125 I2
Banderas Mex. 166 D2
Banderas, Bahía de *b.* Mex. 168 C4
Band-e Sar Qom Iran 110 D3
Band-e Torkestān *mts* Afgh. 111 F3
Bandhi Pak. 111 H5
Bandhogarh India 104 E5
Bandi *r.* India 104 C4
Bandiagara Mali 120 C3
Bandikui India 104 D4
Bandipur National Park India 106 C4
Bandırma Turkey 69 L4
Bandjarmasin *Kalimantan* Indon. *see* **Banjarmasin**
Bandon Ireland 61 D6
Bandon *r.* Ireland 61 D6
Ban Don Thai. *see* **Surat Thani**
Bandon U.S.A. 156 B4
Band Qīr Iran 110 C4
Bandra India 106 B2
Bandundu Dem. Rep. Congo 122 B4
Bandung *Jawa* Indon. 85 D4
Bandya Australia 135 C6
Bāneh Iran 110 B3
Banemo *Halmahera* Indon. 83 D2
Banera India 104 C4
Banes Cuba 169 I4
Banff Canada 150 H5
Banff U.K. 60 G3
Banff National Park Canada 150 G5
Banfora Burkina Faso 120 C3
Bang, Gunung *mt.* Indon. 85 F2
Banga Dem. Rep. Congo 123 C4
Banga *Mindanao* Phil. 82 D5
Banga *r. Mindanao* Phil. 82 D5
Bangai Point *Mindanao* Phil. 82 D5
Bangalore India 106 C3
Bangalow Australia 138 F2
Banganga *r.* India 99 B8
Bangaon India 105 G5
Bangar Brunei 85 F1
Bangar *Luzon* Phil. 82 C2
Bangassou Cent. Afr. Rep. 122 C3
Bangdag Co *salt l.* China 99 C6
Banggai *Sulawesi* Indon. 83 B3
Banggai, Kepulauan *is* Indon. 81 G7
Banggai, Kepulauan *is* Indon. 83 B3
Banggi *i.* Malaysia 85 G1
Banghāzī Libya *see* **Benghazi**
Banghiang, Xé *r.* Laos 86 D3
Bangil *Jawa* Indon. 85 F4
Bangka *i.* Indon. 83 C2
Bangka *i.* Indon. 84 D3
Bangka, Selat *sea chan.* Indon. 83 C2
Bangka, Selat *sea chan.* Indon. 84 D3
Bangka-Belitung *prov.* Indon. 84 D3
Bangkal *Kalimantan* Indon. 85 F3
Bangkala, Teluk *b.* Indon. 83 A4
Bangkalan *Jawa* Indon. 85 F4
Bangkalan *i.* Indon. 83 B3
Bangkaru *i.* Indon. 84 B2
Bangkinang *Sumatera* Indon. 84 C2
Bangkir *Sulawesi* Indon. 83 B2
Bangko *Sumatera* Indon. 84 C3
Bangkog Co *salt l.* China 99 E7

▶**Bangkok** Thai. 87 C4
Capital of Thailand.

Bangkok, Bight of *b.* Thai. 87 C4
Bangkor *Xizang* China 99 D7
Bangkuang *Kalimantan* Indon. 85 F3
Bangkulu *i.* Indon. 83 B3
Bangkulua *Sumbawa* Indon. 85 G5
Bangla *state* India *see* **West Bengal**

▶**Bangladesh** *country* Asia 105 G4
7th most populous country in the world.

Bang Lang, Ang Kep Nam Thai. 84 C1
Bangluo *Gansu* China 94 F5
Bangma Shan *mts* China 96 C4
Bang Mun Nak Thai. 86 C3
Ba Ngoi Vietnam 87 E5
Bangolo Côte d'Ivoire 120 C4
Bangong Co *salt l.* China/India 104 D2
Bangor Ireland 61 C3
Bangor *Northern Ireland* U.K. 61 G3
Bangor *Wales* U.K. 58 C5
Bangor *ME* U.S.A. 162 G2
Bangor *MI* U.S.A. 164 B2
Bangor *PA* U.S.A. 165 H3
Bangs, Mount U.S.A. 159 G3
Bangsalsepulun *Kalimantan* Indon. 85 G3
Bang Saphan Yai Thai. 87 B5
Bangsund Norway 54 G4
Bangued *Luzon* Phil. 82 C2

▶**Bangui** Cent. Afr. Rep. 122 B3
Capital of the Central African Republic.

Bangui *Luzon* Phil. 82 C2
Bangunpurba *Sumatera* Indon. 84 B2
Bangweulu, Lake Zambia 123 C5
Banhā Egypt 112 C5
Banhine, Parque Nacional de *nat. park* Moz. 125 K2
Ban Hin Heup Laos 86 C3
Ban Houei Sai Laos *see* **Huayxay**
Ban Huai Khon Thai. 86 C3
Ban Huai Yang Thai. 87 B5
Bani *Luzon* Phil. 82 B2
Bani, Jbel *ridge* Morocco 64 C6
Bania Cent. Afr. Rep. 122 B3
Bani-Bangou Niger 120 D3
Banifing *r.* Mali 120 C3
Banī Forūr, Jazīreh-ye *i.* Iran 110 D5
Banihal Pass and Tunnel India 104 C2
Bani Point *Luzon* Phil. 82 B3
Banister *r.* U.S.A. 164 F5
Banī Suwayf Egypt 112 C5
Banī Walīd Libya 121 E1
Banī Wuţayfān *well* Saudi Arabia 110 C5
Bāniyās *Al Qunayţirah* Syria 107 B3
Bāniyās *Ţarţūs* Syria 107 B2
Bani Yas *reg.* U.A.E. 110 D6
Banja Luka Bos.-Herz. 68 G2
Banjarmasin *Kalimantan* Indon. 85 F3
Banjes, Liqeni i *resr* Albania 69 I4
Banjiegou *Xinjiang* China 98 E4
Banjieta *Hebei* China 95 I3

▶**Banjul** Gambia 120 B3
Capital of The Gambia.

Banka India 105 F4
Banka Banka Australia 134 F4
Bankapur India 106 B3
Bankass Mali 120 C3
Ban Kengkabao Laos 86 D3
Ban Khao Yoi Thai. 87 B4
Ban Khok Kloi Thai. 87 B5
Bankilaré Niger 120 D3
Bankobankoang *i.* Indon. 85 G4
Banks Island *B.C.* Canada 149 O5
Banks Island *N.W.T.* Canada 146 F2
Banks Islands Vanuatu 133 G3
Banks Lake Canada 151 M2
Banks Lake U.S.A. 156 D3
Banks Peninsula N.Z. 139 D6
Banks Strait Australia 137 [inset]
Bankura India 105 F5
Ban Lamduan Thai. 87 C4
Banlan China 97 F3
Ban Mae La Luang Thai. 86 B3
Banmaw Myanmar *see* **Bhamo**
Banmo Myanmar *see* **Bhamo**
Bann *r.* Ireland 61 F5
Bann *r.* U.K. 61 F2
Ban Nakham Laos 86 D3
Bannerman Town Bahamas 163 E7
Banning U.S.A. 158 E5
Banningville Dem. Rep. Congo *see* **Bandundu**
Ban Noi Myanmar 86 B3
Ban Nong Kung Thai. 86 D3
Bannu Pak. 111 H3
Bano India 105 F5
Bañolas Spain *see* **Banyoles**
Ban Phai Thai. 86 C3
Ban Phôn Laos *see* **Lamam**
Ban Phôn-Hông Laos 86 C3
Banqiao *Gansu* China 94 E4
Banqiao *Yunnan* China 96 C3
Banqiao *Yunnan* China 96 E3
Ban Sanam Chai Thai. 84 C1
Bansgaon *Uttar Prad.* India 99 C8
Bansi *Bihar* India 105 F4
Bansi *Rajasthan* India 104 C4
Bansi *Uttar Prad.* India 104 D4
Bansi *Uttar Prad.* India 105 E4
Bansihari India 105 G4
Banská Bystrica Slovakia 57 Q6
Banspani India 105 F5
Bansur India 104 D4
Ban Sut Ta Thai. 86 B3
Ban Suwan Wari Thai. 86 D4
Banswara India 104 C5
Banta *i.* Indon. 83 A5
Bantaeng *Sulawesi* Indon. 83 A4
Bantayan *i.* Phil. 82 C4
Banteer Ireland 61 D5
Banten *prov.* Indon. 84 D4
Ban Tha Song Yang Thai. 86 B3
Banthat *mts* Cambodia/Thai. *see* **Cardamom Range**
Ban Tha Tum Thai. 86 C4
Ban Thepha Thai. 84 C1
Ban Tôp Laos 86 D3
Bantry Ireland 61 C6
Bantry Bay Ireland 61 C6
Bantul Indon. 85 E4
Bantval India 106 B3
Ban Wang Chao Thai. 86 B3
Ban Woen Laos 86 C3
Ban Xepian Laos 86 D4
Banyak, Pulau-pulau *is* Indon. 84 B2
Ban Yang Yong Thai. 87 B4
Banyo Cameroon 120 E4
Banyoles Spain 67 H2
Banyuasin *r.* Indon. 84 D3
Banyuwangi *Jawa* Indon. 85 F5
Banzare Coast Antarctica 188 G2
Banzare Seamount *sea feature* Indian Ocean 185 N9
Banzart Tunisia *see* **Bizerte**
Banzkow Germany 63 L1
Banzyville Dem. Rep. Congo *see* **Mobayi-Mbongo**
Bao'an China *see* **Shenzhen**
Bao'an *Qinghai* China 94 E5
Bao'an *Shaanxi* China *see* **Zhidan**
Baochang *Nei Mongol* China 95 H3
Baocheng China 96 E1
Baodi *Tianjin* China 95 I4
Baoding *Hebei* China 95 H4
Baofeng China 97 G1
Baohe China *see* **Weixi**
Baoji *Shaanxi* China 95 F5
Baoji *Shaanxi* China 95 F5
Baokang *Hubei* China 97 F2
Baokang *Nei Mongol* China 95 J2
Bao Lac Vietnam 86 D2
Baolin China 90 C3
Bao Lôc Vietnam 87 D5
Baoqing China 90 D3
Baoro Cent. Afr. Rep. 122 B3
Baoshan China 96 C3
Baotou *Nei Mongol* China 95 G3
Baotou Shan *mt.* China/N. Korea 90 C4
Baoulé *r.* Mali 120 C3
Baoxing China 96 D2
Baoying China 97 H1
Baoyou China *see* **Ledong**
Bap India 104 C4
Bapatla India 106 D3
Bapaume France 62 C4
Baptiste Lake Canada 165 F1
Bapu China *see* **Meigu**
Baq'ā' *oasis* Saudi Arabia 113 F6
Baqbaq Egypt *see* **Buqbuq**
Baqên *Xizang* China 99 F6
Baqên *Xizang* China 99 F7
Baqiu China 97 G3
Ba'qūbah Iraq 113 G4
Bar Montenegro 69 H3
Bar Rus. Fed. 95 F1
Bara *Buru* Indon. 83 C3
Bara Sudan 108 D7
Baraawe Somalia 122 E3
Barabai *Kalimantan* Indon. 85 F3
Barabanki India 104 E4
Bara Banki India *see* **Barabanki**
Baraboo U.S.A. 160 F3
Baracaju *r.* Brazil 179 A1
Baracaldo Spain *see* **Barakaldo**
Baracoa Cuba 169 J4
Baradá, Nahr *r.* Syria 107 C3
Baradine Australia 138 D3
Baradine *r.* Australia 138 D3
Baragarh India *see* **Bargarh**
Barahona Dom. Rep. 169 J5
Barahoti *Uttaranchal* India 99 B7
Barail Range *mts* India 105 H4
Baraka *watercourse* Eritrea/Sudan 121 G3
Barakaldo Spain 67 E2
Barakī Barak Afgh. 111 H3
Baralaba Australia 136 E5
Bara Lacha Pass India 104 D2
Baralzon Lake Canada 151 L3
Baram India 105 F5
Baram *r.* Malaysia 85 F1
Baram, Tanjung *pt* Malaysia 85 F1
Baramati India 106 B2
Baramula India *see* **Baramulla**
Baramulla India 104 C2
Baran India 104 D4
Baran *r.* Pak. 111 H5
Bārān, Kūh-e *mts* Iran 111 F3
Baranavichy Belarus 55 O10
Barang, Dasht-i *des.* Afgh. 111 F3
Baranikha Rus. Fed. 77 R3
Baranīs Egypt 108 E5
Barannda India 104 E4
Baranof *AK* U.S.A. 149 N4
Baranof Island *AK* U.S.A. 149 N4
Baranovichi Belarus *see* **Baranavichy**
Baranowicze Belarus *see* **Baranavichy**
Baraouéli Mali 120 C3
Baraque de Fraiture *hill* Belgium 62 F4
Barasat India 105 G5
Barat Daya, Kepulauan *is Maluku* Indon. 83 C4
Barati *Timor* Indon. 83 B5
Baraut India 104 D3
Barbacena Brazil 179 C3
Barbados *country* West Indies 169 M6
Barbar, Gebel el *mt.* Egypt *see* **Barbar, Jabal**
Barbar, Jabal *mt.* Egypt 107 A5
Barbara Lake Canada 152 D4
Barbastro Spain 67 G2
Barbate Spain 67 D5
Barbechitos Mex. 166 D3
Barberton S. Africa 125 J3
Barberton U.S.A. 164 E3
Barbezieux-St-Hilaire France 66 D4
Barbour Bay Canada 151 M2
Barbourville U.S.A. 164 D5
Barboza *Panay* Phil. 82 C4
Barbuda *i.* Antigua and Barbuda 169 L5
Barby (Elbe) Germany 63 L3
Barcaldine Australia 136 D4
Barce Libya *see* **Al Marj**
Barcelona Spain 67 H3
Barcelona Venez. 176 F1
Barcelonnette France 66 H4
Barcelos Brazil 176 F4
Barchfeld Germany 63 K4
Barcino Spain *see* **Barcelona**
Barclay de Tolly *atoll* Fr. Polynesia *see* **Raroia**
Barclayville Liberia 120 C4
Barcoo *watercourse* Australia 136 C5
Barcoo Creek *watercourse* Australia *see* **Cooper Creek**
Barcoo National Park Australia *see* **Welford National Park**
Barcs Hungary 68 G2
Bärdä Azer. 113 G2
Bárðarbunga *mt.* Iceland 54 [inset]
Bardaskan Iran 110 E3
Bardawil, Khabrat al *salt pan* Saudi Arabia 107 D4
Bardawīl, Sabkhat al *lag.* Egypt 107 A4
Barddhaman India 105 F5
Bardejov Slovakia 53 D6
Bardera Somalia *see* **Baardheere**
Bardhaman India *see* **Barddhaman**
Bardsey Island U.K. 59 C6
Bardsīr Iran 110 E4
Barðsneshorn *pt* Iceland 50 D2
Bardstown U.S.A. 164 C5
Barduli Italy *see* **Barletta**
Bardwell U.S.A. 161 F4
Bareilly India 104 D3
Barellan Australia 138 C5
Barentin France 59 H9
Barentsburg Svalbard 76 C2
Barents Sea Arctic Ocean 52 I1
Barentu Eritrea 108 E6
Bareo *Sarawak* Malaysia 85 F2
Barfleur, Pointe de *pt* France 59 F9
Barga *Xizang* China 99 C7
Bargāh Iran 110 E5
Bargarh India 105 E5
Barghamad Iran 110 E2
Bargrennan U.K. 60 E5
Bargteheide Germany 63 K1
Barguna Bangl. 105 G5
Barhaj India 105 E4
Barham Australia 138 B5
Bari Italy 68 G4
Bari Doab *lowland* Pak. 111 I4
Barika Alg. 64 F4
Barinas Venez. 176 D2
Baripada India 105 F5
Bariri Brazil 179 A3
Bari Sadri India 104 C4
Barisal Bangl. 105 G5
Barisan, Pegunungan *mts* Indon. 84 C3
Barito *r.* Indon. 85 F3
Barium Italy *see* **Bari**
Barkal Bangl. 105 H5
Barkam China 96 D2
Barkan, Ra's-e *pt* Iran 110 C4
Barkava Latvia 55 O8
Bark Lake Canada 165 G1
Barkly East S. Africa 125 H6
Barkly Homestead Australia 136 A3
Barkly-Oos S. Africa *see* **Barkly East**
Barkly Tableland *reg.* Australia 136 A3
Barkly-Wes S. Africa *see* **Barkly West**
Barkly West S. Africa 124 G5
Barkol *Xinjiang* China 94 C3
Barkol Hu *salt l. Xinjiang* China 94 C3
Barla Turkey 69 N5
Bârlad Romania 69 L1
Barlag Gol *watercourse* Mongolia 94 C2
Bar-le-Duc France 62 F6
Barlee, Lake *salt flat* Australia 135 B7
Barlee Range *hills* Australia 135 A5
Barletta Italy 68 G4
Barlow *Y.T.* Canada 149 M3
Barlow Lake Canada 151 K2
Barmah Forest Australia 138 B5
Barmedman Australia 138 C5
Barmen-Elberfeld Germany *see* **Wuppertal**
Barmer India 104 B4
Barm Fīrūz, Kūh-e *mt.* Iran 110 C4
Barmouth U.K. 59 C6
Barnala India 104 C3
Barnard, Mount Canada/U.S.A. 149 M4
Barnard Castle U.K. 58 F4
Barnato Australia 138 B3
Barnaul Rus. Fed. 88 E2
Barnegat Bay U.S.A. 165 H4
Barnes Icecap Canada 147 K2
Barnesville *GA* U.S.A. 163 D5
Barnesville *MN* U.S.A. 160 D2
Barneveld Neth. 62 F2
Barneville-Carteret France 59 F9
Barneys Lake *imp. l.* Australia 138 B4
Barney Top *mt.* U.S.A. 159 H3
Barnhart *TX* U.S.A. 167 E2
Barnsley U.K. 58 F5
Barnstable U.S.A. 165 J3
Barnstaple U.K. 59 C7
Barnstaple Bay U.K. 59 C7
Barnstorf Germany 63 I2
Barnum Bay Palau 82 [inset]
Baro Nigeria 120 D4
Baroda *Gujarat* India *see* **Vadodara**
Baroda *Madh. Prad.* India 104 D4
Barong China 96 C2
Barons Range *hills* Australia 135 D6
Barowghīl, Kowtal-e Afgh. 111 I2
Barpathar India 96 B3
Barpeta India 105 G4
Bar Pla Soi Thai. *see* **Chon Buri**
Barques, Point Aux U.S.A. 164 D1
Barquisimeto Venez. 176 E1
Barra Brazil 177 J6
Barra *i.* U.K. 60 B4
Barra, Ponta da *pt* Moz. 125 L2
Barra, Sound of *sea chan.* U.K. 60 B3
Barraba Australia 138 E3
Barra Bonita Brazil 179 A3
Barracão do Barreto Brazil 177 G5
Barra de Navidad Mex. 166 D5
Barra do Bugres Brazil 177 G7
Barra do Corda Brazil 177 I5
Barra do Cuieté Brazil 179 C2
Barra do Garças Brazil 177 H7
Barra do Piraí Brazil 179 C3
Barra do São Manuel Brazil 177 G5
Barra do Turvo Brazil 179 A4
Barra Falsa, Ponta da *pt* Moz. 125 L2
Barraigh *i.* U.K. *see* **Barra**
Barra Kruta Hond. 166 [inset] J6
Barra Mansa Brazil 179 B3
Barrana Pak. 111 I4
Barranca Peru 176 C4
Barranca del Cobre, Parque Natural *nature res.* Mex. 166 D3
Barranqueras Arg. 178 E3
Barranquilla Col. 176 D1
Barre *MA* U.S.A. 165 I2
Barre *VT* U.S.A. 165 I1
Barre des Écrins *mt.* France 66 H4
Barreiras Brazil 177 J6

Barreirinha Brazil 177 G4
Barreirinhas Brazil 177 J4
Barreiro Port. 67 B4
Barreiros Brazil 177 K5
Barren Island India 87 A4
Barren Island Kiribati see Starbuck Island
Barren Islands AK U.S.A. 148 I4
Barren River Lake U.S.A. 164 B5
Barretos Brazil 179 A3
Barrett, Mount hill Australia 134 D4
Barrhead Canada 150 H4
Barrhead U.K. 60 E5
Barrie Canada 164 F1
Barrier Bay Antarctica 188 E2
Barrière Canada 150 F5
Barrier Range hills Australia 137 C6
Barrier Reef Belize 167 H5
Barrington Canada 153 I6
Barrington, Mount Australia 138 E4
Barrington Tops National Park Australia 138 E4
Barringun Australia 138 B2
Barro Alto Brazil 179 A1
Barrocão Brazil 179 C2
Barron U.S.A. 160 F2
Barroterán Mex. 167 E3
Barrow r. Ireland 61 F5
Barrow AK U.S.A. 148 H1
Barrow, Point pt AK U.S.A. 148 H1
Barrow Creek Australia 134 F5
Barrow-in-Furness U.K. 58 D4
Barrow Island Australia 134 A5
Barrow Range hills Australia 135 D6
Barrow Strait Canada 147 I2
Barr Smith Range hills Australia 135 C6
Barry U.K. 59 D7
Barrydale S. Africa 124 E7
Barry Mountains Australia 138 C6
Barrys Bay Canada 165 G1
Barryville U.S.A. 165 H3
Barsalpur India 104 C3
Barshatas Kazakh. 102 E2
Barshi India see Barsi
Barsi India 106 B2
Barsinghausen Germany 63 J2
Barstow U.S.A. 158 E4
Barsur India 106 D2
Bar-sur-Aube France 66 G2
Bartang Tajik. 111 H2
Barter Island AK U.S.A. 149 L1
Barth Germany 57 N3
Bartica Guyana 177 G2
Bartın Turkey 112 D2
Bartle Frere, Mount Australia 136 D3
Bartlett U.S.A. 160 D3
Bartlett Reservoir U.S.A. 159 H5
Barton U.S.A. 165 I1
Barton-upon-Humber U.K. 58 G5
Bartoszyce Poland 57 R3
Bartow U.S.A. 163 D7
Barú, Volcán vol. Panama 169 H7
Barumun r. Indon. 84 C2
Barun Qinghai China 94 D4
Barung i. Indon. 85 F5
Barunga Australia see Bamyili
Barun-Torey, Ozero l. Rus. Fed. 95 H1
Barus Sumatera Indon. 84 B2
Baruunbayan-Ulaan Mongolia 94 E2
Baruunbüren Mongolia 94 F1
Baruunharaa Mongolia see Bayangol
Baruunsuu Mongolia see Tsogttsetsiy
Baruunturuun Mongolia 94 C1
Baruun-Urt Mongolia 95 H2
Baruva India 106 E2
Barwani India 104 C5
Barwéli Mali see Baraouéli
Barwon r. Australia 138 C3
Barygaza India see Bharuch
Barykova, Mys hd Rus. Fed. 148 B3
Barysaw Belarus 55 P9
Barysh Rus. Fed. 53 J5
Basaga Turkm. 111 G2
Basăk, Tônlé r. Cambodia 87 D5
Basalt r. Australia 136 D3
Basalt Island H.K. China 97 [inset]
Basankusu Dem. Rep. Congo 122 B3
Basar India 106 C2
Basarabi Romania 69 M2
Basargechar Armenia see Vardenis
Basay Negros Phil. 82 C4
Basco Phil. 82 C1
Bascuñán, Cabo c. Chile 178 B3
Basel Switz. 66 H3
Basey Samar Phil. 82 D4
Bashäkerd, Kūhhā-ye mts Iran 110 E5
Bashanta Rus. Fed. see Gorodovikovsk
Bashaw Canada 150 H4
Bashee r. S. Africa 125 I7
Bāshī Iran 110 C4
Bashi Channel sea chan. Phil./Taiwan 97 I4
Bashkaus r. Rus. Fed. 98 D2
Bashmakovo Rus. Fed. 53 I5
Bāsht Iran 110 C4
Bashtanka Ukr. 53 G7
Basi Punjab India 104 D3
Basi Rajasthan India 104 D4
Basia India 105 F5
Basilan i. Phil. 82 C5
Basilan Strait Phil. 82 C5
Basildon U.K. 59 H7
Basile, Pico mt. Equat. Guinea 120 D4
Basin U.S.A. 156 F3
Basingstoke U.K. 59 F7
Basin Lake Canada 151 J4
Basirhat India 105 G5
Basīţ, Ra's al pt Syria 107 B2
Başkale Turkey 113 G3
Baskatong, Réservoir resr Canada 152 G5
Baskerville, Cape Australia 134 C4
Başkomutan Tarıhı Milli Parkı nat. park Turkey 69 N5
Başköy Turkey 107 A1
Baskunchak, Ozero l. Rus. Fed. 53 J6
Basle Switz. see Basel
Basmat India 106 C2
Baso i. Indon. 84 C3
Basoko Dem. Rep. Congo 122 C3
Basra Iraq 113 G5
Bassano Canada 151 H5
Bassano del Grappa Italy 68 D2
Bassar Togo 120 D4
Bassas da India reef Indian Ocean 123 D6
Bassas de Pedro Padua Bank sea feature India 106 B3
Bassein Myanmar 86 A3
Bassein r. Myanmar 86 A3
Basse-Normandie admin. reg. France 59 F9
Bassenthwaite Lake U.K. 58 D4
Basse Santa Su Gambia 120 B3

▶Basse-Terre Guadeloupe 169 L5
Capital of Guadeloupe.

▶Basseterre St Kitts and Nevis 169 L5
Capital of St Kitts and Nevis.

Bassett NE U.S.A. 160 D3
Bassett VA U.S.A. 164 F5
Bassikounou Mauritania 120 C3
Bass Rock i. U.K. 60 G4
Bass Strait Australia 137 D8
Bassum Germany 63 I2
Basswood Lake Canada 152 C4
Båstad Sweden 55 H8
Bästänäbäd Iran 110 B2
Bastheim Germany 63 K4
Basti India 105 E4
Bastia Corsica France 66 I5
Bastioes r. Brazil 177 K5
Bastogne Belgium 62 F4
Bastrop LA U.S.A. 161 F5
Bastrop TX U.S.A. 161 D6
Basu, Tanjung pt Indon. 84 C3
Basul r. Pak. 111 G5
Basuo China see Dongfang
Basutoland country Africa see Lesotho
Başyayla Turkey 107 A1
Bata Equat. Guinea 120 D4
Bataan Peninsula Luzon Phil. 82 C3
Batabanó, Golfo de b. Cuba 169 H4
Batac Luzon Phil. 82 C2
Batagay Rus. Fed. 77 O3
Batakan Kalimantan Indon. 85 F4
Batala India 104 C3
Batalha Port. 67 B4
Batam i. Indon. 84 D2
Batamay Rus. Fed. 77 N3
Batamshinskiy Kazakh. 102 A1
Batamshy Kazakh. see Batamshinskiy
Batan Jiangsu China 97 I1
Batan Qinghai China 96 D1
Batan i. Phil. 82 C1
Batan i. Phil. 82 D3
Batan is Phil. 82 C1
Batang China 96 C2
Batang Jawa Indon. 85 E4
Batangafo Cent. Afr. Rep. 122 B3
Batang Ai National Park Malaysia 85 F2
Batangas Luzon Phil. 82 C3
Batanghari r. Indon. 84 D3
Batangpele i. Papua Indon. 83 D3
Batangtarang Kalimantan Indon. 85 E2
Batangtoru Sumatera Indon. 84 B2
Batan Islands Phil. 82 C1
Batanta i. Papua Indon. 83 D3
Batavia Jawa Indon. see Jakarta
Batavia NY U.S.A. 165 F2
Batavia OH U.S.A. 164 C4
Bataysk Rus. Fed. 53 H7
Batbatan i. Phil. 82 C4
Batchawana Mountain hill Canada 152 D5
Bătdâmbâng Cambodia 87 C4
Bateemeucica, Gunung mt. Indon. 84 A1
Batéké, Plateaux Congo 122 B4
Batemans Bay Australia 138 E5
Bates Range hills Australia 135 C6
Batesville AR U.S.A. 161 F5
Batesville IN U.S.A. 164 C4
Batesville MS U.S.A. 161 F5
Batetskiy Rus. Fed. 52 F4
Bath N.B. Canada 153 I5
Bath Ont. Canada 165 G1
Bath U.K. 59 E7
Bath ME U.S.A. 165 K2
Bath NY U.S.A. 165 G2
Bath PA U.S.A. 165 H3
Batha watercourse Chad 121 E3
Bathgate U.K. 60 F5
Bathinda India 104 C3
Bathurst Australia 138 D4
Bathurst Canada 153 I5
Bathurst Gambia see Banjul
Bathurst S. Africa 125 H7
Bathurst, Cape N.W.T. Canada 149 P1
Bathurst, Lake Australia 138 D5
Bathurst Inlet inlet Canada 146 H3
Bathurst Inlet (abandoned) Canada 146 H3
Bathurst Island Australia 134 E2
Bathurst Island Canada 147 I2
Bathyz Döwlet Gorugy nature res. Turkm. 111 F3
Batié Burkina Faso 120 C4
Batikala, Tanjung pt Indon. 83 B3
Batı Menteşe Dağları mts Turkey 69 L6
Batı Toroslar mts Turkey 69 N6
Batken Kyrg. 102 D4
Batkes Indon. 134 E1
Bāţlāq-e Gavkhūnī marsh Iran 110 D3
Batley U.K. 58 F5
Batlow Australia 138 D5
Batman Turkey 113 F3
Batna Alg. 64 F4
Batnorov Mongolia 95 G2
Batō Japan 93 G2
Batok, Bukit hill Sing. 87 [inset]
Bat-Öldziy Mongolia 94 E2
Batong, Ko i. Thai. 84 B1

▶Baton Rouge U.S.A. 161 F6
Capital of Louisiana.

Batopilas Mex. 166 D3
Batouri Cameroon 121 E4
Batrā' tourist site Jordan see Petra
Batrā', Jabal al mt. Jordan 107 B5
Batroûn Lebanon 107 B2
Båtsfjord Norway 54 P1
Batshireet Mongolia 95 G1
Batsümber Töv Mongolia 94 F1
Battambang Cambodia see Bătdâmbâng
Batticaloa Sri Lanka 106 D5
Batti Malv i. India 87 A5
Battipaglia Italy 68 F4
Battle r. Canada 151 I4
Battle Creek U.S.A. 164 C2
Battleford Canada 151 I4
Battle Mountain U.S.A. 158 E1
Battle Mountain mt. U.S.A. 158 E1
Battsengel Arhangay Mongolia 94 E2
Battura Glacier Pak. 104 C1
Batu mt. Eth. 122 D3
Batu, Bukit mt. Malaysia 85 F2
Batu, Pulau-pulau is Indon. 84 B3
Batu, Tanjung pt Indon. 85 G2
Batuata i. Indon. 83 B4
Batubetumbang Indon. 84 D3
Batu Bora, Bukit mt. Malaysia 85 F2
Batudaka i. Indon. 83 B3
Batu Gajah Malaysia 84 C1
Batuhitam, Tanjung pt Indon. 83 B3
Batui Sulawesi Indon. 83 B3
Batulaki Mindanao Phil. 82 D5
Batulicin Kalimantan Indon. 85 G3
Batulilangmebang, Gunung mt. Indon. 85 F2
Batum Georgia see Bat'umi
Bat'umi Georgia 113 F2
Batumonga Indon. 84 C3
Batu Pahat Malaysia 84 C2
Batu Putih, Gunung mt. Malaysia 84 C1
Baturaja Sumatera Indon. 84 D4
Baturetno Jawa Indon. 85 E5
Baturité Brazil 177 K4
Batusangkar Sumatera Indon. 84 C3
Batyrevo Rus. Fed. 53 J5
Batys Qazaqstan admin. div. Kazakh. see Zapadnyy Kazakhstan
Bau Sarawak Malaysia 85 E2
Baubau Sulawesi Indon. 83 B4
Baucau East Timor 83 C5
Bauchi Nigeria 120 D3
Bauda India see Boudh
Baudette U.S.A. 160 E1
Baudh India see Boudh
Baugé France 66 D3
Bauhinia Australia 136 E5
Baukau East Timor see Baucau
Baula Sulawesi Indon. 83 B4
Bauld, Cape Canada 153 L4
Baume-les-Dames France 66 H3
Baunach r. Germany 63 K5
Baundal India 104 C2
Baura Bangl. 105 G4
Bauru Brazil 179 A3
Bausendorf Germany 62 G4
Bauska Latvia 55 N8
Bautino Kazakh. 113 H1
Bautzen Germany 57 O5
Bavānāt Iran 110 D4
Bavaria land Germany see Bayern
Bavaria reg. Germany 63 L6
Bavda India 106 B2
Baviaanskloofberge mts S. Africa 124 F7
Bavispe Mex. 166 C2
Bavispe r. Mex. 166 C2
Bavla India 104 C5
Bavly Rus. Fed. 51 Q5
Baw Myanmar 86 A2
Bawal India 104 D3
Bawal i. Indon. 85 E3
Bawan Kalimantan Indon. 85 F3
Bawang, Tanjung pt Indon. 85 E3
Baw Baw National Park Australia 138 C6
Bawdeswell U.K. 59 I6
Bawdwin Myanmar 86 B2
Bawean i. Indon. 85 F4
Bawinkel Germany 63 H2
Bawlake Myanmar 86 B3
Bawolung China 96 D2
Baxi China 96 D1
Baxian Hebei China see Bazhou
Baxkorgan Xinjiang China 98 E5
Baxley U.S.A. 163 D6
Baxoi China 96 C2
Baxter Mountain U.S.A. 159 J2
Bay Xinjiang China see Baicheng
Bay, Laguna de lag. Luzon Phil. 82 C3
Bayamo Cuba 169 I4
Bayan Heilong. China 90 B3
Bayan Qinghai China 94 D5
Bayan Qinghai China see Hualong
Bayan Lombok Indon. 85 G5
Bayan Arhangay Mongolia see Hashaat
Bayan Govĭ-Altay Mongolia see Bayan-Uul
Bayan Töv Mongolia 95 F2
Bayana India 104 D4
Bayan-Adraga Hentiy Mongolia 95 G1
Bayanaul Kazakh. 102 E1
Bayanbulag Bayanhongor Mongolia 94 D2
Bayanbulag Bayanhongor Mongolia see Bayantsagaan
Bayanbulag Hentiy Mongolia see Ömnödelger
Bayanbulak Xinjiang China 98 D3
Bayanbulak Xinjiang China 98 D4
Bayanchandmanĭ Mongolia 94 F1
Bayandalay Mongolia 94 E3
Bayanday Rus. Fed. 88 J2
Bayandelger Mongolia 95 H2
Bayandelger Mongolia 95 G2
Bayandun Dornod Mongolia 95 H1
Bayang, Pegunungan mts Indon. 85 E2
Bayan Gol Nei Mongol China see Dengkou
Bayangol Mongolia see Bugat
Bayangol Mongolia 94 F1
Bayangol Rus. Fed. 94 E1
Bayan Har Shan mts China 94 C5
Bayan Har Shankou pass Qinghai China 94 D5
Bayanhongor Mongolia 94 E2
Bayanhongor prov. Mongolia 94 D2
Bayan Hot Nei Mongol China 94 F4
Bayanhushuu Mongolia see Galuut
Bayanjargalan Mongolia 95 F2
Bayanlig Mongolia 94 E2
Bayan Mod Nei Mongol China 94 F3
Bayanmönh Mongolia 95 G2
Bayan Nuru Nei Mongol China 94 F3
Bayannuur Mongolia 94 F2
Bayan Obo Nei Mongol China 95 G3
Bayan-Ölgiy prov. Mongolia 94 B1
Bayan-Öndör Mongolia 94 F2
Bayan-Önjüül Mongolia 94 F2
Bayan-Ovoo Govĭ-Altay Mongolia see Altay
Bayan-Ovoo Hentiy Mongolia see Dadal
Bayan-Ovoo Hentiy Mongolia 95 H2
Bayan-Ovoo Ömnögovĭ Mongolia 94 F3
Bayan Qagan Nei Mongol China 95 H3
Bayan Qagan Nei Mongol China 95 J2
Bayansayr Mongolia see Baatsagaan
Bayan Shan mt. China 94 D4
Bayansumküre Xinjiang China 98 D4
Bayan Tal Nei Mongol China 95 I1
Bayanteeg Mongolia 94 E2
Bayan Tohoi Nei Mongol China 95 I1
Bayantöhöm Mongolia see Büren
Bayantsagaan Bayanhongor Mongolia 94 D2
Bayantsagaan Mongolia 95 F2
Bayan Ul Hot Nei Mongol China 95 I2
Bayan Us Nei Mongol China 95 G3
Bayan-Uul Mongolia 95 H1
Bayan-Uul Govĭ-Altay Mongolia 94 C2
Bayan Uul mts Mongolia 94 B1
Bayard U.S.A. 159 I5
Bayasgalant Mongolia see Mönhaan
Bayat Turkey 69 N5
Bayawan Negros Phil. 82 C4
Bayāz Iran 110 E4
Baybay Leyte Phil. 82 D4
Bayboro U.S.A. 163 E5
Bayburt Turkey 113 F2
Bay Canh, Hon i. Vietnam 87 D5
Bay City MI U.S.A. 164 D2
Bay City TX U.S.A. 161 D6
Baydaratskaya Guba Rus. Fed. 76 H3
Baydhabo Somalia 122 E3
Baydrag Mongolia see Dzag
Baydrag Gol r. Mongolia 94 D2
Bayerischer Wald mts Germany 63 M5
Bayerischer Wald nat. park Germany 63 M5
Bayerischer Wald, Nationalpark nat. park Germany 57 N6
Bayern land Germany 63 L6
Bayeux France 59 G9
Bayfield Canada 164 E2
Bayiji Jiangsu China 95 I5
Bayındır Turkey 69 L5
Bay Islands is Hond. see Bahía, Islas de la
Bayizhen Xizang China 99 F7
Bayjī Iraq 113 F4
Baykal, Ozero Rus. Fed. see Baikal, Lake
Baykal-Amur Magistral Rus. Fed. 90 C1
Baykal Range mts Rus. Fed. see Baykal'skiy Khrebet
Baykal'sk Rus. Fed. 94 F1
Baykal'skiy Khrebet mts Rus. Fed. 89 J2
Baykal'skiy Zapovednik nature res. Rus. Fed. 94 F1
Baykan Turkey 113 F3
Bay-Khaak Rus. Fed. 102 H1
Baykibashevo Rus. Fed. 51 R4
Baykonur Kazakh. see Baykonyr
Baykonyr Kazakh. 102 B2
Baymak Rus. Fed. 76 G4
Bay Minette U.S.A. 163 C6
Baynūna'h reg. U.A.E. 110 D6
Bayombong Luzon Phil. 82 C2
Bayona Spain see Baiona
Bayonne France 66 D5
Bayonne U.S.A. 165 H3
Bayo Point Panay Phil. 82 C4
Bay Point Phil. 82 B4
Bay Port U.S.A. 164 D2
Bayqongyr Kazakh. see Baykonyr
Bayram-Ali Turkm. see Baýramaly
Baýramaly Turkm. 111 F2
Bayramiç Turkey 69 L5
Bayreuth Germany 63 L5
Bayrūt Lebanon see Beirut
Bays, Lake of Canada 164 F1
Bayshore U.S.A. 164 C1
Bay Shore U.S.A. 165 I3
Bay Springs U.S.A. 161 F6
Bayston Hill U.K. 59 E6
Baysun Uzbek. see Boysun
Baytik Shan mts China 94 B2
Bayt Lahm West Bank see Bethlehem
Baytown U.S.A. 161 E6
Bayu Sulawesi Indon. 83 B3
Bayunglincir Sumatera Indon. 84 C3
Bay View N.Z. 139 F4
Bayy al Kabīr, Wādī watercourse Libya 121 E1
Baza Spain 67 E5
Baza, Sierra de mts Spain 67 E5
Bazar watercourse Kazakh. 98 C2
Bāzārak Afgh. 111 G3
Bazardüzü Dağı mt. Azer./Rus. Fed. see Bazardyuzyu, Gora
Bazardyuzyu, Gora mt. Azer./Rus. Fed. 113 G2
Bāzār-e Māsāl Iran 110 C2
Bazarnyy Karabulak Rus. Fed. 53 J5
Bazaruto, Ilha do i. Moz. 123 D6
Bazdar Pak. 111 G5
Bazhong China 96 E2
Bazhou Hebei China 95 I4
Bazhou China see Bazhong
Bazin r. Canada 152 G5
Bazmān Iran 111 F5
Bazmān, Kūh-e mt. Iran 111 F4
Bcharré Lebanon 107 C2
Be, Sông r. Vietnam 87 D5
Beach U.S.A. 160 C2
Beachy Head hd U.K. 59 H8
Beacon U.S.A. 165 I3
Beacon Bay S. Africa 125 H7
Beaconsfield U.K. 59 G7
Beagle, Canal sea chan. Arg. 178 C8
Beagle Bank reef Australia 134 C3
Beagle Bay Australia 134 C4
Beagle Gulf Australia 134 E3
Bealanana Madag. 123 E5
Béal an Átha Ireland see Ballina
Béal an Mhuirthead Ireland 61 C3
Béal Átha na Sluaighe Ireland see Ballinasloe
Beale, Lake India 106 B2
Beaminster U.K. 59 E8
Bear r. U.S.A. 156 E4
Bearalváhki Norway see Berlevåg
Bear Cove Point Canada 151 O2
Beardmore Canada 152 D4
Beardmore Glacier Antarctica 188 H1
Bear Island Arctic Ocean see Bjørnøya
Bear Island Canada 152 E3
Bear Lake l. Canada 152 A3
Bear Lake U.S.A. 164 B1
Bear Lake l. U.S.A. 156 F4
Bearma r. India 104 D4
Bear Mountain U.S.A. 160 C3
Bearnaraigh i. U.K. see Berneray
Bear Paw Mountain U.S.A. 156 F2
Bearpaw Mountains U.S.A. 156 F2
Bearskin Lake Canada 151 N4
Beas Dam India 104 C3
Beata, Cabo c. Dom. Rep. 169 J5
Beatrice U.S.A. 160 D3
Beatrice, Cape Australia 136 B2
Beatton r. Canada 150 F3
Beatton River Canada 150 F3
Beatty U.S.A. 158 E3
Beattyville Canada 152 F4
Beattyville U.S.A. 164 D5
Beaucaire France 66 G5
Beauchene Island Falkland Is 178 E8
Beaufort Australia 138 A6
Beaufort Sabah Malaysia 85 F1
Beaufort NC U.S.A. 163 E5
Beaufort SC U.S.A. 163 D5
Beaufort Island H.K. China 97 [inset]
Beaufort Lagoon AK U.S.A. 149 L1
Beaufort Sea Canada/U.S.A. 146 D2
Beaufort West S. Africa 124 F7
Beaulieu r. Canada 151 H2
Beauly U.K. 60 E3
Beauly r. U.K. 60 E3
Beaumaris U.K. 58 C5
Beaumont Belgium 62 E4
Beaumont N.Z. 139 B7
Beaumont MS U.S.A. 161 F6
Beaumont TX U.S.A. 161 E6
Beaune France 66 G3
Beaupréau France 66 D3
Beauquesne France 62 C4
Beauraing Belgium 62 E4
Beauséjour Canada 151 L5
Beauvais France 62 C5
Beauval France 62 C4
Beaver r. Alberta/Saskatchewan Canada 151 J4
Beaver r. Ont. Canada 152 D3
Beaver r. Y.T. Canada 150 E3
Beaver r. Y.T. Canada 149 N3
Beaver AK U.S.A. 149 K2
Beaver OK U.S.A. 161 C4
Beaver PA U.S.A. 164 E3
Beaver UT U.S.A. 159 G2
Beaver r. U.S.A. 159 G2
Beaver Creek Y.T. Canada 149 L3
Beavercreek U.S.A. 164 C4
Beaver Creek r. AK U.S.A. 149 K2
Beaver Creek r. MT U.S.A. 160 B1
Beaver Creek r. ND U.S.A. 160 C2
Beaver Dam KY U.S.A. 164 B5
Beaver Dam WI U.S.A. 160 F3
Beaver Falls U.S.A. 164 E3
Beaverhead Mountains U.S.A. 156 E3
Beaverhill Lake Alta Canada 151 H4
Beaver Hill Lake Canada 151 M4
Beaverhill Lake N.W.T. Canada 151 J2
Beaver Island U.S.A. 162 C2
Beaverlodge Canada 150 G4
Beaver Mountains AK U.S.A. 148 H3
Beaverton Canada 164 F1
Beaverton MI U.S.A. 164 C2
Beaverton OR U.S.A. 156 C3
Beawar India 104 C4
Beazley Arg. 178 C4
Bebedouro Brazil 179 A3
Bebington U.K. 58 D5
Bebra Germany 63 J4
Bêca China 96 C2
Bécard, Lac l. Canada 153 G1
Beccles U.K. 59 I6
Bečej Serbia 69 I2
Becerreá Spain 67 C2
Béchar Alg. 64 D5
Becharof Lake AK U.S.A. 148 H4
Becharof National Wildlife Refuge nature res. AK U.S.A. 148 H4
Bechevin Bay AK U.S.A. 148 G5
Bechhofen Germany 63 K5
Bechuanaland country Africa see Botswana
Beckley U.S.A. 164 E5
Beckum Germany 63 I3
Becky Peak U.S.A. 159 F2
Beco East Timor 83 C5
Bečov nad Teplou Czech Rep. 63 M4
Bedale U.K. 58 F4
Bedburg Germany 62 G4
Bedel', Pereval pass China/Kyrg. see Bedel Pass
Bedelē Eth. 122 D3
Bedel Pass China/Kyrg. 98 B4
Bedford N.S. Canada 153 J5
Bedford Que. Canada 165 I1
Bedford E. Cape S. Africa 125 H7
Bedford Kwazulu-Natal S. Africa 125 J5
Bedford U.K. 59 G6
Bedford IN U.S.A. 164 B4
Bedford KY U.S.A. 164 C4
Bedford PA U.S.A. 165 F3
Bedford VA U.S.A. 164 F5
Bedford, Cape Australia 136 D2
Bedford Downs Australia 134 D4
Bedgerebong Australia 138 C4
Bedi India 104 B5
Bedinggong Indon. 84 D3
Bedla India 104 C4
Bedlington U.K. 58 F3
Bedok Sing. 87 [inset]
Bedok Jetty Sing. 87 [inset]
Bedok Reservoir Sing. 87 [inset]
Bedou China 97 F3
Bedourie Australia 136 B5
Bedum Neth. 62 G1
Bedworth U.K. 59 F6
Beechworth Australia 138 C6
Beechy Canada 151 J5
Beecroft Peninsula Australia 138 E5
Beed India see Bid
Beelitz Germany 63 M2
Beenleigh Australia 138 F1
Beernem Belgium 62 D3
Beersheba Israel 107 B4
Be'ér Sheva' Israel see Beersheba
Be'ér Sheva' watercourse Israel 107 B4
Beervlei Dam S. Africa 124 F7
Beerwah Australia 138 F1
Beetaloo Australia 134 F4
Beethoven Peninsula Antarctica 188 L2
Beeville U.S.A. 161 D6
Befori Dem. Rep. Congo 122 C3
Beg, Lough l. U.K. 61 F3
Bega Australia 138 D6
Bega Maluku Indon. 83 C3
Begari r. Pak. 111 H4
Begicheva, Ostrov i. Rus. Fed. see Bol'shoy Begichev, Ostrov
Begur, Cap de c. Spain 67 H3
Begusarai India 105 F4
Béhague, Pointe pt Fr. Guiana 177 H3
Behbehān Iran 110 C4
Behchokǫ̀ N.W.T. Canada 149 R3
Behleg Qinghai China 99 E5
Behrendt Mountains Antarctica 188 L2
Behrūsī Iran 110 D4
Behshahr Iran 110 D2
Behsūd Afgh. 111 G3
Bei'an China 90 B2
Bei'ao China see Dongtou
Beibei China 96 E2
Beichuan China 96 E2
Beida Libya see Al Bayḍā'
Beida Shan mts Nei Mongol China 94 E4
Beigang Taiwan see Peikang
Beihai China 97 F4
Bei Hulsan Hu salt l. Qinghai China 99 F5

▶Beijing Beijing China 95 I4
Capital of China.

Beijing mun. China 95 I3
Beik Myanmar see Myeik
Beilen Neth. 62 G2
Beiliu China 97 F4
Beilngries Germany 63 L5
Beilu He r. Qinghai China 99 F6
Beiluheyan Qinghai China 94 C5
Beining Liaoning China 95 J3
Beinn an Oir hill U.K. 60 D5
Beinn an Tuirc hill U.K. 60 D5
Beinn Bheigeir hill U.K. 60 C5
Beinn Bhreac hill U.K. 60 D4
Beinn Dearg mt. U.K. 60 E3
Beinn Heasgarnich mt. U.K. 60 E4
Beinn Mholach hill U.K. 60 C2
Beinn Mhòr hill U.K. 60 B3
Beinn na Faoghlia i. U.K. see Benbecula
Beipan Jiang r. China 96 E3
Beipiao Liaoning China 95 J3
Beira Moz. 123 D5
Beiru He r. China 95 H5

▶Beirut Lebanon 107 B3
Capital of Lebanon.

Beishan Nei Mongol China 94 D3
Bei Shan mts China 94 C3
Beitai Ding mts China 95 H4
Beitbridge Zimbabwe 123 C6
Beith U.K. 60 E5
Beit Jālā West Bank 107 B4
Beitun Xinjiang China 98 D3
Beizhen Liaoning China see Beining
Beja Port. 67 C4
Béja Tunisia 68 C6
Bejaïa Alg. 67 I5
Béjar Spain 67 D3
Beji r. Pak. 102 C6
Bejucos Mex. 167 E5
Bekaa valley Lebanon see El Béqaa
Bekasi Jawa Indon. 84 D4
Békés Hungary 69 I1
Békéscsaba Hungary 69 I1
Bekily Madag. 123 E6
Bekkai Japan 90 G4
Bēkma, Sadd dam Iraq 113 G3
Bekovo Rus. Fed. 53 I5
Bekwai Ghana 120 C4
Bela India 105 E4
Bela Pak. 111 G5
Belab r. Pak. 111 H4
Bela-Bela S. Africa 125 I3
Bélabo Cameroon 120 E4
Bela Crkva Serbia 69 I2
Belaga Sarawak Malaysia 85 F2
Bel'agash Kazakh. 98 C2
Bel Air U.S.A. 165 G4
Belalcázar Spain 67 D4
Bělá nad Radbuzou Czech Rep. 63 M5
Belang Sulawesi Indon. 83 C2
Belangbelang i. Maluku Indon. 83 C3
Belapur India 106 B2
Belarus country Europe 53 E5
Belau country N. Pacific Ocean see Palau
Bela Vista Brazil 178 E2
Bela Vista Moz. 125 K4
Bela Vista de Goiás Brazil 179 A2
Belawan Sumatera Indon. 84 B2
Belaya r. Rus. Fed. 77 S3
also known as Bilo
Belaya, Gora mt. Rus. Fed. 148 A2
Belaya Glina Rus. Fed. 53 I7
Belaya Kalitva Rus. Fed. 53 I6
Belaya Kholunitsa Rus. Fed. 52 K4
Belayan r. Indon. 85 G3
Belayan, Gunung mt. Indon. 85 F2
Belaya Tserkva Ukr. see Bila Tserkva
Belbédji Niger 120 D3
Bełchatów Poland 57 Q5
Belcher U.S.A. 164 D5
Belcher Islands Canada 152 F2
Belchiragh Afgh. 111 G3
Belcoo U.K. 61 E3
Belden U.S.A. 158 C1
Belding U.S.A. 164 C2
Beleapani reef India see Cherbaniani Reef
Belebey Rus. Fed. 51 Q5
Beledweyne Somalia 122 E3
Belém Brazil 177 I4
Belém Novo Brazil 179 A5
Belén Arg. 178 C3
Belen Antalya Turkey 107 A1
Belen Hatay Turkey 107 C1
Belen U.S.A. 157 G6
Belep, Îles is New Caledonia 133 G3
Belev Rus. Fed. 53 H5
Belfast S. Africa 125 J3

▶Belfast U.K. 61 G3
Capital of Northern Ireland.

Belfast U.S.A. 162 G2
Belfast Lough inlet U.K. 61 G3
Bēlfodiyo Eth. 122 D2
Belford U.K. 58 F3
Belfort France 66 H3
Belgaum India 106 B3
Belgern Germany 63 N3
Belgian Congo country Africa see Congo, Democratic Republic of the
België country Europe see Belgium
Belgique country Europe see Belgium
Belgium country Europe 62 E4
Belgorod Rus. Fed. 53 H6
Belgorod-Dnestrovskyy Ukr. see Bilhorod-Dnistrovs'kyy

▶Belgrade Serbia 69 I2
Capital of Serbia.

Belgrade ME U.S.A. 165 K1
Belgrade MT U.S.A. 156 F3
Belgrano II research station Antarctica 188 A1
Belice r. Sicily Italy 68 E6
Beliliou i. Palau see Peleliu
Belimbing Sumatera Indon. 84 D4
Belinskiy Rus. Fed. 53 I5
Belinyu Indon. 84 D3
Belitung i. Indon. 85 E3
Belize Angola 123 B4

▶Belize Belize 167 H5
Former capital of Belize.

Belize country Central America 167 H5
Beljak Austria see Villach
Belkina, Mys pt Rus. Fed. 90 E3
Belkofski AK U.S.A. 148 G5
Bel'kovskiy, Ostrov i. Rus. Fed. 77 O2
Bell Australia 138 E1
Bell r. Australia 138 D4
Bell r. Canada 152 F4
Bell r. Y.T. Canada 149 M2
Bella Bella Canada 150 D4
Bellac France 66 E3
Bella Coola Canada 150 E4
Bellaire U.S.A. 164 C1
Bellaire TX U.S.A. 167 G2
Bellary India 106 C3
Bellata Australia 138 D2
Bella Unión Uruguay 178 E4
Bella Vista U.S.A. 158 B1
Bellbrook Australia 138 F3
Bell Cay reef Australia 136 E4
Belledonne mts France 66 G4
Bellefontaine U.S.A. 164 D3
Bellefonte U.S.A. 165 G3
Belle Fourche U.S.A. 160 C2
Belle Fourche r. U.S.A. 160 C2
Belle Glade U.S.A. 163 D7
Belle-Île i. France 66 C3
Belle Isle i. Canada 153 L4
Belle Isle, Strait of Canada 153 K4
Belleville Canada 165 G1
Belleville IL U.S.A. 160 F4
Belleville KS U.S.A. 160 D4
Bellevue IA U.S.A. 160 F3
Bellevue MI U.S.A. 164 C2
Bellevue OH U.S.A. 164 D3
Bellevue WA U.S.A. 156 C3
Bellin Canada see Kangirsuk
Bellingham U.K. 58 E3
Bellingham U.S.A. 156 C2
Bellingshausen research station Antarctica 188 A2
Bellingshausen Sea Antarctica 188 L2
Bellinzona Switz. 66 I3
Bellows Falls U.S.A. 165 I2
Bellpat Pak. 111 H4
Belluno Italy 68 E1
Belluru India 106 C3
Bell Ville Arg. 178 D4
Bellville S. Africa 124 D7
Belm Germany 63 I2
Belmont Australia 138 E4
Belmont U.K. 60 [inset]
Belmont U.S.A. 165 F2
Belmonte Brazil 179 D1

▶Belmopan Belize 167 H5
Capital of Belize.

Belmore, Mount hill Australia 138 F2
Belmullet Ireland see Béal an Mhuirthead
Belo Madag. 123 E6
Belo Campo Brazil 179 C1
Belœil Belgium 62 D4
Belogorsk Rus. Fed. 90 C2
Belogorsk Ukr. see Bilohirs'k
Beloha Madag. 123 E6
Belo Horizonte Brazil 179 C2
Beloit KS U.S.A. 160 D4
Beloit WI U.S.A. 160 F3
Belokurikha Rus. Fed. 102 F1
Belo Monte Brazil 177 H4
Belomorsk Rus. Fed. 52 G2
Belonia India 105 G5
Belopa Sulawesi Indon. 83 B3
Belorechensk Rus. Fed. 113 E1
Belorechenskaya Rus. Fed. see Belorechensk
Belören Turkey 112 D3
Beloretsk Rus. Fed. 76 G4
Belorussia country Europe see Belarus
Belorusskaya S.S.R. country Europe see Belarus
Belostok Poland see Białystok
Belot, Lac l. N.W.T. Canada 149 P2
Belo Tsiribihina Madag. 123 E5
Belousovka Kazakh. 98 C2
Belovo Rus. Fed. 88 F2
Beloyarskiy Rus. Fed. 51 T3
Beloye, Ozero l. Rus. Fed. 52 H3
Beloye More sea Rus. Fed. see White Sea
Belozersk Rus. Fed. 52 H3
Belpre U.S.A. 164 E4
Beltana Australia 137 B6
Belted Range mts U.S.A. 158 E3
Beltes Gol r. Mongolia 94 D1
Belton U.S.A. 161 D6
Bel'ts' Moldova see Bălţi
Bel'tsy Moldova see Bălţi
Beluga Lake AK U.S.A. 149 J3
Belukha, Gora mt. Kazakh./Rus. Fed. 102 G2
Beluran Sabah Malaysia 85 G1
Belush'ye Rus. Fed. 52 J2
Belvidere IL U.S.A. 160 F3
Belvidere NJ U.S.A. 165 H3
Belyaka, Kosa spit Rus. Fed. 148 D2
Belyando r. Australia 136 D4
Belyayevka Ukr. see Bilyayivka
Belyy Rus. Fed. 52 G5
Belyy, Ostrov i. Rus. Fed. 76 I2
Belyy Bom Rus. Fed. 98 D2
Belzig Germany 63 M2
Belzoni U.S.A. 161 F5
Bemaraha, Plateau du Madag. 123 E5
Bembe Angola 123 B4
Bemidji U.S.A. 160 E2
Béna Burkina Faso 120 C3
Bena Dibele Dem. Rep. Congo 122 C4
Benagin Kalimantan Indon. 85 F3
Ben Alder mt. U.K. 60 E4
Benalla Australia 138 B6
Benares India see Varanasi
Ben Arous Tunisia 68 D6
Benavente Spain 67 D2
Ben Avon mt. U.K. 60 F3
Benbane Head hd U.K. 61 F2
Benbecula i. U.K. 60 B3
Ben Boyd National Park Australia 138 E6
Benburb U.K. 61 F3
Bencha China 97 I1
Bencheng Hebei China see Luannan
Ben Chonzie hill U.K. 60 F4
Ben Cleuch hill U.K. 60 F4
Ben Cruachan mt. U.K. 60 D4
Bend U.S.A. 156 C3
Bendearg mt. S. Africa 125 H6
Bendeleben, Mount AK U.S.A. 148 F2
Bendeleben Mountains AK U.S.A. 148 F2
Bender Moldova see Tighina
Bender-Bayla Somalia 122 F3
Bendery Moldova see Tighina
Bendigo Australia 138 B6
Bendoc Australia 138 D6
Bene Moz. 123 D5
Benedict, Mount hill Canada 153 K3
Benenitra Madag. 123 E6
Benešov Czech Rep. 57 O6
Bénestroff France 62 G6
Benevento Italy 68 F4
Beneventum Italy see Benevento
Benezette U.S.A. 165 F3
Beng, Nam r. Laos 86 C3
Bengal, Bay of sea Indian Ocean 103 G8
Bengamisa Dem. Rep. Congo 122 C3
Bengbu China 97 H1
Benghazi Libya 121 F1
Beng He r. China 95 I5
Bengkalis Sumatera Indon. 84 C2
Bengkalis i. Indon. 84 C2
Bengkayang Kalimantan Indon. 85 E2
Bengkulu Sumatera Indon. 84 C3
Bengkulu prov. Indon. 84 C3
Bengkung Kalimantan Indon. 85 G3
Bengoi Seram Indon. 83 D3
Bengtsfors Sweden 55 H7
Benguela Angola 123 B5
Benha Egypt see Banhā
Ben Hiant hill U.K. 60 C4
Ben Hope hill U.K. 60 E2
Ben Horn hill U.K. 60 E2
Beni r. Bol. 176 E6
Beni Dem. Rep. Congo 122 C3
Beni Nepal 105 E3
Beni Abbès Alg. 64 D5
Beniah Lake Canada 151 H2
Benidorm Spain 67 F4
Beni Mellal Morocco 64 C5
Benin country Africa 120 D4
Benin, Bight of g. Africa 120 D4
Benin City Nigeria 120 D4
Beni Saf Alg. 67 F6
Beni Snassen, Monts des mts Morocco 67 E6
Beni Suef Egypt see Banī Suwayf
Benito, Islas is Mex. 166 B2
Benito Juárez Arg. 178 E5
Benito Juárez Mex. 159 F5
Benito Soliven Luzon Phil. 82 C2
Benjamim Constant Brazil 176 E4
Benjamin U.S.A. 161 D5
Benjamín Hill Mex. 166 C2
Benjina Indon. 81 I8
Benkelman U.S.A. 160 C3
Ben Klibreck hill U.K. 60 E2
Ben Lavin Nature Reserve S. Africa 125 I2
Ben Lawers mt. U.K. 60 E4
Ben Lomond mt. Australia 138 E3
Ben Lomond hill U.K. 60 E4
Ben Lomond National Park Australia 137 [inset]
Ben Macdui mt. U.K. 60 F3
Benmara Australia 136 B3
Ben More hill U.K. 60 C4
Ben More mt. U.K. 60 E4
Benmore, Lake N.Z. 139 C7
Ben More Assynt hill U.K. 60 E2
Bennetta, Ostrov i. Rus. Fed. 77 P2
Bennett Island Rus. Fed. see Bennetta, Ostrov
Bennett Lake B.C. Canada 149 N4
Bennettsville U.S.A. 163 E5
Ben Nevis mt. U.K. 60 D4
Bennington NH U.S.A. 165 J2
Bennington VT U.S.A. 165 I2
Benoni S. Africa 125 I4
Ben Rinnes hill U.K. 60 F3
Bensheim Germany 63 I5
Benson AZ U.S.A. 159 H6
Benson MN U.S.A. 160 E2
Benta Seberang Malaysia 84 C1
Benteng Sulawesi Indon. 83 B4
Bentinck Island Myanmar 87 B5
Bentiu Sudan 108 C8
Bent Jbaïl Lebanon 107 B3
Bentley U.K. 58 F5
Bento Gonçalves Brazil 179 A5
Benton AR U.S.A. 161 E5
Benton CA U.S.A. 158 D3
Benton IL U.S.A. 160 F4
Benton KY U.S.A. 161 F4
Benton LA U.S.A. 161 E5
Benton MO U.S.A. 161 F4
Benton PA U.S.A. 165 G3
Bentong Malaysia see Bentung
Benton Harbor U.S.A. 164 B2
Bentonville U.S.A. 161 E4
Bên Tre Vietnam 87 D5
Bentung Malaysia 84 C2
Benua Sulawesi Indon. 83 B4
Benua i. Indon. 84 D2
Benuamartinus Kalimantan Indon. 85 F2
Benue r. Nigeria 120 D4
Benum, Gunung mt. Malaysia 84 C2
Ben Vorlich hill U.K. 60 E4
Benwee Head hd Ireland 61 C3
Benwood U.S.A. 164 E3
Ben Wyvis mt. U.K. 60 E3
Benxi Liaoning China 90 B4
Benxi Liaoning China 95 J3
Beo Sulawesi Indon. 83 C1
Beograd Serbia see Belgrade
Béoumi Côte d'Ivoire 120 C4
Bepagut, Gunung mt. Indon. 84 C4
Beppu Japan 91 C6
Béqaa valley Lebanon see El Béqaa
Bera, Tasik l. Malaysia 84 C2
Berach r. India 104 C4
Beraketa Madag. 123 E6
Berangas Kalimantan Indon. 85 G3
Bérard, Lac l. Canada 153 H2
Berasia India 104 D5
Berastagi Sumatera Indon. 84 B2
Berat Albania 69 H4
Beratus, Gunung mt. Indon. 85 G3
Berau r. Indon. 85 G2
Beravina Madag. 123 E5
Berbak, Taman Nasional nat. park Indon. 84 D3
Berber Sudan 108 D6
Berbera Somalia 122 E2
Berbérati Cent. Afr. Rep. 122 B3
Berchtesgaden, Nationalpark nat. park Germany 57 N7
Berck France 62 B4
Berdichev Ukr. see Berdychiv
Berdigestyakh Rus. Fed. 77 N3
Berdyans'k Ukr. 53 H7
Berdychiv Ukr. 53 F6
Berea KY U.S.A. 164 C5
Berea OH U.S.A. 164 E3
Berebere Maluku Indon. 83 D2
Beregovo Ukr. see Berehove
Beregovoy Rus. Fed. 90 B1
Berehove Ukr. 53 D6
Bereina P.N.G. 81 L8
Bere Island Ireland 61 C6
Bereket Turkm. 110 D2
Berekum Ghana 120 C4
Berel' Kazakh. 98 D2
Berenice Egypt see Baranīs
Berenice Libya see Benghazi
Berens r. Canada 151 L4
Berens Island Canada 151 L4
Berens River Canada 151 L4
Beresford U.S.A. 160 D3
Bereza Belarus see Byaroza
Berezino Belarus see Byerazino
Berezivka Ukr. 53 F7
Berezne Ukr. 53 E6
Bereznik Rus. Fed. 52 I3
Berezniki Rus. Fed. 51 R4
Berezov Rus. Fed. see Berezovo
Berezovka Rus. Fed. 90 B2
Berezovka Ukr. see Berezivka
Berezovo Rus. Fed. 51 T3
Berezovyy Rus. Fed. 90 D2
Berga Germany 63 L3
Berga Spain 67 G2
Bergama Turkey 69 L5
Bergamo Italy 68 C2
Bergby Sweden 55 J6
Bergen Mecklenburg-Vorpommern Germany 57 N3
Bergen Niedersachsen Germany 63 J2
Bergen Norway 55 D6
Bergen U.S.A. 165 G2
Bergen op Zoom Neth. 62 E3
Bergerac France 66 E4
Bergères-lès-Vertus France 62 E6
Bergheim (Erft) Germany 62 G4
Bergisches Land reg. Germany 63 H4
Bergisch Gladbach Germany 62 H4
Bergland Namibia 124 C2
Bergomum Italy see Bergamo
Bergoo U.S.A. 164 E4
Bergsjö Sweden 55 J6
Bergsviken Sweden 54 L4
Bergtheim Germany 63 K5
Bergues France 62 C4
Bergum Neth. see Burgum
Bergville S. Africa 125 I5
Berh Mongolia 95 G2
Berhala, Selat sea chan. Indon. 84 C3
Berhampur India see Baharampur
Berikat, Tanjung pt Indon. 84 D3
Beringa, Ostrov i. Rus. Fed. 77 R4
Beringen Belgium 62 F3
Bering Glacier AK U.S.A. 148 H4
Bering Glacier AK U.S.A. 149 L3
Bering Lake AK U.S.A. 149 K3
Bering Land Bridge National Preserve nature res. AK U.S.A. 148 F2
Beringovskiy Rus. Fed. 77 S3
Bering Sea N. Pacific Ocean 77 S4
Bering Strait Rus. Fed./U.S.A. 148 E2
Berīs, Ra's pt Iran 111 F5
Berislav Ukr. see Beryslav
Berkåk Norway 54 G5
Berkane Morocco 67 E6
Berkel r. Neth. 62 G2
Berkeley U.S.A. 158 B3
Berkeley Springs U.S.A. 165 F4
Berkhout Neth. 62 F2
Berkner Island Antarctica 188 A1
Berkovitsa Bulg. 69 J3
Berkshire Downs hills U.K. 59 F7
Berkshire Hills U.S.A. 165 I2
Berland r. Canada 150 G4
Berlare Belgium 62 E3
Berlevåg Norway 54 P1

▶Berlin Germany 63 N2
Capital of Germany.

Berlin land Germany 63 N2
Berlin MD U.S.A. 165 H4
Berlin NH U.S.A. 165 J1
Berlin PA U.S.A. 165 F4
Berlin Lake U.S.A. 164 E3
Bermagui Australia 138 E6
Bermejíllo Mex. 166 E3
Bermejo r. Arg./Bol. 178 E3
Bermejo Bol. 176 F8
Bermen, Lac l. Canada 153 H3

▶Bermuda terr. N. Atlantic Ocean 169 L2
United Kingdom Overseas Territory.

Bermuda Rise sea feature N. Atlantic Ocean 184 D4

▶Bern Switz. 66 H3
Capital of Switzerland.

Bernalillo U.S.A. 157 G6
Bernardino de Campos Brazil 179 A3
Bernardo O'Higgins, Parque Nacional nat. park Chile 178 B7
Bernasconi Arg. 178 D5
Bernau Germany 63 N2
Bernburg (Saale) Germany 63 L3
Berne Germany 63 I1
Berne Switz. see Bern
Berne U.S.A. 164 C3
Berner Alpen mts Switz. 66 H3
Berneray i. Scotland U.K. 60 B3
Berneray i. Scotland U.K. 60 B4
Bernier Island Australia 135 A6
Bernina Pass Switz. 66 J3
Bernkastel-Kues Germany 62 H5
Beroea Greece see Veroia
Beroea Syria see Aleppo
Beroroha Madag. 123 E6
Beroun Czech Rep. 57 O6
Berounka r. Czech Rep. 57 O6
Berovina Madag. see Beravina
Berri Australia 137 C7
Berriane Alg. 64 E5
Berridale Australia 138 D6
Berriedale U.K. 60 F2
Berrigan Australia 138 B5
Berrima Australia 138 E5
Berrouaghia Alg. 67 H5
Berry Australia 138 E5
Berry U.S.A. 164 C4
Berryessa, Lake U.S.A. 158 B2
Berry Head hd U.K. 59 D8
Berry Islands Bahamas 163 E7
Berryville U.S.A. 165 G4
Berseba Namibia 124 C4
Bersenbrück Germany 63 H2
Bertam Malaysia 84 C1
Berté, Lac l. Canada 153 H4
Berthoud Pass U.S.A. 156 G5
Bertolinía Brazil 177 J5
Bertoua Cameroon 120 E4
Bertraghboy Bay Ireland 61 C4
Beru atoll Kiribati 133 H2
Beruri Brazil 176 F4
Beruwala Sri Lanka 106 C5
Berwick Australia 138 B7
Berwick U.S.A. 165 G3
Berwick-upon-Tweed U.K. 58 E3
Berwyn hills U.K. 59 D6
Beryslav Ukr. 69 O1
Berytus Lebanon see Beirut
Besah Kalimantan Indon. 85 G2
Besalampy Madag. 123 E5
Besançon France 66 H3
Besar i. Indon. 83 B5
Besar, Gunung mt. Indon. 85 F3
Besar, Gunung mt. Malaysia 87 C7
Besbay Kazakh. 102 A2
Besboro Island AK U.S.A. 148 G2
Beserah Malaysia 84 C2
Beshkent Uzbek. 111 G2
Beshneh Iran 110 D4
Besikama Timor Indon. 83 C5
Besitang Sumatera Indon. 84 B1
Beskra Alg. see Biskra
Beslan Rus. Fed. 113 G2
Besnard Lake Canada 151 J4
Besni Turkey 112 E3
Besoba Kazakh. 98 A2
Besor watercourse Israel 107 B4
Beşparmak Dağları mts Cyprus see Pentadaktylos Range
Bessbrook U.K. 61 F3
Bessemer U.S.A. 163 C5
Besshoky, Gora hill Kazakh. 113 I1
Besskorbnaya Rus. Fed. 53 I7
Bessonovka Rus. Fed. 53 J5
Bestamak Vostochnyy Kazakhstan Kazakh. 98 B2
Betanzos Spain 67 B2
Betet i. Indon. 84 D3
Bethal S. Africa 125 I4
Bethanie Namibia 124 C4
Bethany U.S.A. 160 E3
Bethari Nepal 99 C8
Bethel AK U.S.A. 148 G3
Bethel U.S.A. 153 H5
Bethel Park U.S.A. 164 E3
Bethesda U.K. 58 C5
Bethesda MD U.S.A. 165 G4
Bethesda OH U.S.A. 164 E3
Bethlehem S. Africa 125 I5
Bethlehem U.S.A. 165 H3
Bethlehem West Bank 107 B4
Bethulie S. Africa 125 G6
Béthune France 62 C4
Beti Pak. 111 H4
Betim Brazil 179 B2
Betiri, Gunung mt. Indon. 85 F5
Bet Lehem West Bank see Bethlehem
Betma India 104 C5
Betong Sarawak Malaysia 85 E2
Betong Thai. 87 C6
Betoota Australia 136 C5
Betpak-Dala plain Kazakh. 102 D2
Betroka Madag. 123 E6
Bet She'an Israel 107 B3
Betsiamites Canada 153 H4
Betsiamites r. Canada 153 H4
Betsu-zan mt. Japan 92 C2
Bettiah India 105 F4
Bettles AK U.S.A. 149 J2
Bettyhill U.K. 60 E2
Bettystown Ireland 61 F4
Betul India 104 D5
Betun Timor Indon. 83 C5
Betung Kerihun, Taman Nasional Indon. 85 F2
Betwa r. India 104 D4
Betws-y-coed U.K. 59 D5
Betzdorf Germany 63 H4
Beulah Australia 137 C7
Beulah MI U.S.A. 164 B1
Beulah ND U.S.A. 160 C2
Beult r. U.K. 59 H7
Beuthen Poland see Bytom
Bever r. Germany 63 H2
Beverley U.K. 58 G5
Beverley, Lake AK U.S.A. 148 H4
Beverly MA U.S.A. 165 J2
Beverly OH U.S.A. 164 E4
Beverly Hills U.S.A. 158 D4
Beverly Lake Canada 151 K1
Beverstedt Germany 63 I1
Beverungen Germany 63 J3
Beverwijk Neth. 62 E2
Bewani P.N.G. 81 K7
Bexbach Germany 63 H5
Bexhill U.K. 59 H8
Bexley, Cape Canada 146 G3
Beyānlū Iran 110 B3
Beyce Turkey see Orhaneli
Bey Dağları mts Turkey 69 N6
Beykoz Turkey 69 M4
Beyla Guinea 120 C4
Beylagan Azer. see Beyläqan
Beyläqan Azer. 113 G3
Beyneu Kazakh. 100 E2
Beypazarı Turkey 69 N4
Beypınarı Turkey 112 E3
Beypore India 106 B4
Beyrouth Lebanon see Beirut
Beyşehir Turkey 112 C3
Beyşehir Gölü l. Turkey 112 C3
Beytonovo Rus. Fed. 90 B1
Beytüşşebap Turkey 113 F3
Bezameh Iran 110 E3
Bezbozhnik Rus. Fed. 52 K4
Bezhanitsy Rus. Fed. 52 F4
Bezhetsk Rus. Fed. 52 H4
Béziers France 66 F5
Bezmein Turkm. see Abadan
Bezwada India see Vijayawada
Bhabha India see Bhabhua
Bhabhar India 104 B4
Bhabhua India 105 E4
Bhabua India see Bhabhua
Bhachau India 104 B5
Bhachbhar India 104 B4
Bhadarwah India 99 A6
Bhadgaon Nepal see Bhaktapur
Bhadohi India 105 E4
Bhadra India 104 C3
Bhadrachalam Road Station India see Kottagudem
Bhadrak India 105 F5
Bhadrakh India see Bhadrak
Bhadravati India 106 B3
Bhag Pak. 111 G4
Bhaga r. India 99 B6
Bhagalpur India 105 F4
Bhainsa India 106 C2
Bhainsdehi India 104 D5
Bhairab Bazar Bangl. 105 G4
Bhairi Hol mt. Pak. 111 G5
Bhaktapur Nepal 105 F4
Bhalki India 106 C2
Bhamo Myanmar 86 B1
Bhamragarh India 106 D2
Bhandara India 104 D5
Bhanjanagar India 106 E2
Bhanrer Range hills India 104 D5
Bhaptiahi India 105 F4
Bharat country Asia see India
Bharatpur India 104 D4
Bhareli r. India 105 H4
Bharuch India 104 C5
Bhatapara India 105 E5
Bhatarsaigh i. U.K. see Vatersay
Bhatghar Lake India 106 B2
Bhatinda India see Bathinda
Bhatnair India see Hanumangarh
Bhatpara India 105 G5
Bhaunagar India see Bhavnagar
Bhavani r. India 106 C4
Bhavani Sagar l. India 106 C4
Bhavnagar India 104 C5
Bhawana Pak. 111 I4
Bhawanipatna India 106 D2
Bhearnaraigh, Eilean i. U.K. see Berneray
Bheemavaram India see Bhimavaram
Bhekuzulu S. Africa 125 J4
Bhera Pak. 111 I3
Bheri r. Nepal 99 C7
Bhigvan India 106 B2
Bhikhna Thori Nepal 105 F4
Bhilai India 104 E5
Bhildi India 104 C4
Bhilwara India 104 C4
Bhima r. India 106 C2
Bhimar India 104 B4
Bhimavaram India 106 D2
Bhimlath India 104 E5
Bhimphedi Nepal 99 D8
Bhind India 104 D4
Bhinga India 105 E4
Bhisho S. Africa 125 H7
Bhiwandi India 106 B2
Bhiwani India 104 D3
Bhogaipur India 104 D4
Bhojpur Nepal 105 F4
Bhola Bangl. 105 G5
Bhongweni S. Africa 125 I6
Bhopal India 104 D5
Bhopalpatnam India 106 D2
Bhrigukaccha India see Bharuch
Bhuban India 106 E1
Bhubaneshwar India 106 E1
Bhubaneswar India see Bhubaneshwar
Bhuj India 104 B5
Bhusawal India 104 C5
Bhutan country Asia 105 G4
Bhuttewala India 104 B4
Bia r. Ghana 120 C4
Bia, Phou mt. Laos 86 C3
Bīabān mts Iran 110 E5
Biafo Glacier Pak. 104 C2
Biafra, Bight of g. Africa see Benin, Bight of
Biak Indon. 81 J7
Biak Sulawesi Indon. 83 B3
Biak i. Indon. 81 J7
Biała Podlaska Poland 53 D5
Białogard Poland 57 O4
Białystok Poland 53 D5
Bianco, Monte mt. France/Italy see Blanc, Mont
Biandangang Kou r. mouth China 95 J5
Bianzhao Jilin China 95 J2
Bianzhuang Shandong China see Cangshan
Biao Mindanao Phil. 82 D5
Biaora India 104 D5
Biaro i. Indon. 83 C2
Biarritz France 66 D5
Bi'ār Tabrāk well Saudi Arabia 110 B5
Bibai Japan 90 F4
Bibbenluke Australia 138 D6
Bibbiena Italy 68 D3
Bibby Island Canada 151 M2
Biberach an der Riß Germany 57 L6
Bibile Sri Lanka 106 D5
Biblis Germany 63 I5
Biblos Lebanon see Jbail
Bicas Brazil 179 C3
Biçer Turkey 69 N5
Bicester U.K. 59 F7
Bichabhera India 104 C4
Bicheng China see Bishan
Bichevaya Rus. Fed. 90 D3
Bichi r. Rus. Fed. 90 E1
Bichraltar Nepal 99 D8
Bichura Rus. Fed. 95 F1
Bickerton Island Australia 136 B2
Bickleigh U.K. 59 D8
Bicknell U.S.A. 164 B4
Bicoli Halmahera Indon. 83 D2
Bicuari, Parque Nacional do nat. park Angola 123 B5
Bid India 106 B2
Bida Nigeria 120 D4
Bidadari, Tanjung pt Malaysia 85 G1
Bidar India 106 C2
Biddeford U.S.A. 165 J2
Biddinghuizen Neth. 62 F2
Bidean nam Bian mt. U.K. 60 D4
Bideford U.K. 59 C7
Bideford Bay U.K. see Barnstaple Bay
Bidokht Iran 110 E3
Bidzhan Rus. Fed. 90 C3
Bié Angola see Kuito
Bié, Planalto do Angola 123 B5
Biebrzański Park Narodowy nat. park Poland 55 M10
Biedenkopf Germany 63 I4
Biel Switz. 66 H3
Bielawa Poland 57 P5
Bielefeld Germany 63 I2
Bielitz Poland see Bielsko-Biała
Biella Italy 68 C2
Bielsko-Biała Poland 57 Q6
Bielstein hill Germany 63 J3
Bienenbüttel Germany 63 K1
Biên Hoa Vietnam 87 D5
Bienne Switz. see Biel
Bienville, Lac l. Canada 153 G3
Bierbank Australia 138 B1
Biesiesvlei S. Africa 125 G4
Bietigheim-Bissingen Germany 63 J6
Bièvre Belgium 62 F5
Bifoun Gabon 122 B4
Big r. Canada 153 K3
Big r. AK U.S.A. 148 I3
Biga Turkey 69 L4
Bigadiç Turkey 69 M5
Biga Yarımadası pen. Turkey 69 L5
Big Baldy Mountain U.S.A. 156 F3
Big Bar Creek Canada 150 F5
Big Bear Lake U.S.A. 158 E4
Big Belt Mountains U.S.A. 156 F3
Big Bend Swaziland 125 J4
Big Bend National Park U.S.A. 161 C6
Big Black r. MS U.S.A. 167 H1
Bigbury-on-Sea U.K. 59 D8
Big Canyon watercourse U.S.A. 161 C6
Big Delta AK U.S.A. 149 K2
Biger Govĭ-Altay Mongolia 94 D2
Biger Nuur salt l. Mongolia 94 D2
Big Falls U.S.A. 160 E1
Big Fork r. U.S.A. 160 E1
Biggar Canada 151 J4
Biggar U.K. 60 F5
Biggar, Lac l. Canada 152 G4
Bigge Island Australia 134 D3
Biggenden Australia 137 F5
Bigger, Mount B.C. Canada 149 M4
Biggesee l. Germany 63 H3
Biggleswade U.K. 59 G6
Biggs CA U.S.A. 158 C2
Biggs OR U.S.A. 156 C3
Big Hole r. U.S.A. 156 E3
Bighorn r. U.S.A. 156 G3
Bighorn Mountains U.S.A. 156 G3
Big Island Nunavut Canada 147 K3
Big Island N.W.T. Canada 150 G2
Big Island Ont. Canada 151 M5
Big Kalzas Lake Y.T. Canada 149 N3
Big Koniuji Island AK U.S.A. 148 H5
Big Lake l. Canada 151 H1
Big Lake AK U.S.A. 149 J3
Big Lake U.S.A. 161 C6
Bignona Senegal 120 B3
Big Pine U.S.A. 158 D3
Big Pine Peak U.S.A. 158 D4
Big Raccoon r. U.S.A. 164 B4
Big Rapids U.S.A. 164 C2
Big River Canada 151 J4
Big Sable Point U.S.A. 164 B1
Big Salmon r. Y.T. Canada 149 N3
Big Salmon (abandoned) Y.T. Canada 149 N3
Big Sand Lake Canada 151 L3
Big Sandy r. U.S.A. 156 F4
Big Sandy Lake Canada 151 J4
Big Smokey Valley U.S.A. 158 E2
Big South Fork National River and Recreation Area park U.S.A. 164 C5
Big Spring U.S.A. 161 C5
Big Stone Canada 151 I5
Big Stone Gap U.S.A. 164 D5
Bigstone Lake Canada 151 M4
Big Timber U.S.A. 156 F3
Big Trout Lake Canada 151 N4
Big Trout Lake l. Canada 151 N4
Big Valley Canada 151 H4
Big Water U.S.A. 159 H3
Bihać Bos.-Herz. 68 F2
Bihar state India 105 F4
Bihariganj India 105 F4
Bihar Sharif India 105 F4
Bihor, Vârful mt. Romania 69 J1
Bihoro Japan 90 G4
Bijagós, Arquipélago dos is Guinea-Bissau 120 B3
Bijainagar India 104 C4
Bijapur India 106 B2
Bījār Iran 110 B3
Bijbehara India 104 C2
Bijeljina Bos.-Herz. 69 H2
Bijelo Polje Montenegro 69 H3
Bijeraghogarh India 104 E5
Bijiang China see Zhiziluo
Bijie China 96 E3
Bijji India 106 D2
Bijnor India 104 D3
Bijnore India see Bijnor
Bijnot Pak. 111 H4
Bijrān well Saudi Arabia 110 C5
Bijrān, Khashm hill Saudi Arabia 110 C5
Bikampur India 104 C4
Bikaner India 104 C3
Bikhūyeh Iran 110 D5
Bikin Rus. Fed. 90 D3
Bikin r. Rus. Fed. 90 D3
Bikini atoll Marshall Is 186 H5
Bikori Sudan 108 D7
Bikoro Dem. Rep. Congo 122 B4

Bikou China 96 E1
Bikramganj India 105 F4
Bilaa Point Mindanao Phil. 82 D4
Bilād Banī Bū 'Alī Oman 109 I5
Bilaigarh India 106 D1
Bilangbilangan i. Indon. 85 G2
Bilara India 104 C4
Bilaspur Chhattisgarh India 105 E5
Bilaspur Hima. Prad. India 104 D3
Biläsuvar Azer. 113 H3
Bila Tserkva Ukr. 53 F6
Bilauktaung Range mts Myanmar/Thai. 87 B4
Bilbao Spain 67 E2
Bilbays Egypt 112 C5
Bilbeis Egypt see Bilbays
Bilbo Spain see Bilbao
Bil'chir Rus. Fed. 95 G1
Bilecik Turkey 69 M4
Biłgoraj Poland 53 D6
Bilharamulo Tanz. 122 D4
Bilhaur India 104 E4
Bilhorod-Dnistrovs'kyy Ukr. 69 N1
Bili Dem. Rep. Congo 122 C3
Bilibino Rus. Fed. 77 R3
Bilin Myanmar 86 B3
Biliran i. Phil. 82 D4
Bilit Sabah Malaysia 85 G1
Bill U.S.A. 156 G4
Billabalong Australia 135 A6
Billabong Creek r. Australia see Moulamein Creek
Billericay U.K. 59 H7
Billiluna Australia 134 D4
Billingham U.K. 58 F4
Billings U.S.A. 156 F3
Billiton i. Indon. see Belitung
Bill Moores AK U.S.A. 148 G3
Bill of Portland hd U.K. 59 E8
Bill Williams r. U.S.A. 159 F4
Bill Williams Mountain U.S.A. 159 G4
Bilma Niger 120 E3
Bilo r. Rus. Fed. see Belaya
Biloela Australia 136 E5
Bilohirs'k Ukr. 112 D1
Bilohir"ya Ukr. 53 E6
Biloku Guyana 177 G3
Biloli India 106 C2
Bilovods'k Ukr. 53 H6
Biloxi U.S.A. 161 F6
Bilpa Morea Claypan salt flat Australia 136 B5
Bilston U.K. 60 F5
Biltine Chad 121 F3
Bilto Norway 54 L2
Bilugyun Island Myanmar 86 B3
Bilungala Sulawesi Indon. 83 B2
Bilwascarma Nicaragua 166 [inset] J6
Bilyayivka Ukr. 69 N1
Bilzen Belgium 62 F4
Bima Sumbawa Indon. 85 G5
Bima, Teluk b. Sumbawa Indon. 85 G5
Bimberi, Mount Australia 138 D5
Bimbo 121 E4
Bimini Islands Bahamas 163 E7
Bimlipatam India 106 D2
Bināb Iran 110 C2
Bina-Etawa India 104 D4
Binaija, Gunung mt. Seram Indon. 83 D3
Binalbagan Negros Phil. 82 C4
Bīnālūd, Kūh-e mts Iran 110 E2
Binatang Sarawak Malaysia 85 E2
Binboğa Daği mt. Turkey 112 E3
Bincheng Shandong China see Binzhou
Bincheng Shandong China 95 I4
Binchuan China 96 D3
Bindebango Australia 138 C1
Binder Mongolia 95 G1
Bindle Australia 138 D1
Bindu Dem. Rep. Congo 123 B4
Bindura Zimbabwe 123 D5
Binefar Spain 67 G3
Binga Zimbabwe 123 C5
Binga, Monte mt. Moz. 123 D5
Bingara Australia 138 E2
Bingaram i. India 106 B4
Bing Bong Australia 136 B2
Bingcaowan Gansu China 94 E4
Bingen am Rhein Germany 63 H5
Bingham U.S.A. 165 K1
Binghamton U.S.A. 165 H2
Bingmei China see Congjiang
Bingöl Turkey 113 F3
Bingol Dağı mt. Turkey 113 F3
Bingxi China see Yushan
Bingzhongluo China 96 C2
Binh Gia Vietnam 86 D2
Binicuil Negros Phil. 82 C4
Binika India 105 E5
Binjai Sumatera Indon. 84 B2
Bin Mürkhan well U.A.E. 110 D5
Binnaway Australia 138 D3
Binongko i. Indon. 83 C4
Binpur India 105 F5
Bintan i. Indon. 84 D2
Bintang, Bukit mts Malaysia 84 C1
Bint Jbeil Lebanon see Bent Jbaïl
Bintuan Phil. 82 C3
Bintuhan Sumatera Indon. 84 C4
Bintulu Sarawak Malaysia 85 F2
Binubusan Luzon Phil. 82 C3
Binxian Heilong. China 90 B3
Binxian Shaanxi China 95 G5
Binxian Shandong China see Bincheng
Binya Australia 138 C5
Binyang China 97 F4
Bin-Yauri Nigeria 120 D3
Binzhou Guangxi China see Binyang
Binzhou Heilong. China see Binxian
Binzhou Shandong China 95 I4
Bioco i. Equat. Guinea 120 D4
Biograd na Moru Croatia 68 F3
Bioko i. Equat. Guinea see Bioco
Biokovo mts Croatia 68 G3
Bi Qu r. Qinghai China 99 F6
Biquinhas Brazil 179 B2
Bir India see Bid
Bira Rus. Fed. 90 D2
Bi'r Abū Jady oasis Syria 107 D1
Bīrag, Kūh-e mts Iran 111 F5
Birāk Libya 121 E2
Birakan Rus. Fed. 90 C2
Bi'r al 'Abd Egypt 107 A4
Bi'r al Ḥalbā well Syria 107 D2
Bi'r al Jifjāfah well Egypt 107 A4
Bi'r al Khamsah well Egypt 112 B5
Bi'r al Māliḥah well Egypt 107 A5
Bi'r al Mulūsi Iraq 113 F4
Bi'r al Munbaṭiḥ well Syria 107 D2
Bi'r al Qaṭrānī well Egypt 112 B5
Bi'r al Ubbayiḍ well Egypt 112 B6
Birandozero Rus. Fed. 52 H3
Bi'r an Nuṣf well Egypt see Bi'r an Nuṣṣ
Bi'r an Nuṣṣ well Egypt 112 B5
Bir Anzarane W. Sahara 120 B2
Birao Cent. Afr. Rep. 122 C2
Bi'r ar Rābiyah well Egypt 112 B5
Birata Turkm. 111 F1
Biratar Bulak spring China 98 E4
Biratnagar Nepal 105 F4
Bi'r aṭ Ṭarfāwī well Libya 112 B5
Bi'r Başīrī well Syria 107 C2
Bi'r Bayḍā' well Egypt 107 B4
Bi'r Baylī well Egypt 112 B5
Bîr Beiḍa well Egypt see Bi'r Bayḍā'
Bi'r Buṭaymān Syria 113 E3
Birch r. Canada 151 H3
Birch Creek AK U.S.A. 149 K2
Birch Creek r. AK U.S.A. 149 K2
Birches AK U.S.A. 148 I2
Birch Hills Canada 151 J4
Birch Island Canada 150 G5
Birch Lake N.W.T. Canada 150 G2
Birch Lake Ont. Canada 151 M5
Birch Lake Sask. Canada 151 I4
Birch Mountains Canada 150 H3
Birch River U.S.A. 164 E4
Birch Run U.S.A. 164 D2
Bircot Eth. 122 E3
Birdaard Neth. see Burdaard
Bîr Dignâsh well Egypt see Bi'r Diqnāsh
Bi'r Diqnāsh well Egypt 112 B5
Bird Island N. Mariana Is see Farallon de Medinilla
Birdseye U.S.A. 159 H2
Birdsville Australia 137 B5
Birecik Turkey 112 E3
Bîr el 'Abd Egypt see Bi'r al 'Abd
Bir el Arbi well Alg. 67 I6
Bîr el Istabl well Egypt see Bi'r Iṣṭabl
Bîr el Khamsa well Egypt see Bi'r al Khamsah
Bîr el Nuṣṣ well Egypt see Bi'r an Nuṣṣ
Bîr el Obeiyiḍ well Egypt see Bi'r al Ubbayiḍ
Bîr el Qaṭrâni well Egypt see Bi'r al Qaṭrānī
Bîr el Râbia well Egypt see Bi'r ar Rābiyah
Birendranagar Nepal see Surkhet
Bir en Natrûn well Sudan 108 C6
Bireun Sumatera Indon. 84 B1
Bi'r Fāḍil well Saudi Arabia 110 C6
Bi'r Fajr well Saudi Arabia 112 E5
Bi'r Fu'ād well Egypt 112 B5
Bîr Gifgâfa well Egypt see Bi'r al Jifjāfah
Bi'r Ḥajal well Syria 107 D2
Birhan mt. Eth. 122 D2
Bi'r Ḥasanah well Egypt 107 A4
Bi'r Ḥayzān well Saudi Arabia 112 E6
Biri i. Phil. 82 D3
Bi'r Ibn Hirmās Saudi Arabia see Al Bi'r
Bir Ibn Juhayyim Saudi Arabia 110 C6
Birigüi Brazil 179 A3
Bīrīn Syria 107 C2
Bi'r Iṣṭabl well Egypt 112 B5
Bīrjand Iran 110 E3
Bi'r Jubnī well Libya 112 B5
Birkát Hamad well Iraq 113 G5
Birkenfeld Germany 63 H5
Birkenhead U.K. 58 D5
Birkirkara Malta 68 F7
Birksgate Range hills Australia 135 E6
Bîrlad Romania see Bârlad
Bi'r Lahfān well Egypt 107 A4
Birlik Kazakh. 102 D3
Birlik Zhambylskaya Oblast' Kazakh. 98 A3
Birmal reg. Afgh. 111 H3
Birmingham U.K. 59 F6
Birmingham U.S.A. 163 C5
Bîr Mogreïn Mauritania 120 B2
Bi'r Muḥaymid al Wazwaz well Syria 107 D2
Bi'r Nāḥid oasis Egypt 112 C5
Birnin-Gwari Nigeria 120 D3
Birnin-Kebbi Nigeria 120 D3
Birnin Konni Niger 120 D3
Birobidzhan Rus. Fed. 90 D2
Birong Palawan Phil. 82 B4
Bi'r Qaṣīr as Sirr well Egypt 112 B5
Birr Ireland 61 E4
Bi'r Rawḍ Sālim well Egypt 107 A4
Birrie r. Australia 138 C2
Birrindudu Australia 134 E4
Bîr Rôḍ Sâlim well Egypt see Bi'r Rawḍ Sālim
Birsay U.K. 60 F1
Bi'r Shalatayn Egypt 108 E5
Bîr Shalatein Egypt see Bi'r Shalatayn
Birsk Rus. Fed. 51 R4
Birstall U.K. 59 F6
Birstein Germany 63 J4
Bir Ṭalḥah well Saudi Arabia 110 B6
Birthday Mountain hill Australia 136 C2
Birtle Canada 151 K5
Biru Xizang China 99 F7
Birur India 106 B3
Bi'r Usaylīlah well Saudi Arabia 110 B6
Biržai Lith. 55 N8
Bisa India 86 A1
Bisa i. Maluku Indon. 83 C3
Bisai Japan 92 C3
Bisalpur India 104 D3
Bisau India 104 C3
Bisbee U.S.A. 157 F7
Biscay, Bay of sea France/Spain 66 B4
Biscay Abyssal Plain sea feature N. Atlantic Ocean 184 H3
Biscayne National Park U.S.A. 163 D7
Biscoe Islands Antarctica 188 L2
Biscotasi Lake Canada 152 E5
Biscotasing Canada 152 E5
Bisezhai China 96 D4
Bishan China 96 E2
Bishbek Kyrg. see Bishkek
Bishenpur India see Bishnupur
▶Bishkek Kyrg. 102 D3
Capital of Kyrgyzstan.
Bishnath India 96 B3
Bishnupur Manipur India 105 H4
Bishnupur W. Bengal India 105 F5
Bishop U.S.A. 158 D3
Bishop Auckland U.K. 58 F4
Bishop Lake Canada 150 G1
Bishop's Stortford U.K. 59 H7
Bishopville U.S.A. 163 D5
Bishrī, Jabal hills Syria 107 D2
Bishui Heilong. China 90 A1
Bishui Henan China see Biyang
Biskra Alg. 64 F5
Bislig Mindanao Phil. 82 D4
Bislig Bay Mindanao Phil. 82 D4
▶Bismarck U.S.A. 160 C2
Capital of North Dakota.
Bismarck Archipelago is P.N.G. 81 L7
Bismarck Range mts P.N.G. 81 K7
Bismarck Sea P.N.G. 81 L7
Bismark (Altmark) Germany 63 L2
Bismil Turkey 113 F3
Bismo Norway 54 F6
Bison U.S.A. 160 C2
Bīsotūn Iran 110 B3
Bispgården Sweden 54 J5
Bispingen Germany 63 K1
Bissa, Djebel mt. Alg. 67 G5
Bissamcuttak India 106 D2
▶Bissau Guinea-Bissau 120 B3
Capital of Guinea-Bissau.
Bissaula Nigeria 120 E4
Bissett Canada 151 M5
Bistcho Lake Canada 150 G3
Bistriţa Romania 69 K1
Bistriţa r. Romania 69 L1
Bisucay i. Phil. 82 C4
Bitburg Germany 62 G5
Bitche France 63 H5
Bithur India 104 E4
Bithynia reg. Turkey 69 M4
Bitkine Chad 121 E3
Bitlis Turkey 113 F3
Bitola Macedonia 69 I4
Bitolj Macedonia see Bitola
Bitonto Italy 68 G4
Bitrān, Jabal hill Saudi Arabia 110 B6
Bitra Par reef India 106 B4
Bitter Creek r. U.S.A. 159 I2
Bitterfeld Germany 63 M3
Bitterfontein S. Africa 124 D6
Bitter Lakes Egypt 112 D5
Bitterroot r. U.S.A. 156 E3
Bitterroot Range mts U.S.A. 156 E3
Bitterwater U.S.A. 158 C3
Bittkau Germany 63 L2
Bitung Sulawesi Indon. 83 C2
Biu Nigeria 120 E3
Biwa-ko l. Japan 92 B3
Biwa-ko Kokutei-kōen park Japan 92 C3
Biwmaris U.K. see Beaumaris
Biyang China 97 G1
Bīye K'obē Eth. 122 E2
Biysk Rus. Fed. 88 F2
Bizana S. Africa 125 I6
Bizerta Tunisia see Bizerte
Bizerte Tunisia 68 C6
Bīzhanābād Iran 110 E5
▶Bjargtangar hd Iceland 54 [inset]
Most westerly point of Europe.
Bjästa Sweden 54 K5
Bjelovar Croatia 68 G2
Bjerkvik Norway 54 J2
Bjerringbro Denmark 55 F8
Bjørgan Norway 54 G5
Björkliden Sweden 54 K2
Björklinge Sweden 55 J6
Bjorli Norway 54 F5
Björna Sweden 54 K5
Björneborg Fin. see Pori
▶Bjørnøya i. Arctic Ocean 76 C2
Part of Norway.
Bjurholm Sweden 54 K5
Bla Mali 120 C3
Black r. Man. Canada 151 L5
Black r. Ont. Canada 152 E4
Black r. Canada/U.S.A. 149 K2
Black AK U.S.A. 148 F3
Black r. AR U.S.A. 161 F5
Black r. AR U.S.A. 161 F5
Black r. AZ U.S.A. 159 H5
Black r. Vietnam 86 D2
Blackadder Water r. U.K. 60 G5
Blackall Australia 136 D5
Blackbear r. Canada 151 N4
Black Birch Lake Canada 151 J3
Black Bourton U.K. 59 F7
Blackbull Australia 136 C3
Blackburn U.K. 58 E5
Blackburn, Mount AK U.S.A. 149 L3
Blackbutt Australia 138 F1
Black Butte mt. U.S.A. 158 B2
Black Butte Lake U.S.A. 158 B2
Black Canyon gorge U.S.A. 159 F4
Black Canyon of the Gunnison National Park U.S.A. 159 J2
Black Combe hill U.K. 58 D4
Black Creek watercourse U.S.A. 159 I4
Black Donald Lake Canada 165 G1
Blackdown Tableland National Park Australia 136 E4
Blackduck U.S.A. 160 E2
Blackfalds Canada 150 H4
Blackfoot U.S.A. 156 E4
Black Foot r. U.S.A. 156 E3
Black Forest mts Germany 57 L7
Black Hill hill U.K. 58 F5
Black Hills SD U.S.A. 154 G3
Black Hills SD U.S.A. 156 G3
Black Island Canada 151 L5
Black Lake Canada 151 J3
Black Lake l. Canada 151 J3
Black Lake l. U.S.A. 164 C1
Black Mesa mt. U.S.A. 159 I5
Black Mesa ridge U.S.A. 159 H3
Black Mountain Pak. 111 I3
Black Mountain hill U.K. 59 D7
Black Mountain AK U.S.A. 148 G1
Black Mountain CA U.S.A. 158 E4
Black Mountain KY U.S.A. 164 D5
Black Mountain NM U.S.A. 159 I5
Black Mountains hills U.K. 59 D7
Black Mountains U.S.A. 159 F4
Black Nossob watercourse Namibia 124 D2
Black Pagoda India see Konarka
Blackpool U.K. 58 D5
Black Range mts U.S.A. 159 I5
Black Rapids AK U.S.A. 149 K3
Black River MI U.S.A. 164 D1
Black River NY U.S.A. 165 H1
Black River Falls U.S.A. 160 F2
Black Rock hill Jordan see 'Unāb, Jabal al
Black Rock Desert U.S.A. 156 D4
Blacksburg U.S.A. 164 E5
Black Sea Asia/Europe 53 H8
Blacks Fork r. U.S.A. 156 F4
Blackshear U.S.A. 163 D6
Blacksod Bay Ireland 61 B3
Black Springs U.S.A. 158 D2
Blackstairs Mountains hills Ireland 61 F5
Blackstone r. Y.T. Canada 149 M2
Blackstone U.S.A. 165 F5
Black Sugarloaf mt. Australia 138 E3
Black Tickle Canada 153 L3
Blackville Australia 138 E3
Blackwater Australia 136 E4
Blackwater Ireland 61 F5
Blackwater r. Ireland 61 E5
Blackwater r. Ireland/U.K. 61 F3
Blackwater watercourse U.S.A. 161 C5
Blackwater Lake N.W.T. Canada 149 Q3
Blackwater Reservoir U.K. 60 E4
Blackwood r. Australia 135 A8
Blackwood National Park Australia 136 D4
Bladensburg National Park Australia 136 C4
Blaenavon U.K. 59 D7
Blagodarnoye Kazakh. 98 C3
Blagodarnyy Rus. Fed. 113 F1
Blagoevgrad Bulg. 69 J3
Blagoveshchensk Amurskaya Oblast' Rus. Fed. 90 B2
Blagoveshchensk Respublika Bashkortostan Rus. Fed. 51 R4
Blaikiston, Mount Canada 150 H5
Blaine Lake Canada 151 J4
Blair U.S.A. 160 D3
Blair Athol Australia 136 D4
Blair Atholl U.K. 60 F4
Blairgowrie U.K. 60 F4
Blairsden U.S.A. 158 C2
Blairsville U.S.A. 163 D5
Blakang Mati, Pulau i. Sing. see Sentosa
Blakely U.S.A. 163 C6
Blakeney U.K. 59 I6
Blambangan, Semenanjung pen. Indon. 85 F5
▶Blanc, Mont mt. France/Italy 66 H4
5th highest mountain in Europe.
Blanca, Bahía b. Arg. 178 D5
Blanca, Sierra mt. U.S.A. 157 G6
Blanca Peak U.S.A. 157 G5
Blanche, Lake salt flat S.A. Australia 137 B6
Blanche, Lake salt flat W.A. Australia 134 C5
Blanchester U.S.A. 164 D4
Blanc Nez, Cap c. France 62 B4
Blanco r. Bol. 176 F6
Blanco U.S.A. 159 J3
Blanco, Cabo c. Costa Rica 166 [inset] I7
Blanco, Cape U.S.A. 156 B4
Blanc-Sablon Canada 153 K4
Bland r. Australia 138 C4
Bland U.S.A. 164 E5
Blanda r. Iceland 54 [inset]
Blandford Forum U.K. 59 E8
Blanding U.S.A. 159 I3
Blanes Spain 67 H3
Blangah, Telok Sing. 87 [inset]
Blangkejeren Sumatera Indon. 84 B2
Blangpidie Sumatera Indon. 84 B2
Blankenberge Belgium 62 D3
Blankenheim Germany 62 G4
Blanquilla, Isla i. Venez. 176 F1
Blansko Czech Rep. 57 P6
Blantyre Malawi 123 D5
Blarney Ireland 61 D6
Blau Sulawesi Indon. 83 B2
Blaufelden Germany 63 J5
Blåviksjön Sweden 54 K4
Blaye France 66 D4
Blayney Australia 138 D4
Blaze, Point Australia 134 E3
Bleckede Germany 63 K1
Blega Jawa Indon. 85 F4
Bleilochtalsperre resr Germany 63 L4
Blenheim Canada 164 E2
Blenheim N.Z. 139 D5
Blenheim Palace tourist site U.K. 59 F7
Blerick Neth. 62 G3
Blessington Lakes Ireland 61 F4
Bletchley U.K. 59 G6
Blida Alg. 67 H5
Blies r. Germany 63 H5
Bligh Water b. Fiji 133 H3
Blind River Canada 152 E5
Bliss U.S.A. 156 E4
Blissfield U.S.A. 164 D3
Blitar Jawa Indon. 85 F5
Blitta Togo 120 D4
Blocher U.S.A. 164 C4
Block Island U.S.A. 165 J3
Block Island Sound sea chan. U.S.A. 165 J3
Bloemfontein S. Africa 125 H5
Bloemhof S. Africa 125 G4
Bloemhof Dam S. Africa 125 G4
Bloemhof Dam Nature Reserve S. Africa 125 G4
Blomberg Germany 63 J3
Blönduós Iceland 54 [inset]
Blongas Lombok Indon. 85 G5
Bloods Range mts Australia 135 E6
Bloodsworth Island U.S.A. 165 G4
Bloodvein r. Canada 151 L5
Bloody r. N.W.T. Canada 149 Q2
Bloody Foreland pt Ireland 61 D2
Bloomer U.S.A. 160 F2
Bloomfield Canada 165 G2
Bloomfield IA U.S.A. 160 E3
Bloomfield IN U.S.A. 164 B4
Bloomfield MO U.S.A. 161 F4
Bloomfield NM U.S.A. 159 J3
Blooming Prairie U.S.A. 160 E3
Bloomington IL U.S.A. 160 F3
Bloomington IN U.S.A. 164 B4
Bloomington MN U.S.A. 160 E2
Bloomsburg U.S.A. 165 G3
Blora Jawa Indon. 85 E4
Blossburg U.S.A. 165 G3
Blosseville Kyst coastal area Greenland 147 P3
Blouberg S. Africa 125 I2
Blouberg Nature Reserve S. Africa 125 I2
Blountstown U.S.A. 163 C6
Blountville U.S.A. 164 D5
Blow r. Y.T. Canada 149 M1
Bloxham U.K. 59 F6
Blue r. B.C. Canada 149 O4
Blue watercourse U.S.A. 159 I5
Blue Bell Knoll mt. U.S.A. 159 H2
Blueberry r. Canada 150 F3
Blue Creek r. Mex. see Azul
Blue Diamond U.S.A. 159 F3
Blue Earth U.S.A. 160 E3
Bluefield VA U.S.A. 162 D4
Bluefield WV U.S.A. 164 E5
Bluefields Nicaragua 166 [inset] J6
Blue Hills Turks and Caicos Is 163 F8
Blue Knob hill U.S.A. 165 F3
Blue Mesa Reservoir U.S.A. 159 J2
Blue Mountain hill Canada 153 K4
Blue Mountain India 105 H5
Blue Mountain Lake U.S.A. 165 H2
Blue Mountain Pass Lesotho 125 H5
Blue Mountains Australia 138 D4
Blue Mountains U.S.A. 156 D3
Blue Mountains National Park Australia 138 E4
Blue Nile r. Eth./Sudan 108 D6
also known as Ābay Wenz (Ethiopia), Bahr el Azraq (Sudan)
Bluenose Lake Nunavut Canada 149 R1
Blue Ridge GA U.S.A. 163 C5
Blue Ridge VA U.S.A. 164 F5
Blue Ridge mts U.S.A. 164 E5
Blue Stack hill Ireland 61 D3
Blue Stack Mts hills Ireland 61 D3
Bluestone Lake U.S.A. 164 E5
Bluewater U.S.A. 159 J4
Bluff N.Z. 139 B8
Bluff U.S.A. 159 I3
Bluffdale U.S.A. 159 H1
Bluff Island H.K. China 97 [inset]
Bluff Knoll mt. Australia 135 B8
Bluffton IN U.S.A. 164 C3
Bluffton OH U.S.A. 164 D3
Blumenau Brazil 179 A4
Blustry Mountain Canada 156 C2
Blyde River Canyon Nature Reserve S. Africa 125 J3
Blying Sound sea channel AK U.S.A. 149 J4
Blyth Canada 164 E2
Blyth England U.K. 58 F3
Blyth England U.K. 58 F5
Blythe U.S.A. 159 F5
Blytheville U.S.A. 161 F5
Bø Norway 55 F7
Bo Sierra Leone 120 B4
Boac Phil. 82 C3
Boaco Nicaragua 166 [inset] I6
Boa Esperança Brazil 179 B3
Bo'ai Henan China 95 H5
Bo'ai Yunnan China 96 E4
Boali Cent. Afr. Rep. 122 B3
Boalsert Neth. see Bolsward
Boane Moz. 125 K4
Boano i. Maluku Indon. 83 C3
Boano, Selat sea chan. Maluku Indon. 83 C3
Boa Nova Brazil 179 C1
Boardman U.S.A. 164 E3
Boatlaname Botswana 125 G2
Boa Viagem Brazil 177 K5
Boa Vista Brazil 176 F3
Boa Vista i. Cape Verde 120 [inset]
Bobadah Australia 138 C4
Bobai China 97 F4
Bobaomby, Tanjona c. Madag. 123 E5
Bobbili India 106 D2
Bobcaygeon Canada 165 F1
Bobo-Dioulasso Burkina Faso 120 C3
Bobon Samar Phil. 82 D3
Bobotov Kuk mt. Montenegro see Durmitor
Bobriki Rus. Fed. see Novomoskovsk
Bobrinets Ukr. see Bobrynets'
Bobrov Rus. Fed. 53 I6
Bobrovitsa Ukr. see Bobrovytsya
Bobrovytsya Ukr. 53 F6
Bobruysk Belarus see Babruysk
Bobrynets' Ukr. 53 G6
Bobs Lake Canada 165 G1
Bobuk Sudan 108 D7
Bobures Venez. 176 D2
Boby mt. Madag. 123 E6
Boca del Río Mex. 167 F5
Boca de Macareo Venez. 176 F2
Boca do Acre Brazil 176 E5
Boca do Jari Brazil 177 H4
Bocaiúva Brazil 179 C2
Bocaranga Cent. Afr. Rep. 122 B3
Boca Raton U.S.A. 163 D7
Bocas del Toro Panama 166 [inset] J7
Bocas del Toro, Archipiélago de is Panama 166 [inset] J7
Bochnia Poland 57 R6
Bocholt Germany 62 G3
Bochum Germany 63 H3
Bochum S. Africa see Senwabarwana
Bockenem Germany 63 K2
Bocoio Angola 123 B5
Bocoyna Mex. 166 D3
Boda Cent. Afr. Rep. 122 B3
Bodalla Australia 138 E6
Bodallin Australia 135 B7
Bodaybo Rus. Fed. 77 M4
Boddam U.K. 60 H3
Bode r. Germany 63 L3
Bodega Head hd U.S.A. 158 B2
Bodélé reg. Chad 121 E3
Boden Sweden 54 L4
Bodenham U.K. 59 E6
Bodensee l. Germany/Switz. see Constance, Lake
Bodenteich Germany 63 K2
Bodenwerder Germany 63 J3
Bodie (abandoned) U.S.A. 158 D2
Bodinayakkanur India 106 C4
Bodmin U.K. 59 C8
Bodmin Moor moorland U.K. 59 C8
Bodø Norway 54 I3
Bodonchiyn Gol watercourse Mongolia 94 C2
Bodoquena Brazil 177 G7
Bodoquena, Serra da hills Brazil 178 E2
Bodrum Turkey 69 L6
Bodträskfors Sweden 54 L3
Boechout Belgium 62 E3
Boende Dem. Rep. Congo 121 F5
Bo Epinang Sulawesi Indon. 83 B4
Boerne U.S.A. 161 D6
Boeuf r. U.S.A. 161 F6
Boffa Guinea 120 B3
Bogalay Myanmar see Bogale
Bogale Myanmar 86 A3
Bogale r. Myanmar 86 A4
Bogalusa U.S.A. 161 F6
Bogan r. Australia 138 C2
Bogandé Burkina Faso 120 C3
Bogan Gate Australia 138 C4
Bogani Nani Wartabone, Taman Nasional nat. park Indon. 83 B2
Boğazlıyan Turkey 112 D3
Bogcang Zangbo r. Xizang China 99 D7
Bogd Mongolia 94 E2
Bogd Övörhangay Mongolia 94 E2
Bogda Feng mt. Xinjiang China 98 E4
Bogda Shan mts China 94 B3
Boggabilla Australia 138 E2
Boggabri Australia 138 E3
Boggeragh Mts hills Ireland 61 C5
Boghar Alg. 67 H6
Boghari Alg. see Ksar el Boukhari
Bognor Regis U.K. 59 G8
Bogo Cebu Phil. 82 D4
Bogodukhov Ukr. see Bohodukhiv
Bog of Allen reg. Ireland 61 E4
Bogong, Mount Australia 138 C6
Bogopol' Rus. Fed. 90 D3
Bogor Jawa Indon. 84 D4
Bogoroditsk Rus. Fed. 53 H5
Bogorodsk Rus. Fed. 52 I4
Bogorodskoye Khabarovskiy Kray Rus. Fed. 90 F1
Bogorodskoye Kirovskaya Oblast' Rus. Fed. 52 K4
Bogoslof Island AK U.S.A. 148 E5
▶Bogotá Col. 176 D3
Capital of Colombia. 4th most populous city in South America.
Bogotol Rus. Fed. 76 J4
Bogoyavlenskoye Rus. Fed. see Pervomayskiy
Bogra Bangl. 105 G4
Boguchany Rus. Fed. 77 K4
Boguchar Rus. Fed. 53 I6
Bogué Mauritania 120 B3
Boh r. Indon. 85 F2
Bo Hai g. China 95 I4
Bohai Haixia sea chan. China 95 J4
Bohain-en-Vermandois France 62 D5
Bohai Wan b. China 78 D4
Bohemian Forest mts Germany see Böhmer Wald
Böhlen Germany 63 M3
Bohlokong S. Africa 125 I5
Böhme r. Germany 63 J2
Böhmer Wald mts Germany 63 M5
Bohmte Germany 63 I2
Bohodukhiv Ukr. 53 G6
Bohol i. Phil. 82 D4
Bohol Sea Phil. 82 D4
Bohol Strait Phil. 82 C4
Bohu Xinjiang China 98 D4
Boiaçu Brazil 176 F4
Boichoko S. Africa 124 F5
Boigu Island Australia 81 K8
Boikhutso S. Africa 125 H4
Boileau, Cape Australia 134 C4
Boim Brazil 177 G4
Boipeba, Ilha i. Brazil 179 D1
Bois r. Brazil 179 A2
Bois, Lac des l. N.W.T. Canada 149 P2
Bois Blanc Island U.S.A. 162 C2
▶Boise U.S.A. 156 D4
Capital of Idaho.
Boise City U.S.A. 161 C4
Boissevain Canada 151 K5
Boitumelong S. Africa 125 G4
Boizenburg Germany 63 K1
Bojd Iran 110 E3
Bojeador, Cape Luzon Phil. 82 C2
Bojnūrd Iran 110 E2
Bojonegoro Jawa Indon. 85 E4
Bojong Jawa Indon. 84 D4
Bokaak atoll Marshall Is see Taongi
Bokajan India 105 H4
Bokaro India 105 F5
Bokaro Reservoir India 105 F5
Bokat Sulawesi Indon. 83 B2
Bokatola Dem. Rep. Congo 122 B4
Boké Guinea 120 B3
Boke Kazakh. 98 C2
Bokele Dem. Rep. Congo 122 C4
Bokhara r. Australia 138 C2
Bo Kheo Cambodia see Bâ Kêv
Boknafjorden sea chan. Norway 55 D7
Bokoko Dem. Rep. Congo 122 C3
Bökönbaev Kyrg. 98 B4
Bokoro Chad 121 E3
Bokovskaya Rus. Fed. 53 I6
Bokspits S. Africa 124 E4
Boktor Rus. Fed. 90 E2
Bokurdak Turkm. 110 E2
Bol Chad 121 E3
Bolaang Sulawesi Indon. 83 B3
Bolaiti Dem. Rep. Congo 121 F5
Bolama Guinea-Bissau 120 B3
Bolangir India 106 D1
Bolan Pass Pak. 111 G4
Bolavén, Phouphiang plat. Laos 86 D4
Bolbec France 66 E2
Bole Xinjiang China 98 C3
Bole Ghana 120 C4
Boleko Dem. Rep. Congo 122 B4
Bolen Rus. Fed. 90 D2
Bolgar Rus. Fed. 53 K5
Bolgatanga Ghana 120 C3
Bolgrad Ukr. see Bolhrad
Bolhrad Ukr. 69 M2
Boli China 90 C3
Bolia Dem. Rep. Congo 122 B4
Boliden Sweden 54 L4
Bolinao Luzon Phil. 82 B2
Bolingbrook U.S.A. 164 A3
Bolintin-Vale Romania 69 K2
Bolívar Peru 176 C5
Bolivar NY U.S.A. 165 F2
Bolivar TN U.S.A. 161 F5

Bolívar, Pico mt. Venez. 176 D2
Bolivia Cuba 163 E8

▶Bolivia country S. America 176 E7
5th largest country in South America.

Bolkhov Rus. Fed. 53 H5
Bollène France 66 G4
Bollnäs Sweden 55 J6
Bollon Australia 138 C2
Bollstabruk Sweden 54 J5
Bolmen l. Sweden 55 H8
Bolo Panay Phil. 82 C4
Bolobo Dem. Rep. Congo 122 B4
Bolod Islands Phil. 82 C5
Bologna Italy 68 D2
Bolognesi Peru 176 D5
Bologoye Rus. Fed. 52 G4
Bolokanang S. Africa 125 G5
Bolomba Dem. Rep. Congo 122 B3
Bolon' Rus. Fed. see Achan
Bolong Mindanao Phil. 82 C5
Bolpur India 105 F5
Bolsena, Lago di l. Italy 68 D3
Bol'shakovo Rus. Fed. 55 L9
Bol'shaya Chernigovka Rus. Fed. 51 Q5
Bol'shaya Glushitsa Rus. Fed. 53 K5
Bol'shaya Imandra, Ozero l. Rus. Fed. 54 R3
Bol'shaya Martinovka Rus. Fed. 53 I7
Bol'shaya Osinovaya r. Rus. Fed. 148 A2
Bol'shaya Tsarevshchina Rus. Fed. see Volzhskiy
Bol'shaya Vladimirovka Kazakh. 98 B2
Bol'shenarymskoye Kazakh. 102 F2
Bol'shevik, Ostrov i. Rus. Fed. 77 L2
Bol'shezemel'skaya Tundra lowland Rus. Fed. 52 L2
Bol'shiye Barsuki, Peski des. Kazakh. 102 A2
Bol'shiye Chirki Rus. Fed. 52 J3
Bol'shiye Kozly Rus. Fed. 52 H2
Bol'shoy Aksu Kazakh. 98 B4
Bol'shoy Begichev, Ostrov i. Rus. Fed. 189 E2
Bol'shoy Bukon' Kazakh. 98 C2
Bol'shoye Murashkino Rus. Fed. 52 J5
Bol'shoy Irgiz r. Rus. Fed. 53 J6
Bol'shoy Kamen' Rus. Fed. 90 D4
Bol'shoy Kavkaz mts Asia/Europe see Caucasus
Bol'shoy Kundysh r. Rus. Fed. 52 J4
Bol'shoy Lyakhovskiy, Ostrov i. Rus. Fed. 77 P2
Bol'shoy Tokmak Kyrg. see Tokmok
Bol'shoy Tokmak Ukr. see Tokmak
Bolsón de Mapimí des. Mex. 166 D3
Bolsward Neth. 62 F1
Bolton Canada 164 F2
Bolton Mindanao Phil. 82 D5
Bolton U.K. 58 E5
Bolu Turkey 69 N4
Boluntay Qinghai China 99 F5
Boluo China 97 G4
Bolus Head hd Ireland 61 B6
Bolvadin Turkey 69 N5
Bolzano Italy 68 D1
Boma Dem. Rep. Congo 123 B4
Bomaderry Australia 138 E5
Bombala Australia 138 D6
Bombay India see Mumbai
Bombay Beach U.S.A. 159 F5
Bomberai, Semenanjung pen. Indon. 81 I7
Bömbögör Mongolia 94 D2
Bomboma Dem. Rep. Congo 122 B3
Bom Comércio Brazil 176 E5
Bomdila India 105 H4
Bomi Xizang China 99 F7
Bomili Dem. Rep. Congo 122 C3
Bom Jardim Brazil 179 D1
Bom Jardim de Goiás Brazil 179 A2
Bom Jesus Brazil 179 A5
Bom Jesus da Gurgueia, Serra do hills Brazil 177 J5
Bom Jesus da Lapa Brazil 179 C1
Bom Jesus do Norte Brazil 179 C3
Bømlo i. Norway 55 D7
Bomokandi r. Dem. Rep. Congo 122 C3
Bom Retiro Brazil 179 A4
Bom Sucesso Brazil 179 B3
Bon, Cap c. Tunisia 68 D6
Bon, Ko i. Thai. 87 B5
Bona Alg. see Annaba
Bona, Mount AK U.S.A. 149 L3
Bonāb Iran 110 B2
Bon Air U.S.A. 165 G5
Bonaire i. Caribbean Sea 169 K6
Bonandolok Sumatera Indon. 84 B2
Bonanza Nicaragua 166 [inset] I6
Bonanza Peak U.S.A. 156 C2
Bonaparte Archipelago is Australia 134 D3
Bonaparte Lake Canada 150 F5
Bonar Bridge U.K. 60 E3
Bonasila Dome hill AK U.S.A. 148 G3
Bonavista Canada 153 L4
Bonavista Bay Canada 153 L4
Bonchester Bridge U.K. 60 G5
Bondo Dem. Rep. Congo 122 C3
Bondoc Peninsula Luzon Phil. 82 C3
Bondokodi Sumba Indon. 83 A5
Bondoukou Côte d'Ivoire 120 C4
Bondowoso Jawa Indon. 85 F4
Bonduel U.S.A. 164 A1
Bondyuzhskiy Rus. Fed. see Mendeleyevsk
Bône Alg. see Annaba
Bone Sulawesi Indon. 83 B4
Bone, Teluk b. Indon. 83 B4
Bonelipu Sulawesi Indon. 83 B4
Bönen Germany 63 H3
Bonerate Sulawesi Indon. 83 B4
Bonerate i. Indon. 83 B4
Bonerate, Kepulauan is Indon. 83 B4
Bo'ness U.K. 60 F4
Bonete, Cerro mt. Arg. 178 C3
Bonga Eth. 122 D3
Bongabong Mindoro Phil. 82 C3
Bongaigaon India 105 G4
Bongandanga Dem. Rep. Congo 122 C3
Bongani S. Africa 124 F5
Bongao Phil. 82 B5
Bongba Xizang China 99 C6
Bong Co l. China 99 E7
Bongka r. Indon. 83 B3
Bongo i. Phil. 82 D5
Bongo, Massif des mts Cent. Afr. Rep. 122 C3
Bongo, Serra do mts Angola 123 B4
Bongolava mts Madag. 123 E5
Bongor Chad 121 E3
Bông Sơn Vietnam 87 E4
Bonham U.S.A. 161 D5
Bonheiden Belgium 62 E3
Boni Mali 120 C3
Bonifacio Corsica France 66 I6
Bonifacio, Bocche di strait France/Italy see Bonifacio, Strait of
Bonifacio, Bouches de strait France/Italy see Bonifacio, Strait of
Bonifacio, Strait of France/Italy 66 I6

▶Bonin Islands Japan 91 F8
Part of Japan.

Bonjol Sumatera Indon. 84 C2

▶Bonn Germany 62 H4
Former capital of Germany.

Bonna Germany see Bonn
Bonnåsjøen Norway 54 I3
Bonners Ferry U.S.A. 156 D2
Bonnet, Lac du resr Canada 151 M5
Bonnet Plume r. Y.T. Canada 149 N2
Bonneville France 66 H3
Bonneville Salt Flats U.S.A. 159 G1
Bonnières-sur-Seine France 62 B5
Bonnie Rock Australia 135 B7
Bonnieville U.S.A. 164 C5
Bonnyrigg U.K. 60 F5
Bonnyville Canada 151 I4
Bonobono Palawan Phil. 82 B4
Bononia Italy see Bologna
Bonorva Sardinia Italy 68 C4
Bonshaw Australia 138 E2
Bontang Kalimantan Indon. 85 G2
Bontebok National Park S. Africa 124 E8
Bonthe Sierra Leone 120 B4
Bontoc Luzon Phil. 82 C2
Bontomatane Sulawesi Indon. 83 B4
Bontosunggu Sulawesi Indon. 83 A4
Bontrug S. Africa 125 G7
Bonvouloir Islands P.N.G. 136 E1
Bonwapitse Botswana 125 H2
Boo, Kepulauan is Papua Indon. 83 D3
Book Cliffs ridge U.S.A. 159 I2
Booker U.S.A. 161 C4
Boolba Australia 138 D2
Booligal Australia 138 B4
Boomer U.S.A. 164 E4
Boomi Australia 138 D2
Boon U.S.A. 164 C1
Boonah Australia 138 F1
Boone CO U.S.A. 157 G5
Boone IA U.S.A. 160 E3
Boone NC U.S.A. 162 D4
Boone Lake U.S.A. 164 D5
Boones Mill U.S.A. 164 F5
Booneville AR U.S.A. 161 E5
Booneville KY U.S.A. 164 D5
Booneville MS U.S.A. 161 F5
Böön Tsagaan Nuur salt l. Mongolia 94 D2
Boonville CA U.S.A. 158 B2
Boonville IN U.S.A. 164 B4
Boonville MO U.S.A. 160 E4
Boonville NY U.S.A. 165 H2
Boorabin National Park Australia 135 C7
Boorama Somalia 122 E3
Booroorban Australia 138 B5
Boorowa Australia 138 D5
Boort Australia 138 A6
Boothby, Cape Antarctica 188 D2
Boothia, Gulf of Canada 147 J3
Boothia Peninsula Canada 147 I2
Bootle U.K. 58 E5
Booué Gabon 122 B4
Boppard Germany 63 H4
Boqê Xizang China 99 E7
Boqueirão, Serra do hills Brazil 177 J6
Boquilla, Presa de la resr Mex. 166 D3
Boquillas del Carmen Mex. 166 E2
Bor Czech Rep. 63 M5
Bor Rus. Fed. 52 J4
Bor Serbia 69 J2
Bor Sudan 121 G4
Bor Turkey 112 D3
Boraha, Nosy i. Madag. 123 F5
Borah Peak U.S.A. 156 E3
Borai India 106 D1
Borakalalo Nature Reserve S. Africa 125 H3
Boran Kazakh. see Buran
Boraphet, Bung l. Thai. 86 C4
Boraphet, Nong l. Thai. see Boraphet, Bung
Borås Sweden 55 H8
Borasambar India 106 D1
Borāzjān Iran 110 C4
Borba Brazil 177 G4
Borba China 96 C1
Borbon Cebu Phil. 82 D4
Borborema, Planalto da plat. Brazil 177 K5
Borchen Germany 63 I3
Borçka Turkey 113 F2
Bor Dağı mt. Turkey 69 M6
Bordeaux France 66 D4
Borden Island Canada 147 G2
Borden Peninsula Canada 147 J2
Border Ranges National Park Australia 138 F2
Borðeyri Iceland 54 [inset]
Bordj Bou Arréridj Alg. 67 I5
Bordj Bounaama Alg. 67 G6
Bordj Flye Ste-Marie Alg. 120 C2
Bordj Messaouda Alg. 64 F5
Bordj Mokhtar Alg. 120 D2
Bordj Omar Driss Alg. see Bordj Omer Driss
Bordj Omer Driss Alg. 120 D2
Bordu Kyrg. 98 A4
Boreas Abyssal Plain sea feature Arctic Ocean 189 H1
Borel r. Canada 153 H2
Borgå Fin. see Porvoo
Borgarfjörður Iceland 54 [inset]
Borgarnes Iceland 54 [inset]
Børgefjell Nasjonalpark nat. park Norway 54 H4
Borger U.S.A. 161 C5
Borgholm Sweden 55 J8
Borgne, Lake b. U.S.A. 161 F6
Borgo San Lorenzo Italy 68 D3
Bori India 106 C1
Bori r. India 104 C5
Borikhan Laos 86 C3
Borislav Ukr. see Boryslav
Borisoglebsk Rus. Fed. 53 I6
Borisov Belarus see Barysaw
Borisovka Rus. Fed. 53 H6
Borispol' Ukr. see Boryspil'
Bo River Post Sudan 121 F4
Borja Peru 176 C4
Borken Germany 62 G3
Borkenes Norway 54 J2
Borkovskaya Rus. Fed. 52 K2
Borkum Germany 62 G1
Borkum i. Germany 62 G1
Borlänge Sweden 55 I6
Borlaug Norway 55 E6
Borlu Turkey 69 M5
Borna Germany 63 M3
Born-Berge hill Germany 63 K3
Borndiep sea chan. Neth. 62 F1
Borne Neth. 62 G2

▶Borneo i. Asia 80 E6
Largest island in Asia, and 3rd in the world.

Bornholm county Denmark 189 H3
Bornholm i. Denmark 55 I9
Bornova Turkey 69 L5
Borobudur tourist site Indon. 85 E4
Borodino Rus. Fed. 76 J3
Borodinskoye Rus. Fed. 55 P6
Borogontsy Rus. Fed. 77 O3
Borohoro Shan mts China 98 C3
Boroko Sulawesi Indon. 83 B2
Borok-Sulezhskiy Rus. Fed. 52 H4
Boromo Burkina Faso 120 C3
Boron U.S.A. 158 E4
Borondi India 106 D2
Borongan Samar Phil. 82 D4
Boroughbridge U.K. 58 F4
Borovichi Rus. Fed. 52 G4
Borovoy Kirovskaya Oblast' Rus. Fed. 52 K4
Borovoy Respublika Kareliya Rus. Fed. 54 R4
Borovoy Respublika Komi Rus. Fed. 52 L3
Borpeta India see Barpeta
Borrisokane Ireland 61 D5
Borroloola Australia 136 B3
Børsa Norway 54 G5
Borşa Romania 53 E7
Borsakelmas sho'rxogi salt marsh Uzbek. 113 J2
Borshchiv Ukr. 53 E6
Borshchovochnyy Khrebet mts Rus. Fed. 95 G1
Bortala Xinjiang China see Bole
Bortala He r. China 98 C3
Borton U.S.A. 164 B4
Bor-Üdzüür Mongolia see Altay
Borūjen Iran 110 C4
Borūjerd Iran 110 C3
Bor Ul Shan mts China 94 D3
Borun Iran 110 E3
Borve U.K. 60 C3
Boryslav Ukr. 53 D6
Boryspil' Ukr. 53 F6
Borzna Ukr. 53 G6
Borzya Rus. Fed. 95 I1
Borzya r. Rus. Fed. 95 H1
Bosaga Kazakh. 98 A3
Bosanska Dubica Bos.-Herz. 68 G2
Bosanska Gradiška Bos.-Herz. 68 G2
Bosanska Krupa Bos.-Herz. 68 G2
Bosanski Novi Bos.-Herz. 68 G2
Bosansko Grahovo Bos.-Herz. 68 G2
Boscawen Island Tonga see Niuatoputopu
Bose China 96 E4
Bosencheve, Parque Nacional nat. park Mex. 167 E5
Boshof S. Africa 125 G5
Boshruyeh Iran 110 E3
Bosna i Hercegovina country Europe see Bosnia-Herzegovina
Bosna Saray Bos.-Herz. see Sarajevo
Bosnia-Herzegovina country Europe 68 G2
Bosobogolo Pan salt pan Botswana 124 F3
Bosobolo Dem. Rep. Congo 122 B3
Bōsō-hantō pen. Japan 93 G3
Bosporus strait Turkey 69 M4
Bossaga Turkm. see Basaga
Bossangoa Cent. Afr. Rep. 122 B3
Bossembélé Cent. Afr. Rep. 122 B3
Bossier City U.S.A. 161 E5
Bossiesvlei Namibia 124 C3
Bossut, Cape Australia 134 C4
Bostan Xinjiang China 99 D5
Bostān Iran 110 B4
Bostan Pak. 111 G4
Bostāneh, Ra's-e pt Iran 110 D5
Bosten Hu l. China 98 D4
Boston U.K. 59 G6

▶Boston U.S.A. 165 J2
Capital of Massachusetts.

Boston Mountains U.S.A. 161 E5
Boston Spa U.K. 58 F5
Boswell U.S.A. 164 B3
Botad India 104 B5
Botany Bay Australia 138 E4
Botev mt. Bulg. 69 K3
Botevgrad Bulg. 69 J3
Bothaville S. Africa 125 H4
Bothnia, Gulf of Fin./Sweden 55 K6
Bothwell Canada 164 E2
Botkins U.S.A. 164 C3
Botlikh Rus. Fed. 113 G2
Botoşani Romania 53 E7
Botou Hebei China 95 I4
Botshabelo S. Africa 125 H5
Botswana country Africa 123 C6
Botte Donato, Monte mt. Italy 68 G5
Bottesford U.K. 58 G5
Bottrop Germany 62 G3
Botucatu Brazil 179 A3
Botuporã Brazil 179 C1
Botwood Canada 153 L4
Bouaflé Côte d'Ivoire 120 C4
Bouaké Côte d'Ivoire 120 C4
Bouar Cent. Afr. Rep. 122 B3
Bouârfa Morocco 64 D5
Bouba Ndjida, Parc National de nat. park Cameroon 121 E4
Bouca Cent. Afr. Rep. 122 B3
Boucaut Bay Australia 134 F3
Bouchain France 62 D4
Bouctouche Canada 153 I5
Boudh India 106 E1
Bougaa Alg. 67 I5
Bougainville, Cape Australia 134 D3
Bougainville, Selat sea chan. Papua Indon. 83 D3
Bougainville Island P.N.G. 132 F2
Bougainville Reef Australia 136 D2
Boughessa Mali 120 D3
Bougie Alg. see Bejaïa
Bougouni Mali 120 C3
Bougtob Alg. 64 E5
Bouillon Belgium 62 F5
Bouira Alg. 67 H5
Bou Izakarn Morocco 120 C2
Boujdour W. Sahara 120 B2
Boulder Australia 135 C7
Boulder CO U.S.A. 156 G4
Boulder MT U.S.A. 156 E3
Boulder UT U.S.A. 159 H3
Boulder Canyon gorge U.S.A. 159 F3
Boulder City U.S.A. 159 F4
Boulevard U.S.A. 158 E5
Boulia Australia 136 B4
Boulogne France see Boulogne-sur-Mer
Boulogne-Billancourt France 62 C6
Boulogne-sur-Mer France 62 B4
Boumerdes Alg. 67 H5
Bouna Côte d'Ivoire 120 C4
Bou Naceur, Jbel mt. Morocco 64 D5
Boû Nâga Mauritania 120 B3
Boundary AK U.S.A. 149 L2
Boundary Mountains U.S.A. 165 J1
Boundary Peak U.S.A. 158 D3
Boundiali Côte d'Ivoire 120 C4
Boundji Congo 122 B4
Boun Nua Laos 86 C2
Bountiful U.S.A. 159 H1
Bounty Islands N.Z. 133 H6
Bounty Trough sea feature S. Pacific Ocean 186 H9
Bourail New Caledonia 133 G4
Bourbon reg. France see Bourbonnais
Bourbon terr. Indian Ocean see Réunion
Bourbon U.S.A. 164 B3
Bourbonnais reg. France 66 F3
Bourem Mali 120 C3
Bouressa Mali see Boughessa
Bourg-Achard France 59 H9
Bourganeuf France 66 E4
Bourg-en-Bresse France 66 G3
Bourges France 66 F3
Bourget Canada 165 H1
Bourgogne reg. France see Burgundy
Bourgogne, Canal de France 66 G3
Bourke Australia 138 B3
Bourne U.K. 59 G6
Bournemouth U.K. 59 F8
Bourtoutou Chad 121 F3
Bou Saâda Alg. 67 I6
Bou Salem Tunisia 68 C6
Bouse U.S.A. 159 F5
Bouse Wash watercourse U.S.A. 159 F4
Boussu Belgium 62 D4
Boutilimit Mauritania 120 B3
Bouvet Island terr. S. Atlantic Ocean see Bouvetøya

▶Bouvetøya terr. S. Atlantic Ocean 184 I9
Dependency of Norway.

Bouy France 62 E5
Bova Marina Italy 68 F6
Bovenden Germany 63 J3
Boven Kapuas Mountains Indon./Malaysia see Kapuas Hulu, Pegunungan
Bow r. Alta Canada 151 I5
Bow r. Alta Canada 156 F2
Bowa China see Muli
Bowbells U.S.A. 160 C1
Bowden U.S.A. 164 F4
Bowditch atoll Tokelau see Fakaofo
Bowen Australia 136 E4
Bowen, Mount Australia 138 D6
Bowenville Australia 138 E1
Bowers Ridge sea feature Bering Sea 186 H2
Bowie Australia 136 D4
Bowie AZ U.S.A. 159 I5
Bowie TX U.S.A. 161 D5
Bow Island Canada 151 I5
Bowling Green KY U.S.A. 164 B5
Bowling Green MO U.S.A. 160 F4
Bowling Green OH U.S.A. 164 D3
Bowling Green VA U.S.A. 165 G4
Bowling Green Bay National Park Australia 136 D3
Bowman U.S.A. 160 C2
Bowman, Mount Canada 156 C2
Bowman Island Antarctica 188 F2
Bowman Peninsula Antarctica 188 L2
Bowmore U.K. 60 C5
Bowo Xizang China see Bomi
Bowral Australia 138 E5
Bowser Lake B.C. Canada 149 O4
Boxberg Germany 63 J5
Box Elder U.S.A. 160 C2
Box Elder r. U.S.A. 160 C2
Boxing Shandong China 95 I4
Boxtel Neth. 62 F3
Boyabat Turkey 112 D2
Boyana tourist site Bulg. 69 J3
Boyang China 97 H2
Boyd r. Australia 138 F2
Boyd Lagoon salt flat Australia 135 D6
Boyd Lake Canada 151 K2
Boydton U.S.A. 165 F5
Boyers U.S.A. 164 F3
Boykins U.S.A. 165 G5
Boyle Canada 151 H4
Boyle Ireland 61 D4
Boyne r. Ireland 61 F4
Boyne City U.S.A. 164 C1
Boysen Reservoir U.S.A. 156 F4
Boysun Uzbek. 111 G2
Boyuibe Bol. 176 F8
Böyük Qafqaz mts Asia/Europe see Caucasus
Bozanbay Kazakh. 98 C2

▶Bozcaada i. Turkey 69 L5
Most westerly point of Asia.

Bozdağ mt. Turkey 69 L5
Bozdağ mt. Turkey 107 C1
Boz Dağları mts Turkey 69 L5
Bozdoğan Turkey 69 M6
Bozeat U.K. 59 G6
Bozeman U.S.A. 156 F3
Bozen Italy see Bolzano
Bozhou China 97 G1
Bozoum Cent. Afr. Rep. 122 B3
Bozova Turkey 112 E3
Bozqūsh, Kūh-e mts Iran 110 B2
Bozüyük Turkey 69 N5
Bozyazı Turkey 107 A1
Bra Italy 68 B2
Brač i. Croatia 68 G3
Bracadale U.K. 60 C3
Bracadale, Loch b. U.K. 60 C3
Bracara Port. see Braga
Bracciano, Lago di l. Italy 68 E3
Bracebridge Canada 164 F1
Bräcke Sweden 54 I5
Brackenheim Germany 63 J5
Brackettville U.S.A. 161 C6
Bracknell U.K. 59 G7
Bradano r. Italy 68 G4
Bradenton U.S.A. 163 D7

▶Brades Montserrat 169 L5
Temporary capital of Montserrat. Plymouth was abandoned in 1997 owing to volcanic activity.

Bradford Canada 164 F1
Bradford U.K. 58 F5
Bradford OH U.S.A. 164 C3
Bradford PA U.S.A. 165 F3
Bradley U.S.A. 164 B3
Brady U.S.A. 161 D6
Brady Glacier U.S.A. 150 B3
Brae U.K. 60 [inset]
Braemar U.K. 60 F3
Braga Port. 67 B3
Bragado Arg. 178 D5
Bragança Brazil 177 I4
Bragança Port. 67 C3
Bragança Paulista Brazil 179 B3
Brahin Belarus 53 F6
Brahlstorf Germany 63 K1
Brahmanbaria Bangl. 105 G5
Brahmapur India 106 E2
Brahmaputra r. Asia 105 H4
also known as Dihang (India), Siang (India) or Yarlung Zangbo (China)
Brahmaur India 104 D2
Brăila Romania 69 L2
Braine France 62 D5
Braine-le-Comte Belgium 62 E4
Brainerd U.S.A. 160 E2
Braintree U.K. 59 H7
Braithwaite Point Australia 134 F2
Brak r. S. Africa 125 I2
Brake (Unterweser) Germany 63 I1
Brakel Belgium 62 D4
Brakel Germany 63 J3
Brakwater Namibia 124 C2
Bramfield Australia 135 F8
Bramming Denmark 55 F9
Brämön i. Sweden 54 J5
Brampton Canada 164 F2
Brampton England U.K. 58 E4
Brampton England U.K. 59 I6
Bramsche Germany 63 I2
Bramwell Australia 136 C2
Brancaster U.K. 59 H6
Branch Canada 153 L5
Branco r. Brazil 176 F4
Brandberg mt. Namibia 123 B6
Brandbu Norway 55 G6
Brande Denmark 55 F9
Brandenburg Germany 63 M2
Brandenburg land Germany 63 N2
Brandenburg U.S.A. 164 B5
Brandfort S. Africa 125 H5
Brandis Germany 63 N3
Brandon Canada 151 L5
Brandon U.K. 59 H6
Brandon MS U.S.A. 161 F5
Brandon VT U.S.A. 165 I2
Brandon Head hd Ireland 61 B5
Brandon Mountain hill Ireland 61 B5
Brandvlei S. Africa 124 E6
Braniewo Poland 57 Q3
Bransfield Strait Antarctica 188 L2
Branson U.S.A. 161 C4
Brantas r. Indon. 85 F4
Brantford Canada 164 E2
Branxton Australia 138 E4
Bras d'Or Lake Canada 153 J5
Brasil country S. America see Brazil
Brasil, Planalto do plat. Brazil see Brazilian Highlands
Brasileia Brazil 176 E6

▶Brasília Brazil 179 B1
Capital of Brazil.

Brasília de Minas Brazil 179 B2
Braslav Belarus see Braslaw
Braslaw Belarus 55 O9
Braşov Romania 69 K2
Brassey, Banjaran mts Malaysia 85 G1
Brassey, Mount Australia 135 F5
Brassey Range hills Australia 135 C6
Brasstown Bald mt. U.S.A. 163 D5

▶Bratislava Slovakia 57 P6
Capital of Slovakia.

Bratsk Rus. Fed. 88 I1
Bratskoye Vodokhranilishche resr Rus. Fed. 88 I1
Brattleboro U.S.A. 165 I2
Braulio Carrillo, Parque Nacional nat. park Costa Rica 166 [inset] J7
Braunau am Inn Austria 57 N6
Braunfels Germany 63 I4
Braunlage Germany 63 K3
Braunsbedra Germany 63 L3
Braunschweig Germany 63 K2
Brava i. Cape Verde 120 [inset]
Brave U.S.A. 164 E4
Bråviken inlet Sweden 55 J7
Bravo, Cerro mt. Bol. 176 F7
Bravo del Norte, Río r. Mex./U.S.A. see Rio Grande
Brawley U.S.A. 159 F5
Bray Ireland 61 F4
Bray Island Canada 147 K3
Brazeau r. Canada 150 H4
Brazeau, Mount Canada 150 G4

▶Brazil country S. America 177 G5
Largest and most populous country in South America, and 5th largest and 5th most populous in the world.

Brazil U.S.A. 164 B4
Brazil Basin sea feature S. Atlantic Ocean 184 G7
Brazilian Highlands plat. Brazil 179 B2
Brazos r. U.S.A. 161 E6

▶Brazzaville Congo 123 B4
Capital of Congo.

Brčko Bos.-Herz. 68 H2
Bré Ireland see Bray
Breadalbane Australia 136 B4
Breaksea Sound inlet N.Z. 139 A7
Bream Bay N.Z. 139 E2
Brebes Jawa Indon. 85 E4
Brebes, Tanjung pt Indon. 85 E4
Brechfa U.K. 59 C7
Brechin U.K. 60 G4
Brecht Belgium 62 E3
Breckenridge MI U.S.A. 164 C2
Breckenridge MN U.S.A. 160 D2
Breckenridge TX U.S.A. 161 D5
Břeclav Czech Rep. 57 P6
Brecon U.K. 59 D7
Brecon Beacons reg. U.K. 59 D7
Brecon Beacons National Park U.K. 59 D7
Breda Neth. 62 E3
Bredasdorp S. Africa 124 E8
Bredbo Australia 138 D5
Breddin Germany 63 M2
Bredevoort Neth. 62 G3
Bredviken Sweden 54 I3
Bree Belgium 62 F3
Breed U.S.A. 164 A1
Bregenz Austria 57 L7
Breiðafjörður b. Iceland 54 [inset]
Breiðdalsvík Iceland 54 [inset]
Breidenbach Germany 63 I4
Breien U.S.A. 160 C2
Breitenfelde Germany 63 K1
Breitengüßbach Germany 63 K5
Breiter Luzinsee l. Germany 63 N1
Breivikbotn Norway 54 M1
Breizh reg. France see Brittany
Brejo Velho Brazil 179 C1
Brekstad Norway 54 F5
Bremen Germany 63 I1
Bremen land Germany 63 I1
Bremen IN U.S.A. 164 B3
Bremen OH U.S.A. 164 D4
Bremer Bay Australia 135 B8
Bremerhaven Germany 63 I1
Bremer Range hills Australia 135 C8
Bremersdorp Swaziland see Manzini
Bremervörde Germany 63 J1
Bremm Germany 62 H4
Bremner r. AK U.S.A. 149 K3
Brenham U.S.A. 161 D6
Brenna Norway 54 H4
Brennero, Passo di pass Austria/Italy see Brenner Pass
Brenner Pass Austria/Italy 68 D1
Brennerpaß pass Austria/Italy see Brenner Pass
Brentwood U.K. 59 H7
Brescia Italy 68 D2
Breslau Poland see Wrocław
Bresle r. France 62 B4
Brésolles, Lac l. Canada 153 H3
Bressanone Italy 68 D1
Bressay i. U.K. 60 [inset]
Bressuire France 66 D3
Brest Belarus 55 M10
Brest France 66 B2
Brest-Litovsk Belarus see Brest
Bretagne reg. France see Brittany
Breteuil France 62 C5
Brétigny-sur-Orge France 62 C6
Breton Canada 150 H4
Breton Sound b. U.S.A. 161 F6
Brett, Cape N.Z. 139 E2
Bretten Germany 63 I5
Bretton U.K. 58 E5
Breueh, Pulau i. Indon. 84 A1
Brevard U.S.A. 163 D5
Breves Brazil 177 H4
Brevig Mission AK U.S.A. 148 F2
Brewarrina Australia 138 C2
Brewer U.S.A. 162 G2
Brewster NE U.S.A. 160 D3
Brewster OH U.S.A. 164 E3
Brewster, Kap c. Greenland see Kangikajik
Brewster, Lake imp. l. Australia 138 B4
Brewton U.S.A. 163 C6
Breyten S. Africa 125 I4
Breytovo Rus. Fed. 52 H4
Brezhnev Rus. Fed. see Naberezhnyye Chelny
Brezno Slovakia 57 Q6
Brezovo Bulg. 69 K3
Brezovo Polje hill Croatia 68 G2
Bria Cent. Afr. Rep. 122 C3
Briançon France 66 H4
Brian Head mt. U.S.A. 159 G3
Bribbaree Australia 138 C5
Bribie Island Australia 138 F1
Briceni Moldova 53 E6
Brichany Moldova see Briceni
Brichen' Moldova see Briceni
Bridgend U.K. 59 D7
Bridge of Orchy U.K. 60 E4
Bridgeport CA U.S.A. 158 D2
Bridgeport CT U.S.A. 165 I3
Bridgeport IL U.S.A. 164 B4
Bridgeport NE U.S.A. 160 C3
Bridgeport TX U.S.A. 167 F1
Bridger Peak U.S.A. 156 G4
Bridgeton U.S.A. 165 H4
Bridgetown Australia 135 B8

▶Bridgetown Barbados 169 M6
Capital of Barbados.

Bridgetown Canada 153 I5
Bridgeville U.S.A. 165 H4
Bridgewater Canada 153 I5
Bridgewater U.S.A. 165 H2
Bridgnorth U.K. 59 E6
Bridgton U.S.A. 165 J1
Bridgwater U.K. 59 D7

Bridgwater Bay U.K. 59 D7
Bridlington U.K. 58 G4
Bridlington Bay U.K. 58 G4
Bridport Australia 137 [inset]
Bridport U.K. 59 E8
Brie reg. France 66 F2
Brie-Comte-Robert France 62 C6
Brieg Poland see Brzeg
Briery Knob mt. U.S.A. 164 E4
Brig Switz. 66 H3
Brigg U.K. 58 G5
Brigham City U.S.A. 156 E4
Brightlingsea U.K. 59 I7
Brighton Canada 165 G1
Brighton U.K. 59 G8
Brighton CO U.S.A. 156 G5
Brighton MI U.S.A. 164 D2
Brighton NY U.S.A. 165 G2
Brighton WV U.S.A. 164 D4
Brignoles France 66 H5
Brikama Gambia 120 B3
Brillion U.S.A. 164 A1
Brilon Germany 63 I3
Brindisi Italy 68 G4
Brinkley U.S.A. 161 F5
Brion, Île i. Canada 153 J5
Brioude France 66 F4
Brisay Canada 153 H3

▶Brisbane Australia 138 F1
Capital of Queensland. 3rd most populous city in Oceania.

Brisbane Ranges National Park Australia 138 B6
Bristol U.K. 59 E7
Bristol CT U.S.A. 165 I3
Bristol FL U.S.A. 163 C6
Bristol NH U.S.A. 165 J2
Bristol RI U.S.A. 165 J3
Bristol TN U.S.A. 164 D5
Bristol VT U.S.A. 165 I1
Bristol Bay AK U.S.A. 148 G4
Bristol Channel est. U.K. 59 C7
Bristol Lake U.S.A. 159 F4
Britannia Island New Caledonia see Maré
British Antarctic Territory reg. Antarctica 188 L2
British Columbia prov. Canada 150 F5
British Empire Range mts Canada 147 J1
British Guiana country S. America see Guyana

▶British Indian Ocean Territory terr. Indian Ocean 185 M6
United Kingdom Overseas Territory.

British Isles Europe 56 D3
British Mountains Canada/U.S.A. 149 L1
British Solomon Islands country S. Pacific Ocean see Solomon Islands
Brito Godins Angola see Kiwaba N'zogi
Brits S. Africa 125 H3
Britstown S. Africa 124 F6
Brittany reg. France 66 C2
Britton U.S.A. 160 D2
Brive-la-Gaillarde France 66 E4
Briviesca Spain 67 E2
Brixham U.K. 59 D8
Brixia Italy see Brescia
Brlik Kazakh. see Birlik
Brno Czech Rep. 57 P6
Broach India see Bharuch
Broad r. U.S.A. 163 D5
Broadalbin U.S.A. 165 H2
Broad Arrow Australia 135 C7
Broadback r. Canada 152 F4
Broad Bay U.K. see Tuath, Loch a'
Broadford Australia 138 B6
Broadford Ireland 61 D5
Broadford U.K. 60 D3
Broad Law hill U.K. 60 F5
Broadmere Australia 136 A3
Broad Pass AK U.S.A. 149 J3
Broad Peak China/Pak. 111 J3
Broad Sound sea chan. Australia 136 E4
Broadstairs U.K. 59 I7
Broadus U.S.A. 156 G3
Broadview Canada 151 K5
Broadway U.S.A. 165 F4
Broadwood N.Z. 139 D2
Brochet Canada 151 K3
Brochet, Lac l. Canada 151 K3
Brochet, Lac au l. Canada 153 H4
Brock r. N.W.T. Canada 149 Q1
Brocken mt. Germany 63 K3
Brockman, Mount Australia 134 B5
Brockport NY U.S.A. 165 G2
Brockport PA U.S.A. 165 F3
Brockton U.S.A. 165 J2
Brockville Canada 165 H1
Brockway U.S.A. 165 F3
Brodeur Peninsula Canada 147 J2
Brodhead U.S.A. 164 C5
Brodick U.K. 60 D5
Brodnica Poland 57 Q4
Brody Ukr. 53 E6
Broken Arrow U.S.A. 161 E4
Broken Bay Australia 138 E4
Broken Bow NE U.S.A. 160 D3
Broken Bow OK U.S.A. 161 E5
Brokenhead r. Canada 151 L5
Broken Hill Australia 137 C6
Broken Hill Zambia see Kabwe
Broken Plateau sea feature Indian Ocean 185 O8
Brokopondo Suriname 177 G2
Brokopondo Stuwmeer resr Suriname see Professor van Blommestein Meer
Bromberg Poland see Bydgoszcz
Brome Germany 63 K2
Bromo Tengger Semeru, Taman Nasional nat. park Indon. 85 F4
Bromsgrove U.K. 59 E6
Brønderslev Denmark 55 F8
Brønnøysund Norway 54 H4
Bronson FL U.S.A. 163 D6
Bronson MI U.S.A. 164 C3
Brooke U.K. 59 I6
Brooke's Point Palawan Phil. 82 B4
Brookfield U.S.A. 164 A2
Brookhaven U.S.A. 161 F6
Brookings OR U.S.A. 156 B4
Brookings SD U.S.A. 160 D2
Brookline U.S.A. 165 J2
Brooklyn U.S.A. 164 C2
Brooklyn Park U.S.A. 160 E2
Brookneal U.S.A. 165 F5
Brooks Canada 151 I5
Brooks Brook Y.T. Canada 149 N3
Brooks Mountain hill AK U.S.A. 148 F2
Brooks Range mts AK U.S.A. 149 K1
Brookston U.S.A. 164 B3
Brooksville FL U.S.A. 163 D6
Brooksville KY U.S.A. 164 C4
Brookton Australia 135 B8
Brookville IN U.S.A. 164 C4
Brookville PA U.S.A. 164 F3
Brookville Lake U.S.A. 164 C4
Broom, Loch inlet U.K. 60 D3
Broome Australia 134 C4
Brora U.K. 60 F2
Brora r. U.K. 60 F2
Brösarp Sweden 55 I9
Brosna r. Ireland 61 E4
Brosville U.S.A. 164 F5
Brothers is India 87 A5
Brough U.K. 58 E4
Brough Ness pt U.K. 60 G2
Broughshane U.K. 61 F3
Broughton Island Canada see Qikiqtarjuaq
Broughton Islands Australia 138 F4
Brovary Ukr. 53 F6
Brovinia Australia 137 E5
Brovst Denmark 55 F8
Brown City U.S.A. 164 D2
Brown Deer U.S.A. 164 B2
Browne Range hills Australia 135 D6
Brownfield U.S.A. 161 C5
Browning U.S.A. 156 E2
Brown Mountain U.S.A. 158 E4
Brownstown U.S.A. 164 B4
Brownsville KY U.S.A. 164 B5
Brownsville PA U.S.A. 164 F3
Brownsville TN U.S.A. 161 F5
Brownsville TX U.S.A. 161 D7
Brownwood U.S.A. 161 D6
Brownwood, Lake TX U.S.A. 167 F2
Browse Island Australia 134 C3
Bruay-la-Bussière France 62 C4
Bruce Peninsula Canada 164 E1
Bruce Peninsula National Park Canada 164 E1
Bruce Rock Australia 135 B7
Bruchsal Germany 63 I5
Brück Germany 63 M2
Bruck an der Mur Austria 57 O7
Brue r. U.K. 59 E7
Bruges Belgium see Brugge
Brugge Belgium 62 D3
Brühl Baden-Württemberg Germany 63 I5
Brühl Nordrhein-Westfalen Germany 62 G4
Bruin KY U.S.A. 164 D4
Bruin PA U.S.A. 164 F3
Bruin Point mt. U.S.A. 159 H2
Bruint India 105 I3
Brûk, Wâdi el watercourse Egypt see Burūk, Wādī al
Brukkaros Namibia 124 D3
Brûlé Canada 150 G4
Brûlé, Lac l. Canada 153 J3
Brûly Belgium 62 E5
Brumado Brazil 179 C1
Brumath France 63 H6
Brumunddal Norway 55 G6
Brunau Germany 63 L2
Brundisium Italy see Brindisi
Bruneau U.S.A. 156 E4
Brunei country Asia 85 F1
Brunei Brunei see Bandar Seri Begawan
Brunei Bay Malaysia 85 F1
Brunette Downs Australia 136 A3
Brunflo Sweden 54 I5
Brunico Italy 68 D1
Brünn Czech Rep. see Brno
Brunner, Lake N.Z. 139 C6
Bruno Canada 151 J4
Brunswick Germany see Braunschweig
Brunswick GA U.S.A. 163 D6
Brunswick MD U.S.A. 165 G4
Brunswick ME U.S.A. 165 K2
Brunswick, Península de pen. Chile 178 B8
Brunswick Bay Australia 134 D3
Brunswick Lake Canada 152 E4
Bruntál Czech Rep. 57 P6
Brunt Ice Shelf Antarctica 188 B2
Bruntville S. Africa 125 J5
Bruny Island Australia 137 [inset]
Brusa Turkey see Bursa
Brusenets Rus. Fed. 52 I3
Brushton U.S.A. 165 H1
Brusque Brazil 179 A4
Brussel Belgium see Brussels

▶Brussels Belgium 62 E4
Capital of Belgium.

Bruthen Australia 138 C6
Bruxelles Belgium see Brussels
Bruzual Venez. 176 E2
Bryan OH U.S.A. 164 C3
Bryan TX U.S.A. 161 D6
Bryan, Mount hill Australia 137 B7
Bryan Coast Antarctica 188 L2
Bryansk Rus. Fed. 53 G5
Bryanskoye Rus. Fed. 113 G1
Bryant Pond U.S.A. 165 J1
Bryantsburg U.S.A. 164 C4
Bryce Canyon National Park U.S.A. 159 G3
Bryce Mountain U.S.A. 159 I5
Brynbuga U.K. see Usk
Bryne Norway 55 D7
Bryukhovetskaya Rus. Fed. 53 H7
Brzeg Poland 57 P5
Brześć nad Bugiem Belarus see Brest
Bua r. Malawi 123 D5
Bu'aale Somalia 122 E3
Buala Solomon Is 133 F2
Buang i. Indon. 83 C2
Buatan Sumatera Indon. 84 C2
Bu'ayj well Saudi Arabia 110 C5
Būbiyān, Jazīrat Kuwait 110 C4
Bubuan i. Phil. 82 C5
Bucak Turkey 69 N6
Bucaramanga Col. 176 D2
Bucas Grande i. Phil. 82 D4
Buccaneer Archipelago is Australia 134 C4
Buchanan Liberia 120 B4
Buchanan MI U.S.A. 164 B3
Buchanan VA U.S.A. 164 F5
Buchanan, Lake salt flat Australia 136 D4
Buchanan, Lake TX U.S.A. 167 F2
Buchan Gulf Canada 147 K2

▶Bucharest Romania 69 L2
Capital of Romania.

Büchen Germany 63 K1
Buchen (Odenwald) Germany 63 J5
Buchholz Germany 63 M1
Bucholz in der Nordheide Germany 63 J1
Buchon, Point U.S.A. 158 C4
Buchy France 62 B5
Bucin, Pasul pass Romania 69 K1
Buckambool Mountain hill Australia 138 B3
Bückeburg Germany 63 J2
Bücken Germany 63 J2
Buckeye U.S.A. 159 G5
Buckhannon U.S.A. 164 E4
Buckhaven U.K. 60 F4
Buckhorn Lake Canada 165 F1
Buckie U.K. 60 G3
Buckingham U.K. 59 G6
Buckingham U.S.A. 165 F5
Buckingham Bay Australia 79 F9
Buckland AK U.S.A. 148 G2
Buckland r. AK U.S.A. 148 G2
Buckland Tableland reg. Australia 136 E5
Buckleboo Australia 135 G8
Buckle Island Antarctica 188 H2
Buckley watercourse Australia 136 B4
Buckley Bay Antarctica 188 G2
Bucklin U.S.A. 160 D4
Buckskin Mountains U.S.A. 159 G4
Bucks Mountain U.S.A. 158 C2
Bucksport U.S.A. 153 H5
Bückwitz Germany 63 M2
Bucureşti Romania see Bucharest
Bucyrus U.S.A. 164 D3
Buda-Kashalyova Belarus 53 F5
Budalin Myanmar 86 A2

▶Budapest Hungary 69 H1
Capital of Hungary.

Budaun India 104 D3
Budawang National Park Australia 138 E5
Budda Australia 138 B3
Budd Coast Antarctica 188 F2
Budduso Sardinia Italy 68 C4
Bude U.K. 59 C8
Bude U.S.A. 161 F6
Budennovsk Rus. Fed. 113 G1
Buderim Australia 138 F1
Būding Iran 110 E5
Büdingen Germany 63 J4
Budīyah, Jabal hills Egypt 107 A5
Budongquan Qinghai China 94 C5
Budoni Sardinia Italy 68 C4
Budū, Ḥadabat al plain Saudi Arabia 110 C6
Budū', Sabkhat al salt pan Saudi Arabia 110 C6
Budweis Czech Rep. see České Budějovice
Buenaventura Col. 176 C3
Buenaventura Mex. 166 D2
Buena Vista i. N. Mariana Is see Tinian
Buenavista Mindanao Phil. 82 D4
Buenavista Phil. 82 C3
Buena Vista CO U.S.A. 156 G5
Buena Vista VA U.S.A. 164 F5
Buendia, Embalse de resr Spain 67 E3

▶Buenos Aires Arg. 178 E4
Capital of Argentina. 2nd most populous city in South America.

Buenos Aires Costa Rica 166 [inset] J7
Buenos Aires, Lago l. Arg./Chile 178 B7
Buenos Aires National Wildlife Refuge nature res. AZ U.S.A. 166 C2
Buerarema Brazil 179 D1
Buet r. Canada 153 H1
Búfalo Mex. 166 D3
Buffalo r. Canada 150 H2
Buffalo KY U.S.A. 164 C5
Buffalo MO U.S.A. 160 E4
Buffalo NY U.S.A. 165 F2
Buffalo OK U.S.A. 161 D4
Buffalo SD U.S.A. 160 C2
Buffalo TX U.S.A. 161 D6
Buffalo WY U.S.A. 156 G3
Buffalo Head Hills Canada 150 G3
Buffalo Head Prairie Canada 150 G3
Buffalo Hump mt. U.S.A. 156 E3
Buffalo Lake Alta Canada 151 H4
Buffalo Lake N.W.T. Canada 150 H2
Buffalo Narrows Canada 151 I4
Buffels watercourse S. Africa 124 C5
Buffels Drift S. Africa 125 H2
Buftea Romania 69 K2
Bug r. Poland 57 S5
Buga Col. 176 C3
Buga Mongolia see Dörvöljin
Bugaldie Australia 138 D3
Bugant Mongolia 95 F1
Bugat Mongolia 94 C2
Bugdaýly Turkm. 110 D2
Bugel, Tanjung pt Indon. 85 E4
Buggenhout Belgium 62 E3
Bugojno Bos.-Herz. 68 G2
Bugrino Rus. Fed. 52 K1
Bugsuk i. Phil. 82 B4
Bugt Nei Mongol China 95 J1
Buguey Luzon Phil. 82 C2
Bugul'ma Rus. Fed. 51 Q5
Bugun' Kazakh. 102 B2
Bügür Xinjiang China see Luntai
Buguruslan Rus. Fed. 51 Q5
Bühābād Iran 110 D4
Buḥayrat Dahūk resr. Iraq 113 F3
Buhera Zimbabwe 123 D5
Buh He r. China 94 D4
Buhi Luzon Phil. 82 C3
Bühl Germany 63 I6
Buhuşi Romania 69 L1
Buick Canada 150 F3
Builth Wells U.K. 59 D6
Bui National Park Ghana 120 C4
Buinsk Rus. Fed. 53 K5
Bu'in Zahrā Iran 110 C3
Buir Nur l. Mongolia 95 I2
Buitepos Namibia 124 D2
Bujanovac Serbia 69 I3

▶Bujumbura Burundi 122 C4
Capital of Burundi.

Bukachacha Rus. Fed. 89 L2
Buka Daban mt. Qinghai/Xinjiang China 99 E5
Buka Island P.N.G. 132 F2
Būkān Iran 110 B2
Būkand Iran 110 D4
Bukavu Dem. Rep. Congo 122 C4
Bukhara Buxoro Uzbek. see Buxoro
Bukhoro Uzbek. see Buxoro
Bukhtarminskoye Vodokhranilishche resr Kazakh. 98 D2
Bukide i. Indon. 83 C2
Bukit Baka-Bukit Raya, Taman Nasional nat. park Indon. 85 F3
Bukitlidi Kalimantan Indon. 85 F3
Bukit Timah Sing. 87 [inset]
Bukittinggi Sumatera Indon. 84 C3
Bukkapatnam India 106 C3
Bukoba Tanz. 122 D4
Bükreş Romania see Bucharest
Buku, Tanjung pt Indon. 84 D3
Bukukun Rus. Fed. 95 G1
Būl, Kūh-e mt. Iran 110 D4
Bula Seram Indon. 83 D3
Bula P.N.G. 81 K8
Bülach Switz. 66 I3
Bulag Mongolia see Möngönmorït
Bulagtay Mongolia see Hüder
Bulan i. Indon. 84 C2
Bulan Luzon Phil. 82 C3
Bulan i. Phil. 82 C5
Bulancak Turkey 112 E2
Bulandshahr India 104 D3
Bulanık Turkey 113 F3
Bulava Rus. Fed. 90 F2
Bulawa, Gunung mt. Indon. 83 B2
Bulawayo Zimbabwe 123 C6
Buldan Turkey 69 M5
Buldana India see Buldhana
Buldhana India 106 C1
Buldir Island AK U.S.A. 149 [inset]
Buldur Hima. Prad. India 99 B7
Buleda reg. Pak. 111 F5
Bulembu Swaziland 125 J3
Bulgan Bayan-Ölgiy Mongolia 94 B2
Bulgan Bulgan Mongolia 94 E1
Bulgan Mongolia 95 H1
Bulgan Mongolia 94 B2
Bulgan Hovd Mongolia see Darvi
Bulgan Hövsgöl Mongolia see Tsagaan-Üür
Bulgan Ömnögovĭ Mongolia 94 E2
Bulgan prov. Mongolia 94 E1
Bulgan Gol r. Mongolia 94 B2
Bulgar Rus. Fed. see Bolgar
Bulgaria country Europe 69 K3
Bŭlgariya country Europe see Bulgaria
Buli Halmahera Indon. 83 D2
Buli, Teluk b. Halmahera Indon. 83 D2
Buliluyan, Cape Palawan Phil. 82 B4
Bulkley Ranges mts B.C. Canada 149 O5
Bullawarra, Lake salt flat Australia 138 A1
Bullen r. Canada 151 K1
Bullen AK U.S.A. 149 K1
Buller r. N.Z. 139 C5
Buller, Mount Australia 138 C6
Bullering National Park Australia 136 C3
Bullfinch Australia 135 B7
Bullhead City U.S.A. 159 F4
Bulli Australia 138 E5
Bullion Mountains U.S.A. 158 E4
Bullo r. Australia 134 E3
Bulloo Downs Australia 137 C6
Bulloo Lake salt flat Australia 137 C6
Büllsport Namibia 124 C3
Bully Choop Mountain U.S.A. 158 B1
Bulman Australia 134 F3
Bulman Gorge Australia 134 F3
Bulmer Lake Canada 150 F2
Buloh, Pulau i. Sing. 87 [inset]
Buloke, Lake dry lake Australia 138 A6
Bulolo P.N.G. 81 L8
Bulsar India see Valsad
Bultfontein S. Africa 125 H5
Bulu, Gunung mt. Indon. 85 G2
Buluan Mindanao Phil. 82 D5
Bulubulu Sulawesi Indon. 83 B4
Bulukumba Sulawesi Indon. 83 B4
Bulun Rus. Fed. 77 N2
Bulungu Dem. Rep. Congo 123 C4
Bulung'ur Uzbek. 111 G2
Bumba Dem. Rep. Congo 122 C3
Bümbah Libya 112 A4
Bumbah, Khalīj b. Libya 112 A4
Bumbat Nei Mongol China 94 F3
Bumbat Mongolia see Bayan-Öndör
Bumhkang Myanmar 86 B1
Bumpha Bum mt. Myanmar 86 B1
Buna Dem. Rep. Congo 122 B4
Buna Kenya 122 D3
Bunayyān well Saudi Arabia 110 C6
Bunazi Tanz. 122 D4
Bunbeg Ireland see An Bun Beag
Bunbury Australia 135 A8
Bunclody Ireland 61 F5
Buncrana Ireland 61 E2
Bunda Tanz. 122 D4
Bundaberg Australia 136 F5
Bundaleer Australia 138 C2
Bundarra Australia 138 E3
Bundi India 104 C4
Bundjalung National Park Australia 138 F2
Bundoran Ireland 61 D3
Bunduqiya Sudan 121 G4
Buner reg. Pak. 111 I3
Bunga-dake mt. Japan 92 B3
Bungalaut, Selat sea chan. Indon. 84 B3
Bungay U.K. 59 I6
Bungendore Australia 138 D5
Bunger Hills Antarctica 188 F2
Bungi Sulawesi Indon. 83 B4
Bungku Sulawesi Indon. 83 B3
Bungle Bungle National Park Australia see Purnululu National Park
Bungona'og Xizang China 99 E6
Bungo-suidō sea chan. Japan 91 D6
Bunguran, Kepulauan is Indon. see Natuna, Kepulauan
Bunguran, Pulau i. Indon. see Natuna Besar
Buni, Ci r. Indon. 84 D4
Bunia Dem. Rep. Congo 122 D3
Bunianga Dem. Rep. Congo 122 C4
Buningonia well Australia 135 C7
Bunji Pak. 104 C2
Bunker Group atolls Australia 136 F4
Bunker Hill AK U.S.A. 148 F2
Bunkeya Dem. Rep. Congo 123 C5
Bunkie LA U.S.A. 167 G2
Bunnell U.S.A. 163 D6
Bünsum Xizang China 99 C7
Buntok Kalimantan Indon. 85 F3
Buntokecil Kalimantan Indon. 85 F3
Bunya Mountains National Park Australia 138 E1
Bünyan Turkey 112 D3
Bunyu i. Indon. 85 G2
Buôn Đôn Vietnam 87 D4
Buôn Ma Thuột Vietnam 87 E4
Buorkhaya, Guba b. Rus. Fed. 77 O2
Bup r. China 99 D7
Buqayq Saudi Arabia see Abqaiq
Buqbuq Egypt 112 B5
Bura Kenya 122 D4
Buraan Somalia 122 E2
Buram Sudan 121 F3
Buran Kazakh. 102 G2
Burang Xizang China 99 C7
Buranhaém Brazil 179 C2
Buranhaém r. Brazil 179 D2
Burāq Syria 107 C3
Burauen Leyte Phil. 82 D4
Buray r. India 104 C5
Buraydah Saudi Arabia 108 F4
Burbach Germany 63 I4
Burbank U.S.A. 158 D4
Burcher Australia 138 C4
Burco Somalia 122 E3
Bürd Mongolia 94 E2
Burdaard Neth. 62 F1
Burdalyk Turkm. 111 G2
Burdigala France see Bordeaux
Burdur Turkey 69 N6
Burdur Gölü l. Turkey 69 N6
Burdwan India see Barddhaman
Burē Eth. 122 D2
Bure r. U.K. 59 I6
Bureå Sweden 54 L4
Bureinskiy Khrebet mts Rus. Fed. 90 D2
Bureinskiy Zapovednik nature res. Rus. Fed. 90 D2
Büren Mongolia 94 F2
Bürentsogt Mongolia 95 G2
Bureya r. Rus. Fed. 90 C2
Bureya Range mts Rus. Fed. see Bureinskiy Khrebet
Burford Canada 164 E2
Burgaltay Mongolia see Baruunbüren
Burgas Bulg. 69 L3
Burgaw U.S.A. 163 E5
Burg bei Magdeburg Germany 63 L2
Burgbernheim Germany 63 K5
Burgdorf Germany 63 K2
Burgeo Canada 153 K5
Burgersdorp S. Africa 125 H6
Burgersfort S. Africa 125 J3
Burges, Mount hill Australia 135 C7
Burgess, Mount Y.T. Canada 149 M2
Burgess Hill U.K. 59 G8
Burghaun Germany 63 J4
Burghausen Germany 57 N6
Burghead U.K. 60 F3
Burgh-Haamstede Neth. 62 D3
Burgio, Serra di hill Sicily Italy 68 F6
Burglengenfeld Germany 63 M5
Burgos Mex. 167 F3
Burgos Spain 67 E2
Burgstädt Germany 63 M4
Burgsvik Sweden 55 K8
Burgum Neth. 62 G1
Burgundy reg. France 66 G3
Burhan Budai Shan mts China 94 C5
Burhaniye Turkey 69 L5
Burhanpur India 104 D5
Burhar-Dhanpuri India 105 E5
Burhi Gandak r. India 99 D8
Buri Brazil 179 A3
Buriai Indon. 84 C3
Burias i. Phil. 82 C3
Buriat-Mongol Republic aut. rep. Rus. Fed. see Buryatiya, Respublika
Burica, Punta pt Costa Rica 166 [inset] J7
Buri Gandak r. Nepal 99 C8
Burin Canada 153 L5
Burin Peninsula Canada 153 L5
Buriram Thai. 86 C4
Buritama Brazil 179 A3
Buriti Alegre Brazil 179 A2
Buriti Bravo Brazil 177 J5
Buritirama Brazil 177 J6
Buritis Brazil 179 B1
Burjay Xinjiang China 98 E4
Burj Aziz Khan Pak. 111 G4
Burkan-Suu r. Kyrg. 98 B4
Burke U.S.A. 160 D3
Burke Island Antarctica 188 K2
Burke Pass N.Z. see Burkes Pass
Burkes Pass N.Z. 139 C7
Burkesville U.S.A. 164 C5
Burketown Australia 136 B3
Burkeville U.S.A. 165 F5
Burkina Faso country Africa see Burkina Faso
Burkina Faso country Africa 120 C3
Burk's Falls Canada 152 F5
Burkutty Kazakh. 98 B2
Burley U.S.A. 156 E4
Burlington Canada 164 F2
Burlington CO U.S.A. 160 C4
Burlington IA U.S.A. 160 F3
Burlington KS U.S.A. 160 E4
Burlington KY U.S.A. 164 C4
Burlington VT U.S.A. 165 I1
Burlington WI U.S.A. 164 A2
Burmantovo Rus. Fed. 51 S3
Burnaby Canada 150 F5
Burnet U.S.A. 161 D6
Burney U.S.A. 158 C1
Burney, Monte vol. Chile 178 B8
Burnham U.S.A. 165 G3
Burnie Australia 137 [inset]
Burniston U.K. 58 G4
Burnley U.K. 58 E5
Burns U.S.A. 156 D4
Burnside r. Canada 146 H3
Burnside U.S.A. 164 C5
Burnside, Lake salt flat Australia 135 C6
Burns Junction U.S.A. 156 D4
Burns Lake Canada 150 E4
Burntisland U.K. 60 F4
Burnt Lake Canada see Brûlé, Lac
Burntwood r. Canada 151 L4
Burog Co l. Xizang China 99 D6
Buron r. Canada 153 H2
Burovoy Uzbek. 111 F1
Burqin Xinjiang China 98 D3
Burqin He r. China 98 D3
Burqu' Jordan 107 D3
Burra Australia 137 B7
Burra i. U.K. 60 [inset]
Burravoe U.K. 60 [inset]
Burrel Albania 69 I4
Burrel U.S.A. 158 D3
Burren reg. Ireland 61 C4
Burrendong, Lake Australia 138 D4
Burren Junction Australia 138 D3
Burrewarra Point Australia 138 E5
Burrinjuck Australia 138 D5
Burrinjuck Reservoir Australia 138 D5
Burro, Serranías del mts Mex. 167 E2
Burr Oak Reservoir U.S.A. 164 D4
Burro Creek watercourse U.S.A. 159 G4
Burro Peak U.S.A. 159 I5
Burrowa Pine Mountain National Park Australia 138 C6
Burrow Head hd U.K. 60 E6
Burrows U.S.A. 164 B3
Burrundie Australia 134 E3
Bursa Turkey 69 M4
Bûr Safâga Egypt see Bûr Safājah
Būr Safājah Egypt 108 D4
Bûr Sa'îd Egypt see Port Said
Bûr Sa'îd Egypt see Port Said
Būr Sa'īd governorate Egypt 107 A4
Bûr Sa'îd governorate Egypt see Būr Sa'īd
Bursinskoye Vodokhranilishche resr Rus. Fed. 90 C2
Bürstadt Germany 63 I5
Būr Sudan Sudan see Port Sudan
Burt Lake U.S.A. 162 C2
Burton U.S.A. 164 D2
Burton, Lac l. Canada 152 F3
Burtonport Ireland see Ailt an Chorráin
Burton upon Trent U.K. 59 F6
Burträsk Sweden 54 L4
Burt Well Australia 135 F5
Buru i. Maluku Indon. 83 C3
Burubaytal Kazakh. 98 A3
Burūk, Wādī al watercourse Egypt 107 A4
Burullus, Baḥra el lag. Egypt see Burullus, Lake
Burullus, Buḥayrat al lag. Egypt see Burullus, Lake
Burullus, Lake lag. Egypt 112 C5
Burultokay Xinjiang China see Fuhai
Burūn, Ra's pt Egypt 107 A4
Burundi country Africa 122 C4
Burunniy Rus. Fed. see Tsagan Aman
Bururi Burundi 122 C4
Burwash Landing Y.T. Canada 149 M3
Burwick U.K. 60 G2
Buryatia aut. rep. Rus. Fed. see Buryatiya, Respublika
Buryatiya, Respublika aut. rep. Rus. Fed. 94 E1
Buryatskaya Mongolskaya A.S.S.R. aut. rep. Rus. Fed. see Buryatiya, Respublika
Buryn' Ukr. 53 G6
Bury St Edmunds U.K. 59 H6
Burzil Pass Pak. 104 C2
Busan S. Korea see Pusan
Busan Bay Mindanao Phil. 82 C5
Busanga Dem. Rep. Congo 122 C4
Busby U.S.A. 156 G3
Buseire Syria see Al Buşayrah
Bush r. U.K. 61 F2
Būshehr Iran 110 C4
Bushêngcaka China 105 E2
Bushenyi Uganda 122 D4
Bushire Iran see Būshehr
Bushmills U.K. 61 F2
Bushnell U.S.A. 163 D6
Businga Dem. Rep. Congo 122 C3
Busobuso Maluku Indon. 83 D2
Buşrá ash Shām Syria 107 C3
Busse Rus. Fed. 90 B2
Busselton Australia 135 A8
Bussum Neth. 62 F2
Bustamante Nuevo León Mex. 167 E3
Bustillos, Lago l. Mex. 166 D2
Busto Arsizio Italy 68 C2
Busuanga Phil. 82 B3
Busuanga i. Phil. 82 B3
Buta Dem. Rep. Congo 122 C3
Butare Rwanda 122 C4
Butaritari atoll Kiribati 186 H5
Bute Australia 137 B7
Bute i. U.K. 60 D5
Butedale Canada 150 D4
Butha Buthe Lesotho 125 I5
Butha Qi Nei Mongol China see Zalantun
Buthidaung Myanmar 86 A2
Butler AL U.S.A. 161 F5
Butler GA U.S.A. 163 C5
Butler IN U.S.A. 164 C3
Butler KY U.S.A. 164 C4
Butler MO U.S.A. 160 E4
Butler PA U.S.A. 164 F3
Butlers Bridge Ireland 61 E3
Buton i. Indon. 83 B4
Buton, Selat sea chan. Indon. 83 B4
Bütow Germany 63 M1
Butte MT U.S.A. 156 E3
Butte NE U.S.A. 160 D3
Buttelstedt Germany 63 L3
Butterworth Malaysia 84 C1
Butterworth S. Africa 125 I7
Buttes, Sierra mt. U.S.A. 158 C2
Buttevant Ireland 61 D5
Butt of Lewis hd U.K. 60 C2
Button Bay Canada 151 M3
Butuan Mindanao Phil. 82 D4
Butuan Bay Mindanao Phil. 82 D4
Butuo China 96 D3
Buturlinovka Rus. Fed. 53 I6
Butwal Nepal 105 E4
Butzbach Germany 63 I4
Buulobarde Somalia 122 E3
Buur Gaabo Somalia 122 E4
Buurhabaka Somalia 122 E3
Buutsagaan Bayanhongor Mongolia 94 D2
Buxar India 105 F4
Buxoro Uzbek. 111 G2
Buxtehude Germany 63 J1
Buxton U.K. 58 F5

Buy Rus. Fed. 52 I4
Buyant Bayanhongor Mongolia see **Buutsagaan**
Buyant Bayan-Ölgiy Mongolia 94 B1
Buyant Hentiy Mongolia see **Galshar**
Buyant Gol r. Mongolia 94 D2
Buyant Gol r. Mongolia 98 E2
Buyant-Ovoo Mongolia 95 F2
Buyant-Uhaa Mongolia 95 G2
Buynaksk Rus. Fed. 113 G2
Büyükçekmece Turkey 112 C2
Büyük Egri Dağ mt. Turkey 107 A1
Büyükmenderes r. Turkey 69 L6
Buyun Shan mt. Liaoning China 95 J3
Buzancy France 62 E5
Buzău Romania 69 L2
Buzdyak Rus. Fed. 51 Q5
Búzi Moz. 123 D5
Büzmeýin Turkm. see **Abadan**
Buzuluk Rus. Fed. 51 Q5
Buzuluk r. Rus. Fed. 53 I6
Buzzards Bay U.S.A. 165 J3
Byakar Bhutan see **Jakar**
Byala Bulg. 69 K3
Byala Slatina Bulg. 69 J3
Byalynichy Belarus 53 F5
Byarezina r. Belarus 53 F5
Byaroza Belarus 55 N10
Byblos tourist site Lebanon 107 B2
Bydgoszcz Poland 57 Q4
Byelorussia country Europe see **Belarus**
Byerazino Belarus 53 F5
Byers U.S.A. 156 G5
Byeshankovichy Belarus 53 F5
Byesville U.S.A. 164 E4
Bygland Norway 55 E7
Bykhaw Belarus 53 F5
Bykhov Belarus see **Bykhaw**
Bykle Norway 55 E7
Bykovo Rus. Fed. 53 J6
Bylas U.S.A. 159 H5
Bylkyldak Kazakh. 98 A2
Bylot Island Canada 147 K2
Byramgore Reef India 106 A4
Byrd Glacier Antarctica 188 H1
Byrdstown U.S.A. 164 C5
Byrka Rus. Fed. 95 I1
Byrkjelo Norway 55 E6
Byrock Australia 138 C3
Byron U.S.A. 165 J1
Byron, Cape Australia 138 F2
Byron Bay Australia 138 F2
Byron Island Kiribati see **Nikunau**
Byrranga, Gory mts Rus. Fed. 77 K2
Byske Sweden 54 L4
Byssa Rus. Fed. 90 C1
Byssa r. Rus. Fed. 90 C1
Bystrinskiy Golets, Gora mt. Rus. Fed. 95 G1
Bytom Poland 57 Q5
Bytów Poland 57 P3
Byurgyutli Turkm. 110 D2
Byzantium Turkey see **İstanbul**

C

Ca, Sông r. Vietnam 86 D3
Caacupé Para. 178 E3
Caatinga Brazil 179 B2
Caazapá Para. 178 E3
Cabaiguán Cuba 163 E8
Caballas Peru 176 C6
Caballococha Peru 176 D4
Caballo Reservoir NM U.S.A. 166 D1
Caballos Mesteños, Llano de los plain Mex. 166 D2
Cabanaconde Peru 176 D7
Cabanatuan Luzon Phil. 82 C3
Cabano Canada 153 H5
Cabdul Qaadir Somalia 122 E2
Cabeceira Rio Manso Brazil 177 G7
Cabeceiras Brazil 179 B1
Cabeza del Buey Spain 67 D4
Cabeza Prieta National Wildlife Refuge nature res. AZ U.S.A. 166 B1
Cabezas Bol. 176 F7
Cabimas Venez. 176 D1
Cabinda Angola 123 B4
Cabinda prov. Angola 123 B5
Cabinet Inlet Antarctica 188 L2
Cabinet Mountains U.S.A. 156 E2
Cabingan i. Phil. 82 C5
Cabistra Turkey see **Ereğli**
Cabo Frio Brazil 179 C3
Cabo Frio, Ilha do i. Brazil 179 C3
Cabonga, Réservoir resr Canada 152 F5
Cabool U.S.A. 161 E4
Caboolture Australia 138 F1
Cabo Orange, Parque Nacional de nat. park Brazil 177 H3
Cabo Pantoja Peru 176 C4
Cabora Bassa, Lake resr Moz. 123 D5
Cabo Raso Arg. 178 C6
Caborca Mex. 166 B2
Cabot Head hd Canada 164 E1
Cabot Strait Canada 153 J5
Cabourg France 59 G9
Cabo Verde country N. Atlantic Ocean see **Cape Verde**
Cabo Verde, Ilhas do is N. Atlantic Ocean 120 [inset]
Cabo Yubi Morocco see **Tarfaya**
Cabra i. Phil. 82 C3
Cabral, Serra do mts Brazil 179 B2
Cäbrayıl Azer. 113 G3
Cabrera, Illa de i. Spain 67 H4
Cabri Canada 151 I5
Cabugao Luzon Phil. 82 C2
Cabulauan i. Phil. 82 C4
Cabullona Mex. 166 C2
Cabutunan Point Luzon Phil. 82 C2
Caçador Brazil 179 A4
Cacagoin China see **Qagca**
Cacahuatepec Mex. 167 F5
Čačak Serbia 69 I3
Caccia, Capo c. Sardinia Italy 68 C4
Çäçe Turkm. 111 F2
Cacequi Brazil 178 F3
Cáceres Brazil 177 G7
Cáceres Spain 67 C4
Cache Creek Canada 150 F5
Cache Peak U.S.A. 156 E4
Cacheu Guinea-Bissau 120 B3
Cachi, Nevados de mts Arg. 178 C2
Cachimbo, Serra do hills Brazil 177 H5
Cachoeira Brazil 179 D1
Cachoeira Alta Brazil 179 A2
Cachoeira de Goiás Brazil 179 A2
Cachoeira do Arari Brazil 177 I4
Cachoeiro de Itapemirim Brazil 179 C3
Cacine Guinea-Bissau 120 B3
Caciporé, Cabo c. Brazil 177 H3
Cacolo Angola 123 B5
Caconda Angola 123 B5
Cacongo Angola 123 B4
Cactus U.S.A. 161 C4
Caçu Brazil 179 A2
Caculé Brazil 179 C1
Čadca Slovakia 57 Q6
Caddo Lake TX U.S.A. 167 G1
Cadereyta Nuevo León Mex. 167 E3
Cadibarrawirracanna, Lake salt flat Australia 137 A6
Cadig Mountains Luzon Phil. 82 C3
Cadillac Canada 151 J5
Cadillac U.S.A. 164 C1
Cadiz Negros Phil. 82 C4
Cádiz Spain 67 C5
Cadiz IN U.S.A. 164 C4
Cadiz KY U.S.A. 162 C4
Cadiz OH U.S.A. 164 E3
Cádiz, Golfo de g. Spain 67 C5
Cadiz Lake U.S.A. 159 F4
Cadomin Canada 150 G4
Cadotte r. Canada 150 G3
Cadotte Lake Canada 150 G3
Caen France 66 D2
Caerdydd U.K. see **Cardiff**
Caerffili U.K. see **Caerphilly**
Caerfyrddin U.K. see **Carmarthen**
Caergybi U.K. see **Holyhead**
Caernarfon U.K. 59 C5
Caernarfon Bay U.K. 59 C5
Caernarvon U.K. see **Caernarfon**
Caerphilly U.K. 59 D7
Caesaraugusta Spain see **Zaragoza**
Caesarea Alg. see **Cherchell**
Caesarea Cappadociae Turkey see **Kayseri**
Caesarea Philippi Syria see **Bāniyās**
Caesarodunum France see **Tours**
Caesaromagus U.K. see **Chelmsford**
Caetité Brazil 179 C1
Cafayate Arg. 178 C3
Cafelândia Brazil 179 A3
Caffa Ukr. see **Feodosiya**
Cagayan i. Phil. 82 C4
Cagayan r. Luzon Phil. 82 C2
Cagayan de Oro Mindanao Phil. 82 D4
Cagayan de Tawi-Tawi i. Phil. 82 B5
Cagayan Islands Phil. 82 C4
Cagles Mill Lake U.S.A. 164 B4
Cagli Italy 68 E3
Cagliari Sardinia Italy 68 C5
Cagliari, Golfo di b. Sardinia Italy 68 C5
Cagua, Mount vol. Phil. 82 C2
Çagyl Turkm. 113 I2
Cahama Angola 123 B5
Caha Mts hills Ireland 61 C6
Cahermore Ireland 61 B6
Cahir Ireland 61 E5
Cahirsiveen Ireland 61 B6
Cahora Bassa, Lago de resr Moz. see **Cabora Bassa, Lake**
Cahore Point Ireland 61 F5
Cahors France 66 E4
Cahuapanas Peru 176 C5
Cahuita, Punta pt Costa Rica 166 [inset] J7
Cahul Moldova 69 M2
Caia Moz. 123 D5
Caiabis, Serra dos hills Brazil 177 G6
Caianda Angola 123 C5
Caiapó r. Brazil 179 A1
Caiapó, Serra do mts Brazil 179 A2
Caiapônia Brazil 179 A2
Caibarién Cuba 163 E8
Cai Bâu, Đao i. Vietnam 86 D2
Caicara Venez. 176 E2
Caicos Islands Turks and Caicos Is 169 J4
Caicos Passage Bahamas/Turks and Caicos Is 163 F8
Caidian China 97 G2
Caiguna Australia 135 D8
Caimanero, Laguna del lag. Mex. 166 D4
Caiman Point Luzon Phil. 82 B3
Caimodorro mt. Spain 67 F3
Cainnyigoin China 96 D1
Cains Store U.S.A. 164 C5
Caipe Arg. 178 C2
Caird Coast Antarctica 188 B1
Cairngorm Mountains U.K. 60 F3
Cairngorms National Park 60 F3
Cairn Mountain AK U.S.A. 148 I3
Cairnryan U.K. 60 D6
Cairns Australia 136 D3
Cairnsmore of Carsphairn hill U.K. 60 E5

▶**Cairo** Egypt 112 C5
Capital of Egypt. 2nd most populous city in Africa.

Cairo U.S.A. 163 C6
Caisleán an Bharraigh Ireland see **Castlebar**
Caiundo Angola 123 B5
Caiwarro (abandoned) Australia 138 B2
Caiyuanzhen China see **Shengsi**
Caizi Hu l. China 97 H2
Cajamarca Peru 176 C5
Cajati Brazil 179 A4
Cajidiocan Phil. 82 C3
Cajuru Brazil 179 B3
Caka Qinghai China 94 D4
Caka'lho China see **Yanjing**
Čakovec Croatia 68 G1
Çal Denizli Turkey 69 M5
Çal Hakkâri Turkey see **Çukurca**
Cala S. Africa 125 H6
Calabar Nigeria 120 D4
Calabogie Canada 165 G1
Calabria, Parco Nazionale della nat. park Italy 68 G5
Calafat Romania 69 J3
Calagnaan i. Phil. 82 C4
Calagua Mex. 166 C3
Calagua Islands Phil. 82 C3
Calagurris Spain see **Calahorra**
Calahorra Spain 67 F2
Calai Angola 123 B5
Calais France 62 B4
Calais U.S.A. 153 I5
Calakmus tourist site Mex. 167 H5
Calalasteo, Sierra de mts Arg. 178 C3
Calama Brazil 176 F5
Calama Chile 178 C2
Calamajué Mex. 157 E7
Calamar Col. 176 D1
Calamian Group is Phil. 82 B4
Calamocha Spain 67 F3
Calandagan i. Phil. 82 C4
Calandula Angola 123 B4
Calang Sumatera Indon. 84 A1
Calapan Mindoro Phil. 82 C3
Călărași Romania 69 L2
Calatayud Spain 67 F3
Calauag Luzon Phil. 82 C3
Calavite Passage Phil. 82 C3
Calawit i. Phil. 82 B3
Calayan i. Phil. 82 C2
Calbayog Samar Phil. 82 D3
Calbe (Saale) Germany 63 L3
Calbiga Samar Phil. 82 D4
Calcasieu r. LA U.S.A. 167 G2
Calcasieu Lake LA U.S.A. 167 G2
Calçoene Brazil 177 H3
Calcutta India see **Kolkata**
Caldas da Rainha Port. 67 B4
Caldas Novas Brazil 177 I7
Calden Germany 63 J3
Calder r. Canada 150 G1
Caldera Chile 178 B3
Calderitas Mex. 167 H5
Caldervale Australia 136 D5
Caldew r. U.K. 58 E4
Caldwell ID U.S.A. 156 D4
Caldwell KS U.S.A. 161 D4
Caldwell OH U.S.A. 164 E4
Caldwell TX U.S.A. 161 D6
Caledon r. Lesotho/S. Africa 125 H6
Caledon S. Africa 124 D8
Caledon Bay Australia 136 B2
Caledonia Canada 164 F2
Caledonia admin. div. U.K. see **Scotland**
Caledonia U.S.A. 165 G2
Caleta el Cobre Chile 178 B2
Calexico U.S.A. 159 F5
Calf of Man i. Isle of Man 58 C4
Calgary Canada 150 H5
Calhoun U.S.A. 164 B5
Cali Col. 176 C3
Calicoan i. Phil. 82 D4
Calicut India 106 B4
Caliente U.S.A. 159 F3
California U.S.A. 164 F3
California state U.S.A. 157 C4
California, Golfo de g. Mex. 166 B2
California Aqueduct canal U.S.A. 158 C3
Cälilabad Azer. 113 H3
Calingasta Arg. 178 C4
Calipatria U.S.A. 159 F5
Calistoga U.S.A. 158 B2
Calkiní Mex. 167 H4
Callabonna, Lake salt flat Australia 137 C6
Callaghan, Mount U.S.A. 158 E2
Callan Ireland 61 E5
Callan r. U.K. 61 F3
Callander Canada 152 F5
Callander U.K. 60 E4
Callang Luzon Phil. 82 C2
Callao Peru 176 C6
Callao U.S.A. 159 G2
Calles Mex. 167 F4
Callicoon U.S.A. 165 H3
Calling Lake Canada 150 H4
Callington U.K. 59 C8
Calliope Australia 136 E5
Callipolis Turkey see **Gallipoli**
Calmar U.S.A. 160 F3
Calobre Panama 166 [inset] J7
Caloosahatchee r. U.S.A. 163 D7
Calotmul Mex. 167 H4
Caloundra Australia 138 F1
Calpulálpan Mex. 167 F5
Caltagirone Sicily Italy 68 F6
Caltanissetta Sicily Italy 68 F6
Calucinga Angola 123 B5
Calulo Angola 123 B4
Calunga Angola 123 B5
Caluquembe Angola 123 B5
Calusa i. Phil. 82 C4
Caluula Somalia 122 F2
Caluula, Raas pt Somalia 122 F2
Caluya i. Phil. 82 C4
Calvert Hills Australia 136 B3
Calvert Island Canada 150 D5
Calvi Corsica France 66 I5
Calvià Spain 67 H4
Calvinia S. Africa 124 D6
Calvo, Monte mt. Italy 68 F4
Cam r. U.K. 59 H6
Camaçari Brazil 179 D1
Camache Reservoir U.S.A. 158 C2
Camachigama r. Canada 152 F5
Camacho Mex. 161 C7
Camacuio Angola 123 B5
Camacupa Angola 123 B5
Camagüey Cuba 169 I4
Camagüey, Archipiélago de is Cuba 169 I4
Camamu Brazil 179 D1
Camana Peru 176 D7
Camanongue Angola 123 C5
Camapuã Brazil 177 H7
Camaquã Brazil 178 F4
Çamardı Turkey 112 D3
Camargo Bol. 176 E8
Camargo Mex. 167 F3
Camargo, Parque Natural nature res. Mex. 167 F3
Camargue reg. France 66 G5
Camarillo U.S.A. 158 D4
Camarón, Cabo c. Hond. 166 [inset] I6
Camarones Arg. 178 C6
Camarones, Bahía b. Arg. 178 C6
Camas r. U.S.A. 156 E4
Ca Mau Vietnam 87 D5
Cambay India see **Khambhat**
Cambay, Gulf of India see **Khambhat, Gulf of**
Camberley U.K. 59 G7
Cambodia country Asia 87 D4
Camboriú Brazil 179 A4
Camborne U.K. 59 B8
Cambrai France 62 D4
Cambria admin. div. U.K. see **Wales**
Cambrian Mountains hills U.K. 59 D6
Cambridge Canada 164 E2
Cambridge N.Z. 139 E3
Cambridge U.K. 59 H6
Cambridge MA U.S.A. 165 J2
Cambridge MD U.S.A. 165 G4
Cambridge MN U.S.A. 160 E2
Cambridge NY U.S.A. 165 I2
Cambridge OH U.S.A. 164 E3
Cambridge Bay Canada 147 H3
Cambridge City U.S.A. 164 C4
Cambridge Springs U.S.A. 164 E3
Cambrien, Lac l. Canada 153 H2
Cambulo Angola 123 C4
Cambundi-Catembo Angola 123 B5
Cambuquira Brazil 179 B3
Cam Co l. Xizang China 99 C6
Camdeboo National Park S. Africa 124 G7
Camden AL U.S.A. 163 C5
Camden AR U.S.A. 161 E5
Camden NJ U.S.A. 165 H4
Camden NY U.S.A. 165 H2
Camden SC U.S.A. 163 D5
Camden Bay AK U.S.A. 149 K1
Camdenton U.S.A. 160 E4
Cameia Angola 123 C5
Cameia, Parque Nacional da nat. park Angola 123 C5
Cameron AZ U.S.A. 159 H4
Cameron LA U.S.A. 161 E6
Cameron MO U.S.A. 160 E4
Cameron TX U.S.A. 161 D6
Cameron Highlands mts Malaysia 84 C1
Cameron Hills Canada 150 G3
Cameron Island Canada 147 H2
Cameron Park U.S.A. 158 C2
Cameroon country Africa 120 E4
Cameroon, Mount vol. Cameroon see **Cameroun, Mont**
Cameroon Highlands slope Cameroon/Nigeria 120 E4
Cameroun country Africa see **Cameroon**
Cameroun, Mont vol. Cameroon 120 D4
Cametá Brazil 177 I4
Camiguin i. Phil. 82 C2
Camiguin i. Phil. 82 D4
Camiling Luzon Phil. 82 C3
Camiña Chile 176 E7
Camiri Bol. 176 F8
Camisea Peru 176 D6
Camocim Brazil 177 J4
Camooweal Australia 136 B3
Camooweal Caves National Park Australia 136 B4
Camorta i. India 103 H10
Camotes Sea g. Phil. 82 D4
Campamento Hond. 166 [inset] I6
Campana Mex. 166 E3
Campana, Isla i. Chile 178 A7
Campania Island Canada 150 D4
Campbell S. Africa 124 F5
Campbell, Cape N.Z. 139 E5
Campbell, Mount hill Australia 134 E5
Campbellford Canada 165 G1
Campbell Hill hill U.S.A. 164 D3
Campbell Island N.Z. 186 H9
Campbell Lake Canada 151 J2
Campbell Lake N.W.T. Canada 149 N1
Campbell Plateau sea feature S. Pacific Ocean 186 H9
Campbell Range hills Australia 134 D3
Campbell River Canada 150 E5
Campbellsville U.S.A. 164 C5
Campbellton Canada 153 I5
Campbelltown Australia 138 E5
Campbeltown U.K. 60 D5
Campeche Mex. 167 H5
Campeche state Mex. 167 H5
Campeche, Bahía de g. Mex. 168 F5
Camperdown Australia 138 A7
Câmpina Romania 69 K2
Campina Grande Brazil 177 K5
Campinas Brazil 179 B3
Campina Verde Brazil 179 A2
Camplong Timor Indon. 83 B5
Campo Cameroon 120 D4
Campobasso Italy 68 F4
Campo Belo Brazil 179 B3
Campo Belo do Sul Brazil 179 A4
Campo de Diauarum Brazil 177 H6
Campo Florido Brazil 179 A2
Campo Gallo Arg. 178 D3
Campo Grande Brazil 178 F2
Campo Largo Brazil 179 A4
Campo Maior Brazil 177 J4
Campo Maior Port. 67 C4
Campo Mourão Brazil 178 F2
Campos Brazil 179 C3
Campos Altos Brazil 179 B2
Campos Novos Brazil 179 A4
Campos Sales Brazil 177 J5
Campton U.S.A. 164 D5
Câmpulung Romania 69 K2
Câmpulung Moldovenesc Romania 69 K1
Camp Verde U.S.A. 159 H4
Camrose Canada 151 H4
Camrose U.K. 59 B7
Camsell Lake Canada 151 I2
Camsell Portage Canada 151 I3
Camsell Range mts Canada 150 F2
Camulodunum U.K. see **Colchester**
Çan Turkey 69 L4
Ca Na, Mui hd Vietnam 87 E5
Canaan r. Canada 153 I5
Canaan U.S.A. 165 I2
Canaan Peak U.S.A. 159 H3
Canabrava Brazil 179 B2
Canabungan i. Phil. 82 B4
Canacona India 106 B3

▶**Canada** country N. America 146 H4
Largest country in North America and 2nd in the world. 3rd most populous country in North America.

Canada Basin sea feature Arctic Ocean 189 A1
Canadian U.S.A. 161 C5
Canadian r. U.S.A. 161 E5
Canadian Abyssal Plain sea feature Arctic Ocean 189 A1
Cañadon Grande, Sierra mts Arg. 178 C7
Canaima, Parque Nacional nat. park Venez. 176 F2
Çanakkale Turkey 69 L4
Çanakkale Boğazı strait Turkey see **Dardanelles**
Canalejas Arg. 178 C5
Cañamares Spain 67 E3
Canandaigua U.S.A. 165 G2
Cananea Mex. 166 C2
Cananéia Brazil 179 B4
Canápolis Brazil 179 A2
Cañar Ecuador 176 C4
Canarias terr. N. Atlantic Ocean see **Canary Islands**
Canárias, Ilha das i. Brazil 177 J4
Canarias, Islas terr. N. Atlantic Ocean see **Canary Islands**

▶**Canary Islands** terr. N. Atlantic Ocean 120 B2
Autonomous Community of Spain.

Canasayab Mex. 167 H5
Canaseraga U.S.A. 165 G2
Canastota U.S.A. 165 H2
Canastra, Serra da mts Brazil 179 B2
Canastra, Serra da mts Brazil 179 A1
Canatiba Brazil 179 C1
Canatlán Mex. 161 B7
Canaveral, Cape U.S.A. 163 D6
Cañaveras Spain 67 E3
Canavieiras Brazil 179 D1
Cañazas Panama 166 [inset] J7
Canbelego Australia 138 C3

▶**Canberra** Australia 138 D5
Capital of Australia and Australian Capital Territory.

Cancún Mex. 167 I4
Çandar Turkey see **Kastamonu**
Çandarlı Turkey 69 L5
Candela Mex. 167 E3
Candela r. Mex. 161 C7
Candelaria Campeche Mex. 167 H5
Candelaria Chihuahua Mex. 166 D2
Candia Greece see **Iraklion**
Cândido de Abreu Brazil 179 A4
Çandır Turkey 112 D2
Candle AK U.S.A. 148 G2
Candle Lake Canada 151 J4
Candlewood, Lake U.S.A. 165 I3
Cando U.S.A. 160 D1
Candon Luzon Phil. 82 C2
Candon Point Luzon Phil. 82 C2
Cane r. Australia 134 A5
Canea Greece see **Chania**
Canela Brazil 179 A5
Canelones Uruguay 178 E4
Cane Valley U.S.A. 164 C5
Cangallo Peru 176 D6
Cangamba Angola 123 B5
Cangandala, Parque Nacional de nat. park Angola 123 B4
Canglun Malaysia see **Changlun**
Cango Caves S. Africa 124 F7
Cangola Angola 123 B4
Cangshan Shandong China 95 I5
Canguaretama Brazil 177 K5
Canguçu Brazil 178 F4
Canguçu, Serra do hills Brazil 178 F4
Cangwu China 97 F4
Cangzhou Hebei China 95 I4
Caniapiscau Canada 153 H3
Caniapiscau r. Canada 153 H2
Caniapiscau, Réservoir de l. Canada 153 H3
Caniçado Moz. see **Guija**
Canicattì Sicily Italy 68 E6
Canigao Channel Phil. 82 D4
Canim Lake Canada 150 F5
Canindé Brazil 177 K4
Canisteo U.S.A. 165 G2
Canisteo r. U.S.A. 165 G2
Canisteo Peninsula Antarctica 188 K2
Cañitas de Felipe Pescador Mex. 161 C8
Çankırı Turkey 112 D2
Canlaon Negros Phil. 82 C4
Canna Australia 135 A7
Canna i. U.K. 60 C3
Cannanore India 106 B4
Cannanore Islands India 106 B4
Cannelton U.S.A. 164 B5
Cannes France 66 H5
Canning r. AK U.S.A. 149 K1
Cannock U.K. 59 E6
Cannon Beach U.S.A. 156 C3
Cann River Australia 138 D6
Canoas Brazil 179 A5
Canoas, Rio das r. Brazil 179 A4
Canoeiros Brazil 179 B2
Canoe Lake Canada 151 I4
Canoe Lake l. Canada 151 I4
Canoinhas Brazil 179 A4
Canon City U.S.A. 157 G5
Cañón del Sumidero, Parque Nacional nat. park Mex. 167 G5
Cañon Largo watercourse U.S.A. 159 J3
Canoona Australia 136 E4
Canora Canada 151 K5
Canowindra Australia 138 D4
Canso Canada 153 J5
Canso, Cape Canada 153 J5
Cantabrian Mountains Spain see **Cantábrica, Cordillera**
Cantábrica, Cordillera mts Spain 67 D2
Cantábrico, Mar sea Spain 67 C2
Canterbury U.K. 59 I7
Canterbury Bight b. N.Z. 139 C7
Canterbury Plains N.Z. 139 C6
Cần Thơ Vietnam 87 D5
Cantil U.S.A. 158 E4
Cantilan Mindanao Phil. 82 D4
Canton GA U.S.A. 163 C5
Canton IL U.S.A. 160 F3
Canton MO U.S.A. 160 F3
Canton MS U.S.A. 161 F5
Canton NY U.S.A. 165 H1
Canton OH U.S.A. 164 E3
Canton PA U.S.A. 165 G3
Canton SD U.S.A. 160 D3
Canton TX U.S.A. 161 E5
Canton Island atoll Kiribati see **Kanton**
Cantuaria U.K. see **Canterbury**
Cantwell AK U.S.A. 149 J3
Canunda National Park Australia 137 C8
Canutama Brazil 176 F5
Canutillo Mex. 157 G8
Canvey Island U.K. 59 H7
Canwood Canada 151 J4
Cany-Barville France 59 H9
Canyon U.S.A. 161 C5
Canyon (abandoned) Y.T. Canada 149 M3
Canyon City U.S.A. 156 D3
Canyondam U.S.A. 158 C1
Canyon de Chelly National Monument nat. park U.S.A. 159 I3
Canyon Ferry Lake U.S.A. 156 F3
Canyon Lake U.S.A. 159 H5
Canyonlands National Park U.S.A. 159 I2
Canyon Ranges mts N.W.T. Canada 149 P3
Canyons of the Ancients National Monument nat. park U.S.A. 159 I3
Canyonville U.S.A. 156 C4
Cao Bằng Vietnam 86 D2
Caocheng Shandong China see **Caoxian**
Cao Daban Qinghai China 94 E4
Caohai China see **Weining**
Caohe China see **Qichun**
Caohu Xinjiang China 98 D4
Caohu Xinjiang China 98 D4
Caojiahe China see **Qichun**
Caojian China 96 C3
Caoshi China 90 B4
Caoxian Shandong China 95 H5
Caozhou Shandong China see **Heze**
Cap i. Phil. 82 C5
Capac U.S.A. 164 D2
Çapakçur Turkey see **Bingöl**
Capalulu, Selat sea chan. Indon. 83 C3
Capanaparo r. Venez. 176 E2
Capanema Brazil 177 I4
Capão Bonito Brazil 179 A4
Caparaó, Serra do mts Brazil 179 C3
Capas Luzon Phil. 82 C3
Cap-aux-Meules Canada 153 J5
Cap-de-la-Madeleine Canada 153 G5
Cape r. Australia 136 D4
Cape Arid National Park Australia 135 C8
Cape Barren Island Australia 137 [inset]
Cape Basin sea feature S. Atlantic Ocean 184 I8
Cape Breton Highlands National Park Canada 153 J5
Cape Breton Island Canada 153 J5
Cape Charles Canada 153 L3
Cape Charles U.S.A. 165 G5
Cape Coast Ghana 120 C4
Cape Coast Castle Ghana see **Cape Coast**
Cape Cod Bay U.S.A. 165 J3
Cape Cod National Seashore nature res. U.S.A. 165 K3
Cape Coral U.S.A. 163 D7
Cape Crawford Australia 136 A3
Cape Dorset Canada 147 K3
Cape Fanshaw AK U.S.A. 149 N4
Cape Fear r. U.S.A. 163 E5
Cape George Canada 153 J5
Cape Girardeau U.S.A. 161 F4
Cape Johnson Depth sea feature N. Pacific Ocean 186 E5
Cape Juby Morocco see **Tarfaya**
Cape Krusenstern National Monument nat. park AK U.S.A. 148 G2
Capel Australia 135 A8
Cape Le Grand National Park Australia 135 C8
Capelinha Brazil 179 C2
Capella Australia 136 E4
Capelle aan de IJssel Neth. 62 E3
Capelongo Angola see **Kuvango**
Cape May U.S.A. 165 H4
Cape May Court House U.S.A. 165 H4
Cape May Point U.S.A. 165 H4
Cape Melville National Park Australia 136 D2
Capenda-Camulemba Angola 123 B4
Cape of Good Hope Nature Reserve S. Africa 124 D8
Cape Palmerston National Park Australia 136 E4
Cape Range National Park Australia 134 A5
Cape St George Canada 153 K4

▶**Cape Town** S. Africa 124 D7
Legislative capital of South Africa.

Cape Tribulation National Park Australia 136 D2
Cape Upstart National Park Australia 136 D3
Cape Verde country N. Atlantic Ocean 120 [inset]
Cape Verde Basin sea feature N. Atlantic Ocean 184 F5
Cape Verde Plateau sea feature N. Atlantic Ocean 184 F4
Cape Vincent U.S.A. 165 G1
Cape Yakataga AK U.S.A. 149 L3
Cape York Peninsula Australia 136 C2
Cap-Haïtien Haiti 169 J5
Capim r. Brazil 177 I4
Capitán Arturo Prat research station Antarctica 188 A2

▶**Capitol Hill** N. Mariana Is 81 L3
Capital of the Northern Mariana Islands, on Saipan.

Capitol Reef National Park U.S.A. 159 H2
Capivara, Represa resr Brazil 179 A3
Čapljina Bos.-Herz. 68 G3
Cappoquin Ireland 61 E5
Capraia, Isola di i. Italy 68 C3
Caprara, Punta pt Sardinia Italy 68 C4
Capri, Isola di i. Italy 68 F4
Capricorn Channel Australia 136 E4
Capricorn Group atolls Australia 136 F4
Caprivi Strip reg. Namibia 123 C5
Cap Rock Escarpment U.S.A. 161 C5
Capsa Tunisia see **Gafsa**
Captain Cook U.S.A. 157 [inset]
Captina r. U.S.A. 164 E4
Capuava Brazil 179 B4
Caquetá r. Col. 176 E4
Carabao i. Phil. 82 C3
Caracal Romania 69 K2

▶**Caracas** Venez. 176 E1
Capital of Venezuela.

Caraga Mindanao Phil. 82 D5
Caraguatatuba Brazil 179 B3
Caraí Brazil 179 C2
Carajás Brazil 177 H5
Carajás, Serra dos hills Brazil 177 H5
Carales Sardinia Italy see **Cagliari**
Caralis Sardinia Italy see **Cagliari**
Caramoan Peninsula Luzon Phil. 82 C3
Carandaí Brazil 179 C3
Caransebeș Romania 69 J2

Caraquet Canada 153 I5
Carat, Tanjung pt Indon. 84 D3
Caratasca Hond. 166 [inset] J6
Caratasca, Laguna de lag. Hond. 166 [inset] J6
Caratinga Brazil 179 C2
Carauari Brazil 176 E4
Caravaca de la Cruz Spain 67 F4
Caravelas Brazil 179 D2
Carberry Canada 151 L5
Carbó Mex. 166 C2
Carbon, Cap hd Alg. 67 F6
▶Carbón, Laguna del l. Arg. 178 C7
Lowest point in South America.
Carbonara, Capo c. Sardinia Italy 68 C5
Carbondale CO U.S.A. 159 J2
Carbondale PA U.S.A. 165 H3
Carboneras Mex. 161 D7
Carbonia Sardinia Italy 68 C5
Carbonita Brazil 179 C2
Carcaixent Spain 67 F4
Carcajou Canada 150 G3
Carcajou r. N.W.T. Canada 149 O2
Carcar Cebu Phil. 82 C4
Carcassonne France 66 F5
Carcross Y.T. Canada 149 N3
Cardamomes, Chaîne des mts Cambodia/Thai. see Cardamom Range
Cardamom Hills India 106 C4
Cardamom Range mts Cambodia/Thai. 87 C4
Cárdenas Cuba 169 H4
Cárdenas Mex. 168 E4
Cárdenas Tabasco Mex. 167 G5
Cardenyabba watercourse Australia 138 A2
Çardi Turkey see Harmancık
Cardiel, Lago l. Arg. 178 B7
▶Cardiff U.K. 59 D7
Capital of Wales.
Cardiff U.S.A. 165 G4
Cardigan U.K. 59 C6
Cardigan Bay U.K. 59 C6
Cardinal Lake Canada 150 G3
Cardington U.S.A. 164 D3
Cardón, Cerro hill Mex. 166 B3
Cardoso Brazil 179 A3
Cardoso, Ilha do i. Brazil 179 B4
Cardston Canada 150 H5
Careen Lake Canada 151 I3
Carei Romania 69 J1
Carentan France 66 D2
Carey U.S.A. 164 D3
Carey, Lake salt flat Australia 135 C7
Carey Lake Canada 151 K2
Cargados Carajos Islands Mauritius 185 L7
Carhaix-Plouguer France 66 C2
Cariacica Brazil 179 C3
Cariamanga Ecuador 176 C4
Caribbean Sea N. Atlantic Ocean 169 H5
Cariboo Mountains Canada 150 F4
Caribou r. Man. Canada 151 M3
Caribou r. N.W.T. Canada 149 P3
Caribou r. Y.T. Canada 149 N2
Caribou AK U.S.A. 149 K2
Caribou U.S.A. 162 G2
Caribou Lake Canada 147 J4
Caribou Mountains Canada 150 H3
Carichic Mex. 166 D3
Carigara Leyte Phil. 82 D4
Carignan France 62 F5
Carinda Australia 138 C3
Cariñena Spain 67 F3
Carinhanha r. Brazil 179 C1
Carlabhagh U.K. see Carloway
Carleton U.S.A. 164 D2
Carleton, Mount hill Canada 153 I5
Carletonville S. Africa 125 H4
Carlin U.S.A. 158 E1
Carlingford Lough inlet Ireland/U.K. 61 F3
Carlinville U.S.A. 160 F4
Carlisle U.K. 58 E4
Carlisle IN U.S.A. 164 B4
Carlisle KY U.S.A. 164 C4
Carlisle NY U.S.A. 165 H2
Carlisle PA U.S.A. 165 G3
Carlisle Lakes salt flat Australia 135 D7
Carlit, Pic mt. France 66 E5
Carlos Chagas Brazil 179 C2
Carlow Ireland 61 F5
Carloway U.K. 60 C2
Carlsbad Czech Rep. see Karlovy Vary
Carlsbad CA U.S.A. 158 E5
Carlsbad NM U.S.A. 157 G6
Carlsbad TX U.S.A. 167 E2
Carlsbad Caverns National Park U.S.A. 157 G6
Carlsberg Ridge sea feature Indian Ocean 185 L5
Carlson Inlet Antarctica 188 L1
Carlton U.S.A. 160 E2
Carlton Hill Australia 134 E3
Carluke U.K. 60 F5
Carlyle Canada 151 K5
Carmacks Y.T. Canada 149 M3
Carmagnola Italy 68 B2
Carman Canada 151 L5
Carmana Iran see Kermān
Carmarthen U.K. 59 C7
Carmarthen Bay U.K. 59 C7
Carmaux France 66 F4
Carmel IN U.S.A. 164 B4
Carmel NY U.S.A. 165 I3
Carmel, Mount hill Israel 107 B3
Carmel Head hd U.K. 58 C5
Carmelita Guat. 167 H5
Carmel Valley U.S.A. 158 C3
Carmen Mex. 167 E3
Carmen r. Mex. 166 D2
Carmen Bohol Phil. 82 D4
Carmen U.S.A. 157 F7
Carmen, Isla i. Mex. 166 C3
Carmen, Isla del i. Mex. 167 H5
Carmen de Patagones Arg. 178 D6
Carmi U.S.A. 160 F4
Carmichael U.S.A. 158 C2
Carmo da Cachoeira Brazil 179 B3
Carmo do Paranaíba Brazil 179 B2
Carmona Angola see Uíge
Carmona Hond. 166 [inset] I7
Carmona Spain 67 D5
Carnac France 66 C3
Carnamah Australia 135 A7
Carnarvon Australia 135 A6
Carnarvon S. Africa 124 F6
Carnarvon National Park Australia 136 D5
Carnarvon Range hills Australia 135 C6
Carnarvon Range mts Australia 136 E5
Carn Dearg hill U.K. 60 E3
Carndonagh Ireland 61 E2
Carnegie Australia 135 C6
Carnegie, Lake salt flat Australia 135 C6
Carn Eige mt. U.K. 60 D3
Carnes Australia 135 F7
Carney Island Antarctica 188 J2
Carnforth U.K. 58 E4
Carn Glas-choire hill U.K. 60 F3
Car Nicobar i. India 87 A5
Carnlough U.K. 61 G3
Carn nan Gabhar mt. U.K. 60 F4
Carn Odhar hill U.K. 60 E3
Carnot Cent. Afr. Rep. 122 B3
Carnoustie U.K. 60 G4
Carnsore Point Ireland 61 F5
Carnwath r. N.W.T. Canada 149 O1
Carnwath U.K. 60 F5
Caro AK U.S.A. 149 J2
Caro U.S.A. 164 D2
Carola Cay reef Australia 136 F3
Carol City U.S.A. 163 D7
Carolina Brazil 177 I5
Carolina S. Africa 125 J4
Carolina Beach U.S.A. 163 E5
Caroline Canada 150 H4
Caroline Island atoll Kiribati 187 J6
Caroline Islands N. Pacific Ocean 81 K5
Caroline Peak N.Z. 139 A7
Caroline Range hills Australia 134 D4
Caroní r. Venez. 176 F2
Carp Canada 165 G1
Carpathian Mountains Europe 53 C6
Carpații mts Europe see Carpathian Mountains
Carpații Meridionali mts Romania see Transylvanian Alps
Carpații Occidentali mts Romania 69 J2
Carpentaria, Gulf of Australia 136 B2
Carpentras France 66 G4
Carpi Italy 68 D2
Carpinteria U.S.A. 158 D4
Carpio U.S.A. 160 C1
Carra, Lough l. Ireland 61 C4
Carraig na Siuire Ireland see Carrick-on-Suir
Carraig Thuathail Ireland see Carrigtohill
Carrantuohill mt. Ireland 61 C6
Carrara Italy 68 D2
Carrasco, Parque Nacional nat. park Bol. 176 F7
Carrathool Australia 138 B5
Carrhae Turkey see Harran
Carrickfergus U.K. 61 G3
Carrickmacross Ireland 61 F4
Carrick-on-Shannon Ireland 61 D4
Carrick-on-Suir Ireland 61 E5
Carrigallen Ireland 61 E4
Carrigtohill Ireland 61 D6
Carrillo Mex. 166 E3
Carrington U.S.A. 160 D2
Carrizal Mex. 166 D2
Carrizal Bajo Chile 178 B3
Carrizo U.S.A. 159 H4
Carrizo Creek r. U.S.A. 161 C4
Carrizos Mex. 167 F3
Carrizo Springs U.S.A. 161 D6
Carrizo Wash watercourse U.S.A. 159 I4
Carrizozo U.S.A. 157 G6
Carroll U.S.A. 160 E3
Carrollton AL U.S.A. 161 F5
Carrollton GA U.S.A. 163 C5
Carrollton IL U.S.A. 160 F4
Carrollton KY U.S.A. 164 C4
Carrollton MO U.S.A. 160 E4
Carrollton OH U.S.A. 164 E3
Carrolltown U.S.A. 165 F3
Carron r. U.K. 60 E3
Carrot r. Canada 151 K4
Carrothers U.S.A. 164 D3
Carrot River Canada 151 K4
Carrowmore Lake Ireland 61 C3
Carrsville U.S.A. 165 G5
Carruthers Lake Canada 151 K2
Carruthersville U.S.A. 161 F4
Carry Falls Reservoir U.S.A. 165 H1
Çarşamba Turkey 112 E2
Carson r. U.S.A. 158 D2
Carson City MI U.S.A. 164 C2
▶Carson City NV U.S.A. 158 D2
Capital of Nevada.
Carson Escarpment Australia 134 D3
Carson Lake U.S.A. 158 D2
Carson Sink l. U.S.A. 158 D2
Carstensz Pyramid mt. Indon. see Jaya, Puncak
Carstensz-top mt. Indon. see Jaya, Puncak
Carswell Lake Canada 151 I3
Cartagena Col. 176 C1
Cartagena Spain 67 F5
Cartago Costa Rica 166 [inset] J7
Carteret Group is P.N.G. see Kilinailau Islands
Carteret Island Solomon Is see Malaita
Cartersville U.S.A. 163 C5
Carthage tourist site Tunisia 68 D6
Carthage MO U.S.A. 161 E4
Carthage NC U.S.A. 163 E5
Carthage NY U.S.A. 165 H2
Carthage TX U.S.A. 161 E5
Carthago tourist site Tunisia see Carthage
Carthago Nova Spain see Cartagena
Cartier Island Australia 134 C3
Cartmel U.K. 58 E4
Cartwright Man. Canada 151 L5
Cartwright Nfld. and Lab. Canada 153 K3
Caruarú Brazil 177 K5
Carúpano Venez. 176 F1
Carver U.S.A. 164 D5
Carvin France 62 C4
Cary U.S.A. 162 E5
Caryapundy Swamp Australia 137 C6
Casablanca Morocco 64 C5
Casa Branca Brazil 179 B3
Casa de Janos Mex. 166 C2
Casadepaga AK U.S.A. 148 F2
Casa de Piedra, Embalse resr Arg. 178 C5
Casa Grande U.S.A. 159 H5
Casale Monferrato Italy 68 C2
Casalmaggiore Italy 68 D2
Casares Nicaragua 166 [inset] I7
Casas Grandes Mex. 166 D2
Casas Grandes r. Mex. 166 D2
Casca Brazil 179 A5
Cascada de Bassaseachic, Parque Nacional nat. park Mex. 166 C2
Cascade Australia 135 C8
Cascade r. N.Z. 139 B7
Cascade ID U.S.A. 156 D3
Cascade MT U.S.A. 156 F3
Cascade Point N.Z. 139 B7
Cascade Range mts Canada/U.S.A. 156 C4
Cascade Reservoir U.S.A. 156 D3
Cascais Port. 67 B4
Cascal, Paso del pass Nicaragua 166 [inset] I7
Cascavel Brazil 178 F2
Casco Bay U.S.A. 165 K2
Caserta Italy 68 F4
Casey research station Antarctica 188 F2
Casey Bay Antarctica 188 D2
Caseyr, Raas c. Somalia see Gwardafuy, Gees
Cashel Ireland 61 E5
Cashmere Australia 138 D1
Casiguran Luzon Phil. 82 C2
Casiguran Sound sea chan. Luzon Phil. 82 C2
Casino Australia 138 F2
Casiquiare, Canal r. Venez. 176 E3
Casita Mex. 157 F7
Casnewydd U.K. see Newport
Casogoran Bay Phil. 82 D4
Caspe Spain 67 F3
Casper U.S.A. 156 G4
Caspian Lowland Kazakh./Rus. Fed. 100 D2
▶Caspian Sea l. Asia/Europe 113 H1
Largest lake in the world and in Asia/Europe, and lowest point in Europe.
Cass U.S.A. 164 F4
Cass r. U.S.A. 164 D2
Cassacatiza Moz. 123 D5
Cassadaga U.S.A. 164 F2
Cassaigne Alg. see Sidi Ali
Cassamba Angola 123 C5
Cass City U.S.A. 164 D2
Cassel France 62 C4
Casselman Canada 165 H1
Cássia Brazil 179 B3
Cassiar B.C. Canada 149 O4
Cassiar Mountains B.C. Canada 149 O4
Cassilândia Brazil 179 A2
Cassilis Australia 138 D4
Cassino Italy 68 E4
Cassley r. U.K. 60 E3
Cassongue Angola 123 B5
Cassopolis U.S.A. 164 B3
Cassville U.S.A. 161 E4
Castanhal Brazil 177 I4
Castanho Brazil 176 F5
Castaños Mex. 167 E3
Castelfranco Veneto Italy 68 D2
Castell-nedd U.K. see Neath
Castell Newydd Emlyn U.K. see Newcastle Emlyn
Castellón Spain see Castellón de la Plana
Castellón de la Plana Spain 67 F4
Castelo Branco Port. 67 C4
Castelo de Vide Port. 67 C4
Casteltermini Sicily Italy 68 E6
Castelvetrano Sicily Italy 68 E6
Castiglione della Pescaia Italy 68 D3
Castignon, Lac l. Canada 153 H2
Castilla y León reg. Spain 66 B6
Castlebar Ireland 61 C4
Castlebay U.K. 60 B4
Castlebellingham Ireland 61 F4
Castleblayney Ireland 61 F3
Castlebridge Ireland 61 F5
Castle Carrock U.K. 58 E4
Castle Cary U.K. 59 E7
Castle Dale U.S.A. 159 H2
Castlederg U.K. 61 E3
Castledermot Ireland 61 F5
Castle Dome Mountains U.S.A. 159 F5
Castle Donington U.K. 59 F6
Castle Douglas U.K. 60 F6
Castleford U.K. 58 F5
Castlegar Canada 150 G5
Castlegregory Ireland 61 B5
Castle Island Bahamas 163 F8
Castleisland Ireland 61 C5
Castlemaine Australia 138 B6
Castlemaine Ireland 61 C5
Castlemartyr Ireland 61 D6
Castle Mountain Alta Canada 150 H5
Castle Mountain Y.T. Canada 149 N2
Castle Mountain U.S.A. 158 C4
Castle Peak hill H.K. China 97 [inset]
Castle Peak Bay H.K. China 97 [inset]
Castlepoint N.Z. 139 F5
Castlepollard Ireland 61 E4
Castlerea Ireland 61 D4
Castlereagh r. Australia 138 C3
Castle Rock U.S.A. 156 G5
Castletown Ireland 61 E5
Castletown Isle of Man 58 C4
Castor Canada 151 I4
Castor r. U.S.A. 161 F4
Castor, Rivière du r. Canada 152 F3
Castra Regina Germany see Regensburg
Castres France 66 F5
Castricum Neth. 62 E2
▶Castries St Lucia 169 L6
Capital of St Lucia.
Castro Brazil 179 A4
Castro Chile 178 B6
Castro Alves Brazil 179 D1
Castro Verde Port. 67 B5
Castroville U.S.A. 158 C3
Cast Uul mt. Mongolia 94 B1
Caswell AK U.S.A. 149 J3
Çat Turkey 113 F3
Catacamas Hond. 166 [inset] I6
Catacaos Peru 176 B5
Cataguases Brazil 179 C3
Catahoula Lake U.S.A. 161 E6
Cataiñgan Masbate Phil. 82 C3
Çatak Turkey 113 F3
Catalão Brazil 179 B2
Çatalca Yarımadası pen. Turkey 69 M4
Catalina U.S.A. 159 H5
Catalonia aut. comm. Spain see Cataluña
Cataluña aut. comm. Spain 67 G3
Catalunya aut. comm. Spain see Cataluña
Catamarca Arg. 178 C3
Catana Sicily Italy see Catania
Catanauan Luzon Phil. 82 C3
Catanduanes i. Phil. 82 D3
Catanduva Brazil 179 A3
Catania Sicily Italy 68 F6
Catanzaro Italy 68 G5
Cataract Creek watercourse U.S.A. 159 G3
Catarina U.S.A. 161 D6
Catarino Rodríguez Mex. 167 E3
Catarman Samar Phil. 82 D3
Catarman Point Mindanao Phil. 82 D5
Catastrophe, Cape Australia 137 A7
Catawba r. U.S.A. 163 D5
Cataxa Moz. 123 D5
Cat Ba, Đao i. Vietnam 86 D2
Catbalogan Samar Phil. 82 D4
Cateel Mindanao Phil. 82 D5
Cateel Bay Mindanao Phil. 82 D5
Catemaco Mex. 167 G5
Catembe Moz. 125 K4
Catengue Angola 123 B5
Catete Angola 123 B4
Cathair Dónall Ireland 61 B6
Cathair Saidhbhín Ireland see Cahirsiveen
Cathcart Australia 138 D6
Cathcart S. Africa 125 H7
Cathedral Peak S. Africa 125 I5
Cathedral Rock National Park Australia 138 F3
Catherdaniel Ireland see Cathair Dónall
Catherine, Mount U.S.A. 159 G2
Catheys Valley U.S.A. 158 C3
Cathlamet U.S.A. 156 C3
Catió Guinea-Bissau 120 B3
Catisimiña Venez. 176 F3
Cat Island Bahamas 163 F7
Cat Lake Canada 151 N5
Catlettsburg U.S.A. 164 D4
Catoche, Cabo c. Mex. 167 I4
Cato Island and Bank reef Australia 136 F4
Catorce Mex. 167 E4
Catriló Arg. 178 D5
Cats, Mont des hill France 62 C4
Catskill U.S.A. 165 I2
Catskill Mountains U.S.A. 165 H2
Catuane Moz. 125 K4
Cauayan Negros Phil. 82 C4
Caubvick, Mount Canada 153 J2
Cauca r. Col. 169 J7
Caucaia Brazil 177 K4
Caucasia Col. 176 C2
Caucasus mts Asia/Europe 113 F2
Cauchon Lake Canada 151 L4
Caudry France 62 D4
Câu Giat Vietnam 86 D3
Cauit Point Mindanao Phil. 82 D4
Caulonia Italy 68 G5
Caungula Angola 123 B4
Cauquenes Chile 178 B5
Causapscal Canada 153 I4
Căușeni Moldova 69 M1
Cavaglià Italy 68 C2
Cavalcante, Serra do hills Brazil 179 B1
Cavalier U.S.A. 160 D1
Cavan Ireland 61 E4
Çavdır Turkey 69 M6
Cave City U.S.A. 164 C5
Cave Creek U.S.A. 159 H5
Caveira r. Brazil 179 C1
Cavern Island Myanmar 87 B5
Cave Run Lake U.S.A. 164 D4
Caviana, Ilha i. Brazil 177 H3
Cavili rf Phil. 82 C4
Cavite Luzon Phil. 82 C3
Cawdor U.K. 60 F3
Cawnpore India see Kanpur
Cawston U.K. 59 I6
Caxias Brazil 177 J4
Caxias do Sul Brazil 179 A5
Caxito Angola 123 B4
Çay Turkey 69 N5
Cayambe, Volcán vol. Ecuador 176 C3
Çaybaşı Turkey see Çayeli
Çaycuma Turkey 69 O4
Çayeli Turkey 113 F2
▶Cayenne Fr. Guiana 177 H3
Capital of French Guiana.
Cayeux-sur-Mer France 62 B4
Çayırhan Turkey 69 N4
Cayman Brac i. Cayman Is 169 I5
▶Cayman Islands terr. West Indies 169 H5
United Kingdom Overseas Territory.
Cayman Trench sea feature Caribbean Sea 184 C4
Caynabo Somalia 122 E3
Cay Sal i. Bahamas 163 D8
Cay Sal Bank sea feature Bahamas 163 D8
Cay Santa Domingo i. Bahamas 163 F8
Cayucos U.S.A. 158 C4
Cayuga Canada 164 F2
Cayuga Lake U.S.A. 165 G2
Cay Verde i. Bahamas 163 F8
Cazê Xizang China 99 D7
Cazenovia U.S.A. 165 H2
Cazombo Angola 123 C5
Ceadâr-Lunga Moldova see Ciadîr-Lunga
Ceanannus Mór Ireland see Kells
Ceann a Deas na Hearadh pen. U.K. see South Harris
Ceará Brazil see Fortaleza
Ceara Abyssal Plain sea feature S. Atlantic Ocean 184 F6
Ceatharlach Ireland see Carlow
Ceballos Mex. 166 D3
Ceboruco, Volcán vol. Mex. 166 D4
Cebu Cebu Phil. 82 C4
Cebu i. Phil. 82 C4
Čechy reg. Czech Rep. 57 N6
Cecil Plains Australia 138 E1
Cecil Rhodes, Mount hill Australia 135 C6
Cecina Italy 68 D3
Cedar r. ND U.S.A. 160 C2
Cedar r. NE U.S.A. 160 D3
Cedar City U.S.A. 159 G3
Cedar Creek Reservoir TX U.S.A. 167 F1
Cedaredge U.S.A. 159 J2
Cedar Falls U.S.A. 160 E3
Cedar Grove U.S.A. 164 B2
Cedar Hill NM U.S.A. 159 J3
Cedar Hill TN U.S.A. 164 B5
Cedar Island U.S.A. 165 H5
Cedar Lake Canada 151 K4
Cedar Point U.S.A. 164 D3
Cedar Rapids U.S.A. 160 F3
Cedar Run U.S.A. 165 H4
Cedar Springs U.S.A. 164 C2
Cedartown U.S.A. 163 C5
Cedarville S. Africa 125 I6
Cedeño Hond. 166 [inset] I6
Cedral Quintana Roo Mex. 167 I4
Cedral San Luis Potosí Mex. 167 E4
Cedros Hond. 166 [inset] I6
Cedros Sonora Mex. 166 C3
Cedros Zacatecas Mex. 167 E3
Cedros, Cerro mt. Mex. 157 E7
Cedros, Isla i. Mex. 166 B2
Ceduna Australia 135 F8
Ceeldheere Somalia 122 E3
Ceerigaabo Somalia 122 E2
Cefalù Sicily Italy 68 F5
Cegléd Hungary 69 H1
Cêgnê Xizang China 99 F6
Ceheng China 96 E3
Çekerek Turkey 112 D2
Çekiçler Turkm. 110 D2
Celah, Gunung mt. Malaysia see Mandi Angin, Gunung
Celaque, Parque Nacional nat. park Hond. 167 H6
Celaya Mex. 168 D4
Celbridge Ireland 61 F4
Celebes i. Indon. 83 B3
Celebes Basin sea feature Pacific Ocean 186 E5
Celebes Sea Indon./Phil. 81 G6
Celestún Mex. 167 H4
Celina OH U.S.A. 164 C3
Celina TN U.S.A. 164 C5
Celje Slovenia 68 F1
Celle Germany 63 K2
Celovec Austria see Klagenfurt
Celtic Sea Ireland/U.K. 56 D5
Celtic Shelf sea feature N. Atlantic Ocean 184 H2
Cemaru, Gunung mt. Indon. 85 F2
Çemenibit Turkm. 111 F3
Cempi, Teluk b. Sumbawa Indon. 85 G5
Cenderawasih, Teluk b. Indon. 81 J7
Çendir r. Turkm. 110 D2
Cenrana Sulawesi Barat Indon. 83 A3
Centane S. Africa see Kentani
Centenary Zimbabwe 123 D5
Center NE U.S.A. 160 D3
Center TX U.S.A. 161 E6
Centereach U.S.A. 165 I3
Center Point U.S.A. 163 C5
Centerville IA U.S.A. 160 E3
Centerville MO U.S.A. 161 F4
Centerville TX U.S.A. 161 E6
Centerville WV U.S.A. 164 E4
Centrafricaine, République country Africa see Central African Republic
Central admin. dist. Botswana 125 H2
Central AK U.S.A. 149 K2
Central U.S.A. 159 I5
Central, Cordillera mts Col. 176 C3
Central, Cordillera mts Panama 166 [inset] J7
Central, Cordillera mts Peru 176 C6
Central, Cordillera mts Luzon Phil. 82 C2
Central African Empire country Africa see Central African Republic
Central African Republic country Africa 122 B3
Central Brahui Range mts Pak. 111 G4
Central Butte Canada 156 G2
Central City U.S.A. 160 D3
Centralia IL U.S.A. 160 F4
Centralia WA U.S.A. 156 C3
Central Kalahari Game Reserve nature res. Botswana 124 F2
Central Kara Rise sea feature Arctic Ocean 189 F1
Central Makran Range mts Pak. 111 G5
Central Mount Stuart hill Australia 134 F5
Central Pacific Basin sea feature Pacific Ocean 186 H5
Central Provinces state India see Madhya Pradesh
Central Range mts P.N.G. 81 K7
Central Russian Upland hills Rus. Fed. 53 H5
Central Siberian Plateau Rus. Fed. 77 M3
Central Square U.S.A. 165 G2
Centre U.S.A. 163 C5
Centreville AL U.S.A. 163 C5
Centreville U.S.A. 165 G4
Cenxi China 97 F4
Cenyang China see Hengfeng
Ceos i. Greece see Tzia
Cephaloedium Sicily Italy see Cefalù
Cephalonia i. Greece 69 I5
Cepu Jawa Indon. 85 E4
Ceram i. Maluku Indon. see Seram
Ceram Sea Indon. see Seram, Laut
Cerbat Mountains U.S.A. 159 F4
Čerchov mt. Czech Rep. 63 M5
Ceres Arg. 178 D3
Ceres Brazil 179 A1
Ceres S. Africa 124 D7
Ceres U.S.A. 158 C3
Céret France 66 F5
Cerezo de Abajo Spain 67 E3
Cêri Xizang China 99 D7
Cerignola Italy 68 F4
Cerigo i. Greece see Kythira
Cêringgolêb Xizang China see Dongco
Çerkeş Turkey 112 D2
Çerkeşli Turkey 69 M4
Çermik Turkey 113 E3
Cernăuți Ukr. see Chernivtsi
Cernavodă Romania 69 M2
Cerralvo Mex. 167 F3
Cerralvo, Isla i. Mex. 166 C3
Cërrik Albania 69 H4
Cerritos Mex. 168 D4
Cerro Azul Brazil 179 A4
Cerro Azul Mex. 167 F4
Cerro de Pasco Peru 176 C6
Cerro Hoya, Parque Nacional nat. park Panama 166 [inset] J8
Cerro Prieto Mex. 166 D3
Cerros Colorados, Embalse resr Arg. 178 C5
Cervantes, Cerro mt. Arg. 178 B8
Cervati, Monte mt. Italy 68 F4
Cervione Corsica France 66 I5
Cervo Spain 67 C2
Cesena Italy 68 E2
Cēsis Latvia 55 N8
Česká Republika country Europe see Czech Republic
České Budějovice Czech Rep. 57 O6
Českomoravská vysočina hills Czech Rep. 57 O6
Český Krumlov Czech Rep. 57 O6
Český les mts Czech Rep./Germany 63 M5
Çeşme Turkey 69 L5
Cessnock Australia 138 E4
Cetaceo, Mount Phil. 82 C2
Cêtar Qinghai China 94 E4
Cetatea Albă Ukr. see Bilhorod-Dnistrovs'kyy
Cetinje Montenegro 68 H3
Cetraro Italy 68 F5
▶Ceuta N. Africa 67 D6
Autonomous Community of Spain.
Ceva-i-Ra reef Fiji 133 H4
Cévennes mts France 66 F5
Cévennes, Parc National des nat. park France 66 F4
Cevizli Turkey 107 C1
Cevizlik Turkey see Maçka
Ceyhan Turkey 112 D3
Ceyhan r. Turkey 107 B1
Ceyhan Boğazı r. mouth Turkey 107 B1
Ceylanpınar Turkey 113 F3
Ceylon country Asia see Sri Lanka
Chābahār Iran 111 F5
Chablé Mex. 167 H5
Chabrol i. New Caledonia see Lifou
Chabug Xizang China 99 C6
Chabyêr Caka salt l. China 99 D7
Chachapoyas Peru 176 C5
Chacharan Pak. 111 H4
Chäche Turkm. see Çäçe
Chachoengsao Thai. 87 C4
Chachro Pak. 111 H5
Chaco r. U.S.A. 159 I3
Chaco Boreal reg. Para. 178 E2
Chaco Culture National Historical Park U.S.A. 159 J3
Chaco Mesa plat. U.S.A. 159 J4
▶Chad country Africa 121 E3
5th largest country in Africa.
Chad, Lake Africa 121 E3
Chadaasan Mongolia 94 E2
Chadan Rus. Fed. 102 H1
Chadibe Botswana 125 H2
Chadron U.S.A. 160 C3
Chadyr-Lunga Moldova see Ciadîr-Lunga
Chae Hom Thai. 86 B3
Chaek Kyrg. 98 A4
Chaeryŏng N. Korea 91 B5
Chae Son National Park Thai. 86 B3
Chagai Pak. 111 G4
Chagai Hills Afgh./Pak. 111 F4
Chagan Kazakh. 98 B2
Chaganuzun Rus. Fed. 98 E2
Chagdo Kangri mt. China 105 F2
Chaggur Qinghai China 99 F6
Chaghā Khūr mt. Iran 110 C4
Chaghcharān Afgh. 111 G3
Chagny France 66 G3
Chagoda Rus. Fed. 52 G4
Chagos Archipelago is B.I.O.T. 185 M6
Chagos-Laccadive Ridge sea feature Indian Ocean 185 M6
Chagos Trench sea feature Indian Ocean 185 M6
Chagoyan Rus. Fed. 90 C1
Chagrayskoye Plato plat. Kazakh. see Shagyray, Plato
Chagres, Parque Nacional nat. park Panama 166 [inset] K7
Chāh Ākhvor Iran 111 E3
Chāh 'Ali Akbar Iran 110 E3
Chahbounia Alg. 67 H6
Chahchaheh Turkm. 111 F2
Chāh-e Āb Afgh. 111 H2
Chāh-e Bāgh well Iran 110 D4
Chāh-e Bāzargānī Iran 110 D4
Chāh-e Dow Chāhī Iran 110 D4
Chāh-e Gonbad well Iran 110 D3
Chāh-e Kavīr well Iran 110 E3
Chāh-e Khorāsān well Iran 110 D3
Chāh-e Khoshāb Iran 110 E3
Chāh-e Malek well Iran 110 D3
Chāh-e Malek Mīrzā well Iran 110 D4
Chāh-e Mūjān well Iran 110 D3
Chāh-e Qeyṣar well Iran 110 D4
Chāh-e Qobād well Iran 110 D3
Chāh-e Rāh Iran 110 D4
Chāh-e Raḥmān well Iran 111 E4
Chāh-e Shūr well Iran 110 D3
Chāh-e Tūnī well Iran 110 E3
Chāh Kūh Iran 110 D4
Chāh Lak Iran 110 E5
Chāh Pās well Iran 110 D3
Chah Sandan Pak. 111 F4
Chahuites Mex. 167 G5
Chaibasa India 105 F5
Chaigneau, Lac l. Canada 153 I3
Chaigoubu Hebei China see Huai'an
Chaihe Nei Mongol China 95 J2
Chainat Thai. 86 C4
Chainjoin Co l. Xizang China 99 D6
Chai Prakan Thai. 86 B3
Chaitén Chile 178 B6
Chai Wan H.K. China 97 [inset]
Chaiwopu Xinjiang China 98 D4
Chaiya Thai. 87 B5
Chaiyaphum Thai. 86 C4
Chajarí Arg. 178 E4
Chakachamna Lake AK U.S.A. 148 I3
Chakai India 105 F4
Chak Amru Pak. 111 I3
Chakar r. Pak. 111 H4
Chakaria Bangl. 105 H5
Chakdarra Pak. 111 I3
Chakku Pak. 111 G5
Chakonipau, Lac l. Canada 153 H2
Chakoria Bangl. see Chakaria
Ch'ak'vi Georgia 113 F2
Chala Peru 176 D7
Chalap Dalan mts Afgh. 111 G3
Chalatenango El Salvador 166 [inset] H6
Chaláua Moz. 123 D5

Chalaxung Qinghai China 94 D5
Chalcedon Turkey see Kadıköy
Chalengkou Qinghai China 99 F5
Chaleur Bay inlet Canada 153 I4
Chaleurs, Baie des inlet Canada see Chaleur Bay
Chali China 96 C2
Chaling China 97 G3
Chalisgaon India 106 B1
Chalki i. Greece 69 L6
Chalkida Greece 69 J5
Chalkyitsik AK U.S.A. 149 L2
Challakere India 106 C3
Challans France 66 D3
Challapata Bol. 176 E7

▶Challenger Deep sea feature N. Pacific Ocean 186 F5
Deepest point in the world (Mariana Trench).

Challenger Fracture Zone sea feature S. Pacific Ocean 186 M8
Challis U.S.A. 156 E3
Chalmette U.S.A. 161 F6
Châlons-en-Champagne France 62 E6
Châlons-sur-Marne France see Châlons-en-Champagne
Chalon-sur-Saône France 66 G3
Chaltan Pass Azer. 113 H2
Chālūs Iran 110 C2
Cham Germany 63 M5
Cham, Kūh-e hill Iran 110 C3
Chamah, Gunung mt. Malaysia 84 C1
Chamaico Arg. 178 D5
Chamais Bay Namibia 124 B4
Chaman Pak. 100 F3
Chaman Bid Iran 110 E2
Chamao, Khao mt. Thai. 87 C4
Chamba India 104 D2
Chamba Tanz. 123 D5
Chambal r. India 104 D4
Chambas Cuba 163 E8
Chambeaux, Lac l. Canada 153 H3
Chamberlain r. Australia 134 D4
Chamberlain Canada 151 J5
Chamberlain U.S.A. 160 D3
Chamberlain Lake U.S.A. 162 G2
Chamberlin, Mount AK U.S.A. 149 K1
Chambers U.S.A. 159 I4
Chambersburg U.S.A. 165 G4
Chambers Island U.S.A. 164 B1
Chambéry France 66 G4
Chambeshi r. Zambia 123 C5
Chambi, Jebel mt. Tunisia 68 C7
Chamda Xizang China 99 E7
Chamdo China see Qamdo
Chame Panama 166 [inset] K7
Chamechaude mt. France 66 G4
Chamela Mex. 166 D5
Chamiss Bay Canada 150 E5
Chamoli India see Gopeshwar
Chamonix-Mont-Blanc France 66 H4
Champa India 105 E5
Champagne Y.T. Canada 149 M3
Champagne-Ardenne admin. reg. France 62 E6
Champagne Castle mt. S. Africa 125 I5
Champagne Humide reg. France 66 G2
Champagne Pouilleuse reg. France 66 F2
Champagnole France 66 G3
Champagny Islands Australia 134 D3
Champaign U.S.A. 160 F3
Champasak Laos 86 D4
Champdoré, Lac l. Canada 153 I3
Champhai India 105 H5
Champion Canada 150 H5
Champlain U.S.A. 165 G4
Champlain, Lake Canada/U.S.A. 165 I1
Champotón Mex. 167 H5
Chamrajnagar India 106 C4
Chamu Co l. Qinghai China 99 E6
Chamzinka Rus. Fed. 53 J5
Chana Thai. 87 C6
Chanak Turkey see Çanakkale
Chanal Mex. 167 G5
Chañaral Chile 178 B3
Chanārān Iran 110 E2
Chanchén Mex. 167 H5
Chanda India see Chandrapur
Chandalar AK U.S.A. 149 J2
Chandalar r. AK U.S.A. 149 K2
Chandalar, East Fork r. AK U.S.A. 149 K2
Chandalar, Middle Fork r. AK U.S.A. 149 J2
Chandalar, North Fork r. AK U.S.A. 149 J2
Chandalar Lake AK U.S.A. 149 J2
Chandausi India 104 D3
Chandbali India 105 F5
Chandeleur Islands U.S.A. 161 F6
Chanderi India 104 D4
Chandigarh India 104 D3
Chandil India 105 F5
Chandir Uzbek. 111 G2
Chandler Canada 153 I4
Chandler AZ U.S.A. 159 H5
Chandler IN U.S.A. 164 B4
Chandler OK U.S.A. 161 D5
Chandler r. AK U.S.A. 149 J1
Chandler Lake AK U.S.A. 148 I1
Chandmanī Mongolia see Yaruu
Chandmanī Mongolia 94 D2
Chandod India 104 C5
Chandos Lake Canada 165 G1
Chandpur Bangl. 105 G5
Chandpur India 104 D3
Chandragiri India 106 C3
Chandrapur India 106 C2
Chandvad India 106 B1
Chang, Ko i. Thai. 87 C4
Chang'an Shaanxi China 95 G5
Changane r. Moz. 125 K3
Changbai China 90 C4
Changbai Shan mts China/N. Korea 90 B4
Chang Cheng research station Antarctica see Great Wall
Changcheng China 97 F5
Changchow Fujian China see Zhangzhou
Changchow Jiangsu China see Changzhou
Changchun China 90 B4
Changchunling China 90 B3
Changdao Shandong China 95 J4
Changde China 97 F2
Changgang China 97 G3
Changge Henan China 95 H5
Changgi-ap pt S. Korea 91 C5
Changgo Xizang China 99 D7
Chang Hu l. China 97 G2
Changhua Taiwan 97 I3
Changhŭng S. Korea 91 B6
Changhwa Taiwan see Changhua
Changi Sing. 87 [inset]
Changji Xinjiang China 98 D4
Changjiang China 97 F5
Chang Jiang r. China 97 I2 see Yangtze
Changjiang Kou China see Mouth of the Yangtze
Changjin-ho resr N. Korea 91 B4
Changkiang China see Zhanjiang
Changlang India 105 H4
Changleng China see Xinjian
Changli Hebei China 95 I4
Changling Jilin China 95 J2
Changliushui Nei Mongol China 94 F4
Changlun Malaysia 84 C1
Changlung India 109 M3
Changma Gansu China 94 D4
Changmar Xizang China 99 C6
Changning Jiangxi China see Xunwu
Changning Sichuan China 96 E2
Changnyŏn N. Korea 91 B5
Ch'ang-pai Shan mts China/N. Korea see Changbai Shan
Changping Beijing China 95 I3
Changpu China see Suining
Changp'yŏng S. Korea 91 C5
Changsan-got pt N. Korea 91 B5
Changsha China 97 G2
Changshan China 97 H2
Changshan Qundao is China 95 J4
Changshi China 96 E3
Changshoujie China 97 G2
Changshu China 97 I2
Changtai China 97 H3
Changteh China see Changde
Changting Fujian China 97 H3
Changting Heilong. China 90 C3
Changuinola Panama 166 [inset] J7
Changweiliang Qinghai China 99 F5
Ch'angwŏn S. Korea 91 C6
Changwu Shaanxi China 95 F5
Changxing China 97 H2
Changxing Dao i. China 95 J4
Changyang China 97 F2
Changyi Shandong China 95 I4
Changyŏn N. Korea 91 B5
Changyuan Henan China 95 H5
Changzhi Shanxi China 95 H4
Changzhi Shanxi China 95 H5
Changzhou China 97 H2
Chañi, Nevado de mt. Arg. 178 C2
Chania Greece 69 K7
Chanion, Kolpos b. Greece 69 J7
Chankou Gansu China 94 F5
Channahon U.S.A. 164 A3
Channapatna India 106 C3
Channel Islands English Chan. 59 E9
Channel Islands U.S.A. 158 D5
Channel Islands National Park U.S.A. 158 D4
Channel-Port-aux-Basques Canada 153 K5
Channel Rock i. Bahamas 163 E8
Channel Tunnel France/U.K. 59 I7
Channing U.S.A. 161 C5
Chantada Spain 67 C2
Chantal'skiy mt. Rus. Fed. 148 B2
Chantal'vergyrgyn r. Rus. Fed. 148 C2
Chanthaburi Thai. 87 C4
Chantilly France 62 C5
Chanumla India 87 A5
Chanute U.S.A. 160 E4
Chanuwala Pak. 111 I3
Chany, Ozero salt l. Rus. Fed. 76 I4
Chaohu China 97 H2
Chao Hu l. China 97 H2
Chaor Nei Mongol China 95 J1
Chaouèn Morocco 67 D6
Chaowula Shan mt. China 96 C1
Chaoyang Guangdong China 97 H4
Chaoyang Heilong. China see Jiayin
Chaoyang Liaoning China 95 J3
Chaoyangcun Nei Mongol China 95 K1
Chaoyang Hu l. Xizang China 99 D6
Chaozhong Nei Mongol China 95 J1
Chaozhou China 97 H4
Chapada Diamantina, Parque Nacional nat. park Brazil 179 C1
Chapada dos Veadeiros, Parque Nacional da nat. park Brazil 179 B1
Chapais Canada 152 G4
Chapak Guzar Afgh. 111 G2
Chapala Mex. 166 E4
Chapala, Laguna de l. Mex. 168 D4
Chāpārī, Kowtal-e Afgh. 111 G3
Chapayevo Kazakh. 100 E1
Chapayevsk Rus. Fed. 53 K5
Chapecó Brazil 178 F3
Chapecó r. Brazil 178 F3
Chapel-en-le-Frith U.K. 58 F5
Chapelle-lez-Herlaimont Belgium 62 E4
Chapeltown U.K. 58 F5
Chapleau Canada 152 E5
Chaplin Canada 151 J5
Chaplin Lake Canada 151 J5
Chaplino Rus. Fed. 148 D2
Chaplygin Rus. Fed. 53 H5
Chapman, Mount Canada 150 G5
Chapmanville U.S.A. 164 D5
Chappell U.S.A. 160 C3
Chappell Islands Australia 137 [inset]
Chapra Bihar India see Chhapra
Chapra Jharkhand India see Chatra
Chaqmaqtīn, Kowl-e Afgh. 111 I2
Charagua Bol. 176 F7
Charay Mex. 166 C3
Charcas Mex. 168 D4
Charcot Island Antarctica 188 L2
Chard Canada 151 I4
Chard U.K. 59 E8
Chardara Kazakh. see Shardara
Chardara, Step' plain Kazakh. 102 C3
Chardon U.S.A. 164 E3
Chardzhev Turkm. see Türkmenabat
Chardzhou Turkm. see Türkmenabat
Charef Alg. 67 H6
Charef, Oued watercourse Morocco 64 D5
Charente r. France 66 D4
Chari r. Cameroon/Chad 121 E3
Chārī Iran 110 E4
Chārīkār Afgh. 111 H3
Chariot AK U.S.A. 148 F1
Chariton U.S.A. 160 E3
Chärjew Turkm. see Türkmenabat
Charkayuvom Rus. Fed. 52 L2
Chār Kent Afgh. 111 G2
Charkhlik Xinjiang China see Ruoqiang
Charleroi Belgium 62 E4
Charles, Cape U.S.A. 165 H5
Charlesbourg Canada 153 H5
Charles City IA U.S.A. 160 E3
Charles City VA U.S.A. 165 G5
Charles Hill Botswana 124 E2
Charles Island Galápagos Ecuador see Santa María, Isla
Charles Lake Canada 151 I3
Charles Point Australia 134 E3
Charleston N.Z. 139 C5
Charleston IL U.S.A. 160 F4
Charleston MO U.S.A. 161 F4
Charleston SC U.S.A. 163 E5

▶Charleston WV U.S.A. 164 E4
Capital of West Virginia.

Charleston Peak U.S.A. 159 F3
Charlestown Ireland 61 D4
Charlestown IN U.S.A. 164 C4
Charlestown NH U.S.A. 165 I2
Charlestown RI U.S.A. 165 J3
Charles Town U.S.A. 165 G4
Charleville Australia 137 D5
Charleville Ireland 61 D5
Charleville-Mézières France 62 E5
Charlevoix U.S.A. 164 C1
Charley r. AK U.S.A. 149 L2
Charlie Lake Canada 150 F3
Charlotte MI U.S.A. 164 C2
Charlotte NC U.S.A. 163 D5
Charlotte TN U.S.A. 164 B5

▶Charlotte Amalie Virgin Is (U.S.A.) 169 L5
Capital of the U.S. Virgin Islands.

Charlotte Bank sea feature S. China Sea 85 D1
Charlotte Harbor b. U.S.A. 163 D7
Charlotte Lake Canada 150 E4
Charlottesville U.S.A. 165 F4

▶Charlottetown Canada 153 J5
Capital of Prince Edward Island.

Charlton Australia 138 A6
Charlton Island Canada 152 F3
Charron Lake Canada 151 M4
Charsadda Pak. 111 H3
Charshanga Turkm. see Köýtendag
Charshangngy Turkm. see Köýtendag
Charters Towers Australia 136 D4
Chartres France 66 E2
Charyn Kazakh. 98 B4
Charyn r. Kazakh. 98 B4
Chas India 105 F5
Chase Canada 150 G5
Chase U.S.A. 164 C2
Chase City U.S.A. 165 F5
Chashmeh Nūrī Iran 110 E3
Chashmeh-ye Ab-e Garm spring Iran 110 E3
Chashmeh-ye Magu well Iran 110 E3
Chashmeh-ye Mūkīk spring Iran 110 E3
Chashmeh-ye Palasi Iran 110 D3
Chashmeh-ye Safid spring Iran 110 E3
Chashmeh-ye Shotoran well Iran 110 D3
Chashniki Belarus 53 F5
Chaska U.S.A. 160 E2
Chaslands Mistake c. N.Z. 139 B8
Chasŏng N. Korea 90 B4
Chasseral mt. Switz. 57 K7
Chassiron, Pointe de pt France 66 D3
Chastab, Kūh-e mts Iran 110 D3
Chāt Iran 110 D2
Chatanika AK U.S.A. 149 K2
Chatanika r. AK U.S.A. 149 J2
Châteaubriant France 66 D3
Château-du-Loir France 66 E3
Châteaudun France 66 E2
Chateaugay U.S.A. 165 H1
Châteauguay Canada 165 I1
Châteauguay r. Canada 153 H2
Châteauguay, Lac l. Canada 153 H2
Châteaulin France 66 B2
Châteaumeillant France 66 F3
Châteauneuf-en-Thymerais France 62 B6
Châteauneuf-sur-Loire France 66 F3
Chateau Pond l. Canada 153 K3
Châteauroux France 66 E3
Château-Salins France 62 G6
Château-Thierry France 62 D5
Chateh Canada 150 G3
Châtelet Belgium 62 E4
Châtellerault France 66 E3
Chatfield U.S.A. 152 B6
Chatham Canada 164 D2
Chatham U.K. 59 H7
Chatham AK U.S.A. 149 N4
Chatham MA U.S.A. 165 K3
Chatham NY U.S.A. 165 I2
Chatham PA U.S.A. 165 H4
Chatham VA U.S.A. 164 F5
Chatham, Isla i. Chile 178 B8
Chatham Island Galápagos Ecuador see San Cristóbal, Isla
Chatham Island N.Z. 133 I6
Chatham Island Samoa see Savai'i
Chatham Islands N.Z. 133 I6
Chatham Rise sea feature S. Pacific Ocean 186 I8
Chatham Sound sea channel B.C. Canada 149 O5
Chatham Strait AK U.S.A. 149 N4
Châtillon-sur-Seine France 66 G3
Chatkal Range mts Kyrg./Uzbek. 102 D3
Chatom U.S.A. 161 F6
Chatra India 105 F4
Chatra Nepal 105 F4
Chatsworth Canada 164 E1
Chatsworth U.S.A. 165 H4
Chattagam Bangl. see Chittagong
Chattanooga U.S.A. 163 C5
Chattarpur India see Chhatarpur
Chatteris U.K. 59 H6
Chattisgarh state India see Chhattisgarh
Chatturat Thai. 86 C4
Chatyr-Köl l. Kyrg. 98 A4
Chatyr-Tash Kyrg. 102 E3
Châu Đốc Vietnam 87 D5
Chauhtan India 104 B4
Chauk Myanmar 86 A2
Chauka r. India 99 C8
Chaukhamba mts Uttaranchal India 99 B7
Chaumont France 66 G2
Chauncey U.S.A. 164 D4
Chaungzon Myanmar 86 B3
Chaunskaya Guba b. Rus. Fed. 77 R3
Chauny France 62 D5
Chau Phu Vietnam see Châu Đốc
Chausu-yama mt. Japan 92 D3
Chausy Belarus see Chavusy
Chautauqua, Lake U.S.A. 164 F2
Chauter Pak. 111 G4
Chauvin Canada 151 I4
Chavakachcheri Sri Lanka 106 D4
Chaves Port. 67 C3
Chavigny, Lac l. Canada 152 G2
Chavusy Belarus 53 F5
Chawal r. Pak. 111 G4
Chay, Sông r. Vietnam 86 D2
Chayatyn, Khrebet ridge Rus. Fed. 90 E1
Chayevo Rus. Fed. 52 H4
Chaykovskiy Rus. Fed. 51 Q4
Chäyul Xizang China see Qayü
Chazhegovo Rus. Fed. 52 L3
Chazy U.S.A. 165 I1
Cheadle U.K. 59 F6
Cheaha Mountain hill U.S.A. 163 C5
Cheat r. U.S.A. 164 F4
Cheatham Lake U.S.A. 164 B5
Cheb Czech Rep. 63 M4
Chebba Tunisia 68 D7
Cheboksarskoye Vodokhranilishche resr Rus. Fed. 52 J5
Cheboksary Rus. Fed. 52 J4
Cheboygan U.S.A. 162 C2
Chechen Rus. Fed. 148 D2
Chechen', Ostrov i. Rus. Fed. 113 G2
Chech'ŏn S. Korea 91 C5
Chedabucto Bay Canada 153 J5
Chedao Shandong China 95 J4
Cheddar U.K. 59 E7
Cheduba Myanmar see Man-aung
Cheduba Island i. Myanmar see Man-aung Kyun
Chée r. France 62 E6
Cheektowaga U.S.A. 165 F2
Cheepie Australia 138 B1
Cheetham, Cape Antarctica 188 H2
Chefoo Shandong China see Yantai
Chefornak AK U.S.A. 148 F3
Chefu Moz. 125 K2
Chegdomyn Rus. Fed. 90 D2
Chegga Mauritania 120 C2
Chegitun' Rus. Fed. 148 E2
Chegitun' r. Rus. Fed. 148 E2
Chegutu Zimbabwe 123 D5
Chehalis U.S.A. 156 C3
Chehar Burj Iran 110 E2
Chehardeh Iran 110 E3
Chehel Chashmeh, Kūh-e hill Iran 110 B3
Chehel Dokhtarān, Kūh-e mt. Iran 111 F4
Chehell'āyeh Iran 110 E4
Cheju S. Korea 91 B6
Cheju-do i. S. Korea 91 B6
Cheju-haehyŏp sea chan. S. Korea 91 B6
Chek Chue H.K. China see Stanley
Chekhov Moskovskaya Oblast' Rus. Fed. 53 H5
Chekhov Sakhalinskaya Oblast' Rus. Fed. 90 F3
Chekiang prov. China see Zhejiang
Chekichler Turkm. see Çekiçler
Chek Lap Kok reg. H.K. China 97 [inset]
Chek Mun Hoi Hap H.K. China see Tolo Channel
Chekunda Rus. Fed. 90 D2
Chela, Serra da mts Angola 123 B5
Chelan, Lake U.S.A. 156 C2
Chelatna Lake AK U.S.A. 149 J3
Cheleken Turkm. see Hazar
Cheline Moz. 125 L2
Chelkar Kazakh. see Shalkar
Chełm Poland 53 D6
Chelmer r. U.K. 59 H7
Chełmno Poland 57 Q4
Chelmsford U.K. 59 H7
Chelsea MI U.S.A. 164 C2
Chelsea VT U.S.A. 165 I2
Cheltenham U.K. 59 E7
Chelva Spain 67 F4
Chelyabinsk Rus. Fed. 76 H4
Chelyuskin Rus. Fed. 189 E1
Chemax Mex. 167 I4
Chemba Moz. 123 D5
Chêm Co l. China 99 B6
Chemnitz Germany 63 M4
Chemulpo S. Korea see Inch'ŏn
Chemyndy Naryn Kyrg. 98 A4
Chena r. AK U.S.A. 149 K2
Chenab r. India/Pak. 104 B3
Chenachane, Oued watercourse Alg. 120 C2
Chena Hot Springs AK U.S.A. 149 K2
Chenderoh, Tasik resr Malaysia 84 C1
Chendir r. Turkm. see Çendir
Chenega AK U.S.A. 149 J3
Cheney U.S.A. 156 D3
Cheney Reservoir U.S.A. 160 D4
Chengalpattu India 106 D3
Cheng'an Hebei China 95 H4
Chengbu China 97 F3
Chengcheng Shaanxi China 95 G5
Chengchow Henan China see Zhengzhou
Chengde Hebei China 95 I3
Chengde Hebei China 95 I3
Chengdu China 96 E2
Chengele India 96 C2
Chenggong China 96 D3
Chenghai China 97 H4
Cheng Hai l. China 96 D3
Chengjiang China see Taihe
Chengmai China 97 F5
Chengqian Shandong China 95 I5
Chengtu China see Chengdu
Chengwu Shandong China 95 H5
Chengxian China 96 E1
Chengxiang Chongqing China see Wuxi
Chengxiang Jiangxi China see Quannan
Chengyang Shandong China see Juxian
Chengzhong China see Ningming
Cheniu Shan i. China 95 I5
Chenkaladi Sri Lanka 106 D5
Chennai India 106 D3
Chenqian Shan i. China 97 I2
Chenqing China 90 B2
Chenqingqiao China see Chenqing
Chenstokhov Poland see Częstochowa
Chentejn Nuruu mts Mongolia 95 F1
Chenxi China 97 F3
Chenyang China see Chenxi
Chenying China see Wannian
Chenzhou China 97 G3
Chenzhuang Hebei China 95 H4
Chepén Peru 176 C5
Chepes Arg. 178 C4
Chepo Panama 166 [inset] K7
Chepstow U.K. 59 E7
Cheptsa r. Rus. Fed. 52 K4
Chequamegon Bay U.S.A. 160 F2
Cher r. France 66 E3
Chera state India see Kerala
Cherán Mex. 167 E5
Cheraw U.S.A. 163 E5
Cherbaniani Reef India 106 A3
Cherbourg France 66 D2
Cherchell Alg. 67 H5
Cherchen Xinjiang China see Qiemo
Cherdakly Rus. Fed. 53 K5
Cherdoyak Kazakh. 98 C2
Cherdyn' Rus. Fed. 51 R3
Chereapani reef India see Byramgore Reef
Cheremkhovo Rus. Fed. 88 I2
Cheremshany Rus. Fed. 90 D3
Cheremukhovka Rus. Fed. 52 K4
Cherepanovo Rus. Fed. 88 E2
Cherepovets Rus. Fed. 52 H4
Cherevkovo Rus. Fed. 52 J3
Chergui, Chott ech imp. l. Alg. 64 D5
Chéria Alg. 68 B7
Cheriton U.S.A. 165 H5
Cheriyam atoll India 106 B4
Cherkassy Ukr. see Cherkasy
Cherkasy Ukr. 53 G6
Cherkessk Rus. Fed. 113 F1
Cherla India 106 D2
Chernabura Island AK U.S.A. 148 H5
Chernaya Rus. Fed. 52 M1
Chernaya r. Rus. Fed. 52 M1
Chernigov Ukr. see Chernihiv
Chernigovka Rus. Fed. 90 D3
Chernihiv Ukr. 53 F6
Cherninivka Ukr. 53 H7
Chernivtsi Ukr. 53 E6
Chernobyl' Ukr. see Chornobyl'
Chernogorsk Rus. Fed. 88 G2
Chernovtsy Ukr. see Chernivtsi
Chernoye More sea Asia/Europe see Black Sea
Chernushka Rus. Fed. 51 R4
Chernyakhiv Ukr. 53 F6
Chernyakhovsk Rus. Fed. 55 L9
Chernyanka Rus. Fed. 53 H6
Chernyayeve Rus. Fed. 90 B1
Chernyshevsk Rus. Fed. 89 L2
Chernyshevskiy Rus. Fed. 77 M3
Chernyshkovskiy Rus. Fed. 53 I6
Chernyye Zemli reg. Rus. Fed. 53 J7
Chernyy Irtysh r. China/Kazakh. see Ertix He
Chernyy Porog Rus. Fed. 52 G3
Chernyy Yar Rus. Fed. 53 J6
Cherokee U.S.A. 160 E3
Cherokee Sound Bahamas 163 E7

▶Cherrapunji India 105 G4
Highest recorded annual rainfall in the world.

Cherry Creek r. U.S.A. 160 C2
Cherry Creek Mountains U.S.A. 159 F1
Cherry Hill U.S.A. 165 H4
Cherry Island Solomon Is 133 G3
Cherry Lake U.S.A. 158 D2
Cherskiy Rus. Fed. 189 C2
Cherskiy Range mts Rus. Fed. see Cherskogo, Khrebet
Cherskogo, Khrebet mts Rus. Fed. 77 P3
Cherskogo, Khrebet mts Rus. Fed. 95 G1
Chertkov Ukr. see Chortkiv
Chertkovo Rus. Fed. 53 I6
Cherven Bryag Bulg. 69 K3
Chervonoarmeyskoye Ukr. see Vil'nyans'k
Chervonoarmiys'k Donets'ka Oblast' Ukr. see Krasnoarmiys'k
Chervonoarmiys'k Rivnens'ka Oblast' Ukr. see Radyvyliv
Chervonograd Ukr. see Chervonohrad
Chervonohrad Ukr. 53 E6
Chervyen' Belarus 53 F5
Cherwell r. U.K. 59 F7
Cherykaw Belarus 53 F5
Chesapeake U.S.A. 165 G5
Chesapeake Bay U.S.A. 165 G4
Chesham U.K. 59 G7
Cheshire Plain U.K. 58 E5
Cheshme Vtoroy Turkm. 111 F2
Cheshskaya Guba b. Rus. Fed. 52 J2
Cheshtebe Tajik. 111 I2
Cheshunt U.K. 59 G7
Chesnokovka Rus. Fed. see Novoaltaysk
Chester Canada 153 I5
Chester U.K. 58 E5
Chester CA U.S.A. 158 C1
Chester IL U.S.A. 160 F4
Chester MT U.S.A. 156 F2
Chester OH U.S.A. 164 E4
Chester SC U.S.A. 163 D5
Chester r. U.S.A. 165 G4
Chesterfield U.K. 58 F5
Chesterfield U.S.A. 165 G5
Chesterfield, Îles is New Caledonia 133 F3
Chesterfield Inlet Canada 151 N2
Chesterfield Inlet inlet Canada 151 M2
Chester-le-Street U.K. 58 F4
Chestertown MD U.S.A. 165 G4
Chestertown NY U.S.A. 165 I2
Chesterville Canada 165 H1
Chestnut Ridge U.S.A. 164 F3
Chesuncook Lake U.S.A. 162 G2
Chetaïbi Alg. 68 B6
Chéticamp Canada 153 J5
Chetlat i. India 106 B4
Chetumal Mex. 167 H5
Chetwynd Canada 150 F4
Cheung Chau H.K. China 97 [inset]
Chevak AK U.S.A. 148 F3
Chevelon Creek r. U.S.A. 159 H4
Cheviot N.Z. 139 D6
Cheviot Hills U.K. 58 E3
Cheviot Range hills Australia 136 C5
Chevreulx r. Canada 152 G3
Cheyenne OK U.S.A. 161 D5

▶Cheyenne WY U.S.A. 156 G4
Capital of Wyoming.

Cheyenne r. U.S.A. 160 C2
Cheyenne Wells U.S.A. 160 C4
Cheyne Bay Australia 135 B8
Cheyur India 106 D3
Chezacut Canada 150 E4
Chhapra India 105 F4
Chhata India 104 D4
Chhatak Bangl. 105 G4
Chhatarpur Jharkhand India 105 F4
Chhatarpur Madh. Prad. India 104 D4
Chhatr Pak. 111 H4
Chhatrapur India 106 E2
Chhattisgarh state India 105 E5
Chhay Arêng, Stœng r. Cambodia 87 C5
Chhindwara India 104 D5
Chhitkul India 104 D3
Chhukha Bhutan 105 G4
Chi, Lam r. Thai. 87 C4
Chi, Mae Nam r. Thai. 86 D4
Chiai Taiwan 97 I4
Chiamboni Somalia 122 E4
Chiange Angola 123 B5
Chiang Kham Thai. 86 C3
Chiang Khan Thai. 86 C3
Chiang Mai Thai. 86 B3
Chiang Rai Thai. 86 B3
Chiang Saen Thai. 86 C2
Chiapa Mex. 167 G5
Chiapas state Mex. 167 G5
Chiapilla Mex. 167 G5
Chiari Italy 68 C2
Chiautla Mex. 168 E5
Chiavenna Italy 68 C1
Chiayi Taiwan see Chiai
Chiba Japan 93 G3
Chiba pref. Japan 93 G3
Chibi China 97 G2
Chibia Angola 123 B5
Chibit Rus. Fed. 98 D2
Chibizovka Rus. Fed. see Zherdevka
Chiboma Moz. 123 D6
Chibougamau Canada 152 G4
Chibougamau, Lac l. Canada 152 G4
Chibuto Moz. 125 K3
Chicacole India see Srikakulam

▶Chicago U.S.A. 164 B3
4th most populous city in North America.

Chic-Chocs, Monts mts Canada 153 I4
Chichagof AK U.S.A. 149 M4
Chichagof Island AK U.S.A. 149 N4
Chichak r. Pak. 111 G5
Chichaoua Morocco 64 C5
Chichatka Rus. Fed. 90 A1
Chicheng Hebei China 95 H3
Chicheng China see Pengxi
Chichén Itzá tourist site Mex. 167 H4
Chichester U.K. 59 G8
Chichester Range mts Australia 134 B5
Chichgarh India 106 D1
Chichibu Japan 93 F3
Chichibu-gawa r. Japan 93 F2
Chichibu-Tama Kokuritsu-kōen nat. park Japan 93 E3
Chichijima-rettō is Japan 91 F8
Chickaloon AK U.S.A. 149 J3
Chickasawhay r. MS U.S.A. 167 H2
Chickasha U.S.A. 161 D5
Chicken AK U.S.A. 149 L2
Chiclana de la Frontera Spain 67 C5
Chiclayo Peru 176 C5
Chico r. Arg. 178 C6
Chico U.S.A. 158 C2
Chicomo Moz. 125 L3
Chicomucelo Mex. 167 G6
Chicopee U.S.A. 165 I2
Chico Sapocoy, Mount Luzon Phil. 82 C2
Chicoutimi Canada 153 H4
Chicualacuala Moz. 125 J2
Chidambaram India 106 C4
Chidenguele Moz. 125 L3
Chidley, Cape Canada 147 L3
Chido Xizang China see Sêndo
Chido S. Korea 91 B6
Chiducuane Moz. 125 L3
Chiefland U.S.A. 163 D6
Chiemsee l. Germany 57 N7
Chiengmai Thai. see Chiang Mai
Chiers r. France 62 F5
Chieti Italy 68 F3
Chifeng Nei Mongol China 95 I3
Chifre, Serra do mts Brazil 179 C2
Chiganak Kazakh. 102 D2
Chigasaki Japan 93 F3
Chiginagak Volcano, Mount U.S.A. 146 C4
Chigmit Mountains AK U.S.A. 148 I3
Chignik AK U.S.A. 148 H4
Chignik Bay AK U.S.A. 148 H4
Chignik Lagoon AK U.S.A. 148 H4
Chignik Lake AK U.S.A. 148 H4
Chigu Xizang China 99 E7
Chigubo Moz. 125 K2
Chigu Co l. China 99 E7
Chihuahua Mex. 166 D2
Chihuahua state Mex. 166 D2
Chihuahua, Desierto de des Mex. 157 G7
Chiili Kazakh. 102 C3
Chijinpu Gansu China 94 D3
Chikalda India 104 D5
Chikan China 97 F4
Chikaskia r. U.S.A. 161 D4
Chikhali Kalan Parasia India 104 D5
Chikhli India 106 C1
Chikishlyar Turkm. see Çekiçler
Chikmagalur India 106 B3
Chikodi India 106 B2
Chikoy Rus. Fed. 94 F1
Chikoy r. Rus. Fed. 95 F1
Chikuma-gawa r. Japan 93 E1
Chikuminuk Lake AK U.S.A. 148 H3
Chikura Japan 93 F4
Chilanko r. Canada 150 F4
Chilapa Guerrero Mex. 167 F5
Chilas Pak. 104 C2
Chilaw Sri Lanka 106 C5
Chilcotin r. Canada 150 F5
Childers Australia 136 F5
Childress U.S.A. 161 C5
Chile country S. America 178 B4

Chile Basin *sea feature* S. Pacific Ocean **187** O8
Chile Chico Chile **178** B7
Chile Rise *sea feature* S. Pacific Ocean **187** O8
Chilgir Rus. Fed. **53** J7
Chilhowie U.S.A. **164** E5
Chilia-Nouă Ukr. *see* **Kiliya**
Chilik Kazakh. **102** E3
Chilik *r.* Kazakh. **98** B4
Chilika Lake India **106** E2
Chililabombwe Zambia **123** C5
Chilko *r.* Canada **150** F4
Chilko Lake Canada **150** E5
Chilkoot Pass Canada/U.S.A. **149** N4
Chilkoot Trail National Historic Site *nat. park* B.C. Canada **149** N4
Chillán Chile **178** B5
Chillicothe *MO* U.S.A. **160** E4
Chillicothe *OH* U.S.A. **164** D4
Chilliwack Canada **150** F5
Chilo India **104** C4
Chiloé, Isla de *i.* Chile **178** B6
Chiloé, Isla Grande de *i.* Chile *see* **Chiloé, Isla de**
Chilpancingo Mex. **168** E5
Chilpancingo de los Bravos Mex. *see* **Chilpancingo**
Chilpi Pak. **104** C1
Chiltern Hills U.K. **59** G7
Chilton U.S.A. **164** A1
Chiluage Angola **123** C4
Chilubi Zambia **123** C5
Chilung Taiwan **97** I3
Chilwa, Lake Malawi **123** D5
Chimala Tanz. **123** D4
Chimalapa Mex. **167** G5
Chimaltenango Guat. **167** H6
Chimán Panama **166** [inset] K7
Chi Ma Wan *H.K.* China **97** [inset]
Chimay Belgium **62** E4
Chimbas Arg. **178** C4
Chimbay Uzbek. *see* **Chimboy**
Chimborazo *mt.* Ecuador **176** C4
Chimbote Peru **176** C5
Chimboy Uzbek. **102** A3
Chimian Pak. **111** I4
Chimishliya Moldova *see* **Cimişlia**
Chimkent Kazakh. *see* **Shymkent**
Chimney Rock U.S.A. **159** J3
Chimoio Moz. **123** D5
Chimtargha, Qullai *mt.* Tajik. **111** H2
Chimtorga, Gora *mt.* Tajik. *see* **Chimtargha, Qullai**

▶**China** *country* Asia **88** H5
Most populous country in the world and in Asia. 2nd largest country in Asia and 4th largest in the world.

China Mex. **167** F3
China, Republic of *country* Asia *see* **Taiwan**
China Bakir *r.* Myanmar *see* **To**
Chinacates Mex. **166** D3
Chinajá Guat. **167** H5
China Lake *CA* U.S.A. **158** E4
China Lake *ME* U.S.A. **165** K1
Chinandega Nicaragua **166** [inset] I6
China Point U.S.A. **158** D5
Chinati Peak U.S.A. **161** B6
Chincha Alta Peru **176** C6
Chinchaga *r.* Canada **150** G3
Chinchilla Australia **138** E1
Chincholi India **106** C2
Chinchorro, Banco *sea feature* Mex. **167** I5
Chincoteague Bay U.S.A. **165** H5
Chinde Moz. **123** D5
Chindo S. Korea **91** B6
Chin-do *i.* S. Korea **91** B6
Chindwin *r.* Myanmar **86** A2
Chinese Turkestan *aut. reg.* China *see* **Xinjiang Uygur Zizhiqu**
Chinghai *prov.* China *see* **Qinghai**
Chingiz-Tau, Khrebet *mts* Kazakh. **102** E2
Chingleput India *see* **Chengalpattu**
Chingola Zambia **123** C5
Chinguar Angola **123** B5
Chinguetti Mauritania **120** B2
Chinhae S. Korea **91** C6
Chinhoyi Zimbabwe **123** D5
Chini India *see* **Kalpa**
Chiniak *AK* U.S.A. **148** I4
Chiniak, Cape *AK* U.S.A. **148** I4
Chining *Shandong* China *see* **Jining**
Chiniot Pak. **111** I4
Chinipas Mex. **166** C3
Chinit, Stœng *r.* Cambodia **87** D4
Chinju S. Korea **91** C6
Chinle U.S.A. **159** I3
Chinmen Taiwan **97** H3
Chinmen Tao *i.* Taiwan **97** H3
Chinnamp'o N. Korea *see* **Namp'o**
Chinnur India **106** C2
Chino Japan **93** E3
Chino Creek *watercourse* U.S.A. **159** G4
Chinon France **66** E3
Chinook U.S.A. **156** F2
Chinook Trough *sea feature* N. Pacific Ocean **186** I3
Chino Valley U.S.A. **159** G4
Chin-shan China *see* **Zhujing**
Chintamani India **106** C3
Chioggia Italy **68** E2
Chios Greece **69** L5
Chios *i.* Greece **69** K5
Chipam Guat. **167** H6
Chipata Zambia **123** D5
Chip Chap *r.* China/India **99** B6
Chipchihua, Sierra de *mts* Arg. **178** C6
Chiphu Cambodia **87** D5
Chipindo Angola **123** B5
Chiping *Shandong* China **95** I4
Chipinga Zimbabwe *see* **Chipinge**
Chipinge Zimbabwe **123** D6
Chipley U.S.A. **163** C6
Chipman Canada **153** I5
Chippenham U.K. **59** E7
Chippewa, Lake U.S.A. **160** F2
Chippewa Falls U.S.A. **160** F2
Chipping Norton U.K. **59** F7
Chipping Sodbury U.K. **59** E7
Chipurupalle *Andhra Prad.* India **106** D2
Chipurupalle *Andhra Prad.* India **106** D2
Chiquibul National Park Belize **167** H5
Chiquilá Mex. **167** I4
Chiquimula Guat. **167** H6
Chiquinquira Col. **176** D2
Chir *r.* Rus. Fed. **53** I6
Chirada India **106** D3
Chirala India **106** D3
Chiras Afgh. **111** G3
Chirchiq Uzbek. **102** C3
Chiredzi Zimbabwe **123** D6
Chirfa Niger **120** E2
Chiricahua National Monument *nat. park* U.S.A. **159** I5
Chiricahua Peak U.S.A. **159** I6
Chirikof Island *AK* U.S.A. **148** I5
Chiriquí, Golfo de *b.* Panama **166** [inset] J7
Chiriquí, Laguna de *b.* Panama **166** [inset] J7
Chiriquí, Volcán de *vol.* Panama *see* **Barú, Volcán**
Chiriquí Grande Panama **166** [inset] J7
Chiri-san *mt.* S. Korea **91** B6
Chirk U.K. **59** D6
Chirnside U.K. **60** G5
Chirripó *mt.* Costa Rica **169** H7
Chirripó, Parque Nacional *nat. park* Costa Rica **166** [inset] J7
Chiryū Japan **92** D3
Chisamba Zambia **123** C5
Chisana *AK* U.S.A. **149** L3
Chisana *r. AK* U.S.A. **149** L3
Chisana Glacier *AK* U.S.A. **149** J3
Chisasibi Canada **152** F3
Chisec Guat. **167** H6
Chishima-retto *is* Rus. Fed. *see* **Kuril Islands**
Chisholm Canada **150** H4
Chishtian Mandi Pak. **111** I4
Chishui China **96** E2
Chishuihe China **96** E3
Chisimaio Somalia *see* **Kismaayo**

▶**Chişinău** Moldova **69** M1
Capital of Moldova.

Chistochina *AK* U.S.A. **149** K3
Chistopol' Rus. Fed. **52** K5
Chita Japan **92** C4
Chita Rus. Fed. **89** K2
Chitado Angola **123** B5
Chita-hantō *pen.* Japan **92** C4
Chitaldrug India *see* **Chitradurga**
Chitalwana India **104** B4
Chitambo Zambia **123** D5
Chitanana *r. AK* U.S.A. **149** J2
Chitanga Rus. Fed. **95** G1
Chita Oblast *admin. div.* Rus. Fed. *see* **Chitinskaya Oblast'**
Chitato Angola **123** C4
Chita-wan *b.* Japan **92** C4
Chitek Lake Canada **151** J4
Chitek Lake *l.* Canada **151** L4
Chitembo Angola **123** B5
Chitina *AK* U.S.A. **149** K3
Chitina *r. AK* U.S.A. **149** K3
Chitinskaya Oblast' *admin. div.* Rus. Fed. **90** A1
Chitipa Malawi **123** D4
Chitkul India *see* **Chhitkul**
Chitobe Moz. **123** D6
Chitoor India *see* **Chittoor**
Chitor India *see* **Chittaurgarh**
Chitose Japan **90** F4
Chitradurga India **106** C3
Chitrakoot India **104** E4
Chitrakut India *see* **Chitrakoot**
Chitral Pak. **111** H3
Chitral *r.* Pak. **111** H3
Chitravati *r.* India **106** C3
Chitré Panama **166** [inset] J8
Chitrod India **104** B5
Chittagong Bangl. **105** G5
Chittaurgarh India **104** C4
Chittoor India **106** C3
Chittor India *see* **Chittoor**
Chittorgarh India *see* **Chittaurgarh**
Chittur India **106** C4
Chitungwiza Zimbabwe **123** D5
Chiu Lung *H.K.* China *see* **Kowloon**
Chiume Angola **123** C5
Chivasso Italy **68** B2
Chivato, Punta *pt* Mex. **166** C3
Chivela Mex. **167** G5
Chivhu Zimbabwe **123** D5
Chixi China **97** G4
Chiyoda *Gunma* Japan **93** F2
Chiyoda *Ibaraki* Japan **93** G2
Chiyogawa Japan **93** F2
Chizarira National Park Zimbabwe **123** C5
Chizha Vtoraya Kazakh. **53** K6
Chizhou China **97** H2
Chizu Japan **91** D6
Chkalov Rus. Fed. *see* **Orenburg**
Chkalovsk Rus. Fed. **52** I4
Chkalovskoye Rus. Fed. **90** D3
Chlef Alg. **67** G5
Chlef, Oued *r.* Alg. **67** G5
Chloride U.S.A. **159** F4
Chlya, Ozero *l.* Rus. Fed. **90** F1
Choa Chu Kang Sing. **87** [inset]
Choa Chu Kang *hill* Sing. **87** [inset]
Chobe National Park Botswana **123** C5
Chodov Czech Rep. **63** M4
Chodro Rus. Fed. **98** E2
Choele Choel Arg. **178** C5
Chōfu Japan **93** F3
Chogar *r.* Rus. Fed. **90** D1
Chogo Lungma Glacier Pak. **99** A6
Chogori Feng *mt.* China/Pak. *see* **K2**
Chograyskoye Vodokhranilishche *resr* Rus. Fed. **53** J7
Choiseul *i.* Solomon Is **133** F2
Choix Mex. **166** C3
Chojnice Poland **57** P4
Chōkai-san *vol.* Japan **91** F5
Ch'ok'ē *mts* Eth. **122** D2
Ch'ok'ē Mountains Eth. *see* **Ch'ok'ē**
Chokola *mt.* China **104** E3
Chokpar Kazakh. **98** A4
Choksum China **105** F3
Chok-Tal Kyrg. **98** B4
Chokue Moz. *see* **Chókwé**
Chokurdakh Rus. Fed. **77** P2
Chókwé Moz. **125** K3
Cho La *pass* China **96** C2
Cholame U.S.A. **158** C4
Chola Shan *mts* China **96** C1
Cholet France **66** D3
Choloma Hond. **166** [inset] I6
Cholpon Kyrg. **98** A4
Cholpon-Ata Kyrg. **102** E3
Cholula Mex. **167** F5
Choluteca Hond. **166** [inset] I6
Choma Zambia **123** C5
Chomo Ganggar *mt. Xizang* China **99** E7
Chơ Moi Vietnam **86** D2
Chomo Lhari *mt.* China/Bhutan **105** G4
Chom Thong Thai. **86** B3
Chomun *Rajasthan* India **99** A8
Chomutov Czech Rep. **57** N5
Chŏnan Japan **93** G3
Ch'ŏnan S. Korea **91** B5
Chon Buri Thai. **87** C4
Ch'ŏnch'ŏn N. Korea **90** B4
Chone Ecuador **176** B4
Ch'ŏngch'ŏn-gang *r.* N. Korea **91** B5
Ch'ongdo S. Korea **91** C6
Chonggye *Xizang* China *see* **Qonggyai**
Ch'ŏngjin N. Korea **90** C4
Ch'ŏngju S. Korea **91** B5
Chŏng Kal Cambodia **87** C4
Chongkü China **96** C2
Chongli *Hebei* China **95** H3
Chonglong China *see* **Zizhong**
Chongming Dao *i.* China **97** I2
Chongoroi Angola **123** B5
Chŏngp'yŏng N. Korea **91** B5
Chongqing China **96** E2
Chongqing *municipality* China **96** E2
Chonguene Moz. **125** K3
Chŏngŭp S. Korea **91** B6
Chongyang China **97** G2
Chongyi China **97** G3
Chongzuo China **96** E4
Chŏnju S. Korea **91** B6
Chonogol Mongolia *see* **Erdenetsagaan**
Chontalpa Mex. **167** G5

▶**Cho Oyu** *mt.* China/Nepal **105** F3
6th highest mountain in the world and in Asia.

Chopda India **104** C5
Chor Pak. **111** H5
Chora Sfakion Greece **69** K7
Chorley U.K. **58** E5
Chornobyl' Ukr. **53** F6
Chornomors'ke Ukr. **69** O2
Chortkiv Ukr. **53** E6
Ch'osan N. Korea **90** B4
Chōshi Japan **93** G3
Chosŏn *country* Asia *see* **South Korea**
Chosŏn-minjujuŭi-inmin-konghwaguk *country* Asia *see* **North Korea**
Choszczno Poland **57** O4
Chota Peru **176** C5
Chota Sinchula *hill* India **105** G4
Choteau U.S.A. **156** E3
Choti Pak. **111** H4
Choûm Mauritania **120** B2
Chowchilla U.S.A. **158** C3
Chowghat India **106** B4
Chown, Mount Canada **150** G4
Choybalsan Mongolia **95** H2
Choyr Mongolia **95** G2
Chrétiens, Île aux *i.* Canada *see* **Christian Island**
Chřiby *hills* Czech Rep. **57** P6
Chrisman U.S.A. **164** B4
Chrissiesmeer S. Africa **125** J4
Christchurch N.Z. **139** D6
Christchurch U.K. **59** F8
Christian *AK* U.S.A. **149** K2
Christian *r. AK* U.S.A. **149** K2
Christian, Cape Canada **147** L2
Christiana S. Africa **125** G4
Christiania Norway *see* **Oslo**
Christian Island Canada **164** E1
Christiansburg U.S.A. **164** E5
Christianshåb Greenland *see* **Qasigiannguit**
Christie Bay Canada **151** I2
Christie Island Myanmar **87** B5
Christina *r.* Canada **151** I3
Christina, Mount N.Z. **139** B7

▶**Christmas Island** *terr.* Indian Ocean **80** D9
Australian External Territory.

Christopher, Lake *salt flat* Australia **135** D6
Chrudim Czech Rep. **57** O6
Chrysi *i. Kriti* Greece *see* **Gaïdouronisi**
Chrysochou Bay Cyprus **107** A2
Chrysochous, Kolpos *b.* Cyprus *see* **Chrysochou Bay**
Chu Kazakh. *see* **Shu**
Chu *r.* Kazakh./Kyrg. **102** C3
Chuadanga Bangl. **105** G5
Chuali, Lago *l.* Moz. **125** K3
Chuanhui China *see* **Zhoukou**
Chuansha China **97** I2
Chuathbaluk *AK* U.S.A. **148** H3
Chubalung China **96** C2
Chubarovka Ukr. *see* **Polohy**
Chubartau Kazakh. *see* **Barshatas**
Chūbu *airport Aichi* Japan **92** C4
Chūbu-Sangaku Kokuritsu-kōen *nat. park* Japan **92** D2
Chubxi *Qinghai* China **94** D5
Chu-ching China *see* **Zhujing**
Chuchkovo Rus. Fed. **53** I5
Chuckwalla Mountains U.S.A. **159** F5
Chucunaque *r.* Panama **166** [inset] K7
Chudniv Ukr. **53** F6
Chudovo Rus. Fed. **52** F4
Chudskoye, Ozero *l.* Estonia/Rus. Fed. *see* **Peipus, Lake**
Chugach Mountains *AK* U.S.A. **149** K3
Chuginadak Island *AK* U.S.A. **148** E5
Chūgoku-sanchi *mts* Japan **91** D6
Chuguchak *Xinjiang* China *see* **Tacheng**
Chugqênsumdo China *see* **Jigzhi**
Chuguyev Ukr. *see* **Chuhuyiv**
Chuguyevka Rus. Fed. **90** D3
Chugwater U.S.A. **156** G4
Chuhai China *see* **Zhuhai**
Chuhuyiv Ukr. **53** H6
Chu-Iliyskiye Gory *mts* Kazakh. **102** D3
Chuimatan *Gansu* China *see* **Jishishan**
Chujiang China *see* **Shimen**
Chukai Malaysia *see* **Cukai**
Chukchagirskoye, Ozero *l.* Rus. Fed. **90** E1
Chukchi Abyssal Plain *sea feature* Arctic Ocean **189** B1
Chukchi Plateau *sea feature* Arctic Ocean **189** B1
Chukchi Sea Rus. Fed./U.S.A. **148** E1
Chukhloma Rus. Fed. **52** I4
Chukotskiy, Mys *c.* Rus. Fed. **148** D2
Chukotskiy Khrebet *mts* Rus. Fed. **148** B2
Chukotskiy Poluostrov *pen.* Rus. Fed. **148** D2
Chulakkurgan Kazakh. *see* **Sholakkorgan**
Chulaktau Kazakh. *see* **Karatau**
Chulasa Rus. Fed. **52** J2
Chula Vista U.S.A. **158** E5
Chulitna *AK* U.S.A. **149** J3
Chuloonawick *AK* U.S.A. **148** F3
Chulucanas Peru **176** B5
Chulung Pass Pak. **104** D2
Chuluut Gol *r.* Mongolia **94** E1
Chulym Rus. Fed. **76** J4
Chulyshman *r.* Rus. Fed. **98** D2
Chumar India **104** D2
Chumbicha Arg. **178** C3
Chumda China **96** C1
Chumek Kazakh. **98** D2
Chumikan Rus. Fed. **77** O4
Chum Phae Thai. **86** C3
Chumphon Thai. **87** B5
Chum Saeng Thai. **86** C4
Chunar India **105** E4
Ch'unch'ŏn S. Korea **91** B5
Chunchura India **105** G5
Chundzha Kazakh. **102** E3
Chunga Zambia **123** C5
Chung-hua Jen-min Kung-ho-kuo *country* Asia *see* **China**
Chung-hua Min-kuo *country* Asia *see* **Taiwan**
Ch'ungju S. Korea **91** B5
Chungking China *see* **Chongqing**
Ch'ungmu S. Korea *see* **T'ongyŏng**
Chŭngsan N. Korea **91** B5
Chungyang Shanmo *mts* Taiwan **97** I4
Chunhua *Shaanxi* China **95** G5
Chunhuhux Mex. **167** H5
Chunskiy Rus. Fed. **88** H1
Chunya *r.* Rus. Fed. **77** K3
Chuōi, Hon *i.* Vietnam **87** D5
Chuosijia China *see* **Guanyinqiao**
Chupa Rus. Fed. **54** R3
Chūplū Iran **110** B2
Chuquicamata Chile **178** C2
Chur Switz. **66** I3
Churachandpur India **105** H4
Chūrān Iran **110** D4
Churapcha Rus. Fed. **77** O3
Churchill Canada **151** M3
Churchill *r. Man.* Canada **151** M3
Churchill *r. Nfld. and Lab.* Canada **153** J3
Churchill, Cape Canada **151** M3
Churchill Falls Canada **153** J3
Churchill Lake Canada **151** I4
Churchill Mountains Antarctica **188** H1
Churchill Sound *sea chan.* Canada **152** F2
Churchs Ferry U.S.A. **160** D1
Churchville U.S.A. **164** F4
Churek-Dag, Gora *mt.* Rus. Fed. **94** B1
Churia Ghati Hills Nepal **105** F4
Churu India **104** C3
Churubusco U.S.A. **164** C3
Churumuco Mex. **167** E5
Churún-Merú *waterfall* Venez. *see* **Angel Falls**
Chushul India **104** D2
Chuska Mountains U.S.A. **159** I3
Chusovaya *r.* Rus. Fed. **51** R4
Chusovoy Rus. Fed. **51** R4
Chust Ukr. *see* **Khust**
Chute-des-Passes Canada **153** H4
Chutia *Assam* India **105** H4
Chutia *Jharkhand* India **105** F5
Chutung Taiwan **97** I3
Chuuk *is* Micronesia **186** G5
Chuxiong China **96** D3
Chüy *r.* Kazakh./Kyrg. *see* **Chu**
Chüy *admin. div.* Kyrg. **98** A4
Chư Yang Sin *mt.* Vietnam **87** E4
Chūzenji-ko *l.* Japan **93** F2
Chuzhou *Anhui* China **97** H1
Chuzhou *Jiangsu* China **97** H1
Chūzu Japan **92** C3
Chymyshliya Moldova *see* **Cimişlia**
Chyulu Hills National Park Kenya **122** D4
Ciadâr-Lunga Moldova *see* **Ciadîr-Lunga**
Ciadîr-Lunga Moldova **69** M1
Ciamis *Jawa* Indon. **85** E4
Cianjur *Jawa* Indon. **84** D4
Cianorte Brazil **178** F2
Cibadak *Jawa* Indon. **84** D4
Cibatu *Jawa* Indon. **85** E4
Cibecue U.S.A. **159** H4
Cibinong *Jawa* Indon. **84** D4
Cibolo Creek *r.* U.S.A. **161** D6
Cibuta Mex. **166** C2
Cibuta, Sierra *mt.* Mex. **166** C2
Čićarija *mts* Croatia **68** E2
Cicero U.S.A. **164** B3
Cidaun *Jawa* Indon. **84** D4
Cide Turkey **112** D2
Ciechanów Poland **57** R4
Ciego de Ávila Cuba **169** I4
Ciénaga Col. **176** D1
Ciénega Mex. **167** E3
Ciénega de Flores Mex. **161** C7
Cieneguillas Mex. **166** D3
Cienfuegos Cuba **169** H4
Cieza Spain **67** F4
Çiftlik Turkey *see* **Kelkit**
Cifuentes Spain **67** E3
Cigeulis *Jawa* Indon. **84** D4
Cigüela *r.* Spain **67** E4
Cihanbeyli Turkey **112** D3
Cihuatlán Mex. **166** D5
Cijara, Embalse de *resr* Spain **67** D4
Cikalong *Jawa* Indon. **85** E4
Cilacap *Jawa* Indon. **85** E4
Cilangkahan *Jawa* Indon. **84** D4
Çıldır Turkey **113** F2
Çıldır Gölü *l.* Turkey **113** F2
Çıldıroba Turkey **107** C1
Ciledug *Jawa* Indon. **85** E4
Cilento e del Vallo di Diano, Parco Nazionale del *nat. park* Italy **68** F4
Cili China **97** F2
Cilician Gates *pass* Turkey *see* **Gülek Boğazı**
Cill Airne Ireland *see* **Killarney**
Cill Chainnigh Ireland *see* **Kilkenny**
Cill Mhantáin Ireland *see* **Wicklow**
Çilmämmetgum *des.* Turkm. **110** D1
Cilo Dağı *mt.* Turkey **113** G3
Çilov Adası *i.* Azer. **113** H2
Cimahi *Jawa* Indon. **84** D4
Cimarron *CO* U.S.A. **159** J2
Cimarron *KS* U.S.A. **160** C4
Cimarron *NM* U.S.A. **157** G5
Cimarron *r.* U.S.A. **161** D4
Cimişlia Moldova **69** M1
Cimone, Monte *mt.* Italy **68** D2
Cîmpina Romania *see* **Câmpina**
Cîmpulung Romania *see* **Câmpulung**
Cîmpulung Moldovenesc Romania *see* **Câmpulung Moldovenesc**
Cina, Tanjung *c.* Indon. **84** D4
Çınar Turkey **113** F3
Cinaruco-Capanaparo, Parque Nacional *nat. park* Venez. **176** E2
Cinca *r.* Spain **67** G3
Cincinnati U.S.A. **164** C4
Cinco de Outubro Angola *see* **Xá-Muteba**
Cinderford U.K. **59** E7
Çine Turkey **69** M6
Ciney Belgium **62** F4
Cintalapa Mex. **168** F5
Cinto, Monte *mt.* France **66** I5
Cipatuja *Jawa* Indon. **85** E4
Ciping China *see* **Jinggangshan**
Cirata, Waduk *resr Jawa* Indon. **84** D4
Circeo, Parco Nazionale del *nat. park* Italy **68** E4
Circle *AK* U.S.A. **149** K2
Circle *MT* U.S.A. **156** G3
Circle Hot Springs *AK* U.S.A. **149** K2
Circleville *OH* U.S.A. **164** D4
Circleville *UT* U.S.A. **159** G2
Cirebon *Jawa* Indon. **85** E4
Cirencester U.K. **59** F7
Cirenti *Sumatera* Indon. **84** C3
Cirò Marina Italy **68** G5
Cirta Alg. *see* **Constantine**
Cisco U.S.A. **159** I2
Cisne, Islas del *is* Caribbean Sea **169** H5
Citlaltépetl *vol.* Mex. *see* **Orizaba, Pico de**
Čitluk Bos.-Herz. **68** G3
Citronelle U.S.A. **161** F6
Citrus Heights U.S.A. **158** C2
Città di Castello Italy **68** E3
Ciucaş, Vârful *mt.* Romania **69** K2
Ciudad Acuña Mex. **167** E2
Ciudad Altamirano Mex. **168** D5
Ciudad Bolívar Venez. **176** F2
Ciudad Camargo Mex. **166** D3
Ciudad Constitución *Baja California Sur* Mex. **166** C3
Ciudad Cuauhtémoc Mex. **167** H6
Ciudad del Carmen Mex. **167** H5
Ciudad Delicias Mex. **166** D2
Ciudad del Maíz Mex. **167** F4
Ciudad de Valles Mex. **168** E4
Ciudad Guayana Venez. **176** F2
Ciudad Guerrero Mex. **157** G7
Ciudad Guzmán Mex. **168** D5
Ciudad Hidalgo Mex. **167** E5
Ciudad Ixtepec Mex. **167** G5
Ciudad Juárez Mex. **166** D2
Ciudad Lerdo Mex. **166** E3
Ciudad Madero Mex. **167** F4
Ciudad Mante Mex. **168** E4
Ciudad Manuel Doblado Mex. **167** E4
Ciudad Mendoza Mex. **167** F5
Ciudad Mier Mex. **167** F3
Ciudad Obregón Mex. **166** C3
Ciudad Real Spain **67** E4
Ciudad Río Bravo Mex. **167** F3
Ciudad Rodrigo Spain **67** C3
Ciudad Tecún Uman Guat. **167** G6
Ciudad Trujillo Dom. Rep. *see* **Santo Domingo**
Ciudad Victoria Mex. **161** D8
Ciutadella Spain **67** H3
Civa Burnu *pt* Turkey **112** E2
Cividale del Friuli Italy **68** E1
Civitanova Marche Italy **68** E3
Civitavecchia Italy **68** D3
Çivril Turkey **69** M5
Cixi China **97** I2
Cixian *Hebei* China **95** H4
Ciyao *Shandong* China **95** I5
Cizhou *Hebei* China *see* **Cixian**
Cizre Turkey **113** F3
Clacton-on-Sea U.K. **59** I7
Clady U.K. **61** E3
Claire, Lake Canada **151** H3
Clairfontaine Alg. *see* **El Aouinet**
Clamecy France **66** F3
Clam Gulch *AK* U.S.A. **149** J3
Clane Ireland **61** F4
Clanton U.S.A. **163** C5
Clanwilliam Dam S. Africa **124** D7
Clara Ireland **61** E4
Clara Island Myanmar **87** B5
Claraville Australia **136** C3
Clare *N.S.W.* Australia **138** A4
Clare *S.A.* Australia **137** B7
Clare *r.* Ireland **61** C4
Clare U.S.A. **164** C2
Clarecastle Ireland **61** D5
Clare Island Ireland **61** B4
Claremont U.S.A. **165** I2
Claremore U.S.A. **161** E4
Claremorris Ireland **61** D4
Clarence *r.* Australia **138** F2
Clarence N.Z. **139** D6
Clarence Island Antarctica **188** A2
Clarence Strait Iran *see* **Khūran**
Clarence Strait *AK* U.S.A. **149** N4
Clarence Town Bahamas **163** F8
Clarendon *AR* U.S.A. **161** F5
Clarendon *PA* U.S.A. **164** F3
Clarendon *TX* U.S.A. **161** C5
Clarenville Canada **153** L4
Claresholm Canada **150** H5
Clarie Coast Antarctica *see* **Wilkes Coast**
Clarinda U.S.A. **160** E3
Clarington U.S.A. **164** E4
Clarion *IA* U.S.A. **160** E3
Clarion *PA* U.S.A. **164** F3
Clarion *r.* U.S.A. **164** F3
Clarión, Isla *i.* Mex. **168** B5
Clark U.S.A. **160** D2
Clark, Lake *AK* U.S.A. **148** I3
Clark, Mount *N.W.T.* Canada **149** Q2
Clarkdale U.S.A. **159** G4
Clarkebury S. Africa **125** I6
Clarke Range *mts* Australia **136** D4
Clarke River Australia **136** D3
Clarke's Head Canada **153** L4
Clark Mountain U.S.A. **159** F4
Clark Point Canada **164** E1
Clarksburg U.S.A. **164** E4
Clarksdale U.S.A. **161** F5
Clarks Hill U.S.A. **164** B3
Clarks Point *AK* U.S.A. **148** H4
Clarksville *AR* U.S.A. **161** E5
Clarksville *TN* U.S.A. **164** B5
Clarksville *TX* U.S.A. **161** E5
Clarksville *VA* U.S.A. **165** F5
Claro *r. Goiás* Brazil **179** A2
Claro *r. Mato Grosso* Brazil **179** A1
Clashmore Ireland **61** E5
Claude U.S.A. **161** C5
Claudy U.K. **61** E3
Claveria *Luzon* Phil. **82** C2
Clavier Belgium **62** F4
Claxton U.S.A. **163** D5
Clay U.S.A. **164** E4
Clayburg U.S.A. **165** I1
Clay Center *KS* U.S.A. **160** D4
Clay Center *NE* U.S.A. **160** D3
Clay City *IN* U.S.A. **164** B4
Clay City *KY* U.S.A. **164** D5
Clayhole Wash *watercourse* U.S.A. **159** G3
Claypool U.S.A. **159** H5
Clay Springs U.S.A. **159** H4
Clayton *DE* U.S.A. **165** H4
Clayton *GA* U.S.A. **163** D5
Clayton *MI* U.S.A. **164** C3
Clayton *MO* U.S.A. **160** F4
Clayton *NM* U.S.A. **161** C4
Clayton *NY* U.S.A. **165** G1
Claytor Lake U.S.A. **164** E5
Clay Village U.S.A. **164** C4
Clear, Cape Ireland **61** C6
Clearco U.S.A. **164** E4
Clear Creek Canada **164** E2
Clear Creek *r.* U.S.A. **159** H4
Cleare, Cape U.S.A. **146** D4
Clearfield *PA* U.S.A. **165** F3
Clearfield *UT* U.S.A. **156** E4
Clear Fork Brazos *r.* U.S.A. **161** D5
Clear Hills Canada **150** G3
Clear Island Ireland **61** C6
Clear Lake *IA* U.S.A. **160** E3
Clear Lake *SD* U.S.A. **160** D2
Clear Lake *l. CA* U.S.A. **158** B2
Clear Lake *l. UT* U.S.A. **159** G2
Clearmont U.S.A. **156** G3
Clearwater Canada **150** G5
Clearwater *r. Alberta/Saskatchewan* Canada **151** I3
Clearwater *r. Alberta* Canada **150** H4
Clearwater U.S.A. **163** D7
Clearwater Lake Canada **151** K4
Clearwater Mountains U.S.A. **156** E3
Cleaton U.S.A. **164** B5
Cleburne U.S.A. **161** D5
Cleethorpes U.K. **58** G5
Clementi Sing. **87** [inset]
Clendenin U.S.A. **164** E4
Clendening Lake U.S.A. **164** E3
Cleopatra Needle *mt. Palawan* Phil. **82** B4
Clères France **62** B5
Clerf Lux. *see* **Clervaux**
Clerke Reef Australia **134** B4
Clermont Australia **136** D4
Clermont France **62** C5
Clermont-en-Argonne France **62** F5
Clermont-Ferrand France **66** F4
Clervaux Lux. **62** G4
Cles Italy **68** D1
Clevedon U.K. **59** E7
Cleveland *MS* U.S.A. **161** F5
Cleveland *OH* U.S.A. **164** E3
Cleveland *TN* U.S.A. **163** C5
Cleveland *TX* U.S.A. **167** G2
Cleveland *UT* U.S.A. **159** H2
Cleveland *WI* U.S.A. **164** B2
Cleveland, Cape Australia **136** D3
Cleveland, Mount U.S.A. **156** E2
Cleveland Heights U.S.A. **164** E3
Cleveland Hills U.K. **58** F4
Cleveleys U.K. **58** D5
Cleves Germany *see* **Kleve**
Clew Bay Ireland **61** C4
Clifden Ireland **61** B4
Cliff U.S.A. **159** I5
Cliffoney Ireland **61** D3
Clifton Australia **138** E1
Clifton U.S.A. **159** I5
Clifton Beach Australia **136** D3
Clifton Forge U.S.A. **164** F5
Clifton Park U.S.A. **165** I2
Climax Canada **151** I5
Climax U.S.A. **164** C2
Clinch Mountain *mts* U.S.A. **164** D5
Cline River Canada **150** G4
Clinton *B.C.* Canada **150** F5
Clinton *Ont.* Canada **164** E2
Clinton *IA* U.S.A. **160** F3
Clinton *IL* U.S.A. **160** F3
Clinton *IN* U.S.A. **164** B4
Clinton *KY* U.S.A. **161** F4
Clinton *MI* U.S.A. **164** D2
Clinton *MO* U.S.A. **160** E4
Clinton *MS* U.S.A. **161** F5
Clinton *NC* U.S.A. **163** E5
Clinton *OK* U.S.A. **161** D5
Clinton-Colden Lake Canada **151** J1
Clinton Creek (abandoned) *Y.T.* Canada **149** L2
Clintwood U.S.A. **164** D5

▶**Clipperton, Île** *terr.* N. Pacific Ocean **187** M5
French Overseas Territory. Most easterly point of Oceania.

Clisham *hill* U.K. **60** C3
Clitheroe U.K. **58** E5
Clive Lake Canada **150** G2
Cliza Bol. **176** E7
Clocolan S. Africa **125** H5
Cloghan Ireland **61** E4
Clonakilty Ireland **61** D6
Clonbern Ireland **61** D4
Cloncurry Australia **136** C4
Cloncurry *r.* Australia **136** C3
Clones Ireland **61** E3
Clonmel Ireland **61** E5
Clonygowan Ireland **61** E4
Cloonbannin Ireland **61** C5

Help me

Clooneagh Ireland 61 E4
Cloppenburg Germany 63 I2
Cloquet U.S.A. 160 E2
Cloquet r. U.S.A. 160 E2
Cloud Peak WY U.S.A. 154 F3
Cloud Peak WY U.S.A. 156 G3
Clova Canada 152 G4
Clover U.S.A. 159 G1
Cloverdale CA U.S.A. 158 B2
Cloverdale IN U.S.A. 164 B4
Cloverport U.S.A. 164 B5
Clovis CA U.S.A. 158 D3
Clovis NM U.S.A. 161 C5
Cloyne Canada 165 G1
Cluain Meala Ireland see Clonmel
Cluanie, Loch l. U.K. 60 D3
Cluff Lake Mine Canada 151 I3
Cluj-Napoca Romania 69 J1
Clun U.K. 59 D6
Clunes Australia 138 A6
Cluny Australia 136 B5
Cluses France 66 H3
Cluster Springs U.S.A. 165 F5
Clut Lake Canada 150 G1
Clutterbuck Head hd Canada 153 H1
Clutterbuck Hills hill Australia 135 D6
Clwydian Range hills U.K. 58 D5
Clyde Canada 150 H4
Clyde r. U.K. 60 E5
Clyde NY U.S.A. 165 G2
Clyde OH U.S.A. 164 D3
Clyde, Firth of est. U.K. 60 E5
Clydebank U.K. 60 E5
Clyde River Canada 147 L2
Côa r. Port. 67 C3
Coachella U.S.A. 158 E5
Coahuayutla de Guerrero Mex. 167 E5
Coahuila state Mex. 166 E3
Coal r. Y.T. Canada 149 P4
Coal City U.S.A. 164 A3
Coalcomán Mex. 166 E5
Coaldale U.S.A. 158 E2
Coalgate U.S.A. 161 D5
Coal Harbour Canada 150 E5
Coalinga U.S.A. 158 C3
Coalport U.S.A. 165 F3
Coal River B.C. Canada 149 P4
Coal Valley U.S.A. 159 F3
Coalville U.K. 59 F6
Coalville U.S.A. 159 H1
Coari Brazil 176 F4
Coari r. Brazil 176 F4
Coarsegold U.S.A. 158 D3
Coastal Plain U.S.A. 161 E6
Coast Mountains Canada 150 E4
Coast Range hills Australia 137 E5
Coast Ranges mts U.S.A. 158 B1
Coatbridge U.K. 60 E5
Coatepec Mex. 167 F5
Coatepeque Guat. 167 H6
Coatesville U.S.A. 165 H4
Coaticook Canada 165 J1
Coatlán Mex. 167 F5
Coats Island Canada 151 P2
Coats Land reg. Antarctica 188 A1
Coatzacoalcos Mex. 168 F5
Cobán Guat. 167 H6
Cobar Australia 138 B3
Cobargo Australia 138 D6
Cobden Australia 138 A7
Cobh Ireland 61 D6
Cobham r. Canada 151 M4
Cobija Bol. 176 E6
Coblenz Germany see Koblenz
Cobleskill U.S.A. 165 H2
Cobos Mex. 167 F4
Cobourg Peninsula Australia 134 F2
Cobra Australia 135 B6
Cobram Australia 138 B5
Coburg Germany 63 K4
Coburg Island Canada 147 K2
Coca Ecuador 176 C4
Coca Spain 67 D3
Cocalinho Brazil 179 A1
Cocanada India see Kakinada
Cochabamba Bol. 176 E7
Cochem Germany 63 H4
Cochin India 106 C4
Cochin reg. Vietnam 87 D5
Cochinos, Bahía de b. Cuba see Pigs, Bay of
Cochise U.S.A. 159 I5
Cochise Head mt. U.S.A. 159 I5
Cochrane Alta Canada 150 H5
Cochrane Ont. Canada 152 E4
Cochrane r. Canada 151 K3
Cockburn Australia 137 C7
Cockburnspath U.K. 60 G5
Cockburn Town Bahamas 163 F7
Cockburn Town Turks and Caicos Is see Grand Turk
Cockermouth U.K. 58 D4
Cocklebiddy Australia 135 D8
Cockscomb mt. S. Africa 124 G7
Coclé del Norte Panama 166 [inset] J7
Coco r. Hond./Nicaragua 166 [inset] J6
Coco, Cayo i. Cuba 163 E8
Coco, Isla de i. N. Pacific Ocean 169 G7
Cocobeach Gabon 122 A3
Coco Channel India 87 A4
Cocomórachic Mex. 166 D2
Coconino Plateau U.S.A. 159 G4
Cocopara National Park Australia 138 C5
Cocoro i. Phil. 82 C4
Cocos Brazil 179 B1
Cocos Basin sea feature Indian Ocean 185 O5

▶Cocos Islands terr. Indian Ocean 80 B9
Australian External Territory.

Cocos Ridge sea feature N. Pacific Ocean 187 O5
Cocula Mex. 166 E4
Cocuy, Sierra Nevada del mt. Col. 176 D2
Cod, Cape U.S.A. 165 J3
Codajás Brazil 176 F4
Coderre Canada 151 J5
Codfish Island N.Z. 139 A8
Codigoro Italy 68 E2
Cod Island Canada 153 J2
Codlea Romania 69 K2
Codó Brazil 177 J4
Codsall U.K. 59 E6
Cod's Head hd Ireland 61 B6
Cody U.S.A. 156 F3
Coeburn U.S.A. 164 D5
Coen Australia 136 C2
Coesfeld Germany 63 H3
Coeur d'Alene U.S.A. 156 D3
Coeur d'Alene Lake U.S.A. 156 D3
Coevorden Neth. 62 G2
Coffee Bay S. Africa 125 I6
Coffeyville U.S.A. 161 E4
Coffin Bay Australia 137 A7
Coffin Bay National Park Australia 137 A7
Coffs Harbour Australia 138 F3
Cofimvaba S. Africa 125 H7
Cofradía Hond. 166 [inset] H6
Cofre de Perote, Parque Nacional nat. park Mex. 167 F5
Cognac France 66 D4
Cogo Equat. Guinea 120 D4
Coguno Moz. 125 L3
Cohoes U.S.A. 165 I2
Cohuna Australia 138 B5
Coiba, Isla de i. Panama 166 [inset] J8
Coigeach, Rubha pt U.K. 60 D2
Coihaique Chile 178 B7
Coimbatore India 106 C4
Coimbra Port. 67 B3
Coipasa, Salar de salt flat Bol. 176 E7
Coire Switz. see Chur
Colac Australia 138 A7
Colair Lake India see Kolleru Lake
Colatina Brazil 179 C2
Colbitz Germany 63 L2
Colborne Canada 165 G2
Colby U.S.A. 160 C4
Colchester U.K. 59 H7
Colchester U.S.A. 165 I3
Cold Bay AK U.S.A. 148 G5
Cold Bay AK U.S.A. 148 G5
Coldfoot AK U.S.A. 149 J2
Coldingham U.K. 60 G5
Colditz Germany 63 M3
Cold Lake Canada 151 I4
Cold Lake l. Canada 151 I4
Coldspring U.S.A. 161 E6
Coldstream Canada 150 G5
Coldstream U.K. 60 G5
Coldwater Canada 164 F1
Coldwater KS U.S.A. 161 D4
Coldwater MI U.S.A. 164 C3
Coldwater r. U.S.A. 161 F5
Coleambally Australia 138 B5
Colebrook U.S.A. 165 J1
Coleen r. AK U.S.A. 149 L2
Coleman r. Australia 136 C2
Coleman U.S.A. 161 D6
Çölemerik Turkey see Hakkâri
Colenso S. Africa 125 I5
Cole Peninsula Antarctica 188 L2
Coleraine Australia 137 C8
Coleraine U.K. 61 F2
Coles, Punta de pt Peru 176 D7
Coles Bay Australia 137 [inset]
Colesberg S. Africa 125 G6
Coleville Canada 151 I5
Colfax CA U.S.A. 158 C2
Colfax LA U.S.A. 161 E6
Colfax WA U.S.A. 156 D3
Colhué Huapí, Lago l. Arg. 178 C7
Coligny S. Africa 125 H4
Colima Mex. 168 D5
Colima state Mex. 166 E5
Colima, Nevado de vol. Mex. 168 D5
Coll i. U.K. 60 C4
Collado Villalba Spain 67 E3
Collarenebri Australia 138 D2
College AK U.S.A. 149 K2
College Station U.S.A. 161 D6
Collerina Australia 138 C2
Collie N.S.W. Australia 138 D3
Collie W.A. Australia 135 B8
Collier Bay Australia 134 D4
Collier Range National Park Australia 135 B6
Collingwood Canada 164 E1
Collingwood N.Z. 139 D5
Collins U.S.A. 161 F6
Collins Glacier Antarctica 188 E2
Collinson Peninsula Canada 147 H2
Collipulli Chile 178 B5
Collmberg hill Germany 63 N3
Collooney Ireland 61 D3
Colmar France 66 H2
Colmenar Viejo Spain 67 E3
Colmonell U.K. 60 E5
Colne r. U.K. 59 H7
Cologne Germany 62 G4
Coloma U.S.A. 164 B2
Colomb-Béchar Alg. see Béchar
Colômbia Brazil 179 A3
Colombia Mex. 167 F3

▶Colombia country S. America 176 D3
2nd most populous and 4th largest country in South America.

Colombian Basin sea feature S. Atlantic Ocean 184 C5

▶Colombo Sri Lanka 106 C5
Former capital of Sri Lanka.

Colomiers France 66 E5
Colón Buenos Aires Arg. 178 D4
Colón Entre Ríos Arg. 178 E4
Colón Cuba 163 D8
Colón Panama 166 [inset] K7
Colon U.S.A. 164 C3
Colón, Archipiélago de is Ecuador see Galapagos Islands
Colón, Isla de i. Panama 166 [inset] J7
Colona Australia 135 F7
Colonelganj India 105 E4
Colonel Hill Bahamas 163 F8
Colonet, Cabo c. Mex. 166 A2
Colônia r. Brazil 179 D1
Colonia Micronesia 81 J5
Colonia Agrippina Germany see Cologne
Colonia Díaz Mex. 166 C2
Colonia Julia Fenestris Italy see Fano
Colonia Las Heras Arg. 178 C7
Colonial Heights U.S.A. 165 G5
Colonna, Capo c. Italy 68 G5
Colonsay i. U.K. 60 C4
Colorado r. Arg. 178 D5
Colorado r. Mex./U.S.A. 166 B2
Colorado r. U.S.A. 161 D6
Colorado state U.S.A. 156 G5
Colorado City AZ U.S.A. 159 G3
Colorado City TX U.S.A. 161 C5
Colorado Desert U.S.A. 158 E5
Colorado National Monument nat. park U.S.A. 159 I2
Colorado Plateau U.S.A. 159 I3
Colorado River Aqueduct canal U.S.A. 159 F4
Colorado Springs U.S.A. 156 G5
Colossae Turkey see Honaz
Colotlán Mex. 168 D4
Cölpin Germany 63 N1
Colquiri Bol. 176 E7
Colquitt U.S.A. 163 C6
Colson U.S.A. 164 D5
Colsterworth U.K. 59 G6
Colstrip U.S.A. 156 G3
Coltishall U.K. 59 I6
Colton CA U.S.A. 158 E4
Colton NY U.S.A. 165 H1
Colton UT U.S.A. 159 H2
Columbia KY U.S.A. 164 C5
Columbia LA U.S.A. 161 E5
Columbia MD U.S.A. 165 G4
Columbia MO U.S.A. 160 E4
Columbia MS U.S.A. 161 F6
Columbia NC U.S.A. 162 E5
Columbia PA U.S.A. 165 G3

▶Columbia SC U.S.A. 163 D5
Capital of South Carolina.

Columbia TN U.S.A. 162 C5
Columbia r. U.S.A. 156 C3
Columbia, District of admin. dist. U.S.A. 165 G4
Columbia, Mount Canada 150 G4
Columbia, Sierra mts Mex. 166 B2
Columbia City U.S.A. 164 C3
Columbia Lake Canada 150 H5
Columbia Mountains Canada 150 F4
Columbia Plateau U.S.A. 156 D3
Columbine, Cape S. Africa 124 C7
Columbus GA U.S.A. 163 C5
Columbus IN U.S.A. 164 C4
Columbus MS U.S.A. 161 F5
Columbus MT U.S.A. 156 F3
Columbus NC U.S.A. 163 D5
Columbus NE U.S.A. 160 D3
Columbus NM U.S.A. 157 G7

▶Columbus OH U.S.A. 164 D4
Capital of Ohio.

Columbus TX U.S.A. 161 D6
Columbus Grove U.S.A. 164 C3
Columbus Salt Marsh U.S.A. 158 D2
Colusa U.S.A. 158 B2
Colville N.Z. 139 E3
Colville U.S.A. 156 D2
Colville r. AK U.S.A. 149 J1
Colville Channel N.Z. 139 E3
Colville Lake N.W.T. Canada 149 P2
Colwyn Bay U.K. 58 D5
Comacchio Italy 68 E2
Comacchio, Valli di lag. Italy 68 E2
Comai Xizang China 99 E7
Comalcalco Mex. 167 G5
Comanche U.S.A. 161 D6
Comandante Ferraz research station Antarctica 188 A2
Comandante Salas Arg. 178 C4
Comănești Romania 69 L1
Comayagua Hond. 166 [inset] I6
Combahee r. U.S.A. 163 D5
Combarbalá Chile 178 B4
Comber U.K. 61 G3
Combermere Bay Myanmar 86 A3
Combles France 62 C4
Combol i. Indon. 84 C2
Combomune Moz. 125 K2
Combooyne Australia 138 F3
Comencho, Lac l. Canada 152 G4
Comendador Dom. Rep. see Elías Piña
Comendador Gomes Brazil 179 A2
Comeragh Mountains hills Ireland 61 E5
Comercinho Brazil 179 C2
Cometela Moz. 125 L1
Comfort U.S.A. 161 D6
Comilla Bangl. 105 G5
Comines Belgium 62 C4
Comino, Capo c. Sardinia Italy 68 C4
Comitán de Domínguez Mex. 167 G5
Commack U.S.A. 165 I3
Commentry France 66 F3
Committee Bay Canada 147 J3
Commonwealth Territory admin. div. Australia see Jervis Bay Territory
Como Italy 68 C2
Como, Lago di Italy see Como, Lake
Como, Lake Italy 68 C2
Como Chamling l. China 99 E7
Comodoro Rivadavia Arg. 178 C7
Comonfort Mex. 167 E4
Comores country Africa see Comoros
Comorin, Cape India 106 C4
Comoro Islands country Africa see Comoros
Comoros country Africa 123 E5
Compiègne France 62 C5
Compostela Mex. 166 D4
Compostela Mindanao Phil. 82 D5
Comprida, Ilha i. Brazil 179 B4
Comrat Moldova 69 M1
Comrie U.K. 60 F4
Comstock U.S.A. 161 C6
Côn, Sông r. Vietnam 87 E4
Cona Xizang China 99 E8

▶Conakry Guinea 120 B4
Capital of Guinea.

Cona Niyeo Arg. 178 C6
Conceição r. Brazil 179 B2
Conceição da Barra Brazil 179 D2
Conceição do Araguaia Brazil 177 I5
Conceição do Mato Dentro Brazil 179 C2
Concepción Chile 178 B5
Concepción Mex. 161 C7
Concepción r. Mex. 166 B2
Concepción Para. 178 E2
Concepción, Punta pt Mex. 166 C3
Concepción de la Vega Dom. Rep. see La Vega
Conception, Point U.S.A. 158 C4
Conception Island Bahamas 163 F8
Concha Mex. 166 D4
Conchas U.S.A. 157 G6
Conchas Lake U.S.A. 157 G6
Concho Mex. 166 D3
Concho U.S.A. 159 I4
Conchos r. Nuevo León/Tamaulipas Mex. 167 F3
Conchos r. Mex. 166 D2
Concord CA U.S.A. 158 B3
Concord NC U.S.A. 163 D5

▶Concord NH U.S.A. 165 J2
Capital of New Hampshire.

Concord VT U.S.A. 165 J1
Concordia Arg. 178 E4
Concordiá Mex. 161 B8
Concordia Peru 176 D4
Concordia S. Africa 124 C5
Concordia KS U.S.A. 160 D4
Concordia KY U.S.A. 164 B4
Concordia 188 G2
Concord Peak Afgh. 111 I2
Con Cuông Vietnam 86 D3
Condamine Australia 138 E1
Condamine r. Australia 138 D1
Côn Đao Vietnam 87 D5
Condega Nicaragua 166 [inset] I6
Condeúba Brazil 179 C1
Condobolin Australia 138 C4
Condom France 66 E5
Condon U.S.A. 156 C3
Condor, Cordillera del mts Ecuador/Peru 176 C4
Condroz reg. Belgium 62 E4
Conecuh r. U.S.A. 163 C6
Conegliano Italy 68 E2
Conejos Mex. 166 E3
Conejos U.S.A. 157 G5
Conemaugh r. U.S.A. 164 F3
Cone Mountain AK U.S.A. 148 H2
Conestogo Lake Canada 164 E2
Conesus Lake U.S.A. 165 G2
Conflict Group is P.N.G. 136 E1
Confoederatio Helvetica country Europe see Switzerland
Confusion Range mts U.S.A. 159 G2
Congdü Xizang China 99 D7
Conghua China 97 G4
Congjiang China 97 F3
Congleton U.K. 58 E5
Congo country Africa 122 B4

▶Congo r. Congo/Dem. Rep. Congo 122 B4
2nd longest river in Africa, and 8th in the world. Formerly known as Zaïre.

Congo (Brazzaville) country Africa see Congo
Congo (Kinshasa) country Africa see Congo, Democratic Republic of the

▶Congo, Democratic Republic of the country Africa 122 C4
3rd largest and 4th most populous country in Africa.

Congo, Republic of country Africa see Congo
Congo Basin Dem. Rep. Congo 122 C4
Congo Cone sea feature S. Atlantic Ocean 184 I6
Congo Free State country Africa see Congo, Democratic Republic of the
Congonhas Brazil 179 C3
Congress U.S.A. 159 G4
Conhuas Mex. 167 H5
Conimbla National Park Australia 138 D4
Coningsby U.K. 59 G5
Coniston Canada 152 E5
Coniston U.K. 58 D4
Conjuboy Australia 136 D3
Conkal Mex. 167 H4
Conklin Canada 151 I4
Conn r. Canada 152 F3
Conn, Lough l. Ireland 61 C3
Connacht reg. Ireland see Connaught
Connaught reg. Ireland 61 C4
Conneaut U.S.A. 164 E3
Connecticut state U.S.A. 165 I3
Connemara reg. Ireland 61 C4
Connemara National Park Ireland 61 C4
Connersville U.S.A. 164 C4
Connolly, Mount Y.T. Canada 149 N3
Connors Range hills Australia 136 E4
Conoble Australia 138 B4
Conquista Brazil 179 B2
Conrad U.S.A. 156 F2
Conrad Rise sea feature Southern Ocean 185 K9
Conroe U.S.A. 161 E6
Conroe, Lake TX U.S.A. 167 G2
Consejo Belize 167 H5
Conselheiro Lafaiete Brazil 179 C3
Consett U.K. 58 F4
Consolación del Sur Cuba 163 D8
Côn Sơn, Đao i. Vietnam 87 D5
Consort Canada 151 I4
Constance Germany see Konstanz
Constance, Lake Germany/Switz. 57 L7
Constância dos Baetas Brazil 176 F5
Constanța Romania 69 M2
Constantia tourist site Cyprus see Salamis
Constantia Germany see Konstanz
Constantina Spain 67 D5
Constantine Alg. 64 F4
Constantine, Cape AK U.S.A. 148 H4
Constantine Harbor AK U.S.A. 149 [inset]
Constantinople Turkey see İstanbul
Constitución de 1857, Parque Nacional nat. park Mex. 166 B1
Consul Canada 151 I5
Contact U.S.A. 156 E4
Contagalo Brazil 179 C3
Contamana Peru 176 C5
Contas r. Brazil 179 D1
Contoy, Isla i. Mex. 167 I4
Contria Brazil 179 B2
Contwoyto Lake Canada 151 I1
Convención Col. 176 D2
Convent U.S.A. 161 F6
Conway U.K. see Conwy
Conway AR U.S.A. 161 E5
Conway ND U.S.A. 160 D1
Conway NH U.S.A. 165 J2
Conway SC U.S.A. 163 E5
Conway, Cape Australia 136 E4
Conway, Lake salt flat Australia 137 A6
Conway National Park Australia 136 E4
Conway Reef Fiji see Ceva-i-Ra
Conwy U.K. 58 D5
Conwy r. U.K. 59 D5
Coober Pedy Australia 135 F7
Cooch Behar India see Koch Bihar
Coochbehar India see Koch Bihar
Cook Australia 135 E7
Cook, Cape Canada 150 E5
Cook, Grand Récif de reef New Caledonia 133 G3
Cook, Mount Canada/U.S.A. 149 M3
Cook, Mount N.Z. see Aoraki
Cookes Peak U.S.A. 157 G6
Cookeville U.S.A. 162 C4
Cookhouse S. Africa 125 G7
Cook Ice Shelf Antarctica 188 H2
Cook Inlet sea channel AK U.S.A. 148 I3
Cook Islands terr. S. Pacific Ocean 186 J7
Cooksburg U.S.A. 165 H2
Cooks Passage Australia 136 D2
Cookstown U.K. 61 F3
Cook Strait N.Z. 139 E5
Cooktown Australia 136 D2
Coolabah Australia 138 C3
Cooladdi Australia 138 B1
Coolah Australia 138 D3
Coolamon Australia 138 C5
Coolgardie Australia 135 C7
Coolibah Australia 134 E3
Coolidge U.S.A. 159 H5
Cooloola National Park Australia 137 F5
Coolum Beach Australia 137 F5
Cooma Australia 138 D6
Coombah Australia 137 C7
Coonabarabran Australia 138 D3
Coonamble Australia 138 D3
Coondambo Australia 137 A6
Coondapoor India see Kundapura
Coongoola Australia 138 B1
Coon Rapids U.S.A. 160 E2
Cooper Creek watercourse Australia 137 B6
Cooper Mountain Canada 150 G5
Coopernook Australia 138 F3
Cooper's Town Bahamas 163 E7
Cooperstown ND U.S.A. 160 D2
Cooperstown NY U.S.A. 165 H2
Coopracambra National Park Australia 138 D6
Coorabie Australia 135 F7
Coorong National Park Australia 137 B8
Coorow Australia 135 B7
Coosa r. U.S.A. 163 C5
Coos Bay U.S.A. 156 B4
Coos Bay b. U.S.A. 156 B4
Cootamundra Australia 138 D5
Cootehill Ireland 61 E3
Cooyar Australia 138 E1
Copainalá Mex. 167 G5
Copala Mex. 168 E5
Copán tourist site Hond. 166 [inset] H6
Cope U.S.A. 160 C4
Copemish U.S.A. 164 C1

▶Copenhagen Denmark 55 H9
Capital of Denmark.

Copenhagen U.S.A. 165 H2
Copertino Italy 68 H4
Copeton Reservoir Australia 138 E2
Cô Pi, Phou mt. Laos/Vietnam 86 D3
Copiapó Chile 178 B3
Copley Australia 137 B6
Copparo Italy 68 D2
Copper r. AK U.S.A. 149 K3
Copper Cliff Canada 152 E5
Copper Harbor U.S.A. 162 C2
Coppermine Canada see Kugluktuk
Coppermine r. Canada 150 H1
Coppermine Point Canada 152 D5
Copperton S. Africa 124 F5
Copp Lake Canada 150 H2
Coqên Xizang China 99 D7
Coqên Xizang China 99 D7
Coquilhatville Dem. Rep. Congo see Mbandaka
Coquille i. Micronesia see Pikelot
Coquille U.S.A. 156 B4
Coquimbo Chile 178 B3
Coquitlam Canada 150 F5
Corabia Romania 69 K3
Coração de Jesus Brazil 179 B2
Coracesium Turkey see Alanya
Coraki Australia 138 F2
Coral Bay Australia 135 A5
Coral Bay Palawan Phil. 82 B4
Coral Harbour Canada 147 J3
Coral Sea S. Pacific Ocean 132 F3
Coral Sea Basin S. Pacific Ocean 186 G6

▶Coral Sea Islands Territory terr. Australia 132 F3
Australian External Territory.

Corangamite, Lake Australia 138 A7
Corat Azer. 113 H2
Corbeny France 62 D5
Corbett Inlet Canada 151 M2
Corbett National Park India 104 D3
Corbie France 62 C5
Corbin U.S.A. 164 C5
Corby U.K. 59 G6
Corcaigh Ireland see Cork
Corcoran U.S.A. 158 D3
Corcovado, Golfo de sea chan. Chile 178 B6
Corcovado, Parque Nacional nat. park Costa Rica 166 [inset] J7
Corcyra i. Greece see Corfu
Cordele U.S.A. 163 D6
Cordelia U.S.A. 158 B2
Cordell U.S.A. 161 D5
Cordilheiras, Serra das hills Brazil 177 I5
Cordillera Azul, Parque Nacional nat. park Peru 176 C5
Cordillera de los Picachos, Parque Nacional nat. park Col. 176 D3
Cordilleras Range mts Panay Phil. 82 C4
Cordillo Downs Australia 137 C5
Cordisburgo Brazil 179 B2
Córdoba Arg. 178 D4
Córdoba Durango Mex. 166 E3
Córdoba Veracruz Mex. 168 E5
Córdoba Spain 67 D5
Córdoba, Sierras de mts Arg. 178 D4
Cordova Spain see Córdoba
Cordova AK U.S.A. 149 K3
Cordova Peak AK U.S.A. 149 K3
Corduba Spain see Córdoba
Corfu i. Greece 69 H5
Coria Spain 67 C4
Coribe Brazil 179 B1
Coricudgy mt. Australia 138 E4
Corigliano Calabro Italy 68 G5
Coringa Islands Australia 136 E3
Corinium U.K. see Cirencester
Corinth Greece 69 J6
Corinth KY U.S.A. 164 C4
Corinth MS U.S.A. 161 F5
Corinth NY U.S.A. 165 I2
Corinth, Gulf of sea chan. Greece 69 J5
Corinthus Greece see Corinth
Corinto Brazil 179 B2
Corinto Nicaragua 166 [inset] I6
Cork Ireland 61 D6
Corleone Sicily Italy 68 E6
Çorlu Turkey 69 L4
Cormeilles France 59 H9
Cormoran Reef Palau 82 [inset]
Cornelia S. Africa 125 I4
Cornélio Procópio Brazil 179 A3
Cornélios Brazil 179 A5
Cornell U.S.A. 160 F2
Corner Brook Canada 153 K4
Corner Inlet b. Australia 138 C7
Corner Seamounts sea feature N. Atlantic Ocean 184 E3
Corneto Italy see Tarquinia
Cornillet, Mont hill France 62 E5
Corning AR U.S.A. 161 F4
Corning CA U.S.A. 158 B2
Corning NY U.S.A. 165 G2
Cornish watercourse Australia 136 D4
Corn Islands is Nicaragua see Maíz, Islas del
Corno, Monte mt. Italy 68 E3
Corno di Campo mt. Italy/Switz. 66 J3
Cornwall Canada 165 H1
Cornwallis Island Canada 147 I2
Cornwall Island Canada 147 I2
Coro Venez. 176 E1
Coroaci Brazil 179 C2
Coroatá Brazil 177 J4
Corofin Ireland 61 C5
Coromandel Brazil 179 B2
Coromandel Coast India 106 D4
Coromandel Peninsula N.Z. 139 E3
Coromandel Range hills N.Z. 139 E3
Coron Phil. 82 C3
Corona CA U.S.A. 158 E5
Corona NM U.S.A. 157 G6
Coronado U.S.A. 158 E5
Coronado, Bahía de b. Costa Rica 166 [inset] J7
Coronado Bay Mindanao Phil. 82 C5
Coronation Canada 151 I4
Coronation Gulf Canada 146 G3
Coronation Island S. Atlantic Ocean 188 A2
Coronation Island AK U.S.A. 149 N5
Coron Bay Phil. 82 C4
Coronda Arg. 178 D4
Coronel Fabriciano Brazil 179 C2
Coronel Oviedo Para. 178 E3
Coronel Pringles Arg. 178 D5
Coronel Suárez Arg. 178 D5
Çorovodë Albania 69 I4
Corowa Australia 138 C5
Corozal Belize 167 H5
Corpus Christi U.S.A. 161 D7
Corpus Christi, Lake TX U.S.A. 167 F2
Corque Bol. 176 E7
Corral de Cantos mt. Spain 67 D4
Corrales Mex. 157 G8
Corralilla Cuba 163 D8
Corrandibby Range hills Australia 135 A6
Corrente Brazil 177 I6
Corrente r. Bahia Brazil 179 C1
Corrente r. Minas Gerais Brazil 179 A2
Correntes Brazil 177 H7
Correntina Brazil 179 B1
Correntina r. Brazil see Éguas
Corrib, Lough l. Ireland 61 C4
Corrientes Arg. 178 E3
Corrientes, Cabo c. Col. 176 C2
Corrientes, Cabo c. Cuba 163 C8
Corrientes, Cabo c. Mex. 168 C4
Corrigan TX U.S.A. 167 G2
Corrigin Australia 135 B8
Corris U.K. 59 D6
Corry U.S.A. 164 F3
Corse i. France see Corsica
Corse, Cap c. Corsica France 66 I5
Corsham U.K. 59 E7
Corsica i. France 66 I5
Corsicana U.S.A. 161 D5
Corte Corsica France 66 I5
Cortegana Spain 67 C5
Cortes, Sea of g. Mex. see California, Golfo de
Cortez U.S.A. 159 I3
Cortina d'Ampezzo Italy 68 E1
Cortland U.S.A. 165 G2
Corton U.K. 59 I6
Cortona Italy 68 D3
Coruche Port. 67 B4
Çoruh Turkey see Artvin
Çoruh r. Turkey 113 F2
Çorum Turkey 112 D2
Corumbá Brazil 177 G7
Corumbá r. Brazil 179 A2
Corumbá de Goiás Brazil 179 A1
Corumbaíba Brazil 179 A2
Corumbaú, Ponta pt Brazil 179 D2
Corunna Spain see A Coruña
Corunna U.S.A. 164 C2
Corvallis U.S.A. 156 C3
Corwen U.K. 59 D6
Corydon IA U.S.A. 160 E3
Corydon IN U.S.A. 164 B4
Coryville U.S.A. 165 F3
Cos i. Greece see Kos
Cosalá Mex. 166 D3
Cosamaloapan Mex. 167 G5
Cosentia Italy see Cosenza
Cosenza Italy 68 G5
Coshocton U.S.A. 164 E3
Cosne-Cours-sur-Loire France 66 F3
Costa Blanca coastal area Spain 67 F4
Costa Brava coastal area Spain 67 H3
Costa de la Luz coastal area Spain 67 C5
Costa del Sol coastal area Spain 67 D5
Costa de Mosquitos coastal area Nicaragua 166 [inset] J6

Costa Marques Brazil 176 F6
Costa Rica Brazil 177 H7
Costa Rica country Central America 169 H6
Costa Rica Mex. 166 D3
Costa Verde coastal area Spain 67 C2
Costermansville Dem. Rep. Congo see Bukavu
Costeşti Romania 69 K2
Costigan Lake Canada 151 J3
Coswig Germany 63 M3
Cotabato Mindanao Phil. 82 D5
Cotagaita Bol. 176 E8
Cotahuasi Peru 176 D7
Cote, Mount AK U.S.A. 149 O4
Coteau des Prairies slope U.S.A. 160 D2
Coteau du Missouri slope ND U.S.A. 160 C1
Côte d'Azur coastal area France 66 H5
Côte d'Ivoire country Africa 120 C4
Côte Française de Somalis country Africa see Djibouti
Cotentin pen. France 59 F9
Côtes de Meuse ridge France 62 E5
Cothi r. U.K. 59 C7
Cotiaeum Turkey see Kütahya
Cotiella mt. Spain 67 G2
Cotonou Benin 120 D4
Cotopaxi, Volcán vol. Ecuador 176 C4
Cotswold Hills U.K. 59 E7
Cottage Grove U.S.A. 156 C4
Cottbus Germany 57 O5
Cottenham U.K. 59 H6
Cottian Alps mts France/Italy 66 H4
Cottica Suriname 177 H3
Cottiennes, Alpes mts France/Italy see Cottian Alps
Cottonwood AZ U.S.A. 159 G4
Cottonwood CA U.S.A. 158 B1
Cottonwood r. U.S.A. 160 D4
Cottonwood Falls U.S.A. 160 D4
Cotulla U.S.A. 161 D6
Coudersport U.S.A. 165 F3
Couedic, Cape du Australia 137 B8
Coulee City U.S.A. 156 D3
Coulee Dam U.S.A. 156 D3
Coulman Island Antarctica 188 H2
Coulogne France 62 B4
Coulommiers France 62 D6
Coulonge r. Canada 152 F5
Coulterville U.S.A. 158 C3
Council AK U.S.A. 148 G2
Council U.S.A. 156 D3
Council Bluffs U.S.A. 160 E3
Council Grove U.S.A. 160 D4
Councillor Island Australia 137 [inset]
Counselor U.S.A. 159 J3
Coupeville U.S.A. 156 C2
Courageous Lake Canada 151 I1
Courland Lagoon b. Lith./Rus. Fed. 55 L9
Courtenay Canada 150 E5
Courtland U.S.A. 165 G5
Courtmacsherry Ireland 61 D6
Courtmacsherry Bay Ireland 61 D6
Courtown Ireland 61 F5
Courtrai Belgium see Kortrijk
Coushatta U.S.A. 161 E5
Coutances France 66 D2
Coutts Canada 151 I5
Couture, Lac l. Canada 152 G2
Couvin Belgium 62 E4
Cove Fort U.S.A. 159 G2
Cove Island Canada 164 E1
Cove Mountains hills U.S.A. 165 F4
Coventry U.K. 59 F6
Covered Wells U.S.A. 159 G5
Covesville U.S.A. 165 F5
Covilhã Port. 67 C3
Coville, Lake AK U.S.A. 148 I4
Covington GA U.S.A. 163 D5
Covington IN U.S.A. 164 B3
Covington KY U.S.A. 164 C4
Covington LA U.S.A. 161 F6
Covington MI U.S.A. 160 F2
Covington TN U.S.A. 161 F5
Covington VA U.S.A. 164 E5
Cowal, Lake dry lake Australia 138 C4
Cowan, Lake salt flat Australia 135 C7
Cowansville Canada 165 I1
Cowargarzê China 96 C1
Cowcowing Lakes salt flat Australia 135 B7
Cowdenbeath U.K. 60 F4
Cowell Australia 137 B7
Cowes U.K. 59 F8
Cowichan Lake Canada 150 E5
Cowley Australia 138 B1
Cowper Point Canada 147 G2
Cowra Australia 138 D4
Cox r. Australia 136 A2
Coxá r. Brazil 179 B1
Coxen Hole Hond. see Roatán
Coxilha de Santana hills Brazil/Uruguay 178 E4
Coxilha Grande hills Brazil 178 F3
Coxim Brazil 177 H7
Cox's Bazar Bangl. 105 G5
Coyame Mex. 161 B6
Coyhaique Chile see Coihaique
Coyote, Punta pt Mex. 166 C3
Coyote Lake U.S.A. 158 E4
Coyote Peak hill U.S.A. 159 F5
Coyotitán Mex. 166 D4
Coyuca de Benitez Mex. 167 E5
Cozhê China 105 F2
Cozie, Alpi mts France/Italy see Cottian Alps
Cozumel Mex. 167 I4
Cozumel, Isla de i. Mex. 167 I4
Craboon Australia 138 D4
Cracovia Poland see Kraków
Cracow Australia 136 E5
Cracow Poland see Kraków
Cradle Mountain Lake St Clair National Park Australia 137 [inset]
Cradock S. Africa 125 G7
Craig U.K. 60 D3
Craig AK U.S.A. 149 N5
Craig CO U.S.A. 159 J1
Craigavon U.K. 61 F3
Craigieburn Australia 138 B6
Craig Island Taiwan see Mienhua Yü
Craignure U.K. 60 D4
Craigsville U.S.A. 164 E4
Crail U.K. 60 G4
Crailsheim Germany 63 K5
Craiova Romania 69 J2
Cramlington U.K. 58 F3
Cranberry Junction B.C. Canada 149 O5
Cranberry Lake U.S.A. 165 H1
Cranberry Portage Canada 151 K4
Cranborne Chase for. U.K. 59 E8
Cranbourne Australia 138 B7
Cranbrook Canada 150 H5
Crandon U.S.A. 160 F2
Crane TX U.S.A. 166 E2
Crane Lake Canada 151 I5
Cranston KY U.S.A. 164 D4
Cranston RI U.S.A. 165 J3
Cranz Rus. Fed. see Zelenogradsk
Crary Ice Rise Antarctica 188 I1
Crary Mountains Antarctica 188 J1
Crater Lake National Park U.S.A. 156 C4
Crater Peak U.S.A. 158 C1
Craters of the Moon National Monument nat. park U.S.A. 156 E4
Crateús Brazil 177 J5
Crato Brazil 177 K5
Crawford CO U.S.A. 159 J2
Crawford NE U.S.A. 160 C3
Crawford Point Palawan Phil. 82 B4
Crawfordsville U.S.A. 164 B3
Crawfordville FL U.S.A. 163 C6
Crawfordville GA U.S.A. 163 D5
Crawley U.K. 59 G7
Crazy Mountains AK U.S.A. 149 K2
Crazy Mountains U.S.A. 156 F3
Creag Meagaidh mt. U.K. 60 E4
Crécy-en-Ponthieu France 62 B4
Credenhill U.K. 59 E6
Crediton U.K. 59 D8
Cree r. Canada 151 J3
Creel Mex. 157 G8
Cree Lake Canada 151 J3
Creemore Canada 164 E1
Creighton Canada 151 K4
Creil France 62 C5
Creil Neth. 62 F2
Crema Italy 68 C2
Cremlingen Germany 63 K2
Cremona Canada 150 H5
Cremona Italy 68 D2
Crépy-en-Valois France 62 C5
Cres i. Croatia 68 F2
Crescent U.S.A. 156 C4
Crescent City CA U.S.A. 156 B4
Crescent City FL U.S.A. 163 D6
Crescent Group is Paracel Is 80 E3
Crescent Head Australia 138 F3
Crescent Junction U.S.A. 159 I2
Crescent Valley U.S.A. 158 E1
Cressy Australia 138 A7
Cresta, Mount Phil. 82 C2
Crest Hill hill H.K. China 97 [inset]
Crestline U.S.A. 164 D3
Creston Canada 150 G5
Creston IA U.S.A. 160 E3
Creston WY U.S.A. 156 G4
Crestview U.S.A. 163 C6
Creswick Australia 138 A6
Creta i. Greece see Crete
Crete i. Greece 69 K7
Crete U.S.A. 160 D3
Creus, Cap de c. Spain 67 H2
Creuse r. France 66 E3
Creußen Germany 63 L5
Creutzwald France 62 G5
Creuzburg Germany 63 K3
Crevasse Valley Glacier Antarctica 188 J1
Crewe U.K. 59 E5
Crewe U.S.A. 165 F5
Crewkerne U.K. 59 E8
Crianlarich U.K. 60 E4
Criccieth U.K. 59 C6
Criciúma Brazil 179 A5
Crieff U.K. 60 F4
Criffel hill U.K. 60 F6
Criffell hill U.K. see Criffel
Crikvenica Croatia 68 F2
Crillon, Mount AK U.S.A. 149 M4
Crimea pen. Ukr. 112 D1
Crimmitschau Germany 63 M4
Crimond U.K. 60 H3
Cripple Landing AK U.S.A. 148 H3
Crisfield U.S.A. 165 H5
Cristalândia Brazil 177 I6
Cristalina Brazil 179 B2
Cristalino r. Brazil see Mariembero
Cristóbal Colón, Pico mt. Col. 176 D1
Crixás Brazil 179 A1
Crixás Açu r. Brazil 179 A1
Crixás Mirim r. Brazil 179 A1
Crna Gora aut. rep. Europe see Montenegro
Crni Vrh mt. Serbia 69 J2
Črnomelj Slovenia 68 F2
Croagh Patrick hill Ireland 61 C4
Croajingolong National Park Australia 138 D6
Croatia country Europe 68 G2
Crocker, Banjaran mts Malaysia 85 F1
Crocker Range National Park Malaysia 85 G1
Crockett U.S.A. 161 E6
Crofton KY U.S.A. 164 B5
Crofton NE U.S.A. 160 D3
Croghan U.S.A. 165 H2
Croisilles France 62 C4
Croker r. Nunavut Canada 149 R1
Croker, Cape Canada 164 E1
Croker Island Australia 134 F2
Cromarty U.K. 60 E3
Cromarty Firth est. U.K. 60 E3
Cromer U.K. 59 I6
Crook U.K. 58 F4
Crooked Creek AK U.S.A. 148 H3
Crooked Creek AK U.S.A. 149 L2
Crooked Harbour b. H.K. China 97 [inset]
Crooked Island Bahamas 163 F8
Crooked Island H.K. China 97 [inset]
Crooked Island Passage Bahamas 163 F8
Crookston U.S.A. 160 D2
Crooksville U.S.A. 164 D4
Crookwell Australia 138 D5
Croom Ireland 61 D5
Croppa Creek Australia 138 E2
Crosby U.K. 58 D5
Crosby MN U.S.A. 160 E2
Crosby ND U.S.A. 160 C1
Crosbyton U.S.A. 161 C5
Cross Bay Canada 151 M2
Cross City U.S.A. 163 D6
Cross Fell hill U.K. 58 E4
Crossfield Canada 150 H5
Crossgar U.K. 61 G3
Crosshaven Ireland 61 D6
Cross Inn U.K. 59 C6
Cross Lake Canada 151 L4
Cross Lake l. Canada 151 L4
Cross Lake l. U.S.A. 165 G2
Crossley Lakes N.W.T. Canada 149 O1
Crossmaglen U.K. 61 F3
Crossman Peak U.S.A. 159 F4
Cross Sound sea channel AK U.S.A. 149 M4
Crossville U.S.A. 162 C5
Crotch Lake Canada 165 G1
Croton Italy see Crotone
Crotone Italy 68 G5
Crouch r. U.K. 59 H7
Crow r. Canada 150 E3
Crow Agency U.S.A. 156 G3
Crowal watercourse Australia 138 C3
Crowborough U.K. 59 H7
Crowdy Bay National Park Australia 138 F3
Crowell U.S.A. 161 D5
Crowland U.K. 59 G6
Crowley U.S.A. 161 E6
Crowley, Lake U.S.A. 158 D3
Crown Point IN U.S.A. 164 B3
Crownpoint U.S.A. 159 I4
Crown Point NY U.S.A. 165 I2
Crown Prince Olav Coast Antarctica 188 D2
Crown Princess Martha Coast Antarctica 188 B1
Crows Nest Australia 138 F1
Crowsnest Pass Canada 150 H5
Crowsnest Pass pass Canada 150 H5
Crow Wing r. U.S.A. 160 E2
Croydon Australia 136 C3
Crozet U.S.A. 165 F4
Crozet, Îles is Indian Ocean 185 L9
Crozet Basin sea feature Indian Ocean 185 M8
Crozet Plateau sea feature Indian Ocean 185 K8
Crozon France 66 B2
Cruces Cuba 163 D8
Cruden Bay U.K. 60 H3
Cruillas Mex. 161 D7
Crum U.S.A. 164 D5
Crumlin U.K. 61 F3
Crusheen Ireland 61 D5
Cruz Alta Brazil 178 F3
Cruz del Eje Arg. 178 D4
Cruzeiro Brazil 179 B3
Cruzeiro do Sul Brazil 176 D5
Cruz Grande Mex. 167 F5
Cry Lake B.C. Canada 149 O4
Crysdale, Mount Canada 150 F4
Crystal U.S.A. 159 I3
Crystal City Canada 151 L5
Crystal City U.S.A. 161 D6
Crystal Falls U.S.A. 160 F2
Crystal Lake U.S.A. 164 A2
Crystal River U.S.A. 163 D6
Csongrád Hungary 69 I1
Cửa Lớn, Sông r. Vietnam 87 D5
Cuamba Moz. 123 D5
Cuando r. Angola/Zambia 123 C5
Cuangar Angola 123 B5
Cuango Angola 123 B4
Cuanza r. Angola 123 B4
Cuatro Ciénegas Mex. 166 E3
Cuauhtémoc Chihuahua Mex. 166 D2
Cuautla Mex. 167 F5
Cuba NM U.S.A. 157 G5
Cuba NY U.S.A. 165 F2

▶Cuba country West Indies 169 H4
5th largest island and 5th most populous country in North America.

Cubal Angola 123 B5
Cubango r. Angola/Namibia 123 C5
Cubatão Brazil 179 B3
Cub Hills Canada 151 J4
Çubuk Turkey 112 D2
Cubulco Guat. 167 H6
Cucapa, Sierra mts Mex. 159 F5
Cuchi Angola 123 B5
Cuchilla Grande hills Uruguay 178 E4
Cucuí Brazil 176 E3
Cucurpe Mex. 166 C2
Cúcuta Col. 176 D2
Cudal Australia 138 D4
Cuddalore India 106 C4
Cuddapah India 106 C3
Cuddeback Lake U.S.A. 158 E4
Cue Australia 135 B6
Cuéllar Spain 67 D3
Cuemba Angola 123 B5
Cuenca Ecuador 176 C4
Cuenca Luzon Phil. 82 C3
Cuenca Spain 67 E3
Cuenca, Serranía de mts Spain 67 E3
Cuencamé Mex. 166 E3
Cuernavaca Mex. 168 E5
Cuero U.S.A. 161 D6
Cuervos Mex. 159 F5
Cugir Romania 69 J2
Cuiabá Amazonas Brazil 177 G5
Cuiabá Mato Grosso Brazil 177 G7
Cuiabá r. Brazil 177 G7
Cuicatlan Mex. 167 F5
Cuihua China see Daguan
Cuijiang China see Ninghua
Cuijk Neth. 62 F3
Cuilapa Guat. 167 H6
Cuilcagh hill Ireland/U.K. 61 E3
Cuillin Hills U.K. 60 C3
Cuillin Sound sea chan. U.K. 60 C3
Cuilo Angola 123 B4
Cuiluan China 90 C3
Cuité r. Brazil 179 C2
Cuitláhuac Mex. 167 F5
Cuito r. Angola 123 C5
Cuito Cuanavale Angola 123 B5
Cuitzeo, Laguna de l. Mex. 167 E5
Cujangan i. Phil. 82 C5
Cukai Malaysia 84 C1
Çukurca Turkey 110 A2
Çukurova plat. Turkey 107 B1
Culai Shan mt. Shandong China 95 I4
Cu Lao Cham i. Vietnam 86 E4
Cu Lao Xanh i. Vietnam 87 E4
Culasi Panay Phil. 82 C4
Culcairn Australia 138 C5
Culfa Azer. 113 G3
Culgoa r. Australia 138 C2
Culiacán Mex. 166 D3
Culion Phil. 82 B4
Culion i. Phil. 82 B4
Cullen U.K. 60 G3
Cullen Point Australia 136 C1
Cullera Spain 67 F4
Cullivoe U.K. 60 [inset]
Cullman U.S.A. 163 C5
Cullybackey U.K. 61 F3
Cul Mòr hill U.K. 60 D2
Culpeper U.S.A. 165 G4
Culuene r. Brazil 177 H6
Culver, Point Australia 135 D8
Culverden N.Z. 139 D6
Cumaná Venez. 176 F1
Cumari Brazil 179 A2
Cumbal, Nevado de vol. Col. 176 C3
Cumberland KY U.S.A. 164 D5
Cumberland MD U.S.A. 165 F4
Cumberland VA U.S.A. 165 F5
Cumberland r. U.S.A. 162 C4
Cumberland, Lake U.S.A. 164 C5
Cumberland Lake Canada 151 K4
Cumberland Mountains U.S.A. 164 D5
Cumberland Peninsula Canada 147 L3
Cumberland Plateau U.S.A. 162 C5
Cumberland Point U.S.A. 160 F2
Cumberland Sound sea chan. Canada 147 L3
Cumbernauld U.K. 60 F5
Cumbres de Majalca, Parque Nacional nat. park Mex. 166 D2
Cumbres de Monterey, Parque Nacional nat. park Mex. 167 E3
Cumbum India 106 C3
Cumlosen Germany 63 L1
Cummings U.S.A. 158 B2
Cummins Australia 137 A7
Cummins Range hills Australia 134 D4
Cumnock Australia 138 D4
Cumnock U.K. 60 E5
Cumpas Mex. 166 C2
Çumra Turkey 112 D3
Cumuripa Mex. 166 C2
Cumuruxatiba Brazil 179 D2
Cunagua Cuba see Bolivia
Cunderdin Australia 135 B7
Cunén Guat. 167 H6
Cunene r. Angola 123 B5
also known as Kunene
Cuneo Italy 68 B2
Cung Sơn Vietnam 87 E4
Cunnamulla Australia 138 B2
Cunningsburgh U.K. 60 [inset]
Cupar U.K. 60 F4
Cupica, Golfo de b. Col. 176 C2
Cupula, Pico mt. Mex. 166 C3
Curaçá Brazil 177 K5
Curaçá r. Brazil 176 D4
Curaçao terr. Caribbean Sea 169 K6
Curaray r. Ecuador 176 D4
Curdlawidny Lagoon salt flat Australia 137 B6
Curia Switz. see Chur
Curicó Chile 178 B4
Curitiba Brazil 179 A4
Curitibanos Brazil 179 A4
Curlewis Australia 138 E3
Curlew Lake AK U.S.A. 148 G3
Curnamona Australia 137 B6
Currabubula Australia 138 E3
Currais Novos Brazil 177 K5
Curran U.S.A. 164 D1
Currane, Lough l. Ireland 61 B6
Currant U.S.A. 159 F2
Curranyalpa Australia 138 B3
Currawilla Australia 136 C5
Currawinya National Park Australia 138 B2
Currie Australia 132 E5
Currie U.S.A. 159 F1
Currituck U.S.A. 165 G5
Currockbilly, Mount Australia 138 E5
Curry AK U.S.A. 149 J3
Curtis Channel Australia 136 F5
Curtis Island Australia 136 E4
Curtis Island N.Z. 133 I5
Curuá r. Brazil 177 H5
Curup Sumatera Indon. 84 C3
Curupira, Serra mts Brazil/Venez. 176 F3
Cururupu Brazil 177 J4
Curvelo Brazil 179 B2
Curwood, Mount hill U.S.A. 160 F2
Cusco Peru 176 D6
Cushendall U.K. 61 F2
Cushendun U.K. 61 F2
Cushing U.S.A. 161 D4
Cusseta U.S.A. 163 C5
Custer MT U.S.A. 156 G3
Custer SD U.S.A. 160 C3
Cut Bank U.S.A. 156 E2
Cuthbert U.S.A. 163 C6
Cuthbertson Falls Australia 134 F3
Cut Knife Canada 151 I4
Cutler Ridge U.S.A. 163 D7
Cut Off LA U.S.A. 167 H2
Cuttaburra Creek r. Australia 138 B2
Cuttack India 106 E1
Cuvelai Angola 123 B5
Cuxhaven Germany 57 L4
Cuya Chile 176 D7
Cuyahoga Falls U.S.A. 164 E3
Cuyama U.S.A. 158 D4
Cuyama r. U.S.A. 158 C4
Cuyapo Luzon Phil. 82 C3
Cuyo Phil. 82 C4
Cuyo i. Phil. 82 C4
Cuyo East Passage Phil. 82 C4
Cuyo Islands Phil. 82 C4
Cuyo West Passage Phil. 82 C4
Cuyuni r. Guyana 177 G2
Cuyutingni Nicaragua see Kuyu Tingni
Cuzco Peru see Cusco
Cwmbrân U.K. 59 D7
Cyangugu Rwanda 122 C4
Cyclades is Greece 69 K6
Cydonia Greece see Chania
Cygnet U.S.A. 164 D3
Cymru admin. div. U.K. see Wales
Cynthiana U.S.A. 164 C4
Cypress Hills Canada 151 I5
Cyprus country Asia 107 A2
Cyrenaica reg. Libya 121 F2
Cythera i. Greece see Kythira
Czar Canada 151 I4
Czechia country Europe see Czech Republic
Czech Republic country Europe 57 O6
Czernowitz Ukr. see Chernivtsi
Czersk Poland 57 P4
Częstochowa Poland 57 Q5

D

Đa, Sông r. Vietnam see Black
Da'an Jilin China 95 K2
Daanbantayan Phil. 82 C4
Daba Xizang China 99 B7
Ḍabāb, Jabal aḍ mt. Jordan 107 B4
Dabakala Côte d'Ivoire 120 C4
Daban Nei Mongol China 95 I3
Daban Shan mts China 94 E4
Dabao China 96 D2
Daba Shan mts China 97 F1
Dabba China see Daocheng
Dabein Myanmar 86 B3
Dabhoi India 104 C5
Ḍab'ī, Wādī aḍ watercourse Jordan 107 C4
Dabiegai Gansu China 94 C4
Dabie Shan mts China 97 G2
Dablana India 104 C4
Dabola Guinea 120 B3
Dabqig Nei Mongol China 95 G4
Dąbrowa Górnicza Poland 57 Q5
Dabsan Qinghai China 94 C4
Dabsan Hu salt l. Qinghai China 99 F5
Dabs Nur l. China 90 A3
Dabu Guangdong China 97 H3
Dabu Guangxi China see Liucheng
Dabusu Pao l. China see Dabs Nur
Dacca Bangl. see Dhaka
Dachau Germany 57 M6
Dachechang Nei Mongol China 94 E4
Dachengzi Liaoning China 95 I3
Dachuan China see Dazhou
Dacre Canada 165 G1
Dadal Hentiy Mongolia 95 G1
Daday Turkey 112 D2
Dade City U.S.A. 163 D6
Dadeville U.S.A. 163 C5
Dādkān Iran 111 F5
Dadong China see Donggang
Dadra India see Achalpur
Dadu Pak. 111 G5
Daegu S. Korea see Taegu
Daejŏn S. Korea see Taejŏn
Daet Luzon Phil. 82 C3
Dafang China 96 E3
Dafeng China 97 I1
Dafengman China 90 B4
Dafla Hills India 105 H4
Dafoe Canada 151 J5
Dafoe r. Canada 151 M4
Dagana Senegal 120 B3
Dagasuli i. Maluku Indon. 83 C2
Dagcagoin China see Zoigê
Dagcanglhamo Gansu China 94 E5
Dage Hebei China see Fengning
Dagezhen Hebei China see Fengning
Daghmar Oman 110 E6
Dağlıq Qarabağ aut. reg. Azer. 113 G3
Daglung Xizang China 99 E7
Dagma Xizang China 99 F7
Dagö i. Estonia see Hiiumaa
Dagon Myanmar see Rangoon
Dagrag Zangbo r. Xizang China 99 D7
Dagu Tianjin China 95 I4
Daguan China 96 D3
Daguokui Shan hill China 90 C3
Dagupan Luzon Phil. 82 C2
Dagur Qinghai China 94 C4
Dagxoi Sichuan China see Yidun
Dagxoi Sichuan China see Sowa
Dagzê Xizang China 99 E7
Dagzê Co salt l. China 99 D7
Dagzhuka Xizang China 99 E7
Dahadinni r. N.W.T. Canada 149 P3
Dahalach, Isole is Eritrea see Dahlak Archipelago
Dahana des. Saudi Arabia see Ad Dahnā'
Dahe China see Ziyuan
Daheba Qinghai China 94 D5
Daheiding Shan mt. China 90 C3
Dahei Shan mt. Xinjiang China 94 C3
Dahei Shan mts China 90 B4
Dahej India 104 C5
Daheng China 97 H3
Daheyan Xinjiang China see Turpan Zhan
Dahezhen China 90 D3
Da Hinggan Ling mts China 95 I3
Dahlak Archipelago is Eritrea 108 F6
Dahlak Marine National Park Eritrea 108 F6
Daḥl al Furayy well Saudi Arabia 110 B5
Dahlem Germany 62 G4
Dahlenburg Germany 63 K1
Dahm, Ramlat des. Saudi Arabia/Yemen 108 G6
Dahmani Tunisia 68 C7
Dahme Germany 63 N3
Dahn Germany 63 H5
Dahnā' plain Saudi Arabia 110 B5
Dahod India 104 C5
Dahomey country Africa see Benin
Dahongliutan Aksai Chin 99 B6
Dahra Senegal see Dara
Dähre Germany 63 K2
Dahūk Iraq 113 F3
Dahūk, Buḥayrat resr Iraq 113 F3
Dai i. Maluku Indon. 83 D4
Daibosatsu-rei mt. Japan 93 E3
Daicheng Hebei China 95 I4
Daigo Japan 93 G2
Daik Indon. 84 D3
Daik-U Myanmar 86 B3
Đai Lanh, Mui pt Vietnam 87 E4
Dailekh Nepal 105 E3
Dailly U.K. 60 E5
Daimiel Spain 67 E4
Daimon Japan 92 D2
Daimon-tōge pass Japan 93 E2
Daimugen-zan mt. Japan 93 E3
Dainichiga-take vol. Japan 92 C2
Dainichi-gawa r. Japan 92 C2
Dainichi-zan mt. Japan 92 C2
Dainkog China 96 C1
Dainkognubma China 96 C1
Daintree National Park Australia 136 D3
Daiō Japan 92 D4
Daiō-zaki pt Japan 92 C4
Dair, Jebel ed mt. Sudan 108 D7
Dairen Liaoning China see Dalian
Dai-sen vol. Japan 91 D6
Daisetsu-zan Kokuritsu-kōen Japan 90 F4
Daishan China 97 I2
Daitō Ōsaka Japan 92 B4
Daitō Shizuoka Japan 93 E4
Daiya-gawa r. Japan 93 F2
Daiyue Shanxi China see Shanyin
Daiyun Shan mts China 97 H3
Dajan Japan 92 C3
Dajarra Australia 136 B4
Dajin Chuan r. China 96 D2
Dajing Gansu China 94 E4
Da Juh Qinghai China 94 C4

▶Dakar Senegal 120 B3
Capital of Senegal.

Dākhilah, Wāḥāt ad oasis Egypt 108 C4
Dakhla W. Sahara see Ad Dakhla
Dakhla Oasis oasis Egypt see Dākhilah, Wāḥāt ad
Dakituy Rus. Fed. 95 G1
Đăk Lăk, Cao Nguyên plat. Vietnam 87 E4
Dakoank India 87 A6
Dakol'ka r. Belarus 53 F5
Dakor India 104 C5
Dakoro Niger 120 D3
Dakota City IA U.S.A. 160 E3
Dakota City NE U.S.A. 160 D3
Đakovica Kosovo see Gjakovë
Đakovo Croatia 68 H2
Daktuy Rus. Fed. 90 B1
Dala Angola 123 C5
Dalaba Guinea 120 B3
Dalad Qi Nei Mongol China see Shulinzhao
Dalai Jilin China see Da'an
Dalain Hob Nei Mongol China 94 E3
Dalai Nur l. China 95 I3
Dālakī Iran 110 C4
Dalälven r. Sweden 55 J6
Dalamamiao Nei Mongol China 95 H3
Dalaman Turkey 69 M6
Dalandzadgad Mongolia 94 F3
Dalanganem Islands Phil. 82 C4
Dalaoba Xinjiang China 98 C4
Dalap-Uliga-Darrit Marshall Is see Delap-Uliga-Djarrit
Dalat Sarawak Malaysia 85 E2
Đa Lat Vietnam 87 E5
Dalatando Angola see N'dalatando
Dalaud India 104 C5
Dalauda India 104 C5
Dalay Mongolia see Bayandalay
Dalbandin Pak. 111 G4
Dalbeattie U.K. 60 F6
Dalbeg Australia 136 D4
Dalby Australia 138 E1
Dalby Isle of Man 58 C4
Dale Hordaland Norway 55 D6
Dale Sogn og Fjordane Norway 55 D6
Dale City U.S.A. 165 G4
Dale Hollow Lake U.S.A. 164 C5
Dalen Neth. 62 G2
Dalet Myanmar 86 A3
Daletme Myanmar 86 A2
Dalfors Sweden 55 I6
Dalgān Iran 110 E5
Dalgety Australia 138 D6
Dalgety r. Australia 135 A6
Dalhart U.S.A. 161 C4
Dalhousie Canada 153 I4
Dalhousie, Cape N.W.T. Canada 149 O1
Dali Shaanxi China 95 G5
Dali Yunnan China 96 D3
Dalian Liaoning China 95 J4
Daliang China see Shunde
Daliang Qinghai China 94 E4
Daliang Shan mts China 96 D2
Dalian Wan b. China 95 J4
Dali He r. China 95 G4
Daliji China 97 H1
Dalin Nei Mongol China 95 J3
Dalinghe Liaoning China see Linghai
Daling He r. China 95 J3
Dalizi China 90 B4
Dalkeith U.K. 60 F5
Dall, Mount AK U.S.A. 148 I3
Dallas OR U.S.A. 156 C3
Dallas TX U.S.A. 161 D5
Dalles City U.S.A. see The Dalles
Dall Island AK U.S.A. 149 N5
Dall Lake AK U.S.A. 148 G3
Dall Mountain AK U.S.A. 149 J2
Dalmā i. U.A.E. 110 D5
Dalmacija reg. Bos.-Herz./Croatia see Dalmatia
Dalmas, Lac l. Canada 153 H3
Dalmatia reg. Bos.-Herz./Croatia 100 A2
Dalmau India 104 E4
Dalmellington U.K. 60 E5
Dalmeny Canada 151 J4
Dalmi India 105 F5
Dal'negorsk Rus. Fed. 90 D3
Dal'nerechensk Rus. Fed. 90 D3
Dal'niye Zelentsy Rus. Fed. 52 H1
Dalny Liaoning China see Dalian
Daloa Côte d'Ivoire 120 C4

▶Dalol Eth. 108 F7
Highest recorded annual mean temperature in the world.

Daloloia Group is P.N.G. 136 E1
Dalou Shan mts China 96 E3
Dalqān well Saudi Arabia 110 B5
Dalry U.K. 60 E5
Dalrymple U.K. 60 E5
Dalrymple, Lake Australia 136 D4
Daltenganj India 105 F4
Dalton Canada 152 D4
Dalton S. Africa 125 J5
Dalton GA U.S.A. 163 C5
Dalton MA U.S.A. 165 I2
Dalton PA U.S.A. 165 H3
Daltonganj India see Daltenganj
Dalton-in-Furness U.K. 58 D4
Daludalu Sumatera Indon. 84 C2
Daluo China 96 D4
Dalupiri i. Phil. 82 C2
Daly r. Australia 134 E3
Daly City U.S.A. 158 B3
Daly River Australia 134 E3
Daly Waters Australia 134 F4
Damagaram Takaya Niger 120 D3
Daman India 106 B1
Daman and Diu union terr. India 106 A1
Damanhūr Egypt 112 C5
Damanhūr Egypt see Damanhūr
Damant Lake Canada 151 J2

Damão India see Daman
Damaqun Shan mts China 95 H3
Damar Sulawesi Indon. 83 C2
Damar i. Maluku Indon. 83 D3
Damar i. Maluku Indon. 83 D4
Damara Cent. Afr. Rep. 122 B3
Damaraland reg. Namibia 123 B6
Damas Syria see Damascus

▶Damascus Syria 107 C3
Capital of Syria.

Damascus U.S.A. 164 E5
Damaturu Nigeria 120 E3
Damāvand Iran 110 D3
Damāvand, Qolleh-ye mt. Iran 110 D3
Dambulla Sri Lanka 106 D5
Damdy Kazakh. 102 B1
Damghan Iran 110 D2
Damianópolis Brazil 179 B1
Damietta Egypt see Dumyāţ
Daming Hebei China 95 H4
Daming Shan mt. China 97 F4
Dāmiyā Jordan 107 B3
Damjong China 96 B1
Damlasu Turkey 107 D1
Dammam Saudi Arabia 108 H4
Damme Belgium 62 D3
Damme Germany 63 I2
Damoh India 104 D5
Damour Lebanon 107 B3
Dampar, Tasik l. Malaysia 84 C2
Dampelas, Tanjung pt Indon. 83 A2
Dampier Archipelago is Australia 134 B5
Dampier Island P.N.G. see Karkar Island
Dampier Land reg. Australia 134 C4
Dampier Strait P.N.G. 81 L8
Dampir, Selat sea chan. Papua Indon. 83 D3
Damqoq Zangbo r. Xizang China see Maquan He
Dam Qu r. Qinghai China 99 F6
Dâmrei, Chuŏr Phnum mts Cambodia 87 D5
Damroh India 96 B2
Damwâld Neth. see Damwoude
Damwoude Neth. 62 G1
Damxoi Xizang China see Comai
Damxung Xizang China 99 E7
Dana i. Indon. 83 B5
Ḑānā Jordan 107 B4
Dana Nepal 105 E3
Danakil reg. Africa see Denakil
Danané Côte d'Ivoire 120 C4
Đa Năng Vietnam 86 E3
Đa Năng, Vung b. Vietnam 86 E3
Dananhu Xinjiang China 94 C3
Danao Cebu Phil. 82 D4
Danata Turkm. 110 D2
Danau Sentarum, Taman Nasional nature res. Kalimantan Indon. 85 F2
Danba China 96 D2
Danbazhai Shaanxi China 95 G4
Danbury CT U.S.A. 165 I3
Danbury NC U.S.A. 162 D4
Danby U.S.A. 165 I2
Danby Lake U.S.A. 159 F4
Dancheng Henan China 95 H5
Dandaragan Australia 135 A7
Dande Eth. 122 D3
Dandeldhura Nepal 104 E3
Dandeli India 106 B3
Dandong China 91 B4
Dando-san mt. Japan 92 D3
Dandot Pak. 111 I3
Dandridge U.S.A. 162 D4
Dane r. U.K. 58 E5
Daneborg Greenland 189 I2
Danese U.S.A. 164 E5
Danfeng China see Shizong
Dangan Liedao i. China 97 G4
Dangara Tajik. see Danghara
Dangbizhen Rus. Fed. 90 C3
Dangchang Gansu China 94 F5
Dangchengwan Gansu China see Subei
Danger Islands atoll Cook Is see Pukapuka
Danger Point S. Africa 124 D8
Danghara Tajik. 111 H2
Dang He r. Gansu China 94 C3
Danghe Nanshan mts China 94 C4
Dangjin Shankou pass Gansu/Qinghai China 98 F5
Dangla Shan mts Xizang China see Tanggula Shan
Dangqên Xizang China 99 E7
Dângrêk, Chuŏr Phnum mts Cambodia/Thai. see Phanom Dong Rak, Thiu Khao
Dangriga Belize 167 H5
Dangshan Anhui China 95 I5
Dangtu China 97 H2
Daniel's Harbour Canada 153 K4
Daniëlskuil S. Africa 124 F5
Danilov Rus. Fed. 52 I4
Danilovka Rus. Fed. 53 J6
Danilovskaya Vozvyshennost' hills Rus. Fed. 52 H4
Daning Shanxi China 95 G4
Danjiang China see Leishan
Danjiangkou China 97 F1
Danjiangkou Shuiku resr China 97 F1
Danjo-guntō is Japan 91 C6
Ḑank Oman 110 E6
Dankhar India 104 D2
Dankov Rus. Fed. 53 H5
Dankova, Pik mt. Kyrg. 98 B4
Danlí Hond. 166 [inset] I6
Danmark country Europe see Denmark
Dannebrog Ø i. Greenland see Qillak
Dannenberg (Elbe) Germany 63 L1
Dannenwalde Germany 63 N1
Dannevirke N.Z. 139 F5
Dannhauser S. Africa 125 J5
Dano Burkina Faso 120 C3
Danshui Taiwan see Tanshui
Dansville U.S.A. 165 G2
Danta India 104 C4
Dantan India 105 F5
Dantevada India see Dantewara
Dantewada India see Dantewara
Dantewara India 106 D2
Dantu China see Zhenjiang
Danube r. Europe 57 P6
Also spelt Donau (Austria/Germany), Duna (Hungary), Dunaj (Slovakia), Dunărea (Romania), Dunav (Bulgaria/Croatia/Serbia) or Dunay (Ukraine).
Danube Delta Romania/Ukr. 69 M2
Danubyu Myanmar 86 A3
Danumparai Kalimantan Indon. 85 F2
Danum Valley Conservation Area nature res. Malaysia 85 G1
Danville IL U.S.A. 164 B3
Danville IN U.S.A. 164 B4
Danville KY U.S.A. 164 C5
Danville OH U.S.A. 164 D3
Danville PA U.S.A. 165 G3
Danville VA U.S.A. 164 F5
Danville VT U.S.A. 165 I1
Danxian China see Danzhou
Danzhai China 96 E3
Danzhou Guangxi China 97 F3
Danzhou Hainan China 97 F5
Danzhou Shaanxi China see Yichuan
Danzig Poland see Gdańsk
Danzig, Gulf of Poland/Rus. Fed. see Gdańsk, Gulf of
Dao Panay Phil. 82 C4
Daocheng China 96 D2
Daokou Henan China see Huaxian
Daotanghe Qinghai China 94 E4
Dao Tay Sa is S. China Sea see Paracel Islands
Daoud Alg. see Aïn Beïda
Daoukro Côte d'Ivoire 120 C4
Daozhen China 96 E2
Dapa Phil. 82 D4
Dapaong Togo 120 D3
Dapeng Wan b. H.K. China see Mirs Bay
Daphabum mt. India 105 I4
Dapiak, Mount Mindanao Phil. 82 C4
Dapitan Mindanao Phil. 82 C4
Daporijo India 105 H4
Dapu China see Liucheng
Da Qaidam Zhen Qinghai China 99 F5
Daqiao China 96 D3
Daqing China 90 B3
Daqinghe Hebei China 95 I4
Daqing Shan mts China 95 G3
Daqin Tal Nei Mongol China 95 J3
Daqiu China 97 H3
Dāq Mashī Iran 110 E3
Daqq-e Patargān salt flat Iran 111 F3
Daqq-e Sorkh, Kavīr-e salt flat Iran 110 D3
Daqq-e Tundi, Dasht-e imp. l. Afgh. 111 F3
Daquan Gansu China 98 F4
Daquanwan Xinjiang China 94 C3
Daqu Shan i. China 97 I2
Dara Senegal 120 B3
Dar'ā Syria 107 C3
Dâra, Gebel mt. Egypt see Dārah, Jabal
Dārāb Iran 110 D4
Daraga Luzon Phil. 82 C3
Darāgāh Iran 110 D4
Dārah, Jabal mt. Egypt 112 D6
Daraj Libya 120 E1
Dārākūyeh Iran 110 D4
Dārān Iran 110 C3
Daraut-Korgon Kyrg. 111 I2
Darazo Nigeria 120 E3
Darband, Kūh-e mt. Iran 110 E4
Darband-e Hajjī Boland Turkm. 111 F2
Darbhanga India 105 F4
Darby, Cape AK U.S.A. 148 G2
Darby Mountains AK U.S.A. 148 G2
Darcang China 96 C1
Dardanelle U.S.A. 161 E5
Dardanelles strait Turkey 69 L4
Dardesheim Germany 63 K3
Dardo China see Kangding
Dar el Beida Morocco see Casablanca
Darende Turkey 112 E3

▶Dar es Salaam Tanz. 123 D4
Former capital of Tanzania.

Darfo Boario Terme Italy 68 D2
Dargai Pak. 111 H3
Dargaville N.Z. 139 D2
Dargo Australia 138 C6
Dargo Zangbo r. China 105 F3
Darhan Mongolia 94 F1
Darhan Muminggan Lianheqi Nei Mongol China see Bailingmiao
Darien U.S.A. 163 D6
Darién, Golfo del g. Col. 176 C2
Darién, Parque Nacional de nat. park Panama 166 [inset] K8
Darién, Serranía del mts Panama 166 [inset] K7
Dariga Pak. 111 G5
Dariganga Mongolia 95 H2
Dar'inskiy Kazakh. 98 A2
Darío Nicaragua 166 [inset] I6
Darjeeling India see Darjiling
Darjiling India 105 G4
Darkhazīneh Iran 110 C4
Darlag China 96 C1

▶Darling r. Australia 138 B3
2nd longest river in Oceania, and a major part of the longest (Murray-Darling)

Darling Downs hills Australia 138 D1
Darling Range hills Australia 135 A8
Darlington U.K. 58 F4
Darlington U.S.A. 160 F3
Darlington Point Australia 138 C5
Darlot, Lake salt flat Australia 135 C6
Darłowo Poland 57 P3
Darma Pass China/India 99 C7
Darmstadt Germany 63 I5
Darnah Libya 112 A4
Darnall S. Africa 125 J5
Darnick Australia 138 A4
Darnley, Cape Antarctica 188 E2
Darnley Bay N.W.T. Canada 149 P1
Daroca Spain 67 F3
Daroot-Korgon Kyrg. see Daraut-Korgon
Darovskoy Rus. Fed. 52 J4
Darr watercourse Australia 136 C4
Darreh Bīd Iran 110 E3
Darreh-ye Bāhābād Iran 110 D4
Darreh-ye Shahr Iran 110 B3
Darsi India 106 C3
Dart r. U.K. 59 D8
Dartang Xizang China see Baqên
Dartford U.K. 59 H7
Dartmoor Australia 137 C8
Dartmoor hills U.K. 59 C8
Dartmoor National Park U.K. 59 D8
Dartmouth Canada 153 J5
Dartmouth U.K. 59 D8
Dartmouth, Lake salt flat Australia 137 D5
Dartmouth Reservoir Australia 138 C6
Darton U.K. 58 F5
Daru P.N.G. 81 K8
Daru Sierra Leone 120 B4
Daruba Maluku Indon. 83 D2
Daruga-mine mt. Japan 92 A3
Darvaza Turkm. see Derweze
Darvi Govĭ-Altay Mongolia 94 C2
Darvi Hovd Mongolia 94 C2
Darvoz, Qatorkŭhi mts Tajik. 111 H2
Darwazgai Afgh. 111 G4
Darwen U.K. 58 E5
Darweshan Afgh. 111 G4

▶Darwin Australia 134 E3
Capital of Northern Territory.

Darwin, Monte mt. Chile 178 C8
Daryācheh-ye Orūmīyeh salt l. Iran see Urmia, Lake
Dar'yalyktakyr, Ravnina plain Kazakh. 102 B2
Dar"yoi Amu r. Asia see Amudar'ya
Darzhuo Xizang China 99 E6
Dārzīn Iran 110 E4
Dās i. U.A.E. 110 D5
Dasada India 104 B5
Dashbalbar Mongolia 95 H1
Dashennongjia mt. China see Shennong Ding
Dashetai Nei Mongol China 95 G3
Dashhowuz Turkm. see Daşoguz
Dashiqiao Liaoning China 95 J3
Dashitou Xinjiang China 94 B3
Dashizhai Nei Mongol China 95 J2
Dashkesan Azer. see Daşkäsän
Dashkhovuz Turkm. see Daşoguz
Dashköpri Turkm. see Daşköpri
Dashoguz Daşoguz Turkm. see Daşoguz
Dasht Iran 110 E2
Dashtiari Iran 111 F5
Dashuikeng Ningxia China 94 F4
Dashuiqiao Qinghai China 94 D4
Dashuitou Gansu China 94 F4
Daska Pak. 111 I3
Daşkäsän Azer. 113 G2
Daşköpri Turkm. 111 F2
Daşoguz Turkm. 109 I1
Dasongshu China 96 E3
Daspar mt. Pak. 111 I2
Dassalan i. Phil. 82 C5
Dassel Germany 63 J3
Dastgardān Iran 110 E3
Datadian Kalimantan Indon. 85 F2
Datça Turkey 69 L6
Date Japan 90 F4
Date Creek watercourse U.S.A. 159 G4
Dateland U.S.A. 159 G5
Datha India 104 C5
Datia India 104 D4
Datian China 97 H3
Datian Ding mt. China 97 F4
Datil U.S.A. 159 J4
Datong Anhui China 97 H2
Datong Heilong. China 90 B3
Datong Qinghai China 94 E4
Datong Shanxi China 95 H3
Datong He r. China 94 E4
Datong Shan mts China 94 D4
Dattapur India 106 C1
Datu i. Indon. 85 E2
Datu, Tanjung c. Indon./Malaysia 85 E2
Datuk, Tanjung pt Indon. 84 C3
Datu Piang Mindanao Phil. 82 D5
Daudkandi Bangl. 105 G5
Daugava r. Latvia 55 N8
Daugavpils Latvia 55 O9
Daulatabad India 106 B2
Daulatabad Iran see Malāyer
Daulatpur Bangl. 105 G5
Daun Germany 62 G4
Daungyu r. Myanmar 86 A2
Dauphin Canada 151 K5
Dauphiné reg. France 66 G4
Dauphiné, Alpes du mts France 66 G4
Dauphin Island AL U.S.A. 167 H2
Dauphin Lake Canada 151 L5
Daurie Creek r. Australia 135 A6
Dauriya Rus. Fed. 95 I1
Daurskiy Khrebet mts Rus. Fed. 95 G1
Dausa India 104 D4
Dâu Tiêng, Hô resr Vietnam 87 D5
Dava U.K. 60 F3
Däväçi Azer. 113 H2
Davanagere India see Davangere
Davangere India 106 B3
Davao Mindanao Phil. 82 D5
Davao Gulf Mindanao Phil. 82 D5
Dāvarī Iran 110 E5
Dāvarzan Iran 110 E2
Davel S. Africa 125 I4
Davenport IA U.S.A. 160 F3
Davenport WA U.S.A. 156 D3
Davenport Downs Australia 136 C5
Davenport Range hills Australia 134 F5
Daventry U.K. 59 F6
Daveyton S. Africa 125 I4
David Panama 166 [inset] J7
David City U.S.A. 160 D3
Davidson Canada 151 J5
Davidson, Mount hill Australia 134 E5
Davidson Mountains AK U.S.A. 149 L1
Davis research station Antarctica 188 E2
Davis r. Australia 134 C5
Davis i. Myanmar see Than Kyun
Davis CA U.S.A. 158 C2
Davis WV U.S.A. 164 F4
Davis, Mount hill U.S.A. 164 F4
Davis Bay Antarctica 188 G2
Davis Dam U.S.A. 159 F4
Davis Inlet (abandoned) Canada 153 J3
Davis Sea Antarctica 188 F2
Davis Strait Canada/Greenland 147 M3
Davlekanovo Rus. Fed. 51 Q5
Davos Switz. 66 I3
Davy Lake Canada 151 I3
Dawa Liaoning China 95 J3
Dawa Co l. Xizang China 99 D7
Dawa Wenz r. Eth. 122 E3
Dawaxung Xizang China 99 D7
Dawê China 96 D2
Dawei Myanmar see Tavoy
Dawei r. mouth Myanmar see Tavoy
Daweloor i. Maluku Indon. 83 D4
Dawera i. Maluku Indon. 83 D4
Dawna Range mts Myanmar/Thai. 86 B3
Dawna Taungdan mts Myanmar/Thai. see Dawna Range
Dawo Qinghai China see Maqên
Dawqah Oman 109 H6
Dawson r. Australia 136 E4
Dawson Y.T. Canada 149 M2
Dawson GA U.S.A. 163 C6
Dawson ND U.S.A. 160 D2
Dawson, Mount Canada 150 G5
Dawson Bay Canada 151 K4
Dawson Creek Canada 150 F4
Dawson Inlet Canada 151 M2
Dawson Range mts Y.T. Canada 149 L3
Dawsons Landing Canada 150 E5
Dawu Hubei China 97 G2
Dawu Taiwan see Tawu
Dawukou Ningxia China see Shizuishan
Dawu Shan hill China 97 G2
Dawusi Qinghai China 99 E5
Dax France 66 D5
Daxian China see Dazhou
Daxiang Ling mts China 96 D2
Daxihaizi Shuiku resr China 98 D4
Daxin China 96 E4
Daxing Yunnan China see Ninglang
Daxing Yunnan China see Lüchun
Daxue Shan mt. China 94 D4
Da Xueshan mts China 96 D2
Dayan China see Lijiang
Dayang r. India 99 F8
Dayangshu Nei Mongol China 95 K1
Dayan Nuur l. Mongolia 94 B1
Dayao China 96 D3
Dayao Shan mts China 97 F4
Daye China 97 G2
Daying China 96 E2
Daying Jiang r. China 96 C3
Dayishan Jiangsu China see Guanyun
Dāykundī Afgh. 111 G3
Daylesford Australia 138 B6
Daylight Pass U.S.A. 158 E3
Dayong China see Zhangjiajie
Dayr Abū Sa'īd Jordan 107 B3
Dayr az Zawr Syria 113 F4
Dayr Ḥāfir Syria 107 C1
Daysland Canada 151 H4
Dayton OH U.S.A. 164 C4
Dayton TN U.S.A. 162 C5
Dayton TX U.S.A. 167 G2
Dayton VA U.S.A. 165 F4
Dayton WA U.S.A. 156 D3
Daytona Beach U.S.A. 163 D6
Dayu Kalimantan Indon. 85 F3
Dayu Ling mts China 97 G3
Da Yunhe canal China 95 I5
Dayyer Iran 110 C5
Dayyīna i. U.A.E. 110 D5
Dazhai Shanxi China 95 H4
Dazhongji China see Dafeng
Dazhou China 96 E2
Dazhou Dao i. China 97 F5
Dazhu China 96 E2
Dazigou Xinjiang China 94 C3
Dazu China 96 E2
Dazu Rock Carvings tourist site China 96 E2
Ddhaw Gro Habitat Protection Area nature res. Y.T. Canada 149 N3
De Aar S. Africa 124 G6
Dead r. Ireland 61 D5
Deadhorse AK U.S.A. 149 J1
Deadman Lake U.S.A. 158 E4
Deadman's Cay Bahamas 163 F8
Dead Mountains U.S.A. 159 F4

▶Dead Sea salt l. Asia 107 B4
Lowest point in the world and in Asia.

Deadwood U.S.A. 160 C2
Deakin Australia 135 E7
Deal U.K. 59 I7
Dealesville S. Africa 125 G5
De'an China 97 G2
Dean, Forest of U.K. 59 E7
Deán Funes Arg. 178 D4
Deanuvuotna inlet Norway see Tanafjorden
Dearborn U.S.A. 164 D2
Dearne r. U.K. 58 F5
Deary U.S.A. 156 D3
Dease r. B.C. Canada 149 O4
Dease Arm b. N.W.T. Canada 149 Q2
Dease Inlet AK U.S.A. 148 I1
Dease Lake B.C. Canada 149 O4
Dease Lake B.C. Canada 149 O4
Dease Strait Canada 146 H3

▶Death Valley depr. U.S.A. 158 E3
Lowest point in the Americas.

Death Valley Junction U.S.A. 158 E3
Death Valley National Park U.S.A. 158 E3
Deauville France 66 E2
Deaver U.S.A. 156 F3
De Baai S. Africa see Port Elizabeth
Debak Sarawak Malaysia 85 E2
Debao China 96 E4
Debar Macedonia 69 I4
Debauch Mountain AK U.S.A. 148 H2
Debden Canada 151 J4
Debenham U.K. 59 I6
De Beque U.S.A. 159 I2
De Biesbosch, Nationaal Park nat. park Neth. 62 E3
Débo, Lac l. Mali 120 C3
Deborah, Mount AK U.S.A. 149 K3
Deborah East, Lake salt flat Australia 135 B7
Deborah West, Lake salt flat Australia 135 B7
Debrecen Hungary 69 I1
Debre Markos Eth. 108 E7
Debre Tabor Eth. 108 E7
Debre Zeyit Eth. 122 D3
Deçan Kosovo 69 I3
Dečani Kosovo see Deçan
Decatur AL U.S.A. 163 C5
Decatur GA U.S.A. 163 C5
Decatur IL U.S.A. 160 F4
Decatur IN U.S.A. 164 C3
Decatur MI U.S.A. 164 C2
Decatur MS U.S.A. 161 F5
Decatur TX U.S.A. 161 D5

▶Deccan plat. India 106 C2
Plateau making up most of southern and central India.

Deception Bay Australia 138 F1
Dechang China 96 D3
Děčín Czech Rep. 57 O5
Decker U.S.A. 156 G3
Decorah U.S.A. 160 F3
Dedap i. Indon. see Penasi, Pulau
Dedaye Myanmar 86 A3
Deddington U.K. 59 F7
Dedegöl Dağları mts Turkey 69 N6
Dedeleben Germany 63 K2
Dedelstorf Germany 63 K2
Dedemsvaart Neth. 62 G2
Dedo de Deus mt. Brazil 179 B4
Dédougou Burkina Faso 120 C3
Dedovichi Rus. Fed. 52 F4
Dedu China see Wudalianchi
Dee r. Ireland 61 F4
Dee est. U.K. 58 D5
Dee r. England/Wales U.K. 59 D5
Dee r. Scotland U.K. 60 G3
Deel r. Ireland 61 D5
Deel r. Ireland 61 F4
Deep Bay H.K. China 97 [inset]
Deep Creek Lake U.S.A. 164 F4
Deep Creek Range mts U.S.A. 159 G2
Deep River Canada 152 F5
Deepwater Australia 138 E2
Deeri Somalia 122 E3
Deering AK U.S.A. 148 G2
Deering, Mount Australia 135 E6
Deer Island AK U.S.A. 148 G5
Deer Lake Canada 151 M4
Deer Lake l. Canada 151 M4
Deer Lodge U.S.A. 156 E3
Deerpass Bay N.W.T. Canada 149 Q2
Deesa India see Disa
Deeth U.S.A. 156 E4
Defeng China see Liping
Defensores del Chaco, Parque Nacional nat. park Para. 178 D2
Defiance U.S.A. 164 C3
Defiance Plateau U.S.A. 159 I4
De Funiak Springs FL U.S.A. 167 I2
Degana India 104 C4
Degeh Bur Eth. 122 E3
Degema Nigeria 120 D4
Deggendorf Germany 63 M6
Degh r. Pak. 111 I4
De Grey r. Australia 134 B5
De Groote Peel, Nationaal Park nat. park Neth. 62 F3
Degtevo Rus. Fed. 53 I6
De Haan Belgium 62 D3
Dehak Iran 111 F4
De Hamert, Nationaal Park nat. park Neth. 62 G3
Deh-Dasht Iran 110 C4
Deheq Iran 110 C3
Dehestān Iran 110 D4
Deh Golān Iran 110 B3
Dehgon Afgh. 111 F3
Dehi Afgh. 111 G3
Dehkūyeh Iran 110 D5
Dehlorān Iran 110 B3
De Hoge Veluwe, Nationaal Park nat. park Neth. 62 F2
De Hoop Nature Reserve S. Africa 124 E8
Dehqonobod Uzbek. 111 G2
Dehra Dun India 104 D3
Dehradun India see Dehra Dun
Dehri India 105 F4
Deh Shū Afgh. 111 F4
Deim Zubeir Sudan 121 F4
Deinze Belgium 62 D4
Deir-ez-Zor Syria see Dayr az Zawr
Dej Romania 69 J1
Deji Xizang China see Rinbung
Dejiang China 97 F2
De Jouwer Neth. see Joure
De Kalb IL U.S.A. 160 F3
De Kalb MS U.S.A. 161 F5
De Kalb TX U.S.A. 161 E5
De Kalb Junction U.S.A. 165 H1
De-Kastri Rus. Fed. 90 F2
Dekemhare Eritrea 108 E6
Dekhkanabad Uzbek. see Dehqonobod
Dekina Nigeria 120 D4
Dékoa Cent. Afr. Rep. 122 B3
De Koog Neth. 62 E1
De Kooy Neth. 62 E2
Delaki Indon. 83 C5
Delamar Lake U.S.A. 159 F3
De Land U.S.A. 163 D6
Delano U.S.A. 158 D4
Delano Peak U.S.A. 159 G2

▶Delap-Uliga-Djarrit Marshall Is 186 H5
Capital of the Marshall Islands, on Majuro atoll.

Delārām Afgh. 111 F3
Delareyville S. Africa 125 G4
Delarof Islands AK U.S.A. 149 [inset]
Delaronde Lake Canada 151 J4
Delavan U.S.A. 152 C6
Delaware U.S.A. 164 D3
Delaware r. U.S.A. 165 H4
Delaware state U.S.A. 165 H4
Delaware, East Branch r. U.S.A. 165 H3
Delaware Bay U.S.A. 165 H4
Delaware Lake U.S.A. 164 D3
Delaware Water Gap National Recreational Area park U.S.A. 165 H3
Delay r. Canada 153 H2
Delbarton U.S.A. 164 D5
Delbrück Germany 63 I3
Delburne Canada 150 H4
Délèg Xizang China 99 D7
Delegate Australia 138 D6
De Lemmer Neth. see Lemmer
Delémont Switz. 66 H3
Delevan CA U.S.A. 158 B2
Delevan NY U.S.A. 165 F2
Delfinópolis Brazil 179 B3
Delft Neth. 62 E2
Delfzijl Neth. 62 G1
Delgada, Point U.S.A. 158 A1
Delgado, Cabo c. Moz. 123 E5
Delger Mongolia 94 D2
Delgerhaan Töv Mongolia 94 F2
Delgerhangay Mongolia 94 F2
Delgermörön Mongolia see Hüreemaral
Delger Mörön r. Mongolia 94 E1
Delgertsogt Mongolia 94 F2
Delhi Canada 164 E2
Delhi Qinghai China 94 D4

▶Delhi India 104 D3
3rd most populous city in Asia and 6th in the world.

Delhi admin. div. India 99 B7
Delhi CO U.S.A. 157 G5
Delhi LA U.S.A. 161 F5
Delhi NY U.S.A. 165 H2
Deli i. Indon. 84 D4
Delice Turkey 112 D3
Delice r. Turkey 112 D2
Delījān Iran 110 C3
Déljne N.W.T. Canada 149 Q2
Delingha Qinghai China see Delhi
Delisle Canada 151 J5
Delitua Sumatera Indon. 84 B2
Delitzsch Germany 63 M3
Delligsen Germany 63 J3
Dell Rapids U.S.A. 160 D3
Dellys Alg. 67 H5
Del Mar U.S.A. 158 E5
Delmenhorst Germany 63 I1
Delnice Croatia 68 F2
Del Norte U.S.A. 157 G5
Delong China see Ande
De-Longa, Ostrova is Rus. Fed. 77 Q2
De Long Islands Rus. Fed. see De-Longa, Ostrova
De Long Mountains AK U.S.A. 148 G1
De Long Strait Rus. Fed. see Longa, Proliv
Deloraine Canada 151 K5
Delphi U.S.A. 164 B3
Delphos U.S.A. 164 C3
Delportshoop S. Africa 124 G5
Delray Beach U.S.A. 163 D7
Delrey U.S.A. 164 A3
Del Río Mex. 166 C2
Del Rio U.S.A. 161 C6
Delsbo Sweden 55 J6
Delta CO U.S.A. 159 I2
Delta OH U.S.A. 164 C3
Delta UT U.S.A. 159 G2
Delta r. AK U.S.A. 149 K2
Delta Downs Australia 136 C3
Delta Junction AK U.S.A. 149 K2
Deltona U.S.A. 163 D6
Delungra Australia 138 E2
Delüün Bayan-Ölgiy Mongolia 94 B2
Delvin Ireland 61 E4
Delvinë Albania 69 I5
Delwara India 104 C4
Demak Jawa Indon. 85 E4
Demarcation Point pt AK U.S.A. 149 L1
Demavend mt. Iran see Damāvand, Qolleh-ye
Demba Dem. Rep. Congo 123 C4
Dembī Dolo Eth. 108 D8
Demerara Guyana see Georgetown
Demerara Abyssal Plain sea feature S. Atlantic Ocean 184 E5
Demidov Rus. Fed. 53 F5
Deming U.S.A. 157 G6
Demirci Turkey 69 M5
Demirköy Turkey 69 L4
Demirtaş Turkey 107 A1
Demmin Germany 57 N4
Demopolis U.S.A. 163 C5
Demotte U.S.A. 164 B3
Dempo, Gunung vol. Indon. 84 C4
Dempster Highway Canada 149 M2
Dêmqog China 104 D2
Demta Indon. 81 K7
Dem'yanovo Rus. Fed. 52 J3
De Naawte S. Africa 124 E6
Denakil reg. Africa 122 E2
Denali AK U.S.A. 149 K3
Denali AK U.S.A. see McKinley, Mount
Denali Highway AK U.S.A. 149 K3
Denali National Park and Preserve AK U.S.A. 149 J3
Denan Eth. 122 E3
Denbigh Canada 165 G1
Denbigh U.K. 58 D5
Denbigh, Cape AK U.S.A. 148 G2
Den Bosch Neth. see 's-Hertogenbosch
Den Burg Neth. 62 E1
Den Chai Thai. 86 C3
Dendang Indon. 85 D3
Dendâra Mauritania 120 C3
Dendermonde Belgium 62 E3
Dendi mt. Eth. 122 D3
Dendre r. Belgium 62 E3
Dendron S. Africa see Mogwadi
Denezhkin Kamen', Gora mt. Rus. Fed. 51 R3
Denges Passage Palau 82 [inset]
Dengfeng Henan China 95 H5
Dênggar Xizang China 99 D7
Dêngka Gansu China see Têwo
Dêngkagoin Gansu China see Têwo
Dengkou Nei Mongol China 95 F3
Dêngqên Xizang China 99 F7
Dengta China 97 G4
Dengxian China see Dengzhou
Dêngzê Xizang China 99 C6
Dengzhou China 97 G1
Dengzhou Shandong China see Penglai
Den Haag Neth. see The Hague
Denham Australia 135 A6
Denham r. Australia 134 E3
Den Ham Neth. 62 G2
Denham Range mts Australia 136 E4
Den Helder Neth. 62 E2
Denholm Canada 151 I4
Denia Spain 67 G4
Denial Bay Australia 137 A7
Deniliquin Australia 138 B5
Denio U.S.A. 156 D4
Denison IA U.S.A. 160 E3
Denison TX U.S.A. 161 D5
Denison, Cape Antarctica 188 G2
Denison Plains Australia 134 E4
Deniyaya Sri Lanka 106 D5
Denizli Turkey 69 M6
Denman Australia 138 E4
Denman Glacier Antarctica 188 F2
Denmark Australia 132 B5
Denmark country Europe 55 G8
Denmark U.S.A. 164 B1
Denmark Strait Greenland/Iceland 50 A2
Dennis, Lake salt flat Australia 134 E5
Dennison IL U.S.A. 164 B4
Dennison OH U.S.A. 164 E3
Denny U.K. 60 F4
Denov Uzbek. 111 G2

I was Here
2014 3rd year Baby cya future you i If you have read this you have wasted 10 sec of your life.

Denow Uzbek. see Denov
Denpasar *Bali* Indon. 85 F5
Densongi *Sulawesi* Indon. 83 B3
Denton *MD* U.S.A. 165 H4
Denton *TX* U.S.A. 161 D5
D'Entrecasteaux, Point Australia 135 A8
D'Entrecasteaux, Récifs *reef* New Caledonia 133 G3
D'Entrecasteaux Islands P.N.G. 132 F2
D'Entrecasteaux National Park Australia 135 A8

▶Denver *CO* U.S.A. 156 G5
Capital of Colorado.

Denver *PA* U.S.A. 165 G3
Denys *r.* Canada 152 F3
Deo India 105 F4
Deoband India 104 D3
Deogarh *Jharkhand* India see Deoghar
Deogarh *Odisha* India 105 F5
Deogarh *Rajasthan* India 104 C4
Deogarh *Uttar Prad.* India 104 D4
Deogarh *mt.* India 105 E5
Deoghar India 105 F4
Deolali India 106 B2
Deoli India 105 F5
Deori *Madh. Prad.* India 104 D5
Deoria India 105 E4
Deosai, Plains of Pak. 104 C2
Deosil India 105 E5
Deothang Bhutan 105 G4
De Panne Belgium 62 C3
De Pere U.S.A. 164 A1
Deposit U.S.A. 165 H2
Depsang Point *hill* Aksai Chin 99 B6
Deputatskiy Rus. Fed. 77 O3
Dêqên *Xizang* China see Dagzê
Dêqên *Xizang* China 99 E7
Dêqên *Xizang* China 99 E7
De Queen U.S.A. 161 E5
De Quincy *LA* U.S.A. 167 G2
Dera Ghazi Khan Pak. 111 H4
Dera Ismail Khan Pak. 111 H4
Derajat *reg.* Pak. 111 H4
Derawar Fort Pak. 111 H4
Derbent Rus. Fed. 113 H2
Derbesiye Turkey see Şenyurt
Derbur China 90 A2
Derby Australia 134 C4
Derby U.K. 59 F6
Derby *CT* U.S.A. 165 I3
Derby *KS* U.S.A. 161 D4
Derby *NY* U.S.A. 165 F2
Dereham U.K. 59 H6
Derg *r.* Ireland/U.K. 61 E3
Derg, Lough *l.* Ireland 61 D5
Dergachi Rus. Fed. 53 K6
Dergachi Ukr. see Derhachi
Derhachi Ukr. 53 H6
De Ridder U.S.A. 161 E6
Derik Turkey 113 F3
Derm Namibia 124 D2
Derna Libya see Darnah
Dernberg, Cape Namibia 124 B4
Dêrong China 96 C2
Derravaragh, Lough *l.* Ireland 61 E4
Derry U.K. see Londonderry
Derry U.S.A. 165 J2
Derryveagh Mts *hills* Ireland 61 D3
Derst *Nei Mongol* China 95 H3
Derstei *Nei Mongol* China 94 E3
Dêrub *Xizang* China 99 B6
Derudeb Sudan 108 E6
De Rust S. Africa 124 F7
Derventa Bos.-Herz. 68 G2
Derwent *r. England* U.K. 58 F6
Derwent *r. England* U.K. 58 G5
Derwent Water *l.* U.K. 58 D4
Derweze Turkm. 110 E1
Derzhavinsk Kazakh. 102 C1
Derzhavinskiy Kazakh. see Derzhavinsk
Desaguadero *r.* Arg. 178 C4
Désappointement, Îles du *is* Fr. Polynesia 187 K6
Desatoya Mountains U.S.A. 158 E2
Deschambault Lake Canada 151 K4
Deschutes *r.* U.S.A. 156 C3
Desē Eth. 122 D2
Deseado Arg. 178 C7
Deseado *r.* Arg. 178 C7
Desemboque Mex. 166 B2
Desengaño, Punta *pt* Arg. 178 C7
Deseret U.S.A. 159 G2
Deseret Peak U.S.A. 159 G1
Deseronto Canada 165 G1
Desert Canal Pak. 111 H4
Desert Center U.S.A. 159 F5
Desert Lake U.S.A. 159 F3
Desert View U.S.A. 159 H3
Deshler U.S.A. 164 D3
Desierto Central de Baja California, Parque Natural del *nature res.* Mex. 166 B2
De Smet U.S.A. 160 D2

▶Des Moines *IA* U.S.A. 160 E3
Capital of Iowa.

Des Moines *NM* U.S.A. 161 C4
Des Moines *r.* U.S.A. 160 F3
Desna *r.* Rus. Fed./Ukr. 53 F6
Desnogorsk Rus. Fed. 53 G5
Desolación, Isla *i.* Chile 178 B8
Desolation Point Phil. 82 D4
Despen Rus. Fed. 94 C1
Des Plaines U.S.A. 164 B2
Dessau Germany 63 M3
Dessye Eth. see Desē
Destelbergen Belgium 62 D3
Destruction Bay Canada 189 A2
Desvres France 62 B4
Detah Canada 150 H2
Dete Zimbabwe 123 C5
Detmold Germany 63 I3
Detrital Wash *watercourse* U.S.A. 159 F3
Detroit U.S.A. 164 D2
Detroit Lakes U.S.A. 160 E2
Dett Zimbabwe see Dete
Deua National Park Australia 138 D5
Deuben Germany 63 M3
Deurne Neth. 62 F3
Deutschland *country* Europe see Germany
Deutschlandsberg Austria 57 O7
Deutzen Germany 63 M3
Deva Romania 69 J2
Deva U.K. see Chester
Devana U.K. see Aberdeen
Devangere India see Davangere
Devanhalli India 106 C3
Deve Bair *pass* Bulg./Macedonia see Velbŭzhdki Prokhod
Develi Turkey 112 D3
Deventer Neth. 62 G2
Deveron *r.* U.K. 60 G3
Devét Skal *hill* Czech Rep. 57 P6
Devgarh India 106 B2
Devghar India see Deoghar
Devikot India 104 B4
Devil Mountain *hill AK* U.S.A. 148 F2
Devil's Bridge U.K. 59 D6
Devil's Gate *pass* U.S.A. 158 D2
Devil's Lake U.S.A. 160 D1
Devil's Lake *l. TX* U.S.A. 167 E2
Devil's Paw *mt. AK* U.S.A. 149 N4
Devil's Peak U.S.A. 158 D3
Devil's Point Bahamas 163 F7
Devil's Thumb *mt.* Canada/U.S.A. 149 N4
Devine U.S.A. 161 D6
Devizes U.K. 59 F7
Devli India 104 C4
Devnya Bulg. 69 L3
Devon *r.* U.K. 60 F4
Devon Island Canada 147 I2
Devonport Australia 137 [inset]
Devrek Turkey 69 N4
Devrukh India 106 B2
Dewa, Tanjung *pt* Indon. 84 A2
Dewakang Besar *i.* Indon. 85 G4
Dewas India 104 D5
De Weerribben, Nationaal Park *nat. park* Neth. 62 G2
Dewetsdorp S. Africa 125 H5
De Witt *AR* U.S.A. 161 F5
De Witt *IA* U.S.A. 160 F3
Dewsbury U.K. 58 F5
Dexing *Jiangxi* China 97 H2
Dêxing *Xizang* China 99 F7
Dexter *ME* U.S.A. 165 K1
Dexter *MI* U.S.A. 164 D2
Dexter *MO* U.S.A. 161 F4
Dexter *NM* U.S.A. 157 G6
Dexter *NY* U.S.A. 165 G1
Deyang China 96 E2
Dey-Dey Lake *salt flat* Australia 135 E7
Deyhuk Iran 110 E3
Deyong, Tanjung *pt* Indon. 81 J8
Dez *r.* Iran 108 G3
Dezadeash Lake *Y.T.* Canada 149 M3
Dezfūl Iran 110 C3
Dezhneva, Mys *c.* Rus. Fed. 148 E2
Dezhou *Shandong* China 95 I4
Dezhou *Sichuan* China see Dechang
Dezh Shāhpūr Iran see Marīvān
Dhabarau India 105 E4
Dhahab, Wādī adh *r.* Syria 107 B3
Dhāhiriya West Bank 107 B4
Dhahran Saudi Arabia 110 C5

▶Dhaka Bangl. 105 G5
Capital of Bangladesh. 10th most populous city in the world.

Dhalbhum *reg.* India 105 F5
Dhalgaon India 106 B2
Dhamār Yemen 108 F7
Dhamoni India 104 D4
Dhamtari India 106 D1
Dhana Pak. 111 H5
Dhana Sar Pak. 111 H4
Dhanbad India 105 F5
Dhanera India 104 C4
Dhang Range *mts* Nepal 105 E3
Dhankuta Nepal 105 F4
Dhansia India 104 C3
Dhar India 104 C5
Ḍhar Adrar *hills* Mauritania 120 B3
Dharampur India 106 B1
Dharan Bazar Nepal 105 F4
Dharashiv India see Osmanabad
Dhari India 104 B5
Dharmapuri India 106 C3
Dharmavaram India 106 C3
Dharmsala *Hima. Prad.* India see Dharmshala
Dharmsala *Odisha* India 105 F5
Dharmshala India 104 D2
Dharnaoda India 104 D4
Ḍhar Oualâta *hills* Mauritania 120 C3
Ḍhar Tîchît *hills* Mauritania 120 C3
Dharug National Park Australia 138 E4
Dharur India 106 C2
Dharwad India 106 B3
Dharwar India see Dharwad
Dharwas India 104 D2
Dhasan *r.* India 104 D4
Dhāt al Ḥājj Saudi Arabia 112 E5

▶Dhaulagiri *mt.* Nepal 105 E3
7th highest mountain in the world and in Asia.

Dhaulpur India see Dholpur
Dhaura India 104 D4
Dhaurahra India 104 E4
Dhawlagiri *mt.* Nepal see Dhaulagiri
Dhebar Lake India see Jaisamand Lake
Dhekelia Sovereign Base Area *military base* Cyprus 107 A2
Dhemaji India 105 H4
Dhenkanal India 106 E1
Dhībān Jordan 107 B4
Dhidhimótikhon Greece see Didymoteicho
Dhing India 105 H4
Dhirwah, Wādī adh *watercourse* Jordan 107 C4
Dhodhekánisos *is* Greece see Dodecanese
Dhola India 104 B5
Dholera India 104 C5
Dholpur India 104 D4
Dhomokós Greece see Domokos
Dhone India 106 C3
Dhoraji India 104 B5
Dhori India 104 B5
Dhrangadhra India 104 B5
Dhubāb Yemen 108 F7
Dhubri India 105 G4
Dhuburi India see Dhubri
Dhudial Pak. 111 I3
Dhule India 106 B1
Dhulia India see Dhule
Dhulian India 105 F4
Dhulian Pak. 111 I3
Dhuma India 104 D5
Dhund *r.* India 104 D4
Dhurwai India 104 D4
Dhuusa Marreeb Somalia 122 E3
Dia *i.* Greece 69 K7
Diablo, Mount U.S.A. 158 C3
Diablo, Picacho del *mt.* Mex. 166 B2
Diablo Range *mts* U.S.A. 158 C3
Diagbe Dem. Rep. Congo 122 C3
Diamante Arg. 178 D4
Diamantina *watercourse* Australia 136 B5
Diamantina Brazil 179 C2
Diamantina, Chapada *plat.* Brazil 179 C1
Diamantina Deep *sea feature* Indian Ocean 185 O8
Diamantina Gates National Park Australia 136 C4
Diamantino Brazil 177 G6
Diamond Islets Australia 136 E3
Diamond Peak U.S.A. 159 F2
Dianbai China 97 F4
Diancang Shan *mt.* China 96 D3
Dian Chi *l.* China 96 D3
Diandioumé Mali 120 C3
Diane Bank *sea feature* Australia 136 E2
Dianjiang China 96 E2
Dianópolis Brazil 177 I6
Dianyang China see Shidian
Diaobingshan *Liaoning* China 95 J3
Diaokou *Shandong* China 95 I4
Diaoling China 90 C3
Diapaga Burkina Faso 120 D3
Diarizos *r.* Cyprus 107 A2
Diavolo, Mount *hill* India 87 A4
Diaz Point Namibia 124 B4
Dibaya Dem. Rep. Congo 123 C4
Dibella *well* Niger 120 E3
Dibeng S. Africa 124 F4
Dibete Botswana 125 H2
Dibrugarh India 105 H4
Dibse Syria see Dibsī
Dibsī Syria 107 D2
Dickens U.S.A. 161 C5
Dickinson U.S.A. 160 C2
Dicle *r.* Turkey 113 F3 see Tigris
Dīdēsa Wenz *r.* Eth. 122 D3
Didicas *i.* Phil. 82 C2
Didiéni Mali 120 C3
Didsbury Canada 150 H5
Didwana India 104 C4
Didymoteicho Greece 69 L4
Die France 66 G4
Dieblich Germany 63 H4
Diébougou Burkina Faso 120 C3
Dieburg Germany 63 I5
Diedenhofen France see Thionville
Diefenbaker, Lake Canada 151 I5
Diego de Almagro, Isla *i.* Chile 178 A8
Diégo Suarez Madag. see Antsirañana
Diekirch Lux. 62 G5
Diéma Mali 120 C3
Diemel *r.* Germany 63 J3
Điên Biên Vietnam see Điên Biên Phu
Điên Biên Phu Vietnam 86 C2
Diên Châu Vietnam 86 D3
Diên Khanh Vietnam 87 E4
Diepholz Germany 63 I2
Dieppe France 62 B5
Dierks U.S.A. 161 E5
Di'er Songhua Jiang *r.* China 90 B3
Diessen Neth. 62 F3
Diest Belgium 62 F4
Dietikon Switz. 66 I3
Dietrich Camp *AK* U.S.A. 149 J2
Diez Germany 63 I4
Diffa Niger 120 E3
Digby Canada 153 I5
Diggi India 104 C4
Diglur India 106 C2
Digne France see Digne-les-Bains
Digne-les-Bains France 66 H4
Digoin France 66 F3
Digollorin Point *Luzon* Phil. 82 C2
Digos *Mindanao* Phil. 82 D5
Digras India 106 C1
Digri Pak. 111 H5
Digul *r.* Indon. 81 K8
Diguojiadan *Qinghai* China 94 D4
Digya National Park Ghana 120 C4
Dihang *r.* India 105 H4 see Brahmaputra
Dihōk Iraq see Dahūk
Dihourse, Lac *l.* Canada 153 I2
Diinsoor Somalia 122 E3
Dijon France 66 G3
Dik Chad 121 E4
Diken India 104 C4
Dikhil Djibouti 108 F7
Dikho *r.* India 99 F8
Dikili Turkey 69 L5
Diklosmta *mt.* Rus. Fed. 53 J8
Diksmuide Belgium 62 C3
Dikson Rus. Fed. 76 J2
Dīla Eth. 122 D3
Dilaram Iran 110 E4

▶Dili East Timor 83 C5
Capital of East Timor.

Di Linh Vietnam 87 E5
Dillenburg Germany 63 I4
Dilley U.S.A. 161 D6
Dillingen (Saar) Germany 62 G5
Dillingen an der Donau Germany 57 M6
Dillingham *AK* U.S.A. 148 H4
Dillon *r.* Canada 151 I4
Dillon *MT* U.S.A. 156 E3
Dillon *SC* U.S.A. 163 E5
Dillwyn U.S.A. 165 F5
Dilolo Dem. Rep. Congo 123 C5
Dilsen Belgium 62 F3
Dimapur India 105 H4
Dimas Mex. 166 D4
Dimashq Syria see Damascus
Dimbokro Côte d'Ivoire 120 C4
Dimboola Australia 137 C8
Dime Landing *AK* U.S.A. 148 G2
Dimitrov Ukr. see Dymytrov
Dimitrovgrad Bulg. 69 K3
Dimitrovgrad Rus. Fed. 53 K5
Dimitrovo Bulg. see Pernik
Dimmitt U.S.A. 161 C5
Dīmona Israel 107 B4
Dimpho Pan *salt pan* Botswana 124 E3
Dinagat *i.* Phil. 82 D4
Dinajpur Bangl. 105 G4
Dinan France 66 C2
Dinant Belgium 62 E4
Dinapur India 105 F4
Dinar Turkey 69 N5
Dīnār, Kūh-e *mt.* Iran 110 C4
Dinara Planina *mts* Bos.-Herz./Croatia see Dinaric Alps
Dinaric Alps *mts* Bos.-Herz./Croatia 68 G2
Dinbych U.K. see Denbigh
Dinbych-y-pysgod U.K. see Tenby
Dinder National Park Sudan 121 G3
Dindi *r.* India 106 C2
Dindigul India 106 C4
Dindima Nigeria 120 E3
Dindiza Moz. 125 K2
Dindori India 104 E5
Dingalan Bay *Luzon* Phil. 82 C3
Dingbian *Shaanxi* China 95 F4
Dingcheng China see Dingyuan
Dingelstädt Germany 63 K3
Dinggo *Xizang* China 99 D6
Dingin, Bukit *mt.* Indon. 84 C3
Dingla Nepal 105 F4
Dingle Ireland see An Daingean
Dingle Bay Ireland 61 B5
Dingnan China 97 G3
Dingo Australia 136 E4
Dingolfing Germany 63 M6
Dingping China see Linshui
Dingras *Luzon* Phil. 82 C2
Dingshan *Xinjiang* China 98 D3
Dingtao *Shandong* China 95 H5
Dinguiraye Guinea 120 B3
Dingwall U.K. 60 E3
Dingxi *Gansu* China 94 F5
Dingxian *Hebei* China see Dingzhou
Dingxin *Gansu* China 94 D3
Dingxing *Hebei* China 95 H4
Dingyuan China 97 H1
Dingzhou *Hebei* China 95 H4
Dingzi Gang *b.* China 95 J4
Dingzikou *Qinghai* China 98 F5
Dinh Lâp Vietnam 86 D2
Dinkelsbühl Germany 63 K5
Dinngyê *Xizang* China 99 D7
Dinokwe Botswana 125 H2
Dinosaur U.S.A. 159 I1
Dinosaur National Monument *nat. park* U.S.A. 159 I1
Dinslaken Germany 62 G3
Dintiteladas *Sumatera* Indon. 84 D4
Dinwiddie U.S.A. 165 G5
Dioïla Mali 120 C3
Diomede *AK* U.S.A. 148 E2
Diomede Islands Rus. Fed./U.S.A. 148 E2
Dionísio Cerqueira Brazil 178 F3
Diorama Brazil 179 A2
Dioscurias Georgia see Sokhumi
Diouloulou Senegal 120 B3
Diourbel Senegal 120 B3
Dipayal 104 E3
Diphu India 105 H4
Dipkarpaz Cyprus see Rizokarpason
Diplo Pak. 111 H5
Dipolog *Mindanao* Phil. 82 C4
Dipperu National Park Australia 136 E4
Dipu China see Anji
Dir *reg.* Pak. 111 I3
Dirang India 105 H4
Diré Mali 120 C3
Direction, Cape Australia 136 C2
Dirē Dawa Eth. 122 E3
Diriamba Nicaragua 166 [inset] I7
Dirico Angola 123 C5
Dirk Hartog Island Australia 135 A6
Dirranbandi Australia 138 D2
Ḍirs Saudi Arabia 122 E2
Dirschau Poland see Tczew
Dirty Devil *r.* U.S.A. 159 H3
Disa India 104 C4
Disang *r.* India 105 H4
Disappointment, Cape S. Georgia 178 I8
Disappointment, Cape U.S.A. 156 B3
Disappointment, Lake *salt flat* Australia 135 C5
Disappointment Islands Fr. Polynesia see Désappointement, Îles du
Disappointment Lake Canada 153 J3
Disaster Bay Australia 138 D6
Discovery Bay Australia 137 C8
Dishna *r. AK* U.S.A. 148 H3
Disko *i.* Greenland see Qeqertarsuaq
Disko Bugt *b.* Greenland see Qeqertarsuup Tunua
Dismal Swamp U.S.A. 162 E4
Dispur India 105 G4
Disputanta U.S.A. 165 G5
Disraëli Canada 153 H5
Diss U.K. 59 I6
Distrito Federal *admin. dist.* Brazil 179 B1
Distrito Federal *admin. dist.* Mex. 167 F5
Disūq Egypt 112 C5
Dit *i.* Phil. 82 C4
Ditloung S. Africa 124 F5
Dittaino *r. Sicily* Italy 68 F6
Diu India 106 A1
Diuata Mountains *Mindanao* Phil. 82 D4
Diuata Point *Mindanao* Phil. 82 D4
Dīvān Darreh Iran 110 B3
Divehi *country* Indian Ocean see Maldives
Divi, Point India 106 D3
Divichi Azer. see Däväçi
Divide Mountain *AK* U.S.A. 149 L3
Divilacan Bay *Luzon* Phil. 82 C2
Divinópolis Brazil 179 B3
Divnoye Rus. Fed. 53 I7
Divo Côte d'Ivoire 120 C4
Divriği Turkey 112 E3
Diwana Pak. 111 G5
Diwaniyah Iraq see Ad Dīwānīyah
Dixfield U.S.A. 165 J1
Dixon *CA* U.S.A. 158 C2
Dixon *IL* U.S.A. 160 F3
Dixon *KY* U.S.A. 164 B5
Dixon *MT* U.S.A. 156 E3
Dixon Entrance *sea channel* Canada/U.S.A. 149 N5
Dixonville Canada 150 G3
Dixville Canada 165 J1
Diyadin Turkey 113 F3
Diyarbakır Turkey 113 F3
Diz Pak. 111 F5
Diz Chah Iran 110 D3
Dize Turkey see Yüksekova
Dizney U.S.A. 164 D5
Djado Niger 120 E2
Djado, Plateau du Niger 120 E2
Djaja, Puntjak *mt.* Indon. see Jaya, Puncak
Djakarta *Jawa* Indon. see Jakarta
Djakovica Kosovo see Gjakovë
Djakovo Croatia see Đakovo
Djambala Congo 122 B4
Djanet Alg. 120 D2
Djarrit-Uliga-Dalap Marshall Is see Delap-Uliga-Djarrit
Djelfa Alg. 67 H6
Djéma Cent. Afr. Rep. 122 C3
Djenné Mali 120 C3
Djerdap *nat. park* Serbia 69 J2
Djibo Burkina Faso 120 C3
Djibouti *country* Africa 108 F7

▶Djibouti Djibouti 108 F7
Capital of Djibouti.

Djidjelli Alg. see Jijel
Djizak Uzbek. see Jizzax
Djougou Benin 120 D4
Djoum Cameroon 120 E4
Djourab, Erg du *des.* Chad 121 E3
Djúpivogur Iceland 54 [inset]
Djurås Sweden 55 I6
Djurdjura, Parc National du Alg. 67 I5
Dmitriya Lapteva, Proliv *sea chan.* Rus. Fed. 77 P2
Dmitriyev-L'govskiy Rus. Fed. 53 G5
Dmitriyevsk Ukr. see Makiyivka
Dmitrov Rus. Fed. 52 H4
Dmytriyevs'k Ukr. see Makiyivka
Dnepr *r.* Rus. Fed. 53 F5 see Dnieper
Dneprodzerzhinsk Ukr. see Dniprodzerzhyns'k
Dnepropetrovsk Ukr. see Dnipropetrovs'k

▶Dnieper *r.* Europe 53 G7
3rd longest river in Europe. Also spelt Dnepr (Rus. Fed.), Dnipro (Ukraine) or Dnyapro (Belarus).

Dniester *r.* Ukr. 53 F6
also spelt Dnister (Ukraine) or Nistru (Moldova)
Dnipro *r.* Ukr. 53 G7 see Dnieper
Dniprodzerzhyns'k Ukr. 53 G6
Dnipropetrovs'k Ukr. 53 G6
Dnister *r.* Ukr. 53 F6 see Dniester
Dno Rus. Fed. 52 F4
Dnyapro *r.* Belarus 53 F6 see Dnieper
Doāb Afgh. 111 G3
Doaba Pak. 111 H3
Doangdoangan Besar *i.* Indon. 85 G4
Doangdoangan Kecil *i.* Indon. 85 G4
Doan Hung Vietnam 86 D2
Doba Chad 121 E4
Dobdain *Qinghai* China 94 E5
Dobele Latvia 55 M8
Döbeln Germany 63 N3
Doberai, Jazirah *pen.* Indon. 81 I7
Doberai Peninsula Indon. see Doberai, Jazirah
Dobo Indon. 81 I8
Doboj Bos.-Herz. 68 H2
Do Borjī Iran 110 D4
Döbraberg *hill* Germany 63 L4
Dobrich Bulg. 69 L3
Dobrinka Rus. Fed. 53 I5
Dobroye Rus. Fed. 53 H5
Dobrudja *reg.* Romania see Dobruja
Dobruja *reg.* Romania 69 L3
Dobrush Belarus 53 F5
Dobryanka Rus. Fed. 51 R4
Dobzha *Xizang* China 99 E7
Doc Can *rf* Phil. 82 B5
Doce *r.* Brazil 179 D2
Dochart *r.* U.K. 60 E4
Do China Qala Afgh. 111 H4
Docking U.K. 59 H6
Doctor Arroyo Mex. 167 E4
Doctor Belisario Domínguez Mex. 166 D2
Doctor Hicks Range *hills* Australia 135 D7
Doctor Pedro P. Peña Para. 178 D2
Doda India 104 C2
Doda Betta *mt.* India 106 C4
Dod Ballapur India 106 C3
Dodê *Xizang* China 99 E7
Dodecanese *is* Greece 69 L7
Dodekanisa *is* Greece see Dodecanese
Dodekanisos *is* Greece see Dodecanese
Dodge City U.S.A. 160 C4
Dodgeville U.S.A. 160 F3
Dodman Point U.K. 59 C8

▶Dodoma Tanz. 123 D4
Capital of Tanzania.

Dodsonville U.S.A. 164 D4
Doetinchem Neth. 62 G3
Dofa *Maluku* Indon. 83 C3
Dog *r.* Canada 152 C4
Dogai Coring *salt l.* China 99 E6
Dogaicoring Qangco *salt l.* China 99 E6
Doğanşehir Turkey 112 E3
Dogên Co *l. Xizang* China see Bam Tso
Dogên Co *l.* China 99 E7
Dōgen-ko *l.* Japan 93 F2
Doghārūn Iran 111 F3
Dog Island Canada 153 J2
Dog Lake *Man.* Canada 151 L5
Dog Lake *Ont.* Canada 152 C4
Dog Lake *Ont.* Canada 152 D4
Dōgo *i.* Japan 91 D5
Dogondoutchi Niger 120 D3
Dog Rocks *is* Bahamas 163 E7
Doğubeyazıt Turkey 113 G3
Doğu Menteşe Dağları *mts* Turkey 69 M6
Dogxung Zangbo *r. Xizang* China 99 D7
Do'gyaling China 105 G3

▶Doha Qatar 110 C5
Capital of Qatar.

Dohad India see Dahod
Dohazari Bangl. 105 H5
Dohrighat *Uttar Prad.* India 99 C8
Doi *i.* Fiji 133 I4
Doi *i. Maluku* Indon. 83 C2
Doi Inthanon National Park Thai. 86 B3
Doijang *Xizang* China 99 E7
Doi Luang National Park Thai. 86 B3
Doire U.K. see Londonderry
Doi Saket Thai. 86 B3
Dois Irmãos, Serra dos *hills* Brazil 177 J5
Dokan, Sadd Iraq 113 G4
Dok-dō *i.* N. Pacific Ocean see Liancourt Rocks
Dokhara, Dunes de *des.* Alg. 64 F5
Dokka Norway 55 G6
Dokkum Neth. 62 F1
Dokog He *r.* China 96 D2
Dokri Pak. 111 H5
Dokshukino Rus. Fed. see Nartkala
Dokshytsy Belarus 55 O9
Dokuchayeva, Mys *c.* Rus. Fed. 90 G3
Dokuchayevka Kazakh. see Karamendy
Dokuchayevs'k Ukr. 53 H7
Dolbeau-Mistassini Canada 153 G4
Dolbenmaen U.K. 59 C6
Dol-de-Bretagne France 66 D2
Dole France 66 G3
Dolgellau U.K. 59 D6
Dolgen Germany 63 N1
Dolgiy, Ostrov *i.* Rus. Fed. 52 L1
Dolgorukovo Rus. Fed. 53 H5
Dolina Ukr. see Dolyna
Dolinsk Rus. Fed. 90 F3
Dolisie Congo see Loubomo
Dolit *Halmahera* Indon. 83 C3
Dolleman Island Antarctica 188 L2
Dollnstein Germany 63 L6
Dolo *Sulawesi* Indon. 83 A3
Dolok, Pulau *i.* Indon. 81 J8
Dolomites *mts* Italy 68 D2
Dolomiti *mts* Italy see Dolomites
Dolomiti Bellunesi, Parco Nazionale delle *nat. park* Italy 68 D1
Dolomitiche, Alpi *mts* Italy see Dolomites
Dolon Ashuusu *pass* Kyrg. 98 A4
Dolonnur *Nei Mongol* China 95 I3
Dolo Odo Eth. 122 E3
Doloon Mongolia see Tsogt-Ovoo
Dolores Arg. 178 E5
Dolores Guat. 167 H5
Dolores Mex. 166 C3
Dolores Uruguay 178 E4
Dolores U.S.A. 159 I3
Dolores Hidalgo Mex. 167 E4
Dolphin and Union Strait Canada 146 G3
Dolphin Head *hd* Namibia 124 B3
Đô Lương Vietnam 86 D3
Dolyna Ukr. 53 D6
Domaila India 104 D3
Domaniç Turkey 69 M5
Domar Bangl. 99 E8
Domar *Xizang* China 99 C6
Domartang *Xizang* China 99 F7
Domažlice Czech Rep. 63 M5
Domba *Qinghai* China 99 F6
Dom Bākh Iran 110 B3
Dombås Norway 54 F5
Dombóvár Hungary 68 H1
Dombrau Poland see Dąbrowa Górnicza
Dombrovitsa Ukr. see Dubrovytsya
Dombrowa Poland see Dąbrowa Górnicza
Domda China see Qingshuihe
Dome Argus *ice feature* Antarctica 188 E1
Dome Charlie *ice feature* Antarctica 188 F2
Dome Creek Canada 150 F4
Dome Rock Mountains U.S.A. 159 F5
Domeyko Chile 178 B3
Domfront France 66 D2
Dominica *country* West Indies 169 L5
Dominicana, República *country* West Indies see Dominican Republic
Dominican Republic *country* West Indies 169 J5
Dominion, Cape Canada 147 K3
Dominique *i.* Fr. Polynesia see Hiva Oa
Dömitz Germany 63 L1
Dom Joaquim Brazil 179 C2
Dommel *r.* Neth. 62 F3
Domo Eth. 122 E3
Domokos Greece 69 J5
Dompu *Sumbawa* Indon. 85 G5
Domuyo, Volcán *vol.* Arg. 178 B5
Domville, Mount *hill* Australia 138 E2
Don Mex. 166 C3

▶Don *r.* Rus. Fed. 53 H7
5th longest river in Europe.

Don *r.* U.K. 60 G3
Don, Xé *r.* Laos 86 D4
Donaghadee U.K. 61 G3
Donaghmore U.K. 61 F3
Donald Australia 138 A6
Donaldsonville U.S.A. 161 F6
Donalsonville U.S.A. 163 C6
Doñana, Parque Nacional de *nat. park* Spain 67 C5
Donau *r.* Austria/Germany 57 P6 see Danube
Donauwörth Germany 63 K6
Don Benito Spain 67 D4
Doncaster U.K. 58 F5
Dondo Angola 123 B4
Dondo Moz. 123 D5
Dondo, Tanjung *pt* Indon. 83 B2
Dondo, Teluk *b.* Indon. 83 B2
Dondonay *i.* Phil. 82 C4
Dondra Head *hd* Sri Lanka 106 D5
Donegal Ireland 61 D3
Donegal Bay Ireland 61 D3
Donets'k Ukr. 53 H7
Donetsko-Amrovsiyevka Ukr. see Amvrosiyivka
Donets'kyy Kryazh *hills* Rus. Fed./Ukr. 53 H6
Donga *r.* Cameroon/Nigeria 120 D4
Dong'an China 97 F3
Dongane, Lagoa *lag.* Moz. 125 L3
Dongara Australia 135 A7
Dongbatu *Gansu* China 98 F4
Dongbei Pingyuan *plain* China 95 J3
Dongbo *Xizang* China see Mêdog
Dongchuan *Yunnan* China 96 D3
Dongchuan *Yunnan* China see Yao'an
Dongco *Xizang* China 99 D6
Dong Co *l. Xizang* China 99 D6
Dongcun *Shandong* China see Haiyang
Dongcun *Shanxi* China see Lanxian
Dong'e *Shandong* China 95 I4
Dongfang China 97 F5
Dongfanghong China 90 D3

Donggala *Sulawesi* Indon. **83** A3
Donggang China **91** B5
Donggang *Shandong* China **95** I5
Donggi Conag *l. Qinghai* China **94** D5
Donggou China see Donggang
Donggou *Qinghai* China **94** E5
Donggu China **97** G3
Dongguan China **97** G4
Donghai *Jiangsu* China **95** I5
Dong Hai *sea* N. Pacific Ocean see
East China Sea
Donghaiba *Ningxia* China **94** F4
Dongxiang China **97** H2
Đông Hới Vietnam **86** D3
Donghuachi *Gansu* China **95** G4
Donghuang China see Xishui
Dongjiang Shuiku *resr* China **97** G3
Dongjug China **96** B2
Dongkait, Tanjung *pt* Indon. **83** A3
Dongkar *Xizang* China **99** E7
Dongkou China **97** F3
Donglan China **96** E3
Dongle *Gansu* China **94** E4
Dongliao He *r.* China **95** J3
Donglük *Xizang* China **98** E5
Dongmen China see Luocheng
Dongming *Shandong* China **95** H5
Dongminzhutun China **90** A3
Dongning China **90** C3
Dongo Angola **123** B5
Dongo Dem. Rep. Congo **122** B3
Dongola Sudan **108** D6
Dongou Congo **122** B3
Dong Phraya Yen *esc.* Thai. **86** C4
Dongping *Guangdong* China **97** G4
Dongping *Hunan* China see Anhua
Dongping Hu *l.* China **95** I4
Dongpo China see Meishan
Dongqiao *Xizang* China **99** E7
Dongqinghu *Nei Mongol* China **94** F4
Dong Qu *r. Qinghai* China **99** F6
Dongquan *Xinjiang* China **94** C3
Dongshan *Fujian* China **97** H4
Dongshan *Jiangsu* China see Shangyou
Dongshan *Jiangxi* China see Shangyou
Dongshao China **97** G3
Dongsha Qundao *is* China **80** F2
Dongsheng *Nei Mongol* China see Ordos
Dongsheng *Sichuan* China see Shuangliu
Dongshuan China see Tangdan
Dongtai China **97** I1
Dong Taijnar Hu *l. Qinghai* China **99** F5
Dongting Hu *l.* China **97** G2
Dongtou China **97** I3
Đông Triều Vietnam **86** D2
Dong Ujimqin Qi *Nei Mongol* China see
Uliastai
Đông Văn Vietnam **86** D2
Dongxiang China **97** H2
Dongxiangzu *Gansu* China **94** E5
Dongxi Liandao *i.* China **97** H1
Dongxing *Guangxi* China **96** E4
Dongxing *Heilong.* China **90** B3
Dongyang China **97** I2
Dongying *Shandong* China **95** I4
Dongzhen *Gansu* China **94** E4
Dongzhi China **97** H2
Donkerbroek Neth. **62** G1
Donnacona Canada **153** H5
Donnelly *AK* U.S.A. **149** K3
Donnellys Crossing N.Z. **139** D2
Donner Pass U.S.A. **158** C2
Donnersberg *hill* Germany **63** H5
Donostia Spain see San Sebastián
Donousa *i.* Greece **69** K6
Donoussa *i.* Greece see Donousa
Donskoye Rus. Fed. **53** I7
Donsol *Luzon* Phil. **82** C3
Donyztau, Sor *dry lake* Kazakh. **102** A2
Dooagh Ireland **61** B4
Doomadgee Australia **136** B3
Doon *r.* U.K. **60** E5
Doon, Loch *l.* U.K. **60** E5
Doonbeg *r.* Ireland **61** C5
Doonerak, Mount *AK* U.S.A. **149** J2
Doorn Neth. **62** F2
Door Peninsula U.S.A. **164** B1
Doorwerth Neth. **62** F2
Dooxo Nugaaleed *valley* Somalia **122** E3
Doqêmo *Xizang* China **99** F7
Doqoi *Xizang* China **99** E7
Do Qu *r. Qinghai* China **99** F6
Dor *watercourse* Afgh. **111** F4
Dor Israel **107** B3
Dora *r.* Italy **61** C5
Dora, Lake *salt flat* Australia **134** C5
Dorah Pass Pak. **111** H2
Doran Lake Canada **151** I2
Dorbiljin *Xinjiang* China see Emin
Dorbod Qi *Nei Mongol* China see Ulan Hua
Dorchester U.K. **59** E8
Dordabis Namibia **124** C2
Dordogne *r.* France **66** D4
Dordrecht Neth. **62** E3
Dordrecht S. Africa **125** H6
Doreenville Namibia **124** D2
Doré Lake Canada **151** J4
Doré Lake *l.* Canada **151** J4
Dores do Indaiá Brazil **179** B2
Dorgê Co *l. Qinghai* China **94** C5
Dörgön Mongolia **94** C1
Dori *r.* Afgh. **111** G3
Dori Burkina Faso **120** C3
Doring *r.* S. Africa **124** D6
Dorisvale Australia **134** E3
Dorking U.K. **59** G7
Dormagen Germany **62** G3
Dormans France **62** D5
Dormidontovka Rus. Fed. **90** D3
Dornburg Germany **63** I5
Dornie U.K. **60** D3
Dornoch U.K. **60** E3
Dornoch Firth *est.* U.K. **60** E3
Dornogovĭ *prov.* Mongolia **95** G2
Dornum Germany **63** H1
Doro Mali **120** C3
Dorogobuzh Rus. Fed. **53** G5
Dorohoi Romania **69** L3
Dörööö Nuur *salt l.* Mongolia **94** C2
Dorostol Bulg. see Silistra
Dorotea Sweden **54** J4
Dorpat Estonia see Tartu
Dorre Island Australia **135** A6

Dorrigo Australia **138** F3
Dorris U.S.A. **156** C4
Dorset Canada **165** F1
Dorsoidong Co *l. Xizang* China **99** E6
Dortmund Germany **63** H3
Dörtyol Turkey **107** C1
Dorum Germany **63** I1
Doruma Dem. Rep. Congo **122** C3
Dorüneh, Küh-e *mts* Iran **110** E3
Dörverden Germany **63** J2
Dörvöljin Mongolia **94** C2
Dorylaeum Turkey see Eskişehir
Dos Bahías, Cabo *c.* Arg. **178** C6
Dos de Mayo Peru **176** C5
Doshakh, Koh-i- *mt.* Afgh. see
Do Shākh, Kūh-e
Do Shākh, Kūh-e *mt.* Afgh. **111** F3
Dōshi Japan **93** F3
Dos Lagunos Guat. **167** H5
Dos Palos U.S.A. **158** C3
Dosse *r.* Germany **63** M2
Dosso Niger **120** D3
Dostyk Kazakh. **98** C3
Dothan U.S.A. **163** C6
Dot Lake *AK* U.S.A. **149** K3
Dotsero U.S.A. **159** J2
Douai France **62** D4
Douala Cameroon **120** D4
Douarnenez France **66** B2
Double Headed Shot Cays *is* Bahamas
163 D8
Double Island *H.K.* China **97** [inset]
Double Island Point Australia **137** F5
Double Mountain Fork *r.* U.S.A. **161** C5
Double Peak *AK* U.S.A. **148** I3
Double Peak U.S.A. **158** D4
Double Point Australia **136** D3
Double Springs U.S.A. **163** C5
Doubs *r.* France/Switz. **66** G3
Doubtful Sound *inlet* N.Z. **139** A7
Doubtless Bay N.Z. **139** D2
Doucan *Shaanxi* China see Fuping
Douentza Mali **120** C3
Dougga *tourist site* Tunisia **68** C6

► Douglas Isle of Man **58** C4
Capital of the Isle of Man.

Douglas S. Africa **124** F5
Douglas U.K. **60** F5
Douglas *AZ* U.S.A. **157** F7
Douglas *GA* U.S.A. **163** D6
Douglas *WY* U.S.A. **156** G4
Douglas, Cape *AK* U.S.A. **148** I4
Douglas Reef *i.* Japan see Okino-Tori-shima
Douglasville U.S.A. **163** C5
Douhudi China see Gong'an
Doulatpur Bangl. see Daulatpur
Douliu Taiwan see Touliu
Doullens France **62** C4
Douna *l.* Mali **120** C3
Doune U.K. **60** E4
Doupovské hory *mts* Czech Rep. **63** N4
Dourada, Serra *hills* Brazil **179** A2
Dourada, Serra *mts* Brazil **179** A1
Dourados Brazil **178** F2
Douro *r.* Port. **67** B3
also known as Duero (Spain)
Doushi China see Gong'an
Doushui Shuiku *resr* China **97** G3
Douve *r.* France **59** F9
Douzy France **62** F5
Dove *r.* U.K. **59** F6
Dove Brook Canada **153** K3
Dove Creek U.S.A. **159** I3
Dover U.K. **59** I7

► Dover *DE* U.S.A. **165** H4
Capital of Delaware.

Dover *NH* U.S.A. **165** J2
Dover *NJ* U.S.A. **165** H3
Dover *OH* U.S.A. **164** E3
Dover *TN* U.S.A. **162** C4
Dover, Strait of France/U.K. **66** L1
Dover-Foxcroft U.S.A. **165** K1
Dovey *r.* U.K. see Dyfi
Dovrefjell Nasjonalpark *nat. park* Norway
54 F5
Dowagiac U.S.A. **164** B3
Dowi, Tanjung *pt* Indon. **84** B2
Dowlaiswaram India **106** D2
Dowlatābād Afgh. **110** F3
Dowlatābād *Fārs* Iran **110** C4
Dowlatābād *Fārs* Iran **110** C4
Dowlatābād *Khorāsān* Iran **110** E2
Dowlatābād *Khorāsān* Iran **111** F2
Dowl at Yār Afgh. **111** G3
Downieville U.S.A. **158** C2
Downpatrick U.K. **61** G3
Downs U.S.A. **165** H2
Doxong *Xizang* China **99** F7
Doyle U.S.A. **158** C1
Doylestown U.S.A. **165** H3
Dozdān *r.* Iran **110** E5
Dözen *is* Japan **91** D5
Dozois, Réservoir *resr* Canada **152** F5
Dozulé France **59** G9
Drâa, Hamada du *plat.* Alg. **64** C6
Dracena Brazil **179** A3
Drachten Neth. **62** G1
Drăgăneşti-Olt Romania **69** K2
Drăgăşani Romania **69** K2
Dragonera, Isla *i.* Spain see Sa Dragonera
Dragoon U.S.A. **159** H5
Dragsfjärd Fin. **55** M6
Draguignan France **66** H5
Drahichyn Belarus **55** N10
Drake Australia **138** F2
Drake U.S.A. **160** C2
Drakensberg *mts* S. Africa **125** I3
Drake Passage S. Atlantic Ocean **184** D9
Drakes Bay U.S.A. **158** B3
Drama Greece **69** K4
Drammen Norway **55** G7
Drang, Prêk *r.* Cambodia **87** D4
Drangedal Norway **55** F7
Drangme Chu *r.* Bhutan **99** E8
Dransfeld Germany **63** J3
Draper, Mount *AK* U.S.A. **149** M4
Draperstown U.K. **61** F3
Drapsaca Afgh. see Kunduz
Dras India **104** C2

Drasan Pak. **111** I2
Drau *r.* Austria **57** O7 see Drava
Drava *r.* Europe **68** H2
*also known as Drau (Austria), Drave or Dráva
(Hungary)*
Dráva *r.* Hungary see Drava
Drave *r.* Slovenia/Croatia see Drava
Drayton Valley Canada **150** H4
Drazinda Pak. **111** H4
Dréan Alg. **68** B6
Dreistelzberge *hill* Germany **63** J4
Drentse Hoofdvaart *canal* Neth. **62** G2
Drepano, Akra *pt* Greece see
Laimos, Akrotirio
Dresden Canada **164** D2
Dresden Germany **57** N5
Dreux France **62** B6
Drevsjø Norway **55** H6
Drewryville U.S.A. **165** G5
Dri China **96** C2
Driffield U.K. **58** G4
Driftwood U.S.A. **165** F3
Driggs U.S.A. **156** F4
Drillham Australia **138** E1
Drimoleague Ireland **61** C6
Drina *r.* Bosnia-Herzegovina/Serbia **69** H2
Driscoll Island Antarctica **188** J1
Drissa Belarus see Vyerkhnyadzvinsk
Drniš Croatia **68** G3
Drobeta-Turnu Severin Romania **69** J2
Drochtersen Germany **63** J1
Drogheda Ireland **61** F4
Drogichin Belarus see Drahichyn
Drogobych Ukr. see Drohobych
Drohobych Ukr. **53** D6
Droichead Átha Ireland see Drogheda
Droichead Nua Ireland see Newbridge
Droitwich U.K. see Droitwich Spa
Droitwich Spa U.K. **59** E6
Dromdara, Cape Australia **138** E6
Dromod Ireland **61** E4
Dromore *Northern Ireland* U.K. **61** E3
Dromore *Northern Ireland* U.K. **61** F3
Dronfield U.K. **59** F5
Dronning Louise Land *reg.* Greenland **189** I1
Dronning Maud Land *reg.* Antarctica see
Queen Maud Land
Dronten Neth. **62** F2
Drovyanaya Rus. Fed. **95** H1
Druk-Yul *country* Asia see Bhutan
Drumheller Canada **151** H5
Drummond *atoll* Kiribati see Tabiteuea
Drummond U.S.A. **156** E3
Drummond, Lake U.S.A. **165** G5
Drummond Island Kiribati see McKean
Drummond Range *hills* Australia **136** D5
Drummondville Canada **153** G5
Drummore U.K. **60** E6
Drury Lake Canada **150** C2
Druskieniki Lith. see Druskininkai
Druskininkai Lith. **55** N10
Druzhina Rus. Fed. **77** P3
Druzhnaya Gorka Rus. Fed. **55** Q7
Dry *r.* Australia **134** F3
Dryanovo Bulg. **69** K3
Dryberry Lake Canada **151** M5
Dry Creek *AK* U.S.A. **149** K3
Dry Creek U.S.A. **138** E2
Dryden Canada **151** M5
Dryden U.S.A. **165** G2
Dry Fork *r.* U.S.A. **156** F4
Drygalski Ice Tongue Antarctica **188** H1
Drygalski Island Antarctica **188** F2
Dry Lake U.S.A. **159** F3
Dry Lake *l.* U.S.A. **160** D1
Drymen U.K. **60** E4
Dry Ridge U.S.A. **164** C4
Drysdale *r.* Australia **134** D3
Drysdale River National Park Australia
134 D3
Dry Tortugas *is* U.S.A. **163** D7
Du'an China **97** F4
Duancun *Shanxi* China see Wuxiang
Duaringa Australia **136** E4
Duars *reg.* Assam India **99** E8
Duarte, Pico *mt.* Dom. Rep. **169** J5
Duartina Brazil **179** A3
Ḏubā Saudi Arabia **108** E4
Dubai U.A.E. **110** D5
Dubakella Mountain U.S.A. **158** B1
Dubăsari Moldova **53** F7
Dubawnt *r.* Canada **151** L2
Dubawnt Lake Canada **151** K2
Dubayy U.A.E. see Dubai
Dubbo Australia **138** D4
Dubin Kazakh. **98** C4
Dublán Mex. **166** D2

► Dublin Ireland **61** F4
Capital of Ireland.

Dublin U.S.A. **163** D5
Dubna Rus. Fed. **52** H4
Dubno Ukr. **53** E6
Dubois *ID* U.S.A. **156** E3
Dubois *IN* U.S.A. **164** B4
Du Bois U.S.A. **165** F3
Dubovka Rus. Fed. **53** J6
Dubovskoye Rus. Fed. **53** I7
Dubréka Guinea **120** B4
Dubris U.K. see Dover
Dubrovnik Croatia **68** H3
Dubrovytsya Ukr. **53** E6
Dubuque U.S.A. **160** F3
Dubysa *r.* Lith. **55** M9
Đực Bôn Vietnam **87** D5
Duc de Gloucester, Îles du *is* Fr. Polynesia
187 K7
Duchang China **97** H2
Ducheng China see Yunan
Duchesne U.S.A. **159** H1
Duchess Australia **136** B4
Duchess Canada **151** I5
Ducie Island *atoll* Pitcairn Is **187** L7
Duck Bay Canada **151** K4
Duck Creek *r.* Australia **134** B5
Duck Lake Canada **151** J4
Duckwater Peak U.S.A. **159** F2
Duc Tho Vietnam **86** D3
Ducun *Shanxi* China see Fuping
Dudelange Lux. **62** G5
Duderstadt Germany **63** K3
Dudhi India **105** E4
Dudhwa India **104** D3
Dudinka Rus. Fed. **76** J3

Dudley U.K. **59** E6
Dudleyville U.S.A. **159** H5
Dudna *r.* India **106** C2
Dudu India **104** C4
Duékoué Côte d'Ivoire **120** C4
Duen, Bukit *vol.* Indon. **84** C3
Duero *r.* Spain **67** C3
also known as Douro (Portugal)
Duffel Belgium **62** E3
Dufferin, Cape Canada **152** F2
Duffer Peak U.S.A. **156** D4
Duff Islands Solomon Is **133** G2
Dufftown U.K. **60** F3
Dufourspitze *mt.* Italy/Switz. **66** H4
Dufrost, Pointe *pt* Canada **152** F1
Dugi Otok *i.* Croatia **68** F2
Dugi Rat Croatia **68** G3
Dugui Qarag *Nei Mongol* China **95** G4
Du He *r.* China **97** F1
Duida-Marahuaca, Parque Nacional *nat. park*
Venez. **176** E3
Duisburg Germany **62** G3
Duiwelskloof S. Africa **125** J2
Dujiangyan China **96** D2
Dukathole S. Africa **125** H6
Duke Island Antarctica **188** J1
Duke of Clarence *atoll* Tokelau see Nukunonu
Duke of Gloucester Islands Fr. Polynesia see
Duc de Gloucester, Îles du
Duke of York *atoll* Tokelau see Atafu
Duk Fadiat Sudan **121** G4
Dukhovnitskoye Rus. Fed. **53** K5
Duki Pak. **111** H4
Duki Rus. Fed. **90** D2
Duki *r.* Rus. Fed. **90** D2
Dukou China see Panzhihua
Dūkštas Lith. **55** O9
Dulaanhaan Mongolia **94** F1
Dulac U.S.A. **161** F6
Dulan *Qinghai* China **94** D4
Dulawan *Mindanao* Phil. see Datu Piang
Dulbi *r. AK* U.S.A. **148** I2
Dulce U.S.A. **157** G5
Dulce, Golfo *b.* Costa Rica **166** [inset] J7
Dulce Nombre de Culmí Hond.
166 [inset] I6
Dul'durga Rus. Fed. **95** H1
Dulhunty *r.* Australia **136** C1
Dulishi Hu *salt l.* China **99** C6
Dülmen Germany **63** H3
Dulmera India **104** C3
Dulovo Bulg. **69** L3
Duluth U.S.A. **160** E2
Dulverton U.K. **59** D7
Dūmā Syria **107** C3
Dumaguete *Negros* Phil. **82** C4
Dumai *Sumatera* Indon. **84** C2
Dumanquilas Bay *Mindanao* Phil. **82** C5
Dumaran *i.* Phil. **82** C4
Dumaresq *r.* Australia **138** E2
Dumas U.S.A. **161** C5
Dumat al Jandal Saudi Arabia **113** C5
Ḏumayr, Jabal *mts* Syria **107** C3
Dumbakh Iran see Dom Bākh
Dumbarton U.K. **60** E5
Dumbe S. Africa **125** J4
Ḏumbier *mt.* Slovakia **57** Q6
Dumchele India **104** D2
Dum-Dum India **105** G5
Duma Duma India **105** H4
Dumfries U.K. **60** F5
Dumka India **105** F4
Dumoga *Sulawesi* Indon. **83** C2
Dumont d'Urville *research station* Antarctica
188 G2
Dumont d'Urville Sea Antarctica **188** G2
Dümpelfeld Germany **62** G4
Dumyāṭ Egypt **112** C5
Dumyāṭ Egypt see Dumyāṭ
Duna *r.* Hungary **68** H2 see Danube
Dünaburg Latvia see Daugavpils
Dunaj *r.* Slovakia see Danube
Dunajská Streda Slovakia **57** P7
Dunakeszi Hungary **69** H1
Dunany Point Ireland **61** F4
Dunărea *r.* Romania **69** L2 see Danube
Dunării, Delta Romania/Ukr. see
Danube Delta
Dunaújváros Hungary **68** H1
Dunav *r.* Bulg./Croatia/Serbia **68** L2 see
Danube
Dunay *r.* Ukr. see Danube
Dunayivtsi Ukr. **53** E6
Dunbar Australia **136** C3
Dunbar U.K. **60** G4
Dunbar *AK* U.S.A. **149** J2
Dunblane U.K. **60** F4
Dunboyne Ireland **61** F4
Duncan Canada **150** F5
Duncan *AZ* U.S.A. **159** I5
Duncan *OK* U.S.A. **161** D5
Duncan, Cape Canada **152** E3
Duncan, Lac *l.* Canada **152** F3
Duncan Passage India **87** A5
Duncansby Head *hd* U.K. **60** F2
Duncan Town Bahamas **163** F8
Duncormick Ireland **61** F5
Dundaga Latvia **55** M8
Dundalk Ireland **61** F3
Dundalk U.S.A. **165** G4
Dundalk Bay Ireland **61** F4
Dundas Canada **164** F2
Dundas Greenland **147** K2
Dundas, Lake *salt flat* Australia **135** C8
Dundas Island *B.C.* Canada **149** O5
Dundas Strait Australia **134** E2
Dundbürd Mongolia see Batnorov
Dún Dealgan Ireland see Dundalk
Dundee S. Africa **125** J5
Dundee *MI* U.S.A. **164** D3
Dundee *NY* U.S.A. **165** G2
Dundgovĭ *prov.* Mongolia **94** F2
Dund Hot *Nei Mongol* China **95** I3
Dundonald U.K. **61** G3

Dundoo Australia **138** B1
Dundrennan U.K. **60** F6
Dundrum U.K. **61** G3
Dundrum Bay U.K. **61** G3
Dundwa Range *mts* India/Nepal **105** E4
Dune, Lac *l.* Canada **152** G2
Dunedin N.Z. **139** C7
Dunedin U.S.A. **163** D6
Dunenbay Kazakh. **98** C2
Dunfermline U.K. **60** F4
Dungannon U.K. **61** F3
Dungarpur India **104** C5
Dungarvan Ireland **61** E5
Dung Co *l. Xizang* China **99** E7
Dungeness *hd* U.K. **59** H8
Dungeness, Punta *pt* Arg. **178** C8
Düngenheim Germany **63** H4
Dungiven U.K. **61** F3
Dungloe Ireland see An Clochán Liath
Dungu Dem. Rep. Congo **122** C3
Dungun Malaysia **84** C1
Dungunab Sudan **108** E5
Dunhua China **90** C4
Dunhuang *Gansu* China **98** F4
Dunkeld Australia **138** D1
Dunkeld U.K. **60** F4
Dunkellin *r.* Ireland **61** C6
Dunkerque France see Dunkirk
Dunkery Hill *hill* U.K. **59** D7
Dunkirk France **62** C3
Dunkirk U.S.A. **164** F2
Dún Laoghaire Ireland **61** F4
Dunlap *IA* U.S.A. **160** E3
Dunlap *TN* U.S.A. **162** C5
Dunlavin Ireland **61** F4
Dunleer Ireland **61** F4
Dunloy U.K. **61** F2
Dunmanway Ireland **61** C6
Dunmarra Australia **134** F4
Dunmor U.S.A. **164** B5
Dunmore Ireland **61** D4
Dunmore U.S.A. **165** H3
Dunmore Town Bahamas **163** E7
Dunmurry U.K. **61** G3
Dunnet Head *hd* U.K. **60** F2
Dunnigan U.S.A. **158** C2
Dunning U.S.A. **160** C3
Dunnville Canada **164** F2
Dunolly Australia **138** A6
Dunoon U.K. **60** E5
Dunphy U.S.A. **158** E1
Duns U.K. **60** G5
Dunseith U.S.A. **160** C1
Dunstable U.K. **59** G7
Dunstan Mountains N.Z. **139** B7
Dun-sur-Meuse France **62** F5
Duntroon N.Z. **139** C7
Dunvegan Lake Canada **151** J2
Dunyapur Pak. **111** H4
Duobukur He *r.* China **95** K1
Duolun *Nei Mongol* China see Dolonnur
Duomula *Xizang* China **99** C6
Dupang Ling *mts* China **97** F3
Duperré Alg. see Aïn Defla
Dupnitsa Bulg. **69** J3
Dupree U.S.A. **160** C2
Duque de Bragança Angola see Calandula
Dūrā West Bank **107** B4
Durack *r.* Australia **134** D3
Durack Range *hills* Australia **134** D4
Dura Europos Syria see Aş Şālihīyah
Durağan Turkey **112** D2
Durance *r.* France **66** G5
Durand U.S.A. **160** F2
Durango Mex. **161** B7
Durango *state* Mex. **161** B7
Durango Spain **67** E2
Durango U.S.A. **159** J3
Durani *reg.* Afgh. **111** G4
Durant U.S.A. **161** D5
Durazno Uruguay **178** E4
Durazzo Albania see Durrës
Durban S. Africa **125** J5
Durban-Corbières France **66** F5
Durbanville S. Africa **124** D7
Durbin U.S.A. **164** F4
Durbuy Belgium **62** F4
Düren Germany **62** G4
Düren Iran **110** E3
Düren, Kūh-e *mt.* Iran **110** E3
Durg India **104** D3
Durgapur Bangl. **105** G4
Durgapur India **105** F5
Durham Canada **164** E1
Durham U.K. **58** F4
Durham U.S.A. **162** E5
Durham Downs Australia **137** C5
Duri *Sumatera* Indon. **84** C2
Durlas Ireland see Thurles
Durlești Moldova **69** M1
Durmersheim Germany **63** I6
Durmitor *mt.* Montenegro **69** H3
Durmitor *nat. park* Montenegro **68** H3
Durness U.K. **60** E2
Durocortorum France see Reims
Durong South Australia **137** E5
Durostorum Bulg. see Silistra
Durour Island P.N.G. see Aua Island
Durrës Albania **69** H4
Durrie Australia **136** C5
Durrington U.K. **59** F7
Dursey Island Ireland **61** B6
Dursunbey Turkey **69** M5
Duru China see Wuchuan
Durūz, Jabal ad *mt.* Syria **107** C3
Durukhsi Somalia **122** E3
Durusu Gölü *l.* Turkey **69** M4
Durūz, Jabal ad *mt.* Syria **107** C3
D'Urville, Tanjung *pt* Indon. **81** J7
D'Urville Island N.Z. **139** D5
Durzab Afgh. **111** G3
Duşak Turkm. **111** E2
Dushai Pak. **111** G5
Dushan China **96** E3

► Dushanbe Tajik. **111** H2
Capital of Tajikistan.

Dushanzi *Xinjiang* China **98** D3
Dushet'i Georgia **113** G2
Dushikou *Hebei* China **95** H3
Dushore U.S.A. **165** G3
Dusse-Alin', Khrebet *mts* Rus. Fed. **90** D2
Düsseldorf Germany **62** G3
Dusty *NM* U.S.A. **159** J5
Dusty *WA* U.S.A. **156** D3
Dutch East Indies *country* Asia see Indonesia
Dutch Guiana *country* S. America see
Suriname
Dutch Mountain U.S.A. **159** G1
Dutch New Guinea *prov.* Indon. see Papua
Dutch West Indies *terr.* Caribbean
Sea/West Indies see Netherlands Antilles
Dutlwe Botswana **124** F2
Dutse Nigeria **120** D3
Dutsin-Ma Nigeria **120** D3
Dutton *r.* Australia **136** C4
Dutton Canada **164** E2
Dutton U.S.A. **156** F3
Dutton, Lake *salt flat* Australia **137** B6
Dutton, Mount U.S.A. **159** G2
Duval Canada **151** J5
Duvert, Lac *l.* Canada **153** H2
Duvno Bos.-Herz. see Tomislavgrad
Duwa *Xinjiang* China **99** B5
Duwin Iraq **113** G3
Düxanbibazar *Xinjiang* China **99** C5
Duyun China **96** E3
Duzab Pak. **111** F5
Düzce Turkey **69** N4
Duzdab Iran see Zāhedān
Dvina *r.* Europe see Zapadnaya Dvina
Dvina *r.* Rus. Fed. see Severnaya Dvina
Dvinsk Latvia see Daugavpils
Dvinskaya Guba *g.* Rus. Fed. **52** H2
Dwarka India **104** B5
Dwarsberg S. Africa **125** H3
Dwingelderveld, Nationaal Park *nat. park*
Neth. **62** G2
Dworshak Reservoir U.S.A. **156** E3
Dwyka S. Africa **124** E7
Dyat'kovo Rus. Fed. **53** G5
Dyce U.K. **60** G3
Dyer, Cape Canada **147** L3
Dyer Bay Canada **164** E1
Dyersburg U.S.A. **161** F4
Dyffryn U.K. see Valley
Dyfi *r.* U.K. see Dovey
Dyfrdwy *r. England/Wales* U.K. see Dee
Dyje *r.* Austria/Czech Rep. **57** P6
Dyke U.K. **60** F3

► Dykh-Tau, Gora *mt.* Rus. Fed. **113** F2
2nd highest mountain in Europe.

Dyle *r.* Belgium **62** E4
Dyleň *hill* Czech Rep. **63** M5
Dylewska Góra *hill* Poland **57** Q4
Dymytrov Ukr. **53** H6
Dynevor Downs Australia **138** B2
Dyoki S. Africa **125** I6
Dyrrhachium Albania see Durrës
Dysart Australia **136** E4
Dysselsdorp S. Africa **124** F7
Dyurtyuli Rus. Fed. **51** Q4
Dzaanhushuu Mongolia see Ihtamir
Dzadgay Mongolia see Bömbögör
Dzag Mongolia **94** D2
Dzalaa Mongolia see Shinejinst
Dzamīn Üüd Mongolia **95** G3
Dzanga-Ndoki, Parc National de *nat. park*
Cent. Afr. Rep. **122** B3

► Dzaoudzi Mayotte **123** E5
Capital of Mayotte.

Dzaudzhikau Rus. Fed. see Vladikavkaz
Dzavhan Mongolia **94** C1
Dzavhan *prov.* Mongolia **94** C1
Dzavhan Gol *r.* Mongolia **94** C1
Dzavhanmandal Mongolia **94** C1
Dzegstey Mongolia see Ögiynuur
Dzelter Mongolia **94** F1
Dzerzhinsk Belarus see Dzyarzhynsk
Dzerzhinsk Rus. Fed. **52** I4
Dzhagdy, Khrebet *mts* Rus. Fed. **90** C1
Dzhaki-Unakhta Yakbyyana, Khrebet *mts*
Rus. Fed. **90** D2
Dzhalalabad Azer. see Cälilabad
Dzhalal-Abad Kyrg. see Jalal-Abad
Dzhalil' Rus. Fed. **51** Q4
Dzhalinda Rus. Fed. **90** A1
Dzhaltyr Kazakh. see Zhaltyr
Dzhambeyty Kazakh. see Zhympity
Dzhambul Kazakh. see Taraz
Dzhangala Kazakh. **51** Q6
Dzhankoy Ukr. **53** G7
Dzhansugurov Kazakh. **98** B3
Dzhanybek Kazakh. see Zhanibek
Dzharkent Kazakh. see Zharkent
Dzhava Georgia see Java
Dzhetygara Kazakh. see Zhitikara
Dzhezkazgan Kazakh. see Zhezkazgan
Dzhida Rus. Fed. **94** F1
Dzhida *r.* Rus. Fed. **94** F1
Dzhidinskiy, Khrebet *mts* Mongolia/Rus. Fed.
94 F1
Dzhirgatal' Tajik. see Jirgatol
Dzhizak Uzbek. see Jizzax
Dzhokhar Ghala Rus. Fed. see Groznyy
Dzhubga Rus. Fed. **112** E1
Dzhugdzhur, Khrebet *mts* Rus. Fed. **77** O4
Dzhul'fa Azer. see Culfa
Dzhuma Uzbek. see Juma
Dzhungarskiy Alatau, Khrebet *mts*
China/Kazakh. **102** E3
Dzhungarskiye Vorota *pass* Kazakh. **98** C3
Dzhungarskiye Vorota *val.* Kazakh. **98** C3
Dzhusaly Kazakh. **102** B2
Działdowo Poland **57** R4
Dzibalchén Mex. **167** H5
Dzilam de Bravo Mex. **167** H4
Dzitás Mex. **167** H4
Dzogsool Mongolia see Bayantsagaan
Dzöölön Mongolia see Rénchinlhümbe
Dzūkija *nat. park* Lith. **55** N9
Dzungarian Basin China see Junggar Pendi
Dzungarian Gate *pass* China/Kazakh. **102** E3
Dzur Mongolia see Tes
Dzüünbayan Mongolia **95** G2
Dzüünharaa Mongolia **94** F1

Dzuunmod Mongolia 94 F2
Dzüyl Mongolia see Tonhil
Dzyaniskavichy Belarus 55 O10
Dzyarzhynsk Belarus 55 O10
Dzyatlavichy Belarus 55 O10

E

Eabamet Lake Canada 152 D4
Eads U.S.A. 160 C4
Eagar U.S.A. 159 I4
Eagle r. Canada 153 K3
Eagle r. Y.T. Canada 149 M2
Eagle AK U.S.A. 146 D3
Eagle CO U.S.A. 156 G5
Eagle Cap mt. U.S.A. 156 D3
Eagle Crags mt. U.S.A. 158 E4
Eagle Creek r. Canada 151 J4
Eagle Lake Canada 151 M5
Eagle Lake CA U.S.A. 158 C1
Eagle Lake ME U.S.A. 162 G2
Eagle Mountain U.S.A. 159 F5
Eagle Mountain hill U.S.A. 160 F2
Eagle Mountain Lake TX U.S.A. 167 F1
Eagle Pass U.S.A. 161 C6
Eagle Peak U.S.A. 157 G7
Eagle Plain Y.T. Canada 149 M2
Eagle Plains Y.T. Canada 149 M2
Eagle River AK U.S.A. 149 J3
Eagle River U.S.A. 160 F2
Eagle Rock U.S.A. 164 F5
Eaglesham Canada 150 G4
Eagle Summit pass AK U.S.A. 149 K2
Eagle Village AK U.S.A. 149 L2
Eap i. Micronesia see Yap
Ear Falls Canada 151 M5
Earlimart U.S.A. 158 D4
Earl's Seat hill U.K. 60 E4
Earlston U.K. 60 G5
Earn r. U.K. 60 F4
Earn, Loch l. U.K. 60 E4
Earn Lake Y.T. Canada 149 N3
Earp U.S.A. 159 F4
Earth U.S.A. 161 C5
Easington U.K. 58 H5
Easley U.S.A. 163 D5
East Alligator r. Australia 134 F3
East Antarctica reg. Antarctica 188 F1
East Ararat U.S.A. 165 H3
East Aurora U.S.A. 165 F2
East Bay LA U.S.A. 167 H2
East Bay inlet U.S.A. 163 C6
East Bengal country Asia see Bangladesh
Eastbourne U.K. 59 H8
East Branch Clarion River Reservoir U.S.A. 165 F3
East Caicos i. Turks and Caicos Is 163 G8
East Cape N.Z. 139 G3
East Cape AK U.S.A. 149 [inset]
East Carbon City U.S.A. 159 H2
East Caroline Basin sea feature N. Pacific Ocean 186 F5
East Channel watercourse N.W.T. Canada 149 N1
East China Sea N. Pacific Ocean 89 N6
East Coast Bays N.Z. 139 E3
East Dereham England U.K. see Dereham
Eastend Canada 151 I5
East Entrance sea chan. Palau 82 [inset]

▶Easter Island S. Pacific Ocean 187 M7
Part of Chile.

Eastern Cape prov. S. Africa 125 H6
Eastern Desert Egypt 108 D4
Eastern Fields reef Australia 136 D1
Eastern Ghats mts India 106 C4

▶Eastern Island U.S.A. 186 I4
Most northerly point of Oceania.

Eastern Nara canal Pak. 111 H5
Eastern Samoa terr. S. Pacific Ocean see American Samoa
Eastern Sayan Mountains Rus. Fed. see Vostochnyy Sayan
Eastern Taurus plat. Turkey see Güneydoğu Toroslar
Eastern Transvaal prov. S. Africa see Mpumalanga
Easterville Canada 151 L4
Easterwâlde Neth. see Oosterwolde
East Falkland i. Falkland Is 178 E8
East Falmouth U.S.A. 165 J3
East Frisian Islands Germany 57 K4
Eastgate U.S.A. 158 E2
East Greenwich U.S.A. 165 J3
East Grinstead U.K. 59 G7
Easthampton U.S.A. 165 I2
East Hampton U.S.A. 165 I3
East Hartford U.S.A. 165 I3
East Indiaman Ridge sea feature Indian Ocean 185 O7
East Jordan U.S.A. 164 C1
East Kilbride U.K. 60 E5
Eastlake U.S.A. 164 E3
East Lamma Channel H.K. China 97 [inset]
Eastland U.S.A. 161 D5
East Lansing U.S.A. 164 C2
Eastleigh U.K. 59 F8
East Liverpool U.S.A. 164 E3
East London S. Africa 125 H7
East Lynn Lake U.S.A. 164 D4
Eastmain Canada 152 F3
Eastmain r. Canada 152 F3
Eastman U.S.A. 163 D5
East Mariana Basin sea feature N. Pacific Ocean 186 G5
Eastmere Australia 136 D4
East Naples U.S.A. 163 D7
Easton MD U.S.A. 165 G4
Easton PA U.S.A. 165 H3
East Orange U.S.A. 165 H3
East Pacific Rise sea feature N. Pacific Ocean 187 M4
East Pakistan country Asia see Bangladesh
East Palestine U.S.A. 164 E3
East Park Reservoir U.S.A. 158 B2
East Point Canada 153 J5
East Porcupine r. Y.T. Canada 149 M2
Eastport U.S.A. 162 H2
East Providence U.S.A. 165 J3
East Range mts U.S.A. 158 E1
East Retford U.K. see Retford
East St Louis U.S.A. 160 F4
East Sea N. Pacific Ocean see Japan, Sea of
East Shoal Lake Canada 151 L5
East Siberian Sea Rus. Fed. 77 P2
East Side Canal r. U.S.A. 158 D4
East Stroudsburg U.S.A. 165 H3
East Tavaputs Plateau U.S.A. 159 I2

▶East Timor country Asia 83 C5
Former Portuguese territory. Gained independence from Indonesia in 2002.

East Tons r. India 99 D8
East Toorale Australia 138 B3
East Troy U.S.A. 164 A2
East Verde r. U.S.A. 159 H4
Eastville U.S.A. 165 H5
East-Vlylân Neth. see Oost-Vlieland
East York Canada 164 F2
Eaton U.S.A. 164 C4
Eatonia Canada 151 I5
Eaton Rapids U.S.A. 164 C2
Eatonton U.S.A. 163 D5
Eau Claire U.S.A. 160 F2
Eauripik atoll Micronesia 81 K5
Eauripik Rise-New Guinea Rise sea feature N. Pacific Ocean 186 F5
Eauripyg atoll Micronesia see Eauripik
Ebano Mex. 167 F4
Ebbw Vale U.K. 59 D7
Ebebiyin Equat. Guinea 120 E4
Ebenerde Namibia 124 C3
Ebensburg U.S.A. 165 F3
Eber Gölü l. Turkey 69 N5
Ebergötzen Germany 63 K3
Eberswalde-Finow Germany 57 N4
Ebetsu Japan 90 F4
Ebian China 96 D2
Ebina Japan 93 F3
Ebi Nor salt l. China see Ebinur Hu
Ebinur Hu salt l. China 98 C3
Eboli Italy 68 F4
Ebolowa Cameroon 120 E4
Ebony Namibia 124 B2
Ebre r. Spain see Ebro
Ebro r. Spain 67 G3
Ebstorf Germany 63 K1
Eburacum U.K. see York
Ebusus i. Spain see Ibiza
Ecbatana Iran see Hamadān
Eceabat Turkey 69 L4
Echague Luzon Phil. 82 C2
Ech Chélif Alg. see Chlef
Echegárate, Puerto pass Spain 67 E2
Echeng China see Ezhou
Echeverria, Pico mt. Mex. 166 B2
Echigawa Japan 92 C3
Echigo-Sanzan-Tadami Kokutei-kōen park Japan 93 F1
Echizen Japan 92 C3
Echizen-dake mt. Japan 93 E3
Echizen-Kaga-kaigan Kokutei-kōen park Japan 92 C2
Echizen-misaki pt Japan 92 B3
Echmiadzin Armenia see Ejmiatsin
Echo U.S.A. 156 D3
Echo Bay N.W.T. Canada 150 G1
Echo Bay Ont. Canada 152 D5
Echo Cliffs U.S.A. 159 H3
Echoing r. Canada 151 M4
Echt Neth. 62 F3
Echternach Lux. 62 G5
Echuca Australia 138 B6
Echzell Germany 63 I4
Écija Spain 67 D5
Eckental Germany 63 L5
Eckernförde Germany 57 L3
Eclipse Sound sea chan. Canada 147 J2
Écrins, Parc National des nat. park France 66 H4
Ecuador country S. America 176 C4
Écueils, Pointe aux pt Canada 152 F2
Ed Eritrea 108 F7
Ed Sweden 55 G7
Edam Neth. 62 F2
Eday i. U.K. 60 G1
Ed Da'ein Sudan 121 F3
Ed Damazin Sudan 108 D7
Ed Damer Sudan 108 D6
Ed Debba Sudan 108 D6
Eddies Cove Canada 153 K4
Ed Dueim Sudan 108 D7
Eddystone Point Australia 137 [inset]
Eddyville U.S.A. 161 F4
Ede Neth. 62 F2
Edéa Cameroon 120 E4
Edehon Lake Canada 151 L2
Edéia Brazil 179 A2
Eden Australia 138 D6
Eden r. U.K. 58 D4
Eden NC U.S.A. 164 F5
Eden TX U.S.A. 161 D6
Eden, Tanjung pt Maluku Indon. 83 C4
Edenburg S. Africa 125 G5
Edendale N.Z. 139 B8
Edenderry Ireland 61 E4
Edenton U.S.A. 162 E4
Edenville S. Africa 125 H4
Eder r. Germany 63 J3
Eder-Stausee resr Germany 63 I3
Edessa Greece 69 J4
Edessa Turkey see Şanlıurfa
Edewecht Germany 63 H1
Edfu Egypt see Idfū
Edgar Ranges hills Australia 134 C4
Edgartown U.S.A. 165 J3
Edgecumbe Island Solomon Is see Utupua
Edgefield U.S.A. 163 D5
Edge Island Svalbard see Edgeøya
Edgemont U.S.A. 160 C3
Edgeøya i. Svalbard 76 D2
Edgerton Canada 151 I4
Edgerton U.S.A. 160 E3
Edgeworthstown Ireland 61 E4
Édhessa Greece see Edessa
Edina U.S.A. 160 E3
Edinboro U.S.A. 164 E3
Edinburg TX U.S.A. 161 D7
Edinburg VA U.S.A. 165 F4

▶Edinburgh U.K. 60 F5
Capital of Scotland.

Edineț Moldova 53 F7
Edirne Turkey 69 L4
Edith, Mount U.S.A. 156 F3
Edith Cavell, Mount Canada 150 G4
Edith Ronne Land ice feature Antarctica see Ronne Ice Shelf
Edjeleh Libya 120 D2
Edjudina Australia 135 C7
Edku Egypt see Idkū
Edmond U.S.A. 161 D5
Edmonds U.S.A. 156 C3

▶Edmonton Canada 150 H4
Capital of Alberta.

Edmonton U.S.A. 164 C5
Edmore MI U.S.A. 164 C2
Edmore ND U.S.A. 160 D1
Edmund Lake Canada 151 M4
Edmundston Canada 153 H5
Edna U.S.A. 161 D6
Edna Bay AK U.S.A. 149 N5
Edo Japan see Tōkyō
Edo-gawa r. Japan 93 F3
Edom reg. Israel/Jordan 107 B4
Edosaki Japan 93 G3
Édouard, Lac l. Dem. Rep. Congo/Uganda see Edward, Lake
Edremit Turkey 69 L5
Edremit Körfezi b. Turkey 69 L5
Edrengiyn Nuruu mts Mongolia 94 D2
Edsbyn Sweden 55 I6
Edson Canada 150 G4
Eduni, Mount N.W.T. Canada 149 O2
Edward r. N.S.W. Australia 138 B5
Edward r. Qld Australia 136 C2
Edward, Lake Dem. Rep. Congo/Uganda 122 C4
Edward, Mount Antarctica 188 L1
Edwardesabad Pak. see Bannu
Edwards U.S.A. 165 H1
Edward's Creek Australia 137 A6
Edwards Plateau U.S.A. 161 C6
Edwardsville U.S.A. 160 F4
Edward VII Peninsula Antarctica 188 I1
Edziza, Mount B.C. Canada 149 O4
Eek AK U.S.A. 148 G3
Eek r. AK U.S.A. 148 G3
Eeklo Belgium 62 D3
Eel r. U.S.A. 158 A1
Eel, South Fork r. U.S.A. 158 B1
Eem r. Neth. 62 F2
Eemshaven pt Neth. 62 G1
Eenrum Neth. 62 G1
Eenzamheid Pan salt pan S. Africa 124 E4
Eesti country Europe see Estonia
Éfaté i. Vanuatu 133 G3
Effingham U.S.A. 160 F4
Efsus Turkey see Afşin
Eg Mongolia see Batshireet
Egadi, Isole is Sicily Italy 68 D5
Egan Range mts U.S.A. 159 F2
Eganville Canada 165 G1
Egavik AK U.S.A. 148 G2
Egedesminde Greenland see Aasiaat
Egegik Bay AK U.S.A. 148 H4
Eger r. Germany 63 M4
Eger Hungary 57 R7
Egersund Norway 55 E7
Egerton, Mount hill Australia 135 B6
Eggegebirge hills Germany 63 I3
Egg Island AK U.S.A. 148 G3
Egg Lake Canada 151 J4
Eggolsheim Germany 63 L5
Eghezée Belgium 62 E4
Egilsstaðir Iceland 54 [inset]
Eğin Turkey see Kemaliye
Eğirdir Turkey 69 N6
Eğirdir Gölü l. Turkey 69 N6
Egiyn Gol r. Mongolia 94 E1
Eglinton U.K. 61 E2
Egmond aan Zee Neth. 62 E2
Egmont, Cape N.Z. 139 D4
Egmont, Mount vol. N.Z. see Taranaki, Mount
Egmont National Park N.Z. 139 E4
eGoli S. Africa see Johannesburg
Eğriğöz Dağı mts Turkey 69 M5
Egton U.K. 58 G4
Éguas r. Brazil 179 B1
Egvekinot Rus. Fed. 148 C2

▶Egypt country Africa 108 C4
3rd most populous country in Africa.

Ehden Lebanon 107 B2
Ehen Hudag Nei Mongol China 94 E4
Ehingen (Donau) Germany 57 L6
Ehle r. Germany 63 L2
Ehra-Lessien Germany 63 K2
Ehrenberg U.S.A. 159 F5
Ehrenberg Range hills Australia 135 E5
Eibelstadt Germany 63 K5
Eibergen Neth. 62 G2
Eichenzell Germany 63 J4
Eichstätt Germany 63 L6
Eidfjord Norway 55 E6
Eidsvold Australia 136 E5
Eidsvoll Norway 55 G6
Eifel hills Germany 62 G4
Eigenji Japan 92 C3
Eigg i. U.K. 60 C4
Eight Degree Channel India/Maldives 106 B5
Eights Coast Antarctica 188 K2
Eighty Mile Beach Australia 134 C4
Eiheiji Japan 92 C2
Eilat Israel 107 B5
Eildon Australia 138 B6
Eildon, Lake Australia 138 C6
Eileen Lake Canada 151 J2
Eilenburg Germany 63 M3
Eil Malk i. Palau 82 [inset]
Eimke Germany 63 K2
Einasleigh Australia 136 D3
Einasleigh r. Australia 136 C3
Einbeck Germany 63 J3
Eindhoven Neth. 62 F3
Einme Myanmar 86 A3
Einsiedeln Switz. 66 I3
Éire country Europe see Ireland
Eirik Ridge sea feature N. Atlantic Ocean 184 F2
Eiriosgaigh i. U.K. see Eriskay
Eirunepé Brazil 176 E5
Eisberg hill Germany 63 J3
Eiseb watercourse Namibia 123 C5
Eisenach Germany 63 K4
Eisenberg Germany 63 L4
Eisenhower, Mount Canada see Castle Mountain
Eisenhüttenstadt Germany 57 O4
Eisenstadt Austria 57 P7
Eisfeld Germany 63 K4
Eisleben Lutherstadt Germany 63 L3
Eite, Loch inlet U.K. see Etive, Loch
Eiterfeld Germany 63 J4
Eivissa Spain see Ibiza
Eivissa i. Spain see Ibiza
Ejea de los Caballeros Spain 67 F2
Ejeda Madag. 123 E6
Ejin Horo Qi Nei Mongol China see Altan Shiret
Ejin Qi Nei Mongol China see Dalain Hob
Ejmiadzin Armenia see Ejmiatsin
Ejmiatsin Armenia 113 G2
Ejutla Mex. 167 F5
Ekalaka U.S.A. 156 G3
Ekenäs Fin. 55 M7
Ekerem Turkm. 110 D2
Ekeren Belgium 62 E3
Eketahuna N.Z. 139 E5
Ekibastuz Kazakh. 102 E1
Ekimchan Rus. Fed. 90 D1
Ekinyazı Turkey 107 D1
Ekityki, Ozero l. Rus. Fed. 148 B2
Ekka Island N.W.T. Canada 149 Q2
Ekonda Rus. Fed. 77 L3
Ekostrovskaya Imandra, Ozero l. Rus. Fed. 54 R3
Ekshärad Sweden 55 H6
Eksjö Sweden 55 I8
Eksteenfontein S. Africa 124 C5
Ekström Ice Shelf Antarctica 188 B2
Ekuk AK U.S.A. 148 H4
Ekwan r. Canada 152 E3
Ekwan Point Canada 152 E3
Ekwok AK U.S.A. 148 H4
Ela Myanmar 86 B3
El Aaiún W. Sahara see Laâyoune
Elafonisou, Steno sea chan. Greece 69 J6
El 'Agrûd well Egypt see Al 'Ajrūd
Elaia, Cape Cyprus 107 B2
El 'Alamein Egypt see Al 'Alamayn
El Alamo Mex. 166 A2
El 'Âmirîya Egypt see Al 'Āmirīyah
Elands r. S. Africa 125 I3
Elandsdoorn S. Africa 125 I3
El Aouinet Alg. 68 B7
Elar Armenia see Abovyan
El Araïche Morocco see Larache
El Arco Mex. 166 B2
El Ariana Tunisia see L'Ariana
El Aricha Alg. 64 D5
El 'Arîsh Egypt see Al 'Arīsh
El Arrouch Alg. 68 B6
El Ashmûnein Egypt see Al Ashmūnayn
El Asnam Alg. see Chlef
Elassona Greece 69 J5
Elat Israel see Eilat
Elato atoll Micronesia 81 L5
Elazığ Turkey 113 E3
Elba U.S.A. 163 C6
Elba, Isola d' i. Italy 68 D3
El'ban Rus. Fed. 90 E2
El Barco de Valdeorras Spain see O Barco
El Barreal salt l. Mex. 166 D2
Elbasan Albania 69 I4
El Batroun Lebanon see Batroûn
El Baúl Venez. 176 E2
El Bawîti Egypt see Al Bawīṭī
El Bayadh Alg. 64 E5
Elbe r. Germany 63 J1
also known as Labe (Czech Republic)
Elbe-Havel-Kanal canal Germany 63 L2
El Béqaa valley Lebanon 107 C2
Elbert, Mount U.S.A. 156 G5
Elberta U.S.A. 159 H2
Elberton U.S.A. 163 D5
Elbeuf France 66 E2
Elbeyli Turkey 107 C1
El Billete, Cerro mt. Mex. 167 E5
Elbing Poland see Elbląg
Elbistan Turkey 112 E3
Elbląg Poland 57 Q3
El Bluff Nicaragua 166 [inset] J6
El Boulaïda Alg. see Blida
Elbow Canada 151 J5
Elbow Lake U.S.A. 160 D2
El Bozal Mex. 161 C8
El Brasil Mex. 167 E3

▶El'brus mt. Rus. Fed. 113 F2
Highest mountain in Europe.

Elburg Neth. 62 F2
El Burgo de Osma Spain 67 E3
Elburz Mountains Iran 110 C2
El Cajon U.S.A. 158 E5
El Cajón, Represa dam Hond. 166 [inset] I6
El Callao Venez. 176 F2
El Campo U.S.A. 161 D6
El Capitan Mountain U.S.A. 157 G6
El Capulín r. Mex. 161 C7
El Casco Mex. 166 D3
El Cebú, Cerro mt. Mex. 167 G6
El Centro U.S.A. 159 F5
El Cerro Bol. 176 F7
Elche Spain see Elche-Elx
Elche-Elx Spain 67 F4
El Chichónal vol. Mex. 167 G5
El Chilicote Mex. 166 D2
Elcho Island Australia 136 A1
El Coca Orellana Ecuador see Coca
El Coca Ecuador see Coca
El Cocuy, Parque Nacional nat. park Col. 176 D2
El Cuyo Mex. 167 I4
Elda Spain 67 F4
El Dátil Mex. 166 B2
El Desemboque Mex. 157 E7
El Diamante Mex. 166 E2
El'dikan Rus. Fed. 77 O3
El Djezair country Africa see Algeria
El Djezair Alg. see Algiers
El Doctor Mex. 166 B2
Eldon U.S.A. 160 E4
Eldorado Arg. 178 F3
Eldorado Brazil 179 A4
El Dorado Col. 176 D3
El Dorado Mex. 166 D3
El Dorado AR U.S.A. 161 E5
El Dorado KS U.S.A. 160 D4
Eldorado U.S.A. 161 C6
El Dorado Venez. 176 F2
Eldorado Mountains U.S.A. 159 F4
Eldoret Kenya 122 D3
Eldridge, Mount AK U.S.A. 149 L2
Elea, Cape Cyprus see Elaia, Cape
Eleanor U.S.A. 164 E4
Electric Peak U.S.A. 156 F3
Elefantes r. Moz. see Olifants
El Eglab plat. Alg. 120 C2
El Ejido Spain 67 E5
Elemi Triangle terr. Africa see Ilemi Triangle
El Encanto Col. 176 D4
Elend Germany 63 K3
Elephanta Caves tourist site India 106 B2
Elephant Butte Reservoir U.S.A. 157 G6
Elephant Island Antarctica 188 A2
Elephant Pass Sri Lanka 106 D4
Elephant Point Bangl. 105 H5
Elephant Point AK U.S.A. 148 G2
Eleşkirt Turkey 113 F3
El Estor Guat. 167 H6
El Eulma Alg. 64 F4
Eleuthera i. Bahamas 163 E7
Eleven Point r. U.S.A. 161 F4
El Fahs Tunisia 68 C6
El Faiyûm Egypt see Al Fayyūm
El Fasher Sudan 121 F3
El Ferrol Spain see Ferrol
El Ferrol del Caudillo Spain see Ferrol
Elfershausen Germany 63 J4
El Fud Eth. 122 E3
El Fuerte Mex. 166 C3
El Gara Egypt see Qārah
El Geneina Sudan 121 F3
El Geteina Sudan 108 D7
El Ghardaqa Egypt see Al Ghurdaqah
El Ghor plain Jordan/West Bank see Al Ghawr
Elgin U.K. 60 F3
Elgin IL U.S.A. 160 F3
Elgin ND U.S.A. 160 C2
Elgin NV U.S.A. 159 F3
Elgin TX U.S.A. 161 D6
El'ginskiy Rus. Fed. 77 P3
El Gîza Egypt see Giza
El Goléa Alg. 64 E5
El Golfo de Santa Clara Mex. 166 B2
Elgon, Mount Kenya/Uganda 100 C6
El Grullo Tamaulipas Mex. 167 F3
El Guante Mex. 166 D2
El Hadjar Alg. 68 B6
El Ḥammâm Egypt see Al Ḥammām
El Ḥammâmi reg. Mauritania 120 B2
El Ḥank esc. Mali/Mauritania 120 C2
El Ḥarra Egypt see Al Ḥarrah
El Hazim Jordan see Al Hazīm
El Ḥeiz Egypt see Al Ḥayz
El Hierro i. Canary Is 120 B2
El Higo Mex. 167 F4
El Homr Alg. 64 E6
El Homra Sudan 108 D7
Eliase Maluku Indon. 83 D5
Elías Piña Dom. Rep. 169 J5
Elichpur India see Achalpur
Elida U.S.A. 164 C3
Elie U.K. 60 G4
Elila r. Dem. Rep. Congo 122 C4
Elim AK U.S.A. 148 G2
Elimberrum France see Auch
Eling China see Yinjiang
Elingampangu Dem. Rep. Congo 122 C4
Eliot, Mount Canada 153 J2
Élisabethville Dem. Rep. Congo see Lubumbashi
Eliseu Martins Brazil 177 J5
El Iskandarîya Egypt see Alexandria
Elista Rus. Fed. 53 J7
Elixku Xinjiang China 98 B5
Elizabeth NJ U.S.A. 165 H3
Elizabeth WV U.S.A. 164 E4
Elizabeth, Mount hill Australia 134 D4
Elizabeth Bay Namibia 124 B4
Elizabeth City U.S.A. 162 E4
Elizabeth Island Pitcairn Is see Henderson Island
Elizabeth Point Namibia 124 B4
Elizabethton U.S.A. 162 D4
Elizabethtown IL U.S.A. 160 F4
Elizabethtown KY U.S.A. 164 C5
Elizabethtown NC U.S.A. 163 E5
Elizabethtown NY U.S.A. 165 I1
El Jadida Morocco 64 C5
El Jaralito Mex. 166 D3
El Jem Tunisia 68 D7
El Jicaro Nicaragua 166 [inset] I6
El Juile Mex. 167 G5
Elk r. Canada 150 H5
Ełk Poland 57 S4
Elk r. U.S.A. 165 H4
El Kaa Lebanon see Qaa
El Kab Sudan 108 D6
Elkader U.S.A. 160 F3
El Kala Alg. 68 C6
Elk City U.S.A. 161 D5
Elkedra Australia 136 A4
Elkedra watercourse Australia 136 B4
El Kef Tunisia see Le Kef
El Kelaâ des Srarhna Morocco 64 C5
Elkford Canada 150 H5
Elk Grove U.S.A. 158 C2
El Khalil West Bank see Hebron
El Khandaq Sudan 108 D6
El Khârga Egypt see Al Khārijah
El Kharrûba Egypt see Al Kharrūbah
Elkhart IN U.S.A. 164 C3
Elkhart KS U.S.A. 161 C4
El Khartûm Sudan see Khartoum
El Khenachich esc. Mali see El Khnâchîch
El Khnâchîch esc. Mali 120 C2
Elkhorn U.S.A. 160 F3
Elkhorn City U.S.A. 164 D5
Elkhovo Bulg. 69 L3
Elki Turkey see Beytüşşebap
Elkin U.S.A. 162 D4
Elkins U.S.A. 164 F4
Elk Island National Park Canada 151 H4
Elk Lake Canada 152 E5
Elk Lake l. U.S.A. 164 C1
Elkland U.S.A. 165 G3
Elk Mountain U.S.A. 156 G4
Elk Mountains U.S.A. 159 J2
Elko Canada 150 H5
Elko U.S.A. 159 F1
Elk Point Canada 151 I4
Elk Point U.S.A. 160 D3
Elk Springs U.S.A. 159 I1
Elkton MD U.S.A. 165 H4
Elkton VA U.S.A. 165 F4
El Kûbri Egypt see Al Kūbrī
El Kuntilla Egypt see Al Kuntillah
Elkview U.S.A. 164 E4
Ellas country Europe see Greece
Ellaville U.S.A. 163 C5
Ell Bay Canada 151 O1
Ellef Ringnes Island Canada 147 H2
Ellen, Mount U.S.A. 159 H2
Ellenburg Depot U.S.A. 165 I1
Ellendale U.S.A. 160 D2
Ellensburg U.S.A. 156 C3
Ellenville U.S.A. 165 H3
El León, Cerro mt. Mex. 161 B7
Ellesmere, Lake N.Z. 139 D6

▶Ellesmere Island Canada 147 J2
4th largest island in North America, and 10th in the world.

Ellesmere Island National Park Reserve Canada see Quttinirpaaq National Park
Ellesmere Port U.K. 58 E5
Ellettsville U.S.A. 164 B4
Ellice r. Canada 151 K1
Ellice Island N.W.T. Canada 149 N1
Ellice Island atoll Tuvalu see Funafuti
Ellice Islands country S. Pacific Ocean see Tuvalu
Ellicott City U.S.A. 165 G4
Ellijay U.S.A. 163 C5
El Limón Tamaulipas Mex. 167 F4
Ellingen Germany 63 K5
Elliot S. Africa 125 H6
Elliot, Mount Australia 136 D3
Elliotdale S. Africa 125 I6
Elliot Knob mt. U.S.A. 164 F4
Elliot Lake Canada 152 E5
Elliott Australia 134 F4
Elliott Highway AK U.S.A. 149 J2
Elliston U.S.A. 164 E5
Ellon U.K. 60 G3
Ellora Caves tourist site India 106 B1
Ellsworth KS U.S.A. 160 D4
Ellsworth ME U.S.A. 162 G2
Ellsworth NE U.S.A. 160 C3
Ellsworth WI U.S.A. 160 E2
Ellsworth Land reg. Antarctica 188 K1
Ellsworth Mountains Antarctica 188 L1
Ellwangen (Jagst) Germany 63 K6
El Maghreb country Africa see Morocco
Elmakuz Dağı mt. Turkey 107 A1
Elmalı Turkey 69 M6
El Malpais National Monument nat. park U.S.A. 159 J4
El Manşûra Egypt see Al Manşūrah
El Maṭarîya Egypt see Al Maṭarīyah
El Mazâr Egypt see Al Mazār
El Médano Mex. 166 C3
El Meghaïer Alg. 64 F5
El Milia Alg. 64 F4
El Minya Egypt see Al Minyā
Elmira Ont. Canada 164 E2
Elmira P.E.I. Canada 153 J5
Elmira MI U.S.A. 164 C1
Elmira NY U.S.A. 165 G2
El Mirage U.S.A. 159 G5
El Moral Mex. 167 E2
El Moral Spain 67 E5
Elmore Australia 138 B6
El Mreyyé reg. Mauritania 120 C3
Elmshorn Germany 63 J1
El Muglad Sudan 108 C7
Elmvale Canada 164 F1
Elnesvågen Norway 54 E5
El Nevado, Cerro mt. Col. 176 D3
El Nido Palawan Phil. 82 B4
El Oasis Mex. 159 F5
El Obeid Sudan 108 D7
El Ocote, Parque Natural nature res. Mex. 167 G5
El Odaiya Sudan 108 C7
El Oro Coahuila Mex. 166 E3
Elorza Venez. 176 E2
Elota Mex. 166 D4
El Oued Alg. 64 F5
Eloy U.S.A. 159 H5
El Palmito Mex. 166 D3
Elpaputih, Teluk b. Seram Indon. 83 D3
El Paso IL U.S.A. 160 F3
El Paso KS U.S.A. see Derby
El Paso TX U.S.A. 157 G7
El Peñasco Mex. 167 E4
Elphin U.K. 60 D2
Elphinstone i. Myanmar see Thayawthadangyi Kyun
El Pino, Sierra mts Mex. 166 E2
El Portal U.S.A. 158 D3
El Porvenir Mex. 166 D2
El Porvenir Panama 166 [inset] K7
El Prat de Llobregat Spain 67 H3
El Progreso Guat. see Guastatoya
El Progreso Hond. 166 [inset] I6
El Puente Nicaragua 166 [inset] I6
El Puerto de Santa María Spain 67 C5
El Qâhira Egypt see Cairo
El Qasimiye r. Lebanon 107 B3
El Quds Israel/West Bank see Jerusalem
El Quseima Egypt see Al Quşaymah
El Quşeir Egypt see Al Quşayr
El Qûşîya Egypt see Al Qūşīyah
El Real Panama 166 [inset] K7
El Regocijo Mex. 161 B8
El Reno U.S.A. 161 D5
El Retorno Mex. 167 E4
Elrose Canada 151 I5
El Rucio Zacatecas Mex. 166 E4
Elsa Y.T. Canada 149 N3
El Sabinal, Parque Nacional nat. park Mex. 167 F3
El Şaff Egypt see Aş Şaff
El Sahuaro Mex. 166 B2
El Salado Mex. 161 C7
El Salto Mex. 161 B8
El Salvador country Central America 167 H6
El Salvador Chile 178 C3
El Salvador Mex. 161 C7
Elsass reg. France see Alsace
El Sauz Chihuahua Mex. 166 D2
Else r. Germany 63 I2
El Sellûm Egypt see As Sallūm
Elsey Australia 134 F3
El Shallûfa Egypt see Ash Shallūfah

El Sharana Australia 134 F3
El Shatt Egypt see Ash Shatt
Elsie U.S.A. 164 C2
Elsinore Denmark see Helsingør
Elsinore CA U.S.A. 158 E5
Elsinore UT U.S.A. 159 G2
Elsinore Lake U.S.A. 158 E5
El Socorro Mex. 166 E3
Elson Lagoon AK U.S.A. 148 H1
El Sueco Mex. 166 D2
El Suweis Egypt see Suez
El Suweis governorate Egypt see As Suways
El Tajín tourist site Mex. 167 F4
El Tama, Parque Nacional nat. park Venez. 176 D2
El Tarf Alg. 68 C6
El Teleno mt. Spain 67 C2
El Temascal Mex. 161 D7
El Ter r. Spain 67 H2
El Thamad Egypt see Ath Thamad
El Tigre Venez. 176 F2
El Tigre, Parque Nacional nat. park Guat. 167 H5
Eltmann Germany 63 K5
El'ton Rus. Fed. 53 J6
El'ton, Ozero l. Rus. Fed. 53 J6
El Tren Mex. 166 B2
El Triunfo Mex. 166 C4
El Tuparro, Parque Nacional nat. park Col. 176 E2
El Ṭûr Egypt see Aṭ Ṭūr
El Turbio Arg. 178 B8
El Uqṣur Egypt see Luxor
Eluru India 106 D2
Elva Estonia 55 O7
El Vallecillo Mex. 166 C2
Elvanfoot U.K. 60 F5
Elvas Port. 67 C4
Elverum Norway 55 G6
El Vigía, Cerro mt. Mex. 166 D4
Elvira Brazil 176 D5
El Wak Kenya 122 E3
El Wâṭya well Egypt see Al Wāṭiyah
Elwood IN U.S.A. 164 C3
Elwood NE U.S.A. 160 D3
El Wuz Sudan 108 D7
Elx Spain see Elche-Elx
Elxleben Germany 63 K3
Ely U.K. 59 H6
Ely MN U.S.A. 160 F2
Ely NV U.S.A. 159 F2
Elyria U.S.A. 164 D3
Elz Germany 63 I4
El Zacatón, Cerro mt. Mex. 167 F5
El Zagâzîg Egypt see Az Zaqāzīq
El Zape Mex. 166 D3
Elze Germany 63 J2
Émaé i. Vanuatu 133 G3
Emāmrūd Iran 110 D2
Emām Ṣaḩēb Afgh. 111 H2
Emām Taqī Iran 110 E2
Emån r. Sweden 55 J8
E. Martínez Mex. see Emiliano Martínez
Emas, Parque Nacional das nat. park Brazil 177 H7
Emazar Kazakh. 98 C3
Emba Kazakh. 102 A2
Emba r. Kazakh. 102 A2
Embalenhle S. Africa 125 I4
Embarcación Arg. 178 D2
Embarras Portage Canada 151 I3
Embi Kazakh. see Emba
Embira r. Brazil see Envira
Emborcação, Represa de resr Brazil 179 B2
Embrun Canada 165 H1
Embu Kenya 122 D4
Emden Germany 63 H1
Emden Deep sea feature N. Pacific Ocean see Cape Johnson Depth
Emei China see Emeishan
Emeishan China 96 D2
Emei Shan mt. China 96 D2
Emel' r. Kazakh. 98 C3
Emerald Australia 136 E4
Emeril Canada 153 I3
Emerita Augusta Spain see Mérida
Emerson Canada 151 L5
Emerson U.S.A. 164 D4
Emery U.S.A. 159 H2
Emesa Syria see Homs
Emet Turkey 69 M5
eMgwenya S. Africa 125 J3
Emigrant Pass U.S.A. 158 E1
Emigrant Valley U.S.A. 159 F3
Emi Koussi mt. Chad 121 E3
Emile r. Canada 150 G2
Emiliano Martínez Mex. 166 D3
Emiliano Zapata Chiapas Mex. 167 H5
Emin Xinjiang China 98 C3
Emine, Nos pt Bulg. 69 L3
Eminence U.S.A. 164 C4
Emin He r. China 98 C3
Eminska Planina hills Bulg. 69 L3
Emirdağ Turkey 69 N5
Emir Dağı mt. Turkey 69 N5
Emir Dağları mts Turkey 69 N5
eMjindini S. Africa 125 J3
Emmaboda Sweden 55 I8
Emmahaven Sumatera Indon. see Telukbayur
Emmaste Estonia 55 M7
Emmaville Australia 138 E2
Emmeloord Neth. 62 F2
Emmelshausen Germany 63 H4
Emmen Neth. 62 G2
Emmen Switz. 66 I3
Emmerich Germany 62 G3
Emmet Australia 136 D5
Emmetsburg U.S.A. 160 E3
Emmett U.S.A. 156 D4
Emmiganuru India 106 C3
Emmonak AK U.S.A. 148 F3
Emo Canada 151 M5
Emona Slovenia see Ljubljana
Emory Peak U.S.A. 161 C6
Empalme Mex. 166 C3
Empangeni S. Africa 125 J5
Emperor Seamount Chain sea feature N. Pacific Ocean 186 H2
Emperor Trough sea feature N. Pacific Ocean 186 H2
Empingham Reservoir U.K. see Rutland Water
Emplawas Maluku Indon. 83 D5
Empoli Italy 68 D3
Emporia KS U.S.A. 160 D4
Emporia VA U.S.A. 165 G5
Emporium U.S.A. 165 F3
Empress Canada 151 I5
Empty Quarter des. Saudi Arabia see Rub' al Khālī
Ems r. Germany 63 H1
Emsdale Canada 164 F1
Emsdetten Germany 63 H2
Ems-Jade-Kanal canal Germany 63 H1
eMzinoni S. Africa 125 I4
Ena Japan 92 D3
Enafors Sweden 54 H5
Ena-san mt. Japan 92 D3
Enbek Kazakh. 98 B2
Encantadas, Serra das hills Brazil 178 F4
Encanto, Cape Luzon Phil. 82 C3
Encarnación Mex. 166 E4
Encarnación Para. 178 E3
Enchi Ghana 120 C4
Encinal U.S.A. 161 D6
Encinitas U.S.A. 158 E5
Encino U.S.A. 157 G6
Encruzilhada Brazil 179 C1
Endako Canada 150 E4
Endau r. Malaysia 84 C2
Endau-Rompin National Park nat. park Malaysia 87 C7
Ende Flores Indon. 83 B5
Ende i. Indon. 83 B5
Endeavour Strait Australia 136 C1
Enderby Canada 150 G5
Enderby atoll Micronesia see Puluwat
Enderby Land reg. Antarctica 188 D2
Endicott U.S.A. 165 G2
Endicott Mountains AK U.S.A. 148 I2
EnenKio terr. N. Pacific Ocean see Wake Island
Energodar Ukr. see Enerhodar
Enerhodar Ukr. 53 G7
Enewetak atoll Marshall Is 186 G5
Enez Turkey 69 L4
Enfe Lebanon 107 B2
Enfião, Ponta do pt Angola 123 B5
Enfidaville Tunisia 68 D6
Enfield U.S.A. 162 E4
Engan Norway 54 F5
Engaru Japan 90 F3
Engcobo S. Africa 125 H6
En Gedi Israel 107 B4
Engelhard U.S.A. 162 F5
Engel's Rus. Fed. 53 J6
Engelschmangat sea chan. Neth. 62 E1
Enggano i. Indon. 84 C4
Enghien Belgium 62 E4
England admin. div. U.K. 59 E6
Englee Canada 153 L4
Englehart Canada 152 F5
Englewood FL U.S.A. 163 D7
Englewood OH U.S.A. 164 C4
English r. Canada 151 M5
English U.S.A. 164 B4
English Bazar India see Ingraj Bazar
English Channel France/U.K. 59 F9
English Coast Antarctica 188 L2
Engozero Rus. Fed. 52 G2
Enhlalakahle S. Africa 125 J5
Enid U.S.A. 161 D4
Eniwa Japan 90 F4
Eniwetok atoll Marshall Is see Enewetak
Enjiang China see Yongfeng
Enkeldoorn Zimbabwe see Chivhu
Enkhuizen Neth. 62 F2
Enköping Sweden 55 J7
Enmelen Rus. Fed. 148 D2
Enna Sicily Italy 68 F6
Ennadai Lake Canada 151 K2
En Nahud Sudan 108 C7
Ennedi, Massif mts Chad 121 F3
Ennell, Lough l. Ireland 61 E4
Enngonia Australia 138 B2
Enning U.S.A. 160 C2
Ennis Ireland 61 D5
Ennis MT U.S.A. 156 F3
Ennis TX U.S.A. 161 D5
Enniscorthy Ireland 61 F5
Enniskillen U.K. 61 E3
Ennistymon Ireland 61 C5
Enn Nâqoûra Lebanon 107 B3
Enns r. Austria 57 O6
Eno Fin. 54 Q5
Enoch U.S.A. 159 G3
Enok Sumatera Indon. 84 C3
Enontekiö Fin. 54 M2
Enosburg Falls U.S.A. 165 I1
Enosville U.S.A. 164 B4
Enping China 97 G4
Enrekang Sulawesi Indon. 83 A3
Enrile Luzon Phil. 82 C2
Ens Neth. 62 F2
Ensay Australia 138 C6
Enschede Neth. 62 G2
Ense Germany 63 I3
Ensenada Baja California Mex. 166 A2
Ensenada Baja California Sur Mex. 166 C4
Enshi China 97 F2
Enshū-nada g. Japan 92 D4
Ensley U.S.A. 163 C6
Entebbe Uganda 122 D3
Enterprise Canada 150 G2
Enterprise AL U.S.A. 163 C6
Enterprise OR U.S.A. 156 D3
Enterprise UT U.S.A. 159 G3
Enterprise Point Palawan Phil. 82 B4
Entimau, Bukit hill Malaysia 85 F2
Entre Ríos Bol. 176 F8
Entre Rios Brazil 177 H5
Entre Rios de Minas Brazil 179 B3
Entroncamento Port. 67 B4
Enugu Nigeria 120 D4
Enurmino Rus. Fed. 148 E2
Envira Brazil 176 D5
Envira r. Brazil 176 D5
'En Yahav Israel 107 B4
Enyamba Dem. Rep. Congo 122 C4
Enzan Japan 93 E3
Eochaill Ireland see Youghal
Epe Neth. 62 F2
Epéna Congo 122 B3
Épernay France 62 D5
Ephraim U.S.A. 159 H2
Ephrata U.S.A. 165 G3
Epi i. Vanuatu 133 G3
Epidamnus Albania see Durrës
Épinal France 66 H2
Episkopi Bay Cyprus 107 A2
Episkopis, Kolpos b. Cyprus see Episkopi Bay
ePitoli S. Africa see Pretoria
Epomeo, Monte hill Italy 68 E4
Epping U.K. 59 H7
Epping Forest National Park Australia 136 D4
Eppstein Germany 63 I4
Eppynt, Mynydd hills U.K. 59 D6
Epsom U.K. 59 G7
Epte r. France 62 B5
Eqlīd Iran 110 D4
Equatorial Guinea country Africa 120 D4
Équeurdreville-Hainneville France 59 F9
Erac Creek watercourse Australia 138 B1
Eran Palawan Phil. 82 B4
Eran Bay Palawan Phil. 82 B4
Erandol India 106 B1
Erawadi r. Myanmar see Irrawaddy
Erawan National Park Thai. 87 B4
Erbaa Turkey 112 E2
Erbendorf Germany 63 M5
Erbeskopf hill Germany 62 H5
Ercan airport Cyprus 107 A2
Erciş Turkey 113 F3
Erciyes Dağı mt. Turkey 112 D3
Érd Hungary 68 H1
Erdaobaihe China see Baihe
Erdaogou Qinghai China 94 C5
Erdao Jiang r. China 90 B4
Erdek Turkey 69 L4
Erdemli Turkey 107 B1
Erdene Dornogovĭ Mongolia 95 G2
Erdenedalay Mongolia 94 F2
Erdenemandal Arhangay Mongolia 94 E1
Erdenesant Mongolia 94 F2
Erdenet Hövsgöl Mongolia see Shine-Ider
Erdenet Orhon Mongolia 94 F1
Erdenetsagaan Mongolia 95 H2
Erdenetsogt Bayanhongor Mongolia 94 E2
Erdenetsogt Ömnögovĭ Mongolia see Bayan-Ovoo
Erdi reg. Chad 121 F3
Erdniyevskiy Rus. Fed. 53 J7

▶Erebus, Mount vol. Antarctica 188 H1
Highest active volcano in Antarctica.

Erechim Brazil 178 F3
Ereentsav Mongolia 95 H1
Ereğli Konya Turkey 112 D3
Ereğli Zonguldak Turkey 69 N4
Erego Moz. 123 D5
Erei, Monti mts Sicily Italy 68 F6
Ereke Sulawesi Indon. 83 B4
Erementaü Kazakh. see Yereymentau
Eréndira Mex. 167 E5
Erenhaberga Shan mts China 98 D4
Erenhot Nei Mongol China 95 H3
Erepucu, Lago de l. Brazil 177 G4
Erevan Armenia see Yerevan
Erfurt Germany 63 L4
Erfurt airport Germany 63 K4
Ergani Turkey 113 E3
'Erg Chech des. Alg./Mali 120 C2
Ergel Mongolia see Hatanbulag
Ergene r. Turkey 69 L4
Ērgli Latvia 55 N8
Ergu China 90 C3
Ergun Nei Mongol China 95 J1
Ergun He r. China/Rus. Fed. see Argun'
Ergun Youqi Nei Mongol China see Ergun
Ergun Zuoqi China see Genhe
Ergveyem r. Rus. Fed. 148 C2
Er Hai l. China 96 D3
Erhulai China 90 B4
Eriboll, Loch inlet U.K. 60 E2
Ericht r. U.K. 60 F4
Ericht, Loch l. U.K. 60 E4
Erickson Canada 151 L5
Erie KS U.S.A. 161 E4
Erie PA U.S.A. 164 E2
Erie, Lake Canada/U.S.A. 164 E2
'Erîgât des. Mali 120 C3
Erik Eriksenstretet sea chan. Svalbard 76 D2
Eriksdale Canada 151 L5
Erimo-misaki c. Japan 90 F4
Erin Canada 164 E2
Erinpura Road India 104 C4
Eriskay i. U.K. 60 B3
Eritrea country Africa 108 E6
Erlangen Germany 63 L5
Erlangping China 97 F1
Erldunda Australia 135 F6
Erlistoun watercourse Australia 135 C6
Erlong Shan mt. China 90 C4
Erlongshan Shuiku resr China 90 B4
Ermak Kazakh. see Aksu
Ermana, Khrebet mts Rus. Fed. 95 H1
Ermelo Neth. 62 F2
Ermelo S. Africa 125 I4
Ermenek Turkey 107 A1
Ermenek r. Turkey 107 A1
Ermont Egypt see Armant
Ermoupoli Greece 69 K6
Ernakulam India 106 C4
Erne r. Ireland/U.K. 61 D3
Ernest Giles Range hills Australia 135 C6
Erode India 106 C4
Eromanga Australia 137 C5
Erongo admin. reg. Namibia 124 B1
Erp Neth. 62 F3
Erpu Xinjiang China 94 C3
Erqu Shaanxi China see Zhouzhi
Errabiddy Hills Australia 135 A6
Er Rachidia Morocco 64 D5
Er Raoui des. Alg. 64 D6
Errego Moz. 123 D5
Er Remla Tunisia 68 D7
Er Renk Sudan 108 D7
Errigal hill Ireland 61 D2
Errinundra National Park Australia 138 D6
Erris Head hd Ireland 61 B3
Errol U.S.A. 165 J1
Erromango i. Vanuatu 133 G3
Erronan i. Vanuatu see Futuna
Erseka Albania see Ersekë
Ersekë Albania 69 I4
Erskine U.S.A. 160 D2
Ersmark Sweden 54 L5
Ertai Xinjiang China 94 B2
Ertil' Rus. Fed. 53 I6
Ertis r. Kazakh./Rus. Fed. see Irtysh
Ertix He r. China/Kazakh. 102 G2
Ērtra country Africa see Eritrea
Eruh Turkey 113 F3
Erwin U.S.A. 162 D4
Erwitte Germany 63 I3
Erxleben Sachsen-Anhalt Germany 63 L2
Erxleben Sachsen-Anhalt Germany 63 L2
Eryuan China 96 C3
Erzerum Turkey see Erzurum
Erzgebirge mts Czech Rep./Germany 63 N4
Erzhan China 90 B2
Erzin Rus. Fed. 94 C1
Erzin Turkey 107 C1
Erzincan Turkey 113 E3
Erzurum Turkey 113 F3
Esa-ala P.N.G. 136 E1
Esan-misaki pt Japan 90 F4
Esashi Japan 90 F3
Esbjerg Denmark 55 F9
Esbo Fin. see Espoo
Escalante Negros Phil. 82 C4
Escalante U.S.A. 159 H3
Escalante r. U.S.A. 159 H3
Escalante Desert U.S.A. 159 G3
Escalón Mex. 166 D3
Escambia r. U.S.A. 163 C6
Escanaba U.S.A. 162 C2
Escárcega Mex. 167 H5
Escarpada Point Luzon Phil. 82 C2
Escatrón Spain 67 F3
Escaut r. Belgium 62 D4
Esch Neth. 62 F3
Eschede Germany 63 K2
Eschscholtz atoll Marshall Is see Bikini
Eschscholtz Bay AK U.S.A. 148 G2
Esch-sur-Alzette Lux. 62 F5
Eschwege Germany 63 K3
Eschweiler Germany 62 G4
Escondido r. Mex. 161 C6
Escondido r. Nicaragua 166 [inset] J6
Escondido U.S.A. 158 E5
Escudilla mt. U.S.A. 159 I5
Escuinapa Mex. 168 C4
Escuintla Guat. 167 H6
Escuintla Mex. 167 G6
Eséka Cameroon 120 E4
Eşen Turkey 69 M6
Esenguly Turkm. 110 D2
Esenguly Döwlet Gorugy nature res. Turkm. 110 D2
Esens Germany 63 H1
Eşfahān Iran 110 C3
Esfarayen, Reshteh-ye mts Iran 110 E2
Esfideh Iran 111 E3
Eshan China 96 D3
Eshāqābād Iran 110 E3
Eshkamesh Afgh. 111 H2
Eshkanān Iran 110 D5
Eshowe S. Africa 125 J5
Esikhawini S. Africa 125 K5
Esil Kazakh. see Yesil'
Esil r. Kazakh./Rus. Fed. see Ishim
Esk Australia 138 F1
Esk r. Australia 137 [inset]
Esk r. U.K. 58 D4
Eskdalemuir U.K. 60 F5
Esker Canada 153 I3
Eskifjörður Iceland 54 [inset]
Eski Gediz Turkey 69 M5
Eskilstuna Sweden 55 J7
Eskimo Lakes N.W.T. Canada 149 O1
Eskimo Point Canada see Arviat
Eskipazar Turkey 112 D2
Eskişehir Turkey 69 N5
Eski-Yakkabog' Uzbek. 111 G2
Esla r. Spain 67 C3
Eslāmābād-e Gharb Iran 110 B3
Esler Dağı mt. Turkey 69 M6
Eslohe (Sauerland) Germany 63 I3
Eslöv Sweden 55 H9
Esmā'īlī-ye Soflá Iran 110 E4
Eşme Turkey 69 M5
Esmeraldas Ecuador 176 C3
Esmont U.S.A. 165 F5
Esnagami Lake Canada 152 D4
Esnes France 62 D4
Espakeh Iran 111 F5
Espalion France 66 F4
España country Europe see Spain
Espanola Canada 152 E5
Espanola U.S.A. 161 B4
Esparta Hond. 166 [inset] I6
Espe Kazakh. 98 A4
Espelkamp Germany 63 I2
Espenberg, Cape AK U.S.A. 148 G2
Esperance Australia 135 C8
Esperance Bay Australia 135 C8
Esperanza research station Antarctica 188 A2
Esperanza Arg. 178 B8
Esperanza Sonora Mex. 166 C3
Esperanza Masbate Phil. 82 D4
Esperanza, Sierra de la mts Hond. 166 [inset] I6
Espichel, Cabo c. Port. 67 B4
Espigão, Serra do mts Brazil 179 A4
Espigüete mt. Spain 67 D2
Espinazo Mex. 167 E3
Espinhaço, Serra do mts Brazil 179 C2
Espinosa Brazil 179 C1
Espírito Santo Brazil see Vila Velha
Espírito Santo state Brazil 179 C2
Espiritu Luzon Phil. 82 C2
Espíritu Santo i. Vanuatu 133 G3
Espíritu Santo, Isla i. Mex. 166 C3
Espita Mex. 167 H4
Espoo Fin. 55 N6
Espuña mt. Spain 67 F5
Esqueda Mex. 166 C2
Esquel Arg. 178 B6
Esquimalt Canada 150 F5
Essang Sulawesi Indon. 83 C1
Essaouira Morocco 120 C1
Es Semara W. Sahara 120 B2
Essen Belgium 62 E3
Essen Germany 62 H3
Essen (Oldenburg) Germany 63 H2
Essequibo r. Guyana 177 G2
Essex Canada 164 D2
Essex CA U.S.A. 159 F4
Essex MD U.S.A. 165 G4
Essex NY U.S.A. 165 I1
Essexville U.S.A. 164 D2
Esslingen am Neckar Germany 63 J6
Esso Rus. Fed. 77 Q4
Essoyla Rus. Fed. 52 G3
Estagno Point Luzon Phil. 82 C2
Eşţahbān Iran 110 D4
Estância Brazil 177 K6
Estancia U.S.A. 157 G6
Estand, Kūh-e mt. Iran 111 F4
Estats, Pic d' mt. France/Spain 66 E5
Estcourt S. Africa 125 I5
Este r. Germany 63 J1
Estelí Nicaragua 166 [inset] I6
Estella Spain 67 E2
Estepa Spain 67 D5
Estepona Spain 67 D5
Ester AK U.S.A. 149 K2
Esteras de Medinaceli Spain 67 E3
Esterhazy Canada 151 K5
Estero Bay U.S.A. 158 C4
Esteros Mex. 167 F4
Esteros Para. 178 D2
Este Sudeste, Cayos del is Col. 166 [inset] J6
Estevan Canada 151 K5
Estevan Group is Canada 150 D4
Estherville U.S.A. 160 E3
Estill U.S.A. 163 D5
Eston Canada 151 I5
Estonia country Europe 55 N7
Estonskaya S.S.R. country Europe see Estonia
Estrées-St-Denis France 62 C5
Estrela Brazil 179 A5
Estrela, Serra da mts Port. 67 C3
Estrela do Sul Brazil 179 B2
Estrella mt. Spain 67 E4
Estrella, Punta pt Mex. 166 B2
Estremoz Port. 67 C4
Estrondo, Serra hills Brazil 177 I5
Etadunna Australia 137 B6
Etah India 104 D4
Étain France 62 F5
Étamamiou Canada 153 K4
Étampes France 66 F2
Étaples France 62 B4
Etawah Rajasthan India 104 D4
Etawah Uttar Prad. India 104 D4
Etchojoa Mex. 166 C3
Ethandakukhanya S. Africa 125 J4
Ethelbert Canada 151 K5
Ethel Creek Australia 135 C5
E'Thembini S. Africa 124 F5

▶Ethiopia country Africa 122 D3
2nd most populous country in Africa.

Etimesğut Turkey 112 D3
Etive, Loch inlet U.K. 60 D4
Etivluk r. AK U.S.A. 148 H1

▶Etna, Mount vol. Sicily Italy 68 F6
Highest active volcano in Europe.

Etne Norway 55 D7
Etobicoke Canada 164 F2
Etolin Strait AK U.S.A. 148 F3
Etorofu-tō i. Rus. Fed. see Iturup, Ostrov
Etosha National Park Namibia 123 B5
Etosha Pan salt pan Namibia 123 B5
Etoumbi Congo 122 B3
Etrek r. Iran/Turkm. see Atrek
Etrek Turkm. 110 D2
Étrépagny France 62 B5
Étretat France 59 H9
Ettelbruck Lux. 62 G5
Etten-Leur Neth. 62 E3
Ettlingen Germany 63 I6
Ettrick Water r. U.K. 60 F5
Etzatlán Mex. 166 D4
Euabalong Australia 138 C4
Euboea i. Greece see Evvoia
Eucla Australia 135 E7
Euclid U.S.A. 164 E3
Euclides da Cunha Brazil 177 K6
Eucumbene, Lake Australia 138 D6
Eudistes, Lac des l. Canada 153 I4
Eudora U.S.A. 161 F5
Eudunda Australia 137 B7
Eufaula AL U.S.A. 163 C6
Eufaula OK U.S.A. 161 E5
Eufaula Lake resr U.S.A. 161 E5
Eugene U.S.A. 156 C3
Eugenia, Punta pt Mex. 166 B3
Eugowra Australia 138 D4
Eulo Australia 138 B2
Eumungerie Australia 138 D3
Eungella Australia 136 E4
Eungella National Park Australia 136 E4
Eunice LA U.S.A. 161 E6
Eunice NM U.S.A. 161 C5
Eupen Belgium 62 G4

▶Euphrates r. Asia 113 G5
Longest river in western Asia.
Also known as Al Furāt (Iraq/Syria) or Fırat (Turkey).

Eura Fin. 55 M6
Eure r. France 62 B5
Eureka AK U.S.A. 149 J2
Eureka CA U.S.A. 156 B4
Eureka KS U.S.A. 160 D4
Eureka MT U.S.A. 156 E2
Eureka NV U.S.A. 159 F2
Eureka OH U.S.A. 164 D4
Eureka SD U.S.A. 160 D2
Eureka UT U.S.A. 159 G2
Eureka Roadhouse AK U.S.A. 149 K3
Eureka Sound sea chan. Canada 147 J2
Eureka Springs U.S.A. 161 E4
Eureka Valley U.S.A. 158 E3
Euriowie Australia 137 C6
Euroa Australia 138 B6
Eurombah Australia 137 E5
Eurombah Creek r. Australia 137 E5
Europa, Île i. Indian Ocean 123 E6
Europa, Punta de pt Gibraltar see Europa Point
Europa Point Gibraltar 67 D5
Euskirchen Germany 62 G4
Eutaw U.S.A. 163 C5
Eutsuk Lake Canada 150 E4
Eutzsch Germany 63 M3
Eva Downs Australia 134 F4
Evans, Lac l. Canada 152 F4
Evans, Mount U.S.A. 156 G5
Evansburg Canada 150 H4
Evans City U.S.A. 164 E3
Evans Head Australia 138 F2
Evans Head hd Australia 138 F2
Evans Ice Stream Antarctica 188 L1
Evans Strait Canada 151 P2
Evanston IL U.S.A. 164 B2
Evanston WY U.S.A. 156 F4
Evansville Canada 152 E5
Evansville AK U.S.A. 149 J2
Evansville IN U.S.A. 164 B5
Evansville WY U.S.A. 156 G4
Evant U.S.A. 161 D6
Eva Perón Arg. see La Plata
Evart U.S.A. 164 C2
Evaton S. Africa 125 H4
Evaz Iran 110 D5
Evening Shade U.S.A. 161 F4
Evensk Rus. Fed. 77 Q3
Everard, Cape Australia see Hicks, Point
Everard, Lake salt flat Australia 137 A6
Everard, Mount Australia 135 F5
Everard Range hills Australia 135 F6
Everdingen Neth. 62 F3
Everek Turkey see Develi

▶Everest, Mount China/Nepal 105 F4
Highest mountain in the world and in Asia.

Everett PA U.S.A. 165 F3
Everett WA U.S.A. 156 C3
Evergem Belgium 62 D3
Everglades swamp U.S.A. 163 D7
Everglades National Park U.S.A. 163 D7
Evergreen U.S.A. 163 C6
Evesham Australia 136 C4
Evesham U.K. 59 F6
Evesham, Vale of valley U.K. 59 F6
Evijärvi Fin. 54 M5
Evje Norway 55 E7
Évora Port. 67 C4
Evoron, Ozero l. Rus. Fed. 90 E2
Évreux France 62 B5
Evros r. Greece/Turkey see Maritsa
Evrotas r. Greece 69 J6
Évry France 62 C6
Evrychou Cyprus 107 A2
Evrykhou Cyprus see Evrychou
Evvoia i. Greece 69 K5
Ewan Australia 136 D3
Ewaso Ngiro r. Kenya 122 E3
Ewe, Loch b. U.K. 60 D3
Ewenkizu Zizhiqi Nei Mongol China see Bayan Tohoi
Ewing U.S.A. 164 D5
Ewirgol Xinjiang China 98 D4
Ewo Congo 122 B4
Exaltación Bol. 176 E6
Excelsior S. Africa 125 H5
Excelsior Mountain U.S.A. 158 D2
Excelsior Mountains U.S.A. 158 D2
Exe r. U.K. 59 D8
Exeter Australia 138 E5
Exeter Canada 164 E2
Exeter U.K. 59 D8
Exeter CA U.S.A. 158 D3
Exeter NH U.S.A. 165 J2
Exeter Lake Canada 151 I1
Exloo Neth. 62 G2
Exminster U.K. 59 D8
Exmoor hills U.K. 59 D7
Exmoor National Park U.K. 59 D7
Exmore U.S.A. 165 H5
Exmouth Australia 134 A5
Exmouth U.K. 59 D8
Exmouth, Mount Australia 138 D3
Exmouth Gulf Australia 134 A5
Exmouth Lake Canada 150 H1
Exmouth Plateau sea feature Indian Ocean 185 P7
Expedition National Park Australia 136 E5
Expedition Range mts Australia 136 E5
Exploits r. Canada 153 L4
Exton U.S.A. 165 H3
Extremadura aut. comm. Spain 67 D4
Exuma Cays is Bahamas 163 E7
Exuma Sound sea chan. Bahamas 163 F7
Eyasi, Lake salt l. Tanz. 122 D4
Eyawadi r. Myanmar see Irrawaddy
Eye U.K. 59 I6
Eyeberry Lake Canada 151 J2
Eyelenoborsk Rus. Fed. 51 S3
Eyemouth U.K. 60 G5
Eyjafjörður inlet Iceland 54 [inset]
Eyl Somalia 122 E3
Eylau Rus. Fed. see Bagrationovsk
Eynsham U.K. 59 F7

▶Eyre (North), Lake Australia 137 B6
Largest lake in Oceania, and lowest point.

Eyre (South), Lake Australia 137 B6
Eyre, Lake Australia 137 B6
Eyre Creek watercourse Australia 136 B5
Eyre Mountains N.Z. 139 B7
Eyre Peninsula Australia 137 A7
Eystrup Germany 63 J2
Eysturoy i. Faroe Is 54 [inset]
Ezakheni S. Africa 125 J5
Ezel U.S.A. 164 D5
Ezenzeleni S. Africa 125 I4
Ezequiel Ramos Mexía, Embalse resr Arg. 178 C5
Ezhou China 97 G2
Ezhva Rus. Fed. 52 K3
Ezine Turkey 69 L5
Ezo i. Japan see Hokkaidō
Ezousa r. Cyprus 107 A2

F

Faaborg Denmark 55 G9
Faadhippolhu Atoll Maldives 106 B5
Faafxadhuun Somalia 122 E3
Fabens U.S.A. 157 G7
Faber, Mount hill Sing. 87 [inset]
Faber Lake Canada 150 G2
Fåborg Denmark see Faaborg
Fabriano Italy 68 E3
Faches-Thumesnil France 62 D4
Fachi Niger 120 E3
Fada Chad 121 F3
Fada-N'Gourma Burkina Faso 120 D3
Fadghāmī Syria 113 F4
Fadiffolu Atoll Maldives see Faadhippolhu Atoll
Fadippolu Atoll Maldives see Faadhippolhu Atoll
Faenza Italy 68 D2
Færoerne terr. N. Atlantic Ocean see Faroe Islands

Faeroes terr. N. Atlantic Ocean see **Faroe Islands**
Fafanlap Papua Indon. **83** D3
Făgăraş Romania **69** K2

▶**Fagatogo** American Samoa **133** I3
Capital of American Samoa.

Fagersta Sweden **55** I7
Fagita Papua Indon. **83** D3
Fagne reg. Belgium **62** E4
Fagurhólsmýri Iceland **54** [inset]
Fagwir Sudan **108** D8
Fahraj Iran **110** D4
Fā'id Egypt **112** D5
Fairbanks AK U.S.A. **149** K2
Fairborn U.S.A. **164** C4
Fairbury U.S.A. **160** D3
Fairchance U.S.A. **164** F4
Fairfax U.S.A. **165** G4
Fairfield CA U.S.A. **158** B2
Fairfield IA U.S.A. **160** F3
Fairfield ID U.S.A. **156** E4
Fairfield IL U.S.A. **160** F4
Fairfield OH U.S.A. **164** C4
Fairfield TX U.S.A. **161** D6
Fair Haven U.S.A. **165** I2
Fair Head hd U.K. **61** F2
Fairie Queen Shoal sea feature Phil. **82** B4
Fair Isle i. U.K. **60** H1
Fairlee U.S.A. **165** I2
Fairlie **139** C7
Fairmont MN U.S.A. **160** E3
Fairmont WV U.S.A. **164** E4
Fair Oaks U.S.A. **164** B3
Fairplay, Mount AK U.S.A. **149** L3
Fairview Australia **136** D2
Fairview Canada **150** G3
Fairview MI U.S.A. **164** C1
Fairview OK U.S.A. **161** D4
Fairview PA U.S.A. **164** E2
Fairview UT U.S.A. **159** H2
Fairview Park H.K. China **97** [inset]
Fairweather, Cape AK U.S.A. **149** M4
Fairweather, Mount Canada/U.S.A. **149** M4
Fais i. Micronesia **81** K5
Faisalabad Pak. **111** I4
Faissault France **62** E5
Faith U.S.A. **160** C2
Faizabad Afgh. see **Feyzābād**
Faizabad India **105** E4
Fakaofo atoll Tokelau **133** I2
Fakaofu atoll Tokelau see **Fakaofo**
Fakenham U.K. **59** H6
Fåker Sweden **54** I5
Fakfak Indon. **81** I7
Fakhrābād Iran **110** D4
Fakiragram India **105** G4
Fako vol. Cameroon see **Cameroun, Mont**
Faku Liaoning China **95** J3
Fal r. U.K. **59** C8
Falaba Sierra Leone **120** B4
Falaise Lake Canada **150** G2
Falam Myanmar **86** A2
Falavarjan Iran **110** C3
Falcon Lake Canada **151** M5
Falcon Lake I. Mex./U.S.A. **167** F3
Falenki Rus. Fed. **52** K4
Falfurrias U.S.A. **161** D7
Falher Canada **150** G4
Falkenberg Germany **63** N3
Falkenberg Sweden **55** H8
Falkenhagen Germany **63** M1
Falkenhain Germany **63** M3
Falkensee Germany **63** N2
Falkenstein Germany **63** M5
Falkirk U.K. **60** F5
Falkland U.K. **60** F4
Falkland Escarpment sea feature S. Atlantic Ocean **184** E9

▶**Falkland Islands** terr. S. Atlantic Ocean **178** E8
United Kingdom Overseas Territory.

Falkland Plateau sea feature S. Atlantic Ocean **184** E9
Falkland Sound sea chan. Falkland Is **178** D8
Falköping Sweden **55** H7
Fallbrook U.S.A. **158** E5
Fallieres Coast Antarctica **188** L2
Fallingbostel Germany **63** J2
Fallon U.S.A. **158** D2
Fall River U.S.A. **165** J3
Fall River Pass U.S.A. **156** G4
Falls City U.S.A. **160** E3
Falmouth U.K. **59** B8
Falmouth KY U.S.A. **164** C4
Falmouth VA U.S.A. **165** G4
False r. Canada **153** H2
False Bay S. Africa **124** D8
False Pass AK U.S.A. **148** G5
False Point India **105** F5
Falso, Cabo c. Hond. **166** [inset] J6
Falster i. Denmark **55** G9
Fălticeni Romania **53** E7
Falun Sweden **55** I6
Fam, Kepulauan is Papua Indon. **83** D3
Famagusta Cyprus **107** A2
Famagusta Bay Cyprus see **Ammochostos Bay**
Fameck France **62** G5
Famenin Iran **110** C3
Fame Range hills Australia **135** C6
Family Lake Canada **151** M5
Family Well Australia **134** D5
Fāmūr, Daryācheh-ye l. Iran **110** C4
Fana Mali **120** C3
Fanad Head hd Ireland **61** E2
Fandriana Madag. **123** E6
Fane r. Ireland **61** F4
Fang Thai. **86** B3
Fangcheng Guangxi China see **Fangchenggang**
Fangcheng Henan China **97** G1
Fangchenggang China **97** F4
Fangdou Shan mts China **97** F2
Fangliao Taiwan **97** I4
Fangshan Taiwan **97** I4
Fangxian China **97** F1
Fangzheng China **90** C3
Fankuai China **97** F2
Fankuaidian China see **Fankuai**
Fanling H.K. China **97** [inset]
Fannich, Loch l. U.K. **60** D3
Fannūj Iran **111** E5
Fano Italy **68** E3
Fanshan Anhui China **97** H2
Fanshan Zhejiang China **97** I3
Fanshi Shanxi China **95** H4
Fanum Fortunae Italy see **Fano**
Faqīh Aḥmadān Iran **110** C4
Farab Turkm. see **Farap**
Faraba Mali **120** B3
Faradofay Madag. see **Tôlañaro**
Farafangana Madag. **123** E6
Farāfirah, Wāḥāt al oasis Egypt **108** C4
Farafra Oasis oasis Egypt see **Farāfirah, Wāḥāt al**
Farāh Afgh. **111** F3
Farahābād Iran see **Khezerābād**
Farallon de Medinilla i. N. Mariana Is **81** L3
Farallon de Pajaros vol. N. Mariana Is **81** K2
Farallones de Cali, Parque Nacional nat. park Col. **176** C3
Faranah Guinea **120** B3
Farap Turkm. **111** F2
Fararah Oman **109** I6
Farasān, Jazā'ir is Saudi Arabia **108** F6
Faraulep atoll Micronesia **81** K5
Fareham U.K. **59** F8
Farewell AK U.S.A. **148** I3
Farewell, Cape Greenland **147** N3
Farewell, Cape N.Z. **139** D5
Farewell Spit N.Z. **139** D5
Färgelanda Sweden **55** H7
Farghona Uzbek. see **Farg'ona**
Fargo U.S.A. **160** D2
Farg'ona Uzbek. **109** L1
Faribault U.S.A. **160** E2
Faribault, Lac l. Canada **153** H2
Faridabad India **104** D3
Faridkot India **104** C3
Faridpur Bangl. **105** G5
Farīmān Iran **111** E3
Farkhar Afgh. see **Farkhato**
Farkhato Afgh. **111** H2
Farkhor Tajik. **111** H2
Farmahin Iran **110** C3
Farmer Island Canada **152** E2
Farmerville U.S.A. **161** E5
Farmington Canada **150** F4
Farmington ME U.S.A. **165** J1
Farmington MO U.S.A. **160** F4
Farmington NH U.S.A. **165** J2
Farmington NM U.S.A. **159** I3
Farmington Hills U.S.A. **164** D2
Far Mountain Canada **150** E4
Farmville U.S.A. **165** F5
Farnborough U.K. **59** G7
Farne Islands U.K. **58** F3
Farnham U.K. **59** G7
Farnham, Lake salt flat Australia **135** D6
Farnham, Mount Canada **150** G5
Faro Brazil **177** G4
Faro Y.T. Canada **149** N3
Faro Port. **67** C5
Fårö i. Sweden **55** K8
Faroe - Iceland Ridge sea feature Arctic Ocean **189** I2

▶**Faroe Islands** terr. N. Atlantic Ocean **54** [inset]
Self-governing Danish territory.

Fårösund Sweden **55** K8
Farquhar Group is Seychelles **123** F5
Farquharson Tableland hills Australia **135** C6
Farrāshband Iran **110** D4
Farr Bay Antarctica **188** F2
Farristown U.S.A. **164** C5
Farrukhabad India see **Fatehgarh**
Fārsī Afgh. **111** F3
Farsund Norway **55** E7
Fārūj Iran **110** E2
Farwell MI U.S.A. **164** C2
Farwell TX U.S.A. **161** C5
Fasā Iran **110** D4
Fasano Italy **68** G4
Faşikan Geçidi pass Turkey **107** A1
Faßberg Germany **63** K2
Fastiv Ukr. **53** F6
Fastov Ukr. see **Fastiv**
Fatehabad India **104** C3
Fatehgarh India **104** D4
Fatehpur Rajasthan India **104** C4
Fatehpur Uttar Prad. India **104** E4
Fatick Senegal **120** B3
Fattoilep atoll Micronesia see **Faraulep**
Faughan r. U.K. **61** E2
Faulkton U.S.A. **160** D2
Faulquemont France **62** G5
Fauresmith S. Africa **125** G5
Fauske Norway **54** I3
Faust Canada **150** H4
Fawcett Canada **150** H4
Fawley U.K. **59** F8
Fawn r. Canada **151** N4
Faxaflói b. Iceland **54** [inset]
Faxälven r. Sweden **54** J5
Faya Chad **121** E3
Fayette AL U.S.A. **163** C5
Fayette MO U.S.A. **160** E4
Fayette MS U.S.A. **161** F6
Fayette OH U.S.A. **164** C3
Fayetteville AR U.S.A. **161** E4
Fayetteville NC U.S.A. **163** E5
Fayetteville TN U.S.A. **163** C5
Fayetteville WV U.S.A. **164** E4
Fâyid Egypt see **Fā'id**
Faylakah i. Kuwait **110** C4
Fazao Malfakassa, Parc National de nat. park Togo **120** D4
Fazilka India **104** C3
Fazrān, Jabal hill Saudi Arabia **110** C5
Fdérik Mauritania **120** B2
Fead Group is P.N.G. see **Nuguria Islands**
Feale r. Ireland **61** C5
Fear, Cape U.S.A. **163** E5
Featherston N.Z. **139** E5
Feathertop, Mount Australia **138** C6
Fécamp France **66** E2
Federal District admin. dist. Brazil see **Distrito Federal**
Federalsburg U.S.A. **165** H4
Fedusar India **104** C4
Fehet Lake Canada **151** M1
Fehmarn i. Germany **57** M3
Fehrbellin Germany **63** M2
Feia, Lagoa lag. Brazil **179** C3
Feicheng Shandong China see **Feixian**
Feijó Brazil **176** D5
Feilding N.Z. **139** E5
Fei Ngo Shan hill H.K. China see **Kowloon Peak**
Feio r. Brazil see **Aguapeí**
Feira de Santana Brazil **179** D1
Feixi China **97** H2
Feixian Shandong China **95** I5
Feixiang Hebei China **95** H4
Fejd el Abiod pass Alg. **68** B6
Feke Turkey **112** D3
Felanitx Spain **67** H4
Feldberg Germany **63** N1
Feldberg mt. Germany **57** L7
Feldkirch Austria **57** L7
Feldkirchen in Kärnten Austria **57** O7
Felidhu Atoll Maldives **103** D11
Felidu Atoll Maldives see **Felidhu Atoll**
Felipe C. Puerto Mex. **167** H5
Felixlândia Brazil **179** B2
Felixstowe U.K. **59** I7
Felixton S. Africa **125** J5
Fellowsville U.S.A. **164** F4
Felsina Italy see **Bologna**
Felton U.S.A. **165** H4
Feltre Italy **68** D1
Femunden l. Norway **54** G5
Femundsmarka Nasjonalpark nat. park Norway **54** H5
Fenaio, Punta del pt Italy **68** D3
Fence Lake U.S.A. **159** I4
Fener Burnu hd Turkey **107** B1
Fénérive Madag. see **Fenoarivo Atsinanana**
Fengari mt. Greece **69** K4
Fengcheng Fujian China see **Lianjiang**
Fengcheng Fujian China see **Yongding**
Fengcheng Fujian China see **Anxi**
Fengcheng Guangdong China see **Xinfeng**
Fengcheng Guangxi China see **Fengshan**
Fengcheng Guizhou China see **Tianzhu**
Fengcheng Jiangxi China **97** G2
Fenggang Fujian China see **Shaxian**
Fenggang Guizhou China **96** E3
Fenggang Jiangxi China see **Yihuang**
Fenggeling Gansu China **94** F5
Fengguang China **90** B3
Fenghuang China **97** F3
Fengjiaba China see **Wangcang**
Fengjie China **97** F2
Fengkai China **97** F4
Fenglin Taiwan **97** I4
Fengming Shaanxi China see **Qishan**
Fengming Sichuan China see **Pengshan**
Fengnan Hebei China **95** I4
Fengning Hebei China **95** I3
Fengqi Shaanxi China see **Luochuan**
Fengqing China **96** C3
Fengqiu Henan China **95** H5
Fengrun Hebei China **95** I4
Fengshan Fujian China see **Luoyuan**
Fengshan Guangxi China **96** E3
Fengshan Hubei China see **Luotian**
Fengshan Yunnan China see **Fengqing**
Fengshuba Shuiku resr China **97** G3
Fengshui Shan mt. China **90** A1
Fengtongzhai Giant Panda Reserve nature res. China **96** D2
Fengxian Jiangsu China **95** I5
Fengxian Shanghai China **96** E1
Fengxiang Heilong. China see **Luobei**
Fengxiang Yunnan China see **Lincang**
Fengyang China **97** H1
Fengyuan Shaanxi China **95** G5
Fengyüan Taiwan **97** I3
Fengzhen Nei Mongol China **95** H3
Feni Bangl. **105** G5
Feniak Lake AK U.S.A. **148** H1
Feni Islands P.N.G. **132** F2
Fenimore Pass sea channel AK U.S.A. **149** [inset]
Fennville U.S.A. **164** B2
Feno, Capo di c. Corsica France **66** I6
Fenoarivo Atsinanana Madag. **123** E5
Fenshui Guan pass China **97** H3
Fenton U.S.A. **164** D2
Fenua Ura atoll Fr. Polynesia see **Manuae**
Fenxiang Shaanxi China **95** F5
Fenyang Shanxi China **95** G4
Fenyi China **97** G3
Feodosiya Ukr. **112** D1
Fer, Cap de c. Alg. **68** B6
Férai Greece see **Feres**
Ferdows Iran **110** E3
Fère-Champenoise France **62** D6
Feres Greece **69** L4
Fergus Canada **164** E2
Fergus Falls U.S.A. **160** D2
Ferguson Lake Canada **151** L2
Fergusson Island P.N.G. **132** F2
Fériana Tunisia **68** C7
Ferijaz Kosovo **69** I3
Ferkessédougou Côte d'Ivoire **120** C4
Fermo Italy **68** E3
Fermont Canada **153** I3
Fermoselle Spain **67** C3
Fermoy Ireland **61** D5
Fernandina, Isla i. Galápagos Ecuador **176** [inset]
Fernandina Beach U.S.A. **163** D6
Fernando de Magallanes, Parque Nacional nat. park Chile **178** B8
Fernando de Noronha i. Brazil **184** F6
Fernandópolis Brazil **179** A3
Fernando Poó i. Equat. Guinea see **Bioco**
Fernão Dias Brazil **179** B2
Ferndale U.S.A. **158** A1
Ferndown U.K. **59** F8
Fernlee Australia **138** C2
Fernley U.S.A. **158** D2
Ferns Ireland **61** F5
Ferozepore India see **Firozpur**
Ferrara Italy **68** D2
Ferreira-Gomes Brazil **177** H3
Ferriday LA U.S.A. **167** H2
Ferro, Capo c. Sardinia Italy **68** C4
Ferrol Spain **67** B2
Ferron U.S.A. **159** H2
Ferros Brazil **179** C2
Ferry AK U.S.A. **149** J2
Ferryland Canada **153** L5
Ferryville Tunisia see **Menzel Bourguiba**
Fertő-tavi nat. park Hungary **68** G1
Ferwerd Neth. see **Ferwert**
Ferwert Neth. **62** F1
Fès Morocco **64** D5
Feshi Dem. Rep. Congo **123** B4
Fessenden U.S.A. **160** D2
Festus U.S.A. **160** F4
Fet Dom, Tanjung pt Papua Indon. **83** D3
Fété Bowé Senegal **120** B3
Fethard Ireland **61** E5
Fethiye Malatya Turkey see **Yazıhan**
Fethiye Muğla Turkey **69** M6
Fethiye Körfezi b. Turkey **69** M6
Fetisovo Kazakh. **113** I2
Fetlar i. U.K. **60** [inset]
Fettercairn U.K. **60** G4
Feucht Germany **63** L5
Feuchtwangen Germany **63** K5
Feuilles, Rivière aux r. Canada **153** H2
Fevral'sk Rus. Fed. **90** C1
Fevzipaşa Turkey **112** E3
Feyzābād Afgh. **111** H2
Feyzābād Kermān Iran **110** D4
Feyzābād Khorāsān Iran **110** E3
Fez Morocco see **Fès**
Ffestiniog U.K. **59** D6
Fianarantsoa Madag. **123** E6
Fichē Eth. **122** D3
Fichtelgebirge hills Germany **63** M4
Field U.S.A. **164** D5
Fier Albania **69** H4
Fiery Creek r. Australia **136** B3
Fife Lake U.S.A. **164** C1
Fife Ness pt U.K. **60** G4
Fifield Australia **138** C4
Fifth Meridian Canada **150** H3
Figeac France **66** F4
Figueira da Foz Port. **67** B3
Figueras Spain see **Figueres**
Figueres Spain **67** H2
Figuig Morocco **64** D5
Figuil Cameroon **121** E4

▶**Fiji** country S. Pacific Ocean **133** H3
4th most populous and 5th largest country in Oceania.

Fīk' Eth. **122** E3
Filadelfia Para. **178** D2
Filchner Ice Shelf Antarctica **188** A1
Filey U.K. **58** G4
Filibe Bulg. see **Plovdiv**
Filingué Niger **120** D3
Filipinas country Asia see **Philippines**
Filippiada Greece **69** I5
Filipstad Sweden **55** I7
Fillan Norway **54** F5
Fillmore CA U.S.A. **158** D4
Fillmore UT U.S.A. **159** G2
Fils r. Germany **63** J6
Filtu Eth. **122** E3
Fimbull Ice Shelf Antarctica **188** C2
Fin Iran **110** C3
Finch Canada **165** H1
Findhorn r. U.K. **60** F3
Fındık Turkey **110** A2
Findlay U.S.A. **164** D3
Fine U.S.A. **165** H1
Finger Lake Canada **151** M4
Finger Lakes U.S.A. **165** G2
Finike Turkey **69** N6
Finike Körfezi b. Turkey **69** N6
Finisterre Spain see **Fisterra**
Finisterre, Cabo c. Spain see **Finisterre, Cape**
Finisterre, Cape Spain **67** B2
Fink Creek AK U.S.A. **148** G2
Finke watercourse Australia **136** A5
Finke, Mount hill Australia **135** F7
Finke Bay Australia **134** E3
Finke Gorge National Park Australia **135** F6
Finland country Europe **54** O5
Finland, Gulf of Europe **55** M7

▶**Finlay** r. Canada **150** E3
Part of the Mackenzie-Peace-Finlay, the 2nd longest river in North America.

Finlay, Mount Canada **150** E3
Finlay Forks Canada **150** F4
Finley U.S.A. **160** D2
Finn r. Ireland **61** E3
Finne ridge Germany **63** L3
Finnigan, Mount Australia **136** D2
Finniss, Cape Australia **135** F8
Finnmarksvidda reg. Norway **54** H2
Finnsnes Norway **54** J2
Fins Oman **110** E6
Finschhafen P.N.G. **81** L8
Finspång Sweden **55** I7
Fintona U.K. **61** E3
Fintown Ireland see **Baile na Finne**
Finucane Range hills Australia **136** C4
Fionn Loch l. U.K. **60** D3
Fionnphort U.K. **60** C4
Fiordland National Park N.Z. **139** A7
Fir reg. Saudi Arabia **110** B4
Firat r. Turkey **112** E3 see **Euphrates**
Firebaugh U.S.A. **158** C3
Firedrake Lake Canada **151** J2
Fire Island AK U.S.A. **149** J3
Firenze Italy see **Florence**
Fireside B.C. Canada **149** P4
Firk, Sha'ib watercourse Iraq **113** G5
Firmat Arg. **178** D4
Firminy France **66** G4
Firmum Italy see **Fermo**
Firmum Picenum Italy see **Fermo**
Firovo Rus. Fed. **52** G4
Firozabad India **104** D4
Firozkoh reg. Afgh. **111** G3
Firozpur Haryana India **99** B8
Firozpur Punjab India **104** C3
Firth r. Y.T. Canada **149** M1
Fīrūzābād Iran **110** D4
Fīrūzkūh Iran **110** D3
Firyuza Turkm. see **Pöwrize**
Fischbach Germany **63** H5
Fischersbrunn Namibia **124** B3
Fish watercourse Namibia **124** C5
Fisher (abandoned) Australia **135** E7
Fisher Bay Antarctica **188** G2
Fisher Glacier Antarctica **188** E2
Fisher River Canada **151** L5
Fishers U.S.A. **164** B4
Fishers Island U.S.A. **165** J3
Fisher Strait Canada **147** J3
Fishguard U.K. **59** C7
Fishing Branch Wilderness Territorial Park Reserve nature res. Y.T. Canada **149** M2
Fishing Creek U.S.A. **165** G4
Fishing Lake Canada **151** M4
Fish Lake Canada **150** F2
Fish Lake AK U.S.A. **149** J2
Fish Point U.S.A. **164** D2
Fish Ponds H.K. China **97** [inset]
Fiske, Cape Antarctica **188** L2
Fiskenæsset Greenland see **Qeqertarsuatsiaat**
Fismes France **62** D5
Fisterra Spain **67** B2
Fisterra, Cabo c. Spain see **Finisterre, Cape**
Fitchburg U.S.A. **160** F3
Fitri, Lac l. Chad **121** E3
Fitton, Mount Y.T. Canada **149** M1
Fitzgerald Canada **151** I3
Fitzgerald U.S.A. **163** D6
Fitzgerald River National Park Australia **135** B8
Fitz Hugh Sound sea chan. Canada **150** D5
Fitz Roy Arg. **178** C7
Fitzroy r. Australia **134** C4
Fitz Roy, Cerro mt. Arg. **178** B7
Fitzroy Crossing Australia **134** D4
Fitzwilliam Island Canada **164** E1
Fiume Croatia see **Rijeka**
Fivemiletown U.K. **61** E3
Five Points U.S.A. **158** C3
Fizi Dem. Rep. Congo **123** C4
Fizuli Azer. see **Füzuli**
Flå Norway **55** F6
Flagstaff S. Africa **125** I6
Flagstaff U.S.A. **159** H4
Flagstaff Lake U.S.A. **162** G2
Flaherty Island Canada **152** F2
Flambeau r. U.S.A. **160** F2
Flamborough Head hd U.K. **58** G4
Fläming hills Germany **63** M2
Flaming Gorge Reservoir U.S.A. **156** F4
Flaminksvlei salt pan S. Africa **124** E6
Flanagan r. Canada **151** M4
Flandre reg. France **62** C4
Flannagan Lake U.S.A. **164** D5
Flannan Isles U.K. **60** B2
Flåsjön l. Sweden **54** I4
Flat r. N.W.T. Canada **149** P3
Flat AK U.S.A. **148** H3
Flat r. U.S.A. **164** C2
Flat Creek Y.T. Canada **149** M3
Flathead r. U.S.A. **154** E2
Flathead Lake U.S.A. **156** E3
Flatiron mt. U.S.A. **156** E3
Flat Island S. China Sea **80** F4
Flat Lick U.S.A. **164** D5
Flattery, Cape Australia **136** D2
Flattery, Cape U.S.A. **156** B2
Flat Top mt. Y.T. Canada **149** M3
Flatwillow Creek r. U.S.A. **156** G3
Flatwoods U.S.A. **164** E4
Fleetmark Germany **63** L2
Fleetwood Australia **136** D4
Fleetwood U.K. **58** D5
Fleetwood U.S.A. **165** H3
Flekkefjord Norway **55** E7
Flemingsburg U.S.A. **164** D4
Flemington U.S.A. **165** H3
Flen Sweden **55** J7
Flensburg Germany **57** L3
Flers France **66** D2
Flesherton Canada **164** E1
Flesko, Tanjung pt Indon. **83** C2
Fletcher Lake Canada **151** I2
Fletcher Peninsula Antarctica **188** L2
Fleur de Lys Canada **153** K4
Fleur-de-May, Lac l. Canada **153** I4
Flinders r. Australia **136** C3
Flinders Chase National Park Australia **137** B7
Flinders Group National Park Australia **136** D2
Flinders Island Australia **137** [inset]
Flinders Passage Australia **136** E3
Flinders Ranges mts Australia **137** B7
Flinders Ranges National Park Australia **137** B6
Flinders Reefs Australia **136** E3
Flin Flon Canada **151** K4
Flint U.K. **58** D5
Flint U.S.A. **164** D2
Flint r. U.S.A. **163** C6
Flint Island Kiribati **187** J6
Flinton Australia **138** D1
Flisa Norway **55** H6

▶**Flissingskiy, Mys** c. Rus. Fed. **76** H2
Most easterly point of Europe.

Flixecourt France **62** C4
Flodden U.K. **58** E3
Flöha Germany **63** N4
Flood Range mts Antarctica **188** J1
Flora r. Australia **134** E3
Flora U.S.A. **164** B3
Florac France **66** F4
Florala U.S.A. **163** C6
Florange France **62** G5
Flora Reef Australia **136** D3
Florence Italy **68** D3
Florence AL U.S.A. **163** C5
Florence AZ U.S.A. **159** H5
Florence CO U.S.A. **157** G5
Florence OR U.S.A. **156** B4
Florence SC U.S.A. **163** E5
Florence WI U.S.A. **160** F2
Florence Junction U.S.A. **159** H5
Florencia Col. **176** C3
Florennes Belgium **62** E4
Florentia Italy see **Florence**
Florentino Ameghino, Embalse resr Arg. **178** C6
Flores r. Arg. **178** E5
Flores Guat. **167** H5
Flores i. Indon. **83** B5
Flores, Laut sea Indon. **83** A4
Flores Island Canada **150** E5
Flores Sea Indon. see **Flores, Laut**
Floresta Brazil **177** K5
Floresville U.S.A. **161** D6
Floriano Brazil **177** J5
Florianópolis Brazil **179** A4
Florida Uruguay **178** E4
Florida state U.S.A. **163** D6
Florida, Straits of Bahamas/U.S.A. **163** D8
Florida Bay U.S.A. **163** D7
Florida City U.S.A. **163** D7
Florida Islands Solomon Is **133** G2
Florida Keys is U.S.A. **163** D7
Florin U.S.A. **158** C2
Florina Greece **69** I4
Florissant U.S.A. **160** F4
Florø Norway **55** D6
Flour Lake Canada **153** I3
Floyd U.S.A. **164** E5
Floyd, Mount U.S.A. **159** G4
Floydada U.S.A. **161** C5
Fluessen l. Neth. **62** F2
Fluk Maluku Indon. **83** C3
Flushing Neth. see **Vlissingen**
Fly r. P.N.G. **81** K8
Flying Fish, Cape Antarctica **188** K2
Flying Mountain U.S.A. **159** I6
Flylân i. Neth. see **Vlieland**
Foam Lake Canada **151** K5
Foča Bos.-Herz. **68** H3
Foça Turkey **69** L5
Fochabers U.K. **60** F3
Focşani Romania **69** L2
Fogang China **97** G4
Foggia Italy **68** F4
Fogi Buru Indon. **83** C3
Fogo i. Cape Verde **120** [inset]
Fogo Island Canada **153** L4
Foinaven hill U.K. **60** E2
Foix France **66** E5
Folda sea chan. Norway **54** I3
Foldereid Norway **54** H4
Foldfjorden sea chan. Norway **54** G4
Folegandros i. Greece **69** K6
Foleyet Canada **152** E4
Foley Island Canada **147** K3
Folger AK U.S.A. **148** H3
Foligno Italy **68** E3
Folkestone U.K. **59** I7
Folkingham U.K. **59** G6
Folkston U.S.A. **163** D6
Folldal Norway **54** G5
Follonica Italy **68** D3
Folsom Lake U.S.A. **158** C2
Fomboni Comoros **123** E5
Fomento Cuba **163** E8
Fomin Rus. Fed. **53** I7
Fominskaya Rus. Fed. **52** K2
Fominskoye Rus. Fed. **52** I4
Fonda U.S.A. **165** H2
Fond-du-Lac Canada **151** J3
Fond du Lac r. Canada **151** J3
Fond du Lac U.S.A. **164** A2
Fondevila Spain **67** B3
Fondi Italy **68** E4
Fonni Sardinia Italy **68** C4
Fonsagrada Spain see **A Fonsagrada**
Fonseca, Golfo do b. Central America **166** [inset] H6
Fontaine Lake Canada **151** J3
Fontanges Canada **153** H3
Fontas Canada **150** F3
Fontas r. Canada **150** F3
Fonte Boa Brazil **176** E4
Fonteneau, Lac l. Canada **153** J4
Fontur pt Iceland **54** [inset]
Foochow China see **Fuzhou**
Foot's Bay Canada **164** F1
Foping China **97** F1
Foraker, Mount AK U.S.A. **149** J3
Foraulep atoll Micronesia see **Faraulep**
Forbes Australia **138** D4
Forbes, Mount Canada **150** G4
Forchheim Germany **63** L5
Ford r. U.S.A. **162** C2
Ford City U.S.A. **158** D4
Førde Norway **55** D6
Forde Lake Canada **151** L2
Fordham U.K. **59** H6
Fordingbridge U.K. **59** F8
Ford Range mts Antarctica **188** J1
Fords Bridge Australia **138** B2
Fordsville U.S.A. **164** B5
Fordyce U.S.A. **161** E5
Forécariah Guinea **120** B4
Forel, Mont mt. Greenland **147** O3
Foreland hd U.K. **59** F8
Foreland Point U.K. **59** D7
Foremost Canada **156** F2
Foresight Mountain Canada **150** E4
Forest Canada **164** E2
Forest MS U.S.A. **161** F5
Forest OH U.S.A. **164** D3
Forestburg Canada **151** H4
Forest Creek r. Australia **136** C3
Forest Hill Australia **138** C5
Forest Ranch U.S.A. **158** C2
Forestville Canada **153** H4
Forestville CA U.S.A. **158** B2
Forestville MI U.S.A. **164** D2
Forfar U.K. **60** G4
Forgan U.S.A. **161** C4
Forges-les-Eaux France **62** B5
Forillon, Parc National de nat. park Canada **153** I4
Forked River U.S.A. **165** H4
Forks U.S.A. **156** B3
Fork Union U.S.A. **165** F5
Forlì Italy **68** E2
Forman U.S.A. **160** D2
Formby U.K. **58** D5
Formentera i. Spain **67** G4
Formentor, Cap de c. Spain **67** H4
Formerie France **62** B5
Former Yugoslav Republic of Macedonia country Europe see **Macedonia**
Formiga Brazil **179** B3
Formosa Arg. **178** E3
Formosa country Asia see **Taiwan**
Formosa Brazil **179** B1
Formosa, Serra hills Brazil **177** G6
Formosa Bay Kenya see **Ungwana Bay**
Formosa Strait China/Taiwan see **Taiwan Strait**
Formoso r. Bahia Brazil **179** B1
Formoso r. Tocantins Brazil **179** A1
Fornos Moz. **125** L2
Forres U.K. **60** F3
Forrest Vic. Australia **138** A7
Forrest W.A. Australia **135** E7
Forrestal Range mts Antarctica **188** A1
Forrest City U.S.A. **161** F5
Forrester Island AK U.S.A. **149** N5
Forrest Lake Canada **151** I3
Forrest Lakes salt flat Australia **135** E7

Fors Sweden 54 J5
Forsayth Australia 136 C3
Forsnäs Sweden 54 M3
Forssa Fin. 55 M6
Forster Australia 138 F4
Forsyth GA U.S.A. 163 D5
Forsyth MT U.S.A. 156 G3
Forsyth Range hills Australia 136 C4
Fort Abbas Pak. 111 I4
Fort Albany Canada 152 E3
Fortaleza Brazil 177 K4
Fort Amsterdam U.S.A. see New York
Fort Archambault Chad see Sarh
Fort Ashby U.S.A. 165 F4
Fort Assiniboine Canada 150 H4
Fort Augustus U.K. 60 E3
Fort Beaufort S. Africa 125 H7
Fort Benton U.S.A. 156 F3
Fort Bragg U.S.A. 158 B2
Fort Branch U.S.A. 164 B4
Fort Carillon U.S.A. see Ticonderoga
Fort Charlet Alg. see Djanet
Fort Chimo Canada see Kuujjuaq
Fort Chipewyan Canada 151 I3
Fort Collins U.S.A. 156 G4
Fort-Coulonge Canada 152 F5
Fort Crampel Cent. Afr. Rep. see Kaga Bandoro
Fort-Dauphin Madag. see Tôlañaro
Fort Davis U.S.A. 161 C6

▶Fort-de-France Martinique 169 L6
Capital of Martinique.

Fort de Kock Sumatera Indon. see Bukittinggi
Fort de Polignac Alg. see Illizi
Fort Deposit AL U.S.A. 167 I1
Fort Dodge U.S.A. 160 E3
Fort Duchesne U.S.A. 159 I1
Fort Edward U.S.A. 165 I2
Fortescue r. Australia 134 B5
Forte Veneza Brazil 177 H5
Fort Flatters Alg. see Bordj Omer Driss
Fort Foureau Cameroon see Kousséri
Fort Franklin N.W.T. Canada see Déljne
Fort Gardel Alg. see Zaouatallaz
Fort Gay U.S.A. 164 D4
Fort George Canada see Chisasibi
Fort Glenn AK U.S.A. 148 F5
Fort Good Hope N.W.T. Canada 149 O2
Fort Gouraud Mauritania see Fdérik
Forth r. U.K. 60 F4
Forth, Firth of est. U.K. 60 F4
Fort Hancock TX U.S.A. 166 D2
Fort Hertz Myanmar see Putao
Fortification Range mts U.S.A. 159 F2
Fortín General Mendoza Para. 178 D2
Fortín Leonida Escobar Para. 178 D2
Fortín Madrejón Para. 178 E2
Fortín Pilcomayo Arg. 178 D2
Fortín Ravelo Bol. 176 F7
Fortín Sargento Primero Leyes Arg. 178 E2
Fortín Suárez Arana Bol. 176 F7
Fortín Teniente Juan Echauri López Para. 178 D2
Fort Jameson Zambia see Chipata
Fort Johnston Malawi see Mangochi
Fort Kent U.S.A. 162 G2
Fort Lamy Chad see Ndjamena
Fort Laperrine Alg. see Tamanrasset
Fort Laramie U.S.A. 156 G4
Fort Lauderdale U.S.A. 163 D7
Fort Liard Canada 150 F2
Fort Mackay Canada 151 I3
Fort Macleod Canada 150 H5
Fort Madison U.S.A. 160 F3
Fort Manning Malawi see Mchinji
Fort McMurray Canada 151 I3
Fort McPherson N.W.T. Canada 149 N2
Fort Meyers Beach U.S.A. 163 D7
Fort Morgan U.S.A. 160 C3
Fort Munro Pak. 111 H4
Fort Myers U.S.A. 163 D7
Fort Nelson Canada 150 F3
Fort Nelson r. Canada 150 F3
Fort Norman N.W.T. Canada see Tulita
Fort Orange U.S.A. see Albany
Fort Payne U.S.A. 163 C5
Fort Peck U.S.A. 156 G2
Fort Peck Reservoir U.S.A. 156 G3
Fort Pierce U.S.A. 163 D7
Fort Portal Uganda 122 D3
Fort Providence Canada 150 G2
Fort Resolution Canada 150 H2
Fortrose N.Z. 139 B8
Fortrose U.K. 60 E3
Fort Rosebery Zambia see Mansa
Fort Rousset Congo see Owando
Fort Rupert Canada see Waskaganish
Fort St James Canada 150 E4
Fort St John Canada 150 F3
Fort Sandeman Pak. see Zhob
Fort Saskatchewan Canada 150 H4
Fort Scott U.S.A. 160 E4
Fort Severn Canada 152 D2
Fort-Shevchenko Kazakh. 100 E2
Fort Simpson Canada 150 F2
Fort Smith Canada 151 H2
Fort Smith U.S.A. 161 E5
Fort Stockton U.S.A. 161 C6
Fort Sumner U.S.A. 157 G6
Fort Supply U.S.A. 161 D4
Fort Thomas U.S.A. 159 I5
Fort Trinquet Mauritania see Bîr Mogreïn
Fortuna U.S.A. 160 C1
Fortune Bay Canada 153 L5
Fort Valley U.S.A. 163 D5
Fort Vermilion Canada 150 G3
Fort Victoria Zimbabwe see Masvingo
Fort Walton Beach FL U.S.A. 167 I2
Fort Ware Canada see Ware
Fort Wayne U.S.A. 164 C3
Fort William U.K. 60 D4
Fort Worth U.S.A. 161 D5
Fort Yates U.S.A. 160 C2
Fortymile r. Canada/U.S.A. 149 L2
Fortymile, Middle Fork r. AK U.S.A. 149 L2
Fortymile, West Fork r. AK U.S.A. 149 L2
Fort Yukon AK U.S.A. 149 K2
Forum Iulii France see Fréjus
Forūr, Jazīreh-ye i. Iran 110 D5
Forvik Norway 54 H4
Foshan China 97 G4
Fo Shek Chau H.K. China see Basalt Island
Fossano Italy 68 B2
Fossil U.S.A. 156 C3
Fossil Downs Australia 134 D4
Foster Australia 138 C7
Foster U.S.A. 164 C4
Foster, Mount Canada/U.S.A. 149 N4
Foster Lakes Canada 151 J3
Fostoria U.S.A. 164 D3
Fotadrevo Madag. 123 E6
Fotherby U.K. 58 G5
Fotokol Cameroon 121 E3
Fotuna i. Vanuatu see Futuna
Fougères France 66 D2
Foula i. U.K. 60 [inset]
Foul Island Myanmar 86 A3
Foulness Point U.K. 59 H7
Foul Point Sri Lanka 106 D4
Foumban Cameroon 120 E4
Foundation Ice Stream glacier Antarctica 188 L1
Fount U.S.A. 164 D5
Fountains Abbey and Royal Water Garden (NT) tourist site U.K. 58 F4
Fourches, Mont des hill France 66 G2
Four Corners U.S.A. 158 E4
Fouriesburg S. Africa 125 I5
Fourmies France 62 E4
Four Mountains, Islands of the AK U.S.A. 148 E5
Fournier, Lac l. Canada 153 I4
Fournoi i. Greece 69 L6
Fourpeaked Mountain AK U.S.A. 148 I4
Fouta Djallon reg. Guinea 120 B3
Foveaux Strait N.Z. 139 A8
Fowey r. U.K. 59 C8
Fowler CO U.S.A. 157 G5
Fowler IN U.S.A. 164 B3
Fowler Ice Rise Antarctica 188 L1
Fowlers Bay Australia 132 D5
Fowlers Bay b. Australia 135 F8
Fowlerville U.S.A. 164 C2
Fox r. B.C. Canada 150 E3
Fox r. Man. Canada 151 M3
Fox r. U.S.A. 160 F3
Fox Creek Canada 150 G4
Fox Creek U.S.A. 164 C5
Foxdale Isle of Man 58 C4
Foxe Basin g. Canada 147 K3
Foxe Channel Canada 147 J3
Foxe Peninsula Canada 147 K3
Fox Glacier N.Z. 139 C6
Fox Islands AK U.S.A. 148 E5
Fox Lake Canada 150 H3
Fox Mountain Y.T. Canada 149 N3
Fox Valley Canada 151 I5
Foyers U.K. 60 E3
Foyle r. Ireland/U.K. 61 E3
Foyle, Lough b. Ireland/U.K. 61 E2
Foynes Ireland 61 C5
Foz de Areia, Represa de resr Brazil 179 A4
Foz do Cunene Angola 123 B5
Foz do Iguaçu Brazil 178 F3
Fraga Spain 67 G3
Frakes, Mount Antarctica 188 K1
Framingham U.S.A. 165 J2
Framnes Mountains Antarctica 188 E2
Franca Brazil 179 B3
Français, Récif des reef New Caledonia 133 G3
Francavilla Fontana Italy 68 G4

▶France country Europe 66 F3
3rd largest and 3rd most populous country in Europe.

Frances Australia 137 C8
Frances r. Y.T. Canada 149 O3
Frances Lake Canada 150 D2
Frances Lake Y.T. Canada 149 O3
Franceville Gabon 122 B4
Francis Canada 151 K5
Francis atoll Kiribati see Beru
Francis, Lake U.S.A. 165 J1
Francisco de Orellana Orellana Ecuador see Coca
Francisco de Orellana Ecuador see Coca
Francisco I. Madero Coahuila Mex. 166 E3
Francisco I. Madero Durango Mex. 161 B7
Francisco Zarco Mex. 166 A1
Francistown Botswana 123 C6
Francois Canada 153 K5
François Lake Canada 150 E4
Francois Peron National Park Australia 135 A6
Francs Peak U.S.A. 156 F4
Franeker Neth. 62 F1
Frankenberg Germany 63 N4
Frankenberg (Eder) Germany 63 I3
Frankenhöhe hills Germany 57 M6
Frankenmuth U.S.A. 164 D2
Frankenthal (Pfalz) Germany 63 I5
Frankenwald mts Germany 63 L4
Frankford Canada 165 G1
Frankfort IN U.S.A. 164 B3

▶Frankfort KY U.S.A. 164 C4
Capital of Kentucky.

Frankfort MI U.S.A. 164 B1
Frankfort OH U.S.A. 164 D4
Frankfurt Germany see Frankfurt am Main
Frankfurt am Main Germany 63 I4
Frankfurt an der Oder Germany 57 O4
Frank Hann National Park Australia 135 C8
Frankin Lake U.S.A. 159 F1
Fränkische Alb hills Germany 63 K6
Fränkische Schweiz reg. Germany 63 L5
Frankland, Cape Australia 137 [inset]
Franklin AZ U.S.A. 159 I5
Franklin GA U.S.A. 163 C5
Franklin IN U.S.A. 164 B4
Franklin KY U.S.A. 164 B5
Franklin LA U.S.A. 161 F6
Franklin MA U.S.A. 165 J2
Franklin NC U.S.A. 163 D5
Franklin NE U.S.A. 160 D3
Franklin NH U.S.A. 165 J2
Franklin PA U.S.A. 164 F3
Franklin TN U.S.A. 162 C5
Franklin TX U.S.A. 161 D6
Franklin VA U.S.A. 165 G5
Franklin WV U.S.A. 164 F4
Franklin, Point pt AK U.S.A. 148 H1
Franklin Bay N.W.T. Canada 149 P1
Franklin D. Roosevelt Lake resr U.S.A. 156 D2
Franklin Furnace U.S.A. 164 D4
Franklin-Gordon National Park Australia 137 [inset]
Franklin Island Antarctica 188 H1
Franklin Mountains N.W.T. Canada 149 Q3
Franklin Mountains AK U.S.A. 149 K1
Franklin Strait Canada 147 I2
Franklinton U.S.A. 161 F6
Franklinville U.S.A. 165 F2
Frankston Australia 138 B7
Fränsta Sweden 54 J5
Frantsa-Iosifa, Zemlya is Rus. Fed. 76 G2
Franz Canada 152 D4
Franz Josef Glacier N.Z. 139 C6
Frasca, Capo della c. Sardinia Italy 68 C5
Frascati Italy 68 E4
Fraser r. Australia 134 C4
Fraser r. B.C. Canada 150 F5
Fraser r. Nfld. and Lab. Canada 153 J2
Fraser, Mount hill Australia 135 B6
Fraserburg S. Africa 124 E6
Fraserburgh U.K. 60 G3
Fraserdale Canada 152 E4
Fraser Island Australia 136 F5
Fraser Island National Park Australia 136 F5
Fraser Lake Canada 150 E4
Fraser National Park Australia 138 B6
Fraser Plateau Canada 150 E4
Fraser Range hills Australia 135 C8
Frauenfeld Switz. 66 I3
Fray Bentos Uruguay 178 E4
Frazeysburg U.S.A. 164 D3
Frechen Germany 62 G4
Freckleton U.K. 58 E5
Frederic U.S.A. 164 C1
Frederica U.S.A. 165 H4
Fredericia Denmark 55 F9
Frederick MD U.S.A. 165 G4
Frederick OK U.S.A. 161 D5
Frederick Reef Australia 136 F4
Fredericksburg TX U.S.A. 161 D6
Fredericksburg VA U.S.A. 165 G4
Frederick Sound sea channel AK U.S.A. 149 N4
Fredericktown U.S.A. 160 F4

▶Fredericton Canada 153 I5
Capital of New Brunswick.

Frederikshåb Greenland see Paamiut
Frederikshavn Denmark 55 G8
Frederiksværk Denmark 55 H9
Fredonia AZ U.S.A. 159 G3
Fredonia KS U.S.A. 161 E4
Fredonia NY U.S.A. 164 F2
Fredonia WI U.S.A. 164 B2
Fredrika Sweden 54 K4
Fredrikshamn Fin. see Hamina
Fredrikstad Norway 55 G7
Freedonyer Peak U.S.A. 158 C1
Freehold U.S.A. 165 H3
Freeland U.S.A. 165 H3
Freeling Heights hill Australia 137 B6
Freel Peak U.S.A. 158 D2
Freels, Cape Canada 153 L4
Freeman U.S.A. 160 D3
Freeman, Lake U.S.A. 164 B3
Freeport FL U.S.A. 163 C6
Freeport IL U.S.A. 160 F3
Freeport TX U.S.A. 161 E6
Freeport City Bahamas 163 E7
Freer U.S.A. 161 D7
Freesoil U.S.A. 164 B1
Free State prov. S. Africa 125 H5

▶Freetown Sierra Leone 120 B4
Capital of Sierra Leone.

Fregenal de la Sierra Spain 67 C4
Fregon Australia 135 F6
Fréhel, Cap c. France 66 C2
Frei (Chile) research station Antarctica 188 A2
Freiberg Germany 63 N4
Freiburg Switz. see Fribourg
Freiburg im Breisgau Germany 57 K6
Freisen Germany 63 H5
Freising Germany 57 M6
Freistadt Austria 57 O6
Fréjus France 66 H5
Fremantle Australia 135 A8
Fremont CA U.S.A. 158 C3
Fremont IN U.S.A. 164 C3
Fremont MI U.S.A. 164 C2
Fremont NE U.S.A. 160 D3
Fremont OH U.S.A. 164 D3
Fremont r. U.S.A. 159 H2
Fremont Junction U.S.A. 159 H2
Frenchburg U.S.A. 164 D5
French Cay i. Turks and Caicos Is 163 F8
French Congo country Africa see Congo

▶French Guiana terr. S. America 177 H3
French Overseas Department.

French Guinea country Africa see Guinea
French Island Australia 138 B7
French Lick U.S.A. 164 B4
Frenchman r. U.S.A. 156 G2
Frenchman Lake CA U.S.A. 158 C2
Frenchman Lake NV U.S.A. 159 F3
Frenchpark Ireland 61 D4
French Pass N.Z. 139 D5

▶French Polynesia terr. S. Pacific Ocean 187 K7
French Overseas Country.

French Somaliland country Africa see Djibouti

▶French Southern and Antarctic Lands terr. Indian Ocean 185 M8
French Overseas Territory.

French Sudan country Africa see Mali
French Territory of the Afars and Issas country Africa see Djibouti
Frenda Alg. 67 G6
Frentsjer Neth. see Franeker
Freren Germany 63 H2
Fresco r. Brazil 177 H5
Freshford Ireland 61 E5
Fresnillo Mex. 168 D4
Fresno U.S.A. 158 D3
Fresno r. U.S.A. 158 C3
Fresno Reservoir U.S.A. 156 F2
Fressel, Lac l. Canada 152 G3
Freu, Cap des c. Spain 67 H4
Freudenberg Germany 63 H4
Freudenstadt Germany 57 L6
Frévent France 62 C4
Frew watercourse Australia 136 A4
Frewena Australia 136 A3
Freycinet Estuary inlet Australia 135 A6
Freycinet Peninsula Australia 137 [inset]
Freyenstein Germany 63 M1
Freyming-Merlebach France 62 G5
Fria Guinea 120 B3
Fria, Cape Namibia 123 B5
Friant U.S.A. 158 D3
Frias Arg. 178 C3
Fribourg Switz. 66 H3
Friday Harbor U.S.A. 156 C2
Friedeburg Germany 63 H1
Friedens U.S.A. 165 F3
Friedland Rus. Fed. see Pravdinsk
Friedrichshafen Germany 57 L7
Friedrichskanal canal Germany 63 L2
Friend U.S.A. 160 D3
Friendly Islands country S. Pacific Ocean see Tonga
Friendship U.S.A. 160 F3
Friesack Germany 63 M2
Friese Wad tidal flat Neth. 62 F1
Friesoythe Germany 63 H1
Frinton-on-Sea U.K. 59 I7
Frio r. U.S.A. 161 D6
Frio watercourse U.S.A. 161 C5
Frisco Mountain U.S.A. 159 G2
Frissell, Mount hill U.S.A. 165 I2
Fritzlar Germany 63 J3
Frjentsjer Neth. see Franeker
Frobisher Bay Canada see Iqaluit
Frobisher Bay b. Canada 147 L3
Frobisher Lake Canada 151 I3
Frohavet b. Norway 54 F5
Frohburg Germany 63 M3
Froissy France 62 C5
Frolovo Rus. Fed. 53 I6
Frome watercourse Australia 137 B6
Frome U.K. 59 E7
Frome r. U.K. 59 E8
Frome, Lake salt flat Australia 137 B6
Frome Downs Australia 137 B6
Fröndenberg Germany 63 H3
Frontera Coahuila Mex. 167 E3
Frontera Tabasco Mex. 167 G5
Frontera, Punta pt Mex. 167 G5
Fronteras Mex. 166 C2
Front Royal U.S.A. 165 F4
Frosinone Italy 68 E4
Frostburg U.S.A. 165 F4
Frøya i. Norway 54 F5
Fruges France 62 C4
Fruita U.S.A. 159 I2
Fruitland U.S.A. 159 H1
Fruitvale U.S.A. 159 I2
Frunze Kyrg. see Bishkek
Frusino Italy see Frosinone
Fruška Gora nat. park Serbia 69 H2
Frýdek-Místek Czech Rep. 57 Q6
Fu'an China 97 H3
Fucheng Anhui China see Fengyang
Fucheng Shaanxi China see Fuxian
Fuchū Japan 93 F3
Fuchū Toyama Japan 92 D2
Fuchuan China 97 F3
Fuchun Jiang r. China 97 I2
Fude China 97 H3
Fuding China 97 I3
Fudul reg. Saudi Arabia 110 B6
Fuenlabrada Spain 67 E3
Fuerte r. Mex. 157 F8
Fuerte Olimpo Para. 178 E2
Fuerteventura i. Canary Is 120 B2
Fufeng China 96 E1
Fuga i. Phil. 82 C2
Fugong China 96 C3
Fugou China 97 G1
Fugu Shaanxi China 95 G4
Fuguo Shandong China see Zhanhua
Fuhai Xinjiang China 98 D3
Fuhai Linchang Xinjiang China 98 E3
Fuḩaymī Iraq 113 F4
Fujairah U.A.E. 110 E5
Fujeira U.A.E. see Fujairah
Fuji Japan 93 E3
Fujian prov. China 97 H3
Fujieda Japan 93 E4
Fuji-Hakone-Izu Kokuritsu-kōen nat. park Japan 93 F4
Fujihashi Japan 92 C3
Fujiidera Japan 92 B4
Fujikawa Japan 93 E3
Fuji-kawa r. Japan 93 E3
Fujimi Nagano Japan 93 E3
Fujimi Saitama Japan 93 F3
Fujin China 90 C3
Fujino Japan 93 F3
Fujinomiya Japan 93 E3
Fujioka Aichi Japan 92 D3
Fujioka Gunma Japan 93 F2
Fujioka Tochigi Japan 93 F2
Fuji-san vol. Japan 93 E3
Fujisawa Japan 93 F3
Fujishiro Japan 93 G3
Fujiwara Mie Japan 92 C3
Fujiwara Tochigi Japan 93 F2
Fujiyoshida Japan 93 E3
Fūka Egypt see Fūkah
Fūkah Egypt 112 B5
Fukang Xinjiang China 98 D3
Fukaya Japan 93 F2
Fukiage Japan 93 F2
Fukien prov. China see Fujian
Fukuchiyama Japan 92 B3
Fukude Japan 93 D4
Fukue-jima i. Japan 91 C6
Fukui Japan 92 C2
Fukui pref. Japan 92 C3
Fukumitsu Japan 92 C2
Fukuno Japan 92 C2
Fukuoka Japan 91 C6
Fukuoka Gifu Japan 92 D3
Fukuoka Toyama Japan 92 C2
Fukuroi Japan 93 D4
Fukusaki Japan 92 A4
Fukushima Japan 91 F5
Fukuyama Japan 91 C7
Fûl, Gebel hill Egypt see Fūl, Jabal
Fūl, Jabal hill Egypt 107 A5
Fulchhari Bangl. 105 G4
Fulda Germany 63 J4
Fulda r. Germany 63 J3
Fulham U.K. 59 G7
Fuli China see Jixian
Fuliji China 97 H1
Fuling China 96 E2
Fulitun China see Jixian
Fullerton CA U.S.A. 158 E5
Fullerton NE U.S.A. 160 D3
Fullerton, Cape Canada 151 N2
Fulton IN U.S.A. 164 B3
Fulton MO U.S.A. 160 F4
Fulton MS U.S.A. 161 F5
Fulton NY U.S.A. 165 G2
Fumane Moz. 125 K3
Fumay France 62 E5
Fumin China 96 D3
Funabashi Chiba Japan 93 F3
Funabashi Toyama Japan 92 D2
Funafuti atoll Tuvalu 133 H2
Funan China 97 G1

▶Funchal Madeira 120 B1
Capital of Madeira.

Fundão Brazil 179 C2
Fundão Port. 67 C3
Fundi Italy see Fondi
Fundición Mex. 166 C3
Fundy, Bay of g. Canada 153 I5
Fundy National Park Canada 153 I5
Fünen i. Denmark see Fyn
Funeral Peak U.S.A. 158 E3
Fünfkirchen Hungary see Pécs
Fung Wong Shan hill H.K. China see Lantau Peak
Funhalouro Moz. 125 L2
Funing Jiangsu China 97 H1
Funing Yunnan China 96 E4
Funiu Shan mts China 97 F1
Funtua Nigeria 120 D3
Funzie U.K. 60 [inset]
Fuping Hebei China 95 H4
Fuping Shaanxi China 95 G5
Fuqing China 97 H3
Fūrgun, Kūh-e mt. Iran 110 E5
Furmanov Rus. Fed. 52 I4
Furmanovka Kazakh. see Moyynkum
Furmanovo Kazakh. see Zhalpaktal
Furnás hill Spain 67 G4
Furnas, Represa resr Brazil 179 B3
Furneaux Group is Australia 137 [inset]
Furnes Belgium see Veurne
Furong China see Wan'an
Fürstenau Germany 63 H2
Fürstenberg Germany 63 N1
Fürstenwalde Germany 57 O4
Fürth Germany 63 K5
Furth im Wald Germany 63 M5
Furudono Japan 93 G1
Furukawa Gifu Japan 92 D2
Furukawa Japan 91 F5
Fury and Hecla Strait Canada 147 J3
Fusan S. Korea see Pusan
Fushan Shandong China 95 J4
Fushan Shanxi China 95 G5
Fushimi Japan 92 B4
Fushun Liaoning China 95 J3
Fushuncheng Liaoning China see Shuncheng
Fuso Japan 92 C3
Fusong China 90 B4
Fussa Japan 93 F3
Futaba Japan 93 E3
Futagawa Japan 92 D4
Futago-yama mt. Japan 93 E2
Futami Japan 92 C4
Fu Tau Pun Chau i. H.K. China 97 [inset]
Futtsu Japan 93 F3
Futtsu-misaki pt Japan 93 F3
Futuna i. Vanuatu 133 H3
Futuna Islands Wallis and Futuna Is see Hoorn, Îles de
Fuxian Liaoning China see Wafangdian
Fuxian Shaanxi China 95 G5
Fuxian Hu l. China 96 D3
Fuxin Liaoning China 95 J3
Fuxin Liaoning China 95 J3
Fuxing China see Wangmo
Fuxinzhen Liaoning China see Fuxin
Fuyang Anhui China 97 G1
Fuyang Guangxi China see Fuchuan
Fuyang Zhejiang China 97 H2
Fuyang He r. China 95 I4
Fuying Dao i. China 97 I3
Fuyu Anhui China see Susong
Fuyu Heilong. China 95 K2
Fuyu Jilin China see Songyuan
Fuyu Jilin China 90 B3
Fuyuan Heilong. China 90 D2
Fuyuan Yunnan China 96 E3
Fuyun Xinjiang China 94 B2
Fuzhou Fujian China 97 H3
Fuzhou Jiangxi China 97 H3
Füzuli Azer. 113 G3
Fyn i. Denmark 55 G9
Fyne, Loch inlet U.K. 60 D5
F.Y.R.O.M. (Former Yugoslav Republic of Macedonia) country Europe see Macedonia

G

Gaaf Atoll Maldives see Huvadhu Atoll
Gaâfour Tunisia 68 C6
Gaalkacyo Somalia 122 E3
Gaat r. Malaysia 85 F2
Gabakly Turkm. 111 F2
Gabasumdo Qinghai China see Tongde
Gabbs U.S.A. 158 E2
Gabbs Valley Range mts U.S.A. 158 D2
Gabd Pak. 111 F5
Gabela Angola 123 B5
Gaberones Botswana see Gaborone
Gabès Tunisia 64 G5
Gabès, Golfe de g. Tunisia 64 G5
Gabo Island Australia 138 D6
Gabon country Africa 122 B4

▶Gaborone Botswana 125 G3
Capital of Botswana.

Gābrīk Iran 110 E5
Gabrovo Bulg. 69 K3
Gabú Guinea-Bissau 120 B3
Gadag India 106 B3
Gadaisu P.N.G. 136 E1
Gadap Pak. 111 G5
Gadchiroli India 106 D1
Gäddede Sweden 54 I4
Gadê China 96 C1
Gades Spain see Cádiz
Gadhka India 111 H6
Gadhra India 104 B5
Gadra Pak. 111 H5
Gadsden U.S.A. 163 C5
Gadsden AZ U.S.A. 166 B1
Gadwal India 106 C2
Gadyach Ukr. see Hadyach
Gaer U.K. 59 D7
Găeşti Romania 69 K2
Gaeta Italy 68 E4
Gaeta, Golfo di g. Italy 68 E4
Gaferut i. Micronesia 81 L5
Gaffney U.S.A. 163 D5
Gafsa Tunisia 68 C7
Gag i. Papua Indon. 83 D3
Gagarin Rus. Fed. 53 G5
Gagnoa Côte d'Ivoire 120 C4
Gagnon Canada 153 H4
Gago Coutinho Angola see Lumbala N'guimbo
Gagra Georgia 53 I8
Gahai Qinghai China 94 D4
Gaiab watercourse Namibia 124 D5
Gaibanda Bangl. see Gaibandha
Gaibandha Bangl. 105 G4
Gaïdouronisi i. Greece 69 K7
Gaifi, Wâdi el watercourse Egypt see Jayfī, Wādī al
Gail U.S.A. 161 C5
Gaildorf Germany 63 J6
Gaillac France 66 E5
Gaillimh Ireland see Galway
Gaillon France 62 B5
Gaindainqoinkor Xizang China 99 E7
Gainesboro U.S.A. 164 C5
Gainesville FL U.S.A. 163 D6
Gainesville GA U.S.A. 163 D5
Gainesville MO U.S.A. 161 E4
Gainesville TX U.S.A. 161 D5
Gainsborough U.K. 58 G5
Gairdner, Lake salt flat Australia 137 A6
Gairloch U.K. 60 D3
Gair Loch b. U.K. 60 D3
Gaixian Liaoning China see Gaizhou
Gaizhou Liaoning China 95 J3
Gajah Hutan, Bukit hill Malaysia 84 C1
Gajipur India see Ghazipur
Gajol India 105 G4
Gakarosa mt. S. Africa 124 F4
Gakona AK U.S.A. 149 K3
Gala Xizang China 99 E7
Galaasiya Uzbek. see Galaosiyo
Gala Co l. China 99 E7
Galâla el Bahariya, Gebel el plat. Egypt see Jalālah al Baḩrīyah, Jabal
Galana r. Kenya 122 E4
Galang Besar i. Indon. 84 D2
Galanta Slovakia 57 P6
Galaosiyo Uzbek. 111 G2

▶Galapagos Islands is Ecuador 187 O6
Part of Ecuador. Most westerly point of South America.

Galapagos Rise sea feature Pacific Ocean 187 N6
Galashiels U.K. 60 G5
Galaţi Romania 69 M2
Galatina Italy 68 H4
Gala Water r. U.K. 60 G5
Galax U.S.A. 164 E5
Galaýmor Turkm. 111 F3
Galaymor Turkm. see Galaýmor
Galbally Ireland 61 D5
Galdhøpiggen mt. Norway 55 F6
Galeana Chihuahua Mex. 166 D2
Galeana Nuevo León Mex. 167 E3
Galela Halmahera Indon. 83 C2
Galena AK U.S.A. 148 H2
Galena IL U.S.A. 160 F3
Galena MD U.S.A. 165 H4
Galena MO U.S.A. 161 E4
Galera, Punta pt Chile 178 B6
Galera, Punta pt Mex. 167 F6
Galesburg IL U.S.A. 160 F3
Galesburg MI U.S.A. 164 C2
Galeshewe S. Africa 124 G5
Galeton U.S.A. 165 G3
Galey r. Ireland 61 C5
Galheirão r. Brazil 179 B1
Galiano Island Canada 150 F5
Galich Rus. Fed. 52 I4
Galichskaya Vozvyshennost' hills Rus. Fed. 52 I4
Galicia aut. comm. Spain 67 C2
Galičica nat. park Macedonia 69 I4
Galilee, Lake salt flat Australia 136 D4
Galilee, Sea of l. Israel 107 B3
Galion U.S.A. 164 D3
Galiuro Mountains U.S.A. 159 H5
Galizia aut. comm. Spain see Galicia
Gallabat Sudan 108 E7
G'allaorol Uzbek. 111 G1
Gallatin MO U.S.A. 160 E4
Gallatin TN U.S.A. 164 B5
Galle Sri Lanka 106 D5
Gallego Rise sea feature Pacific Ocean 187 M6
Gallegos r. Arg. 178 C8
Gallia country Europe see France

▶Gallinas, Punta pt Col. 176 D1
Most northerly point of South America.

Gallipoli Italy 68 H4
Gallipoli Turkey 69 L4
Gallipolis U.S.A. 164 D4
Gällivare Sweden 54 L3
Gällö Sweden 54 I5
Gallo Island U.S.A. 165 G2
Gallo Mountains U.S.A. 159 I4
Gallup U.S.A. 159 I4
Galmisdale U.K. 60 C4
Galong Australia 138 D5
Galoya Sri Lanka 106 D4
Gal Oya National Park Sri Lanka 106 D5

Galshar *Hentiy* Mongolia **95** G2
Galston U.K. **60** E5
Galt Mongolia **94** D1
Galt U.S.A. **158** C2
Galtat Zemmour W. Sahara **120** B2
Galtee Mountains *hills* Ireland **61** D5
Galtymore *hill* Ireland **56** C4
Galūgāh, Kūh-e *mts* Iran **110** D4
Galuut Mongolia **94** E2
Galveston *IN* U.S.A. **164** B3
Galveston *TX* U.S.A. **161** E6
Galveston Bay U.S.A. **161** E6
Galwa Nepal **105** E3
Galway Ireland **61** C4
Galway Bay Ireland **61** C4
Gam *i. Papua* Indon. **83** D3
Gam *i. Papua* Indon. **83** D3
Gâm, Sông *r.* Vietnam **86** D2
Gamagōri Japan **92** D4
Gamalakhe S. Africa **125** J6
Gamalama *vol. Maluku* Indon. **83** C2
Gamay Bay *Samar* Phil. **82** D3
Gamba *Xizang* China *see* **Gongbalou**
Gamba Gabon **122** A4
Gambēla Eth. **122** D3
Gambēla National Park Eth. **122** D3
Gambell *AK* U.S.A. **148** E3
Gambella Eth. *see* **Gambēla**
Gambia, The *country* Africa **120** B3
Gambier, Îles *is* Fr. Polynesia **187** L7
Gambier Islands Australia **137** B7
Gambier Islands Fr. Polynesia *see* **Gambier, Îles**
Gambo Canada **153** L4
Gamboma Congo **122** B4
Gamboola Australia **136** C3
Gamboula Cent. Afr. Rep. **122** B3
Gamda China *see* **Zamtang**
Gamêtî *N.W.T.* Canada **149** R2
Gamkunoro, Gunung *vol. Halmahera* Indon. **83** C2
Gamlakarleby Fin. *see* **Kokkola**
Gamleby Sweden **55** J8
Gammelstaden Sweden **54** M4
Gammon Ranges National Park Australia **137** B6
Gamō Japan **92** C3
Gamova, Mys *pt* Rus. Fed. **90** C4
Gamshadzai Kūh *mts* Iran **111** F4
Gamtog China **96** C2
Gamud *mt.* Eth. **122** D3
Gamzigrad-Romuliana *tourist site* Serbia **69** J3
Gana China **96** D1
Ganado U.S.A. **159** I4
Gananoque Canada **165** G1
Gäncä Azer. **113** G2
Gancaohu *Xinjiang* China **98** E4
Gancheng China **97** F5
Ganda Angola **123** B5
Ganda *Xizang* China **99** F7
Gandadiwata, Bukit *mt.* Indon. **83** A3
Gandaingoin China **105** G3
Gandajika Dem. Rep. Congo **123** C4
Gandak Barrage Nepal **105** E4
Gandari Mountain Pak. **111** H4
Gandava Pak. **111** G4
Gander Canada **153** L4
Ganderkesee Germany **63** I1
Gandesa Spain **67** G3
Gandhidham India **104** B5
Gandhinagar India **104** C5
Gandhi Sagar *resr* India **104** C4
Gandia Spain **67** F4
Gandu *Qinghai* China **94** E5
Gandzha Azer. *see* **Gäncä**
Ganes Creek *AK* U.S.A. **148** H3
Ganga *r.* Bangl./India **105** G5 *see* **Ganges**
Ganga Cone *sea feature* Indian Ocean *see* **Ganges Cone**
Gangán Arg. **178** C6
Ganganagar India **104** C3
Gangapur India **104** D4
Ganga Sera India **104** B4
Gangaw Myanmar **86** A2
Gangawati India **106** C3
Gangaw Range *mts* Myanmar **86** B2
Gangca *Qinghai* China **94** E4
Gangdisê Shan *mts Xizang* China **99** C7
Ganges *r.* Bangl./India **105** G5 *also known as* *Ganga*
Ganges France **66** F5
Ganges, Mouths of the Bangl./India **105** G5
Ganges Cone *sea feature* Indian Ocean **185** N4
Gangou *Qinghai* China **94** D4
Gangouyi *Gansu* China **94** F5
Gangra Turkey *see* **Çankırı**
Gangtok India **105** G4
Gangu *Gansu* China **94** F5
Gangziyao *Hebei* China **95** H4
Gan He *r.* China **95** K1
Ganhezi *Xinjiang* China **98** E3
Gani *Halmahera* Indon. **83** D3
Gan Jiang *r.* China **97** H2
Ganjig *Nei Mongol* China **95** J3
Ganjing *Shaanxi* China **95** G5
Ganjur Sum *Nei Mongol* China **95** H2
Ganluo China **96** D2
Ganmain Australia **138** C5
Gannan *Heilong.* China **95** J2
Gannat France **66** F3
Gannett Peak U.S.A. **156** F4
Ganq *Qinghai* China **99** F5
Ganquan *Shaanxi* China **95** G4
Ganshui China **96** E2
Gansu *prov.* China **94** D3
Gantang *Nei Mongol* China **94** F4
Gantheaume Point Australia **134** C4
Ganting *Shaanxi* China *see* **Huxian**
Gantsevichi Belarus *see* **Hantsavichy**
Gantung Indon. **85** E3
Ganxian China **97** G3
Ganye Nigeria **120** E4
Ganyu *Jiangsu* China **95** I5
Ganyushkino Kazakh. **51** P6
Ganzhou China **97** G3
Ganzi Sudan **121** G4
Gao Mali **120** C3
Gaoba *Gansu* China **94** E4
Gaocheng *Hebei* China **95** H4
Gaocheng China *see* **Litang**
Gaocun China *see* **Mayang**
Gaohe China *see* **Huaining**
Gaohebu China *see* **Huaining**
Gaolan *Gansu* China **94** E4
Gaoleshan China *see* **Xianfeng**
Gaoliangjian China *see* **Hongze**
Gaoling *Shaanxi* China **95** G5
Gaomi *Shandong* China **95** I4
Gaomutang China **97** F3
Gaoping *Shanxi* China **95** H5
Gaoqing *Shandong* China **95** I4
Gaotai *Gansu* China **94** D4
Gaotang *Shandong* China **95** I4
Gaoth Dobhair Ireland **61** D2
Gaoting China *see* **Daishan**
Gaotingzhen China *see* **Daishan**
Gaotouyao *Nei Mongol* China **95** G4
Gaoua Burkina Faso **120** C3
Gaoual Guinea **120** B3
Gaoxiong Taiwan *see* **Kaohsiung**
Gaoyang *Hebei* China **95** H4
Gaoyao China *see* **Zhaoqing**
Gaoyi *Hebei* China **95** H4
Gaoyou China **97** H1
Gaoyou Hu *l.* China **97** H1
Gap France **66** H4
Gapan *Luzon* Phil. **82** C3
Gapuwiyak Australia **136** A2
Gaqoi *Xizang* China **99** C7
Gaqung *Xizang* China **99** D7
Gar China **104** E2
Gar Pak. **111** F5
Gar' *r.* Rus. Fed. **90** C1
Gara, Lough *l.* Ireland **61** D4
Garabekevyul Turkm. *see* **Garabekewül**
Garabekewül Turkm. **111** G2
Garabil Belentligi *hills* Turkm. **111** F2
Garabogaz Turkm. **113** I2
Garabogaz Aylagy *b.* Turkm. *see* **Garabogazköl Aýlagy**
Garabogazköl Aýlagy *b.* Turkm. **113** I2
Garabogazköl Aylagy *b.* Turkm. *see* **Garabogazköl Aýlagy**
Garabogazköl Bogazy *sea chan.* Turkm. **113** I2
Garachiné Panama **166** [inset] K7
Garachiné, Punta *pt* Panama **166** [inset] K7
Garägheh Iran **111** F4
Garagum *des.* Turkm. **110** E2
Garagum *des.* Turkm. *see* **Karakum Desert**
Garagum Kanaly *canal* Turkm. **111** F2
Garah Australia **138** D2
Garalo Mali **120** C3
Garamätnyýaz Turkm. **111** G2
Garamätnyyaz Turkm. *see* **Garamätnyýaz**
Garamba *r.* Dem. Rep. Congo **122** C3
Garang *Qinghai* China **94** E4
Garanhuns Brazil **177** K5
Ga-Rankuwa S. Africa **125** H3
Garapuava Brazil **179** B2
Gárasavvon Sweden *see* **Karesuando**
Garautha India **104** D4
Garba China *see* **Jiulong**
Garbahaarrey Somalia **122** E3
Garba Tula Kenya **122** D3
Garberville U.S.A. **158** B1
Garbsen Germany **63** J2
Garça Brazil **179** A3
Garco China **105** G2
Garda, Lago di Italy *see* **Garda, Lake**
Garda, Lake Italy **68** D2
Garde, Cap de *c.* Alg. **68** B6
Gardelegen Germany **63** L2
Garden City U.S.A. **160** C4
Garden Hill Canada **151** M4
Garden Mountain U.S.A. **164** E5
Gardeyz Afgh. *see* **Gardēz**
Gardēz Afgh. **111** H3
Gardinas Belarus *see* **Hrodna**
Gardiner U.S.A. **165** K1
Gardiner, Mount Australia **134** F5
Gardiner Range *hills* Australia **134** E4
Gardiners Island U.S.A. **165** I3
Gardīz Afgh. *see* **Gardēz**
Gardner *atoll* Micronesia *see* **Faraulep**
Gardner U.S.A. **165** J2
Gardner Inlet Antarctica **188** L1
Gardner Island *atoll* Kiribati *see* **Nikumaroro**
Gardner Pinnacles *is* U.S.A. **186** I4
Gáregasnjárga Fin. *see* **Karigasniemi**
Garelochhead U.K. **60** E4
Gareloi Island *AK* U.S.A. **149** [inset]
Garet el Djenoun *mt.* Alg. **120** D2
Gargano, Parco Nazionale del *nat. park* Italy **68** F4
Gargantua, Cape Canada **152** D5
Gargunsa China *see* **Gar**
Gargždai Lith. **55** L9
Garhchiroli India *see* **Gadchiroli**
Garhi *Madh. Prad.* India **106** C1
Garhi *Rajasthan* India **104** C5
Garhi Khairo Pak. **111** G4
Garhmuktesar *Uttar Prad.* India **99** B7
Garhwa India **105** E4
Gari Rus. Fed. **51** S4
Gariau Indon. **81** I7
Garibaldi, Mount Canada **150** F5
Gariep Dam *resr* S. Africa **125** G6
Garies S. Africa **124** C6
Garigliano *r.* Italy **68** E4
Garissa Kenya **122** D4
Garkalne Latvia **55** N8
Garkung Caka *l. Xizang* China **99** D6
Garland U.S.A. **161** D5
Garm Tajik. *see* **Gharm**
Garm Āb Iran **111** E3
Garmāb Iran **110** E3
Garm Āb, Chashmeh-ye *spring* Iran **110** E3
Garmī Iran **110** C2
Garmsar Iran **110** D3
Garmsel *reg.* Afgh. **111** F4
Garner *IA* U.S.A. **160** E3
Garner *KY* U.S.A. **164** D5
Garnett U.S.A. **160** E4
Garnpung Lake *imp. l.* Australia **138** A4
Garo Hills India **105** G4
Garonne *r.* France **66** D4
Garoowe Somalia **122** E3
Garopaba Brazil **179** A5
Garoua Cameroon **120** E4
Garoua Boulai Cameroon **121** E4
Gar Qu *r. Qinghai* China **99** F6
Garqu Yan *Qinghai* China **99** F6
Garré Arg. **178** D5
Garrett U.S.A. **164** C3
Garrison U.S.A. **160** E2
Garruk Pak. **111** G4
Garry *r.* U.K. **60** E3
Garrychyrla Turkm. *see* **Garryçyrla**
Garryçyrla Turkm. **111** F2
Garry Island *N.W.T.* Canada **149** N1
Garry Lake Canada **151** K1
Garrynahine U.K. **60** C2
Garsen Kenya **122** E4
Garshy Turkm. *see* **Garşy**
Garsila Sudan **121** F3
Garşy Turkm. **113** I2
Gartar China *see* **Qianning**
Garth U.K. **59** D6
Gartog China *see* **Markam**
Gartok *Xizang* China *see* **Garyarsa**
Gartow Germany **63** L1
Garub Namibia **124** C4
Garusuun Palau **82** [inset]
Garut *Jawa* Indon. **85** D4
Garvagh U.K. **61** F3
Garve U.K. **60** E3
Garwa India *see* **Garhwa**
Garwha India *see* **Garhwa**
Gar Xincun *Xizang* China **99** C6
Gary *IN* U.S.A. **164** B3
Gary *WV* U.S.A. **164** E5
Garyarsa *Xizang* China **99** C7
Garyi China **96** C2
Garyū-zan *mt.* Japan **91** D6
Garza García Mex. **161** C7
Garzê China **96** C2
Gar Zangbo *r.* China **99** B6
Gasan-Kuli Turkm. *see* **Esenguly**
Gas City U.S.A. **164** C3
Gascogne *reg.* France *see* **Gascony**
Gascogne, Golfe de *g.* France *see* **Gascony, Gulf of**
Gascony *reg.* France **66** D5
Gascony, Gulf of France **66** C5
Gascoyne *r.* Australia **135** A6
Gascoyne Junction Australia **135** A6
Gase *Xizang* China **99** D7
Gasherbrum I *mt.* China/Pak. **104** D2
Gas Hu *salt l.* China **99** E5
Gashua Nigeria **120** E3
Gask Iran **111** E3
Gaspar Cuba **163** E8
Gaspar, Selat *sea chan.* Indon. **84** D3
Gaspé Canada **153** I4
Gaspé, Cap *c.* Canada **153** I4
Gaspésie, Péninsule de la *pen.* Canada **153** I4
Gassan *vol.* Japan **91** F5
Gassaway U.S.A. **164** E4
Gasselte Neth. **62** G2
Gasteiz Spain *see* **Vitoria-Gasteiz**
Gastello Rus. Fed. **90** F2
Gaston U.S.A. **165** G5
Gaston, Lake U.S.A. **165** G5
Gastonia U.S.A. **163** D5
Gata, Cabo de *c.* Spain **67** E5
Gata, Cape Cyprus **107** A2
Gata, Sierra de *mts* Spain **67** C3
Gataga *r. B.C.* Canada **149** P4
Gatas, Akra *c.* Cyprus *see* **Gata, Cape**
Gatchina Rus. Fed. **55** Q7
Gate City U.S.A. **164** D5
Gatehouse of Fleet U.K. **60** E6
Gatentiri Indon. **81** K8
Gateshead U.K. **58** F4
Gates of the Arctic National Park and Preserve *AK* U.S.A. **148** I2
Gatesville U.S.A. **161** D6
Gateway U.S.A. **159** I2
Gatineau Canada **165** H1
Gatineau *r.* Canada **152** G5
Gatong China *see* **Jomda**
Gatooma Zimbabwe *see* **Kadoma**
Gatton Australia **138** F1
Gatvand Iran **110** C3
Gatyana S. Africa *see* **Willowvale**
Gau *i.* Fiji **133** H3
Gauer Lake Canada **151** L3
Gauhati India *see* **Guwahati**
Gaujas nacionālais parks *nat. park* Latvia **55** N8
Gaul *country* Europe *see* **France**
Gaula *r.* Norway **54** G5
Gaume *reg.* Belgium **62** F5
Gaurama Brazil **179** A4
Gauribidanur India **106** C3
Gauteng *prov.* S. Africa **125** I4
Gavarr Armenia **113** G2
Gāvbandī Iran **110** D5
Gāvbūs, Kūh-e *mts* Iran **110** D5

▶**Gavdos** *i.* Greece **69** K7
Most southerly point of Europe.

Gavião *r.* Brazil **179** C1
Gavīleh Iran **110** B3
Gav Khūnī Iran **110** D3
Gävle Sweden **55** J6
Gavrilovka Vtoraya Rus. Fed. **53** I5
Gavrilov-Yam Rus. Fed. **52** H4
Gawachab Namibia **124** C4
Gawai Myanmar **96** C3
Gawan India **105** F4
Gawilgarh Hills India **104** D5
Gawler Australia **137** B7
Gawler Ranges *hills* Australia **137** A7
Gaxun Nur *salt l. Nei Mongol* China **94** E3
Gaya India **105** F4
Gaya *i.* Malaysia **85** G1
Gaya *i.* Malaysia **85** G1
Gaya Niger **120** D3
Gaya He *r.* China **90** C4
Gayam *Jawa* Indon. **85** F4
Gayéri Burkina Faso **120** D3
Gaylord U.S.A. **164** C1
Gayndah Australia **137** E5
Gayny Rus. Fed. **52** L3
Gaysin Ukr. *see* **Haysyn**
Gayutino Rus. Fed. **52** H4
Gaz Iran **110** C3

▶**Gaza** *terr.* Asia **107** B4
Semi-autonomous region.

▶**Gaza** Gaza **107** B4
Capital of Gaza.

Gaza *prov.* Moz. **125** K2
Gazan Pak. **111** G4
Gazandzhyk Turkm. *see* **Bereket**
Gazanjyk Turkm. *see* **Bereket**
Gaza Strip *terr.* Asia *see* **Gaza**
Gaziantep Turkey **112** E3
Gaziantep *prov.* Turkey **107** C1
Gazibenli Turkey *see* **Yahyalı**
Gazīk Iran **111** F3
Gazimağusa Cyprus *see* **Famagusta**
Gazimuro-Ononskiy Khrebet *mts* Rus. Fed. **95** G1
Gazimurskiy Khrebet *mts* Rus. Fed. **89** L2
Gazimurskiy Zavod Rus. Fed. **89** L2
Gazipaşa Turkey **107** A1
Gazli Uzbek. **111** F1
Gaz Māhū Iran **110** E5
Gbadolite Dem. Rep. Congo **122** C3
Gbarnga Liberia **120** C4
Gboko Nigeria **120** D4
Gcuwa S. Africa *see* **Butterworth**
Gdańsk Poland **57** Q3
Gdańsk, Gulf of Poland/Rus. Fed. **57** Q3
Gdańska, Zatoka *g.* Poland/Rus. Fed. *see* **Gdańsk, Gulf of**
Gdingen Poland *see* **Gdynia**
Gdov Rus. Fed. **55** O7
Gdynia Poland **57** Q3
Geaidnovuohppi Norway **54** M2
Gearhart Mountain U.S.A. **156** C4
Gearraidh na h-Aibhne U.K. *see* **Garrynahine**
Gebe *i. Maluku* Indon. **83** D2
Gebesee Germany **63** K3
Geçitkale Cyprus *see* **Lefkonikon**
Gedang, Gunung *mt.* Indon. **84** C3
Gedaref Sudan **108** E7
Gedern Germany **63** J4
Gedinne Belgium **62** E5
Gediz *r.* Turkey **69** L5
Gedney Drove End U.K. **59** H6
Gedong *Sarawak* Malaysia **85** E2
Gedong, Tanjong *pt* Sing. **87** [inset]
Gedser Denmark **55** G9
Gedungpakuan *Sumatera* Indon. **84** D4
Geel Belgium **62** F3
Geelong Australia **138** B7
Geelvink Channel Australia **135** A7
Geel Vloer *salt pan* S. Africa **124** E5
Gees Gwardafuy *c.* Somalia *see* **Gwardafuy, Gees**
Geeste Germany **63** H2
Geesthacht Germany **63** K1
Gê'gyai *Xizang* China **99** C6
Ge Hu *l.* China **97** H2
Geidam Nigeria **120** E3
Geiersberg *hill* Germany **63** J5
Geikie *r.* Canada **151** K3
Geilenkirchen Germany **62** G4
Geilo Norway **55** F6
Geinō Japan **92** C4
Geiranger Norway **54** E5
Geislingen an der Steige Germany **63** J6
Geisûm, Gezâ'ir *is* Egypt *see* **Qaysūm, Juzur**
Geita Tanz. **122** D4
Geithain Germany **63** M3
Gejiu China **96** D4
Geka, Mys *hd* Rus. Fed. **148** B2
Geka, Mys *hd* Rus. Fed. **148** B2
Gëkdepe Turkm. **110** E2
Gela *Sicily* Italy **68** F6
Gêladaindong *mt. Qinghai* China **99** E6
Geladī Eth. **122** E3
Gelam *i.* Indon. **85** E3
Gelang, Tanjung *pt* Malaysia **87** C7
Geldern Germany **62** G3
Gelendzhik Rus. Fed. **112** E1
Gelibolu Turkey *see* **Gallipoli**
Gelidonya Burnu *pt* Turkey *see* **Yardımcı Burnu**
Gelincik Dağı *mt.* Turkey **69** N5
Gelmord Iran **110** E3
Gelnhausen Germany **63** J4
Gelsenkirchen Germany **62** H3
Gelumbang *Sumatera* Indon. **84** D3
Gemas Malaysia **84** C2
Gemena Dem. Rep. Congo **122** B3
Geminokağı Cyprus *see* **Karavostasi**
Gemlik Turkey **69** M4
Gemona del Friuli Italy **68** E1
Gemsa Egypt *see* **Jamsah**
Gemsbok National Park Botswana **124** E3
Gemsbokplein *well* S. Africa **124** E4
Gemuk Mountain *AK* U.S.A. **148** H3
Genalē Wenz *r.* Eth. **122** E3
Genappe Belgium **62** E4
Genāveh Iran **110** C4
General Acha Arg. **178** D5
General Alvear Arg. **178** C5
General Belgrano II *research station* Antarctica *see* **Belgrano II**
General Bravo Mex. **161** D7

▶**General Carrera, Lago** *l.* Arg./Chile **178** B7
Deepest lake in South America.

General Conesa Arg. **178** D6
General Escobeda Mex. **167** E3
General Freire Angola *see* **Muxaluando**
General Juan Madariaga Arg. **178** E5
General La Madrid Arg. **178** D5
General Luna Phil. **82** D4
General MacArthur *Samar* Phil. **82** D4
General Machado Angola *see* **Camacupa**
General Pico Arg. **178** D5
General Pinedo Arg. **178** D3
General Roca Arg. **178** C5
General Salgado Brazil **179** A3
General San Martín *research station* Antarctica *see* **San Martín**
General Santos *Mindanao* Phil. **82** D5
General Simón Bolívar Mex. **161** C7
General Terán Mex. **167** F3
General Trías Mex. **166** D2
General Villegas Arg. **178** D5
Genesee U.S.A. **165** G3
Geneseo U.S.A. **165** G2
Geneva S. Africa **125** H4
Geneva Switz. **66** H3
Geneva *AL* U.S.A. **163** C6
Geneva *IL* U.S.A. **164** A3
Geneva *NE* U.S.A. **160** D3
Geneva *NY* U.S.A. **165** G2
Geneva *OH* U.S.A. **164** E3
Geneva, Lake France/Switz. **66** H3
Genève Switz. *see* **Geneva**
Genf Switz. *see* **Geneva**
Gengda China *see* **Gana**
Gengma China **96** C4
Gengxuan China *see* **Gengma**
Genhe China **90** A2
Gen He *r.* China **95** I1
Genichesk Ukr. *see* **Heniches'k**
Genji India **104** C5
Genk Belgium **62** F4
Gennep Neth. **62** F3
Genoa Australia **138** D6
Genoa Italy **68** C2
Genoa, Gulf of Italy **68** C2
Genova Italy *see* **Genoa**
Genova, Golfo di Italy *see* **Genoa, Gulf of**
Gent Belgium *see* **Ghent**
Genteng *Jawa* Indon. **84** D4
Genteng *i.* Indon. **85** F4
Genthin Germany **63** M2
Genting Highlands Malaysia **84** C2
Gentioux, Plateau de France **66** F4
Genua Italy *see* **Genoa**
Geographe Bay Australia **135** A8
Geographical Society Ø *i.* Greenland **147** P2
Geok-Tepe Turkm. *see* **Gëkdepe**
George, Zemlya *i.* Rus. Fed. **76** F1
George *r.* Canada **153** I2
George S. Africa **124** F7
George, Lake Australia **138** D5
George, Lake *AK* U.S.A. **149** K3
George, Lake *FL* U.S.A. **163** D6
George, Lake *NY* U.S.A. **165** I2
George Land *i.* Rus. Fed. *see* **Georga, Zemlya**
Georges Mills U.S.A. **165** I2
George Sound *inlet* N.Z. **139** A7
Georgetown Australia **136** C3

▶**George Town** Cayman Is **169** H5
Capital of the Cayman Islands.

Georgetown Gambia **120** B3

▶**Georgetown** Guyana **177** G2
Capital of Guyana.

George Town Malaysia **84** C1
Georgetown *AK* U.S.A. **148** H3
Georgetown *DE* U.S.A. **165** H4
Georgetown *GA* U.S.A. **163** C6
Georgetown *IL* U.S.A. **164** B4
Georgetown *KY* U.S.A. **164** C4
Georgetown *OH* U.S.A. **164** D4
Georgetown *SC* U.S.A. **163** E5
Georgetown *TX* U.S.A. **161** D6
George VI Sound *sea chan.* Antarctica **188** L2
George V Land *reg.* Antarctica **188** G2
George West U.S.A. **161** D6
Georgia *country* Asia **113** F2
Georgia *state* U.S.A. **163** D5
Georgia, Strait of Canada **150** E5
Georgiana U.S.A. **161** E1
Georgian Bay Canada **164** E1
Georgian Bay Islands National Park Canada **164** F1
Georgienne, Baie *b.* Canada *see* **Georgian Bay**
Georgina *watercourse* Australia **136** B5
Georgiu-Dezh Rus. Fed. *see* **Liski**
Georgiyevka *Vostochnyy Kazakhstan* Kazakh. **102** F2
Georgiyevka *Zhambylskaya Oblast'* Kazakh. *see* **Korday**
Georgiyevsk Rus. Fed. **113** F1
Georgiyevskoye Rus. Fed. **52** J4
Georg von Neumayer *research station* Antarctica *see* **Neumayer**
Gera Germany **63** M4
Geraardsbergen Belgium **62** D4
Geral, Serra *mts* Brazil **179** A4
Geral de Goiás, Serra *hills* Brazil **179** B1
Geraldine N.Z. **139** C7
Geral do Paraná, Serra *hills* Brazil **179** B1
Geraldton Australia **135** A7
Gerama *i.* Indon. **83** C1
Gerar *watercourse* Israel **107** B4
Gerber U.S.A. **158** B1
Gercüş Turkey **113** F3
Gerdine, Mount *AK* U.S.A. **148** I3
Gerede Turkey **112** D2
Gereshk Afgh. **111** G4
Gerik Malaysia **84** C1
Gerlach U.S.A. **158** D1
Gerlachovský štít *mt.* Slovakia **57** R6
Germaine, Lac *l.* Canada **153** I3
German Bight *g.* Denmark/Germany **57** K3
Germania *country* Europe *see* **Germany**
Germanicea Turkey *see* **Kahramanmaraş**
Germansen Landing Canada **150** E4
German South-West Africa *country* Africa *see* **Namibia**
Germantown *OH* U.S.A. **164** C4
Germantown *WI* U.S.A. **164** A2

▶**Germany** *country* Europe **57** L5
2nd most populous country in Europe.

Germersheim Germany **63** I5
Gernsheim Germany **63** I5
Gero Japan **92** D3
Gerolstein Germany **62** G4
Gerolzhofen Germany **63** K5
Gerona Spain *see* **Girona**
Gerrit Denys *is* P.N.G. *see* **Lihir Group**
Gers *r.* France **66** E4
Gersfeld (Rhön) Germany **63** J4
Gersoppa India **106** B3
Gerstungen Germany **63** K4
Gerwisch Germany **63** L2
Géryville Alg. *see* **El Bayadh**
Gêrzê *Xizang* China **99** D6
Gerze Turkey **112** D2
Gescher Germany **62** H3
Gesoriacum France *see* **Boulogne-sur-Mer**
Gessie U.S.A. **164** B3
Getai *Shaanxi* China **95** G5
Gete *r.* Belgium **62** F4
Gettysburg *PA* U.S.A. **165** G4
Gettysburg *SD* U.S.A. **160** D2
Gettysburg National Military Park *nat. park* U.S.A. **165** G4
Getz Ice Shelf Antarctica **188** J2
Geumapang *r.* Indon. **84** B2
Geumpang *Sumatera* Indon. **84** B1
Geureudong, Gunung *vol.* Indon. **84** B1
Geurie Australia **138** D4
Gevaş Turkey **113** F3
Gevgelija Macedonia **69** J4
Gexianzhuang *Hebei* China *see* **Qinghe**
Gexto Spain *see* **Algorta**
Gey Iran *see* **Nīkshahr**
Geyikli Turkey **69** L5
Geylegphug Bhutan **105** G4
Geysdorp S. Africa **125** G4
Geyserville U.S.A. **158** B2
Geyve Turkey **69** N4
Gezidong *Qinghai* China **94** E4
Gezīr Iran **110** D5
Ghaap Plateau S. Africa **124** F4
Ghāb, Wādī al *r.* Syria **107** C2
Ghabāghib Syria **107** C3
Ghabeish Sudan **108** C7
Ghadaf, Wādī al *watercourse* Jordan **107** C4
Ghadamès Libya *see* **Ghadāmis**
Ghadāmis Libya **120** D1
Gha'em Shahr Iran **110** D2
Ghaghara *r.* India **105** F4
Ghaibi Dero Pak. **111** G5
Ghalend Iran **111** F4
Ghallaorol Uzbek. *see* **G'allaorol**
Ghana *country* Africa **120** C4
Ghanādah, Rās *pt* U.A.E. **110** D5
Ghantila India **104** B5
Ghanwā Saudi Arabia **108** G4
Ghanzi Botswana **123** C6
Ghanzi *admin. dist.* Botswana **124** F2
Ghap'an Armenia *see* **Kapan**
Ghār, Ras al *pt* Saudi Arabia **110** C5
Ghardaïa Alg. **64** E5
Gharghoda India **106** D1
Ghārib, Gebel *mt.* Egypt *see* **Ghārib, Jabal**
Ghārib, Jabal *mt.* Egypt **112** D5
Gharm Tajik. **111** H2
Gharq Ābād Iran **110** C3
Gharwa India *see* **Garhwa**
Gharyān Libya **121** E1
Ghāt Libya **120** E2
Ghatgan India **105** F5
Ghatol India **104** C5
Ghawdex *i.* Malta *see* **Gozo**
Ghazal, Bahr el *watercourse* Chad **121** E3
Ghazaouet Alg. **67** F6
Ghaziabad India **104** D3
Ghazi Ghat Pak. **111** H4
Ghazipur India **105** E4
Ghazna Afgh. *see* **Ghaznī**
Ghaznī Afgh. **111** H3
Ghaznī *r.* Afgh. **111** G3
Ghazoor Afgh. **111** G3
Ghazzah Gaza *see* **Gaza**
Ghebar Gumbad Iran **110** E3
Ghent Belgium **62** D3
Gheorghe Gheorghiu-Dej Romania *see* **Onești**
Gheorgheni Romania **69** K1
Gherla Romania **69** J1
Ghijduwon Uzbek. *see* **G'ijduvon**
Ghilzai *reg.* Afgh. **111** G4
Ghīnah, Wādī al *watercourse* Saudi Arabia **107** D4
Ghisonaccia *Corsica* France **66** I5
Ghorak Afgh. **111** G3
Ghost Lake Canada **150** H2
Ghotaru India **104** B4
Ghotki Pak. **111** H5
Ghudamis Libya *see* **Ghadāmis**
Ghugri *r.* India **105** F4
Ghurayfah *hill* Saudi Arabia **107** C4
Ghūrī Iran **110** D4
Ghurian Afgh. **111** F3
Ghurrab, Jabal *hill* Saudi Arabia **110** B5
Ghuzor Uzbek. *see* **G'uzor**
Ghyvelde France **62** C3
Giaginskaya Rus. Fed. **113** F1
Gialias *r.* Cyprus **107** A2
Gia Nghia Vietnam **87** D4
Gianisada *i.* Greece **69** L7
Giannitsa Greece **69** J4
Giant's Castle *mt.* S. Africa **125** I5
Giant's Causeway *lava field* U.K. **61** F2
Gianysada *i. Kriti* Greece *see* **Gianisada**
Gia Rai Vietnam **87** D5
Giarre *Sicily* Italy **68** F6
Gibb *r.* Australia **134** D3
Gibbonsville U.S.A. **156** E3
Gibeon Namibia **124** C3
Gibraltar *terr.* Europe **67** D5

▶**Gibraltar** Gibraltar **184** H3
United Kingdom Overseas Territory.

Gibraltar, Strait of Morocco/Spain **67** C6
Gibraltar Range National Park Australia **138** F2
Gibson Australia **135** C8
Gibson City U.S.A. **164** A3
Gibson Desert Australia **135** C6
Gichgeniyn Nuruu *mts* Mongolia **94** C2
Gidar Pak. **111** G4
Giddalur India **106** C3
Giddi, Gebel el *hill* Egypt *see* **Jiddī, Jabal al**
Giddings U.S.A. **161** D6
Gīdolē Eth. **121** G4
Gien France **66** F3
Gießen Germany **63** I4
Gīfan Iran **110** E2
Gifford *r.* Canada **147** J2
Gifhorn Germany **63** K2
Gift Lake Canada **150** H4
Gifu Japan **92** C3
Gifu *pref.* Japan **92** C3
Giganta, Cerro *mt.* Mex. **166** C3
Gigha *i.* U.K. **60** D5
Gīgīga Eth. *see* **Jijiga**
G'ijduvon Uzbek. **111** G1
Gijón Spain *see* **Gijón-Xixón**
Gijón-Xixón Spain **67** D2
Gila *r.* U.S.A. **159** F5
Gila, Tanjung *pt Maluku* Indon. **83** D2
Gila Bend U.S.A. **159** G5
Gila Bend Mountains U.S.A. **159** G5
Gīlān-e Gharb Iran **110** B3
Gilbert *r.* Australia **136** C3
Gilbert *AZ* U.S.A. **159** H5
Gilbert *WV* U.S.A. **164** E5
Gilbert, Mount *AK* U.S.A. **149** J3
Gilbert Islands Kiribati **186** H5
Gilbert Islands *country* Pacific Ocean *see* **Kiribati**
Gilbert Peak U.S.A. **159** H1
Gilbert Ridge *sea feature* Pacific Ocean **186** H6
Gilbert River Australia **136** C3
Gilbués Brazil **177** I5
Gil Chashmeh Iran **110** E3

Gilé Moz. 123 D5
Giles Creek r. Australia 134 E4
Gilford Island Canada 150 E5
Gilgai Australia 138 E2
Gilgandra Australia 138 D3
Gil Gil Creek r. Australia 138 D2
Gilgit Pak. 104 C2
Gilgit r. Pak. 109 L2
Gilgit-Baltistan admin. div. Pak. 111 I2
Gilgunnia Australia 138 C4
Gili Iyang i. Indon. 85 F4
Gilimanuk Bali Indon. 85 F5
Gılındire Turkey see Aydıncık
Gillam Canada 151 M3
Gillen, Lake salt flat Australia 135 D6
Gilles, Lake salt flat Australia 137 B7
Gillett U.S.A. 165 G3
Gillette U.S.A. 156 G3
Gilliat Australia 136 C4
Gillingham England U.K. 59 E7
Gillingham England U.K. 59 H7
Gilling West U.K. 58 F4
Gillon Point pt AK U.S.A. 148 [inset]
Gilman U.S.A. 164 B3
Gilmer U.S.A. 161 E5
Gilmour Island Canada 152 F2
Gilroy U.S.A. 158 C3
Gīmbī Eth. 122 D3
Gimhae S. Korea see Kimhae
Gimli Canada 151 L5
Gimol'skoye, Ozero l. Rus. Fed. 52 G3
Ginebra, Laguna l. Bol. 176 E6
Gineifa Egypt see Junayfah
Gin Gin Australia 136 E5
Gingin Australia 135 A7
Gingoog Mindanao Phil. 82 D4
Gīnīr Eth. 122 E3
Ginosa Italy 68 G4
Ginzo de Limia Spain see Xinzo de Limia
Gioia del Colle Italy 68 G4
Gipouloux r. Canada 152 G3
Gippsland reg. Australia 138 B7
Girā, Wādī watercourse Egypt see Jirā', Wādī
Gīrān Rīg mt. Iran 110 E4
Girard U.S.A. 164 E2
Girardin, Lac l. Canada 153 I2
Girdab Iran 110 E3
Girdwood AK U.S.A. 149 J3
Giresun Turkey 112 E2
Girgenti Sicily Italy see Agrigento
Giridh India see Giridih
Giridih India 105 F4
Girilambone Australia 138 C3
Girna r. India 104 C5
Gir National Park India 104 B5
Girne Cyprus see Kyrenia
Girón Ecuador 176 C4
Giron Sweden see Kiruna
Girona Spain 67 H3
Gironde est. France 66 D4
Girot Pak. 111 I3
Girral Australia 138 C4
Girraween National Park Australia 138 E2
Girvan U.K. 60 E5
Girvas Rus. Fed. 52 G3
Gisasa r. AK U.S.A. 148 H2
Gisborne N.Z. 139 G4
Giscome Canada 150 F4
Gislaved Sweden 55 H8
Gisors France 62 B5
Gissar Tajik. see Hisor
Gissar Range mts Tajik./Uzbek. 111 G2
Gissarskiy Khrebet mts Tajik./Uzbek. see Gissar Range
Gitarama Rwanda 122 C4
Gitega Burundi 122 C4
Giuba r. Somalia see Jubba
Giulianova Italy 68 E3
Giurgiu Romania 69 K3
Giuvala, Pasul pass Romania 69 K2
Givar Iran 110 E2
Givet France 62 E4
Givors France 66 G4
Givry-en-Argonne France 62 E6
Giyani S. Africa 125 J2
Giza Egypt 112 C5
Gizhiga Rus. Fed. 77 R3
Gjakovë Kosovo 69 I3
Gjilan Kosovo 69 I3
Gjirokastër Albania 69 I4
Gjirokastra Albania see Gjirokastër
Gjoa Haven Canada 147 I3
Gjøra Norway 54 F5
Gjøvik Norway 55 G6
Gkinas, Akrotirio pt Greece 69 M6
Glace Bay Canada 153 K5
Glacier Bay AK U.S.A. 149 N4
Glacier Bay National Park and Preserve AK U.S.A. 149 M4
Glacier National Park Canada 150 G5
Glacier National Park U.S.A. 156 E2
Glacier Peak vol. U.S.A. 156 C2
Gladstad Norway 54 G4
Gladstone Australia 136 E4
Gladstone Canada 151 L5
Gladwin U.S.A. 164 C2
Gladys U.S.A. 164 F5
Gladys Lake Canada 150 C3
Glamis U.K. 60 F4
Glamis U.S.A. 159 F5
Glamoč Bos.-Herz. 68 G2
Glan r. Germany 63 H5
Glan Mindanao Phil. 82 D5
Glandorf Germany 63 I2
Glanton U.K. 58 F3
Glasgow U.K. 60 E5
Glasgow KY U.S.A. 164 C5
Glasgow MT U.S.A. 156 G2
Glasgow VA U.S.A. 164 F5
Glaslyn Canada 151 I4
Glass, Loch l. U.K. 60 E3
Glass Mountain U.S.A. 158 D3
Glass Peninsula AK U.S.A. 149 N4
Glastonbury U.K. 59 E7
Glauchau Germany 63 M4
Glazov Rus. Fed. 52 L4
Gleiwitz Poland see Gliwice
Glen U.S.A. 165 J1
Glen Allen U.S.A. 165 G5
Glen Alpine Dam S. Africa 125 I2
Glenamaddy Ireland 61 D4
Glenamoy r. Ireland 61 C3
Glen Arbor U.S.A. 164 C1
Glenbawn, Lake Australia 138 E4
Glenboro Canada 151 L5
Glen Canyon gorge U.S.A. 159 H3
Glen Canyon Dam U.S.A. 159 H3
Glencoe Canada 164 E2
Glencoe S. Africa 125 J5
Glencoe U.S.A. 160 E2
Glendale AZ U.S.A. 159 G5
Glendale CA U.S.A. 158 D4
Glendale UT U.S.A. 159 G3
Glendale Lake U.S.A. 165 F3
Glen Davis Australia 138 E4
Glenden Australia 136 E4
Glendive U.S.A. 156 G3
Glendon Canada 151 I4
Glendo Reservoir U.S.A. 156 G4
Glenfield U.S.A. 165 H2
Glengavlen Ireland 61 E3
Glengyle Australia 136 B5
Glen Innes Australia 138 E2
Glenluce U.K. 60 E6
Glen Lyon U.S.A. 165 G3
Glenlyon Peak Y.T. Canada 149 N3
Glen More valley U.K. 60 E3
Glenmorgan Australia 138 D1
Glenn U.S.A. 158 B2
Glennallen AK U.S.A. 149 K3
Glenn Highway AK U.S.A. 149 K3
Glennie U.S.A. 164 D1
Glenns Ferry U.S.A. 156 E4
Glenora B.C. Canada 149 O4
Glenore Australia 136 C3
Glenormiston Australia 136 B4
Glenreagh Australia 138 F3
Glen Rose U.S.A. 161 D5
Glenrothes U.K. 60 F4
Glens Falls U.S.A. 165 I2
Glen Shee valley U.K. 60 F4
Glenties Ireland 61 D3
Glenveagh National Park Ireland 61 E2
Glenville U.S.A. 164 E4
Glenwood AR U.S.A. 161 E5
Glenwood IA U.S.A. 160 E3
Glenwood MN U.S.A. 160 E2
Glenwood NM U.S.A. 159 I5
Glenwood Springs U.S.A. 159 J2
Glevum U.K. see Gloucester
Glinde Germany 63 K1
Glittertinden mt. Norway 55 F6
Gliwice Poland 57 Q5
Globe U.S.A. 159 H5
Glogau Poland see Głogów
Głogów Poland 57 P5
Glomfjord Norway 54 H3
Glomma r. Norway 54 G7
Glommersträsk Sweden 54 K4
Glorieuses, Îles is Indian Ocean 123 E5
Glorioso Islands Indian Ocean see Glorieuses, Îles
Glory of Russia Cape AK U.S.A. 148 D3
Gloster U.S.A. 161 F6
Gloucester Australia 138 E3
Gloucester U.K. 59 E7
Gloucester MA U.S.A. 165 J2
Gloucester VA U.S.A. 165 G5
Glover Reef Belize 167 I5
Gloversville U.S.A. 165 H2
Glovertown Canada 153 L4
Glöwen Germany 63 M2
Glubinnoye Rus. Fed. 90 D3
Glubokiy Krasnoyarskiy Kray Rus. Fed. 88 H2
Glubokiy Rostovskaya Oblast' Rus. Fed. 53 I6
Glubokoye Belarus see Hlybokaye
Glubokoye Kazakh. 102 F1
Gluggarnir hill Faroe Is 54 [inset]
Glukhov Ukr. see Hlukhiv
Glusburn U.K. 58 F5
Glynebwy U.K. see Ebbw Vale
Gmelinka Rus. Fed. 53 J6
Gmünd Austria 57 O6
Gmunden Austria 57 N7
Gnarp Sweden 55 J5
Gnarrenburg Germany 63 J1
Gnesen Poland see Gniezno
Gniezno Poland 57 P4
Gnjilane Kosovo see Gjilan
Gnowangerup Australia 135 B8
Gnows Nest Range hills Australia 135 B7
Goa India 106 B3
Goa state India 106 B3
Goageb Namibia 124 C4
Goalen Head hd Australia 138 E6
Goalpara India 105 G4
Goang Flores Indon. 83 A5
Goat Fell hill U.K. 60 D5
Goba Eth. 122 E3
Gobabis Namibia 124 D2
Gobannium U.K. see Abergavenny
Gobas Namibia 124 D4
Gobi Desert des. China/Mongolia 88 J4
Gobindpur India 105 F5
Gobles U.S.A. 164 C2
Gobō Japan 92 B5
Goch Germany 62 G3
Gochas Namibia 124 D3
Go Công Vietnam 87 D5
Godalming U.K. 59 G7
Godavari r. India 106 D2
Godavari, Cape India 106 D2
Godda India 105 F4
Godē Eth. 122 E3
Godere Eth. 122 E3
Goderich Canada 164 E2
Goderville France 59 H9
Godhavn Greenland see Qeqertarsuaq
Godhra India 104 C5
Godia Creek b. India 111 H6
Gōdo Japan 92 C3
Godo, Gunung mt. Indon. 83 C3
Gods r. Canada 151 M3
Gods Lake Canada 151 M4
God's Mercy, Bay of Canada 151 O2
Godthåb Greenland see Nuuk
Godwin-Austen, Mount China/Pak. see K2
Goedereede Neth. 62 D3
Goedgegun Swaziland see Nhlangano
Goegap Nature Reserve S. Africa 124 D5
Goélands, Lac aux l. Canada 153 J3
Goes Neth. 62 D3
Gogama Canada 152 E5
Gogebic Range hills U.S.A. 160 F2
Gogra r. India see Ghaghara
Goiana Brazil 177 L5
Goiandira Brazil 179 A2
Goianésia Brazil 179 A1
Goiânia Brazil 179 A2
Goiás Brazil 179 A1
Goiás state Brazil 179 A2
Goicangmai Xizang China 99 C6
Goikul Palau 82 [inset]
Goincang Qinghai China 94 E5
Goinsargoin China 96 C2
Goio-Erê Brazil 178 F2
Gojō Japan 92 B4
Gojra Pak. 111 I4
Goka Japan 93 F2
Gokak India 106 B2
Gokarn India 106 B3
Gök Çay r. Turkey 107 A1
Gökçeada i. Turkey 69 K4
Gökdepe Turkm. see Gëkdepe
Gökdere r. Turkey 107 A1
Goklenkuy, Solonchak salt l. Turkm. 110 E1
Gökova Körfezi b. Turkey 69 L6
Gokprosh Hills Pak. 111 F5
Göksun Turkey 112 E3
Goksu Parkı Turkey 107 A1
Gokteik Myanmar 86 B2
Gokwe Zimbabwe 123 C5
Gol Norway 55 F6
Golaghat India 105 H4
Golbāf Iran 110 E4
Gölbaşı Turkey 112 E3
Golconda U.S.A. 165 E1
Gölcük Turkey 69 M4
Gold U.S.A. 165 G3
Gołdap Poland 57 S3
Gold Beach U.S.A. 156 B4
Goldberg Germany 63 M1
Gold Coast country Africa see Ghana
Gold Coast Australia 138 F2
Gold Creek AK U.S.A. 149 J3
Golden U.S.A. 156 G5
Golden Bay N.Z. 139 D5
Goldendale U.S.A. 156 C3
Goldene Aue reg. Germany 63 K3
Golden Gate Highlands National Park S. Africa 125 I5
Golden Hinde mt. Canada 150 E5
Golden Lake Canada 165 G1
Golden Meadow LA U.S.A. 167 H2
Golden Prairie Canada 151 I5
Goldenstedt Germany 63 I2
Goldfield U.S.A. 158 E3
Goldsand Lake Canada 151 K3
Goldsboro U.S.A. 163 E5
Goldstone Lake U.S.A. 158 E4
Goldsworthy (abandoned) Australia 134 B5
Goldthwaite U.S.A. 161 D6
Goldvein U.S.A. 165 G4
Göle Turkey 113 F2
Golestān Afgh. 111 F3
Goleta U.S.A. 158 D4
Golets-Davydov, Gora mt. Rus. Fed. 89 J2
Golfito Costa Rica 166 [inset] J7
Golfo di Orosei Gennargentu e Asinara, Parco Nazionale del nat. park Sardinia Italy 68 C4
Gölgeli Dağları mts Turkey 69 M6
Goliad U.S.A. 161 D6
Golin Baixing Nei Mongol China 95 J2
Gölköy Turkey 112 E2
Gollel Swaziland see Lavumisa
Golm Germany 63 M2
Golmberg hill Germany 63 N2
Golmud Qinghai China 94 C4
Golmud He r. China 94 C4
Golovin AK U.S.A. 148 G2
Golovin Bay AK U.S.A. 148 G2
Golovnino Rus. Fed. 90 G4
Golpāyegān Iran 110 C3
Gölpazarı Turkey 69 N4
Golsovia AK U.S.A. 148 G3
Golspie U.K. 60 F3
Gol Vardeh Iran 111 F3
Golyama Syutkya mt. Bulg. 69 K4
Golyam Persenk mt. Bulg. 69 K4
Golyshi Rus. Fed. see Vetluzhskiy
Golzow Germany 63 M2
Goma Dem. Rep. Congo 122 C4
Gomang Co salt l. China 99 E7
Gomangxung Qinghai China 94 E5
Gomanodan-zan mt. Japan 92 B4
Gomati r. India 109 N4
Gombak, Bukit hill Sing. 87 [inset]
Gombe Nigeria 120 E3
Gombe r. Tanz. 123 D4
Gombi Nigeria 120 E3
Gombroon Iran see Bandar-e 'Abbās
Gomel' Belarus see Homyel'
Gómez Palacio Mex. 166 E3
Gomīshān Iran 110 D2
Gommern Germany 63 L2
Gomo Xizang China 99 D6
Gomo Co salt l. China 99 D6
Gomumu i. Maluku Indon. 83 C3
Gonābād Iran 110 E2
Gonaïves Haiti 169 J5
Gonarezhou National Park Zimbabwe 123 D6
Gonbad-e Kavus Iran 110 D2
Gonda India 105 E4
Gondal India 104 B5
Gondar Eth. see Gonder
Gonder Eth. 122 D2
Gondia India 104 E5
Gondiya India see Gondia
Gönen Turkey 69 L4
Gonfreville-l'Orcher France 59 H9
Gong'an China 97 G2
Gongbalou Xizang China 99 E7
Gongbo'gyamda Xizang China 99 F7
Gongchakou Gansu China 94 D4
Gongchang Gansu China see Longxi
Gongcheng China 97 F3
Gonggar Xizang China 99 E7
Gongga Shan mt. China 96 D2
Gonghe Qinghai China 94 E4
Gonghe Yunnan China see Mouding
Gonghui Hebei China 95 H3
Gongjiang China see Yudu
Gongliu Xinjiang China 98 C4
Gongogi r. Brazil 179 D1
Gongolgon Australia 138 C3
Gongpoquan Gansu China 94 D3
Gongquan China 96 E2
Gongwang Shan mts China 96 D3
Gongxian Henan China see Gongyi
Gongxian China see Gongquan
Gongyi Henan China 95 H5
Gonjo China see Kasha
Gonzáles Mex. 167 F4
Gonzales CA U.S.A. 158 C3
Gonzales TX U.S.A. 161 D6
Gonzha Rus. Fed. 90 B1
Goochland U.S.A. 165 G5
Goodenough, Cape Antarctica 188 G2
Goodenough, Mount hill N.W.T. Canada 149 N2
Goodenough Island P.N.G. 132 F2
Gooderham Canada 165 F1
Good Hope, Cape of S. Africa 124 D8
Goodhope Bay AK U.S.A. 148 G2
Good Hope Mountain Canada 156 B2
Gooding U.S.A. 156 E4
Goodland IN U.S.A. 164 B3
Goodland KS U.S.A. 160 C4
Goodlettsville U.S.A. 164 B5
Goodnews AK U.S.A. 148 G4
Goodnews Bay b. AK U.S.A. 148 G4
Goodooga Australia 138 C2
Goodpaster r. AK U.S.A. 149 K2
Goodspeed Nunataks Antarctica 188 E2
Goole U.K. 58 G5
Goolgowi Australia 138 B5
Goolma Australia 138 D4
Gooloogong Australia 138 D4
Goomalling Australia 135 B7
Goombalie Australia 138 B2
Goondiwindi Australia 138 E2
Goongarrie, Lake salt flat Australia 135 C7
Goongarrie National Park Australia 135 C7
Goonyella Australia 136 D4
Goorly, Lake salt flat Australia 135 B7
Goose Bay Canada see Happy Valley-Goose Bay
Goose Creek U.S.A. 163 D5
Goose Lake U.S.A. 156 C4
Gooty India 106 C3
Gopalganj Bangl. 105 G5
Gopalganj India 105 F4
Gopeshwar India 104 D3
Göppingen Germany 63 J6
Gorakhpur India 105 E4
Goražde Bos.-Herz. 68 H3
Gorbernador U.S.A. 159 J3
Gorczański Park Narodowy nat. park Poland 57 R6
Gorda, Punta pt Nicaragua 166 [inset] J6
Gorda, Punta pt U.S.A. 158 A1
Gördes Turkey 69 M5
Gordil Cent. Afr. Rep. 122 C3
Gordon r. Canada 151 O1
Gordon U.K. 60 G5
Gordon AK U.S.A. 149 L1
Gordon U.S.A. 160 C3
Gordon, Lake Australia 137 [inset]
Gordon Downs (abandoned) Australia 134 E4
Gordon Lake Canada 151 I3
Gordon Lake U.S.A. 165 F4
Gordonsville U.S.A. 165 F4
Goré Chad 121 E4
Gorē Eth. 122 D3
Gore N.Z. 139 B8
Gore U.S.A. 165 F4
Gorebridge U.K. 60 F5
Gore Point pt AK U.S.A. 149 J4
Gorey Ireland 61 F5
Gorg Iran 111 E4
Gorgān Iran 110 D2
Gorgān, Khalīj-e Iran 110 D2
Gorge Range hills Australia 134 B5
Gorgona, Isla i. Col. 176 C3
Gorham U.S.A. 165 J1
Gori Georgia 108 F1
Gorinchem Neth. 62 E3
Goris Armenia 113 G3
Gorizia Italy 68 E2
Gorki Belarus see Horki
Gor'kiy Rus. Fed. see Nizhniy Novgorod
Gor'kovskoye Vodokhranilishche resr Rus. Fed. 52 I4
Gorlice Poland 53 D6
Görlitz Germany 57 O5
Gorlovka Ukr. see Horlivka
Gorna Dzhumaya Bulg. see Blagoevgrad
Gorna Oryakhovitsa Bulg. 69 K3
Gornji Milanovac Serbia 69 I2
Gornji Vakuf Bos.-Herz. 68 G3
Gorno-Altaysk Rus. Fed. 102 G1
Gorno-Altayskaya Avtonomnaya Oblast' aut. rep. Rus. Fed. see Altay, Respublika
Gornotrakiyska Nizina lowland Bulg. 69 K3
Gornozavodsk Permskaya Oblast' Rus. Fed. 51 R4
Gornozavodsk Sakhalinskaya Oblast' Rus. Fed. 90 F3
Gornyak Altayskiy Kray Rus. Fed. 98 C2
Gornyy Rus. Fed. 53 K6
Gornyy Altay aut. rep. Rus. Fed. see Altay, Respublika
Gornyye Klyuchi Rus. Fed. 90 D3
Goro i. Fiji see Koro
Gorodenka Ukr. see Horodenka
Gorodets Rus. Fed. 52 I4
Gorodishche Penzenskaya Oblast' Rus. Fed. 53 J5
Gorodishche Volgogradskaya Oblast' Rus. Fed. 53 J6
Gorodok Belarus see Haradok
Gorodok Rus. Fed. see Zakamensk
Gorodok Khmel'nyts'ka Oblast' Ukr. see Horodok
Gorodok L'vivs'ka Oblast' Ukr. see Horodok
Gorodovikovsk Rus. Fed. 53 I7
Goroka P.N.G. 81 L8
Gorokhovets Rus. Fed. 52 I4
Gorom Gorom Burkina Faso 120 C3
Gorong, Kepulauan is Indon. 81 I7
Gorongosa mt. Moz. 123 D5
Gorongosa, Parque Nacional de nat. park Moz. 123 D5
Gorontalo Sulawesi Indon. 83 B2
Gorontalo prov. Indon. 83 B2
Gorshechnoye Rus. Fed. 53 H6
Gort Ireland 61 D4
Gortahork Ireland see Gort an Choirce
Gort an Choirce Ireland 61 D2
Gorutuba r. Brazil 179 C1
Gorveh Iran 110 E4
Goryachiy Klyuch Rus. Fed. 113 E1
Görzke Germany 63 M2
Gorzów Wielkopolski Poland 57 O4
Gosainthan mt. Xizang China see Xixabangma Feng
Gose Japan 92 B4
Gosforth U.K. 58 F3
Goshen CA U.S.A. 158 D3
Goshen IN U.S.A. 164 C3
Goshen NH U.S.A. 165 I2
Goshen NY U.S.A. 165 H3
Goshen VA U.S.A. 164 F5
Goshiki Japan 92 A4
Goshoba Turkm. see Goşoba
Goslar Germany 63 K3
Goşoba Turkm. 113 I2
Gospić Croatia 68 F2
Gosport U.K. 59 F8
Gossi Mali 120 C3
Gostivar Macedonia 69 I4
Gosu China 96 C1
Göteborg Sweden see Gothenburg
Gotemba Shizuoka Japan see Gotenba
Gotenba Shizuoka Japan 93 E3
Götene Sweden 55 H7
Gotenhafen Poland see Gdynia
Gotha Germany 63 K4
Gothenburg Sweden 55 G8
Gothenburg U.S.A. 160 C3
Gotland i. Sweden 55 K8
Gotō-rettō is Japan 91 C6
Gotse Delchev Bulg. 69 J4
Gotska Sandön i. Sweden 55 K7
Gōtsu Japan 91 D6
Göttingen Germany 63 J3
Gott Peak Canada 150 F5
Gottwaldow Czech Rep. see Zlín
Gouda Neth. 62 E2
Goudiri Senegal 120 B3
Goudoumaria Niger 120 E3
Goûgaram Niger 120 D3
▶Gough Island S. Atlantic Ocean 184 H8
Dependency of St Helena.
Gouin, Réservoir resr Canada 152 G4
Goulburn Australia 138 D5
Goulburn r. N.S.W. Australia 138 E4
Goulburn r. Vic. Australia 138 B6
Goulburn Islands Australia 134 F2
Goulburn River National Park Australia 138 E4
Gould Coast Antarctica 188 J1
Goulou atoll Micronesia see Ngulu
Goundam Mali 120 C3
Goundi Chad 121 E4
Goupil, Lac l. Canada 153 H3
Gouraya Alg. 67 G5
Gourcy Burkina Faso 120 C3
Gourdon France 66 E4
Gouré Niger 120 E3
Gouripur Bangl. 105 G4
Gourits r. S. Africa 124 E8
Gourma-Rharous Mali 120 C3
Gournay-en-Bray France 62 B5
Goussainville France 62 C5
Gouverneur U.S.A. 165 H1
Governador Valadares Brazil 179 C2
Governor Generoso Mindanao Phil. 82 D5
Governor's Harbour Bahamas 163 E7
Govĭ-Altay prov. Mongolia 94 C2
Govĭ Altayn Nuruu mts Mongolia 94 D2
Govind Ballash Pant Sagar resr India 105 E4
Govind Sagar resr India 99 B7
Govĭ-Ugtaal Mongolia 95 F2
Gowanda U.S.A. 165 F2
Gowan Range hills Australia 136 D5
Gowaqungo Xizang China 99 D7
Gowārān Afgh. 111 G4
Gowd-e Mokh l. Iran 110 D4
Gowd-e Zereh plain Afgh. 111 F4
Gowmal Kalay Afgh. 111 H3
Gowna, Lough l. Ireland 61 E4
Goya Arg. 178 E3
Göyçay Azer. 113 G2
Goyder watercourse Australia 135 F6
Goýmatdag hills Turkm. 110 D1
Goymatdag hills Turkm. see Goýmatdag
Göynük Turkey 69 N4
Goyoum Cameroon 120 E4
Gozareh Afgh. 111 F3
Goz-Beïda Chad 121 F3
Gozen-yama Japan 93 G2
Gozha Co salt l. China 99 C6
Gözkaya Turkey 107 C1
Gozo i. Malta 68 F6
Graaff-Reinet S. Africa 124 G7
Grabfeld plain Germany 63 K4
Grabo Côte d'Ivoire 120 C4
Grabouw S. Africa 124 D8
Grabow Germany 63 L1
Gračac Croatia 68 F2
Gracefield Canada 152 F5
Gracey U.S.A. 164 B5
Grachi Kazakh. 98 B2
Gracias Hond. 166 [inset] H6
Gradaús, Serra dos hills Brazil 177 H5
Gradiška Bos.-Herz. see Bosanska Gradiška
Grady U.S.A. 161 C5
Gräfenhainichen Germany 63 M3
Grafenwöhr Germany 63 L5
Grafton Australia 138 F2
Grafton ND U.S.A. 160 D1
Grafton WI U.S.A. 164 B2
Grafton WV U.S.A. 164 E4
Grafton, Cape Australia 136 D3
Grafton, Mount U.S.A. 159 F2
Grafton Passage Australia 136 D3
Graham NC U.S.A. 162 E4
Graham TX U.S.A. 161 D5
Graham, Mount U.S.A. 159 I5
Graham Bell Island Rus. Fed. see Greem-Bell, Ostrov
Graham Island B.C. Canada 149 N5
Graham Island Nunavut Canada 147 I2
Graham Land reg. Antarctica 188 L2
Grahamstown S. Africa 125 H7
Grahovo Bos.-Herz. see Bosansko Grahovo
Graigue Ireland 61 F5
Grajagan Jawa Indon. 85 F5
Grajaú Brazil 177 I5
Grajaú r. Brazil 177 J4
Grammont Belgium see Geraardsbergen
Grammos mt. Greece 69 I4
Grampian Mountains U.K. 60 E4
Grampians National Park Australia 137 C8
Granada Nicaragua 166 [inset] I7
Granada Spain 67 E5
Granada U.S.A. 160 C4
Granard Ireland 61 E4
Granbury U.S.A. 161 D5
Granby Canada 153 G5
Gran Canaria i. Canary Is 120 B2
Gran Chaco reg. Arg./Para. 178 D3
Grand r. MO U.S.A. 164 B2
Grand r. SD U.S.A. 160 C2
Grand Atlas mts Morocco see Haut Atlas
Grand Bahama i. Bahamas 163 E7
Grand Ballon mt. France 57 K7
Grand Bank Canada 153 L5
Grand Banks of Newfoundland sea feature N. Atlantic Ocean 184 E3
Grand-Bassam Côte d'Ivoire 120 C4
Grand Bay-Westfield Canada 153 I5
Grand Bend Canada 164 E2
Grand Blanc U.S.A. 164 D2
Grand Canal Ireland 61 E4
Grand Canary i. Canary Is see Gran Canaria
Grand Canyon U.S.A. 159 G3
Grand Canyon gorge U.S.A. 159 G3
Grand Canyon National Park U.S.A. 159 G3
Grand Canyon - Parashant National Monument nat. park U.S.A. 159 G3
Grand Cayman i. Cayman Is 169 H5
Grand Drumont mt. France 57 K7
Grande r. Bahia Brazil 179 B1
Grande r. São Paulo Brazil 179 A3
Grande r. Nicaragua 166 [inset] J6
Grande, Bahía b. Arg. 178 C8
Grande, Cerro mt. Mex. 167 F5
Grande, Ilha i. Brazil 179 B3
Grande Cache Canada 150 G4
Grande Comore i. Comoros see Njazidja
Grande Prairie Canada 150 G4
Grand Erg de Bilma des. Niger 120 E3
Grand Erg Occidental des. Alg. 64 D5
Grand Erg Oriental des. Alg. 64 F6
Grande-Rivière Canada 153 I4
Grandes, Salinas salt marsh Arg. 178 C4
Gran Desierto del Pinacate, Parque Natural del nature res. Mex. 166 B2
Grande-Vallée Canada 153 I4
Grand Falls N.B. Canada 153 I5
Grand Falls-Windsor Nfld. and Lab. Canada 153 L4
Grand Forks Canada 150 G5
Grand Forks U.S.A. 160 D2
Grand Gorge U.S.A. 165 H2
Grand Haven U.S.A. 164 B2
Grandin, Lac l. Canada 150 G1
Grandioznyy, Pik mt. Rus. Fed. 88 H2
Grand Island U.S.A. 160 D3
Grand Isle U.S.A. 161 F6
Grand Junction U.S.A. 159 I2
Grand Lac Germain l. Canada 153 I4
Grand-Lahou Côte d'Ivoire 120 C4
Grand Lake N.B. Canada 153 I5
Grand Lake Nfld. and Lab. Canada 153 J3
Grand Lake Nfld. and Lab. Canada 153 K4
Grand Lake LA U.S.A. 161 E6
Grand Lake MI U.S.A. 164 D1
Grand Lake St Marys U.S.A. 164 C3
Grand Ledge U.S.A. 164 C2
Grand Manan Island Canada 153 I5
Grand Marais MI U.S.A. 162 C2
Grand Marais MN U.S.A. 160 F2
Grand-Mère Canada 153 G5
Grand Mesa U.S.A. 159 J2
Grândola Port. 67 B4
Grand Passage New Caledonia 133 G3
Grand Rapids Canada 151 L4
Grand Rapids MI U.S.A. 164 C2
Grand Rapids MN U.S.A. 160 E2
Grand-Sault Canada see Grand Falls
Grand Staircase-Escalante National Monument nat. park U.S.A. 159 H3
Grand St-Bernard, Col du pass Italy/Switz. see Great St Bernard Pass
Grand Teton mt. U.S.A. 156 F4
Grand Teton National Park U.S.A. 156 F4
Grand Traverse Bay U.S.A. 164 C1
▶Grand Turk Turks and Caicos Is 169 J4
Capital of the Turks and Caicos Islands.
Grandville U.S.A. 164 C2
Grandvilliers France 62 B5
Grand Wash Cliffs mts U.S.A. 159 F4
Grange Ireland 61 E6
Grängesberg Sweden 55 I6
Grangeville U.S.A. 156 D3
Granisle Canada 150 E4
Granite Falls U.S.A. 160 E2
Granite Mountain hill AK U.S.A. 148 G2
Granite Mountain hill AK U.S.A. 148 H3
Granite Mountain U.S.A. 158 E1
Granite Mountains CA U.S.A. 159 F4
Granite Mountains CA U.S.A. 159 F5
Granite Peak MT U.S.A. 156 F3
Granite Peak UT U.S.A. 159 G1
Granite Range mts AK U.S.A. 149 K4
Granite Range mts NV U.S.A. 158 D1
Granitola, Capo c. Sicily Italy 68 E6
Granja Brazil 177 J4
Gran Laguna Salada l. Arg. 178 C6
Gränna Sweden 55 I7
Gran Paradiso mt. Italy 68 B2
Gran Paradiso, Parco Nazionale del nat. park Italy 68 B2
Gran Pilastro mt. Austria/Italy 57 M7
Gran San Bernardo, Colle del pass Italy/Switz. see Great St Bernard Pass
Gran Sasso e Monti della Laga, Parco Nazionale del nat. park Italy 68 E3
Granschütz Germany 63 M3
Gransee Germany 63 N1
Grant U.S.A. 160 C3
Grant, Mount U.S.A. 158 E2
Grant Creek AK U.S.A. 148 I2
Grantham U.K. 59 G6
Grant Island Antarctica 188 J2
Grant Lake Canada 150 G1
Grantown-on-Spey U.K. 60 F3
Grant Range mts U.S.A. 159 F2
Grants U.S.A. 159 J4
Grants Pass U.S.A. 156 C4
Grantsville UT U.S.A. 159 G1
Grantsville WV U.S.A. 164 E4
Granville France 66 D2
Granville AZ U.S.A. 159 I5
Granville NY U.S.A. 165 I2
Granville TN U.S.A. 164 C5
Granville (abandoned) Y.T. Canada 149 M3
Granville Lake Canada 151 K3
Grão Mogol Brazil 179 C2

If you are Reading this I'm a 300 year old Alien and if you read this im coming to find you.

Grapevine Mountains U.S.A. 158 E3
Gras, Lac de *l.* Canada 151 I1
Graskop S. Africa 125 J3
Grasplatz Namibia 124 B4
Grass *r.* Canada 151 L3
Grass *r.* U.S.A. 165 H1
Grasse France 66 H5
Grassflat U.S.A. 165 F3
Grassington U.K. 58 F4
Grasslands National Park Canada 151 J5
Grassrange U.S.A. 156 F3
Grass Valley U.S.A. 158 C2
Grassy Butte U.S.A. 160 C2
Grästorp Sweden 55 H7
Gratz U.S.A. 164 C4
Graudenz Poland *see* **Grudziądz**
Graus Spain 67 G2
Gravataí Brazil 179 A5
Grave, Pointe de *pt* France 66 D4
Gravelbourg Canada 151 J5
Gravel Hill Lake Canada 151 K2
Gravelines France 62 C4
Gravelotte S. Africa 125 J2
Gravenhurst Canada 164 F1
Grave Peak U.S.A. 156 E3
Gravesend Australia 138 E2
Gravesend U.K. 59 H7
Gravina in Puglia Italy 68 G4
Grawn U.S.A. 164 C1
Gray France 66 G3
Gray *GA* U.S.A. 163 D5
Gray *KY* U.S.A. 164 C5
Gray *ME* U.S.A. 165 J2
Grayback Mountain U.S.A. 156 C4
Gray Lake Canada 151 I2
Grayling *r.* Canada 150 E3
Grayling *AK* U.S.A. 148 G3
Grayling U.S.A. 164 C1
Grayling Fork *r.* Canada/U.S.A. 149 L2
Grays U.K. 59 H7
Grays Harbor *inlet* U.S.A. 156 B3
Grays Lake U.S.A. 156 F4
Grayson U.S.A. 164 D4
Graz Austria 57 O7
Greasy Lake Canada 150 F2
Great Abaco *i.* Bahamas 163 E7
Great Australian Bight *g.* Australia 135 E8
Great Baddow U.K. 59 H7
Great Bahama Bank *sea feature* Bahamas 163 E7
Great Barrier Island N.Z. 139 E3
Great Barrier Reef Australia 136 D1
Great Barrier Reef Marine Park (Cairns Section) Australia 136 D3
Great Barrier Reef Marine Park (Capricorn Section) Australia 136 E4
Great Barrier Reef Marine Park (Central Section) Australia 136 E3
Great Barrier Reef Marine Park (Far North Section) Australia 136 D2
Great Barrington U.S.A. 165 I2
Great Basalt Wall National Park Australia 136 D3
Great Basin U.S.A. 158 E2
Great Basin National Park U.S.A. 159 F2
Great Bear *r.* N.W.T. Canada 149 P2

▶**Great Bear Lake** Canada 150 G1
4th largest lake in North America, and 7th in the world.

Great Belt *sea chan.* Denmark 55 G9
Great Bend U.S.A. 160 D4
Great Bitter Lake Egypt 107 A4
Great Blasket Island Ireland 61 B5

▶**Great Britain** *i.* U.K. 56 G4
Largest island in Europe, and 8th in the world.

Great Clifton U.K. 58 D4
Great Coco Island Cocos Is 80 A4
Great Cumbrae *i.* U.K. 60 E5
Great Dismal Swamp National Wildlife Refuge *nature res.* U.S.A. 165 G5
Great Dividing Range *mts* Australia 138 B6
Great Eastern Erg *des.* Alg. *see* **Grand Erg Oriental**
Greater Antarctica *reg.* Antarctica *see* **East Antarctica**
Greater Antilles *is* Caribbean Sea 169 H4
Greater Khingan Mountains China *see* **Da Hinggan Ling**
Greater St Lucia Wetland Park *nature res.* S. Africa 125 K4
Greater Sunda Islands Indon. 80 B7
Greater Tunb *i.* The Gulf 110 D5
Great Exuma *i.* Bahamas 163 F8
Great Falls U.S.A. 156 F3
Great Fish *r.* S. Africa 125 H7
Great Fish Point S. Africa 125 H7
Great Fish River Reserve Complex *nature res.* S. Africa 125 H7
Great Gandak *r.* India 105 F4
Great Ganges *atoll* Cook Is *see* **Manihiki**
Great Guana Cay *i.* Bahamas 163 E7
Great Inagua *i.* Bahamas 169 J4
Great Karoo *plat.* S. Africa 124 F7
Great Kei *r.* S. Africa 125 I7
Great Lake Australia 137 [inset]
Great Limpopo Transfrontier Park 125 J2
Great Malvern U.K. 59 E6
Great Meteor Tablemount *sea feature* N. Atlantic Ocean 184 G4
Great Namaqualand *reg.* Namibia 124 C4
Great Nicobar *i.* India 87 A6
Great Ormes Head *hd* U.K. 58 D5
Great Ouse *r.* U.K. 59 H6
Great Oyster Bay Australia 137 [inset]
Great Palm Islands Australia 136 D3
Great Plain of the Koukdjuak Canada 147 K3
Great Plains U.S.A. 160 C3
Great Point U.S.A. 165 J3
Great Rift Valley Africa 122 D4
Great Ruaha *r.* Tanz. 123 D4
Great Sacandaga Lake U.S.A. 165 H2
Great St Bernard Pass Italy/Switz. 68 B2
Great Salt Lake U.S.A. 159 G1
Great Salt Lake Desert U.S.A. 159 G1
Great Sand Dunes National Park U.S.A. 157 G5
Great Sand Hills Canada 151 I5
Great Sand Sea *des.* Egypt/Libya 112 B5
Great Sandy Desert Australia 134 C5
Great Sandy Island Australia *see* **Fraser Island**
Great Sea Reef Fiji 133 H3
Great Sitkin Island *AK* U.S.A. 149 [inset]

▶**Great Slave Lake** Canada 150 H2
Deepest and 5th largest lake in North America and 10th largest in the world.

Great Smoky Mountains U.S.A. 163 C5
Great Smoky Mountains National Park U.S.A. 162 D5
Great Snow Mountain Canada 150 E3
Greatstone-on-Sea U.K. 59 H8
Great Stour *r.* U.K. 59 I7
Great Torrington U.K. 59 C8
Great Victoria Desert Australia 135 E7
Great Wall *research station* Antarctica 188 A2
Great Wall *tourist site* China 95 I3
Great Waltham U.K. 59 H7
Great Western Erg *des.* Alg. *see* **Grand Erg Occidental**
Great West Torres Islands Myanmar 87 B5
Great Whernside *hill* U.K. 58 F4
Great Yarmouth U.K. 59 I6
Grebenkovskiy Ukr. *see* **Hrebinka**
Grebyonka Ukr. *see* **Hrebinka**
Greco, Cape Cyprus *see* **Greko, Cape**
Gredos, Sierra de *mts* Spain 67 D3
Greece *country* Europe 69 I5
Greece U.S.A. 165 G2
Greeley U.S.A. 156 G4
Greely Center U.S.A. 160 D3
Greem-Bell, Ostrov *i.* Rus. Fed. 76 H1
Green *r. KY* U.S.A. 164 B5
Green *r. WY* U.S.A. 159 I2
Green Bay U.S.A. 164 A1
Green Bay *b.* U.S.A. 164 B1
Greenbrier U.S.A. 164 B5
Greenbrier *r.* U.S.A. 164 E5
Green Cape Australia 138 E6
Greencastle Bahamas 163 E7
Greencastle U.K. 61 F3
Greencastle U.S.A. 164 B4
Green Cove Springs U.S.A. 163 D6
Greene *ME* U.S.A. 165 J1
Greene *NY* U.S.A. 165 H2
Greeneville U.S.A. 162 D4
Greenfield *CA* U.S.A. 158 C3
Greenfield *IN* U.S.A. 164 C4
Greenfield *MA* U.S.A. 165 I2
Greenfield *OH* U.S.A. 164 D4
Green Head *hd* Australia 135 A7
Greenhill Island Australia 134 F2
Green Island Taiwan *see* **Lü Tao**
Green Island Bay *Palawan* Phil. 82 B4
Green Lake Canada 151 J4

▶**Greenland** *terr.* N. America 147 N3
Self-governing Danish territory. Largest island in North America and in the world, and 3rd largest political entity in North America.

Greenland Basin *sea feature* Arctic Ocean 189 I2
Greenland Fracture Zone *sea feature* Arctic Ocean 189 I1
Greenland Sea Greenland/Svalbard 76 A2
Greenlaw U.K. 60 G5
Green Mountains U.S.A. 165 I1
Greenock U.K. 60 E5
Greenore Ireland 61 F3
Greenough, Mount *AK* U.S.A. 149 L1
Greenport U.S.A. 165 I3
Green River P.N.G. 81 K7
Green River *UT* U.S.A. 159 H2
Green River *WY* U.S.A. 156 F4
Green River Lake U.S.A. 164 C5
Greensboro U.S.A. 163 D5
Greensburg *IN* U.S.A. 164 C4
Greensburg *KS* U.S.A. 160 D4
Greensburg *KY* U.S.A. 164 C5
Greensburg *LA* U.S.A. 161 F6
Greensburg *PA* U.S.A. 164 F3
Greens Peak U.S.A. 159 I4
Greenstone Point U.K. 60 D3
Green Swamp U.S.A. 163 E5
Greentown U.S.A. 164 C3
Greenup *IL* U.S.A. 160 F4
Greenup *KY* U.S.A. 164 D4
Green Valley Canada 165 H1
Green Valley *AZ* U.S.A. 166 C2
Greenville *B.C.* Canada *see* **Laxgalts'ap**
Greenville Liberia 120 C4
Greenville *AL* U.S.A. 163 C6
Greenville *IL* U.S.A. 160 F4
Greenville *KY* U.S.A. 164 B5
Greenville *ME* U.S.A. 162 G2
Greenville *MI* U.S.A. 164 C2
Greenville *MS* U.S.A. 161 F5
Greenville *NC* U.S.A. 162 E5
Greenville *NH* U.S.A. 165 J2
Greenville *OH* U.S.A. 164 C3
Greenville *PA* U.S.A. 164 E3
Greenville *SC* U.S.A. 163 D5
Greenville *TX* U.S.A. 161 D5
Greenwich *atoll* Micronesia *see* **Kapingamarangi**
Greenwich *CT* U.S.A. 165 I3
Greenwich *OH* U.S.A. 164 D3
Greenwood *AR* U.S.A. 161 E5
Greenwood *IN* U.S.A. 164 B4
Greenwood *MS* U.S.A. 161 F5
Greenwood *SC* U.S.A. 163 D5
Gregory *r.* Australia 136 B3
Gregory, Lake *salt flat S.A.* Australia 137 B6
Gregory, Lake *salt flat W.A.* Australia 134 D5
Gregory, Lake *salt flat W.A.* Australia 135 B6
Gregory Downs Australia 136 B3
Gregory National Park Australia 134 E4
Gregory Range *hills Qld* Australia 136 C3
Gregory Range *hills W.A.* Australia 134 C5
Greifswald Germany 57 N3
Greiz Germany 63 M4
Greko, Cape Cyprus 107 B2
Gremikha Rus. Fed. 189 G2
Gremyachinsk Rus. Fed. 51 R4
Grenå Denmark 55 G8
Grenaa Denmark *see* **Grenå**
Grenada U.S.A. 161 F5
Grenada *country* West Indies 169 L6
Grenade France 66 E5
Grenen *spit* Denmark 55 G8
Grenfell Australia 138 D4
Grenfell Canada 151 K5
Grenoble France 66 G4
Grense-Jakobselv Norway 54 Q2
Grenville, Cape Australia 136 C1
Grenville Island Fiji *see* **Rotuma**
Greshak Pak. 111 G5
Gresham U.S.A. 156 C3
Gresik *Jawa* Indon. 85 F4
Gressåmoen Nasjonalpark *nat. park* Norway 54 H4
Greta *r.* U.K. 58 E4
Gretna U.K. 60 F6
Gretna *LA* U.S.A. 161 F6
Gretna *VA* U.S.A. 164 F5
Greußen Germany 63 K3
Grevelingen *sea chan.* Neth. 62 D3
Greven Germany 63 H2
Grevena Greece 69 I4
Grevenbicht Neth. 62 F3
Grevenbroich Germany 62 G3
Grevenmacher Lux. 62 G5
Grevesmühlen Germany 57 M4
Grey, Cape Australia 136 B2
Greybull U.S.A. 156 F3
Greybull *r.* U.S.A. 156 F3
Grey Hunter Peak *Y.T.* Canada 149 N3
Grey Islands Canada 153 L4
Greylock, Mount U.S.A. 165 I2
Greymouth N.Z. 139 C6
Grey Range *hills* Australia 138 A2
Grey's Plains Australia 135 A6
Greytown S. Africa 125 J5
Grez-Doiceau Belgium 62 E4
Gribanovskiy Rus. Fed. 53 I6
Gridley U.S.A. 158 C2
Griffin U.S.A. 163 C5
Griffin Point *pt AK* U.S.A. 149 L1
Griffith Australia 138 C5
Grigan *i.* N. Mariana Is *see* **Agrihan**
Grik Malaysia *see* **Gerik**
Grim, Cape Australia 137 [inset]
Grimari Cent. Afr. Rep. 122 C3
Grimma Germany 63 M3
Grimmen Germany 57 N3
Grimnitzsee *l.* Germany 63 N2
Grimsby U.K. 58 G5
Grímsey *i.* Iceland 54 [inset]
Grimshaw Canada 150 G3
Grímsstaðir Iceland 54 [inset]
Grimstad Norway 55 F7
Grindavík Iceland 54 [inset]
Grindsted Denmark 55 F9
Grind Stone City U.S.A. 164 D1
Grindul Chituc *spit* Romania 69 M2
Grinnell Peninsula Canada 147 I2
Griqualand East *reg.* S. Africa 125 I6
Griqualand West *reg.* S. Africa 124 F5
Griquatown S. Africa 124 F5
Grise Fiord Canada 147 J2
Grishino Ukr. *see* **Krasnoarmiys'k**
Grisik *Sumatera* Indon. 84 C3
Gris Nez, Cap *c.* France 62 B4
Gritley U.K. 60 G2
Grizzly Bear Mountain *hill* Canada 150 F1
Grmeč *mts* Bos.-Herz. 68 G2
Grobbendonk Belgium 62 E3
Groblersdal S. Africa 125 I3
Groblershoop S. Africa 124 F5
Grodno Belarus *see* **Hrodna**
Groen *watercourse* S. Africa 124 F6
Groen *watercourse* S. Africa 124 C6
Groix, Île de *i.* France 66 C3
Grombalia Tunisia 68 D6
Gronau (Westfalen) Germany 62 H2
Grong Norway 54 H4
Groningen Neth. 62 G1
Groninger Wad *tidal flat* Neth. 62 G1
Grønland *terr.* N. America *see* **Greenland**
Groom Lake U.S.A. 159 F3
Groot-Aar Pan *salt pan* S. Africa 124 E4
Groot Berg *r.* S. Africa 124 D7
Groot Brakrivier S. Africa 124 F8
Grootdraaidam *dam* S. Africa 125 I4
Grootdrink S. Africa 124 E5
Groote Eylandt *i.* Australia 136 B2
Grootfontein Namibia 123 B5
Groot Karas Berg *plat.* Namibia 124 D4
Groot Letaba *r.* S. Africa 125 J2
Groot Marico S. Africa 125 H3
Groot Swartberge *mts* S. Africa 124 E7
Grootvloer *salt pan* S. Africa 124 E5
Groot Winterberg *mt.* S. Africa 125 H7
Gros Morne National Park Canada 153 K4
Gross Barmen Namibia 124 C2
Große Aue *r.* Germany 63 J2
Große Laaber *r.* Germany 63 M6
Großengottern Germany 63 K3
Großenkneten Germany 63 I2
Großenlüder Germany 63 J4
Großer Arber *mt.* Germany 63 N5
Großer Beerberg *hill* Germany 63 K4
Großer Eyberg *hill* Germany 63 H5
Großer Gleichberg *hill* Germany 63 K4
Großer Kornberg *hill* Germany 63 M4
Großer Osser *mt.* Czech Rep./Germany 63 N5
Großer Rachel *mt.* Germany 57 N6
Grosser Speikkogel *mt.* Austria 57 O7
Grosseto Italy 68 D3
Grossevichi Rus. Fed. 90 E3
Groß-Gerau Germany 63 I5
Großglockner *mt.* Austria 57 N7
Groß Oesingen Germany 63 K2
Großrudestedt Germany 63 L3
Groß Schönebeck Germany 63 N2
Gross Ums Namibia 124 D2
Großvenediger *mt.* Austria 57 N7
Gros Ventre Range *mts* U.S.A. 156 F4
Groswater Bay Canada 153 K3
Groton U.S.A. 160 D2
Grottoes U.S.A. 165 F4
Grou Neth. 62 F1
Groundhog *r.* Canada 152 E4
Grouw Neth. *see* **Grou**
Grove U.S.A. 161 E4
Grove City U.S.A. 164 D4
Grove Hill U.S.A. 163 C6
Grove Mountains Antarctica 188 E2
Grover Beach U.S.A. 158 C4
Grovertown U.S.A. 164 B3
Groveton *NH* U.S.A. 165 J1
Groveton *TX* U.S.A. 161 E6
Growler Mountains U.S.A. 159 G5
Groznyy Rus. Fed. 113 G2
Grubišno Polje Croatia 68 G2
Grudovo Bulg. *see* **Sredets**
Grudziądz Poland 57 Q4
Grünau Namibia 124 D4
Grünberg Poland *see* **Zielona Góra**
Grundarfjörður Iceland 54 [inset]
Grundy U.S.A. 164 D5
Gruñidora Mex. 161 C7
Grünstadt Germany 63 I5
Gruver U.S.A. 161 C4
Gruzinskaya S.S.R. *country* Asia *see* **Georgia**
Gryazi Rus. Fed. 53 H5
Gryazovets Rus. Fed. 52 I4
Gryfice Poland 57 O4
Gryfino Poland 57 O4
Gryfów Śląski Poland 57 O5
Gryllefjord Norway 54 J2
Grytviken S. Georgia 178 I8
Gua India 105 F5
Guacanayabo, Golfo de *b.* Cuba 169 I4
Guachochi Mex. 157 G8
Guadajoz *r.* Spain 67 D5
Guadalajara Mex. 168 D4
Guadalajara Spain 67 E3
Guadalcanal *i.* Solomon Is 133 G2
Guadalete *r.* Spain 67 C5
Guadalope *r.* Spain 67 F3
Guadalquivir *r.* Spain 67 C5
Guadalupe *Nuevo León* Mex. 167 E3
Guadalupe *Zacatecas* Mex. 166 E4
Guadalupe *i.* Mex. 166 A2
Guadalupe *watercourse* Mex. 158 E5
Guadalupe U.S.A. 158 C4
Guadalupe *r. TX* U.S.A. 167 F2
Guadalupe, Sierra de *mts* Spain 67 D4
Guadalupe Aguilera Mex. 161 B7
Guadalupe Bravos Mex. 157 G7
Guadalupe Mountains National Park U.S.A. 157 G7
Guadalupe Peak U.S.A. 157 G7
Guadalupe Victoria *Baja California* Mex. 159 F5
Guadalupe Victoria *Durango* Mex. 161 B7
Guadalupe y Calvo Mex. 166 D3
Guadarrama, Sierra de *mts* Spain 67 D3

▶**Guadeloupe** *terr.* West Indies 169 L5
French Overseas Department.

Guadeloupe Passage Caribbean Sea 169 L5
Guadiana *r.* Port./Spain 67 C5
Guadix Spain 67 E5
Guafo, Isla *i.* Chile 178 B6
Guagua *Luzon* Phil. 82 C3
Guaíba Brazil 179 A5
Guaiçuí Brazil 179 B2
Guaíra Brazil 178 F2
Guaizihu *Nei Mongol* China 94 E3
Guajaba, Cayo *i.* Cuba 163 E8
Guaje, Laguna de *l.* Mex. 166 E2
Guaje, Llano de *plain* Mex. 166 E3
Gualala U.S.A. 158 B2
Gualán Guat. 167 H6
Gualeguay Arg. 178 E4
Gualeguaychu Arg. 178 E4
Gualicho, Salina *salt flat* Arg. 178 C6

▶**Guam** *terr.* N. Pacific Ocean 81 K4
United States Unincorporated Territory.

Guamblin, Isla *i.* Chile 178 A6
Guampí, Sierra de *mts* Venez. 176 E2
Guamúchil Mex. 166 C3
Gua Musang Malaysia 84 C1
Gu'an *Hebei* China 95 I4
Guanabacoa Cuba 163 D8
Guanacaste, Cordillera de *mts* Costa Rica 166 [inset] I7
Guanacaste, Parque Nacional *nat. park* Costa Rica 166 [inset] I7
Guanacevi Mex. 166 D3
Guanahacabibes, Península de *pen.* Cuba 163 C8
Guanaja Hond. 166 [inset] I5
Guanajay Cuba 163 D8
Guanajuato Mex. 168 D4
Guanajuato *state* Mex. 167 E4
Guanambi Brazil 179 C1
Guanare Venez. 176 E2
Guandaokou *Henan* China 95 G5
Guandi Shan *mt. Shanxi* China 95 G4
Guandu China 97 G3
Guane Cuba 169 H4
Guang'an China 96 E2
Guangchang China 97 H3
Guangdong *prov.* China 97 [inset]
Guanghai China 97 G4
Guanghan China 96 E2
Guanghua China *see* **Laohekou**
Guangling *Shanxi* China 95 H4
Guangming China *see* **Xide**
Guangming Ding *mt.* China 97 H2
Guangnan China 96 E3
Guangning *Liaoning* China *see* **Beining**
Guangrao *Shandong* China 95 I4
Guangshan China 97 G2
Guangxi *aut. reg.* China *see* **Guangxi Zhuangzu Zizhiqu**
Guangxi Zhuangzu Zizhiqu *aut. reg.* China 96 F4
Guangyuan China 96 E1
Guangze China 97 H3
Guangzhou China 97 G4
Guangzong *Hebei* China 95 H4
Guanhães Brazil 179 C2
Guan He *r.* China 95 I5
Guanhe Kou *r. mouth* China 95 I5
Guanipa *r.* Venez. 176 F2
Guanling China 96 E3
Guanmian Shan *mts* China 97 F2
Guannan China 97 H1
Guanpo China 97 F1
Guanshui China 90 B4
Guansuo China *see* **Guanling**
Guantánamo Cuba 169 I4
Guantao *Hebei* China 95 H4
Guanting *Qinghai* China 94 E5
Guanxian China *see* **Dujiangyan**
Guanyang China 97 F3
Guanyinqiao China 96 D2
Guanyun *Jiangsu* China 95 I5
Guapé Brazil 179 B3
Guapí Col. 176 C3
Guápiles Costa Rica 166 [inset] J7
Guaporé *r.* Bol./Brazil 176 E6
Guaporé Brazil 179 A5
Guaqui Bol. 176 E7
Guará *r.* Brazil 179 B1
Guarabira Brazil 177 K5
Guaranda Ecuador 176 C4
Guarapari Brazil 179 C3
Guarapuava Brazil 179 A4
Guararapes Brazil 179 A3
Guaratinguetá Brazil 179 B3
Guaratuba Brazil 179 A4
Guaratuba, Baía de *b.* Brazil 179 A4
Guarda Port. 67 C3
Guardafui, Cape Somalia *see* **Gwardafuy, Gees**
Guardiagrele Italy 68 F3
Guardo Spain 67 D2
Guárico, del Embalse *resr* Venez. 176 E2
Guarujá Brazil 179 B3
Guasave Mex. 166 C3
Guasdualito Venez. 176 D2
Guastatoya Guat. 167 H6

▶**Guatemala** *country* Central America 167 H6
4th most populous country in North America.

Guatemala Guat. *see* **Guatemala City**

▶**Guatemala City** Guat. 167 H6
Capital of Guatemala.

Guaviare *r.* Col. 176 E3
Guaxupé Brazil 179 B3
Guayaquil Ecuador 176 C4
Guayaquil, Golfo de *g.* Ecuador 176 B4
Guaymas Mex. 166 C3
Guazacapán Guat. 167 H6
Guazhou *Gansu* China 94 C3
Guba Eth. 122 D2
Gubakha Rus. Fed. 51 R4
Gubat *Luzon* Phil. 82 D3
Gubbi India 106 C3
Gubeikou *Beijing* China 95 I3
Gubio Nigeria 120 E3
Gubkin Rus. Fed. 53 H6
Gucheng *Gansu* China 94 D3
Gucheng *Gansu* China 94 E4
Gucheng *Hebei* China 95 H4
Gucheng China 97 F1
Gucheng *Shanxi* China 95 G5
Guchin-Us Mongolia 94 E2
Gudari India 106 D2
Gudbrandsdalen *valley* Norway 55 F6
Gudermes Rus. Fed. 113 G2
Gudivada India 106 D2
Gudiyattam India 106 C3
Gudur *Andhra Prad.* India 106 C3
Gudur *Andhra Prad.* India 106 C3
Gudvangen Norway 55 E6
Gudzhal *r.* Rus. Fed. 90 D2
Gué, Rivière du *r.* Canada 153 H2
Guecho Spain *see* **Algorta**
Guéckédou Guinea 120 B4
Guelma Alg. 68 B6
Guelmine Morocco 120 B2
Guelph Canada 164 E2
Guémez Mex. 161 D8
Guénange France 62 G5
Guerara Alg. 64 E5
Guérard, Lac *l.* Canada 153 I2
Guercif Morocco 64 D5
Guéret France 66 E3

▶**Guernsey** *terr.* Channel Is 59 E9
United Kingdom Crown Dependency.

Guernsey U.S.A. 156 G4
Guérou Mauritania 120 B3
Guerrah Et-Tarf *salt pan* Alg. 68 B7
Guerrero *Tamaulipas* Mex. 167 F3
Guerrero *state* Mex. 167 E5
Guerrero Negro Mex. 166 B3
Guers, Lac *l.* Canada 153 I2
Gueugnon France 66 G3
Gufeng China *see* **Pingnan**
Gufu China *see* **Xingshan**
Gugē *mt.* Eth. 122 D3
Gügerd, Küh-e *mts* Iran 110 D3
Guguan *i.* N. Mariana Is 81 L3
Guhakolak, Tanjung *pt* Indon. 84 D4
Guhe China 97 H2
Güh Küh *mt.* Iran 110 E5
Guhuai China *see* **Pingyu**
Guiana Basin *sea feature* N. Atlantic Ocean 184 E5
Guiana Highlands *mts* S. America 176 E2
Guichi China *see* **Chizhou**
Guichicovi Mex. 167 G5
Guidan-Roumji Niger 120 D3
Guide *Qinghai* China 94 E5
Guider Cameroon 121 E4
Guiding China 96 E3
Guidong China 97 G3
Guidonia-Montecelio Italy 68 E4
Guigang China 97 F4
Guiglo Côte d'Ivoire 120 C4
Guignicourt France 62 D5
Guija Moz. 125 K3
Guiji Shan *mts* China 97 I2
Guildford U.K. 59 G7
Guilford U.S.A. 162 G2
Guilherme Capelo Angola *see* **Cacongo**
Guilin China 97 F3
Guillaume-Delisle, Lac *l.* Canada 152 F2
Guimarães Brazil 177 J4
Guimarães Port. 67 B3
Guimaras *i.* Phil. 82 C4
Guimaras Strait Phil. 82 C4
Guimeng Ding *mt. Shandong* China 95 I5
Guinan *Qinghai* China 94 E5
Guindulman *Bohol* Phil. 82 D4
Guinea *country* Africa 120 B3
Guinea, Gulf of Africa 120 D4
Guinea Basin *sea feature* N. Atlantic Ocean 184 H5
Guinea-Bissau *country* Africa 120 B3
Guinea-Conakry *country* Africa *see* **Guinea**
Guinea Ecuatorial *country* Africa *see* **Equatorial Guinea**
Guiné-Bissau *country* Africa *see* **Guinea-Bissau**
Guinée *country* Africa *see* **Guinea**
Güines Cuba 169 H4
Guînes France 62 B4
Guines, Lac *l.* Canada 153 J3
Guingamp France 66 C2
Guiones, Punta *pt* Costa Rica 166 [inset] I7
Guipavas France 66 B2
Guiping China 97 F4
Güira de Melena Cuba 163 D8
Guiratinga Brazil 177 H7
Guiscard France 62 D5
Guise France 62 D5
Guishan China *see* **Xinping**
Guishun China 96 E3
Guiuan *Samar* Phil. 82 D4
Guixi *Chongqing* China *see* **Dianjiang**
Guixi *Jiangxi* China 97 H2
Guiyang *Guizhou* China 96 E3
Guiyang *Hunan* China 97 G3
Guizhou *prov.* China 96 E3
Guizi China 97 F4
Gujarat *state* India 104 C5
Gujar Khan Pak. 111 I3
Gujerat *state* India *see* **Gujarat**
Gujiao *Shanxi* China 95 H4
Gujranwala Pak. 111 I3
Gujrat Pak. 111 I3
Gukovo Rus. Fed. 53 H6
Gulabgarh India 104 D2
Gulang *Gansu* China 94 E4
Gulbarga India 106 C2
Gulbene Latvia 55 O8
Gul'cha Kyrg. *see* **Gülchö**
Gülchö Kyrg. 102 D3
Gülcihan Turkey 107 B1
Gülek Boğazı *pass* Turkey 112 D3
Gulf, The Asia 110 C4
Gulf of Chihli China *see* **Bo Hai**
Gulfport U.S.A. 161 F6
Gulian China 90 A1
Gulin China 96 E3
Gulistan Uzbek. *see* **Guliston**
Guliston Uzbek. 102 C3
Gulitel *hill* Palau 82 [inset]
Gülitz Germany 63 L1
Guliya Shan *mt. Nei Mongol* China 95 J1
Gulja *Xinjiang* China *see* **Yining**
Gul Kach Pak. 111 H4
Gulkana *AK* U.S.A. 149 K3
Gul'kevichi Rus. Fed. 113 F1
Gull Lake Canada 151 I5
Gullrock Lake Canada 151 M5
Gullträsk Sweden 54 L3
Güllük Körfezi *b.* Turkey 69 L6
Gülnar Turkey 107 A1
Gul'shat Kazakh. 98 A3
Gulü China *see* **Xincai**
Gulu Uganda 122 D3
Guluwuru Island Australia 136 B1
Gulyayevskiye Koshki, Ostrova *is* Rus. Fed. 52 L1
Guma *Xinjiang* China *see* **Pishan**
Gumal *r.* Pak. 111 H4
Gumare Botswana 123 C5
Gumbaz Pak. 111 H4
Gumbinnen Rus. Fed. *see* **Gusev**
Gumdag Turkm. 110 D2
Gumel Nigeria 120 D3
Gümgüm Turkey *see* **Varto**
Gumla India 105 F5
Gumma Japan *see* **Gunma**
Gumma *pref.* Japan *see* **Gunma**
Gummersbach Germany 63 H3
Gumpang *r.* Indon. 84 B1
Gümüşhacıköy Turkey 112 D2
Gümüşhane Turkey 113 E2
Guna India 104 D4
Gunan China *see* **Qijiang**
Guna Terara *mt.* Eth. 108 E7
Gunbar Australia 138 B5
Gunbower Australia 138 B5
Güncang China 96 B2
Gund *r.* Tajik. *see* **Gunt**
Gundagai Australia 138 D5
Gundelsheim Germany 63 J5
Güney Turkey 69 M5
Güneydoğu Toroslar *plat.* Turkey 112 F3
Gunglilap Myanmar 86 B1
Gungu Dem. Rep. Congo 123 B4
Gunib Rus. Fed. 113 G2
Gunisao *r.* Canada 151 L4
Gunisao Lake Canada 151 L4
Gunma Japan 93 F2
Gunma *pref.* Japan 93 E2
Gunnaur India 104 D3
Gunnbjørn Fjeld *nunatak* Greenland 147 P3
Gunnedah Australia 138 E3
Gunnerus Ridge *sea feature* Antarctica 188 D2
Gunning Australia 138 D5
Gunnison U.S.A. 157 G5
Gunnison *r.* U.S.A. 159 I2
Gunong Ayer *Sarawak* Malaysia *see* **Gunung Ayer**
Güns Hungary *see* **Kőszeg**
Gunt *r.* Tajik. 111 H2
Guntakal India 106 C3
Güntersberge Germany 63 K3
Guntur India 106 D2
Gunungapi *i. Maluku* Indon. 83 C4
Gunung Ayer *Sarawak* Malaysia 85 E2
Gunungbatubesar *Kalimantan* Indon. 85 G3
Gunung Gading National Park Malaysia 85 E2
Gunung Gede Pangrango, Taman Nasional *nat. park* Indon. 84 D4
Gunung Halimun, Taman Nasional *nat. park* Indon. 84 D4
Gunung Leuser, Taman Nasional *nat. park* Indon. 84 B2
Gunung Mulu National Park Malaysia 85 F1
Gunung Niyut, Suaka Margasatwa *nature res.* Indon. 85 E2
Gunung Palung, Taman Nasional *nat. park* Indon. 85 E3
Gunung Rinjani, Taman Nasional *nat. park Lombok* Indon. 85 G5
Gunungsitoli Indon. 84 B2
Gunungsugih *Sumatera* Indon. 84 D4
Gunungtua *Sumatera* Indon. 84 B2
Günyüzü Turkey 112 C3
Gunza Angola *see* **Porto Amboim**
Günzburg Germany 57 M6
Gunzenhausen Germany 63 K5
Guochengyi *Gansu* China 94 F4
Guo He *r.* China 97 H1
Guo He *r.* China 95 H5
Guojia *Gansu* China 94 F5
Guojiatun *Hebei* China 95 I3
Guoluezhen *Henan* China *see* **Lingbao**
Guovdageaidnu Norway *see* **Kautokeino**
Guoyang *Anhui* China 95 I5
Guozhen *Shaanxi* China *see* **Baoji**
Gupis Pak. 104 C1
Gurban Obo *Nei Mongol* China 95 H3

Gurbantünggüt Shamo des. China 98 D3
Gurdaspur India 104 C2
Gurdon U.S.A. 161 E5
Gurdzhaani Georgia see Gurjaani
Güre Turkey 69 M5
Gurgan Iran see Gorgān
Gurgaon India 104 D3
Gurgei, Jebel mt. Sudan 121 F3
Gurha India 104 B4
Guri, Embalse de resr Venez. 176 F2
Gurig National Park Australia 134 F2
Gurinhatã Brazil 179 A2
Gurjaani Georgia 113 G2
Gur Khar Iran 111 E4
Guro Moz. 123 D5
Gurşunmagdan Kärhanasy Turkm. 111 G2
Guru China 105 G3
Gürün Turkey 112 E3
Gurupá Brazil 177 H4
Gurupi Brazil 177 I6
Gurupi r. Brazil 177 I4
Gurupi, Serra do hills Brazil 177 I4
Guru Sikhar mt. India 104 C4
Guruzala India 106 C2
Gurvandzagal Mongolia 95 H1
Gurvan Sayan Uul mts Mongolia 94 E3
Gurvansayhan Mongolia 95 F2
Gurvantes Mongolia 94 E3
Gur'yev Kazakh. see Atyrau
Gur'yevsk Rus. Fed. 55 L9
Gur'yevskaya Oblast' admin. div. Kazakh. see Atyrauskaya Oblast'
Gurz Afgh. 111 G3
Gusau Nigeria 120 D3
Güsen Germany 63 L2
Gusev Rus. Fed. 55 M9
Gushan China 91 A5
Gushgy Turkm. see Serhetabat
Gushi China 97 G1
Gusino Rus. Fed. 53 F5
Gusinoozersk Rus. Fed. 94 F1
Gusinoye, Ozero l. Rus. Fed. 94 F1
Gus'-Khrustal'nyy Rus. Fed. 52 I5
Guspini Sardinia Italy 68 C5
Gustav Holm, Kap c. Greenland see Tasiilap Karra
Gustavo Sotelo Mex. 166 B2
Gustavus AK U.S.A. 149 N4
Güsten Germany 63 L3
Gustine U.S.A. 158 C3
Güstrow Germany 57 N4
Gutang Xizang China 99 F7
Gütersloh Germany 63 I3
Guthrie AZ U.S.A. 159 I5
Guthrie KY U.S.A. 164 B5
Guthrie OK U.S.A. 161 D5
Guthrie TX U.S.A. 161 C5
Gutian Fujian China 97 H3
Gutian Fujian China 97 H3
Guting Shandong China see Yutai
Gutsuo China 105 F3
Guwahati India 105 G4
Guwēr Iraq 113 F3
Guwlumaýak Turkm. 110 D1
Guwlumayak Turkm. see Guwlumaýak
Guxhagen Germany 63 J3
Guxian China 97 G3
Guyana country S. America 177 G2
Guyane Française terr. S. America see French Guiana
Guyang Hunan China see Guzhang
Guyang Nei Mongol China 95 G3
Guyenne reg. France 66 D4
Guy Fawkes River National Park Australia 138 F3
Guyi China see Sanjiang
Guymon U.S.A. 161 C4
Guyot Glacier Canada/U.S.A. 149 L3
Guyra Australia 138 E3
Guysborough Canada 153 J5
Guyuan Hebei China 95 H3
Guyuan Ningxia China 94 F5
Güzeloluk Turkey 107 B1
Güzelyurt Cyprus see Morfou
Guzhang China 97 F2
Guzhen China 97 H1
Guzhou China see Rongjiang
Guzmán Mex. 166 D2
Guzmán, Lago de l. Mex. 166 D2
G'uzor Uzbek. 111 G2
Gvardeysk Rus. Fed. 55 L9
Gvasyugi Rus. Fed. 90 E3
Gwa Myanmar 86 A3
Gwabegar Australia 138 D3
Gwadar West Bay Pak. 111 F5
Gwaii Haanas National Park Reserve B.C. Canada 149 O5
Gwaldam Uttaranchal India 99 B7
Gwal Haidarzai Pak. 111 H4
Gwalior India 104 D4
Gwanda Zimbabwe 123 C6
Gwane Dem. Rep. Congo 122 C3
Gwardafuy, Gees c. Somalia 122 F2
Gwash Pak. 111 G4
Gwatar Bay Pak. 111 F5
Gwedaukkon Myanmar 86 A1
Gweebarra Bay Ireland 61 D3
Gweedore Ireland see Gaoth Dobhair
Gwelo Zimbabwe see Gweru
Gweru Zimbabwe 123 C5
Gweta Botswana 123 C6
Gwinner U.S.A. 160 D2
Gwoza Nigeria 120 E3
Gwydir r. Australia 138 D2
Gyablung Xizang China 99 F7
Gyaca Xizang China 99 F7
Gyaco Xizang China 99 C6
Gyagartang China 96 D1
Gyaijêpozhanggê Qinghai China see Zhidoi
Gyai Qu r. Xizang China 99 F7
Gyairong China 96 C1
Gyaisi China see Jiulong
Gyali i. Greece 69 L6
Gyamug Xizang China 99 C6
Gyandzha Azer. see Gäncä
Gyangnyi Caka salt l. China 99 D6
Gyangrang Xizang China 99 D7
Gyangtse Xizang China see Gyangzê
Gyangzê Xizang China 99 E7
Gya'nyima Xizang China 99 C7
Gyaring Qinghai China 94 D5
Gyaring Co l. China 99 E7
Gyaring Hu l. Qinghai China 94 D5
Gyarishing India 96 B2
Gyaros i. Greece 69 K6
Gyarubtang China 96 B2
Gydan, Khrebet mts Rus. Fed. see Kolymskiy, Khrebet
Gydan Peninsula Rus. Fed. 76 I2
Gydanskiy Poluostrov pen. Rus. Fed. see Gydan Peninsula
Gyêgu China see Yushu
Gyêmdong Xizang China 99 F7
Gyêsar Co l. Xizang China 99 D7
Gyêwa Xizang China see Zabqung
Gyigang China 96 C2
Gyimda Xizang China 99 F7
Gyipug Xizang China 99 C6
Gyirong Xizang China 99 D7
Gyirong Xizang China 99 D7
Gyixong Xizang China see Gonggar
Gyiza Qinghai China 99 F6
Gyldenløve Fjord inlet Greenland see Umiiviip Kangertiva
Gympie Australia 137 F5
Gyobingauk Myanmar 86 A3
Gyōda Japan 93 F2
Gyöngyös Hungary 57 Q7
Győr Hungary 68 G1
Gypsum Point Canada 150 H2
Gypsumville Canada 151 L5
Gyrfalcon Islands Canada 153 H2
Gytheio Greece 69 J6
Gyula Hungary 69 I1
Gyulafehérvár Romania see Alba Iulia
Gyümai China see Darlag
Gyumri Armenia 113 F2
Gyungcang Xizang China 99 B6
Gyzylarbat Turkm. see Serdar
Gyzylbaýdak Turkm. 111 F2
Gyzylbaydak Turkm. see Gyzylbaýdak
Gzhatsk Rus. Fed. see Gagarin

H

Ha Bhutan 105 G4
Haa-Alif Atoll Maldives see Ihavandhippolhu Atoll
Haanhöhiy Uul mts Mongolia 94 C1
Ha'apai Group is Tonga 133 I3
Haapajärvi Fin. 54 N5
Haapavesi Fin. 54 N4
Haapsalu Estonia 55 M7
Ha 'Arava watercourse Israel/Jordan see 'Arabah, Wādī al
Ha'Arava, Naḥal watercourse Israel/Jordan see Jayb, Wādī al
Haarlem Neth. 62 E2
Haarlem S. Africa 124 F7
Haarstrang ridge Germany 63 H3
Hab r. Pak. 111 G5
Habahe Xinjiang China 98 D2
Habana Cuba see Havana
Habarane Sri Lanka 106 D4
Habarōn well Saudi Arabia 110 C6
Habaswein Kenya 122 D3
Habay Canada 150 G3
Habbān Yemen 108 G7
Ḥabbānīyah, Hawr al l. Iraq 113 F4
Hab Chauki Pak. 111 G5
Habiganj Bangl. 105 G4
Habikino Japan 92 B4
Habirag Nei Mongol China 95 H3
Habra India 105 G5
Hachibuse-yama mt. Japan 93 E2
Hachijō-jima i. Japan 91 E6
Hachikai Japan 92 C3
Hachiman Japan 92 C3
Hachiman-misaki c. Japan 93 G3
Hachimori-yama mt. Japan 92 D2
Hachinohe Japan 90 F4
Hachiōji Japan 93 F3
Hachita U.S.A. 159 I6
Hacıköy Turkey see Çekerek
Hack, Mount Australia 137 B6
Hackberry U.S.A. 159 G4
Hackensack U.S.A. 165 H3
Hacufera Moz. 123 D6
Ḥadabat al Jilf al Kabīr plat. Egypt see Jilf al Kabīr, Haḍabat al
Hadadong Xinjiang China 98 C4
Hadagalli India 106 B3
Hada Mountains Afgh. 111 G4
Hadano Japan 93 F3
Hadapu Gansu China 94 F5
Hadat Nei Mongol China 95 I1
Hadayang Nei Mongol China 95 K1
Ḥadd, Ra's al pt Oman 111 E6
Haddington U.K. 60 G5
Haddumati Atoll Maldives see Hadhdhunmathi Atoll
Haddunmahti Atoll Maldives see Hadhdhunmathi Atoll
Hadejia Nigeria 120 E3
Ḥadera Israel 107 B3
Ḥadera r. Israel 107 B3
Haderslev Denmark 55 F9
Hadhdhunmathi Atoll Maldives 103 D11
Hadhramaut reg. Yemen see Ḥaḍramawt
Ḥādī, Jabal al mts Jordan 107 C4
Hadilik Xinjiang China 99 D5
Hadım Turkey 112 D3
Hadleigh U.K. 59 H6
Hadong S. Korea 91 B6
Ḥadraj, Wādī watercourse Saudi Arabia 107 C4
Ḥaḍramawt reg. Yemen 122 E2
Hadranum Sicily Italy see Adrano
Hadrian's Wall tourist site U.K. 58 E3
Hadrumetum Tunisia see Sousse
Hadsund Denmark 55 G8
Hadweenzic r. AK U.S.A. 149 K2
Hadyach Ukr. 53 G6
Haeju N. Korea 91 B5
Haeju-man b. N. Korea 91 B5
Haenam S. Korea 91 B6
Haenertsburg S. Africa 125 I2
Ha'erbin China see Harbin
Ḥafar al 'Atk well Saudi Arabia 110 B5
Ḥafar al Bāṭin Saudi Arabia 108 G4
Hafford Canada 151 J4
Hafik Turkey 112 E3
Ḥafīrah, Qā' al salt pan Jordan 107 C4
Hafirat Nasah Saudi Arabia 110 B5
Hafizabad Pak. 111 I3
Haflong India 105 H4
Hafnarfjörður Iceland 54 [inset]
Hafren r. U.K. see Severn
Haft Gel Iran 110 C4
Hafursfjörður b. Iceland 54 [inset]
Haga Myanmar see Haka
Hagachi-zaki pt Japan 93 E4
Hagar Nish Plateau Eritrea 108 E6

▶Hagåtña Guam 81 K4
Capital of Guam.

Hagelberg hill Germany 63 M2
Hagemeister Island AK U.S.A. 148 G4
Hagemeister Strait AK U.S.A. 148 G4
Hagen Germany 63 H3
Hagenow Germany 63 L1
Hagerhill U.S.A. 164 D5
Hagerstown U.S.A. 165 G4
Hagfors Sweden 55 H6
Haggin, Mount U.S.A. 156 E3
Hagi Japan 91 C6
Ha Giang Vietnam 86 D2
Hagiwara Japan 92 D3
Hagley U.K. 59 E6
Hag's Head hd Ireland 61 C5
Hague U.S.A. 165 I2
Haguenau France 63 H6
Hahajima-rettō is Japan 91 F8
Hai Tanz. 121 G5
Hai, Ko i. Thai. 84 B1
Hai'an China 97 F4
Haib watercourse Namibia 124 C5
Haibara Nara Japan 92 B4
Haibara Shizuoka Japan 93 E4
Haibowan Nei Mongol China see Wuhai
Haicheng Guangdong China see Haifeng
Haicheng Liaoning China 95 J3
Haicheng Ningxia China see Haiyuan
Haiding Hu salt l. Qinghai China 94 C5
Hai Dương Vietnam 86 D2
Haifa Israel 107 B3
Haifa, Bay of Israel 107 B3
Haifeng China 97 G4
Haig Australia 135 D7
Haiger Germany 63 I4
Haihu Qinghai China 94 E4
Haikakan country Asia see Armenia
Haikang China see Leizhou
Haikou China 97 F4
Ḥā'il Saudi Arabia 113 F6
Ḥā'il, Wādī watercourse Saudi Arabia 113 F6
Hailar Nei Mongol China see Hulun Buir
Hailey U.S.A. 156 E4
Haileybury Canada 152 F5
Hailin China 90 C3
Hailong China see Meihekou
Hails Nei Mongol China 95 I3
Hailsham U.K. 59 H8
Hailun China 90 B3
Hailuoto Fin. 54 N4
Hainan i. China 97 F5
Hainan prov. China 97 F5
Hai-nang Myanmar 86 B2
Hainan Strait China 97 F5
Hainaut reg. France 62 D4
Haines AK U.S.A. 149 N4
Haines Junction Y.T. Canada 149 M3
Haines Road Canada/U.S.A. 149 M3
Hainichen Germany 63 N4
Hainleite ridge Germany 63 K3
Hai Phong Vietnam 86 D2
Haiphong Vietnam see Hai Phong
Haiqing China 90 D3
Hairag Qinghai China 94 E4
Haitan Dao i. China 97 H3
Haiti country West Indies 169 J5
Haitou China 97 F5
Hai Triêu Vietnam 87 E4
Haiwee Reservoir U.S.A. 158 E3
Haiya Sudan 108 E6
Haiyan Qinghai China 94 E4
Haiyan Zhejiang China 97 I2
Haiyang China see Xiuning
Haiyang Shandong China 95 J4
Haiyang Dao i. China 91 A5
Haiyou China see Sanmen
Haiyuan Ningxia China 94 F4
Haizhou Wan b. China 95 I5
Hāj Ali Qoli, Kavīr-e salt l. Iran 110 D3
Hajdúböszörmény Hungary 69 I1
Hajeb El Ayoun Tunisia 68 C7
Ḥajhir mt. Yemen 109 H7
Haji Mahesar Pak. 111 G4
Hajipur India 105 F4
Hajir reg. Saudi Arabia 110 C5
Ḥajjah Yemen 108 F6
Ḥājjīābād Fārs Iran 110 D4
Ḥājjīābād Hormozgan Iran 110 D4
Ḥājjīābād Iran 110 D3
Haju Nei Mongol China 94 D3
Hajuu-Us Mongolia see Govĭ-Ugtaal
Haka Myanmar 86 A2
Hakha Myanmar see Haka
Hakkâri Turkey 113 F3
Hakkas Sweden 54 L3
Hakken-zan mt. Japan 92 B4
Hakkō-san hill Japan 93 E2
Hakodate Japan 90 F4
Hakkō-dake mt. Japan 90 F3
Hakone Japan 93 F3
Hakone-tōge pass Japan 93 F3
Hakos Mountains Namibia 124 C2
Hakseen Pan salt pan S. Africa 124 E4
Hakuba Japan 93 D2
Hakui Japan 92 C2
Hakusan Japan 92 C4
Haku-san vol. Japan 92 C2
Haku-san Kokuritsu-kōen nat. park Japan 92 C2
Hakushū Japan 93 E3
Hal Belgium see Halle
Hala Pak. 111 H5
Ḥalab Syria see Aleppo
Ḥalabja Iraq 113 G4
Halaç Turkm. 111 G2
Halaç Turkm. see Halaç
Halachó Mex. 167 H4
Halaha China 90 B3
Halahai China 90 B3
Halaib Egypt 108 E5

▶Halaib Triangle terr. Egypt/Sudan 108 E5
Disputed territory (Egypt/Sudan) administered by Egypt.

Halāl, Gebel hill Egypt see Hilāl, Jabal
Ha Lam Vietnam 86 E4
Ḥalāniyāt, Juzur al is Oman 109 I6
Hālawa U.S.A. 157 [inset]
Halba Lebanon 107 C2
Halban Hövsgöl Mongolia see Tsetserleg
Halberstadt Germany 63 L3
Halcon, Mount Mindoro Phil. 82 C3
Haldane r. N.W.T. Canada 149 Q2
Halden Norway 55 G7
Haldensleben Germany 63 L2
Haldwani India 104 D3
Hale watercourse Australia 136 A5
Hale Nei Mongol China 95 G3
Hale U.S.A. 164 D1
Hāleh Iran 110 D5
Haleparki Deresi r. Syria/Turkey see Quwayq, Nahr
Halesowen U.K. 59 E6
Halesworth U.K. 59 I6
Half Assini Ghana 120 C4
Halfmoon Bay N.Z. 139 B8
Halfway r. Canada 150 F3
Halfway Ireland 61 D6
Halfway Mountain hill AK U.S.A. 148 I3
Halfweg Neth. 62 E2
Halhgol Dornod Mongolia 95 I2
Halhgol Mongolia 95 I2
Halia India 105 E4
Ḥalībīyah Syria 113 E4
Haliburton Canada 165 F1
Haliburton Highlands hills Canada 165 F1
Halicarnassus Turkey see Bodrum

▶Halifax Canada 153 J5
Capital of Nova Scotia.

Halifax U.K. 58 F5
Halifax NC U.S.A. 162 E4
Halifax VA U.S.A. 165 F5
Halifax, Mount Australia 136 D3
Halik Shan mts Xinjiang China 98 C4
Halilulik Timor Indon. 83 C5
Ḥalīmah mt. Lebanon/Syria 107 C2
Haliut Nei Mongol China 95 G3
Halkett, Cape AK U.S.A. 148 I1
Halkirk U.K. 60 F2
Hall U.S.A. 164 C5
Hälla Sweden 54 J5
Halladale r. U.K. 60 F2
Halla-san National Park S. Korea 91 B6
Hall Beach Canada 147 J3
Halle Belgium 62 E4
Halle Neth. 62 G3
Halle (Saale) Germany 63 L3
Halleck U.S.A. 159 F1
Hällefors Sweden 55 I7
Hallein Austria 57 N7
Halle-Neustadt Germany 63 L3
Hallett, Cape Antarctica 188 H2
Hallettsville U.S.A. 161 D6
Halley research station Antarctica 188 B1
Hallgreen, Mount Antarctica 188 B2
Halliday U.S.A. 160 C2
Halliday Lake Canada 151 I2
Hall Island AK U.S.A. 148 D3
Hall Islands Micronesia 186 G5
Hällnäs Sweden 54 K4
Hallock U.S.A. 160 D1
Hall Peninsula Canada 147 L3
Hallsberg Sweden 55 I7
Halls Creek Australia 134 D4
Halls Gap U.S.A. 164 C5
Halls Lake Canada 165 F1
Hallstead U.S.A. 165 H3
Halluin Belgium 62 D4
Hallviken Sweden 54 I5
Halmahera i. Maluku Indon. 83 D2
Halmahera, Laut sea Maluku Indon. 83 D3
Halmahera Sea Maluku Indon. see Halmahera, Laut
Halmstad Sweden 55 H8
Ha Long Vietnam 86 D2
Hals Denmark 55 G8
Hälsingborg Sweden see Helsingborg
Halsua Fin. 54 N5
Haltang He r. China 94 C4
Haltern Germany 63 H3
Haltunchén Mex. 167 H5
Haltwhistle U.K. 58 E4
Ḥālūl i. Qatar 110 D5
Halura i. Indon. 83 B5
Ḥalvān Iran 110 E3
Halver Germany 63 H3
Haly, Mount hill Australia 138 E1
Ham France 62 D5
Hamada Japan 91 D6
Hamâda El Ḥaricha des. Mali 120 C2
Hamadān Iran 110 C3
Ḥamādat Murzuq plat. Libya 122 B1
Ḥamāh Syria 107 C2
Hamajima Japan 92 C4
Hamakita Japan 93 D4
Hamam Turkey 107 C1
Hamamatsu Japan 92 D4
Hamana-ko l. Japan 92 D4
Hamaoka Japan 93 E4
Hamar Norway 55 G6
Hamarøy Norway 54 I2
Ḥamāṭa, Gebel mt. Egypt see Ḥamāṭah, Jabal
Ḥamāṭah, Jabal mt. Egypt 108 D5
Hamatonbetsu Japan 90 F3
Hambantota Sri Lanka 106 D5
Hambergen Germany 63 I1
Hambleton Hills U.K. 58 F4
Hamburg Germany 63 J1
Hamburg land Germany 63 J1
Hamburg S. Africa 125 H7
Hamburg AR U.S.A. 161 F5
Hamburg NY U.S.A. 165 F2
Hamburgisches Wattenmeer, Nationalpark nat. park Germany 57 L4
Ḥamḍ, Wādī al watercourse Saudi Arabia 108 E4
Hamden U.S.A. 165 I3
Hämeenlinna Fin. 55 N6
HaMelaḥ, Yam salt l. Asia see Dead Sea
Hamelin Australia 135 A6
Hameln Germany 63 J2
Hamersley Lakes salt flat Australia 135 B7
Hamersley Range mts Australia 134 B5
Hamhŭng N. Korea 91 B5
Hami Xinjiang China 94 C3
Hamid Sudan 108 D5
Hamilton Qld Australia 136 C4
Hamilton S.A. Australia 137 A5
Hamilton Vic. Australia 137 C8
Hamilton watercourse Qld Australia 136 B4
Hamilton watercourse S.A. Australia 137 A5

▶Hamilton Bermuda 169 L2
Capital of Bermuda.

Hamilton Canada 164 F2
Hamilton r. Canada see Churchill
Hamilton N.Z. 139 E3
Hamilton U.K. 60 E5
Hamilton AK U.S.A. 148 G3
Hamilton AL U.S.A. 163 C5
Hamilton CO U.S.A. 159 J1
Hamilton MI U.S.A. 164 B2
Hamilton MT U.S.A. 156 E3
Hamilton NY U.S.A. 165 H2
Hamilton OH U.S.A. 164 C4
Hamilton TX U.S.A. 161 D6
Hamilton, Mount AK U.S.A. 148 H3
Hamilton, Mount CA U.S.A. 158 C3
Hamilton, Mount NV U.S.A. 159 F2
Hamilton City U.S.A. 158 B2
Hamilton Inlet Canada 153 K3
Hamilton Mountain hill U.S.A. 165 H2
Ḥamīm, Wādī al watercourse Libya 65 I5
Hamina Fin. 55 O6
Hamirpur Hima. Prad. India 104 D3
Hamirpur Uttar Prad. India 104 E4
Hamitabat Turkey see Isparta
Hamju N. Korea 91 B5
Hamlet U.S.A. 163 E5
Hamlin TX U.S.A. 161 C5
Hamlin WV U.S.A. 164 D4
Hamm Germany 63 H3
Ḥammām al 'Alīl Iraq 113 F3
Hammam Boughrara Alg. 67 F6
Hammamet Tunisia 68 D6
Hammamet, Golfe de g. Tunisia 68 D6
Ḥammār, Hawr al imp. l. Iraq 113 G5
Hammarstrand Sweden 54 J5
Hammelburg Germany 63 J4
Hammerdal Sweden 54 I5
Hammerfest Norway 54 M1
Hamminkeln Germany 62 G3
Hammond U.S.A. 164 B3
Hammond LA U.S.A. 167 H2
Hammone, Lac l. Canada 153 K4
Hammonton U.S.A. 165 H4
Ham Ninh Vietnam 87 D5
Hamoir Belgium 62 F4
Hampden Sydney U.S.A. 165 F5
Hampshire Downs hills U.K. 59 F7
Hampton AR U.S.A. 161 E5
Hampton IA U.S.A. 160 E3
Hampton NH U.S.A. 165 J2
Hampton SC U.S.A. 163 D5
Hampton VA U.S.A. 165 G5
Hampton Tableland reg. Australia 135 D8
Ḥamrā, Birkat al well Saudi Arabia 113 F5
Hamra, Vâdii watercourse Syria/Turkey see Ḥimār, Wādī al
Ḥamrā Jūdah plat. Saudi Arabia 110 C5
Hamrat esh Sheikh Sudan 108 C7
Ham Tân Vietnam 87 D5
Hamta Pass India 104 D2
Hāmūn-e Jaz Mūrīān salt marsh Iran 110 E5
Hāmūn-e Lowrah dry lake Afgh./Pak. see Hamun-i-Lora
Hāmūn Helmand salt flat Afgh./Iran 111 F4
Hamun-i-Lora dry lake Afgh./Pak. 111 G4
Hamun-i-Mashkel salt flat Pak. 111 F4
Hamunt Kūh hill Iran 111 F5
Hamur Turkey 113 F3
Hamura Japan 93 F3
Hamwic U.K. see Southampton
Hāna U.S.A. 157 [inset]
Hanábana r. Cuba 163 D8
Hanahai watercourse Botswana/Namibia 124 F2
Ḥanak Saudi Arabia 108 E4
Hanakpınar Turkey see Çınar
Hanalei U.S.A. 157 [inset]
Hanamaki Japan 91 F5
Hanamigawa Japan 93 G3
Hanang mt. Tanz. 123 D4
Hanau Germany 63 I4
Hanawa Japan 93 G2
Hanbin China see Ankang
Hanbogd Mongolia 95 F3
Hanchang China see Pingjiang
Hancheng Shaanxi China 95 G5
Hanchuan China 97 G2
Hancock MD U.S.A. 165 F4
Hancock NY U.S.A. 165 H3
Handa Japan 92 C4
Handa Island U.K. 60 D2
Handan Hebei China 95 H4
Handeni Tanz. 123 D4
Handian Shanxi China see Changzhi
Haneda airport Japan 93 F3
HaNegev des. Israel see Negev
HaNeqarot watercourse Israel 107 B4
Hanfeng China see Kaixian
Hanford U.S.A. 158 D3
Hangan Myanmar 86 B4
Hangayn Nuruu mts Mongolia 94 D1
Hangchow China see Hangzhou
Hangchuan China see Guangze
Hanggin Houqi Nei Mongol China see Xamba
Hanggin Qi Nei Mongol China see Xin
Hangō Fin. see Hanko
Hangu Tianjin China 95 I4
Hanguang China 97 G3
Hangya Qinghai China 94 D4
Hangzhou China 97 I2
Hangzhou Wan b. China 97 I2
Hani Turkey 113 F3
Hanish Kabir i. Yemen see Suyūl Ḥanīsh
Hanji Gansu China see Linxia
Hanjia China see Pengshui
Hanjiaoshui Ningxia China 94 F4
Hankensbüttel Germany 63 K2
Hankey S. Africa 124 G7
Hanko Fin. 55 M7
Hanksville U.S.A. 159 H2
Hanle India 104 D2
Hanley Canada 151 J5
Hann, Mount hill Australia 134 D3
Hanna Canada 151 I5
Hannagan Meadow U.S.A. 159 I5
Hannah Bay Canada 152 E4
Hannibal MO U.S.A. 160 F4
Hannibal NY U.S.A. 165 G2
Hannō Japan 93 F3
Hannover Germany 63 J2
Hannoversch Münden Germany 63 J3
Hann Range mts Australia 135 F5
Hannut Belgium 62 F4
Hanöbukten b. Sweden 55 I9

▶Ha Nôi Vietnam 86 D2
Capital of Vietnam.

Hanoi Vietnam see Ha Nôi
Hanover Canada 164 E1
Hanover Germany see Hannover
Hanover S. Africa 124 G6
Hanover NH U.S.A. 165 I2
Hanover PA U.S.A. 165 G4
Hanover VA U.S.A. 165 G5
Hansen Mountains Antarctica 188 D2
Hanshou China 97 F2
Han Shui r. China 97 G2
Hansi India 104 D3
Hansnes Norway 54 K2
Hanstholm Denmark 55 F8
Han Sum Nei Mongol China 95 I2
Han-sur-Nied France 62 G6
Hantsavichy Belarus 55 O10
Hanumangarh India 104 C3
Hanuy Gol r. Mongolia 94 E1
Hanwood Australia 138 C5
Hanxia Gansu China 94 D4
Hanyang China see Caidian
Hanyang Feng mt. China 97 G2
Hanyin China 97 F1
Hanyū Japan 93 F2
Hanzhong China 96 E1
Hao atoll Fr. Polynesia 187 K7
Haomen Qinghai China see Menyuan
Haora India 105 G5
Haparanda Sweden 54 N4
Happy Jack U.S.A. 159 H4
Happy Valley-Goose Bay Canada 153 J3
Hapur Uttar Prad. India 99 B7
Ḥaql Saudi Arabia 107 B5
Haqshah well Saudi Arabia 110 C6
Hara Japan 93 E3
Ḥaraḍ well Saudi Arabia 110 C5
Ḥarad, Jabal al mt. Jordan 107 B5
Haraḏh Saudi Arabia 108 G5
Haradok Belarus 53 F5
Haramachi Japan 91 F5
Haramgai Xinjiang China 98 D3
Haramukh mt. India 104 C2
Haran Turkey see Harran
Harappa Road Pak. 111 I4
Harar Eth. see Hārer

▶Harare Zimbabwe 123 D5
Capital of Zimbabwe.

Ḥarāsīs, Jiddat al des. Oman 109 I6
Harāt Iran 110 D4
Har-Ayrag Mongolia 95 G2
Haraze-Mangueigne Chad 121 F3
Harb, Jabal mt. Saudi Arabia 112 D6
Harbin China 90 B3
Harboi Hills Pak. 111 G4
Harbor Beach U.S.A. 164 D2
Harchoka India 105 E5
Harda India 104 D5
Harda Khas India see Harda
Hardangerfjorden sea chan. Norway 55 D7
Hardangervidda plat. Norway 55 E6
Hardangervidda Nasjonalpark nat. park Norway 55 E6
Hardap admin. reg. Namibia 124 C3
Hardap nature res. Namibia 124 C3
Hardap Dam Namibia 124 C3
Harden, Bukit mt. Indon. 85 F1
Hardenberg Neth. 62 G2
Harderwijk Neth. 62 F2
Hardeveld mts S. Africa 124 D6
Hardheim Germany 63 J5
Hardin U.S.A. 156 G3
Harding r. Nunavut Canada 149 R1
Harding S. Africa 125 I6
Harding Ice Field AK U.S.A. 149 J3
Harding Range hills Australia 135 B6
Hardinsburg IN U.S.A. 164 B4
Hardinsburg KY U.S.A. 164 B5
Hardoi India 104 E4
Hardwar India see Haridwar
Hardwick U.S.A. 165 I1
Hardy U.S.A. 161 F4
Hardy Reservoir U.S.A. 164 C2
Hare Bay Canada 153 L4
Hareiḍin, Wâdi watercourse Egypt see Ḥuraydin, Wādī
Hare Indian r. N.W.T. Canada 149 O2
Harelbeke Belgium 62 D4
Haren Neth. 62 G1
Haren (Ems) Germany 63 H2
Hārer Eth. 122 E3
Harf el Mreffi mt. Lebanon 107 B3
Hargant Nei Mongol China 95 I1
Hargeisa Somalia see Hargeysa
Hargele Eth. 122 E3
Hargeysa Somalia 122 E3
Harghita-Mădăraș, Vârful mt. Romania 69 K1
Harhatan Nei Mongol China 95 F4
Harhorin Mongolia 94 E2
Har Hu l. Qinghai China 94 D4
Haridwar India 104 D3
Ḥarif, Har mt. Israel 107 B4
Harihar India 106 B3
Harihari N.Z. 139 C6
Hariharpur India 106 B3
Ḥārim Syria 107 C1
Harīm, Jabal al mt. Oman 110 E5
Harima Japan 92 A4
Harima-nada b. Japan 92 A4
Haringhat r. Bangl. 105 G5
Haringvliet est. Neth. 62 E3
Harinoki-dake mt. Japan 92 D2
Ḥarīr, Wādī adh r. Syria 107 C3
Hari Rūd r. Afgh./Iran 111 F2
Harjavalta Fin. 55 M6
Harlan IA U.S.A. 160 E3
Harlan KY U.S.A. 164 D5
Harlan County Lake U.S.A. 160 D3
Harlech U.K. 59 C6
Harleston U.K. 59 I6
Harlingen Neth. 62 F1
Harlingen U.S.A. 161 D7
Harlow U.K. 59 H7
Harlowton U.S.A. 156 F3

Harly France 62 D5
Harman U.S.A. 164 F4
Harmancık Turkey 69 M5
Harmony U.S.A. 165 K1
Harmsdorf Germany 63 K1
Harnai India 106 B2
Harnai Pak. 111 G4
Harnes France 62 C4
Harney Basin U.S.A. 156 D4
Harney Lake U.S.A. 156 D4
Härnösand Sweden 54 J5
Harns Neth. see Harlingen
Har Nuden Nei Mongol China 95 I1
Har Nuur l. Mongolia 94 C1
Har Nuur l. Mongolia 94 D1
Haroldswick U.K. 60 [inset]
Harper Liberia 120 C4
Harper U.S.A. 161 D4
Harper, Mount Y.T. Canada 149 M2
Harper, Mount AK U.S.A. 149 L2
Harper Bend reg. AK U.S.A. 149 J2
Harper Creek r. Canada 150 H3
Harper Lake U.S.A. 158 E4
Harp Lake Canada 153 J3
Harpstedt Germany 63 I2
Harqin Qi Nei Mongol China see Jinshan
Harqin Zuoqi Mongolzu Zizhixian Liaoning China see Dachengzi
Harquahala Mountains U.S.A. 157 E6
Harrai India 104 D5
Harran Turkey 107 D1
Harrand Pak. 111 H4
Harricana, Rivière d' r. Canada 152 F4
Harrington Australia 138 F3
Harrington U.S.A. 165 H4
Harris, Lake salt flat Australia 137 A6
Harris, Mount Australia 135 E6
Harris, Sound of sea chan. U.K. 60 B3
Harrisburg AR U.S.A. 161 F5
Harrisburg IL U.S.A. 160 F4
Harrisburg NE U.S.A. 160 C3

▶Harrisburg PA U.S.A. 165 G3
Capital of Pennsylvania.

Harrismith Australia 135 B8
Harrison AR U.S.A. 161 E4
Harrison MI U.S.A. 164 C1
Harrison NE U.S.A. 160 C3
Harrison OH U.S.A. 164 C4
Harrison, Cape Canada 153 K3
Harrison Bay AK U.S.A. 149 J1
Harrisonburg LA U.S.A. 161 F6
Harrisonburg VA U.S.A. 165 F4
Harrisonville U.S.A. 160 E4
Harriston Canada 164 E2
Harrisville MI U.S.A. 164 D1
Harrisville NY U.S.A. 165 H1
Harrisville PA U.S.A. 164 E3
Harrisville WV U.S.A. 164 E4
Harrodsburg IN U.S.A. 164 B4
Harrodsburg KY U.S.A. 164 C5
Harrodsville N.Z. see Otorohanga
Harrogate U.K. 58 F5
Harrowsmith Canada 165 G1
Harry S. Truman Reservoir U.S.A. 160 E4
Har Sai Shan mt. Qinghai China 94 D5
Harsefeld Germany 63 J1
Harsīn Iran 110 B3
Harşit r. Turkey 112 E2
Hârşova Romania 69 L2
Harstad Norway 54 J2
Harsud India 104 D5
Harsum Germany 63 J2
Hart r. Canada 146 E3
Hart U.S.A. 164 B2
Hartao Liaoning China 95 J3
Hartbees watercourse S. Africa 124 E5
Hartberg Austria 57 O7
Harteigan mt. Norway 55 E6
Harter Fell hill U.K. 58 E4

▶Hartford CT U.S.A. 165 I3
Capital of Connecticut.

Hartford KY U.S.A. 164 B5
Hartford MI U.S.A. 164 B2
Hartford City U.S.A. 164 C3
Hartland U.K. 59 C8
Hartland U.S.A. 165 K1
Hartland Point U.K. 59 C7
Hartlepool U.K. 58 F4
Hartley U.S.A. 161 C5
Hartley Zimbabwe see Chegutu
Hartley Bay Canada 150 D4
Hartola Fin. 55 O6
Harts r. S. Africa 125 G5
Härtsfeld hills Germany 63 K6
Harts Range mts Australia 135 F5
Hartsville U.S.A. 164 B5
Hartswater S. Africa 124 G4
Hartville U.S.A. 161 E4
Hartwell U.S.A. 163 D5
Harue Japan 92 C2
Haruku i. Maluku Indon. 83 D3
Haruna Japan 93 E2
Haruno Japan 93 D3
Har Us Nuur l. Mongolia 94 C2
Har Us Nuur salt l. Mongolia 94 C1
Haruuhin Gol r. Mongolia 94 F1
Harūz-e Bālā Iran 110 E4
Harvard, Mount U.S.A. 156 G5
Harvey Australia 135 A8
Harvey U.S.A. 160 C2
Harvey Mountain U.S.A. 158 C1
Harwich U.K. 59 I7
Haryana state India 104 D3
Harz hills Germany 57 M5
Har Zin Israel 107 B4
Ḩaşāh, Wādī al watercourse Jordan 107 B4
Ḩaşāh, Wādī al watercourse Jordan/Saudi Arabia 107 C4
Hasalbag Xinjiang China 99 B5
Ḩasanah, Wādī watercourse Egypt 107 A4
Hasan Dağı mts Turkey 112 D3
Hasan Guli Turkm. see Esenguly
Hasankeyf Turkey 113 F3
Hasan Küleh Afgh. 111 F3
Hasanur India 106 C4
Hasardag mt. Turkm. 110 E2
Hasbaïya Lebanon 107 B3
Hasbaya Lebanon see Hasbaïya
Hase r. Germany 63 H2
Hase Japan 93 E3
Haselünne Germany 63 H2
Hashaat Arhangay Mongolia 94 E2
Hashaat Mongolia see Delgerhangay
Hashak Iran 111 F5
HaSharon plain Israel 107 B3
Hashima Japan 92 C3
Hashimoto Japan 92 B4
Hashtgerd Iran 110 C3
Hashtpar Iran 110 C2
Hashtrud Iran 110 B2
Haskell U.S.A. 161 D5
Haslemere U.K. 59 G7
Hăşmaşul Mare mt. Romania 69 K1
Ḩaşş, Jabal al hills Syria 107 C1
Hassan India 106 C3
Hassayampa watercourse U.S.A. 159 G5
Haßberge hills Germany 63 K4
Hasselt Belgium 62 F4
Hasselt Neth. 62 G2
Hassi Bel Guebbour Alg. 120 D2
Hassi Messaoud Alg. 64 F5
Hässleholm Sweden 55 H8
Hastings Australia 138 B7
Hastings r. Australia 138 F3
Hastings Canada 165 G1
Hastings N.Z. 139 F4
Hastings U.K. 59 H8
Hastings MI U.S.A. 164 C2
Hastings MN U.S.A. 160 E2
Hastings NE U.S.A. 160 D3
Hasuda Japan 93 F3
Hasunuma Japan 93 G3
Hata India 105 E4
Hata Japan 93 D2
Hatanbulag Mongolia 95 G3
Hatansuudal Mongolia see Bayanlig
Hatashō Japan 92 C3
Hatay Turkey see Antakya
Hatay prov. Turkey 107 C1
Hatch U.S.A. 159 G3
Hatches Creek (abandoned) Australia 136 A4
Hatchet Lake Canada 151 K3
Hatfield Australia 138 A4
Hatfield U.K. 58 G5
Hatgal Mongolia 94 E1
Hath India 106 D1
Hat Head National Park Australia 138 F3
Hathras India 104 D4
Ha Tiên Vietnam 87 D5
Ha Tinh Vietnam 86 D3
Hatisar Bhutan see Geylegphug
Hatod India 104 C5
Hato Hud East Timor see Hatudo
Hatra Iraq 113 F4
Hatsu-shima i. Japan 93 F3
Hattah Australia 137 C7
Hattah Kulkyne National Park Australia 137 C7
Hatteras, Cape U.S.A. 163 F5
Hatteras Abyssal Plain sea feature S. Atlantic Ocean 184 D4
Hattfjelldal Norway 54 H4
Hattiesburg U.S.A. 161 F6
Hattingen Germany 63 H3
Hatton, Gunung hill Malaysia 85 G1
Hattori-gawa r. Japan 92 C4
Hattras Passage Myanmar 87 B4
Hatudo East Timor 83 C5
Hat Yai Thai. 87 C6
Hau Bon Vietnam see A Yun Pa
Haubstadt U.S.A. 164 B4
Haud reg. Eth. 122 E3
Hauge Norway 55 E7
Haugesund Norway 55 D7
Haukeligrend Norway 55 E7
Haukipudas Fin. 54 N4
Haukivesi l. Fin. 54 P5
Haultain r. Canada 151 J4
Hauraki Gulf N.Z. 139 E3
Haut Atlas mts Morocco 64 C5
Haute-Normandie admin. reg. France 62 B5
Haute-Volta country Africa see Burkina Faso
Haut-Folin hill France 66 G3
Hauts Plateaux Alg. 64 D5

▶Havana Cuba 169 H4
Capital of Cuba.

Havana U.S.A. 160 F3
Havant U.K. 59 G8
Havasu, Lake U.S.A. 159 F4
Havel r. Germany 63 L2
Havelange Belgium 62 F4
Havelberg Germany 63 M2
Havelock Canada 165 G1
Havelock N.Z. 139 D5
Havelock Swaziland see Bulembu
Havelock U.S.A. 163 E5
Havelock Falls Australia 134 F3
Havelock Island India 87 A5
Havelock North N.Z. 139 F4
Haverfordwest U.K. 59 C7
Haverhill U.S.A. 165 J2
Haveri India 106 B3
Haversin Belgium 62 F4
Havixbeck Germany 63 H3
Havlíčkův Brod Czech Rep. 57 O6
Havøysund Norway 54 N1
Havran Turkey 69 L5
Havre U.S.A. 156 F2
Havre Aubert, Île du i. Canada 153 J5
Havre Rock i. Kermadec Is 133 I5
Havre-St-Pierre Canada 153 J4
Havza Turkey 112 D2
Hawai'i i. U.S.A. 157 [inset]
Hawai'ian Islands N. Pacific Ocean 186 I4
Hawaiian Ridge sea feature N. Pacific Ocean 186 I4
Hawai'i Volcanoes National Park U.S.A. 157 [inset]
Ḩawallī Kuwait 110 C4
Hawar i. Bahrain see Ḩuwār
Hawarden U.K. 58 D5
Hawea, Lake N.Z. 139 B7
Hawera N.Z. 139 E4
Hawes U.K. 58 E4
Hawesville U.S.A. 164 B5
Hāwī U.S.A. 157 [inset]
Hawick U.K. 60 G5
Ḩawīzah, Hawr al imp. l. Iraq 113 G5
Hawkdun Range mts N.Z. 139 B7
Hawke Bay N.Z. 139 F4
Hawkes Bay Canada 153 K4
Hawkins Peak U.S.A. 159 G3
Hawlēr Iraq see Arbīl
Hawley U.S.A. 165 H3
Hawng Luk Myanmar 86 B2
Ḩawrān, Wādī watercourse Iraq 113 F4
Ḩawshah, Jibāl al mts Saudi Arabia 110 B6
Hawston S. Africa 124 D8
Hawthorne U.S.A. 158 D2
Haxat China 90 B3
Haxat Hudag Nei Mongol China 95 H2
Haxby U.K. 58 F4
Hay Australia 138 B5
Hay watercourse Australia 136 B5
Hay r. Canada 150 H2
Haya Seram Indon. 83 D3
Hayachine-san mt. Japan 91 F5
Haya-gawa r. Japan 93 D1
Hayakawa Japan 93 E3
Haya-kawa r. Japan 93 E3
Hayama Japan 93 F3
Hayastan country Asia see Armenia
Haycock AK U.S.A. 148 G2
Haydān, Wādī al r. Jordan 107 B4
Hayden AZ U.S.A. 159 H5
Hayden CO U.S.A. 159 J1
Hayden IN U.S.A. 164 C4
Hayes r. Man. Canada 151 M3
Hayes r. Nunavut Canada 147 I3
Hayes, Mount AK U.S.A. 149 K3
Hayes Halvø pen. Greenland 147 L2
Hayfield Reservoir U.S.A. 159 F5
Hayfork U.S.A. 158 B1
Hayl, Wādī watercourse Syria 107 C3
Hayl, Wādī al watercourse Syria 107 D2
Haylaastay Mongolia see Sühbaatar
Hayle U.K. 59 B8
Haymā' Oman 109 I6
Haymana Turkey 112 D3
Haymarket U.S.A. 165 G4
Hay-on-Wye U.K. 59 D6
Hayrabolu Turkey 69 L4
Hayrhandulaan Mongolia 94 E2
Hay River Canada 146 G3
Hay River Reserve Canada 150 H2
Hays KS U.S.A. 160 D4
Hays MT U.S.A. 156 F2
Ḩays Yemen 108 F7
Haysville U.S.A. 161 D4
Haysyn Ukr. 53 F6
Ḩayṭān, Jabal hill Egypt 107 A4
Hayward CA U.S.A. 158 B3
Hayward WI U.S.A. 160 F2
Haywards Heath U.K. 59 G8
Hazar Turkm. 110 D2
Hazarajat reg. Afgh. 111 G3
Hazard U.S.A. 164 D5
Hazaribag India see Hazaribagh
Hazaribagh India 105 F5
Hazaribagh Range mts India 105 E5
Hazār Masjed, Kūh-e mts Iran 110 E2
Hazebrouck France 62 C4
Hazelton Canada 150 E4
Hazen Bay AK U.S.A. 148 F3
Hazen Strait Canada 147 G2
Hazerswoude-Rijndijk Neth. 62 E2
Hazhdanahr reg. Afgh. 111 G2
Hazlehurst MS U.S.A. 167 H2
Hazleton IN U.S.A. 164 B4
Hazleton PA U.S.A. 165 H3
Hazlett, Lake salt flat Australia 134 E5
Ḩaẓrat-e Solṭān Afgh. 111 G2
Hazu Japan 92 D4
Hazumi-saki pt Japan 92 C4
H. Bouchard Arg. 178 D4
Headford Ireland 61 C4
Headingly Australia 136 B4
Head of Bight b. Australia 135 E7
Healdsburg U.S.A. 158 B2
Healesville Australia 138 B6
Healy AK U.S.A. 149 J3
Healy Lake AK U.S.A. 149 K3
Heanor U.K. 59 F5
Heard Island Indian Ocean 185 M9

▶Heard Island and McDonald Islands terr. Indian Ocean 185 M9
Australian External Territory.

Hearne U.S.A. 161 D6
Hearne Lake Canada 151 H2
Hearrenfean Neth. see Heerenveen
Hearst Canada 152 E4
Hearst Island Antarctica 188 L2
Heart r. U.S.A. 160 C2
Heart of Neolithic Orkney tourist site U.K. 60 F1
Heathcote Australia 138 B6
Heathfield U.K. 59 H8
Heathsville U.S.A. 165 G5
Hebbardsville U.S.A. 164 B5
Hebbronville U.S.A. 161 D7
Hebei prov. China 95 H4
Hebel Australia 138 C2
Heber U.S.A. 159 H4
Heber City U.S.A. 159 H1
Heber Springs U.S.A. 161 E5
Hebi Henan China 95 H5
Hebian Shanxi China 95 H4
Hebron Canada 153 J2
Hebron U.S.A. 160 D3
Hebron West Bank 107 B4
Hecate Strait B.C. Canada 149 O5
Hecelchakán Mex. 167 H4
Hecheng Jiangxi China see Zixi
Hecheng Zhejiang China see Qingtian
Hechi China 97 F3
Hechuan Chongqing China 96 E2
Hechuan Jiangxi China see Yongxing
Hecla Island Canada 151 L5
Heda Japan 93 E4
Hede China see Sheyang
Hede Sweden 54 H5
Hedemora Sweden 55 I6
He Devil Mountain U.S.A. 156 D3
Hedionda Grande Mex. 167 E3
Hedi Shuiku resr China 97 F4
Heech Neth. see Heeg
Heeg Neth. 62 F2
Heek Germany 62 H2
Heer Belgium 62 E4
Heerde Neth. 62 G2
Heerenveen Neth. 62 F2
Heerhugowaard Neth. 62 E2
Heerlen Neth. 62 F4
Hefa Israel see Haifa
Hefa, Mifraz Israel see Haifa, Bay of
Hefei China 97 H2
Hefeng China 97 F2
Heflin U.S.A. 163 C5
Hegang China 90 C3
Heho Myanmar 86 B2
Heidan r. Jordan see Haydān, Wādī al
Heidberg hill Germany 63 L3
Heide Germany 57 L3
Heide Namibia 124 C2
Heidelberg Germany 63 I5
Heidelberg S. Africa 125 I4
Heidenheim an der Brenz Germany 63 K6
Heihe China 90 B2
Heilbron S. Africa 125 H4
Heilbronn Germany 63 J5
Heiligenhafen Germany 57 M3
Hei Ling Chau i. H.K. China 97 [inset]
Heilongjiang prov. China 95 J2
Heilong Jiang r. China 90 D2
also known as Amur (Rus. Fed.)
Heilong Jiang r. Rus. Fed. see Amur
Heilsbronn Germany 63 K5
Heilungkiang prov. China see Heilongjiang
Heimahe Qinghai China 94 D4
Heinola Fin. 55 O6
Heinze Islands Myanmar 87 B4
Heiquan Gansu China 94 D4
Heirnkut Myanmar 86 A1
Heishan Liaoning China 95 J3
Heishantou Nei Mongol China 95 I1
Heishantou Xinjiang China 94 B2
Heishi Beihu l. Xizang China 99 C6
Heishui China 96 D1
Heisker Islands U.K. see Monach Islands
Heist-op-den-Berg Belgium 62 E3
Ḩeiṭân, Gebel hill Egypt see Ḩayṭān, Jabal
Heituo Shan mt. Shanxi China 95 H4
Hejaz reg. Saudi Arabia see Hijaz
Hejian Hebei China 95 I4
Hejiang China 96 E2
He Jiang r. China 97 F4
Hejiao Nei Mongol China 95 G3
Hejin Shanxi China 95 G5
Hejing Xinjiang China 98 D4
Hekimhan Turkey 112 E3
Hekinan Japan 92 C4
Hekla vol. Iceland 54 [inset]
Heko-san mt. Japan 92 C3
Hekou Gansu China 94 E4
Hekou Hubei China 97 G2
Hekou Jiangxi China see Yanshan
Hekou Sichuan China see Yajiang
Hekou Yunnan China 96 D4
Helagsfjället mt. Sweden 54 H5
Helam India 96 B3
Helan Shan mts China 94 F4
Helbra Germany 63 L3
Helen atoll Palau 81 I6
Helena AR U.S.A. 161 F5

▶Helena MT U.S.A. 156 E3
Capital of Montana.

Helen Reef Palau 81 I6
Helensburgh U.K. 60 E4
Helen Springs Australia 134 F4
Ḩeleẓ Israel 107 B4
Helgoland i. Germany 57 K3
Helgoländer Bucht g. Germany 57 L3
Heligoland i. Germany see Helgoland
Heligoland Bight g. Germany see Helgoländer Bucht
Heliopolis Lebanon see Ba'albek
Helixi China see Ningguo
Hella Iceland 54 [inset]
Helland Norway 54 J2
Hellas country Europe see Greece
Helleh r. Iran 110 C4
Hellespont strait Turkey see Dardanelles
Hellevoetsluis Neth. 62 E3
Hellhole Gorge National Park Australia 136 D5
Hellín Spain 67 F4
Hellinikon tourist site Greece 112 A3
Hells Canyon gorge U.S.A. 156 D3
Hell-Ville Madag. see Andoany
Helmand prov. Afgh. 111 F4
Helmand r. Afgh. 111 F4
Helmantica Spain see Salamanca
Helmbrechts Germany 63 L4
Helme r. Germany 63 L3
Helmeringhausen Namibia 124 C3
Helmet Mountain AK U.S.A. 149 K2
Helmond Neth. 62 F3
Helmsdale U.K. 60 F2
Helmsdale r. U.K. 60 F2
Helmstedt Germany 63 L2
Helong China 90 C4
Helper U.S.A. 159 H2
Helpter Berge hills Germany 63 N1
Helsingborg Sweden 55 H8
Helsingfors Fin. see Helsinki
Helsingør Denmark 55 H8

▶Helsinki Fin. 55 N6
Capital of Finland.

Helston U.K. 59 B8
Helvécia Brazil 179 D2
Helvetic Republic country Europe see Switzerland
Ḩelwân Egypt see Ḩulwān
Hemel Hempstead U.K. 59 G7
Hemet U.S.A. 158 E5
Hemingford U.S.A. 160 C3
Hemlock Lake U.S.A. 165 G2
Hemmingen Germany 63 J2
Hemmingford Canada 165 I1
Hemmoor Germany 63 J1
Hempstead U.S.A. 161 D6
Hemsby U.K. 59 I6
Hemse Sweden 55 K8
Henan Qinghai China 94 E5
Henan prov. China 97 G1
Henares r. Spain 67 E3
Henashi-zaki pt Japan 91 E4
Henbury Australia 135 F6
Hendek Turkey 69 N4
Henderson KY U.S.A. 164 B5
Henderson NC U.S.A. 162 E4
Henderson NV U.S.A. 159 F3
Henderson NY U.S.A. 165 G2
Henderson TN U.S.A. 161 F5
Henderson TX U.S.A. 161 E5
Henderson Island Pitcairn Is 187 L7
Hendersonville NC U.S.A. 163 D5
Hendersonville TN U.S.A. 164 B5
Henderville atoll Kiribati see Aranuka
Hendon U.K. 59 G7
Hendorābī i. Iran 110 D5
Hendy-Gwyn U.K. see Whitland
Hengām Iran 111 E5
Hengduan Shan mts China 96 C2
Hengelo Neth. 62 G2
Hengfeng China 97 H2
Hengnan China see Hengyang
Hengshan China 90 C3
Hengshan Shaanxi China 95 G4
Heng Shan mt. China 97 G3
Heng Shan mts China 95 H4
Hengshui Hebei China 95 H4
Hengshui Jiangxi China see Chongyi
Hengxian China 97 F4
Hengyang Hunan China 97 G3
Hengyang Hunan China 97 G3
Hengzhou China see Hengxian
Heniches'k Ukr. 53 G7
Henley N.Z. 139 C7
Henley-on-Thames U.K. 59 G7
Henlopen, Cape U.S.A. 165 H4
Hennef (Sieg) Germany 63 H4
Hennenman S. Africa 125 H4
Hennepin U.S.A. 160 F3
Hennessey U.S.A. 161 D4
Hennigsdorf Berlin Germany 63 N2
Henniker U.S.A. 165 J2
Henning U.S.A. 164 B3
Henrietta U.S.A. 161 D5
Henrietta Maria, Cape Canada 152 E3
Henrieville U.S.A. 159 H3
Henrique de Carvalho Angola see Saurimo
Henry, Cape U.S.A. 165 G5
Henry Ice Rise Antarctica 188 A1
Henryk Arctowski research station Antarctica see Arctowski
Henry Kater, Cape Canada 147 L3
Henry Mountains U.S.A. 159 H2
Hensall Canada 164 E2
Henshaw, Lake U.S.A. 158 E5
Hentiesbaai Namibia 124 B2
Hentiy prov. Mongolia 95 G2
Henty Australia 138 C5
Henzada Myanmar see Hinthada
Heping Guangdong China 97 G3
Heping Guizhou China see Huishui
Heping Guizhou China see Yanhe
Hepo China see Jiexi
Heppner U.S.A. 156 D3
Heptanesus is Ionia Nisia Greece see Ionian Islands
Heptanesus is Greece see Ionian Islands
Hepu China 97 F4
Heqiao Gansu China 94 E4
Heqing China 96 D3
Hequ Shanxi China 95 G4
Heraclea Turkey see Ereğli
Heraclea Pontica Turkey see Ereğli
Heraklion Greece see Iraklion
Herald Cays atolls Australia 136 E3
Herāt Afgh. 111 F3
Hérault r. France 66 F5
Herbertabad India 87 A5
Herbert Downs Australia 136 B4
Herbert Island AK U.S.A. 148 E5
Herbert River Falls National Park Australia 136 D3
Herbert Wash salt flat Australia 135 D6
Herborn Germany 63 I4
Herbstein Germany 63 J4
Hercules Dome ice feature Antarctica 188 K1
Herdecke Germany 63 H3
Herdorf Germany 63 H4
Heredia Costa Rica 166 [inset] I7
Hereford U.K. 59 E6
Hereford U.S.A. 161 C5
Héréhérétué atoll Fr. Polynesia 187 K7
Herent Belgium 62 E4
Herford Germany 63 I2
Heringen (Werra) Germany 63 K4
Herington U.S.A. 160 D4
Herīs Iran 110 B2
Herisau Switz. 66 I3
Herkimer U.S.A. 165 H2
Herlen Mongolia 95 G2
Herlen Gol r. China/Mongolia 89 L3
Herlen He r. China/Mongolia see Herlen Gol
Herleshausen Germany 63 K3
Herlong U.S.A. 158 C1
Herm i. Channel Is 59 E9
Hermanas Mex. 167 E3
Herma Ness hd U.K. 60 [inset]
Hermann U.S.A. 160 F4
Hermannsburg Germany 63 K2
Hermanus S. Africa 124 D8
Hermel Lebanon 107 C2
Hermes, Cape S. Africa 125 I6
Hermidale Australia 138 C3
Hermiston U.S.A. 156 D3
Hermitage MO U.S.A. 160 E4
Hermitage PA U.S.A. 164 E3
Hermitage Bay Canada 153 K5
Hermite, Islas is Chile 178 C9
Hermit Islands P.N.G. 81 L7
Hermon, Mount Lebanon/Syria 107 B3
Hermonthis Egypt see Armant
Hermopolis Magna Egypt see Al Ashmūnayn
Hermosa U.S.A. 159 J3
Hermosillo Mex. 166 C2
Hernandarias Para. 178 F3
Hernando U.S.A. 161 F5
Herndon CA U.S.A. 158 D3
Herndon PA U.S.A. 165 G3
Herndon WV U.S.A. 164 E5
Herne Germany 63 H3
Herne Bay U.K. 59 I7
Herning Denmark 55 F8
Heroica Nogales Mex. see Nogales
Heroica Puebla de Zaragoza Mex. see Puebla
Hérouville-St-Clair France 59 G9
Herowābād Iran see Khalkhāl
Herradura Mex. 167 E4
Herrera del Duque Spain 67 D4
Herrero, Punta pt Mex. 167 I5
Herrieden Germany 63 K5
Herschel Y.T. Canada 149 M1
Herschel Island Y.T. Canada 149 M1
Hershey U.S.A. 165 G3
Hertford U.K. 59 G7
Hertzogville S. Africa 125 G5
Herve Belgium 62 F4
Hervé, Lac l. Canada 153 H3
Hervey Islands Cook Is 187 J7
Herzberg Brandenburg Germany 63 M2
Herzberg Brandenburg Germany 63 N3
Herzlake Germany 63 H2
Herzliyya Israel 107 B3
Herzogenaurach Germany 63 K5
Herzsprung Germany 63 M1
Ḩeşār Iran 110 C4
Ḩeşār Iran 110 E5
Hesdin France 62 C4
Hesel Germany 63 H1
Heshan China 97 F4
Heshengqiao China 97 G2
Heshui Gansu China 95 G5
Heshun Shanxi China 95 H4
Hesperia U.S.A. 158 E4
Hesperus U.S.A. 159 I3
Hesperus, Mount AK U.S.A. 148 I3
Hesperus Peak U.S.A. 159 I3
Hesquiat Canada 150 E5
Hess r. Y.T. Canada 149 N3
Hess Creek r. AK U.S.A. 149 J2
Heßdorf Germany 63 K5
Hesse land Germany see Hessen
Hesselberg hill Germany 63 K5
Hessen land Germany 63 J4
Hessisch Lichtenau Germany 63 J3
Hess Mountains Y.T. Canada 149 N3
Het r. Laos 86 D2
Heteren Neth. 62 F3
Hetou China 97 F4
Hettinger U.S.A. 160 C2
Hetton U.K. 58 E4
Hettstedt Germany 63 L3
Heung Kong Tsai H.K. China see Aberdeen
Ḩevron West Bank see Hebron
Hexham U.K. 58 E4
Hexian Anhui China 97 H2
Hexian Guangxi China see Hezhou
Hexigten Qi Nei Mongol China see Jingpeng
Hexipu Gansu China 94 E4
Heyang Shaanxi China 95 G5
Ḩeydarābād Iran 110 B2
Ḩeydarābād Iran 111 F4
Heydebreck Poland see Kędzierzyn-Koźle
Heyin Qinghai China see Guide
Heysham U.K. 58 E4
Heyshope Dam S. Africa 125 J4
Heyuan China 97 G4
Heywood U.K. 58 E5
Heze Shandong China 95 H5
Hezhang China 96 E3
Hezheng Gansu China 94 E5
Hezhou China 97 F3
Hezuo Gansu China 94 E5
Hialeah U.S.A. 163 D7
Hiawassee U.S.A. 163 D5
Hiawatha U.S.A. 160 E4
Hibbing U.S.A. 160 E2
Hibbs, Point Australia 137 [inset]
Hibernia Reef Australia 134 C3
Hīchān Iran 111 F5
Hichisō Japan 92 D3
Hicks, Point Australia 138 D6
Hicks Bay N.Z. 139 G3
Hicks Cays is Belize 167 H5
Hicks Lake Canada 151 K2
Hicksville U.S.A. 164 C3
Hico U.S.A. 161 D5
Hida-gawa r. Japan 92 D3
Hidaka Hyōgo Japan 92 A3
Hidaka Saitama Japan 93 F3
Hidaka Wakayama Japan 92 B5
Hidaka-gawa r. Japan 92 B5
Hidaka-sanmyaku mts Japan 90 F4
Hida-Kiso-gawa Kokutei-kōen park Japan 92 D3
Hida-kōchi plat. Japan 92 C2
Hidalgo Coahuila Mex. 167 F3
Hidalgo Mex. 161 D7
Hidalgo state Mex. 167 F4
Hidalgo del Parral Mex. 166 D3
Hidalgotitlán Mex. 167 G5
Hida-sanmyaku mts Japan 92 D2
Hidrolândia Brazil 179 A2
Hierosolyma Israel/West Bank see Jerusalem
Higashi Japan 93 G1
Higashiizu Japan 93 F4
Higashi-Matsuyama Japan 93 F2
Higashimurayama Japan 93 F3
Higashi-Ōsaka Japan 92 B4
Higashi-Shirakawa Japan 92 D3
Higashi-suidō sea chan. Japan 91 C6
Higashiura Aichi Japan 92 C4
Higashiura Hyōgo Japan 92 A4
Higashi-yama mt. Japan 93 D2
Higgins U.S.A. 161 C4
Higgins Bay U.S.A. 165 H2
Higgins Lake U.S.A. 164 C1
High Atlas mts Morocco see Haut Atlas
High Desert U.S.A. 156 C4
High Island i. H.K. China 97 [inset]
High Island U.S.A. 161 E6
High Island Reservoir H.K. China 97 [inset]
Highland Peak CA U.S.A. 158 D2
Highland Peak NV U.S.A. 159 F3
Highlands U.S.A. 165 I3
Highland Springs U.S.A. 165 G5
High Level Canada 150 G3
Highmore U.S.A. 160 D2
High Point U.S.A. 162 E5
High Point hill U.S.A. 165 H3
High Prairie Canada 150 G4
High River Canada 150 H5
Highrock Lake Man. Canada 151 K4
Highrock Lake Sask. Canada 151 J3
High Springs U.S.A. 163 D6
High Tatras mts Poland/Slovakia see Tatra Mountains
High Wycombe U.K. 59 G7
Higuera de Abuya Mex. 166 D3
Higuera de Zaragoza Mex. 166 C3
Higüey Dom. Rep. 169 K5
Higuri-gawa r. Japan 93 F3
Hiiumaa i. Estonia 55 M7
Hijānah, Buḩayrat al imp. l. Syria 107 C3
Hijau, Gunung mt. Indon. 84 C3
Hijaz reg. Saudi Arabia 108 E4
Hijiri-dake mt. Japan 93 E3
Hikabo-yama mt. Japan 93 E2
Hikami Japan 92 B3
Hikata Japan 93 G3
Hiki-gawa r. Japan 92 B5
Ḩikmah, Ra's al pt Egypt 112 B5

Hiko U.S.A. 159 F3
Hikone Japan 92 C3
Hikurangi mt. N.Z. 139 G3
Hila Maluku Indon. 83 C4
Hilahila Sulawesi Indon. 83 B4
Hilāl, Jabal hill Egypt 107 A4
Hilāl, Ra's al pt Libya 108 B3
Hilary Coast Antarctica 188 H1
Hildale U.S.A. 159 G3
Hildburghausen Germany 63 K4
Hilders Germany 63 K4
Hildesheim Germany 63 J2
Hillah Iraq 113 G4
Hill Bank Belize 167 H5
Hill City U.S.A. 160 D4
Hillegom Neth. 62 E2
Hill End Australia 138 D4
Hillerød Denmark 55 H9
Hillgrove Australia 136 D3
Hill Island Lake Canada 151 I2
Hillman U.S.A. 164 D1
Hillsboro ND U.S.A. 160 D2
Hillsboro NM U.S.A. 157 G6
Hillsboro OH U.S.A. 164 D4
Hillsboro OR U.S.A. 156 C3
Hillsboro TX U.S.A. 161 D5
Hillsdale IN U.S.A. 164 B4
Hillsdale MI U.S.A. 164 C3
Hillside Australia 134 B5
Hillston Australia 138 B4
Hillsville U.S.A. 164 E5
Hilo U.S.A. 157 [inset]
Hilton Australia 136 B4
Hilton S. Africa 125 J5
Hilton U.S.A. 165 G2
Hilton Head Island U.S.A. 163 D5
Hilvan Turkey 112 E3
Hilversum Neth. 62 F2
Himachal Pradesh state India 104 D3
Himaga-shima i. Japan 92 D4
Himalaya mts Asia 104 D2
Himalchul mt. Nepal 105 F3
Himanka Fin. 54 M4
Ḥimār, Wādī al watercourse Syria/Turkey 107 D1
Himarë Albania 69 H4
Himatnagar India 104 C5
Hime-gawa r. Japan 93 D1
Himeji Japan 92 A4
Himi Japan 92 C2
Ḥimş Syria see Homs
Ḥimş, Baḥrat resr Syria see Qaṭṭīnah, Buḥayrat
Hinako i. Indon. 84 B2
Hinatuan Mindanao Phil. 82 D4
Hinatuan Passage Phil. 82 D4
Hîncești Moldova 69 M1
Hinchinbrook Entrance sea channel AK U.S.A. 149 K3
Hinchinbrook Island Australia 136 D3
Hinchinbrook Island AK U.S.A. 149 K3
Hinckley U.K. 59 F6
Hinckley MN U.S.A. 160 E2
Hinckley UT U.S.A. 159 G2
Hinckley Reservoir U.S.A. 165 H2
Hindan r. India 99 B7
Hindaun India 104 D4
Hinderwell U.K. 58 G4
Hindley U.K. 58 E5
Hindman U.S.A. 164 D5
Hindmarsh, Lake dry lake Australia 137 C8
Hindu Kush mts Afgh./Pak. 111 G3
Hindupur India 106 C3
Hines Creek Canada 150 G3
Hinesville U.S.A. 163 D6
Hinganghat India 106 C1
Hingoli India 106 C2
Hınıs Turkey 113 F3
Hinnøya i. Norway 54 I2
Hino Shiga Japan 92 C3
Hino Tōkyō Japan 93 F3
Hinobaan Negros Phil. 82 C4
Hinoemata Japan 93 F1
Hino-gawa r. Japan 92 C2
Hino-gawa r. Japan 92 C3
Hinojosa del Duque Spain 67 D4
Hino-misaki pt Japan 92 B5
Hinsdale U.S.A. 165 I2
Hinte Germany 63 H1
Hinthada Myanmar 86 A3
Hinton Canada 150 G4
Hinton U.S.A. 164 E5
Hi-numa l. Japan 93 G2
Hiort i. U.K. see St Kilda
Hippolytushoef Neth. 62 E2
Hipponium Italy see Vibo Valentia
Hippo Regius Alg. see Annaba
Hippo Zarytus Tunisia see Bizerte
Hirabit Dağ mt. Turkey 113 G3
Hiraga-take mt. Japan 93 F1
Hirakata Japan 92 B4
Hirakud Dam India 105 E5
Hirakud Reservoir India 105 E5
Hirapur India 104 D4
Hiratsuka Japan 93 F3
Hiraya Japan 92 D3
Hiriyur India 106 C3
Hirokawa Japan 92 B4
Hirosaki Japan 90 F4
Hiroshima Japan 91 D6
Hirschaid Germany 63 L5
Hirschberg Germany 63 L4
Hirschberg mt. Germany 57 M7
Hirschberg Poland see Jelenia Góra
Hirschenstein mt. Germany 63 M6
Hirson France 62 E5
Hîrşova Romania see Hârşova
Hirta is U.K. see St Kilda
Hirtshals Denmark 55 F8
Hiruga-take mt. Japan 93 F3
Hirukawa Japan 92 D3
Hisai Japan 92 C4
Hisar India 104 C3
Hisar Iran 110 C2
Hisarköy Turkey see Domaniç
Hisarönü Turkey 69 O4
Ḥisb, Sha'īb watercourse Iraq 113 G5
Ḥisbān Jordan 107 B4
Hishig-Öndör Bulgan Mongolia 94 E1
Hisiu P.N.G. 81 L8
Hisor Tajik. 111 H2
Hisor Tizmasi mts Tajik./Uzbek. see Gissar Range
Hispalis Spain see Seville
Hispania country Europe see Spain

▶Hispaniola i. Caribbean Sea 169 J4
Consists of the Dominican Republic and Haiti.

Hispur Glacier Pak. 104 C1
Hissar India see Hisar
Hisua India 105 F4
Ḥisyah Syria 107 C2
Hīt Iraq 113 F4
Hitachi Japan 93 G2
Hitachinaka Japan 93 G2
Hitachi-Ōta Japan 93 G2
Hitra i. Norway 54 F5
Hitzacker Germany 63 L1
Hiuchiga-take vol. Japan 93 F2
Hiva Oa i. Fr. Polynesia 187 K6
Hixon Canada 150 F4
Hixson Cay reef Australia 136 F4
Hiyoshi Kyōto Japan 92 B3
Hiyoshi Nagano Japan 92 D3
Hiyyon watercourse Israel 107 B4
Hizan Turkey 113 F3
Hjälmaren l. Sweden 55 I7
Hjerkinn Norway 54 F5
Hjo Sweden 55 I7
Hjørring Denmark 55 G8
Hkakabo Razi mt. China/Myanmar 96 C2
Hlaingdet Myanmar 86 B2
Hlako Kangri mt. Xizang China see Lhagoi Kangri
Hlane Royal National Park Swaziland 125 J4
Hlatikulu Swaziland 125 J4
Hlegu Myanmar 86 B3
Hlohlowane S. Africa 125 H5
Hlotse Lesotho 125 I5
Hluhluwe-Umfolozi Park nature res. S. Africa 125 J5
Hlukhiv Ukr. 53 G6
Hlung-Tan Myanmar 86 B2
Hlusha Belarus 53 F5
Hlybokaye Belarus 55 O9
Ho Ghana 120 D4
Hoa Binh Vietnam 86 D2
Hoa Binh Vietnam 86 D3
Hoachanas Namibia 124 D2
Hoagland U.S.A. 164 C3
Hoang Liên Sơn mts Vietnam 86 C2
Hoang Sa is S. China Sea see Paracel Islands
Hoan Lao Vietnam 86 D3

▶Hobart Australia 137 [inset]
Capital of Tasmania.

Hobart U.S.A. 161 D5
Hobbs U.S.A. 161 C5
Hobbs Coast Antarctica 188 J1
Hobe Sound U.S.A. 163 D7
Hobiganj Bangl. see Habiganj
Hoboksar Xinjiang China 98 D3
Hobor Nei Mongol China 95 H3
Hobro Denmark 55 F8
Hobyo Somalia 122 E3
Hoceima, Baie d'Al b. Morocco 67 E6
Hochandochtla Mountain hill AK U.S.A. 148 I2
Höchberg Germany 63 J5
Hochfeiler mt. Austria/Italy see Gran Pilastro
Hochfeld Namibia 123 B6
Hochharz nat. park Germany 63 K3
Hô Chi Minh Vietnam see Ho Chi Minh City
Ho Chi Minh City Vietnam 87 D5
Hochschwab mt. Austria 57 O7
Hochschwab mts Austria 57 O7
Hockenheim Germany 63 I5
Ḥôḍ reg. Mauritania 120 C3
Hodal Haryana India 99 B8
Hōdatsu-san hill Japan 92 C2
Hoddesdon U.K. 59 G7
Hodeidah Yemen 108 F7
Hodgenville U.S.A. 164 C5
Hodgson Downs Australia 134 F3
Hódmezővásárhely Hungary 69 I1
Hodna, Chott el salt l. Alg. 67 I6
Hodo-dan pt N. Korea 91 B5
Hödrögö Mongolia see Nömrög
Hodzana r. AK U.S.A. 149 K2
Hoek van Holland Neth. see Hook of Holland
Hoensbroek Neth. 62 F4
Hoeryŏng N. Korea 90 C4
Hof Germany 63 L4
Hoffman Mountain U.S.A. 165 I2
Hofheim in Unterfranken Germany 63 K4
Hofmeyr S. Africa 125 G6
Höfn Iceland 54 [inset]
Hofors Sweden 55 J6
Hofsjökull ice cap Iceland 54 [inset]
Hofsós Iceland 54 [inset]
Hōfu Japan 91 C6
Hofūf Saudi Arabia 108 G4
Höganäs Sweden 55 H8
Hogan Group is Australia 138 C7
Hogansburg U.S.A. 165 H1
Hogatza AK U.S.A. 148 I2
Hogatza r. AK U.S.A. 148 I2
Hogback Mountain U.S.A. 160 C3
Hoge Vaart canal Neth. 62 F2
Hogg, Mount Y.T. Canada 149 N3
Hoggar plat. Alg. 120 D2
Hog Island U.S.A. 165 H5
Högsby Sweden 55 J8
Hohenloher Ebene plain Germany 63 J5
Hohenmölsen Germany 63 M3
Hohennauen Germany 63 M2
Hohensalza Poland see Inowrocław
Hohenwald U.S.A. 162 C5
Hohenwartetalsperre resr Germany 63 L4
Hoher Dachstein mt. Austria 57 N7
Hoh Ereg Nei Mongol China see Wuchuan
Hohe Rhön mts Germany 63 J4
Hohe Tauern mts Austria 57 N7
Hohe Venn moorland Belgium 62 G4
Hohhot Nei Mongol China 95 G3
Höhmorit Mongolia 94 C2
Hohneck mt. France 66 H2
Hoholitna r. AK U.S.A. 148 H3
Hoh Sai Hu l. Qinghai China 94 C5
Hoh Xil Hu salt l. China 99 E6
Hoh Xil Shan mts China 99 E6
Hoh Yanhu salt l. Qinghai China 94 D4
Hôi An Vietnam 86 E4
Hoika Qinghai China 94 D5
Hoima Uganda 122 D3
Hoit Taria Qinghai China 94 D4
Hojagala Turkm. 110 E2
Hojai India 105 H4
Hojambaz Turkm. 111 G2
Højryggen mts Greenland 147 M2
Hōki-gawa r. Japan 93 G2
Hokitika N.Z. 139 C6
Hokkaidō i. Japan 90 F4
Hokksund Norway 55 F7
Hokota Japan 93 G2
Hokudan Japan 92 A4
Hokunō Japan 92 C3
Hokusei Japan 92 C3
Hol Norway 55 F6
Holbæk Denmark 55 G9
Holbeach U.K. 59 H6
Holbrook Australia 138 C5
Holbrook U.S.A. 159 H4
Holden U.S.A. 159 G2
Holdenville U.S.A. 161 D5
Holdrege U.S.A. 160 D3
Holgate U.S.A. 164 C3
Holguín Cuba 169 I4
Holikachuk AK U.S.A. 148 H3
Holitna r. AK U.S.A. 148 H3
Höljes Sweden 55 H6
Holland country Europe see Netherlands
Holland MI U.S.A. 164 B2
Holland NY U.S.A. 165 F2
Hollandia Indon. see Jayapura
Hollick-Kenyon Peninsula Antarctica 188 L2
Hollick-Kenyon Plateau Antarctica 188 K1
Hollidaysburg U.S.A. 165 F3
Hollis AK U.S.A. 149 N5
Hollis OK U.S.A. 161 D5
Hollister U.S.A. 158 C3
Holly U.S.A. 164 D2
Hollyhill U.S.A. 164 C5
Holly Springs U.S.A. 161 F5
Hollywood CA U.S.A. 159 D4
Hollywood FL U.S.A. 163 D7
Holm Norway 54 H4
Holman Canada see Ulukhaktok
Holmes Reef Australia 136 D3
Holmestrand Norway 55 G7
Holmgard Rus. Fed. see Velikiy Novgorod
Holm Ø i. Greenland see Kiatassuaq
Holmön i. Sweden 54 L5
Holmsund Sweden 54 L5
Holokuk Mountain hill AK U.S.A. 148 H3
Ḥolon Israel 107 B3
Holoog Namibia 124 C4
Holothuria Banks reef Australia 134 D3
Holroyd r. Australia 136 C2
Holstebro Denmark 55 F8
Holstein U.S.A. 160 E3
Holsteinsborg Greenland see Sisimiut
Holston r. U.S.A. 162 D4
Holsworthy U.K. 59 C8
Holt U.K. 59 I6
Holt U.S.A. 164 C2
Holton U.S.A. 164 B2
Holwerd Neth. 62 F1
Holwert Neth. see Holwerd
Holycross Ireland 61 E5
Holy Cross AK U.S.A. 148 H3
Holy Cross, Mount of the U.S.A. 156 G5
Holyhead U.K. 58 C5
Holyhead Bay U.K. 58 C5
Holy Island England U.K. 58 F3
Holy Island Wales U.K. 58 C5
Holyoke U.S.A. 160 C3
Holy See Europe see Vatican City
Holywell U.K. 58 D5
Holzhausen Germany 63 M3
Holzkirchen Germany 57 M7
Holzminden Germany 63 J3
Homand Iran 111 E3
Homāyūnshahr Iran see Khomeynīshahr
Homberg (Efze) Germany 63 J3
Hombori Mali 120 C3
Homburg Germany 63 H5
Home Bay Canada 147 L3
Homécourt France 62 F5
Homer AK U.S.A. 149 J4
Homer GA U.S.A. 163 D5
Homer LA U.S.A. 161 E5
Homer MI U.S.A. 164 C2
Homer NY U.S.A. 165 G2
Homerville U.S.A. 163 D6
Homestead Australia 136 D4
Homnabad India 106 C2
Homoine Moz. 125 L2
Homs Libya see Al Khums
Homs Syria 107 C2
Homyel' Belarus 53 F5
Honan prov. China see Henan
Honavar India 106 B3
Honaz Turkey 69 M6
Hon Chông Vietnam 87 D5
Honda Bay Palawan Phil. 82 B4
Hondeklipbaai S. Africa 124 C6
Hondo r. Belize/Mex. 167 H5
Hondo U.S.A. 161 D6
Hondsrug reg. Neth. 62 G1
Honduras country Central America 169 G6
Honduras, Gulf of Belize/Hond. 166 [inset] I5
Hønefoss Norway 55 G6
Honesdale U.S.A. 165 H3
Honey Mex. 167 F4
Honey Lake salt l. U.S.A. 158 C1
Honeyoye Lake U.S.A. 165 G2
Honfleur France 66 E2
Hong, Mouths of the Vietnam see Red River, Mouths of the
Hông, Sông r. Vietnam see Red
Hongchengzi Gansu China 94 E4
Hongchuan China see Hongya
Hongde Gansu China 95 F4
Honggouzi Qinghai China 98 E5
Honggu Gansu China 94 E4
Hongguo China see Panxian
Honghai Wan b. China 97 G4
Honghe China 96 D4
Hong He r. China 97 G1
Honghu China 97 G2
Hongjialou Shandong China see Licheng
Hongjiang Hunan China 97 F3
Hongjiang Sichuan China see Wangcang
Hong Kong H.K. China 97 [inset]
Hong Kong aut. reg. China 97 [inset]
Hong Kong Harbour sea chan. H.K. China 97 [inset]
Hong Kong Island H.K. China 97 [inset]
Hongliu Daquan well Nei Mongol China 94 D3
Hongliuhe Gansu China 94 C3
Hongliu He r. China 95 G4
Hongliuquan Qinghai China 98 E5
Hongliuwan Gansu China see Aksay
Hongliuyuan Gansu China 94 E4
Hongliuyuan Gansu China 98 F4
Hongor Nei Mongol China 95 H2
Hongor Mongolia see Naran
Hongqiao China see Qidong
Hongqicun Xinjiang China 94 C3
Hongqizhen Hainan China see Wuzhishan
Hongqizhen China see Wuzhishan
Hongshansi Nei Mongol China 94 F4
Hongshi China 90 B4
Hongshui He r. China 96 F4
Hongtong Shanxi China 95 G4
Honguedo, Détroit d' sea chan. Canada 153 I4
Hongwansi Gansu China see Sunan
Hongwŏn N. Korea 91 B4
Hongxing Jilin China 95 J2
Hongya China 96 D2
Hongyashan Shuiku resr Gansu China 94 E4
Hongyuan China 96 D1
Hongze China 97 H1
Hongze Hu l. China 97 H1

▶Honiara Solomon Is 133 F2
Capital of the Solomon Islands.

Honiton U.K. 59 D8
Honjō Japan 91 F5
Honjo Japan 93 D2
Honjō Saitama Japan 93 F2
Honkajoki Fin. 55 M6
Honkawane Japan 93 E3
Honningsvåg Norway 54 N1
Honoka'a U.S.A. 157 [inset]

▶Honolulu U.S.A. 157 [inset]
Capital of Hawaii.

▶Honshū i. Japan 91 D6
Largest island in Japan, 3rd largest in Asia and 7th in the world.

Honwad India 106 B2
Hood, Mount vol. U.S.A. 156 C3
Hood Bay AK U.S.A. 149 N4
Hood Point Australia 135 B8
Hood Point P.N.G. 136 D1
Hood River U.S.A. 156 C3
Hoogeveen Neth. 62 G2
Hoogezand-Sappemeer Neth. 62 G1
Hooghly r. mouth India see Hugli
Hooker U.S.A. 161 C4
Hook Head hd Ireland 61 F5
Hook of Holland Neth. 62 E3
Hook Reef Australia 136 E3
Hoolt Mongolia see Tögrög
Hoonah AK U.S.A. 149 N4
Hooper Bay AK U.S.A. 148 F3
Hooper Bay AK U.S.A. 148 F3
Hooper Island U.S.A. 165 G4
Hoopeston U.S.A. 164 B3
Hoopstad S. Africa 125 G4
Höör Sweden 55 H9
Hoorn Neth. 62 F2
Hoorn, Îles de is Wallis and Futuna Is 133 I3
Hōō-san mt. Japan 93 E3
Hoosick U.S.A. 165 I2
Hoover Dam U.S.A. 159 F3
Hoover Memorial Reservoir U.S.A. 164 D3
Höövör Mongolia see Baruunbayan-Ulaan
Hopa Turkey 113 F2
Hope Canada 150 F5
Hope r. N.Z. 139 D6
Hope AK U.S.A. 149 J3
Hope AR U.S.A. 161 E5
Hope IN U.S.A. 164 C4
Hope, Lake salt flat Australia 135 C8
Hope, Point pt AK U.S.A. 148 F1
Hopedale Canada 153 J3
Hopefield S. Africa 124 D7
Hopei prov. China see Hebei
Hopelchén Mex. 167 H5
Hope Mountains Canada 153 J3
Hope Saddle pass N.Z. 139 D5
Hopes Advance, Baie b. Canada 153 H2
Hopes Advance, Cap c. Canada 147 L3
Hopes Advance Bay Canada see Aupaluk
Hopetoun Australia 137 C7
Hopetown S. Africa 124 G5
Hopewell U.S.A. 165 G5
Hopewell Islands Canada 152 F2
Hopin Myanmar 86 B1
Hopkins r. Australia 137 C8
Hopkins, Lake salt flat Australia 135 E6
Hopkinsville U.S.A. 164 B5
Hopland U.S.A. 158 B2
Hoquiam U.S.A. 156 C3
Hor Qinghai China 94 E5
Hor Xizang China 99 C7
Horace Mountain AK U.S.A. 149 J2
Horado Japan 92 C3
Hōrai Japan 92 D4
Hōraiji-san hill Japan 92 D4
Horasan Turkey 113 F2
Hörby Sweden 55 H9
Horcasitas Mex. 166 D2
Horgo Mongolia see Tariat
Hörh Uul mts Mongolia 94 F3
Horigane Japan 93 D2
Horinger Nei Mongol China 95 G3
Horiult Mongolia see Bogd

▶Horizon Deep sea feature S. Pacific Ocean 186 I7
Deepest point in the Tonga Trench, and 2nd in the world.

Horki Belarus 53 F5
Horlick Mountains Antarctica 188 K1
Horlivka Ukr. 53 H6
Hormoz i. Iran 110 E5
Hormoz, Kūh-e mt. Iran 110 D5
Hormuz, Strait of Iran/Oman 110 E5
Horn Austria 57 O6
Horn r. Canada 150 G2
Horn c. Iceland 54 [inset]

▶Horn, Cape Chile 178 C9
Most southerly point of South America.

Hornaday r. N.W.T. Canada 149 Q1
Hornavan l. Sweden 54 J3
Hornbeck LA U.S.A. 167 G2
Hornbrook U.S.A. 156 C4
Hornburg Germany 63 K2
Horncastle U.K. 58 G5
Horndal Sweden 55 J6
Horne, Îles de is Wallis and Futuna Is see Hoorn, Îles de
Horneburg Germany 63 J1
Hörnefors Sweden 54 K5
Hornell U.S.A. 165 G2
Hornepayne Canada 152 D4
Hornillos Mex. 166 C3
Hornisgrinde mt. Germany 57 L6
Horn Island MS U.S.A. 167 H2
Hornkranz Namibia 124 C2
Horn Mountains Canada 150 F2
Horn Mountains AK U.S.A. 148 H3
Hornos, Cabo de Chile see Horn, Cape
Hornoy-le-Bourg France 62 B5
Horn Peak Y.T. Canada 149 O3
Hornsby Australia 138 E4
Hornsea U.K. 58 G5
Hornslandet pen. Sweden 55 J6
Horodenka Ukr. 53 E6
Horodnya Ukr. 53 F6
Horodok Khmel'nyts'ka Oblast' Ukr. 53 E6
Horodok L'vivs'ka Oblast' Ukr. 53 D6
Horokanai Japan 90 F3
Horo Shan mts China 98 C4
Horoshiri-dake mt. Japan 90 F4
Horqin Shadi reg. China 95 J3
Horqin Youyi Qianqi Nei Mongol China see Ulanhot
Horqin Zuoyi Houqi Nei Mongol China see Ganjig
Horqin Zuoyi Zhongqi Nei Mongol China see Baokang
Horrabridge U.K. 59 C8
Horrocks Australia 135 A7
Horru Xizang China 99 E7
Horse Cave U.S.A. 164 C5
Horsefly Canada 150 F4
Horseheads U.S.A. 165 G2
Horse Islands Canada 153 L4
Horseleap Ireland 61 D4
Horsens Denmark 55 F9
Horseshoe Bend Australia 135 F6
Horseshoe Reservoir U.S.A. 159 H4
Horseshoe Seamounts sea feature N. Atlantic Ocean 184 G3
Horsham Australia 137 C8
Horsham U.K. 59 G7
Horšovský Týn Czech Rep. 63 M5
Horst hill Germany 63 J4
Hörstel Germany 63 H2
Horten Norway 55 G7
Hortobágyi nat. park Hungary 69 I1
Horton r. N.W.T. Canada 149 P1
Horwood Lake Canada 152 E4
Hōryūji tourist site Japan 92 B4
Hösbach Germany 63 J4
Hose, Pegunungan mts Malaysia 85 F2
Ḥoseynābād Iran 110 B3
Ḥoseynīyeh Iran 110 C4
Hoshab Pak. 111 F5
Hoshangabad India 104 D5
Hoshiarpur India 104 C3
Hōshööt Arhangay Mongolia see Öldziyt
Hōshööt Bayan-Ölgiy Mongolia see Tsengel
Hosoe Japan 92 D4
Hospet India 106 C3
Hospital Ireland 61 D5
Hosséré Vokre mt. Cameroon 120 E4
Hosta Butte mt. U.S.A. 159 I4
Hotagen r. Sweden 54 I5
Hotahudo East Timor see Hatudo
Hotaka Japan 93 D2
Hotaka-dake mt. Japan 92 D2
Hotaka-yama mt. Japan 93 F2
Hotan Xinjiang China 99 C5
Hotan He watercourse China 98 C4
Hotazel S. Africa 124 F4
Hot Creek Range mts U.S.A. 158 E2
Hotgi India 106 C2
Hotham r. Australia 135 B8
Hotham Inlet AK U.S.A. 148 G2
Hoti Seram Indon. 83 D3
Hoting Sweden 54 J4
Hot Springs AR U.S.A. 161 E5
Hot Springs NM U.S.A. see Truth or Consequences
Hot Springs SD U.S.A. 160 C3
Hot Sulphur Springs U.S.A. 156 G4
Hottah Lake Canada 150 G1
Hottentots Bay Namibia 124 B4
Hottentots Point Namibia 124 B4
Houdan France 62 B6
Houffalize Belgium 62 F4
Hougang Sing. 87 [inset]
Houghton MI U.S.A. 160 F2
Houghton NY U.S.A. 165 F2
Houghton Lake U.S.A. 164 C1
Houghton Lake l. U.S.A. 164 C1
Houghton le Spring U.K. 58 F4
Houie Moc, Phou mt. Laos 86 C2
Houlton U.S.A. 162 H2
Houma Shanxi China 95 G5
Houma U.S.A. 161 F6
Houmen China 97 G4
Hourl Qinghai China 94 D4
House Range mts U.S.A. 159 G2
Houston Canada 150 E4
Houston AK U.S.A. 149 J3
Houston MO U.S.A. 161 F4
Houston MS U.S.A. 161 F5
Houston TX U.S.A. 161 E6
Hout r. S. Africa 125 I2
Houtman Abrolhos is Australia 135 A7
Houton U.K. 60 F2
Houwater S. Africa 124 F6
Houxia Xinjiang China 98 D4
Houzihe Qinghai China 94 E4
Hovd Hovd Mongolia 94 B2
Hovd Övörhangay Mongolia see Bogd
Hovd prov. Mongolia 94 C2
Hovd Gol r. Mongolia 94 C1
Hove U.K. 59 G8
Hoveton U.K. 59 I6
Hovmantorp Sweden 55 I8
Hövsgöl Mongolia 95 G3
Hövsgöl prov. Mongolia 94 E1
Hövsgöl Nuur l. Mongolia 94 E1
Hövüün Mongolia see Noyon
Howar, Wadi watercourse Sudan 108 C6
Howard Australia 136 F5
Howard PA U.S.A. 165 G3
Howard SD U.S.A. 160 D2
Howard WI U.S.A. 164 A1
Howard City U.S.A. 164 C2
Howard Lake Canada 151 J2
Howard Pass AK U.S.A. 148 H1
Howden U.K. 58 G5
Howe, Cape Australia 138 D6
Howe, Mount Antarctica 188 J1
Howell U.S.A. 164 D2
Howick Canada 165 I1
Howick S. Africa 125 J5
Howland U.S.A. 162 G2

▶Howland Island terr. N. Pacific Ocean 133 I1
United States Unincorporated Territory.

Howlong Australia 138 C5
Howrah India see Haora
Howth Ireland 61 F4
Ḥowz well Iran 110 E3
Ḥowz-e Khān well Iran 110 E3
Ḥowz-e Panj Iran 110 E4
Ḥowz-e Panj waterhole Iran 110 D3
Howz i-Mian i-Tak Iran 110 D3
Hô Xa Vietnam 86 D3
Höxter Germany 63 J3
Hoxtolgay Xinjiang China 98 D3
Hoxud Xinjiang China 98 D4
Hoy i. U.K. 60 F2
Hoya Germany 63 J2
Hōya Japan 93 F3
Høyanger Norway 55 E6
Hoyerswerda Germany 57 O5
Høylandet Norway 54 H4
Hoym Germany 63 L3
Hoyor Amt Nei Mongol China 94 F3
Höytiäinen l. Fin. 54 P5
Hoyt Peak U.S.A. 159 H1
Hozu-gawa r. Japan 92 B3
Hpa-an Myanmar 86 B3
Hpapun Myanmar 86 B3
Hradec Králové Czech Rep. 57 O5
Hradiště hill Czech Rep. 63 N4
Hrasnica Bos.-Herz. 68 H3
Hrazdan Armenia 113 G2
Hrebinka Ukr. 53 G6
Hrodna Belarus 55 M10
Hrvatska country Europe see Croatia
Hrvatsko Grahovo Bos.-Herz. see Bosansko Grahovo
Hsenwi Myanmar 86 B2
Hsiang Chang i. H.K. China see Hong Kong Island
Hsiang Kang H.K. China see Hong Kong
Hsi-hseng Myanmar 86 B2
Hsin-chia-p'o country Asia see Singapore
Hsin-chia-p'o Sing. see Singapore
Hsin-chia-p'o Sing. see Singapore
Hsinchu Taiwan 97 I3
Hsinking China see Changchun
Hsinying Taiwan 97 I4
Hsipaw Myanmar 86 B2
Hsi-sha Ch'ün-tao is S. China Sea see Paracel Islands
Hsiyüp'ing Yü i. Taiwan 97 H4
Hsüeh Shan mt. Taiwan 97 I3
Huab watercourse Namibia 123 B6
Huabei Pingyuan plain China 95 H4
Huachi Gansu China 95 G4
Huachinera Mex. 166 C2
Huacho Peru 176 C6
Huachuan China 90 C3
Huade Nei Mongol China 95 H3
Huadian China 90 B4
Huadu China 97 G4
Huahai Gansu China 94 D3
Huahaizi Qinghai China 98 F5
Hua Hin Thai. 87 B4
Huai'an Hebei China 95 H3
Huai'an Jiangsu China 97 H1
Huai'an Jiangsu China see Chuzhou
Huaibei China 97 H1
Huaibin China 97 G1
Huaicheng Guangdong China see Huaiji
Huaicheng Jiangsu China see Chuzhou
Huaidezhen China 90 B4
Huaidian China see Shenqiu
Huai Had National Park Thai. 86 D3
Huaihua China 97 F3
Huaiji China 97 G4
Huai Kha Khaeng Wildlife Reserve nature res. Thai. 86 B4
Huailai Hebei China 95 H3
Huaillas mt. Peru 176 C5
Huainan China 97 H1
Huaining Anhui China 97 H2
Huaining Anhui China see Shipai
Huairen Shanxi China 95 H4
Huairou Beijing China 95 I3
Huaiyang China 97 G1
Huaiyin Jiangsu China 97 H1
Huaiyin Jiangsu China see Huai'an
Huaiyuan China 97 H1
Huajialing Gansu China 94 F5
Huajuápan de León Mex. 168 E5
Huaki Maluku Indon. 83 C4
Hualahuises Mex. 167 F3
Hualapai Peak U.S.A. 159 G4
Hualian Taiwan see Hualien
Hualien Taiwan 97 I3
Huallaga r. Peru 176 C5
Hualong Qinghai China 94 E4
Huambo Angola 123 B5
Huanan China 90 C3
Huancane Peru 176 E7
Huancavelica Peru 176 C6
Huancayo Peru 176 C6
Huancheng Gansu China see Huanxian
Huangbei China 97 G3
Huangcaoba China see Xingyi
Huangcheng Gansu China 94 E4
Huang-chou Hubei China see Huanggang
Huangchuan China 97 G1
Huanggang China 97 G2
Huang Hai sea N. Pacific Ocean see Yellow Sea
Huang He r. China see Yellow
Huanghe Kou r. mouth China 95 I4
Huanghua Hebei China 95 I4
Huangjiajian China 97 I1
Huang-kang Hubei China see Huanggang

Huangling Shaanxi China 95 G5
Huangliu China 97 F5
Huanglong Shaanxi China 95 G5
Huanglongsi Henan China see Kaifeng
Huangmao Jian mt. China 97 H3
Huangmei China 97 G2
Huangpu China 97 G4
Huangqi China 97 H3
Huangshan China 97 H2
Huangshi China 97 G2
Huangtu Gaoyuan plat. China 95 F4
Huangxian Shandong China 95 J4
Huangyan China 97 I2
Huangyang Gansu China 94 E4
Huangyuan Qinghai China 94 E4
Huangzhong Qinghai China 94 E4
Huangzhou Hubei China see Huanggang
Huaning China 96 D3
Huaniushan Gansu China 94 C3
Huanjiang China 97 F3
Huanren China 90 B4
Huanshan China see Yuhuan
Huantai Shandong China 95 I4
Huánuco Peru 176 C5
Huanxian Gansu China 95 F4
Huaping China 96 D3
Huap'ing Yü i. Taiwan 97 I3
Huaqiao China 96 E2
Huaqiaozhen China see Huaqiao
Huaráz Peru 176 C5
Huarmey Peru 176 C6
Huarong China 97 G2
Huascarán, Nevado de mt. Peru 176 C5
Huasco Chile 178 B3
Hua Shan mt. Shaanxi China 95 G5
Huashaoying Hebei China 95 H3
Huashixia Qinghai China 94 D5
Huashugou Gansu China see Jingtieshan
Huashulinzi China 90 B4
Huatabampo Mex. 166 C3
Huatong Liaoning China 95 J3
Huatusco Mex. 167 F5
Huauchinango Mex. 167 F4
Huaxian Guangdong China see Huadu
Huaxian Henan China 95 H5
Huaxian Shaanxi China 95 G5
Huayacocotla Mex. 167 F4
Huayang China see Jixi
Huayin China 97 F1
Huayuan China 97 F2
Huayxay Laos 86 C2
Huazangsi Gansu China see Tianzhu
Huazhaizi Gansu China 94 E4
Hubbard, Mount Canada/U.S.A. 149 M3
Hubbard, Pointe pt Canada 153 I2
Hubbard Lake U.S.A. 164 D1
Hubbart Point Canada 151 M3
Hubei prov. China 97 G2
Hubli India 106 B3
Hückelhoven Germany 62 G3
Hucknall U.K. 59 F5
Huddersfield U.K. 58 F5
Huder Nei Mongol China 95 J1
Hüder Mongolia 95 F1
Hudiksvall Sweden 55 J6
Hudson MA U.S.A. 165 J2
Hudson MD U.S.A. 165 G4
Hudson MI U.S.A. 164 C3
Hudson NH U.S.A. 165 J2
Hudson NY U.S.A. 165 I2
Hudson r. U.S.A. 165 I3
Hudson, Baie d' sea Canada see Hudson Bay
Hudson, Détroit d' strait Canada see Hudson Strait
Hudson Bay Canada 151 K4
Hudson Bay sea Canada 151 O3
Hudson Falls U.S.A. 165 I2
Hudson Island Tuvalu see Nanumanga
Hudson Mountains Antarctica 188 K2
Hudson's Hope Canada 150 F3
Hudson Strait Canada 147 K3
Huê Vietnam 86 D3
Huehuetán Mex. 167 G6
Huehuetenango Guat. 167 H6
Huehueto, Cerro mt. Mex. 161 B7
Huejuquilla Mex. 166 E4
Huejutla Mex. 167 F4
Huelva Spain 67 C5
Huentelauquén Chile 178 B4
Huépac Mex. 166 C2
Huércal-Overa Spain 67 F5
Huertecillas Mex. 161 C7
Huesca Spain 67 F2
Huéscar Spain 67 E5
Huétamo Mex. 167 E5
Huggins Island AK U.S.A. 148 I2
Hughenden Australia 136 D4
Hughes r. Canada 151 K3
Hughes AK U.S.A. 148 I2
Hughes (abandoned) Australia 135 E7
Hughson U.S.A. 158 C3
Hugli r. mouth India 105 F5
Hugo CO U.S.A. 160 C4
Hugo OK U.S.A. 161 E5
Hugo Lake U.S.A. 161 E5
Hugoton U.S.A. 161 C4
Huhehot Nei Mongol China see Hohhot
Huhhot Nei Mongol China see Hohhot
Huhudi S. Africa 124 G4
Hui'an China 97 H3
Hui'anpu Ningxia China 94 F4
Huiarau Range mts N.Z. 139 F4
Huib-Hoch Plateau Namibia 124 C4
Huichang China 97 G3
Huicheng Anhui China see Shexian
Huicheng Guangdong China see Huilai
Huicholes, Sierra de los mts Mex. 166 D4
Huidong China 96 D3
Huihe Nei Mongol China 95 I1
Huijbergen Neth. 62 E3
Huiji He r. China 95 H5
Huila, Nevado de vol. Col. 176 C3
Huíla, Planalto da Angola 123 B5
Huilai China 97 H4
Huili China 96 D3
Huimanguillo Mex. 167 G5
Huimin Shandong China 95 I4
Huinan China see Nanhui
Huining Gansu China 94 F5
Huinong Ningxia China 94 F4
Huishi Gansu China see Huining
Huishui China 96 E3
Huiten Nur l. China 94 B5
Huitong China 97 F3
Huittinen Fin. 55 M6
Huitupan Mex. 167 G5
Huixian Gansu China 96 E1
Huixian Henan China 95 H5
Huixtla Mex. 167 G6
Huiyang China see Huizhou
Huize China 96 D3
Huizhou China 97 G4
Hujirt Arhangay Mongolia see Tsetserleg
Hujirt Övörhangay Mongolia 94 E2
Hujirt Töv Mongolia see Delgerhaan
Hujr Saudi Arabia 108 F4
Hukawng Valley Myanmar 86 B1
Hukuntsi Botswana 124 E2
Hulahula r. AK U.S.A. 149 K1
Hulan China 90 B3
Hulan Ergi Heilong. China 95 J2
Ḩulayfah Saudi Arabia 108 F4
Ḩulayḩilah well Syria 107 D2
Huliao China see Dabu
Hulilan Iran 110 B3
Hulin China 90 D3
Hulingol Nei Mongol China 95 J2
Hulin Gol r. China 90 B3
Hull Canada 165 H1
Hull U.K. see Kingston upon Hull
Hull Island atoll Kiribati see Orona
Hultsfred Sweden 55 I8
Huludao Liaoning China 95 J3
Hulu Hu salt l. Qinghai China 99 E6
Hulun Buir Nei Mongol China 95 I1
Hulun Nur l. China 95 I1
Ḩulwān Egypt 112 C5
Huma China 90 B2
Humahuaca Arg. 178 C2
Humaitá Brazil 176 F5
Humaya r. Mex. 157 G8
Humaym well U.A.E. 110 D6
Humayyān, Jabal hill Saudi Arabia 110 B5
Humber, Mouth of the U.K. 58 H5
Humboldt Canada 151 J4
Humboldt AZ U.S.A. 159 G4
Humboldt NE U.S.A. 160 E3
Humboldt NV U.S.A. 158 D1
Humboldt r. U.S.A. 158 D1
Humboldt Bay U.S.A. 156 B4
Humboldt Range mts U.S.A. 158 D1
Humbolt Salt Marsh U.S.A. 158 E2
Hume r. N.W.T. Canada 149 O2
Humeburn Australia 138 B1
Hu Men sea chan. China 97 G4
Hume Reservoir Australia 138 C5
Humphrey Island atoll Cook Is see Manihiki
Humphreys, Mount U.S.A. 158 D3
Humphreys Peak U.S.A. 159 H4
Hūn Libya 121 E2
Húnaflói b. Iceland 54 [inset]
Hunan prov. China 97 F3
Hundeluft Germany 63 M3
Hunedoara Romania 69 J2
Hünfeld Germany 63 J4
Hungary country Europe 65 H2
Hungerford Australia 138 B2
Hung Fa Leng hill H.K. China see Robin's Nest
Hüngiy Gol r. Mongolia 94 C1
Hŭngnam N. Korea 91 B5
Hung Shui Kiu H.K. China 97 [inset]
Hưng Yên Vietnam 86 D2
Hun He r. China 95 J3
Hunjiang China see Baishan
Huns Mountains Namibia 124 C4
Hunstanton U.K. 59 H6
Hunte r. Germany 63 I1
Hunter r. Australia 138 E4
Hunter, Mount AK U.S.A. 149 J3
Hunter Island Australia 137 [inset]
Hunter Island Canada 150 D5
Hunter Island S. Pacific Ocean 133 H4
Hunter Islands Australia 137 [inset]
Huntingburg U.S.A. 164 B4
Huntingdon Canada 165 H1
Huntingdon U.K. 59 G6
Huntingdon PA U.S.A. 165 G3
Huntingdon TN U.S.A. 161 F4
Huntington IN U.S.A. 164 C3
Huntington OR U.S.A. 156 D3
Huntington WV U.S.A. 164 D4
Huntington Beach U.S.A. 158 D5
Huntington Creek r. U.S.A. 159 F1
Huntly N.Z. 139 E3
Huntly U.K. 60 G3
Hunt Mountain U.S.A. 156 G3
Huntsville Canada 164 F1
Huntsville AL U.S.A. 163 C5
Huntsville AR U.S.A. 161 E4
Huntsville TN U.S.A. 164 C5
Huntsville TX U.S.A. 161 E6
Hunucmá Mex. 167 H4
Hunyuan Shanxi China 95 H4
Hunza reg. Pak. 104 C1
Hunza r. Pak. 99 A6
Huocheng Xinjiang China 98 C3
Huoer Xizang China see Hor
Huojia Henan China 95 H5
Huolin He r. China see Hulin Gol
Huolongmen China 90 B2
Huolu Hebei China see Luquan
Hương Khê Vietnam 86 D3
Huonville Australia 137 [inset]
Huoqiu China 97 H1
Huoshan China 97 H2
Huo Shan mt. China see Baima Jian
Huoshao Tao i. Taiwan see Lü Tao
Huoxian Shanxi China see Huozhou
Huozhou Shanxi China 95 G4
Hupeh prov. China see Hubei
Hupnik r. Turkey 107 C1
Hupu India 96 B2
Ḩūr Iran 110 E4
Hurault, Lac l. Canada 153 H3
Ḩuraydīn, Wādī watercourse Egypt 107 A4
Huraysān reg. Saudi Arabia 110 B6
Hurd, Cape Canada 164 E1
Hurd Island Kiribati see Arorae
Hure Nei Mongol China 95 J3
Hüreemaral Mongolia 94 D2
Hüremt Mongolia see Sayhan
Hürent Mongolia see Taragt
Hure Qi Nei Mongol China see Hure
Hurghada Egypt see Al Ghurdaqah
Hurleg Qinghai China 94 D4
Hurleg Hu l. Qinghai China 94 D4
Hurler's Cross Ireland 61 D5
Hurley NM U.S.A. 159 I5
Hurley WI U.S.A. 160 F2
Hurmagai Pak. 111 G4
Huron CA U.S.A. 158 C3
Huron SD U.S.A. 160 D2

▶Huron, Lake Canada/U.S.A. 164 D1
2nd largest lake in North America, and 4th in the world.

Hurricane U.S.A. 159 G3
Hursley U.K. 59 F7
Hurst Green U.K. 59 H7
Hurung, Gunung mt. Indon. 85 F2
Husain Nika Pak. 111 H4
Húsavík Norðurland eystra Iceland 54 [inset]
Húsavík Vestfirðir Iceland 54 [inset]
Huseyinabat Turkey see Alaca
Huseyınli Turkey see Kızılırmak
Hushan Zhejiang China 97 H2
Hushan Zhejiang China see Wuyi
Hushan Zhejiang China see Cixi
Huşi Romania 69 M1
Huskvarna Sweden 55 I8
Huslia AK U.S.A. 148 H2
Huslia r. AK U.S.A. 148 H2
Husn Jordan see Al Ḩişn
Ḩuşn Āl 'Abr Yemen 108 G6
Husnes Norway 55 D7
Husum Germany 57 L3
Husum Sweden 54 K5
Hutag Mongolia see Hutag-Öndör
Hutag-Öndör Mongolia 94 E1
Hutanopan Sumatera Indon. 84 B2
Hutchinson KS U.S.A. 160 D4
Hutchinson MN U.S.A. 160 E2
Hutch Mountain U.S.A. 159 H4
Hutou China 90 D3
Hutsonville U.S.A. 164 B4
Hutton, Mount hill Australia 137 E5
Hutton Range hills Australia 135 C6
Hutubi Xinjiang China 98 D3
Hutubi He r. China 98 D3
Hutuo He r. China 95 I4
Huvadhu Atoll Maldives 103 D11
Hüvek Turkey see Bozova
Hūvīān, Kūh-e mts Iran 111 E5
Ḩuwār i. Bahrain 110 C5
Huwaytat reg. Saudi Arabia 107 C5
Huxi China 97 G3
Huxian Shaanxi China 95 G5
Huzhong China 90 A2
Huzhou China 97 I2
Huzhu Qinghai China 94 E4
Hvannadalshnúkur vol. Iceland 54 [inset]
Hvar i. Croatia 68 G3
Hvide Sande Denmark 55 F8
Hvíta r. Iceland 54 [inset]
Hwange Zimbabwe 123 C5
Hwange National Park Zimbabwe 123 C5
Hwang Ho r. China see Yellow
Hwedza Zimbabwe 123 D5
Hwlffordd U.K. see Haverfordwest
Hyakuriga-take hill Japan 92 B3
Hyannis MA U.S.A. 165 J3
Hyannis NE U.S.A. 160 C3
Hyargas Nuur salt l. Mongolia 94 C1
Hyco Lake U.S.A. 164 F5
Hyde N.Z. 139 C7
Hyden Australia 135 B8
Hyden U.S.A. 164 D5
Hyde Park U.S.A. 165 I1
Hyder AK U.S.A. 149 O5
Hyderabad India 106 C2
Hyderabad Pak. 111 H5
Hydra i. Greece see Ydra
Hyères France 66 H5
Hyères, Îles d' is France 66 H5
Hyesan N. Korea 90 C4
Hyland r. Y.T. Canada 149 O4
Hyland, Mount Australia 138 F3
Hyland Post Canada 150 D3
Hyllestad Norway 55 D6
Hyltebruk Sweden 55 H8
Hyndman Peak U.S.A. 156 E4
Hyōgo pref. Japan 92 A3
Hyōno-sen mt. Japan 91 D6
Hyrcania Iran see Gorgān
Hyrynsalmi Fin. 54 P4
Hysham U.S.A. 156 G3
Hythe Canada 150 G4
Hythe U.K. 59 I7
Hyūga Japan 91 C6
Hyvinkää Fin. 55 N6

I

Iaciara Brazil 179 B1
Iaco r. Brazil 176 E5
Iaçu Brazil 179 C1
Iadera Croatia see Zadar
Iaeger U.S.A. 164 E5
Iakora Madag. 123 E6
Ialomiţa r. Romania 69 L2
Ianca Romania 69 L2
Iaşi Romania 69 L1
Iba Luzon Phil. 82 B3
Ibadan Nigeria 120 D4
Ibagué Col. 176 C3
Ibaiti Brazil 179 A3
Ibapah U.S.A. 159 G1
Ibaraki Ibaraki Japan 93 G2
Ibaraki Ōsaka Japan 92 B4
Ibaraki pref. Japan 93 G2
Ibarra Ecuador 176 C3
Ibb Yemen 108 F7
Ibbenbüren Germany 63 H2
Iberá, Esteros del marsh Arg. 178 E3
Iberia Peru 176 E6

▶Iberian Peninsula Europe 67
Consists of Portugal, Spain and Gibraltar.

Iberville, Lac d' l. Canada 153 G3
Ibeto Nigeria 120 D3
iBhayi S. Africa see Port Elizabeth
Ibi Sumatera Indon. 84 B1
Ibi Nigeria 120 D4
Ibiá Brazil 179 B2
Ibiaí Brazil 179 B2
Ibiapaba, Serra da hills Brazil 177 J4
Ibiassucê Brazil 179 C1
Ibicaraí Brazil 179 D1
Ibigawa Japan 92 C3
Ibi-gawa r. Japan 92 C3
Ibiquera Brazil 179 C1
Ibirama Brazil 179 A4
Ibiranhém Brazil 179 C2
Ibi-Sekigahara-Yōrō Kokutei-kōen park Japan 92 C3
Ibitinga Brazil 179 A3
Ibiza Spain 67 G4
Ibiza i. Spain 67 G4
Iblei, Monti mts Sicily Italy 68 F6
Ibn Buşayyiş well Saudi Arabia 110 B5
Ibotirama Brazil 177 J6
Iboundji, Mont hill Gabon 122 B4
Ibrā' Oman 110 E6
İbradı Turkey 112 C3
Ibrī Oman 110 E6
Ibu Halmahera Indon. 83 C2
Ibuhos i. Phil. 82 C1
Ibuki Japan 92 C3
Ibuki-sanchi mts Japan 92 C3
Ibuki-yama mt. Japan 92 C3
Ica Peru 176 C6
Ica r. Peru see Putumayo
Icaiché Mex. 167 H5
Içana Brazil 176 E3
Içana r. Brazil 176 E3
Icaria i. Greece see Ikaria
Icatu Brazil 177 J4
Iceberg Canyon gorge U.S.A. 159 F3
İçel Mersin Turkey see Mersin

▶Iceland country Europe 54 [inset]
2nd largest island in Europe.

Iceland Basin sea feature N. Atlantic Ocean 184 G2
Icelandic Plateau sea feature N. Atlantic Ocean 189 I2
Ichalkaranji India 106 B2
Ichifusa-yama mt. Japan 91 C6
Ichihara Japan 93 G3
Ichikai Japan 93 G2
Ichikawa Chiba Japan 93 F3
Ichikawa Hyōgo Japan 92 A3
Ichi-kawa r. Japan 92 A4
Ichikawadaimon Japan 93 E3
Ichinomiya Aichi Japan 92 C3
Ichinomiya Aichi Japan 92 D4
Ichinomiya Chiba Japan 93 G3
Ichinomiya Hyōgo Japan 92 A4
Ichinomiya Yamanashi Japan 93 E3
Ichinoseki Japan 91 F5
Ichinskaya Sopka vol. Rus. Fed. 77 Q4
Ichishi Japan 92 C4
Ichkeul, Parc National de l' Tunisia 68 C6
Ichnya Ukr. 53 G6
Ichtegem Belgium 62 D3
Ichtershausen Germany 63 K4
Icó Brazil 177 K5
Iconha Brazil 179 C3
Iconium Turkey see Konya
Icosium Alg. see Algiers
Iculisma France see Angoulême
Icy Bay AK U.S.A. 149 K4
Icy Bay AK U.S.A. 149 L4
Icy Cape AK U.S.A. 148 G1
Icy Strait AK U.S.A. 149 N4
İd Turkey see Narman
Idabel U.S.A. 161 E5
Ida Grove U.S.A. 160 E3
Idah Nigeria 120 D4
Idaho state U.S.A. 156 E3
Idaho City U.S.A. 156 E4
Idaho Falls U.S.A. 156 E4
Idalia National Park Australia 136 D5
Idar India 104 C5
Idar-Oberstein Germany 63 H5
Ide Japan 92 B4
Ider Mongolia see Galt
Ideriyn Gol r. Mongolia 94 E1
Idfū Egypt 108 D5
Idhān Awbārī des. Libya 120 E2
Idhān Murzūq des. Libya 120 E2
Idhra i. Greece see Ydra
Idi Amin Dada, Lake Dem. Rep. Congo/Uganda see Edward, Lake
Idiofa Dem. Rep. Congo 123 B4
Iditarod AK U.S.A. 148 H3
Iditarod r. AK U.S.A. 148 H3
Idivuoma Sweden 54 M2
Idkū Egypt 112 C5
Idle r. U.K. 58 G5
Idlewild airport U.S.A. see John F. Kennedy
Idlib Syria 107 C2
Idra i. Greece see Ydra
Idre Sweden 55 H6
Idstein Germany 63 I4
Idutywa S. Africa 125 I7
Idzhevan Armenia see Ijevan
Iecava Latvia 55 N8
Iepê Brazil 179 A3
Ieper Belgium 62 C4
Ierapetra Greece 69 K7
Ierissou, Kolpos b. Greece 69 J4
Iešjávri l. Norway 54 N2
Ifakara Tanz. 123 D4
Ifalik atoll Micronesia 81 K5
Ifaluk atoll Micronesia see Ifalik
Ifanadiana Madag. 123 E6
Ife Nigeria 120 D4
Ifenat Chad 121 E3
Iferouâne Niger 120 D3
Iffley Australia 136 C3
Ifjord Norway 54 O1
Ifôghas, Adrar des hills Mali 120 D3
Iforas, Adrar des hills Mali see Ifôghas, Adrar des
Iga Japan 92 C4
Igan Sarawak Malaysia 85 E2
Igan r. Malaysia 85 E2
Iganga Uganda 121 G4
Igarapava Brazil 179 B3
Igarka Rus. Fed. 76 J3
Igatpuri India 106 B2
Igbeti Nigeria see Igbetti
Igbetti Nigeria 120 D4
Igdir Iran 110 B2
Iğdır Turkey 113 G3
Igel'veyem r. Rus. Fed. 148 D2
Iggesund Sweden 55 J6
Igikpak, Mount AK U.S.A. 148 I2
Igiugig AK U.S.A. 148 I4
Igizyar China 111 J2
Iglesias Sardinia Italy 68 C5
Iglesiente reg. Sardinia Italy 68 C5
Igloolik Canada 147 J3
Igluligaarjuk Canada see Chesterfield Inlet
Ignace Canada 151 N5
Ignacio Zaragosa Mex. 166 D2
Ignacio Zaragoza Tamaulipas Mex. 167 F4
Ignacio Zaragoza Mex. 161 C8
Ignalina Lith. 55 O9
İğneada Turkey 69 L4
İğneada Burnu pt Turkey 69 M4
Ignoitijala India 87 A5
iGoli S. Africa see Johannesburg
Igom Papua Indon. 83 D3
Igoumenitsa Greece 69 I5
Igra Rus. Fed. 51 Q4
Igrim Rus. Fed. 51 S3
Iguaçu r. Brazil 179 A4
Iguaçu, Saltos do waterfall Arg./Brazil see Iguaçu Falls
Iguaçu Falls Arg./Brazil 178 F3
Iguaí Brazil 179 C1
Iguala Mex. 168 E5
Igualada Spain 67 G3
Iguape Brazil 179 B4
Iguaraçu Brazil 179 A3
Iguatama Brazil 179 B3
Iguatemi Brazil 178 F2
Iguatu Brazil 177 K5
Iguazú, Cataratas do waterfall Arg./Brazil see Iguaçu Falls
Iguéla Gabon 122 A4
Iguidi, Erg des. Alg./Mauritania 120 C2
Igunga Tanz. 123 D4
Iharaña Madag. 123 E5
Ihavandhippolhu Atoll Maldives 106 B5
Ihavandiffulu Atoll Maldives see Ihavandhippolhu Atoll
Ih Bogd Uul mt. Mongolia 102 J3
Ihbulag Mongolia see Hanbogd
Ihhayrhan Mongolia see Bayan-Önjüül
Ihosy Madag. 123 E6
Ih Tal Nei Mongol China 95 J3
Ihtamir Mongolia 94 E2
Ih-Uul Mongolia 94 E1
Iida Japan 93 D3
Iide-san mt. Japan 91 E5
Iijärvi l. Fin. 54 O2
Iijima Japan 93 D3
Iijoki r. Fin. 54 N4
Iinan Japan 92 C4
Iioka Japan 93 G3
Iisalmi Fin. 54 O5
Iitaka Japan 92 C4
Iiyama Japan 93 E2
Iizuka Japan 91 C6
Ijebu-Ode Nigeria 120 D4
Ijen-Merapi-Maelang, Cagar Alam nature res. Jawa Indon. 85 F5
Ijevan Armenia 113 G2
IJmuiden Neth. 62 E2
IJssel r. Neth. 62 F2
IJsselmeer l. Neth. 62 F2
IJzer r. Belgium see Yser
Ikaahuk Canada see Sachs Harbour
Ikaalinen Fin. 55 M6
Ikageleng S. Africa 125 H3
Ikageng S. Africa 125 H4
Ikaho Japan 93 E2
iKapa S. Africa see Cape Town
Ikare Nigeria 120 D4
Ikaria i. Greece 69 L6
Ikaruga Japan 92 B4
Ikast Denmark 55 F8
Ikawa Japan 93 E3
Ikeda Fukui Japan 92 C3
Ikeda Japan 90 F4
Ikeda Nagano Japan 93 D2
Ikeda Ōsaka Japan 92 B3
Ikegoya-yama mt. Japan 92 C4
Ikela Dem. Rep. Congo 122 C4
Ikhtiman Bulg. 69 J3
Ikhutseng S. Africa 124 G5
Iki-Burul Rus. Fed. 53 J7
Ikom Nigeria 120 D4
Ikoma Japan 92 B4
Ikpikpuk r. AK U.S.A. 148 I1
Iksan S. Korea 91 B6
Ikuji-hana pt Japan 92 D2
Ikungu Tanz. 123 D4
Ikuno Japan 92 A3
Ikusaka Japan 93 D2
Ilagan Luzon Phil. 82 C2
Ilaisamis Kenya 122 D3
Īlām Iran 110 B3
Ilam Nepal 105 F4
Ilan Taiwan 97 I3
Ilave Peru 176 E7
Iława Poland 57 Q4
Ilazārān, Kūh-e mt. Iran 110 E4
Il Bogd Uul mts Mongolia 94 D2
Île-à-la-Crosse Canada 151 J4
Île-à-la-Crosse, Lac l. Canada 151 J4
Ilebo Dem. Rep. Congo 123 C4
Île-de-France admin. reg. France 62 C6
Île Europa i. Indian Ocean see Europa, Île
Ilek Kazakh. 51 Q5

▶Ilemi Triangle terr. Africa 122 D3
Disputed territory (Ethiopia/Kenya/Sudan) administered by Kenya.

Ilen r. Ireland 61 C6
Ileret Kenya 122 D3
Ileza Rus. Fed. 52 I3
Ilfeld Germany 63 K3
Ilford Canada 151 M3
Ilford U.K. 59 H7
Ilfracombe Australia 136 D4
Ilfracombe U.K. 59 C7
Ilgaz Turkey 112 D2
Ilgın Turkey 112 C3
Ilha Grande, Represa resr Brazil 178 F2
Ilha Solteíra, Represa resr Brazil 179 A3
Ílhavo Port. 67 B3
Ilhéus Brazil 179 D1
Ili Kazakh. see Kapchagay
Iliamna AK U.S.A. 148 I4
Iliamna Lake AK U.S.A. 148 I4
Iliamna Volcano AK U.S.A. 148 I3
İliç Turkey 112 E3
Il'ichevsk Azer. see Şärur
Il'ichevsk Ukr. see Illichivs'k
Ilici Spain see Elche-Elx
Iligan Mindanao Phil. 82 D4
Iligan Bay Mindanao Phil. 82 D4
Iligan Point Luzon Phil. 82 C2
Ilimananngip Nunaa i. Greenland 147 P2
Il'inka Rus. Fed. 53 J7
Il'inka Respublika Tyva Rus. Fed. 94 C1
Il'inskiy Permskaya Oblast' Rus. Fed. 51 R4
Il'inskiy Sakhalinskaya Oblast' Rus. Fed. 90 F3
Il'insko-Podomskoye Rus. Fed. 52 J3
Ilin Strait Phil. 82 C3
Iliomar East Timor 83 C5
Ilion U.S.A. 165 H2
Ilium tourist site Turkey see Troy
Ilivit Mountains AK U.S.A. 148 G3
Iliysk Kazakh. see Kapchagay
Ilkal India 106 C3
Ilkeston U.K. 59 F6
Ilkley U.K. 58 F5
Illana Bay Mindanao Phil. 82 C5
Illapel Chile 178 B4
Illéla Niger 120 D3
Iller r. Germany 57 L6
Illichivs'k Ukr. 69 N1
Illimani, Nevado de mt. Bol. 176 E7
Illinois r. U.S.A. 160 F4
Illinois state U.S.A. 164 A3
Illizi Alg. 120 D2
Illogwa watercourse Australia 136 A5
Ilm r. Germany 63 L3
Ilmajoki Fin. 54 M5
Il'men', Ozero l. Rus. Fed. 52 F4
Ilmenau Germany 63 K4
Ilmenau r. Germany 63 K1
Ilminster U.K. 59 E8
Ilnik AK U.S.A. 148 H4
Ilo Peru 176 D7
Iloc i. Phil. 82 B4
Iloilo Panay Phil. 82 C4
Iloilo Strait Phil. 82 C4
Ilomantsi Fin. 54 Q5
Ilong India 96 B3
Ilorin Nigeria 120 D4
Ilovlya Rus. Fed. 53 I6
Ilsede Germany 63 K2
Iluka Australia 138 F2
Ilulissat Greenland 147 M3
Iluppur India 106 C4
Ilva i. Italy see Elba, Isola d'
Imabari Japan 91 D6
Imadate Japan 92 C3
Imaichi Japan 93 F2
Imajō Japan 92 C3
Imala Moz. 123 D5
Imam-baba Turkm. 111 F2
İmamoğlu Turkey 112 D3
Iman Rus. Fed. see Dal'nerechensk
Iman r. Rus. Fed. 90 D3
Imari Japan 91 C6
Imaruí Brazil 179 A5
Imataca, Serranía de mts Venez. 176 F2
Imatra Fin. 55 P6
Imazu Japan 92 C3
Imba-numa l. Japan see Inba-numa
Imbituva Brazil 179 A4
imeni 26 Bakinskikh Komissarov Azer. see Uzboy
imeni Babushkina Rus. Fed. 52 I4
imeni Chapayevka Turkm. see S. A. Nyýazow Adyndaky
imeni Kalinina Tajik. see Cheshtebe
imeni Kirova Kazakh. see Kopbirlik
imeni Petra Stuchki Latvia see Aizkraukle
imeni Poliny Osipenko Rus. Fed. 90 E1
imeni Tel'mana Rus. Fed. 90 D2
Īmī Eth. 122 E3
Imishli Azer. see İmişli
İmişli Azer. 113 H3
Imit Pak. 104 C1
Imja-do i. S. Korea 91 B6
Imlay U.S.A. 158 D1
Imlay City U.S.A. 164 D2
Imola Italy 68 D2
iMonti S. Africa see East London
Impendle S. Africa 125 I5
Imperatriz Brazil 177 I5
Imperia Italy 68 C3
Imperial CA U.S.A. 159 F5
Imperial NE U.S.A. 160 C3
Imperial Beach U.S.A. 158 E5
Imperial Dam U.S.A. 159 F5
Imperial Valley plain U.S.A. 159 F5
Imperieuse Reef Australia 134 B4
Impfondo Congo 122 B3
Imphal India 105 H4
İmralı Adası i. Turkey 69 M4
İmroz Turkey 69 K4
İmroz i. Turkey see Gökçeada
Imtān Syria 107 C3
Imuris Mex. 166 C2
Imuruan Bay Palawan Phil. 82 B4
Imuruk Basin l. AK U.S.A. 148 F2
Imuruk Lake AK U.S.A. 148 G2
In r. Rus. Fed. 90 D2
Ina Ibaraki Japan 93 G3
Ina Nagano Japan 93 D3
Inabe Japan 92 C3
Inabu Japan 92 D3
Inae Japan 92 C3
Inagauan Palawan Phil. 82 B4
Inagawa Japan 92 B4
Ina-gawa r. Japan 92 B4
Inage Japan 93 G3
Inagi Japan 93 F3
Inalik U.S.A. see Diomede
Inambari r. Peru 176 E6
Inami Hyōgo Japan 92 A4
Inami Toyama Japan 92 C2
Inanam Sabah Malaysia 85 G1
Inanda S. Africa 125 J5
Inanudak Bay AK U.S.A. 148 E5
Inari Fin. 54 O2
Inarijärvi l. Fin. 54 O2
Inarijoki r. Fin./Norway 54 N2
Inasa Japan 92 D4
Inazawa Japan 92 C3
Inba Japan 93 G3
Inba-numa l. Japan 93 G3
Inca Spain 67 H4
İnce Burnu pt Turkey 69 L4
İnce Burun pt Turkey 112 D2
Inch Ireland 61 F5
Inchard, Loch b. U.K. 60 D2
Incheon S. Korea see Inch'ŏn
Inchicronan Lough l. Ireland 61 D5
Inch'ŏn S. Korea 91 B5
Inchoun Rus. Fed. 148 E2
Incirli Turkey see Karasu
Indaal, Loch b. U.K. 60 C5
Indalsälven r. Sweden 54 J5

Indalstø Norway 55 D6
Inda Silasē Eth. 122 D2
Indaw Myanmar 86 A2
Indawgyi, Lake Myanmar 96 C3
Indé Mex. 166 D3
Indefatigable Island Galápagos Ecuador see Santa Cruz, Isla
Independence CA U.S.A. 158 D3
Independence IA U.S.A. 160 F3
Independence KS U.S.A. 161 E4
Independence KY U.S.A. 164 C4
Independence MO U.S.A. 160 E4
Independence VA U.S.A. 164 E5
Independence Mountains U.S.A. 156 D4
Inder Nei Mongol China 95 J2
Inderborskiy Kazakh. 100 E2
Indi India 106 C2
▶India country Asia 103 E7
2nd most populous country in the world and in Asia. 3rd largest country in Asia, and 7th in the world.
Indian r. Y.T. Canada 149 M3
Indiana U.S.A. 164 F3
Indiana state U.S.A. 164 B3
Indian-Antarctic Ridge sea feature Southern Ocean 186 D9
▶Indianapolis U.S.A. 164 B4
Capital of Indiana.
Indian Cabins Canada 150 G3
Indian Desert India/Pak. see Thar Desert
Indian Harbour Canada 153 K3
Indian Head Canada 151 K5
Indian Lake U.S.A. 165 H2
Indian Lake l. NY U.S.A. 165 H2
Indian Lake l. OH U.S.A. 164 D3
Indian Lake l. PA U.S.A. 165 F3
Indian Mountain AK U.S.A. 148 I2
▶Indian Ocean 185
3rd largest ocean in the world.
Indianola IA U.S.A. 160 E3
Indianola MS U.S.A. 161 F5
Indian Peak U.S.A. 159 G2
Indian Springs IN U.S.A. 164 B4
Indian Springs NV U.S.A. 159 F3
Indian Wells U.S.A. 159 H4
Indiga Rus. Fed. 52 K2
Indigirka r. Rus. Fed. 77 P2
Indigskaya Guba b. Rus. Fed. 52 K2
Inđija Serbia 69 I2
Indin Lake Canada 150 H1
Indio r. Nicaragua 166 [inset] J7
Indio U.S.A. 158 E5
Indira Point India see Pygmalion Point
Indira Priyadarshini Pench National Park India 104 D5
Indispensable Reefs Solomon Is 133 G3
Indjija Serbia see Inđija
Indo-China reg. Asia 86 D3
▶Indonesia country Asia 80 E7
4th most populous country in the world and 3rd in Asia.
Indore India 104 C5
Indragiri r. Indon. 84 C3
Indramayu Jawa Indon. 85 E4
Indramayu, Tanjung pt Indon. 85 E4
Indrapura Sumatera Indon. 84 C3
Indrapura, Gunung vol. Indon. see Kerinci, Gunung
Indrapura, Tanjung pt Indon. 84 C3
Indravati r. India 106 D2
Indre r. France 66 E3
Indulkana Australia 135 F6
Indur India see Nizamabad
Indus r. China/Pakistan 111 G6
also known as Sênggê Zangbo (China) or Shiquan He (China)
Indus, Mouths of the Pak. 111 G5
Indus Cone sea feature Indian Ocean 185 M4
Indwe S. Africa 125 H6
Ine Japan 92 B3
İnebolu Turkey 112 D2
İnegöl Turkey 69 M4
Inerie vol. Flores Indon. 83 B5
Inevi Turkey see Cihanbeyli
Inez U.S.A. 164 D5
Infantes Spain see Villanueva de los Infantes
Infiernillo, Presa resr Mex. 168 D5
Ing, Nam Mae r. Thai. 86 C2
Inga Rus. Fed. 54 S3
Ingalls, Mount U.S.A. 158 C2
Ingelmunster Belgium 62 D4
Ingenika r. Canada 150 E3
Ingersoll Canada 164 E2
Ingettolgoy Mongolia see Selenge
Inggelang i. Maluku Indon. 83 D2
Ingham Australia 136 D3
Ingichka Uzbek. 111 G2
Ingleborough hill U.K. 58 E4
Inglefield Land reg. Greenland 147 K2
Ingleton U.K. 58 E4
Inglewood Qld Australia 138 E2
Inglewood Vic. Australia 138 A6
Inglewood U.S.A. 158 D5
Ingoda r. Rus. Fed. 95 H1
Ingoka Pum mt. Myanmar 86 B1
Ingoldmells U.K. 58 H5
Ingolstadt Germany 63 L6
Ingomar Australia 135 F7
Ingomar U.S.A. 156 G3
Ingonish Canada 153 J5
Ingraj Bazar India 105 G4
Ingram U.S.A. 164 F5
Ingray Lake Canada 150 G1
Ingrid Christensen Coast Antarctica 188 E2
Ingwavuma S. Africa 125 K4
Ingwavuma r. S. Africa/Swaziland see Ngwavuma
Ingwiller France 63 H6
Inhaca Moz. 125 K3
Inhaca, Península pen. Moz. 125 K4
Inhambane Moz. 125 L2
Inhambane prov. Moz. 125 L2
Inhaminga Moz. 123 D5
Inharrime Moz. 125 L3
Inhassoro Moz. 123 D6
Inhaúmas Brazil 179 B1
Inhobim Brazil 179 C1
Inhumas Brazil 179 A2
Inielika vol. Flores Indon. 83 B5
Inis Ireland see Ennis
Inis Córthaidh Ireland see Enniscorthy
Inishark i. Ireland 61 B4
Inishbofin i. Ireland 61 B4
Inisheer i. Ireland 61 C4
Inishkea North i. Ireland 61 B3
Inishkea South i. Ireland 61 B3
Inishmaan i. Ireland 61 C4
Inishmore i. Ireland 61 C4
Inishmurray i. Ireland 61 D3
Inishowen pen. Ireland 61 E2
Inishowen Head hd Ireland 61 F2
Inishtrahull i. Ireland 61 E2
Inishturk i. Ireland 61 B4
Injgan Sum Nei Mongol China 95 I2
Injune Australia 137 E5
Inkerman Australia 136 C3
Inklin Canada 150 C3
Inklin r. B.C. Canada 149 N4
Inkylap Turkm. 111 F2
Inland Kaikoura Range mts N.Z. 139 D6
Inland Lake AK U.S.A. 148 H2
Inland Sea Japan see Seto-naikai
Inlet U.S.A. 165 H2
Inman r. Nunavut Canada 149 R1
Inn r. Europe 57 M7
Innaanganeq c. Greenland 147 L2
Innamincka Australia 137 C5
Innamincka Regional Reserve nature res. Australia 137 C5
Inndyr Norway 54 I3
Inner Mongolia aut. reg. China see Nei Mongol Zizhiqu
Inner Sound sea chan. U.K. 60 D3
Innes National Park Australia 137 B7
Innisfail Australia 136 D3
Innisfail Canada 150 H4
Innokent'yevka Rus. Fed. 90 C2
Innoko r. AK U.S.A. 148 H3
Innoko National Wildlife Refuge nature res. AK U.S.A. 148 H3
Innsbruck Austria 57 M7
Innuksuak r. Canada 152 F2
Inny r. Ireland 61 E4
Inobonto Sulawesi Indon. 83 C2
Inocência Brazil 179 A2
Inokuchi Japan 92 C2
Inongo Dem. Rep. Congo 122 B4
İnönü Turkey 69 N5
Inoucdjouac Canada see Inukjuak
Inowrocław Poland 57 Q4
In Salah Alg. 120 D2
Insch U.K. 60 G3
▶Inscription, Cape Australia 136 B3
Most westerly point of Oceania.
Insein Myanmar 86 B3
Insterburg Rus. Fed. see Chernyakhovsk
Inta Rus. Fed. 51 S2
Interamna Italy see Teramo
Interlaken Switz. 66 H3
International Falls U.S.A. 160 E1
Interview Island India 87 A4
Intracoastal Waterway canal U.S.A. 161 E6
Intutu Peru 176 D4
Inubō-zaki pt Japan 91 F6
Inukjuak Canada 152 F2
Inuvik N.W.T. Canada 149 N1
Inuyama Japan 92 C3
Inveraray U.K. 60 D4
Inverbervie U.K. 60 G4
Invercargill N.Z. 139 B8
Inverell Australia 138 E2
Invergordon U.K. 60 E3
Inverkeithing U.K. 60 F4
Inverleigh Australia 136 C3
Invermay Canada 151 K5
Inverness Canada 153 J5
Inverness U.K. 60 E3
Inverness CA U.S.A. 158 B2
Inverness FL U.S.A. 163 D6
Inverurie U.K. 60 G3
Investigator Channel Myanmar 87 B4
Investigator Group is Australia 135 F8
Investigator Ridge sea feature Indian Ocean 185 O6
Investigator Strait Australia 137 B7
Inwood U.S.A. 165 F4
Inya Rus. Fed. 98 D2
Inyanga Zimbabwe see Nyanga
Inyangani mt. Zimbabwe 123 D5
Inyokern U.S.A. 158 E4
Inyo Mountains U.S.A. 158 D3
Inyonga Tanz. 123 D4
Inza Rus. Fed. 53 J5
Inzai Japan 93 G3
Inzhavino Rus. Fed. 53 I5
Ioannina Greece 69 I5
Iokanga r. Rus. Fed. 52 H2
Iola U.S.A. 160 E4
Iolgo, Khrebet mts Rus. Fed. 102 G1
Iolotan' Turkm. see Ýolöten
Iona Canada 153 J5
Iona i. U.K. 60 C4
Iona, Parque Nacional do nat. park Angola 123 B5
Ione U.S.A. 158 E2
Iongo Angola 123 B4
Ionia U.S.A. 164 C2
Ionia Nisia is Ionia Nisia Greece see Ionian Islands
Ionian Islands Greece 69 H5
Ionian Sea Greece/Italy 68 H5
Ionioi Nisoi is Ionia Nisia Greece see Ionian Islands
Ionioi Nisoi is Greece see Ionian Islands
Ioniveyem r. Rus. Fed. 148 D2
Iōno Japan 93 G2
Ios i. Greece 69 K6
Iowa state U.S.A. 160 E3
Iowa City U.S.A. 160 F3
Iowa Falls U.S.A. 160 E3
Iō-zan hill Japan 92 C2
Ipameri Brazil 179 A2
Ipanema Brazil 179 C2
Iparía Peru 176 D5
Ipatinga Brazil 179 C2
Ipatovo Rus. Fed. 53 I7
Ipelegeng S. Africa 125 G4
Ipewik r. AK U.S.A. 148 F1
Ipiales Col. 176 C3
Ipiaú Brazil 179 D1
Ipirá Brazil 179 D1
Ipiranga Brazil 179 A4
iPitoli S. Africa see Pretoria
Ipixuna r. Brazil 176 F5
Ipoh Malaysia 84 C1
Iporá Brazil 179 A2
Ippy Cent. Afr. Rep. 122 C3
İpsala Turkey 69 L4
Ipswich Australia 138 F1
Ipswich U.K. 59 I6
Ipswich U.S.A. 160 D2
Ipu Brazil 177 J4
Ipuh Sumatera Indon. 84 C3
▶Iqaluit Canada 147 L3
Capital of Nunavut.
Iqe Qinghai China 94 C4
Iqe He r. China 99 F5
Iquique Chile 178 B2
Iquiri r. Brazil see Ituxi
Iquitos Peru 176 D4
Īrafshān reg. Iran 111 F5
Irago-misaki pt Japan 92 D4
Irago-suidō str. Japan 92 C4
Irai Brazil 178 F3
Irakleio Greece see Iraklion
Iraklion Greece 69 K7
Iramaia Brazil 179 C1
Iran country Asia 110 D3
Iran, Pegunungan mts Indon. 85 F2
Īrānshahr Iran 111 F5
Irapuato Mex. 168 D4
Iraq country Asia 113 F4
Irara Brazil 179 D1
Irati Brazil 179 A4
Irayel' Rus. Fed. 52 L2
Irazú, Volcán vol. Costa Rica 166 [inset] J7
Irbid Jordan 107 B3
Irbil Iraq see Arbīl
Irbit Rus. Fed. 76 H4
Irecê Brazil 177 J6
Ireland country Europe 61 E4
▶Ireland i. Ireland/U.K. 61
4th largest island in Europe.
Irema Dem. Rep. Congo 122 C4
Irgiz Kazakh. 102 B2
Irgiz r. Kazakh. 102 B2
Iri S. Korea see Iksan
Irian, Teluk b. Indon. see Cenderawasih, Teluk
Irian Barat prov. Indon. see Papua
Irian Jaya prov. Indon. see Papua
Iriba Chad 121 F3
Īrī Dāgh mt. Iran 110 B2
Iriga Luzon Phil. 82 C3
Irîgui reg. Mali/Mauritania 120 C3
Iringa Tanz. 123 D4
Iriri r. Brazil 177 H4
Irish Free State country Europe see Ireland
Irish Sea Ireland/U.K. 61 G4
Irituia Brazil 177 I4
'Irj well Saudi Arabia 110 C5
Irkutsk Rus. Fed. 88 I2
Irma Canada 151 I4
Irmak Turkey 112 D3
Irminger Basin sea feature N. Atlantic Ocean 184 F2
Iron Baron Australia 137 B7
Iron Creek AK U.S.A. 148 F2
Irondequoit U.S.A. 165 G2
Iron Mountain U.S.A. 160 F2
Iron Mountain mt. U.S.A. 159 G3
Iron Range National Park Australia 136 C2
Iron River U.S.A. 160 F2
Ironton MO U.S.A. 160 F4
Ironton OH U.S.A. 164 D4
Ironwood Forest National Monument nat. park U.S.A. 159 H5
Iroquois r. N.W.T. Canada 149 O1
Iroquois r. U.S.A. 164 B3
Iroquois Falls Canada 152 E4
Irosin Luzon Phil. 82 D3
Irō-zaki pt Japan 93 E4
Irpen' Ukr. see Irpin'
Irpin' Ukr. 53 F6
'Irq al Ḩarūrī des. Saudi Arabia 110 B5
'Irq Banbān des. Saudi Arabia 110 B5
Irrawaddy r. Myanmar 86 A4
Irrawaddy, Mouths of the Myanmar 86 A4
Irshad Pass Afgh./Pak. 111 I2
Irta Rus. Fed. 52 K3
Irthing r. U.K. 58 E4
▶Irtysh r. Kazakh./Rus. Fed. 102 E1
5th longest river in Asia and 10th in the world, and a major part of the 2nd longest in Asia (Ob'-Irtysh).
Iruma Japan 93 F3
Iruma-gawa r. Japan 93 F3
Irun Spain 67 F2
Iruña Spain see Pamplona
Iruñea Spain see Pamplona
Irvine U.K. 60 E5
Irvine CA U.S.A. 158 E5
Irvine KY U.S.A. 164 D5
Irvine Glacier Antarctica 188 L2
Irving U.S.A. 161 D5
Irvington U.S.A. 164 B5
Irwin r. Australia 135 A7
Irwinton U.S.A. 163 D5
Isa Nigeria 120 D3
Isaac r. Australia 136 E4
Isabel U.S.A. 160 C2
Isabela Negros Phil. 82 C4
Isabela Phil. 82 C5
Isabela, Isla i. Galápagos Ecuador 176 [inset]
Isabelia, Cordillera mts Nicaragua 166 [inset] I6
Isabella Lake U.S.A. 158 D4
Isachsen, Cape Canada 147 H2
Ísafjarðardjúp est. Iceland 54 [inset]
Ísafjörður Iceland 54 [inset]
Isa Khel Pak. 111 H3
Isar r. Germany 63 M6
Isarog, Mount Phil. 82 C3
Isawa Japan 93 E3
Isbister U.K. 60 [inset]
Ischia, Isola d' i. Italy 68 E4
Ise Japan 92 C4
Isehara Japan 93 F3
Isère r. France 66 G4
Isère, Pointe pt Fr. Guiana 177 H2
Iserlohn Germany 63 H3
Isernhagen Germany 63 J2
Isernia Italy 68 F4
Isesaki Japan 93 F2
Ise-shima Kokuritsu-kōen nat. park Japan 92 C4
Ise-wan b. Japan 92 C4
Iseyin Nigeria 120 D4
Isfahan Iran see Eşfahān
Isfana Kyrg. 111 H2
Isheyevka Rus. Fed. 53 K5
Ishibe Japan 92 C3
Ishigaki Japan 89 M8
Ishige Japan 93 F2
Ishikari-wan b. Japan 90 F4
Ishikawa pref. Japan 92 C2
Ishim r. Kazakh./Rus. Fed. 102 D1
Ishinomaki Japan 91 F5
Ishinomaki-wan b. Japan 89 Q5
Ishioka Japan 93 G2
Ishkoshim Tajik. 111 H2
Ishpeming U.S.A. 162 C2
Ishtikhon Uzbek. see Ishtixon
Ishtixon Uzbek. 111 G2
Ishtragh Afgh. 111 H2
Ishurdi Bangl. 105 G4
Ishwardi Bangl. see Ishurdi
Isiboro Sécure, Parque Nacional nat. park Bol. 176 E7
Isigny-sur-Mer France 59 F9
Işıklar Dağı mts Turkey 69 L4
Işıklı Turkey 69 M5
Isil'kul' Rus. Fed. 76 I4
Isipingo S. Africa 125 J5
Isiro Dem. Rep. Congo 122 C3
Isisford Australia 136 D5
Iskateley Rus. Fed. 52 L2
İskenderun Turkey 107 C1
İskenderun Körfezi b. Turkey 107 B1
İskilip Turkey 112 D2
Iskitim Rus. Fed. 76 J4
Iskŭr r. Bulg. 69 K3
Iskushuban Somalia 122 F2
Iskut r. B.C. Canada 149 O4
Isla r. Scotland U.K. 60 F4
Isla r. Scotland U.K. 60 G3
Isla Gorge National Park Australia 136 E5
İslahiye Turkey 112 E3
Islamabad India see Anantnag
▶Islamabad Pak. 111 I3
Capital of Pakistan.
Islamgarh Pak. 111 H5
Islamkot Pak. 111 H5
Island r. Canada 150 F2
Ísland country Europe see Iceland
Island U.S.A. 164 B5
Island Bay Palawan Phil. 82 B4
Island Falls U.S.A. 162 G2
Island Lagoon salt flat Australia 137 B6
Island Lake Canada 151 M4
Island Lake l. Canada 151 M4
Island Magee pen. U.K. 61 G3
Island Pond U.S.A. 165 J1
Islands, Bay of N.Z. 139 E2
Islas de Bahá, Parque Nacional nat. park Hond. 166 [inset] I5
Islay i. U.K. 60 C5
Isle of Man terr. Irish Sea 58 C4
Isle of Wight U.S.A. 165 G5
Isle Royale National Park U.S.A. 160 F2
Ismail Ukr. see Izmayil
Ismā'īlīya Egypt see Al Ismā'īlīyah
Ismā'īlīya governorate Egypt see Al Ismā'īlīyah
Ismailly Azer. see İsmayıllı
İsmayıllı Azer. 113 H2
Isobe Japan 92 C4
Isogo Japan 93 F3
Isojoki Fin. 54 L5
Isoka Zambia 123 D5
Isokylä Fin. 54 O3
Isokyrö Fin. 54 M5
Isola di Capo Rizzuto Italy 68 G5
Ispahan Iran see Eşfahān
Isparta Turkey 69 N6
Isperikh Bulg. 69 L3
Ispikan Pak. 111 F5
İspir Turkey 113 F2
Ispisar Tajik. see Khŭjand
Isplinji Pak. 111 G4
Israel country Asia 107 B4
Israelite Bay Australia 135 C8
Isra'īl country Asia see Israel
Isselburg Germany 62 G3
Isshiki Japan 92 D4
Issia Côte d'Ivoire 120 C4
Issimu Sulawesi Indon. 83 B2
Issoire France 66 F4
Issyk-Kul' Kyrg. see Balykchy
Issyk-Kul', Ozero salt l. Kyrg. see Ysyk-Köl
Istalif Afgh. 111 H3
▶İstanbul Turkey 69 M4
2nd most populous city in Europe.
İstanbul Boğazı strait Turkey see Bosporus
Īstgāh-e Eznā Iran 110 C3
Istiaia Greece 69 J5
Istik r. Tajik. 111 I2
Istočni Drvar Bos.-Herz. 68 G2
Istra pen. Croatia see Istria
Istres France 66 G5
Istria pen. Croatia 68 E2
Isumi Japan 93 G3
Isumi-gawa r. Japan 93 G3
Isüüj Mongolia see Bayanchandmanī
Iswardi Bangl. see Ishurdi
Itabapoana r. Brazil 179 C3
Itaberá Brazil 179 A3
Itaberaba Brazil 179 C1
Itaberaí Brazil 179 A2
Itabira Brazil 179 C2
Itabirito Brazil 179 C3
Itabuna Brazil 179 D1
Itacajá Brazil 177 I5
Itacarambi Brazil 179 B1
Itacoatiara Brazil 177 G4
Itadori Japan 92 C3
Itaetê Brazil 179 C1
Itagmatana Iran see Hamadān
Itaguaçu Brazil 179 C2
Itaí Brazil 179 A3
Itaiópolis Brazil 179 A4
Itäisen Suomenlahden kansallispuisto nat. park Fin. 55 O6
Itaituba Brazil 177 G4
Itajaí Brazil 179 A4
Itajubá Brazil 179 B3
Itajuipe Brazil 179 D1
Itako Japan 93 G3
Itakura Gunma Japan 93 F2
Itakura Niigata Japan 93 E1
Italia country Europe see Italy
Italia, Laguna l. Bol. 176 F6
▶Italy country Europe 68 E3
5th most populous country in Europe.
Itamarandiba Brazil 179 C2
Itambé Brazil 179 C1
Itambé, Pico de mt. Brazil 179 C2
It Amelân i. Neth. see Ameland
Itami Japan 92 B4
Itami airport Japan 92 B4
Itampolo Madag. 123 E6
Itanagar India 105 H4
Itanguari r. Brazil 179 B1
Itanhaém Brazil 179 B4
Itanhém Brazil 179 C2
Itanhém r. Brazil 179 D2
Itaobím Brazil 179 C2
Itapaci Brazil 179 A1
Itapajipe Brazil 179 A2
Itapebi Brazil 179 D1
Itapecerica Brazil 179 B3
Itapemirim Brazil 179 C3
Itaperuna Brazil 179 C3
Itapetinga Brazil 179 C1
Itapetininga Brazil 179 A3
Itapeva Brazil 179 A3
Itapeva, Lago l. Brazil 179 A5
Itapicuru Brazil 177 J6
Itapicuru, Serra de hills Brazil 177 I5
Itapicuru Mirim Brazil 177 J4
Itapipoca Brazil 177 K4
Itapira Brazil 179 B3
Itaporanga Brazil 179 A3
Itapuã Brazil 179 A5
Itaqui Brazil 178 E3
Itararé Brazil 179 A4
Itarsi India 104 D5
Itarumã Brazil 179 A2
Itatiba Brazil 179 B3
Itatuba Brazil 176 F5
Itaúna Brazil 179 B3
Itaúnas Brazil 179 D2
Itbayat i. Phil. 82 C1
Itchen Lake Canada 151 H1
Itea Greece 69 J5
Ithaca MI U.S.A. 164 C2
Ithaca NY U.S.A. 165 G2
It Hearrenfean Neth. see Heerenveen
iThekweni S. Africa see Durban
Ith Hils ridge Germany 63 J2
Ithrah Saudi Arabia 107 C4
Itilleq Greenland 147 M3
Itimbiri r. Dem. Rep. Congo 122 C3
Itinga Brazil 179 C2
Itiquira Brazil 177 H7
Itiruçu Brazil 179 C1
Itiúba, Serra de hills Brazil 177 K6
Itkillik r. AK U.S.A. 149 J1
Itō Japan 93 F4
Itoigawa Japan 93 D1
Itonuki Japan 92 C3
iTswane S. Africa see Pretoria
Ittiri Sardinia Italy 68 C4
Ittoqqortoormiit Greenland 147 P2
Itu Brazil 179 B3
Itu Abu Island Spratly Is 80 E4
Ituaçu Brazil 179 C1
Ituberá Brazil 179 D1
Ituí r. Brazil 176 D4
Ituiutaba Brazil 179 A2
Itumbiara Brazil 179 A2
Itumbiara, Barragem resr Brazil 179 A2
Ituni Guyana 177 G2
Itupiranga Brazil 177 I5
Ituporanga Brazil 179 A4
Iturama Brazil 179 A2
Iturbide Campeche Mex. 167 H5
Iturbide Mex. 161 D7
Ituri r. Dem. Rep. Congo 122 C3
Iturup, Ostrov i. Rus. Fed. 90 G3
Itutinga Brazil 179 B3
Ituxi r. Brazil 176 F5
Ityop'ia country Africa see Ethiopia
Itz r. Germany 63 K5
Itzehoe Germany 57 L4
Iuka U.S.A. 161 F5
Iul'tin Rus. Fed. 148 C2
Ivalo Fin. 54 O2
Ivalojoki r. Fin. 54 O2
Ivanava Belarus 55 N10
Ivanhoe Australia 138 B4
Ivanhoe U.S.A. 160 D2
Ivanhoe Lake Canada 151 J2
Ivankiv Ukr. 53 F6
Ivankovtsy Rus. Fed. 90 D2
Ivanof Bay AK U.S.A. 148 H5
Ivano-Frankivs'k Ukr. 53 E6
Ivano-Frankovsk Ukr. see Ivano-Frankivs'k
Ivanovka Rus. Fed. 90 B2
Ivanovo Belarus see Ivanava
Ivanovo tourist site Bulg. 69 K3
Ivanovo Rus. Fed. 52 I4
Ivanovskiy Khrebet mts Kazakh. 98 C2
Ivanteyevka Rus. Fed. 53 K5
Ivantsevichi Belarus see Ivatsevichy
Ivatsevichy Belarus 55 N10
Ivaylovgrad Bulg. 69 L4
Ivdel' Rus. Fed. 51 S3
Ivishak r. AK U.S.A. 149 J1
Ivittuut Greenland 147 N3
Iviza i. Spain see Ibiza
Ivory Coast country Africa see Côte d'Ivoire
Ivrea Italy 68 B2
İvrindi Turkey 69 L5
Ivris Ugheltekhili pass Georgia 113 G2
Ivry-la-Bataille France 62 B6
Ivugivik Canada see Ivujivik
Ivujivik Canada 147 K3
Ivvavik National Park Y.T. Canada 149 M1
Ivyanyets Belarus 55 O10
Ivydale U.S.A. 164 E4
Iwade Japan 92 B4
Iwafune Japan 93 F2
Iwai Japan 93 F2
Iwaki Japan 93 G1
Iwaki-san vol. Japan 90 F4
Iwakuni Japan 91 D6
Iwakura Japan 92 C3
Iwama Japan 93 G2
Iwamizawa Japan 90 F4
Iwamura Japan 92 D3
Iwamurada Japan 93 E2
Iwan r. Indon. 85 F2
Iwase Japan 93 G2
Iwasehama Japan 92 D2
Iwasuge-yama vol. Japan 93 E2
Iwata Japan 93 D4
Iwataki Japan 92 B3
Iwatsuki Japan 93 F3
Iwo Nigeria 120 D4
Iwye Belarus 55 N10
Ixcamilpa Mex. 167 F5
Ixelles Belgium 62 E4
Ixhuatlán Veracruz Mex. 167 F4
Ixiamas Bol. 176 E6
Ixmiquilpán Mex. 168 E4
Ixopo S. Africa 125 J6
Ixtacomitán Mex. 167 G5
Ixtapa, Punta pt Mex. 167 E5
Ixtlán Mex. 168 D4
Ixtlán Oaxaca Mex. 167 F5
Ixworth U.K. 59 H6
Iya i. Indon. 83 B5
İyirmi Altı Bakı Komissarı Azer. see Uzboy
Izabal Guat. 166 [inset] H6
Izabal, Lago de l. Guat. 167 H6
Izamal Mex. 167 H4
Izapa tourist site Mex. 167 G6
Izberbash Rus. Fed. 113 G2
Izegem Belgium 62 D4
Īzeh Iran 110 C4
Izembek National Wildlife Refuge nature res. AK U.S.A. 148 G5
Izgal Pak. 111 I3
Izhevsk Rus. Fed. 51 Q4
Izhma Respublika Komi Rus. Fed. 52 L2
Izhma Respublika Komi Rus. Fed. see Sosnogorsk
Izhma r. Rus. Fed. 52 L2
Izigan, Cape AK U.S.A. 148 F5
Izmail Ukr. see Izmayil
Izmayil Ukr. 69 M2
İzmir Turkey 69 L5
İzmir Körfezi g. Turkey 69 L5
İzmit Turkey 69 M4
İzmit Körfezi b. Turkey 69 M4
Izozog Bol. 176 F7
Izra' Syria 107 C3
Iztochni Rodopi mts Bulg. 69 K4
Izúcar de Matamoros Mex. 167 F5
Izu-hantō pen. Japan 93 E4
Izuhara Japan 91 C6
Izumi Fukui Japan 92 C3
Izumi Fukushima Japan 93 G2
Izumi Kanagawa Japan 93 F3
Izumi Ōsaka Japan 92 B4
Izumiōtsu Japan 92 B4
Izumisano Japan 92 B4
Izumo Japan 91 D6
Izunagaoka Japan 93 E3
▶Izu-Ogasawara Trench sea feature N. Pacific Ocean 186 F3
5th deepest trench in the world.
Izushi Japan 92 A3
Izu-shotō is Japan 93 F4
Izyaslav Ukr. 53 E6
Iz"yayu Rus. Fed. 52 M2
Izyum Ukr. 53 H6

J

Jabal Dab Saudi Arabia 110 C6
Jabalón r. Spain 67 D4
Jabalpur India 104 D5
Jabbūl, Sabkhat al salt flat Syria 107 C2
Jabir reg. Oman 110 E6
Jabiru Australia 134 F3
Jablah Syria 107 B2
Jablanica Bos.-Herz. 68 G3
Jaboatão Brazil 177 L5
Jaboticabal Brazil 179 A3
Jabung, Tanjung pt Indon. 84 D3
Jacala Mex. 167 F4
Jacaltenango Guat. 167 H6
Jacaraci Brazil 179 C1
Jacareacanga Brazil 177 G5
Jacareí Brazil 179 B3
Jacarézinho Brazil 179 A3
Jáchymov Czech Rep. 63 M4
Jacinto Brazil 179 C2
Jack r. Australia 136 D2
Jack Lake Canada 165 F1
Jackman U.S.A. 162 G2
Jacksboro U.S.A. 161 D5
Jackson Australia 138 D1
Jackson AL U.S.A. 163 C6
Jackson CA U.S.A. 158 C2
Jackson GA U.S.A. 163 D5
Jackson KY U.S.A. 164 D5
Jackson MI U.S.A. 164 C2
Jackson MN U.S.A. 160 E3
▶Jackson MS U.S.A. 161 F5
Capital of Mississippi.
Jackson NC U.S.A. 162 E4
Jackson OH U.S.A. 164 D4
Jackson TN U.S.A. 161 F5
Jackson WY U.S.A. 156 F4
Jackson, Mount Antarctica 188 L2
Jackson Head hd N.Z. 139 B6
Jacksonville AR U.S.A. 161 E5
Jacksonville FL U.S.A. 163 D6
Jacksonville IL U.S.A. 160 F4
Jacksonville NC U.S.A. 163 E5
Jacksonville OH U.S.A. 164 D4
Jacksonville TX U.S.A. 161 E6
Jacksonville Beach U.S.A. 163 D6
Jack Wade U.S.A. 146 D3
Jacmel Haiti 169 J5
Jaco i. East Timor 83 C5
Jacobabad Pak. 111 H4
Jacobina Brazil 177 J6
Jacob Lake U.S.A. 159 G3

Jacobsdal S. Africa 124 G5
Jacques-Cartier, Détroit de *sea chan.* Canada 153 I4
Jacques-Cartier, Mont *mt.* Canada 153 I4
Jacques Cartier Passage Canada *see* Jacques-Cartier, Détroit de
Jacuí Brazil 179 B3
Jacuípe *r.* Brazil 177 K6
Jacunda Brazil 177 I4
Jaddangi India 106 D2
Jaddi, Ras *pt* Pak. 111 F5
Jadebusen *b.* Germany 63 I1
J. A. D. Jensen Nunatakker *nunataks* Greenland 147 N3
Jadotville Dem. Rep. Congo *see* Likasi
Jādū Libya 120 E1
Jaen *Luzon* Phil. 82 C3
Jaén Spain 67 E5
Ja'farābād Iran 110 E2
Jaffa, Cape Australia 137 B8
Jaffna Sri Lanka 106 C4
Jafr, Qā' al *imp. l.* Jordan 107 C4
Jagadhri India 104 D3
Jagalur India 106 C3
Jagatsinghapur India *see* Jagatsinghpur
Jagatsinghpur India 105 F5
Jagdalpur India 106 D2
Jagdaqi *Nei Mongol* China 95 K1
Jagersfontein S. Africa 125 G5
Jaggang *Xizang* China 99 B6
Jaggayyapeta India 106 D2
Jaghīn Iran 110 E5
Jagok Tso *salt l.* China *see* Urru Co
Jagsamka China *see* Luding
Jagst *r.* Germany 63 J5
Jagtial India 106 C2
Jaguariaíva Brazil 179 A4
Jaguaripe Brazil 179 D1
Jagüey Grande Cuba 163 D8
Jahām, 'Irq *des.* Saudi Arabia 110 B5
Jahanabad India *see* Jehanabad
Jahmah *well* Iraq 113 G5
Jahrom Iran 110 D4
Jaicós Brazil 177 J5
Jaigarh India 106 B2
Jailolo *Halmahera* Indon. 83 C2
Jailolo, Selat *sea chan. Maluku* Indon. 83 D3
Jailolo Gilolo *i. Maluku* Indon. *see* Halmahera
Jainca *Qinghai* China 94 E5
Jainpur India 105 E4
Jaintiapur Bangl. *see* Jaintiapur
Jaintiapur Bangl. 105 H4
Jainzhug *Xizang* China *see* Gutang
Jaipur India 104 C4
Jaipurhat Bangl. *see* Joypurhat
Jais India 105 E4
Jaisalmer India 104 B4
Jaisamand Lake India 104 C4
Jaitaran India 104 C4
Jaitgarh *hill* India 106 C1
Jajapur India *see* Jajpur
Jajarkot Nepal 109 N4
Jajce Bos.-Herz. 68 G2
Jajnagar *state* India *see* Odisha
Jajpur India 105 F5
Jakar Bhutan 105 G4

▶Jakarta *Jawa* Indon. 84 D4
Capital of Indonesia. 9th most populous city in the world.

Jakes Corner Y.T. Canada 149 N3
Jakhau India 104 B5
Jakin *mt.* Afgh. 111 G4
Jakkī Kowr Iran 111 F5
Jäkkvik Sweden 54 J3
Jakliat India 104 C3
Jako *i.* East Timor *see* Jaco
Jakobshavn Greenland *see* Ilulissat
Jakobstad Fin. 54 M5
Jal U.S.A. 161 C5
Jalaid *Nei Mongol* China *see* Inder
Jalājil Saudi Arabia 110 B5
Jalālābād Afgh. 111 H3
Jalalabad *Uttar Prad.* India 99 B8
Jalal-Abad Kyrg. 102 D3
Jalal-Abad *admin. div.* Kyrg. 98 A4
Jalālah al Baḩrīyah, Jabal *plat.* Egypt 112 C5
Jalalpur Pirwala Pak. 111 H4
Jalāmid, Ḩazm al *ridge* Saudi Arabia 113 E5
Jalandhar India 104 C3
Jalapa Guat. 167 H6
Jalapa Mex. 167 G5
Jalapa Mex. 168 E5
Jalapa Nicaragua 166 [inset] I6
Jalapa Enríquez Mex. *see* Jalapa
Jalasjärvi Fin. 54 M5
Jalaun India 104 D4
Jalawlā' Iraq 113 G4
Jaldak Afgh. 111 G4
Jaldhaka *r.* Bangl. 99 E8
Jaldrug India 106 C2
Jales Brazil 179 A3
Jalesar India 104 D4
Jalgaon India 104 C5
Jalībah Iraq 113 G5
Jalingo Nigeria 120 E4
Jalisco *state* Mex. 166 D5
Jallābī Iran 110 E5
Jalna India 106 B2
Jālo Iran 111 F5
Jalón *r.* Spain 67 F3
Jalor India *see* Jalore
Jalore India 104 C4
Jalostotitlán Mex. 166 E4
Jalpa *Guanajuato* Mex. 167 E4
Jalpa Mex. 168 D4
Jalpaiguri India 105 G4
Jalpan Mex. 167 F4
Jālū Libya 121 F2
Jalūlā Iraq *see* Jalawlā'
Jām *reg.* Iran 111 F3
Jamaica *country* West Indies 169 I5
Jamaica Channel Haiti/Jamaica 169 I5
Jamalpur Bangl. 105 G4
Jamalpur India 105 F4
Jamanxim *r.* Brazil 177 G4
Jamati *Xinjiang* China 98 C3
Jambi *Sumatera* Indon. 84 C3
Jambi *prov.* Indon. 84 C3
Jambin Australia 136 E5
Jambo India 104 C4
Jamboaye *r.* Indon. 84 B1
Jambongan *i.* Malaysia 85 G1
Jambu *Kalimantan* Indon. 85 G3
Jambuair, Tanjung *pt* Indon. 84 B1
Jamda India 105 F5
Jamekunte India 106 C2
James *r. N. Dakota/S. Dakota* U.S.A. 160 D3
James *r. VA* U.S.A. 165 G5
James, Baie *b.* Canada *see* James Bay
Jamesabad Pak. 111 H5
James Bay Canada 152 E3
Jamesburg U.S.A. 165 H3
James Island *Galápagos* Ecuador *see* San Salvador, Isla
Jameson Land *reg.* Greenland 147 P2
James Peak N.Z. 139 B7
James Ranges *mts* Australia 135 F6
James Ross Island Antarctica 188 A2
James Ross Strait Canada 147 I3
Jamestown Australia 137 B7
Jamestown Canada *see* Wawa
Jamestown S. Africa 125 H6

▶Jamestown St Helena 184 H7
Capital of St Helena.

Jamestown *ND* U.S.A. 160 D2
Jamestown *NY* U.S.A. 164 F2
Jamestown *TN* U.S.A. 164 C5
Jamkhed India 106 B2
Jammu India 104 C2

▶Jammu and Kashmir *terr.* Asia 104 D2
Disputed territory (India/Pakistan).

Jamnagar India 104 B5
Jampang Kulon *Jawa* Indon. 84 D4
Jampur Pak. 111 H4
Jamrud Pak. 111 H3
Jämsä Fin. 55 N6
Jamsah Egypt 112 D6
Jämsänkoski Fin. 54 N6
Jamshedpur India 105 F5
Jamtai *Xinjiang* China 98 C4
Jamtari Nigeria 120 E4
Jamui India 105 F4
Jamuk, Gunung *mt.* Indon. 85 G2
Jamuna *r.* Bangl. *see* Raimangal
Jamuna *r.* Bangl. *see* Yamuna
Jamuna *r.* India 99 F8
Janā *i.* Saudi Arabia 110 C5
Janāb, Wādī al *watercourse* Jordan 107 C4
Janakpur India 105 E5
Janaúba Brazil 179 C1
Jand Pak. 111 I3
Jandaia Brazil 179 A2
Jandaq Iran 110 D3
Jandola Pak. 111 H3
Jandowae Australia 138 E1
Janesville *CA* U.S.A. 158 C1
Janesville *WI* U.S.A. 160 F3
Jang, Tanjung *pt* Indon. 84 D3
Jangada Brazil 179 A4
Jangal Iran 110 E3
Jangamo Moz. 125 L3
Jangaon India 106 C2
Jangco *Xizang* China 99 E7
Jangipur India 105 G4
Jangnga Turkm. *see* Jaňňa
Jangngai Ri *mts Xizang* China 99 D6
Jangngai Zangbo *r. Xizang* China 99 D6
Jänickendorf Germany 63 N2
Jani Khel Pak. 111 H3

▶Jan Mayen *terr.* Arctic Ocean 189 I2
Part of Norway.

Jan Mayen Fracture Zone *sea feature* Arctic Ocean 189 I2
Jaňňa Turkm. 110 D1
Janos Mex. 166 C2
Jans Bay Canada 151 I4
Jansenville S. Africa 124 G7
Januária Brazil 179 B1
Janūb Sīnā' *governorate* Egypt 107 A5
Janūb Sīnā' *governorate* Egypt *see* Janūb Sīnā'
Janzar *mt.* Pak. 111 F5
Jaodar Pak. 111 F5

▶Japan *country* Asia 91 D5
10th most populous country in the world.

Japan, Sea of N. Pacific Ocean 91 D5
Japan Alps National Park Japan *see* Chūbu-Sangaku Kokuritsu-kōen
Japan Trench *sea feature* N. Pacific Ocean 186 F3
Japiim Brazil 176 D5
Japón Hond. 166 [inset] I6
Japurá *r.* Brazil 176 F4
Japvo Mount India 105 H4
Jaqué Panama 166 [inset] K8
Jarābulus Syria 107 D1
Jaraguá Brazil 179 A1
Jaraguá, Serra *mts* Brazil 179 A4
Jaraguá do Sul Brazil 179 A4
Jarash Jordan 107 B3
Jarboesville U.S.A. *see* Lexington Park
Jardine River National Park Australia 136 C1
Jardinésia Brazil 179 A2
Jardinópolis Brazil 179 B3
Jargalang China 90 A4
Jargalant *Arhangay* Mongolia *see* Battsengel
Jargalant *Bayanhongor* Mongolia 94 D2
Jargalant *Bayan-Ölgiy* Mongolia *see* Bulgan
Jargalant *Dornod* Mongolia *see* Matad
Jargalant *Govĭ-Altay* Mongolia *see* Biger
Jargalant *Hovd* Mongolia *see* Hovd
Jargalant Mongolia 94 D1
Jargalant *Töv* Mongolia 94 F1
Jargalant Hayrhan *mt.* Mongolia 94 C2
Jargalthaan Mongolia 95 G2
Jari *r.* Brazil 177 H4
Järna Sweden 55 J7
Jarocin Poland 57 P5
Jarosław Poland 53 D6
Järpen Sweden 54 H5
Jarqo'rg'on Uzbek. 111 G2
Jarqŭrghon Uzbek. *see* Jarqo'rg'on
Jarrettsville U.S.A. 165 G4
Jartai *Nei Mongol* China 94 F4
Jartai Yanchi *salt l. Nei Mongol* China 94 F4
Jarú Brazil 176 F6
Jarud *Nei Mongol* China *see* Lubei
Järvakandi Estonia 55 N7
Järvenpää Fin. 55 N6

▶Jarvis Island *terr.* S. Pacific Ocean 186 J6
United States Unincorporated Territory.

Jarwa India 105 E4
Jashpurnagar India 105 F5
Jäsk Iran 110 E5
Jäsk-e Kohneh Iran 110 E5
Jasliq Uzbek. 113 J2
Jasło Poland 53 D6
Jasol India 104 C4
Jason Islands Falkland Is 178 D8
Jason Peninsula Antarctica 188 L2
Jasonville U.S.A. 164 B4
Jasper Canada 150 G4
Jasper *AL* U.S.A. 163 C5
Jasper *FL* U.S.A. 163 D6
Jasper *GA* U.S.A. 163 C5
Jasper *IN* U.S.A. 164 B4
Jasper *NY* U.S.A. 165 G2
Jasper *TN* U.S.A. 163 C5
Jasper *TX* U.S.A. 161 E6
Jasper National Park Canada 150 G4
Jasrasar India 104 C4
Jaşşān Iraq 113 G4
Jassy Romania *see* Iaşi
Jastrzębie-Zdrój Poland 57 Q6
Jaswantpura India 104 C4
Jászberény Hungary 69 H1
Jataí Brazil 179 A2
Jatapu *r.* Brazil 177 G4
Jath India 106 B2
Jati Pak. 111 H5
Jatibarang *Jawa* Indon. 85 E4
Jatibonico Cuba 163 E8
Jatiluhur, Waduk *resr Jawa* Indon. 84 D4
Játiva Spain *see* Xàtiva
Jatiwangi *Jawa* Indon. 85 E4
Jatoi Pak. 111 H4
Jat Poti Afgh. 111 G4
Jaú Brazil 179 A3
Jaú *r.* Brazil 176 F4
Jaú, Parque Nacional do *nat. park* Brazil 176 F4
Jaua Sarisariñama, Parque Nacional *nat. park* Venez. 176 F3
Jauja Peru 176 C6
Jaumave Mex. 167 F4
Jaunlutriņi Latvia 55 M8
Jaunpiebalga Latvia 55 O8
Jaunpur India 105 E4
Jauri Iran 111 F4
Java Georgia 113 F2

▶Java *i.* Indon. 85 E4
5th largest island in Asia.

Javaés *r.* Brazil *see* Formoso
Javand Afgh. 111 G3
Javari *r.* Brazil/Peru *see* Yavari
Java Ridge *sea feature* Indian Ocean 185 P6
Javarthushuu Mongolia *see* Bayan-Uul
Java Sea Indon. *see* Jawa, Laut

▶Java Trench *sea feature* Indian Ocean 186 C6
Deepest point in the Indian Ocean.

Jävenitz Germany 63 L2
Jävre Sweden 54 L4
Jawa *i.* Indon. *see* Java
Jawa, Laut *sea* Indon. 85 E4
Jawa Barat *prov.* Indon. 84 D4
Jawa Tengah *prov.* Indon. 85 E4
Jawa Timur *prov.* Indon. 85 F4
Jawhar India 106 B2
Jawhar Somalia 122 E3
Jawor Poland 57 P5
Jay U.S.A. 161 E4

▶Jaya, Puncak *mt.* Indon. 81 J7
Highest mountain in Oceania.

Jayakusumu *mt.* Indon. *see* Jaya, Puncak
Jayakwadi Sagar *l.* India 106 B2
Jayantiapur Bangl. *see* Jaintiapur
Jayapura Indon. 81 K7
Jayawijaya, Pegunungan *mts* Indon. 81 J7
Jayb, Wādī al *watercourse* Israel/Jordan 107 B4
Jayfī, Wādī al *watercourse* Egypt 107 B4
Jaypur India 106 D2
Jayrūd Syria 107 C3
Jayton U.S.A. 161 C5
Jazīreh-ye Shīf Iran 110 C4
Jazminal Mex. 167 E3
Jbail Lebanon 107 B2
J. C. Murphey Lake U.S.A. 164 B3
Jean U.S.A. 159 F4
Jean Marie River Canada 150 F2
Jeannin, Lac *l.* Canada 153 I2
Jebāl Bārez, Kūh-e *mts* Iran 110 E4
Jebel, Bahr el *r.* Sudan/Uganda *see* White Nile
Jebel Abyad Plateau Sudan 108 C6
Jebus Indon. 84 D3
Jech Doab *lowland* Pak. 111 I4
Jedburgh U.K. 60 G5
Jeddah Saudi Arabia 108 E5
Jedeida Tunisia 68 C6
Jeetze *r.* Germany 63 L1
Jefferson *IA* U.S.A. 160 E3
Jefferson *NC* U.S.A. 162 D4
Jefferson *OH* U.S.A. 164 E3
Jefferson *TX* U.S.A. 161 E5
Jefferson, Mount U.S.A. 158 E2
Jefferson, Mount *vol.* U.S.A. 156 C3

▶Jefferson City U.S.A. 160 E4
Capital of Missouri.

Jeffersonville *GA* U.S.A. 163 D5
Jeffersonville *IN* U.S.A. 164 C4
Jeffersonville *OH* U.S.A. 164 D4
Jeffreys Bay S. Africa 124 G8
Jehanabad India 105 F4
Jeju S. Korea *see* Cheju
Jejuí Guazú *r.* Para. 178 E2
Jēkabpils Latvia 55 N8
Jelbart Ice Shelf Antarctica 188 B2
Jelenia Góra Poland 57 O5
Jelep La *pass* China/India 99 E8
Jelgava Latvia 55 M8
Jellico U.S.A. 164 C5
Jellicoe Canada 152 D4
Jelloway U.S.A. 164 D3
Jemaja *i.* Indon. 84 D2
Jember *Jawa* Indon. 85 F5
Jeminay *Xinjiang* China 98 D3
Jeminay Kazakh. 98 D3
Jempang, Danau *l.* Indon. 85 G3
Jena Germany 63 L4
Jena U.S.A. 161 E6
Jendouba Tunisia 68 C6
Jengish Chokusu *mt.* China/Kyrg. *see* Pobeda Peak
Jenīn West Bank 107 B3
Jenkins U.S.A. 164 D5
Jênlung *Xizang* China 99 D7
Jenne Mali *see* Djenné
Jenner Canada 151 I5
Jennings *r. B.C.* Canada 149 N4
Jennings U.S.A. 161 E6
Jenolan Caves Australia 138 E4
Jenpeg Canada 151 L4
Jensen U.S.A. 159 I1
Jens Munk Island Canada 147 K3
Jepara *Jawa* Indon. 85 E4
Jeparit Australia 137 C8
Jequié Brazil 179 C1
Jequitaí *r.* Brazil 179 B2
Jequitinhonha Brazil 179 C2
Jequitinhonha *r.* Brazil 179 D1
Jerantut Malaysia 84 C2
Jerba, Île de *i.* Tunisia 64 G5
Jerbar Sudan 121 G4
Jereh Iran 110 C4
Jérémie Haiti 169 J5
Jerez Mex. 168 D4
Jerez de la Frontera Spain 67 C5
Jergol Norway 54 N2
Jergucat Albania 69 I5
Jericho Australia 136 D4
Jericho West Bank 107 B4
Jerichow Germany 63 M2
Jerid, Chott el *salt l.* Tunisia 64 F5
Jerijeh, Tanjung *pt* Malaysia 85 E2
Jerilderie Australia 138 B5
Jerimoth Hill *hill* U.S.A. 165 J3
Jeroaquara Brazil 179 A1
Jerome U.S.A. 156 E4
Jerruck Pak. 111 H5

▶Jersey *terr.* Channel Is 59 E9
United Kingdom Crown Dependency.

Jersey City U.S.A. 165 H3
Jersey Shore U.S.A. 165 G3
Jerseyville U.S.A. 160 F4
Jerumenha Brazil 177 J5

▶Jerusalem Israel/West Bank 107 B4
De facto capital of Israel, disputed.

Jervis Bay Australia 138 E5
Jervis Bay *b.* Australia 138 E5
Jervis Bay Territory *admin. div.* Australia 138 E5
Jesenice Slovenia 68 F1
Jesenice, Vodní nádrž *resr* Czech Rep. 63 M4
Jesi Italy 68 E3
Jesselton *Sabah* Malaysia *see* Kota Kinabalu
Jessen Germany 63 M3
Jessheim Norway 55 G6
Jessore Bangl. 105 G5
Jesteburg Germany 63 J1
Jesu Maria Island P.N.G. *see* Rambutyo Island
Jesup U.S.A. 163 D6
Jesús Carranza Mex. 167 G5
Jesús María, Barra *spit* Mex. 161 D7
Jeti-Ögüz Kyrg. 98 B4
Jetmore U.S.A. 160 D4
Jetpur India 104 B5
Jever Germany 63 H1
Jewell Ridge U.S.A. 164 E5
Jewish Autonomous Oblast *admin. div.* Rus. Fed. *see* Yevreyskaya Avtonomnaya Oblast'
Jeypur India *see* Jaypur
Jezzine Lebanon 107 B3
Jhabua India 104 C5
Jhajhar India *see* Jhajjar
Jhajjar India 104 D3
Jhal Pak. 111 G4
Jhalawar India 104 D4
Jhal Jhao Pak. 111 G5
Jhang Pak. 111 I4
Jhansi India 104 D4
Jhanzi *r.* India 86 A1
Jhapa Nepal 105 F4
Jharia India 105 F5
Jharkhand *state* India 105 F5
Jharsuguda India 105 F5
Jhawani Nepal 105 F4
Jhelum *r.* India/Pak. 111 I4
Jhelum Pak. 111 I3
Jhenaidah Bangl. 105 G5
Jhenaidaha Bangl. *see* Jhenaidah
Jhenida Bangl. *see* Jhenaidah
Jhimpir Pak. 111 H5
Jhudo Pak. 111 H5
Jhumritilaiya India 105 F4
Jhund India 104 B5
Jhunjhunun India 104 C3
Jiachuan China 96 E1
Jiachuanzhen China *see* Jiachuan
Jiading *Jiangxi* China *see* Xinfeng
Jiading *Shanghai* China 97 I2
Jiahe China 97 G3
Jiajiang China 96 D2
Jialing Jiang *r. Sichuan* China 94 F6
Jialu *Shaanxi* China *see* Jiaxian
Jialu He *r.* China 95 H5
Jiamusi China 90 C3
Ji'an *Jiangxi* China 97 G3
Ji'an *Jilin* China 90 B4
Jianchang *Liaoning* China 95 I3
Jianchuan China 96 C3
Jiande China 97 H2
Jiangbei China *see* Yubei
Jiangbiancun China 97 G3
Jiangcheng China 96 D4
Jiangcun China 97 G3
Jiangdu China 97 H1
Jiange China *see* Pu'an
Jianghong China 97 F4
Jiangjiapo *Shandong* China 95 J4
Jiangjin China 96 E2
Jiangjunmiao *Xinjiang* China 94 B2
Jiangjunmu *Hebei* China 95 H4
Jiangjuntai *Gansu* China 94 D3
Jiangkou *Guangdong* China *see* Fengkai
Jiangkou *Guizhou* China 97 F3
Jiangkou *Shaanxi* China 96 E1
Jiangling China *see* Jingzhou
Jiangluozhen China 96 E1
Jiangmen China 97 G4
Jiangna China *see* Yanshan
Jiangshan China 97 H2
Jiangsi China *see* Dejiang
Jiangsu *prov.* China 97 H1
Jiangtaibu *Ningxia* China 94 F5
Jiangxi *prov.* China 97 G3
Jiangxia China 97 G2
Jiangxian *Shanxi* China 95 G5
Jiangxigou *Qinghai* China 94 E4
Jiangyan China 97 I1
Jiangyin China 97 I2
Jiangyou China 96 E2
Jiangyu *Shandong* China 95 I4
Jiangzhesongrong *Xizang* China 99 D7
Jianhu *Jiangsu* China 95 I5
Jianjun *Shaanxi* China *see* Yongshou
Jiankang China 96 D3
Jianli China 97 G2
Jian'ou China 97 H3
Jianping China *see* Langxi
Jianping *Liaoning* China 95 I3
Jianping *Liaoning* China 95 I3
Jianqiao *Hebei* China 95 I4
Jianshe *Qinghai* China 94 D5
Jianshe China *see* Baiyü
Jianshi China 97 F2
Jianshui China 96 D4
Jianshui Hu *l. Xizang* China 99 C6
Jianxing China 96 E2
Jianyang *Fujian* China 97 H3
Jianyang *Sichuan* China 96 E2
Jiaochang China 96 D1
Jiaochangba China *see* Jiaochang
Jiaocheng China *see* Jiaoling
Jiaocheng *Shanxi* China 95 H4
Jiaohe *Hebei* China 95 I4
Jiaohe China 90 B4
Jiaojiang China *see* Taizhou
Jiaokou *Shanxi* China 95 G4
Jiaokui China *see* Yiliang
Jiaolai He *r.* China 95 J3
Jiaoling China 97 H3
Jiaonan *Shandong* China 95 I5
Jiaopingdu China 96 D3
Jiaowei China 97 H3
Jiaozhou *Shandong* China 95 J4
Jiaozuo *Henan* China 95 H5
Jiarsu *Qinghai* China 94 C4
Jiasa China 96 D3
Jiashan China *see* Mingguang
Jiashi *Xinjiang* China 98 B5
Jia Tsuo La *pass Xizang* China 99 D7
Jiawang China 97 H1
Jiaxian China 97 G1
Jiaxian *Shaanxi* China 95 G4
Jiaxing China 97 I2
Jiayi Taiwan *see* Chiai
Jiayin China 90 C2
Jiayuguan *Gansu* China 94 D4
Jiazi China 97 H4
Jibūtī *country* Africa *see* Djibouti
Jibuti Djibouti *see* Djibouti
Jiddah Saudi Arabia *see* Jeddah
Jiddī, Jabal al *hill* Egypt 107 A4
Jidong China 90 C3
Jiehkkevárri *mt.* Norway 54 K2
Jiehu *Shandong* China *see* Yinan
Jieshi China 97 G4
Jieshipu *Gansu* China 94 F5
Jieshi Wan *b.* China 97 G4
Jiexi China 97 G4
Jiexiu *Shanxi* China 95 G4
Jieyang China 97 H4
Jieznas Lith. 55 N9
Jigzhi China 96 D1
Jiḩār, Wādī al *watercourse* Syria 107 C2
Jihlava Czech Rep. 57 O6
Jija Sarai Afgh. 111 F3
Jijel Alg. 64 F4
Jijiga Eth. 122 E3
Jījīrud Iran 110 C3
Jijitai *Gansu* China 94 D3
Jijū China 96 D3
Jil'ād *reg.* Jordan 107 B3
Jilf al Kabīr, Haḑabat al *plat.* Egypt 108 C5
Jilh al 'Ishār *plain* Saudi Arabia 110 B5
Jilib Somalia 122 E3
Jili Hu *l.* China 98 D3
Jilin China 90 B4
Jilin *prov.* China 95 K3
Jiling *Gansu* China 94 E4
Jilin Hada Ling *mts* China 90 B4
Jiliu He *r.* China 90 A2
Jilo India 104 C4
Jilong Taiwan *see* Chilung
Jīma Eth. 122 D3
Jimda China *see* Zindo
Jiménez *Chihuahua* Mex. 166 D3
Jiménez *Coahuila* Mex. 167 E2
Jiménez *Tamaulipas* Mex. 161 D7
Jimeng *Qinghai* China 94 D4
Jimía, Cerro *mt.* Hond. 168 G5
Jimo *Shandong* China 95 J4
Jimokuji Japan 92 C3
Jimsar *Xinjiang* China 98 E4
Jim Thorpe U.S.A. 165 H3
Jinan *Shandong* China 95 I4
Jin'an China *see* Songpan
Jinbi China *see* Dayao
Jinchang *Gansu* China 94 E4
Jincheng *Shanxi* China 95 H5
Jincheng *Sichuan* China *see* Yilong
Jincheng *Yunnan* China *see* Wuding
Jinchengjiang China *see* Hechi
Jinchuan *Gansu* China *see* Jinchang
Jinchuan *Jiangxi* China *see* Xingan
Jind India 104 D3
Jinding China *see* Lanping
Jindřichův Hradec Czech Rep. 57 O6
Jin'e China *see* Longchang
Jinfosi *Gansu* China 94 D4
Jing Xinjiang China *see* Jinghe
Jingbian *Shaanxi* China 95 G4
Jingchuan *Gansu* China 95 F5
Jingde China 97 H2
Jingdezhen China 97 H2
Jingellic Australia 138 C5
Jinggangshan China 97 G3
Jinggang Shan *hill* China 97 G3
Jinggongqiao China 97 H2
Jinggu *Gansu* China 94 E5
Jinggu China 96 D4
Jinghai *Tianjin* China 95 I4
Jinghe *Xinjiang* China 98 C3
Jing He *r.* China 95 G5
Jinghong China 96 D4
Jingle *Shanxi* China 95 H4
Jingmen China 97 G2
Jingning *Gansu* China 94 F5
Jingpeng *Nei Mongol* China 95 I3
Jingpo China 90 C4
Jingpo Hu *resr* China 90 C4
Jingsha China *see* Jingzhou
Jingtai *Gansu* China 94 E4
Jingtieshan *Gansu* China 94 D4
Jingxi China 96 E4
Jingxian *Anhui* China 97 H2
Jingxian *Hunan* China *see* Jingzhou
Jingyang China *see* Jingde
Jingyu China 90 B4
Jingyuan *Gansu* China 94 F4
Jingzhou *Hubei* China 97 G2
Jingzhou *Hubei* China 97 G2
Jingzhou *Hunan* China 97 F3
Jinhe *Nei Mongol* China 90 A2
Jinhe *Yunnan* China *see* Jinping
Jinhu China 97 H1
Jinhua *Yunnan* China *see* Jianchuan
Jinhua *Zhejiang* China 97 H2
Jining *Nei Mongol* China 95 H3
Jining *Shandong* China 95 I5
Jinja Uganda 122 D3
Jinjiang *Hainan* China *see* Chengmai
Jinjiang *Yunnan* China 96 D3
Jin Jiang *r.* China 97 G2
Jinka Eth. 122 D3
Jinmen Taiwan *see* Chinmen
Jinmen Dao *i.* Taiwan *see* Chinmen Tao
Jinmu Jiao *pt* China 97 F5
Jinning China 96 D3
Jinotega Nicaragua 166 [inset] I6
Jinotepe Nicaragua 166 [inset] I7
Jinping *Guizhou* China 97 F3
Jinping *Yunnan* China 96 D4
Jinping *Yunnan* China *see* Qiubei
Jinping Shan *mts* China 96 D3
Jinsen S. Korea *see* Inch'ŏn
Jinsha China 96 E3
Jinsha Jiang *r.* China 96 E2 *see* Yangtze
Jinshan *Nei Mongol* China *see* Guyang
Jinshan *Nei Mongol* China 95 I3
Jinshan China *see* Zhujing
Jinshan *Yunnan* China *see* Lufeng
Jinshi *Hunan* China 97 F2
Jinshi *Hunan* China *see* Xinning
Jinta *Gansu* China 94 D4
Jintotolo *i.* Phil. 82 C4
Jintotolo Channel Phil. 82 C4
Jintur India 106 C2
Jinxi *Anhui* China *see* Taihu
Jinxi *Jiangxi* China 97 H3
Jinxi *Liaoning* China *see* Lianshan
Jin Xi *r.* China 97 H3
Jinxian China 97 H2
Jinxian *Liaoning* China *see* Linghai
Jinxiang *Shandong* China 95 I5
Jinyun China 97 I2
Jinz, Qā' al *salt flat* Jordan 107 C4
Jinzhai China 97 G2
Jinzhong *Shanxi* China 95 H4
Jinzhou *Liaoning* China 95 J3
Jinzhou *Liaoning* China 95 J4
Jinzhou Wan *b.* China 95 J4
Jinzhu China *see* Daocheng
Jinzū-gawa *r.* Japan 92 D2
Ji-Paraná Brazil 176 F6
Jipijapa Ecuador 176 B4
Ji Qu *r. Qinghai* China 99 G7
Jiquilisco El Salvador 166 [inset] H6
Jiquiriçá Brazil 179 D1
Jiquitaia Brazil 179 D2
Jirā', Wādī *watercourse* Egypt 107 A5
Jirānīyāt, Shi'bān al *watercourse* Saudi Arabia 107 D4
Jirgatol Tajik. 111 H2
Jiri *r.* India 86 A1
Jirin Gol *Nei Mongol* China 95 I2
Jīroft Iran 110 E4
Jirriiban Somalia 122 E3
Jirwān Saudi Arabia 110 C6
Jirwan *well* Saudi Arabia 110 C6
Jishan *Shanxi* China 95 G5
Jishi *Qinghai* China *see* Xunhua
Jishishan *Gansu* China 94 E5
Jishou China 97 F2
Jisr ash Shughūr Syria 107 C2
Jitian China *see* Lianshan
Jitotol Mex. 167 G5
Jitra Malaysia 84 C1
Jiu *r.* Romania 69 J3
Jiuchenggong *Shaanxi* China *see* Linyou
Jiudengkou *Nei Mongol* China 94 F4
Jiuding Shan *mt.* China 96 D2
Jiujiang *Jiangxi* China 97 G2
Jiujiang *Jiangxi* China 97 H2
Jiulian China *see* Mojiang
Jiuling Shan *mts* China 97 G2
Jiulong H.K. China *see* Kowloon
Jiulong *Sichuan* China 96 D2
Jiumiao *Liaoning* China 95 J3
Jiuqian China 97 F3
Jiuquan *Gansu* China 94 D4
Jiurongcheng *Shandong* China 95 J4
Jiuxian *Shanxi* China 95 G4
Jiuxu China 96 E3
Jiuzhou Jiang *r.* China 97 F4
Jiwani Pak. 111 F5
Jiwen *Nei Mongol* China 95 J1
Jixi *Anhui* China 97 H2
Jixi *Heilong.* China 90 C3
Jixian *Hebei* China *see* Jizhou
Jixian China 90 C3
Jixian *Henan* China *see* Weihui
Jixian *Shanxi* China 95 G4
Jiyuan *Henan* China 95 H5
Jīzah, Ahrāmāt al *tourist site* Egypt *see* Pyramids of Giza
Jīzān Saudi Arabia 108 F6
Jizhou *Hebei* China 95 H4
Jizō-dake *mt.* Japan 93 F2

Jizzakh Uzbek. see Jizzax
Jizzax Uzbek. 111 G1
Joaçaba Brazil 179 A4
Joaíma Brazil 179 C2
João Belo Moz. see Xai-Xai
João de Almeida Angola see Chibia
João Pessoa Brazil 177 L5
João Pinheiro Brazil 179 B2
Joaquin V. González Arg. 178 D3
Jōban Japan 93 G2
Jobo Point Mindanao Phil. 82 D4
Job Peak U.S.A. 158 D2
Jocketa Germany 63 M4
Jocotán Guat. 167 H6
Joda India 105 F5
Jodhpur India 104 C4
Jodiya India 104 B5
Joensuu Fin. 54 P5
Jōetsu Japan 93 E1
Jofane Moz. 123 D6
Joffre, Mount Canada 150 H5
Jōganji-gawa r. Japan 92 D2
Jōga-shima i. Japan 93 F3
Jogbura Nepal 104 E3
Jõgeva Estonia 55 O7
Jogjakarta Indon. see Yogyakarta
Jōhana Japan 92 C2
Johannesburg S. Africa 125 H4
Johannesburg U.S.A. 158 E4
Johan Peninsula Canada 147 K2
Johi Pak. 111 G5
John r. AK U.S.A. 149 J2
John Day U.S.A. 156 D3
John Day r. U.S.A. 156 C3
John D'Or Prairie Canada 150 H3
John F. Kennedy airport U.S.A. 165 I3
John H. Kerr Reservoir U.S.A. 165 F5
John Jay, Mount Canada/U.S.A. 149 O4
John o'Groats U.K. 60 F2
Johnson U.S.A. 160 C4
Johnsonburg U.S.A. 165 F3
Johnson City NY U.S.A. 165 H2
Johnson City TN U.S.A. 162 D4
Johnson City TX U.S.A. 161 D6
Johnsondale U.S.A. 158 D4
Johnson Draw watercourse U.S.A. 161 C6
Johnson's Crossing Y.T. Canada 149 N3
Johnston, Lake salt flat Australia 135 C8
Johnston and Sand Islands terr. N. Pacific Ocean see Johnston Atoll

▶Johnston Atoll terr. N. Pacific Ocean 186 I4
United States Unincorporated Territory.

Johnstone U.K. 60 E5
Johnstone Lake Canada see Old Wives Lake
Johnston Range hills Australia 135 B7
Johnstown Ireland 61 E5
Johnstown NY U.S.A. 165 H2
Johnstown PA U.S.A. 165 F3
Jōhoku Japan 93 G2
Johor state Malaysia 84 C2
Johor, Selat strait Malaysia/Sing. 87 [inset]
Johor, Sungai r. Malaysia 87 [inset]
Johor Bahru Malaysia 84 C2
Jõhvi Estonia 55 O7
Joinville Brazil 179 A4
Joinville France 66 G2
Joinville Island Antarctica 188 A2
Jojutla Mex. 167 F5
Jokkmokk Sweden 54 K3
Jökulsá r. Iceland 54 [inset]
Jökulsá á Fjöllum r. Iceland 54 [inset]
Jökulsá í Fljótsdal r. Iceland 54 [inset]
Jolfa Iran 110 B2
Joliet U.S.A. 164 A3
Joliet, Lac l. Canada 152 F4
Joliette Canada 153 G5
Jolly Lake Canada 151 H1
Jolo Phil. 82 C5
Jolo i. Phil. 82 C5
Jomalig i. Phil. 82 C3
Jombang Jawa Indon. 85 F4
Jomda China 96 C2
Jōmine-san mt. Japan 93 F2
Jonancy U.S.A. 164 D5
Jonathan Point Belize 167 H5
Jonava Lith. 55 N9
Jonê Gansu China 94 E5
Jōnen-dake mt. Japan 92 D2
Jonesboro AR U.S.A. 161 F5
Jonesboro LA U.S.A. 161 E5
Jones Islands AK U.S.A. 149 J1
Jones Sound sea chan. Canada 147 J2
Jonesville MI U.S.A. 164 C3
Jonesville VA U.S.A. 164 D5
Jonglei Canal Sudan 108 D8
Jönköping Sweden 55 I8
Jonquière Canada 153 H4
Jonuta Mex. 167 G5
Joplin U.S.A. 161 E4
Joppa Israel see Tel Aviv-Yafo
Jora India 104 D4
Jordan country Asia 107 C4
Jordan r. Asia 107 B4
Jordan U.S.A. 156 G3
Jordan r. U.S.A. 156 D4
Jordânia Brazil 179 C1
Jordet Norway 55 H6
Jorhat India 105 H4
Jor Hu l. China 98 B5
Jork Germany 63 J1
Jorm Afgh. 111 H2
Jörn Sweden 54 L4
Joroinen Fin. 54 O5
Jorong Kalimantan Indon. 85 F3
Jørpeland Norway 55 E7
Jos Nigeria 120 D4
Jose Abad Santos Mindanao Phil. 82 D5
José Cardel Mex. 167 F5
José de San Martín Arg. 178 B6
Jose Pañganiban Luzon Phil. 82 C3
Joseph, Lac l. Canada 153 I3
Joseph Bonaparte Gulf Australia 134 E3
Joseph City U.S.A. 159 H4
Joshimath India 104 D3
Jōshinetsu-kōgen Kokuritsu-kōen nat. park Japan 93 E2
Joshipur India 106 E1
Joshua Tree National Park U.S.A. 159 F5
Jos Plateau Nigeria 120 D4
Jostedalsbreen Nasjonalpark nat. park Norway 55 E6
Jotunheimen Nasjonalpark nat. park Norway 55 F6
Jouaiya Lebanon 107 B3
Joubertina S. Africa 124 F7
Jouberton S. Africa 125 H4
Jõuga Estonia 55 O7
Joûnié Lebanon 107 B3
Joure Neth. 62 F2
Joutsa Fin. 55 O6
Joutseno Fin. 55 P6
Jouy-aux-Arches France 62 G5
Jovellanos Cuba 163 D8
Jowai India 105 H4
Jowr Deh Iran 110 C2
Jowzak Iran 111 F4
Joy, Mount Y.T. Canada 149 N3
Joya de Cerén tourist site El Salvador 167 H6
Joyce's Country reg. Ireland 61 C4
Jōyō Japan 92 B4
Joypurhat Bangl. 105 G4
Juan Aldama Mex. 161 C7
Juancheng Shandong China 95 H5
Juan de Fuca Strait Canada/U.S.A. 154 C2
Juan Escutia Mex. 166 D4
Juan Fernández, Archipiélago is S. Pacific Ocean 187 O8
Juan Fernández Islands S. Pacific Ocean see Juan Fernández, Archipiélago
Juanjuí Peru 176 C5
Juankoski Fin. 54 P5
Juan Mata Ortíz Mex. 166 C2
Juaréz Mex. 167 E3
Juárez, Sierra de mts Mex. 166 A1
Juàzeiro Brazil 177 J5
Juàzeiro do Norte Brazil 177 K5
Juba r. Somalia see Jubba
Juba Sudan 121 G4
Jubany research station Antarctica 188 A2
Jubba r. Somalia 122 E4
Jubbah Saudi Arabia 113 F5
Jubbulpore India see Jabalpur
Jubilee Lake salt flat Australia 135 D7
Juby, Cap c. Morocco 120 B2
Juchatengo Mex. 167 F5
Juchitán Mex. 168 E5
Jucuruçu Brazil 179 D2
Jucuruçu r. Brazil 179 D2
Judaberg Norway 55 D7
Judaidat al Hamir Iraq 113 F5
Judayyidat 'Ar'ar well Iraq 113 F5
Judenburg Austria 57 O7
Judian China 96 C3
Judith Gap U.S.A. 156 F3
Juegang China see Rudong
Juelsminde Denmark 55 G9
Juerana Brazil 179 D2
Jugar China see Sêrxü
Juh Nei Mongol China 95 G4
Juhongtu Qinghai China 94 D4
Juigalpa Nicaragua 166 [inset] I6
Juillet, Lac l. Canada 153 J3
Juína Brazil 177 G6
Juist i. Germany 62 H1
Juiz de Fora Brazil 179 C3
Jujuhan r. Indon. 84 C3
Ju Ju Klu Turkm. 111 F2
Jukkoku-tōge pass Japan 93 E2
Julaca Bol. 176 E8
Julesburg U.S.A. 160 C3
Julia Brazil 176 E4
Juliaca Peru 176 D7
Julia Creek Australia 136 C4
Julian U.S.A. 158 E5
Julian, Lac l. Canada 152 F3
Julianadorp Neth. 62 E2
Julian Alps mts Slovenia see Julijske Alpe
Julianatop mt. Indon. see Mandala, Puncak
Juliana Top mt. Suriname 177 G3
Julianehåb Greenland see Qaqortoq
Jülich Germany 62 G4
Julijske Alpe mts Slovenia 68 E1
Julimes Mex. 166 D2
Juliomagus France see Angers
Julius, Lake Australia 136 B4
Jullundur India see Jalandhar
Juma Uzbek. 111 G2
Jumbilla Peru 176 C5
Jumilla Spain 67 F4
Jumla Nepal 105 E3
Jümme r. Germany 63 H1
Jumna r. India see Yamuna
Jump r. U.S.A. 160 F2
Junagadh India 104 B5
Junagarh India 106 D2
Junan Shandong China 95 I5
Junayfah Egypt 107 A4
Junbuk Iran 110 E3
Jun Bulen Nei Mongol China 95 I2
Junction TX U.S.A. 161 D6
Junction UT U.S.A. 159 G2
Junction City KS U.S.A. 160 D4
Junction City KY U.S.A. 164 C5
Junction City OR U.S.A. 156 C3
Jundiaí Brazil 179 B3
Jundian China 97 F1

▶Juneau AK U.S.A. 149 N4
Capital of Alaska.

Juneau WI U.S.A. 160 F3
Juneau Icefield B.C. Canada 149 N4
Junee Australia 138 C5
Jûn el Khudr b. Lebanon 107 B3
Jungar Qi Nei Mongol China see Xuejiawan
Jungfrau mt. Switz. 66 H3
Junggar Pendi basin China 102 G2
Jungsi Xizang China 99 E6
Juniata r. U.S.A. 165 G3
Junín Arg. 178 D4
Junín Peru 176 C6
Junior U.S.A. 164 F4
Juniper Mountain U.S.A. 159 I1
Juniper Mountains U.S.A. 159 G4
Junipero Serro Peak U.S.A. 158 C3
Junlian China 96 E2
Junmenling China 97 G3
Juno U.S.A. 161 C6
Junsele Sweden 54 J5
Junshan Hu l. China 97 H2
Junxi China see Datian
Junxian China see Danjiangkou
Ju'nyung China 96 C1
Ju'nyunggoin China see Ju'nyung
Jūō Japan 93 G2
Juodupė Lith. 55 N8
Jupiá Brazil 179 A3
Jupía, Represa resr Brazil 179 A3
Jupiter U.S.A. 163 D7
Juquiá r. Brazil 179 B4
Jur r. Sudan 108 C8
Jura mts France/Switz. 66 G4
Jura i. U.K. 60 D4
Jura, Sound of sea chan. U.K. 60 D5
Juraci Brazil 179 C1
Juradó Col. 166 [inset] K8
Jurbarkas Lith. 55 M9
Jurf ad Darāwīsh Jordan 107 B4
Jürgenstorf Germany 63 M1
Jurh Nei Mongol China 95 J2
Jurh Nei Mongol China 95 J2
Jūrmala Latvia 55 M8
Jurmu Fin. 54 O4
Jurong Sing. 87 [inset]
Jurong, Sungai r. Sing. 87 [inset]
Jurong Island reg. Sing. 87 [inset]
Juruá r. Brazil 176 E4
Juruena r. Brazil 177 G5
Juruena, Parque Nacional do nat. park Brazil 177 G5
Juruti Brazil 177 G4
Jurva Fin. 54 L5
Jūshiyama Japan 92 C3
Jūshqān Iran 110 E2
Jūsīyah Syria 107 C2
Jussara Brazil 179 A1
Justice U.S.A. 164 E5
Jutaí Brazil 176 E5
Jutaí r. Brazil 176 E4
Jüterbog Germany 63 N3
Jutiapa Guat. 167 H6
Jutiapa Hond. 166 [inset] I6
Juticalpa Hond. 166 [inset] I6
Jutis Sweden 54 J3
Jutland pen. Denmark 55 F8
Juuka Fin. 54 P5
Juva Fin. 54 O6
Juwain Afgh. 111 F4
Juwana Jawa Indon. 85 E4
Juxian Shandong China 95 I5
Juye Shandong China 95 I5
Jūyom Iran 110 D4
Južnoukrajinsk Ukr. see Yuzhnoukrayinsk
Jwaneng Botswana 124 G3
Jylland pen. Denmark see Jutland
Jyrgalang Kyrg. 98 B4
Jyväskylä Fin. 54 N5

K

▶K2 mt. China/Pak. 104 D2
2nd highest mountain in Asia and in the world.

Ka r. Nigeria 120 D3
Kaafu Atoll Maldives see Male Atoll
Kaa-Iya del Gran Chaco, Parque Nacional nat. park Bol. 176 F7
Kaakhka Turkm. see Kaka
Ka'ala mt. U.S.A. 157 [inset]
Kaapstad S. Africa see Cape Town
Kaarina Fin. 55 M6
Kaarßen Germany 63 L1
Kaarst Germany 62 G3
Kaavi Fin. 54 P5
Kaba Xinjiang China see Habahe
Kaba r. China/Kazakh. 98 D3
Kabaena i. Indon. 83 B4
Kabakly Turkm. see Gabakly
Kabala Sierra Leone 120 B4
Kabale Uganda 122 C4
Kabalega Falls National Park Uganda see Murchison Falls National Park
Kabalo Dem. Rep. Congo 123 C4
Kabambare Dem. Rep. Congo 123 C4
Kabanbay Kazakh. 102 F2
Kabangu Dem. Rep. Congo 123 C5
Kabanjahe Sumatera Indon. 84 B2
Kabara i. Fiji 133 I3
Kabarai Papua Indon. 83 D3
Kabarega National Park Uganda see Murchison Falls National Park
Kabasalan Mindanao Phil. 82 C5
Kaba-san hill Japan 93 G2
Kabaw Valley Myanmar 86 A2
Kabbani r. India 106 C3
Kåbdalis Sweden 54 L3
Kabetan i. Indon. 83 B2
Kabinakagami r. Canada 152 D4
Kabinakagami Lake Canada 152 D4
Kabinda Dem. Rep. Congo 123 C4
Kabir Indon. 83 C5
Kabīr r. Syria 107 B2
Kabīrkūh mts Iran 110 B3
Kabo Cent. Afr. Rep. 122 B3
Kābol Afgh. see Kābul
Kabompo r. Zambia 123 C5
Kabong Sarawak Malaysia 85 E2
Kabongo Dem. Rep. Congo 123 C4
Kabūdeh Iran 111 F3
Kabūd Gonbad Iran 111 E2
Kabūd Rāhang Iran 110 C3
Kabugao Luzon Phil. 82 C2

▶Kābul Afgh. 111 H3
Capital of Afghanistan.

Kābul r. Afgh. 111 I3
Kabuli P.N.G. 81 L7
Kabunda Dem. Rep. Congo 123 C5
Kabunduk Sumba Indon. 83 A5
Kabura-gawa r. Japan 93 F2
Kaburuang i. Indon. 83 C2
Kabūtar Khān Iran 110 E4
Kabwe Zambia 123 C5
Kacepi Maluku Indon. 83 D3
Kacha Kuh mts Iran/Pak. 111 F4
Kachalinskaya Rus. Fed. 53 J6
Kachchh, Great Rann of marsh India see Kachchh, Rann of
Kachchh, Gulf of India 104 B5
Kachchh, Little Rann of marsh India 104 B5
Kachchh, Rann of marsh India 104 B4
Kachemak Bay AK U.S.A. 149 J4
Kachia Nigeria 120 D4
Kachiry Kazakh. 88 D2
Kachkanar Rus. Fed. 51 R4
Kachret'i Georgia 113 G2
Kachug Rus. Fed. 88 J2
Kaçkar Dağı mt. Turkey 113 F2
Kada Japan 92 B4
Kadaingti Myanmar 86 B3
Kadaiyanallur India 106 C4
Kadanai r. Afgh./Pak. 111 G4
Kadan Kyun i. Myanmar 87 B4
Kadapongan i. Indon. 85 F4
Kadatuang i. Indon. 83 B4
Kadavu i. Fiji 133 H3
Kadavu Passage Fiji 133 H3
Kadaya Rus. Fed. 95 I1
Kaddam l. India 106 C2
Kade Ghana 120 C4
Kādhimain Iraq 113 G4
Kadi India 104 C5
Kadıköy Turkey 69 M4
Kadınhanı Turkey 112 D3
Kadiolo Mali 120 C3
Kadiri India 106 C3
Kadirli Turkey 112 E3
Kadirpur Pak. 111 I4
Kadiyevka Ukr. see Stakhanov
Kadmat atoll India 106 B4
Ka-do i. N. Korea 91 B5
Kadok Malaysia 84 C1
Kadoka U.S.A. 160 C3
Kadoma Zimbabwe 123 C5
Kadonkani Myanmar 86 A4
Kadu Myanmar 86 B1
Kadugli Sudan 108 C7
Kaduna Nigeria 120 D3
Kaduna r. Nigeria 120 D4
Kadusam mt. China/India 105 I3
Kaduy Rus. Fed. 52 H4
Kadyy Rus. Fed. 52 I4
Kadzherom Rus. Fed. 52 L2
Kaédi Mauritania 120 B3
Kaélé Cameroon 121 E3
Kaeng Krachan National Park Thai. 87 B4
Kaesŏng N. Korea 91 B5
Kāf Saudi Arabia 107 C4
Kafa Ukr. see Feodosiya
Kafakumba Dem. Rep. Congo 123 C4
Kafan Armenia see Kapan
Kafanchan Nigeria 120 D4

▶Kaffeklubben Ø i. Greenland 189 I1
Most northerly point of North America.

Kafiau i. Papua Indon. 83 D3
Kafireas, Akra pt Greece see Ntoro, Kavo
Kafiristan reg. Pak. 111 H3
Kafr ash Shaykh Egypt 112 C5
Kafr el Sheikh Egypt see Kafr ash Shaykh
Kafue Zambia 123 C5
Kafue r. Zambia 123 C5
Kafue National Park Zambia 123 C5
Kaga Japan 92 C2
Kaga Bandoro Cent. Afr. Rep. 122 B3
Kagan Pak. 111 I3
Kagan Uzbek. see Kogon
Kagang Qinghai China 94 E5
Kaganovichabad Tajik. see Kolkhozobod
Kaganovichi Pervyye Ukr. see Polis'ke
Kagarlyk Ukr. see Kaharlyk
Kåge Sweden 54 L4
Kağızman Turkey 113 F2
Kaglik Lake N.W.T. Canada 149 O1
Kagmar Sudan 108 D7
Kagologolo Indon. 84 B3
Kagosaka-tōge pass Japan 93 E3
Kagoshima Japan 91 C7
Kagoshima pref. Japan 91 C7
Kagul Moldova see Cahul
Kaguyak AK U.S.A. 148 I4
Kahama Tanz. 122 D4
Kaharlyk Ukr. 53 F6
Kahatola i. Maluku Indon. 83 C2
Kahayan r. Indon. 85 F3
Kaherekoau Mountains N.Z. 139 A7
Kahla Germany 63 L4
Kahnūj Iran 110 E4
Kahoka U.S.A. 160 F3
Kahoku-gata l. Japan 92 C2
Kaho'olawe i. U.S.A. 157 [inset]
Kahperusvaarat mts Fin. 54 L2
Kahramanmaraş Turkey 112 E3
Kahror Pak. 111 H4
Kâhta Turkey 112 E3
Kahuku U.S.A. 157 [inset]
Kahuku Point U.S.A. 157 [inset]
Kahulaui i. U.S.A. see Kaho'olawe
Kahurangi National Park N.Z. 139 D5
Kahurangi Point N.Z. 139 D5
Kahuta Pak. 111 I3
Kahuzi-Biega, Parc National du nat. park Dem. Rep. Congo 122 C4
Kai, Kepulauan is Indon. 81 I8
Kaiapoi N.Z. 139 D6
Kaibab U.S.A. 159 G3
Kaibab Plateau U.S.A. 159 G3
Kaibamardang Qinghai China 94 D4
Kaibara Japan 92 B3
Kai Besar i. Indon. 81 I8
Kaibito Plateau U.S.A. 159 H3
Kaida Japan 92 D3
Kaidu He r. China 98 D4
Kaifeng Henan China 95 H5
Kaifeng Henan China 95 H5
Kaihua Yunnan China see Wenshan
Kaihua Zhejiang China 97 H2
Kaiingveld reg. S. Africa 124 E5
Kaijiang China 96 E2
Kai Kecil i. Indon. 81 I8
Kai Keung Leng H.K. China 97 [inset]
Kaikoura N.Z. 139 D6
Kailas mt. Xizang China see Kangrinboqê Feng
Kailasahar India see Kailashahar
Kailashahar India 105 H4
Kailas Range mts Xizang China see Gangdisê Shan
Kaili China 96 E3
Kailu Nei Mongol China 95 J3
Kailua U.S.A. 157 [inset]
Kailua-Kona U.S.A. 157 [inset]
Kaimana Indon. 81 I7
Kaimanawa Mountains N.Z. 139 E4
Kaimar China 96 B1
Kaimganj Uttar Prad. India 99 B8
Kaimur Range hills India 104 E4
Käina Estonia 55 M7
Kainan Wakayama Japan 92 B4
Kainda Kyrg. see Kayyngdy
Kaindy Kyrg. see Kayyngdy
Kainji Lake National Park Nigeria 120 D4
Kaipara Harbour N.Z. 139 E3
Kaiparowits Plateau U.S.A. 159 H3
Kaiping China 97 G4
Kaipokok Bay Canada 153 K3
Kairana India 104 D3
Kairatu Seram Indon. 83 D3
Kairiru Island P.N.G. 81 K7
Kaironi Indon. 81 I7
Kairouan Tunisia 68 D7
Kaiserslautern Germany 63 H5
Kaiser Wilhelm II Land reg. Antarctica 188 E2
Kait, Tanjung pt Indon. 84 D3
Kaitaia N.Z. 139 D2
Kaitangata N.Z. 139 B8
Kaitawa N.Z. 139 F4
Kaithal India 104 D3
Kaitong Jilin China see Tongyu
Kaitum Sweden 54 L3
Kaiwatu Maluku Indon. 83 C5
Kaiwi Channel U.S.A. 157 [inset]
Kaixian China 97 F2
Kaiyang China 96 E3
Kaiyuan Liaoning China 95 K3
Kaiyuan Yunnan China 96 D4
Kaiyuh Mountains AK U.S.A. 148 H3
Kaizu Japan 92 C3
Kaizuka Japan 92 B4
Kajaani Fin. 54 O4
Kajabbi Australia 136 C4
Kajaki Afgh. 111 G3
Kajang Malaysia 84 C2
Kajarabie, Lake Australia 138 D1
Kajikazawa Japan 93 E3
Kajrān Afgh. 111 G3
Kajy-Say Kyrg. 98 B4
Kaka Turkm. 111 E2
Kakaban i. Indon. 85 G2
Kakabeka Falls Canada 152 C4
Kakabia i. Indon. 83 B4
Kakadu National Park Australia 134 F3
Kakagi Lake Canada 151 M5
Kakal r. Mindanao Phil. 82 D5
Kakali Sulawesi Barat Indon. 83 A3
Kakamas S. Africa 124 E5
Kakamega Kenya 122 D3
Kakamigahara Japan 92 C3
Kakana India 87 A5
Kakar Pak. 111 G5
Kakata Liberia 120 B4
Kake AK U.S.A. 149 N4
Kakegawa Japan 93 E4
Kakenge Dem. Rep. Congo 123 C4
Kakerbeck Germany 63 L2
Kakhi Azer. see Qax
Kakhonak AK U.S.A. 148 I4
Kakhovka Ukr. 69 O1
Kakhovs'ke Vodoskhovyshche resr Ukr. 53 G7
Kakhul Moldova see Cahul
Kākī Iran 110 C4
Kakinada India 106 D2
Kakisa Canada 150 G2
Kakisa r. Canada 150 G2
Kakisa Lake Canada 150 G2
Kakogawa Japan 92 A4
Kako-gawa r. Japan 92 A4
Kakori India 104 E4
Kakpak Kuduk well Xinjiang China 94 B2
Kakshaal-Too mts China/Kyrg. 102 E3
Kaktovik AK U.S.A. 149 L1
Kakul Pak. 111 I3
Kakus r. Malaysia 85 F2
Kakwa r. Canada 150 G4
Kala Pak. 111 H4
Kala Tanz. 123 D4
Kalaâ Kebira Tunisia 68 D7
Kalaallit Nunaat terr. N. America see Greenland
Kalabahi Indon. 83 C5
Kalabáka Greece see Kalampaka
Kalabakan Sabah Malaysia 85 G1
Kalabgur India 106 C2
Kalabo Zambia 123 C5
Kalach Rus. Fed. 53 I6
Kalacha Dida Kenya 122 D3
Kalach-na-Donu Rus. Fed. 53 I6
Kaladan r. India/Myanmar 86 A2
Kaladar Canada 165 G1
Ka Lae pt U.S.A. 157 [inset]
Kalaena r. Indon. 83 B3
Kalagwe Myanmar 86 B2
Kalahari Desert Africa 124 F2
Kalahari Gemsbok National Park S. Africa 124 E3
Kalaikhum Tajik. see Qal'aikhum
Kalai-Khumb Tajik. see Qal'aikhum
Kalajoki Fin. 54 M4
Kalalé Benin 120 D3
Kalaliok Sulawesi Indon. 83 B3
Kalalusu i. Indon. 83 C1
Kalam India 106 C1
Kalam Pak. 111 I3
Kalámai Greece see Kalamata
Kalamare Botswana 125 H2
Kalamaria Greece 69 J4
Kalamata Greece 69 J6
Kalamazoo U.S.A. 164 C2
Kalambau i. Indon. 85 F4
Kalampaka Greece 69 I5
Kalanchak Ukr. 69 O1
Kalandi Pak. 111 F4
Kalandula Angola see Calandula
Kalanguy Rus. Fed. 95 I1
Kalannie Australia 135 B7
Kalanshiyū ar Ramlī al Kabīr, Sarīr des. Libya 108 B3
Kalān Zīād Iran 111 E5
Kalao i. Indon. 83 B4
Kalaong Mindanao Phil. 82 D5
Kalaotoa i. Indon. 83 B4
Kalapa Indon. 84 D3
Kalapana (abandoned) U.S.A. 157 [inset]
Kalār Iraq 113 G4
Kalasin Thai. 86 C3
Kalāt Afgh. 111 G3
Kalāt Khorāsān Iran see Kabūd Gonbad
Kalāt Sīstān va Balūchestān Iran 111 E5
Kalat Balochistan Pak. 111 G4
Kalat Balochistan Pak. 111 G5
Kalat, Kūh-e mt. Iran 110 E3
Kalaupapa U.S.A. 157 [inset]
Kalaus r. Rus. Fed. 53 J7
Kalaw Myanmar 86 B2
Kälbäcär Azer. 113 G2
Kalbarri Australia 135 A6
Kalbarri National Park Australia 135 A6
Kalbe (Milde) Germany 63 L2
Kalbinskiy Khrebet mts Kazakh. 98 C2
Kale Turkey 69 M6
Kalecik Turkey 112 D2
Kaledupa i. Indon. 83 B4
Kalefeld Germany 63 K3
Kaleindaung inlet Myanmar 86 A3
Kalemie Dem. Rep. Congo 123 C4
Kalemyo Myanmar 86 A2
Kāl-e Namak Iran 110 D3
Kalevala Rus. Fed. 54 Q4
Kalewa Myanmar 86 A2
Kaleybar Iran 110 B2
Kalga Rus. Fed. 95 I1
Kalgan Hebei China see Zhangjiakou
Kalghatgi India 106 B3
Kalgoorlie Australia 135 C7
Kāl Gūsheh Iran 110 E4
Kali Croatia 68 F2
Kali r. India/Nepal 104 E3
Kaliakra, Nos pt Bulg. 69 M3
Kalianda Sumatera Indon. 84 D4
Kalibo Panay Phil. 82 C4
Kaliet Indon. 84 B3
Kali Gandaki r. Nepal 105 F4
Kaligiri India 106 C3
Kalikata India see Kolkata
Kalima Dem. Rep. Congo 122 C4
Kalimantan reg. Indon. 85 E3
Kalimantan Barat prov. Indon. 85 E2
Kalimantan Selatan prov. Indon. 85 F3
Kalimantan Tengah prov. Indon. 85 F3
Kalimantan Timur prov. Indon. 85 G2
Kálimnos i. Greece see Kalymnos
Kali Nadi r. India 99 C8
Kalinin Rus. Fed. see Tver'
Kalinin Adyndaky Tajik. see Cheshtebe
Kaliningrad Rus. Fed. 55 L9
Kalinino Armenia see Tashir
Kalinino Rus. Fed. 52 I4
Kalininsk Rus. Fed. 53 J6
Kalininskaya Rus. Fed. 53 H7
Kalinjara India 104 C5
Kalinkavichy Belarus 53 F5
Kalinkovichi Belarus see Kalinkavichy
Kalisat Jawa Indon. 85 F5
Kalisch Poland see Kalisz
Kalispell U.S.A. 156 E2
Kalisz Poland 57 Q5
Kalitva r. Rus. Fed. 53 I6
Kaliua Tanz. 123 D4
Kaliujar India 104 E4
Kalix Sweden 54 M4
Kalkalighat India 105 H4
Kalkalpen, Nationalpark nat. park Austria 57 O7
Kalkan Turkey 69 M6
Kalkaska U.S.A. 164 C1
Kalkfeld Namibia 123 B6
Kalkfonteindam dam S. Africa 125 G5
Kalkudah Sri Lanka 106 D5
Kall Germany 62 G4
Kallang r. Sing. 87 [inset]
Kallaste Estonia 55 O7
Kallavesi l. Fin. 54 O5
Kallsedet Sweden 54 H5
Kallsjön l. Sweden 54 H5
Kallur India 106 C2
Kalmar Sweden 55 J8
Kalmarsund sea chan. Sweden 55 J8
Kalmit hill Germany 63 I5
Kalmükh Qal'eh Iran 110 E2
Kalmunai Sri Lanka 106 D5
Kalmykia aut. rep. Rus. Fed. see Kalmykiya-Khalm'g-Tangch, Respublika
Kalmykiya-Khalm'g-Tangch, Respublika aut. rep. Rus. Fed. 113 G1
Kalmykovo Kazakh. see Taypak
Kalmytskaya Avtonomnaya Oblast' aut. rep. Rus. Fed. see Kalmykiya-Khalm'g-Tangch, Respublika
Kalnai India 105 E5
Kalodnaye Belarus 55 O11
Kalol India 104 C5
Kaloma i. Indon. 83 C2
Kalomo Zambia 123 C5
Kalone Peak Canada 150 E4
Kalongan Sulawesi Indon. 83 C1
Kalpa India 104 D3
Kalpeni atoll India 106 B4
Kalpetta India 106 C4
Kalpi India 104 D4
Kalpin Xinjiang China 98 B4
Kalsi Uttaranchal India 99 B7
Kaltag AK U.S.A. 148 H2
Kaltensundheim Germany 63 K4
Kaltukatjara Australia 135 E6
Kalu India 111 I4
Kaluga Rus. Fed. 53 H5
Kalukalukuang i. Indon. 85 G4
Kaluku Sulawesi Barat Indon. 83 A3
Kalulong, Bukit mt. Malaysia 85 F2
Kalundborg Denmark 55 G9
Kalupis Falls Malaysia 85 G1
Kalush Ukr. 53 E6
Kalvakol India 106 C2
Kälviä Fin. 54 M5
Kal'ya Rus. Fed. 51 R3
Kalyan India 106 B2
Kalyandurg India 109 M7
Kalyansingapuram India 106 D2
Kalyazin Rus. Fed. 52 H4
Kalymnos i. Greece 69 L6
Kama Dem. Rep. Congo 122 C4
Kama Myanmar 86 A3

▶Kama r. Rus. Fed. 52 L4
4th longest river in Europe.

Kamagaya Japan 93 F3
Kamaishi Japan 91 F5
Kamakura Japan 93 F3
Kamalia Pak. 111 I4
Kaman Rajasthan India 99 B8
Kaman Turkey 112 D3
Kamanashi-gawa r. Japan 93 E3
Kamanashi-yama mt. Japan 93 E3
Kamaniskeg Lake Canada 165 G1
Kamanjab Namibia 123 B5
Kamarān i. Yemen 108 F6
Kamaran Island Yemen see Kamarān
Kamard reg. Afgh. 111 G3
Kamarod Pak. 111 F5
Kamaron Sierra Leone 120 B4

Kamashi Uzbek. see Qamashi
Kamasin India 104 E4
Kambaiti Myanmar 86 B1
Kambalda Australia 135 C7
Kambam India 106 C4
Kambang Sumatera Indon. 84 C3
Kambangan i. Indon. 85 E5
Kambara i. Fiji see Kabara
Kambara Japan see Kanbara
Kambardi Xinjiang China 98 C4
Kambia Sierra Leone 120 B4
Kambing, Pulau i. East Timor see Ataúro, Ilha de
Kambo-san mt. N. Korea see Kwanmo-bong
Kambove Dem. Rep. Congo 123 C5
Kambuno, Bukit mt. Indon. 83 B3
Kambūt Libya 112 B5
Kamchatka, Poluostrov pen. Rus. Fed. see Kamchatka Peninsula
Kamchatka Basin sea feature Bering Sea 186 H2
Kamchatka Peninsula Rus. Fed. 77 Q4
Kamchiya r. Bulg. 69 L3
Kameia, Parque Nacional de nat. park Angola see Cameia, Parque Nacional da
Kamelik r. Rus. Fed. 53 K5
Kamen Germany 63 H3
Kamen', Gory mt. Rus. Fed. 76 K3
Kamenets-Podol'skiy Ukr. see Kam"yanets'-Podil's'kyy
Kamenitsa mt. Bulg. 69 J4
Kamenjak, Rt pt Croatia 68 E2
Kamenka Kazakh. 51 Q5
Kamenka Arkhangel'skaya Oblast' Rus. Fed. 52 J2
Kamenka Penzenskaya Oblast' Rus. Fed. 53 J5
Kamenka Primorskiy Kray Rus. Fed. 90 E3
Kamenka-Bugskaya Ukr. see Kam"yanka-Buz'ka
Kamenka-Strumilovskaya Ukr. see Kam"yanka-Buz'ka
Kamen'-na-Obi Rus. Fed. 88 E2
Kamennogorsk Rus. Fed. 55 P6
Kamennomostskiy Rus. Fed. 113 F1
Kamenolomni Rus. Fed. 53 I7
Kamenongue Angola see Camanongue
Kamen'-Rybolov Rus. Fed. 90 D3
Kamenskoye Rus. Fed. 77 R3
Kamenskoye Ukr. see Dniprodzerzhyns'k
Kamensk-Shakhtinskiy Rus. Fed. 53 I6
Kamensk-Ural'skiy Rus. Fed. 76 H4
Kameoka Japan 92 B3
Kamet mt. Xizang China 99 B7
Kameyama Japan 92 C4
Kami Hyōgo Japan 92 A3
Kami Nagano Japan 93 D3
Kamichi Japan 92 D2
Kamiesberge mts S. Africa 124 D6
Kamieskroon S. Africa 124 C6
Kamifukuoka Japan 93 F3
Kami-ishizu Japan 92 C3
Kami-jima i. Japan 92 C4
Kamikawa Saitama Japan 93 F2
Kamikawachi Japan 93 F2
Kamikitayama Japan 92 B4
Kamikuishiki Japan 93 E3
Kamileroi Australia 136 C3
Kamilukuak Lake Canada 151 K2
Kamina Dem. Rep. Congo 123 C4
Kaminaka Japan 92 B3
Kaminak Lake Canada 151 M2
Kaminoho Japan 92 D3
Kaminokawa Japan 93 F2
Kaminuriak Lake Canada see Qamanirjuaq Lake
Kamioka Japan 92 D2
Kamishak Bay AK U.S.A. 148 I4
Kamishihi Japan 92 C2
Kamishihoro Japan 90 F4
Kamisu Japan 93 G3
Kami-taira Japan 92 C2
Kami-takara Japan 92 D2
Kami-yahagi Japan 92 D3
Kamiyamada Japan 93 E2
Kamla r. India 99 F8
Kamloops Canada 150 F5
Kammuri-jima i. Japan see Kanmuri-jima
Kammuri-yama mt. Japan see Kanmuri-yama
Kamo Armenia see Gavarr
Kamo Kyōto Japan 92 B4
Kamo Yamanashi Japan 93 E4
Kamogawa Japan 93 G3
Kamoke Pak. 111 I4
Kamonia Dem. Rep. Congo 123 C4
Kampa Indon. 84 D3

►Kampala Uganda 122 D3
Capital of Uganda.

Kampar r. Indon. 84 C2
Kampar Malaysia 84 C1
Kampara India 106 D1
Kamparkiri r. Indon. 84 C2
Kampen Neth. 62 F2
Kampene Dem. Rep. Congo 122 C4
Kamphaeng Phet Thai. 86 B3
Kampinoski Park Narodowy nat. park Poland 57 R4
Kâmpóng Cham Cambodia 87 D5
Kâmpóng Chhnăng Cambodia 87 D4
Kâmpóng Khleăng Cambodia 87 D4
Kâmpóng Saôm Cambodia see Sihanoukville
Kâmpóng Spœ Cambodia 87 D5
Kâmpóng Thum Cambodia 87 D4
Kâmpóng Trâbêk Cambodia 87 D5
Kâmpôt Cambodia 87 D5
Kamptee India see Kamthi
Kampuchea country Asia see Cambodia
Kamrau, Teluk b. Indon. 81 I7
Kamsack Canada 151 K5
Kamskoye Vodokhranilishche resr Rus. Fed. 51 R4
Kamsuuma Somalia 122 E3
Kamthi India 104 D5
Kamuchawie Lake Canada 151 K3
Kamuli Uganda 122 D3
Kam"yanets'-Podil's'kyy Ukr. 53 E6
Kam"yanka-Buz'ka Ukr. 53 E6
Kamyanyets Belarus 55 M10
Kāmyārān Iran 110 B3
Kamyshin Rus. Fed. 53 J6
Kamystybas, Ozero l. Kazakh. 102 B2
Kamyzyak Rus. Fed. 53 K7
Kamzar Oman 110 E5
Kanaaupscow r. Canada 152 F3
Kanab U.S.A. 159 G3
Kanab Creek r. U.S.A. 159 G3
Kanae Japan 93 D3
Kanaga Island AK U.S.A. 149 [inset]
Kanagawa pref. Japan 93 F3
Kanairiktok r. Canada 153 K3
Kanak Pak. 111 G4
Kanakanak AK U.S.A. 148 H4
Kananga Dem. Rep. Congo 123 C4
Kanangio, Mount vol. P.N.G. 81 L7
Kanangra-Boyd National Park Australia 138 E4
Kanarak India see Konarka
Kanarraville U.S.A. 159 G3
Kanas watercourse Namibia 124 C4
Kanasagō Japan 93 G2
Kanash Rus. Fed. 52 J5
Kanas Köl l. China 98 D2
Kanatak AK U.S.A. 148 H4
Kanauj India see Kannauj
Kanaya Shizuoka Japan 93 E4
Kanaya Wakayama Japan 92 B4
Kanayama Japan 92 D3
Kanayka Kazakh. 98 C2
Kanazawa Ishikawa Japan 92 C2
Kanazawa Kanagawa Japan 93 F3
Kanazu Japan 92 C2
Kanbalu Myanmar 86 A2
Kanbara Japan 93 E3
Kanchalan Rus. Fed. 148 B2
Kanchalan r. Rus. Fed. 148 B2
Kanchanaburi Thai. 87 B4
Kanchanjanga mt. India/Nepal see Kangchenjunga
Kanchipuram India 106 C3
Kand mt. Pak. 111 G4
Kanda Pak. 111 G4
Kandahār Afgh. 111 G4
Kandalaksha Rus. Fed. 54 R3
Kandalakshskiy Zaliv g. Rus. Fed. 54 R3
Kandang Sumatera Indon. 84 B2
Kandangan Kalimantan Indon. 85 F3
Kandar Indon. 134 E2
Kandavu i. Fiji see Kadavu
Kandavu Passage Fiji see Kadavu Passage
Kandé Togo 120 D4
Kandh Kot Pak. 111 H4
Kandi Benin 120 D3
Kandi India 106 C2
Kandi, Tanjung pt Indon. 83 B2
Kandiaro Pak. 111 H5
Kandik r. Canada/U.S.A. 149 L2
Kandıra Turkey 69 N4
Kandos Australia 138 D4
Kandreho Madag. 123 E5
Kandrian P.N.G. 81 L8
Kandukur India 106 C3
Kandy Sri Lanka 106 D5
Kandyagash Kazakh. 102 A2
Kane U.S.A. 165 F3
Kane Bassin b. Greenland 189 K1
Kaneh watercourse Iran 110 D5
Kanektok r. AK U.S.A. 148 G4
Kāne'ohe U.S.A. 157 [inset]
Kaneti Pak. 111 G4
Kanevskaya Rus. Fed. 53 H7
Kaneyama Gifu Japan 92 D3
Kang Afgh. 111 F4
Kang Botswana 124 F2
Kangaamiut Greenland 147 M3
Kangaarsussuaq c. Greenland 147 K2
Kangaba Mali 120 C3
Kangal Turkey 112 E3
Kangān Būshehr Iran 110 D5
Kangān Hormozgan Iran 110 E5
Kangandala, Parque Nacional de nat. park Angola see Cangandala, Parque Nacional de
Kangar Malaysia 84 C1
Kangaroo Island Australia 137 B7
Kangaroo Point Australia 136 B3
Kangaslampi Fin. 54 P5
Kangasniemi Fin. 54 O6
Kangāvar Iran 110 B3
Kangbao Hebei China 95 H3

►Kangchenjunga mt. India/Nepal 105 G4
3rd highest mountain in Asia and in the world.

Kangding China 96 D2
Kangean, Kepulauan is Indon. 85 F4
Kangen r. Sudan 121 G4
Kangerlussuaq Greenland 147 M3
Kangerlussuaq inlet Greenland 147 M3
Kangerlussuaq inlet Greenland 189 J2
Kangersuatsiaq Greenland 147 M2
Kangertittivaq sea chan. Greenland 147 P2
Kanggye N. Korea 90 B4
Kanghwa S. Korea 91 B5
Kangikajik c. Greenland 147 P2
Kangiqsualujjuaq Canada 153 I2
Kangirsuk Canada 153 H1
Kang Krung National Park Thai. 87 B5
Kangle Gansu China 94 E5
Kangle Jiangxi China see Wanzai
Kanglong China 96 C1
Kangmar Xizang China 105 F3
Kangmar Xizang China 99 E7
Kangnŭng S. Korea 91 C5
Kango Gabon 122 B3
Kangping Liaoning China 95 J3
Kangri Karpo Pass China/India 105 I3
Kangrinboqê Feng mt. Xizang China 99 C7
Kangro Xizang China 99 D6
Kangsangdobdê Xizang China see Xainza
Kang Tipayan Dakula i. Phil. 85 H1
Kangto mt. China/India 99 F8
Kangtog Xizang China 99 D6
Kangxian China 96 E1
Kangxiwar Xinjiang China 99 B5
Kani Japan 92 D3
Kanibongan Sabah Malaysia 85 G1
Kanie Japan 92 C3
Kanifing Gambia 120 B3
Kanigiri India 106 C3
Kanin, Poluostrov pen. Rus. Fed. 52 J2
Kanin Nos Rus. Fed. 189 G2
Kanin Nos, Mys c. Rus. Fed. 52 I1
Kaninskiy Bereg coastal area Rus. Fed. 52 I2
Kanjiroba mt. Nepal 105 E3
Kankaanpää Fin. 55 M6
Kankakee U.S.A. 164 B3
Kankan Guinea 120 C3
Kanker India 106 D1
Kankesanturai Sri Lanka 106 D4
Kankossa Mauritania 120 B3
Kanlaon, Mount vol. Phil. 82 C4
Kanmaw Kyun i. Myanmar 87 B5
Kanmuri-jima i. Japan 92 B3
Kanmuri-yama mt. Japan 92 C3
Kanna-gawa r. Japan 93 F2
Kannami Japan 93 E3
Kannauj India 104 D4
Kanniya Kumari c. India see Comorin, Cape
Kannonkoski Fin. 54 N5
Kannon-zaki pt Japan 92 D1
Kannur India see Cannanore
Kannus Fin. 54 M5
Kano i. Indon. 83 C3
Kano Nigeria 120 D3
Kano-gawa r. Japan 93 E3
Kanonerka Kazakh. 98 B2
Kanonpunt pt S. Africa 124 E8
Kanosh U.S.A. 159 G2
Kanovlei Namibia 123 B5
Kanowit Sarawak Malaysia 85 F2
Kanoya Japan 91 C7
Kanpur Odisha India 106 E1
Kanpur Uttar Prad. India 104 E4
Kanra Japan 93 E2
Kanrach reg. Pak. 111 G5
Kansai airport Japan 92 B4
Kansas U.S.A. 164 B4
Kansas r. U.S.A. 160 E4
Kansas state U.S.A. 160 D4
Kansas City KS U.S.A. 160 E4
Kansas City MO U.S.A. 160 E4
Kansk Rus. Fed. 77 K4
Kansu Xinjiang China 98 A5
Kansu prov. China see Gansu
Kantang Thai. 87 B6
Kantara hill Cyprus 107 A2
Kantaralak Thai. 87 D4
Kantavu i. Fiji see Kadavu
Kantchari Burkina Faso 120 D3
Kantemirovka Rus. Fed. 53 H6
Kanthi India 105 F5
Kantishna AK U.S.A. 149 J3
Kantishna r. AK U.S.A. 149 J2
Kantli r. India 99 A7
Kantō-heiya plain Japan 93 F3
Kanton atoll Kiribati 133 I2
Kanto-sanchi mts Japan 93 E3
Kantulong Myanmar 86 B3
Kanturk Ireland 61 D5
Kanuku Mountains Guyana 177 G3
Kanuma Japan 93 F2
Kanur India 106 C3
Kanus Namibia 124 D4
Kanuti r. AK U.S.A. 148 I2
Kanuti National Wildlife Refuge nature res. AK U.S.A. 149 J2
Kanyakubja India see Kannauj
Kanyamazane S. Africa 125 J3
Kanye Botswana 125 G3
Kanzaki Japan 92 A3
Kao Halmahera Indon. 83 C2
Kao, Teluk b. Halmahera Indon. 83 C2
Kaôh Pring i. Cambodia 87 C5
Kaohsiung Taiwan 97 I4
Kaôh Smăch i. Cambodia 87 C5
Kaôh Tang i. Cambodia 87 C5
Kaokoveld plat. Namibia 123 B5
Kaolack Senegal 120 B3
Kaoma Zambia 123 C5
Kaouadja Cent. Afr. Rep. 122 C3
Kapa S. Africa see Cape Town
Kapa'a U.S.A. 157 [inset]
Kapa'au U.S.A. 157 [inset]
Kapal Kazakh. 98 B3
Kapalabuaya Maluku Indon. 83 C3
Kapan Armenia 113 G3
Kapanga Dem. Rep. Congo 123 C4
Kaparhā Iran 110 C4
Kapatu Zambia 123 D4
Kapchagay Kazakh. 102 E3
Kapchagayskoye Vodokhranilishche resr Kazakh. 102 E3
Kap Dan Greenland see Kulusuk
Kapellen Belgium 62 E3
Kapello, Akra pt Attiki Greece see Kapello, Akrotirio
Kapello, Akrotirio pt Greece 69 J6
Kapellskär Sweden 55 K7
Kapelskär Sweden see Kapellskär
Kapili r. India 105 G4
Kapingamarangi atoll Micronesia 186 G5
Kapingamarangi Rise sea feature N. Pacific Ocean 186 G5
Kapıorman Dağları mts Turkey 69 N4
Kapip Pak. 111 H4
Kapiri Mposhi Zambia 123 C5
Kapisillit Greenland 147 M3
Kapiskau r. Canada 152 E3
Kapit Sarawak Malaysia 85 F2
Kapiti Island N.Z. 139 E5
Kaplamada, Gunung mt. Buru Indon. 83 C3
Kaplankyr, Chink hills Asia 113 I2
Kaplankyr Döwlet Gorugy nature res. Turkm. 110 E1
Kapoeta Sudan 121 G4
Kapondai, Tanjung pt Flores Indon. 83 B5
Kaposvár Hungary 68 G1
Kappel Germany 63 H5
Kappeln Germany 57 L3
Kapsukas Lith. see Marijampolė
Kaptai Bangl. 105 H5
Kaptsegaytuy Rus. Fed. 95 I1
Kapuas r. Indon. 85 E3
Kapuas r. Indon. 85 F3
Kapuas Hulu, Pegunungan mts Indon./Malaysia 85 F2
Kapuriya India 104 C4
Kapurthala India 104 C3
Kapuskasing Canada 152 E4
Kapustin Yar Rus. Fed. 53 J6
Kaputar mt. Australia 138 E3
Kaputir Kenya 122 D3
Kapuvár Hungary 68 G1
Kapydzhik, Gora mt. Armenia/Azer. see Qazangödağ
Kapyl' Belarus 55 O10
Ka Qu r. Xizang China 99 F7
Kaqung China 111 J2
Kara India 104 E4
Kara Togo 120 D4
Kara r. Turkey 113 F3
Kara Art Pass Xinjiang China 98 A5
Kara-Balta Kyrg. 102 D3
Karabalyk Kazakh. 100 F1
Karabas Kazakh. 98 A2
Karabekaul' Turkm. see Garabekewül
Karabiga Turkey 69 L4
Karabil', Vozvyshennost' hills Turkm. see Garabil Belentligi
Kara-Bogaz-Gol, Proliv sea chan. Turkm. see Garabogazköl Bogazy
Kara-Bogaz-Gol'skiy Zaliv b. Turkm. see Garabogazköl Aýlagy
Karabük Turkey 112 D2
Karabulak Almatinskaya Oblast' Kazakh. 98 B3
Karabulak Vostochnyy Kazakhstan Kazakh. 98 D3
Karabulakskaya Kazakh. 98 A2
Karabura Xinjiang China see Yumin
Karaburun Turkey 69 L5
Karabutak Kazakh. 102 B2
Karacabey Turkey 69 M4
Karacaköy Turkey 69 M4
Karacalı Dağ mt. Turkey 113 E3
Karaçal Tepe mt. Turkey 107 A1
Karacasu Turkey 69 M6
Karaca Yarımadası pen. Turkey 69 N6
Karachayevsk Rus. Fed. 113 F2
Karachev Rus. Fed. 53 G5
Karachi Pak. 111 G5
Karacurun Turkey see Hilvan
Karad India 106 B2
Kara Dağ hill Turkey 107 D1
Kara Dağ mt. Turkey 112 D3
Kara-Dar'ya Uzbek. see Payshanba
Kara Deniz sea Asia/Europe see Black Sea
Karagan Rus. Fed. 90 A1
Karaganda Kazakh. 102 D2
Karagandinskaya Oblast' admin. div. Kazakh. 98 A2
Karagash Kazakh. 98 B3
Karagayly Kazakh. 102 E2
Karagaylybulak Kazakh. 98 D2
Karaginskiy Zaliv b. Rus. Fed. 77 R4
Karagiye, Vpadina depr. Kazakh. 113 H2
Karagola India 105 F4
Karaguzhikha Kazakh. 98 C2
Karahallı Turkey 69 M5
Karahasanlı Turkey 112 D3
Karaikal India 106 C4
Karaikkudi India 106 C4
Kara Irtysh r. Kazakh. 98 D3
Karaisalı Turkey 112 D3
Karaitan Kalimantan Indon. 85 G2
Karaj Iran 110 C3
Karak Jordan see Al Karak
Karakalli Turkey see Özalp
Karakax Xinjiang China see Moyu
Karakax He r. China 99 C5
Karakax Shan mts Xinjiang China 99 C6
Karakelong i. Indon. 83 C1
Karaki Xinjiang China 99 C5
Karakitang i. Indon. 83 C2
Karaklis Armenia see Vanadzor
Karakoçan Turkey 113 F3
Kara-Köl Kyrg. 102 D3
Karakol Kyrg. 102 E3
Karakol Ysyk-Köl Kyrg. 98 B4
Karakoram Pass China/India 104 D2
Karakoram Range mts Asia 101 G3
Karakoram Range mts Asia 111 I2
Kara K'orē Eth. 122 D2
Karakorum Range mts Asia see Karakoram Range
Karakorum Range mts Asia see Karakoram Range
Karaköse Turkey see Ağrı
Kara Kul' Kyrg. see Kara-Köl
Karakul', Ozero l. Tajik. see Qarokŭl
Karakum Kazakh. 98 B3
Kara Kum des. Turkm. see Garagum
Kara Kum des. Turkm. see Karakum Desert
Karakum, Peski Kazakh. see Karakum Desert
Karakum Desert Kazakh. 100 E2
Karakum Desert Turkm. see Garagum
Karakum Desert Turkm. 110 F2
Karakumskiy Kanal canal Turkm. see Garagum Kanaly
Kara Kumy des. Turkm. see Garagum
Karakurt Turkey 113 F2
Karakuş Dağı ridge Turkey 69 N5
Karal Chad 121 E3
Karala Estonia 55 L7
Karalundi Australia 135 B6
Karama r. Indon. 83 A3
Karamagay Xinjiang China see Haramgai
Karaman Turkey 112 D3
Karaman prov. Turkey 107 A1
Karamanlı Turkey 69 M6
Karamay Xinjiang China 98 D3
Karambar Pass Afgh./Pak. 111 I2
Karambu Kalimantan Indon. 85 G3
Karamea N.Z. 139 D5
Karamea Bight b. N.Z. 139 C5
Karamendy Kazakh. 102 B1
Karamian i. Indon. 85 F4
Karamiran Xinjiang China 99 D5
Karamiran He r. China 99 D5
Karamiran Shankou pass Xinjiang China 99 D5
Karamürsel Turkey 69 M4
Karamyshevo Rus. Fed. 55 P8
Karān i. Saudi Arabia 110 C5
Karang, Tanjung pt Indon. 83 A3
Karangagung Sumatera Indon. 84 D3
Karangan Sumatera Indon. 84 D4
Karangasem Bali Indon. 85 F5
Karangbolong, Tanjung pt Indon. 85 E5
Karangetang vol. Indon. 83 C2
Karanja India 106 C1
Karanjia India 104 E5
Karaoy Almatinskaya Oblast' Kazakh. 98 A3
Karaoy Almatinskaya Oblast' Kazakh. 98 A3
Karapınar Gaziantep Turkey 107 C1
Karapınar Konya Turkey 112 D3
Karaqi Xinjiang China 98 B4
Karas admin. reg. Namibia 124 C4
Karasay Xinjiang China 99 C5
Kara-Say Kyrg. 98 B4
Karasburg Namibia 124 D5
Kara Sea Rus. Fed. 76 I2
Kárášjohka Finnmark Norway see Karasjok
Karasjok Norway 54 N2
Karasor, Ozero salt l. Kazakh. 98 A2
Kara Strait Rus. Fed. see Karskiye Vorota, Proliv
Karasu Japan 92 C4
Karasu Karagandinskaya Oblast' Kazakh. 98 A3
Karasu r. Syria/Turkey 107 C1
Karasu Bitlis Turkey see Hizan
Karasu Sakarya Turkey 69 N4
Karasu r. Turkey 113 F3
Karasubazar Ukr. see Bilohirs'k
Karasu-gawa r. Japan 93 F2
Karasuk Rus. Fed. 76 I4
Karasuyama Japan 93 G2
Karāt Iran 111 F3
Karatal Kazakh. 98 D3
Karataş Turkey 107 B1
Karataş Burnu hd Turkey see Fener Burnu
Karatau Kazakh. 102 D3
Karatau, Khrebet mts Kazakh. 102 C3
Karatepe Turkey 107 A1
Karathuri Myanmar 87 B5
Karativu i. Sri Lanka 106 C4
Karatol r. Kazakh. 98 B3
Karatsu Japan 91 C6
Karatung i. Indon. 83 C1
Karatüngü Xinjiang China 94 B2
Karaudanawa Guyana 177 G3
Karaul Kazakh. 98 C2
Karauli India 104 D4
Karavan Kyrg. see Kerben
Karavostasi Cyprus 107 A2
Karawang Jawa Indon. 84 D4
Karaxahar r. China see Kaidu He
Karayılan Turkey 107 C1
Karayulgan Xinjiang China 98 C4
Karazhal Kazakh. 102 D2
Karazhingil Kazakh. 98 A3
Karbalā' Iraq 113 G4
Karben Germany 63 I4
Karbushevka Kazakh. 98 A2
Karcag Hungary 69 I1
Karden Germany 63 H4
Kardhítsa Greece see Karditsa
Karditsa Greece 69 I5
Kärdla Estonia 55 M7
Karee S. Africa 125 H5
Kareeberge mts S. Africa 124 E6
Kareima Sudan 108 D6
Kareli India 104 D5
Karelia aut. rep. Rus. Fed. see Kareliya, Respublika
Kareliya, Respublika aut. rep. Rus. Fed. 54 R5
Karel'skaya A.S.S.R. aut. rep. Rus. Fed. see Kareliya, Respublika
Karel'skiy Bereg coastal area Rus. Fed. 54 R3
Karema Tanz. 123 D4
Karera India 104 D4
Karesuando Sweden 54 M2
Karevāndar Iran 111 F5
Kargalinskaya Rus. Fed. 113 G2
Kargalinski Rus. Fed. see Kargalinskaya
Kargaly Kazakh. 98 A2
Kargapazarı Dağları mts Turkey 113 F3
Karghalik Xinjiang China see Yecheng
Kargı Turkey 112 D2
Kargil India 104 D2
Kargilik Xinjiang China see Yecheng
Kargıpınarı Turkey 107 B1
Kargopol' Rus. Fed. 52 H3
Kari Nigeria 120 E3
Karīān Iran 110 E5
Kariba Zimbabwe 123 C5
Kariba, Lake resr Zambia/Zimbabwe 123 C5
Kariba Dam Zambia/Zimbabwe 123 C5
Kariba-yama vol. Japan 90 E4
Karibib Namibia 124 B1
Karigasniemi Fin. 54 N2
Karijini National Park Australia 135 B5
Karijoki Fin. 54 L5
Karikachi-tōge pass Japan 90 F4
Karikari, Cape N.Z. 139 D2
Karimata i. Indon. 85 E3
Karimata, Pulau-pulau is Indon. 85 E3
Karimata, Selat str. Indon. 85 E3
Karimganj India 105 H4
Karimnagar India 106 C2
Karimun Besar i. Indon. 84 C2
Karimunjawa i. Indon. 85 E4
Karimunjawa, Pulau-pulau is Indon. 85 E4
Káristos Greece see Karystos
Kariya Japan 92 C4
Karjat Mahar. India 106 B2
Karjat Mahar. India 106 B2
Karkaralinsk Kazakh. 102 E2
Karkaralong, Kepulauan is Indon. 82 D5
Karkar Island P.N.G. 81 L7
Karkh Pak. 111 G5
Karkinits'ka Zatoka g. Ukr. 69 O2
Kärkölä Fin. 55 N6
Karkonoski Park Narodowy nat. park Czech Rep./Poland see Krkonošský národní park
Karksi-Nuia Estonia 55 N7
Karkük Iraq see Kirkūk
Karlachi Pak. 111 H3
Karlholmsbruk Sweden 55 J6
Karlik Shan mts Xinjiang China 94 C3
Karlıova Turkey 113 F3
Karlivka Ukr. 53 G6
Karl Marks, Qullai mt. Tajik. 111 I2
Karl-Marx-Stadt Germany see Chemnitz
Karlovac Croatia 68 F2
Karlovka Ukr. see Karlivka
Karlovo Bulg. 69 K3
Karlovy Vary Czech Rep. 63 M4
Karlsbad Germany 63 I6
Karlsborg Sweden 55 I7
Karlsburg Romania see Alba Iulia
Karlshamn Sweden 55 I8
Karlskoga Sweden 55 I7
Karlskrona Sweden 55 I8
Karlsruhe Germany 63 I5
Karlstad Sweden 55 H7
Karlstad U.S.A. 160 D1
Karlstadt Germany 63 J5
Karluk AK U.S.A. 148 I4
Karlyk Turkm. 111 G2
Karmala India 106 B2
Karmel, Har hill Israel see Carmel, Mount
Karmona Spain see Córdoba
Karmøy i. Norway 55 D7
Karmpur Pak. 111 I4
Karnafuli Reservoir Bangl. 105 H5
Karnal India 104 D3
Karnali r. Nepal 99 C7
Karnataka state India 106 B3
Karnavati India see Ahmadabad
Karnes City U.S.A. 161 D6
Karnobat Bulg. 69 L3
Karodi Pak. 111 G5
Karoi Zimbabwe 123 C5
Karokpi Myanmar 86 B4
Karo La pass Xizang China 99 E7
Karompalompo i. Indon. 83 B4
Karong India 105 H4
Karonga Malawi 123 D4
Karonie Australia 135 C7
Karool-Döbö Kyrg. 98 B4
Karoo National Park S. Africa 124 F7
Karoo Nature Reserve S. Africa see Camdeboo National Park
Karoonda Australia 137 B7
Karora Eritrea 108 E6
Káros i. Greece see Keros
Karossa Sulawesi Barat Indon. 83 A3
Karossa, Tanjung pt Sumba Indon. 85 G5
Karow Germany 63 M1
Karpasia pen. Cyprus 107 B2
Karpas Peninsula Cyprus see Karpasia
Karpathos i. Greece 69 L7
Karpathou, Steno sea chan. Greece 69 L6
Karpaty mts Europe see Carpathian Mountains
Karpenisi Greece 69 I5
Karpilovka Belarus see Aktsyabrski
Karpinsk Rus. Fed. 51 S4
Karpogory Rus. Fed. 52 J2
Karpuz r. Turkey 107 A1
Karratha Australia 134 B5
Karroo plat. S. Africa see Great Karoo
Karrychirla Turkm. see Garryçyrla
Kars Turkey 113 F2
Kärsämäki Fin. 54 N5
Kārsava Latvia 55 O8
Karshi Qashqadaryo Uzbek. see Qarshi
Karskiye Vorota, Proliv strait Rus. Fed. 76 G3
Karskoye More sea Rus. Fed. see Kara Sea
Karstädt Germany 63 L1
Karstula Fin. 54 N5
Karsu Turkey 107 C1
Karsun Rus. Fed. 53 J5
Kartal Turkey 69 M4
Kartaly Rus. Fed. 76 H4
Kartayel' Rus. Fed. 52 L2
Karttula Fin. 54 O5
Karuizawa Japan 93 E2
Karumba Australia 136 C3
Karumbhar Island India 104 B5
Karun, Kūh-e hill Iran 110 C4
Kārūn, Rūd-e r. Iran 110 C4
Karuni Sumba Indon. 83 A5
Karur India 106 C4
Karvia Fin. 54 M5
Karviná Czech Rep. 57 Q6
Karwar India 106 B3
Karyagino Azer. see Füzuli
Karymskoye Rus. Fed. 89 K2
Karynzharyk, Peski des. Kazakh. 113 I2
Karystos Greece 69 K5
Kaş Turkey 69 M6
Kasa India 106 B2
Kasaba Turkey see Turgutlu
Kasabonika Canada 152 C3
Kasabonika Lake Canada 152 C3
Kasaga-dake mt. Japan 92 D2
Kasagi Japan 92 B4
Kasagi-yama mt. Japan 92 D3
Kasahara Japan 92 D3
Kasaï r. Dem. Rep. Congo 122 B4
also known as Kwa
Kasai Japan 92 A4
Kasaï, Plateau du Dem. Rep. Congo 123 C4
Kasaji Dem. Rep. Congo 123 C5
Kasama Japan 93 G2
Kasama Zambia 123 D5
Kasamatsu Japan 92 C3
Kasan Uzbek. see Koson
Kasane Botswana 123 C5
Kasano-misaki pt Japan 92 C2
Kasaragod India 106 B3
Kasargod India see Kasaragod
Kasargode India see Kasaragod
Kasatkino Rus. Fed. 90 C2
Kasatori-yama hill Japan 92 C4
Kasba Lake Canada 151 K2
Kasba Tadla Morocco 64 C5
Kasegaluk Lagoon AK U.S.A. 148 G1
Kasenga Dem. Rep. Congo 123 C5
Kasengu Dem. Rep. Congo 123 C4
Kasese Dem. Rep. Congo 122 C4
Kasese Uganda 122 D3
Kasevo Rus. Fed. see Neftekamsk
Kasganj India 104 D4
Kasha China 96 C2
Kashabowie Canada 152 C4
Kāshān Iran 110 C3
Kashary Rus. Fed. 53 I6
Kashechewan Canada 152 E3
Kashega AK U.S.A. 148 F5
Kashegelok AK U.S.A. 148 H3
Kashgar Xinjiang China see Kashi
Kashi Xinjiang China 98 B5
Kashiba Japan 92 B4
Kashihara Japan 92 B4
Kashima Ibaraki Japan 93 G3
Kashima Ishikawa Japan 92 C2
Kashima-nada b. Japan 93 G3
Kashimayaria-dake mt. Japan 92 D2
Kashimo Japan 92 D3
Kashin Rus. Fed. 52 H4
Kashipur India 104 D3
Kashira Rus. Fed. 53 H5
Kashiwa Japan 93 F3
Kashiwara Japan 92 B4
Kashiwazaki Japan 91 E5
Kashkanteniz Kazakh. 98 A3
Kashkarantsy Rus. Fed. 52 H2
Kashku'iyeh Iran 110 D4
Kāshmar Iran 110 E3
Kashmir terr. Asia see Jammu and Kashmir
Kashmir, Vale of reg. India 104 C2
Kashunuk r. AK U.S.A. 148 F3
Kashyukulu Dem. Rep. Congo 123 C4
Kasi India see Varanasi
Kasigar Afgh. 111 H3
Kasigluk AK U.S.A. 148 G3
Kasimbar Sulawesi Indon. 83 A3
Kasimov Rus. Fed. 53 I5
Kasiruta i. Maluku Indon. 83 C3
Kaskattama r. Canada 151 N3
Kaskelen Kazakh. 98 B4
Kaskinen Fin. 54 L5
Kas Klong i. Cambodia see Kŏng, Kaôh
Kaskö Fin. see Kaskinen
Kaslo Canada 150 G5

Kasmere Lake Canada **151** K3
Kasongan *Kalimantan* Indon. **85** F3
Kasongo Dem. Rep. Congo **123** C4
Kasongo-Lunda Dem. Rep. Congo **123** B4
Kasos *i.* Greece **69** L7
Kaspiy Mangy Oypaty *lowland* Kazakh./Rus. Fed. *see* **Caspian Lowland**
Kaspiysk Rus. Fed. **113** G2
Kaspiyskiy Rus. Fed. *see* **Lagan'**
Kaspiyskoye More *l.* Asia/Europe *see* **Caspian Sea**
Kassa Slovakia *see* **Košice**
Kassala Sudan **108** E6
Kassandras, Akra *pt* Greece *see* **Kassandras, Akrotirio**
Kassandras, Akrotirio *pt* Greece **69** J5
Kassandras, Kolpos *b.* Greece **69** J4
Kassel Germany **63** J3
Kasserine Tunisia **68** C7
Kastag Pak. **111** F5
Kastamonu Turkey **112** D2
Kastellaun Germany **63** H4
Kastelli *Kriti* Greece *see* **Kissamos**
Kastéllion Greece *see* **Kissamos**
Kastéllion *Kriti* Greece *see* **Kissamos**
Kastellorizon *i.* Greece *see* **Megisti**
Kasterlee Belgium **62** E3
Kastoria Greece **69** I4
Kastornoye Rus. Fed. **53** H6
Kastsyukovichy Belarus **53** G5
Kasuga *Gifu* Japan **92** C3
Kasuga *Hyōgo* Japan **92** B3
Kasugai Japan **92** C3
Kasukabe Japan **93** F3
Kasukawa Japan **93** F2
Kasulu Tanz. **123** D4
Kasumigaura Japan **93** G2
Kasumiga-ura *l.* Japan **93** G2
Kasumkent Rus. Fed. **113** H2
Kasungu Malawi **123** D5
Kasungu National Park Malawi **123** D5
Kasur Pak. **111** I4
Katâdtlit Nunât *terr.* N. America *see* **Greenland**
Katahdin, Mount U.S.A. **162** G2
Kataklik India **104** D2
Katako-Kombe Dem. Rep. Congo **122** C4
Katakwi Uganda **122** D3
Katalla *AK* U.S.A. **149** K3
Katana India **104** C5
Katangi India **104** D5
Katanning Australia **135** B8
Katano Japan **92** B4
Katashina Japan **93** F2
Katashina-gawa *r.* Japan **93** F2
Katata Japan **92** B3
Katavi National Park Tanz. **123** D4
Katawaz *reg.* Afgh. **111** G3
Katchall *i.* India **87** A6
Katea Dem. Rep. Congo **123** C4
Kateel *r. AK* U.S.A. **148** H2
Katerini Greece **69** J4
Katesh Tanz. **123** D4
Kate's Needle *mt.* Canada/U.S.A. **149** N4
Katete Zambia **123** D5
Katherîna, Gebel *mt.* Egypt *see* **Kātrīnā, Jabal**
Katherine Australia **134** F3
Katherine Gorge National Park Australia *see* **Nitmiluk National Park**
Kathi India **111** I6
Kathiawar *pen.* India **104** B5
Kathihar India *see* **Katihar**
Kathiraveli Sri Lanka **106** D4
Kathiwara India **104** C5
Kathleen Falls Australia **134** E3

▶**Kathmandu** Nepal **105** F4
Capital of Nepal.

Kathu S. Africa **124** F4
Kathua India **104** C2
Kati Mali **120** C3
Katibas *r.* Malaysia **85** F2
Katihar India **105** F4
Katikati S. Africa **125** H7
Katima Mulilo Namibia **123** C5
Katimik Lake Canada **151** L4
Katiola Côte d'Ivoire **120** C4
Kā Tiritiri o te Moana *mts* N.Z. *see* **Southern Alps**
Katkop Hills S. Africa **124** E6
Katlehong S. Africa **125** I4
Katma *Xinjiang* China **99** D5
Katmai National Park and Preserve U.S.A. **146** C4
Katmandu Nepal *see* **Kathmandu**
Kato Achaïa Greece **69** I5
Kat O Chau *H.K.* China *see* **Crooked Island**
Kat O Hoi *b. H.K.* China *see* **Crooked Harbour**
Katon-Karagay Kazakh. **98** D2
Katoomba Australia **138** E4
Katoposa, Gunung *mt.* Indon. **83** B3
Katowice Poland **57** Q5
Katoya India **105** G5
Katrancık Dağı *mts* Turkey **69** M6
Kātrīnā, Jabal *mt.* Egypt **112** D5
Katrine, Loch *l.* U.K. **60** E4
Katrineholm Sweden **55** J7
Katse Dam Lesotho **125** I5
Katsina Nigeria **120** D3
Katsina-Ala Nigeria **120** D4
Katsunuma Japan **93** E3
Katsura-gawa *r.* Japan **93** F3
Katsuragi-san *hill* Japan **92** B4
Katsuura Japan **93** G3
Katsuyama *Fukui* Japan **92** C2
Kattaktoc, Cap *c.* Canada **153** I2
Kattamudda Well Australia **134** D5
Kattaqo'rg'on Uzbek. **111** G2
Kattaqŭrghon Uzbek. *see* **Kattaqo'rg'on**
Kattasang Hills Afgh. **111** G3
Kattegat *strait* Denmark/Sweden **55** G8
Kattowitz Poland *see* **Katowice**
Katumbar India **104** D4
Katun' *r.* Rus. Fed. **98** D1
Katunino Rus. Fed. **52** J4
Katunskiy Khrebet *mts* Rus. Fed. **98** D2
Katuri Pak. **111** H4
Katwa India *see* **Katoya**
Katwijk aan Zee Neth. **62** E2
Katzenbuckel *hill* Germany **63** J5
Kaua'i *i.* U.S.A. **157** [inset]
Kaua'i Channel U.S.A. **157** [inset]
Kaub Germany **63** H4
Kaufungen Germany **63** J3
Kauhajoki Fin. **54** M5
Kauhava Fin. **54** M5
Kaukauna U.S.A. **164** A1
Kaukkwè Hills Myanmar **86** B1
Kaukonen Fin. **54** N3
Ka'ula *i.* U.S.A. **157** [inset]
Kaulakahi Channel U.S.A. **157** [inset]
Kaumajet Mountains Canada **153** J2
Kaunakakai U.S.A. **157** [inset]
Kaunas Lith. **55** M9
Kaunata Latvia **55** O8
Kaundy, Vpadina *depr.* Kazakh. **113** I2
Kaunia Bangl. **105** G4
Kaura-Namoda Nigeria **120** D3
Kau Sai Chau *i. H.K.* China **97** [inset]
Kaustinen Fin. **54** M5
Kautokeino Norway **54** M2
Kau-ye Kyun *i.* Myanmar **87** B5
Kavadarci Macedonia **69** J4
Kavak Turkey **112** E2
Kavaklıdere Turkey **69** M6
Kavala Greece **69** K4
Kavalas, Kolpos *b.* Greece **69** K4
Kavalerovo Rus. Fed. **90** D3
Kavali India **106** D3
Kavār Iran **110** D4
Kavaratti India **106** B4
Kavaratti *atoll* India **106** B4
Kavarna Bulg. **69** M3
Kavendou, Mont *mt.* Guinea **120** B3
Kaveri *r.* India **106** C4
Kavīr Iran **110** C3
Kavīr, Dasht-e *des.* Iran **110** D3
Kavīr Kūshk *well* Iran **110** E3
Kavkasioni *mts* Asia/Europe *see* **Caucasus**
Kawa *Seram* Indon. **83** D3
Kawa Myanmar **86** B3
Kawabe *Gifu* Japan **92** D3
Kawabe *Wakayama* Japan **92** B5
Kawachi *Ibaraki* Japan **93** G3
Kawachi *Ishikawa* Japan **92** C2
Kawachi *Tochigi* Japan **93** F2
Kawachi-Nagano Japan **92** B4
Kawagama Lake Canada **165** F1
Kawage Japan **92** C4
Kawagoe Japan **93** F3
Kawaguchi *Saitama* Japan **93** F3
Kawaguchiko Japan **93** E3
Kawaguchi-ko *l.* Japan **93** E3
Kawai *Gifu* Japan **92** D2
Kawaihae U.S.A. **157** [inset]
Kawaikini U.S.A. **157** [inset]
Kawakami *Nagano* Japan **93** E3
Kawakami *Nara* Japan **92** B4
Kawakawa N.Z. **139** E2
Kawakita Japan **92** C2
Kawambwa Zambia **123** C4
Kawamoto Japan **93** F2
Kawana Zambia **123** C5
Kawanakajima Japan **93** E2
Kawana-zaki *pt* Japan **93** F4
Kawane Japan **93** E4
Kawangkoan *Sulawesi* Indon. **83** C2
Kawanishi Japan **92** B3
Kawarazawa-gawa *r.* Japan **93** F2
Kawardha India **104** E5
Kawartha Lakes Canada **165** F1
Kawasaki Japan **93** F3
Kawashima Japan **92** C3
Kawato *Sulawesi* Indon. **83** B3
Kawaue Japan **92** D3
Kawau Island N.Z. **139** E3
Kawawachikamach Canada **153** I3
Kawazu Japan **93** E4
Kawdut Myanmar **86** B4
Kawe *i. Papua* Indon. **83** D2
Kawerau N.Z. **139** F4
Kawhia N.Z. **139** E4
Kawhia Harbour N.Z. **139** E4
Kawich Peak U.S.A. **158** E3
Kawich Range *mts* U.S.A. **158** E3
Kawinaw Lake Canada **151** L4
Kawinda *Sumbawa* Indon. **85** G5
Kawio *i.* Indon. **83** C1
Kaw Lake U.S.A. **161** D4
Kawlin Myanmar **86** A2
Kawm Umbū Egypt **108** D5
Kawngmeum Myanmar **86** B2
Kawthaung Myanmar **87** B5
Kaxgar *Xinjiang* China *see* **Kashi**
Kaxgar He *r.* China **98** B4
Kax He *r.* China **98** C4
Kaxtax Shan *mts* China **99** C5
Kaya Burkina Faso **120** C3
Kayadibi Turkey **112** E3
Kayaga-take *mt.* Japan **93** E3
Kayak Island *AK* U.S.A. **149** K4
Kayan *r.* Indon. **85** E3
Kayan *r.* Indon. **85** G2
Kayangel Atoll Palau **82** [inset]
Kayangel Passage Palau **82** [inset]
Kayankulam India **106** C4
Kayan Mentarang, Taman Nasional *nat. park* Indon. **85** F2
Kayar India **106** C2
Kayasa *Halmahera* Indon. **83** C2
Kaycee U.S.A. **156** G4
Kaydak, Sor *dry lake* Kazakh. **113** I1
Kaydanovo Belarus *see* **Dzyarzhynsk**
Kayembe-Mukulu Dem. Rep. Congo **123** C4
Kayenta U.S.A. **159** H3
Kayes Mali **120** B3
Kayigyalik Lake *AK* U.S.A. **148** G3
Kaymaz Turkey **69** N5
Kaynar Kazakh. **102** E2
Kaynar *Zhambylskaya Oblast'* Kazakh. **98** A4
Kaynar Turkey **112** E3
Kaynupil'gyn, Laguna *lag.* Rus. Fed. **148** B3
Kayo Japan **92** B3
Kayoa *i. Maluku* Indon. **83** C2
Kay Point *pt Y.T.* Canada **149** M1
Kayseri Turkey **112** D3
Kayuadi *i.* Indon. **83** B4
Kayuagung *Sumatera* Indon. **84** D3
Kayuyu Dem. Rep. Congo **122** C4
Kayyngdy Kyrg. **102** D3
Kazach'ye Rus. Fed. **77** O2
Kazakh Azer. *see* **Qazax**
Kazakhskaya S.S.R. *country* Asia *see* **Kazakhstan**
Kazakhskiy Melkosopochnik *plain* Kazakh. **102** D1
Kazakhskiy Zaliv *b.* Kazakh. **113** I2

▶**Kazakhstan** *country* Asia **100** F2
4th largest country in Asia, and 9th in the world.

Kazakhstan Kazakh. *see* **Aksay**
Kazakstan *country* Asia *see* **Kazakhstan**
Kazan *r.* Canada **151** M2
Kazan' Rus. Fed. **52** K5
Kazanchunkur Kazakh. **98** C2
Kazandzhik Turkm. *see* **Bereket**
Kazanka *r.* Rus. Fed. **52** K5
Kazanlı Turkey **107** B1
Kazanlŭk Bulg. **69** K3
Kazan-rettō *is* Japan *see* **Volcano Islands**
Kazatin Ukr. *see* **Kozyatyn**

▶**Kazbek** *mt.* Georgia/Rus. Fed. **53** J8
4th highest mountain in Europe.

Kaz Dağı *mts* Turkey **69** L5
Kāzerūn Iran **110** C4
Kazhim Rus. Fed. **52** K3
Kazidi Tajik. *see* **Qozideh**
Kazi Magomed Azer. *see* **Qazımämmäd**
Kazincbarcika Hungary **53** D6
Kaziranga National Park India **105** H4
Kazo Japan **93** F2
Kazret'i Georgia **113** G2
Kaztalovka Kazakh. **51** P6
Kazusa Japan **93** G3
Kazy Turkm. **110** E2
Kazym *r.* Rus. Fed. **51** T3
Kazymskiy Mys Rus. Fed. **51** T3
Keady U.K. **61** F3
Keams Canyon U.S.A. **159** H4
Kéamu *i.* Vanuatu *see* **Anatom**
Kearney U.S.A. **160** D3
Kearny U.S.A. **159** H5
Keban Turkey **112** E3
Keban Barajı *resr* Turkey **112** E3
Kebatu *i.* Indon. **85** E3
Kébémèr Senegal **120** B3
Kebili Tunisia **64** F5
Kebīr, Nahr al *r.* Lebanon/Syria **107** B2
Kebkabiya Sudan **121** F3
Kebnekaise *mt.* Sweden **54** K3
Kebock Head *hd* U.K. **60** C2
K'ebrī Dehar Eth. **122** E3
Kebumen *Jawa* Indon. **85** E4
Kebur *Sumatera* Indon. **84** C3
Kech *reg.* Pak. **111** F5
Kecheng *Qinghai* China **94** D4
Kechika *r. B.C.* Canada **149** P4
Keçiborlu Turkey **69** N6
Kecskemét Hungary **69** H1
K'eda Georgia **113** F2
Kedah *state* Malaysia **84** C1
Kėdainiai Lith. **55** M9
Kedairu Passage Fiji *see* **Kadavu Passage**
Kedarnath Peak *Uttaranchal* India **99** B7
Kedgwick Canada **153** I5
Kedian China **97** G2
Kediri *Jawa* Indon. **85** F4
Kedong China **90** B3
Kedva *r.* Rus. Fed. **52** L2
Kędzierzyn-Koźle Poland **57** Q5
Keele *r. Y.T.* Canada **149** P2
Keele Peak *Y.T.* Canada **149** O3
Keeler U.S.A. **158** E3
Keeley Lake Canada **151** I4
Keeling Islands *terr.* Indian Ocean *see* **Cocos Islands**
Keen, Mount *hill* U.K. **60** G4
Keenapusan *i.* Phil. **82** B5
Keene *CA* U.S.A. **158** D4
Keene *KY* U.S.A. **164** C5
Keene *NH* U.S.A. **165** I2
Keene *OH* U.S.A. **164** E3
Keeper Hill *hill* Ireland **61** D5
Keepit, Lake *resr* Australia **138** E3
Keep River National Park Australia **134** E3
Keerbergen Belgium **62** E3
Keer-weer, Cape Australia **136** C2
Keetmanshoop Namibia **124** D4
Keewatin Canada **151** M5
Kefallinía *i.* Greece *see* **Cephalonia**
Kefallonia *i.* Greece *see* **Cephalonia**
Kefamenanu *Timor* Indon. **83** C5
Kefe Ukr. *see* **Feodosiya**
Keffi Nigeria **120** D4
Keflavík Iceland **54** [inset]
Kê Ga, Mui *pt* Vietnam **87** E5
Kegalla Sri Lanka **106** D5
Kegen Kazakh. **102** E3
Kegeti Kyrg. **98** A4
Keglo, Baie de *b.* Canada **153** I2
Keg River Canada **150** G3
Kegul'ta Rus. Fed. **53** J7
Kehra Estonia **55** N7
Kehsi Mansam Myanmar **86** B2
Keighley U.K. **58** F5
Keihoku Japan **92** B3
Keila Estonia **55** N7
Keimoes S. Africa **124** E5
Keitele Fin. **54** O5
Keitele *l.* Fin. **54** O5
Keith Australia **137** C8
Keith U.K. **60** G3
Keith Arm *b. N.W.T.* Canada **149** Q2
Kejimkujik National Park Canada **153** I5
Kekachi-yama *mt.* Japan **92** D2
Kekaha U.S.A. **157** [inset]
Kékes *mt.* Hungary **57** R7
Kekik *i. Maluku* Indon. **83** D3
Keklau Palau **82** [inset]
Kekri India **104** C4
K'elafo Eth. **122** E3
Kelai *i.* Maldives **106** B5
Kelan *Shanxi* China **95** G4
Kelang *i. Maluku* Indon. **83** C3
Kelang Malaysia *see* **Klang**
Kelantan *r.* Malaysia **84** C1
Kelantan *state* Malaysia **84** C1
Kelapa *i. Maluku* Indon. **83** D5
Kelara *r.* Indon. **83** A4
Kelawar *i.* Indon. **85** E3
Kelberg Germany **62** G4
Kelheim Germany **63** L6
Kelibia Tunisia **68** D6
Kelif Uzboýy *marsh* Turkm. **111** F2
Kelīrī Iran **110** E5
Kelkheim (Taunus) Germany **63** I4
Kelkit Turkey **113** E2
Kelkit *r.* Turkey **112** E2
Kéllé Congo **122** B4
Keller Lake Canada **150** F2
Kellett, Cape Canada **146** F2
Kelleys Island U.S.A. **164** D3
Kelliher Canada **151** K5
Kelloselkä Fin. **54** P3
Kells Ireland **61** F4
Kells *r.* U.K. **61** F3
Kelly U.S.A. **164** B5
Kelly *r. AK* U.S.A. **148** G2
Kelly, Mount *hill AK* U.S.A. **148** G1
Kelly Lake *N.W.T.* Canada **149** P2
Kelly Range *hills* Australia **135** C6
Kelmė Lith. **55** M9
Kelmis Belgium **62** G4
Kélo Chad **121** E4
Kelowna Canada **150** G5
Kelp Head *hd* Canada **150** E5
Kelseyville U.S.A. **158** B2
Kelso U.K. **60** G5
Kelso *CA* U.S.A. **159** F4
Kelso *WA* U.S.A. **156** C3
Keluang Malaysia **84** C2
Kelvington Canada **151** K4
Kem' Rus. Fed. **52** G2
Kem' *r.* Rus. Fed. **52** G2
Kemabung *Sabah* Malaysia **85** F1
Ke Macina Mali *see* **Massina**
Kemah Turkey **112** E3
Kemaliye Turkey **112** E3
Kemalpaşa Turkey **69** L5
Kemano (abandoned) Canada **150** E4
Kemasik Malaysia **84** C1
Kembayan *Kalimantan* Indon. **85** E2
Kembé Cent. Afr. Rep. **122** C3
Kemeneshát *hills* Hungary **68** G1
Kemer *Antalya* Turkey **69** N6
Kemer *Muğla* Turkey **69** M6
Kemer Barajı *resr* Turkey **69** M6
Kemerovo Rus. Fed. **76** J4
Kemi Fin. **54** N4
Kemijärvi Fin. **54** O3
Kemijärvi *l.* Fin. **54** O3
Kemijoki *r.* Fin. **54** N4
Kemin Kyrg. **98** A4
Kemiö Fin. *see* **Kimito**
Kemir Turkm. *see* **Keymir**
Kemmerer U.S.A. **156** F4
Kemnath Germany **63** L5
Kemnay U.K. **60** G3
Kemp Coast *reg.* Antarctica *see* **Kemp Land**
Kempele Fin. **54** N4
Kempen Germany **62** G3
Kempisch Kanaal *canal* Belgium **62** F3
Kemp Land *reg.* Antarctica **188** D2
Kemp Peninsula Antarctica **188** A2
Kemp's Bay Bahamas **163** E7
Kempsey Australia **138** F3
Kempt, Lac *l.* Canada **152** G5
Kempten (Allgäu) Germany **57** M7
Kempton U.S.A. **164** B3
Kempton Park S. Africa **125** I4
Kemptville Canada **165** H1
Kemujan *i.* Indon. **85** E4
Ken *r.* India **104** E4
Kenai *AK* U.S.A. **149** J3
Kenai Fiords National Park *AK* U.S.A. **149** J4
Kenai Lake *AK* U.S.A. **149** J3
Kenai Mountains *AK* U.S.A. **149** J4
Kenai National Wildlife Refuge *nature res. AK* U.S.A. **149** J3
Kenai Peninsula *AK* U.S.A. **149** J3
Kenam, Tanjung *pt* Indon. **84** D4
Kenamu *r.* Canada **153** K3
Kenansville U.S.A. **163** E5
Kenâyis, Râs el *pt* Egypt *see* **Ḥikmah, Ra's al**
Kenbridge U.S.A. **165** F5
Kencong *Jawa* Indon. **85** F5
Kendal *Jawa* Indon. **85** E4
Kendal U.K. **58** E4
Kendall Australia **138** F3
Kendall, Cape Canada **147** J3
Kendall Island Bird Sanctuary *nature res. N.W.T.* Canada **149** N1
Kendallville U.S.A. **164** C3
Kendari *Sulawesi* Indon. **83** B3
Kendawangan *Kalimantan* Indon. **85** E3
Kendawangan *r.* Indon. **85** E3
Kendégué Chad **121** E3
Kendrapara India **105** F5
Kendraparha India *see* **Kendrapara**
Kendrick Peak U.S.A. **159** H4
Kendujhar India *see* **Keonjhar**
Kendujhargarh India *see* **Keonjhar**
Kendyktas *mts* Kazakh. **98** A4
Kendyrli-Kayasanskoye, Plato *plat.* Kazakh. **113** I2
Kendyrlisor, Solonchak *salt l.* Kazakh. **113** I2
Kenebri Australia **138** D3
Kenedy U.S.A. **161** D6
Kenema Sierra Leone **120** B4
Kenepai, Gunung *mt.* Indon. **85** E2
Kenge Dem. Rep. Congo **123** B4
Keng Lap Myanmar **86** C2
Kengtung Myanmar **86** B2
Kenhardt S. Africa **124** E5
Kéniéba Mali **120** B3
Kénitra Morocco **64** C5
Kenli *Shandong* China **95** I4
Kenmare Ireland **61** C6
Kenmare U.S.A. **160** C1
Kenmare River *inlet* Ireland **61** B6
Kenmore U.S.A. **165** F2
Kenn Germany **62** G5
Kenna U.S.A. **161** C5
Kennebec U.S.A. **160** D3
Kennebec *r.* U.S.A. **162** G2
Kennebunkport U.S.A. **165** J2
Kennedy, Cape U.S.A. *see* **Canaveral, Cape**
Kennedy Entrance *sea channel AK* U.S.A. **148** I4
Kennedy Range National Park Australia **135** A6
Kennedy Town *H.K.* China **97** [inset]
Kenner U.S.A. **161** F6
Kennet *r.* U.K. **59** G7
Kenneth Range *hills* Australia **135** B5
Kennett U.S.A. **161** F4
Kennewick U.S.A. **156** D3
Kennicott *AK* U.S.A. **149** L3
Kenn Reef Australia **136** F4
Kenny Lake *AK* U.S.A. **149** K3
Kenogami *r.* Canada **152** D4
Keno Hill *Y.T.* Canada **149** N3
Kenora Canada **151** M5
Kenosha U.S.A. **164** B2
Kenozero, Ozero *l.* Rus. Fed. **52** H3
Kent *r.* U.K. **58** E4
Kent *OH* U.S.A. **164** E3
Kent *TX* U.S.A. **161** B6
Kent *VA* U.S.A. **164** E5
Kent *WA* U.S.A. **156** C3
Kentani S. Africa **125** I7
Kent Group *is* Australia **137** [inset]
Kentland U.S.A. **164** B3
Kenton U.S.A. **164** D3
Kent Peninsula Canada **146** H3
Kentucky *state* U.S.A. **164** C5
Kentucky Lake U.S.A. **161** F4
Kentwood *LA* U.S.A. **167** H2
Kenya *country* Africa **122** D3

▶**Kenya, Mount** Kenya **122** D4
2nd highest mountain in Africa.

Kenyir, Tasik *resr* Malaysia **84** C1
Ken-zaki *pt* Japan **93** F3
Keokuk U.S.A. **160** F3
Keoladeo National Park India **104** D4
Keonjhar India **105** F5
Keonjhargarh India *see* **Keonjhar**
Keosauqua U.S.A. **160** F3
Keowee, Lake *resr* U.S.A. **163** D5
Kepahiang *Sumatera* Indon. **84** C3
Kepina *r.* Rus. Fed. **52** I2
Keppel Bay Australia **136** E4
Kepsut Turkey **69** M5
Kepulauan Bangka-Belitung *prov.* Indon. *see* **Bangka-Belitung**
Kera India **105** F5
Kerāh Iran **110** E4
Kerala *state* India **106** B4
Kerang Australia **138** A5
Kerava Fin. **55** N6
Kerba Alg. **67** G5
Kerbau, Tanjung *pt* Indon. **84** C3
Kerbela Iraq *see* **Karbalā'**
Kerben Kyrg. **102** D3
Kerbi *r.* Rus. Fed. **90** E1
Kerbodot, Lac *l.* Canada **153** I3
Kerch Ukr. **112** E1
Kerchem'ya Rus. Fed. **52** L3
Kerema P.N.G. **81** L8
Keremeos Canada **150** G5
Kerempe Burun *pt* Turkey **112** D2
Keren Eritrea **108** E6
Kerewan Gambia **120** B3
Kergeli Turkm. **110** E2
Kerguélen, Îles *is* Indian Ocean **185** M9
Kerguelen Islands Indian Ocean *see* **Kerguélen, Îles**
Kerguelen Plateau *sea feature* Indian Ocean **185** M9
Kericho Kenya **122** D4
Kerihun *mt.* Indon. **85** F2
Kerikeri N.Z. **139** D2
Kerimäki Fin. **54** P6
Kerinci, Danau *l.* Indon. **84** C3
Kerinci, Gunung *vol.* Indon. **84** C3
Kerinci Seblat, Taman Nasional *nat. park* Indon. **84** C3
Kerintji *vol.* Indon. *see* **Kerinci, Gunung**
Keriya *Xinjiang* China *see* **Yutian**
Keriya He *watercourse* China **99** C5
Keriya Shankou *pass Xinjiang* China **99** C6
Kerken Germany **62** G3
Kerkennah, Îles *is* Tunisia **68** D7
Kerkiçi Turkm. **111** G2
Kerkini, Limni *l.* Greece **69** J4
Kerkinitis, Limni *l.* Greece *see* **Kerkini, Limni**
Kérkira *i.* Greece *see* **Corfu**
Kerkouane *tourist site* Tunisia **68** D6
Kerkyra Greece **69** H5
Kerkyra *i.* Greece *see* **Corfu**
Kerma Sudan **108** D6
Kermadec Islands S. Pacific Ocean **133** I5

▶**Kermadec Trench** *sea feature* S. Pacific Ocean **186** I8
4th deepest trench in the world.

Kermān Iran **110** E4
Kerman U.S.A. **158** C3
Kermān, Bīābān-e Iran **110** E4
Kermānshāh Iran **110** B3
Kermānshāhān Iran **110** D4
Kermine Uzbek. *see* **Navoiy**
Kermit U.S.A. **161** C6
Kern *r.* U.S.A. **158** D4
Kernertut, Cap *c.* Canada **153** I2
Keroh Malaysia *see* **Pengkalan Hulu**
Keros *i.* Greece **69** K6
Keros Rus. Fed. **52** L3
Kérouané Guinea **120** C4
Kerpen Germany **62** G4
Kerr, Cape Antarctica **188** H1
Kerrobert Canada **151** I5
Kerrville U.S.A. **161** D6
Kerry Head *hd* Ireland **61** C5
Kerteh Malaysia **84** C1
Kerteminde Denmark **55** G9
Kertosono *Jawa* Indon. **85** F4
Keruak *Lombok* Indon. **85** G5
Kerulen *r.* China/Mongolia *see* **Herlen Gol**
Kerumutan, Suaka Margasatwa *nature res.* Indon. **84** C3
Kerur India **106** B2
Keryneia Cyprus *see* **Kyrenia**
Kerzaz Alg. **120** C2
Kerzhenets *r.* Rus. Fed. **52** J4
Kesagami Lake Canada **152** E4
Kesälahti Fin. **54** P6
Keşan Turkey **69** L4
Keşap Turkey **53** H8
Kesariya India **105** F4
Kesennuma Japan **91** F5
Keshan China **90** B2
Keshem Afgh. **111** H2
Keshena U.S.A. **164** A1
Keshendeh-ye Bala Afgh. **111** G2
Keshod India **104** B5
Keshvar Iran **110** C3
Keskin Turkey **112** D3
Keskozero Rus. Fed. **52** G3
Kesova Gora Rus. Fed. **52** H4
Kessel Neth. **62** G3
Kestell S. Africa **125** I5
Kesten'ga Rus. Fed. **54** Q4
Kestilä Fin. **54** O4
Keswick Canada **164** F1
Keswick U.K. **58** D4
Keszthely Hungary **68** G1
Ketahun *Sumatera* Indon. **84** C3
Ketapang *Jawa* Indon. **85** F4
Ketapang *Kalimantan* Indon. **85** E3
Ketchikan *AK* U.S.A. **149** O5
Ketian *Qinghai* China **99** E6
Keti Bandar Pak. **111** G5
Ketik *r. AK* U.S.A. **148** H1
Ketlkede Mountain *hill AK* U.S.A. **148** H2
Ketmen', Khrebet *mts* China/Kazakh. **102** F3
Kettering U.K. **59** G6
Kettering U.S.A. **164** C4
Kettle *r.* Canada **150** G5
Kettle Creek *r.* U.S.A. **165** G3
Kettle Falls U.S.A. **156** D2
Kettleman City U.S.A. **158** D3
Kettle River Range *mts* U.S.A. **156** D2
Ketungau *r.* Indon. **85** E2
Keuka U.S.A. **165** G2
Keuka Lake U.S.A. **165** G2
Keumgang, Mount N. Korea *see* **Kumgang-san**
Keumsang, Mount N. Korea *see* **Kumgang-san**
Keuruu Fin. **54** N5
Kew Turks and Caicos Is **163** F8
Kewanee U.S.A. **160** F3
Kewapante *Flores* Indon. **83** B5
Kewaunee U.S.A. **164** B1
Keweenaw Bay U.S.A. **160** F2
Keweenaw Peninsula U.S.A. **160** F2
Keweenaw Point U.S.A. **162** C2
Key, Lough *l.* Ireland **61** D3
Keyala Sudan **121** G4
Keyano Canada **153** G3
Keya Paha *r.* U.S.A. **160** D3
Key Harbour Canada **152** E5
Keyi *Xinjiang* China **98** C4
Keyihe *Nei Mongol* China **95** J1
Key Largo U.S.A. **163** D7
Keymir Turkm. **110** D2
Keynsham U.K. **59** E7
Keyser U.S.A. **165** F4
Keystone Lake U.S.A. **161** D4
Keystone Peak U.S.A. **159** H6
Keysville U.S.A. **165** F5
Keytesville U.S.A. **160** E4
Keyvy, Vozvyshennost' *hills* Rus. Fed. **52** H2
Key West U.S.A. **163** D7
Kez Rus. Fed. **51** Q4
Kezi Zimbabwe **123** C6
Kgalagadi *admin. dist.* Botswana **124** E3
Kgalagadi Transfrontier National Park **125** D2
Kgalazadi *admin. dist.* Botswana *see* **Kgalagadi**
Kgatlen *admin. dist.* Botswana *see* **Kgatleng**
Kgatleng *admin. dist.* Botswana **125** H3
Kgomofatshe Pan *salt pan* Botswana **124** E2
Kgoro Pan *salt pan* Botswana **124** G3
Kgotsong S. Africa **125** H4
Kgun Lake *AK* U.S.A. **148** G3
Khabab Syria **107** C3
Khabar Iran **110** D4
Khabarikha Rus. Fed. **52** L2
Khabarovsk Rus. Fed. **90** D2
Khabarovskiy Kray *admin. div.* Rus. Fed. **90** D2
Khabarovsk Kray *admin. div.* Rus. Fed. *see* **Khabarovskiy Kray**
Khabary Rus. Fed. **88** D2
Khabis Iran *see* **Shahdād**
Khabody Pass Afgh. **111** F3
Khachmas Azer. *see* **Xaçmaz**
Khadar, Jabal *mt.* Oman **110** E6
Khadro Pak. **111** H5
Khadzhiolen Turkm. **110** E2
Khafs Banbān *well* Saudi Arabia **110** B5
Khagaria India **105** F4
Khagrachari Bangl. **105** G5
Khagrachhari Bangl. *see* **Khagrachari**
Khairgarh Pak. **111** H4
Khairpur *Punjab* Pak. **111** I4
Khairpur *Sindh* Pak. **111** H5
Khāīz, Kūh-e *mt.* Iran **110** C4
Khaja Du Koh *hill* Afgh. **111** G2
Khajuha India **104** E4
Khāk-e Jabbar Afgh. **111** H3
Khakhea Botswana **124** F3
Khak-rēz Afgh. **111** G4
Khakriz *reg.* Afgh. **111** G4
Khalajestan *reg.* Iran **110** C3
Khalatse India **104** D2
Khalifat *mt.* Pak. **111** G4
Khalīj Surt *g.* Libya *see* **Sirte, Gulf of**
Khalilabad India **105** E4
Khalīlī Iran **110** D5
Khalkabad Turkm. **111** F1
Khalkhāl Iran **110** C2
Khálki *i.* Greece *see* **Chalki**
Khalkís Greece *see* **Chalkida**
Khallikot India **106** E2
Khalturin Rus. Fed. *see* **Orlov**
Khamar-Daban, Khrebet *mts* Rus. Fed. **94** E1
Khamaria India **106** D1
Khambhat India **104** C5
Khambhat, Gulf of India **106** A2
Khamgaon India **106** C1
Khamir Yemen **108** F6
Khamis Mushayṭ Saudi Arabia **108** F6
Khamkkeut Laos **86** D3
Khamma *well* Saudi Arabia **110** B5
Khammam India **106** D2
Khammouan Laos *see* **Thakèk**
Khamra Rus. Fed. **77** M3
Khamseh *reg.* Iran **110** C3
Khan Afgh. **111** H3
Khan, Nam *r.* Laos **86** C3
Khānābād Afgh. **111** H2
Khān al Baghdādī Iraq **113** F4
Khān al Mashāhidah Iraq **113** G4
Khān al Muşallá Iraq **113** G4
Khanapur India **106** B2
Khān ar Raḥbah Iraq **113** G5
Khanasur Pass Iran/Turkey **113** G3
Khanbalik *Beijing* China *see* **Beijing**
Khānch Iran **110** B2
Khandagayty Rus. Fed. **94** C1
Khandu India **111** I6
Khandwa India **104** D5
Khandyga Rus. Fed. **77** O3
Khanewal Pak. **111** H4

Khan Hung Vietnam see Soc Trăng
Khaniá Greece see Chania
Khānī Yek Iran 110 D4
Khanka, Lake China/Rus. Fed. 90 D3
Khanka, Ozero l. China/Rus. Fed. see Khanka, Lake
Khankendi Azer. see Xankändi
Khanna India 104 D3
Khannā, Qā' salt pan Jordan 107 C3
Khanpur Pak. 111 H4
Khanpur Pak. 111 H4
Khān Ruḩābah Iraq see Khān ar Raḩbah
Khansar Pak. 111 H4
Khān Shaykhūn Syria 107 C2
Khantau Kazakh. 98 A3
Khantayskoye, Ozero l. Rus. Fed. 76 K3
Khan-Tengri, Pik mt. Kazakh./Kyrg. 98 C4
Khanthabouli Laos see Savannakhét
Khanty-Mansiysk Rus. Fed. 76 H3
Khān Yūnis Gaza 107 B4
Khanzi admin. dist. Botswana see Ghanzi
Khao Ang Rua Nai Wildlife Reserve nature res. Thai. 87 C4
Khao Banthat Wildlife Reserve nature res. Thai. 87 B6
Khao Chum Thong Thai. 87 B5
Khaoen Si Nakarin National Park Thai. 87 B4
Khao Laem, Ang Kep Nam Thai. 86 B4
Khao Laem National Park Thai. 86 B4
Khao Luang National Park Thai. 87 B5
Khao Pu-Khao Ya National Park Thai. 87 B6
Khao Soi Dao Wildlife Reserve nature res. Thai. 87 C4
Khao Sok National Park Thai. 87 B5
Khao Yai National Park Thai. 87 C4
Khapcheranga Rus. Fed. 95 H1
Khaplu Pak. 102 E4
Khaptad National Park Nepal 104 E3
Kharabali Rus. Fed. 53 J7
Kharagpur Bihar India 105 F4
Kharagpur W. Bengal India 105 F5
Khārān r. Iran 109 I4
Kharanor Rus. Fed. 95 I1
Kharari India see Abu Road
Kharda India 106 B2
Khardi India 104 C6
Khardong La pass India see Khardung La
Khardung La pass India 104 D2
Kharez Ilias Afgh. 111 F3
Kharfiyah Iraq 113 G5
Kharga Egypt see Al Khārijah
Kharga r. Rus. Fed. 90 D1
Khârga, El Wâḥât el oasis Egypt see Khārijah, Wāḥāt al
Kharga Oasis Egypt see Khārijah, Wāḥāt al
Kharg Islands Iran 110 C4
Khargon India 104 C5
Khari r. Rajasthan India 104 C4
Khari r. Rajasthan India 104 C4
Kharian Pak. 111 I3
Khariar India 106 D1
Khārijah, Wāḥāt al oasis Egypt 108 D5
Kharîm, Gebel hill Egypt see Kharīm, Jabal
Kharīm, Jabal hill Egypt 107 A4
Kharkhara r. India 104 E5
Kharkhauda Haryana India 99 B7
Kharkiv Ukr. 53 H6
Khar'kov Ukr. see Kharkiv
Khār Kūh mt. Iran 110 D4
Kharlovka Rus. Fed. 52 H1
Kharlu Rus. Fed. 54 Q6
Kharmanli Bulg. 69 K4
Kharoti reg. Afgh. 111 H3
Kharovsk Rus. Fed. 52 I4
Kharsia India 105 E5

▶Khartoum Sudan 108 D6
Capital of Sudan. 4th most populous city in Africa.

Kharwar reg. Afgh. 111 H3
Khasavyurt Rus. Fed. 113 G2
Khash Afgh. 111 F4
Khāsh Iran 111 F4
Khāsh, Dasht-e Afgh. 111 F4
Khashgort Rus. Fed. 51 T2
Khashm el Girba Sudan 108 E7
Khashm Şana' Saudi Arabia 112 E6
Khash Rūd r. Afgh. 111 F4
Khashuri Georgia 113 F2
Khasi Hills India 105 G4
Khaskovo Bulg. 69 K4
Khatanga Rus. Fed. 77 L2
Khatanga, Gulf of Rus. Fed. see Khatangskiy Zaliv
Khatangskiy Zaliv b. Rus. Fed. 77 L2
Khatayakha Rus. Fed. 52 M2
Khatinza Pass Pak. 111 H2
Khatmat al Malāha Oman 110 E5
Khatyrka Rus. Fed. 77 S3
Khāvāk, Khowtal-e Afgh. 111 H3
Khavda India 104 B5
Khayamnandi S. Africa 125 G6
Khaybar Saudi Arabia 108 E4
Khayelitsha S. Africa 124 D8
Khayrān, Ra's al pt Oman 110 E6
Khedrī Iran 110 E3
Khefa Israel see Haifa
Khehuene, Ponta pt Moz. 125 L2
Khemis Miliana Alg. 67 H5
Khemmarat Thai. 86 D3
Khenchela Alg. 68 B7
Khenifra Morocco 64 C5
Kherāmeh Iran 110 D4
Kherrata Alg. 67 I5
Kherreh Iran 110 D5
Khersan r. Iran 110 C4
Kherson Ukr. 69 O1
Kheta r. Rus. Fed. 77 L2
Kheyrābād Iran 110 D4
Khezerābād Iran 110 D2
Khiching India 105 F5
Khilok Rus. Fed. 95 G1
Khilok r. Rus. Fed. 95 F1
Khinganskiy Zapovednik nature res. Rus. Fed. 90 C2
Khinsar Pak. 111 H5
Khíos i. Greece see Chios
Khipro Pak. 111 H5
Khirbat Isrīyah Syria 107 C2
Khitai Dawan pass Aksai Chin 99 B6
Khīyāv Iran 110 B2
Khiytola Rus. Fed. 55 P6
Khlevnoye Rus. Fed. 53 H5
Khlong, Mae r. Thai. 87 C4
Khlong Saeng Wildlife Reserve nature res. Thai. 87 B5
Khlong Wang Chao National Park Thai. 86 B3
Khlung Thai. 87 C4
Khmel'nik Ukr. see Khmil'nyk
Khmel'nitskiy Ukr. see Khmel'nyts'kyy
Khmel'nyts'kyy Ukr. 53 E6
Khmer Republic country Asia see Cambodia
Khmil'nyk Ukr. 53 E6
Khoai, Hon i. Vietnam 87 D5
Khobda Kazakh. 102 A1
Khobi Georgia 113 F2
Khodā Āfarīd spring Iran 110 E3
Khodzha-Kala Turkm. see Hojagala
Khodzhambaz Turkm. see Hojambaz
Khodzhent Tajik. see Khŭjand
Khodzheyli Qoraqalpog'iston Respublikasi Uzbek. see Xo'jayli
Khojand Tajik. see Khŭjand
Khokhowe Pan salt pan Botswana 124 E3
Khokhropar Pak. 111 H5
Khoksar India 104 D2
Kholm Afgh. 111 G2
Kholm Poland see Chełm
Kholm Rus. Fed. 52 F4
Kholmsk Rus. Fed. 90 F3
Kholon Israel see Holon
Kholtoson Rus. Fed. 94 E1
Kholzun, Khrebet mts Kazakh./Rus. Fed. 98 D2
Khomas admin. reg. Namibia 124 C2
Khomas Highland hills Namibia 124 B2
Khomeyn Iran 110 C3
Khomeynīshahr Iran 110 C3
Khong, Ménam r. Laos/Thai. 86 D4 see Mekong
Khonj Iran 110 D5
Khonj, Kūh-e mts Iran 110 D5
Khon Kaen Thai. 86 C3
Khon Kriel Cambodia see Phumĭ Kon Kriel
Khonsa India 105 H4
Khonuu Rus. Fed. 77 P3
Khoper r. Rus. Fed. 53 I6
Khor Rus. Fed. 90 D3
Khor r. Rus. Fed. 90 D3
Khorat Plateau Thai. 86 C3
Khorda India see Khurda
Khordha India see Khurda
Khoreyver Rus. Fed. 52 M2
Khorinsk Rus. Fed. 89 J2
Khorixas Namibia 123 B6
Khormūj, Kūh-e mt. Iran 110 C4
Khorog Tajik. see Khorugh
Khorol Rus. Fed. 90 D3
Khorol Ukr. 53 G6
Khoroslū Dāgh hills Iran 110 B2
Khorramābād Iran 110 C3
Khorramshahr Iran 110 C4
Khorugh Tajik. 111 H2
Khosheutovo Rus. Fed. 53 J7
Khōst reg. Afgh./Pak. 111 H3
Khōst 111 H3
Khosūyeh Iran 110 D4
Khotan Xinjiang China see Hotan
Khotang Nepal 99 D8
Khotol Mountain hill AK U.S.A. 148 H2
Khouribga Morocco 64 C5
Khovaling Tajik. 111 H2
Khowrjān Iran 110 D4
Khowrnag, Kūh-e mt. Iran 110 D3
Khreum Myanmar 86 A2
Khri r. India 99 E8
Khroma r. Rus. Fed. 77 P2
Khromtau Kazakh. 102 A1
Khru r. India 99 F8
Khrushchev Ukr. see Svitlovods'k
Khrysokhou Bay Cyprus see Chrysochou Bay
Khrystynivka Ukr. 53 F6
Khuar Pak. 111 I3
Khudumelapye Botswana 124 G2
Khudzhand Tajik. see Khŭjand
Khufaysah, Khashm al hill Saudi Arabia 110 B6
Khugiana Afgh. see Pirzada
Khuis Botswana 124 E4
Khŭjand Tajik. 102 C3
Khŭjayli Qoraqalpog'iston Respublikasi Uzbek. see Xo'jayli
Khŭjayli Uzbek. see Xo'jayli
Khu Khan Thai. 87 D4
Khulays Saudi Arabia 108 E5
Khulkhuta Rus. Fed. 53 J7
Khulm r. Afgh. 111 G2
Khulna Bangl. 105 G5
Khulo Georgia 113 F2
Khuma S. Africa 125 H4
Khŭm Batheay Cambodia 87 D5
Khunayzīr, Jabal al mts Syria 107 C2
Khūnīk Bālā Iran 110 E3
Khūnīnshahr Iran see Khorramshahr
Khunjerab Pass China/Pak. 104 C1
Khunsar Iran 110 C3
Khun Yuam Thai. 86 B3
Khūr Iran 110 E3
Khūran sea chan. Iran 110 D5
Khuraỹs Saudi Arabia 108 G4
Khurd, Koh-i- mt. Afgh. 111 G3
Khurda India 106 E1
Khurdha India see Khurda
Khurja India 104 D3
Khurmalik Afgh. 111 F3
Khurmuli Rus. Fed. 90 E2
Khūrrāb Iran 110 D4
Khurz Iran 110 D3
Khushab Pak. 111 I3
Khushalgarh Pak. 111 H3
Khushshah, Wādī al watercourse Jordan/Saudi Arabia 107 C5
Khust Ukr. 53 D6
Khutse Game Reserve nature res. Botswana 124 G2
Khutsong S. Africa 125 H4
Khutu r. Rus. Fed. 90 E2
Khuzdar Pak. 111 G5
Khvāf Iran 111 F3
Khvāf reg. Iran 111 F3
Khvājeh Iran 110 B2
Khvalynsk Rus. Fed. 53 K5
Khvodrān Iran 110 D4
Khvord Nārvan Iran 110 E3
Khvormūj Iran 110 C4
Khvoy Iran 110 B2
Khvoynaya Rus. Fed. 52 G4
Khwaja Amran mt. Pak. 111 G4
Khwaja Muhammad Range mts Afgh. 111 H2
Khyber Pakhtunkhwa prov. Pak. 111 H3
Khyber Pass Afgh./Pak. 111 H3
Kiama Australia 138 E5
Kiamba Mindanao Phil. 82 D5
Kiamichi r. U.S.A. 161 E5
Kiana AK U.S.A. 148 G2
Kiangsi prov. China see Jiangxi
Kiangsu prov. China see Jiangsu
Kiantajärvi l. Fin. 54 P4
Kiari India 99 B6
Kīāseh Iran 110 D2
Kiatassuaq i. Greenland 147 M2
Kibaha Tanz. 123 D4
Kibali r. Dem. Rep. Congo 122 C3
Kibangou Congo 122 B4
Kibawe Mindanao Phil. 82 D5
Kibaya Tanz. 123 D4
Kibi Japan 92 B4
Kiboga Uganda 122 D3
Kibombo Dem. Rep. Congo 122 C4
Kibondo Tanz. 122 D4
Kibre Mengist Eth. 121 G4
Kıbrıs country Asia see Cyprus
Kibungo Rwanda 122 D4
Kičevo Macedonia 69 I4
Kichmengskiy Gorodok Rus. Fed. 52 J4
Kiçik Qafqaz mts Asia see Lesser Caucasus
Kicking Horse Pass Canada 150 G5
Kidal Mali 120 D3
Kidderminster U.K. 59 E6
Kidepo Valley National Park Uganda 122 D3
Kidira Senegal 120 B3
Kidmang India 104 D2
Kidnappers, Cape N.Z. 139 F4
Kidsgrove U.K. 59 E5
Kidurong, Tanjung pt Malaysia 85 F2
Kiel Germany 57 M3
Kiel U.S.A. 164 A2
Kiel Canal Germany 57 L3
Kielce Poland 57 R5
Kielder Water resr U.K. 58 E3
Kieler Bucht b. Germany 57 M3
Kienge Dem. Rep. Congo 123 C5
Kierspe Germany 63 H3

▶Kiev Ukr. 53 F6
Capital of Ukraine.

Kiffa Mauritania 120 B3
Kifisia Greece 69 J5
Kifrī Iraq 113 G4

▶Kigali Rwanda 122 D4
Capital of Rwanda.

Kigalik r. AK U.S.A. 148 I1
Kiğı Turkey 113 F3
Kiglapait Mountains Canada 153 J2
Kigluaik Mountains AK U.S.A. 148 F2
Kigoma Tanz. 123 C4
Kihambatang Kalimantan Indon. 85 F3
Kihlanki Fin. 54 M3
Kihniö Fin. 54 M5
Kīholo U.S.A. 157 [inset]
Kii-hantō pen. Japan 92 B5
Kiik Kazakh. 98 A3
Kiiminki Fin. 54 N4
Kii-Nagashima Japan 92 C4
Kii-sanchi mts Japan 92 B5
Kii-suidō sea chan. Japan 89 O6
Kijimadaira Japan 93 E2
Kikerino Rus. Fed. 55 P7
Kikiakrorak r. AK U.S.A. 149 J1
Kikinda Serbia 69 I2
Kikki Pak. 111 F5
Kikládhes is Greece see Cyclades
Kikmiktalikamiut AK U.S.A. 148 F3
Kiknur Rus. Fed. 52 J4
Kikonai Japan 90 F4
Kikori P.N.G. 81 K8
Kikori r. P.N.G. 81 K8
Kikugawa Japan 93 E4
Kikwit Dem. Rep. Congo 123 B4
Kilafors Sweden 55 J6
Kilar India 104 D2
Kilauea U.S.A. 157 [inset]
Kilauea Crater U.S.A. 157 [inset]
Kilbon Seram Indon. 83 D3
Kilbuck Mountains AK U.S.A. 148 H3
Kilchu N. Korea 90 C4
Kilcoole Ireland 61 F4
Kilcormac Ireland 61 E4
Kilcoy Australia 138 F1
Kildare Ireland 61 F4
Kil'dinstroy Rus. Fed. 54 R2
Kilekale Lake N.W.T. Canada 149 Q2
Kilemary Rus. Fed. 52 J4
Kilembe Dem. Rep. Congo 123 B4
Kilfinan U.K. 60 D5
Kilgore U.S.A. 161 E5
Kilham U.K. 58 E3
Kilia Ukr. see Kiliya
Kılıç Dağı mt. Syria/Turkey see Aqra', Jabal al
Kilifi Kenya 122 D4
Kilik Pass Xinjiang China 99 A5

▶Kilimanjaro vol. Tanz. 122 D4
Highest mountain in Africa.

Kilimanjaro National Park Tanz. 122 D4
Kilinailau Islands P.N.G. 132 F2
Kilindoni Tanz. 123 D4
Kilingi-Nõmme Estonia 55 N7
Kilis Turkey 107 C1
Kilis prov. Turkey 107 C1
Kiliuda Bay AK U.S.A. 148 I4
Kiliya Ukr. 69 M2
Kilkee Ireland 61 C5
Kilkeel U.K. 61 G3
Kilkenny Ireland 61 E5
Kilkhampton U.K. 59 C8
Kilkis Greece 69 J4
Killala Ireland 61 C3
Killala Bay Ireland 61 C3
Killaloe Ireland 61 D5
Killam Canada 151 I4
Killarney N.T. Australia 134 E4
Killarney Qld Australia 138 F2
Killarney Canada 152 E5
Killarney Ireland 61 C5
Killarney National Park Ireland 61 C6
Killary Harbour b. Ireland 61 C4
Killbuck U.S.A. 164 E3
Killeen U.S.A. 161 D6
Killenaule Ireland 61 E5
Killik r. AK U.S.A. 148 I1
Killimor Ireland 61 D4
Killin U.K. 60 E4
Killinchy U.K. 61 G3
Killíni mt. Greece see Kyllini
Killinick Ireland 61 F5
Killorglin Ireland 61 C5
Killurin Ireland 61 F5
Killybegs Ireland 61 D3
Kilmacrenan Ireland 61 E2
Kilmaine Ireland 61 C4
Kilmallock Ireland 61 D5
Kilmaluag U.K. 60 C3
Kilmarnock U.K. 60 E5
Kilmelford U.K. 60 D4
Kil'mez' Rus. Fed. 52 K4
Kil'mez' r. Rus. Fed. 52 K4
Kilmona Ireland 61 D6
Kilmore Australia 138 B6
Kilmore Quay Ireland 61 F5
Kilosa Tanz. 123 D4
Kilpisjärvi Fin. 54 L2
Kilrea U.K. 61 F3
Kilrush Ireland 61 C5
Kilsyth U.K. 60 E5
Kiltan atoll India 106 B4
Kiltullagh Ireland 61 D4
Kilwa Masoko Tanz. 123 D4
Kilwinning U.K. 60 E5
Kim U.S.A. 161 C4
Kimanis, Teluk b. Malaysia 85 F1
Kimba Australia 135 G8
Kimba Congo 122 B4
Kimball U.S.A. 160 C3
Kimball, Mount AK U.S.A. 149 K3
Kimbe P.N.G. 132 F2
Kimberley S. Africa 124 G5
Kimberley Plateau Australia 134 D4
Kimberley Range hills Australia 135 B6
Kimch'aek N. Korea 91 C4
Kimch'ŏn S. Korea 91 C5
Kimhae S. Korea 91 C6
Kimhandu mt. Tanz. 123 D4
Kimhwa S. Korea 91 B5
Kími Greece see Kymi
Kimito Fin. 55 M6
Kimitsu Japan 93 F3
Kimmirut Canada 147 L3
Kimolos i. Greece 69 K6
Kimovsk Rus. Fed. 53 H5
Kimpese Dem. Rep. Congo 123 B4
Kimpoku-san mt. Japan see Kinpoku-san
Kimry Rus. Fed. 52 H4
Kimsquit Canada 150 E4
Kimvula Dem. Rep. Congo 123 B4
Kinabalu, Gunung mt. Sabah Malaysia 85 G1
Kinabalu National Park Malaysia 85 G1
Kinabatangan r. Malaysia 85 G1
Kinabatangan, Kuala r. mouth Malaysia 85 G1
Kinango Kenya 123 D4
Kinasa Japan 93 E2
Kinaskan Lake B.C. Canada 149 O4
Kinbasket Lake Canada 150 G4
Kinbrace U.K. 60 F2
Kincaid Canada 151 J5
Kincardine Canada 164 E1
Kincardine U.K. 60 F4
Kinchega National Park Australia 137 C7
Kincolith B.C. Canada 149 O5
Kinda Dem. Rep. Congo 123 C4
Kindat Myanmar 86 A2
Kinde U.S.A. 164 D2
Kinder LA U.S.A. 167 G2
Kinder Scout hill U.K. 58 F5
Kindersley Canada 151 I5
Kindia Guinea 120 B3
Kindu Dem. Rep. Congo 122 C4
Kinegnak AK U.S.A. 148 G4
Kinel' Rus. Fed. 53 K5
Kineshma Rus. Fed. 52 I4
Kingaroy Australia 138 E1
King Christian Island Canada 147 H2
King City U.S.A. 158 C3
King Cove AK U.S.A. 148 G5
King Edward VII Land pen. Antarctica see Edward VII Peninsula
Kingfield U.S.A. 165 J1
Kingfisher U.S.A. 161 D5
King George U.S.A. 165 G4
King George, Mount Canada 156 E2
King George Island Antarctica 188 A2
King George Islands Canada 152 F2
King George Islands Fr. Polynesia see Roi Georges, Îles du
King Hill hill Australia 134 C5
Kingisepp Rus. Fed. 55 P7
King Island Australia 137 [inset]
King Island Canada 150 E4
King Island Myanmar see Kadan Kyun
King Island AK U.S.A. 148 E2
Kingisseppa Estonia see Kuressaare
Kinglake National Park Australia 138 B6
King Leopold and Queen Astrid Coast Antarctica 188 E2
King Leopold Range National Park Australia 134 D4
King Leopold Ranges hills Australia 134 D4
Kingman U.S.A. 159 F4

▶Kingman Reef terr. N. Pacific Ocean 186 J5
United States Unincorporated Territory.

King Mountain B.C. Canada 149 O4
King Mountain hill U.S.A. 161 C6
Kingoonya Australia 137 A6
King Peak Antarctica 188 L1
King Peninsula Antarctica 188 K2
Kingri Pak. 111 H4
Kings r. Ireland 61 E5
Kings r. CA U.S.A. 158 C3
Kings r. NV U.S.A. 156 D4
King Salmon AK U.S.A. 148 H4
King Salmon r. AK U.S.A. 148 H4
Kingsbridge U.K. 59 D8
Kingsburg U.S.A. 158 D3
Kings Canyon National Park U.S.A. 158 D3
Kingscliff Australia 138 F2
Kingscote Australia 137 B7
Kingscourt Ireland 61 F4
King Sejong research station Antarctica 188 A2
King's Lynn U.K. 59 H6
Kingsmill Group is Kiribati 133 H2
Kingsnorth U.K. 59 H7
King Sound b. Australia 134 C4
Kings Peak U.S.A. 159 H1
Kingsport U.S.A. 162 D4
Kingston Australia 137 [inset]
Kingston Canada 165 G1

▶Kingston Jamaica 169 I5
Capital of Jamaica.

▶Kingston Norfolk I. 133 G4
Capital of Norfolk Island.

Kingston MO U.S.A. 160 E4
Kingston NY U.S.A. 165 H3
Kingston OH U.S.A. 164 D4
Kingston PA U.S.A. 165 H3
Kingston Peak U.S.A. 159 F4
Kingston South East Australia 137 B8
Kingston upon Hull U.K. 58 G5

▶Kingstown St Vincent 169 L6
Capital of St Vincent.

Kingstree U.S.A. 163 E5
Kingsville U.S.A. 161 D7
Kingswood U.K. 59 E7
Kington U.K. 59 D6
Kingungi Dem. Rep. Congo 123 B4
Kingurutik r. Canada 153 J2
Kingussie U.K. 60 E3
King William U.S.A. 165 G5
King William Island Canada 147 I3
King William's Town S. Africa 125 H7
Kingwood TX U.S.A. 161 E6
Kingwood WV U.S.A. 164 F4
Kinloch N.Z. 139 B7
Kinloss U.K. 60 F3
Kinmen Taiwan see Chinmen
Kinmen i. Taiwan see Chinmen Tao
Kinmount Canada 165 F1
Kinna Sweden 55 H8
Kinnegad Ireland 61 E4
Kinneret, Yam l. Israel see Galilee, Sea of
Kinniyai Sri Lanka 106 D4
Kinnula Fin. 54 N5
Kinoje r. Canada 152 E3
Kino-kawa r. Japan 92 B4
Kinomoto Japan 92 C3
Kinoosao Canada 151 K3
Kinosaki Japan 92 A3
Kinpoku-san mt. Japan 91 E5
Kinross U.K. 60 F4
Kinsale Ireland 61 D6
Kinsale U.S.A. 165 G4

▶Kinshasa Dem. Rep. Congo 123 B4
Capital of the Democratic Republic of the Congo. 3rd most populous city in Africa.

Kinsley U.S.A. 160 D4
Kinsman U.S.A. 164 E3
Kinston U.S.A. 163 E5
Kintom Sulawesi Indon. 83 B3
Kintop Kalimantan Indon. 85 F3
Kintore U.K. 60 G3
Kintyre pen. U.K. 60 D5
Kin-U Myanmar 86 A2
Kinu-gawa r. Japan 93 G3
Kinunuma-yama mt. Japan 93 F2
Kinushseo r. Canada 152 E3
Kinyeti mt. Sudan 121 G4
Kinzig r. Germany 63 I4
Kiowa CO U.S.A. 156 G5
Kiowa KS U.S.A. 161 D4
Kipahigan Lake Canada 151 K4
Kiparissía Greece see Kyparissia
Kipawa, Lac l. Canada 152 F5
Kipchak Pass Xinjiang China 98 B4
Kipling Canada 151 K5
Kipling Station Canada see Kipling
Kipnuk AK U.S.A. 148 F4
Kiptopeke U.S.A. 165 H5
Kipungo Angola see Quipungo
Kipushi Dem. Rep. Congo 123 C5
Kira Japan 92 D4
Kirakira Solomon Is 133 G3
Kirandul India 106 D2
Kirchdorf Germany 63 I2
Kirchheim-Bolanden Germany 63 I5
Kirchheim unter Teck Germany 63 J6
Kircubbin U.K. 61 G3
Kirdimi Chad 121 E3
Kirenga r. Rus. Fed. 89 J1
Kirensk Rus. Fed. 77 L4
Kireyevsk Rus. Fed. 53 H5
Kirghizia country Asia see Kyrgyzstan
Kirghiz Range mts Kazakh./Kyrg. 102 D3
Kirgizskaya S.S.R. country Asia see Kyrgyzstan
Kirgizskiy Khrebet mts Kazakh./Kyrg. see Kirghiz Range
Kirgizstan country Asia see Kyrgyzstan
Kiri Dem. Rep. Congo 122 B4
Kiribati country Pacific Ocean 186 I6
Kiriga-mine mt. Japan 93 E2
Kırıkhan Turkey 107 C1
Kırıkkale Turkey 112 D3
Kirikkuduk Xinjiang China 94 B2
Kirillov Rus. Fed. 52 H4
Kirillovo Rus. Fed. 90 F3
Kirin China see Jilin
Kirin prov. China see Jilin
Kirinda Sri Lanka 106 D5
Kirinyaga mt. Kenya see Kenya, Mount
Kirishi Rus. Fed. 52 G4
Kirishima-Yaku Kokuritsu-kōen Japan 91 C7
Kirishima-yama vol. Japan 91 C7
Kiritimati atoll Kiribati 187 J5
Kiriwina Islands P.N.G. see Trobriand Islands
Kırkağaç Turkey 69 L5
Kirk Bulāg Dāgi mt. Iran 110 B2
Kirkby U.K. 58 E5
Kirkby in Ashfield U.K. 59 F5
Kirkby Lonsdale U.K. 58 E4
Kirkby Stephen U.K. 58 E4
Kirkcaldy U.K. 60 F4
Kirkcolm U.K. 60 D6
Kirkcudbright U.K. 60 E6
Kirkenær Norway 55 H6
Kirkenes Norway 54 Q2
Kirkfield Canada 165 F1
Kirkintilloch U.K. 60 E5
Kirkkonummi Fin. 55 N6
Kirkland U.S.A. 159 G4
Kirkland Lake Canada 152 E4
Kırklareli Turkey 69 L4
Kirklin U.S.A. 164 B3
Kirk Michael Isle of Man 58 C4
Kirkoswald U.K. 58 E4
Kirkpatrick, Mount Antarctica 188 H1
Kirksville U.S.A. 160 E3
Kirkūk Iraq 113 G4
Kirkwall U.K. 60 G2
Kirkwood S. Africa 125 G7
Kirman Iran see Kermān
Kirn Germany 63 H5
Kirov Kaluzhskaya Oblast' Rus. Fed. 53 G5
Kirov Kirovskaya Oblast' Rus. Fed. 52 K4
Kirova, Zaliv b. Azer. see Qızılağac Körfäzi
Kirovabad Azer. see Gäncä
Kirovabad Tajik. see Panj
Kirovakan Armenia see Vanadzor
Kirovo Ukr. see Kirovohrad
Kirovo-Chepetsk Rus. Fed. 52 K4
Kirovo-Chepetskiy Rus. Fed. see Kirovo-Chepetsk
Kirovograd Ukr. see Kirovohrad
Kirovohrad Ukr. 53 G6
Kirovsk Leningradskaya Oblast' Rus. Fed. 52 F4
Kirovsk Murmanskaya Oblast' Rus. Fed. 54 R3
Kirovsk Turkm. see Badabaýhan
Kirovs'ke Ukr. 112 D1
Kirovskiy Rus. Fed. 90 D3
Kirovskoye Ukr. see Kirovs'ke
Kırpaşa pen. Cyprus see Karpasia
Kirpili Turkm. 110 E2
Kirriemuir U.K. 60 F4
Kirs Rus. Fed. 52 L4
Kirsanov Rus. Fed. 53 I5
Kırşehir Turkey 112 D3
Kirthar National Park Pak. 111 G5
Kirthar Range mts Pak. 111 G5
Kirtland U.S.A. 159 I3
Kirtorf Germany 63 J4
Kiruna Sweden 54 L3
Kirundu Dem. Rep. Congo 122 C4
Kirwan Escarpment Antarctica 188 B2
Kiryū Japan 93 F2
Kisa Sweden 55 I8
Kisama, Parque Nacional de nat. park Angola see Quiçama, Parque Nacional do
Kisandji Dem. Rep. Congo 123 B4
Kisangani Dem. Rep. Congo 122 C3
Kisantu Dem. Rep. Congo 123 B4
Kisar i. Maluku Indon. 83 C5
Kisaralik r. AK U.S.A. 148 G3
Kisaran Sumatera Indon. 84 B2
Kisarazu Japan 93 F3
Kisei Japan 92 C4
Kiselevsk Rus. Fed. 88 F2
Kisel'ovka Rus. Fed. 90 E2
Kish i. Iran 110 D5
Kishanganj India 105 F4
Kishangarh Madh. Prad. India 104 D4
Kishangarh Rajasthan India 104 B4
Kishangarh Rajasthan India 104 C4
Kishangarh Rajasthan India 104 D4
Kishi Nigeria 120 D4
Kishigawa Japan 92 B4
Kishi-gawa r. Japan 92 B4
Kishinev Moldova see Chişinău
Kishiwada Japan 92 B4
Kishkenekol' Kazakh. 101 G1
Kishoreganj Bangl. 105 G4
Kishorganj Bangl. see Kishoreganj
Kisi Nigeria see Kishi
Kisii Kenya 122 D4
Kiska Island AK U.S.A. 149 [inset]
Kiskittogisu Lake Canada 151 L4
Kiskitto Lake Canada 151 L4
Kiskunfélegyháza Hungary 69 H1
Kiskunhalas Hungary 69 H1
Kiskunsági nat. park Hungary 69 H1
Kislovodsk Rus. Fed. 113 F2
Kismaayo Somalia 122 E4
Kismayu Somalia see Kismaayo
Kiso Japan 93 D3
Kisofukushima Japan 92 D3
Kisogawa Japan 92 C3
Kiso-gawa r. Japan 92 C3
Kiso-gawa r. Japan 93 E3
Kisoro Uganda 121 F5
Kisosaki Japan 92 C3
Kiso-sanmyaku mts Japan 93 D3
Kispiox Canada 150 E4
Kispiox r. Canada 150 E4
Kissamos Greece 69 J7
Kisseraing Island Myanmar see Kanmaw Kyun
Kissidougou Guinea 120 B4
Kissimmee U.S.A. 163 D6
Kissimmee, Lake U.S.A. 163 D7
Kississing Lake Canada 151 K4
Kistendey Rus. Fed. 53 I5
Kistigan Lake Canada 151 M4
Kistna r. India see Krishna
Kisumu Kenya 122 D4
Kisykkamys Kazakh. see Dzhangala
Kita Hyōgo Japan 92 B4
Kita Kyōto Japan 92 B3
Kita Mali 120 C3
Kitab Uzbek. see Kitob
Kita-Daitō-jima i. Japan 89 O7
Kitagata Japan 92 C3
Kitaibaraki Japan 93 G2
Kita-Iō-jima vol. Japan 81 K1
Kitakami Japan 91 F5
Kita-Kyūshū Japan 91 C6
Kitale Kenya 122 D3
Kitami Japan 90 F4
Kitamimaki Japan 93 E2
Kitamoto Japan 93 F3
Kitatachibana Japan 93 F2
Kitaura Ibaraki Japan 93 G2
Kita-ura l. Japan 93 G3
Kitayama Japan 92 B5
Kit Carson U.S.A. 160 C4
Kitchener Canada 164 E2
Kitchigama r. Canada 152 F4
Kitee Fin. 54 Q5
Kitgum Uganda 122 D3
Kíthira i. Greece see Kythira
Kíthnos i. Greece see Kythnos
Kiti, Cape Cyprus see Kition, Cape
Kitimat Canada 150 D4
Kitinen r. Fin. 54 O3
Kition, Cape Cyprus 107 A2
Kitiou, Akra c. Cyprus see Kition, Cape

Kitkatla B.C. Canada 149 O5
Kitob Uzbek. 111 G2
Kitsault B.C. Canada 149 O5
Kitsuregawa Japan 93 G2
Kittanning U.S.A. 164 F3
Kittatinny Mountains hills U.S.A. 165 H3
Kittery U.S.A. 165 J2
Kittilä Fin. 54 N3
Kittur India 106 B3
Kitty Hawk U.S.A. 162 F4
Kitui Kenya 122 D4
Kitwanga Canada 150 D4
Kitwe Zambia 123 C5
Kitzbüheler Alpen mts Austria 57 N7
Kitzingen Germany 63 K5
Kitzscher Germany 63 M3
Kiukpalik Island AK U.S.A. 148 I4
Kiu Lom, Ang Kep Nam Thai. 86 B3
Kiunga P.N.G. 81 K8
Kiuruvesi Fin. 54 O5
Kivak Rus. Fed. 148 D2
Kivalina AK U.S.A. 148 F2
Kividlo AK U.S.A. 148 F2
Kivijärvi Fin. 54 N5
Kiviõli Estonia 55 O7
Kivu, Lake Dem. Rep. Congo/Rwanda 122 C4
Kiwaba N'zogi Angola 123 B4
Kiwai Island P.N.G. 81 K8
Kiwalik AK U.S.A. 148 G2
Kiwalik r. AK U.S.A. 148 G2
Kiyev Ukr. see Kiev
Kiyevskoye Vodokhranilishche resr Ukr. see Kyyivs'ke Vodoskhovyshche
Kıyıköy Turkey 69 M4
Kiyomi Japan 92 D2
Kiyosumi-yama hill Japan 93 G3
Kiyotsu-gawa r. Japan 93 E1
Kizel Rus. Fed. 51 R4
Kizema Rus. Fed. 52 J3
Kizha Rus. Fed. 95 G1
Kizil Xinjiang China 98 C4
Kizilawat Xinjiang China 98 B5
Kızılcadağ Turkey 69 M6
Kızılca Dağ mt. Turkey 112 C3
Kızılcahamam Turkey 112 D2
Kızıldağ mt. Turkey 107 A1
Kızıldağ mt. Turkey 107 B1
Kızıl Dağı mt. Turkey 112 E3
Kızılırmak Turkey 112 D2
Kızılırmak r. Turkey 112 D2
Kızıltepe Turkey 113 F3
Kizilyurt Rus. Fed. 113 G2
Kızkalesi Turkey 107 B1
Kizlyar Rus. Fed. 113 G2
Kizlyarskiy Zaliv b. Rus. Fed. 113 G1
Kizner Rus. Fed. 52 K4
Kizu Japan 92 B4
Kizu-gawa r. Japan 92 B4
Kizyl-Arbat Turkm. see Serdar
Kizyl-Atrek Turkm. see Etrek
Kizyl Jilga Aksai Chin 99 B6
Kjøllefjord Norway 54 O1
Kjøpsvik Norway 54 J2
Kladno Czech Rep. 57 O5
Klagan Sabah Malaysia 85 G1
Klagenfurt Austria 57 O7
Klagetoh U.S.A. 159 I4
Klaipėda Lith. 55 L9
Klaksvík Faroe Is 54 [inset]
Klamath U.S.A. 156 B4
Klamath r. U.S.A. 146 F5
Klamath Falls U.S.A. 156 C4
Klamath Mountains U.S.A. 156 C4
Klampo Kalimantan Indon. 85 G2
Klang Malaysia 84 C2
Klappan r. B.C. Canada 149 O4
Klarälven r. Sweden 55 H7
Klaten Jawa Indon. 85 E4
Klatovy Czech Rep. 57 N6
Klawer S. Africa 124 D6
Klawock AK U.S.A. 149 N5
Klazienaveen Neth. 62 G2
Kleides Islands Cyprus 107 B2
Kleinbegin S. Africa 124 E5
Klein Karas Namibia 124 D4
Klein Nama Land reg. S. Africa see Namaqualand
Klein Roggeveldberge mts S. Africa 124 E7
Kleinsee S. Africa 124 C5
Klemtu Canada 150 D4
Klerksdorp S. Africa 125 H4
Klery Creek AK U.S.A. 148 G2
Kletnya Rus. Fed. 53 G5
Kletsk Belarus see Klyetsk
Kletskaya Rus. Fed. 53 I6
Kletskiy Rus. Fed. see Kletskaya
Kleve Germany 62 G3
Klichka Rus. Fed. 95 I1
Klidhes Islands Cyprus see Kleides Islands
Klimkovka Rus. Fed. 52 K4
Klimovo Rus. Fed. 53 G5
Klin Rus. Fed. 52 H4
Kling Mindanao Phil. 82 D5
Klingenberg am Main Germany 63 J5
Klingenthal Germany 63 M4
Klingkang, Banjaran mts Indon./Malaysia 85 E2
Klink Germany 63 M1
Klínovec mt. Czech Rep. 63 N4
Klintehamn Sweden 55 K8
Klintsy Rus. Fed. 53 G5
Ključ Bos.-Herz. 68 G2
Kłodzko Poland 57 P5
Klondike r. Y.T. Canada 149 M2
Klondike Gold Rush National Historical Park nat. park AK U.S.A. 149 N4
Kloosterhaar Neth. 62 G2
Klosterneuburg Austria 57 P6
Klotz, Mount Y.T. Canada 149 L2
Klötze (Altmark) Germany 63 L2
Kluane Game Sanctuary nature res. Y.T. Canada 149 L3
Kluane Lake Y.T. Canada 149 M3
Kluane National Park Y.T. Canada 149 M3
Kluang Malaysia see Keluang
Kluang, Tanjung pt Indon. 85 E3
Kluczbork Poland 57 Q5
Klukhori Rus. Fed. see Karachayevsk
Klukhorskiy, Pereval Georgia/Rus. Fed. 113 F2
Klukwan AK U.S.A. 149 N4
Klumpang, Teluk b. Indon. 85 G3
Klungkung Bali Indon. 85 F5
Klutina Lake AK U.S.A. 149 K3
Klyetsk Belarus 55 O10
Klyosato Japan 93 E1
Klyuchevskaya, Sopka vol. Rus. Fed. 77 R4
Klyuchi Rus. Fed. 90 B2
Knåda Sweden 55 I6
Knaresborough U.K. 58 F4
Knee Lake Man. Canada 151 M4
Knee Lake Sask. Canada 151 J4
Knetzgau Germany 63 K5
Knife r. U.S.A. 160 C2
Knight Inlet Canada 150 E5
Knighton U.K. 59 D6
Knights Landing U.S.A. 158 C2
Knightstown U.S.A. 164 C4
Knin Croatia 68 G2
Knittelfeld Austria 57 O7
Knjaževac Serbia 69 J3
Knob Lake Canada see Schefferville
Knob Lick U.S.A. 164 C5
Knob Peak hill Australia 134 E3
Knock Ireland 61 D4
Knockalongy hill Ireland 61 D3
Knockalough Ireland 61 C5
Knockanaffrin hill Ireland 61 E5
Knockboy hill Ireland 61 C6
Knock Hill hill U.K. 60 G3
Knockmealdown Mts hills Ireland 61 D5
Knocknaskagh hill Ireland 61 D5
Knokke-Heist Belgium 62 D3
Knorrendorf Germany 63 N1
Knowle U.K. 59 F6
Knowlton Canada 165 I1
Knox IN U.S.A. 164 B3
Knox PA U.S.A. 164 F3
Knox, Cape B.C. Canada 149 N5
Knox Coast Antarctica 188 F2
Knoxville GA U.S.A. 163 D5
Knoxville TN U.S.A. 162 D5
Knud Rasmussen Land reg. Greenland 147 L2
Knysna S. Africa 124 F8
Ko, Gora mt. Rus. Fed. 90 E3
Koartac Canada see Quaqtaq
Koba Indon. 84 D3
Kobbfoss Norway 54 P2
Kobe Halmahera Indon. 83 C2
Kōbe Japan 92 B4
København Denmark see Copenhagen
Kobenni Mauritania 120 C3
Kobi Seram Indon. 83 D3
Koblenz Germany 63 H4
Koboldo Rus. Fed. 90 D1
Kobrin Belarus see Kobryn
Kobroör i. Indon. 81 I8
Kobryn Belarus 55 N10
Kobuchizawa Japan 93 E3
Kobuk AK U.S.A. 148 H2
Kobuk r. AK U.S.A. 148 G2
Kobuk Valley National Park AK U.S.A. 148 H2
K'obulet'i Georgia 113 F2
Kobushiga-take mt. Japan 93 E3
Kocaeli Turkey see İzmit
Kocaeli Yarımadası pen. Turkey 69 M4
Kočani Macedonia 69 J4
Kocasu r. Turkey 69 M4
Kocê Gansu China 94 E5
Kočevje Slovenia 68 F2
Koch Bihar India 105 G4
Kocher r. Germany 63 J5
Kochevo Rus. Fed. 51 Q4
Kochi India see Cochin
Kōchi Japan 91 D6
Koçhisar Turkey see Kızıltepe
Koch Island Canada 147 K3
Kochkor Kyrg. 102 E3
Kochkorka Kyrg. see Kochkor
Kochkurovo Rus. Fed. 53 J5
Kochubeyevskoye Rus. Fed. 113 F1
Kod India 106 B3
Kodaira Japan 93 F3
Kodala India 106 E2
Kodama Japan 93 F2
Kodarma India 105 F4
Kōdera Japan 92 A4
Koderma India see Kodarma
Kodiak AK U.S.A. 148 I4
Kodiak Island AK U.S.A. 148 I4
Kodiak National Wildlife Refuge nature res. AK U.S.A. 148 I4
Kodibeleng Botswana 125 H2
Kodino Rus. Fed. 52 H3
Kodiyakkarai India 106 C4
Kodok Sudan 108 D8
Kodyma Ukr. 53 F6
Kodzhaele mt. Bulg./Greece 69 K4
Koedoesberg mts S. Africa 124 E7
Koegrabie S. Africa 124 E5
Koekenaap S. Africa 124 D6
Koersel Belgium 62 F3
Koës Namibia 124 D3
Kofa Mountains U.S.A. 159 G5
Koffiefontein S. Africa 124 G5
Koforidua Ghana 120 C4
Kōfu Yamanashi Japan 93 E3
Koga Japan 93 F2
Kogaluc r. Canada 152 F2
Kogaluc, Baie de b. Canada 152 F2
Kogaluk r. Canada 153 J2
Kogan Australia 138 E1
Køge Denmark 55 H9
Kogon r. Guinea 120 B3
Kogon Uzbek. 111 G2
Kohan Pak. 111 G5
Kohat Pak. 111 H3
Kohestānāt Afgh. 111 G3
Kohila Estonia 55 N7
Kohima India 105 H4
Kohistan reg. Afgh. 111 H3
Kohistan reg. Pak. 111 I3
Kohler Range mts Antarctica 188 K2
Kohlu Pak. 111 H4
Kohsan Afgh. 111 F3
Kohtla-Järve Estonia 55 O7
Kohŭng S. Korea 91 B6
Koidern Y.T. Canada 149 L3
Koidern Mountain Y.T. Canada 149 L3
Koidu Sierra Leone see Sefadu
Koihoa India 87 A5
Koikyim Qu r. Qinghai China 99 F6
Koilkonda India 106 C2
Koin N. Korea 91 B4
Koin r. Rus. Fed. 52 K3
Koi Sanjaq Iraq 113 G3
Koito-gawa r. Japan 93 F3
Kōje-do i. S. Korea 91 C6
Kojonup Australia 135 B8
Kōka Japan 92 C4
Kokai-gawa r. Japan 93 G3
Kokand Farg'ona Uzbek. see Qo'qon
Kökar Fin. 55 L7
Kök-Art Osh Kyrg. 98 A4
Kokawa Japan 92 B4
Kök-Aygyr Kyrg. 98 A4
Kokchetav Kazakh. see Kokshetau
Kokemäenjoki r. Fin. 55 L6
Kokerboom Namibia 124 D5
Ko Kha Thai. 86 B3
Kokkilai Sri Lanka 106 D4
Kokkola Fin. 54 M5
Kok Kuduk well Xinjiang China 98 D3
Koko Nigeria 120 D3
Kokoda P.N.G. 81 L8
Kokolik r. AK U.S.A. 148 G1
Kokomo U.S.A. 164 B3
Kokong Botswana 124 F3
Kokos i. Indon. 87 A7
Kokosi S. Africa 125 H4
Kokpekti Kazakh. 102 F2
Kokrines AK U.S.A. 148 I2
Kokrines Hills AK U.S.A. 148 I2
Kokruagarok AK U.S.A. 148 I1
Koksan N. Korea 91 B5
Kokshaal-Tau, Khrebet mts China/Kyrg. see Kakshaal-Too
Koksharka Rus. Fed. 52 J4
Kokshetau Kazakh. 101 F1
Koksoak r. Canada 153 H2
Kokstad S. Africa 125 I6
Koksu Almatinskaya Oblast' Kazakh. 98 B3
Koksu Kazakh. 98 B3
Koktal Kazakh. 102 E3
Kokterek Almatinskaya Oblast' Kazakh. 98 B3
Kokterek Kazakh. 53 K6
Koktokay Xinjiang China see Fuyun
Koktokay Xinjiang China 94 B2
Koktuma Kazakh. 98 C3
Koku, Tanjung pt Indon. 83 B4
Kokubunji Japan 93 F2
Kokufu Japan 92 D2
Kokushiga-take mt. Japan 93 E3
Koküy Xinjiang China 94 B2
Kokyar Xinjiang China 99 B5
Kokzhayyk Kazakh. 98 C2
Kola i. Indon. 81 I8
Kola Rus. Fed. 54 R2
Kolachi r. Pak. 111 G5
Kolahoi mt. India 104 C2
Kolaka Sulawesi Indon. 83 B4
Kolambugan Mindanao Phil. 82 C4
Kolana Indon. 83 C5
Ko Lanta Thai. 87 B6
Kola Peninsula Rus. Fed. 52 H2
Kolar Chhattisgarh India 106 D2
Kolar Karnataka India 106 C3
Kolaras India 104 D4
Kolar Gold Fields India 106 C3
Kolari Fin. 54 M3
Kolarovgrad Bulg. see Shumen
Kolasib India 105 H4
Kolayat India 104 C4
Kolbano Timor Indon. 83 C5
Kolberg Poland see Kołobrzeg
Kol'chugino Rus. Fed. 52 H4
Kolda Senegal 120 B3
Kolding Denmark 55 F9
Kole Kasaï-Oriental Dem. Rep. Congo 122 C4
Kole Orientale Dem. Rep. Congo 122 C3
Koléa Alg. 67 H5
Kolekole mt. U.S.A. 157 [inset]
Koler Sweden 54 L4
Kolguyev, Ostrov i. Rus. Fed. 52 K1
Kolhan reg. India 105 F5
Kolhapur India 106 B2
Kolhumadulu Atoll Maldives 103 D11
Koliganek AK U.S.A. 148 H4
Kolikata India see Kolkata
Kõljala Estonia 55 M7
Kolkasrags pt Latvia 55 M8

▶Kolkata India 105 G5
5th most populous city in Asia and 8th in the world.

Kolkhozabad Khatlon Tajik. see Vose
Kolkhozabad Khatlon Tajik. see Kolkhozobod
Kolkhozobod Tajik. 111 H2
Kollam India see Quilon
Kolleru Lake India 106 D2
Kollum Neth. 62 G1
Kolmanskop (abandoned) Namibia 124 B4
Köln Germany see Cologne
Köln-Bonn airport Germany 63 H4
Kołobrzeg Poland 57 O3
Kologriv Rus. Fed. 52 J4
Kolokani Mali 120 C3
Kolombangara i. Solomon Is 133 F2
Kolomea Ukr. see Kolomyya
Kolomna Rus. Fed. 53 H5
Kołomyja Ukr. see Kolomyya
Kolomyya Ukr. 53 E6
Kolondiéba Mali 120 C3
Kolonedale Sulawesi Indon. 83 B3
Koloni Cyprus 107 A2
Kolonkwaneng Botswana 124 E4
Kolono Sulawesi Indon. 83 B4
Kolowana Watobo, Teluk b. Indon. 83 B4
Kolozsvár Romania see Cluj-Napoca
Kolpashevo Rus. Fed. 76 J4
Kolpos Messaras b. Greece 69 K7
Kol'skiy Poluostrov pen. Rus. Fed. see Kola Peninsula
Kölük Turkey see Kâhta
Koluli Eritrea 108 F7
Kolumadulu Atoll Maldives see Kolhumadulu Atoll
Kolva r. Rus. Fed. 52 M2
Kolvan India 106 B2
Kolvereid Norway 54 G4
Kolvik Norway 54 N1
Kolvitskoye, Ozero l. Rus. Fed. 54 R3
Kolwa reg. Pak. 111 G5
Kolwezi Dem. Rep. Congo 123 C5
Kolyma r. Rus. Fed. 77 R3
Kolyma Lowland Rus. Fed. see Kolymskaya Nizmennost'
Kolyma Range mts Rus. Fed. see Kolymskiy, Khrebet
Kolymskaya Nizmennost' lowland Rus. Fed. 77 Q3
Kolymskiy, Khrebet mts Rus. Fed. 77 R3
Kolyshley Rus. Fed. 53 J5
Kolyuchaya, Gora mt. Rus. Fed. 148 A2
Kolyuchin, Ostrov i. Rus. Fed. 148 D2
Kolyuchinskaya Guba b. Rus. Fed. 148 D2
Kol'zhat Kazakh. 98 C4
Kom mt. Bulg. 69 J3
Kom Xinjiang China 98 D2
Komadugu-gana watercourse Nigeria 120 E3
Komae Japan 93 F3
Komaga-dake mt. Japan 93 D3
Komagane Japan 93 D3
Komaga-take mt. Japan 93 F1
Komaggas S. Africa 124 C5
Komaio P.N.G. 81 K8
Komaki Japan 92 C3
Komandnaya, Gora mt. Rus. Fed. 90 E2
Komandorskiye Ostrova is Rus. Fed. 77 R4
Komárno Slovakia 57 Q7
Komati r. Swaziland 125 J3
Komatipoort S. Africa 125 J3
Komatsu Japan 92 C2
Komba i. Indon. 83 B4
Kombakomba Sulawesi Indon. 83 B3
Komebail Lagoon Palau 82 [inset]
Komering r. Indon. 84 D3
Komga S. Africa 125 H7
Komintern Ukr. see Marhanets'
Kominternivs'ke Ukr. 69 N1
Komiža Croatia 68 G3
Komló Hungary 68 H1
Kommunarsk Ukr. see Alchevs'k
Komodo i. Indon. 83 A5
Komodo, Taman Nasional nat. park Indon. 83 A5
Kôm Ombo Egypt see Kawm Umbū
Komono Congo 122 B4
Komono Japan 92 C3
Komoran i. Indon. 81 J8
Komoro Japan 93 E2
Komotini Greece 69 K4
Kompong Cham Cambodia see Kâmpóng Cham
Kompong Chhnang Cambodia see Kâmpóng Chhnăng
Kompong Kleang Cambodia see Kâmpóng Khleăng
Kompong Som Cambodia see Sihanoukville
Kompong Speu Cambodia see Kâmpóng Spœ
Kompong Thom Cambodia see Kâmpóng Thum
Komrat Moldova see Comrat
Komsberg mts S. Africa 124 E7
Komsomol Kazakh. see Karabalyk
Komsomolabad Tajik. see Komsomolobod
Komsomolets Kazakh. see Karabalyk
Komsomolets, Ostrov i. Rus. Fed. 76 K1
Komsomolobod Tajik. 111 H2
Komsomol's'k Ukr. 53 G6
Komsomol'skiy Chukotskiy Avtonomnyy Okrug Rus. Fed. 189 C2
Komsomol'skiy Khanty-Mansiyskiy Avtonomnyy Okrug Rus. Fed. see Yugorsk
Komsomol'skiy Respublika Kalmykiya - Khalm'g-Tangch Rus. Fed. 53 J7
Komsomol'sk-na-Amure Rus. Fed. 90 E2
Komsomol'skoye Kazakh. 102 B1
Komsomol'skoye Rus. Fed. 53 J6
Kömürlü Turkey 113 F2
Kon India 105 E4
Konacık Turkey 107 B1
Konada India 106 D2
Kōnan Aichi Japan 92 C3
Kōnan Shiga Japan 92 C4
Konarak India see Konarka
Konarka India 105 F6
Konch India 104 D4
Konda Japan 92 B3
Kondagaon India 106 D2
Kondinin Australia 135 B8
Kondinskoye Rus. Fed. see Oktyabr'skoye
Kondoa Tanz. 123 D4
Kondol' Rus. Fed. 53 J5
Kondopoga Rus. Fed. 52 G3
Kondoz Afgh. see Kunduz
Kondrovo Rus. Fed. 53 G5
Konergino Rus. Fed. 148 C2
Köneürgenç Turkm. 109 I1
Köneürgenç Turkm. see Köneürgenç
Kong Cameroon 120 E4
Kŏng, Kaôh i. Cambodia 87 C5
Kông, Tônlé r. Cambodia 87 D4
Kong, Xé r. Laos 86 D4
Kongakut r. AK U.S.A. 149 L1
Kongauru i. Palau 82 [inset]
Kong Christian IX Land reg. Greenland 147 O3
Kong Christian X Land reg. Greenland 147 P2
Kongelab atoll Marshall Is see Rongelap
Kong Frederik IX Land reg. Greenland 147 M3
Kong Frederik VI Kyst coastal area Greenland 147 N3
Kongiganak AK U.S.A. 148 G4
Kong Kat hill Indon. 85 G2
Kongkemul mt. Indon. 85 G2
Kongōdo-san mt. Japan 92 D2
Kongō-Ikoma Kokutei-kōen park Japan 92 B4
Kongolo Dem. Rep. Congo 123 C4
Kongor Sudan 121 G4
Kong Oscars Fjord inlet Greenland 147 P2
Kongoussi Burkina Faso 120 C3
Kongsberg Norway 55 F7
Kongsvinger Norway 55 H6
Kongur Shan mt. Xinjiang China 98 A5
Königsberg Rus. Fed. see Kaliningrad
Königsee Germany 63 L4
Königswinter Germany 63 H4
Königs Wusterhausen Germany 63 N2
Konimekh Uzbek. see Konimex
Konimex Uzbek. 111 G1
Konin Poland 57 Q4
Konjic Bos.-Herz. 68 G3
Konkiep watercourse Namibia 124 C5
Könnern Germany 63 L3
Konnevesi Fin. 54 O5
Kōno Japan 92 C3
Konosha Rus. Fed. 52 I3
Kōnosu Japan 93 F2
Konotop Ukr. 53 G6
Konpara India 105 E5
Kon Plông Vietnam 87 E4
Konqi He r. China 98 E4
Konrei Palau 82 [inset]
Konsei-tōge pass Japan 93 F2
Konso Eth. 122 D3
Konstantinograd Ukr. see Krasnohrad
Konstantinovka Rus. Fed. 90 B2
Konstantinovka Ukr. see Kostyantynivka
Konstantinovy Lázně Czech Rep. 63 M5
Konstanz Germany 57 L7
Kontha Myanmar 86 B2
Kontiolahti Fin. 54 P5
Konttila Fin. 54 O4
Kon Tum Vietnam 87 D4
Kon Tum, Cao Nguyên Vietnam 87 E4
Könugard Ukr. see Kiev
Konus mt. Rus. Fed. 148 B2
Konushin, Mys pt Rus. Fed. 52 I2
Konya Turkey 112 D3
Konyrat Kazakh. 98 A3
Konyrolen Kazakh. 98 B3
Konz Germany 62 G5
Konzhakovskiy Kamen', Gora mt. Rus. Fed. 51 R4
Koocanusa, Lake resr Canada/U.S.A. 150 H5
Kooch Bihar India see Koch Bihar
Kookynie Australia 135 C7
Koolyanobbing Australia 135 B7
Koondrook Australia 138 B5
Koorawatha Australia 138 D5
Koordarrie Australia 134 A5
Kootenay r. Canada 150 G5
Kootenay Lake Canada 150 G5
Kootenay National Park Canada 150 G5
Kootjieskolk S. Africa 124 E6
Koozata Lagoon AK U.S.A. 148 E3
Kopa Almatinskaya Oblast' Kazakh. 98 A4
Kopa Vostochnyy Kazakhstan Kazakh. 98 B3
Kópasker Iceland 54 [inset]
Kopbirlik Kazakh. 102 E2
Koper Slovenia 68 E2
Kopet Dag mts Iran/Turkm. 110 E2
Kopet-Dag, Khrebet mts Iran/Turkm. see Kopet Dag
Köpetdag Gershi mts Iran/Turkm. see Kopet Dag
Köping Sweden 55 J7
Köpmanholmen Sweden 54 K5
Kopong Botswana 125 G3
Koppal India 106 C3
Koppang Norway 55 G6
Kopparberg Sweden 55 I7
Koppeh Dāgh mts Iran/Turkm. see Kopet Dag
Köppel hill Germany 63 H4
Koppi r. Rus. Fed. 90 F2
Koppies S. Africa 125 H4
Koppieskraal Pan salt pan S. Africa 124 E4
Koprivnica Croatia 68 G1
Köprülü Turkey 107 A1
Köprülü Kanyon Milli Parkı nat. park Turkey 69 N6
Kopyl' Belarus see Kapyl'
Kora India 104 E4
Kōra Japan 92 C3
Korablino Rus. Fed. 53 I5
K'orahē Eth. 122 E3
Korak Pak. 111 G5
Koramlik Xinjiang China 99 D5
Korangal India 106 C2
Korangi Pak. 111 G5
Korān va Monjan Afgh. 111 H2
Koraput India 106 D2
Korat Thai. see Nakhon Ratchasima
Koratla India 106 C2
Korba India 105 E5
Korbach Germany 63 I3
Korbu, Gunung mt. Malaysia 84 C1
Korçë Albania 69 I4
Korčula Croatia 68 G3
Korčula i. Croatia 68 G3
Korčulanski Kanal sea chan. Croatia 68 G3
Korday Kazakh. 102 D3
Kord Küy Iran 110 D2
Kords reg. Iran 111 F5
Korea, North country Asia 91 B5
Korea, South country Asia 91 B5
Korea Bay g. China/N. Korea 91 B5
Korea Strait Japan/S. Korea 91 C6
Koregaon India 106 B2
Korenovsk Rus. Fed. 113 E1
Korenovskaya Rus. Fed. see Korenovsk
Korepino Rus. Fed. 51 R3
Korets' Ukr. 53 E6
Körfez Turkey 69 M4
Korff Ice Rise Antarctica 188 L1
Korfovskiy Rus. Fed. 90 D2
Korgalzhyn Kazakh. 102 D1
Korgas Xinjiang China 98 C3
Korgen Norway 54 H3
Korhogo Côte d'Ivoire 120 C4
Koribundu Sierra Leone 120 B4
Kori Creek inlet India 104 B5
Korinthiakos Kolpos sea chan. Greece see Corinth, Gulf of
Korinthos Greece see Corinth
Kőris-hegy hill Hungary 68 G1
Koritnik mt. Albania 69 I3
Koritsa Albania see Korçë
Kōriyama Japan 91 F5
Korkuteli Turkey 69 N6
Korla Xinjiang China 98 D4
Kormakitis, Cape Cyprus 107 A2
Körmend Hungary 68 G1
Kornat nat. park Croatia 68 F3
Korneyevka Karagandinskaya Oblast' Kazakh. 98 A2
Korneyevka Rus. Fed. 53 K6
Koro Côte d'Ivoire 120 C4
Koro i. Fiji 133 H3
Koro r. Indon. 83 B3
Koro Mali 120 C3
Koroc r. Canada 153 I2
Köroğlu Dağları mts Turkey 69 O4
Köroğlu Tepesi mt. Turkey 112 D2
Korogwe Tanz. 123 D4
Koroneia, Limni l. Greece 69 J4
Korong Vale Australia 138 A6
Koronia, Limni l. Greece see Koroneia, Limni

▶Koror Palau 82 [inset]
Former capital of Palau.

Koror i. Palau 82 [inset]
Koro Sea b. Fiji 133 H3
Korosten' Ukr. 53 F6
Korostyshiv Ukr. 53 F6
Koro Toro Chad 121 E3
Korovin Bay AK U.S.A. 149 [inset]
Korovin Volcano AK U.S.A. 149 [inset]
Korpilahti Fin. 54 N5
Korpo Fin. 55 L6
Korppoo Fin. see Korpo
Korsakov Rus. Fed. 90 F3
Korsnäs Fin. 54 L5
Korsør Denmark 55 G9
Korsun'-Shevchenkivs'kyy Ukr. 53 F6
Korsun'-Shevchenkovskiy Ukr. see Korsun'-Shevchenkivs'kyy
Korsze Poland 57 R3
Kortesjärvi Fin. 54 M5
Korti Sudan 108 D6
Kortkeros Rus. Fed. 52 K3
Kortrijk Belgium 62 D4
Korvala Fin. 54 O3
Koryakskaya, Sopka vol. Rus. Fed. 77 Q4
Koryakskoye Nagor'ye mts Rus. Fed. 77 S3
Koryazhma Rus. Fed. 52 J3
Kōryō Japan 92 B4
Koryŏng S. Korea 91 C6
Kos i. Greece 69 L6
Kosa Rus. Fed. 51 Q4
Kosai Japan 92 D4
Kosam India 104 E4
Kosan N. Korea 91 B5
Kościan Poland 57 P4
Kosciusko, Mount Australia see Kosciuszko, Mount
Kosciuszko, Mount Australia 138 D6
Kosciuszko National Park Australia 138 D6
Köse Turkey 113 E2
Köseçobanlı Turkey 107 A1
Kōsei Japan 92 C3
Kosgi India 106 C2
Kosh-Agach Rus. Fed. 94 B1
Kosh-Döbö Kyrg. 98 A4
Koshigaya Japan 93 F3
Koshikijima-rettō is Japan 91 C7
Koshino Japan 92 C2
Koshk Afgh. 111 F3
Koshkarkol', Ozero l. Kazakh. 98 C3
Koshk-e Kohneh Afgh. 111 F3
Koshki Rus. Fed. 53 K5
Kōshoku Japan 93 E2
Kosi r. India 99 B7
Kosi Bay S. Africa 125 K4
Košice Slovakia 53 D6
Kosigi India 106 C3
Kosi Reservoir Nepal 99 D8
Koskuduk Kazakh. 98 B3
Koskullskulle Sweden 54 L3
Köslin Poland see Koszalin
Kosma r. Rus. Fed. 52 K2
Koson Uzbek. 111 G2
Kosŏng N. Korea 91 C5
Kosova country Europe see Kosovo

▶Kosovo country Europe 69 I3
World's newest independent country. Gained independence from Serbia in February 2008.

Kosovska Mitrovica Kosovo see Mitrovicë
Kosrae atoll Micronesia 186 G5
Kosrap Xinjiang China 99 B5
Kösseine hill Germany 63 L5
Kossol Passage Palau 82 [inset]
Kossol Reef Palau 82 [inset]
Kosta-Khetagurovo Rus. Fed. see Nazran'
Kostanay Kazakh. 100 F1
Kostenets Bulg. 69 J3
Kosti Sudan 108 D7
Kostinbrod Bulg. 69 J3
Kostino Rus. Fed. 76 J3
Kostomuksha Rus. Fed. 54 Q4
Kostopil' Ukr. 53 E6
Kostopol' Ukr. see Kostopil'
Kostroma Rus. Fed. 52 I4
Kostrzyn Poland 57 O4
Kostyantynivka Ukr. 53 H6
Kostyukovichi Belarus see Kastsyukovichy
Kosuge Japan 93 E3
Kosugi Japan 92 D2
Kos'yu Rus. Fed. 51 R2
Koszalin Poland 57 P3
Kőszeg Hungary 68 G1
Kota Andhra Prad. India 106 D3
Kota Chhattisgarh India 105 E5
Kota Rajasthan India 104 C4
Kōta Japan 92 D4
Kotaagung Sumatera Indon. 84 D4
Kota Baharu Malaysia see Kota Bharu
Kotabaru Kalimantan Indon. 85 E3
Kotabaru Kalimantan Indon. 85 G3
Kotabaru Sumatera Indon. 84 B2
Kota Belud Sabah Malaysia 85 G1
Kotabesi Kalimantan Indon. 85 F3
Kota Bharu Malaysia 84 C1
Kotabumi Sumatera Indon. 84 D4
Kotabunan Sulawesi Indon. 83 C2
Kot Addu Pak. 111 H4
Kota Kinabalu Sabah Malaysia 85 G1
Kotamobagu Sulawesi Indon. 83 C2
Kotaneelee Range mts Canada 150 E2
Kotanemel', Gora mt. Kazakh. 98 B3
Kotaparh India 106 D2
Kotapinang Sumatera Indon. 84 C2
Kota Samarahan Sarawak Malaysia 85 E2
Kotatengah Sumatera Indon. 84 C2
Kota Tinggi Malaysia 84 C2
Kotawaringin Kalimantan Indon. 85 E3
Kotcho r. Canada 150 F3
Kotcho Lake Canada 150 F3
Kot Diji Pak. 111 H5
Kotdwara Uttaranchal India 99 B7
Kotel'nich Rus. Fed. 52 K4
Kotel'nikovo Rus. Fed. 53 I7
Kotel'nyy, Ostrov i. Rus. Fed. 77 O2
Kotgar India 106 D2
Kotgarh India 104 D3
Kothagudem India see Kottagudem
Köthen (Anhalt) Germany 63 L3
Kotido Uganda 121 G4
Kotikovo Rus. Fed. 90 D3
Kot Imamgarh Pak. 111 H5
Kotka Fin. 55 O6
Kot Kapura India 104 C3
Kotkino Rus. Fed. 52 K2
Kotlas Rus. Fed. 52 J3
Kotli Pak. 111 I3
Kotlik AK U.S.A. 148 G3
Kötlutangi pt Iceland 54 [inset]
Kotly Rus. Fed. 55 P7
Kotō Japan 92 C3
Kotorkoshi Nigeria 120 D3
Kotovo Rus. Fed. 53 J6
Kotovsk Rus. Fed. 53 I5
Kotra India 104 C4

Kotra Pak. 111 G4
Kotri r. India 106 D2
Kot Sarae Pak. 111 G6
Kottagudem India 106 D2
Kottarakara India 106 C4
Kottayam India 106 C4
Kotte Sri Lanka see Sri Jayewardenepura Kotte
Kotto r. Cent. Afr. Rep. 122 C3
Kotturu India 106 C3
Kotuy r. Rus. Fed. 77 L2
Kotzebue AK U.S.A. 148 G2
Kotzebue Sound sea channel AK U.S.A. 148 G2
Kötzting Germany 63 M5
Kouango Cent. Afr. Rep. 122 C3
Koubia Guinea 120 B3
Kouchibouguac National Park Canada 153 I5
Koudougou Burkina Faso 120 C3
Kouebokkeveld mts S. Africa 124 D7
Koufey Niger 120 E3
Koufonisi i. Greece 69 L7
Kougaberge mts S. Africa 124 F7
Koukourou r. Cent. Afr. Rep. 122 B3
Koulen Cambodia see Kulen
Koulikoro Mali 120 C3
Koumac New Caledonia 133 G4
Koumenzi Xinjiang China 94 C3
Koumi Japan 93 E2
Koumpentoum Senegal 120 B3
Koundâra Guinea 120 B3
Kounradskiy Karagandinskaya Oblast' Kazakh. 98 A3
Kountze U.S.A. 161 E6
Koupéla Burkina Faso 120 C3
Kourou Fr. Guiana 177 H2
Kouroussa Guinea 120 C3
Kousséri Cameroon 121 E3
Koutiala Mali 120 C3
Kouvola Fin. 55 O6
Kovallberget Sweden 54 J4
Kovdor Rus. Fed. 54 Q3
Kovdozero, Ozero l. Rus. Fed. 54 R3
Kovel' Ukr. 53 E6
Kovernino Rus. Fed. 52 I4
Kovilpatti India 106 C4
Kovno Lith. see Kaunas
Kovriga, Gora hill Rus. Fed. 52 K2
Kovrov Rus. Fed. 52 I4
Kovylkino Rus. Fed. 53 I5
Kovzhskoye, Ozero l. Rus. Fed. 52 H3
Kowangge Sumbawa Indon. 85 G5
Kowanyama Australia 136 C2
Kowloon H.K. China 97 [inset]
Kowloon Peak hill H.K. China 97 [inset]
Kowloon Peninsula H.K. China 97 [inset]
Kowŏn N. Korea 91 B5
Kox Kuduk well Xinjiang China 94 C3
Koxlax Xinjiang China 99 C5
Koxtag Xinjiang China 99 B5
Kōya Japan 92 B4
Kōyaguchi Japan 92 B4
Kōyama-misaki pt Japan 91 C6
Kōya-Ryūjin Kokutei-kōen park Japan 92 B4
Köyceğiz Turkey 69 M6
Koyginveyem r. Rus. Fed. 148 A2
Koygorodok Rus. Fed. 52 K3
Koyna Reservoir India 106 B2
Köýtendag Turkm. 111 G2
Koyuk AK U.S.A. 148 G2
Koyuk r. AK U.S.A. 148 G2
Koyukuk AK U.S.A. 148 H2
Koyukuk r. AK U.S.A. 148 H2
Koyukuk, Middle Fork r. AK U.S.A. 149 J2
Koyukuk, North Fork r. AK U.S.A. 149 J2
Koyukuk, South Fork r. AK U.S.A. 149 J2
Koyukuk Island AK U.S.A. 148 H2
Koyukuk National Wildlife Refuge nature res. AK U.S.A. 148 H2
Koyulhisar Turkey 112 E2
Kozağacı Turkey see Günyüzü
Kozakai Japan 92 D4
Kōzaki Japan 93 G3
Kō-zaki pt Japan 91 C6
Kozan Turkey 112 D3
Kozani Greece 69 I4
Kozara mts Bos.-Herz. 68 G2
Kozara nat. park Bos.-Herz. 68 G2
Kozarska Dubica Bos.-Herz. see Bosanska Dubica
Kozelets' Ukr. 53 F6
Kozel'sk Rus. Fed. 53 G5
Kozhikode India see Calicut
Kozhva Rus. Fed. 52 M2
Kozlu Turkey 69 N4
Koz'modem'yansk Rus. Fed. 52 J4
Kožuf mts Greece/Macedonia 69 J4
Kōzu-shima i. Japan 93 F4
Kozyatyn Ukr. 53 F6
Kpalimé Togo 120 D4
Kpandae Ghana 120 C4
Kpungan Pass India/Myanmar 86 B1
Kra, Isthmus of Thai. 87 B5
Krabi Thai. 87 B5
Kra Buri Thai. 87 B5
Krâchéh Cambodia 87 D4
Kraddsele Sweden 54 J4
Kragan Jawa Indon. 85 E4
Kragerø Norway 55 F7
Kraggenburg Neth. 62 F2
Kragujevac Serbia 69 I2

▶Krakatau i. Indon. 84 D4
2nd deadliest recorded volcanic eruption (1883).

Krakatau vol. Indon. 80 D8
Krakatau, Taman Nasional nat. park Indon. 84 D4
Krakau Poland see Kraków
Kraków Poland 57 Q5
Krakower See l. Germany 63 M1
Krâlănh Cambodia 87 C4
Kralendijk Bonaire 169 K6
Kramators'k Ukr. 53 H6
Kramfors Sweden 54 J5
Krammer est. Neth. 62 E3
Kranidi Greece 69 J6
Kranj Slovenia 68 F1
Kranji Reservoir Sing. 87 [inset]
Kranskop S. Africa 125 J5
Krasavino Rus. Fed. 52 J3
Krasilov Ukr. see Krasyliv
Krasino Rus. Fed. 76 G2
Kraskino Rus. Fed. 90 C4
Krāslava Latvia 55 O9
Kraslice Czech Rep. 63 M4
Krasnaya Gorbatka Rus. Fed. 52 I5
Krasnaya Polyana Kazakh. 98 A2
Krasnaya Yaranga Rus. Fed. 148 D2
Krasnaya Zarya Rus. Fed. 53 H5
Krasnoarmeysk Rus. Fed. 53 J6
Krasnoarmeysk Ukr. see Krasnoarmiys'k
Krasnoarmiys'k Ukr. 53 H6
Krasnoborsk Rus. Fed. 52 J3
Krasnodar Rus. Fed. 112 E1
Krasnodar Kray admin. div. Rus. Fed. see Krasnodarskiy Kray
Krasnodarskiy Kray admin. div. Rus. Fed. 112 E1
Krasnodon Ukr. 53 H6
Krasnogorodskoye Rus. Fed. 55 P8
Krasnogorsk Rus. Fed. 90 F2
Krasnogorskoye Rus. Fed. 52 L4
Krasnograd Ukr. see Krasnohrad
Krasnogvardeysk Uzbek. see Bulung'ur
Krasnogvardeyskoye Rus. Fed. 53 I7
Krasnohrad Ukr. 53 G6
Krasnohvardiys'ke Ukr. 53 G7
Krasnokamensk Rus. Fed. 95 I1
Krasnokamsk Rus. Fed. 51 R4
Krasnoperekops'k Ukr. 53 G7
Krasnopol'ye Rus. Fed. 90 F2
Krasnorechenskiy Rus. Fed. 90 D3
Krasnoslobodsk Rus. Fed. 53 I5
Krasnotur'insk Rus. Fed. 51 S4
Krasnoufimsk Rus. Fed. 51 R4
Krasnovishersk Rus. Fed. 51 R3
Krasnovodsk Turkm. see Türkmenbaşy
Krasnovodsk, Mys pt Turkm. 110 D2
Krasnovodskoye Plato plat. Turkm. 113 I2
Krasnowodsk Aylagy b. Turkm. see Türkmenbaşy Aýlagy
Krasnoyarovo Rus. Fed. 90 C2
Krasnoyarsk Rus. Fed. 76 K4
Krasnoyarskoye Vodokhranilishche resr Rus. Fed. 88 G2
Krasnoye Lipetskaya Oblast' Rus. Fed. 53 H5
Krasnoye Respublika Kalmykiya - Khalm'g-Tangch Rus. Fed. see Ulan Erge
Krasnoznamenskiy Kazakh. see Yegindykol'
Krasnoznamenskoye Kazakh. see Yegindykol'
Krasnyy Rus. Fed. 53 F5
Krasnyy Chikoy Rus. Fed. 95 G1
Krasnyye Baki Rus. Fed. 52 J4
Krasnyy Kamyshanik Rus. Fed. see Komsomol'skiy
Krasnyy Kholm Rus. Fed. 52 H4
Krasnyy Kut Rus. Fed. 53 J6
Krasnyy Luch Ukr. 53 H6
Krasnyy Lyman Ukr. 53 H6
Krasnyy Oktyabr' Kazakh. 98 B3
Krasnyy Yar Rus. Fed. 53 K7
Krasyliv Ukr. 53 E6
Kratie Cambodia see Krâchéh
Kratke Range mts P.N.G. 81 L8
Kraulshavn Greenland see Nuussuaq
Krâvanh, Chuŏr Phnum mts Cambodia/Thai. see Cardamom Range
Kraynovka Rus. Fed. 113 G2
Krefeld Germany 62 G3
Krekatok Island AK U.S.A. 148 F3
Kremenchug Ukr. see Kremenchuk
Kremenchugskoye Vodokhranilishche resr Ukr. see Kremenchuts'ka Vodoskhovyshche
Kremenchuk Ukr. 53 G6
Kremenchuts'ka Vodoskhovyshche resr Ukr. 53 G6
Křemešník hill Czech Rep. 57 O6
Kremges Ukr. see Svitlovods'k
Kremmidi, Akra pt Greece see Kremmydi, Akrotirio
Kremmydi, Akrotirio pt Greece 69 J6
Krems Austria see Krems an der Donau
Krems an der Donau Austria 57 O6
Krenitzin Islands AK U.S.A. 148 F5
Kresta, Zaliv g. Rus. Fed. 148 C2
Kresttsy Rus. Fed. 52 G4
Kretinga Lith. 55 L9
Kreuzau Germany 62 G4
Kreuztal Germany 63 H4
Kreva Belarus 55 O9
Kribi Cameroon 120 D4
Krichev Belarus see Krychaw
Kriel S. Africa 125 I4
Krikellos Greece 69 I5
Kril'on, Mys c. Rus. Fed. 90 F3
Krishna India 106 C2
Krishna r. India 106 D2
Krishnanagar India 105 G5
Krishnaraja Sagara l. India 106 C3
Kristiania Norway see Oslo
Kristiansand Norway 55 E7
Kristianstad Sweden 55 I8
Kristiansund Norway 54 E5
Kristiinankaupunki Fin. see Kristinestad
Kristinehamn Sweden 55 I7
Kristinestad Fin. 54 L5
Kristinopol' Ukr. see Chervonohrad
Kriti i. Greece see Crete
Kritiko Pelagos sea Greece 69 K6
Krivoy Rog Ukr. see Kryvyy Rih
Križevci Croatia 68 G1
Krk i. Croatia 68 F2
Krkonošský narodní park nat. park Czech Rep./Poland 57 O5
Krokom Sweden 54 I5
Krokstadøra Norway 54 F5
Krokstranda Norway 54 I3
Krolevets' Ukr. 53 G6
Kronach Germany 63 L4
Krŏng Kaôh Kŏng Cambodia 87 C5
Kronoby Fin. 54 M5
Kronprins Christian Land reg. Greenland 189 I1
Kronprins Frederik Bjerge nunataks Greenland 147 O3
Kronshtadt Rus. Fed. 55 P7
Kronstadt Romania see Braşov
Kronstadt Rus. Fed. see Kronshtadt
Kronwa Myanmar 86 B4
Kroonstad S. Africa 125 H4
Kropotkin Rus. Fed. 113 F1
Kropstädt Germany 63 M3
Krosno Poland 53 D6
Krotoszyn Poland 57 P5
Kroya Jawa Indon. 85 E4
Kruger National Park S. Africa 125 J2
Kruglikovo Rus. Fed. 90 D2
Krugloi Point pt AK U.S.A. 148 [inset]
Kruglyakov Rus. Fed. see Oktyabr'skiy
Krui Sumatera Indon. 84 C4
Kruisfontein S. Africa 124 G8
Kruja Albania see Krujë
Krujë Albania 69 H4
Krumovgrad Bulg. 69 K4
Krungkao Thai. see Ayutthaya
Krung Thep Thai. see Bangkok
Krupa Bos.-Herz. see Bosanska Krupa
Krupa na Uni Bos.-Herz. see Bosanska Krupa
Krupki Belarus 53 F5
Krusenstern, Cape AK U.S.A. 148 G2
Kruševac Serbia 69 I3
Krušné hory mts Czech Rep. 63 M4
Kruzof Island AK U.S.A. 149 N4
Krychaw Belarus 53 F5
Krylov Seamount sea feature N. Atlantic Ocean 184 G4
Krym' pen. Ukr. see Crimea
Krymsk Rus. Fed. 112 E1
Krymskaya Rus. Fed. see Krymsk
Kryms'kyy Pivostriv pen. Ukr. see Crimea
Krypsalo Kazakh. 98 A3
Krystynopol Ukr. see Chervonohrad
Krytiko Pelagos sea Greece see Kritiko Pelagos
Kryvyy Rih Ukr. 53 G7
Ksabi Alg. 64 D6
Ksar Chellala Alg. 67 H6
Ksar el Boukhari Alg. 67 H6
Ksar el Kebir Morocco 67 D6
Ksar-es-Souk Morocco see Er Rachidia
Ksenofontova Rus. Fed. 51 R3
Kshirpai India 105 F5
Ksour Essaf Tunisia 68 D7
Kstovo Rus. Fed. 52 J4
Kū', Jabal al hill Saudi Arabia 108 G4
Kuah Malaysia 84 B1
Kuaidamao China see Tonghua
Kuala Belait Brunei 85 F1
Kuala Dungun Malaysia see Dungun
Kualajelai Kalimantan Indon. 85 E3
Kuala Kangsar Malaysia 84 C1
Kualakapuas Kalimantan Indon. 85 F3
Kuala Kerai Malaysia 84 C1
Kualakuayan Kalimantan Indon. 85 F3
Kuala Kubu Baharu Malaysia 84 C2
Kualakurun Kalimantan Indon. 85 F3
Kualalangsa Sumatera Indon. 84 B1
Kuala Lipis Malaysia 84 C1

▶Kuala Lumpur Malaysia 84 C2
Joint capital (with Putrajaya) of Malaysia.

Kuala Nerang Malaysia 84 C1
Kualapembuang Kalimantan Indon. 85 F3
Kuala Penyu Sabah Malaysia 85 F1
Kuala Pilah Malaysia 84 C2
Kuala Rompin Malaysia 84 C2
Kualasampit Indon. 85 F3
Kuala Selangor Malaysia 84 C2
Kualasimpang Sumatera Indon. 84 B1
Kuala Terengganu Malaysia 84 C1
Kualatungal Sumatera Indon. 84 C3
Kuamut Sabah Malaysia 85 G1
Kuamut r. Malaysia 85 G1
Kuancheng Hebei China 95 I3
Kuandian China 90 B4
Kuantan Malaysia 84 C2
Kuba Azer. see Quba
Kuban' r. Rus. Fed. 53 H7
Kubār Syria 113 E4
Kubaybāt Syria 107 C2
Kubaysah Iraq 113 F4
Kubenskoye, Ozero l. Rus. Fed. 52 H4
Kubrat Bulg. 69 L3
Kubu Bali Indon. 85 F5
Kubu Kalimantan Indon. 85 E3
Kubuang Kalimantan Indon. 85 F2
Kubukhay Rus. Fed. 95 H1
Kubumesaäi Kalimantan Indon. 85 F2
Kuchaman Road India 111 I5
Kuchema Rus. Fed. 52 I2
Kuching Sarawak Malaysia 85 E2
Kuchino-Erabu-shima i. Japan 91 C7
Kucing Sarawak Malaysia see Kuching
Kuçovë Albania 69 H4
Kuda India 104 B5
Kudal India 106 B3
Kudangan Kalimantan Indon. 85 E3
Kudap Sumatera Indon. 84 C2
Kudara-Somon Rus. Fed. 95 F1
Kudat Sabah Malaysia 85 G1
Kudiakof Islands AK U.S.A. 148 G5
Kudligi India 106 C3
Kudobin Islands AK U.S.A. 148 G4
Kudoyama Japan 92 B4
Kudremukh mt. India 106 B3
Kudus Jawa Indon. 85 E4
Kudymkar Rus. Fed. 51 Q4
Kueishan Tao i. Taiwan 97 I3
Kūfah Iraq 112 G4
Kufar Seram Indon. 83 D3
Kufstein Austria 57 N7
Kugaaruk Canada 147 J3
Kugaluk r. N.W.T. Canada 149 O1
Kugaly Kazakh. 98 B3
Kugesi Rus. Fed. 52 J4
Kugka Lhai Xizang China 99 E7
Kugluktuk Canada 189 L2
Kugmallit Bay N.W.T. Canada 149 N1
Kugri Qinghai China 94 D5
Kuguno Japan 92 D2
Kūh, Ra's-al- pt Iran 110 E5
Kūhak Iran 111 F5
Kuhanbokano mt. China 105 E3
Kuhbier Germany 63 M1
Kūhdasht Iran 110 B3
Kūhīn Iran 110 C2
Kūhīrī Iran 111 F5
Kuhmo Fin. 54 P4
Kuhmoinen Fin. 55 N6
Kūhpāyeh mt. Iran 110 E4
Kūhrān, Kūh-e mt. Iran 110 E5
Kühren Germany 63 M3
Kui Buri Thai. 87 B4
Kuile He r. China 95 K1
Kuis Namibia 124 C3
Kuiseb watercourse Namibia 124 B2
Kuitan China 97 G4
Kuito Angola 123 B5
Kuitun Xinjiang China see Kuytun
Kuiu Island AK U.S.A. 149 N4
Kuivaniemi Fin. 54 N4
Kujang N. Korea 91 B5
Kuji Japan 91 F4
Kuji-gawa r. Japan 93 G2
Kujikuri Japan 93 G3
Kujūkuri-hama coastal area Japan 93 G3
Kujū-san vol. Japan 91 C6
Kuk r. AK U.S.A. 148 G1
Kukaklek Lake AK U.S.A. 148 I4
Kukālār, Kūh-e hill Iran 110 C4
Kukan Rus. Fed. 90 D2
Kukës Albania 69 I3
Kukesi Albania see Kukës
Kuki Japan 93 F2
Kukizaki Japan 93 G3
Kuki-zaki pt Japan 92 C4
Kukmor Rus. Fed. 52 K4
Kukpowruk r. AK U.S.A. 148 G1
Kukpuk r. AK U.S.A. 148 F1
Kukshi India 104 C5
Kukunuru India 106 D2
Kukup Malaysia 84 C2
Kükürtli Turkm. 110 E2
Kukusan, Gunung hill Indon. 85 F3
Kūl r. Iran 110 D5
Kula Turkey 69 M5
Kulabu, Gunung mt. Indon. 84 B2
Kulaisila India 105 F5
Kula Kangri mt. China/Bhutan 105 G3
Kulanak Kyrg. 98 A4
Kulandy Kazakh. 102 A2
Kulaneh reg. Pak. 111 F5
Kular Rus. Fed. 77 O2
Kulassein i. Phil. 82 C5
Kulat, Gunung mt. Indon. 85 G2
Kulawi Sulawesi Indon. 83 A3
Kuldīga Latvia 55 L8
Kuldja Xinjiang China see Yining
Kul'dur Rus. Fed. 90 C2
Kule Botswana 124 E2
Kulebaki Rus. Fed. 53 I5
Kulen Cambodia 87 D4
Kulgera Australia 135 F6
Kulikovka Kazakh. 98 B4
Kulikovo Rus. Fed. 52 J3
Kulim Malaysia 84 C1
Kulin Australia 135 B8
Kulja Australia 135 B7
Kulkyne watercourse Australia 138 B3
Kullu India 104 D3
Kulmbach Germany 63 L4
Kŭlob Tajik. 111 H2
Kuloy Rus. Fed. 52 I3
Kuloy r. Rus. Fed. 52 I2
Kulp Turkey 113 F3
Kul'sary Kazakh. 100 E2
Külsheim Germany 63 J5
Kulu India see Kullu
Kulu Turkey 112 D3
Kulunda Rus. Fed. 88 D2
Kulundinskaya Step' plain Kazakh./Rus. Fed. 88 D2
Kulundinskoye, Ozero salt l. Rus. Fed. 88 D2
Kulusuk Greenland 147 O3
Kulusutay Rus. Fed. 95 H1
Kulwin Australia 137 C7
Kulyab Tajik. see Kŭlob
Kuma r. Rus. Fed. 53 J7
Kumagaya Japan 93 F2
Kumai Kalimantan Indon. 85 E3
Kumai, Teluk b. Indon. 85 E3
Kumakhta Rus. Fed. 95 H1
Kumalar Dağı mts Turkey 69 N5
Kumamoto Japan 91 C6
Kumano Japan 91 E6
Kumanovo Macedonia 69 I3
Kumara Rus. Fed. 90 B2
Kumasi Ghana 120 C4
Kumayri Armenia see Gyumri
Kumba Cameroon 120 D4
Kumbakonam India 106 C4
Kumbe Indon. 81 K8
Kümbet Turkey 69 N5
Kumbharli Ghat mt. India 106 B2
Kumbher Nepal 99 C7
Kumbla India 106 B3
Kumchuru Botswana 124 F2
Kum-Dag Turkm. see Gumdag
Kumdah Saudi Arabia 108 G5
Kumel well Iran 110 D3
Kumeny Rus. Fed. 52 K4
Kumertau Rus. Fed. 76 G4
Kumgang-san mt. N. Korea 91 C5
Kumguri India 105 G4
Kumi S. Korea 91 C5
Kumi Uganda 121 G4
Kumihama Japan 92 A3
Kumihama-wan l. Japan 92 A3
Kumiyama Japan 92 B4
Kum Kuduk well Xinjiang China 98 E4
Kumla Sweden 55 I7
Kumlu Turkey 107 C1
Kummersdorf-Alexanderdorf Germany 63 N2
Kumo Nigeria 120 E3
Kŭmŏ-do i. S. Korea 91 B6
Kumon Range mts Myanmar 86 B1
Kumotori-yama mt. Japan 93 E3
Kumozu-gawa r. Japan 92 C4
Kumphawapi Thai. 86 C3
Kums Namibia 124 D5
Kumta India 106 B3
Kumu Dem. Rep. Congo 122 C3
Kumukh Rus. Fed. 113 G2
Kumul Xinjiang China see Hami
Kumund India 106 D1
Kümüx Xinjiang China 98 E4
Kumylzhenskaya Rus. Fed. see Kumylzhenskiy
Kumylzhenskiy Rus. Fed. 53 I6
Kun r. Myanmar 86 B3
Kuna r. AK U.S.A. 148 H1
Kunar r. Afgh. 111 H3
Kunashir, Ostrov i. Rus. Fed. 90 G3
Kunashirskiy Proliv sea chan. Japan/Rus. Fed. see Nemuro-kaikyō
Kunchaung Myanmar 86 B2
Kunchuk Tso salt l. China 105 E2
Kunda Estonia 55 O7
Kunda India 105 E4
Kundapura India 106 B3
Kundelungu, Parc National de nat. park Dem. Rep. Congo 123 C5
Kundelungu Ouest, Parc National de nat. park Dem. Rep. Congo 123 C5
Kundia India 104 C4
Kundur i. Indon. 84 C2
Kunduz Afgh. 111 H2
Kunene r. Angola see Cunene
Kuneneng admin. dist. Botswana see Kweneng
Künes Xinjiang China see Xinyuan
Künes Chang Xinjiang China 98 C4
Künes He r. China 98 C4
Künes Linchang Xinjiang China 98 D4
Kungälv Sweden 55 G8
Kungar-Tuk Rus. Fed. 94 D1
Kungei Alatau mts Kazakh./Kyrg. 98 B4
Kunggar Xizang China see Maizhokunggar
Kunghit Island B.C. Canada 149 O5
Kungsbacka Sweden 55 H8
Kungshamn Sweden 55 G7
Kungu Dem. Rep. Congo 122 B3
Kungur mt. Xinjiang China see Kongur Shan
Kungur Rus. Fed. 51 R4
Kunhing Myanmar 86 B2
Kuni r. India 106 C2
Kuni Japan 93 E2
Kūnīch Iran 110 E5
Kunié i. New Caledonia see Pins, Île des
Kunigai India 106 C3
Kunimi-dake hill Japan 92 C2
Kunimi-dake mt. Japan 91 C6
Kuningan Jawa Indon. 85 E4
Kunkavav India 104 B5
Kunlong Myanmar 86 B2
Kunlui r. India/Nepal 99 E8

▶Kunlun Shan mts China 94 B5
Location of highest active volcano in Asia.

Kunlun Shankou pass Qinghai China 94 C5
Kunming China 96 D3
Kuno r. India 99 B8
Kunsan S. Korea 91 B6
Kunshan China 97 I2
Kununurra Australia 134 E3
Kunwak r. Canada 151 L2
Kunwari r. India 99 B8
Kun'ya Rus. Fed. 52 F4
Kunyang Yunnan China see Jinning
Kunyang Zhejiang China see Pingyang
Kunya-Urgench Turkm. see Köneürgenç
Kunyu Shan mts China 95 J4
Künzelsau Germany 63 J5
Künzels-Berg hill Germany 63 L3
Kuocang Shan mts China 97 I2
Kuohijärvi l. Fin. 55 N6
Kuolayarvi Rus. Fed. 54 P3
Kuopio Fin. 54 O5
Kuortane Fin. 54 M5
Kupa r. Croatia/Slovenia 68 G2
Kupang Timor Indon. 83 B5
Kupang, Teluk b. Timor Indon. 83 B5
Kupari India 105 F5
Kuparuk r. AK U.S.A. 149 J1
Kupiškis Lith. 55 N9
Kupreanof Island AK U.S.A. 149 N4
Kupreanof Point pt AK U.S.A. 148 H5
Kupreanof Strait AK U.S.A. 148 I4
Kupwara India 104 C2
Kup"yans'k Ukr. 53 H6
Kuqa Xinjiang China 98 C4
Kur r. Rus. Fed. 90 D2
also known as Kür (Georgia), Kura
Kura r. Georgia 113 G2
also known as Kur (Russian Federation), Kura
Kuragino Rus. Fed. 88 G2
Kurai-yama mt. Japan 92 D2
Kurakh Rus. Fed. 53 J8
Kurama Range mts Asia 109 K1
Kurama-yama hill Japan 92 B3
Kuraminskiy Khrebet mts Asia see Kurama Range
Kūrān Dap Iran 111 E5
Kurashiki Japan 91 D6
Kurasia India 105 E5
Kurayn i. Saudi Arabia 110 C5
Kurayoshi Japan 91 D6
Kurayskiy Khrebet mts Rus. Fed. 94 B1
Kurchatov Rus. Fed. 53 G6
Kurchum Kazakh. 102 F2
Kurchum r. Kazakh. 98 C2
Kürdämir Azer. 113 H2
Kurday Kazakh. 98 A4
Kŭrdzhali Bulg. 69 K4
Kure Japan 91 D6
Küre Turkey 112 D2
Kure Atoll U.S.A. 186 I4
Kuressaare Estonia 55 M7
Kurgal'dzhino Kazakh. see Korgalzhyn
Kurgal'dzhinskiy Kazakh. see Korgalzhyn
Kurgan Rus. Fed. 76 H4
Kurganinsk Rus. Fed. 113 F1
Kurgannaya Rus. Fed. see Kurganinsk
Kurgantyube Tajik. see Qŭrghonteppa
Kuri Afgh. 111 H2
Kuri India 104 B4
Kuria Muria Islands Oman see Ḥalāniyāt, Juzur al
Kuridala Australia 136 C4
Kurigram Bangl. 105 G4
Kurihama Japan 93 F3
Kurihashi Japan 93 F2
Kurikka Fin. 54 M5
Kuril Basin sea feature Sea of Okhotsk 186 F2
Kuril Islands Rus. Fed. 90 H3
Kurilovka Rus. Fed. 53 K6
Kuril'sk Rus. Fed. 90 G3
Kuril'skiye Ostrova is Rus. Fed. see Kuril Islands
Kuril Trench sea feature N. Pacific Ocean 186 F3
Kurimoto Japan 93 G3
Kuriyama Tochigi Japan 93 F2
Kurkino Rus. Fed. 53 H5
Kurmashkino Kazakh. see Kurchum
Kurmuk Sudan 108 D7
Kurnool India 106 C3
Kurobane Japan 93 G2
Kurobe Japan 92 D2
Kurobe-gawa r. Japan 92 D2
Kurobe-ko resr Japan 92 D2
Kurodashō Japan 92 B3
Kurohime-yama mt. Japan 93 D2
Kurohone Japan 93 F2
Kuroiso Japan 93 G2
Kurort Schmalkalden Germany 63 K4
Kuro-shima i. Japan 92 B4
Kuroso-yama mt. Japan 92 C4
Kurovskiy Rus. Fed. 90 B1
Kurow N.Z. 139 C7
Kurram Pak. 111 H3
Kurri Kurri Australia 138 E4
Kursavka Rus. Fed. 113 F1
Kürshim Kazakh. see Kurchum
Kurshskiy Zaliv b. Lith./Rus. Fed. see Courland Lagoon
Kuršių marios b. Lith./Rus. Fed. see Courland Lagoon
Kursk Rus. Fed. 53 H6
Kurskaya Rus. Fed. 113 G1
Kurskiy Zaliv b. Lith./Rus. Fed. see Courland Lagoon
Kurşunlu Turkey 112 D2
Kurtalan Turkey 113 F3
Kurtoğlu Burnu pt Turkey 69 M6
Kurtpınar Turkey 107 B1
Kurtty r. Kazakh. 98 B3
Kurucaşile Turkey 112 D2
Kuruçay Turkey 112 E3
Kurukshetra India 104 D3
Kuruktag mts China 98 D4
Kuruman S. Africa 124 F4
Kuruman watercourse S. Africa 124 E4
Kurume Japan 91 C6
Kurumkan Rus. Fed. 89 K2
Kurunegala Sri Lanka 106 D5
Kurunzulay Rus. Fed. 95 I1
Kurupa r. AK U.S.A. 148 I1
Kurupam India 106 D2
Kurupkan Rus. Fed. 148 D2
Kurush, Jebel hills Sudan 108 D5
Kur'ya Rus. Fed. 51 R3
Kuryk Kazakh. 113 H2
Kuşadası Turkey 69 L6
Kuşadası Körfezi b. Turkey 69 L6
Kusaie atoll Micronesia see Kosrae
Kusary Azer. see Qusar
Kusatsu Gunma Japan 93 E2
Kusatsu Shiga Japan 92 B3
Kuşcenneti nature res. Turkey 107 B1
Kuschke Nature Reserve S. Africa 125 I3
Kusel Germany 63 H5
Kuş Gölü l. Turkey 69 L4
Kushalgarh India 104 C5
Kushchevskaya Rus. Fed. 53 H7
Kushida-gawa r. Japan 92 C4
Kushigata Japan 93 E3
Kushihara Japan 92 D3
Kushimoto Japan 91 D6
Kushiro Japan 90 G4
Kushka Turkm. see Serhetabat
Kushkopola Rus. Fed. 52 J3
Kushmurun Kazakh. 100 F1
Kushtagi India 106 C3
Kushtia Bangl. 105 G5
Kushtih Iran 111 E4
Kuskan Turkey 107 A1
Kuskokwim r. AK U.S.A. 148 G3
Kuskokwim, North Fork r. AK U.S.A. 148 I3
Kuskokwim, South Fork r. AK U.S.A. 148 I3
Kuskokwim Bay AK U.S.A. 148 F4
Kuskokwim Mountains AK U.S.A. 148 I2
Kuşluyan Turkey see Gölköy
Kusŏng N. Korea 91 B5
Kustanay Kazakh. see Kostanay
Kustatan AK U.S.A. 149 J3
Küstence Romania see Constanţa
Küstenkanal canal Germany 63 H1
Kustia Bangl. see Kushtia
Kusu Halmahera Indon. 83 C2
Kusu Japan 92 C4
Kut Iran 110 C4
Kut, Ko i. Thai. 87 C5
Kuta Bali Indon. 85
Kutabagok Sumatera Indon. 84 B1
Kūt 'Abdollāh Iran 110 C4
Kutacane Sumatera Indon. 84 B2
Kütahya Turkey 69 M5
Kutai, Taman Nasional nat. park Indon. 85 G2
K'ut'aisi Georgia 113 F2
Kut-al-Imara Iraq see Al Kūt
Kutan Rus. Fed. 113 G1
Kutanibong Indon. 87 B7
Kutaraja Sumatera Indon. see Banda Aceh
Kutayfat Ţurayf vol. Saudi Arabia 107 D4
Kutch, Gulf of India see Kachchh, Gulf of
Kutch, Rann of marsh India see Kachchh, Rann of
Kutchan Japan 90 F4
Kutina Croatia 68 G2
Kutjevo Croatia 68 G2
Kutkai Myanmar 86 B2
Kutno Poland 57 Q4
Kutru India 106 D2
Kutsuki Japan 92 B3
Kutu Dem. Rep. Congo 122 B4
Kutubdia Island Bangl. 105 G5
Kutum Sudan 121 F3
Kutztown U.S.A. 165 H3
Kuujjua r. Canada 146 G2
Kuujjuaq Canada 153 H2
Kuujjuarapik Canada 152 F3
Kuusamo Fin. 54 P4
Kuusankoski Fin. 55 O6
Kuvango Angola 123 B5
Kuvshinovo Rus. Fed. 52 G4
Kuwait country Asia 110 B4

▶Kuwait Kuwait 110 B4
Capital of Kuwait.

Kuwajleen atoll Marshall Is see Kwajalein
Kuwana Japan 92 C3
Kuybyshev Novosibirskaya Oblast' Rus. Fed. 76 I4
Kuybyshev Respublika Tatarstan Rus. Fed. see Bolgar
Kuybyshev Samarskaya Oblast' Rus. Fed. see Samara
Kuybysheve Ukr. 53 H7
Kuybyshevka-Vostochnaya Rus. Fed. see Belogorsk
Kuybyshevskoye Vodokhranilishche resr Rus. Fed. 53 K5
Kuyeda Rus. Fed. 51 R4
Kuye He r. China 95 G4
Kuygan Kazakh. 102 D2
Küysu Xinjiang China 94 C3
Kuytun Xinjiang China 98 D3
Kuytun Rus. Fed. 88 I2
Kuytun He r. China 98 C3
Kuyucak Turkey 69 M6

Kuyus Rus. Fed. 98 D2
Kuyu Tingni Nicaragua 166 [inset] J6
Kuze Japan 92 C3
Kuzino Rus. Fed. 51 R4
Kuzitrin r. AK U.S.A. 148 F2
Kuznechnoye Rus. Fed. 55 P6
Kuznetsk Rus. Fed. 53 J5
Kuznetsovo Rus. Fed. 90 E3
Kuznetsovs'k Ukr. 53 E6
Kuzovatovo Rus. Fed. 53 J5
Kuzuryū-gawa r. Japan 92 C2
Kuzuryū-ko resr Japan 92 C3
Kuzuu Japan 93 F2
Kvænangen sea chan. Norway 54 L1
Kvaløya i. Norway 54 K2
Kvalsund Norway 54 M1
Kvarnerić sea chan. Croatia 68 F2
Kvichak AK U.S.A. 148 H4
Kvichak r. AK U.S.A. 148 H4
Kvichak Bay AK U.S.A. 148 H4
Kvitøya ice feature Svalbard 76 E2
Kwa r. Dem. Rep. Congo see Kasaï
Kwabhaca S. Africa see Mount Frere
Kwadelen atoll Marshall Is see Kwajalein
Kwajalein atoll Marshall Is 186 H5
Kwala Sumatera Indon. 84 B2
Kwale Nigeria 120 D4
KwaMashu S. Africa 125 J5
KwaMhlanga S. Africa 125 I3
Kwa Mtoro Tanz. 123 D4
Kwandang Sulawesi Indon. 83 B2
Kwangch'ŏn S. Korea 91 B5
Kwangchow China see Guangzhou
Kwangju S. Korea 91 B6
Kwangsi Chuang Autonomous Region aut. reg. China see Guangxi Zhuangzu Zizhiqu
Kwangtung prov. China see Guangdong
Kwanmo-bong mt. N. Korea 90 C4
Kwanobuhle S. Africa 125 G7
KwaNojoli S. Africa 125 G7
Kwanonqubela S. Africa 125 H7
KwaNonzame S. Africa 124 G6
Kwanza r. Angola see Cuanza
Kwatinidubu S. Africa 125 H7
KwaZamokuhle S. Africa 125 I4
KwaZamukucinga S. Africa 124 G7
Kwazamuxolo S. Africa 124 G6
KwaZanele S. Africa 125 I4
KwaZulu-Natal prov. S. Africa 125 J5
Kweichow prov. China see Guizhou
Kweiyang China see Guiyang
Kwekwe Zimbabwe 123 C5
Kweneng admin. dist. Botswana 124 G2
Kwenge r. Dem. Rep. Congo 123 B4
Kwetabohigan r. Canada 152 E4
Kwethluk AK U.S.A. 148 G3
Kwethluk r. AK U.S.A. 148 G3
Kwezi-Naledi S. Africa 125 H6
Kwidzyn Poland 57 Q4
Kwigillingok AK U.S.A. 148 G4
Kwiguk AK U.S.A. 148 F3
Kwikila P.N.G. 81 L8
Kwilu r. Angola/Dem. Rep. Congo 123 B4
Kwo Chau Kwan To is H.K. China see Ninepin Group
Kwoka mt. Indon. 81 I7
Kyabra Australia 137 C5
Kyabram Australia 138 B6
Kyadet Myanmar 86 A2
Kyaikkami Myanmar 86 B3
Kyaiklat Myanmar 86 A3
Kyaikto Myanmar 86 B3
Kyakhta Rus. Fed. 94 F1
Kyalite Australia 138 A5
Kyancutta Australia 135 F8
Kyangin Myanmar 86 B3
Kyangngoin Xizang China 99 F7
Kyaukhnyat Myanmar 86 B3
Kyaukkyi Myanmar 86 B3
Kyaukme Myanmar 86 B2
Kyaukpadaung Myanmar 86 A2
Kyaukpyu Myanmar 86 A3
Kyaukse Myanmar 86 B2
Kyauktaw Myanmar 86 A2
Kyaunggon Myanmar 86 A3
Kybartai Lith. 55 M9
Kyebogyi Myanmar 86 B3
Kyêbxang Co l. China 105 G2
Kyeikdon Myanmar 86 B3
Kyeikywa Myanmar 86 B3
Kyeintali Myanmar 86 A3
Kyela Tanz. 123 D4
Kyelang India 104 D2
Kyidaunggan Myanmar 86 B3
Kyikug Qinghai China 94 E4
Kyiv Ukr. see Kiev
Kyklades is Greece see Cyclades
Kyle Canada 151 I5
Kyle of Lochalsh U.K. 60 D3
Kyll r. Germany 62 G5
Kyllini mt. Greece 69 J6
Kymi Greece 69 K5
Kymis, Akra pt Greece see Kymis, Akrotirio
Kymis, Akrotirio pt Greece 69 K5
Kyneton Australia 138 B6
Kynuna Australia 136 C4
Kyoga, Lake Uganda 122 D3
Kyōga-dake mt. Japan 92 C2
Kyōga-dake mt. Japan 93 D3
Kyōga-misaki pt Japan 92 B3
Kyogle Australia 138 F2
Kyonan Japan 93 F3
Kyong Myanmar 86 B2
Kyŏngju S. Korea 91 C6
Kyonpyaw Myanmar 86 A3
Kyōtanabe Japan 92 B4
Kyōto Japan 92 B4
Kyōto pref. Japan 92 B3
Kyōwa Ibaraki Japan 93 G2
Kyparissia Greece 69 I6
Kypros country Asia see Cyprus
Kypshak, Ozero salt l. Kazakh. 101 F1
Kyra Rus. Fed. 95 H1
Kyra Panagia i. Greece 69 K5
Kyrenia Cyprus 107 A2
Kyrenia Mountains Cyprus see Pentadaktylos Range
Kyrgyz Ala-Too mts Kazakh./Kyrg. see Kirghiz Range
Kyrgyzstan country Asia 102 D3
Kyritz Germany 63 M2
Kyrksæterøra Norway 54 F5
Kyrta Rus. Fed. 51 R3
Kyssa Rus. Fed. 52 J2
Kytalyktakh Rus. Fed. 77 O3
Kythira i. Greece 69 J6
Kythnos i. Greece 69 K6
Kyunglung Xizang China 99 C7
Kyunhla Myanmar 86 A2
Kyun Pila i. Myanmar 87 B5
Kyuquot Canada 150 E5
Kyurdamir Azer. see Kürdämir
Kyūshū i. Japan 91 C7
Kyushu-Palau Ridge sea feature N. Pacific Ocean 186 F4
Kyustendil Bulg. 69 J3
Kywebwe Myanmar 86 B3
Kywong Australia 138 C5
Kyyev Ukr. see Kiev
Kyyiv Ukr. see Kiev
Kyyivs'ke Vodoskhovyshche resr Ukr. 53 F6
Kyyjärvi Fin. 54 N5
Kyzyl Rus. Fed. 102 H1
Kyzylagash Kazakh. 98 B3
Kyzyl-Art, Pereval pass Kyrg./Tajik. see Kyzylart Pass
Kyzylart Pass Kyrg./Tajik. 111 I2
Kyzyl-Burun Azer. see Siyäzän
Kyzylkesek Kazakh. 98 C3
Kyzyl-Khaya Rus. Fed. 94 B1
Kyzyl-Kiya Kyrg. see Kyzyl-Kyya
Kyzylkum, Peski des. Kazakh./Uzbek. see Kyzylkum Desert
Kyzylkum Desert Kazakh./Uzbek. 102 B3
Kyzyl-Kyya Kyrg. 102 D3
Kyzyl-Mazhalyk Rus. Fed. 102 H1
Kyzylorda Kazakh. 102 C3
Kyzylrabot Tajik. see Qizilrabot
Kyzylsay Kazakh. 113 I2
Kyzyl-Suu Kyrg. 98 B4
Kyzylysor Kazakh. 113 H1
Kyzylzhar Kazakh. 102 C2
Kzyl-Dzhar Kazakh. see Kyzylzhar
Kzyl-Orda Kazakh. see Kyzylorda
Kzyltu Kazakh. see Kishkenekol'

L

Laagri Estonia 55 N7
La Aguja Mex. 166 C4
Laam Atoll Maldives see Hadhdhunmathi Atoll
La Amistad, Parque Internacional nat. park Costa Rica/Panama 166 [inset] J7
La Angostura, Presa de resr Mex. 167 G6
Laanila Fin. 54 O2
La Ardilla, Cerro mt. Mex. 166 E4
Laascaanood Somalia 122 E3
La Ascensión, Bahía de b. Mex. 169 G5
Laasgoray Somalia 122 E2

▶Laâyoune W. Sahara 120 B2
Capital of Western Sahara.

La Babia Mex. 166 E2
La Baie Canada 153 H4
Labala Indon. 83 B5
La Baleine, Grande Rivière de r. Canada 152 F3
La Baleine, Petite Rivière de r. Canada 152 F3
La Baleine, Rivière à r. Canada 153 I2
La Banda Arg. 178 D3
Labang Sarawak Malaysia 85 F2
La Barge U.S.A. 156 F4
Labasa Fiji 133 H3
La Baule-Escoublac France 66 C3
Labazhskoye Rus. Fed. 52 L2
Labe r. Czech Rep. see Elbe
Labé Guinea 120 B3
La Belle U.S.A. 163 D7
Labengke i. Indon. 83 B3
La Bénoué, Parc National de nat. park Cameroon 121 E4
Laberge, Lake Y.T. Canada 149 N3
Labi Brunei 85 F1
Labian, Tanjung pt Malaysia 85 G1
La Biche, Lac l. Canada 151 H4
Labinsk Rus. Fed. 113 F1
Labis Malaysia 84 C2
La Biznaga Mex. 166 C2
Labo Luzon Phil. 82 C3
Labobo i. Indon. 83 B3
La Boquilla Mex. 166 D3
La Boucle du Baoulé, Parc National de nat. park Mali 120 C3
Labouheyre France 66 D4
Laboulaye Arg. 178 D4
Labrador reg. Canada 153 J3
Labrador City Canada 153 I3
Labrador Sea Canada/Greenland 147 M3
Labrang Gansu China see Xiahe
Lábrea Brazil 176 F5
Labuan Malaysia 85 F1
Labuan i. Malaysia 85 F1
Labuan state Malaysia 85 F1
Labuanbajo Sulawesi Indon. 83 B3
Labudalin Nei Mongol China see Ergun
La Bufa, Cerro mt. Mex. 166 E5
Labuhan Jawa Indon. 84 D4
Labuhanbajo Flores Indon. 83 A5
Labuhanbilik Sumatera Indon. 84 C2
Labuhanhaji Sumatera Indon. 84 B2
Labuhanmeringgai Sumatera Indon. 84 D4
Labuhanruku Sumatera Indon. 84 B2
Labuk r. Malaysia 85 G1
Labuk, Teluk b. Malaysia 85 G1
Labuna Maluku Indon. 83 C3
Labutta Myanmar 86 A3
Labyrinth, Lake salt flat Australia 137 A6
Labytnangi Rus. Fed. 76 H3
Laç Albania 69 H4
La Cabrera, Sierra de mts Spain 67 C2
La Cadena Mex. 166 D3
Lac-Allard Canada 153 J4
La Calle Alg. see El Kala
Lacandón, Parque Nacional nat. park Guat. 167 H5
La Cañiza Spain see A Cañiza
Lacantún r. Mex. 167 H5
La Capelle France 62 D5
La Carlota Arg. 178 D4
La Carlota Negros Phil. 82 C4
La Carolina Spain 67 E4
Lăcăuţi, Vârful mt. Romania 69 L2
Laccadive, Minicoy and Amindivi Islands union terr. India see Lakshadweep
Laccadive Islands India 106 B4
Lac du Bonnet Canada 151 L5
Lacedaemon Greece see Sparti
La Ceiba Hond. 166 [inset] I6
Lacepede Bay Australia 137 B8
Lacepede Islands Australia 134 C4
Lacha, Ozero l. Rus. Fed. 52 H3
Lachendorf Germany 63 K2
Lachine U.S.A. 164 D1

▶Lachlan r. Australia 138 A5
5th longest river in Oceania.

La Chorrera Panama 166 [inset] K7
Lachute Canada 152 G5
Laçın Azer. 113 G3
La Ciotat France 66 G5
La Ciudad Mex. 166 D4
Lac La Biche Canada 151 I4
Lac la Martre N.W.T. Canada see Whatî
Lacolle Canada 165 I1
La Colorada Sonora Mex. 166 C2
La Colorada Zacatecas Mex. 161 C8
Lacombe Canada 150 H4
La Comoé, Parc National de nat. park Côte d'Ivoire 120 C4
La Concepción Panama 166 [inset] J7
La Concordia Mex. 167 G5
Laconi Sardinia Italy 68 C5
Laconia U.S.A. 165 J2
La Corey Canada 151 I4
La Coruña Spain see A Coruña
La Corvette, Lac de l. Canada 152 G3
La Coubre, Pointe de pt France 66 D4
La Crete Canada 150 G3
La Crosse KS U.S.A. 160 D4
La Crosse VA U.S.A. 165 F5
La Crosse WI U.S.A. 160 F3
La Cruz Costa Rica 166 [inset] I7
La Cruz Chihuahua Mex. 166 D3
La Cruz Sinaloa Mex. 166 D4
La Cruz Tamaulipas Mex. 167 F3
La Cruz Nicaragua 166 [inset] I6
La Cruz, Cerro mt. Mex. 167 E5
La Cuesta Coahuila Mex. 166 E2
La Culebra, Sierra de mts Spain 67 C3
La Cygne U.S.A. 160 E4
Lada, Teluk b. Indon. 84 D4
Ladainha Brazil 179 C2
Ladakh reg. India/Pak. 104 D2
Ladakh Range mts India 104 D2
Ladang, Ko i. Thai. 87 B6
La Demajagua Cuba 163 D8
La Demanda, Sierra de mts Spain 67 E2
La Democracia Guat. 167 H6
La Déroute, Passage de strait Channel Is/France 59 E9
Ladik Turkey 112 D2
Lādīz Iran 111 F4
Ladnun India 104 C4

▶Ladoga, Lake Rus. Fed. 52 F3
2nd largest lake in Europe.

Ladong China 97 F3
Ladozhskoye Ozero l. Rus. Fed. see Ladoga, Lake
Ladrones terr. N. Pacific Ocean see Northern Mariana Islands
Ladrones, Islas is Panama 166 [inset] J8
Ladu mt. India 105 H4
Ladue r. Canada/U.S.A. 149 L3
La Dura Mex. 166 C2
Ladva-Vetka Rus. Fed. 52 G3
Ladybank U.K. 60 F4
Ladybrand S. Africa 125 H5
Lady Frere S. Africa 125 H6
Lady Grey S. Africa 125 H6
Ladysmith S. Africa 125 I5
Ladysmith U.S.A. 160 F2
Ladzhanurges Georgia see Lajanurpekhi
Lae P.N.G. 81 L8
Laem Ngop Thai. 87 C4
Lærdalsøyri Norway 55 E6
La Esmeralda Bol. 176 F8
Læsø i. Denmark 55 G8
La Esperanza Hond. 166 [inset] H6
Lafayette Alg. see Bougaa
La Fayette AL U.S.A. 163 C5
Lafayette IN U.S.A. 164 B3
Lafayette LA U.S.A. 161 E6
Lafayette TN U.S.A. 164 B5
Lafé Cuba 163 C8
La Fère France 62 D5
Laferte r. Canada 150 G2
La Ferté-Gaucher France 62 D6
La-Ferté-Milon France 62 D5
La Ferté-sous-Jouarre France 62 D6
Lafia Nigeria 120 D4
Lafiagi Nigeria 120 D4
Laflamme r. Canada 152 F4
Lafleche Canada 151 J5
La Flèche France 66 D3
La Follette U.S.A. 164 C5
La Forest, Lac l. Canada 153 H3
Laforge Canada 153 G3
Laforge r. Canada 153 G3
La Frégate, Lac de l. Canada 152 G3
Lāft Iran 110 D5
Laful India 87 A6
La Galissonnière, Lac l. Canada 153 J4

▶La Galite i. Tunisia 68 C6
Most northerly point of Africa.

La Galite, Canal de sea chan. Tunisia 68 C6
La Gallega Mex. 166 D3
Lagan' Rus. Fed. 53 J7
Lagan r. U.K. 61 G3
La Garamba, Parc National de nat. park Dem. Rep. Congo 122 C3
Lagarto Brazil 177 K6
Lage Germany 63 I3
Lågen r. Norway 55 G7
Lage Vaart canal Neth. 62 F2
Lagg U.K. 60 D5
Laggan U.K. 60 E3
Lagh Bor watercourse Kenya/Somalia 122 E3
Laghouat Alg. 64 E5
Lagkor Co salt l. China 99 D6
La Gloria Mex. 161 D7
Lago Agrio Ecuador 176 C3
Lagoa Santa Brazil 179 C2
Lagoa Vermelha Brazil 179 A5
Lagodekhi Georgia 113 G2
Lagolândia Brazil 179 A1
La Gomera i. Canary Is 120 B2
La Gomera Guat. 167 H6
La Gonâve, Île de i. Haiti 169 J5
Lagong i. Indon. 85 E2
Lagonoy Gulf Luzon Phil. 82 C3

▶Lagos Nigeria 120 D4
Former capital of Nigeria. Most populous city in Africa.

Lagos Port. 67 B5
Lagosa Tanz. 123 C4
Lagos de Moreno Mex. 167 E4
La Grande r. Canada 152 F3
La Grande U.S.A. 156 D3
La Grande 3, Réservoir resr Canada 152 G3
La Grande 4, Réservoir resr Que. Canada 147 K4
La Grande 4, Réservoir resr Que. Canada 153 G3
La Grange Australia 134 C4
La Grange CA U.S.A. 158 C3
La Grange GA U.S.A. 163 C5
Lagrange U.S.A. 164 C3
La Grange KY U.S.A. 164 C4
La Grange TX U.S.A. 161 D6
La Gran Sabana plat. Venez. 176 F2
La Grita Venez. 176 D2
La Guajira, Península de pen. Col. 176 D1
Laguna Brazil 179 A5
Laguna, Picacho de la mt. Mex. 166 C4
Laguna Dam U.S.A. 159 F5
Laguna de Perlas Nicaragua 166 [inset] J6
Laguna de Temascal, Parque Natural nature res. Mex. 167 F5
Laguna Lachua, Parque Nacional nat. park Guat. 167 H6
Laguna Mountains U.S.A. 158 E5
Laguna Ojo de Liebre, Parque Natural de la nature res. Mex. 166 B3
Lagunas Chile 178 C2
Laguna San Rafael, Parque Nacional nat. park Chile 178 B7
Lagunas de Catemaco, Parque Natural nature res. Mex. 167 G5
Lagunas de Chacahua, Parque Nacional nat. park Mex. 167 F6
Lagunas de Montebello, Parque Nacional nat. park Mex. 167 H5
Laha Heilong. China 95 K1
La Habana Cuba see Havana
La Habra U.S.A. 158 E5
Lahad Datu Sabah Malaysia 85 G1
Lahad Datu, Teluk b. Malaysia 85 G1
La Hague, Cap de c. France 66 D2
Lahar Madh. Prad. India 99 B8
Laharpur India 104 E4
Lahat Sumatera Indon. 84 C3
Lahe Myanmar 86 A1
Lahemaa rahvuspark nat. park Estonia 55 N7
La Hève, Cap de c. France 59 H9
Lahewa Indon. 84 B2
Laḥij Yemen 108 F7
Lāhījān Iran 110 C2
Lahn r. Germany 63 H4
Lahnstein Germany 63 H4
Laholm Sweden 55 H8
Lahontan Reservoir U.S.A. 158 D2
Lahore Pak. 111 I4
Lahri Pak. 111 H4
Lahti Fin. 55 N6
La Huerta Mex. 166 D5
Laï Chad 121 E4
Lai'an China 97 H1
Laibach Slovenia see Ljubljana
Laibin China 97 F4
Laidley Australia 138 F1
Laifeng China 97 F2
L'Aigle France 66 E2
Laihia Fin. 54 M5
Lai-hka Myanmar 86 B2
Lai-Hsak Myanmar 86 B2
Laimakuri India 105 H4
Laimos, Akrotirio pt Greece 69 J5
Laingsburg S. Africa 124 E7
Laingsburg U.S.A. 164 C2
Lainioälven r. Sweden 54 M3
Lair U.S.A. 164 C4
L'Aïr, Massif de mts Niger 120 D3
Lairg U.K. 60 E2
Lais Sumatera Indon. 84 C3
Lais Mindanao Phil. 82 D5
La Isabela Cuba 163 D8
Laishevo Rus. Fed. 52 K5
Laishui Hebei China 95 H4
Laitila Fin. 55 L6
Laives Italy 68 D1
Laiwu Shandong China 95 I4
Laiwui Maluku Indon. 83 C3
Laixi Shandong China 95 J4
Laiyang Shandong China 95 J4
Laiyuan Hebei China 95 H4
Laizhou Shandong China 95 I4
Laizhou Wan b. China 95 I4
Lajamanu Australia 134 E4
Lajanurpekhi Georgia 113 F2
Lajeado Brazil 179 A5
Lajes Rio Grande do Norte Brazil 177 K5
Lajes Santa Catarina Brazil 179 A4
La Joya Chihuahua Mex. 166 D3
La Junta Mex. 166 D2
La Junta U.S.A. 160 C4
La Juventud, Isla de la i. Cuba 169 H4
Lakadiya India 104 B5
La Kagera, Parc National de nat. park Rwanda see Akagera National Park
L'Akagera, Parc National de nat. park Rwanda see Akagera National Park
Lake U.S.A. 164 D5
Lake Andes U.S.A. 160 D3
Lakeba i. Fiji 133 I3
Lake Bardawil Reserve nature res. Egypt 107 A4
Lake Bolac Australia 138 A6
Lake Butler U.S.A. 163 D6
Lake Cargelligo Australia 138 C4
Lake Cathie Australia 138 F3
Lake Charles U.S.A. 161 E6
Lake City CO U.S.A. 159 J3
Lake City FL U.S.A. 163 D6
Lake City MI U.S.A. 164 C1
Lake Clark National Park and Preserve AK U.S.A. 148 I3
Lake Clear U.S.A. 165 H1
Lake District National Park U.K. 58 D4
Lake Eyre National Park Australia 137 B6
Lakefield Australia 136 D2
Lakefield Canada 165 F1
Lakefield National Park Australia 136 D2
Lake Forest U.S.A. 164 B2
Lake Gairdner National Park Australia 137 B7
Lake Geneva U.S.A. 160 F3
Lake George MI U.S.A. 164 C2
Lake George NY U.S.A. 165 I2
Lake Grace Australia 135 B8
Lake Harbour Canada see Kimmirut
Lake Havasu City U.S.A. 159 F4
Lakehurst U.S.A. 165 H3
Lake Isabella U.S.A. 158 D4
Lake Jackson U.S.A. 161 E6
Lake King Australia 135 B8
Lake Kopiago P.N.G. 81 K8
Lakeland FL U.S.A. 163 D7
Lakeland GA U.S.A. 163 D6
Lake Louise Canada 150 G5
Lakemba i. Fiji see Lakeba
Lake Mills U.S.A. 160 E3
Lake Minchumina AK U.S.A. 148 I3
Lake Nash Australia 136 B4
Lake Odessa U.S.A. 164 C2
Lake Paringa N.Z. 139 B6
Lake Placid FL U.S.A. 163 D7
Lake Placid NY U.S.A. 165 I1
Lake Pleasant U.S.A. 165 H2
Lakeport CA U.S.A. 158 B2
Lakeport MI U.S.A. 164 D2
Lake Providence U.S.A. 161 F5
Lake Range mts U.S.A. 158 D1
Lake River Canada 152 E3
Lakes Entrance Australia 138 D6
Lakeside AZ U.S.A. 159 I4
Lakeside VA U.S.A. 165 G5
Lake Tabourie Australia 138 E5
Lake Tekapo N.Z. 139 C7
Lake Torrens National Park Australia 137 B6
Lakeview MI U.S.A. 164 C2
Lakeview OH U.S.A. 164 D3
Lakeview OR U.S.A. 156 C4
Lake Village U.S.A. 161 F5
Lake Wales U.S.A. 163 D7
Lakewood CO U.S.A. 156 G5
Lakewood NJ U.S.A. 165 H3
Lakewood NY U.S.A. 164 F2
Lakewood OH U.S.A. 164 E3
Lake Worth U.S.A. 163 D7
Lakha India 104 B4
Lakhdenpokh'ya Rus. Fed. 54 Q6
Lakhimpur Assam India see North Lakhimpur
Lakhimpur Uttar Prad. India 104 E4
Lakhisarai India 105 F4
Lakhish r. Israel 107 B4
Lakhnadon India 104 D5
Lakhpat India 104 B5
Lakhtar India 104 B5
Lakin U.S.A. 160 C4
Lakitusaki r. Canada 152 E3
Lakki Marwat Pak. 111 H3
Lakohembi Sumba Indon. 83 B5
Lakonikos Kolpos b. Greece 69 J6
Lakor i. Maluku Indon. 83 D5
Lakota Côte d'Ivoire 120 C4
Lakota U.S.A. 160 D1
Laksefjorden sea chan. Norway 54 O1
Lakselv Norway 54 N1
Lakshadweep is India see Laccadive Islands
Lakshadweep union terr. India 106 B4
Lakshettipet India 106 C2
Lakshmipur Bangl. 105 G5
Laksmipur Bangl. see Lakshmipur
Lala Mindanao Phil. 82 C5
Lalaghat India 105 H4
Lalbara India 106 D1
L'Alcora Spain 67 F3
Lāleh Zār, Kūh-e mt. Iran 110 E4
Lalganj India 105 F4
Lālī Iran 110 C3
La Libertad El Salvador 167 H6
La Libertad Guat. 167 H5
La Libertad Nicaragua 166 [inset] I6
La Ligua Chile 178 B4
Laliki Maluku Indon. 83 C4
Lalimboee Sulawesi Indon. 83 B3
Lalin China 90 B3
Lalín Spain 67 B2
La Línea de la Concepción Spain 67 D5
Lalin He r. China 90 B3
Lalitpur India 104 D4
Lalitpur Nepal see Patan
Lal-Lo Luzon Phil. 82 C2
Lalmanirhat Bangl. see Lalmonirhat
Lalmonirhat Bangl. 105 G4
Laloa Sulawesi Indon. 83 B4
La Loche Canada 151 I3
La Loche, Lac l. Canada 151 I3
La Louvière Belgium 62 E4
Lal'sk Rus. Fed. 52 J3
Laluin i. Maluku Indon. 83 C3
Lalung La pass Xizang China 99 D7
Lama Bangl. 105 H5
La Macarena, Parque Nacional nat. park Col. 176 D3
La Maddalena Sardinia Italy 68 C4
La Madeleine, Îles de is Canada 153 J5
La Madeleine, Monts de mts France 66 F3
Lamadian Heilong. China 95 K2
Lamadianzi Heilong. China see Lamadian
Lamag Sabah Malaysia 85 G1
La Maiko, Parc National de nat. park Dem. Rep. Congo 122 C4
Lamakera Indon. 83 B5
La Malbaie Canada 153 H5
La Malinche, Parque Nacional nat. park Mex. 167 F5
Lamam Laos 86 D4
La Mancha Mex. 166 E3
La Mancha reg. Spain 67 E4
La Manche strait France/U.K. see English Channel
La Máquina Mex. 166 D2
Lamar CO U.S.A. 160 C4
Lamar MO U.S.A. 161 E4
Lamard Iran 110 D5
La Margeride, Monts de mts France 66 F4
La Marmora, Punta mt. Sardinia Italy 68 C5
La Marne au Rhin, Canal de France 62 G6
La Marque U.S.A. 161 E6
La Martre, Lac l. Canada 150 G2
Lamas r. Turkey 107 B1
La Masica Hond. 166 [inset] I6
La Mauricie, Parc National de nat. park Canada 153 G5
Lamawan Nei Mongol China 95 G3
Lambaréné Gabon 122 B4
Lambasa Fiji see Labasa
Lambasina i. Indon. 83 B4
Lambayeque Peru 176 C5
Lambay Island Ireland 61 G4
Lambeng Kalimantan Indon. 85 F3
Lambert atoll Marshall Is see Ailinglaplap

▶Lambert Glacier Antarctica 188 E2
Largest series of glaciers in the world.

Lambert's Bay S. Africa 124 D7
Lambeth Canada 164 E2
Lambi India 104 C3
Lambourn Downs hills U.K. 59 F7
Lame Sumatera Indon. 84 B2
La Medjerda, Monts de la mts Alg. 68 B6
Lamego Port. 67 C3
Lamèque, Île i. Canada 153 I5
La Merced Arg. 178 C3
La Merced Peru 176 C6
Lameroo Australia 137 C7
La Mesa U.S.A. 158 E5
Lamesa U.S.A. 161 C5
Lamia Greece 69 J5
Lamigan Point Mindanao Phil. 82 D5
Lamington National Park Australia 138 F2
La Misa Mex. 166 C2
La Misión Mex. 158 E5
Lamitan Phil. 82 C5
Lamlam Papua Indon. 83 D3
Lamma Island H.K. China 97 [inset]
Lammerlaw Range mts N.Z. 139 B7
Lammermuir Hills U.K. 60 G5
Lammhult Sweden 55 I8
Lammi Fin. 55 N6
Lamon Bay Phil. 82 C3
Lamongan Jawa Indon. 85 F4
Lamont CA U.S.A. 158 D4
Lamont WY U.S.A. 156 G4
La Montagne d'Ambre, Parc National de nat. park Madag. 123 E5
La Montaña de Covadonga, Parque Nacional de nat. park Spain see Los Picos de Europa, Parque Nacional de
La Mora Mex. 166 E3
La Morita Chihuahua Mex. 166 D2
La Morita Coahuila Mex. 161 C6
Lamotrek atoll Micronesia 81 L5
La Moure U.S.A. 160 D2
Lampang Thai. 86 B3
Lam Pao, Ang Kep Nam Thai. 86 C3
Lampasas U.S.A. 161 D6
Lampazos Mex. 167 E3
Lampedusa, Isola di i. Sicily Italy 68 E7
Lampeter U.K. 59 C6
Lamphun Thai. 86 B3
Lampsacus Turkey see Lâpseki
Lampung prov. Indon. 84 D4
Lampung, Teluk b. Indon. 84 D4
Lam Tin H.K. China 97 [inset]
Lamu Kenya 122 E4
Lamu Myanmar 86 A3
Lāna'i i. U.S.A. 157 [inset]
Lāna'i City U.S.A. 157 [inset]
La Nao, Cabo de c. Spain 67 G4
Lanao, Lake Mindanao Phil. 82 D5
Lanark Canada 165 G1
Lanark U.K. 60 F5
Lanas Sabah Malaysia 85 G1
Lanbi Kyun i. Myanmar 87 B5
Lanboyan Point Mindanao Phil. 82 C4
Lancang China 96 C4
Lancang Jiang r. China 96 C2
Lancaster Canada 165 H1
Lancaster U.K. 58 E4
Lancaster CA U.S.A. 158 D4
Lancaster KY U.S.A. 164 C5
Lancaster MO U.S.A. 160 E3
Lancaster NH U.S.A. 165 J1
Lancaster OH U.S.A. 164 D4
Lancaster PA U.S.A. 165 G3
Lancaster SC U.S.A. 163 D5
Lancaster VA U.S.A. 165 G5
Lancaster WI U.S.A. 160 F3
Lancaster Canal U.K. 58 E5
Lancaster Sound strait Canada 147 J2
Lancun Shandong China 95 J4
Landak r. Indon. 85 E3
Landana Angola see Cacongo
Landau an der Isar Germany 63 M6
Landau in der Pfalz Germany 63 I5
Landeck Austria 57 M7
Lander watercourse Australia 134 E5
Lander U.S.A. 156 F4
Landesbergen Germany 63 J2
Landfall Island India 87 A4
Landhi Pak. 111 G5
Landik, Gunung mt. Indon. 84 C3
Landis Canada 151 I4
Landor Australia 135 B6
Landsberg Poland see Gorzów Wielkopolski
Landsberg am Lech Germany 57 M6
Land's End pt U.K. 59 B8
Landshut Germany 63 M6
Landskrona Sweden 55 H9
Landstuhl Germany 63 H5
Land Wursten reg. Germany 63 I1
Lanesborough Ireland 61 E4
Lanfeng Henan China see Lankao
La'nga Co l. China 99 C7
Langao China 97 F1
Langar Afgh. 111 H3
Langara Sulawesi Indon. 83 B4
Langberg mts S. Africa 124 F5
Langdon U.S.A. 160 D1
Langeac France 66 F4
Langeberg mts S. Africa 124 D7
Langeland i. Denmark 55 G9
Längelmäki Fin. 55 N6
Langelsheim Germany 63 K3
Langen Germany 63 I1
Langenburg Canada 151 K5
Langenhagen Germany 63 J2
Langenhahn Germany 63 H4
Langenlonsheim Germany 63 H5
Langenthal Switz. 66 H3
Langenweddingen Germany 63 L2
Langeoog Germany 63 H1
Langesund Norway 55 F7
Langfang Hebei China 95 I4
Langgam Sumatera Indon. 84 C2

Langgapayung Sumatera Indon. 84 C2
Langgar Xizang China 99 F7
Langgöns Germany 63 I4
Langjan Nature Reserve S. Africa 125 I2
Langjökull ice cap Iceland 54 [inset]
Langka Sumatera Indon. 84 B1
Langkawi i. Malaysia 84 B1
Langkesi, Kepulauan is Indon. 83 C4
Lang Kha Toek, Khao mt. Thai. 87 B5
Langklip S. Africa 124 E5
Langkon Sabah Malaysia 85 G1
Langley Canada 150 F5
Langley U.S.A. 164 D5
Langlo Crossing Australia 137 D5
Langmusi Gansu China see Dagcanglhamo
Langong, Xé r. Laos 86 D3
Langøya i. Norway 54 I2
Langphu mt. China 105 F3
Langport U.K. 59 E7
Langqên Zangbo r. China 99 B7
Langqi China 97 H3
Langres France 66 G3
Langres, Plateau de France 66 G3
Langru Xinjiang China 99 B5
Langsa Sumatera Indon. 84 B1
Langsa, Teluk b. Indon. 84 B1
Långsele Sweden 54 J5
Langshan Nei Mongol China 95 F3
Lang Shan mts China 95 F3
Lang Sơn Vietnam 86 D2
Langtang National Park Nepal 105 F3
Langtao Myanmar 86 B1
Langting India 105 H4
Langtoft U.K. 58 G4
Langtoutun Nei Mongol China 95 J2
Langtry U.S.A. 161 C6
Languan Shaanxi China see Lantian
Languedoc reg. France 66 E5
Langundu, Tanjung pt Sumbawa Indon. 85 G5
Långvattnet Sweden 54 L4
Langwedel Germany 63 J2
Langxi China 97 H2
Langya Shan mt. Hebei China 95 H4
Langzhong China 96 E2
Lanigan Canada 151 J5
Lanín, Parque Nacional nat. park Arg. 178 B5
Lanín, Volcán vol. Arg./Chile 178 B5
Lanjak, Bukit mt. Malaysia 85 E2
Lanji India 104 E5
Lanka country Asia see Sri Lanka
Lankao Henan China 95 H5
Länkäran Azer. 113 H3
Lannion France 66 C2
La Noria Mex. 166 D4
Lanping China 96 C3
Lansån Sweden 54 M3
L'Anse U.S.A. 160 F2
Lanshan China 97 G3
▶Lansing U.S.A. 164 C2
Capital of Michigan.
Lanta, Ko i. Thai. 87 B6
Lantau Island H.K. China 97 [inset]
Lantau Peak hill H.K. China 97 [inset]
Lantian Shaanxi China 95 G5
Lanuza Bay Mindanao Phil. 82 D4
Lanxi Heilong. China 90 B3
Lanxi Zhejiang China 97 H2
Lanxian Shanxi China 95 G4
Lan Yü i. Taiwan 97 I4
Lanzarote i. Canary Is 120 B2
Lanzhou Gansu China 94 E4
Lanzijing Jilin China 95 J2
Laoag Luzon Phil. 82 C2
Laoang Phil. 82 D3
Laobie Shan mts China 96 C4
Laobukou China 97 F3
Lao Cai Vietnam 86 C2
Laodicea Syria see Latakia
Laodicea Turkey see Denizli
Laodicea ad Lycum Turkey see Denizli
Laodicea ad Mare Syria see Latakia
Laofengkou Xinjiang China 98 C3
Laoha He r. China 95 J3
Laohekou China 97 F1
Laohutun Liaoning China 95 J4
Laojie China see Yongping
Laojunmiao Gansu China see Yumen
La Okapi, Parc National de nat. park Dem. Rep. Congo 122 C3
Lao Ling mts China 90 B4
Laon France 62 D5
Laoqitai Xinjiang China 94 B3
La Oroya Peru 176 C6
Laos country Asia 86 C3
Laoshan Shandong China 95 J4
Laoshawan Xinjiang China 98 D3
Laotieshan Shuidao sea chan. China see Bohai Haixia
Laotougou China 90 C4
Laotuding Shan hill China 90 B4
Laowohi pass India see Khardung La
Laoximiao Nei Mongol China 94 E3
Laoyacheng Qinghai China 94 E4
Laoye Ling mts Heilongjiang/Jilin China 90 B4
Laoye Ling mts Heilongjiang/Jilin China 90 C4
Laoyemiao Xinjiang China 94 C2
Lapa Brazil 179 A4
Lapac i. Phil. 82 C5
La Palma i. Canary Is 120 B2
La Palma Guat. 167 H5
La Palma Panama 166 [inset] K7
La Palma U.S.A. 159 H5
La Palma del Condado Spain 67 C5
La Panza Range mts U.S.A. 158 C4
La Paragua Venez. 176 F2
Laparan i. Phil. 82 B5
La Parilla Mex. 161 B8
La Paya, Parque Nacional nat. park Col. 176 D3
La Paz Arg. 178 E4
▶La Paz Bol. 176 E7
Official capital of Bolivia.
La Paz Hond. 166 [inset] I6
La Paz Mex. 166 C3
La Paz Nicaragua 166 [inset] I6
La Paz, Bahía b. Mex. 166 C3
La Pedrera Col. 176 E4
Lapeer U.S.A. 164 D2
La Pendjari, Parc National de nat. park Benin 120 D3
La Perla Mex. 166 D2
La Pérouse Strait Japan/Rus. Fed. 90 F3
La Pesca Mex. 161 D8
La Piedad Mex. 166 E4
Lapinig Samar Phil. 82 D3
Lapinlahti Fin. 54 O5
La Pintada Panama 166 [inset] J7
Lapithos Cyprus 107 A2
Laplace LA U.S.A. 167 H2
Lap Lae Thai. 86 C3
La Plant U.S.A. 160 C2
La Plata Arg. 178 E4
La Plata MD U.S.A. 165 G4
La Plata MO U.S.A. 160 E3
La Plata, Isla i. Ecuador 176 B4
▶La Plata, Río de sea chan. Arg./Uruguay 178 E4
Part of the Rìo de la Plata - Paraná, 2nd longest river in South America, and 9th in the world.
La Plonge, Lac l. Canada 151 J4
Lapmežciems Latvia 55 M8
Lapominka Rus. Fed. 52 I2
La Porte U.S.A. 164 B3
Laporte U.S.A. 165 G3
Laporte, Mount Y.T. Canada 149 P3
Laposo, Bukit mt. Indon. 83 A4
La Potherie, Lac l. Canada 153 G2
La Poza Grande Mex. 166 B3
Lappajärvi Fin. 54 M5
Lappajärvi l. Fin. 54 M5
Lappeenranta Fin. 55 P6
Lappersdorf Germany 63 M5
Lappi Fin. 55 L6
Lappland reg. Europe 54 K3
La Pryor U.S.A. 161 D6
Lâpseki Turkey 69 L4
Laptevo Rus. Fed. see Yasnogorsk
Laptev Sea Rus. Fed. 77 N2
Lapua Fin. 54 M5
Lapuko Sulawesi Indon. 83 B4
Lapu-Lapu Phil. 82 C4
Lapurdum France see Bayonne
La Purísima Mex. 166 B3
Laqiya Arbain well Sudan 108 C5
La Quiaca Arg. 178 C2
L'Aquila Italy 68 E3
La Quinta U.S.A. 158 E5
Lār Iran 110 D5
Larache Morocco 67 C6
Lārak i. Iran 110 E5
Laramie U.S.A. 156 G4
Laramie r. U.S.A. 156 G4
Laramie Mountains U.S.A. 156 G4
Laranda Turkey see Karaman
Laranjal Paulista Brazil 179 B3
Laranjeiras do Sul Brazil 178 F3
Laranjinha r. Brazil 179 A3
Larantuka Flores Indon. 83 B5
Larat Indon. 134 E1
Larat i. Indon. 134 E1
Larba Alg. 67 H5
Lärbro Sweden 55 K8
L'Archipélago de Mingan, Réserve du Parc National de nat. park Canada 153 J4
L'Ardenne, Plateau de plat. Belgium see Ardennes
Laredo Spain 67 E2
Laredo U.S.A. 161 D7
La Reforma Veracruz Mex. 167 F4
La Reina Adelaida, Archipiélago de is Chile 178 B8
Largeau Chad see Faya
Largo U.S.A. 163 D7
Largs U.K. 60 E5
Lārī Iran 110 B2
L'Ariana Tunisia 68 D6
Lariang Sulawesi Barat Indon. 83 A3
Lariang r. Indon. 83 A3
Larimore U.S.A. 160 D2
La Rioja Arg. 178 C3
La Rioja aut. comm. Spain 67 E2
Larisa Greece 69 J5
Larissa Greece see Larisa
Laristan reg. Iran 110 E5
Larkana Pak. 111 H5
Lark Harbour Canada 153 K4
Lar Koh mt. Afgh. 111 F3
Lark Passage Australia 136 D2
L'Arli, Parc National de nat. park Burkina Faso 120 D3
Larnaca Cyprus 107 A2
Larnaka Cyprus see Larnaca
Larnaka Bay Cyprus 107 A2
Larnakos, Kolpos b. Cyprus see Larnaka Bay
Larne U.K. 61 G3
Larned U.S.A. 160 D4
La Robe Noire, Lac de l. Canada 153 J4
La Robla Spain 67 D2
La Roche-en-Ardenne Belgium 62 F4
La Rochelle France 66 D3
La Roche-sur-Yon France 66 D3
La Roda Spain 67 E4
La Romana Dom. Rep. 169 K5
La Ronge Canada 151 J4
La Ronge, Lac l. Canada 151 J4
La Rosa Mex. 167 E3
La Rosita Mex. 167 E2
Larrey Point Australia 134 B4
Larrimah Australia 134 F3
Lars Christensen Coast Antarctica 188 E2
Larsen Bay AK U.S.A. 148 I4
Larsen Ice Shelf Antarctica 188 L2
Larsmo Fin. 54 M5
Larvik Norway 55 G7
Las Adjuntas, Presa de resr Mex. 161 D8
Lasahau Sulawesi Indon. 83 B4
La Sal U.S.A. 159 I2
LaSalle Canada 165 I1
La Salle U.S.A. 152 C6
La Salonga Nord, Parc National de nat. park Dem. Rep. Congo 122 C4
La Sambre à l'Oise, Canal de France 62 D5
Lasan Kalimantan Indon. 85 F2
Las Animas U.S.A. 160 C4
Las Ánimas, Punta pt Mex. 166 B2
Las Anod Somalia see Laascaanood
La Sarre Canada 152 F4
Las Avispas Mex. 166 C2
La Savonnière, Lac l. Canada 153 G3
La Scie Canada 153 L4
Las Cruces Mex. 166 D2
Las Cruces CA U.S.A. 158 C4
Las Cruces NM U.S.A. 157 G6
La Selle, Pic mt. Haiti 169 J5
La Serena Chile 178 B3
Las Esperanças Mex. 167 E3
La Seu d'Urgell Spain 67 G2
Las Flores Arg. 178 E5
Las Guacamatas, Cerro mt. Mex. 157 F7
Lāshār r. Iran 111 F5
Lashburn Canada 151 I4
Las Heras Arg. 178 C4
Las Herreras Mex. 166 D3
Lashio Myanmar 86 B2
Lashkar India 104 D4
Lashkar Gāh Afgh. 111 G4
Las Juntas Chile 178 C3
Las Lavaderos Mex. 167 F4
Las Lomitas Arg. 178 D2
Las Marismas marsh Spain 67 C5
Las Martinetas Arg. 178 C7
Las Mesteñas Mex. 166 D2
Las Minas, Cerro de mt. Hond. 167 H6
Las Mulatas is Panama see San Blas, Archipiélago de
Las Nieves Mex. 166 D3
Las Nopaleras, Cerro mt. Mex. 166 E3
La Société, Archipel de is Fr. Polynesia see Society Islands
Lasolo, Teluk b. Indon. 83 B3
La Somme, Canal de France 62 C5
Las Palmas watercourse Mex. 158 E5
Las Palmas Panama 166 [inset] J7
Las Palmas de Gran Canaria Canary Is 120 B2
Las Petas Bol. 177 G7
La Spezia Italy 68 C2
Las Piedras, Río de r. Peru 176 E6
Las Planchas Hond. 166 [inset] I6
Las Plumas Arg. 178 C6
Laspur Pak. 111 I2
Lassance Brazil 179 B2
Lassen Peak vol. U.S.A. 158 C1
Lassen Volcanic National Park U.S.A. 158 C1
Las Tablas Mex. 167 F4
Las Tablas Panama 166 [inset] J8
Las Tablas de Daimiel, Parque Nacional de nat. park Spain 67 E4
Last Chance U.S.A. 160 C4
Las Termas Arg. 178 D3
Last Mountain Lake Canada 151 J5
Las Tórtolas, Cerro mt. Chile 178 C3
Lastoursville Gabon 122 B4
Lastovo i. Croatia 68 G3
Las Tres Vírgenes, Volcán vol. Mex. 166 B3
Lastrup Germany 63 H2
Las Tunas Cuba 169 I4
Las Varas Chihuahua Mex. 166 D2
Las Varas Nayarit Mex. 168 C4
Las Varillas Arg. 178 D4
Las Vegas NM U.S.A. 157 G6
Las Vegas NV U.S.A. 159 F3
Las Viajas, Isla de i. Peru 176 C6
Las Villuercas mt. Spain 67 D4
La Tabatière Canada 153 K4
Latacunga Ecuador 176 C4
Latady Island Antarctica 188 L2
Latakia Syria 107 B2
Latalata i. Maluku Indon. 83 C3
La Teste-de-Buch France 66 D4
La Tetilla, Cerro mt. Mex. 166 D4
Latham Australia 135 B7
Lathen Germany 63 H2
Latheron U.K. 60 F2
Lathi India 104 B4
Latho India 104 D2
Lathrop U.S.A. 158 C3
Latina Italy 68 E4
La Tortuga, Isla i. Venez. 176 E1
Latouche AK U.S.A. 149 K3
Latouche Island AK U.S.A. 149 K3
La Trinidad Nicaragua 166 [inset] I6
La Trinidad Luzon Phil. 82 C2
La Trinitaria Mex. 167 G5
Latrobe U.S.A. 164 F3
Latrun West Bank 107 B4
Lattaquié Syria see Latakia
Lattrop Neth. 62 G2
La Tuque Canada 153 G5
Latur India 106 C2
Latvia country Europe 55 N8
Latvija country Europe see Latvia
Latviyskaya S.S.R. country Europe see Latvia
Lauca, Parque Nacional nat. park Chile 176 E7
Lauchhammer Germany 57 N5
Lauder U.K. 60 G5
Laudio Spain see Llodio
Lauenbrück Germany 63 J1
Lauenburg (Elbe) Germany 63 K1
Lauf an der Pegnitz Germany 63 L5
Laufen Switz. 66 H3
Lauge Koch Kyst reg. Greenland 147 L2
Laughlen, Mount Australia 135 F5
Laughlin Peak U.S.A. 157 G5
Lauka Estonia 55 M7
Launceston Australia 137 [inset]
Launceston U.K. 59 C8
Laune r. Ireland 61 C5
Launggyaung Myanmar 86 B1
Launglon Myanmar 87 B4
Launglon Bok Islands Myanmar 87 B4
La Unidad Mex. 167 G6
La Unión Bol. 176 F7
La Unión El Salvador 166 [inset] I6
La Unión Hond. 166 [inset] I6
La Unión Mex. 167 E5
Laur Luzon Phil. 82 C3
Laura Australia 136 D2
Laurel DE U.S.A. 165 H4
Laurel MS U.S.A. 161 F6
Laurel MT U.S.A. 156 F3
Laureldale U.S.A. 165 H3
Laurel Hill hills U.S.A. 164 F4
Laurencekirk U.K. 60 G4
Laurieton Australia 138 F3
Laurinburg U.S.A. 163 E5
Lauru i. Solomon Is see Choiseul
Lausanne Switz. 66 H3
Laut i. Indon. 85 E1
Laut i. Indon. 85 E3
Laut i. Indon. 85 G3
Laut, Selat sea chan. Indon. 85 F3
Lautem East Timor 83 C5
Lautersbach (Hessen) Germany 63 J4
Laut Kecil, Kepulauan is Indon. 85 F4
Lautoka Fiji 133 H3
Lauttawar, Danau l. Indon. 84 B1
Lauvuskylä Fin. 54 P5
Lauwersmeer l. Neth. 62 G1
Lava Beds National Monument nat. park U.S.A. 156 C4
Laval Canada 152 G5
Laval France 66 D2
La Vall d'Uixó Spain 67 F4
Lāvān i. Iran 110 D5
La Vanoise, Massif de mts France 66 H4
La Vanoise, Parc National de nat. park France 66 H4
Lavapié, Punta pt Chile 178 B5
Lāvar Iran 110 C4
Laveaga Peak U.S.A. 158 C3
La Vega Dom. Rep. 169 J5
La Venta Hond. 166 [inset] I6
Laverne U.S.A. 161 D4
Laverton Australia 135 C7
La Víbora Mex. 166 E3
La Vila Joíosa Spain see Villajoyosa-La Vila Joíosa
La Viña Peru 176 C5
Lavongai i. P.N.G. see New Hanover
Lavras Brazil 179 B3
Lavrentiya Rus. Fed. 148 E2
Lavumisa Swaziland 125 J4
Lavushi-Manda National Park Zambia 123 D5
Lawa India 104 C4
Lawa Myanmar 86 B1
Lawa Pak. 111 H3
Lawang i. Indon. 85 G5
Lawas Sarawak Malaysia 85 F1
Lawashi r. Canada 152 E3
Law Dome ice feature Antarctica 188 F2
Lawele Sulawesi Indon. 83 B4
Lawin i. Maluku Indon. 83 D3
Lawit, Gunung mt. Indon./Malaysia 85 F2
Lawit, Gunung mt. Malaysia 84 C1
Lawksawk Myanmar 86 B2
Lawn Hill National Park Australia 136 B3
La Woëvre, Plaine de plain France 62 F5
Lawra Ghana 120 C3
Lawrence IN U.S.A. 164 B4
Lawrence KS U.S.A. 160 E4
Lawrence MA U.S.A. 165 J2
Lawrenceburg IN U.S.A. 164 C4
Lawrenceburg KY U.S.A. 164 C4
Lawrenceburg TN U.S.A. 162 C5
Lawrenceville GA U.S.A. 163 D5
Lawrenceville IL U.S.A. 164 B4
Lawrenceville VA U.S.A. 165 G5
Lawrence Wells, Mount hill Australia 135 C6
Lawton U.S.A. 161 D5
Lawu, Gunung vol. Indon. 85 E4
Lawz, Jabal al mt. Saudi Arabia 112 D5
Laxå Sweden 55 I7
Laxey Isle of Man 58 C4
Laxgalts'ap B.C. Canada 149 O5
Lax Kw'alaams B.C. Canada 149 O5
Laxo U.K. 60 [inset]
Laxong Co l. Xizang China 99 D6
Laya r. Rus. Fed. 52 M2
Layar, Tanjung pt Indon. 85 G4
Laydennyy, Mys c. Rus. Fed. 52 J1
Layeni Maluku Indon. 83 D4
Laylá Saudi Arabia 108 G5
Layla salt pan Saudi Arabia 107 D4
Laysan Island U.S.A. 186 I4
Laysu Xinjiang China 98 C4
Laytonville U.S.A. 158 B2
Layyah Pak. 111 H4
Laza Myanmar 86 B1
La Zacatosa, Picacho mt. Mex. 166 C4
Lazarev Rus. Fed. 90 F1
Lazarevac Serbia 69 I2
Lázaro Cárdenas Baja California Mex. 166 B2
Lázaro Cárdenas Baja California Mex. 166 B2
Lázaro Cárdenas Mex. 168 D5
Lazcano Uruguay 178 F4
Lazdijai Lith. 55 M9
Lazhuglung Xizang China 99 C6
Lazikou China 96 D1
Lazo Primorskiy Kray Rus. Fed. 90 D4
Lazo Respublika Sakha (Yakutiya) Rus. Fed. 77 O3
Lead U.S.A. 160 C2
Leader Water r. U.K. 60 G5
Leadville Australia 138 D4
Leaf r. U.S.A. 161 F6
Leaf Bay Canada see Tasiujaq
Leaf Rapids Canada 151 K3
Leakey U.S.A. 161 D6
Leaksville U.S.A. see Eden
Leamington Canada 164 D2
Leamington Spa, Royal U.K. 59 F6
Leane, Lough l. Ireland 61 C5
Leap Ireland 61 C6
Leatherhead U.K. 59 G7
L'Eau Claire, Lac à l. Canada 152 G2
L'Eau Claire, Rivière à r. Canada 152 G2
L'Eau d'Heure l. Belgium 62 E4
Leavenworth IN U.S.A. 164 B4
Leavenworth KS U.S.A. 160 E4
Leavenworth WA U.S.A. 156 C3
Leavitt Peak U.S.A. 158 D2
Lebach Germany 62 G5
Lebak Mindanao Phil. 82 D5
Lebanon country Asia 107 B2
Lebanon IN U.S.A. 164 B3
Lebanon KY U.S.A. 164 C5
Lebanon MO U.S.A. 160 E4
Lebanon NH U.S.A. 165 I2
Lebanon OH U.S.A. 164 C4
Lebanon OR U.S.A. 156 C3
Lebanon PA U.S.A. 165 G3
Lebanon TN U.S.A. 162 C4
Lebanon VA U.S.A. 164 D5
Lebanon Junction U.S.A. 164 C5
Lebanon Mountains Lebanon see Liban, Jebel
Lebbeke Belgium 62 E3
Lebec U.S.A. 158 D4
Lebedyan' Rus. Fed. 53 H5
Lebel-sur-Quévillon Canada 152 F4
Le Blanc France 66 E3
Lebo Sulawesi Indon. 83 B4
Lębork Poland 57 P3
Lebowakgomo S. Africa 125 I3
Lebrija Spain 67 C5
Łebsko, Jezioro lag. Poland 57 P3
Lebu Chile 178 B5
Lebyazh'ye Kazakh. see Akku
Lebyazh'ye Rus. Fed. 52 K4
Le Caire Egypt see Cairo
Le Cateau-Cambrésis France 62 D4
Le Catelet France 62 D4
Lecce Italy 68 H4
Lecco Italy 68 C2
Lech r. Austria/Germany 57 M7
Lechaina Greece 69 I6
Lechang China 97 G3
Le Chasseron mt. Switz. 66 H3
Le Chesne France 62 E5
Lechtaler Alpen mts Austria 57 M7
Leck Germany 57 L3
Lecompte U.S.A. 161 E6
Le Creusot France 66 G3
Le Crotoy France 62 B4
Lectoure France 66 E5
Ledang, Gunung mt. Malaysia 84 C2
Ledbury U.K. 59 E6
Ledesma Spain 67 D3
Ledmore U.K. 60 E2
Ledmozero Rus. Fed. 54 R4
Ledo Kalimantan Indon. 85 E2
Ledong Hainan China 86 E3
Ledong Hainan China 97 F5
Le Dorat France 66 E3
Ledu Qinghai China 94 E4
Leduc Canada 150 H4
Lee r. Ireland 61 D6
Lee IN U.S.A. 164 B3
Lee MA U.S.A. 165 I2
Leech Lake U.S.A. 160 E2
Leeds U.K. 58 F5
Leedstown U.K. 59 B8
Leek Neth. 62 G1
Leek U.K. 59 E5
Leende Neth. 62 F3
Leer (Ostfriesland) Germany 63 H1
Leesburg FL U.S.A. 163 D6
Leesburg GA U.S.A. 163 C6
Leesburg OH U.S.A. 164 D4
Leesburg VA U.S.A. 165 G4
Leese Germany 63 J2
Lee Steere Range hills Australia 135 C6
Leesville U.S.A. 161 E6
Leesville Lake OH U.S.A. 164 E3
Leesville Lake VA U.S.A. 164 F5
Leeton Australia 138 C5
Leeu-Gamka S. Africa 124 E7
Leeuwarden Neth. 62 F1
Leeuwin, Cape Australia 135 A8
Leeuwin-Naturaliste National Park Australia 135 A8
Lee Vining U.S.A. 158 D3
Leeward Islands Caribbean Sea 169 L5
Lefka Cyprus 107 A2
Lefkada Greece 69 I5
Lefkada i. Greece 69 I5
Lefkás Greece see Lefkada
Lefke Cyprus see Lefka
Lefkimmi Greece 69 I5
Lefkoniko Cyprus see Lefkonikon
Lefkonikon Cyprus 107 A2
Lefkoşa Cyprus see Nicosia
Lefkosia Cyprus see Nicosia
Lefroy r. Canada 153 H2
Lefroy, Lake salt flat Australia 135 C7
Legarde r. Canada 152 D4
Legaspi Luzon Phil. 82 C3
Legden Germany 62 H2
Legges Tor mt. Australia 137 [inset]
Leghorn Italy see Livorno
Legnago Italy 68 D2
Legnica Poland 57 P5
Legohli N.W.T. Canada see Norman Wells
Le Grand U.S.A. 158 C3
Legune Australia 134 E3
Leh India 104 D2
Le Havre France 66 E2
Lehi U.S.A. 159 H1
Lehighton U.S.A. 165 H3
Lehmo Fin. 54 P5
Lehre Germany 63 K2
Lehrte Germany 63 J2
Lehtimäki Fin. 54 M5
Lehututu Botswana 124 E2
Leibnitz Austria 57 O7
Leicester U.K. 59 F6
Leichhardt r. Australia 132 B3
Leichhardt Falls Australia 136 B3
Leichhardt Range mts Australia 136 D4
Leiden Neth. 62 E2
Leie r. Belgium 62 D3
Leigh N.Z. 139 E3
Leigh U.K. 58 E5
Leighton Buzzard U.K. 59 G7
Leiktho Myanmar 86 B3
Leimen Germany 63 I5
Leine r. Germany 63 J2
Leinefelde Germany 63 K3
Leinster Australia 135 C6
Leinster reg. Ireland 61 F4
Leinster, Mount hill Ireland 61 F5
Leipsic U.S.A. 164 D3
Leipsoi i. Greece 69 L6
Leipzig Germany 63 M3
Leipzig-Halle airport Germany 63 M3
Leiranger Norway 54 I3
Leiria Port. 67 B4
Leirvik Norway 55 D7
Leishan China 97 F3
Leisler, Mount hill Australia 135 E5
Leisnig Germany 63 M3
Leitchfield U.S.A. 164 B5
Leith Hill hill U.K. 59 G7
Leiva, Cerro mt. Col. 176 D3
Leixlip Ireland 61 F4
Leiyang China 97 G3
Leizhou China 97 F4
Leizhou Bandao pen. China 97 F4
Leizhou Wan b. China 97 F4
Lek r. Neth. 62 E3
Leka Norway 54 G4
Lékana Congo 122 B4
Le Kef Tunisia 68 C6
Lekhainá Greece see Lechaina
Lekitobi Maluku Indon. 83 C3
Lekkersing S. Africa 124 C5
Lékoni Gabon 122 B4
Leksand Sweden 55 I6
Leksozero, Ozero l. Rus. Fed. 54 Q5
Leksula Buru Indon. 83 C3
Lelai, Tanjung pt Halmahera Indon. 83 D2
Leland U.S.A. 164 C1
Leli China see Tianlin
Leling Shandong China 95 I4
Lelinta Papua Indon. 83 D3
Lelogama Timor Indon. 83 B5
Lélouma Guinea 120 B3
Lelystad Neth. 62 F2
Le Maire, Estrecho de sea chan. Arg. 178 C9
Léman, Lac l. France/Switz. see Geneva, Lake
Le Mans France 66 E2
Le Mars U.S.A. 160 D3
Lembeh i. Indon. 83 C2
Lemberg France 63 H5
Lemberg Ukr. see L'viv
Lembruch Germany 63 I2
Lembu Kalimantan Indon. 85 G2
Lembu, Gunung mt. Indon. 84 B1
Lembubut Kalimantan Indon. 85 G1
Lemdiyya Alg. see Médéa
Leme Brazil 179 B3
Lemele Neth. 62 G2
Lemesos Cyprus see Limassol
Lemgo Germany 63 I2
Lemhi Range mts U.S.A. 156 E3
Lemi Fin. 55 O6
Lemieux Islands Canada 147 L3
Lemmenjoen kansallispuisto nat. park Fin. 54 N2
Lemmer Neth. 62 F2
Lemmon U.S.A. 160 C2
Lemmon, Mount U.S.A. 159 H5
Lemnos i. Greece see Limnos
Lemoncove U.S.A. 158 D3
Lemoore U.S.A. 158 D3
Le Moyne, Lac l. Canada 153 H2
Lemro r. Myanmar 86 A2
Lemtybozh Rus. Fed. 51 R3
Lemukutan i. Indon. 85 E2
Le Murge hills Italy 68 G4
Lemvig Denmark 55 F8
Lem"yu r. Rus. Fed. 52 M3
Lena r. Rus. Fed. 88 J1
Lena U.S.A. 164 A1
Lena, Mount U.S.A. 159 I1
Lenadoon Point Ireland 61 C3
Lenangguar Sumbawa Indon. 85 G5
Lenchung Tso salt l. China 105 E2
Lencóis Brazil 179 C1
Lençóis Maranhenses, Parque Nacional dos nat. park Brazil 177 J4
Lendeh Iran 110 C4
Lendery Rus. Fed. 54 Q5
Le Neubourg France 59 H9
Lengerich Germany 63 H2
Lenghuzhen Qinghai China 98 F5
Lenglong Ling mts China 94 E4
Lengshuijiang China 97 F3
Lengshuitan China 97 F3
Lenham U.K. 59 H7
Lenhovda Sweden 55 I8
Lenin Tajik. 111 H2
Lenin, Qullai mt. Kyrg./Tajik. see Lenin Peak
Lenina, Pik mt. Kyrg./Tajik. see Lenin Peak
Leninabad Tajik. see Khŭjand
Leninakan Armenia see Gyumri
Lenin Atyndagy Choku mt. Kyrg./Tajik. see Lenin Peak
Lenine Ukr. 112 D1
Leningrad Rus. Fed. see St Petersburg
Leningrad Tajik. 111 H2
Leningrad Oblast admin. div. Rus. Fed. see Leningradskaya Oblast'
Leningradskaya Rus. Fed. 53 H7
Leningradskaya Oblast' admin. div. Rus. Fed. 55 R7
Leningradskiy Rus. Fed. 77 S3
Leningradskiy Tajik. see Leningrad
Lenino Ukr. see Lenine
Leninobod Tajik. see Khŭjand
Lenin Peak Kyrg./Tajik. 111 I2
Leninsk Kazakh. see Baykonyr
Leninsk Rus. Fed. 53 J6
Leninskiy Rus. Fed. 53 H5
Leninsk-Kuznetskiy Rus. Fed. 76 J4
Leninskoye Kazakh. 53 K6
Leninskoye Kirovskaya Oblast' Rus. Fed. 52 J4
Leninskoye Yevreyskaya Avtonomnaya Oblast' Rus. Fed. 90 D3
Lenkoran' Azer. see Länkäran
Lenne r. Germany 63 H3
Lennoxville Canada 165 J1
Lenoir U.S.A. 162 D5
Lenore U.S.A. 164 D5
Lenore Lake Canada 151 J4
Lenox U.S.A. 165 I2
Lens France 62 C4
Lensk Rus. Fed. 77 M3
Lenti Hungary 68 G1
Lentini Sicily Italy 68 F6
Lenya Myanmar 87 B5
Lenzen Germany 63 L1
Léo Burkina Faso 120 C3
Leoben Austria 57 O7
Leodhais, Eilean i. U.K. see Lewis, Isle of
Leok Sulawesi Indon. 83 B2
Leominster U.K. 59 E6
Leominster U.S.A. 165 J2
León Mex. 166 D4
León Nicaragua 166 [inset] I6
León Spain 67 D2
Leon r. U.S.A. 161 D6
Leonardtown U.S.A. 165 G4
Leonardville Namibia 124 D2
Leona Vicario Mex. 167 I4
Leongatha Australia 138 B7
Leonidi Peloponnisos Greece see Leonidio
Leonidio Greece 69 J6
Leonidovo Rus. Fed. 90 F2
Leonora Australia 135 C7
Leontovich, Cape AK U.S.A. 148 G5
Leopold U.S.A. 164 E4
Leopold and Astrid Coast Antarctica see King Leopold and Queen Astrid Coast
Léopold II, Lac l. Dem. Rep. Congo see Mai-Ndombe, Lac
Leopoldina Brazil 179 C3
Leopoldo de Bulhões Brazil 179 A2
Léopoldville Dem. Rep. Congo see Kinshasa
Leoti U.S.A. 160 C4
Leoville Canada 151 J4
Lepalale S. Africa see Lephalale
Lepar i. Indon. 84 D3
Lepaya Latvia see Liepāja
Lepel' Belarus see Lyepyel'
Lepellé r. Canada 153 H1
Lephalala r. S. Africa 125 H2
Lephalale S. Africa 125 H2
Lephepe Botswana 125 G2

Lephoi S. Africa 125 G6
Leping China 97 H2
Lepontine, Alpi mts Italy/Switz. 68 C1
Leppävirta Fin. 54 O5
Lepreau, Point Canada 153 I5
Lepsa Kazakh. see Lepsy
Lepsinsk Kazakh. 98 C3
Lepsy Kazakh. 102 E2
Lepsy r. Kazakh. 98 B3
Le Puy France see Le Puy-en-Velay
Le Puy-en-Velay France 66 F4
Le Quesnoy France 62 D4
Lerala Botswana 125 H2
Leratswana S. Africa 125 H5
Léré Mali 120 C3
Lereh Indon. 81 J7
Lereh, Tanjung pt Indon. 83 A3
Leribe Lesotho see Hlotse
Lérida Col. 176 D4
Lérida Spain see Lleida
Lerik Azer. 113 H3
Lerma Mex. 167 H5
Lerma Spain 67 E2
Lermontov Rus. Fed. 113 F1
Lermontovka Rus. Fed. 90 D3
Lermontovskiy Rus. Fed. see Lermontov
Leros i. Greece 69 L6
Le Roy U.S.A. 165 G2
Le Roy, Lac l. Canada 152 G2
Lerum Sweden 55 H8
Lerwick U.K. 60 [inset]
Les Amirantes is Seychelles see Amirante Islands
Lesbos i. Greece 69 K5
Les Cayes Haiti 169 J5
Leshan China 96 D2
Leshou Hebei China see Xianxian
Leshukonskoye Rus. Fed. 52 J2
Lesi watercourse Sudan 121 F4
Leskhimstroy Ukr. see Syeverodonets'k
Leskovac Serbia 69 I3
Leslie U.S.A. 164 C2
Lesneven France 66 B2
Lesnoy Kirovskaya Oblast' Rus. Fed. 52 L4
Lesnoy Murmanskaya Oblast' Rus. Fed. see Umba
Lesnoye Rus. Fed. 52 G4
Lesogorsk Rus. Fed. 90 F2
Lesopil'noye Rus. Fed. 90 D3
Lesosibirsk Rus. Fed. 76 K4
Lesotho country Africa 125 I5
Lesozavodsk Rus. Fed. 90 D3
L'Espérance Rock i. Kermadec Is 133 I5
Les Pieux France 59 F9
Les Sables-d'Olonne France 66 D3
Lesse r. Belgium 62 E4
Lesser Antarctica reg. Antarctica see West Antarctica
Lesser Antilles is Caribbean Sea 169 K6
Lesser Caucasus mts Asia 113 F2
Lesser Himalaya mts India/Nepal 104 D3
Lesser Khingan Mountains China see Xiao Hinggan Ling
Lesser Slave Lake Canada 150 H4
Lesser Sunda Islands Indon. 80 F8
Lesser Tunb i. The Gulf 110 D5
Lessines Belgium 62 D4
L'Est, Canal de France 62 G6
L'Est, Île de i. Canada 153 J5
L'Est, Pointe de pt Canada 153 J4
Lester U.S.A. 164 E5
Lestijärvi Fin. 54 N5
Lesung, Bukit mt. Indon. 85 F2
Les Vans France 66 G4
Lesvos i. Greece see Lesbos
Leszno Poland 57 P5
Letaba S. Africa 125 J2
Letchworth Garden City U.K. 59 G7
Le Télégraphe hill France 66 G3
Leteri India 104 D4
Letha Range mts Myanmar 86 A2
Lethbridge Alta Canada 151 H5
Lethbridge Nfld. and Lab. Canada 153 L4
Leti i. Maluku Indon. 83 C5
Leti, Kepulauan is Maluku Indon. 83 C5
Leticia Col. 176 E4
Leting Hebei China 95 I4
Letlhakeng Botswana 125 G3
Letnerechenskiy Rus. Fed. 52 G2
Letniy Navolok Rus. Fed. 52 H2
Letoda Maluku Indon. 83 D5
Le Touquet-Paris-Plage France 62 B4
Letpadan Myanmar 86 A3
Le Tréport France 62 B4
Letsitele S. Africa 125 J2
Letsopa S. Africa 125 G4
Letterkenny Ireland 61 E3
Letung Indon. 84 D2
Letwurung Maluku Indon. 83 D4
Lëtzebuerg country Europe see Luxembourg
Letzlingen Germany 63 L2
Léua Angola 123 C5
Leucas Greece see Lefkada
Leucate, Étang de l. France 66 F5
Leuchars U.K. 60 G4
Leukas Greece see Lefkada
Leung Shuen Wan Chau i. H.K. China see High Island
Leunovo Rus. Fed. 52 I2
Leupp U.S.A. 159 H4
Leupung Indon. 87 A6
Leura Australia 136 E4
Leusden Neth. 62 F2
Leuser, Gunung mt. Indon. 84 B2
Leutershausen Germany 63 K5
Leuven Belgium 62 E4
Levadeia Sterea Ellada Greece see Livadeia
Levan U.S.A. 159 H2
Levanger Norway 54 G5
Levante, Riviera di coastal area Italy 68 C2
Levanto Italy 68 C2
Levashi Rus. Fed. 113 G2
Levelland U.S.A. 161 C5
Levelock AK U.S.A. 148 H4
Leven England U.K. 58 G5
Leven Scotland U.K. 60 G4
Leven, Loch l. U.K. 60 F4
Lévêque, Cape Australia 134 C4
Leverkusen Germany 62 G3
Lévézou mts France 66 F4
Levice Slovakia 57 Q6
Levin N.Z. 139 E5
Lévis Canada 153 H5
Levitha i. Greece 69 L6
Levittown NY U.S.A. 165 I3
Levittown PA U.S.A. 165 H3
Levkás i. Greece see Lefkada
Levkímmi Greece see Lefkimmi
Levskigrad Bulg. see Karlovo
Lev Tolstoy Rus. Fed. 53 H5
Lévy, Cap c. France 59 F9
Lewa Sumba Indon. 83 A5
Lewe Myanmar 86 B3
Lewerberg mt. S. Africa 124 C5
Lewes U.K. 59 H8
Lewes U.S.A. 165 H4
Lewis CO U.S.A. 159 I3
Lewis IN U.S.A. 164 B4
Lewis KS U.S.A. 160 D4
Lewis, Isle of i. U.K. 60 C2
Lewis, Lake salt flat Australia 134 F5
Lewisburg KY U.S.A. 164 B5
Lewisburg PA U.S.A. 165 G3
Lewisburg WV U.S.A. 164 E5
Lewis Cass, Mount Canada/U.S.A. 149 O4
Lewis Hills hill Canada 153 K4
Lewis Pass N.Z. 139 D6
Lewis Range hills Australia 134 E5
Lewis Range mts U.S.A. 156 E2
Lewis Smith, Lake U.S.A. 163 C5
Lewiston ID U.S.A. 156 D3
Lewiston ME U.S.A. 165 J1
Lewistown IL U.S.A. 160 F3
Lewistown MT U.S.A. 156 F3
Lewistown PA U.S.A. 165 G3
Lewisville U.S.A. 161 E5
Lewoleba Indon. 83 B5
Lewotobi, Gunung vol. Flores Indon. 83 B5
Lexington KY U.S.A. 164 C4
Lexington MI U.S.A. 164 D2
Lexington NC U.S.A. 162 D5
Lexington NE U.S.A. 160 D3
Lexington TN U.S.A. 161 F5
Lexington VA U.S.A. 164 F5
Lexington Park U.S.A. 165 G4
Leyden Neth. see Leiden
Leye China 96 E3
Leyla Dāgh mt. Iran 110 B2
Leyte i. Phil. 82 D4
Leyte Gulf Phil. 82 D4
Lezha Albania see Lezhë
Lezhë Albania 69 H4
Lezhi China 96 E2
Lezhu China 97 G4
L'gov Rus. Fed. 53 G6
Lhagoi Kangri mt. Xizang China 99 D7
Lhari Xizang China see Si'erdingka
Lhari Xizang China 99 F7
Lharigarbo Xizang China 99 E6
Lhasa Xizang China 99 E7
Lhasa He r. China 99 E7
Lhasoi Xizang China 99 F7
Lhatog China 96 C2
Lhaviyani Atoll Maldives see Faadhippolhu Atoll
Lhazê Xizang China 99 D7
Lhazê Xizang China 99 F7
Lhazhong China 105 F3
Lhokkruet Sumatera Indon. 84 A1
Lhokseumawe Sumatera Indon. 84 B1
Lhoksukon Sumatera Indon. 84 B1
Lhomar Xizang China 99 E7
Lhorong Xizang China 99 F7

▶Lhotse mt. China/Nepal 105 F4
4th highest mountain in the world and in Asia.

Lhozhag Xizang China 99 E7
Lhuntshi Bhutan 105 G4
Lhünzê Xizang China see Xingba
Lhünzê Xizang China 99 F7
Liakoura mt. Greece 69 J5
Liancheng China see Guangnan
Liancourt France 62 C5
Liancourt Rocks i. N. Pacific Ocean 91 C5
Liandu China see Lishui
Liang Sulawesi Indon. 83 B3
Lianga Mindanao Phil. 82 D4
Lianga Bay Mindanao Phil. 82 D4
Liangcheng Nei Mongol China 95 H3
Liangdang China 96 E1
Liangdaohe Xizang China 99 E7
Lianghe Chongqing China 97 F2
Lianghe Yunnan China 96 C3
Lianghekou Chongqing China see Lianghe
Lianghekou Gansu China 96 E1
Lianghekou Sichuan China 96 D2
Liangping China 96 E2
Liangpran, Bukit mt. Indon. 85 F2
Liangshan China see Liangping
Liang Shan mt. Myanmar 86 B1
Liangshi China see Shaodong
Liangtian China 97 F4
Liang Timur, Gunung mt. Malaysia 84 C2
Liangzhen Shaanxi China 95 G4
Liangzhou Gansu China see Wuwei
Liangzi Hu l. China 97 G2
Lianhe China see Qianjiang
Lianhua China 97 G3
Lianhua Shan mts China 97 G4
Lianjiang Fujian China 97 H3
Lianjiang Jiangxi China see Xingguo
Liannan China 97 G3
Lianping China 97 G3
Lianran China see Anning
Lianshan Guangdong China 97 G3
Lianshan Liaoning China 95 J3
Lianshui China 97 H1
Liant, Cape i. Thai. see Samae San, Ko
Liantang China see Nanchang
Lianxian China see Lianzhou
Lianyin China 90 A1
Lianyungang Jiangsu China 95 I5
Lianzhou Guangdong China 97 G3
Lianzhou Guangxi China see Hepu
Liaocheng Shandong China 95 H4
Liaodong Bandao pen. China 95 J3
Liaodong Wan b. China 95 J3
Liaodun Xinjiang China 94 C3
Liaodunzhan Xinjiang China 94 C3
Liaogao China see Songtao
Liao He r. China 95 J3
Liaoning prov. China 95 J3
Liaoyang Liaoning China 95 J3
Liaoyuan China 90 B4
Liaozhong Liaoning China 95 J3
Liapades Greece 69 H5
Liard r. Canada 150 F2
Liard Highway Canada 150 F2
Liard Plateau B.C./Y.T. Canada 149 P3
Liard River B.C. Canada 149 P4
Liari Pak. 111 G5
Liat i. Indon. 84 D3
Liathach mt. U.K. 60 D3
Liban country Asia see Lebanon
Liban, Jebel mts Lebanon 107 C2
Libau Latvia see Liepāja
Libby U.S.A. 156 E2
Libenge Dem. Rep. Congo 122 B3
Liberal U.S.A. 161 C4
Liberdade Brazil 179 B3
Liberec Czech Rep. 57 O5
Liberia country Africa 120 C4
Liberia Costa Rica 166 [inset] I7
Liberty AK U.S.A. 149 L2
Liberty IN U.S.A. 164 C4
Liberty KY U.S.A. 164 C5
Liberty ME U.S.A. 165 K1
Liberty MO U.S.A. 160 E4
Liberty MS U.S.A. 161 F6
Liberty NY U.S.A. 165 H3
Liberty TX U.S.A. 161 E6
Liberty Lake U.S.A. 165 G4
Libin Belgium 62 F5
Libmanan Luzon Phil. 82 C3
Libni, Gebel hill Egypt see Libnī, Jabal
Libnī, Jabal hill Egypt 107 A4
Libo China 96 E3
Libobo, Tanjung pt Halmahera Indon. 83 D3
Libode S. Africa 125 I6
Libong, Ko i. Thai. 87 B6
Libourne France 66 D4
Libral Well Australia 134 D5
Libre, Sierra mts Mex. 166 C2

▶Libreville Gabon 122 A3
Capital of Gabon.

Libuganon r. Mindanao Phil. 82 D5

▶Libya country Africa 121 E2
4th largest country in Africa.

Libyan Desert Egypt/Libya 108 C5
Libyan Plateau Egypt 112 B5
Licantén Chile 178 B4
Licata Sicily Italy 68 E6
Lice Turkey 113 F3
Lich Germany 63 I4
Lichas pen. Greece 69 J5
Licheng Guangxi China see Lipu
Licheng Jiangsu China see Jinhu
Licheng Shandong China 95 I4
Licheng Shanxi China 95 H4
Lichfield U.K. 59 F6
Lichinga Moz. 123 D5
Lichte Germany 63 L4
Lichtenau Germany 63 I3
Lichtenburg S. Africa 125 H4
Lichtenfels Germany 63 L4
Lichtenvoorde Neth. 62 G3
Lichuan Hubei China 97 F2
Lichuan Jiangxi China 97 H3
Licun Shandong China see Laoshan
Lida Belarus 55 N10
Liddel Water r. U.K. 60 G5
Lidfontein Namibia 124 D3
Lidköping Sweden 55 H7
Lidsjöberg Sweden 54 I4
Liebenau Germany 63 J2
Liebenburg Germany 63 K2
Liebenwalde Germany 63 N2
Liebig, Mount Australia 135 E5
Liechtenstein country Europe 66 I3
Liège Belgium 62 F4
Liegnitz Poland see Legnica
Lieksa Fin. 54 Q5
Lielupe r. Latvia 55 N8
Lielvārde Latvia 55 N8
Lienart Dem. Rep. Congo 122 C3
Lienchung i. Taiwan see Matsu Tao
Liên Nghia Vietnam 87 E5
Liên Sơn Vietnam 87 E4
Lienz Austria 57 N7
Liepāja Latvia 55 L8
Liepaya Latvia see Liepāja
Lier Belgium 62 E3
Lierre Belgium see Lier
Lieshout Neth. 62 F3
Lietuva country Europe see Lithuania
Liévin France 62 C4
Lièvre, Rivière du r. Canada 152 G5
Liezen Austria 57 O7
Lifamatola i. Indon. 83 C3
Liffey r. Ireland 61 F4
Lifford Ireland 61 E3
Lifi Mahuida mt. Arg. 178 C6
Lifou i. New Caledonia 133 G4
Lifu i. New Caledonia see Lifou
Ligao Luzon Phil. 82 C3
Līgatne Latvia 55 N8
Lighthouse Reef Belize 167 I5
Lightning Ridge Australia 138 C2
Ligny-en-Barrois France 62 F6
Ligonha r. Moz. 123 D5
Ligonier U.S.A. 164 C3
Ligui Mex. 166 C3
Ligure, Mar sea France/Italy see Ligurian Sea
Ligurian Sea France/Italy 68 C3
Ligurienne, Mer sea France/Italy see Ligurian Sea
Ligurta U.S.A. 159 F5
Lihir Group is P.N.G. 132 F2
Lihou Reef and Cays Australia 136 E3
Liivi laht b. Estonia/Latvia see Riga, Gulf of
Lijiang Yunnan China 96 D3
Lijiang Yunnan China see Yuanjiang
Lijiazhai China 97 G2
Lika reg. Croatia 68 F2
Likasi Dem. Rep. Congo 123 C5
Likati Dem. Rep. Congo 122 C3
Likely Canada 150 F4
Likhachevo Ukr. see Pervomays'kyy
Likhachyovo Ukr. see Pervomays'kyy
Likhapani India 105 H4
Likhás pen. Greece see Lichas
Likhoslavl' Rus. Fed. 52 G4
Likisia East Timor see Liquiçá
Liku Kalimantan Indon. 85 E2
Liku Sarawak Malaysia 85 F1
Likupang Sulawesi Indon. 83 C2
Likurga Rus. Fed. 52 I4
L'Île-Rousse Corsica France 66 I5
Lilienthal Germany 63 I1
Liling China 97 G3
Lilla Pak. 111 I3
Lilla Edet Sweden 55 H7
Lille Belgium 62 E3
Lille France 62 D4
Lille (Lesquin) airport France 62 D4
Lille Bælt sea chan. Denmark see Little Belt
Lillebonne France 59 H9
Lillehammer Norway 55 G6
Lillers France 62 C4
Lillesand Norway 55 F7
Lillestrøm Norway 55 G7
Lilley U.S.A. 164 C2
Lillholmsjö Sweden 54 I5
Lillian, Point hill Australia 135 D6
Lillington U.S.A. 163 E5
Lillooet Canada 150 F5
Lillooet r. Canada 150 F5
Lillooet Range mts Canada 150 F5

▶Lilongwe Malawi 123 D5
Capital of Malawi.

Liloy Mindanao Phil. 82 C4
Lilydale Australia 137 B7

▶Lima Peru 176 C6
Capital of Peru. 5th most populous city in South America.

Lima MT U.S.A. 156 E3
Lima NY U.S.A. 165 G2
Lima OH U.S.A. 164 C3
Lima Duarte Brazil 179 C3
Lima Islands China see Wanshan Qundao
Liman Rus. Fed. 53 J7
Limar Maluku Indon. 83 C4
Limas Indon. 84 D2
Limassol Cyprus 107 A2
Limavady U.K. 61 F2
Limay r. Arg. 178 C5
Limbang Sarawak Malaysia 85 F1
Limbaži Latvia 55 N8
Limboto Sulawesi Indon. 83 B2
Limboto, Danau l. Indon. 83 B2
Limbung Sulawesi Indon. 83 A4
Limbungan Kalimantan Indon. 85 F3
Limbunya Australia 134 E4
Limburg an der Lahn Germany 63 I4
Lim Chu Kang hill Sing. 87 [inset]
Lime Acres S. Africa 124 F5
Lime Hills AK U.S.A. 148 I3
Limeira Brazil 179 B3
Limerick Ireland 61 D5
Limestone Point Canada 151 L4
Lime Village AK U.S.A. 148 I3
Limingen Norway 54 H4
Limingen l. Norway 54 H4
Limington U.S.A. 165 J2
Liminka Fin. 54 N4
Limmen Bight b. Australia 136 B2
Limnos i. Greece 69 K5
Limoeiro Brazil 177 K5
Limoges Canada 165 H1
Limoges France 66 E4
Limón Hond. 166 [inset] I6
Limon U.S.A. 160 C4
Limonlu Turkey 107 B1
Limonum France see Poitiers
Limousin reg. France 66 E4
Limoux France 66 F5
Limpopo prov. S. Africa 125 I2
Limpopo r. S. Africa/Zimbabwe 125 K3
Limpopo National Park 125 J2
Limu China 97 F3
Līnah well Saudi Arabia 113 F5
Linakhamari Rus. Fed. 54 Q2
Lin'an China see Jianshui
Linao Bay Mindanao Phil. 82 D5
Linapacan i. Phil. 82 B4
Linapacan Strait Phil. 82 B4
Linares Chile 178 B5
Linares Mex. 167 F3
Linares Spain 67 E4
Linau Balui plat. Malaysia 85 F2
Lincang China 96 D4
Lincheng Hainan China see Lingao
Lincheng Hunan China see Huitong
Linchuan China see Fuzhou
Linck Nunataks nunataks Antarctica 188 K1
Lincoln Arg. 178 D4
Lincoln U.K. 58 G5
Lincoln CA U.S.A. 158 C2
Lincoln IL U.S.A. 160 F3
Lincoln MI U.S.A. 164 D1

▶Lincoln NE U.S.A. 160 D3
Capital of Nebraska.

Lincoln City IN U.S.A. 164 B4
Lincoln City OR U.S.A. 156 B3
Lincoln Island Paracel Is 80 E3
Lincoln National Park Australia 137 A7
Lincoln Sea Canada/Greenland 189 J1
Lincolnshire Wolds hills U.K. 58 G5
Lincolnton U.S.A. 163 D5
Linda, Serra hills Brazil 179 C1
Linda Creek watercourse Australia 136 B4
Lindau Germany 63 M2
Lindau (Bodensee) Germany 57 L7
Lindeman Group is Australia 136 E4
Linden Canada 150 H5
Linden Germany 63 I4
Linden Guyana 177 G2
Linden AL U.S.A. 163 C5
Linden MI U.S.A. 164 D2
Linden TN U.S.A. 162 C5
Linden TX U.S.A. 161 E5
Linden Grove U.S.A. 160 E2
Lindern (Oldenburg) Germany 63 H2
Lindesnes c. Norway 55 E7
Lindhos Greece see Lindos
Lindi r. Dem. Rep. Congo 122 C3
Lindi Tanz. 123 D4
Lindian Heilong. China 95 K2
Lindisfarne i. U.K. see Holy Island
Lindley S. Africa 125 H4
Lindong Nei Mongol China 95 I3
Lindos Greece 65 J4
Lindos, Akra pt Notio Aigaio Greece see Gkinas, Akrotirio
Lindsay Canada 165 F1
Lindsay CA U.S.A. 158 D3
Lindsay MT U.S.A. 156 G3
Lindsborg U.S.A. 160 D4
Lindside U.S.A. 164 E5
Lindum U.K. see Lincoln
Line Islands Kiribati 187 J5
Linesville U.S.A. 164 E3
Linfen Shanxi China 95 G4
Lingampet India 106 C2
Linganamakki Reservoir India 106 B3
Lingao China 97 F5
Lingayen Luzon Phil. 82 C2
Lingayen Gulf Luzon Phil. 82 C2
Lingbao Henan China 95 G5
Lingbi China 97 H1
Lingcheng Anhui China see Lingbi
Lingcheng Guangxi China see Lingshan
Lingcheng Hainan China see Lingshui
Lingcheng Shandong China see Lingxian
Lingchuan Guangxi China 97 F3
Lingchuan Shanxi China 95 H5
Lingelethu S. Africa 125 H7
Lingen (Ems) Germany 63 H2
Lingga i. Indon. 84 D3
Lingga Sarawak Malaysia 85 E2
Lingga, Kepulauan is Indon. 84 D3
Linggo Co l. Xizang China 99 E6
Linghai Liaoning China 95 J3
Lingig Mindanao Phil. 82 D5
Lingkabau Sabah Malaysia 85 G1
Lingkas Kalimantan Indon. 85 G2
Lingle U.S.A. 156 G4
Lingomo Dem. Rep. Congo 122 C3
Lingqiu Shanxi China 95 H4
Lingshan China 97 F4
Lingshan Wan b. China 95 J5
Lingshi Shanxi China 95 G4
Lingshui China 97 F5
Lingshui Wan b. China 97 F5
Lingsugur India 106 C2
Lingtai Gansu China 95 F5
Linguère Senegal 120 B3
Lingui China 97 F3
Lingxi China see Yongshun
Lingxian China see Yanling
Lingxian Shandong China 95 I4
Lingxiang China 97 G2
Lingyang China see Cili
Lingyuan Liaoning China 95 I3
Lingyun China 96 E3
Lingzi Tang reg. Aksai Chin 99 B6
Linhai China 97 I2
Linhares Brazil 179 C2
Linhe Nei Mongol China 95 F3
Linhpa Myanmar 86 A1
Linjiang China 90 B4
Linjin China 97 F1
Linköping Sweden 55 I7
Linkou China 90 C3
Linli China 97 F2
Linlithgow U.K. 60 F5
Linlü Shan mt. Henan China 95 H4
Linmingguan Hebei China see Yongnian
Linn MO U.S.A. 160 F4
Linn TX U.S.A. 161 D7
Linn, Mount U.S.A. 158 B1
Linnansaaren kansallispuisto nat. park Fin. 54 P5
Linnhe, Loch inlet U.K. 60 D4
Linnich Germany 62 G4
Linosa, Isola di i. Sicily Italy 68 E7
Linpo Myanmar 86 B2
Linqing Shandong China 95 H4
Linquan China 97 G1
Linru Henan China see Ruzhou
Linruzhen Henan China 95 H5
Lins Brazil 179 A3
Linshu China 97 H1
Linshui China 96 E2
Lintah, Selat sea chan. Indon. 83 A5
Lintan Gansu China 94 E5
Lintao Gansu China 94 E5
Linton IN U.S.A. 164 B4
Linton ND U.S.A. 160 C2
Lintong Shaanxi China 95 G5
Linwu China 97 G3
Linxi Nei Mongol China 95 I3
Linxia Gansu China 94 E5
Linxia Gansu China 94 E5
Linxian Henan China see Linzhou
Linxian Shanxi China 95 G4
Linxiang China 97 G2
Linyi Shandong China 95 I4
Linyi Shandong China 95 I5
Linyi Shanxi China 95 G5
Linying China 97 G1
Linyou Shaanxi China 95 F5
Linz Austria 57 O6
Linze Gansu China 94 E4
Linzhou Henan China 95 H4
Lio Matoh Sarawak Malaysia 85 F2
Lion, Golfe du g. France 66 F5
Lions, Gulf of France see Lion, Golfe du
Lions Bay Canada 150 F5
Lioppa Maluku Indon. 83 C4
Lioua Chad 121 E3
Lipa Luzon Phil. 82 C3
Lipang i. Indon. 83 C2
Lipari Sicily Italy 68 F5
Lipari, Isole is Italy 68 F5
Lipatkain Sumatera Indon. 84 C2
Lipetsk Rus. Fed. 53 H5
Lipin Bor Rus. Fed. 52 H3
Liping China 97 F3
Lipova Romania 69 I1
Lipovtsy Rus. Fed. 90 C3
Lippe r. Germany 63 G3
Lippstadt Germany 63 I3
Lipsoí i. Greece see Leipsoi
Lipti Lekh pass Nepal 104 E3
Liptrap, Cape Australia 138 B7
Lipu China 97 F3
Liquiçá East Timor 83 C5
Liquissa East Timor see Liquiçá
Lira Uganda 122 D3
Liran i. Maluku Indon. 83 C4
Liranga Congo 122 B4
Lircay Peru 176 D6
Lirung Sulawesi Indon. 83 C2
Lisala Dem. Rep. Congo 122 C3
L'Isalo, Massif de mts Madag. 123 E6
L'Isalo, Parc National de nat. park Madag. 123 E6
Lisbellaw U.K. 61 E3
Lisboa Port. see Lisbon

▶Lisbon Port. 67 B4
Capital of Portugal.

Lisbon ME U.S.A. 165 J1
Lisbon NH U.S.A. 165 J1
Lisbon OH U.S.A. 164 E3
Lisburn U.K. 61 F3
Lisburne, Cape AK U.S.A. 148 F1
Liscannor Bay Ireland 61 C5
Lisdoonvarna Ireland 61 C4
Lishan Shaanxi China see Lintong
Lishan Taiwan 97 I3
Lishe Jiang r. China 96 D3
Lishi Jiangxi China see Dingnan
Lishi Shanxi China 95 G4
Lishu China 90 B4
Lishui China 97 H2
Li Shui r. China 97 F2
Lisichansk Ukr. see Lysychans'k
Lisieux France 66 E2
Liskeard U.K. 59 C8
Liski Rus. Fed. 53 H6
L'Isle-Adam France 62 C5
Lismore Australia 138 F2
Lismore Ireland 61 E5
Lisnarrick U.K. 61 E3
Lisnaskea U.K. 61 E3
Liss mt. Saudi Arabia 107 D4
Lissa Poland see Leszno
Lister, Mount Antarctica 188 H1
Listowel Canada 164 E2
Listowel Ireland 61 C5
Listvyaga, Khrebet mts Kazakh./Rus. Fed. 98 D2
Lit Sweden 54 I5
Litang Guangxi China 97 F4
Litang Sichuan China 96 D2
Līṭānī, Nahr el r. Lebanon 107 B3
Litchfield CA U.S.A. 158 C1
Litchfield CT U.S.A. 165 I3
Litchfield IL U.S.A. 160 F4
Litchfield MI U.S.A. 164 C2
Litchfield MN U.S.A. 160 E2
Lit-et-Mixe France 66 D4
Lithgow Australia 138 E4
Lithino, Akra pt Kriti Greece see Lithino, Akrotirio
Lithino, Akrotirio pt Greece 69 K7
Lithuania country Europe 55 M9
Lititz U.S.A. 165 G3
Litoměřice Czech Rep. 57 O5
Litovko Rus. Fed. 90 D2
Litovskaya S.S.R. country Europe see Lithuania
Little r. U.S.A. 161 E6
Little Abaco i. Bahamas 163 E7
Little Abitibi r. Canada 152 E4
Little Abitibi Lake Canada 152 E4
Little Andaman i. India 87 A5
Little Bahama Bank sea feature Bahamas 163 E7
Little Barrier i. N.Z. 139 E3
Little Belt sea chan. Denmark 55 F9
Little Belt Mountains U.S.A. 156 F3
Little Bitter Lake Egypt 107 A4
Little Black r. AK U.S.A. 149 K2
Little Cayman i. Cayman Is 169 H5
Little Churchill r. Canada 151 M3
Little Chute U.S.A. 164 A1
Little Coco Island Cocos Is 87 A4
Little Colorado r. U.S.A. 159 H3
Little Creek Peak U.S.A. 159 G3
Little Current Canada 152 E5
Little Current r. Canada 152 D4
Little Desert National Park Australia 137 C8
Little Diomede i. AK U.S.A. 148 E2
Little Egg Harbor inlet U.S.A. 165 H4
Little Exuma i. Bahamas 163 F8
Little Falls U.S.A. 160 E2
Littlefield AZ U.S.A. 159 G3
Littlefield TX U.S.A. 161 C5
Little Fork r. U.S.A. 160 E1
Little Grand Rapids Canada 151 M4
Littlehampton U.K. 59 G8
Little Inagua Island Bahamas 163 F8
Little Karas Berg plat. Namibia 124 D4
Little Karoo plat. S. Africa 124 E7
Little Lake U.S.A. 158 E4
Little Mecatina Island Canada see Petit Mécatina, Île du
Little Minch sea chan. U.K. 60 B3
Little Missouri r. U.S.A. 160 C2
Little Namaqualand reg. S. Africa see Namaqualand
Little Nicobar i. India 87 A6
Little Ouse r. U.K. 59 H6
Little Pamir mts Asia 111 I2
Little Rancheria r. Canada 150 D2
Little Red River Canada 150 H3

▶Little Rock U.S.A. 161 E5
Capital of Arkansas.

Littlerock U.S.A. 158 E4
Little Sable Point U.S.A. 164 B2
Little Salmon Lake Y.T. Canada 149 N3
Little Salt Lake U.S.A. 159 G3
Little Sandy Desert Australia 135 B5
Little San Salvador i. Bahamas 163 F7
Little Sitkin Island AK U.S.A. 149 [inset]
Little Smoky Canada 150 G4
Little Tibet reg. India/Pak. see Ladakh
Littleton U.S.A. 156 G5
Little Valley U.S.A. 165 F2
Little Wind r. U.S.A. 156 F4
Litunde Moz. 123 D5
Liu'an China see Lu'an
Liuba China 96 E1
Liucheng China 97 F3
Liuchiu Yü i. Taiwan 97 I4
Liuchong He r. China 96 E3
Liuchow China see Liuzhou
Liugong Dao i. China 95 J4
Liuhe China 90 B4
Liuheng Dao i. China 97 I2
Liujiachang China 97 F2
Liujiaxia Gansu China see Yongjing
Liujiaxia Shuiku resr China 96 D1
Liukesong China 90 B3
Liulin Gansu China see Jonê
Liulin Shanxi China 95 G4
Liupan Shan mts China 94 F5
Liupanshui China see Lupanshui
Liuquan Jiangsu China 95 I5

Liure Hond. 166 [inset] I6
Liushuquan *Xinjiang* China 94 C3
Liuwa Plain National Park Zambia 123 C5
Liuyang China 97 G2
Liuyuan *Gansu* China 98 F4
Liuzhan *Heilong.* China 95 K1
Liuzhangzhen *Shanxi* China *see* Yuanqu
Liuzhou China 97 F3
Livadeia Greece 69 J5
Līvāni Latvia 55 O8
Livengood *AK* U.S.A. 149 J2
Live Oak U.S.A. 163 D6
Liveringa Australia 132 C3
Livermore *CA* U.S.A. 158 C3
Livermore *KY* U.S.A. 164 B5
Livermore, Mount U.S.A. 161 B6
Livermore Falls U.S.A. 165 J1
Liverpool Australia 138 E4
Liverpool Canada 153 I5
Liverpool U.K. 58 E5
Liverpool Bay *N.W.T.* Canada 149 O1
Liverpool Plains Australia 138 E3
Liverpool Range *mts* Australia 138 D3
Livia U.S.A. 164 B5
Livingston Guat. 167 H6
Livingston U.K. 60 F5
Livingston *AL* U.S.A. 161 F5
Livingston *KY* U.S.A. 164 C5
Livingston *MT* U.S.A. 156 F3
Livingston *TN* U.S.A. 164 C5
Livingston *TX* U.S.A. 161 E6
Livingston, Lake U.S.A. 161 E6
Livingstone Zambia 123 C5
Livingston Island Antarctica 188 L2
Livingston Manor U.S.A. 165 H3
Livno Bos.-Herz. 68 G3
Livny Rus. Fed. 53 H5
Livojoki *r.* Fin. 54 O4
Livonia *MI* U.S.A. 164 D2
Livonia *NY* U.S.A. 165 G2
Livorno Italy 68 D3
Livramento do Brumado Brazil 179 C1
Liwā Oman 110 E5
Liwā', Wādī al *watercourse* Syria 107 C3
Liwale Tanz. 123 D4
Liwu *Hebei* China *see* Lixian
Lixian *Gansu* China 94 F5
Lixian *Hebei* China 95 H4
Lixian *Sichuan* China 96 D2
Lixus Morocco *see* Larache
Liyang China *see* Hexian
Liyuan China *see* Sangzhi
Lizard U.K. 59 B9
Lizarda Brazil 177 I5
Lizard Point U.K. 59 B9
Lizarra Spain *see* Estella
Lizemores U.S.A. 164 E4
Liziping China 96 D2
Lizy-sur-Ourcq France 62 D5
Ljouwert Neth. *see* Leeuwarden

▶Ljubljana Slovenia 68 F1
Capital of Slovenia.

Ljugarn Sweden 55 K8
Ljungan *r.* Sweden 54 J5
Ljungaverk Sweden 54 J5
Ljungby Sweden 55 H8
Ljusdal Sweden 55 J6
Ljusnan *r.* Sweden 55 J6
Ljusne Sweden 55 J6
Llaima, Volcán *vol.* Chile 178 B5
Llanandras U.K. *see* Presteigne
Llanbadarn Fawr U.K. 59 C6
Llanbedr Pont Steffan U.K. *see* Lampeter
Llanbister U.K. 59 D6
Llandeilo U.K. 59 D7
Llandissilio U.K. 59 C7
Llandovery U.K. 59 D7
Llandrindod Wells U.K. 59 D6
Llandudno U.K. 58 D5
Llandysul U.K. 59 C6
Llanegwad U.K. 59 C7
Llanelli U.K. 59 C7
Llanfair Caereinion U.K. 59 D6
Llanfair-ym-Muallt U.K. *see* Builth Wells
Llangefni U.K. 58 C5
Llangollen U.K. 59 D6
Llangurig U.K. 59 D6
Llanllyfni U.K. 59 C5
Llannerch-y-medd U.K. 58 C5
Llannor U.K. 59 C6
Llano Mex. 166 C2
Llano U.S.A. 161 D6
Llano *r.* U.S.A. 161 D6
Llano Estacado *plain* U.S.A. 161 C5
Llano Grande *Durango* Mex. 166 D4
Llanos *plain* Col./Venez. 176 E2
Llanquihue, Lago *l.* Chile 178 B6
Llanrhystud U.K. 59 C6
Llantrisant U.K. 59 D7
Llanuwchllyn U.K. 59 D6
Llanwnog U.K. 59 D6
Llanymddyfri U.K. *see* Llandovery
Llay U.K. 59 D5
Lleida Spain 67 G3
Llerena Spain 67 C4
Llíria Spain 67 F4
Llodio Spain 67 E2
Lloyd George, Mount Canada 150 E3
Lloyd Lake Canada 151 I3
Lloydminster Canada 151 I4
Lluchmayor Spain *see* Llucmajor
Llucmajor Spain 67 H4

▶Llullaillaco, Volcán *vol.* Chile 178 C2
Highest active volcano in the world and South America.

Lô, Sông *r.* China/Vietnam 86 D2
Loa *r.* Chile 178 B2
Loa U.S.A. 159 H2
Loagan Bunut National Park Malaysia 85 F2
Loakulu *Kalimantan* Indon. 85 G3
Loay *Bohol* Phil. 82 D4
Loban' *r.* Rus. Fed. 52 K4
Lobata *Sulawesi* Indon. 83 B3
Lobatejo *mt.* Spain 67 D5
Lobatse Botswana 125 G3
Lobaye *r.* Cent. Afr. Rep. 122 B3
Löbejün Germany 63 L3
Löbenberg *hill* Germany 63 M3
Loberia Arg. 178 E5
Lobi, Mount *vol.* Phil. 82 D4
Lobito Angola 123 B5
Lobos Arg. 178 E5
Lobos, Cabo *c.* Mex. 166 B2
Lobos, Isla *i.* Mex. 166 C3
Lobos, Isla de *i.* Mex. 167 F4
Lobos de Tierra, Isla *i.* Peru 176 B5
Loburg Germany 63 M2
Lôc Binh Vietnam 86 D2
Lochaline U.K. 60 D4
Lo Chau *H.K.* China *see* Beaufort Island
Loch Baghasdail U.K. *see* Lochboisdale
Lochboisdale U.K. 60 B3
Lochcarron U.K. 60 D3
Lochearnhead U.K. 60 E4
Lochem Neth. 62 G2
Lochern National Park Australia 136 C5
Loches France 66 E3
Loch Garman Ireland *see* Wexford
Lochgelly U.K. 60 F4
Lochgilphead U.K. 60 D4
Lochinver U.K. 60 D2
Loch Lomond and Trossachs National Park U.K. 60 E4
Lochmaddy U.K. 60 B3
Lochnagar *mt.* U.K. 60 F4
Loch nam Madadh U.K. *see* Lochmaddy
Loch Raven Reservoir U.S.A. 165 G4
Lochy, Loch *l.* U.K. 60 E4
Lock Australia 137 A7
Lockerbie U.K. 60 F5
Lockhart Australia 138 C5
Lockhart U.S.A. 161 D6
Lock Haven U.S.A. 165 G3
Löcknitz *r.* Germany 63 L1
Lockport U.S.A. 165 F2
Lockwood Hills *AK* U.S.A. 148 H2
Lôc Ninh Vietnam 87 D5
Lod Israel 107 B4
Loddon *r.* Australia 138 A5
Lodève France 66 F5
Lodeynoye Pole Rus. Fed. 52 G3
Lodge, Mount Canada/U.S.A. 149 M4
Lodhikheda India 104 D5
Lodhran Pak. 111 H4
Lodi Italy 68 C2
Lodi *CA* U.S.A. 158 C2
Lodi *OH* U.S.A. 164 D3
Lødingen Norway 54 I2
Lodja Dem. Rep. Congo 122 C4
Lodomeria Rus. Fed. *see* Vladimir
Lodrani India 104 B5
Lodwar Kenya 122 D3
Łódź Poland 57 Q5
Loei Thai. 86 C3
Loeriesfontein S. Africa 124 D6
Lofoten *is* Norway 54 H2
Lofusa Sudan 121 G4
Log Rus. Fed. 53 I6
Loga Niger 120 D3
Logan *IA* U.S.A. 160 E3
Logan *OH* U.S.A. 164 D4
Logan *UT* U.S.A. 156 F4
Logan *WV* U.S.A. 164 E5

▶Logan, Mount *Y.T.* Canada 149 L3
2nd highest mountain in North America.

Logan, Mount U.S.A. 156 C2
Logan Creek *r.* Australia 136 D4
Logan Lake Canada 150 F5
Logan Mountains *N.W.T./Y.T.* Canada 149 O3
Logansport *IN* U.S.A. 164 B3
Logansport *LA* U.S.A. 161 E6
Logatec Slovenia 68 F2
Logpung *Qinghai* China 94 E5
Logroño Spain 67 E2
Logtak Lake India 105 H4
Lohardaga India 105 F5
Loharu India 104 C3
Lohatlha S. Africa 124 F5
Lohawat India 104 C4
Lohfelden Germany 63 J3
Lohil *r.* China/India *see* Zayü Qu
Lohiniva Fin. 54 N3
Lohjanjärvi *l.* Fin. 55 M6
Löhne Germany 63 I2
Lohne (Oldenburg) Germany 63 I2
Lohtaja Fin. 54 M4
Loi, Nam *r.* Myanmar 86 C2
Loikaw Myanmar 86 B3
Loi Lan *mt.* Myanmar/Thai. 86 B3
Loi-lem Myanmar 86 B2
Loi Lun Myanmar 86 B2
Loimaa Fin. 55 M6
Loipyet Hills Myanmar 86 B1
Loire *r.* France 66 C3
Loi Sang *mt.* Myanmar 86 B2
L'Oise à l'Aisne, Canal de France 62 D5
Loi Song *mt.* Myanmar 86 B2
Loja Ecuador 176 C4
Loja Spain 67 D5
Lokan *r.* Malaysia 85 G1
Lokan tekojärvi *l.* Fin. 54 O3
Lokchim *r.* Rus. Fed. 52 K3
Lokeren Belgium 62 E3
Lokgwabe Botswana 124 E3
Lokichar Kenya 100 C6
Lokichokio Kenya 122 D3
Lokilalaki, Gunung *mt.* Indon. 83 B3
Løkken Denmark 55 F8
Løkken Norway 54 F5
Loknya Rus. Fed. 52 F4
Lokoja Nigeria 120 D4
Lokolama Dem. Rep. Congo 122 B4
Lokossa Benin 120 D4
Lokot' Rus. Fed. 53 G5
Lol Sudan 121 F4
Lola Guinea 120 C4
Lola, Mount U.S.A. 158 C2
Loleta U.S.A. 158 A1
Lolland *i.* Denmark 55 G9
Lollondo Tanz. 122 D4
Lolo U.S.A. 156 E3
Lolobata *Halmahera* Indon. 83 D2
Loloda *Halmahera* Indon. 83 C2
Loloda Utara, Kepulauan *is Maluku* Indon. 83 C2
Lolo Pass U.S.A. 156 E3
Lolotoi East Timor 83 C5
Lolowau Indon. 84 B2
Lolwane S. Africa 124 F4
Lom Bulg. 69 J3
Lom Norway 55 F6
Loma U.S.A. 159 I2
Lomami *r.* Dem. Rep. Congo 122 C3
Lomar Pass Afgh. 111 G3
Lomas, Bahía de *b.* Chile 178 C8
Lomas de Zamora Arg. 178 E4
Lombarda, Serra *hills* Brazil 177 H3
Lomblen *i.* Indon. 83 B5
Lombok *Lombok* Indon. 85 G5
Lombok *i.* Indon. 85 G5
Lombok, Selat *sea chan.* Indon. 85 F5

▶Lomé Togo 120 D4
Capital of Togo.

Lomela Dem. Rep. Congo 122 C4
Lomela *r.* Dem. Rep. Congo 121 F5
Lomira U.S.A. 164 A2
Lomme France 62 C4
Lommel Belgium 62 F3
Lomond Canada 153 K4
Lomond, Loch *l.* U.K. 60 E4
Lomonosov Rus. Fed. 55 P7
Lomonosov Ridge *sea feature* Arctic Ocean 189 B1
Lomovoye Rus. Fed. 52 I2
Lomphat Cambodia *see* Lumphăt
Lompobatang, Hutan Lindung *nature res. Sulawesi* Indon. 83 A4
Lompobattang, Gunung *mt.* Indon. 83 A4
Lompoc U.S.A. 158 C4
Lom Sak Thai. 86 C3
Łomża Poland 57 S4
Lơn, Hon *i.* Vietnam 87 E4
Lonar India 106 C2
Londa Bangl. 105 G5
Londa India 106 B3
Londinières France 62 B5
Londinium U.K. *see* London
Londoko Rus. Fed. 90 D2
London Canada 164 E2

▶London U.K. 59 G7
Capital of the United Kingdom and of England. 4th most populous city in Europe.

London *KY* U.S.A. 164 C5
London *OH* U.S.A. 164 D4
Londonderry U.K. 61 E3
Londonderry *OH* U.S.A. 164 D4
Londonderry *VT* U.S.A. 165 I2
Londonderry, Cape Australia 134 D3
Londrina Brazil 179 A3
Lone Pine U.S.A. 158 D3
Long Thai. 86 B3
Long *AK* U.S.A. 148 I2
Longa Angola 123 B5
Longa, Proliv *sea chan.* Rus. Fed. 77 S2
Longagung *Kalimantan* Indon. 85 F2
Long Akah *Sarawak* Malaysia 85 F2
Long'an China 96 E4
Long'anqiao *Heilong.* China 95 K2
Long Ashton U.K. 59 E7
Longbawan *Kalimantan* Indon. 85 F2
Long Bay U.S.A. 163 E5
Longbeach N.Z. 139 C7
Long Beach U.S.A. 158 D5
Longberini *Kalimantan* Indon. 85 F2
Longbia *Kalimantan* Indon. 85 G2
Longbo China *see* Shuangpai
Longboh *Kalimantan* Indon. 85 F2
Long Branch U.S.A. 165 I3
Longchang China 96 E2
Longcheng *Anhui* China *see* Xiaoxian
Longcheng *Guangdong* China *see* Longmen
Longcheng *Yunnan* China *see* Chenggong
Longchuan China *see* Nanhua
Longchuan Jiang *r.* China 96 C4
Long Creek *r.* Canada 151 K5
Long Creek U.S.A. 156 D3
Longde *Ningxia* China 94 F5
Long Eaton U.K. 59 F6
Longford Ireland 61 E4
Longgang *Chongqing* China *see* Dazu
Longgang *Guangdong* China 97 G4
Longgi *r.* Indon. 85 G2
Longhoughton U.K. 58 F3
Longhua *Hebei* China 95 I3
Longhui China 97 F3
Longhurst, Mount Antarctica 188 H1
Longibau *Kalimantan* Indon. 85 G2
Longikis *Kalimantan* Indon. 85 G3
Longiram *Kalimantan* Indon. 85 F3
Long Island Bahamas 163 F8
Long Island *N.S.* Canada 153 I5
Long Island *Nunavut* Canada 152 F3
Long Island India 87 A4
Long Island P.N.G. 81 L8
Long Island U.S.A. 165 I3
Long Island Sound *sea chan.* U.S.A. 165 I3
Longjiang *Heilong.* China 95 J2
Longjin China *see* Qingliu
Longju China 96 B2
Longkou *Shandong* China 95 J4
Longlac Canada 152 D4
Long Lake *l.* Canada 152 D4
Long Lake U.S.A. 165 H2
Long Lake *l. ME* U.S.A. 162 G2
Long Lake *l. MI* U.S.A. 164 D1
Long Lake *l. ND* U.S.A. 160 C2
Long Lake *l. NY* U.S.A. 165 H1
Long Lama *Sarawak* Malaysia 85 F2
Longli China 96 E3
Longlin China 96 E3
Longling China 96 C3
Longmeadow U.S.A. 165 I2
Long Melford U.K. 59 H6
Longmen *Guangdong* China 97 G4
Longmen *Heilong.* China 90 B2
Longmen Shan *hill* China 97 F1
Longmen Shan *mts* China 96 E1
Longming China 96 E4
Longmont U.S.A. 156 G4
Long Murum *Sarawak* Malaysia 85 F2
Longnan China 96 E1
Longnan China 97 G3
Longnawan *Kalimantan* Indon. 85 F2
Longpahangai *Kalimantan* Indon. 85 F2
Long Phu Vietnam 87 D5
Longping China *see* Luodian
Long Point *Ont.* Canada 164 E2
Long Point *Man.* Canada 151 L4
Long Point *Ont.* Canada 164 E2
Long Point N.Z. 139 B8
Long Point Bay Canada 164 E2
Long Prairie U.S.A. 160 E2
Long Preston U.K. 58 E4
Longpujungan *Kalimantan* Indon. 85 F2
Longquan *Guizhou* China *see* Danzhai
Longquan *Guizhou* China *see* Fenggang
Longquan *Hunan* China *see* Xintian
Longquan Xi *r.* China 97 I2
Long Range Mountains *Nfld. and Lab.* Canada 153 K4
Long Range Mountains *Nfld. and Lab.* Canada 153 K5
Longreach Australia 136 D4
Longriba China 96 D1
Longshan *Guizhou* China *see* Longli
Longshan *Hunan* China 97 F2
Longshan *Yunnan* China *see* Longling
Long Shan *mts* China 94 F5
Longsheng China 97 F3
Longshou Shan *mts* China 94 E4
Longs Peak U.S.A. 156 G4
Long Stratton U.K. 59 I6
Long Teru *Sarawak* Malaysia 85 F2
Longtom Lake Canada 150 G1
Longtou *Nei Mongol* China 95 J1
Longtown U.K. 58 E3
Longue-Pointe-de-Mingan Canada 153 I4
Longueuil Canada 152 G5
Longuyon France 62 F5
Longvale U.S.A. 158 B2
Longview *TX* U.S.A. 161 E5
Longview *WA* U.S.A. 156 C3
Longwai *Kalimantan* Indon. 85 G2
Longwangmiao China 90 D3
Longwei Co *l. Xizang* China 99 E6
Longxi *Gansu* China 94 F5
Longxian *Guangdong* China *see* Wengyuan
Longxian *Shaanxi* China 94 F5
Longxingchang *Nei Mongol* China *see* Wuyuan
Longxi Shan *mt.* China 97 H3
Longxu China *see* Cangwu
Long Xuyên Vietnam 87 D5
Longyan China 97 H3
Longyao *Hebei* China 95 H4

▶Longyearbyen Svalbard 76 C2
Capital of Svalbard.

Longzhen China 90 B2
Longzhou China 96 E4
Longzhouping China *see* Changyang
Löningen Germany 63 H2
Lonoke U.S.A. 161 F5
Lönsboda Sweden 55 I8
Lons-le-Saunier France 66 G3
Lontar *i. Maluku* Indon. 83 D4
Lonton Myanmar 86 B1
Looc Phil. 82 C3
Loochoo Islands Japan *see* Ryukyu Islands
Loogootee U.S.A. 164 B4
Lookout, Cape Canada 152 E3
Lookout, Cape U.S.A. 163 E5
Lookout, Point Australia 138 F1
Lookout, Point U.S.A. 164 D1
Lookout Mountain U.S.A. 159 I4
Lookout Point Australia 135 B8
Lookout Ridge *AK* U.S.A. 148 H1
Loolmalasin *vol. crater* Tanz. 122 D4
Loon Canada 152 C4
Loon *r.* Canada 150 H3
Loongana Australia 135 D7
Loon Lake Canada 151 I4
Loop Head *hd* Ireland 61 C5
Lop *Xinjiang* China 99 C5
Lopasnya Rus. Fed. *see* Chekhov
Lopatina, Gora *mt.* Rus. Fed. 90 F2
Lop Buri Thai. 86 C4
Lopé, Parc National de la *nat. park* Gabon 122 B4
Lopez *Luzon* Phil. 82 C3
Lopez, Cap *c.* Gabon 122 A4
Lopnur *Xinjiang* China *see* Yuli
Lop Nur *salt flat* China 98 E4
Lopphavet *b.* Norway 54 L1
Loptyuga Rus. Fed. 52 K3
Lora Pak. 111 G5
Lora *r.* Venez. 176 D2
Lora del Río Spain 67 D5
Lorain U.S.A. 164 D3
Loralai Pak. 111 H4
Loralai *r.* Pak. 111 H4
Loramie, Lake U.S.A. 164 C3
Lorana *Sulawesi* Indon. 83 B3
Lorca Spain 67 F5
Lorch Germany 63 H4
Lord Auckland Shoal *sea feature* Phil. 82 B4
Lordegān Iran 110 C4
Lord Howe Atoll Solomon Is *see* Ontong Java Atoll
Lord Howe Island Australia 133 F5
Lord Howe Rise *sea feature* S. Pacific Ocean 186 G7
Lord Loughborough Island Myanmar 87 B5
Lordsburg U.S.A. 159 I5
Lore East Timor 83 C5
Lore Lindu, Taman Nasional *nat. park* Indon. 83 B3
Lorena Brazil 179 B3
Lorengau P.N.G. 81 L7
Lorentz, Taman Nasional Indon. 81 J7
Lorenzo del Real Mex. 167 F4
Loreto Brazil 177 I5
Loreto *Baja California Sur* Mex. 166 C3
Loreto Phil. 82 D4
Lorient France 66 C3
Lorillard *r.* Canada 151 N1
Loring U.S.A. 156 G2
Lorino Rus. Fed. 148 E2
Lorn, Firth of *est.* U.K. 60 D4
Lorne Australia 136 D5
Lorne *watercourse* Australia 136 B3
Loro *r.* China 99 F7
Lorrain, Plateau France 63 G6
Lorraine Australia 136 B3
Lorraine *admin. reg.* France 62 G6
Lorraine *reg.* France 62 F5
Lorsch Germany 63 I5
Lorup Germany 63 H2
Losal India 104 C4
Los Alamos *CA* U.S.A. 158 C4
Los Alamos *NM* U.S.A. 157 G6
Los Aldamas Mex. 167 F3
Los Alerces, Parque Nacional *nat. park* Arg. 178 B6
Los Ángeles Chile 178 B5

▶Los Angeles U.S.A. 158 D4
3rd most populous city in North America.

Los Angeles Aqueduct *canal* U.S.A. 158 D4
Los Arabos Cuba 163 D8
Los Baños Mex. 166 D3
Los Banos U.S.A. 158 C3
Los Blancos Arg. 178 D2
Los Canarreos, Archipiélago de *is* Cuba 169 H4
Los Cerritos *watercourse* Mex. 157 F8
Los Chiles Costa Rica 166 [inset] I7
Los Chonos, Archipiélago de *is* Chile 178 A6
Los Coronados, Islas *is* Mex. 158 E5
Los Desventurados, Islas de *is* S. Pacific Ocean 187 O7
Los Estados, Isla de *i.* Arg. 178 D8
Los Gigantes, Llanos de *plain* Mex. 161 B6
Los Glaciares, Parque Nacional *nat. park* Arg. 178 B8
Losheim Germany 62 G5
Los Hoyos Mex. 166 C2
Lošinj *i.* Croatia 68 F2
Los Jardines de la Reina, Archipiélago de *is* Cuba 169 I4
Los Juríes Arg. 178 D3
Los Katios, Parque Nacional *nat. park* Col. 169 I7
Loskop Dam S. Africa 125 I3
Los Leones Mex. 166 D2
Los Lunas U.S.A. 157 G6
Los Mármoles, Parque Nacional *nat. park* Mex. 167 F4
Los Menucos Arg. 178 C6
Los Mochis Mex. 166 C3
Los Molinos U.S.A. 158 B1
Losombo Dem. Rep. Congo 122 B3
Los Palacios Cuba 163 D8
Lospatos East Timor 83 C5
Los Picos de Europa, Parque Nacional de *nat. park* Spain 67 D2
Los Remedios *r.* Mex. 161 B7
Los Reyes Mex. 166 E5
Los Roques, Islas *is* Venez. 176 E1
Losser Neth. 62 G2
Lossie *r.* U.K. 60 F3
Lossiemouth U.K. 60 F3
Lößnitz Germany 63 M4
Lost Creek *KY* U.S.A. 164 D5
Lost Creek *WV* U.S.A. 164 E4
Los Teques Venez. 176 E1
Los Testigos *is* Venez. 176 F1
Lost Hills U.S.A. 158 D4
Lost Trail Pass U.S.A. 156 E3
Lostwithiel U.K. 59 C8
Los Vidrios Mex. 159 G6
Los Vilos Chile 178 B4
Lot *r.* France 66 E4
Lota Chile 178 B5
Loṭfābād Turkm. 110 E2
Lothringen *reg.* France *see* Lorraine
Lotikipi Plain Kenya/Sudan 122 D3
Loto Dem. Rep. Congo 122 C4
Lotsane *r.* Botswana 125 I2
Lot's Wife *i.* Japan *see* Sōfu-gan
Lotta *r.* Fin./Rus. Fed. 54 Q2
also known as Lutto
Lotte Germany 63 H2
Louangnamtha Laos 86 C2
Louangphabang Laos 86 C3
Loubomo Congo 123 B4
Loudéac France 66 C2
Loudi China 97 F3
L'Ouest, Pointe de *pt* Canada 153 I4
Loufan *Shanxi* China 95 G4
Louga Senegal 120 B3
Loughborough U.K. 59 F6
Lougheed Island Canada 147 H2
Loughor *r.* U.K. 59 C7
Loughrea Ireland 61 D4
Loughton U.K. 59 H7
Louhans France 66 G3
Louisa *KY* U.S.A. 164 D4
Louisa *VA* U.S.A. 165 G4
Louisbourg Canada 153 K5
Louisburg Canada *see* Louisbourg
Louisburgh Ireland 61 C4
Louise, Lake *AK* U.S.A. 149 K3
Louise Falls Canada 150 G2
Louis-Gentil Morocco *see* Youssoufia
Louisiade Archipelago *is* P.N.G. 136 F1
Louisiana U.S.A. 160 F4
Louisiana *state* U.S.A. 161 F6
Louis Trichardt S. Africa *see* Makhado
Louisville *GA* U.S.A. 163 D5
Louisville *IL* U.S.A. 160 F4
Louisville *KY* U.S.A. 164 C4
Louisville *MS* U.S.A. 161 F5
Louisville Ridge *sea feature* S. Pacific Ocean 186 I8
Louis-XIV, Pointe *pt* Canada 152 F3
Loukhi Rus. Fed. 54 R3
Loukoléla Congo 122 B4
Loukouo Congo 121 E5
Loulé Port. 67 B5
Loum Cameroon 120 D4
Louny Czech Rep. 57 N5
Loup *r.* U.S.A. 160 D3
Loups Marins, Lacs des *lakes* Canada 152 G2
Loups Marins, Petit lac des *l.* Canada 153 G2
Lourdes Canada 153 K4
Lourdes France 66 D5
Lourenço Marques Moz. *see* Maputo
Lousã Port. 67 B3
Loushan China 90 C3
Loushanguan China *see* Tongzi
Louth Australia 138 B3
Louth U.K. 58 G5
Loutra Aidipsou Greece 69 J5
Louvain Belgium *see* Leuven
Louviers France 62 B5
Louwater-Suid Namibia 124 C2
Louwsburg S. Africa 125 J4
Lövånger Sweden 54 L4
Lovat' *r.* Rus. Fed. 52 F4
Lovech Bulg. 69 K3
Lovell U.S.A. 165 J1
Lovelock U.S.A. 158 D1
Lovendegem Belgium 62 D3
Lovers' Leap *mt.* U.S.A. 164 E5
Loviisa Fin. 55 O6
Lovington U.S.A. 161 C5
Lovozero Rus. Fed. 52 G1
Lóvua Angola 123 C4
Lóvua Angola 123 C5
Low, Cape Canada 147 J3
Lowa Dem. Rep. Congo 122 C4
Lowa *r.* Dem. Rep. Congo 122 C4
Lowarai Pass Pak. 111 H3
Lowell *IN* U.S.A. 164 B3
Lowell *MA* U.S.A. 165 J2
Lower Arrow Lake Canada 150 G5
Lower California *pen.* Mex. *see* Baja California
Lower Glenelg National Park Australia 137 C8
Lower Granite Gorge U.S.A. 159 G4
Lower Hutt N.Z. 139 E5
Lower Laberge *Y.T.* Canada 149 N3
Lower Lake U.S.A. 158 B2
Lower Lough Erne *l.* U.K. 61 E3
Lower Post *B.C.* Canada 149 O4
Lower Red Lake U.S.A. 160 E2
Lower Saxony *land* Germany *see* Niedersachsen
Lower Tunguska *r.* Rus. Fed. *see* Nizhnyaya Tunguska
Lower Zambezi National Park Zambia 123 C5
Lowestoft U.K. 59 I6
Łowicz Poland 57 Q4
Low Island Kiribati *see* Starbuck Island
Lowkhi Afgh. 111 F4
Lowther Hills U.K. 60 F5
Lowville U.S.A. 165 H2
Loxicha Mex. 167 F5
Loxstedt Germany 63 I1
Loxton Australia 137 C7
Loyal, Loch *l.* U.K. 60 E2
Loyalsock Creek *r.* U.S.A. 165 G3
Loyalton U.S.A. 158 C2
Loyalty Islands New Caledonia *see* Loyauté, Îles
Loyang *Henan* China *see* Luoyang
Loyauté, Îles *is* New Caledonia 133 G4
Loyev Belarus *see* Loyew
Loyew Belarus 53 F6
Lozère, Mont *mt.* France 66 F4
Loznica Serbia 69 H2
Lozova Ukr. 53 H6
Lozovaya Ukr. *see* Lozova
Lua *r.* Dem. Rep. Congo 122 B3
Luacano Angola 123 C5
Lu'an China 97 H2
Luân Châu Vietnam 86 C2
Luanchuan China 97 F1

▶Luanda Angola 123 B4
Capital of Angola.

Luang *i. Maluku* Indon. 83 D5
Luang, Khao *mt.* Thai. 87 B5
Luang, Thale *lag.* Thai. 87 C6
Luang Namtha Laos *see* Louangnamtha
Luang Phrabang, Thiu Khao *mts* Laos/Thai. 86 C3
Luang Prabang Laos *see* Louangphabang
Luanhaizi *Qinghai* China 94 C5
Luan He *r.* China 95 I4
Luannan *Hebei* China 95 I4
Luanping *Hebei* China 95 I3
Luanshya Zambia 123 C5
Luanxian *Hebei* China 95 I4
Luanza Dem. Rep. Congo 123 C4
Luanzhou *Hebei* China *see* Luanxian
Luao Angola *see* Luau
Luar, Danau *l.* Indon. 85 F2
Luarca Spain 67 C2
Luashi Dem. Rep. Congo 123 C5
Luau Angola 123 C5
Luba Equat. Guinea 120 D4
Lubaczów Poland 53 D6
Lubalo Angola 123 B4
Lubānas ezers *l.* Latvia 55 O8
Lubang Phil. 82 C3
Lubang *i.* Phil. 82 C3
Lubang Islands Phil. 82 B3
Lubango Angola 123 B5
Lubao Dem. Rep. Congo 123 C4
Lubartów Poland 53 D6
Lübbecke Germany 63 I2
Lubbeskolk *salt pan* S. Africa 124 D5
Lubbock U.S.A. 161 C5
Lübbow Germany 63 L2
Lübeck Germany 57 M4
Lubeck U.S.A. 164 E4
Lubefu Dem. Rep. Congo 123 C4
Lubei *Nei Mongol* China 95 J2
Lüben Poland *see* Lubin
Lubersac France 66 E4
Lubin Poland 57 P5
Lublin Poland 53 D6
Lubnān *country* Asia *see* Lebanon
Lubnān, Jabal *mts* Lebanon *see* Liban, Jebel
Lubny Ukr. 53 G6
Lubok Antu *Sarawak* Malaysia 85 E2
Lübtheen Germany 63 L1
Lubuagan *Luzon* Phil. 82 C2
Lubudi Dem. Rep. Congo 123 C4
Lubukbalang *Sumatera* Indon. 84 D3
Lubuklinggau *Sumatera* Indon. 84 C3
Lubukpakam *Sumatera* Indon. 84 B2
Lubuksikaping *Sumatera* Indon. 84 C2
Lubumbashi Dem. Rep. Congo 123 C5
Lubutu Dem. Rep. Congo 122 C4
Lübz Germany 63 M1
Lucala Angola 123 B4
Lucan Canada 164 E2
Lucan Ireland 61 F4
Lucania, Mount *Y.T.* Canada 149 L3
Lücaoshan *Qinghai* China 99 F5
Lucapa Angola 123 C4
Lucas U.S.A. 164 B5
Lucasville U.S.A. 164 D4
Lucca Italy 68 D3
Luce Bay U.K. 60 E6
Lucedale U.S.A. 161 F6
Lucélia Brazil 179 A3
Lucena *Luzon* Phil. 82 C3
Lucena Spain 67 D5
Lučenec Slovakia 57 Q6
Lucera Italy 68 F4
Lucerne Switz. 66 I3
Lucerne Valley U.S.A. 158 E4
Lucero Mex. 166 D2
Luchegorsk Rus. Fed. 90 D3
Lucheng *Guangxi* China *see* Luchuan
Lucheng *Shanxi* China 95 H4
Lucheng *Sichuan* China *see* Kangding
Luchuan China 97 F4
Lüchun China 96 D4
Lucipara, Kepulauan *is Maluku* Indon. 83 C4
Łuck Ukr. *see* Luts'k

Luckeesarai India *see* **Lakhisarai**
Luckenwalde Germany **63** N2
Luckhoff S. Africa **124** G5
Lucknow Canada **164** E2
Lucknow India **104** E4
Lücongpo China **97** F2
Lucrecia, Cabo *c.* Cuba **169** I4
Lucusse Angola **123** C5
Lucy Creek Australia **136** B4
Lüda *Liaoning* China *see* **Dalian**
Lüdenscheid Germany **63** H3
Lüderitz Namibia **124** B4
Ludewa Tanz. **123** D5
Ludhiana India **104** C3
Ludian China **96** D3
Luding China **96** D2
Ludington U.S.A. **164** B2
Ludlow U.K. **59** E6
Ludlow U.S.A. **158** E4
Ludogorie *reg.* Bulg. **69** L3
Ludowici U.S.A. **163** D6
Ludvika Sweden **55** I6
Ludwigsburg Germany **63** J6
Ludwigsfelde Germany **63** N2
Ludwigshafen am Rhein Germany **63** I5
Ludwigslust Germany **63** L1
Ludza Latvia **55** O8
Luebo Dem. Rep. Congo **123** C4
Luena Angola **123** B5
Luena Flats *plain* Zambia **123** C5
Lüeyang China **96** E1
Lufeng *Guangdong* China **97** G4
Lufeng *Yunnan* China **96** D3
Lufkin U.S.A. **161** E6
Lufu China *see* **Shilin**
Luga Rus. Fed. **55** P7
Luga *r.* Rus. Fed. **55** P7
Lugano Switz. **66** I3
Lugansk Ukr. *see* **Luhans'k**
Lugau Germany **63** M4
Lügde Germany **63** J3
Lugdunum France *see* **Lyon**
Lugg *r.* U.K. **59** E6
Luggudontsen *mt. Xizang* China **99** E7
Lugnaquilla *hill* Ireland **61** F5
Lugo Italy **68** D2
Lugo Spain **67** C2
Lugoj Romania **69** I2
Lugu *Xizang* China **99** D6
Lugus *i.* Phil. **82** C5
Luhans'k Ukr. **53** H6
Luhe China **97** H1
Lu He *r.* China **95** G4
Luhe *r.* Germany **63** K1
Luḥfi, Wādī *watercourse* Jordan **107** C3
Luhin Sum *Nei Mongol* China **95** I2
Luhit *r.* China/India *see* **Zayü Qu**
Luhit *r.* India **105** H4
Luhua China *see* **Heishui**
Luhuo China **96** D2
Luhyny Ukr. **53** F6
Luia Angola **123** C4
Luiana Angola **123** C5
Luichow Peninsula China *see* **Leizhou Bandao**
Luik Belgium *see* **Liège**
Luimneach Ireland *see* **Limerick**
Luiro *r.* Fin. **54** O3
Luis Echeverría Álvarez Mex. **158** E5
Luis L. León, Presa *resr* Mex. **166** D2
Luis Moya *Zacatecas* Mex. **166** E4
Luitpold Coast Antarctica **188** A1
Luiza Dem. Rep. Congo **123** C4
Lujiang China **97** H2
Lüjing *Gansu* China **94** F5
Lukachek Rus. Fed. **90** D1
Lukapa Angola *see* **Lucapa**
Lukavac Bos.-Herz. **68** H2
Lukenga, Lac *l.* Dem. Rep. Congo **123** C4
Lukenie *r.* Dem. Rep. Congo **122** B4
Lukeville *AZ* U.S.A. **166** B2
Lukh *r.* Rus. Fed. **52** I4
Lukhovitsy Rus. Fed. **53** H5
Luk Keng *H.K.* China **97** [inset]
Lukou China *see* **Zhuzhou**
Lukovit Bulg. **69** K3
Łuków Poland **53** D6
Lukoyanov Rus. Fed. **53** J5
Lükqün *Xinjiang* China **98** E4
Luksagu *Sulawesi* Indon. **83** B3
Luksuzi National Park Zambia **123** D5
Luleå Sweden **54** M4
Luleälven *r.* Sweden **54** M4
Lüleburgaz Turkey **69** L4
Luliang China **96** D3
Lüliang Shan *mts* China **95** G4
Lulimba Dem. Rep. Congo **123** C4
Luling U.S.A. **161** D6
Lulong *Hebei* China **95** I4
Lulonga *r.* Dem. Rep. Congo **122** B3
Luluabourg Dem. Rep. Congo *see* **Kananga**
Lülung *Xizang* China **99** D7
Lumachomo *Xizang* China **99** D7
Lumajang *Jawa* Indon. **85** F5
Lumajangdong Co *salt l.* China **99** C6
Lumbala *Moxico* Angola *see* **Lumbala Kaquengue**
Lumbala *Moxico* Angola *see* **Lumbala N'guimbo**
Lumbala Kaquengue Angola **123** C5
Lumbala N'guimbo Angola **123** C5
Lumberton U.S.A. **163** E5
Lumbini Nepal **105** E4
Lumbis *Kalimantan* Indon. **85** G1
Lumbrales Spain **67** C3
Lumezzane Italy **68** D2
Lumi P.N.G. **81** K7
Lumphăt Cambodia **87** D4
Lumpkin U.S.A. **163** C5
Lumsden Canada **151** J5
Lumsden N.Z. **139** B7
Lumut Malaysia **84** C1
Lumut, Gunung *mt.* Indon. **85** F3
Lumut, Tanjung *pt* Indon. **84** D3
Lün Mongolia **94** F2
Luna *Luzon* Phil. **82** C2
Luna U.S.A. **159** I5
Lunan China *see* **Shilin**
Lunan Bay U.K. **60** G4
Lunan Lake Canada **151** M1
Lunan Shan *mts* China **96** D3
Luna Pier U.S.A. **164** D3
Lund Pak. **111** H5
Lund Sweden **55** H9
Lund *NV* U.S.A. **159** F2
Lund *UT* U.S.A. **159** G2
Lundar Canada **151** L5
Lundu *Sarawak* Malaysia **85** E2
Lundy U.K. **59** C7
Lune *r.* Germany **63** I1
Lune *r.* U.K. **58** E4
Lüneburg Germany **63** K1
Lüneburger Heide *reg.* Germany **63** K1
Lünen Germany **63** H3
Lunenburg U.S.A. **165** F5
Lunéville France **66** H2
Lunga *r.* Zambia **123** C5
Lungdo China **105** E2
Lunggar *Xizang* China **99** C7
Lunggar Shan *mts Xizang* China **99** C7
Lung Kwu Chau *i. H.K.* China **97** [inset]
Lungleh India *see* **Lunglei**
Lunglei India **105** H5
Lungmari *mt. Xizang* China **99** D7
Lungmu Co *salt l.* China **99** C6
Lungwebungu *r.* Zambia **123** C5
Lunh Nepal **105** E3
Luni India **104** C4
Luni *r.* India **104** B4
Luni *r.* Pak. **111** H4
Luninets Belarus *see* **Luninyets**
Luning U.S.A. **158** D2
Luninyets Belarus **55** O10
Lunkaransar India **104** C3
Lunkha India **104** C3
Lünne Germany **63** H2
Lunsar Sierra Leone **120** B4
Lunsklip S. Africa **125** I3
Luntai *Xinjiang* China **98** D4
Lunyuk *Sumbawa* Indon. **85** G5
Luobei China **90** C3
Luobuzhuang *Xinjiang* China **98** E5
Luocheng *Fujian* China *see* **Hui'an**
Luocheng *Gansu* China **94** D4
Luocheng *Guangxi* China **97** F3
Luochuan *Shaanxi* China **95** G5
Luodian China **96** E3
Luoding China **97** F4
Luodou Sha *i.* China **97** F4
Luohe China **97** G1
Luo He *r. Henan* China **95** H5
Luo He *r. Shaanxi* China **95** G5
Luoma Hu *l.* China **95** I5
Luonan *Shaanxi* China **95** G5
Luoning *Henan* China **95** G5
Luoping China **96** E3
Luotian China **97** G2
Luoto Fin. *see* **Larsmo**
Luotuoquan *Gansu* China **94** D3
Luoxiao Shan *mts* China **97** G3
Luoxiong China *see* **Luoping**
Luoyang *Guangdong* China *see* **Boluo**
Luoyang *Henan* China **95** H5
Luoyang *Zhejiang* China *see* **Taishun**
Luoyuan China **97** H3
Luozigou China **90** C4
Lupane Zimbabwe **123** C5
Lupanshui China **96** E3
Lupar *r.* Malaysia **85** E2
L'Upemba, Parc National de *nat. park* Dem. Rep. Congo **123** C4
Lupeni Romania **69** J2
Lupilichi Moz. **123** D5
Lupon *Mindanao* Phil. **82** D5
Lupton U.S.A. **159** I4
Luqiao China *see* **Luding**
Luqu *Gansu* China **94** E5
Lu Qu *r.* China *see* **Tao He**
Luquan *Hebei* China **95** H4
Luquan China **86** C1
Luray U.S.A. **165** F4
Luremo Angola **123** B4
Lurgan U.K. **61** F3
Lúrio Moz. **123** E5
Lurio *r.* Moz. **123** E5

▶**Lusaka** Zambia **123** C5
Capital of Zambia.

Lusambo Dem. Rep. Congo **123** C4
Lusancay Islands and Reefs P.N.G. **132** F2
Lusangi Dem. Rep. Congo **123** C4
Luseland Canada **151** I4
Lush, Mount *hill* Australia **134** D4
Lushar *Qinghai* China *see* **Huangzhong**
Lushi *Henan* China **95** G5
Lushnja Albania *see* **Lushnjë**
Lushnjë Albania **69** H4
Lushui China *see* **Luzhang**
Lushuihe China **90** B4
Lüshun *Liaoning* China **95** J4
Lüsi China **97** I1
Lusi *r.* Indon. **85** E4
Lusikisiki S. Africa **125** I6
Lusk U.S.A. **156** G4
Luso Angola *see* **Luena**
Lussvale Australia **138** C1
Lut, Bahrat *salt l.* Asia *see* **Dead Sea**
Lut, Dasht-e *des.* Iran **110** E4
Lutai *Tianjin* China *see* **Ninghe**
Lü Tao *i.* Taiwan **97** I4
Lutetia France *see* **Paris**
Lüt-e Zangī Aḥmad *des.* Iran **110** E4
Luther U.S.A. **164** C1
Luther Lake Canada **164** E2
Lutherstadt Wittenberg Germany **63** M3
Luton U.K. **59** G7
Lutong *Sarawak* Malaysia **85** F1
Łutselk'e Canada **151** I2
Luts'k Ukr. **53** E6
Luttelgeest Neth. **62** F2
Luttenberg Neth. **62** G2
Lutto *r.* Fin./Rus. Fed. *see* **Lotta**
Lutz U.S.A. **163** D6
Lützelbach Germany **63** J5
Lützow-Holm Bay Antarctica **188** D2
Lutzputs S. Africa **124** E5
Lutzville S. Africa **124** D6
Luuk Phil. **82** C5
Luumäki Fin. **55** O6
Luuq Somalia **122** E3
Luverne *AL* U.S.A. **163** C6
Luverne *MN* U.S.A. **160** D3
Luvuei Angola **123** C5
Luvuvhu *r.* S. Africa **125** J2
Luwero Uganda **122** D3
Luwingu Zambia **123** C5
Luwuhuyu *Kalimantan* Indon. **85** E3
Luwuk *Sulawesi* Indon. **83** B3
Luxembourg *country* Europe **62** G5

▶**Luxembourg** Lux. **62** G5
Capital of Luxembourg.

Luxemburg *country* Europe *see* **Luxembourg**
Luxeuil-les-Bains France **66** H3
Luxi *Hunan* China *see* **Wuxi**
Luxi *Yunnan* China **96** C3
Luxi *Yunnan* China **96** D3
Luxolweni S. Africa **125** G6
Luxor Egypt **108** D4
Luya Shan *mts* China **95** G4
Luyi China **97** G1
Luyksgestel Neth. **62** F3
Luyuan *Shaanxi* China *see* **Gaoling**
Luza Rus. Fed. **52** J3
Luza *r.* Rus. Fed. **52** J3
Luza *r.* Rus. Fed. **52** M2
Luzern Switz. *see* **Lucerne**
Luzhai China **97** F3
Luzhang China **96** C3
Luzhi China **96** E3
Luzhou China **96** E2
Luziânia Brazil **179** B2
Luzon *i.* Phil. **82** C3
Luzon Strait Phil. **82** C1
Luzy France **66** F3
L'viv Ukr. **53** E6
L'vov Ukr. *see* **L'viv**
Lwów Ukr. *see* **L'viv**
Lyady Rus. Fed. **55** P7
Lyakhavichy Belarus **55** O10
Lyakhovichi Belarus *see* **Lyakhavichy**
Lyallpur Pak. *see* **Faisalabad**
Lyamtsa Rus. Fed. **52** H2
Lycia *reg.* Turkey **69** M6
Lyck Poland *see* **Ełk**
Lycksele Sweden **54** K4
Lycopolis Egypt *see* **Asyūṭ**
Lydd U.K. **59** H8
Lydda Israel *see* **Lod**
Lyddan Island Antarctica **188** B2
Lydenburg S. Africa *see* **Mashishing**
Lydia *reg.* Turkey **69** L5
Lydney U.K. **59** E7
Lyel'chytsy Belarus **53** F6
Lyell, Mount U.S.A. **158** D3
Lyell Brown, Mount *hill* Australia **135** E5
Lyell Island *B.C.* Canada **149** O5
Lyepyel' Belarus **55** P9
Lykens U.S.A. **165** G3
Lyman U.S.A. **156** F4
Lyme Bay U.K. **59** E8
Lyme Regis U.K. **59** E8
Lymington U.K. **59** F8
Lynchburg *OH* U.S.A. **164** D4
Lynchburg *TN* U.S.A. **162** C5
Lynchburg *VA* U.S.A. **164** F5
Lynchville U.S.A. **165** J1
Lyndhurst *N.S.W.* Australia **138** D4
Lyndhurst *Qld* Australia **136** D3
Lyndhurst *S.A.* Australia **137** B6
Lyndon Australia **135** A5
Lyndon *r.* Australia **135** A5
Lyndonville U.S.A. **165** I1
Lyne *r.* U.K. **58** D4
Lyness U.K. **60** F2
Lyngdal Norway **55** E7
Lynn U.K. *see* **King's Lynn**
Lynn *IN* U.S.A. **164** C3
Lynn *MA* U.S.A. **165** J2
Lynndyl U.S.A. **159** G2
Lynn Lake Canada **151** K3
Lynton U.K. **59** D7
Lynx Lake Canada **151** J2
Lyon France **66** G4
Lyon *r.* U.K. **60** F4
Lyon Mountain U.S.A. **165** I1
Lyons Australia **135** F7
Lyons France *see* **Lyon**
Lyons *GA* U.S.A. **163** D5
Lyons *NY* U.S.A. **165** G2
Lyons Falls U.S.A. **165** H2
Lyozna Belarus **53** F5
Lyra Reef P.N.G. **132** F2
Lys *r.* France **62** D4
Lysekil Sweden **55** G7
Lyskovo Rus. Fed. **52** J4
Ly Sơn, Đao *i.* Vietnam **86** E4
Lys'va Rus. Fed. **51** R4
Lysychans'k Ukr. **53** H6
Lysyye Gory Rus. Fed. **53** J6
Lytham St Anne's U.K. **58** D5
Lytton Canada **150** F5
Lyuban' Belarus **55** P10
Lyubertsy Rus. Fed. **51** N4
Lyubeshiv Ukr. **53** E6
Lyubim Rus. Fed. **52** I4
Lyubytino Rus. Fed. **52** G4
Lyudinovo Rus. Fed. **53** G5
Lyunda *r.* Rus. Fed. **52** J4
Lyzha *r.* Rus. Fed. **52** M2

M

Ma *r.* Myanmar **86** B2
Ma, Nam *r.* Laos **86** C2
Ma'agan Israel **107** B3
Maale Maldives *see* **Male**
Maale Atholhu *atoll* Maldives *see* **Male Atoll**
Maalhosmadulu Atholhu Uthuruburi *atoll* Maldives *see* **North Maalhosmadulu Atoll**
Maalhosmadulu Atoll Maldives **106** B5
Ma'ān Jordan **107** B4
Maan Turkey *see* **Nusratiye**
Maaninka Fin. **54** O5
Maaninkavaara Fin. **54** P3
Maanĭt *Bulgan* Mongolia *see* **Hishig-Öndör**
Maanĭt *Töv* Mongolia *see* **Bayan**
Ma'anshan China **97** H2
Maardu Estonia **55** N7
Maarianhamina Fin. *see* **Mariehamn**
Ma'arrat an Nu'mān Syria **107** C2
Maarssen Neth. **62** F2
Maas *r.* Neth. **62** E3
also known as Meuse (Belgium/France)
Maaseik Belgium **62** F3
Maasin *Leyte* Phil. **82** D4
Maasmechelen Belgium **62** F4
Maas-Schwalm-Nette *nat. park* Germany/Neth. **62** F3
Maastricht Neth. **62** F4
Maaza Plateau Egypt **112** C6
Maba *Guangdong* China *see* **Qujiang**
Maba *Jiangsu* China **97** H1
Maba *Halmahera* Indon. **83** D2
Mabai China *see* **Maguan**
Mabalacat *Luzon* Phil. **82** C3
Mabalane Moz. **125** K2
Mabana Dem. Rep. Congo **122** C3
Mabaruma Guyana **176** G2
Mabein Myanmar **86** B2
Mabel Creek Australia **135** F7
Mabel Downs Australia **134** D4
Mabella Canada **152** C4
Mabel Lake Canada **150** G5
Maberly Canada **165** G1
Mabian China **96** D2
Mabja *Xizang* China **99** D7
Mablethorpe U.K. **58** H5
Mabopane S. Africa **125** I3
Mabote Moz. **125** L2
Mabou Canada **153** J5
Mabrak, Jabal *mt.* Jordan **107** B4
Mabuasehube Game Reserve *nature res.* Botswana **124** F3
Mabudis *i.* Phil. **82** C1
Mabule Botswana **124** G3
Mabutsane Botswana **124** F3
Macá, Monte *mt.* Chile **178** B7
Macadam Plains Australia **135** B6
Macaé Brazil **179** C3
Macajalar Bay *Mindanao* Phil. **82** D4
Macajuba Brazil **179** C1
Macaloge Moz. **123** D5
MacAlpine Lake Canada **147** H3
Macamic Canada **152** F4
Macan, Kepulauan *atolls* Indon. *see* **Taka'Bonerate, Kepulauan**
Macandze Moz. **125** K2
Macao China **97** G4
Macao *Special Administrative Region.* China **97** G4
Macapá Brazil **177** H3
Macará Ecuador **176** C4
Macaracas Panama **166** [inset] J8
Macarani Brazil **179** C1
Macas Ecuador **176** C4
Macassar *Sulawesi* Indon. *see* **Makassar**
Macassar Strait Indon. *see* **Makassar, Selat**
Macau Brazil **177** K5
Macau *aut. reg.* China *see* **Macao**
Macaúba Brazil **177** H6
Macauley Island N.Z. **133** I5
Macau *aut. reg.* China *see* **Macao**
Maccaretane Moz. **125** K3
Macclenny U.S.A. **163** D6
Macclesfield U.K. **58** E5
Macdiarmid Canada **152** C4
Macdonald, Lake *salt flat* Australia **135** E5
Macdonald Range *hills* Australia **134** D3
Macdonnell Ranges *mts* Australia **135** E5
MacDowell Lake Canada **151** M4
Macduff U.K. **60** G3
Macedo de Cavaleiros Port. **67** C3
Macedon *mt.* Australia **138** B6
Macedon *country* Europe *see* **Macedonia**
Macedonia *country* Europe **69** I4
Macedonia *reg.* Greece/Macedonia **69** J4
Maceió Brazil **177** K5
Macenta Guinea **120** C4
Macerata Italy **68** E3
Macfarlane, Lake *salt flat* Australia **137** B7
Macgillycuddy's Reeks *mts* Ireland **61** C6
Machachi Ecuador **176** C4
Machaila Moz. **125** K2
Machakos Kenya **122** D4
Machala Ecuador **176** C4
Machali *Qinghai* China *see* **Madoi**
Machan *Sarawak* Malaysia **85** F2
Machanga Moz. **123** D6
Machar Marshes Sudan **108** D8
Machattie, Lake *salt flat* Australia **136** B5
Machatuine Moz. **125** K3
Machault France **62** E5
Machaze Moz. *see* **Chitobe**
Macheng China **97** G2
Macherla India **106** C2
Machhagan India **105** F5
Machhakund Reservoir India **106** D2
Machias *ME* U.S.A. **162** H2
Machias *NY* U.S.A. **165** F2
Machida Japan **93** F3
Machilipatnam India **106** D2
Machiques Venez. **176** D1
Māch Kowr Iran **111** F5
Machrihanish U.K. **60** D5
Machu Picchu *tourist site* Peru **176** D6
Machynlleth U.K. **59** D6
Macia Moz. **125** K3
Macias Nguema *i.* Equat. Guinea *see* **Bioco**
Măcin Romania **69** M2
Macintyre *r.* Australia **138** E2
Macintyre Brook *r.* Australia **138** E2
Mack U.S.A. **159** I2
Maçka Turkey **113** E2
Mackay Australia **136** E4
MacKay *r.* Canada **151** I3
Mackay U.S.A. **156** E3
Mackay, Lake *salt flat* Australia **134** E5
MacKay Lake Canada **151** I2
Mackenzie *r.* Australia **136** E4
Mackenzie Canada **150** F4

▶**Mackenzie** *r. N.W.T.* Canada **149** N1
Part of the Mackenzie-Peace-Finlay, the 2nd longest river in North America.

Mackenzie Guyana *see* **Linden**
Mackenzie *atoll* Micronesia *see* **Ulithi**
Mackenzie Bay Antarctica **188** E2
Mackenzie Bay *N.W.T./Y.T.* Canada **149** M1
Mackenzie Highway Canada **150** G2
Mackenzie King Island Canada **147** G2
Mackenzie Mountains *N.W.T./Y.T.* Canada **149** N2

▶**Mackenzie-Peace-Finlay** *r.* Canada **146** E3
2nd longest river in North America

Mackillop, Lake *salt flat* Australia *see* **Yamma Yamma, Lake**
Mackintosh Range *hills* Australia **135** D6
Macklin Canada **151** I4
Macksville Australia **138** F3
Maclean Australia **138** F2
Maclear S. Africa **125** I6
MacLeod Canada *see* **Fort Macleod**
MacLeod, Lake *imp. l.* Australia **135** A6
Macmillan *r. Y.T.* Canada **149** N3
Macmillan Pass *Y.T.* Canada **149** O3
Macomb U.S.A. **160** F3
Macomer *Sardinia* Italy **68** C4
Mâcon France **66** G3
Macon *GA* U.S.A. **163** D5
Macon *MO* U.S.A. **160** E4
Macon *MS* U.S.A. **161** F5
Macon *OH* U.S.A. **164** D4
Macondo Angola **123** C5
Macoun Lake Canada **151** K3
Macpherson Robertson Land *reg.* Antarctica *see* **Mac. Robertson Land**
Macpherson's Strait India **87** A5
Macquarie *r.* Australia **138** C3
Macquarie, Lake *b.* Australia **138** E4

▶**Macquarie Island** S. Pacific Ocean **186** G9
Part of Australia. Most southerly point of Oceania.

Macquarie Marshes Australia **138** C3
Macquarie Mountain Australia **138** D4
Macquarie Ridge *sea feature* S. Pacific Ocean **186** G9
MacRitchie Reservoir Sing. **87** [inset]
Mac. Robertson Land *reg.* Antarctica **188** E2
Macroom Ireland **61** D6
Mactún Mex. **167** H5
Macumba Australia **137** A5
Macumba *watercourse* Australia **137** B5
Macuspana Mex. **167** G5
Macuzari, Presa *resr* Mex. **166** C3
Mādabā Jordan **107** B4
Madadeni S. Africa **125** J4

▶**Madagascar** *country* Africa **123** E6
Largest island in Africa and 4th in the world.

Madagascar Basin *sea feature* Indian Ocean **185** L7
Madagascar Ridge *sea feature* Indian Ocean **185** K8
Madagasikara *country* Africa *see* **Madagascar**
Madakasira India **106** C3
Madalai Palau **82** [inset]
Madama Niger **121** E2
Madan Bulg. **69** K4
Madanapalle India **106** C3
Madang P.N.G. **81** L8
Madaoua Niger **120** D3
Madaripur Bangl. **105** G5
Madau Turkm. *see* **Madaw**
Madaw Turkm. **110** D2
Madawaska Canada **165** G1
Madawaska *r.* Canada **165** G1
Madaya Myanmar **86** B2
Madded India **106** D2

▶**Madeira** *r.* Brazil **176** G4
4th longest river in South America.

▶**Madeira** *terr.* N. Atlantic Ocean **120** B1
Autonomous Region of Portugal.

Madeira, Arquipélago da *terr.* N. Atlantic Ocean *see* **Madeira**
Maden Turkey **113** E3
Madeniyet Kazakh. **98** B3
Madera Mex. **166** C2
Madera U.S.A. **158** C3
Madgaon India **106** B3
Madha India **106** B2
Madhavpur India **104** B5
Madhepura India **105** F4
Madhipura India *see* **Madhepura**
Madhubani India **105** F4
Madhya Pradesh *state* India **104** D5
Madi, Dataran Tinggi *plat.* Indon. **85** F2
Madibogo S. Africa **125** G4
Madidi *r.* Bol. **176** E6
Madikeri India **106** B3
Madikwe Game Reserve *nature res.* S. Africa **125** H3
Madill U.S.A. **161** D5
Madīnat ath Thawrah Syria **107** D2
Madingo-Kayes Congo **123** B4
Madingou Congo **123** B4
Madison *FL* U.S.A. **163** D6
Madison *GA* U.S.A. **163** D5
Madison *IN* U.S.A. **164** C4
Madison *ME* U.S.A. **165** K1
Madison *NE* U.S.A. **160** D3
Madison *SD* U.S.A. **160** D2
Madison *VA* U.S.A. **165** F4

▶**Madison** *WI* U.S.A. **160** F3
Capital of Wisconsin.

Madison *WV* U.S.A. **164** E4
Madison *r.* U.S.A. **156** F3
Madison Heights U.S.A. **164** F5
Madisonville *KY* U.S.A. **164** B5
Madisonville *TX* U.S.A. **161** E6
Madita *Sumba* Indon. **83** B5
Madiun *Jawa* Indon. **85** E4
Madley, Mount *hill* Australia **135** C6
Madoc Canada **165** G1
Mado Gashi Kenya **122** D3
Madoi *Qinghai* China **94** D5
Madona Latvia **55** O8
Madpura India **104** B4
Madra Dağı *mts* Turkey **69** L5
Madrakah Saudi Arabia **108** E5
Madrakah, Ra's *c.* Oman **109** I6
Madras India *see* **Chennai**
Madras *state* India *see* **Tamil Nadu**
Madras U.S.A. **156** C3
Madre, Laguna *lag.* Mex. **161** D7
Madre, Laguna *lag.* U.S.A. **161** D7
Madre, Sierra *mt. Luzon* Phil. **82** C2
Madre de Chiapas, Sierra *mts* Mex. **167** G5
Madre de Dios *r.* Peru **176** E6
Madre de Dios, Isla *i.* Chile **178** A8
Madre del Sur, Sierra *mts* Mex. **168** D5
Madre Mountain U.S.A. **159** J4
Madre Occidental, Sierra *mts* Mex. **157** F7
Madre Oriental, Sierra *mts* Mex. **161** C7
Madrid *Mindanao* Phil. **82** D4

▶**Madrid** Spain **67** E3
Capital of Spain. 5th most populous city in Europe.

Madridejos Phil. **82** C4
Madridejos Spain **67** E4
Madruga Cuba **163** D8
Madu *i.* Indon. **83** B4
Madugula India **106** D2
Madura *i.* Indon. **85** F4
Madura, Selat *sea chan.* Indon. **85** F4
Madurai India **106** C4
Madurantakam India **106** C3
Madvār, Kūh-e *mt.* Iran **110** D4
Madwas India **105** E4
Maé *i.* Vanuatu *see* **Émaé**
Maebashi Japan **93** F2
Mae Hong Son Thai. **86** B3
Maelang *Sulawesi* Indon. **83** B2
Mae Ping National Park Thai. **86** B3
Mae Ramat Thai. **86** B3
Mae Sai Thai. **86** B2
Mae Sariang Thai. **86** B3
Mae Sot Thai. **86** B3
Maestre de Campo *i.* Phil. **82** C3
Mae Suai Thai. **86** B3
Mae Tuen Wildlife Reserve *nature res.* Thai. **86** B3
Maevatanana Madag. **123** E5
Maéwo *i.* Vanuatu **133** G3
Mae Wong National Park Thai. **86** B4
Mae Yom National Park Thai. **86** C3
Mafa *Halmahera* Indon. **83** C2
Mafeking Canada **151** K4
Mafeking S. Africa *see* **Mafikeng**
Mafeteng Lesotho **125** H5
Maffra Australia **138** C6
Mafia Island Tanz. **123** D4
Mafikeng S. Africa **125** G3
Mafinga Tanz. **123** D4
Mafra Brazil **179** A4
Mafraq Jordan *see* **Al Mafraq**
Magabeni S. Africa **125** J6
Magadan Rus. Fed. **77** Q4
Magadi Kenya **122** D4
Magaiza Moz. **125** K2
Magallanes Chile *see* **Punta Arenas**
Magallanes *Luzon* Phil. **82** C3
Magallanes, Estrecho de Chile *see* **Magellan, Strait of**
Magangue Col. **176** D2
Mağara Dağı *mt.* Turkey **107** A1
Magaramkent Rus. Fed. **113** H2
Magaria Niger **120** D3
Magarida P.N.G. **136** E1
Magas Rus. Fed. **113** G2
Magat *r. Luzon* Phil. **82** C2
Magazine Mountain *hill* U.S.A. **161** E5
Magdagachi Rus. Fed. **90** B1
Magdalena Bol. **176** F6
Magdalena *r.* Col. **176** D1
Magdalena *Baja California Sur* Mex. **166** B3
Magdalena *Sonora* Mex. **166** C2
Magdalena *r.* Mex. **166** C2
Magdalena, Bahía *b.* Mex. **166** C3
Magdalena, Isla *i.* Chile **178** B6
Magdalena, Isla *i.* Mex. **166** B3
Magdaline, Gunung *mt.* Malaysia **85** G1
Magdeburg Germany **63** L2
Magdelaine Cays *atoll* Australia **136** E3
Magelang *Jawa* Indon. **85** E4
Magellan, Strait of Chile **178** B8
Magellan Seamounts *sea feature* N. Pacific Ocean **186** F4
Magenta, Lake *salt flat* Australia **135** B8
Magerøya *i.* Norway **54** N1
Maggiorasca, Monte *mt.* Italy **68** C2
Maggiore, Lago Italy *see* **Maggiore, Lake**
Maggiore, Lake Italy **68** C2
Maghâgha Egypt *see* **Maghāghah**
Maghāghah Egypt **112** C5
Maghama Mauritania **120** B3
Maghâra, Gebel *hill* Egypt *see* **Magharah, Jabal**
Magharah, Jabal *hill* Egypt **107** A4
Maghera U.K. **61** F3
Magherafelt U.K. **61** F3
Maghnia Alg. **67** F6
Maghor Afgh. **111** F3
Maghull U.K. **58** E5
Magilligan Point U.K. **61** F2
Magiscatzín Mex. **167** F4
Magitang *Qinghai* China *see* **Jainca**
Magma U.S.A. **159** H5
Magna Grande *mt. Sicily* Italy **68** F6
Magnetic Island Australia **136** D3
Magnetic Passage Australia **136** D3
Magnetity Rus. Fed. **54** R2
Magnitogorsk Rus. Fed. **76** G4
Magnolia *AR* U.S.A. **161** E5
Magnolia *MS* U.S.A. **161** F6
Magny-en-Vexin France **62** B5
Mago Rus. Fed. **90** F1
Màgoé Moz. **123** D5
Magog Canada **165** I1
Mago National Park Eth. **122** D3
Magosa Cyprus *see* **Famagusta**
Magozal Mex. **167** F4
Magpie *r.* Canada **153** I4
Magpie, Lac *l.* Canada **153** I4
Magta' Lahjar Mauritania **120** B3
Magu Tanz. **122** D4
Magu, Khrebet *mts* Rus. Fed. **90** E1
Maguan China **96** E4
Magude Moz. **125** K3
Magueyal Mex. **166** E3
Magura Bangl. **105** G5
Maguse Lake Canada **151** M2
Magway Myanmar *see* **Magwe**
Magwe Myanmar **86** A2
Magyar Köztársaság *country* Europe *see* **Hungary**
Magyichaung Myanmar **86** A2
Mahābād Iran **110** B2
Mahabharat Range *mts* Nepal **105** F4
Mahaboobnagar India *see* **Mahbubnagar**
Mahad India **106** B2
Mahadeo Hills India **104** D5
Mahaffey U.S.A. **165** F3
Mahai *Qinghai* China **99** F5
Mahajamba *r.* Madag. **123** E5
Mahajan India **104** C3
Mahajanga Madag. **123** E5
Mahakam *r.* Indon. **85** G3

Mahalapye Botswana 125 H2
Mahale Mountains National Park Tanz. 123 C4
Mahalevona Madag. 123 E5
Mahallāt Iran 110 C3
Māhān Iran 110 E4
Mahanadi r. India 106 E1
Mahanoro Madag. 123 E5
Maha Oya Sri Lanka 106 D5
Maharajganj Bihar India 99 D8
Maharajganj Uttar Prad. India 99 C8
Maharashtra state India 106 B2
Maha Sarakham Thai. 86 C3
Mahasham, Wâdi el watercourse Egypt see **Muhashsham, Wādī al**
Mahaxai Laos 86 D3
Mahbubabad India 106 D2
Mahbubnagar India 106 C2
Mahd adh Dhahab Saudi Arabia 108 F5
Mahdia Alg. 67 G6
Mahdia Guyana 177 G2
Mahdia Tunisia 68 D7
Mahe Gansu China 94 F5
Mahé i. Seychelles 185 L6
Mahendragiri mt. India 106 E2
Mahenge Tanz. 123 D4
Mahesana India 104 C5
Mahgawan Madh. Prad. India 99 B8
Mahi r. India 104 C5
Mahia Peninsula N.Z. 139 F4
Mahilyow Belarus 53 F5
Mahim India 106 B2
Mah Jān Iran 110 D4
Mahlabatini S. Africa 125 J5
Mahlsdorf Germany 63 L2
Maḥmūdābād Iran 110 D2
Maḥmūd-e 'Erāqī Afgh. see **Maḥmūd-e Rāqī**
Maḥmūd-e Rāqī Afgh. 111 H3
Mahnomen U.S.A. 160 D2
Maho Sri Lanka 106 D5
Mahoba India 104 D4
Maholi India 104 E4
Mahón Spain 67 I4
Mahony Lake N.W.T. Canada 149 P2
Mahrauni India 104 D4
Mahrès Tunisia 68 D7
Māhrūd Iran 111 F3
Mahsana India see **Mahesana**
Mahuanggou Qinghai China 99 F5
Mahudaung mts Myanmar 86 A2
Māhukona U.S.A. 157 [inset]
Mahur India 106 C2
Mahuva India 104 B5
Mahwa India 104 D4
Mahya Dağı mt. Turkey 69 L4
Mai i. Maluku Indon. 83 C4
Mai i. Vanuatu see **Émaé**
Maiaia Moz. see **Nacala**
Maibang India 86 A1
Maicao Col. 176 D1
Maicasagi r. Canada 152 F4
Maicasagi, Lac l. Canada 152 F4
Maichen China 97 F4
Maidenhead U.K. 59 G7
Maidi Halmahera Indon. 83 C2
Maidstone Canada 151 I4
Maidstone U.K. 59 H7
Maiduguri Nigeria 120 E3
Maiella, Parco Nazionale della nat. park Italy 68 F3
Mai Gudo mt. Eth. 122 D3
Maigue r. Ireland 61 D5
Maihar India 104 E4
Maihara Japan 92 C3
Maiji Gansu China 94 F5
Maiji Shan mt. China 96 E1
Maikala Range hills India 104 E5
Maiko r. Dem. Rep. Congo 122 C3
Mailan Hill mt. India 105 E5
Mailani Uttar Prad. India 99 C7
Maileppe Indon. 84 B3
Mailly-le-Camp France 62 E6
Mailsi Pak. 111 I4
Main r. Germany 63 I4
Main r. U.K. 61 F3
Main Brook Canada 153 L4
Mainburg Germany 63 L6
Main Channel lake channel Canada 164 E1
Maindargi India 106 C2
Mai-Ndombe, Lac l. Dem. Rep. Congo 122 B4
Main-Donau-Kanal canal Germany 63 K5
Main Duck Island Canada 165 G2
Maine state U.S.A. 165 K1
Maine, Gulf of Canada/U.S.A. 165 K2
Maîné Hanari, Cerro hill Col. 176 D4
Maïné-Soroa Niger 120 E3
Maingkaing Myanmar 86 A1
Maingkwan Myanmar 86 B1
Maingy Island Myanmar 87 B4
Mainhardt Germany 63 J5
Mainit Mindanao Phil. 82 D4
Mainit, Lake Mindanao Phil. 82 D4
Mainkung China 96 C2
Mainland i. Scotland U.K. 60 F1
Mainland i. Scotland U.K. 60 [inset]
Mainleus Germany 63 L4
Mainling Xizang China 99 F7
Mainoru Australia 134 F3
Mainpat reg. India 105 E5
Mainpuri India 104 D4
Main Range National Park Australia 138 F2
Maintenon France 62 B6
Maintirano Madag. 123 E5
Mainz Germany 63 I4
Maio i. Cape Verde 120 [inset]
Maipú Arg. 178 E5
Maisaka Japan 92 D4
Maiskhal Island Bangl. 105 G5
Maisons-Laffitte France 62 C6
Maitengwe Botswana 123 C6
Maitland N.S.W. Australia 138 E4
Maitland S.A. Australia 137 B7
Maitland r. Australia 134 B5
Maitland, Banjaran mts Malaysia 85 G1
Maitland Point pt N.W.T. Canada 149 O1
Maitri research station Antarctica 188 C2
Maiwo i. Vanuatu see **Maéwo**
Maiyu, Mount hill Australia 134 E4
Maíz, Islas del is Nicaragua 166 [inset] J6
Maizar Pak. 111 H3
Maizhokunggar Xizang China 99 E7
Maizuru Japan 92 B3
Maja Jezercë mt. Albania 69 H3
Majdel Aanjar tourist site Lebanon 107 B3
Majene Sulawesi Barat Indon. 83 A3
Majestic U.S.A. 164 D5
Majhūd well Saudi Arabia 110 C6
Majī Eth. 122 D3
Majia He r. China 95 I4
Majiang Guangxi China 97 F4
Majiang Guizhou China 96 E3
Majiawan Ningxia China see **Huinong**
Majiazi China 90 B2
Majōl country N. Pacific Ocean see **Marshall Islands**
Major, Puig mt. Spain 67 H4
Majorca i. Spain 67 H4
Mājro atoll Marshall Is see **Majuro**
Majuli Island India 99 F8
Majunga Madag. see **Mahajanga**
Majuro atoll Marshall Is 186 H5
Majwemasweu S. Africa 125 H5
Makabana Congo 122 B4
Makabe Japan 93 G2
Makale Sulawesi Indon. 83 A3
Makalehi i. Indon. 83 C2

▶**Makalu** mt. China/Nepal 105 F4
5th highest mountain in the world and in Asia.

Makalu Barun National Park Nepal 105 F4
Makanchi Kazakh. 102 F2
Makanpur India 104 E4
Makari Mountain National Park Tanz. see **Mahale Mountains National Park**
Makarov Rus. Fed. 90 F2
Makarov Basin sea feature Arctic Ocean 189 B1
Makarska Croatia 68 G3
Makarwal Pak. 111 H3
Makar'ye Rus. Fed. 52 K4
Makar'yev Rus. Fed. 52 I4
Makassar Sulawesi Indon. 83 A4
Makassar, Selat str. Indon. 83 A3
Makat Kazakh. 100 E2
Makatini Flats lowland S. Africa 125 K4
Makedonija country Europe see **Macedonia**
Makelulu hill Palau 82 [inset]
Makeni Sierra Leone 120 B4
Makete Tanz. 123 D4
Makeyevka Ukr. see **Makiyivka**
Makgadikgadi depr. Botswana 123 C6
Makgadikgadi Pans National Park Botswana 123 C6
Makhachkala Rus. Fed. 113 G2
Makhad Pak. 111 H3
Makhado S. Africa 125 I2
Makhāzin, Kathīb al des. Egypt 107 A4
Makhâzin, Kathîb el des. Egypt see **Makhāzin, Kathīb al**
Makhazine, Barrage El dam Morocco 67 D6
Makhmūr Iraq 113 F4
Makhtal India 106 C2
Maki Japan 93 E1
Makian vol. Maluku Indon. 83 C2
Makihata-yama mt. Japan 93 E2
Makin atoll Kiribati see **Butaritari**
Makindu Kenya 122 D4
Makino Japan 92 C3
Makinsk Kazakh. 101 G1
Makioka Japan 93 E3
Makira i. Solomon Is see **San Cristobal**
Makiyivka Ukr. 53 H6
Makkah Saudi Arabia see **Mecca**
Makkovik Canada 153 K3
Makkovik, Cape Canada 153 K3
Makkum Neth. 62 F1
Makó Hungary 69 I1
Makokou Gabon 122 B3
Makopong Botswana 124 F3
Makotipoko Congo 121 E5
Makran reg. Iran/Pak. 111 F5
Makrana India 104 C4
Makran Coast Range mts Pak. 111 F5
Makri India 106 D2
Maksatikha Rus. Fed. 52 G4
Maksi India 104 D5
Maksimovka Rus. Fed. 90 E3
Maksotag Iran 111 F4
Maksudangarh India 104 D5
Mākū Iran 110 B2
Makunguwiro Tanz. 123 D5
Makurdi Nigeria 120 D4
Makushin Bay AK U.S.A. 148 F5
Makwassie S. Africa 125 G4
Mal India 105 G4
Mala Ireland see **Mallow**
Mala i. Solomon Is see **Malaita**
Malå Sweden 54 K4
Mala, Punta pt Panama 166 [inset] J8
Malabang Mindanao Phil. 82 D5
Malabar Coast India 106 B3

▶**Malabo** Equat. Guinea 120 D4
Capital of Equatorial Guinea.

Malabuñgan Palawan Phil. 82 B4
Malaca Spain see **Málaga**
Malacca Malaysia see **Melaka**
Malacca state Malaysia see **Melaka**
Malacca, Strait of Indon./Malaysia 84 B1
Malad City U.S.A. 156 E4
Maladzyechna Belarus 55 O9
Malá Fatra nat. park Slovakia 57 Q6
Málaga Spain 67 D5
Malaga U.S.A. 161 B5
Malagasy Republic country Africa see **Madagascar**
Malahar Sumba Indon. 83 B5
Málainn Mhóir Ireland 61 D3
Malaita i. Solomon Is 133 G2
Malaka mt. Sumbawa Indon. 85 G5
Malakal Palau 82 [inset]
Malakal Sudan 108 D8
Malakal Passage Palau 82 [inset]
Malakanagiri India see **Malkangiri**
Malakheti Nepal 104 E3
Malakula i. Vanuatu 133 G3
Malamala Sulawesi Indon. 83 B3
Malampaya Sound sea chan. Palawan Phil. 82 B4
Malan, Ras pt Pak. 111 G5
Malang Jawa Indon. 85 F4
Malangana Nepal see **Malangwa**
Malange Angola see **Malanje**
Malangwa Nepal 105 F4
Malanje Angola 123 B4
Malappuram India 106 C4
Mälaren l. Sweden 55 J7
Malargüe Arg. 178 C5
Malartic Canada 152 F4
Malasoro, Teluk b. Indon. 83 A4
Malaspina Glacier AK U.S.A. 149 L4
Malatayur, Tanjung pt Indon. 85 F3
Malatya Turkey 112 E3
Malavalli India 106 C3
Malawali i. Malaysia 85 G1
Malawi country Africa 123 D5
Malawi, Lake Africa see **Nyasa, Lake**
Malawi National Park Zambia see **Nyika National Park**
Malaya pen. Malaysia see **Malaysia, Semenanjung**
Malaya Pera Rus. Fed. 52 L2
Malaya Vishera Rus. Fed. 52 G4
Malaybalay Mindanao Phil. 82 D4
Malāyer Iran 110 C3
Malay Peninsula Asia 87 B4
Malay Reef Australia 136 E3
Malay Sary Kazakh. 98 B3
Malaysia country Asia 84 F2
Malaysia, Semenanjung pen. Malaysia see **Peninsular Malaysia**
Malazgirt Turkey 113 F3
Malbon Australia 136 C4
Malbork Poland 57 Q3
Malborn Germany 62 G5
Malchin Germany 57 N4
Malcolm Australia 135 C7
Malcolm, Point Australia 135 C8
Malcolm Island Myanmar 87 B5
Maldegem Belgium 62 D3
Malden U.S.A. 161 F4
Malden Island Kiribati 187 J6
Maldives country Indian Ocean 103 D10
Maldon Australia 138 B6
Maldon U.K. 59 H7
Maldonado Uruguay 178 F4
Maldonado, Punta pt Mex. 167 F5

▶**Male** Maldives 103 D11
Capital of the Maldives.

Maleas, Akra pt Peloponnisos Greece see **Maleas, Akrotirio**
Maleas, Akrotirio pt Greece 69 J6
Male Atoll Maldives 103 D11
Malebogo S. Africa 125 G5
Malegaon Mahar. India 106 B1
Malegaon Mahar. India 106 C2
Malé Karpaty hills Slovakia 57 P6
Malek Sīāh, Kūh-e mt. Afgh. 111 F4
Malele Dem. Rep. Congo 123 B4
Maler Kotla India 104 C3
Maleševske Planine mts Bulg./Macedonia 69 J4
Maleta Rus. Fed. 95 G1
Malgobek Rus. Fed. 113 G2
Malgomaj l. Sweden 54 J4
Malḥa, Naqb mt. Egypt see **Māliḥah, Naqb**
Malhada Brazil 179 C1
Malheur r. U.S.A. 156 D3
Malheur Lake U.S.A. 156 D4
Mali country Africa 120 C3
Mali Dem. Rep. Congo 122 C4
Mali Guinea 120 B3
Maliana East Timor 83 C5
Malianjing Gansu China 94 C3
Malianjing Gansu China 94 E4
Maligay Bay Mindanao Phil. 82 C5
Malihabad Uttar Prad. India 99 C8
Māliḥah, Naqb mt. Egypt 107 A5
Malik Naro mt. Pak. 111 F4
Maliku Sulawesi Indon. 83 B3
Mali Kyun i. Myanmar 87 B4
Malili Sulawesi Indon. 83 B3
Malin Ukr. see **Malyn**
Malindi Kenya 122 E4
Malines Belgium see **Mechelen**
Maling Gansu China 95 F4
Malin Head hd Ireland 61 E2
Malin More Ireland see **Málainn Mhóir**
Malino Sulawesi Indon. 83 A4
Malino, Gunung mt. Indon. 83 B2
Malipo China 96 E4
Mali Raginac mt. Croatia 68 F2
Malita Mindanao Phil. 82 D5
Malitbog Leyte Phil. 82 D4
Malka r. Rus. Fed. 113 G2
Malkangiri India 106 D2
Malkapur India 106 B2
Malkara Turkey 69 L4
Mal'kavichy Belarus 55 O10
Malkhanskiy Khrebet mts Rus. Fed. 95 G1
Malko Tŭrnovo Bulg. 69 L4
Mallacoota Australia 138 D6
Mallacoota Inlet b. Australia 138 D6
Mallaig U.K. 60 D4
Mallani reg. India 111 H5
Mallawī Egypt 112 C6
Mallee Cliffs National Park Australia 137 C7
Mallery Lake Canada 151 L1
Mallét Brazil 179 A4
Mallorca i. Spain see **Majorca**
Mallow Ireland 61 D5
Mallowa Well Australia 134 D5
Mallwyd U.K. 59 D6
Malm Norway 54 G4
Malmberget Sweden 54 L3
Malmédy Belgium 62 G4
Malmesbury S. Africa 124 D7
Malmesbury U.K. 59 E7
Malmö Sweden 55 H9
Malmyzh Rus. Fed. 52 K4
Malo i. Indon. 83 C1
Maloca Brazil 177 G3
Malolos Luzon Phil. 82 C3
Malone U.S.A. 165 H1
Malonje mt. Tanz. 123 D4
Maloshuyka Rus. Fed. 52 H3
Malosmadulu Atoll Maldives see **Maalhosmadulu Atoll**
Måløy Norway 54 D6
Maloyaroslavets Rus. Fed. 53 H5
Malozemel'skaya Tundra lowland Rus. Fed. 52 K2
Malpaso Mex. 166 E4
Malpelo, Isla de i. N. Pacific Ocean 169 H8
Malprabha r. India 106 C2
Malta country Europe 68 F7
Malta Latvia 55 O8
Malta ID U.S.A. 156 E4
Malta MT U.S.A. 156 G2
Malta Channel Italy/Malta 68 F6
Maltahöhe Namibia 124 C3
Maltby U.K. 58 F5
Maltby le Marsh U.K. 58 H5
Malton U.K. 58 G4
Maluku is Indon. see **Moluccas**
Maluku prov. Indon. 83 D3
Maluku, Laut sea Indon. 83 C3
Maluku Utara prov. Indon. 83 C3
Ma'lūlā, Jabal mts Syria 107 C3
Malung Sweden 55 H6
Maluti Mountains Lesotho 125 I5
Malu'u Solomon Is 133 G2
Malvan India 106 B2
Malvasia Greece see **Monemvasia**
Malvern U.K. see **Great Malvern**
Malvern U.S.A. 161 E5
Malvérnia Moz. see **Chicualacuala**
Malvinas, Islas terr. S. Atlantic Ocean see **Falkland Islands**
Malyn Ukr. 53 F6
Malyy Anyuy r. Rus. Fed. 77 R3
Malyye Derbety Rus. Fed. 53 J7
Malyy Kavkaz mts Asia see **Lesser Caucasus**
Malyy Kunaley Rus. Fed. 95 F1
Malyy Lyakhovskiy, Ostrov i. Rus. Fed. 77 P2
Malyy Uzen' r. Kazakh./Rus. Fed. 53 K6
Mamadysh Rus. Fed. 52 K5
Mamafubedu S. Africa 125 I4
Mamasa Sulawesi Barat Indon. 83 A3
Mamatān Nāvar l. Afgh. 111 G4
Mamba Xizang China 99 F7
Mamba Japan see **Manba**
Mambahenauhan i. Phil. 82 B5
Mambai Brazil 179 B1
Mambajao Phil. 82 D4
Mambasa Dem. Rep. Congo 122 C3
Mambi Sulawesi Barat Indon. 83 A3
Mamburao Mindoro Phil. 82 C3
Mamelodi S. Africa 125 I3
Mamfe Cameroon 120 D4
Mamit India 105 H5
Mammoth U.S.A. 159 H5
Mammoth Cave National Park U.S.A. 164 B5
Mammoth Reservoir U.S.A. 158 D3
Mamonas Brazil 179 C1
Mamoré r. Bol./Brazil 176 E6
Mamou Guinea 120 B3
Mampikony Madag. 123 E5
Mampong Ghana 120 C4
Mamuju Sulawesi Barat Indon. 83 A3
Mamuno Botswana 124 E2
Man Côte d'Ivoire 120 C4
Man India 106 B2
Man r. India 106 B2
Man U.S.A. 164 E5
Man, Isle of terr. Irish Sea 58 C4
Manacapuru Brazil 176 F4
Manacor Spain 67 H4
Manado Sulawesi Indon. 83 C2
Manadotua i. Indon. 83 C2

▶**Managua** Nicaragua 166 [inset] I6
Capital of Nicaragua.

Managua, Lago de l. Nicaragua 166 [inset] I6
Manakara Madag. 123 E6
Manakau mt. N.Z. 139 D6
Manākhah Yemen 108 F6

▶**Manama** Bahrain 110 C5
Capital of Bahrain.

Manamadurai India 106 C4
Mana Maroka National Park S. Africa 125 H5
Manamelkudi India 106 C4
Manam Island P.N.G. 81 L7
Mananara Avaratra Madag. 123 E5
Manangoora Australia 136 B3
Mananjary Madag. 123 E6
Manantali, Lac de l. Mali 120 B3
Manantenina Madag. 123 E6
Mana Pass China/India 99 B7
Mana Pools National Park Zimbabwe 123 C5

▶**Manapouri, Lake** N.Z. 139 A7
Deepest lake in Oceania.

Manas Xinjiang China 98 D3
Manasa India 104 C4
Manas He r. China 98 D3
Manas Hu l. China 98 D3
Manāṣīr reg. U.A.E. 110 D6

▶**Manaslu** mt. Nepal 105 F3
8th highest mountain in the world and in Asia.

Manassas U.S.A. 165 G4
Manastir Macedonia see **Bitola**
Manas Wildlife Sanctuary nature res. Bhutan 105 G4
Manatang Indon. 83 C5
Manatsuru Japan 93 F3
Manatuto East Timor 83 C5
Man-aung Myanmar 86 A3
Man-aung Kyun Myanmar 86 A3
Manaus Brazil 176 F4
Manavgat Turkey 112 C3
Manay Mindanao Phil. 82 D5
Manazuru-misaki pt Japan 93 F3
Manba Japan 93 E2
Manbazar India 105 F5
Manbij Syria 107 C1
Manby U.K. 58 H5
Mancelona U.S.A. 164 C1
Manchar India 106 B2
Manchester U.K. 58 E5
Manchester CT U.S.A. 165 I3
Manchester IA U.S.A. 160 F3
Manchester KY U.S.A. 164 D5
Manchester MD U.S.A. 165 G4
Manchester MI U.S.A. 164 C2
Manchester NH U.S.A. 165 J2
Manchester OH U.S.A. 164 D4
Manchester TN U.S.A. 162 C5
Manchester VT U.S.A. 165 I2
Mancılık Turkey 112 E3
Mand Pak. 111 F5
Mand, Rūd-e r. Iran 110 C4
Manda Tanz. 123 D4
Manda, Jebel mt. Sudan 121 F4
Manda, Parc National de nat. park Chad 121 E4
Mandabe Madag. 123 E6
Mandah Sumatera Indon. 84 C3
Mandah Mongolia 95 G2
Mandai Sing. 87 [inset]
Mandal Bulgan Mongolia see **Orhon**
Mandal Töv Mongolia see **Batsümber**
Mandal Norway 55 E7

▶**Mandala, Puncak** mt. Indon. 81 K7
3rd highest mountain in Oceania.

Mandalay Myanmar 86 B2
Mandale Myanmar see **Mandalay**
Mandalgovĭ Mongolia 94 F2
Mandalī Iraq 113 G4
Mandal-Ovoo Mongolia 94 F2
Mandalt Nei Mongol China 95 H3
Mandalt Sum Nei Mongol China 95 H2
Mandan U.S.A. 160 C2
Mandaon Masbate Phil. 82 C3
Mandar, Teluk b. Indon. 83 A3
Mandas Sardinia Italy 68 C5
Mandasa India 106 E2
Mandasor India see **Mandsaur**
Mandav Hills India 104 B5
Mandel Afgh. 111 F3
Mandera Kenya 122 E3
Manderfield U.S.A. 159 G2
Manderscheid Germany 62 G4
Mandeville Jamaica 169 I5
Mandeville N.Z. 139 B7
Mandha India 104 B4
Mandhoúdhíon Greece see **Mantoudi**
Mandi India 104 D3
Mandiana Guinea 120 C3
Mandi Angin, Gunung mt. Malaysia 84 C1
Mandi Burewala Pak. 111 I4
Mandié Moz. 123 D5
Mandini S. Africa 125 J5
Mandioli i. Maluku Indon. 83 C3
Mandira Dam India 105 F5
Mandla India 104 E5
Mandleshwar India 104 C5
Mandor Kalimantan Indon. 85 E2
Mandor, Cagar Alam nature res. Indon. 85 E2
Mandrael India 104 D4
Mandritsara Madag. 123 E5
Mandsaur India 104 C4
Mandul i. Indon. 85 G2
Mandurah Australia 135 A8
Manduria Italy 68 G4
Mandvi India 104 B5
Mandya India 106 C3
Manerbio Italy 68 D2
Manevychi Ukr. 53 E6
Manfalūṭ Egypt 112 C6
Manfredonia Italy 68 F4
Manfredonia, Golfo di g. Italy 68 G4
Manga Brazil 179 C1
Manga Burkina Faso 120 C3
Mangabeiras, Serra das hills Brazil 177 I6
Mangai Dem. Rep. Congo 122 B4
Mangaia i. Cook Is 187 J7
Mangakino N.Z. 139 E4
Mangalagiri India 106 D2
Mangaldai India 86 A1
Mangaldoi India see **Mangaldai**
Mangalia Romania 69 M3
Mangalmé Chad 121 E3
Mangalore India 106 B3
Mangaon India 106 B2
Mangareva Islands Fr. Polynesia see **Gambier, Îles**
Mangaung Free State S. Africa 125 H5
Mangaung Free State S. Africa see **Bloemfontein**
Mangawan India 105 E4
Ma'ngê Gansu China see **Luqu**
Mangea i. Cook Is see **Mangaia**
Manggar Indon. 85 E3
Mangghyshlaq Kazakh. see **Mangystau**
Mangghystaū Kazakh. see **Mangystau**
Mangghystaū admin. div. Kazakh. see **Mangistauskaya Oblast'**
Mangghyt Uzbek. see **Mang'it**
Manghit Uzbek. see **Mang'it**
Mangin Range mts Myanmar see **Mingin Range**
Mangistau Kazakh. see **Mangystau**
Mangistauskaya Oblast' admin. div. Kazakh. 113 I2
Mang'it Uzbek. 102 B3
Mangkalihat, Tanjung pt Indon. 85 G2
Mangkutup r. Indon. 85 F3
Mangla Bangl. see **Mongla**
Mangla Pak. 111 I3
Mangnai Qinghai China 99 E5
Mangnai Zhen Qinghai China 99 E5
Mangochi Malawi 123 D5
Mangoky r. Madag. 123 E6
Mangole i. Indon. 83 C3
Mangole, Selat sea chan. Indon. 83 C3
Mangoli India 106 B2
Mangotsfield U.K. 59 E7
Mangqystaū Shyghanaghy b. Kazakh. see **Mangyshlakskiy Zaliv**
Mangra Qinghai China see **Guinan**
Mangral India 104 B5
Mangrul India 106 C1
Mangshi China see **Luxi**
Mangualde Port. 67 C3
Manguéni, Plateau du Niger 120 E2
Mangui China 90 A2
Mangula Zimbabwe see **Mhangura**
Mangulile Hond. 166 [inset] I6
Mangum U.S.A. 161 D5
Mangupung i. Indon. 83 C1
Mangut Rus. Fed. 95 H1
Mangyshlak Kazakh. see **Mangystau**
Mangyshlak, Poluostrov pen. Kazakh. 113 H1
Mangyshlak Oblast admin. div. Kazakh. see **Mangistauskaya Oblast'**
Mangyshlakskaya Oblast' admin. div. Kazakh. see **Mangistauskaya Oblast'**
Mangyshlakskiy Zaliv b. Kazakh. 113 H1
Mangystau Kazakh. 113 H2
Manhā Brazil 179 B1
Manhan Mongolia 94 C2
Manhan Hövsgöl Mongolia see **Alag-Erdene**
Manhattan U.S.A. 160 D4
Manhica Moz. 125 K3
Manhoca Moz. 125 K4
Manhuaçu Brazil 179 C3
Manhuaçu r. Brazil 179 C2
Mani Xizang China 99 D6
Mania r. Madag. 123 E5
Maniago Italy 68 E1
Manicouagan Canada 153 H4
Manicouagan r. Canada 153 H4
Manicouagan, Réservoir resr Canada 153 H4
Manic Trois, Réservoir resr Canada 153 H4
Manīfah Saudi Arabia 110 C5
Maniganggo China 96 C2
Manigotagan Canada 151 L5
Manihiki atoll Cook Is 186 J6
Maniitsoq Greenland 147 M3
Manikchhari Bangl. 105 H5
Manikgarh India see **Rajura**

▶**Manila** Luzon Phil. 82 C3
Capital of the Philippines.

Manila U.S.A. 156 F4
Manila Bay Luzon Phil. 82 C3
Manildra Australia 138 D4
Manilla Australia 138 E3
Manimbaya, Tanjung pt Indon. 83 A3
Maningrida Australia 134 F3
Maninjau, Danau l. Indon. 84 C3
Manipa i. Maluku Indon. 83 C3
Manipa, Selat sea chan. Maluku Indon. 83 C3
Manipur India see **Imphal**
Manipur state India 105 H4
Manisa Turkey 69 L5
Manismata Kalimantan Indon. 85 E3
Manistee U.S.A. 164 B1
Manistee r. U.S.A. 164 B1
Manistique U.S.A. 162 C2
Manitoba prov. Canada 151 L4
Manitoba, Lake Canada 151 L5
Manito Lake Canada 151 I4
Manitou Canada 151 L5
Manitou, Lake U.S.A. 164 B3
Manitou Beach U.S.A. 165 G2
Manitou Falls Canada 151 M5
Manitou Islands U.S.A. 164 B1
Manitoulin Island Canada 152 E5
Manitouwadge Canada 152 D4
Manitowoc U.S.A. 164 B1
Maniwaki Canada 152 G5
Manizales Col. 176 C2
Manja Madag. 123 E6
Manjarabad India 106 B3
Manjeri India 106 C4
Manjhand Pak. 111 H5
Manjhi India 105 F4
Manjra r. India 106 C2
Man Kabat Myanmar 86 B1
Mankaiana Swaziland see **Mankayane**
Mankato KS U.S.A. 160 D4
Mankato MN U.S.A. 160 E2
Mankayane Swaziland 125 J4
Mankera Pak. 111 H4
Mankono Côte d'Ivoire 120 C4
Mankota Canada 151 J5
Manlay Mongolia 94 F2
Manley Hot Springs AK U.S.A. 149 J2
Manmad India 106 B1
Mann r. Australia 134 F3
Mann, Mount Australia 135 E6
Manna Sumatera Indon. 84 C4
Man Na Myanmar 86 B2
Mannahill Australia 137 B7
Mannar Sri Lanka 106 C4
Mannar, Gulf of India/Sri Lanka 106 C4
Manneru r. India 106 D3
Mannessier, Lac l. Canada 153 H3
Mannheim Germany 63 I5
Mannicolo Islands Solomon Is see **Vanikoro Islands**
Manning r. Australia 138 F3
Manning Canada 150 G3
Manning U.S.A. 163 D5
Mannington U.S.A. 164 E4
Manningtree U.K. 59 I7
Mann Ranges mts Australia 135 E6
Mannsville KY U.S.A. 164 C5
Mannsville NY U.S.A. 165 G2
Mannu, Capo c. Sardinia Italy 68 C4
Mannville Canada 151 I4
Man-of-War Rocks is U.S.A. see **Gardner Pinnacles**
Manoharpur Rajasthan India 99 B8
Manohar Thana India 104 D4
Manokotak AK U.S.A. 148 H4
Manokwari Indon. 81 I7
Manoron Myanmar 87 B5
Manosque France 66 G5
Manouane r. Canada 153 H4
Manouane, Lac l. Canada 153 H4
Man Pan Myanmar 86 B2
Manp'o N. Korea 90 B4
Manra i. Kiribati 133 I2
Manresa Spain 67 G3
Mansa Gujarat India 104 C5
Mansa Punjab India 104 C3
Mansa Zambia 123 C5
Mansa Konko Gambia 120 B3
Mansalean Sulawesi Indon. 83 B3
Man Sam Myanmar 86 B2
Mansehra Pak. 109 L3
Mansel Island Canada 147 K3
Mansfield Australia 138 C6
Mansfield U.K. 59 F5
Mansfield LA U.S.A. 161 E5
Mansfield OH U.S.A. 164 D3
Mansfield PA U.S.A. 165 G3
Mansfield, Mount U.S.A. 165 I1
Man Si Myanmar 86 B1
Mansi Myanmar 86 A1
Manso r. Brazil see **Mortes, Rio das**
Mansuela Seram Indon. 83 D3
Manta Ecuador 176 B4
Mantalingajan, Mount Palawan Phil. 82 B4
Mantarara Maluku Indon. 83 C3
Mantaro r. Peru 176 D6
Manteca U.S.A. 158 C3
Mantehage i. Indon. 83 C2
Mantena Brazil 179 C2
Manteo U.S.A. 162 F5
Mantes-la-Jolie France 62 B6
Mantiqueira, Serra da mts Brazil 179 B3
Manto Hond. 166 [inset] I6
Manton U.S.A. 164 C1
Mantoudi Greece 69 J5
Mantova Italy see **Mantua**
Mäntsälä Fin. 55 N6
Mänttä Fin. 54 N5
Mantua Cuba 163 C8

Mantua Italy 68 D2
Mantuan Downs Australia 136 D5
Manturovo Rus. Fed. 52 J4
Mäntyharju Fin. 55 O6
Mäntyjärvi Fin. 54 O3
Manú Peru 176 D6
Manu, Parque Nacional nat. park Peru 176 D6
Manuae atoll Fr. Polynesia 187 J7
Manu'a Islands American Samoa 133 I3
Manuel Ribas Brazil 179 A4
Manuel Vitorino Brazil 179 C1
Manuelzinho Brazil 177 H5
Manui i. Indon. 83 B3
Manuk i. Maluku Indon. 83 D4
Manukan Mindanao Phil. 82 C4
Manukau N.Z. 139 E3
Manukau Harbour N.Z. 139 E3
Manuk Manka i. Phil. 82 B5
Manunda watercourse Australia 137 B7
Manusela, Taman Nasional nat. park Seram Indon. 83 D3
Manus Island P.N.G. 81 L7
Manvi India 106 C3
Many U.S.A. 161 E6
Manyana Botswana 125 G3
Manyas Turkey 69 L4
Manyas Gölü l. Turkey see Kuş Gölü
Manych-Gudilo, Ozero l. Rus. Fed. 53 I7
Many Island Lake Canada 151 I5
Manyoni Tanz. 123 D4
Manzai Pak. 111 H3
Manzanares Spain 67 E4
Manzanillo Cuba 169 I4
Manzanillo Mex. 168 D5
Manzanillo, Punta pt Panama 166 [inset] K7
Manzhouli Nei Mongol China 95 I1
Manzini Swaziland 125 J4
Mao Chad 121 E3
Maó Spain see Mahón
Maoba Guizhou China 96 E3
Maoba Hubei China 97 F2
Maocifan China 97 G2
Mao'ergai China 96 D1
Maojiachuan Gansu China 94 F4
Maojing Gansu China 94 F4
Maoke, Pegunungan mts Indon. 81 J7
Maokeng S. Africa 125 H4
Maokui Shan mt. China 90 A4
Maolin Jilin China 95 J3
Maomao Shan mt. Gansu China 94 E4
Maoming China 97 F4
Maoniupo Xizang China 99 D6
Maoniushan Qinghai China 94 D4
Ma On Shan hill H.K. China 97 [inset]
Maopi T'ou c. Taiwan 97 I4
Maopora i. Maluku Indon. 83 C4
Maotou Shan mt. China 96 D3
Mapai Moz. 125 J2
Mapam Yumco l. China 99 C7
Mapane Sulawesi Indon. 83 B3
Mapanza Zambia 123 C5
Mapastepec Mex. 167 G6
Maphodi S. Africa 125 G6
Mapimí Mex. 166 E3
Mapinhane Moz. 125 L2
Mapiri Bol. 176 E7
Maple r. MI U.S.A. 164 C2
Maple r. ND U.S.A. 160 D2
Maple Creek Canada 151 I5
Maple Heights U.S.A. 164 E3
Maple Peak U.S.A. 159 I5
Mapmakers Seamounts sea feature N. Pacific Ocean 186 H4
Mapoon Australia 136 C1
Mapor i. Indon. 84 D2
Mapoteng Lesotho 125 H5
Maprik P.N.G. 81 K7
Mapuera r. Brazil 177 G4
Mapulanguene Moz. 125 K3
Mapungubwe National Park S. Africa 125 I2

▶Maputo Moz. 125 K3
Capital of Mozambique.

Maputo prov. Moz. 125 K3
Maputo r. Moz./S. Africa 125 K4
Maputo, Baía de b. Moz. 125 K4
Maputsoe Lesotho 125 H5
Maqanshy Kazakh. see Makanchi
Maqar an Na'am well Iraq 113 F5
Maqat Kazakh. see Makat
Maqên Qinghai China 94 E5
Maqên Xizang China 99 E7
Maqên Kangri mt. Qinghai China 94 D5
Maqiao Xinjiang China 98 D3
Maqnā Saudi Arabia 112 D5
Maqteïr reg. Mauritania 120 B2
Maqu China 96 D1
Ma Qu r. China see Huang He
Maquan He r. Xizang China 99 D7
Maqueda Channel Phil. 82 C3
Maquela do Zombo Angola 123 B4
Maquinchao Arg. 178 C6
Mar r. Pak. 111 G5
Mar, Serra do mts Rio de Janeiro/São Paulo Brazil 179 B3
Mar, Serra do mts Rio Grande do Sul/Santa Catarina Brazil 179 A5
Mara r. Canada 151 I1
Mara India 105 E5
Mara S. Africa 125 I2
Maraã Brazil 176 E4
Marabá Brazil 177 I5
Marabahan Kalimantan Indon. 85 F3
Marabatua i. Indon. 85 F4
Maraboon, Lake resr Australia 136 E4
Maracá, Ilha de i. Brazil 177 H3
Maracaibo Venez. 176 D1
Maracaibo, Lago de Venez. see Maracaibo, Lake
Maracaibo, Lake Venez. 176 D2
Maracaju Brazil 178 E2
Maracaju, Serra de hills Brazil 178 E2
Maracanda Uzbek. see Samarqand
Maracás Brazil 179 C1
Maracás, Chapada de hills Brazil 179 C1
Maracay Venez. 176 E1
Marādah Libya 121 E2
Maradi Niger 120 D3
Marāgheh Iran 110 B2
Maragondon Luzon Phil. 82 C3
Marahuaca, Cerro mt. Venez. 176 E3
Marajó, Baía de est. Brazil 177 I4
Marajó, Ilha de i. Brazil 177 H4
Marakele National Park S. Africa 125 H3
Maralal Kenya 122 D3
Maralbashi Xinjiang China see Bachu
Maralinga Australia 135 E7
Maralwexi Xinjiang China see Bachu
Maramasike i. Solomon Is 133 G2
Maramba Zambia see Livingstone
Marambio research station Antarctica 188 A2
Marampit i. Indon. 83 C1
Maran Malaysia 84 C2
Maran mt. Pak. 111 G4
Marana U.S.A. 159 H5
Marand Iran 110 B2
Marandellas Zimbabwe see Marondera
Marang Malaysia 84 C1
Marang Myanmar 87 B5
Maranhão r. Brazil 179 A1
Maranoa r. Australia 138 D1
Marañón r. Peru 176 D4
Marão Moz. 125 L3
Marão mt. Port. 67 C3
Marapi, Gunung vol. Sumatera Indon. 84 C3
Mara Rosa Brazil 179 A1
Maraş Turkey see Kahramanmaraş
Marasende i. Indon. 85 G4
Marathon Canada 152 D4
Marathon FL U.S.A. 163 D7
Marathon NY U.S.A. 165 G2
Marathon TX U.S.A. 161 C6
Maratua i. Indon. 85 G2
Maraú Brazil 179 D1
Marau Kalimantan Indon. 85 E3
Maravillas Creek watercourse U.S.A. 161 C6
Marawi Mindanao Phil. 82 D4
Märäzä Azer. 113 H2
Marbella Spain 67 D5
Marble Bar Australia 134 B5
Marble Canyon U.S.A. 159 H3
Marble Canyon gorge U.S.A. 159 H3
Marble Hall S. Africa 125 I3
Marble Hill U.S.A. 161 F4
Marble Island Canada 151 N2
Marbul Pass India 104 C2
Marburg S. Africa 125 J6
Marburg Slovenia see Maribor
Marburg an der Lahn Germany 63 I4
Marca, Ponta do pt Angola 123 B5
Marcala Hond. 166 [inset] H6
Marcali Hungary 68 G1
Marcelino Ramos Brazil 179 A4
March U.K. 59 H6
Marche reg. France 66 E3
Marche-en-Famenne Belgium 62 F4
Marchena Spain 67 D5
Marchinbar Island Australia 136 B1
Mar Chiquita, Laguna l. Arg. 178 D4
Marchtrenk Austria 57 O6
Marco U.S.A. 163 D7
Marcoing France 62 D4
Marcona Peru 176 C7
Marcopeet Islands Canada 152 F2
Marcus Baker, Mount AK U.S.A. 149 K3
Marcy, Mount U.S.A. 165 I1
Mardan Pak. 111 I3
Mar del Plata Arg. 178 E5
Mardīān Afgh. 111 G2
Mardin Turkey 113 F3
Mardzad Mongolia see Hayrhandulaan
Maré i. New Caledonia 133 G4
Maree, Loch l. U.K. 60 D3
Mareh Iran 111 E5
Marengo IA U.S.A. 160 E3
Marengo IN U.S.A. 164 B4
Marevo Rus. Fed. 52 G4
Marfa U.S.A. 161 B6
Margai Caka l. Xizang China 99 D6
Margam Ri mts Xizang China 99 D6
Marganets Ukr. see Marhanets'
Margao India see Madgaon
Margaret r. Australia 134 D4
Margaret watercourse Australia 137 B6
Margaret, Mount hill Australia 134 B5
Margaret Lake Alta Canada 150 H3
Margaret Lake N.W.T. Canada 150 G1
Margaret River Australia 135 A8
Margaretville U.S.A. 165 H2
Margarita, Isla de i. Venez. 176 F1
Margaritovo Rus. Fed. 90 D4
Margate U.K. 59 I7
Margherita, Lake Eth. see Abaya, Lake

▶Margherita Peak Dem. Rep. Congo/Uganda 122 C3
3rd highest mountain in Africa.

Marghilon Uzbek. see Marg'ilon
Marg'ilon Uzbek. 102 D3
Märgo, Dasht-i des. Afgh. see Märgow, Dasht-e
Margog Caka l. Xizang China 99 D6
Margosatubig Mindanao Phil. 82 C5
Märgow, Dasht-e des. Afgh. 111 F4
Margraten Neth. 62 F4
Marguerite Canada 150 F4
Marguerite, Pic mt. Dem. Rep. Congo/Uganda see Margherita Peak
Marguerite Bay Antarctica 188 L2
Margyang Xizang China 99 E7
Marhaj Khalīl Iraq 113 G4
Marhanets' Ukr. 53 G7
Marhoum Alg. 64 D5
Mari Myanmar 86 B1
Maria atoll Fr. Polynesia 187 J7
María Cleofas, Isla i. Mex. 166 D4
María Elena Chile 178 C2
Maria Island Australia 136 A2
Maria Island Myanmar 87 B5
Maria Island National Park Australia 137 [inset]
Mariala National Park Australia 137 D5
María Madre, Isla i. Mex. 166 D4
María Magdelena, Isla i. Mex. 166 D4
Mariana Brazil 179 C3
Marianao Cuba 163 D8
Mariana Ridge sea feature N. Pacific Ocean 186 F4

▶Mariana Trench sea feature N. Pacific Ocean 186 F5
Deepest trench in the world.

Mariani India 105 H4
Mariánica, Cordillera mts Spain see Morena, Sierra
Marian Lake Canada 150 G2
Marianna AR U.S.A. 161 F5
Marianna FL U.S.A. 163 C6
Mariano Machado Angola see Ganda
Mariánské Lázně Czech Rep. 63 M5
Marias r. U.S.A. 156 F3
Marías, Islas is Mex. 168 C4

▶Mariato, Punta pt Panama 166 [inset] J8
Most southerly point of North America.

Maria van Diemen, Cape N.Z. 139 D2
Ma'rib Yemen 108 G6
Maribor Slovenia 68 F1
Marica r. Bulg. see Maritsa
Maricopa AZ U.S.A. 159 G5
Maricopa CA U.S.A. 158 D4
Maricopa Mountains U.S.A. 159 G5
Maridi Sudan 121 F4
Marie Byrd Land reg. Antarctica 188 J1
Marie-Galante i. Guadeloupe 169 L5
Mariehamn Fin. 55 K6
Mariembero r. Brazil 179 A1
Marienbad Czech Rep. see Mariánské Lázně
Marienberg Germany 63 N4
Marienburg Poland see Malbork
Marienhafe Germany 63 H1
Mariental Namibia 124 C3
Marienwerder Poland see Kwidzyn
Mariestad Sweden 55 H7
Mariet r. Canada 152 F2
Marietta GA U.S.A. 163 C5
Marietta OH U.S.A. 164 E4
Marietta OK U.S.A. 161 D5
Marignane France 66 G5
Marii, Mys pt Rus. Fed. 78 G2
Mariinsk Rus. Fed. 76 J4
Mariinskiy Posad Rus. Fed. 52 J4
Marijampolė Lith. 55 M9
Marília Brazil 179 A3
Marillana Australia 134 B5
Marimba Angola 123 B4
Marimun Kalimantan Indon. 85 F3
Marín Mex. 167 E3
Marín Spain 67 B2
Marina U.S.A. 158 C3
Marina di Gioiosa Ionica Italy 68 G5
Mar''ina Gorka Belarus see Mar''ina Horka
Mar''ina Horka Belarus 55 P10
Marinduque i. Phil. 82 C3
Marinette U.S.A. 164 B1
Maringá Brazil 179 A3
Maringa r. Dem. Rep. Congo 122 B3
Maringo U.S.A. 164 D3
Marinha Grande Port. 67 B4
Marion AL U.S.A. 163 C5
Marion AR U.S.A. 161 F5
Marion IL U.S.A. 160 F4
Marion IN U.S.A. 164 C3
Marion KS U.S.A. 160 D4
Marion MI U.S.A. 164 C1
Marion NY U.S.A. 165 G2
Marion OH U.S.A. 164 D3
Marion SC U.S.A. 163 E5
Marion VA U.S.A. 164 E5
Marion, Lake U.S.A. 163 D5
Marion Reef Australia 136 F3
Maripa Venez. 176 E2
Mariposa U.S.A. 158 D3
Marisa Sulawesi Indon. 83 B2
Mariscala Mex. 167 F5
Mariscal José Félix Estigarribia Para. 178 D2
Maritime Alps mts France/Italy 66 H4
Maritime Kray admin. div. Rus. Fed. see Primorskiy Kray
Maritimes, Alpes mts France/Italy see Maritime Alps
Maritsa r. Bulg. 69 L4
also known as Evros (Greece/Turkey), Marica (Bulgaria), Meriç (Turkey)
Marittime, Alpi mts France/Italy see Maritime Alps
Mariupol' Ukr. 53 H7
Mariusa nat. park Venez. 176 F2
Marīvān Iran 110 B3
Marjan Afgh. see Wazi Khwa
Marjayoûn Lebanon 107 B3
Marka Somalia 122 E3
Markakol', Ozero l. Kazakh. 98 D2
Markala Mali 120 C3
Markam China 96 C2
Markaryd Sweden 55 H8
Markdale Canada 164 E1
Marken S. Africa 125 I2
Markermeer l. Neth. 62 F2
Market Deeping U.K. 59 G6
Market Drayton U.K. 59 E6
Market Harborough U.K. 59 G6
Markethill U.K. 61 F3
Market Weighton U.K. 58 G5
Markha r. Rus. Fed. 77 M3
Markham Canada 164 F2
Markit Xinjiang China 98 B5
Markkleeberg Germany 63 M3
Markleeville U.S.A. 158 D2
Marklohe Germany 63 J2
Markog Qu r. China 96 D1
Markounda Cent. Afr. Rep. 122 B3
Markovo Rus. Fed. 189 C2
Markranstädt Germany 63 M3
Marks Rus. Fed. 53 J6
Marks U.S.A. 161 F5
Marksville U.S.A. 161 E6
Marktheidenfeld Germany 63 J5
Marktredwitz Germany 63 M4
Marl Germany 62 H3
Marla Australia 135 F6
Marlborough Downs hills U.K. 59 F7
Marle France 62 D5
Marlette U.S.A. 164 D2
Marlin U.S.A. 161 D6
Marlinton U.S.A. 164 E4
Marlo Australia 138 D6
Marmagao India 106 B3
Marmande France 66 E4
Marmara, Sea of g. Turkey 69 M4
Marmara Denizi g. Turkey see Marmara, Sea of
Marmara Gölü l. Turkey 69 M5
Marmarica reg. Libya 112 B5
Marmaris Turkey 69 M6
Marmarth U.S.A. 160 C2
Marmê Xizang China 99 C6
Marmet U.S.A. 164 E4
Marmion, Lake salt l. Australia 135 C7
Marmion Lake Canada 151 N5
Marmolada mt. Italy 68 D1
Marmot Bay AK U.S.A. 148 I4
Marmot Island AK U.S.A. 149 J4
Marne r. France 62 C6
Marne-la-Vallée France 62 C6
Marnitz Germany 63 L1
Maroantsetra Madag. 123 E5
Maroc country Africa see Morocco
Marol Pak. 104 D2
Marol Pak. 111 I4
Maroldsweisach Germany 63 K4
Maromokotro mt. Madag. 123 E5
Marondera Zimbabwe 123 D5
Maroochydore Australia 138 F1
Maroonah Australia 135 A5
Maroon Peak U.S.A. 156 G5
Maros Sulawesi Indon. 83 A4
Maros r. Indon. 83 A4
Marosvásárhely Romania see Târgu Mureş
Maroua Cameroon 121 E3
Marovoay Madag. 123 E5
Marowali Sulawesi Indon. 83 B3
Marqādah Syria 113 F4
Mar Qu r. China see Markog Qu
Marquard S. Africa 125 H5
Marquesas Islands Fr. Polynesia 187 K6
Marquesas Keys is U.S.A. 163 D7
Marquês de Valença Brazil 179 C3
Marquette U.S.A. 162 C2
Marquez U.S.A. 161 D6
Marquion France 62 D4
Marquise France 62 B4
Marquises, Îles is Fr. Polynesia see Marquesas Islands
Marra Australia 138 A3
Marra r. Australia 138 C3
Marra, Jebel mt. Sudan 121 F3
Marra, Jebel Sudan 121 F3
Marracuene Moz. 125 K3
Marrakech Morocco 64 C5
Marrakesh Morocco see Marrakech
Marrangua, Lagoa l. Moz. 125 L3
Marrar Australia 138 C5
Marrawah Australia 137 [inset]
Marree Australia 137 B6
Marrowbone U.S.A. 164 C5
Marruecos country Africa see Morocco
Marrupa Moz. 123 D5
Marryat Australia 135 F6
Marsá al 'Alam Egypt 108 D4
Marsa 'Alam Egypt see Marsá al 'Alam
Marsa al Burayqah Libya 121 E1
Marsabit Kenya 122 D3
Marsala Sicily Italy 68 E6
Marsá Maṭrūḥ Egypt 112 B5
Marsberg Germany 63 I3
Marsciano Italy 68 E3
Marsden Australia 138 C4
Marsden Canada 151 I4
Marsdiep sea chan. Neth. 62 E2
Marseille France 66 G5
Marseilles France see Marseille
Marsfjället mt. Sweden 54 I4
Marshall watercourse Australia 136 B4
Marshall AK U.S.A. 148 G3
Marshall AR U.S.A. 161 E5
Marshall IL U.S.A. 164 B4
Marshall MI U.S.A. 164 C2
Marshall MN U.S.A. 160 E2
Marshall MO U.S.A. 160 E4
Marshall TX U.S.A. 161 E5
Marshall Islands country N. Pacific Ocean 186 H5
Marshalltown U.S.A. 160 E3
Marshfield MO U.S.A. 161 E4
Marshfield WI U.S.A. 160 F2
Marsh Harbour Bahamas 163 E7
Mars Hill U.S.A. 162 H2
Marsh Island U.S.A. 161 F6
Marsh Lake Y.T. Canada 149 N3
Marsh Lake Y.T. Canada 149 N3
Marsh Peak U.S.A. 159 I1
Marsh Point Canada 151 M3
Marsing U.S.A. 156 D4
Märsta Sweden 55 J7
Marsyaty Rus. Fed. 51 S3
Martaban, Gulf of g. Myanmar see Mottama, Gulf of
Martanai Besar i. Malaysia 85 G1
Martapura Kalimantan Indon. 85 F3
Martapura Sumatera Indon. 84 D4
Marten River Canada 152 F5
Marte R. Gómez, Presa resr Mex. 167 F3
Martha's Vineyard i. U.S.A. 165 J3
Martigny Switz. 66 H3
Martim Vaz, Ilhas is S. Atlantic Ocean see Martin Vas, Ilhas
Martin r. Canada 150 F2
Martin Slovakia 57 Q6
Martin MI U.S.A. 164 C2
Martin SD U.S.A. 160 C3
Martínez Mex. 167 F4
Martinez Lake U.S.A. 159 F5
Martinho Campos Brazil 179 B2

▶Martinique terr. West Indies 169 L6
French Overseas Department.

Martinique Passage Dominica/Martinique 169 L5
Martin Peninsula Antarctica 188 K2
Martin Point pt AK U.S.A. 149 L1
Martinsburg U.S.A. 165 G4
Martins Ferry U.S.A. 164 E3
Martinsville IL U.S.A. 164 B4
Martinsville IN U.S.A. 164 B4
Martinsville VA U.S.A. 164 F5

▶Martin Vas, Ilhas is S. Atlantic Ocean 184 G7
Most easterly point of South America.

Martin Vaz Islands S. Atlantic Ocean see Martin Vas, Ilhas
Martök Kazakh. see Martuk
Marton N.Z. 139 E5
Martorell Spain 67 G3
Martos Spain 67 E5
Martuk Kazakh. 100 E1
Martuni Armenia 113 G2
Maru Gansu China 94 E5
Marudi Sarawak Malaysia 85 F1
Marudu, Teluk b. Malaysia 85 G1
Maruf Afgh. 111 G4
Maruim Brazil 177 K6
Marukhis Ugheltekhili pass Georgia/Rus. Fed. 113 F2
Maruko Japan 93 E2
Marulan Australia 138 D5
Maruoka Japan 92 C2
Marusthali reg. India 111 H5
Maruyama Japan 93 F3
Maruyama-gawa r. Japan 92 A3
Marvast Iran 110 D4
Marv Dasht Iran 110 D4
Marvejols France 66 F4
Marvine, Mount U.S.A. 159 H2
Marwayne Canada 151 I4
Mary r. Australia 134 E3
Mary Turkm. 111 F2
Maryborough Qld Australia 137 F5
Maryborough Vic. Australia 138 A6
Marydale S. Africa 124 F5
Mary Frances Lake Canada 151 J2
Mary Lake Canada 151 K2
Maryland state U.S.A. 165 G4
Maryport U.K. 58 D4
Mary's Harbour Canada 153 L3
Marys Igloo AK U.S.A. 148 F2
Marysvale U.S.A. 159 G2
Marysville CA U.S.A. 158 C2
Marysville KS U.S.A. 160 D4
Marysville OH U.S.A. 164 D3
Maryvale N.T. Australia 135 F6
Maryvale Qld Australia 136 D3
Maryville MO U.S.A. 160 E3
Maryville TN U.S.A. 162 D5
Marzagão Brazil 179 A2
Marzahna Germany 63 M2
Masachapa Nicaragua 166 [inset] I7
Masada tourist site Israel 107 B4
Masagua Guat. 167 H6
Masāhūn, Kūh-e mt. Iran 110 D4
Masai Steppe plain Tanz. 123 D4
Masaka Uganda 122 D4
Masakhane S. Africa 125 H6
Masalembu Besar i. Indon. 85 F4
Masalembu Kecil i. Indon. 85 F4
Masallı Azer. 113 H3
Masamba Sulawesi Indon. 83 B3
Masamba mt. Indon. 83 B3
Masan S. Korea 91 C6
Masapun Maluku Indon. 83 C4
Masasi Tanz. 123 D5
Masavi Bol. 176 F7
Masaya Nicaragua 166 [inset] I7
Masaya, Volcán vol. Nicaragua 166 [inset] I7
Masbate Masbate Phil. 82 C3
Masbate i. Phil. 82 C3
Mascara Alg. 67 G6
Mascarene Basin sea feature Indian Ocean 185 L7
Mascarene Plain sea feature Indian Ocean 185 L7
Mascarene Ridge sea feature Indian Ocean 185 L6
Mascota Mex. 166 D4
Mascote Brazil 179 D1
Masein Myanmar 86 A2
Ma Sekatok b. Indon. 85 G2
Masela Maluku Indon. 83 D5
Masela i. Maluku Indon. 83 D5
Masepe i. Indon. 83 B3

▶Maseru Lesotho 125 H5
Capital of Lesotho.

Mashai Lesotho 125 I5
Mashan China 97 F4
Masherbrum mt. Pak. 104 D2
Mashhad Iran 111 E2
Mashiko Japan 93 G2
Mashishing S. Africa 125 J3
Mashket r. Pak. 111 F5
Mashki Chah Pak. 111 F4
Masi Norway 54 M2
Masiáca Mex. 166 C3
Masibambane S. Africa 125 H6
Masīlah, Wādī al watercourse Yemen 108 H6
Masilo S. Africa 125 H5
Masi-Manimba Dem. Rep. Congo 123 B4
Masimbu Sulawesi Barat Indon. 83 A3
Masindi Uganda 122 D3
Masinloc Luzon Phil. 82 B3
Masinyusane S. Africa 124 F6
Masira, Gulf of Oman see Maṣīrah, Khalīj
Maṣīrah, Jazīrat i. Oman 109 I5
Maṣīrah, Khalīj b. Oman 109 I6
Masira Island Oman see Maṣīrah, Jazīrat
Masiwang r. Seram Indon. 83 D3
Masjed Soleymān Iran 110 C4
Mask, Lough l. Ireland 61 C4
Maskūtān Iran 111 E5
Maslovo Rus. Fed. 51 S3
Masoala, Tanjona c. Madag. 123 F5
Masohi Seram Indon. 83 D3
Mason MI U.S.A. 164 C2
Mason OH U.S.A. 164 C4
Mason TX U.S.A. 161 D6
Mason, Lake salt flat Australia 135 B6
Mason Bay N.Z. 139 A8
Mason City U.S.A. 160 E3
Masoni i. Indon. 83 C3
Masontown U.S.A. 164 F4
Masqaṭ Oman see Muscat
Masqaṭ reg. Oman see Muscat
'Masrūg well Oman 110 D6
Massa Italy 68 D2
Massachusetts state U.S.A. 165 I2
Massachusetts Bay U.S.A. 165 J2
Massadona U.S.A. 159 I1
Massafra Italy 68 G4
Massakory Chad 121 E3
Massa Marittimo Italy 68 D3
Massangena Moz. 123 D6
Massango Angola 123 B4
Massawa Eritrea 108 E6
Massawippi, Lac l. Canada 165 I1
Massena U.S.A. 165 H1
Massenya Chad 121 E3
Masset B.C. Canada 149 N5
Massieville U.S.A. 164 D4
Massif Central mts France 66 F4
Massilia France see Marseille
Massillon U.S.A. 164 E3
Massina Mali 120 C3
Massinga Moz. 125 L2
Massingir Moz. 125 K2
Massingir, Barragem de resr Moz. 125 K2
Masson Island Antarctica 188 F2
Mastchoh Tajik. 111 H2
Masterton N.Z. 139 E5
Masticho, Akra pt Voreio Aigaio Greece see Oura, Akrotirio
Mastung Pak. 100 F4
Mastūrah Saudi Arabia 108 E5
Masty Belarus 55 N10
Masuda Japan 91 C6
Masuho Japan 93 E3
Masuku Gabon see Franceville
Masulipatam India see Machilipatnam
Masulipatnam India see Machilipatnam
Masuna i. American Samoa see Tutuila
Masurai, Bukit mt. Indon. 84 C3
Masvingo Zimbabwe 123 D6
Masvingo prov. Zimbabwe 125 J1
Maswa Tanz. 122 D4
Maswaar i. Indon. 81 I7
Maşyāf Syria 107 C2
Mat, Nam r. Laos 86 D3
Mata Myanmar 86 B1
Matabeleland South prov. Zimbabwe 125 I1
Matachewan Canada 152 E5
Matachic Mex. 166 D2
Matad Dornod Mongolia 95 H2
Matadi Dem. Rep. Congo 123 B4
Matador U.S.A. 161 C5
Matagalpa Nicaragua 166 [inset] I6
Matagami Canada 152 F4
Matagami, Lac l. Canada 152 F4
Matagorda TX U.S.A. 167 F2
Matagorda Island U.S.A. 161 D6
Mataigou Ningxia China see Taole
Matak i. Indon. 84 D2
Matak Kazakh. 98 A2
Matakana Island N.Z. 139 F3
Matala Angola 123 B5
Maţāli', Jabal hill Saudi Arabia 113 F6
Matam Senegal 120 B3
Matamey Niger 120 D3
Matamoras U.S.A. 165 H3
Matamoros Coahuila Mex. 166 E3
Matamoros Tamaulipas Mex. 167 F3
Matana, Danau l. Indon. 83 B3
Matanal Point Phil. 82 C5
Matandu r. Tanz. 123 D4
Matane Canada 153 I4
Matanuska AK U.S.A. 149 J3
Matanzas Cuba 169 H4
Matapalo, Cabo c. Costa Rica 166 [inset] J7
Matapan, Cape pt Greece see Tainaro, Akrotirio
Matapédia, Lac l. Canada 153 I4
Maţār well Saudi Arabia 110 B5
Matara Sri Lanka 106 D5
Mataram Lombok Indon. 85 G5
Matarani Peru 176 D7
Mataranka Australia 134 F3
Matarape, Teluk b. Indon. 83 B3
Matarinao Bay Samar Phil. 82 D4
Mataripe Brazil 179 D1
Mataró Spain 67 H3
Matarombea r. Indon. 83 B3
Matasiri i. Indon. 85 F4
Matatiele S. Africa 125 I6
Matatila Reservoir India 104 D4
Mataura N.Z. 139 B8

▶Matā'utu Wallis and Futuna Is 133 I3
Capital of Wallis and Futuna Islands.

Mata-Utu Wallis and Futuna Is see Matā'utu
Matawai N.Z. 139 F4
Matay Kazakh. 102 E2
Matcha Tajik. see Mastchoh
Mat Con, Hon i. Vietnam 86 D3
Mategua Bol. 176 F6
Matehuala Mex. 161 C8
Matemanga Tanz. 123 D5
Matera Italy 68 G4
Mateur Tunisia 68 C6
Mathaji India 104 B4
Matheson Canada 152 E4
Mathews U.S.A. 165 G5
Mathis U.S.A. 161 D6
Mathoura Australia 138 B5
Mathura India 104 D4
Mati Mindanao Phil. 82 D5
Matiali India 105 G4
Matias Cardoso Brazil 179 C1
Matías Romero Mex. 168 E5
Matimekosh Canada 153 I3
Matin India 105 E5
Matina Costa Rica 166 [inset] J7
Matinenda Lake Canada 152 E5
Matizi China 96 D1
Matla r. India 105 G5
Matlabas r. S. Africa 125 H2
Matli Pak. 111 H5
Matlock U.K. 59 F5
Mato, Cerro mt. Venez. 176 E2
Matobo Hills Zimbabwe 123 C6
Mato Grosso Brazil 176 G7
Mato Grosso state Brazil 179 A1
Matopo Hills Zimbabwe see Matobo Hills
Matos Costa Brazil 179 A4
Matosinhos Port. 67 B3
Mato Verde Brazil 179 C1
Maṭraḥ Oman 110 E6
Matroosberg mt. S. Africa 124 D7
Matsesta Rus. Fed. 113 E2
Matsubara Japan 92 B4
Matsuda Japan 93 F3
Matsudai Japan 93 E1
Matsudo Japan 93 F3
Matsue Japan 91 D6
Matsuida Japan 93 E2
Matsukawa Nagano Japan 93 D2
Matsukawa Nagano Japan 93 D3
Matsumoto Japan 93 D2
Matsunoyama Japan 93 E1
Matsuo Japan 93 G3
Matsuoka Japan 92 C2
Matsusaka Japan 92 C4
Matsushiro Japan 93 E2
Matsu Tao i. Taiwan 97 I3
Matsuyama Japan 91 D6
Matsuzaki Japan 93 E4
Mattagami r. Canada 152 E4
Mattamuskeet, Lake U.S.A. 162 E5
Mattawa Canada 152 F5
Matterhorn mt. Italy/Switz. 68 B2
Matterhorn mt. U.S.A. 156 E4
Matthew Town Bahamas 169 J4

Maţţī, Sabkhat salt pan Saudi Arabia 110 D6
Mattō Japan 92 C2
Mattoon U.S.A. 160 F4
Matturai Sri Lanka see Matara
Matu Sarawak Malaysia 85 E2
Matuku i. Fiji 133 H3
Matumbo Angola 123 B5
Maturín Venez. 176 F2
Matusadona National Park Zimbabwe 123 C5
Matutuang i. Indon. 83 C1
Matutum, Mount vol. Phil. 82 D5
Matwabeng S. Africa 125 H5
Maty Island P.N.G. see Wuvulu Island
Mau India see Maunath Bhanjan
Maúa Moz. 123 D5
Maubeuge France 62 D4
Maubin Myanmar 86 A3
Ma-ubin Myanmar 86 B1
Maubourguet France 66 E5
Mauchline U.K. 60 E5
Maudaha India 104 E4
Maude Australia 137 D7
Maud Seamount sea feature S. Atlantic Ocean 184 I10
Mau-é-ele Moz. see Marão
Maués Brazil 177 G4
Maughold Head hd Isle of Man 58 C4
Maug Islands N. Mariana Is 81 L2
Maui i. U.S.A. 157 [inset]
Maukkadaw Myanmar 86 A2
Maulbronn Germany 63 I6
Maule r. Chile 178 B5
Maulvi Bazar Bangl. see Moulvibazar
Maumee U.S.A. 164 D3
Maumee Bay U.S.A. 164 D3
Maumere Flores Indon. 83 B5
Maumturk Mts hills Ireland 61 C4
Maun Botswana 123 C5
Mauna Kea vol. U.S.A. 157 [inset]
Mauna Loa vol. U.S.A. 157 [inset]
Maunath Bhanjan India 105 E4
Maunatlala Botswana 125 H2
Mauneluk r. AK U.S.A. 148 H2
Maungaturoto N.Z. 139 E3
Maungdaw Myanmar 86 A2
Maungmagan Islands Myanmar 87 B4
Maunoir, Lac l. N.W.T. Canada 149 P2
Maurepas, Lake U.S.A. 161 F6
Mauriac France 66 F4
Maurice country Indian Ocean see Mauritius
Maurice, Lake salt flat Australia 135 E7
Maurik Neth. 62 F3
Mauritania country Africa 120 B3
Mauritanie country Africa see Mauritania
Mauritius country Indian Ocean 185 L7
Maurs France 66 F4
Mauston U.S.A. 160 F3
Mava Dem. Rep. Congo 122 C3
Mavago Moz. 123 D5
Mavan, Kūh-e hill Iran 110 E3
Mavanza Moz. 125 L2
Mavinga Angola 123 C5
Mavrovo nat. park Macedonia 69 I4
Mavume Moz. 125 L2
Mavuya S. Africa 125 H6
Mawa, Bukit mt. Indon. 85 F2
Ma Wan i. H.K. China 97 [inset]
Māwān, Khashm hill Saudi Arabia 110 B6
Mawana India 104 D3
Mawanga Dem. Rep. Congo 123 B4
Ma Wang Dui tourist site China 97 G2
Mawasangka Sulawesi Indon. 83 B4
Mawei China 97 H3
Mawjib, Wādī al r. Jordan 107 B4
Mawkmai Myanmar 86 B2
Mawlaik Myanmar 86 A2
Mawlamyaing Myanmar 86 B3
Mawlamyine Myanmar see Mawlamyaing
Mawqaq Saudi Arabia 113 F6
Mawson research station Antarctica 188 E2
Mawson Coast Antarctica 188 E2
Mawson Escarpment Antarctica 188 E2
Mawson Peninsula Antarctica 188 H2
Maw Taung mt. Myanmar 87 B5
Mawza Yemen 108 F7
Maxán Arg. 178 C3
Maxcanú Mex. 167 H4
Maxhamish Lake Canada 150 F3
Maxia, Punta mt. Sardinia Italy 68 C5
Maxixe Moz. 125 L2
Maxmo Fin. 54 M5
May, Isle of i. U.K. 60 G4
Maya i. Indon. 85 E3
Maya r. Rus. Fed. 77 O3
Mayaguana i. Bahamas 163 F8
Mayaguana Passage Bahamas 163 F8
Mayagüez Puerto Rico 169 K5
Mayahi Niger 120 D3
Mayak Rus. Fed. 90 E2
Mayakovskiy, Qullai mt. Tajik. 111 H2
Mayakovskogo, Pik mt. Tajik. see Mayakovskiy, Qullai
Mayalibit, Teluk b. Papua Indon. 83 D3
Mayama Congo 122 B4
Maya Mountains Belize/Guat. 167 H5
Mayan Gansu China see Mayanhe
Mayang China 97 F3
Mayanhe Gansu China 94 F5
Mayar hill U.K. 60 F4
Maya-san hill Japan 92 B4
Maybeury U.S.A. 164 E5
Maybole U.K. 60 E5
Maych'ew Eth. 122 D2
Maydān Shahr Afgh. see Meydān Shahr
Maydh Somalia 108 G7
Maydos Turkey see Eceabat
Mayen Germany 63 H4
Mayenne France 66 D2
Mayenne r. France 66 D3
Mayer U.S.A. 159 G4
Mayêr Kangri mt. Xizang China 99 D6
Mayersville U.S.A. 161 F5
Mayerthorpe Canada 150 H4
Mayfield N.Z. 139 C6
Mayhan Mongolia see Sant
Mayhill NM U.S.A. 166 D1
Mayi He r. China 90 C3
Maykamys Kazakh. 98 B3
Maykop Rus. Fed. 113 F1
Maymanah Afgh. 111 G3
Mayna Respublika Khakasiya Rus. Fed. 76 K4
Mayna Ul'yanovskaya Oblast' Rus. Fed. 53 J5
Mayni India 106 B2
Maynooth Canada 165 G1
Mayo Y.T. Canada 149 N3
Mayo r. Mex. 166 C3
Mayo U.S.A. 163 D6
Mayo Alim Cameroon 120 E4
Mayoko Congo 122 B4
Mayo Lake Y.T. Canada 149 N3
Mayon vol. Luzon Phil. 82 C3
Mayor, Puig mt. Spain see Major, Puig
Mayor Island N.Z. 139 F3
Mayor Pablo Lagerenza Para. 178 D1

▶Mayotte terr. Africa 123 E5
French Departmental Collectivity.

Mayraira Point Luzon Phil. 82 C2
Mayskiy Amurskaya Oblast' Rus. Fed. 90 C1
Mayskiy Kabardino-Balkarskaya Respublika Rus. Fed. 113 G2
Mays Landing U.S.A. 165 H4
Mayson Lake Canada 151 J3
Maysville U.S.A. 164 D4
Maytag Xinjiang China see Dushanzi
Mayu i. Maluku Indon. 83 C2
Mayumba Gabon 122 B4
Mayum La pass Xizang China 99 C7
Mayuram India 106 C4
Mayville MI U.S.A. 164 D2
Mayville ND U.S.A. 160 D2
Mayville NY U.S.A. 164 F2
Mayville WI U.S.A. 164 A2
Mazabuka Zambia 123 C5
Mazaca Turkey see Kayseri
Mazagan Morocco see El Jadida
Mazapil Mex. 167 E3
Mazar Xinjiang China 99 B5
Mazar, Koh-i- mt. Afgh. 111 G3
Mazara, Val di valley Sicily Italy 68 E6
Mazara del Vallo Sicily Italy 68 E6
Mazār-e Sharīf Afgh. 111 G2
Mazārī' reg. U.A.E. 110 D6
Mazartag Xinjiang China 98 C5
Mazartag mt. Xinjiang China 98 B5
Mazatán Mex. 166 C2
Mazatenango Guat. 167 H6
Mazatlán Mex. 168 C4
Mazatzal Peak U.S.A. 159 H4
Mazdaj Iran 113 H4
Maze Japan 92 D3
Maze-gawa r. Japan 92 D3
Mažeikiai Lith. 55 M8
Mazhūr, 'Irq al des. Saudi Arabia 110 A5
Mazīm Oman 110 E6
Mazocahui Mex. 166 C2
Mazocruz Peru 176 E7
Mazomora Tanz. 123 D4
Mazong Shan mt. Gansu China 94 D3
Mazong Shan mts China 94 C3
Mazu Dao i. Taiwan see Matsu Tao
Mazunga Zimbabwe 123 C6
Mazyr Belarus 53 F5
Mazzouna Tunisia 68 C7

▶Mbabane Swaziland 125 J4
Capital of Swaziland.

Mbahiakro Côte d'Ivoire 120 C4
Mbaïki Cent. Afr. Rep. 122 B3
Mbakaou, Lac de l. Cameroon 120 E4
Mbala Zambia 123 D4
Mbale Uganda 122 D3
Mbalmayo Cameroon 120 E4
Mbam r. Cameroon 120 E4
Mbandaka Dem. Rep. Congo 122 B4
M'banza Congo Angola 123 B4
Mbarara Uganda 121 G5
Mbari r. Cent. Afr. Rep. 122 C3
Mbaswana S. Africa 125 K4
Mbemkuru r. Tanz. 123 D4
Mbeya Tanz. 123 D4
Mbinga Tanz. 123 D5
Mbini Equat. Guinea 120 D4
Mbizi Zimbabwe 123 D6
Mboki Cent. Afr. Rep. 122 C3
Mbomo Congo 122 B3
Mbouda Cameroon 120 E4
Mbour Senegal 120 B3
Mbout Mauritania 120 B3
Mbozi Tanz. 123 D4
Mbrès Cent. Afr. Rep. 122 B3
Mbuji-Mayi Dem. Rep. Congo 123 C4
Mbulu Tanz. 122 D4
Mburucuyá Arg. 178 E3
McAdam Canada 153 I5
McAlester U.S.A. 161 E5
McAlister mt. Australia 138 D5
McAllen U.S.A. 161 D7
McArthur r. Australia 136 B2
McArthur U.S.A. 164 D4
McArthur Mills Canada 165 G1
McBain U.S.A. 164 C1
McBride Canada 150 F4
McCall U.S.A. 156 D3
McCamey U.S.A. 161 C6
McCammon U.S.A. 156 E4
McCarthy AK U.S.A. 149 L3
McCauley Island B.C. Canada 149 O5
McClintock, Mount Antarctica 188 H1
McClintock Channel Canada 147 H2
McClintock Range hills Australia 134 D4
McClure, Lake U.S.A. 158 C3
McClure Strait Canada 146 G2
McClusky U.S.A. 160 C2
McComb U.S.A. 161 F6
McConaughy, Lake U.S.A. 160 C3
McConnell Range mts N.W.T. Canada 149 P2
McConnellsburg U.S.A. 165 G4
McConnelsville U.S.A. 164 E4
McCook U.S.A. 160 C3
McCormick U.S.A. 163 D5
McCrea r. Canada 150 H2
McCreary Canada 151 L5
McCullum, Mount Y.T. Canada 149 M2
McDame Canada 150 D3
McDermitt U.S.A. 156 D4
McDonald Islands Indian Ocean 185 M9
McDonald Peak U.S.A. 156 E3
McDonough U.S.A. 163 C5
McDougall AK U.S.A. 149 J3
McDougall's Bay S. Africa 124 C5
McDowell Peak U.S.A. 159 H5
McFarland U.S.A. 158 D4
McGill U.S.A. 159 F2
McGivney Canada 153 I5
McGrath AK U.S.A. 148 I3
McGrath MN U.S.A. 160 E2
McGraw U.S.A. 165 G2
McGregor r. Canada 150 F4
McGregor S. Africa 124 D7
McGregor, Lake Canada 150 H5
McGregor Range hills Australia 137 C5
McGuire, Mount U.S.A. 156 E3
Mchinga Tanz. 123 D4
Mchinji Malawi 123 D5
McIlwraith Range hills Australia 136 C2
McInnes Lake Canada 151 M4
McIntosh U.S.A. 160 C2
McKay Range hills Australia 134 C5
McKean i. Kiribati 133 I2
McKee U.S.A. 164 C5
McKenzie r. U.S.A. 156 C3
McKinlay r. Australia 136 C4

▶McKinley, Mount AK U.S.A. 149 J3
Highest mountain in North America.

McKinley Park AK U.S.A. 149 J3
McKinney U.S.A. 161 D5
McKittrick U.S.A. 158 D4
McLaughlin U.S.A. 160 C2
McLeansboro U.S.A. 160 F4
McLennan Canada 150 G4
McLeod r. Canada 150 H4
McLeod Bay Canada 151 I2
McLeod Lake Canada 150 F4
McLoughlin, Mount U.S.A. 156 C4
McMillan, Lake U.S.A. 161 B5
McMinnville OR U.S.A. 156 C3
McMinnville TN U.S.A. 162 C5
McMurdo research station Antarctica 188 H1
McMurdo Sound b. Antarctica 188 H1
McNary U.S.A. 159 I4
McNaughton Lake Canada see Kinbasket Lake
McPherson U.S.A. 160 D4
McQuesten r. Y.T. Canada 149 M3
McRae U.S.A. 163 D5
McTavish Arm b. Canada 150 G1
McVeytown U.S.A. 165 G3
McVicar Arm b. Canada 150 F1
Mdantsane S. Africa 125 H7
M'Daourouch Alg. 68 B6
M'Đrak Vietnam 87 E4
Mê, Hon i. Vietnam 86 D3
Mead, Lake resr U.S.A. 159 F3
Meade U.S.A. 161 C4
Meade r. U.S.A. 146 C2
Meade r. AK U.S.A. 148 H1
Meade r. AK U.S.A. 148 H1
Meadow Australia 135 A6
Meadow SD U.S.A. 160 C2
Meadow UT U.S.A. 159 G2
Meadow Lake Canada 151 I4
Meadville MS U.S.A. 161 F6
Meadville PA U.S.A. 164 E3
Meaford Canada 164 E1
Meaken-dake vol. Japan 90 G4
Mealhada Port. 67 B3
Mealy Mountains Canada 153 K3
Meandarra Australia 138 D1
Meander River Canada 150 G3
Meares i. Indon. 83 C1
Meaux France 62 C6
Mebulu, Tanjung pt Indon. 85 F5
Mecca Saudi Arabia 108 E5
Mecca CA U.S.A. 158 E5
Mecca OH U.S.A. 164 E3
Mechanic Falls U.S.A. 165 J1
Mechanicsville U.S.A. 165 G5
Mechelen Belgium 62 E3
Mechelen Neth. 62 F4
Mecherchar i. Palau see Eil Malk
Mecheria Alg. 64 D5
Mechernich Germany 62 G4
Mechigmen Rus. Fed. 148 D2
Mecitözü Turkey 112 D2
Meckenheim Germany 62 H4
Mecklenburger Bucht b. Germany 57 M3
Mecklenburg-Vorpommern land Germany 63 M1
Mecklenburg - West Pomerania land Germany see Mecklenburg-Vorpommern
Meda r. Australia 134 C4
Meda Port. 67 C3
Medak India 106 C2
Medan Sumatera Indon. 84 B2
Medang i. Indon. 85 G5
Medanosa, Punta pt Arg. 178 C7
Médanos de Coro, Parque Nacional nat. park Venez. 176 E1
Medawachchiya Sri Lanka 106 D4
Médéa Alg. 67 H5
Medebach Germany 63 I3
Medellín Col. 176 C2
Meden r. U.K. 58 G5
Medenine Tunisia 64 G5
Mederdra Mauritania 120 B3
Medford NY U.S.A. 165 I3
Medford OK U.S.A. 161 D4
Medford OR U.S.A. 156 C4
Medford WI U.S.A. 160 F2
Medfra AK U.S.A. 148 I3
Medgidia Romania 69 M2
Media U.S.A. 165 H4
Mediaş Romania 69 K1
Medicine Bow r. U.S.A. 156 G4
Medicine Bow Mountains U.S.A. 156 G4
Medicine Bow Peak U.S.A. 156 G4
Medicine Hat Canada 151 I5
Medicine Lake U.S.A. 156 G2
Medicine Lodge U.S.A. 161 D4
Medina Brazil 179 C2
Medina Saudi Arabia 108 E5
Medina ND U.S.A. 160 D2
Medina NY U.S.A. 165 F2
Medina OH U.S.A. 164 E3
Medinaceli Spain 67 E3
Medina del Campo Spain 67 D3
Medina de Rioseco Spain 67 D3
Medina Lake U.S.A. 161 D6
Medinipur India 105 F5
Mediolanum Italy see Milan
Mediterranean Sea 64 K5
Mednyy, Ostrov i. Rus. Fed. 186 H2
Médoc reg. France 66 D4
Mêdog Xizang China 99 F7
Medora U.S.A. 160 C2
Medstead Canada 151 I4
Medu Kongkar Xizang China see Maizhokunggar
Meduro atoll Marshall Is see Majuro
Medvedevo Rus. Fed. 52 J4
Medveditsa r. Rus. Fed. 53 I6
Medvednica mts Croatia 68 F2
Medvezh'i, Ostrova is Rus. Fed. 77 R2
Medvezh'ya vol. Rus. Fed. 90 H3
Medvezh'ya, Gora mt. Rus. Fed. 90 E3
Medvezh'yegorsk Rus. Fed. 52 G3
Medway r. U.K. 59 H7
Meekatharra Australia 135 B6
Meeker CO U.S.A. 159 J1
Meeker OH U.S.A. 164 D3
Meelpaeg Reservoir Canada 153 K4
Meemu Atoll Maldives see Mulaku Atoll
Meerane Germany 63 M4
Meerlo Neth. 62 G3
Meerut India 104 D3
Mega i. Indon. 84 C3
Mega Escarpment Eth./Kenya 122 D3
Megalopoli Greece 69 J6
Megamo Indon. 81 I7
Mégantic, Lac l. Canada 153 H5
Megara Greece 69 J5
Megezez mt. Eth. 122 D3

▶Meghalaya state India 105 G4
Highest mean annual rainfall in the world.

Meghasani mt. India 105 F5
Meghri Armenia 113 G3
Megin Turkm. 110 E2
Megisti i. Greece 69 M6
Megri Armenia see Meghri
Mehamn Norway 54 O1
Mehar Pak. 111 G5
Meharry, Mount Australia 135 B5
Mehbubnagar India see Mahbubnagar
Mehdia Tunisia see Mahdia
Meherpur Bangl. 105 G5
Meherrin U.S.A. 165 F5
Meherrin r. U.S.A. 165 G5
Mehlville U.S.A. 160 F4
Mehrakān salt marsh Iran 110 D5
Mehrān Hormozgan Iran 110 D5
Mehrān Īlām Iran 110 B3
Mehren Germany 62 G4
Mehriz Iran 110 D4
Mehsana India see Mahesana
Mehtar Lām Afgh. 111 H3
Meia Ponte r. Brazil 179 A2
Meicheng China see Minqing
Meichuan Gansu China 94 F5
Meiganga Cameroon 121 E4
Meighen Island Canada 147 I2
Meigu China 96 D2
Meihekou China 90 B4
Meihō Japan 92 D3
Meikeng China 97 G3
Meikle r. Canada 150 G3
Meikle Says Law hill U.K. 60 G5
Meiktila Myanmar 86 A2
Meilin China see Ganxian
Meilleur r. Canada 150 E2
Meilu China 97 F4
Meine Germany 63 K2
Meinersen Germany 63 K2
Meiningen Germany 63 K4
Meishan Anhui China see Jinzhai
Meishan Sichuan China 96 D2
Meishan Shuiku resr China 97 G2
Meißen Germany 57 N5
Meister r. Y.T. Canada 149 O3
Meitan China 96 E3
Meiwa Gunma Japan 93 F2
Meiwa Mie Japan 92 C4
Meixi China 90 D3
Meixian China see Meizhou
Meixian Shaanxi China 95 F5
Meixing China see Xiaojin
Meizhou China 97 H3
Mej r. India 104 D4
Mejicana mt. Arg. 178 C3
Mejillones Chile 178 B2
Mékambo Gabon 122 B3
Mek'elē Eth. 122 D2
Mekelle Eth. see Mek'elē
Mékhé Senegal 120 B3
Mekhtar Pak. 111 H4
Meknassy Tunisia 68 C7
Meknès Morocco 64 C5
Mekong r. Asia 86 D4
also known as Ménam Khong (Laos/Thailand)
Mekong, Mouths of the Vietnam 87 D5
Mekoryuk AK U.S.A. 148 F3
Melaka Malaysia 84 C2
Melaka state Malaysia 84 C2
Melalap Sabah Malaysia 85 F1
Melalo, Tanjung pt Indon. 84 D3
Melanau, Gunung hill Indon. 87 E7
Melanesia is Pacific Ocean 186 G6
Melanesian Basin sea feature Pacific Ocean 186 G5
Melawi r. Indon. 85 E2

▶Melbourne Australia 138 B6
Capital of Victoria. 2nd most populous city in Oceania.

Melbourne U.S.A. 163 D6
Melby U.K. 60 [inset]
Melchor de Mencos Guat. 167 H5
Melchor Ocampo Mex. 167 E3
Meldorf Germany 57 L3

▶Melekeok Palau 82 [inset]
Capital of Palau.

Melekess Rus. Fed. see Dimitrovgrad
Melenki Rus. Fed. 53 I5
Melet Turkey see Mesudiye
Mélèzes, Rivière aux r. Canada 153 H2
Melfa U.S.A. 165 H5
Melfi Chad 121 E3
Melfi Italy 68 F4
Melfort Canada 151 J4
Melhus Norway 54 G5
Meliadine Lake Canada 151 M2
Meliau Kalimantan Indon. 85 E3
Melide Spain 67 C2
Melilis i. Indon. 83 B3

▶Melilla N. Africa 67 E6
Autonomous Community of Spain.

Melimoyu, Monte mt. Chile 178 B6
Melintang, Danau l. Indon. 85 G3
Meliskerke Neth. 62 D3
Melita Canada 151 K5
Melitene Turkey see Malatya
Melitopol' Ukr. 53 G7
Melk Austria 57 O6
Melka Guba Eth. 122 D3
Melksham U.K. 59 E7
Mellakoski Fin. 54 N3
Mellansel Sweden 54 K5
Melle Germany 63 I2
Mellerud Sweden 55 H7
Mellette U.S.A. 160 D2
Mellid Spain see Melide
Mellilia N. Africa see Melilla
Mellor Glacier Antarctica 188 E2
Mellrichstadt Germany 63 K4
Mellum i. Germany 63 I1
Melmoth S. Africa 125 J5
Mel'nichoye Rus. Fed. 90 D3
Melo Uruguay 178 F4
Meloco Moz. 123 D5
Melolo Sumba Indon. 83 B5
Melozitna r. AK U.S.A. 148 I2
Melrhir, Chott salt l. Alg. 64 F5
Melrose Australia 135 C6
Melrose U.K. 60 G5
Melrose U.S.A. 160 E2
Melsungen Germany 63 J3
Melta, Mount Malaysia see Tawai, Bukit
Melton Australia 138 B6
Melton Mowbray U.K. 59 G6
Meluan Sarawak Malaysia 85 E2
Melun France 66 F2
Melville Canada 151 K5
Melville, Cape Australia 136 D2
Melville, Cape Phil. 82 B5
Melville, Lake Canada 153 K3
Melville Bugt b. Greenland see Qimusseriarsuaq
Melville Hills Nunavut Canada 149 Q1
Melville Island Australia 134 E2
Melville Island Canada 147 H2
Melville Peninsula Canada 147 J3
Melvin U.S.A. 164 A3
Melvin, Lough l. Ireland/U.K. 61 D3
Mêmar Co salt l. China 99 C6
Memba Moz. 123 E5
Memberamo r. Indon. 81 J7
Memboro Sumba Indon. 83 A5
Memel Lith. see Klaipėda
Memel S. Africa 125 I4
Memmelsdorf Germany 63 K5
Memmingen Germany 57 M7
Mempawah Kalimantan Indon. 85 E2
Memphis tourist site Egypt 112 C5
Memphis MI U.S.A. 164 D2
Memphis TN U.S.A. 161 F5
Memphis TX U.S.A. 161 C5
Memphrémagog, Lac l. Canada 165 I1
Mena Timor Indon. 83 C5
Mena Ukr. 53 G6
Mena U.S.A. 161 E5
Ménaka Mali 120 D3
Menanga Maluku Indon. 83 C3
Menard U.S.A. 161 D6
Menasha U.S.A. 164 A1
Mendanau i. Indon. 84 D3
Mendanha Brazil 179 C2
Mendarik i. Indon. 84 D2
Mendawai Kalimantan Indon. 85 F3
Mendawai r. Indon. 85 F3
Mende France 66 F4
Mendefera Eritrea 108 E7
Mendeleyev Ridge sea feature Arctic Ocean 189 B1
Mendeleyevsk Rus. Fed. 52 L5
Mendenhall U.S.A. 161 F6
Mendenhall, Cape AK U.S.A. 148 F4
Mendenhall Glacier AK U.S.A. 149 N4
Méndez Tamaulipas Mex. 167 F3
Mendez-Nuñez Luzon Phil. 82 C3
Mendī Eth. 122 D3
Mendi P.N.G. 81 K8
Mendip Hills U.K. 59 E7
Mendocino U.S.A. 158 B2
Mendocino, Cape U.S.A. 158 A1
Mendocino, Lake U.S.A. 158 B2
Mendooran Australia 138 D3
Mendota CA U.S.A. 158 C3
Mendota IL U.S.A. 160 F3
Mendoza Arg. 178 C4
Menemen Turkey 69 L5
Menengiyn Tal plain Mongolia 95 H2
Ménerville Alg. see Thenia
Mengalum i. Malaysia 85 F1
Mengba Gansu China 95 F5
Mengban China 96 D4
Mengcheng China 97 H1
Menggala Sumatera Indon. 84 D4
Menghai China 96 D4
Mengjin China 97 G1
Mengkatip Kalimantan Indon. 85 F3
Mengkiang r. Indon. 85 E2
Mengkoka, Gunung mt. Indon. 83 B3
Mengla China 96 D4
Menglang China see Lancang
Menglie China see Jiangcheng
Mengxian Henan China see Mengzhou
Mengyang China see Mingshan
Mengyin Shandong China 95 I5
Mengzhou Henan China 95 H5
Mengzi China 96 D4
Menihek Canada 153 I3
Menihek Lakes Canada 153 I3
Menindee Australia 137 C7
Menindee, Lake Australia 137 C7
Ménistouc, Lac l. Canada 153 I3
Menkere Rus. Fed. 77 N3
Mennecy France 62 C6
Menominee U.S.A. 164 B1
Menomonee Falls U.S.A. 164 A2
Menomonie U.S.A. 160 F2
Menongue Angola 123 B5
Menorca i. Spain see Minorca
Mensalong Kalimantan Indon. 85 G2
Mentakab Malaysia 84 C2
Mentarang r. Indon. 85 G2
Mentasta Lake AK U.S.A. 149 L3
Mentasta Mountains AK U.S.A. 149 K3
Mentawai, Kepulauan is Indon. 84 B3
Mentawai, Selat sea chan. Indon. 84 C3
Mentaya r. Indon. 85 F3
Menteroda Germany 63 K3
Mentmore U.S.A. 159 I4
Mentok Indon. 84 D3
Menton France 66 H5
Mentone U.S.A. 161 C6
Mentuba r. Indon. 85 F3
Menuf Egypt see Minūf
Menukung Kalimantan Indon. 85 F3
Menuma Japan 93 F2
Menunu Sulawesi Indon. 83 B2
Menyapa, Gunung mt. Indon. 85 G2
Menyuan Qinghai China 94 E4
Menza Rus. Fed. 95 G1
Menza r. Rus. Fed. 95 G1
Menzel Bourguiba Tunisia 68 C6
Menzelet Barajı resr Turkey 112 E3
Menzelinsk Rus. Fed. 51 Q4
Menzel Temime Tunisia 68 D6
Menzies Australia 135 C7
Menzies, Mount Antarctica 188 E2
Meobbaai b. Namibia 124 B3
Meoqui Mex. 166 D2
Meppel Neth. 62 G2
Meppen Germany 63 H2
Mepuze Moz. 125 K2
Meqheleng S. Africa 125 H5
Mequon U.S.A. 164 B2
Merah Kalimantan Indon. 85 G2
Merak Jawa Indon. 84 D4
Meråker Norway 54 G5
Merano Italy 68 D1
Merapi, Gunung vol. Jawa Indon. 85 E4
Meratswe r. Botswana 124 G2
Meratus, Pegunungan mts Indon. 85 F3
Merauke Indon. 81 K8
Merbau Sumatera Indon. 84 C2
Merca Somalia see Marka
Mercantour, Parc National du nat. park France 66 H4
Merced U.S.A. 158 C3
Merced r. U.S.A. 158 C3
Mercedes Arg. 178 E3
Mercedes Uruguay 178 E4
Mercer ME U.S.A. 165 K1
Mercer PA U.S.A. 164 E3
Mercer WI U.S.A. 160 F2
Mercês Brazil 179 C3
Mercury Islands N.Z. 139 E3
Mercy, Cape Canada 147 L3
Merdenik Turkey see Göle
Mere Belgium 62 D4
Mere U.K. 59 E7
Meredith U.S.A. 165 J2
Meredith, Lake U.S.A. 161 C5
Merefa Ukr. 53 H6
Merga Oasis Sudan 108 C6
Mergui Myanmar see Myeik
Mergui Archipelago is Myanmar 87 B5
Meriç r. Turkey 69 L4
also known as Evros (Greece/Turkey), Marica (Bulgaria), Maritsa (Bulgaria)
Mérida Mex. 167 H4
Mérida Spain 67 C4
Mérida Venez. 176 D2
Mérida, Cordillera de mts Venez. 176 D2
Meriden U.S.A. 165 I3
Meridian MS U.S.A. 161 F5
Meridian TX U.S.A. 161 D6
Mérignac France 66 D4
Merijärvi Fin. 54 N4
Merikarvia Fin. 55 L6
Merimbula Australia 138 D6
Merín, Laguna l. Brazil/Uruguay see Mirim, Lagoa
Meringur Australia 137 C7
Merir i. Palau 81 I6
Merit Sarawak Malaysia 85 F2
Merjayoun Lebanon see Marjayoûn
Merkel U.S.A. 161 C5
Merluna Australia 136 C2
Mermaid Reef Australia 134 B4
Meron, Har mt. Israel 107 B3
Merowe Sudan 108 D6
Mêrqung Co l. China 105 F3
Merredin Australia 135 B7
Merrick hill U.K. 60 E5
Merrickville Canada 165 H1
Merrill MI U.S.A. 164 C2
Merrill WI U.S.A. 160 F2
Merrill, Mount Canada 150 E2
Merrillville U.S.A. 164 B3
Merriman U.S.A. 160 C3
Merritt Canada 150 F5
Merritt Island U.S.A. 163 D6
Merriwa Australia 138 E4
Merrygoen Australia 138 D3
Mersa Fatma Eritrea 108 F7
Mersa Maţrûḥ Egypt see Marsá Maţrūḥ
Mersch Lux. 62 G5
Merseburg (Saale) Germany 63 L3
Mersey est. U.K. 58 E5
Mersin Turkey 107 B1
Mersin prov. Turkey 107 A1
Mersing Malaysia 84 C2
Mersing, Bukit mt. Malaysia 85 F2
Mērsrags Latvia 55 M8
Merta India 104 C4
Merthyr Tydfil U.K. 59 D7
Mértola Port. 67 C5
Mertz Glacier Antarctica 188 G2
Mertz Glacier Tongue Antarctica 188 G2
Mertzon U.S.A. 161 C6
Méru France 62 C5

▶Meru vol. Tanz. 122 D4
4th highest mountain, and highest active volcano, in Africa.

Meru Betiri, Taman Nasional nat. park Indon. 85 F5
Merui Pak. 111 F4
Merutai Sabah Malaysia 85 G1
Merv Turkm. see Mary
Merweville S. Africa 124 E7
Merzifon Turkey 112 D2
Merzig Germany 62 G5
Merz Peninsula Antarctica 188 L2
Mesa Halmahera Indon. 83 D2
Mesa AZ U.S.A. 159 H5
Mesa NM U.S.A. 157 G6
Mesabi Range hills U.S.A. 160 E2
Mesagne Italy 68 G4
Mesa Mountain hill AK U.S.A. 148 I3
Mesanak i. Indon. 84 D2
Mesa Negra mt. U.S.A. 159 J4
Mesara, Ormos b. Kriti Greece see Kolpos Messaras

Mesara, Ormos b. Kriti Greece see Kolpos Messaras
Mesa Verde National Park U.S.A. 159 I3
Mescalero Apache Indian Reservation res. NM U.S.A. 166 D1
Meschede Germany 63 I3
Mese Myanmar 86 B3
Meselefors Sweden 54 J4
Mesgouez, Lac Canada 152 G4
Meshed Iran see Mashhad
Meshkān Iran 110 E2
Meshra'er Req Sudan 108 C8
Mesick U.S.A. 164 C1
Mesimeri Greece 69 J4
Mesolongi Greece 69 I5
Mesolóngion Greece see Mesolongi
Mesopotamia reg. Iraq 113 F4
Mesquita Brazil 179 C2
Mesquite NV U.S.A. 159 F3
Mesquite TX U.S.A. 161 D5
Mesquite Lake U.S.A. 159 F4
Messaad Alg. 64 E5
Messana Sicily Italy see Messina
Messina Sicily Italy 68 F5
Messina, Strait of Italy 68 F5
Messina, Stretta di Italy see Messina, Strait of
Messini Greece 69 J6
Messiniakos Kolpos b. Greece 69 J6
Mesta r. Bulg. 69 K4
Mesta r. Greece see Nestos
Mesta, Akrotirio pt Greece 69 K5
Mestghanem Alg. see Mostaganem
Mestlin Germany 63 L1
Meston, Akra pt Voreio Aigaio Greece see Mesta, Akrotirio
Mestre Italy 68 E2
Mesudiye Turkey 112 E2
Mesuji r. Indon. 84 D4
Meta r. Col./Venez. 176 E2
Métabetchouan Canada 153 H4
Meta Incognita Peninsula Canada 147 L3
Metairie U.S.A. 161 F6
Metallifere, Colline mts Italy 68 D3
Metán Arg. 178 C3
Metangai Kalimantan Indon. 85 F3
Metapán El Salvador 167 H6
Meteghan Canada 153 I5
Meteor Depth sea feature S. Atlantic Ocean 184 G9
Methoni Greece 69 I6
Methuen U.S.A. 165 J2
Methven U.K. 60 F4
Metionga Lake Canada 152 C4
Metković Croatia 68 G3
Metlaoui Tunisia 64 F5
Metoro Moz. 123 D5
Metro Sumatera Indon. 84 D4
Metropolis U.S.A. 161 F4
Metsada tourist site Israel see Masada
Metter U.S.A. 163 D5
Mettet Belgium 62 E4
Mettingen Germany 63 H2
Mettler U.S.A. 158 D4
Mettur India 106 C4
Metu Eth. 122 D3
Metz France 62 G5
Metz U.S.A. 164 C3
Meulaboh Sumatera Indon. 84 B1
Meureudu Sumatera Indon. 84 B1
Meuse r. Belgium/France 62 F3
also known as Maas (Netherlands)
Meuselwitz Germany 63 M3
Mevagissey U.K. 59 C8
Mêwa China 96 D1
Mexcala Mex. 167 F5
Mexia U.S.A. 161 D6
Mexiana, Ilha i. Brazil 177 I3
Mexicali Mex. 166 B1
Mexican Hat U.S.A. 159 I3
Mexicanos, Lago de los l. Mex. 166 D2
Mexican Water U.S.A. 159 I3

▶Mexico country Central America 166 B2
2nd most populous and 3rd largest country in North America.

México Mex. see Mexico City
México state Mex. 167 F5
Mexico ME U.S.A. 165 J1
Mexico MO U.S.A. 160 F4
Mexico NY U.S.A. 165 G2
Mexico, Gulf of Mex./U.S.A. 155 H6

▶Mexico City Mex. 168 E5
Capital of Mexico. Most populous city in North America, and 2nd in the world.

Meybod Iran 110 D3
Meydanī, Ra's-e pt Iran 110 E5
Meydān Shahr Afgh. 111 H3
Meyenburg Germany 63 M1
Meyersdale U.S.A. 164 F4
Meymeh Iran 110 C3
Meynypil'gyno Rus. Fed. 189 C2
Mezada tourist site Israel see Masada
Mezcalapa Mex. 167 G5
Mezcalapa r. Mex. 167 G5
Mezdra Bulg. 69 J3
Mezen' Rus. Fed. 52 J2
Mezen' r. Rus. Fed. 52 J2
Mézenc, Mont mt. France 66 G4
Mezenskaya Guba b. Rus. Fed. 52 I2
Mezhdurechensk Kemerovskaya Oblast' Rus. Fed. 88 F2
Mezhdurechensk Respublika Komi Rus. Fed. 52 K3
Mezhdurechnye Rus. Fed. see Shali
Mezhdusharskiy, Ostrov i. Rus. Fed. 76 G2
Mezitli Turkey 107 B1
Mezőtúr Hungary 69 I1
Mezquital Mex. 166 D4
Mezquital r. Mex. 166 D4
Mezquitic Mex. 166 E4
Mežvidi Latvia 55 O8
Mhàil, Rubh' a' pt U.K. 60 C5
Mhangura Zimbabwe 123 D5
Mhlume Swaziland 125 J4
Mhow India 104 C5
Mi r. Myanmar 105 H5
Miahuatlán Mex. 168 E5
Miajadas Spain 67 D4
Miaméré Cent. Afr. Rep. 122 B3
Miami AZ U.S.A. 159 H5

▶Miami FL U.S.A. 163 D7
5th most populous city in North America.

Miami OK U.S.A. 161 E4
Miami Beach U.S.A. 163 D7
Miancaowan Qinghai China 94 D5
Mianchi Henan China 95 G5
Mīāndehī Iran 110 E3
Mīāndowāb Iran 110 B2
Miandrivazo Madag. 123 E5
Mianduhe Nei Mongol China 95 J1
Mīāneh Iran 110 B2
Miang, Phu mt. Thai. 86 C3
Miangas i. Phil. 82 D5
Miani India 111 I4
Miani Hor b. Pak. 111 G5
Mianjoi Afgh. 111 G3
Mianning China 96 D2
Mianwali Pak. 111 H3
Mianxian China 96 E1
Mianyang Hubei China see Xiantao
Mianyang Shaanxi China see Mianxian
Mianyang Sichuan China 96 E2
Mianzhu China 96 E2
Miaodao Liedao is China 95 J4
Miao'ergou Xinjiang China 98 C3
Miaoli Taiwan 97 I3
Miarinarivo Madag. 123 E5
Miarritze France see Biarritz
Miasa Japan 93 D2
Miass Rus. Fed. 76 H4
Miboro-ko l. Japan 92 C2
Mibu Japan 93 F2
Mibu-gawa r. Japan 93 D3
Mica Creek Canada 150 G4
Mica Mountain U.S.A. 159 H5
Micang Shan mts China 96 E1
Michalovce Slovakia 53 D6
Michel Canada 151 I4
Michelau in Oberfranken Germany 63 L4
Michelson, Mount AK U.S.A. 149 K1
Michelstadt Germany 63 J5
Michendorf Germany 63 N2
Micheng China see Midu
Michigan state U.S.A. 164 C2

▶Michigan, Lake U.S.A. 164 B2
3rd largest lake in North America, and 5th in the world.

Michigan City U.S.A. 164 B3
Michinberi India 106 D2
Michipicoten Bay Canada 152 D5
Michipicoten Island Canada 152 D5
Michipicoten River Canada 152 D5
Michoacán state Mex. 167 E5
Michurin Bulg. see Tsarevo
Michurinsk Rus. Fed. 53 I5
Mico r. Nicaragua 166 [inset] I6
Micronesia country N. Pacific Ocean see Micronesia, Federated States of
Micronesia is Pacific Ocean 186 F5
Micronesia, Federated States of country N. Pacific Ocean 186 G5
Midai i. Indon. 85 D2
Mid-Atlantic Ridge sea feature Atlantic Ocean 184 E4
Mid-Atlantic Ridge sea feature Atlantic Ocean 184 G8
Middelburg Neth. 62 D3
Middelburg E. Cape S. Africa 125 G6
Middelburg Mpumalanga S. Africa 125 I3
Middelfart Denmark 55 F9
Middelharnis Neth. 62 E3
Middelwit S. Africa 125 H3
Middle Alkali Lake U.S.A. 156 C4
Middle America Trench sea feature N. Pacific Ocean 187 N5
Middle Andaman i. India 87 A4
Middle Atlas mts Morocco see Moyen Atlas
Middle Bay Canada 153 K4
Middlebourne U.S.A. 164 E4
Middleburg U.S.A. 165 G3
Middleburgh U.S.A. 165 H2
Middlebury IN U.S.A. 164 C3
Middlebury VT U.S.A. 165 I1
Middle Caicos i. Turks and Caicos Is 163 G8
Middle Channel watercourse N.W.T. Canada 149 N1
Middle Concho r. U.S.A. 161 C6
Middle Congo country Africa see Congo
Middle Island Thai. see Tasai, Ko
Middle Loup r. U.S.A. 160 D3
Middlemarch N.Z. 139 C7
Middlemount Australia 136 E4
Middle River U.S.A. 165 G4
Middlesbrough U.K. 58 F4
Middle Strait India see Andaman Strait
Middleton Australia 136 C4
Middleton Canada 153 I5
Middleton Island atoll American Samoa see Rose Island
Middleton Island AK U.S.A. 149 K4
Middletown CA U.S.A. 158 B2
Middletown CT U.S.A. 165 I3
Middletown NY U.S.A. 165 H3
Middletown VA U.S.A. 165 F4
Midelt Morocco 64 D5
Midhurst U.K. 59 G8
Midi, Canal du France 66 F5
Mid-Indian Basin sea feature Indian Ocean 185 N6
Mid-Indian Ridge sea feature Indian Ocean 185 M7
Midland Canada 165 F1
Midland CA U.S.A. 159 F5
Midland IN U.S.A. 164 B4
Midland MI U.S.A. 164 C2
Midland SD U.S.A. 160 C2
Midland TX U.S.A. 161 C5
Midleton Ireland 61 D6
Midnapore India see Medinipur
Midnapur India see Medinipur
Midongy Atsimo Madag. 123 E6
Midori Japan 93 F3
Mid-Pacific Mountains sea feature N. Pacific Ocean 186 G4
Midu China 96 D3
Miðvágur Faroe Is 54 [inset]
Midway Oman see Thamarīt

▶Midway Islands terr. N. Pacific Ocean 186 I4
United States Unincorporated Territory.

Midway Islands AK U.S.A. 149 J1
Midway Well Australia 135 C5
Midwest U.S.A. 156 G4
Midwest City U.S.A. 161 D5
Midwoud Neth. 62 F2
Midyat Turkey 113 F3
Midye Turkey see Kıyıköy
Mid Yell U.K. 60 [inset]
Midzhur mt. Bulg./Serbia 112 A2
Mie pref. Japan 92 C4
Miehikkälä Fin. 55 O6
Miekojärvi l. Fin. 54 N3
Mielec Poland 53 D6
Mienhua Yü i. Taiwan 97 I3
Mieraslompolo Fin. 54 O2
Mierašluoppal Fin. see Mieraslompolo
Miercurea-Ciuc Romania 69 K1
Mieres Spain 67 D2
Mieres del Camín Spain see Mieres
Mī'ēso Eth. 122 E3
Mieste Germany 63 L2
Mifflinburg U.S.A. 165 G3
Mifflintown U.S.A. 165 G3
Migang Shan mt. Gansu/Ningxia China 94 F5
Migdol S. Africa 125 G4
Miging India 96 B2
Migriggyangzham Co l. Qinghai China 99 E6
Miguel Alemán, Presa resr Mex. 167 F5
Miguel Auza Mex. 161 C7
Miguel de la Borda Panama 166 [inset] J7
Miguel Hidalgo, Presa resr Mex. 166 C3
Mihalıççık Turkey 69 N5
Mihama Aichi Japan 92 C4
Mihama Fukui Japan 92 B3
Mihama Wakayama Japan 92 B5
Mihara Japan 91 D6
Mihara Hyōgo Japan 92 A4
Mihara-yama vol. Japan 93 F4
Mihintale Sri Lanka 106 D4
Mihmandar Turkey 107 B1
Mihō Japan 93 G3
Mijares r. Spain see Millárs
Mijdrecht Neth. 62 E2
Mikata Japan 92 B3
Mikata-ko l. Japan 92 B3
Mikawa Japan 92 C2
Mikawa-wan b. Japan 92 D4
Mikawa-wan Kokutei-kōen park Japan 92 D4
Mikhalkino Rus. Fed. 77 R3
Mikhaylov Rus. Fed. 53 H5
Mikhaylovgrad Bulg. see Montana
Mikhaylov Island Antarctica 188 E2
Mikhaylovka Amurskaya Oblast' Rus. Fed. 90 C2
Mikhaylovka Primorskiy Kray Rus. Fed. 90 D4
Mikhaylovka Tul'skaya Oblast' Rus. Fed. see Kimovsk
Mikhaylovka Volgogradskaya Oblast' Rus. Fed. 53 I6
Mikhaylovskiy Rus. Fed. 102 E1
Mikhaylovskoye Rus. Fed. see Shpakovskoye
Mikhrot Timna Israel 107 B5
Miki Japan 92 A4
Mikir Hills India 105 H4
Miki-zaki pt Japan 92 C5
Mikkabi Japan 92 D4
Mikkeli Fin. 55 O6
Mikkelin mlk Fin. 55 O6
Mikkwa r. Canada 150 H3
Míkonos i. Greece see Mykonos
Mikoyan Armenia see Yeghegnadzor
Mikulkin, Mys c. Rus. Fed. 52 J2
Mikumi National Park Tanz. 123 D4
Mikumo Japan 92 C4
Mikun' Rus. Fed. 52 K3
Mikuni Japan 92 C2
Mikuni-sanmyaku mts Japan 93 E2
Mikuni-yama mt. Japan 93 E3
Mikura-jima i. Japan 91 E6
Milaca U.S.A. 160 E2
Miladhunmadulu Atoll Maldives 106 B5
Miladummadulu Atoll Maldives see Miladhunmadulu Atoll
Milan Italy 68 C2
Milan MI U.S.A. 164 D2
Milan MO U.S.A. 160 E3
Milan OH U.S.A. 164 D3
Milange Moz. 123 D5
Milano Italy see Milan
Milas Turkey 69 L6
Milazzo Sicily Italy 68 F5
Milazzo, Capo di c. Sicily Italy 68 F5
Milbank U.S.A. 160 D2
Milbridge U.S.A. 162 H2
Milde r. Germany 63 L2
Mildenhall U.K. 59 H6
Mildura Australia 137 C7
Mile China 96 D3
Mileiz, Wâdi el watercourse Egypt see Mulayz, Wādī al
Miles Australia 138 E1
Miles City U.S.A. 156 G3
Milestone Ireland 61 D5
Miletto, Monte mt. Italy 68 F4
Mileura Australia 135 B6
Milford Ireland 61 E2
Milford DE U.S.A. 165 H4
Milford IL U.S.A. 164 B3
Milford MA U.S.A. 165 J2
Milford MI U.S.A. 164 D2
Milford NE U.S.A. 160 D3
Milford NH U.S.A. 165 J2
Milford PA U.S.A. 165 H3
Milford UT U.S.A. 159 G2
Milford VA U.S.A. 165 G4
Milford Haven U.K. 59 B7
Milford Sound N.Z. 139 A7
Milford Sound inlet N.Z. 139 A7
Milgarra Australia 136 C3
Milh, Bahr al l. Iraq see Razāzah, Buḥayrat ar
Miliana Alg. 67 H5
Milid Turkey see Malatya
Milikapiti Australia 134 E2
Miling Australia 135 B7
Milk r. U.S.A. 156 G2
Milk, Wadi el watercourse Sudan 108 D6
Mil'kovo Rus. Fed. 77 Q4
Millaa Millaa Australia 136 D3
Millárs r. Spain 67 F4
Millau France 66 F4
Millbrook Canada 165 F1
Mill Creek r. U.S.A. 158 B1
Milledgeville U.S.A. 163 D5
Mille Lacs lakes U.S.A. 160 E2
Mille Lacs, Lac des l. Canada 147 I5
Millen U.S.A. 163 D5
Millennium Island atoll Kiribati see Caroline Island
Miller U.S.A. 160 D2
Miller, Mount AK U.S.A. 149 L3
Miller Lake Canada 164 E1
Millerovo Rus. Fed. 53 I6
Millersburg OH U.S.A. 164 E3
Millersburg PA U.S.A. 165 G3
Millers Creek U.S.A. 164 D5
Millersville U.S.A. 165 G4
Millerton Lake U.S.A. 158 D3
Millet Canada 150 H4
Milleur Point U.K. 60 D5
Mill Hall U.S.A. 165 G3
Millicent Australia 137 C8
Millington MI U.S.A. 164 D2
Millington TN U.S.A. 161 F5
Millinocket U.S.A. 162 G2
Mill Island Canada 147 K3
Millmerran Australia 138 E1
Millom U.K. 58 D4
Millport U.K. 60 E5
Millsboro U.S.A. 165 H4
Mills Creek watercourse Australia 136 C4
Mills Lake Canada 150 G2
Millstone KY U.S.A. 164 D5
Millstone WV U.S.A. 164 E4
Millstream-Chichester National Park Australia 134 B5
Millthorpe Australia 138 D4
Milltown Canada 153 I5
Milltown U.S.A. 156 E3
Milltown Malbay Ireland 61 C5
Millungera Australia 136 C3
Millville U.S.A. 165 H4
Millwood U.S.A. 164 B5
Millwood Lake U.S.A. 161 E5
Milly Milly Australia 135 B6
Milne Land i. Greenland see Ilimananngip Nunaa
Milner U.S.A. 159 J1
Milo r. Guinea 120 C3
Milogradovo Rus. Fed. 90 D4
Miloli'i U.S.A. 157 [inset]
Milos i. Greece 69 K6
Milparinka Australia 137 C6
Milpitas U.S.A. 158 C3
Milroy U.S.A. 165 G3
Milton N.Z. 139 B8
Milton DE U.S.A. 165 H4
Milton FL U.S.A. 167 I2
Milton NH U.S.A. 165 J2
Milton WV U.S.A. 164 D4
Milton Keynes U.K. 59 G6
Miluo China 97 G2
Milverton Canada 164 E2
Milwaukee U.S.A. 164 B2

▶Milwaukee Deep sea feature Caribbean Sea 184 D4
Deepest point in the Puerto Rico Trench and in the Atlantic.

Milybulabk Kazakh. 98 A2
Mimbres watercourse U.S.A. 159 J5
Mimili Australia 135 F6
Mimisal India 106 C4
Mimizan France 66 D4
Mimongo Gabon 122 B4
Mimosa Rocks National Park Australia 138 E6
Mina Mex. 167 E3
Mina U.S.A. 158 D2
Mīnāb Iran 110 E5
Minaçu Brazil 179 A1
Minahasa, Semenanjung pen. Indon. 83 B2
Minahassa Peninsula Indon. see Minahasa, Semenanjung
Minakami Japan 93 E2
Minaker Canada see Prophet River
Mīnākh Syria 107 C1
Minaki Canada 151 M5
Minakuchi Japan 92 C4
Minami Japan 92 C3
Minamia Australia 134 F3
Minami-arupusu Kokuritsu-kōen nat. park Japan 93 E3
Minamiashigara Japan 93 F3
Minami-Bōsō Kokutei-kōen park Japan 93 F4
Minamichita Japan 92 C4
Minami-Daitō-jima i. Japan 89 O7
Minami-gawa r. Japan 92 B3
Minami-Iō-jima vol. Japan 81 K2
Minamiizu Japan 93 E4
Minami-kawara Japan 93 F2
Minamimaki Japan 93 E2
Minamiminowa Japan 93 D3
Minaminasu Japan 93 G2
Minamishinano Japan 93 D3
Min'an China see Longshan
Minano Japan 93 F2
Minaret of Jam tourist site Afgh. 111 G3
Minas Sumatera Indon. 84 C2
Minas Uruguay 178 E4
Minas, Sierra de las mts Guat. 167 H6
Minas de Matahambre Cuba 163 D8
Minas Gerais state Brazil 179 B2
Minas Novas Brazil 179 C2
Minatitlán Mex. 168 F5
Minbu Myanmar 86 A2
Minbya Myanmar 86 A2
Minchinmávida vol. Chile 178 B6
Minchumina, Lake AK U.S.A. 148 I3
Mindanao i. Phil. 82 D5
Mindanao r. Mindanao Phil. 82 D5
Mindanao Trench sea feature N. Pacific Ocean see Philippine Trench
Mindelo Cape Verde 120 [inset]
Minden Canada 165 F1
Minden Germany 63 I2
Minden LA U.S.A. 161 E5
Minden NE U.S.A. 154 H3
Minden NV U.S.A. 158 D2
Mindon Myanmar 86 A3
Mindoro i. Phil. 82 C3
Mindoro Strait Phil. 82 B3
Mindouli Congo 122 B4
Mine Head hd Ireland 61 E6
Minehead U.K. 59 D7
Mineola U.S.A. 165 I3
Mineola TX U.S.A. 167 G1
Miner r. N.W.T. Canada 149 O1
Miner r. Y.T. Canada 149 M2
Mineral U.S.A. 165 G4
Mineral'nyye Vody Rus. Fed. 113 F1
Mineral Wells U.S.A. 161 D5
Mineralwells U.S.A. 164 E4
Minersville PA U.S.A. 165 G3
Minersville UT U.S.A. 159 G2
Minerva U.S.A. 164 E3
Minerva Reefs Fiji 133 I4
Mineyama Japan 92 B3
Minfeng Xinjiang China 99 C5
Minga Dem. Rep. Congo 123 C5
Mingäçevir Azer. 113 G2
Mingäçevir Su Anbarı resr Azer. 113 G2
Mingala Cent. Afr. Rep. 122 C3
Mingan, Îles de is Canada 153 J4
Mingan Archipelago National Park Reserve Canada see L'Archipélago de Mingan, Réserve du Parc National de
Mingbuloq Uzbek. 102 B3
Mingechaur Azer. see Mingäçevir
Mingechaurskoye Vodokhranilishche resr Azer. see Mingäçevir Su Anbarı
Mingenew Australia 135 A7
Mingfeng China see Yuan'an
Minggang China 97 G1
Mingguang China 97 H1
Mingin Range mts Myanmar 86 A2
Ming-Kush Kyrg. 98 A4
Minglanilla Spain 67 F4
Mingoyo Tanz. 123 D5
Mingshan China 96 D2
Mingshui Gansu China 94 D3
Mingshui Heilong. China 90 B3
Mingteke Xinjiang China 99 A5
Mingulay i. U.K. 60 B4
Mingxi China 97 H3
Mingzhou Hebei China see Weixian
Mingzhou Shaanxi China see Suide
Minhe China see Jinxian
Minhla Magwe Myanmar 86 A3
Minhla Pegu Myanmar 86 A3
Minho r. Port./Spain see Miño
Minicoy atoll India 106 B4
Minigwal, Lake salt flat Australia 135 C7
Minilya Australia 135 A5
Minilya r. Australia 135 A5
Minipi Lake Canada 153 J3
Miniss Lake Canada 151 N5
Minitonas Canada 151 K4
Minjian China see Mabian
Min Jiang r. Sichuan China 96 E2
Min Jiang r. China 97 H3
Minkébé, Parc National de nat. park Gabon 122 B3
Minle Gansu China 94 E4
Minna Nigeria 120 D4
Minna Bluff pt Antarctica 188 H1
Minne Sweden 54 I5
Minneapolis KS U.S.A. 160 D4
Minneapolis MN U.S.A. 160 E2
Minnedosa Canada 151 L5
Minnehaha Springs U.S.A. 164 F4
Minneola U.S.A. 161 C4
Minnesota r. U.S.A. 160 E2
Minnesota state U.S.A. 160 E2
Minnewaukan U.S.A. 160 D1
Minnitaki Lake Canada 151 N5
Mino Japan 92 C3
Miño r. Port./Spain 67 B3
also known as Minho
Minobu Japan 93 E3
Minobu-san mt. Japan 93 E3
Minobu-sanchi mts Japan 93 E4
Minokamo Japan 92 D3
Mino-Mikawa-kōgen reg. Japan 92 D3
Minoo Japan 92 B4
Minorca i. Spain 67 H3
Minori Japan 93 G2
Minot U.S.A. 160 C1
Minowa Japan 93 D3
Minqār, Ghadīr imp. l. Syria 107 C3
Minqin Gansu China 94 E4
Minqing China 97 H3
Minquan Henan China 95 H5
Min Shan mts China 96 D1
Minsin Myanmar 86 A1

▶Minsk Belarus 55 O10
Capital of Belarus.

Mińsk Mazowiecki Poland 57 R4
Minsterley U.K. 59 E6
Mintaka Pass China/Pak. 104 C1
Mintang Qinghai China 94 E5
Minto AK U.S.A. 149 J2
Minto, Lac l. Canada 152 G2
Minto, Mount Antarctica 188 H2
Minto Inlet Canada 146 G2
Minton Canada 151 J5
Mīnudasht Iran 110 D2
Minūf Egypt 112 C5
Minusinsk Rus. Fed. 88 G2
Minvoul Gabon 122 B3
Minxian Gansu China 94 F5
Minya Konka mt. China see Gongga Shan
Minywa Myanmar 86 A2
Minzong India 105 I4
Mio U.S.A. 164 C1
Miquan Xinjiang China 98 D4
Miquelon Canada 152 F4
Miquelon i. St Pierre and Miquelon 153 K5
Mirabad Afgh. 111 F4
Mirabela Brazil 179 B2
Mirador-Dos Lagunos-Río Azul, Parque Nacional nat. park Guat. 167 H5
Miraflores Mex. 166 C4
Mīrah, Wādī al watercourse Iraq/Saudi Arabia 113 F4
Miraí Brazil 179 C3
Miraj India 106 B2
Miramar Arg. 178 E5
Miramar, Lago l. Mex. 167 H5
Miramichi Canada 153 I5
Miramichi Bay Canada 153 I5
Mirampellou, Kolpos b. Greece 69 K7
Mirampelou, Kolpos b. Kriti Greece see Mirampellou, Kolpos
Miran Xinjiang China 98 E5
Miranda Brazil 178 E2
Miranda Moz. see Macaloge
Miranda U.S.A. 158 B1
Miranda, Lake salt flat Australia 135 C6
Miranda de Ebro Spain 67 E2
Mirandela Port. 67 C3
Mirandola Italy 68 D2
Mirante Brazil 179 C1
Mirante, Serra do hills Brazil 179 A3
Mirassol Brazil 179 A3
Mir-Bashir Azer. see Tärtär
Mirbāṭ Oman 109 H6
Mirboo North Australia 138 C7
Mirepoix France 66 E5
Mirgarh Pak. 111 I4
Mirgorod Ukr. see Myrhorod
Miri Sarawak Malaysia 85 F1
Miri mt. Pak. 111 F4
Mirialguda India 106 C2
Miri Hills India 105 H4
Mirim, Lagoa l. Brazil/Uruguay 178 F4
Mirim, Lagoa do l. Brazil 179 A5
Mirintu watercourse Australia 138 A2
Mirjan India 106 B3
Mirny research station Antarctica 188 F2
Mirnyy Arkhangel'skaya Oblast' Rus. Fed. 52 I3
Mirnyy Respublika Sakha (Yakutiya) Rus. Fed. 77 M3
Mirond Lake Canada 151 K4
Mironovka Ukr. see Myronivka
Mirow Germany 63 M1
Mirpur Khas Pak. 111 H5
Mirpur Sakro Pak. 111 G5
Mirsali Xinjiang China 98 D4
Mirs Bay H.K. China 97 [inset]
Mirtoan Sea Greece see Myrtoo Pelagos
Mirtoö Pelagos sea Greece see Myrtoo Pelagos
Miryalaguda India see Mirialguda
Miryang S. Korea 91 C6
Mirzachirla Turkm. see Murzechirla
Mirzachul Uzbek. see Guliston
Mirzapur India 105 E4
Mirzawal India 104 C3
Misaka Japan 93 E3
Misaki Chiba Japan 93 G3
Misaki Ōsaka Japan 92 B4
Misakubo Japan 93 D3
Misalay Xinjiang China 99 C5
Misantla Mex. 167 F5
Misato Gunma Japan 93 E2
Misato Mie Japan 92 C4
Misato Nagano Japan 93 D2
Misato Saitama Japan 93 F2
Misato Saitama Japan 93 F3
Misato Wakayama Japan 92 B4
Misaw Lake Canada 151 K3
Miscou Island Canada 153 I5
Misehkow r. Canada 152 C4
Mīsh, Kūh-e hill Iran 110 E3
Misha India 87 A6
Mishāsh al Ashāwī well Saudi Arabia 110 C5
Mishāsh az Zuayyinī well Saudi Arabia 110 C5
Mishawaka U.S.A. 164 B3
Misheguk Mountain AK U.S.A. 148 G1
Mishicot U.S.A. 164 B1
Mishima Japan 93 E3
Mi-shima i. Japan 91 C6
Mishmi Hills India 105 H3
Mishvan' Rus. Fed. 52 L2
Misima Island P.N.G. 136 F1
Misis Dağ hills Turkey 107 B1
Miskin Oman 110 E6
Miskitos, Cayos is Nicaragua 166 [inset] J6
Miskitos, Costa de coastal area Nicaragua see Costa de Mosquitos
Miskolc Hungary 53 D6
Mismā, Tall al hill Jordan 107 C3
Misoöl i. Papua Indon. 83 D3
Misquah Hills U.S.A. 160 F2
Misr country Africa see Egypt
Misraç Turkey see Kurtalan
Miṣrātah Libya 121 E1
Missinaibi r. Canada 152 E4
Mission TX U.S.A. 167 F3
Mission Beach Australia 136 D3
Mission Viejo U.S.A. 158 E5
Missisa r. Canada 152 D3
Missisa Lake Canada 152 D3
Missisicabi r. Canada 152 F4
Mississauga Canada 164 F2
Mississinewa Lake U.S.A. 164 C3

▶Mississippi r. U.S.A. 161 F6
4th longest river in North America, and a major part of the longest (Mississippi-Missouri).

Mississippi state U.S.A. 161 F5
Mississippi Delta U.S.A. 161 F6
Mississippi Lake Canada 165 G1

▶Mississippi-Missouri r. U.S.A. 155 I4
Longest river in North America, and 4th in the world.

Mississippi Sound sea chan. U.S.A. 161 F6
Missolonghi Greece see Mesolongi
Missoula U.S.A. 156 E3

▶Missouri r. U.S.A. 160 F4
3rd longest river in North America, and a major part of the longest (Mississippi-Missouri).

Missouri state U.S.A. 160 E4
Mistanipisipou r. Canada 153 J4
Mistassibi r. Canada 147 K5
Mistassini r. Canada 153 G4
Mistassini, Lac l. Canada 152 G4
Mistastin Lake Canada 153 J3
Mistelbach Austria 57 P6
Mistinibi, Lac l. Canada 153 J2
Mistissini Canada 152 G4
Misty Fiords National Monument Wilderness nat. park U.S.A. 149 O5
Misugi Japan 92 C4
Misumba Dem. Rep. Congo 123 C4
Misurata Libya see Miṣrātah
Mita, Punta de pt Mex. 166 D4
Mitaka Japan 93 F3
Mitake Gifu Japan 92 D3
Mitake Nagano Japan 92 D3
Mitchell Australia 137 D5
Mitchell r. N.S.W. Australia 138 F2
Mitchell r. Qld Australia 136 C2

Mitchell r. Vic. Australia 138 C6
Mitchell Canada 164 E2
Mitchell IN U.S.A. 164 B4
Mitchell OR U.S.A. 156 C3
Mitchell SD U.S.A. 160 D3
Mitchell, Lake Australia 136 D3
Mitchell, Mount U.S.A. 162 D5
Mitchell and Alice Rivers National Park Australia 136 C2
Mitchell Island Cook Is see Nassau
Mitchell Island atoll Tuvalu see Nukulaelae
Mitchell Point Australia 134 E2
Mitchelstown Ireland 61 D5
Mīt Ghamr Egypt 112 C5
Mit Ghamr Egypt see Mīt Ghamr
Mithi Pak. 111 H5
Mithrau Pak. 111 H5
Mithri Pak. 111 G4
Miti i. Maluku Indon. 83 D2
Mitilíni Greece see Mytilini
Mitkof Island AK U.S.A. 149 N4
Mito Aichi Japan 92 D4
Mito Ibaraki Japan 93 G2
Mitole Tanz. 123 D4
Mitomi Japan 93 E3
Mitre mt. N.Z. 139 E5
Mitre Island Solomon Is 133 H3
Mitrofania Island AK U.S.A. 148 H5
Mitrofanovka Rus. Fed. 53 H6
Mitrovica Kosovo see Mitrovicë
Mitrovicë Kosovo 69 I3
Mitsinjo Madag. 123 E5
Mits'iwa Eritrea see Massawa
Mitsue Japan 92 C4
Mitsukaidō Japan 93 F2
Mitsumatarenge-dake mt. Japan 92 D2
Mitsutōge-yama mt. Japan 93 E3
Mitta Mitta Australia 138 C6
Mittellandkanal canal Germany 63 I2
Mitterteich Germany 63 M5
Mittimatalik Canada see Pond Inlet
Mittweida Germany 63 M4
Mitú Col. 176 D3
Mitumba, Chaîne des mts Dem. Rep. Congo 123 C5
Mitzic Gabon 122 B3
Miughalaigh i. U.K. see Mingulay
Miura Japan 93 F3
Miura-hantō pen. Japan 93 F3
Miwa Fukushima Japan 93 G1
Miwa Ibaraki Japan 93 G2
Miwa Kyōto Japan 92 B3
Mixian Henan China see Xinmi
Miya Japan 92 D2
Miyada Japan 93 D3
Miyagase-ko resr Japan 93 F3
Miyagawa Gifu Japan 92 D2
Miyagawa Mie Japan 92 C4
Miya-gawa r. Japan 92 C4
Miya-gawa r. Japan 92 D2
Miyake-jima i. Japan 93 F4
Miyako Japan 91 F5
Miyakonojō Japan 91 C7
Miyama Fukui Japan 92 C2
Miyama Gifu Japan 92 C3
Miyama Kyōto Japan 92 B3
Miyama Mie Japan 92 C4
Miyama Wakayama Japan 92 B5
Miyamae Japan 93 F3
Miyang China see Mile
Miyani India 104 B5
Miyazaki Fukui Japan 92 C3
Miyazaki Japan 91 C7
Miyazu Japan 92 B3
Miyazu-wan b. Japan 92 B3
Miyi China 96 D3
Miyoshi Aichi Japan 92 D3
Miyoshi Chiba Japan 93 F3
Miyoshi Japan 91 D6
Miyota Japan 93 E2
Miyun Beijing China 95 I3
Miyun Shuiku resr China 95 I3
Mīzāni Afgh. 111 G3
Mīzan Teferī Eth. 122 D3
Mizdah Libya 121 E1
Mizen Head hd Ireland 61 C6
Mizhhir"ya Ukr. 53 D6
Mizhi Shaanxi China 95 G4
Mizo Hills state India see Mizoram
Mizoram state India 105 H5
Mizpé Ramon Israel 107 B4
Mizugaki-yama mt. Japan 93 E3
Mizuhashi Japan 92 D2
Mizuho Kyōto Japan 92 B3
Mizuho Tōkyō Japan 93 F3
Mizunami Japan 92 D3
Mizuno-gawa r. Japan 93 F2
Mizusawa Japan 91 F5
Mjölby Sweden 55 I7
Mkata Tanz. 123 D4
Mkushi Zambia 123 C5
Mladá Boleslav Czech Rep. 57 O5
Mladenovac Serbia 69 I2
Mława Poland 57 R4
Mlilwane Nature Reserve Swaziland 125 J4
Mljet i. Croatia 68 G3
Mlungisi S. Africa 125 H6
Mmabatho S. Africa 125 G3
Mmamabula Botswana 125 H2
Mmathethe Botswana 125 G3
Mo Norway 55 D6
Moa i. Maluku Indon. 83 D5
Moab reg. Jordan 107 B4
Moab U.S.A. 159 I2
Moa Island Australia 136 C1
Moala i. Fiji 133 H3
Mo'alla Iran 110 D3
Moamba Moz. 125 K3
Moanda Gabon 122 B4
Moapa U.S.A. 159 F3
Moate Ireland 61 E4
Mobara Japan 93 G3
Mobārakeh Iran 110 C3
Mobayembongo Dem. Rep. Congo see Mobayi-Mbongo
Mobayi-Mbongo Dem. Rep. Congo 122 C3
Moberly U.S.A. 160 E4
Moberly Lake Canada 150 F4
Mobha India 104 C5
Mobile AL U.S.A. 161 F6
Mobile AZ U.S.A. 159 G5
Mobile Bay U.S.A. 161 F6
Mobile Point AL U.S.A. 167 I2
Moble watercourse Australia 138 B1
Mobo Masbate Phil. 82 C3
Mobridge U.S.A. 160 C2
Mobutu, Lake Dem. Rep. Congo/Uganda see Albert, Lake
Mobutu Sese Seko, Lake Dem. Rep. Congo/Uganda see Albert, Lake
Moca Geçidi pass Turkey 107 A1
Moçambique country Africa see Mozambique
Moçambique Moz. 123 E5
Moçâmedes Angola see Namibe
Môc Châu Vietnam 86 D2
Mocha Yemen 108 F7
Mocha, Isla i. Chile 178 B5
Mochicahui Mex. 166 C3
Mochirma, Parque Nacional nat. park Venez. 176 F1
Mochudi Botswana 125 H3
Mochudi admin. dist. Botswana see Kgatleng
Mocimboa da Praia Moz. 123 E5
Möckern Germany 63 L2
Möckmühl Germany 63 J5
Mockträsk Sweden 54 L4
Mocoa Col. 176 C3
Mococa Brazil 179 B3
Mocoduene Moz. 125 L2
Mocorito Mex. 166 D3
Moctezuma Chihuahua Mex. 166 D2
Moctezuma San Luis Potosí Mex. 168 D4
Moctezuma Sonora Mex. 166 C2
Mocuba Moz. 123 D5
Mocun China 97 G4
Modan Indon. 81 I7
Modane France 66 H4
Modder r. S. Africa 125 G5
Modena Italy 68 D2
Modena U.S.A. 159 G3
Modesto U.S.A. 158 C3
Modesto Lake U.S.A. 158 C3
Modimolle S. Africa 125 I3
Modot Mongolia see Tsenhermandal
Modung China 96 C2
Moe Australia 138 C7
Moel Sych hill U.K. 59 D6
Moelv Norway 55 G6
Moen Norway 54 K2
Moenkopi U.S.A. 159 H3
Moenkopi Wash r. U.S.A. 159 H4
Moeraki Point N.Z. 139 C7
Moero, Lake Dem. Rep. Congo/Zambia see Mweru, Lake
Moers Germany 62 G3
Moffat U.K. 60 F5
Moga India 104 C3

▶Mogadishu Somalia 122 E3
Capital of Somalia.

Mogador Morocco see Essaouira
Mogadore Reservoir U.S.A. 164 E3
Moganyaka S. Africa 125 I3
Mogao Ku Gansu China 98 F5
Mogaung Myanmar 86 B1
Mogdy Rus. Fed. 90 D2
Mögelin Germany 63 M2
Mogilev Belarus see Mahilyow
Mogilev Podol'skiy Ukr. see Mohyliv Podil's'kyy
Mogi-Mirim Brazil 179 B3
Mogiquiçaba Brazil 179 D2
Mogocha Rus. Fed. 89 L2
Mogod mts Tunisia 68 C6
Mogoditshane Botswana 125 G3
Mogollon Mountains U.S.A. 159 I5
Mogollon Plateau U.S.A. 159 H4
Mogontiacum Germany see Mainz
Mogoytuy Rus. Fed. 95 H1
Mogroum Chad 121 E3
Moguqi Nei Mongol China 95 J2
Mogwadi S. Africa 125 I2
Mogwase S. Africa 125 H3
Mogzon Rus. Fed. 89 K2
Mohács Hungary 68 H2
Mohaka r. N.Z. 139 F4
Mohala India 106 D1
Mohale Dam Lesotho 125 I5
Mohale's Hoek Lesotho 125 H6
Mohall U.S.A. 160 C1
Mohammad Iran 110 E3
Mohammadia Alg. 67 G6
Mohan r. India/Nepal 104 E3
Mohana India 104 D4
Mohave, Lake U.S.A. 159 F4
Mohawk r. U.S.A. 165 I2
Mohawk Mountains U.S.A. 159 G5
Mohenjo Daro tourist site Pak. 111 H5
Moher, Cliffs of Ireland 61 C5
Mohican, Cape AK U.S.A. 148 F3
Mohill Ireland 61 E4
Möhne r. Germany 63 H3
Möhnetalsperre resr Germany 63 I3
Mohon Peak U.S.A. 159 G4
Mohoro Tanz. 123 D4
Mohyliv Podil's'kyy Ukr. 53 E6
Moi Norway 55 E7
Moijabana Botswana 125 H2
Moincêr Xizang China 99 C7
Moinda Xizang China 99 E7
Moindawang Arun. Prad. India 99 E8
Moine Moz. 125 K3
Moinești Romania 69 L1
Mointy Kazakh. see Moyynty
Mo i Rana Norway 54 I3
Moirang India 96 B3
Mõisaküla Estonia 55 N7
Moisie Canada 153 I4
Moisie r. Canada 153 I4
Moissac France 66 E4
Mojave U.S.A. 158 D4
Mojave r. U.S.A. 158 E4
Mojave Desert U.S.A. 158 E4
Mojiang China 96 D4
Moji das Cruzes Brazil 179 B3
Mojokerto Jawa Indon. 85 F4
Mojos, Llanos de plain Bol. 176 E6
Moju r. Brazil 177 I4
Mōka Japan 93 G2
Mokama India 105 F4
Mokau N.Z. 139 E4
Mokau r. N.Z. 139 E4
Mokelumne r. U.S.A. 158 C2
Mokelumne Aqueduct canal U.S.A. 158 C2
Mokhoabong Pass Lesotho 125 I5
Mokhotlong Lesotho 125 I5
Mokhtārān Iran 110 E3
Moknine Tunisia 68 D7
Mokohinau Islands N.Z. 139 E2
Mokokchung India 105 H4
Mokolo Cameroon 121 E3
Mokolo r. S. Africa 125 H2
Mokopane S. Africa 125 I3
Mokp'o S. Korea 91 B6
Mokrous Rus. Fed. 53 J6
Moksha r. Rus. Fed. 53 I5
Mokshan Rus. Fed. 53 J5
Möksy Fin. 54 N5
Môktama Myanmar see Mottama
Môktama, Gulf of Myanmar see Mottama, Gulf of
Mokundurra India see Mukandwara
Mokwa Nigeria 120 D4
Molango Mex. 167 F4
Molatón mt. Spain 67 F4
Moldary Kazakh. 98 B2
Moldavia country Europe see Moldova
Moldavskaya S.S.R. country Europe see Moldova
Molde Norway 54 E5
Moldjord Norway 54 I3
Moldova country Europe 53 F7
Moldoveanu, Vârful mt. Romania 69 K2
Moldovei de Sud, Cîmpia plain Moldova 69 M1
Molega Lake Canada 153 I5
Molen r. S. Africa 125 I4
Mole National Park Ghana 120 C4
Molepolole Botswana 125 G3
Molėtai Lith. 55 N9
Molfetta Italy 68 G4
Molière Alg. see Bordj Bounaama
Molihong Shan mt. China see Morihong Shan
Molina de Aragón Spain 67 F3
Moline U.S.A. 161 D4
Molkom Sweden 55 H7
Mollagara Turkm. 110 D2
Mollakara Turkm. see Mollagara
Mol Len mt. India 105 H4
Möllenbeck Germany 63 N1
Mollendo Peru 176 D7
Mölln Germany 63 K1
Mölnlycke Sweden 55 H8
Molochnyy Rus. Fed. 54 R2
Molodechno Belarus see Maladzyechna
Molodezhnaya research station Antarctica 188 D2
Moloka'i i. U.S.A. 157 [inset]
Moloma r. Rus. Fed. 52 K4
Molong Australia 138 D4
Molopo watercourse Botswana/S. Africa 124 E5
Molotov Rus. Fed. see Perm'
Molotovsk Kyrg. see Kayyngdy
Molotovsk Arkhangel'skaya Oblast' Rus. Fed. see Severodvinsk
Molotovsk Kirovskaya Oblast' Rus. Fed. see Nolinsk
Moloundou Cameroon 121 E4
Molson Lake Canada 151 L4
Molu i. Indon. 81 I8
Moluccas is Indon. 83 C3
Molucca Sea Indon. see Maluku, Laut
Moma Moz. 123 D5
Moma r. Rus. Fed. 77 P3
Momba Australia 138 A3
Mombaça Brazil 177 K5
Mombasa Kenya 122 D4
Mombetsu Hokkaidō Japan see Monbetsu
Mombetsu Hokkaidō Japan see Monbetsu
Mombi New India 105 H4
Mombum Indon. 81 J8
Momchilgrad Bulg. 69 K4
Momence U.S.A. 164 B3
Momi, Ra's pt Yemen 109 H7
Momotombo, Volcán vol. Nicaragua 166 [inset] I6
Momoyama Japan 92 B4
Mompog Passage Phil. 82 C3
Mompós Col. 176 D2
Møn i. Denmark 55 H9
Mon India 105 H4
Mona terr. Irish Sea see Isle of Man
Mona U.S.A. 159 H2
Monaca U.S.A. 164 E3
Monach, Sound of sea chan. U.K. 60 B3
Monach Islands U.K. 60 B3
Monaco country Europe 66 H5
Monaco Basin sea feature N. Atlantic Ocean 184 G4
Monadhliath Mountains U.K. 60 E3
Monaghan Ireland 61 F3
Monahans U.S.A. 161 C6
Mona Passage Dom. Rep./Puerto Rico 169 K5
Monapo Moz. 123 E5
Monar, Loch l. U.K. 60 D3
Monarch Mountain Canada 150 E5
Monarch Pass U.S.A. 157 G5
Mona Reservoir U.S.A. 159 H2
Monashee Mountains Canada 150 G5
Monastir Macedonia see Bitola
Monastir Tunisia 68 D7
Monastyrishche Ukr. see Monastyryshche
Monastyryshche Ukr. 53 F6
Monbetsu Hokkaidō Japan 90 F3
Monbetsu Hokkaidō Japan 90 F4
Moncalieri Italy 68 B2
Monchegorsk Rus. Fed. 54 R3
Mönchengladbach Germany 62 G3
Monchique Port. 67 B5
Moncks Corner U.S.A. 163 D5
Monclova Mex. 167 E3
Moncouche, Lac l. Canada 153 H4
Moncton Canada 153 I5
Mondego r. Port. 67 B3
Mondlo S. Africa 125 J4
Mondo Chad 121 E3
Mondovì Italy 68 B2
Mondragone Italy 68 E4
Mondy Rus. Fed. 88 I2
Monemvasia Greece 69 J6
Monessen U.S.A. 164 F3
Moneta U.S.A. 156 G4
Moneygall Ireland 61 E5
Moneymore U.K. 61 F3
Monfalcone Italy 68 E2
Monfalut Egypt see Manfalūţ
Monforte de Lemos Spain 67 C2
Monga Dem. Rep. Congo 122 C3
Mongala r. Dem. Rep. Congo 122 B3
Mongar Bhutan 105 G4
Mongbwalu Dem. Rep. Congo 122 D3
Mông Cai Vietnam 86 D2
Mongers Lake salt flat Australia 135 B7
Monggon Qulu Nei Mongol China 95 I1
Mong Hang Myanmar 86 B2
Mong Hkan Myanmar 86 C2
Mong Hpayak Myanmar 86 B2
Mong Hsat Myanmar 86 B2
Mong Hsawk Myanmar 86 B2
Mong Hsu Myanmar 86 B2
Monghyr India see Munger
Mong Kung Myanmar 86 B2
Mong Kyawt Myanmar 86 B3
Mongla Bangl. 105 G5
Mong Lin Myanmar 86 C2
Mong Loi Myanmar 86 C2
Mong Long Myanmar 86 B2
Mong Nai Myanmar 86 B2
Mong Nawng Myanmar 86 B2
Mongo Chad 121 E3
Mongolia country Asia 88 I3
Mongolküre Xinjiang China see Zhaosu
Mongol Uls country Asia see Mongolia
Möngönmorīt Mongolia 95 G1
Mongonu Nigeria 120 E3
Mongora Pak. 111 I3
Mongour hill U.K. 60 G4
Mong Pan Myanmar 86 B2
Mong Ping Myanmar 86 B2
Mong Pu Myanmar 86 B2
Mong Pu-awn Myanmar 86 B2
Mongrove, Punta pt Mex. 166 E5
Mong Si Myanmar 86 B2
Mongu Zambia 123 C5
Mong Un Myanmar 86 C2
Mong Yai Myanmar 86 B2
Mong Yang Myanmar 86 B2
Mong Yawn Myanmar 86 B2
Mong Yawng Myanmar 86 C2
Mönhaan Mongolia 95 H2
Mönhbulag Mongolia see Yösöndzüyl
Mönh Hayrhan Uul mt. Mongolia 94 B2
Moniaive U.K. 60 F5
Monitor Mountain U.S.A. 158 E2
Monitor Range mts U.S.A. 158 E2
Monivea Ireland 61 D4
Monkey Bay Malawi 123 D5
Monkira Australia 136 C5
Monkton Canada 164 E2
Monmouth U.K. 59 E7
Monmouth U.S.A. 160 F3
Monmouth Mountain Canada 150 F5
Monnow r. U.K. 59 E7
Mono, Punta del pt Nicaragua 166 [inset] J7
Mono Lake U.S.A. 158 D2
Monolithos Greece 69 L6
Monomoy Point U.S.A. 165 J3
Monon U.S.A. 164 B3
Monopoli Italy 68 G4
Monreal del Campo Spain 67 F3
Monreale Sicily Italy 68 E5
Monroe IN U.S.A. 164 C3
Monroe LA U.S.A. 161 E5
Monroe MI U.S.A. 164 D3
Monroe NC U.S.A. 163 D5
Monroe WI U.S.A. 160 F3
Monroe Center U.S.A. 160 F2
Monroe Lake U.S.A. 164 B4
Monroeton U.S.A. 165 G3
Monroeville AL U.S.A. 167 I2

▶Monrovia Liberia 120 B4
Capital of Liberia.

Mons Belgium 62 D4
Monschau Germany 62 G4
Monselice Italy 68 D2
Montabaur Germany 63 H4
Montagu S. Africa 124 E7
Montague Canada 153 J5
Montague MI U.S.A. 164 B2
Montague TX U.S.A. 161 D5
Montague Island AK U.S.A. 149 K3
Montague Range hills Australia 135 B6
Montague Strait AK U.S.A. 149 J4
Montalat r. Indon. 85 F3
Montalto mt. Italy 68 F5
Montalto Uffugo Italy 68 G5
Montana Bulg. 69 J3
Montana AK U.S.A. 149 J3
Montana state U.S.A. 156 F3
Montaña de Comayagua, Parque Nacional nat. park Hond. 166 [inset] I6
Montaña de Cusuco, Parque Nacional nat. park Hond. 167 H6
Montaña de Yoro nat. park Hond. 166 [inset] I6
Montañas de Colón mts Hond. 166 [inset] I6
Montanhas do Tumucumaque, Parque Nacional 177 H3
Montargis France 66 F3
Montauban France 66 E4
Montauk U.S.A. 165 J3
Montauk Point U.S.A. 165 J3
Mont-aux-Sources mt. Lesotho 125 I5
Montbard France 66 G3
Mont Blanc mt. France/Italy 66 H4
Montblanc Spain 67 G3
Montblanch Spain see Montblanc
Montbrison France 66 G4
Montceau-les-Mines France 66 G3
Montcornet France 62 E5
Mont-de-Marsan France 66 D5
Montdidier France 62 C5
Monte Alban tourist site Mex. 167 F5
Monte Alegre Brazil 177 H4
Monte Alegre de Goiás Brazil 179 B1
Monte Alegre de Minas Brazil 179 A2
Monte Azul Brazil 179 C1
Monte Azul Paulista Brazil 179 A3
Montebello Canada 152 G5
Montebello Islands Australia 134 A5
Montebelluna Italy 68 E2
Monte-Carlo Monaco 66 H5
Monte Cristi Dom. Rep. 169 J5
Monte Cristo S. Africa 125 H2
Monte Dourado Brazil 177 H4
Monte Escobedo Mex. 166 E4
Monte Falterona, Campigna e delle Foreste Casentinesi, Parco Nazionale del nat. park Italy 68 D3
Montego Bay Jamaica 169 I5
Montélimar France 66 G4
Monte Lindo r. Para. 178 E2
Montello U.S.A. 160 F3
Montemorelos Mex. 167 F3
Montemor-o-Novo Port. 67 B4
Montenegro country Europe 68 H2
Montepulciano Italy 68 D3
Monte Quemado Arg. 178 D3
Montereau-Fault-Yonne France 66 F2
Monterey Mex. see Monterrey
Monterey CA U.S.A. 158 C3
Monterey VA U.S.A. 164 F4
Monterey Bay U.S.A. 158 B3
Montería Col. 176 C2
Monteros Arg. 178 C3
Monterrey Baja California Mex. 159 F5
Monterrey Nuevo León Mex. 167 E3
Montesano U.S.A. 156 C3
Montesano sulla Marcellana Italy 68 F4
Monte Santo Brazil 177 K6
Monte Santu, Capo di c. Sardinia Italy 68 C4
Montes Claros Brazil 179 C2
Montesilvano Italy 68 F3
Montevarchi Italy 68 D3

▶Montevideo Uruguay 178 E4
Capital of Uruguay.

Montevideo U.S.A. 160 E2
Montezuma U.S.A. 160 E3
Montezuma Creek U.S.A. 159 I3
Montezuma Peak U.S.A. 158 E3
Montfort Neth. 62 F3
Montgomery U.K. 59 D6

▶Montgomery AL U.S.A. 163 C5
Capital of Alabama.

Montgomery WV U.S.A. 164 E4
Montgomery Islands Australia 134 C3
Monthey Switz. 66 H3
Monticello AR U.S.A. 161 F5
Monticello FL U.S.A. 163 D6
Monticello IN U.S.A. 164 B3
Monticello KY U.S.A. 164 C5
Monticello MO U.S.A. 160 F3
Monticello NY U.S.A. 165 H3
Monticello UT U.S.A. 159 I3
Montignac France 66 E4
Montignies-le-Tilleul Belgium 62 E4
Montigny-lès-Metz France 62 G5
Montilla Spain 67 D5
Monti Sibillini, Parco Nazionale dei nat. park Italy 68 E3
Montividiu Brazil 179 A2
Montivilliers France 59 H9
Mont-Joli Canada 153 H4
Mont-Laurier Canada 152 G5
Montluçon France 66 F3
Montmagny Canada 153 H5
Montmédy France 62 F5
Montmirail France 62 D6
Montmorillon France 66 E3
Montmort-Lucy France 62 D6
Monto Australia 136 E5
Montour Falls U.S.A. 165 G2
Montoursville U.S.A. 165 G3
Montpelier ID U.S.A. 156 F4

▶Montpelier VT U.S.A. 165 I1
Capital of Vermont.

Montpellier France 66 F5
Montréal Canada 152 G5
Montreal r. Ont. Canada 152 D5
Montreal r. Ont. Canada 152 F5
Montreal Lake Canada 151 J4
Montreal Lake l. Canada 151 J4
Montréal-Mirabel airport Canada 152 G5
Montreal River Canada 152 D5
Montréal-Trudeau airport Canada 152 G5
Montreuil France 62 B4
Montreux Switz. 66 H3
Montrose well S. Africa 124 E4
Montrose U.K. 60 G4
Montrose CO U.S.A. 159 J2
Montrose PA U.S.A. 165 H3
Montross U.S.A. 165 G4
Monts, Pointe des pt Canada 153 I4
Mont-St-Aignan France 59 I9

▶Montserrat terr. West Indies 169 L5
United Kingdom Overseas Territory.

Montuosa, Isla i. Panama 166 [inset] J8
Montviel, Lac l. Canada 153 H3
Monument Mountain hill AK U.S.A. 148 G2
Monument Valley reg. U.S.A. 159 H3
Monywa Myanmar 86 A2
Monza Italy 68 C2
Monze, Cape pt Pak. see Muari, Ras
Monzón Spain 67 G3
Mooi r. S. Africa 125 J5
Mooifontein Namibia 124 C4
Mookane Botswana 125 H2
Mookgopong S. Africa see Naboomspruit
Moolawatana Australia 137 B6
Moomba Australia 137 C6
Moomin Creek r. Australia 138 D2
Moonaree Australia 137 A6
Moonbi Range mts Australia 138 E3
Moonda Lake salt flat Australia 137 C5
Moonie Australia 138 E1
Moonie r. Australia 138 D2
Moora Australia 135 B7
Mooraberree Australia 136 C5
Moorcroft U.S.A. 156 G3
Moore r. Australia 135 A7
Moore U.S.A. 156 F3
Moore, Lake salt flat Australia 135 B7
Moore Creek AK U.S.A. 148 H3
Moore Embayment b. Antarctica 188 H1
Moorefield U.S.A. 165 F4
Moore Haven U.S.A. 163 D7
Moore Reef Australia 136 E3
Moore Reservoir U.S.A. 165 J1
Moore River National Park Australia 135 A7
Moores Island Bahamas 163 E7
Moorfoot Hills U.K. 60 F5
Moorhead U.S.A. 160 D2
Moorman U.S.A. 164 B5
Moornanyah Lake imp. l. Australia 138 A4
Mooroopna Australia 138 B6
Moorreesburg S. Africa 124 D7
Moorrinya National Park Australia 136 D4
Moose r. Canada 152 E4
Moose Creek AK U.S.A. 149 K2
Moose Factory Canada 152 E4
Moosehead Lake U.S.A. 162 G2
Moose Jaw Canada 151 J5
Moose Jaw r. Canada 151 J5
Moose Lake U.S.A. 160 E2
Mooselookmeguntic Lake U.S.A. 165 J1
Moose Mountain Creek r. Canada 151 K5
Moose Pass AK U.S.A. 149 J3
Moosilauke, Mount U.S.A. 165 J1
Moosomin Canada 151 K5
Moosonee Canada 152 E4
Mootwingee National Park Australia 137 C6
Mopane S. Africa 125 I2
Mopeia Moz. 123 D5
Mopipi Botswana 123 C6
Mopti Mali 120 C3
Moqor Afgh. 111 G3
Moquegua Peru 176 D7
Mora Cameroon 121 E3
Mora Spain 67 E4
Mora Sweden 55 I6
Mora MN U.S.A. 160 E2
Mora NM U.S.A. 157 G6
Mora r. U.S.A. 157 G6
Moradabad India 104 D3
Morada Nova Brazil 177 K5
Moraine Lake Canada 151 J1
Moraleda, Canal sea chan. Chile 178 B6
Morales Guat. 166 [inset] H6
Moram India 106 C2
Moramanga Madag. 123 E5
Moran U.S.A. 156 F4
Moranbah Australia 136 E4
Morang Nepal see Biratnagar
Morar, Loch l. U.K. 60 D4
Morari, Tso l. India 104 D2
Moratuwa Sri Lanka 106 C5
Morava reg. Czech Rep. 57 P6
Moravia U.S.A. 165 G2
Morawa Australia 135 A7
Moray Firth b. U.K. 60 E3
Moray Range hills Australia 134 E3
Morbach Germany 62 H5
Morbeng S. Africa see Soekmekaar
Morbi India 104 B5
Morcenx France 66 D4
Morcillo Mex. 161 B7
Mordaga China 89 M2
Mor Dağı mt. Turkey 113 G3
Morden Canada 151 L5
Mordovo Rus. Fed. 53 I5
Mordvinof, Cape AK U.S.A. 148 F5
Moreau r. U.S.A. 160 C2
Moreau, South Fork r. U.S.A. 160 C2
Morecambe U.K. 58 E4
Morecambe Bay U.K. 58 D4
Moree Australia 138 D2
Morehead P.N.G. 81 K8
Morehead U.S.A. 164 D4
Morehead City U.S.A. 169 I2
Morel r. India 99 B8
Moreland U.S.A. 164 C5
More Laptevykh sea Rus. Fed. see Laptev Sea
Morelia Mex. 168 D5
Morella Australia 136 C4
Morella Spain 67 F3
Morelos Mex. 157 G8
Morelos state Mex. 167 F5
Morena India 104 D4
Morena, Sierra mts Spain 67 C5
Morenci AZ U.S.A. 159 I5
Morenci MI U.S.A. 164 C3
Moreni Romania 69 K2
Moreno Mex. 166 C2
Moreno Valley U.S.A. 158 E5
Moresby, Mount B.C. Canada 149 N5
Moresby Island B.C. Canada 149 N5
Moreswe Pan salt pan Botswana 124 G2
Moreton Bay Australia 138 F1
Moreton-in-Marsh U.K. 59 F7
Moreton Island Australia 138 F1
Moreton Island National Park Australia 138 F1
Moreuil France 62 C5
Morez France 66 H3
Morfou Cyprus 107 A2
Morfou Bay Cyprus 107 A2
Morgan U.S.A. 156 F4
Morgan City U.S.A. 161 F6
Morgan Hill U.S.A. 158 C3
Morganton U.S.A. 162 D5
Morgantown KY U.S.A. 164 B5
Morgantown WV U.S.A. 164 F4
Morgenzon S. Africa 125 I4
Morges Switz. 66 H3
Morgh, Kowtal-e Afgh. 111 H3
Morghāb r. Afgh. 111 F3
Morghāb reg. Afgh. 111 F3
Morhar r. India 105 F4
Mori Xinjiang China 94 B3
Mori Japan 90 F4
Mori Shizuoka Japan 93 D4
Moriah, Mount U.S.A. 159 F2
Moriarty's Range hills Australia 138 B2
Morice Lake Canada 150 E4
Morichal Col. 176 D3
Moriguchi Japan 92 B4
Morihong Shan mt. China 90 B4
Morija Lesotho 125 H5
Morin Dawa Nei Mongol China see Nirji
Moringen Germany 63 J3
Morioka Japan 91 F5
Moris Mex. 166 C2
Morisset Australia 138 E4
Moriya Japan 93 F3
Moriyama Japan 92 C3
Moriyoshi-zan vol. Japan 91 F5
Morjärv Sweden 54 M3
Morjen r. Pak. 111 F4
Morki Rus. Fed. 52 K4
Morlaix France 66 C2
Morley U.K. 58 F5
Mormam Flat Dam U.S.A. 159 H5
Mormant France 62 C6
Mormon Lake U.S.A. 159 H4
Mormugao India see Marmagao
Morne Diablotins vol. Dominica 169 L5
Morney watercourse Australia 136 C5
Mornington, Isla i. Chile 178 A7
Mornington Abyssal Plain sea feature S. Atlantic Ocean 184 C9
Mornington Island Australia 136 B3
Mornington Peninsula National Park Australia 138 B7

Moro Pak. 111 G5
Moro U.S.A. 156 C3
Morobe P.N.G. 81 L8
Morocco country Africa 120 C1
Morocco U.S.A. 164 B3
Morococala mt. Bol. 176 E7
Morogoro Tanz. 123 D4
Moro Gulf Phil. 82 C5
Morojaneng S. Africa 125 H5
Morokweng S. Africa 124 F4
Moroleón Mex. 167 E4
Moromaho i. Indon. 83 C4
Morombe Madag. 123 E6
Morón Cuba 163 E8
Mörön Mongolia 94 E1
Morondava Madag. 123 E6
Morón de la Frontera Spain 67 D5
▶Moroni Comoros 123 E5

Capital of the Comoros.

Moroni U.S.A. 159 H2
Morotai i. Maluku Indon. 83 D2
Morotai, Selat sea chan. Maluku Indon. 83 C2
Moroto Uganda 122 D3
Morowali, Cagar Alam nature res. Indon. 83 B3
Morozovsk Rus. Fed. 53 I6
Morpeth Canada 164 E2
Morpeth U.K. 58 F3
Morphou Cyprus see Morfou
Morrill U.S.A. 164 C5
Morrilton U.S.A. 161 E5
Morrin Canada 151 H5
Morrinhos Brazil 179 A2
Morris Canada 151 L5
Morris IL U.S.A. 160 F3
Morris MN U.S.A. 160 E2
Morris PA U.S.A. 165 G3
Morris Jessup, Kap c. Greenland 189 I1
Morrison U.S.A. 160 F3
Morristown AZ U.S.A. 159 G5
Morristown NJ U.S.A. 165 H3
Morristown NY U.S.A. 165 H1
Morristown TN U.S.A. 162 D4
Morrisville U.S.A. 165 H2
Morro Brazil 179 B2
Morro Bay U.S.A. 158 C4
Morro d'Anta Brazil 179 D2
Morro de Papanoa hd Mex. 167 E5
Morro de Petatlán hd Mex. 167 E5
Morro do Chapéu Brazil 177 J6
Morro Grande hill Brazil 177 H4
Morrosquillo, Golfo de b. Col. 176 C2
Morrumbene Moz. 125 L2
Morschen Germany 63 J3
Morse Canada 151 J5
Morse U.S.A. 161 C4
Morse, Cape Antarctica 188 G2
Morse Reservoir U.S.A. 164 B3
Morshanka Rus. Fed. 53 I5
Morshansk Rus. Fed. see Morshanka
Morsott Alg. 68 C7
Mort watercourse Australia 136 C4
Mortagne-au-Perche France 66 E2
Mortagne-sur-Sèvre France 66 D3
Mortara Italy 68 C2
Mortehoe U.K. 59 C7
Morteros Arg. 178 D4
Mortes, Rio das r. Brazil 179 A1
Mortimer's Bahamas 163 F8
Mortlake Australia 138 A7
Mortlock Islands Micronesia 186 G5
Mortlock Islands P.N.G. see Takuu Islands
Morton U.K. 59 G6
Morton TX U.S.A. 161 C5
Morton WA U.S.A. 156 C3
Morton National Park Australia 138 E5
Morundah Australia 138 C5
Morupule Botswana 125 H2
Moruroa atoll Fr. Polynesia see Mururoa
Moruya Australia 138 E5
Morven Australia 137 D5
Morven hill U.K. 60 F2
Morvern reg. U.K. 60 D4
Morvi India see Morbi
Morwell Australia 138 C7
Morzhovets, Ostrov i. Rus. Fed. 52 I2
Morzhovoi Bay AK U.S.A. 148 G5
Mosbach Germany 63 J5
Mosborough U.K. 58 F5
Mosby U.S.A. 156 G3
▶Moscow Rus. Fed. 52 H5

Capital of the Russian Federation. Most populous city in Europe.

Moscow ID U.S.A. 156 D3
Moscow PA U.S.A. 165 H3
Moscow University Ice Shelf Antarctica 188 G2
Mosel r. Germany 63 H4
Moselebe watercourse Botswana 124 F3
Moselle r. France 62 G5
Möser Germany 63 L2
Moses, Mount U.S.A. 158 E1
Moses Lake U.S.A. 156 D3
Moses Point AK U.S.A. 148 G2
Mosgiel N.Z. 139 C7
Moshaweng watercourse S. Africa 124 F4
Moshchnyy, Ostrov i. Rus. Fed. 55 O7
Moshi Tanz. 122 D4
Mosh'yuga Rus. Fed. 52 L2
Mosi-oa-Tunya waterfall Zambia/Zimbabwe see Victoria Falls
Mosjøen Norway 54 H4
Moskal'vo Rus. Fed. 90 F1
Moskenesøy i. Norway 54 H3
Moskva Rus. Fed. see Moscow
Moskva Tajik. 111 H2
Mosonmagyaróvár Hungary 57 P7
Mosquera Col. 176 C3
Mosquero U.S.A. 157 G6
Mosquitia reg. Hond. 166 [inset] J6
Mosquito r. Brazil 179 C1
Mosquito Creek Lake U.S.A. 164 E3
Mosquito Lake Canada 151 K2
Mosquito Mountain hill AK U.S.A. 148 H3
Mosquitos, Golfo de los b. Panama 166 [inset] J7
Moss Norway 55 G7
Mossâmedes Angola see Namibe
Mossat U.K. 60 G3
Mossburn N.Z. 139 B7
Mosselbaai S. Africa see Mossel Bay
Mossel Bay S. Africa 124 F8
Mossel Bay b. S. Africa 124 F8
Mossgiel Australia 138 B4
Mossman Australia 136 D3
Mossoró Brazil 177 K5
Moss Vale Australia 138 E5
Mossy r. Canada 151 K4
Most Czech Rep. 57 N5
Mostaganem Alg. 67 G6
Mostar Bos.-Herz. 68 G3
Mostoos Hills Canada 151 I4
Mostovskoy Rus. Fed. 113 F1
Mosty Belarus see Masty
Mostyn Sabah Malaysia 85 G1
Mosul Iraq 113 F3
Mosuowan Xinjiang China 98 D3
Møsvatnet l. Norway 55 F7
Motagua r. Guat. 167 H6
Motala Sweden 55 I7
Motaze Moz. 125 K3
Motegi Japan 93 G2
Motetema S. Africa 125 I3
Moth India 104 D4
Motherwell U.K. 60 F5
Moti i. Maluku Indon. 83 C2
Motian Ling hill China 90 A4
Motihari India 105 F4
Motilla del Palancar Spain 67 F4
Motiti Island N.Z. 139 F3
Motokwe Botswana 124 F3
Motono Japan 93 G3
Motosu Japan 92 C3
Motosu-ko l. Japan 93 E3
Motozintla Mex. 167 G6
Motril Spain 67 E5
Motru Romania 69 J2
Mott U.S.A. 160 C2
Mottama Myanmar 86 B3
Mottama, Gulf of Myanmar 86 B3
Motu Ihupuku i. N.Z. see Campbell Island
Motul Mex. 167 H4
Mouaskar Alg. see Mascara
Mouding China 96 D3
Moudjéria Mauritania 120 B3
Moudros Greece 69 K5
Mouhijärvi Fin. 55 M6
Mouila Gabon 122 B4
Moukalaba Doudou, Parc National de nat. park Gabon 122 A4
Moulamein Australia 138 B5
Moulamein Creek r. Australia 138 A5
Moulavibazar Bangl. see Moulvibazar
Mould Bay Canada 146 G2
Moulèngui Binza Gabon 122 B4
Moulins France 66 F3
Moulmein Myanmar see Mawlamyaing
Moulouya r. Morocco 64 D4
Moultrie U.S.A. 163 D6
Moultrie, Lake U.S.A. 163 E5
Moulvibazar Bangl. 105 G4
Mound City KS U.S.A. 160 E4
Mound City SD U.S.A. 160 C2
Moundou Chad 121 E4
Moundsville U.S.A. 164 E4
Moŭng Roessei Cambodia 87 C4
Mount Abu India 104 C4
Mountain r. N.W.T. Canada 149 O2
Mountainair U.S.A. 157 G6
Mountain Brook U.S.A. 163 C5
Mountain City U.S.A. 164 E5
Mountain Home AR U.S.A. 161 E4
Mountain Home ID U.S.A. 156 E4
Mountain Home UT U.S.A. 159 H1
Mountain Lake Park U.S.A. 164 F4
Mountain View U.S.A. 161 E5
Mountain Village AK U.S.A. 148 G3
Mountain Zebra National Park S. Africa 125 G7
Mount Airy U.S.A. 164 E5
Mount Aspiring National Park N.Z. 139 B7
Mount Assiniboine Provincial Park Canada 150 H5
Mount Ayliff S. Africa 125 I6
Mount Ayr U.S.A. 160 E3
Mountbellew Ireland 61 D4
Mount Buffalo National Park Australia 138 C6
Mount Carmel U.S.A. 164 B4
Mount Carmel Junction U.S.A. 159 G3
Mount Coolon Australia 136 D4
Mount Darwin Zimbabwe 123 D5
Mount Denison Australia 134 F5
Mount Desert Island U.S.A. 162 G2
Mount Dutton Australia 137 A5
Mount Eba Australia 137 A6
Mount Elgon National Park Uganda 122 D3
Mount Fletcher S. Africa 125 I6
Mount Forest Canada 164 E2
Mount Frankland National Park Australia 135 B8
Mount Frere S. Africa 125 I6
Mount Gambier Australia 137 C8
Mount Gilead U.S.A. 164 D3
Mount Hagen P.N.G. 81 K8
Mount Holly U.S.A. 165 H4
Mount Hope Australia 138 B4
Mount Hope U.S.A. 164 E5
Mount Howitt Australia 137 C5
Mount Isa Australia 136 B4
Mount Jackson U.S.A. 165 F4
Mount Jewett U.S.A. 165 F3
Mount Joy U.S.A. 165 G3
Mount Kaputar National Park Australia 138 E3
Mount Keith Australia 135 C6
Mount Lofty Range mts Australia 137 B7
Mount Magnet Australia 135 B7
Mount Manara Australia 138 A4
Mount McKinley National Park U.S.A. see Denali National Park and Preserve
Mount Meadows Reservoir U.S.A. 158 C1
Mountmellick Ireland 61 E4
Mount Moorosi Lesotho 125 H6
Mount Morgan Australia 136 E4
Mount Morris MI U.S.A. 164 D2
Mount Morris NY U.S.A. 165 G2
Mount Murchison Australia 138 A3
Mount Nebo U.S.A. 164 E4
Mount Olivet U.S.A. 164 C4
Mount Pearl Canada 153 L5
Mount Pleasant Canada 153 I5
Mount Pleasant IA U.S.A. 160 F3
Mount Pleasant MI U.S.A. 164 C2
Mount Pleasant TX U.S.A. 161 E5
Mount Pleasant UT U.S.A. 159 H2
Mount Rainier National Park U.S.A. 156 C3
Mount Remarkable National Park Australia 137 B7
Mount Revelstoke National Park Canada 150 G5
Mount Robson Provincial Park Canada 150 G4
Mount Rogers National Recreation Area park U.S.A. 164 E5
Mount St Helens National Volcanic Monument nat. park U.S.A. 156 C3
Mount Sanford Australia 134 E4
Mount's Bay U.K. 59 B8
Mount Shasta U.S.A. 156 C4
Mountsorrel U.K. 59 F6
Mount Sterling U.S.A. 164 D4
Mount Swan Australia 136 A4
Mount Union U.S.A. 165 G3
Mount Vernon Australia 135 B6
Mount Vernon AL U.S.A. 167 H2
Mount Vernon IL U.S.A. 160 F4
Mount Vernon IN U.S.A. 162 C4
Mount Vernon KY U.S.A. 164 C5
Mount Vernon MO U.S.A. 161 E4
Mount Vernon OH U.S.A. 164 D3
Mount Vernon TX U.S.A. 161 E5
Mount Vernon WA U.S.A. 156 C2
Mount William National Park Australia 137 [inset]
Mount Willoughby Australia 135 F6
Moura Australia 136 E5
Moura Brazil 176 F4
Moura Port. 67 C4
Mourdi, Dépression du depr. Chad 121 F3
Mourdiah Mali 120 C3
Mourne r. U.K. 61 E3
Mourne Mountains hills U.K. 61 F3
Mousa i. U.K. 60 [inset]
Mouscron Belgium 62 D4
Mousgougou Chad 122 B2
Moussafoyo Chad 121 E4
Moussoro Chad 121 E3
Moutamba Congo 122 B4
Mouth of the Yangtze China 97 I2
Moutong Sulawesi Indon. 83 B2
Mouy France 62 C5
Mouydir, Monts du plat. Alg. 120 D2
Mouzon France 62 F5
Movas Mex. 166 C2
Mowbullan, Mount Australia 138 E1
Moxey Town Bahamas 163 E7
Moy r. Ireland 61 C3
Moyahua Mex. 166 E4
Moyale Eth. 122 D3
Moyen Atlas mts Morocco 64 C5
Moyen Congo country Africa see Congo
Moyeni Lesotho 125 H6
Moynalyk Rus. Fed. 102 I1
Moynaq Uzbek. see Mo'ynoq
Mo'ynoq Uzbek. 102 A3
Moyo i. Indon. 85 G5
Moyobamba Peru 176 C5
Moyock U.S.A. 165 G5
Moyola r. U.K. 61 F3
Moyu Xinjiang China 99 B5
Moyynkum Kazakh. 102 D3
Moyynkum, Peski des. Kazakh. 102 C3
Moyynty Kazakh. 102 D2
Mozambique country Africa 123 D6
Mozambique Channel Africa 123 E6
Mozambique Ridge sea feature Indian Ocean 185 K7
Mozdok Rus. Fed. 113 G2
Mozdūrān Iran 111 F2
Mozhaysk Rus. Fed. 53 H5
Mozhga Rus. Fed. 52 L4
Mozhnābād Iran 111 F3
Mozo Myanmar 96 B4
Mozyr' Belarus see Mazyr
Mpaathutlwa Pan salt pan Botswana 124 E3
Mpanda Tanz. 123 D4
Mpen India 105 I4
Mpika Zambia 123 D5
Mpolweni S. Africa 125 J5
Mporokoso Zambia 123 D4
Mpulungu Zambia 123 D4
Mpumalanga prov. S. Africa 125 I4
Mpunde mt. Tanz. 123 D4
Mpwapwa Tanz. 123 D4
Mqanduli S. Africa 125 I6
Mqinvartsveri mt. Georgia/Rus. Fed. see Kazbek
Mrauk-U Myanmar 86 A2
Mrewa Zimbabwe see Murehwa
Mrkonjić-Grad Bos.-Herz. 68 G2
M'Saken Tunisia 68 D7
Mshinskaya Rus. Fed. 55 P7
M'Sila Alg. 67 I6
Msta r. Rus. Fed. 52 F4
Mstislavl' Belarus see Mstsislaw
Mstsislaw Belarus 53 F5
Mtelo Kenya 122 D3
Mtoko Zimbabwe see Mutoko
Mtorwi Tanz. 123 D4
Mtsensk Rus. Fed. 53 H5
Mts'ire Kavkasioni Asia see Lesser Caucasus
Mtubatuba S. Africa 125 K5
Mtunzini S. Africa 125 J5
Mtwara Tanz. 123 E5
Mu r. Myanmar 86 A2
Mu'āb, Jibāl reg. Jordan see Moab
Muanda Dem. Rep. Congo 123 B4
Muang Ham Laos 86 D2
Muang Hiam Laos 86 C2
Muang Hinboun Laos 86 D3
Muang Hôngsa Laos 86 C3
Muang Khi Laos 86 C3
Muang Không Laos 87 D4
Muang Khoua Laos 86 C2
Muang Lamam Laos see Lamam
Muang Mok Laos 86 D3
Muang Ngoy Laos 86 C2
Muang Ou Nua Laos 86 C2
Muang Pakbeng Laos 86 C3
Muang Paktha Laos 86 C2
Muang Pakxan Laos see Pakxan
Muang Phalan Laos 80 D3
Muang Phin Laos 86 D3
Muang Sam Sip Thai. 86 D4
Muang Sing Laos 86 C2
Muang Soum Laos 86 C3
Muang Souy Laos 86 C3
Muang Thadua Laos 86 C3
Muang Thai country Asia see Thailand
Muang Va Laos 86 C2
Muang Vangviang Laos 86 C3
Muang Xon Laos 86 C2
Muar Malaysia 84 C2
Muar r. Malaysia 84 C2
Muara Brunei 85 F1
Muaraancalong Kalimantan Indon. 85 G2
Muaraatap Kalimantan Indon. 85 G2
Muarabeliti Sumatera Indon. 84 C3
Muarabulian Sumatera Indon. 84 C3
Muarabungo Sumatera Indon. 84 C3
Muaradua Sumatera Indon. 84 D4
Muaraenim Sumatera Indon. 84 C3
Muarainu Kalimantan Indon. 85 F3
Muarajawa Kalimantan Indon. 85 G3
Muarakaman Kalimantan Indon. 85 G3
Muara Kaman Sedulang, Cagar Alam nature res. Kalimantan Indon. 85 G2
Muaralabuh Sumatera Indon. 84 C3
Muaralakitan Sumatera Indon. 84 C3
Muaralaung Kalimantan Indon. 85 F3
Muaralesan Kalimantan Indon. 85 G2
Muaramayang Kalimantan Indon. 85 G2
Muaranawai Kalimantan Indon. 85 G2
Muararupit Sumatera Indon. 84 C3
Muarasabak Sumatera Indon. 84 C3
Muarasiberut Indon. 84 B3
Muarasipongi Sumatera Indon. 84 B2
Muarasoma Sumatera Indon. 84 B2
Muaras Reef Indon. 85 G2
Muaratebo Sumatera Indon. 84 C3
Muaratembesi Sumatera Indon. 84 C3
Muarateweh Kalimantan Indon. 85 F3
Muara Tuang Sarawak Malaysia see Kota Samarahan
Muarawahau Kalimantan Indon. 85 G2
Muari i. Maluku Indon. 83 C3
Muari, Ras pt Pak. 111 G5
Mu'ayqil, Khashm al hill Saudi Arabia 110 C5
Mubarek Uzbek. see Muborak
Mubarraz well Saudi Arabia 113 F5
Mubende Uganda 122 D3
Mubi Nigeria 120 E3
Muborak Uzbek. 111 G2
Mubur i. Indon. 84 D2
Mucajaí, Serra do mts Brazil 176 F3
Mucalic r. Canada 153 I2
Muccan Australia 134 C5
Much Germany 63 H4
Mucheng Henan China see Wuzhi
Muchinga Escarpment Zambia 123 D5
Muchuan China 96 D2
Muck i. U.K. 60 C4
Mucojo Moz. 123 E5
Muconda Angola 123 C5
Mucubela Moz. 123 D5
Mucugê Brazil 179 C1
Mucur Turkey 112 D3
Mucuri Brazil 179 D2
Mucuri r. Brazil 179 D2
Muda r. Malaysia 84 C1
Mudabidri India 106 B3
Mudan Shandong China see Heze
Mudanjiang China 90 C3
Mudan Jiang r. China 90 C3
Mudan Ling mts China 90 B4
Mudanya Turkey 69 M4
Muḍaybī Oman 110 E6
Mudaysīsāt, Jabal al hill Jordan 107 C4
Muddus nationalpark nat. park Sweden 54 K3
Muddy r. U.S.A. 159 F3
Muddy Gap U.S.A. 156 G4
Muddy Peak U.S.A. 159 F3
Mūd-e Dahanāb Iran 110 E3
Mudersbach Germany 63 H4
Mudgal India 106 C3
Mudgee Australia 138 D4
Mudhol India 106 B2
Mudigere India 106 B3
Mudjatik r. Canada 151 J3
Mud Lake U.S.A. 158 E3
Mudraya country Africa see Egypt
Mudurnu Turkey 69 N4
Mud'yuga Rus. Fed. 52 H3
Mueda Moz. 123 D5
Mueller Range hills Australia 134 D4
Muerto, Mar lag. Mex. 167 G5
Muertos Cays is Bahamas 163 D7
Muftyuga Rus. Fed. 52 J2
Mufulira Zambia 123 C5
Mufumbwe Zambia 123 C5
Mufu Shan mts China 97 G2
Muğan Düzü lowland Azer. 113 H3
Mugarripug China 105 F2
Mugegawa Japan 92 C3
Mughalbhin Pak. see Jati
Mughal Kot Pak. 111 H4
Mughal Sarai India 105 E4
Mūghār Iran 110 D3
Mughayrā' Saudi Arabia 107 C5
Mughayrā' Saudi Arabia 110 B5
Mugi Gifu Japan 92 D3
Muğla Turkey 69 M6
Mugodzhary, Gory mts Kazakh. 102 A2
Mug Qu r. Qinghai China 94 C5
Mugu Karnali r. Nepal 99 C7
Mugur-Aksy Rus. Fed. 94 B1
Mugxung Qinghai China 99 F6
Mūḩ, Sabkhat imp. l. Syria 107 D2
Muhala Xinjiang China see Yutian
Muhammad Ashraf Pak. 111 H5
Muhammad Qol Sudan 108 E5
Muhammarah Iran see Khorramshahr
Muhar Qinghai China 94 D4
Muhashsham, Wādī al watercourse Egypt 107 B4
Muḩaysh, Wādī al watercourse Jordan 107 C5
Muhaysin Syria 107 D1
Mühlanger Germany 63 M3
Mühlberg Germany 63 N3
Mühlhausen (Thüringen) Germany 63 K3
Mühlig-Hofmann Mountains Antarctica 188 C2
Muhos Fin. 54 N4
Muḩradah Syria 107 C2
Mui Bai Bung c. Vietnam see Mui Ca Mau
Mui Ba Lang An pt Vietnam 86 E4
Mui Ca Mau c. Vietnam 87 D5
Mui Đôc pt Vietnam 86 D3
Muié Angola 123 C5
Muika Japan 93 E1
Muiliyk i. Maluku Indon. 83 D3
Muineachán Ireland see Monaghan
Muine Bheag Ireland see Bagenalstown
Muir U.S.A. 164 C2
Muirkirk U.K. 60 E5
Muir of Ord U.K. 60 E3
Mui Ron hd Vietnam 86 D3
Muite Moz. 123 D5
Mujeres, Isla i. Mex. 167 I4
Muji Xinjiang China 99 B5
Mujong r. Malaysia 85 F2
Muju S. Korea 91 B5
Mukacheve Ukr. 53 D6
Mukachevo Ukr. see Mukacheve
Mukah Sarawak Malaysia 85 F2
Mukah r. Malaysia 85 F2
Mukalla Yemen 108 G7
Mukandwara India 104 D4
Mukawa Yamanashi Japan 93 E3
Mukdahan Thai. 86 D3
Mukden Liaoning China see Shenyang
Mukeru Palau 82 [inset]
Muketei r. Canada 152 D3
Mukhen Rus. Fed. 90 E2
Mukhino Rus. Fed. 90 B1
Mukhorshibir' Rus. Fed. 95 G1
Mukhtuya Rus. Fed. see Lensk
Mukinbudin Australia 135 B7
Mukō Japan 92 B4
Mu Ko Chang Marine National Park Thai. 87 C5
Mukojima-rettō is Japan 91 F8
Mukomuko Sumatera Indon. 84 C3
Mukry Turkm. 111 G2
Muktsar India 104 C3
Mukur Vostochnyy Kazakhstan Kazakh. 98 C2
Mukutawa r. Canada 151 L4
Mukwonago U.S.A. 164 A2
Mula r. India 106 B2
Mulakatholhu atoll Maldives see Mulaku Atoll
Mulaku Atoll Maldives 103 D11
Mulaly Kazakh. 98 B3
Mulan China 90 C3
Mulanay Luzon Phil. 82 C3
Mulanje, Mount Malawi 123 D5
Mulapula, Lake salt flat Australia 137 B6
Mulatos Mex. 166 C2
Mula-tupo Panama 166 [inset] K7
Mulayḩ Saudi Arabia 110 B5
Mulayḩah, Jabal hill U.A.E. 110 D5
Mulayz, Wādī al watercourse Egypt 107 A4
Mulchatna r. AK U.S.A. 148 H3
Mulde r. Germany 63 M3
Mule Creek NM U.S.A. 159 I5
Mule Creek WY U.S.A. 156 G4
Mulegé Mex. 166 B3
Muleshoe U.S.A. 161 C5
Mulga Park Australia 135 E6
Mulgathing Australia 135 F7
Mulgrave Hills AK U.S.A. 148 G2
Mulhacén mt. Spain 67 E5
Mülhausen France see Mulhouse
Mülheim an der Ruhr Germany 62 G3
Mulhouse France 66 H3
Muli China 96 D3
Muli Rus. Fed. see Vysokogorniy
Mulia Indon. 81 J7
Muling Heilong. China 90 C3
Muling Heilong. China 90 C3
Muling He r. China 90 D3
Mull i. U.K. 60 D4
Mull, Sound of sea chan. U.K. 60 C4
Mullaghcleevaun hill Ireland 61 F4
Mullaittivu Sri Lanka 106 D4
Mullaley Australia 138 D3
Mullengudgery Australia 138 C3
Mullens U.S.A. 164 E5
Muller watercourse Australia 134 F5
Muller, Pegunungan mts Indon. 85 F2
Mullett Lake U.S.A. 164 C1
Mullewa Australia 135 A7
Mullica r. U.S.A. 165 H4
Mullingar Ireland 61 E4
Mullion Creek Australia 138 D4
Mull of Galloway c. U.K. 60 E6
Mull of Kintyre hd U.K. 60 D5
Mull of Oa hd U.K. 60 C5
Mullumbimby Australia 138 F2
Mulobezi Zambia 123 C5
Mulshi Lake India 106 B2
Multai India 104 D5
Multan Pak. 111 H4
Multia Fin. 54 N5
Multien reg. France 62 C6
Mulu, Gunung mt. Malaysia 85 F1
Mulug India 106 C2
▶Mumbai India 106 B2

2nd most populous city in Asia and 3rd in the world.

Mumbil Australia 138 D4
Mumbwa Zambia 123 C5
Muminabad Tajik. see Leningrad
Mŭ'minobod Tajik. see Leningrad
Mun, Mae Nam r. Thai. 86 D4
Muna i. Indon. 83 B4
Muna Mex. 167 H4
Muna r. Rus. Fed. 77 N3
Munabao Pak. 111 H5
Munaðarnes Iceland 54 [inset]
Münchberg Germany 63 L4
München Germany see Munich
München-Gladbach Germany see Mönchengladbach
Münchhausen Germany 63 I4
Muncho Lake Canada 150 E3
Muncie U.S.A. 164 C3
Muncoonie West, Lake salt flat Australia 136 B5
Muncy U.S.A. 165 G3
Munda Pak. 111 H4
Mundel Lake Sri Lanka 106 C5
Mundesley U.K. 59 I6
Mundford U.K. 59 H6
Mundiwindi Australia 135 C5
Mundra India 104 B5
Mundrabilla Australia 132 C5
Munds Park U.S.A. 159 H4
Mundubbera Australia 137 E5
Mundwa India 104 C4
Munfordville U.S.A. 164 C5
Mungallala Australia 137 D5
Mungana Australia 136 D3
Mungári Moz. 123 D5
Mungbere Dem. Rep. Congo 122 C3
Mungeli India 105 E5
Munger India 105 F4
Mu Nggava i. Solomon Is see Rennell
Munggaresak, Tanjung pt Indon. 85 E2
Mungindi Australia 138 D2
Mungla Bangl. see Mongla
Mungo Angola 123 B5
Mungo, Lake Australia 138 A4
Mungo National Park Australia 138 A4
Munich Germany 57 M6
Munising U.S.A. 162 C2
Munjpur India 104 B5
Munkács Ukr. see Mukacheve
Munkebakken Norway 54 P2
Munkedal Sweden 55 G7
Munkfors Sweden 55 H7
Munkhafaḍ al Qaṭṭārah depr. Egypt see Qattara Depression
Munku-Sardyk, Gora mt. Mongolia/Rus. Fed. 94 E1
Münnerstadt Germany 63 K4
Munnik S. Africa 125 I2
Munroe Lake Canada 151 L3
Munsan S. Korea 91 B5
Munse Sulawesi Indon. 83 B4
Münster Hessen Germany 63 I5
Münster Niedersachsen Germany 63 K2
Münster Nordrhein-Westfalen Germany 63 H3
Munster reg. Ireland 61 D5
Münsterland reg. Germany 63 H3
Muntadgin Australia 135 B7
Munte Sulawesi Indon. 83 A2
Muntervary hd Ireland 61 C6
Munyal-Par sea feature India see Bassas de Pedro Padua Bank
Munzur Vadisi Milli Parkı nat. park Turkey 65 L4
Muojärvi l. Fin. 54 P4
Mương Nhe Vietnam 86 C2
Muong Sai Laos see Oudômxai
Muonio Fin. 54 M3
Muonioälven r. Fin./Sweden 54 M3
Muonionjoki r. Fin./Sweden see Muonioälven
Muor i. Maluku Indon. 83 D2
Mupa, Parque Nacional da nat. park Angola 123 B5
Muping Shandong China 95 J4
Muping China see Baoxing
Muqaynimah well Saudi Arabia 110 C6
Muqdisho Somalia see Mogadishu
Muquem Brazil 179 A1
Muqui Brazil 179 C3
Mur r. Austria 57 P7

also known as Mura (Croatia/Slovenia)

Mura r. Croatia/Slovenia see Mur
Murai, Tanjong pt Sing. 87 [inset]
Murai Reservoir Sing. 87 [inset]
Murakami Japan 91 E5
Murallón, Cerro mt. Chile 178 B7
Muramvya Burundi 122 C4
Murashi Rus. Fed. 52 K4
Murat r. Turkey 113 E3
Muratlı Turkey 69 L4
Muraysah, Ra's al pt Libya 112 B5
Murchison watercourse Australia 135 A6
Murchison, Mount Antarctica 188 H2
Murchison, Mount hill Australia 135 B6
Murchison Falls National Park Uganda 122 D3
Murcia Spain 67 F5
Murcia aut. comm. Spain 67 F5
Murcielagos Bay Mindanao Phil. 82 C4
Murdo U.S.A. 160 C3
Mure Japan 93 E2
Murehwa Zimbabwe 123 D5
Mureşul r. Romania 69 I1
Muret France 66 E5
Murewa Zimbabwe see Murehwa
Murfreesboro AR U.S.A. 161 E5
Murfreesboro TN U.S.A. 162 C5
Murg r. Germany 63 I6
Murgab Tajik. see Murghob
Murgab Turkm. see Murgap
Murgab r. Turkm. see Murgap
Murgap Turkm. 111 F2
Murgap r. Turkm. 109 J2
Murgha Kibzai Pak. 111 H4
Murghob Tajik. 111 I2
Murgon Australia 137 E5
Murgoo Australia 135 B6
Muri Qinghai China 94 D4
Muri Qinghai China 94 E4
Muri India 105 F5
Muria, Gunung mt. Indon. 85 E4
Muriaé Brazil 179 C3
Murid Pak. 111 G4
Muriege Angola 123 C4
Murih, Pulau i. Indon. 85 E2
Müritz l. Germany 63 M1
Müritz, Nationalpark nat. park Germany 63 N1
Murmansk Rus. Fed. 54 R2
Murmanskaya Oblast' admin. div. Rus. Fed. 54 S2
Murmanskiy Bereg coastal area Rus. Fed. 52 G1
Murmansk Oblast admin. div. Rus. Fed. see Murmanskaya Oblast'
Muro Japan 92 C4
Muro, Capo di c. Corsica France 66 I6
Murō-Akame-Aoyama Kokutei-kōen park Japan 92 C4
Murom Rus. Fed. 52 I5
Muromagi-gawa r. Japan 92 D2
Muroran Japan 90 F4
Muros Spain 67 B2
Muroto Japan 91 D6
Muroto-zaki pt Japan 91 D6
Murphy ID U.S.A. 156 D4
Murphy NC U.S.A. 163 D5
Murphysboro U.S.A. 160 F4
Murrah reg. Saudi Arabia 110 C6
Murrah al Kubrá, Al Buḩayrah al l. Egypt see Great Bitter Lake
Murrah aş Şughrá, Al Buḩayrah al l. Egypt see Little Bitter Lake
Murramarang National Park 138 I5
Murra Murra Australia 138 C2
Murrat el Kubra, Buheirat l. Egypt see Great Bitter Lake
Murrat el Sughra, Buheirat l. Egypt see Little Bitter Lake
▶Murray r. S.A. Australia 137 B7

3rd longest river in Oceania, and a major part of the longest (Murray-Darling).

Murray *r. W.A.* Australia **135** A8
Murray *KY* U.S.A. **161** F4
Murray *UT* U.S.A. **159** H1
Murray, Lake P.N.G. **81** K8
Murray, Lake U.S.A. **163** D5
Murray, Mount Y.T. Canada **149** O3
Murray Bridge Australia **137** B7

▶**Murray-Darling** *r.* Australia **132** E5
Longest river in Oceania.

Murray Downs Australia **134** F5
Murray Range *hills* Australia **135** E6
Murraysburg S. Africa **124** F6
Murray Sunset National Park Australia **137** C7
Murrhardt Germany **63** J6
Murrieta U.S.A. **158** E5
Murringo Australia **138** D5
Murrisk *reg.* Ireland **61** C4
Murroogh Ireland **61** C4

▶**Murrumbidgee** *r.* Australia **138** A5
4th longest river in Oceania.

Murrumburrah Australia **138** D5
Murrurundi Australia **138** E3
Mursan India **104** D4
Murshidabad India **105** G4
Murska Sobota Slovenia **68** G1
Mürt Iran **111** F5
Murtoa Australia **137** C8
Murua *i.* P.N.G. *see* **Woodlark Island**
Murud India **106** B2
Murud, Gunung *mt.* Indon. **85** F2
Murui *r.* Indon. **85** F3
Muruin Sum Shuiku *resr* China **95** J3
Murung *r.* Indon. **85** F3
Murung *r.* Indon. **85** F3
Murunkan Sri Lanka **106** D4
Murupara N.Z. **139** F4
Mururoa *atoll* Fr. Polynesia **187** K7
Murviedro Spain *see* **Sagunto**
Murwara India **104** E5
Murwillumbah Australia **138** F2
Murzechirla Turkm. **111** F2
Murzūq Libya **121** E2
Mürzzuschlag Austria **57** O7
Muş Turkey **113** F3
Mūsā, Khowr-e *b.* Iran **110** C4
Musakhel Pak. **111** H4
Musala *mt.* Bulg. **69** J3
Musala *i.* Indon. **84** B2
Musan N. Korea **90** C4
Musandam Peninsula Oman/U.A.E. **110** E5
Mūsā Qal'eh, Rūd-e *r.* Afgh. **111** G3
Musashino Japan **93** F3
Musay'īd Qatar *see* **Umm Sa'id**

▶**Muscat** Oman **110** E6
Capital of Oman.

Muscat *reg.* Oman **110** E5
Muscat and Oman *country* Asia *see* **Oman**
Muscatine U.S.A. **160** F3
Musgrave Australia **136** C2
Musgrave Harbour Canada **153** L4
Musgrave Ranges *mts* Australia **135** E6
Mushāsh al Kabid *well* Jordan **107** C5
Mushayyish, Wādī al *watercourse* Jordan **107** C4
Mushie Dem. Rep. Congo **122** B4
Mushkaf Pak. **111** G4
Musi *r.* Indon. **84** D3
Music Mountain U.S.A. **159** G4
Musina S. Africa **125** J2
Musinia Peak U.S.A. **159** H2
Muskeg *r.* Canada **150** F2
Muskeget Channel U.S.A. **165** J3
Muskegon *MI* U.S.A. **162** C3
Muskegon *MI* U.S.A. **164** B2
Muskegon *r.* U.S.A. **164** B2
Muskegon Heights U.S.A. **164** B2
Muskeg River Canada **150** G4
Muskogee U.S.A. **161** E5
Muskoka, Lake Canada **164** F1
Muskrat Dam Lake Canada **151** N4
Musmar Sudan **108** E6
Musoma Tanz. **122** D4
Musquanousse, Lac *l.* Canada **153** J4
Musquaro, Lac *l.* Canada **153** J4
Mussau Island P.N.G. **81** L7
Musselburgh U.K. **60** F5
Musselkanaal Neth. **62** H2
Musselshell *r.* U.S.A. **156** G3
Mussende Angola **123** B5
Mustafabad *Uttar Prad.* India **99** C8
Mustafakemalpaşa Turkey **69** M4
Mustau, Gora *mt. Xinjiang* China **98** D3
Mustjala Estonia **55** M7
Mustvee Estonia **55** O7
Musu-dan *pt* N. Korea **90** C4
Muswellbrook Australia **138** E4
Mūţ Egypt **108** C4
Mut Turkey **107** A1
Mutá, Ponta do *pt* Brazil **179** D1
Mutare Zimbabwe **123** D5
Mutayr *reg.* Saudi Arabia **110** B5
Mutina Italy *see* **Modena**
Muting Indon. **81** K8
Mutis Col. **176** C2
Mutis, Gunung *mt. Timor* Indon. **83** C5
Mutnyy Materik Rus. Fed. **52** L2
Mutoko Zimbabwe **123** D5
Mutsamudu Comoros **123** E5
Mutsu Japan **90** F4
Mutsuzawa Japan **93** G3
Muttaburra Australia **136** D4
Mutton Island Ireland **61** C5
Muttukuru India **106** D3
Muttupet India **106** C4
Mutum Brazil **179** C2
Mutunópolis Brazil **179** A1
Mutur Sri Lanka **106** D4
Mutusjärvi *r.* Fin. **54** O2
Muurola Fin. **54** N3
Mu Us Shamo *des.* China **95** G4
Muxaluando Angola **123** B4
Muxi China *see* **Muchuan**
Muxima Angola **123** B4
Muyezerskiy Rus. Fed. **54** R5
Muyinga Burundi **122** D4
Mŭynoq Uzbek. *see* **Mo'ynoq**
Muyumba Dem. Rep. Congo **123** C4
Muyunkum, Peski *des.* Kazakh. *see* **Moyynkum, Peski**
Muyuping China **97** F2
Muzaffarabad Pak. **111** I3
Muzaffargarh Pak. **111** H4
Muzaffarnagar India **104** D3
Muzaffarpur India **105** F4
Muzamane Moz. **125** K2
Muzat He *r.* China **98** C4
Muzhi Rus. Fed. **51** S2
Mūzīn Iran **111** F5
Muzon, Cape *AK* U.S.A. **149** N5
Múzquiz Mex. **167** E3
Muztag *mt. Xinjiang* China **99** C6
Muz Tag *mt. Xinjiang* China **99** D5
Muztagata *mt. Xinjiang* China **98** A5
Muztor Kyrg. *see* **Toktogul**
Mvadi Gabon **122** B3
Mvolo Sudan **121** F4
Mvuma Zimbabwe **123** D5
Mwanza Malawi **123** D5
Mwanza Tanz. **122** D4
Mwaro Burundi **122** C4
Mweelrea *hill* Ireland **61** C4
Mweka Dem. Rep. Congo **123** C4
Mwene-Ditu Dem. Rep. Congo **123** C4
Mwenezi Zimbabwe **123** D6
Mwenga Dem. Rep. Congo **122** C4
Mweru, Lake Dem. Rep. Congo/Zambia **123** C4
Mweru Wantipa National Park Zambia **123** C4
Mwimba Dem. Rep. Congo **123** C4
Mwinilunga Zambia **123** C5
Myadaung Myanmar **86** B2
Myadzyel Belarus **55** O9
Myajlar India **104** B4
Myall Lakes National Park Australia **138** F4
Myanaung Myanmar **86** A3
Myanmar *country* Asia **86** A2
Myauk-U Myanmar *see* **Mrauk-U**
Myaungmya Myanmar **86** A3
Myawadi Thai. **86** B3
Mybster U.K. **60** F2
Myebon Myanmar **86** A2
Myede Myanmar *see* **Aunglan**
Myeik Myanmar **87** B4
Myingyan Myanmar **86** A2
Myinkyado Myanmar **86** B2
Myinmoletkat *mt.* Myanmar **87** B4
Myitkyina Myanmar **86** B1
Myitson Myanmar **86** B2
Myitta Myanmar **87** B4
Myittha Myanmar **86** B2
Mykolayiv Ukr. **69** O1
Mykonos *i.* Greece **69** K6
Myla Rus. Fed. **52** K2
Myla *r.* Rus. Fed. **52** K2
Mylae *Sicily* Italy *see* **Milazzo**
Mylasa Turkey *see* **Milas**
Mymensing Bangl. *see* **Mymensingh**
Mymensingh Bangl. **105** G4
Mynämäki Fin. **55** M6
Mynaral Kazakh. **98** A3
Myōgi Japan **93** E2
Myōgi-Arafune-Saku-kōgen Kokutei-kōen *park* Japan **93** E2
Myōgi-san *mt.* Japan **93** E2
Myōken-yama *hill* Japan **92** A4
Myōkō Japan **93** E2
Myōkō-kōgen Japan **93** E2
Myŏnggan N. Korea **90** C4
Myory Belarus **55** O9
My Phước Vietnam **87** D5
Mýrdalsjökull *ice cap* Iceland **54** [inset]
Myre Norway **54** I2
Myrheden Sweden **54** L4
Myrhorod Ukr. **53** G6
Myrnam Canada **151** I4
Myronivka Ukr. **53** F6
Myrtle Beach U.S.A. **163** E5
Myrtleford Australia **138** C6
Myrtle Point U.S.A. **156** B4
Myrtoo Pelagos *sea* Greece **69** J6
Mysia *reg.* Turkey **69** L5
Mys Lazareva Rus. Fed. *see* **Lazarev**
Myślibórz Poland **57** O4
My Son Sanctuary *tourist site* Vietnam **86** E4
Mysore India **106** C3
Mysore *state* India *see* **Karnataka**
Mys Shmidta Rus. Fed. **77** T3
Mysy Rus. Fed. **52** L3
My Tho Vietnam **87** D5
Mytikas *mt.* Greece *see* **Olympus, Mount**
Mytilene *i.* Greece *see* **Lesbos**
Mytilini Greece **69** L5
Mytilini Strait Greece/Turkey **69** L5
Mytishchi Rus. Fed. **52** H5
Myton U.S.A. **159** H1
Myyeldino Rus. Fed. **52** L3
Mzamomhle S. Africa **125** H6
Mže *r.* Czech Rep. **63** M5
Mzimba Malawi **123** D5
Mzuzu Malawi **123** D5

N

Naab *r.* Germany **63** M5
Nā'ālehu U.S.A. **157** [inset]
Naantali Fin. **55** M6
Naas Ireland **61** F4
Naba Myanmar **86** B1
Nababeep S. Africa **124** C5
Nababganj Bangl. *see* **Nawabganj**
Nabadwip India *see* **Navadwip**
Nabarangapur India **106** D2
Nabarangpur India *see* **Nabarangapur**
Nabari Japan **92** C4
Nabari-gawa *r.* Japan **92** C4
Nabas *Panay* Phil. **82** C4
Nabatîyé et Tahta Lebanon **107** B3
Nabatiyet et Tahta Lebanon *see* **Nabatîyé et Tahta**
Nabberu, Lake *salt flat* Australia **135** C6
Nabburg Germany **63** M5
Naberera Tanz. **123** D4
Naberezhnyye Chelny Rus. Fed. **51** Q4
Nabesna *AK* U.S.A. **149** L3
Nabesna *r. AK* U.S.A. **149** L3
Nabesna Glacier *AK* U.S.A. **148** I3
Nabesna Village *AK* U.S.A. **149** L3
Nabeul Tunisia **68** D6
Nabha India **104** D3
Nabil'skiy Zaliv *lag.* Rus. Fed. **90** F2
Nabire Indon. **81** J7
Nabi Younés, Ras en *pt* Lebanon **107** B3
Nāblus West Bank **107** B3
Naboomspruit S. Africa **125** I3
Nabq Reserve *nature res.* Egypt **112** D5
Nābulus West Bank *see* **Nāblus**
Nacajuca Mex. **167** G5
Nacala Moz. **123** E5
Nacaome Hond. **166** [inset] I6
Nachalovo Rus. Fed. **53** K7
Nachicapau, Lac *l.* Canada **153** I2
Nachingwea Tanz. **123** D5
Nachna India **104** B4
Nachuge India **87** A5
Nacimiento Reservoir U.S.A. **158** C4
Naco U.S.A. **157** F7
Nacogdoches U.S.A. **161** E6
Nacozari de García Mex. **166** C2
Nada China *see* **Danzhou**
Nadachi Japan **93** E1
Nadaleen *r.* Canada **150** C2
Nadbai *Rajasthan* India **99** B8
Nådendal Fin. *see* **Naantali**
Nadezhdinskoye Rus. Fed. **90** D2
Nadiad India **104** C5
Nadol India **104** C4
Nador Morocco **67** E6
Nadqān, Qalamat *well* Saudi Arabia **110** C6
Nadūshan Iran **110** D3
Nadvirna Ukr. **53** E6
Nadvoitsy Rus. Fed. **52** G3
Nadvornaya Ukr. *see* **Nadvirna**
Nadym Rus. Fed. **76** I3
Næstved Denmark **55** G9
Nafarroa *aut. comm.* Spain *see* **Navarra**
Nafas, Ra's an *mt.* Egypt **107** B5
Nafḩa, Har *hill* Israel **107** B4
Nafpaktos Greece **69** I5
Nafplio Greece **69** J6
Naftalan Azer. **113** G2
Naft-e Safīd Iran **110** C4
Naft-e Shāh Iran *see* **Naft Shahr**
Naft Shahr Iran **110** B3
Nafūd ad Daḩl *des.* Saudi Arabia **110** B6
Nafūd al Ghuwayţah *des.* Saudi Arabia **107** D5
Nafūd al Jur'ā *des.* Saudi Arabia **110** B5
Nafūd as Sirr *des.* Saudi Arabia **110** B5
Nafūd as Surrah *des.* Saudi Arabia **110** A6
Nafūd Qunayfidhah *des.* Saudi Arabia **110** B5
Nafūsah, Jabal *hills* Libya **120** E1
Nafy Saudi Arabia **108** F4
Nag, Co *l.* China **99** E6
Naga Japan **92** B4
Naga *Luzon* Phil. **82** C3
Nagagami *r.* Canada **152** D4
Nagagami Lake Canada **152** D4
Nagahama Japan **91** D6
Nagahama *Shiga* Japan **92** C3
Naga Hills India **105** H4
Naga Hills *state* India *see* **Nagaland**
Nagai Island *AK* U.S.A. **148** G5
Nagaizumi Japan **93** E3
Nagakute Japan **92** D3
Nagaland *state* India **105** H4
Nagamangala India **106** C3
Nagambie Australia **138** B6
Nagano Japan **93** E2
Nagano *pref.* Japan **93** D2
Naganohara Japan **93** E2
Nagaoka Japan **91** E5
Nagaokakyō Japan **92** B4
Nagaon India **105** H4
Nagapatam India *see* **Nagapattinam**
Nagapattinam India **106** C4
Nagar *r.* Bangl./India **99** E8
Nagar *Hima. Prad.* India **109** M3
Nagar *Karnataka* India **106** B3
Nagara Japan **93** G3
Nagara-gawa *r.* Japan **92** C3
Nagaram India **106** D2
Nagareyama Japan **93** F3
Nagari Hills India **106** C3
Nagarjuna Sagar Reservoir India **106** C2
Nagar Parkar Pak. **111** H5
Nagar Untari India **105** E4
Nagarzê *Xizang* China **99** E7
Nagasaka Japan **93** E3
Nagasaki Japan **91** C6
Nagashima *Mie* Japan **92** C3
Nagato *Nagano* Japan **93** E2
Nagato Japan **91** C6
Nagatoro Japan **93** F2
Nagaur India **104** C4
Nagawa Japan **92** D2
Nagbhir India **106** C1
Nagda India **104** C5
Nageezi U.S.A. **159** J3
Nagercoil India **106** C4
Nagha Kalat Pak. **111** G5
Nag' Ḩammādī Egypt *see* **Naj' Ḩammādī**
Nagina India **104** D3
Nagiso Japan **92** D3
Nagjog *Xizang* China **99** G7
Nagold *r.* Germany **63** I6
Nagong Chu *r. Xizang* China *see* **Parlung Zangbo**
Nagorno-Karabakh *aut. reg.* Azer. *see* **Dağlıq Qarabağ**
Nagornyy Rus. Fed. **148** B3
Nagornyy Karabakh *aut. reg.* Azer. *see* **Dağlıq Qarabağ**
Nagorsk Rus. Fed. **52** K4
Nagoya Japan **92** C3
Nagpur India **104** D5
Nagqu *Xizang* China **99** F7
Nag Qu *r. Xizang* China **99** F7
Nagurskoye Rus. Fed. **76** F1
Nagyatád Hungary **68** G1
Nagybecskerek Serbia *see* **Zrenjanin**
Nagyenyed Romania *see* **Aiud**
Nagykanizsa Hungary **68** G1
Nagyvárad Romania *see* **Oradea**
Naha Japan **89** N7
Nahan India **104** D3
Nahanni Butte Canada **150** F2
Nahanni National Park Reserve N.W.T. Canada **149** P3
Nahanni Range *mts* Canada **150** F2
Naharāyim Jordan **107** B3
Nahariyya Israel **107** B3
Nahāvand Iran **110** C3
Nahr Dijlah *r.* Iraq/Syria **113** G5 *see* **Tigris**
Nahuel Huapi, Parque Nacional *nat. park* Arg. **178** B6
Nahunta U.S.A. **163** D6
Naic *Luzon* Phil. **82** C3
Naica Mex. **166** D3
Nai Ga Myanmar **96** C3
Naij Tal *Qinghai* China **94** C5
Naikliu *Timor* Indon. **83** B5
Nailung *Xizang* China **99** F7
Naiman Qi *Nei Mongol* China *see* **Daqin Tal**
Naimin Shuiquan *well Xinjiang* China **94** B2
Nain Canada **153** J2
Nā'īn Iran **110** D3
Nainital India **104** D3
Naini Tal India *see* **Nainital**
Nairn U.K. **60** F3
Nairn *r.* U.K. **60** F3

▶**Nairobi** Kenya **122** D4
Capital of Kenya.

Naissus Serbia *see* **Niš**
Naivasha Kenya **122** D4
Najaf Iraq **113** G5
Najafābād Iran **110** C3
Na'jān Saudi Arabia **110** B5
Najd *reg.* Saudi Arabia **108** F4
Nájera Spain **67** E2
Naj' Ḩammādī Egypt **108** D4
Naji *Nei Mongol* China **95** J1
Najibabad India **104** D3
Najin N. Korea **90** C4
Najitun *Nei Mongol* China *see* **Naji**
Najrān Saudi Arabia **108** F6
Naka *Hyōgo* Japan **92** A3
Naka *Ibaraki* Japan **93** G2
Nakadōri-shima *i.* Japan **91** C6
Na Kae Thai. **86** D3
Nakagawa *Nagano* Japan **93** D3
Naka-gawa *r.* Japan **93** G2
Nakagō Japan **93** E2
Nakai Japan **93** F3
Nakaizu Japan **93** F4
Nakajima *Fukushima* Japan **93** G1
Nakajima *Ishikawa* Japan **92** C1
Nakajō Japan **93** E2
Nakakawane Japan **93** E3
Nakambé *r.* Burkina Faso/Ghana *see* **White Volta**
Nakamichi Japan **93** E3
Nakaminato Japan **93** G2
Nakanbe *r.* Burkina Faso/Ghana *see* **White Volta**
Nakanno Rus. Fed. **77** L3
Nakano Japan **93** E2
Nakanojō Japan **93** E2
Nakano-take *mt.* Japan **93** F1
Nakasato *Gunma* Japan **93** E2
Nakasato *Niigata* Japan **93** E1
Nakasongola Uganda **121** G4
Nakatomi Japan **93** E3
Nakatsu Japan **91** C6
Nakatsu *Wakayama* Japan **92** B5
Nakatsugawa Japan **92** D3
Nakatsu-gawa *r.* Japan **93** E2
Nakfa Eritrea **108** E6
Nakhichevan' Azer. *see* **Naxçıvan**
Nakhl Egypt **107** A5
Nakhodka Rus. Fed. **90** D4
Nakhola India **105** H4
Nakhon Nayok Thai. **87** C4
Nakhon Pathom Thai. **87** C4
Nakhon Phanom Thai. **86** D3
Nakhon Ratchasima Thai. **86** C4
Nakhon Sawan Thai. **86** C4
Nakhon Si Thammarat Thai. **87** B5
Nakhtarana India **104** B5
Nakina Canada **152** D4
Nakina *r. B.C.* Canada **149** N4
Naknek *AK* U.S.A. **148** H4
Naknek Lake *AK* U.S.A. **148** H4
Nakodar *Punjab* India **99** A7
Nakonde Zambia **123** D4
Nakoso Japan **93** G2
Nakskov Denmark **55** G9
Naktong-gang *r.* S. Korea **91** C6
Nakuru Kenya **122** D4
Nakusp Canada **150** G5
Nal Pak. **111** G5
Nal *r.* Pak. **111** G5
Na-lang Myanmar **86** B2
Nalayh Mongolia **95** F2
Nalázi Moz. **125** K3
Nalbari India **105** G4
Nal'chik Rus. Fed. **113** F2
Naldurg India **106** C2
Nalgonda India **106** C2
Naliya India **104** B5
Nallamala Hills India **106** C3
Nallıhan Turkey **69** N4
Nālūt Libya **120** E1
Namaa, Tanjung *pt Seram* Indon. **83** D3
Namaacha Moz. **125** K3
Namacurra Moz. **123** D5
Namadgi National Park Australia **138** D5
Namahadi S. Africa **125** I4
Namai Bay Palau **82** [inset]
Namak, Daryācheh-ye *salt flat* Iran **110** C3
Namak, Kavīr-e *salt flat* Iran **110** E3
Namakkal India **106** C4
Namakwaland *reg.* Namibia *see* **Great Namaqualand**
Namakzar-e Shadad *salt flat* Iran **110** E4
Namaland *reg.* Namibia *see* **Great Namaqualand**
Namang Indon. **84** D3
Namangan Uzbek. **102** D3
Namaqualand *reg.* Namibia *see* **Great Namaqualand**
Namaqualand *reg.* S. Africa **124** C5
Namaqua National Park S. Africa **124** C6
Namas Indon. **81** K8
Namatanai P.N.G. **132** F2
Nambour Australia **138** F1
Nambu Japan *see* **Nanbu**
Nambucca Heads Australia **138** F3
Nambung National Park Australia **135** A7
Năm Căn Vietnam **87** D5
Namcha Barwa *mt. Xizang* China *see* **Namjagbarwa Feng**
Namche Bazar Nepal **105** F4
Namco *Xizang* China **99** E7
Nam Co *salt l.* China **99** E7
Namdalen *valley* Norway **54** H4
Namdalseid Norway **54** G4
Nam Định Vietnam **86** D2
Namegawa Japan **93** F2
Namelakl Passage Palau **82** [inset]
Namen Belgium *see* **Namur**
Namerikawa Japan **92** D2
Nam-gang *r.* N. Korea **91** B5
Namhae-do *i.* S. Korea **91** B6
Namhsan Myanmar **86** B2
Namiai Japan **92** D3
Namib Desert Namibia **124** B3
Namibe Angola **123** B5
Namibia *country* Africa **123** B6
Namibia Abyssal Plain *sea feature* N. Atlantic Ocean **184** I8
Namib-Naukluft Game Park *nature res.* Namibia **124** B3
Namie Japan **91** F5
Namīn Iran **113** H3
Namjagbarwa Feng *mt. Xizang* China **99** F7
Namka *Xizang* China **99** E7
Namlan Myanmar **86** B2
Namlang *r.* Myanmar **86** B2
Namlea *Buru* Indon. **83** C3
Namling *Xizang* China **99** E7
Nam Loi *r.* Myanmar *see* **Nanlei He**
Nam Nao National Park Thai. **86** C3
Nam Ngum Reservoir Laos **86** C3
Namoding *Xizang* China **99** D7
Namoi *r.* Australia **138** D3
Namoku Japan **93** E2
Namonuito *atoll* Micronesia **81** L5
Nampa *mt.* Nepal **104** E3
Nampa U.S.A. **156** D4
Nampala Mali **120** C3
Nam Phong Thai. **86** C3
Namp'o N. Korea **91** B5
Nampula Moz. **123** D5
Namrole *Buru* Indon. **83** C3
Namsai Myanmar **86** B1
Namsang Myanmar **86** B2
Namsen *r.* Norway **54** G4
Nam She Tsim *hill H.K.* China *see* **Sharp Peak**
Namsos Norway **54** G4
Namti Myanmar **86** B1
Namtok Myanmar **86** B3
Namtok Chattakan National Park Thai. **86** C3
Namton Myanmar **86** B2
Namtsy Rus. Fed. **77** N3
Namtu Myanmar **86** B2
Namu Canada **150** E5
Namuli, Monte *mt.* Moz. **123** D5
Namuno Moz. **123** D5
Namur Belgium **62** E4
Namutoni Namibia **123** B5
Namwŏn S. Korea **91** B6
Namya Ra Myanmar **86** B1
Namyit Island S. China Sea **80** E4
Nan Thai. **86** C3
Nana Bakassa Cent. Afr. Rep. **122** B3
Nanaimo Canada **150** F5
Nanakai Japan **93** G2
Nanam N. Korea **90** C4
Nan'an China **97** H3
Nanango Australia **138** F1
Nananib Plateau Namibia **124** C3
Nanao Japan **92** C1
Nanatsuka Japan **92** C2
Nanatsu-shima *i.* Japan **91** E5
Nanbai China *see* **Zunyi**
Nanbaxian *Qinghai* China **99** F5
Nanbin China *see* **Shizhu**
Nanbu China **96** E2
Nanbu Japan **93** E3
Nancha China **90** C3
Nanchang *Jiangxi* China **97** G2
Nanchang *Jiangxi* China **97** G2
Nanchangshan *Shandong* China *see* **Changdao**
Nanchong China **96** E2
Nanchuan China **96** E2
Nancowry *i.* India **87** A6
Nancun *Henan* China **95** H5
Nancun *Shanxi* China *see* **Zezhou**
Nancy France **62** G6
Nancy (Essey) *airport* France **62** G6
Nanda Devi *mt.* India **104** E3
Nanda Kot *mt.* India **104** E3
Nandan China **96** E3
Nandapur India **106** D2
Nanded India **106** C2
Nander India *see* **Nanded**
Nandewar Range *mts* Australia **138** E3
Nandod India **106** B1
Nandurbar India **104** C5
Nandyal India **106** C3
Nanfeng *Guangdong* China **97** F4
Nanfeng *Jiangxi* China **97** H3
Nang *Xizang* China **99** F7
Nanga Eboko Cameroon **120** E4
Nangah Dedai *Kalimantan* Indon. **85** E3
Nangahembaloh *Kalimantan* Indon. **85** F2
Nangahkemangai *Kalimantan* Indon. **85** F3
Nangahketungau *Kalimantan* Indon. **85** E2
Nangahmau *Kalimantan* Indon. **85** E3
Nangah Merakai *Kalimantan* Indon. **85** E2
Nangahpinoh *Kalimantan* Indon. **85** E3
Nangahsuruk *Kalimantan* Indon. **85** F2
Nangahtempuai *Kalimantan* Indon. **85** F2
Nangalao *i.* Phil. **82** C4

▶**Nanga Parbat** *mt.* Pak. **104** C2
9th highest mountain in the world and in Asia.

Nangar National Park Australia **138** D4
Nangataman *Kalimantan* Indon. **85** E3
Nangatayap *Kalimantan* Indon. **85** E3
Nangdoi *Qinghai* China **94** E4
Nangin Myanmar **87** B5
Nangnim-sanmaek *mts* N. Korea **91** B4
Nangong *Hebei* China **95** H4
Nangqên China **96** C1
Nangsin Sum *Nei Mongol* China **95** G4
Nangulangwa Tanz. **123** D4
Nanguneri India **106** C4
Nanhu *Gansu* China **98** F5
Nanhua *Gansu* China **94** D4
Nanhua China **96** D3
Nanhui China **97** I2
Nanjian China **96** D3
Nanjiang China **96** E1
Nanjing China **97** H1
Nanji Shan *i.* China **97** I3
Nanjō Japan **92** C3
Nanka Jiang *r.* China **96** C4
Nankang China **97** G3
Nanking China *see* **Nanjing**
Nankova Angola **123** B5
Nanle *Henan* China **95** H4
Nanlei He *r.* China **96** C4
also known as Nam Loi (Myanmar)
Nanling China **97** H2
Nan Ling *mts* China **97** F3
Nanliu Jiang *r.* China **97** F4
Nanlong China *see* **Nanbu**
Nanma *Shandong* China *see* **Yiyuan**
Nanmulingzue *Xizang* China *see* **Namling**
Nannilam India **106** C4
Nannine Australia **135** B6
Nanning China **97** F4
Nanniwan *Shaanxi* China **95** G4
Nannō Japan **92** C3
Nannup Australia **135** A8
Na Noi Thai. **86** C3
Nanortalik Greenland **147** N3
Nanouki *atoll* Kiribati *see* **Nonouti**
Nanouti *atoll* Kiribati *see* **Nonouti**
Nanpan Jiang *r.* China **96** E3
Nanpi *Hebei* China **95** I4
Nanpiao *Liaoning* China **95** J3
Nanping China **97** H3
Nanpu China *see* **Pucheng**
Nanri Dao *i.* China **97** H3
Nansei Japan **92** C4
Nansei-shotō *is* Japan *see* **Ryukyu Islands**
Nansei-shotō Trench *sea feature* N. Pacific Ocean *see* **Ryukyu Trench**
Nansen Basin *sea feature* Arctic Ocean **189** H1
Nansen Sound *sea chan.* Canada **147** I1
Nan-sha Ch'ün-tao *is* S. China Sea *see* **Spratly Islands**
Nanshan Island S. China Sea **80** F4
Nanshankou *Qinghai* China **94** C4
Nanshankou *Xinjiang* China **94** C3
Nansha Qundao *is* S. China Sea *see* **Spratly Islands**
Nansio Tanz. **122** D4
Nantai-san *hill* Japan **93** G2
Nantai-san *mt.* Japan **93** F2
Nantes France **66** D3
Nantes à Brest, Canal de France **66** C3
Nanteuil-le-Haudouin France **62** C5
Nanthi Kadal *lag.* Sri Lanka **106** D4
Nanticoke Canada **164** E2
Nanticoke U.S.A. **165** H4
Nantō Japan **92** C4
Nantong China **97** I2
Nantou China **97** [inset]
Nant'ou Taiwan **97** I4
Nantucket U.S.A. **165** J3
Nantucket Island U.S.A. **165** K3
Nantucket Sound *g.* U.S.A. **165** J3
Nantwich U.K. **59** E5
Nanumaga *i.* Tuvalu *see* **Nanumanga**
Nanumanga *i.* Tuvalu **133** H2
Nanumea *atoll* Tuvalu **133** H2
Nanuque Brazil **179** C2
Nanusa, Kepulauan *is* Indon. **83** C1
Nanushuk *r. AK* U.S.A. **149** J1
Nanxi China **96** E2
Nanxian China **97** G2
Nanxiong China **97** G3
Nanyang China **97** G1
Nanyuki Kenya **122** D4
Nanzamu *Liaoning* China **95** K3
Nanzhang China **97** F2
Nanzhao China *see* **Zhao'an**
Nanzhou China *see* **Nanxian**
Naococane, Lac *l.* Canada **153** H3
Naoero *country* S. Pacific Ocean *see* **Nauru**
Naogaon Bangl. **105** G4
Naoli He *r.* China **90** D3
Naomid, Dasht-e *des.* Afgh./Iran **111** F3
Naong, Bukit *mt.* Malaysia **85** F2
Naoshera India **104** C2
Napa U.S.A. **158** B2
Napaimiut *AK* U.S.A. **148** H3
Napakiak *AK* U.S.A. **148** G3
Napaktulik Lake Canada **151** H1
Napanee Canada **165** G1
Napaskiak *AK* U.S.A. **148** G3
Napasoq Greenland **147** M3
Naperville U.S.A. **164** A3
Napier N.Z. **139** F4
Napier Range *hills* Australia **134** D4
Napierville Canada **165** I1
Naples Italy **68** F4
Naples *FL* U.S.A. **163** D7
Naples *ME* U.S.A. **165** J2
Naples *TX* U.S.A. **161** E5
Naples *UT* U.S.A. **159** I1
Napo China **96** E4
Napo *r.* Ecuador **176** D4
Napoleon *IN* U.S.A. **164** C4
Napoleon *ND* U.S.A. **160** D2
Napoleon *OH* U.S.A. **164** C3
Napoli Italy *see* **Naples**
Naqadeh Iran **110** B2
Nara India **104** B5
Nara Japan **92** B4
Nara *pref.* Japan **92** B4
Nara Mali **120** C3
Narach Belarus **55** O9
Naracoorte Australia **137** C8
Naradhan Australia **138** C4
Narai-gawa *r.* Japan **93** D2
Narainpur India **106** D2
Narakawa Japan **93** D3
Naralua India **105** F4
Naran Mongolia **95** H2
Naranbulag *Dornod* Mongolia *see* **Bayandun**
Naranbulag *Uvs* Mongolia **94** C1
Naranjal Ecuador **176** C4
Naranjo Mex. **157** F8
Naranjos Mex. **167** F4
Naran Sebstein Bulag *spring Gansu* China **94** D3
Narasapur India **106** D2
Narasaraopet India **106** D2
Narashino Japan **93** G3
Narasinghapur India **106** E1
Narasun Rus. Fed. **95** H1
Narat *Xinjiang* China **98** D4
Narathiwat Thai. **87** C6
Narat Shan *mts* China **98** C4
Nara Visa U.S.A. **161** C5
Narayanganj Bangl. **105** G5
Narayanganj India **104** E5
Narayangarh India **104** C4
Narbada *r.* India *see* **Narmada**

Narberth U.K. 59 C7
Narbo France see Narbonne
Narbonne France 66 F5
Narborough Island Galápagos Ecuador see Fernandina, Isla
Narcea r. Spain 67 C2
Narcondam Island India 87 A4
Nardò Italy 68 H4
Narechi r. Pak. 111 H4
Narembeen Australia 135 B8
Nares Abyssal Plain sea feature S. Atlantic Ocean 184 D4
Nares Deep sea feature N. Atlantic Ocean 184 D4
Nares Strait Canada/Greenland 147 K2
Naretha Australia 135 D7
Narew r. Poland 57 R4
Narib Namibia 124 C3
Narikel Jinjira i. Bangl. see St Martin's Island
Narimanov Rus. Fed. 53 J7
Narimskiy Khrebet mts Kazakh. see Narymskiy Khrebet
Narin Afgh. 111 H2
Narin reg. Afgh. 111 H2
Narin Nei Mongol China 95 G4
Narince Turkey 112 E3
Narin Gol watercourse China 99 F5
Narita Japan 93 G3
Narita airport Japan 93 G3
Nariu-misaki pt Japan 92 B3
Nariynteel Mongolia 94 E2
Narizon, Punta pt Mex. 166 C3
Narkher India 104 D5
Narmada r. India 104 C5
Narman Turkey 113 F2
Narnaul India 104 D3
Narni Italy 68 E3
Narnia Italy see Narni
Narodnaya, Gora mt. Rus. Fed. 51 S3
Naro-Fominsk Rus. Fed. 53 H5
Narok Kenya 122 D4
Narooma Australia 138 E6
Narovchat Rus. Fed. 53 I5
Narowlya Belarus 53 F6
Närpes Fin. 54 L5
Narrabri Australia 138 D3
Narragansett Bay U.S.A. 165 J3
Narran r. Australia 138 C2
Narrandera Australia 138 C5
Narran Lake Australia 138 C2
Narrogin Australia 135 B8
Narromine Australia 138 D4
Narrows U.S.A. 164 E5
Narrowsburg U.S.A. 165 H3
Narsapur India 106 C2
Narsaq Greenland 147 N3
Narshingdi Bangl. see Narsingdi
Narsimhapur India see Narsinghpur
Narsingdi Bangl. 105 G5
Narsinghpur India 104 D5
Narsipatnam India 106 D2
Nart Nei Mongol China 95 H3
Nart Mongolia see Orhon
Nartkala Rus. Fed. 113 F2
Narusawa Japan 93 E3
Narutō Japan 93 G3
Naruto Japan 91 D6
Narva Estonia 55 P7
Narva Bay Estonia/Rus. Fed. 55 O7
Narvacan Luzon Phil. 82 C2
Narva laht b. Estonia/Rus. Fed. see Narva Bay
Narva Reservoir resr Estonia/Rus. Fed. see Narvskoye Vodokhranilishche
Narva veehoidla resr Estonia/Rus. Fed. see Narvskoye Vodokhranilishche
Narvik Norway 54 J2
Narvskiy Zaliv b. Estonia/Rus. Fed. see Narva Bay
Narvskoye Vodokhranilishche resr Estonia/Rus. Fed. 55 P7
Narwana India 104 D3
Nar'yan-Mar Rus. Fed. 52 L2
Narymskiy Khrebet mts Kazakh. 102 F2
Naryn Kyrg. 102 E3
Naryn admin. div. Kyrg. 98 A4
Naryn r. Kyrg./Uzbek. 98 A4
Naryn Rus. Fed. 94 C1
Narynkol Kazakh. 98 C4
Näsåker Sweden 54 J5
Na Scealaga is Ireland see The Skelligs
Nash Harbor AK U.S.A. 148 F3
Nashik India 106 B1
Nashua U.S.A. 165 J2
Nashville AR U.S.A. 161 E5
Nashville GA U.S.A. 163 D6
Nashville IN U.S.A. 164 B4
Nashville NC U.S.A. 162 E5
Nashville OH U.S.A. 164 D3

▶Nashville TN U.S.A. 162 C4
Capital of Tennessee.

Naşīb Syria 107 C3
Näsijärvi l. Fin. 55 M6
Nasik India see Nashik
Nasilat Kalimantan Indon. 85 E2
Nasir Pak. 111 H4
Nasir Sudan 108 D8
Nasirabad Bangl. see Mymensingh
Nasirabad India 104 C4
Nāşirīyah Iraq 113 G5
Naskaupi r. Canada 153 J3
Naşr Egypt 112 C5
Nasratabad Iran see Zābol
Naşrīān-e Pā'īn Iran 110 B3
Nass r. B.C. Canada 149 O5
Nassau r. Australia 136 C2

▶Nassau Bahamas 163 E7
Capital of The Bahamas.

Nassau i. Cook Is 133 J3
Nassau U.S.A. 165 I2
Nassawadox U.S.A. 165 H5
Nasser, Lake resr Egypt 108 D5
Nässjö Sweden 55 I8
Nassuttooq inlet Greenland 147 M3
Nastapoca r. Canada 152 F2
Nastapoka Islands Canada 152 F2
Nasu Japan 93 G1
Nasu-dake vol. Japan 93 F1
Nasugbu Luzon Phil. 82 C3
Nasva Rus. Fed. 52 F4
Nata Botswana 123 C6
Nataboti Buru Indon. 83 C3
Natal Brazil 177 K5
Natal Sumatera Indon. 84 B2
Natal prov. S. Africa see KwaZulu-Natal
Natal Basin sea feature Indian Ocean 185 K8
Naţanz Iran 110 C3
Natashō Japan 92 B3
Natashquan Canada 153 J4
Natashquan r. Canada 153 J4
Natazhat, Mount AK U.S.A. 149 L3
Natchez U.S.A. 161 F6
Natchitoches U.S.A. 161 E6
Nathalia Australia 138 B6
Nathia Gali Pak. 111 I3
Nati, Punta pt Spain 67 H3
Natillas Mex. 167 E3
Nation AK U.S.A. 149 L2
National City U.S.A. 158 E5
National West Coast Tourist Recreation Area park Namibia 124 B2
Natitingou Benin 120 D3
Natividad, Isla i. Mex. 166 B3
Natividade Brazil 177 I6
Natkyizin Myanmar 86 B4
Natla r. N.W.T. Canada 149 O3
Natmauk Myanmar 86 A2
Nator Bangl. see Natore
Nátora Mex. 157 F7
Natore Bangl. 105 G4
Natori Japan 91 F5
Natron, Lake salt l. Tanz. 122 D4
Nattai National Park Australia 138 E5
Nattalin Myanmar 86 A3
Nattaung mt. Myanmar 86 B3
Na'tū Iran 111 F3
Natuashish 153 J3
Natuna, Kepulauan is Indon. 85 D1
Natuna Besar i. Indon. 85 E1
Natural Bridges National Monument nat. park U.S.A. 159 H3
Naturaliste, Cape Australia 135 A8
Naturaliste Plateau sea feature Indian Ocean 185 P8
Naturita U.S.A. 159 I2
Nauchas Namibia 124 C2
Nau Co l. Xizang China 99 C6
Nauen Germany 63 M2
Naufragados, Ponta dos pt Brazil 179 A4
Naujan Mindoro Phil. 82 C3
Naujoji Akmenė Lith. 55 M8
Naukh India 104 C4
Naukot Pak. 111 H5
Naumburg (Hessen) Germany 63 J3
Naumburg (Saale) Germany 63 L3
Naunglon Myanmar 86 B3
Naungpale Myanmar 86 B3
Naupada India 106 E2
Na'ūr Jordan 107 B4
Nauroz Kalat Pak. 111 G4
Naurskaya Rus. Fed. 113 G2
Nauru i. Nauru 133 G2
Nauru country S. Pacific Ocean 133 G2
Naushki Rus. Fed. 94 F1
Naustdal Norway 55 D6
Nauta Peru 176 D4
Nautaca Uzbek. see Qarshi
Nautanwa Uttar Prad. India 99 C8
Naute Dam Namibia 124 C4
Nautla Mex. 167 F4
Nauzad Afgh. 111 G3
Nava Mex. 167 E2
Navadwip India 105 G5
Navahrudak Belarus 55 N10
Navajo Lake U.S.A. 159 J3
Navajo Mountain U.S.A. 159 H3
Naval Phil. 82 D4
Navalmoral de la Mata Spain 67 D4
Navalvillar de Pela Spain 67 D4
Navan Ireland 61 F4
Navangar India see Jamnagar
Navapolatsk Belarus 55 P9
Nāvar, Dasht-e depr. Afgh. 111 G3
Navarin, Mys c. Rus. Fed. 77 S3
Navarra aut. comm. Spain 67 F2
Navarra, Comunidad Foral de aut. comm. Spain see Navarra
Navarre Australia 138 A6
Navarre aut. comm. Spain see Navarra
Navarro r. U.S.A. 158 B2
Navashino Rus. Fed. 52 I5
Navasota U.S.A. 161 D6
Navasota r. TX U.S.A. 167 F2

▶Navassa Island terr. West Indies 169 I5
United States Unincorporated Territory.

Naver r. U.K. 60 E2
Näverede Sweden 54 I5
Navi Mumbai 106 B2
Navlakhi India 104 B5
Navlya Rus. Fed. 53 G5
Năvodari Romania 69 M2
Navoi Uzbek. see Navoiy
Navoiy Uzbek. 111 G1
Navojoa Mex. 166 C3
Navolato Mex. 166 D3
Návpaktos Greece see Nafpaktos
Návplion Greece see Nafplio
Navşar Turkey see Şemdinli
Navsari India 106 B1
Navy Town AK U.S.A. 148 [inset]
Nawá Syria 107 C3
Nawabganj Bangl. 105 G4
Nawabshah Pak. 111 H5
Nawada India 105 F4
Nāwah Afgh. 111 G3
Nawalgarh India 104 C4
Nawanshahr India 104 D3
Nawan Shehar India see Nawanshahr
Nawar, Dasht-i depr. Afgh. see Nāvar, Dasht-e
Nawarangpur India see Nabarangapur
Nawngcho Myanmar see Nawnghkio
Nawnghkio Myanmar 86 B2
Nawng Hpa Myanmar 86 B2
Nawngleng Myanmar 86 B2
Nawoiy Uzbek. see Navoiy
Naxçıvan Azer. 113 G3
Naxos i. Greece 69 K6
Nayag Xizang China 99 F6
Nayagarh India 106 E1
Nayak Afgh. 111 G3
Nayar Mex. 168 D4
Nayarit state Mex. 166 D4
Nāy Band, Kūh-e mt. Iran 110 E3
Nayong China 96 E3
Nayoro Japan 90 F3

▶Nay Pyi Taw Myanmar 86 B3
Joint capital (with Rangoon) of Myanmar.

Nazaré Brazil 179 D1
Nazareno Mex. 166 E3
Nazareth Israel 107 B3
Nazário Brazil 179 A2
Nazas Mex. 166 D3
Nazas r. Mex. 166 D3
Nazca Peru 176 D6
Nazca Ridge sea feature S. Pacific Ocean 187 O7
Nazerat Israel see Nazareth
Nāzīl Iran 111 F4
Nazilli Turkey 69 M6
Nazimabad Pak. 111 G5
Nazımiye Turkey 113 E3
Nazir Hat Bangl. 105 G5
Nazko Canada 150 F4
Nazran' Rus. Fed. 113 G2
Nazrēt Eth. 122 D3
Nazwá Oman 110 E6
Ncojane Botswana 124 E2
N'dalatando Angola 123 B4
Ndao i. Indon. 83 B5
Ndélé Cent. Afr. Rep. 122 C3
Ndendé Gabon 122 B4
Ndende i. Solomon Is see Ndeni
Ndeni i. Solomon Is 133 G3

▶Ndjamena Chad 121 E3
Capital of Chad.

N'Djamena Chad see Ndjamena
Ndjouani i. Comoros see Nzwani
Ndoi i. Fiji see Doi
Ndola Zambia 123 C5
Nduke i. Solomon Is see Kolombangara
Ndwedwe S. Africa 125 J5
Ne, Hon i. Vietnam 86 D3
Neabul Creek r. Australia 138 C1
Neagari Japan 92 C2
Neagh, Lough l. U.K. 61 F3
Neah Bay U.S.A. 156 B2
Neale, Lake salt flat Australia 135 E6
Nea Liosia Greece 69 J5
Neapoli Greece 69 J6
Neapolis Italy see Naples
Near Islands AK U.S.A. 148 [inset]
Nea Roda Greece 69 J4
Neath U.K. 59 D7
Neath r. U.K. 59 D7
Neba Japan 92 D3
Nebbi Uganda 122 D3
Nebesnaya, Gora mt. Xinjiang China 98 C4
Nebine Creek r. Australia 138 C2
Neblina, Pico da mt. Brazil 176 E3
Nebo Australia 136 E4
Nebo, Mount U.S.A. 159 H2
Nebolchi Rus. Fed. 52 G4
Nebraska state U.S.A. 160 C3
Nebraska City U.S.A. 160 E3
Nebrodi, Monti mts Sicily Italy 68 F6
Neches r. U.S.A. 161 E6
Nechisar National Park Eth. 122 D3
Nechranice, Vodní nádrž resr Czech Rep. 63 N4
Neckar r. Germany 63 I5
Neckarsulm Germany 63 J5
Necker Island U.S.A. 186 J4
Necochea Arg. 178 E5
Nederland country Europe see Netherlands
Nederlandse Antillen terr. Caribbean Sea/West Indies see Netherlands Antilles
Neder Rijn r. Neth. 62 F3
Nedlouc, Lac l. Canada 153 G2
Nedluk Lake Canada see Nedlouc, Lac
Nedre Soppero Sweden 54 L2
Nédroma Alg. 67 F6
Neeba-san mt. Japan 93 E2
Needle Mountain U.S.A. 156 F3
Needles U.S.A. 159 F4
Neemach India see Neemuch
Neemuch India 104 C4
Neenah U.S.A. 164 A1
Neepawa Canada 151 L5
Neergaard Lake Canada 147 J2
Neerijnen Neth. 62 F3
Neerpelt Belgium 62 F3
Neftçala Azer. 113 H3
Neftechala Azer. see Uzboy
Neftechala Azer. see Neftçala
Neftegorsk Sakhalinskaya Oblast' Rus. Fed. 90 F1
Neftegorsk Samarskaya Oblast' Rus. Fed. 53 K5
Neftekamsk Rus. Fed. 51 Q4
Neftekumsk Rus. Fed. 113 G1
Nefteyugansk Rus. Fed. 76 I3
Neftezavodsk Turkm. see Seýdi
Neftezawodsk Turkm. see Seýdi
Nefyn U.K. 59 C6
Nefza Tunisia 68 C6
Negage Angola 123 B4
Negār Iran 110 E4
Negara Bali Indon. 85 F5
Negara Kalimantan Indon. 85 F3
Negara r. Indon. 85 F3
Negēlē Eth. 122 D3
Negeri Sembilan state Malaysia 84 C2
Negev des. Israel 107 B4
Negomane Moz. 123 D5
Negombo Sri Lanka 106 C5
Negotino Macedonia 69 J4
Negra, Cordillera mts Peru 176 C5
Negra, Punta pt Peru 176 B5
Negra, Serra mts Brazil 179 C2
Negrais, Cape Myanmar 86 A4
Négrine Alg. 68 B7
Negri Sembilan state Malaysia see Negeri Sembilan
Negro r. Arg. 178 D6
Negro r. Brazil 177 G7
Negro r. Brazil 179 A4
Negro r. S. America 176 G4
Negro, Cabo c. Morocco 67 D6
Negroponte i. Greece see Evvoia
Negros i. Phil. 82 C4
Negru Vodă, Podişul plat. Romania 69 M3
Nehbandān Iran 111 F4
Nehe Heilong. China 95 K1
Neiguanying Gansu China 94 F5
Neijiang China 96 E2
Neilburg Canada 151 I4
Neimenggu aut. reg. China see Nei Mongol Zizhiqu
Nei Mongol Zizhiqu aut. reg. China 95 E3
Neinstedt Germany 63 L3
Neiqiu Hebei China 95 H4
Neiva Col. 176 C3
Neixiang China 97 F1
Nejanilini Lake Canada 151 L3
Nejapa Mex. 167 G5
Nejd reg. Saudi Arabia see Najd
Neka Iran 110 D2
Nek'emtē Eth. 122 D3
Neko-zaki pt Japan 92 A3
Nekrasovskoye Rus. Fed. 52 I4
Neksø Denmark 55 I9
Nelang India 104 D3
Nelia Australia 136 C4
Nelidovo Rus. Fed. 52 G4
Neligh U.S.A. 160 D3
Nel'kan Rus. Fed. 77 P3
Nellore India 106 C3
Nelluz watercourse Turkey 107 D1
Nel'ma Rus. Fed. 90 E3
Nelson Canada 150 G5
Nelson r. Canada 151 M3
Nelson N.Z. 139 D5
Nelson U.K. 58 E5
Nelson U.S.A. 159 G4
Nelson, Cape Australia 137 C8
Nelson, Cape P.N.G. 81 L8
Nelson, Estrecho strait Chile 178 A8
Nelson Bay Australia 138 F4
Nelson Forks Canada 150 F3
Nelsonia U.S.A. 165 H5
Nelson Island AK U.S.A. 148 F3
Nelson Lagoon AK U.S.A. 148 G5
Nelson Lakes National Park N.Z. 139 D6
Nelson Reservoir U.S.A. 156 G2
Nelspruit S. Africa 125 J3
Néma Mauritania 120 C3
Nema Rus. Fed. 52 K4
Neman r. Belarus/Lith. see Nyoman
Neman Rus. Fed. 55 M9
Nemausus France see Nîmes
Nemawar India 104 D5
Nemed Rus. Fed. 52 L3
Nementcha, Monts des mts Alg. 68 B7
Nemetocenna France see Arras
Nemetskiy, Mys c. Rus. Fed. 54 Q2
Nemirov Ukr. see Nemyriv
Nemiscau r. Canada 152 F4
Nemiscau, Lac l. Canada 152 F4
Nemor He r. China 95 K1
Nemours Alg. see Ghazaouet
Nemours France 66 F2
Nemrut Dağı mt. Turkey 113 F3
Nemunas r. Lith. see Nyoman
Nemuro Japan 90 G4
Nemuro-kaikyō sea chan. Japan/Rus. Fed. 90 G4
Nemyriv Ukr. 53 F6
Nenagh Ireland 61 D5
Nenan Heilong. China 95 K1
Nenana AK U.S.A. 149 J2
Nenana r. AK U.S.A. 149 J2
Nene r. U.K. 59 H6
Nenjiang Heilong. China 95 K1
Nen Jiang r. China 95 K2
Neo Japan 92 C3
Neo-gawa r. Japan 92 C3
Neosho U.S.A. 161 E4
Nepal country Asia 105 E3
Nepalganj Nepal 105 E3
Nepean Canada 165 H1
Nepean, Point Australia 138 B7
Nephi U.S.A. 159 H2
Nephin hill Ireland 61 C3
Nephin Beg Range hills Ireland 61 C3
Nepisiguit r. Canada 153 I5
Nepoko r. Dem. Rep. Congo 122 C3
Nérac France 66 E4
Neragon Island AK U.S.A. 148 F3
Nerang Australia 138 F1
Nera Tso l. China 105 H3
Nerchinsk Rus. Fed. 89 L2
Nerekhta Rus. Fed. 52 I4
Néret, Lac l. Canada 153 H3
Neretva r. Bos.-Herz./Croatia 68 G3
Nêri Pünco l. Xizang China 99 E7
Neriquinha Angola 123 C5
Neris r. Lith. 55 M9
also known as Viliya (Belarus/Lithuania)
Nerl' r. Rus. Fed. 52 H4
Nerópolis Brazil 179 A2
Neryungri Rus. Fed. 77 N4
Nes Neth. 62 F1
Nes Norway 55 F6
Nes' Rus. Fed. 52 J2
Nesbyen Norway 55 F6
Neshkan Rus. Fed. 148 D2
Neshkenpil'khyn, Laguna lag. Rus. Fed. 148 D2
Neskaupstaður Iceland 54 [inset]
Nesle France 62 C5
Nesna Norway 54 H3
Nesri India 106 B2
Ness r. U.K. 60 E3
Ness, Loch l. U.K. 60 E3
Ness City U.S.A. 160 D4
Nesse r. Germany 63 K4
Nesselrode, Mount Canada/U.S.A. 149 N4
Nestor Falls Canada 151 M5
Nestos r. Greece 69 K4
also known as Mesta
Nesvizh Belarus see Nyasvizh
Netanya Israel 107 B3
Netherlands country Europe 62 F2

▶Netherlands Antilles terr. Caribbean Sea/West Indies dissolved in 2010. (Formerly consisted of Aruba, Bonaire, Curaçao, Saba, Sint Eustatius, and Sint Maarten)

Netphen Germany 63 I4
Netrakona Bangl. 105 G4
Netrokona Bangl. see Netrakona
Nettilling Lake Canada 147 K3
Neubrandenburg Germany 63 N1
Neuburg an der Donau Germany 63 L6
Neuchâtel Switz. 66 H3
Neuchâtel, Lac de l. Switz. 66 H3
Neuendettelsau Germany 63 K5
Neuenhaus Germany 62 G2
Neuenkirchen Germany 63 J1
Neuenkirchen (Oldenburg) Germany 63 I2
Neufchâteau Belgium 62 F5
Neufchâteau France 66 G2
Neufchâtel-en-Bray France 62 B5
Neufchâtel-Hardelot France 62 B4
Neuharlingersiel Germany 63 H1
Neuhausen Rus. Fed. see Gur'yevsk
Neuhof Germany 63 J4
Neu Kaliß Germany 63 L1
Neukirchen Hessen Germany 63 J4
Neukirchen Sachsen Germany 63 M4
Neukuhren Rus. Fed. see Pionerskiy
Neumarkt in der Oberpfalz Germany 63 L5
Neumayer research station Antarctica 188 B2
Neumünster Germany 57 L3
Neunburg vorm Wald Germany 63 M5
Neunkirchen Austria 57 P7
Neunkirchen Germany 63 H5
Neuquén Arg. 178 C5
Neuruppin Germany 63 M2
Neu Sandez Poland see Nowy Sącz
Neuse r. U.S.A. 163 E5
Neusiedler See l. Austria/Hungary 57 P7
Neusiedler See Seewinkel, Nationalpark nat. park Austria 57 P7
Neuss Germany 62 G3
Neustadt (Wied) Germany 63 H4
Neustadt am Rübenberge Germany 63 J2
Neustadt an der Aisch Germany 63 K5
Neustadt an der Hardt Germany see Neustadt an der Weinstraße
Neustadt an der Waldnaab Germany 63 M5
Neustadt an der Weinstraße Germany 63 I5
Neustadt bei Coburg Germany 63 L4
Neustadt-Glewe Germany 63 L1
Neustrelitz Germany 63 N1
Neutraubling Germany 63 M6
Neuville-lès-Dieppe France 62 B5
Neuwied Germany 63 H4
Neu Wulmstorf Germany 63 J1
Nevada IA U.S.A. 160 E3
Nevada MO U.S.A. 160 E4
Nevada state U.S.A. 156 D5
Nevada, Sierra mts Spain 67 E5
Nevada, Sierra mts U.S.A. 158 C1
Nevada City U.S.A. 158 C2
Nevado, Cerro mt. Arg. 178 C5
Nevado, Sierra del mts Arg. 178 C5
Nevado de Colima, Parque Nacional nat. park Mex. 166 E5
Nevasa India 106 B2
Nevatim Israel 107 B4
Nevdubstroy Rus. Fed. see Kirovsk
Nevel' Rus. Fed. 52 F4
Nevel'sk Rus. Fed. 90 F3
Never Rus. Fed. 90 B1
Nevers France 66 F3
Nevertire Australia 138 C3
Nevesinje Bos.-Herz. 68 H3
Nevinnomyssk Rus. Fed. 113 F1
Nevşehir Turkey 112 D3
Nevskoye Rus. Fed. 90 D3
New r. CA U.S.A. 159 F5
New r. WV U.S.A. 164 E5
Newala Tanz. 123 D5
New Albany IN U.S.A. 164 C4
New Albany MS U.S.A. 161 F5
New Amsterdam Guyana 177 G2
New Amsterdam U.S.A. see New York
New Angledool Australia 138 C2
Newark DE U.S.A. 165 H4
Newark NJ U.S.A. 165 H3
Newark NY U.S.A. 165 G2
Newark OH U.S.A. 164 D3
Newark airport U.S.A. 162 F3
Newark Lake U.S.A. 159 F2
Newark-on-Trent U.K. 59 G5
New Bedford U.S.A. 165 J3
Newberg U.S.A. 156 C3
New Berlin U.S.A. 165 H2
New Bern U.S.A. 163 E5
Newberry IN U.S.A. 164 B4
Newberry MI U.S.A. 162 C2
Newberry SC U.S.A. 163 D5
Newberry National Volcanic Monument nat. park U.S.A. 156 C4
Newberry Springs U.S.A. 158 E4
New Bethlehem U.S.A. 164 F3
Newbiggin-by-the-Sea U.K. 58 F3
New Bight Bahamas 163 F7
New Bloomfield U.S.A. 165 G3
New Bombay see Navi Mumbai
Newboro Canada 165 G1
New Boston OH U.S.A. 164 D4
New Boston TX U.S.A. 161 E5
New Braunfels U.S.A. 161 D6
Newbridge Ireland 61 F4
New Britain i. P.N.G. 81 L8
New Britain U.S.A. 165 I3
New Britain Trench sea feature S. Pacific Ocean 186 G6
New Brunswick prov. Canada 153 I5
New Brunswick U.S.A. 165 H3
New Buffalo U.S.A. 164 B3
Newburgh Canada 165 G1
Newburgh U.K. 60 G3
Newburgh U.S.A. 165 H3
Newbury U.K. 59 F7
Newburyport U.S.A. 165 J2
Newby Bridge U.K. 58 E4

▶New Caledonia terr. S. Pacific Ocean 133 G4
French Overseas Collectivity.

New Caledonia Trough sea feature Tasman Sea 186 G7
New Carlisle Canada 153 I4
Newcastle Australia 138 E4
Newcastle Canada 165 F2
Newcastle Ireland 61 F4
Newcastle S. Africa 125 I4
Newcastle U.K. 61 G3
New Castle CO U.S.A. 159 J2
New Castle IN U.S.A. 164 C4
New Castle KY U.S.A. 164 C4
New Castle PA U.S.A. 164 E3
Newcastle UT U.S.A. 159 G3
New Castle VA U.S.A. 164 E5
Newcastle WY U.S.A. 156 G4
Newcastle Emlyn U.K. 59 C6
Newcastle-under-Lyme U.K. 59 E5
Newcastle upon Tyne U.K. 58 F4
Newcastle Waters Australia 134 F4
Newcastle West Ireland 61 C5
Newchwang Liaoning China see Yingkou
New City U.S.A. 165 I3
Newcomb U.S.A. 159 I3
New Concord U.S.A. 164 E4
New Cumberland U.S.A. 164 E3
New Cumnock U.K. 60 E5
New Deer U.K. 60 G3

▶New Delhi India 104 D3
Capital of India.

New Don Pedro Reservoir U.S.A. 158 C3
Newell U.S.A. 160 C2
Newell, Lake salt flat Australia 135 D6
Newell, Lake Canada 151 I5
New England National Park Australia 138 F3
New England Range mts Australia 138 E3
New England Seamounts sea feature N. Atlantic Ocean 184 E3
Newenham, Cape AK U.S.A. 148 G4
Newent U.K. 59 E7
New Era U.S.A. 164 B2
Newfane NY U.S.A. 165 F2
Newfane VT U.S.A. 165 I2
New Forest National Park 59 F8
Newfoundland i. Canada 153 K4
Newfoundland prov. Canada see Newfoundland and Labrador
Newfoundland and Labrador prov. Canada 153 K3
Newfoundland Evaporation Basin salt l. U.S.A. 159 G1
New Galloway U.K. 60 E5
New Georgia i. Solomon Is 133 F2
New Georgia Islands Solomon Is 133 F2
New Georgia Sound sea chan. Solomon Is 133 F2
New Glasgow Canada 153 J5

▶New Guinea i. Indon./P.N.G. 81 K8
Largest island in Oceania, and 2nd in the world.

Newhalen AK U.S.A. 148 I4
New Halfa Sudan 108 E6
New Hamilton AK U.S.A. 148 G3
New Hampshire state U.S.A. 165 J1
New Hampton U.S.A. 160 E3
New Hanover i. P.N.G. 132 F2
New Haven CT U.S.A. 165 I3
New Haven IN U.S.A. 164 C3
New Haven WV U.S.A. 164 E4
New Hebrides country S. Pacific Ocean see Vanuatu
New Hebrides Trench sea feature S. Pacific Ocean 186 H7
New Holstein U.S.A. 164 A2
New Iberia U.S.A. 161 F6
Newington S. Africa 125 J3
Newinn Ireland 61 E5
New Ireland i. P.N.G. 132 F2
New Jersey state U.S.A. 165 H4
New Kensington U.S.A. 164 F3
New Kent U.S.A. 165 G5
Newkirk U.S.A. 161 D4
New Lanark U.K. 60 F5
Newland Range hills Australia 135 C7
New Lexington U.S.A. 164 D4
New Liskeard Canada 152 F5
New London CT U.S.A. 165 I3
New London MO U.S.A. 160 F4
New Madrid U.S.A. 161 F4
Newman Australia 135 B5
Newman U.S.A. 158 C3
Newmarket Canada 164 F1
Newmarket Ireland 61 C5
Newmarket U.K. 59 H6
New Market U.S.A. 165 F4
Newmarket-on-Fergus Ireland 61 D5
New Martinsville U.S.A. 164 E4
New Meadows U.S.A. 156 D3
New Mexico state U.S.A. 157 G6
New Miami U.S.A. 164 C4
New Milford U.S.A. 165 H3
Newnan U.S.A. 163 C5
New Orleans U.S.A. 161 F6
New Paris IN U.S.A. 164 C3
New Paris OH U.S.A. 164 C4
New Philadelphia U.S.A. 164 E3
New Pitsligo U.K. 60 G3
New Plymouth N.Z. 139 E4
Newport Mayo Ireland 61 C4
Newport Tipperary Ireland 61 D5
Newport England U.K. 59 E6
Newport England U.K. 59 F8
Newport Wales U.K. 59 D7
Newport AR U.S.A. 161 F5
Newport IN U.S.A. 164 B4
Newport KY U.S.A. 164 C4
Newport MI U.S.A. 164 D3
Newport NH U.S.A. 165 I2
Newport NJ U.S.A. 165 H4
Newport OR U.S.A. 156 B3
Newport RI U.S.A. 165 J3
Newport VT U.S.A. 165 I1
Newport WA U.S.A. 156 D2
Newport Beach U.S.A. 158 E5
Newport News U.S.A. 165 G5
Newport Pagnell U.K. 59 G6
New Port Richey U.S.A. 163 D6
New Providence i. Bahamas 163 E7
Newquay U.K. 59 B8
New Roads U.S.A. 161 F6
New Rochelle U.S.A. 165 I3
New Rockford U.S.A. 160 D2
New Romney U.K. 59 H8
New Ross Ireland 61 F5
Newry Australia 134 E4
Newry U.K. 61 F3
New Siberia Islands Rus. Fed. 77 P2
New Smyrna Beach U.S.A. 163 D6
New South Wales state Australia 138 C4
New Stanton U.S.A. 164 F3
New Stuyahok AK U.S.A. 148 H4
Newtok AK U.S.A. 148 F3
Newton U.K. 58 E5
Newton GA U.S.A. 163 C6
Newton IA U.S.A. 160 E3
Newton IL U.S.A. 160 F4
Newton KS U.S.A. 160 D4
Newton MA U.S.A. 165 J2
Newton MS U.S.A. 161 F5
Newton NC U.S.A. 162 D5
Newton NJ U.S.A. 165 H3

Newton TX U.S.A. 161 E6
Newton Abbot U.K. 59 D8
Newton Mearns U.K. 60 E5
Newton Stewart U.K. 60 E6
Newtown Ireland 61 D5
Newtown England U.K. 59 E6
Newtown Wales U.K. 59 D6
Newtown U.S.A. 164 C4
New Town U.S.A. 160 C1
Newtownabbey U.K. 61 G3
Newtownards U.K. 61 G3
Newtownbarry Ireland see Bunclody
Newtownbutler U.K. 61 E3
Newtown Mount Kennedy Ireland 61 F4
Newtown St Boswells U.K. 60 G5
Newtownstewart U.K. 61 E3
New Ulm U.S.A. 160 E2
Newville U.S.A. 165 G3
New World Island Canada 153 L4

▶New York U.S.A. 165 I3
2nd most populous city in North America, and 5th in the world.

New York state U.S.A. 165 H2

▶New Zealand country Oceania 139 D5
3rd largest and 3rd most populous country in Oceania.

Neya Rus. Fed. 52 I4
Neyagawa Japan 92 B4
Ney Bīd Iran 110 E4
Neyrīz Iran 110 D4
Neyshābūr Iran 110 E2
Nezahualcóyotl, Presa resr Mex. 167 G5
Nezhin Ukr. see Nizhyn
Nezperce U.S.A. 156 D3
Ngabang Kalimantan Indon. 85 E2
Ngabé Congo 122 B4
Nga Chong, Khao mt. Myanmar/Thai. 86 B4
Ngadubolu Sumba Indon. 83 A5
Ngagahtawng Myanmar 96 C3
Ngagau mt. Tanz. 123 D4
Ngajangel i. Palau 82 [inset]
Ngalipaëng Sulawesi Indon. 83 C2
Ngalu Sumba Indon. 83 B5
Ngamegei Passage Palau 82 [inset]
Ngamring Xizang China 99 D7
Ngangla Ringco salt l. China 99 C7
Nganglong Kangri mt. Xizang China 99 C6
Nganglong Kangri mts Xizang China 99 C6
Ngangzê Co salt l. China 99 D7
Ngangzê Shan mts Xizang China 99 D7
Nganjuk Jawa Indon. 85 E4
Ngân Sơn Vietnam 86 D2
Ngaoundal Cameroon 120 E4
Ngaoundéré Cameroon 121 E4
Ngape Myanmar 86 A2
Ngaputaw Myanmar 86 A3
Ngaras Sumatera Indon. 84 D4
Ngardmau Palau 82 [inset]
Ngardmau Bay Palau 82 [inset]
Ngaregur i. Palau 82 [inset]
Ngariungs i. Palau 82 [inset]
Ngateguil, Point Palau 82 [inset]
Ngathainggyaung Myanmar 86 A3
Ngau i. Fiji see Gau
Ngawa China see Aba
Ngawi Jawa Indon. 85 E4
Ngcheangel atoll Palau see Kayangel Atoll
Ngeaur i. Palau see Angaur
Ngemelachel Palau see Malakal
Ngemelis Islands Palau 82 [inset]
Ngergoi i. Palau 82 [inset]
Ngeruangel i. Palau 81 I5
Ngesebus i. Palau 82 [inset]
Ngga Pulu mt. Indon. see Jaya, Puncak
Ngiap r. Laos 86 C3
Ngilmina Timor Indon. 83 C5
Ngimbang Jawa Indon. 85 F4
Ngiva Angola see Ondjiva
Ngo Congo 122 B4
Ngoako Ramalepe S. Africa see Duiwelskloof
Ngobasangel i. Palau 82 [inset]
Ngofakiaha Maluku Indon. 83 C2
Ngoichogê Xizang China 99 F7
Ngoin, Co salt l. China 99 E7
Ngok Linh mt. Vietnam 86 D4
Ngoko r. Cameroon/Congo 121 E4
Ngola Shan mts Qinghai China 94 D4
Ngola Shankou pass Qinghai China 94 D5
Ngom Qu r. Xizang China 99 G7
Ngong Shuen Chau pen. H.K. China see Stonecutters' Island
Ngoqumaima Xizang China 99 D6
Ngoring Qinghai China 94 D5
Ngoring Hu l. Qinghai China 94 D5
Ngourti Niger 120 E3
Nguigmi Niger 120 E3
Nguiu Australia 134 E2
Ngükang Xizang China 99 F7
Ngukurr Australia 134 F3
Ngulu atoll Micronesia 81 J5
Ngunju, Tanjung pt Sumba Indon. 83 B5
Ngunza Angola see Sumbe
Ngunza-Kabolu Angola see Sumbe
Ngura Gansu China 94 E5
Nguru Nigeria 120 E3
Ngwaketse admin. dist. Botswana see Southern
Ngwane country Africa see Swaziland
Ngwathe S. Africa 125 H4
Ngwavuma r. S. Africa/Swaziland 125 K4
Ngwelezana S. Africa 125 J5
Nhachengue Moz. 125 L2
Nhamalabué Moz. 123 D5
Nha Trang Vietnam 87 E4
Nhecolândia Brazil 177 G7
Nhill Australia 137 C8
Nhlangano Swaziland 125 J4
Nho Quan Vietnam 86 D2
Nhow i. Fiji see Gau
Nhulunbuy Australia 136 B2
Niacam Canada 151 J4
Niafounké Mali 120 C3
Niagara U.S.A. 162 C2
Niagara Falls Canada 164 F2
Niagara Falls U.S.A. 164 F2
Niagara-on-the-Lake Canada 164 F2
Niagzu Aksai Chin 99 B6
Niah Sarawak Malaysia 85 F2
Niakaramandougou Côte d'Ivoire 120 C4

▶Niamey Niger 120 D3
Capital of Niger.

Nīām Kand Iran 110 E5
Niampak Indon. 81 H6
Nianbai Qinghai China see Ledu
Niangara Dem. Rep. Congo 122 C3
Niangay, Lac l. Mali 120 C3
Nianyuwan Liaoning China see Xingangzhen
Nianzishan Heilong. China 95 J2
Nias i. Indon. 84 B2
Niassa, Lago l. Africa see Nyasa, Lake
Niaur i. Palau see Angaur
Nīāzābād Iran 111 F3
Nibil Well Australia 134 D5
Nīca Latvia 55 L8

▶Nicaragua country Central America 169 G6
5th largest country in North America.

Nicaragua, Lago de l. Nicaragua 166 [inset] I7
Nicaragua, Lake Nicaragua see Nicaragua, Lago de
Nicastro Italy 68 G5
Nice France 66 H5
Nice U.S.A. 158 B2
Nicephorium Syria see Ar Raqqah
Niceville U.S.A. 163 C6
Nichicun, Lac l. Canada 153 H3
Nicholas Channel Bahamas/Cuba 163 D8
Nicholasville U.S.A. 164 C5
Nichols U.S.A. 164 A1
Nicholson r. Australia 136 B3
Nicholson Lake Canada 151 K2
Nicholson Range hills Australia 135 B6
Nicholville U.S.A. 165 H1
Nicobar Islands India 87 A5
Nicolás Bravo Mex. 167 H5
Nicolaus U.S.A. 158 C2
Nicomedia Kocaeli Turkey see İzmit

▶Nicosia Cyprus 107 A2
Capital of Cyprus.

Nicoya Costa Rica 166 [inset] I7
Nicoya, Golfo de b. Costa Rica 166 [inset] I7
Nicoya, Península de pen. Costa Rica 166 [inset] I7
Nida Lith. 55 L9
Nidagunda India 106 C2
Nidd r. U.K. 58 F4
Nidda Germany 63 J4
Nidder r. Germany 63 I4
Nidzica Poland 57 R4
Niebüll Germany 57 L3
Nied r. France 62 G5
Niederanven Lux. 62 G5
Niederaula Germany 63 J4
Niedere Tauern mts Austria 57 N7
Niedersachsen land Germany 63 I2
Niedersächsisches Wattenmeer, Nationalpark nat. park Germany 62 G1
Niefang Equat. Guinea 120 E4
Niellé Côte d'Ivoire 120 C3
Nienburg (Weser) Germany 63 J2
Niers r. Germany 62 F3
Nierstein Germany 63 I5
Nieuwe-Niedorp Neth. 62 E2
Nieuwerkerk aan de IJssel Neth. 62 E3
Nieuw Nickerie Suriname 177 G2
Nieuwolda Neth. 62 G1
Nieuwoudtville S. Africa 124 D6
Nieuwpoort Belgium 62 C3
Nieuw-Vossemeer Neth. 62 E3
Nif Seram Indon. 83 D3
Niğde Turkey 112 D3
Niger country Africa 120 D3

▶Niger r. Africa 120 D4
3rd longest river in Africa.

Niger, Mouths of the Nigeria 120 D4
Niger Cone sea feature S. Atlantic Ocean 184 I5

▶Nigeria country Africa 120 D4
Most populous country in Africa, and 8th in the world.

Nighthawk Lake Canada 152 E4
Nightmute AK U.S.A. 148 F3
Nigrita Greece 69 J4
Nihing Pak. 111 G4
Nihon country Asia see Japan
Niigata Japan 91 E5
Niigata pref. Japan 91 E5
Niigata-yake-yama vol. Japan 93 E2
Niihama Japan 91 D6
Niihari Japan 93 G2
Ni'ihau i. U.S.A. 157 [inset]
Nii-jima i. Japan 93 F4
Niimi Japan 91 D6
Niitsu Japan 91 E5
Nijil, Wādī watercourse Jordan 107 B4
Nijkerk Neth. 62 F2
Nijmegen Neth. 62 F3
Nijverdal Neth. 62 G2
Nikel' Rus. Fed. 54 Q2
Nikiniki Timor Indon. 83 C5
Nikiski AK U.S.A. 149 J3
Nikki Benin 120 D4
Nikkō Japan 93 F2
Nikkō Kokuritsu-kōen nat. park Japan 93 F2
Nikolaevsk AK U.S.A. 149 J4
Nikolai AK U.S.A. 148 I3
Nikolayev Ukr. see Mykolayiv
Nikolayevka Rus. Fed. 53 J5
Nikolayevsk Rus. Fed. 53 J6
Nikolayevskiy Rus. Fed. see Nikolayevsk
Nikolayevsk-na-Amure Rus. Fed. 90 F1
Nikol'sk Rus. Fed. 52 J4
Nikolski AK U.S.A. 148 E5
Nikol'skiy Kazakh. see Satpayev
Nikol'skoye Kamchatskaya Oblast' Rus. Fed. 77 R4
Nikol'skoye Vologod. Obl. Rus. Fed. see Sheksna
Nikopol' Ukr. 53 G7
Niksar Turkey 112 E2
Nīkshahr Iran 111 F5
Nikšić Montenegro 68 H3
Nīkū Jahān Iran 111 F5
Nikumaroro atoll Kiribati 133 I2
Nikunau i. Kiribati 133 H2
Nīl, Bahr el r. Africa see Nile
Nila vol. Maluku Indon. 83 D4
Nilagiri India 105 F5
Niland U.S.A. 159 F5
Nilande Atoll Maldives see Nilandhoo Atoll
Nilandhe Atoll Maldives see Nilandhoo Atoll
Nilandhoo Atoll Maldives 103 D11
Nilang India see Nelang
Nilanga India 106 C2
Nilaveli Sri Lanka 106 D4

▶Nile r. Africa 112 C5
Longest river in the world.

Niles MI U.S.A. 164 B3
Niles OH U.S.A. 164 E3
Nilgiri Hills India 106 C4
Nīlī 111 G3
Nilka Xinjiang China 98 C4
Nīl Kowtal Afgh. 111 G3
Nilphamari Bangl. 105 G4
Nilsiä Fin. 54 P5
Nimach India see Neemuch
Niman r. Rus. Fed. 90 D2
Nimba, Monts mts Africa see Nimba, Mount
Nimba, Mount Africa 120 C4
Nimbal India 106 B2
Nimberra Well Australia 135 C5
Nimelen r. Rus. Fed. 90 E1
Nîmes France 66 G5
Nimmitabel Australia 137 E8
Nimrod Glacier Antarctica 188 H1
Nimu India 104 D2
Nimule Sudan 121 G4
Nimwegen Neth. see Nijmegen
Nindigully Australia 138 D2
Nine Degree Channel India 106 B4
Nine Islands P.N.G. see Kilinailau Islands
Ninepin Group is H.K. China 97 [inset]
Ninetyeast Ridge sea feature Indian Ocean 185 N8
Ninety Mile Beach Australia 138 C7
Ninety Mile Beach N.Z. 139 D2
Nineveh U.S.A. 165 H2
Ning'an China 90 C3
Ningbo China 97 I2
Ningcheng Nei Mongol China 95 I3
Ningde China 97 H3
Ning'er China see Pu'er
Ningguo China 97 H2
Ninghai China 97 I2
Ninghe Tianjin China 95 I4
Ninghsia Hui Autonomous Region aut. reg. China see Ningxia Huizu Zizhiqu
Ninghua China 97 H3
Ninging India 105 H3
Ningjiang China see Songyuan
Ningjing Shan mts China 96 C2
Ninglang China 96 D3
Ningling Henan China 95 H5
Ningming China 96 E4
Ningnan China 96 D3
Ningqiang China 96 E1
Ningwu Shanxi China 95 H4
Ningxia aut. reg. China see Ningxia Huizu Zizhiqu
Ningxia Huizu Zizhiqu aut. reg. China 94 F4
Ningxian Gansu China 95 F5
Ningxiang China 97 G2
Ningyang Shandong China 95 I5
Ningzhou China see Huaning
Ninh Binh Vietnam 86 D2
Ninh Hoa Vietnam 87 E4
Ninigo Group atolls P.N.G. 81 K7
Ninilchik AK U.S.A. 149 J3
Ninnis Glacier Antarctica 188 G2
Ninnis Glacier Tongue Antarctica 188 H2
Ninohe Japan 91 F4
Ninomiya Kanagawa Japan 93 F3
Ninomiya Tochigi Japan 93 F2
Niobrara r. U.S.A. 160 D3
Nioko Arun. Prad. India 99 F8
Niokolo Koba, Parc National du nat. park Senegal 120 B3
Niono Mali 120 C3
Nioro Mali 120 C3
Niort France 66 D3
Nipani India 106 B2
Nipanipa, Tanjung pt Indon. 83 B3
Nipawin Canada 151 J4
Niphad India 106 B1
Nipigon Canada 147 J5
Nipigon, Lake Canada 147 J5
Nipishish Lake Canada 153 J3
Nipissing, Lake Canada 152 F5
Nippon country Asia see Japan
Nippon Hai sea N. Pacific Ocean see Japan, Sea of
Nipton U.S.A. 159 F4
Niquelândia Brazil 179 A1
Nir Ardabīl Iran 110 B2
Nir Yazd Iran 110 D4
Nira r. India 106 B2
Nirasaki Japan 93 E3
Nirayama Japan 93 E3
Nirji Nei Mongol China 95 K1
Nirmal India 106 C2
Nirmali India 105 F4
Nirmal Range hills India 106 C2
Niš Serbia 69 I3
Nisa Port. 67 C4
Nisa tourist site Turkm. 110 E2
Nisarpur India 106 B1
Niscemi Sicily Italy 68 F6
Nishan Xizang China 99 D6
Nīshāpūr Iran see Neyshābūr
Nishiaizu Japan 92 C3
Nishiizu Japan 93 E4
Nishikata Tochigi Japan 93 F2
Nishikatsura Japan 93 E3
Nishi-maizuru Japan 92 B3
Nishinasuno Japan 93 F2
Nishinomiya Japan 92 B4
Nishino-shima vol. Japan 91 F8
Nishio Japan 92 D4
Nishi-Sonogi-hantō pen. Japan 91 C6
Nishiwaki Japan 92 A4
Nishiyoshino Japan 92 B4
Nisibis Turkey see Nusaybin
Nisiharu Japan 92 C3
Nísiros i. Greece see Nisyros
Niskibi r. Canada 151 N3
Nisling r. Y.T. Canada 149 M3
Nispen Neth. 62 E3
Nissan r. Sweden 55 H8
Nisshin Japan 92 D3
Nistru r. Moldova 69 N1 see Dniester
Nisutlin r. Y.T. Canada 149 N3
Nisyros i. Greece 69 L6
Niṭā Saudi Arabia 110 C5
Nitchequon Canada 153 H3
Nitendi i. Solomon Is see Ndeni
Niterói Brazil 179 C3
Nith r. U.K. 60 F5
Nitibe East Timor 83 C5
Niti Pass China/India 104 D3
Niti Shankou pass China/India see Niti Pass
Nitmiluk National Park Australia 134 F3
Nitra Slovakia 57 Q6
Nitro U.S.A. 164 E4
Nitta Japan 93 F2
Niuafo'ou i. Tonga 133 I3
Niuatoputopu i. Tonga 133 I3
Niubiziliang Qinghai China 98 F5

▶Niue terr. S. Pacific Ocean 133 J3
Self-governing New Zealand Overseas Territory.

Niujing China see Binchuan
Niulakita i. Tuvalu 133 H3
Niur, Pulau i. Indon. 84 C3
Niushan Jiangsu China see Donghai
Niutao i. Tuvalu 133 H2
Niutoushan China 97 H2
Niuzhuang Liaoning China 95 J3
Nivala Fin. 54 N5
Nive watercourse Australia 136 D5
Nivelles Belgium 62 E4
Niwai India 104 C4
Niwas India 104 E5
Nixia China see Sêrxü
Nixon U.S.A. 158 D2
Niya Xinjiang China see Minfeng
Niya He r. China 99 C5
Niyut, Gunung mt. Indon. 85 E2
Niza Japan 93 F3
Nizamabad India 106 C2
Nizam Sagar l. India 106 C2
Nizhnedevitsk Rus. Fed. 53 H6
Nizhnekamsk Rus. Fed. 52 K5
Nizhnekamskoye Vodokhranilishche resr Rus. Fed. 51 Q4
Nizhnekolymsk Rus. Fed. 77 R3
Nizhnetambovskoye Rus. Fed. 90 E2
Nizhneudinsk Rus. Fed. 88 H2
Nizhnevartovsk Rus. Fed. 76 I3
Nizhnevolzhsk Rus. Fed. see Narimanov
Nizhneyansk Rus. Fed. 77 O2
Nizhneye Giryunino Rus. Fed. 95 I1
Nizhniy Baskunchak Rus. Fed. 53 J6
Nizhniye Kayrakty Kazakh. 98 A2
Nizhniye Kresty Rus. Fed. see Cherskiy
Nizhniy Lomov Rus. Fed. 53 I5
Nizhniy Novgorod Rus. Fed. 52 I4
Nizhniy Odes Rus. Fed. 52 L3
Nizhniy Pyandzh Tajik. see Panji Poyon
Nizhniy Tagil Rus. Fed. 51 R4
Nizhniy Tsasuchey Rus. Fed. 95 H1
Nizhnyaya Mola Rus. Fed. 52 J2
Nizhnyaya Omra Rus. Fed. 52 L3
Nizhnyaya Pirenga, Ozero l. Rus. Fed. 54 R3
Nizhnyaya Tunguska r. Rus. Fed. 76 J3
Nizhnyaya Tura Rus. Fed. 51 R4
Nizhyn Ukr. 53 F6
Nizina r. AK U.S.A. 150 A2
Nizina Mazowiecka reg. Poland 57 R4
Nizip Turkey 107 C1
Nízke Tatry nat. park Slovakia 57 Q6
Nizkiy, Mys hd Rus. Fed. 148 B2
Nizwā Oman see Nazwá
Nizza France see Nice
Njallavarri mt. Norway 54 L2
Njavve Sweden 54 K3
Njazidja i. Comoros 123 E5
Njombe Tanz. 123 D4
Njurundabommen Sweden 54 J5
Nkambe Cameroon 120 E4
Nkandla S. Africa 125 J5
Nkawkaw Ghana 120 C4
Nkhata Bay Malawi 123 D5
Nkhotakota Malawi 123 D5
Nkondwe Tanz. 123 D4
Nkongsamba Cameroon 120 D4
Nkululeko S. Africa 125 H6
Nkwenkwezi S. Africa 125 H7
Noakhali Bangl. 105 G5
Noatak AK U.S.A. 148 G2
Noatak r. AK U.S.A. 148 G2
Noatak National Preserve nature res. AK U.S.A. 148 H1
Nobber Ireland 61 F4
Nobeoka Japan 91 C6
Noblesville U.S.A. 164 B3
Noboribetsu Japan 90 F4
Noccundra Australia 137 C5
Nochistlán Mex. 166 E4
Nochixtlán Mex. 167 F5
Nockatunga Australia 137 C5
Nocona U.S.A. 161 D5
Noda Japan 93 F3
Nodagawa Japan 92 B3
Noel Kempff Mercado, Parque Nacional nat. park Bol. 176 F6
Noelville Canada 152 E5
Nogales Mex. 166 C2
Nogales U.S.A. 157 F7
Nōgata Japan 91 C6
Nogent-le-Rotrou France 66 E2
Nogent-sur-Oise France 62 C5
Nogi Japan 93 F2
Noginsk Rus. Fed. 52 H5
Nogliki Rus. Fed. 90 F2
Nogoa r. Australia 136 E4
Nōgōhaku-san mt. Japan 92 C3
Nogon Toli Nei Mongol China 94 F4
Noguchigorō-dake mt. Japan 92 D2
Nohalal Mex. 167 H5
Nohar India 104 C3
Noheji Japan 90 F4
Nohfelden Germany 62 H5
Nohoit Qinghai China 94 C4
Noida India 104 D3
Noirmoutier, Île de i. France 66 C3
Noirmoutier-en-l'Île France 66 C3
Noisseville France 62 G5
Nojima-zaki c. Japan 93 F4
Nojiri-ko l. Japan 93 E2
Nokami Japan 92 B4
Nokhowch, Kūh-e mt. Iran 111 F5
Nōkis Uzbek. see Nukus
Nok Kundi Pak. 111 F4
Nokomis Canada 151 J5
Nokomis Lake Canada 151 K3
Nokou Chad 121 E3
Nokrek Peak India 105 G4
Nola Cent. Afr. Rep. 122 B3
Nolin River Lake U.S.A. 164 B5
Nolinsk Rus. Fed. 52 K4
No Mans Land i. U.S.A. 165 J3
Nome AK U.S.A. 148 F2
Nome, Cape AK U.S.A. 148 F2
Nomgon Mongolia 94 F3
Nomhon Qinghai China 94 D4
Nomhon He r. Qinghai China 94 C4
Nomin Gol r. China 95 K1
Nomoi Islands Micronesia see Mortlock Islands
Nomonde S. Africa 125 H6
Nömrög Mongolia 94 D1
Nomto Rus. Fed. 94 F1
Nomugi-tōge pass Japan 92 D2
Nomzha Rus. Fed. 52 I4
Nonacho Lake Canada 151 I2
Nondalton AK U.S.A. 148 I4
Nondweni S. Africa 125 J5
Nong'an China 90 B3
Nông Hèt Laos 86 D3
Nonghui China see Guang'an
Nong Khai Thai. 86 C3
Nongoma S. Africa 125 J4
Nongstoin India 105 G4
Nonidas Namibia 124 B2
Nonni r. China see Nen Jiang
Nonning Australia 137 B7
Nonnweiler Germany 62 G5
Nonoava Mex. 166 D3
Nonoichi Japan 92 C2
Nonouti atoll Kiribati 133 H2
Nonthaburi Thai. 87 C4
Nonvianuk Lake AK U.S.A. 148 I4
Nonzwakazi S. Africa 124 G6
Noolyeanna Lake salt flat Australia 137 B5
Noondie, Lake salt flat Australia 135 B7
Noonkanbah Australia 134 D4
Noonthorangee Range hills Australia 137 C6
Noorama Creek watercourse Australia 138 B1
Noordbeveland i. Neth. 62 D3
Noorderhaaks i. Neth. 62 E2
Noordoost Polder Neth. 62 F2
Noordwijk-Binnen Neth. 62 E2
Noorvik AK U.S.A. 148 G2
Nootka Island Canada 150 E5
Nora r. Rus. Fed. 90 C2
Norak Tajik. 111 H2
Norak, Obanbori resr Tajik. 111 H2
Norala Mindanao Phil. 82 D5
Noranda Canada 152 F4
Nor-Bayazet Armenia see Gavarr
Norberg Sweden 55 I6
Norcang Xizang China 99 D7
Nord Greenland see Station Nord
Nord, Canal du France 62 D4
Nordaustlandet i. Svalbard 76 D2
Nordegg Canada 150 G4
Norden Germany 63 H1
Nordenshel'da, Arkhipelag is Rus. Fed. 76 K2
Nordenskjold Archipelago is Rus. Fed. see Nordenshel'da, Arkhipelag
Norderney Germany 63 H1
Norderstedt Germany 63 K1
Nordfjordeid Norway 54 D6
Nordfold Norway 54 I3
Nordfriesische Inseln Germany see North Frisian Islands
Nordhausen Germany 63 K3
Nordholz Germany 63 I1
Nordhorn Germany 62 H2
Nordkapp c. Norway see North Cape
Nordkinnhalvøya i. Norway 54 O1
Nordkjosbotn Norway 54 K2
Nordli Norway 54 H4
Nördlingen Germany 63 K6
Nordmaling Sweden 54 K5
Nord- og Østgrønland, Nationalparken i nat. park Greenland 147 O2

▶Nordøstrundingen c. Greenland 189 I1
Most easterly point of North America.

Nord-Ostsee-Kanal Germany see Kiel Canal
Norðoyar i. Faroe Is 50 E3
Nord-Pas-de-Calais admin. reg. France 62 C4
Nordpfälzer Bergland reg. Germany 63 H5
Nordre Strømfjord inlet Greenland see Nassuttooq
Nordrhein-Westfalen land Germany 63 H3
Nordvik Rus. Fed. 77 M2
Nore r. Ireland 61 F5
Nore, Pic de mt. France 66 F5
Noreg country Europe see Norway
Norfolk NE U.S.A. 160 D3
Norfolk NY U.S.A. 165 H1
Norfolk VA U.S.A. 165 G5

▶Norfolk Island terr. S. Pacific Ocean 133 G4
Territory of Australia.

Norfolk Island Ridge sea feature Tasman Sea 186 H7
Norfork Lake U.S.A. 161 E4
Norg Neth. 62 G1
Norge country Europe see Norway
Norheimsund Norway 55 E6
Norikura-dake vol. Japan 92 D2
Noril'sk Rus. Fed. 76 J3
Norkyung Xizang China 99 E7
Norland Canada 165 F1
Norma Co l. Xizang China 99 E6
Norman U.S.A. 161 D5
Norman, Lake resr U.S.A. 162 D5
Normanby Island P.N.G. 136 E1
Normandes, Îles is English Chan. see Channel Islands
Normandia Brazil 177 G3
Normandie reg. France see Normandy
Normandie, Collines de hills France 66 D2
Normandy reg. France 66 D2
Normanton Australia 136 C3
Norman Wells N.W.T. Canada 149 P2
Norogachic Mex. 166 D3
Norovlin Mongolia 95 G1
Norquay Canada 151 K5
Ñorquinco Arg. 178 B6
Norra Kvarken strait Fin./Sweden 54 L5
Norra Storfjället mts Sweden 54 I4
Norrent-Fontes France 62 C4
Norris Lake U.S.A. 164 D5
Norristown U.S.A. 165 H3
Norrköping Sweden 55 J7
Norrtälje Sweden 55 K7
Norseman Australia 135 C8
Norsjö Sweden 54 K4
Norsk Rus. Fed. 90 C1
Norsup Vanuatu 133 G3
Norte, Punta pt Arg. 178 E5
Norte, Serra do hills Brazil 177 G6
Nortelândia Brazil 177 G6
Nörten-Hardenberg Germany 63 J3
North, Cape Antarctica 188 H2
North, Cape Canada 153 J5
Northallerton U.K. 58 F4
Northam Australia 135 B7
Northampton Australia 132 B4
Northampton U.K. 59 G6
Northampton MA U.S.A. 165 I2
Northampton PA U.S.A. 165 H3
North Andaman i. India 87 A4
North Anna r. U.S.A. 165 G5
North Arm b. Canada 150 H2
North Atlantic Ocean Atlantic Ocean 155 O4
North Augusta U.S.A. 163 D5
North Aulatsivik Island Canada 153 J2
North Australian Basin sea feature Indian Ocean 185 P6
North Balabac Strait Phil. 82 B4
North Baltimore U.S.A. 164 D3
North Battleford Canada 151 I4
North Bay Canada 152 F5
North Belcher Islands Canada 152 F2
North Berwick U.K. 60 G4
North Berwick U.S.A. 165 J2
North Borneo state Malaysia see Sabah
North Bourke Australia 138 B3
North Branch U.S.A. 160 E2
North Caicos i. Turks and Caicos Is 163 G8
North Canton U.S.A. 164 E3
North Cape Canada 153 I5
North Cape Norway 54 N1
North Cape N.Z. 139 D2
North Cape AK U.S.A. 149 [inset]
North Caribou Lake Canada 151 N4
North Carolina state U.S.A. 162 E4
North Cascades National Park U.S.A. 156 C2
North Channel lake channel Canada 152 E5
North Channel U.K. 61 G2
North Charleston U.S.A. 163 E5
North Chicago U.S.A. 164 B2
North China Plain plain China see Huabei Pingyuan
Northcliffe Glacier Antarctica 188 F2
North Collins U.S.A. 165 F2
North Concho r. U.S.A. 161 C6
North Conway U.S.A. 165 J1
North Dakota state U.S.A. 160 C2
North Downs hills U.K. 59 G7
North East U.S.A. 164 F2
Northeast Cape AK U.S.A. 148 E3
Northeast Foreland c. Greenland see Nordøstrundingen
North-East Frontier Agency state India see Arunachal Pradesh
Northeast Pacific Basin sea feature N. Pacific Ocean 187 J4
Northeast Point Bahamas 163 F8
Northeast Providence Channel Bahamas 163 E7
North Edwards U.S.A. 158 E4
Northeim Germany 63 J3
North Entrance sea chan. Palau 82 [inset]
Northern prov. S. Africa see Limpopo
Northern Areas admin. div. Pak. see Gilgit-Baltistan
Northern Cape prov. S. Africa 124 D5
Northern Donets r. Rus. Fed./Ukr. see Severskiy Donets
Northern Dvina r. Rus. Fed. see Severnaya Dvina
Northern Indian Lake Canada 151 L3
Northern Ireland prov. U.K. 61 F3
Northern Lau Group is Fiji 133 I3
Northern Light Lake Canada 152 C4

▶Northern Mariana Islands terr. N. Pacific Ocean 81 K3
United States Commonwealth.

Northern Rhodesia country Africa see Zambia
Northern Sporades is Greece see Voreies Sporades
Northern Sporades is Greece see Voreies Sporades
Northern Territory admin. div. Australia 132 D3
Northern Transvaal prov. S. Africa see Limpopo
North Esk r. U.K. 60 G4
Northfield MN U.S.A. 160 E2
Northfield VT U.S.A. 165 I1
North Foreland c. U.K. 59 I7
North Fork U.S.A. 158 D3
North Fork Pass Y.T. Canada 149 M2
North French r. Canada 152 E4
North Frisian Islands Germany 57 L3
North Geomagnetic Pole (2008) Canada 189 K1
North Grimston U.K. 58 G4
North Haven U.S.A. 165 I3
North Head hd N.Z. 139 E3
North Henik Lake Canada 151 L2
North Hero U.S.A. 165 I1
North Horr Kenya 122 D3
North Island India 106 B4

▶North Island N.Z. 139 D4
3rd largest island in Oceania.

North Island Phil. 82 C1
North Islet rf Phil. 82 C4
North Jadito Canyon gorge U.S.A. 159 H4
North Judson U.S.A. 164 B3
North Kingsville U.S.A. 164 E3
North Knife r. Canada 151 M3
North Knife Lake Canada 151 L3
North Korea country Asia 91 B5
North Lakhimpur India 105 H4
North Las Vegas U.S.A. 159 F3

North Little Rock U.S.A. **161** E5
North Loup r. U.S.A. **160** D3
North Luangwa National Park Zambia **123** D5
North Maalhosmadulu Atoll Maldives **106** B5
North Magnetic Pole (2008) Arctic Ocean **189** A1
North Malosmadulu Atoll Maldives *see* **North Maalhosmadulu Atoll**
North Mam Peak U.S.A. **159** J2
North Muskegon U.S.A. **164** B2
North Palisade *mt.* U.S.A. **158** D3
North Perry U.S.A. **164** E3
North Platte U.S.A. **160** C3
North Platte r. U.S.A. **160** C3
North Pole Arctic Ocean **189** I1
North Pole *AK* U.S.A. **149** K2
North Port U.S.A. **163** D7
North Reef Island India **87** A4
North Rhine-Westphalia *land* Germany *see* **Nordrhein-Westfalen**
North Rim U.S.A. **159** G3
North Rona *i.* U.K. *see* **Rona**
North Ronaldsay *i.* U.K. **60** G1
North Ronaldsay Firth *sea chan.* U.K. **60** G1
North Saskatchewan r. Canada **151** J4
North Schell Peak U.S.A. **159** F2
North Sea Europe **56** H2
North Seal r. Canada **151** L3
North Sentinel Island India **87** A5
North Shields U.K. **58** F3
North Shoal Lake Canada **151** L5
North Shoshone Peak U.S.A. **158** E2
North Siberian Lowland Rus. Fed. **76** L2
North Siberian Lowland Rus. Fed. **189** E2
North Simlipal National Park India **105** F5
North Sinai *governorate* Egypt *see* **Shamāl Sīnā'**
North Slope *plain AK* U.S.A. **149** J1
North Somercotes U.K. **58** H5
North Spirit Lake Canada **151** M4
North Stradbroke Island Australia **138** F1
North Sunderland U.K. **58** F3
North Syracuse U.S.A. **165** G2
North Taranaki Bight *b.* N.Z. **139** E4
North Terre Haute U.S.A. **164** B4
Northton U.K. **60** B3
North Tonawanda U.S.A. **165** F2
North Trap *reef* N.Z. **139** A8
North Troy U.S.A. **165** I1
North Tyne r. U.K. **58** E4
North Ubian *i.* Phil. **82** C5
North Uist *i.* U.K. **60** B3
Northumberland National Park U.K. **58** E3
Northumberland Strait Canada **153** I5
North Vancouver Canada **150** F5
North Verde *i.* Phil. **82** B4
North Vernon U.S.A. **164** C4
Northville U.S.A. **165** H2
North Wabasca Lake Canada **150** H3
North Walsham U.K. **59** I6
Northway Junction *AK* U.S.A. **149** L3
North West *prov.* S. Africa **124** G4
Northwest Atlantic Mid-Ocean Channel N. Atlantic Ocean **184** E1
North West Cape Australia **134** A5
Northwest Cape *AK* U.S.A. **148** E3
North West Frontier *prov.* Pak. *see* **Khyber Pakhtunkhwa**
North West Nelson Forest Park *nat. park* N.Z. *see* **Kahurangi National Park**
Northwest Pacific Basin *sea feature* N. Pacific Ocean **186** G3
Northwest Providence Channel Bahamas **163** E7
North West River Canada **153** K3
Northwest Territories *admin. div.* Canada **150** J2
Northwich U.K. **58** E5
North Wildwood U.S.A. **165** H4
North Windham U.S.A. **165** J2
Northwind Ridge *sea feature* Arctic Ocean **189** B1
Northwood U.S.A. **165** J2
North York Canada **164** F2
North York Moors *moorland* U.K. **58** G4
North York Moors National Park U.K. **58** G4
Norton U.K. **58** G4
Norton *KS* U.S.A. **160** D4
Norton *VA* U.S.A. **164** D5
Norton *VT* U.S.A. **165** J1
Norton Bay *AK* U.S.A. **148** G2
Norton de Matos Angola *see* **Balombo**
Norton Shores U.S.A. **164** B2
Norton Sound *sea channel AK* U.S.A. **148** G3
Nortonville U.S.A. **164** B5
Norutak Lake *AK* U.S.A. **148** I2
Norvegia, Cape Antarctica **188** B2
Norwalk *CT* U.S.A. **165** I3
Norwalk *OH* U.S.A. **164** D3
Norway *country* Europe **54** E6
Norway U.S.A. **165** J1
Norway House Canada **151** L4
Norwegian Basin *sea feature* N. Atlantic Ocean **184** H1
Norwegian Bay Canada **147** I2
Norwegian Sea N. Atlantic Ocean **189** H2
Norwich Canada **164** E2
Norwich U.K. **59** I6
Norwich *CT* U.S.A. **165** I3
Norwich *NY* U.S.A. **165** H2
Norwood *CO* U.S.A. **159** I2
Norwood *NY* U.S.A. **165** H1
Norwood *OH* U.S.A. **164** C4
Norzagaray *Luzon* Phil. **82** C3
Nosaka Japan **93** G3
Nose Japan **92** B4
Nosegawa Japan **92** B4
Nose Lake Canada **151** I1
Noshiro Japan **91** F4
Nosovaya Rus. Fed. **52** L1
Noşratābād Iran **111** E4
Noss, Isle of *i.* U.K. **60** [inset]
Nossebro Sweden **55** H7
Nossen Germany **63** N3
Nossob *watercourse* Africa **124** D2 *also known as Nosop*
Nossob *watercourse* Africa **124** D2 *also known as Nossob*
Notakwanon r. Canada **153** J2
Notch Peak U.S.A. **159** G2
Noteć r. Poland **57** O4
Notikewin r. Canada **150** G3
Noto, Golfo di *g. Sicily* Italy **68** F6
Notodden Norway **55** F7
Notogawa Japan **92** C3
Noto-hantō *pen.* Japan **89** P5
Notojima Japan **92** D1
Noto-jima *i.* Japan **92** D1
Notre-Dame, Monts *mts* Canada **153** H5
Notre Dame Bay Canada **153** L4
Notre-Dame-de-Koartac Canada *see* **Quaqtaq**
Nottawasaga Bay Canada **164** E1
Nottaway r. Canada **152** F4
Nottingham U.K. **59** F6
Nottingham Island Canada **147** K3
Nottoway r. U.S.A. **165** G5
Nottuln Germany **63** H3
Notukeu Creek r. Canada **151** J5
Nou Japan **93** D1
Nouabalé-Ndoki, Parc National *nat. park* Congo **122** B3
Nouâdhibou Mauritania **120** B2
Nouâdhibou, Râs *c.* Mauritania **120** B2

▶**Nouakchott** Mauritania **120** B3
Capital of Mauritania.

Nouâmghâr Mauritania **120** B3
Nouei Vietnam **86** D4

▶**Nouméa** New Caledonia **133** G4
Capital of New Caledonia.

Nouna Burkina Faso **120** C3
Noupoort S. Africa **124** G6
Nousu Fin. **54** P3
Nouveau-Brunswick *prov.* Canada *see* **New Brunswick**
Nouveau-Comptoir Canada *see* **Wemindji**
Nouvelle Calédonie *i.* S. Pacific Ocean **133** G4
Nouvelle Calédonie *terr.* S. Pacific Ocean *see* **New Caledonia**
Nouvelle-France, Cap de *c.* Canada **147** K3
Nouvelles Hébrides *country* S. Pacific Ocean *see* **Vanuatu**
Nova América Brazil **179** A1
Nova Chaves Angola *see* **Muconda**
Nova Freixa Moz. *see* **Cuamba**
Nova Friburgo Brazil **179** C3
Nova Gaia Angola *see* **Cambundi-Catembo**
Nova Goa India *see* **Panaji**
Nova Gradiška Croatia **68** G2
Nova Iguaçu Brazil **179** C3
Nova Kakhovka Ukr. **69** O1
Nova Lima Brazil **179** C2
Nova Lisboa Angola *see* **Huambo**
Novalukoml' Belarus **53** F5
Nova Mambone Moz. **123** D6
Nova Nabúri Moz. **123** D5
Nova Odesa Ukr. **53** F7
Nova Paraiso Brazil **176** F3
Nova Pilão Arcado Brazil **177** J5
Nova Ponte Brazil **179** B2
Nova Ponte, Represa *resr* Brazil **179** B2
Novara Italy **68** C2
Nova Roma Brazil **179** B1
Nova Scotia *prov.* Canada **153** I6
Nova Sento Sé Brazil **177** J5
Novato U.S.A. **158** B2
Nova Trento Brazil **179** A4
Nova Venécia Brazil **179** C2
Nova Xavantino Brazil **177** H6
Novaya Kakhovka Ukr. *see* **Nova Kakhovka**
Novaya Kazanka Kazakh. **51** P6
Novaya Ladoga Rus. Fed. **52** G3
Novaya Lyalya Rus. Fed. **51** S4
Novaya Odessa Ukr. *see* **Nova Odesa**
Novaya Sibir', Ostrov *i.* Rus. Fed. **77** P2
Novaya Ussura Rus. Fed. **90** E2

▶**Novaya Zemlya** *is* Rus. Fed. **76** G2
3rd largest island in Europe.

Nova Zagora Bulg. **69** L3
Novelda Spain **67** F4
Nové Zámky Slovakia **57** Q7
Novgorod Rus. Fed. *see* **Velikiy Novgorod**
Novgorod-Severskiy Ukr. *see* **Novhorod-Sivers'kyy**
Novgorod-Volynskiy Ukr. *see* **Novohrad-Volyns'kyy**
Novhorod-Sivers'kyy Ukr. **53** G6
Novi Grad Bos.-Herz. *see* **Bosanski Novi**
Novi Iskŭr Bulg. **69** J3
Novikovo Rus. Fed. **90** F3
Novi Kritsim Bulg. *see* **Stamboliyski**
Novi Ligure Italy **68** C2
Novillero Mex. **166** D4
Novi Pazar Bulg. **69** L3
Novi Pazar Serbia **69** I3
Novi Sad Serbia **69** H2
Novo Acre Brazil **179** C1
Novoalekseyevka Kazakh. *see* **Khobda**
Novoaltaysk Rus. Fed. **88** E2
Novoanninskiy Rus. Fed. **53** I6
Novo Aripuanã Brazil **176** F5
Novoazovs'k Ukr. **53** H7
Novocheboksarsk Rus. Fed. **52** J4
Novocherkassk Rus. Fed. **53** I7
Novo Cruzeiro Brazil **179** C2
Novodoroninskoye Rus. Fed. **95** H1
Novodugino Rus. Fed. **52** G5
Novodvinsk Rus. Fed. **52** I2
Novoekonomicheskoye Ukr. *see* **Dymytrov**
Novogeorgiyevka Rus. Fed. **90** B2
Novogrudok Belarus *see* **Navahrudak**
Novo Hamburgo Brazil **179** A5
Novohradské hory *mts* Czech Rep. **57** O6
Novohrad-Volyns'kyy Ukr. **53** E6
Novokhopersk Rus. Fed. **53** I6
Novokiyevskiy Uval Rus. Fed. **90** C2
Novokubansk Rus. Fed. **113** F1
Novokubanskiy Rus. Fed. *see* **Novokubansk**
Novokuybyshevsk Rus. Fed. **53** K5
Novokuznetsk Rus. Fed. **88** F2
Novolazarevskaya *research station* Antarctica **188** C2
Novolukoml' Belarus *see* **Novalukoml'**
Novo Mesto Slovenia **68** F2
Novomikhaylovskiy Rus. Fed. **112** E1
Novomoskovsk Rus. Fed. **53** H5
Novomoskovs'k Ukr. **53** G6
Novonikolayevsk Rus. Fed. *see* **Novosibirsk**
Novonikolayevskiy Rus. Fed. **53** I6
Novooleksiyivka Ukr. **53** G7
Novopashiyskiy Rus. Fed. *see* **Gornozavodsk**
Novopavlovka Rus. Fed. **95** G1
Novopokrovka *Vostochnyy Kazakhstan* Kazakh. **98** C2
Novopokrovka Rus. Fed. **90** D3
Novopokrovskaya Rus. Fed. **53** I7
Novopolotsk Belarus *see* **Navapolatsk**
Novopskov Ukr. **53** H6
Novo Redondo Angola *see* **Sumbe**
Novorossiyka Rus. Fed. **90** C1
Novorossiysk Rus. Fed. **112** E1
Novorybnaya Rus. Fed. **77** L2
Novorzhev Rus. Fed. **52** F4
Novoselenginsk Rus. Fed. **94** F1
Novoselovo Rus. Fed. **88** G1
Novoselskoye Rus. Fed. *see* **Achkhoy-Martan**
Novosel'ye Rus. Fed. **55** P7
Novosergiyevka Rus. Fed. **51** Q5
Novoshakhtinsk Rus. Fed. **53** H7
Novosheshminsk Rus. Fed. **52** K5
Novosibirsk Rus. Fed. **76** J4
Novosibirskiye Ostrova *is* Rus. Fed. *see* **New Siberia Islands**
Novosil' Rus. Fed. **53** H5
Novosokol'niki Rus. Fed. **52** F4
Novospasskoye Rus. Fed. **53** J5
Novotroyits'ke Ukr. **53** G7
Novoukrainka Ukr. *see* **Novoukrayinka**
Novoukrayinka Ukr. **53** F6
Novouzensk Rus. Fed. **53** K6
Novovolyns'k Ukr. **53** E6
Novovoronezh Rus. Fed. **53** H6
Novovoronezhskiy Rus. Fed. *see* **Novovoronezh**
Novovoskresenovka Rus. Fed. **90** B1
Novovoznesenovka Kyrg. **98** B4
Novoye Chaplino Rus. Fed. **148** D2
Novozybkov Rus. Fed. **53** F5
Nový Jičín Czech Rep. **57** P6
Novyy Afon Georgia *see* **Akhali Ap'oni**
Novyy Bor Rus. Fed. **52** L2
Novyy Donbass Ukr. *see* **Dymytrov**
Novyye Petushki Rus. Fed. *see* **Petushki**
Novyy Kholmogory Rus. Fed. *see* **Archangel**
Novyy Margelan Uzbek. *see* **Farg'ona**
Novyy Nekouz Rus. Fed. **52** H4
Novyy Oskol Rus. Fed. **53** H6
Novyy Port Rus. Fed. **76** I3
Novyy Urengoy Rus. Fed. **76** I3
Novyy Urgal Rus. Fed. **90** D2
Novyy Uzen' Kazakh. *see* **Zhanaozen**
Novyy Zay Rus. Fed. **52** L5
Now Iran **110** D4
Nowabganj Bangl. *see* **Nawabganj**
Nowata U.S.A. **161** E4
Nowdī Iran **110** C2
Nowgong India *see* **Nagaon**
Nowitna r. *AK* U.S.A. **148** I2
Nowitna National Wildlife Refuge *nature res. AK* U.S.A. **148** I2
Now Kharegan Iran **110** D2
Nowleye Lake Canada **151** K2
Nowogard Poland **57** O4
Noworadomsk Poland *see* **Radomsko**
Nowra Australia **138** E5
Nowrangapur India *see* **Nabarangapur**
Nowshera Pak. **111** I3
Nowyak Lake Canada **151** L2
Nowy Sącz Poland **57** R6
Nowy Targ Poland **57** R6
Noxen U.S.A. **165** G3
Noy, Xé r. Laos **86** D3
Noyabr'sk Rus. Fed. **76** I3
Noyes Island *AK* U.S.A. **149** N5
Noyon France **62** C5
Noyon Mongolia **94** E3
Nozawaonsen-mura Japan **93** E2
Nozizwe S. Africa **125** G6
Nqamakwe S. Africa **125** H7
Nqutu S. Africa **125** J5
Nsanje Malawi **123** D5
Nsombo Zambia **123** C5
Nsukka Nigeria **120** D4
Nsumbu National Park Zambia *see* **Sumbu National Park**
Ntambu Zambia **123** C5
Ntha S. Africa **125** H4
Ntoro, Kavo *pt* Greece **69** K5
Ntoum Gabon **122** A3
Ntungamo Uganda **122** D4
Nuanetsi Zimbabwe *see* **Mwenezi**
Nuangan *Sulawesi* Indon. **83** C2
Nu'aym *reg.* Oman **110** D6
Nuba Mountains Sudan **108** D7
Nubian Desert Sudan **108** D5
Nubra r. India **99** B6
Nüden Mongolia *see* **Ulaanbadrah**
Nudo Coropuna *mt.* Peru **176** D7
Nueces r. U.S.A. **161** D7
Nueltin Lake Canada **151** L2
Nueva Arcadia Hond. **166** [inset] H6
Nueva Ciudad Guerrero Mex. **161** D7
Nueva Gerona Cuba **169** H4
Nueva Harberton Arg. **178** C8
Nueva Imperial Chile **178** B5
Nueva Loja Ecuador *see* **Lago Agrio**
Nueva Ocotepeque Hond. **166** [inset] H6
Nueva Rosita Mex. **167** E3
Nueva San Salvador El Salvador **167** H6
Nueva Villa de Padilla Mex. **161** D7
Nueve de Julio Arg. *see* **9 de Julio**
Nuevitas Cuba **169** I4
Nuevo, Cayo *i.* Mex. **167** H4
Nuevo, Golfo *g.* Arg. **178** D6
Nuevo Casas Grandes Mex. **166** D2
Nuevo Ideal Mex. **166** D3
Nuevo Laredo Mex. **167** F3
Nuevo León Mex. **159** F5
Nuevo León *state* Mex. **161** D7
Nuevo Rocatuerte Ecuador **176** C4
Nuga Mongolia *see* **Dzavhanmandal**
Nugaal *watercourse* Somalia **122** E3
Nugget Point N.Z. **139** B8
Nugur India **106** D2
Nuguria Islands P.N.G. **132** F2
Nuh, Ras *pt* Pak. **111** F5
Nuhaka N.Z. **139** F4
Nui *atoll* Tuvalu **133** H2
Nui Con Voi r. Vietnam *see* **Red**
Nuiqsut *AK* U.S.A. **149** J1
Nui Thanh Vietnam **86** E4
Nui Ti On *mt.* Vietnam **86** D4
Nujiang China **96** C2
Nu Jiang r. China/Myanmar *see* **Salween**
Nukata Japan **92** D4
Nukey Bluff *hill* Australia **137** A7
Nukha Azer. *see* **Şäki**

▶**Nuku'alofa** Tonga **133** I4
Capital of Tonga.

Nukufetau *atoll* Tuvalu **133** H2
Nuku Hiva *i.* Fr. Polynesia **187** K6
Nukuhiva *i.* Fr. Polynesia *see* **Nuku Hiva**
Nukuhu P.N.G. **81** L8
Nukulaelae *atoll* Tuvalu **133** H2
Nukulailai *atoll* Tuvalu *see* **Nukulaelae**
Nukumanu Islands P.N.G. **133** F2
Nukunau *i.* Kiribati *see* **Nikunau**
Nukunono *atoll* Tokelau *see* **Nukunonu**
Nukunonu *atoll* Tokelau **133** I2
Nukus Uzbek. **102** A3
Nulato *AK* U.S.A. **148** H2
Nullagine Australia **134** C5
Nullarbor Australia **135** E7
Nullarbor National Park Australia **135** E7
Nullarbor Plain Australia **135** E7
Nullarbor Regional Reserve *park* Australia **135** E7
Nuluarniavik, Lac *l.* Canada **152** F2
Nulu'erhu Shan *mts* China **95** I3
Num *i.* Indon. **81** J7
Num Nepal **99** D8
Numalla, Lake *salt flat* Australia **138** B2
Numan Nigeria **122** B3
Numanuma P.N.G. **136** E1
Numata *Gunma* Japan **93** F2
Numazu Japan **93** E3
Numbulwar Australia **136** A2
Numedal *valley* Norway **55** F6
Numfoor *i.* Indon. **81** I7
Numin He r. China **90** B3
Numurkah Australia **138** B6
Nunachuak *AK* U.S.A. **148** H4
Nunaksaluk Island Canada **153** J3
Nunakuluut *i.* Greenland **147** N3
Nunap Isua *c.* Greenland *see* **Farewell, Cape**
Nunapitchuk *AK* U.S.A. **148** G3
Nunarsuit *i.* Greenland *see* **Nunakuluut**
Nunavakpak Lake *AK* U.S.A. **148** G3
Nunavaugaluk, Lake *AK* U.S.A. **148** H4
Nunavik *reg.* Canada **152** G1
Nunavut *admin. div.* Canada **151** L2
Nunda U.S.A. **165** G2
Nundle Australia **138** E3
Nuneaton U.K. **59** F6
Nungba India **105** H4
Nungesser Lake Canada **151** M5
Nungnain Sum *Nei Mongol* China **95** I2
Nunivak Island *AK* U.S.A. **148** F4
Nunkapasi India **106** E1
Nunkun *mt.* India **104** D2
Nunligran Rus. Fed. **148** D2
Nuñomoral Spain **67** C3
Nunspeet Neth. **62** F2
Nunukan *i.* Indon. **85** G2
Nunyamo Rus. Fed. **148** E2
Nuojiang China *see* **Tongjiang**
Nuoro *Sardinia* Italy **68** C4
Nupani *i.* Solomon Is **133** G3
Nuqrah Saudi Arabia **108** F4
Nur *Xinjiang* China **99** C5
Nur r. Iran **110** D2
Nura *Almatinskaya Oblast'* Kazakh. **98** B4
Nura Kazakh. **98** A2
Nura r. Kazakh. **98** A2
Nūrābād Iran **110** C4
Nurakita *i.* Tuvalu *see* **Niulakita**
Nurata Uzbek. *see* **Nurota**
Nur Dağları *mts* Turkey **107** B1
Nurek Tajik. *see* **Norak**
Nurek Reservoir Tajik. *see* **Norak, Obanbori**
Nurekskoye Vodokhranilishche *resr* Tajik. *see* **Norak, Obanbori**
Nuremberg Germany **63** L5
Nūrestān **109** K3
Nuri Mex. **166** C2
Nuri, Teluk *b.* Indon. **85** E3
Nurla India **104** D2
Nurlat Rus. Fed. **53** K5
Nurmes Fin. **54** P5
Nurmo Fin. **54** M5
Nürnberg Germany *see* **Nuremberg**
Nurota Uzbek. **102** C3
Nurri, Mount *hill* Australia **138** C3
Nur Turu *Qinghai* China **99** F5
Nusa Kambangan, Cagar Alam *nature res. Jawa* Indon. **85** E4
Nusa Laut *i. Maluku* Indon. **83** D3
Nusa Tenggara Barat *prov.* Indon. **85** G5
Nusawulan Indon. **81** I7
Nusaybin Turkey **113** F3
Nusela, Kepulauan *is Papua* Indon. **83** D3
Nushagak r. *AK* U.S.A. **148** H4
Nushagak Bay *AK* U.S.A. **148** H4
Nushagak Peninsula *AK* U.S.A. **148** H4
Nu Shan *mts* China **96** C3
Nu-shima *i.* Japan **92** A4
Nushki Pak. **111** G4
Nusratiye Turkey **107** D1
Nutak Canada **153** J2
Nutarawit Lake Canada **151** L2
Nutauge, Laguna *lag.* Rus. Fed. **148** C2
Nutepel'men Rus. Fed. **148** D2
Nutrioso U.S.A. **159** I5
Nuttal Pak. **111** H4
Nutwood Downs Australia **134** F3
Nutzotin Mountains *AK* U.S.A. **149** K2

▶**Nuuk** Greenland **147** M3
Capital of Greenland.

Nuupas Fin. **54** O3
Nuussuaq Greenland **147** M2
Nuussuaq *pen.* Greenland **147** M2
Nuwaybi' al Muzayyinah Egypt **112** D5
Nuweiba el Muzeina Egypt *see* **Nuwaybi' al Muzayyinah**
Nuwerus S. Africa **124** D6
Nuweveldberge *mts* S. Africa **124** E7
Nuwuk *AK* U.S.A. **148** H1
Nuyakuk r. *AK* U.S.A. **148** H4
Nuyakuk Lake *AK* U.S.A. **148** H4
Nuyts, Point Australia **135** B8
Nuyts Archipelago *is* Australia **135** F8
Nuzvid India **106** D2
Nwanedi Nature Reserve S. Africa **125** J2
Nxai Pan National Park Botswana **123** C5
Nyaän, Bukit *hill* Indon. **85** F2
Nyac *AK* U.S.A. **148** H3
Nyagan' Rus. Fed. **51** T3
Nyagquka China *see* **Yajiang**
Nyagrong China *see* **Xinlong**
Nyahururu Kenya **122** D3
Nyah West Australia **138** A5
Nyaimai *Xizang* China **99** F7
Nyainqêntanglha Feng *mt. Xizang* China **99** E7
Nyainqêntanglha Shan *mts Xizang* China **99** E7
Nyainrong *Xizang* China **99** F6
Nyåker Sweden **54** K5
Nyakh Rus. Fed. *see* **Nyagan'**
Nyaksimvol' Rus. Fed. **51** S3
Nyala Sudan **121** F3
Nyalam *Xizang* China *see* **Congdü**
Nyalikungu Tanz. *see* **Maswa**
Nyamandhiovu Zimbabwe **123** C5
Nyamtumbo Tanz. **123** D5
Nyande Zimbabwe *see* **Masvingo**
Nyandoma Rus. Fed. **52** I3
Nyandomskiy Vozvyshennost' *hills* Rus. Fed. **52** H3
Nyanga Congo **122** B4
Nyanga Zimbabwe **123** D5
Nyangbo *Xizang* China **99** F7
Nyang Qu r. China **99** F7
Nyapa, Gunung *mt.* Indon. **85** G2
Nyar r. India **99** B7
Nyarling r. Canada **150** H2

▶**Nyasa, Lake** Africa **123** D4
3rd largest lake in Africa, and 9th in the world.

Nyasaland *country* Africa *see* **Malawi**
Nyashabozh Rus. Fed. **52** L2
Nyasvizh Belarus **55** O10
Nyaungdon Myanmar *see* **Yandoon**
Nyaunglebin Myanmar **86** B3
Nyborg Denmark **55** G9
Nyborg Norway **54** P1
Nybro Sweden **55** I8
Nyeboe Land *reg.* Greenland **147** M1
Nyêmo *Xizang* China **99** E7
Nyenchen Tanglha Range *mts Xizang* China *see* **Nyainqêntanglha Shan**
Nyeri Kenya **122** D4
Nygchigen, Mys *c.* Rus. Fed. **148** D2
Nyi, Co *l. Xizang* China **99** D6
Nyika National Park Zambia **123** D5
Nyima *Xizang* China **99** D7
Nyima *Xizang* China **99** F7
Nyimba Zambia **123** D5
Nyingchi *Xizang* China **99** F7
Nyingzhong *Xizang* China **99** E7
Nyinma China *see* **Maqu**
Nyíregyháza Hungary **53** D7
Nyiru, Mount Kenya **122** D3
Nykarleby Fin. **54** M5
Nykøbing Denmark **55** G9
Nykøbing Sjælland Denmark **55** G9
Nyköping Sweden **55** J7
Nyland Sweden **54** J5
Nylsvley *nature res.* S. Africa **125** I3
Nymagee Australia **138** C4
Nymboida National Park Australia **138** F2
Nynäshamn Sweden **55** J7
Nyngan Australia **138** C3
Nyogzê *Xizang* China **99** C7
Nyohō-san *mt.* Japan **93** F2
Nyoman r. Belarus/Lith. **55** M10 *also known as Neman or Nemunas*
Nyon Switz. **66** H3
Nyons France **66** G4
Nýřany Czech Rep. **63** N5
Nyrob Rus. Fed. **51** R3
Nysa Poland **57** P5
Nysh Rus. Fed. **90** F2
Nyssa U.S.A. **156** D4
Nystad Fin. *see* **Uusikaupunki**
Nytva Rus. Fed. **51** R4
Nyūgasa-yama *mt.* Japan **93** E3
Nyūkawa Japan **92** D2
Nyuksenitsa Rus. Fed. **52** J3
Nyunzu Dem. Rep. Congo **123** C4
Nyurba Rus. Fed. **77** M3
Nyūzen Japan **92** D2
Nyyskiy Zaliv *lag.* Rus. Fed. **90** F1
Nzambi Congo **122** B4
Nzega Tanz. **123** D4
Nzérékoré Guinea **120** C4
N'zeto Angola **123** B4
Nzwani *i.* Comoros **123** E5

O

Oahe, Lake U.S.A. **160** C2
O'ahu *i.* U.S.A. **157** [inset]
Oaitupu *i.* Tuvalu *see* **Vaitupu**
Oak Bluffs U.S.A. **165** J3
Oak City U.S.A. **159** G2
Oak Creek U.S.A. **159** J1
Oakdale U.S.A. **161** E6
Oakes U.S.A. **160** D2
Oakey Australia **138** E1
Oak Grove *KY* U.S.A. **164** B5
Oak Grove *LA* U.S.A. **161** F5
Oak Grove *MI* U.S.A. **164** C1
Oakham U.K. **59** G6
Oak Harbor U.S.A. **164** D3
Oak Hill *OH* U.S.A. **164** D4
Oak Hill *WV* U.S.A. **164** E5
Oakhurst U.S.A. **158** D3
Oak Lake Canada **151** K5
Oakland *CA* U.S.A. **158** B3
Oakland *MD* U.S.A. **164** F4
Oakland *ME* U.S.A. **165** K1
Oakland *NE* U.S.A. **160** D3
Oakland *OR* U.S.A. **156** C4
Oakland *airport* U.S.A. **158** B3
Oakland City U.S.A. **164** B4
Oaklands Australia **138** C5
Oak Lawn U.S.A. **164** B3
Oakley U.S.A. **160** C4
Oakover r. Australia **134** C5
Oak Park *IL* U.S.A. **164** B3
Oak Park *MI* U.S.A. **164** C2
Oak Park Reservoir U.S.A. **159** I1
Oakridge U.S.A. **156** C4
Oak Ridge U.S.A. **162** C4
Oakvale Australia **137** C7
Oak View U.S.A. **158** D4
Oakville Canada **164** F2
Oakwood *OH* U.S.A. **164** C3
Oakwood *TN* U.S.A. **164** B5
Oamaru N.Z. **139** C7
Ōamishirasato Japan **93** G3
Ōarai Japan **93** G2
Oaro N.Z. **139** D6
Ōashi-gawa r. Japan **93** F2
Oasis *CA* U.S.A. **158** E3
Oasis *NV* U.S.A. **156** E4
Oates Coast *reg.* Antarctica *see* **Oates Land**
Oates Land *reg.* Antarctica **188** H2
Oaxaca Mex. **168** E5
Oaxaca *state* Mex. **167** F5
Oaxaca de Juárez Mex. *see* **Oaxaca**

▶**Ob'** r. Rus. Fed. **88** E2
Part of the Ob'-Irtysh, the 2nd longest river in Asia.

Ob, Gulf of *sea chan.* Rus. Fed. *see* **Obskaya Guba**
Oba Canada **152** D4
Oba *i.* Vanuatu *see* **Aoba**
Obako-dake *mt.* Japan **92** B4
Obala Cameroon **120** E4
Obama Japan **92** B3
Obama-wan *b.* Japan **92** B3
Oban U.K. **60** D4
Obara Japan **92** D3
O Barco Spain **67** C2
Obata Japan **92** C4
Obbia Somalia *see* **Hobyo**
Obdorsk Rus. Fed. *see* **Salekhard**
Óbecse Serbia *see* **Bečej**
Obed Canada **150** G4
Oberaula Germany **63** J4
Oberdorla Germany **63** K3
Oberhausen Germany **62** G3
Oberlin *KS* U.S.A. **160** C4
Oberlin *LA* U.S.A. **161** E6
Oberlin *OH* U.S.A. **164** D3
Obermoschel Germany **63** H5
Oberon Australia **138** D4
Oberpfälzer Wald *mts* Germany **63** M5
Obersinn Germany **63** J4
Oberthulba Germany **63** J4
Obertshausen Germany **63** I4
Oberwälder Land *reg.* Germany **63** J3
Obi *i. Maluku* Indon. **83** C3
Obi, Kepulauan *is Maluku* Indon. **83** C3
Obi, Selat *sea chan. Maluku* Indon. **83** C3
Óbidos Brazil **177** G4
Obihiro Japan **90** F4
Obilatu *i. Maluku* Indon. **83** C3
Obil'noye Rus. Fed. **53** J7

▶**Ob'-Irtysh** r. Rus. Fed. **76** H3
2nd longest river in Asia, and 5th in the world.

Obitsu-gawa r. Japan **93** F3
Obluch'ye Rus. Fed. **90** C2
Obninsk Rus. Fed. **53** H5
Obo Cent. Afr. Rep. **122** C3
Obo *Qinghai* China **94** E4
Obock Djibouti **108** F7
Ŏbŏk N. Korea **90** C4
Obokote Dem. Rep. Congo **122** C4
Obo Liang *Qinghai* China **98** F5
Obong, Gunung *mt.* Malaysia **85** F1
Obouya Congo **122** B4
Oboyan' Rus. Fed. **53** H6
Obozerskiy Rus. Fed. **52** I3
Obregón, Presa *resr* Mex. **166** C3
Obrenovac Serbia **69** I2
Obruk Turkey **112** D3
Observatory Hill *hill* Australia **135** F7
Obshchiy Syrt *hills* Rus. Fed. **51** Q5
Obskaya Guba *sea chan.* Rus. Fed. **76** I3
Ōbu Japan **92** C3
Obuasi Ghana **120** C4
Obuse Japan **93** E2
Ob''yachevo Rus. Fed. **52** K3
Ocala U.S.A. **163** D6
Ocampo *Chihuahua* Mex. **166** C2
Ocampo *Coahuila* Mex. **166** E3
Ocaña Col. **176** D2
Ocaña Spain **67** E4
Occidental, Cordillera *mts* Chile **176** E7
Occidental, Cordillera *mts* Col. **176** C3
Occidental, Cordillera *mts* Peru **176** D7
Oceana U.S.A. **164** E5
Ocean Cape *AK* U.S.A. **149** M4
Ocean Cay *i.* Bahamas **163** E7
Ocean City *MD* U.S.A. **165** H4
Ocean City *NJ* U.S.A. **165** H4
Ocean Falls Canada **150** E4
Ocean Island Kiribati *see* **Banaba**
Ocean Island *atoll* U.S.A. *see* **Kure Atoll**
Oceanside U.S.A. **158** E5
Ocean Springs U.S.A. **161** F6
Ochakiv Ukr. **69** N1
Och'amch'ire Georgia **113** F2
Ocher Rus. Fed. **51** Q4
Ochiishi-misaki *pt* Japan **90** G4
Ochil Hills U.K. **60** F4
Ochrida, Lake Albania/Macedonia *see* **Ohrid, Lake**
Ochsenfurt Germany **63** K5
Ochtrup Germany **63** H2
Ocilla U.S.A. **163** D6
Ockelbo Sweden **55** J6
Ocolaşul Mare, Vârful *mt.* Romania **69** K1
Oconomowoc U.S.A. **164** A2
Oconto U.S.A. **164** B1
Ocoroni Mex. **166** C3
Ocos Guat. **167** G6
Ocosingo Mex. **167** G5
Ocotal Nicaragua **166** [inset] I6
Ocotlán *Oaxaca* Mex. **167** F5
Ocozocoautla Mex. **167** G5
Octeville-sur-Mer France **59** H9
October Revolution Island Rus. Fed. *see* **Oktyabr'skoy Revolyutsii, Ostrov**
Ocú Panama **166** [inset] J8
Oda, Jebel *mt.* Sudan **108** E5
Ódáðahraun *lava field* Iceland **54** [inset]
Ŏdaejin N. Korea **90** C4
Odae-san National Park S. Korea **91** C5
Ōdai Japan **92** C4
Ōdaigahara-zan *mt.* Japan **92** C4
Odaira-tōge *pass* Japan **92** D3

Ōdate Japan 91 F4
Odawara Japan 93 F3
Odda Norway 55 E6
Odei r. Canada 151 L3
Odell U.S.A. 164 B3
Odem U.S.A. 161 D7
Odemira Port. 67 B5
Ödemiş Turkey 69 L5
Ödenburg Hungary see Sopron
Odense Denmark 55 G9
Odenwald reg. Germany 63 I5
Oder r. Germany 63 J3
also known as Odra (Poland)
Oderbucht b. Germany 57 O3
Oder-Havel-Kanal canal Germany 63 N2
Odesa Ukr. see Odessa
Ödeshog Sweden 55 I7
Odessa Ukr. 69 N1
Odessa TX U.S.A. 161 C6
Odessa WA U.S.A. 156 D3
Odessus Bulg. see Varna
Odiel r. Spain 67 C5
Odienné Côte d'Ivoire 120 C4
Odintsovo Rus. Fed. 52 H5
Ôdôngk Cambodia 87 D5
Odra r. Germany/Pol. 57 Q6
also known as Oder (Germany)
Odzala, Parc National d' nat. park Congo 122 B3
Ōe Japan 92 B3
Oea Libya see Tripoli
Oeiras Brazil 177 J5
Oelsnitz Germany 63 M4
Oenkerk Neth. 62 F1
Oenpelli Australia 134 F3
Oesel i. Estonia see Hiiumaa
Oeufs, Lac des l. Canada 153 G3
Ōe-yama hill Japan 92 B3
Of Turkey 113 F2
O'Fallon r. U.S.A. 156 G3
Ofanto r. Italy 68 G4
Ofaqim Israel 107 B4
Offa Nigeria 120 D4
Offenbach am Main Germany 63 I4
Offenburg Germany 57 K6
Oga r. Indon. 85 F2
Oga Japan 91 E5
Oga-dake mt. Japan 93 F1
Ogadēn reg. Eth. 122 E3
Oga-hantō pen. Japan 91 E5
Ōgaki Japan 92 C3
Ogallala U.S.A. 160 C3
Ogan r. Indon. 84 D3
Ogano Japan 93 F2
Ogasa Japan 93 E4
Ogasawara-shotō is Japan see Bonin Islands
Ōga-tō mt. Japan 93 E2
Ogawa Ibaraki Japan 93 G2
Ogawa Ibaraki Japan 93 G2
Ogawa Nagano Japan 93 D2
Ogawa Saitama Japan 93 F2
Ōgawa Japan 93 G2
Ogbomosho Nigeria 120 D4
Ogbomosho Nigeria see Ogbomosho
Ogden IA U.S.A. 160 E3
Ogden UT U.S.A. 156 F4
Ogden, Mount B.C. Canada 149 N4
Ogdensburg U.S.A. 165 H1
Ogidaki Canada 152 D5
Ogilvie r. Y.T. Canada 149 M2
Ogilvie Mountains Y.T. Canada 149 L2
Ögiynuur Mongolia 94 E2
Oglala Pass sea channel AK U.S.A. 149 [inset]
Oglethorpe, Mount U.S.A. 163 C5
Oglio r. Italy 68 D2
Oglongi Rus. Fed. 90 E1
Ogmore Australia 136 E4
Ōgo Japan 93 F2
Ogoamas, Gunung mt. Indon. 83 B2
Ogōchi-damu dam Japan 93 F3
Ogodzha Rus. Fed. 90 D1
Ogoja Nigeria 120 D4
Ogoki r. Canada 152 D4
Ogoki Lake Canada 160 G1
Ogoki Reservoir Canada 152 C4
Ogoron Rus. Fed. 90 C1
Ogose Japan 93 F3
Ogosta r. Bulg. 69 J3
Ogre Latvia 55 N8
Ōguchi Japan 92 C3
Ogulin Croatia 68 F2
Ogurchinskiy, Ostrov i. Turkm. see Ogurjaly Adasy
Ogurjaly Adasy i. Turkm. 110 D2
Oğuzeli Turkey 107 C1
Ohai N.Z. 139 A7
Ohakune N.Z. 139 E4
Ohanet Alg. 120 D2
Ōhara Japan 93 G3
Ōhata Japan 90 F4
Ohcejohka Fin. see Utsjoki
O'Higgins (Chile) research station Antarctica 188 A2
O'Higgins, Lago l. Chile 178 B7
Ohio r. U.S.A. 164 A5
Ohio state U.S.A. 164 D3
Ōhira Japan 93 F2
Ōhito Japan 93 E3
Ohm r. Germany 63 I4
Ohogamiut AK U.S.A. 148 G3
Ohrdruf Germany 63 K4
Ohře r. Czech Rep. 63 N4
Ohre r. Germany 63 L2
Ohrid Macedonia 69 I4
Ohrid, Lake Albania/Macedonia 69 I4
Ohridsko Ezero l. Albania/Macedonia see Ohrid, Lake
Ohrigstad S. Africa 125 J3
Öhringen Germany 63 J5
Ohrit, Liqeni i l. Albania/Macedonia see Ohrid, Lake
Ohura N.Z. 139 E4
Ōi Fukui Japan 92 B3
Oich r. U.K. 60 E3
Oiga Xizang China 99 F7
Ōigawa Japan 93 E4
Ōi-gawa r. Japan 92 B3
Ōi-gawa r. Japan 93 E4
Oignies France 62 C4
Oil City U.S.A. 164 F3
Oise r. France 62 C6
Ōiso Japan 93 F3
Ōita Japan 91 C6
Oiti mt. Greece 69 J5
Ōizumi Yamanashi Japan 93 E3
Oizuruga-dake mt. Japan 92 C2
Ojai U.S.A. 158 D4
Ojalava i. Samoa see 'Upolu
Ōji Japan 92 B4
Ojinaga Mex. 166 D2
Ojitlán Mex. 167 F5
Ojiya Japan 91 E5
Ojo Caliente U.S.A. 157 G5
Ojo de Laguna Mex. 166 D2
Ojo de Liebre, Lago b. Mex. 166 B3

▶Ojos del Salado, Nevado mt. Arg./Chile 178 C3
2nd highest mountain in South America.

Ojuelos de Jalisco Mex. 167 E4
Oka r. Rus. Fed. 53 I4
Oka r. Rus. Fed. 88 I1
Okabe Saitama Japan 93 F2
Okabe Shizuoka Japan 93 E4
Okahandja Namibia 124 C1
Okahukura N.Z. 139 E4
Okakarara Namibia 123 B6
Okak Islands Canada 153 J2
Okanagan Lake Canada 150 G5
Okanda Sri Lanka 106 D5
Okano r. Gabon 122 B4
Okanogan U.S.A. 156 D2
Okanogan r. U.S.A. 156 D2
Okara Pak. 111 I4
Okarem Turkm. see Ekerem
Okataina vol. N.Z. see Tarawera, Mount
Okaukuejo Namibia 123 B5
Okavango r. Africa 123 C5

▶Okavango Delta swamp Botswana 123 C5
Largest oasis in the world.

Okavango Swamps Botswana see Okavango Delta
Ōkawachi Japan 92 A3
Okaya Japan 93 E2
Okayama Japan 91 D6
Okazaki Japan 92 D4
Okeechobee U.S.A. 163 D7
Okeechobee, Lake U.S.A. 163 D7
Okeene U.S.A. 161 D4
Okefenokee Swamp U.S.A. 163 D6
Okegawa Japan 93 F2
Okehampton U.K. 59 C8
Okemah U.S.A. 161 D5
Oker r. Germany 63 K2
Okha India 104 B5
Okha Rus. Fed. 90 F1
Okha Rann marsh India 104 B5
Okhotsk Rus. Fed. 77 P4
Okhotsk, Sea of Japan/Rus. Fed. 90 G3
Okhotskoye More sea Japan/Rus. Fed. see Okhotsk, Sea of
Okhtyrka Ukr. 53 G6
Okinawa i. Japan 91 B8
Okinawa-guntō is Japan see Okinawa-shotō
Okinawa-shotō is Japan 91 B8
Okino-Daitō-jima i. Japan 89 O8
Okino-shima i. Japan 92 B4
Okino-Tori-shima i. Japan 89 P8
Oki-shotō is Japan 89 O5
Oki-shotō is Japan 91 D5
Okkan Myanmar 86 A3
Oklahoma state U.S.A. 161 D5

▶Oklahoma City U.S.A. 161 D5
Capital of Oklahoma.

Okmok sea feature N. Pacific Ocean 148 E5
Okmulgee U.S.A. 161 D5
Okolona KY U.S.A. 164 C4
Okolona MS U.S.A. 161 F5
Okondja Gabon 122 B4
Okovskiy Les for. Rus. Fed. 52 G5
Okoyo Congo 122 B4
Okpeti, Gora mt. Kazakh. 98 C3
Øksfjord Norway 54 M1
Oktemberyan Armenia see Armavir
Oktwin Myanmar 86 B3
Oktyabr' Kazakh. see Kandyagash
Oktyabr'sk Kazakh. see Kandyagash
Oktyabr'skiy Belarus see Aktsyabrski
Oktyabr'skiy Amurskaya Oblast' Rus. Fed. 90 C1
Oktyabr'skiy Arkhangel'skaya Oblast' Rus. Fed. 52 I3
Oktyabr'skiy Kamchatskaya Oblast' Rus. Fed. 77 Q4
Oktyabr'skiy Respublika Bashkortostan Rus. Fed. 51 Q5
Oktyabr'skiy Volgogradskaya Oblast' Rus. Fed. 53 I7
Oktyabr'skoye Rus. Fed. 51 T3
Oktyabr'skoy Revolyutsii, Ostrov i. Rus. Fed. 77 K2
Okuchi Japan 92 C2
Okulovka Rus. Fed. 52 G4
Oku-sangai-dake mt. Japan 92 D3
Okushiri-tō i. Japan 90 E4
Okuta Nigeria 120 D4
Okutadami-ko resr Japan 93 F1
Okutama Japan 93 F3
Okutama-ko l. Japan 93 F3
Okutango-hantō pen. Japan 92 B3
Okutone-ko resr Japan 93 F2
Ōkuwa Japan 92 D3
Okwa watercourse Botswana 124 G1
Ólafsvík Iceland 54 [inset]
Olakkur India 106 C3
Olancha U.S.A. 158 D3
Olancha Peak U.S.A. 158 D3
Olanchito Hond. 166 [inset] I6
Öland i. Sweden 55 J8
Olary Australia 137 C7
Olathe CO U.S.A. 159 J2
Olathe KS U.S.A. 160 E4
Olavarría Arg. 178 D5
Oława Poland 57 P5
Olbernhau Germany 63 N4
Olbia Sardinia Italy 68 C4
Old Bahama Channel Bahamas/Cuba 163 E8
Old Bastar India 106 D2
Oldcastle Ireland 61 E4
Old Cork Australia 136 C4
Old Crow Y.T. Canada 149 M2
Old Crow r. Y.T. Canada 149 M2
Oldeboorn Neth. see Aldeboarn
Oldenburg Germany 63 I1
Oldenburg in Holstein Germany 57 M3
Oldenzaal Neth. 62 G2
Olderdalen Norway 54 L2
Old Forge U.S.A. 165 H2
Old Gidgee Australia 135 B6
Oldham U.K. 58 E5
Old Harbor AK U.S.A. 148 I4
Old Head of Kinsale hd Ireland 61 D6
Old John Lake AK U.S.A. 149 K1
Oldman r. Canada 150 I5
Oldmeldrum U.K. 60 G3
Old Perlican Canada 153 L5
Old Rampart AK U.S.A. 149 L2
Old River U.S.A. 158 D4
Olds Canada 150 H5
Old Speck Mountain U.S.A. 165 J1
Old Station U.S.A. 158 C1
Old Wives Lake Canada 151 J5
Öldziyt Arhangay Mongolia 94 E1
Öldziyt Arhangay Mongolia see Erdenemandal
Öldziyt Bayanhongor Mongolia 94 E2
Öldziyt Dornogovĭ Mongolia see Sayhandulaan
Öldziyt Dundgovĭ Mongolia 94 F2
Olean U.S.A. 165 F2
Olecko Poland 57 S3
Olekma r. Rus. Fed. 77 N3
Olekminsk Rus. Fed. 77 N3
Olekminskiy Stanovik mts Rus. Fed. 89 M2
Oleksandrivs'k Ukr. see Zaporizhzhya
Oleksandriya Ukr. 53 G6
Ølen Norway 55 D7
Olenegorsk Rus. Fed. 54 R2
Olenek Rus. Fed. 77 M3
Olenek r. Rus. Fed. 77 M2
Olenek Bay Rus. Fed. see Olenekskiy Zaliv
Olenekskiy Zaliv b. Rus. Fed. 77 N2
Olenino Rus. Fed. 52 G4
Olenitsa Rus. Fed. 52 G2
Olenivs'ki Kar"yery Ukr. see Dokuchayevs'k
Olentuy Rus. Fed. 95 H1
Olenya Rus. Fed. see Olenegorsk
Oleshky Ukr. see Tsyurupyns'k
Olet Tongo mt. Sumbawa Indon. 85 G5
Olevs'k Ukr. 53 E6
Ol'ga Rus. Fed. 90 D4
Olga, Lac l. Canada 152 F4
Olga, Mount Australia 135 E6
Ol'ginsk Rus. Fed. 90 D1
Olginskoye Rus. Fed. see Kochubeyevskoye
Ölgiy Mongolia 94 B1
Olhão Port. 67 C5
Olia Chain mts Australia 135 E6
Olifants r. Moz./S. Africa 125 J3
also known as Elefantes
Olifants watercourse Namibia 124 D3
Olifants S. Africa 125 J2
Olifants r. W. Cape S. Africa 124 D6
Olifants r. W. Cape S. Africa 124 E7
Olifantshoek S. Africa 124 F4
Olifantsrivierberge mts S. Africa 124 D7
Olimarao atoll Micronesia 81 L5
Olimbos hill Cyprus see Olympos
Olimbos mt. Greece see Olympus, Mount
Olimpos Beydağları Milli Parkı nat. park Turkey 69 N6
Olinalá Mex. 167 F5
Olinda Brazil 177 L5
Olinga Moz. 123 D5
Olio Australia 136 C4
Oliphants Drift S. Africa 125 H3
Olisipo Port. see Lisbon
Oliva Spain 67 F4
Oliva, Cordillera de mts Arg./Chile 178 C3
Olivares, Cerro de mt. Arg./Chile 178 C4
Olive Hill U.S.A. 164 D4
Olivehurst U.S.A. 158 C2
Oliveira dos Brejinhos Brazil 179 C1
Olivença Moz. see Lupilichi
Olivenza Spain 67 C4
Oliver Lake Canada 151 K3
Olivet MI U.S.A. 164 C2
Olivet SD U.S.A. 160 D3
Olivia U.S.A. 160 E2
Oljoq Nei Mongol China 95 F4
Ol'khovka Rus. Fed. 53 J6
Ollagüe Chile 178 C2
Ollombo Congo 122 B4
Olmaliq Uzbek. 102 C3
Olmos Peru 176 C5
Olmütz Czech Rep. see Olomouc
Olney U.K. 59 G6
Olney IL U.S.A. 160 F4
Olney MD U.S.A. 165 G4
Olney TX U.S.A. 161 D5
Olofström Sweden 55 I8
Olomane r. Canada 153 J4
Olomouc Czech Rep. 57 P6
Olonets Rus. Fed. 52 G3
Olongapo Luzon Phil. 82 C3
Olongliko Kalimantan Indon. 85 F3
Oloron-Ste-Marie France 66 D5
Olosenga atoll American Samoa see Swains Island
Olot Spain 67 H2
Olot Uzbek. 111 F2
Olovyannaya Rus. Fed. 95 H1
Olovyannaya Rus. Fed. 148 C2
Oloy r. Rus. Fed. 77 Q3
Oloy, Qatorkŭhi mts Asia see Alai Range
Olpe Germany 63 H3
Olsztyn Poland 57 R4
Olt r. Romania 69 K3
Olten Switz. 66 H3
Oltenița Romania 69 L2
Oltu Turkey 113 F2
Oluan Pi c. Taiwan 97 I4
Olutanga i. Phil. 82 C5
Ol'viopol' Ukr. see Pervomays'k
Olymbos hill Cyprus see Olympos

▶Olympia U.S.A. 156 C3
Capital of Washington state.

Olympic National Park U.S.A. 156 C3
Olympos hill Cyprus 107 A2
Olympos Greece see Olympus, Mount
Olympos mt. Greece see Olympus, Mount
Olympos nat. park Greece see Olympou, Ethnikos Drymos
Olympou, Ethnikos Drymos nat. park Greece 69 J4
Olympus, Mount Greece 69 J4
Olympus, Mount U.S.A. 156 C3
Olyutorskiy Rus. Fed. 189 C2
Olyutorskiy, Mys c. Rus. Fed. 77 S4
Olyutorskiy Zaliv b. Rus. Fed. 77 R4
Olzheras Rus. Fed. see Mezhdurechensk
Oma Xizang China 99 C6
Oma r. Rus. Fed. 52 J2
Ōmachi Japan 93 D2
Omaezaki Japan 93 E4
Omae-zaki pt Japan 93 E4
Omagh U.K. 61 E3
Omaha U.S.A. 160 E3
Omaheke admin. reg. Namibia 124 D2
Omal'skiy Khrebet mts Rus. Fed. 90 E1
Ōmama Japan 93 F2
Oman country Asia 109 I6
Oman, Gulf of Asia 110 E5
Omaruru Namibia 123 B6
Omate Peru 176 D7
Omaweneno Botswana 124 F3
Omba i. Vanuatu see Aoba
Ombai, Selat sea chan. Indon. 83 C5
Ombalantu Namibia see Uutapi
Ombolata Indon. 84 B2
Omboué Gabon 122 A4
Ombu Xizang China 99 D7
Omdraaisvlei S. Africa 124 F6
Omdurman Sudan 108 D6
Ōme Japan 93 F3
Omeo Australia 138 C6
Omer U.S.A. 164 D1
Ometepe, Isla de i. Nicaragua 166 [inset] I7
Ometepec Mex. 168 E5
Omgoy Wildlife Reserve nature res. Thai. 86 B3
Om Hajēr Eritrea 108 E7
Ōmi Japan 93 E2
Ōmi Niigata Japan 93 D1
Ōmi Shiga Japan 92 C3
Omīdīyeh Iran 110 C4
Omigawa Japan 93 G3
Ōmihachiman Japan 92 C3
Omineca Mountains Canada 150 E3
Omitara Namibia 124 C2
Ōmiya Ibaraki Japan 93 G2
Ōmiya Kyōto Japan 92 B3
Ōmiya Mie Japan 92 C4
Ōmiya Saitama Japan 93 F3
Ommaney, Cape AK U.S.A. 149 N4
Ommen Neth. 62 G2
Ömnödelger Hentiy Mongolia 95 G2
Ömnögovĭ prov. Mongolia 94 F3
Omōi-gawa r. Japan 93 F2
Omolon Rus. Fed. 77 R3
Omo National Park Eth. 122 D3
Omotegō Japan 93 G1
Omsk Rus. Fed. 76 I4
Omsukchan Rus. Fed. 77 Q3
Ōmū Japan 90 F3
O-mu Myanmar 86 B2
Omu, Vârful mt. Romania 69 K2
Ōmura Japan 91 C6
Ōmuro-yama hill Japan 93 F4
Ōmuro-yama mt. Japan 93 E3
Ōmuro-yama mt. Japan 93 F3
Omutninsk Rus. Fed. 52 L4
Onaman Lake Canada 152 D4
Onamia U.S.A. 160 E2
Onancock U.S.A. 165 H5
Onang Sulawesi Barat Indon. 83 A3
Onangué, Lac l. Gabon 122 B4
Onaping Lake Canada 152 E5
Onatchiway, Lac l. Canada 153 H4
Onavas Mex. 166 C2
Onawa U.S.A. 160 D3
Onaway U.S.A. 164 C1
Onbingwin Myanmar 87 B4
Oncativo Arg. 178 D4
Onchan Isle of Man 58 C4
Oncócua Angola 123 B5
Öncül Turkey 107 D1
Ondal India see Andal
Ondangwa Namibia 123 B5
Onderstedorings S. Africa 124 E6
Ondjiva Angola 123 B5
Ondo Nigeria 120 D4
Öndörhaan Mongolia 95 G2
Ondor Had Nei Mongol China 95 J2
Öndörhushuu Mongolia see Bulgan
Ondorkara Xinjiang China 94 B2
Ondor Mod Nei Mongol China 94 F3
Öndörshil Mongolia 95 G2
Ondor Sum Nei Mongol China 95 H3
Öndör-Ulaan Mongolia 94 E1
Ondozero Rus. Fed. 52 G3
One Botswana 124 E2
One and a Half Degree Channel Maldives 103 D11
Onega Rus. Fed. 52 H3
Onega r. Rus. Fed. 52 H3
Onega, Lake l. Rus. Fed. see Onezhskoye Ozero

▶Onega, Lake Rus. Fed. 52 G3
3rd largest lake in Europe.

Onega Bay g. Rus. Fed. see Onezhskaya Guba
One Hundred and Fifty Mile House Canada see 150 Mile House
One Hundred Mile House Canada see 100 Mile House
Oneida NY U.S.A. 165 H2
Oneida TN U.S.A. 164 C5
Oneida Lake U.S.A. 165 H2
O'Neill U.S.A. 160 D3
Onekama U.S.A. 164 B1
Onekotan, Ostrov i. Rus. Fed. 77 Q5
Oneonta AL U.S.A. 163 C5
Oneonta NY U.S.A. 165 H2
Onești Romania 69 L1
Onezhskaya Guba g. Rus. Fed. 52 G2
Onezhskoye Ozero Rus. Fed. 51 N3
Onezhskoye Ozero l. Rus. Fed. see Onega, Lake
Ong r. India 106 D1
Onga Gabon 122 B4
Ongers watercourse S. Africa 124 F5
Ongi Dundgovĭ Mongolia see Sayhan-Ovoo
Ongi Övörhangay Mongolia see Uyanga
Ongiyn Gol r. Mongolia 94 E2
Ongjin N. Korea 91 B5
Ongniud Qi Nei Mongol China see Wudan
Ongole India 106 D3
Ongon Mongolia see Bürd
Onguday Rus. Fed. 98 D2
Onida U.S.A. 160 C2
Oniishi Japan 93 F2
Onilahy r. Madag. 123 E6
Onistagane, Lac l. Canada 153 H4
Onitsha Nigeria 120 D4
Onjati Mountain Namibia 124 C2
Onjiva Angola see Ondjiva
Onjuku Japan 93 G3
Ōno Fukui Japan 92 C3
Ōno Gifu Japan 92 C3
Ono Hyōgo Japan 92 A4
Ōnohara-jima i. Japan 93 F4
Ono-i-Lau i. Fiji 133 I4
Onomichi Japan 91 D6
Onon atoll Micronesia see Namonuito
Onon Mongolia see Binder
Onon r. Rus. Fed. 95 H1
Onon Gol r. Mongolia 95 H1
Onor, Gora mt. Rus. Fed. 90 F2
Onotoa atoll Kiribati 133 H2
Onseepkans S. Africa 124 D5
Onslow Australia 134 A5
Onslow Bay U.S.A. 163 E5
Onstwedde Neth. 62 H1
Ontake-san vol. Japan 92 D3
Ontaratue r. N.W.T. Canada 149 O2
Ontario prov. Canada 151 N5
Ontario U.S.A. 158 E4
Ontario, Lake Canada/U.S.A. 165 G2
Ontong Java Atoll Solomon Is 133 F2
Onutu atoll Kiribati see Onotoa
Onverwacht Suriname 177 G2
Onyx U.S.A. 158 D4
Oodnadatta Australia 137 A5
Oodweyne Somalia 122 E3
Ōoka Japan 93 D2
Oolambeyan National Park 138 F5
Ooldea Australia 135 E7
Ooldea Range hills Australia 135 E7
Oologah Lake resr U.S.A. 161 E4
Ooratippra r. Australia 136 B4
Oos-Londen S. Africa see East London
Oostburg Neth. 62 D3
Oostende Belgium see Ostend
Oostendorp Neth. 62 F2
Oosterhout Neth. 62 E3
Oosterschelde est. Neth. 62 D3
Oosterwolde Neth. 62 G2
Oostvleteren Belgium 62 C4
Oost-Vlieland Neth. 62 F1
Ootacamund India see Udagamandalam
Ootsa Lake Canada 150 E4
Ootsa Lake l. Canada 150 E4
Opal Mex. 161 C7
Opala Dem. Rep. Congo 122 C4
Oparino Rus. Fed. 52 K4
Oparo i. Fr. Polynesia see Rapa
Opasatika r. Canada 152 E4
Opasatika Lake Canada 152 E4
Opasquia Canada 151 M4
Opataca, Lac l. Canada 152 G4
Opava Czech Rep. 57 P6
Opel hill Germany 63 H5
Opelika U.S.A. 163 C5
Opelousas U.S.A. 161 E6
Opeongo Lake Canada 152 F5
Opheim U.S.A. 156 G2
Ophir, Gunung vol. Indon. 84 C2
Opienge Dem. Rep. Congo 122 C3
Opin Seram Indon. 83 D3
Opinaca r. Canada 152 F3
Opinaca, Réservoir resr Canada 152 F3
Opinnagau r. Canada 152 E3
Opiscotéo, Lac l. Canada 153 H3
Op Luang National Park Thai. 86 B3
Opmeer Neth. 62 E2
Opochka Rus. Fed. 55 P8
Opocopa, Lac l. Canada 153 I3
Opodepe Mex. 166 C2
Opole Poland 57 P5
Oporto Port. 67 B3
Opotiki N.Z. 139 F4
Opp U.S.A. 163 C6
Oppdal Norway 54 F5
Oppeln Poland see Opole
Opportunity U.S.A. 156 D3
Opunake N.Z. 139 D4
Opuwo Namibia 123 B5
Oqsu r. Tajik. 111 I2
Oquitoa Mex. 166 C2
Ōra Japan 93 F2
Oracle U.S.A. 159 H5
Oradea Romania 69 I1
Orahovac Kosovo see Rahovec
Orai India 104 D4
Oraibi U.S.A. 159 H4
Oraibi Wash watercourse U.S.A. 159 H4
Oral Kazakh. see Ural'sk
Oran Alg. 67 F6
Orán Arg. 178 D2
O Rang Cambodia 87 D4
Orang India 105 H4
Ŏrang N. Korea 90 C4
Orange Australia 138 D4
Orange France 66 G4
Orange r. Namibia/S. Africa 124 C5
Orange CA U.S.A. 158 E5
Orange MA U.S.A. 165 I2
Orange TX U.S.A. 161 E6
Orange VA U.S.A. 165 F4
Orange, Cabo c. Brazil 177 H3
Orangeburg U.S.A. 163 D5
Orange City U.S.A. 160 D3
Orange Cone sea feature S. Atlantic Ocean 184 I8
Orange Free State prov. S. Africa see Free State
Orangeville Canada 164 E2
Orange Walk Belize 167 H5
Orani Luzon Phil. 82 C3
Oranienburg Germany 63 N2
Oranje r. Namibia/S. Africa see Orange
Oranje Gebergte hills Suriname 177 G3
Oranjemund Namibia 124 C5

▶Oranjestad Aruba 169 J6
Capital of Aruba.

Oranmore Ireland 61 D4
Orapa Botswana 123 C6
Oras Samar Phil. 82 D3
Oras Bay Samar Phil. 82 D3
Orăștie Romania 69 J2
Orașul Stalin Romania see Brașov
Oratia, Mount AK U.S.A. 148 G4
Oravais Fin. 54 M5
Orba Co l. China 99 C6
Orbetello Italy 68 D3
Orbost Australia 138 D6
Orca Bay AK U.S.A. 149 K3
Orcadas research station S. Atlantic Ocean 188 A2
Orchard City U.S.A. 159 J2
Orchha India 104 D4
Orchila, Isla i. Venez. 176 E1
Orchy r. U.K. 60 D4
Orcutt U.S.A. 158 C4
Ord r. Australia 134 E3
Ord U.S.A. 160 D3
Ord, Mount hill Australia 134 D4
Órdenes Spain see Ordes
Orderville U.S.A. 159 G3
Ordes Spain 67 B2
Ordesa-Monte Perdido, Parque Nacional nat. park Spain 67 G2
Ord Mountain U.S.A. 158 E4
Ordos Nei Mongol China 95 G4
Ord River Dam Australia 134 E4
Ordu Hatay Turkey see Yayladağı
Ordu Ordu Turkey 112 E2
Ordubad Azer. 113 G3
Ordway U.S.A. 160 C4
Ordzhonikidze Rus. Fed. see Vladikavkaz
Ore Nigeria 120 D4
Oreana U.S.A. 158 D1
Örebro Sweden 55 I7
Oregon IL U.S.A. 160 F3
Oregon OH U.S.A. 164 D3
Oregon state U.S.A. 156 C4
Oregon City U.S.A. 156 C3
Orekhov Ukr. see Orikhiv
Orekhovo-Zuyevo Rus. Fed. 52 H5
Orel Rus. Fed. 53 H5
Orel, Gora mt. Rus. Fed. 90 E1
Orel', Ozero l. Rus. Fed. 90 E1
Orem U.S.A. 159 H1
Ore Mountains Czech Rep./Germany see Erzgebirge
Orenburg Rus. Fed. 76 G4
Orense Spain see Ourense
Oreor Palau see Koror
Oreor i. Palau see Koror
Orepuki N.Z. 139 A8
Öresund strait Denmark/Sweden 55 H9
Oretana, Cordillera mts Spain see Toledo, Montes de
Orewa N.Z. 139 E3
Oreye Belgium 62 F4
Orfanou, Kolpos b. Greece 69 J4
Orford Australia 137 [inset]
Orford U.K. 59 I6
Orford Ness hd U.K. 59 I6
Organabo Fr. Guiana 177 H2
Organ Pipe Cactus National Monument nat. park U.S.A. 159 G5
Orge r. France 62 C6
Orgil Mongolia see Jargalant
Orgon Tal Nei Mongol China 95 H3
Orgūn Afgh. 111 H3
Orhaneli Turkey 69 M5
Orhangazi Turkey 69 M4
Orhei Moldova 53 F7
Orhon Bulgan Mongolia 94 E1
Orhon Mongolia 94 F1
Orhon Gol r. Mongolia 94 F1
Orhontuul Mongolia 94 F1
Orichi Rus. Fed. 52 K4
Oriental, Cordillera mts Bol. 176 E7
Oriental, Cordillera mts Col. 176 D2
Oriental, Cordillera mts Peru 176 E6
Orihuela Spain 67 F4
Orikhiv Ukr. 53 G7
Orillia Canada 164 F1
Orimattila Fin. 55 N6
Orin U.S.A. 156 G4
Orinoco r. Col./Venez. 176 F2
Orinoco Delta Venez. 176 F2
Orissa state India see Odisha
Orissaare Estonia 55 M7
Oristano Sardinia Italy 68 C5
Orivesi Fin. 55 N6
Orivesi l. Fin. 54 P5
Oriximiná Brazil 177 G4
Orizaba Mex. 168 E5

▶Orizaba, Pico de vol. Mex. 168 E5
Highest active volcano and 3rd highest mountain in North America.

Orizona Brazil 179 A2
Orkanger Norway 54 F5
Örkelljunga Sweden 55 H8
Orkhon Valley tourist site Mongolia 94 E2
Orkla r. Norway 54 F5
Orkney S. Africa 125 H4
Orkney Islands is U.K. 60 F1
Orla U.S.A. 161 C6
Orland U.S.A. 158 B2
Orlândia Brazil 179 B3
Orlando U.S.A. 163 D6
Orland Park U.S.A. 164 B3
Orleaes Brazil 179 A5
Orléans France 66 E3
Orleans IN U.S.A. 164 B4
Orleans VT U.S.A. 165 I1
Orléans, Île d' i. Canada 153 H5
Orléansville Alg. see Chlef
Orlik Rus. Fed. 88 H2
Orlov Rus. Fed. 52 K4
Orlov Gay Rus. Fed. 53 K6
Orlovskiy Rus. Fed. 53 I7
Ormara Pak. 111 G5
Ormara, Ras hd Pak. 111 G5
Ormiston Canada 151 J5
Ormoc Leyte Phil. 82 D4
Ormskirk U.K. 58 E5
Ormstown Canada 165 I1
Ornach Pak. 111 G5
Ornain r. France 62 E6
Orne r. France 66 D2
Ørnes Norway 54 H3
Örnsköldsvik Sweden 54 K5
Orobie, Alpi mts Italy 68 C1
Orobo, Serra do hills Brazil 179 C1
Orodara Burkina Faso 120 C3
Orofino U.S.A. 156 D3
Orog Nuur salt l. Mongolia 94 E2
Oro Grande U.S.A. 158 E4
Orogrande U.S.A. 157 G6
Orol Dengizi salt l. Kazakh./Uzbek. see Aral Sea

Oromocto Canada 153 I5
Oromocto Lake Canada 153 I5
Oron Israel 107 B4
Orona atoll Kiribati 133 I2
Orono U.S.A. 162 G2
Orontes r. Asia 112 E3 see 'Āṣī, Nahr al
Orontes r. Lebanon/Syria 107 C2
Oroqen Zizhiqi Nei Mongol China see Alihe
Oroquieta Mindanao Phil. 82 C4
Orós, Açude resr Brazil 177 K5
Orosei, Golfo di b. Sardinia Italy 68 C4
Orosháza Hungary 69 I1
Oroville U.S.A. 158 C2
Oroville, Lake U.S.A. 158 C2
Orqohan Nei Mongol China 95 J1
Orr U.S.A. 160 E1
Orsa Sweden 55 I6
Orsha Belarus 53 F5
Orshanka Rus. Fed. 52 J4
Orsk Rus. Fed. 76 G4
Ørsta Norway 54 E5
Orta Toroslar plat. Turkey 107 A1
Ortegal, Cabo c. Spain 67 C2
Orthez France 66 D5
Ortigueira Spain 67 C2
Ortíz Mex. 166 C2
Ortles mt. Italy 68 D1
Orton U.K. 58 E4
Ortona Italy 68 F3
Ortonville U.S.A. 160 D2
Ortospana Afgh. see Kābul
Orto-Tokoy Kyrg. 98 A4
Orukuizu i. Palau 82 [inset]
Orulgan, Khrebet mts Rus. Fed. 77 N3
Orumbo Namibia 124 C2
Orūmīyeh Iran see Urmia
Oruro Bol. 176 E7
Orūzgān Afgh. 111 G3
Orvieto Italy 68 E3
Orville Coast Antarctica 188 L1
Orwell OH U.S.A. 164 E3
Orwell VT U.S.A. 165 I2
Orxon Gol r. China 95 I1
Oryol Rus. Fed. see Orel
Os Norway 54 G5
Osa Rus. Fed. 51 R4
Osa, Península de pen. Costa Rica 166 [inset] J7
Osage IA U.S.A. 160 E3
Osage WV U.S.A. 164 E4
Osage WY U.S.A. 156 G3
Osaka Japan 92 D3
Ōsaka Japan 92 B4
Ōsaka pref. Japan 92 B4
Osakarovka Kazakh. 102 D1
Ōsakasayama Japan 92 B4
Ōsaka-wan b. Japan 92 B4
Ōsawano Japan 92 D2
Osawatomie U.S.A. 160 E4
Osborn, Mount AK U.S.A. 148 F2
Osborne U.S.A. 160 D4
Osby Sweden 55 H8
Osceola IA U.S.A. 160 E3
Osceola MO U.S.A. 160 E4
Osceola NE U.S.A. 160 D3
Oschatz Germany 63 N3
Oschersleben (Bode) Germany 63 L2
Oschiri Sardinia Italy 68 C4
Ösel i. Estonia see Hiiumaa
Osetr r. Rus. Fed. 53 H5
Ōse-zaki pt Japan 91 C6
Ōse-zaki pt Japan 93 E3
Osgoode Canada 165 H1
Osgood Mountains U.S.A. 156 D4
Osh Kyrg. 102 D3
Oshakati Namibia 123 B5
Oshawa Canada 165 F2
Ōshika Japan 93 E3
Oshika-hantō pen. Japan 91 F5
Ōshima Niigata Japan 93 E1
Ōshima Tōkyō Japan 93 F4
Ōshima Toyama Japan 92 D2
Ō-shima i. Japan 90 E4
Ō-shima i. Japan 92 C2
Ō-shima i. Japan 93 F4
Oshimizu Japan 92 C2
Oshino Japan 93 E3
Oshkosh NE U.S.A. 160 C3
Oshkosh WI U.S.A. 164 A1
Oshmyany Belarus see Ashmyany
Oshnovīyeh Iran 110 B2
Oshogbo Nigeria 120 D4
Oshtorān Kūh mt. Iran 110 C3
Oshwe Dem. Rep. Congo 122 B4
Osijek Croatia 68 H2
Osilinka r. Canada 150 E3
Osimo Italy 68 E3
Osinovka Rus. Fed. 95 G1
Osipenko Ukr. see Berdyans'k
Osipovichi Belarus see Asipovichy
Osiyan India 104 C4
Osizweni S. Africa 125 J4
Osječenica mts Bos.-Herz. 68 G2
Ösjön l. Sweden 54 I5
Oskaloosa U.S.A. 160 E3
Oskarshamn Sweden 55 J8
Öskemen Kazakh. see Ust'-Kamenogorsk

▶Oslo Norway 55 G7
Capital of Norway.

Oslob Cebu Phil. 82 C4
Oslofjorden sea chan. Norway 55 G7
Osmanabad India 106 C2
Osmancık Turkey 112 D2
Osmaneli Turkey 69 M4
Osmaniye Turkey 112 E3
Osmannagar India 106 C2
Os'mino Rus. Fed. 55 P7
Osnabrück Germany 63 I2
Osnaburg atoll Fr. Polynesia see Mururoa
Osogbo Nigeria see Oshogbo
Osogovska Planina mts Bulg./Macedonia 69 J3
Osogovske Planine mts Bulg./Macedonia see Osogovska Planina
Osogovski Planini mts Bulg./Macedonia see Osogovska Planina
Osorno Chile 178 B6
Osorno Spain 67 D2
Osoyoos Canada 150 G5
Osøyri Norway 55 D6
Osprey Reef Australia 136 D2
Oss Neth. 62 F3
Ossa, Mount Australia 137 [inset]
Osseo U.S.A. 152 C5
Ossineke U.S.A. 164 D1
Ossining U.S.A. 165 I3
Ossipee U.S.A. 165 J2
Ossipee Lake U.S.A. 165 J2
Oßmannstedt Germany 63 L3
Ossokmanuan Lake Canada 153 I3
Ossora Rus. Fed. 77 R4
Ossu East Timor 83 C5
Ostashkov Rus. Fed. 52 G4
Ostbevern Germany 63 H2
Oste r. Germany 63 J1
Ostend Belgium 62 C3
Ostende Belgium see Ostend
Osterburg (Altmark) Germany 63 L2
Österbymo Sweden 55 I8
Österdalälven l. Sweden 55 H6
Østerdalen valley Norway 55 G5
Osterfeld Germany 63 L3
Osterholz-Scharmbeck Germany 63 I1
Osterode am Harz Germany 63 K3
Österreich country Europe see Austria
Östersund Sweden 54 I5
Osterwieck Germany 63 K3
Ostfriesische Inseln Germany see East Frisian Islands
Ostfriesland reg. Germany 63 H1
Östhammar Sweden 55 K6
Ostrava Czech Rep. 57 Q6
Ostróda Poland 57 Q4
Ostrogozhsk Rus. Fed. 53 H6
Ostrov Czech Rep. 63 M4
Ostrov Rus. Fed. 55 P8
Ostrovets Poland see Ostrowiec Świętokrzyski
Ostrovskoye Rus. Fed. 52 I4
Ostrów Poland see Ostrów Wielkopolski
Ostrowiec Poland see Ostrowiec Świętokrzyski
Ostrowiec Świętokrzyski Poland 53 D6
Ostrów Mazowiecka Poland 57 R4
Ostrowo Poland see Ostrów Wielkopolski
Ostrów Wielkopolski Poland 57 P5
Ōsuka Japan 93 D4
O'Sullivan Lake Canada 152 D4
Osŭm r. Bulg. 69 K3
Ōsumi-shotō is Japan 91 C7
Osuna Spain 67 D5
Oswego KS U.S.A. 161 E4
Oswego NY U.S.A. 165 G2
Oswestry U.K. 59 D6
Ota Japan 92 C3
Ōta Japan 93 F2
Otago Peninsula N.Z. 139 C7
Otahiti i. Fr. Polynesia see Tahiti
Ōtake Japan 92 D3
Ōtake-san mt. Japan 93 F3
Ōtaki Chiba Japan 93 G3
Ōtaki Saitama Japan 93 E3
Otaki N.Z. 139 E5
Otanmäki Fin. 54 O4
Otar Kazakh. 98 A4
Otari Japan 93 D2
Otaru Japan 90 F4
Otavi Namibia 123 B5
Ōtawara Japan 93 G2
Otdia atoll Marshall Is see Wotje
Otegen Batyr Kazakh. 98 B4
Otelnuc, Lac l. Canada 153 H2
Otematata N.Z. 139 C7
Otepää Estonia 55 O7
Oteros r. Mex. 166 C3
Otgon Tenger Uul mt. Mongolia 94 D2
Oti Sulawesi Indon. 83 A3
Otinapa Mex. 161 B7
Otira N.Z. 139 C6
Otis U.S.A. 160 C3
Otish, Monts hills Canada 153 H4
Otjinene Namibia 123 B6
Otjiwarongo Namibia 123 B6
Otjozondjupa admin. reg. Namibia 124 C1
Otley U.K. 58 F5
Ōto Japan 92 B4
Otog Qi Nei Mongol China see Ulan
Otorohanga N.Z. 139 E4
Otoskwin r. Canada 151 N5
Otowa Japan 92 D4
Otpan, Gora hill Kazakh. 113 H1
Otpor Rus. Fed. see Zabaykal'sk
Otradnoye Rus. Fed. see Otradnyy
Otradnyy Rus. Fed. 53 K5
Otranto Italy 68 H4
Otranto, Strait of Albania/Italy 68 H4
Otrogovo Rus. Fed. see Stepnoye
Otrozhnyy Rus. Fed. 77 S3
Otsego Lake U.S.A. 165 H2
Ōtsu Ibaraki Japan 93 G2
Ōtsu Shiga Japan 92 B3
Ōtsuki Japan 93 E3
Otta Norway 55 F6

▶Ottawa Canada 165 H1
Capital of Canada.

Ottawa r. Canada 152 G5
also known as Rivière des Outaouais
Ottawa IL U.S.A. 160 F3
Ottawa KS U.S.A. 160 E4
Ottawa OH U.S.A. 164 C3
Ottawa Islands Canada 152 E2
Otter r. U.K. 59 D8
Otterbein U.S.A. 164 B3
Otterburn U.K. 58 E3
Otter Island AK U.S.A. 148 E4
Otter Rapids Canada 152 E4
Ottersberg Germany 63 J1
Ottignies Belgium 62 E4
Ottuk Kyrg. 98 A4
Ottumwa U.S.A. 160 E3
Ottweiler Germany 63 H5
Otukpo Nigeria 120 D4
Oturkpo Nigeria see Otukpo
Otuzco Peru 176 C5
Otway, Cape Australia 138 A7
Otway National Park Australia 138 A7
Ouachita r. U.S.A. 161 F6
Ouachita, Lake U.S.A. 161 E5
Ouachita Mountains Arkansas/Oklahoma U.S.A. 155 I5
Ouachita Mountains Arkansas/Oklahoma U.S.A. 161 E5
Ouadda Cent. Afr. Rep. 122 C3
Ouaddaï reg. Chad 121 F3

▶Ouagadougou Burkina Faso 120 C3
Capital of Burkina Faso.

Ouahigouya Burkina Faso 120 C3
Ouahran Alg. see Oran
Ouaka r. Cent. Afr. Rep. 122 B3
Oualâta Mauritania 120 C3
Ouallam Niger 120 D3
Ouanda-Djallé Cent. Afr. Rep. 122 C3
Ouando Cent. Afr. Rep. 122 C3
Ouango Cent. Afr. Rep. 122 C3
Ouara r. Cent. Afr. Rep. 122 C3
Ouarâne reg. Mauritania 120 C2
Ouargaye Burkina Faso 120 D3
Ouargla Alg. 64 F5
Ouarogou Burkina Faso see Ouargaye
Ouarzazate Morocco 64 C5
Ouasiemsca r. Canada 153 G4
Oubangui r. Cent. Afr. Rep./Dem. Rep. Congo see Ubangi
Oubergpas pass S. Africa 124 G7
Ōuchiyama Japan 92 C4
Ouda Japan 92 B4
Oudenaarde Belgium 62 D4
Oudômxai Laos 86 C2
Oudtshoorn S. Africa 124 F7
Oud-Turnhout Belgium 62 E3
Oued Tlélat Alg. 67 F6
Oued Zem Morocco 64 C5
Oued Zénati Alg. 68 B6
Ouessant, Île d' i. France 66 B2
Ouesso Congo 122 B3
Ouezzane Morocco 67 D6
Oughter, Lough l. Ireland 61 E3
Ougo-gawa r. Japan 92 A4
Ouguati Namibia 124 B1
Ougura-yama mt. Japan 93 E2
Ouiriego Mex. 166 C3
Ouistreham France 59 G9
Oujda Morocco 67 F6
Oujeft Mauritania 120 B3
Oulainen Fin. 54 N4
Oulangan kansallispuisto nat. park Fin. 54 P3
Ouled Djellal Alg. 67 I6
Ouled Farès Alg. 67 G5
Ouled Naïl, Monts des mts Alg. 67 H6
Oulu Fin. 54 N4
Oulujärvi l. Fin. 54 O4
Oulujoki r. Fin. 54 N4
Oulunsalo Fin. 54 N4
Oulx Italy 68 B2
Oum-Chalouba Chad 121 F3
Oum el Bouaghi Alg. 68 B7
Oum-Hadjer Chad 121 E3
Ounasjoki r. Fin. 54 N3
Oundle U.K. 59 G6
Oungre Canada 151 K5
Ounianga Kébir Chad 121 F3
Oupeye Belgium 62 F4
Our r. Lux. 62 G5
Oura, Akrotirio pt Greece 69 L5
Ouray CO U.S.A. 159 J2
Ouray UT U.S.A. 159 I1
Ourcq r. France 62 D5
Ourense Spain 67 C2
Ouricuri Brazil 177 J5
Ourinhos Brazil 179 A3
Ouro r. Brazil 179 A1
Ouro Preto Brazil 179 C3
Ourthe r. Belgium 62 F4
Our Valley valley Germany/Lux. 62 G5
Ous Rus. Fed. 51 S3
Ouse r. England U.K. 58 G5
Ouse r. England U.K. 59 H8
Outaouais, Rivière des r. Canada 152 G5 see Ottawa
Outardes, Rivière aux r. Canada 153 H4
Outardes Quatre, Réservoir resr Canada 153 H4
Outer Hebrides is U.K. 60 B3
Outer Mongolia country Asia see Mongolia
Outer Santa Barbara Channel U.S.A. 158 D5
Outjo Namibia 123 B6
Outlook Canada 151 J5
Outokumpu Fin. 54 P5
Out Skerries is U.K. 60 [inset]
Ouvéa atoll New Caledonia 133 G4
Ouyanghai Shuiku resr China 97 G3
Ouyen Australia 137 C7
Ouzel r. U.K. 59 G6
Ouzinkie AK U.S.A. 148 I4
Ovace, Punta d' mt. Corsica France 66 I6
Ovacık Turkey 107 A1
Ovada Italy 68 C2
Ovalle Chile 178 B4
Ovamboland reg. Namibia 123 B5
Ovan Gabon 122 B3
Ovar Port. 67 B3
Overath Germany 63 H4
Överkalix Sweden 54 M3
Overlander Roadhouse Australia 135 A6
Overland Park U.S.A. 160 E4
Overton U.S.A. 159 F3
Övertorneå Sweden 54 M3
Överum Sweden 55 J8
Overveen Neth. 62 E2
Ovid CO U.S.A. 160 C3
Ovid NY U.S.A. 165 G2
Oviedo Spain 67 D2
Övögdiy Mongolia see Telmen
Ovoot Mongolia see Dariganga
Övörhangay prov. Mongolia 94 E2
Øvre Anárjohka Nasjonalpark nat. park Norway 54 N2
Øvre Dividal Nasjonalpark nat. park Norway 54 K2
Øvre Rendal Norway 55 G6
Ovruch Ukr. 53 F6
Ovsyanka Rus. Fed. 90 B1
Övt Mongolia see Bat-Öldziy
Owando Congo 122 B4
Owa Rafa i. Solomon Is see Santa Ana
Owasco Lake U.S.A. 165 G2
Owase Japan 92 C4
Owase-wan b. Japan 92 C4
Owatonna U.S.A. 160 E2
Owbeh Afgh. 111 F3
Owego U.S.A. 165 G2
Owel, Lough l. Ireland 61 E4
Owen Island Myanmar 87 B5
Owenmore r. Ireland 61 C3
Owenreagh r. U.K. 61 E3
Owen River N.Z. 139 D5
Owens r. U.S.A. 158 E3
Owensboro U.S.A. 164 B5
Owen Sound Canada 164 E1
Owen Sound inlet Canada 164 E1
Owen Stanley Range mts P.N.G. 81 L8
Owenton U.S.A. 164 C4
Owerri Nigeria 120 D4
Owikeno Lake Canada 150 E5
Owingsville U.S.A. 164 D4
Owkal Afgh. 111 F3
Owl r. Canada 151 M3
Owl Creek Mountains U.S.A. 156 F4
Owo Nigeria 120 D4
Owosso U.S.A. 164 C2
Owyhee U.S.A. 156 D4
Owyhee r. U.S.A. 156 D4
Owyhee Mountains U.S.A. 156 D4
Öxarfjörður b. Iceland 54 [inset]
Oxbow Canada 151 K5
Ox Creek r. U.S.A. 160 C1
Oxelösund Sweden 55 J7
Oxford N.Z. 139 D6
Oxford U.K. 59 F7
Oxford IN U.S.A. 164 B3
Oxford MA U.S.A. 165 J2
Oxford MD U.S.A. 165 G4
Oxford MS U.S.A. 161 F5
Oxford NC U.S.A. 162 E4
Oxford NY U.S.A. 165 H2
Oxford OH U.S.A. 164 C4
Oxford House Canada 151 M4
Oxford Lake Canada 151 M4
Oxkutzcab Mex. 167 H4
Oxley Australia 138 B5
Oxleys Peak Australia 138 E3
Oxley Wild Rivers National Park Australia 138 F3
Ox Mountains hills Ireland 61 D3
Oxnard U.S.A. 158 D4
Oxtongue Lake Canada 165 F1
Oxus r. Asia see Amudar'ya
Oya Sarawak Malaysia 85 E2
Øya Norway 54 H3
Oyabe Japan 92 C2
Oyabe-gawa r. Japan 92 D2
Oyama Shizuoka Japan 93 E3
Oyama Tochigi Japan 93 F2
Ōyama Japan 92 D2
Ō-yama mt. Japan 93 F3
Ō-yama vol. Japan 93 F4
Ōyamada Japan 92 C4
Ōyamazaki Japan 92 B4
Oyapock r. Brazil/Fr. Guiana 177 H3
Oychilik Kazakh. 98 C3
Oyem Gabon 122 B3
Oyen Canada 151 I5
Oygon Mongolia see Tüdevtey
Oykel r. U.K. 60 E3
Oyo Nigeria 120 D4
Ōyodo Japan 92 B4
Oyonnax France 66 G3
Oyster Rocks is India 106 B3
Oy-Tal Kyrg. 98 A4
Oyten Germany 63 J1
Oytograk Xinjiang China 99 C5
Oyukludağı mt. Turkey 107 A1
Özalp Turkey 113 G3
Ozamiz Mindanao Phil. 82 C4
Ozark AL U.S.A. 163 C6
Ozark AR U.S.A. 161 E5
Ozark MO U.S.A. 161 E4
Ozark Plateau U.S.A. 161 E4
Ozarks, Lake of the U.S.A. 160 E4
O'zbekiston country Asia see Uzbekistan
Özen Kazakh. see Kyzylsay
Ozernovskiy Rus. Fed. 77 Q4
Ozernyy Rus. Fed. 148 C2
Ozernyy Rus. Fed. 53 G5
Ozerpakh Rus. Fed. 90 F1
Ozersk Rus. Fed. 55 M9
Ozerskiy Rus. Fed. 90 F3
Ozery Rus. Fed. 53 H5
Ozeryane Rus. Fed. 90 C2
Ozieri Sardinia Italy 68 C4
Ozinki Rus. Fed. 53 K6
Oznachennoye Rus. Fed. see Sayanogorsk
Ozona U.S.A. 161 C6
Ozuki Japan 91 C6
Ozuluama Mex. 167 F4

P

Paamiut Greenland 147 N3
Pa-an Myanmar see Hpa-an
Paanopa i. Kiribati see Banaba
Paarl S. Africa 124 D7
Paatsjoki r. Europe see Patsoyoki
Paballelo S. Africa 124 E5
P'abal-li N. Korea 90 C4
Pabbay i. U.K. 60 B3
Pabianice Poland 57 Q5
Pabianitz Poland see Pabianice
Pabna Bangl. 105 G4
Pabradė Lith. 55 N9
Pab Range mts Pak. 111 G5
Pacaás Novos, Parque Nacional nat. park Brazil 176 F6
Pacaraimã, Serra mts S. America see Pakaraima Mountains
Pacasmayo Peru 176 C5
Pacaya, Volcán de vol. Guat. 167 H6
Pachagarh Bangl. see Panchagarh
Pacheco Chihuahua Mex. 166 C2
Pacheco Zacatecas Mex. 161 C7
Pachikha Rus. Fed. 52 J3
Pachino Sicily Italy 68 F6
Pachmarhi India 104 D5
Pachor India 104 D5
Pachora India 106 B1
Pachpadra India 104 C4
Pachuca Mex. 168 E4
Pachuca de Soto Mex. see Pachuca
Pacific-Antarctic Ridge sea feature S. Pacific Ocean 187 J9
Pacific Grove U.S.A. 158 C3

▶Pacific Ocean 186
Largest ocean in the world.

Pacific Rim National Park Canada 150 E5
Pacijan i. Phil. 82 D4
Pacinan, Tanjung pt Indon. 85 F4
Pacitan Jawa Indon. 85 E5
Packsaddle Australia 137 C6
Pacoval Brazil 177 H4
Pacuí r. Brazil 179 B2
Paczków Poland 57 P5
Padada Mindanao Phil. 82 D5
Padalere Sulawesi Indon. 83 B3
Padali Rus. Fed. see Amursk
Padamarang i. Indon. 83 B4
Padampur India 104 C3
Padang Kalimantan Indon. 85 E3
Padang Sulawesi Indon. 83 B4
Padang Sumatera Indon. 84 C3
Padang i. Indon. 84 C2
Padang Endau Malaysia 84 C2
Padang Luwai, Cagar Alam nature res. Kalimantan Indon. 85 G3
Padangpanjang Sumatera Indon. 84 C3
Padangsidimpuan Sumatera Indon. 84 B2
Padangtikar Kalimantan Indon. 85 E3
Padangtikar i. Indon. 85 E3
Padany Rus. Fed. 52 G3
Padas r. Malaysia 85 F1
Padatha, Kūh-e mt. Iran 110 C3
Padaung Myanmar 86 A3
Padcaya Bol. 176 F8
Paddington Australia 138 B4
Padeabesar i. Indon. 83 B3
Paden City U.S.A. 164 E4
Paderborn Germany 63 I3
Paderborn/Lippstadt airport Germany 63 I3
Padeşu, Vârful mt. Romania 69 J2
Padibyu Myanmar 86 B2
Padilla Bol. 176 F7
Padjelanta nationalpark nat. park Sweden 54 J3
Padova Italy see Padua
Padrão, Ponta pt Angola 123 B4
Padrauna India 105 F4
Padre Island U.S.A. 161 D7
Padstow U.K. 59 C8
Padsvillye Belarus 55 O9
Padua India 106 D2
Padua Italy 68 D2
Paducah KY U.S.A. 161 F4
Paducah TX U.S.A. 161 C5
Padum India 104 D2
Paegam N. Korea 90 C4
Paektu-san mt. China/N. Korea see Baotou Shan
Paengnyŏng-do i. S. Korea 91 B5
Paete Luzon Phil. 82 C3
Pafos Cyprus see Paphos
Pafuri Moz. 125 J2
Pag Croatia 68 F2
Pag i. Croatia 68 F2
Paga Flores Indon. 83 B5
Pagadenbaru Jawa Indon. 85 D4
Pagadian Mindanao Phil. 82 C5
Pagai Selatan i. Indon. 84 C3
Pagai Utara i. Indon. 84 C3
Pagalu i. Equat. Guinea see Annobón
Pagan i. N. Mariana Is 81 L3
Pagaralam Sumatera Indon. 84 C3
Pagasitikos Kolpos b. Greece 69 J5
Pagatan Kalimantan Indon. 85 F3
Pagatan Kalimantan Indon. 85 F3
Page U.S.A. 159 H3
Page, Mount Y.T. Canada 149 L1
Pagerdewa Sumatera Indon. 84 D3
Paget, Mount S. Georgia 178 I8
Paget Cay reef Australia 136 F3
Pagon i. N. Mariana Is see Pagan
Pagosa Springs U.S.A. 157 G5
Pagqên China see Gadê
Pagri Xizang China 99 E8
Pagwa River Canada 152 D4
Pagwi P.N.G. 81 K7
Pah r. AK U.S.A. 148 H2
Pāhala U.S.A. 157 [inset]
Pahang r. Malaysia 84 C2
Pahang state Malaysia 84 C2
Pahauman Kalimantan Indon. 85 E2
Pahlgam India 104 C2
Pāhoa U.S.A. 157 [inset]
Pahokee U.S.A. 163 D7
Pahra Kariz Afgh. 111 F3
Pahranagat Range mts U.S.A. 159 F3
Pahrump U.S.A. 159 F3
Pahuj r. India 104 D4
Pahute Mesa plat. U.S.A. 158 E3
Pai Thai. 86 B3
Paicines U.S.A. 158 C3
Paide Estonia 55 N7
Paignton U.K. 59 D8
Päijänne l. Fin. 55 N6
Paikü Co l. China 99 D7
Pailin Cambodia 87 C4
Pailolo Channel U.S.A. 157 [inset]
Paimio Fin. 55 M6
Paimiut AK U.S.A. 148 F3
Paimiut AK U.S.A. 148 G3
Painan Sumatera Indon. 84 C3
Painel Brazil 179 A4
Painesville U.S.A. 164 E3
Pains Brazil 179 B3
Painted Desert U.S.A. 159 H3
Painted Rock Dam U.S.A. 159 G5
Paint Hills Canada see Wemindji
Paint Rock U.S.A. 161 D6
Paintsville U.S.A. 164 D5
Paisley U.K. 60 E5
Paita Peru 176 B5
Paitan, Teluk b. Malaysia 85 G1
Paitou China 97 I2
Paiva Couceiro Angola see Quipungo
Paixban Mex. 167 H5
Paizhou China 97 G2
Pajala Sweden 54 M3
Paka Malaysia 84 C1
Pakal i. Maluku Indon. 83 D2
Pakala India 106 C3
Pakanbaru Sumatera Indon. see Pekanbaru
Pakangyi Myanmar 86 A2
Pakaraima Mountains Guyana 169 M8
Pakaraima Mountains S. America 176 F3
Pakaur India 105 F4
Pakesley Canada 152 E5
Pakhachi Rus. Fed. 77 R3
Pakhoi China see Beihai
Paki Nigeria 120 D3

▶Pakistan country Asia 111 H4
4th most populous country in Asia, and 6th in the world.

Pakkat Sumatera Indon. 84 B2
Paknampho Thai. see Nakhon Sawan
Pakokku Myanmar 86 A2
Pakowki Lake imp. l. Canada 151 I5
Pakpattan Pak. 111 I4
Pak Phanang Thai. 87 C5
Pak Phayun Thai. 87 C6
Pakruojis Lith. 55 M9
Paks Hungary 68 H1
Pakse Laos see Pakxé
Pak Tam Chung H.K. China 97 [inset]
Pak Thong Chai Thai. 86 C4
Paku r. Malaysia 85 F2
Paku, Tanjung pt Indon. 84 D3
Pakue Sulawesi Indon. 83 B3
Pakur India see Pakaur
Pakxan Laos 86 C3
Pakxé Laos 86 D4
Pakxeng Laos 86 C2
Pala Chad 121 E4
Pala Myanmar 87 B4
Palabuhanratu Jawa Indon. 84 D4
Palabuhanratu, Teluk b. Indon. 84 D4
Palaestinia reg. Asia see Palestine
Palaiochora Greece 69 J7
Palaiseau France 62 C6
Palakkad India see Palghat
Palakkat India see Palghat
Palamakoloi Botswana 124 F2
Palamau India see Palamu
Palamea Maluku Indon. 83 C3
Palamós Spain 67 H3
Palamu India 105 F5
Palana Rus. Fed. 77 Q4
Palanan Luzon Phil. 82 C2
Palanan Point Luzon Phil. 82 C2
Palandur India 106 D1
Palangān, Kūh-e mts Iran 111 F4
Palangkaraya Kalimantan Indon. 85 F3
Palani India 106 C4
Palanpur India 104 C4
Palanro Sulawesi Indon. 83 A4
Palantak Pak. 111 G5
Palapag Samar Phil. 82 D3
Palapye Botswana 125 H2
Palasa Sulawesi Indon. 83 B2
Palatka Rus. Fed. 77 Q3
Palatka U.S.A. 163 D6
Palau country N. Pacific Ocean 82 [inset]
Palau Hatta i. Maluku Indon. 83 D4
Palaui i. Phil. 82 C2
Palauig Luzon Phil. 82 B3
Palau Islands Palau 81 I5
Palauk Myanmar 87 B4
Palausekopong, Tanjung pt Indon. 84 D4
Palaw Myanmar 87 B4
Palawan i. Phil. 82 B4
Palawan Passage str. Phil. 82 B4
Palawan Trough sea feature N. Pacific Ocean 186 D5
Palayan Luzon Phil. 82 C3
Palayankottai India 106 C4
Palchal Lake India 106 D2
Paldiski Estonia 55 N7
Palekh Rus. Fed. 52 I4
Paleleh Sulawesi Indon. 83 B2
Palembang Sumatera Indon. 84 D3
Palena Chile 178 B6
Palencia Spain 67 D2
Palermo Sicily Italy 68 E5
Palestine reg. Asia 107 B3
Palestine U.S.A. 161 E6
Paletwa Myanmar 86 A2
Palezgir Chauki Pak. 111 H4
Palghat India 106 C4
Palgrave, Mount hill Australia 135 A5
Palhoca Brazil 179 A4
Pali Chhattisgarh India 106 D1
Pali Mahar. India 106 B2
Pali Rajasthan India 104 C4
Pali India 105 E5
Paliat i. Indon. 85 F4

▶Palikir Micronesia 186 G5
Capital of Micronesia.

Palimbang Mindanao Phil. 82 D5
Palinuro, Capo c. Italy 68 F4
Paliouri, Akra pt Greece see Paliouri, Akrotirio
Paliouri, Akra pt Greece see Paliouri, Akrotirio
Paliouri, Akrotirio pt Greece 69 J5
Palisade U.S.A. 159 I2
Paliseul Belgium 62 F5
Palitana India 104 B5
Palivere Estonia 55 M7
Palk Bay Sri Lanka 106 C4
Palkino Rus. Fed. 55 P8
Palkonda Range mts India 106 C3
Palk Strait India/Sri Lanka 106 C4
Palla Bianca mt. Austria/Italy see Weißkugel
Pallamallawa Australia 138 E2
Pallas Green New Ireland 61 D5
Pallasovka Rus. Fed. 53 J6
Pallas-Yllästunturin kansallispuisto nat. park Fin. 54 M2
Pallavaram India 106 D3
Palliser, Cape N.Z. 139 E5
Palliser, Îles is Fr. Polynesia 187 K7
Palliser Bay N.Z. 139 E5
Pallu India 104 C3
Palma r. Brazil 179 B1
Palma del Río Spain 67 D5
Palma de Mallorca Spain 67 H4
Palmaner India 106 C3
Palmares Brazil 177 K5
Palmares do Sul Brazil 179 A5
Palmas Brazil 179 A4
Palmas 176 I6
Palmas, Cape Liberia 120 C4
Palm Bay U.S.A. 163 D7
Palmdale U.S.A. 158 D4
Palmeira Brazil 179 A4
Palmeira das Missões Brazil 178 F3
Palmeira dos Índios Brazil 177 K5
Palmeirais Brazil 177 J5
Palmeiras Brazil 179 C1
Palmeirinhas, Ponta das pt Angola 123 B4
Palmer research station Antarctica 188 L2
Palmer r. Australia 136 C3
Palmer watercourse Australia 135 F6
Palmer AK U.S.A. 149 J3
Palmer Land reg. Antarctica 188 L2
Palmerston N.T. Australia 134 E3
Palmerston N.T. Australia see Darwin

Palmerston Canada 164 E2
Palmerston atoll Cook Is 133 J3
Palmerston N.Z. 139 C7
Palmerston North N.Z. 139 E5
Palmerton U.S.A. 165 H3
Palmerville Australia 136 D2
Palmetto Point Bahamas 163 E7
Palmi Italy 68 F5
Palmillas Mex. 167 F4
Palmira Col. 176 C3
Palmira Cuba 163 D8
Palm Springs U.S.A. 158 E5
Palmyra Syria see Tadmur
Palmyra MO U.S.A. 160 F4
Palmyra PA U.S.A. 165 G3
Palmyra VA U.S.A. 165 F5
▶Palmyra Atoll terr. N. Pacific Ocean 186 J5
United States Unincorporated Territory.
Palmyras Point India 105 F5
Palni Hills India 106 C4
Palo Alto U.S.A. 158 B3
Palo Blanco Mex. 167 E3
Palo Chino watercourse Mex. 157 E7
Palo de las Letras Col. 166 [inset] K8
Palo Duro watercourse U.S.A. 161 C5
Paloh Sarawak Malaysia 85 E2
Paloich Sudan 108 D7
Palojärvi Fin. 54 M2
Palojoensuu Fin. 54 M2
Palomaa Fin. 54 O2
Palomares Mex. 167 G5
Palomar Mountain U.S.A. 158 E5
Paloncha India 106 D2
Palo Pinto U.S.A. 161 D5
Palopo Sulawesi Indon. 83 B3
Palos, Cabo de c. Spain 67 F5
Palo Verde U.S.A. 159 F5
Palo Verde, Parque Nacional nat. park Costa Rica 166 [inset] I7
Palpetu, Tanjung pt Buru Indon. 83 C3
Paltamo Fin. 54 O4
Palu Sulawesi Indon. 83 A3
Palu i. Indon. 83 B5
Palu r. Indon. 83 A3
Palu Turkey 113 E3
Paluan Mindoro Phil. 82 C3
Paluan Bay Mindoro Phil. 82 C3
Pal'vart Turkm. 111 G2
Palwal India 104 D3
Palwancha India see Paloncha
Palyeskaya Nizina marsh Belarus/Ukr. see Pripet Marshes
▶Pamana i. Indon. 83 B5
Most southerly point of Asia.
Pamana Besar i. Indon. 83 B5
Pamanukan Jawa Indon. 85 D4
Pambarra Moz. 125 L1
Pambero Sulawesi Indon. 83 A2
Pambula Australia 138 D6
Pamekasan Jawa Indon. 85 F4
Pameungpeuk Jawa Indon. 85 D4
Pamidi India 106 C3
Pamiers France 66 E5
Pamir mts Asia 111 I2
Pamlico Sound sea chan. U.S.A. 163 E5
Pamouscachiou, Lac l. Canada 153 H4
Pampa U.S.A. 161 C5
Pampa de Infierno Arg. 178 D3
Pampanua Sulawesi Indon. 83 B4
Pampas reg. Arg. 178 D5
Pampeluna Spain see Pamplona
Pamphylia reg. Turkey 69 N6
Pamplin U.S.A. 165 F5
Pamplona Col. 176 D2
Pamplona Negros Phil. 82 C4
Pamplona Spain 67 F2
Pampow Germany 63 L1
Pamukan, Teluk b. Indon. 85 G3
Pamukova Turkey 69 N4
Pamzal India 104 D2
Pana U.S.A. 160 F4
Panabá Mex. 167 H4
Panabo Mindanao Phil. 82 D5
Panabutan Bay Mindanao Phil. 82 C5
Panaca U.S.A. 159 F3
Panache, Lake Canada 152 E5
Panagtaran Point Palawan Phil. 82 B4
Panagyurishte Bulg. 69 K3
Panaitan i. Indon. 84 D4
Panaji India 106 B3
Panama country Central America 169 H7
Panamá Panama see Panama City
Panamá, Bahía de b. Panama 166 [inset] K7
Panama Canal Panama 166 [inset] K7
▶Panama City Panama 166 [inset] K7
Capital of Panama.
Panama City U.S.A. 163 C6
Panamá, Golfo de g. Panama 166 [inset] K8
Panama, Gulf of Panama see Panamá, Golfo de
Panama, Isthmus of Panama 169 I7
Panamá, Istmo de Panama see Panama, Isthmus of
Panamint Range mts U.S.A. 158 E3
Panamint Valley U.S.A. 158 E3
Pananjung Pangandaran, Taman Wisata nat. park Indon. 85 E4
Panao Peru 176 C5
Panar r. India 99 E8
Panarea, Isola i. Italy 68 F5
Panarik Indon. 85 E2
Panarukan Jawa Indon. 85 F4
Panay i. Phil. 82 C4
Panayarvi Natsional'nyy Park nat. park Rus. Fed. 54 Q3
Panay Gulf Phil. 82 C4
Pancake Range mts U.S.A. 159 F2
Pančevo Serbia 69 I2
Panchagarh Bangl. 105 G4
Pancingapan, Bukit mt. Indon. 85 F2
Pancsova Serbia see Pančevo
Pancurbatu Sumatera Indon. 84 B2
Panda Moz. 125 L3
Pandan Panay Phil. 82 C4
Pandan Phil. 82 D3
Pandan, Selat strait Sing. 87 [inset]
Pandan Bay Panay Phil. 82 C4
Pandang Kalimantan Indon. 85 F3
Pandan Reservoir Sing. 87 [inset]
Pandeglang Jawa Indon. 84 D4
Pandeiros r. Brazil 179 B1
Pandharpur India 106 B2
Pandora Costa Rica 166 [inset] J7
Pandy U.K. 59 E7
Paneas Syria see Bāniyās
Panevėžys Lith. 55 N9
Panfilov Kazakh. see Zharkent
Pang, Nam r. Myanmar 86 B2
Pangandaran Jawa Indon. 85 E4
Pañganiban Phil. 82 D3
Pangean Sulawesi Barat Indon. 83 A3
Panghsang Myanmar 86 B2
Pangi Range mts Pak. 111 I3
Pangjiabu Hebei China 95 H3
Pangkah, Tanjung pt Indon. 85 F4
Pangkajene Sulawesi Indon. 83 A4
Pangkalanbuun Kalimantan Indon. 85 E3
Pangkalanlunang Sumatera Indon. 84 B2
Pangkalansusu Sumatera Indon. 84 B1
Pangkal Kalong Malaysia 84 C1
Pangkalpinang Indon. 84 D3
Pangkalsiang, Tanjung pt Indon. 83 B3
Panglang Myanmar 86 B1
Panglao i. Phil. 82 C4
Pangman Canada 151 J5
Pangnirtung Canada 147 L3
Pangody Rus. Fed. 76 I3
Pangong Tso salt l. China/India see Bangong Co
Pangrango vol. Indon. 84 D4
Pang Sida National Park Thai. 87 C4
Pang Sua, Sungai r. Sing. 87 [inset]
Pangtara Myanmar 96 C4
Pangu He r. China 90 B1
Panguitch U.S.A. 159 G3
Pangujon, Tanjung pt Indon. 85 E3
Panguruan Sumatera Indon. 84 B2
Pangutaran i. Phil. 82 C5
Pangutaran Group is Phil. 82 C5
Panhandle U.S.A. 161 C5
Panipat India 104 D3
Panir Pak. 111 G4
Panitan Palawan Phil. 82 B4
Panj Tajik. 111 H2
Panjāb Afgh. 111 G3
Panjakent Tajik. 111 G2
Panjang Sumatera Indon. 84 D4
Panjang i. Indon. 85 E2
Panjang i. Indon. 85 G2
Panjang, Bukit Sing. 87 [inset]
Panjang, Selat sea chan. Indon. 84 C2
Panjgur Pak. 111 G5
Panjim India see Panaji
Panjin Liaoning China see Panshan
Panji Poyon Tajik. 111 H2
Panjnad r. Pak. 111 H4
Panjshīr reg. Afgh. 111 H3
Pankakoski Fin. 54 Q5
Pankof, Cape AK U.S.A. 148 G5
Panlian China see Miyi
Panna India 104 E4
Panna reg. India 104 D4
Pannawonica Australia 134 B5
Pano Lefkara Cyprus 107 A2
Panopah Kalimantan Indon. 85 E3
Panorama Brazil 179 A3
Panormus Sicily Italy see Palermo
Panshan Liaoning China 95 J3
Panshi China 90 B4
Panshui China see Pu'an
Pantai Kalimantan Indon. 85 G3
Pantaicermin, Gunung mt. Indon. 84 C3
▶Pantanal marsh Brazil 177 G7
Largest area of wetlands in the world.
Pantanal Matogrossense, Parque Nacional do nat. park Brazil 177 G7
Pantano U.S.A. 159 H6
Pantar i. Indon. 83 C5
Pantelaria Sicily Italy see Pantelleria
Pantelleria Sicily Italy 68 D6
Pantelleria, Isola di i. Sicily Italy 68 E6
Pante Macassar East Timor 83 C5
Pantemakassar East Timor see Pante Macassar
Pantha Myanmar 86 A2
Panther r. U.S.A. 164 B5
Panth Piploda India 104 C5
Panticapaeum Ukr. see Kerch
Pantonlabu Sumatera Indon. 84 B1
Pantukan Mindanao Phil. 82 D5
Panua, Cagar Alam nature res. Indon. 83 B2
Pánuco Sinaloa Mex. 161 B8
Pánuco Veracruz Mex. 168 E4
Pánuco r. Mex. 167 F4
Panwari India 104 D4
Panxian China 96 E3
Panyu China 97 G4
Panzhihua China 96 D3
Panzi Dem. Rep. Congo 123 B4
Panzos Guat. 167 H6
Paola Italy 68 G5
Paola U.S.A. 160 E4
Paoli U.S.A. 164 B4
Paoni Seram Indon. 83 D3
Paoua Cent. Afr. Rep. 122 B3
Paôy Pêt Cambodia 87 C4
Pápa Hungary 68 G1
Papa, Monte del mt. Italy 68 F4
Papagni r. India 106 C3
Pāpa'ikou U.S.A. 157 [inset]
Papakura N.Z. 139 E3
Papanasam India 106 C4
Papanoa Mex. 167 E5
Papantla Mex. 168 E4
Papar Sabah Malaysia 85 F1
Paparoa National Park N.Z. 139 C6
Papa Stour i. U.K. 60 [inset]
Papa Westray i. U.K. 60 G1
Papay i. U.K. see Papa Westray
▶Papeete Fr. Polynesia 187 K7
Capital of French Polynesia.
Papenburg Germany 63 H1
Paphos Cyprus 107 A2
Paphus Cyprus see Paphos
Papillion U.S.A. 160 D3
Papoose Lake U.S.A. 159 F3
Pappenheim Germany 63 K6
Papua prov. Indon. 83 D3
Papua, Gulf of P.N.G. 81 K8
▶Papua New Guinea country Oceania 132 E2
2nd largest and 2nd most populous country in Oceania.
Pa Qal'eh Iran 110 D4
Par U.K. 59 C8
Pará r. Brazil 179 B2
Para i. Indon. 83 C2
Pará, Rio do r. Brazil 177 I4
Paraburdoo Australia 135 B5
Paracale Luzon Phil. 82 C3
Paracatu Brazil 179 B2
Paracatu r. Brazil 179 B2
Paracel Islands S. China Sea 80 E3
Parachilna Australia 137 B6
Parachute U.S.A. 159 I2
Paraćin Serbia 69 I3
Paracuru Brazil 177 K4
Pará de Minas Brazil 179 B2
Paradis Canada 152 F4
Paradise r. Canada 153 K3
Paradise AK U.S.A. 148 G3
Paradise U.S.A. 158 C2
Paradise Hill Canada 151 I4
Paradise Peak U.S.A. 158 E2
Paradise River Canada 153 K3
Parado Sumbawa Indon. 85 G5
Paradwip India 105 F5
Paraetonium Egypt see Marsá Maṭrūḥ
Paragominas Brazil 177 I4
Paragould U.S.A. 161 F4
Paragua i. Phil. see Palawan
Paraguaçu Paulista Brazil 179 A3
Paraguay r. Arg./Para. 178 E3
Paraguay country S. America 178 E2
Paraíba do Sul r. Brazil 179 C3
Parainen Fin. see Pargas
Paraíso Campeche Mex. 167 G5
Paraíso Tabasco Mex. 167 G5
Paraíso do Norte Brazil 177 I6
Paraisópolis Brazil 179 B3
Parak Iran 110 D5
Parakou Benin 120 D4
Paralakhemundi India 106 E2
Paralkot India 106 D2
Paramagudi India see Paramakkudi
Paramakkudi India 106 C4
▶Paramaribo Suriname 177 G2
Capital of Suriname.
Paramillo, Parque Nacional nat. park Col. 176 C2
Paramirim Brazil 179 C1
Paramo Frontino mt. Col. 176 C2
Paramus U.S.A. 165 H3
Paramushir, Ostrov i. Rus. Fed. 77 Q4
Paran watercourse Israel 107 B4
Paraná Arg. 178 D4
Paranã Brazil 179 B1
Paraná r. Brazil 179 A1
Paraná state Brazil 179 A4
▶Paraná r. S. America 178 E4
Part of the Río de la Plata - Paraná, 2nd longest river in South America.
Paraná, Serra do hills Brazil 179 B1
Paranaguá Brazil 179 A4
Paranaíba Brazil 179 A2
Paranaíba r. Brazil 179 A3
Paranapiacaba, Serra mts Brazil 179 A4
Paranavaí Brazil 178 F2
Parang i. Indon. 85 E4
Parang Phil. 82 C5
Parangi Aru r. Sri Lanka 106 D4
Parang Pass India 104 D2
Parângul Mare, Vârful mt. Romania 69 J2
Paranthan Sri Lanka 106 D4
Paraopeba Brazil 179 B2
Parapara Halmahera Indon. 83 C2
Pārapāra Iraq 113 G4
Paraparaumu N.Z. 139 E5
Paras Mex. 161 D7
Paras Pak. 111 I3
Paraspori, Akra pt Greece see Paraspori, Akrotirio
Paraspori, Akrotirio pt Greece 69 L7
Parateca Brazil 179 C1
Paratinga Brazil 179 C1
Parāū, Kūh-e mt. Iraq 113 G4
Paraúna Brazil 179 A2
Parbhani India 106 C2
Parchim Germany 63 L1
Parding China 105 G2
Pardo r. Bahia Brazil 179 D1
Pardo r. Mato Grosso do Sul Brazil 178 F2
Pardo r. São Paulo Brazil 179 A3
Pardoo Australia 134 B5
Pardubice Czech Rep. 57 O5
Parece Vela i. Japan see Okino-Tori-shima
Pare Chu r. China 99 B6
Parecis, Serra dos hills Brazil 176 F6
Paredón Coahuila Mex. 167 E3
Pareh Iran 110 B2
Parenda India 106 B2
Parenggean Kalimantan Indon. 85 F3
Parent Canada 152 G5
Parent, Lac l. Canada 152 F4
Pareora N.Z. 139 C7
Parepare Sulawesi Indon. 83 A4
Parga Greece 69 I5
Pargas Fin. 55 M6
Parghelia Italy 68 F5
Pargi India 106 C2
Paria, Gulf of Trin. and Tob./Venez. 169 L6
Paria, Península de pen. Venez. 176 F1
Pariaman Sumatera Indon. 84 C3
Paria Plateau U.S.A. 159 G3
Parida, Isla i. Panama 166 [inset] J7
Parigi Sulawesi Indon. 83 B3
Parikkala Fin. 55 P6
Parikud Islands India 106 E2
Parima, Serra mts Brazil 176 F3
Parima-Tapirapecó, Parque Nacional nat. park Venez. 176 F3
Parintins Brazil 177 G4
Paris Canada 164 E2
▶Paris France 62 C6
Capital of France. 3rd most populous city in Europe.
Paris IL U.S.A. 164 B4
Paris KY U.S.A. 164 C4
Paris MO U.S.A. 160 E4
Paris TN U.S.A. 161 F4
Paris TX U.S.A. 161 E5
Paris (Charles de Gaulle) airport France 62 C5
Paris (Orly) airport France 62 C6
Paris Crossing U.S.A. 164 C4
Parit Buntar Malaysia 84 C1
Pārīz Iran 110 D4
Pārk Iran 111 F5
Park U.K. 61 E3
Parkano Fin. 55 M5
Park City U.S.A. 164 B5
Parke Lake Canada 153 K3
Parker AZ U.S.A. 159 F4
Parker CO U.S.A. 156 G5
Parker Dam U.S.A. 159 F4
Parker Lake Canada 151 M2
Parker Range hills Australia 135 B8
Parkersburg U.S.A. 164 E4
Parkers Lake U.S.A. 164 C5
Parkes Australia 138 D4
Park Falls U.S.A. 160 F2
Park Forest U.S.A. 164 B3
Parkhar Tajik. see Farkhor
Parkhill Canada 164 E2
Park Rapids U.S.A. 160 E2
Parkutta Pak. 104 D2
Park Valley U.S.A. 156 E4
Parla Kimedi India see Paralakhemundi
Parlakimidi India see Paralakhemundi
Parli Vaijnath India 106 C2
Parlung Zangbo r. China 96 B2
Parma Italy 68 D2
Parma ID U.S.A. 156 D4
Parma OH U.S.A. 164 E3
Parnaíba Brazil 177 J4
Parnaíba r. Brazil 177 J4
Parnassus N.Z. 139 D6
Parnassus, Mount mt. Greece see Liakoura
Parner India 106 B2
Parnon mts Greece see Parnonas
Parnon mts Greece see Parnonas
Parnonas mts Greece 69 J6
Pärnu Estonia 55 N7
Pärnu-Jaagupi Estonia 55 N7
Paro Bhutan 105 G4
Paroikia Greece 69 K6
Parona Turkey see Fındık
Paroo watercourse Australia 138 A3
Paroo Channel watercourse Australia 138 A3
Paroo-Darling National Park 138 E3
Paropamisus mts Afgh. see Safīd Kūh
Paroreang, Bukit mt. Indon. 83 A3
Paros Notio Aigaio Greece see Paroikia
Paros i. Greece 69 K6
Parowan U.S.A. 159 G3
Parral Chile 178 B5
Parramatta Australia 138 E4
Parramore Island U.S.A. 165 H5
Parras Mex. 166 E3
Parrett r. U.K. 59 D7
Parrita Costa Rica 166 [inset] I7
Parry, Cape N.W.T. Canada 149 P1
Parry, Kap c. Greenland see Kangaarsussuaq
Parry, Lac l. Canada 152 G2
Parry Bay Canada 147 J3
Parry Channel Canada 147 G2
Parry Islands Canada 147 G2
Parry Peninsula N.W.T. Canada 149 P1
Parry Range hills Australia 134 A5
Parry Sound Canada 164 E1
Parsnip Peak U.S.A. 159 F2
Parsons KS U.S.A. 161 E4
Parsons WV U.S.A. 164 F4
Parsons Lake N.W.T. Canada 149 N1
Parsons Range hills Australia 134 F3
Parta Xizang China 99 E7
Partabgarh India 106 B2
Partabpur India 105 E5
Partenstein Germany 63 J4
Parthenay France 66 D3
Partida, Isla i. Mex. 166 C3
Partizansk Rus. Fed. 90 D4
Partney U.K. 58 H5
Partridge r. Canada 152 E4
Partry Ireland 61 C4
Partry Mts hills Ireland 61 C4
Paru r. Brazil 177 H4
Pārūd Iran 111 F5
Paryang Xizang China 99 C7
Parygino Kazakh. 98 D2
Parys S. Africa 125 H4
Pasa Dağı mt. Turkey 112 D3
Pasadena CA U.S.A. 158 D4
Pasadena TX U.S.A. 161 E6
Pasado, Cabo c. Ecuador 176 B4
Pa Sang Thai. 86 B3
Pasangkayu Sulawesi Barat Indon. 83 A3
Pasarbantal Sumatera Indon. 84 C3
Pasarseblat Sumatera Indon. 84 C3
Pasarseluma Sumatera Indon. 84 C4
Pasarwajo Sulawesi Indon. 83 B4
Pasawng Myanmar 86 B3
Pascagama r. Canada 152 G4
Pascagoula U.S.A. 161 F6
Pascagoula r. U.S.A. 161 F6
Paşcani Romania 69 L1
Pasco U.S.A. 156 D3
Pascoal, Monte hill Brazil 179 D2
Pascua, Isla de i. S. Pacific Ocean see Easter Island
Pascual Phil. 82 C3
Pas de Calais strait France/U.K. see Dover, Strait of
Pasewalk Germany 57 O4
Pasfield Lake Canada 151 J3
Pasha Rus. Fed. 52 G3
Pashih Haihsia sea chan. Phil./Taiwan see Bashi Channel
Pashkovo Rus. Fed. 90 C2
Pashkovskiy Rus. Fed. 53 H7
Pashtun Zarghun Afgh. 111 F3
Pashū'īyeh Iran 110 E4
Pasig Luzon Phil. 82 C3
Pasi Ga Myanmar 86 B1
Pasige i. Indon. 83 C2
Pasighat India 105 H3
Pasinler Turkey 113 F3
Pasir Gudang Malaysia 87 [inset]
Pasirian Jawa Indon. 85 F5
Pasir Mas Malaysia 84 C1
Pasirpangarayan Sumatera Indon. 84 C2
Pasir Putih Malaysia 84 C1
Pasitelu, Pulau-pulau is Indon. 83 B4
Paskūh Iran 111 F5
Pasni Pak. 185 M4
Paso Caballos Guat. 167 H5
Paso de los Toros Uruguay 178 E4
Paso de San Antonio Mex. 161 C6
Pasok Myanmar 86 A2
Paso Real Hond. 166 [inset] I6
Paso Robles U.S.A. 158 C4
Pasquia Hills Canada 151 K4
Passaic U.S.A. 165 H3
Passa Tempo Brazil 179 B3
Passau Germany 57 N6
Passi Panay Phil. 82 C4
Passo del San Gottardo Switz. see St Gotthard Pass
Passo Fundo Brazil 178 F3
Passos Brazil 179 B3
Passur r. Bangl. see Pusur
Passuri Nadi r. Bangl. see Pusur
Pastavy Belarus 55 O9
Pastaza r. Peru 176 C4
Pasto Col. 176 C3
Pastol Bay AK U.S.A. 148 G3
Pastora Peak U.S.A. 159 I3
Pastos Bons Brazil 177 J5
Pasu Pak. 104 C1
Pasuquin Luzon Phil. 82 C2
Pasur Turkey see Kulp
Pasuruan Jawa Indon. 85 F4
Pasvalys Lith. 55 N8
Pasvikelva r. Europe see Patsoyoki
Pata i. Phil. 82 C5
Patache, Punta pt Chile 178 B2
Patagonia reg. Arg. 178 B8
Pataliputra India see Patna
Patan Gujarat India see Somnath
Patan Gujarat India 104 C5
Patan Mahar. India 106 B2
Patan Nepal 105 F4
Patan Pak. 111 I3
Patandar, Koh-i- mt. Pak. 111 G5
Patani Halmahera Indon. 83 D2
Patavium Italy see Padua
Patea N.Z. 139 E4
Patea inlet N.Z. see Doubtful Sound
Pate Island Kenya 122 E4
Pateley Bridge U.K. 58 F4
Patensie S. Africa 124 G7
Patera India 104 D4
Paterson Australia 138 E4
Paterson r. Australia 138 C2
Paterson U.S.A. 165 H3
Paterson Range hills Australia 134 C5
Pathanamthitta India 106 C4
Pathankot India 104 C2
Pathari India 104 D5
Pathein Myanmar see Bassein
Pathfinder Reservoir U.S.A. 156 G4
Pathiu Thai. 87 B5
Pathum Thani Thai. 87 C4
Pati Jawa Indon. 85 E4
Patía r. Col. 176 C3
Patiala India 104 D3
Patinti, Selat sea chan. Maluku Indon. 83 C3
Patiro, Tanjung pt Indon. 83 B4
Patkai Bum mts India/Myanmar 105 H4
Patkaklik Xinjiang China 99 D5
Patmos i. Greece 69 L6
Patna India 105 F4
Patna Odisha India 105 F5
Patnagarh India 105 E5
Patnanongan i. Phil. 82 C3
Patnos Turkey 113 F3
Pato Branco Brazil 178 F3
Patoda India 106 B2
Patoka r. U.S.A. 164 B4
Patoka Lake U.S.A. 164 B4
Patos Albania 69 H4
Patos Brazil 177 K5
Patos, Lagoa dos l. Brazil 178 F4
Patos de Minas Brazil 179 B2
Patquía Arg. 178 C4
Patra Greece see Patras
Patrae Greece see Patras
Pátrai Greece see Patras
Patras Greece 69 I5
Patreksfjörður Iceland 54 [inset]
Patricio Lynch, Isla i. Chile 178 A7
Patrick Creek watercourse Australia 136 D4
Patrimônio Brazil 179 A2
Patrocínio Brazil 179 B2
Paṭrū Iran 111 E3
Patsoyoki r. Europe 54 Q2
Pattadakal tourist site India 106 B2
Pattani Thai. 87 C6
Pattani, Mae Nam r. Thai. 84 C1
Pattaya Thai. 87 C4
Pattensen Germany 63 J2
Patterson CA U.S.A. 158 C3
Patterson LA U.S.A. 161 F6
Patterson, Mount Y.T. Canada 149 N2
Patti India 105 E4
Patti Maluku Indon. 83 C5
Pattijoki Fin. 54 N4
Pättikkä Fin. 54 L2
Patton U.S.A. 165 F3
Pattullo, Mount B.C. Canada 149 O4
Patu Brazil 177 K5
Patuakhali Bangl. 105 G5
Patuanak Canada 151 J4
Patuca r. Hond. 166 [inset] I6
Patuca, Punta pt Hond. 166 [inset] I6
Patucas, Parque Nacional nat. park Hond. 166 [inset] I6
Patur India 106 C1
Patuxent r. U.S.A. 165 G4
Patuxent Range mts Antarctica 188 L1
Patvinsuon kansallispuisto nat. park Fin. 54 Q5
Pátzcuaro Mex. 167 E5
Pau France 66 D5
Pauhunri mt. China/India 105 G4
Pauillac France 66 D4
Pauini Brazil 176 E5
Pauiní r. Brazil 176 E5
Pauk Myanmar 86 A2
Paukkaung Myanmar 86 A3
Paulatuk N.W.T. Canada 149 Q1
Paulatuuq N.W.T. Canada see Paulatuk
Paulden U.S.A. 159 G4
Paulding U.S.A. 164 C3
Paulicéia Brazil 179 A3
Paulis Dem. Rep. Congo see Isiro
Paul Island Canada 153 J2
Paulo Afonso Brazil 177 K5
Paulo de Faria Brazil 179 A3
Pauloff Harbor AK U.S.A. 148 G5
Paulpietersburg S. Africa 125 J4
Paul Roux S. Africa 125 H5
Pauls Valley U.S.A. 161 D5
Paumotu, Îles is Fr. Polynesia see Tuamotu Islands
Paung Myanmar 86 B3
Paungbyin Myanmar 86 A1
Paungde Myanmar 86 A3
Pauni India 106 C1
Pauri India 104 D3
Pavagada India 106 C3
Pavão Brazil 179 C2
Pāveh Iran 110 B3
Pavia Italy 68 C2
Pāvilosta Latvia 55 L8
Pavino Rus. Fed. 52 J4
Pavlikeni Bulg. 69 K3
Pavlodar Kazakh. 102 E1
Pavlodarskaya Oblast' admin. div. Kazakh. 98 B1
Pavlof Bay AK U.S.A. 148 G5
Pavlof Islands AK U.S.A. 148 G5
Pavlof Volcano AK U.S.A. 149 [inset]
Pavlograd Ukr. see Pavlohrad
Pavlohrad Ukr. 53 G6
Pavlovka Rus. Fed. 53 J5
Pavlovo Rus. Fed. 52 I5
Pavlovsk Altayskiy Kray Rus. Fed. 88 E2
Pavlovsk Voronezhskaya Oblast' Rus. Fed. 53 I6
Pavlovskaya Rus. Fed. 53 H7
Pawahku Myanmar 86 B1
Pawai India 104 E4
Pawan r. Indon. 85 E3
Pawayan Uttar Prad. India 99 C7
Pawnee U.S.A. 161 D4
Pawnee r. U.S.A. 160 D4
Pawnee City U.S.A. 160 D3
Paw Paw MI U.S.A. 164 C2
Paw Paw WV U.S.A. 165 F4
Pawtucket U.S.A. 165 J3
Pawut Myanmar 87 B4
Paxson AK U.S.A. 149 K3
Paxton U.S.A. 164 A3
Payahe Halmahera Indon. 83 C2
Payakumbuh Sumatera Indon. 84 C3
Paya Lebar Sing. 87 [inset]
Payette U.S.A. 156 D3
Pay-Khoy, Khrebet hills Rus. Fed. 76 H3
Payne Canada see Kangirsuk
Payne, Lac l. Canada 152 G2
Paynes Creek U.S.A. 158 C1
Payne's Find Australia 135 B7
Paynesville U.S.A. 160 E2
Paysandú Uruguay 178 E4
Pays de Bray reg. France 62 B5
Payshanba Uzbek. 111 G1
Payson U.S.A. 159 H4
Payung, Tanjung pt Malaysia 85 F2
Payzawat Xinjiang China see Jiashi
Pazar Turkey 113 F2
Pazarcık Turkey 112 E3
Pazardzhik Bulg. 69 K3
Pazin Croatia 68 E2
Pe Myanmar 87 B4
Peabody KS U.S.A. 160 D4
Peabody MA U.S.A. 165 J2
▶Peace r. Canada 150 I3
Part of the Mackenzie-Peace-Finlay, the 2nd longest river in North America.
Peace Point Canada 151 H3
Peace River Canada 150 G3
Peach Creek U.S.A. 164 E5
Peach Springs U.S.A. 159 G4
Peacock Hills Canada 151 I1
Peak Charles hill Australia 135 C8
Peak Charles National Park Australia 135 C8
Peak District National Park U.K. 58 F5
Peake watercourse Australia 137 B6
Peaked Mountain hill U.S.A. 162 G2
Peak Hill N.S.W. Australia 138 D4
Peak Hill W.A. Australia 135 B6
Peale, Mount U.S.A. 159 I2
Peanut U.S.A. 158 B1
Pearce U.S.A. 159 I6
Pearce Point Australia 134 E3
Peard Bay AK U.S.A. 148 H1
Pearisburg U.S.A. 164 E5
Pearl r. U.S.A. 161 F6
Pearl Harbor inlet U.S.A. 157 [inset]
Pearsall U.S.A. 161 D6
Pearson U.S.A. 163 D6
Pearston S. Africa 125 G7
Peary Channel Canada 147 I2
Peary Land reg. Greenland 189 J1
Pease r. U.S.A. 161 D5
Peawanuck Canada 152 D3
Pebane Moz. 123 D5
Pebas Peru 176 D4
Pebengko Sulawesi Indon. 83 B3
Peć Kosovo see Pejë
Peçanha Brazil 179 C2
Pecan Island LA U.S.A. 167 G2
Peças, Ilha das i. Brazil 179 A4
Pechenga Rus. Fed. 54 Q2
Pechora Rus. Fed. 52 M2
Pechora r. Rus. Fed. 52 L1
Pechora Sea Rus. Fed. see Pechorskoye More
Pechorskaya Guba b. Rus. Fed. 52 L1
Pechorskoye More sea Rus. Fed. 189 G2
Pechory Rus. Fed. 55 O8
Peck U.S.A. 164 D2
Peck, Mount B.C. Canada 150 E3
Pecos U.S.A. 161 C6
Pecos r. U.S.A. 161 C6
Pécs Hungary 68 H1
Pedasí Panama 166 [inset] J8
Pedda Vagu r. India 106 C2
Pedder, Lake Australia 137 [inset]
Peddie S. Africa 125 H7
Pedernales Dom. Rep. 169 J5
Pedersöre Fin. 54 M5
Pediaios r. Cyprus 107 A2
Pediva Angola 123 B5
Pediwang Halmahera Indon. 83 C2
Pedra Azul Brazil 179 C1
Pedra Preta, Serra da mts Brazil 179 A1
Pedras de Maria da Cruz Brazil 179 B1
Pedregal Panama 166 [inset] J7

Pedregulho Brazil 179 B3
Pedreiras Brazil 177 J4
Pedriceña Mex. 166 E3
Pedro, Point Sri Lanka 106 D4
Pedro Bay AK U.S.A. 148 I4
Pedro Betancourt Cuba 163 D8
Pedro II, Ilha reg. Brazil/Venez. 176 E3
Pedro Juan Caballero Para. 178 E2
Peebles U.K. 60 F5
Peebles U.S.A. 164 D4
Pee Dee r. U.S.A. 163 E5
Peekskill U.S.A. 165 I3
Peel r. Australia 138 E3
Peel r. N.W.T./Y.T. Canada 149 N1
Peel Isle of Man 58 C4
Peel River Game Preserve nature res. N.W.T./Y.T. Canada 149 N2
Peer Belgium 62 F3
Peera Peera Poolanna Lake salt flat Australia 137 B5
Peerless Lake Canada 150 H3
Peerless Lake l. Canada 150 H3
Peers Canada 150 G4
Peery Lake salt flat Australia 138 A3
Pegasus Bay N.Z. 139 D6
Pegnitz Germany 63 L5
Pegu Myanmar 86 B3
Pegunungan Latimojong nature res. Indon. 83 B3
Pegunungan Peruhumpenai nature res. Indon. 83 B3
Pegu Yoma mts Myanmar 86 A3
Pegysh Rus. Fed. 52 K3
Pehuajó Arg. 178 D5
Peikang Taiwan 97 I4
Peine Chile 178 C2
Peine Germany 63 K2
Peint India 106 B1
Peipsi järv l. Estonia/Rus. Fed. see Peipus, Lake
Peipus, Lake Estonia/Rus. Fed. 55 O7
Peiraias Greece see Piraeus
Pei Shan mts China see Bei Shan
Peißen Germany 63 L3
Peixe Brazil 177 I6
Peixe r. Brazil 179 A1
Peixian Jiangsu China see Pizhou
Peixian Jiangsu China 95 I5
Peixoto de Azevedo Brazil 177 H6
Pejantan i. Indon. 84 D2
Pejë Kosovo 69 I3
Pèk Laos see Phônsavan
Peka Lesotho 125 H5
Pekabata Sulawesi Indon. 83 A3
Pekalongan Jawa Indon. 85 E4
Pekan Malaysia 84 C2
Pekanbaru Sumatera Indon. 84 C2
Pekin U.S.A. 160 F3
Peking Beijing China see Beijing
Pekinga Benin 120 D3
Pelabuhan Klang Malaysia 84 C2
Pelagie, Isole is Sicily Italy 68 E7
Pelaihari Kalimantan Indon. 85 F3
Pelalawan Sumatera Indon. 84 C2
Pelapis i. Indon. 85 E3
Pelawanbesar Kalimantan Indon. 85 G2
Peleaga, Vârful mt. Romania 69 J2
Pelee Island Canada 164 D3
Pelee Point Canada 164 D3
Peleliu i. Palau 82 [inset]
Peleng i. Indon. 83 B3
Peleng, Selat sea chan. Indon. 83 B3
Peleng, Teluk b. Indon. 83 B3
Peles Rus. Fed. 52 K3
Pélican, Lac du l. Canada 153 G2
Pelican Lake Canada 151 K4
Pelican Lake U.S.A. 160 E1
Pelican Narrows Canada 151 K4
Pelkosenniemi Fin. 54 O3
Pella S. Africa 124 D5
Pellatt Lake Canada 151 I1
Pelleluhu Islands P.N.G. 81 K7
Pello Fin. 54 M3
Pelly r. Canada 150 C2
Pelly Crossing Y.T. Canada 149 M3
Pelly Island N.W.T. Canada 149 N1
Pelly Lake Canada 151 K1
Pelly Mountains Y.T. Canada 149 N3
Pelokang is Indon. 85 G4
Peloponnese admin. reg. Greece 69 J6
Pelopónnesos admin. reg. Greece see Peloponnese
Peloponnisos admin. reg. Greece see Peloponnese
Pelotas Brazil 178 F4
Pelotas, Rio das r. Brazil 179 A4
Pelusium tourist site Egypt 107 A4
Pelusium, Bay of Egypt see Ţīnah, Khalīj aţ
Pemalang Jawa Indon. 85 E4
Pemangkat Kalimantan Indon. 85 E2
Pemarung, Pulau i. Indon. 85 G3
Pematangsiantar Sumatera Indon. 84 B2
Pemba Moz. 123 E5
Pemba Island Tanz. 123 D4
Pemberton Canada 150 F5
Pembina r. Canada 150 H4
Pembina r. U.S.A. 160 D1
Pembine U.S.A. 162 C2
Pembre Indon. 81 J8
Pembroke Canada 152 F5
Pembroke U.K. 59 C7
Pembroke U.S.A. 163 D5
Pembrokeshire Coast National Park U.K. 59 B7
Pembuanghulu Kalimantan Indon. 85 F3
Pemuar Kalimantan Indon. 85 E3
Pen India 106 B2
Peña Cerredo mt. Spain see Torrecerredo
Peñalara mt. Spain 67 E3
Penamar Brazil 179 C1
Penambo Range mts Malaysia see Tama Abu, Banjaran
Penampang Sabah Malaysia 85 G1
Peña Nevada, Cerro mt. Mex. 168 E4
Penang state Malaysia see Pinang
Penápolis Brazil 179 A3
Peñaranda de Bracamonte Spain 67 D3
Penarie Australia 138 A5
Penarlâg U.K. see Hawarden
Peñarroya mt. Spain 67 F3
Peñarroya-Pueblonuevo Spain 67 D4
Penarth U.K. 59 D7
Peñas, Cabo de c. Spain 67 D2
Penas, Golfo de g. Chile 178 A7
Peñas Blancas Nicaragua 166 [inset] I7
Penasi, Pulau i. Indon. 87 A6
Peña Ubiña mt. Spain 67 D2
Pender U.S.A. 160 D3
Pendle Hill hill U.K. 58 E5
Pendleton U.S.A. 156 D3
Pendleton Bay Canada 150 E4
Pendopo Sumatera Indon. 84 C3
Pend Oreille r. U.S.A. 156 D2
Pend Oreille Lake U.S.A. 156 D2
Pendra India 105 E5
Penduv India 106 B2
Pendzhikent Tajik. see Panjakent
Penebangan i. Indon. 85 E3
Peneda Gerês, Parque Nacional da nat. park Port. 67 B3
Penetanguishene Canada 164 F1
Penfro U.K. see Pembroke
Peng'an China 96 E2
Penganga r. India 106 C2
Peng Chau i. H.K. China 97 [inset]
P'engchia Yü i. Taiwan 97 I3
Penge Dem. Rep. Congo 123 C4
Penge S. Africa 125 J3
P'enghu Ch'üntao is Taiwan 97 H4
P'enghu Liehtao is Taiwan see P'enghu Ch'üntao
P'enghu Tao i. Taiwan 97 H4
Pengiki i. Indon. 85 E2
Pengkalan Hulu Malaysia 84 C1
Peng Kang hill Sing. 87 [inset]
Penglai Shandong China 95 J4
Penglaizhen China see Daying
Pengshan China 96 D2
Pengshui China 97 F2
Pengwa Myanmar 86 A2
Pengxi China 96 E2
Penha Brazil 179 A4
Penhoek Pass S. Africa 125 H6
Penhook U.S.A. 164 F5
Peniche Port. 67 B4
Penicuik U.K. 60 F5
Penida i. Indon. 85 F5
Penig Germany 63 M4
Peninga Rus. Fed. 54 R5
Peninsular Malaysia Malaysia 84 C2
Penitente, Serra do hills Brazil 177 I5
Penn U.S.A. see Penn Hills
Pennell Coast Antarctica 188 H2
Penn Hills U.S.A. 164 F3
Pennine, Alpi mts Italy/Switz. 68 B2
Pennine Alps mts Italy/Switz. see Pennine, Alpi
Pennines hills U.K. 58 E4
Pennington Gap U.S.A. 164 D5
Pennsburg U.S.A. 165 H3
Penns Grove U.S.A. 165 H4
Pennsville U.S.A. 165 H4
Pennsylvania state U.S.A. 164 F3
Pennville U.S.A. 164 C3
Penn Yan U.S.A. 165 G2
Penny Icecap Canada 147 L3
Penny Point Antarctica 188 H1
Penola Australia 137 C8
Peñón Blanco Mex. 166 D3
Penong Australia 135 F7
Penonomé Panama 166 [inset] J7
Penrhyn atoll Cook Is 187 J6
Penrhyn Basin sea feature S. Pacific Ocean 187 J6
Penrith Australia 138 E4
Penrith U.K. 58 E4
Pensacola U.S.A. 163 C6
Pensacola Mountains Antarctica 188 L1
Pensiangan Sabah Malaysia 85 G1
Pensi La pass India 104 D2
Pentadaktylos Range mts Cyprus 107 A2
Pentakota India 106 D2
Pentecost Island Vanuatu 133 G3
Pentecôte, Île i. Vanuatu see Pentecost Island
Penticton Canada 150 G5
Pentire Point U.K. 59 B8
Pentland Australia 136 D4
Pentland Firth sea chan. U.K. 60 F2
Pentland Hills U.K. 60 F5
Pentwater U.S.A. 164 B2
Penuba Indon. 84 D3
Penuguan Sumatera Indon. 84 D3
Penunjuk, Tanjung pt Malaysia 84 C1
Penwegon Myanmar 86 B3
Pen-y-Bont ar Ogwr U.K. see Bridgend
Penygadair hill U.K. 59 D6
Penylan Lake Canada 151 J2
Penyu, Kepulauan is Maluku Indon. 83 C4
Penza Rus. Fed. 53 J5
Penzance U.K. 59 B8
Penzhinskaya Guba b. Rus. Fed. 77 R3
Peoria AZ U.S.A. 159 G5
Peoria IL U.S.A. 160 F3
Peotone U.S.A. 164 B3
Peper, Teluk b. Indon. see Lada, Teluk
Pequeña, Punta pt Mex. 166 B3
Pequop Mountains U.S.A. 159 F1
Peradeniya Sri Lanka 106 D5
Pera Head hd Australia 136 C2
Perak i. Malaysia 84 B1
Perak r. Malaysia 84 C1
Perak state Malaysia 84 C1
Perales del Alfambra Spain 67 F3
Perambalur India 106 C4
Perämeren kansallispuisto nat. park Fin. 54 N4
Peranap Sumatera Indon. 84 C3
Peräseinäjoki Fin. 54 M5
Percé Canada 153 I4
Percival Lakes salt flat Australia 134 D5
Percy U.S.A. 165 J1
Percy Isles Australia 136 E4
Percy Reach l. Canada 165 G1
Perdizes Brazil 179 B2
Perdu, Lac l. Canada 153 H4
Peregrebnoye Rus. Fed. 51 T3
Pereira Col. 176 C3
Pereira Barreto Brazil 179 A3
Pereira de Eça Angola see Ondjiva
Pere Marquette r. U.S.A. 164 B2
Peremul Par reef India 106 B4
Peremyshlyany Ukr. 53 E6
Perenjori Australia 135 B7
Pereslavl'-Zalesskiy Rus. Fed. 52 H4
Pereslavskiy Natsional'nyy Park nat. park Rus. Fed. 52 H4
Pereyaslavka Rus. Fed. 90 D3
Pereyaslav-Khmel'nitskiy Ukr. see Pereyaslav-Khmel'nyts'kyy
Pereyaslav-Khmel'nyts'kyy Ukr. 53 F6
Perforated Island Thai. see Bon, Ko
Pergamino Arg. 178 D4
Perhentian Besar, Pulau i. Malaysia 84 C1
Perho Fin. 54 N5
Péribonka, Lac l. Canada 153 H4
Perico Arg. 178 C2
Pericos Sinaloa Mex. 166 D3
Peridot U.S.A. 159 H5
Périgueux France 66 E4
Perijá, Parque Nacional nat. park Venez. 176 D2
Perija, Sierra de mts Venez. 176 D2
Peringat Malaysia 84 C1
Periyar India see Erode
Perkasie U.S.A. 165 H3
Perkat, Tanjung pt Indon. 84 D3
Perlas, Archipiélago de las is Panama 166 [inset] K7
Perlas, Laguna de lag. Nicaragua 166 [inset] J6
Perlas, Punta de pt Nicaragua 166 [inset] J6
Perleberg Germany 63 L1
Perlis state Malaysia 84 C1
Perm' Rus. Fed. 51 R4
Permas Rus. Fed. 52 J4
Pernambuco Brazil see Recife
Pernambuco Plain sea feature S. Atlantic Ocean 184 G6
Pernatty Lagoon salt flat Australia 137 B6
Pernem India 106 B3
Pernik Bulg. 69 J3
Pernov Estonia see Pärnu
Perojpur Bangl. see Pirojpur
Peron Islands Australia 134 E3
Péronne France 62 C5
Perote Mex. 167 F5
Perpignan France 66 F5
Perranporth U.K. 59 B8
Perrégaux Alg. see Mohammadia
Perris U.S.A. 158 E5
Perros-Guirec France 66 C2
Perrot, Île i. Canada 165 I1
Perry FL U.S.A. 163 D6
Perry GA U.S.A. 163 D5
Perry MI U.S.A. 164 C2
Perry OK U.S.A. 161 D4
Perry Lake U.S.A. 160 E4
Perryton U.S.A. 161 C4
Perryville AK U.S.A. 148 H5
Perryville MO U.S.A. 160 F4
Perseverancia Bol. 176 F6
Pershore U.K. 59 E6
Persia country Asia see Iran
Persian Gulf Asia see The Gulf
Pertek Turkey 113 E3

▶Perth Australia 135 A7
Capital of Western Australia. 4th most populous city in Oceania.

Perth Canada 165 G1
Perth U.K. 60 F4
Perth Amboy U.S.A. 165 H3
Perth-Andover Canada 153 I5
Perth Basin sea feature Indian Ocean 185 P7
Pertominsk Rus. Fed. 52 H2
Pertunmaa Fin. 55 O6
Pertusato, Capo c. Corsica France 66 I6
Peru atoll Kiribati see Beru

▶Peru country S. America 176 D6
3rd largest and 4th most populous country in South America.

Peru IL U.S.A. 160 F3
Peru IN U.S.A. 164 B3
Peru NY U.S.A. 165 I1
Peru-Chile Trench sea feature S. Pacific Ocean 187 O6
Perugia Italy 68 E3
Peruru India 106 C3
Perusia Italy see Perugia
Péruwelz Belgium 62 D4
Pervomay Kyrg. 98 A4
Pervomaysk Rus. Fed. 53 I5
Pervomays'k Ukr. 53 F6
Pervomayskiy Kazakh. 102 F1
Pervomayskiy Arkhangel'skaya Oblast' Rus. Fed. see Novodvinsk
Pervomayskiy Tambovskaya Oblast' Rus. Fed. 53 I5
Pervomays'kyy Ukr. 53 H6
Pervorechenskiy Rus. Fed. 77 R3
Pesaguan Kalimantan Indon. 85 E3
Pesaguan r. Indon. 85 E3
Pesaro Italy 68 E3
Pescadores is Taiwan see P'enghu Ch'üntao
Pescara Italy 68 F3
Pescara r. Italy 68 F3
Peschanokopskoye Rus. Fed. 53 I7
Peschanoye Rus. Fed. see Yashkul'
Peschanyy, Mys pt Kazakh. 113 H2
Pesé Panama 166 [inset] J8
Pesha r. Rus. Fed. 52 J2
Peshanjan Afgh. 111 F3
Peshawar Pak. 111 H3
Peshkopi Albania 69 I4
Peshtera Bulg. 69 K3
Peski Turkm. 111 F2
Peski Karakumy des. Turkm. see Karakum Desert
Peskovka Rus. Fed. 52 L4
Pesnica Slovenia 68 F1
Pespire Hond. 166 [inset] I6
Pesqueira Mex. 166 C2
Pessac France 66 D4
Pessin Germany 63 M2
Pestovo Rus. Fed. 52 G4
Pestravka Rus. Fed. 53 K5
Petah Tiqwa Israel 107 B3
Petäjävesi Fin. 54 N5
Petak, Tanjung pt Halmahera Indon. 83 D2
Petaling Jaya Malaysia 87 C7
Petalion, Kolpos sea chan. Greece 69 K5
Petaluma U.S.A. 158 B2
Pétange Lux. 62 F5
Petangis Kalimantan Indon. 85 F3
Petatlán Mex. 168 D5
Petauke Zambia 123 D5
Petén Itzá, Lago l. Guat. 167 H5
Petenwell Lake U.S.A. 160 F2
Peterbell Canada 152 E4
Peterborough Australia 137 B7
Peterborough Canada 165 F1
Peterborough U.K. 59 G6
Peterborough U.S.A. 165 J2
Peterculter U.K. 60 G3
Peterhead U.K. 60 H3
Peter I Island Antarctica 188 K2
Peter I Øy i. Antarctica see Peter I Island
Peter Lake Canada 151 M2
Peterlee U.K. 58 F4
Petermann Bjerg nunatak Greenland 147 P2
Petermann Ranges mts Australia 135 E6
Peter Pond Lake Canada 151 I4
Peters, Lac l. Canada 153 H2
Petersberg Germany 63 J4
Petersburg AK U.S.A. 149 N4
Petersburg IL U.S.A. 160 F4
Petersburg IN U.S.A. 164 B4
Petersburg NY U.S.A. 165 I2
Petersburg VA U.S.A. 165 G5
Petersburg WV U.S.A. 164 F4
Petersfield U.K. 59 G7
Petershagen Germany 63 I2
Petersville AK U.S.A. 149 J3
Peter the Great Bay Rus. Fed. see Petra Velikogo, Zaliv
Peth India 106 B2
Petilia Policastro Italy 68 G5
Petit Atlas mts Morocco see Anti Atlas
Petitcodiac Canada 153 I5
Petitjean Morocco see Sidi Kacem
Petit Lac Manicouagan l. Canada 153 I3
Petit Mécatina r. Nfld. and Lab./Que. Canada 153 K4
Petit Mécatina, Île du i. Canada 153 K4
Petit Morin r. France 62 D6
Petitot r. Canada 150 F2
Petit St-Bernard, Col du pass France 66 H4
Petit Saut, Barrage du resr Fr. Guiana 177 H3
Peto Mex. 167 H4
Petoskey U.S.A. 162 C2
Petra tourist site Jordan 107 B4
Petra Velikogo, Zaliv b. Rus. Fed. 90 C4
Petre, Point Canada 165 G2
Petrich Bulg. 69 J4
Petrified Forest National Park U.S.A. 159 I4
Petrikau Poland see Piotrków Trybunalski
Petrikov Belarus see Pyetrykaw
Petrinja Croatia 68 G2
Petroaleksandrovsk Uzbek. see To'rtko'l
Petrograd Rus. Fed. see St Petersburg
Petrokhanski Prokhod pass Bulg. 69 J3
Petrokov Poland see Piotrków Trybunalski
Petrolia Canada 164 D2
Petrolia U.S.A. 158 A1
Petrolina Brazil 177 J5
Petrolina de Goiás Brazil 179 A2
Petropavl Kazakh. see Petropavlovsk
Petropavlovsk Kazakh. 98 C3
Petropavlovsk Respublika Buryatiya Rus. Fed. 94 F1
Petropavlovsk Kazakh. 101 F1
Petropavlovsk Rus. Fed. see Petropavlovsk-Kamchatskiy
Petropavlovsk-Kamchatskiy Rus. Fed. 77 Q4
Petrópolis Brazil 179 C3
Petroşani Romania 69 J2
Petrovsk Rus. Fed. 53 J5
Petrovskoye Rus. Fed. see Svetlograd
Petrovsk-Zabaykal'skiy Rus. Fed. 95 G1
Petrozavodsk Rus. Fed. 52 G3
Petrus Steyn S. Africa 125 I4
Petrusville S. Africa 124 G6
Petsamo Rus. Fed. see Pechenga
Pettau Slovenia see Ptuj
Petten Neth. 62 E2
Pettigo U.K. 61 E3
Petukhovo Rus. Fed. 76 H4
Petushki Rus. Fed. 52 H5
Petzeck mt. Austria 57 N7
Peuetsagu, Gunung vol. Indon. 84 B1
Peureula Sumatera Indon. 84 B1
Pevek Rus. Fed. 77 S3
Pêxung Xizang China 99 F6
Pey Ostān Iran 110 E3
Peza r. Rus. Fed. 52 J2
Pezinok Slovakia 57 P6
Pezu Pak. 111 H3
Pfälzer Wald hills Germany 63 H5
Pforzheim Germany 63 I6
Pfungstadt Germany 63 I5
Phagameng Limpopo S. Africa 125 I3
Phagwara India 104 C3
Phahameng Free State S. Africa 125 H5
Phalaborwa S. Africa 125 J2
Phalodi India 104 C4
Phalsund India 104 B4
Phalta India 105 G5
Phaluai, Ko i. Thai. 87 B5
Phalut Peak India/Nepal 105 G4
Phan Thai. 86 B3
Phanat Nikhom Thai. 87 C4
Phangan, Ko i. Thai. 87 C5
Phang Hoei, San Khao mts Thai. 86 C3
Phangnga Thai. 87 B5
Phăng Xi Păng mt. Vietnam 86 C2
Phanom Dong Rak, Thiu Khao mts Cambodia/Thai. 87 D4
Phan Rang-Thap Cham Vietnam 87 E5
Phan Thiêt Vietnam 87 E5
Phapon Myanmar see Pyapon
Phat Diêm Vietnam 86 D2
Phatthalung Thai. 87 C6
Phayam, Ko i. Thai. 87 B5
Phayao Thai. 86 B3
Phayuhakhiri Thai. 86 C4
Phek India 105 H4
Phelps Lake Canada 151 K3
Phen Thai. 86 C3
Phenix U.S.A. 165 F5
Phenix City U.S.A. 163 C5
Phet Buri Thai. 87 B4
Phetchabun Thai. 86 C3
Phiafai Laos 86 D4
Phichai Thai. 86 C3
Phichit Thai. 86 C3
Philadelphia Jordan see 'Ammān
Philadelphia Turkey see Alaşehir
Philadelphia MS U.S.A. 161 F5
Philadelphia NY U.S.A. 165 H1
Philadelphia PA U.S.A. 165 H4
Philip U.S.A. 160 C2
Philip Atoll Micronesia see Sorol
Philippeville Alg. see Skikda
Philippeville Belgium 62 E4
Philippi U.S.A. 164 E4
Philippi, Lake salt flat Australia 136 B5
Philippine Neth. 62 D3
Philippine Basin sea feature N. Pacific Ocean 186 E4
Philippines country Asia 82 C3
Philippine Sea N. Pacific Ocean 81 G3

▶Philippine Trench sea feature N. Pacific Ocean 186 E4
3rd deepest trench in the world.

Philippolis S. Africa 125 G6
Philippopolis Bulg. see Plovdiv
Philippsburg Germany 63 I5
Philipsburg MT U.S.A. 156 E3
Philipsburg PA U.S.A. 165 F3
Philip Smith Mountains AK U.S.A. 149 J2
Philipstown S. Africa 124 G6
Phillip Island Australia 138 B7
Phillips ME U.S.A. 165 J1
Phillips WI U.S.A. 160 F2
Phillipsburg U.S.A. 160 D4
Phillips Range hills Australia 134 D4
Philmont U.S.A. 165 I2
Philomelium Turkey see Akşehir
Phiritona S. Africa 125 H4
Phitsanulok Thai. 86 C3

▶Phnom Penh Cambodia 87 D5
Capital of Cambodia.

Phnum Pénh Cambodia see Phnom Penh
Pho, Laem pt Thai. 87 C6
Phoenicia U.S.A. 165 H2

▶Phoenix U.S.A. 157 E6
Capital of Arizona.

Phoenix Island Kiribati see Rawaki
Phoenix Islands Kiribati 133 I2
Phoenix Islands Protected Area Kiribati 133 I2
Phô Lu Vietnam 86 D2
Phon Thai. 86 C4
Phong Nha Vietnam 86 D3
Phôngsali Laos 86 C2
Phong Saly Laos see Phôngsali
Phong Thô Vietnam 86 C2
Phon Phisai Thai. 86 C3
Phônsavan Laos 86 C3
Phon Thong Thai. 86 C3
Phosphate Hill Australia 136 C4
Phrae Thai. 86 C3
Phra Nakhon Si Ayutthaya Thai. see Ayutthaya
Phrao Thai. 86 B3
Phra Saeng Thai. 87 B5
Phrom Phiram Thai. 86 C3
Phsar Ream Cambodia 87 C5
Phu Bai Vietnam 86 D3
Phuchong-Nayoi National Park Thai. 87 D4
Phu Cuong Vietnam see Thu Dâu Môt
Phuket Thai. 87 B6
Phuket, Ko i. Thai. 87 B6
Phu-khieo Wildlife Reserve nature res. Thai. 86 C3
Phulabani India see Phulbani
Phulbani India 106 E1
Phulchhari Ghat Bangl. see Fulchhari
Phulji Pak. 111 G5
Phu Lôc Vietnam 86 D3
Phu Lôc Vietnam 87 D5
Phu Luang National Park Thai. 86 C3
Phu Ly Vietnam 86 D2
Phumĭ Bŏeng Mealea Cambodia 87 D4
Phumĭ Chhlong Cambodia 87 D4
Phumĭ Kaôh Kŏng Cambodia 87 C5
Phumĭ Kon Kriel Cambodia 87 C4
Phumĭ Mlu Prey Cambodia 87 D4
Phumĭ Moŭng Cambodia 87 C4
Phumiphon, Khuan Thai. 86 B3
Phumĭ Prêk Kak Cambodia 87 D4
Phumĭ Sâmraông Cambodia 87 C4
Phumĭ Trâm Kak Cambodia 87 D5
Phumĭ Veal Renh Cambodia 87 C5
Phu My Vietnam 87 E4
Phung Hiêp Vietnam 87 D5
Phước Bưu Vietnam 87 D5
Phước Hai Vietnam 87 D5
Phu Phac Mo mt. Vietnam 86 C2
Phu Phan National Park Thai. 86 C3
Phu Quôc, Đao i. Vietnam 87 C5
Phu Quy, Đao i. Vietnam 87 E5
Phu Tho Vietnam 86 D2
Phu Vinh Vietnam see Tra Vinh
Phyu Myanmar 86 B3
Piabung, Gunung mt. Indon. 85 F2
Piaca Brazil 177 I5
Piacenza Italy 68 C2
Piacouadie, Lac l. Canada 153 H4
Piagochioui r. Canada 152 F3
Piai, Tanjung pt Malaysia 84 C2
Pian r. Australia 138 D3
Pianguan Shanxi China 95 G4
Pianosa, Isola i. Italy 68 D3
Piatra Neamţ Romania 69 L1
Piave r. Italy 68 E2
Pibor Post Sudan 121 G4
Pic r. Canada 152 D4
Picacho U.S.A. 159 H5
Picachos, Cerro dos mt. Mex. 166 B2
Picardie admin. reg. France 62 C5
Picardie reg. France see Picardy
Picardy admin. reg. France see Picardie
Picardy reg. France 62 B5
Picauville France 59 F9
Picayune U.S.A. 161 F6
Piceance Creek r. U.S.A. 159 I1
Pich Mex. 167 H5
Picháchic Mex. 166 D2
Pichanal Arg. 178 D2
Pichhor India 104 D4
Pichilemu Chile 178 B4
Pichilingue Mex. 166 C3
Pichucalco Mex. 167 G5
Pickens U.S.A. 164 E4
Pickering Canada 164 F2
Pickering U.K. 58 G4
Pickering, Vale of valley U.K. 58 G4
Pickle Lake Canada 147 I4
Pico Bonito, Parque Nacional nat. park Hond. 166 [inset] I6
Pico da Neblina, Parque Nacional do nat. park Brazil 176 E3
Pico de Orizaba, Parque Nacional nat. park Mex. 167 F5
Pico de Tancítaro, Parque Nacional nat. park Mex. 166 E5
Picos Brazil 177 J5
Pico Truncado Arg. 178 C7
Picton Australia 138 E5
Picton Canada 165 G2
Picton N.Z. 139 E5
Pictou Canada 153 J5
Picture Butte Canada 151 H5
Pidarak Pak. 111 F5
Pidurutalagala mt. Sri Lanka 106 D5
Piedade Brazil 179 B3
Piedra de Águila Arg. 178 B6
Piedras, Punta pt Arg. 178 E5
Piedras Blancas Point U.S.A. 158 C4
Piedras Negras Guat. 167 H5
Piedras Negras Coahuila Mex. 167 E2
Piedras Negras Veracruz Mex. 167 F5
Pie Island Canada 152 C4
Pieksämäki Fin. 54 O5
Pielavesi Fin. 54 O5
Pielinen l. Fin. 54 P5
Pieljekaise nationalpark nat. park Sweden 54 J3
Pienaarsrivier S. Africa 125 I3
Pieniński Park Narodowy nat. park Poland 57 R6
Pieninský nat. park Slovakia 57 R6
Pierce U.S.A. 160 D3
Pierce Lake Canada 151 M4
Pierceland Canada 151 I4
Pierceton U.S.A. 164 C3
Pieria mts Greece 69 J4
Pierowall U.K. 60 G1
Pierpont U.S.A. 164 E3

▶Pierre U.S.A. 160 C2
Capital of South Dakota.

Pierrelatte France 66 G4
Pietermaritzburg S. Africa 125 J5
Pietersaari Fin. see Jakobstad
Pietersburg Limpopo S. Africa see Polokwane
Pie Town U.S.A. 159 I4
Pietra Spada, Passo di pass Italy 68 G5
Piet Retief S. Africa 125 J4
Pietrosa mt. Romania 69 K1
Pigeon U.S.A. 164 D2
Pigeon Bay Canada 164 D3
Pigeon Lake Canada 150 H4
Piggott U.S.A. 161 F4
Pigg's Peak Swaziland 125 J3
Pigs, Bay of Cuba 163 D8
Piguicas mt. Mex. 167 F4
Pihij India 104 C5
Pihkva järv l. Estonia/Rus. Fed. see Pskov, Lake
Pihlajavesi l. Fin. 54 P6
Pihlava Fin. 55 L6
Pihtipudas Fin. 54 N5
Piippola Fin. 54 N4
Piispajärvi Fin. 54 P4
Pijijiapan Mex. 167 G6
Pikalevo Rus. Fed. 52 G4
Pike U.S.A. 164 E4
Pike Bay Canada 164 E1
Pikelot i. Micronesia 81 L5
Pikes Peak U.S.A. 156 G5
Piketon U.S.A. 164 D4
Pikeville KY U.S.A. 164 D5
Pikeville TN U.S.A. 162 C5
Pikinni atoll Marshall Is see Bikini
Pikmiktalik AK U.S.A. 148 G3
Pikou Liaoning China 95 J4
Piła Poland 57 P4
Pilanesberg National Park S. Africa 125 H3
Pilar Arg. 178 E4
Pilar Para. 178 E3
Pilar Phil. 82 D4
Pilar de Goiás Brazil 179 A1
Pilas i. Phil. 82 C5
Pilas Channel Phil. 82 C5
Pilaya r. Bol. 176 F8
Pilcomayo r. Bol./Para. 176 F8
Pile Bay Village AK U.S.A. 148 I4
Piler India 106 C3
Pilgrim Springs AK U.S.A. 148 F2
Pili Luzon Phil. 82 C3
Pili, Cerro mt. Chile 178 C2
Pilibangan India 104 C3
Pilibhit India 104 D3
Pilipinas country Asia see Philippines
Pillau Rus. Fed. see Baltiysk
Pillcopata Peru 176 D6
Pilliga Australia 138 D3
Pillsbury, Lake U.S.A. 158 B2
Pil'na Rus. Fed. 52 J5
Pil'nya, Ozero l. Rus. Fed. 52 M1
Pilões, Serra dos mts Brazil 179 B2
Pilos Greece see Pylos
Pilot Knob mt. U.S.A. 156 E3
Pilot Peak U.S.A. 158 E2
Pilot Point AK U.S.A. 148 H4
Pilot Station AK U.S.A. 148 G3
Pilottown LA U.S.A. 167 H2
Pilsen Czech Rep. see Plzeň
Piltene Latvia 55 L8
Pil'tun, Zaliv lag. Rus. Fed. 90 F1
Pilu Pak. 111 H5
Pima U.S.A. 159 I5
Pimenta Bueno Brazil 176 F6
Pimento U.S.A. 164 B4
Pimpalner India 106 B1
Pin r. India 104 D2
Pin r. Myanmar 86 A2
Pinahat India 104 D4
Pinaleno Mountains U.S.A. 159 H5
Pinamalayan Mindoro Phil. 82 C3
Pinamar Arg. 178 E5
Pinang Malaysia see George Town
Pinang i. Malaysia 84 C1
Pinang state Malaysia 84 C1
Pinangah Sabah Malaysia 85 G1
Pınarbaşı Turkey 112 E3
Pinar del Río Cuba 169 H4
Pinarhisar Turkey 69 L4
Piñas Ecuador 176 C4
Pincher Creek Canada 150 H5
Pinckneyville U.S.A. 160 F4
Pinconning U.S.A. 164 D2
Pińczów Poland 57 R5
Pindaí Brazil 179 C1
Pindamonhangaba Brazil 179 B3
Pindar Australia 135 A7
Pindar r. India 99 B7

Pindaré r. Brazil 177 J4
Píndhos Óros mts Greece see Pindus Mountains
Pindos mts Greece see Pindus Mountains
Pindrei India 104 E5
Pindus Mountains Greece 69 I5
Pine watercourse Australia 137 C7
Pine r. MI U.S.A. 164 C1
Pine r. MI U.S.A. 164 C2
Pine Bluff U.S.A. 161 E5
Pine Bluffs U.S.A. 156 G4
Pine Creek Australia 134 E3
Pine Creek r. U.S.A. 165 G3
Pinecrest U.S.A. 158 C2
Pinedale NM U.S.A. 159 I4
Pinedale WY U.S.A. 156 F4
Pine Dock Canada 151 L5
Pine Falls Canada 151 L5
Pine Flat Lake U.S.A. 158 D3
Pinega Rus. Fed. 52 I2
Pinega r. Rus. Fed. 52 I2
Pinegrove Australia 135 A6
Pine Grove U.S.A. 165 G3
Pine Hills FL U.S.A. 163 D6
Pinehouse Lake Canada 151 J4
Pinehouse Lake l. Canada 151 J4
Pineimuta r. Canada 151 N4
Pineios r. Greece 69 J5
Pine Island Bay Antarctica 187 N10
Pine Island Glacier Antarctica 188 K1
Pine Islands FL U.S.A. 163 D7
Pine Islands FL U.S.A. 163 D7
Pine Knot U.S.A. 164 C5
Pineland U.S.A. 161 E6
Pine Mountain U.S.A. 158 C4
Pine Peak U.S.A. 159 G4
Pine Point pt Canada 150 H2
Pine Point (abandoned) Canada 150 H2
Pineridge U.S.A. 158 D3
Pine Ridge U.S.A. 160 C3
Pinerolo Italy 68 B2
Pines, Akrotirio pt Greece 69 K4
Pines, Isle of i. Cuba see La Juventud, Isla de
Pines, Isle of i. New Caledonia see Pins, Île des
Pines, Lake o' the TX U.S.A. 167 G1
Pinetop U.S.A. 159 I4
Pinetown S. Africa 125 J5
Pine Valley U.S.A. 165 G2
Pineville KY U.S.A. 164 D5
Pineville LA U.S.A. 167 G2
Pineville MO U.S.A. 161 E4
Pineville WV U.S.A. 164 E5
Ping, Mae Nam r. Thai. 86 C4
Ping'an Qinghai China 94 E4
Ping'anyi Qinghai China see Ping'an
Pingba China 96 E3
Pingbian China 96 D4
Ping Dao i. China 95 I5
Pingding Shanxi China 95 H4
Pingdingbu Hebei China see Guyuan
Pingdingshan China 97 G1
Pingdong Taiwan see P'ingtung
Pingdu Jiangxi China see Anfu
Pingdu Shandong China 95 I4
Pinggang China 90 B4
Pinggu Beijing China 95 I3
Pinghe China 97 H3
Pinghu China see Pingtang
Pingjiang China 97 G2
Pingjinpu China 96 E2
Pingle China 97 F3
Pingli China 97 F1
Pingliang Gansu China 94 F5
Pinglu Shanxi China 95 G5
Pingluo Ningxia China 94 F4
Pingma China see Tiandong
Pingnan China 97 H3
Pingqiao China 97 G1
Pingquan Hebei China 95 I3
Pingshan Hebei China 95 H4
Pingshan Sichuan China 96 E2
Pingshan Yunnan China see Luquan
Pingshi China 97 G3
Pingshu Hebei China see Daicheng
Pingtan China 97 H3
Pingtan Dao i. China see Haitan Dao
Pingtang China 96 E3
P'ingtung Taiwan 97 I4
Pingxi China see Yuping
Pingxiang Gansu China see Tongwei
Pingxiang Guangxi China 96 E4
Pingxiang Jiangxi China 97 G3
Pingyang Heilong. China 95 K1
Pingyang Zhejiang China 97 I3
Pingyao Shanxi China 95 H4
Pingyi Shandong China 95 I5
Pingyin Shandong China 95 I4
Pingyu China 97 G1
Pingyuan Shandong China 95 I4
Pingyuanjie China 96 D4
Pingzhai China 97 F3
Pinhal Brazil 179 B3
Pinheiro Brazil 177 I4
Pinhoe U.K. 59 D8
Pini i. Indon. 84 B2
Piniós r. Greece see Pineios
Pinjin Australia 135 C7
Pink Mountain Canada 150 F3
Pinlaung Myanmar 86 B2
Pinlebu Myanmar 86 A1
Pinnacle hill U.S.A. 165 F4
Pinnacle Island AK U.S.A. 148 D3
Pinnacles National Monument nat. park U.S.A. 158 C3
Pinnau r. Germany 63 J1
Pinneberg Germany 63 J1
Pinnes, Akra pt Greece see Pines, Akrotirio
Pinoh r. Indon. 85 E3
Pinon Hills CA U.S.A. 158 E4
Pinos, Isla de i. Cuba see La Juventud, Isla de
Pinos, Mount U.S.A. 158 D4
Pinotepa Nacional Mex. 168 E5
Pinrang Sulawesi Indon. 83 A3
Pinrang Sulawesi Indon. 83 B3
Pins, Île des i. New Caledonia 133 G4
Pins, Pointe aux pt Canada 164 E2
Pinsk Belarus 55 O10
Pinta, Sierra hill U.S.A. 159 G5
Pintada Creek watercourse U.S.A. 157 G6
Pintados Chile 178 C2
Pintasan Sabah Malaysia 85 G1
Pintura U.S.A. 159 G3
Pioche U.S.A. 159 F3
Piodi Dem. Rep. Congo 123 C4
Pioneer Mountains U.S.A. 156 E3
Pioner, Ostrov i. Rus. Fed. 76 K2
Pionerskiy Kaliningradskaya Oblast' Rus. Fed. 55 L9
Pionerskiy Khanty-Mansiyskiy Avtonomnyy Okrug Rus. Fed. 51 S3
Pionki Poland 57 R5
Piopio N.Z. 139 E4
Piopiotahi inlet N.Z. see Milford Sound
Piorini, Lago l. Brazil 176 F4
Piotrków Trybunalski Poland 57 Q5
Pipa Dingzi mt. China 90 C4
Pipar India 104 C4
Pipar Road India 104 C4
Piperi i. Greece 69 K5
Piper Peak U.S.A. 158 E3
Pipestone Canada 151 K5
Pipestone r. Canada 151 N4
Pipestone U.S.A. 160 D3
Pipli India 104 C3
Pipmuacan, Réservoir resr Canada 153 H4
Piqan Xinjiang China see Shanshan
Piqanlik Xinjiang China 98 C4
Piqua U.S.A. 164 C3
Piquiri r. Brazil 179 A4
Pira Benin 120 D4
Piracanjuba Brazil 179 A2
Piracicaba Brazil 179 B3
Piracicaba r. Brazil 179 C2
Piraçununga Brazil 179 B3
Piracuruca Brazil 177 J4
Piraeus Greece 69 J6
Piraí do Sul Brazil 179 A4
Piráievs Greece see Piraeus
Piraju Brazil 179 A3
Pirajuí Brazil 179 A3
Pirallahı Adası Azer. 113 H2
Piranhas Bahia Brazil 179 C1
Piranhas Goiás Brazil 177 H7
Piranhas r. Rio Grande do Norte Brazil 177 K5
Piranhas r. Brazil 179 A2
Pirapora Brazil 179 B2
Pirari Nepal 99 D8
Piraube, Lac l. Canada 153 H4
Pirawa India 104 D4
Pirenópolis Brazil 179 A1
Pires do Rio Brazil 179 A2
Pírgos Greece see Pyrgos
Pirin nat. park Bulg. 69 J4
Pirineos mts Europe see Pyrenees
Piripiri Brazil 177 J4
Pirlerkondu Turkey see Taşkent
Pirmasens Germany 63 H5
Pirojpur Bangl. 105 G5
Pir Panjal Pass India 104 C2
Pir Panjal Range mts India/Pak. 111 I3
Piru Seram Indon. 83 D3
Piru, Teluk b. Seram Indon. 83 D3
Piryatin Ukr. see Pyryatyn
Pirzada Afgh. 111 G4
Pisa Italy 68 D3
Pisae Italy see Pisa
Pisagua Chile 176 D7
Pisang i. Maluku Indon. 83 D3
Pisang, Kepulauan is Indon. 81 I7
Pisau, Tanjung pt Malaysia 85 G1
Pisaurum Italy see Pesaro
Pisco Peru 176 C6
Písek Czech Rep. 57 O6
Pisha China see Ningnan
Pishan Xinjiang China 99 B5
Pīshīn Iran 102 B6
Pishin Pak. 111 G4
Pishin Lora r. Pak. 111 G4
Pishpek Kyrg. see Bishkek
Pisidia reg. Turkey 112 C3
Pising Sulawesi Indon. 83 B4

▶Pissis, Cerro Arg. 178 C3
4th highest mountain in South America.

Pisté Mex. 167 H4
Pisticci Italy 68 G4
Pistoia Italy 68 D3
Pistoriae Italy see Pistoia
Pisuerga r. Spain 67 D3
Pita Guinea 120 B3
Pitaga Canada 153 I3
Pital Mex. 167 H5
Pitanga Brazil 179 A4
Pitangui Brazil 179 B2
Pitar India 104 B5
Pitarpunga Lake imp. l. Australia 138 A5
Pitcairn, Henderson, Ducie and Oeno Islands terr. S. Pacific Ocean see Pitcairn Islands
Pitcairn Island Pitcairn Islands 187 L7

▶Pitcairn Islands terr. S. Pacific Ocean 187 L7
United Kingdom Overseas Territory.

Piteå Sweden 54 L4
Piteälven r. Sweden 54 L4
Pitelino Rus. Fed. 53 I5
Piterka Rus. Fed. 53 J6
Pitești Romania 69 K2
Pithoragarh India 104 E3
Pitihra India 104 D5
Pitiquito Mex. 166 B2
Pitkas Point AK U.S.A. 148 G3
Pitkyaranta Rus. Fed. 52 F3
Pitlochry U.K. 60 F4
Pitong China see Pixian
Pitsane Siding Botswana 125 G3
Pitti i. India 106 B4
Pitt Island B.C. Canada 149 O5
Pitt Island N.Z. 133 I6
Pitt Islands Solomon Is see Vanikoro Islands
Pittsboro U.S.A. 161 F5
Pittsburg KS U.S.A. 161 E4
Pittsburg TX U.S.A. 161 E5
Pittsburgh U.S.A. 164 F3
Pittsfield MA U.S.A. 165 I2
Pittsfield ME U.S.A. 165 K1
Pittsfield VT U.S.A. 165 I2
Pittston U.S.A. 165 H3
Pittsworth Australia 138 E1
Pitz Lake Canada 151 L2
Piumhí Brazil 179 B3
Piura Peru 176 B5
Piute Mountains U.S.A. 159 F4
Piute Peak U.S.A. 158 D4
Piute Reservoir U.S.A. 159 G2
Piuthan Nepal 105 E3
Pivabiska r. Canada 152 E4
Pivka Slovenia 68 F2
Pixa Xinjiang China 99 B5
Pixariá mt. Greece see Pyxaria
Pixian China 96 D2
Pixley U.S.A. 158 D4
Pixoyal Mex. 167 H5
Piz Bernina mt. Italy/Switz. 68 C1
Piz Buin mt. Austria/Switz. 57 M7
Pizhanka Rus. Fed. 52 K4
Pizhi Nigeria 120 D4
Pizhma Rus. Fed. 52 J4
Pizhma r. Rus. Fed. 52 K4
Pizhma r. Rus. Fed. 52 L2
Pizhou Jiangsu China 95 I5
Pkulagalid Point Palau 82 [inset]
Pkulagasemieg pt Palau 82 [inset]
Pkulngril pt Palau 82 [inset]
Pkurengei pt Palau 82 [inset]
Placentia Canada 153 L5
Placentia Italy see Piacenza
Placentia Bay Canada 153 L5
Placer Masbate Phil. 82 C4
Placer Mindanao Phil. 82 D4
Placerville CA U.S.A. 158 C2
Placerville CO U.S.A. 159 I2
Placetas Cuba 163 E8
Plácido de Castro Brazil 176 E6
Plain Dealing U.S.A. 161 E5
Plainfield CT U.S.A. 165 J3
Plainfield IN U.S.A. 164 B4
Plainfield VT U.S.A. 165 I1
Plains KS U.S.A. 161 C4
Plains TX U.S.A. 161 C5
Plainview U.S.A. 161 C5
Plainville IN U.S.A. 164 B4
Plainville KS U.S.A. 160 D4
Plainwell U.S.A. 164 C2
Plaju Sumatera Indon. 84 D3
Plaka, Akra pt Kriti Greece see Plaka, Akrotirio
Plaka, Akrotirio pt Greece 69 L7
Plakoti, Cape Cyprus 107 B2
Plamondon Canada 151 H4
Plampang Sumbawa Indon. 85 G5
Planá Czech Rep. 63 M5
Plana Cays is Bahamas 163 F8
Planada U.S.A. 158 C3
Planaltina Brazil 179 B1
Plane r. Germany 63 M2
Plankinton U.S.A. 160 D3
Plano U.S.A. 161 D5
Planura Brazil 179 A3
Plaquemine U.S.A. 161 F6
Plasencia Spain 67 C3
Plaster City U.S.A. 159 F5
Plaster Rock Canada 153 I5
Plastun Rus. Fed. 90 E3
Platani r. Sicily Italy 68 E6
Platberg mt. S. Africa 125 I5

▶Plateau Antarctica
Lowest recorded annual mean temperature in the world.

Plateros Mex. 166 E4
Platina U.S.A. 158 B1
Platinum AK U.S.A. 148 G4
Plato Col. 176 D2
Platón Sánchez Mex. 167 F4
Platte r. U.S.A. 160 E3
Platte City U.S.A. 160 E4
Plattling Germany 63 M6
Plattsburgh U.S.A. 165 I1
Plattsmouth U.S.A. 160 E3
Plau Germany 63 M1
Plauen Germany 63 M4
Plauer See l. Germany 63 M1
Plavsk Rus. Fed. 53 H5
Playa Azul Mex. 166 E5
Playa Noriega, Lago l. Mex. 157 F7
Playas Ecuador 176 B4
Playas Lake U.S.A. 159 I6
Plây Ku Vietnam 87 E4
Playón Mex. 166 C3
Pleasant, Lake U.S.A. 159 G5
Pleasant Bay U.S.A. 165 K3
Pleasant Grove U.S.A. 159 H1
Pleasant Hill Lake U.S.A. 164 D3
Pleasanton U.S.A. 161 D6
Pleasant Point N.Z. 139 C7
Pleasantville U.S.A. 165 H4
Pleasure Ridge Park U.S.A. 164 C4
Pleaux France 66 F4
Pledger Lake Canada 152 E4
Plei Doch Vietnam 87 D4
Pleihari Martapura, Suaka Margasatwa nature res. Indon. 85 F3
Pleihari Tanah, Suaka Margasatwa nature res. Kalimantan Indon. 85 F4
Plei Kân Vietnam 86 D4
Pleinfeld Germany 63 K5
Pleiße r. Germany 63 M3
Plenty watercourse Australia 136 B5
Plenty, Bay of g. N.Z. 139 F3
Plentywood U.S.A. 156 G2
Plesetsk Rus. Fed. 52 I3
Pleshchenitsy Belarus see Plyeshchanitsy
Plétipi, Lac l. Canada 153 H4
Plettenberg Germany 63 H3
Plettenberg Bay S. Africa 124 F8
Pleven Bulg. 69 K3
Plevna Bulg. see Pleven
Plieran r. Malaysia 85 F2
Pljevlja Montenegro 69 H3
Płock Poland 57 Q4
Pločno mt. Bos.-Herz. 68 G3
Plodovoye Rus. Fed. 52 F3
Ploemeur France 66 C3
Ploești Romania see Ploiești
Ploiești Romania 69 L2
Plomb du Cantal mt. France 66 F4
Ploskoye Rus. Fed. see Stanovoye
Płoty Poland 57 O4
Ploudalmézeau France 66 B2
Plouzané France 66 B2
Plovdiv Bulg. 69 K3
Plover Cove Reservoir H.K. China 97 [inset]
Plover Islands AK U.S.A. 148 I1
Płozk Poland see Płock
Plum U.S.A. 164 F3
Plumridge Lakes salt flat Australia 135 D7
Plungė Lith. 55 L9
Plutarco Elías Calles, Presa resr Mex. 157 F7
Plutarco Elís Calles, Presa resr Mex. 166 C2
Pluto, Lac l. Canada 153 H3
Plyeshchanitsy Belarus 55 O9
Ply Huey Wati, Khao mt. Myanmar/Thai. 86 B3
Plymouth U.K. 59 C8
Plymouth CA U.S.A. 158 C2
Plymouth IN U.S.A. 164 B3
Plymouth MA U.S.A. 165 J3
Plymouth NC U.S.A. 162 E5
Plymouth NH U.S.A. 165 J2
Plymouth WI U.S.A. 164 B2

▶Plymouth Montserrat 169 L5
Capital of Montserrat, abandoned in 1997 owing to volcanic activity. Temporary capital established at Brades.

Plymouth Bay U.S.A. 165 J3
Plynlimon hill U.K. 59 D6
Plyussa Rus. Fed. 55 P7
Plzeň Czech Rep. 57 N6
Pô Burkina Faso 120 C3
Po r. Italy 68 E2
Pô, Parc National de nat. park Burkina Faso 120 C3
Po, Tanjung pt Malaysia 85 E2
Poás, Volcán vol. Costa Rica 166 [inset] I7
Poat i. Indon. 83 B3
Pobeda Peak China/Kyrg. 98 C4
Pobedy, Pik mt. China/Kyrg. see Pobeda Peak
Pocahontas U.S.A. 161 F4
Pocatello U.S.A. 156 E4
Pochala Sudan 121 G4
Pochayiv Ukr. 53 E6
Pochep Rus. Fed. 53 G5
Pochinki Rus. Fed. 53 J5
Pochinok Rus. Fed. 53 G5
Pochutla Mex. 168 E5
Pock, Gunung hill Malaysia 85 G1
Pocking Germany 57 N6
Pocklington U.K. 58 G5
Poções Brazil 179 C1
Pocomoke City U.S.A. 165 H4
Pocomoke Sound b. U.S.A. 165 H5
Poconé Brazil 177 G7
Pocono Mountains hills U.S.A. 165 H3
Pocono Summit U.S.A. 165 H3
Poco Ranakah vol. Flores Indon. 83 B5
Poços de Caldas Brazil 179 B3
Podanur India 106 C4
Poddor'ye Rus. Fed. 52 F4
Podgorenskiy Rus. Fed. 53 H6

▶Podgorica Montenegro 69 H3
Capital of Montenegro

Podgornoye Rus. Fed. 76 J4
Podile India 106 C3
Podișul Transilvaniei plat. Romania see Transylvanian Basin
Podkamennaya Tunguska r. Rus. Fed. 77 K3
Podocarpus, Parque Nacional nat. park Ecuador 176 C4
Podol'sk Rus. Fed. 53 H5
Podporozh'ye Rus. Fed. 52 G3
Podujevë Kosovo 69 I3
Podujevo Kosovo see Podujevë
Podz' Rus. Fed. 52 K3
Poelela, Lagoa l. Moz. 125 L3
Poeppel Corner salt flat Australia 137 B5
Poetovio Slovenia see Ptuj
Pofadder S. Africa 124 D5
Pogar Rus. Fed. 53 G5
Poggibonsi Italy 68 D3
Poggio di Montieri mt. Italy 68 D3
Pogradec Albania 69 I4
Pogranichnik Afgh. 111 F3
Pogranichnyy Rus. Fed. 90 C3
Poh Sulawesi Indon. 83 B3
Po Hai g. China see Bo Hai
P'ohang S. Korea 91 C5
Pohnpei atoll Micronesia 186 G5
Pohri India 104 D4
Poi India 105 H4
Poiana Mare Romania 69 J3
Poigar Sulawesi Indon. 83 C2
Poinsett, Cape Antarctica 188 F2
Point Arena U.S.A. 158 B2
Point au Fer Island U.S.A. 161 F6
Pointe a la Hache U.S.A. 161 F6
Pointe-à-Pitre Guadeloupe 169 L5
Pointe-Noire Congo 123 B4
Point Hope AK U.S.A. 148 F1
Point Lake Canada 150 H1
Point Lay AK U.S.A. 148 G1
Point of Rocks U.S.A. 156 F4
Point Pelee National Park Canada 164 D3
Point Pleasant NJ U.S.A. 165 H3
Point Pleasant WV U.S.A. 164 D4
Poitiers France 66 E3
Poitou reg. France 66 E3
Poix-de-Picardie France 62 B5
Pojuca r. Brazil 179 D1
Pokaran India 104 B4
Pokataroo Australia 138 D2
Pokcha Rus. Fed. 51 R3
Pokhara Nepal 105 E3
Pokhran Landi Pak. 111 G5
Pokhvistnevo Rus. Fed. 51 Q5
Pok Liu Chau i. H.K. China see Lamma Island
Poko Dem. Rep. Congo 122 C3
Poko Mountain hill AK U.S.A. 148 G1
Pokosnoye Rus. Fed. 88 I1
P'ok'r Kovkas mts Asia see Lesser Caucasus
Pokrovka Chitinskaya Oblast' Rus. Fed. 90 A1
Pokrovka Primorskiy Kray Rus. Fed. 90 C4
Pokrovsk Respublika Sakha (Yakutiya) Rus. Fed. 77 N3
Pokrovsk Saratovskaya Oblast' Rus. Fed. see Engel's
Pokrovskoye Rus. Fed. 53 H7
Pokshen'ga r. Rus. Fed. 52 J3
Pol India 104 C5
Pola Croatia see Pula
Pola Mindoro Phil. 82 C3
Polacca Wash watercourse U.S.A. 159 H4
Pola de Lena Spain 67 D2
Pola de Siero Spain 67 D2
Poland country Europe 50 J5
Poland NY U.S.A. 165 H2
Poland OH U.S.A. 164 E3
Polar Plateau Antarctica 188 A1
Polatlı Turkey 112 D3
Polatsk Belarus 55 P9
Polavaram India 106 D2
Polcirkeln Sweden 54 L3
Pol-e 'Alam 111 H3
Polee i. Papua Indon. 83 D3
Pol-e Fāsā Iran 110 D4
Pol-e Khatum Iran 111 F2
Pol-e Khomrī Afgh. 111 H3
Pol-e Safid Iran 110 D2
Polessk Rus. Fed. 55 L9
Poles'ye marsh Belarus/Ukr. see Pripet Marshes
Polewali Sulawesi Barat Indon. 83 A3
Polgahawela Sri Lanka 106 D5
Poli Shandong China 95 I5
Poli Cyprus see Polis
Políaigos i. Greece see Polyaigos
Police Poland 57 O4
Policoro Italy 68 G4
Poligny France 66 G3
Polikastron Greece see Polykastro
Polillo i. Phil. 82 C3
Polillo Islands Phil. 82 C3
Polillo Strait Phil. 82 C3
Polis Cyprus 107 A2
Polis'ke Ukr. 53 F6
Polis'kyy Zapovidnyk nature res. Ukr. 53 F6
Polkan Rus. Fed. 52 K2
Políyiros Greece see Polygyros
Polkowice Poland 57 P5
Pollachi India 106 C4
Pollard Islands U.S.A. see Gardner Pinnacles
Polle Germany 63 J3
Pollino, Monte mt. Italy 68 G5
Pollino, Parco Nazionale del nat. park Italy 68 G5
Polloc Harbour b. Mindanao Phil. 82 C5
Pollock Pines U.S.A. 158 C2
Pollock Reef Australia 135 C8
Polmak Norway 54 O1
Polnovat Rus. Fed. 51 T3
Polo Fin. 54 P4
Poloat atoll Micronesia see Puluwat
Pologi Ukr. see Polohy
Polohy Ukr. 53 H7
Polokwane S. Africa 125 I2
Polomoloc Mindanao Phil. 82 D5
Polonne Ukr. 53 E6
Polonnoye Ukr. see Polonne
Polotsk Belarus see Polatsk
Polperro U.K. 59 C8
Polska country Europe see Poland
Polson U.S.A. 156 E3
Polta r. Rus. Fed. 52 I2
Poltava Ukr. 53 G6
Poltoratsk Turkm. see Aşgabat
Põltsamaa Estonia 55 N7
Polunochnoye Rus. Fed. 51 S3
Põlva Estonia 55 O7
Polvadera U.S.A. 157 G6
Polvijärvi Fin. 54 P5
Polvoxal Mex. 167 H5
Polyaigos i. Greece 69 K6
Polyanovgrad Bulg. see Karnobat
Polyarnyy Chukotskiy Avtonomnyy Okrug Rus. Fed. 77 S3
Polyarnyy Murmanskaya Oblast' Rus. Fed. 54 R2
Polyarnyye Zori Rus. Fed. 54 R3
Polyarnyy Ural mts Rus. Fed. 51 S2
Polygyros Greece 69 J4
Polykastro Greece 69 J4
Polynesia is Pacific Ocean 186 I6
Polynésie Française terr. S. Pacific Ocean see French Polynesia
Pom Indon. 81 J7
Pomarkku Fin. 55 M6
Pombal Pará Brazil 177 H4
Pombal Paraíba Brazil 177 K5
Pombal Port. 67 B4
Pomene Moz. 125 L2
Pomeranian Bay Poland 57 O3
Pomeroy S. Africa 125 J5
Pomeroy U.K. 61 F3
Pomeroy OH U.S.A. 164 D4
Pomeroy WA U.S.A. 156 D3
Pomezia Italy 68 E4
Pomfret S. Africa 124 F3
Pomona Belize 167 H5
Pomona Namibia 124 B4
Pomona U.S.A. 158 E4
Pomorie Bulg. 69 L3
Pomorskie, Pojezierze reg. Poland 57 O4
Pomorskiy Bereg coastal area Rus. Fed. 52 G2
Pomorskiy Proliv sea chan. Rus. Fed. 52 K1
Pomos Point Cyprus 107 A2
Pomo Tso l. China see Puma Yumco
Pomou, Akra pt Cyprus see Pomos Point
Pomozdino Rus. Fed. 52 L3
Pompain Xizang China 99 F7
Pompano Beach U.S.A. 163 D7
Pompei Italy 68 F4
Pompéia Brazil 179 A3
Pompey France 62 G6
Pompeyevka Rus. Fed. 90 C2
Ponape atoll Micronesia see Pohnpei
Ponask Lake Canada 151 M4
Ponazyrevo Rus. Fed. 52 J4
Ponca City U.S.A. 161 D4
Ponce Puerto Rico 169 K5
Ponce de Leon Bay U.S.A. 163 D7
Poncheville, Lac l. Canada 152 F4
Pondicherry India see Puducherry
Pondicherry union terr. India see Puducherry
Pondichéry India see Puducherry
Pond Inlet Canada 189 K2
Ponds Bay Canada see Pond Inlet
Poneloya Nicaragua 166 [inset] I6
Ponente, Riviera di coastal area Italy 68 B3
Poneto U.S.A. 164 C3
Ponferrada Spain 67 C2
Pongara, Pointe pt Gabon 122 A3
Pongaroa N.Z. 139 F5
Pongda Xizang China 99 F7
Pongo watercourse Sudan 121 F4
Pongola r. S. Africa 125 K4
Pongolapoort Dam l. S. Africa 125 J4
Poniki, Gunung mt. Indon. 83 B2
Ponindilisa, Tanjung pt Indon. 83 B3
Ponnagyun Myanmar 86 A2
Ponnaivar r. India 106 C4
Ponnampet India 106 B3
Ponnani India 106 B4
Ponnyadaung Range mts Myanmar 86 A2
Pono Indon. 81 I8
Ponoka Canada 150 H4
Ponorogo Jawa Indon. 85 E4
Ponoy r. Rus. Fed. 52 I2
Pons r. Canada 153 H2

▶Ponta Delgada Arquipélago dos Açores 184 G3
Capital of the Azores.

Ponta Grossa Brazil 179 A4
Pontal Brazil 179 A3
Pontalina Brazil 179 A2
Pont-à-Mousson France 62 G6
Ponta Porã Brazil 178 E2
Pontarfynach U.K. see Devil's Bridge
Pont-Audemer France 59 H9
Pontault-Combault France 62 C6
Pontax r. Canada 152 F4
Pontchartrain, Lake U.S.A. 161 F6
Pont-de-Loup Belgium 62 E4
Ponte Alta do Norte Brazil 177 I6
Ponte de Sor Port. 67 B4
Ponte Firme Brazil 179 B2
Pontefract U.K. 58 F5
Ponteix Canada 151 J5
Ponteland U.K. 58 F3
Ponte Nova Brazil 179 C3
Pontes-e-Lacerda Brazil 177 G7
Pontevedra Spain 67 B2
Ponthierville Dem. Rep. Congo see Ubundu
Pontiac IL U.S.A. 160 F3
Pontiac MI U.S.A. 164 D2
Pontiae is Italy see Ponziane, Isole
Pontianak Kalimantan Indon. 85 E3
Pontine Islands is Italy see Ponziane, Isole
Pont-l'Abbé France 66 B3
Pontoise France 62 C5
Ponton watercourse Australia 135 C7
Ponton Canada 151 L4
Pontotoc U.S.A. 161 F5
Pont-Ste-Maxence France 62 C5
Pontypool U.K. 59 D7
Pontypridd U.K. 59 D7
Ponza, Isola di i. Italy 68 E4
Ponziane, Isole is Italy 68 E4
Poochera Australia 135 F8
Poole U.K. 59 F8
Poole U.S.A. 164 B5
Poolowanna Lake salt flat Australia 137 B5
Poona India see Pune
Pooncarie Australia 137 C7
Poonch India see Punch
Poopelloe Lake salt l. Australia 138 B3
Poopó, Lago de l. Bol. 176 E7
Poor Knights Islands N.Z. 139 E2
Poorman AK U.S.A. 148 I2
Popayán Col. 176 C3
Poperinge Belgium 62 C4
Popigay r. Rus. Fed. 77 L2
Popiltah Australia 137 C7
Popilta Lake imp. l. Australia 137 C7
Poplar r. Canada 151 L4
Poplar U.S.A. 156 G2
Poplar Bluff U.S.A. 161 F4
Poplar Camp U.S.A. 164 E5
Poplarville U.S.A. 161 F6

▶Popocatépetl, Volcán vol. Mex. 168 E5
5th highest mountain in North America.

Popoh Jawa Indon. 85 E5
Popokabaka Dem. Rep. Congo 123 B4
Popondetta P.N.G. 81 L8
Popovichskaya Rus. Fed. see Kalininskaya
Popovo Bulg. 69 L3
Popovo Polje plain Bos.-Herz. 68 G3
Poppberg hill Germany 63 L5
Poppenberg hill Germany 63 K3
Poprad Slovakia 57 R6
Poptún Guat. 167 H5
Poquoson U.S.A. 165 G5
Porali r. Pak. 111 G5
Porangahau N.Z. 139 F5
Porangatu Brazil 179 A1
Porbandar India 104 B5
Porcher Island B.C. Canada 149 O5
Porcos r. Brazil 179 B1
Porcupine r. Canada/U.S.A. 149 K2
Porcupine, Cape Canada 153 K3
Porcupine Abyssal Plain sea feature N. Atlantic Ocean 184 G2
Porcupine Gorge National Park Australia 136 D4
Porcupine Hills Canada 151 K4
Porcupine Mountains U.S.A. 160 F2
Poreč Croatia 68 E2
Porecatu Brazil 179 A3
Poretskoye Rus. Fed. 53 J5
Porgyang Xizang China 99 C6
Pori Fin. 55 L6
Porirua N.Z. 139 E5
Porkhov Rus. Fed. 55 P8
Porlamar Venez. 176 F1
Pormpuraaw Australia 136 C2
Pornic France 66 C3
Poro i. Phil. 82 D4
Poronaysk Rus. Fed. 90 F2
Porong Xizang China 99 E7
Poros Greece 69 J6
Porosozero Rus. Fed. 52 G3
Porpoise Bay Antarctica 188 G2
Porsangerfjorden sea chan. Norway 54 N1
Porsangerhalvøya pen. Norway 54 N1
Porsgrunn Norway 55 F7
Porsuk r. Turkey 69 N5
Portadown U.K. 61 F3
Portaferry U.K. 61 G3
Portage MI U.S.A. 164 C2
Portage PA U.S.A. 165 F3
Portage WI U.S.A. 160 F3
Portage Creek AK U.S.A. 148 H4
Portage Lakes U.S.A. 164 E3
Portage la Prairie Canada 151 L5
Portal U.S.A. 160 C1
Port Alberni Canada 150 E5
Port Albert Australia 138 C7
Portalegre Port. 67 C4
Portales U.S.A. 161 C5
Port-Alfred Canada see La Baie
Port Alfred S. Africa 125 H7
Port Alice Canada 150 E5
Port Allegany U.S.A. 165 F3
Port Allen U.S.A. 161 F6
Port Alma Australia 136 E4
Port Alsworth AK U.S.A. 148 I3
Port Angeles U.S.A. 156 C2
Port Antonio Jamaica 169 I5

Portarlington Ireland 61 E4
Port Arthur Australia 137 [inset]
Port Arthur *Liaoning* China *see* Lüshun
Port Arthur U.S.A. 161 E6
Port Askaig U.K. 60 C5
Port Augusta Australia 137 B7

▶Port-au-Prince Haiti 169 J5
Capital of Haiti.

Port Austin U.S.A. 164 D1
Port aux Choix Canada 153 K4
Portavogie U.K. 61 G3
Port Barton *b. Palawan* Phil. 82 B4
Port Beaufort S. Africa 124 E8
Port Blair India 87 A5
Port Bolster Canada 164 F1
Portbou Spain 67 H2
Port Brabant *N.W.T.* Canada *see* Tuktoyaktuk
Port Burwell Canada 164 E2
Port Campbell Australia 138 A7
Port Campbell National Park Australia 138 A7
Port Carling Canada 164 F1
Port-Cartier Canada 153 I4
Port Chalmers N.Z. 139 C7
Port Charlotte U.S.A. 163 D7
Port Clarence *b. AK* U.S.A. 148 F2
Port Clements *B.C.* Canada 149 N5
Port Clinton U.S.A. 164 D3
Port Credit Canada 164 F2
Port-de-Paix Haiti 169 J5
Port Dickson Malaysia 84 C2
Port Douglas Australia 136 D3
Port Edward *B.C.* Canada 149 O5
Port Edward S. Africa 125 J6
Porteira Brazil 177 G4
Porteirinha Brazil 179 C1
Portel Brazil 177 H4
Port Elgin Canada 164 E1
Port Elizabeth S. Africa 125 G7
Port Ellen U.K. 60 C5
Port Erin Isle of Man 58 C4
Porter Lake *N.W.T.* Canada 151 J2
Porter Lake *Sask.* Canada 151 J3
Porter Landing *B.C.* Canada 149 O4
Porterville S. Africa 124 D7
Porterville U.S.A. 158 D3
Port Étienne Mauritania *see* Nouâdhibou
Port Everglades U.S.A. *see* Fort Lauderdale
Port Fitzroy N.Z. 139 E3
Port Francqui Dem. Rep. Congo *see* Ilebo
Port-Gentil Gabon 122 A4
Port Gibson *MS* U.S.A. 167 H2
Port Glasgow U.K. 60 E5
Port Graham *AK* U.S.A. 149 J4
Port Harcourt Nigeria 120 D4
Port Harrison Canada *see* Inukjuak
Porthcawl U.K. 59 D7
Port Hedland Australia 134 B5
Port Heiden *AK* U.S.A. 148 H4
Port Heiden *b. AK* U.S.A. 148 H4
Port Henry U.S.A. 165 I1
Port Herald Malawi *see* Nsanje
Porthleven U.K. 59 B8
Porthmadog U.K. 59 C6
Port Hope Canada 165 F2
Port Hope Simpson Canada 153 L3
Port Hueneme U.S.A. 158 D4
Port Huron U.S.A. 164 D2
Portimão Port. 67 B5
Port Jackson Australia *see* Sydney
Port Jackson *inlet* Australia 138 E4
Port Keats Australia *see* Wadeye
Port Klang Malaysia *see* Pelabuhan Klang
Port Láirge Ireland *see* Waterford
Portland *N.S.W.* Australia 138 D4
Portland *Vic.* Australia 137 C8
Portland *IN* U.S.A. 164 C3
Portland *ME* U.S.A. 165 J2
Portland *MI* U.S.A. 164 C2
Portland *OR* U.S.A. 156 C3
Portland *TN* U.S.A. 164 B5
Portland, Isle of *pen.* U.K. 59 E8
Portland Bill *hd* U.K. *see* Bill of Portland
Portland Creek Pond *l.* Canada 153 K4
Portland Roads Australia 136 C2
Port-la-Nouvelle France 66 F5
Portlaoise Ireland 61 E4
Port Lavaca U.S.A. 161 D6
Portlaw Ireland 61 E5
Portlethen U.K. 60 G3
Port Lincoln Australia 137 A7
Port Lions *AK* U.S.A. 148 I4
Portlock *AK* U.S.A. 149 J4
Port Loko Sierra Leone 120 B4

▶Port Louis Mauritius 185 L7
Capital of Mauritius.

Port-Lyautey Morocco *see* Kénitra
Port Macquarie Australia 138 F3
Portmadoc U.K. *see* Porthmadog
Port McNeill Canada 150 E5
Port-Menier Canada 153 I4
Port Moller *AK* U.S.A. 148 G5
Port Moller *b. AK* U.S.A. 148 G5

▶Port Moresby P.N.G. 81 L8
Capital of Papua New Guinea.

Portnaguran U.K. 60 C2
Portnahaven U.K. 60 C5
Port nan Giúran U.K. *see* Portnaguran
Port Neill Australia 137 B7
Portneuf *r.* Canada 153 H4
Port Nis *Scotland* U.K. *see* Port of Ness
Port Nis U.K. *see* Port of Ness
Port Noarlunga Australia 137 B7
Port Nolloth S. Africa 124 C5
Port Norris U.S.A. 165 H4
Port-Nouveau-Québec Canada *see* Kangiqsualujjuaq
Porto Port. *see* Oporto
Porto Acre Brazil 176 E5
Porto Alegre Brazil 179 A5
Porto Alexandre Angola *see* Tombua
Porto Amboim Angola 123 B5
Porto Amélia Moz. *see* Pemba
Porto Artur Brazil 177 G6
Porto Belo Brazil 179 A4
Portobelo Panama 166 [inset] K7
Portobelo, Parque Nacional *nat. park* Panama 166 [inset] K7
Port O'Brien *AK* U.S.A. 148 I4
Porto de Moz Brazil 177 H4
Porto de Santa Cruz Brazil 179 C1
Porto dos Gaúchos Óbidos Brazil 177 G6
Porto Esperança Brazil 177 G7
Porto Esperidião Brazil 177 G7
Portoferraio Italy 68 D3
Port of Ness U.K. 60 C2
Porto Franco Brazil 177 I5

▶Port of Spain Trin. and Tob. 169 L6
Capital of Trinidad and Tobago.

Porto Grande Brazil 177 H3
Portogruaro Italy 68 E2
Porto Jofre Brazil 177 G7
Portola U.S.A. 158 C2
Portomaggiore Italy 68 D2
Porto Mendes Brazil 178 F2
Porto Murtinho Brazil 178 E2
Porto Nacional Brazil 177 I6

▶Porto-Novo Benin 120 D4
Capital of Benin.

Porto Novo Cape Verde 120 [inset]
Porto Primavera, Represa *resr* Brazil 178 F2
Port Orchard U.S.A. 156 C3
Port Orford U.S.A. 156 B4
Porto Rico Angola 123 B4
Porto Santo, Ilha de *i.* Madeira 120 B1
Porto Seguro Brazil 179 D2
Porto Tolle Italy 68 E2
Porto Torres *Sardinia* Italy 68 C4
Porto União Brazil 179 A4
Porto-Vecchio *Corsica* France 66 I6
Porto Velho Brazil 176 F5
Portoviejo Ecuador 176 B4
Porto Wálter Brazil 176 D5
Portpatrick U.K. 60 D6
Port Perry Canada 165 F1
Port Phillip Bay Australia 138 B7
Port Pirie Australia 137 B7
Port Radium Canada *see* Echo Bay
Portreath U.K. 59 B8
Portree U.K. 60 C3
Port Rexton Canada 153 L4
Port Royal U.S.A. 165 G4
Port Royal Sound *inlet* U.S.A. 163 D5
Portrush U.K. 61 F2
Port Safaga Egypt *see* Būr Safājah
Port Safety *AK* U.S.A. 148 F2
Port Said Egypt 107 A4
Port St Joe U.S.A. 163 C6
Port St Lucie City U.S.A. 163 D7
Port St Mary Isle of Man 58 C4
Portsalon Ireland 61 E2
Port Sanilac U.S.A. 164 D2
Port Severn Canada 164 F1
Port Shepstone S. Africa 125 J6
Port Simpson *B.C.* Canada *see* Lax Kw'alaams
Portsmouth U.K. 59 F8
Portsmouth *NH* U.S.A. 165 J2
Portsmouth *OH* U.S.A. 164 D4
Portsmouth *VA* U.S.A. 165 G5
Portsoy U.K. 60 G3
Port Stanley Falkland Is *see* Stanley
Port Stephens *b.* Australia 138 F4
Portstewart U.K. 61 F2
Port Sudan Sudan 108 E6
Port Sulphur *LA* U.S.A. 167 H2
Port Swettenham Malaysia *see* Pelabuhan Klang
Port Talbot U.K. 59 D7
Port Tambang *b. Luzon* Phil. 82 C3
Porttipahdan tekojärvi *l.* Fin. 54 O2
Port Townsend U.S.A. 156 C2
Portugal *country* Europe 67 C4
Portugalete Spain 67 E2
Portugália Angola *see* Chitato
Portuguese East Africa *country* Africa *see* Mozambique
Portuguese Guinea *country* Africa *see* Guinea-Bissau
Portuguese Timor *country* Asia *see* East Timor
Portuguese West Africa *country* Africa *see* Angola
Portumna Ireland 61 D4
Portus Herculis Monoeci *country* Europe *see* Monaco
Port-Vendres France 66 F5

▶Port Vila Vanuatu 133 G3
Capital of Vanuatu.

Portville U.S.A. 165 F2
Port Vladimir Rus. Fed. 54 R2
Port Waikato N.Z. 139 E3
Port Washington U.S.A. 164 B2
Port William U.K. 60 E6
Porvenir Bol. 176 E6
Porvenir Chile 178 B8
Porvoo Fin. 55 N6
Posada Spain 67 D2
Posada de Llanera Spain *see* Posada
Posadas Arg. 178 E3
Posen Poland *see* Poznań
Posen U.S.A. 164 D1
Poseyville U.S.A. 164 B4
Poshekhon'ye Rus. Fed. 52 H4
Poshekon'ye-Volodarsk Rus. Fed. *see* Poshekhon'ye
Posht-e Badam Iran 110 D3
Poshteh-ye Chaqvīr *hill* Iran 110 E4
Posht-e Kūh *mts* Iran 110 B3
Posht-e Rūd-e Zamindavar *reg.* Afgh. *see* Zamīndāvar
Posht Kūh *hill* Iran 110 C2
Posio Fin. 54 P3
Poskam *Xinjiang* China *see* Zepu
Poso *Sulawesi* Indon. 83 B3
Poso *r.* Indon. 83 B3
Poso, Danau *l.* Indon. 83 B3
Poso, Teluk *b.* Indon. 83 B3
Posof Turkey 113 F2
Posŏng S. Korea 91 B6
Possession Island Namibia 124 B4
Pößneck Germany 63 L4
Possum Kingdom Lake *TX* U.S.A. 167 F1
Post U.S.A. 161 C5
Postavy Belarus *see* Pastavy
Poste-de-la-Baleine Canada *see* Kuujjuarapik
Poste Weygand Alg. 120 D2
Postmasburg S. Africa 124 F5
Poston U.S.A. 159 F4
Postville Canada 153 K3
Postville U.S.A. 152 C6
Postysheve Ukr. *see* Krasnoarmiys'k
Pota *Flores* Indon. 83 B5
Pótam Mex. 166 C3
Poté Brazil 179 C2
Poteau U.S.A. 161 E5
Potegaon India 106 D2
Potentia Italy *see* Potenza
Potenza Italy 68 F4
Poth U.S.A. 161 D6
P'ot'i Georgia 113 F2
Potikal India 106 D2
Potiraguá Brazil 179 D1
Potiskum Nigeria 120 E3
Potlatch U.S.A. 156 D3
Pot Mountain U.S.A. 156 E3
Po Toi *i. H.K.* China 97 [inset]
Potomac *r.* U.S.A. 165 G4
Potomana, Gunung *mt.* Indon. 83 C5
Potosí Bol. 176 E7
Potosi U.S.A. 160 F4
Potosi Mountain U.S.A. 159 F4
Pototan *Panay* Phil. 82 C4
Potrerillos Chile 178 C3
Potrerillos Hond. 166 [inset] I6
Potrero del Llano *Chihuahua* Mex. 166 D2
Potsdam Germany 63 N2
Potsdam U.S.A. 165 H1
Potter U.S.A. 160 C3
Potterne U.K. 59 E7
Potters Bar U.K. 59 G7
Potter Valley U.S.A. 158 B2
Pottstown U.S.A. 165 H3
Pottsville U.S.A. 165 G3
Pottuvil Sri Lanka 106 D5
Potwar *reg.* Pak. 111 I3
Pouch Cove Canada 153 L5
Poughkeepsie U.S.A. 165 I3
Poulin de Courval, Lac *l.* Canada 153 H4
Poulton-le-Fylde U.K. 58 E5
Pouso Alegre Brazil 179 B3
Poŭthĭsăt Cambodia 87 C4
Poŭthĭsăt, Stœng *r.* Cambodia 87 D4
Považská Bystrica Slovakia 57 Q6
Povenets Rus. Fed. 52 G3
Poverty Bay N.Z. 139 F4
Povlen *mt.* Serbia 69 H2
Póvoa de Varzim Port. 67 B3
Povorino Rus. Fed. 53 I6
Povorotnyy, Mys *hd* Rus. Fed. 90 D4
Poway U.S.A. 158 E5
Powder *r.* U.S.A. 156 G3
Powder, South Fork *r.* U.S.A. 156 G4
Powder River U.S.A. 156 G4
Powell *r.* U.S.A. 164 D5
Powell, Lake *resr* U.S.A. 159 H3
Powell Lake Canada 150 E5
Powell Mountain U.S.A. 158 D2
Powell Point Bahamas 163 E7
Powell River Canada 150 E5
Powhatan *AR* U.S.A. 161 F4
Powhatan *VA* U.S.A. 165 G5
Powo China 96 C1
Pōwrize Turkm. 110 E2
Poxoréu Brazil 177 H7
Poyang China *see* Boyang
Poyang Hu *l.* China 97 H2
Poyan Reservoir Sing. 87 [inset]
Poyarkovo Rus. Fed. 90 C2
Pozantı Turkey 112 D3
Požarevac Serbia 69 I2
Poza Rica Mex. 168 E4
Pozdeyevka Rus. Fed. 90 C2
Požega Croatia 68 G2
Požega Serbia 69 I3
Pozharskoye Rus. Fed. 90 D3
Poznań Poland 57 P4
Pozoblanco Spain 67 D4
Pozo Colorado Para. 178 E2
Pozo Nuevo Mex. 166 C2
Pozsony Slovakia *see* Bratislava
Pozzuoli Italy 68 F4
Prabumulih *Sumatera* Indon. 84 D3
Prachatice Czech Rep. 57 O6
Prachi *r.* India 105 F6
Prachin Buri Thai. 87 C4
Prachuap Khiri Khan Thai. 87 B5
Prades France 66 F5
Prado Brazil 179 D2

▶Prague Czech Rep. 57 O5
Capital of the Czech Republic.

Praha Czech Rep. *see* Prague

▶Praia Cape Verde 120 [inset]
Capital of Cape Verde.

Praia do Bilene Moz. 125 K3
Prainha Brazil 177 H4
Prairie Australia 136 D4
Prairie *r.* U.S.A. 160 E2
Prairie Dog Town Fork *r.* U.S.A. 161 C5
Prairie du Chien U.S.A. 160 F3
Prairie River Canada 151 K4
Pram, Khao *mt.* Thai. 87 B5
Pran *r.* Thai. 87 C4
Pran Buri Thai. 87 B4
Prapat *Sumatera* Indon. 84 B2
Prasonisi, Akra *pt Notio Aigaio* Greece *see* Prasonisi, Akrotirio
Prasonisi, Akrotirio *pt* Greece 69 L7
Prata Brazil 179 A2
Prata *r.* Brazil 179 A2
Prat de Llobregat Spain *see* El Prat de Llobregat
Prathes Thai *country* Asia *see* Thailand
Prato Italy 68 D3
Pratt U.S.A. 160 D4
Prattville U.S.A. 163 C5
Pravdinsk Rus. Fed. 55 L9
Praya *Lombok* Indon. 85 G5
Preah, Prêk *r.* Cambodia 87 D4
Preăh Vihéar Cambodia 87 D4
Preble U.S.A. 165 G2
Prechistoye *Smolenskaya Oblast'* Rus. Fed. 53 G5
Prechistoye *Yaroslavskaya Oblast'* Rus. Fed. 52 I4
Precipice National Park Australia 136 E5
Preeceville Canada 151 K5
Pregolya *r.* Rus. Fed. 55 L9
Preiļi Latvia 55 O8
Prelate Canada 151 I5
Premer Australia 138 D3
Prémery France 66 F3
Premnitz Germany 63 M2
Prentiss U.S.A. 161 F6
Prenzlau Germany 57 N4
Preparis Island Cocos Is 80 A4
Preparis North Channel Cocos Is 80 A4
Preparis South Channel Cocos Is 80 A4
Přerov Czech Rep. 57 P6
Presa de la Amistad, Parque Natural *nature res.* Mex. 167 E2
Presa San Antonio Mex. 167 E3
Prescelly Mts *hills* U.K. *see* Preseli, Mynydd
Prescott Canada 165 H1
Prescott *AR* U.S.A. 161 E5
Prescott *AZ* U.S.A. 159 G4
Prescott Valley U.S.A. 159 G4
Preseli, Mynydd *hills* U.K. 59 C7
Preševo Serbia 69 I3
Presidencia Roque Sáenz Peña Arg. 178 D3
Presidente Dutra Brazil 177 J5
Presidente Hermes Brazil 176 F6
Presidente Olegário Brazil 179 B2
Presidente Prudente Brazil 179 A3
Presidente Venceslau Brazil 179 A3
Presidio U.S.A. 161 B6
Preslav Bulg. *see* Veliki Preslav
Prešov Slovakia 53 D6
Prespa, Lake Europe 69 I4
Prespansko Ezero *l.* Europe *see* Prespa, Lake
Prespes *nat. park* Greece 69 I4
Prespës, Liqeni i *l.* Europe *see* Prespa, Lake
Presque Isle *ME* U.S.A. 162 G2
Presque Isle *MI* U.S.A. 164 D1
Pressburg Slovakia *see* Bratislava
Presteigne U.K. 59 D6
Preston U.K. 58 E5
Preston *ID* U.S.A. 156 F4
Preston *MN* U.S.A. 160 E3
Preston *MO* U.S.A. 160 E4
Preston, Cape Australia 134 B5
Prestonpans U.K. 60 G5
Prestonsburg U.S.A. 164 D5
Prestwick U.K. 60 E5
Preto *r. Bahia* Brazil 177 J6
Preto *r. Minas Gerais* Brazil 179 B2
Preto *r.* Brazil 179 D1

▶Pretoria S. Africa 125 I3
Official capital of South Africa.

Pretoria-Witwatersrand-Vereeniging *prov.* S. Africa *see* Gauteng
Pretzsch Germany 63 M3
Preussisch-Eylau Rus. Fed. *see* Bagrationovsk
Preußisch Stargard Poland *see* Starogard Gdański
Preveza Greece 69 I5
Prewitt U.S.A. 159 I4
Prey Vêng Cambodia 87 D5
Priaral'skiye Karakumy, Peski *des.* Kazakh. 102 B2
Priargunsk Rus. Fed. 95 I1
Pribilof Islands *AK* U.S.A. 148 E4
Priboj Serbia 69 H3
Price *r.* Australia 134 E3
Price *NC* U.S.A. 164 F5
Price *UT* U.S.A. 159 H2
Price *r.* U.S.A. 159 H2
Price Island Canada 150 D4
Prichard *AL* U.S.A. 161 F6
Prichard *WV* U.S.A. 164 D4
Pridorozhnoye Rus. Fed. *see* Khulkhuta
Priekule Latvia 55 L8
Priekuļi Latvia 55 N8
Priel'brus'ye, Natsional'nyy Park *nat. park* Rus. Fed. 53 I8
Prienai Lith. 55 M9
Prieska S. Africa 124 F5
Prievidza Slovakia 57 Q6
Prignitz *reg.* Germany 63 M1
Prijedor Bos.-Herz. 68 G2
Prijepolje Serbia 69 H3
Prikaspiyskaya Nizmennost' *lowland* Kazakh./Rus. Fed. *see* Caspian Lowland
Prilep Macedonia 69 I4
Priluki Ukr. *see* Pryluky
Přimda Czech Rep. 63 M5
Primero de Enero Cuba 163 E8
Primorsk Rus. Fed. 55 P6
Primorsk Ukr. *see* Prymors'k
Primorskiy Kray *admin. div.* Rus. Fed. 90 D3
Primorsko-Akhtarsk Rus. Fed. 53 H7
Primo Tapia Mex. 166 A1
Primrose Lake Canada 151 I4
Prims *r.* Germany 62 G5
Prince Albert Canada 151 J4
Prince Albert S. Africa 124 F7
Prince Albert Mountains Antarctica 188 H1
Prince Albert National Park Canada 151 J4
Prince Albert Peninsula Canada 146 G2
Prince Albert Road S. Africa 124 E7
Prince Alfred, Cape Canada 146 F2
Prince Alfred Hamlet S. Africa 124 D7
Prince Charles Island Canada 147 K3
Prince Charles Mountains Antarctica 188 E2
Prince Edward Island *prov.* Canada 153 J5

▶Prince Edward Islands Indian Ocean 185 K9
Part of South Africa.

Prince Edward Point Canada 165 G2
Prince Frederick U.S.A. 165 G4
Prince George Canada 150 F4
Prince Harald Coast Antarctica 188 D2
Prince of Wales, Cape *AK* U.S.A. 148 E2
Prince of Wales Island Australia 136 C1
Prince of Wales Island Canada 147 I2
Prince of Wales Island *AK* U.S.A. 149 N5
Prince of Wales Strait Canada 146 G2
Prince Patrick Island Canada 146 G2
Prince Regent Inlet *sea chan.* Canada 147 I2
Prince Rupert *B.C.* Canada 149 O5
Princess Anne U.S.A. 165 H4
Princess Astrid Coast Antarctica 188 C2
Princess Charlotte Bay Australia 136 C2
Princess Elizabeth Land *reg.* Antarctica 188 E2
Princess Mary Lake Canada 151 L1
Princess Ragnhild Coast Antarctica 188 C2
Princess Royal Island Canada 150 D4
Princeton Canada 150 F5
Princeton *CA* U.S.A. 158 B2
Princeton *IL* U.S.A. 160 F3
Princeton *IN* U.S.A. 164 B4
Princeton *MO* U.S.A. 160 E3
Princeton *NJ* U.S.A. 165 H3
Princeton *WV* U.S.A. 164 E5
Prince William Sound *b. AK* U.S.A. 149 K3
Príncipe *i.* São Tomé and Príncipe 120 D4
Prindle, Mount *AK* U.S.A. 149 K2
Prineville U.S.A. 156 C3
Prins Harald Kyst *coastal area* Antarctica *see* Prince Harald Coast
Prinzapolca Nicaragua 166 [inset] J6
Priozersk Rus. Fed. 55 Q6
Priozyorsk Rus. Fed. *see* Priozersk
Pripet *r.* Belarus/Ukr. 53 F6
also spelt Pryp"yat' (Ukraine) or Prypyats' (Belarus)
Pripet Marshes Belarus/Ukr. 53 E6
Prirechnyy Rus. Fed. 54 Q2

▶Prishtinë Kosovo 69 I3
Capital of Kosovo

Priština Kosovo *see* Prishtinë
Pritzier Germany 63 L1
Pritzwalk Germany 63 M1
Privas France 66 G4
Privlaka Croatia 68 F2
Privolzhsk Rus. Fed. 52 I4
Privolzhskaya Vozvyshennost' *hills* Rus. Fed. 53 J6
Privolzhskiy Rus. Fed. 53 J6
Privolzh'ye Rus. Fed. 53 K5
Priyutnoye Rus. Fed. 53 I7
Prizren Kosovo 69 I3
Probolinggo *Jawa* Indon. 85 F4
Probstzella Germany 63 L4
Probus U.K. 59 C8
Proddatur India 106 C3
Professor van Blommestein Meer *resr* Suriname 177 G3
Progreso *Coahuila* Mex. 167 E3
Progreso *Hidalgo* Mex. 167 F4
Progreso *Yucatán* Mex. 167 H4
Progress Rus. Fed. 90 C2
Project City U.S.A. 156 C4
Prokhladnyy Rus. Fed. 113 G2
Prokop'yevsk Rus. Fed. 88 F2
Prokuplje Serbia 69 I3
Proletarsk Rus. Fed. 53 I7
Proletarskaya Rus. Fed. *see* Proletarsk
Prome Myanmar *see* Pyè
Promissão Brazil 179 A3
Promissão, Represa *resr* Brazil 179 A3
Prophet *r.* Canada 150 F3
Prophet River Canada 150 F3
Propriá Brazil 177 K6
Proskurov Ukr. *see* Khmel'nyts'kyy
Prosperidad *Mindanao* Phil. 82 D4
Prosser U.S.A. 156 D3
Protem S. Africa 124 E8
Provadiya Bulg. 69 L3
Prøven Greenland *see* Kangersuatsiaq
Provence *reg.* France 66 G5
Providence *KY* U.S.A. 164 B5
Providence *MD* U.S.A. *see* Annapolis

▶Providence *RI* U.S.A. 165 J3
Capital of Rhode Island.

Providence, Cape N.Z. 139 A8
Providence, Cape *AK* U.S.A. 148 H4
Providencia, Isla de *i.* Caribbean Sea 169 H6
Provideniya Rus. Fed. 148 D2
Provincetown U.S.A. 165 J2
Provo U.S.A. 159 H1
Provost Canada 151 I4
Prudentópolis Brazil 179 A4
Prudhoe Bay *AK* U.S.A. 149 J1
Prudhoe Bay *AK* U.S.A. 149 J1
Prüm Germany 62 G4
Prüm *r.* Germany 62 G5
Prunelli-di-Fiumorbo *Corsica* France 66 I5
Pruntytown U.S.A. 164 E4
Prusa Turkey *see* Bursa
Prushkov Poland *see* Pruszków
Pruszków Poland 57 R4
Prut *r.* Europe 53 F7
Prydz Bay Antarctica 188 E2
Pryluky Ukr. 53 G6
Prymors'k Ukr. 53 H7
Prymors'ke Ukr. *see* Sartana
Pryp"yat' *r.* Ukr. 53 F6 *see* Pripet
Pryp"yat' (abandoned) Ukr. 53 F6
Prypyats' *r.* Belarus 51 L5 *see* Pripet
Przemyśl Poland 53 D6
Przheval'sk Kyrg. *see* Karakol
Przheval'sk Pristany Kyrg. 98 B4
Psara *i.* Greece 69 K5
Pskov Rus. Fed. 55 P8
Pskov, Lake Estonia/Rus. Fed. 55 O7
Pskov Oblast *admin. div.* Rus. Fed. *see* Pskovskaya Oblast'
Pskovskaya Oblast' *admin. div.* Rus. Fed. 55 P8
Pskovskoye Ozero *l.* Estonia/Rus. Fed. *see* Pskov, Lake
Ptolemaïda Greece 69 I4
Ptolemais Israel *see* 'Akko
Ptuj Slovenia 68 F1
Pu *r.* Indon. 84 C3
Pua Thai. 86 C3
Puaka *hill* Sing. 87 [inset]
Pu'an *Guizhou* China 96 E3
Pu'an *Sichuan* China 96 E2
Puan S. Korea 91 B6
Pucallpa Peru 176 D5
Pucheng *Fujian* China 97 H3
Pucheng *Shaanxi* China 95 G5
Puchezh Rus. Fed. 52 I4
Puch'ŏn S. Korea 91 B5
Pucio Point *Panay* Phil. 82 C4
Puck Poland 57 Q3
Pudai *watercourse* Afgh. *see* Dor
Pūdanū Iran 110 D3
Pudasjärvi Fin. 54 O4
Pudi *Kalimantan* Indon. 85 G3
Pudimoe S. Africa 124 G4
Pudong China 96 E4
Pudozh Rus. Fed. 52 H3
Pudsey U.K. 58 F5
Pudu China *see* Suizhou
Puducherri India *see* Puducherry
Puducherry India 106 C4
Puducherry *union terr.* India 106 C4
Pudukkottai India 106 C4
Puebla *Baja California* Mex. 159 F5
Puebla *Puebla* Mex. 168 E5
Puebla *state* Mex. 167 F5
Puebla de Sanabria Spain 67 C2
Puebla de Zaragoza Mex. *see* Puebla
Pueblo U.S.A. 157 G5
Pueblo Nuevo Mex. 166 D4
Pueblo Nuevo Nicaragua 166 [inset] I6
Pueblo Viejo, Laguna de *lag.* Mex. 167 F4
Pueblo Yaqui Mex. 166 C3
Puelches Arg. 178 C5
Puelén Arg. 178 C5
Puente de Ixtla Mex. 167 F5
Puente-Genil Spain 67 D5
Pu'er China 96 D4
Puerco *watercourse* U.S.A. 159 H4
Puerto Acosta Bol. 176 E7
Puerto Alegre Bol. 176 F6
Puerto Ángel Mex. 167 F6
Puerto Arista Mex. 167 G6
Puerto Armuelles Panama 166 [inset] J7
Puerto Ayacucho Venez. 176 E2
Puerto Bahía Negra Para. *see* Bahía Negra
Puerto Baquerizo Moreno *Galápagos* Ecuador 176 [inset]
Puerto Barrios Guat. 166 [inset] H6
Puerto Cabello Venez. 176 E1
Puerto Cabezas Nicaragua 166 [inset] J6
Puerto Cabo Gracias á Dios Nicaragua 166 [inset] J6
Puerto Carreño Col. 176 E2
Puerto Casado Para. 178 E2
Puerto Cavinas Bol. 176 E6
Puerto Coig Arg. 178 C8
Puerto Cortés Costa Rica 166 [inset] J7
Puerto Cortés Hond. 166 [inset] I6
Puerto Cortés Mex. 166 C3
Puerto de Lobos Mex. 166 B2
Puerto de Los Ángeles, Parque Natural *nature res.* Mex. 166 D4
Puerto de Morelos Mex. 167 I4
Puerto Escondido Mex. 168 E5
Puerto Francisco de Orellana Ecuador *see* Coca
Puerto Frey Bol. 176 F6
Puerto Génova Bol. 176 E6
Puerto Guarani Para. 178 E2
Puerto Heath Bol. 176 E6
Puerto Huitoto Col. 176 D3
Puerto Inírida Col. 176 E3
Puerto Isabel Bol. 177 G7
Puerto Juáres Mex. 167 I4
Puerto Leguizamo Col. 176 D4
Puerto Lempira Hond. 166 [inset] J6
Puerto Libertad Mex. 166 B2
Puerto Limón Costa Rica 166 [inset] J7
Puertollano Spain 67 D4
Puerto Lobos Arg. 178 C6
Puerto Madero Mex. 167 G6
Puerto Madryn Arg. 178 C6
Puerto Magdalena Mex. 166 B3
Puerto Maldonado Peru 176 E6
Puerto Máncora Peru 176 B4
Puerto México Mex. *see* Coatzacoalcos
Puerto Montt Chile 178 B6
Puerto Morazán Nicaragua 166 [inset] I6
Puerto Natales Chile 178 B8
Puerto Nuevo Col. 176 E2
Puerto Peñasco Mex. 166 B2
Puerto Pirámides Arg. 178 D6
Puerto Plata Dom. Rep. 169 J5
Puerto Portillo Peru 176 D5
Puerto Prado Peru 176 D6
Puerto Princesa *Palawan* Phil. 82 B4
Puerto Quepos Costa Rica 166 [inset] I7
Puerto Quetzal Guat. 166 H6
Puerto Real Mex. 167 H5
Puerto Rico Arg. 178 E3
Puerto Rico Bol. 176 E6

▶Puerto Rico *terr.* West Indies 169 K5
United States Commonwealth.

▶Puerto Rico Trench *sea feature* Caribbean Sea 184 D4
Deepest trench in the Atlantic Ocean.

Puerto Sandino Nicaragua 166 [inset] I6
Puerto San José Guat. 167 H6
Puerto Santa Cruz Arg. 178 C8
Puerto Sastre Para. 178 E2
Puerto Saucedo Bol. 176 F6
Puerto Somoza Nicaragua *see* Puerto Sandino
Puerto Suárez Bol. 177 G7
Puerto Supe Peru 176 C6
Puerto Vallarta Mex. 168 C4
Puerto Victoria Peru 176 D5
Puerto Visser Arg. 178 C7
Puerto Williams Chile 178 C8
Puerto Yartou Chile 178 B8
Puerto Ybapobó Para. 178 E2
Pugachev Rus. Fed. 53 K5
Pugal India 104 C3
Puge China 96 D3
Puger *Jawa* Indon. 85 F5
Pūhāl-e Khamīr, Kūh-e *mts* Iran 110 D5
Puhiwaero *c.* N.Z. *see* South West Cape
Puigmal *mt.* France/Spain 66 F5
Pui O Wan *b. H.K.* China 97 [inset]
Pujada Bay *Mindanao* Phil. 82 D5
Puji *Shaanxi* China *see* Wugong
Puji China *see* Puge
Pukaki, Lake N.Z. 139 C7
Pukapuka *atoll* Cook Is 133 J3
Pukaskwa National Park Canada 152 D4
Pukatawagan Canada 151 K4
Pukchin N. Korea 91 B4
Pukch'ŏng N. Korea 91 C4
Pukekohe N.Z. 139 E3
Puketeraki Range *mts* N.Z. 139 D6
Pukeuri Junction N.Z. 139 C7
Puksubaek-san *mt.* N. Korea 90 B4
Pula Croatia 68 E2
Pula *Sardinia* Italy 68 C5
Pulandian *Liaoning* China 95 J4
Pulandian Wan *b.* China 95 J4
Pulangi *r. Mindanao* Phil. 82 D5
Pulangpisau *Kalimantan* Indon. 85 F3
Pulap *atoll* Micronesia 81 L5
Pulasi *i.* Indon. 83 B4
Pulaski *NY* U.S.A. 165 G2
Pulaski *VA* U.S.A. 164 E5
Pulaski *WI* U.S.A. 164 A1
Pulaukijang *Sumatera* Indon. 84 C3
Pulau Pinang *state* Malaysia *see* Pinang

Pulau Simeulue, Suaka Margasatwa *nature res.* Indon. **87** A7
Pulheim Germany **62** G3
Pulicat Lake *inlet* India **106** D3
Pulivendla India **106** C3
Pulkkila Fin. **54** N4
Pullman U.S.A. **156** D3
Pulo Anna *i.* Palau **81** I6
Pulog, Mount *Luzon* Phil. **82** C2
Pulozero Rus. Fed. **54** R2
Púlpito, Punta *pt* Mex. **166** C3
Pulu *Xinjiang* China **99** C5
Pülümür Turkey **113** E3
Pulusuk *atoll* Micronesia **81** L5
Pulutan *Sulawesi* Indon. **83** C1
Puluwat *atoll* Micronesia **81** L5
Pulwama India **111** I3
Pumasillo, Cerro *mt.* Peru **176** D6
Puma Yumco *l.* China **99** E7
Pumiao China *see* **Yongning**
Puná, Isla *i.* Ecuador **176** B4
Punakha Bhutan **105** G4
Punch India **104** C2
Punchaw Canada **150** F4
Punda Maria S. Africa **125** J2
Pundri India **104** D3
Pune India **106** B2
P'ungsan N. Korea **90** C4
Puning China **97** H4
Punjab *state* India **104** C3
Punjab *prov.* Pak. **111** H4
Punmah Glacier Pak. **104** D2
Puno Peru **176** D7
Punta, Cerro de *mt.* Puerto Rico **169** K5
Punta Abreojos Mex. **157** E8
Punta Alta Arg. **178** D5
Punta Arenas Chile **178** B8
Punta Balestrieri *mt.* Italy **68** C4
Punta del Este Uruguay **178** F5
Punta Delgada Arg. **178** D6
Punta Gorda Belize **166** [inset] H5
Punta Gorda Nicaragua **166** [inset] J7
Punta Gorda U.S.A. **163** D7
Punta Norte Arg. **178** D6
Punta Prieta Mex. **166** B2
Puntarenas Costa Rica **166** [inset] I7
Punuk Islands *AK* U.S.A. **148** E3
Punxsutawney U.S.A. **165** F3
Puokio Fin. **54** O4
Puolanka Fin. **54** O4
Puqi China *see* **Chibi**
Pur *r.* Rus. Fed. **76** I3
Puracé, Volcán de *vol.* Col. **176** C3
Purbalingga *Jawa* Indon. **85** E4
Purcell U.S.A. **161** D5
Purcell Mountain *AK* U.S.A. **148** H2
Purcell Mountains Canada **150** G5
Pur Co *l.* China **99** C6
Purgadala *Xizang* China **99** D6
Purgatoire *r.* U.S.A. **160** C4
Puri India **106** E2
Purmerend Neth. **62** E2
Purna *r. Mahar.* India **104** D5
Purna *r. Mahar.* India **106** C2
Purnea India *see* **Purnia**
Purnia India **105** F4
Purnululu National Park Australia **134** E4
Pursat Cambodia *see* **Poŭthĭsăt**
Puruandíro Mex. **167** E4
Purukcahu *Kalimantan* Indon. **85** F3
Puruliya India **105** F5

▶**Purus** *r.* Peru **176** F4
3rd longest river in South America.

Puruvesi *l.* Fin. **54** P6
Purvis *MS* U.S.A. **167** H2
Purwakarta *Jawa* Indon. **84** D4
Purwareja *Jawa* Indon. **85** E4
Purwodadi *Jawa* Indon. **85** E4
Purwokerto *Jawa* Indon. **85** E4
Puryŏng N. Korea **90** C4
Pusa *Bihar* India **99** D8
Pusa *Sarawak* Malaysia **85** E2
Pusad India **106** C2
Pusan S. Korea **91** C6
Pusan Point *Mindanao* Phil. **82** D5
Pusatlı Dağı *mt.* Turkey **107** A1
Pushchino Rus. Fed. **53** H5
Pushemskiy Rus. Fed. **52** J3
Pushkin Rus. Fed. **55** Q7
Pushkino Azer. *see* **Biläsuvar**
Pushkinskaya, Gora *mt.* Rus. Fed. **90** F3
Pushkinskiye Gory Rus. Fed. **55** P8
Pusht-i-Rud *reg.* Afgh. *see* **Zamīndāvar**
Pustoshka Rus. Fed. **52** F4
Pusur *r.* Bangl. **105** G5
Putahow Lake Canada **151** K3
Putain *Timor* Indon. **83** C5
Putao Myanmar **86** B1
Puteoli Italy *see* **Pozzuoli**
Puteran *i.* Indon. **85** F4
Puthein Myanmar *see* **Bassein**
Putian China **97** H3
Puting China *see* **De'an**
Puting, Tanjung *pt* Indon. **85** E3
Putintsevo Kazakh. **98** D2
Putla Mex. **167** F5
Putlitz Germany **63** M1
Putna *r.* Romania **69** L2
Putney U.S.A. **165** I2
Putoi *i.* H.K. China *see* **Po Toi**
Putorana, Gory *mts* Rus. Fed. **189** E2

▶**Putrajaya** Malaysia **84** C2
Joint capital (with Kuala Lumpur) of Malaysia.

Putre Chile **176** E7
Putsonderwater S. Africa **124** E5
Puttalam Sri Lanka **106** C4
Puttalam Lagoon Sri Lanka **106** C4
Puttelange-aux-Lacs France **62** G5
Putten Neth. **62** F2
Puttershoek Neth. **62** E3
Puttgarden Germany **57** M3
Putumayo *r.* Col. **176** D4
also known as Ica (Peru)
Putuo China *see* **Shenjiamen**
Putusibau *Kalimantan* Indon. **85** F2
Puumala Fin. **55** P6
Pu'uwai U.S.A. **157** [inset]
Puvirnituq Canada **152** F1
Puxian *Shanxi* China **95** G4
Puyallup U.S.A. **156** C3
Puyang *Henan* China **95** H5
Puy de Sancy *mt.* France **66** F4
Puyehue, Parque Nacional *nat. park* Chile **178** B6
Puysegur Point N.Z. **139** A8
Puzak, Hāmūn-e *marsh* Afgh. **111** F4
Puzla Rus. Fed. **52** L3
Pweto Dem. Rep. Congo **123** C4
Pwinbyu Myanmar **86** A2
Pwllheli U.K. **59** C6
Pyal'ma Rus. Fed. **52** G3
Pyalo Myanmar **86** A3
Pyamalaw *r.* Myanmar **86** A4
Pyandzh Tajik. *see* **Panj**
Pyaozero, Ozero *l.* Rus. Fed. **54** Q3
Pyaozerskiy Rus. Fed. **54** Q4
Pyapali India **106** C3
Pyapon Myanmar **86** A3
Pyasina *r.* Rus. Fed. **76** J2
Pyatigorsk Rus. Fed. **113** F1
Pyatikhatki Ukr. *see* **P"yatykhatky**
P"yatykhatky Ukr. **53** G6
Pyay Myanmar *see* **Pyè**
Pychas Rus. Fed. **52** L4
Pyè Myanmar **86** A3
Pye, Mount *hill* N.Z. **139** B8
Pye Islands *AK* U.S.A. **149** J4
Pyetrykaw Belarus **53** F5
Pygmalion Point India **87** A6
Pyhäjoki Fin. **54** N4
Pyhäjoki *r.* Fin. **54** N4
Pyhäntä Fin. **54** O4
Pyhäsalmi Fin. **54** N5
Pyhäselkä *l.* Fin. **54** P5
Pyi Myanmar *see* **Pyè**
Pyin Myanmar *see* **Pyè**
Pyingaing Myanmar **86** A2
Pyinmana Myanmar **86** B3
Pyin-U-Lwin Myanmar **86** B2
Pyle U.K. **59** D7
Pyl'karamo Rus. Fed. **76** J3
Pylos Greece **69** I6
Pymatuning Reservoir U.S.A. **164** E3
Pyŏktong N. Korea **90** B4
P'yŏnggang N. Korea **91** B5
P'yŏnghae S. Korea **91** C5
P'yŏngsong N. Korea **91** B5
P'yŏngt'aek S. Korea **91** B5

▶**P'yŏngyang** N. Korea **91** B5
Capital of North Korea.

Pyramid Hill Australia **138** B6
Pyramid Lake U.S.A. **158** D1
Pyramid Peak U.S.A. **159** J1
Pyramid Range *mts* U.S.A. **158** D2
Pyramids of Giza *tourist site* Egypt **112** C5
Pyrénées *mts* Europe *see* **Pyrenees**
Pyrenees *mts* Europe **67** H2
Pyrénées, Parc National des *nat. park* France/Spain **66** D5
Pyre Peak *vol. AK* U.S.A. **149** [inset]
Pyrgos Greece **69** I6
Pyryatyn Ukr. **53** G6
Pyrzyce Poland **57** O4
Pyshchug Rus. Fed. **52** J4
Pytalovo Rus. Fed. **55** O8
Pyxaria *mt.* Greece **69** J5

Q

Qaa Lebanon **107** C2
Qaanaaq Greenland *see* **Thule**
Qabātiya West Bank **107** B3
Qabnag *Xizang* China **99** F7
Qabqa *Qinghai* China *see* **Gonghe**
Qacentina Alg. *see* **Constantine**
Qacha's Nek Lesotho **125** I6
Qādes Afgh. **111** F3
Qādisīyah, Sadd *dam* Iraq **113** F4
Qadisiyah Dam Iraq *see* **Qādisīyah, Sadd**
Qā'emābād Iran **111** F4
Qagan *Nei Mongol* China **95** I1
Qagan Ders *Nei Mongol* China **94** F3
Qagan Nur *Nei Mongol* China **95** G4
Qagan Nur *Nei Mongol* China **95** H3
Qagan Nur *Nei Mongol* China **95** H3
Qagan Nur *Qinghai* China **94** D4
Qagan Nur *Xinjiang* China **98** D4
Qagan Nur *l.* China **95** K2
Qagan Nur *resr* China **95** H3
Qagan Obo *Nei Mongol* China **95** G2
Qagan Qulut *Nei Mongol* China **95** I2
Qagan Teg *Nei Mongol* China **95** H3
Qagan Tohoi *Qinghai* China **94** C5
Qagan Us *Nei Mongol* China **89** K4
Qagan Us *Qinghai* China *see* **Dulan**
Qagan Us He *r.* China **94** D4
Qagbasêrag China **96** B2
Qagca China **96** C1
Qagcaka China **105** E2
Qagchêng China *see* **Xiangcheng**
Qahar Youyi Houqi *Nei Mongol* China *see* **Bayan Qagan**
Qahar Youyi Qianqi *Nei Mongol* China *see* **Togrog Ul**
Qahar Youyi Zhongqi *Nei Mongol* China *see* **Hobor**
Qahremānshahr Iran *see* **Kermānshāh**
Qaidam He *r.* China **94** C4
Qaidam Pendi *basin* China **94** C4
Qaidam Shan *mts Qinghai* China **94** C4
Qaidar *Qinghai* China *see* **Cêtar**
Qainaqangma *Xizang* China **99** E6
Qaisar, Koh-i- *mt.* Afgh. *see* **Qeyṣār, Kūh-e**
Qakar *Xinjiang* China **99** C5
Qalā Diza Iraq **113** G3
Qalagai Afgh. **111** H3
Qala-i-Kang Afgh. *see* **Kang**
Qal'aikhum Tajik. **111** H2
Qala Jamal Afgh. **111** F3
Qalansīyah Yemen **109** H7
Qala Shinia Takht Afgh. **111** G3
Qalāt Afgh. *see* **Kalāt**
Qal'at al Ḥiṣn Syria **107** C2
Qal'at al Mu'aẓẓam Saudi Arabia **112** E6
Qal'at Bīshah Saudi Arabia **108** F5
Qal'at Muqaybirah, Jabal *mt.* Syria **107** D2
Qal'at Ṣahyūn *tourist site* Syria **107** C2
Qal'eh Dāgh *mt.* Iran **110** B2
Qal'eh Tirpul Afgh. **111** F3
Qal'eh-ye Bost Afgh. **111** G4
Qal'eh-ye Now Afgh. **111** F3
Qal'eh-ye Shūrak *well* Iran **110** E3
Qalgar *Nei Mongol* China **94** F4
Qalhāt Oman **110** E6
Qalib Bāqūr *well* Iraq **113** G5
Qalluviartuuq, Lac *l.* Canada **152** G2
Qalyūb Egypt **112** C5
Qalyūb Egypt *see* **Qalyūb**
Qamalung *Qinghai* China **94** D5
Qamanirjuaq Lake Canada **151** M2
Qamanittuaq Canada *see* **Baker Lake**
Qamashi Uzbek. **111** G2
Qamata S. Africa **125** H6
Qamdo China **96** C2
Qandahar Afgh. *see* **Kandahār**
Qandarānbāshī, Kūh-e *mt.* Iran **110** B2
Qandyaghash Kazakh. *see* **Kandyagash**
Qangdin Sum *Nei Mongol* China **95** H3
Qangdoi *Xizang* China **99** C6
Qangzê *Xizang* China **99** B7
Qapan Iran **110** D2
Qapqal *Xinjiang* China **98** C4
Qapshagay Kazakh. *see* **Kapchagay**
Qapshagay Bögeni *resr* Kazakh. *see* **Kapchagayskoye Vodokhranilishche**
Qaqortoq Greenland **147** N3
Qara Āghach *r.* Iran *see* **Mand, Rūd-e**
Qarabutaq Kazakh. *see* **Karabutak**
Qaraçala Azer. **110** C2
Qara Ertis *r.* China/Kazakh. *see* **Ertix He**
Qaraghandy Kazakh. *see* **Karaganda**
Qaraghayly Kazakh. *see* **Karagayly**
Qārah Egypt **112** B5
Qārah Saudi Arabia **113** F5
Qarah Bāgh Afgh. **111** H3
Qarak China **111** J2
Qaraqum *des.* Turkm. *see* **Garagum**
Qaraqum *des.* Turkm. *see* **Karakum Desert**
Qara Quzi Iran **110** D2
Qarasu Azer. **113** H2
Qara Şū Chāy *r.* Syria/Turkey *see* **Karasu**
Qara Tarai *mt.* Afgh. **111** G3
Qarataū Kazakh. *see* **Karatau**
Qarataū Zhotasy *mts* Kazakh. *see* **Karatau, Khrebet**
Qara Tikan Iran **110** C2
Qarazhal Kazakh. *see* **Karazhal**
Qardho Somalia **122** E3
Qareh Chāy *r.* Iran **110** C3
Qareh Sū *r.* Iran **110** B2
Qareh Tekān Iran **111** F2
Qarhan *Qinghai* China **94** C4
Qarkilik *Xinjiang* China *see* **Ruoqiang**
Qarn al Kabsh, Jabal *mt.* Egypt **112** D5
Qarnayn *i.* U.A.E. **110** D5
Qarnein *i.* U.A.E. *see* **Qarnayn**
Qarn el Kabsh, Gebel *mt.* Egypt *see* **Qarn al Kabsh, Jabal**
Qarnobcho'l cho'li *plain* Uzbek. **111** G2
Qarokŭl *l.* Tajik. **111** I2
Qarqan *Xinjiang* China *see* **Qiemo**
Qarqan He *r.* China **98** D5
Qarqaraly Kazakh. *see* **Karkaralinsk**
Qarqi *Xinjiang* China **98** C4
Qarqi *Xinjiang* China **98** D4
Qarshi Uzbek. **111** G2
Qarshi cho'li *plain* Uzbek. **111** G2
Qarshi Chŭli *plain* Uzbek. *see* **Qarshi cho'li**
Qartaba Lebanon **107** B2
Qārūh, Jazīrat *i.* Kuwait **110** C4
Qārūn, Birkat *l.* Egypt **112** C5
Qârûn, Birket *l.* Egypt *see* **Qārūn, Birkat**
Qaryat al Gharab Iraq **113** G5
Qaryat al Ulyā Saudi Arabia **110** B5
Qasa Murg *mts* Afgh. **111** F3
Qāsemābād Iran **110** E3
Qash Qai *reg.* Iran **110** C4
Qasigiannguit Greenland **147** M3
Qasq *Nei Mongol* China **95** G3
Qaṣr al Azraq Jordan **107** C4
Qaṣr al Farāfirah Egypt **112** B6
Qaṣr al Kharānah Jordan **107** C4
Qaṣr al Khubbāz Iraq **113** F4
Qaṣr 'Amrah *tourist site* Jordan **107** C4
Qaṣr Burqu' *tourist site* Jordan **107** C3
Qaṣr-e Shīrīn Iran **110** B3
Qaṣr Farâfra Egypt *see* **Qaṣr al Farāfirah**
Qassimiut Greenland **147** N3
Qaṭanā Syria **107** C3
Qatar *country* Asia **110** C5
Qaṭmah Syria **107** C1
Qatrūyeh Iran **110** D4
Qaṭṭāfī, Wādī al *watercourse* Jordan **107** C4
Qaṭṭâra, Râs *esc.* Egypt *see* **Qaṭṭārah, Ra's**
Qattara Depression Egypt **112** B5
Qaṭṭārah, Ra's *esc.* Egypt **112** B5
Qaṭṭīnah, Buḥayrat *resr* Syria **107** C2
Qax Azer. **113** G2
Qaxi *Xinjiang* China **98** C4
Qāyen Iran **110** E3
Qaynar Kazakh. *see* **Kaynar**
Qaysār, Kuh-i- *mt.* Afgh. **111** G3
Qaysīyah, Qā' al *imp. l.* Jordan **107** C4
Qaysūm, Juzur is Egypt **112** D6
Qayū *Xizang* China **99** F7
Qayyārah Iraq **113** F4
Qazangödağ *mt.* Armenia/Azer. **113** G3
Qazaq Shyghanaghy *b.* Kazakh. *see* **Kazakhskiy Zaliv**
Qazaqstan *country* Asia *see* **Kazakhstan**
Qazax Azer. **108** G1
Qazi Ahmad Pak. **111** H5
Qazımämmäd Azer. **113** H2
Qazvīn Iran **110** C2
Qedir *Xinjiang* China **98** D4
Qeh *Nei Mongol* China **94** E3
Qeisûm, Gezâ'ir *is* Egypt *see* **Qaysūm, Juzur**
Qeisum Islands Egypt *see* **Qaysūm, Juzur**
Qena Egypt *see* **Qinā**
Qeqertarsuaq Greenland **147** M3
Qeqertarsuaq *i.* Greenland **147** M3
Qeqertarsuatsiaat Greenland **147** M3
Qeqertarsuup Tunua *b.* Greenland **147** M3
Qeshm Iran **110** E5
Qeydār Iran **110** C2
Qeydū Iran **110** C3
Qeyṣār, Kūh-e *mt.* Afgh. **111** G3
Qezel Owzan, Rūdkhāneh-ye *r.* Iran **110** C2
Qeẓi'ot Israel **107** B4
Qian'an *Hebei* China **95** I4
Qian'an *Jilin* China **95** K2
Qianfo Dong *Gansu* China *see* **Mogao Ku**
Qianfodong *Xinjiang* China **98** C4
Qian Gorlos China *see* **Qianguozhen**
Qianguozhen China **90** B3
Qiangwei He *r.* China **95** I5
Qian He *r.* China **95** F5
Qianjiang *Chongqing* China **97** F2
Qianjiang *Hubei* China **97** G2
Qianjin *Heilong.* China **90** D3
Qianjin *Jilin* China **90** C3
Qianning China **96** D2
Qianqihao *Jilin* China **95** J2
Qian Shan *mts* China **95** J3
Qianshanlaoba *Xinjiang* China **98** D3
Qianxi China **96** E3
Qianxi *Hebei* China **95** I3
Qianxian *Shaanxi* China **95** G5
Qianyang *Shaanxi* China **95** F5
Qiaocheng China *see* **Bozhou**
Qiaocun *Shanxi* China **95** H4
Qiaojia China **96** D3
Qiaoshan *Shaanxi* China *see* **Huangling**
Qiaotou *Qinghai* China *see* **Datong**
Qiaowa China *see* **Muli**
Qiaowan *Gansu* China **94** D3
Qiaozhuang China *see* **Qingchuan**
Qibā' Saudi Arabia **113** G6
Qibing S. Africa **125** H5
Qichun China **97** G2
Qidong China **97** G3
Qidukou China **96** B1
Qiemo *Xinjiang* China **99** D5
Qihe *Shandong* China **95** I4
Qi He *r.* China **95** H5
Qijiang China **96** E2
Qijiaojing *Xinjiang* China **94** B3
Qikiqtarjuaq Canada **147** L3
Qiktim *Xinjiang* China **94** B3
Qila Ladgasht Pak. **111** F5
Qilaotu Shan *mts* China **95** I3
Qila Saifullah Pak. **111** H4
Qilian *Qinghai* China **94** E4
Qilian Shan *mt.* China **94** D4
Qilian Shan *mts* China **94** D4
Qilizhen *Gansu* China **98** F4
Qillak *i.* Greenland **147** O3
Qiman *Xinjiang* China **98** C4
Qiman Tag *mts* China **99** E5
Qimusseriarsuaq *b.* Greenland **147** L2
Qinā Egypt **108** D4
Qin'an *Gansu* China **94** F5
Qincheng China *see* **Nanfeng**
Qincheng *Xinjiang* China **94** C3
Qing'an China **90** B3
Qingaq Canada *see* **Bathurst Inlet (abandoned)**
Qingcheng *Gansu* China *see* **Qingyang**
Qingchuan China **96** E1
Qingdao *Shandong* China **95** J4
Qinggang China **90** B3
Qinggil *Xinjiang* China *see* **Qinghe**
Qinggilik *Xinjiang* China **99** D5
Qinghai *prov.* China **94** D4
Qinghai Hu *salt l. Qinghai* China **94** E4
Qinghai Nanshan *mts* China **94** D4
Qinghe *Hebei* China **95** H4
Qinghe *Heilong.* China **90** C3
Qinghe *Xinjiang* China **94** B2
Qinghecheng China **90** B4
Qinghua *Henan* China *see* **Bo'ai**
Qingjian *Shaanxi* China **95** G4
Qingjiang *Jiangsu* China *see* **Huai'an**
Qingjiang *Jiangxi* China *see* **Zhangshu**
Qing Jiang *r.* China **97** F2
Qingkou *Jiangsu* China *see* **Ganyu**
Qinglan China **97** F5
Qingliu China **97** H3
Qinglong *Hebei* China **95** I3
Qinglung *Xizang* China **99** E7
Qingpu China **97** I2
Qingquan China *see* **Xishui**
Qingshan China *see* **Wudalianchi**
Qingshizui *Qinghai* China **94** E4
Qingshui *Gansu* China *see* **Qingshuipu**
Qingshui *Gansu* China **94** F5
Qingshuihe *Nei Mongol* China **95** G4
Qingshuihe *Qinghai* China **96** C1
Qingshuihezi *Xinjiang* China **98** C3
Qingshuihezi *Xinjiang* China **98** D4
Qingshuipu *Gansu* China **94** D4
Qingtian China **97** I2
Qingtongxia *Ningxia* China **94** F4
Qingxian *Hebei* China **95** I4
Qingxu *Shanxi* China **95** H4
Qingyang *Anhui* China **97** H2
Qingyang *Gansu* China **95** F4
Qingyang *Gansu* China **95** F5
Qingyang *Jiangsu* China *see* **Sihong**
Qingyuan *Gansu* China *see* **Weiyuan**
Qingyuan *Guangdong* China **97** G4
Qingyuan *Guangxi* China *see* **Yizhou**
Qingyuan *Liaoning* China **90** B4
Qingyuan *Shanxi* China *see* **Qingxu**
Qingyuan *Zhejiang* China **97** H3
Qingyun *Shandong* China **95** I4
Qingzang Gaoyuan *plat. Xizang* China *see* **Tibet, Plateau of**
Qingzhen China **96** E3
Qingzhou *Hebei* China *see* **Qingxian**
Qingzhou *Shandong* China **95** I4
Qinhuangdao *Hebei* China **95** I4
Qinjiang China *see* **Shicheng**
Qin Ling *mts* China **96** E1
Qinshui *Shanxi* China **95** H5
Qinting China *see* **Lianhua**
Qinxian *Shanxi* China **95** H4
Qinyang *Henan* China **95** H5
Qinyuan *Shanxi* China **95** H4
Qinzhou China **97** F4
Qionghai China **97** F5
Qiongjiexue *Xizang* China *see* **Qonggyai**
Qionglai China **96** D2
Qionglai Shan *mts* China **96** D2
Qiongxi China *see* **Hongyuan**
Qiongzhong China **97** F5
Qiongzhou Haixia *strait* China *see* **Hainan Strait**
Qiping *Gansu* China **94** D4
Qiqian China **90** A1
Qiqihar *Heilong.* China **95** J2
Qiquanhu *Xinjiang* China **98** E4
Qīr Iran **110** D4
Qira *Xinjiang* China **99** C5
Qîraîya, Wâdi *watercourse* Egypt *see* **Qurayyah, Wādī**
Qiryat Israel **107** B3
Qiryat Shemona Israel **107** B3
Qishan *Shaanxi* China **95** F5
Qishon *r.* Israel **107** B3
Qitab ash Shāmah *vol. crater* Saudi Arabia **107** C4
Qitai *Xinjiang* China **98** E4
Qitaihe China **90** C3
Qiubei China **96** E3
Qiujin China **97** G2
Qixia *Shandong* China **95** J4
Qixian *Henan* China **95** H5
Qixian *Henan* China **95** H5
Qixian *Shanxi* China **95** H4
Qixing He *r.* China **90** D3
Qiyang China **97** F3
Qiying *Ningxia* China **94** F4
Qizhou Liedao *i.* China **97** F5
Qızılağac Körfəzi *b.* Azer. **110** C2
Qizil-Art, Aghbai *pass* Kyrg./Tajik. *see* **Kyzylart Pass**
Qizilqum *des.* Kazakh./Uzbek. *see* **Kyzylkum Desert**
Qizilrabot Tajik. **111** I2
Qobustan Qoruğu *nat. res.* Azer. **113** H2
Qogir Feng *mt.* China/Pak. *see* **K2**
Qog Ul *Nei Mongol* China **95** I2
Qoigargoinba *Qinghai* China **94** E5
Qoijê *Qinghai* China **94** D4
Qoltag *mts* China **98** E4
Qom Iran **110** C3
Qomdo *Xizang* China *see* **Qumdo**
Qomīsheh Iran *see* **Shahrezā**
Qomolangma Feng *mt.* China/Nepal *see* **Everest, Mount**
Qomsheh Iran *see* **Shahrezā**
Qonāq, Kūh-e *hill* Iran **110** C3
Qondūz Afgh. *see* **Kunduz**
Qonggyai *Xizang* China **99** E7
Qo'ng'irot Uzbek. **102** A3
Qongj *Nei Mongol* China **95** G3
Qongkol *Xinjiang* China **98** D4
Qong Muztag *mt. Xinjiang/Xizang* China **99** C6
Qongrat Uzbek. *see* **Qo'ng'irot**
Qonj *Qinghai* China **94** D4
Qoornoq Greenland **147** M3
Qoqek *Xinjiang* China *see* **Tacheng**
Qo'qon Uzbek. **102** D3
Qorako'l Uzbek. **111** F2
Qorghalzhyn Kazakh. *see* **Korgalzhyn**
Qornet es Saouda *mt.* Lebanon **107** C2
Qorovulbozor Uzbek. **111** G2
Qorowulbozor Uzbek. *see* **Qorovulbozor**
Qorveh Iran **110** B3
Qo'shrabot Uzbek. **111** G1
Qosh Tepe Iraq **113** F3
Qostanay Kazakh. *see* **Kostanay**
Qoubaiyat Lebanon **107** C2
Qowowuyag *mt.* China/Nepal *see* **Cho Oyu**
Qozideh Tajik. **111** H2
Quabbin Reservoir U.S.A. **165** I2
Quadra Island Canada **150** E5
Quadros, Lago dos *l.* Brazil **179** A5
Quaidabad Pak. **111** H3
Quail Mountains U.S.A. **158** E4
Quairading Australia **135** B8
Quakenbrück Germany **63** H2
Quakertown U.S.A. **165** H3
Quambatook Australia **138** A5
Quambone Australia **138** C3
Quamby Australia **136** C4
Quanah U.S.A. **161** D5
Quanbao Shan *mt. Henan* China **95** G5
Quan Dao Hoang Sa *is* S. China Sea *see* **Paracel Islands**
Quân Đao Nam Du *i.* Vietnam **87** D5
Quan Dao Truong Sa *is* S. China Sea *see* **Spratly Islands**
Quang Ha Vietnam **86** D2
Quang Ngai Vietnam **86** E4
Quang Tri Vietnam **86** D3
Quan Hoa Vietnam **86** D2
Quan Long Vietnam *see* **Ca Mau**
Quannan China **97** G3
Quan Phu Quoc *i.* Vietnam *see* **Phu Quôc, Đao**
Quanshuigou Aksai Chin **99** B6
Quantock Hills U.K. **59** D7
Quanwan H.K. China *see* **Tsuen Wan**
Quanzhou *Fujian* China **97** H3
Quanzhou *Guangxi* China **97** F3
Qu'Appelle *r.* Canada **151** K5
Quaqtaq Canada **147** L3
Quarry Bay H.K. China **97** [inset]
Quartu Sant'Elena *Sardinia* Italy **68** C5
Quartzite Mountain U.S.A. **158** E3
Quartzsite U.S.A. **159** F5
Quba Azer. **113** H2
Quchan Iran **110** E2
Qudaym Syria **107** D2
Queanbeyan Australia **138** D5

▶**Québec** Canada **153** H5
Capital of Québec.

Québec *prov.* Canada **165** I1
Quebra Anzol *r.* Brazil **179** B2
Quedlinburg Germany **63** L3
Queen Adelaide Islands Chile *see* **La Reina Adelaida, Archipiélago de**
Queen Anne U.S.A. **165** H4
Queen Bess, Mount Canada **156** B2
Queen Charlotte B.C. Canada **149** N5
Queen Charlotte Islands B.C. Canada **149** N5
Queen Charlotte Sound *sea chan.* Canada **150** D5
Queen Charlotte Strait Canada **150** E5
Queen Creek U.S.A. **159** H5
Queen Elizabeth Islands Canada **147** H2
Queen Elizabeth National Park Uganda **122** C4
Queen Mary, Mount *Y.T.* Canada **149** M3
Queen Mary Land *reg.* Antarctica **188** F2
Queen Maud Gulf Canada **147** H3
Queen Maud Land *reg.* Antarctica **184** G10
Queen Maud Land *reg.* Antarctica **188** C2
Queen Maud Mountains Antarctica **188** J1
Queenscliff Australia **138** B7
Queensland *state* Australia **138** B1
Queenstown Australia **137** [inset]
Queenstown Ireland *see* **Cobh**
Queenstown N.Z. **139** B7
Queenstown S. Africa **125** H6
Queenstown Sing. **87** [inset]
Queets U.S.A. **156** B3
Queimada, Ilha *i.* Brazil **177** H4
Quelimane Moz. **123** D5
Quelite Mex. **166** D4
Quellón Chile **178** B6
Quelpart Island S. Korea *see* **Cheju-do**
Quemado U.S.A. **159** I4
Quemoy *i.* Taiwan *see* **Chinmen Tao**
Que Que Zimbabwe *see* **Kwekwe**
Querétaro Mex. **168** D4
Querétaro *state* Mex. **167** F4
Querétaro de Arteaga Mex. *see* **Querétaro**
Querfurt Germany **63** L3
Querobabi Mex. **166** C2
Quesnel Canada **150** F4
Quesnel Lake Canada **150** F4
Quetta Pak. **111** G4
Quetzaltenango Guat. **167** H6
Queuco Chile **178** B5
Quezaltepeque El Salvador **167** H6
Quezon *Palawan* Phil. **82** B4

▶**Quezon City** *Luzon* Phil. **82** C3
Former capital of the Philippines.

Qufu *Shandong* China **95** I5
Quibala Angola **123** B5
Quibaxe Angola **123** B4
Quibdó Col. **176** C2
Quiberon France **66** C3
Quiçama, Parque Nacional do *nat. park* Angola **123** B4
Qui Châu Vietnam **86** D3
Quiet Lake *Y.T.* Canada **149** N3
Quilá Mex. **166** D3
Quilalí Nicaragua **166** [inset] I6
Quilengues Angola **123** B5
Quillabamba Peru **176** D6
Quillacollo Bol. **176** E7
Quillan France **66** F5
Quill Lakes Canada **151** J5
Quilmes Arg. **178** E4
Quilon India **106** C4
Quilpie Australia **138** B1
Quilpué Chile **178** B4
Quimbele Angola **123** B4
Quimilí Arg. **178** D3
Quimper France **66** B3
Quimperlé France **66** C3
Quinag *hill* U.K. **60** D2
Quinalasag *i.* Phil. **82** C3
Quincy *CA* U.S.A. **158** C2
Quincy *FL* U.S.A. **163** C6
Quincy *IL* U.S.A. **160** F4
Quincy *IN* U.S.A. **164** B4
Quincy *MA* U.S.A. **165** J2
Quincy *MI* U.S.A. **164** C3
Quincy *OH* U.S.A. **164** D3
Quines Arg. **178** C4
Quinga Moz. **123** E5
Quinggir *Xinjiang* China **98** E4
Quinhagak *AK* U.S.A. **148** G4
Quiniluban *i.* Phil. **82** C4
Quinn Canyon Range *mts* U.S.A. **159** F3
Quintana Roo *state* Mex. **167** H5
Quinto Spain **67** F3
Quionga Moz. **123** E5
Quiotepec Mex. **167** F5
Quipungo Angola **123** B5
Quiriguá *tourist site* Guat. **166** [inset] H6
Quirima Angola **123** B5
Quirimbas, Parque Nacional das **123** E5
Quirindi Australia **138** E3
Quirinópolis Brazil **179** A2
Quissanga Moz. **123** E5
Quissico Moz. **125** L3
Quitapa Angola **123** B5
Quitilipi Arg. **178** D3
Quitman *GA* U.S.A. **163** D6
Quitman *MS* U.S.A. **161** F5

▶**Quito** Ecuador **176** C4
Capital of Ecuador.

Quitovac Mex. **166** B2
Quixadá Brazil **177** K4
Quixeramobim Brazil **177** K5
Qujiang *Guangdong* China **97** G3
Qujiang *Sichuan* China *see* **Quxian**
Qujie China **97** F4
Qujing China **96** D3
Qulandy Kazakh. *see* **Kulandy**
Qulbān Layyah *well* Iraq **110** B4
Qulho *Xizang* China **99** D7
Qulin Gol *r.* China **95** J2
Qulsary Kazakh. *see* **Kul'sary**
Qulyndy Zhazyghy *plain* Kazakh./Rus. Fed. *see* **Kulundinskaya Step'**
Qulzum, Baḥr al Egypt *see* **Suez Bay**
Qumar He *r.* China **94** C5
Qumarheyan *Qinghai* China **94** C5
Qumarlêb *Qinghai* China **99** F6
Qumarrabdün China **96** B1
Qumbu S. Africa **125** I6
Qumdo *Xizang* China **99** F7
Qumigxung *Xizang* China **99** D7
Qumqo'rg'on Uzbek. **111** G2
Qumqŭrghon Uzbek. *see* **Qumqo'rg'on**
Qumrha S. Africa **125** H7
Qumulangma *mt.* China/Nepal *see* **Everest, Mount**
Qunayy *well* Saudi Arabia **110** B6
Qundūz Afgh. *see* **Kunduz**
Qŭnghirot Uzbek. *see* **Qo'ng'irot**
Qu'ngoin *r. Qinghai* China **94** E5
Quntamari *Xizang* China **99** E6
Qu'nyido China **96** C2
Quoich *r.* Canada **151** M1
Quoich, Loch *l.* U.K. **60** D3
Quoile *r.* U.K. **61** G3
Quoin Point S. Africa **124** D8
Quoxo *r.* Botswana **124** G2
Qŭqon Uzbek. *see* **Qo'qon**
Qurama, Qatorkŭhi *mts* Asia *see* **Kurama Range**
Qurama Tizmasi *mts* Asia *see* **Kurama Range**
Qurayyah, Wādī *watercourse* Egypt **107** B4
Qurayyat al Milḥ *l.* Jordan **107** C4
Qŭrghonteppa Tajik. **111** H2
Qusar Azer. **113** H2
Qushan China *see* **Beichuan**
Qŭshrabot Uzbek. *see* **Qo'shrabot**
Qusmuryn Kazakh. *see* **Kushmurun**
Qusum *Xizang* China **99** B6
Qusum *Xizang* China **99** F7
Quthing Lesotho *see* **Moyeni**
Quttinirpaaq National Park Canada **147** K1
Quwayq, Nahr *r.* Syria/Turkey **107** C2
Quwo *Shanxi* China **95** G5
Quwu Shan *mts* China **94** F4
Quxian *Sichuan* China **96** E2

Quxian Zhejiang China see Quzhou
Qüxü Xizang China 99 E7
Quyang China see Jingzhou
Quyghan Kazakh. see Kuygan
Quy Nhơn Vietnam 87 E4
Quyon Canada 165 G1
Qüyün Eshek i. Iran 110 B2
Quzhou Hebei China 95 H4
Quzhou China 97 H2
Quzi Gansu China 95 F4
Qypshaq Köli salt l. Kazakh. see Kypshak, Ozero
Qyrghyz Zhotasy mts Kazakh./Kyrg. see Kirghiz Range
Qyteti Stalin Albania see Kuçovë
Qyzylorda Kazakh. see Kyzylorda
Qyzylqum des. Kazakh./Uzbek. see Kyzylkum Desert
Qyzyltü Kazakh. see Kishkenekol'
Qyzylzhar Kazakh. see Kyzylzhar

R

Raa Atoll Maldives see North Maalhosmadulu Atoll
Raab r. Austria 57 P7
Raab Hungary see Győr
Raahe Fin. 54 N4
Rääkkylä Fin. 54 P5
Raalte Neth. 62 G2
Raanujärvi Fin. 54 N3
Raas i. Indon. 85 F4
Raasay i. U.K. 60 C3
Raasay, Sound of sea chan. U.K. 60 C3
Raba Sumbawa Indon. 85 G5
Rabang Xizang China 99 C6
Rabat Gozo Malta see Victoria
Rabat Malta 68 F7

▶Rabat Morocco 64 C5
Capital of Morocco.

Rabaul P.N.G. 132 F2
Rabbath Ammon Jordan see 'Ammān
Rabbit r. B.C. Canada 149 P4
Rabbit Flat Australia 134 E5
Rabbitskin r. Canada 150 F2
Rabia Papua Indon. 83 D3
Rābigh Saudi Arabia 108 E5
Rabinal Guat. 167 H6
Rabnabad Islands Bangl. 105 G5
Râbniţa Moldova see Rîbniţa
Rabocheostrovsk Rus. Fed. 52 G2
Racaka China 96 C2
Raccoon Cay i. Bahamas 163 F8
Race, Cape Canada 153 L5
Raceland LA U.S.A. 167 H2
Race Point U.S.A. 165 J2
Rachaïya Lebanon 107 B3
Rachal U.S.A. 161 D7
Racha Noi, Ko i. Thai. 84 B1
Rachaya Lebanon see Rachaïya
Racha Yai, Ko i. Thai. 84 B1
Rachel U.S.A. 159 F3
Rach Gia Vietnam 87 D5
Rach Gia, Vinh b. Vietnam 87 D5
Racibórz Poland 57 Q5
Racine WI U.S.A. 164 B2
Racine WV U.S.A. 164 E4
Rădăuţi Romania 53 E7
Radcliff U.S.A. 164 C5
Radde Rus. Fed. 90 C2
Rádeyilikóé N.W.T. Canada see Fort Good Hope
Radford U.S.A. 164 E5
Radili Ko N.W.T. Canada see Fort Good Hope
Radisson Que. Canada 152 F3
Radisson Sask. Canada 151 J4
Radlinski, Mount Antarctica 188 K1
Radnevo Bulg. 69 K3
Radom Poland 57 R5
Radom Sudan 121 F4
Radomir Bulg. 69 J3
Radom National Park Sudan 121 F4
Radomsko Poland 57 Q5
Radoviš Macedonia 112 A2
Radstock U.K. 59 E7
Radstock, Cape Australia 135 F8
Radun' Belarus 55 N9
Radviliškis Lith. 55 M9
Radyvyliv Ukr. 53 E6
Rae Bareli India 104 E4
Raecreek r. Y.T. Canada 149 M2
Rae-Edzo N.W.T. Canada see Behchokò
Rae Lakes N.W.T. Canada see Gamètì
Raeside, Lake salt flat Australia 135 C7
Raetihi N.Z. 139 E4
Rāf hill Saudi Arabia 113 E5
Rafaela Arg. 178 D4
Rafaḩ Gaza see Rafiah
Rafaï Cent. Afr. Rep. 122 C3
Rafḩā' Saudi Arabia 113 F5
Rafiah Gaza 107 B4
Rafsanjān Iran 110 D4
Raft r. U.S.A. 156 E4
Raga Sudan 121 F4
Ragang, Mount vol. Mindanao Phil. 82 D5
Ragay Gulf Luzon Phil. 82 C3
Rägelin Germany 63 M1
Ragged, Mount hill Australia 135 C8
Ragged Island Bahamas 163 F8
Rāgh Afgh. 111 H2
Rago Nasjonalpark nat. park Norway 54 J3
Ragösen Germany 63 M2
Ragueneau Canada 153 H4
Raguhn Germany 63 M3
Ragusa Croatia see Dubrovnik
Ragusa Sicily Italy 68 F6
Ragxi Xizang China 99 F7
Ra'gyagoinba Qinghai China 94 E5
Raha Sulawesi Indon. 83 B4
Rahachow Belarus 53 F5
Rahad r. Sudan 108 D7
Rahaeng Thai. see Tak
Rahden Germany 63 I2
Rahimyar Khan Pak. 111 H4
Rahovec Kosovo 69 I3
Rahuri India 106 B2
Rai, Hon i. Vietnam 87 D5
Raiatea i. Fr. Polynesia 187 J7
Raibu i. Indon. see Air
Raichur India 106 C2
Raiganj India 105 G4
Raigarh Chhattisgarh India 105 E5
Raigarh Odisha India 106 D2
Raijua i. Indon. 83 B5
Railroad City AK U.S.A. 148 H3
Railroad Pass U.S.A. 158 E2
Railroad Valley U.S.A. 159 F2
Raimangal r. Bangl. 105 G5
Raimbault, Lac l. Canada 153 H3
Rainbow Lake Canada 150 G3
Raine Island Australia 136 D1
Rainelle U.S.A. 164 E5
Raini r. Pak. 111 H4
Rainier, Mount vol. U.S.A. 156 C3
Rainis Sulawesi Indon. 83 C1
Rainy r. Canada/U.S.A. 151 M5
Rainy Lake Canada/U.S.A. 155 I2
Rainy River Canada 151 M5
Raipur Chhattisgarh India 105 E5
Raipur W. Bengal India 105 F5
Raisen India 104 D5
Raisio Fin. 55 M6
Raismes France 62 D4
Raitalai India 104 D5
Raivavae i. Fr. Polynesia 187 K7
Raiwind Pak. 111 I4
Raja i. Indon. 85 F4
Raja, Ujung pt Indon. 84 B2
Rajaampat, Kepulauan is Papua Indon. 83 D3
Rajabasa, Gunung vol. Indon. 84 D4
Rajahmundry India 106 D2
Raja-Jooseppi Fin. 54 P2
Rajang Sarawak Malaysia 85 E2
Rajang r. Malaysia 85 E2
Rajanpur Pak. 111 H4
Rajapalaiyam India 106 C4
Rajapur India 106 B2
Rajasthan state India 104 C4
Rajasthan Canal India 104 C3
Rajauri India see Rajouri
Rajevadi India 106 B2
Rajgarh India 104 D4
Räjijovsset Fin. see Raja-Jooseppi
Rajik Indon. 84 D3
Rajkot India 104 B5
Raj Mahal India 104 C4
Rajmahal Hills India 105 F4
Raj Nandgaon India 104 E5
Rajouri India 104 C2
Rajpipla India 104 C5
Rajpur India 104 C5
Rajpura India 104 D3
Rajputana Agency state India see Rajasthan
Rajsamand India 104 C4
Rajshahi Bangl. 105 G4
Rājū Syria 107 C1
Rajula India 106 A1
Rajur India 106 C1
Rajura India 106 C2
Raka Xizang China 99 D7
Rakan, Ra's pt Qatar 110 C5
Rakaposhi mt. Pak. 104 C1
Raka Zangbo r. Xizang China see Dogxung Zangbo
Rakhiv Ukr. 53 E6
Rakhni Pak. 111 H4
Rakhni r. Pak. 111 H4
Rakhshan r. Pak. 111 F5
Rakit i. Indon. 85 E4
Rakit i. Indon. 85 G5
Rakitnoye Belgorodskaya Oblast' Rus. Fed. 53 G6
Rakitnoye Primorskiy Kray Rus. Fed. 90 D3
Rakiura i. N.Z. see Stewart Island
Rakke Estonia 55 O7
Rakkestad Norway 55 G7
Rakmanovskie Klyuchi Kazakh. 98 D2
Rakovski Bulg. 69 K3
Rakushechnyy, Mys pt Kazakh. 113 H2
Rakvere Estonia 55 O7

▶Raleigh U.S.A. 162 E5
Capital of North Carolina.

Ralla Sulawesi Indon. 83 A4
Ralston U.S.A. 165 G3
Ram r. Canada 150 F2
Rama Nicaragua 166 [inset] I6
Ramādī Iraq 113 F4
Ramagiri India 106 E2
Ramah U.S.A. 159 I4
Ramalho, Serra do hills Brazil 179 B1
Rāmallāh West Bank 107 B4
Ramanagaram India 106 C3
Ramanathapuram India 106 C4
Ramapo Deep sea feature N. Pacific Ocean 186 F3
Ramapur India 106 D1
Ramas, Cape India 106 B3
Ramatlabama S. Africa 125 G3
Rambhapur India 104 C5
Rambouillet France 62 B6
Rambutyo Island P.N.G. 81 L7
Rame Head hd Australia 138 D6
Rame Head hd U.K. 59 C8
Rameshki Rus. Fed. 52 H4
Ramezān Kalak Iran 111 F5
Ramganga r. India 99 B8
Ramgarh Jharkhand India 105 F5
Ramgarh Rajasthan India 104 B4
Ramgarh Rajasthan India 104 C3
Ramgul reg. Afgh. 111 H3
Rāmhormoz Iran 110 C4
Ramingining Australia 134 F3
Ramitan Uzbek. see Romiton
Ramla Israel 107 B4
Ramlat Rabyānah des. Libya see Rebiana Sand Sea
Ramm, Jabal mts Jordan 107 B5
Ramnad India see Ramanathapuram
Râmnicu Sărat Romania 69 L2
Râmnicu Vâlcea Romania 69 K2
Ramon' Rus. Fed. 53 H6
Ramona U.S.A. 158 E5
Ramos r. Mex. 161 B7
Ramos Arizpe Mex. 167 E3
Ramotswa Botswana 125 G3
Rampart AK U.S.A. 149 J2
Rampart of Genghis Khan tourist site Asia 95 H1
Ramparts r. N.W.T. Canada 149 O2
Rampur Hima. Prad. India 99 B7
Rampur India 104 D3
Rampur Uttar Prad. India 99 B7
Rampur Boalia Bangl. see Rajshahi
Ramree Myanmar 86 A3
Ramree Island Myanmar 86 A3
Rāmsar Iran 110 C2
Ramsele Sweden 54 J5
Ramsey Isle of Man 58 C4
Ramsey U.K. 59 G6
Ramsey U.S.A. 165 H3
Ramsey Bay Isle of Man 58 C4
Ramsey Island U.K. 59 B7
Ramsey Lake Canada 152 E5
Ramsgate U.K. 59 I7
Rāmshir Iran 110 C4
Ramsing mt. India 105 H3
Ramu Bangl. 105 H5
Ramusio, Lac l. Canada 153 J3
Ramygala Lith. 55 N9
Ranaghat India 105 G5
Ranai i. U.S.A. see Lāna'i
Rana Pratap Sagar resr India 104 C4
Ranapur India 104 C5
Ranasar India 104 B4
Ranau Sabah Malaysia 85 G1
Ranau, Danau l. Indon. 84 C4
Rancagua Chile 178 B4
Rancharia Brazil 179 A3
Rancheria Y.T. Canada 149 O3
Rancheria r. Y.T. Canada 149 O3
Ranchi India 105 F5
Rancho Grande Mex. 166 E4
Ranco, Lago l. Chile 178 B6
Rand Australia 138 C5
Randalstown U.K. 61 F3
Randers Denmark 55 G8
Randijaure l. Sweden 54 K3
Randolph ME U.S.A. 165 K1
Randolph UT U.S.A. 156 F4
Randolph VT U.S.A. 165 I2
Randsjö Sweden 54 H5
Råneå Sweden 54 M4
Ranérou Senegal 120 B3
Ranfurly N.Z. 139 C7
Ranga r. India 99 F8
Rangae Thai. 87 C6
Rangamati Bangl. 105 H5
Rangapara India 105 H4
Rangas, Tanjung pt Indon. 83 A3
Rangasa, Tanjung pt Indon. 83 A3
Rangeley Lake U.S.A. 165 J1
Rangely U.S.A. 159 I1
Ranger Lake Canada 152 E5
Rangiora N.Z. 139 D6
Rangitata r. N.Z. 139 C7
Rangitikei r. N.Z. 139 E5
Rangkasbitung Jawa Indon. 84 D4
Rangke China see Zamtang
Rangkŭl Tajik. 111 I2
Rangôn Myanmar see Rangoon

▶Rangoon Myanmar 86 B3
Joint capital (with Nay Pyi Taw) of Myanmar.

Rangoon r. Myanmar 86 B3
Rangpur Bangl. 105 G4
Rangsang i. Indon. 84 C2
Rangse Myanmar 86 A1
Ranibennur India 106 B3
Raniganj India 105 F5
Ranipur Pak. 111 H5
Raniwara India 104 C4
Rankin U.S.A. 161 C6
Rankin Inlet Canada 151 M2
Rankin's Springs Australia 138 C4
Ranna Estonia 55 O7
Rannes Australia 136 E5
Rannoch, Loch U.K. 60 E4
Ranong Thai. 87 B5
Ranot Thai. 87 C6
Ranpur India 104 B5
Ränsa Iran 110 C3
Ransby Sweden 55 H6
Rantasalmi Fin. 54 P5
Rantau Kalimantan Indon. 85 F3
Rantau i. Indon. 84 C2
Rantaukampar Sumatera Indon. 84 C2
Rantaupanjang Kalimantan Indon. 85 F3
Rantaupanjang Kalimantan Indon. 85 G2
Rantauprapat Sumatera Indon. 84 B2
Rantaupulut Kalimantan Indon. 85 F3
Rantemario, Gunung mt. Indon. 83 B3
Rantepao Sulawesi Indon. 83 A3
Rantoul U.S.A. 164 A3
Rantsila Fin. 54 N4
Ranua Fin. 54 O4
Rānya Iraq 113 G3
Ranyah, Wādī watercourse Saudi Arabia 108 F5
Rao Go mt. Laos/Vietnam 86 D3
Raohe China 90 D3
Raoul Island Kermadec Is 133 I4
Rapa i. Fr. Polynesia 187 K7
Rapa-iti i. Fr. Polynesia see Rapa
Rapallo Italy 68 C2
Rapar India 104 B5
Raphoe Ireland 61 E3
Rapidan r. U.S.A. 165 G4
Rapid City U.S.A. 160 C2
Rapid River U.S.A. 162 C2
Rapla Estonia 55 N7
Rappang Sulawesi Indon. 83 A3
Rapti r. India 99 C8
Rapur Andhra Prad. India 106 C3
Rapur Gujarat India 104 B5
Rapurapu i. Phil. 82 D3
Raqqa Syria see Ar Raqqah
Raquette Lake U.S.A. 165 H2
Rara National Park Nepal 105 E3
Raritan Bay U.S.A. 165 H3
Rarkan Pak. 111 H4
Raroia atoll Fr. Polynesia 187 K7
Rarotonga i. Cook Is 187 J7
Ras India 104 C4
Rasa i. Phil. 82 B4
Rasa, Punta pt Arg. 178 D6
Ra's ad Daqm Oman 109 I6
Ra's al Ḩikmah Egypt 112 B5
Ras al Khaimah U.A.E. see Ra's al Khaymah
Ra's al Khaymah U.A.E. 110 D5
Ra's an Naqb Jordan 107 B4
Ras Dashen mt. Eth. see Ras Dejen

▶Ras Dejen mt. Eth. 122 D2
5th highest mountain in Africa.

Raseiniai Lith. 55 M9
Rās el Hikma Egypt see Ra's al Ḩikmah
Ra's Ghārib Egypt 112 D5
Rashaant Bayan-Ölgiy Mongolia see Delüün
Rashaant Dundgovĭ Mongolia see Öldziyt
Rashad Sudan 108 D7
Rashīd Egypt 112 C5
Rashīd Egypt see Rashīd
Rashid Qala Afgh. 111 G4
Rashm Iran 110 D3
Rasht Iran 110 C2
Raskam mts China 99 A5
Ras Koh mt. Pak. 111 G4
Raskoh mts Pak. 111 G4
Raso, Cabo c. Arg. 178 C6
Raso da Catarina hills Brazil 177 K5
Rason Lake salt flat Australia 135 D7
Rasony Belarus 55 P9
Raspberry Island AK U.S.A. 148 I4
Rasra India 105 E4
Rasshua, Ostrov i. Rus. Fed. 89 S3
Rass Jebel Tunisia 68 D6
Rasskazovo Rus. Fed. 53 I5
Rastatt Germany 63 I6
Rastede Germany 63 I1
Rastow Germany 63 L1
Rasūl watercourse Iran 110 D5
Rasul Pak. 111 I3
Ratae U.K. see Leicester
Ratai, Gunung mt. Indon. 84 D4
Rätan Sweden 54 I5
Ratanda S. Africa 125 I4
Ratangarh India 104 C3
Rätansbyn Sweden 54 I5
Rat Buri Thai. 87 B4
Rathangan Ireland 61 F4
Rathbun Lake U.S.A. 160 E3
Rathdowney Ireland 61 E5
Rathdrum Ireland 61 F5
Rathedaung Myanmar 86 A2
Rathenow Germany 63 M2
Rathfriland U.K. 61 F3
Rathkeale Ireland 61 D5
Rathlin Island U.K. 61 F2
Ratibor Poland see Racibórz
Ratingen Germany 62 G3
Ratisbon Germany see Regensburg
Rat Island AK U.S.A. 149 [inset]
Rat Islands AK U.S.A. 149 [inset]
Ratiya India 104 C3
Rat Lake Canada 151 L3
Ratlam India 104 C5
Ratmanova, Ostrov i. Rus. Fed. 148 E2
Ratnagiri India 106 B2
Ratnapura Sri Lanka 106 D5
Ratne Ukr. 53 E6
Ratno Ukr. see Ratne
Raton U.S.A. 157 G5
Rattray Head hd U.K. 60 H3
Rättvik Sweden 55 I6
Ratz, Mount B.C. Canada 149 N4
Ratzeburg Germany 63 K1
Rau i. Maluku Indon. 83 D2
Raub Malaysia 84 C2
Rauðamýri Iceland 54 [inset]
Raudhatain Kuwait 110 B4
Rauenstein Germany 63 L4
Raufarhöfn Iceland 54 [inset]
Raukumara Range mts N.Z. 139 F4
Raul Soares Brazil 179 C3
Rauma Fin. 55 L6
Raupelyan Rus. Fed. 148 E2
Raurkela India 105 F5
Rauschen Rus. Fed. see Svetlogorsk
Rausu Japan 90 G3
Rautavaara Fin. 54 P5
Rautjärvi Fin. 55 P6
Ravänsar Iran 110 B3
Rävar Iran 110 E4
Ravat Kyrg. 111 H2
Ravels Belgium 62 E3
Ravena U.S.A. 165 I2
Ravenglass U.K. 58 D4
Ravenna Italy 68 E2
Ravenna NE U.S.A. 160 D3
Ravenna OH U.S.A. 164 E3
Ravensburg Germany 57 L7
Ravenshoe Australia 136 D3
Ravenswood Australia 136 D4
Ravi r. Pak. 111 H4
Ravnina Turkm. see Rawnina
Rawa Aopa Watumohai, Taman Nasional nat. park Indon. 83 B4
Rāwah Iraq 113 F4
Rawaki i. Kiribati 133 I2
Rawalpindi Pak. 111 I3
Rawalpindi Lake Canada 150 H1
Rawāndiz Iraq 113 G3
Rawas r. Indon. 84 C3
Rawi, Ko i. Thai. 87 B6
Rawicz Poland 57 P5
Rawlinna Australia 135 D7
Rawlins U.S.A. 156 G4
Rawlinson Range hills Australia 135 E6
Rawnina Maryyskaya Oblast' Turkm. 111 F2
Rawnina Maryyskaya Oblast' Turkm. 111 F2
Rawson Arg. 178 C6
Rawu China 96 C2
Raxón, Cerro mt. Guat. 168 G5
Ray, Cape Canada 153 K5
Raya, Bukit mt. Kalimantan Indon. 85 E3
Rayachoti India 106 C3
Rayadurg India 106 C3
Rayagada India 106 D2
Rayagarha India see Rayagada
Rayak Lebanon 107 C3
Raychikhinsk Rus. Fed. 90 C2
Raydah Yemen 108 F6
Rayes Peak U.S.A. 158 D4
Rayevskiy Rus. Fed. 51 Q5
Rayleigh U.K. 59 H7
Raymond U.S.A. 165 J2
Raymond Terrace Australia 138 E4
Raymondville U.S.A. 161 D7
Raymore Canada 151 J5
Ray Mountains AK U.S.A. 148 I2
Rayner Glacier Antarctica 188 D2
Rayones Mex. 167 E3
Rayong Thai. 87 C4
Raystown Lake U.S.A. 165 F3
Rayü Xizang China 99 F7
Raz, Pointe du pt France 66 B2
Razan Iran 110 C3
Rāzān Iran 110 C3
Razani Pak. 111 H3
Razāzah, Buḩayrat ar l. Iraq 113 F4
Razdan Armenia see Hrazdan
Razdel'naya Ukr. see Rozdil'na
Razdol'noye Rus. Fed. 90 C4
Razeh Iran 110 C3
Razgrad Bulg. 69 L3
Razhêng Zangbo r. Xizang China 99 E7
Razim, Lacul lag. Romania 69 M2
Razisi China 96 D1
Razlog Bulg. 69 J4
Razmak Pak. 111 H3
Raz"yezd 3km Rus. Fed. see Novyy Urgal
Ré, Île de i. France 66 D3
Reading U.K. 59 G7
Reading MI U.S.A. 164 C3
Reading OH U.S.A. 164 C4
Reading PA U.S.A. 165 H3
Reagile S. Africa 125 H3
Realicó Arg. 178 D5
Réalmont France 66 F5
Reăng Kesei Cambodia 87 C4
Reata Mex. 167 E3
Reate Italy see Rieti
Rebais France 62 D6
Rebecca, Lake salt flat Australia 135 C7
Rebiana Sand Sea des. Libya 121 F2
Reboly Rus. Fed. 54 Q5
Rebrikha Rus. Fed. 88 E2
Rebun-tō i. Japan 90 F3
Recherche, Archipelago of the is Australia 135 C8
Rechitsa Belarus see Rechytsa
Rechna Doab lowland Pak. 111 I4
Rechytsa Belarus 53 F5
Recife Brazil 177 L5
Recife, Cape S. Africa 125 G8
Recklinghausen Germany 63 H3
Reconquista Arg. 178 E3
Recreo Arg. 178 C3
Rectorville U.S.A. 164 D4
Red r. Australia 136 C3
Red r. Canada 150 E3
Red r. Canada/U.S.A. 160 D1
Red r. TN U.S.A. 164 B5
Red r. U.S.A. 161 F6
Red r. Vietnam 86 D2
Redang i. Malaysia 84 C1
Red Bank NJ U.S.A. 165 H3
Red Bank TN U.S.A. 163 C5
Red Basin China see Sichuan Pendi
Red Bay Canada 153 K4
Redberry Lake Canada 151 J4
Red Bluff U.S.A. 158 B1
Red Bluff Lake U.S.A. 161 C6
Red Butte mt. U.S.A. 159 G4
Redcar U.K. 58 F4
Redcliff Canada 156 F2
Redcliffe, Mount hill Australia 135 C7
Red Cliffs Australia 137 C7
Red Cloud U.S.A. 160 D3
Red Deer Canada 150 H4
Red Deer r. Alberta/Saskatchewan Canada 151 I5
Red Deer r. Man./Sask. Canada 151 K4
Red Deer Lake Canada 151 K4
Reddersburg S. Africa 125 H5
Red Devil AK U.S.A. 148 H3
Redding U.S.A. 158 B1
Redditch U.K. 59 F6
Rede r. U.K. 58 E3
Redenção Brazil 177 H5
Redeyef Tunisia 68 C7
Redfield U.S.A. 160 D2
Red Granite Mountain Y.T. Canada 149 M3
Red Hills U.S.A. 161 D4
Red Hook U.S.A. 165 I3
Red Idol Gorge China 99 E7
Red Indian Lake Canada 153 K4
Redkey U.S.A. 164 C3
Redkino Rus. Fed. 52 H4
Redknife r. Canada 150 G2
Red Lake Canada 151 M5
Red Lake U.S.A. 159 G4
Red Lake r. U.S.A. 160 D2
Red Lake Falls U.S.A. 151 L6
Red Lakes U.S.A. 160 E1
Redlands U.S.A. 158 E4
Red Lion U.S.A. 165 G4
Red Lodge U.S.A. 156 F3
Redmesa U.S.A. 159 I3
Redmond OR U.S.A. 156 C3
Redmond UT U.S.A. 159 H2
Red Oak U.S.A. 160 E3
Redonda Island Canada 150 E5
Redondo Port. 67 C4
Redondo Beach U.S.A. 158 D5
Redoubt Volcano AK U.S.A. 148 I3
Red Peak U.S.A. 156 E3
Red River, Mouths of the Vietnam 86 D2
Red Rock Canada 152 C4
Red Rock AZ U.S.A. 159 H5
Redrock U.S.A. 159 I5
Red Rock PA U.S.A. 165 G3
Redrock Lake Canada 150 H1
Red Sea Africa/Asia 108 D4
Redstone r. N.W.T. Canada 149 P2
Red Sucker Lake Canada 151 M4
Reduzum Neth. 62 F1
Redwater Canada 150 H4
Redway U.S.A. 158 B1
Red Wing U.S.A. 160 E2
Redwood City U.S.A. 158 B3
Redwood Falls U.S.A. 160 E2
Redwood National Park U.S.A. 156 B4
Redwood Valley U.S.A. 158 B2
Ree, Lough l. Ireland 61 E4
Reed U.S.A. 164 B5
Reed City U.S.A. 164 C2
Reedley U.S.A. 158 D3
Reedsport U.S.A. 156 B4
Reedsville U.S.A. 164 E4
Reedville U.S.A. 165 G5
Reedy U.S.A. 164 E4
Reedy Glacier Antarctica 188 J1
Reefton N.Z. 139 C6
Rees Germany 62 G3
Reese U.S.A. 164 D2
Reese r. U.S.A. 158 E1
Refahiye Turkey 112 E3
Refugio U.S.A. 161 D6
Regen Germany 63 N6
Regen r. Germany 63 M5
Regência Brazil 179 D2
Regensburg Germany 63 M5
Regenstauf Germany 63 M5
Reggane Alg. 120 D2
Reggio Calabria Italy see Reggio di Calabria
Reggio Emilia-Romagna Italy see Reggio nell'Emilia
Reggio di Calabria Italy 68 F5
Reggio Emilia Italy see Reggio nell'Emilia
Reggio nell'Emilia Italy 68 D2
Reghin Romania 69 K1
Regi Afgh. 111 G3

▶Regina Canada 151 J5
Capital of Saskatchewan.

Régina Fr. Guiana 177 H3
Registān reg. Afgh. 111 G4
Registro Brazil 178 G2
Registro do Araguaia Brazil 179 A1
Regium Lepidum Italy see Reggio nell'Emilia
Regozero Rus. Fed. 54 Q4
Rehau Germany 63 M4
Rehburg (Rehburg-Loccum) Germany 63 J2
Rehli India 104 D5
Rehoboth Namibia 124 C2
Rehoboth Bay U.S.A. 165 H4
Rehovot Israel 107 B4
Reïbell Alg. see Ksar Chellala
Reibitz Germany 63 M3
Reichenbach Germany 63 M4
Reichshoffen France 63 H6
Reid Australia 135 E7
Reidh, Rubha pt U.K. 60 D3
Reidsville U.S.A. 162 E4
Reigate U.K. 59 G7
Reiley Peak U.S.A. 159 H5
Reims France 62 E5
Reinbek Germany 63 K1
Reindeer r. Canada 151 K4
Reindeer Grazing Reserve nature res. N.W.T. Canada 149 O1
Reindeer Island Canada 151 L4
Reindeer Lake Canada 151 K3
Reine Norway 54 H3
Reinosa Spain 67 D2
Reinsfeld Germany 62 G5
Reiphólsfjöll hill Iceland 54 [inset]
Reisaelva r. Norway 54 L2
Reisa Nasjonalpark nat. park Norway 54 M2
Reisjärvi Fin. 54 N5
Reitz S. Africa 125 I4
Rekapalle India 106 D2
Reken Germany 62 H3
Reliance Canada 151 I2
Relizane Alg. 67 G6
Rellano Mex. 166 D3
Rellingen Germany 63 J1
Remagen Germany 63 H4
Remarkable, Mount hill Australia 137 B7
Rembang Jawa Indon. 85 E4
Remedios Cuba 163 E8
Remedios, Punta pt El Salvador 167 H6
Remeshk Iran 110 E5
Remhoogte Pass Namibia 124 C2
Remi France see Reims
Remmel Mountain U.S.A. 156 C2
Rempang i. Indon. 84 C2
Remscheid Germany 63 H3
Rena Norway 55 G6
Renaix Belgium see Ronse
Renam Myanmar 96 C3
Renapur India 106 C2
Renchinlhümbe Mongolia 94 D1
Rendsburg Germany 57 L3
René-Levasseur, Île i. Canada 153 H4
Renews Canada 153 L5
Renfrew Canada 165 G1
Renfrew U.K. 60 E5
Rengali Reservoir India 105 F5
Rengat Sumatera Indon. 84 C3
Rengo Chile 178 B4
Ren He r. China 97 F1
Renheji China 97 G2
Renhou Hebei China see Tangxian
Renhua China 97 G3
Reni Ukr. 69 M2
Renick U.S.A. 164 E5
Renland reg. Greenland see Tuttut Nunaat
Rennell i. Solomon Is 133 G3
Rennerod Germany 63 I4
Rennes France 66 D2
Rennick Glacier Antarctica 188 H2
Rennie Canada 151 M5
Reno r. Italy 68 E2
Reno U.S.A. 158 D2
Renovo U.S.A. 165 G3
Renqiu Hebei China 95 I4
Rensselaer U.S.A. 164 B3
Renswoude Neth. 62 F2
Renton U.S.A. 156 C3
Réo Burkina Faso 120 C3
Reo Flores Indon. 83 B5
Repalle India 106 D2
Repetek Turkm. 111 F2
Repetek Döwlet Gorugy nature res. Turkm. 111 F2
Repolka Rus. Fed. 55 P7
Republic U.S.A. 156 D2
Republican r. U.S.A. 160 D4
Republic of South Africa country Africa 124 F5
Repulse Bay b. Australia 136 E4
Repulse Bay Canada 147 J3
Requena Peru 176 D5
Requena Spain 67 F4
Reşadiye Turkey 112 E2
Resag, Gunung mt. Indon. 84 D4
Reserva Brazil 179 A4
Reserve U.S.A. 159 I5
Reshi China 97 F2
Reshteh-ye Alborz mts Iran see Elburz Mountains
Reshui Qinghai China 94 E4
Resistencia Arg. 178 E3
Reşiţa Romania 69 I2
Resolute Canada 147 I2
Resolute Bay Nunavut Canada see Resolute
Resolution Island Canada 147 L3
Resolution Island N.Z. 139 A7
Resplendor Brazil 179 C2
Restigouche r. Canada 153 I5
Resülayn Turkey see Ceylanpınar
Retalhuleu Guat. 167 H6
Retezat, Parcul Naţional nat. park Romania 69 J2
Retford U.K. 58 G5
Rethel France 62 E5
Rethem (Aller) Germany 63 J2
Réthimnon Greece see Rethymno
Rethymno Greece 69 K7

Retreat Australia 136 C5
Reuden Germany 63 M2

▶Réunion *terr.* Indian Ocean 185 L7
French Overseas Department.

Reus Spain 67 G3
Reusam, Pulau *i.* Indon. 84 B2
Reutlingen Germany 57 L6
Reval Estonia *see* Tallinn
Revda Rus. Fed. 54 S3
Revel Estonia *see* Tallinn
Revel France 66 F5
Revelstoke Canada 150 G5
Revigny-sur-Ornain France 62 E6
Revillagigedo, Islas *is* Mex. 168 B5
Revillagigedo Island *AK* U.S.A. 149 O5
Revin France 62 E5
Revivim Israel 107 B4
Revolyutsii, Pik *mt.* Tajik. *see* Revolyutsiya, Qullai
Revolyutsiya, Qullai *mt.* Tajik. 111 I2
Rewa India 104 E4
Rewari India 104 D3
Rex *AK* U.S.A. 149 J2
Rexburg U.S.A. 156 F4
Rexton Canada 153 I5
Rey, Isla del *i.* Panama 166 [inset] K7
Reyes, Point U.S.A. 158 B2
Reyhanlı Turkey 107 C1
Reykir Iceland 54 [inset]
Reykjanes Ridge *sea feature* N. Atlantic Ocean 184 F2
Reykjanestá *pt* Iceland 54 [inset]

▶Reykjavík Iceland 54 [inset]
Capital of Iceland.

Reyneke, Ostrov *i.* Rus. Fed. 90 E1
Reynoldsburg U.S.A. 164 D4
Reynolds Range *mts* Australia 134 F5
Reynosa Mex. 167 F3
Rezā Iran 110 D3
Reẕā'īyeh Iran *see* Urmia
Reẕā'īyeh, Daryācheh-ye *salt l.* Iran *see* Urmia, Lake
Rēzekne Latvia 55 O8
Rezvān Iran 111 F4
Rezvāndeh Iran *see* Rezvānshahr
Rezvānshahr Iran 110 C2
R. F. Magón Mex. *see* Ricardo Flores Magón
Rhaeader Gwy U.K. *see* Rhayader
Rhayader U.K. 59 D6
Rheda-Wiedenbrück Germany 63 I3
Rhede Germany 62 G3
Rhegium Italy *see* Reggio di Calabria
Rheims France *see* Reims
Rhein *r.* Germany 63 G3 *see* Rhine
Rheine Germany 63 H2
Rheinland-Pfalz *land* Germany 63 H5
Rheinsberg Germany 63 M1
Rheinstetten Germany 63 I6
Rhemilès *well* Alg. 120 C2
Rhin *r.* France 63 I6 *see* Rhine
Rhine *r.* Germany 63 G3
also spelt Rhein (Germany) or Rhin (France)
Rhinebeck U.S.A. 165 I3
Rhinelander U.S.A. 160 F2
Rhineland-Palatinate *land* Germany *see* Rheinland-Pfalz
Rhinkanal *canal* Germany 63 M2
Rhinow Germany 63 M2
Rhiwabon U.K. *see* Ruabon
Rho Italy 68 C2
Rhode Island *state* U.S.A. 165 J3
Rhodes Greece 69 M6
Rhodes *i.* Greece 69 M6
Rhodesia *country* Africa *see* Zimbabwe
Rhodes Peak U.S.A. 156 E3
Rhodope Mountains Bulg./Greece 69 J4
Rhodus *i.* Greece *see* Rhodes
Rhône *r.* France/Switz. 66 G5
Rhum *i.* U.K. *see* Rum
Rhuthun U.K. *see* Ruthin
Rhydaman U.K. *see* Ammanford
Rhyl U.K. 58 D5
Riachão Brazil 177 I5
Riacho Brazil 179 C2
Riacho de Santana Brazil 179 C1
Riacho dos Machados Brazil 179 C1
Rialma Brazil 179 A1
Rialto U.S.A. 158 E4
Riam *Kalimantan* Indon. 85 E3
Riasi India 104 C2
Riau *prov.* Indon. 84 C2
Riau, Kepulauan *is* Indon. 84 D2
Ribadeo Spain 67 C2
Ribadesella Spain 67 D2
Ribas do Rio Pardo Brazil 178 F2
Ribat Afgh. 111 H2
Ribat-i-Shur *waterhole* Iran 110 E3
Ribáuè Moz. 123 D5
Ribble *r.* U.K. 58 E5
Ribblesdale *valley* U.K. 58 E4
Ribe Denmark 55 F9
Ribécourt-Dreslincourt France 62 C5
Ribeira *r.* Brazil 179 B4
Ribeirão Preto Brazil 179 B3
Ribemont France 62 D5
Ribérac France 66 E4
Riberalta Bol. 176 E6
Rîbniţa Moldova 53 F7
Ribnitz-Damgarten Germany 57 N3
Říčany Czech Rep. 57 O6
Ricardo Flores Magón Mex. 166 D2
Rice U.S.A. 165 F5
Rice Lake Canada 165 F1
Richards Bay S. Africa 125 K5
Richards Inlet Antarctica 188 H1
Richards Island *N.W.T.* Canada 149 N1
Richardson *r.* Canada 151 I3
Richardson *AK* U.S.A. 149 K2
Richardson U.S.A. 161 D5
Richardson Highway *AK* U.S.A. 149 K3
Richardson Island Canada 150 G1
Richardson Lakes U.S.A. 165 J1
Richardson Mountains *N.W.T./Y.T.* Canada 149 N2
Richardson Mountains N.Z. 139 B7
Richfield U.S.A. 159 G2
Richfield Springs U.S.A. 165 H2
Richford *NY* U.S.A. 165 G2
Richford *VT* U.S.A. 165 I1
Richgrove U.S.A. 158 D4
Richland U.S.A. 156 D3
Richland Center U.S.A. 160 F3
Richmond *N.S.W.* Australia 138 E4
Richmond *Qld* Australia 136 C4
Richmond Canada 165 H1
Richmond N.Z. 139 D5
Richmond *KwaZulu-Natal* S. Africa 125 J5
Richmond *N. Cape* S. Africa 124 F6
Richmond U.K. 58 F4
Richmond *CA* U.S.A. 158 B3
Richmond *IN* U.S.A. 164 C4
Richmond *KY* U.S.A. 164 C5
Richmond *MI* U.S.A. 164 D2
Richmond *MO* U.S.A. 160 E4
Richmond *TX* U.S.A. 161 E6

▶Richmond *VA* U.S.A. 165 G5
Capital of Virginia.

Richmond Dale U.S.A. 164 D4
Richmond Hill U.S.A. 163 D6
Richmond Range *hills* Australia 138 F2
Richoi *Xizang* China 99 D7
Richtersveld Cultural and Botanical Landscape *tourist site* S. Africa 124 C5
Richtersveld National Park S. Africa 124 C5
Richvale U.S.A. 158 C2
Richwood U.S.A. 164 E4
Rico U.S.A. 159 I3
Ricomagus France *see* Riom
Riddell Nunataks Antarctica 188 E2
Ridder Kazakh. 98 C2
Rideau Lakes Canada 165 G1
Ridge *r.* Canada 152 D4
Ridgecrest U.S.A. 158 E4
Ridge Farm U.S.A. 164 B4
Ridgeland *MS* U.S.A. 161 F5
Ridgeland *SC* U.S.A. 163 D5
Ridgetop U.S.A. 164 B5
Ridgetown Canada 164 E2
Ridgeway *OH* U.S.A. 164 D3
Ridgeway *VA* U.S.A. 164 F5
Ridgway *CO* U.S.A. 159 J2
Ridgway *PA* U.S.A. 165 F3
Riding Mountain National Park Canada 151 K5
Riecito Venez. 176 E1
Riemst Belgium 62 F4
Riesa Germany 63 N3
Riesco, Isla *i.* Chile 178 B8
Riet *watercourse* S. Africa 124 E6
Rietavas Lith. 55 L9
Rietfontein S. Africa 124 E4
Rieti Italy 68 E3
Rifā'ī, Tall *mt.* Jordan/Syria 107 C3
Rifeng China *see* Lichuan
Rifle U.S.A. 159 J2
Rifstangi *pt* Iceland 54 [inset]
Rift Valley Lakes National Park Eth. *see* Abijatta-Shalla National Park

▶Rīga Latvia 55 N8
Capital of Latvia.

Riga, Gulf of Estonia/Latvia 55 M8
Rigain Pünco *l. Xizang* China 99 D6
Rīgān Iran 110 E4
Rīgas jūras līcis *b.* Estonia/Latvia *see* Riga, Gulf of
Rigby U.S.A. 156 F4
Rīgestān *reg.* Afgh. *see* Registān
Rigolet Canada 153 K3
Rigside U.K. 60 F5
Riia laht *b.* Estonia/Latvia *see* Riga, Gulf of
Riihimäki Fin. 55 N6
Riiser-Larsen Ice Shelf Antarctica 188 B2
Riito Mex. 166 B1
Rijau Nigeria 120 D3
Rijeka Croatia 68 F2
Rikā, Wādī ar *watercourse* Saudi Arabia 110 B6
Rikitgaib *Sumatera* Indon. 84 B1
Rikor India 96 B2
Rikuchū-kaigan Kokuritsu-kōen Japan 91 F5
Rikuzen-takata Japan 91 F5
Rila *mts* Bulg. 69 J3
Rila *Xizang* China 99 D7
Riley U.S.A. 156 D4
Rileyville U.S.A. 165 F4
Rillieux-la-Pape France 66 G4
Rillito U.S.A. 159 H5
Rimah, Wādī al *watercourse* Saudi Arabia 108 F4
Rimau, Pulau *i.* Indon. 84 D3
Rimavská Sobota Slovakia 57 R6
Rimbey Canada 150 H4
Rimini Italy 68 E2
Rîmnicu Sărat Romania *see* Râmnicu Sărat
Rîmnicu Vîlcea Romania *see* Râmnicu Vâlcea
Rimo Glacier India 99 B6
Rimouski Canada 153 H4
Rimpar Germany 63 J5
Rimsdale, Loch *l.* U.K. 60 E2
Rinbung *Xizang* China 99 E7
Rinca *i.* Indon. 83 A5
Rincão Brazil 179 A3
Rincón de Romos Mex. 166 E4
Rind *r.* India 99 C8
Rindal Norway 54 F5
Rindü *Xizang* China 99 E7
Ringarooma Bay Australia 137 [inset]
Ringas India 104 C4
Ringe Germany 62 G2
Ringebu Norway 55 G6
Ringhkung Myanmar 86 B1
Ringkøbing Denmark 55 F8
Ringsend U.K. 61 F2
Ringsted Denmark 55 G9
Ringtor *Xizang* China 99 C7
Ringvassøya *i.* Norway 54 K2
Ringwood Australia 138 B6
Ringwood U.K. 59 F8
Rinjani, Gunung *vol.* Indon. 80 F8
Rinns Point U.K. 60 C5
Rinqênzê China 105 G3
Rinteln Germany 63 J2
Río Abiseo, Parque Nacional *nat. park* Peru 176 C5
Rio Azul Brazil 179 A4
Riobamba Ecuador 176 C4
Rio Blanco U.S.A. 159 J2
Rio Bonito Brazil 179 C3
Rio Branco Brazil 176 E6
Rio Branco, Parque Nacional do *nat. park* Brazil 176 F3
Río Bravo, Parque Internacional del *nat. park* Mex. 166 E2
Rio Brilhante Brazil 178 F2
Río Casca Brazil 179 C3
Rio Claro Brazil 179 B3
Río Colorado Arg. 178 D5
Río Cuarto Arg. 178 D4
Rio das Pedras Moz. 125 L2
Rio de Contas Brazil 179 C1

▶Rio de Janeiro Brazil 179 C3
Former capital of Brazil. 3rd most populous city in South America.

Rio de Janeiro *state* Brazil 179 C3
Río de Jesús Panama 166 [inset] J8

▶Río de la Plata-Paraná *r.* S. America 178 E4
2nd longest river in South America, and 9th in the world.

Rio Dell U.S.A. 158 A1
Rio do Sul Brazil 179 A4
Río Frío Costa Rica 166 [inset] J7
Río Gallegos Arg. 178 C8
Río Grande Arg. 178 C8
Rio Grande Brazil 178 F4
Río Grande Mex. 161 C8
Rio Grande *r.* Mex./U.S.A. 154 H6
also known as Bravo de Norte, Río
Rio Grande City U.S.A. 161 D7
Rio Grande do Sul *state* Brazil 179 A5
Rio Grande Rise *sea feature* S. Atlantic Ocean 184 F8
Ríohacha Col. 176 D1
Río Hato Panama 166 [inset] J7
Río Hondo, Embalse *resr* Arg. 178 C3
Rioja Peru 176 C5
Río Lagartos Mex. 167 H4
Rio Largo Brazil 177 K5
Riom France 66 F4
Rio Manso, Represa do *resr* Brazil 177 G6
Río Mulatos Bol. 176 E7
Río Muni *reg.* Equat. Guinea 120 E4
Río Negro, Embalse del *resr* Uruguay 178 E4
Rioni *r.* Georgia 113 F2
Rio Novo Brazil 179 C3
Rio Pardo de Minas Brazil 179 C1
Río Plátano, Reserva Biósfera del *nature res.* Hond. 166 [inset] I6
Rio Preto Brazil 179 C3
Rio Preto, Serra do *hills* Brazil 179 B2
Rio Rancho U.S.A. 157 G6
Ríosucio Col. 166 [inset] K8
Río Tigre Ecuador 176 C4
Rio Tuba *Palawan* Phil. 82 B4
Riou Lake Canada 151 J3
Rio Verde Brazil 179 A2
Río Verde *Quintana Roo* Mex. 167 H5
Río Verde *San Luis Potosí* Mex. 167 F4
Rio Verde de Mato Grosso Brazil 177 H7
Rio Vista U.S.A. 158 C2
Ripky Ukr. 53 F6
Ripley *England* U.K. 58 F4
Ripley *England* U.K. 59 F5
Ripley *NY* U.S.A. 164 F2
Ripley *OH* U.S.A. 164 D4
Ripley *WV* U.S.A. 164 E4
Ripoll Spain 67 H2
Ripon U.K. 58 F4
Ripon U.S.A. 158 C3
Ripu India 105 G4
Risca U.K. 59 D7
Rishiri-tō *i.* Japan 90 F3
Rishon LeZiyyon Israel 107 B4
Rish Pish Iran 111 F5
Rising Sun *IN* U.S.A. 164 C4
Rising Sun *MD* U.S.A. 165 G4
Risle *r.* France 59 H9
Risør Norway 55 F7
Rissa Norway 54 F5
Ristiina Fin. 55 O6
Ristijärvi Fin. 54 P4
Ristikent Rus. Fed. 54 Q2
Risum *Xizang* China 99 B6
Ritan *r.* Indon. 85 F2
Ritang *Xizang* China 99 F7
Ritchie S. Africa 124 G5
Ritchie's Archipelago *is* India 87 A4
Ritch Island *N.W.T.* Canada 149 R2
Ritscher Upland *mts* Antarctica 188 B2
Ritsem Sweden 54 J3
Ritter, Mount U.S.A. 158 D3
Ritterhude Germany 63 I1
Rittō Japan 92 B3
Ritzville U.S.A. 156 D3
Riu, Laem *pt* Thai. 87 B5
Riva del Garda Italy 68 D2
Rivas Nicaragua 166 [inset] I7
Rivera Arg. 178 D5
Rivera Uruguay 178 E4
River Cess Liberia 120 C4
Riverhead U.S.A. 165 I3
Riverhurst Canada 151 J5
Riverina Australia 135 C7
Riverina *reg.* Australia 138 B5
Riversdale S. Africa 124 E8
Riverside S. Africa 125 I6
Riverside U.S.A. 158 E5
Rivers Inlet Canada 150 E5
Riversleigh Australia 136 B3
Riverton N.Z. 139 B8
Riverton *VA* U.S.A. 165 F4
Riverton *WY* U.S.A. 156 F4
Riverview Canada 153 I5
Rivesaltes France 66 F5
Riviera Beach U.S.A. 163 D7
Rivière-du-Loup Canada 153 H5
Rivière-Pentecôte Canada 153 I4
Rivière-Pigou Canada 153 I4
Rivne Ukr. 53 E6
Rivungo Angola 123 C5
Riwaka N.Z. 139 D5
Riwoqê China *see* Racaka

▶Riyadh Saudi Arabia 108 G5
Capital of Saudi Arabia.

Riyan India 111 I5
Riyue Shankou *pass Qinghai* China 94 E4
Riza *well* Iran 110 D3
Rizal *Luzon* Phil. 82 C3
Rize Turkey 113 F2
Rizhao *Shandong* China *see* Donggang
Rizhao *Shandong* China 95 I5
Rizokarpaso Cyprus *see* Rizokarpason
Rizokarpason Cyprus 107 B2
Rīzū *well* Iran 110 E3
Rīzū'īyeh Iran 110 E4
Rjukan Norway 55 F7
Rjuvbrokkene *mt.* Norway 55 E7
Rkîz Mauritania 120 B3
Roa Norway 55 G6
Roachdale U.S.A. 164 B4
Roach Lake U.S.A. 159 F4
Roade U.K. 59 G6
Roads U.S.A. 164 D4

▶Road Town Virgin Is (U.K.) 169 L5
Capital of the British Virgin Islands.

Roan Norway 54 G4
Roan Fell *hill* U.K. 60 G5
Roan High Knob *mt.* U.S.A. 162 D4
Roanne France 66 G3
Roanoke *IN* U.S.A. 164 C3
Roanoke *VA* U.S.A. 164 F5
Roanoke *r.* U.S.A. 162 E4
Roanoke Rapids U.S.A. 162 E4
Roan Plateau U.S.A. 159 I2
Roaring Spring U.S.A. 165 F3
Roaringwater Bay Ireland 61 C6
Roatán Hond. 166 [inset] I5
Röbäck Sweden 54 L5
Robat *r.* Afgh. 111 F4
Robāţe Tork Iran 110 C3
Robāţ Karīm Iran 110 C3
Robāt-Sang Iran 110 E3
Robb Canada 150 G4
Robbins Island Australia 137 [inset]
Robbinsville U.S.A. 163 D5
Robe Australia 137 B8
Robe *r.* Australia 134 A5
Robe *r.* Ireland 61 C4
Röbel Germany 63 M1
Robert-Bourassa, Réservoir *resr* Canada 152 F3
Robert Glacier Antarctica 188 D2
Robert Lee U.S.A. 161 C6
Roberts U.S.A. 156 E4
Roberts, Mount Australia 138 F2
Robertsburg U.S.A. 164 E4
Roberts Butte *mt.* Antarctica 188 H2
Roberts Creek Mountain U.S.A. 158 E2
Robertsfors Sweden 54 L4
Robertsganj India 105 E4
Robertson S. Africa 124 D7
Robertson, Lac *l.* Canada 153 K4
Robertson Bay Antarctica 188 H2
Robertson Island Antarctica 188 A2
Robertson Range *hills* Australia 135 C5
Robertsport Liberia 120 B4
Roberval Canada 153 G4
Robhanais, Rubha *hd* U.K. *see* Butt of Lewis
Robin Hood's Bay U.K. 58 G4
Robin's Nest *hill H.K.* China 97 [inset]
Robinson *Y.T.* Canada 149 N3
Robinson U.S.A. 164 B4
Robinson Mountains *AK* U.S.A. 148 I4
Robinson Mountains *AK* U.S.A. 149 L3
Robinson Range *hills* Australia 135 B6
Robinson River Australia 136 B3
Robles Pass U.S.A. 159 H5
Roblin Canada 151 K5
Robsart Canada 151 I5
Robson, Mount Canada 150 G4
Robstown U.S.A. 161 D7
Roby U.S.A. 161 C5
Roçadas Angola *see* Xangongo
Roca Partida, Punta *pt* Mex. 167 G5
Rocas Alijos *is* Mex. 166 B3
Rocca Busambra *mt. Sicily* Italy 68 E6
Rocha Uruguay 178 F4
Rochdale U.K. 58 E5
Rochechouart France 66 E4
Rochefort Belgium 62 F4
Rochefort France 66 D4
Rochefort, Lac *l.* Canada 153 G2
Rochegda Rus. Fed. 52 I3
Rochester Australia 138 B6
Rochester U.K. 59 H7
Rochester *IN* U.S.A. 164 B3
Rochester *MN* U.S.A. 160 E2
Rochester *NH* U.S.A. 165 J2
Rochester *NY* U.S.A. 165 G2
Rochford U.K. 59 H7
Rochlitz Germany 63 M3
Roc'h Trévezel *hill* France 66 C2
Rock *r. Y.T.* Canada 149 M2
Rock *r. Y.T.* Canada 149 P3
Rockall *i.* N. Atlantic Ocean 50 D4
Rockall Bank *sea feature* N. Atlantic Ocean 184 G2
Rock Creek *Y.T.* Canada 149 M2
Rock Creek U.S.A. 164 E3
Rock Creek *r.* U.S.A. 156 G2
Rockdale U.S.A. 161 D6
Rockefeller Plateau Antarctica 188 J1
Rockford *AL* U.S.A. 163 C5
Rockford *IL* U.S.A. 160 F3
Rockford *MI* U.S.A. 164 C2
Rockglen Canada 151 J5
Rockhampton Australia 136 E4
Rockhampton Downs Australia 134 F4
Rock Hill U.S.A. 163 D5
Rockingham Australia 135 A8
Rockingham U.S.A. 163 E5
Rockingham Bay Australia 136 D3
Rockinghorse Lake Canada 151 H1
Rock Island Canada 165 I1
Rock Island U.S.A. 160 F3
Rocklake U.S.A. 160 D1
Rockland *MA* U.S.A. 165 J2
Rockland *ME* U.S.A. 162 G2
Rocknest Lake Canada 150 H1
Rockport *IN* U.S.A. 164 B5
Rockport *TX* U.S.A. 161 D7
Rock Rapids U.S.A. 160 D3
Rock River U.S.A. 156 G4
Rock Sound Bahamas 163 E7
Rock Springs *MT* U.S.A. 156 G3
Rocksprings U.S.A. 161 C6
Rock Springs *WY* U.S.A. 156 F4
Rockstone Guyana 177 G2
Rockville *CT* U.S.A. 165 I3
Rockville *IN* U.S.A. 164 B4
Rockville *MD* U.S.A. 165 G4
Rockwell City U.S.A. 160 E3
Rockwood *MI* U.S.A. 164 D2
Rockwood *PA* U.S.A. 164 F4
Rockyford Canada 150 H5
Rocky Harbour Canada 153 K4
Rocky Hill U.S.A. 164 D4
Rocky Island Lake Canada 152 E5
Rocky Lane Canada 150 G3
Rocky Mount U.S.A. 164 F5
Rocky Mountain House Canada 150 H4
Rocky Mountain National Park U.S.A. 156 G4
Rocky Mountains Canada/U.S.A. 154 F3
Rocky Point *pt AK* U.S.A. 148 G2
Rocourt-St-Martin France 62 D5
Rocroi France 62 E5
Rodberg Norway 55 F6
Rødbyhavn Denmark 55 G9
Roddickton Canada 153 L4
Rodeio Brazil 179 A4
Rodel U.K. 60 C3
Roden Neth. 62 G1
Rödental Germany 63 L4
Rodeo Arg. 178 C4
Rodeo Mex. 166 D3
Rodeo U.S.A. 157 F7
Rodez France 66 F4
Ródhos *i.* Greece *see* Rhodes
Rodi *i.* Greece *see* Rhodes
Roding Germany 63 M5
Rodney, Cape *AK* U.S.A. 148 F2
Rodniki Rus. Fed. 52 I4
Rodolfo Sanchez Toboada Mex. 166 A2
Rodopi Planina *mts* Bulg./Greece *see* Rhodope Mountains
Rodos Greece *see* Rhodes
Rodos *i.* Greece *see* Rhodes
Rodosto Turkey *see* Tekirdağ
Rodrigues Island Mauritius 185 M7
Roe *r.* U.K. 61 F2
Roebourne Australia 134 B5
Roebuck Bay Australia 134 C4
Roedtan S. Africa 125 I3
Roe Plains Australia 135 D7
Roermond Neth. 62 F3
Roeselare Belgium 62 D4
Roes Welcome Sound *sea chan.* Canada 147 J3
Rogachev Belarus *see* Rahachow
Rogätz Germany 63 L2
Rogers U.S.A. 161 E4
Rogers, Mount U.S.A. 164 E5
Rogers City U.S.A. 164 D1
Rogers Lake U.S.A. 158 E4
Rogerson U.S.A. 156 E4
Rogersville U.S.A. 164 D5
Roggan *r.* Canada 152 F3
Roggan, Lac *l.* Canada 152 F3
Roggeveen Basin *sea feature* S. Pacific Ocean 187 O8
Roggeveld *plat.* S. Africa 124 E7
Roggeveldberge *esc.* S. Africa 124 E7
Roghadal U.K. *see* Rodel
Rognan Norway 54 I3
Rögnitz *r.* Germany 63 K1
Rogue *r.* U.S.A. 156 B4
Roha India 106 B2
Rohnert Park U.S.A. 158 B2
Rohrbach in Oberösterreich Austria 57 N6
Rohrbach-lès-Bitche France 63 H5
Rohri Sangar Pak. 111 H5
Rohtak India 104 D3
Roi Et Thai. 86 C3
Roi Georges, Îles du *is* Fr. Polynesia 187 K6
Rois-Bheinn *hill* U.K. 60 D4
Roisel France 62 D5
Roja Latvia 55 M8
Rojas Arg. 178 D4
Rojo, Cabo *c.* Mex. 167 F4
Rokan *r.* Indon. 84 C2
Rokeby Australia 136 C2
Rokeby National Park Australia 136 C2
Rokiškis Lith. 55 N9
Roknäs Sweden 54 L4
Rokugō Japan 93 E3
Rokuriga-hara *plain* Japan 93 E2
Rokusei Japan 92 C2
Rokytne Ukr. 53 E6
Rola Co *l. Xizang* China 99 E6
Rolagang *Xizang* China 99 E6
Rola Kangri *mt. Xizang* China 99 E6
Rolândia Brazil 179 A3
Rolim de Moura Brazil 176 F6
Roll *AZ* U.S.A. 159 G5
Roll *IN* U.S.A. 164 C3
Rolla *MO* U.S.A. 160 F4
Rolla *ND* U.S.A. 160 D1
Rollag Norway 55 F6
Rolleston Australia 136 E5
Rolleville Bahamas 163 F8
Rolling Fork U.S.A. 161 F5
Rollins U.S.A. 156 E3
Roma Australia 137 E5
Roma Italy *see* Rome
Roma Lesotho 125 H5
Roma Sweden 55 K8
Roma *TX* U.S.A. 167 F3
Roma, Pulau *i. Maluku* Indon. *see* Romang, Pulau
Romain, Cape U.S.A. 163 E5
Romaine *r.* Canada 153 J4
Roman Romania 69 L1
Română, Câmpia *plain* Romania 69 J2
Romanche Gap *sea feature* S. Atlantic Ocean 184 G6
Romanet, Lac *l.* Canada 153 I2
Romang, Pulau *i. Maluku* Indon. 83 C4
Romania *country* Europe 69 K2
Roman-Kosh *mt.* Ukr. 112 D1
Romano, Cape U.S.A. 163 D7
Romanovka Rus. Fed. 89 K2
Romans-sur-Isère France 66 G4
Romanzof, Cape *AK* U.S.A. 148 F3
Romanzof Mountains *AK* U.S.A. 149 K1
Rombas France 62 G5
Romblon Phil. 82 C3
Romblon *i.* Phil. 82 C3
Romblon Passage Phil. 82 C3

▶Rome Italy 68 E4
Capital of Italy.

Rome *GA* U.S.A. 163 C5
Rome *ME* U.S.A. 165 K1
Rome *NY* U.S.A. 165 H2
Rome *TN* U.S.A. 164 B5
Rome City U.S.A. 164 C3
Romeo U.S.A. 164 D2
Romford U.K. 59 H7
Romilly-sur-Seine France 66 F2
Romiton Uzbek. 111 G2
Romney U.S.A. 165 F4
Romney Marsh *reg.* U.K. 59 H7
Romny Ukr. 53 G6
Rømø *i.* Denmark 55 F9
Romodanovo Rus. Fed. 53 J5
Romorantin-Lanthenay France 66 E3
Rompin *r.* Malaysia 84 C2
Romsey U.K. 59 F8
Romu *mt. Sumbawa* Indon. 85 G5
Romulus U.S.A. 164 D2
Ron India 106 B3
Rona *i.* U.K. 60 D1
Ronas Hill *hill* U.K. 60 [inset]
Roncador, Serra do *hills* Brazil 177 H6
Roncador Reef Solomon Is 133 F2
Ronda Spain 67 D5
Ronda, Serranía de *mts* Spain 67 D5
Rondane Nasjonalpark *nat. park* Norway 55 F6
Rondon Brazil 178 F2
Rondonópolis Brazil 177 H7
Rondout Reservoir U.S.A. 165 H3
Rongcheng *Anhui* China *see* Qingyang
Rongcheng *Guangxi* China *see* Rongxian
Rongcheng *Hubei* China *see* Jianli
Rongcheng *Shandong* China 95 J4
Rongcheng Wan *b.* China 95 J4
Rong Chu *r.* China 99 E7
Rongelap *atoll* Marshall Is 186 H5
Rongjiang *Guizhou* China 97 F3
Rongjiang *Jiangxi* China *see* Nankang
Rongjiawan China *see* Yueyang
Rongklang Range *mts* Myanmar 86 A2
Rongmei China *see* Hefeng
Rongshui China 97 F3
Rongwo *Qinghai* China *see* Tongren
Rongxian China 97 F4
Rongyul China 96 C2
Rongzhag China *see* Danba
Rönlap *atoll* Marshall Is *see* Rongelap
Rønne Denmark 55 I9
Ronneby Sweden 55 I8
Ronne Entrance *strait* Antarctica 188 L2
Ronne Ice Shelf Antarctica 188 L1
Ronnenberg Germany 63 J2
Ronse Belgium 62 D4
Roodepoort S. Africa 125 H4
Roodeschool Neth. 62 G1
Rooke Island P.N.G. *see* Umboi
Roordahuizum Neth. *see* Reduzum
Roorkee India 104 D3
Roosendaal Neth. 62 E3
Roosevelt *AZ* U.S.A. 159 H5
Roosevelt *UT* U.S.A. 159 I1
Roosevelt, Mount Canada 150 E3
Roosevelt Island Antarctica 188 I1
Root *r.* Canada 150 F2
Root *r.* U.S.A. 160 F3
Ropar India *see* Rupnagar
Roper *r.* Australia 136 A2
Roper Bar Australia 134 F3
Roquefort France 66 D4
Roraima, Mount Guyana 176 F2
Rorey Lake *N.W.T.* Canada 149 O2
Rori India 104 C3
Rori Indon. 81 J7
Røros Norway 54 G5
Rørvik Norway 54 G4
Rosa, Punta *pt* Mex. 166 C3
Rosales Mex. 166 D2
Rosalia U.S.A. 156 D3
Rosamond U.S.A. 158 D4
Rosamond Lake U.S.A. 158 D4
Rosamorada Mex. 166 D4
Rosario Arg. 178 D4
Rosário Brazil 177 J4
Rosario *Baja California* Mex. 166 B2
Rosario *Coahuila* Mex. 166 E3
Rosario *Sinaloa* Mex. 168 C4
Rosario *Sonora* Mex. 166 C3
Rosario *Zacatecas* Mex. 161 C7
Rosario *Luzon* Phil. 82 C2
Rosario *Luzon* Phil. 82 C3
Rosario Venez. 176 D1
Rosário do Sul Brazil 178 F4
Rosário Oeste Brazil 177 G6
Rosarito *Baja California* Mex. 166 A1
Rosarito *Baja California* Mex. 166 B2
Rosarito *Baja California Sur* Mex. 166 C3
Rosarno Italy 68 F5
Roscoe *r. N.W.T.* Canada 149 Q1
Roscoff France 66 C2
Roscommon Ireland 61 D4
Roscommon U.S.A. 164 C1
Roscrea Ireland 61 E5
Rose *r.* Australia 136 A2
Rose, Mount U.S.A. 158 D2
Rose Atoll American Samoa *see* Rose Island

▶Roseau Dominica 169 L5
Capital of Dominica.

Roseau U.S.A. 160 E1
Roseau *r.* U.S.A. 160 D1
Roseberth Australia 137 B5
Rose Blanche Canada 153 K5
Rosebud *r.* Canada 150 H5
Rosebud U.S.A. 156 G3
Roseburg U.S.A. 156 C4
Rose City U.S.A. 164 C1
Rosedale U.S.A. 161 F5
Rosedale Abbey U.K. 58 G4
Roseires Reservoir Sudan 108 D7
Rose Island *atoll* American Samoa 133 J3
Rosenberg U.S.A. 161 E6
Rosendal Norway 55 E7
Rosendal S. Africa 125 H5
Rosenheim Germany 57 N7
Rose Peak U.S.A. 159 I5
Rose Point *pt B.C.* Canada 149 O5
Roseto degli Abruzzi Italy 68 F3
Rosetown Canada 151 J5
Rosetta Egypt *see* Rashīd
Rose Valley Canada 151 K4
Roseville *CA* U.S.A. 158 C2
Roseville *MI* U.S.A. 164 D2
Roseville *OH* U.S.A. 164 D4
Rosewood Australia 138 F1
Roshchino Rus. Fed. 55 P6
Rosh Pinah Namibia 124 C4

Roshtkala Tajik. see Roshtqal'a
Roshtqal'a Tajik. 111 H2
Rosignano Marittimo Italy 68 D3
Roşiori de Vede Romania 69 K2
Roskilde Denmark 55 H9
Roskruge Mountains U.S.A. 159 H5
Roslavl' Rus. Fed. 53 G5
Roslyakovo Rus. Fed. 54 R2
Roslyatino Rus. Fed. 52 J4
Ross r. Y.T. Canada 149 N3
Ross N.Z. 139 C6
Ross, Mount hill N.Z. 139 E5
Rossano Italy 68 G5
Rossan Point Ireland 61 D3
Ross Barnett Reservoir U.S.A. 161 F5
Ross Bay Junction Canada 153 I3
Rosscarbery Ireland 61 C6
Ross Dependency reg. Antarctica 188 I2
Rosseau, Lake Canada 164 F1
Rossel Island P.N.G. 136 F1
Ross Ice Shelf Antarctica 188 I1
Rossignol, Lac l. Canada 152 G3
Rössing Namibia 124 B2
Ross Island Antarctica 188 H1
Rossiyskaya Sovetskaya Federativnaya Sotsialisticheskaya Respublika country Asia/Europe see Russian Federation
Rossland Canada 150 G5
Rosslare Ireland 61 F5
Rosslare Harbour Ireland 61 F5
Roßlau Germany 63 M3
Rosso Mauritania 120 B3
Ross-on-Wye U.K. 59 E7
Rossony Belarus see Rasony
Rossosh' Rus. Fed. 53 H6
Ross River Y.T. Canada 149 N3
Ross Sea Antarctica 188 H1
Roßtal Germany 63 K5
Røssvatnet l. Norway 54 I4
Rossville U.S.A. 164 B3
Roßwein Germany 63 N3
Rosswood Canada 150 D4
Rostāq Afgh. 111 H2
Rostāq Iran 110 D5
Rosthern Canada 151 J4
Rostock Germany 57 N3
Rostov Rus. Fed. 52 H4
Rostov-na-Donu Rus. Fed. 53 H7
Rostov-on-Don Rus. Fed. see Rostov-na-Donu
Rosvik Sweden 54 L4
Roswell U.S.A. 157 G6
Rota i. N. Mariana Is 81 L4
Rot am See Germany 63 K5
Rotch Island Kiribati see Tamana
Rote i. Indon. 83 B5
Rotenburg (Wümme) Germany 63 J1
Roth Germany 63 L5
Rothaargebirge hills Germany 63 I4
Rothbury U.K. 58 F3
Rothenburg ob der Tauber Germany 63 K5
Rother r. U.K. 59 G8
Rothera research station Antarctica 188 L2
Rotherham U.K. 58 F5
Rothes U.K. 60 F3
Rothesay U.K. 60 D5
Rothwell U.K. 59 G6
Roti Indon. 83 B5
Roti i. Indon. see Rote
Roti, Selat sea chan. Indon. 83 B5
Roto Australia 138 B4
Rotomagus France see Rouen
Rotomanu N.Z. 139 C6
Rotondo, Monte mt. Corsica France 66 I5
Rotorua N.Z. 139 F4
Rotorua, Lake N.Z. 139 F4
Röttenbach Germany 63 L5
Rottendorf Germany 63 K5
Rottenmann Austria 57 O7
Rotterdam Neth. 62 E3
Rottleberode Germany 63 K3
Rottnest Island Australia 135 A8
Rottumeroog i. Neth. 62 G1
Rottweil Germany 57 L6
Rotuma i. Fiji 133 H3
Rotung India 96 B2
Rötviken Sweden 54 I5
Rötz Germany 63 M5
Roubaix France 62 D4
Rouen France 62 B5
Rough River Lake U.S.A. 164 B5
Roulers Belgium see Roeselare
Roumania country Europe see Romania
Roundeyed Lake Canada 153 H3
Round Hill hill U.K. 58 F4
Round Mountain Australia 138 F3
Round Rock AZ U.S.A. 159 I3
Round Rock TX U.S.A. 161 D6
Roundup U.S.A. 156 F3
Rousay i. U.K. 60 F1
Rouses Point U.S.A. 165 I1
Routh Bank sea feature Phil. see Seahorse Bank
Rouxville S. Africa 125 H6
Rouyn-Noranda Canada 152 F4
Rouyuan Gansu China see Huachi
Rouyuanchengzi Gansu China see Huachi
Rovaniemi Fin. 54 N3
Roven'ki Rus. Fed. 53 H6
Rovereto Italy 68 D2
Rôviĕng Tbong Cambodia 87 D4
Rovigo Italy 68 D2
Rovinj Croatia 68 E2
Rovno Ukr. see Rivne
Rovnoye Rus. Fed. 53 J6
Rovuma r. Moz./Tanz. see Ruvuma
Rowena Australia 138 D2
Rowley Island Canada 147 K3
Rowley Shoals sea feature Australia 134 B4
Równe Ukr. see Rivne
Roxas Luzon Phil. 82 C2
Roxas Mindanao Phil. 82 C4
Roxas Mindoro Phil. 82 C3
Roxas Palawan Phil. 82 B4
Roxas Panay Phil. 82 C4
Roxboro U.S.A. 162 E4
Roxburgh N.Z. 139 B7
Roxburgh Island Cook Is see Rarotonga
Roxby Downs Australia 137 B6
Roxo, Cabo c. Senegal 120 B3
Roy MT U.S.A. 156 F3
Roy NM U.S.A. 157 G5
Royal Canal Ireland 61 E4
Royal Chitwan National Park Nepal 105 F4
Royale, Île i. Canada see Cape Breton Island
Royale, Isle i. U.S.A. 160 F1
Royal Natal National Park S. Africa 125 I5
Royal National Park Australia 138 E5
Royal Oak U.S.A. 164 D2
Royal Sukla Phanta Wildlife Reserve Nepal 104 E3
Royan France 66 D4
Roye France 62 C5
Roy Hill Australia 134 B5
Royston U.K. 59 G6
Rozdil'na Ukr. 69 N1
Rozivka Ukr. 53 H7
Rtishchevo Rus. Fed. 53 I5
Rua, Tanjung pt Sumba Indon. 83 A5
Ruabon U.K. 59 D6
Ruaha National Park Tanz. 123 D4
Ruahine Range mts N.Z. 139 F5
Ruanda country Africa see Rwanda
Ruang i. Indon. 83 C2

▶Ruapehu, Mount vol. N.Z. 139 E4
Highest active volcano in Oceania.

Ruapuke Island N.Z. 139 B8
Ruatoria N.Z. 139 G3
Ruba Belarus 53 F5

▶Rub' al Khālī des. Saudi Arabia 108 G6
Largest uninterrupted stretch of sand in the world.

Rubaydā reg. Saudi Arabia 110 C5
Rubtsovsk Rus. Fed. 102 F1
Ruby AK U.S.A. 148 I2
Ruby Dome mt. U.S.A. 159 F1
Ruby Mountains U.S.A. 159 F1
Rubys Inn U.S.A. 159 G3
Ruby Valley U.S.A. 159 F1
Rucheng China 97 G3
Ruckersville U.S.A. 165 F4
Rudall River National Park Australia 134 C5
Rudarpur India 105 E4
Ruda Śląska Poland 57 Q5
Rudauli India 105 E4
Rūdbār Iran 110 C2
Rudkøbing Denmark 55 G9
Rudnaya Pristan' Rus. Fed. 90 D3
Rudnichnyy Rus. Fed. 52 L4
Rudnik Ingichka Uzbek. see Ingichka
Rudnya Smolenskaya Oblast' Rus. Fed. 53 F5
Rudnya Volgogradskaya Oblast' Rus. Fed. 53 J6
Rudnyy Kazakh. 100 F1
Rudolf, Lake salt l. Eth./Kenya see Turkana, Lake

▶Rudol'fa, Ostrov i. Rus. Fed. 76 G1
Most northerly point of Europe.

Rudolph Island Rus. Fed. see Rudol'fa, Ostrov
Rudolstadt Germany 63 L4
Rudong China 97 I1
Rūdsar Iran 110 C2
Rue France 62 B4
Rufiji r. Tanz. 123 D4
Rufino Arg. 178 D4
Rufisque Senegal 120 B3
Rufrufua Indon. 81 I7
Rufunsa Zambia 123 C5
Rufus Lake N.W.T. Canada 149 O1
Rugao China 97 I1
Rugby U.K. 59 F6
Rugby U.S.A. 160 C1
Rugeley U.K. 59 F6
Rügen i. Germany 57 N3
Rugged Mountain Canada 150 E5
Rügland Germany 63 K5
Ruḩayyat al Ḩamr'ā' waterhole Saudi Arabia 110 B5
Ruhengeri Rwanda 122 C4
Ruhnu i. Estonia 55 M8
Ruhr r. Germany 63 G3
Ruhuna National Park Sri Lanka 106 D5
Rui'an China 97 I3
Rui Barbosa Brazil 179 C1
Ruicheng China 97 F1
Ruijin China 97 G3
Ruili China 96 C3
Ruin Point Canada 151 P2
Ruipa Tanz. 123 D4
Ruiz Mex. 168 C4
Ruiz, Nevado del vol. Col. 176 C3
Rujaylah, Ḩarrat ar lava field Jordan 107 C3
Rūjiena Latvia 55 N8
Ruk is Micronesia see Chuuk
Rukanpur Pak. 111 I4
Rukumkot Nepal 105 E3
Rukuwa Sulawesi Indon. 83 C4
Rukwa, Lake Tanz. 123 D4
Rulin China see Chengbu
Rulong China see Xinlong
Rum i. U.K. 60 C4
Rum, Jebel mts Jordan see Ramm, Jabal
Ruma Serbia 69 H2
Rumāh Saudi Arabia 108 G4
Rumania country Europe see Romania
Rumbai Sulawesi Indon. 83 C2
Rumbek Sudan 121 F4
Rumberpon i. Indon. 81 I7
Rum Cay i. Bahamas 163 F8
Rum Jungle Australia 134 E3
Rummānā hill Syria 107 D3
Rumphi Malawi 123 D5
Run i. Maluku Indon. 83 D4
Runan China 97 G1
Runaway, Cape N.Z. 139 F3
Runcorn U.K. 58 E5
Rundu Namibia 123 B5
Runduma i. Indon. 83 C4
Rundvik Sweden 54 K5
Rŭng, Kaôh i. Cambodia 87 C5
Rungan r. Indon. 85 F3
Rungwa Tanz. 123 D4
Rungwa r. Tanz. 123 D4
Runheji China 97 H1
Runing China see Runan
Runton Range hills Australia 135 C5
Ruokolahti Fin. 55 P6
Ruoqiang Xinjiang China 98 E5
Ruoqiang He r. China 98 E5
Ruo Shui watercourse China 94 E3
Rupa India 105 H4
Rupat i. Indon. 84 C2
Rupert r. Canada 152 F4
Rupert ID U.S.A. 156 E4
Rupert WV U.S.A. 164 E5
Rupert Bay Canada 152 F4
Rupert Coast Antarctica 188 J1
Rupert House Canada see Waskaganish
Rupnagar India 104 D3
Rupshu reg. India 104 D2
Ruqqād, Wādī ar watercourse Israel 107 B3
Rural Retreat U.S.A. 164 E5
Rusaddir N. Africa see Melilla
Rusape Zimbabwe 123 D5
Ruschuk Bulg. see Ruse
Ruse Bulg. 69 K3
Rusera India 105 F4
Rush U.S.A. 164 D4
Rushan Shandong China 95 J4
Rush Creek r. U.S.A. 160 C4
Rushden U.K. 59 G6
Rushinga Zimbabwe 123 D5
Rushui He r. China 94 F5
Rushville IL U.S.A. 160 F3
Rushville IN U.S.A. 164 C4
Rushville NE U.S.A. 160 C3
Rushworth Australia 138 B6
Rusk U.S.A. 161 E6
Russell Man. Canada 151 K5
Russell Ont. Canada 165 H1
Russell N.Z. 139 E2
Russell KS U.S.A. 160 D4
Russell PA U.S.A. 164 F3
Russell, Mount AK U.S.A. 149 J3
Russell Bay Antarctica 188 J2
Russell Lake Man. Canada 151 K3
Russell Lake N.W.T. Canada 150 H2
Russell Lake Sask. Canada 151 J3
Russell Range hills Australia 135 C8
Russell Springs U.S.A. 164 C5
Russellville AL U.S.A. 161 G5
Russellville AR U.S.A. 161 E5
Russellville KY U.S.A. 164 B5
Rüsselsheim Germany 63 I4
Russia country Asia/Europe see Russian Federation
Russian r. U.S.A. 158 B2

▶Russian Federation country Asia/Europe 76 I3
Largest country in the world, Europe and Asia. Most populous country in Europe, 5th in Asia and 9th in the world.

Russian Mission AK U.S.A. 148 G3
Russian Mountains AK U.S.A. 148 H3
Russian Soviet Federal Socialist Republic country Asia/Europe see Russian Federation
Russkaya Koshka, Kosa spit Rus. Fed. 148 B2
Russkiy, Ostrov i. Rus. Fed. 90 C4
Russkiy Kameshkir Rus. Fed. 53 J5
Rust'avi Georgia 113 G2
Rustburg U.S.A. 164 F5
Rustenburg S. Africa 125 H3
Ruston U.S.A. 161 E5
Ruta Maluku Indon. 83 C3
Rutanzige, Lake Dem. Rep. Congo/Uganda see Edward, Lake
Ruteng Flores Indon. 83 B5
Ruth U.S.A. 159 F2
Rüthen Germany 63 I3
Rutherglen Australia 138 C6
Ruther Glen U.S.A. 165 G5
Ruthin U.K. 59 D5
Ruthiyai India 104 D4
Ruth Reservoir U.S.A. 158 B1
Rutka r. Rus. Fed. 52 J4
Rutland U.S.A. 165 I2
Rutland Water resr U.K. 59 G6
Rutledge Lake Canada 151 I2
Rutog Xizang China 99 B6
Rutog Xizang China 99 D7
Rutog Xizang China 99 F7
Rutul Rus. Fed. 113 G2
Ruukki Fin. 54 N4
Ruvuma r. Moz./Tanz. 123 E5
also known as Rovuma
Ruwayshid, Wādī watercourse Jordan 107 C3
Ruwayṭah, Wādī watercourse Jordan 107 C5
Ruweis U.A.E. 110 D5
Ruwenzori National Park Uganda see Queen Elizabeth National Park
Ruza Rus. Fed. 52 H5
Ruzayevka Kazakh. 100 F1
Ruzayevka Rus. Fed. 53 J5
Ruzhou Henan China 95 H5
Ružomberok Slovakia 57 Q6
Rwanda country Africa 122 C4
Ryābād Iran 110 D2
Ryan, Loch b. U.K. 60 D5
Ryazan' Rus. Fed. 53 H5
Ryazhsk Rus. Fed. 53 I5
Rybachiy, Poluostrov pen. Rus. Fed. 54 R2
Rybach'ye Kazakh. 98 C3
Rybach'ye Kyrg. see Balykchy
Rybinsk Rus. Fed. 52 H4

▶Rybinskoye Vodokhranilishche resr Rus. Fed. 52 H4
5th largest lake in Europe

Rybnik Poland 57 Q5
Rybnitsa Moldova see Rîbnița
Rybnoye Rus. Fed. 53 H5
Rybreka Rus. Fed. 52 G3
Ryd Sweden 55 I8
Rydberg Peninsula Antarctica 188 L2
Ryde U.K. 59 F8
Rye U.K. 59 H8
Rye r. U.K. 58 G4
Rye Bay U.K. 59 H8
Ryegate U.S.A. 156 F3
Rye Patch Reservoir U.S.A. 158 D1
Rykovo Ukr. see Yenakiyeve
Ryl'sk Rus. Fed. 53 G6
Rylstone Australia 138 D4
Ryn-Peski des. Kazakh. 51 P6
Ryōgami-san mt. Japan 93 E2
Ryōhaku-sanchi mts Japan 92 C3
Ryojun Liaoning China see Lüshun
Ryōkami Japan 93 E2
Ryōzen-zan mt. Japan 92 C3
Ryūga-dake mt. Japan 92 C3
Ryūgasaki Japan 93 G3
Ryukyu Islands Japan 91 B8
Ryūkyū-rettō is Japan see Ryukyu Islands
Ryukyu Trench sea feature N. Pacific Ocean 186 E4
Ryūō Shiga Japan 92 C3
Ryūō Yamanashi Japan 93 E3
Ryūsō-san mt. Japan 93 E3
Ryūyō Japan 93 D4
Rzeszów Poland 53 D6
Rzhaksa Rus. Fed. 53 I5
Rzhev Rus. Fed. 52 G4

S

Sa'ādah al Barṣā' pass Saudi Arabia 107 C5
Sa'ādatābād Iran 110 D4
Saal an der Donau Germany 63 L6
Saale r. Germany 63 L3
Saalfeld Germany 63 L4
Saanich Canada 150 F5
Saar land Germany see Saarland
Saar r. Germany 62 G5
Saarbrücken Germany 62 G5
Saaremaa i. Estonia 55 M7
Saarenkylä Fin. 54 N3
Saargau reg. Germany 62 G5
Saarijärvi Fin. 54 N5
Saari-Kämä Fin. 54 O3
Saarikoski Fin. 54 L2
Saaristomeren kansallispuisto nat. park Fin. see Skärgårdshavets nationalpark
Saarland land Germany 62 G5
Saarlouis Germany 62 G5
Saatlı Azer. 113 H3
Saatly Azer. see Saatlı
Sab'a Egypt see Saba'ah
Saba'ah Egypt 107 A4
Sab' Ābār Syria 107 C3
Šabac Serbia 69 H2
Sabadell Spain 67 H3
Sabae Japan 92 C3
Sabah state Malaysia 85 G1
Sabak Malaysia 84 C2
Sabalana i. Indon. 83 A4
Sabalana, Kepulauan is Indon. 83 A4
Sabalgarh Madh. Prad. India 99 B8
Sabana, Archipiélago de is Cuba 169 H4
Sabanagrande Hond. 166 [inset] I6
Sabang Aceh Indon. 84 A1
Sabang Sulawesi Indon. 83 A2
Sabang Sulawesi Indon. 83 B3
Şabanözü Turkey 112 D2
Sabará Brazil 179 C2
Sabaru i. Indon. 83 A4
Sabastiya West Bank 107 B3
Sab'atayn, Ramlat as des. Yemen 108 G6
Sabaudia Italy 68 E4
Sabaya Bol. 176 E7
Sabdê China 96 D2
Sabelo S. Africa 124 F6
Sāberi, Hāmūn-e marsh Afgh./Iran 111 F4
Şabḩā Jordan 107 C3
Sabhā Libya 121 E2
Şabḩā' Saudi Arabia 110 B6
Sabhrai India 104 B5
Sabi r. India 104 D3
Sabi r. Moz./Zimbabwe see Save
Sabie Moz. 125 K3
Sabie r. Moz./S. Africa 125 K3
Sabie S. Africa 125 J3
Sabina U.S.A. 164 D4
Sabinal Mex. 166 D2
Sabinal, Cayo i. Cuba 163 E8
Sabinas Mex. 167 E3
Sabinas r. Mex. 161 C7
Sabinas Hidalgo Mex. 167 E3
Sabine r. U.S.A. 161 E6
Sabine Lake U.S.A. 161 E6
Sabine Pass U.S.A. 161 E6
Sabini, Monti mts Italy 68 E3
Sabirabad Azer. 113 H2
Sabkhat al Bardawīl Reserve nature res. Egypt see Lake Bardawil Reserve
Sablayan Mindoro Phil. 82 C3
Sable, Cape Canada 153 I6
Sable, Cape U.S.A. 163 D7
Sable, Lac du l. Canada 153 I3
Sable Island Canada 153 K6
Sabon Kafi Niger 120 D3
Sabrātah Libya 121 E1
Sabrina Coast Antarctica 188 F2
Sabtang i. Phil. 82 C1
Sabugal Port. 67 C3
Sabulu Sulawesi Indon. 83 B3
Sabunten i. Indon. 85 F4
Saburyū-yama mt. Japan 93 E2
Sabzawar Afgh. see Shīndand
Sabzevār Iran 110 E2
Sabzvārān Iran see Jīroft
Sacalinul Mare, Insula i. Romania 69 M2
Sacaton U.S.A. 159 H5
Sac City U.S.A. 160 E3
Săcele Romania 69 K2
Sachigo r. Canada 151 N4
Sachigo Lake Canada 151 M4
Sachin India 104 C5
Sach'on S. Korea 91 C6
Sach Pass India 104 D2
Sachsen land Germany 63 N3
Sachsen-Anhalt land Germany 63 L2
Sachsenheim Germany 63 J6
Sachs Harbour Canada 146 F2
Sacirsuyu r. Syria/Turkey see Sājūr, Nahr
Sackpfeife hill Germany 63 I4
Sackville Canada 153 I5
Saco ME U.S.A. 165 J2
Saco MT U.S.A. 156 G2
Sacol i. Phil. 82 C5
Sacramento Brazil 179 B2

▶Sacramento U.S.A. 158 C2
Capital of California.

Sacramento r. U.S.A. 158 C2
Sacramento Mountains U.S.A. 157 G6
Sacramento Valley U.S.A. 158 B1
Sacxán Mex. 167 H5
Sada S. Africa 125 H7
Sádaba Spain 67 F2
Sá da Bandeira Angola see Lubango
Şadad Syria 107 C2
Şa'dah Yemen 108 F6
Sadang r. Indon. 83 A3
Sadao Thai. 87 C6
Saddat al Hindīyah Iraq 113 G4
Saddleback Mesa mt. U.S.A. 161 C5
Saddle Hill hill Australia 136 D2
Saddle Peak hill India 87 A4
Sa Đec Vietnam 87 D5
Sadêng China 96 B2
Sadieville U.S.A. 164 C4
Sadīj watercourse Iran 110 E5
Sadiola Mali 120 B3
Sadiqabad Pak. 111 H4
Sad Istragh mt. Afgh./Pak. 111 I2
Sa'dīyah, Hawr as imp. l. Iraq 113 G4
Sa'diyyat i. U.A.E. 110 D5
Sado r. Port. 67 B4
Sadoga-shima i. Japan 91 E5
Sadong r. Malaysia 85 E2
Sadot Egypt see Sadūt
Sadovoye Rus. Fed. 53 J7
Sa Dragonera i. Spain 67 H4
Sadras India 106 D3
Sadūt Egypt 107 B4
Sadût Egypt see Sadūt
Sæby Denmark 55 G8
Saena Julia Italy see Siena
Safad Israel see Ẓefat
Safāshahr Iran 110 D4
Safayal Maqūf well Iraq 113 G5
Safed Khirs mts Afgh. 111 H2
Safed Koh mts Afgh. 111 G3
Safed Koh mts Afgh./Pak. 111 H3
Saffānīyah, Ra's as pt Saudi Arabia 110 C4
Säffle Sweden 55 H7
Safford U.S.A. 159 I5
Saffron Walden U.K. 59 H6
Safi Morocco 64 C5
Safīdār, Kūh-e mt. Iran 110 D4
Safīd Kūh mts Afgh. 111 F3
Safīd Sagak Iran 111 F3
Safiras, Serra das mts Brazil 179 C2
Şāfītā Syria 107 C2
Safonovo Arkhangel'skaya Oblast' Rus. Fed. 52 K2
Safonovo Smolenskaya Oblast' Rus. Fed. 53 G5
Safrā' al Asyāḩ esc. Saudi Arabia 110 A5
Safrā' as Sark esc. Saudi Arabia 108 F4
Safranbolu Turkey 112 D2
Saga Xizang China 99 D7
Saga Japan 91 C6
Saga Kazakh. 102 B1
Sagaing Myanmar 86 A2
Sagamihara Japan 93 F3
Sagamiko Japan 93 F3
Sagami-nada g. Japan 93 F4
Sagami-wan b. Japan 93 F3
Sagamore U.S.A. 164 F3
Saganthit Kyun i. Myanmar 87 B4
Sagar Karnataka India 106 B3
Sagar Karnataka India 106 C2
Sagar Madh. Prad. India 104 D5
Sagara Japan 93 E4
Sagaredzho Georgia see Sagarejo
Sagarejo Georgia 113 G2
Sagar Island India 105 G5
Sagarmatha National Park Nepal 105 F4
Sagastyr Rus. Fed. 77 N2
Sagavanirktok r. AK U.S.A. 149 J1
Sage U.S.A. 156 F4
Saggi, Har mt. Israel 107 B4
Saghand Iran 110 D3
Sagigik Island AK U.S.A. 148 D6
Saginaw U.S.A. 164 D2
Saginaw Bay U.S.A. 164 D2
Saglek Bay Canada 153 J2
Saglouc Canada see Salluit
Sagly Rus. Fed. 94 B1
Sagone, Golfe de b. Corsica France 66 I5
Sagres Port. 67 B5
Sagsay watercourse Mongolia 94 D2
Sagthale India 104 C5
Saguache U.S.A. 157 G5
Sagua la Grande Cuba 169 H4
Saguaro Lake U.S.A. 159 H5
Saguaro National Park U.S.A. 159 H5
Saguenay r. Canada 153 H4
Saguling, Waduk resr Jawa Indon. 84 D4
Sagunt Spain see Sagunto
Sagunto Spain 67 F4
Saguntum Spain see Sagunto
Sagwon AK U.S.A. 149 J1
Sahabab Uttar Prad. India 99 B7
Sahagún Spain 67 D2
Sahand, Kūh-e mt. Iran 110 B2
Sahara des. Africa 120 D3
Şaḩara el Gharbîya des. Egypt see Western Desert
Şaḩara el Sharqîya des. Egypt see Eastern Desert
Saharan Atlas mts Alg. see Atlas Saharien
Saharanpur India 104 D3
Sahara Well Australia 134 C5
Saharsa India 105 F4
Sahaswan India 104 D3
Sahat, Kūh-e hill Iran 110 D3
Sahatwar India 105 F4
Şahbuz Azer. 113 G3
Sahdol India see Shahdol
Sahebganj India see Sahibganj
Sahebgunj India see Sahibganj
Saheira, Wâdi el watercourse Egypt see Suhaymī, Wādī as
Sahel reg. Africa 120 C3
Sahibganj India 105 F4
Sahiwal Pak. 111 I4
Sahlābād Iran 111 E3
Şaḩm Oman 110 E5
Şaḩneh Iran 110 B3
Şaḩrā al Ḩijārah reg. Iraq 113 G5
Sahu Qinghai China see Zadoi
Sahu Halmahera Indon. 83 C2
Sahuaripa Mex. 166 C2
Sahuayo Mex. 168 D4
Sa Huynh Vietnam 87 E4
Sahyadri mts India see Western Ghats
Sahyadriparvat Range hills India 106 B1
Şahyūn, Qal'at tourist site Syria 107 C2
Sai r. India 105 E4
Sai Buri Thai. 87 C6
Sai Buri, Mae Nam r. Thai. 84 C1
Saïda Alg. 67 G6
Saïda Lebanon see Sidon
Sai Dao Tai, Khao mt. Thai. 87 C4
Saïdia Morocco 67 E6
Sa'īdīyeh Iran see Solṭānīyeh
Saidpur Bangl. 105 G4
Sai-gawa r. Japan 92 C2
Sai-gawa r. Japan 93 E2
Saiha India 105 H5
Saihan Tal Nei Mongol China 95 H3
Saihan Toroi Nei Mongol China 94 E3
Saijō Japan 91 D6
Saikai Kokuritsu-kōen Japan 91 C6
Saiki Japan 91 C6
Sai Kung H.K. China 97 [inset]
Sailana India 104 C5
Sailolof Papua Indon. 83 D3
Saimaa l. Fin. 55 P6
Saimbeyli Turkey 112 E3
Saindak Pak. 111 F4
Sa'īndezh Iran 110 B2
Sa'īn Qal'eh Iran see Sa'īndezh
St Abb's Head hd U.K. 60 G5
St Agnes U.K. 59 B8
St Agnes i. U.K. 59 A9
St Alban's Canada 153 L5
St Albans U.K. 59 G7
St Albans VT U.S.A. 165 I1
St Albans WV U.S.A. 164 E4
St Alban's Head hd England U.K. see St Aldhelm's Head
St Albert Canada 150 H4
St Aldhelm's Head hd U.K. 59 E8
St-Amand-les-Eaux France 62 D4
St-Amand-Montrond France 66 F3
St-Amour France 66 G3
St-André, Cap pt Madag. see Vilanandro, Tanjona
St Andrews U.K. 60 G4
St Andrew Sound inlet U.S.A. 163 D6
St Anne U.S.A. 164 B3
St Ann's Bay Jamaica 169 I5
St Anthony Canada 153 L4
St Anthony U.S.A. 156 F4
St-Arnaud Alg. see El Eulma
St Arnaud Australia 138 A6
St Arnaud Range mts N.Z. 139 D6
St-Arnoult-en-Yvelines France 62 B6
St Asaph Bay N.T. Australia 83 D5
St-Augustin Canada 153 K4
St Augustin r. Canada 153 K4
St Augustine U.S.A. 163 D6
St Austell U.K. 59 C8
St-Avertin France 66 E3
St-Avold France 62 G5
St Barbe Canada 153 K4

▶St-Barthélemy i. West Indies 169 L5
French Overseas Collectivity.

St Bees U.K. 58 D4
St Bees Head hd U.K. 58 D4
St Bride's Bay U.K. 59 B7
St-Brieuc France 66 C2
St Catharines Canada 164 F2
St Catherines Island U.S.A. 163 D6
St Catherine's Point U.K. 59 F8
St-Céré France 66 E4
St-Chamond France 66 G4
St Charles ID U.S.A. 156 F4
St Charles MD U.S.A. 165 G4
St Charles MI U.S.A. 164 C2
St Charles MO U.S.A. 160 F4
St-Chély-d'Apcher France 66 F4
St Christopher and Nevis country West Indies see St Kitts and Nevis
St Clair r. Canada/U.S.A. 164 D2
St Clair, Lake Canada/U.S.A. 164 D2
St-Claude France 66 G3
St Clears U.K. 59 C7
St Cloud U.S.A. 160 E2
St Croix r. U.S.A. 152 B5
St Croix Falls U.S.A. 160 E2
St David U.S.A. 159 H6
St David's Head hd U.K. 59 B7
St-Denis France 62 C6

▶St-Denis Réunion 185 L7
Capital of Réunion.

St-Denis-du-Sig Alg. see Sig
St-Dié France 66 H2
St-Dizier France 62 E6
St-Domingue country West Indies see Haiti
Sainte Anne Canada 151 L5
Ste-Anne, Lac l. Canada 153 I4
St Elias, Cape AK U.S.A. 149 K4

▶St Elias, Mount AK U.S.A. 149 L3
4th highest mountain in North America.

St Elias Mountains Y.T. Canada 149 L3
Ste-Marguerite r. Canada 153 I4
Ste-Marie, Cap c. Madag. see Vohimena, Tanjona
Sainte-Marie, Île i. Madag. see Boraha, Nosy
Ste-Maxime France 66 H5
Sainte Rose du Lac Canada 151 L5
Saintes France 66 D4
Sainte Thérèse, Lac l. Canada 150 F1
St-Étienne France 66 G4
St-Étienne-du-Rouvray France 62 B5
St-Fabien Canada 153 H4
St-Félicien Canada 153 G4
Saintfield U.K. 61 G3
St-Florent Corsica France 66 I5
St-Florent-sur-Cher France 66 F3
St-Floris, Parc National nat. park Cent. Afr. Rep. 122 C3
St-Flour France 66 F4
St Francesville U.S.A. 161 F6
St Francis U.S.A. 160 C4
St Francis r. U.S.A. 161 F5
St Francis Isles Australia 135 F8
St-François r. Canada 153 G5
St-François, Lac l. Canada 153 H5
St-Gaudens France 66 E5
St George Australia 138 D2
St George r. Australia 136 D3
St George AK U.S.A. 148 E5
St George SC U.S.A. 163 D5
St George UT U.S.A. 159 G3
St George, Point U.S.A. 156 B4
St George Island AK U.S.A. 148 E4
St George Range hills Australia 134 D4
St-Georges Canada 153 H5

▶St George's Grenada 169 L6
Capital of Grenada.

St George's Bay Nfld. and Lab. Canada 153 K4
St George's Bay N.S. Canada 153 J5

St George's Cay i. Belize 167 I5
St George's Channel Ireland/U.K. 61 F6
St George's Channel P.N.G. 132 F2
St George's Head hd Australia 138 E5
St Gotthard Hungary see Szentgotthárd
St Gotthard Pass Switz. 66 I3
St Govan's Head hd U.K. 59 C7
St Helen U.S.A. 164 C1
St Helena i. S. Atlantic Ocean 184 H7
St Helena U.S.A. 158 B2
St Helena, Ascension and Tristan de Cunha terr. S. Atlantic Ocean 184 H7
St Helena Bay S. Africa 124 D7
St Helens Australia 137 [inset]
St Helens U.K. 58 E5
St Helens U.S.A. 156 C3
St Helens, Mount vol. U.S.A. 156 C3
St Helens Point Australia 137 [inset]

▶St Helier Channel Is 59 E9
Capital of Jersey.

Sainthiya India 105 F5
St-Hubert Belgium 62 F4
St-Hyacinthe Canada 153 G5
St Ignace U.S.A. 162 C2
St Ignace Island Canada 152 D4
St Ishmael U.K. 59 C7
St Ives England U.K. 59 B8
St Ives England U.K. 59 G6
St-Jacques, Cap Vietnam see Vung Tau
St-Jacques-de-Dupuy Canada 152 F4
St James MN U.S.A. 160 E3
St James MO U.S.A. 160 F4
St James, Cape B.C. Canada 149 O6
St-Jean r. Canada 153 I4
St-Jean, Lac l. Canada 153 G4
St-Jean-d'Acre Israel see 'Akko
St-Jean-d'Angély France 66 D4
St-Jean-de-Monts France 66 C3
St-Jean-sur-Richelieu Canada 165 I1
St-Jérôme Canada 152 G5
St Joe r. U.S.A. 156 D3
Saint John Canada 153 I5
St John U.S.A. 160 D4
St John r. U.S.A. 162 H2
St John, Cape Canada 153 L4
St John Bay Canada 153 K4
St John Island Canada 153 K4

▶St John's Antigua and Barbuda 169 L5
Capital of Antigua and Barbuda.

▶St John's Canada 153 L5
Capital of Newfoundland and Labrador.

St Johns AZ U.S.A. 159 I4
St Johns MI U.S.A. 164 C2
St Johns OH U.S.A. 164 C3
St Johns r. U.S.A. 163 D6
St Johnsbury U.S.A. 165 I1
St John's Chapel U.K. 58 E4
St Joseph IL U.S.A. 164 A3
St Joseph LA U.S.A. 161 F6
St Joseph MI U.S.A. 164 B2
St Joseph MO U.S.A. 160 E4
St Joseph r. U.S.A. 164 C3
St Joseph, Lake Canada 151 N5
St-Joseph-d'Alma Canada see Alma
St Joseph Island Canada 152 E5
St Joseph Island TX U.S.A. 167 F3
St-Junien France 66 E4
St Just U.K. 59 B8
St-Just-en-Chaussée France 62 C5
St Keverne U.K. 59 B8
St Kilda i. U.K. 50 E4
St Kilda is U.K. 56 C2
St Kitts and Nevis country West Indies 169 L5
St-Laurent inlet Canada see St Lawrence
St-Laurent, Golfe du g. Canada see St Lawrence, Gulf of
St-Laurent-du-Maroni Fr. Guiana 177 H2
St Lawrence Canada 153 L5
St Lawrence inlet Canada 153 H4
St Lawrence, Cape Canada 153 J5
St Lawrence, Gulf of Canada 153 J4
St Lawrence Island AK U.S.A. 148 B3
St Lawrence Islands National Park Canada 165 H1
St Lawrence Seaway sea chan. Canada/U.S.A. 165 H1
St-Léonard Canada 153 G5
St Leonard U.S.A. 165 G4
St Lewis r. Canada 153 K3
St-Lô France 66 D2
St-Louis Senegal 120 B3
St Louis MI U.S.A. 164 C2
St Louis MO U.S.A. 160 F4
St Louis r. U.S.A. 152 B5
St Lucia country West Indies 169 L6
St Lucia, Lake S. Africa 125 K5
St Lucia Estuary S. Africa 125 K5
St Luke's Island Myanmar see Zadetkale Kyun
St Magnus Bay U.K. 60 [inset]
St-Maixent-l'École France 66 D3
St-Malo France 66 C2
St-Malo, Golfe de g. France 66 C2
St-Marc Haiti 169 J5
St Maries U.S.A. 156 D3
St Marks S. Africa 125 H7
St Mark's S. Africa see Cofimvaba
St-Martin i. West Indies see Sint Maarten

▶St-Martin i. West Indies 169 L5
French Overseas Collectivity. The southern part of the island is the Dutch territory of Sint Maarten.

St Martin, Cape S. Africa 124 C7
St Martin, Lake Canada 151 L5
St Martin's i. U.K. 59 A9
St Martin's Island Bangl. 86 A2
St Mary Peak Australia 137 B6
St Mary Reservoir Canada 150 H5
St Mary's Canada 164 E2
St Mary's U.K. 60 G2
St Mary's i. U.K. 59 A9
St Marys AK U.S.A. 148 G3
St Marys PA U.S.A. 165 F3
St Marys WV U.S.A. 164 E4
St Marys r. U.S.A. 164 C3
St Mary's, Cape Canada 153 L5
St Mary's Bay Canada 153 L5
St Marys City U.S.A. 165 G4
St Matthew Island AK U.S.A. 148 D3
St Matthews U.S.A. 164 C4
St Matthew's Island Myanmar see Zadetkyi Kyun
St Matthias Group is P.N.G. 81 L7
St-Maurice r. Canada 153 G5
St Mawes U.K. 59 B8
St-Médard-en-Jalles France 66 D4
St Meinrad U.S.A. 164 B4
St Michael AK U.S.A. 148 G3
St Michaels U.S.A. 165 G4
St Michael's Bay Canada 153 L3
St-Mihiel France 62 F6
St-Nazaire France 66 C3
St Neots U.K. 59 G6
St-Nicolas Belgium see Sint-Niklaas
St-Nicolas, Mont hill Lux. 62 G5
St-Nicolas-de-Port France 66 H2
St-Omer France 62 C4
Saintonge reg. France 66 D4
St-Pacôme Canada 153 H5
St-Palais France 66 D5
St Paris U.S.A. 164 D3
St-Pascal Canada 153 H5
St Paul r. Canada 153 K4
St-Paul atoll Fr. Polynesia see Hereheretue
St Paul AK U.S.A. 148 E4

▶St Paul MN U.S.A. 160 E2
Capital of Minnesota.

St Paul NE U.S.A. 160 D3
St-Paul, Île i. Indian Ocean 185 N8
St Paul Island AK U.S.A. 148 E4
St Paul Subterranean River National Park Phil. 82 B4
St Peter and St Paul Rocks is N. Atlantic Ocean see São Pedro e São Paulo

▶St Peter Port Channel Is 59 E9
Capital of Guernsey.

St Peter's N.S. Canada 153 J5
St Peters P.E.I. Canada 153 J5
St Petersburg Rus. Fed. 55 Q7
St Petersburg U.S.A. 163 D7
St-Pierre mt. France 66 G5

▶St-Pierre St Pierre and Miquelon 153 L5
Capital of St Pierre and Miquelon.

▶St Pierre and Miquelon terr. N. America 153 K5
French Territorial Collectivity.

St-Pierre-d'Oléron France 66 D4
St-Pierre-le-Moûtier France 66 F3
St-Pol-sur-Ternoise France 62 C4
St-Pourçain-sur-Sioule France 66 F3
St-Quentin France 62 D5
St Regis U.S.A. 156 E3
St Regis Falls U.S.A. 165 H1
St-Rémi Canada 165 I1
St-Saëns France 62 B5
St Sebastian Bay S. Africa 124 E8
St-Siméon Canada 153 H5
St Simons Island U.S.A. 163 D6
St Theresa Point Canada 151 M4
St Thomas Canada 164 E2
St-Trond Belgium see Sint-Truiden
St-Tropez France 66 H5
St-Tropez, Cap de c. France 66 H5
St-Vaast-la-Hougue France 59 F9
St-Valery-en-Caux France 59 H9
St-Véran France 66 H4
St Vincent U.S.A. 160 D1
St Vincent country West Indies see St Vincent and the Grenadines
St Vincent, Cape Australia 137 [inset]
St Vincent, Cape Port. see São Vicente, Cabo de
St Vincent, Gulf Australia 137 B7
St Vincent and the Grenadines country West Indies 169 L6
St Vincent Passage St Lucia/St Vincent 169 L6
St-Vith Belgium 62 G4
St Walburg Canada 151 I4
St Williams Canada 164 E2
St-Yrieix-la-Perche France 66 E4
Sain Us Nei Mongol China 95 F3
Saioa mt. Spain 67 F2
Saipal mt. Nepal 104 E3
Saipan i. N. Mariana Is 81 L3
Saipan Palau 82 [inset]
Sai Pok Liu Hoi Hap H.K. China see West Lamma Channel
Saitama Japan 89 P5
Saitama pref. Japan 93 E3
Saiteli Turkey see Kadınhanı
Saitlai Myanmar 86 A2
Saittanulkki hill Fin. 54 N3
Sai Yok National Park Thai. 87 B4
Sajam Indon. 81 I7
Sajama, Nevado mt. Bol. 176 E7
Sājir Saudi Arabia 110 B5
Sājūr, Nahr r. Syria/Turkey 107 D1
Sajzī Iran 110 D3
Sak watercourse S. Africa 124 E5
Sakado Japan 93 F3
Sakae Chiba Japan 93 G3
Sakae Nagano Japan 93 E2
Sakai Fukui Japan 92 C2
Sakai Gunma Japan 93 F2
Sakai Ibaraki Japan 93 F2
Sakai Nagano Japan 93 E2
Sakai Ōsaka Japan 92 B4
Sakaide Japan 91 D6
Sakaigawa Japan 93 E3
Sakākah Saudi Arabia 113 F5
Sakakawea, Lake U.S.A. 160 C2
Sakaki Japan 93 E2
Sakakita Japan 93 E2
Sakala i. Indon. 85 G4
Sakami Canada 152 G3
Sakami r. Canada 152 F3
Sakami-gawa r. Japan 93 F3
Sakami Lake Canada 152 F3
Sakar mts Bulg. 69 L4
Sakaraha Madag. 123 E6
Sak'art'velo country Asia see Georgia
Sakarya Sakarya Turkey see Adapazarı
Sakarya r. Turkey 69 N4
Sakashita Japan 92 D3
Sakassou Côte d'Ivoire 120 C4
Sakata Japan 91 E5
Sakauchi Japan 92 C3
Sakchu N. Korea 91 B4
Saken Seyfullin Kazakh. 98 A2
Sakesar Pak. 111 I3
Sakhalin i. Rus. Fed. 90 F2
Sakhalin Oblast admin. div. Rus. Fed. see Sakhalinskaya Oblast'
Sakhalinskaya Oblast' admin. div. Rus. Fed. 90 F2
Sakhalinskiy Zaliv b. Rus. Fed. 90 F1
Sakhi India 104 C3
Sakhile S. Africa 125 I4
Şäki Azer. 113 G2
Saki Nigeria see Shaki
Saki Ukr. see Saky
Šakiai Lith. 55 M9
Sakir mt. Pak. 111 G4
Sakishima-shotō is Japan 89 M8
Sakoli India 104 D5
Sakon Nakhon Thai. 86 D3
Sakrivier S. Africa 124 E6
Saku Nagano Japan 93 E2
Saku Nagano Japan 93 E2
Sakuma Japan 93 D3
Sakura Japan 93 G3
Sakuragawa Japan 93 G3
Sakura-gawa r. Japan 93 G2
Sakurai Japan 92 B4
Saku-shima i. Japan 92 D4
Saky Ukr. 112 D1
Säkylä Fin. 55 M6
Sal i. Cape Verde 120 [inset]
Sal r. Rus. Fed. 53 I7
Sal, Punta pt Hond. 166 [inset] I6
Sala Sweden 55 J7
Salabangka, Kepulauan is Indon. 83 B3
Salaberry-de-Valleyfield Canada 165 H1
Salacgrīva Latvia 55 N8
Sala Consilina Italy 68 F4
Salada, Laguna salt l. Mex. 166 B1
Saladas Arg. 178 E3
Salado r. Buenos Aires Arg. 178 E5
Salado r. Santa Fé Arg. 178 D4
Salado r. Arg. 178 C5
Salado r. Mex. 167 F3
Salaga Ghana 120 C4
Salairskiy Kryazh ridge Rus. Fed. 88 E2
Salajwe Botswana 124 G2
Şalālah Oman 109 H6
Salamá Guat. 167 H6
Salamá Hond. 166 [inset] I6
Salamanca Mex. 168 D4
Salamanca Spain 67 D3
Salamanca U.S.A. 165 F2
Salamanga Moz. 125 K4
Salamantica Spain see Salamanca
Salamat, Bahr r. Chad 121 E4
Salamban Kalimantan Indon. 85 F3
Salāmī Iran 111 E3
Salamina i. Greece 69 J6
Salamis tourist site Cyprus 107 A2
Salamís i. Greece see Salamina
Salamīyah Syria 107 C2
Salamonie r. U.S.A. 164 C3
Salamonie Lake U.S.A. 164 C3
Salang, Tūnel-e Afgh. 111 H3
Salantai Lith. 55 L8
Salaqi Nei Mongol China 95 G3
Salar de Pocitos Arg. 178 C2
Salari Pak. 111 G5
Salas Spain 67 C2
Salaspils Latvia 55 N8
Salatiga Jawa Indon. 85 E4
Salavan Laos 86 D4
Salawati i. Papua Indon. 83 D3
Salawin, Mae Nam r. China/Myanmar see Salween
Salay Mindanao Phil. 82 D4
Salaya India 104 B5
Salayar i. Indon. 83 B4
Salayar, Selat sea chan. Indon. 83 B4
Sala y Gómez, Isla i. S. Pacific Ocean 187 M7
Salazar Angola see N'dalatando
Salbris France 66 F3
Šalcha r. AK U.S.A. 149 K2
Šalčininkai Lith. 55 N9
Salcombe U.K. 59 D8
Saldae Alg. see Bejaïa
Saldaña Spain 67 D2
Saldanha S. Africa 124 C7
Saldanha Bay S. Africa 124 C7
Saldus Latvia 55 M8
Sale Australia 138 C7
Salea Sulawesi Indon. 83 B3
Saleh, Teluk b. Sumbawa Indon. 85 G5
Şāleḩābād Iran 110 C3
Salekhard Rus. Fed. 76 H3
Salem India 106 C4
Salem AR U.S.A. 161 F4
Salem IL U.S.A. 160 F4
Salem IN U.S.A. 164 B4
Salem MA U.S.A. 165 J2
Salem MO U.S.A. 160 F4
Salem NJ U.S.A. 165 H4
Salem NY U.S.A. 165 I2
Salem OH U.S.A. 164 E3

▶Salem OR U.S.A. 156 C3
Capital of Oregon.

Salem SD U.S.A. 160 D3
Salem VA U.S.A. 164 E5
Salen Scotland U.K. 60 D4
Salen Scotland U.K. 60 D4
Salerno Italy 68 F4
Salerno, Golfo di g. Italy 68 F4
Salernum Italy see Salerno
Salford U.K. 58 E5
Salgótarján Hungary 57 Q6
Salgueiro Brazil 177 K5
Salian Afgh. 111 F4
Salibabu i. Indon. 83 C2
Salida U.S.A. 157 G5
Salies-de-Béarn France 66 D5
Salihli Turkey 69 M5
Salihorsk Belarus 55 O10
Salima Malawi 123 D5
Salimbatu Kalimantan Indon. 85 G2
Salina KS U.S.A. 160 D4
Salina UT U.S.A. 159 H2
Salina, Isola i. Italy 68 F5
Salina Cruz Mex. 168 E5
Salinas Brazil 179 C2
Salinas Ecuador 176 B4
Salinas Mex. 168 D4
Salinas r. Mex. 161 D7
Salinas U.S.A. 158 C3
Salinas r. U.S.A. 158 C3
Salinas, Cabo de c. Spain see Ses Salines, Cap de
Salinas, Ponta das pt Angola 123 B5
Salinas Peak U.S.A. 157 G6
Saline U.S.A. 164 D2
Saline r. U.S.A. 160 D4
Saline Valley depr. U.S.A. 158 E3
Salinópolis Brazil 177 I4
Salinosó Lachay, Punta pt Peru 176 C6
Salisbury U.K. 59 F7
Salisbury MD U.S.A. 165 H4
Salisbury NC U.S.A. 162 D5
Salisbury Zimbabwe see Harare
Salisbury, Mount AK U.S.A. 149 K1
Salisbury Plain U.K. 59 E7
Şalkhad Syria 107 C3
Salla Fin. 54 P3
Sallisaw U.S.A. 161 E5
Salluit Canada 189 K2
Sallum, Khalīj as b. Egypt 112 B5
Sallyana Nepal 105 E3
Salmās Iran 110 B2
Salmi Rus. Fed. 52 F3
Salmo Canada 150 G5
Salmon U.S.A. 156 E3
Salmon r. U.S.A. 156 D3
Salmon Arm Canada 150 G5
Salmon Falls Creek r. U.S.A. 156 E4
Salmon Fork r. Canada/U.S.A. 149 L2
Salmon Gums Australia 135 C8
Salmon Reservoir U.S.A. 165 H2
Salmon River Mountains U.S.A. 156 E3
Salmon Village AK U.S.A. 149 L2
Salmtal Germany 62 G5
Salo Fin. 55 M6
Salome U.S.A. 159 G5
Salon India 104 E4
Salon-de-Provence France 66 G5
Salonica Greece see Thessaloniki
Salonika Greece see Thessaloniki
Salpausselkä reg. Fin. 55 N6
Salqīn Syria 107 C1
Salses, Étang de l. France see Leucate, Étang de
Sal'sk Rus. Fed. 53 I7
Salsomaggiore Terme Italy 68 C2
Salt Jordan see As Salṭ
Salt watercourse S. Africa 124 F7
Salt r. U.S.A. 159 G5
Salta Arg. 178 C2
Saltaire U.K. 58 F5
Saltash U.K. 59 C8
Saltcoats U.K. 60 E5
Saltee Islands Ireland 61 F5
Saltfjellet Svartisen Nasjonalpark nat. park Norway 54 I3
Saltfjorden sea chan. Norway 54 H3
Salt Flat TX U.S.A. 166 D2
Salt Fork Arkansas r. U.S.A. 161 D4
Salt Fork Lake U.S.A. 164 E3
Saltillo Mex. 167 E3
Salt Lake India 111 I5

▶Salt Lake City U.S.A. 159 H1
Capital of Utah.

Salt Lick U.S.A. 164 D4
Salto Brazil 179 B3
Salto Uruguay 178 E4
Salto da Divisa Brazil 179 D2
Salto de Agua Chiapas Mex. 167 G5
Salto Grande Brazil 179 A3
Salton Sea salt l. U.S.A. 159 F5
Salto Santiago, Represa de resr Brazil 178 F3
Salt Range hills Pak. 111 I3
Salt River Canada 151 H2
Saluda U.S.A. 165 G5
Saluebesar i. Indon. 83 B3
Saluekecil i. Indon. 83 B3
Salue Timpaus, Selat sea chan. Indon. 83 B3
Salûm Egypt see As Sallūm
Salûm, Khalîg el b. Egypt see Sallum, Khalīj as
Saluq, Kūh-e mt. Iran 110 E2
Salur India 106 D2
Saluzzo Italy 68 B2
Salvador Brazil 179 D1
Salvador, Lake U.S.A. 161 F6
Salvaleón de Higüey Dom. Rep. see Higüey
Salvatierra Mex. 167 E4
Salvation Creek r. U.S.A. 159 H2
Salwah Saudi Arabia 122 F1
Salwah, Dawḩat b. Qatar/Saudi Arabia 110 C5
Salween r. China/Myanmar 96 C5
also known as Mae Nam Salawin, Nu Jiang (China) or Thanlwin (Myanmar)
Salyan Azer. 113 H3
Salyan Nepal see Sallyana
Sal'yany Azer. see Salyan
Salyersville U.S.A. 164 D5
Salzbrunn Namibia 124 C3
Salzburg Austria 57 N7
Salzgitter Germany 63 K2
Salzhausen Germany 63 K1
Salzkotten Germany 63 I3
Salzmünde Germany 63 L3
Salzwedel Germany 63 L2
Sam India 104 B4
Samae San, Ko i. Thai. 87 C4
Samagaltay Rus. Fed. 94 C1
Samāh well Saudi Arabia 110 B4
Samaida Iran see Someydeh
Samaixung Xizang China 99 C6
Samak, Tanjung pt Indon. 84 D3
Samakhixai Laos see Attapu
Samal i. Phil. 82 D5
Samalanga Sumatera Indon. 84 B1
Samalantan Kalimantan Indon. 85 E2
Samalayuca Mex. 166 D2
Samales Group is Phil. 82 C5
Samalga Pass sea channel AK U.S.A. 148 E5
Samalkot India 106 D2
Samālūṭ Egypt 112 C5
Samâlûṭ Egypt see Samālūṭ
Samana Cay i. Bahamas 163 F8
Samanala mt. Sri Lanka see Adam's Peak
Samandağı Turkey 107 B1
Samangān Afgh. see Āybak
Samangān Iran 111 F3
Samani Japan 90 F4
Samanlı Dağları mts Turkey 69 M4
Samar Kazakh. see Samarskoye
Samar i. Phil. 82 D4
Samara Rus. Fed. 53 K5
Samara r. Rus. Fed. 51 Q5
Samarahan Sarawak Malaysia see Sri Aman
Samarga Rus. Fed. 90 E3
Samarinda Kalimantan Indon. 85 G3
Samarka Rus. Fed. 90 D3
Samarkand Uzbek. see Samarqand
Samarkand, Pik mt. Tajik. see Samarqand, Qullai
Samarobriva France see Amiens
Samarqand Uzbek. 111 G2
Samarqand, Qullai mt. Tajik. 111 H2
Sāmarrā' Iraq 113 F4
Samar Sea g. Phil. 82 D4
Samarskoye Kazakh. 102 F2
Samarz Nei Mongol China 95 H2
Samasata Pak. 111 H4
Samastipur India 105 F4
Samate Papua Indon. 83 D3
Şamaxı Azer. 113 H2
Samba r. Indon. 85 F3
Samba India 104 C2
Sambaliung mts Indon. 85 G2
Sambalpur India 105 E5
Sambar, Tanjung pt Indon. 85 E3
Sambas Kalimantan Indon. 85 E2
Sambat Ukr. see Kiev
Sambava Madag. 123 F5
Sambha India 105 G4
Sambhajinagar India see Aurangabad
Sambhal India 104 D3
Sambhar Lake India 104 C4
Sambiat Sulawesi Indon. 83 B3
Sambir Ukr. 53 D6
Sambit i. Indon. 85 G2
Sambito r. Brazil 177 J5
Sambo Sulawesi Barat Indon. 83 A3
Samboja Kalimantan Indon. 85 G3
Sâmbor Cambodia 87 D4
Sambor Ukr. see Sambir
Samborombón, Bahía b. Arg. 178 E5
Sambre r. Belgium/France 62 E4
Sambu Japan see Sanbu
Samch'ŏk S. Korea 91 C5
Samch'ŏnp'o S. Korea see Sach'on
Same Tanz. 122 D4
Samegawa Japan 93 G1
Samer France 62 B4
Sami India 104 B5
Samia, Tanjung pt Indon. 83 B2
Samīrah Saudi Arabia 108 F4
Samirum Iran see Yazd-e Khvāst
Samizu Japan 93 E2
Samjiyŏn N. Korea 90 C4
Şämkir Azer. 113 G2
Sam Neua Laos see Xam Nua
Samoa country S. Pacific Ocean 133 I3
Samoa Basin sea feature S. Pacific Ocean 186 I7
Samoa i Sisifo country S. Pacific Ocean see Samoa
Samobor Croatia 68 F2
Samoded Rus. Fed. 52 I3
Samokov Bulg. 69 J3
Šamorín Slovakia 57 P6
Samos i. Greece 69 L6
Samosir i. Indon. 84 B2
Samothrace i. Greece see Samothraki
Samothraki i. Greece 69 K4
Samoylovka Rus. Fed. 53 I6
Sampaga Sulawesi Barat Indon. 83 A3
Sampang Jawa Indon. 85 F4
Sampê China see Xiangcheng
Sampit Kalimantan Indon. 85 F3
Sampit r. Indon. 85 F3
Sampit, Teluk b. Indon. 85 F3
Sampolawa Sulawesi Indon. 83 B4
Sam Rayburn Reservoir U.S.A. 161 E6
Samrong Cambodia see Phumĭ Sâmraông
Samsang Xizang China 99 C7
Sam Sao, Phou mts Laos/Vietnam 86 C2
Samson U.S.A. 163 C6
Sâm Sơn Vietnam 86 D3
Samsun Turkey 112 E2
Samsy Kazakh. 98 B4
Samti Afgh. 111 H2
Samui, Ko i. Thai. 87 C5
Samukawa Japan 93 F3
Samut Prakan Thai. 87 C4
Samut Sakhon Thai. 87 C4
Samut Songkhram Thai. 87 C4
Samyai Xizang China 99 E7
San Mali 120 C3
San, Phou mt. Laos 86 C3
San, Tônlé r. Cambodia 87 D4

▶Şan'ā' Yemen 108 F6
Capital of Yemen.

Sanaa Yemen see Şan'ā'
Sanada Japan 93 E2
SANAE IV research station Antarctica 188 B2
Sanage Japan 92 D3
San Agostín U.S.A. see St Augustine
San Agustin, Cape Mindanao Phil. 82 D5
San Agustin, Plains of U.S.A. 159 I5
Sanak AK U.S.A. 148 G5
Sanak Island AK U.S.A. 148 G5
Sanana Maluku Indon. 83 C3
Sanandaj Iran 110 B3
San Andreas U.S.A. 158 C2
San Andrés Guat. 167 H5
San Andres Phil. 82 D3
San Andrés, Isla de i. Caribbean Sea 169 H6
San Andres Mountains U.S.A. 157 G6
San Andrés Tuxtla Mex. 167 G5
San Angelo U.S.A. 161 C6
San Antonio Belize 167 H5
San Antonio Chile 178 B4
San Antonio Hond. 166 [inset] I6
San Antonio Luzon Phil. 82 C3
San Antonio NM U.S.A. 157 G6
San Antonio TX U.S.A. 161 D6
San Antonio r. U.S.A. 161 D6
San Antonio, Cabo c. Cuba 169 H4
San Antonio Bay Palawan Phil. 82 B4
San Antonio del Mar Mex. 166 A2
San Antonio de Oriente Hond. 166 [inset] I6
San Antonio Oeste Arg. 178 D6
San Antonio Reservoir U.S.A. 158 C4
San Augustín de Valle Fértil Arg. 178 C4
San Augustine U.S.A. 161 E6
San Bartolo Mex. 167 E4
San Benedetto del Tronto Italy 68 E3
San Benedicto, Isla i. Mex. 168 B5
San Benito Guat. 167 H5
San Benito U.S.A. 161 D7
San Benito r. U.S.A. 158 C3
San Benito Mountain U.S.A. 158 C3
San Bernardino U.S.A. 158 E4
San Bernardino Mountains U.S.A. 158 E4
San Bernardino Strait Phil. 82 D3
San Bernardo Chile 178 B4
San Bernardo Mex. 166 D3
San Blas Nayarit Mex. 166 D4
San Blas Sinaloa Mex. 166 C3
San Blas, Archipiélago de is Panama 166 [inset] K7
San Blas, Cape U.S.A. 163 C6
San Blas, Cordillera de mts Panama 166 [inset] K7
San Borja Bol. 176 E6
Sanbornville U.S.A. 165 J2
Sanbu China see Kaiping
Sanbu Japan 93 G3
San Buenaventura Mex. 167 E3
San Carlos Chile 178 B5
San Carlos Equat. Guinea see Luba
San Carlos Coahuila Mex. 167 E2
San Carlos Tamaulipas Mex. 161 D7
San Carlos Nicaragua 166 [inset] I7
San Carlos Luzon Phil. 82 C3
San Carlos Negros Phil. 82 C4
San Carlos U.S.A. 159 H5
San Carlos Venez. 176 E2
San Carlos de Bariloche Arg. 178 B6
San Carlos de Bolívar Arg. 178 D5
San Carlos Indian Reservation res. AZ U.S.A. 166 C1
San Carlos Lake U.S.A. 159 H5
Sancha Gansu China 94 F5
Sancha Shanxi China 95 G4
Sanchahe China see Fuyu
Sancha He r. China 96 E3
Sanchakou Xinjiang China 98 B5
Sanchi India 104 D5
San Chien Pau mt. Laos 86 C2
Sanchor India 104 B4
San Ciro de Acosta Mex. 167 F4
San Clemente U.S.A. 158 E5
San Clemente Island U.S.A. 158 D5
Sanclêr U.K. see St Clears
Sanco Point Mindanao Phil. 82 D4
San Cristóbal Verapaz Guat. 167 H6
San Cristóbal Arg. 178 D4
San Cristobal i. Solomon Is 133 G3
San Cristóbal Venez. 176 D2
San Cristóbal, Isla i. Galápagos Ecuador 176 [inset]
San Cristóbal, Volcán vol. Nicaragua 166 [inset] I6
San Cristóbal de las Casas Mex. 167 G5
Sancti Spíritus Cuba 169 I4
Sand r. S. Africa 125 J2
Sanda Japan 92 B4
Sandagou Rus. Fed. 90 D4
Sandai Kalimantan Indon. 85 E3
Sanda Island U.K. 60 D5
Sandakan Sabah Malaysia 85 G1
Sandakan, Pelabuhan inlet Malaysia 85 G1
Sandakphu Peak Sikkim India 99 E8
Sândăn Cambodia 87 D4
Sandane Norway 54 E6
Sandanski Bulg. 69 J4
Sandaohezi Xinjiang China see Shawan
Sandaré Mali 120 B3
Sandau Germany 63 M2
Sanday i. U.K. 60 G1
Sandbach U.K. 59 E5
Sandborn U.S.A. 164 B4
Sand Cay reef India 106 B4
Sandefjord Norway 55 G7
Sandercock Nunataks Antarctica 188 D2
Sanders U.S.A. 159 I4
Sandersleben Germany 63 L3
Sanderson U.S.A. 161 C6
Sandfire Roadhouse Australia 134 C4
Sand Fork U.S.A. 164 E4
Sandgate Australia 138 F1
Sandhead U.K. 60 E6
Sand Hill r. U.S.A. 160 D2
Sand Hills U.S.A. 160 C3
Sandia Peru 176 E6
San Diego Chihuahua Mex. 166 D2
San Diego CA U.S.A. 158 E5
San Diego TX U.S.A. 161 D7
San Diego, Sierra mts Mex. 166 C2
Sandıklı Turkey 69 N5
Sandila India 104 E4
Sanding i. Indon. 84 C3
Sand Islands AK U.S.A. 148 F3
Sand Lake Canada 152 D5
Sand Lake l. Canada 151 M5
Sandnes Norway 55 D7
Sandnessjøen Norway 54 H3
Sandoa Dem. Rep. Congo 123 C4
Sandomierz Poland 53 D6
San Donà di Piave Italy 68 E2
Sandover watercourse Australia 136 B4
Sandovo Rus. Fed. 52 H4
Sandoway Myanmar see Thandwè
Sandown U.K. 59 F8
Sandoy i. Faroe Is 54 [inset]
Sand Point AK U.S.A. 148 G5
Sandpoint U.S.A. 156 D2
Sandray i. U.K. 60 B4
Sandringham Australia 136 B5
Şandrul Mare, Vârful mt. Romania 69 L1
Sandsjö Sweden 55 I6
Sandspit B.C. Canada 149 O5
Sand Springs U.S.A. 161 D4
Sand Springs Salt Flat U.S.A. 158 D2
Sandstone Australia 135 B6
Sandstone U.S.A. 160 E2
Sandu Guizhou China 96 E3
Sandu Hunan China 97 G3
Sandur Faroe Is 54 [inset]
Sandusky MI U.S.A. 164 D2
Sandusky OH U.S.A. 164 D3
Sandveld mts S. Africa 124 D6
Sandverhaar Namibia 124 C4
Sandvika Akershus Norway 55 G7
Sandvika Nord-Trøndelag Norway 54 H5
Sandviken Sweden 55 J6
Sandwich Bay Canada 153 K3
Sandwich Island Vanuatu see Éfaté

Sandwich Islands is N. Pacific Ocean see Hawai'ian Islands
Sandwick U.K. 60 [inset]
Sandwip Bangl. 105 G5
Sandy U.S.A. 159 H1
Sandy r. U.S.A. 165 K1
Sandy Bay Canada 151 K4
Sandy Cape Qld Australia 136 F5
Sandy Cape Tas. Australia 137 [inset]
Sandy Hook U.S.A. 164 D4
Sandy Hook pt U.S.A. 165 H3
Sandy Island Australia 134 C3
Sandykgachy Turkm. see Sandykgaçy
Sandykgaçy Turkm. 111 F2
Sandykly Gumy des. Turkm. 111 F2
Sandy Lake Alta Canada 150 H4
Sandy Lake Ont. Canada 151 M4
Sandy Lake l. Canada 151 M4
Sandy Springs U.S.A. 163 C5
San Estanislao Para. 178 E2
San Esteban, Isla i. Mex. 166 B2
San Felipe Chile 178 B4
San Felipe Baja California Mex. 166 B2
San Felipe Chihuahua Mex. 166 D3
San Felipe Guanajuato Mex. 167 E4
San Felipe Venez. 176 E1
San Felipe, Cayos de is Cuba 163 D8
San Felipe de Puerto Plata Dom. Rep. see Puerto Plata
San Fernando Chile 178 B4
San Fernando Baja California Mex. 166 B2
San Fernando Tamaulipas Mex. 167 F3
San Fernando watercourse Mex. 157 E7
San Fernando Luzon Phil. 82 C2
San Fernando Luzon Phil. 82 C3
San Fernando Spain 67 C5
San Fernando Trin. and Tob. 169 L6
San Fernando U.S.A. 158 D4
San Fernando de Apure Venez. 176 E2
San Fernando de Atabapo Venez. 176 E3
San Fernando de Monte Cristi Dom. Rep. see Monte Cristi
Sanford FL U.S.A. 163 D6
Sanford ME U.S.A. 165 J2
Sanford MI U.S.A. 164 C2
Sanford NC U.S.A. 162 E5
Sanford, Mount AK U.S.A. 149 K3
Sanford Lake U.S.A. 164 C2
San Francisco Arg. 178 D4
San Francisco Sonora Mex. 166 B2
San Francisco U.S.A. 158 B3
San Francisco, Cabo de c. Ecuador 176 B3
San Francisco, Passo de pass Arg./Chile 178 C3
San Francisco, Sierra mts Mex. 166 B3
San Francisco Bay inlet U.S.A. 158 B3
San Francisco del Oro Mex. 166 D3
San Francisco de Paula, Cabo c. Arg. 178 C7
San Francisco el Alto Mex. 167 F4
San Francisco Gotera El Salvador 166 [inset] H6
San Francisco Javier Spain 67 G4
San Gabriel, Punta pt Mex. 166 B2
San Gabriel Mountains U.S.A. 158 D4
Sangachaly Azer. see Sanqaçal
Sangaigerong Sumatera Indon. 84 D3
Sangameshwar India 106 B2
Sangamon r. U.S.A. 160 F3
Sangan, Koh-i- mt. Afgh. see Sangān, Kūh-e
Sangān, Kūh-e mt. Afgh. 111 G3
Sangar Rus. Fed. 77 N3
Sangareddi India 106 C2
Sangareddy India see Sangareddi
Sangasanga Kalimantan Indon. 85 G3
Sanga Sanga i. Phil. 82 B5
San Gavino Monreale Sardinia Italy 68 C5
Sangay, Parque Nacional nat. park Ecuador 176 C4
Sangba Xizang China 99 F7
Sangboy Islands Phil. 82 C5
Sangbur Afgh. 111 F3
Sangeang i. Indon. 83 A5
Sangejing Nei Mongol China 94 F3
Sangequanzi Xinjiang China 94 B3
Sanger U.S.A. 158 D3
Sangerfield U.S.A. 165 H2
Sangerhausen Germany 63 L3
Sang-e Surakh Iran 110 E2
Sanggar, Teluk b. Sumbawa Indon. 85 G5
Sanggarmai China 96 D1
Sanggau Kalimantan Indon. 85 E2
Sanggeluhang i. Indon. 83 C2
Sanggou Wan b. China 95 J4
Sangilen, Nagor'ye mts Rus. Fed. 94 C1
San Giovanni in Fiore Italy 68 G5
Sangir India 104 C5
Sangir i. Indon. 83 C2
Sangir, Kepulauan is Indon. 83 C2
Sangiyn Dalay Mongolia see Erdenedalay
Sangiyn Dalay Nuur salt l. Mongolia 94 D1
Sangkapura Jawa Indon. 85 F4
Sangkarang, Kepulauan is Indon. 83 A4
Sangkulirang Kalimantan Indon. 85 G2
Sangkulirang, Teluk b. Indon. 85 G2
Sangli India 106 B2
Sangmai China see Dêrong
Sangmélima Cameroon 120 E4
Sangngagqoiling Xizang China 99 F7
Sango Zimbabwe 123 D6
Sangole India 106 B2
San Gorgonio Mountain U.S.A. 158 E4
Sangowo Maluku Indon. 83 D2
Sangpi China see Xiangcheng
Sangre de Cristo Range mts U.S.A. 157 G5
Sangri Xizang China 99 F7
Sangrur India 104 C3
Sangsang Xizang China 99 D7
Sangu r. Bangl. 105 G5
Sanguem India 106 B3
Sangutane r. Moz. 125 K3
Sangyuan Hebei China see Wuqiao
Sangzhi China 97 F2
Sanhe China see Sandu
Sanhe Nei Mongol China 95 J1
San Hilario Mex. 166 C3
San Hipólito, Punta pt Mex. 166 B3
Sanhūr Egypt 112 C5
Sanhūr Egypt see Sanhūr
San Ignacio Belize 167 H5
San Ignacio Beni Bol. 176 E6
San Ignacio Santa Cruz Bol. 176 F7
San Ignacio Santa Cruz Bol. 176 F7
San Ignacio Baja California Mex. 166 B2
San Ignacio Baja California Sur Mex. 166 B3
San Ignacio Durango Mex. 161 C7
San Ignacio Sonora Mex. 166 C2
San Ignacio Para. 178 E3
San Ignacio, Laguna l. Mex. 166 B3
Sanikiluaq Canada 152 F2
San Ildefonso Peninsula Luzon Phil. 82 C2
Sanin-kaigan Kokuritsu-kōen nat. park Japan 92 A3
San Jacinto Masbate Phil. 82 C3
San Jacinto U.S.A. 158 E5
San Jacinto Peak U.S.A. 158 E5
San Javier Bol. 176 F7
Sanjiang Guangdong China see Liannan
Sanjiang Guangxi China 97 F3
Sanjiang Guizhou China see Jinping
Sanjiangkou Liaoning China 95 J3
Sanjiaocheng Qinghai China see Haiyan
Sanjiaoping China 97 F2
Sanjō Japan 91 E5
San Joaquin r. U.S.A. 158 C2
San Joaquin Valley U.S.A. 158 C3
Sanjoli India 104 C5
San Jon U.S.A. 161 C5
San Jorge, Golfo de g. Arg. 178 C7
San Jorge, Golfo de g. Spain see Sant Jordi, Golf de

▶San José Costa Rica 166 [inset] I7
Capital of Costa Rica.

San Jose Luzon Phil. 82 C3
San Jose Mindoro Phil. 82 C3
San Jose Mindoro Phil. 82 C3
San Jose CA U.S.A. 158 C3
San Jose NM U.S.A. 157 G6
San Jose watercourse U.S.A. 159 J4
San José, Isla i. Mex. 166 C3
San José de Amacuro Venez. 176 F2
San José de Bavicora Mex. 166 D2
San Jose de Buenavista Panay Phil. 82 C4
San José de Chiquitos Bol. 176 F7
San José de Comondú Mex. 166 C3
San José de Gracia Baja California Sur Mex. 166 B3
San José de Gracia Sinaloa Mex. 166 D3
San José de Gracia Sonora Mex. 166 C2
San Josée la Brecha Mex. 166 C3
San José del Cabo Mex. 166 C4
San José del Guaviare Col. 176 D3
San José de Mayo Uruguay 178 E4
San José de Raíces Mex. 161 C7
Sanju Xinjiang China 99 B5
San Juan Arg. 178 C4
San Juan r. Costa Rica/Nicaragua 166 [inset] J7
San Juan mt. Cuba 163 D8
San Juan Chihuahua Mex. 166 D3
San Juan Coahuila Mex. 167 E3
San Juan r. Mex. 161 D7
San Juan Leyte Phil. 82 D4
San Juan Mindanao Phil. 82 D4

▶San Juan Puerto Rico 169 K5
Capital of Puerto Rico.

San Juan U.S.A. 159 J5
San Juan r. U.S.A. 159 H3
San Juan, Cabo c. Arg. 178 D8
San Juan, Cabo c. Equat. Guinea 120 D4
San Juan, Punta pt El Salvador 166 [inset] H6
San Juan Bautista Para. 178 E3
San Juan Bautista de las Misiones Para. see San Juan Bautista
San Juancito Hond. 166 [inset] I6
San Juan de Guadalupe Mex. 161 C7
San Juan del Norte Nicaragua 166 [inset] J7
San Juan del Norte, Bahía de b. Nicaragua 166 [inset] J7
San Juan de los Morros Venez. 176 E2
San Juan del Río Durango Mex. 166 D3
San Juan del Río Querétaro Mex. 167 F4
San Juan del Sur Nicaragua 166 [inset] I7
San Juan Evangelista Mex. 167 G5
San Juanico, Punta pt Mex. 166 B3
San Juanito Mex. 166 D3
San Juanito, Isla i. Mex. 166 D4
San Juan Ixcoy Guat. 167 H6
San Juan Mountains U.S.A. 159 J3
San Juan y Martínez Cuba 163 D8
Sanju He watercourse China 99 B5
San Julián Arg. 178 C7
San Justo Arg. 178 D4
Sankari Drug India 106 C4
Sankh r. India 103 F7
Sankhu India 104 C3
Sankra Chhattisgarh India 106 D1
Sankra Rajasthan India 104 B4
Sankt Augustin Germany 63 H4
Sankt Gallen Switz. 66 I3
Sankt-Peterburg Rus. Fed. see St Petersburg
Sankt Pölten Austria 57 O6
Sankt Veit an der Glan Austria 57 O7
Sankt Vith Belgium see St-Vith
Sankt Wendel Germany 63 H5
Sanku India 104 D2
San Lázaro, Cabo c. Mex. 166 B3
San Lázaro, Sierra de mts Mex. 166 C4
Şanlıurfa Turkey 112 E3
Şanlıurfa prov. Turkey 107 D1
San Lorenzo Arg. 178 D4
San Lorenzo Beni Bol. 176 E7
San Lorenzo Tarija Bol. 176 F8
San Lorenzo Ecuador 176 C3
San Lorenzo Hond. 166 [inset] I6
San Lorenzo Mex. 166 D2
San Lorenzo mt. Spain 67 E2
San Lorenzo, Cerro mt. Arg./Chile 178 B7
San Lorenzo, Isla i. Mex. 166 B2
Sanlúcar de Barrameda Spain 67 C5
San Lucas Baja California Sur Mex. 166 B3
San Lucas Baja California Sur Mex. 166 C4
San Lucas, Cabo c. Mex. 166 C4
San Lucas, Serranía de mts Col. 176 D2
San Luis Arg. 178 C4
San Luis Guat. 167 H5
San Luis Guerrero Mex. 167 E5
San Luis AZ U.S.A. 159 F5
San Luis AZ U.S.A. 159 H5
San Luis CO U.S.A. 161 B4
San Luís, Isla i. Mex. 166 B2
San Luis de la Paz Mex. 167 E4
San Luis Gonzaga Mex. 166 C3
San Luisito Mex. 166 B2
San Luis Obispo U.S.A. 158 C4
San Luis Obispo Bay U.S.A. 158 C4
San Luis Pajón Hond. 166 [inset] H6
San Luis Potosí Mex. 168 D4
San Luis Potosí state Mex. 167 E4
San Luis Reservoir U.S.A. 158 C3
San Luis Río Colorado Mex. 166 B1
San Manuel U.S.A. 159 H5
San Marcial, Punta pt Mex. 166 C3
San Marcos Guat. 167 H6
San Marcos Hond. 166 [inset] I6
San Marcos Guerrero Mex. 167 F5
San Marcos U.S.A. 161 D6
San Marcos, Isla i. Mex. 166 B3
San Marino country Europe 68 E3

▶San Marino San Marino 68 E3
Capital of San Marino.

San Martín research station Antarctica 188 L2
San Martín Catamarca Arg. 178 C3
San Martín Mendoza Arg. 178 C4
San Martín, Lago l. Arg./Chile 178 B7
San Martín, Volcán vol. Mex. 167 G5
San Martin de Bolaños Mex. 166 E4
San Martín de los Andes Arg. 178 B6
San Mateo U.S.A. 158 B3
San Mateo Mountains U.S.A. 159 J4
San Matías Bol. 177 G7
San Matías, Golfo g. Arg. 178 D6
Sanmen China 97 I2
Sanmen Wan b. China 97 I2
Sanmenxia Henan China 95 G5
San Miguel El Salvador 166 [inset] H6
San Miguel Panama 166 [inset] K7
San Miguel Luzon Phil. 82 C3
San Miguel U.S.A. 158 C4
San Miguel r. U.S.A. 159 I2
San Miguel Bay Luzon Phil. 82 C3
San Miguel de Allende Mex. 167 E4
San Miguel de Cruces Mex. 166 D3
San Miguel de Horcasitas r. Mex. 166 C2
San Miguel de Huachi Bol. 176 E7
San Miguel de Tucumán Arg. 178 C3
San Miguel do Araguaia Brazil 179 A1
San Miguel el Alto Mex. 166 E4
San Miguel Island U.S.A. 158 C4
San Miguel Islands Phil. 82 B5
San Miguelito Panama 166 [inset] K7
San Miguel Sola de Vega Mex. 167 F5
Sanming China 97 H3
Sannan Japan 92 B3
San Narciso Luzon Phil. 82 C3
Sanndatti India 106 B3
Sanndraigh i. U.K. see Sandray
Sannicandro Garganico Italy 68 F4
San Nicolás Durango Mex. 157 G8
San Nicolás Guerrero Mex. 167 F5
San Nicolás Tamaulipas Mex. 161 D7
San Nicolas Luzon Phil. 82 C2
San Nicolas Island U.S.A. 158 D5
Sannieshof S. Africa 125 G4
Sanniquellie Liberia 120 C4
Sano Japan 93 F2
Sanok Poland 53 D6
San Pablo Bol. 176 E8
San Pablo Mex. 167 F4
San Pablo Luzon Phil. 82 C3
San Pablo de Manta Ecuador see Manta
San Pedro Arg. 178 D2
San Pedro Belize 167 I5
San Pedro Bol. 176 F7
San Pedro Chile 178 C2
San-Pédro Côte d'Ivoire 120 C4
San Pedro Baja California Sur Mex. 166 C4
San Pedro Chihuahua Mex. 166 D2
San Pedro Para. see San Pedro de Ycuamandyyú
San Pedro Mindoro Phil. 82 C3
San Pedro watercourse U.S.A. 159 H5
San Pedro, Punta pt Costa Rica 166 [inset] J7
San Pedro, Sierra de mts Spain 67 C4
San Pedro Carchá Guat. 167 H6
San Pedro Channel U.S.A. 158 D5
San Pedro de Arimena Col. 176 D3
San Pedro de Atacama Chile 178 C2
San Pedro de las Colonias Mex. 166 E3
San Pedro de Macorís Dom. Rep. 169 K5
San Pedro de Ycuamandyyú Para. 178 E2
San Pedro el Saucito Mex. 166 C2
San Pedro Martir, Parque Nacional nat. park Mex. 166 B2
San Pedro Sula Hond. 166 [inset] H6
San Pierre U.S.A. 164 B3
San Pietro, Isola di i. Sardinia Italy 68 C5
San Pitch r. U.S.A. 159 H2
Sanpu Gansu China 94 E4
Sanqaçal Azer. 113 H2
Sanquhar U.K. 60 F5
Sanquianga, Parque Nacional nat. park Col. 176 C3
San Quintín, Cabo c. Mex. 166 A2
San Rafael Arg. 178 C4
San Rafael CA U.S.A. 158 B3
San Rafael NM U.S.A. 159 J4
San Rafael r. U.S.A. 159 H2
San Rafael del Norte Nicaragua 166 [inset] I6
San Rafael Knob mt. U.S.A. 159 H2
San Rafael Mountains U.S.A. 158 C4
San Ramón Bol. 176 F6
Sanrao China 97 H3
San Remo Italy 68 B3
San Roque Spain 67 B2
San Roque, Punta pt Mex. 166 B3
San Saba U.S.A. 161 D6
San Saba r. TX U.S.A. 167 F2
San Salvador i. Bahamas 163 F7

▶San Salvador El Salvador 167 H6
Capital of El Salvador.

San Salvador, Isla i. Galápagos Ecuador 176 [inset]
San Salvador de Jujuy Arg. 178 C2
Sansanné-Mango Togo 120 D3
San Sebastián Arg. 178 C8
San Sebastián Spain 67 F2
San Sebastián de los Reyes Spain 67 E3
Sansepolcro Italy 68 E3
San Severo Italy 68 F4
San Simon U.S.A. 159 I5
Sanski Most Bos.-Herz. 68 G2
Sansoral Islands Palau see Sonsorol Islands
Sansui China 97 F3
Sant Mongolia 94 E2
Santa r. Peru 176 C5
Santa Amelia Guat. 167 H5
Santa Ana Bol. 176 E7
Santa Ana El Salvador 167 H6
Santa Ana Sonora Mex. 166 C2
Santa Ana i. Solomon Is 133 G3
Santa Ana U.S.A. 158 E5
Santa Ana de Yacuma Bol. 176 E6
Santa Anita Baja California Sur Mex. 166 C4
Santa Anna U.S.A. 161 D6
Santa Bárbara Brazil 179 C2
Santa Bárbara Cuba see La Demajagua
Santa Bárbara Hond. 166 [inset] H6
Santa Bárbara Chihuahua Mex. 166 D3
Santa Barbara U.S.A. 158 D4
Santa Bárbara, Ilha i. Brazil 179 D2
Santa Barbara Channel U.S.A. 158 C4
Santa Bárbara d'Oeste Brazil 179 B3
Santa Barbara Island U.S.A. 158 D5
Santa Catalina Panama 166 [inset] J7
Santa Catalina, Gulf of U.S.A. 158 E5
Santa Catalina, Isla i. Mex. 166 C3
Santa Catalina de Armada Spain 67 B2
Santa Catalina Island U.S.A. 158 D5
Santa Catarina state Brazil 179 A4
Santa Catarina Baja California Mex. 166 B2
Santa Catarina Nuevo León Mex. 167 E3
Santa Catarina, Ilha de i. Brazil 179 A4
Santa Clara Col. 176 E4
Santa Clara Cuba 169 I4
Santa Clara Chihuahua Mex. 166 D2
Santa Clara r. Mex. 166 D2
Santa Clara CA U.S.A. 158 C3
Santa Clara UT U.S.A. 159 G3
Santa Clarita U.S.A. 158 D4
Santa Clotilde Peru 176 D4
Santa Comba Angola see Waku-Kungo
Santa Croce, Capo c. Sicily Italy 68 F6
Santa Cruz Bol. 176 F7
Santa Cruz Brazil 177 K5
Santa Cruz Costa Rica 166 [inset] I7
Santa Cruz Sonora Mex. 166 C2
Santa Cruz Luzon Phil. 82 B3
Santa Cruz Luzon Phil. 82 C2
Santa Cruz Luzon Phil. 82 C3
Santa Cruz U.S.A. 158 B3
Santa Cruz watercourse U.S.A. 159 G5
Santa Cruz, Isla i. Galápagos Ecuador 176 [inset]
Santa Cruz, Isla i. Mex. 166 C3
Santa Cruz Barillas Guat. 167 H6
Santa Cruz Cabrália Brazil 179 D2
Santa Cruz de Goiás Brazil 179 A2
Santa Cruz de la Palma Canary Is 120 B2
Santa Cruz del Sur Cuba 169 I4
Santa Cruz de Moya Spain 67 F4
Santa Cruz de Tenerife Canary Is 120 B2
Santa Cruz de Yojoa Hond. 166 [inset] I6
Santa Cruz do Sul Brazil 178 F3
Santa Cruz Island U.S.A. 158 D4
Santa Cruz Islands Solomon Is 133 G3
Santa Elena, Bahía de b. Ecuador 176 B4
Santa Elena, Cabo c. Costa Rica 166 [inset] I7
Santa Elena, Punta pt Ecuador 176 B4
Santa Eudóxia Brazil 179 B3
Santa Eufemia, Golfo di g. Italy 68 G5
Santa Eulalia Mex. 167 E2
Santa Fé Arg. 178 D4
Santa Fé Cuba 163 D8
Santa Fé Panama 166 [inset] J7
Santa Fe Phil. 82 C3

▶Santa Fe U.S.A. 157 G6
Capital of New Mexico.

Santa Fé de Bogotá Col. see Bogotá
Santa Fé de Minas Brazil 179 B2
Santa Fé do Sul Brazil 179 A3
Santa Gertrudis Mex. 166 D3
Santa Helena Brazil 177 I4
Santa Helena de Goiás Brazil 179 A2
Santai Sichuan China 96 E2
Santai Xinjiang China 98 C3
Santai Xinjiang China 98 E3
Santai Yunnan China 96 D3
Santa Inês Brazil 177 I4
Santa Inés, Isla i. Chile 178 L3
Santa Isabel Arg. 178 C5
Santa Isabel Equat. Guinea see Malabo
Santa Isabel i. Solomon Is 133 F2
Santa Isabel, Sierra mts Mex. 166 B2
Santa Juliana Brazil 179 B2
Santalpur India 104 B5
Santa Lucia Guat. 167 H6
Santa Lucia Range mts U.S.A. 158 C3
Santa Margarita U.S.A. 158 C4
Santa Margarita, Isla i. Mex. 166 C3
Santa María Arg. 178 C3
Santa Maria Amazonas Brazil 177 G4
Santa Maria Rio Grande do Sul Brazil 178 F3
Santa Maria Cape Verde 120 [inset]
Santa María Mex. 167 H5
Santa María r. Mex. 166 D2
Santa María Peru 176 D4
Santa Maria U.S.A. 158 C4
Santa Maria r. U.S.A. 159 G4
Santa Maria, Cabo de c. Moz. 125 K4
Santa Maria, Cabo de c. Port. 67 C5
Santa Maria, Chapadão de hills Brazil 179 B1
Santa María, Isla i. Galápagos Ecuador 176 [inset]
Santa Maria, Serra de hills Brazil 179 B1
Santa Maria da Vitória Brazil 179 B1
Santa María de Cuevas Mex. 166 D3
Santa María del Oro Mex. 166 D3
Santa María del Río Mex. 167 E4
Santa Maria do Suaçuí Brazil 179 C2
Santa Maria Island Vanuatu 133 G3
Santa Maria Madalena Brazil 179 C3
Santa Maria Mountains U.S.A. 159 G4
Santa Marta Col. 176 D1
Santa Marta, Cabo de c. Angola 123 B5
Santa Marta Grande, Cabo de c. Brazil 179 A5
Santa Martha, Cerro mt. Mex. 167 G5
Santa Maura i. Greece see Lefkada
Santa Monica U.S.A. 158 D4
Santa Monica, Pico mt. Mex. 157 E8
Santa Monica Bay U.S.A. 158 D5
Santan Kalimantan Indon. 85 G3
Santana Brazil 179 C1
Santana r. Brazil 179 A2
Santana do Araguaia Brazil 177 H5
Santander Spain 67 E2
Santa Nella U.S.A. 158 C3
Santanghu Xinjiang China 94 C2
Santanilla, Islas is Caribbean Sea see Cisne, Islas del
Santan Mountain hill U.S.A. 159 H5
Sant'Antioco Sardinia Italy 68 C5
Sant'Antioco, Isola di i. Sardinia Italy 68 C5
Sant Antoni de Portmany Spain 67 G4
Santapilly India 106 D2
Santaquin U.S.A. 159 H2
Santa Quitéria Brazil 177 J4
Santarém Brazil 177 H4
Santarém Port. 67 B4
Santa Rita Coahuila Mex. 167 E3
Santa Rosa Arg. 178 D5
Santa Rosa Acre Brazil 176 D5
Santa Rosa Rio Grande do Sul Brazil 178 F3
Santa Rosa Mex. 161 C7
Santa Rosa Quintana Roo Mex. 167 H5
Santa Rosa CA U.S.A. 158 B2
Santa Rosa NM U.S.A. 157 G6
Santa Rosa de Copán Hond. 166 [inset] H6
Santa Rosa de la Roca Bol. 176 F7
Santa Rosa Island U.S.A. 158 C5
Santa Rosalía Mex. 166 B3
Santa Rosa Range mts U.S.A. 156 D4
Santa Rosa Wash watercourse U.S.A. 159 G5
Santa Sylvina Arg. 178 D3
Santa Teresa Australia 135 F6
Santa Teresa r. Brazil 179 A1
Santa Teresa Nayarit Mex. 166 D4
Santa Teresa Tamaulipas Mex. 167 F3
Santa Vitória Brazil 179 A2
Santa Ynez r. U.S.A. 158 C4
Santa Ysabel i. Solomon Is see Santa Isabel
Santee U.S.A. 158 E5
Santee r. U.S.A. 163 E5
San Telmo Mex. 166 A2
Santiago Brazil 178 F3
Santiago i. Cape Verde 120 [inset]

▶Santiago Chile 178 B4
Capital of Chile.

Santiago Dom. Rep. 169 J5
Santiago Baja California Sur Mex. 166 C4
Santiago Panama 166 [inset] J7
Santiago Luzon Phil. 82 C2
Santiago, Cerro mt. Panama 166 [inset] J7
Santiago, Río Grande de r. Mex. 166 D4
Santiago Astata Mex. 167 G5
Santiago de Compostela Spain 67 B2
Santiago de Cuba Cuba 169 I4
Santiago del Estero Arg. 178 D3
Santiago de los Caballeros Dom. Rep. see Santiago
Santiago Ixcuintla Mex. 166 D4
Santiaguillo, Laguna de l. Mex. 161 B7
Santianna Point Canada 151 P2
Santigi Sulawesi Indon. 83 B2
Santiki, Tanjung pt Indon. 83 B2
Santipur India see Shantipur
Sant Jordi, Golf de g. Spain 67 G3
Santō Hyōgo Japan 92 A3
Santō Shiga Japan 92 C3
Santo Amaro Brazil 179 D1
Santo Amaro de Campos Brazil 179 C3
Santo Anastácio Brazil 179 A3
Santo André Brazil 179 B3
Santo Angelo Brazil 178 F3

▶Santo Antão i. Cape Verde 120 [inset]
Most westerly point of Africa.

Santo Antônio Brazil 176 F4
Santo Antônio r. Brazil 179 C2
Santo Antônio São Tomé and Príncipe 120 D4
Santo Antônio, Cabo c. Brazil 179 D1
Santo Antônio da Platina Brazil 179 A3
Santo Antônio de Jesus Brazil 179 D1
Santo Antônio do Içá Brazil 176 E4
Santo Corazón Bol. 177 G7
Santo Domíngo Cuba 163 D8

▶Santo Domingo Dom. Rep. 169 K5
Capital of the Dominican Republic.

Santo Domingo Guat. 167 H6
Santo Domingo Baja California Mex. 166 B2
Santo Domingo Baja California Sur Mex. 166 C3
Santo Domingo San Luis Potosí Mex. 167 E4
Santo Domingo Nicaragua 166 [inset] I6
Santo Domingo country West Indies see Dominican Republic
Santo Domingo de Guzmán Dom. Rep. see Santo Domingo
Santo Domingo Tehuantepec Mex. 167 G5
Santo Hipólito Brazil 179 B2
Santorini i. Greece 69 K6
Santos Brazil 179 B3
Santos Dumont Brazil 179 C3
Santos Plateau sea feature S. Atlantic Ocean 184 E7
Santo Tomás Mex. 157 E7
Santo Tomás Nicaragua 166 [inset] I6
Santo Tomás Peru 176 D6
Santo Tomé Arg. 178 E3
Sanup Plateau U.S.A. 159 G3
San Valentín, Cerro mt. Chile 178 B7
San Vicente El Salvador 166 [inset] H6
San Vicente Baja California Mex. 166 A2
San Vicente Luzon Phil. 82 C2
San Vicente de Baracaldo Spain see Barakaldo
San Vicente de Cañete Peru 176 C6
San Vincenzo Italy 68 D3
San Vito, Capo c. Sicily Italy 68 E5
Sanwa Ibaraki Japan 93 F2
Sanwa Niigata Japan 93 E1
Sanwer India 104 C5
Sanxia Shuiku resr China see Three Gorges Reservoir
Sanya China 97 F5
Sanyuan Shaanxi China 95 G5
S. A. Nyýazow Adyndaky Turkm. 111 F2
Sanza Pombo Angola 123 B4
Sao, Phou mt. Laos 86 C3
São Bernardo do Campo Brazil 179 B3
São Borja Brazil 178 E3
São Carlos Brazil 179 B3
São Domingos Brazil 179 B1
São Felipe, Serra de hills Brazil 179 B1
São Félix Bahia Brazil 179 D1
São Félix Mato Grosso Brazil 177 H6
São Félix Pará Brazil 177 H5
São Fidélis Brazil 179 C3
São Francisco Brazil 179 B1

▶São Francisco r. Brazil 179 C1
5th longest river in South America.

São Francisco, Ilha de i. Brazil 179 A4
São Francisco de Paula Brazil 179 A5
São Francisco de Sales Brazil 179 A2
São Francisco do Sul Brazil 179 A4
São Gabriel Brazil 178 F4
São Gonçalo Brazil 179 C3
São Gonçalo do Abaeté Brazil 179 B2
São Gonçalo do Sapucaí Brazil 179 B3
São Gotardo Brazil 179 B2
São João, Ilhas de is Brazil 177 J4
São João da Barra Brazil 179 C3
São João da Boa Vista Brazil 179 B3
São João da Madeira Port. 67 B3
São João da Ponte Brazil 179 B1
São João del Rei Brazil 179 B3
São João do Paraíso Brazil 179 C1
São Joaquim Brazil 179 A5
São Joaquim da Barra Brazil 179 B3
São José Amazonas Brazil 176 E4
São José Santa Catarina Brazil 179 A4
São José do Rio Preto Brazil 179 A3
São José dos Campos Brazil 179 B3
São José dos Pinhais Brazil 179 A4
São Leopoldo Brazil 179 A5
São Lourenço Brazil 179 B3
São Lourenço r. Brazil 177 G7
São Luís Brazil 177 J4
São Luís Brazil 177 G4
São Luís de Montes Belos Brazil 179 A2
São Manuel Brazil 179 A3
São Marcos r. Brazil 179 B2
São Mateus Brazil 179 D2
São Mateus do Sul Brazil 179 A4
São Miguel i. Arquipélago dos Açores 184 G3
São Miguel r. Brazil 179 B2
São Miguel do Tapuio Brazil 177 J5
Saône r. France 66 G4
Saoner India 104 D5
São Nicolau i. Cape Verde 120 [inset]

▶São Paulo Brazil 179 B3
Most populous city in South America and 4th in the world.

São Paulo state Brazil 179 A3
São Paulo de Olivença Brazil 176 E4
São Pedro da Aldeia Brazil 179 C3
São Pedro e São Paulo is N. Atlantic Ocean 184 G5
São Pires r. Brazil see Teles Pires
São Raimundo Nonato Brazil 177 J5
Saori Japan 92 C3
São Romão Amazonas Brazil 176 E5
São Romão Minas Gerais Brazil 179 B2
São Roque Brazil 179 B3
São Roque, Cabo de c. Brazil 177 K5
São Salvador Angola see M'banza Congo
São Salvador do Congo Angola see M'banza Congo
São Sebastião Brazil 179 B3
São Sebastião, Ilha do i. Brazil 179 B3
São Sebastião do Paraíso Brazil 179 B3
São Sebastião dos Poções Brazil 179 B1
São Simão Minas Gerais Brazil 177 H7
São Simão São Paulo Brazil 179 B3
São Simão, Barragem de resr Brazil 179 A2
Sao-Siu Maluku Indon. 83 C2
São Tiago i. Cape Verde see Santiago

▶São Tomé São Tomé and Príncipe 120 D4
Capital of São Tomé and Príncipe.

São Tomé i. São Tomé and Príncipe 120 D4
São Tomé, Cabo de c. Brazil 179 C3
São Tomé, Pico de mt. São Tomé and Príncipe 120 D4
São Tomé and Príncipe country Africa 120 D4
Saoura, Oued watercourse Alg. 64 D6
São Vicente Brazil 179 B3
São Vicente i. Cape Verde 120 [inset]
São Vicente, Cabo de c. Port. 67 B5
Sapako Indon. 84 B3
Sapanca Turkey 69 N4
Saparua Maluku Indon. 83 D3
Saparua i. Maluku Indon. 83 D3
Sapaul India see Supaul
Sape, Selat sea chan. Indon. 83 A5
Sape, Teluk b. Sumbawa Indon. 85 G5
Şaphane Dağı mt. Turkey 69 N5
Sapo, Serranía del mts Panama 166 [inset] K8
Sapo National Park Liberia 120 C4
Sapouy Burkina Faso 120 C3
Sapozhok Rus. Fed. 53 I5
Sappa Creek r. U.S.A. 160 D3
Sapporo Japan 90 F4
Sapudi i. Indon. 85 F4
Sapulpa U.S.A. 161 D4
Sapulu Jawa Indon. 85 F4
Sapulut Sabah Malaysia 85 G1
Sāqī Iran 110 E3
Saqqez Iran 110 B2
Sarā Iran 110 B2
Sarāb Iran 110 B2
Sara Buri Thai. 87 C4
Saradiya India 104 B5
Saragossa Spain see Zaragoza
Saragt Turkm. 111 F2
Saraguro Ecuador 176 C4
Sarahs Turkm. see Saragt
Sarai Afgh. 111 G3
Sarai Sidhu Pak. 111 I4

▶Sarajevo Bos.-Herz. 68 H3
Capital of Bosnia-Herzegovina.

Sarakhs Iran 111 F2
Saraktash Rus. Fed. 76 G4
Saraland U.S.A. 161 F6
Saramati mt. India/Myanmar 86 A1
Saran' Kazakh. 102 D2
Saran, Gunung mt. Indon. 85 E3
Saranac U.S.A. 164 C2
Saranac r. U.S.A. 165 I1
Saranac Lake U.S.A. 165 H1
Saranda Albania see Sarandë
Sarandë Albania 69 I5
Sarandib country Asia see Sri Lanka

Sarangani i. Phil. 82 D5
Sarangani Bay Mindanao Phil. 82 D5
Sarangani Islands Phil. 82 D5
Sarangani Strait Phil. 82 D5
Sarangpur India 104 D5
Saransk Rus. Fed. 53 J5
Sara Peak Nigeria 120 D4
Saraphi Thai. 86 B3
Sarapul Rus. Fed. 51 Q4
Sarāqib Syria 107 C2
Sarasota U.S.A. 163 D7
Saraswati r. India 111 H6
Sarata Ukr. 69 M1
Saratoga CA U.S.A. 158 B3
Saratoga WY U.S.A. 156 G4
Saratoga Springs U.S.A. 162 F3
Saratok Sarawak Malaysia 85 E2
Saratov Rus. Fed. 53 J6
Saratovskoye Vodokhranilishche resr Rus. Fed. 53 J5
Saratsina, Akrotirio pt Greece 69 K5
Saravan Iran 111 F5
Sarawak state Malaysia 85 E2
Saray Turkey 69 L4
Sarayköy Turkey 69 M6
Sarayönü Turkey 112 D3
Sarbāz Iran 109 J4
Sarbāz reg. Iran 111 F5
Sarbhang Bhutan 105 G4
Sarbīsheh Iran 109 I3
Sarbulak Xinjiang China 94 B2
Sarda r. India/Nepal 99 C7
Sarda r. Nepal 105 E3
Sard Āb Afgh. 111 H2
Sardarshahr India 104 C3
Sar Dasht Iran 110 B2
Sardegna i. Sardinia Italy see Sardinia
Sardica Bulg. see Sofia
Sardinia Costa Rica 166 [inset] I7
Sardinia i. Sardinia Italy 68 C4
Sardis MS U.S.A. 161 F5
Sardis WV U.S.A. 164 E4
Sardis Lake resr U.S.A. 161 F5
Sar-e Būm Afgh. 111 G3
Sareks nationalpark nat. park Sweden 54 J3
Sarektjåkkå mt. Sweden 54 J3
Sarempaka, Gunung mt. Indon. 85 F3
Sar-e Pol Afgh. 111 G2
Sar-e Pol-e Ẕahāb Iran 110 B3
Sar Eskandar Iran see Hashtrud
Sare Yazd Iran 110 D4
Sargasso Sea N. Atlantic Ocean 187 P4
Sargodha Pak. 111 I3
Sarh Chad 121 E4
Sarhad reg. Iran 111 F4
Sārī Iran 110 D2
Saria i. Greece 69 L7
Sar-i-Bum Afgh. see Sar-e Būm
Sáric Mex. 166 C2
Sarigan i. N. Mariana Is 81 L3
Sarigh Jilganang Kol salt l. Aksai Chin 104 D2
Sarıgöl Turkey 69 M5
Sarıkamış Turkey 113 F2
Sarikei Sarawak Malaysia 85 E2
Sarikül, Qatorkŭhi mts China/Tajik. see Sarykol Range
Sarila India 104 D4
Sarina Australia 136 E4
Sarıoğlan Kayseri Turkey 112 D3
Sarıoğlan Konya Turkey see Belören
Sariqamish Kuli salt l. Turkm./Uzbek. see Sarykamyshskoye Ozero
Sarīr Tibesti des. Libya 121 E2
Sarita U.S.A. 161 D7
Sarıveliler Turkey 107 A1
Sariwŏn N. Korea 91 B5
Sarıyar Barajı resr Turkey 69 N5
Sarıyer Turkey 69 M4
Sarız Turkey 112 E3
Sark i. Channel Is 59 E9
Sarkand Kazakh. 102 E2
Şarkikaraağaç Turkey 69 N5
Şarkışla Turkey 112 E3
Şarköy Turkey 69 L4
Sarlath Range mts Afgh./Pak. 111 G4
Sarmi Indon. 81 J7
Särna Sweden 55 H6
Sarneh Iran 110 B3
Sarnen Switz. 66 I3
Sarni India see Amla
Sarnia Canada 164 D2
Sarny Ukr. 53 E6
Saroako Sulawesi Indon. 83 B3
Sarolangun Sumatera Indon. 84 C3
Saroma-ko l. Japan 90 F3
Saronikos Kolpos g. Greece 69 J6
Saros Körfezi b. Turkey 69 L4
Sarova Rus. Fed. 53 I5
Sarowbī Afgh. 111 H3
Sarpa, Ozero l. Rus. Fed. 53 J6
Sarpan i. N. Mariana Is see Rota
Sar Passage Palau 82 [inset]
Sarpsborg Norway 55 G7
Sarqant Kazakh. see Sarkand
Sarre r. France 62 H5
Sarrebourg France 62 H6
Sarreguemines France 62 H5
Sarria Spain 67 C2
Sarry France 62 E6
Sartana Ukr. 53 H7
Sartanahu Pak. 111 H5
Sartène Corsica France 66 I6
Sarthe r. France 66 D3
Sartokay Xinjiang China 94 B2
Sartu China see Daqing
Saruna Pak. 111 G5
Sarupsar India 104 C3
Şärur Azer. 113 G3
Saru Tara tourist site Afgh. 111 F4
Sarv Iran 110 D3
Sarvābād Iran 110 B3
Sárvár Hungary 68 G1
Sarwar India 104 C4
Sary-Bulak Kyrg. 98 A4
Sarygamysh Köli salt l. Turkm./Uzbek. see Sarykamyshskoye Ozero
Sary-Ishikotrau, Peski des. Kazakh. see Saryyesik-Atyrau, Peski
Sary-Jaz r. Kyrg. 98 B4
Sarykamyshskoye Ozero salt l. Turkm./Uzbek. 113 J2
Sarykol Range mts China/Tajik. 111 I2
Sarykomey Kazakh. 98 A3
Saryozek Kazakh. 102 E3
Saryshagan Kazakh. 102 D2
Sarysu watercourse Kazakh. 102 C2
Sarytash Kazakh. 113 H1
Sary-Tash Kyrg. 111 I2
Sary-Ter, Gora mt. Kyrg. 98 B4
Saryýazy Suw Howdany resr Turkm. 111 F2
Saryyesik-Atyrau, Peski des. Kazakh. 102 E2
Saryzhaz Kazakh. 98 B4
Sarzha Kazakh. 113 H2
Sarzhal Kazakh. 98 B2
Sasak Sumatera Indon. 84 B2
Sasar, Tanjung pt Sumba Indon. 83 A5
Sasaram India 105 F4
Sasayama Japan 92 B3
Sasebo Japan 91 C6
Sashima Japan 93 F2
Saskatchewan prov. Canada 151 J4
Saskatchewan r. Canada 151 K4
Saskatoon Canada 151 J4
Saskylakh Rus. Fed. 77 M2
Saslaya mt. Nicaragua 166 [inset] I6
Saslaya, Parque Nacional nat. park Nicaragua 166 [inset] I6
Sasoi r. India 104 B5
Sasolburg S. Africa 125 H4
Sasovo Rus. Fed. 53 I5
Sass r. Canada 150 H2
Sassandra Côte d'Ivoire 120 C4
Sassari Sardinia Italy 68 C4
Sassenberg Germany 63 I3
Sassnitz Germany 57 N3
Sass Town Liberia 120 C4
Sasykkol', Ozero l. Kazakh. 102 F2
Sasykoli Rus. Fed. 53 J7
Sasyqköl l. Kazakh. see Sasykkol', Ozero
Satahual i. Micronesia see Satawal
Sata-misaki c. Japan 91 C7
Satana India 106 B1
Satan Pass U.S.A. 159 I4
Satara India 106 B2
Satara S. Africa 125 J3
Satawal i. Micronesia 81 L5
Sätbaev Kazakh. see Satpayev
Satengar i. Indon. 85 G4
Satevó Mex. 166 D3
Satevo r. Mex. 157 G8
Satırlar Turkey see Yeşilova
Satkania Bangl. 105 H5
Satkhira Bangl. 105 G5
Satluj r. India/Pak. see Sutlej
Satmala Range hills India 106 C2
Satna India 104 E4
Satomi Japan 93 G2
Satonda i. Indon. 85 G5
Satpayev Kazakh. 102 C2
Satpura Range mts India 104 C5
Satsuma-hantō pen. Japan 91 C7
Sattahip Thai. 87 C4
Satte Japan 93 F2
Satteldorf Germany 63 K5
Satthwa Myanmar 86 A3
Satu Mare Romania 53 D7
Satun Thai. 87 C6
Satwas India 104 D5
Saubi i. Indon. 85 F4
Sauceda Mountains U.S.A. 159 G5
Saucillo Mex. 166 D2
Sauda Norway 55 E7
Sauðárkrókur Iceland 54 [inset]

▶Saudi Arabia country Asia 108 F4
5th largest country in Asia.

Sauer r. France 63 I6
Saug r. Mindanao Phil. 82 D5
Saugatuck U.S.A. 164 B2
Saugeen r. Canada 164 E1
Sāūjbolāgh Iran see Mahābād
Sauk Center U.S.A. 160 E2
Saulieu France 66 G3
Saulnois reg. France 62 G6
Sault Sainte Marie Canada 152 D5
Sault Sainte Marie U.S.A. 162 C2
Saumalkol' Kazakh. 100 F1
Saumarez Reef Australia 136 F4
Saumlakki Indon. 134 E2
Saumur France 66 D3
Saunders, Mount hill Australia 134 E3
Saunders Coast Antarctica 188 J1
Saur, Khrebet mts China/Kazakh. 98 D3
Saurimo Angola 123 C4
Sausu Sulawesi Indon. 83 B3
Sautar Angola 123 B5
Sauvolles, Lac l. Canada 153 G3
Sava r. Europe 68 I2
Savá Hond. 166 [inset] I6
Savage River Australia 137 [inset]
Savai'i i. Samoa 133 I3
Savala r. Rus. Fed. 53 I6
Savalou Benin 120 D4
Savanat Iran see Eşţahbān
Savane r. Canada 153 H4
Savanna U.S.A. 160 F3
Savannah GA U.S.A. 163 D5
Savannah OH U.S.A. 164 D3
Savannah TN U.S.A. 161 F5
Savannah r. U.S.A. 163 D5
Savannah Sound Bahamas 163 E7
Savannakhét Laos 86 D3
Savanna-la-Mar Jamaica 169 I5
Savant Lake Canada 152 C4
Savant Lake l. Canada 152 C4
Savanur India 106 B3
Sävar Sweden 54 L5
Savaştepe Turkey 69 L5
Savè Benin 120 D4
Save r. Moz./Zimbabwe 123 D6
Sāveh Iran 110 C3
Saverne France 63 H6
Saverne, Col de pass France 63 H6
Saviaho Fin. 54 P5
Savinskiy Rus. Fed. 52 I3
Savitri r. India 106 B2
Savli India 104 C5
Savoie reg. France see Savoy
Savona Italy 68 C2
Savonlinna Fin. 54 P6
Savonranta Fin. 54 P5
Savoonga AK U.S.A. 148 E3
Savoy reg. France 66 H3
Şavşat Turkey 113 F2
Sävsjö Sweden 55 I8
Savu i. Indon. 83 B5
Savukoski Fin. 54 P3
Savur Turkey 113 F3
Savu Sea Indon. see Sawu, Laut
Savvo-Borzya Rus. Fed. 95 I1
Saw Myanmar 86 A2
Sawahlunto Sumatera Indon. 84 C3
Sawai, Teluk b. Seram Indon. 83 D3
Sawai Madhopur India 104 D4
Sawan Kalimantan Indon. 85 F3
Sawan Myanmar 86 B1
Sawar India 104 C4
Sawara Japan 93 G3
Sawatch Range mts U.S.A. 156 G5
Sawel Mountain hill U.K. 61 E3
Sawi, Ao b. Thai. 87 B5
Sawn Myanmar 86 B2
Sawtell Australia 138 F3
Sawtooth Mountain AK U.S.A. 149 J2
Sawtooth Mountains MN U.S.A. 160 F2
Sawtooth Range mts U.S.A. 156 C2
Sawu Indon. 83 B5
Sawu i. Indon. see Savu
Sawu, Laut sea Indon. 83 B5
Sawyer Myanmar 86 B2
Sawyer U.S.A. 164 B3
Saxilby U.K. 58 G5
Saxman AK U.S.A. 149 O5
Saxmundham U.K. 59 I6
Saxnäs Sweden 54 I4
Saxony land Germany see Sachsen
Saxony-Anhalt land Germany see Sachsen-Anhalt
Saxton U.S.A. 165 F3
Say Niger 120 D3
Saya Japan 92 C3
Sayabouri Laos see Xaignabouli
Sayafi i. Maluku Indon. 83 D2
Sayak Kazakh. 102 E2
Sayama Japan 93 F3
Sayang i. Papua Indon. 83 D2
Sayanogorsk Rus. Fed. 88 G2
Sayano-Shushenskoye Vodokhranilishche resr Rus. Fed. 88 G2
Sayansk Rus. Fed. 88 I2
Sayaq Kazakh. see Sayak
Saýat Turkm. 111 F2
Sayat Turkm. see Saýat
Sayaxché Guat. 167 H5
Şaydā Lebanon see Sidon
Sāyen Iran 110 D4
Sayer Island Thai. see Similan, Ko
Sayghān Afgh. 111 G3
Sayhan Mongolia 94 E1
Sayhandulaan Dornogovĭ Mongolia 95 G2
Sayhan-Ovoo Dundgovĭ Mongolia 94 E2
Sayḥūt Yemen 108 H6
Sayingpan China 96 D3
Saykhin Kazakh. 51 P6
Saylac Somalia 121 H3
Saylan country Asia see Sri Lanka
Saylyugem, Khrebet mts Rus. Fed. 98 E2
Saynshand Mongolia 95 G2
Sayn-Ust Mongolia see Höhmorĭt
Sayoa mt. Spain see Saioa
Sayot Turkm. see Saýat
Şayqal, Baḩr imp. l. Syria 107 C3
Sayqyn Kazakh. see Saykhin
Sayram Hu salt l. China 98 C3
Sayre OK U.S.A. 161 D5
Sayre PA U.S.A. 165 G3
Sayreville U.S.A. 165 H3
Saysu Xinjiang China 94 C3
Sayula Jalisco Mex. 166 E5
Sayula Mex. 168 F5
Sayyod Turkm. see Saýat
Sazdy Kazakh. 53 K7
Sazin Pak. 111 I3
Sbaa Alg. 64 D6
Sbeitla Tunisia 68 C7
Scaddan Australia 135 C8
Scafell Pike hill U.K. 58 D4
Scalasaig U.K. 60 C4
Scalea Italy 68 F5
Scalloway U.K. 60 [inset]
Scalpaigh, Eilean i. U.K. see Scalpay
Scalpay i. U.K. 60 C3
Scammon Bay AK U.S.A. 148 F3
Scapa Flow inlet U.K. 60 F2
Scarba i. U.K. 60 D4
Scarborough Canada 164 F2
Scarborough Trin. and Tob. 169 L6
Scarborough U.K. 58 G4
Scarborough Shoal sea feature S. China Sea 80 F3
Scariff Island Ireland 61 B6
Scarp i. U.K. 60 B2
Scarpanto i. Greece see Karpathos
Scawfell Shoal sea feature S. China Sea 84 D1
Schaale r. Germany 63 K1
Schaalsee l. Germany 63 K1
Schaerbeek Belgium 62 E4
Schaffhausen Switz. 66 I3
Schafstädt Germany 63 L3
Schagen Neth. 62 E2
Schagerbrug Neth. 62 E2
Schakalskuppe Namibia 124 C4
Schärding Austria 57 N6
Scharendijke Neth. 62 D3
Scharteberg hill Germany 62 G4
Schaumburg U.S.A. 164 A2
Schebheim Germany 63 K5
Scheeßel Germany 63 J1
Schefferville Canada 153 I3
Scheibbs Austria 57 O6
Schelde r. Belgium see Scheldt
Scheldt r. Belgium 62 E3
Schell Creek Range mts U.S.A. 159 F2
Schellerten Germany 63 K2
Schellville U.S.A. 158 B2
Schenectady U.S.A. 165 I2
Schenefeld Germany 63 J1
Schermerhorn Neth. 62 E2
Schertz U.S.A. 161 D6
Schierling Germany 63 M6
Schiermonnikoog Neth. 62 G1
Schiermonnikoog i. Neth. 62 G1
Schiermonnikoog Nationaal Park nat. park Neth. 62 G1
Schiffdorf Germany 63 I1
Schinnen Neth. 62 F4
Schio Italy 68 D2
Schkeuditz Germany 63 M3
Schleiden Germany 62 G4
Schleiz Germany 63 L4
Schleswig Germany 57 L3
Schleswig-Holstein land Germany 63 K1
Schleswig-Holsteinisches Wattenmeer, Nationalpark nat. park Germany 57 L3
Schleusingen Germany 63 K4
Schlitz Germany 63 J4
Schloss Holte-Stukenbrock Germany 63 I3
Schloss Wartburg tourist site Germany 63 K3
Schlüchtern Germany 63 J4
Schlüsselfeld Germany 63 K5
Schmallenberg Germany 63 I3
Schmidt Island Rus. Fed. see Shmidta, Ostrov
Schmidt Peninsula Rus. Fed. see Shmidta, Poluostrov
Schneeberg Germany 63 M4
Schneidemühl Poland see Piła
Schneidlingen Germany 63 L3
Schneverdingen Germany 63 J1
Schoharie U.S.A. 165 H2
Schönebeck Germany 63 M1
Schönebeck (Elbe) Germany 63 L2
Schönefeld airport Germany 63 N2
Schöningen Germany 63 K2
Schöntal Germany 63 J5
Schoolcraft U.S.A. 164 C2
Schoonhoven Neth. 62 E3
Schopfloch Germany 63 K5
Schöppenstedt Germany 63 K2
Schortens Germany 63 H1
Schouten Island Australia 137 [inset]
Schouten Islands P.N.G. 81 K7
Schrankogel mt. Austria 57 M7
Schreiber Canada 152 D4
Schroon Lake U.S.A. 165 I2
Schröttersburg Poland see Płock
Schulenburg U.S.A. 161 D6
Schuler Canada 151 I5
Schull Ireland 61 C6
Schultz Lake Canada 151 L1
Schüttorf Germany 63 H2
Schuyler U.S.A. 160 D3
Schuyler Lake U.S.A. 165 H2
Schuylkill Haven U.S.A. 165 G3
Schwabach Germany 63 L5
Schwäbische Alb mts Germany 57 L7
Schwäbisch Gmünd Germany 63 J6
Schwäbisch Hall Germany 63 J5
Schwaförden Germany 63 I2
Schwalm r. Germany 63 J3
Schwalmstadt-Ziegenhain Germany 63 J4
Schwandorf Germany 63 M5
Schwaner, Pegunungan mts Indon. 85 F3
Schwanewede Germany 63 I1
Schwarmstedt Germany 63 J2
Schwarze Elster r. Germany 63 M3
Schwarzenbek Germany 63 K1
Schwarzenberg Germany 63 M4
Schwarzer Mann hill Germany 62 G4
Schwarzrand mts Namibia 124 C3
Schwarzwald mts Germany see Black Forest
Schwatka, Mount AK U.S.A. 149 K2
Schwatka Mountains AK U.S.A. 148 H2
Schwaz Austria 57 M7
Schwedt an der Oder Germany 57 O4
Schwegenheim Germany 63 I5
Schweich Germany 62 G5
Schweinfurt Germany 63 K4
Schweinitz Germany 63 N3
Schweinrich Germany 63 M1
Schweiz country Europe see Switzerland
Schweizer-Reneke S. Africa 125 G4
Schwelm Germany 63 H3
Schwerin Germany 63 L1
Schweriner See l. Germany 63 L1
Schwetzingen Germany 63 I5
Schwyz Switz. 66 I3
Sciacca Sicily Italy 68 E6
Scicli Sicily Italy 68 F6
Science Hill U.S.A. 164 C5
Scilly, Île atoll Fr. Polynesia see Manuae
Scilly, Isles of U.K. 59 A9
Scioto r. U.S.A. 164 D4
Scipio U.S.A. 159 G2
Scobey U.S.A. 156 G2
Scodra Albania see Shkodër
Scofield Reservoir U.S.A. 159 H2
Scole U.K. 59 I6
Scone Australia 138 E4
Scone U.K. 60 F4
Scoresby Land reg. Greenland 147 P2
Scoresbysund Greenland see Ittoqqortoormiit
Scoresby Sund sea chan. Greenland see Kangertittivaq
Scorno, Punta dello pt Sardinia Italy see Caprara, Punta
Scorpion Bight b. Australia 135 D8
Scotia Ridge sea feature S. Atlantic Ocean 184 E9
Scotia Ridge sea feature S. Atlantic Ocean 188 A2
Scotia Sea S. Atlantic Ocean 184 F9
Scotland Canada 164 E2
Scotland admin. div. U.K. 60 F3
Scotland U.S.A. 165 G4
Scotstown Canada 153 H5
Scott U.S.A. 164 C3
Scott, Cape Australia 134 E3
Scott, Cape Canada 150 D5
Scott, Mount hill U.S.A. 161 D5
Scott Base research station Antarctica 188 H1
Scottburgh S. Africa 125 J6
Scott City U.S.A. 160 C4
Scott Coast Antarctica 188 H1
Scott Glacier Antarctica 188 I1
Scott Island Antarctica 188 H2
Scott Islands Canada 150 D5
Scott Lake Canada 151 J3
Scott Mountains Antarctica 188 D2
Scott Reef Australia 134 C3
Scottsbluff U.S.A. 160 C3
Scottsboro U.S.A. 163 C5
Scottsburg U.S.A. 164 C4
Scottsville KY U.S.A. 164 B5
Scottsville VA U.S.A. 165 F5
Scourie U.K. 60 D2
Scousburgh U.K. 60 [inset]
Scrabster U.K. 60 F2
Scranton U.S.A. 165 H3
Scunthorpe U.K. 58 G5
Scuol Switz. 66 J3
Scupi Macedonia see Skopje
Scutari Albania see Shkodër
Scutari, Lake Albania/Montenegro 69 H3
Seaboard U.S.A. 165 G5
Seabrook, Lake salt flat Australia 135 B7
Seaford U.K. 59 H8
Seaforth Canada 164 E2
Seahorse Shoal sea feature Phil. 82 B4
Seal r. Canada 151 M3
Seal, Cape S. Africa 124 F8
Sea Lake Australia 137 C7
Seal Lake Canada 153 J3
Sealy U.S.A. 161 D6
Seaman U.S.A. 164 D4
Seaman Range mts U.S.A. 159 F3
Seamer U.K. 58 G4
Searchlight U.S.A. 159 F4
Searcy U.S.A. 161 F5
Searles Lake U.S.A. 158 E4
Seaside CA U.S.A. 157 C5
Seaside OR U.S.A. 156 C3
Seaside Park U.S.A. 165 H4
Seattle U.S.A. 156 C3
Seattle, Mount Canada/U.S.A. 149 M3
Seaview Range mts Australia 136 D3
Seba Indon. 83 B5
Sebaco Nicaragua 166 [inset] I6
Sebago Lake U.S.A. 165 J2
Sebakung Kalimantan Indon. 85 G3
Sebangan, Teluk b. Indon. 85 F3
Sebangka i. Indon. 84 D2
Sebastea Turkey see Sivas
Sebastian U.S.A. 163 D7
Sebastián Vizcaíno, Bahía b. Mex. 166 B2
Sebasticook r. U.S.A. 165 K1
Sebasticook Lake U.S.A. 165 K1
Sebastopol Ukr. see Sevastopol'
Sebastopol U.S.A. 158 B2
Sebatik i. Indon. 85 G1
Sebauh Sarawak Malaysia 85 F2
Sebayan, Bukit mt. Indon. 85 E3
Sebba Burkina Faso 120 D3
Seben Turkey 69 N4
Sebenico Croatia see Šibenik
Sebeş Romania 69 J2
Sebesi i. Indon. 84 D4
Sebewaing U.S.A. 164 D2
Sebezh Rus. Fed. 55 P8
Şebinkarahisar Turkey 112 E2
Seblat, Gunung mt. Indon. 84 C3
Sebree U.S.A. 164 B5
Sebring U.S.A. 163 D7
Sebrovo Rus. Fed. 53 I6
Sebta N. Africa see Ceuta
Sebuku i. Indon. 85 G3
Sebuku r. Indon. 85 G1
Sebuku, Teluk b. Indon. 85 G2
Sebuku-Sembakung, Taman Nasional nat. park Kalimantan Indon. 85 G1
Sebuyau Sarawak Malaysia 85 E2
Sechelt Canada 150 F5
Sechenovo Rus. Fed. 53 J5
Sechura Peru 176 B5
Sechura, Bahía de b. Peru 176 B5
Seckach Germany 63 J5
Second Mesa U.S.A. 159 H4
Secretary Island N.Z. 139 A7
Secunda S. Africa 125 I4
Secunderabad India 106 C2
Sedalia U.S.A. 160 E4
Sedam India 106 C2
Sedan France 62 E5
Sedan U.S.A. 161 D4
Sedan Dip Australia 136 C3
Sedanka Island AK U.S.A. 148 F5
Seddon N.Z. 139 E5
Seddonville N.Z. 139 C5
Sedeh Iran 110 E3
Sederot Israel 107 B4
Sedlčany Czech Rep. 57 O6
Sedlets Poland see Siedlce
Sedom Israel 107 B4
Sedona U.S.A. 159 H4
Sédrata Alg. 68 B6
Sedulang Kalimantan Indon. 85 G2
Šeduva Lith. 55 M9
Seedorf Germany 63 K1
Seehausen Germany 63 L2
Seehausen (Altmark) Germany 63 L2
Seeheim Namibia 124 C4
Seeheim-Jugenheim Germany 63 I5
Seela Pass Y.T. Canada 149 M2
Seelig, Mount Antarctica 188 K1
Seelze Germany 63 J2
Seenu Atoll Maldives see Addu Atoll
Sées France 66 E2
Seesen Germany 63 K3
Seevetal Germany 63 K1
Sefadu Sierra Leone 120 B4
Sefare Botswana 125 H2
Seferihisar Turkey 69 L5
Sefīd, Kūh-e mt. Iran 110 C3
Sefophe Botswana 125 H2
Segalstad Norway 55 G6
Segama r. Malaysia 85 G1
Segamat Malaysia 84 C2
Ségbana Benin 120 D3
Segeletz Germany 63 M2
Segeri Sulawesi Indon. 83 A4
Segezha Rus. Fed. 52 G3
Seghnān Afgh. 111 H2
Segontia U.K. see Caernarfon
Segontium U.K. see Caernarfon
Segorbe Spain 67 F4
Ségou Mali 120 C3
Segovia r. Hond./Nicaragua see Coco
Segovia Spain 67 D3
Segozerskoye, Ozero resr Rus. Fed. 52 G3
Seguam Island AK U.S.A. 148 D5
Seguam Pass sea channel AK U.S.A. 149 [inset]
Séguédine Niger 120 E2
Séguéla Côte d'Ivoire 120 C4
Seguin U.S.A. 161 D6
Segula Island AK U.S.A. 149 [inset]
Segura r. Spain 67 F4
Segura, Sierra de mts Spain 67 E5
Sehithwa Botswana 123 C6
Sehlabathebe National Park Lesotho 125 I5
Seho i. Indon. 83 C3
Sehore India 104 D5
Sehwan Pak. 111 G5
Seibert U.S.A. 160 C4
Seignelay r. Canada 153 H4
Seika Japan 92 B4
Seikphyu Myanmar 86 A2
Seiland i. Norway 54 M1
Seille r. France 62 G5
Seinaiji Japan 92 D3
Seinäjoki Fin. 54 M5
Seine r. Canada 151 N5
Seine r. France 62 A5
Seine, Baie de b. France 66 D2
Seine, Val de valley France 66 F2
Seipinang Kalimantan Indon. 85 F3
Seistan reg. Iran see Sīstān
Seiwa Japan 92 C4
Sejaka Kalimantan Indon. 85 G3
Sejangkung Kalimantan Indon. 85 E2
Sejny Poland 55 M9
Sekadau Kalimantan Indon. 85 E2
Sekanak, Teluk b. Indon. 84 D3
Sekatak Bengara Kalimantan Indon. 85 G2
Sekayu Sumatera Indon. 84 C3
Seke China see Sêrtar
Seki Gifu Japan 92 C3
Seki Mie Japan 92 C4
Sekicau, Gunung vol. Indon. 84 D4
Sekidō-san hill Japan 92 C2
Sekigahara Japan 92 C3
Sekijō Japan 93 F2
Sekiyado Japan 93 F2
Sekoma Botswana 124 F3
Sekondi Ghana 120 C4
Sek'ot'a Eth. 122 D2
Sekura Kalimantan Indon. 85 E2
Şela Rus. Fed. see Shali
Selagan r. Indon. 84 C3
Selakau Kalimantan Indon. 85 E2
Selama Malaysia 87 C6
Selangor state Malaysia 84 C2
Selaru i. Maluku Indon. 83 D5
Selassi Indon. 81 I7
Selatan, Tanjung pt Indon. 85 F4
Selatpanjang Sumatera Indon. 84 C2
Selawik AK U.S.A. 148 G2
Selawik r. AK U.S.A. 148 G2
Selawik Lake AK U.S.A. 148 G2
Selawik National Wildlife Refuge nature res. AK U.S.A. 148 H2
Selb Germany 63 M4
Selbekken Norway 54 F5
Selbu Norway 54 G5
Selby U.K. 58 F5
Selby U.S.A. 160 C2
Selby, Lake AK U.S.A. 148 I2
Selbyville U.S.A. 165 H4
Selden U.S.A. 160 C4
Seldovia AK U.S.A. 149 J4
Sele Papua Indon. 83 D3
Sele, Selat sea chan. Papua Indon. 83 D3
Selebi-Phikwe Botswana 123 C6
Selebi-Pikwe Botswana see Selebi-Phikwe
Selemdzha r. Rus. Fed. 90 C1
Selemdzhinsk Rus. Fed. 90 C1
Selemdzhinskiy Khrebet mts Rus. Fed. 90 D1
Selendi Turkey 69 M5
Selenduma Rus. Fed. 94 F1

▶Selenga r. Mongolia/Rus. Fed. 88 J2
Part of the Yenisey-Angara-Selenga, 3rd longest river in Asia.
Also known as Selenga Mörön.

Selenga r. Rus. Fed. 94 G1
Selenga Mörön r. Mongolia see Selenga
Selenge Mongolia 94 E1
Selenge Mongolia see Ih-Uul
Selenge prov. Mongolia 94 F1
Selenge Mörön r. Mongolia 94 F1
Sêlêpug Xizang China 99 C7
Seletar Sing. 87 [inset]
Seletar Reservoir Sing. 87 [inset]
Selety r. Kazakh. see Sileti
Seletyteniz, Ozero salt l. Kazakh. see Siletiteniz, Ozero
Seleucia Turkey see Silifke
Seleucia Pieria Turkey see Samandağı
Selfridge U.S.A. 160 C2
Sel'gon Stantsiya Rus. Fed. 90 D2
Selib Rus. Fed. 52 K3
Sélibabi Mauritania 120 B3
Selibe-Phikwe Botswana see Selebi-Phikwe
Seligenstadt Germany 63 I4
Seliger, Ozero l. Rus. Fed. 52 G4
Seligman U.S.A. 159 G4
Selikhino Rus. Fed. 90 E2
Selîma Oasis Sudan 108 C5
Selimbau Kalimantan Indon. 85 F2
Selimiye Turkey 69 L6
Selinsgrove U.S.A. 165 G3
Seliu i. Indon. 85 D3
Selizharovo Rus. Fed. 52 G4
Seljord Norway 55 F7
Selkirk Canada 151 L5
Selkirk U.K. 60 G5
Selkirk Mountains Canada 150 G4
Sellafield U.K. 58 D4
Sellersburg U.S.A. 164 C4
Sellore Island Myanmar see Saganthit Kyun
Sells U.S.A. 159 H6
Selm Germany 63 H3
Selma AL U.S.A. 163 C5
Selma CA U.S.A. 158 D3
Selmer U.S.A. 161 F5
Selong Lombok Indon. 85 G5
Selous, Mount Y.T. Canada 149 N3
Selseleh-ye Pīr Shūrān mts Iran 111 F4
Selsey Bill hd U.K. 59 G8
Sel'tso Rus. Fed. 53 G5
Selty Rus. Fed. 52 L4
Selu i. Indon. 134 E1
Seluan i. Indon. 85 D1
Selvas reg. Brazil 176 D5
Selvin U.S.A. 164 B4
Selway r. U.S.A. 156 E3
Selwyn Lake Canada 151 J2
Selwyn Mountains N.W.T./Y.T. Canada 149 O2
Selwyn Range hills Australia 136 B4
Selz r. Germany 63 I5
Semangka, Teluk b. Indon. 84 D4
Semarang Jawa Indon. 85 E4
Sematan Sarawak Malaysia 85 E2
Semau i. Indon. 83 B5
Semayang, Danau l. Indon. 85 G3
Sembakung r. Indon. 85 G2
Sembawang Sing. 87 [inset]
Sembé Congo 122 B3
Şemdinli Turkey 113 G3
Semendire Serbia see Smederevo
Semenivka Ukr. 53 G5
Semenov Rus. Fed. 52 J4
Semenovka Ukr. see Semenivka
Semeru, Gunung vol. Indon. 84 E4
Semey Kazakh. see Semipalatinsk
Semidi Islands AK U.S.A. 148 H4
Semikarakorsk Rus. Fed. 53 I7

Semiluki Rus. Fed. 53 H6
Seminoe Reservoir U.S.A. 156 G4
Seminole U.S.A. 161 C5
Semipalatinsk Kazakh. 102 F1
Semirara i. Phil. 82 C3
Semirara Islands Phil. 82 C4
Semīrom Iran 110 C4
Semitau Kalimantan Indon. 85 E2
Semiyarka Kazakh. 98 B2
Semizbuga Kazakh. 98 A2
Sem Kolodezey Ukr. see Lenine
Semnān Iran 110 D3
Semnān va Dāmghān reg. Iran 110 D3
Sêmnyi Qinghai China 94 E4
Semois r. Belgium/France 62 E5
Semois, Vallée de la valley Belgium/France 62 E5
Semporna Sabah Malaysia 85 G1
Sempu i. Indon. 85 F5
Semyonovskoye Arkhangel'skaya Oblast' Rus. Fed. see Bereznik
Semyonovskoye Kostromskaya Oblast' Rus. Fed. see Ostrovskoye
Sena Bol. 176 E6
Senaja Sabah Malaysia 85 G1
Sena Madureira Brazil 176 E5
Senanga Zambia 123 C5
Senaning Kalimantan Indon. 85 E2
Sendai Kagoshima Japan 91 C7
Sendai Miyagi Japan 91 F5
Sêndo Xizang China 99 F7
Senduruhan Kalimantan Indon. 85 E3
Senebui, Tanjung pt Indon. 84 C2
Seneca KS U.S.A. 160 D4
Seneca OR U.S.A. 156 D3
Seneca Lake U.S.A. 165 G2
Seneca Rocks U.S.A. 164 F4
Senecaville Lake U.S.A. 164 E4
Senegal country Africa 120 B3
Sénégal r. Mauritania/Senegal 120 B3
Seney U.S.A. 160 G2
Senftenberg Germany 57 O5
Senga Hill Zambia 123 D4
Sengar r. India 99 B8
Sengata Kalimantan Indon. 85 G2
Sêngdoi Xizang China 99 C7
Sengerema Tanz. 122 D4
Sengeyskiy, Ostrov i. Rus. Fed. 52 K1
Sênggê Zangbo r. China 104 D2 see Indus
Sengiley Rus. Fed. 53 K5
Sengirli, Mys pt Kazakh. see Syngyrli, Mys
Sêngli Co l. Xizang China 99 D7
Senhor do Bonfim Brazil 177 J6
Senigallia Italy 68 E3
Senj Croatia 68 F2
Senja i. Norway 54 J2
Senjōga-dake mt. Japan 92 B4
Senjōga-dake mt. Japan 93 E3
Sen'kina Rus. Fed. 52 K2
Şenköy Turkey 107 C1
Senlac S. Africa 124 F3
Senlin Shan mt. China 90 C4
Senlis France 62 C5
Senmonorom Cambodia 87 D4
Sennan Japan 92 B4
Sennar Sudan 108 D7
Sennen U.K. 59 B8
Senneterre Canada 152 F4
Sennokura-yama mt. Japan 93 E2
Senqu r. Lesotho 125 H6
Sens France 66 F2
Sensuntepeque El Salvador 166 [inset] H6
Senta Serbia 69 I2
Sentas Kazakh. 98 C2
Senthal India 104 D3
Sentinel U.S.A. 159 G5
Sentinel Peak Canada 150 F4
Sentispac Mex. 166 D4
Sentosa i. Sing. 87 [inset]
Senwabarwana S. Africa 125 I2
Senyiur Kalimantan Indon. 85 G2
Şenyurt Turkey 113 F3
Seo de Urgell Spain see La Seu d'Urgell
Seonath r. India 106 D1
Seoni India 104 D5
Seorinarayan India 105 E5

▶Seoul S. Korea 91 B5
Capital of South Korea.

Sepanjang i. Indon. 85 F4
Separation Well Australia 134 C5
Sepasu Kalimantan Indon. 85 G2
Sepauk Kalimantan Indon. 85 E2
Sepik r. P.N.G. 81 K7
Sepinang Kalimantan Indon. 85 G2
Seping r. Malaysia 85 F2
Sep'o N. Korea 91 B5
Sepon India 105 H4
Seppa India 105 H4
Sept-Îles Canada 153 I4
Seputih r. Indon. 84 D4
Sequoia National Park U.S.A. 158 D3
Serafimovich Rus. Fed. 53 I6
Sêraitang China see Baima
Seram i. Maluku Indon. 83 D3
Seram, Laut sea Indon. 83 D3
Serang Jawa Indon. 84 D4
Serangoon Harbour b. Sing. 87 [inset]
Serapi, Gunung hill Indon. 87 E7
Serapong, Mount hill Sing. 87 [inset]
Serasan i. Indon. 85 E2
Serasan, Selat sea chan. Indon. 85 E2
Seraya i. Indon. 83 A5
Seraya i. Indon. 85 E2
Serbâl, Gebel mt. Egypt see Sirbāl, Jabal

▶Serbia country Europe 69 I2
Formerly known as Yugoslavia and as Serbia and Montenegro. Up to 1993 included Bosnia-Herzegovina, Croatia, Macedonia, Montenegro and Slovenia. Became independent from Montenegro in June 2006. Kosovo declared independence in February 2008.

Sêrbug Co l. Xizang China 99 E6
Sêrca Xizang China 99 F7
Serchhip India 105 H5
Serdar Turkm. 110 E2
Serdica Bulg. see Sofia
Serdo Eth. 122 E2
Serdoba r. Rus. Fed. 53 J5
Serdobsk Rus. Fed. 53 J5
Serdtse-Kamen', Mys c. Rus. Fed. 148 E2
Serebryansk Kazakh. 102 F2
Seredka Rus. Fed. 55 P7
Şereflikoçhisar Turkey 112 D3
Seremban Malaysia 84 C2
Serengeti National Park Tanz. 122 D4
Serenje Zambia 123 D5
Serezha r. Rus. Fed. 52 I5
Sergach Rus. Fed. 52 J5
Sergelen Dornod Mongolia 95 H1
Sergelen Sühbaatar Mongolia see Tüvshinshiree
Sergeyevka Rus. Fed. 90 B2
Sergiyev Posad Rus. Fed. 52 H4
Sergo Ukr. see Stakhanov
Serh Qinghai China 94 D4
Serhetabat Turkm. 111 F3
Seria Brunei 85 F1
Serian Sarawak Malaysia 85 E2
Seribu, Kepulauan is Indon. 84 D4
Serifos i. Greece 69 K6
Sérigny r. Canada 153 H3
Sérigny, Lac l. Canada 153 H3
Serik Turkey 112 C3
Serikbuya Xinjiang China 98 B5
Serikkembelo Seram Indon. 83 C3
Seringapatam Reef Australia 134 C3
Sêrkang Xizang China see Nyainrong
Sermata i. Maluku Indon. 83 D5
Sermata, Kepulauan is Maluku Indon. 83 D5
Sermersuaq glacier Greenland 147 M2
Sermilik inlet Greenland 147 O3
Sernovodsk Rus. Fed. 53 K5
Sernur Rus. Fed. 52 K4
Sernyy Zavod Turkm. see Kükürtli
Seronga Botswana 123 C5
Serov Rus. Fed. 51 S4
Serowe Botswana 125 H2
Serpa Port. 67 C5
Serpa Pinto Angola see Menongue
Serpentine Hot Springs AK U.S.A. 148 F2
Serpentine Lakes salt flat Australia 135 E7
Serpukhov Rus. Fed. 53 H5
Serra Brazil 179 C3
Serra Alta Brazil 179 A4
Serrachis r. Cyprus 107 A2
Serra da Bocaina, Parque Nacional da nat. park Brazil 179 B3
Serra da Bodoquena, Parque Nacional da nat. park Brazil 177 G8
Serra da Canastra, Parque Nacional da nat. park Brazil 179 B3
Serra da Mesa, Represa resr Brazil 179 A1
Serra das Araras Brazil 179 B1
Serra do Divisor, Parque Nacional da nat. park Brazil 176 D5
Sérrai Greece see Serres
Serranía de la Neblina, Parque Nacional nat. park Venez. 176 E3
Serraria, Ilha i. Brazil see Queimada, Ilha
Serra Talhada Brazil 177 K5
Serre r. France 62 D5
Serres Greece 69 J4
Serrinha Brazil 177 K6
Sêrro Brazil 179 C2
Sers Tunisia 68 C6
Sertanópolis Brazil 179 A3
Sertãozinho Brazil 179 B3
Sêrtar China 96 D1
Sertavul Geçidi pass Turkey 107 A1
Sertolovo Rus. Fed. 55 Q6
Serua vol. Maluku Indon. 83 D4
Seruai Sumatera Indon. 84 B1
Serui Indon. 81 J7
Serule Botswana 123 C6
Seruna India 104 C3
Serutu i. Indon. 85 E3
Seruyan r. Indon. 85 F3
Serwaru Maluku Indon. 83 C5
Sêrwolungwa Qinghai China 94 C5
Sêrxü China 96 C1
Serykh Gusey, Ostrova is Rus. Fed. 148 D2
Seryshevo Rus. Fed. 90 C2
Sesayap Kalimantan Indon. 85 G2
Sesayap r. Indon. 85 G2
Seseganaga Lake Canada 152 C4
Sese Islands Uganda 122 D4
Sesel country Indian Ocean see Seychelles
Sesepe Maluku Indon. 83 C3
Sesfontein Namibia 123 B5
Seshachalam Hills India 106 C3
Seshan Rus. Fed. 148 E2
Sesheke Zambia 123 C5
Sesostris Bank sea feature India 106 A3
Ses Salines, Cap de c. Spain 67 H4
Sestri Levante Italy 68 C2
Sestroretsk Rus. Fed. 55 P6
Set, Phou mt. Laos 86 D4
Sète France 66 F5
Sete Lagoas Brazil 179 B2
Setermoen Norway 54 K2
Setesdal valley Norway 55 E7
Seti r. Nepal 104 E3
Sétif Alg. 64 F4
Seto Japan 92 D3
Seto-naikai sea Japan 89 O6
Seto-naikai Kokuritsu-kōen Japan 91 D6
Setsan Myanmar 86 A3
Settat Morocco 64 C5
Settepani, Monte mt. Italy 68 C2
Settle U.K. 58 E4
Setúbal Port. 67 B4
Setúbal, Baía de b. Port. 67 B4
Seul, Lac l. Canada 151 M5
Seulimeum Sumatera Indon. 84 A1
Sevan Armenia 113 G2
Sevan, Lake Armenia 113 G2
Sevan, Ozero l. Armenia see Sevan, Lake
Sevana Lich l. Armenia see Sevan, Lake
Sevastopol' Ukr. 112 D1
Seven Islands Canada see Sept-Îles
Seven Islands Bay Canada 153 J2
Sevenoaks U.K. 59 H7
Seventy Mile House Canada see 70 Mile House
Sévérac-le-Château France 66 F4
Severn r. Australia 138 E2
Severn r. Canada 151 O4
Severn S. Africa 124 F4
Severn r. U.K. 59 E7
also known as Hafren
Severnaya Dvina r. Rus. Fed. 52 I2
Severnaya Sos'va r. Rus. Fed. 51 T3
Severnaya Zemlya is Rus. Fed. 77 L1
Severn Lake Canada 151 N4
Severnoye Rus. Fed. 51 Q5
Severnyy Nenetskiy Avtonomnyy Okrug Rus. Fed. 52 K1
Severnyy Respublika Komi Rus. Fed. 76 H3
Severobaykal'sk Rus. Fed. 89 J1
Severo-Baykal'skoye Nagor'ye mts Rus. Fed. 77 M4
Severo-Chuyskiy Khrebet mts Rus. Fed. 98 D2
Severodonetsk Ukr. see Syeverodonets'k
Severodvinsk Rus. Fed. 52 H2
Severo-Kuril'sk Rus. Fed. 77 Q4
Severomorsk Rus. Fed. 54 R2
Severoonezhsk Rus. Fed. 52 H3
Severo-Sibirskaya Nizmennost' lowland Rus. Fed. see North Siberian Lowland
Severoural'sk Rus. Fed. 51 R3
Severo-Yeniseyskiy Rus. Fed. 76 K3
Severskaya Rus. Fed. 112 E1
Severskiy Donets r. Rus. Fed./Ukr. 53 I7
also known as Northern Donets, Sivers'kyy Donets'
Sevier U.S.A. 159 G2
Sevier r. U.S.A. 159 G2
Sevier Desert U.S.A. 159 G2
Sevier Lake U.S.A. 159 G2
Sevierville U.S.A. 162 D5
Sevilla Col. 176 C3
Sevilla Spain see Seville
Seville Spain 67 D5
Sevlyush Ukr. see Vynohradiv
Sêwa Xizang China 99 E6
Sewani India 104 C3
Seward AK U.S.A. 149 J3
Seward NE U.S.A. 160 D3
Seward Mountains Antarctica 188 L2
Seward Peninsula AK U.S.A. 148 F2
Sexi Spain see Almuñécar
Sexsmith Canada 150 G4
Sextín Mex. 166 D3
Sextín r. Mex. 166 D3
Seya Japan 93 F3
Seyah Band Koh mts Afgh. 111 F3
Seyakha Rus. Fed. 189 F2
Seybaplaya Mex. 167 H5
Seychelles country Indian Ocean 185 L6
Seýdi Turkm. 111 F2
Seydişehir Turkey 112 C3
Seyðisfjörður Iceland 54 [inset]
Seyhan Turkey see Adana
Seyhan r. Turkey 107 B1
Seyitgazi Turkey 69 N5
Seym r. Rus. Fed./Ukr. 53 G6
Seymchan Rus. Fed. 77 Q3
Seymour Australia 138 B6
Seymour S. Africa 125 H7
Seymour IN U.S.A. 164 C4
Seymour TX U.S.A. 161 D5
Seymour Inlet Canada 150 E5
Seymour Range mts Australia 135 F6
Seypan i. N. Mariana Is see Saipan
Seyyedābād Afgh. 111 H3
Sézanne France 62 D6
Sfakia Kriti Greece see Chora Sfakion
Sfântu Gheorghe Romania 69 K2
Sfax Tunisia 68 D7
Sfikia, Limni resr Greece see Sfikias, Limni
Sfikias, Limni resr Greece 69 J4
Sfîntu Gheorghe Romania see Sfântu Gheorghe
Sgiersch Poland see Zgierz
's-Graveland Neth. 62 F2
's-Gravenhage Neth. see The Hague
Sgurr Alasdair hill U.K. 60 C3
Sgurr Dhomhnuill hill U.K. 60 D4
Sgurr Mòr mt. U.K. 60 D3
Sgurr na Ciche mt. U.K. 60 D3
Shaanxi prov. China 95 G5
Shaartuz Tajik. see Shahrtuz
Shaban Pak. 111 G4
Shabani Zimbabwe see Zvishavane
Shabestar Iran 110 B2
Shabībī, Jabal ash mt. Jordan 107 B5
Shabla, Nos pt Bulg. 69 M3
Shabogamo Lake Canada 153 I3
Shabunda Dem. Rep. Congo 122 C4
Shache Xinjiang China 98 B5
Shacheng Hebei China see Huailai
Shackleton Coast Antarctica 188 H1
Shackleton Glacier Antarctica 188 I1
Shackleton Ice Shelf Antarctica 188 F2
Shackleton Range mts Antarctica 188 A1
Shadaogou China 97 F2
Shadaw Myanmar 86 B3
Shādegān Iran 110 C4
Shadihar Pak. 111 G4
Shady Grove U.S.A. 156 C4
Shady Spring U.S.A. 164 E5
Shafer, Lake U.S.A. 164 B3
Shafer Peak Antarctica 188 H2
Shafter U.S.A. 158 D4
Shaftesbury U.K. 59 E7
Shagamu r. Canada 152 D3
Shagan watercourse Kazakh. 98 B2
Shagedu Nei Mongol China 95 G4
Shageluk AK U.S.A. 148 H3
Shaghyray Üstirti plat. Kazakh. see Shagyray, Plato
Shagonar Rus. Fed. 102 H1
Shag Point N.Z. 139 C7
Shag Rocks is S. Georgia 178 H8
Shagyray, Plato plat. Kazakh. 102 A2
Shahabad Karnataka India 106 C2
Shahabad Rajasthan India 104 D4
Shāhābād Uttar Prad. India 104 E4
Shāhābād Iran see Eslāmābād-e Gharb
Shah Alam Malaysia 84 C2
Shah Bandar Pak. 111 G5
Shahdād Iran 110 E4
Shahdol India 104 E5
Shahe China 97 F2
Shahe Shandong China 95 I4
Shahe Xinjiang China see Jiujiang
Shahepu Gansu China see Linze
Shahezhen Gansu China see Linze
Shahezhen China see Jiujiang
Shah Fuladi mt. Afgh. 111 G3
Shahid, Ras pt Pak. 111 F5
Shāhīn Dezh Iran see Sa'īndezh
Shah Ismail Afgh. 111 G4
Shahjahanpur India 104 D4
Shāh Jehān, Kūh-e mts Iran 110 E2
Shāh Jūy Afgh. 111 G3
Shāh Kūh mt. Iran 110 E4
Shahousuo Liaoning China 95 J3
Shāhpūr Iran see Salmās
Shahrak Afgh. 111 G3
Shāhrakht Iran 111 F3
Shahr-e Bābak Iran 110 D4
Shahr-e Kord Iran 110 C3
Shahr-e Şafā Afgh. 111 G4
Shahrezā Iran 110 C3
Shahrig Pak. 111 G4
Shahrisabz Uzbek. 111 G2
Shahriston Tajik. 111 H2
Shahr Rey Iran 110 C3
Shahr Sultan Pak. 111 H4
Shahrtuz Tajik. 111 H2
Shāhrūd Iran see Emāmrūd
Shāhrūd, Rūdkhāneh-ye r. Iran 110 C2
Shāh Savārān, Kūh-e mts Iran 110 E4
Shāh Taqī Iran see Emām Taqī
Shaighalu Pak. 111 H4
Shaikh Husain mt. Pak. 111 G4
Shaikhpura India see Sheikhpura
Shā'īr, Jabal mts Syria 107 C2
Sha'īra, Gebel mt. Egypt see Sha'īrah, Jabal
Sha'īrah, Jabal mt. Egypt 107 B5
Shaj'ah, Jabal hill Saudi Arabia 110 C5
Shajapur India 104 D5
Shajianzi China 90 B4
Shakaga-dake mt. Japan 92 B4
Shakaville S. Africa 125 J5
Shakh Tajik. see Shoh
Shakhbuz Azer. see Şahbuz
Shākhen Iran 111 E3
Shakhovskaya Rus. Fed. 52 G4
Shakhrisabz Uzbek. see Shahrisabz
Shakhristan Tajik. see Shahriston
Shakhtinsk Kazakh. 102 D2
Shakhty Respublika Buryatiya Rus. Fed. see Gusinoozersk
Shakhty Rostovskaya Oblast' Rus. Fed. 53 I7
Shakhun'ya Rus. Fed. 52 J4
Shaki Nigeria 120 D4
Shakotan-hantō pen. Japan 90 F4
Shaktoolik AK U.S.A. 148 G2
Shalakusha Rus. Fed. 52 I3
Shalang China 97 F4
Shali Rus. Fed. 113 G2
Shaliangzi Qinghai China 94 C4
Shaliuhe Qinghai China see Gangca
Shalkar India 104 D3
Shalkar Kazakh. 102 A2
Shalkarteniz, Solonchak salt marsh Kazakh. 102 B2
Shalkode Kazakh. 98 B4
Shallow Bay N.W.T. Canada 149 M1
Shalqar Kazakh. see Shalkar
Shaluli Shan mts China 96 C2
Shaluni mt. India 105 I3
Shama r. Tanz. 123 D4
Shamāl Sīnā' governorate Egypt 107 A4
Shamāl Sīnā' governorate Egypt see Shamāl Sīnā'
Shamalzā'ī Afgh. 111 G4
Shāmat al Akbād des. Saudi Arabia 113 F5
Shamattawa Canada 151 N4
Shamattawa r. Canada 152 D3
Shambār Iran 110 C3
Shamgong Bhutan see Shemgang
Shamīl Iran 110 E5
Shāmīyah des. Iraq/Syria 107 D2
Shamkhor Azer. see Şämkir
Shamrock U.S.A. 161 C5
Shancheng Fujian China see Taining
Shancheng Shandong China see Shanxian
Shand Afgh. 111 F4
Shandan Gansu China 94 E4
Shandian He r. China 95 I3
Shandong prov. China 95 I4
Shandong Bandao pen. China 95 J4
Shandur Pass Pak. 111 I2
Shangchao China 97 F3
Shangcheng China 97 G2
Shang Chu r. China 99 E7
Shangchuan Dao i. China 97 G4
Shangdu Nei Mongol China 95 H3
Shangganling China 90 C3

▶Shanghai China 97 I2
4th most populous city in Asia and 7th in the world.

Shanghai municipality China 97 I2
Shanghe Shandong China 95 I4
Shangji China see Xichuan
Shangjie China see Yangbi
Shangjin China 97 F1
Shangkuli Nei Mongol China 95 J1
Shangluo China 97 F1
Shangmei China see Xinhua
Shangnan China 97 F1
Shangpa China see Fugong
Shangpai China see Feixi
Shangpaihe China see Feixi
Shangqiu Henan China 95 H5
Shangrao China 97 H2
Shangsanshilipu Xinjiang China 98 C3
Shangshui China 97 G1
Shangyou China 97 G3
Shangyou Shuiku resr China 98 C4
Shangyu China 97 I2
Shangzhi China 90 B3
Shangzhou Shaanxi China see Shangluo
Shangzhou Shaanxi China see Shangluo
Shanhaiguan Hebei China 95 I3
Shanhe Gansu China see Zhengning
Shanhetun China 90 B3
Shankou China 97 F4
Shankou Xinjiang China 94 C3
Shanlaragh Ireland 61 C6
Shannon airport Ireland 61 D5
Shannon est. Ireland 61 D5
Shannon r. Ireland 61 D5
Shannon, Mouth of the Ireland 61 C5
Shannon National Park Australia 135 B8
Shannon Ø i. Greenland 189 I1
Shan Plateau Myanmar 86 B2
Shanshan Xinjiang China 94 B3
Shanshanzhan Xinjiang China 94 B3
Shansi prov. China see Shanxi
Shan Teng hill H.K. China see Victoria Peak
Shantipur India 105 G5
Shantou China 97 H4
Shantung prov. China see Shandong
Shanwei China 97 G4
Shanxi prov. China 95 G4
Shanxian Shandong China 95 I5
Shanyang China 97 F1
Shanyin Shanxi China 95 H4
Shaodong China 97 F3
Shaoguan China 97 G3
Shaowu China 97 H3
Shaoxing China 97 I2
Shaoyang China 97 F3
Shap U.K. 58 E4
Shapa China 97 F4
Shaping China see Ebian
Shapinsay i. U.K. 60 G1
Shapkina r. Rus. Fed. 52 L2
Shapshal'skiy Khrebet mts Rus. Fed. 98 E2
Shaqiuhe Xinjiang China 98 E3
Shaqrā' Saudi Arabia 108 G4
Shaquanzi Xinjiang China 98 C3
Shar Kazakh. 98 C2
Shār, Jabal mt. Saudi Arabia 112 D6
Sharaf well Iraq 113 F5
Sharalday Rus. Fed. 95 F1
Sharan 111 H3
Sharan Jogizai Pak. 111 H4
Shārb Māh Iran 110 E4
Sharbulag Mongolia see Dzavhan
Shardara Kazakh. 102 C3
Shardara, Step' plain Kazakh. see Chardara, Step'
Sharga Govĭ-Altay Mongolia 94 C2
Sharga Mongolia see Tsagaan-Uul
Sharhulsan Mongolia see Mandal-Ovoo
Shari r. Cameroon/Chad see Chari
Shārī, Buḩayrat imp. l. Iraq 113 G4
Shari-dake vol. Japan 90 G4
Sharīfah Syria 107 C2
Sharjah U.A.E. 110 D5
Sharka-leb La pass Xizang China 99 E7
Sharkawshchyna Belarus 55 O9
Shark Bay Australia 135 A6
Shark Reef Australia 136 D2
Sharlyk Rus. Fed. 51 Q5
Sharm ash Shaykh Egypt 112 D6
Sharm el Sheikh Egypt see Sharm ash Shaykh
Sharon U.S.A. 164 E3
Sharon Springs U.S.A. 160 C4
Sharpe Lake Canada 151 M4
Sharp Mountain Y.T. Canada 149 M2
Sharp Peak hill H.K. China 97 [inset]
Sharqat Iraq see Ash Sharqāţ
Sharqī, Jabal ash mts Lebanon/Syria 107 B3
Sharqiy Ustyurt Chink esc. Uzbek. 102 A3
Sharur Azer. see Şärur
Shar Us Gol r. Mongolia 94 D2
Shar'ya Rus. Fed. 52 J4
Shashe r. Botswana/Zimbabwe 123 C6
Shashemenē Eth. 122 D3
Shashi China see Jingzhou
Shashubay Kazakh. 98 A3
Shasta U.S.A. 158 B1
Shasta, Mount vol. U.S.A. 156 C4
Shasta Lake U.S.A. 158 B1
Shatilki Belarus see Svyetlahorsk
Sha Tin H.K. China 97 [inset]
Shatki Rus. Fed. 53 J5
Shaţnat as Salmās, Wādī watercourse Syria 107 D2
Sha Tong Hau Shan H.K. China see Bluff Island
Shatoy Rus. Fed. 113 G2
Shatsk Rus. Fed. 53 I5
Shaţţ al 'Arab r. Iran/Iraq 113 H5
Shatura Rus. Fed. 53 H5
Shaubak Jordan see Ash Shawbak
Shaunavon Canada 151 I5
Shaver Lake U.S.A. 158 D3
Shaviovik r. AK U.S.A. 149 K1
Shaw r. Australia 134 B5
Shawan Xinjiang China 98 D3
Shawangunk Mountains hills U.S.A. 165 H3
Shawano U.S.A. 164 A1
Shawano Lake U.S.A. 164 A1
Shawinigan Canada 153 G5
Shawnee OK U.S.A. 161 D5
Shawnee WY U.S.A. 156 G4
Shawneetown U.S.A. 160 F4
Shaxian China 97 H3
Shay Gap (abandoned) Australia 134 C5
Shaykh, Jabal ash mt. Lebanon/Syria see Hermon, Mount
Shaykh Miskīn Syria 107 C3
Shaytūr Iran 110 D4
Shāzand Iran 110 C3
Shazaoyuan Gansu China 98 F5
Shaz̧āz̧, Jabal mt. Saudi Arabia 113 F6
Shazud Tajik. 111 I2
Shchekino Rus. Fed. 53 H5
Shchel'yayur Rus. Fed. 52 L2
Shcherbakov Rus. Fed. see Rybinsk
Shchigry Rus. Fed. 53 H6
Shchors Ukr. 53 F6
Shchuchin Belarus see Shchuchyn
Shchuchyn Belarus 55 N10
Shebalino Rus. Fed. 102 G1
Shebekino Rus. Fed. 53 H6
Sheberghān Afgh. 111 G2
Sheboygan U.S.A. 164 B2
Shebshi Mountains Nigeria 120 E4
Shebunino Rus. Fed. 90 F3
Shecheng Hebei China see Shexian
Shediac Canada 153 I5
Shedin Peak Canada 150 E4
Shedok Rus. Fed. 113 F1
Sheelin, Lough l. Ireland 61 E4
Sheenjek r. AK U.S.A. 149 K2
Sheep Haven b. Ireland 61 E2
Sheepmoor S. Africa 125 J4
Sheep Mountain U.S.A. 159 J2
Sheep Peak U.S.A. 159 F3
Sheep's Head hd Ireland see Muntervary
Sheerness U.K. 59 H7
Sheet Harbour Canada 153 J5
Shefar'am Israel 107 B3
Sheffield N.Z. 139 D6
Sheffield U.K. 58 F5
Sheffield AL U.S.A. 163 C5
Sheffield PA U.S.A. 164 F3
Sheffield TX U.S.A. 161 C6
Sheffield Lake Canada 153 K4
Shegah Afgh. 111 G4
Shegmas Rus. Fed. 52 K2
Shehong China 96 E2
Sheikh, Jebel esh mt. Lebanon/Syria see Hermon, Mount
Sheikhpura India 105 F4
Sheikhupura Pak. 111 I4
Shekak r. Canada 152 D4
Shekār Āb Iran 110 D3
Shekhawati reg. India 111 I5
Shekhem West Bank see Nāblus
Shekhpura India see Sheikhpura
Sheki Azer. see Şäki
Shekka Ch'ün-Tao H.K. China see Soko Islands
Shek Kwu Chau i. H.K. China 97 [inset]
Shekou China 97 [inset]
Sheksna Rus. Fed. 52 H4
Sheksninskoye Vodokhranilishche resr Rus. Fed. 52 H4
Shek Uk Shan mt. H.K. China 97 [inset]
Shela Xizang China 99 F7
Shelagskiy, Mys pt Rus. Fed. 77 S2
Shelbina U.S.A. 160 E4
Shelburn U.S.A. 164 B4
Shelburne N.S. Canada 153 I6
Shelburne Ont. Canada 164 E1
Shelburne Bay Australia 136 C1
Shelby MI U.S.A. 164 B2
Shelby MS U.S.A. 161 F5
Shelby MT U.S.A. 156 F2
Shelby NC U.S.A. 163 D5
Shelbyville IL U.S.A. 160 F4
Shelbyville IN U.S.A. 164 C4
Shelbyville KY U.S.A. 164 C4
Shelbyville TN U.S.A. 162 C5
Sheldon IA U.S.A. 160 E3
Sheldon IL U.S.A. 164 B3
Sheldon Point AK U.S.A. 148 F3
Sheldrake Canada 153 I4
Shelek Kazakh. see Chilik
Shelikhova, Zaliv g. Rus. Fed. 77 Q3
Shelikof Strait AK U.S.A. 148 I4
Shell U.S.A. 160 B2
Shellbrook Canada 151 J4
Shelley U.S.A. 156 E4
Shellharbour Australia 138 E5
Shell Lake Canada 151 J4
Shell Lake U.S.A. 160 F2
Shell Mountain U.S.A. 158 B1
Shelter Bay Canada see Port-Cartier
Shelter Island U.S.A. 165 I3
Shelter Point N.Z. 139 B8
Shelton U.S.A. 156 C3
Shemakha Azer. see Şamaxı
Shemgang Bhutan 105 G4
Shemonaikha Kazakh. 98 C2
Shemordan Rus. Fed. 52 K4
Shenandoah IA U.S.A. 160 E3
Shenandoah PA U.S.A. 165 G3
Shenandoah r. U.S.A. 165 G4
Shenandoah Mountains U.S.A. 164 F4
Shenandoah National Park U.S.A. 165 F4
Shenchi Shanxi China 95 H4
Shendam Nigeria 120 D4
Shending Shan hill China 90 D3
Shengel'dy Almatinskaya Oblast' Kazakh. 98 B3
Shengena mt. Tanz. 123 D4
Shengli China 97 G2
Shengli Daban pass Xinjiang China 98 D4
Shengli Feng mt. China/Kyrg. see Jengish Chokusu
Shengli Qichang Xinjiang China 98 B4
Shengli Shibachang Xinjiang China 98 C4
Shengping China 90 B3
Shengrenjian Shanxi China see Pinglu
Shengsi China 97 I2
Shengsi Liedao is China 97 I2
Shenjiamen China 97 I2
Shen Khan Bandar Afgh. 111 H2
Shenkursk Rus. Fed. 52 I3
Shenmu Shaanxi China 95 G4
Shennong Ding mt. China 97 F2
Shennongjia China 97 F2
Shenqiu China 97 G1
Shenshu China 90 C3
Shensi prov. China see Shaanxi
Shentala Rus. Fed. 53 K5
Shenton, Mount hill Australia 135 C7
Shenxian Hebei China see Shenzhou
Shenxian Shandong China 95 H4
Shenyang Liaoning China 95 J3
Shenzhen China 97 G4
Shenzhen Wan b. H.K. China see Deep Bay
Shenzhou Hebei China 95 H4
Sheopur India 104 D4
Shepetivka Ukr. 53 E6
Shepetovka Ukr. see Shepetivka
Shepherd Islands Vanuatu 133 G3
Shepherdsville U.S.A. 164 C5
Shepparton Australia 138 B6
Sheppey, Isle of i. U.K. 59 H7
Sheqi China 97 G1
Sherabad Uzbek. see Sherobod
Sherborne U.K. 59 E8
Sherbro Island Sierra Leone 120 B4
Sherbrooke Canada 153 H5
Sherburne U.S.A. 165 H2
Shercock Ireland 61 F4
Shereiq Sudan 108 D6
Shergaon India 105 H4
Shergarh India 104 C4
Sheridan AR U.S.A. 161 E5
Sheridan WY U.S.A. 156 G3
Sheringham U.K. 59 I6
Sherlovaya Gora Rus. Fed. 95 I1
Sherman U.S.A. 161 D5
Sherman Mountain U.S.A. 159 F1
Sherobod Uzbek. 111 G2
Sherpur Dhaka Bangl. 105 G4
Sherpur Rajshahi Bangl. 105 G4
Sherridon Canada 151 K4
's-Hertogenbosch Neth. 62 F3
Sherwood Forest reg. U.K. 59 F5
Sherwood Lake Canada 151 K2
Sheslay B.C. Canada 149 O4
Sheslay r. B.C. Canada 149 N4
Shethanei Lake Canada 151 L3
Shetland Islands is U.K. 60 [inset]
Shetpe Kazakh. 100 E2
Sheung Shui H.K. China 97 [inset]
Sheung Sze Mun sea chan. H.K. China 97 [inset]
Shevchenko Kazakh. see Aktau
Shevli r. Rus. Fed. 90 D1
Shexian China 97 H2
Shexian Hebei China 95 H4
Sheyang China 97 I1
Sheyenne r. U.S.A. 160 D2
Shey Phoksundo National Park Nepal 105 E3
Shiant Islands U.K. 60 C3
Shiashkotan, Ostrov i. Rus. Fed. 77 Q5
Shibakawa Japan 93 E3
Shibām Yemen 108 G6
Shibandong Jing well China 94 C3

Shiban Jing *well* China **94** D3
Shibaocheng *Gansu* China **94** D4
Shibar, Kowtal-e Afgh. **111** H3
Shibata Japan **91** E5
Shibayama Japan **93** G3
Shibayama-gata *l.* Japan **92** C2
Shibazhan China **90** B1
Shibh Jazīrat Sīnā' *pen.* Egypt *see* **Sinai**
Shibīn al Kawm Egypt **112** C5
Shibîn el Kôm Egypt *see* **Shibīn al Kawm**
Shibogama Lake Canada **152** C3
Shibotsu-jima *i.* Rus. Fed. *see* **Zelenyy, Ostrov**
Shibukawa Japan **93** F2
Shibu-tōge *pass* Japan **93** E2
Shibutsu-san *mt.* Japan **93** F2
Shicheng *Fujian* China *see* **Zhouning**
Shicheng *Jiangxi* China **97** H3
Shicheng Dao *i.* China **95** J4
Shichimen-zan *mt.* Japan **93** E3
Shicun *Shanxi* China *see* **Xiangfen**
Shidād al Mismā' *hill* Saudi Arabia **107** D4
Shidao *Shandong* China **95** J4
Shidao Wan *b.* China **95** J4
Shidian China **96** C3
Shidongsi *Gansu* China *see* **Gaolan**
Shiel, Loch *l.* U.K. **60** D4
Shield, Cape Australia **136** B2
Shieli Kazakh. *see* **Chiili**
Shifa, Jabal ash *mts* Saudi Arabia **112** D5
Shifang China **96** E2
Shiga *Nagano* Japan **93** D2
Shiga *Shiga* Japan **92** B3
Shiga *pref.* Japan **92** B3
Shigaraki Japan **92** C4
Shigatse *Xizang* China *see* **Xigazê**
Shigong *Gansu* China **98** F4
Shiguai *Nei Mongol* China **95** G3
Shiguaigou *Nei Mongol* China *see* **Shiguai**
Shiḥān *mt.* Jordan **107** B4
Shihezi *Xinjiang* China **98** D3
Shihkiachwang *Hebei* China *see* **Shijiazhuang**
Shijiao China *see* **Fogang**
Shijiazhuang *Hebei* China **95** H4
Shijiu Hu *l.* China **97** H2
Shijiusuo *Shandong* China *see* **Rizhao**
Shika Japan **92** C1
Shikag Lake Canada **152** C4
Shikar *r.* Pak. **111** F4
Shikarpur Pak. **111** H5
Shikengkong *mt.* China **97** G3
Shikhany Rus. Fed. **53** J5
Shiki Japan **93** F3
Shikine-jima *i.* Japan **93** F4
Shikishima Japan **93** E3
Shikohabad India **104** D4
Shikoku *i.* Japan **91** D6
Shikoku-sanchi *mts* Japan **91** D6
Shikotan, Ostrov *i.* Rus. Fed. **90** G4
Shikotan-tō *i.* Rus. Fed. *see* **Shikotan, Ostrov**
Shikotsu-Tōya Kokuritsu-kōen Japan **90** F4
Shildon U.K. **58** F4
Shilega Rus. Fed. **52** J2
Shilianghe Shuiku *resr* China **95** I5
Shiliguri India **105** G4
Shilin China **96** D3
Shilipu China **97** G2
Shiliu China *see* **Changjiang**
Shilla *mt.* India **104** D2
Shillelagh Ireland **61** F5
Shillo *r.* Israel **107** B3
Shillong India **105** G4
Shilou *Shanxi* China **95** G4
Shilovo Rus. Fed. **53** I5
Shilüüstey Mongolia **94** D2
Shima Japan **92** C4
Shima *spring* Japan **93** E2
Shimada Japan **93** E4
Shimagahara Japan **92** C4
Shima-hantō *pen.* Japan **92** C4
Shimamoto Japan **92** B4
Shimanovsk Rus. Fed. **90** B1
Shimbiris *mt.* Somalia **122** E2
Shimen *Gansu* China **96** D1
Shimen *Hunan* China **97** F2
Shimen *Yunnan* China *see* **Yunlong**
Shimizu *Fukui* Japan **92** C2
Shimizu *Shizuoka* Japan **93** E3
Shimizu *Shizuoka* Japan **93** E3
Shimizu *Wakayama* Japan **92** B4
Shimla India **104** D3
Shimminato Japan *see* **Shinminato**
Shimo Japan **92** D2
Shimobe Japan **93** E3
Shimoda Japan **93** E4
Shimodate Japan **93** F2
Shimofusa Japan **93** G3
Shimoga India **106** B3
Shimoichi Japan **92** B4
Shimojō Japan **93** D3
Shimokita-hantō *pen.* Japan **90** F4
Shimokitayama Japan **92** B4
Shimoni Kenya **123** D4
Shimonita Japan **93** E2
Shimonoseki Japan **91** C6
Shimosuwa Japan **93** E2
Shimotsu Japan **92** B4
Shimotsuma Japan **93** F2
Shimoyama Japan **92** D3
Shimsk Rus. Fed. **52** F4
Shin Japan **93** F2
Shin, Loch *l.* U.K. **60** E2
Shināfiyah Iraq *see* **Ash Shanāfiyah**
Shinan China *see* **Xingye**
Shinano Japan **93** E2
Shin-asahi Japan **92** C3
Shīndand Afgh. **111** F3
Shine-Ider *Hövsgöl* Mongolia **94** D1
Shinejinst Mongolia **94** D2
Shingbwiyang Myanmar **86** B1
Shing-gai Myanmar **86** B1
Shinghshal Pass Pak. **111** I2
Shingletown U.S.A. **158** C1
Shingozha Kazakh. **98** C3
Shingū Japan **91** E6
Shingwedzi S. Africa **125** J2
Shingwedzi *r.* S. Africa **125** J2
Shinkāy Afgh. **111** G4
Shinkay Ghar Afgh. **111** H3
Shinminato Japan **92** D2
Shinnston U.S.A. **164** E4
Shino-jima *i.* Japan **92** C4
Shinonoi Japan **93** E2
Shinsei Japan **92** C3
Shinshār Syria **107** C2
Shinshiro Japan **92** D4
Shinshūshin Japan **93** E2
Shintō Japan **93** E2
Shintone Japan **93** G3
Shinyanga Tanz. **122** D4
Shio Japan **92** C2
Shiobara Japan **93** F2
Shiocton U.S.A. **164** A1
Shiogama Japan **91** F5
Shiojiri Japan **93** D2
Shiomi-dake *mt.* Japan **93** E3
Shiono-misaki *c.* Japan **91** D6
Shioya Japan **93** F2
Shioya-zaki *pt* Japan **93** G1
Shiozawa Japan **93** E1
Shipai China **97** H2
Shiping China **96** D4
Shipki Pass China/India **99** B7
Shipman U.S.A. **165** F5
Shippegan Island Canada **153** I5
Shippensburg U.S.A. **165** G3
Shippō Japan **92** C3
Shiprock U.S.A. **159** I3
Shiprock Peak U.S.A. **159** I3
Shipu *Shaanxi* China *see* **Huanglong**
Shipu China **97** I2
Shipunovo Rus. Fed. **88** E2
Shiqian China **97** F3
Shiqiao China *see* **Panyu**
Shiqizhen China *see* **Zhongshan**
Shiquan China **97** F1
Shiquanhe *Xizang* China *see* **Gar**
Shiquanhe *Xizang* China *see* **Ali**
Shiquan He *r.* China **104** D2 *see* **Indus**
Shiquan Shuiku *resr* China **97** F1
Shira Rus. Fed. **88** F2
Shīrābād Iran **110** C2
Shirahama *Chiba* Japan **93** F4
Shirai-san *hill* Japan **92** C4
Shirakawa *Fukushima* Japan **93** G1
Shirakawa *Gifu* Japan **92** C2
Shirakawa *Gifu* Japan **92** D3
Shirakawa-go and Gokayama *tourist site* Japan **91** E5
Shirake-mine *mt.* Japan **92** D2
Shirako Japan **93** G3
Shirakura-yama *mt.* Japan **92** D3
Shirama-yama *hill* Japan **92** B4
Shiramine Japan **92** C2
Shirane Japan **93** E3
Shirane-san *mt.* Japan **93** E2
Shirane-san *mt.* Japan **93** E3
Shirane-san *vol.* Japan **93** F2
Shirasawa Japan **93** F2
Shirase Coast Antarctica **188** J1
Shirase Glacier Antarctica **188** D2
Shīrāz Iran **110** D4
Shire *r.* Malawi **123** D5
Shireet Mongolia *see* **Bayandelger**
Shireza Pak. **111** G5
Shirīn Tagāb Afgh. **111** G2
Shiriya-zaki *c.* Japan **90** F4
Shirkala *reg.* Kazakh. **102** A2
Shīr Kūh *mt.* Iran **110** D4
Shiroi Japan **93** G3
Shirokura-yama *mt.* Japan **93** D3
Shiroro Reservoir Nigeria **120** D3
Shirotori Japan **92** C3
Shirouma-dake *mt.* Japan **92** D2
Shiroyama Japan **93** F3
Shirpur India **104** C5
Shirten Holoy Gobi *des.* China **94** D3
Shīrvān Iran **110** E2
Shisanjianfang *Xinjiang* China **94** B3
Shisanzhan China **90** B2
Shishaldin Volcano U.S.A. **146** B4
Shisha Pangma *mt. Xizang* China *see* **Xixabangma Feng**
Shishmaref *AK* U.S.A. **148** F2
Shishmaref Inlet *AK* U.S.A. **148** F2
Shishou China **97** G2
Shisui Japan **93** G3
Shitan China **97** G3
Shitang China **97** I2
Shitanjing *Ningxia* China **94** F4
Shitara Japan **92** D3
Shithāthah Iraq **113** F4
Shiv India **104** B4
Shiveluch, Sopka *vol.* Rus. Fed. **77** R4
Shivpuri India **104** D4
Shivwits U.S.A. **159** G3
Shivwits Plateau U.S.A. **159** G3
Shiwan *Shaanxi* China **95** G4
Shiwan Dashan *mts* China **96** E4
Shiwa Ngandu Zambia **123** D5
Shixing China **97** G3
Shiyan China **97** F1
Shizhu China **97** F2
Shizi *Gansu* China **95** F5
Shizilu *Shandong* China *see* **Junan**
Shizipu China **97** H2
Shizong China **96** D3
Shizuishan *Ningxia* China **94** F4
Shizuishanzhan *Ningxia* China **94** F4
Shizuoka Japan **93** E4
Shizuoka *pref.* Japan **93** E4

▶**Shkhara** *mt.* Georgia/Rus. Fed. **113** F2
3rd highest mountain in Europe.

Shklov Belarus *see* **Shklow**
Shklow Belarus **53** F5
Shkodër Albania **69** H3
Shkodra Albania *see* **Shkodër**
Shkodrës, Liqeni i *l.* Albania/Montenegro *see* **Scutari, Lake**
Shmidta, Ostrov *i.* Rus. Fed. **76** K1
Shmidta, Poluostrov *pen.* Rus. Fed. **90** F1
Shoal Lake Canada **151** K5
Shoals U.S.A. **164** B4
Shōbara Japan **91** D6
Shōgawa Japan **92** D2
Shō-gawa *r.* Japan **92** D2
Shoh Tajik. **111** H2
Shohi Pass Pak. *see* **Tal Pass**
Shokanbetsu-dake *mt.* Japan **90** F4
Shōkawa Japan **92** C2
Sholakkorgan Kazakh. **102** C3
Sholapur India *see* **Solapur**
Sholaqorghan Kazakh. *see* **Sholakkorgan**
Shomba *r.* Rus. Fed. **54** R4
Shomvukva Rus. Fed. **52** K3
Shōmyō-gawa *r.* Japan **92** D2
Shona Ridge *sea feature* S. Atlantic Ocean **184** I9
Shonzha Kazakh. *see* **Chundzha**
Shor India **104** D2
Shorap Pak. **111** G5
Shorapur India **106** C2
Shorawak *reg.* Afgh. **111** G4
Sho'rchi Uzbek. **111** G2
Shorewood *IL* U.S.A. **164** A3
Shorewood *WI* U.S.A. **164** B2
Shorkot Pak. **111** I4
Shorkozakhly, Solonchak *salt flat* Turkm. **113** J2
Shoshone *CA* U.S.A. **158** E4
Shoshone *ID* U.S.A. **156** E4
Shoshone *r.* U.S.A. **156** F3
Shoshone Mountains U.S.A. **158** E2
Shoshone Peak U.S.A. **158** E3
Shoshong Botswana **125** H2
Shoshoni U.S.A. **156** F4
Shostka Ukr. **53** G6
Shotor Khūn Afgh. **111** G3
Shouguang *Shandong* China **95** I4
Shouyang *Shanxi* China **95** H4
Shouyang Shan *mt.* China **97** F1
Shōwa Japan **93** F2
Showak Sudan **108** E7
Show Low U.S.A. **159** H4
Shoyna Rus. Fed. **52** J2
Shpakovskoye Rus. Fed. **113** F1
Shpola Ukr. **53** F6
Shqipëria *country* Europe *see* **Albania**
Shreve U.S.A. **164** D3
Shreveport U.S.A. **161** E5
Shrewsbury U.K. **59** E6
Shri Lanka *country* Asia *see* **Sri Lanka**
Shri Mohangarh India **104** B4
Shrirampur India **105** G5
Shu Kazakh. **102** D3
Shū *r.* Kazakh./Kyrg. *see* **Chu**
Shu'ab, Ra's *pt* Yemen **109** H7
Shuajingsi China **96** D1
Shuangbai China **96** D3
Shuangcheng *Fujian* China *see* **Zherong**
Shuangcheng *Heilong.* China **90** B3
Shuanghe China **97** G2
Shuanghechang China **96** E2
Shuanghedagang China **90** C2
Shuanghu *Xizang* China **99** D6
Shuanghuyu *Shaanxi* China *see* **Zizhou**
Shuangjiang *Guizhou* China *see* **Jiangkou**
Shuangjiang *Hunan* China *see* **Tongdao**
Shuangjiang *Yunnan* China *see* **Eshan**
Shuangliao *Jilin* China **95** J3
Shuangliu China **96** D2
Shuangpai China **97** F3
Shuangshanzi *Hebei* China **95** I3
Shuangshipu China *see* **Fengxian**
Shuangxi China *see* **Shunchang**
Shuangyang China **90** B4
Shuangyashan China **90** C3
Shubarkuduk Kazakh. **102** A2
Shubayh *well* Saudi Arabia **107** D4
Shublik Mountains *AK* U.S.A. **149** K1
Shufu *Xinjiang* China **98** A5
Shugozero Rus. Fed. **52** G4
Shu He *r.* China **95** I5
Shuicheng China *see* **Lupanshui**
Shuiding *Xinjiang* China *see* **Huocheng**
Shuidong China *see* **Dianbai**
Shuiji *Shandong* China *see* **Laixi**
Shuijing China **96** E1
Shuijingkuang *Qinghai* China **99** E6
Shuikou China **97** F3
Shuikouguan China **96** E4
Shuikoushan China **97** G3
Shuiluocheng *Gansu* China *see* **Zhuanglang**
Shuiquan *Gansu* China **94** F4
Shuiquanzi *Gansu* China **94** E4
Shuizhai China *see* **Wuhua**
Shuizhan *Qinghai* China **99** E5
Shulakpachak Peak *AK* U.S.A. **148** I2
Shulan China **90** B3
Shule *Xinjiang* China **98** B5
Shulehe *Gansu* China **98** G4
Shule He *r.* China **94** C3
Shule Nanshan *mts* China **94** D4
Shulinzhao *Nei Mongol* China **95** G3
Shulu *Hebei* China *see* **Xinji**
Shumagin Islands *AK* U.S.A. **148** G5
Shumba Zimbabwe **123** C5
Shumen Bulg. **69** L3
Shumerlya Rus. Fed. **52** J5
Shumilina Belarus **53** F5
Shumyachi Rus. Fed. **53** G5
Shunchang China **97** H3
Shuncheng China **90** A4
Shunde China **97** G4
Shungnak *AK* U.S.A. **148** H2
Shunyi *Beijing* China **95** I3
Shuoxian *Shanxi* China *see* **Shuozhou**
Shuozhou *Shanxi* China **95** H4
Shuqrah Yemen **108** G7
Shūr *r.* Iran **110** D4
Shūr *r.* Iran **111** F3
Shūr *watercourse* Iran **110** D5
Shur *watercourse* Iran **110** E3
Shūr, Rūd-e *watercourse* Iran **110** E4
Shūr Āb *watercourse* Iran **110** D4
Shūrjestān Iran **110** D4
Shūrū Iran **111** F4
Shuryshkarskiy Sor, Ozero *l.* Rus. Fed. **51** T2
Shūsh Iran **110** C3
Shusha Azer. *see* **Şuşa**
Shushtar Iran **110** C3
Shutfah, Qalamat *well* Saudi Arabia **110** D6
Shuwaysh, Tall ash *hill* Jordan **107** C4
Shuya *Ivanovskaya Oblast'* Rus. Fed. **52** I4
Shuya *Respublika Kareliya* Rus. Fed. **52** G3
Shuyak Island *AK* U.S.A. **148** I4
Shuyang *Jiangsu* China **95** I5
Shuyskoye Rus. Fed. **52** I4
Shuzenji Japan **93** E4
Shwebo Myanmar **86** A2
Shwedwin Myanmar **86** A1
Shwegun Myanmar **86** B3
Shwegyin Myanmar **86** B3
Shweudaung *mt.* Myanmar **86** B2
Shyghanaq Kazakh. *see* **Chiganak**
Shygys Konyrat Kazakh. **98** A3
Shymkent Kazakh. **102** C3
Shyok *r.* India **99** A6
Shyok India **104** D2
Shypuvate Ukr. **53** H6
Shyroke Ukr. **53** G7
Sia Indon. **81** I8
Siabu *Sumatera* Indon. **84** B2
Siachen Glacier India/Pak. **99** B6
Siahan Range *mts* Pak. **111** F5
Sīah Chashmeh Iran **110** B2
Siahgird Afgh. **111** G2
Siah Koh *mts* Afgh. **111** G3
Siak *r.* Indon. **84** C2
Siak Sri Inderapura *Sumatera* Indon. **84** C2
Sialkot Pak. **111** I3
Siam *country* Asia *see* **Thailand**
Sian *Shaanxi* China *see* **Xi'an**
Sian Rus. Fed. **90** B1
Siang *r.* India *see* **Brahmaputra**
Siantan *i.* Indon. **84** D2
Siargao *i.* Phil. **82** D4
Siasi Phil. **82** C5
Siasi *i.* Phil. **82** C5
Siaton *Negros* Phil. **82** C4
Siau *i.* Indon. **83** C2
Šiauliai Lith. **55** M9
Siayan *i.* Phil. **97** I4
Siazan' Azer. *see* **Siyäzän**
Si Bai, Lam *r.* Thai. **86** D4
Sibasa S. Africa **125** J2
Sibati *Xinjiang* China *see* **Xibet**
Sibay *i.* Phil. **82** C4
Sibayi, Lake S. Africa **125** K4
Sibda China **96** C2
Šibenik Croatia **68** F3
Siberia *reg.* Rus. Fed. **77** M3
Siberut *i.* Indon. **84** B3
Siberut, Selat *sea chan.* Indon. **84** B3
Siberut, Taman Nasional *nat. park* Indon. **84** B3
Sibi Pak. **111** G4
Sibidiri P.N.G. **81** K8
Sibigo Indon. **84** A2
Sibiloi National Park Kenya **122** D3
Sibir' *reg.* Rus. Fed. *see* **Siberia**
Sibiti Congo **122** B4
Sibiu Romania **69** K2
Sibley U.S.A. **160** E3
Siboa *Sulawesi* Indon. **83** B2
Sibolga *Sumatera* Indon. **84** B2
Siborongborong *Sumatera* Indon. **84** B2
Sibsagar India **105** H4
Sibu *Sarawak* Malaysia **85** E2
Sibuco *Mindanao* Phil. **82** C5
Sibuco Bay *Mindanao* Phil. **82** C5
Sibuguey *r. Mindanao* Phil. **82** C5
Sibuguey Bay *Mindanao* Phil. **82** C5
Sibut Cent. Afr. Rep. **122** B3
Sibuti *Sarawak* Malaysia **85** F1
Sibutu *i.* Phil. **82** B5
Sibutu Passage Phil. **82** B5
Sibuyan *i.* Phil. **82** C3
Sibuyan Sea Phil. **82** C3
Sicamous Canada **150** G5
Sicapoo *mt. Luzon* Phil. **82** C2
Sicayac *Mindanao* Phil. **82** C4
Sicca Veneria Tunisia *see* **Le Kef**
Siccus *watercourse* Australia **137** B6
Sicheng *Anhui* China *see* **Sixian**
Sicheng *Guangxi* China *see* **Lingyun**
Sichon Thai. **87** B5
Sichuan *prov.* China **96** D2
Sichuan Pendi *basin* China **96** E2
Sicié, Cap *c.* France **66** G5
Sicilia *i.* Italy *see* **Sicily**
Sicilian Channel Italy/Tunisia **68** E6
Sicily *i.* Italy **68** F5
Sicuani Peru **176** D6
Sidangoli *Halmahera* Indon. **83** C2
Siddhapur India **104** C5
Siddipet India **106** C2
Sidenreng, Danau *l.* Indon. **83** A3
Sideros, Akra *pt Kriti* Greece *see* **Sideros, Akrotirio**
Sideros, Akrotirio *pt* Greece **69** L7
Sidesaviwa S. Africa **124** F7
Sidhauli India **104** E4
Sidhi India **105** E4
Sidhpur India *see* **Siddhapur**
Sidi Aïssa Alg. **67** H6
Sidi Ali Alg. **67** G5
Sīdī Barrānī Egypt **112** B5
Sidi Bel Abbès Alg. **67** F6
Sidi Bennour Morocco **64** C5
Sidi Bou Sa'id Tunisia *see* **Sidi Bouzid**
Sidi Bouzid Tunisia **68** C7
Sidi el Barrâni Egypt *see* **Sīdī Barrānī**
Sidi El Hani, Sebkhet de *salt pan* Tunisia **68** D7
Sidi Ifni Morocco **120** B2
Sidi Kacem Morocco **64** C5
Sidikalang *Sumatera* Indon. **84** B2
Sidi Khaled Alg. **64** E5
Sid Lake Canada **151** J2
Sidlaw Hills U.K. **60** F4
Sidley, Mount Antarctica **188** J1
Sidli India **105** G4
Sidmouth U.K. **59** D8
Sidney *IA* U.S.A. **160** E3
Sidney *MT* U.S.A. **156** G3
Sidney *NE* U.S.A. **160** C3
Sidney *OH* U.S.A. **164** C3
Sidney Lanier, Lake U.S.A. **163** D5
Sidoan *Sulawesi* Indon. **83** B2
Sidoan *Sulawesi* Indon. **83** B2
Sidoarjo *Jawa* Indon. **85** F4
Sidoktaya Myanmar **86** A2
Sidon Lebanon **107** B3
Sidr Egypt *see* **Sudr**
Siedlce Poland **53** D5
Sieg *r.* Germany **63** H4
Siegen Germany **63** I4
Siĕmréab Cambodia **87** C4
Siem Reap Cambodia *see* **Siĕmréab**
Si'en China *see* **Huanjiang**
Siena Italy **68** D3
Sieradz Poland **57** Q5
Si'erdingka *Xizang* China **99** F7
Sierra Blanca U.S.A. **157** G7
Sierra Colorada Arg. **178** C6
Sierra Grande Arg. **178** C6
Sierra Leone *country* Africa **120** B4
Sierra Leone Basin *sea feature* N. Atlantic Ocean **184** G5
Sierra Leone Rise *sea feature* N. Atlantic Ocean **184** G5
Sierra Madre Mountains U.S.A. **158** C4
Sierra Mojada Mex. **166** E3
Sierra Nevada, Parque Nacional *nat. park* Venez. **176** D2
Sierra Nevada de Santa Marta, Parque Nacional *nat. park* Col. **176** D1
Sierraville U.S.A. **158** C2
Sierra Vista U.S.A. **157** F7
Sierre Switz. **66** H3
Sievi Fin. **54** N5
Sifang Ling *mts* China **96** E4
Sifangtai China **90** B3
Sīfenī Eth. **122** E2
Sifnos *i.* Greece **69** K6
Sig Alg. **67** F6
Sigep, Tanjung *pt* Indon. **84** B3
Sigguup Nunaa *pen.* Greenland **147** M2
Sighetu Marmaţiei Romania **53** D7
Sighişoara Romania **69** K1
Siglap Sing. **87** [inset]
Sigli *Sumatera* Indon. **84** A1
Siglufjörður Iceland **54** [inset]
Sigma *Panay* Phil. **82** C4
Signal de Botrange *hill* Belgium **62** G4
Signal de la Ste-Baume *mt.* France **66** G5
Signal Peak U.S.A. **159** F5
Signy-l'Abbaye France **62** E5
Sigoisooinan Indon. **84** B3
Sigourney U.S.A. **160** E3
Sigri, Akra *pt Voreio Aigaio* Greece *see* **Saratsina, Akrotirio**
Sigsbee Deep *sea feature* G. of Mexico **187** N4
Siguatepeque Hond. **167** I6
Sigüenza Spain **67** E3
Siguiri Guinea **120** C3
Sigulda Latvia **55** N8
Sigurd U.S.A. **159** H2
Sihanoukville Cambodia **87** C5
Sihaung Myauk Myanmar **86** A2
Sihawa India **106** D1
Sihong China **97** H1
Sihora India **104** E5
Sihou *Shandong* China *see* **Changdao**
Sihui China **97** G4
Siikajoki Fin. **54** N4
Siilinjärvi Fin. **54** O5
Siirt Turkey **113** F3
Sijawal Pak. **104** B4
Sijunjung *Sumatera* Indon. **84** C3
Sikaka Saudi Arabia *see* **Sakākah**
Sikakap Indon. **84** C3
Sikandra Rao India **104** D4
Sikanni Chief Canada **150** F3
Sikanni Chief *r.* Canada **150** F3
Sikar India **104** C4
Sikaram *mt.* Afgh. **111** H3
Sikasso Mali **120** C3
Sikaw Myanmar **86** B2
Sikeli *Sulawesi* Indon. **83** B4
Sikeston U.S.A. **161** F4
Sikhote-Alin' *mts* Rus. Fed. **90** D4
Sikhote-Alinskiy Zapovednik *nature res.* Rus. Fed. **90** E3
Sikinos *i.* Greece **69** K6
Sikka India **104** B5
Sikkim *state* India **105** G4
Siknik Cape *AK* U.S.A. **148** E3
Siko *i. Maluku* Indon. **83** C2
Siksjö Sweden **54** J4
Sikuaishi *Liaoning* China **95** J4
Sikuati *Sabah* Malaysia **85** G1
Sil *r.* Spain **67** C2
Şila' *i.* Saudi Arabia **112** D6
Silago *Leyte* Phil. **82** D4
Šilalė Lith. **55** M9
Si Lanna National Park Thai. **86** B3
Sila Point *Samar* Phil. **82** D3
Silas U.S.A. **161** F6
Silavatturai Sri Lanka **106** C4
Silawaih Agam *vol.* Indon. **84** A1
Silay *Negros* Phil. **82** C4
Silberberg *hill* Germany **63** J1
Silchar India **105** H4
Şile Turkey **69** M4
Sileru *r.* India **106** D2
Silesia *reg.* Czech Rep./Poland **57** P5
Sileti *r.* Kazakh. **88** C2
Siletiteniz, Ozero *salt l.* Kazakh. **101** G1
Silghat India **105** H4
Siliana Tunisia **68** C6
Silifke Turkey **107** A1
Siliguri India *see* **Shiliguri**
Siling Co *salt l.* China **99** E7
Silipur India **104** D4
Silistra Bulg. **69** L2
Silistria Bulg. *see* **Silistra**
Silivri Turkey **69** M4
Siljan *l.* Sweden **55** I6
Silkeborg Denmark **55** F8
Sillajhuay *mt.* Chile **176** E7
Sillamäe Estonia **55** O7
Sille Turkey **112** D3
Silli India **105** F5
Sillod India **106** B1
Silobela S. Africa **125** J4
Silsbee *TX* U.S.A. **167** G2
Silsby Lake Canada **151** M4
Silt U.S.A. **159** J2
Siltaharju Fin. **54** O3
Siluas *Kalimantan* Indon. **85** E2
Sīlūp *r.* Iran **111** F5
Šilutė Lith. **55** L9
Silvan Turkey **113** F3
Silvânia Brazil **179** A2
Silvassa India **106** B1
Silver Bank Passage Turks and Caicos Is **169** J4
Silver Bay U.S.A. **160** F2
Silver City *NM* U.S.A. **159** I5
Silver City *NV* U.S.A. **158** D2
Silver City (abandoned) *Y.T.* Canada **149** M3
Silver Creek *r.* U.S.A. **159** H4
Silver Lake U.S.A. **156** C4
Silver Lake *l.* U.S.A. **158** E4
Silvermine Mts *hills* Ireland **61** D5
Silver Peak Range *mts* U.S.A. **158** E3
Silver Spring U.S.A. **165** G4
Silver Springs U.S.A. **158** D2
Silverthrone Mountain Canada **150** E5
Silvertip Mountain Canada **150** F5
Silverton U.K. **59** D8
Silverton *CO* U.S.A. **159** J3
Silverton *TX* U.S.A. **161** C5
Silvituc Mex. **167** H5
Sima *Xizang* China **99** E7
Simao China **96** D4
Simara *i.* Phil. **82** C3
Simard, Lac *l.* Canada **152** F5
Simaria India **105** F4
Simatang *i.* Indon. **83** B2
Simav Turkey **69** M5
Simav Dağları *mts* Turkey **69** M5
Simawat *Xinjiang* China **99** C5
Simba Dem. Rep. Congo **122** C3
Simbirsk Rus. Fed. *see* **Ul'yanovsk**
Simcoe Canada **164** E2
Simcoe, Lake Canada **164** F1
Simdega India **106** E1
Simēn *mts* Eth. **122** D2
Simēn Mountains Eth. *see* **Simēn**
Simeonof Island *AK* U.S.A. **148** H5
Simeulue *i.* Indon. **84** B2
Simferopol' Ukr. **112** D1
Simi *i.* Greece *see* **Symi**
Simikot Nepal **105** E3
Similan, Ko *i.* Thai. **87** B5
Simi Valley U.S.A. **158** D4
Simla India *see* **Shimla**
Simla U.S.A. **156** G5
Şimleu Silvaniei Romania **69** J1
Simmerath Germany **62** G4
Simmern (Hunsrück) Germany **63** H5
Simmesport U.S.A. **161** F6
Simms U.S.A. **156** F3
Simojärvi *l.* Fin. **54** O3
Simon Mex. **161** C7
Simonette *r.* Canada **150** G4
Simon Wash *watercourse* U.S.A. **159** I5
Simoom Sound Canada **150** E5
Simoom Sound Canada *see* **Simoom Sound**
Simpang *Sumatera* Indon. **84** D3
Simpang Mangayau, Tanjung *pt* Malaysia **80** F5
Simplício Mendes Brazil **177** J5
Simplon Pass Switz. **66** I3
Simpson Canada **151** J5
Simpson U.S.A. **156** F2
Simpson Desert Australia **136** B5
Simpson Desert National Park Australia **136** B5
Simpson Desert Regional Reserve *nature res.* Australia **137** B5
Simpson Islands Canada **151** H2
Simpson Lake *N.W.T.* Canada **149** P1
Simpson Park Mountains U.S.A. **158** E2
Simpson Peninsula Canada **147** J3
Simrishamn Sweden **55** I9
Simuk *i.* Indon. **84** B3
Simulubek Indon. **84** B3
Simunjan *Sarawak* Malaysia **85** E2
Simunul *i.* Phil. **82** B5
Simushir, Ostrov *i.* Rus. Fed. **89** S3
Sina *r.* India **106** B2
Sinabang Indon. **84** B2
Sinabung *vol.* Indon. **84** B2
Sinai *pen.* Egypt **107** A5
Sinai, Mont *hill* France **62** E5
Sinai al Janûbîya *governorate* Egypt *see* **Janūb Sīnā'**
Sinai ash Shamâlîya *governorate* Egypt *see* **Shamāl Sīnā'**
Si Nakarin, Ang Kep Nam Thai. **86** B4
Sinaloa *state* Mex. **157** F8
Sinalunga Italy **68** D3
Sinan China **97** F3
Sinancha Rus. Fed. *see* **Cheremshany**
Sinbo Myanmar **86** B1
Sinbyubyin Myanmar **87** B4
Sinbyugyun Myanmar **86** A2
Sincan Turkey **112** E3
Sincelejo Col. **176** C2
Sinchu Taiwan *see* **T'aoyüan**
Sinclair Mills Canada **150** F4
Sincora, Serra do *hills* Brazil **179** C1
Sind *r.* India **104** D4
Sind Pak. *see* **Thul**
Sind *prov.* Pak. *see* **Sindh**
Sinda Rus. Fed. **90** E2
Sindañgan *Mindanao* Phil. **82** C4
Sindangan Bay *Mindanao* Phil. **82** C4
Sindangbarang *Jawa* Indon. **84** D4
Sindari India **104** B4
Sindeh, Teluk *b. Flores* Indon. **83** B5
Sindelfingen Germany **63** I6
Sindh *prov.* Pak. **111** H5
Sindhuli Garhi Nepal **105** F4
Sindhulimadi Nepal *see* **Sindhuli Garhi**
Sındırgı Turkey **69** M5
Sindor Rus. Fed. **52** K3
Sindou Burkina Faso **120** C3
Sindri India **105** F5
Sind Sagar Doab *lowland* Pak. **111** H4
Sinel'nikovo Ukr. *see* **Synel'nykove**
Sines Port. **67** B5
Sines, Cabo de *c.* Port. **67** B5
Sinettä Fin. **54** N3
Sinfra Côte d'Ivoire **120** C4
Sing Myanmar **86** B2
Singa Sudan **108** D7
Singanallur India **106** C4
Singapore *country* Asia **84** D2

▶**Singapore** Sing. **87** [inset]
Capital of Singapore.

Singapore *r.* Sing. **87** [inset]
Singapore, Strait of Indon./Sing. **87** [inset]
Singapura *country* Asia *see* **Singapore**
Singapura Sing. *see* **Singapore**
Singapura Sing. *see* **Singapore**
Singapuru India **106** D2
Singaraja *Bali* Indon. **85** F5
Sing Buri Thai. **86** C4
Singgimtay *Xinjiang* China **98** E4
Singhampton Canada **164** E1
Singhana India **104** C3
Singida Tanz. **123** D4
Singidunum Serbia *see* **Belgrade**
Singim *Xinjiang* China *see* **Singgimtay**
Singkaling Hkamti Myanmar **86** A1
Singkang *Sulawesi* Indon. **83** B4
Singkarak *Sumatera* Indon. **84** C3
Singkawang *Kalimantan* Indon. **85** E2
Singkep *i.* Indon. **84** D3
Singkil *Sumatera* Indon. **84** B2
Singkuang *Sumatera* Indon. **84** B2
Singleton Australia **138** E4
Singleton, Mount *hill N.T.* Australia **134** E5
Singleton, Mount *hill W.A.* Australia **135** B7
Singora Thai. *see* **Songkhla**
Sin'gosan N. Korea *see* **Kosan**
Singra India **105** G4
Singri India **105** H4
Singu Myanmar **96** B4
Singwara India **106** D1

Sin'gye N. Korea **91** B5
Sinhala *country* Asia *see* **Sri Lanka**
Sinhkung Myanmar **86** B1
Siniloan *Luzon* Phil. **82** C3
Sining *Qinghai* China *see* **Xining**
Sinio, Gunung *mt.* Indon. **83** A3
Siniscola *Sardinia* Italy **68** C4
Sinj Croatia **68** G3
Sinjai *Sulawesi* Indon. **83** B4
Sinjār, Jabal *mt.* Iraq **113** F3
Sinkat Sudan **108** E6
Sinkiang *aut. reg.* China *see* **Xinjiang Uygur Zizhiqu**
Sinkiang Uighur Autonomous Region *aut. reg.* China *see* **Xinjiang Uygur Zizhiqu**
Sinmi-do *i.* N. Korea **91** B5
Sinn Germany **63** I4
Sinnamary Fr. Guiana **177** H2
Sinn Bishr, Gebel *hill* Egypt *see* **Sinn Bishr, Jabal**
Sinn Bishr, Jabal *hill* Egypt **107** A5
Sinneh Iran *see* **Sanandaj**
Sinoia Zimbabwe *see* **Chinhoyi**
Sinop Brazil **177** G6
Sinop Turkey **112** D2
Sinope Turkey *see* **Sinop**
Sinoquipe Mex. **166** C2
Sinp'a N. Korea **90** B4
Sinp'o N. Korea **91** C4
Sinsang N. Korea **91** B5
Sinsheim Germany **63** I5
Sintang *Kalimantan* Indon. **85** E2
Sint Eustatius *i.* West Indies **169** L5
Sint-Laureins Belgium **62** D3

▶**Sint Maarten** *terr.* West Indies **169** L5
Self-governing Netherlands territory. The northern part of the island is the French Overseas Collectivity of St Martin.

Sint-Niklaas Belgium **62** E3
Sinton U.S.A. **161** D6
Sintra Port. **67** B4
Sint-Truiden Belgium **62** F4
Sinŭiju N. Korea **91** B4
Sinuk *AK* U.S.A. **148** F2
Sinzig Germany **63** H4
Siocon *Mindanao* Phil. **82** C5
Siófok Hungary **68** H1
Sioma Ngwezi National Park Zambia **123** C5
Sion Switz. **66** H3
Sion Mills U.K. **61** E3
Siorapaluk Greenland **147** K2
Sioux Center U.S.A. **155** H3
Sioux City U.S.A. **160** D3
Sioux Falls U.S.A. **160** D3
Sioux Lookout Canada **151** N5
Sipacate Guat. **167** H6
Sipadan, Pulau *i. Sabah* Malaysia **85** G1
Sipalay *Negros* Phil. **82** C4
Sipang, Tanjung *pt* Malaysia **85** E2
Siphaqeni S. Africa *see* **Flagstaff**
Siping China **90** B4
Sipitang *Sabah* Malaysia **85** F1
Sipiwesk Canada **151** L4
Sipiwesk Lake Canada **151** L4
Siple, Mount Antarctica **188** J2
Siple Coast Antarctica **188** I1
Siple Island Antarctica **188** J2
Siponj Tajik. *see* **Bartang**
Sipsey *r.* U.S.A. **161** F5
Sipura *i.* Indon. **84** B3
Sipura, Selat *sea chan.* Indon. **84** B3
Sīq, Wādī as *watercourse* Egypt **107** A5
Siquia *r.* Nicaragua **166** [inset] I6
Siquijor Phil. **82** C4
Siquijor *i.* Phil. **82** C4
Sir *r.* Pak. **111** H6
Sir, Dar'yoi *r.* Asia *see* **Syrdar'ya**
Sira India **106** C3
Sira *r.* Norway **55** E7
Şīr Abū Nu'āyr *i.* U.A.E. **110** D5
Siracusa *Sicily* Italy *see* **Syracuse**
Siraha Nepal *see* **Sirha**
Sirajganj Bangl. **105** G4
Sir Alexander, Mount Canada **150** F4
Şiran Turkey **113** E2
Sirbāl, Jabal *mt.* Egypt **112** D5
Şīr Banī Yās *i.* U.A.E. **110** D5
Sircilla India *see* **Sirsilla**
Sirdaryo *r.* Asia *see* **Syrdar'ya**
Sirdaryo Uzbek. **102** C3
Sir Edward Pellew Group *is* Australia **136** B2
Sireniki Rus. Fed. **148** D2
Sirha Nepal **105** F4
Sirḩān, Wādī as *watercourse* Jordan/Saudi Arabia **107** C4
Sirik, Tanjung *pt* Malaysia **85** E2
Siri Kit, Khuan Thai. **86** C3
Sírina *i.* Greece *see* **Syrna**
Sīrjā Iran **111** F5
Sir James MacBrien, Mount *N.W.T.* Canada **149** P3
Sīrjān Iran **110** D4
Sīrjān *salt flat* Iran **110** D4
Sirkazhi India **106** C4
Sirmilik National Park Canada **147** K2
Şırnak Turkey **113** F3
Sirohi India **104** C4
Sirombu Indon. **84** B2
Sirong *Sulawesi* Indon. **83** B3
Sironj India **104** D4
Síros *i.* Greece *see* **Syros**
Sirpur India **106** C2
Sirretta Peak U.S.A. **158** D4
Sīrrī, Jazīreh-ye *i.* Iran **110** D5
Sirsa India **104** C3
Sir Sandford, Mount Canada **150** G5
Sirsi *Karnataka* India **106** B3
Sirsi *Madh. Prad.* India **104** D4
Sirsi *Uttar Prad.* India **104** D3
Sirsilla India **106** C2
Sirte Libya **121** E1
Sirte, Gulf of Libya **121** E1
Sir Thomas, Mount *hill* Australia **135** E6
Siruguppa India **106** C3
Sirur India **106** B2
Şirvan Turkey **113** F3
Sirvel India **106** C3
Širvintai Lith. *see* **Širvintos**
Širvintos Lith. **55** N9
Sīrwān *r.* Iraq **113** G4
Sir Wilfrid Laurier, Mount Canada **150** G4
Sis Turkey *see* **Kozan**
Sisak Croatia **68** G2
Sisaket Thai. **86** D4
Sisal Mex. **167** H4
Sischu Mountain *AK* U.S.A. **148** I2
Siscia Croatia *see* **Sisak**
Sishen S. Africa **124** F4
Sishilipu *Gansu* China **94** F5
Sishuang Liedao *is* China **97** I3
Sisian Armenia **113** G3
Sisimiut Greenland **147** M3
Sisipuk Lake Canada **151** K4
Sisogúichic Mex. **166** D3
Sisŏphŏn Cambodia **87** C4
Sissano P.N.G. **81** K7
Sisseton U.S.A. **160** D2
Sīstān *reg.* Iran **111** F4
Sisteron France **66** G4
Sisters *is* India **87** A5
Sīt Iran **110** E5
Sitamarhi India **105** F4
Sitang China *see* **Sinan**
Sitangkai Phil. **82** B5
Sitapur India **104** E4
Siteia Greece **69** L7
Siteki Swaziland **125** J4
Sithonia *pen.* Greece *see* **Sithonias, Chersonisos**
Sithonias, Chersonisos *pen.* Greece **69** J4
Sitía Greece *see* **Siteia**
Sitian *Xinjiang* China **94** C3
Sitidgi Lake *N.W.T.* Canada **149** N1
Sitila Moz. **125** L2
Siting China **96** E3
Sítio do Mato Brazil **179** C1
Sitka *AK* U.S.A. **149** N4
Sitka National Historical Park *nat. park AK* U.S.A. **149** N4
Sitkinak Island *AK* U.S.A. **148** I4
Sitkinak Strait *AK* U.S.A. **148** I4
Sitra *oasis* Egypt *see* **Sitrah**
Sitrah *oasis* Egypt **112** B5
Sittang *r.* Myanmar *see* **Sittaung**
Sittard Neth. **62** F4
Sittaung Myanmar **86** A1
Sittaung *r.* Myanmar **86** B3
Sittensen Germany **63** J1
Sittingbourne U.K. **59** H7
Sittoung *r.* Myanmar *see* **Sittaung**
Sittwe Myanmar **86** A2
Situbondo *Jawa* Indon. **85** F4
Siumpu *i.* Indon. **83** B4
Siuna Nicaragua **166** [inset] I6
Siuri India **105** F5
Sivaganga India **106** C4
Sivakasi India **106** C4
Sivaki Rus. Fed. **90** B1
Sivan India *see* **Siwan**
Sivas Turkey **112** E3
Sivaslı Turkey **69** M5
Siverek Turkey **113** E3
Siverskiy Rus. Fed. **55** Q7
Sivers'kyy Donets' *r.* Rus. Fed./Ukr. *see* **Severskiy Donets**
Sivomaskinskiy Rus. Fed. **51** S2
Sivrice Turkey **113** E3
Sivrihisar Turkey **69** N5
Sivukile S. Africa **125** I4
Sīwa Egypt *see* **Sīwah**
Siwa *Sulawesi* Indon. **83** B3
Sīwah Egypt **112** B5
Sīwah, Wāḩāt *oasis* Egypt **112** B5
Siwalik Range *mts* India/Nepal **104** D3
Siwan India **105** F4
Siwana India **104** C4
Siwa Oasis *oasis* Egypt *see* **Sīwah, Wāḩāt**
Sixian China **97** H1
Sixmilecross U.K. **61** E3
Sixtymile *Y.T.* Canada **149** L2
Siyabuswa S. Africa **125** I3
Siyang *Jiangsu* China **95** I5
Siyäzän Azer. **113** H2
Siyitang *Nei Mongol* China **95** G3
Siyunī Iran **110** D3
Siziwang Qi *Nei Mongol* China *see* **Ulan Hua**
Sjælland *i.* Denmark *see* **Zealand**
Sjenica Serbia **69** I3
Sjöbo Sweden **55** H9
Sjøvegan Norway **54** J2
Skadarsko Jezero *nat. park* Montenegro **69** H3
Skadovs'k Ukr. **69** O1
Skaftárós *r. mouth* Iceland **54** [inset]
Skagafjörður *inlet* Iceland **54** [inset]
Skagen Denmark **55** G8
Skagerrak *strait* Denmark/Norway **55** F8
Skagit *r.* U.S.A. **156** C2
Skagway *AK* U.S.A. **149** N4
Skaidi Norway **54** N1
Skaland Norway **54** J2
Skalmodal Sweden **54** I4
Skanderborg Denmark **55** F8
Skaneateles Lake U.S.A. **165** G2
Skara Sweden **55** H7
Skardarsko Jezero *l.* Albania/Montenegro *see* **Scutari, Lake**
Skardu Pak. **104** C2
Skärgårdshavets nationalpark *nat. park* Fin. **55** L7
Skarnes Norway **55** G6
Skarżysko-Kamienna Poland **57** R5
Skaulo Sweden **54** L3
Skawina Poland **57** Q6
Skeena *r. B.C.* Canada **149** O5
Skeena Mountains *B.C.* Canada **149** O4
Skegness U.K. **58** H5
Skellefteå Sweden **54** L4
Skellefteälven *r.* Sweden **54** L4
Skelleftehamn Sweden **54** L4
Skelmersdale U.K. **58** E5
Skerries Ireland **61** F4
Ski Norway **55** G7
Skiathos *i.* Greece **69** J5
Skibbereen Ireland **61** C6
Skibotn Norway **54** L2
Skiddaw *hill* U.K. **58** D4
Skien Norway **55** F7
Skiermûntseach Neth. *see* **Schiermonnikoog**
Skiermûntseach *i.* Neth. *see* **Schiermonnikoog**
Skierniewice Poland **57** R5
Skikda Alg. **68** B6
Skipsea U.K. **58** G5
Skipton Australia **138** A6
Skipton U.K. **58** E5
Skirlaugh U.K. **58** G5
Skíros *i.* Greece *see* **Skyros**
Skive Denmark **55** F8
Skjern Denmark **55** F9
Skjolden Norway **55** E6
Skobelev Uzbek. *see* **Farg'ona**
Skobeleva, Pik *mt.* Kyrg. **111** I2
Skodje Norway **54** E5
Skoganvarri Norway **54** N2
Skokie U.S.A. **164** B2
Skomer Island U.K. **59** B7
Skopelos *i.* Greece **69** J5
Skopin Rus. Fed. **53** H5

▶**Skopje** Macedonia **69** I4
Capital of Macedonia.

Skoplje Macedonia *see* **Skopje**
Skövde Sweden **55** H7
Skovorodino Rus. Fed. **90** A1
Skowhegan U.S.A. **165** K1
Skrunda Latvia **55** M8
Skukum, Mount *Y.T.* Canada **149** N3
Skukuza S. Africa **125** J3
Skull Valley U.S.A. **159** G4
Skuodas Lith. **55** L8
Skurup Sweden **55** H9
Skutskär Sweden **55** J6
Skvyra Ukr. **53** F6
Skwentna *r. AK* U.S.A. **149** J3
Skye *i.* U.K. **60** C3
Skylge *i.* Neth. *see* **Terschelling**
Skyring, Seno *b.* Chile **178** B8
Skyros Greece **69** K5
Skyros *i.* Greece **69** K5
Skytrain Ice Rise Antarctica **188** L1
Slættaratindur *hill* Faroe Is **54** [inset]
Slagelse Denmark **55** G9
Slagnäs Sweden **54** K4
Slamet, Gunung *vol.* Indon. **85** E4
Slana *AK* U.S.A. **149** L3
Slane Ireland **61** F4
Slaney *r.* Ireland **61** F5
Slantsy Rus. Fed. **55** P7
Slapovi Krke *nat. park* Croatia **68** F3
Slashers Reefs Australia **136** D3
Slatina Croatia **68** G2
Slatina Romania **69** K2
Slaty Fork U.S.A. **164** E4
Slava Rus. Fed. **90** C1
Slave *r.* Canada **151** H2
Slave Coast Africa **120** D4
Slave Lake Canada **150** H4
Slave Point Canada **150** H2
Slavgorod Belarus *see* **Slawharad**
Slavgorod Rus. Fed. **88** D2
Slavkovichi Rus. Fed. **55** P8
Slavonska Požega Croatia *see* **Požega**
Slavonski Brod Croatia **68** H2
Slavuta Ukr. **53** E6
Slavutych Ukr. **53** F6
Slavyanka Rus. Fed. **90** C4
Slavyansk Ukr. *see* **Slov"yans'k**
Slavyanskaya Rus. Fed. *see* **Slavyansk-na-Kubani**
Slavyansk-na-Kubani Rus. Fed. **112** E1
Slawharad Belarus **53** F5
Sławno Poland **57** P3
Slayton U.S.A. **160** E3
Sleaford U.K. **59** G5
Slea Head *hd* Ireland **61** B5
Sleat Neth. *see* **Sloten**
Sleat, Sound of *sea chan.* U.K. **60** D3
Sledge Island *AK* U.S.A. **148** F2
Sled Lake Canada **151** J4
Sleeper Islands Canada **152** F2
Sleeping Bear Dunes National Lakeshore *nature res.* U.S.A. **164** B1
Sleetmute *AK* U.S.A. **148** H3
Sleman Indon. **85** E4
Slessor Glacier Antarctica **188** B1
Slick Rock U.S.A. **159** I2
Slidell *LA* U.S.A. **167** H2
Slide Mountain U.S.A. **165** H3
Slieve Bloom Mts *hills* Ireland **61** E5
Slieve Car *hill* Ireland **61** C3
Slieve Donard *hill* U.K. **61** G3
Slieve Gamph *hills* Ireland *see* **Ox Mountains**
Slievekimalta *hill* Ireland *see* **Keeper Hill**
Slieve Mish Mts *hills* Ireland **61** B5
Slieve Snaght *hill* Ireland **61** E2
Sligachan U.K. **60** C3
Sligeach Ireland *see* **Sligo**
Sligo Ireland **61** D3
Sligo U.S.A. **164** F3
Sligo Bay Ireland **61** D3
Slinger U.S.A. **164** A2
Slippery Rock U.S.A. **164** E3
Slite Sweden **55** K8
Sliven Bulg. **69** L3
Sloan U.S.A. **159** F4
Sloat U.S.A. **158** C2
Sloboda Rus. Fed. *see* **Ezhva**
Slobodchikovo Rus. Fed. **52** K3
Slobodskoy Rus. Fed. **52** K4
Slobozia Romania **69** L2
Slochteren Neth. **62** G1
Slonim Belarus **55** N10
Slootdorp Neth. **62** E2
Sloten Neth. **62** F2
Slough U.K. **59** G7
Slovakia *country* Europe **50** J6
Slovenia *country* Europe **68** F2
Slovenija *country* Europe *see* **Slovenia**
Slovenj Gradec Slovenia **68** F1
Slovensko *country* Europe *see* **Slovakia**
Slovenský raj *nat. park* Slovakia **57** R6
Slov"yans'k Ukr. **53** H6
Słowiński Park Narodowy *nat. park* Poland **57** P3
Sluch *r.* Ukr. **53** E6
S'Lung, B'Nom *mt.* Vietnam **87** D5
Słupsk Poland **57** P3
Slussfors Sweden **54** J4
Slutsk Belarus **55** O10
Slyne Head *hd* Ireland **61** B4
Slyudyanka Rus. Fed. **88** I2
Small Point U.S.A. **165** K2
Smallwood Reservoir Canada **153** I3
Smalyavichy Belarus **55** P9
Smalyenskaya Wzvyshsha *hills* Belarus/Rus. Fed. *see* **Smolensko-Moskovskaya Vozvyshennost'**
Smarhon' Belarus **55** O9
Smeaton Canada **151** J4
Smederevo Serbia **69** I2
Smederevska Palanka Serbia **69** I2
Smela Ukr. *see* **Smila**
Smethport U.S.A. **165** F3
Smidovich Rus. Fed. **90** D2
Smila Ukr. **53** F6
Smilde Neth. **62** G2
Smiltene Latvia **55** N8
Smirnykh Rus. Fed. **90** F2
Smith Canada **150** H4
Smith Arm *b. N.W.T.* Canada **149** Q2
Smith Bay *AK* U.S.A. **148** I1
Smith Center U.S.A. **160** D4
Smithfield S. Africa **125** H6
Smithfield *NC* U.S.A. **162** E5
Smithfield *UT* U.S.A. **156** F4
Smith Glacier Antarctica **188** K1
Smith Island India **87** A4
Smith Island *MD* U.S.A. **165** G4
Smith Island *VA* U.S.A. **165** H5
Smith Mountain Lake U.S.A. **164** F5
Smith River *B.C.* Canada **149** P4
Smiths Falls Canada **165** G1
Smithton Australia **137** [inset]
Smithtown Australia **138** F3
Smithville *OK* U.S.A. **161** E5
Smithville *WV* U.S.A. **164** E4
Smoke Creek Desert U.S.A. **158** D1
Smoking Mountains *N.W.T.* Canada **149** P1
Smoky Bay Australia **135** F8
Smoky Cape Australia **138** F3
Smoky Falls Canada **152** E4
Smoky Hill *r.* U.S.A. **160** C4
Smoky Hills *KS* U.S.A. **154** H4
Smoky Hills *KS* U.S.A. **160** D4
Smoky Lake Canada **151** H4
Smoky Mountains U.S.A. **156** E4
Smøla *i.* Norway **54** E5
Smolenka Rus. Fed. **53** K6
Smolensk Rus. Fed. **53** G5
Smolensk-Moscow Upland *hills* Belarus/Rus. Fed. *see* **Smolensko-Moskovskaya Vozvyshennost'**
Smolensko-Moskovskaya Vozvyshennost' *hills* Belarus/Rus. Fed. **53** G5
Smolevichi Belarus *see* **Smalyavichy**
Smolyan Bulg. **69** K4
Smooth Rock Falls Canada **152** E4
Smoothrock Lake Canada **152** C4
Smoothstone Lake Canada **151** J4
Smørfjord Norway **54** N1
Smorgon' Belarus *see* **Smarhon'**
Smyley Island Antarctica **188** L2
Smyrna Turkey *see* **İzmir**
Smyrna U.S.A. **165** H4
Smyth Island *atoll* Marshall Is *see* **Taongi**
Snæfell *mt.* Iceland **54** [inset]
Snaefell *hill* Isle of Man **58** C4
Snag (abandoned) *Y.T.* Canada **149** L3
Snake *r. N.W.T./Y.T.* Canada **149** N2
Snake *r.* U.S.A. **156** D3
Snake Island Australia **138** C7
Snake Range *mts* U.S.A. **159** F2
Snake River Canada **150** F3
Snake River Plain U.S.A. **156** E4
Snare *r.* Canada **150** G2
Snare Lake Canada **151** J3
Snare Lakes Canada *see* **Wekweêtì**
Snares Islands N.Z. **133** G6
Snåsa Norway **54** H4
Sneedville U.S.A. **164** D5
Sneek Neth. **62** F1
Sneem Ireland **61** C6
Sneeuberge *mts* S. Africa **124** G6
Snegamook Lake Canada **153** J3
Snegurovka Ukr. *see* **Tetiyiv**
Snelling U.S.A. **158** C3
Snettisham U.K. **59** H6
Snezhnogorsk Rus. Fed. **76** J3
Snežnik *mt.* Slovenia **68** F2
Sniečkus Lith. *see* **Visaginas**
Snihurivka Ukr. **53** G7
Snits Neth. *see* **Sneek**
Snizort, Loch *b.* U.K. **60** C3
Snoqualmie Pass U.S.A. **156** C3
Snøtinden *mt.* Norway **54** H3
Snoul Cambodia *see* **Snuŏl**
Snover U.S.A. **164** D2
Snovsk Ukr. *see* **Shchors**
Snowbird Lake Canada **151** K2
Snowcap Mountain *AK* U.S.A. **148** I3
Snowcrest Mountain Canada **150** G5
Snowdon *mt.* U.K. **59** C5
Snowdonia National Park U.K. **59** D6
Snowdrift Canada *see* **Łutselk'e**
Snowdrift *r.* Canada **151** I2
Snowflake U.S.A. **159** H4
Snow Hill U.S.A. **165** H4
Snow Lake Canada **151** K4
Snowville U.S.A. **156** E4
Snow Water Lake U.S.A. **159** F1
Snowy *r.* Australia **138** D6
Snowy Mountain U.S.A. **165** H2
Snowy Mountains Australia **138** C6
Snowy Peak *AK* U.S.A. **149** L2
Snowy River National Park Australia **138** D6
Snug Corner Bahamas **163** F8
Snug Harbour *Nfld. and Lab.* Canada **153** L3
Snug Harbour *Ont.* Canada **164** E1
Snuŏl Cambodia **87** D4
Snyder U.S.A. **161** C5
Soabuwe *Seram* Indon. **83** D3
Soalala Madag. **123** E5
Soalara Madag. **123** E6
Soanierana-Ivongo Madag. **123** E5
Soan-kundo *is* S. Korea **91** B6
Soavinandriana Madag. **123** E5
Sobat *r.* Sudan **108** D8
Sobatsubu-yama *mt.* Japan **93** E3
Sobger *r.* Indon. **81** K7
Sobinka Rus. Fed. **52** I5
Sobradinho, Barragem de *resr* Brazil **177** J6
Sobral Brazil **177** J4
Sobue Japan **92** C3
Sochi Rus. Fed. **113** E2
Sŏch'ŏn S. Korea **91** B5
Society Islands Fr. Polynesia **187** J7
Socorro Brazil **179** B3
Socorro Col. **176** D2
Socorro U.S.A. **157** G6
Socorro, Isla *i.* Mex. **168** B5
Socotra *i.* Yemen **109** H7
Soc Trăng Vietnam **87** D5
Socuéllamos Spain **67** E4
Soda Lake *CA* U.S.A. **158** D4
Soda Lake *CA* U.S.A. **158** E4
Sodankylä Fin. **54** O3
Soda Plains Aksai Chin **99** B6
Soda Springs U.S.A. **156** F4
Sodegaura Japan **93** F3
Söderhamn Sweden **55** J6
Söderköping Sweden **55** J7
Södertälje Sweden **55** J7
Sodiri Sudan **108** C7
Sodo Eth. **122** D3
Södra Kvarken *strait* Fin./Sweden **55** K6
Sodus U.S.A. **165** G2
Soë *Timor* Indon. **83** C5
Soekarno, Puntjak *mt.* Indon. *see* **Jaya, Puncak**
Soekmekaar S. Africa **125** I2
Soerabaia *Jawa* Indon. *see* **Surabaya**
Soerendonk Neth. **62** F3
Soest Germany **63** I3
Soest Neth. **62** F2
Sofala Australia **138** D4

▶**Sofia** Bulg. **69** J3
Capital of Bulgaria.

Sofiya Bulg. *see* **Sofia**
Sofiyevka Ukr. *see* **Vil'nyans'k**
Sofiysk *Khabarovskiy Kray* Rus. Fed. **90** D1
Sofiysk *Khabarovskiy Kray* Rus. Fed. **90** E2
Sofporog Rus. Fed. **54** Q4
Sofrana *i.* Greece **69** L6
Softa Kalesi *tourist site* Turkey **107** A1
Sōfu-gan *i.* Japan **91** F7
Sog *Xizang* China **99** F7
Soğanlı Dağları *mts* Turkey **113** E2
Sogat *Xinjiang* China **98** D4
Sogda Rus. Fed. **90** D2
Sögel Germany **63** H2
Sogma *Xizang* China **99** C6
Sogmai *Xizang* China **99** B6
Søgne Norway **55** E7
Sognefjorden *inlet* Norway **55** D6
Sogod *Leyte* Phil. **82** D4
Sogod Bay *Leyte* Phil. **82** D4
Sogo Nur *l. Nei Mongol* China **94** E3
Sog Qu *r. Xizang* China **99** F6
Sogruma China **96** D1
Söğüt Turkey **69** N4
Söğüt Dağı *mts* Turkey **69** M6
Soh Iran **110** C3
Sohâg Egypt *see* **Sūhāj**
Sohagpur India **104** D5
Soham U.K. **59** H6
Sohan *r.* Pak. **111** H3
Sohano P.N.G. **132** F2
Sohar Oman *see* **Şuḩār**
Sohawal India **104** E4
Sohela India **105** E5
Sohng Gwe, Khao *hill* Myanmar/Thai. **87** B4
Sŏho-ri N. Korea **91** C4
Sohŭksan-do *i.* S. Korea **91** B6
Soignies Belgium **62** E4
Soila China **96** C2
Soini Fin. **54** N5
Soissons France **62** D5
Sojat India **104** C4
Sojat Road India **104** C4
Sojoton Point *Negros* Phil. **82** C4
Sok *r.* Rus. Fed. **53** K5
Sōka Japan **93** F3
Sokal' Ukr. **53** E6
Sokch'o S. Korea **91** C5
Söke Turkey **69** L6
Sokhondo, Gora *mt.* Rus. Fed. **95** G1
Sokhor, Gora *mt.* Rus. Fed. **94** F1
Sokhumi Georgia **113** F2
Sokiryany Ukr. *see* **Sokyryany**
Sokodé Togo **120** D4
Soko Islands *H.K.* China **97** [inset]
Sokol Rus. Fed. **52** I4
Sokolo Mali **120** C3
Sokolov Czech Rep. **63** M4
Sokoto Nigeria **120** D3
Sokoto *r.* Nigeria **120** D3
Sokyryany Ukr. **53** E6
Sola Cuba **163** E8
Sola *i.* Tonga *see* **Ata**
Solan India **104** D3
Solana Beach U.S.A. **158** E5
Solander Island N.Z. **139** A8
Solano *Luzon* Phil. **82** C2
Solapur India **106** B2
Soldotna *AK* U.S.A. **149** J3
Soledad U.S.A. **158** C3
Soledad de Doblado Mex. **167** F5
Soledade Brazil **178** F3
Solenoye Rus. Fed. **53** I7
Solfjellsjøen Norway **54** H3
Solginskiy Rus. Fed. **52** I3
Solhan Turkey **113** F3
Soligalich Rus. Fed. **52** I4
Soligorsk Belarus *see* **Salihorsk**
Solihull U.K. **59** F6
Solikamsk Rus. Fed. **51** R4
Sol'-Iletsk Rus. Fed. **76** G4
Solimões *r.* S. America *see* **Amazon**
Solimón, Punta *pt* Mex. **167** I5
Solingen Germany **62** H3
Solitaire Namibia **124** B2
Sol-Karmala Rus. Fed. *see* **Severnoye**
Şollar Azer. **113** H2
Sollefteå Sweden **54** J5
Söllichau Germany **63** M3
Solling *hills* Germany **63** J3
Sollstedt Germany **63** K3
Sollum, Gulf of Egypt *see* **Sallum, Khalīj as**
Solms Germany **63** I4
Solnechnogorsk Rus. Fed. **52** H4
Solnechnyy *Amurskaya Oblast'* Rus. Fed. **90** A1
Solnechnyy *Khabarovskiy Kray* Rus. Fed. **90** E2
Solo *r.* Indon. **83** B3
Solo *r.* Indon. **85** F4
Solok *Sumatera* Indon. **84** C3
Sololá Guat. **167** H6
Solomon *AK* U.S.A. **148** F2
Solomon U.S.A. **159** I5
Solomon, North Fork *r.* U.S.A. **160** D4

▶**Solomon Islands** *country* S. Pacific Ocean **133** G2
4th largest and 5th most populous country in Oceania.

Solomon Sea S. Pacific Ocean **132** F2
Solon *Nei Mongol* China **95** J2
Solon U.S.A. **165** K1
Solon Springs U.S.A. **160** F2
Solor *i.* Indon. **83** B5
Solor, Kepulauan *is* Indon. **83** B5
Solothurn Switz. **66** H3
Solovetskiye Ostrova *is* Rus. Fed. **52** G2
Solov'yevsk Mongolia **95** H1
Solov'yevsk Rus. Fed. **90** B1
Šolta *i.* Croatia **68** G3
Solţānābād *Kermān* Iran **110** E4
Solţānābād *Khorāsān* Iran **111** E3
Solţānābād Iran **110** C3
Solţānīyeh Iran **110** C2
Soltau Germany **63** J2
Sol'tsy Rus. Fed. **52** F4
Solvay U.S.A. **165** G2
Sölvesborg Sweden **55** I8
Solway Firth *est.* U.K. **60** F6
Solwezi Zambia **123** C5
Soma Turkey **69** L5
Somain France **62** D4
Somalia *country* Africa **122** E3
Somali Basin *sea feature* Indian Ocean **185** L6
Somaliland *reg.* Somalia **122** E3
Somali Republic *country* Africa *see* **Somalia**
Somba, Gunung *mt.* Indon. **85** G2
Sombo Angola **123** C4
Sombor Serbia **69** H2
Sombrerete Mex. **166** E4
Sombrero Channel India **87** A6
Sombrio, Lago do *l.* Brazil **179** A5
Somero Fin. **55** M6
Somerset *KY* U.S.A. **164** C5
Somerset *MI* U.S.A. **164** C2
Somerset *OH* U.S.A. **164** D4
Somerset *PA* U.S.A. **164** F4
Somerset, Lake Australia **138** F1
Somerset East S. Africa **125** G7
Somerset Island Canada **147** I2
Somerset Reservoir U.S.A. **165** I2
Somerset West S. Africa **124** D8
Somersworth U.S.A. **165** J2
Somerton U.S.A. **159** F5
Somerville *NJ* U.S.A. **165** H3
Somerville *TN* U.S.A. **161** F5
Somerville Reservoir *TX* U.S.A. **167** F2
Someydeh Iran **110** B3
Somme *r.* France **62** B4
Sommen *l.* Sweden **55** I7
Sömmerda Germany **63** L3
Sommet, Lac du *l.* Canada **153** H3
Somnath India **104** B5
Somotillo Nicaragua **166** [inset] I6
Somoto Nicaragua **166** [inset] I6
Somutu Myanmar **86** B1
Son *r.* India **105** F4
Soná Panama **166** [inset] J8
Sonag *Qinghai* China *see* **Zêkog**
Sonapur India **106** D1
Sonar *r.* India **104** D4
Sŏnbong N. Korea **90** C4
Sŏnch'ŏn N. Korea **91** B5
Sønderborg Denmark **55** F9
Sondershausen Germany **63** K3
Søndre Strømfjord Greenland *see* **Kangerlussuaq**
Søndre Strømfjord *inlet* Greenland *see* **Kangerlussuaq**
Sondrio Italy **68** C1
Sonepat India *see* **Sonipat**
Sonepur India *see* **Sonapur**
Song *Sarawak* Malaysia **85** F2
Songa *Maluku* Indon. **83** C3
Songbai China *see* **Shennongjia**
Songbu China **97** G2
Sông Câu Vietnam **87** E4
Songcheng China *see* **Xiapu**
Sông Đa, Hô *resr* Vietnam **86** D2
Songea Tanz. **123** D5
Songhua Hu *resr* China **90** B4
Songhua Jiang *r. Heilongjiang/Jilin* China **90** D3
Songhua Jiang *r. Jilin* China *see* **Di'er Songhua Jiang**
Songjiachuan *Shaanxi* China *see* **Wubu**
Songjiang China **97** I2
Songjianghe China **90** B4
Sŏngjin N. Korea *see* **Kimch'aek**
Songkan China **96** E2
Songkhla Thai. **87** C6
Songköl *l.* Kyrg. **98** A4
Song Ling *mts* China **95** I3
Songlong Myanmar **86** B2
Sŏngnam S. Korea **91** B5
Songnim N. Korea **91** B5
Songo Angola **123** B4
Songo Moz. **123** D5
Songpan China **96** D1
Songshan *Gansu* China **94** E4
Songshan China *see* **Ziyun**
Song Shan *mt. Henan* China **95** H5
Songtao China **97** F2
Songxi China **97** H3
Songxian *Henan* China **95** H5
Songyuan *Fujian* China *see* **Songxi**
Songyuan *Jilin* China **90** B3
Songzi China **97** F2
Sơn Hai Vietnam **87** E5
Soni Japan **92** C4
Sonid Youqi *Nei Mongol* China *see* **Saihan Tal**
Sonid Zuoqi *Nei Mongol* China *see* **Mandalt**
Sonipat India **104** D3
Sonkajärvi Fin. **54** O5
Sonkovo Rus. Fed. **52** H4
Sơn La Vietnam **86** C2
Sonmiani Pak. **111** G5
Sonmiani Bay Pak. **111** G5
Sonneberg Germany **63** L4
Sono *r. Minas Gerais* Brazil **179** B2
Sono *r. Tocantins* Brazil **177** I5
Sonobe Japan **92** B3
Sonoma U.S.A. **158** B2
Sonoma Peak U.S.A. **158** E1
Sonora *r.* Mex. **166** C2
Sonora *state* Mex. **166** C2
Sonora *CA* U.S.A. **158** C3
Sonora *KY* U.S.A. **164** C5
Sonora *TX* U.S.A. **161** C6
Sonoran Desert U.S.A. **159** G5
Sonoran Desert National Monument *nat. park* U.S.A. **157** E6
Sonoran Desert National Monument *nat. park AZ* U.S.A. **166** B1
Sonqor Iran **110** B3
Sonsonate El Salvador **167** H6
Sonsorol Islands Palau **81** I5

Sơn Tây Vietnam 86 D2
Sonwabile S. Africa 125 I6
Soochow China see Suzhou
Sooghmeghat AK U.S.A. 148 E3
Soomaaliya country Africa see Somalia
Sopi, Tanjung pt Maluku Indon. 83 D2
Sopo watercourse Sudan 121 F4
Sopot Bulg. 69 K3
Sopot Poland 57 Q3
Sop Prap Thai. 86 B3
Sopron Hungary 68 G1
Sopur India 104 C2
Soputan, Gunung vol. Indon. 83 C2
Sora Italy 68 E4
Sorab India 106 B3
Sorada India 106 E2
Söråker Sweden 54 J5
Sŏrak-san mt. S. Korea 91 C5
Sorak-san National Park S. Korea 91 C5
Sorel Canada 153 G5
Soreq r. Israel 107 B4
Sorgun Turkey 112 D3
Sorgun r. Turkey 107 B1
Soria Spain 67 E3
Sorikmarapi vol. Indon. 84 B2
Sorkh, Kūh-e mts Iran 110 D3
Sorkhān Iran 110 E4
Sorkheh Iran 110 D3
Sørli Norway 54 H4
Sorø Denmark 57 M3
Soro India 105 F5
Soroca Moldova 53 F6
Sorocaba Brazil 179 B3
Soroki Moldova see Soroca
Sorol atoll Micronesia 81 K5
Sorong Papua Indon. 83 D3
Soroti Uganda 122 D3
Sørøya i. Norway 54 M1
Sorraia r. Port. 67 B4
Sørreisa Norway 54 K2
Sorrento Italy 68 F4
Sorsele Sweden 54 J4
Sorsogon Luzon Phil. 82 D3
Sortavala Rus. Fed. 54 Q6
Sortland Norway 54 I2
Sortopolovskaya Rus. Fed. 52 K3
Sorvizhi Rus. Fed. 52 K4
Sŏsan S. Korea 91 B5
Sosenskiy Rus. Fed. 53 G5
Soshanguve S. Africa 125 I3
Sosna r. Rus. Fed. 53 H5
Sosneado mt. Arg. 178 C4
Sosnogorsk Rus. Fed. 52 L3
Sosnovka Kyrg. 98 A4
Sosnovka Arkhangel'skaya Oblast' Rus. Fed. 52 J3
Sosnovka Kaliningradskaya Oblast' Rus. Fed. 51 K5
Sosnovka Murmanskaya Oblast' Rus. Fed. 52 I2
Sosnovka Tambovskaya Oblast' Rus. Fed. 53 I5
Sosnovo Rus. Fed. 55 Q6
Sosnovo-Ozerskoye Rus. Fed. 89 K2
Sosnovyy Rus. Fed. 54 R4
Sosnovyy Bor Rus. Fed. 55 P7
Sosnowiec Poland 57 Q5
Sosnowitz Poland see Sosnowiec
Sos'va Khanty-Mansiyskiy Avtonomnyy Okrug Rus. Fed. 51 S3
Sos'va Sverdlovskaya Oblast' Rus. Fed. 51 S4
Sotang Xizang China 99 F7
Sotara, Volcán vol. Col. 176 C3
Sotkamo Fin. 54 P4
Soto la Marina Mex. 167 F4
Sotteville-lès-Rouen France 62 B5
Sotuta Mex. 167 H4
Souanké Congo 122 B3
Soubré Côte d'Ivoire 120 C4
Souderton U.S.A. 165 H3
Soufflenheim France 63 H6
Soufli Greece 69 L4
Soufrière St Lucia 169 L6
Soufrière vol. St Vincent 169 L6
Sougueur Alg. 67 G6
Souillac France 66 E4
Souilly France 62 F5
Souk Ahras Alg. 68 B6
Souk el Arbaâ du Rharb Morocco 64 C5
Sŏul S. Korea see Seoul
Soulac-sur-Mer France 66 D4
Soulom France 66 D5
Sounding Creek r. Canada 151 I4
Souni Cyprus 107 A2
Soûr Lebanon see Tyre
Sourdough AK U.S.A. 149 K3
Soure Brazil 177 I4
Sour el Ghozlane Alg. 67 H5
Souris Canada 151 K5
Souris r. Canada 151 L5
Souriya country Asia see Syria
Sousa Brazil 177 K5
Sousa Lara Angola see Bocoio
Sousse Tunisia 68 D7
Soustons France 66 D5

▶South Africa, Republic of country Africa 124 F5
5th most populous country in Africa.

Southampton Canada 164 E1
Southampton U.K. 59 F8
Southampton U.S.A. 165 I3
Southampton, Cape Canada 147 J3
Southampton Island Canada 151 O1
South Andaman i. India 87 A5
South Anna r. U.S.A. 165 G5
South Anston U.K. 58 F5
South Aulatsivik Island Canada 153 J2
South Australia state Australia 132 D5
South Australian Basin sea feature Indian Ocean 185 P8
Southaven U.S.A. 161 F5
South Baldy mt. U.S.A. 157 G6
South Bank U.K. 58 F4
South Bass Island U.S.A. 164 D3
South Bend IN U.S.A. 164 B3
South Bend WA U.S.A. 156 C3
South Bluff pt Bahamas 163 F8
South Boston U.S.A. 165 F5
South Brook Canada 153 K4
South Cape pt U.S.A. see Ka Lae
South Carolina state U.S.A. 163 D5
South Charleston OH U.S.A. 164 D4
South Charleston WV U.S.A. 164 E4
South China Sea N. Pacific Ocean 80 F4
South Coast Town Australia see Gold Coast
South Dakota state U.S.A. 160 C2
South Downs hills U.K. 59 G8
South-East admin. dist. Botswana 125 G3
South East Cape Australia 137 [inset]
Southeast Cape AK U.S.A. 148 E3
Southeast Indian Ridge sea feature Indian Ocean 185 N8
South East Isles Australia 135 C8
Southeast Pacific Basin sea feature S. Pacific Ocean 187 M10
South East Point Australia 138 C7
Southend Canada 151 K3
Southend U.K. 60 D5
Southend-on-Sea U.K. 59 H7
Southern admin. dist. Botswana 124 G3
Southern Alps mts N.Z. 139 C6
Southern Cross Australia 135 B7
Southern Indian Lake Canada 151 L3
Southern Lau Group is Fiji 133 I3
Southern National Park Sudan 121 F4
Southern Ocean 188 C2
Southern Pines U.S.A. 163 E5
Southern Rhodesia country Africa see Zimbabwe
Southern Uplands hills U.K. 60 E5
South Esk r. U.K. 60 F4
South Esk Tableland reg. Australia 134 D4
Southey Canada 151 J5
Southfield U.S.A. 164 D2
South Fiji Basin sea feature S. Pacific Ocean 186 H7
South Fork U.S.A. 158 B1
South Geomagnetic Pole (2008) Antarctica 188 F1
South Georgia i. S. Atlantic Ocean 178 I8

▶South Georgia and the South Sandwich Islands terr. S. Atlantic Ocean 178 I8
United Kingdom Overseas Territory

South Harris pen. U.K. 60 B3
South Haven U.S.A. 164 B2
South Henik Lake Canada 151 L2
South Hill U.S.A. 165 F5
South Honshu Ridge sea feature N. Pacific Ocean 186 F3
South Indian Lake Canada 151 L3
South Island India 106 B4

▶South Island N.Z. 139 D7
2nd largest island in Oceania.

South Islet rf Phil. 82 B4
South Junction Canada 151 M5
South Korea country Asia 91 B5
South Lake Tahoe U.S.A. 158 C2
South Luangwa National Park Zambia 123 D5
South Magnetic Pole (2008) Antarctica 188 G2
South Mills U.S.A. 165 G5
Southminster U.K. 59 H7
South Mountains hills U.S.A. 165 G4
South Nahanni r. N.W.T. Canada 150 F2
South Naknek AK U.S.A. 148 H4
South New Berlin U.S.A. 165 H2
South Orkney Islands S. Atlantic Ocean 184 F10
South Paris U.S.A. 165 J1
South Platte r. U.S.A. 160 C3
South Point Bahamas 163 F8
South Pole Antarctica 188 C1
Southport Qld Australia 138 F1
Southport Tas. Australia 137 [inset]
Southport U.K. 58 D5
Southport U.S.A. 165 G2
South Portland U.S.A. 165 J2
South Ronaldsay i. U.K. 60 G2
South Royalton U.S.A. 165 I2
South Salt Lake U.S.A. 159 H1
South Sand Bluff pt S. Africa 125 J6

▶South Sandwich Islands S. Atlantic Ocean 184 G9
United Kingdom Overseas Territory.

South Sandwich Trench sea feature S. Atlantic Ocean 184 G9
South San Francisco U.S.A. 158 B3
South Saskatchewan r. Canada 151 J4
South Seal r. Canada 151 L3
South Shetland Islands Antarctica 188 A2
South Shetland Trough sea feature S. Atlantic Ocean 188 L2
South Shields U.K. 58 F3
South Sinai governorate Egypt see Janūb Sīnā'
South Solomon Trench sea feature S. Pacific Ocean 186 G6
South Taranaki Bight b. N.Z. 139 E4
South Tasman Rise sea feature Southern Ocean 186 F9
South Tent mt. U.S.A. 159 H2
South Tons r. India 105 E4
South Twin Island Canada 152 F3
South Tyne r. U.K. 58 E4
South Uist i. U.K. 60 B3
South Wellesley Islands Australia 136 B3
South-West Africa country Africa see Namibia
South West Cape N.Z. 139 A8
Southwest Cape AK U.S.A. 148 E3
South West Entrance sea chan. P.N.G. 136 E1
Southwest Indian Ridge sea feature Indian Ocean 185 K8
South West National Park Australia 137 [inset]
Southwest Pacific Basin sea feature S. Pacific Ocean 186 I8
Southwest Peru Ridge sea feature S. Pacific Ocean see Nazca Ridge
South West Rocks Australia 138 F3
South Whitley U.S.A. 164 C3
South Wichita r. U.S.A. 161 D5
South Windham U.S.A. 165 J2
Southwold U.K. 59 I6
Southwood National Park Australia 138 E1
Soutpansberg mts S. Africa 125 I2
Souttouf, Adrar mts W. Sahara 120 B2
Soverato Italy 68 G5
Sovereign Mountain AK U.S.A. 149 J3
Sovetsk Kaliningradskaya Oblast' Rus. Fed. 55 L9
Sovetsk Kirovskaya Oblast' Rus. Fed. 52 K4
Sovetskaya Gavan' Rus. Fed. 90 F2
Sovetskiy Khanty-Mansiyskiy Avtonomnyy Okrug Rus. Fed. 51 S3
Sovetskiy Leningradskaya Oblast' Rus. Fed. 55 P6
Sovetskiy Respublika Mariy El Rus. Fed. 52 K4
Sovetskoye Chechenskaya Respublika Rus. Fed. see Shatoy
Sovetskoye Stavropol'skiy Kray Rus. Fed. see Zelenokumsk
Sovyets'kyy Ukr. 112 D1
Sowa China 96 C2
Sōwa Japan 93 F2
Soweto S. Africa 125 H4
So'x Tajik. 111 H2
Sōya-kaikyō strait Japan/Rus. Fed. see La Pérouse Strait
Sōya-misaki c. Japan 90 F3
Soyana r. Rus. Fed. 52 I2
Soyma r. Rus. Fed. 52 K2
Soyopa Mex. 157 F7
Sozh r. Europe 53 F6
Sozopol Bulg. 69 L3
Spa Belgium 62 F4

▶Spain country Europe 67 E3
4th largest country in Europe.

Spalato Croatia see Split
Spalatum Croatia see Split
Spalding U.K. 59 G6
Spanish Canada 152 E5
Spanish Fork U.S.A. 159 H1
Spanish Guinea country Africa see Equatorial Guinea
Spanish Netherlands country Europe see Belgium
Spanish Sahara terr. Africa see Western Sahara
Spanish Town Jamaica 169 I5
Sparks U.S.A. 158 D2
Sparta Greece see Sparti
Sparta GA U.S.A. 163 D5
Sparta KY U.S.A. 164 C4
Sparta MI U.S.A. 164 C2
Sparta NC U.S.A. 164 E5
Sparta TN U.S.A. 162 C5
Spartanburg U.S.A. 163 D5
Sparti Greece 69 J6
Spartivento, Capo c. Italy 68 G6
Spas-Demensk Rus. Fed. 53 G5
Spas-Klepiki Rus. Fed. 53 I5
Spassk-Dal'niy Rus. Fed. 90 D3
Spassk-Ryazanskiy Rus. Fed. 53 I5
Spatha, Akra pt Kriti Greece see Spatha, Akrotirio
Spatha, Akrotirio pt Greece 69 J7
Spearman U.S.A. 161 C4
Speedway U.S.A. 164 B4
Spence Bay Canada see Taloyoak
Spencer IA U.S.A. 160 E3
Spencer ID U.S.A. 156 E3
Spencer IN U.S.A. 164 B4
Spencer NE U.S.A. 160 D3
Spencer WV U.S.A. 164 E4
Spencer, Cape AK U.S.A. 149 M4
Spencer, Point pt AK U.S.A. 148 F2
Spencer Bay Namibia 124 B3
Spencer Gulf est. Australia 137 B7
Spencer Range hills Australia 134 E3
Spennymoor U.K. 58 F4
Sperrin Mountains hills U.K. 61 E3
Sperryville U.S.A. 165 F4
Spessart reg. Germany 63 J5
Spétsai i. Greece see Spetses
Spetses i. Greece 69 J6
Spey r. U.K. 60 F3
Speyer Germany 63 I5
Spezand Pak. 111 G4
Spice Islands Indon. see Maluku
Spider Crater tourist site Australia 134 D4
Spijk Neth. 62 G1
Spijkenisse Neth. 62 E3
Spike Mountain AK U.S.A. 149 L2
Spilimbergo Italy 68 E1
Spilsby U.K. 58 H5
Spīn Böldak Afgh. 111 G4
Spintangi Pak. 111 H4
Spirit Lake U.S.A. 160 E3
Spirit River Canada 150 G4
Spirovo Rus. Fed. 52 G4
Spišská Nová Ves Slovakia 53 D6
Spiti r. India 104 D3

▶Spitsbergen i. Svalbard 76 C2
5th largest island in Europe.

Spittal an der Drau Austria 57 N7
Spitzbergen i. Svalbard see Spitsbergen
Split Croatia 68 G3
Split Lake Canada 151 L3
Split Lake I. Canada 151 L3
Spokane U.S.A. 156 D3
Spoletium Italy see Spoleto
Spoleto Italy 68 E3
Spóng Cambodia 87 D4
Spoon r. U.S.A. 160 F3
Spooner U.S.A. 160 F2
Spornitz Germany 63 L1
Spotsylvania U.S.A. 165 G4
Spotted Horse U.S.A. 156 G3
Spranger, Mount Canada 150 F4
Spratly Islands S. China Sea 80 E4
Spray U.S.A. 156 D3
Spree r. Germany 57 N4
Sprimont Belgium 62 F4
Springbok S. Africa 124 C5
Springdale Canada 153 L4
Springdale U.S.A. 164 C4
Springe Germany 63 J2
Springer U.S.A. 157 G5
Springerville U.S.A. 159 I4
Springfield CO U.S.A. 160 C4

▶Springfield IL U.S.A. 160 F4
Capital of Illinois.

Springfield KY U.S.A. 164 C5
Springfield MA U.S.A. 165 I2
Springfield MO U.S.A. 161 E4
Springfield OH U.S.A. 164 D4
Springfield OR U.S.A. 156 C3
Springfield TN U.S.A. 164 B5
Springfield VT U.S.A. 165 I2
Springfield WV U.S.A. 165 F4
Springfontein S. Africa 125 G6
Spring Glen U.S.A. 159 H2
Spring Grove U.S.A. 164 A2
Springhill Canada 153 I5
Spring Hill U.S.A. 163 D6
Springhouse Canada 150 F5
Spring Mountains U.S.A. 159 F3
Springs Junction N.Z. 139 D6
Springsure Australia 136 E5
Spring Valley MN U.S.A. 160 E3
Spring Valley NY U.S.A. 165 H3
Springview U.S.A. 160 D3
Springville CA U.S.A. 158 D3
Springville NY U.S.A. 165 F2
Springville PA U.S.A. 165 H3
Springville UT U.S.A. 159 H1
Sprowston U.K. 59 I6
Spruce Grove Canada 150 H4
Spruce Knob mt. U.S.A. 162 E4
Spruce Mountain CO U.S.A. 159 I2
Spruce Mountain NV U.S.A. 159 F1
Spurn Head hd U.K. 58 H5
Spurr, Mount vol. AK U.S.A. 148 I3
Spuzzum Canada 150 F5
Squam Lake U.S.A. 165 J2
Square Lake U.S.A. 153 H5
Squaw Harbor AK U.S.A. 148 G5
Squillace, Golfo di g. Italy 68 G5
Squires, Mount hill Australia 135 D6
Sragen Jawa Indon. 85 E4
Srbinje Bos.-Herz. see Foča
Srê Âmběl Cambodia 87 C5
Srebrenica 69 H2
Sredets Burgas Bulg. 69 L3
Sredets Sofiya-Grad Bulg. see Sofia
Sredinnyy Khrebet mts Rus. Fed. 77 Q4
Sredna Gora mts Bulg. 69 J3
Srednekolymsk Rus. Fed. 77 Q3
Sredne-Russkaya Vozvyshennost' hills Rus. Fed. see Central Russian Upland
Sredne-Sibirskoye Ploskogor'ye plat. Rus. Fed. see Central Siberian Plateau
Sredneye Kuyto, Ozero l. Rus. Fed. 54 Q4
Sredniy Ural mts Rus. Fed. 51 R4
Srednogorie Bulg. 69 K3
Srednyaya Akhtuba Rus. Fed. 53 J6
Sreepur Bangl. see Sripur
Sre Khtum Cambodia 87 D4
Srê Noy Cambodia 87 D4
Sretensk Rus. Fed. 89 L2
Sri Aman Sarawak Malaysia 85 E2
Sriharikota Island India 106 D3

▶Sri Jayewardenepura Kotte Sri Lanka 106 C5
Capital of Sri Lanka.

Srikakulam India 106 E2
Sri Kalahasti India 106 C3
Sri Lanka country Asia 106 D5
Srinagar India 104 C2
Sri Pada mt. Sri Lanka see Adam's Peak
Sripur Bangl. 105 G4
Srirangam India 106 C4
Sri Thep tourist site Thai. 86 C3
Srivardhan India 106 B2
Staaten r. Australia 136 C3
Staaten River National Park Australia 136 C3
Stabroek Guyana see Georgetown
Stade Germany 63 J1
Staden Belgium 62 D4
Stadskanaal Neth. 62 G2
Stadtallendorf Germany 63 J4
Stadthagen Germany 63 J2
Stadtilm Germany 63 L4
Stadtlohn Germany 62 G3
Stadtoldendorf Germany 63 J3
Stadtroda Germany 63 L4
Staffa i. U.K. 60 C4
Staffelberg hill Germany 63 L4
Staffelstein Germany 63 K4
Stafford U.K. 59 E6
Stafford U.S.A. 165 G4
Stafford Creek Bahamas 163 E7
Stafford Springs U.S.A. 165 I3
Stagen Kalimantan Indon. 85 G3
Stagg Lake Canada 150 H2
Staicele Latvia 55 N8
Staines U.K. 59 G7
Stakhanov Ukr. 53 H6
Stakhanovo Rus. Fed. see Zhukovskiy
Stalbridge U.K. 59 E8
Stalham U.K. 59 I6
Stalin Bulg. see Varna
Stalinabad Tajik. see Dushanbe
Stalingrad Rus. Fed. see Volgograd
Staliniri Georgia see Ts'khinvali
Stalino Ukr. see Donets'k
Stalinogorsk Rus. Fed. see Novomoskovsk
Stalinogród Poland see Katowice
Stalinsk Rus. Fed. see Novokuznetsk
Stalowa Wola Poland 53 D6
Stamboliyski Bulg. 69 K3
Stamford Australia 136 C4
Stamford U.K. 59 G6
Stamford CT U.S.A. 165 I3
Stamford NY U.S.A. 165 H2
Stamford TX U.S.A. 167 F1
Stampalia i. Greece see Astypalaia
Stampriet Namibia 124 D3
Stamsund Norway 54 H2
Stanardsville U.S.A. 165 F4
Stanberry U.S.A. 160 E3
Stancomb-Wills Glacier Antarctica 188 B1
Standard Canada 150 H5
Standdaarbuiten Neth. 62 E3
Standerton S. Africa 125 I4
Standish U.S.A. 164 D2
Stanfield U.S.A. 159 H5
Stanford KY U.S.A. 164 C5
Stanford MT U.S.A. 156 F3
Stanger S. Africa 125 J5
Stanislaus r. U.S.A. 158 C3
Stanislav Ukr. see Ivano-Frankivs'k
Stanke Dimitrov Bulg. see Dupnitsa
Staňkov Czech Rep. 63 N5
Stanley Australia 137 [inset]
Stanley H.K. China 97 [inset]

▶Stanley Falkland Is 178 E8
Capital of the Falkland Islands.

Stanley U.K. 58 F4
Stanley ID U.S.A. 156 E3
Stanley KY U.S.A. 164 B5
Stanley ND U.S.A. 160 C1
Stanley VA U.S.A. 165 F4
Stanley, Mount hill N.T. Australia 134 E5
Stanley, Mount hill Tas. Australia 137 [inset]
Stanley, Mount Dem. Rep. Congo/Uganda see Margherita Peak
Stanleyville Dem. Rep. Congo see Kisangani
Stann Creek Belize see Dangriga
Stannington U.K. 58 F3
Stanovoye Rus. Fed. 53 H5
Stanovoye Nagor'ye mts Rus. Fed. 89 L1
Stanovoy Khrebet mts Rus. Fed. 77 N4
Stansmore Range hills Australia 134 E5
Stanthorpe Australia 138 E2
Stanton U.K. 59 H6
Stanton KY U.S.A. 164 D5
Stanton MI U.S.A. 164 C2
Stanton ND U.S.A. 160 C2
Stanton TX U.S.A. 161 C5
Stapleton U.S.A. 160 C3
Starachowice Poland 57 R5
Stara Planina mts Bulg./Serbia see Balkan Mountains
Staraya Russa Rus. Fed. 52 F4
Stara Zagora Bulg. 69 K3
Starbuck Island Kiribati 187 J6
Star City U.S.A. 164 B3
Starcke National Park Australia 136 D2
Stargard in Pommern Poland see Stargard Szczeciński
Stargard Szczeciński Poland 57 O4
Staritsa Rus. Fed. 52 G4
Starke U.S.A. 163 D6
Starkville U.S.A. 161 F5
Star Lake U.S.A. 165 H1
Starnberger See l. Germany 57 M7
Staroaleyskoye Rus. Fed. 98 C2
Starobel'sk Ukr. see Starobil's'k
Starobil's'k Ukr. 53 H6
Starogard Gdański Poland 57 Q4
Starokonstantinov Ukr. see Starokostyantyniv
Starokostyantyniv Ukr. 53 E6
Starominskaya Rus. Fed. 53 H7
Staroshcherbinovskaya Rus. Fed. 53 H7
Star Peak U.S.A. 158 D1
Start Point U.K. 59 D8
Starve Island Kiribati see Starbuck Island
Staryya Darohi Belarus 53 F5
Staryye Dorogi Belarus see Staryya Darohi
Staryy Kayak Rus. Fed. 77 L2
Staryy Oskol Rus. Fed. 53 H6
Staßfurt Germany 63 L3
State College U.S.A. 165 G3
State Line U.S.A. 161 F6
Staten Island Arg. see Los Estados, Isla de
Statenville U.S.A. 163 D6
Statesboro U.S.A. 163 D5
Statesville U.S.A. 162 D5
Statia i. West Indies see Sint Eustatius
Station U.S.A. 164 C4
Station Nord Greenland 189 I1
Stauchitz Germany 63 N3
Staufenberg Germany 63 I4
Staunton U.S.A. 164 F4
Stavanger Norway 55 D7
Staveley U.K. 58 F5
Stavropol' Rus. Fed. 113 F1
Stavropol Kray admin. div. Rus. Fed. see Stavropol'skiy Kray
Stavropol'-na-Volge Rus. Fed. see Tol'yatti
Stavropol'skaya Vozvyshennost' hills Rus. Fed. 113 F1
Stavropol'skiy Kray admin. div. Rus. Fed. 113 F1
Stayner Canada 164 E1
Stayton U.S.A. 156 C3
Steadville S. Africa 125 I5
Steamboat Springs U.S.A. 156 G4
Stearns U.S.A. 164 C5
Stebbins AK U.S.A. 148 G3
Steele Creek AK U.S.A. 149 L2
Steele Island Antarctica 188 L2
Steelville U.S.A. 160 F4
Steen r. Canada 150 G3
Steenderen Neth. 62 G2
Steenkampsberge mts S. Africa 125 J3
Steen River Canada 150 G3
Steens Mountain U.S.A. 156 D4
Steenstrup Gletscher glacier Greenland see Sermersuaq
Steenvoorde France 62 C4
Steenwijk Neth. 62 G2
Steese Highway AK U.S.A. 149 K2
Stefansson Island Canada 147 H2
Stegi Swaziland see Siteki
Steigerwald mts Germany 63 K5
Stein Germany 63 L5
Steinach Germany 63 L4
Steinaker Reservoir U.S.A. 159 I1
Steinbach Canada 151 L5
Steinfeld (Oldenburg) Germany 63 I2
Steinfurt Germany 63 H2
Steinhausen Namibia 123 B6
Steinheim Germany 63 J3
Steinkjer Norway 54 G4
Steinkopf S. Africa 124 C5
Steinsdalen Norway 54 G4
Stella S. Africa 124 G4
Stella Maris Bahamas 163 F8
Stellenbosch S. Africa 124 D7
Steller, Mount AK U.S.A. 149 L3
Stello, Monte mt. Corsica France 66 I5
Stelvio, Parco Nazionale dello nat. park Italy 68 D1
Stenay France 62 F5
Stendal Germany 63 L2
Stenhousemuir U.K. 60 F4
Stenungsund Sweden 55 G7
Steornabhagh U.K. see Stornoway
Stepanakert Azer. see Xankändi
Stephens, Cape N.Z. 139 D5
Stephens City U.S.A. 165 F4
Stephens Lake Canada 151 M3
Stephenville U.S.A. 161 D5
Stepnoy Kyrg. 98 A4
Stepnoy Rus. Fed. see Elista
Stepnoye Rus. Fed. 53 J6
Stepovak Bay AK U.S.A. 148 G5
Sterkfontein Dam resr S. Africa 125 I5
Sterkstroom S. Africa 125 H6
Sterlet Lake Canada 151 I1
Sterlibashevo Rus. Fed. 51 R5
Sterling S. Africa 124 E6
Sterling CO U.S.A. 160 C3
Sterling IL U.S.A. 160 F3
Sterling MI U.S.A. 164 C1
Sterling UT U.S.A. 159 H2
Sterling City U.S.A. 161 C6
Sterling Heights U.S.A. 164 D2
Sterlitamak Rus. Fed. 76 G4
Stettin Poland see Szczecin
Stettler Canada 151 H4
Steubenville KY U.S.A. 164 C5
Steubenville OH U.S.A. 164 E3
Stevenage U.K. 59 G7
Stevenson U.S.A. 156 C3
Stevenson Entrance sea channel AK U.S.A. 148 I4
Stevenson Lake Canada 151 L4
Stevens Point U.S.A. 160 F2
Stevens Village AK U.S.A. 149 J2
Stevensville MI U.S.A. 164 B2
Stevensville PA U.S.A. 165 G3
Stewart B.C. Canada 149 O5
Stewart r. Y.T. Canada 149 M3
Stewart, Isla i. Chile 178 B8
Stewart Crossing Y.T. Canada 149 M3
Stewart Island N.Z. 139 A8
Stewart Islands Solomon Is 133 G2
Stewart Lake Canada 147 J3
Stewarton U.K. 60 E5
Stewarts Point U.S.A. 158 B2
Stewiacke Canada 153 J5
Steynsburg S. Africa 125 G6
Steyr Austria 57 O6
Steytlerville S. Africa 124 G7
Stiens Neth. 62 F1
Stif Alg. see Sétif
Stigler U.S.A. 161 E5
Stikine r. B.C. Canada 149 N4
Stikine Plateau B.C. Canada 149 O4
Stikine Ranges mts B.C. Canada 149 O4
Stikine Strait U.S.A. 150 C3
Stilbaai S. Africa 124 E8
Stiles U.S.A. 164 A1
Stillwater MN U.S.A. 160 E2
Stillwater OK U.S.A. 161 D4
Stillwater Range mts U.S.A. 158 D2
Stillwell U.S.A. 164 B3
Stilton U.K. 59 G6
Stilwell U.S.A. 161 E5
Stinnett U.S.A. 161 C5
Štip Macedonia 69 J4
Stirling Australia 134 F5
Stirling Canada 165 G1
Stirling U.K. 60 F4
Stirling Creek r. Australia 134 E4
Stirling Range National Park Australia 135 B8
Stittsville Canada 165 H1
Stjørdalshalsen Norway 54 G5
Stockbridge U.S.A. 164 C2
Stockerau Austria 57 P6
Stockheim Germany 63 L4

▶Stockholm Sweden 55 K7
Capital of Sweden.

Stockinbingal Australia 138 C5
Stockport U.K. 58 E5
Stockton CA U.S.A. 158 C3
Stockton KS U.S.A. 160 D4
Stockton MO U.S.A. 160 E4
Stockton UT U.S.A. 159 G1
Stockton Islands AK U.S.A. 149 K1
Stockton Lake U.S.A. 160 E4
Stockton-on-Tees U.K. 58 F4
Stockton Plateau TX U.S.A. 166 E2
Stockville U.S.A. 160 C3
Stod Czech Rep. 63 N5
Stœng Trêng Cambodia 87 D4
Stoer, Point of U.K. 60 D2
Stoke-on-Trent U.K. 59 E5
Stokesley U.K. 58 F4
Stokes Point Australia 137 [inset]
Stokes Range hills Australia 134 E4
Stokkseyri Iceland 54 [inset]
Stokkvågen Norway 54 H3
Stokmarknes Norway 54 I2
Stolac Bos.-Herz. 68 G3
Stolberg (Rheinland) Germany 62 G4
Stolboukha Vostochnyy Kazakhstan Kazakh. 98 D2
Stolbovoy Rus. Fed. 189 G2
Stolbtsy Belarus see Stowbtsy
Stolin Belarus 55 O11
Stollberg Germany 63 M4
Stolp Poland see Słupsk
Stolzenau Germany 63 J2
Stone U.K. 59 E6
Stoneboro U.S.A. 164 E3
Stonecliffe Canada 152 F5
Stonecutters' Island pen. H.K. China 97 [inset]
Stonehaven U.K. 60 G4
Stonehenge Australia 136 C5
Stonehenge tourist site U.K. 59 F7
Stoner U.S.A. 159 I3
Stonewall Canada 151 L5
Stonewall Jackson Lake U.S.A. 164 E4
Stony r. AK U.S.A. 148 H3
Stony Creek U.S.A. 165 G5
Stony Lake Canada 151 L3
Stony Point U.S.A. 165 G2
Stony Rapids Canada 151 J3
Stony River U.S.A. 146 C3
Stooping r. Canada 152 E3
Stora Lulevatten l. Sweden 54 K3
Stora Sjöfallets nationalpark nat. park Sweden 54 J3
Storavan l. Sweden 54 K4
Store Bælt sea chan. Denmark see Great Belt
Støren Norway 54 G5
Storfjordbotn Norway 54 O1
Storforshei Norway 54 I3
Storjord Norway 54 I3
Storkerson Peninsula Canada 147 H2
Storm Bay Australia 137 [inset]
Stormberg S. Africa 125 H6
Storm Lake U.S.A. 160 E3
Stornosa mt. Norway 54 E6
Stornoway U.K. 60 C2
Storozhevsk Rus. Fed. 52 L3
Storozhynets' Ukr. 53 E6
Storrs U.S.A. 165 I3
Storseleby Sweden 54 J4
Storsjön l. Sweden 54 I5
Storskrymten mt. Norway 54 F5
Storslett Norway 54 L2
Stortemelk sea chan. Neth. 62 F1
Storuman Sweden 54 J4
Storuman l. Sweden 54 J4

Storvik Sweden 55 J6
Storvorde Denmark 55 G8
Storvreta Sweden 55 J7
Story U.S.A. 156 G3
Stotfold U.K. 59 G6
Stoughton Canada 151 K5
Stour r. England U.K. 59 F6
Stour r. England U.K. 59 F8
Stour r. England U.K. 59 I7
Stour r. England U.K. 59 I7
Stourbridge U.K. 59 E6
Stourport-on-Severn U.K. 59 E6
Stout Lake Canada 151 M4
Stowbtsy Belarus 55 O10
Stowe U.S.A. 165 I1
Stowmarket U.K. 59 H6
Stoyba Rus. Fed. 90 C1
Strabane U.K. 61 E3
Stradbally Ireland 61 E4
Stradbroke U.K. 59 I6
Stradella Italy 68 C2
Strakonice Czech Rep. 57 N6
Stralsund Germany 57 N3
Strand S. Africa 124 D8
Stranda Norway 54 E5
Strangford U.K. 61 G3
Strangford Lough inlet U.K. 61 G3
Strangways r. Australia 134 F3
Stranraer U.K. 60 D6
Strasbourg France 66 H2
Strasburg Germany 63 N1
Strasburg U.S.A. 165 F4
Strassburg France see Strasbourg
Stratford Australia 138 C6
Stratford Canada 164 E2
Stratford CA U.S.A. 158 D3
Stratford TX U.S.A. 161 C4
Stratford-upon-Avon U.K. 59 F6
Strathaven U.K. 60 E5
Strathmore Canada 150 H5
Strathmore r. U.K. 60 E2
Strathnaver Canada 150 F4
Strathroy Canada 164 E2
Strathspey valley U.K. 60 F3
Strathy U.K. 60 F2
Stratton U.K. 59 C8
Stratton U.S.A. 165 J1
Stratton Mountain U.S.A. 165 I2
Straubing Germany 63 M6
Straumnes pt Iceland 54 [inset]
Strawberry U.S.A. 159 H4
Strawberry Mountain U.S.A. 156 D3
Strawberry Reservoir U.S.A. 159 H1
Streaky Bay Australia 135 F8
Streaky Bay b. Australia 135 F8
Streator U.S.A. 160 F3
Street U.K. 59 E7
Streetsboro U.S.A. 164 E3
Strehaia Romania 69 J2
Strehla Germany 63 N3
Streich Mound hill Australia 135 C7
Strelka Rus. Fed. 77 Q3
Strel'na r. Rus. Fed. 52 H2
Strenči Latvia 55 N8
Streymoy i. Faroe Is 54 [inset]
Stříbro Czech Rep. 63 M5
Strichen U.K. 60 G3
Strimonas r. Greece see Strymonas
Stroeder Arg. 178 D6
Strokestown Ireland 61 D4
Stroma, Island of U.K. 60 F2
Stromboli, Isola i. Italy 68 F5
Stromness S. Georgia 178 I8
Stromness U.K. 60 F2
Strömstad Sweden 55 G7
Strömsund Sweden 54 I5
Strongsville U.S.A. 164 E3
Stronsay i. U.K. 60 G1
Stroud Australia 138 E4
Stroud U.K. 59 E7
Stroud Road Australia 138 E4
Stroudsburg U.S.A. 165 H3
Struer Denmark 55 F8
Struga Macedonia 69 I4
Strugi-Krasnyye Rus. Fed. 55 P7
Struis Bay S. Africa 124 E8
Strullendorf Germany 63 K5
Struma r. Bulg. 69 J4
also known as Strymonas (Greece)
Strumble Head hd U.K. 59 B6
Strumica Macedonia 69 J4
Struthers U.S.A. 164 E3
Stryama r. Bulg. 69 K3
Strydenburg S. Africa 124 F5
Strymonas r. Greece 69 J4
also known as Struma (Bulgaria)
Stryn Norway 54 E6
Stryy Ukr. 53 D6
Strzelecki, Mount hill Australia 134 F5
Strzelecki Desert Australia 137 C6
Strzelecki Regional Reserve nature res. Australia 137 B6
Stuart FL U.S.A. 163 D7
Stuart NE U.S.A. 160 D3
Stuart VA U.S.A. 164 E5
Stuart Island AK U.S.A. 148 G3
Stuart Lake Canada 150 E4
Stuart Range hills Australia 137 A6
Stuarts Draft U.S.A. 164 F4
Stuart Town Australia 138 D4
Stuchka Latvia see Aizkraukle
Stučka Latvia see Aizkraukle
Studholme Junction N.Z. 139 C7
Studsviken Sweden 54 K5
Study Butte TX U.S.A. 166 E2
Stukely, Lac l. Canada 165 I1
Stung Treng Cambodia see Stœ̆ng Trêng
Stupart r. Canada 151 M4
Stupino Rus. Fed. 53 H5
Sturge Island Antarctica 188 H2
Sturgeon r. Ont. Canada 152 F5
Sturgeon r. Sask. Canada 151 J4
Sturgeon Bay b. Canada 151 L4
Sturgeon Bay U.S.A. 164 B1
Sturgeon Bay Canal lake channel U.S.A. 164 B1
Sturgeon Falls Canada 152 F5
Sturgeon Lake Ont. Canada 151 N5
Sturgeon Lake Ont. Canada 165 F1
Sturgis MI U.S.A. 164 C3
Sturgis SD U.S.A. 160 C2
Sturt, Mount hill Australia 137 C6
Sturt Creek watercourse Australia 134 D4
Sturt National Park Australia 137 C6
Sturt Stony Desert Australia 137 C6
Stutterheim S. Africa 125 H7
Stuttgart Germany 63 J6
Stuttgart U.S.A. 161 F5
Stuver, Mount AK U.S.A. 149 J1
Stykkishólmur Iceland 54 [inset]
Styr r. Belarus/Ukr. 53 E5
Suaçuí Grande r. Brazil 179 C2
Suai East Timor 83 C5
Suai Sarawak Malaysia 85 F2
Suakin Sudan 108 E6
Suao Taiwan 97 I3
Suaqui Grande Mex. 166 C2
Suau P.N.G. 136 E1
Subačius Lith. 55 N9
Subang Jawa Indon. 85 D4
Subankhata India 105 G4
Subansiri r. India 99 F8
Subarnapur India see Sonapur
Sūbāshī Iran 110 C3
Subay reg. Saudi Arabia 110 B5
Şubayḩah Saudi Arabia 107 D4
Subei Gansu China 98 F5
Subi Besar i. Indon. 85 E2
Subi Kecil i. Indon. 85 E2
Sublette U.S.A. 161 C4
Subotica Serbia 69 H1
Success, Lake U.S.A. 158 D3
Succiso, Alpi di mts Italy 68 D2
Suceava Romania 53 E7
Suchan Rus. Fed. see Partizansk
Suck r. Ireland 61 D4
Suckling, Cape AK U.S.A. 149 L3
Suckling, Mount P.N.G. 136 E1
Suckow Germany 63 L1

▶Sucre Bol. 176 E7
Legislative capital of Bolivia.

Suczawa Romania see Suceava
Sud, Grand Récif du reef New Caledonia 133 G4
Suda Rus. Fed. 52 H4
Sudak Ukr. 112 D1
Sudama Japan 93 E3

▶Sudan country Africa 121 F3
Largest country in Africa, and 10th largest in the world.

Suday Rus. Fed. 52 I4
Sudayr reg. Saudi Arabia 110 B5
Sudbury Canada 152 E5
Sudbury U.K. 59 H6
Sudd swamp Sudan 108 C8
Sude r. Germany 63 K1
Sudest Island P.N.G. see Tagula Island
Sudetenland mts Czech Rep./Poland see Sudety
Sudety mts Czech Rep./Poland 57 O5
Sudislavl' Rus. Fed. 52 I4
Sudlersville U.S.A. 165 H4
Süd-Nord-Kanal canal Germany 62 H2
Sudogda Rus. Fed. 52 I5
Sudr Egypt 107 A5
Suðuroy i. Faroe Is 54 [inset]
Sue watercourse Sudan 121 F4
Sueca Spain 67 F4
Suez Egypt 107 A5
Suez, Gulf of Egypt 107 A5
Suez Bay Egypt 107 A5
Suez Canal Egypt 107 A4
Suffolk U.S.A. 165 G5
Sugarbush Hill hill U.S.A. 160 F2
Sugarloaf Mountain U.S.A. 165 J1
Sugarloaf Point Australia 138 F4
Suga-shima i. Japan 92 C4
Sugbuhan Point Phil. 82 D4
Süget Xinjiang China see Sogat
Sugi i. Indon. 84 C2
Sugun Xinjiang China 98 B5
Sugut r. Malaysia 85 G1
Sugut, Tanjung pt Malaysia 85 G1
Suhai Hu l. Qinghai China 98 F5
Suhai Obo Nei Mongol China 94 F3
Suhait Nei Mongol China 94 F4
Sūhāj Egypt 108 D4
Şuḩār Oman 110 E5
Suhaymī, Wādī as watercourse Egypt 107 A4
Sühbaatar Mongolia 94 F1
Sühbaatar Mongolia 95 H2
Sühbaatar prov. Mongolia 95 H2
Suheli Par i. India 106 B4
Suhl Germany 63 K4
Suhlendorf Germany 63 K2
Suhul reg. Saudi Arabia 110 B6
Suhūl al Kidan plain Saudi Arabia 110 D6
Şuhut Turkey 69 N5
Sui Pak. 111 H4
Sui, Laem pt Thai. 87 B5
Suibin China 90 C3
Suid-Afrika country Africa see Republic of South Africa
Suide Shaanxi China 95 G4
Suidzhikurmsy Turkm. see Madaw
Suifenhe China 90 C3
Suifu Japan 93 G2
Suigetsu-ko l. Japan 92 B3
Suigō-Tsukuba Kokutei-kōen park Japan 93 G2
Suihua China 90 B3
Suileng China 90 B3
Suining Hunan China 97 F3
Suining Jiangsu China 97 H1
Suining Sichuan China 96 E2
Suippes France 62 E5
Suir r. Ireland 61 E5
Suisse country Europe see Switzerland
Suita Japan 92 B4
Sui Vehar Pak. 111 H4
Suixi China 97 H1
Suixian Henan China 95 H5
Suixian Hubei China see Suizhou
Suiyang Guizhou China 96 E3
Suiyang Henan China 95 H5
Suiza country Europe see Switzerland
Suizhong Liaoning China 95 J3
Suizhou China 97 G2
Suj Nei Mongol China 95 F3
Sujangarh India 104 C4
Sujawal Pak. 111 H5
Suk atoll Micronesia see Pulusuk
Sukabumi Jawa Indon. 84 D4
Sukadana Kalimantan Indon. 85 E3
Sukadana Sumatera Indon. 84 D4
Sukadana, Teluk b. Indon. 85 E3
Sukagawa Japan 91 F5
Sukanegara Jawa Indon. 84 D4
Sukaraja Kalimantan Indon. 85 E3
Sukaramai Kalimantan Indon. 85 E3
Sukarnapura Indon. see Jayapura
Sukarno, Puncak mt. Indon. see Jaya, Puncak
Sukau Sabah Malaysia 85 G1
Sukchŏn N. Korea 91 B5
Sukhinichi Rus. Fed. 53 G5
Sukhona r. Rus. Fed. 52 J3
Sukhothai Thai. 86 B3
Sukhumi Georgia see Sokhumi
Sukhum-Kale Georgia see Sokhumi
Sukkertoppen Greenland see Maniitsoq
Sukkozero Rus. Fed. 52 G3
Sukkur Pak. 111 H5
Sukma India 106 D2
Sukpay Rus. Fed. 90 E3
Sukpay r. Rus. Fed. 90 E3
Sukri r. India 104 C4
Suktel r. India 106 D1
Sukun i. Indon. 83 B5
Sula i. Norway 55 D6
Sula r. Rus. Fed. 52 K2
Sula, Kepulauan is Indon. 83 C3
Sulabesi i. Indon. 83 C3
Sulaiman Range mts Pak. 111 H4
Sulak Rus. Fed. 113 G2
Sülär Iran 110 C4
Sula Sgeir i. U.K. 60 C1
Sulasih, Gunung vol. Indon. 84 C3
Sulat i. Indon. 85 G5
Sulat Samar Phil. 82 D4
Sulatna Crossing AK U.S.A. 148 I2
Sulawesi i. Indon. see Celebes
Sulawesi Barat prov. Indon. 83 A3
Sulawesi Selatan prov. Indon. 83 A3
Sulawesi Tengah prov. Indon. 83 B3
Sulawesi Tenggara prov. Indon. 83 B4
Sulawesi Utara prov. Indon. 83 C2
Sulaymān Beg Iraq 113 G4
Sulaymānīyah Iraq 113 G4
Sulayyimah Saudi Arabia 110 B6
Sulci Sardinia Italy see Sant'Antioco
Sulcis Sardinia Italy see Sant'Antioco
Suledeh Iran 110 C2
Suleman, Teluk b. Indon. 85 G2
Sule Skerry i. U.K. 60 E1
Sule Stack i. U.K. 60 E1
Suliki Sumatera Indon. 84 C3
Sulingen Germany 63 I2
Sulin Gol r. Qinghai China 94 C4
Sulitjelma Norway 54 J3
Sulkava Fin. 54 P6
Sullana Peru 176 B4
Sullivan IL U.S.A. 160 F4
Sullivan IN U.S.A. 164 B4
Sullivan Bay Canada 150 E5
Sullivan Island Myanmar see Lanbi Kyun
Sullivan Lake Canada 151 I5
Sulmo Italy see Sulmona
Sulmona Italy 68 E3
Sulphur LA U.S.A. 161 E6
Sulphur OK U.S.A. 161 D5
Sulphur r. U.S.A. 161 E5
Sulphur Springs U.S.A. 161 E5
Sultan Canada 152 E5
Sultan, Koh-i- mts Pak. 111 F4
Sultanabad India see Osmannagar
Sultanabad Iran see Arāk
Sultan Dağları mts Turkey 69 N5
Sultanıye Turkey see Karapınar
Sultanpur India 105 E4
Suluan i. Phil. 82 D4
Sulu Archipelago is Phil. 82 C5
Sulu Basin sea feature N. Pacific Ocean 186 E5
Sülüklü Turkey 112 D3
Sülüktü Kyrg. 111 H2
Sulusaray Turkey 112 E3
Sulu Sea N. Pacific Ocean 80 F5
Suluvvaulik, Lac l. Canada 153 G2
Sulyukta Kyrg. see Sülüktü
Sulzbach-Rosenberg Germany 63 L5
Sulzberger Bay Antarctica 188 I1
Suma Japan 92 B4
Sumāil Oman 110 E6
Sumalata Sulawesi Indon. 83 B2
Sumampa Arg. 178 D3
Sumangat, Tanjung pt Malaysia 85 G1
Sumapaz, Parque Nacional nat. park Col. 176 D3
Sümär Iran 110 B3
Sumatera i. Indon. see Sumatra
Sumatera Barat prov. Indon. 84 C3
Sumatera Selatan prov. Indon. 84 C3
Sumatera Utara prov. Indon. 84 B2

▶Sumatra i. Indon. 84 B2
2nd largest island in Asia, and 6th in the world.

Šumava nat. park Czech Rep. 57 N6
Sumba i. Indon. 83 B5
Sumba, Selat sea chan. Indon. 83 A5
Sumbar r. Turkm. 110 D2
Sumbawa i. Indon. 83 A5
Sumbawabesar Sumbawa Indon. 85 G5
Sumbawanga Tanz. 123 D4
Sumbe Angola 123 B5
Sumbing, Gunung vol. Indon. 84 C3
Sumbu National Park Zambia 123 D4
Sumburgh U.K. 60 [inset]
Sumburgh Head hd U.K. 60 [inset]
Sumdo Aksai Chin 99 B6
Sumdo China 96 D2
Sumdum, Mount AK U.S.A. 149 N4
Sumedang Jawa Indon. 85 D4
Sume'eh Sarā Iran 110 C2
Sumeih Sudan 108 C8
Sumenep Jawa Indon. 85 F4
Sumgait Azer. see Sumqayıt
Sumisu-jima i. Japan 89 Q6
Sümiyn Bulag Mongolia see Gurvandzagal
Summēl Iraq 113 F3
Summer Beaver Canada 152 C3
Summerford Canada 153 L4
Summer Island U.S.A. 162 C2
Summer Isles U.K. 60 D2
Summerland Canada 150 G5
Summersville U.S.A. 164 E4
Summit AK U.S.A. 149 J3
Summit Lake Canada 150 F4
Summit Lake AK U.S.A. 149 K3
Summit Mountain U.S.A. 158 E2
Summit Peak U.S.A. 157 G5
Sumnal Aksai Chin 99 B6
Sumner N.Z. 139 D6
Sumner, Lake N.Z. 139 D6
Sumon-dake mt. Japan 91 E5
Sumoto Japan 92 A4
Sumpangbinangae Sulawesi Indon. 83 A4
Šumperk Czech Rep. 57 P6
Sumpu Japan see Shizuoka
Sumqayıt Azer. 113 H2
Sumskiy Posad Rus. Fed. 52 G2
Sumter U.S.A. 163 D5
Sumur India 104 D2
Sumxi Xizang China 99 C6
Sumy Ukr. 53 G6
Sumzom China 96 C2
Suna Rus. Fed. 52 K4
Sunaj India 104 D4
Sunam India 104 C3
Sunamganj Bangl. 105 G4
Sunami Japan 92 C3
Sunan Gansu China 94 D4
Sunart, Loch inlet U.K. 60 D4
Şunaynah Oman 110 D6
Sunburst U.S.A. 156 F2
Sunbury Australia 138 B6
Sunbury OH U.S.A. 164 D3
Sunbury PA U.S.A. 165 G3
Sunch'ŏn S. Korea 91 B6
Sun City S. Africa 125 H3
Sun City AZ U.S.A. 159 G5
Sun City CA U.S.A. 158 E5
Sunda, Selat str. Indon. 84 D4
Sunda Kalapa Jawa Indon. see Jakarta
Sundance U.S.A. 156 G3
Sundarbans coastal area Bangl./India 105 G5
Sundarbans National Park Bangl./India 105 G5
Sundargarh India 105 F5
Sunda Shelf sea feature Indian Ocean 185 P5
Sunda Strait Indon. see Sunda, Selat
Sunda Trench sea feature Indian Ocean see Java Trench
Sunderland U.K. 58 F4
Sundern (Sauerland) Germany 63 I3
Sündiken Dağları mts Turkey 69 N5
Sundown National Park Australia 138 E2
Sundre Canada 150 H5
Sundridge Canada 152 F5
Sundsvall Sweden 54 J5
Sundukli, Peski des. Turkm. see Sandykly Gumy
Sundumbili S. Africa 125 J5
Sunduyka Rus. Fed. 95 G1
Sungaiapit Sumatera Indon. 84 C2
Sungaiguntung Sumatera Indon. 84 C2
Sungaikabung Sumatera Indon. 84 C2
Sungaikakap Kalimantan Indon. 85 E3
Sungailiat Sumatera Indon. 84 D3
Sungaipenuh Sumatera Indon. 84 C3
Sungai Petani Malaysia 84 C1
Sungaipinyuh Kalimantan Indon. 85 E2
Sungaiselan Indon. 84 D3
Sungari r. China see Songhua Jiang
Sungei Seletar Reservoir Sing. 87 [inset]
Sungguminasa Sulawesi Indon. 83 A4
Sungkiang China see Songjiang
Sung Kong i. H.K. China 97 [inset]
Sungqu China see Songpan
Sungsang Sumatera Indon. 84 D3
Sungurlu Turkey 112 D2
Sunkar, Gora mt. Kazakh. 98 A3
Sun Kosi r. Nepal 105 F4
Sunman U.S.A. 164 C4
Sunndal Norway 55 E6
Sunndalsøra Norway 54 F5
Sunne Sweden 55 H7
Sunnyside U.S.A. 156 D3
Sunnyvale U.S.A. 158 B3
Suno-saki pt Japan 93 F4
Sun Prairie U.S.A. 160 F3
Sunset House Canada 150 G4
Sunset Peak hill H.K. China 97 [inset]
Suntar Rus. Fed. 77 M3
Suntsar Pak. 111 F5
Sunwi-do i. N. Korea 91 B5
Sunwu China 90 B2
Sunyani Ghana 120 C4
Suolijärvet l. Fin. 54 P3
Suomi country Europe see Finland
Suomussalmi Fin. 54 P4
Suō-nada b. Japan 91 C6
Suonenjoki Fin. 54 O5
Suong r. Laos 86 C3
Suoyarvi Rus. Fed. 52 G3
Suozhen Shandong China see Huantai
Supa India 106 B3
Supaul India 105 F4
Superior AZ U.S.A. 159 H5
Superior MT U.S.A. 156 E3
Superior NE U.S.A. 160 D3
Superior WI U.S.A. 160 E2
Superior, Laguna lag. Mex. 167 G5

▶Superior, Lake Canada/U.S.A. 155 J2
Largest lake in North America, and 2nd in the world.

Suphan Buri Thai. 87 C4
Süphan Dağı mt. Turkey 113 F3
Supiori i. Indon. 81 J7
Suponevo Rus. Fed. 53 G5
Support Force Glacier Antarctica 188 A1
Sūq ash Shuyūkh Iraq 113 G5
Suqian China 97 H1
Suquṭrā i. Yemen see Socotra
Şūr Oman 111 E6
Sur, Point U.S.A. 158 C3
Sur, Punta pt Arg. 178 E5
Sura r. Rus. Fed. 53 J4
Şuraabad Azer. 113 H2
Surabaya Jawa Indon. 85 F4
Sūrak Iran 110 E5
Surakarta Jawa Indon. 85 E4
Suramana Sulawesi Indon. 83 A3
Sūrān Iran 111 F5
Şūrān Syria 107 C2
Surat Australia 138 D1
Surat India 104 C5
Suratgarh India 104 C3
Surat Thani Thai. 87 B5
Surazh Rus. Fed. 53 G5
Surbiton Australia 136 D4
Surdulica Serbia 69 J3
Sûre r. Lux. 62 G5
Surendranagar India 104 B5
Suretka Costa Rica 166 [inset] J7
Surf U.S.A. 158 C4
Surgut Rus. Fed. 76 I3
Suri India see Siuri
Suriapet India 106 C2
Surigao Mindanao Phil. 82 D4
Surigao Strait Phil. 82 D4
Surin Thai. 86 C4
Surinam country S. America see Suriname
Suriname country S. America 177 G3
Surin Nua, Ko i. Thai. 87 B5
Surkhduz Afgh. 111 G4
Surkhet Nepal 105 E3
Surkhon Uzbek. see Surxon
Sürmene Turkey 113 F2
Surovikino Rus. Fed. 53 I6
Surprise B.C. Canada 149 N4
Surprise Lake B.C. Canada 149 N4
Surpura India 104 C4
Surrey Canada 150 F5
Surry U.S.A. 165 G5
Surskoye Rus. Fed. 53 J5
Surt Libya see Sirte
Surtsey i. Iceland 54 [inset]
Sürü Hormozgan Iran 110 E5
Sürü Sīstān va Balūchestān Iran 110 E5
Suruç Turkey 107 D1
Surud, Raas pt Somalia 122 E2
Surud Ad mt. Somalia see Shimbiris
Suruga-wan b. Japan 93 E4
Surulangun Sumatera Indon. 84 C3
Surup Mindanao Phil. 82 D5
Survey Pass AK U.S.A. 148 I2
Surwold Germany 63 H2
Surxon Uzbek. 111 G2
Suryapet India see Suriapet
Şuşa Azer. 113 G3
Susah Tunisia see Sousse
Susaki Japan 91 D6
Susan U.S.A. 165 G5
Süsangerd Iran 110 C4
Susanino Rus. Fed. 90 F1
Susanville U.S.A. 158 C1
Suşehri Turkey 112 E2
Susitna r. AK U.S.A. 149 J3
Susitna, Mount AK U.S.A. 149 J3
Susitna Lake AK U.S.A. 149 K3
Suso Thai. 87 B6
Susobana-gawa r. Japan 93 E2
Susong China 97 H2
Susono Japan 93 E3
Susquehanna U.S.A. 165 H3
Susquehanna r. U.S.A. 165 G4
Susquehanna, West Branch r. U.S.A. 165 G3
Susques Arg. 178 C2
Sussex U.S.A. 165 G5
Susua Sulawesi Indon. 83 B3
Susul Sabah Malaysia 85 G1
Susuman Rus. Fed. 77 P3
Susupu Halmahera Indon. 83 C2
Susurluk Turkey 69 M5
Sutak India 104 D2
Sutay Uul mt. Mongolia 94 C2
Sutherland Australia 138 E5
Sutherland S. Africa 124 E7
Sutherland U.S.A. 160 C3
Sutherland Range hills Australia 135 D6
Sutjeska nat. park Bos.-Herz. 68 H3
Sutlej r. India/Pak. 104 B3
Sütlüce Turkey 107 A1
Sutter U.S.A. 158 C2
Sutterton U.K. 59 G6
Sutton Canada 165 I1
Sutton r. Canada 152 E3
Sutton U.K. 59 H6
Sutton AK U.S.A. 149 J3
Sutton NE U.S.A. 160 D3
Sutton WV U.S.A. 164 E4
Sutton Coldfield U.K. 59 F6
Sutton in Ashfield U.K. 59 F5
Sutton Lake Canada 152 D3
Sutton Lake U.S.A. 164 E4
Suttor r. Australia 136 D4
Suttsu Japan 90 F4
Sutwik Island AK U.S.A. 148 H4
Sutyr' r. Rus. Fed. 90 D2
Suugant Mongolia see Gurvansayhan
Suusamyr Kyrg. 98 A4

▶Suva Fiji 133 H3
Capital of Fiji.

Suvadiva Atoll Maldives see Huvadhu Atoll
Suvalki Poland see Suwałki
Suvorov atoll Cook Is see Suwarrow
Suvorov Rus. Fed. 53 H5
Suwa Japan 93 E2
Suwa-ko l. Japan 93 E2
Suwakong Kalimantan Indon. 85 F3
Suwałki Poland 53 D5
Suwannaphum Thai. 86 C4
Suwannee r. U.S.A. 163 D6
Suwanose-jima i. Japan 91 C7
Suwaran, Gunung mt. Indon. 85 G2
Suwarrow atoll Cook Is 133 J3
Suwayliḩ Jordan 107 B3
Suwayr well Saudi Arabia 113 F5
Suways, Khalīj as g. Egypt see Suez, Gulf of
Suways, Qanāt as canal Egypt see Suez Canal
Suweilih Jordan see Suwayliḩ
Suweis, Khalîg el g. Egypt see Suez, Gulf of
Suweis, Qanâ el canal Egypt see Suez Canal
Suwŏn S. Korea 91 B5
Suxik Qinghai China 94 C4
Suykbulak Kazakh. 98 C2
Suyūl Ḩanīsh i. Yemen 108 F7
Suz, Mys pt Kazakh. 113 I2
Suzaka Japan 93 E2
Suzdal' Rus. Fed. 52 I4
Suzhou Anhui China 97 H1
Suzhou Gansu China see Jiuquan
Suzhou Jiangsu China 97 I2
Suzi He r. China 90 B4
Suzuka Japan 92 C4
Suzuka-gawa r. Japan 92 C4
Suzuka Kokutei-kōen park Japan 92 C3
Suzuka-sanmyaku mts Japan 92 C4
Suzu-misaki pt Japan 91 E5
Sværholthalvøya pen. Norway 54 O1

▶Svalbard terr. Arctic Ocean 76 C2
Part of Norway.

Svappavaara Sweden 54 L3
Svartenhuk Halvø pen. Greenland see Sigguup Nunaa
Svatove Ukr. 53 H6
Svay Chék Cambodia 87 C4
Svay Riĕng Cambodia 87 D5
Svecha Rus. Fed. 52 J4
Sveg Sweden 55 I5
Sveķi Latvia 55 O8
Svelgen Norway 54 D6
Svellingen Norway 54 F5
Švenčionėliai Lith. 55 N9
Švenčionys Lith. 55 O9
Svendborg Denmark 55 G9
Svensbu Norway 54 K2
Svenstavik Sweden 54 I5
Sverdlovsk Rus. Fed. see Yekaterinburg
Sverdlovs'k Ukr. 53 H6
Sverdrup Islands Canada 147 I2
Sverige country Europe see Sweden
Sveti Nikole Macedonia 69 I4
Svetlaya Rus. Fed. 90 E3
Svetlogorsk Belarus see Svyetlahorsk
Svetlogorsk Kaliningradskaya Oblast' Rus. Fed. 55 L9
Svetlogorsk Krasnoyarskiy Kray Rus. Fed. 76 J3
Svetlograd Rus. Fed. 113 F1
Svetlovodsk Ukr. see Svitlovods'k
Svetlyy Kaliningradskaya Oblast' Rus. Fed. 55 L9
Svetlyy Orenburgskaya Oblast' Rus. Fed. 102 B1
Svetlyy Yar Rus. Fed. 53 J6
Svetogorsk Rus. Fed. 55 P6
Sviahnúkar vol. Iceland 54 [inset]
Svilaja mts Croatia 68 G3
Svilengrad Bulg. 69 L4
Svinecea Mare, Vârful mt. Romania 69 J2
Svir Belarus 55 O9
Svir' r. Rus. Fed. 52 G3
Svishtov Bulg. 69 K3
Svitava r. Czech Rep. 57 P6
Svitavy Czech Rep. 57 P6
Svitlovods'k Ukr. 53 G6
Sviyaga r. Rus. Fed. 52 K5
Svizzer, Parc Naziunal Switz. 68 D1
Svizzera country Europe see Switzerland
Svobodnyy Rus. Fed. 90 C2
Svolvær Norway 54 I2
Svrljiške Planine mts Serbia 69 J3
Svyatoy Nos, Mys c. Rus. Fed. 52 K2
Svyetlahorsk Belarus 53 F5
Swadlincote U.K. 59 F6
Swaffham U.K. 59 H6
Swain Reefs Australia 136 F4
Swainsboro U.S.A. 163 D5
Swains Island atoll American Samoa 133 I3
Swakop watercourse Namibia 124 B2
Swakopmund Namibia 124 B2
Swale r. U.K. 58 F4
Swallow Islands Solomon Is 133 G3
Swamihalli India 106 C3
Swampy r. Canada 153 H2
Swan r. Australia 135 A7
Swan r. Man./Sask. Canada 151 K4
Swan r. Ont. Canada 152 E3
Swanage U.K. 59 F8
Swandale U.S.A. 164 E4
Swan Hill Australia 138 A5
Swan Hills Canada 150 H4
Swan Islands is Caribbean Sea see Cisne, Islas del
Swan Lake B.C. Canada 149 O5
Swan Lake Man. Canada 151 K4
Swanley U.K. 59 H7
Swanquarter U.S.A. 163 E5
Swan Reach Australia 137 B7
Swan River Canada 151 K4
Swansea U.K. 59 D7
Swansea Bay U.K. 59 D7
Swanton CA U.S.A. 158 B3
Swanton VT U.S.A. 165 I1
Swartbergpas pass S. Africa 124 F7
Swart Nossob watercourse Namibia see Black Nossob
Swartruggens S. Africa 125 H3
Swartz Creek U.S.A. 164 D2
Swasey Peak U.S.A. 159 G2
Swat Kohistan reg. Pak. 111 I3
Swatow China see Shantou
Swayzee U.S.A. 164 C3
Swaziland country Africa 125 J4

▶Sweden country Europe 54 I5
5th largest country in Europe.

Sweet Home U.S.A. 156 C3
Sweet Springs U.S.A. 164 E5
Sweetwater U.S.A. 161 C5
Sweetwater r. U.S.A. 156 G4
Swellendam S. Africa 124 E8
Świdnica Poland 57 P5
Świdwin Poland 57 O4
Świebodzin Poland 57 O4
Świecie Poland 57 Q4
Swift r. AK U.S.A. 148 H3
Swift Current Canada 151 J5
Swiftcurrent Creek r. Canada 151 J5
Swift Fork r. AK U.S.A. 148 I3
Swilly r. Ireland 61 E3
Swilly, Lough inlet Ireland 61 E2
Swindon U.K. 59 F7
Swinford Ireland 61 D4
Świnoujście Poland 57 O4
Swinton U.K. 60 G5
Swiss Confederation country Europe see Switzerland
Switzerland country Europe 66 I3
Swords Ireland 61 F4
Swords Range hills Australia 136 C4
Syamozero, Ozero l. Rus. Fed. 52 G3
Syamzha Rus. Fed. 52 I3
Syang Nepal 105 E3
Syas'troy Rus. Fed. 52 G3
Sychevka Rus. Fed. 52 G5
Sydenham atoll Kiribati see Nonouti

▶Sydney Australia 138 E4
Capital of New South Wales. Most populous city in Oceania.

Sydney Canada 153 J5
Sydney Island Kiribati see Manra
Sydney Lake Canada 151 M5

Sydney Mines Canada 153 J5
Syedra tourist site Turkey 107 A1
Syeverodonets'k Ukr. 53 H6
Syke Germany 63 I2
Sykesville U.S.A. 165 F3
Syktyvkar Rus. Fed. 52 K3
Sylarna mt. Norway/Sweden 54 H5
Sylhet Bangl. 105 G4
Syloga Rus. Fed. 52 I3
Sylt i. Germany 57 L3
Sylva U.S.A. 163 D5
Sylvania GA U.S.A. 163 D5
Sylvania OH U.S.A. 164 D3
Sylvan Lake Canada 150 H4
Sylvester U.S.A. 163 D6
Sylvester, Lake salt flat Australia 136 A3
Sylvia, Mount Canada 150 E3
Symerton U.S.A. 164 A3
Symi i. Greece 69 L6
Synel'nykove Ukr. 53 G6
Syngyrli, Mys pt Kazakh. 113 I2
Synya Rus. Fed. 51 R2
Syowa research station Antarctica 188 D2
Syracusae Sicily Italy see Syracuse
Syracuse Sicily Italy 68 F6
Syracuse KS U.S.A. 160 C4
Syracuse NY U.S.A. 165 G2
Syrdar'ya r. Asia 102 C3
Syrdar'ya Uzbek. see Sirdaryo
Syrdaryinskiy Uzbek. see Sirdaryo
Syria country Asia 112 E4
Syriam Myanmar see Thanlyin
Syrian Desert Asia 112 E4
Syrna i. Greece 69 L6
Syros i. Greece 69 K6
Syrskiy Rus. Fed. 53 H5
Sysmä Fin. 55 N6
Sysola r. Rus. Fed. 52 K3
Syumsi Rus. Fed. 52 K4
Syurkum Rus. Fed. 90 F2
Syurkum, Mys pt Rus. Fed. 90 F2
Syzran' Rus. Fed. 53 K5
Szabadka Serbia see Subotica
Szczecin Poland 57 O4
Szczecinek Poland 57 P4
Szczytno Poland 57 R4
Szechwan prov. China see Sichuan
Szeged Hungary 69 I1
Székesfehérvár Hungary 68 H1
Szekszárd Hungary 68 H1
Szentes Hungary 69 I1
Szentgotthárd Hungary 68 G1
Szigetvár Hungary 68 G1
Szolnok Hungary 69 I1
Szombathely Hungary 68 G1
Sztálinváros Hungary see Dunaújváros

T

Taagga Duudka reg. Somalia 122 E3
Taal, Lake Luzon Phil. 82 C3
Tabaco Luzon Phil. 82 C3
Tābah Saudi Arabia 108 F4
Tabajara Brazil 176 F5
Tabakhmela Georgia see Kazret'i
Tabalo P.N.G. 81 L7
Tabanan Bali Indon. 85 F5
Tabang Kalimantan Indon. 85 G2
Tabang r. Indon. 85 F2
Tabankulu S. Africa 125 I6
Ţabaqah Ar Raqqah Syria 107 D2
Ţabaqah Ar Raqqah Syria see Madīnat ath Thawrah
Tabar Islands P.N.G. 132 F2
Tabarka Tunisia 68 C6
Ţabas Iran 111 F3
Tabasco Mex. 166 E4
Tabasco state Mex. 167 G5
Tabāsin Iran 110 E4
Tābask, Kūh-e mt. Iran 110 C4
Tabatinga Amazonas Brazil 176 E4
Tabatinga São Paulo Brazil 179 A3
Tabatinga, Serra da hills Brazil 177 J6
Tabatsquri, Tba l. Georgia 113 F2
Tabayama Japan 93 E3
Tabayin Myanmar 86 A2
Tabayoo, Mount Luzon Phil. 82 C2
Tabbita Australia 138 B5
Tabelbala Alg. 64 D6
Taber Canada 151 H5
Tabet, Nam r. Myanmar 86 B1
Tabia Tsaka salt l. China 99 D7
Tabin Wildlife Reserve nature res. Malaysia 85 G1
Tabir r. Indon. 84 C3
Tabiteuea atoll Kiribati 133 H2
Tabivere Estonia 55 O7
Tablas i. Phil. 82 C3
Tablas Strait Phil. 82 C3
Table Cape N.Z. 139 F4
Table Mountain AK U.S.A. 149 L1
Table Point Palawan Phil. 82 B4
Tabligbo Togo 120 D4
Tábor Czech Rep. 57 O6
Tabora Tanz. 123 D4
Tabou Côte d'Ivoire 120 C4
Tabrīz Iran 110 B2
Tabuaeran atoll Kiribati 187 J5
Tabūk Saudi Arabia 112 E5
Tabulam Australia 138 F2
Tabulan Sulawesi Indon. 83 B3
Tabuyung Sumatera Indon. 84 B2
Tabwémasana, Mount Vanuatu 133 G3
Täby Sweden 55 K7
Tacalé Brazil 177 H3
Tacámbaro Mex. 167 E5
Tacaná, Volcán de vol. Mex. 167 G6
Tachakou Xinjiang China 98 D3
Tacheng Xinjiang China 98 C3
Tachie Canada 150 E4
Tachikawa Tōkyō Japan 93 F3
Tachov Czech Rep. 63 M5
Tacipi Sulawesi Indon. 83 B4
Tacloban Leyte Phil. 82 D4
Tacna Peru 176 D7
Tacna AZ U.S.A. 166 B1
Tacoma U.S.A. 156 C3
Taco Pozo Arg. 178 D3
Tacuarembó Uruguay 178 E4
Tacupeto Mex. 166 C2
Tadcaster U.K. 58 F5
Tademaït, Plateau du Alg. 64 E6
Tadenet Lake N.W.T. Canada 149 P1
Tadin New Caledonia 133 G4
Tadjikistan country Asia see Tajikistan
Tadjourah Djibouti 108 F7
Tadmur Syria 107 D2
Tado Japan 92 C3
Tadohae Haesang National Park S. Korea 91 B6
Tadoule Lake Canada 151 L3
Tadoussac Canada 153 H4
Tadpatri India 106 C3
Tadwale India 106 C2
Tadzhikskaya S.S.R. country Asia see Tajikistan
T'aean Haean National Park S. Korea 91 B5
Taech'ŏng-do i. S. Korea 91 B5
Taedasa-do N. Korea 91 B5
Taedong-man b. N. Korea 91 B5
Taegu S. Korea 91 C6
Taehan-min'guk country Asia see South Korea
Taehŭksan-kundo is S. Korea 91 B6
Taejŏn S. Korea 91 B5
Taejŏng S. Korea 91 B6
T'aepaek S. Korea 91 C5
Ta'erqi Nei Mongol China 95 J2
Taf r. U.K. 59 C7
Tafahi i. Tonga 133 I3
Tafalla Spain 67 F2
Tafeng China see Lanshan
Tafila Jordan see Aţ Ţafīlah
Tafi Viejo Arg. 178 C3
Tafresh Iran 110 C3
Taft Iran 110 D4
Taft U.S.A. 158 D4
Taftān, Kūh-e mt. Iran 111 F4
Taftanāz Syria 107 C2
Tafwap India 87 A6
Taga Japan 92 C3
Tagagawik r. AK U.S.A. 148 H2
Taganrog Rus. Fed. 53 H7
Taganrog, Gulf of Rus. Fed./Ukr. 53 H7
Taganrogskiy Zaliv b. Rus. Fed./Ukr. see Taganrog, Gulf of
Tagarev, Gora mt. Iran/Turkm. 110 E2
Tagarkaty, Pereval pass Tajik. 111 I2
Tagaung Myanmar 86 B2
Tagbilaran Bohol Phil. 82 C4
Tagchagpu Ri mt. Xizang China 99 C6
Tagdempt Alg. see Tiaret
Taghmon Ireland 61 F5
Tagish Y.T. Canada 149 N3
Tagish Lake B.C. Canada 149 N4
Tagoloan r. Mindanao Phil. 82 D4
Tagtabazar Turkm. 111 F3
Taguchi-zaki pt Japan 92 B4
Tagudin Luzon Phil. 82 C2
Tagula P.N.G. 136 F1
Tagula Island P.N.G. 136 F1
Tagum Mindanao Phil. 82 D5
Tagus r. Port. 67 B4
also known as Tajo (Portugal) or Tejo (Spain)
Taha Heilong. China 95 K2
Tahaetkun Mountain Canada 150 G5
Tahan, Gunung mt. Malaysia 84 C1
Tahanroz'ka Zatoka b. Rus. Fed./Ukr. see Taganrog, Gulf of
Tahara Japan 92 D4
Tahat, Mont mt. Alg. 120 D2
Tahaurawe i. U.S.A. see Kaho'olawe
Tahe China 90 B1
Taheke N.Z. 139 D2
Tahilt Mongolia see Tsogt
Tahiti i. Fr. Polynesia 187 K7
Tahlab r. Iran/Pak. 111 F4
Tahlab, Dasht-i- plain Pak. 111 F4
Tahlequah U.S.A. 161 E5
Tahltan B.C. Canada 149 O4
Tahoe, Lake U.S.A. 158 C2
Tahoe Lake Canada 147 H3
Tahoe Vista U.S.A. 158 C2
Tahoka U.S.A. 161 C5
Tahoua Niger 120 D3
Tahrūd Iran 110 E4
Tahrūd r. Iran 110 E4
Tahtsa Peak Canada 150 E4
Tahulandang i. Indon. 83 C2
Tahuna Sulawesi Indon. 83 C2
Taï, Parc National de nat. park Côte d'Ivoire 120 C4
Tai'an Liaoning China 95 J3
Tai'an Shandong China 95 I4
Taibai Gansu China 95 G4
Taibai Shaanxi China 95 F5
Taibai Shan mt. China 96 E1
Taibei Taiwan see T'aipei
Taibus Qi Nei Mongol China see Baochang
T'aichung Taiwan 97 I3
Taidong Taiwan see T'aitung
Taiei Japan 93 G3
Taigong China see Taijiang
Taigu Shanxi China 95 H4
Taihang Shan mts China 95 H4
Taihang Shan mts China 95 H4
Taihape N.Z. 139 E4
Taihe Jiangxi China 97 G3
Taihe Sichuan China see Shehong
Taihezhen China see Shehong
Tai Ho Wan H.K. China 97 [inset]
Taihu China 97 H2
Tai Hu l. China 97 I2
Taihuai Shanxi China 95 H4
Taijiang China 97 F3
Taikang Heilong. China 95 K2
Taikang Henan China 95 H5
Taiko-yama hill Japan 92 B3
Tailaco East Timor 83 C5
Tailai Heilong. China 95 J2
Tai Lam Chung Shui Tong resr H.K. China 97 [inset]
Taileleo Indon. 84 B3
Tailem Bend Australia 137 B7
Tai Long Wan b. H.K. China 97 [inset]
Taimani reg. Afgh. 111 F3
Tai Mo Shan hill H.K. China 97 [inset]
Tain U.K. 60 F2
T'ainan Taiwan 97 I4
T'ainan Taiwan see Hsinying
Tainaro, Akra pt Greece see Tainaro, Akrotirio
Tainaro, Akrotirio pt Greece 69 J6
Taining China 97 H3
Tai O H.K. China 97 [inset]
Taiobeiras Brazil 179 C1
Taipa Sulawesi Indon. 83 B3
Tai Pang Wan b. H.K. China see Mirs Bay
▶T'aipei Taiwan 97 I3
Capital of Taiwan.
Taiping Guangdong China see Shixing
Taiping Guangxi China see Chongzuo
Taiping Guangxi China 97 F4
Taiping Malaysia 84 C1
Taipingchuan Jilin China 95 J2
Taiping Ling mt. Nei Mongol China 95 J2
Tai Po H.K. China 97 [inset]
Tai Po Hoi b. H.K. China see Tolo Harbour
Tai Poutini National Park N.Z. see Westland National Park
Taiqian Henan China 95 H5
Taira Toyama Japan 92 C2
Tairbeart U.K. see Tarbert
Tai Rom Yen National Park Thai. 87 B5
Tairuq Iran 110 B3
Tais Sumatera Indon. 84 C4
Tais P.N.G. 81 K8
Taishaku-san mt. Japan 93 F2
Taishan China 97 G4
Taishun China 97 H3
Tai Siu Mo To is H.K. China see The Brothers
Taissy France 62 E5
Taitaitanopo i. Indon. 84 C3
Taitao, Península de pen. Chile 178 B7
Tai Tapu N.Z. 139 D6
Tai To Yan mt. H.K. China 97 [inset]
Taitō-zaki pt Japan 93 G3
T'aitung Taiwan 97 I4
Tai Tung Shan hill H.K. China see Sunset Peak
Taivalkoski Fin. 54 P4
Taivaskero hill Fin. 54 N2
Taiwan country Asia 97 I4
T'aiwan Haihsia strait China/Taiwan see Taiwan Strait
Taiwan Haixia strait China/Taiwan see Taiwan Strait
Taiwan Shan mts Taiwan see Chungyang Shanmo
Taiwan Strait China/Taiwan 97 H4
Taixian China see Jiangyan
Taixing China 97 I1
Taiyuan Shanxi China 95 H4
Tai Yue Shan i. H.K. China see Lantau Island
Taiyue Shan mts China 95 G4
Taizhao Xizang China 99 F7
Taizhong Taiwan see T'aichung
Taizhong Taiwan see Fengyüan
Taizhou Jiangsu China 97 H1
Taizhou Zhejiang China 97 I2
Taizhou Liedao i. China 97 I2
Taizhou Wan b. China 97 I2
Taizi He r. China 90 B4
Ta'izz Yemen 108 F7
Tājābād Iran 110 E4
Tajal Pak. 111 H5
Tajamulco, Volcán de vol. Guat. 167 H6
Tajem, Gunung hill Indon. 85 D3
Tajerouine Tunisia 68 C7
Tajikistan country Asia 111 H2
Tajimi Japan 92 D3
Tajiri Japan 92 B4
Tajitos Mex. 166 B2
Tajo r. Spain 67 C4 see Tagus
Tajrīsh Iran 110 C3
Tak Thai. 86 B3
Takāb Iran 110 B2
Takabba Kenya 122 E3
Taka'Bonerate, Kepulauan atolls Indon. 83 B4
Taka Bonerate, Taman Nasional nat. park Indon. 83 B4
Takagi Japan 93 D3
Takahagi Japan 93 G2
Takahama Aichi Japan 92 C4
Takahama Fukui Japan 92 B3
Takahara-gawa r. Japan 92 D2
Takahashi Japan 91 D6
Takaishi Japan 92 B4
Takaiwa-misaki pt Japan 92 C1
Takamatsu Ishikawa Japan 92 C2
Takamatsu Japan 91 D6
Takami-yama mt. Japan 92 C4
Takamori Nagano Japan 93 D3
Takane Gifu Japan 92 D2
Takane Yamanashi Japan 93 E3
Takanezawa Japan 93 F2
Takaoka Japan 92 D2
Takapuna N.Z. 139 E3
Takarazuka Japan 92 B4
Ta karpo China 105 G4
Takasago Japan 92 A4
Takasaki Japan 93 F2
Takashima Japan 92 C3
Takashōzu-yama mt. Japan 92 C2
Takasu Japan 92 C3
Takasuma-yama mt. Japan 93 E2
Takasuzu-san hill Japan 93 G2
Takatō Japan 93 E3
Takatokwane Botswana 124 G3
Takatomi Japan 92 C3
Takatori Japan 92 B4
Takatshwaane Botswana 124 E2
Takatsuki Ōsaka Japan 92 B4
Takatsuki Shiga Japan 92 C3
Takatsuki-yama mt. Japan 91 D6
Takayama Gifu Japan 92 D2
Takayama Gunma Japan 93 E2
Tak Bai Thai. 87 C6
Takefu Japan 92 C3
Takengon Sumatera Indon. 84 B1
Takeno Japan 92 A3
Takeo Cambodia see Takêv
Takeshi Japan 93 E2
Take-shima i. N. Pacific Ocean see Liancourt Rocks
Takestān Iran 110 C2
Taketoyo Japan 92 C4
Takêv Cambodia 87 D5
Takhemaret Alg. 67 G6
Takhini Hotspring Y.T. Canada 149 N3
Ta Khli Thai. 86 C4
Ta Khmau Cambodia 87 D5
Takhta-Bazar Turkm. see Tagtabazar
Takht Apān, Kūh-e mt. Iran 110 C3
Takhteh Iran 110 D4
Takhteh Pol Afgh. 111 G4
Takht-e Soleymān mt. Iran 110 C2
Takht-e Soleymān tourist site Iran 110 B2
Takht-i-Bahi tourist site Pak. 111 H3
Takht-i-Sulaiman mt. Pak. 111 H4
Taki Mie Japan 92 C4
Takijuq Lake Canada see Napaktulik Lake
Takino Japan 92 A4
Takinoue Japan 90 F3
Takisung Kalimantan Indon. 85 F3
Takla Lake Canada 150 E4
Takla Landing Canada 150 E4
Takla Makan des. China see Taklimakan Shamo
Taklimakan Desert China see Taklimakan Shamo
Taklimakan Shamo des. China 98 C5
Tako Japan 93 G3
Takotna AK U.S.A. 148 H3
Takpa Shiri mt. Xizang China 99 F7
Takslesluk Lake AK U.S.A. 148 G3
Taku Canada 150 C3
Taku r. Canada/U.S.A. 149 N4
Takum Nigeria 120 D4
Takuu Islands P.N.G. 133 F2
Talachyn Belarus 53 F5
Talaja India 104 C5
Talakan Amurskaya Oblast' Rus. Fed. 90 C2
Talakan Khabarovskiy Kray Rus. Fed. 90 D2
Talamanca, Cordillera de mts Costa Rica 166 [inset] J7
Talandzha Rus. Fed. 90 C2
Talang, Gunung vol. Indon. 84 C3
Talangbatu Sumatera Indon. 84 D3
Talangbetutu Sumatera Indon. 84 D3
Talara Peru 176 B4
Talar-i-Band mts Pak. see Makran Coast Range
Talas Kyrg. 102 D3
Talas Ala-Too mts Kyrg. 102 D3
Talas Range mts Kyrg. see Talas Ala-Too
Talasskiy Alatau, Khrebet mts Kyrg. see Talas Ala-Too
Talatakoh i. Indon. 83 B3
Ţal'at Mūsá mt. Lebanon/Syria 107 C2
Talaud, Kepulauan is Indon. 83 C1
Talavera de la Reina Spain 67 D4
Talawgyi Myanmar 86 B1
Talaya Rus. Fed. 77 Q3
Talayan Mindanao Phil. 82 D5
Talbehat India 104 D4
Talbīsah Syria 107 C2
Talbot, Mount hill Australia 135 D6
Talbotton U.S.A. 163 C5
Talbragar r. Australia 138 D4
Talca Chile 178 B5
Talcahuano Chile 178 B5
Taldan Rus. Fed. 90 B1
Taldom Rus. Fed. 52 H4
Taldykorgan Kazakh. 102 E3
Taldy-Kurgan Kazakh. see Taldykorgan
Taldyqorghan Kazakh. see Taldykorgan
Taldy-Suu Kyrg. 98 B4
Tālesh Iran see Hashtpar
Talgar Kazakh. 98 B4
Talgar, Pik mt. Kazakh. 98 B4
Talgarth U.K. 59 D7
Talguppa India 106 B3
Talia Australia 137 A7
Taliabu i. Indon. 83 C3
Talibon Bohol Phil. 82 D4
Talikota India 106 C2
Talikud i. Phil. 82 D5
Talimakan Desert China. 98 C5
Talimakan Shamo des. China see Talimakan Desert
Talimardzhan Uzbek. see Tollimarjon
Talin Hiag Heilong. China 95 K2
Taliparamba India 106 B3
Talisay Cebu Phil. 82 C4
Talisayan Kalimantan Indon. 85 G2
Talisayan Mindanao Phil. 82 D4
Talış Dağları mts Azer./Iran 110 C2
Taliséi i. Indon. 83 C2
Talitsa Rus. Fed. 52 J4
Taliwang Sumbawa Indon. 85 G5
Talkeetna AK U.S.A. 149 J3
Talkeetna r. AK U.S.A. 149 J3
Talkeetna Mountains AK U.S.A. 149 J3
Talkh Āb Iran 110 E3
Tallacootra, Lake salt flat Australia 135 F7
Talladega U.S.A. 163 C5
▶Tallahassee U.S.A. 163 C6
Capital of Florida.
Tall al Aḩmar Syria 107 D1
Tallassee AL U.S.A. 167 I1
Tall Baydar Syria 113 F3
Tall-e Ḩalāl Iran 110 D4
▶Tallinn Estonia 55 N7
Capital of Estonia.
Tall Kalakh Syria 107 C2
Tall Kayf Iraq 113 F3
Tall Kūjik Syria 113 F3
Tallow Ireland 61 D5
Tallulah U.S.A. 161 F5
Tall 'Uwaynāt Iraq 113 F3
Tallymerjen Uzbek. see Tollimarjon
Tal'ne Ukr. 53 F6
Tal'noye Ukr. see Tal'ne
Taloda India 104 C5
Talodi Sudan 108 D7
Taloga U.S.A. 161 D4
Talon, Lac l. Canada 153 I3
Ta-long Myanmar 86 B2
Tāloqān Afgh. 111 H2
Talos Dome ice feature Antarctica 188 H2
Ta Loung San mt. Laos 86 C2
Talovaya Rus. Fed. 53 I6
Taloyoak Canada 147 I3
Talpa Mex. 166 D4
Tal Pass Pak. 111 I3
Talshand Mongolia see Chandmanī
Talsi Latvia 55 M8
Tal Sīyāh Iran 111 F4
Taltal Chile 178 B3
Taltson r. Canada 151 H2
Talu Xizang China 99 F7
Talu Sumatera Indon. 84 B2
Taludaa Sulawesi Indon. 83 B2
Taluti, Teluk b. Seram Indon. 83 D3
Talvik Norway 54 M1
Talwood Australia 138 D2
Talyshskiye Gory mts Azer./Iran see Talış Dağları
Talyy Rus. Fed. 52 L2
Tama Japan 93 F3
Tama Abu, Banjaran mts Malaysia 85 F2
Tamabo Range mts Malaysia see Tama Abu, Banjaran
Tama-gawa r. Japan 93 F3
Tamaki Japan 92 C4
Tamala Australia 135 A6
Tamala Rus. Fed. 53 I5
Tamale Ghana 120 C4
Tamalung Kalimantan Indon. 85 F3
Tamamura Japan 93 F2
Tamana i. Kiribati 133 H2
Taman Negara National Park Malaysia 84 C1
Tamano Japan 91 D6
Tamanrasset Alg. 120 D2
Tamanthi Myanmar 86 A1
Tamaqua U.S.A. 165 H3
Tamar India 105 F5
Tamar Syria see Tadmur
Tamar r. U.K. 59 C8
Tamari Japan 93 G2
Tamarugal, Pampa de plain Chile 176 E7
Tamasane Botswana 125 H2
Tamatave Madag. see Toamasina
Tamatsukuri Japan 93 G2
Tamaulipas state Mex. 161 D7
Tamaulipas, Sierra de mts Mex. 167 F4
Tamazula Durango Mex. 166 D3
Tamazula Jalisco Mex. 166 E5
Tamazulápam Mex. 167 F5
Tamazunchale Mex. 167 F4
Tamba Japan see Tanba
Tambacounda Senegal 120 B3
Tamba-kōchi plat. Japan see Tanba-kōchi
Tambalongang i. Indon. 83 B4
Tambangmunjul Kalimantan Indon. 85 E3
Tambangsawah Sumatera Indon. 84 C3
Tambaqui Brazil 176 F5
Tambar Springs Australia 138 D3
Tambea Sulawesi Indon. 83 B4
Tambelan, Kepulauan is Indon. 84 D2
Tambelan Besar i. Indon. 85 D2
Tamberu Jawa Indon. 85 F4
Tambisan Sabah Malaysia 85 G1
Tambo r. Australia 138 C6
Tambohorano Madag. 123 E5
Tamboli Sulawesi Indon. 83 B3
Tambor Mex. 166 D3
▶Tambora, Gunung vol. Sumbawa Indon. 85 G5
Deadliest recorded volcanic eruption (1815).
Tamboritha mt. Australia 138 C6
Tambov Rus. Fed. 53 I5
Tambovka Rus. Fed. 90 C2
Tambu, Teluk b. Indon. 83 A2
Tambulanan, Bukit hill Malaysia 85 G1
Tambunan Sabah Malaysia 85 G1
Tambura Sudan 121 F4
Tamburi Brazil 179 C1
Tambuyukon, Gunung mt. Malaysia 85 G1
Tâmchekket Mauritania 120 B3
Tamdybulak Uzbek. see Tomdibuloq
Tâmega r. Port. 67 B3
Tamenghest Alg. see Tamanrasset
Tamenglong India 105 H4
Tamerza Tunisia 68 B7
Tamgak, Adrar mt. Niger 120 D3
Tamgué, Massif du mt. Guinea 120 B3
Tamiahua Mex. 167 F4
Tamiahua, Laguna de lag. Mex. 168 E4
Tamiang r. Indon. 84 B1
Tamiang, Ujung pt Indon. 84 B1
Tamil Nadu state India 106 C4
Tamirin Gol r. Mongolia 94 E2
Tamitsa Rus. Fed. 52 H2
Ţâmîya Egypt see Ţāmīyah
Ţāmīyah Egypt 112 C5
Tamkuhi India 105 F4
Tam Ky Vietnam 86 E4
Tammarvi r. Canada 151 K1
Tammerfors Fin. see Tampere
Tammisaari Fin. see Ekenäs
Tampa U.S.A. 163 D7
Tampa Bay U.S.A. 163 D7
Tampang Sumatera Indon. 84 D4
Tampere Fin. 55 M6
Tampico Mex. 168 E4
Tampin Malaysia 84 C2
Tampines Sing. 87 [inset]
Tampo Sulawesi Indon. 83 B4
Tamsagbulag Mongolia 95 I2
Tamsag Muchang Nei Mongol China 94 E3
Tamsweg Austria 57 N7
Tamu Myanmar 86 A1
Tamuín Mex. 167 F4
Tamworth Australia 138 E3
Tamworth U.K. 59 F6
Tan Kazakh. 98 B2
Tana r. Fin./Norway see Tenojoki
Tana r. Kenya 122 E4
Tana Madag. see Antananarivo
Tana r. AK U.S.A. 149 L3
Tana i. Vanuatu see Tanna
Tana, Lake Eth. 122 D2
Tanabe Japan 91 D6
Tanabi Brazil 179 A3
Tana Bru Norway 54 P1
Tanacross AK U.S.A. 149 L3
Tanadak Island AK U.S.A. 148 D5
Tanada Lake U.S.A. 150 A2
Tanafjorden inlet Norway 54 P1
Tanaga vol. AK U.S.A. 149 [inset]
Tanaga Island AK U.S.A. 149 [inset]
Tanaga Pass sea channel AK U.S.A. 149 [inset]
Tanagura Japan 93 G1
Tanah, Tanjung pt Indon. 85 E4
T'ana Hāyk' l. Eth. see Tana, Lake
Tanahbala i. Indon. 84 B3
Tanahgrogot Kalimantan Indon. 85 G3
Tanahjampea i. Indon. 83 B4
Tanahmasa i. Indon. 84 B3
Tanahmerah Kalimantan Indon. 85 G2
Tanah Merah Malaysia 84 C1
Tanahputih Sumatera Indon. 84 C2
Tanah Rata Malaysia 84 C1
Tanakeke i. Indon. 83 A4
Tanambung Sulawesi Barat Indon. 83 A3
Tanami Australia 134 E4
Tanami Desert Australia 134 E4
Tân An Vietnam 87 D5
Tanana AK U.S.A. 148 I2
Tanana r. AK U.S.A. 148 I2
Tananarive Madag. see Antananarivo
Tanandava Madag. 123 E6
Tanauan Leyte Phil. 82 D4
Tanba Japan 92 B3
Tanba-kōchi plat. Japan 92 B3
Tanbu Shandong China 95 I5
Tancheng China see Pingtan
Tancheng Shandong China 95 I5
Tanch'ŏn N. Korea 91 C4
Tanda Côte d'Ivoire 120 C4
Tanda Uttar Prad. India 104 D3
Tanda Uttar Prad. India 105 E4
Tandag Mindanao Phil. 82 D4
Ţăndărei Romania 69 L2
Tandaué Angola 123 B5
Tandek Sabah Malaysia 85 G1
Tandi India 104 D2
Tandil Arg. 178 E5
Tando Adam Pak. 111 H5
Tando Allahyar Pak. 111 H5
Tando Bago Pak. 111 H5
Tandou Lake imp. l. Australia 137 C7
Tandragee U.K. 61 F3
Tandubatu i. Phil. 82 C5
Tandur India 106 C2
Tanduri Pak. 111 G4
Tanega-shima i. Japan 91 C7
Tanen Taunggyi mts Thai. 86 B3
Tanezrouft reg. Alg./Mali 120 C2
Ţanf, Jabal aţ hill Syria 107 D3
Tang, Ra's-e pt Iran 111 E5
Tanga Rus. Fed. 95 G1
Tanga Tanz. 123 D4
Tangail Bangl. 105 G4
Tanga Islands P.N.G. 132 F2
Tanganyika country Africa see Tanzania
▶Tanganyika, Lake Africa 123 C4
Deepest and 2nd largest lake in Africa, and 6th largest in the world.
Tangará Brazil 179 A4
Tangasseri India 106 C4
Tangdan China 96 D3
Tangdê Xizang China 99 F7
Tangeli Iran 110 D2
Tanger Morocco see Tangier
Tangerang Jawa Indon. 84 D4
Tangerhütte Germany 63 L2
Tangermünde Germany 63 L2
Tang-e Sarkheh Iran 111 E5
Tanggarma Qinghai China 94 D4
Tanggo Xizang China 99 E7
Tanggor China 96 D1
Tanggu Tianjin China 95 I4
Tanggulashan Qinghai China 94 C5
Tanggula Shan mt. Qinghai/Xizang China 99 E6
Tanggula Shan mts Xizang China 99 E6
Tanggula Shankou pass Xizang China 99 E6
Tangguo Xizang China 99 D7
Tanghai Hebei China 95 I4
Tanghe China 97 G1
Tangier Morocco 67 D6
Tangiers Morocco see Tangier
Tangkelemboko, Gunung mt. Indon. 83 B3
Tangkittebak, Gunung mt. Indon. 84 D4
Tang La pass Xizang China 99 E8
Tangla India 105 G4
Tanglag China 96 C1
Tanglin Sing. 87 [inset]
Tangmai Xizang China 99 F7
Tangnag Qinghai China 94 E5
Tango Japan 92 B3
Tangorin Australia 136 D4
Tangra Yumco salt l. China 99 D7
Tangse Sumatera Indon. 84 A1
Tangshan Guizhou China see Shiqian
Tangshan Hebei China 95 I4
Tangte mt. Myanmar 86 B2
Tangtse India see Tanktse
Tangub Mindanao Phil. 82 C4
Tangwan China 97 F3
Tangwanghe China 90 C2
Tangxian Hebei China 95 H4
Tangyin Henan China 95 H5
Tangyuan China 90 C3
Tangyung Tso salt l. China 105 F3
Tanhaçu Brazil 179 C1
Tanhua Fin. 54 O3
Tani Cambodia 87 D5
Taniantaweng Shan mts China 96 B2
Tanigawa-dake mt. Japan 93 E2
Tanigumi Japan 92 C3
Tanimbar, Kepulauan is Indon. 134 E1
Taninthari Myanmar see Tenasserim
Tanintharyi Myanmar see Tenasserim
Taninthayi Myanmar see Tenasserim
Taniwel Seram Indon. 83 D3
Tanjah Morocco see Tangier
Tanjay Negros Phil. 82 C4
Tanjiajing Gansu China 94 E4
Tanjore India see Thanjavur
Tanjung Kalimantan Indon. 85 F3
Tanjung Sumatera Indon. 84 D3
Tanjungbalai Sumatera Indon. 84 B2
Tanjungbalai Sumatera Indon. 84 C2
Tanjungbaliha Maluku Indon. 83 C3
Tanjungbatu Kalimantan Indon. 85 G2
Tanjungbatu Sumatera Indon. 84 C3
Tanjungbuayabuaya, Pulau i. Indon. 85 G2
Tanjungenim Sumatera Indon. 84 C3
Tanjunggaru Kalimantan Indon. 85 G3
Tanjungkarang-Telukbetung Sumatera Indon. see Bandar Lampung
Tanjungpandan Indon. 85 D3
Tanjungpinang Indon. 84 D2
Tanjungpura Sumatera Indon. 84 B2
Tanjung Puting, Taman Nasional nat. park Indon. 85 F3
Tanjungraja Sumatera Indon. 84 D3
Tanjungredeb Kalimantan Indon. 85 G2
Tanjungsaleh i. Indon. 85 E3
Tanjungsatai Kalimantan Indon. 85 E3
Tanjungselor Kalimantan Indon. 85 G2
Tankhoy Rus. Fed. 94 F1
Tankse India see Tanktse
Tanktse India 104 D2
Tankwa-Karoo National Park S. Africa 124 D7
Tanna i. Vanuatu 133 G3
Tannadice U.K. 60 G4
Tannan Japan 92 B3
Tännäs Sweden 54 H5
Tanner, Mount Canada 150 G5
Tannu-Ola, Khrebet mts Rus. Fed. 94 B1
Tannu Tuva aut. rep. Rus. Fed. see Tyva, Respublika
Tañon Strait Phil. 82 C4

Tanot India 104 B4
Tanout Niger 120 D3
Tanquian Mex. 167 F4
Tansen Nepal 105 E4
Tanshui Taiwan 97 I3
Tansyk Kazakh. 98 B3
Ţanţā Egypt 112 C5
Ęanţa Egypt see Ţanţā
Tan-Tan Morocco 120 B2
Tantō Japan 92 A3
Tantoyuca Mex. 167 F4
Tantu Jilin China 95 J2
Tanuku India 106 D2
Tanuma Japan 93 F2
Tanumbirini Australia 134 F4
Tanumshede Sweden 55 G7
Tanyurer r. Rus. Fed. 148 A2
Tanzania country Africa 123 D4
Tanzawa-Ōyama Kokutei-kōen park Japan 93 F3
Tanzilla r. B.C. Canada 149 O4
Tao, Ko i. Thai. 87 B5
Tao'an Jilin China see Taonan
Taobh Tuath U.K. see Northton
Taocheng China see Daxin
Taocun Shandong China 95 J4
Tao'er He r. China 95 J2
Tao He r. China 94 E5
Taohong China see Longhui
Taohuajiang China see Taojiang
Taohuaping China see Longhui
Taojiang China 97 G2
Taolanaro Madag. see Tôlañaro
Taole Ningxia China 94 F4
Taonan Jilin China 95 J2
Taongi atoll Marshall Is 186 H5
Taos U.S.A. 157 G5
Taounate Morocco 64 D5
Taourirt Morocco 64 D5
Taoxi China 97 H3
Taoyang Gansu China see Lintao
Taoyuan China 97 F2
T'aoyüan Taiwan 97 I3
Tapa Estonia 55 N7
Tapaan Passage Phil. 82 C5
Tapachula Mex. 167 G6
Tapah Malaysia 87 C6
Tapajós r. Brazil 177 H4
Tapaktuan Sumatera Indon. 84 B2
Tapan Sumatera Indon. 84 C3
Tapanatepec Mex. 167 G5
Tapanuli, Teluk b. Indon. 84 B2
Tapat i. Maluku Indon. 83 C3
Tapauá Brazil 176 F5
Tapauá r. Brazil 176 F5
Taperoá Brazil 179 D1
Tapi r. India 104 C5
Tapiau Rus. Fed. see Gvardeysk
Tapijulapa Mex. 167 G5
Tapinbini Kalimantan Indon. 85 E3
Tapis, Gunung mt. Malaysia 84 C1
Tapisuelas Mex. 166 C3
Taplejung Nepal 105 F4
Tap Mun Chau i. H.K. China 97 [inset]
Ta-pom Myanmar 86 B2
Tappahannock U.S.A. 165 G5
Tappal Uttar Prad. India 99 B7
Tappalang Sulawesi Indon. 85 G3
Tappeh, Kūh-e hill Iran 110 C3
Taprobane country Asia see Sri Lanka
Tapuaenuku mt. N.Z. 139 D5
Tapul Phil. 82 C5
Tapul Group is Phil. 82 C5
Tapulonanjing mt. Indon. 84 B2
Tapung r. Indon. 84 C2
Tapurucuara Brazil 176 E4
Taputeouea atoll Kiribati see Tabiteuea
Ţaqţaq Iraq 113 G4
Taquara Brazil 179 A5
Taquarí Rio Grande do Sul Brazil 179 A5
Taquarí r. Brazil 177 G7
Taquaritinga Brazil 179 A3
Tar r. Ireland 61 E5
Tara Australia 138 E1
Ţarābulus Lebanon see Tripoli
Ţarābulus Libya see Tripoli
Taragt Mongolia 94 E2
Tarahuwan India 104 E4
Tarai reg. India 105 G4
Tarakan Kalimantan Indon. 85 G2
Tarakan i. Indon. 85 G2
Tarakki reg. Afgh. 111 G3
Taraklı Turkey 69 N4
Taran, Mys pt Rus. Fed. 55 K9
Tarana Australia 138 D4
Taranagar India 104 C3
Taranaki, Mount vol. N.Z. 139 E4
Tarancón Spain 67 E3
Tarangambadi India 106 C4
Tarangire National Park Tanz. 122 D4
Taranto Italy 68 G4
Taranto, Golfo di g. Italy 68 G4
Taranto, Gulf of Italy see Taranto, Golfo di
Tarapoto Peru 176 C5
Tarapur India 106 B2
Tararua Range mts N.Z. 139 E5
Tarascon-sur-Ariège France 66 E5
Tarasovskiy Rus. Fed. 53 I6
Tarauacá Brazil 176 D5
Tarauacá r. Brazil 176 E5
Tarawera N.Z. 139 F4
Tarawera, Mount vol. N.Z. 139 F4
Taraz Kazakh. 102 D3
Tarazona Spain 67 F3
Tarazona de la Mancha Spain 67 F4
Tarbagatay Kazakh. 98 C3
Tarbagatay Rus. Fed. 95 F1
Tarbagatay, Khrebet mts Kazakh. 102 F2
Tarbat Ness pt U.K. 60 F3
Tarbert Ireland 61 C5
Tarbert Scotland U.K. 60 C3
Tarbert Scotland U.K. 60 D5
Tarbes France 66 E5
Tarboro U.S.A. 162 E5
Tarcoola Australia 135 F7
Tarcoon Australia 138 C3
Tarcoonyinna watercourse Australia 135 F6
Tarcutta Australia 138 C5
Tardoki-Yani, Gora mt. Rus. Fed. 90 E2
Taree Australia 138 F3
Tarella Australia 137 C6
Tarentum Italy see Taranto
Ţarfā', Baţn aţ depr. Saudi Arabia 110 C6
Tarfaya Morocco 120 B2
Targa well Niger 120 D3
Targan Heilong. China see Talin Hiag
Targhee Pass U.S.A. 156 F3
Târgovişte Romania 69 K2
Targuist Morocco 67 D6
Târgu Jiu Romania 69 J2
Târgu Mureş Romania 69 K1
Târgu Neamţ Romania 69 L1
Târgu Secuiesc Romania 69 L1
Targyailing Xizang China 99 D7
Targyn Kazakh. 98 C2
Tarhūnah Libya 121 E1
Tari P.N.G. 81 K8
Tarian Gol Nei Mongol China 95 G4
Tariat Mongolia 94 D1
Tarif U.A.E. 110 D5
Tarifa Spain 67 D5
Tarifa, Punta de pt Spain 67 D5
Tarigtig Point Luzon Phil. 82 C2
Tarija Bol. 176 F8
Tarikere India 106 B3
Tariku r. Indon. 81 J7
Tarim Xinjiang China 98 C4
Tarīm Yemen 108 G6
Tarim Basin China 98 C5
Tarime Tanz. 122 D4
Tarim He r. China 98 D4
Tarim Liuchang Xinjiang China 98 D4
Tarim Pendi basin China see Tarim Basin
Tarim Qichang Xinjiang China 98 D4
Tarīn Kowt Afgh. 111 G3
Taritatu r. Indon. 81 J7
Taritipan Sabah Malaysia see Tandek
Tarka r. S. Africa 125 G7
Tarkastad S. Africa 125 H7
Tarkio U.S.A. 160 E3
Tarko-Sale Rus. Fed. 76 I3
Tarkwa Ghana 120 C4
Tarlac Luzon Phil. 82 C3
Tarlac r. Luzon Phil. 82 C2
Tarlauly Kazakh. 98 B3
Tarlo River National Park Australia 138 D5
Tarma Peru 176 C6
Tarmar Xizang China 99 E7
Tarmstedt Germany 63 J1
Tarn r. France 66 E4
Tärnaby Sweden 54 I4
Tarnak r. Afgh. 111 G4
Târnăveni Romania 69 K1
Tarnobrzeg Poland 53 D6
Tarnogskiy Gorodok Rus. Fed. 52 I3
Tarnopol Ukr. see Ternopil'
Tarnów Poland 53 D6
Tarnowitz Poland see Tarnowskie Góry
Tarnowskie Góry Poland 57 Q5
Taro Co salt l. China 99 C7
Ţārom Iran 110 D4
Taroom Australia 137 E5
Tarō-san mt. Japan 93 F2
Taroudannt Morocco 64 C5
Tarpaulin Swamp Australia 136 B3
Tarq Iran 110 C3
Tarquinia Italy 68 D3
Tarquinii Italy see Tarquinia
Tarrabool Lake salt flat Australia 136 A3
Tarraco Spain see Tarragona
Tarrafal Cape Verde 120 [inset]
Tarragona Spain 67 G3
Tårrajaur Sweden 54 K3
Tarran Hills hill Australia 138 C4
Tarrant Point Australia 136 B3
Tàrrega Spain 67 G3
Tarso Emissi mt. Chad 121 E2
Tarsus Turkey 107 B1
Tart Qinghai China 99 F5
Tärtär Azer. 113 G2
Tartu Estonia 55 O7
Ţarţūs Syria 107 B2
Tarui Japan 92 C3
Tarumovka Rus. Fed. 113 G1
Tarung Hka r. Myanmar 86 B1
Tarutao, Ko i. Thai. 87 B6
Tarutao National Park Thai. 87 B6
Tarutung Sumatera Indon. 84 B2
Tarvisium Italy see Treviso
Tarys-Arzhan Rus. Fed. 94 D1
Tarz Iran 110 E4
Tasai, Ko i. Thai. 87 B5
Tasaral Kazakh. 98 A3
Taschereau Canada 152 F4
Taseko Mountain Canada 150 F5
Tashauz Turkm. see Daşoguz
Tash-Bashat Kyrg. 98 B4
Tashi Gansu China 94 C3
Tashi Chho Bhutan see Thimphu
Tashigang Bhutan 105 G4
Tashino Rus. Fed. see Pervomaysk
Tashir Armenia 113 G2
Tashk, Daryācheh-ye l. Iran 110 D4
Tashkent Toshkent Uzbek. see Toshkent
Tāshqurghān Afgh. see Kholm
Tashtagol Rus. Fed. 88 F2
Tashtyp Rus. Fed. 88 F2
Tasialujjuaq, Lac l. Canada 153 G2
Tasiat, Lac l. Canada 152 G2
Tasiilap Karra c. Greenland 147 O3
Tasiilaq Greenland see Ammassalik
Tasikmalaya Jawa Indon. 85 E4
Tasīl Syria 107 B3
Tasiujaq Canada 153 H2
Tasiusaq Greenland 147 M2
Taşkent Turkey 107 A1
Tasker Niger 120 E3
Taskesken Kazakh. 102 F2
Taşköprü Turkey 112 D2
Tasman Abyssal Plain sea feature Tasman Sea 186 G8
Tasman Basin sea feature Tasman Sea 186 G8
Tasman Bay N.Z. 139 D5

▶Tasmania state Australia 137 [inset]
4th largest island in Oceania.

Tasman Islands P.N.G. see Nukumanu Islands
Tasman Mountains N.Z. 139 D5
Tasman Peninsula Australia 137 [inset]
Tasman Sea S. Pacific Ocean 132 H6
Taşova Turkey 112 D2
Tassara Niger 120 D3
Tassialouc, Lac l. Canada 152 G2
Tassili du Hoggar plat. Alg. 120 D2
Tassili n'Ajjer plat. Alg. 120 D2
Tasty Kazakh. 102 C3
Taşucu Turkey 107 A1
Tas-Yuryakh Rus. Fed. 77 M3
Tata Morocco 64 C6
Tataba Sulawesi Indon. 83 B3
Tatabánya Hungary 68 H1
Tatalin Gol r. Qinghai China 94 C4
Tatamailau, Foho mt. East Timor 83 C5
Tataouine Tunisia 64 G5
Tatarbunary Ukr. 69 M2
Tatarsk Rus. Fed. 76 I4
Tatarskiy Proliv strait Rus. Fed. 90 F2
Tatar Strait Rus. Fed. see Tatarskiy Proliv
Tatau Sarawak Malaysia 85 F2
Tate r. Australia 136 C3
Tatebayashi Japan 93 F2
Tateishi-misaki pt Japan 92 C3
Tateiwa Japan 93 F1
Tateshina Japan 93 E2
Tateshina-yama mt. Japan 93 E2
Tateyama Chiba Japan 93 F4
Tateyama Toyama Japan 92 D2
Tate-yama vol. Japan 92 D2
Tathlina Lake Canada 150 G2
Tathlīth Saudi Arabia 108 F6
Tathlīth, Wādī watercourse Saudi Arabia 108 F5
Tathra Australia 138 D6
Tatinnai Lake Canada 151 L2
Tatishchevo Rus. Fed. 53 J6
Tatitlek AK U.S.A. 149 K3
Tatkon Myanmar 86 B2
Tatla Lake Canada 150 E5
Tatla Lake l. Canada 150 E5
Tatlayoko Lake Canada 150 E5
Tatnam, Cape Canada 151 N3
Tatomi Japan 93 E3
Tatra Mountains Poland/Slovakia 57 Q6
Tatrang Xinjiang China 99 D5
Tatry mts Poland/Slovakia see Tatra Mountains
Tatrzański Park Narodowy nat. park Poland 57 Q6
Tatshenshini r. B.C. Canada 149 M4
Tatshenshini-Alsek Provincial Wilderness Park Canada 150 B3
Tatsinskiy Rus. Fed. 53 I6
Tatsuno Nagano Japan 93 D3
Tatsunokuchi Japan 92 C2
Tatsuruhama Japan 92 C1
Tatsuyama Japan 93 D4
Tatuí Brazil 179 B3
Tatuk Mountain Canada 150 E4
Tatum U.S.A. 161 C5
Tatvan Turkey 113 F3
Tau Norway 55 D7
Taua Brazil 177 J5
Tauapeçaçu Brazil 176 F4
Taubaté Brazil 179 B3
Tauber r. Germany 63 J5
Tauberbischofsheim Germany 63 J5
Taucha Germany 63 M3
Taufstein hill Germany 63 J4
Taukum, Peski des. Kazakh. 102 D3
Taumarunui N.Z. 139 E4
Taumaturgo Brazil 176 D5
Taung S. Africa 124 G4
Taungdwingyi Myanmar 86 A2
Taunggyi Myanmar 86 B2
Taunglau Myanmar 86 B2
Taung-ngu Myanmar 86 B3
Taungnyo Range mts Myanmar 86 B3
Taungtha Myanmar 86 A2
Taungup Myanmar 96 B5
Taunton U.K. 59 D7
Taunton U.S.A. 165 J3
Taunus hills Germany 63 H4
Taupo N.Z. 139 F4
Taupo, Lake N.Z. 139 E4
Tauragė Lith. 55 M9
Tauranga N.Z. 139 F3
Taurasia Italy see Turin
Taureau, Réservoir resr Canada 152 G5
Taurianova Italy 68 G5
Tauroa Point N.Z. 139 D2
Taurus Mountains Turkey 107 A1
Taute r. France 59 F9
Tauz Azer. see Tovuz
Tavas Turkey 69 M6
Tavastehus Fin. see Hämeenlinna
Tavayvaam r. Rus. Fed. 148 B2
Taverham U.K. 59 I6
Taveuni i. Fiji 133 I3
Tavildara Tajik. 111 H2
Tavira Port. 67 C5
Tavistock Canada 164 E2
Tavistock U.K. 59 C8
Tavoy Myanmar 87 B4
Tavoy r. mouth Myanmar 87 B4
Tavoy Island Myanmar see Mali Kyun
Tavoy Point Myanmar 87 B4
Tavricheskoye Kazakh. 98 C2
Tavşanlı Turkey 69 M5
Taw r. U.K. 59 C7
Tawai, Bukit mt. Malaysia 85 G1
Tawakoni, Lake TX U.S.A. 167 G1
Tawang India 105 G4
Tawaramoto Japan 92 B4
Tawas City U.S.A. 164 D1
Tawau Sabah Malaysia 85 G1
Tawau, Teluk b. Malaysia 85 G1
Tawè Myanmar see Tavoy
Tawe r. U.K. 59 D7
Tawi r. India 99 A6
Ţawī Ḩafīr well U.A.E. 110 D5
Ţawī Murra well U.A.E. 110 D5
Tawi-Tawi i. Phil. 82 B5
Tawmaw Myanmar 86 B1
Tawu Taiwan 97 I4
Taxco Mex. 167 F5
Taxkorgan Xinjiang China 99 A5
Tay r. Y.T. Canada 149 N3
Tay r. U.K. 60 F4
Tay, Firth of est. U.K. 60 F4
Tay, Lake salt flat Australia 135 C8
Tay, Loch l. U.K. 60 E4
Tayabas Bay Luzon Phil. 82 C3
Tayan Kalimantan Indon. 85 E2
Tayandu, Kepulauan is Indon. 81 I8
Taybola Rus. Fed. 54 R2
Taycheedah U.S.A. 164 A2
Taygan Mongolia see Delger
Tayinloan U.K. 60 D5
Taylor Canada 150 F3
Taylor AK U.S.A. 148 F2
Taylor MI U.S.A. 164 D2
Taylor NE U.S.A. 160 D3
Taylor TX U.S.A. 161 D6
Taylor, Mount U.S.A. 159 J4
Taylor Mountains AK U.S.A. 148 H3
Taylorsville U.S.A. 164 C4
Taylorville U.S.A. 160 F4
Taymā' Saudi Arabia 112 E6
Taymura r. Rus. Fed. 77 K3
Taymyr, Ozero l. Rus. Fed. 77 L2
Taymyr, Poluostrov pen. Rus. Fed. see Taymyr Peninsula
Taymyr Peninsula Rus. Fed. 76 J2
Tây Ninh Vietnam 87 D5
Tayoltita Mex. 166 D3
Taypak Kazakh. 51 Q6
Taypaq Kazakh. see Taypak
Tayshet Rus. Fed. 88 H1
Tayshir Mongolia 94 D2
Taytay Luzon Phil. 82 C3
Taytay Palawan Phil. 82 B4
Taytay Bay Palawan Phil. 82 B4
Taytay Point Leyte Phil. 82 D4
Tayu Jawa Indon. 85 E4
Tayuan China 90 B2
Tayyebād Iran 111 F3
Taz r. Rus. Fed. 76 I3
Taza Morocco 64 D5
Tāza Khurmātū Iraq 113 G4
Tazawa Japan 93 D2
Taze Myanmar 86 A2
Tazewell TN U.S.A. 164 D5
Tazewell VA U.S.A. 164 E5
Tazimina Lakes AK U.S.A. 148 I3
Tazin r. Canada 151 I2
Tazin Lake Canada 151 I3
Tāzirbū Libya 121 F2
Tazlina AK U.S.A. 149 K3
Tazlina Lake AK U.S.A. 149 K3
Tazmalt Alg. 67 I5
Tazovskaya Guba sea chan. Rus. Fed. 76 I3
Tbessa Alg. see Tébessa

▶T'bilisi Georgia 113 G2
Capital of Georgia.

Tbilisskaya Rus. Fed. 53 I7
Tchabal Mbabo mt. Cameroon 120 E4
Tchad country Africa see Chad
Tchamba Togo 120 D4
Tchibanga Gabon 122 B4
Tchigaï, Plateau du Niger 121 E2
Tchin-Tabaradene Niger 120 D3
Tcholliré Cameroon 121 E4
Tchula U.S.A. 161 F5
Tczew Poland 57 Q3
Te, Prêk r. Cambodia 87 D4
Teacapán Mex. 166 D4
Teague, Lake salt flat Australia 135 C6
Te Anau N.Z. 139 A7
Te Anau, Lake N.Z. 139 A7
Teapa Mex. 167 G5
Te Araroa N.Z. 139 G3
Teate Italy see Chieti
Te Awamutu N.Z. 139 E4
Teba Indon. 81 J7
Tébarat Niger 120 D3
Tebas Kalimantan Indon. 85 E2
Tebay U.K. 58 E4
Tebedu Sarawak Malaysia 85 E2
Tebesjuak Lake Canada 151 L2
Tébessa Alg. 68 C7
Tébessa, Monts de mts Alg. 68 C7
Tebingtinggi Sumatera Indon. 84 B2
Tebingtinggi Sumatera Indon. 84 C3
Tebo r. Indon. 84 C3
Tébourba Tunisia 68 C6
Téboursouk Tunisia 68 C6
Tebulos Mt'a Georgia/Rus. Fed. 113 G2
Tecalitlán Mex. 166 E5
Tecate Mex. 166 A1
Tece Turkey 107 B1
Techiman Ghana 120 C4
Tecka Arg. 178 B6
Tecklenburger Land reg. Germany 63 H2
Tecolutla Mex. 167 F4
Tecomán Mex. 166 E5
Tecoripa Mex. 166 C2
Técpan Mex. 168 D5
Tecuala Mex. 168 C4
Tecuci Romania 69 L2
Tecumseh MI U.S.A. 164 D3
Tecumseh NE U.S.A. 160 D3
Tedori-gawa r. Japan 92 C2
Tedzhen Turkm. see Tejen
Teec Nos Pos U.S.A. 159 I3
Teel Mongolia see Öndör-Ulaan
Teeli Rus. Fed. 98 E2
Tees r. U.K. 58 F4
Teeswater Canada 164 E1
Teet'lit Zhen N.W.T. Canada see Fort McPherson
Tefé r. Brazil 176 F4
Tefenni Turkey 69 M6
Tegal Jawa Indon. 85 E4
Tegel airport Germany 63 N2
Tegid, Llyn l. Wales U.K. see Bala Lake
Tegineneng Sumatera Indon. 84 D4

▶Tegucigalpa Hond. 166 [inset] I6
Capital of Honduras.

Teguidda-n-Tessoumt Niger 120 D3
Tehachapi U.S.A. 158 D4
Tehachapi Mountains U.S.A. 158 D4
Tehachapi Pass U.S.A. 158 D4
Tehek Lake Canada 151 M1
Teheran Iran see Tehrān
Tehery Lake Canada 151 M1
Téhini Côte d'Ivoire 120 C4
Tehoru Seram Indon. 83 D3

▶Tehrān Iran 110 C3
Capital of Iran.

Tehri India see Tikamgarh
Tehuacán Mex. 168 E5
Tehuantepec, Golfo de g. Mex. 167 G6
Tehuantepec, Gulf of Mex. see Tehuantepec, Golfo de
Tehuantepec, Istmo de isthmus Mex. 168 F5
Tehuitzingo Mex. 167 F5
Teide, Pico del vol. Canary Is 120 B2
Teifi r. U.K. 59 C6
Teignmouth U.K. 59 D8
Teixeira de Sousa Angola see Luau
Teixeiras Brazil 179 C3
Teixeira Soares Brazil 179 A4
Tejakula Bali Indon. 85 F5
Tejen Turkm. 111 F2
Tejo r. Port. 67 B4 see Tagus
Tejon Pass U.S.A. 158 D4
Tejupan, Punta pt Mex. 166 E5
Tekapo, Lake N.Z. 139 C6
Tekari-dake mt. Japan 93 E3
Tekax Mex. 167 H4
Tekeli Kazakh. 102 E3
Tekes Xinjiang China 98 C4
Tekes Kazakh. 98 C4
Tekes He r. China 98 C4
Tekiliktag mt. Xinjiang China 99 C5
Tekin Rus. Fed. 90 D2
Tekirdağ Turkey 69 L4
Tekka India 106 D2
Tekkali India 106 E2
Teknaf Bangl. 105 H5
Tekong Kechil, Pulau i. Sing. 87 [inset]
Teku Sulawesi Indon. 83 B3
Te Kuiti N.Z. 139 E4
Tel r. India 106 D1
Tela Hond. 166 [inset] I6
Télagh Alg. 67 F6
Telan i. Indon. 84 C2
Telanaipura Sumatera Indon. see Jambi
Telaquana Lake AK U.S.A. 148 I3
Telashi Hu salt l. Qinghai China 99 F6
Tel Ashqelon tourist site Israel 107 B4
Télataï Mali 120 D3
Tel Aviv-Yafo Israel 107 B3
Telč Czech Rep. 57 O6
Telchac Puerto Mex. 167 H4
Telegapulang Kalimantan Indon. 85 F3
Telekhany Belarus see Tsyelyakhany
Telêmaco Borba Brazil 179 A4
Telen r. Indon. 85 G2
Teleorman r. Romania 69 K3
Telertheba, Djebel mt. Alg. 120 D2
Telescope Peak U.S.A. 158 E3
Teles Pires r. Brazil 177 G5
Telford U.K. 59 E6
Telgte Germany 63 H3
Tel Hazor tourist site Israel 107 B3
Telica, Volcán vol. Nicaragua 166 [inset] I6
Telida AK U.S.A. 148 I3
Télimélé Guinea 120 B3
Teljo, Jebel mt. Sudan 108 C7
Telkwa Canada 150 E4
Tell Atlas mts Alg. see Atlas Tellien
Tell City U.S.A. 164 B5
Teller AK U.S.A. 148 F2
Tell es Sultan West Bank see Jericho
Tellicherry India 106 B4
Tellin Belgium 62 F4
Telloh Iraq 113 G5
Telluride U.S.A. 159 J3
Telmen Mongolia 94 D1
Telmen Nuur salt l. Mongolia 94 D1
Tel'novskiy Rus. Fed. 90 F2
Telo Indon. 84 B3
Teloloapán Mex. 167 F5
Telo Martius France see Toulon
Telpoziz, Gora mt. Rus. Fed. 51 R3
Telsen Arg. 178 C6
Telšiai Lith. 55 M9
Teltow Germany 63 N2
Teluk Anson Malaysia see Teluk Intan
Telukbajur Sumatera Indon. see Telukbayur
Telukbatang Kalimantan Indon. 85 E3
Telukbayur Sumatera Indon. 84 C3
Telukbetung Sumatera Indon. see Bandar Lampung
Teluk Cenderawasih, Taman Nasional nat. park Indon. 81 I7
Telukdalam Indon. 84 B2
Teluk Intan Malaysia 84 C1
Telukkuantan Sumatera Indon. 84 C3
Telukmelano Kalimantan Indon. 85 E3
Teluknaga Jawa Indon. 84 D4
Telukpakedai Kalimantan Indon. 85 E3
Temagami Lake Canada 152 F5
Temaju i. Indon. 85 E2
Temanggung Jawa Indon. 85 E4
Temapache Mex. 167 F4
Têmarxung Xizang China 99 E6
Temax Mex. 167 H4
Temba S. Africa 125 I3
Tembagapura Indon. 81 J7
Tembenchi r. Rus. Fed. 77 K3
Tembesi r. Indon. 84 C3
Tembilahan Sumatera Indon. 84 C3
Tembisa S. Africa 125 I4
Tembo Aluma Angola 123 B4
Teme r. U.K. 59 E6
Temecula U.S.A. 158 E5
Temenchula, Gora mt. Rus. Fed. 94 D1
Temengor, Tasik resr Malaysia 84 C1
Temerluh Malaysia 84 C2
Temiang, Bukit mt. Malaysia 84 C1
Teminabuan Indon. 81 I7
Temirtau Kazakh. 102 D1
Témiscamie r. Canada 153 G4
Témiscamie, Lac l. Canada 153 G4
Témiscaming Canada 152 F5
Témiscamingue, Lac l. Canada 152 F5
Témiscouata, Lac l. Canada 153 H5
Temiyang i. Indon. 84 D2
Temmes Fin. 54 N4
Temnikov Rus. Fed. 53 I5
Temora Australia 138 C5
Temósachic Mex. 166 D2
Tempe U.S.A. 159 H5
Tempe, Danau l. Indon. 83 A4
Tempe Downs Australia 135 F6
Tempelhof airport Germany 63 N2
Tempino Sumatera Indon. 84 C3
Temple MI U.S.A. 164 C1
Temple TX U.S.A. 161 D6
Temple Bar U.K. 59 C6
Temple Dera Pak. 111 H4
Templemore Ireland 61 E5
Templer Bank sea feature Phil. 82 B4
Temple Sowerby U.K. 58 E4
Templeton watercourse Australia 136 B4
Templin Germany 63 N1
Tempoal Mex. 167 F4
Tempué Angola 123 B5
Têmpung Qinghai China 94 D4
Temryuk Rus. Fed. 112 E1
Temryukskiy Zaliv b. Rus. Fed. 53 H7
Temuco Chile 178 B5
Temuka N.Z. 139 C7
Temuli China see Butuo
Tena Ecuador 176 C4
Tenabo Mex. 167 H4
Tenabo, Mount U.S.A. 158 E1
Tenakee Springs AK U.S.A. 149 N4
Tenali India 106 D2
Tenango México Mex. 167 F5
Tenasserim Myanmar 87 B4
Tenasserim r. Myanmar 87 B4
Tenbury Wells U.K. 59 E6
Tenby U.K. 59 C7
Tendaho Eth. 122 E2
Tende, Col de pass France/Italy 66 H4
Ten Degree Channel India 87 A5
Tendō Japan 91 F5
Tenedos i. Turkey see Bozcaada
Ténenkou Mali 120 C3
Ténéré reg. Niger 120 D3
Ténéré du Tafassâsset des. Niger 120 E2
Tenerife i. Canary Is 120 B2
Ténès Alg. 67 G5
Teng, Nam r. Myanmar 86 B3
Tengah, Kepulauan is Indon. 85 G4
Tengah, Sungai r. Sing. 87 [inset]
Tengahdai Flores Indon. 83 B5
Tengcheng China see Tengxian
Tengchong China 96 C3
Tengeh Reservoir Sing. 87 [inset]
Tenggarong Kalimantan Indon. 85 G3
Tengger Els Nei Mongol China 94 F4
Tengger Shamo des. Nei Mongol China 94 F4
Tenggul i. Malaysia 84 C1
Tengiz, Ozero salt l. Kazakh. 102 C1
Tengqiao China 97 F5
Tengréla Côte d'Ivoire 120 C3
Ten'gushevo Rus. Fed. 53 I5
Tengxian China 97 F4
Tengxian Shandong China see Tengzhou
Tengzhou Shandong China 95 I5
Teni India see Theni
Teniente Jubany research station Antarctica see Jubany
Tenille U.S.A. 163 D6
Tenkanyy, Khrebet ridge Rus. Fed. 148 D2
Tenkawa Japan 92 B4
Tenke Dem. Rep. Congo 123 C5
Tenkeli Rus. Fed. 77 P2
Tenkergynpil'gyn, Laguna lag. Rus. Fed. 148 C1
Tenkodogo Burkina Faso 120 C3
Ten Mile Lake salt flat Australia 135 C6
Ten Mile Lake Canada 153 K4
Tennant Creek Australia 134 F4
Tennessee r. U.S.A. 161 F4
Tennessee state U.S.A. 164 C5
Tennessee Pass U.S.A. 156 G5
Tennevoll Norway 54 J2
Tenojoki r. Fin./Norway 54 P1
Tenom Sabah Malaysia 85 F1
Tenosique Mex. 167 H5
Tenpaku Japan 92 C3
Tenri Japan 92 B4
Tenryū Nagano Japan 93 D3
Tenryū Shizuoka Japan 93 D4
Tenryū-gawa r. Japan 93 D3
Tenryū-Okumikawa Kokutei-kōen park Japan 93 D3
Tenteno Sulawesi Indon. 83 B3
Tenterden U.K. 59 H7
Tenterfield Australia 138 F2
Ten Thousand Islands U.S.A. 163 D7
Tentolomatinan, Gunung mt. Indon. 83 B2
Tentudia mt. Spain 67 C4
Tentulia Bangl. see Tetulia
Teocelo Mex. 167 F5
Teodoro Sampaio Brazil 178 F2
Teófilo Otôni Brazil 179 C2
Teomabal i. Phil. 82 C5
Teopisca Mex. 167 G5
Teotihuacán tourist site Mex. 167 F5
Tepa Maluku Indon. 83 D4
Tepache Mex. 166 C2
Te Paki N.Z. 139 D2
Tepatitlán Mex. 168 D4
Tepehuanes Mex. 166 D3
Tepeji Mex. 167 F5
Tepeköy Turkey see Karakoçan
Tepelenë Albania 69 I4
Tepelmeme de Morelos Mex. 167 F5
Tepelská vrchovina hills Czech Rep. 63 M5
Tepequem, Serra mts Brazil 169 L8
Tepianlangsat Kalimantan Indon. 85 G2
Tepic Mex. 168 D4
Te Pirita N.Z. 139 C6
Teplá r. Czech Rep. 63 M4
Teplice Czech Rep. 57 N5
Teplogorka Rus. Fed. 52 L3
Teploozersk Rus. Fed. 90 C2
Teploye Rus. Fed. 53 H5
Teploye Ozero Rus. Fed. see Teploozersk
Tepoca, Cabo c. Mex. 157 E7
Tepopa, Punta pt Mex. 166 B2
Tequila Mex. 168 D4
Tequisistlán Mex. 167 G5
Tequisquiapan Mex. 167 F4
Téra Niger 120 D3
Terai Japan 92 C2
Teram Kangri mt. China 99 B6
Teramo Italy 68 E3
Terang Australia 138 A7
Ter Apel Neth. 62 H2
Teratani r. Pak. 111 H4
Terbang Selatan i. Maluku Indon. 83 D4
Terbang Utara i. Maluku Indon. 83 D4
Tercan Turkey 113 F3
Terebovlya Ukr. 53 E6
Tere-Khol' Rus. Fed. 94 C1
Tere-Khol', Ozero l. Rus. Fed. 94 D1
Terektinskiy Khrebet mts Rus. Fed. 98 D2
Terekty Kazakh. 102 G2
Terengganu r. Malaysia 84 C1
Terengganu state Malaysia 84 C1
Terentang Kalimantan Indon. 85 E3
Terentang, Pulau i. Indon. 85 G3
Teresa Cristina Brazil 179 A4
Tereshka r. Rus. Fed. 53 J6
Teresina Brazil 177 J5
Teresina de Goias Brazil 179 B1
Teresita Col. 176 E3
Teresópolis Brazil 179 C3
Teressa Island India 87 A5
Terezinha Brazil 177 H3
Tergeste Italy see Trieste
Tergnier France 62 D5
Tergun Daba Shan mts Qinghai China 94 C4
Terhiyn Tsagaan Nuur l. Mongolia 94 D1
Teriberka Rus. Fed. 54 S2

Tering Xizang China 99 E7
Termez Uzbek. see Termiz
Termini Imerese Sicily Italy 68 E6
Términos, Laguna de lag. Mex. 167 H5
Termit-Kaoboul Niger 120 E3
Termiz Uzbek. 111 G2
Termo U.S.A. 158 C1
Termoli Italy 68 F4
Termonde Belgium see Dendermonde
Tern r. U.K. 59 E6
Ternate Maluku Indon. 83 C2
Ternate i. Maluku Indon. 83 C2
Terneuzen Neth. 62 D3
Terney Rus. Fed. 90 E3
Terni Italy 68 E3
Ternopil' Ukr. 53 E6
Ternopol' Ukr. see Ternopil'
Terpeniya, Mys c. Rus. Fed. 90 G2
Terpeniya, Zaliv g. Rus. Fed. 90 F2
Terra Alta U.S.A. 164 F4
Terra Bella U.S.A. 158 D4
Terrace Canada 150 D4
Terrace Bay Canada 152 D4
Terra Firma S. Africa 124 F3
Terråk Norway 54 H4
Terralba Sardinia Italy 68 C5
Terra Nova Bay Antarctica 188 H1
Terra Nova National Park Canada 153 L4
Terrazas Mex. 166 D2
Terre Adélie reg. Antarctica see Adélie Land
Terrebonne Bay U.S.A. 161 F6
Terre Haute U.S.A. 164 B4
Terrell TX U.S.A. 167 F1
Terre-Neuve prov. Canada see Newfoundland and Labrador
Terre-Neuve-et-Labrador prov. Canada see Newfoundland and Labrador
Terrero Mex. 166 D2
Terres Australes et Antarctiques Françaises terr. Indian Ocean see French Southern and Antarctic Lands
Terry U.S.A. 156 G3
Terschelling i. Neth. 62 F1
Terskey Ala-Too mts Kyrg. 98 B4
Terskiy Bereg coastal area Rus. Fed. 52 H2
Tertenia Sardinia Italy 68 C5
Terter Azer. see Tärtär
Teruel Spain 67 F3
Tervola Fin. 54 N3
Tes Mongolia 94 C1
Tešanj Bos.-Herz. 68 G2
Teseney Eritrea 108 E6
Tesha r. Rus. Fed. 53 I5
Teshekpuk Lake AK U.S.A. 148 I1
Teshio Japan 90 F3
Teshio-gawa r. Japan 90 F3
Tesiyn Gol r. Mongolia 94 C1
Teslin Y.T. Canada 149 N3
Teslin r. Y.T. Canada 149 N3
Teslin Lake B.C./Y.T. Canada 149 N3
Tesouras r. Brazil 179 A1
Tessalit Mali 120 D2
Tessaoua Niger 120 D3
Tessolo Moz. 125 L1
Test r. U.K. 59 F8
Testour Tunisia 68 C6
Tetachuck Lake Canada 150 E4
Tetas, Punta pt Chile 178 B2
Tete Moz. 123 D5
Tetehosi Indon. 84 B2
Te Teko N.Z. 139 F4
Teteriv r. Ukr. 53 F6
Teterow Germany 57 N4
Tetiyev Ukr. see Tetiyiv
Tetiyiv Ukr. 53 F6
Tetlin AK U.S.A. 149 L3
Tetlin Junction AK U.S.A. 149 L3
Tetlin Lake AK U.S.A. 149 L3
Tetlin National Wildlife Refuge nature res. AK U.S.A. 149 L3
Tetney U.K. 58 G5
Teton r. U.S.A. 156 F3
Tétouan Morocco 67 D6
Tetovo Macedonia 69 I3
Tetsyeh Mountain AK U.S.A. 149 K1
Tetuán Morocco see Tétouan
Tetulia Bangl. 105 G4
Tetulia sea chan. Bangl. 105 G5
Tetyukhe Rus. Fed. see Dal'negorsk
Tetyukhe-Pristan' Rus. Fed. see Rudnaya Pristan'
Tetyushi Rus. Fed. 53 K5
Teuco r. Arg. 178 D2
Teufelsbach Namibia 124 C2
Teul de González Ortega Mex. 166 E4
Teun vol. Maluku Indon. 83 D4
Teunom Sumatera Indon. 84 A1
Teunom r. Indon. 84 A1
Teutoburger Wald hills Germany 63 I2
Teuva Fin. 54 L5
Tevere r. Italy see Tiber
Teverya Israel see Tiberias
Teviot r. U.K. 60 G5
Te Waewae Bay N.Z. 139 A8
Tewah Kalimantan Indon. 85 F3
Te Waipounamu i. N.Z. see South Island
Tewane Botswana 125 H2
Tewantin Australia 137 F5
Teweh r. Indon. 85 F3
Tewkesbury U.K. 59 E7
Têwo Gansu China 94 E5
Têwo Sichuan China 94 E5
Texarkana AR U.S.A. 161 E5
Texarkana TX U.S.A. 161 E5
Texas Australia 138 E2
Texas state U.S.A. 161 D6
Texas City TX U.S.A. 167 G2
Texcoco Mex. 167 F5
Texel i. Neth. 62 E1
Texhoma U.S.A. 161 C4
Texoma, Lake U.S.A. 161 D5
Teyateyaneng Lesotho 125 H5
Teykovo Rus. Fed. 52 I4
Teza r. Rus. Fed. 52 I4
Teziutlán Mex. 167 F5
Tezpur India 105 H4
Tezu India 105 I4
Tha, Nam r. Laos 86 C2
Thaa Atoll Maldives see Kolhumadulu Atoll
Tha-anne r. Canada 151 M2
Thabana-Ntlenyana mt. Lesotho 125 I5
Thaba Nchu S. Africa 125 H5
Thaba Putsoa mt. Lesotho 125 H5
Thaba-Tseka Lesotho 125 I5
Thabazimbi S. Africa 125 H3
Thab Lan National Park Thai. 87 C4
Tha Bo Laos 86 C3
Thabong S. Africa 125 H4
Thabyedaung Myanmar 96 C4
Thade r. Myanmar 86 A3
Thagyettaw Myanmar 87 B4
Tha Hin Thai. see Lop Buri
Thai Binh Vietnam 86 D2
Thailand country Asia 86 C4
Thailand, Gulf of Asia 87 C5
Thai Muang Thai. 87 B5
Thai Nguyên Vietnam 86 D2
Thaj Saudi Arabia 110 C5
Thakèk Laos 86 D3
Thakurgaon Bangl. 105 G4
Thakurtola India 104 E5
Thal Germany 63 K4
Thala Tunisia 68 C7
Thalang Thai. 87 B5
Thalassery India see Tellicherry
Thal Desert Pak. 111 H4
Thale (Harz) Germany 63 L3
Thaliparamba India see Taliparamba
Thallon Australia 138 D2
Thalo Pak. 111 G4
Thamaga Botswana 125 G3
Thamar, Jabal mt. Yemen 108 G7
Thamarīt Oman 109 H6
Thame r. U.K. 59 F7
Thames r. Ont. Canada 155 K3
Thames r. Ont. Canada 164 D2
Thames N.Z. 139 E3
Thames est. U.K. 59 H7
Thames r. U.K. 59 H7
Thamesford Canada 164 E2
Thana India see Thane
Thanatpin Myanmar 86 B3
Thandwè Myanmar 86 A3
Thane India 106 B2
Thanet, Isle of pen. U.K. 59 I7
Thangoo Australia 134 C4
Thangra India 104 D2
Thanh Hoa Vietnam 86 D3
Thanjavur India 106 C4
Than Kyun i. Myanmar 87 B5
Thanlwin r. China/Myanmar see Salween
Thanlyin Myanmar 86 B3
Thaolintoa Lake Canada 151 L2
Tha Pla Thai. 86 C3
Thap Put Thai. 87 B5
Thapsacus Syria see Dibsī
Thap Sakae Thai. 87 B5
Tharabwin Myanmar 87 B4
Tharad Gujarat India 104 B4
Tharad Gujarat India 104 B4
Thar Desert India/Pak. 111 H5
Thargomindah Australia 138 A1
Tharrawaw Myanmar 86 A3
Tharthār, Buḥayrat ath l. Iraq 113 F4
Tharwāniyyah U.A.E. 110 D6
Thasos i. Greece 69 K4
Thatcher U.S.A. 159 I5
Thât Khê Vietnam 86 D2
Thaton Myanmar 86 B3
Thatta Pak. 111 G5
Thaungdut Myanmar 86 A1
Tha Uthen Thai. 86 D3
Thayatal, Nationalpark nat. park Austria/Czech Rep. 57 O5
Thayawthadangyi Kyun i. Myanmar 87 B4
Thayetmyo Myanmar 86 A3
Thazi Magwe Myanmar 86 A3
Thazi Mandalay Myanmar 105 I5
Thazzik Mountain AK U.S.A. 149 K2
The Aldermen Islands N.Z. 139 F3
Theba U.S.A. 159 G5
The Bahamas country West Indies 163 E7
Thebes Greece see Thiva
The Bluff Bahamas 163 E7
The Broads nat. park U.K. 59 I6
The Brothers is H.K. China 97 [inset]
The Calvados Chain is P.N.G. 136 F1
The Cheviot hill U.K. 58 E3
The Dalles U.S.A. 156 C3
Thedford U.S.A. 160 C3
The Entrance Australia 138 E4
The Faither stack U.K. 60 [inset]
The Fens reg. U.K. 59 G6
The Gambia country Africa 120 B3
Thegon Myanmar 86 A3
The Grampians mts Australia 137 C8
The Great Oasis oasis Egypt see Khārijah, Wāḥāt al
The Grenadines is St Vincent 169 L6
The Gulf Asia 110 C4

▶The Hague Neth. 62 E2
Seat of government of the Netherlands.

The Hunters Hills N.Z. 139 C7
Thekulthili Lake Canada 151 I2
The Lakes National Park Australia 138 C6
Thelon r. Canada 151 L1
The Lynd Junction Australia 136 D3
Themar Germany 63 K4
Thembalihle S. Africa 125 I4
The Minch sea chan. U.K. 60 C2
The Naze c. Norway see Lindesnes
The Needles stack U.K. 59 F8
Theni India 106 C4
Thenia Alg. 67 H5
Theniet El Had Alg. 67 H6
The North Sound sea chan. U.K. 60 G1
Theodore Australia 136 E5
Theodore Canada 151 K5
Theodore Roosevelt Lake U.S.A. 159 H5
Theodore Roosevelt National Park U.S.A. 160 C2
Theodosia Ukr. see Feodosiya
The Old Man of Coniston hill U.K. 58 D4
The Paps hill Ireland 61 C5
The Pas Canada 151 K4
The Pilot mt. Australia 138 D6
Thera i. Greece see Santorini
Thérain r. France 62 C5
Theresa U.S.A. 165 H1
Thermaïkos Kolpos g. Greece 69 J4
Thermopolis U.S.A. 156 F4
The Rock Australia 138 C5
Thérouanne France 62 C4
The Salt Lake salt flat Australia 137 C6

▶The Settlement Christmas I. 80 D9
Capital of Christmas Island.

The Sisters hill AK U.S.A. 148 G3
The Skaw spit Denmark see Grenen
The Skelligs is Ireland 61 B6
The Slot sea chan. Solomon Is see New Georgia Sound
The Solent strait U.K. 59 F8
Thessalon Canada 152 E5
Thessalonica Greece see Thessaloniki
Thessaloniki Greece 69 J4
The Storr hill U.K. 60 C3
Thet r. U.K. 59 H6
The Teeth mt. Palawan Phil. 82 B4
The Terraces hills Australia 135 C7
Thetford U.K. 59 H6
Thetford Mines Canada 153 H5
Thetkethaung r. Myanmar 86 A4
The Triangle mts Myanmar 86 B1
The Trossachs hills U.K. 60 E4
The Twins Australia 137 A6
Theva-i-Ra reef Fiji see Ceva-i-Ra

▶The Valley Anguilla 169 L5
Capital of Anguilla.

Thevenard Island Australia 134 A5
Thévenet, Lac l. Canada 153 H2
Theveste Alg. see Tébessa
The Wash b. U.K. 59 H6
The Weald reg. U.K. 59 H7
The Woodlands U.S.A. 161 E6
Thibodaux U.S.A. 161 F6
Thicket Portage Canada 151 L4
Thief River Falls U.S.A. 160 D1
Thiel Neth. see Tiel
Thiel Mountains Antarctica 188 K1
Thielsen, Mount U.S.A. 156 C4
Thielt Belgium see Tielt
Thiérache reg. France 62 D5
Thiers France 66 F4
Thiès Senegal 120 B3
Thika Kenya 122 D4
Thiladhunmathi Atoll Maldives 106 B5
Thiladunmathi Atoll Maldives see Thiladhunmathi Atoll
Thimbu Bhutan see Thimphu

▶Thimphu Bhutan 105 G4
Capital of Bhutan.

Thionville France 62 G5
Thira i. Greece see Santorini
Thirsk U.K. 58 F4
Thirty Mile Lake Canada 151 L2
Thiruvananthapuram India see Trivandrum
Thiruvannamalai India see Tiruvannamalai
Thiruvarur India 106 C4
Thiruvattiyur India see Tiruvottiyur
Thisted Denmark 55 F8
Thistle Creek Y.T. Canada 149 M3
Thistle Lake Canada 151 I1
Thityabin Myanmar 86 A2
Thiu Khao Luang Phrabang mts Laos/Thai. see Luang Phrabang, Thiu Khao
Thiva Greece 69 J5
Thívai Greece see Thiva
Thlewiaza r. Canada 151 M2
Thoa r. Canada 151 I2
Thô Chu, Đao i. Vietnam 87 C5
Thoen Thai. 96 C5
Thoeng Thai. 86 C3
Thohoyandou S. Africa 125 J2
Tholen Neth. 62 E3
Tholen i. Neth. 62 E3
Tholey Germany 62 H5
Thomas Hill Reservoir U.S.A. 160 E4
Thomas Hubbard, Cape Canada 147 I1
Thomaston CT U.S.A. 165 I3
Thomaston GA U.S.A. 163 C5
Thomastown Ireland 61 E5
Thomasville AL U.S.A. 163 C6
Thomasville GA U.S.A. 163 D6
Thommen Belgium 62 G4
Thompson Canada 151 L4
Thompson r. Canada 150 F5
Thompson U.S.A. 159 I2
Thompson r. U.S.A. 154 I4
Thompson Falls U.S.A. 156 E3
Thompson Peak U.S.A. 157 G6
Thompson's Falls Kenya see Nyahururu
Thompson Sound Canada 150 E5
Thomson U.S.A. 163 D5
Thon Buri Thai. 87 C4
Thonokied Lake Canada 151 I1
Thoothukudi India see Tuticorin
Thoreau U.S.A. 159 I4
Thorn Neth. 62 F3
Thorn Poland see Toruń
Thornaby-on-Tees U.K. 58 F4
Thornapple r. U.S.A. 164 C2
Thornbury U.K. 59 E7
Thorne U.K. 58 G5
Thorne U.S.A. 158 D2
Thornton r. Australia 136 B3
Thorold Canada 164 F2
Thorshavnfjella reg. Antarctica see Thorshavnheiane
Thorshavnheiane reg. Antarctica 188 C2
Thota-ea-Moli Lesotho 125 H5
Thôt Nôt Vietnam 87 D5
Thouars France 66 D3
Thoubal India 105 H4
Thourout Belgium see Torhout
Thousand Islands Canada/U.S.A. 165 G1
Thousand Lake Mountain U.S.A. 159 H2
Thousand Oaks U.S.A. 158 D4
Thousandsticks U.S.A. 164 D5
Thrace reg. Europe 69 L4
Thraki reg. Europe see Thrace
Thrakiko Pelagos sea Greece 69 K4
Three Gorges Reservoir China 101 J3
Three Hills Canada 150 H5
Three Hummock Island Australia 137 [inset]
Three Kings Islands N.Z. 139 D2
Three Oaks U.S.A. 164 B3
Three Pagodas Pass Myanmar/Thai. 86 B4
Three Points, Cape Ghana 120 C4
Three Rivers U.S.A. 164 C3
Three Rivers TX U.S.A. 167 F2
Three Sisters mt. U.S.A. 156 C3
Three Springs Australia 135 A7
Thrissur India see Trichur
Throckmorton U.S.A. 161 D5
Throssell, Lake salt flat Australia 135 D6
Throssel Range hills Australia 134 C5
Thrushton National Park Australia 138 C1
Thu Ba Vietnam 87 D5
Thubun Lakes Canada 151 I2
Thu Dâu Môt Vietnam 87 D5
Thuddungra Australia 138 D5
Thu Đuc Vietnam 87 D5
Thuin Belgium 62 E4
Thul Pak. 111 H4
Thulaythawāt Gharbī, Jabal hill Syria 107 D2
Thule Greenland 147 L2
Thun Switz. 66 H3
Thunder Bay Canada 147 J5
Thunder Bay b. U.S.A. 164 D1
Thunder Creek r. Canada 151 J5
Thüngen Germany 63 J5
Thung Salaeng Luang National Park Thai. 86 C3
Thung Song Thai. 87 B5
Thung Wa Thai. 84 B1
Thung Yai Naresuan Wildlife Reserve nature res. Thai. 86 B4
Thüringen land Germany 63 K3
Thüringer Becken reg. Germany 63 L3
Thüringer Wald mts Germany 63 K4
Thuringia land Germany see Thüringen
Thuringian Forest mts Germany see Thüringer Wald
Thurles Ireland 61 E5
Thurn, Pass Austria 57 N7
Thursday Island Australia 136 C1
Thurso U.K. 60 F2
Thurso r. U.K. 60 F2
Thurston Island Antarctica 188 K2
Thurston Peninsula i. Antarctica see Thurston Island
Thüster Berg hill Germany 63 J2
Thuthukudi India see Tuticorin
Thwaite U.K. 58 E4
Thwaites Glacier Tongue Antarctica 188 K1
Thyatira Turkey see Akhisar
Thyborøn Denmark 55 F8
Thymerais reg. France 62 B6
Tiancang Gansu China 94 D3
Tianchang China 97 H1
Tiancheng Gansu China 94 D4
Tiancheng China see Chongyang
Tianchi Gansu China 95 F4
Tianchi China see Lezhi
Tiandeng China 96 E4
Tiandong China 96 E4
T'ianet'i Georgia 113 G2
Tianfanjie China 97 H2
Tianguistengo Mex. 167 F4
Tianjin Tianjin China 95 I4
Tianjin mun. China 95 I4
Tianjun Qinghai China 94 D4
Tianlin China 96 E3
Tianma China see Changshan
Tianmen China 97 G2
Tianqiaoling China 90 C4
Tianquan China 96 D2
Tianshan Nei Mongol China 95 J3
Tian Shan mts China/Kyrg. see Tien Shan
Tianshui Gansu China 94 F5
Tianshuibu Gansu China 94 F4
Tianshuihai Aksai Chin 99 B6
Tianshuijing Gansu China 98 F4
Tiantai China 97 I2
Tiantaiyong Nei Mongol China 95 I3
Tiantang China see Yuexi
Tianyang China 96 E4
Tianyi Nei Mongol China see Ningcheng
Tianzhen Shandong China see Gaoqing
Tianzhen Shanxi China 95 H3
Tianzhou China see Tianyang
Tianzhu Gansu China 94 E4
Tianzhu Guizhou China 97 F3
Tiaret Alg. 67 G6
Tiassalé Côte d'Ivoire 120 C4
Tibabar Sabah Malaysia see Tambunan
Tibagi Brazil 179 A4
Tibal, Wādī watercourse Iraq 113 F4
Tibati Cameroon 120 E4
Tibba Pak. 111 H4
Tibé, Pic de mt. Guinea 120 C4
Tiber r. Italy 68 E4
Tiberias Israel 107 B3
Tiberias, Lake Israel see Galilee, Sea of
Tiber Reservoir U.S.A. 156 F2
Tibesti mts Chad 121 E2
Tibet aut. reg. China see Xizang Zizhiqu
Tibet, Plateau of Xizang China 99 D6
Tibi India 111 I4
Tibooburra Australia 137 C6
Tibrikot Nepal 105 E3
Tibro Sweden 55 I7
Tibur Italy see Tivoli
Tiburón, Isla i. Mex. 166 B2
Ticao i. Phil. 82 C3
Ticehurst U.K. 59 H7
Tichborne Canada 165 G1
Tichégami r. Canada 153 G4
Tîchît Mauritania 120 C3
Tichla W. Sahara 120 B2
Ticinum Italy see Pavia
Ticonderoga U.S.A. 165 I2
Ticul Mex. 167 H4
Tidaholm Sweden 55 H7
Tiddim Myanmar 86 A2
Tiden India 87 A6
Tidjikja Mauritania 120 B3
Tidore i. Maluku Indon. 83 C2
Tiechanggou Xinjiang China 98 D3
Tiefa Liaoning China see Diaobingshan
Tiel Neth. 62 F3
Tieli China 90 B3
Tieling Liaoning China 95 J3
Tielongtan Aksai Chin 99 B6
Tielt Belgium 62 D4
Tienen Belgium 62 E4
Tien Shan mts China/Kyrg. 88 D4
Tientsin Tianjin China see Tianjin
Tientsin mun. China see Tianjin
Tiên Yên Vietnam 86 D2
Tierp Sweden 55 J6
Tierra Amarilla U.S.A. 157 G5
Tierra Blanca Mex. 167 F5
Tierra Colorada Mex. 167 F5

▶Tierra del Fuego, Isla Grande de i. Arg./Chile 178 C8
Largest island in South America.

Tierra del Fuego, Parque Nacional nat. park Arg. 178 C8
Tiétar r. Spain 67 D4
Tiétar, Valle de valley Spain 67 D3
Tietê r. Brazil 179 A3
Tieyon Australia 135 F6
Tiffin U.S.A. 164 D3
Tiflis Georgia see T'bilisi
Tifore i. Maluku Indon. 83 C2
Tifton U.S.A. 163 D6
Tifu Buru Indon. 83 C3
Tiga i. Malaysia 85 F1
Tigalda Island AK U.S.A. 148 F5
Tigapuluh, Pegunungan mts Indon. 84 C3
Tiga Reservoir Nigeria 120 D3
Tigen Kazakh. 113 H1
Tīgh Āb Iran 111 F5
Tigheciului, Dealurile hills Moldova 69 M2
Tighina Moldova 69 M1
Tigiretskiy Khrebet mts Kazakh./Rus. Fed. 98 C2
Tigiria India 106 E1
Tignère Cameroon 120 E4
Tignish Canada 153 I5
Tigranocerta Turkey see Siirt
Tigre r. Venez. 176 F2
Tigre, Cerro del mt. Mex. 167 F4
Tigris r. Asia 113 G5
also known as Dicle (Turkey) or Nahr Dijlah (Iraq/Syria)
Tigrovaya Balka Zapovednik nature res. Tajik. 111 H2
Tiguidit, Falaise de esc. Niger 120 D3
Tīh, Gebel el plat. Egypt see Tīh, Jabal at
Tīh, Jabal at plat. Egypt 107 A5
Tihāmat 'Asīr reg. Saudi Arabia 100 D4
Tihuatlán Mex. 167 F4
Tijuana Mex. 166 A1
Tikal tourist site Guat. 167 H5
Tikal, Parque Nacional nat. park Guat. 167 H5
Tikamgarh India 104 D4
Tikanlik Xinjiang China 98 D4
Tikchik Lake AK U.S.A. 148 H4
Tikhoretsk Rus. Fed. 53 I7
Tikhvin Rus. Fed. 52 G4
Tikhvinskaya Gryada ridge Rus. Fed. 52 G4
Tiki Basin sea feature S. Pacific Ocean 187 L7
Tikokino N.Z. 139 F4
Tikopia i. Solomon Is 133 G3
Tikrīt Iraq 113 F4
Tikse India 104 D2
Tikshozero, Ozero l. Rus. Fed. 54 R3
Tiksi Rus. Fed. 77 N2
Tila r. Nepal 99 C7
Tiladummati Atoll Maldives see Thiladhunmathi Atoll
Tilaiya Reservoir India 105 F4
Tilamuta Sulawesi Indon. 83 B2
Tilbeşar Ovasi plain Turkey 107 C1
Tilbooroo Australia 138 B1
Tilburg Neth. 62 F3
Tilbury Canada 164 D2
Tilbury U.K. 59 H7
Tilcara Arg. 178 C2
Tilcha Creek watercourse Australia 137 C6
Tilden U.S.A. 161 D6
Tilemsès Niger 120 D3
Tilemsi, Vallée du watercourse Mali 120 D3
Tilhar India 104 D4
Tilimsen Alg. see Tlemcen
Tilin Myanmar 86 A2
Tillabéri Niger 120 D3
Tillamook U.S.A. 156 C3
Tillanchong Island India 87 A5
Tillia Niger 120 D3
Tillicoultry U.K. 60 F4
Tillsonburg Canada 164 E2
Tillyfourie U.K. 60 G3
Tilonia India 111 I5
Tilos i. Greece 69 L6
Tilothu India 105 F4
Tilpa Australia 138 B3
Tilsit Rus. Fed. see Sovetsk
Tilt r. U.K. 60 F4
Tilton IL U.S.A. 164 B3
Tilton NH U.S.A. 165 J2
Tilu, Bukit mt. Indon. 83 B3
Tim Rus. Fed. 53 H6
Tīmā Egypt 108 D4
Timah, Bukit hill Sing. 87 [inset]
Timakara i. India 106 B4
Timanskiy Kryazh ridge Rus. Fed. 52 K2
Timar Turkey 113 F3
Timaru N.Z. 139 C7
Timashevsk Rus. Fed. 53 H7
Timashevskaya Rus. Fed. see Timashevsk
Timbalier Bay LA U.S.A. 167 H2
Timbedgha Mauritania 120 C3
Timber Creek Australia 132 D3
Timber Mountain U.S.A. 158 E3
Timberville U.S.A. 165 F4
Timbuktu Mali 120 C3
Timbun Mata i. Malaysia 85 G1
Timétrine reg. Mali 120 C3
Timiaouine Alg. 120 D2
Timimoun Alg. 64 E6
Timirist, Râs pt Mauritania 120 B3
Timiskaming, Lake Canada see Témiscamingue, Lac
Timişoara Romania 69 I2
Timmins Canada 152 E4
Timms Hill hill U.S.A. 160 F2
Timon Brazil 177 J5
Timor i. Indon. 83 C5
Timor Sea Australia/Indon. 132 C3
Timor Timur country Asia see East Timor
Timpaus i. Indon. 83 C3
Timperley Range hills Australia 135 C6
Timrå Sweden 54 J5
Tîn, Ra's at pt Libya 112 A4
Ëina, Khalîg el b. Egypt see Ţīnah, Khalīj aţ
Tīnah Syria 107 D1
Ţīnah, Khalīj aţ b. Egypt 107 A4
Tin Can Bay Australia 137 F5
Tindivanam India 106 C3
Tindouf Alg. 64 C6
Ti-n-Essako Mali 120 D3
Tinggi i. Malaysia 84 D2
Tingha Australia 138 E2
Tingis Morocco see Tangier
Tingo María Peru 176 C5
Tingréla Côte d'Ivoire see Tengréla
Tingri Xizang China 99 D7
Tingsryd Sweden 55 I8
Tingvoll Norway 54 F5
Tingwall U.K. 60 F1
Tingzhou China see Changting
Tinharé, Ilha de i. Brazil 179 D1
Tinh Gia Vietnam 86 D3
Tinian i. N. Mariana Is 81 L4
Tini Heke is N.Z. see Snares Islands
Tinjar r. Malaysia 85 F2
Tinjil i. Indon. 84 D4
Tinnelvelly India see Tirunelveli
Tinogasta Arg. 178 C3
Tinompo Sulawesi Indon. 83 B2
Tinos Greece 69 K6
Tinos i. Greece 69 K6
Tinqueux France 62 D5
Tinrhert, Hamada de Alg. 120 D2
Tinsukia India 105 H4
Tintagel U.K. 59 C8
Ëinţâne Mauritania 120 B3
Tintina Arg. 178 D3
Tintinara Australia 137 C7
Tioga U.S.A. 160 C1
Tioman i. Malaysia 84 D2
Tionesta U.S.A. 164 F3
Tionesta Lake U.S.A. 164 F3
Tipasa Alg. 67 H5
Tiphsah Syria see Dibsī
Tipitapa Nicaragua 166 [inset] I6
Tipperary Ireland 61 D5
Tiptala Bhanjyang pass Nepal 99 D8
Tipton CA U.S.A. 158 D3
Tipton IA U.S.A. 160 F3
Tipton IN U.S.A. 164 B3
Tipton MO U.S.A. 160 E4
Tipton, Mount U.S.A. 159 F4
Tiptop U.S.A. 164 E5
Tip Top Hill hill Canada 152 D4
Tiptree U.K. 59 H7
Tiptur India 106 C3
Tipturi India see Tiptur
Tiquisate Guat. 167 H6
Tiracambu, Serra do hills Brazil 177 I4
Tirah reg. Pak. 111 H3

▶Tirana Albania 69 H4
Capital of Albania.

Tiranë Albania see Tirana
Tirano Italy 68 D1
Tirari Desert Australia 137 B5
Tiraspol Moldova 69 M1
Tiraz Mountains Namibia 124 C4
Tire Turkey 69 L5
Tirebolu Turkey 113 E2
Tiree i. U.K. 60 C4
Tîrgovişte Romania see Târgovişte
Tîrgu Jiu Romania see Târgu Jiu
Tîrgu Mureş Romania see Târgu Mureş
Tîrgu Neamţ Romania see Târgu Neamţ
Tîrgu Secuiesc Romania see Târgu Secuiesc
Tiri Pak. 111 G4
Tirich Mir mt. Pak. 111 H2
Tirlemont Belgium see Tienen
Tirna r. India 106 C2
Tîrnăveni Romania see Târnăveni
Tírnavos Greece see Tyrnavos
Tiros Brazil 179 B2
Tirourda, Col de pass Alg. 67 I5
Tirreno, Mare sea France/Italy see Tyrrhenian Sea
Tirso r. Sardinia Italy 68 C5
Tirthahalli India 106 B3
Tiruchchendur India 106 C4
Tiruchchirappalli India 106 C4
Tiruchengodu India 106 C4
Tirunelveli India 106 C4
Tirupati India 106 C3
Tiruppattur Tamil Nadu India 106 C3
Tiruppattur Tamil Nadu India 106 C4
Tiruppur India 106 C4
Tiruttani India 106 C3
Tirutturaippundi India 106 C4
Tiruvallur India 106 C3
Tiruvannamalai India 106 C3
Tiruvottiyur India 106 D3
Tiru Well Australia 134 D5
Tisa r. Serbia 69 I2
also known as Tisza (Hungary) or Tysa (Ukraine)
Tisdale Canada 151 J4
Tishomingo U.S.A. 161 D5
Ţisīyah Syria 107 C3
Tissemsilt Alg. 67 G6
Tista r. India 99 E8
Tisza r. Hungary see Tisa
Titabar Assam India 99 F8
Titaluk r. AK U.S.A. 148 I1
Titalya Bangl. see Tetulia
Titan Dome ice feature Antarctica 188 H1
Titao Burkina Faso 120 C3
Tit-Ary Rus. Fed. 77 N2
Titawin Morocco see Tétouan
Titicaca, Lago Bol./Peru see Titicaca, Lake

▶Titicaca, Lake Bol./Peru 176 E7
Largest lake in South America.

Titi Islands N.Z. 139 A8
Titiea mt. N.Z. see Aspiring, Mount
Titlagarh India 106 D1
Titograd Montenegro see Podgorica
Titova Mitrovica Kosovo see Mitrovicë
Titovo Užice Serbia see Užice
Titovo Velenje Slovenia see Velenje
Titov Veles Macedonia see Veles
Titov Vrbas Serbia see Vrbas
Ti Tree Australia 134 F5
Titu Romania 69 K2
Titusville FL U.S.A. 163 D6
Titusville PA U.S.A. 164 F3
Tiu Chung Chau i. H.K. China 97 [inset]
Tiumpain, Rubha an hd U.K. see Tiumpan Head
Tiumpan Head hd U.K. 60 C2
Tiva watercourse Kenya 122 D4
Tivari India 104 C4
Tiverton Canada 164 E1
Tiverton U.K. 59 D8
Tivoli Italy 68 E4
Ţīwī Oman 110 E6
Tiwi Aboriginal Land res. N.T. Australia 83 D5
Tiworo, Selat sea chan. Indon. 83 B4
Tixtla Mex. 167 F5
Ti-ywa Myanmar 87 B4
Tizi El Arba hill Alg. 67 H5
Tizimín Mex. 167 H4

Tizi N'Kouilal *pass* Alg. 67 I5
Tizi Ouzou Alg. 67 I5
Tiznap He *r.* China 99 B5
Tiznit Morocco 120 C2
Tizoc Mex. 166 E3
Tiztoutine Morocco 67 E6
Tjaneni Swaziland 125 J3
Tjappsåive Sweden 54 K4
Tjeukemeer *l.* Neth. 62 F2
Tjirebon *Jawa* Indon. *see* Cirebon
Tjolotjo Zimbabwe *see* Tsholotsho
Tjorhom Norway 55 E7
Tkibuli Georgia *see* Tqibuli
Tlacotalpán Mex. 167 G5
Tlacotepec, Cerro *mt.* Mex. 167 E5
Tlahualilo Mex. 166 E3
Tlalnepantla Mex. 167 F5
Tlancualpican Mex. 167 F5
Tlapa Mex. 167 F5
Tlapacoyan Mex. 167 F5
Tlaxcala Mex. 168 E5
Tlaxcala *state* Mex. 167 F5
Tlaxco Mex. 167 F5
Tlaxiaco Mex. 167 F5
Tl'ell *B.C.* Canada 149 O5
Tlemcen Alg. 67 F6
Tlhakalatlou S. Africa 124 F5
Tlholong S. Africa 125 I5
Tlokweng Botswana 125 G3
Tlyarata Rus. Fed. 113 G2
Tnekveyem *r.* Rus. Fed. 148 B2
To *r.* Myanmar 86 B3
Toad *r.* Canada 150 E3
Toad River Canada 150 E3
Toagel Mlungui Palau 82 [inset]
Toamasina Madag. 123 E5
Toana *mts* U.S.A. 159 F1
Toano U.S.A. 165 G5
Toa Payoh Sing. 87 [inset]
Toba China 96 C2
Toba Japan 92 C4
Toba, Danau *l.* Indon. 84 B2
Toba, Lake Indon. *see* Toba, Danau
Toba and Kakar Ranges *mts* Pak. 111 G4
Toba Gargaji Pak. 111 I4
Tobago *i.* Trin. and Tob. 169 L6
Tobar an Choire Ireland *see* Tobercurry
Tobelo *Halmahera* Indon. 83 C2
Tobercurry Ireland 61 D3
Tobermorey Australia 136 B4
Tobermory Australia 138 A1
Tobermory Canada 164 E1
Tobermory U.K. 60 C4
Tobi *i.* Palau 81 I6
Tobin, Lake *salt flat* Australia 134 D5
Tobin, Mount U.S.A. 158 E1
Tobin Lake Canada 151 K4
Tobin Lake *l.* Canada 151 K4
Tobishima Japan 92 C3
Tobi-shima *i.* Japan 91 E5
Toboali Indon. 84 D3
Tobol *r.* Kazakh./Rus. Fed. 100 F1
Tobol'sk Rus. Fed. 76 H4
Toboso *Negros* Phil. 82 C4
Tobruk Libya *see* Tubruq
Tobseda Rus. Fed. 52 L1
Tōbu Japan 93 E2
Tobyl *r.* Kazakh./Rus. Fed. *see* Tobol
Tobysh *r.* Rus. Fed. 52 K2
Tocache Nuevo Peru 176 C5
Tocantinópolis Brazil 177 I5
Tocantins *r.* Brazil 179 A1
Tocantins *state* Brazil 179 A1
Tocantinzinha *r.* Brazil 179 A1
Toccoa U.S.A. 163 D5
Tochi *r.* Pak. 111 H3
Tochigi Japan 93 F2
Tochigi *pref.* Japan 93 F2
Töcksfors Sweden 55 G7
Tocoa Hond. 166 [inset] I6
Tocopilla Chile 178 B2
Tocumwal Australia 138 B5
Tod, Mount Canada 150 G5
Toda Japan 93 F3
Todd *watercourse* Australia 136 A5
Todi Italy 68 E3
Todog *Xinjiang* China 98 C3
Todoga-saki *pt* Japan 91 F5
Todok *Xinjiang* China *see* Todog
Todos Santos Mex. 166 C4
Toe Head *hd* U.K. 60 B3
Tōei Japan 92 D3
Tofino Canada 150 E5
Toft U.K. 60 [inset]
Tofua *i.* Tonga 133 I3
Toga Japan 92 D2
Tōgane Japan 93 G3
Togatax *Xinjiang* China 99 C6
Togi Japan 92 C1
Togiak *AK* U.S.A. 148 G4
Togiak *r. AK* U.S.A. 148 G4
Togiak Bay *AK* U.S.A. 148 G4
Togiak Lake *AK* U.S.A. 148 H4
Togiak National Wildlife Refuge *nature res. AK* U.S.A. 148 G4
Togian *i.* Indon. 83 B3
Togian, Kepulauan *is* Indon. 83 B3
Togliatti Rus. Fed. *see* Tol'yatti
Togo *country* Africa 120 D4
Tōgō *Aichi* Japan 92 D3
Tograsay He *r.* China 99 E5
Tögrög *Hovd* Mongolia *see* Manhan
Tögrög Mongolia 94 E2
Togrog Ul *Nei Mongol* China 95 H3
Togtoh *Nei Mongol* China 95 G3
Togton He *r.* China 99 F6
Togura Japan 93 E2
Tohatchi U.S.A. 159 I4
Tohenbatu *mt.* Malaysia 85 F2
Tohoku Japan 92 C3
Toholampi Fin. 54 N5
Tohom *Nei Mongol* China 94 F3
Töhöm Mongolia *see* Mandah
Tohono O'Odham (Papago) Indian Reservation *res. AZ* U.S.A. 166 B1
Toi *Shizuoka* Japan 93 E4
Toiba *Xizang* China 99 E7
Toibalewe India 87 A5
Toide Japan 92 C2
Toijala Fin. 55 M6
Toili *Sulawesi* Indon. 83 B3
Toi-misaki *pt* Japan 91 C7
Toin Japan 92 C3
Toineke *Timor* Indon. 83 C5
Toivakka Fin. 54 O5
Toiyabe Range *mts* U.S.A. 158 E2
Toja *Sulawesi* Indon. 83 B3
Tojikiston *country* Asia *see* Tajikistan
Tōjō *Hyōgo* Japan 92 B4
Tok *AK* U.S.A. 149 L3
Tōkai *Aichi* Japan 92 C3
Tōkai *Ibaraki* Japan 93 G2
Tokala, Gunung *mt.* Indon. 83 B3
Tōkamachi Japan 93 E1
Tokar Sudan 108 E6
Tokara-rettō *is* Japan 91 C7
Tokarevka Kazakh. 98 A2
Tokarevka Rus. Fed. 53 I6
Tokat Turkey 112 E2
Tŏkchŏk-to *i.* S. Korea 91 B5
Tokdo *i.* N. Pacific Ocean *see* Liancourt Rocks

▶Tokelau *terr.* S. Pacific Ocean 133 I2
New Zealand Overseas Territory.

Toki Japan 92 D3
Tokigawa Japan 93 F2
Toki-gawa *r.* Japan 92 C3
Tokkuztara *Xinjiang* China *see* Gongliu
Toklat *AK* U.S.A. 149 J2
Toklat *r. AK* U.S.A. 149 J2
Tokmak Kyrg. *see* Tokmok
Tokmak Ukr. 53 G7
Tokmok Kyrg. 102 E3
Tokomaru Bay N.Z. 139 G4
Tokoname Japan 92 C4
Tokoroa N.Z. 139 E4
Tokorozawa Japan 93 F3
Tokoza S. Africa 125 I4
Toksook Bay *AK* U.S.A. 148 F3
Toksu *Xinjiang* China *see* Xinhe
Toksun *Xinjiang* China 98 E4
Tok-tō *i.* N. Pacific Ocean *see* Liancourt Rocks
Toktogul Kyrg. 102 D3
Tokto-ri *i.* N. Pacific Ocean *see* Liancourt Rocks
Tokty Kazakh. 98 C3
Tokur Rus. Fed. 90 D1
Tokushima Japan 91 D6
Tokuyama Japan 91 C6

▶Tōkyō Japan 93 F3
Capital of Japan. Most populous city in the world and in Asia.

Tōkyō *mun.* Japan 93 F3
Tōkyō-wan *b.* Japan 93 F3
Tokyrau *watercourse* Kazakh. 98 A3
Tokzār Afgh. 111 G3
Tolaga Bay N.Z. 139 G4
Tôlañaro Madag. 123 E6
Tolbo Mongolia 94 B1
Tolbukhin Bulg. *see* Dobrich
Tolbuzino Rus. Fed. 90 B1
Tolé Panama 166 [inset] J7
Tole Bi Kazakh. 98 A4
Toledo Brazil 178 F2
Toledo Spain 67 D4
Toledo *IA* U.S.A. 160 E3
Toledo *OH* U.S.A. 164 D3
Toledo *OR* U.S.A. 156 C3
Toledo, Montes de *mts* Spain 67 D4
Toledo Bend Reservoir U.S.A. 161 E6
Toletum Spain *see* Toledo
Toli *Xinjiang* China 98 C3
Toliara Madag. 123 E6
Tolitoli *Sulawesi* Indon. 83 B2
Tol'ka Rus. Fed. 76 J3
Tolleson U.S.A. 159 G5
Tollimarjon Uzbek. 111 G2
Tolmachevo Rus. Fed. 55 P7
Tolo Dem. Rep. Congo 122 B4
Toloa Creek Hond. 166 [inset] I6
Tolo Channel *H.K.* China 97 [inset]
Tolochin Belarus *see* Talachyn
Tolo Harbour *b. H.K.* China 97 [inset]
Tolonuu *i. Maluku* Indon. 83 D2
Tolosa France *see* Toulouse
Tolosa Spain 67 E2
Tolovana *r. AK* U.S.A. 149 J2
Toluca Mex. 168 E5
Toluca de Lerdo Mex. *see* Toluca
Tol'yatti Rus. Fed. 53 K5
Tom' *r.* Rus. Fed. 90 B2
Tomaga-shima *i.* Japan 92 B4
Tomagashima-suidō *sea chan.* Japan 92 A4
Tomah U.S.A. 160 F3
Tomakomai Japan 90 F4
Tomales U.S.A. 158 B2
Tomali Indon. 81 G7
Tomamae Japan 90 F3
Tomani *Sabah* Malaysia 85 F1
Tomanivi *mt.* Fiji 133 H3
Tomar Brazil 176 F4
Tomar Port. 67 B4
Tomari Rus. Fed. 90 F3
Tomarza Turkey 112 D3
Tomaszów Lubelski Poland 53 D6
Tomaszów Mazowiecki Poland 57 R5
Tomatin U.K. 60 F3
Tomatlán Mex. 168 C5
Tomazina Brazil 179 A3
Tombador, Serra do *hills* Brazil 177 G6
Tombigbee *r.* U.S.A. 163 C6
Tomboco Angola 123 B4
Tombouctou Mali *see* Timbuktu
Tombstone U.S.A. 157 F7
Tombua Angola 123 B5
Tom Burke S. Africa 125 H2
Tomdibuloq Uzbek. 102 B3
Tome Moz. 125 L2
Tomea *i.* Indon. 83 B4
Tomelilla Sweden 55 H9
Tomelloso Spain 67 E4
Tomi Romania *see* Constanța
Tomika Japan 92 C3
Tomingley Australia 138 D4
Tomini, Teluk *g.* Indon. 83 B3
Tominian Mali 120 C3
Tomintoul U.K. 60 F3
Tomioka *Gunma* Japan 93 E2
Tomisato Japan 93 G3
Tomislavgrad Bos.-Herz. 68 G3
Tomiura Japan 93 F3
Tomiyama *Aichi* Japan 93 D3
Tomiyama *Chiba* Japan 93 F3
Tomizawa Japan 93 E3
Tomkinson Ranges *mts* Australia 135 E6
Tømmerneset Norway 54 I3
Tommot Rus. Fed. 77 N4
Tomo *r.* Col. 176 E2
Tomobe Japan 93 G2
Tomóchic Mex. 166 D2
Tomorlog *Qinghai* China 99 E5
Tomort *mt* China 94 C3
Tomortei *Nei Mongol* China 95 H3
Tompira *Sulawesi* Indon. 83 B3
Tompkinsville U.S.A. 164 C5
Tompo *Sulawesi* Indon. 83 A3
Tom Price Australia 134 B5
Tomra *Xizang* China 99 D7
Tomsk Rus. Fed. 76 J4
Toms River U.S.A. 165 H4
Tomtabacken *hill* Sweden 55 I8
Tomtor Rus. Fed. 77 P3
Tomur Feng *mt.* China/Kyrg. *see* Jengish Chokusu
Tomuzlovka *r.* Rus. Fed. 53 J7
Tom White, Mount *AK* U.S.A. 149 L3
Tonalá Mex. 168 F5
Tonalá *Veracruz* Mex. 167 G5
Tonami Japan 92 C2
Tonantins Brazil 176 E4
Tonb-e Bozorg, Jazīreh-ye *i.* The Gulf *see* Greater Tunb
Tonb-e Küchek, Jazīreh-ye *i.* The Gulf *see* Lesser Tunb
Tonbridge U.K. 59 H7
Tondabayashi Japan 92 B4
Tondano *Sulawesi* Indon. 83 C2
Tønder Denmark 55 F9
Tondi India 106 C4
Tone *Gunma* Japan 93 F2
Tone *Ibaraki* Japan 93 G3
Tone *r.* U.K. 59 E7
Tone-gawa *r.* Japan 93 G3
Toney Mountain Antarctica 188 K1
Tonga *country* S. Pacific Ocean 133 I4
Tongaat S. Africa 125 J5
Tongariro National Park N.Z. 139 E4
Tongatapu Group *is* Tonga 133 I4

▶Tonga Trench *sea feature* S. Pacific Ocean 186 I7
2nd deepest trench in the world.

Tongbai Shan *mts* China 97 G1
Tongcheng China 97 H2
Tongcheng *Shandong* China *see* Dong'e
T'ongch'ŏn N. Korea 91 B5
Tongchuan *Shaanxi* China 95 G5
Tongchuan *Sichuan* China *see* Santai
Tongdao China 97 F3
Tongde *Qinghai* China 94 E5
Tongduch'ŏn S. Korea 91 B5
Tongeren Belgium 62 F4
Tonggu China 97 G2
Tongguan *Shaanxi* China 95 G5
Tongguzbasti *Xinjiang* China 98 C5
Tonggu Zui *pt* China 97 F5
Tonghae S. Korea 91 C5
Tonghai China 96 D3
Tonghe China 90 C3
Tonghua *Jilin* China 90 B4
Tonghua *Jilin* China 90 B4
Tongi Bangl. *see* Tungi
Tongjiang *Heilong.* China 90 D3
Tongjiang *Sichuan* China 96 E2
Tongking, Gulf of China/Vietnam 86 E2
Tongko *Sulawesi* Indon. 83 B3
Tongle China *see* Leye
Tongliang China 96 E2
Tongliao *Nei Mongol* China 95 J3
Tongling China 97 H2
Tonglu China 97 H2
Tongo Australia 138 A3
Tongo Lake *salt flat* Australia 138 A3
Tongquil *i.* Phil. 82 C5
Tongren *Guizhou* China 97 F3
Tongren *Qinghai* China 94 E5
Tongres Belgium *see* Tongeren
Tongsa Bhutan 105 G4
Tongshan *Jiangsu* China *see* Xuzhou
Tongshi *Hainan* China *see* Wuzhishan
Tongta Myanmar 86 B2
Tongtian He *r. Qinghai* China 96 C1 *see* Yangtze
Tongtian He *r. Qinghai* China 99 G6
Tongue U.K. 60 E2
Tongue *r.* U.S.A. 156 G3
Tongue of the Ocean *sea chan.* Bahamas 163 E7
Tongwei *Gansu* China 94 F5
Tongxin *Ningxia* China 94 F4
T'ongyŏng S. Korea 91 C6
Tongyu *Jilin* China 95 J2
Tongzhou *Beijing* China 95 I4
Tongzi China 96 E2
Tonhil Mongolia 94 C2
Tónichi Mex. 166 C2
Tonila Mex. 166 E5
Tonk India 104 C4
Tonkābon Iran 110 C2
Tonki Cape *AK* U.S.A. 149 J4
Tonkin *reg.* Vietnam 86 D2
Tônlé Repou *r.* Laos 87 D4
Tônlé Sab *l.* Cambodia *see* Tonle Sap

▶Tonle Sap *l.* Cambodia 87 C4
Largest lake in southeast Asia.

Tōno *Fukushima* Japan 93 G1
Tonopah *AZ* U.S.A. 159 G5
Tonopah *NV* U.S.A. 158 E2
Tonoshō *Chiba* Japan 93 G3
Tonosí Panama 166 [inset] J8
Tonota Botswana 123 C6
Tons *r.* India 99 B7
Tønsberg Norway 55 G7
Tonsina *AK* U.S.A. 149 K3
Tonstad Norway 55 E7
Tonto Creek *watercourse* U.S.A. 159 H5
Tonvarjeh Iran 110 E3
Tonzang Myanmar 86 A2
Tonzi Myanmar 86 A1
Toobeah Australia 138 D2
Toobli Liberia 120 C4
Tooele U.S.A. 159 G1
Toogoolawah Australia 138 F1
Toolik *r. AK* U.S.A. 149 J1
Tooma *r.* Australia 138 D6
Toompine Australia 138 B1
Toora Australia 138 C7
Tooraweenah Australia 138 D3
Toorberg *mt.* S. Africa 124 G7
Toowoomba Australia 138 E1
Tooxin Somalia 122 F2
Top Afgh. 111 H3
Topagoruk *r. AK* U.S.A. 148 I1
Top Boğazı Geçidi *pass* Turkey 107 C1

▶Topeka U.S.A. 160 E4
Capital of Kansas.

Topia Mex. 166 D3
Toplana, Gunung *mt. Seram* Indon. 83 D3
Töplitz Germany 63 M2
Topoľčany Slovakia 57 Q6
Topolobampo Mex. 166 C3
Topolovgrad Bulg. 69 L3
Topozero, Ozero *l.* Rus. Fed. 54 R4
Topsfield U.S.A. 162 H2
Tor Eth. 121 G4
Torahime Japan 92 C3
Toranggekuduk *Xinjiang* China 94 B2
Tor Baldak *mt.* Afgh. 111 G4
Torbalı Turkey 69 L5
Torbat-e Heydarīyeh Iran 110 E3
Torbat-e Jām Iran 111 F3
Torbay Bay Australia 135 B8
Torbert, Mount *AK* U.S.A. 148 I3
Torbeyevo Rus. Fed. 53 I5
Torch *r.* Canada 151 K4
Tordesillas Spain 67 D3
Tordesilos Spain 67 F3
Töre Sweden 54 M4
Torelló Spain 67 H2
Torenberg *hill* Neth. 62 F2
Toreo *Sulawesi* Indon. 83 B3
Toretam Kazakh. *see* Baykonyr
Torey Rus. Fed. 94 F1
Torgau Germany 63 M3
Torghay Kazakh. *see* Turgay
Torgun *r.* Rus. Fed. 53 J6
Torhout Belgium 62 D3
Toride Japan 93 G3
Torigakubi-misaki *pt* Japan 93 E1
Torigoe Japan 92 C2
Torii-tōge *pass* Japan 93 D3
Torii-tōge *pass* Japan 93 E2
Torikabuto-yama *mt.* Japan 93 E2
Torino Italy *see* Turin
Tori-shima *i.* Japan 91 F7
Torit Sudan 121 G4
Toriya Japan 92 C2
Torkamān Iran 110 B2
Torkovichi Rus. Fed. 52 F4
Tornado Mountain Canada 150 H5
Torneå Fin. *see* Tornio
Torneälven *r.* Sweden 54 N4
Torneträsk *l.* Sweden 54 K2
Torngat, Monts *mts* Canada *see* Torngat Mountains
Torngat Mountains Canada 153 I2
Torngat Mountains National Park Reserve Canada 153 J2
Tornio Fin. 54 N4
Toro Spain 67 D3
Toro, Pico del *mt.* Mex. 161 C7
Torobuku *Sulawesi* Indon. 83 B4
Torom Rus. Fed. 90 D1

▶Toronto Canada 164 F2
Capital of Ontario.

Toro Peak U.S.A. 158 E5
Toropets Rus. Fed. 52 F4
Tororo Uganda 122 D3
Toros Dağları *mts* Turkey *see* Taurus Mountains
Torphins U.K. 60 G3
Torquay Australia 138 B7
Torquay U.K. 59 D8
Torrance U.S.A. 158 D5
Torrão Port. 67 B4
Torre *mt.* Port. 67 C3
Torreblanca Spain 67 G3
Torre Blanco, Cerro *mt.* Mex. 166 B1
Torrecerredo *mt.* Spain 67 D2
Torre del Greco Italy 68 F4
Torre de Moncorvo Port. 67 C3
Torrelavega Spain 67 D2
Torremolinos Spain 67 D5

▶Torrens, Lake *imp. l.* Australia 137 B6
2nd largest lake in Oceania.

Torrens Creek Australia 136 D4
Torrent Spain 67 F4
Torrente Spain *see* Torrent
Torreón Mex. 166 E3
Torres Brazil 179 A5
Torres Mex. 166 C2
Torres del Paine, Parque Nacional *nat. park* Chile 178 B8
Torres Islands Vanuatu 133 G3
Torres Novas Port. 67 B4
Torres Strait Australia 132 E2
Torres Vedras Port. 67 B4
Torrevieja Spain 67 F5
Torrey U.S.A. 159 H2
Torridge *r.* U.K. 59 C8
Torridon, Loch *b.* U.K. 60 D3
Torrijos Spain 67 D4
Torrington Australia 138 E2
Torrington *CT* U.S.A. 162 F3
Torrington *WY* U.S.A. 156 G4
Torsa Chhu *r.* Bhutan 99 E8
Torsby Sweden 55 H6

▶Tórshavn Faroe Is 54 [inset]
Capital of the Faroe Islands.

Tortilla Flat U.S.A. 159 H5
To'rtko'l Uzbek. 102 B3
Törtköl Uzbek. *see* To'rtko'l
Tortoli *Sardinia* Italy 68 C5
Tortona Italy 68 C2
Tortosa Spain 67 G3
Tortuga, Laguna *l.* Mex. 167 F4
Tortuguero, Parque Nacional *nat. park* Costa Rica 166 [inset] J7
Tortum Turkey 113 F2
Toru-Aygyr Kyrg. 98 B4
Ţorūd Iran 110 D3
Torue *Sulawesi* Indon. 83 B3
Torugart, Pereval *pass* China/Kyrg. *see* Turugart Pass
Torul Turkey 113 E2
Toruń Poland 57 Q4
Tory Island Ireland 61 D2
Tory Sound *sea chan.* Ireland 61 D2
Torzhok Rus. Fed. 52 G4
Tosa Japan 91 D6
Tosbotn Norway 54 H4
Tosca S. Africa 124 F3
Tosca, Punta *pt* Mex. 166 C3
Toscano, Arcipelago *is* Italy 68 C3
Tosham India 104 C3
Tōshi-jima *i.* Japan 92 C4
To-shima *i.* Japan 93 F4
Tōshima-yama *mt.* Japan 91 F4

▶Toshkent Uzbek. 102 C3
Capital of Uzbekistan.

Tosno Rus. Fed. 52 F4
Toson Hu *l. Qinghai* China 94 D4
Tosontsengel Mongolia 94 D1
Tosontsengel Mongolia 94 E1
Tostado Arg. 178 D3
Tostedt Germany 63 J1
Tosya Turkey 112 D2
Totapola *mt.* Sri Lanka 106 D5
Tôtes France 62 B5
Tot'ma Rus. Fed. 52 I4
Totness Suriname 177 G2
Totolapan Mex. 167 F5
Totonicapán Guat. 167 H6
Totsuka Japan 93 F3
Totsukawa Japan 92 B4
Totsu-kawa *r.* Japan 92 B5
Tottenham Australia 138 C4
Totton U.K. 59 F8
Tottori Japan 91 D6
Touba Côte d'Ivoire 120 C4
Touba Senegal 120 B3
Toubkal, Jbel *mt.* Morocco 64 C5
Toubkal, Parc National du *nat. park* Morocco 64 C5
Touboro Cameroon 121 E4
Toudaohu *Nei Mongol* China 94 F4
Tougan Burkina Faso 120 C3
Touggourt Alg. 64 F5
Tougué Guinea 120 B3
Touil Mauritania 120 B3
Toul France 62 F6
Touliu Taiwan 97 I4
Toulon France 66 G5
Toulon U.S.A. 160 F3
Toulouse France 66 E5
Toumodi Côte d'Ivoire 120 C4
Toupai China 97 F3
Tourane Vietnam *see* Đa Nẵng
Tourcoing France 62 D4
Tourgis Lake Canada 151 J1
Tourlaville France 59 F9
Tournai Belgium 62 D4
Tournon-sur-Rhône France 66 G4
Tournus France 68 A1
Touros Brazil 177 K5
Tours France 66 E3
Tousside, Pic *mt.* Chad 121 E2
Toussoro, Mont *mt.* Cent. Afr. Rep. 122 C3
Toutai China 90 B3
Touwsrivier S. Africa 124 E7
Toužim Czech Rep. 63 M4
Töv *prov.* Mongolia 94 F2
Tovarkovo Rus. Fed. 53 G5
Tovil'-Dora Tajik. *see* Tavildara
Tovuz Azer. 113 G2
Towada Japan 90 F4
Towak Mountain *hill AK* U.S.A. 148 F3
Towanda U.S.A. 165 G3
Towaoc U.S.A. 159 I3
Towari *Sulawesi* Indon. 83 B4
Towcester U.K. 59 G6
Tower Ireland 61 D6
Towner U.S.A. 160 C1
Townes Pass U.S.A. 158 E3
Townsend U.S.A. 156 F3
Townsend, Mount Australia 138 D6
Townshend Island Australia 136 E4
Townsville Australia 136 D3
Towori, Teluk *b.* Indon. 83 B3
Towot Sudan 121 G4
Towr Kham Afgh. 111 H3
Towson U.S.A. 165 G4
Towuti, Danau *l.* Indon. 83 B3
Towyn U.K. *see* Tywyn
Toxkan He *r.* China 98 C4
Toy U.S.A. 158 D1
Toyah U.S.A. 161 C6
Toyama Japan 92 D2
Toyama *pref.* Japan 92 D2
Toyama-wan *b.* Japan 92 D1
Toyêma *Qinghai* China 94 E5
Toygunen Rus. Fed. 148 D2
Toyoake Japan 92 D3
Toyoda Japan 93 D4
Toyohashi Japan 92 D4
Toyokawa Japan 92 D4
Toyo-kawa *r.* Japan 92 D4
Toyonaka Japan 92 B4
Toyone Japan 92 D3
Toyono *Nagano* Japan 93 E2
Toyono *Ōsaka* Japan 92 B4
Toyooka *Hyōgo* Japan 92 A3
Toyooka *Nagano* Japan 93 D3
Toyooka *Shizuoka* Japan 93 D4
Toyoshina Japan 93 D2
Toyota Japan 92 D3
Toyoyama Japan 92 C3
Tozanlı Turkey *see* Almus
Tozê Kangri *mt. Xizang* China 99 C6
Tozeur Tunisia 64 F5
Tozi, Mount *AK* U.S.A. 149 J2
Tozitna *r. AK* U.S.A. 148 I2
Tqibuli Georgia 113 F2
Traben Germany 62 H5
Trâblous Lebanon *see* Tripoli
Trabotivište Macedonia 69 J4
Trabzon Turkey 113 E2
Tracy *CA* U.S.A. 158 C3
Tracy *MN* U.S.A. 160 E2
Trading *r.* Canada 152 C4
Traer U.S.A. 160 E3
Trafalgar U.S.A. 164 B4
Trafalgar, Cabo *c.* Spain 67 C5
Traffic Mountain *Y.T.* Canada 149 O3
Trail Canada 150 G5
Tràille, Rubha na *pt* U.K. 60 D5
Traill Island Greenland *see* Traill Ø
Traill Ø *i.* Greenland 147 P2
Trainor Lake Canada 150 F2
Trajectum Neth. *see* Utrecht
Trakai Lith. 55 N9
Tra Khuc, Sông *r.* Vietnam 86 E4
Trakiya *reg.* Europe *see* Thrace
Trakt Rus. Fed. 52 K3
Trakya *reg.* Europe *see* Thrace
Tralee Ireland 61 C5
Tralee Bay Ireland 61 C5
Trá Li Ireland *see* Tralee
Tramandaí Brazil 179 A5
Tramán Tepuí *mt.* Venez. 176 F2
Trá Mhór Ireland *see* Tramore
Tramore Ireland 61 E5
Tranås Sweden 55 I7
Trancas Arg. 178 C3
Trancoso Brazil 179 D2
Tranemo Sweden 55 H8
Tranent U.K. 60 G5
Trang Thai. 87 B6
Trangan *i.* Indon. 134 F1
Trangie Australia 138 C4
Trân Ninh, Cao Nguyên Laos 86 C3
Transantarctic Mountains Antarctica 188 H2
Trans Canada Highway Canada 151 H5
Transylvanian Alps *mts* Romania 69 J2
Transylvanian Basin *plat.* Romania 69 K1
Trapani *Sicily* Italy 68 E5
Trapezus Turkey *see* Trabzon
Trapper Creek *AK* U.S.A. 149 J3
Trapper Peak U.S.A. 156 E3
Trappes France 62 C6
Traralgon Australia 138 C7
Trashigang Bhutan *see* Tashigang
Trasimeno, Lago *l.* Italy 68 E3
Trasvase, Canal de Spain 67 E4
Trat Thai. 87 C4
Traunsee *l.* Austria 57 N7
Traunstein Germany 57 N7
Travaillant Lake *N.W.T.* Canada 149 O2
Travellers Lake *imp. l.* Australia 137 C7
Travers, Mount N.Z. 139 D6
Traverse City U.S.A. 164 C1
Traverse Peak *hill AK* U.S.A. 148 H2
Tra Vinh Vietnam 87 D5
Travis, Lake *TX* U.S.A. 167 F2
Travnik Bos.-Herz. 68 G2
Trbovlje Slovenia 68 F1
Tre, Hon *i.* Vietnam 87 E4
Treasury Islands Solomon Is 132 F2
Treat Island *AK* U.S.A. 148 I2
Trebbin Germany 63 N2
Trebević *nat. park* Bos.-Herz. 68 H3
Třebíč Czech Rep. 57 O6
Trebinje Bos.-Herz. 68 H3
Trebišov Slovakia 53 D6
Trebizond Turkey *see* Trabzon
Trebnje Slovenia 68 F2
Trebur Germany 63 I5
Tree Island India 106 B4
Trefaldwyn U.K. *see* Montgomery
Treffurt Germany 63 K3
Treffynnon U.K. *see* Holywell
Trefyclawdd U.K. *see* Knighton
Trefynwy U.K. *see* Monmouth
Tregosse Islets and Reefs Australia 136 E3
Treinta y Tres Uruguay 178 F4
Trelew Arg. 178 C6
Trelleborg Sweden 55 H9
Trélon France 62 E4
Tremblant, Mont *hill* Canada 152 G5
Trembleur Lake Canada 150 E4
Tremiti, Isole *is* Italy 68 F3
Tremont U.S.A. 165 G3
Tremonton U.S.A. 156 E4
Tremp Spain 67 G2
Trenance U.K. 59 B8
Trenary U.S.A. 162 C2
Trenche *r.* Canada 153 G5
Trenčín Slovakia 57 Q6
Trendelburg Germany 63 J3
Trêng Cambodia 87 C4
Trenggalek *Jawa* Indon. 85 E5
Trengganu *state* Malaysia *see* Terengganu
Trenque Lauquén Arg. 178 D5
Trent Italy *see* Trento
Trent *r.* U.K. 59 G5
Trento Italy 68 D1
Trenton Canada 165 G1
Trenton *FL* U.S.A. 163 D6
Trenton *GA* U.S.A. 163 C5
Trenton *KY* U.S.A. 164 B5
Trenton *MO* U.S.A. 160 E3
Trenton *NC* U.S.A. 163 E5
Trenton *NE* U.S.A. 160 C3

▶Trenton *NJ* U.S.A. 165 H3
Capital of New Jersey.

Treorchy U.K. 59 D7
Trepassey Canada 153 L5
Tres Arroyos Arg. 178 D5
Tresco *i.* U.K. 59 A9
Três Corações Brazil 179 B3
Tres Esquinas Col. 176 C3
Tres Forcas, Cabo *c.* Morocco *see* Trois Fourches, Cap des
Três Lagoas Brazil 179 A3
Três Marias, Represa *resr* Brazil 179 B2
Tres Picachos, Sierra *mts* Mex. 157 G7
Tres Picos, Cerro *mt.* Arg. 178 D5
Tres Picos, Cerro *mt.* Mex. 167 G5
Três Pontas Brazil 179 B3
Tres Puntas, Cabo *c.* Arg. 178 C7
Três Rios Brazil 179 C3
Tres Zapotes *tourist site* Mex. 167 G5
Tretten Norway 55 G6
Tretyy Severnyy Rus. Fed. *see* 3-y Severnyy
Treuchtlingen Germany 63 K6
Treuenbrietzen Germany 63 M2
Treungen Norway 55 F7
Treves Germany *see* Trier
Treviglio Italy 68 C2
Treviso Italy 68 E2
Trevose Head *hd* U.K. 59 B8
Tri An, Hồ *resr* Vietnam 87 D5
Triánda Greece *see* Trianta
Triangle U.S.A. 165 G4
Trianta Greece 69 M6
Tribal Areas *admin. div.* Pak. 111 H3

Tri Brata, Gora hill Rus. Fed. 90 F1
Tribune U.S.A. 160 C4
Tricase Italy 68 H5
Trichinopoly India see Tiruchchirappalli
Trichur India 106 C4
Tricot France 62 C5
Trida Australia 138 B4
Tridentum Italy see Trento
Trier Germany 62 G5
Trieste Italy 68 E1
Trieste, Golfo di g. Europe see Trieste, Gulf of
Trieste, Gulf of Europe 68 E2
Triglav mt. Slovenia 68 E1
Triglavski narodni park nat. park Slovenia 68 E1
Trikala Greece 69 I5
Trikkala Greece see Trikala

▶ Trikora, Puncak mt. Indon. 81 J7
2nd highest mountain in Oceania.

Trim Ireland 61 F4
Trincheras Mex. 166 C2
Trindade Brazil 179 A2
Trindade, Ilha da i. S. Atlantic Ocean 184 G7
Trinidad Bol. 176 F6
Trinidad Cuba 169 I4
Trinidad i. Trin. and Tob. 169 L6
Trinidad Uruguay 178 E4
Trinidad U.S.A. 157 G5
Trinidad country West Indies see Trinidad and Tobago
Trinidad and Tobago country West Indies 169 L6
Trinity U.S.A. 161 E6
Trinity r. CA U.S.A. 158 B1
Trinity r. TX U.S.A. 161 E6
Trinity Bay Canada 153 L5
Trinity Islands AK U.S.A. 148 I4
Trinity Range mts U.S.A. 158 D1
Trinkat Island India 87 A5
Trionto, Capo c. Italy 68 G5
Tripa r. Indon. 84 B2
Tripkau Germany 63 L1
Tripoli Greece see Tripoli
Tripoli Lebanon 107 B2

▶ Tripoli Libya 121 E1
Capital of Libya.

Trípolis Greece see Tripoli
Trípolis Lebanon see Tripoli
Tripunittura India 106 C4
Tripura state India 105 G5
Tristan da Cunha i. S. Atlantic Ocean 184 H8
Trisul mt. India 104 D3
Triton Canada 153 L4
Triton Island atoll Paracel Is 80 E3
Trittau Germany 63 K1
Trittenheim Germany 62 G5
Triunfo Hond. 166 [inset] I6
Trivandrum India 106 C4
Trivento Italy 68 F4
Trnava Slovakia 57 P6
Trobriand Islands P.N.G. 132 F2
Trochu Canada 150 H5
Trofors Norway 54 H4
Trogir Croatia 68 G3
Troia Italy 68 F4
Troisdorf Germany 63 H4
Trois Fourches, Cap des c. Morocco 67 E6
Trois-Ponts Belgium 62 F4
Trois-Rivières Canada 153 G5
Troitsko-Pechorsk Rus. Fed. 52 R3
Troitskoye Altayskiy Kray Rus. Fed. 88 E2
Troitskoye Khabarovskiy Kray Rus. Fed. 90 E2
Troitskoye Respublika Kalmykiya - Khalm'g-Tangch Rus. Fed. 53 J7
Troll 188 B2
Trollhättan Sweden 55 H7
Trombetas r. Brazil 177 G4
Tromelin, Île i. Indian Ocean 185 L7
Tromelin Island Micronesia see Fais
Tromen, Volcán vol. Arg. 178 B5
Tromie r. U.K. 60 E3
Trompsburg S. Africa 125 G6
Tromsø Norway 54 K2
Trona U.S.A. 158 E4
Tronador, Monte mt. Arg. 178 B6
Trondheim Norway 54 G5
Trondheimsfjorden sea chan. Norway 54 F5
Trongsa Bhutan see Tongsa
Trongsa Chhu r. Bhutan 99 E8
Troödos, Mount Cyprus 107 A2
Troödos Mountains Cyprus 107 A2
Troon U.K. 60 E5
Tropeiros, Serra dos hills Brazil 179 B1
Tropic U.S.A. 159 G3
Tropic of Cancer 161 B8
Tropic of Capricorn 136 G4
Trosh Rus. Fed. 52 L2
Trostan hill U.K. 61 F2
Trout r. B.C. Canada 150 F3
Trout r. N.W.T. Canada 150 G2
Trout Lake Alta Canada 150 H3
Trout Lake l. N.W.T. Canada 150 F2
Trout Lake l. Ont. Canada 151 M5
Trout Peak U.S.A. 156 F3
Trout Run U.S.A. 165 G3
Trouville-sur-Mer France 59 H9
Trowbridge U.K. 59 E7
Troy tourist site Turkey 69 L5
Troy AL U.S.A. 163 C6
Troy KS U.S.A. 160 E4
Troy MI U.S.A. 164 D2
Troy MO U.S.A. 160 F4
Troy MT U.S.A. 156 E2
Troy NH U.S.A. 165 I2
Troy NY U.S.A. 165 I2
Troy OH U.S.A. 164 C3
Troy PA U.S.A. 165 G3
Troyan Bulg. 69 K3
Troyes France 66 G2
Troy Lake U.S.A. 158 E4
Troy Peak U.S.A. 159 F2
Trstenik Serbia 69 I3
Truc Giang Vietnam see Bên Tre
Trucial Coast country Asia see United Arab Emirates
Trucial States country Asia see United Arab Emirates
Trud Rus. Fed. 52 G4
Trufanovo Rus. Fed. 52 J2

Trujillo Hond. 166 [inset] I6
Trujillo Peru 176 C5
Trujillo Spain 67 D4
Trujillo Venez. 176 D2
Trujillo, Monte mt. Dom. Rep. see Duarte, Pico
Truk is Micronesia see Chuuk
Trulben Germany 63 H5
Trumann U.S.A. 161 F5
Trumbull, Mount U.S.A. 159 G3
Trumon Sumatera Indon. 84 B2
Trundle Australia 138 C4
Truong Sa is S. China Sea see Spratly Islands
Truro Canada 153 J5
Truro U.K. 59 B8
Trusan Sarawak Malaysia 85 F1
Trusan r. Malaysia 85 F1
Truskmore hill Ireland 61 D3
Trus Madi, Gunung mt. Malaysia 85 G1
Trutch Canada 150 F3
Truth or Consequences U.S.A. 157 G6
Trutnov Czech Rep. 57 O5
Truva tourist site Turkey see Troy
Trypiti, Akra pt Kriti Greece see Trypiti, Akrotirio
Trypiti, Akrotirio pt Greece 69 K7
Trysil Norway 55 H6
Trzebiatów Poland 57 O3
Tsagaanburgad Bayan-Ölgiy Mongolia 94 B3
Tsagaannuur Dornod Mongolia see Halhgol
Tsagaan Nuur salt l. Mongolia 94 E2
Tsagaan-Olom Mongolia see Tayshir
Tsagaan-Ovoo Mongolia 95 H1
Tsagaan-Ovoo Mongolia see Nariynteel
Tsagaan-Uul Hövsgöl Mongolia 94 D1
Tsagaan-Üür Hövsgöl Mongolia 94 E1
Tsagan Aman Rus. Fed. 53 J7
Tsagan-Nur Rus. Fed. 53 J7
Tsaidam Basin basin China see Qaidam Pendi
Tsaka La Jammu and Kashmir/India 104 D2
Tsalenjikha Georgia 113 F2
Tsaratanana, Massif du mts Madag. 123 E5
Tsarevo Bulg. 69 L3
Tsaris Mountains Namibia 124 C3
Tsaritsyn Rus. Fed. see Volgograd
Tsaukaib Namibia 124 B4
Tsavo East National Park Kenya 122 D4
Tsavo West National Park Africa 122 D4
Tseel Mongolia 94 C2
Tsefat Israel see Zefat
Tselinograd Kazakh. see Astana
Tsengel Bayan-Ölgiy Mongolia 94 B1
Tsengel Mongolia see Tosontsengel
Tsenhermandal Mongolia 95 G2
Tsenogora Rus. Fed. 52 J2
Tses Namibia 124 D3
Tsetseg Mongolia 94 C2
Tsetsegnuur Mongolia see Tsetseg
Tsetseng Botswana 124 F2
Tsetserleg Arhangay Mongolia 94 E1
Tsetserleg Arhangay Mongolia 94 E2
Tsetserleg Mongolia 94 D1
Tshabong Botswana 124 F3
Tshane Botswana 124 E3
Tshela Dem. Rep. Congo 123 B4
Tshibala Dem. Rep. Congo 123 C4
Tshikapa Dem. Rep. Congo 123 C4
Tshing S. Africa 125 J3
Tshipise S. Africa 125 J2
Tshofa Dem. Rep. Congo 123 C4
Tshokwane S. Africa 125 J3
Tsholotsho Zimbabwe 123 C5
Tshootsha Botswana 124 E2
Tshuapa r. Dem. Rep. Congo 121 F5
Tshwane S. Africa see Pretoria
Tsiigehtchic N.W.T. Canada 149 N2
Tsil'ma r. Rus. Fed. 52 K2
Tsimlyansk Rus. Fed. 53 I7
Tsimlyanskoye Vodokhranilishche resr Rus. Fed. 53 I7
Tsinan Shandong China see Jinan
Tsineng S. Africa 124 F4
Tsinghai prov. China see Qinghai
Tsing Shan Wan H.K. China see Castle Peak Bay
Tsingtao Shandong China see Qingdao
Tsing Yi i. H.K. China 97 [inset]
Tsining Nei Mongol China see Jining
Tsiombe Madag. 123 E6
Tsiroanomandidy Madag. 123 E5
Tsitsihar Heilong. China see Qiqihar
Tsitsikamma Forest and Coastal National Park S. Africa 124 G8
Tsitsutl Peak Canada 150 E4
Tsivil'sk Rus. Fed. 52 J5
Tskhaltubo Georgia see Tsqaltubo
Ts'khinvali Georgia 113 F2
Tsna r. Rus. Fed. 53 I5
Tsnori Georgia 113 G2
Tsogt Mongolia 94 D2
Tsogt-Ovoo Mongolia 94 F3
Tsogttsetsiy Mongolia 94 F3
Tsokar Chumo l. India 104 D2
Tsolo S. Africa 125 I6
Tsomo S. Africa 125 H7
Tsqaltubo Georgia 113 F2
Tsu Japan 92 C4
Tsubata Japan 92 C2
Tsuchiura Japan 93 G2
Tsuchiyama Japan 92 C4
Tsuen Wan H.K. China 97 [inset]
Tsuga Japan 93 F2
Tsugarū-kaikyō strait Japan 90 F4
Tsuge Japan 92 C4
Tsugu Japan 92 D3
Tsukechi Japan 92 D3
Tsukigata Japan 90 F4
Tsukiyono Japan 93 F2
Tsukuba Japan 93 G2
Tsukude Japan 92 D4
Tsukui Japan 93 F3
Tsul-Ulaan Mongolia see Bayannuur
Tsumagoi Japan 93 E3
Tsumeb Namibia 123 B5
Tsumeki-zaki pt Japan 93 E4
Tsumis Park Namibia 124 C2
Tsumkwe Namibia 123 C5
Tsuna Japan 92 A4

Tsunan Japan 93 E1
Tsunega-misaki pt Japan 92 B3
Tsuru Japan 93 E3
Tsuruga Japan 92 C3
Tsuruga-wan b. Japan 92 B3
Tsurugi Japan 92 C3
Tsurugi-dake mt. Japan 92 D2
Tsurukhaytuy Rus. Fed. see Priargunsk
Tsuruoka Japan 91 E5
Tsushima Japan 92 C3
Tsushima is Japan 91 C6
Tsushima-kaikyō strait Japan/S. Korea see Korea Strait
Tsuyama Japan 91 D6
Tswaane Botswana 124 E2
Tswaraganang S. Africa 125 G5
Tswelelang S. Africa 125 G4
Tsyelyakhany Belarus 55 N10
Tsyp-Navolok Rus. Fed. 54 R2
Tsyurupyns'k Ukr. 69 O1
Tthedzeh Koe N.W.T. Canada see Wrigley
Tthenaagoo Canada see Nahanni Butte
Tua Dem. Rep. Congo 122 B4
Tua, Tanjung pt Indon. 84 D4
Tual Indon. 81 I8
Tuam Ireland 61 D4
Tuamotu, Archipel des is Fr. Polynesia see Tuamotu Islands
Tuamotu Islands Fr. Polynesia 187 K6
Tuân Giao Vietnam 86 C2
Tuangku i. Indon. 84 B2
Tuapse Rus. Fed. 112 E1
Tuaran Sabah Malaysia 85 G1
Tuas Sing. 87 [inset]
Tuath, Loch a' b. U.K. 60 C2
Tuba City U.S.A. 159 H3
Tubalai i. Maluku Indon. 83 D3
Tuban Jawa Indon. 85 F4
Tubarão Brazil 179 A5
Tubarjal Saudi Arabia 107 D4
Tubau Sarawak Malaysia 85 F1
Tubbataha Reefs Phil. 82 B4
Tubbergen Neth. 62 G2
Tübingen Germany 57 L6
Tubmanburg Liberia 120 B4
Tubod Mindanao Phil. 82 C4
Tubruq Libya 112 A4
Tubu r. Indon. 85 G2
Tubuai i. Fr. Polynesia 187 K7
Tubuai Islands Fr. Polynesia 187 J7
Tubutama Mex. 166 C2
Tucano Brazil 177 K6
Tucavaca Bol. 177 G7
Tüchen Germany 63 M1
Tuchheim Germany 63 M2
Tuchitua Y.T. Canada 149 O3
Tuchodi r. Canada 150 F3
Tuckerton U.S.A. 165 H4
Tucopia i. Solomon Is see Tikopia
Tucson U.S.A. 159 H5
Tucson Mountains U.S.A. 159 H5
Tuctuc r. Canada 153 J3
Tucumán Arg. see San Miguel de Tucumán
Tucumcari U.S.A. 161 C5
Tucupita Venez. 176 F2
Tucuruí Brazil 177 I4
Tucuruí, Represa resr Brazil 177 I4
Tudela Spain 67 F2
Tuder Italy see Todi
Tüdevtey Mongolia 94 D1
Tuela r. Port. 67 C3
Tuen Mun H.K. China 97 [inset]
Tuensang India 105 H4
Tufts Abyssal Plain sea feature N. Pacific Ocean 187 K2
Tugela r. S. Africa 125 J5
Tugidak Island AK U.S.A. 148 I4
Tuglung Xizang China 99 F7
Tuguan Maputi r. Indon. 83 A2
Tugubun Point Mindanao Phil. 82 D5
Tuguegarao Luzon Phil. 82 C2
Tugur Rus. Fed. 90 E1
Tugyl Kazakh. 98 D3
Tuhemberua Indon. 84 B2
Tujiabu China see Yongxiu
Tujuh, Kepulauan is Indon. 84 D3
Tujung Kalimantan Indon. 85 G2
Tukangbesi, Kepulauan is Indon. 83 B4
Tukarak Island Canada 152 F2
Tukituki r. N.Z. 139 F4
Tuklung AK U.S.A. 148 H4
Tuktoyaktuk N.W.T. Canada 149 N1
Tuktut Nogait National Park N.W.T./Nunavut Canada 149 Q1
Tuktuujaartuq N.W.T. Canada see Tuktoyaktuk
Tukums Latvia 55 M8
Tukung, Bukit mt. Indon. 85 F2
Tukuringra, Khrebet mts Rus. Fed. 90 B1
Tukuyu Tanz. 123 D4
Tula Tamaulipas Mex. 167 F4
Tula Rus. Fed. 53 H5
Tulach Mhór Ireland see Tullamore
Tulagt Ar Gol r. China 99 F5
Tulai Gansu China 99 F5
Tulai Nanshan mts China 94 D4
Tulai Shan mts China 94 D4
Tulak Afgh. 111 F3
Tulameen Canada 150 F5
Tula Mountains Antarctica 188 D2
Tulancingo Mex. 168 E4
Tulangbawang r. Indon. 84 D4
Tulare U.S.A. 158 D3
Tulare Lake Bed U.S.A. 158 D4
Tularosa N.M. U.S.A. 157 G6
Tularosa Mountains U.S.A. 159 I5
Tulasi mt. India 106 D2
Tulbagh S. Africa 124 D7
Tulcán Ecuador 176 C3
Tulcea Romania 69 M2
Tule r. U.S.A. 161 C5
Tuléar Madag. see Toliara
Tulehu Maluku Indon. 83 D3
Tulemalu Lake Canada 151 L2
Tule Mod Nei Mongol China 95 J2
Tulia U.S.A. 161 C5
Tulihe Nei Mongol China 95 J1
Tulita N.W.T. Canada 149 O2
Tulkarem West Bank see Ŧulkarm
Ŧulkarm West Bank 107 B3
Tulla Ireland 61 D5
Tullahoma U.S.A. 162 C5
Tullamore Australia 138 C4

Tullamore Ireland 61 E4
Tulle France 66 E4
Tulleråsen Sweden 54 I5
Tullibigeal Australia 138 C4
Tullos LA U.S.A. 167 G2
Tullow Ireland 61 F5
Tully Australia 136 D3
Tully r. Australia 136 D3
Tully U.K. 61 E3
Tulos Rus. Fed. 54 R5
Tulqarem West Bank see Ŧulkarm
Tulsa U.S.A. 161 E4
Tulsipur Nepal 105 E3
Tuluá Col. 176 C3
Tuluksak AK U.S.A. 148 G3
Tulūl al Ashāqif hills Jordan 107 C3
Tulum tourist site Mex. 167 I4
Tulun Rus. Fed. 88 I2
Tulungagung Jawa Indon. 85 E5
Tulu Welel mt. Eth. 122 D3
Tuma r. Nicaragua 166 [inset] I6
Tuma Rus. Fed. 53 I5
Tumahole S. Africa 125 H4
Tumain Xizang China 99 E6
Tumannyy Rus. Fed. 54 S2
Tumasik Sing. see Singapore
Tumasik Sing. see Singapore
Tumba Dem. Rep. Congo 122 C4
Tumba Sweden 55 J7
Tumba, Lac l. Dem. Rep. Congo 122 B4
Tumbangmiri Kalimantan Indon. 85 F3
Tumbangsamba Kalimantan Indon. 85 F3
Tumbangsenamang Kalimantan Indon. 85 F3
Tumbao Mindanao Phil. 82 D5
Tumbarumba Australia 138 D5
Tumbes Peru 176 B4
Tumbiscatío Mex. 166 E5
Tumbler Ridge Canada 150 F4
Tumby Bay Australia 137 B7
Tumcha r. Fin./Rus. Fed. 54 Q3
also known as Tuntsajoki
Tumd Youqi Nei Mongol China see Salaqi
Tumd Zuoqi Nei Mongol China see Qasq
Tumen Jilin China 90 C4
Tumen Shaanxi China 97 F1
Tumen r. China/N. Korea see Tumen
Tumereng Guyana 176 F2
Tumindao i. Phil. 82 B5
Tumkur India 106 C3
Tummel r. U.K. 60 F4
Tummel, Loch l. U.K. 60 F4
Tummin Rus. Fed. 90 F2
Tump Pak. 111 F5
Tumpah Kalimantan Indon. 85 F3
Tumpat Malaysia 84 C1
Tumpôr, Phnum mt. Cambodia 87 C4
Tumpu, Gunung mt. Indon. 83 B3
Tumputiga, Gunung mt. Indon. 83 B3
Tumshuk Uzbek. 111 G2
Tumu Ghana 120 C3
Tumucumaque, Parque Indígena do res. Brazil 177 G3
Tumucumaque, Serra hills Brazil 177 G3
Tumudibandh India 106 D2
Tumushuke Xinjiang China 98 C4
Tumut Australia 138 D5
Tuna Fin. 55 J6
Tuna Bay Mindanao Phil. 82 D5
Ṭunb al Kubrá i. The Gulf see Greater Tunb
Ṭunb aş Şughrá i. The Gulf see Lesser Tunb
Tunbridge Wells, Royal U.K. 59 H7
Tunceli Turkey 113 E3
Tunchang China 97 F5
Tuncurry Australia 138 F4
Tundun-Wada Nigeria 120 D3
Tunduru Tanz. 123 D5
Tunes Tunisia see Tunis
Tunga Nigeria 120 D4
Tungabhadra Reservoir India 106 C3
Tungawan Mindanao Phil. 82 C5
Tungi Bangl. 105 G5
Tungku Sabah Malaysia 85 G1
Tungla Nicaragua 166 [inset] I6
Tung Lung Island H.K. China 97 [inset]
Tungnaá r. Iceland 54 [inset]
Tungor Rus. Fed. 90 F1
Tung Pok Liu Hoi Hap H.K. China see East Lamma Channel
Tungsten (abandoned) N.W.T. Canada 149 O3
Tung Wan H.K. China 97 [inset]
Tuni India 106 D2
Tunica U.S.A. 161 F5

▶ Tunis Tunisia 68 D6
Capital of Tunisia.

Tunis, Golfe de g. Tunisia 68 D6
Tunisia country Africa 64 F5
Tunja Col. 176 D2
Tunkhannock U.S.A. 165 H3
Tunki Nicaragua 166 [inset] I6
Tunliu Shanxi China 95 H4
Tunnsjøen l. Norway 54 H4
Tunstall U.K. 59 I6
Tuntsa Fin. 54 P3
Tuntsajoki r. Fin./Rus. Fed. see Tumcha
Tuntutuliak AK U.S.A. 148 G3
Tununak AK U.S.A. 148 G3
Tunulic r. Canada 153 J2
Tunungayualok Island Canada 153 J2
Tunxi Anhui China see Huangshan
Tuodian China see Shuangbai
Tuo He r. China 95 I5
Tuojiang China see Fenghuang
Tuol Khpos Cambodia 87 D4
Tuoniang Jiang r. China 96 E3
Tuoputiereke Xinjiang China see Jeminay
Tuotuoheyan Qinghai China see Tanggulashan
Tüp Kyrg. 102 E3
Tupã Brazil 179 A3
Tupaciguara Brazil 179 A2
Tupanciretã Brazil 178 F3
Tupelo U.S.A. 161 F5
Tupik Rus. Fed. 89 L2
Tupinambarama, Ilha i. Brazil 177 G4
Tupiza Bol. 176 E8
Tupper Canada 150 F4
Tupper Lake U.S.A. 165 H1
Tupper Lake l. U.S.A. 165 H1

Tüpqaraghan Tübegi pen. Kazakh. see Mangyshlak, Poluostrov

▶ Tupungato, Cerro mt. Arg./Chile 178 C4
5th highest mountain in South America.

Tuqayyid well Iraq 110 B4
Tuquan Nei Mongol China 95 J2
Tuqu Wan b. China see Lingshui Wan
Tura Xinjiang China 99 D5
Tura India 105 G4
Tura Rus. Fed. 77 L3
Turabah Saudi Arabia 108 F5
Turakina N.Z. 139 E5
Turan Rus. Fed. 88 G2
Turana, Khrebet mts Rus. Fed. 90 C2
Turan Lowland Asia 102 A4
Turan Oypaty lowland Asia see Turan Lowland
Turan Pasttekisligi lowland Asia see Turan Lowland
Turan Pesligi lowland Asia see Turan Lowland
Turanskaya Nizmennost' lowland Asia see Turan Lowland
Ŧuraq al 'Ilab hills Syria 107 D3
Turar Ryskulov Kazakh. 102 D3
Tura-Ryskulova Kazakh. see Turar Ryskulov
Ŧurayf Saudi Arabia 107 D4
Turba Estonia 55 N7
Turbat Pak. 111 F5
Turbo Col. 176 C2
Turda Romania 69 J1
Türeh Iran 110 C3
Turfan Xinjiang China see Turpan
Turfan Depression China see Turpan Pendi
Turgay Kazakh. 102 B2
Turgayskaya Dolina valley Kazakh. 102 B2
Türgen Uul mt. Mongolia 94 B1
Türgen Uul mts Mongolia 94 B1
Türgovishte Bulg. 69 L3
Turgutlu Turkey 69 L5
Turhal Turkey 112 E2
Türi Estonia 55 N7
Turia r. Spain 67 F4
Turiaçu Brazil 177 I4
Turin Canada 151 H5
Turin Italy 68 B2
Turiy Rog Rus. Fed. 90 C3

▶ Turkana, Lake salt l. Eth./Kenya 122 D3
5th largest lake in Africa.

Turkestan Kazakh. 102 C3
Turkestan Range mts Asia 111 G2
Turkey country Asia/Europe see Turkey
Turkey U.S.A. 164 D5
Turkey r. U.S.A. 160 F3
Turki Rus. Fed. 53 I6
Türkistan Kazakh. see Turkestan
Türkiye country Asia/Europe see Turkey
Turkmenabat Lebap Turkm. see Türkmenabat
Türkmenabat Turkm. 111 F2
Türkmen Adasy i. Turkm. see Ogurjaly Adasy
Türkmen Aýlagy b. Turkm. 110 D2
Türkmen Aýlagy b. Turkm. see Türkmen Aýlagy
Türkmenbaşy Turkm. 110 D1
Türkmenbaşy Aýlagy b. Turkm. 110 D2
Türkmenbaşy Aýlagy b. Turkm. see Türkmenbaşy Aýlagy
Türkmenbaşy Döwlet Gorugy nature res. Turkm. 110 D2
Türkmen Dağı mt. Turkey 69 N5
Turkmenistan country Asia 109 I2
Türkmenostan country Asia see Turkmenistan
Turkmenskaya S.S.R. country Asia see Turkmenistan
Türkoğlu Turkey 112 E3

▶ Turks and Caicos Islands terr. West Indies 169 J4
United Kingdom Overseas Territory.

Turks Island Passage Turks and Caicos Is 163 G5
Turks Islands Turks and Caicos Is 169 J4
Turku Fin. 55 M6
Turkwel watercourse Kenya 122 D3
Turlock U.S.A. 158 C3
Turlock Lake U.S.A. 158 C3
Turmalina Brazil 179 C2
Turnagain r. Canada 150 E3
Turnagain, Cape N.Z. 139 F5
Turnberry U.K. 60 E5
Turnbull, Mount U.S.A. 159 H5
Turneffe Islands atoll Belize 167 I5
Turner U.S.A. 156 D1
Turner Valley Canada 150 H5
Turnhout Belgium 62 E3
Turnor Lake Canada 151 I3
Türnovo Bulg. see Veliko Tŭrnovo
Turnu Măgurele Romania 69 K3
Turnu Severin Romania see Drobeta-Turnu Severin
Turon r. Australia 138 D4
Turones France see Tours
Turovets Rus. Fed. 52 I4

▶ Turpan Pendi depr. China 98 E4
Lowest point in northern Asia.

Turpan Zhan Xinjiang China 98 E4
Turquino, Pico mt. Cuba 169 I4
Turrialba Costa Rica 166 [inset] J7
Turriff U.K. 60 G3
Turris Libisonis Sardinia Italy see Porto Torres
Tursāq Iraq 113 G4
Turtle Island Fiji see Vatoa
Turtle Islands Phil. 82 B5
Turtle Lake Canada 151 I4
Turugart Pass China/Kyrg. 102 E3
Turugart Shankou pass China/Kyrg. see Turugart Pass
Turuvanur India 106 C3
Turvo r. Brazil 179 A2
Turvo r. Brazil 179 A2
Tusayan U.S.A. 159 G4
Tuscaloosa U.S.A. 163 C5
Tuscarawas r. U.S.A. 164 E3
Tuscarora Mountains hills U.S.A. 165 G3
Tuscola IL U.S.A. 160 F4
Tuscola TX U.S.A. 161 D5
Tuscumbia U.S.A. 163 C5
Tuskegee U.S.A. 163 C5
Tussey Mountains hills U.S.A. 165 F3

Tustin U.S.A. 164 C1
Tustumena Lake AK U.S.A. 149 J3
Tutak Turkey 113 F3
Tutayev Rus. Fed. 52 H4
Tutera Spain see Tudela
Tuticorin India 106 C4
Tutoh r. Malaysia 85 F2
Tutong Brunei 85 F1
Tuttle Creek Reservoir U.S.A. 160 D4
Tuttlingen Germany 57 L7
Tuttut Nunaat reg. Greenland 147 P2
Tutuala East Timor 83 C5
Tutubu P.N.G. 136 E1
Tutubu Tanz. 123 D4
Tutuila i. American Samoa 133 I3
Tutume Botswana 123 C6
Tututalak Mountain AK U.S.A. 148 G2
Tututepec Mex. 167 F5
Tuul Gol r. Mongolia 94 F1
Tuul-bong r. N. Korea 90 B4
Tuupovaara Fin. 54 Q5
Tuusniemi Fin. 54 P5
Tuva aut. rep. Rus. Fed. see Tyva, Respublika
Tuva country S. Pacific Ocean 133 H2
Tuvalu country S. Pacific Ocean 133 H2
Tüvshinshiree Sühbaatar Mongolia 95 G2
Tuwau r. Indon. 85 G2
Tuwayq, Jabal hills Saudi Arabia 108 G4
Tuwayq, Jabal mts Saudi Arabia 108 G4
Tuwwal Saudi Arabia 108 E5
Tuxpan Jalisco Mex. 166 E5
Tuxpan Nayarit Mex. 166 D4
Tuxpan Mex. 168 E4
Tuxtla Gutiérrez Mex. 167 G5
Tuya Lake B.C. Canada 149 O4
Tuyên Quang Vietnam 86 D2
Tuy Hoa Vietnam 87 E4
Tuyuk Kazakh. 98 E3
Tuz, Lake salt l. Turkey 112 D3
Tuz Gölü salt l. Turkey see Tuz, Lake
Tuzha Rus. Fed. 52 J4
Tuz Khurmātū Iraq 113 G4
Tuzla Bos.-Herz. 68 H2
Tuzla Turkey 107 B1
Tuzla Gölü lag. Turkey 69 L4
Tuzlov r. Rus. Fed. 53 I7
Tuzu r. Myanmar 86 A1
Tvedestrand Norway 55 F7
Tver' Rus. Fed. 52 G4
Twain Harte U.S.A. 158 C2
Tweed Canada 165 G1
Tweed r. U.K. 60 G5
Tweed Heads Australia 138 F2
Tweedie Canada 151 I4
Tweefontein S. Africa 124 D7
Twee Rivier Namibia 124 D3
Twentekanaal canal Neth. 62 G2
Twentynine Palms U.S.A. 158 E4
Twin Bridges CA U.S.A. 158 C2
Twin Bridges MT U.S.A. 156 E3
Twin Buttes Reservoir U.S.A. 161 C6
Twin Falls Canada 153 I3
Twin Falls U.S.A. 156 E4
Twin Heads hill Australia 134 D5
Twin Hills AK U.S.A. 148 G4
Twin Mountain AK U.S.A. 148 H3
Twin Peak U.S.A. 158 C2
Twistringen Germany 63 I2
Twitchen Reservoir U.S.A. 158 C4
Twitya r. N.W.T. Canada 149 O2
Twizel 139 C7
Twofold Bay Australia 138 D6
Two Harbors U.S.A. 160 F2
Two Hills Canada 151 I4
Two Rivers U.S.A. 164 B1
Tyan' Shan' mts China/Kyrg. see Tien Shan
Tyao r. India/Myanmar 96 B4
Tyatya, Vulkan vol. Rus. Fed. 90 G3
Tydal Norway 54 G5
Tygart Valley U.S.A. 164 F4
Tygda Rus. Fed. 90 B1
Tygda r. Rus. Fed. 90 B1
Tyler U.S.A. 161 E5
Tylertown U.S.A. 161 F6
Tym' r. Rus. Fed. 90 F2
Tymna, Laguna lag. Rus. Fed. 148 S3
Tymovskoye Rus. Fed. 90 F2
Tynda Rus. Fed. 89 M1
Tyndall U.S.A. 160 D3
Tyndinskiy Rus. Fed. see Tynda
Tyne r. U.K. 60 G4
Tynemouth U.K. 58 F3
Tynset Norway 54 G5
Tyone r. AK U.S.A. 149 K3
Tyonek AK U.S.A. 148 J3
Tyoploozyorsk Rus. Fed. see Teploozersk
Tyoploye Ozero Rus. Fed. see Teploozersk
Tyr Lebanon see Tyre
Tyras Ukr. see Bilhorod-Dnistrovs'kyy
Tyre Lebanon 107 B3
Tyree, Mount Antarctica 188 L1
Tyrma Rus. Fed. 90 D2
Tyrma r. Rus. Fed. 90 C2
Tyrnävä Fin. 54 N4
Tyrnavos Greece 69 J5
Tyrnyauz Rus. Fed. 113 F2
Tyrone NM U.S.A. 166 C1
Tyrrell r. Australia 138 A5
Tyrrell, Lake dry lake Australia 137 C7
Tyrrell Lake Canada 151 I2
Tyrrhenian Sea France/Italy 68 D4
Tyrus Lebanon see Tyre
Tysa r. Ukr. see Tisa
Tyukalinsk Rus. Fed. 76 I4
Tyulen'i Ostrova is Kazakh. 113 H1
Tyumen' Rus. Fed. 76 H4
Tyup Kyrg. see Tüp
Tyuratam Kazakh. see Baykonyr
Tyva, Respublika aut. rep. Rus. Fed. 94 D1
Tywi r. U.K. 59 C7
Tywyn U.K. 59 C6
Tzaneen S. Africa 125 J2
Tzia i. Greece 69 K6
Tzucacab Mex. 167 H4

U

Uaco Congo Angola see Waku-Kungo
Ualan atoll Micronesia see Kosrae

Uamanda Angola 123 C5
Uarc, Ras c. Morocco see
Trois Fourches, Cap des
Uaroo Australia 135 A5
Uatumã r. Brazil 177 G4
Uauá Brazil 177 K5
Uaupés r. Brazil 176 E3
Uaxactún Guat. 167 H5
U'aylī, Wādī al watercourse Saudi Arabia 107 D4
U'aywij well Saudi Arabia 110 B4
U'aywij, Wādī al watercourse Saudi Arabia 113 F5
Ubá Brazil 179 C3
Uba r. Kazakh. 98 C2
Ubaí Brazil 179 B2
Ubaitaba Brazil 179 D1
Ubangi r. Cent. Afr. Rep./Dem. Rep. Congo 122 B4
Ubangi-Shari country Africa see
Central African Republic
Ubauro Pak. 111 H4
Ubayyiḍ, Wādī al watercourse Iraq/Saudi Arabia 113 F4
Ube Japan 91 C6
Úbeda Spain 67 E4
Uberaba Brazil 179 B2
Uberlândia Brazil 179 A2
Ubin, Pulau i. Sing. 87 [inset]
Ubly U.S.A. 164 D2
Ubolratna, Ang Kep Nam Thai. 86 C3
Ubombo S. Africa 125 K4
Ubon Ratchathani Thai. 86 D4
Ubstadt-Weiher Germany 63 I5
Ubundu Dem. Rep. Congo 121 F5
Üçajy Turkm. 111 F2
Ucar Azer. 113 G2
Uçarı Turkey 107 A1
Ucayali r. Peru 176 D4
Uch Pak. 111 H4
Üchajy Turkm. see Üçajy
Üchān Iran 110 C2
Ucharal Kazakh. 102 F2
Uchigō Japan 93 G1
Uchihara Japan 93 G2
Uchimura-gawa r. Japan 93 E2
Uchinada Japan 92 C2
Uchita Japan 92 B4
Uchiura-wan b. Japan 90 F4
Uchiyama-tōge pass Japan 93 E2
Uchkeken Rus. Fed. 113 F2
Uchkuduk Uzbek. see Uchquduq
Uchquduq Uzbek. 102 B3
Uchte Germany 63 I2
Uchte r. Germany 63 L2
Uchto r. Pak. 111 G5
Uchur r. Rus. Fed. 77 O4
Uckermark reg. Germany 63 N1
Uckfield U.K. 59 H8
Ucluelet Canada 150 E5
Ucross U.S.A. 156 G3
Uda r. Rus. Fed. 89 J2
Uda r. Rus. Fed. 90 D1
Udachnoye Rus. Fed. 53 J7
Udachnyy Rus. Fed. 189 E2
Udagamandalam India 106 C4
Udaipur Rajasthan India 104 C4
Udaipur Tripura India 105 G5
Udanti r. India/Myanmar 105 E5
Uday r. Ukr. 53 G6
'Udaynān well Saudi Arabia 110 C6
Uddevalla Sweden 55 G7
Uddingston U.K. 60 E5
Uddjaure l. Sweden 54 J4
'Udeid, Khōr al inlet Qatar 110 C5
Uden Neth. 62 F3
Udgir India 106 C2
Udhagamandalam India see
Udagamandalam
Udhampur India 104 C2
Udia-Milai atoll Marshall Is see Bikini
Udimskiy Rus. Fed. 52 J3
Udine Italy 68 E1
Udit India 111 I5
Udjuktok Bay Canada 153 J3
Udmalaippettai India see Udumalaippettai
Udomlya Rus. Fed. 52 G4
Udone-jima i. Japan 93 F4
Udon Thani Thai. 86 C3
Udskaya Guba b. Rus. Fed. 77 O4
Udskoye Rus. Fed. 90 D1
Udumalaippettai India 106 C4
Udupi India 106 B3
Udyl', Ozero l. Rus. Fed. 90 E1
Udzhary Azer. see Ucar
Udzungwa Mountains National Park Tanz. 123 D4
Uéa atoll New Caledonia see Ouvéa
Uebonti Sulawesi Indon. 83 B3
Ueckermünde Germany 57 O4
Ueda Japan 93 E2
Uekuli Sulawesi Indon. 83 B3
Uele r. Dem. Rep. Congo 122 C3
Uelen Rus. Fed. 148 E2
Uel'kal' Rus. Fed. 148 C2
Uelzen Germany 63 K2
Ueno Gunma Japan 93 E2
Ueno Mie Japan 92 C4
Uenohara Japan 93 F3
Uetersen Germany 63 J1
Uettingen Germany 63 J5
Uetze Germany 63 K2
Ufa Rus. Fed. 51 R5
Ufa r. Rus. Fed. 51 R5
Uffenheim Germany 63 K5
Uftyuga r. Rus. Fed. 52 J3
Ugab watercourse Namibia 123 B6
Ugak Bay AK U.S.A. 148 I4
Ugalla r. Tanz. 123 D4
Uganda country Africa 122 D3
Uganik AK U.S.A. 148 I4
Ugashik AK U.S.A. 148 H4
Ugashik Bay AK U.S.A. 148 H4
Ugie S. Africa 125 I6
Ūgīnak Iran 111 F5
Uglegorsk Rus. Fed. 90 F2
Uglich Rus. Fed. 52 H4
Ugljan i. Croatia 68 F2
Uglovoye Rus. Fed. 90 C2
Ugol'naya Rus. Fed. 77 P3
Ugolnyy Rus. Fed. see Beringovskiy
Ugol'nyye Kopi Rus. Fed. 148 B2
Ugra Rus. Fed. 53 G5
Ugtaaltsaydam Mongolia 94 F1
Uher Hudag Nei Mongol China 95 G3
Uherské Hradiště Czech Rep. 57 P6
Úhlava r. Czech Rep. 63 N5
Uhrichsville U.S.A. 164 E3
Uibhist a' Deas i. U.K. see South Uist
Uibhist a' Tuath i. U.K. see North Uist
Uig U.K. 60 C3
Uíge Angola 123 B4
Ŭijŏngbu S. Korea 91 B5
Ŭiju N. Korea 91 B4
Uimaharju Fin. 54 Q5
Uinta Mountains U.S.A. 159 H1
Uis Mine Namibia 123 B6
Uitenhage S. Africa 125 G7
Uithoorn Neth. 62 E2
Uithuizen Neth. 62 G1
Uivak, Cape Canada 153 J2
Ujhani India 104 D4
Uji Japan 92 B4
Uji-gawa r. Japan 92 B4
Uji-guntō is Japan 91 C7
Ujiie Japan 93 F2
Ujitawara Japan 92 B4
Ujiyamada Japan see Ise
Ujjain India 104 C5
Ujohbilang Kalimantan Indon. 85 F2
Ujung Kulon, Taman Nasional nat. park Indon. 84 D4
Ujung Pandang Sulawesi Indon. see Makassar
Újvidék Serbia see Novi Sad
Ukal Sagar l. India 104 C5
Ukata Nigeria 120 D3
'Ukayrishah well Saudi Arabia 110 B5
uKhahlamba-Drakensberg Park nat. park S. Africa 125 I5
Ukholovo Rus. Fed. 53 I5
Ukhrul India 105 H4
Ukhta Respublika Kareliya Rus. Fed. see
Kalevala
Ukhta Respublika Komi Rus. Fed. 52 L3
Ukiah CA U.S.A. 158 B2
Ukiah OR U.S.A. 156 D3
Ukkusiksalik National Park 147 J3
Ukkusissat Greenland 147 M2
Ukmergė Lith. 55 N9

▶Ukraine country Europe 53 F6
2nd largest country in Europe.

Ukrainskaya S.S.R. country Europe see
Ukraine
Ukrayina country Europe see Ukraine
Uku-jima i. Japan 91 C6
Ukwi Botswana 124 E2
Ukwi Pan salt pan Botswana 124 E2
Ul r. India 99 B7
Ulaanbaatar Mongolia see Ulan Bator
Ulaanbaatar mun. Mongolia 94 F2
Ulaanbadrah Mongolia 95 G3
Ulaan-Ereg Mongolia see Bayanmönh
Ulaangom Mongolia 94 C1
Ulaanhudag Mongolia see Erdenesant
Ulaan Nuur salt l. Mongolia 94 E2
Ulaan-Uul Bayanhongor Mongolia see Öldziyt
Ulaan-Uul Dornogovĭ Mongolia see Erdene
Ulak Island AK U.S.A. 149 [inset]
Ulan Australia 138 D4
Ulan Nei Mongol China 95 G4
Ulan Qinghai China 94 D4

▶Ulan Bator Mongolia 94 F2
Capital of Mongolia.

Ulanbel' Kazakh. 102 D3
Ulan Buh Shamo des. China 94 F3
Ulan Erge Rus. Fed. 53 J7
Ulanhad Nei Mongol China see Chifeng
Ulanhot Nei Mongol China 95 J2
Ulan Hua Nei Mongol China 95 G3
Ulan-Khol Rus. Fed. 53 J7
Ulanlinggi Xinjiang China 98 D4
Ulan Mod Nei Mongol China 94 F4
Ulan Suhai Nei Mongol China 94 F3
Ulansuhai Nur l. China 95 G3
Ulan Tohoi Nei Mongol China 94 E3
Ulan-Ude Rus. Fed. 89 J2
Ulan Ul Hu l. China 99 E6
Ulaş Turkey 112 E3
Ulastai Xinjiang China 98 D4
Ulawa Island Solomon Is 133 G2
Ulayyah reg. Saudi Arabia 110 B6
Ul'ba Kazakh. 98 C2
Ul'banskiy Zaliv b. Rus. Fed. 90 E1
Ulchin S. Korea 91 C5
Uldz Mongolia see Norovlin
Uldz r. Mongolia 95 H1
Uleåborg Fin. see Oulu
Ulebsechel i. Palau see Auluptagel
Ulefoss Norway 55 F7
Ulekchin Rus. Fed. 94 F1
Ülenurme Estonia 55 O7
Ulety Rus. Fed. 95 H1
Ulgain Gol r. China 95 I2
Ulhasnagar India 106 B2
Uliastai Nei Mongol China 95 I2
Uliastay Mongolia 94 D2
Uliatea i. Fr. Polynesia see Raiatea
Ulicoten Neth. 62 E3
Ulie atoll Micronesia see Woleai
Ulita r. Rus. Fed. 54 R2
Ulithi atoll Micronesia 81 J4
Ul'ken Sulutor Kazakh. 98 A4
Ulladulla Australia 138 E5
Ullapool U.K. 60 D3
Ulla Ulla, Parque Nacional nat. park Bol. 176 E6
Ullava Fin. 54 M5
Ullersuaq c. Greenland 147 K2
Ullswater l. U.K. 58 E4
Ullŭng-do i. S. Korea 91 C5
Ulm Germany 57 L6
Ulmarra Australia 138 F2
Ulmen Germany 62 G4
Uloowaranie, Lake salt flat Australia 137 B5
Ulricehamn Sweden 55 H8
Ulrum Neth. 62 G1
Ulsan S. Korea 91 C6
Ulsberg Norway 54 F5
Ulster reg. Ireland/U.K. 61 E3
Ulster U.S.A. 165 G3
Ulster Canal Ireland/U.K. 61 E3
Ultima Australia 138 A5
Ulu Sulawesi Indon. 83 C2
Ulúa r. Hond. 166 [inset] I6
Ulubat Gölü l. Turkey 69 M4
Ulubey Turkey 69 M5
Uluborlu Turkey 69 N5
Uludağ mt. Turkey 69 M4
Uludağ Milli Parkı nat. park Turkey 69 M4
Ulugqat Xinjiang China see Wuqia
Ulu Kali, Gunung mt. Malaysia 84 C2
Ulukhaktok Canada 189 L2
Ulukışla Turkey 112 D3
Ulundi S. Africa 125 J5
Ulungur He r. China 98 D3
Ulungur Hu l. China 98 D3
Ulunkhan Rus. Fed. 89 K2
Uluru hill Australia 135 E6
Uluru-Kata Tjuta National Park Australia 135 E6
Uluru National Park Australia see
Uluru-Kata Tjuta National Park
Ulutau Kazakh. see Ulytau
Ulutau, Gory mts Kazakh. see Ulytau, Gory
Ulu Temburong National Park Brunei 85 F1
Uluyatır Turkey 107 C1
Ulva i. U.K. 60 C4
Ulvenhout Neth. 62 E3
Ulverston U.K. 58 D4
Ulvsjön Sweden 55 I6
Ül'yanov Kazakh. see Ul'yanovskiy
Ul'yanovsk Rus. Fed. 53 K5
Ul'yanovskiy Kazakh. 102 D1
Ul'yanovskoye Kazakh. see Ul'yanovskiy
Ulyatuy Rus. Fed. 95 I1
Ulysses KS U.S.A. 160 C4
Ulysses KY U.S.A. 164 D5
Ulytau Kazakh. 102 C2
Ulytau, Gory mts Kazakh. 102 C2
Uma Rus. Fed. 90 A1
Umaltinskiy Rus. Fed. 90 D2
'Umān country Asia see Oman
Umán Mex. 167 H4
Uman' Ukr. 53 F6
Umarao Pak. 111 G4
'Umarī, Qā' al salt pan Jordan 107 C4
Umaria India 104 E5
Umarkhed India 106 C2
Umarkot India 106 D2
Umarkot Pak. 111 H4
Umarkot Pak. 111 H5
Umaroona, Lake salt flat Australia 137 B5
Umarpada India 104 C5
Umatilla U.S.A. 156 D3
Umayan r. Mindanao Phil. 82 D4
Umba Rus. Fed. 52 G2
Umbagog Lake U.S.A. 165 J1
Umbeara Australia 135 F6
Umbele i. Indon. 83 B3
Umboi i. P.N.G. 81 L8
Umeå Sweden 54 L5
Umeälven r. Sweden 54 L5
Umera Maluku Indon. 83 D3
Umfolozi r. S. Africa 125 K5
Umfreville Lake Canada 151 M5
Umhlanga Rocks S. Africa 125 J5
Umiat AK U.S.A. 148 I1
Umi-gawa r. Japan 93 D1
Umiiviip Kangertiva inlet Greenland 147 N3
Umingmaktok (abandoned) Canada 189 L2
Umirzak Kazakh. 113 H2
Umiujaq Canada 152 F2
Umkomaas S. Africa 125 J6
Umkumiut AK U.S.A. 148 F3
Umlaiteng India 105 H4
Umlazi S. Africa 125 J5
Umm ad Daraj, Jabal mt. Jordan 107 B3
Umm al 'Amad Syria 107 C2
Umm al Jamājim well Saudi Arabia 110 B5
Umm al Qaywayn U.A.E. 110 D5
Umm al Qaiwain U.A.E. see Umm al Qaywayn
Umm ar Raqabah, Khabrat imp. l. Saudi Arabia 107 C5
Umm at Qalbān Saudi Arabia 113 F6
Umm az Zumūl well Oman 110 D6
Umm Bāb Qatar 110 C5
Umm Bel Sudan 108 C7
Umm Keddada Sudan 108 C7
Umm Lajj Saudi Arabia 108 E4
Umm Nukhaylah hill Saudi Arabia 107 D5
Umm Qaṣr Iraq 113 G5
Umm Quṣūr i. Saudi Arabia 112 D6
Umm Ruwaba Sudan 108 D7
Umm Sa'ad Libya 112 B5
Umm Sa'id Qatar 110 C5
Umm Shugeira Sudan 108 C7
Umm Wa'āl hill Saudi Arabia 107 D4
Umm Wazīr well Saudi Arabia 110 B6
Umnak Island AK U.S.A. 148 E5
Umnak Pass sea channel AK U.S.A. 148 E5
Um Phang Wildlife Reserve nature res. Thai. 86 B4
Umpqua r. U.S.A. 156 B4
Umpulo Angola 123 B5
Umraniye Turkey 69 N5
Umred India 106 C1
Umri India 104 D4
Umtali Zimbabwe see Mutare
Umtata S. Africa 125 I6
Umtentweni S. Africa 125 J6
Umuahia Nigeria 120 D4
Umuarama Brazil 178 F2
Umvuma Zimbabwe see Mvuma
Umzimkulu S. Africa 125 I6
Una r. Bos.-Herz./Croatia 68 G2
Una Brazil 179 D1
Una India 104 D3
'Unāb, Jabal al hill Jordan 107 C5
'Unāb, Wādī al watercourse Jordan 107 C4
Unaí Brazil 179 B2
Unakami Japan 93 G3
Unalakleet AK U.S.A. 148 G3
Unalakleet r. AK U.S.A. 148 G3
Unalaska AK U.S.A. 148 F5
Unalaska Island AK U.S.A. 148 F5
Unalga Island AK U.S.A. 148 F5
Unapool U.K. 60 D2
Unauna i. Indon. 83 B3
'Unayzah Saudi Arabia 108 F4
'Unayzah, Jabal hill Iraq 113 E4
Unazuki Japan 92 D2
Uncia Bol. 176 E7
Uncompahgre Peak U.S.A. 159 J2
Uncompahgre Plateau U.S.A. 159 I2
Undara National Park Australia 136 D3
Underberg S. Africa 125 I5
Underbool Australia 137 C7
Underwood U.S.A. 164 C4
Undu, Tanjung pt Sumba Indon. 83 B5
Undur Seram Indon. 83 D3
Unecha Rus. Fed. 53 G5
Unga AK U.S.A. 148 G5
Unga Island AK U.S.A. 148 G5
Ungalik AK U.S.A. 148 G2
Ungalik r. AK U.S.A. 148 G2
Ungama Bay Kenya see Ungwana Bay
Ungarie Australia 138 C4
Ungava, Baie d' b. Canada see Ungava Bay
Ungava, Péninsule d' pen. Canada 152 G1
Ungava Bay Canada 153 I2
Ungava Peninsula Canada see
Ungava, Péninsule d'
Ungeny Moldova see Ungheni
Ungheni Moldova 69 L1
Unguana Moz. 125 L2
Unguja i. Tanz. see Zanzibar Island
Unguz, Solonchakovyye Vpadiny salt flat Turkm. 110 E2
Üngüz Angyrsyndaky Garagum des. Turkm. 110 E1
Ungvár Ukr. see Uzhhorod
Ungwana Bay Kenya 122 E4
Uni Rus. Fed. 52 K4
União Brazil 177 J4
União da Vitória Brazil 179 A4
União dos Palmares Brazil 177 K5
Uniara Rajasthan India 99 B8
Unimak Bight b. AK U.S.A. 148 F5
Unimak Island AK U.S.A. 148 F5
Unimak Pass sea channel AK U.S.A. 148 F5
Unini r. Brazil 176 F4
Union MO U.S.A. 160 F4
Union WV U.S.A. 164 E5
Union, Mount U.S.A. 159 G4
Union City OH U.S.A. 164 C3
Union City PA U.S.A. 164 F3
Union City TN U.S.A. 161 F4
Uniondale S. Africa 124 F7
Unión de Reyes Cuba 163 D8

▶Union of Soviet Socialist Republics
Divided in 1991 into 15 independent nations: Armenia, Azerbaijan, Belarus, Estonia, Georgia, Latvia, Kazakhstan, Kyrgyzstan, Lithuania, Moldova, the Russian Federation, Tajikistan, Turkmenistan, Ukraine and Uzbekistan.

Union Springs U.S.A. 163 C5
Uniontown U.S.A. 164 F4
Unionville U.S.A. 165 G3
United Arab Emirates country Asia 110 D6
United Arab Republic country Africa see Egypt

▶United Kingdom country Europe 56 G3
4th most populous country in Europe.

United Provinces state India see
Uttar Pradesh

▶United States of America country
N. America 154 F3
Most populous country in North America, and 3rd most populous in the world. Also 3rd largest country in the world, and 2nd in North America.

United States Range mts Canada 147 L1
Unity Canada 151 I4
Unjha India 104 C5
Unna Germany 63 H3
Unnao India 104 E4
Unoke Japan 92 C2
Ŭnp'a N. Korea 91 B5
Unsan N. Korea 91 B4
Ŭnsan N. Korea 91 B5
Unst i. U.K. 60 [inset]
Unstrut r. Germany 63 L3
Untor, Ozero l. Rus. Fed. 51 T3
Unuk r. Canada/U.S.A. 149 O4
Unuli Horog Qinghai China 94 B5
Unzen-dake vol. Japan 91 C6
Unzha Rus. Fed. 52 J4
Uozu Japan 92 D2
Upalco U.S.A. 159 H1
Upar Ghat reg. India 105 F5
Upemba, Lac l. Dem. Rep. Congo 123 C4
Uperbada India 105 F5
Upernavik Greenland 147 M2
Upi Mindanao Phil. 82 D5
Upington S. Africa 124 E5
Upland U.S.A. 158 E4
Upleta India 104 B5
Upoloksha Rus. Fed. 54 Q3
'Upolu i. Samoa 133 I3
Upper Arlington U.S.A. 164 D3
Upper Arrow Lake Canada 150 G5
Upper Chindwin Myanmar see Mawlaik
Upper Fraser Canada 150 F4
Upper Garry Lake Canada 151 K1
Upper Hutt N.Z. 139 E5
Upper Kalskag AK U.S.A. 148 G3
Upper Klamath Lake U.S.A. 156 C4
Upper Liard Y.T. Canada 149 O3
Upper Lough Erne l. U.K. 61 E3
Upper Marlboro U.S.A. 165 G4
Upper Mazinaw Lake Canada 165 G1
Upper Missouri Breaks National Monument nat. park U.S.A. 160 A2
Upper Peirce Reservoir Sing. 87 [inset]
Upper Red Lake U.S.A. 160 E1
Upper Sandusky U.S.A. 164 D3
Upper Saranac Lake U.S.A. 165 H1
Upper Seal Lake Canada see Iberville, Lac d'
Upper Tunguska r. Rus. Fed. see Angara
Upper Volta country Africa see Burkina Faso
Upper Yarra Reservoir Australia 138 B6
Uppinangadi India 106 B3
Uppsala Sweden 55 J7
Upright, Cape AK U.S.A. 148 D3
Upsala Canada 152 C4
Upshi India 104 D2
Upton U.S.A. 165 J2
'Uqaqah, Wādī watercourse Jordan 107 B4
'Uqayribāt Syria 107 C2
'Uqlat al 'Udhaybah well Iraq 113 G5
Uqturpan Xinjiang China see Wushi
Uracas vol. N. Mariana Is see
Farallon de Pajaros
Urad Qianqi Nei Mongol China see Xishanzui
Urad Zhongqi Nei Mongol China see Haliut
Ūrāf Iran 110 E4
Uraga-suidō sea chan. Japan 93 F3
Uragawara Japan 93 E1
Urakawa Japan 90 F4
Ural hill Australia 138 C4
Ural r. Kazakh./Rus. Fed. 100 E2
Uralla Australia 138 E3
Ural Mountains Rus. Fed. 51 S2
Ural'sk Kazakh. 100 E1
Ural'skaya Oblast' admin. div. Kazakh. see
Zapadnyy Kazakhstan
Ural'skiye Gory mts Rus. Fed. see
Ural Mountains
Ural'skiy Khrebet mts Rus. Fed. see
Ural Mountains
Urambo Tanz. 123 D4
Uran India 106 B2
Urana Australia 138 C5
Urana, Lake Australia 138 C5
Urandangi Australia 136 B4
Urandi Brazil 179 C1
Uranium City Canada 151 I3
Uranquinty Australia 138 C5
Uraricoera r. Brazil 176 F3
Urartu country Asia see Armenia
Ura-Tyube Tajik. see Üroteppa
Uravakonda India 106 C3
Uravan U.S.A. 159 I2
Urawa Japan 93 F3
Urayasu Japan 93 F3
'Urayf an Nāqah, Jabal hill Egypt 107 B4
Uray'irah Saudi Arabia 110 C5
'Urayq ad Duḥūl des. Saudi Arabia 110 B5
'Urayq Sāqān des. Saudi Arabia 110 B5
Urbana IL U.S.A. 160 F3
Urbana OH U.S.A. 164 D3
Urbino Italy 68 E3
Urbinum Italy see Urbino
Urbs Vetus Italy see Orvieto
Urdoma Rus. Fed. 52 K3
Urd Tamir Gol r. Mongolia 94 E2
Urdyuzhskoye, Ozero l. Rus. Fed. 52 K2
Urdzhar Kazakh. 102 F2
Ure r. U.K. 58 F4
Ureki Georgia 113 F2
Urelik Rus. Fed. 148 D2
Uren' Rus. Fed. 52 J4
Urengoy Rus. Fed. 76 I3
Uréparapara i. Vanuatu 133 G3
Ures Mex. 166 C2
Ureshino Japan 92 C4
Urewera National Park N.Z. 139 F4
Urfa Turkey see Şanlıurfa
Urfa prov. Turkey see Şanlıurfa
Urga Mongolia see Ulaanbaatar
Urgal r. Rus. Fed. 90 D2
Urganch Uzbek. 102 B3
Urgench Uzbek. see Urganch
Ürgüp Turkey 112 D3
Urgut Uzbek. 111 G2
Urho Xinjiang China 98 D3
Urho Kekkosen kansallispuisto nat. park Fin. 54 O2
Urie r. U.K. 60 G3
Uril Rus. Fed. 90 C2
Uripitijuata, Cerro mt. Mex. 166 E5
Urique Mex. 166 D3
Urisino Australia 138 A2
Urizura Japan 93 G2
Urjala Fin. 55 M6
Urk Neth. 62 F2
Urkan Rus. Fed. 90 B1
Urkan r. Rus. Fed. 90 B1
Urla Turkey 69 L5
Urlingford Ireland 61 E5
Urluk Rus. Fed. 95 F1
Urmā aş Şughrá Syria 107 C1
Urmai Xizang China 99 D7
Urmia Iran 110 B2
Urmia, Lake salt l. Iran 110 B2
Urmston Road sea chan. H.K. China 97 [inset]
Uromi Nigeria 120 D4
Uroševac Kosovo see Ferijaz
Urosozero Rus. Fed. 52 G3
Üroteppa Tajik. 111 H2
Urru Co salt l. China 99 D7
Urt Mongolia see Gurvantes
Urt Moron Qinghai China 99 F5
Urt Moron r. Qinghai China 94 C4
Uruáchic Mex. 166 C3
Uruaçu Brazil 179 A1
Uruana Brazil 179 A1
Uruapan Baja California Mex. 157 D7
Uruapan Michoacán Mex. 168 D5
Urubamba r. Peru 176 D6
Urucara Brazil 177 G4
Urucu r. Brazil 176 F4
Uruçuca Brazil 179 D1
Uruçuí Brazil 177 J5
Uruçuí, Serra do hills Brazil 177 I5
Urucuia Brazil 179 B2
Urucurituba Brazil 177 G4
Urugi Japan 92 D3
Uruguai r. Arg./Uruguay see Uruguay
Uruguaiana Brazil 178 E3
Uruguay r. Arg./Uruguay 178 E4
also known as Uruguai
Uruguay country S. America 178 E4
Uruhe China 90 B2
Urukthapel i. Palau 82 [inset]
Urumchi Xinjiang China see Ürümqi
Ürümqi Xinjiang China 98 D4
Urundi country Africa see Burundi
Urup, Ostrov i. Rus. Fed. 89 S3
Uru Pass China/Kyrg. 98 B4
Urusha Rus. Fed. 90 A1
Urutaí Brazil 179 A2
Uryl' Kazakh. 102 G2
Uryupino Rus. Fed. 89 M2
Uryupinsk Rus. Fed. 53 I6
Ürzhar Kazakh. see Urdzhar
Urzhum Rus. Fed. 52 K4
Urziceni Romania 69 L2
Usa Japan 91 C6
Usa r. Rus. Fed. 52 M2
Uşak Turkey 69 M5
Usakos Namibia 124 B1
Usarp Mountains Antarctica 188 H2
Usborne, Mount hill Falkland Is 178 E8
Ushakova, Ostrov i. Rus. Fed. 76 I1
Ushanovo Kazakh. 98 C2
Ushant i. France see Ouessant, Île d'
Usharal Kazakh. see Ucharal
Ush-Bel'dyr Rus. Fed. 88 H2
Ushibori Japan 93 G3
Ushiku Japan 93 G2
Ushimawashi-yama mt. Japan 92 B5
Ushkaniy, Gory mts Rus. Fed. 148 B2
Ushtobe Kazakh. 102 E2
Ush-Tyube Kazakh. see Ushtobe
Ushuaia Arg. 178 C8
Ushumun Rus. Fed. 90 B1
Usingen Germany 63 I4
Usinsk Rus. Fed. 51 R2
Usk U.K. 59 E7
Usk r. U.K. 59 E7
Uskhodni Belarus 55 O10
Uskoplje Bos.-Herz. see Gornji Vakuf
Üsküdar Turkey 69 M4
Uslar Germany 63 J3
Usman' Rus. Fed. 53 H5
Usmanabad India see Osmanabad
Usmas ezers l. Latvia 55 M8
Usogorsk Rus. Fed. 52 K3
Usol'ye-Sibirskoye Rus. Fed. 88 I2
Uspenovka Rus. Fed. 90 B1
Uspenskiy Kazakh. 98 A2
Ussel France 66 F4
Ussuri r. China/Rus. Fed. 90 D2
Ussuriysk Rus. Fed. 90 C4
Ust'-Abakanskoye Rus. Fed. see Abakan
Usta Muhammad Pak. 111 H4
Ust'-Balyk Rus. Fed. see Nefteyugansk
Ust'-Donetskiy Rus. Fed. 53 I7
Ust'-Dzheguta Rus. Fed. 113 F1
Ust'-Dzhegutinskaya Rus. Fed. see
Ust'-Dzheguta
Ustica, Isola di i. Sicily Italy 68 E5
Ust'-Ilimsk Rus. Fed. 77 L4
Ust'-Ilimskiy Vodokhranilishche resr Rus. Fed. 77 L4
Ust'-Ilya Rus. Fed. 95 H1
Ust'-Ilych Rus. Fed. 51 R3
Ústí nad Labem Czech Rep. 57 O5
Ustinov Rus. Fed. see Izhevsk
Üstirt plat. Kazakh./Uzbek. see
Ustyurt Plateau
Ustka Poland 57 P3
Ust'-Kamchatsk Rus. Fed. 77 R4
Ust'-Kamenogorsk Kazakh. 102 F2
Ust'-Kan Rus. Fed. 98 D2
Ust'-Koksa Rus. Fed. 98 D2
Ust'-Kulom Rus. Fed. 52 L3
Ust'-Kut Rus. Fed. 77 L4
Ust'-Kuyga Rus. Fed. 77 O2
Ust'-Labinsk Rus. Fed. 113 E1
Ust'-Labinskaya Rus. Fed. see Ust'-Labinsk
Ust'-Lyzha Rus. Fed. 52 M2
Ust'-Maya Rus. Fed. 77 O3
Ust'-Nera Rus. Fed. 77 P3
Ust'-Ocheya Rus. Fed. 52 K3
Ust'-Olenek Rus. Fed. 77 M2
Ust'-Omchug Rus. Fed. 77 P3
Ust'-Ordynskiy Rus. Fed. 88 I2
Ust'-Penzhino Rus. Fed. see Kamenskoye
Ust'-Port Rus. Fed. 76 J3
Ustrem Rus. Fed. 51 T3
Ust'-Tsil'ma Rus. Fed. 52 L2
Ust'-Uda Rus. Fed. 88 I2
Ust'-Ulagan Rus. Fed. 98 D2
Ust'-Umalta Rus. Fed. 90 D2
Ust'-Undurga Rus. Fed. 89 L2
Ust'-Ura Rus. Fed. 52 J3
Ust'-Urgal Rus. Fed. 90 D2
Ust'-Usa Rus. Fed. 52 M2
Ust'-Vayen'ga Rus. Fed. 52 I3
Ust'-Voya Rus. Fed. 51 R3
Ust'-Vyyskaya Rus. Fed. 52 J3
Ust'ya r. Rus. Fed. 52 I3
Ust'ye Rus. Fed. 52 H4
Ustyurt, Plato plat. Kazakh./Uzbek. see
Ustyurt Plateau
Ustyurt Plateau Kazakh./Uzbek. 100 E2
Ustyurt Platosi plat. Kazakh./Uzbek. see
Ustyurt Plateau
Ustyuzhna Rus. Fed. 52 H4
Usu Xinjiang China 98 D3
Usu i. Indon. 83 B5
Usuda Japan 93 E2
Usulután El Salvador 166 [inset] H6
Usumacinta r. Guat./Mex. 167 G5
Usumbura Burundi see Bujumbura
Usun Apau, Dataran Tinggi plat. Malaysia 85 F2
Usvyaty Rus. Fed. 52 F5
Utah state U.S.A. 156 F5
Utah Lake U.S.A. 159 H1
Utajärvi Fin. 54 O4
Utano Japan 92 B4
Utashinai Rus. Fed. see Yuzhno-Kuril'sk
Utata Rus. Fed. 94 E1
'Utaybah, Buḥayrat al imp. l. Syria 107 C3
Utena Lith. 55 N9
Uterlai India 104 B4
Uthai Thani Thai. 86 C4
Uthal Pak. 111 G5
'Uthmānīyah Syria 107 C2
Utiariti Brazil 177 G6
Utica NY U.S.A. 165 H2
Utica OH U.S.A. 164 D3
Utiel Spain 67 F4
Utikuma Lake Canada 150 H4
Utila Hond. 166 [inset] I5
Utlwanang S. Africa 125 G4
Utopia AK U.S.A. 148 I2
Utrecht Neth. 62 F2
Utrecht S. Africa 125 J4
Utrera Spain 67 D5
Utsjoki Fin. 54 O2
Utsugi-dake mt. Japan 93 D3
Utsunomiya Japan 93 F2
Utta Rus. Fed. 53 J7
Uttaradit Thai. 86 C3
Uttarakhand state India see Uttaranchal
Uttaranchal state India 104 D3
Uttarkashi India 104 D3
Uttar Kashi India see Uttarkashi
Uttar Pradesh state India 104 D4
Uttoxeter U.K. 59 F6
Uttranchal state India see Uttaranchal
Utu Xinjiang China see Miao'ergou
Utubulak Xinjiang China 98 D3
Utukok r. AK U.S.A. 148 G1
Utupua i. Solomon Is 133 G3
Uummannaq Greenland see Dundas
Uummannaq Fjord inlet Greenland 189 J2
Uummannarsuaq c. Greenland see
Farewell, Cape
Uurainen Fin. 54 N5
Üüreg Nuur salt l. Mongolia 94 B1
Üür Gol r. Mongolia 94 E1
Uusikaarlepyy Fin. see Nykarleby
Uusikaupunki Fin. 55 L6
Uutapi Namibia 123 B5
Uva Rus. Fed. 52 L4

Uvalde U.S.A. 161 D6
Uval Karabaur *hills* Kazakh./Uzbek. 113 I2
Uval Muzbel' *hills* Kazakh. 113 I2
Uvarovo Rus. Fed. 53 I6
Uvéa *atoll* New Caledonia *see* **Ouvéa**
Uvinza Tanz. 123 D4
Uvs *prov.* Mongolia 94 C1
Uvs Nuur *salt l.* Mongolia 94 C1
Uwajima Japan 91 D6
'Uwayrid, Ḥarrat al *lava field* Saudi Arabia 108 E4
Uwaysiṭ *well* Saudi Arabia 107 D4
Uweinat, Jebel *mt.* Sudan 108 C5
Uwi *i.* Indon. 84 D2
Uxbridge Canada 164 F1
Uxbridge U.K. 59 G7
Uxin Ju *Nei Mongol* China 95 G4
Uxin Qi *Nei Mongol* China *see* **Dabqig**
Uxmal *tourist site* Mex. 167 H4
Uxxaktal *Xinjiang* China 98 D4
Uyak *AK* U.S.A. 148 I4
Uyaly Kazakh. 102 B3
Uyanga *Övörhangay* Mongolia 94 E2
Uyar Rus. Fed. 88 G1
Üydzin Mongolia *see* **Manlay**
Uyo Nigeria 120 D4
Üyönch Mongolia 94 C2
Üyönch Gol *r.* China 94 B2
Uyu Chaung *r.* Myanmar 86 A1
Uyuni Bol. 176 E8
Uyuni, Salar de *salt flat* Bol. 176 E8
Uza *r.* Rus. Fed. 53 J5
Uzbekistan *country* Asia 102 B3
Ŭzbekiston *country* Asia *see* **Uzbekistan**
Uzbekskaya S.S.R. *country* Asia *see* **Uzbekistan**
Uzbek S.S.R. *country* Asia *see* **Uzbekistan**
Uzboy Azer. 113 H3
Uzboý Turkm. 110 D2
Uzen' Kazakh. *see* **Kyzylsay**
Uzhgorod Ukr. *see* **Uzhhorod**
Uzhhorod Ukr. 53 D6
Užhorod Ukr. *see* **Uzhhorod**
Užice Serbia 69 H3
Uzlovaya Rus. Fed. 53 H5
Üzöngü Toosu *mt.* China/Kyrg. 98 B4
Üzümlü Turkey 69 M6
Uzun Uzbek. 111 H2
Uzunagach *Almatinskaya Oblast'* Kazakh. 98 B4
Uzunagach *Almatinskaya Oblast'* Kazakh. 98 B4
Uzunbulak *Xinjiang* China 98 D3
Uzun Bulak *spring Xinjiang* China 98 E4
Uzunköprü Turkey 69 L4
Uzynkair Kazakh. 102 B3

V

Vaaf Atoll Maldives *see* **Felidhu Atoll**
Vaajakoski Fin. 54 N5
Vaal *r.* S. Africa 125 F5
Vaala Fin. 54 O4
Vaalbos National Park S. Africa 124 G5
Vaal Dam S. Africa 125 I4
Vaalwater S. Africa 125 I3
Vaasa Fin. 54 L5
Vaavu Atoll Maldives *see* **Felidhu Atoll**
Vác Hungary 57 Q7
Vacaria Brazil 179 A5
Vacaria, Campo da *plain* Brazil 179 A5
Vacaville U.S.A. 158 C2
Vachon *r.* Canada 153 H1
Vad Rus. Fed. 52 J5
Vad *r.* Rus. Fed. 53 I5
Vada India 106 B2
Vadla Norway 55 E7
Vadodara India 104 C5
Vadsø Norway 54 P1

▶**Vaduz** Liechtenstein 66 I3
Capital of Liechtenstein.

Værøy *i.* Norway 54 H3
Vaga *r.* Rus. Fed. 52 I3
Vågåmo Norway 55 F6
Vaganski Vrh *mt.* Croatia 68 F2
Vágar *i.* Faroe Is 54 [inset]
Vägsele Sweden 54 K4
Vágur Faroe Is 54 [inset]
Váh *r.* Slovakia 57 Q7
Vähäkyrö Fin. 54 M5

▶**Vaiaku** Tuvalu 133 H2
Capital of Tuvalu, on Funafuti atoll.

Vaida Estonia 55 N7
Vaiden U.S.A. 161 F5
Vail U.S.A. 154 F4
Vailly-sur-Aisne France 62 D5
Vaitupu *i.* Tuvalu 133 H2
Vajrakarur India *see* **Kanur**
Vakhsh Tajik. 111 H2
Vakhsh *r.* Tajik. 111 H2
Vakhstroy Tajik. *see* **Vakhsh**
Vakīlābād Iran 110 E4
Valbo Sweden 55 J6
Valcheta Arg. 178 C6
Valdai Hills Rus. Fed. *see* **Valdayskaya Vozvyshennost'**
Valday Rus. Fed. 52 G4
Valdayskaya Vozvyshennost' *hills* Rus. Fed. 52 G4
Valdecañas, Embalse de *resr* Spain 67 D4
Valdemārpils Latvia 55 M8
Valdemarsvik Sweden 55 J7
Valdepeñas Spain 67 E4
Val-de-Reuil France 62 B5
Valdés, Península *pen.* Arg. 178 D6
Valdez *AK* U.S.A. 149 K3
Valdivia Chile 178 B5
Val-d'Or Canada 152 F4
Valdosta U.S.A. 163 D6
Valdres *valley* Norway 55 F6
Vale Georgia 113 F2
Vale U.S.A. 156 D3
Valemount Canada 150 G4
Valença Brazil 179 D1
Valence France 66 G4
València Spain *see* **Valencia**
Valencia Spain 67 F4
Valencia *reg.* Spain 67 F4
Valencia Venez. 176 E1
Valencia, Golfo de *g.* Spain 67 G4
Valencia de Don Juan Spain 67 D2
Valencia Island Ireland 61 B6
Valenciennes France 62 D4
Valensole, Plateau de France 66 H5
Valentia Spain *see* **Valencia**
Valentin Rus. Fed. 90 D4
Valentine U.S.A. 160 C3
Valentine *TX* U.S.A. 166 D2
Valenzuela *Luzon* Phil. 82 C3
Våler Norway 55 G6
Valera Venez. 176 D2
Vale Verde Brazil 179 D2
Val Grande, Parco Nazionale della *nat. park* Italy 68 C1
Valjevo Serbia 69 H2
Valka Latvia 55 O8
Valkeakoski Fin. 55 N6
Valkenswaard Neth. 62 F3
Valky Ukr. 53 G6
Valkyrie Dome *ice feature* Antarctica 188 D1
Valladolid Mex. 167 H4
Valladolid Spain 67 D3
Vallard, Lac *l.* Canada 153 H3
Valle Norway 55 E7
Vallecillos Mex. 167 F3
Vallecito Reservoir U.S.A. 159 J3
Valle de Banderas Mex. 166 D4
Valle de la Pascua Venez. 176 E2
Valle de Olivos Mex. 166 D3
Valle de Santiago Mex. 167 E4
Valle de Zaragoza Mex. 166 D3
Valledupar Col. 176 D1
Vallée-Jonction Canada 153 H5
Valle Fértil, Sierra de *mts* Arg. 178 C4
Valle Grande Bol. 176 F7
Valle Hermoso Mex. 167 F3
Vallejo U.S.A. 158 B2
Valle Nacional Mex. 167 F5
Vallenar Chile 178 B3

▶**Valletta** Malta 68 F7
Capital of Malta.

Valley *r.* Canada 151 L5
Valley U.K. 58 C5
Valley City U.S.A. 160 D2
Valley Head *hd Luzon* Phil. 82 C2
Valleyview Canada 150 G4
Valls Spain 67 G3
Val Marie Canada 151 J5
Valmiera Latvia 55 N8
Valmy U.S.A. 158 E1
Valnera *mt.* Spain 67 E2
Valognes France 59 F9
Valona Albania *see* **Vlorë**
Valozhyn Belarus 55 O9
Val-Paradis Canada 152 F4
Valparai India 106 C4
Valparaíso Chile 178 B4
Valparaíso Mex. 166 E4
Valparaiso *FL* U.S.A. 167 I2
Valparaiso U.S.A. 164 B3
Valpoi India 106 B3
Valréas France 66 G4
Vals, Tanjung *c.* Indon. 81 J8
Valsad India 106 B1
Valspan S. Africa 124 G4
Val'tevo Rus. Fed. 52 J2
Valtimo Fin. 54 P5
Valuyevka Rus. Fed. 53 I7
Valuyki Rus. Fed. 53 H6
Vammala Fin. 55 M6
Van Turkey 113 F3
Van, Lake *salt l.* Turkey 113 F3
Vanadzor Armenia 113 G2
Van Buren *AR* U.S.A. 161 E5
Van Buren *MO* U.S.A. 161 F4
Van Buren *OH* U.S.A. *see* **Kettering**
Vanceburg U.S.A. 164 D4
Vanch Tajik. *see* **Vanj**
Vancleve U.S.A. 164 D5
Vancouver Canada 150 F5
Vancouver U.S.A. 156 C3
Vancouver, Cape *AK* U.S.A. 148 F3
Vancouver, Mount Canada/U.S.A. 149 M3
Vancouver Island Canada 150 E5
Vanda Fin. *see* **Vantaa**
Vandalia *IL* U.S.A. 160 F4
Vandalia *OH* U.S.A. 164 C4
Vandekerckhove Lake Canada 151 K3
Vanderbijlpark S. Africa 125 H4
Vanderbilt U.S.A. 164 C1
Vandergrift U.S.A. 164 F3
Vanderhoof Canada 150 E4
Vanderkloof Dam *resr* S. Africa 124 G6
Vanderlin Island Australia 136 B2
Vanderwagen U.S.A. 159 I4
Van Diemen, Cape *N.T.* Australia 134 E2
Van Diemen, Cape *Qld* Australia 136 B3
Van Diemen Gulf Australia 134 F2
Van Diemen's Land *state* Australia *see* **Tasmania**
Vändra Estonia 55 N7
Väner, Lake Sweden *see* **Vänern**

▶**Vänern** *l.* Sweden 55 H7
4th largest lake in Europe.

Vänersborg Sweden 55 H7
Vangaindrano Madag. 123 E6
Van Gia Vietnam 87 E4
Van Gölü *salt l.* Turkey *see* **Van, Lake**
Van Horn U.S.A. 157 G7
Vanikoro Islands Solomon Is 133 G3
Vanimo P.N.G. 81 K7
Vanino Rus. Fed. 90 F2
Vanivilasa Sagara *resr* India 106 C3
Vaniyambadi India 106 C3
Vanj Tajik. 111 H2
Vankarem Rus. Fed. 148 D2
Vankarem *r.* Rus. Fed. 148 C2
Vankarem, Laguna *lag.* Rus. Fed. 148 D2
Vännäs Sweden 54 K5
Vannes France 66 C3
Vannes, Lac *l.* Canada 153 I3
Vannovka Kazakh. *see* **Turar Ryskulov**
Vannøya *i.* Norway 54 K1
Van Rees, Pegunungan *mts* Indon. 81 J7
Vanrhynsdorp S. Africa 124 D6
Vansant U.S.A. 164 D5
Vansbro Sweden 55 I6
Vansittart Island Canada 147 J3
Van Starkenborgh Kanaal *canal* Neth. 62 G1
Vantaa Fin. 55 N6
Van Truer Tableland *reg.* Australia 135 C6
Vanua Lava *i.* Vanuatu 133 G3
Vanua Levu *i.* Fiji 133 H3
Vanuatu *country* S. Pacific Ocean 133 G3
Van Wert U.S.A. 164 C3
Vanwyksvlei S. Africa 124 E6
Vanwyksvlei *l.* S. Africa 124 E6
Văn Yên Vietnam 86 D2
Van Zylsrus S. Africa 124 F4
Varadero Cuba 163 D8
Varahi India 104 B5
Varakļāni Latvia 55 O8
Varalé Côte d'Ivoire 120 C4
Varāmīn Iran 110 C3
Varanasi India 105 E4
Varandey Rus. Fed. 52 M1
Varangerfjorden *sea chan.* Norway 54 P1
Varangerhalvøya *pen.* Norway 51 L1
Varangerhalvøya *pen.* Norway 54 P1
Varaždin Croatia 68 G1
Varberg Sweden 55 H8
Vardar *r.* Macedonia 69 J4
Varde Denmark 55 F9
Vardenis Armenia 113 G2
Vardø Norway 54 Q1
Varel Germany 63 I1
Varėna Lith. 55 N9
Varese Italy 68 C2
Varfolomeyevka Rus. Fed. 90 D3
Vårgårda Sweden 55 H7
Varginha Brazil 179 B3
Varik Neth. 62 F3
Varillas Chile 178 B2
Varkana Iran *see* **Gorgān**
Varkaus Fin. 54 O5
Varna Bulg. 69 L3
Värnamo Sweden 55 I8
Värnäs Sweden 55 H6
Varnavino Rus. Fed. 52 J4
Várnjárg *pen.* Norway *see* **Varangerhalvøya**
Varpaisjärvi Fin. 54 O5
Várpalota Hungary 68 H1
Varsaj Afgh. 111 H2
Varsh, Ozero *l.* Rus. Fed. 52 J2
Varto Turkey 113 F3
Várzea da Palma Brazil 179 B2
Vasa Fin. *see* **Vaasa**
Vasai India 106 B2
Vashka *r.* Rus. Fed. 52 J2
Vasht Iran *see* **Khāsh**
Vasilkov Ukr. *see* **Vasyl'kiv**
Vasknarva Estonia 55 O7
Vaslui Romania 69 L1
Vassar U.S.A. 164 D2
Vas-Soproni-síkság *hills* Hungary 68 G1
Vastan Turkey *see* **Gevaş**
Västerås Sweden 55 J7
Västerdalälven *r.* Sweden 55 I6
Västerfjäll Sweden 54 J3
Västerhaninge Sweden 55 K7
Västervik Sweden 55 J8
Vasto Italy 68 F3
Vasyl'kiv Ukr. 53 F6
Vatan France 66 E3
Vaté *i.* Vanuatu *see* **Éfaté**
Vatersay *i.* U.K. 60 B4
Vathar India 106 B2
Vathí Greece *see* **Vathy**
Vathy Greece 69 L6

▶**Vatican City** Europe 68 E4
Independent papal state, the smallest country in the world.

Vaticano, Città del Europe *see* **Vatican City**
Vatnajökull *ice cap* Iceland 54 [inset]
Vatnajökull *nat. park* Iceland 54 [inset]
Vatoa *i.* Fiji 133 I3
Vatra Dornei Romania 69 K1
Vätter, Lake Sweden *see* **Vättern**
Vättern *l.* Sweden 55 I7
Vaughn U.S.A. 157 G6
Vaupés *r.* Col. 176 E3
Vauquelin *r.* Canada 152 F3
Vauvert France 66 G5
Vauxhall Canada 151 H5
Vavatenina Madag. 123 E5
Vava'u Group *is* Tonga 133 I3
Vavitao *i.* Fr. Polynesia *see* **Raivavae**
Vavoua Côte d'Ivoire 120 C4
Vavozh Rus. Fed. 52 K4
Vavuniya Sri Lanka 106 D4
Vawkavysk Belarus 55 N10
Växjö Sweden 55 I8
Vay, Đao *i.* Vietnam 87 C5
Vayegi Rus. Fed. 77 S3
Vayenga Rus. Fed. *see* **Severomorsk**
Vazante Brazil 179 B2
Vazáš Sweden *see* **Vittangi**
Veaikevárri Sweden *see* **Svappavaara**
Veal Vêng Cambodia 87 C4
Vecht *r.* Neth. 62 G2
also known as Vechte (Germany)
Vechta Germany 63 I2
Vechte *r.* Germany 63 G2
also known as Vecht (Netherlands)
Veckerhagen (Reinhardshagen) Germany 63 J3
Vedaranniyam India 106 C4
Vedasandur India 106 C4
Veddige Sweden 55 H8
Vedea *r.* Romania 69 K3
Veedersburg U.S.A. 164 B3
Veendam Neth. 62 G1
Veenendaal Neth. 62 F2
Vega *i.* Norway 54 G4
Vega U.S.A. 161 C5
Vega de Alatorre Mex. 167 F4
Vega Point *pt AK* U.S.A. 149 [inset]
Vegreville Canada 151 H4
Vehari Pak. 111 I4
Vehkalahti Fin. 55 O6
Vehoa Pak. 111 H4
Veinticinco de Mayo *Buenos Aires* Arg. *see* **25 de Mayo**
Veinticinco de Mayo *La Pampa* Arg. *see* **25 de Mayo**
Veirwaro Pak. 111 H5
Veitshöchheim Germany 63 J5
Vejle Denmark 55 F9
Vekil'bazar Turkm. *see* **Wekilbazar**
Velardena Mex. 166 E3
Velas, Cabo *c.* Costa Rica 166 [inset] I7
Velbert Germany 62 H3
Velbŭzhdki Prokhod *pass* Bulg./Macedonia 69 J3
Velddrif S. Africa 124 D7
Velebit *mts* Croatia 68 F2
Velen Germany 62 G3
Velenje Slovenia 68 F1
Veles Macedonia 69 I4
Vélez-Málaga Spain 67 D5
Vélez-Rubio Spain 67 E5
Velhas *r.* Brazil 179 B2
Velibaba Turkey *see* **Aras**
Velika Gorica Croatia 68 G2
Velika Plana Serbia 69 I2
Velikaya *r.* Rus. Fed. 52 K4
Velikaya *r.* Rus. Fed. 55 P8
Velikaya *r.* Rus. Fed. 77 S3
Velikaya Kema Rus. Fed. 90 E3
Veliki Preslav Bulg. 69 L3
Velikiye Luki Rus. Fed. 52 F4
Velikiy Novgorod Rus. Fed. 52 F4
Velikiy Ustyug Rus. Fed. 52 J3
Velikonda Range *hills* India 106 C3
Veliko Tŭrnovo Bulg. 69 K3
Velikoye Rus. Fed. 52 H4
Velikoye, Ozero *l.* Rus. Fed. 53 I5
Veli Lošinj Croatia 68 F2
Velizh Rus. Fed. 52 F5
Vella Lavella *i.* Solomon Is 133 F2
Vellar *r.* India 106 C4
Vellberg Germany 63 J5
Vellmar Germany 63 J3
Vellore India 106 C3
Velpke Germany 63 K2
Vel'sk Rus. Fed. 52 I3
Velsuna Italy *see* **Orvieto**
Velten Germany 63 N2
Veluwezoom, Nationaal Park *nat. park* Neth. 62 F2
Velykyy Tokmak Ukr. *see* **Tokmak**
Vel'yu *r.* Rus. Fed. 52 L3
Vemalwada India 106 C2
Vema Seamount *sea feature* S. Atlantic Ocean 184 I8
Vema Trench *sea feature* Indian Ocean 185 M6
Vempalle India 106 C3
Venado, Isla del *i.* Nicaragua 166 [inset] J7
Venado Tuerto Arg. 178 D4
Venafro Italy 68 F4
Venceslau Bráz Brazil 179 A3
Vendinga Rus. Fed. 52 J3
Vendôme France 66 E3
Venegas Mex. 161 C8
Venetia Italy *see* **Venice**
Venetie *AK* U.S.A. 149 K2
Venetie Landing *AK* U.S.A. 149 K2
Venev Rus. Fed. 53 H5
Venezia Italy *see* **Venice**
Venezia, Golfo di *g.* Europe *see* **Venice, Gulf of**

▶**Venezuela** *country* S. America 176 E2
5th most populous country in South America.

Venezuela, Golfo de *g.* Venez. 176 D1
Venezuelan Basin *sea feature* S. Atlantic Ocean 184 D4
Vengurla India 106 B3
Veniaminof Volcano U.S.A. 146 C4
Venice Italy 68 E2
Venice U.S.A. 163 D7
Venice *LA* U.S.A. 167 H2
Venice, Gulf of Europe 68 E2
Vénissieux France 66 G4
Venkatapalem India 106 D2
Venkatapuram India 106 D2
Venlo Neth. 62 G3
Vennesla Norway 55 E7
Venray Neth. 62 F3
Venta *r.* Latvia/Lith. 55 M8
Venta Lith. 55 M8
Ventersburg S. Africa 125 H5
Ventersdorp S. Africa 125 H4
Venterstad S. Africa 125 G6
Ventnor U.K. 59 F8
Ventotene, Isola *i.* Italy 68 E4
Ventoux, Mont *mt.* France 66 G4
Ventspils Latvia 55 L8
Ventura U.S.A. 158 D4
Venus Bay Australia 138 B7
Venustiano Carranza Mex. 161 C7
Venustiano Carranza, Presa *resr* Mex. 167 E3
Vera Arg. 178 D3
Vera Spain 67 F5
Vera Cruz Brazil 179 A3
Veracruz Mex. 168 E5
Vera Cruz Mex. *see* **Veracruz**
Veracruz *state* Mex. 167 F4
Veraval India 104 B5
Verbania Italy 68 C2
Vercelli Italy 68 C2
Vercors *reg.* France 66 G4
Verdalsøra Norway 54 G5
Verde *r. Goiás* Brazil 179 A2
Verde *r. Goiás* Brazil 179 A2
Verde *r. Goiás* Brazil 179 B2
Verde *r. Minas Gerais* Brazil 179 A2
Verde *r. Chihuahua/Durango* Mex. 166 D3
Verde *r.* U.S.A. 159 H5
Verde Island Passage Phil. 82 C3
Verden (Aller) Germany 63 J2
Verde Pequeno *r.* Brazil 179 C1
Verdi U.S.A. 158 D2
Verdon *r.* France 66 G5
Verdun France 62 F5
Vereeniging S. Africa 125 H4
Vereshchagino Rus. Fed. 51 Q4
Vergennes U.S.A. 165 I1
Véria Greece *see* **Veroia**
Verín Spain 67 C3
Veríssimo Brazil 179 A2
Verkhneberezovskiy Kazakh. 98 C2
Verkhneimbatsk Rus. Fed. 76 J3
Verkhnekolvinsk Rus. Fed. 52 M2
Verkhnespasskoye Rus. Fed. 52 J4
Verkhnetulomskiy Rus. Fed. 54 Q2
Verkhnetulomskoye Vodokhranilishche *res.* Rus. Fed. 54 Q2
Verkhnevilyuysk Rus. Fed. 77 N3
Verkhneye Kuyto, Ozero *l.* Rus. Fed. 54 Q4
Verkhnezeysk Rus. Fed. 89 N2
Verkhniy Shergol'dzhin Rus. Fed. 95 G1
Verkhniy Ul'khun Rus. Fed. 95 H1
Verkhniy Vyalozerskiy Rus. Fed. 52 G2
Verkhnyaya Khava Rus. Fed. 53 H6
Verkhnyaya Salda Rus. Fed. 51 S4
Verkhnyaya Tunguska *r.* Rus. Fed. *see* **Angara**
Verkhnyaya Tura Rus. Fed. 51 R4
Verkhoshizhem'ye Rus. Fed. 52 K4
Verkhovazh'ye Rus. Fed. 52 I3
Verkhov'ye Rus. Fed. 53 H5
Verkhoyansk Rus. Fed. 77 O3
Verkhoyanskiy Khrebet *mts* Rus. Fed. 77 N2
Verkhuba Kazakh. 98 C2
Vermand France 62 D5
Vermelho *r.* Brazil 179 A1
Vermilion Canada 151 I4
Vermilion Bay U.S.A. 161 F6
Vermilion Cliffs *AZ* U.S.A. 159 G3
Vermilion Cliffs *UT* U.S.A. 159 G3
Vermilion Cliffs National Monument *nat. park* U.S.A. 159 H3
Vermilion Lake U.S.A. 160 E2
Vermillion U.S.A. 160 D3
Vermillion Bay Canada 151 M5
Vermont *state* U.S.A. 165 I1
Vernadsky *research station* Antarctica 188 L2
Vernal U.S.A. 159 I1
Verner Canada 152 E5
Verneuk Pan *salt pan* S. Africa 124 E5
Vernon Canada 150 G5
Vernon France 62 B5
Vernon *AL* U.S.A. 163 C5
Vernon *IN* U.S.A. 164 C4
Vernon *TX* U.S.A. 161 D5
Vernon *UT* U.S.A. 159 G1
Vernon Islands Australia 134 E3
Vernoye Rus. Fed. 90 C2
Vernyy Kazakh. *see* **Almaty**
Vero Beach U.S.A. 163 D7
Veroia Greece 69 J4
Verona Italy 68 D2
Verona U.S.A. 164 F4
Versailles France 62 C6
Versailles *IN* U.S.A. 164 C4
Versailles *KY* U.S.A. 164 C4
Versailles *OH* U.S.A. 164 C3
Versec Serbia *see* **Vršac**
Versmold Germany 63 I2
Vert, Île *i.* Canada 153 H4
Vertou France 66 D3
Verulam S. Africa 125 J5
Verulamium U.K. *see* **St Albans**
Verviers Belgium 62 F4
Vervins France 62 D5
Verwood Canada 151 J5
Verzy France 62 E5
Vescovato *Corsica* France 66 I5
Vesele Ukr. 53 G7
Veselyy Rus. Fed. 53 I7
Veselyy Yar Rus. Fed. 90 D4
Veshenskaya Rus. Fed. 53 I6
Vesle *r.* France 62 D5
Veslyana *r.* Rus. Fed. 52 L3
Vesontio France *see* **Besançon**
Vesoul France 66 H3
Vessem Neth. 62 F3
Vesterålen *is* Norway 54 H2
Vesterålsfjorden *sea chan.* Norway 54 H2
Vestertana Norway 54 O1
Vestfjorddalen *valley* Norway 55 F7
Vestfjorden *sea chan.* Norway 54 H3
Véstia Brazil 179 A3
Vestmanna Faroe Is 54 [inset]
Vestmannaeyjar Iceland 54 [inset]
Vestmannaeyjar *is* Iceland 54 [inset]
Vestnes Norway 54 E5
Vesturhorn *hd* Iceland 54 [inset]
Vesuvio *vol.* Italy *see* **Vesuvius**
Vesuvius *vol.* Italy 68 F4
Ves'yegonsk Rus. Fed. 52 H4
Veszprém Hungary 68 G1
Veteli Fin. 54 M5
Veteran Canada 151 I4
Vetlanda Sweden 55 I8
Vetluga Rus. Fed. 52 J4
Vetluga *r.* Rus. Fed. 52 J4
Vetluzhskiy *Kostromskaya Oblast'* Rus. Fed. 52 J4
Vetluzhskiy *Nizhegorodskaya Oblast'* Rus. Fed. 52 J4
Vettore, Monte *mt.* Italy 68 E3
Veurne Belgium 62 C3
Vevay U.S.A. 164 C4
Vevey Switz. 66 H3
Vexin Normand *reg.* France 62 B5
Veyo U.S.A. 159 G3
Vézère *r.* France 66 E4
Vezirköprü Turkey 112 D2
Vialar Alg. *see* **Tissemsilt**
Viamao Brazil 179 A5
Viana *Espírito Santo* Brazil 179 C3
Viana *Maranhão* Brazil 177 J4
Viana do Castelo Port. 67 B3
Vianen Neth. 62 F3
Viangchan Laos *see* **Vientiane**
Viangphoukha Laos 86 C2
Viannos Greece 69 K7
Vianópolis Brazil 179 A2
Viareggio Italy 68 D3
Viborg Denmark 55 F8
Viborg Rus. Fed. *see* **Vyborg**
Vibo Valentia Italy 68 G5
Vic Spain 67 H3
Vicam Mex. 166 C3
Vicecomodoro Marambio *research station* Antarctica *see* **Marambio**
Vicente, Point U.S.A. 158 D5
Vicente Guerrero *Baja California* Mex. 166 A2
Vicenza Italy 68 D2
Vich Spain *see* **Vic**
Vichada *r.* Col. 176 E3
Vichadero Uruguay 178 F4
Vichy France 66 F3
Vicksburg *AZ* U.S.A. 159 G5
Vicksburg *MS* U.S.A. 161 F5
Viçosa Brazil 179 C3
Victor, Mount Antarctica 188 D2
Victor Harbor Australia 137 B7
Victoria Arg. 178 D4
Victoria *r.* Australia 134 E3
Victoria *state* Australia 138 B6

▶**Victoria** Canada 150 F5
Capital of British Columbia.

Victoria Chile 178 B5
Victoria Malaysia *see* **Labuan**
Victoria Malta 68 F6
Victoria *Luzon* Phil. 82 C3

▶**Victoria** Seychelles 185 L6
Capital of the Seychelles.

Victoria *TX* U.S.A. 161 D6
Victoria *VA* U.S.A. 165 F5
Victoria *prov.* Zimbabwe *see* **Masvingo**

▶**Victoria, Lake** Africa 122 D4
Largest lake in Africa, and 3rd in the world.

Victoria, Lake Australia 137 C7
Victoria, Mount Fiji *see* **Tomanivi**
Victoria, Mount Myanmar 86 A2
Victoria, Mount P.N.G. 81 L8
Victoria and Albert Mountains Canada 147 K2
Victoria Falls Zambia/Zimbabwe 123 C5
Victoria Harbour *sea chan.* H.K. China *see* **Hong Kong Harbour**

▶**Victoria Island** Canada 146 H2
3rd largest island in North America, and 9th in the world.

Victoria Land *coastal area* Antarctica 188 H2
Victoria Peak Belize 168 G5
Victoria Peak *hill* H.K. China 97 [inset]
Victoria Range *mts* N.Z. 139 D6
Victoria River Downs Australia 134 E4
Victoriaville Canada 153 H5
Victoria West S. Africa 124 F6
Victorica Arg. 178 C5
Víctor Rosales Mex. 166 E4
Victorville U.S.A. 158 E4
Victory Downs Australia 135 F6
Vidalia U.S.A. 161 F6
Vidal Junction U.S.A. 159 F4
Videle Romania 69 K2
Vidisha India 104 D5
Vidlin U.K. 60 [inset]
Vidlitsa Rus. Fed. 52 G3
Viechtach Germany 63 M5
Viedma Arg. 178 D6
Viedma, Lago *l.* Arg. 178 B7
Viejo, Cerro *mt.* Mex. 166 B2
Vielank Germany 63 L1
Vielsalm Belgium 62 F4
Vienenburg Germany 63 K3

▶**Vienna** Austria 57 P6
Capital of Austria.

Vienna *MO* U.S.A. 160 F4
Vienna *WV* U.S.A. 164 E4
Vienne France 66 G4
Vienne *r.* France 66 E3

▶**Vientiane** Laos 86 C3
Capital of Laos.

Vieques *i.* Puerto Rico 169 K5
Vieremä Fin. 54 O5
Viersen Germany 62 G3
Vierzon France 66 F3
Viesca Mex. 166 E3
Viesīte Latvia 55 N8
Vieste Italy 68 G4
Vietas Sweden 54 K3
Vietnam *country* Asia 86 D3
Viêt Nam *country* Asia *see* **Vietnam**
Viêt Quang Vietnam 86 D2
Viêt Tri Vietnam 86 D2
Vieux Comptoir, Lac du *l.* Canada 152 F3
Vieux-Fort Canada 153 K4
Vieux Poste, Pointe du *pt* Canada 153 J4
Vigan *Luzon* Phil. 82 C2
Vigevano Italy 68 C2
Vigia Brazil 177 I4
Vigía Chico Mex. 167 I5
Vignacourt France 62 C4
Vignemale *mt.* France 64 D3
Vignola Italy 68 D2
Vigo Spain 67 B2
Vihanti Fin. 54 N4
Vihti Fin. 55 N6
Viipuri Rus. Fed. *see* **Vyborg**
Viitasaari Fin. 54 N5
Vijayadurg India 106 B2
Vijayanagaram India *see* **Vizianagaram**
Vijayapati India 106 C4
Vijayawada India 106 D2
Vík Iceland 54 [inset]
Vikajärvi Fin. 54 O3
Vikeke East Timor *see* **Viqueque**
Viking Canada 151 I4
Vikna *i.* Norway 54 G4
Vikøyri Norway 55 E6
Vila Vanuatu *see* **Port Vila**
Vila Alferes Chamusca Moz. *see* **Guija**
Vila Bittencourt Brazil 176 E4
Vila Bugaço Angola *see* **Camanongue**
Vila Cabral Moz. *see* **Lichinga**
Vila da Ponte Angola *see* **Kuvango**
Vila de Aljustrel Angola *see* **Cangamba**
Vila de Almoster Angola *see* **Chiange**
Vila de João Belo Moz. *see* **Xai-Xai**
Vila de María Arg. 178 D3
Vila de Trego Morais Moz. *see* **Chókwé**
Vila Fontes Moz. *see* **Caia**
Vila Franca de Xira Port. 67 B4
Vilagarcía de Arousa Spain 67 B2
Vila Gomes da Costa Moz. 125 K3
Vilalba Spain 67 C2
Vila Luísa Moz. *see* **Marracuene**
Vila Marechal Carmona Angola *see* **Uíge**
Vila Miranda Moz. *see* **Macaloge**
Vilanandro, Tanjona *pt* Madag. 123 E5
Vilanculos Moz. 125 L1
Vila Nova de Gaia Port. 67 B3
Vilanova i la Geltrú Spain 67 G3
Vila Pery Moz. *see* **Chimoio**
Vila Real Port. 67 C3
Vilar Formoso Port. 67 C3
Vila Salazar Angola *see* **N'dalatando**
Vila Salazar Zimbabwe *see* **Sango**
Vila Teixeira de Sousa Angola *see* **Luau**
Vila Velha Brazil 179 C3
Vilcabamba, Cordillera *mts* Peru 176 D6
Vil'cheka, Zemlya *i.* Rus. Fed. 76 H1
Vileid' *r.* Rus. Fed. 52 J3
Vileyka Belarus *see* **Vilyeyka**
Vil'gort Rus. Fed. 52 K3
Vilhelmina Sweden 54 J4
Vilhena Brazil 176 F6

Viliya r. Belarus/Lith. see Neris
Viljandi Estonia 55 N7
Viljoenskroon S. Africa 125 H4
Vilkaviškis Lith. 55 M9
Vilkija Lith. 55 M9
Vil'kitskogo, Proliv strait Rus. Fed. 77 K2
Vilkovo Ukr. see Vylkove
Villa Abecia Bol. 176 E8
Villa Ahumada Mex. 166 D2
Villa Ángela Arg. 178 D3
Villa Bella Bol. 176 E6
Villa Bens Morocco see Tarfaya
Villablino Spain 67 C2
Villacañas Spain 67 E4
Villach Austria 57 N7
Villacidro Sardinia Italy 68 C5
Villa Cisneros W. Sahara see Ad Dakhla
Villa Comaltitlán Mex. 167 G6
Villa Coronado Mex. 166 D3
Villa de Álvarez Mex. 166 E5
Villa de Cos Mex. 166 E4
Villa de Guadalupe Campeche Mex. 167 H5
Villa Dolores Arg. 178 C4
Villa Flores Mex. 167 G5
Villagarcía de Arosa Spain see Vilagarcía de Arousa
Villagrán Mex. 161 D7
Villaguay Arg. 178 E4
Villahermosa Mex. 167 G5
Villa Insurgentes Mex. 166 C3
Villajoyosa Spain see Villajoyosa-La Vila Joíosa
Villajoyosa-La Vila Joíosa Spain 67 F4
Villa La Venta Mex. 167 G5
Villaldama Mex. 167 E3
Villa Mainero Mex. 161 D7
Villa María Arg. 178 D4
Villa Montes Bol. 176 F8
Villa Nora S. Africa 125 I2
Villanueva Mex. 166 E4
Villanueva de la Serena Spain 67 D4
Villanueva de los Infantes Spain 67 E4
Villanueva-y-Geltrú Spain see Vilanova i la Geltrú
Villa Ocampo Arg. 178 E3
Villa Ocampo Mex. 166 D3
Villa Ojo de Agua Arg. 178 D3
Villa O. Pereyra Mex. see Villa Orestes Pereyra
Villa Orestes Pereyra Mex. 166 D3
Villaputzu Sardinia Italy 68 C5
Villa Regina Arg. 178 C5
Villarrica Para. 178 E3
Villarrica, Lago l. Chile 178 B5
Villarrica, Parque Nacional nat. park Chile 178 B5
Villarrobledo Spain 67 E4
Villas U.S.A. 165 H4
Villasalazar Zimbabwe see Sango
Villa San Giovanni Italy 68 F5
Villa Sanjurjo Morocco see Al Hoceima
Villa San Martin Arg. 178 D3
Villa Unión Arg. 178 C3
Villa Unión Coahuila Mex. 167 E2
Villa Unión Durango Mex. 161 B8
Villa Unión Sinaloa Mex. 168 C4
Villa Valeria Arg. 178 D4
Villavicencio Col. 176 D3
Villazon Bol. 176 E8
Villefranche-sur-Saône France 66 G4
Ville-Marie Canada see Montréal
Villena Spain 67 F4
Villeneuve-sur-Lot France 66 E4
Villeneuve-sur-Yonne France 66 F2
Ville Platte LA U.S.A. 167 G2
Villers-Cotterêts France 62 D5
Villers-sur-Mer France 59 G9
Villerupt France 62 F5
Villeurbanne France 66 G4
Villiers S. Africa 125 I4
Villingen Germany 57 L6
Villuppuram India see Villupuram
Villupuram India 106 C4
Vilna Canada 151 I4
Vilna Lith. see Vilnius

▶Vilnius Lith. 55 N9
Capital of Lithuania.

Vil'nyans'k Ukr. 53 G7
Vilppula Fin. 54 N5
Vils r. Germany 63 L5
Vils r. Germany 63 N6
Vilvoorde Belgium 62 E4
Vilyeyka Belarus 55 O9
Vilyuy r. Rus. Fed. 77 N3
Vilyuyskoye Vodokhranilishche resr Rus. Fed. 77 M3
Vimmerby Sweden 55 I8
Vimy France 62 C4
Vina r. Cameroon 121 E4
Vina U.S.A. 158 B2
Viña del Mar Chile 178 B4
Vinalhaven Island U.S.A. 162 G2
Vinaròs Spain 67 G3
Vinaroz Spain see Vinaròs
Vincelotte, Lac l. Canada 153 G3
Vincennes U.S.A. 164 B4
Vincennes Bay Antarctica 188 F2
Vinchina Arg. 178 C3
Vindelälven r. Sweden 54 K5
Vindeln Sweden 54 K4
Vindhya Range hills India 104 C5
Vindobona Austria see Vienna
Vine Grove U.S.A. 164 C5
Vineland U.S.A. 165 H4
Vinh Vietnam 86 D3
Vinh Loc Vietnam 86 D2
Vinh Long Vietnam 87 D5
Vinh Thưc, Đao i. Vietnam 86 D2
Vinita U.S.A. 161 E4
Vinjhan India 104 B5
Vinland i. Canada see Newfoundland
Vinnitsa Ukr. see Vinnytsya
Vinnytsya Ukr. 53 F6
Vinogradov Ukr. see Vynohradiv
Vinson Massif mt. Antarctica 188 L1
Vinstra Norway 55 F6
Vintar Luzon Phil. 82 C2
Vinton U.S.A. 160 E3
Vinukonda India 106 C2
Violeta Cuba see Primero de Enero
Vipperow Germany 63 M1
Viqueque East Timor 83 C5
Virac Phil. 82 D3
Viramgam India 104 C5
Viranşehir Turkey 113 E3
Virawah Pak. 111 H5
Virchow, Mount hill Australia 134 B5
Virdel India 104 C5
Virden Canada 151 K5
Virden U.S.A. 159 I5
Vire France 66 D2
Virei Angola 123 B5
Virgem da Lapa Brazil 179 C2
Virgilina U.S.A. 165 F5
Virgin r. U.S.A. 159 F3
Virginia Ireland 61 E4
Virginia S. Africa 125 H5
Virginia U.S.A. 160 F4
Virginia state U.S.A. 164 F5
Virginia Beach U.S.A. 165 H5
Virginia City MT U.S.A. 156 F3
Virginia City NV U.S.A. 158 D2
Virginia Falls N.W.T. Canada 149 P3

▶Virgin Islands (U.K.) terr. West Indies 169 L5
United Kingdom Overseas Territory.

▶Virgin Islands (U.S.A.) terr. West Indies 169 L5
United States Unincorporated Territory.

Virgin Mountains U.S.A. 159 F3
Virginópolis Brazil 179 C2
Virkkala Fin. 55 N6
Virôchey Cambodia 87 D4
Viroqua U.S.A. 160 F3
Virovitica Croatia 68 G2
Virrat Fin. 54 M5
Virton Belgium 62 F5
Virtsu Estonia 55 M7
Virudhunagar India 106 C4
Virudunagar India see Virudhunagar
Virunga, Parc National des nat. park Dem. Rep. Congo 122 C4
Vis i. Croatia 68 G3
Visaginas Lith. 55 O9
Visakhapatnam India see Vishakhapatnam
Visalia U.S.A. 158 D3
Visapur India 106 B2
Visayan Islands Phil. 82 D4
Visayan Sea Phil. 82 C4
Visbek Germany 63 I2
Visby Sweden 55 K8
Viscount Melville Sound sea chan. Canada 147 G2
Visé Belgium 62 F4
Višegrad Bos.-Herz. 69 H3
Viseu Brazil 177 I4
Viseu Port. 67 C3
Vishakhapatnam India 106 D2
Vishera r. Rus. Fed. 51 R4
Vishera r. Rus. Fed. 52 L3
Višķi Latvia 55 O8
Visnagar India 104 C5
Viso, Monte mt. Italy 68 B2
Visoko Bos.-Herz. 68 H3
Visp Switz. 66 H3
Visselhövede Germany 63 J2
Vista U.S.A. 158 E5
Vista Lake U.S.A. 158 D4
Vistonida, Limni lag. Greece 69 K4
Vistula r. Poland 57 Q3
Vitebsk Belarus see Vitsyebsk
Viterbo Italy 68 E3
Vitichi Bol. 176 E8
Vitigudino Spain 67 C3
Viti Levu i. Fiji 133 H3
Vitimskoye Ploskogor'ye plat. Rus. Fed. 89 K2
Vitória Brazil 179 C3
Vitória da Conquista Brazil 179 C1
Vitoria-Gasteiz Spain 67 E2
Vitória Seamount sea feature S. Atlantic Ocean 184 F7
Vitré France 66 D2
Vitry-en-Artois France 62 C4
Vitry-le-François France 62 E6
Vitsyebsk Belarus 53 F5
Vittangi Sweden 54 L3
Vittel France 66 G2
Vittoria Sicily Italy 68 F6
Vittorio Veneto Italy 68 E2
Viveiro Spain 67 C2
Vivero Spain see Viveiro
Vivo S. Africa 125 I2
Vizagapatam India see Vishakhapatnam
Vizcaíno, Desierto de des. Mex. 166 B3
Vizcaíno, Sierra mts Mex. 166 B3
Vize Turkey 69 L4
Vize, Ostrov i. Rus. Fed. 76 I2
Vizhas r. Rus. Fed. 52 J2
Vizianagaram India 106 D2
Vizinga Rus. Fed. 52 K3
Vlaardingen Neth. 62 E3
Vlădeasa, Vârful mt. Romania 69 J1
Vladikavkaz Rus. Fed. 113 G2
Vladimir Primorskiy Kray Rus. Fed. 90 D4
Vladimir Vladimirskaya Oblast' Rus. Fed. 52 I4
Vladimiro-Aleksandrovskoye Rus. Fed. 90 D4
Vladimir-Volynskiy Ukr. see Volodymyr-Volyns'kyy
Vladivostok Rus. Fed. 90 C4
Vlakte S. Africa 125 I3
Vlasotince Serbia 69 J3
Vlas'yevo Rus. Fed. 90 F1
Vlieland i. Neth. 62 E1
Vlissingen Neth. 62 D3
Vlora Albania see Vlorë
Vlorë Albania 69 H4
Vlotho Germany 63 I2
Vlotslavsk Poland see Włocławek
Vltava r. Czech Rep. 57 O5
Vobkent Uzbek. 111 G1
Vöcklabruck Austria 57 N6
Vodlozero, Ozero l. Rus. Fed. 52 H3
Voe U.K. 60 [inset]
Voerendaal Neth. 62 F4
Vogelkop Peninsula Indon. see Doberai, Jazirah
Vogelsberg hills Germany 63 I4
Voghera Italy 68 C2
Vohburg an der Donau Germany 63 L6
Vohémar Madag. see Iharaña
Vohenstrauß Germany 63 M5
Vohibinany Madag. see Ampasimanolotra
Vohimarina Madag. see Iharaña
Vohimena, Tanjona c. Madag. 123 E6
Vohipeno Madag. 123 E6
Vöhl Germany 63 I3
Võhma Estonia 55 N7
Voinjama Liberia 120 C4
Vojens Denmark 55 F9
Vojvodina prov. Serbia 69 H2
Vokhma Rus. Fed. 52 J4
Voknavolok Rus. Fed. 54 Q4
Vol' r. Rus. Fed. 52 L3
Volcán Barú, Parque Nacional nat. park Panama 166 [inset] J7
Volcano Bay Japan see Uchiura-wan

▶Volcano Islands Japan 81 K2
Part of Japan.

Volda Norway 54 E5
Vol'dino Rus. Fed. 52 L3
Volendam Neth. 62 F2
Volga Rus. Fed. 52 H4

▶Volga r. Rus. Fed. 53 J7
Longest river in Europe.

Volga Upland hills Rus. Fed. see Privolzhskaya Vozvyshennost'
Volgodonsk Rus. Fed. 53 I7
Volgograd Rus. Fed. 53 J6
Volgogradskoye Vodokhranilishche resr Rus. Fed. 53 J6
Völkermarkt Austria 57 O7
Volkhov Rus. Fed. 52 G4
Volkhov r. Rus. Fed. 52 G3
Völklingen Germany 62 G5
Volkovysk Belarus see Vawkavysk
Volksrust S. Africa 125 I4
Vol'no-Nadezhdinskoye Rus. Fed. 90 C4
Volnovakha Ukr. 53 H7
Vol'nyansk Ukr. see Vil'nyans'k
Volochanka Rus. Fed. 76 K2
Volochisk Ukr. see Volochys'k
Volochys'k Ukr. 53 E6
Volodars'ke Ukr. 53 H7
Volodarskoye Kazakh. see Saumalkol'
Volodymyr-Volyns'kyy Ukr. 53 E6
Vologda Rus. Fed. 52 H4
Volokolamsk Rus. Fed. 52 G4
Volokovaya Rus. Fed. 52 K2
Volos Greece 69 J5
Volosovo Rus. Fed. 55 P7
Volot Rus. Fed. 52 F4
Volovo Rus. Fed. 53 H5
Volozhin Belarus see Valozhyn
Volsinii Italy see Orvieto
Vol'sk Rus. Fed. 53 J5

▶Volta, Lake resr Ghana 120 D4
4th largest lake in Africa.

Volta Blanche r. Burkina Faso/Ghana see White Volta
Voltaire, Cape Australia 134 D3
Volta Redonda Brazil 179 B3
Volturno r. Italy 68 E4
Volubilis tourist site Morocco 64 C5
Volvi, Limni l. Greece 69 J4
Volzhsk Rus. Fed. 52 K5
Volzhskiy Samarskaya Oblast' Rus. Fed. 53 K5
Volzhskiy Volgogradskaya Oblast' Rus. Fed. 53 J6
Vondanka Rus. Fed. 52 J4
Von Frank Mountain AK U.S.A. 148 I3
Vontimitta India 106 C3
Vopnafjörður Iceland 54 [inset]
Vopnafjörður b. Iceland 54 [inset]
Vörå Fin. 54 M5
Voranava Belarus 55 N9
Voreies Sporades is Greece 69 J5
Voreioi Sporades is Greece see Voreies Sporades
Voring Plateau sea feature N. Atlantic Ocean 184 I1
Vorjing mt. India 105 H3
Vorkuta Rus. Fed. 76 H3
Vormsi i. Estonia 55 M7
Vorona r. Rus. Fed. 53 I6
Voronezh Rus. Fed. 53 H6
Voronezh r. Rus. Fed. 53 H6
Voronov, Mys pt Rus. Fed. 52 I2
Vorontsovo-Aleksandrovskoye Rus. Fed. see Zelenokumsk
Voroshilov Rus. Fed. see Ussuriysk
Voroshilovgrad Ukr. see Luhans'k
Voroshilovsk Rus. Fed. see Stavropol'
Voroshilovsk Ukr. see Alchevs'k
Vorotynets Rus. Fed. 52 J4
Vorozhba Ukr. 53 G6
Vorpommersche Boddenlandschaft, Nationalpark nat. park Germany 57 N3
Vorskla r. Rus. Fed. 53 G6
Võrtsjärv l. Estonia 55 N7
Võru Estonia 55 O8
Vorukh Tajik. 111 H2
Vosburg S. Africa 124 F6
Vose Tajik. 111 H2
Vosges mts France 66 H3
Voskresensk Rus. Fed. 53 H5
Voskresenskoye Rus. Fed. 52 H4
Voss Norway 55 E6
Vostochno-Sakhalinskiy Gory mts Rus. Fed. 90 F2
Vostochno-Sibirskoye More sea Rus. Fed. see East Siberian Sea
Vostochnyy Kirovskaya Oblast' Rus. Fed. 52 L4
Vostochnyy Sakhalinskaya Oblast' Rus. Fed. 90 F2
Vostochnyy Kazakhstan admin. div. Kazakh. 98 D2
Vostochnyy Sayan mts Rus. Fed. 88 G2
Vostok research station Antarctica 188 F1
Vostok Primorskiy Kray Rus. Fed. 90 D3
Vostok Sakhalinskaya Oblast' Rus. Fed. see Neftegorsk
Vostok Island Kiribati 187 J6
Vostroye Rus. Fed. 52 J3
Votkinsk Rus. Fed. 51 Q4
Votkinskoye Vodokhranilishche resr Rus. Fed. 51 R4
Votuporanga Brazil 179 A3
Vouziers France 62 E5
Voves France 66 E2
Voyageurs National Park U.S.A. 160 E1
Voynitsa Rus. Fed. 54 Q4
Vöyri Fin. see Vörå
Voyvozh Rus. Fed. 52 L3
Vozhayel' Rus. Fed. 52 K3
Vozhe, Ozero l. Rus. Fed. 52 H3
Vozhega Rus. Fed. 52 I3
Vozhgaly Rus. Fed. 52 K4
Voznesens'k Ukr. 53 F7
Vozonin Trough sea feature Arctic Ocean 189 F1
Vozrozhdenya Island i. Uzbek. 102 A3
Vozzhayevka Rus. Fed. 90 C2
Vrangel' Rus. Fed. 90 D4
Vrangelya, Mys pt Rus. Fed. 90 E1
Vrangelya, Ostrov i. Rus. Fed. see Wrangel Island
Vranje Serbia 69 I3
Vratnik pass Bulg. 69 L3
Vratsa Bulg. 69 J3
Vrbas Serbia 69 H2
Vrede S. Africa 125 I4
Vredefort S. Africa 125 H4
Vredenburg S. Africa 124 C7
Vredendal S. Africa 124 D6
Vresse Belgium 62 E5
Vriddhachalam India 106 C4
Vries Neth. 62 G1
Vrigstad Sweden 55 I8
Vršac Serbia 69 I2
Vryburg S. Africa 124 G4
Vryheid S. Africa 125 J4
Vsevidof, Mount vol. U.S.A. 146 B4
Vsevolozhsk Rus. Fed. 52 F3
Vu Ban Vietnam 86 D2
Vučitrn Kosovo see Vushtrri
Vukovar Croatia 69 H2
Vuktyl' Rus. Fed. 51 R3
Vukuzakhe S. Africa 125 I4
Vulcan Canada 150 H5
Vulcan Island P.N.G. see Manam Island
Vulcano, Isola i. Italy 68 F5
Vu Liêt Vietnam 86 D3
Vulture Mountains U.S.A. 159 G5
Vung Tau Vietnam 87 D5
Vuntut National Park Y.T. Canada 149 M1
Vuohijärvi Fin. 55 O6
Vuolijoki Fin. 54 O4
Vuollerim Sweden 54 L3
Vuostimo Fin. 54 O3
Vurnary Rus. Fed. 52 J5
Vushtrri Kosovo 69 I3
Vvedenovka Rus. Fed. 90 C2
Vyara India 104 C5
Vyarkhowye Belarus see Ruba
Vyatka Rus. Fed. see Kirov
Vyatka r. Rus. Fed. 52 K5
Vyatskiye Polyany Rus. Fed. 52 K4
Vyazemskiy Rus. Fed. 90 D3
Vyaz'ma Rus. Fed. 53 G5
Vyazniki Rus. Fed. 52 I4
Vyazovka Rus. Fed. 53 J5
Vyborg Rus. Fed. 55 P6
Vychegda r. Rus. Fed. 52 J3
Vychegodskiy Rus. Fed. 52 J3
Vydrino Rus. Fed. 94 F1
Vyerkhnyadzvinsk Belarus 55 O9
Vyetryna Belarus 55 P9
Vygozero, Ozero l. Rus. Fed. 52 G3
Vyksa Rus. Fed. 53 I5
Vylkove Ukr. 69 M2
Vym' r. Rus. Fed. 52 K3
Vynohradiv Ukr. 53 D6
Vypin Island India 106 C4
Vypolzovo Rus. Fed. 52 G4
Vyritsa Rus. Fed. 55 Q7
Vyrnwy, Lake U.K. 59 D6
Vyselki Rus. Fed. 53 H7
Vysha Rus. Fed. 53 I5
Vyshhorod Ukr. 53 F6
Vyshnevolotskaya Gryada ridge Rus. Fed. 52 G4
Vyshniy-Volochek Rus. Fed. 52 G4
Vyškov Czech Rep. 57 P6
Vysokaya Gora Rus. Fed. 52 K5
Vysokogorniy Rus. Fed. 90 E2
Vystupovychi Ukr. 53 F6
Vytegra Rus. Fed. 52 H3
Vyya r. Rus. Fed. 52 J3
Vyžuona r. Lith. 55 N9

W

Wa Ghana 120 C3
Waal r. Neth. 62 E3
Waalwijk Neth. 62 F3
Waat Sudan 108 D8
Wabag P.N.G. 81 K8
Wabakimi Lake Canada 152 C4
Wabasca r. Canada 150 H3
Wabasca-Desmarais Canada 150 H4
Wabash U.S.A. 164 C3
Wabash r. U.S.A. 164 A5
Wabasha U.S.A. 160 E2
Wabassi r. Canada 152 D4
Wabatongushi Lake Canada 152 D4
Wabē Gestro r. Eth. 100 D6

▶Wabē Shebelē Wenz r. Eth. 122 E3
5th longest river in Africa.

Wabigoon Lake Canada 151 M5
Wabowden Canada 151 L4
Wabrah well Saudi Arabia 110 B5
Wabu China 97 H1
Wabuk Point Canada 152 D3
Wabush Canada 153 I3
Waccasassa Bay U.S.A. 163 D6
Wachi Japan 92 B3
Wächtersbach Germany 63 J4
Waco Canada 153 I4
Waco U.S.A. 161 D6
Waconda Lake U.S.A. 160 D4
Wada Japan 93 G3
Wada-misaki pt Japan 92 B4
Wada-tōge pass Japan 93 E2
Wadayama Japan 92 A3
Wadbilliga National Park Australia 138 D6
Waddān Libya 65 H6
Waddell Dam U.S.A. 159 G5
Waddeneilanden Neth. 62 E1
Waddenzee sea chan. Neth. 62 E2
Waddington, Mount Canada 150 E5
Waddinxveen Neth. 62 E2
Wadebridge U.K. 59 C8
Wadena Canada 151 K5
Wadena U.S.A. 160 E2
Wadern Germany 62 G5
Wadesville U.S.A. 164 B4
Wadeye Australia 134 E3
Wadgassen Germany 62 G5
Wadh Pak. 111 G5
Wadhwan India see Surendranagar
Wadi India 106 C2
Wādī as Sīr Jordan 107 B4
Wadi Halfa Sudan 108 D5
Wad Medani Sudan 108 D7
Wad Rawa Sudan 108 D6
Wadsworth U.S.A. 158 D2
Waenhuiskrans S. Africa 124 E8
Wafangdian Liaoning China 95 J4
Wafra Kuwait see Al Wafrah
Wagenfeld Germany 63 I2
Wagenhoff Germany 63 K2
Wagga Wagga Australia 138 C5
Wagner U.S.A. 160 D3
Wagoner U.S.A. 161 E4
Wagon Mound U.S.A. 157 G5
Wah Pak. 111 I3
Wahai Seram Indon. 83 D3
Wāḥāt Jālū Libya 121 F2
Wahemen, Lac l. Canada 153 H3
Wahiawā U.S.A. 157 [inset]
Wahlhausen Germany 63 J3
Wahpeton U.S.A. 160 D2
Wahran Alg. see Oran
Wah Wah Mountains U.S.A. 159 G2
Wai India 106 B2
Waialua U.S.A. 157 [inset]
Waiau N.Z. see Franz Josef Glacier
Waiau r. N.Z. 139 D6
Waiblingen Germany 63 J6
Waidhofen an der Ybbs Austria 57 O7
Waigama Papua Indon. 83 D3
Waigeo i. Papua Indon. 83 D3
Waiheke Island N.Z. 139 E3
Waikabubak Sumba Indon. 83 A5
Waikaia r. N.Z. 139 B7
Waikari N.Z. 139 D6
Waikerie Australia 137 B7
Waiklibang Flores Indon. 83 B5
Waikouaiti N.Z. 139 C7
Wailuku U.S.A. 157 [inset]
Waimangaroa N.Z. 139 C5
Waimarama N.Z. 139 F4
Waimate N.Z. 139 C7
Waimea U.S.A. 157 [inset]
Waimenda Sulawesi Indon. 83 B3
Wainganga r. India 106 C2
Waingapu Sumba Indon. 83 B5
Wainhouse Corner U.K. 59 C8
Waini Point Guyana 177 G2
Wainwright Canada 151 I4
Wainwright AK U.S.A. 148 H1
Waiouru N.Z. 139 E4
Waipahi N.Z. 139 B8
Waipaoa r. N.Z. 139 F4
Waipara N.Z. 139 D6
Waipawa N.Z. 139 F4
Waipukurau N.Z. 139 F4
Wairarapa, Lake N.Z. 139 E5
Wairau r. N.Z. 139 E5
Wairoa N.Z. 139 F4
Wairoa r. N.Z. 139 F4
Wairunu Flores Indon. 83 B5
Waisai Papua Indon. 83 D3
Waitahanui N.Z. 139 F4
Waitahuna N.Z. 139 B7
Waitakaruru N.Z. 139 E3
Waitaki r. N.Z. 139 C7
Waitangi N.Z. 133 I6
Waite River Australia 134 F5
Waiuku N.Z. 139 E3
Waiwera South N.Z. 139 B8
Waiya Seram Indon. 83 D3
Waiyang China 97 H3
Wajima Japan 91 E5
Wajir Kenya 122 E3
Waka Flores Indon. 83 B5
Waka, Tanjung pt Indon. 83 C3
Wakasa-wan b. Japan 92 B3
Wakasa-wan Kokutei-kōen park Japan 92 B3
Wakatipu, Lake N.Z. 139 B7
Wakatobi, Taman Nasional nat. park Indon. 83 B4
Wakaw Canada 151 J4
Wakayama Japan 92 B4
Wakayama pref. Japan 92 B5
Wake Atoll terr. N. Pacific Ocean see Wake Island
WaKeeney U.S.A. 160 D4
Wakefield N.Z. 139 D5
Wakefield U.K. 58 F5
Wakefield MI U.S.A. 160 F2
Wakefield RI U.S.A. 165 J3
Wakefield VA U.S.A. 165 G5

▶Wake Island terr. N. Pacific Ocean 186 H4
United States Unincorporated Territory.

Wakema Myanmar 86 A3
Wakhan reg. Afgh. 111 I2
Wakkanai Japan 90 F3
Wakkerstroom S. Africa 125 J4
Wakool Australia 138 B5
Wakool r. Australia 138 A5
Wakuach, Lac l. Canada 153 I3
Waku-Kungo Angola 123 B5
Wałbrzych Poland 57 P5
Walcha Australia 138 E3
Walcott U.S.A. 156 G4
Walcourt Belgium 62 E4
Wałcz Poland 57 P4
Waldburg Range mts Australia 135 B6
Walden U.S.A. 165 H3
Waldenbuch Germany 63 J6
Waldenburg Poland see Wałbrzych
Waldkraiburg Germany 57 N6
Waldo U.S.A. 164 D3
Waldoboro U.S.A. 165 K1
Waldorf U.S.A. 165 G4
Waldport U.S.A. 156 B3
Waldron U.S.A. 161 E5
Waldron, Cape Antarctica 188 F2
Walea, Selat sea chan. Indon. 83 B3
Waleabahi i. Indon. 83 B3
Waleakodi i. Indon. 83 B3
Walebing Australia 135 B7
Walêg China 96 D2
Wales admin. div. U.K. 59 D6
Wales AK U.S.A. 148 E2
Walgaon India 104 D5
Walgett Australia 138 D3
Walgreen Coast Antarctica 188 K1
Walhalla MI U.S.A. 164 B2
Walhalla ND U.S.A. 160 D1
Walikale Dem. Rep. Congo 121 F5
Walingai P.N.G. 81 L8
Walker r. Australia 136 A2
Walker watercourse Australia 135 F6
Walker MI U.S.A. 164 C2
Walker MN U.S.A. 160 E2
Walker r. U.S.A. 158 D2
Walker Bay S. Africa 124 D8
Walker Creek r. Australia 136 C3
Walker Lake Canada 151 L4
Walker Lake AK U.S.A. 148 I2
Walker Lake U.S.A. 158 D2
Walker Pass U.S.A. 158 D4
Walkersville U.S.A. 165 G4
Walkerton Canada 164 E1
Walkerton U.S.A. 164 B3
Wall, Mount hill Australia 134 B5
Wallaby Island Australia 136 C2
Wallace ID U.S.A. 156 D3
Wallace NC U.S.A. 163 E5
Wallace VA U.S.A. 164 D5
Wallaceburg Canada 164 D2
Wallal Downs Australia 134 C4
Wallangarra Australia 138 E2
Wallaroo Australia 137 B7
Wallasey U.K. 58 D5
Walla Walla Australia 138 C5
Walla Walla U.S.A. 156 D3
Walldürn Germany 63 J5
Wallekraal S. Africa 124 C6
Wallendbeen Australia 138 D5
Wallingford U.K. 59 F7
Wallis, Îles is Wallis and Futuna Is 133 I3

▶Wallis and Futuna Islands terr. S. Pacific Ocean 133 I3
French Overseas Collectivity.

Wallis et Futuna, Îles terr. S. Pacific Ocean see Wallis and Futuna Islands
Wallis Islands Wallis and Futuna Is see Wallis, Îles
Wallis Lake inlet Australia 138 F4
Wallops Island U.S.A. 165 H5
Wallowa Mountains U.S.A. 156 D3
Walls U.K. 60 [inset]
Walls of Jerusalem National Park Australia 137 [inset]
Wallumbilla Australia 137 E5
Walmsley Lake Canada 151 I2
Walney, Isle of i. U.K. 58 D4
Walnut Creek U.S.A. 158 B3
Walnut Grove U.S.A. 158 C2
Walnut Ridge U.S.A. 161 F4
Walong India 105 I3
Walpole U.S.A. 165 I2
Walrus Island AK U.S.A. 148 E4
Walrus Islands AK U.S.A. 148 G4
Walsall U.K. 59 F6
Walsenburg U.S.A. 157 G5
Walsh U.S.A. 161 C4
Walsrode Germany 63 J2
Waltair India 106 D2
Walterboro U.S.A. 163 D5
Walters U.S.A. 161 D5
Walter's Range hills Australia 138 B2
Walthall U.S.A. 161 F5
Waltham U.S.A. 165 J2
Walton IN U.S.A. 164 B3
Walton KY U.S.A. 164 C4
Walton NY U.S.A. 165 H2
Walton WV U.S.A. 164 E4
Walvisbaai Namibia see Walvis Bay
Walvisbaai b. Namibia see Walvis Bay
Walvis Bay Namibia 124 B2
Walvis Bay b. Namibia 124 B2
Walvis Ridge sea feature S. Atlantic Ocean 184 H8
Wama Afgh. 111 H3
Wamba Equateur Dem. Rep. Congo 121 F5
Wamba Orientale Dem. Rep. Congo 122 C3
Wamba Nigeria 120 D4
Wamlana Buru Indon. 83 C3
Wampum U.S.A. 164 E3
Wampusirpi Hond. 166 [inset] I6
Wamsutter U.S.A. 156 G4
Wamulan Buru Indon. 83 C3
Wana Pak. 111 H3
Wanaaring Australia 138 B2
Wanaka N.Z. 139 B7
Wanaka, Lake N.Z. 139 B7
Wan'an China 97 G3
Wanapitei Lake Canada 152 E5
Wanasabari Sulawesi Indon. 83 B4
Wanbi Australia 137 C7
Wanbrow, Cape N.Z. 139 C7
Wanci Sulawesi Indon. 83 B4
Wanda Shan mts China 90 D3
Wandering River Canada 151 H4
Wandersleben Germany 63 K4
Wandlitz Germany 63 N2
Wando S. Korea 91 B6
Wandoan Australia 137 E5
Wanganui N.Z. 139 E4
Wanganui r. N.Z. 139 E4
Wangaratta Australia 138 C6
Wangcang China 96 E1
Wangcun Shandong China 95 J4
Wangda China see Zogang
Wangdain Xizang China 99 E7
Wangdi Phodrang Bhutan 105 G4
Wangdu Hebei China 95 H4
Wanggamet, Gunung mt. Sumba Indon. 83 B5
Wanggao China 97 F3
Wang Gaxun Qinghai China 94 D4
Wanggezhuang Shandong China see Jiaonan
Wangguan China 96 E1
Wangiwangi i. Indon. 83 B4
Wangjiawan Shaanxi China 95 G4
Wangkibila Hond. 166 [inset] I6
Wangkui China 90 B3
Wangmo China 96 E3
Wangqing China 90 C4
Wangwu Shan mts China 97 F1

Wangying China see Huaiyin
Wanham Canada 150 G4
Wan Hsa-la Myanmar 86 B2
Wanie-Rukula Dem. Rep. Congo 122 C3
Wankaner India 104 B5
Wankie Zimbabwe see Hwange
Wanlaweyn Somalia 122 E3
Wanna Germany 63 I1
Wanna Lakes salt flat Australia 135 E7
Wannian China 97 H2
Wanning China 97 F5
Wanouchi Japan 92 C3
Wanroij Neth. 62 F3
Wanrong Shanxi China 95 G5
Wanshan China 97 F3
Wanshan Qundao is China 97 G4
Wansheng China 96 E2
Wanshengchang China see Wansheng
Wantage U.K. 59 F7
Wanxian Chongqing China 97 F2
Wanxian Chongqing China see Shahe
Wanyuan China 97 F1
Wanzai China 97 G2
Wanze Belgium 62 F4
Wapakoneta U.S.A. 164 C3
Wapawekka Lake Canada 151 J4
Wapello U.S.A. 160 F3
Wapikaimaski Lake Canada 152 C4
Wapikopa Lake Canada 152 C3
Wapiti r. Canada 150 G4
Wapotih Buru Indon. 83 C3
Wapusk National Park Canada 151 M3
Waqên China 96 D1
Waqf aş Şawwān, Jibāl hills Jordan 107 C4
War U.S.A. 164 E5
Wara Japan 92 D3
Warab Sudan 108 C8
Warangal India 106 C2
Waranga Reservoir Australia 138 B6
Waratah Bay Australia 138 B7
Warbreccan Australia 136 C5
Warburg Germany 63 J3
Warburton Australia 135 D6
Warburton watercourse Australia 137 B5
Warburton Bay Canada 151 I2
Warche r. Belgium 62 F4
Ward, Mount N.Z. 139 B6
Warden S. Africa 125 I4
Wardenburg Germany 63 I1
Wardha India 106 C1
Wardha r. India 106 C2
Ward Hill hill U.K. 60 F2
Ward Hunt, Cape P.N.G. 81 L8
Ware Canada 150 E3
Ware U.S.A. 165 I2
Wareham U.K. 59 E8
Waremme Belgium 62 F4
Waren Germany 63 M1
Warendorf Germany 63 H3
Warginburra Peninsula Australia 136 E4
Wargla Alg. see Ouargla
Warialda Australia 138 E2
Warin Chamrap Thai. 86 D4
Waring Mountains AK U.S.A. 148 G2
Warkum Neth. see Workum
Warkworth U.K. 58 F3
Warli China see Walêg
Warloy-Baillon France 62 C4
Warman Canada 151 J4
Warmbad Namibia 124 D5
Warmbad S. Africa 125 I3
Warmbaths S. Africa see Warmbad
Warminster U.K. 59 E7
Warminster U.S.A. 165 H3
Warmond Neth. 62 E2
Warm Springs NV U.S.A. 158 E2
Warm Springs VA U.S.A. 164 F4
Warmwaterberg mts S. Africa 124 E7
Warner Canada 151 H5
Warner Lakes U.S.A. 156 D4
Warner Mountains U.S.A. 156 C4
Warnes Bol. 176 F7
Warning, Mount Australia 138 F2
Waronda India 106 C2
Warora India 106 C1
Warra Australia 138 E1
Warragamba Reservoir Australia 138 E5
Warragul Australia 138 B7
Warrambool r. Australia 138 C3
Warrandirinna, Lake salt flat Australia 137 B5
Warrandyte Australia 138 B6
Warrawagine Australia 134 C5
Warrego r. Australia 138 B3
Warrego Range hills Australia 136 D5
Warren Australia 138 C3
Warren AR U.S.A. 161 E5
Warren MI U.S.A. 164 D2
Warren MN U.S.A. 160 D1
Warren OH U.S.A. 164 E3
Warren PA U.S.A. 164 F3
Warren Hastings Island Palau see Merir
Warren Island U.S.A. 150 C4
Warren Point pt N.W.T. Canada 149 N1
Warrenpoint U.K. 61 F3
Warrensburg MO U.S.A. 160 E4
Warrensburg NY U.S.A. 165 I2
Warrenton S. Africa 124 G5
Warrenton GA U.S.A. 163 D5
Warrenton MO U.S.A. 160 F4
Warrenton VA U.S.A. 165 G4
Warri Nigeria 120 D4
Warriners Creek watercourse Australia 137 B6
Warrington N.Z. 139 C7
Warrington U.K. 58 E5
Warrington U.S.A. 163 C6
Warrnambool Australia 137 C8
Warroad U.S.A. 160 E1
Warrumbungle National Park Australia 138 D3

▶Warsaw Poland 57 R4
Capital of Poland.

Warsaw IN U.S.A. 164 C3
Warsaw KY U.S.A. 164 C4
Warsaw MO U.S.A. 160 E4
Warsaw NY U.S.A. 165 F2
Warsaw VA U.S.A. 165 G5
Warshiikh Somalia 122 E3
Warstein Germany 63 I3
Warszawa Poland see Warsaw
Warta r. Poland 57 O4
Waru Kalimantan Indon. 85 G3
Warwick Australia 138 F2
Warwick U.K. 59 F6
Warwick U.S.A. 165 J3
Warzhong China 96 D2
Wasaga Beach Canada 164 E1
Wasatch Range mts U.S.A. 156 F5
Wasbank S. Africa 125 J5
Wasco U.S.A. 158 D4
Washburn ND U.S.A. 160 C2
Washburn WI U.S.A. 160 F2
Washiga-take mt. Japan 92 C3
Washim India 106 C1

▶Washington DC U.S.A. 165 G4
Capital of the United States of America.

Washington GA U.S.A. 163 D5
Washington IA U.S.A. 160 F3
Washington IN U.S.A. 164 B4
Washington MO U.S.A. 160 F4
Washington NC U.S.A. 162 E5
Washington NJ U.S.A. 165 H3
Washington PA U.S.A. 164 E3
Washington UT U.S.A. 159 G3
Washington state U.S.A. 156 C3
Washington, Cape Antarctica 188 H2
Washington, Mount U.S.A. 165 J1
Washington Court House U.S.A. 164 D4
Washington Island U.S.A. 162 C2
Washington Land reg. Greenland 147 L2
Washir Afgh. 111 F3
Washita r. U.S.A. 161 D5
Washpool National Park Australia 138 F2
Washtucna U.S.A. 156 D3
Washuk Pak. 111 G5
Wasi India 106 B2
Wasi' Saudi Arabia 110 B5
Wasi' well Saudi Arabia 110 C6
Wasiri Maluku Indon. 83 C4
Wasisi Buru Indon. 83 C3
Waskaganish Canada 152 F4
Waskagheganish Canada see Waskaganish
Waskaiowaka Lake Canada 151 L3
Waskey, Mount AK U.S.A. 148 H4
Waspán Nicaragua 166 [inset] I6
Wassenaar Neth. 62 E2
Wasser Namibia 124 D4
Wasserkuppe hill Germany 63 J4
Wassertrüdingen Germany 63 K5
Wassuk Range mts U.S.A. 158 D2
Wasua P.N.G. 81 K8
Wasum P.N.G. 81 L8
Waswanipi r. Canada 152 F4
Waswanipi, Lac l. Canada 152 F4
Watam P.N.G. 81 K7
Watambayoli Sulawesi Indon. 83 B3
Watampone Sulawesi Indon. 83 B4
Watana, Mount AK U.S.A. 149 J3
Watansoppeng Sulawesi Indon. 83 A4
Watapi Lake Canada 151 I4
Watarai Japan 92 C4
Watarase-gawa r. Japan 93 F2
Watarrka National Park Australia 135 E6
Watauchi Japan 93 E2
Watenstadt-Salzgitter Germany see Salzgitter
Waterbury CT U.S.A. 165 I3
Waterbury VT U.S.A. 165 I1
Waterbury Lake Canada 151 J3
Water Cays i. Bahamas 163 E8
Waterdown Canada 164 F2
Wateree r. U.S.A. 163 D5
Waterfall AK U.S.A. 149 N5
Waterford Ireland 61 E5
Waterford PA U.S.A. 164 F3
Waterford WI U.S.A. 164 A2
Waterford Harbour Ireland 61 F5
Watergrasshill Ireland 61 D5
Waterhen Lake Canada 151 L4
Waterloo Australia 134 E4
Waterloo Belgium 62 E4
Waterloo Ont. Canada 164 E2
Waterloo Que. Canada 165 I1
Waterloo IA U.S.A. 160 E3
Waterloo IL U.S.A. 160 F4
Waterloo NY U.S.A. 165 G2
Waterlooville U.K. 59 F8
Waterton Lakes National Park Canada 150 H5
Watertown NY U.S.A. 165 H2
Watertown SD U.S.A. 160 D2
Watertown WI U.S.A. 160 F3
Waterval Boven S. Africa 125 J3
Water Valley U.S.A. 161 F5
Waterville ME U.S.A. 165 K1
Waterville WA U.S.A. 156 C3
Watford Canada 164 E2
Watford U.K. 59 G7
Watford City U.S.A. 160 C2
Wathaman r. Canada 151 K3
Wathaman Lake Canada 151 K3
Watheroo National Park Australia 135 A7
Wathlingen Germany 63 K2
Watino Canada 150 G4
Watîr, Wâdi watercourse Egypt 107 B5
Watkins Glen U.S.A. 165 G2
Watling Island Bahamas see San Salvador
Watmuri Indon. 134 E1
Watonga U.S.A. 161 D5
Watowato, Bukit mt. Halmahera Indon. 83 D2
Watrous Canada 151 J5
Watrous U.S.A. 157 G6
Watseka U.S.A. 164 B3
Watsi Kengo Dem. Rep. Congo 121 F5
Watson r. Australia 136 C2
Watson Canada 151 J4
Watson Lake Y.T. Canada 149 O3
Watsontown U.S.A. 165 G3
Watsonville U.S.A. 158 C3
Watten U.K. 60 F2
Watterson Lake Canada 151 L2
Watton U.K. 59 H6
Watts Bar Lake resr U.S.A. 162 C5
Wattsburg U.S.A. 164 F2
Watubela, Kepulauan is Indon. 81 I7
Watuwila, Bukit mt. Indon. 83 B3
Wau P.N.G. 81 L8
Wau Sudan 108 C8
Waubay Lake U.S.A. 160 D2
Wauchope N.S.W. Australia 138 F3
Wauchope N.T. Australia 134 F5
Waukara, Gunung mt. Indon. 83 A3
Waukarina (abandoned) Australia 137 B7
Waukarlycarly, Lake salt flat Australia 134 C5
Waukegan U.S.A. 164 B2
Waukesha U.S.A. 164 A2
Waupaca U.S.A. 160 F2
Waupun U.S.A. 160 F3
Waurika U.S.A. 161 D5
Wausau U.S.A. 160 F2
Wausaukee U.S.A. 162 C2
Wauseon U.S.A. 164 C3
Wautoma U.S.A. 160 F2
Wave Hill Australia 134 E4
Waveney r. U.K. 59 I6
Waverly IA U.S.A. 160 E3
Waverly NY U.S.A. 165 G2
Waverly OH U.S.A. 164 D4
Waverly TN U.S.A. 162 C4
Waverly VA U.S.A. 165 G5
Wavre Belgium 62 E4
Waw Myanmar 86 B3
Wawa Canada 152 D5
Wawalalindu Sulawesi Indon. 83 B3
Wāw al Kabīr Libya 121 E2
Wawasee, Lake U.S.A. 164 C3
Wawo Sulawesi Indon. 83 B3
Wawotebi Sulawesi Indon. 83 B3
Waxahachie U.S.A. 161 D5
Waxü Gansu China 94 E5
Waxxari Xinjiang China 98 D5
Way, Lake salt flat Australia 135 C6
Wayabula Maluku Indon. 83 D2
Wayag i. Papua Indon. 83 D2
Wayamli Halmahera Indon. 83 D2
Wayaobu Shaanxi China see Zichang
Waycross U.S.A. 163 D6
Wayhaya Maluku Indon. 83 C3
Way Kambas, Taman Nasional nat. park Indon. 84 D4
Waykilo Maluku Indon. 83 C3
Wayland KY U.S.A. 164 D5
Wayland MI U.S.A. 164 C2
Wayne NE U.S.A. 160 D3
Wayne WV U.S.A. 164 D4
Waynesboro GA U.S.A. 163 D5
Waynesboro MS U.S.A. 161 F6
Waynesboro TN U.S.A. 162 C5
Waynesboro VA U.S.A. 165 F4
Waynesburg U.S.A. 164 E4
Waynesville MO U.S.A. 160 E4
Waynesville NC U.S.A. 162 D5
Waynoka U.S.A. 161 D4
Waza, Parc National de nat. park Cameroon 121 E3
Wāzah Khwāh Afgh. see Wazi Khwa
Wazi Khwa Afgh. 111 H3
Wazirabad Pak. 111 I3
Wazuka Japan 92 B4
W du Niger, Parcs Nationaux du nat. park Niger 120 D3
We, Pulau i. Indon. 84 A1
Weagamow Lake Canada 151 N4
Weam P.N.G. 81 K8
Wear r. U.K. 58 F4
Weare U.S.A. 165 J2
Weatherford U.S.A. 161 D5
Weaver Lake Canada 151 L4
Weaverville U.S.A. 156 C4
Webb, Mount hill Australia 134 E5
Webequie Canada 152 D3
Weber, Mount B.C. Canada 149 O5
Weber Basin sea feature Laut Banda 186 E6

▶Webi Shebelē r. Somalia 122 E3
5th longest river in Africa.

Webster IN U.S.A. 164 C4
Webster MA U.S.A. 165 J2
Webster SD U.S.A. 160 D2
Webster City U.S.A. 160 E3
Webster Springs U.S.A. 164 E4
Wecho Lake Canada 150 H2
Weda Halmahera Indon. 83 C2
Weda, Teluk b. Halmahera Indon. 83 D2
Wedau P.N.G. 136 E1
Weddell Abyssal Plain sea feature Southern Ocean 188 A2
Weddell Island Falkland Is 178 D8
Weddell Sea Antarctica 188 A2
Wedderburn Australia 138 A6
Weddin Mountains National Park Australia 138 D4
Wedel (Holstein) Germany 63 J1
Wedge Mountain Canada 150 F5
Wedowee U.S.A. 163 C5
Weedville U.S.A. 165 F3
Weeim i. Papua Indon. 83 D3
Weenen S. Africa 125 J5
Weener Germany 63 H1
Weert Neth. 62 F3
Weethalle Australia 138 C4
Wee Waa Australia 138 D3
Wegberg Germany 62 G3
Węgorzewo Poland 57 R3
Weichang Hebei China 95 I3
Weida Germany 63 M4
Weidenberg Germany 63 L5
Weiden in der Oberpfalz Germany 63 M5
Weidongmen China see Qianjin
Weifang Shandong China 95 I4
Weihai Shandong China 95 J4
Wei He r. Henan China 95 H4
Wei He r. Shaanxi China 95 G5
Weihui Henan China 95 H5
Weilburg Germany 63 I4
Weilmoringle Australia 138 C2
Weimar Germany 63 L4
Weinan Shaanxi China 95 G5
Weinheim Germany 63 I5
Weining China 96 E3
Weinsberg Germany 63 J5
Weipa Australia 136 C2
Weiqu Shaanxi China see Chang'an
Weir r. Australia 138 D2
Weirong Gansu China 94 F5
Weir River Canada 151 M3
Weirton U.S.A. 164 E3
Weiser U.S.A. 156 D3
Weishan Shandong China 95 I5
Weishan China 96 D3
Weishan Hu l. China 95 I5
Weishi Henan China 95 H5
Weiße Elster r. Germany 63 L3
Weißenburg in Bayern Germany 63 K5
Weißenfels Germany 63 L3
Weißkugel mt. Austria/Italy 57 M7
Weissrand Mountains Namibia 124 D3
Weiterstadt Germany 63 I5
Weitzel Lake Canada 151 J3
Weixi China 96 C3
Weixian Hebei China 95 H4
Weixin China 96 E3
Weiya Xinjiang China 94 C3
Weiyuan Gansu China 94 F5
Weiyuan Qinghai China see Huzhu
Weiyuan Sichuan China 96 E2
Weiyuan Yunnan China see Jinggu
Weiyuan Jiang r. China 96 D4
Weiz Austria 57 O7
Weizhou Ningxia China 94 F4
Weizhou China see Wenchuan
Weizhou Dao i. China 97 F4
Weizi Liaoning China 95 J3
Wejherowo Poland 57 Q3
Wekilbazar Turkm. 111 F2
Wekusko Canada 151 L4
Wekusko Lake Canada 151 L4
Wekweêtì Canada 150 H1
Welatam Myanmar 86 B1
Welbourn Hill Australia 135 F6
Welch U.S.A. 164 E5
Weld U.S.A. 165 J1
Weldiya Eth. 122 D2
Welford National Park Australia 136 C5
Welgevonden Game Reserve nature res. S. Africa 125 H3
Welk'īt'ē Eth. 122 D3
Welkom S. Africa 125 H4
Welland Canada 164 F2
Welland r. U.K. 59 G6
Welland Canal Canada 164 F2
Wellesley Canada 164 E2
Wellesley Islands Australia 136 B3
Wellesley Lake Y.T. Canada 149 M3
Wellfleet U.S.A. 165 J3
Wellin Belgium 62 F4
Wellingborough U.K. 59 G6
Wellington Australia 138 D4
Wellington Canada 165 G2

▶Wellington N.Z. 139 E5
Capital of New Zealand.

Wellington S. Africa 124 D7
Wellington England U.K. 59 D8
Wellington England U.K. 59 E6
Wellington CO U.S.A. 156 G4
Wellington IL U.S.A. 164 B3
Wellington KS U.S.A. 161 D4
Wellington NV U.S.A. 158 D2
Wellington OH U.S.A. 164 D3
Wellington TX U.S.A. 161 C5
Wellington UT U.S.A. 159 H2
Wellington, Isla i. Chile 178 B7
Wellington Range hills N.T. Australia 134 F3
Wellington Range hills W.A. Australia 135 C6
Wells Canada 150 F4
Wells U.K. 59 E7
Wells U.S.A. 156 E4
Wells, Lake salt flat Australia 135 C6
Wellsboro U.S.A. 165 G3
Wellsburg U.S.A. 164 E3
Wellsford N.Z. 139 E3
Wells-next-the-Sea U.K. 59 H6
Wellston U.S.A. 164 C1
Wellsville U.S.A. 165 G2
Wellton U.S.A. 159 F5
Wels Austria 57 O6
Welshpool U.K. 59 D6
Welsickendorf Germany 63 N3
Welwitschia Namibia see Khorixas
Welwyn Garden City U.K. 59 G7
Welzheim Germany 63 J6
Wem U.K. 59 E6
Wembesi S. Africa 125 I5
Wembley Canada 150 G4
Wemindji Canada 152 F3
Wenatchee U.S.A. 156 C3
Wenatchee Mountains U.S.A. 156 C3
Wenchang Hainan China 97 F5
Wenchang Sichuan China see Zitong
Wenchow China see Wenzhou
Wenchuan China 96 D2
Wendelstein Germany 63 L5
Wenden Germany 63 H4
Wenden Latvia see Cēsis
Wenden U.S.A. 159 G5
Wendeng Shandong China 95 J4
Wendover U.S.A. 159 F1
Wenfengzhen Gansu China 94 F5
Weng'an China 96 E3
Wengshui China 96 C2
Wengyuan China 97 G3
Wenhua China see Weishan
Wenkutu Nei Mongol China 95 J1
Wenlan China see Mengzi
Wenling China 97 I2
Wenlock r. Australia 136 C2
Wenping China see Ludian
Wenquan Guizhou China 96 E2
Wenquan Henan China see Wenxian
Wenquan Hubei China see Yingshan
Wenquan Qinghai China 105 G2
Wenquan Qinghai China 94 D5
Wenquan Qinghai China 99 E6
Wenquan Xinjiang China 98 C3
Wenshan China 96 E4
Wenshui China 96 E2
Wensu Xinjiang China 98 C4
Wensum r. U.K. 59 I6
Wentorf bei Hamburg Germany 63 K1
Wentworth Australia 137 C7
Wenxi China 97 F1
Wenxian Gansu China 96 E1
Wenxian Henan China 97 G1
Wenxing China see Xiangyin
Wenzhou China 97 I3
Wenzlow Germany 63 M2
Wepener S. Africa 125 H5
Wer India 104 D4
Werben (Elbe) Germany 63 L2
Werda Botswana 124 F3
Werdau Germany 63 M4
Werdër Eth. 122 E3
Werder Germany 63 M2
Werdohl Germany 63 H3
Werinama Seram Indon. 83 D3
Werl Germany 63 H3
Wernberg-Köblitz Germany 63 M5
Werne Germany 63 H3
Wernecke Mountains Y.T. Canada 149 M2
Wernigerode Germany 63 K3
Werra r. Germany 63 J3
Werris Creek Australia 138 E3
Wertheim Germany 63 J5
Wervik Belgium 62 D4
Werwaru Maluku Indon. 83 D5
Wesel Germany 62 G3
Wesel-Datteln-Kanal canal Germany 62 G3
Wesenberg Germany 63 M1
Wesendorf Germany 63 K2
Weser r. Germany 63 I1
Weser sea chan. Germany 63 I1
Wesergebirge hills Germany 63 I2
Weslaco U.S.A. 161 D7
Weslemkoon Lake Canada 165 G1
Wesleyville Canada 153 L4
Wessel, Cape Australia 136 B1
Wessel Islands Australia 136 B1
Wesselsbron S. Africa 125 H4
Wesselton S. Africa 125 I4
Wessington Springs U.S.A. 160 D2
West r. N.W.T. Canada 149 P1
Westall, Point Australia 135 F8
West Allis U.S.A. 164 A2
West Antarctica reg. Antarctica 188 J1
West Australian Basin sea feature Indian Ocean 185 O7

▶West Bank terr. Asia 107 B3
Territory occupied by Israel.

West Bay Canada 153 K3
West Bay b. LA U.S.A. 167 H2
West Bay inlet U.S.A. 163 C6
West Bend U.S.A. 164 A2
West Bengal state India 105 F5
West Branch U.S.A. 164 C1
West Bromwich U.K. 59 F6
Westbrook U.S.A. 165 J2
West Burke U.S.A. 165 J1
West Burra i. U.K. see Burra
Westbury U.K. 59 E7
West Caicos i. Turks and Caicos Is 163 F8
West Cape Howe Australia 135 B8
West Caroline Basin sea feature N. Pacific Ocean 186 F5
West Chester U.S.A. 165 H4
Westcliffe U.S.A. 157 G5
West Coast National Park S. Africa 124 D7
West End Bahamas 163 E7
Westerburg Germany 63 H4
Westerholt Germany 63 H1
Westerland Germany 57 L3
Westerlo Belgium 62 E3
Westerly U.S.A. 165 J3
Western r. Canada 151 J1
Western Australia state Australia 135 C6
Western Cape prov. S. Africa 124 E7
Western Desert Egypt 112 C6
Western Dvina r. Europe see Zapadnaya Dvina
Western Ghats mts India 106 B3
Western Lesser Sunda Islands prov. Indon. see Nusa Tenggara Barat
Western Port b. Australia 138 B7

▶Western Sahara terr. Africa 120 B2
Disputed territory (Morocco).

Western Samoa country S. Pacific Ocean see Samoa
Western Sayan Mountains reg. Rus. Fed. see Zapadnyy Sayan
Westerschelde est. Neth. 62 D3
Westerstede Germany 63 H1
Westerville U.S.A. 164 D3
Westerwald hills Germany 63 H4
West Falkland i. Falkland Is 178 D8
West Fargo U.S.A. 160 D2
West Fayu atoll Micronesia 81 L5
Westfield IN U.S.A. 164 B3
Westfield MA U.S.A. 165 I2
Westfield NY U.S.A. 164 F2
Westfield PA U.S.A. 165 G3
West Frisian Islands Neth. see Waddeneilanden
Westgat sea chan. Neth. 62 G1
Westgate Australia 138 C1
West Glacier U.S.A. 156 E2
West Grand Lake U.S.A. 162 H2
West Hartford U.S.A. 165 I3
Westhausen Germany 63 K6
West Haven U.S.A. 165 I3
Westhill U.K. 60 G3
Westhope U.S.A. 160 C1
West Ice Shelf Antarctica 188 E2
West Indies is Caribbean Sea 169 J4
West Irian prov. Indon. see Papua
West Island India 87 A4
Westkapelle Neth. 62 D3
West Kazakhstan Oblast admin. div. Kazakh. see Zapadnyy Kazakhstan
West Kingston U.S.A. 165 J3
West Lafayette U.S.A. 164 B3
West Lamma Channel H.K. China 97 [inset]
Westland Australia 136 C4
Westland National Park N.Z. 139 C6
Westleigh S. Africa 125 H4
Westleton U.K. 59 I6
West Liberty U.S.A. 164 D5
West Linton U.K. 60 F5
West Loch Roag b. U.K. 60 C2
Westlock Canada 150 H4
West Lorne Canada 164 E2
West Lunga National Park Zambia 123 C5
West MacDonnell National Park Australia 135 F5
West Malaysia pen. Malaysia see Malaysia, Semenanjung
Westmalle Belgium 62 E3
Westmar Australia 138 D1
West Mariana Basin sea feature N. Pacific Ocean 186 F4
West Memphis U.S.A. 161 F5
Westminster U.S.A. 165 G4
Westmoreland Australia 136 B3
Westmoreland U.S.A. 164 B5
Westmorland U.S.A. 159 F5
Weston Sabah Malaysia 85 F1
Weston OH U.S.A. 164 D3
Weston WV U.S.A. 164 E4
Weston-super-Mare U.K. 59 E7
West Palm Beach U.S.A. 163 D7
West Papua prov. Indon. see Papua
West Passage Palau see Toagel Mlungui
West Plains U.S.A. 161 F4
West Point pt Australia 137 [inset]
West Point CA U.S.A. 158 C2
West Point KY U.S.A. 164 C5
West Point MS U.S.A. 161 F5
West Point NE U.S.A. 160 D3
West Point VA U.S.A. 165 G5
West Point mt. AK U.S.A. 149 K2
West Point Lake resr U.S.A. 163 C5
Westport Canada 165 G1
Westport Ireland 61 C4
Westport N.Z. 139 C5
Westport CA U.S.A. 158 B2
Westport KY U.S.A. 164 C4
Westport NY U.S.A. 165 I1
Westray Canada 151 K4
Westray i. U.K. 60 F1
Westray Firth sea chan. U.K. 60 F1
Westree Canada 152 E5
West Rutland U.S.A. 165 I2
West Salem U.S.A. 164 D3
West Siberian Plain Rus. Fed. 76 J3
West-Skylge Neth. see West-Terschelling
West Stewartstown U.S.A. 165 J1
West-Terschelling Neth. 62 F1
West Topsham U.S.A. 165 I1
West Union IA U.S.A. 160 F3
West Union IL U.S.A. 164 B4
West Union OH U.S.A. 164 D4
West Union WV U.S.A. 164 E4
West Valley City U.S.A. 159 H1
Westville U.S.A. 164 B3
West Virginia state U.S.A. 164 E4
Westwood U.S.A. 158 C1
West Wyalong Australia 138 C4
West York U.S.A. 165 G4
Westzaan Neth. 62 E2
Wetan i. Maluku Indon. 83 D4
Wetar i. Maluku Indon. 83 C4
Wetar, Selat sea chan. Indon. 83 C5
Wetaskiwin Canada 150 H4
Wete Tanz. 123 D4
Wetter r. Germany 63 I4
Wettin Germany 63 L3
Wetumpka U.S.A. 163 C5
Wetwun Myanmar 86 B2
Wetzlar Germany 63 I4
Wevok AK U.S.A. 148 F1
Wewahitchka U.S.A. 163 C6
Wewak P.N.G. 81 K7
Wewoka U.S.A. 161 D5
Wexford Ireland 61 F5
Wexford Harbour b. Ireland 61 F5
Weyakwin Canada 151 J4
Weybridge U.K. 59 G7
Weyburn Canada 151 K5
Weyhe Germany 63 I2
Weymouth U.K. 59 E8
Weymouth U.S.A. 165 J2
Wezep Neth. 62 G2
Whakaari i. N.Z. 139 F3
Whakatane N.Z. 139 F3
Whalan Creek r. Australia 138 D2
Whale r. Canada see La Baleine, Rivière à
Whalsay i. U.K. 60 [inset]
Whampoa China see Huangpu
Whangamata N.Z. 139 E3
Whanganui National Park N.Z. 139 E4
Whangarei N.Z. 139 E2
Whapmagoostui Canada 152 F3
Wharfe r. U.K. 58 F5
Wharfedale valley U.K. 58 F4
Wharton U.S.A. 161 D6
Wharton Lake Canada 151 L1
Whatì N.W.T. Canada 149 R3
Wheatland IN U.S.A. 164 B4
Wheatland WY U.S.A. 156 G4
Wheaton IL U.S.A. 164 A3
Wheaton MN U.S.A. 160 D2
Wheaton-Glenmont U.S.A. 165 G4
Wheeler U.S.A. 161 C5
Wheeler Lake Canada 150 H2
Wheeler Lake resr U.S.A. 163 C5
Wheeler Peak NM U.S.A. 157 G5
Wheeler Peak NV U.S.A. 159 F2
Wheelersburg U.S.A. 164 D4
Wheeling U.S.A. 164 E3
Whernside hill U.K. 58 E4
Whinham, Mount Australia 135 E6
Whiskey Jack Lake Canada 151 K3
Whitburn U.K. 60 F5
Whitby Canada 165 F2
Whitby U.K. 58 G4
Whitchurch U.K. 59 E6
Whitchurch-Stouffville Canada 164 F2
White r. Canada 152 D4
White r. Canada/U.S.A. 149 M3
White r. AR U.S.A. 155 I5
White r. AR U.S.A. 161 F5
White r. CO U.S.A. 159 I1
White r. IN U.S.A. 164 B4
White r. MI U.S.A. 164 B2
White r. NV U.S.A. 159 F3
White r. SD U.S.A. 160 D3
White r. VT U.S.A. 165 I2
White watercourse U.S.A. 159 H5
White, Lake salt flat Australia 134 E5
White Bay Canada 153 K4
White Butte mt. U.S.A. 160 C2
White Canyon U.S.A. 159 H3
White Cloud U.S.A. 164 C2
Whitecourt Canada 150 H4
Whiteface Mountain U.S.A. 165 I1
Whitefield U.S.A. 165 J1
Whitefish r. N.W.T. Canada 149 P2
Whitefish U.S.A. 156 E2
Whitefish Bay U.S.A. 164 B1
Whitefish Lake Canada 151 J2
Whitefish Lake AK U.S.A. 148 I3
Whitefish Point U.S.A. 162 C2
Whitehall Ireland 61 E5
Whitehall U.K. 60 G1
Whitehall NY U.S.A. 165 I2
Whitehall WI U.S.A. 160 F2
Whitehaven U.K. 58 D4
Whitehead U.K. 61 G3
White Hill hill Canada 153 J5
Whitehill U.K. 59 G7
White Hills AK U.S.A. 149 J1

▶Whitehorse Y.T. Canada 149 N3
Capital of Yukon.

White Horse U.S.A. 159 J4
White Horse, Vale of valley U.K. 59 F7
White Horse Pass U.S.A. 159 F1
White House U.S.A. 164 B5
White Island Antarctica 188 D2
White Island N.Z. see Whakaari
White Lake Ont. Canada 152 D4
White Lake Ont. Canada 165 G1

White Lake LA U.S.A. 161 E6
White Lake MI U.S.A. 164 B2
Whitemark Australia 137 [inset]
White Mountain AK U.S.A. 148 G2
White Mountain Peak U.S.A. 158 D3
White Mountains AK U.S.A. 149 K2
White Mountains U.S.A. 165 J1
White Mountains National Park Australia 136 D4
Whitemouth Lake Canada 151 M5
Whitemud r. Canada 150 G3
White Nile r. Sudan/Uganda 108 D6
also known as Bahr el Abiad or Bahr el Jebel
White Nossob watercourse Namibia 124 D2
White Oak U.S.A. 164 D5
White Otter Lake Canada 151 N5
White Pass Canada/U.S.A. 149 N4
White Pine Range mts U.S.A. 159 F2
White Plains U.S.A. 165 I3
White River Canada 152 D4
Whiteriver U.S.A. 159 I5
White River U.S.A. 160 C3
White River Valley U.S.A. 159 F2
White Rock Peak U.S.A. 159 F2
White Russia country Europe see Belarus
Whitesail Lake Canada 150 E4
White Salmon U.S.A. 156 C3
Whitesand r. Canada 150 H2
White Sands National Monument nat. park U.S.A. 157 G6
Whitesburg U.S.A. 164 D5
White Sea Rus. Fed. 52 H2
Whitestone r. Y.T. Canada 149 M2
White Stone U.S.A. 165 G5
White Sulphur Springs MT U.S.A. 156 F3
White Sulphur Springs WV U.S.A. 164 E5
Whitesville U.S.A. 164 E5
Whiteville U.S.A. 163 E5
White Volta r. Burkina Faso/Ghana 120 C4
also known as Nakambé or Nakanbe or Volta Blanche
Whitewater U.S.A. 159 I2
Whitewater Baldy mt. U.S.A. 159 I5
Whitewater Lake Canada 152 C4
Whitewood Australia 136 C4
Whitewood Canada 151 K5
Whitfield U.K. 59 I7
Whithorn U.K. 60 E6
Whitianga N.Z. 139 E3
Whitland U.K. 59 C7
Whitley Bay U.K. 58 F3
Whitmore Mountains Antarctica 188 K1
Whitney Canada 165 F1
Whitney, Lake TX U.S.A. 167 F2
Whitney, Mount U.S.A. 158 D3
Whitney Point U.S.A. 165 H2
Whitstable U.K. 59 I7
Whitsunday Group is Australia 136 E4
Whitsunday Island National Park Australia 136 E4
Whitsun Island Vanuatu see Pentecost Island
Whittemore U.S.A. 164 D1
Whittier AK U.S.A. 149 J3
Whittlesea Australia 138 B6
Whittlesey U.K. 59 G6
Whitton Australia 138 C5
Wholdaia Lake Canada 151 J2
Why U.S.A. 159 G5
Whyalla Australia 137 B7
Wiang Sa Thai. 86 C3
Wiarton Canada 164 E1
Wibaux U.S.A. 156 G3
Wichelen Belgium 62 D3
Wichita U.S.A. 160 D4
Wichita r. U.S.A. 161 D5
Wichita Falls U.S.A. 161 D5
Wichita Mountains U.S.A. 161 D5
Wick U.K. 60 F2
Wick r. U.K. 60 F2
Wickenburg U.S.A. 159 G5
Wickes U.S.A. 161 E5
Wickford U.K. 59 H7
Wickham r. Australia 134 E4
Wickham, Cape Australia 137 [inset]
Wickham, Mount hill Australia 134 E4
Wickliffe U.S.A. 161 F4
Wicklow Ireland 61 F5
Wicklow Head hd Ireland 61 G5
Wicklow Mountains Ireland 61 F5
Wicklow Mountains National Park Ireland 61 F4
Wide Bay AK U.S.A. 148 H4
Widerøe, Mount Antarctica 188 C2
Widerøefjellet mt. Antarctica see Widerøe, Mount
Widgeegoara watercourse Australia 138 B1
Widgiemooltha Australia 135 C7
Widi, Kepulauan is Maluku Indon. 83 D3
Widnes U.K. 58 E5
Wi-do i. S. Korea 91 B6
Wied r. Germany 63 H4
Wiehengebirge hills Germany 63 I2
Wiehl Germany 63 H4
Wielkopolskie, Pojezierze reg. Poland 57 O4
Wielkopolski Park Narodowy nat. park Poland 57 P4
Wieluń Poland 57 Q5
Wien Austria see Vienna
Wiener Neustadt Austria 57 P7
Wien Lake AK U.S.A. 149 J2
Wierden Neth. 62 G2
Wieren Germany 63 K2
Wieringerwerf Neth. 62 F2
Wiesbaden Germany 63 I4
Wiesenfelden Germany 63 M5
Wiesentheid Germany 63 K5
Wiesloch Germany 63 I5
Wiesmoor Germany 63 H1
Wietze Germany 63 J2
Wietzendorf Germany 63 J2
Wieżyca hill Poland 57 Q3
Wigan U.K. 58 E5
Wiggins U.S.A. 161 F6
Wight, Isle of i. England U.K. 59 F8
Wigierski Park Narodowy nat. park Poland 55 M9
Wignes Lake Canada 151 J2
Wigston U.K. 59 F6
Wigton U.K. 58 D4
Wigtown U.K. 60 E6
Wigtown Bay U.K. 60 E6
Wijchen Neth. 62 F3
Wijhe Neth. 62 G2
Wilberforce, Cape Australia 136 B1
Wilbur U.S.A. 156 D3
Wilburton U.S.A. 161 E5
Wilcannia Australia 138 A3
Wilcox U.S.A. 165 F3
Wilczek Land i. Rus. Fed. see Vil'cheka, Zemlya
Wildberg Germany 63 M2
Wildcat Peak U.S.A. 158 E2
Wild Coast S. Africa 125 I6
Wilderness National Park S. Africa 124 F8
Wildeshausen Germany 63 I2
Wild Horse Hill mt. U.S.A. 160 C3
Wildspitze mt. Austria 57 M7
Wildwood FL U.S.A. 163 D6
Wildwood NJ U.S.A. 165 H4
Wilge r. S. Africa 125 I4
Wilge r. S. Africa 125 I3
Wilgena Australia 135 F7
▶Wilhelm, Mount P.N.G. 81 L8
5th highest mountain in Oceania.
Wilhelm II Land reg. Antarctica see Kaiser Wilhelm II Land
Wilhelmina Gebergte mts Suriname 177 G3
Wilhelmina Kanaal canal Neth. 62 F3
Wilhelmshaven Germany 63 I1
Wilhelmstal Namibia 124 C1
Wilkes-Barre U.S.A. 165 H3
Wilkesboro U.S.A. 162 D4
Wilkes Coast Antarctica 188 G2
Wilkes Land reg. Antarctica 188 G2
Wilkie Canada 151 I4
Wilkins Coast Antarctica 188 L2
Wilkins Ice Shelf Antarctica 188 L2
Wilkinson Lakes salt flat Australia 135 F7
Will, Mount B.C. Canada 149 O4
Willand U.K. 59 D8
Willandra Billabong watercourse Australia 138 B4
Willandra National Park Australia 138 B4
Willapa Bay U.S.A. 156 B3
Willard Mex. 166 C2
Willard NM U.S.A. 157 G6
Willard OH U.S.A. 164 D3
Willcox U.S.A. 159 I5
Willcox Playa salt flat U.S.A. 159 I5
Willebadessen Germany 63 J3
Willebroek Belgium 62 E3
▶Willemstad Curaçao 169 K6
Capital of Curaçao.
Willeroo Australia 134 E3
Willette U.S.A. 164 C5
William, Mount Australia 137 C8
William Creek Australia 137 B6
William Lake Canada 151 L4
Williams AZ U.S.A. 159 G4
Williams CA U.S.A. 158 B2
Williamsburg KY U.S.A. 164 C5
Williamsburg OH U.S.A. 164 C4
Williamsburg VA U.S.A. 165 G5
Williams Lake Canada 150 F4
William Smith, Cap c. Canada 153 I1
Williamson NY U.S.A. 165 G2
Williamson WV U.S.A. 164 D5
Williamsport IN U.S.A. 164 B3
Williamsport PA U.S.A. 165 G3
Williamston U.S.A. 162 E5
Williamstown KY U.S.A. 164 C4
Williamstown NJ U.S.A. 165 H4
Willimantic U.S.A. 165 I3
Willis Group atolls Australia 136 E3
Williston S. Africa 124 E6
Williston ND U.S.A. 160 C1
Williston SC U.S.A. 163 D5
Williston Lake Canada 150 F4
Williton U.K. 59 D7
Willits U.S.A. 158 B2
Willmar U.S.A. 160 E2
Willoughby, Lake U.S.A. 165 I1
Willow AK U.S.A. 149 J3
Willow Beach U.S.A. 159 F4
Willow Bunch Canada 151 J5
Willow Creek AK U.S.A. 149 K3
Willow Hill U.S.A. 165 G3
Willow Lake Canada 150 G2
Willowlake r. Canada 150 F2
Willowmore S. Africa 124 F7
Willowra Australia 134 F5
Willows U.S.A. 158 B2
Willow Springs U.S.A. 161 F4
Willowvale S. Africa 125 I7
Wills, Lake salt flat Australia 134 E5
Wilma U.S.A. 163 C6
Wilmington DE U.S.A. 165 H4
Wilmington NC U.S.A. 163 E5
Wilmington OH U.S.A. 164 D4
Wilmore U.S.A. 164 C5
Wilmslow U.K. 58 E5
Wilno Lith. see Vilnius
Wilnsdorf Germany 63 I4
Wilpattu National Park Sri Lanka 106 D4
Wilseder Berg hill Germany 63 J1
Wilson watercourse Australia 137 C5
Wilson atoll Micronesia see Ifalik
Wilson KS U.S.A. 160 D4
Wilson NC U.S.A. 162 E5
Wilson NY U.S.A. 165 F2
Wilson, Mount CO U.S.A. 159 J3
Wilson, Mount NV U.S.A. 159 F2
Wilson, Mount OR U.S.A. 156 C3
Wilsonia U.S.A. 158 D3
Wilson's Promontory pen. Australia 138 C7
Wilson's Promontory National Park Australia 138 C7
Wilsum Germany 62 G2
Wilton r. Australia 134 F3
Wilton U.S.A. 165 J1
Wiltz Lux. 62 F5
Wiluna Australia 135 C6
Wimereux France 62 B4
Wina r. Cameroon see Vina
Winamac U.S.A. 164 B3
Winbin watercourse Australia 137 D5
Winburg S. Africa 125 H5
Wincanton U.K. 59 E7
Winchester Canada 165 H1
Winchester U.K. 59 F7
Winchester IN U.S.A. 164 C3
Winchester KY U.S.A. 164 C5
Winchester NH U.S.A. 165 I2
Winchester TN U.S.A. 163 C5
Winchester VA U.S.A. 165 F4
Wind r. Y.T. Canada 149 N2
Wind r. U.S.A. 156 F4
Windau Latvia see Ventspils
Windber U.S.A. 165 F3
Wind Cave National Park U.S.A. 160 C3
Windermere U.K. 58 E4
Windermere l. U.K. 58 E4
Windham AK U.S.A. 149 N4
▶Windhoek Namibia 124 C2
Capital of Namibia.
Windigo Lake Canada 151 N4
Windlestraw Law hill U.K. 60 G5
Wind Mountain U.S.A. 157 G6
Windom U.S.A. 160 E3
Windom Peak U.S.A. 159 J3
Windorah Australia 136 C5
Window Rock U.S.A. 159 I4
Wind Point U.S.A. 164 B2
Wind River Range mts U.S.A. 156 F4
Windrush r. U.K. 59 F7
Windsbach Germany 63 K5
Windsor Australia 138 E4
Windsor N.S. Canada 153 I5
Windsor Ont. Canada 164 D2
Windsor U.K. 59 G7
Windsor NC U.S.A. 162 E4
Windsor NY U.S.A. 165 H2
Windsor VA U.S.A. 165 G5
Windsor VT U.S.A. 165 I2
Windsor Locks U.S.A. 165 I3
Windward Islands Caribbean Sea 169 L5
Windward Passage Cuba/Haiti 169 J5
Windy U.S.A. 146 D3
Windy Fork r. AK U.S.A. 148 I3
Winefred Lake Canada 151 I4
Winfield KS U.S.A. 161 D4
Winfield WV U.S.A. 164 E4
Wingate U.K. 58 F4
Wingen Australia 138 E3
Wingene Belgium 62 D3
Wingen-sur-Moder France 63 H6
Wingham Australia 138 F3
Wingham Canada 164 E2
Wini East Timor 83 C5
Winisk r. Canada 152 D3
Winisk (abandoned) Canada 152 D3
Winisk Lake Canada 152 D3
Winkana Myanmar 86 B4
Winkelman U.S.A. 159 H5
Winkler Canada 151 L5
Winlock U.S.A. 156 C3
Winneba Ghana 120 C4
Winnebago, Lake U.S.A. 164 A1
Winnecke Creek watercourse Australia 134 E4
Winnemucca U.S.A. 158 E1
Winnemucca Lake U.S.A. 158 D1
Winner U.S.A. 160 C3
Winnett U.S.A. 156 F3
Winnfield U.S.A. 161 E6
Winnibigoshish, Lake U.S.A. 160 E2
Winnie U.S.A. 161 E6
Winning Australia 135 A5
▶Winnipeg Canada 151 L5
Capital of Manitoba.
Winnipeg r. Canada 151 L5
Winnipeg, Lake Canada 151 L5
Winnipegosis Canada 151 L5
Winnipegosis, Lake Canada 151 K4
Winnipesaukee, Lake U.S.A. 165 J2
Winnsboro LA U.S.A. 167 H1
Winona AZ U.S.A. 159 H4
Winona MN U.S.A. 160 F2
Winona MO U.S.A. 161 F4
Winona MS U.S.A. 161 F5
Winschoten Neth. 62 H1
Winsen (Aller) Germany 63 J2
Winsen (Luhe) Germany 63 K1
Winsford U.K. 58 E5
Winslow AZ U.S.A. 159 H4
Winslow ME U.S.A. 165 K1
Winsop, Tanjung pt Indon. 81 I7
Winsted U.S.A. 165 I3
Winston-Salem U.S.A. 162 D4
Winterberg Germany 63 I3
Winter Haven U.S.A. 163 D6
Winters CA U.S.A. 158 C2
Winters TX U.S.A. 161 D6
Wintersville U.S.A. 164 E3
Winterswijk Neth. 62 G3
Winterthur Switz. 66 I3
Winterton S. Africa 125 I5
Winthrop U.S.A. 165 K1
Winton Australia 136 C4
Winton N.Z. 139 B8
Winton U.S.A. 162 E4
Winwick U.K. 59 G6
Wiralaga Sumatera Indon. 84 D3
Wirral pen. U.K. 58 D5
Wirrulla Australia 137 A7
Wisbech U.K. 59 H6
Wiscasset U.S.A. 165 K1
Wisconsin r. U.S.A. 160 F3
Wisconsin state U.S.A. 164 A1
Wisconsin Rapids U.S.A. 160 F2
Wise U.S.A. 164 D5
Wiseman AK U.S.A. 149 J2
Wishaw U.K. 60 F5
Wisher U.S.A. 160 D2
Wisil Dabarow Somalia 122 E3
Wisła r. Poland see Vistula
Wismar Germany 57 M4
Wistaria Canada 150 E4
Witbank S. Africa 125 I3
Witbooisvlei Namibia 124 D3
Witham U.K. 59 H7
Witham r. U.K. 59 H6
Witherbee U.S.A. 165 I1
Withernsea U.K. 58 H5
Witherspoon, Mount AK U.S.A. 149 K3
Witjira National Park Australia 137 A5
Witmarsum Neth. 62 F1
Witney U.K. 59 F7
Witrivier S. Africa 125 J3
Witry-lès-Reims France 62 E5
Witteberg mts S. Africa 125 H6
Wittenberg Germany see Lutherstadt Wittenberg
Wittenberge Germany 63 L2
Wittenburg Germany 63 L1
Witti, Banjaran mts Malaysia 85 G1
Wittingen Germany 63 K2
Wittlich Germany 62 G5
Wittmund Germany 63 H1
Wittstock Germany 63 M1
Witu Islands P.N.G. 81 L7
Witvlei Namibia 124 D2
Witzenhausen Germany 63 J3
Wivenhoe, Lake Australia 138 F1
Władysławowo Poland 57 Q3
Włocławek Poland 57 Q4
Wobkent Uzbek. see Vobkent
Wodonga Australia 138 C6
Wœrth France 63 H6
Wohlthat Mountains Antarctica 188 C2
Woippy France 62 G5
Wōjjā atoll Marshall Is see Wotje
Wokam i. Indon. 81 I8
Woken He r. China 90 C3
Wokha India 105 H4
Woking U.K. 59 G7
Wokingham watercourse Australia 136 C4
Wokingham U.K. 59 G7
Woko National Park Australia 138 E3
Wolcott IN U.S.A. 164 B3
Wolcott NY U.S.A. 165 G2
Woldegk Germany 63 N1
Wolea atoll Micronesia see Woleai
Woleai atoll Micronesia 81 K5
Wolf r. Y.T. Canada 149 N3
Wolf r. TN U.S.A. 161 F5
Wolf r. WI U.S.A. 160 F2
Wolf Creek MT U.S.A. 156 E3
Wolf Creek OR U.S.A. 156 C4
Wolf Creek Mountain hill AK U.S.A. 148 G3
Wolf Creek Pass U.S.A. 157 G5
Wolfen Germany 63 M3
Wolfenbüttel Germany 63 K2
Wolfhagen Germany 63 J3
Wolf Lake Y.T. Canada 149 O3
Wolf Mountain AK U.S.A. 148 I2
Wolf Point U.S.A. 156 G2
Wolfsberg Austria 57 O7
Wolfsburg Germany 63 K2
Wolfstein Germany 63 H5
Wolfville Canada 153 I5
Wolgast Germany 57 N3
Wolin Poland 57 O4
Wollaston Lake Canada 151 K3
Wollaston Lake l. Canada 151 K3
Wollaston Peninsula Canada 146 G3
Wollemi National Park Australia 138 E4
Wollongong Australia 138 E5
Wolmaransstad S. Africa 125 G4
Wolmirstedt Germany 63 L2
Wolong Reserve nature res. China 96 D2
Wolowaru Flores Indon. 83 B5
Wolseley Australia 137 C8
Wolseley S. Africa 124 D7
Wolsey U.S.A. 160 D2
Wolsingham U.K. 58 F4
Wolvega Neth. 62 G2
Wolvegea Neth. see Wolvega
Wolverhampton U.K. 59 E6
Wolverine r. N.W.T. Canada 149 O1
Wolverine U.S.A. 164 C1
Wolya r. Indon. 84 A1
Womens Bay AK U.S.A. 148 I4
Wommelgem Belgium 62 E3
Womrather Höhe hill Germany 63 H5
Wonarah Australia 136 B3
Wonay, Kowtal-e Afgh. 111 H3
Wondai Australia 137 E5
Wongalarroo Lake salt l. Australia 138 B3
Wongarbon Australia 138 D4
Wong Chuk Hang H.K. China 97 [inset]
Wong Leng hill H.K. China 97 [inset]
Wong Wan Chau H.K. China see Double Island
Wŏnju S. Korea 91 B5
Wonogiri Jawa Indon. 85 E4
Wonosari Indon. 85 E4
Wonosobo Jawa Indon. 85 E4
Wonowon Canada 150 F3
Wonreli Maluku Indon. 83 C5
Wŏnsan N. Korea 91 B5
Wonthaggi Australia 138 B7
Wonyulgunna, Mount hill Australia 135 B6
Woocalla Australia 137 B6
Wood r. AK U.S.A. 149 J2
Wood, Mount Y.T. Canada 149 L3
Woodbine GA U.S.A. 163 D6
Woodbine NJ U.S.A. 165 H4
Woodbridge U.K. 59 I6
Woodbridge U.S.A. 165 G4
Wood Buffalo National Park Canada 150 H3
Woodburn U.S.A. 156 C3
Woodbury NJ U.S.A. 165 H4
Woodbury TN U.S.A. 161 G5
Woodchopper Creek AK U.S.A. 149 L2
Wooded Bluff hd Australia 138 F2
Wood Lake Canada 151 K4
Woodlake U.S.A. 158 D3
Woodland CA U.S.A. 158 C2
Woodland PA U.S.A. 165 F3
Woodland WA U.S.A. 156 C3
Woodlands Sing. 87 [inset]
Woodlark Island P.N.G. 132 F2
Woodridge Canada 151 L5
Woodroffe watercourse Australia 136 B4
Woodroffe, Mount Australia 135 E6
Woodruff UT U.S.A. 156 F4
Woodruff WI U.S.A. 160 F2
Woods, Lake salt flat Australia 134 F4
Woods, Lake of the Canada/U.S.A. 155 I2
Woodsfield U.S.A. 164 E4
Woodside Australia 138 C7
Woodstock N.B. Canada 153 I5
Woodstock Ont. Canada 164 E2
Woodstock IL U.S.A. 160 F3
Woodstock VA U.S.A. 165 F4
Woodstock VT U.S.A. 165 I2
Woodsville U.S.A. 165 I1
Woodville Canada 165 F1
Woodville MS U.S.A. 161 F6
Woodville OH U.S.A. 164 D3
Woodville TX U.S.A. 161 E6
Woodward U.S.A. 161 D4
Woody U.S.A. 158 D4
Woody Island AK U.S.A. 148 I4
Wooler U.K. 58 E3
Woolgoolga Australia 138 F3
Wooli Australia 138 F2
Woollard, Mount Antarctica 188 K1
Woollett, Lac l. Canada 152 G4
Woolyeenyer Hill hill Australia 135 C8
Woomera Australia 137 B6
Woomera Prohibited Area Australia 135 F7
Woonsocket RI U.S.A. 165 J2
Woonsocket SD U.S.A. 160 D2
Woorabinda Australia 136 E5
Wooramel r. Australia 135 A6
Wooster U.S.A. 164 E3
Worbis Germany 63 K3
Worbody Point Australia 136 C2
Worcester S. Africa 124 D7
Worcester U.K. 59 E6
Worcester MA U.S.A. 165 J2
Worcester NY U.S.A. 165 H2
Wörgl Austria 57 N7
Workai i. Indon. 81 I8
Workington U.K. 58 D4
Worksop U.K. 58 F5
Workum Neth. 62 F2
Worland U.S.A. 156 G3
Wörlitz Germany 63 M3
Wormerveer Neth. 62 E2
Worms Germany 63 I5
Worms Head hd U.K. 59 C7
Wortel Namibia 124 C2
Wörth am Rhein Germany 63 I5
Worthing U.K. 59 G8
Worthington IN U.S.A. 164 B4
Worthington MN U.S.A. 160 E3
Wosi Halmahera Indon. 83 C3
Wosu Sulawesi Indon. 83 B3
Wotje atoll Marshall Is 186 H5
Wotu Sulawesi Indon. 83 B3
Woudrichem Neth. 62 E3
Woustviller France 62 H5
Wowoni i. Indon. 83 B4
Wowoni, Selat sea chan. Indon. 83 B3
Wozrojdeniye Oroli i. Uzbek. see Vozrozhdenya Island
Wrangel Island Rus. Fed. 77 T2
Wrangell AK U.S.A. 149 N4
Wrangell, Cape AK U.S.A. 148 [inset]
Wrangell, Mount AK U.S.A. 149 K3
Wrangell Island U.S.A. 150 C3
Wrangell Mountains AK U.S.A. 148 H4
Wrangell-St Elias National Park and Preserve AK U.S.A. 149 L3
Wrath, Cape U.K. 60 D2
Wray U.S.A. 160 C3
Wreake r. U.K. 59 F6
Wreck Point S. Africa 124 C5
Wreck Reef Australia 136 F4
Wrecsam U.K. see Wrexham
Wrestedt Germany 63 K2
Wrexham U.K. 59 E5
Wright Samar Phil. 82 D4
Wrightmyo India 87 A5
Wrightson, Mount U.S.A. 157 F7
Wrightwood U.S.A. 158 E4
Wrigley N.W.T. Canada 149 Q3
Wrigley U.S.A. 164 D4
Wrigley Gulf Antarctica 188 J2
Wrocław Poland 57 P5
Września Poland 57 P4
Wu'an China see Changtai
Wu'an Hebei China 95 H4
Wubin Australia 135 B7
Wubu Shaanxi China 95 G4
Wuchagou Nei Mongol China 95 J2
Wuchang Heilong. China 90 B3
Wuchang Hubei China see Jiangxia
Wuchow China see Wuzhou
Wuchuan Guangdong China see Meilu
Wuchuan Guizhou China 96 E2
Wuchuan Nei Mongol China 95 G3
Wuda Nei Mongol China 94 F4
Wudalianchi China 90 B2
Wuḍām 'Alwā Oman 110 E6
Wudan Nei Mongol China 95 I3
Wudang Shan mt. China 97 F1
Wudao Liaoning China 95 J4
Wudaoliang Qinghai China 94 C5
Wudi Shandong China 95 I4
Wuding China 96 D3
Wuding He r. China 95 G4
Wudinna Australia 135 F8
Wufeng Hubei China 97 F2
Wufeng Yunnan China see Zhenxiong
Wufo Gansu China 94 F4
Wugang China 97 F3
Wugong Shaanxi China 95 G5
Wuhai Nei Mongol China 94 F4
Wuhan China 97 G2
Wuhe China 97 H1
Wuhu China 97 H2
Wuhua China 97 G4
Wuhubei China 97 H2
Wūjang Xizang China 99 B6
Wu Jiang r. China 96 E2
Wujin Jiangsu China see Changzhou
Wujin Sichuan China see Xinjin
Wukari Nigeria 120 D4
Wulang China 96 B2
Wuleidao Wan b. China 95 J4
Wuli Qinghai China 94 C5
Wulian Feng mts China 96 D2
Wuliang Shan mts China 96 D3
Wuliaru i. Indon. 134 E1
Wuli Jiang r. China 97 F4
Wulik r. AK U.S.A. 148 F2
Wuling Shan mts China 97 F2
Wulong China 96 E2
Wulongji China see Huaibin
Wulur Maluku Indon. 83 D4
Wumatang Xizang China 99 E7
Wumeng Shan mts China 96 D3
Wuming China 97 F4
Wümme r. Germany 63 I1
Wundwin Myanmar 86 B2
Wungda China 96 D2
Wuning China 97 G2
Wünnenberg Germany 63 I3
Wunnummin Lake Canada 147 J4
Wunsiedel Germany 63 M4
Wunstorf Germany 63 J2
Wupatki National Monument nat. park U.S.A. 159 H4
Wuping China 97 H3
Wuppertal Germany 63 H3
Wuppertal S. Africa 124 D7
Wuqi Shaanxi China 95 G4
Wuqia Xinjiang China 98 A5
Wuqia Xinjiang China 98 A5
Wuqiang Hebei China 95 H4
Wuqiao Hebei China 95 I4
Wuqing Tianjin China 95 I4
Wuquan China see Wuyang
Wuranga Australia 135 B7
Wurno Nigeria 120 D3
Würzburg Germany 63 J5
Wurzen Germany 63 M3
Wushan Chongqing China 97 F2
Wushan Gansu China 94 F5
Wu Shan mts China 97 F2
Wushi Guangdong China 97 F4
Wushi Xinjiang China 98 B4
Wüstegarten hill Germany 63 J3
Wusuli Jiang r. China/Rus. Fed. see Ussuri
Wutai Shanxi China 95 H4
Wutai Xinjiang China 98 C3
Wutaishan Shanxi China 95 H4
Wutonggou Nei Mongol China 94 D3
Wutonggou Xinjiang China 98 E4
Wutongwozi Quan well Xinjiang China 94 C3
Wuvulu Island P.N.G. 81 K7
Wuwei Gansu China 94 E4
Wuxi Chongqing China 97 F2
Wuxi Hunan China 97 F2
Wuxi Hunan China see Qiyang
Wuxi Jiangsu China 97 I2
Wuxia China see Wushan
Wuxian China see Suzhou
Wuxiang Shanxi China 95 H4
Wuxing China see Huzhou
Wuxu China 97 F4
Wuxuan China 97 F4
Wuxue China 97 G2
Wuyang Guizhou China see Zhenyuan
Wuyang Henan China 97 G1
Wuyang Shanxi China 95 H4
Wuyang Zhejiang China see Wuyi
Wuyi China 97 H2
Wuyiling China 90 C2
Wuyi Shan mts China 97 H3
Wuyuan Jiangxi China 97 H2
Wuyuan Nei Mongol China 95 G3
Wuyuan Zhejiang China see Haiyan
Wuyun China see Jinyun
Wuzhai Shanxi China 95 G4
Wuzhi Henan China 95 H5
Wuzhishan China 97 F5
Wuzhi Shan mts China 97 F5
Wuzhong Ningxia China 94 F4
Wuzhou China 97 F4
Wyalkatchem Australia 135 B7
Wyalong Australia 138 C4
Wyandra Australia 138 B1
Wyangala Reservoir Australia 138 D4
Wyara, Lake salt flat Australia 138 B2
Wycheproof Australia 138 A6
Wylliesburg U.S.A. 165 F5
Wyloo Australia 134 B5
Wylye r. U.K. 59 F7
Wymondham U.K. 59 I6
Wymore U.S.A. 160 D3
Wynbring Australia 135 F7
Wyndham Australia 134 E3
Wyndham-Werribee Australia 138 B6
Wynne U.S.A. 161 F5
Wynyard Canada 151 J5
Wyola Lake salt flat Australia 135 E7
Wyoming U.S.A. 164 C2
Wyoming state U.S.A. 156 G4
Wyoming Peak U.S.A. 156 F4
Wyoming Range mts U.S.A. 156 F4
Wyong Australia 138 E4
Wyperfeld National Park Australia 137 C7
Wysox U.S.A. 165 G3
Wyszków Poland 57 R4
Wythall U.K. 59 F6
Wytheville U.S.A. 164 E5
Wytmarsum Neth. see Witmarsum

X

Xaafuun Somalia 122 F2
▶Xaafuun, Raas pt Somalia 108 H7
Most easterly point of Africa.
Xabyai Xizang China 99 G7
Xabyaisamba China 96 C2
Xaçmaz Azer. 113 H2
Xagjang Xizang China 99 F7
Xagnag Xizang China 99 C6
Xago Xizang China 99 E7
Xagquka Xizang China 99 F7
Xaidulla Xinjiang China 99 B5
Xaignabouli Laos 86 C3
Xaignabouri Laos see Xaignabouli
Xainza Xizang China 99 E7
Xaitongmoin Xizang China 99 E7
Xai-Xai Moz. 125 K3
Xakur Xinjiang China 98 B5
Xal, Cerro de hill Mex. 167 H4
Xalapa Mex. see Jalapa
Xaltianguis Mex. 167 F5
Xamba Nei Mongol China 95 F3
Xambioa Brazil 177 I5
Xam Nua Laos 86 D2
Xá-Muteba Angola 123 B4
Xan r. Laos 86 C3
Xanagas Botswana 124 E2
Xangd Nei Mongol China 94 E3
Xangda China see Nangqên
Xangdin Hural Nei Mongol China 95 G3
Xangdoring Xizang China 99 C6
Xangongo Angola 123 B5
Xangzha Xizang China 99 F7
Xanica Mex. 167 F5
Xankändi Azer. 113 G3
Xanlar Azer. 113 G2
Xanthi Greece 69 K4
Xarag Qinghai China 94 D4
Xarardheere Somalia 122 E3
Xarba La pass Xizang China 99 D7
Xar Burd Nei Mongol China see Bayan Nuru
Xardong Xizang China 99 D7
Xar Hudag Nei Mongol China 95 H2
Xar Moron r. China 95 G3
Xar Moron r. China 95 J3
Xarru Xizang China 99 D7
Xarsingma Xizang China see Yadong
Xàtiva Spain 67 F4
Xavantes, Serra dos hills Brazil 177 I6
Xaxa Xizang China 99 C6
Xayar Xinjiang China 98 C4
Xazgat Xinjiang China 98 D3
Xcalak Mex. 167 I5
X-Can Mex. 167 I4
Xegil Xinjiang China 98 B4

Xekar *Xinjiang* China **98** B5
Xelva Spain *see* **Chelva**
Xenia U.S.A. **164** D4
Xênkyêr *Xizang* China **99** E7
Xero Potamos *r.* Cyprus *see* **Xeros**
Xeros *r.* Cyprus **107** A2
Xhora S. Africa *see* **Elliotdale**
Xia Awat *Xinjiang* China **98** B5
Xiabancheng *Hebei* China *see* **Chengde**
Xia Bazar *Xinjiang* China **98** B5
Xiabole Shan *mt.* China **90** B2
Xiachuan Dao *i.* China **97** G4
Xiacun *Shandong* China *see* **Rushan**
Xia Dawo *Qinghai* China **94** D5
Xiadong *Gansu* China **94** C3
Xiaguan China *see* **Dali**
Xiaguanying *Gansu* China **94** F5
Xiahe *Gansu* China **94** E5
Xiajiang *Xizang* China *see* **Xagjang**
Xiajin *Shandong* China **95** I4
Xiamaya *Xinjiang* China **94** C3
Xiamen China **97** H3
Xi'an *Shaanxi* China **95** G5
Xianfeng China **97** F2
Xiangcheng *Henan* China **95** H5
Xiangcheng *Sichuan* China **96** C2
Xiangcheng *Yunnan* China *see* **Xiangyun**
Xiangfan China **97** G1
Xiangfen *Shanxi* China **95** G5
Xiangfeng China *see* **Laifeng**
Xianggang *H.K.* China *see* **Hong Kong**
Xianggang Tebie Xingzhengqu *aut. reg.* China *see* **Hong Kong**
Xianggelila China **96** C3
Xiangjiang China *see* **Huichang**
Xiangkou China *see* **Wulong**
Xiangning *Shanxi* China **95** G5
Xiangride *Qinghai* China **94** D5
Xiangshan China *see* **Menghai**
Xiangshui *Jiangsu* China **95** I5
Xiangshuiba China **97** F3
Xiangtan China **97** G3
Xiangxiang China **97** G3
Xiangyang China *see* **Xiangfan**
Xiangyang Hu *l. Xizang* China **99** E6
Xiangyin China **97** G2
Xiangyun China **96** D3
Xianju China **97** I2
Xianning China **97** G2
Xiannümiao China *see* **Jiangdu**
Xianshui He *r.* China **96** D2
Xiantao China **97** G2
Xianxia Ling *mts* China **97** H3
Xianxian *Hebei* China **95** I4
Xianyang *Shaanxi* China **95** G5
Xi'anzhou *Ningxia* China **94** F4
Xiaoba *Ningxia* China *see* **Qingtongxia**
Xiaocaohu China **102** G3
Xiaochang *Hebei* China **95** H3
Xiaodong China **97** F4
Xiaodongliang China **96** C1
Xiao'ergou *Nei Mongol* China **95** J1
Xiaofan *Hebei* China *see* **Wuqiang**
Xiaogan China **97** G2
Xiaogang China *see* **Dongxiang**
Xiaoguai *Xinjiang* China **98** D3
Xiaoguan *Gansu* China **95** F4
Xiaohaizi Shuiku *resr Xinjiang* China **98** B5
Xiao Hinggan Ling *mts* China **90** B2
Xiaojin *Gansu* China **95** F5
Xiaojin China **96** D2
Xiaolangdi Shuiku *resr Henan/Shanxi* China **95** H5
Xiaonan *Gansu* China *see* **Dongxiangzu**
Xiaonanchuan *Qinghai* China **94** C5
Xiao Qaidam *Qinghai* China **99** F5
Xiaosanjiang China **97** G3
Xiaoshan China **97** I2
Xiao Shan *mts* China **95** G5
Xiaoshi China *see* **Benxi**
Xiao Surmang China **96** C1
Xiaotao China **97** H3
Xiaowutai Shan *mt. Hebei* China **95** H4
Xiaoxi China *see* **Pinghe**
Xiaoxian *Anhui* China **95** I5
Xiaoxiang Ling *mts* China **96** D2
Xiaoxita China *see* **Yiling**
Xiaoyang Shan *i.* China **97** I2
Xiaoyi *Henan* China *see* **Gongyi**
Xiaoyi *Shanxi* China **95** G4
Xiaoyingpan *Xinjiang* China **98** C3
Xiapu China **97** I3
Xiaqiong China *see* **Batang**
Xiashan China *see* **Zhanjiang**
Xiasifen *Gansu* China **94** E4
Xiatil Mex. **167** H5
Xiaxian *Shanxi* China **95** G5
Xiayang China *see* **Yanling**
Xiayanjing China *see* **Yanjing**
Xiayingpan *Guizhou* China *see* **Luzhi**
Xiayingpan *Guizhou* China *see* **Lupanshui**
Xiayukou China **97** F1
Xiazhen *Shandong* China *see* **Weishan**
Xiazhuang China *see* **Linshu**
Xibdê China **96** C2
Xibet *Xinjiang* China **98** E3
Xibing China **97** H3
Xibu China *see* **Dongshan**
Xichang China **96** D3
Xicheng *Hebei* China *see* **Yangyuan**
Xichou China **96** E4
Xichuan China **97** F1
Xide China **96** D2
Xidu China *see* **Hengyang**
Xiejiaji *Shandong* China *see* **Qingyun**
Xiemahe' China **97** F2
Xieng Khouang Laos *see* **Phônsavan**
Xiêng Lam Vietnam **86** D3
Xieyang Dao *i.* China **97** F4
Xifeng *Gansu* China *see* **Qingyang**
Xifeng *Guizhou* China **96** E3
Xifeng *Liaoning* China **90** B4
Xifengzhen *Gansu* China *see* **Qingyang**
Xigazê *Xizang* China **99** E7
Xihan Shui *r.* China **96** E1
Xihe *Gansu* China **94** F5
Xi He *r.* China **96** E2
Xi He *watercourse* China **94** E3
Xihu *Gansu* China **98** F4
Xihua *Henan* China **95** H5
Xihuachi *Gansu* China *see* **Heshui**
Xiji *Ningxia* China **94** F5
Xi Jiang *r.* China **97** G4
Xijian Quan *well Gansu* China **94** D3
Xijir *Qinghai* China **94** B5
Xijir Ulan Hu *salt l.* China **99** E6
Xijishui *Gansu* China **94** E4
Xil *Nei Mongol* China **95** H3
Xilaotou Shan *mt. Nei Mongol* China **95** J2
Xiliangzi *Qinghai* China **98** F5
Xiliao He *r.* China **95** J3
Xiligou *Qinghai* China *see* **Ulan**
Xilin China **96** E3
Xilinhot *Nei Mongol* China **95** I3
Xilin Qagan Obo *Nei Mongol* China *see* **Qagan Obo**
Ximiao *Nei Mongol* China **94** E3
Xin *Nei Mongol* China **95** G4
Xin'an *Anhui* China *see* **Lai'an**
Xin'an *Guizhou* China *see* **Anlong**
Xin'an *Hebei* China *see* **Anxin**
Xin'an *Henan* China **95** H5
Xin'anjiang China **97** H2
Xin'anjiang Shuiku *resr* China **97** H2
Xinavane Moz. **125** K3
Xin Barag Youqi *Nei Mongol* China *see* **Altan Emel**
Xin Barag Zuoqi *Nei Mongol* China *see* **Amgalang**
Xin Bulag Dong *Nei Mongol* China **95** I1
Xincai China **97** G1
Xinchang *Jiangxi* China *see* **Yifeng**
Xinchang *Zhejiang* China **97** I2
Xincheng *Fujian* China *see* **Gutian**
Xincheng *Gansu* China **94** E4
Xincheng *Guangdong* China *see* **Xinxing**
Xincheng *Guangxi* China **97** F3
Xincheng *Ningxia* China **94** F4
Xincheng *Shanxi* China *see* **Yuanqu**
Xincheng *Sichuan* China *see* **Zhaojue**
Xinchengbu *Shaanxi* China **95** G4
Xinchepaizi *Xinjiang* China **98** D3
Xincun China *see* **Dongchuan**
Xindi *Guangxi* China **97** F4
Xindi *Hubei* China *see* **Honghu**
Xindian *Heilong.* China **95** K2
Xindu *Guangxi* China **97** F4
Xindu *Sichuan* China *see* **Luhuo**
Xindu *Sichuan* China **96** E2
Xinduqiao China **96** D2
Xinfeng *Guangdong* China **97** G3
Xinfeng *Jiangxi* China **97** G3
Xinfengjiang Shuiku *resr* China **97** G4
Xing'an *Guangxi* China **97** F3
Xingan China **97** G3
Xing'an *Shaanxi* China *see* **Ankang**
Xingangzhen *Liaoning* China **95** J4
Xingba *Xizang* China **99** F7
Xingcheng *Hebei* China *see* **Qianxi**
Xingcheng *Liaoning* China **95** J3
Xingdi *Xinjiang* China **98** D4
Xingguo *Gansu* China *see* **Qin'an**
Xingguo *Hubei* China *see* **Yangxin**
Xingguo *Jiangxi* China **97** G3
Xinghai *Qinghai* China **94** D5
Xinghua China **97** H1
Xinghua Wan *b.* China **97** H3
Xingkai China **90** D3
Xingkai Hu *l.* China/Rus. Fed. *see* **Khanka, Lake**
Xinglong *Hebei* China **95** I3
Xinglong China **90** B2
Xinglongzhen *Gansu* China **96** E1
Xinglongzhen *Heilong.* China **90** B3
Xingning *Guangdong* China **97** G3
Xingning *Hunan* China **97** G3
Xingou China **97** G2
Xingping *Shaanxi* China **95** G5
Xingqêngoin China **96** D2
Xingren China **96** E3
Xingrenbu *Ningxia* China **94** F4
Xingsagoinba *Qinghai* China **94** E5
Xingshan *Guizhou* China *see* **Majiang**
Xingshan *Hubei* China **97** F2
Xingtai *Hebei* China **95** H4
Xingtang *Hebei* China **95** H4
Xingu *r.* Brazil **177** H4
Xingu, Parque Indígena do *res.* Brazil **177** H6
Xinguangwu *Shanxi* China **95** H4
Xinguara Brazil **177** H5
Xingxian *Shanxi* China **95** G4
Xingxingxia *Xinjiang* China **94** C3
Xingyang *Henan* China **95** H5
Xingye China **97** F4
Xingyi China **96** E3
Xinhe *Hebei* China **95** H4
Xinhe *Xinjiang* China **98** C4
Xin Hot *Nei Mongol* China **95** H3
Xinhua *Guangdong* China *see* **Huadu**
Xinhua *Hunan* China **97** F3
Xinhua *Yunnan* China *see* **Qiaojia**
Xinhua *Yunnan* China *see* **Funing**
Xinhuang China **97** F3
Xinhui China **97** G4
Xinhui *Nei Mongol* China **95** I3
Xining *Qinghai* China **94** E4
Xinji *Hebei* China **95** H4
Xinjian China **97** G2
Xinjiang *Shanxi* China **95** G5
Xinjiang *aut. reg.* China *see* **Xinjiang Uygur Zizhiqu**
Xinjiangkou China *see* **Songzi**
Xinjiang Uygur Zizhiqu *aut. reg.* China **94** B3
Xinjie *Nei Mongol* China **95** G4
Xinjie *Qinghai* China **96** D1
Xinjie *Yunnan* China **96** C3
Xinjie *Yunnan* China **96** D4
Xinjin *Liaoning* China *see* **Pulandian**
Xinjin China **96** D2
Xinjing China *see* **Jingxi**
Xinkai He *r.* China **95** J3
Xinling China *see* **Badong**
Xinlitun China **90** B2
Xinlong China **96** D2
Xinmi *Henan* China **95** H5
Xinmin China **90** B2
Xinmin *Liaoning* China **95** J3
Xinminzhen *Shaanxi* China **95** G4
Xinning *Gansu* China *see* **Ningxian**
Xinning *Hunan* China **97** F3
Xinning *Jiangxi* China *see* **Wuning**
Xinning *Sichuan* China *see* **Kaijiang**
Xinping China **96** D3
Xinqiao China **97** G1
Xinqing China **90** C2
Xinquan China **97** H3
Xinshan China *see* **Anyuan**
Xinshiba China *see* **Ganluo**
Xinsi China **96** E1
Xintai *Shandong* China **95** I5
Xintanpu China **97** G2
Xintian China **97** G3
Xinxian *Shanxi* China *see* **Xinzhou**
Xinxiang *Henan* China **95** H5
Xinxing China **97** G4
Xinyang *Henan* China **97** G1
Xinyang *Henan* China *see* **Pingqiao**
Xinyang Gang *r.* China **95** J5
Xinye China **97** G1
Xinyi *Guangdong* China **97** F4
Xinyi *Jiangsu* China **95** I5
Xinyi He *r.* China **95** I5
Xinying China **97** F5
Xinying Taiwan *see* **Hsinying**
Xinyu China **97** G3
Xinyuan *Qinghai* China *see* **Tianjun**
Xinyuan *Xinjiang* China **98** C4
Xinzhangfang *Nei Mongol* China **95** J1
Xinzheng *Henan* China **95** H5
Xinzhou *Guangxi* China *see* **Longlin**
Xinzhou *Hubei* China **97** G2
Xinzhou *Shanxi* China **89** K5
Xinzhou *Shanxi* China **95** H4
Xinzhu Taiwan *see* **Hsinchu**
Xinzo de Limia Spain **67** C2
Xiongshan China *see* **Zhenghe**
Xiongshi China *see* **Guixi**
Xiongzhou China *see* **Nanxiong**
Xiping *Henan* China **97** F1
Xiping *Henan* China **97** G1
Xiqing Shan *mts* China **94** E5
Xiqu *Gansu* China **94** E4
Xique Xique Brazil **177** J6
Xisa China *see* **Xichou**
Xishanzui *Nei Mongol* China **95** G3
Xisha Qundao *is* S. China Sea *see* **Paracel Islands**
Xishuangbanna *reg.* China **96** D4
Xishuanghe *Shandong* China *see* **Kenli**
Xishui *Guizhou* China **96** E2
Xishui *Hubei* China **97** G2
Xi Taijnar Hu *l. Qinghai* China **99** F5
Xitianmu Shan *mt.* China **97** H2
Xitieshan *Qinghai* China **94** C4
Xiugu China *see* **Jinxi**
Xi Ujimqin Qi *Nei Mongol* China *see* **Bayan Ul Hot**
Xiuning China **97** H2
Xiushan *Chongqing* China **97** F2
Xiushan *Yunnan* China *see* **Tonghai**
Xiushui China **97** G2
Xiuwen China **96** E3
Xiuwu *Henan* China **95** H5
Xiuyan *Liaoning* China **95** J3
Xiuyan *Shaanxi* China *see* **Qingjian**
Xiuying China **97** F4
Xiwanzi *Hebei* China *see* **Chongli**
Xiwu China **96** C1
Xixabangma Feng *mt. Xizang* China **99** D7
Xixia China **97** F1
Xixian *Shanxi* China **95** G4
Xixiang China **96** E1
Xixiu China *see* **Anshun**
Xixón Spain *see* **Gijón-Xixón**
Xiyang *Shanxi* China **95** H4
Xiyang Dao *i.* China **97** I3
Xiyang Jiang *r.* China **96** E3
Xiying *Gansu* China **94** E4
Xizang *aut. reg.* China *see* **Xizang Zizhiqu**
Xizang Gaoyuan *plat. Xizang* China *see* **Qingzang Gaoyuan**
Xizang Zizhiqu *aut. reg.* China **105** G3
Xizhong Dao *i.* China **95** J4
Xobando *Xizang* China **99** F7
Xoi *Xizang* China *see* **Qüxü**
Xo'jayiryox tog'i *mt.* Uzbek. **111** G2
Xo'jayli Uzbek. **102** A3
Xoka *Xizang* China **99** F7
Xorkol *Xinjiang* China **98** E5
Xortang *Xinjiang* China **99** D5
Xuancheng China **97** H2
Xuan'en China **97** F2
Xuanhua *Hebei* China **95** H3
Xuân Lôc Vietnam **87** D5
Xuanwei China **96** E3
Xuanzhou China *see* **Xuancheng**
Xuchang China **97** G1
Xucheng China *see* **Xuwen**
Xuddur Somalia **122** E3
Xueba *Xizang* China **99** F7
Xuefeng China *see* **Mingxi**
Xuefeng Shan *mts* China **97** F3
Xuehua Shan *hill Shanxi* China **95** G5
Xuejiawan *Nei Mongol* China **95** G4
Xue Shan *mts* China **96** C3
Xugin Gol *r. Qinghai* China **94** C5
Xugou *Jiangsu* China **95** I5
Xugui *Nei Mongol* China **95** J1
Xugui *Qinghai* China **94** C5
Xuguit Qi *Nei Mongol* China *see* **Yakeshi**
Xujiang China *see* **Guangchang**
Xulun Hobot Qagan Qi *Nei Mongol* China *see* **Qagan Nur**
Xulun Hoh Qi *Nei Mongol* China *see* **Dund Hot**
Xümatang China **96** C1
Xunde Qundao *is* Paracel Is *see* **Amphitrite Group**
Xungba *Xizang* China *see* **Xangdoring**
Xungmai *Xizang* China **99** E7
Xung Qu *r. Xizang* China **99** F7
Xungru *Xizang* China **99** D7
Xunhe China **90** B2
Xun He *r.* China **90** C2
Xunhua *Qinghai* China **94** E5
Xun Jiang *r.* China **97** F4
Xunwu China **97** G3
Xunxian *Henan* China **95** H5
Xunyi *Shaanxi* China **95** G5
Xúquer, Riu *r.* Spain **67** F4
Xurgan *Qinghai* China **94** C5
Xuru Co *salt l.* China **99** D7
Xushui *Hebei* China **95** H4
Xuwen China **80** E2
Xuyi China **97** H1
Xuyong China **96** E2
Xuzhou *Jiangsu* China **95** I5

Y

Ya'an China **96** D2
Yaba *Maluku* Indon. **83** C3
Yabanabat Turkey *see* **Kızılcahamam**
Yabēlo Eth. **122** D3
Yablonovyy Khrebet *mts* Rus. Fed. **95** G1
Yabrai Shan *mts* China **94** E4
Yabrai Yanchang *Nei Mongol* China **94** E4
Yabrīn *reg.* Saudi Arabia **110** C6
Yabu Japan **92** A3
Yabuli China **90** C3
Yabuzukahon Japan **93** F2
Yacha China *see* **Baisha**
Yacheng China **97** F5
Yachi He *r.* China **96** E3
Yachimata Japan **93** G3
Yachiyo *Chiba* Japan **93** G3
Yachiyo *Ibaraki* Japan **93** F2
Yacuma *r.* Bol. **176** E6
Yadgir India **106** C2
Yadong *Xizang* China **99** E8
Yadrin Rus. Fed. **52** J5
Yaeyama-rettō *is* Japan **89** M8
Yafa Israel *see* **Tel Aviv-Yafo**
Yafran Libya **121** E1
Yagaba Ghana **120** C3
Yagan *Nei Mongol* China **94** E3
Yağda Turkey *see* **Erdemli**
Yaghan Basin *sea feature* S. Atlantic Ocean **184** D9
Yagi Japan **92** B3
Yagkêng *Qinghai* China **94** D4
Yagman Turkm. **110** D2
Yago Mex. **166** D4
Yagodnoye Rus. Fed. **77** P3
Yagodnyy Rus. Fed. **90** E2
Yagoua Cameroon **121** E3
Yagra *Xizang* China **99** C7
Yagradagzê Shan *mt. Qinghai* China **94** C5
Yaguajay Cuba **163** E8
Yaha Thai. **87** C6
Yahagi-gawa *r.* Japan **92** C4
Yahk Canada **150** G5
Yahualica Mex. **168** D4
Yahyalı Turkey **65** L4
Yai Myanmar *see* **Ye**
Yai, Khao *mt.* Thai. **87** B4
Yaita Japan **93** F2
Yaizu Japan **93** E4
Yajiang China **96** D2
Yakacık Turkey **107** C1
Yakak, Cape *AK* U.S.A. **149** [inset]
Yakatograk *Xinjiang* China **98** D5
Yake-dake *vol.* Japan **92** D2
Yakeshi *Nei Mongol* China **95** J1
Yakhab *waterhole* Iran **110** E3
Yakhehal Afgh. **111** G4
Yakima U.S.A. **156** C3
Yakima *r.* U.S.A. **156** D3
Yakmach Pak. **111** F4
Yako Burkina Faso **120** C3
Yakovlevka Rus. Fed. **90** D3
Yakuno Japan **92** A3
Yaku-shima *i.* Japan **91** C7
Yakutat *AK* U.S.A. **149** M4
Yakutat Bay *AK* U.S.A. **149** L4
Yakutsk Rus. Fed. **77** N3
Yakymivka Ukr. **53** G7
Yala Thai. **87** C6
Yalai *Xizang* China **99** D7
Yala National Park Sri Lanka *see* **Ruhuna National Park**
Yalan Dünya Mağarası *tourist site* Turkey **107** A1
Yale Canada **150** F5
Yale U.S.A. **164** D2
Yalgoo Australia **135** B7
Yalkubul, Punta *pt* Mex. **167** H4
Yalleroi Australia **136** D5
Yaloké Cent. Afr. Rep. **122** B3
Yalova Turkey **69** M4
Yalta Ukr. **112** D1
Yalu He *r.* China **95** J2
Yalu Jiang *r.* China/N. Korea **90** B4
Yalujiang Kou *r. mouth* China/N. Korea **91** B5
Yalvaç Turkey **69** N5
Yamada *Chiba* Japan **93** G3
Yamada *Toyama* Japan **92** D2
Yamagata *Ibaraki* Japan **93** G2
Yamagata *Nagano* Japan **93** D2
Yamagata Japan **91** F5
Yamaguchi *Nagano* Japan **92** D3
Yamaguchi Japan **91** C6
Yamakita Japan **93** F3
Yamal, Poluostrov *pen.* Rus. Fed. *see* **Yamal Peninsula**
Yam-Alin', Khrebet *mts* Rus. Fed. **90** D1
Yamal Peninsula Rus. Fed. **76** H2
Yamanaka Japan **92** C2
Yamanaka-ko *l.* Japan **93** E3
Yamanashi Japan **93** E3
Yamanashi *pref.* Japan **93** E3
Yamanie Falls National Park Australia **136** D3
Yamanokako Japan **93** E3
Yamanouchi Japan **93** E2
Yamansu *Xinjiang* China **94** C3
Yamaoka Japan **92** D3
Yamarovka Rus. Fed. **95** G1
Yamashiro Japan **92** B4
Yamato *Gifu* Japan **92** C3
Yamato *Ibaraki* Japan **93** G2
Yamato *Kanagawa* Japan **93** F3
Yamato-Aogaki Kokutei-kōen *park* Japan **92** B4
Yamato-Kōriyama Japan **92** B4
Yamatotakada Japan **92** B4
Yamatsuri Japan **93** G2
Yamazoe Japan **92** C4
Yamba Australia **138** F2
Yamba Lake Canada **151** I1
Yambarran Range *hills* Australia **134** E3
Yambi, Mesa de *hills* Col. **176** D3
Yambio Sudan **121** F4
Yambol Bulg. **69** L3
Yamdena *i.* Indon. **134** E1
Yamethin Myanmar **86** B2
Y'ami *i.* Phil. **97** I4

▶**Yamin, Puncak** *mt.* Indon. **81** J7
4th highest mountain in Oceania.

Yamizo-san *mt.* Japan **93** G2
Yamkanmardi India **106** B2
Yamkhad Syria *see* **Aleppo**
Yamm Rus. Fed. **55** P7
Yamma Yamma, Lake *salt flat* Australia **137** C5

▶**Yamoussoukro** Côte d'Ivoire **120** C4
Capital of Côte d'Ivoire.

Yampa *r.* U.S.A. **159** I1
Yampil' Ukr. **53** F6
Yampol' Ukr. *see* **Yampil'**
Yamuna *r.* India **104** E4
Yamunanagar India **104** D3
Yamzho Yumco *l.* China **99** E7
Yana *r.* Rus. Fed. **77** O2
Yanam India **106** D2
Yan'an *Shaanxi* China **95** G4
Yanaoca Peru **176** D6
Yanaon India *see* **Yanam**
Yanaul Rus. Fed. **51** Q4
Yanbu' al Baḩr Saudi Arabia **108** E5
Yanceyville U.S.A. **162** E4
Yanchang *Shaanxi* China **95** G4
Yancheng *Henan* China **97** G1
Yancheng *Jiangsu* China **97** I1
Yancheng *Shandong* China *see* **Qihe**
Yanchep Australia **135** A7
Yanchi *Ningxia* China **95** F4
Yanchi *Xinjiang* China **94** C3
Yanchi *Xinjiang* China **98** D3
Yanchiwan *Gansu* China **98** F5
Yanchuan *Shaanxi* China **95** G4
Yanco Australia **138** C5
Yanco Creek *r.* Australia **138** B5
Yanco Glen Australia **137** C6
Yanda *watercourse* Australia **138** B3
Yandama Creek *watercourse* Australia **137** C6
Yandao China *see* **Yingjing**
Yandoon Myanmar **86** A3
Yandrakinot Rus. Fed. **148** D2
Yandun *Xinjiang* China **94** C3
Yanfolila Mali **120** C3
Ya'ngamdo *Xizang* China **99** F7
Ya'ngamdo *Xizang* China **99** F7
Yangbajain *Xizang* China **99** E7
Yangbi China **96** C3
Yangcheng *Guangdong* China *see* **Yangshan**
Yangcheng *Shanxi* China **95** H5
Yangchuan China *see* **Suiyang**
Yangchun China **97** F4
Yangcun China **97** G4
Yangcun *Tianjin* China *see* **Wuqing**
Yangdaxkak *Xinjiang* China **98** E5
Yangdok N. Korea **91** B5
Yanggao *Shanxi* China **95** H3
Yanggu *Shandong* China **95** H4
Yanghe *Ningxia* China *see* **Yongning**
Yang Hu *l. Xizang* China **99** D6
Yangi Davan *pass* Aksai Chin/China **99** B6
Yangi Nishon Uzbek. **111** G2
Yangī Qal'ah Afgh. **111** H2
Yangiqishloq Uzbek. **102** C3
Yangirabot Uzbek. **111** G1
Yangiyo'l Uzbek. **102** C3
Yangjiajiang China **97** G2
Yangjialing *Shaanxi* China **95** G4
Yangjiang China **97** F4
Yangjiaogou *Shandong* China **95** I4
Yangming China *see* **Heping**
Yangôn Myanmar *see* **Rangoon**
Yangping China **97** F2
Yangquan *Shanxi* China **95** H4
Yangquangu *Shanxi* China **95** G4
Yangshan China **97** G3
Yang Talat Thai. **86** C3
Yangtouyan China **96** D3
Yangtze *r. Qinghai* China *see* **Tongtian He**
Yangtze *r.* China **96** E2
Also known as Chang Jiang, Jinsha Jiang, Tongtian He, Yangtze Kiang or Zhi Qu.
Yangtze Kiang *r.* China *see* **Yangtze**
Yanguan *Gansu* China **94** F5
Yangudi Rassa National Park Eth. **122** E2
Yang-Weigang *Jiangsu* China **95** I5
Yangxi China **97** F4
Yangxian China **96** E1
Yangxin China **97** G2
Yangyang S. Korea **91** C5
Yangyuan *Hebei* China **95** H3
Yangzhou *Jiangsu* China **97** H1
Yangzhou *Shaanxi* China *see* **Yangxian**
Yanhe China **97** F2
Yanhu *Xinjiang* China **98** E4
Yanhu *Xizang* China **99** C6
Yanhuqu China **105** E2
Yanishpole Rus. Fed. **52** G3
Yanis''yarvi, Ozero *l.* Rus. Fed. **54** Q5
Yanji China **90** C4
Yanjiang China *see* **Ziyang**
Yanjin *Henan* China **95** H5
Yanjin *Yunnan* China **96** E2
Yanjing *Sichuan* China *see* **Yanyuan**
Yanjing *Xizang* China **96** C2
Yanjing *Yunnan* China *see* **Yanjin**
Yankara National Park Nigeria **120** E4
Yankton U.S.A. **160** D3
Yanling *Henan* China **95** H5
Yanling *Hunan* China **97** G3
Yanling *Sichuan* China *see* **Weiyuan**
Yannina Greece *see* **Ioannina**
Yano-Indigirskaya Nizmennost' *lowland* Rus. Fed. **77** P2
Yanomami, Parque Indígena *res.* Brazil **176** F3
Yanovski, Mount *AK* U.S.A. **149** N4
Yanqi *Xinjiang* China **98** D4
Yanqing *Beijing* China **95** H3
Yanrey *r.* Australia **135** A5
Yanshan *Hebei* China **95** I4
Yanshan *Jiangxi* China **97** H2
Yanshan *Yunnan* China **96** E4
Yan Shan *mts* China **95** I3
Yanshi *Henan* China **95** H5
Yanshiping *Qinghai* China **99** F6
Yanskiy Zaliv *g.* Rus. Fed. **77** O2
Yantabulla Australia **138** B2
Yantai *Shandong* China **95** J4
Yanting China **96** E2
Yantongshan China **90** B4
Yantou China **97** I2
Yanwa China **96** C3
Yany-Kurgan Kazakh. *see* **Zhanakorgan**
Yanyuan China **96** D3
Yanzhou *Shandong* China **95** I5
Yao Chad **121** E3
Yao Japan **92** B4
Yao'an China **96** D3
Yaodian *Shaanxi* China **95** G4
Yaodu China *see* **Dongzhi**
Yaojie *Gansu* China *see* **Honggu**
Yaoli China **97** H2
Yaoquanzi *Gansu* China **94** D4
Yaotsu Japan **92** D3

▶**Yaoundé** Cameroon **120** E4
Capital of Cameroon.

Yaoxian *Shaanxi* China *see* **Yaozhou**
Yaoxiaoling China **90** B2
Yao Yai, Ko *i.* Thai. **87** B6
Yaozhen *Shaanxi* China **95** G4
Yaozhou *Shaanxi* China **95** G5
Yap *i.* Micronesia **81** J5
Yapen *i.* Indon. **81** J7
Yappar *r.* Australia **136** C3
Yap Trench *sea feature* N. Pacific Ocean **186** F5
Yaqui *r.* Mex. **166** C3
Yar Rus. Fed. **52** L4
Yaradzha Turkm. *see* **Ýarajy**
Ýarajy Turkm. **110** E2
Yaraka Australia **136** D5
Yarangüme Turkey *see* **Tavas**
Yaransk Rus. Fed. **52** J4
Yardea Australia **137** A7
Yardımcı Burnu *pt* Turkey **69** N6
Yardımlı Azer. **113** H3
Yardoi *Xizang* China **99** E7
Yardymly Azer. *see* **Yardımlı**
Yare *r.* U.K. **59** I6
Yarega Rus. Fed. **52** L3

▶**Yaren** Nauru **133** G2
Capital of Nauru.

Yarensk Rus. Fed. **52** K3
Yariga-take *mt.* Japan **92** D2
Yarīm Yemen **108** F7
Yarımca Turkey *see* **Körfez**
Yarkand *Xinjiang* China *see* **Shache**
Yarkant *Xinjiang* China *see* **Shache**
Yarkant He *r.* China **99** B5
Yarker Canada **165** G1
Yarkhun *r.* Pak. **111** I2
Yarlung Zangbo *r.* China **99** F7 *see* **Brahmaputra**
Yarmouth Canada **153** I6
Yarmouth *England* U.K. **59** F8
Yarmouth *England* U.K. *see* **Great Yarmouth**
Yarmouth U.S.A. **165** J2
Yarmuk *r.* Asia **107** B3
Yarnell U.S.A. **159** G4
Yaroslavl' Rus. Fed. **52** H4
Yaroslavskiy Rus. Fed. **90** D3
Yarra *r.* Australia **138** B6
Yarra Junction Australia **138** B6
Yarram Australia **138** C7
Yarraman Australia **138** E1
Yarrawonga Australia **138** B6
Yarra Yarra Lakes *salt flat* Australia **135** A7
Yarronvale Australia **138** B1
Yarrowmere Australia **136** D4
Yartö Tra La *pass* China **105** H3
Yartsevo *Krasnoyarskiy Kray* Rus. Fed. **76** J3
Yartsevo *Smolenskaya Oblast'* Rus. Fed. **53** G5
Yaru *r.* China **99** D7
Yarumal Col. **176** C2
Yaruu Mongolia **94** D1
Yarwa China **96** C2
Yarzhong China **96** C2
Yaş Romania *see* **Iaşi**
Yasaka *Kyōto* Japan **92** B3
Yasaka *Nagano* Japan **93** D2
Yasato Japan **93** G2
Yasawa Group *is* Fiji **133** H3
Yashilkŭl *l.* Tajik. **111** I2
Yashira Japan **93** F2
Yashiro Japan **92** A4
Yashkul' Rus. Fed. **53** J7
Yasin Pak. **104** C1
Yasnogorsk Rus. Fed. **53** H5
Yasnyy Rus. Fed. **90** C1
Yasothon Thai. **86** D4
Yass Australia **138** D5
Yass *r.* Australia **138** D5
Yassı Burnu *c.* Cyprus *see* **Plakoti, Cape**
Yasu Japan **92** C3
Yāsūj Iran **110** C4
Yasuní, Parque Nacional *nat. park* Ecuador **176** C4
Yasuoka Japan **93** D3
Yasuzuka Japan **93** E1
Yatağan Turkey **69** M6
Yaté New Caledonia **133** G4
Yates *r.* Canada **150** H2
Yates Center U.S.A. **160** E4
Yathkyed Lake Canada **151** L2
Yatomi Japan **92** C3
Yatou *Shandong* China *see* **Rongcheng**
Yatsuga-take *vol.* Japan **93** E3
Yatsuga-take-Chūshin-kōgen Kokutei-kōen *park* Japan **93** E2
Yatsuo Japan **92** D2
Yatsushiro Japan **91** C6
Yaṭṭa West Bank **107** B4
Yatton U.K. **59** E7
Yauca Peru **176** D7
Yau Tong *b. H.K.* China **97** [inset]
Yauyupe Hond. **166** [inset] I6
Yavan Tajik. *see* **Yovon**
Yavari *r.* Brazil/Peru **176** E4
also known as Javari (Brazil/Peru)
Yávaros Mex. **166** C3
Yavatmal India **106** C1
Yavi Turkey **113** F3
Yaví, Cerro *mt.* Venez. **176** E2
Yavoriv Ukr. **53** D6
Yavuzlu Turkey **107** C1
Yawata Japan **92** B4
Yawatongguz He *r.* China **99** C5
Yawatongguzlangar *Xinjiang* China **99** C5
Yaw Chaung *r.* Myanmar **96** B4
Yaxchilan *tourist site* Guat. **167** H5
Yaxian China *see* **Sanya**
Yay Myanmar *see* **Ye**
Yayladağı Turkey **107** C2
Yazd Iran **110** D4
Yazdān Iran **111** F3
Yazd-e Khvāst Iran **110** D4
Yazıhan Turkey **112** E3
Yazoo *r. MS* U.S.A. **167** H1
Yazoo City U.S.A. **161** F5
Yazukami Japan **93** G2
Y Bala U.K. *see* **Bala**

Yding Skovhøj *hill* Denmark **57** L3
Ydra *i.* Greece **69** J6
Y Drenewydd U.K. *see* **Newtown**
Ye Myanmar **86** B4
Yea Australia **138** B6
Yealmpton U.K. **59** D8
Yebaishou *Liaoning* China *see* **Jianping**
Yebawmi Myanmar **86** A1
Yebbi-Bou Chad **121** E2
Yecheng *Xinjiang* China **99** B5
Yécora Mex. **166** C2
Yedashe Myanmar **86** B3
Yedatore India **106** C3
Yedi Burun Başı *pt* Turkey **69** M6
Yeeda River Australia **134** C4
Yefremov Rus. Fed. **53** H5
Yêgainnyin *Qinghai* China *see* **Henan**
Yeghegnadzor Armenia **113** G3
Yegindybulak Kazakh. **98** B2
Yegindykol' Kazakh. **102** C1
Yegorlykskaya Rus. Fed. **53** I7
Yegorova, Mys *pt* Rus. Fed. **90** E3
Yegor'yevsk Rus. Fed. **53** H5
Yei Sudan **121** G4
Yei *r.* Sudan **121** G4
Yeji China **97** G2
Yejiaji China *see* **Yeji**
Yekaterinburg Rus. Fed. **76** H4
Yekaterinodar Rus. Fed. *see* **Krasnodar**
Yekaterinoslav Ukr. *see* **Dnipropetrovs'k**
Yekaterinoslavka Rus. Fed. **90** C2
Yekhegnadzor Armenia *see* **Yeghegnadzor**
Ye Kyun *i.* Myanmar **86** A3
Yelabuga *Khabarovskiy Kray* Rus. Fed. **90** D2
Yelabuga *Respublika Tatarstan* Rus. Fed. **52** K5
Yelan' Rus. Fed. **53** I6
Yelan' *r.* Rus. Fed. **53** I6
Yelandur India **106** C3
Yelantsy Rus. Fed. **88** J2
Yelarbon Australia **138** E2
Yelbarsli Turkm. **111** F2
Yelenovskiye Kar'yery Ukr. *see* **Dokuchayevs'k**
Yelets Rus. Fed. **53** H5
Yeliguan *Gansu* China **94** E5
Yélimané Mali **120** B3
Yelizavetgrad Ukr. *see* **Kirovohrad**
Yelkhovka Rus. Fed. **53** K5
Yell *i.* U.K. **60** [inset]
Yellabina Regional Reserve *nature res.* Australia **135** F7
Yellandu India **106** D2
Yellapur India **106** B3
Yellowhead Pass Canada **150** G4

▶**Yellowknife** Canada **150** H2
Capital of the Northwest Territories.

Yellowknife *r.* Canada **150** H2
Yellow Mountain *hill* Australia **138** C4

▶**Yellow** *r.* China
4th longest river in Asia, and 7th in the world

Yellow Sea N. Pacific Ocean **89** N5
Yellowstone *r.* U.S.A. **160** C2
Yellowstone Lake U.S.A. **156** F3
Yellowstone National Park U.S.A. **156** F3
Yell Sound *strait* U.K. **60** [inset]
Yeloten Turkm. *see* **Ýolöten**
Yelovo Rus. Fed. **51** Q4
Yel'sk Belarus **53** F6
Yel'tay Kazakh. **98** C3
Yelucá *mt.* Nicaragua **166** [inset] I6
Yelva *r.* Rus. Fed. **52** K3
Yema Nanshan *mts* China **94** C4
Yema Shan *mts* China **98** F5
Yematan *Qinghai* China **94** D4
Yematan *Qinghai* China **94** D5
Yemen *country* Asia **108** G6
Yemetsk Rus. Fed. **52** I3
Yemişenbükü Turkey *see* **Taşova**
Yemmiganur India *see* **Emmiganuru**
Yemtsa Rus. Fed. **52** I3
Yemva Rus. Fed. **52** K3
Yena Rus. Fed. **54** Q3
Yenagoa Nigeria **120** D4
Yenakiyeve Ukr. **53** H6
Yenakiyevo Ukr. *see* **Yenakiyeve**
Yenangyat Myanmar **86** A2
Yenangyaung Myanmar **86** A2
Yenanma Myanmar **86** A3
Yenda Australia **138** C5
Yêndum China *see* **Zhag'yab**
Yengisar *Xinjiang* China **98** B5
Yengisar *Xinjiang* China **98** D4
Yengisu *Xinjiang* China **98** D4
Yengo National Park Australia **138** E4
Yenice Turkey **69** L5
Yenidamlar Turkey *see* **Demirtaş**
Yenihan Turkey *see* **Yıldızeli**
Yenije-i-Vardar Greece *see* **Giannitsa**
Yenişehir Greece *see* **Larisa**
Yenişehir Turkey **69** M4

▶**Yenisey** *r.* Rus. Fed. **76** J2
Part of the Yenisey-Angara-Selenga, 3rd longest river in Asia.

▶**Yenisey-Angara-Selenga** *r.* Rus. Fed. **76** J2
3rd longest river in Asia, and 6th in the world.

Yeniseysk Rus. Fed. **76** K4
Yeniseyskiy Kryazh *ridge* Rus. Fed. **76** K4
Yeniseyskiy Zaliv *inlet* Rus. Fed. **189** F2
Yeniugou *Qinghai* China **94** D4
Yeniugou *Qinghai* China **94** D5
Yeniyol Turkey *see* **Borçka**
Yên Minh Vietnam **86** D2
Yenotayevka Rus. Fed. **53** J7
Yentna *r.* AK U.S.A. **149** J3
Yeola India **106** B1
Yeo Lake *salt flat* Australia **135** D6
Yeotmal India *see* **Yavatmal**
Yeoval Australia **138** D4
Yeovil U.K. **59** E8
Yeo Yeo *r.* Australia *see* **Bland**
Yepachi Mex. **166** C2
Yeppoon Australia **136** E4
Yeraliyev Kazakh. *see* **Kuryk**
Yerbabuena Mex. **167** E4
Yerbent Turkm. **110** E2
Yerbogachen Rus. Fed. **77** L3
Yercaud India **106** C4

▶**Yerevan** Armenia **113** G2
Capital of Armenia.

Yereymentau Kazakh. **102** D1
Yergara India **106** C2
Yergeni *hills* Rus. Fed. **53** J7
Yergoğu Romania *see* **Giurgiu**
Yeriho West Bank *see* **Jericho**
Yerilla Australia **135** C7
Yerington U.S.A. **158** D2
Yerköy Turkey **112** D3
Yerla *r.* India **106** B2
Yermak Kazakh. *see* **Aksu**
Yermakovo Rus. Fed. **90** B1
Yermak Plateau *sea feature* Arctic Ocean **189** H1
Yermentau Kazakh. *see* **Yereymentau**
Yermo Mex. **166** D3
Yermo U.S.A. **158** E4
Yerofey Pavlovich Rus. Fed. **90** A1
Yerres *r.* France **62** C6
Yersa *r.* Rus. Fed. **52** L2
Yershov Rus. Fed. **53** K6
Yertsevo Rus. Fed. **52** I3
Yeruḥam Israel **107** B4
Yerupaja *mt.* Peru **176** C6
Yerushalayim Israel/West Bank *see* **Jerusalem**
Yeruslan *r.* Rus. Fed. **53** J6
Yesagyo Myanmar **86** A2
Yesan S. Korea **91** B5
Yesik Kazakh. **98** B4
Yesil' Kazakh. **100** F1
Yeşilhisar Turkey **112** D3
Yeşilırmak *r.* Turkey **112** E2
Yeşilova *Burdur* Turkey **69** M6
Yeşilova *Yozgat* Turkey *see* **Sorgun**
Yessentuki Rus. Fed. **113** F1
Yessey Rus. Fed. **77** L3
Yes Tor *hill* U.K. **59** C8
Yêtatang *Xizang* China *see* **Baqên**
Yetman Australia **138** E2
Ye-U Myanmar **86** A2
Yeu, Île d' *i.* France **66** C3
Yevdokimovskoye Rus. Fed. *see* **Krasnogvardeyskoye**
Yevlakh Azer. *see* **Yevlax**
Yevlax Azer. **113** G2
Yevpatoriya Ukr. **112** D1
Yevreyskaya Avtonomnaya Oblast' *admin. div.* Rus. Fed. **90** D2
Yexian *Shandong* China *see* **Laizhou**
Yeygen'yevka Kazakh. **98** B4
Yeyik *Xinjiang* China **99** C5
Yeysk Rus. Fed. **53** H7
Yeyungou *Xinjiang* China **98** D4
Yezhou China *see* **Jianshi**
Yezhuga *r.* Rus. Fed. **52** J2
Yezo *i.* Japan *see* **Hokkaidō**
Yezyaryshcha Belarus **52** F5
Y Fenni U.K. *see* **Abergavenny**
Y Fflint U.K. *see* **Flint**
Y Gelli Gandryll U.K. *see* **Hay-on-Wye**
Yialí *i.* Greece *see* **Gyali**
Yi'allaq, Gebel *mt.* Egypt *see* **Yu'alliq, Jabal**
Yialousa Cyprus *see* **Aigialousa**
Yi'an China **90** B3
Yianisádha *i.* Greece *see* **Gianisada**
Yianisádha *i. Kriti* Greece *see* **Gianisada**
Yiannitsá Greece *see* **Giannitsa**
Yibin *Sichuan* China **96** E2
Yibin *Sichuan* China **96** E2
Yibug Caka *salt l.* China **99** D6
Yichang *Hubei* China **97** F2
Yicheng *Henan* China *see* **Zhumadian**
Yicheng *Hubei* China **97** G2
Yicheng *Shanxi* China **95** G5
Yichuan *Henan* China **95** H5
Yichuan *Shaanxi* China **95** G5
Yichun *Heilong.* China **90** C3
Yichun *Jiangxi* China **97** G3
Yidu China *see* **Zhicheng**
Yidu *Shandong* China *see* **Qingzhou**
Yidun China **96** C2
Yifeng China **97** G2
Yiggêtang *Qinghai* China *see* **Sêrwolungwa**
Yiggêtang *Qinghai* China **94** D5
Yihatuoli *Gansu* China **94** D3
Yi He *r. Henan* China **95** H5
Yi He *r. Shandong* China **95** I5
Yihuang China **97** H3
Yijun *Shaanxi* China **95** G5
Yilaha *Heilong.* China **95** K1
Yilan China **90** C3
Yilan Taiwan *see* **Ilan**
Yıldız Dağları *mts* Turkey **69** L4
Yıldızeli Turkey **112** E3
Yilehuli Shan *mts* China **90** A2
Yiliang China **96** E3
Yiling *Hubei* China **97** F2
Yiliping *Qinghai* China **99** F5
Yilong *Heilong.* China **90** B3
Yilong *Sichuan* China **96** E2
Yilong *Yunnan* China *see* **Shiping**
Yilong Hu *l.* China **96** D4
Yimatu He *r.* China **95** I3
Yimianpo China **90** C3
Yimin He *r.* China **95** I1
Yinan *Shandong* China **95** I5
Yinbaing Myanmar **86** B3
Yincheng China *see* **Dexing**
Yinchuan *Ningxia* China **94** F4
Yindarlgooda, Lake *salt flat* Australia **135** C7
Yingcheng China **97** G2
Yingde China **97** G3
Yinggehai China **97** F5
Yinggen China *see* **Qiongzhong**
Ying He *r.* China **97** H1
Yingjing China **96** D2
Yingkou *Liaoning* China **95** J3
Yingkou *Liaoning* China *see* **Dashiqiao**
Yingpanshui *Ningxia* China **94** F4
Yingshan China **97** G2
Yingtan China **97** H2
Yingtaoyuan *Shandong* China **95** H5
Yingxian *Shanxi* China **95** H4
Yining *Jiangxi* China *see* **Xiushui**
Yining *Xinjiang* China **98** C4
Yining *Xinjiang* China **98** C4
Yinjiang China **97** F3
Yinkeng China *see* **Yinkengxu**
Yinkengxu China **97** G3
Yinmabin Myanmar **86** A2
Yinnyein Myanmar **86** B3
Yin Shan *mts* China **95** G3
Yinxian China *see* **Ningbo**
Yi'ong Nongchang *Xizang* China **99** F7
Yi'ong Zangbo *r. Xizang* China **99** F7
Yipinglang China **96** D3
Yiquan China *see* **Meitan**
Yiran Co *l. Qinghai* China **99** F6
Yirga Alem Eth. **122** D3
Yirol Sudan **121** G4
Yirshi *Nei Mongol* China **95** I2
Yirtkuq Bulak *spring Xinjiang* China **98** E4
Yirxie *Nei Mongol* China *see* **Yirshi**
Yisa China *see* **Honghe**
Yishan *Guangxi* China *see* **Yizhou**
Yishan *Jiangsu* China *see* **Guanyun**
Yi Shan *mt. Shandong* China **95** I4
Yishui *Shandong* China **95** I5
Yishun Sing. **87** [inset]
Yíthion Greece *see* **Gytheio**
Yitiaoshan *Gansu* China *see* **Jingtai**
Yitong He *r.* China **90** B3
Yi Tu, Nam *r.* Myanmar **86** B2
Yituline *Nei Mongol* China **95** J1
Yiwanquan *Xinjiang* China **94** C3
Yiwu *Xinjiang* China **94** C3
Yiwu China **96** D4
Yiwulü Shan *mts* China **95** J3
Yixian *Liaoning* China **95** J3
Yixing China **97** H2
Yiyang China **97** G2
Yiyuan *Shandong* China **95** I4
Yizheng China **97** H1
Yizhou China **97** F3
Yizhou *Liaoning* China *see* **Yixian**
Yizra'el *country* Asia *see* **Israel**
Yläne Fin. **55** M6
Ylihärmä Fin. **54** M5
Yli-Ii Fin. **54** N4
Yli-Kärppä Fin. **54** N4
Ylikiiminki Fin. **54** O4
Yli-Kitka *l.* Fin. **54** P3
Ylistaro Fin. **54** M5
Ylitornio Fin. **54** M3
Ylivieska Fin. **54** N4
Ylöjärvi Fin. **55** M6
Ymer Ø *i.* Greenland **147** P2
Ynys Enlli *i.* U.K. *see* **Bardsey Island**
Ynys Môn *i.* U.K. *see* **Anglesey**
Yoakum U.S.A. **161** D6
Yoder U.S.A. **164** C3
Yodo-gawa *r.* Japan **92** B4
Yogan, Cerro *mt.* Chile **178** B8
Yogo Japan **92** C3
Yogyakarta Indon. **85** E4
Yogyakarta *admin. dist.* Indon. **85** E5
Yoho National Park Canada **150** G5
Yoigilanglêb *r. Qinghai* China **99** G6
Yojoa, Lago de *l.* Hond. **166** [inset] I6
Yōka Japan **92** A3
Yokadouma Cameroon **121** E4
Yōkaichi Japan **92** C3
Yōkaichiba Japan **93** G3
Yokawa Japan **92** B4
Yokkaichi Japan **92** C4
Yoko Cameroon **120** E4
Yokohama *Kanagawa* Japan **93** F3
Yokokawa Japan **93** E2
Yokoshiba Japan **93** G3
Yokosuka Japan **93** F3
Yokote Japan **91** F5
Yokoze Japan **93** F3
Yola Nigeria **120** E4
Yolaina, Cordillera de *mts* Nicaragua **166** [inset] I7
Yolo U.S.A. **158** C2
Yolombo Dem. Rep. Congo **122** C4
Ýolöten Turkm. **111** F2
Yoloxóchitl Mex. **167** F5
Yoluk Mex. **167** I4
Yom, Mae Nam *r.* Thai. **86** C4
Yomou Guinea **120** C4
Yomuka Indon. **81** J8
Yonaguni-jima *i.* Japan **97** I3
Yŏnan N. Korea **91** B5
Yonezawa Japan **91** F5
Yong'an *Chongqing* China *see* **Fengjie**
Yong'an *Fujian* China **97** H3
Yongbei China *see* **Yongsheng**
Yongchang *Gansu* China **94** E4
Yongcheng *Henan* China **95** I5
Yongcong China **97** F3
Yongdeng *Gansu* China **94** E4
Yongding *Fujian* China **97** H3
Yongding *Yunnan* China *see* **Yongren**
Yongding *Yunnan* China *see* **Fumin**
Yongding He *r.* China **95** I4
Yongfeng China **97** G3
Yongfengqu *Xinjiang* China **98** D4
Yongfu China **97** F3
Yonghe *Shanxi* China **95** G4
Yŏnghŭng N. Korea **91** B5
Yŏnghŭng-man *b.* N. Korea **91** B5
Yŏngil-man *b.* S. Korea **91** C6
Yongjing *Gansu* China **94** E5
Yongjing *Guizhou* China *see* **Xifeng**
Yongjing *Liaoning* China *see* **Xifeng**
Yŏngjin Qu *r.* China **95** H4
Yŏngju S. Korea **91** C5
Yongkang *Yunnan* China **96** C3
Yongkang *Zhejiang* China **97** I2
Yongle China *see* **Zhen'an**
Yongnian *Hebei* China **95** H4
Yongning *Guangxi* China **97** F4
Yongning *Jiangxi* China *see* **Tonggu**
Yongning *Ningxia* China **94** F4
Yongning *Sichuan* China *see* **Xuyong**
Yongping China **96** C3
Yongqing *Gansu* China *see* **Qingshui**
Yongren China **96** D3
Yongsheng China **96** D3
Yongshou *Shaanxi* China **95** G5
Yongshun China **97** F2
Yongtai China **97** H3
Yongxi China *see* **Nayong**
Yongxing *Hunan* China **97** G3
Yongxing *Jiangxi* China **97** G3
Yongxing *Shaanxi* China **95** G4
Yongxiu China **97** G2
Yongyang China *see* **Weng'an**
Yongzhou China **97** F3
Yonkers U.S.A. **165** I3
Yopal Col. **176** D2
Yopurga *Xinjiang* China **98** B5
Yoquivo Mex. **166** D3
Yordu India **104** C2
Yorii Japan **93** F2
York Australia **135** B7
York Canada **164** F2
York U.K. **58** F5
York *AL* U.S.A. **161** F5
York *NE* U.S.A. **160** D3
York *PA* U.S.A. **165** G4
York, Cape Australia **136** C1
York, Kap *c.* Greenland *see* **Innaanganeq**
York, Vale of *valley* U.K. **58** F4
Yorke Peninsula Australia **137** B7
York Mountains *AK* U.S.A. **148** F2
Yorkshire Dales National Park U.K. **58** E4
Yorkshire Wolds *hills* U.K. **58** G5
Yorkton Canada **151** K5
Yorktown U.S.A. **165** G5
Yorkville U.S.A. **160** F3
Yoro Hond. **166** [inset] I6
Yōrō Japan **92** C3
Yoroi-zaki *pt* Japan **92** C4
Yoronga *i. Maluku* Indon. **83** D3
Yöröö Gol *r.* Mongolia **94** F1
Yorosso Mali **120** C3
Yosemite U.S.A. **164** C5
Yosemite National Park U.S.A. **158** D3
Yoshida *Saitama* Japan **93** F2
Yoshida *Shizuoka* Japan **93** E4
Yoshii *Gunma* Japan **93** E2
Yoshima Japan **93** G1
Yoshino Japan **92** B4
Yoshinodani Japan **92** C2
Yoshino-gawa *r.* Japan **92** B4
Yoshino-Kumano Kokuritsu-kōen *nat. park* Japan **92** C5
Yoshkar-Ola Rus. Fed. **52** J4
Yösöndzüyl Mongolia **94** E2
Yos Sudarso *i.* Indon. *see* **Dolok, Pulau**
Yŏsu S. Korea **91** B6
Yotsukaidō Japan **93** G3
Yotsukura Japan **93** G1
Yotvata Israel **107** B5
Youbou Canada **150** E5
Youdunzi *Qinghai* China **99** E5
Youghal Ireland **61** E6
Youlin *Shandong* China **95** I4
Young Australia **138** D5
Young U.S.A. **159** H4
Younghusband, Lake *salt flat* Australia **137** B6
Younghusband Peninsula Australia **137** B7
Young Island Antarctica **188** H2
Youngstown Canada **151** I5
Youngstown U.S.A. **164** E3
Youshashan *Qinghai* China **99** E5
You Shui *r.* China **97** F2
Youssoufia Morocco **64** C5
Youvarou Mali **120** C3
Youxi China **97** H3
Youxian China **97** G3
Youyang China **97** F2
Youyi China **90** C3
Youyi Feng *mt.* China/Rus. Fed. **98** D2
Yovon Tajik. **111** H2
Yowah *watercourse* Australia **138** B2
Yozgat Turkey **112** D3
Ypres Belgium *see* **Ieper**
Yreka U.S.A. **156** C4
Yrghyz Kazakh. *see* **Irgiz**
Yr Wyddfa *mt.* U.K. *see* **Snowdon**
Yser *r.* France **62** C4
also known as IJzer (Belgium)
Ysselsteyn Neth. **62** F3
Ystad Sweden **55** H9
Ystwyth *r.* U.K. **59** C6
Ysyk-Ata Kyrg. **98** A4
Ysyk-Köl Kyrg. *see* **Balykchy**
Ysyk-Köl *admin. div.* Kyrg. **98** B4

▶**Ysyk-Köl** *salt l.* Kyrg. **102** E3
5th largest lake in Asia.

Ythan *r.* U.K. **60** G3
Y Trallwng U.K. *see* **Welshpool**
Ytyk-Kyuyel' Rus. Fed. **77** O3
Yu *i. Maluku* Indon. **83** D3
Yu'alliq, Jabal *mt.* Egypt **107** A4
Yuan'an China **97** F2
Yuanbaoshan *Nei Mongol* China **95** I3
Yuanbao Shan *mt.* China **97** F3
Yuanjiang *Hunan* China **97** G2
Yuanjiang *Yunnan* China **96** D4
Yuan Jiang *r. Hunan* China **97** F2
Yuan Jiang *r. Yunnan* China **96** D4
Yuanjiazhuang China *see* **Foping**
Yuanlin *Nei Mongol* China **95** J1
Yuanling China **97** F2
Yuanma China *see* **Yuanmou**
Yuanmou China **96** D3
Yuanping *Shanxi* China **95** H4
Yuanqu *Shanxi* China **95** G5
Yuanquan *Gansu* China *see* **Anxi**
Yuanshan China *see* **Lianping**
Yuanshanzi *Gansu* China **94** D4
Yuanyang China *see* **Xinjie**
Yuasa Japan **92** B4
Yub'ā *i.* Saudi Arabia **112** D6
Yuba City U.S.A. **158** C2
Yubei China **96** E2
Yuben' Tajik. **111** I2
Yucatán *pen.* Mex. **167** H5
Yucatán *state* Mex. **167** H4
Yucatan Channel Cuba/Mex. **167** I4
Yucca U.S.A. **159** F4
Yucca Lake U.S.A. **158** E3
Yucca Valley U.S.A. **158** E4
Yucheng *Henan* China **95** H5
Yucheng *Shandong* China **95** I4
Yucheng *Sichuan* China *see* **Ya'an**
Yuci *Shanxi* China *see* **Jinzhong**
Yudi Shan *mt.* China **90** A1
Yudu China **97** G3
Yuelai China *see* **Huachuan**
Yueliang Pao *l.* China **95** J2
Yuendumu Australia **134** E5
Yuen Long *H.K.* China **97** [inset]
Yueqing China **97** I2
Yuexi China **97** H2
Yueyang *Hunan* China **97** G2
Yueyang *Hunan* China **97** G2
Yueyang *Sichuan* China *see* **Anyue**
Yug *r.* Rus. Fed. **52** J3
Yugan China **97** H2
Yugawara Japan **93** F3
Yuge *Qinghai* China **99** F6
Yugorsk Rus. Fed. **51** S3
Yugoslavia *country* Europe *see* **Serbia**

▶**Yugoslavia**
Former European country. Up to 1993 included Bosnia-Herzegovina, Croatia, Macedonia and Slovenia. Renamed as Serbia and Montenegro in 2003. Serbia and Montenegro became separate independent countries in June 2006. Kosovo became independent from Serbia in February 2008.

Yuhang China **97** I2
Yuhu China *see* **Eryuan**
Yuhuan China **97** I2
Yuhuang Ding *mt. Shandong* China **95** I4
Yui Japan **93** E3
Yuin Australia **135** B6
Yu Jiang *r.* China **97** F4
Yukagirskoye Ploskogor'ye *plat.* Rus. Fed. **77** Q3
Yukamenskoye Rus. Fed. **52** L4
Yukarı Sakarya Ovaları *plain* Turkey **69** N5
Yukarısarıkaya Turkey **112** D3
Yūki Japan **93** F2
Yuki *r.* AK U.S.A. **148** H2
Yukon *admin. div.* Canada **149** N3

▶**Yukon** *r.* Canada/U.S.A. **148** F3
5th longest river in North America.

Yukon-Charley Rivers National Preserve *nature res.* AK U.S.A. **149** L2
Yukon Crossing (abandoned) *Y.T.* Canada **149** M3
Yukon Delta *AK* U.S.A. **148** F3
Yukon Flats National Wildlife Refuge *nature res.* AK U.S.A. **149** K2
Yüksekova Turkey **113** G3
Yulara Australia **135** E6
Yule *r.* Australia **134** B5
Yuleba Australia **138** D1
Yulee U.S.A. **163** D6
Yuli *Xinjiang* China **98** D4
Yulin *Guangxi* China **97** F4
Yulin *Shaanxi* China **95** G4
Yulong Xueshan *mt.* China **96** D3
Yuma *AZ* U.S.A. **159** F5
Yuma *CO* U.S.A. **160** C3
Yuma Desert U.S.A. **159** F5
Yumco *Xizang* China **99** D7
Yumen *Gansu* China **94** D4
Yumendongzhan *Gansu* China **94** D4
Yumenguan *Gansu* China **98** F4
Yumenzhen *Gansu* China **94** D3
Yumin *Xinjiang* China **98** C3
Yumt Uul *mt.* Mongolia **94** D2
Yumurtalık Turkey **107** B1
Yuna Australia **135** A7
Yunak Turkey **112** C3
Yunan China **97** F4
Yunaska Island *AK* U.S.A. **148** E5
Yuncheng *Shandong* China **95** H5
Yuncheng *Shanxi* China **95** G5
Yundamindera Australia **135** C7
Yunfu China **97** G4
Yungas *reg.* Bol. **176** E7
Yungui Gaoyuan *plat.* China **96** D3
Yunhe *Jiangsu* China *see* **Pizhou**
Yunhe *Yunnan* China *see* **Heqing**
Yunhe *Zhejiang* China **97** H2
Yunjinghong China *see* **Jinghong**
Yunkai Dashan *mts* China **97** F4
Yünlin Taiwan *see* **Touliu**
Yunling China *see* **Yunxiao**
Yun Ling *mts* China **96** C3
Yunlong China **96** C3
Yunmeng China **97** G2
Yunmenling China *see* **Junmenling**
Yunnan *prov.* China **96** D3
Yunta Australia **137** B7
Yunt Dağı *mt.* Turkey **107** A1
Yunxi *Hubei* China **97** F1
Yunxi *Sichuan* China *see* **Yanting**
Yunxian *Hubei* China **97** F1
Yunxian *Yunnan* China **96** D3
Yunxiao China **97** H4
Yunyang *Chongqing* China **97** F2
Yunyang *Henan* China **97** G1
Yuping *Guizhou* China *see* **Libo**
Yuping *Guizhou* China **97** F3
Yuping *Yunnan* China *see* **Pingbian**
Yuqing China **96** E3
Yura Japan **92** B5
Yura-gawa *r.* Japan **92** B3
Yuraygir National Park Australia **138** F2
Yurba Co *l. Xizang* China **99** D6
Yürekli Turkey **107** B1
Yurga Rus. Fed. **76** J4
Yuriria Mex. **168** D4
Yurungkax He *r.* China **99** C5
Yur'ya Rus. Fed. **52** K4
Yur'yakha *r.* Rus. Fed. **52** L2
Yuryev Estonia *see* **Tartu**
Yur'yevets Rus. Fed. **52** I4
Yur'yev-Pol'skiy Rus. Fed. **52** H4
Yuscarán Hond. **166** [inset] I6
Yushan China **97** H2
Yü Shan *mt.* Taiwan **97** I4
Yushe *Shanxi* China **95** H4
Yushino Rus. Fed. **52** L1
Yushkozero Rus. Fed. **54** R4
Yushu *Jilin* China **90** B3
Yushu *Qinghai* China **96** C1
Yushugou *Xinjiang* China **98** D4
Yushuwan China *see* **Huaihua**
Yusufeli Turkey **113** F2
Yus'va Rus. Fed. **51** Q4
Yuta West Bank *see* **Yatta**
Yutai *Shandong* China **95** I5
Yutan China *see* **Ningxiang**
Yutian *Hebei* China **95** I4
Yutian *Xinjiang* China **99** C5
Yutiangao *Nei Mongol* China **95** I3
Yūtō Japan **92** D4
Yuwang *Ningxia* China **94** F4
Yuxi *Guizhou* China *see* **Daozhen**
Yuxi *Hubei* China **97** F2
Yuxi *Yunnan* China **96** D3
Yuxian *Hebei* China **95** H4
Yuxian *Shanxi* China **95** H4
Yuyangguan China **97** F2
Yuyao China **97** I2
Yuzawa Japan **91** F5
Yuzha Rus. Fed. **52** I4
Yuzhno-Kamyshovyy Khrebet *ridge* Rus. Fed. **90** F3
Yuzhno-Kuril'sk Rus. Fed. **90** G3
Yuzhno-Muyskiy Khrebet *mts* Rus. Fed. **89** K1
Yuzhno-Sakhalinsk Rus. Fed. **90** F3
Yuzhno-Sukhokumsk Rus. Fed. **113** G1
Yuzhnoukrayinsk Ukr. **53** F7
Yuzhnyy Rus. Fed. *see* **Adyk**
Yuzhnyy Altay, Khrebet *mts* Kazakh. **98** D2
Yuzhong *Gansu* China **94** F5
Yuzhou *Chongqing* China *see* **Chongqing**
Yuzhou *Hebei* China *see* **Yuxian**
Yuzhou *Henan* China **95** H5
Yuzovka Ukr. *see* **Donets'k**
Yuzuruha-yama *hill* Japan **92** A4
Yverdon Switz. **66** H3
Yvetot France **66** E2
Ywamun Myanmar **86** A2

Z

Zaamin Uzbek. *see* **Zomin**
Zaandam Neth. **62** E2
Zab, Monts du *mts* Alg. **67** I6
Zabānābād Iran **110** E3
Zabaykal'sk Rus. Fed. **95** I1
Zabīd Yemen **108** F7
Zābol Iran **111** F4
Zabqung *Xizang* China **99** D7
Zacapa Guat. **167** H6
Zacapu Mex. **167** E5
Zacatal Mex. **167** H5
Zacatecas Mex. **168** D4
Zacatecas *state* Mex. **161** C8
Zacatecoluca El Salvador **166** [inset] H6
Zacatepec *Morelos* Mex. **167** F5
Zacatlán Mex. **167** F5
Zacharo Greece **69** I6
Zacoalco Mex. **168** D4
Zacualpán Mex. **167** F5
Zacynthus *i.* Greece *see* **Zakynthos**
Zadar Croatia **68** F2
Zadetkale Kyun *i.* Myanmar **87** B5
Zadetkyi Kyun *i.* Myanmar **87** B5
Zadi Myanmar **87** B4
Zadoi *Qinghai* China **99** F6
Zadonsk Rus. Fed. **53** H5
Zadran *reg.* Afgh. **111** H3
Za'farâna Egypt *see* **Za'farānah**
Za'farānah Egypt **112** D5
Zafer Adaları *is* Cyprus *see* **Kleides Islands**
Zafer Burnu *c.* Cyprus *see* **Apostolos Andreas, Cape**
Zafora *i.* Greece *see* **Sofrana**
Zafra Spain **67** C4
Zagazig Egypt *see* **Az Zaqāzīq**
Zaghdeh *well* Iran **110** E3
Zaghouan Tunisia **68** D6
Zagorsk Rus. Fed. *see* **Sergiyev Posad**

▶**Zagreb** Croatia **68** F2
Capital of Croatia.

Zagros, Kūhhā-ye *mts* Iran *see* **Zagros Mountains**
Zagros Mountains Iran **110** B3
Zagunao China *see* **Lixian**
Za'gya Zangbo *r. Xizang* China **99** E7
Zāhedān Iran **111** F4
Zahir Pir Pak. **111** H4
Zaḥlah Lebanon *see* **Zahlé**
Zahlé Lebanon **107** B3
Zähmet Turkm. **111** F2
Ẓahrān Saudi Arabia **108** F6
Zahrez Chergui *salt pan* Alg. **67** H6
Zahrez Rharbi *salt pan* Alg. **67** H6
Zainlha China *see* **Xiaojin**
Zainsk Rus. Fed. *see* **Novyy Zay**
Zaire *country* Africa *see* **Congo, Democratic Republic of the**
Zaïre *r.* Congo/Dem. Rep. Congo *see* **Congo**
Zaječar Serbia **69** J3
Zaka Zimbabwe **123** D6
Zakamensk Rus. Fed. **94** E1
Zakataly Azer. *see* **Zaqatala**
Zakháro Greece *see* **Zacharo**
Zakhmet Turkm. *see* **Zähmet**
Zākhō Iraq **113** F3
Zakhodnyaya Dzvina *r.* Europe *see* **Zapadnaya Dvina**
Zákinthos *i.* Greece *see* **Zakynthos**
Zakopane Poland **57** Q6
Zakouma, Parc National de *nat. park* Chad **121** E3
Zakwaski, Mount Canada **150** F5
Zakynthos Greece **69** I6
Zakynthos *i.* Greece **69** I6
Zala *Xizang* China **99** F7
Zalaegerszeg Hungary **68** G1
Zalai-domsag *hills* Hungary **68** G1
Zalamea de la Serena Spain **67** D4
Zalantun *Nei Mongol* China **95** J2
Zalari Rus. Fed. **88** I2
Zalău Romania **69** J1
Zaleski U.S.A. **164** D4
Ẓalim Saudi Arabia **108** F5
Zalingei Sudan **121** F3
Ẓalmā, Jabal aẓ *mt.* Saudi Arabia **108** E4
Zama Japan **93** F3
Zama City Canada **150** G3
Zambales Mountains *Luzon* Phil. **82** C3
Zambeze *r.* Africa **123** C5 *see* **Zambezi**

▶**Zambezi** *r.* Africa **123** C5
4th longest river in Africa. Also known as Zambeze.

Zambezi Zambia **123** C5
Zambia *country* Africa **123** C5
Zamboanga *Mindanao* Phil. **82** C5
Zamboanga Peninsula *Mindanao* Phil. **82** C5
Zamboanguita *Negros* Phil. **82** C4
Zamfara *watercourse* Nigeria **120** D3
Zamīndāvar *reg.* Afgh. **111** F4
Zamkog China *see* **Zamtang**
Zamora Ecuador **176** C4
Zamora Spain **67** D3
Zamora de Hidalgo Mex. **168** D5
Zamość Poland **53** D6
Zamost'ye Poland *see* **Zamość**
Zamtang China **96** D1
Zamuro, Sierra del *mts* Venez. **176** F3

Zanaga Congo 122 B4
Zanatepec Mex. 167 G5
Zancle Sicily Italy see Messina
Zanda Xizang China 99 B7
Zandamela Moz. 125 L3
Zandvliet Belgium 62 E3
Zane Hills AK U.S.A. 148 H2
Zanesville U.S.A. 164 D4
Zangguy Xinjiang China 99 B5
Zangsêr Kangri mt. Xizang China 99 D6
Zangskar reg. India see Zanskar
Zangskar Mountains India see Zanskar Mountains
Zanhuang Hebei China 95 H4
Zanjān Iran 110 C2
Zanjān Rūd r. Iran 110 B2
Ẕannah, Jabal aẕ hill U.A.E. 110 D5
Zanskar r. India 99 B6
Zanskar reg. India 104 D2
Zanskar Mountains India 104 D2
Zante i. Greece see Zakynthos
Zanthus Australia 135 C7
Zanughān Iran 110 E3
Zanzibar Tanz. 123 D4
Zanzibar Island Tanz. 123 D4
Zaosheng Gansu China 95 G5
Zaoshi Hubei China 97 G2
Zaoshi Hunan China 97 G3
Zaouatallaz Alg. 120 D2
Zaouet el Kahla Alg. see Bordj Omer Driss
Zaoyang China 97 G1
Zaoyangzhan China 97 G1
Zaoyuan Xinjiang China 98 D3
Zaozernyy Rus. Fed. 77 K4
Zaozhuang Shandong China 95 I5
Zapadnaya Dvina r. Europe 52 F5
also known as Dvina or Zakhodnyaya Dzvina, English form Western Dvina
Zapadnaya Dvina Rus. Fed. 52 G4
Zapadni Rodopi mts Bulg. 69 J4
Zapadno-Kazakhstanskaya Oblast' admin. div. Kazakh. see Zapadnyy Kazakhstan
Zapadno-Sakhalinskiy Khrebet mts Rus. Fed. 90 F2
Zapadno-Sibirskaya Nizmennost' plain Rus. Fed. see West Siberian Plain
Zapadno-Sibirskaya Ravnina plain Rus. Fed. see West Siberian Plain
Zapadnyy Alamedin, Pik mt. Kyrg. 98 A4
Zapadnyy Chink Ustyurta esc. Kazakh. 113 I2
Zapadnyy Kazakhstan admin. div. Kazakh. 51 Q6
Zapadnyy Kil'din Rus. Fed. 54 S2
Zapadnyy Sayan reg. Rus. Fed. 88 F2
Zapata U.S.A. 161 D7
Zapata, Península de pen. Cuba 163 D8
Zapiga Chile 176 E7
Zapolyarnyy Rus. Fed. 54 Q2
Zapol'ye Rus. Fed. 52 H4
Zaporizhzhya Ukr. 53 G7
Zaporozh'ye Ukr. see Zaporizhzhya
Zapug Xizang China 99 C6
Zaqatala Azer. 113 G2
Zaqên Qinghai China 99 F6
Za Qu r. China 96 C2
Zaqungngomar mt. Xizang China 99 E6
Zara Xizang China see Moinda
Zara Croatia see Zadar
Zara Turkey 112 E3
Zarafshan Uzbek. see Zarafshon
Zarafshon Uzbek. 102 B3
Zarafshon, Qatorkŭhi mts Tajik. 111 G2
Zaragoza Coahuila Mex. 167 E2
Zaragoza Spain 67 F3
Zarand Iran 110 E4
Zarang Xizang China 99 B7
Zaranikh Reserve nature res. Egypt 107 B4
Zaranj Afgh. 111 F4
Zarasai Lith. 55 O9
Zárate Arg. 178 E4
Zaraysk Rus. Fed. 53 H5
Zaraza Venez. 176 E2
Zarbdor Uzbek. 111 H1
Zärdab Azer. 53 J8
Zarechensk Rus. Fed. 54 Q3
Zāreh Iran 110 C3
Zarembo Island AK U.S.A. 149 N4
Zargun mt. Pak. 111 G4
Zari Afgh. 111 G3
Zaria Nigeria 120 D3
Zarichne Ukr. 53 E6
Zarifète, Col des pass Alg. 67 F6
Zarinsk Rus. Fed. 88 E2
Zarmardan Afgh. 111 F3
Zarneh Iran 110 B3
Zărnești Romania 69 K2
Zarqā' Jordan see Az Zarqā'
Zarqā', Nahr az r. Jordan 107 B3
Zarubino Rus. Fed. 90 C4
Zaruga-dake mt. Japan 93 E3
Żary Poland 57 O5
Zarzis Tunisia 64 G5
Zashchita Kazakh. 98 C2
Zasheyek Rus. Fed. 54 Q3
Zaskar reg. India see Zanskar
Zaskar Range mts India see Zanskar Mountains
Zaslawye Belarus 55 O9
Zastron S. Africa 125 H6
Za'tarī, Wādī az watercourse Jordan 107 C3
Zaterechnyy Rus. Fed. 53 J7
Zauche reg. Germany 63 M2
Zaunguzskiye Karakumy des. Turkm. see Üngüz Angyrsyndaky Garagum
Zautla Mex. 167 F5
Zavalla U.S.A. 161 E6
Zavetnoye Rus. Fed. 53 I7
Zavety Il'icha Rus. Fed. 90 F2
Zavidoviči Bos.-Herz. 68 H2
Zavitaya Rus. Fed. see Zavitinsk
Zavitinsk Rus. Fed. 90 C2
Zavolzhsk Rus. Fed. 52 I4
Zavolzh'ye Rus. Fed. see Zavolzhsk
Závora, Ponta pt Moz. 125 L3
Zawa Qinghai China 94 E4
Zawa Xinjiang China 99 B5
Zawiercie Poland 57 Q5
Zawīlah Libya 121 E2
Zāwīyah, Jabal az hills Syria 107 C2
Zaxoi Xizang China 99 E7
Zaydī, Wādī az watercourse Syria 107 C3
Zaysan Kazakh. 102 F2
Zaysan, Lake Kazakh. 102 F2
Zaysan, Ozero l. Kazakh. see Zaysan, Lake
Zayü China see Gyigang
Zayü Qu r. China/India 105 I3
Žďar nad Sázavou Czech Rep. 57 O6
Zdolbuniv Ukr. 53 E6
Zdolbunov Ukr. see Zdolbuniv
Zealand i. Denmark 55 G9
Zēbāk Afgh. 104 B1
Zebediela S. Africa 125 I3
Zebulon U.S.A. 164 D5
Zedelgem Belgium 62 D3
Zeebrugge Belgium 62 D3
Zeeland U.S.A. 164 B2
Zeerust S. Africa 125 H3
Ẕefat Israel 107 B3
Zehdenick Germany 63 N2
Zeil, Mount Australia 135 F5
Zeil am Main Germany 63 K4
Zeist Neth. 62 F2
Zeitz Germany 63 M3
Zêkog Qinghai China 94 E5
Zekti Xinjiang China 98 C4
Zela Turkey see Zile
Zelennik Rus. Fed. 52 J3
Zelenoborsk Rus. Fed. 51 S3
Zelenoborskiy Rus. Fed. 54 R3
Zelenodol'sk Rus. Fed. 52 K5
Zelenogorsk Rus. Fed. 55 P6
Zelenograd Rus. Fed. 52 H4
Zelenogradsk Rus. Fed. 55 L9
Zelenokumsk Rus. Fed. 113 F1
Zelentsovo Rus. Fed. 52 J4
Zelenyy, Ostrov i. Rus. Fed. 90 G4
Zelinggou Qinghai China 94 D4
Zell am See Austria 57 N7
Zellingen Germany 63 J5
Zelzate Belgium 62 D3
Žemaitijos nacionalinis parkas nat. park Lith. 55 L8
Zêmdasam China 96 D1
Zemetchino Rus. Fed. 53 I5
Zémio Cent. Afr. Rep. 122 C3
Zemmora Alg. 67 G6
Zempoaltépetl, Nudo de mt. Mex. 168 E5
Zengcheng China 97 G4
Zenica Bos.-Herz. 68 G2
Ẕenifim watercourse Israel 107 B4
Zennor U.K. 59 B8
Zenta Serbia see Senta
Zenzach Alg. 67 H6
Zepu Xinjiang China 99 B5
Zeravshanskiy Khrebet mts Tajik. see Zarafshon, Qatorkŭhi
Zerbst Germany 63 M3
Zerenike Reserve nature res. Egypt see Zaranikh Reserve
Zerf Germany 62 G5
Zernien Germany 63 K1
Zernitz Germany 63 M2
Zernograd Rus. Fed. 53 I7
Zernovoy Rus. Fed. see Zernograd
Zêsum Xizang China 99 E7
Zêtang Xizang China 99 E7
Zetel Germany 63 H1
Zeulenroda Germany 63 L4
Zeven Germany 63 J1
Zevenaar Neth. 62 G3
Zevgari, Cape Cyprus 107 A2
Zeya Rus. Fed. 90 B1
Zeya r. Rus. Fed. 90 B2
Zeydar Iran 110 E2
Zeydī Iran 111 F5
Zeyskiy Zapovednik nature res. Rus. Fed. 90 B1
Zeysko-Bureinskaya Vpadina depr. Rus. Fed. 90 C2
Zeyskoye Vodokhranilishche resr Rus. Fed. 90 B1
Zeytin Burnu c. Cyprus see Elaia, Cape
Zêzere r. Port. 67 B4
Zezhou Shanxi China 95 H5
Zgharta Lebanon 107 B2
Zghorta Lebanon see Zgharta
Zgierz Poland 57 Q5
Zhabinka Belarus 55 N10
Zhaggo China see Luhuo
Zhaglag China 96 C1
Zhag'yab China 96 C2
Zhaksy Sarysu watercourse Kazakh. see Sarysu
Zhalanash Almatinskaya Oblast' Kazakh. 98 B4
Zhalanash Kazakh. see Damdy
Zhalpaktal Kazakh. 51 P6
Zhalpaqtal Kazakh. see Zhalpaktal
Zhaltyr Kazakh. 102 C1
Zhambyl Karagandinskaya Oblast' Kazakh. 102 D2
Zhambyl Zhambylskaya Oblast' Kazakh. see Taraz
Zhambylskaya Oblast' admin. div. Kazakh. 98 A3
Zhameuka Kazakh. 98 C3
Zhamo Xizang China see Bomi
Zhanakorgan Kazakh. 102 C3
Zhanang Xizang China 99 E7
Zhanaortalyk Kazakh. 98 A3
Zhanaozen Kazakh. 100 E2
Zhanatalan Kazakh. 98 B4
Zhanatas Kazakh. 102 C3
Zhanbei China 90 B2
Zhangaözen Kazakh. see Zhanaozen
Zhanga Qazan Kazakh. see Novaya Kazanka
Zhangaqorghan Kazakh. see Zhanakorgan
Zhangatas Kazakh. see Zhanatas
Zhangbei Hebei China 95 H3
Zhangcheng China see Yongtai
Zhangcunpu China 97 H1
Zhangdian Shandong China see Zibo
Zhanggu China see Danba
Zhangguangcai Ling mts China 90 C3
Zhanggutai Liaoning China 95 J3
Zhanghua Taiwan see Changhua
Zhangiztobe Kazakh. 98 C2
Zhangjiabang China 97 G2
Zhangjiachuan Gansu China 94 F5
Zhangjiajie China 97 F2
Zhangjiakou Hebei China 95 H3
Zhangjiang China see Taoyuan
Zhangjiapan Shaanxi China see Jingbian
Zhangla China 96 D1
Zhangling China 90 A1
Zhanglou China 97 H1
Zhangping China 97 H3
Zhangqiangzhen China 90 A4
Zhangqiao China 97 H1
Zhangqiu Shandong China 95 I4
Zhangshu China 97 G2
Zhangwu Liaoning China 95 J3
Zhangxian Gansu China 94 F5
Zhangye Gansu China 94 E4
Zhangzhou China 97 H3
Zhangzi Shanxi China 95 H4
Zhanhe China see Zhanbei
Zhanhua Shandong China 95 I4
Zhanibek Kazakh. 51 P6
Zhanjiang China 97 F4
Zhanjiang Bei China see Chikan
Zhao'an China 97 H4
Zhaodong China 90 B3
Zhaoge Henan China see Qixian
Zhaojue China 96 D2
Zhaoliqiao China 97 G2
Zhaoping China 97 F3
Zhaoqing China 97 G4
Zhaoren Shaanxi China see Changwu
Zhaosu Xinjiang China 98 C4
Zhaosutai He r. China 95 J3
Zhaotong China 96 D3
Zhaoxian Hebei China 95 H4
Zhaoyang Hu l. China 95 I5
Zhaoyuan China 90 B3
Zhaoyuan Shandong China 95 J4
Zhaozhou Hebei China see Zhaoxian
Zhaozhou China 90 B3
Zharbulak Kazakh. 98 C3
Zhari Namco salt l. China 99 D7
Zharkamys Kazakh. 102 A2
Zharkent Kazakh. 102 F3
Zharkovskiy Rus. Fed. 52 G5
Zharma Kazakh. 102 F2
Zharsuat Kazakh. 98 C3
Zharyk Kazakh. 98 C2
Zhashkiv Ukr. 53 F6
Zhashkov Ukr. see Zhashkiv
Zhaslyk Uzbek. see Jasliq
Zhaxi China see Weixin
Zhaxi Co salt l. China 99 D6
Zhaxigang Xizang China 99 B6
Zhaxigang Xizang China 99 E7
Zhaxizê China 96 C2
Zhaxizong Xizang China 99 D7
Zhayü China 96 C2
Zhayyq r. Kazakh./Rus. Fed. see Ural
Zhdanov Ukr. see Mariupol'
Zhdanovsk Azer. see Beyläqan
Zhecheng Henan China 95 H5
Zhedao China see Lianghe
Zhêhor China 96 D2
Zhejiang prov. China 97 I2
Zhekezhal Kazakh. 98 A2
Zhelaniya, Mys c. Rus. Fed. 76 H2
Zheleznodorozhnyy Rus. Fed. see Yemva
Zheleznodorozhnyy Uzbek. see Qo'ng'irot
Zheleznogorsk Rus. Fed. 53 G5
Zhelou China see Ceheng
Zheltorangy Kazakh. 98 A3
Zheltyye Vody Ukr. see Zhovti Vody
Zhem Kazakh. see Emba
Zhen'an China 97 F1
Zhenba China 96 E1
Zhengding Hebei China 95 H4
Zhenghe China 97 H3
Zhengjiakou Hebei China see Gucheng
Zhengjiatun Jilin China see Shuangliao
Zhengkou Hebei China see Gucheng
Zhenglan Qi Nei Mongol China see Dund Hot
Zhenglubu Gansu China 94 E4
Zhengning Gansu China 95 G5
Zhengxiangbai Qi Nei Mongol China see Qagan Nur
Zhengyang China 97 G1
Zhengyangguan China 97 H1
Zhengzhou Henan China 95 H5
Zhenhai China 97 I2
Zhenjiang China 97 H1
Zhenjiangguan China 96 D1
Zhenlai Jilin China 95 J2
Zhenning China 96 E3
Zhenping China 97 F2
Zhenwudong Shaanxi China see Ansai
Zhenxi Jilin China 95 J2
Zhenxiong China 96 E3
Zhenyang China see Zhengyang
Zhenyuan Gansu China 95 F5
Zhenyuan China 97 F3
Zherdevka Rus. Fed. 53 I6
Zherong China 97 H3
Zheshart Rus. Fed. 52 K3
Zhetikara Kazakh. see Zhitikara
Zhêxam Xizang China 99 D7
Zhexi Shuiku resr China 97 F2
Zhezkazgan Kazakh. 102 C2
Zhezqazghan Kazakh. see Zhezkazgan
Zhicheng Hubei China 97 F2
Zhicheng Shandong China see Qingzhou
Zhicheng Zhejiang China see Changxing
Zhidan Shaanxi China 95 G4
Zhidoi Qinghai China 99 F6
Zhifang China see Jiangxia
Zhigalovo Rus. Fed. 88 J2
Zhigansk Rus. Fed. 77 N3
Zhigou Shandong China 95 I5
Zhigung Xizang China 99 E7
Zhijiang Hubei China 97 F2
Zhijiang Hunan China 86 E1
Zhijin China 96 E3
Zhilong China see Yangxi
Zhiluozhen Shaanxi China 95 G5
Zhi Qu r. China see Yangtze
Zhitikara Kazakh. 100 F1
Zhitkovichi Belarus see Zhytkavichy
Zhitkur Rus. Fed. 53 J6
Zhitomir Ukr. see Zhytomyr
Zhīvār Iran 110 B3
Zhiziluo China 96 C3
Zhlobin Belarus 53 F5
Zhmerinka Ukr. see Zhmerynka
Zhmerynka Ukr. 53 F6
Zhob Pak. 111 H4
Zhob r. Pak. 111 H3
Zholnuskay Kazakh. 98 C2
Zhong'an China see Fuyuan
Zhongba Guangdong China 97 G4
Zhongba Sichuan China see Jiangyou
Zhongba Xizang China 99 D7
Zhongduo China see Youyang
Zhongguo country Asia see China
Zhongguo Renmin Gongheguo country Asia see China
Zhonghe China see Xiushan
Zhongmou Henan China 95 H5
Zhongning Ningxia China 94 F4
Zhongping China see Huize
Zhongpu Gansu China 94 E4
Zhongshan research station Antarctica 188 E2
Zhongshan Guangdong China 97 G4
Zhongshan Guangxi China 97 F3
Zhongshan Guizhou China see Lupanshui
Zhongshu Yunnan China see Luxi
Zhongshu Yunnan China see Luliang
Zhongtai Gansu China see Lingtai
Zhongtiao Shan mts China 95 G5
Zhongwei Ningxia China 94 F4
Zhongxin Guangdong China 97 G3
Zhongxin Yunnan China see Xianggelila
Zhongxin Yunnan China see Huaping
Zhongxing Jiangsu China see Siyang
Zhongxingji China 97 H2
Zhongxinzhan Qinghai China 94 D5
Zhongyang Shanxi China 95 G4
Zhongyaozhan China 90 B2
Zhongyicun China 96 D3
Zhongyuan China 97 F5
Zhongzhai China 96 E1
Zhosaly Kazakh. see Dzhusaly
Zhosaly Pavlodarskaya Oblast' Kazakh. 98 B2
Zhoucheng Shandong China 95 I5
Zhoujiajing Gansu China 94 E4
Zhoukou Henan China 97 G1
Zhoukou Sichuan China see Peng'an
Zhoukoudian tourist site China 95 H4
Zhouning China 97 H3
Zhoushan China 97 I2
Zhoushan Dao i. China 97 I2
Zhoushan Qundao is China 97 I2
Zhouzhi Shaanxi China 95 G5
Zhovti Vody Ukr. 53 G6
Zhuanghe Liaoning China 95 J4
Zhuanglang Gansu China 94 F5
Zhubgyügoin China 96 C1
Zhucheng Shandong China 95 I5
Zhudong Taiwan see Chutung
Zhugkyung Qinghai China 94 D4
Zhugla Xizang China 99 F7
Zhugqu China 96 E1
Zhuhai China 97 G4
Zhuji Zhejiang China 97 I2
Zhujing China 97 I2
Zhukeng China 97 G4
Zhukovka Rus. Fed. 53 G5
Zhukovskiy Rus. Fed. 53 H5
Zhulong He r. China 95 H4
Zhumadian China 97 G1
Zhuokeji China 96 D2
Zhuolu Hebei China 95 H3
Zhuozhou Hebei China 95 I4
Zhuozi Nei Mongol China 95 H3
Zhuozishan Nei Mongol China see Zhuozi
Zhusandala, Step' plain Kazakh. 98 A3
Zhushan Hubei China 97 F1
Zhushan Hubei China see Xuan'en
Zhuxi China 97 F1
Zhuxiang China 97 H1
Zhuyang China see Dazhu
Zhuzhou Hunan China 97 G3
Zhuzhou Hunan China 97 G3
Zhydachiv Ukr. 53 E6
Zhympity Kazakh. 51 Q5
Zhytkavichy Belarus 55 O10
Zhytomyr Ukr. 53 F6
Zīā'ābād Iran 110 C3
Žiar nad Hronom Slovakia 57 Q6
Zibā salt pan Saudi Arabia 107 D4
Zibo Shandong China 95 I4
Zichang Shaanxi China 95 G4
Zicheng China see Zijin
Zicuirán Mex. 167 E5
Zidi Pak. 111 G5
Ziel, Mount Australia see Zeil, Mount
Zielona Góra Poland 57 O5
Ziemelkursas augstiene hills Latvia 55 M8
Zierenberg Germany 63 J3
Ziesar Germany 63 M2
Ziftá Egypt 112 C5
Zigê Tangco l. China 99 E6
Zīghan Libya 121 F2
Zigong China 96 E2
Ziguey Chad 121 E3
Ziguinchor Senegal 120 B3
Žīguri Latvia 55 O8
Zihuatanejo Mex. 168 D5
Zijin China 97 G4
Zijpenberg hill Neth. 62 G2
Ziketan Qinghai China see Xinghai
Zile Turkey 112 D2
Žilina Slovakia 57 Q6
Zillah Libya 121 E2
Zima Rus. Fed. 88 I2
Zimapán Mex. 167 F4
Zimatlán Mex. 167 F5
Zimba Zambia 123 C5
Zimbabwe country Africa 123 C5
Zimi Sierra Leone see Zimmi
Zimmerbude Rus. Fed. see Svetlyy
Zimmi Sierra Leone 120 B4
Zimnicea Romania 69 K3
Zimniy Bereg coastal area Rus. Fed. 52 H2
Zimovniki Rus. Fed. 53 I7
Zimrīn Syria 107 B2
Ẕin watercourse Israel 107 B4
Zin Pak. 111 H4
Zinave, Parque Nacional de nat. park Moz. 123 D6
Zinder Niger 120 D3
Zindo China 96 D2
Ziniaré Burkina Faso 120 C3
Zinihu Nei Mongol China 94 F4
Zinjibār Yemen 108 G7
Zinoyevsk Ukr. see Kirovohrad
Zion U.S.A. 164 B2
Zion National Park U.S.A. 159 G3
Zionz Lake Canada 151 N5
Zippori Israel 107 B3
Zi Qu r. Qinghai China 99 G6
Ziqudukou China 96 B1
Zirc Hungary 68 G1
Zirkel, Mount U.S.A. 156 G4
Zirkūh i. U.A.E. 110 D5
Zirndorf Germany 63 K5
Ziro India 105 H4
Zirreh Afgh. 111 F4
Zīr Rūd Iran 110 C4
Zi Shui r. China 89 K7
Zistersdorf Austria 57 P6
Zitácuaro Mex. 168 D5
Zitong China 96 E2
Zittau Germany 57 O5
Zitziana r. AK U.S.A. 149 J2
Zixi China 97 H3
Zixing China see Xingning
Ziyang Jiangxi China see Wuyuan
Ziyang Shaanxi China 97 F1
Ziyang Sichuan China 96 E2
Ziyaret Dağı hill Turkey 107 B1
Ziyuan China 97 F3
Ziyun China 96 E3
Ziz, Oued watercourse Morocco 64 D5
Zizhong China 96 E2
Zizhou Shaanxi China 95 G4
Zlatoustovsk Rus. Fed. 90 D1
Zlín Czech Rep. 57 P6
Zmeinogorsk Rus. Fed. 102 F1
Zmiyevka Rus. Fed. 53 H5
Znamenka Kazakh. 98 B2
Znamenka Rus. Fed. 53 I5
Znamenka Ukr. see Znam"yanka
Znam"yanka Ukr. 53 G6
Znojmo Czech Rep. 57 P6
Zoar S. Africa 124 E7
Zoco Xizang China 99 C6
Zoetermeer Neth. 62 E2
Zogainrawar Qinghai China see Huashixia
Zogang China 96 C2
Zogqên China 96 C1
Zoidê Lhai Xizang China 99 E6
Zoigê China 96 D1
Zoji La pass India 104 C2
Zola S. Africa 125 H7
Zolder Belgium 62 F3
Zolochev Kharkivs'ka Oblast' Ukr. see Zolochiv
Zolochev L'vivs'ka Oblast' Ukr. see Zolochiv
Zolochiv Kharkivs'ka Oblast' Ukr. 53 G6
Zolochiv L'vivs'ka Oblast' Ukr. 53 E6
Zolotonosha Ukr. 53 G6
Zolotoy, Khrebet mts Rus. Fed. 148 B2
Zolotoye Rus. Fed. 53 J6
Zolotukhino Rus. Fed. 53 H5
▶Zomba Malawi 123 D5
Former capital of Malawi.
Zombor Serbia see Sombor
Zomin Uzbek. 111 H2
Zongjiafangzi Qinghai China 94 D4
Zonguldak Turkey 69 N4
Zongxoi China 105 G3
Zongzhai Gansu China 94 D4
Zörbig Germany 63 M3
Zorgho Burkina Faso 120 C3
Zorgo Burkina Faso see Zorgho
Zorn r. France 63 I6
Żory Poland 57 Q5
Zossen Germany 63 N2
Zottegem Belgium 62 D4
Zouar Chad 121 E2
Zoucheng Shandong China 95 I5
Zouérat Mauritania 120 B2
Zoulang Nanshan mts China 94 D4
Zouping Shandong China 95 I4
Zousfana, Oued watercourse Alg. 64 D5
Zoushi China 97 F2
Zouxian Shandong China see Zoucheng
Zrenjanin Serbia 69 I2
Zschopau Germany 63 N4
Zschopau r. Germany 63 N3
Zschornewitz Germany 63 M3
Zubālah, Birkat waterhole Saudi Arabia 113 F5
Zubillaga Arg. 178 D5
Zubova Polyana Rus. Fed. 53 I5
Zubtsov Rus. Fed. 52 G4
Zuénoula Côte d'Ivoire 120 C4
Zug Switz. 66 I3
Zugdidi Georgia 113 F2
Zugspitze mt. Austria/Germany 57 M7
Zugu Nigeria 120 D3
Zuider Zee l. Neth. see IJsselmeer
Zuidhorn Neth. 62 G1
Zuid-Kennemerland Nationaal Park nat. park Neth. 62 E2
Zuitai China see Kangxian
Zuitaizi China see Kangxian
Zuitou Shaanxi China see Taibai
Zújar r. Spain 67 D4
Zuli He r. Gansu China 94 F4
Zülpich Germany 62 G4
Zumba Ecuador 176 C4
Zumpango Mex. 167 F5
Zumpango del Río Mex. 167 F5
Zunheboto India 105 H4
Zunhua Hebei China 95 I3
Zuni U.S.A. 159 I4
Zuni watercourse U.S.A. 159 I4
Zuni Mountains U.S.A. 159 I4
Zun-Torey, Ozero l. Rus. Fed. 95 H1
Zunyi Guizhou China 96 E3
Zunyi Guizhou China 96 E3
Zuo Jiang r. China/Vietnam 86 E2
Zuoquan Shanxi China 95 H4
Zuoyun Shanxi China 95 H4
Županja Croatia 68 H2
Zūrābād Āẕarbāyjān-e Gharbī Iran 110 B2
Zūrābād Khorāsān Iran 111 F3
Zurhen Ul Shan mts China 99 E6
Zürich Switz. 66 I3
Zurmat reg. Afgh. 111 H3
Zuru Nigeria 120 D3
Zurzuna Turkey see Çıldır
Zushi Japan 93 F3
Zutphen Neth. 62 G2
Zuwārah Libya 120 E1
Zuyevka Rus. Fed. 52 K4
Zūzan Iran 111 E3
Zvishavane Zimbabwe 123 D6
Zvolen Slovakia 57 Q6
Zvornik Bos.-Herz. 69 H2
Zwedru Liberia 120 C4
Zweeloo Neth. 62 G2
Zweibrücken Germany 63 H5
Zweletemba S. Africa 124 D7
Zwelitsha S. Africa 125 H7
Zwethau Germany 63 N3
Zwettl Austria 57 O6
Zwickau Germany 63 M4
Zwochau Germany 63 M3
Zwolle Neth. 62 G2
Zwönitz Germany 63 M4
Zyablovo Rus. Fed. 52 L4
Zygi Cyprus 107 A2
Zyryan Kazakh. see Zyryanovsk
Zyryanka Rus. Fed. 77 Q3
Zyryanovsk Kazakh. 102 F2
Zyyi Cyprus see Zygi

Acknowledgements

Maps and data

Maps, design and origination by Collins Geo, HarperCollins Reference, Glasgow.
Illustrations created by HarperCollins Publishers unless otherwise stated.

Cover image: Planetary Visions Ltd/Science Photo Library.

Earthquake data (pp10–11): United States Geological Survey (USGS) National Earthquakes Information Center, Denver, USA.

Population map (pp16–17): 2005. Gridded Population of the World Version 3 (GPWv3). Palisades, NY: Socioeconomic Data and Applications Center (SEDAC), Columbia University. Available at http://sedac.ciesn.columbia.edu/plue/gpw http://www.ciesin.columbia.edu

Internet capacity and telecommunications traffic (pp20–21): ©TeleGeography Research.

Company sales figures (p25): Reprinted by permission of Forbes Magazine ©2008Forbes Inc.

Coral reefs data (p31): UNEP World Conservation Monitoring Centre, Cambridge, UK, and World Resources Institute (WRI), Washington D.C., USA.

Desertification data(p31):U.S. Department of Agriculture Natural Resources Conservation Service.

Antarctica (p152): Antarctic Digital Database (versions1 and 2), ©Scientific Committee on Antarctic research (SCAR), Cambridge, UK (1993,1998).

Photographs and images

Page	Image	Satellite/Sensor	Credit	Page	Image	Satellite/Sensor	Credit	Page	Image	Satellite/Sensor	Credit
6–7	Greenland	MODIS	MODIS/NASA	34	Venice main	MODIS	MODIS/NASA	126–127	Oceania		Blue Marble: Next Generation. NASA's Earth Observatory
8–9	Vatican City	IKONOS	IKONOS satellite imagery courtesy of GeoEye		Venice inset		NASA/GSFC				
				35	Venice main	ASTER	NASA/ASTER	128–129	Heron Island	IKONOS	IKONOS satellite imagery courtesy of GeoEye
12–13	Tropical storm Dina	MODIS	MODIS/NASA/GSFC		Venice insets	IKONOS	IKONOS satellite imagery courtesy of GeoEye	128–129	Banks Peninsula	Space shuttle	NASA
14–15	Tokyo	ASTER	ASTER/NASA	36	Namib Desert	Landsat	USGS EROS Data Center	130–131	Nouméa	ISS	NASA/Johnson Space Center
	Cropland,Consuegra		© Rick Barrentine/Corbis	37	Kamchatka Peninsula	MODIS	MODIS/NASA	130–131	Wellington		NZ Aerial Mapping Ltd www.nzam.com
	Mojave Desert		Keith Moore	38	Kuala Lumpur	IKONOS	IKONOS satellite imagery courtesy of GeoEye	140–141	North America		Blue Marble: Next Generation. NASA's Earth Observatory
	Larsen Ice Shelf	MODIS	MODIS/NASA	39	Cape Canaveral	ASTER	NASA/GSFC/METI/ERSDAC/JAROS, and US/Japan ASTER Science Team	142–143	Mississippi Delta	ASTER	ASTER/NASA
16–17	Singapore		Courtesy of USGS EROS Data Center					142–143	Panama Canal	Landsat	Clifton-Campbell Imaging Inc.
	Kuna Indians		© Danny Lehman/Corbis	40	Songhua River	ASTER	ASTER/NASA	144–145	Mexicali	ASTER	NASA
18–19	Hong Kong		IKONOS satellite imagery courtesy of GeoEye	41	Spider Crater	ASTER	ASTER/NASA	144–145	The Bahamas	MODIS	MODIS/NASA
24–25	Sudanese village		Mark Edwards/Still Pictures	44–45	Europe		Blue Marble: Next Generation. NASA's Earth Observatory	170–171	South America		Blue Marble: Next Generation. NASA's Earth Observatory
26–27	Spratly Islands	IKONOS	IKONOS satellite imagery courtesy of GeoEye	46–47	Iceland	MODIS	MODIS/NASA	172–173	Amazon/Rio Negro	Terra/MISR	NASA
28–29	Colombia		FREDY AMARILES/AFP/Getty Images	48–49	Bosporus	ISS	NASA/Johnson Space Center	172–173	Tierra del Fuego	MODIS	MODIS/NASA
	Kathmandu, Nepal		Harmut Schwarzbach/Still Pictures	70–71	Asia		Blue Marble: Next Generation. NASA's Earth Observatory	174–175	Galapagos Islands	MODIS	MODIS/NASA
30–31	Deforestation, Itaipu	Landsat	Images reproduced by kind permission of UNEP					174–175	Falkland Islands	MODIS	MODIS/NASA
	Aral Sea	Landsat	Images reproduced by kind permission of UNEP	72–73	Yangtze	MODIS	MODIS/NASA	180–181	Antarctica		NRSC Ltd/Science Photo Library and Blue Marble: Next Generation. NASA's Earth Observatory
					Caspian Sea	MODIS	MODIS/NASA				
	Great Barrier Reef	MODIS	MODIS/NASA	74–75	Timor	MODIS	MODIS/NASA	182–183	Larsen Ice Shelf	MODIS	MODIS/NASA
32–33	Lake Chad	Landsat	Images reproduced by kind permission of UNEP		Beijing	MODIS	IKONOS satellite imagery courtesy of GeoEye				
	Tubarjal, Arabian Desert	Landsat	Images reproduced by kind permission of UNEP	114–115	Africa		Blue Marble: Next Generation. NASA's Earth Observatory				
	Palm Islands x3	IKONOS	IKONOS satellite imagery courtesy of GeoEye	116–117	Congo River	Space shuttle	NASA				
	Las Vegas x2	Landsat	Images reproduced by kind permission of UNEP		Lake Victoria	MODIS	MODIS/NASA				
				118–119	Cape Town	IKONOS	IKONOS satellite imagery courtesy of GeoEye				

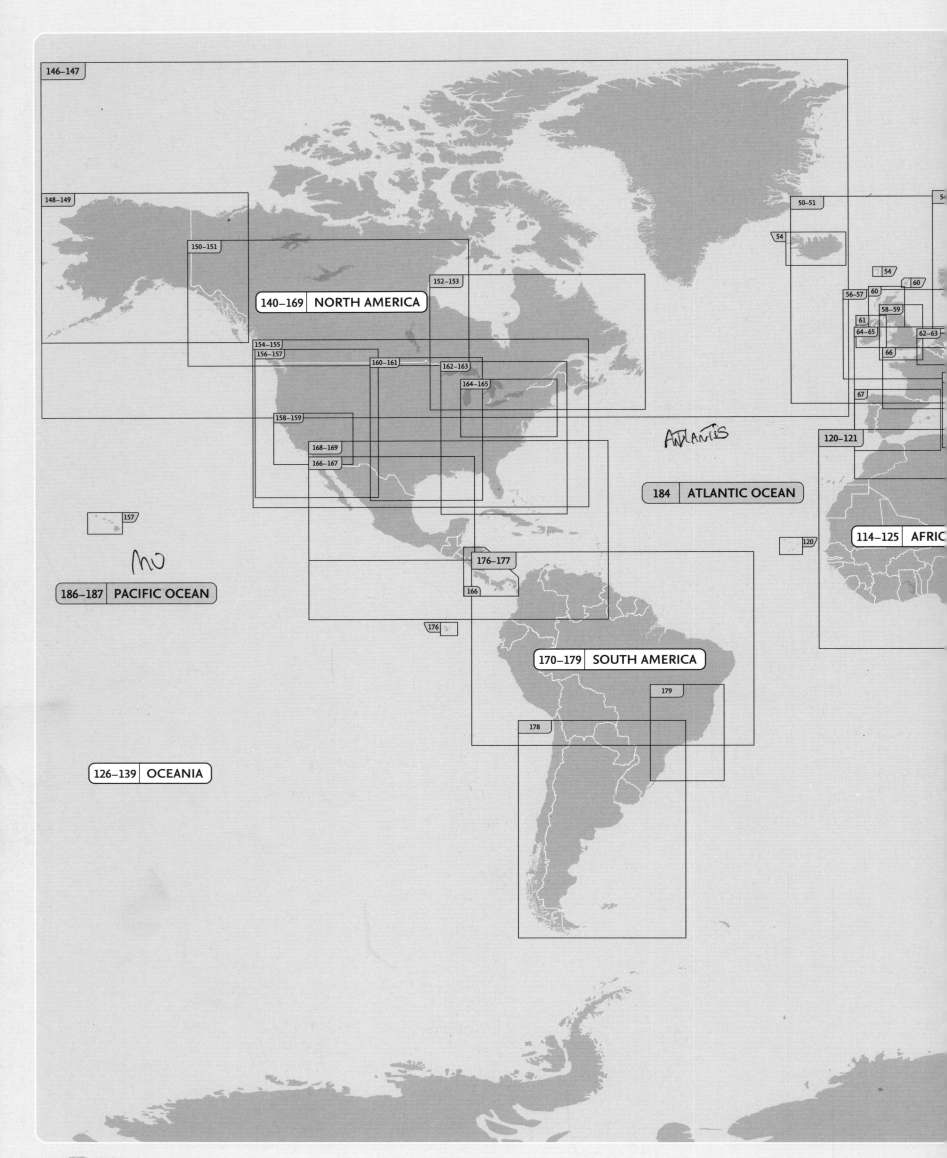

146–147

148–149

150–151

152–153

140–169 NORTH AMERICA

154–155
156–157

160–161

162–163

164–165

158–159

168–169
166–167

157

50–51

54

54

56–57

60

60

58–59

61

64–65

62–63

66

67

120–121

114–125 AFRIC

184 ATLANTIC OCEAN

120

186–187 PACIFIC OCEAN

176–177

166

176

170–179 SOUTH AMERICA

179

178

126–139 OCEANIA

Find your map